C000269090

ISBN 978-0-260-00663-9
PIBN 11027212

[Supplement to *The Builder*, July 9, 1892.]

AN

✣ ILLUSTRATED ✣ WEEKLY ✣ MAGAZINE ✣

FOR THE

CHITECT, ENGINEER, ARCHÆOLOGIST, CONSTRUCTOR, SANITARY REFORMER, AND ART-LOVER.

CONDUCTED BY

H. H. STATHAM,

FELLOW OF THE ROYAL INSTITUTE OF BRITISH ARCHITECTS.

"Every man's proper mansion-house, and home, being the theater of his hospitality, the seate of selfe-fruition, the comfortablest part s own life, the noblest of his sonne's inheritance, a kinde of private princedome, nay, to the possessors thereof, an epitome of the e world, may well deserve, by these attributes, according to the degree of the master, to be decently and delightfully adorned."

"Architecture can want no commendation, where there are noble men, or noble mindes."—SIR HENRY WOTTON.

"Our English word TO BUILD is the Anglo-Saxon Bylban, to confirm, to establish, to make firm and sure and fast, to consolidate. trengthen; and is applicable to all other things as well as to dwelling-places."—DIVERSIONS OF PURLEY.

"Always be ready to speak your mind, and a base man will avoid you."—WILLIAM BLAKE.

VOLUME LXII.—JANUARY TO JUNE, 1892.

FICE: No. 46, CATHERINE STREET, COVENT GARDEN, LONDON, W.C.

Printed at
74-6, Gt. Queen-st., Lincoln's Inn Fields,
London, W.C.

INDEX TO VOLUME LXII.

JANUARY TO JUNE, 1892.

CONTENTS.

Articles and Reviews iii
Notes v
Reports of Meetings, Papers Read, Law Cases, &c. vi
Correspondence: Subjects of Letters viii
Correspondence: Writers of Letters ix
General ix
Architects, &c., of Buildings Illustrated xi
Illustrations xi

ARTICLES AND REVIEWS.

ABBEYS: Kirkstall, 11; Westminster, north transept, 11
Academy, Royal, pictures at, 349
Adam, Robert, centenary of, 174, 228
Album of Academy Drawings, the *Builder*, 42, 186
Amendment of the Building Act, 21
America, Central, sculptures from, 72
Analyses of ancient mortar, 470
Ancient Rome, remains of, 256
Antiquities, Egyptian, 209
Archæology, Greek, 291, 292, 318, 340, 342
Architect, the, and his artists, 403
Architectural: details, Indian, 199; perspective, 84; study by Bramante, 46
Architecture: Dictionary of, 411; military, in Germany, 22; Saracenic, 162
Architecture: at the Paris *Salon*, 369; at the Royal Academy, 333, 353, 373, 394, 414, 432, 454, 460, 475; at the Royal Scottish Academy, 19
Architecture of: the lake dwellings of Europe, 277, 299; of the Teutonic Order of Knights in Prussia, 22
Architecture from a cosmical point of view, 1
Art of the year, French, 395
Art Galleries competition, Glasgow, 317, 335, 342, 357, 502
Artistes Celèbres, 341
Assyria, ancient life in, 26
Asylums for the insane, 197
Athenæum, new offices, 290
Athens; excavations, 318; Parthenon, 205
Atmosphere of railway tunnels, 265
Attic burying-places, 318
Ayr working men's club, 461

BALUSTRADE, copper, Chesterfield-gardens, 502
Band-saw, large, 251
Barrett-Browning Memorial, 415
Bases found at Silchester, 41
Basilicas: St. Peter's, Rome, 2; Silchester, 478
Bath Municipal Buildings, 30, 420
Baths, Cheetham-hill, Manchester, 416
Bedroom fittings, Lennox-gardens, 340
Bell-tower, Rothenburg, 11
Bermondsey Public Library, 60
Birmingham Hospital competn., 217, 246
Bishopsgate, old houses, 135, 304
Blind-fittings, new, 13
Board schools, Kettering, 324
Boilers, hot-water, 126, 145, 271, 293, 311, 326, 342, 363, 385

Books, magazines, pamphlets, &c.: notices, reviews, and articles as to:—
A. A. Notes, 94, 400
Adam, Robert and James, Works in Architecture, 176, 226
"Advertisers' A. B. C.," 85
Album of Academy Architecture, the *Builder*, 42, 186
All the Year Round, 120, 460
Almanacks, 14, 18
American Journal of Archæology, 301
Antiquary, the, 30, 110, 289, 376, 459
Architectural Record (N.Y.), 372, 404
Architectural Review (Boston), 30, 280
Art Journal, 30, 119, 205, 288, 375, 459
Assiter, H. G., Notes on the Public Health Act, 444
Atlantic Monthly, 120, 283, 376, 460
Baker, W. L., Girder Construction, 444
Bath Herald's centenary, 251
Beare, T. H., Building Stones, 351
Berliner *Philologische Wochenshrift* 115
Black and White Academy Guide, 403
Blomfield, R., and Thomas, F. J., The Formal Garden in England, 151
Bolton, A., Mosaic Paving, 72
Bottone, S., Electric Lighting, 403
Bristol and Clifton Pictorial, 210
British Almanac, 18
British Clayworker, the, 329
Builder Album of Academy Architecture, 42, 186
Building Construction, Notes on, 84, 91

Books, Magazines, &c. (continued):—
Bulletin de Correspondance Hellénique, 280
Burdett, H. C., Hospitals and Asylums, 197
Burke, M. D., Brick Pavements, 444
Cartault, A., *Terres Cuites Grecques*, 342
Catalogue: Birmingham Museum, 321; Terra-Cottas, Vienna Museum, 48
Catalogues, trade, 14, 18, 49, 85, 292, 329, 345
Cayley, R. A., Old Basing Church, 14
Century, the, 31, 120, 206, 288, 376, 460
Clark, D. K., Engineers' Pocket-book, 13
Clarke, H., London Improvements, 292
Classical Review, 239
Codrington, T., Macadamised Roads, 105
Construction, Notes on, 84, 91
Contemporary Review, 120, 178, 205
Cornhill Magazine, 206, 289, 460
Cuningham, W. M., Railway through Siberia, 18
Curtius, E., and Adler, F., Olympia, 292
Daremberg's *Dictionnaire des Antiquités*, 301
Dargenty, G., Antoine Watteau, 341
Day, L. F., Nature in Ornament, 39
Denning, D., Cabinet-making, 106
Diaries, 49, 106
Dictionary of Architecture, 411
Dictionary of the World's Press, 49
Directories, Press, 49, 85, 270
Directory, City of London, 270
Douglas, W. D., Geometrical Problem, 342
Dumont, A., *Mélanges d'Archéologie*, 209
Dutton's Essex Almanac, &c., 49
Edinburgh Review, 375
Egypt Exploration Fund: Memoirs, 209
English Illustrated Magazine, 120, 206, 289, 376, 460
Essex Review, 85, 376
Ferguson, F. O., Architectural Perspective, 84
Ferree, B., Christian Thought in Architure, 342
Fire and Water, 274
Forgues, E., Abraham Bosse, 341
Fortnightly Review, 93, 119, 177, 205, 288, 460
Funfzehntes Hallisches Winkelmanns-programm, 292
Garden Oracle, the, 270
Gardner, P., New Chapters in Greek History, 391
Garnier, C., and Ammann, A., *L'Habitation Humaine*, 55
Gazette des Beaux Arts, 119, 205, 288, 375, 459
Gentleman's Magazine, 206
Girard, P., *La Peinture Antique*, 292
Gotch, J. A., Architecture of the Renaissance, 7, 474
Grimshaw, R., Practical Catechism, 49
Handbook for India, Murray's, 208
Harper's Magazine, 30, 120, 206, 289, 460
Harrison, J. P., Pre-Norman Stonework, Oxford, 13
Hasluck, P. N., Milling Machines, 210
Health Record (Dublin), 31
Hellyer, S. S., Plumbing, 84
Heslop, T. H. B., Main Roads, 218
Homolle et Henzey, MM., Works of M. Dumont, 209
Huish, M. B., Year's Art, the, 210
Imray, J., and Biggs, C. H. W., Principles of Mechanical Engineering, 443
Institute *Transactions*, 27
Institution of Civil Engineers: Engineering Education, 18
Jacob, Col., Jeypore Portfolio, 109
Jahrbuch, Prussian Archæological, 280, 320
Jervis, G., *I Tesori Sotterranei dell' Italia*, 208

Books, Magazines, &c. (continued):—
Johnston's Map, England & Wales, 444
Journal, Franklin Institute, 6, 178, 337
Law Almanack, 14
Lawford, G. M., House-drainage, 444
Laxton's Price-book, 443
Lefort, P., Velasquez, 341
Lethaby, W. R., Architecture, Mysticism, and Myth, 1
Lindley, P., New Holidays in Essex, 403
Local Govt. Handy Series, 49, 162
Local Government Journal, 295
Lockwood's Price-book, 443
Lodge, H. C., Boston, U.S., 48
Loftie, W. J., London Suburbs, 496
Longman's Magazine, 206
Ludgate Monthly, 120
Mackay, T., Plea for Liberty, 292
Macdonell, A. A., Camping Out, 444
Macmillan's Magazine, 206
Mackmurdo, A. H., Plain Handicrafts, 341
Magazine of Art, 30, 119, 205, 281, 288, 375, 459
Maguire, T. M., London Householders' Chart, 106
Manufacturers' Export Journal, 85, 387
Maps of London, new, 295, 437
Masner, K., Catalogue of Terra-Cottas Vienna, 48
Maspéro, G., Life in Ancient Egypt and Assyria, 26
Michel, Emile: Gerard Terburg, 341; Les Brueghel, 341
Middleton, Prof., Ancient Rome, 255
Mitchell, F., Building Construction, 291
Mitchell, G. B. Hints to Taxpayers, 214
Mitchell's Press Directory, 270
Mittheilungen of the German Archæological Institute, 73, 257, 495
Murray, A. S., Greek Archæology, 340
Murray's Handbook for India, 208
National Review, 372, 460
Natural Science, 135
Naville, E., Hieroglyphic Papyri, 209
New Review, 120, 205
Nineteenth Century, 31, 120, 178, 205, 288, 376, 460
Notes on Building Construction, 84, 91
Oxborrow and Money-Kent's Office Manual, 342
Pall Mall Guide to Pictures, 475
Palliser's Specification Blanks, 444
Paris, P., Elatée, 291
Phipson, W. W., Memoir of, 210
Planat, P., *Encyclopédie de l'Architecture*, 310
Portfolio, the, 31
Press Directories, 49, 85, 270
Quarterly Review, 73
Quarterly Statement, Palestine Exploration Fund, 120, 370
Redgrave, G. R., History of Water-Colour Painting in England, 403
Revue des Deux Mondes, 205, 459
Revue Générale, 205, 460
Revue Scientifique, 289
Rogers, S. E., *Local Government Annual*, 106
Russell, S. A., Electric Light Cables, 291
Scientific American, 43
Scribner's Magazine, 30, 206, 288, 376, 460
Sell's Dictionary of the Press, 40
Shelley's Press Directory, 270
Shute, John, First and Chiefe Groundes of Architecture, 203
Spon's Price-book, 443
Sprague's Pocket Diary, 49
Stanford's London Water Map, 437
Temple Bar, 120, 289
Timber, 85
Trade catalogues, 14, 18, 49, 85, 202, 329, 345
Transactions, American Society of Civil Engineers, 48, 258, 302, 337
Transactions, Edinburgh Architectural Association, 135
Transactions, Inst. of Architects, 27
Watts, G. F., Plain Handicrafts, 341

Books, Magazines, &c. (continued):—
White, William H., The Architect and his Artists, 403
Wiener Vorlegeblätter für Archäologische, 292
Williams, J., Sketches of Village Buildings, 49
Willing's Press Guide, 270
Wolff, A. R., Ventilation of Bldgs., 291
Zeitschrift für Bauweisen, 281

Bosse, Abraham, 341
Boston, reredos at St. Botolph's, 330
Boston, U.S., history of, 48
Bradford smallpox hospital, 308, 365
Bramante, architectural study by, 46
Brasses: William de Etchingham and William Fienles, 226
Brewer, H. W., on Old St. Peter's, 2
Brickwork, efflorescence in, 321
Bridge, cantilever, Red Rock, U.S.A., 302
Bridge, railway, design for a, 307
Bridge, Tower, 476
Broderers' Company's Hall, 206
"Brooklands," Weybridge, 340
Bronze objects found at Silchester, 41
British Gallery, proposed, 226
Brittany, cemetery erections in, 44
Brueghels, the, 341
Builder Album of Academy Drawings, 42, 186
Builders Price-books, 443
Building Act and the Institute, 21
Building construction, 84, 91, 291
Building Exhibition, Islington, 228
Building stones, 237, 270, 351
Burlington Club, pictures at, 494
Burlington House, Old Masters at, 25
Bury Municipal Bldgs., design for, 380
Bury St. Edmunds, Tudor Memorial Tomb, 381

CABINET-MAKING, art of, 106
Cables, electric light, 291
Caen, tower at, 12
Canals, Russian, 429
Cantilever bridge, Red Rock, 302
Carpenters' Hall, exhibition at, 374
Cartoons for window, Euston Church, 360
Carvings, North Walsham, 62
Castles: German, 22; Grandtully, 206
Cathedrals: Chichester, 186; Ely, 266, 288; Gloucester, 46; Hereford, 102; Lincoln (Wren's Library), 250; Llandaff, 358; Norwich, 288; Oxford, 13, 440, 465; St. Paul's, 10; Old St. Paul's, 11; St. Peter's, Rome, 11; Old St. Peter's, Rome, 2; Peterborough, 451, 487, 509; Victoria, British Columbia, 392
Celtic monastery, Skellig Michael, 141
Cemetery erections, French, 44
Central America, sculptures from, 72
Chalices and patens, 58
Changes at the Institute, 460
Chapels: Radley College, 340; St. James, San Miniato, decoration, 480; Tonbridge School, 380
Chapter-house, design for a, 307
Chart for London householders, 106
Cheetham Baths, 416
Chester, old, 104, 162, 206, 248, 288, 420; Roman hypocaust, 307
Chichester Cathedral, 186
Chimney-piece, East Grinstead, 391
Choirs: Ely Cathedral, 288; Peterborough Cathedral, 451, 487, 509
Christ Church Cathedral, Oxford, 440, 465
Christ Church Priory, Hants, 409
Christian thought in architecture, 342
Church, design for a, 62
Church for a mountainous district, 30
Churches: All Saints', Hertford, 6, 14, 31; Mission, Canterbury-road, S.E., 80; proposed, at Drogheda, 420; Long Clawson, 140; near Peterborough, 268; St. John the Baptist, Kensington, 323; St. Jude's, Preston, 461; St. Mary, Woolnoth, 420; Seascale, 46

ARTICLES AND REVIEWS (continued):—

Church-plate, 58
Churchyard crosses, Brittany, 45
Circulation of water, 50
Cloisters, Radley College, 340
Club, workmen's, Ayr, 461
Coils and radiators, 423
Colleges: Hymers', Hull, 46; Maynooth: mural painting, 307; Radley, 340; St. Cuthbert's, Worksop, 80
Committees on Town-holdings, 493
Competition designs: Barrett-Browning Memorial, 415; Birmingham Hospital, 217, 246; Cathedral, Victoria, B.C., 392, 444; Glasgow Art Galleries, 317, 335, 342, 357, 502; Oxford Municipal Buildings, 491
Composition by Bramante, 46
Composition of ancient mortar, 470
Construction, 84, 91, 291
Construction of lake dwellings, 277, 299
Cranes, safety provision for, 459
Cross, processional, St. Oswald's, Durham, 379
Crypt, old, Chester, 206, 248
Crystal Palace Electrical Exhibition, 113
Cosmical view of architecture, 1
Costessey, sketches at, 62
Country house, study for a, 46
Coutances, tower at, 12

DAILY LIFE in the ancient world, 26
Decoration: Chapel of St. James, San Miniato, 480; Indian, 199, 206
Decorative painting at the *Salon*, 395
Decorative work by the Adams, 174, 226
Delacroix monument, Paris, 12
Design by Bramante, 40
Designs for: Barrett-Browning Memorial, 415; Birmingham General Hospital, 217, 246; British Gallery, 226; Bury Municipal Buildings, 380; Cathedral, Victoria, B.C., 392, 444; chapter-house, 307; church at Drogheda, 420; frieze, 480; Glasgow Art Galleries, 317, 335, 342, 357, 502; large town mansion, 62; mountain church, 30; Oxford Municipal Buildings, 491; public library, 122; sedan-chair, 226; steeple, 288; stone railway bridge, 307, 384; town church, 62; wall-papers, 323
Destructor for sewer-gas, 9
Details, Indian, 199
Directories, 49, 85, 270
Dictionary of Architecture, 411
Discoveries at Silchester, 40
Distribution of: electricity, 291; power from central stations, 131, 166
Domes: St. Paul's, 10; St. Peter's, 11
Domrémy, Memorial of Jeanne d'Arc, 246
Doorways, Norwich, 62
Drawing-room, Weybridge, 340
Drogheda, proposed church, 420
Ducal Palace, original, Venice, 132
Dwelling, woman's influence on the, 57
Dwellings, lake, 277, 299

EARL'S COURT-SQUARE: flats, 502
Early English hall, Lincoln, 374
East Anglia, wayside notes in, 62
East Grinstead, chimney-piece at, 381
Efflorescence in brickwork, 321
Egypt: ancient, life in, 26; Exploration, 209
Elateia, 291
Election, London County Council, 173
Electric: cables, 291; lighting, 403; motors, 131; Electrical Exhibition at the Crystal Palace, 113
Electricity, distribution of, 291
Ely Cathedral, 200, 288
Enamelling, history of, 28
Encyclopédie de l'Architecture, Planat's, 310
English: gardens, 151; iron trade in 1891, 8
Engraving by Bramante, a, 46
Europe, lake dwellings of, 277, 290
Excavations: Athens, 318; Silchester, 40
Exhibitions: Building, at Islington, 238; Carpenters' Hall, 374; Electrical, at the Crystal Palace, 113; Polytechnic Institution, 33; sanitary, at Hornsey, 505
Exploration of Egypt, 209

FACTORY near Malvern, 80
Fellows, election of, at the Institute, 469
Fiennes brass, Hurstmonceaux, 226
Fireplace, old, at Chester, 104
Fittings in bedroom, Lennox-gardens, 340
Fittings for blinds, 13
Fixing portable ranges, 31
Flats, Earl's Court-square, 502
Formal gardens, 151
French: art of the year, 395: cemetery erections, old, 44; encyclopædia of architecture, 310; towers, 12
Frieze, design for a, 480
Furniture, bedroom, 340

GALLERIES, Art, Glasgow, 317, 335, 342, 357, 502
Gallery, proposed British, 226
Gardens, formal, 151
Gardner, J. S., on enamelling, 28
Gas-engines, 131
Gates, garden, 152, 153
Gavarni, 341
Geology of Italy, 208
Geometrical manual, a, 342
German architecture, Mediæval, 22
Geymüller, Baron, on Teutonic architecture, 22
Glasgow Art Galleries competition, 317, 335, 342, 357, 502
Gloucester Cathedral, condition of, 46
Grandtully Castle, 206
Graves, Attic, 318
Grayingham Church, reredos, 461
Great Britain, lake dwellings of, 299
Great St. Helens, old houses, 135, 304
Greek: archæology, 291, 292, 318, 340, 342; history, 391; terra-cottas, 342
Ground-rents, taxation of, 493
Guildhall, Lavenham, 323
Guildhall, Westminster, 376

HABITATION, the human, 55
Hall and staircase, Queen's-gate, 226
Halls: Broderers' Company's, 206; Canterbury-road, S.E., 80; Cheetham, Manchester, 416; Early English, Lincoln, 374
Handbooks: Greek Archæology, 340; India and Ceylon, 208
Handicrafts, plain, 341
Hanover Schools, Grosvenor-square, 140
Heat, radiation of, 15, 34
Hereford Cathedral, 102
Hertford, All Saints' Church, 6, 14, 31
Hieroglyphic papyri, 209
Highgate, sanitary samples at, 505
Historic towns: Boston, U.S., 48
History, Greek, new chapters, 391
History of: enamelling, 28; human habitation, 55; water-colour painting, 403
Holman's sewer-gas exhauster, 9
Hornsey, sanitary exhibition at, 505
Horticultural buildings, heating, 107, 126, 145, 166, 190, 211, 231, 249
Hospitals: Birmingham, competition, 217; Small-pox, Bradford, 308, 365; South London Ophthalmic, 289, 303
Hot-Water, warming by (see "Student's Column").
House, the Jew's, Lincoln, 30, 106
House and shop, Redruth, 104
House and studio, a painter's, 122
Houses: Bromley, 104; Chesterfield-gardens, 502; Chislehurst, 226; country, 46; "Munstead Corner," Godalming, 62; Queen's-gate, 122, 226; Stanmore Park estate, 226; Wiltshire, 480; Wokingham, 122; Wraysbury, 461
Houses of Parliament, Melbourne, 340
Houses, old: Bishopsgate, 135, 304; Chester, 162, 288, 420; Ipswich, 80; Norwich, 62
Human habitation, the, 55
Hurstmonceaux, brass at, 226
Hydraulic motors, 131, 166
Hymers' College, Hull, 46
Hypocaust, Roman, Chester, 307

ILLUSTRATIONS of old Chester, 104, 162, 206, 248, 288, 307, 420
Imperial Institute, 480, 497
Improvements, London-street, 292
India, Murray's Handbook for, 208
Indian architectural details, 199, 206
Industrial Exhibition, Polytechnic, 33
Infirmary, Rotherhithe, 288
Inland navigation in Russia, 429
Insane, asylums for the, 197
Institute of Architects: proposed changes, 469; suggestions for a Building Act, 21
Ipswich, old house at, 80
Ireland, building stones of, 237, 270
Iron trade, English, in 1891, 8
Ispahan, Mosque of Shah Abbas, 140
Italy: lake dwellings of, 278; subterranean treasures of, 208

"JEANNE D'ARC:" Sculptured group for Domrémy, 246
"Jew's House," Lincoln, 30, 106
Jeypore Portfolio, the, 199
Jib-cranes, safety, 459

KIRKSTALL ABBEY, 11
Klingen Thor, Rothenburg, 11

LADY'S BOWER, Watergate Row South, Chester, 420
Lake dwellings, architecture of, 277, 299
Landscape gardener, sins of the, 151
Lanternes des morts, Brittany, 44
Lavenham Guildhall, 323
Ledbury, Barrett-Browning Memorial, 415
Lennox-gardens, bedroom in, 340
Letters, Paris, 7, 95, 179, 263, 354, 434
Liberty, a plea for, 292
Libraries: Bermondsey, 60; design for public, 122; Wren's, Lincoln, 259
Life in ancient Egypt and Assyria, 26
Life of Robert Adam, 174
Lighting, electric, 403
Lincoln: Early English hall, 374: "Jew's House," 30, 106; Wren's Library, 259
Liverpool, hydraulic power in, 132, 166
Llandaff Cathedral, 358
Local Government Annual, the, 106
Lodge at Compton, Sherborne, 324
Log-saw, large, 251
London: County Council Election, 173; street improvements, 292

MACADAMISED roads, 105, 218, 248
Magazines and Reviews, notes on the, 30, 85, 93, 119, 205, 288, 375, 459
Mansion, Stanford Hall, Notts, 162
Mansion, town, design for, 62
Maynooth Chapel, mural painting, 307
Mediæval German architecture, 22
Melbourne Houses of Parliament, 340
Memorial to Mary Tudor, 381
Mersey Tunnel Railway, 48
Metropolitan: Building Acts, 21; Railway, experiments on, 265
Milling machines, 210
Mineral-water factory, Malvern, 80
Mission-church, Canterbury-rd., S.E., 80
Monastery, Skellig Michael, 141
Monumental brasses, Sussex, 226
Monuments: Attic, 318; Delacroix, Paris, 12; Mrs. Rowley, St. Neots, 360
Mortar, ancient, 470
Mosaic pavement, 72, 502
Mosaics in St. Mark's, Venice, 30
Mosque of Shah Abbas, Ispahan, 140
Mountain church, a, 30
"Mountfield," Chislehurst, 226
Municipal Buildings: Bath, 30, 420; Oxford, 491; Sheffield, 400
"Munstead Corner," Godalming, 62
Mural painting, Maynooth Chapel, 307
Murray's Greek Archæology, 340
Murray's Handbook for India, 208
Music-room, Putney Heath, 400
Mysticism and architecture, 1

NATURE in ornament, 39
Navigation, inland, in Russia, 429
New chapters in Greek history, 391
New Gallery exhibition, the, 338
Norwich: Cathedral, 288; sketches in, 62
Notes on: building construction, 84, 91; chalices and patens, 58; the history of enamelling, 28; the magazines and reviews, 30, 85, 93, 119, 205, 288, 375, 459; from Paris, 7, 95, 179, 263, 354, 373, 434

OFFICE-MANUAL, a, 342
Offices for the *Athenæum*, 290
Offices, Copthall-avenue, 246
Old Chester, 104, 162, 206, 248, 288, 307, 420
Old Masters at Burlington House, 25
Old pictures at the Burlington Club, 494
Old St. Paul's, London, 11
Old St. Peter's, Rome, 2
Olympia, 292
Ophthalmic Hospital, Sth. Lndn., 289, 303
Ornament: Indian, 199, 206; nature in, 39; Saracenic, 162, 189
Ossuary, St. Pol de Léon, Finistère, 44
Oxford: Christ Church Cathedral, 13, 440, 465; Municipal Buildings competition, 491

PAINTER'S house and studio, a, 122
Painting, a French Manual on, 292
Painting, mural, Maynooth, 307
Palaces: Bishop Lloyd's, Chester, 104, 288; Ducal, Venice, 132
Paperhangings, designs for, 323
Papyri, hieroglyphic, 209
Paris, letters from, 7, 95, 179, 263, 354, 434
Parliament Houses, Melbourne, 340
Parry, J., on hydraulic power in Liverpool, 132, 166
Parthenon, Athens, 205
Patens and chalices, 58
Pavements, tesselated, at Silchester, 41
Paving, mosaic, 72, 502
Payment of quantity-surveyors, 412
Perspective, architectural, 84
Peterborough: Cathedral: choir, 451, 487, 509; sketches near, 268
Pewsham House, Wilts. 480
Phipson, the late W. W., 210
Pictures: Burlington Club, 494; New Gallery, 338; Old Masters, Burlington House, 25; Royal Academy, 349
Pipes, hot-water, 65, 85, 107, 126, 145, 166, 190, 211, 231, 484
Planat's *Encyclopédie de l'Architecture*, 310
Planning of Asylums, 197
Plates of Building Construction, 291
Plumbing, principles and practice of, 84
Polytechnic Institution exhibition, 33
Portable ranges, fixing, 31
Pottery found at Silchester, 41
Power, hydraulic, 131, 166
Power distribution from centres, 131, 166
Press directories, 49, 85, 270
Price-books, builders', 413
Priory, Christ Church, Hants, 499
Processional cross, St. Oswald's, Durham, 379
Prussia, architecture of the Teutonic order of Knights, 22
Pulpit, San Cesareo, Rome, 480

QUANTITY-SURVEYORS and their fees, 412
Queen's-gate, houses at, 122, 226

RADIATION of heat, 15, 34
Radiators and coils, 423
Radley College, 340
Railway, Mersey Tunnel, 48
Railway bridge, design for a, 307, 384
Railway tunnels, atmosphere of, 265
Ranges, portable, fixing, 31
Ransome's band-saw for large logs, 251
Red Rock cantilever bridge, 302
Reference-books, 49, 85, 270, 295
Remains of ancient Rome, 255
Renishaw Hall, Derbyshire: staircase, 140
Report on Town Holdings, 493
Reredoses: Grayingham Church, 461; St. Botolph's, Boston, 380
Retable, St. Alban's, Teddington, 461
Reviews and magazines, 30, 85, 93, 119, 205, 288, 375, 459
Right of quantity surveyors to fees, 412
Rivers, Russian, 429
Roads, macadamised, 105, 218, 248
Roller-blind fittings, 13
Roman: hypocaust, Chester, 307; remains at Sbeitla, 460; remains at Silchester, 40
Rome: ancient, 255; dome of St. Peter's, 11; Old St. Peter's, 2; pulpit in San Cesareo, 480
Rothenburg, the Klingen Thor, 11
Rotherhithe Infirmary, 288
Rowley *Monument*, St. Neot's Ch., 360
"Rows" of Chester, the, 162, 228
Royal Academy: architecture at, 333, 353, 373, 394, 414, 432, 454, 460, 475; pictures at 349; sculpture at, 416
Royal Academy drawings, *Builder* Album, 180
Royal Scottish Academy, architecture, 19
Ruins, Skellig Michael, 141
Russia, inland navigation in, 429

SAFETY jib-cranes, 459
Saint Alban's Church, Teddington: retable, 461
St. Botolph's, Boston: reredos, 380
St. Cuthbert's College, Worksop, 80
St. John-the-Baptist's, Kensington, 323
St. Jude's Church, Preston, 461
St. Mark's, Venice: mosaics, 30
St. Mary Woolnoth, 420
St. Neot's Ch., Rowley Monument, 360
St. Olave's Infirmary, Rotherhithe, 288
St. Oswald's, Durham: processional cross, 379
St. Paul's Cathedral, 10; Old St. Paul's, 11
St. Peter's, Rome, 11; Old St. Peter's, 2
St. Stephen's Schools, Canonbury, 206
Salon: architecture at the, 369; decorative painting at the, 395
Salon of the Champ de Mars, Paris, 397
Sandstones of Ireland, 237, 270
Sanitary samples at Highgate, 505
Saracenic ornament, 162, 189
Sbeitla, temples at, 460
School Chapel, Tonbridge, 380
Schools: Canonbury, 206; Gilbert-street, Grosvenor-sq., 140; Kettering, 324
Schweppe & Co.'s factory, Malvern, 80
Science of construction, the, 91
Scotch cranes, safety, 459
Sculpture: "Jeanne d'Arc," 246; New Gallery, 339; Royal Academy, 416
Sculptures from Central America, 72
Seascale Church, 46
Sedan-chair, design for, 226
Sessions House, Westminster, 376
Sèvres manufactory, the, 7
Sewer-gas exhauster, Holman's, 9
Sheffield Municipal Buildings, 400
Sherborne tomb, Chichester Cath., 189
Shop, Redruth, Cornwall, 104
Silchester, discoveries at, 40, 478
Skellig Michael, Ireland, 141
Sketches: in East Anglia, 62; near Peterborough, 268
Smallpox hospital, Bradford, 308, 365
South Kensington Museum, sculptures from Central America, 72
South London Ophthalmic Hsptl., 289, 303
Sparrowe's house, Ipswich, 80
Stained-glass windows: Euston Church, 360; St. Mary's, Leigh, 122
Staircases: house in Queen's-gate, 226; Renishaw Hall, Derbyshire, 140; St. Paul's Cathedral, 11; Sheffield Municipal Buildings, 400
Standage, H. C., on efflorescence in brickwork, 321
Stanford Hall, Nottinghamshire, 162, 214
Steam-rolling on main roads, 218, 248
Steeple, design for a, 288
Stone railway bridge, design for, 307, 384
Stones, building, tests of, 351
Street improvements, London, 292
Student's Column, the: Warming Buildings by Hot-water:—15, 34, 50, 65, 85, 107, 126, 145, 166, 190, 211, 231, 249, 271, 293, 311, 326, 342, 363, 385, 404, 423, 444, 463, 484, 507
Studio, a painter's, 122
Study by Bramante, a, 46
Study for a country house, 46
Subterranean treasures of Italy, 208
Suggestions for a new Building Act, 21
Sundials, 152
Sussex brasses, two, 226
Switzerland, lake dwellings of, 277, 299
Symbolism, cosmical, 2
Symbolism in architecture, 342

TATE GALLERY, proposed, 226
Taxation of ground-rents, 493
Temples, three, at Sbeitla, 460
Terburg, 341
Terra-cottas: Greek, 342; Vienna Museum, 48
Tests of building-stones, 351
Teutonic architecture, 22
Tite Prize design for a steeple, 288
Token House, Copthall-avenue, 246
Tombs: Attic, 318; Bishop Sherborne, Chichester Cathedral, 189; Memorial, Mary Tudor, Bury St. Edmunds, 381
Tonbridge School Chapel, 380
Tower Bridge, the, 476
Tower opening, Norwich Cathedral, 288
Towers: Imperial Institute, 480; Rothenburg, 11; St. Etienne, Caen, 12; St Pierre, Coutances, 12
Town Holdings Committee's Report, 493
Town mansion, design for, 62
Treasures, Subterranean, of Italy, 208
Tudor Memorial Tomb, Bury St. Edmunds, 381
Tunnels, railway, atmosphere of, 265

VASES, Greek, 292
Velasquez, 341
Venetian blind-fittings, 13
Venice: Original Ducal Palace, 132; mosaics in St. Mark's, 30
Ventilation of: buildings, 291; sewers, 9
Victoria, British Columbia: proposed cathedral, 392, 444
Vienna Museum, terra-cottas in, 48
Villa residence at Bromley, 104
Volga, the, 429

WALES, lake dwellings of, 290
Wall-decoration, San Miniato, 480
Wall-paper, designs for, 323
Waller, F. S., on Gloucester Cathedral, 47
Warming buildings by hot-water (See "Student's Column")
Water, circulation of, 50
Water-colour painting, history of, 403
Watteau, 341
Wayside Notes in East Anglia, 62
Westminster Abbey: north transept, 11
Westminster: Guildhall, 376
Windows, stained glass: Euston Church, 360; St. Mary's Church, Leigh, 122
Wokingham, house at, 122
Woman, the dwelling as influenced by, 56
Woodwork at Carpenters' Hall, 374
Working Men's Club, Ayr, 461
Works of reference, 49, 85, 270, 295
Works of Robt. and Jas. Adam, 174, 226
Wren's Library, Lincoln Cathedral, 259

NOTES.

A. A. Notes, 94
Abbey Craig, Stirling, 320
Abbey Church, Notre Dame, Fécamp, 42
Academy, Royal: new Associates, 73
Accidents: electric light, 200; to horses on asphalte roads, 372
Advertising architects, 43, 58, 321
Agora, Athens, 134, 257
Air, wet screen for, 74
Albert Palace, Battersea Park, 302
Album of Academy Architecture, the *Builder*, 42
Aldrich's experiments with solenoids, 387
Almshouses, Skinners' Co.'s, 135, 258
Amalgamated Society of Engineers, 154
Ameer of Bokhara as sanitary reformer, 475
America: concrete floors in, 413; height of buildings in, 74
American: National Gallery, proposed, 6; railways, 7; roads, 372; School at Athens, 134
American Journal of Archæology, 301
American Society of Civil Engineers: *Transactions*, 258
Anderson, Dr. Rowand, on technical education, 74
Anniversary of re-building Hamburg, 393
Antiquities: Etruscan, 301; King of Hanover's 337
Apethorpe, 337
Archæology: Greek, 73, 115, 134, 154, 257, 258, 280, 301, 320, 495; nautical, 320
Architekten-Verein, Berlin, 393
Armourers' and Braziers' Exhibition, 372
Artillery-ground, Westminster, 258
Artisans' dwellings competition, Halifax, 200, 210
"Artistic and Literary Association," 58
Architects: advertising, 43, 58, 321; as directors of companies, 394; as shareholders, 302
Architects, remuneration of, 280
Architectural Record, New York, 372, 404
Architectural Review, Boston, 280
Architecture: Assyrian, 320; errors about, 454; Greek, 73, 115, 177, 248; from the painters' and sculptors' standpoint, 94; of the Parthenon, 177; Renaissance, 7, 474; at the Royal Academy, 281
Art, Japanese, 221
Art exhibitions, Berlin, 453
Art galleries: Edinburgh, 116; British, proposed, 200, 269
Art metal-work, 372
Art-needlework, Danish, 353
Arts and industries, home, 497
Ashmolean Museum, Oxford, 474
Asphalte roads, dangers of, 372
Assessors, technical, wanted in the law courts, 74, 155, 302
Assessors in competitions, 200
Associates, new: Royal Academy, 73; Royal Scottish Academy, 201, 281
Assyrian architecture, 320
Athens, excavations at, 134, 257, 258
Australia, competition mania, 221

Bailly, the late A. N., 27
Balfour, A. J., on art, 352
Barclay, E., pictures by, 302
Basilica found at Silchester, 453, 478
Battersea Park: Albert Palace, 302
Battersea Parochial Offices competition, 5
Beaumaris Pier competition, 57
Bedford Estate, overcrowding on the, 220
"Beehive" tomb, Mycenæ, 495
Berlin: Architekten-Verein, 393; art exhibitions, 453; building regulations, 393; cathedral, 135, 200, 220, 239; Exhibition in 1898, 319; extension of boundaries, 371; disturbances at, 178; municipal architects, 320; municipal buildings, 320, 371; Schinkel Medal, 220; school-building rules, 177; street names in German letters, 432; Unter den Linden, 320; water supply, 74, 107
Berliner Philologische Wochenschrift, 115
Bethnal-green Poor's Land, 6
"Betterment" and the County Ccl., 431
Birmingham: railway collision, 453; Water Bill, 5, 199
Bishopsgate: old houses, 135, 304; railway collision, 496
Blunder, a scientific, 6
Board of Trade and railway rates, 27, 473
Boiler insurance and inspection, 412
Bokhara, sanitary measures in, 475
Borough Market, enlargement of, 74
Braziers' Exhibition, the, 372
Bridges: Cromwell-road, 431; Sandwich, 135
Bristol Cathedral, 472
Bristowe, Mr., M.P., death of, 453
British Museum; lectures at, 43, 57, 73, 94, 177, 248; terra-cotta cornice, 116
Brockwell Park, 432, 453
Bronzes, Greek, 73
Builder, the: and American piracy, 372; Album of Academy Architecture, 42
Builders and the School Board, 155
Building Act consolidation, proposed, 7
Building by-laws, 154
Building Exhibition, Islington, 42
Building Regulations: Berlin, 393; Glasgow, 115 128, 156
Building Stones of Texas, 93
Bulletin de Correspondance Hellénique, 280
Butcher, Prof., on art, 352
By-laws: building, 154: under the Public Health Act, 154
Byzantine church in Cilicia, 301

Cable industry, the, 6
Camberwell Church, 201
Campo Santo, Pisa, 27
Carpenters' strike, Canterbury, in 1787, 221
Casings for electric light wires, 337
Castle, Ravenscraig, 43
Castles, Scotch, 135
Catalogue, Birmingham Museum, 321
Catastrophe at Gateshead, 5
Cathedral Song-School, Edinburgh: decoration, 259
Cathedrals, Berlin, 135, 200, 220, 239; Bristol, 472; Lincoln, 301; St. Alban's, Lord Grimthorpe's work at, 384
Cats, Mdme. Ronner's paintings of, 414
Cemetery, Merovingian, at Andresy, 413
Census Report, the, 496
Centenary of death of Sir Joshua Reynolds, 134
Cesspool emptying into the Thames, 7
Chancery-lane, demolitions in, 28, 239
Charcoal-burners of Croydon, 372
Chariot group of Mausoleum, 154, 177
Chatham electric light accident, 200
Cheap trains for workmen, 393
Chicago: collapse of a building in, 394; Exhibition, 320, 337; water supply, 135
Chimney disaster at Cleckheaton, 279
Chipiez's model of Parthenon, 114, 219
Churches: All Saints', Hertford, 6, 14, 31; Byzantine, in Cilicia, 301; City, 154, 155, 336; Notre Dame, Fécamp, 42; St. Anne's, Soho, 474; St. Dunstan-in-the-East, 336; St. Gervais, Paris, 240; St. Giles's, Camberwell, 201; St. Helen's, Bishopsgate, 154, 155; St. Mary, Woolnoth, 7, 154; St. Werburgh, Derby, 353; Wrexham, 393
Churchyards: Spitalfields, 155; Westminster, 240
Cilica, Byzantine church in, 301
City churches, 154, 155, 336
Clarence, Duke of, the late, 42, 64
Classical Review, 239
Classification of railway rates, 27, 257
Cleckheaton chimney disaster, the, 279
Clock, proposed new, for St. Paul's, 94
Clock-tower, Willenhall, 393
Coal-trade strike in the North, 176, 199, 220, 239, 280, 336, 393, 431
Coal-porters, strike of, London, 134
Coffee-houses, old City, 220
Colliers of Croydon, 372
Collisions, railway, Birmingham, 453; Bishopsgate, 496
Commissions, illicit, 115
Commission, Royal, on Metropolitan Water Supply, 220
Commissions, surveyors', 200
Common, West Wickham, 221
Compensation of architects, 280
Competition mania in Australia, 221
Competitions: Artisans' dwellings, Halifax, 200, 210; Battersea Parochial Offices, 5; Beaumaris pier, 57; County Council Buildings, Stafford, 258; drainage of Sofia, 301; Dublin, 454; Llanelly Town-hall, 321; Whitworth Institute, 75, 94
Competitions, assessors in, 200
Concrete floor, monolithic, 413
Consolidation of the Building Act, 7
Contractors and the London County Council, 431
Conversazioni: Institute of Architects, 495; Royal Society, 352, 473
Coode, Sir J., 135, 191
Coombe Wood, Surrey, 372
Cornice, terra-cotta, found at Civita Lavinia, 116
Coroner's jury's verdict in Chicago, 394
County Buildings, Edinburgh, 201
County Council, Middlesex, 155
County Council Buildings, Stafford, 258
Covent-Garden, the "Hummums," 337
Cowl, Wheeler & Sons', 454
Critics, the, and Mr. Whistler, 240
Cromwell-road bridge, 431
Crookes, Prof., on electricity, 93
Croydon Charcoal-burners, 372
Crystal Palace Electrical Exhibition, 42, 75, 136, 177
Cutting off the water supply, 135, 214, 509

Danger of asphalte paving, 372
Danish School of Art Needlework, 353
Davis, H. W. B., pictures by, 58
Death of the Duke of Clarence, 42, 64
Decoration: Edinburgh, 259; Japanese, 221
Demolitions: Her Majesty's Theatre, 394; Chancery-lane, 28, 239
Derby, St. Werburgh's Church, 353
Design of stained glass, 164
Designs for Battersea Parochial Offices, 5
Dinner, Royal Academy, 352
Diphtheria at Wellington College, 42
Disaster, Hampstead Heath Station, 319
Discoveries: in the Athenian Agora, 134, 257; of a basilica at Silchester, 453, 478; of a Merovingian Cemetery, 413
Disturbances at Berlin, 178
Divining-rod, belief in the, 259
Dome, Chicago Exhibition, 337
Domestic sanatoria, 73
Dowdeswell's Galleries, 94, 178
Drainage: Edinburgh Castle, 116; house, 43; Sofia, 301
Drainage-basin of the Irwell, 394
Drawing in elementary schools, 200
Drawings: at the Institute, 57; by W. L. Wyllie, 94
Dublin: competition, 454; Trinity College, 496

Dudley Gallery, 58, 155, 302
Durham coal strike, 176, 199, 220, 239, 280, 336, 393, 431
Dust, 93, 125
Dysart House, Fifeshire, 43

Edinburgh: Architectural Assoc., 135; Castle drainage, 116; Children's Hospital, 281; County Buildings, 201; decoration by Mrs. Traquair, 259; proposed Knox statue, 497; Ramsay Lodge, 432; Scottish National Gallery, 116; public hall, 43
Education, technical: Edinburgh, 74; London, 134
Education Department and the teaching of drawing, 200
Eiffel Tower, Paris, 373
Eiffel Tower, imitation, Wembley, 280
Eight-hours question, the, 393, 496
Egyptology, University College, 474
Election, London County Council, 199
Electric-light: accidents, 200; in omnibuses, 474; in St. Pancras, 281; systems of wiring, 352; in theatres, 413; wire-casings, 337
Electrical: Exhibition, Crystal Palace, 42, 75, 136, 177; experiments, 337
Electricity, possibilities of, 93
Electro-magnetic machinery, 178
Emanuel Hospital, Westminster, 453
Embroidery, Danish, 353
Engineering competitions, 57
Engineering trade dispute in the North, 92, 116, 154
English Renaissance, the, 7, 474
Enteric fever, Foundling Hospital, 93
Epidauros, excavations at, 495
Eretria, excavations at, 301
Errors about Architecture, 454
Etchings, exhibition of, 201
Ether, 431
Etruscan antiquities, 301
Euston Station, 28, 352
Evidence of experts, the, 155
Examinations at the Institute, 4
Excavations: Athens, 134, 257; Epidauros, 495; Eretria, 301; Mycenæ, 495
Exchange, Manchester, 319
Exchange, Works and Construction, 281
Exhibition: Building, Islington, 42; brass and metal work, 372; Chicago, 320, 337; Electrical, Crystal Palace, 42, 75, 136, 177; International, Isle of Man, 135; proposed, Berlin, 319; Vienna, 394
Experiments, electrical, 337

"Faculties" for church work, 258
Farringdon Market, 43, 240, 453
Fécamp, Church of Notre Dame, 42
Fellowship, Institute of Architects, 452
Fever at the Foundling Hospital, 93
Finance of the London County Council, 5
Fine Art Society, 58, 94, 201, 475
Fires: All Saints' Church, Hertford, 6, 14, 31; Hotel Royal, New York, 115
Floor, monolithic concrete, 413
Fog, screen for, 74
Fogs, loss entailed by, 5, 28, 134
Fortnightly Review, 93, 177
Foundling Hospital, fever at, 93
Fountain, Willenhall, 393
Fowler *v.* Walker, 413
French Gallery, the, 259
Frescoes: Manchester, 372; Pisa, 27
Fuel-gas, 6

Gallery of British Art, proposed, 200, 269
Galton, Sir D., on ventilation, 74
Gaol, Horsemonger-lane, 201
Gardner, Prof., on the mausoleum sculptures, 154, 177
Gas as fuel, 6
Gateshead theatre catastrophe, 5
Geological survey of Texas, 92
German: architectural publications, 321; honour for Sir J. Millais, 453; slide-rules, 155
Germany, water supply in, 74
Giddy *v.* Ross, 200
Gladstone, Mr., and eight hours, 496
Glasgow Building Bill, 115, 128, 156
Globe, the, and the *Builder*, 259
Grachen, Mr., and patent-fees, 336, 453
Goupil Gallery, the, 240
Granites, foreign, 5, 93
Graveyard, St. Margaret's, 210
Grease-traps, evils of, 93
Great St. Helens, old houses, 135, 304
Greek: archæology, 73, 115, 134, 154, 257, 258, 280, 301, 320, 495; architecture, 73, 115, 177, 248; sculpture, 57, 154, 177, 248; temple, growth of the, 73
Grimthorpe, Lord, and his work at St. Albans, 384
Guides, popular, to museums, 321
Guildhall, Westminster, 155, 320, 376
Guildhall Museum, 178

Haldane, Mr., Bill for Land Purchase, 371
Hall, public, for Edinburgh, 43
Hamburg, jubilee of rebuilding, 393
Hammer, Prof., on slide-rules, 155
Hampstead, old, 496
Hampstead Heath Station disaster, 319
Handbell Ringers, 495
Hanging Committee, Royal Academy, 281
Hanover antiquities, 337
Hart *v.* Monarch Land Co., Ltd., 155
Hart-Dyke, Sir W., on drawing, 200
Heat and motion, 6
Height of buildings in America, 74
Hellenic Society, 154, 301

Henthorn *v.* Fraser, 496
Hertford, All Saints' Church, 6, 14, 31
Hill, Miss Octavia, and open spaces, 452
Hilly Fields, Lewisham, 178
Holborn to Strand communications, 230
Home Arts and Industries Assoc., 497
Horse Accident Prevention Soc., 372
Horsemonger-lane Gaol, 201
Hospitals: Children's, Edinburgh, 281; infectious diseases, 73; St. Mary's, Paddington, 454
Hotel fire in New York, 115
House of Lords on smoke and fog, 134
House-drainage, 43
House-signs, old London, 178
Houses, old: Great St. Helens, 135, 304; Lincoln, 201; Raleigh's, at Youghal, 258; Sir Joshua Reynolds', 134; Tradescant's, South Lambeth, 474
Hummums, Covent-garden, 337
Hunt, Holman, and frescoes at Pisa, 27
Hygiene of railway carriages, 75
Hypæthral temples of antiquity, 115

Illahun, 239
Illicit commissions, 116
Imperial Institute, 495
Imperial penny postage, 431
Improvements at Euston Station, 28, 352
India-rubber, scarcity of, 6
Industries, home, 497
Influenza, epidemic, the, 73
Inspection of boilers, 412
Institute of Architects: *conversazione*, 495; examinations, 4, 452; Fellowship, 452; Students' drawings, 57; *Transactions*, 27
Institute of Painters in Water Colours, 221
Insurance and height of buildings, 74
Interments: St. Helen's, Bishopsgate, 154, 155; St. Mary Woolnoth, 7, 154
Invention, 497
Inventors, a request to, 136
Irish railway rates, 27
Iron manufacture in the United States, 6
Ironwork, South Kensington Museum, 473
Irwell, pollution of the, 394
Isle of Man, international exhibition, 135

Jackson, Mr.: and the Academy, 73: and the Institute, 4
Jahrbuch, Prussian Archæological, 280, 320
Japanesque, 221
Jerry-building in Chicago, 394
Jerusalem Coffee-house, 220
Johnson, the late R. J., 353
Johnson's Patent Pulley Co., 302
Journal of Franklin Institute, 178, 337
Junior Engineering Society, 474

Kelvin, Lord, 27, 177
Kensington: sanitary condition of, 135; the Terrace, 432
Kensington Museum: ironwork at, 473
King of Hanover's antiquities, 337
King's Cross, 7, 50
Kipling, Rudyard, on American roads, 372
Knox statue, proposed, Edinburgh, 497

Labour question, the, 393
Lambeth Bridge, 473
Lancashire, Derbyshire, and East Coast Railway, 473
Lancet on London water supply, 155, 214
Land purchase, Mr. Haldane's Bill, 371
Langdon Abbey estate, 414
Lavington, Sussex, 394
Law: as to "faculties," 258; of rating the, 393; of light, the, 200, 413
Law Courts, technical assessors wanted, 74, 155, 302
Lectures at the British Museum, 43, 57, 73, 94, 177, 248
Legislation as to fogs, 5, 28, 134
Leicester-sq., house of Sir J. Reynolds, 134
Light and air cases, 200, 413
Lincoln Minster: Queen Eleanor's monument, 74; tower, 301; Wren's library, 201, 220, 247, 250, 257
Line of frontage case, 371
Linlithgow Palace, 413
Litigation as to patents, 74
Liverpool, and railway rates question, 352
Llanelly Town-hall competition, 321
Local Authorities (Purchase of Land) Bill, 371
Lodge, Dr. O., on ether, 431
London: building trades, 473; coal-porters' strike, 134; house-signs, old, 178; population, 496; suburbs, 496; water supply, 5, 7, 73, 135, 155, 214, 220, 432
London, Chatham, & Dover third-class, 177
London County Council: Betterment, 431; Brockwell-park, 432; Contractors and the rate of wages, 431; Cromwell-road Bridge, 431; Election, 199; Finance, 5; Hilly Fields, Lewisham, 178; Lambeth Bridge, 473; Safety chains on the Embankment, 496; Technical Education, 134; Tooting-Bec Common, 28; Vauxhall Bridge, 473; Walworth-road railway station, 247; Weights and Measures Office, Newington, 201; Westminster Bridge tramway, 177, 371
London School Board's builders, 155, 314
Lords, House of, on smoke and fog, 134

Machinery, electro-magnetic, 178
Macleod *v.* Thrupp, 352

NOTES (continued) :—

Madox Brown and the Manchester Town-hall frescoes, 372
Manchester: Royal Exchange, 319, 445; Royal Institution Gallery, 57, 219, 247, 281, 319, 413; Town-hall frescoes, 372; Whitworth Inst. competition, 75, 94
Manchester New College, Oxford, 372
Manchester, Sheffield, and Lincolnshire Railway Bill, 28, 239, 319, 452
Mania for competitions in Australia, 221
Marathon, monument of, 280
Markets: Borough, 74: Farringdon, 453
Mausoleum, chariot group of the, 154, 177
Memorial fountains v. tombstones, 393
Memorials of the dead, 221
Menpes, M., pictures of Venice, 475
Merovingian cemetery, discovery of, 413
Metal-work, Armourers' Exhibition, 372
Metropolitan: Building Act consolidation, 7; water supply, 5, 7, 73, 135, 155, 220, 432
Middlesex County Council House, 155
Midland Railway Co. and third-class dining and sleeping cars, 115
Millais, Sir J., German honour for, 453
Miners' strike in the North, 176, 199, 220, 239, 280, 336, 393, 431
Mittheilungen of the German Archæological Institute, 73, 257, 258 495
Model of the Parthenon, M. Chipiez's, 114, 219
Monolithic concrete floor, 413
Montague-close, Southwark, 94
Monuments: Battle of Marathon, 280; Queen Eleanor's, Lincoln Minster, 74; Wellington, St. Paul's Cathedral, 301
Morris v Brinsmead, case of, 94
Mortality in relation to meteorology, 93
Museum, Ashmolean, 474
Museum lectures, 43
Municipal works, Berlin, 320, 371
Mycenæ, excavations at, 495

National Association for Promotion of Technical Education, 134
National Gallery, proposed American, 6
Natural Science, 135
Nautical archæology, 320
Needlework, Danish, 353
Nemi, Temple of Diana, 115
Nettlefolds' patent case, 74
New English Art Club, 302
New York: hotel fire, 115; model of the Parthenon, 114, 219
Newgate-street: Panyer-alley, 259
Newspapers and "quotation," 259
Nickalls v. Briscoe, 258
Nineteenth Century Art Society, 302
Nixon's School, Oxford, 372
Nottingham chart of mortality in relation to meteorology, 93

Omnibuses, electric lighting in, 474
Open spaces, London, 6, 28, 178, 220, 432, 452, 453, 474
Opera and the electric light, 413
Opera-house, Her Majesty's, 394
Organ-grinding nuisance, the, 178
Overcrowding: on the Bedford Estate, 220; on railways, 239, 258
Oxford: Ashmolean Museum, 474; lull in building operations, 372

Paintings of cats by Mdme. Ronner, 414
Paintings by Mr. Whistler, 240
Palace, Linlithgow, 413
Panic in theatres, 5
Panyer-alley, Newgate-street, 259
Paragraphs, puffing, 94
Paris: Church of St. Gervais, 240; Eiffel Tower, 373; snow in, 156; in the Tuileries gardens, 373
Paris church, Wrexham, 393
Parks and open spaces, London, 6, 28, 178, 220, 432, 453
Parochial Offices, Battersea, 5
Parthenon: architecture of the, 177; model of, New York, 114, 219; pediment figures, 177
Patent-fees, reduction of, 336, 453
Patentees, a hint to, 136
Patents, litigation as to, 74
Paving: asphalte, 372; wood, 413
Payment of architects, 280
Peerage for Sir W. Thomson, 27
Pendarves v. Monro, 413
Perrot, M., on the Vaphio cups, 280
Petrie, Mr., and Hellenic studies, 239
Phillips v. Low, 200
Physical Society, the, 431
Pictures: by Mr. E. Barclay, 302: by Mr. H. W. B. Davis, 58; at Dowdeswell's Galleries, 178; at the Dudley Gallery, 58, 155, 302; Fine Art Society's Gallery, 58, 94, 201, 475; at the French Gallery, 259; Nineteenth Century Art Society, 302; of the tidal Seine, 221; by Mr. Walter Severn, 58; Society of Painters in Water-Colours, 337; of Venice by Mr. Menpes, 475; by Mr. Wimperis, 94
Pier, Beaumaris, competition, 57
Pig-iron manufacture, United States, 6
Piggott, Mr. F. T., on "Japanesque," 221
Piracy by American journals, 43, 372, 404
Pisa, frescoes at, 27
Pitt, William, and Coombe Wood, 372
Plaster-work at Imperial Institute, 495
Pollution: Irwell, 394; Thames, 7
Poor's land, Bethnal-green, 6
Population of London, 496
Possibilities of electricity, 93
Post-office reforms, 431
Potsdam water supply, 74
Powers of the London water companies, 135, 214, 509
Prevention of fogs, 5, 28
Prisons: Horsemonger-lane, 201; Tothill Fields, 43
Prize drawings at the Institute, 57
Properties for sale, 221, 258, 337, 394, 414
Prussian: Academy, the, 453; railway carriages, 75
Public Health Act, the, 154
Publications, German architectural, 321

Quarterly Review and the London water question, 73
Queen Eleanor's monument, Lincoln, 74
"Quotation," 259

Railway bridges, stresses on, 258
Railway carriages: overcrowded, 239, 258; ventilation of, 75
Railway collisions: Birmingham, 453; Bishopsgate, 496
Railway Clearing-House, 27
Railway rates, 27, 257, 352, 473
Railway stations: Hampstead Heath, 319; Walworth-road, 257
Railway time-tables, 336
Railways: American, 7; Lancashire, Derbyshire, and East Coast, 473; Manchester, Sheffield, and Lincolnshire, 28, 239, 319, 452; Midland, and third-class, 115
Railways and second-class, 42
Raleigh's house at Youghal, 258
Ramsay Lodge, Edinburgh, 432
Rating law, 393
Ravenscraig Castle, 43
Record Office, the, 28
Reduction of the patent fees, 336
Reforms, Post-office, 431
Regulations, theatre, 453
Renaissance architecture, 7, 474
Remuneration of architects, 280
Resistance standards, 337
Restoration of Bristol Cathedral, 472
Reynolds, Sir Joshua, centenary, 134
Richmond, W. B., on architecture, 94
Road-paving in St. Pancras, 413
Roads, American, 372
Ronner, Mdme.'s, paintings of cats, 414
Rooms, minimum size of, 154
Rothley Temple estate, 221
Royal Academy: architecture at, 281; new Associates, 73; dinner, 352
Royal Commission on Metropolitan Water Supply, 220, 432
Royal Exchange, Manchester, 319, 445
Royal Institution Gallery, Manchester, 57, 219, 247, 281, 319, 413
Royal Scottish Academy, 281; new Associates, 201
Royal Society of Painter-Etchers, 201
Royal Society's *conversazione*, 352, 473

Safety in theatres, 5, 453
Saint Albans, Ld Grimthorpe's work, 384
St. Anne's Church, Soho, 474
St. Antholin's steeple, 336, 361
St. Dunstan's-in-the-East, 336
St. Gervais, Church of, Paris, 240
St. Giles's Church, Camberwell, 201
St. Helen's, Bishopsgate, 154, 155
St. Margaret's graveyard, 240
St. Mary Woolnoth, 7, 154
St. Mary's Hospital, Paddington, 454
St. Pancras: electric lighting, 281; road-paving, 413; snow clearance, 320
St. Paul's Cathedral: proposed new clock, 94; Wellington monument, 301
St. Werburgh's, Derby, 353
Sale of property, point of law as to, 496
Salford Surveyorship, 496
Salisbury, Lord, on the fog question, 134
Sanatoria, domestic, 73
Sandwich, bridge at, 135
Sanitary: arrangements at Wellington College, 42; condition of the Foundling Hospital, 93; condition of Kensington, 135; measures in Bokhara, 475
Schinkel Medal, Berlin, 240
School Board and its builders, 155
Schools, elementary, Berlin, 177
Scientific American, plagiarism by, 43
Scotch castles, 135
Scottish National Gallery, Edinburgh 116
Screen, wet, for air, 74
Sculpture: Greek, 57, 154, 177; of the Mausoleum, 154, 177
Silchester, basilica found at, 453, 478
Second-class on railways, 42
Seine, pictures of the, 221
Sellers, Miss, lectures, British Museum, 57, 73, 94, 177, 248
Sessions House, Westminster, 155, 320, 376
Severn, Walter, pictures by, 58
Shareholders, architects as, 302
Stirling, the Abbey Craig, 320
Single-trap system of house-drainage, 43
Site of Farringdon Market, 43, 240
Sketches by W. L. Wyllie, 94
Skinners' Company's almshouses, 135, 258
Slide-rules at Stuttgart, 155
Smoke and fog, 134
Snow: in Paris, 156; clearance in St. Pancras, 320
Society of Arts, paper at, 93
Society of Fine Arts, 221
Society of Painter-Etchers, 201
Society of Painters in Water-Colours, 337
Society for Preserving Memorials of the Dead, 221
Sofia, drainage of, 301
Soho, St. Anne's Churchyard, 474
Soirée, Institute of Architects, 495
Solenoids, two-coil, 337
South Kensington Museum, ironwork, 473
Southwark: the Borough Market, 74; Montague-close, 94
Sparta, the site of, 134
Speeches at the Academy dinner, 352
Stafford County Council Buildings, 258
Stained glass, treatment of, 154
Standards, resistance, 337
Statue of George IV., King's Cross, 7, 50
Statue, Knox, Edinburgh, 497
Steam-boiler inspection, 412
Steven's monument of Wellington, 301
Stone: building, Texas, 93; Victoria, 474
Stones, old: King's Cross, 7, 50; Panyer-alley, 259
Stonehenge, pictures of, 302
Strand to Holborn communications, 239
Stresses on railway bridges, 258
Street name-plates in Berlin, 432
Strikes a century ago, 221
Strikes: engineers in the North, 92, 115, 154; London coal-porters, 134; Northern coal-trade, 176, 199, 220, 239, 280, 336, 393, 431
Students' drawings at the Institute, 57
Studniczka, Dr., on a monument of Marathon, 280
Stuttgart, slide rules in, 155
Suburbs, London, 496
Surveyor-architect, a, 43, 58
Surveyors' commission, 200
Surveyorship, Salford, 496

Tait, Lawson, on memorial fountains, 393
Tate, H., offer of an art gallery, 200, 269
Teaching of drawing, the, 200
Teaching University for London, 336
Teale, Dr., on dust, 93, 125
Technical Assessors in the Law Courts, 74, 155, 302
Technical Education: Edinburgh, 74; London, 134
Temple of Diana at Nemi, 115
Temples, hypæthral, 115
Terra-cotta cornice, Civita Lavinia, 116
Terra-cottas, Greek, 73
Terrace, the, Kensington, 432
Texas, Geology of, 92
Thames, pollution of, 7
Theatre: catastrophe at Gateshead, 5; Covent Garden, electric lighting 413; Her Majesty's, 394; regulations, 453
Third-class on the London, Chatham, and Dover line, 177
Third-class dining and sleeping cars, 115.
Thomson, Sir W., 27
Time-tables, railway, 336
Times, the, and tramways, 371
Tothill Fields Prison, 43
Tottenham Court-road, rebuilding in, 222
Touting architects, 48, 58, 321
Towers: Eiffel, at Wembley, 280; Lincoln Minster, 301; City churches, 336
Town-hall, Llanelly, 321
Tooting-Bec Common, 28
Tradescant's "Ark," South Lambeth, 474
Trains, cheap, 393
Tramway, Westminster Bridge, 177, 371
Transactions: American Society of Civil Engineers, 258, 337; Edinburgh Architectural Assoc., 135; Institute of Architects, 27
Traquair, Mrs., decoration by, 259
Treatment of stained glass, 154
Trinity College, Dublin, 496
Tuileries Gardens, Paris, 373
Tyneside engineers' strike, 92, 115, 154

"United Hotel," proposed, 394
United States iron manufacture, 6
University College, Egyptology at, 474
University for London, proposed, 336
Unter den Linden, Berlin, 320

Valuation of property for mortgage, 352
Vaphio cups, the, 280
Vauxhall Bridge, 473
Venice, pictures by Mr. Menpes, 475
Ventilating-cowl, Wheeler's, 454
Ventilation of: railway carriages, 75; Victoria Infirmary, Glasgow, 74
Verdict of a coroner's jury in Chicago, 394
Victoria stone, 474
Vienna Exhibition, 394
Vitality of: errors about architecture, 454; a scientific blunder, 6

Wages: in London building trades, 473; and the London County Council, 431
Wales and West of England Girder Co., 394
Walworth-road railway station, 257
Washington, National Gallery, proposed, 7
Water-colours: at the Dudley Gallery, 155; Institute of, 221; Society of, 337; by Mr. Sutton Palmer, 201
Water companies' powers, 135, 214, 431, 509
Water discovery and the divining rod, 259
Water-gate, York-stairs, Adelphi, 135, 281
Water supply of: Birmingham, 5, 199; Chicago, 135; London, 5, 7, 73, 135, 155, 214, 220, 432; North Germany, 74, 107
Waugh, Mr., report on the Cleckheaton chimney disaster, 279
Weights and Measures Office, Newington, 201
Wellington College, sanitation at, 42
Wellington Monument, St. Paul's, 301
West Wickham Common, 221
Westminster: artillery-ground, 258; Emanuel Hospital, 453; Guildhall or Sessions House, 155, 320, 376; St. Margaret's Church, 240; Tothill Fields Prison, 43
Westminster Bridge tramway, 177, 371
Whitworth Institute competition, 75, 94
Wimperis, Mr., pictures by, 94
Windows: St. Gervais, Paris, 240; St. Margaret's, Westminster, 240
Wires, electric, casings for, 337
Wiring, a new system of, 352
Witnesses, expert, 155
Wood paving, 413
Woolavington, Sussex, 394
Workmen's: cheap trains, 393; combinations a century ago, 221
Works and Construction Stock Exchange, proposed, 281
Wren's: City Churches, 336; library at Lincoln, 201, 220, 247, 250, 257
Wrexham Parish Church, 393
Wyllie, W. L., sketches by, 94

York Water-gate, Adelphi, 135, 281
Youghal, Sir W. Raleigh's house, 258

Zeitschrift für Bauwesen, 281

REPORTS OF MEETINGS, PAPERS READ, LAW CASES, ETC.

Abbey, Newbattle, 183
Addresses to Institute students, 79, 83
Aird, J., on engineering education, 324
Aitchison, Prof.: on Byzantine architecture, 241; on ironwork, 284; on metal-work, 456; on Saracenic architecture, 75, 95, 116, 136, 156, 179; on Signor Beltrami, 283
Alhambra, Granada, 138
Amendment of: Building Acts, 13, 120, 289; Public Health Acts, 381
Amsterdam, new theatre, 240
Anderson, J. Macvicar: address to students, 79, 83; at the Architect's Benevolent Soc., 208; on the late E. A. Freeman, 240; on the Examinations, 240, 282; on planning, 79, 83
Anderton, J., evidence, Labour Commission, 246
Anemometers, 329
Angell, L., on electric lighting, 398
Appleton, E., on professional topics, 321
Arbitrations as to main roads, 30, 382, 447
Archaic and archaistic sculpture, 222
Archæological Societies: — British Archæological Assoc., 48, 165, 207, 251, 305, 339, 422, 463; Exeter Diocesan, 477; Lancashire and Cheshire Antiquarian Soc., 105; Leicester Archæological Soc., 105; Society of Antiquaries of Scotland, 18; Surrey Archæological Society, 225
Architects and craftsmen, 268, 437, 462
Architects in the time of Shakspere, 202
Architects' Benevolent Society, 207
Architectural Association: — Annual Dinner, 443; Design of Technical Colleges and Schools, 61; Discussion Section, 44, 83, 164, 204, 265, 305; Domestic Electric Lighting, 163, 190; Editorship of *A.A. Notes*, 400, 442; Election of Officers, 443; Fashions in Architecture and the kindred arts, 99; How they Built in Shakspere's Time, 202; Literature and Architecture, 284; Members' *Soirée*, 393; Nomination of Committee, 400, 442; Presidency, 281; Recent Developments in Theatre-Planning, 242, 264; Relation of the Architect to the Workman, 437, 462; Spring Visits (see "Visits"); Travelling Student for 1892, 443; Travelling Student's Notes, 442
Architectural Examination, 240, 282, 377
Architectural poetry, 226
Architectural Societies: — Birmingham Architectural Assoc., 83, 206, 323; Carlisle Engineering, Architectural, and Surveying Assoc., 44, 83, 183, 240; Devon and Exeter, 225, 321; Dundee Inst. of Architecture, 60, 323; Edinburgh Architectural Assoc., 104, 142, 183, 225, 268, 306, 346, 356, 383, 447, 462; Glasgow Architectural Assoc., 83, 104, 142, 183, 206, 305, 463, 498; Glasgow Inst. of Architects, 295, 402; Institute, Royal, of British Architects (see "Institute"); Leeds and Yorkshire, 59, 105, 142, 183, 225, 269, 356; Liverpool, 45, 59, 83, 207, 498; Manchester, 59, 414, 498; Northern Architectural Assoc., 83, 402; Sheffield, 45, 123, 207, 492; York Architectural Assoc., 225
Architecture: Byzantine, 241; early Irish, 305; English Renaissance, 59; fashions in, 99; of the human figure,

REPORTS, &c. (continued) :— 142; metal-work in, 434, 455; Saracenic, 75, 95, 116, 136, 156, 179; of Scottish towns, 142; Somersetshire, 442
Architecture and literature, 284
Art, Greek, 57, 73; Art and health, 229; Art of the Low Countries, the, 323
Art of planning, the, 79, 83
Art-Union of London, 339
Artisans' dwellings, 12, 289
Artists' General Benevolent Inst., 337
Ashbee, C. R., on architect and workman, 437
Associations of Master Builders, 84, 173
Association of Municipal Engineers, 295, 355, 381, 399, 416, 482, 499
Association of Sanitary Inspectors, 32, 143, 192, 228, 310, 383
Atmospheric hypothesis of epidemics, 147

Baggallay, F. T.: on building in Shakspeare's time, 204; on fashions in architecture, 101; on literature and architecture, 287; on theatre-planning, 265
Baker, A., on building legislation, 121
Bateman, C. E., on Castle Bromwich Church, 323
Barry, C., on planning, 83
Bars and gates, London, 125, 143, 269
Bartlett, H. H., on the building-trade, 357
Beltrami, Sig., on Milan Cathedral, 282
Berlin: sale of water by meter at, 9; sewage-farms, 304
Berrington, J. A., on cement-testing, 45
Bethnal Green: Poor's Land, 13; slum clearance, 12
Beveridge, J., evidence, Labour Commission, 186
Binnie, A. B., evidence, Water Commission, 481
Blashill, T., on building legislation, 122
Boilers, water supply of, 193
Bolton, R., on electrical hoists, 291
Bonar, T., on Yester Castle, 305
Booth, R., on gas-producers, 147
Boulger, Prof., on timber, 370
Boulnois, H. P., on destructors, 339, 388
Boyle, R., & Son, Ltd., 289
Bracebridge Church, Lincoln, 207
Brady, J., on clerks of works, 144
Bramwell, Sir F., evidence, Water Commission, 421
Brick-burning, improvements in, 193
Bridges: Lambeth, 479; Tower, 244; Vauxhall, 479
Brightmore, A. W., on water-supply, 19
Bristol Cathedral, 472
British Museum lectures, 57, 73, 141, 164, 184, 207, 225
Brodie, C. H., on fashions in architecture, 101
Bronze castings, 435, 455
Brook-street, Limehouse, scheme, 239
Brooke's Market, Holborn, 352
Brough, J., evidence, Labour Commission, 186
Brown, A., on Nottingham works, 355, 399
Bryan, W. B., evidence, Water Commission, 420, 481
Brydon, J. M.: on the English Renaissance, 59; on metal work, 455
Buckham, E., on the Shone system, 500
Buckingham-street watergate, 143
Builder law reports, 316
Builders' Benevolent Institution, 439
Builders' Clerks' Benevolent Inst., 165, 209, 345
Builders' Foremen's Instn., 190
Builders' Institute, the, 124, 357
Building in Shakspere's time, 202
Building Act amendment, 13, 120, 289
Building Act, cases under, 251, 274, 352
Building legislation, London, 120, 280
Building Regulations Bill, Glasgow, 205
Building trade evidence, Labour Commission, 184, 230, 244
Burghley House, the building of, 203
Burnet, J. J., on architect and craftsman, 268
Burrell, W., on literature and architecture, 287
Burt, J. M., on employers' liability, 100
Byzantine Architecture, 211

Cairo: house, 158; mosques, 97, 99, 157
Cane-hill asylum, 506
Carpenter, H., on painted glass, 159
Carpenters' Company's prizes, 17
Case under Public Health Act (London), 295
Cases under the Employers' Liability Act, 68, 110
Cases under the Metropolis Local Management Act, 68, 88, 147, 371
Cases under the Metropolitan Building Act (see "Building Act")
Castings in metal, 434, 455
Castles: Drumlanrig, 463; Pitteadie, 383; Seafield, 383; Yester, 305
Cathedrals: Bristol, 472; Cordova, 136; Milan, 282; Oxford, 165
Cawston, A., on building legislation, 122
Cement and cement testing, 45
Chairmanship, London County Council, 183, 228
Chariot-group of the Mausoleum, 154
Chelsea: Embankment, 13; Water Company, 457
Child, J., evidence, Water Commission, 436
Chipiez's model of the Parthenon, 282
Chit-chat, professional, 321
Churches: Castle Bromwich, 323; Harrow, 477; Perranzabuloe, 165; St. Nicholas, Dalkeith, 183; St. Saviour's Southwark, 207; Suffolk, 83; town, 123
Clark, A. H.: on building in Shakspeare's time, 204; on literature and architecture, 287
Clarke, Max: on electric lighting, 163; on theatre-planning, 264
Clarke, Somers, on Milan Cathedral, 283
Claybury Asylum, 506
Clerks of Works' Association, 144
Club, New Travellers', 356
Cole, R. L., on electric lighting, 164, 190
Colour, Saracenic, 179
Collard, A. O., on building in Shakespere's time, 204
Colleges, technical, design of, 61
Collins, E., evidence, Water Commission, 420
Collins, H. H., on building legislation, 121
Colls, J. H., on builders' foremen, 190
Conference on rating of machinery, 87
Conservators of the Thames and the London water question, 481, 503
Construction, steel in, 208
Corbie, G., evidence at Water Commission, 436
Cordova: cathedral, 136; mosque, 137
Craftsmen, architects and, 268, 437, 462
Cresswell, H. O., on architecture and craftsmen, 462
Crisis at the Architectural Assoc., 400, 442
Crystal Palace School of Engineering, 324

Dalkeith, St. Nicholas Church, 183
Daly, M. César, 120, 213
Davenport, J., on sanitary Inspectors, 310
Dawkins, Boyd, evidence at Water Commission, 421
Dawson, H., on electric lighting, 398
Day, L. F., on stained glass, 102
Dew, G., evidence, Labour Commission, 184
Design in glass painting, 160
Destruction of refuse, 339, 383, 388
Dicksee, B.: on building legislation, 121; on building in Shakspere's time, 204; on theatre planning, 264
Dines, W. H., on anemometer comparisons, 329
Dinners: Architectural Assoc., 443; Assoc. of Sanitary Inspectors, 228; Builders' Clerks' Benevolent Inst., 269; Builders' Foremen and Clerks of Works' Inst., 190; Clerks of Works' Assoc., 144; Institute of Builders, 357
Disfigurement of Somerset House, 377
Disinfection, 143
Dissension at the A.A., 400, 412
Domestic electric lighting, 163
Drainage, Shone system, 501
Drawings at the Institute, 81
Drower, J. E., on builders' clerks, 270
Drumlanrig Castle, 462
Dust, 93, 125

East London Water Company, 420, 481
Edinburgh, Wellington statue, 104, 142
Editorship of *A. A. Notes*, 400
Education, technical, 74, 300
Egypt Exploration Fund, 224
Egyptian: mosques, 97, 117, 157; trellis-work, 180, 181
Electric lighting, 83, 163, 190, 398
Electrical hoisting machinery, 291
Ely, Bishop of, on stained glass, 161
Emanuel Hospital, Westminster, 65
Emmett, A., evidence, Labour Commission, 246
Employers' liability, 68, 110, 190
Enamel painting on glass, 160
Engineering School, Crystal Palace, 324
Engineering Societies:—Association of Birmingham Students, Inst. C.E., 53, 126, 164, 234; Civil and Mechanical Engineers' Soc., 147, 193; Institution of Civil Engineers (see "Institution"); Junior Engineering Soc., 474; Liverpool Engineering Soc., 19, 65, 110, 147, 191, 339, 383; Society of Engineers, 105, 290, 356, 505
Engineers' tests for iron, 147, 191
English Renaissance, the, 59
Epidemics, atmospheric hypothesis, 147
Estimating, approximately, 104
Estimates for 1892, L.C.C., 306
Evidence: Labour Commission, 184, 230, 241; Royal Commission on Metropolitan Water Supply, 418, 435, 456, 480, 503
Examinations: for Inspectors of nuisances, 18, 345, 387; Institute of Architects', 210, 282, 377; Municipal Engineers, 295, 416; at the Surveyors' Institution, 109, 322, 355
Exploration of Egypt, 224

Fairford windows, the, 160
Farrow, F. R., on A.A. matters, 400
Fashions in architecture and the arts, 99
Finance, London County Council, 83
Fleming, O., on fashions in architecture, 101
Flower, Major L., evidence, Water Commission, 436
Ford, O., on bronze casting, 455
Foreign sewage precipitation works, 505
Fountain, Shaftesbury Memorial, 357
Fowler, Sir J., on Egypt exploration, 224
Francis, J., evidence, Water Commission, 418
Fraser, —, evidence, Water Commission, 456
Freeman, E. A., the late, 240
Fulham recreation-ground, 479
Funeral Reform Association, 388

Gardner, Prof., on the Mausoleum sculptures, 154
Gardner, Starkie: on castings in metal, 455; on Renaissance ironwork, 283, 284
Garnett, Prof., on technical schools, 61
Gas-producers, 147
Gasometer, to store 12,000,000 cubic feet, 506
Gasworks, South Metropolitan, 506
Gates and bars, 125, 143
Gill, A. C., evidence, Water Commission, 457
Gill, H., on water meters at Berlin, 9
Gill, J. C., on Peterboro' water-supply, 483
Glasgow, old, 305
Glasgow Building Regulations Bill, 295
Glass, stained and painted, 159
Godfrey, R., on sewer ventilation, 501
Godwin Bursary, 82
Gold Medallist for 1892, 120, 213
Goldsmith, F. T. W.: on A.A. matters, 401; on building in Shakspeare's time, 204; on fashions in architecture, 101; on literature and architecture, 287
Gotch, J. A., on building in Shakspere's time, 202, 205
Gough, J. H., evidence, Water Commission, 481, 503
Government, the, and the London water question, 65
Graham, A., on the history of metal-work in architecture, 455
Grand Junction Water Company, 456
Greek: architecture, 73, 164, 207; art, 57, 73; sculpture, 57, 141, 154, 164, 184, 207, 222, 225
Greek Temple, growth of the, 73
Grueber, H., Egypt Exploration, 224
Guild and School of Handicraft, 437, 462

Hack, R., evidence, Water Commission, 457
Hackney Marsh, 479
Hackney Wick relief sewer, 183
Hall, E. T., on Building Legislation, 120
Hamm, H., evidence, Labour Commission, 246
Handicraft, Guild and School of, 437
Harries, H., on influenza epidemics, 147
Harrow Church and School, 477
Hatfield House, the building of, 202, 203
Health and art, 220
Heaton, C., on glass-painting, 160
Height of buildings in London, 306, 357
Hellenic Society, 164
Heraldry in relation to architecture, 225
Hoists, electrical, 291
Holborn to Strand, new street, 88
Holiday, H., on stained-glass, 161
Hornsey main roads arbitration, 447
Hospital, 8th. London Ophthalmic, 289, 303
House-duty, the, 143
Houses fronting more than one street, 147
Human figure, architecture of the, 142

Imperial Institute, 165, 497
Improvements at Nottingham, 355
Incorporated Association of Municipal and County Engineers:—Examinations, 295, 416; meeting at Nottingham, 355, 381, 399, 425; meeting at Peterborough, 482, 499
Incrustation of boilers, 193
Infection and disinfection, 143
Influenza epidemics, 147
Inhabited House Duty, the, 143
Institute of Builders, 124, 357
Institute, Royal, of British Architects:—Annual Report, 376; Art of Planning, 79; Application of Metals to Architectural Design, 434, 455; Byzantine Architecture 241; Castings in Metal, 434, 455; Chipiez's model of the Parthenon, 282; Construction of the Central Pillars of Milan Cathedral, 282; Disfigurement of Somerset House, 377; Election of Council, 478; Electric Lighting, 398; Examinations, 240, 282, 377; Freeman, the late Prof. E. A., 240; Grant to the Architectural Association, 78; Grissell Gold Medal, 82; Godwin Bursary, the, 82; London Building Legislation, 120; Medals and Prizes, 59, 81, 120, 213, 377; Obituary, 120, 240, 281, 377; President's Address to Students, 79; Pugin Studentship, 81; Renaissance Ironwork, 283; Royal Gold Medallist, 120, 213; Soane Medallion, 82; Stained and Painted Glass, 159; Suggestions for the Conduct of Competitions, 207; Theatre at Amsterdam, 240; Tite Prize, the, 82
Institution of Civil Engineers:—Annual Report, 478; dinner, 179; election of Council, 479; sale of water by meter at Berlin, 9; sewage-farms of Berlin, 304
Inventors' Institute, 193
Irish architecture, early, 305
Iron, tests for, 147, 191
Ironfounding, 435
Ironwork, Renaissance, 283
Isaacs, L. H., on capital and labour, 357
Ispahan, mosques at, 116, 140

Jackson, T. G.: and the A.A., 401; on stained glass, 161

Kaaba at Mecca, the, 76, 95
Kent Water Company, 480
King's College, Cambridge, stained-glass at, 160
Knox, W., evidence, Labour Commission, 185
Krall, C., on work in precious metals, 434

Labour Commission, building trade evidence, 184, 230, 244
Lambeth: Bridge, 479; Water Company, 458
Landlords' liability for sanitary defects, 295
Law reports in the *Builder*, 316
Laying out streets, 381
Lea Conservancy, the, 436
Lectures: by Professor Aitchison to the Students of the Royal Academy on Saracenic Architecture, 75, 95, 116, 136, 156, 179; by Miss Millington-Lathbury, at the British Museum, 73; Dr. Murray's, at the Royal Academy, 222; by Miss Sellers, at the British Museum, 57, 141, 164, 184, 207, 225
Legal:—Arbitrations, 36, 314, 447; Fletcher v. Lewis, Building Act case, 251; Fowler v. Pereira, Building Act case, 274; Fowler v. Walker, light and air case, 413; Gebhardt v. Saunders, case under the Public Health Act (London), 295; Giddy v. Ross, surveyors' commission, 200; Hart v. Monarch Land Co., Limited, damages by adjoining building, 155; Henthorn v. Fraser, sale of property, 496; London, Chatham, and Dover Railway Co. v. Addison, third-class accommodation, 177; London County Council v. Cross: case under the Metropolis Local Management Act, 371; London County Council v. Pearse: case under the Metropolitan Building Act, 352; London County Council v. Pollock: case under the Metropolis Local Management Act, 147; London School Board v. Wall: claim for deviations, 314; Lovegrove v. Parsons: Building Act case, 274; Lovegrove v. Truman, Hanbury, & Co., surveyor's fee for negotiating purchase, 194; Macleod v. Thrupp, valuation of property for mortgage, 352; Morris v. Brinsmead, commission for press notices, 94; Nettlefold's patent case, 74; Nickalls v. Briscoe, "faculty" for church work, 268; Overseers and Churchwardens of Norwood v. Salter, rating law, 393; Patent cases, 74; Patmore v. Kennerley, employers' liability, 68; Pendarves v. Monro, law of light, 413; Phillips v. Low, law of light, 200; Richardson v. Mathews, alleged breach of contract, 425; Wandsworth District Board of works v. Bird, case under Metropolis Local Management Act, 88; Wandsworth District Board of Works v. Lower, case under Metropolis Local Management Act, 68; Willetts v. Watt, employers' liability, 110
Liability, employers', 68, 110, 190
Liability of owner for sanitary defects, 295
Library, Wren's, Lincoln, 250, 257
Lighting, electric, 83, 163, 190, 398
Lime, tenders for, 289
Limit of height of buildings, 306, 357
Lincoln, Wren's Library, 250, 257
Lindsay, J., on estimating, 104
Line of frontage cases, 371
Linlithgow Palace, 104, 142, 207, 225, 356, 413
Literature and architecture, 284
London building legislation, 120
London County Council:—Alexandra Palace and Park, 402; Alterations, Shoreditch Town Hall, 479; Amendment of the Building Acts, 13, 289; Appointment of Assistant Medical Officers, 105, 506; Appointment of a Parks Superintendent, 143; Artisans' dwellings, 12, 289; Banstead Asylum, 105, 506; Bars and gates, 125, 143, 269; Bethnal Green Poor's land, 13; Bethnal Green slum clearance, 12; "Betterment," 244; Blackwall Tunnel, 183, 402; Brockwell Park, 402, 479; Brook-street, Limehouse, scheme, 280; Brooke's Market, Holborn, 382; Building Act Committee, 244; Buildings on the Victoria Embankment vetoed, 507; Bust of the late Mr. Firth, 165; Cane-hill Asylum, 402, 506; Chairmanship, 183, 228, 382; Chelsea Embankment, 13; Claybury Asylum, 506; Committees, 244; Contracts for lime, 289; Date for first meeting of New Council, 64; Electric and cable railway schemes, 382; Emanuel Hospital, Westminster, 65; Estimates, the, 306; Finance, 83, 269, 306, 506; Gallery of British Art, proposed, 289; Goldsmith-sq. site, 12; Hackney Wick Relief Sewer, 183; Inhabited House Duty, 143; Lambeth and Vauxhall Bridges, 479; Lauderdale House, Highgate, 183; Limit of height of buildings, 306, 357; Loans, 83, 269, 306, 402, 479; North Park, Eltham, 402; Palm-house for Battersea-park, 13; Parks and open spaces, 13, 143, 402; Payments to contractors during holidays, 305; Public Buildings, proposed, at Battersea, 306; Purchase of Hackney Marsh, 479; Quantity-surveyors and their remuneration, 382; Railway and other schemes, 125, 382; Recreation-ground, Fulham, 479; Regulations for the safety of theatres, 105; Reorganisation of administrative work, 244, 422; Rosebery-avenue, 13, 357; Salary of the Deputy-Chairman, 269, 289; Sewage precipitation, 165; Sewage-sludge and sludge ships, 402; Shaftesbury Memorial Fountain, Piccadilly, 357; Sites for new Offices, 64; Special Committee on contracts, 439; Technical Education, 306; Tenders, 143, 244, 260, 289, 357, 382, 402, 479, 507; Tenders: return of deposits of money, 64; Theatre regulations, 105, 124, 242, 264, 269, 382; Toole's Theatre, 269; Tottenham-court-road, widening, 506; Vacant seat, 479; Valuation of land, 105; Vote of condolence with the Royal Family, 64; Vote of thanks to the staff, 184; Wages and hours clause in contracts, 357, 402, 422, 439, 506; Walworth-road Railway Station, 269; Water question, 64, 165, 183, 422, 507; Water-closets in Board Schools, 143; York Water-gate, 143
London water question, the, 64, 165, 183, 214, 418, 422, 435, 456, 480, 503, 507
Longden, H.: on iron-founding, 435
Louttit, S. H., evidence, Water Commission, 458
Lowe, E. J., on raindrops, 402
Lubbock, Sir J.: on County Council work, 183; on technical education, 306
Lucas, J., evidence, Water Commission, 458
Lynskey, P., evidence, Labour Commission, 184

MacGregor, D. B., evidence, Labour Commission, 240
Mackay, Sheriff, on Scottish architecture, 142
Machinery, rating of, 87

REPORTS, &c. (continued):—

MacNamara, R. S., evidence, Labour Commission, 184
Main roads arbitrations, 86, 382, 447
Master Builders' Associations, 84, 123
Mathews, J. D., on bldg. legislation, 122
Mausoleum, chariot-group of the, 154
Meade, T. de C., on refuse disposal, 388
Mecca, 76, 77, 95
Medals and prizes at the Institute, 59, 81, 120, 213
Memorials of the dead, preserving, 233
Metal in architectural design, 434, 455
Meteorological Society, 88, 147, 329, 402
Metropolis Local Management Act, cases under, 68, 147
Metropolitan Building Acts, 13, 120
Metropolitan Life Assurance Bldg., 123
Metropolitan Water Supply, 64, 165, 183, 214, 418, 422, 435, 456, 480, 503, 507
Michelangelo, architecture of, 183
Milan Cathedral, central pillars, 282
Miller, A. H., on old Glasgow, 305
Millington-Lathbury, Miss, on Greek art, 78
Model of Parthenon, M. Chipiez's, 282
Mohammedan architecture, 75, 95, 116, 136, 156, 179
Moore, F., evidence, Labour Commission, 244
Morris, E. L., evidence, Water Commission, 420
Morris, T., on tests for iron, 147
Morris, W., evidence, Water Commission, 461
Mosques: Amrou, Cairo, 97; Cordova, 137; Ispahan, 116, 140; Persian, 116, 140; Sultan Hassan, Cairo, 99, 157
Mountford, E. W., on architects and craftsmen, 462
Municipal Engineers, examinations for, 295, 416
Municipal Engineers' Assoc., 205, 355, 381, 399, 416, 482, 499
Municipal works in Nottingham, 355, 390, 425; in Peterborough, 482, 499
Murray, A. S., on archaic and archaistic sculpture, 222
Music School, Harrow, 477

National Assoc. of Master Builders, 123
National Portrait Gallery, 399
Nevill, Ralph, on building legislation, 122
New River Company, the, 418
New Travellers' Club, 356
New York model of the Parthenon, 282
Newbattle Abbey, 183
Newbery, F. H., on the human figure, 142
Newberry, P. E., on Egypt exploration, 224
Newington Weights and Measures Office, 289
Nottingham: Master Builders' Assoc., 84; municipal works at, 355, 381, 425; sewage-farm, 399

Offices, proposed new, for the London County Council, 84
Office of Works and Linlithgow Palace, 104, 142
Open spaces, London, 13, 143, 479
Ophthalmic Hospital, Sth. London, 289, 303
Ornament, Saracenic, 179
Otley, A., evidence, Labour Commission, 184
Oxford Cathedral, Saxon work at, 165

Painted glass, 159
Palace, Linlithgow, 104, 142 207, 225, 356, 413
Palm-house for Battersea Park, 13
Parker, T. F., evidence, Water Commission, 458
Parks, London, 13, 143, 402
Parthenon, M. Chipiez's model, 282
Patrick, C. G., on builders' clerks, 269
Paul, J. B., on heraldry in relation to architecture, 225
Payne, A.: on building legislation, 121; on Byzantine architecture, 241
Peabody Fund, the, 213
Peach, C. S., on electric lighting, 164
Pearson, J. L., on restoration of Bristol Cathedral, 472

Perranzabuloe Church, 165
Persian mosques, 116
Peterborough, municipal engineering at, 482, 499
Phillips, W., evidence, Labour Commission, 245
Phœnix Philanthropic Society of House-Painters, 233
Pite, A. B.: on Michelangelo, 183; on electric lighting, 164
Pitteadie Castle, 383
Planning: art of, 79, 83; technical colleges, 61; theatres, 242, 264
Play, the Architectural Association, 383
Plumbers, registration of, 17, 147, 213, 233, 509
Poetry, architectural, 206
Poor's land, Bethnal Green, 13
Portrait Gallery, National, 399
Poulson, Mr., on water, 383
Powell, J., on glass-painting, 160
Precious metals, works in the, 434
Precipitation of sewage, 165, 505
Preece, W. H., on electric lighting, 398, 399
President of the Institute's address to students, 79
President's address, Soc. of Engineers, 105
Prizes: Art-Union of London, 339; Carpenters' Company's, 17; Institute of British Architects, 59, 81
Professional chit-chat, 321
Pryce, T. E., on A. A. matters, 400
Public Health Act, London, case under, 295
Public Health Acts Amendment, 381
Pugin Studentship, the, 81

Railway Station, Walworth-road, 269
Rain-drops, 383, 402
Randolph, W., on town churches, 123
Rating of machinery, 87
Records of building in Shakspeare's time, 202, 203
Recreation-ground, Fulham, 479
Refuse-destructors, 330, 383, 388
Register House, Edinburgh, 104, 142
Registration of plumbers, 17, 147, 213, 233, 509
Regulations for safety of theatres, 124, 242, 264, 269, 382
Reid, Dr., on infection and disinfection, 143
Relation of architect to workman, 437, 462
Renaissance: English, 59; glass-painting, 160; ironwork, 283
Restler, J. W., evidence, Water Commission, 457
Restorations: Bristol Cathedral, 472; Lincoln Cathedral, 250, 257; Linlithgow Palace, 104, 356
Reynolds, W. B., on electric lighting, 399
Richardson, Dr., on sanitary matters, 82, 220
Roads, maintenance of, 382
Roechling, H. A., on Berlin sewage-farms, 304
Rosebery, Lord, on Linlithgow Palace, 356
Rosebery-avenue, 13, 357
Royal Academy: lectures on architecture, 75, 95, 116, 136, 156, 179; lectures on sculpture, 222
Royal Commission on Labour: building-trade evidence, 184, 230, 244
Royal Commission on Metropolitan Water Supply, 418, 435, 456, 480, 503
Royal Gold Medallist for 1892, 120
Royal Meteorological Soc., 88, 147, 329, 402
Russell, Hon. R., on epidemics, 147

Safety of theatres, 124, 242, 264, 269, 382
Saint Nicholas Church, Dalkeith, 183
St. Saviour's, Southwark, 207
Sakurai, K., on architecture in Somersetshire, 442
Sale of water by meter at Berlin, 9
Salt-market, old, Glasgow, 305
Sanitary Assurance Association, 127
Sanitary Institute's Exams., 18, 345, 387
Sanitary Inspectors' Association, 32, 143, 192, 228, 310, 383
Sanitation, results of, 310
Saracenic architecture, 75, 95, 116, 136, 156, 179

Saxon work at Oxford Cathedral, 165
Scavenging and refuse disposal, 388
School, Harrow, 477
School of Engineering, Crystal Palace, 324
Schools, technical, design of, 61
Sculpture: archaic and archaistic, 222; Greek, 57, 141, 154, 164, 184, 207, 222, 225
Sculptures of the Mausoleum, 154, 184
Seafield Castle, 383
Searle, J., evidence, Water Commission, 419
Sellers, Miss, on Greek art, 57, 141, 164, 184, 207, 225
Sewage-farms: Berlin, 304; Nottingham, 399; Peterborough, 483
Sewage precipitation, 165, 505
Sewer, Hackney Wick, 183
Sewers, ventilation of, 501
Sewerage works, Nottingham, 355
Sewerage and sewage disposal, 44
Shaftesbury Memorial Fountain, the, 357
Shakspeare's time, building in, 202
Shone system of town drainage, 501
Shute, John, 203
Sim, E. H., on literature and architecture, 287
Simmonds, J., evidence, Labour Commission, 184
Simonds, G., on bronze casting, 455
Singer, H., on bronze castings, 435
Slate trade, the, and builders, 425
Slater, J.: on building legislation, 122; on drawings at the Institute, 83; on the late T. H. Eagles, 281; on electric lighting, 398
Smart, W., on brick-burning, 193
Smith, T. T., on electric lighting, 398
Soane Medallion, the, 82
Society of Arts, papers at, 93, 125
Society of Antiquaries, 250, 257
Society of Engineers, 105
Society for Preserving Memorials of the Dead, 233
Soirée, Architectural Association, 383
Somerset House, disfigurement of, 377
Somersetshire architecture, 442
South London Ophthalmic Hosp., 289, 303
South Metropolitan Gasworks, 509
Southwark, St. Saviour's Church, 207
Southwark and Vauxhall Water Co., 457
Speech-Room, Harrow, 477
Spiers, R. Phené, on Byzantine architecture, 241
Spinks, W., on Public Health Acts, 381
Stained and painted glass, 159
Statham, H. H.: on building legislation, 122; on Chipiez's model of the Parthenon, 282; on ironwork, 284; on metal in architecture, 456
Steel applied to construction, 268
Stirk, J., evidence, Labour Commission, 216
Stockdale, J. C.: on building in Shakspeare's time, 204; on literature and architecture, 287
Stokes, L.: on A.A. matters, 401; on architects and handicrafts, 462; on fashions in architecture, 101
Story of a raindrop, 383
Strand to Holborn communication, 88
Street, new, Holborn to the Strand, 88
Streets, laying-out, 381
Students' night at the Institute, 79, 81
Suffolk churches, 83
Suggestions for competitions, 207
Sunley, S., evidence, Labour Commission, 216
Surrey Archæological Society, 225
Surveyors in the time of Shakspeare, 202
Surveyors' and Auctioneers' Clerks' Provident Association, 194
Surveyors' Institution: Examinations, 109, 322, 355; Scientific Study of Timber, 379

Tadema, A., on stained glass, 161
Teale, Dr., on dust, 93, 125
Technical colleges and schools, 61
Technical education: in Edinburgh, 74; and the London County Council, 306
Technicalities of glass painting, 160
Temples, Greek, 73, 207
Temple at Mecca, 76

Tenders at the London County Council, 64, 143, 244, 269, 289, 357, 382, 402, 506, 507
Tests for iron, 147, 191
Thames Conservators and the water question, 481, 503
Theatre-planning developments, 242, 264
Theatre, new, at Amsterdam, 240
Theatres: safety of, 124, 242, 264, 269, 382; Toole's, 269
Thorpe, John, 202
Timber, scientific study of, 379, 402
Tite Prize, the, 82
Topley, W., evidence, Water Commission, 422
Tottenham Court-road widening, 507
Tower Bridge, 244
Town: churches, 123; drainage, Shone system, 501
Townsend, H., on literature and architecture, 284, 287
Travellers' Club, new, 356
Treatment of stained glass, 159
Trellis-work, Egyptian, 180, 181
Turley, A., on sewage disposal, 44

Vacher, S.: on architects and craftsmen, 462; on electric lighting, 398
Vauxhall Bridge, 479
Ventilation of sewers, 501
Visits, Architectural Association's:— Harrow, 477; Imperial Institute, 165; Metropolitan Life Assurance Buildings, 123; New National Portrait Gallery, 399; New Travellers' Club, 356; Newington Weights and Measures Offices, 289; Royal South London Ophthalmic Hospital, 289, 303; St. Saviour's Church, Southwark, 207; Tower Bridge, 244

Wages and hours clause in contracts, 357, 402, 422, 439, 506
Walshaw, J. W., on municipal work at Peterborough, 482
Walworth-road Railway Station, 269
Water-meters in Berlin, 9
Water question, London, 64, 165, 183, 214, 418, 422, 507
Water supply, Berlin, 9
Water supply, London: Royal Commission, 418, 435, 456, 480, 503
Water supply of Peterborough, 483
Water-gate, Buckingham-street, 143
Waterhouse, P.: on fashions in architecture, 101; on Suffolk churches, 83
Webb, Aston: on clerks of works, 144; on students' work at the Institute, 81
Weights and Measures Office, Newington, 289
Wellington statue, Edinburgh, 104, 142
West Middlesex Water Company, 436
Westlake, N. H. J.: on fashions in architecture, 99; on glass painting, 160
Westminster, Emanuel Hospital, 65
Whall, C. W., on stained glass, 162
White, W. H., on Chipiez's model of the Parthenon, 282
Whitelaw, C. E., on Irish architecture, 305
Whitley,—Evidence, Labour Commission, 246
Wilson, J. W., on engineering, 105
Winchester, stained glass at, 160
Windmills as electric motors, 193
Windows, stained glass, 159
Woodrow, E., on theatre-planning, 242
Woodthorpe, E.: on building legislation, 122; on fashions in architecture, 101; on theatre-planning, 264
Wollheim, A., on sewage precipitation, 505
Woolner, T., R.A., on art and health, 229
Workman and the architect, the, 437, 462
Wren's Library at Lincoln, 250, 257

Yester House and Castle, 305
York water-gate, the, 143
Young, W. C., evidence at Water Commission, 436

CORRESPONDENCE.

Subjects of Letters.

Adjoining buildings, 85
Air-bound pipes, 144
Amendment of the Building Act, 33, 49
American journal, piracy by a, 404
Arbitration, Hornsey main roads, 463
Architects' monuments, 107
Architectural Association, 403
Architectural education, 292, 310, 325, 342, 361, 384, 403
Art, Japanese, 271
Art-Galleries competition, Glasgow, 342
Artisans' dwellings, 107, 125, 144, 166, 190; competition, Halifax, 210, 231
Ayr, *insulæ* at, 190
Berlin waterworks, 107
Bolsover colliery competition, 65, 85
Boston Church, 384, 404
Brickwork, computation of, 210, 249
British Museum, lectures at, 248
Building Act for London, future, 33, 49
Building by-laws for London, 65
Building penalty, 444, 463
Building stones in Ireland, 270
Buildings, adjoining, 85
Carpenters' strike, the late, 190, 211
Casings for electric wires, 190

Subjects of Letters (continued):—
Cathedral, St. Albans, work at, 362, 384
Cemetery, Ripon, 271
Changes at the Institute, 507
Chester, crypt in Watergate-street, 248
Chipiez's model of the Parthenon, 230
Christ's Hospital, 363
Churches: Boston, 384, 404; Hertford, 14; Tetnes, 33, 50; Lewisham, 484
Coke-breeze concrete, 125, 144, 210, 230
Competitions: artisans' dwellings, Halifax, 210, 231; Bolsover colliery, 65, 85; Ripon cemetery, 271; Victoria Cathedral, B.C., 444
Computation of brickwork, 210, 249
Concrete: for artisans' dwellings, 107, 125, 144, 166, 190; flooring boards on, 65, 85, 107
Contract, payments on, 230
Crypt, Watergate-street, Chester, 248
Designs: Glasgow Art Galleries, 342; railway bridge, 362, 384
Dust, 125
Education, architectural, 292, 310, 325, 342, 361, 384, 403
Election of Fellows, R.I.B.A., 463
Electric wires, casings for, 190
Evidence, Labour Commission, 230

Subjects of Letters (continued):—
Examinations at the Institute, 14
Firebrick, 444
Fires, extinguishing, 166
Flooring-boards on concrete, 65, 85, 107
Font, ancient, at Northampton, 422
Glasgow Art Galleries competition, 342
Grissell Medal competition, the, 362, 384
Holborn to Strand communication, 229
Hornsey main roads arbitration, 463
Ireland, building-stones of, 270
Institute: Examinations, 14; election of Fellows, 463; status of members at, 507
Institution, Royal, Manchester, 247
Insulæ, Silchester and Ayr, 190
Japanese art, 271
Jew's house, Lincoln, 106
Labour Commission, the, 230
Ladders, safety of, 362
Lectures, British Museum, 248
Lewisham parish church, 484
Lincoln: Cathedral, 247; Jew's house, 106; Wren's Library, 247, 270, 293
Liverpool motive power, 166
London building by-laws, 65
Maintenance of main roads, 248, 311, 326
Manchester Royal Institution, 247
Match-boarding on new walls, 126

Subjects of Letters (continued):—
Measuring brickwork, 210, 249
Metropolitan Building Act, 33, 49
Monuments to architects, 107
Motive-power at Liverpool, 166
Oak-block flooring on concrete, 126
Paint, removing, 293, 311
Parthenon, M. Chipiez's model, 230
Payments on contract, 230
Penalty, building, 444, 463
Pipes, air-bound, 144
Piracy by an American journal, 404
Railway bridge, design for a, 362, 384
"Restoration" at Lincoln Cathedral, 247
Restorations by Scott, 325, 326, 361, 384
Ripon Minster and Sir G. Scott, 326
Road maintenance, 248, 311, 326
Rood-screens, 15, 50
Royal Commission on Labour, 230
Royal Institution, Manchester, 247
Saint Albans Cathedral, work at, 362, 384
St. Antholin's steeple, 361
Scott's restorations, 325, 326, 361, 384
Screens, rood, 15, 50; fourteenth and fifteenth century, 463, 484, 507
Silchester, *insulæ* at, 190
Status of the architect, R.I.B.A., 507
Steam-rolling on main-roads, 248, 311, 326

CORRESPONDENCE—*Subjects of Letters (continued)*:—

Steeple of St. Antholin's, the, 361
Stone, old, found at King's Cross, 50
Stones, building, in Ireland, 270
Strand and Holborn communication, 229
Strike, carpenters', 190, 211
Tar on slates, 50
Tiles, soft, 33
Totnes Church, 33, 50
Valuation, 210
Varnish, 231, 271
Ventilation of workrooms, 507
Victoria (B.C.) Cathedral competn., 444
Watch-house, old, at King's Cross, 50
Waterworks, Berlin, 107
Work at St. Albans Cathedral, 362, 384
Workrooms, ventilation of, 507
Wren's Library at Lincoln, 247, 270, 293

Writers of Letters

Adams, C. A., architectural education, 292, 325, 384
Baker, A., Scott's restorations, 325, 361, 384

Writers of Letters (continued):—
Brodie, C. H., architectural education, 310
Burrell, W., Architectural Association, 403
Clarke, Somers: "restoration at Lincoln," 247, 293; Scott's restorations, 361
Cresswell, H. O.: architectural education, 310; A.A. matters, 403
Deane, T. M., Glasgow Galleries designs, 342
Drew, T., building stones of Ireland, 270
Duncan, L. L., Lewisham Church, 484
Farrow, F. R., Architectural Assoc., 403
Fawkes, F. A., electric wire casings, 190
Ferguson, C. J., Wren's Library, Lincoln, 270
Fleming, O., architectural education, 310
Flower, A. S., measuring, 249
Gale, E. S.: Architectural Association, 403; architectural education, 310
Gill, G. H., Berlin waterworks, 107
Godbolt, G., removing old paint, 311
Goldsmith, F. T. W., A.A. matters, 403
Greenwell, A., steam rolling, 248, 311
Grimthorpe, Lord, on work at St. Albans, 362, 384
Harlock, H., Grissell Medal, 384
Hems, H., 14th and 15th c. screens, 484
Hill, A., Institute examinations, 14

Writers of Letters (continued):—
Humphreys, H. H., Grissell Medal, 362
Hunter, J. K., "*insula*," 190
Jackson, T. G.: architectural education, 361; Institute examinations, 14
Johnson, R., extinguishing fires, 166
Jones, R., computation of brickwork, 210
Kenwood, J. C., firebrick, 444
Knightley, T. E., Building Act, 49
Lottie, W. J.: Scott's restorations, 325; Wren's Library, Lincoln, 270
Lovegrove, H., building penalty, 463
Lunn, W., Scott's restorations, 361
Luscombe, E. G. S., Totnes Church, 50
McArthy, D., removing old paint, 311
Mathews, J. D., St. Antholin's steeple, 301
Medland, J., Scott's restorations, 361
Millard, W., architectural education, 310
Moore, F. A., evidence before the Labour Commission, 230
Mountford, E. W., A.A. matters, 403
Neale, J., piracy by American journal, 404
Nicholl, S. J., watch-house at King's Cross, 50
Parry, J., motive-power at Liverpool, 166
Phillips, R., main roads, 248, 326
Potter, T., concrete, 125, 166

Writers of Letters (continued):—
Pratt, H. W., Architectural Assoc., 403
Pryce, T. E., architectural education, 310
Ruck-Keene, B., screens, 463
Scargill, W., All Saints' Ch., Hertford, 14
Scott, G. G.: font, Northampton, 423; crypt in Watergate-street, 248
Sellers, Miss, lectures, Brit. Museum, 248
Simmons, W., coke breeze concrete, 230
Simpson, F. M.: architectural education, 310; street, Holborn to Strand, 229
Stokes, L., architectural education, 310, 312, 361
Teale, Dr., dust, 125
Vacher, S., membership, R.I.B.A., 507
Venables, E., Jew's house, Lincoln, 106
Weatherley, W. S., Boston Church, 404
White, H. F., removing old paint, 293
White, William H., Chipiez's model of the Parthenon, 230
Wight, N., Japanese art, 271
Williams, H. R., Hornsey main roads arbitration, 463
Woodthorpe, E., Architectural Assoc., 403
Worthington, L., artisans' dwellings competition, Halifax, 231

GENERAL.

Abbey, Bourn, 146
Accidents, railway, in India, 234
Actinograph, Harter & Driffield's, 51
Admiralty buildings, new, 509
"Almack's," 146
Altars: Belchamp St. Paul's, 338; Felton, 50
Amendment of the Building Acts, 86
American: drain-pipes, 169; railway bridges, 128
Antiquities, Danish, 322
Appointments, 51, 251, 395, 402, 506
Architectship, City, Aberdeen, 104, 213
Architectural: books, sale of, 487; Examination and the timber-trade, 329
Art Union of London: plates, 184
Artisans' dwellings: Austria, 53; Dublin, 168; Essen, 425; Manchester, 212
Artisans' Dwellings Co., 170
Aspinall Memorial Hall, Liverpool, 327
Associates, new, of Royal Academy, 87
Assoc. of Municipal Engineers, 213, 295, 344
Asylums: Blackburn, 183; Claybury, 328; Coxlodge, 143, 247; Rossiville, N.S.W., 233, 307; Sunderland, 143, 183
Athenæum Offices, new, 233
Athens, mosaic at, 329
Auction sales in 1891, 36
Australia, electric light in, 168
Austrian law as to artisans' dwellings, 53
Aztec city, discovery of, 397

Bank premises: Adlington, 66; Leeds, 66, 146, 486; Oldham, 192; Rotherham, 386; St. Helens, 446.
Barrett-Browning Memorial, Ledbury, 394
Bath Herald, centenary of, 251
Bath Pump-room, 212, 232, 509
Baths: Aston, 232; Cheetham, 406, 416; Farnworth, 307; Salford, 464; Salisbury, 17; Southampton, 232; Stafford, 364; Stockton, 108; Walsall, 498
Bells, 34, 193, 466
Bexley system of emptying cesspools, 287
Bingley Railway Station, 386
Birmingham: building in, 35, 66; workmen's dwellings, 509
Bishopsgate Girls' School, 16
Bonar Bridge viaduct, Sutherland, 425
Boring tools, square-hole, 295
Bourn Abbey, 146
Brick machine, Kennedy, 365
Bricks, paving, 169
Bricklayers' wages, London, 296
Bridge, suspension, in Iceland, 85
Bridges: Brooklyn, 147; Stockport, 192; Vienna, 293; Writtle, 168
Bristol Cathedral, 313
British Association for the Advancement of Science, 425
British mineral production, 466
British Museum lectures, 14
Broad-gauge, last of the, 407, 425
Brompton Hospital Chapel, 294
Brussels a sea-port, 169
Builders' hardware in France, 357
Building: industry, Mexico, 307; legislation, London, 86
Building Regulations Bill, Glasgow, 128
Building-trade failures in 1891, 18
Building trade in Scotland in 1891, 85
Building-trade wages in Havre, 251
Buildings for the Salvation Army, 344
Burial-ground, Southwark, 110
Bust of the late W. H. Smith, 170

Canals: Finland, 87; Nicaragua, 447
Canterbury Cathedral, 156

Capital and Labour:—Bricklayers, London, 298, 460, 473, 488; Bricklayers' strike at Harrogate, 365; Bricklayers' strike, Redditch, 447; Bricklayers' strike at Worcester, 365; Brickmakers' strike in West London, 425; Building trade in Scotland in 1891, 35; Building-trade strike in Birmingham, 365; Building-trade strike at Cardiff, 365, 466, 488; Building-trade wages in Geneva, 364; Building-trade wages in Havre, 251; Building-trade wages in London, 473, 466, 488; Building trades evidence given before the Royal Commission on Labour, 184, 230, 244; Carpenters' strike, the recent, 190, 211; Coal-porters, London strike of, 134; Coal trade strike in the North, 176, 199, 220, 239, 280, 336, 393; Eight-hours question, the, 393, 496; Engineering trades in the North, 92, 115, 154; Labourers, Blackwall Tunnel works, 183; London County Council and rates of wages, 357, 402, 422, 431, 439; Masons' strike at Harrogate, 365; Masons' strike, Nelson, 447; Workmen's combinations a century ago, 221
Carlisle, Tullie House, 464
Carpenters' Co.: exhibition, 273; prizes, 17
Carpenters' Hall, lectures at, 67
Cambrian Academy of Art, 88
Cambridge: Slade Professorship, 68
Casement window, Sim's, 128
Casing for electric light wires, 314
Cathedrals: Bristol, 313; Canterbury, 156; Dunblane, 424; Lichfield, 127; Lincoln, 312; Norwich, 66; Peterborough, 108; Portsmouth, 294; St. Macartan's Monoghan, 406
Cements: Keene's, 346; Portland, tests for, 274; Robinson's, 345; strong, 272
Cemetery chapels, Northfleet, 207
Cesspool emptying, Bexley system, 287
Changes of address, 212, 233, 274, 295, 503
Chapels: Brompton Hospital, 294; St. Margaret's House, Roath, 364
Chicago: Exhibition, 87, 142, 345, 407, 465; tall building in, 110
Choir-stalls, Christ Church, Clifton, 18
Church of St. Magdalen, 329

Church Building News:—Ambergate, 146; Apperley Bridge, 446; Belfast, 406; Berrow, 487; Blackheath, 87; Bonane, 508; Bridgeton, 232; Brighton, 108; Brignall, 445; Brittol, 127; Camberwell, 201; Cardiff, 232; Chacewater, 104, 122; Clifton, 18; Derby, 353, 405; Edinburgh, 424; Emsworth, 146; Falstone, 446; Felton, 51; Giggleswick, 405; Glasgow, 232; Grayingham, 461; Haddington, 313; Hanmer, 344; Highweek, 192; Hilton, 312; Herringworth, 446; Jedburgh, 328; Jersey, 445; Leytonstone, 273; Lichfield Cathedral, 127; London, 87; Long Clawson, 140; Lulsley, 406; Marcross, 486; Mickleham, 168; Moreton-in-the Marsh, 424; New Kilpatrick, 386; Normacot, 191; Plymouth, 213; Plymstock, 364; Poplar, 509; Portobello, 192; Preston, 461; Ranmoor, 53; Saundby, 213; Shaldon, 66; Smethwick, 424; Staines, 67; Sunderland, 465; Stranraer, 446; Teddington, 461; Torquay, 213; Tottington, 232; Uphill, 406; Waddesdon, 508; Wainfleet, 328; West Bromwich, 191; Wetton, 146; Wimborne Minster, 16; Winterborne Stickland, 273; Woodham Mortimer, 405; Woodleigh, 35; Wybunbury, 364
Churches, city, 329
Circular saws, setting, 68
Circus, Edgehill, 192
Climatology, 53
Clock-tower near Victoria Station, 233
Clocks, 169, 251, 330, 433
Club buildings: Bacup, 344; Chorlton-cum-Hardy, 364; Failsworth, 509; Glasgow, 312; Lincoln, 250; Newmarket, 273; Roath, 386
Coinage, the new, 323
College, R.C., Glasgow, 232
College of Surgeons, Dublin: schools, 127
Columbus, monument, New York, 487
Competitions: Art Galleries, Glasgow, 317, 335, 342, 357, 502; Artisans' dwellings, Halifax, 200, 210, 231; Assessors in, 200; Asylum, Blackburn, 183; Asylum, Coxlodge, 143, 247; Asylum, Rossiville, New South Wales, 233, 307; Asylum, Sunderland, 143, 183; Australia, 221, 233; Baths, Farnworth, 307; Baths, Walsall, 498; Barrett-Browning Memorial, Ledbury, 394; 415; Cathedral, Victoria, British Columbia, 392, 444; Cemetery, Ripon, 271; Cemetery Chapels, Northfleet, 207; Church restoration, Chacewater, 104, 122; Coinage, the new, 323; Cottage Hospital, Galashiels, 480; County Council Buildings, Stafford, 258, 498; Designs for floorcloth and linoleum, 388; Drainage of Sofia, 301, 329; Higher-Grade School, Winchester, 422; Hospital, Birmingham, 207, 217, 246; Hospital (infectious), West Fife, 480; Institute Suggestions, the, 207; Library, Willesden, 422; Municipal Buildings, Bath, 30; Municipal Buildings, Bury, 380; Municipal Buildings, Oxford, 491; Parochial Offices, Battersea, 5; Pier, Beaumaris, 67; Police Station, Shrewsbury, 165; School Board Offices, Keighley, 13; School, houses, &c., Bolsover Colliery, 65, 85; Schools, Burslem, 422; Schools, Chadsmoor, 18; Schools, Goole, 247; Schools, Penrith, 323; Technical School, Aston Manor, 183; Technical Schools, Darwen, 165; Technical Schools, Heywood, 307; Town-hall, Llanelly, 321; Truants' schools, Lichfield, 104; Whitworth Institute, Manchester, 75, 84, 94; Wesleyan Chapel, Barnard Castle, 498; Wesleyan Chapel, Harrogate, 41
Compulsion in sanitary matters, 19
Concentration of population, 407
Concrete-mixing machine, 110
Congress, sanitary, workmen's, 128
Convent, Granard, 344
Conversion of gauge, G.W.R., 407, 425
Co-operative buildings: Bradford, 386; Broomhill, 87; Jarrow, 313; Leeds, 192; Pelaw, 213; Seaton Burn, 250; Shiremoor, 321
Copper-trade in 1891, 67
Cork pavement, 53
County Architectship, Cumberland, 251
County Buildings, Edinburgh, 406
County Council, Cornwall, 194, 314
Court-houses: Birkdale, 313; Glasgow, 167
Coventry-street, 109
Crapper & Co.'s sanitary appliances, 314
Crossbones burial ground, Southwark, 110
Croydon Municipal Buildings, 486
Crush at Hampstead Heath Station, 330
Cutting-off the water supply, 509

Darwen Technical Schools, 165
Debt-recovery and water supply, 214
Decoration, Leeds Town hall, 424
Depôt for Pickford & Co., Queen-st., 192
Diocesan surveyorships, 51
Dissenting Church Building News: Aberdeen, 108; Barnard Castle, 498; Barnstaple, 213; Bedwas (Mon.), 446; Beverley, 168; Blackbrook, St. Helens, 167; Cudworth, 477; Devonport, 87; Edinburgh, 127; Felton, 51; Gateshead, 486; Greenock, 273; Harrogate, 41; Illogan, 127; Laugharne, 424; Launceston, 250; Lichfield, 424; Newtonbreda, 232; Paisley, 327, 386; Ramsey, I.M., 168; Ripley, 446; Salford, 66; Shadwell, 364; Sherwood, 386; West Auckland, 191; Withington, 108; Wolverton, 312
Dissolutions of partnerships, 35, 365, 439
Docks: Antwerp, 52; Liverpool, 487
Drain-pipe test at Nottingham, 425
Drain-pipes, American, 169
Dredging process, a new, 365
Drill-halls, Exeter, 424
Dry-press brick machine, Kennedy, 365
Dublin: Artisans' dwellings, 169; College of Surgeons, 127; Mansion House, 510
Dust-collecting in St. Pancras, 251

Eaton Hall, 295
Edinburgh: County Buildings, 406; General Post Office, 294; new park, 53; new observatory, 204; Restalrig Free Church, 127; Solicitors' Library, 405; Theological College, 508; trades' hall, 68; Trades' Maiden Hospital, 407
Education, engineering, 18
Electric lighting: Australia, 168; Berlin, 169; Copenhagen, 509; Manchester, 408; Nelson, 408; Mansion House, London, 214; South Africa, 193
Electric mains, underground, 407
Electric-wire casings, 314
Emigrants, information for, 345
Enamelled metal, 346
Engineering: education, 18; trades', 37
Engravings, sale of, 169
Euphrates Valley Railway, 314
Examination, architectural, timber-trade, view of, 329
Exchange, Manchester, 445
Exhibitions: Carpenters' Company's, 273; Chicago, 87, 142, 315, 407, 465; electrical, Moscow, 170, 295; Finnish, 290; of Indian metal work, 346; Isle of Man, 251; Lemberg, 329

Factories, warming and ventilating, 330
Factory, Bristol, 424
Failures in the building trade in 1891, 18
Farringdon Market, new, 486
Ferdinand's Bridge, Vienna, 293
Festivities, 365
Fire-engines, 214, 295
Fireproof: construction, 18; paint, 387
Floor-materials, wear of, 314
Floorcloth, designs for, 388
Fog, London, 193

Foreign and Colonial:—Africa, South, 193, 320; Antwerp, 52; Australia, 168, 233, 307, 316; Austria, 53; Belgium, 53, 169; Berlin, 17, 146, 168, 169, 193, 213, 233, 250, 295, 328, 344, 387, 407, 424, 447, 465; Bombay, 487; Brussels, 169; Bulgaria, 387; Cairo, 487; Capetown, 329; Constantinople, 169; Copenhagen, 509; Denmark, 36, 100, 313, 322, 447, 509; Finland, 87, 290; France, 52, 67, 87, 109, 127, 146, 168, 192, 213, 250, 273, 295, 313, 328, 344, 365, 387, 407, 424, 446, 465, 486, 509; Geneva, 364; Gothenburg, 18; Hamburg, 425; Helsingfors, 290; Heidelberg, 193; Holland, 387; Iceland, 85; Information for emigrants, 345; Lemberg, 329; Mexico, 307; Moscow, 170, 295; Munich, 17, 169, 233, 250, 329, 465; New South Wales, 168, 169, 233, 307, 346; New York, 365; Norway, 52, 109, 169, 320, 446; Oldenburg, 193; Paris, 233; Russia, 170, 273, 295, 447; St. Petersburg, 273, 447; Sofia, 329; Stuttgart, 36, 465; Sweden, 16, 17, 18, 52, 68, 127, 193, 313, 405; Switzerland, 193, 250, 345, 465; Sydney, 87; Vienna, 36, 169, 193, 293, 315, 387, 487
Foreshore Improvements, Southport, 447
Foresters' Hall, Plymouth, 250
Footpace, Manchester Cathedral, 214
Fountain presented to Ayr, 480
Foy, Morgan, & Co.'s Wood Report, 52
France, road-making in, 315
Freeholds, Kentish-town, 425
French Embassy, St. Petersburg, 273

Gas companies and gasfitting, 330
Girls' Home, Ballysillan, 465
Girls' Institute, Manchester, 327

GENERAL (continued):—

Glasgow: Art Galleries competition, 357; Buildings Regulations Bill, 128: Court-house, 167; Technical College, 170, 193; tunnels under the Clyde, 344; R.C. College, 234
Grammar School, Horsham, 35
"Gravita" water-meter, 251
Great Western Railway: last of the broad-gauge, 407, 425
Gymnasium, Hulme, 87

Halls: Cardiff, 294; Cwmaman, 87; Liverpool, 327; Plymouth, 250, 344; Salisbury, 108; Silksworth, 445; Warnham, 364
Hampstead Heath Station, 330, 379
Harbours: Ardrossan, 328; Dover, 447
Hardware, builders', in France, 337
Hardwick, the late P.C., 108
Hard-wood trade in 1891, 36
Havre, building-trade wages in, 251
Highest-grade School, Portsmouth, 273
Hints to taxpayers, 214
Homes, sailors', 466
Hospitals: Birmingham, 207; Brentford, 66; Manchester, 312; Stoke Newington, 328; Torbay, 109; West Fife, 480; Wolverhampton, 17
Hospitals, cottage: Galashiels, 480; High Wycombe, 35; Ledbury, 35; Middlesbrough, 87; Willesden, 174
Hotel, Belfast, 192
Hygiene, street, 169
"Hylonite," 466

Improvements: Dewsbury, 509; Nelson, 408; Sheffield, 330; West Hartlepool, 67
Incorporated Association of Municipal and County Engineers, 213, 295, 344
India, railway accidents in, 234
Indian metal-work, 316
Infirmary, Leeds, 232
Information for emigrants, 345
Institutes: Girls', Manchester, 327; workmen's, Deepcar, 327; Woodhouse, Leeds, 364
Institution of Mechanical Engineers, 67
Irish seal, a new, 345
Iron and steel production of Belgium, 53
Iron Trade, English, 33, 52, 68, 85, 110, 123, 147, 170, 194, 214, 234, 251, 273, 280, 329, 345, 365, 379, 408, 434, 460, 479, 493
Isle of Man Exhibition, 251

Keene's cement, early days of, 346
Kennedy dry-press brick machine, 365
Killeen Castle, 109

Land: Chiswick, 425; Hastings, 509; sales of, 1891, 110; Victoria Embankment, 178
Landing-stage, Holyhead, 510
Leary & Co.'s hardwood circular, 36
Lectern, Ranmoor Church, 53
Leeds: Infirmary, 232; street improvement, 53
Legislation, sanitary, and overcrowding, 425
Lens, photographic, 18
Libraries: Birmingham, 498; Solicitors', Edinburgh, 405; Free, Willesden, 422
Library of Mr. Wyatt Papworth, 487
Lift at the Metropolitan Tabernacle, 83
Linoleum, designs for, 398
Liverpool: Aspinall Memorial Hall, 327; docks, 487
London: building legislation, 86; parishes, surveys of, 443; water-question (see "Water Supply")
London County Council and the tramways, 329
London and County Banking Co., 128
Ludgate-hill, widening of, 365
Lyric Theatre, the, 407

Machine for mixing concrete, 110
Mains, electric, 407
Manchester: artisans' dwellings, 212; Cathedral, foot-pace, 214; electric lighting, 408; Exchange alterations, 445; Girls' Institute, 327; Hospital for Consumption, 312; Whitworth Institute, 84, 94
Manchester, Sheffield, and Lincolnshire Railway Bill, 313
Manor-house, Ockwells, 447
Mansion House, London, electric lighting at, 214
Mansion House, Dublin, decorations, 510
Maps of London, new, 295
Market buildings: Abertillery, 232; Farringdon, 486; Gateshead, 364; Halifax, 405; London, 436; Wigan, 273
Marlborough House, 328
Marylebone, sanitary conveniences, 295
Matheson & Grant's engineering trades' report, 37
Medals, Society of Arts, 510
Metal, enamelled, 346
Metal-work, Indian, 346
Metopes found at Selinus, 214
Metropolitan Building Acts, 86
Metropolitan Tabernacle: lift, 83
Metropolitan water-question, 346
Mineral production, British, 466
Miners' Hall, Silksworth, 445
Mission Hall, Cardiff, 294
Mission Hall, Plymouth, 344
Mission Church, Bristol, 127
Monoghan: St. Macartan's Cathedral, 406
Monuments: to Columbus, New York, 487; Kirkintilloch Cemetery, 12
Morning Post Offices, 232
Mosaic at Athens, 329
Municipal Buildings: Bombay, 487; Croydon, 486
Municipal and County Engineers' Association, 213, 295, 344.

Newcastle Cathedral bells, 466
New York: Columbus monument, 487; scavenging in, 365
Nicaragua canal, 447
Nineteenth Century Art Society, 37, 351
Norwich Cathedral, 66
"Novelty" Theatre, the, 345

Obituary:—Audrien, M., 354; Bailly, A. N., 27; Barbedienne, M., 264; Barradale, I., 212; Beadel, W. J., M.P., 294; Beaty, T., 169; Bidlake, G., 361; Blanchard, M. H., 127; Bristowe, T. L., M.P., 453, 479; Bruce, Dr. J. C., 294; Burnell, E. H., 312; Carpenter, Dr. A., 86; Chaffers, W., 327; Chesser, J., 146; Coode, Sir J., 191; Duke of Clarence, 42, 64; Dupont, L. P. H., 95; Eagles, T. H., 281, 294; Edwards, Miss A. B., 327; Foggin, W., 86; Freeman, Prof. E. A., 231, 240; Hammon, H. J., 405; Hardwick, P. C., 108, 120; Hudson, W., 212; Johnson, R. J., 343, 353; Leloir, J. B. A., 264; Melida, E., 355; Monnier, J. E., 355; Morgan, T., F.S.A., 66; Poole, H., 212; Porter, A., 66; Price, J. E., 108; Rhind, J., A.R.S.A., 294; Robinson, F. J., 364; Roper, G. F., 405; Rüntz, J., 16; Sanders, W. B., 86; Shillitoe, J., 16; Smith, W., 16; Stocks, Lumb, 364; Thomson, Dr. J., 386; Watson, 339; Wilkinson, W., 16; Zerffi, G. G., 108
Observatory, new, Edinburgh, 294
Ockwells Manor-house, 447
Oddfellows' Building, Chicago, 110
Offices: Local Board, Felixstowe, 66; *Morning Post*, 232; Slaithwaite, 424
Orphan Working School, 51
Organs, electric, 365
Over-crowding in cities, 425
Oxford-circus sanitary conveniences, 295

Paint, fireproof, 387
Palace, Bishopthorpe, 146
Parish Buildings: Burton-on-Trent, 445; Newcastle, 360; Plymouth, 344
Parks: Dewsbury, 509; Edinburgh, 53
Partnerships, 35, 194, 365, 439
Patent Office, site for, 233
Patent Office Report, 465
Patents, recent:—Bolts, 426; brace-bits, 111; brick-kilns, 53, 252; brick-making machinery, 19, 111, 234, 314, 510; bricks, 37, 274, 275, 314; bridge-flooring, 170; building-blocks, 510; cements, 111, 148, 511; chandeliers, 69; channels, underground, 170; chimney-tops, 53, 69, 89, 274; chimneys, 170, 315; cowls, 274, 366, 448; decorative material, 19; distemper, 467; door-fastenings, 331, 488; door-furniture, 37, 69; door-hooks, 466; door latches, 388; door pivots, 426; door-springs, 488; doors and gates, 69, 129, 195; drain plug, 215; drainage, 195; drain-testing, 89; drain ventilation, 129, 388, 488; drilling-machine, 331; electric-light fittings, 331; facings, architectural, 296; fireplaces, 19, 37, 148, 195, 297; fireproof construction, 215, 275, 331; flooring cramp, 129; floors, 19, 215, 331, 347; flushing cisterns, 129, 170, 234, 296; gasfittings, 274; glazing-bars, 148, 388; grates, 19, 297; gully-traps, 215; heating apparatus, 366; joints for pipes, 215, 252; kilns, 53, 252, 346, 366; knobs and door handles, 37, 331; lathing metallic, 408; lavatory basins, 53; louvre windows, 53; nails, 346; parquetry, 37, 252; pipe-connexions, 456; pipe-hooks, 366; pipe-joints, 215, 252; planes, 426; portable buildings, 111, 488; ranges, 19; roofs, 89, 111; sash cords, 69; sash-fasteners, 170, 252, 296, 321, 366; saw for cutting stone, 37; saws, 274; scaffoldings, 69; screws, metal, 129; sewer ventilation, 488; shutters, swinging, 129; sinks, 215; size-paint, 314; sliding-doors, 426; smoke prevention, 170; solution for damp walls, 389; solution, preservative, 510; staircases, fireproof, 215; stair-treads, 19; stone-cutting, 37; stoves, 37; subways, 170; white lead, 234; tiles, 37, 315, 486, 510; ventilation, 148, 315, 488; ventilation of drains, 129, 388, 488; ventilators, 148, 274, 315, 347, 448, 466; waste-preventing cisterns, 129, 170; water-closets, 19, 53, 89, 298; water-pipes, 89; window-sashes and frames, 19, 37, 69, 148, 195, 234, 408, 448, 466
Pavement, cork, 53
Paving-brick, a strong, 169
Photographic: lens, 18; plates, time measurement for, 51
Pipe-bender, a, 251
Plastering, Robinson's, 345
Plates of the Art Union of London, 184
Police buildings: Cathcart, 405; Great Witley, 191; Shrewsbury, 165
Poor-Law buildings, Croydon, 312
Population, concentration of, 407
Portland cement tests, 274
Post Offices: Edinburgh, 294; Goole, 192
Powers of water companies, 509
Price, the late J. E., 108
Prints and engravings, sale of, 169
Prizes: Carpenters' Company's, 17; Turners' Company's, 446
Production of tin-plates, U.S., 407
Progress at West Hartlepool, 67
Properties for sale, 109, 307, 329, 345, 407, 465
Public Health (London) Act, 18, 295
Pulpit, Bridestone, 167
Pump Room, Bath, 212, 232, 509

Raft, a big, 346
Railway: accidents in India, 234; bridges in America, 128
Railway Stations: Bingley, 386; Hampstead Heath, 330, 379
Railways: electric, in Siam, 407; Euphrates Valley, 314; new, to London, 313; new cross-country, 460; Northern of Sweden, 68; through Siberia, 18; of the world, 273, 314
Removals, 212, 233, 274, 295, 503
Reredoses: Belchamp St. Paul's, 386; Berrow, Somerset, 487; Felton, 50
Restoration of Wimborne Minster, 16
Results of auction sales in 1891, 36
Reynolds, Sir Joshua, 251
Road-making in France, 345
Roman Catholic Church Building News:—Christchurch, Hants, 65; Drogheda, 420; Portsmouth, 294
Royal Academy: new Associates, 87; lectures, 36, 109
Royal Cambrian Academy of Art, 88
Royal Institution, 251
Royal Meteorological Society, 53

Sailors' homes, 466
St. Macartan's Cathedral, Monoghan, 406
St. Margaret's House of Mercy, Roath, 364
St. Mary Magdalene, Church of, 329
St. Pancras, dust-collecting in, 251
St. Petersburg, French Embassy, 273
Sales: of architectural books, 487; prints and engravings, 169; property (see "Property")
Salvation Army buildings, 344
Sanatorium, Ladywell, Eccles, 509
Sanitary: catalogues, 345; Congress, workmen's, 128; conveniences, Marylebone, 295; conveniences near Victoria Station, 233; legislation and overcrowding, 425; matters, compulsion in, 19; specialities at Chelsea, 314
Sanitary Inspectors' Association, 68
Sanitary Institute, 87, 425
Sash, Brett's reversible, 144
Saw-mill, electric, 263
Saws, setting circular, 68
Scavenging: in New York, 365; unseasonable, 69
School Board Offices, Keighley, 13
School Building News:—Baildon, 508; Barking, 51; Barry, 327; Bearpark, 232; Bishopsgate, 16; Brecon, 364; Brighton, 108; Bristol, 424; Bruton, 344; Burslem, 422; Canonbury, 206; Chadsmoor, 13; Crossness, 507; Darnall, 508; Dublin, 127; Edinburgh, 465; Greenheys, 166; Harrogate, 509; Hartlepool, 191; Hastings, 212; Horsham, 35; Idle, 446; Kingswood, 424; Leeds, 446; Lichfield, 104; London, 276; Manchester, 406; Middleton, 445; Northfleet, 109; Percy Main, 36; Poolstock, 508; Portsmouth, 278; Quaker's Yard, 344; Sheffield, 51; Skipton, 67; South Shields, 508; Weston-Super-Mare, 386; Widnes, 386; Wigan, 109, 503; Winchester, 422
Science and Art Schools, Weston-super-Mare, 386
Scotch building trade in 1891, 35
Screw, a perfect, 147
Sea-defences at Lancing, 329
Seal, new, for Ireland, 315
Sessions Court, Great Witley, 191
Setting circular saws, 63
Sewer-pipes, American, 169
Sewerage and Drainage:—Abergwynfy, 364; Accrington, 67; Ash-next-Sandwich, 328; Berlin, 304; Birkdale, 67; Bournemouth, 192; Cape Town, 329; Castle Donnington, 67; Chester-le-Street, 51; Cranleigh, 109; Ellesmere Port, 328; Hayes (Middlesex), 36; Hendon, 406; Hornsey, 386; King's Norton, 424; Knaresborough, 17; Llandaff Yard, 109; London, 140; Loughborough, 273; Ludlow, 406; Nottingham, 355; Orphan Working School, Haverstock Hill, 51; Peasmarsh, 294; Peterborough, 482; Pocklington, 386; Poole, 17; Rawdon, 127; Royton, 294; Sale, 109; Sofia, 301, 329; Stone, 273; Swansea, 168; West Hartlepool, 67; Whitby, 329; Whitchurch, Cardiff, 406; Wincanton, 344
Sexey's Trade School, Bruton, 344
Shops, Cardiff, 167
Siemens' Brothers' works, 337
Slade Professorship, Cambridge, 68
Slate trade in 1891, 36
Slate, waste, use for, 233
Slaughter-houses, Bradford, 386
Smoke and fog, 193
Society of Arts, 87, 510
Society for the Encouragement of the Fine Arts, 34
Sorbonne, Paris, 87
Southport foreshore improvements, 447
Specialties, sanitary, at Chelsea, 314
Square-hole boring tools, 295
Stained Glass and Decoration:—Arbroath, 274; Belgrave, 387; Bodmin, 446; Bradford, 233; Christchurch, Hants, 65; Clifton, 510; Crich, 387; Dublin, 510; Edinburgh, 328; Euston, (Suffolk), 360; Giggleswick, 36; Great Hallingbury, 168; Haworth, 487; Hulme, 328; Idle, 36; Jedburgh, 446; Kirkwall, 328; Langtree, 233; Leeds Town-hall, 424; Leicester, 387; Leigh, Lancashire, 122; Longsight, 406; Manchester, 328, 406, 426, 487; Newcastle, 86; Norton Cuckney, 487; Paris (St. Gervais), 240; Powerstock, 233; Radcliffe, 168, 408; Selby Abbey, 387; Sheffield, 233; South Darley, 233; Thorpe Satchville, 446; West Worlington, 233; Yardley, 440
Staircase, emergency, 87
Stair-tread, "Eiffel," 509
Stalls, Clifton, 18
Stedman & Co.'s copper-trade circular, 67
Steel window-frames, 87
Stone, an artificial, 273
Stove, the "Belvoir," 251
Street hygiene, 169
Studentships, free, Westminster School of Art, 52
Surveyorships: Belfast, 51; Bootle, 314; Cutlers' Company, 167; Diocesan, 51, 281; Dorset, 231; Grantham, 327; Hanwell, 205; Herefordshire, 327; Islington, 212; Leicester, 167; Lincoln, 51; Luton, 67; Neath, 458; Nelson, 405; St. Pancras, 80; Salford, 445, 465, 496; Sheffield, 192; Southampton, 231
Surveys of London parishes, 443

Technical College, Glasgow, 170, 193
Technical Schools: Aston Manor, 183; Darwen, 165; Heywood, 307; Ringsend, near Dublin, 424; Salford, 250
Telephony, 18; long-distance, 16; in Bulgaria, 170
Telephones and infection, 425
Telford Park estate, Streatham, 110
Terra-cotta as a fireproof material, 18
Testimonial, 192
Tests of Portland cement, 274
Theatres: Lyric, 407; "Novelty," 345; ventilation of, 37
Tin-plates, United States, 407
Tobacco-pipes, old, 107
Tower, Waddesdon Church, 508
Townhall, Cleckheaton, 146
Trade festivities, 365
Trade school, Bruton, 344
Trades' hall for Edinburgh, 68
Trades' Maiden Hospital, Edinburgh, 407
Tramways and the County Council, 329
Tree-felling machinery, 343
Truants' schools: Quaker's-yard, 344; Lichfield, 104
Tullie House, Carlisle, 464
Tunnels, Glasgow Harbour, 314
Turners' Company's prizes, 446
Turnstile, in-and-out, 128, 147

University College, lectures at, 334
University Extension Lectures on architecture, 67

Valve, straight-way, 365
Venice at "Olympia," 18
Ventilation: L'Air Froid system, 147, 169; factories, 330; theatres, 37
Ventilators, 18, 321
Viaduct, Bonar Bridge, Sutherland, 425
Vicarage, St. Helens, 213
Victoria Embankment, land on, 178

Wages, building-trade, in Havre, 251
Waste slate, new use for, 233
Water-closet, self-flushing, 425
Water-meter, "Gravita," 251
Water companies' powers, 509
Water Supply: Avington-park, 85; Berlin, 9, 75, 107; Birmingham, 5, 190; Bishop's Castle, 364; Chicago, 135; Cheshunt, 386; Clonmel, 109; Craven Arms, 509; Dynas Powis, 35; East Brook, 35; Gothenburg, 18; Hemsworth, 250; Henley-in-Arden, 386; Leominster, 406; Liverpool, 274; London, 5, 7, 64, 135, 155, 165, 183, 214, 346, 418, 422, 432, 435, 456, 480, 503, 507; Margam, 51; North Germany, 74; Peterborough, 483; Potsdam, 74; Rugeley, 328; Rothesay, 406; Sherborne, 483; Stanford Hall, 214; West Bridgeford, 51
Water supply and debt recovery, 214, 509
Water-tunnel under the Mersey, 274
Well-sinking, 19
Westminster School of Art, 52
White-lead, innocuous, 407
Whitworth Institute, Manchester, 84, 94
Willis's Rooms, St. James's, 146
Wimborne Minster, 16
Window, Sim's casement, 128
Window-frames, steel, 87
Wire-casings for electric light, 314
Wire-rope, large, 170
Wood Report, Foy, Morgan, & Co.'s, 52
Workhouse extension, Patricroft, 300
Workmen's dwellings, Birmingham, 509
Workmen's Institute, Deepcar, 327
Workmen's sanitary congress, a, 128

Yorkshire College, Leeds, 67
Yorkshire Penny Bank, Leeds, 456

Zerffi, the late G. G., 108

ARCHITECTS, ETC., OF BUILDINGS ILLUSTRATED.

Architects of Buildings, and authors and draughtsmen of Designs and works Illustrated :—

Adam, Robert, sedan-chair, 227
Adam, R. and J., decorative works, 174, 176
Aitchison, G., pavement and balustrade, house in Chesterfield-gardens, 503
Allar, A., sculpture, Jeanne d'Arc, 216
Ardron, A., schools, Canonbury, 206, 207
Ayling, S., staircase, St. Paul's Cath., 10
Bartlett, A., design for a library, 123
Begg, J.: design for a chapter-house, 308, 309; transept, Westminster, 11
Blomfield, A. C., mosaics, Venice, 30, 31
Blomfield, R. T., drawing-room, "Brooklands," Weybridge, 340
Booth & Chadwick, baths and public hall, Cheetham, 417, 418
Botterill, Son, & Bilson, Hymers' College, Hull, 46, 47
Bramante, architectural study by, 46
Brewer, H. W.: Old St. Paul's, London, 10; Old St. Peter's, Rome, 3, 11
Briggs, R. A., flats, Earl's Court-sq., 503
Brooks, J., Church of St. John-the-Baptist, Kensington, 325
Brooks, James, & Son, Chapel, Tonbridge School, 380
Brydon, J. M., Municipal Buildings, Bath, 30, 31, 421
Carpenter & Ingelow, St. Cuthbert's College, Worksop, 80
Caröe, W. D.: music-room, Putney Heath, 401; schools, Grosvenor-sq., 141
Cawston, A., bedroom, Lennox-gdns., 340
Cockerell, S. P., Guildhall, Westminster, 376
Collcutt, T. E.: house, Wraysbury, 460, 461; Imperial Institute: tower, 480
Corder, J. S.: sketches in East Anglia, 63, 80, 324; old house, Ipswich, 80; Guildhall Lavenham, 324
Crane, W., designs for wall papers, 324
Dalou, M., Delacroix Monument, 11
Day, L. F., designs for wall-papers, 324
Ferguson, C. J., Seascale Church, 46
Fletcher, W. H., Stanford Hall, 162
Fooks, Miss A., St. Mary Woolnoth, 420
Footitt, W. G., processional cross, St. Oswald's, Durham, 379
Fox, G. E., pavements at Silchester, 41
Freeman, R. K., Church of St. Jude, Preston, 461
Fulleylove, J., St. Peter's, Rome, 11
Gladwin, — north elevation, St. Paul's, 11
Goddard, Paget, & Goddard, house, Stanmore Park, 227
Gotch & Saunders, Schools, Kettering, 325
Graham, A., temples at Sheitla, 460
Gregg, H. A., shop, Redruth, 103
Greenslade, S. K.: Gate, Bishop West's Chapel, Ely, 267; arcading, west porch, Ely, 267; view beneath tower, Norwich Cathedral, 283; exterior of choir, Ely Cathedral, 289
Guillon, A., cemetery erections in Brittany, 44, 45, 46
Gwatkin, A., design for frieze, 480
Harber, W., house at Chislehurst, 227
Harlock, H., railway bridge, 308, 309
Hart, A. H., design for mansion, 62, 63
Hellicar, E., lodge, Sherborne, 325
Henman, W., Hospital, Birmingham, 216
Holman, S., sewer-gas exhauster, 9
Honeyman & Keppie: design for Glasgow Art Gallery, 502, 503
Horsley, G. C.: decoration, Chapel of St. James, San Miniato, 481; Ely Cathedral, 266; pulpit, San Cesareo, Rome, 481
Howitt, J., church, Long Clawson, 141
Hughes, J., F.C.S., illustrations of ancient mortar, 471
Huntly-Gordon, H., Broderers' Hall, 207
Ivison, T. P.: illustrations of Old Chester: fireplace, Bishop Lloyd's Palace, 103; houses, Watergate-street, 162; Crypt, Watergate-street, 206; supports of Bishop Lloyd's Palace, 288; "Lady's Bower," Watergate Row, 420
Jackson, T. G., Radley College, 340
James J. H., plan, Llandaff Cathedral, 358
Johnson, J.: Hereford Cathedral, 102; Public Library, Bermondsey, 60
Jones, Inigo, old houses in Great St. Helens, 304
Kerr, P., Houses of Parliament, Melbourne, 340, 341
Kitsell, T. R., design for steeple, 289
Knight, F. G., houses, Queen's-gate, 122, 123, 226
Lovell, R. J., Mission Church, Canterbury-road, S.E., 81
Lutyens, E. L., house, Godalming, 62
Mallows, C. E., Llandaff Cath., 358, 359
Mitchell, A., sketches in and near Peterborough, 266, 267
Morley & Woodhouse, small-pox hospital, Bradford, 308
Morris, G. Ll., design for a mountain church, 31
Morris & Hunter, Working Men's Club, Ayr, 461
Mountford, E. W., Municipal Buildings, Sheffield, 400, 401
Newberry, J. E., design for church, 63
Newman & Newman, Infirmary, Rotherhithe, 289
Newton, E., house at Wokingham, 123
Paul, R. W.: arms of the See of Hereford, 101; Christ Church Cathedral, Oxford, 440; plan, Ely Cathedral, 266; plan of Hereford Cathedral, 102; sketches at Chichester Cathedral, 185, 186, 187, 188, 189; sketches at Christ Church Cathedral, Oxford, 440, 441, 442; sketches at Ely Cathedral, 268; sketches of ironwork in South Kensington Museum, 473
Pearson, J. L., transept, Westminster, 11
Pite, A. B.: Chichester Cathedral, 184; Klingen-Thor, Rothenburg, 11; plan of ancient rood-screen, Chichester Cathedral, and the old organ-case, 189
Ponting, C. E., Pewsham House, Wilts, 481
Powell, A. H., Jew's House, Lincoln, 31
Price, F. G., sketches at Hereford Cathedral, 103
Pywell, J. A., Priory, Christchurch, Hants, 499, 500
Reid, R. A., towers, Caen and Coutances, 12
Sale, G., Plan of the Temple of Mecca, 76
Sarney, G. G., electric wire casing, 314
Scargill, W., plan, All Saints' Church, Hertford, 31
Sellers, J. H., study for country-house, 47
Shrigley & Hunt, window, Leigh Church, Lancs., 122
Simpson, F. M.: house and studio, 123; plan of street, Holborn to Strand, 229; staircase, Renishaw Hall, 140
Skipworth, A. H.: reredos, Grayingham Church, 461; retable, St. Alban's Church, Teddington, 460
Smith, S. R. J., Gallery of British Art, proposed, 220, 227
Statham, H. H., view of St. Paul's Cath., 10
Street, A. E.: Chimneypiece, St. Margaret's, East Grinstead, 381; Mary Tudor tomb, Bury St. Edmunds, 381
Street, W. C., offices for *Athenæum*, 290
Teather, H., door, Llandaff Cathedral, 360
Thompson, W. H., blind fittings, 13
Thompson & Lea's safety jib crane, 459
Truefitt & Truefitt, factory for Schweppe & Co., Malvern, 81
Tulloch, F. H., design for Municipal Buildings, Bury, 380
Walters, F. A., monument, St. Neots Church, Hunts, 359
Watkins, W. G., Wren's Library, Lincoln Cathedral, 260, 263
Watson, T. L., design for church, Drogheda, 421
Weatherley, W. S., reredos, Beaton, 331
Westlake, N. H. J., mural painting, Maynooth, 308
Williams, T. B., offices, Copthall-avenue, 216
Williams & Hopton, house, Bromley, 193
Williams, West, & Slade, Grandtully Castle, 206
Wooldridge, H. E., window, Euston Church, 359
Wren, Sir C.: St. Paul's Cathedral, 10; Library, Lincoln Cathedral, 260, 263

ILLUSTRATIONS.

[*The Illustrations will be found on, or immediately following or preceding, the pages indicated.*]

ABBEY, Kirkstall, before the Removal of the Ivy, 11; Ground Plan, 11
Abbey, Westminster: North Transept, as Restored by Mr. J. L. Pearson, R.A.; Drawn by John Begg, 11
Alhambra, Granada: Court of the Fishpond, 138; Plan, 139, Wall-Diaper, Hall of the Ambassadors, 163
Arcades: Capilla de Villa Viciosa, Cordova Cathedral, 136; Mosque at Cordova, 137
Arcading, West Porch, Ely; Drawn by S. K. Greenslade, 267
Architectural Study by Bramante, 46
Arms of the See of Hereford, 104
Art Gallery, Glasgow: Design by Messrs. Honeyman & Keppie, 502, 503

BALUSTRADE, Copper, house in Chesterfield gardens: G. Aitchison, Architect, 503
Balustrades, Indian, from the "Jeypore Portfolio," 207
Bases found at Silchester, 41
Basilica, Early Christian, at Silchester: Plan, 478
Basilica of St. Peter, Rome, about A.D. 1500: Drawn by H. W. Brewer, 3, 11
Baths and Public Hall, Cheetham: Booth & Chadwick, Architects, 417, 418
Bedroom, House in Lennox-gardens: A. Cawston, Architect, 340
Bell-Tower, Chichester Cathedral: Drawn by R. W. Paul, 187
Blind-Fittings: Thompson's, 13
Brasses: William de Etchingham, Etchingham, 226; William Fienles, Burstmonceaux, 226
Bridge, Cantilever, Red Rock, U.S.A., 303
Bridge, Railway: Design for, by H. Harlock, 308, 309
Bridge, Tower: Diagrams showing Erection of High-Level Footways, 476
Bronze Objects found at Silchester, 41

CAPITALS, Christchurch Priory, Hants: Drawn by J. A. Pywell, 500
Cartoons for Window, Euston Church, Suffolk: By H. Ellis Wooldridge, 359
Carvings, North Walsham: Sketched by J. S. Corder, 63
Casement, Wren's Library, Lincoln: Drawn by W. G. Watkins, 263
Casing, Sarney's, for Electric-Light Wires, 314
Castle, Grandtully, Perthshire: Additions: Williams, West, and Slade, Architects, 206
Cathedral, Canterbury: Ancient Choir Screen, 362
Cathedral, Cordova: Arcade, Capilla de Villa Viciosa, 136
Cathedral, Lincoln: Wren's Library, Measured and Drawn by W. G. Watkins, 260-263
Cathedral, Norwich: View Beneath Tower Opening: Drawn by S. K. Greenslade, 288,
Cathedral, St. Peter's, Rome: Drawn by John Fulleylove, 11; Old St. Peter's, Rome: Drawn by H. W. Brewer, 3, 11
Cathedrals of England and Wales:—
Chichester: Drawn by A. Beresford Pite, 184; Plan revised to date by A. B. Pite, 185; View Across Nave, 185; Bishop Sherborne's Tomb, 185, 189; Bishop Langton's Tomb, 186; Bell-Tower, 187; Columns and Piers in Presbytery, 188; Ancient Rood-screen and Organ-case before fall of Tower, 189
Christ Church, Oxford: Drawn by R. W. Paul, 440; Plan: Measured and Drawn by R. W. Paul, 440; View across the Lady Chapel, 440; View across the North Transept, 440; the Chapter-House, &c., 440; Remains of the Shrine of St. Frideswide, Measured and Drawn by R. W. Paul, 441; Capitals, 441; Base of Ancient Cross, 441; Slab in Chapter-House, 442; Poppy-heads in Stalls of Latin Chapel, 442
Ely: Drawn by G. C. Horsley, 266; Plan, Measured and Drawn by R. W. Paul, 266; Plan of Foundations of Norman Apse, 266; Gate to Bishop West's Chapel: Drawn by S. K. Greenslade, 267; Bay of Arcading, West Porch, 267; Exterior of Choir, 289
Hereford: Drawn by J. Johnson, 102; Plan, drawn by R. W. Paul, 102; Doorway from Cloisters to Chapter-House, 102: Tomb of Bishop Charlton, drawn by F. G. Price, 103; Tomb of Sir Richard Pembridge, 103; Font, 103; Arms of the See, 104
Llandaff: West Front: Drawn by C. E. Mallows, 358; Plan, measured and drawn by J. H. James, 358; Supposed Chancel-Arch of Bishop Urban's Church, 358; First Bay of the Nave, 358; Chapter-House, 359; West Door, 360
St. Paul's, London: Drawn by the Editor, 10; Plan, 10; Staircase of South-west Tower, drawn by S Ayling, 10; North Elevation, from an Engraving by Gladwin, 11; Old St. Paul's, before the destruction of the Spire, drawn by H. W. Brewer, 10
Cemetery Crosses in Brittany: Drawn by Adolphe Guillon, 45
Chair, Episcopal, Ely Cathedral: Sketched by R. W. Paul, 268
Chapel, Radley College: T. G. Jackson, Architect, 340
Chapel, Tonbridge School: Jas. Brooks & Son, Architects, 380
Chapter-House, Design for, by John Begg, 308, 309
Chapter-House, Christ Church Cathedral, Oxford: Drawn by R. W. Paul, 440
Chapter-House, Llandaff Cathedral: Drawn by C. E. Mallows, 359
Chimney-piece: Design for, by the brothers Adam, 175
Chimney-piece, St. Margaret's, East Grinstead: A. E. Street, Architect, 381
Choir, Ely Cathedral, Exterior: Drawn by S. K. Greenslade, 289
Choir-Screen, Ancient, Canterbury Cathedral, 362
Christ Church Cathedral, Oxford: Drawn by R. W. Paul, 440
Christchurch Priory, Hants: North Transept: Drawn by J. A. Pywell, 499; Capitals, 500
Church, All Saints', Hertford, destroyed by fire: Plan, drawn by W. Scargill, 31
Church, Costessey: Sketches by J. S. Corder, 63
Church: Design for, by J. E. Newberry, Architect, 63
Church, Mission, Canterbury-road, S.E.: R. J. Lovell, Architect, 81
Church for a Mountainous District: Designed by G. Ll. Morris, Architect, 31
Church, proposed, Long Clawson, J. Howitt, Archtect, 141
Church of St. John-the-Baptist, Kensington: James Brooks, Architect, 325
Church of St Jude, Preston: R. K. Freeman, Architect, 461
Church of St. Mary Woolnoth, City: Interior: Drawn by Miss A. Fooks, 420
Church, St. Peter's, Drogheda: Design for: by T. L. Watson, Architect, 421
Church, Seascale,: C. J. Ferguson, Architect, 46
Churches near Peterborough: Sketched by Arnold B. Mitchell (see "Sketches")
Cloister, Lincoln Cathedral: Wren's Library: Drawn by W. G. Watkins, 260
Cloisters, Radley College: T. G. Jackson, Architect, 340
Club, Working Men's Unionist, Ayr: Morris & Hunter, Architects, 461
College, Hymers', Hall: Botterill, Son, & Bilson, Architects, 46, 47
College, Radley: T. G. Jackson, A.R.A., Architect, 340
College, St. Cuthbert's, Worksop: Carpenter & Ingelow, Architects, 80
Composition by Bramante, a, 46
Crane, Safety: Thompson and Lea's Patent, 459
Cross, Processional (Ancient), St. Oswald's Church, Durham: Drawn by W. G. Footitt, 379
Crypt, Watergate-st., Chester: Drawn by T. P. Ivison, 206

DECORATION, Chapel of St. James, San Miniato: Drawn by G. C. Horsley, 481
Decoration of End Wall of a Drawing-room: By Robert and James Adam, 174
Decorative Detail, from the "Jeypore Portfolio," 207
Delacroix Monument, Paris: M. Dalou, Sculptor, 11
Design for a Chapter-House: by John Begg, 308, 309
Design for a Church at Drogheda: By T. L. Watson, Architect, 421
Design for a Frieze: By Mr. Arthur Gwatkin, 480

ILLUSTRATIONS (continued):—

Design for the Proposed Gallery of British Art: By S. R. J. Smith, Architect, 226, 227
Design for Glasgow Art Gallery: Honeyman & Kepple, Architects, 502, 503
Design for Library for County Town: By Arthur Bartlett, 123
Design for a Mountain Church: G. Ll. Morris, Archt., 31
Design for Municipal Buildings, Bury: By F. H. Tulloch, 380
Design for a Tower and Spire: By T. R. Kitsell, 280
Design for Town Church: By J. E. Newberry, Archt., 63
Design for a large Town Mansion, awarded Royal Academy Gold Medal: By A. H. Hart, 62, 63
Designs for Wall-Papers, by Walter Crane and Lewis F. Day, 323, 324
Diagram showing Drainage at Foundling Hospital, 93
Diagrams Illustrating Prof. Aitchison's Lectures at the Royal Academy:—Alhambra, Granada, Section and Plan, 138, 139; Arcade, Capilla de Villa Viciosa, Cordova Cathedral, 136; Arcade, Mosque at Cordova, 137; Dome of Tomb, Karafeh, 163; Door of Mosque at Cairo, 185; Door-head, brick, Saracenic, 18[illegible]; Entrance of the Fountain, Kaid Bey, Cairo, 163; Kaaba at Mecca, from a Tile Panel, 77; Mosaics from Mosque at Cordova, 163; Mosque of Touloun, details, 185; Ornament in Cairo, 185; Ornament, Hall of the Ambassadors, Alhambra, 163; Pavement, marble, Alexandria, 185; Plan of the Alhambra, Granada, 139; Plan of Djuma Mosque, Ispahan, 117; Plan of a House in Cairo, 158; Plan of Mosque of Amru, Cairo, 96; Plan and Section of Mosque of Shah Abbas, Ispahan, 140; Plan of Mosque of Sultan Hassan, Cairo, 97; Plan of the Temple of Mecca, 76; Ruined Tower at Rei, Persia, 119; Section, Mosque of Sultan Hassan, Cairo, 157; Shop at Tantah, Egypt, 163; Trellis, Cairo, 180; Trellis, Rosetta, 181
Diagrams Illustrating Warming by Hot-Water ("Students' Column"), 15, 34, 50, 51, 65, 66, 85, 86, 107, 108, 126, 145, 166, 167, 190, 191 211, 212, 231, 272, 312, 326, 327, 343, 363, 364, 385, 404, 405, 423, 444, 445, 463, 464, 486, 507, 508
Dome of St. Peter's, Rome: Drawn by J. Fulleylove, 11
Dome of Tomb, Karafeh, 163
Door, Mosque of Sultan Daahir Bibars, Cairo, 185
Door, Prior's, Ely Cathedral: Drawn by R. W. Paul, 268
Door, West, Llandaff Cathedral: Drawn by H. Teather, 380
Door, Wren's Library, Lincoln: Drawn by W. G. Watkins, 201
Door-jamb, Carved, Cairo, 185
Doorway from Cloisters to Chapter House, Hereford, 102
Doorway, Fountain Kaid Bey, Cairo, 163
Doorways, Norwich: Sketched by J. S. Corder, 63
Drawing-room, "Brooklands," Weybridge: R. T. Blomfield, Architect, 340

FACTORY for Messrs. Schweppe & Co., Colwall, near Malvern: Trueflitt & Trueflitt, Architects, 81
Fireplace, Bishop Lloyd's Palace, Chester, 103
Fireplace, St. Margaret's, East Grinstead: A. E. Street, Architect, 381
Flats at Earl's Court-square: R. A. Briggs, Architect, 503
Font, Ancient, St. Andrew's Hospital, Northampton, 423
Font, Hereford Cathedral: Drawn by F. G. Price, 103
Frieze: Designed by Mr. Arthur Gwatkin, 480
Furniture, Bedroom, Lennox-gardens: A. Cawston, Architect, 340

GALLERY, Art, Glasgow, Design for, by Messrs. Honeyman & Keppie, 502, 503
Gallery of British Art, Design for, by S. R. J. Smith, Architect, 226, 227
Gate, Garden, Tissington, Derby, 152
Gate-Piers, Canons Ashby, 153
Gateway, Bishop West's Chapel, Ely; Drawn by S. K. Greenslade, 267
Guildhall, Lavenham: Measured and Drawn by J. S. Corder, 324
Guildhall or Sessions House, Westminster: now Demolished; S. P. Cockerell, Architect, 376

HALL of the Broderers' Company: Elevation: H. Huntly-Gordon, Architect, 207
Hall, Early English, Lincoln: Remains of, 374
Hall and Baths, Cheetham: Booth & Chadwick, Architects, 417, 418
Hall and Mission Church, Canterbury-road, Old Kent-road: R. J. Lovell, Architect, 81
Hall and Staircase, House, Queen's Gate: F. G. Knight, Architect, 226
Heraldry: Arms of the See of Hereford, 104; at Ely Cathedral: Sketched by R. W. Paul, 268
Hospital, General, Birmingham: Selected Design; W. Henman, Architect, 246, 247
Hospital, Smallpox, Bradford: Morley & Woodhouse, Architects, 308
House in Cairo, Plan, 158
House, Country, Study for a, by J. H. Sellers, 47
House, Jew's, Lincoln: Drawn by A. H. Powell, 31
House, Chislehurst, W. Harber, Architect, 227
House, Godalming, E. L. Lutyens, Architect, 62
House, Wraysbury, T. E. Collcutt, Architect, 460, 461
House, South Hill Park, Bromley: Williams & Hopton, Architects, 103, 104
House, Sparrowe's, Ipswich: Drawn by J. S. Corder, 80
House, Stanmore Park Estate, Goddard, Paget, & Goddard, Architects, 227
House, Wiltshire: C. E. Ponting, Architect, 481
House, Wokingham: Ernest Newton, Architect, 123
House and Shop, Redruth: H. A. Gregg, Architect, 103
House and Studio for a Painter: Designed by F. M. Simpson, 123
House of the Tradescants and Ashmole, Lambeth, 474
Houses of Parliament, Melbourne: P. Kerr, Architect, 340, 341
Houses, Old, in Great St. Helens, Bishopsgate, attributed to Inigo Jones, and about to be Demolished, 304
Houses, Old, Chester: Drawn by T. P. Ivison, 162, 288, 420
Houses, Old, Norwich: Sketched by J. S. Corder, 63
Houses, Queen's-gate: F. G. Knight, Archt., 122, 123, 226
Hypocaust, Roman, Chester, 307

ILLUSTRATIONS of Old Chester, Drawn by T. P. Ivison: Fireplace, Bishop Lloyd's Palace, 103; Old Houses and "Rows," Watergate-street, 162; Crypt, Watergate-street, 206; Supports under Bishop Lloyd's Palace, 288; "The Lady's Bower," Watergate-Row, South, 420
Imperial Institute: Tower: T. E. Collcutt, Archt., 480
Infirmary, Rotherhithe: Alterations and Additions: Newman & Newman, Architects, 289
Ironwork in South Kensington Museum: Sketched by R. W. Paul, 473

JEW'S House, Lincoln: Drawn by A. H. Powell, 31
Jib-Cranes, Thompson and Lea's Safety, 459

KAABA, the, Mecca: Sale's Plan, 76; View (from a Sixteenth-Century Tile Panel at Esbekieh), 77
Klingen-Thor, Rothenburg: Drawn by A. B. Pite, 11

LANTERNES DES MORTS, Brittany: Drawn by Adolphe Guillon, 44
Library, Bermondsey: J. Johnson, Architect, 60
Library, Lincoln Cathedral: Sir C. Wren, Architect: Measured and Drawn by W. G. Watkins, 260-263
Library for County Town: Designed by A. Bartlett, 123
Lodge, Compton, Sherborne: E. Hellicar, Architect, 325

MANSION, Stanford Hall, Nottinghamshire: W. H. Fletcher, Architect, 102
Mansion, Town: Design by A. H. Hart, awarded the Royal Academy Gold Medal, 62-63
Mansions, Earl's Court-sq.: R. A. Briggs, Architect, 503
Monastery, Early Celtic, Skellig Michael: Plan, 140; View showing Cross and Cells, 141; Remains of the Church, 141; Plans and Sections of Cells, 142
Monument to Delacroix, Paris: M. Dalou, Sculptor, 11
Monument to Mrs. Rowley, St. Neots Church, Hunts: F. A. Walters, Architect, 350
Mortar, Ancient: Illustrations showing Sand in, 471
Mosaics: Mosque of Cordova, 163; in St. Mark's, Venice: Drawn by A. C. Blomfield, 30, 31
Mosques: Amru, Cairo: Plan, 96; Cordova: Arcade, 137; Mosaics, 163; Djûma, Ispahan: Plan, 117; Shah Abbas, Ispahan, 140; Sultan Hassan, Cairo: Plan 97: Section, 157; Mosque of Touloun, Cairo: Detail, 185
Municipal Buildings, Bath: J. M. Brydon, Architect, 30, 31, 421
Municipal Buildings, Bury: Design by F. H. Tulloch, 350
Municipal Buildings, Sheffield: Selected Design: E. W. Mountford, Architect: Grand Staircase, 400; Surrey-street and Churchyard Fronts, 400, 401
Music-Room, "Highlands," Putney Heath: W. D. Carõe, Architect, 401

NEWEL and Baluster, Norwich: Sketched by J. S. Corder, 63

OFFICES for the *Athenæum*: W. C. Street, Architect, 290
Offices, Token House, Copthall-avenue: T. Barnes Williams, Architect, 246
Organ-Case, Chichester Cathedral, before the fall of the Tower, 180
Ornament: Indian, from the "Jeypore Portfolio," 207; Saracenic, Cairo, 163, 180; Saracenic, Cordova, 163
Ossuary, St. Pol de Léon, Finistère, 46

PAINTING, Mural, "Christ before Pilate," Maynooth College Chapel: By N. H. J. Westlake, 308
Panel, Woodwork, Cairo, 185
Parliament-Houses, Melbourne: P. Kerr, Archt., 340, 341
Pavement, Marble, Alexandria, 185
Pavement, Mosaic, House in Chesterfield-gardens: G. Aitchison, Architect, 503
Pavements, Tesselated, found at Silchester: Drawn by G. E. Fox, 41
Plan of a Cairo house, 158
Plan of Basilica found at Silchester, 478
Plan of Old Buildings, Venice, 133
Plan of Proposed Street from Holborn to the Strand: Suggested by F. M. Simpson, 229
Plans of Cathedrals: Chichester, 185; Christ Church, Oxford, 440; Ely, 266; Hereford, 102; Llandaff, 358; St. Paul's, London, 10
Porch, Costessey Church: Sketched by J. S. Corder, 63
Pottery found at Silchester, 41
Priory, Christchurch, Hants: Transept; Drawn by J. A. Pywell, 499, 500
Pulpit, San Cesareo, Rome: Drawn by G. C. Horsley, 481

RAILWAY-BRIDGE, Stone: Designed by H. Harlock, 308, 309
Reredos, Grayingham Church: A. H. Skipworth, Architect, 461
Reredos, Boston: W. S. Weatherley, Architect, 381
Retable for St. Alban's Church, Teddington: A. H. Skipworth, Architect, 460
Rood-Screen, Ancient, Chichester Cathedral: Plan: Drawn by A. B. Pite, 189

SAINT MARK'S, Venice: Mosaics in Baptistery; Drawn by A. C. Blomfield, 30, 31
School, Tonbridge: Chapel: J. Brooks & Son, Architects, 380
Schools, Canonbury: A. Ardron, Architect, 206
Schools, Gilbert-street, Grosvenor-square, W. D. Carõe, Architect, 141
Schools, Kettering: Gotch & Saunders, Architects, 325
Screen, Ancient, Canterbury Cathedral, 362
Sculptured Group: "Jeanne d'Arc entend ses voix," for Church at Domrémy: A. Allar, Sculptor, 246
Sedan Chair: Designed by Robert Adam, 227
Sessions House, Westminster: S. P. Cockerell, Architect, 376
Sewer-gas Exhauster and Destructor, Holman's, 9
Shop, Redruth, H. A. Gregg, Architect, 103
Shop at Tantah, Egypt, 163
Shrine of St. Frideswide, Remains of, Christ Church Cathedral, Oxford: Measured and Drawn by R. W. Paul, 441
Sketches in East Anglia, by J. S. Corder:—Doorways, Norwich, 63; Houses, Norwich, 63; Carvings, North Walsham, 63; Stair Newel and Baluster, Norwich, 63; Porch, Costessey Church, 63; Tower and Spire, Costessey Church, 63
Sketches in and near Peterborough, by Arnold B. Mitchell:—March Church, 266; Palace, Peterborough, 266; Whittlesea Church, 266; Belfry, Ketton Church, 266; Wittering Church, 266; Tickencote Church, 267; Old House, Stamford, 267; St. Leonard's Priory, Stamford, 267; Barnack Church, 267; Rectory, Tickencote, 267
Spire, Design for a, by T. R. Kitsell, 280
Staircase, House, Queen's-gate: F. G. Knight, Archt., 226
Staircase, Renishaw Hall: F. M. Simpson, Architect, 140
Staircase, Sheffield Municipal Buildings: E. W. Mountford, Architect, 400
Staircase in South-West Tower, St. Paul's Cathedral: Drawn by S. Ayling, 10
Statue (lead) of Cupid, Melbourne, Derbyshire, 153
Steeple, Tite Prize Design: By T. R. Kitsell, 289
Studio, Painter's: Designed by F. M. Simpson, 123
Study by Bramante: from an Engraving in the British Museum, 46
Sundial, Wrest, Bedfordshire, 152

TABLE, Wren's Library, Lincoln: Drawn by W. G. Watkins, 262
Temple of Mecca: Plan, by George Sale, 76; View, from a Sixteenth-Century Tile Panel at Esbekieh, 77
Temples at Sbeitla, North Africa: a Restoration by Mr. Alexander Graham, F.S.A., 460
Tomb, Memorial, to Mary Tudor, at St. Mary's Church, Bury St. Edmunds: A. E. Street, Architect, 381
Tomb of Bishop Charlton, Hereford Cathedral; Drawn by F. G. Price, 103
Tomb of Bishop Sherborne, Chichester Cathedral: Drawn by R. W. Paul, 185, 189
Tomb of Sir Richard Pembridge, Hereford Cathedral: Drawn by F. G. Price, 103
Tower, Imperial Institute: T. E. Collcutt, Archt., 480
Tower, Rothenburg: Drawn by A. B. Pite, 11
Tower, ruined, at Rei, Persia, 119
Tower, St. Étienne, Caen: Drawn by R. A. Reid, 12
Tower, St. Pierre, Coutances: Drawn by R. A. Reid, 12
Tower Bridge: Diagrams showing Erection of High-Level Footways, 476
Tower and Spire, Design for, by T. R. Kitsell, 289
Transept, North, of Westminster Abbey: Restored by Mr. J. L. Pearson, R.A.: Drawn by John Begg, 11
Trellis-work, Egyptian, 180, 181

WALL DECORATION, Chapel of St. James, San Miniato: Drawn by G. C. Horsley, 481
Wall-papers, Designs, for, by Walter Crane and L. F. Day, 323, 324
Wayside Notes in East Anglia, by J. S. Cordet (see "Sketches").
Window, Stained Glass, Euston Church, Suffolk: Cartoons by H. Ellis Wooldridge, 359
Window, Stained Glass, St. Mary's Church, Leigh, Lancashire, by Shrigley & Hunt, 122
Window, Wren's Library Lincoln: Drawn by W. G. Watkins, 263

VOL. LXII., No. 2552—SATURDAY, JANUARY 2, 1892.

ILLUSTRATIONS.

Cathedrals of England and Wales: XIII., St. Paul's.—Drawn by the Editor .... *Double-Page Ink-Photo.*
Plan of St. Paul's Cathedral .... *Double-Page Photo-Litho.*
Staircase to South-West Tower, St. Paul's Cathedral, leading to Library.—Drawn by Mr. Stephen Ayling .... *Double-Page Ink-Photo.*
Old St. Paul's Cathedral (before the Destruction of the Spire).—Drawn by Mr. H. W. Brewer .... *Double-Page Photo-Litho.*
Dome of St. Peter's, Rome.—From a Water-Colour Drawing by Mr. John Fulleylove .... *Double-Page Ink-Photo.*
Old St. Peter's, Rome, *circa* A.D. 1450.—Restored from Ancient Authorities by Mr. H. W. Brewer .... *Double-Page Photo-Litho.*
Westminster Abbey: North Transept, as Restored by Mr. J. L. Pearson, R.A.—Drawn by Mr. John Begg .... *Double-Page Ink-Photo.*
The Klingen Thor, Rothenburg.—From a Drawing by Mr. A. Beresford Pite .... *Double-Page Ink-Photo.*
Kirkstall Abbey: From a Photograph taken before the Removal of the Ivy .... *Double-Page Ink-Photo.*
Monument to Delacroix in the Gardens of the Luxembourg, Paris.—M. Dalou, Sculptor: Engraved by J. D. Cooper .... *Double-Page Wood-Engraving.*

Blocks in Text.

North Elevation of St. Paul's Cathedral.—From an Engraving by Gladwin, published in 1828 .... *Double-Page Zincograph.*

Key-Sketch to View of Old St. Peter's at Rome .... Page 3
Holman's "Sewer-Gas Exhauster and Destructor" 9
Plan of Kirkstall Abbey 11
Central Towers, St. Pierre, Coutances, and St. Etienne, Caen .... Page 10
New Blind-Fittings 13
Diagrams in Student's Column: Heating by Hot Water 15

CONTENTS.

Architecture from a Cosmical Point of View 1
Old St. Peter's, Rome 2
Notes 4
Letter from Paris 7
The English Iron Trade in 1891 8
Holman's "Sewer-Gas Exhauster and Destructor" 9
The Sale of Water by Meter at Berlin 9
St. Paul's Cathedral 10
Staircase, St. Paul's Cathedral 11
Old St. Paul's Cathedral from the North-East 11
St. Peter's Dome, from the Piazza della Sagrestia 11
The Klingen Thor, Rothenburg, Bavaria 11
Kirkstall Abbey 11
Old St. Paul's Cathedral from the North-east 11
"Le Temps Portant la Renommée" 12
London County Council 12
New Blind Fittings 13
Competitions 13
Books: D. K. Clark's "Mechanical Engineer's Pocket-book" (London: Crosby Lockwood & Son); J. P. Harrison's "Design and Stonework of Oxford Cathedral" (London: H. Frowde; Oxford: Clarendon Press)? Rev. R. A. Cayley's "Architectural Memoir of Old Basing Church" (Basingstoke: C. J. Jacob); Short Notices 14
Recent Trade Catalogues 14
The Institute and its Examinations 14
All Saints' Church, Hertford 14
Rood Screens 15
Student's Column.—Warming Buildings by Hot Water. I. 15
Obituary 16
General Building News 16
Foreign and Colonial 17
Sanitary and Engineering News 17
Miscellaneous 17
Recent Patents 19
Some Recent Sales of Property 19

Architecture from a Cosmical Point of View.

HE turn of the year, when one thinks what it really means, is an event that may very well draw our thoughts away beyond the mere daily necessities and fashions of architecture to a consideration of the subject in a wider and more abstract sense. To most of us, in our every-day attitude of mind, the New Year is a date merely, a marking off of a fresh division of our time, another milestone in the race of life (which in itself is a serious consideration enough, no doubt); also an excuse for a holiday, a little relaxation of business, a fresh interchange of friendly or neighbourly greetings and hospitalities. But when we think for a moment what it is which has marked out the interval for us,—the traversing by our planet of one more of its elliptical circuits round the sun,—we seem to be carried in thought somewhat beyond the annual amenities of New Year's Day. We are reminded thereby of our connexion with the great mechanism of the solar system, so vast to our perception, so small in comparison with the universe of suns on whose movements we can but partially speculate. Regarded from this point of view, the earth is no more a surface on which cities may grow up, mansions and town-halls be erected, and land laid out for building estates; all these transactions become infinitesimal from the cosmic point of view; trivial and impertinent details, hardly perceptible at all in the general contemplation of our sphere as one among "flying synods of worlds."

There is only one sense in which architecture retains its dignity and importance even from this point of view; so far, namely, as it is the expression of an abstract thought or ideal. Amid the multifarious demands of practical life, and the limiting conditions of practical achievement, it is but seldom—in these bustling and hurrying modern days hardly ever—that architecture can rise entirely above utilitarian considerations and exist solely as an intellectual expression. But so far or so often as it can do this, it is in a certain sense independent of mere scale. Thought is not measurable by a material scale.

> "A sphere is but a sphere;
> Small, Great, are merely terms we bandy here;
> Since to the spirit's absoluteness all
> Are like." *

Ideal architecture in its purest form becomes not the mere construction of a shelter, however elaborate or picturesque, but the expression of an aspiration or a mood of the mind. It may even have a relation with the cosmic spectacle, if it is regarded as the effort of man to express in his own way something of the grandeur and the hidden meaning which he has learned to discern in nature. In such a light the structures raised on the face of a planet by its inhabitants, infinitesimal as they are in comparative scale, may partake somewhat of the greatness and mystery of the scheme of nature which inspired them; and if we could imagine the various planets of our system to be in the same stage of habitability, and could visit them one by one, we might find it not the least interesting part of the investigation to compare the various ways in which mental thought and aspiration expressed themselves in structures raised solely for the satisfaction or embodiment of an ideal; to note, according to Wordsworth's fancy, how

> "Swift Mercury resounds with mirth,
> Great Jove is full of stately bowers."

As a matter of fact, probably, it must be many and many an age before the surface of Jupiter is contracted into ground solid enough for foundations; and an aqueous architecture is at all events beyond our present powers of conception. Nor indeed can we realise the least in imagination what entirely different possibilities of architectural expression may exist in planets of different conditions as to chemical composition and modulus of gravitation. Our forms of architecture seem varied enough; they may however be far more restricted in idea and conception than we are in the least aware of, in comparison with possible combinations which have never

* "Sordello," Book VI.

entered our human conception. Such as they are however, some of them may have a deeper significance than is commonly attached to them, where they have really been the outcome of the effort to give form to an abstract idea, to express a thought which may in a typical sense be indicated in architecture, although in a material sense, like Milton's gate of heaven,

> "Inimitable on earth
> By model or by shading pencil drawn."

If these are deemed profitless speculations, at all events it seems that we are not alone in indulging such, for with the New Year there comes to us a small book* specially concerned with "architecture, mysticism and myth," and by an architect who is no mere speculator, but one of the best draughtsmen and most artistic designers among the younger generation of English architects. The main point of Mr. Lethaby's fanciful but interesting little book, as stated in the introductory chapter, is that the usual history of Architecture, "with its theory of utilitarian origins from the hut and the tumulus," is rather the history of building; that architecture "is thought behind form, embodied and realised for the purpose of its manifestation and transmission."

> "Of the modes of this thought we must again distinguish; some were unconscious and instinctive, as the desire for symmetry, smoothness, sublimity, and the like merely æsthetic qualities, which properly enough belong to true architecture; and others were direct and didactic, speaking by a more or less perfect realisation, or through a code of symbols, accompanied by traditions which explained them. The main purpose and burthen of sacred architecture,—and all architecture, temple, tomb, and palace, was sacred in the early days,—is thus inextricably bound up with a people's thoughts about God and the universe."

The author goes on to urge that there is evidence of a "cosmical symbolism" in the architecture of the early world, and that the intention of the temple idea was "to set up a local reduplication of the temple not made with hands, the World Temple itself." Mr. Lethaby goes on to follow up this idea by tracing out the symbolism of various forms of ancient architecture; and though in his preface he disclaims the possession of the learning which may be thought necessary for the treatment of such a subject, he at all events brings together a great many curious facts and fancies from many writers, and brings out a great many curious resemblances and hints from ancient buildings of different styles and peoples. The relation of the placing and designing of ancient buildings to the sun and the sunrise, of which he gives many examples, is a study which has quite recently passed from the domain of fancy into that of scientific and historical investigation, and probably there are many more facts to be brought to light yet upon this interesting and suggestive subject. Among the chapters is one on "Pavements like the Sea," and a succeeding one on "Ceilings like the Sky." In regard to this last subject Mr. Lethaby observes that "it may be said that at great periods of architecture ceilings were always skies," *i.e.*, studded with stars or with some similar suggestive decoration. This is going perhaps a little too far, unless we are to suppose that the author does not mean to include Greek architecture among great periods of architecture. Such an idea is not in keeping with the genius of Greek architecture; nor, we observe, does he bring forward any suggestion or example of such an idea from Greek buildings or literature. The idea is Egyptian, Byzantine, and Mediæval, but distinctly not Greek, though the placing or orientation of the Greek temples in regard to the position of the heavenly bodies appears likely to be more and more supported by evidence the more the question is looked into. This practice they very probably derived from the Egyptians. In regard to the Egyptian treatment of the ceiling Mr. Lethaby quotes from Champollion: "The Egyptians compared the sky to the ceilings of an edifice, and those of the greater part of the temples are painted blue, powdered with stars. . . . The goddess of the sky is figured under the form of a woman, whose body, placed horizontally, and out of all proportion long, embraces a large space, circumscribed by the legs and arms, which are vertical." A sketch of such a figure is given; we are not told whence it is taken. In a less symbolical and more material, but certainly more architectural sense, it may be rationally supposed that the first idea of the dome, which is a feature more easily treated for internal than for external effect, was a derivation from the dome of the sky. All these ideas, as Mr. Lethaby does not fail to remark, belong essentially to a time when the earth was regarded as a fixed plane with the sky as a solid sphere extending over it, in which the stars were set. The modern scientific cosmogony has made sad work of all these old picturesque ideas of the universe, which lent themselves far better to typification or imitation in architecture than does the modern cosmogony.

In some chapters, as in that on the planetary spheres, the author rides his subject rather too far. The curious fact of the influence of the number seven on the mind of the ancient world is indubitable, but it is not easy to be sure whether it was the cause or the effect of some of the ancient fancies. To commence with the statement that "the number seven is written in the sky," that is, in the supposed seven planets, is a rather curious ignoring of the fact that all this is altered long ago; and in commenting on the fact that the Great Bear, "probably the first known and named of the constellations" is represented by seven stars, the author leaves us in doubt whether he means to imply that the collocation of these seven stars was one of the influences in giving importance to that number, or whether seven stars were selected to define a constellation in consequence of a previous attachment to the number seven. All this about the importance of the number is of course pure mysticism, which has nothing really to do with the typifying of abstract ideas on architecture, though it is interesting to study the various ways in which the worship, as we may call it, of the number seven can be traced. A more interesting subject, because less hackneyed, is that of ancient ideas as to the centre of the earth, by which of course the ancients meant the central spot upon the supposed flat surface of the earth. A diagram is given illustrating the fable of how the true centre of the earth was determined by two eagles being sent by Jupiter to fly, one from the east the other from the west, the spot where they met being the centre; but as in some other cases, the author does not make it clear whether the illustration is taken from any ancient representation or is merely his own way of illustrating the idea in drawing. The drawing, in outline, represents a kind of half-egg-shaped stone with the flat side downwards, and a bird on each side. It may be observed that Browning, whom nothing seems to have escaped, brings in this legend as an illustration in the sixth book of "Sordello"—

> "So, says
> Old fable, the two eagles went two ways
> About the world: where, in the midst, they met,
> Though on a shifting waste of sand, was set
> Jove's temple."

All this is merely mysticism, no doubt, and seems far enough from architecture in any sense; but it takes its part in what the author states is the central object of his book, to show "the influence of the known and imagined facts of the universe on architecture." The moral of this (for there is a moral in the book) is that architecture should still be designed, in its highest forms, under the influence of and with some relation to the known and imagined facts of the universe; in fact, that the highest significance of architecture is not attainable otherwise; that it must have a symbolism, immediately comprehensible by the great body of spectators. But of what kind, and in what relation to the "facts of the universe" as at present "known," Mr. Lethaby does not offer to define. What he does say is rather negative than positive: "No terraced temples of Babylon to reach the skies, no gold-plated palaces of Ecbatana, seven-walled; no ivory palaces of Ahab, nor golden houses of Nero with corridors a mile long," all which were the production of the times of despotism and forced labour. That difference we can all see: architecture was once for the tyrant or aristocrat, and must in future ages be for the people, who have not shown hitherto much longing for architecture poetry and magnificence, for buildings designed in relation to and symbolical of the known facts of the universe. And one difference between the ancient and the modern life seems to be at present, that we have not even time to think of and contemplate architecture in the abstract and ideal spirit: everything is swallowed up in utility. As Matthew Arnold puts it

> "We say that repose has fled
> For ever the banks of the River of Time;
> That cities will crowd to its edge,
> In a blacker incessanter line,
> That the din will be more on its banks,
> Denser the trade on its stream,
> Flatter the plain where it flows
> Fiercer the sun overhead;
> That never will those on its breast
> See an ennobling sight
> Drink of the feeling of quiet again."

So one is often tempted to think now; but we do not know what higher and more widely-distributed education may bring forth in time, and whether the human race in the future may not still rise to the conception that there is something more in architecture than to afford work for the quantity-surveyor and the contractor. Possibly it may be thought that, even in that case, the symbolism of nature is too fanciful and unpractical an element to find favour in these enlightened days. But the fact, which Mr. Lethaby's book reminds us of, that this semi-mystical element and meaning once so largely permeated architecture, is significant in itself, and not without suggestiveness for the present day. Architecture at all events *once* meant more than meets the eye, and was connected in the minds of men with the order of the universe, as they understood it. It is as well to be reminded that such an ideal meaning, such a cosmic significance, was once recognised in architecture, and might again afford it, in a changed form, a new and higher significance than attaches to mere stone and mortar, and pilasters and colonnades. The possibility of the revival of such a higher symbolism in the art at all events forms a not unsuitable subject of speculation for the New Year, when our thoughts naturally turn towards the future developments which Time has in store for every phase of human craft or invention, Architecture among the rest.

OLD ST. PETER'S, ROME.

BY MR. H. W. BREWER.

GRAND as the modern Vatican Basilica undoubtedly *is*, yet the archæologist and historian must always regret that the ancient church, the site of which it occupies, has so entirely disappeared. When one contemplates the fact that down to within four centuries of our own times there existed a vast, complete ecclesiastical edifice of the age of Constantine, very slightly altered from what that Emperor left it,—a building which preserved all the main characteristics of its original design, the largest ancient church of early Christian times, no architectural splendour, not even Michelangelo's glorious dome, can compensate for its loss.

It is a remarkable fact that all through the Middle Ages, down to the dawn of the Renaissance, it never seems to have entered into the minds of the Pontiffs to rebuild the old Vatican Basilica; even the glories of Venice, Milan, and Florence, to say nothing of the noble Gothic cathedrals of the north, could not tempt them to rebuild the great,

* "Architecture, Mysticism, and Myth." By W. R. Lethaby. London: Percival & Co.

REFERENCES.

A. The Quadriporticus.
B. Nave of the Basilica.
C. Space where Paul III. erected the Chapel of the Archconfraternity of S.S. Sacrament.
D. Aisles of the Basilica.
E. Transept of the Basilica, or "Transverse Nave."
F. The Lady Chapel erected by Probus and Proba.
G. Entrance used by the Popes when they resided at the Lateran.
H. Chapel called the Secretarium.
J. Place where Sextus IV. built the Canon's Chapel.
K. Church of "Sta. Maria de Febribus." Afterwards used as the Sacristy of St. Peter's.
L. Church of St. Petronilla.
M. The Vatican Obelisk, called "La Giulia."
N. Chapel and Tomb of St. John Chrisostom.
O. Chapel and Tomb of St. Gregory the Great.
P. The "Jerusalem Church."
Q. Campo Santo.
R. St. Salvator de Ossibus.
S. Monastery of St. Stephen.
T. Ancient Chapel and Cemetery, called "Fons Petri."
V. Ancient buildings of the Vatican.
W. "Orologium," or clock-tower, of the Vatican.
X. Porta Pertusa.
Y. The Belvedere.
Z. Church of St. Gregory in Platea.

1. "Church of St. Appolinaris," or Hospitium for Pilgrims.
2. Entrance Gateway, or Propylæum.
3. Loggia from which the Popes gave Benediction.
4. "Turris Cymbalaria" (Bell-Tower).
5. Platform in front of Basilica.
6. The Five Flights of Marble Steps.
7. The Pine-Cone from the Mausoleum of Hadrian.
8. The Cantharus, or Fountain.

Key Sketch to View of Ancient Basilica of St. Peter, Rome.

rude, and somewhat barbarously-constructed old building.

Grimaldi, in his "History of the Vatican Basilica," refers to these facts.

Of course, various minor alterations and additions took place, from time to time, in the ancient Basilica, but the main fabric remained whole and entire as it had been constructed by Constantine, certainly down to the time of Nicholas V. This Pontiff has been usually accredited with the idea of the erection of the modern St. Peter's and the destruction of the ancient church, but there does not really appear to be any warrant for the statement.

Undoubtedly, in the time of Nicholas V. the old Basilica, which, Grimaldi says, had from the first been hastily constructed, and to a large extent from the materials of old classical buildings, had become decayed; in fact, some portion of it,—I am inclined to think the great apse or tribune,—had fallen down, and Nicholas V. had called in the celebrated architects, Leo Battista Alberti and Carlo Rosellino, who seem to have drawn up a report upon the condition of the building; what else they did is very doubtful. Either, however, in the time of Nicholas V. (whose pontificate extended from 1447 to 1455) or shortly after, the great transept of the church was pulled down, the altars, monuments, and other objects of art which it contained being rebuilt in the nave, evidently with the intention of replacing them in their original situations when the works of restoration or rebuilding had been completed. That this work was partially, if not wholly, carried out, is quite certain, because, on the reverse of a medal struck by Paul II. is a very interesting representation of the tribune or apse of St. Peter's as erected by that Pontiff. The inscription round it reads as follows: "Anno Christi MCCCCLXX has ædes condidit," and in the arch over the tribune is the inscription, "Tribuna S. Petri," and below it the word "Roma." The tribune is here shown with a semi-dome above it, inlaid with mosaic, and a great baldacchino of a simple early form below it. Evidently the whole thing was an attempt to reconstruct the old tribune. There are two very interesting early drawings showing the church at about this period. One has been republished by De Rossi and the other is engraved in the "Nuremberg Chronicle." Both of these show St. Peter's without transepts, but prove that in all other respects the church and its remarkable forecourt, or "quadriporticus," remained pretty much in their original condition. With the pontificate of Julius II., however, an entirely new state of things set in, and in 1506 Bramante commenced the present gigantic edifice, pulling down all the work which had been constructed by Nicholas V., Paul II., and other Pontiffs down to his own time. The great nave and aisles, the quadriporticus, and the lofty campanile were, however, not interfered with, and remained, with certain alterations and additions, down to the time of Paul V. (1605), who, with Carlo Maderno as his architect, perpetrated the terrible mistake of putting up the vast east front of the modern Basilica, which not only destroyed the symmetrical arrangement of Michelangelo's plan, but also necessitated the entire destruction of the old Basilica, which would not have been the case if Michelangelo's short nave had been adhered to.

There are a great number of drawings in existence showing the old church as it stood, with Michelangelo's dome and transepts rising up behind it. Amongst the most interesting are the following. The plan and views by Giulio Ballino (1567); by Marius Kartarus (1575); and a large view of the City of Rome, dedicated to Henry III. of France, by Antonio Lafrario (1577); also a view published in 1580, evidently taken from a much earlier drawing; also in the following works—Ciampini "De Sacris Edificiis a Constantino Magno Constructis," 1688; "Bonanni Templi Vaticani Historia," 1696; and "Fontana de Obilisco Vaticani," &c.

In many of these views we see the quadriporticus and the great nave and aisles of the old church, with the various additions that had been made to it from time to time. Although the eastern and western sides of the quadriporticus were unaltered yet, the north and south had been encroached upon by various structures. Upon the space marked C in our key-sketch, Paul III. (1503), had erected a large chapel with an elaborate Renaissance front projecting right across the south walk of the quadriporticus, and on the opposite side a large building called the "Auditorium Rotæ" was constructed by Innocent VIII. (1484-1492) which must have blocked up a considerable portion of the north walk.

The series of buildings forming the east front of the quadriporticus are shown in the earlier views, as represented in the drawing. To the extreme south-east (see I. in the sketch-plan) stood a quadrangular structure, with open arcades to the upper stories, which is described by Ciampini as the "Church of St. Appolinaris," but Bonanni, with greater probability, says that it was a Hospitium, erected by Leo III. for pilgrims. It was subsequently restored by Paul II., when, in all probability, the Renaissance doorway and windows, shown in the later drawings, were added. The arcaded stories above look like the old work of Leo III.

In the centre of the eastern front of the quadriporticus stood the great entrance gateway (fig. 2, sketch-plan), with three bronze doors. The arches and columns appear to have been Constantine's work, but the upper portion of the building had been covered by mosaic work, and Gothic windows introduced during the fourteenth century. To the north of this was a sort of open loggia (fig. 3). In the earlier views this is shown as a simple arcade with a balcony over it, protected by a penthouse roof, but in the later views, which are made from drawings executed by order of Sextus V., a much more important structure is represented, with regular Renaissance pilasters and friezes; an alteration which was carried out between the pontificates of Sextus IV., 1471, and

Alexander VI., 1503. There is rather an interesting question about this. The view in the "Nuremberg Chronicle," published 1494, shows this structure in its original condition, so that the drawing from which that very interesting engraving was made must have been taken at least a quarter of a century earlier,—I am inclined to think during the pontificate of Pius II. It is corroborated in nearly every detail by the Mediæval view of Rome, published by De Rossi. Immediately behind this loggia rose the lofty campanile, called "Turris Cymbalaria" by earlier writers (fig. 4). Although this was undoubtedly a lofty and beautiful structure, yet, surely, the old writers must have exaggerated its merits when we find Blondus affirming that "Talem Turrim Campanariam omnium primam in orbe terrarem fuisse!" Another writer, Angelus Rocca, states that "it was the loftiest tower in the whole world!!" Ciampini, however, with his usual moderation, speaks of it as "Quidem non humilis Turris." The building is very carefully described in Bonanni, in a quotation from Tiberius Alpharanus, who, in the reign of Sextus V., collected together all the drawings and manuscripts relating to St. Peter's. In fact, as neither Ciampini nor Bonanni themselves saw the ancient church, most of the facts which they state are taken from Tiberius Alpharanus, Turregio, and other earlier writers, whereas their plans and views are copied from drawings, either collected together or prepared under the direction of Tiberius Alpharanus. It is but just to both writers to say that they acknowledge their obligations.

From Bonanni's description of the tower we gather that it stood four stories high above the roof of the quadriporticus, that in each story were eight two-light windows, with double columns and Gothic tracery, but Bonanni says that it was crowned by a dome and not by a spire, and undoubtedly the drawings executed in the pontificate of Sextus V. agree with his description in every particular, but the earlier views agree in showing it crowned by a pyramidal spire; and as Tiberius Alpharanus says, that the tower was restored in 1574, and there can be little doubt that the domical top, which has a very Renaissance appearance about it, was an addition of that date. The tower was constructed originally by Leo IV., in 1303, but, according to a writer of the name of Rutilius Albrinus, it was struck by lightning in the year 1333, when the bells were melted, and the whole was not restored until 1353. It may be a question whether there were not two towers attached to the quadriporticus, as built by Constantine, but there are no means of proving this point.

In front of the quadriporticus, and leading up to the great gate, was a platform (fig. 5) approached by an immensely wide flight of white marble steps, subdivided into five sets, each consisting of seven steps—(fig. 6). Passing through the great gate and entering the quadriporticus, we should have found in the centre of the court-yard, the great Pigna or pine-cone from the mausoleum of Hadrian (fig. 7), preserved beneath an elaborate and beautiful Gothic baldacchino adorned with mosaic work, and a few yards nearer to the church another pine-cone of brass which spouted out water and formed a fountain for the refreshment of pilgrims visiting the church (fig. 8).

The great east front of the church itself, though preserving the outline of Constantine's church, had been covered with mosaics, and its windows filled with Gothic traceries in the fourteenth century. Grimaldi speaks of these windows as being arranged "more Germanico," but they appear to have resembled most Italian Gothic windows of that period. Like all the others in the church, they were divided into three lights, and had three cusped circles in the head.

The church consisted of a long and very wide nave with four aisles. The clearstory was supported by forty-six columns, twenty-three on either side. The transept was not arranged as in Gothic churches, but formed a transverse nave at right-angles to the principal one, so that there was no "crossing." The great apse or tribune opened from the west side of the transept by a large arch called "Arca Triumphalis." To the west of the great apse was the Lady-chapel, erected by Probus and Proba (Prefect of Rome, and his wife), in the sixth century. It really formed a complete little basilica, having its nave, aisle, apse, and campanile, as is shown by the long section of St. Peter's in Fontana's work (see F).

The old basilica of St. Peter was surrounded by chapels and churches. Referring to our key-sketch, at G was the pontifical entrance to St. Peter's, used by the Popes when they lived at the Lateran Palace, and beyond it, at H, was a building called the "secretarium," in which they robed. Some writers have reversed the order of things here, and have created a confusion which seems to have very much troubled Bonanni, inasmuch as it makes the Popes enter the basilica through a chapel without an external doorway to it, and robe themselves upon a public staircase! All along this side of the nave were a series of ancient chapels, but Sextus IV. destroyed all their symmetry and regularity by building what, from the view published in Bonanni, and made in the pontificate of Sextus V., must have been a remarkably ugly chapel (J) for the use of the canons of St. Peter.

Two very curious buildings will be seen at figs. K, L. They are similar in design, forming large rotundas. Fontana appears to think that one, or both, of these were Pagan temples, which stood upon the spina of the old circus of Nero. Ciampini, however, says that the further one, dedicated to St. Petronilla, was erected by Honorius I. According to Fontana, these temples were dedicated to Venus and Mars; and what certainly is a strong argument in favour of Fontana's view is the fact that they stood close to the situation of the old obelisk called "La Giulia" (see M), from its having been brought over by Julius Cæsar, which certainly was in its original position on the spina of the circus, before Fontana removed it to the front of the modern church.

The two rotundas, however, were dedicated under the titles of "St. Petronilla" and "Sta. Maria de Febribus." The former was pulled down before the time of Sextus V., but a very interesting view in Bonanni's work shows the latter as it appeared in the time of that Pontiff, when it came to be used as the sacristy of St. Peter's. Uniting these buildings was a chapel and altar dedicated to St. John Chrisostom, see N, within which that great doctor of the Church was buried. On the opposite side of the basilica, at O, stood the chapel of St. Gregory the Great, containing the tomb of that illustrious Pontiff, and beyond it was a complete basilica church, P, which belonged originally to a monastery called Jerusalem, but after the removal of that monastery was dedicated to St. Vincent, and I cannot help connecting this building with the Jerusalem Chamber at Westminster Abbey. Its position is identical, and its juxtaposition to the tomb of St. Gregory the Great, whom Venerable Bede calls the Apostle of England (see book 2, cap. 1), seems too remarkable to be a mere coincidence.

On the opposite side of a narrow street, on the south side of the Basilica, stood the Campo Santo (Q), with its church dedicated to "S. Salvator de Ossibus" (R), erected by Charlemagne. It had a lofty campanile, and is shown in Ciampini's plan as being very nearly square, standing north and south, and not east and west. It should here be noted that the Basilica of St. Peter itself was *exactly* orientated, but, of course, as in all the old Basilica churches, the Tribune and High Altar were at the west end, the latter having its back towards the congregation, so that when celebrating the priest and the congregation faced each other. So exactly due east and west was the Basilica that, on the vernal equinox, the great doors of the porch of the quadriporticus were thrown open at sunrise, and also the eastern doors of the church itself, and as the sun rose, its rays passed through the outer doors, then through the inner doors, and, penetrating straight through the nave, illuminated the High Altar.

On the right hand side of our view the old buildings of the Vatican are indicated, there is, however, considerable uncertainty about them. Nothing now remains of an earlier date than Nicholas V., except possibly the external walls of the Sistine Chapel, which look as if they might have formed a portion of a great hall or keep, which is shown in early views. Muratori says that Nicholas V. intended to rebuild the whole of the Vatican and St. Peter's. This statement seems to require corroboration, for, as we have previously noticed, his work at St. Peter's must be regarded rather in the light of a restoration than the commencement of a new building. The old Vatican was built, or re-built, by Innocent III. Bonanni, quoting from a manuscript life of Innocent III., says that "in 1200 he caused this house to be made anew, with chapel, chaplin's chambers, kitchen, stables, houses of the chancellors and chamberlains, elemosynarium, &c. He commenced the great hall (probably the building on the site of the Sistine Chapel), completed the loggia, enclosed the palace with walls and built the towers." It appears that Arnolpho di Lapo was one of the architects employed. In 1258 we find it stated that Nicholas III. ordered to be made the great hall, the palace, the chapel, and the ancient buildings to be enlarged. In all probability this hall was the one in the lower court of the Vatican, which is distinctly shown between the two great towers, one of which formed the "Otologium," or clock-tower. John XXIII. built the long gallery which connected the Vatican with the Castle of St. Angelo. It will be noticed at once that the Vatican and the Belvedere formed distinct buildings. It is to be regretted that the antiquarians and writers of the fifteenth and sixteenth centuries did not extend to the Vatican the same care which they exercised in preserving documents and drawings of the church and quadriporticus. As it is, anything like a careful restoration of the palace is impossible, as the views which show it are too vague to be implicitly relied on for such a purpose. As far as the palace itself is concerned, therefore, our restoration must be taken as being merely suggestive.

H. W. B.

NOTES.

FROM our correspondence columns it will be seen that our friend Mr. T. G. Jackson continues to hammer away at the Institute and its examinations, and now concludes with the charge that the Institute is not offering "to a too confiding public" any guarantee of the artistic competence of its members. We do not understand that the Institute ever professed to be able to accomplish such an object by an examination test. What it professes to be accomplishing, or aiming at, is, in the interests of architects, to direct the studies of students to a fixed end, and to raise the general standard of knowledge and education among its members; and in the interests of the public, to ensure that members of its body shall have a competent knowledge of the technique of architecture. That is all the public could demand from it, or could expect to obtain. The question of an architect's artistic power, it has been over and over again pointed out (by "the memorialists" themselves among others), cannot be decided by any infallible test, any more than in any other branch of art. Cultivated public opinion settles that in the long run, as in every other form of art. Membership of the Royal Academy, a purely artistic body, does not settle such a question in the eyes of the public. People who know enough to distinguish between good and bad sculpture or painting are not influenced in their purchases or commissions by the consideration whether the artist is or is not a member of the Royal Academy. They judge the artist on his own merits and the testimony of his known works. The same test of free public opinion would operate equally in deciding the artistic status of an architect. The Institute is not proposing to say to the public, "all our members are men of artistic power;" nor does the public want its advice on that point, any more than it wants that of the Royal Academy. What it proposes is to be able eventually to say, "all our members are men well instructed in the history and technique of architecture, and are up to a certain standard in general education" (the latter not so unimportant a point as some people think). More than this it is impossible that it could accomplish, since there is no infallible test of artistic power. Mr. Jackson blames the Institute for not doing what, in the nature of things, it is impossible that it could do.

THE dreadful catastrophe at Gateshead can hardly come under the chapter of accidents; even the word "catastrophe," which we substituted for "accident," is hardly the expression called for. The deaths unhappily caused by the rush for the exit should really be returned under the heading, "Suicide while in a state of unsound mind," always excepting that of the unfortunate doorkeeper who was killed while doing his best to bring a set of panic-stricken people to reason. It is with a melancholy sense of the hopelessness of average human nature that one has to read once more the discreditable story of hundreds of people losing all courage and presence of mind, and killing each other in a panic flight, because one hysterical woman screamed out "Fire!" The hysterical person, who is usually an element in these cases, has much to answer for, and has not always the excuse of feminine nervousness; and if the next person who started the cry of "Fire"! in such a case could be caught and given a year's imprisonment, perhaps other silly people would think twice before trying to upset the nerves of others on an occasion when coolness is the first requisite. In regard to the exit question it does not appear this has much to do with the matter when people once give way to a panic. The practice of keeping one leaf of the door closed after the house is full is very reprehensible, and may give rise to danger, or at least delay in exit, even when there is no panic; but it does not appear that it would have made any difference in this case if the doors had both been open. The real point in the matter, however, lies in the evidence the event gives of the danger and impropriety of wooden construction in theatres, with hollow spaces where inflammable matter can lodge. Had the gallery been built of iron and concrete, with solid steps, there would have been no crevices in which papers could get lodged and into which matches could be let drop, and the hysterical person would have no temptation to begin his or her death-song. That is the moral of the whole thing from a constructor's point of view. Build the whole gallery of iron and concrete, and set wooden benches, if there are any, on solid steps, and the material for a fire-panic is reduced to a minimum, if not entirely removed. Here the whole material was, as it were, carefully prepared, and only required the match and the hysterical person to set it going.

THE three premiated designs for the proposed new parochial offices at Battersea have been for the past week on view at the new Free Library, Lavender-hill. Considering that this was a "limited" competition, we think it desirable that all the designs sent in should have been exhibited, and not only those awarded the premiums. Ample space was available in the room in which the drawings are hung for a selection at least of the other designs, and such a course would have been distinctly fairer to the other competitors, and would have allowed the general public to form an independent idea of the merits of the several designs submitted. The design sent in by Mr. Mountford, which was placed first, we have already noticed and illustrated (*Builder*, December 19, 1891). Of the various ways which were open to competitors in the arrangement of the blocks (the details as to the arrangement of the various offices having been clearly defined in the conditions) two naturally presented themselves,—either of separating the public hall block from the official block, or combining them in one. Mr. Mountford has chosen the latter, which has the merit of giving communication between them by means of corridors without going into the open air, and is also the more economical of the two arrangements. The fall in the site was considerable at the northern end, and this has enabled Mr. Mountford to place the two smaller halls, which were required by the conditions, below the Public Hall. The Council Chamber is placed centrally, facing Lavender-hill, on the first floor, and the Coroner's Court is on the same floor at the back of the official block, and approached by a separate staircase, as shown on the ground-plan. The angle formed at the junction of the two blocks has been cleverly masked by the introduction of an octagonal vestibule to the public-hall, covered with a glass dome, with the reception-room and lavatories leading directly from it. The design by Mr. Cheers is somewhat unaccountable in its arrangement. On a site which was, compared with many, of a simple character, there is no obvious reason that we can see for the complicated arrangement of the various offices. The first thing that occurred to us on looking at the plans was that it would be apparently very easy to get into the building, and very difficult to get out. The central portion of the façade, which naturally suggested the position for a Council Chamber, has been unnecessarily frittered away in staircase and vestibules, and the Council Chamber finds a resting-place at the extreme rear of the building, where the quiet,—when it was reached,—would be its only recommendation. A large public hall, over 100 ft. in length, occupies the major portion of one side of the front block, although it does not appear on the front elevation. In short, this design is one of those unhappy instances of an exterior which gives no key as to its internal arrangement, and wants that element of simplicity and directness which should be characteristic of a good plan. Messrs. Reed & Macdonald, who were placed third, have adopted the "separate block" system, and the official block has a carriage-way completely surrounding it. The arrangement of the various offices is good. The Council Chamber and Coroner's Court are on the first floor, as in the design submitted by Mr. Mountford. The elevation to Lavender-hill is somewhat tame, and is not improved by the perspective view, which gives an even less satisfactory result than the elevation would lead one to expect.

THE resignation of Lord Lingen and Mr. Cohen of their positions on the Financial Committee of the London County Council has had one good effect, at any rate: it has drawn public attention to the principles of municipal loans. There are two clearly-defined parties in the Council on this point. The one to which Lord Lingen and all clear-headed men of business belong desires to see loans paid off in such a manner that the amount payable each year becomes less and less. The other party, headed by Mr. Charles Harrison, desires to see loans paid off on what is called the annuity principle, by which the amount of principal and interest to be repaid will be the same in the last as in the first year of the debt. It is clear that the first-named is the proper principle, otherwise —as it is certain that fresh improvements will necessitate fresh loans,—in a certain number of years the municipal debt must be largely increased. But when the amount payable diminishes year by year, if fresh loans are required, they can be procured without increasing the burden on the community. Moreover, each generation should, so far as possible, pay for its own work, even if the work should be a benefit to posterity. It is not possible, of course, for a community to pay for extensive operations out of the revenue of a few years. But that is no reason why they should not pay off as much of the money borrowed during present times as is possible. Any other system of finance is both unsound and wanting in courage.

THE Bill which is brought forward by the Corporation of Birmingham for the purpose of obtaining a new water supply from the mountains of Wales is hardly likely to meet with any serious opposition. The principle that large towns are entitled to go to some distant district for the water supply has already been sanctioned in the case of Manchester and Liverpool. Hence the only questions to be set up relate to matters of detail. It has been supposed that a new Standing Order of the House of Commons may entitle the London County Council to oppose this Bill, on the ground that London may some day wish to obtain a supply from the same source. But it is doubtful if the Standing Order in question applies to such a case as this; even if it does give the London County Council a *locus standi*, it is equally clear that a possible, but uncertain, scheme for the supply of London from the mountains of Cardigan, Radnor, and Brecknock cannot be any real ground for refusing the demands of Birmingham. There is a legal and sensible maxim that the first in point of time is the first in point of right, and this principle clearly applies to such a case as this. The amount of the cost of the work, between six and seven millions, is very large, but it is an undertaking which, if successfully carried out, will supply Birmingham with water for generations, and it is well that such a work should, if done at all, be done thoroughly.

THE recent fogs have again drawn public attention to the way in which time, money, and health are lost in consequence of them. There was a time when they hardly caused inconvenience: the growth of London has increased their density and their injurious effects. In truth, they are the modern plague of London. It is annoying that no attempt has yet been made to obtain an authoritative and trustworthy report as to the means for their prevention. A Royal Commission, composed of scientific and practical men, might make a report, which might in its turn lead to beneficial legislation. These winter fogs have now become so great a pest that it is certain they will cause large numbers of persons who are not bound to the metropolis by business ties to leave it in the winter, and will prevent many from coming to London who would otherwise do so. The Metropolitan Members of Parliament should take the matter in hand: they are strong enough to force the matter on the attention of the Government, which, indeed, should not require much pressure to order an investigation into this affliction of the metropolis.

WE have received several samples of polished stone of grey, green, and red tints, and called "Bavarian granites," which the senders are desirous of more fully introducing to the English market. Now, we have nothing much to say against the materials, so far as their utility is concerned, but we do object to having them sent to us as coming from Bavaria, when we find that, as a matter of fact, some come from Sweden, and others from Saxony. Six of the specimens sent are unquestionably of Bavarian origin, and are quarried in the neighbourhood of Bayreuth; these are grey, with the exception of one which is greenish in tint. The Swedish and Saxon samples are of rich red and deep green colours, and when these are interspersed with the true Bavarian stones they decidedly heighten the tone of the whole. A beautiful pink granite was also included amongst the samples, but in answer to an inquiry we find that this "has been withdrawn, as there is very great difficulty in getting any quantity of it." Why, then, was it sent to us? The real Bavarian granites, although of grey tints and not so showy, perhaps, as the remaining specimens, required no bolstering up. They are amongst the best granites we have ever seen; with one exception they are of warm tints, and will doubtless find a ready sale on that account. The nature of the minerals of which they are constituted, no less than the general structure of the stones, and their fine grain, place them at once above the average granites in point of durability. The greenish variety contains rather more iron pyrites than we like to see in a really first-class weather stone, and magnetite is found in small quantities in the more basic kinds, but these deleterious accessory features are more than compensated for by the fine condition of the essential minerals concerned, and do not materially detract from the value of the granites as a whole. The deep red stone from Sweden, which takes a good polish, is coarse-grained, its general tint resulting from the colour of the orthoclase felspar; the quartz is beautifully opalescent, and a dark mineral, resembling hornblende, is abundant. The dark green stone, apparently from Warberg, in Sweden, although handsome, contains such a large proportion of iron that we do not consider it would weather very well. It is not a stranger to the British market; we have seen it commonly in the yards of certain Aberdeen granite merchants. In the red granite from Saxony, alluded to, the orthoclase is pink, and the more or less rounded crystals of quartz which are "smoky" produce an effect much resembling our famous Peterhead granite. All these stones, from their nature and appearance, are eligible for competition in this country, and they will doubtless become conspicuous features in the market.

AT an adjourned meeting on Wednesday, the 23rd ult., the London County Council agreed (as reported in another column) to offer 5,000*l.* for the "Poor's Land," Bethnal-green, in pursuance of a clause in the Charity Commissioners' scheme of February last year:—

"The trustees shall, with the approval of the Charity Commissioners, and upon terms such as to secure a sufficient benefit to the poor of the parish of St. Matthew, Bethnal-green, forthwith grant to the London County Council, or any other public body, all the land held in trust for the charity, provided that the said land be secured and permanently maintained . . . . as a recreation-ground accessible to the inhabitants of the said parish."

This area of about six and a quarter acres is all that now remains of the fifteen acres, waste land of the manor, as conveyed under a deed of 1690 to "trustees for the poor" by certain persons who had bought the land and enclosed the greater part of it "for the prevention of any new buildings thereon, and to be for the yearly relief of the poor," &c. The trustees are empowered to lease the lands for terms of twenty-one years at the longest. Under special Acts they were paid 3,000*l.* Consols for sites for St. John's Chutch and vicarage, and the Museum, opened in 1872, with its adjoining pleasure-ground.* A lease of the remainder to Bethnal House (private lunatic) Asylum, for purposes of a garden, expired at Michaelmas, 1889. The Commissioners drafted three schemes,—one to carry into effect proposals by a majority of the twelve trustees for selling three plots of the vacant land for about 19,500*l.*, to provide sites for a free library, an infirmary, and a new Vestry Hall, with conversion of 2½ acres into an open space. Those projects were opposed by, *inter alios*, the Metropolitan Public Gardens Association. The ultimate scheme was recently petitioned against,—in respect of its clause 30, quoted above,—by a majority of the trustees. They urged that whilst the deed of 1690 had, admittedly, two objects,—provision for the poor, and keeping the land open,—the latter is subordinate to the former, or eleemosynary, trust; and that such a sale would debar them from obtaining a full price for the ground. On July 23 Mr. Justice Chitty gave judgment in court in favour of the scheme, and declined to allow the petitioners' costs as out of the trust. His lordship is reported to have said that, looking to the deed, the contested clause formed, in his opinion, a lawful and *cy pres* appropriation of the property, for the deed, besides setting up a charity, had declared the land was to be kept open. Thus, we gather, a long out-standing question will now, in all likelihood, be determined.

ALL Saints' Church, Hertford, which, as we read, was entirely destroyed by fire last week, stands within a large graveyard in Fore-street, on the south side of the borough. As rebuilt, mainly of flint and chalk overlaid with rough-cast, early in the fifteenth century, it consisted of nave, chancel, transepts, and western tower. Two aisles were added since, and a leaden-covered spire. The interior was decorated, re-pewed, and repaired in 1872-3. This is one of two churches held, together with a house, by Peter de Valoignes, castellan of Hertford, *temp.* the Conqueror,* and assigned by Peter's son, Robert, to the canons at Waltham "for the health of himself and Hawise, his wife." The monks enjoyed this grant, confirmed by Richard I., until 26 Hen. VIII. when the Crown took the vicarage advowson, then rated, together with that of St. John, at 10*l.* 6s. 8½d. per annum. We gather that the organ (1750) and the fine peal of bells are destroyed. The bells were originally five in number. In 1674 William Wake cast the great hell into four smaller bells; the eight were recast 1771, by Pack & Chapman, at the cost of the Society of College Youths, Hertford, who, twenty years later, added two trebles, cast by Bryant, a townsman,—making ten in all. Here were many monuments and memorials of certain county families, including those of Dimsdale, Harrison, Townshend, Battell, Cherry, &c., with inscribed brasses to Isabel de Newmarch, maid-of-honour to Richard II.'s consort Isabella; William Wake, "somtym yeman of John Duc of Bedford's hors, And lat Survayor with King Henry Sixt he was;" and John Prest, "quondam Janitor Hospitii Katharinæ nuper Reginæ Angliæ,"—Henry V.'s queen. The registers are saved: an entry,—

"1666, Nov. 17th, Sir Richard Fanshawe, Lord Im Bassador, was laid in the Vault in the Chansell."

cited in Turnor's "History of Hertford," shows Colley Cibber correctly says that Fanshawe, our Ambassador to Madrid, where he died, was buried in this church. A subsequent entry stands thus:—

"1671, May 18, Sir Richard Fanshawe, Imbassador, was taken out of this Vault, and laid in his Vault at Ware."

A tombstone in the burial-ground recorded the interment of "Black Tom" of the Bull Inn, Bishopsgate-street, in 1696. A view of All Saints', by J. & H. S. Storer, will be found in Lewis Turnor's volume.

AN interesting lecture on "The Development of the Pig-iron Manufacture in the United States" has been lately delivered before the Franklin Institute by Mr. John Birkinbine, and now appears in the *Journal* of the Society for last month. In 1866, the United States only produced as much pig-iron as Great Britain did in 1835, so that she was then thirty-one years behind this country. At the end of 1884, however, she was only twenty-one years behind, and if the same rate of progress of both countries continues, she will produce as much pig-iron as England in 1950. In the United States between 1830 and 1860, the production of iron increased twice as fast as the population, and between 1860 and 1890 it has increased four times as rapidly, the consumption at the present day being at the rate of about 300 lbs. per head, the whole of which is produced in the country. Great Britain, on the other hand, makes more than she consumes, and during 1889 the production reached nearly 500 lbs. per head. As at present the production for the whole world is about 25,000,000 tons per annum, and during the next ten years this supply must be increased by at least 50 per cent., there is a bright future for those engaged in the manufacture of pig-iron and the allied industries.

THE same journal contains a paper on "Fuel Gas," by Mr. Arthur Kitson, in which he describes its production and distribution. The great value of gas for metallurgical work became evident directly Siemens introduced his regenerative furnace. The distinction that is made between fuel gas and illuminating gas arises chiefly from the difference in cost, since the latter makes excellent fuel gas providing it can be sold at a price sufficiently low to allow it being used for the purpose. Since it is possible to obtain about one-half of the total heat of combustion of gas, while only one-sixth of the heat contained in coal can be made serviceable for ordinary domestic purposes, the fact that gas generated from coal contains less energy than the coal itself does not prevent fuel-gas being economical. The author draws attention in his lecture to various methods of making the gas, and describes a producer he has designed, besides giving the results of several experiments he has carried out in connexion with this subject.

IT is extraordinary what vitality a scientific blunder possesses. More than twenty years ago Professor Tait, speaking before the British Association, said:—"Mark, however, that heat is not the mere motions, but the energy of these motions—a very different thing, for heat and kinetic energy in general are no more '*modes of motion*' than potential energy of every kind (including that of unfired gunpowder) is a '*mode of rest.*' In fact, a '*mode of motion*' is, if the word motion be used in its ordinary sense, purely kinematical, not physical,—and, if motion be used in Newton's sense, it refers to momentum, not to energy." This emphatic protest ought to have killed the expression long ago, yet only the other day, not in a popular work, but in a singularly able leading article in the *Electrician*, on the question of the existence of electricity, we came upon the statement that heat is a "mode of motion." This strange persistence of error makes it very important to protest early against any abuse of scientific phrases. Already in three glossaries of electrical terms, we have found the "watt" defined as the unit of electrical energy, and a writer in *Lightning* who made, by implication, the same statement, while acknowledging the error, defends it, as "what in common parlance is done among engineers on every day in the week." If this be so, so much the worse for the engineers; they are preparing trouble for themselves in the future. What is the use of giving special names to definite scientific conceptions, if these names are to be regarded as interchangeable at will?

THE cable industry was threatened with extinction lately from the scarcity of india-rubber. Fortunately a large number of these valuable trees have been discovered in New Guinea, whence they can be transplanted and cultivated in more accessible portions of the globe. We shall, therefore, continue to receive from America early news of depressions, atmospheric and mercantile, and of the sayings and doings of that erratic genius, Mr. Edison.

WE have received a large quarto illustrated pamphlet got up by Mr. Franklin W. Smith, a wealthy inhabitant of Boston (with the help of Messrs. Renwick, Aspinwall, &

---

* Opened by the Office of Works in 1876. To it was added the Green, on the east side of which stood "Blind Beggars' House," built in 1570, it is said, by John Thorpe, the architect, for one John Kirby.

* For account of Hertford Castle see the *Builder*, December 23, 1882.

Russell, architects, of New York) containing the general idea for a great National Gallery of History and Art for America, proposed to be erected on the banks of the Potomac at Washington. The object of the publication is to arouse the public mind in America on the subject, and certainly the scheme proposed by Mr. Smith is magnificent enough to satisfy even a country which always wants to do something bigger than all the rest of the world has done. The idea apparently is that all the leading styles of architecture of the world are to be reproduced in the several halls and galleries; the domain is to be entered by a bridge over a small lake flanked by circular colonnades, and the climax reached at the further side in a kind of modern Acropolis with an imitation Parthenon (to a larger scale) surrounded by great double colonnades. The galleries, we presume, are to be filled with works of art of various types. We should very much doubt so ambitious a scheme being carried out, and fear it would look rather like an enormous museum of curiosities. If the American nation wish to have a National Gallery of Art, they will do more wisely to content themselves with attempting a more reasonable building in a modern style.

WE note the appearance of the third part of Mr. Gotch's work on the "Architecture of the Renaissance in England,"* which includes illustrations and description of Kirby Hall, well known as one of the most interesting buildings of its class. The first two "Parts" of the book we have already noticed at some length. When the whole six "Parts" have been issued we will devote further space to a consideration of the remainder of the work.

IN the matter of the London Building Act Consolidation Bill, the Building Act Committee of the London County Council have suggested a number of amendments, and the Institute of Architects have issued suggestions for a "Draft Bill for the codification and amendment of the Metropolitan Building Acts," printing in double column the existing clauses with the proposed amendments and amplifications opposite. These we shall give full consideration to on another occasion.

THE *Daily News* says that in making the subway between the Great Northern Railway terminus and the King's Cross (Metropolitan) station, the men have found a solid block of concrete several yards square, 2 ft. under the centre of the roadway, a few feet north of the Metropolitan tunnel. Our contemporary goes on to say:

"According to old plans, it is the foundation of the cross erected in 1290, by order of Edward I., as one of the resting-places of the body of Queen Eleanor, on its way from Hornby, in Lincoln (*sic*) where she died, to Westminster Abbey."

We have not seen the old plans referred to; and, at present, are inclined to suspect that, in view of the block's situation, and shallow depth beneath the present surface, it formed rather a foundation for the ridiculous structure, of brick cemented over, consisting of a watch-house (with a pair of Doric-fluted columns at each angle) and clock-tower, surmounted with George IV.'s statue, by Stephen Geary, architect, which was erected on the site (as we have read) of Cromwell's observatory at Battle-bridge sixty years ago. They took down the statue in 1842; the watch-house and tower, having served as a police-station, and then as a tavern with a camera-obscura in the tower, remained until 1845.† Crosses were set up in London to the Queen's memory at Charing-cross, where Charles I.'s statue now stands, and in Cheapside, by the end of Milk-street (or Wood-street). Of the latter there are views in Wilkinson's "Londina," after the Cowdray painting of Edward VI.'s coronation procession, and an original drawing (1606) in the Pepysian Library, at Magdalene College, Cambridge, &c.

THE following paragraph, which appears in the *Times* of Tuesday last, ought to do something to further the movement in favour of an improved source of water supply for London:—

"POLLUTION OF THE THAMES.—At Staines Petty Sessions, yesterday, George and Robert Morgan and William Haimer were summoned by the Thames Conservancy for having emptied the contents of a cesspool into the Thames just above the intakes of the metropolitan water companies. The case was clearly proved by a Conservancy official, and the defendants were fined 50s. each."

We wonder how many cases of this kind escape undetected? The dangers to which London is thus exposed have often been pointed out, and it is appalling to think of the possible consequences in the event of the prevalence of typhoid fever in Staines or other places above it.

FROM a letter of the Rector of St. Mary Woolnoth, in the *Times* of December 26, giving some of the results of Mr. Mark H. Judge's examination into the condition of the building, it seems evident that it is nothing short of a public duty, independently of any consideration of the use of the church by the congregation, to remove from the centre of the city the festering mass of human remains which is enclosed in the basement of the church. That this may be done without permanent injury to Hawksmoor's remarkable building we have no doubt, and we hope we shall bear no more talk of anything so absurd as destroying the church.

IN reviewing a book on American railways some time ago we spoke strongly as to evidence given in it as to the deplorable want of the feeling of responsibility for the public safety, both in the construction of railways and in the performance of duty by officials, which was admitted in a book written by American engineers and railway officials. According to the New York correspondent of the *Times* (December 25) a crucial instance of this criminal light-heartedness on the part of American railway officials was given in the case of the collision between two trains on the New York Central Railway:—

"It is alleged that the brakesman who was sent to stop the St. Louis express reached Hastings Station in ample time to stop the train, but, believing it not to be due for some minutes, he stopped to take a drink with the stationmaster, and while so engaged the express dashed past."

Englishmen who are interested in railway working may be allowed to feel some pride in the reflection that such a deliberate dereliction of duty would be impossible and unheard-of among the humblest officials of a great English railroad.

LETTER FROM PARIS.

SINCE our last letter the question of the Sèvres manufactory has been definitely settled. The Minister of Public Instruction, much embarrassed by the refusal of M. Bracquemond to undertake the directorship, took the advice of the Conseil Supérieur des Beaux-Arts, which has decided a division of power between three distinct sections. The "administration" section will be placed under M. Baumgart, who will be responsible for the working of the manufactory. The section of "Travaux Techniques" will be placed under a distinguished chemist, M. Vogt; and that of "Travaux d'Art" under M. Jules Coutan, the sculptor of the monumental fountain of the great Exhibition.

M. Coutan's talent is well known; he is a conscientious artist in his own work, with a fine eye for form, but nothing in his past career seems to point him out specially for such a post as that at Sèvres. Ceramic art requires a special knowledge and experience, and a director of designi n that art should have also knowledge of the practical processes employed; in fact there is or should be a close connexion between "travaux d'art and travaux techniques" in this class of work. The future will show whether the young sculptor will be able to put any new life into the now rather superannuated form of work put forth, not much to the national credit, from the Sèvres manufactory.

The Minister is also bent on transforming and developing the "Ecole de Sèvres." This institution is organised for giving instruction in ceramics for the benefit of private industry. Henceforward every citizen furnished with an official authorisation can obtain all the instruction he requires in design and manufacture; and funds are reserved for making all researches in regard to the fabrication and design of ceramic work. In short, the Sèvres institution will now be at once an artistic establishment, a centre of scientific research, and a school of advanced study in ceramic art. Such at all events, is the intention of the Minister of Fine Arts. It remains to be seen whether or not the good results anticipated will be realised under the routine system which always clings about a State establishment.

We have referred already to the projected "museum fund," to be furnished by the proceeds of payment on entry, a measure certain to be exceedingly unpopular. Such has been the opinion of the Budget Committee, which has pronounced itself strongly in favour of retaining the present free entry to National Museums. The Committee is, however, in favour of the increase of the annual credit for museums and art galleries, in order to facilitate the purchase of pictures and works of art. The authorised expenditure will probably be raised from 200,000 to 500,000 francs, and this is certainly the best solution of the difficulty, and there is little doubt that Parliament will ratify the proposal.

A good deal has been said in the press about a provincial shop for the manufactory of spurious Millet pictures, said to have been concocted by a former pupil of the artist. The fraud has been carried on for some time, it appears with profitable results. The police have put an end to an enterprise, which at all events showed that the "facture" of the celebrated painter of the "Angelus" was not difficult to imitate, and that the artistic perception of the majority of purchasers leaves great room for improvement.

Fraud however is very rife at present in connexion with artistic work; not only the fabrication of spurious works of art, but of the whole materials with which they are produced, such as pigments, oils, varnishes, &c. A number of painters, all members of the Institut, have felt this so strongly that they have addressed a memorandum to the Prefect of Police praying that all materials of painting offered for sale should be examined at the municipal laboratory and officially stamped.

We are in the season of small private exhibitions. To the usual number is this year added an exhibition with the pompous title of the "Exposition des Peintres Symbolistes." Under this title, perhaps destined to efface that of "Impressionist," are grouped a few young artists of talent, nearly lost in a crowd of mediocrities. Among those whose talents have been long recognised are M. Renoir, with a fine pastel; M. Willette, who has three exceedingly delicate drawings; and M. Lepère with an important landscape. Among those who promise well are MM. Bonnard, Maurice Jenis, Anquetin, Filliger, de Toulouse, Lautrec and Seruzier.

The exhibition organised by M. Antocolski, a Russian sculptor, is also noticeable. He has a great reputation in his own country, and his score or so of statues exhibited enable one to appreciate his merits, but he shows a certain "preciosity" in the handling of the marble which is too much of the modern Italian school, and fatigues one by the *finesse* and multiplicity of detail. This pitfall at least modern French sculpture has avoided, and the exhibition of terra-cottas by the lamented Carrier-Belleuse which is now open forms a notable contrast in this respect with the work of the Russian sculptor.

It may be mentioned here that there is shortly to be an exhibition of the works of the late landscape painter Pelouse, as well as the ninth international exhibition of "Blanc et Noir," which will this year be transferred to the Champ de Mars, and will comprise an important retrospective exhibition of engraving to which many well-known collectors have promised to contribute.

* Published by B. T. Batsford.

† *Vide* prints (1830) of the statue, and woodcuts (1842) of its removal, in the Guildhall Library, and the Grace Collection, British Museum; also Pugin's "Contrasts."

The exhibition of photographs collected by the Commission des Monuments Historiques, at the Trocadéro, should not be overlooked. There may be seen photographs of many of the most curious ancient churches in France: St. Oustrille, Ruan, Uzerche, St. Calais, &c. This fine collection, organised by M. Mieusement, shows the visitor also the Druidic monuments, dolmens, and meuliers, scattered about the districts of Charente, Maine-et-Loire, la Sarthe, and Brittany.

From historic monuments to "bâtiments civils" the transition is easy, since both are under the same administration, and it may be here mentioned that M. Yves Guyot has reconstituted the bureau of "bâtiments civils," which for 1892 will be thus composed: M. Jules Comte, President; MM. Charles Garnier, Daumet, Pascal, Moyaux, Bouvard, Marcel Lambert, Paulin, Vaudremer, Sédille and Blondel.

It is announced that the Direction des Musées Nationaux has decided to put at the disposition of the public plans of large dimensions and variously tinted, to be hung at the two principal entrances of the Louvre, to enable visitors to find their way round without a guide; an excellent innovation, since to strangers the Louvre is a complete labyrinth of which it is difficult to find the clue. The Louvre has just acquired a curious bronze statuette of Dionysos, attributed to Praxiteles, and long reputed among archæologists as one of the finest productions of that period of Greek art. It has also acquired five polychromatic stucco statues of the Italian school of the fifteenth century.

The State Committee of Fine Arts has recently examined the new model executed by M. Rodin for the monument to Victor Hugo in the Pantheon. In the first design, which was refused, the three figures symbolising the inspiring voices of the poet were placed above his head. In the second, the figure of Victor Hugo himself dominates the group. The new design is considered very satisfactory and M. Rodin is commissioned to commence the work.

Since December 25 the public has been admitted to examine the ninety-six designs, at the Champ de Mars, for the decoration of the Salle des Banquets at the Hôtel de Ville. The first selection will not be made till January 5 or 6, and the Jury will have some difficulty, from among these ninety-six, in selecting the five who are to be worthy of entering for the final competition. The spaces for the decoration are three large ceilings and eight door-heads. The sum to be allowed is 49,000 francs, and the Committee charged with the work have set themselves against the eternal "still-life" subjects which form the recognised decoration of dining-halls. Some of the painters have endeavoured to combine the figure with these materials of decoration, by paintings of fish-shops, fruiterers, &c.; but the result is not happy. Others have struck the patriotic chord, and one represents on the ceiling the fraternising of French and Russian sailors at Cronstadt! In spite of some pretentious or absurd work, however, the competition as a whole is up to a high standard.

The Académie des Beaux-Arts will be shortly occupied in filling the place of M. Alphand. M. Philippe Gille is said to be a candidate. He is a well-known journalist and dramatic author. His candidature can hardly be considered serious, yet it is more comprehensible than that of M. Roger Ballu, who is said to have already commenced the customary round of visits; but he is too young a man and with too little artistic achievement to show, to have any chance of entering an institution of which every member is a celebrity.

The Académie des Beaux-Arts will also have shortly to elect two foreign corresponding members in place of MM. Rosa and Vela. M. Fioreli is a candidate "en première ligne," Mr. Alma-Tadema "en seconde ligne;" MM. Hasenauer, Jacobi, and Cuypers are also spoken of.

Public works in Paris offer little of interest at this time of year. We may mention the formation of a new abattoir on the left bank, similar to that of la Villette; and the works necessary for the isolation of the Sainte Chapelle. It is said that the Musée Galliera will soon be inaugurated. We shall have occasion to speak further of this elegant edifice, designed by M. Ginain at the cost of the widow of the Duc de Galliera, and the porticoes of which are adorned with sculpture by MM. Chapu, Thomas, and Cavelier. The art collection of the city of Paris will be infinitely better here than in the Musée d'Auteuil, built hurriedly in an out-of-the-way quarter, and which is, in fact, no more than a store-room, almost unknown to the Parisian public.

The general meeting of the "Société des Artistes Français" was held a few days ago. It appears from the results of the meeting that in spite of the schism which led to the establishment of the rival Salon, the financial condition of the Society is most prosperous; it proposes to spend a portion of its funds in creating a "maison de retraite" for impoverished artists, and has already collected and set aside for this purpose a capital of 113,000 francs; and it will be able in the course of this year to distribute more than 22,000 francs in giving relief to artists or their families. It may be said therefore that the future prospects of the "Société des Artistes Français" are exceedingly satisfactory.

THE ENGLISH IRON TRADE IN 1891.

IT would be vain to deny that 1891 has been a disappointing year to the iron trade. Prospects at its opening were not such as to give rise to sanguine expectations, but they warranted the hope that the coming year would be a fairly favourable one. This, however, has not been the case. The financial troubles towards the close of 1890, further disturbances in our trade relations with South America, the full effects of the tariff changes made in the United States, and a heavy falling-off in the shipments to the colonies, all tended to check our export trade. If it had not been for the comparatively sound character of our home business, the loss experienced by the English iron industry would have been still more severe than it actually has been. Taking things as we find them, and looking at facts broadly, we are confronted by a decline in our export trade such as it has not often been our duty to chronicle.

It will be fully a fortnight yet, from the time of writing, before we shall have the complete returns of our export trade; but the results of the first eleven months of 1891 form a safe indicator what the total deficiency in the year's exports will be. We shipped in the first eleven months of the year now closing 3,018,026 tons of iron and steel, of a total value of 25,007,291*l*., against 3,738,020 tons, valued at 29,313,214*l*., in the corresponding period of 1890. The loss was consequently 719,994 tons, or over 19 per cent., in quantity, and 4,305,923*l*., or 14·7 per cent., in value. Although the decrease is emphatic, it is, nevertheless, a source of comparative satisfaction that the decline in tonnage and value shows no great difference, an indicating that prices have not deteriorated greatly in the year, as will be seen further on. To this loss in iron and steel must be added a falling-off of nearly 9 per cent. in hardware and cutlery, of over 2 per cent. in implements and tools, and of 3·2 per cent. in machinery and mill-work. Unsatisfactory as this may appear, it is somewhat of a consolation to know that it might have been worse, considering all the conditions of business in 1891.

As in the case of our foreign trade, we shall have to wait some time yet before we learn the extent of our production of iron and steel in 1891. The estimated output of pig-iron in the north of England during the year is, in round numbers, 2,630,000 tons, against 2,846,089 tons in 1890, and from this preliminary statement of the production of the chief pig-iron making district in the country, some idea may be formed of what the total decline in the output of 1891 may be, bearing in mind the fact that the production of 1890 was the largest on record. It is an illustration of the changed conditions of the pig-iron trade that the price of Cleveland iron is no longer governed by that of Scotch pig-iron warrants. This is a healthy sign, and due to the fact that the pernicious speculation in Scotch warrants has been put a stop to by their successful "cornering" by what is known in the trade as the London syndicate, which body succeeded, in the course of the year, in getting hold of nearly the whole of the pig-iron warrants, the gambling in which has hitherto had such a baneful effect upon legitimate trade. What the ulterior objects of the syndicate may be is a matter of very little interest; but the good it has done is evident. The cash price of Scotch warrants at the beginning of 1891 was 46s. 2½d., at a time when the strike of the blast furnacemen in Scotland had not yet collapsed, as it subsequently did. The London syndicate managed, owing to the strike and the large purchases it was steadily making, to force up the price in January to 48s. 1½d. It continued manipulating the market, to suit its own ends, throughout the year, the price falling to 42s. 10d. by the end of March, but rising gradually until 59s. was reached on June 1. Since then, the syndicate having obtained all the iron wanted,—that is to say, nearly the whole of the pig-iron warrants in existence,—the price has steadily gone down, and at the close of the year it stands at 47s. 11d., or 1s. 9d. better than at its beginning.

Cleveland pig-iron stood in January at 42s. 6d. per ton, and December finds it at 38s., which shows the decline on the year to have been 4s. 6d. per ton. The comparatively high price of Scotch pig-iron caused large shipments of Cleveland iron to be made to Scotland, the increase in 1891 amounting to over 160,000 tons, counterbalanced to some extent by decreased exports to the Continent, but leaving the year's shipments of Cleveland pig still about 80,000 tons above those of 1890. This fact, no doubt, contributed to the comparative steadiness of Cleveland pig-iron, notwithstanding a reduced consumption. The price of pig-iron in Lancashire has also been comparatively steady, although the tendency, owing to a lessened demand, has been downwards, the decline being about 2s. 6d. per ton, from 48s. 6d. to 49s. 6d. to 46s. to 47s. for Lancashire iron. What are known as district brands have been sold in Lancashire at reductions ranging from 1s. to to 1s. 6d. per ton. Of all the pig-iron-making districts, Staffordshire has been the most favourably placed during the year. Cold-blast pig-iron was in January quoted 100s. per ton; it went up to 105s., but now stands again at 100s. Hot-air iron fell from 65s. to 62s. 6d., but is now again 65s. Part-mine pig has risen from 42s. 6d. to 50s., and common iron from 37s. 6d. to 40s. As the consumption in Staffordshire has been nearly throughout the year in excess of the output, this explains the firmness which prevailed. The hematite pig-iron trade has not been very active, and everywhere a decline on the year's prices has been reported. In the north-west of England mixed numbers of Bessemer pig were quoted by makers 54s. 6d.; they are now 49s. On the east coast hematites fetched 55s. in January, and 48s. in December. In Lancashire, good foundry hematites were at the beginning of the year at 64s., and at present 57s. is the price. It only remains to add that Scotch makers, owing to the strike, sold very little pig during the first four months of the year, but, even after the furnaces were in blast again, there was only a very quiet business doing, and the result has been a decline ranging from 2s. to 9s. per ton, according to brand.

The fortunes of the finished iron trade have varied greatly during the year and in the several districts. In the north of England, although pretty well engaged, makers have had to submit to reductions averaging 9s. per ton on the year. Scotch producers of manufactured iron were, during the first part of the year, employed badly, but they are now doing better, without any really good prospects, however. They had to reduce their prices for bars from 6*l* 7s. 6d. to 6*l*. 5s., and subsequently two other reductions, each of 5s. a ton, had to be made. Later on, however, the price rose to 5*l*. 17s. 6d., at which it now stands. Finished iron makers in Lancashire were in about the same position as those of Scotland. The year opened dull with them, with bars at 6*l*. 2s. 6d. to 6*l*. 5s., hoops at 6*l*. 7s. 6d. to 6*l*. 10s., and sheets at 7*l*. 10s. to 7*l*. 15s. The close of the year finds bars at 6*l*. to 6*l*. 2s. 6d., hoops at the opening rates, and sheets at 7*l*. 7s. 6d. to 7*l*. 10s. The tinplate trade is now in a worse position than it was twelve months ago. The effects of the McKinley tariff did not make themselves felt until after June 30, but since that date the monthly exports have fallen to about one-half. The result has been stagnation in the industry, and a drop of about 4s. per box. Manufacturers of finished hardwares have not had much cause to complain. Their business was necessarily somewhat affected by the adverse conditions ruling in other branches of the iron trade, but there has never been any actual depression with them, and their prospects are better than they were a year ago.

The steel trade has not been nearly so well employed during the past year as in the two preceding ones, and wherever we look, we find a reduction of output and a lowering of prices. The production of steel ingots during the first six months of 1891 was over 100,000 tons less than in the corresponding half-year of 1890, and this fact will explain the drooping tendency of the market. Those who suffered most were the railmakers; manufacturers of steel supplying shipbuilding material being far better off, owing to the generally healthy condition of the shipbuilding trade. In the north of England several works have had to stop from time to time, and the decline in rails has been as much as 10s. per ton, while ship angles and ship and boiler plates only receded 2s. 6d. a ton. In South Wales, where the dulness has, perhaps, been most severely felt, rails have lost 17s. 6d. per ton, while another staple product, tinplate bar, has gone down 20s. a ton. The Scotch steelmakers have been fairly well engaged, and they have now their orderbooks quite full. The decline in ship plates in Scotland has been 5s. a ton, and in boiler plates 15s. a ton, the difference in the reduction of prices plainly showing what kind of material was most called for. The steel trade of Sheffield, especially the heavy branches, has not had much to complain of, and, notwithstanding keen competition, the year will probably prove a fairly prosperous one for most concerns. The steelmakers of the Furness district have been fairly active, but those of West Cumberland have been rather quiet. The decline for the various steel products manufactured in the north-west ranges from 2s. 6d. a ton for ship-plates to 17s. 6d. for rails and 2*l.* for wire rods. Tinplate bars have advanced 5s. per ton, and hoops 20s. The Lancashire steel trade has been dull, and boiler plates, the principal product, have declined 10s. a ton.

As we pointed out above, the shipbuilding industry has been fairly well employed during the year. The total output amounted to 1,268,470 tons, compared with 1,272,263 tons in 1890, comprising 748 steam vessels and 209 sailing ships in 1891. The difference in the tonnage, it will be seen, is not large, but what is more remarkable is that in some of the more important centres there has been a heavy falling-off, while others, hitherto of less importance, have come to the front. The royal dockyards also increased their output considerably. The prospects of shipbuilders are now hardly so bright as they were at the end of 1890, the amount of work in hand being much smaller. Marine engineers, in consequence of the fair activity in the shipbuilding trade, have been very well employed; but it deserves to be noted that in the past year the proportion of sailing vessels built has been far larger than in previous years. Otherwise makers of marine engines would have secured a better business than they actually did. Nevertheless, they have been better off than other departments of the engineering trades, although most engineering firms will enter the year with a fair amount of work in hand.

Happily, there have been no very serious disturbances in the relations between capital and labour. The most serious trouble was that with the engineers in the north-eastern parts, who, not content with quarrelling with their employers, took to fighting amongst themselves. We refer to the dispute between the plumbers and fitters. This, however, was at last settled, as was also the long-pending strike of the Scotch blast-furnacemen, who were utterly defeated. Another passing cloud was the demand for a week of fifty-three hours by the engineers in Lancashire, which, after some resistance by employers, was finally conceded. Sheffield manufacturers of cutlery, owing to depression, had to ask their men for a reduction of 5 per cent. in their wages. Some resisted, and were out for a long time; but others, being endowed with more common-sense, accepted the inevitable. Although not directly connected with the iron trade, the action of the South Wales coal-owners in giving notice to the colliers of the termination of the sliding scale has a bearing upon it. We need not enter into the merits of the case, but we may express the hope that the pending negotiations will end in a compromise; in the contrary case, a very serious rupture and disturbance in the labour market and the coal trade are to be apprehended. We may add that the fictitious cry for an eight hours' working day for miners appears to find divided sympathy even with those most concerned, and when astute politicians decline to express their opinions on such a delicate question, we may hope for seeing it shelved indefinitely, for it ought never to have been raised, British workmen, and especially British miners, having shown by their unions that they are well able to take care of themselves without interference by the legislature.

It is, as we know from experience, a very hazardous undertaking, at any time, to say much, either one way or the other, as to the trade prospects of a coming year. Appearances last year were so promising that we ventured upon a prognostication which would have come true *if* the unforeseen had not happened. As the unexpected is a factor which has to be reckoned with, all we dare venture upon is to say that not too much should be expected of the year we have entered upon. It may, however, be observed that there is a fair amount of work in hand in most branches of the iron trade, and that the good harvests in America ought to give a fillip to business. Should the South American Republics settle down to a more orderly state of things than have prevailed lately, a revival may also arise from that quarter; but great caution will have to be exercised in the immediate future in trading with those countries.

HOLMAN'S "SEWER-GAS EXHAUSTER AND DESTRUCTOR."

MR. STEPHEN HOLMAN, M.Inst.C.E. (formerly of the well-known firm of Tangye Brothers & Holman), has for the last few years been devoting his attention to a means of relieving sewers of their poisonous gases without resort to open grids (which are often a nuisance), or to stack-pipes carried up the sides or fronts of buildings, to which there are often strong objections. Mr. Holman utilises the ordinary street lamp columns as his extracting-shafts and destructors. In the base of the column is placed what is at once the extracting and the destroying apparatus, as shown in the accompanying section, in which A represents a

6-in. pipe leading from the sewer, projecting 3 in. above the brick foundation on which the column rests (such foundation being not less than 21 in. below the ground-line), and within the lower end of the column. B shows the connexion for the gas supply from the street main, C the brass regulating governor of the burner, D the brass atmospheric burner, and E Holman's patent wind-proof burner-protector,—the bottom cup of this protector resting on the collar of the burner, the inner pieces being placed within that bottom cup, and the top part, E, above it. This cup is then surrounded and surmounted by a series of ribbed cones and chambers in cast-iron so arranged as to retain the heat of the burner in what is practically a furnace formed of a series of circuitous passages, through which the sewer air, drawn up the 6 in. pipe leading to the sewer, must pass and be rendered harmless, afterwards passing out by the upper part of the column through the lantern into the open air. After the burner with its protecting cups has been placed in position, the ribbed cones forming the body of the furnace are placed round it, commencing with the bottom cone which surrounds the burner; the flanged cone, F, is then placed on top of the bottom cone, and inside the flanged cone are placed, one after the other, the three cones, G, G, G, after which the central pin is dropped in and the top cone, H, is superposed. The top and bottom cones are covered with asbestos to prevent the radiation of heat. These extractors are in use by the London County Council, the Richmond Corporation, the Hornsey and Acton Local Boards, and many other local authorities, with satisfactory results, according to the testimony of the respective Borough Engineers and Surveyors. The burners are made to consume from six to eight cubic feet of gas per hour, at a cost of from 4½d. to 6d. per day of twenty-four hours. The apparatus, as tested by the anemometer, will extract from 40,000 to 60,000 cubic feet of sewer-air per day. Professor Wanklyn and other chemists speak very favourably of the efficiency of the "furnace" in rendering innocuous the sewer air which passes through it.

For use in connexion with the extractor and destructor at night, Mr. Holman has devised a very ingenious flash-light burner, by the use of which the gas can be lighted or extinguished without opening the lantern.

THE SALE OF WATER BY METER AT BERLIN.

AT the fifth ordinary meeting of the present Session of the Institution of Civil Engineers, on the 8th ult., the President, Mr. George Berkley, in the chair, the paper read was on "The Sale of Water by Measure in Berlin," by Mr. Henry Gill, M.Inst. C.E.

The author drew attention to the fact that the concentration of the population in cities, and the increasing severity of the tests for ascertaining the quality of water supplied to towns, made the difficulty and cost of obtaining sufficient and suitable water for domestic purposes greater each year. In addition, the enforcement of the laws for the protection of rivers against pollution added to the expense and difficulty of the disposal of the waste-water of town populations. These causes made it the interest of the municipalities, as owners of the water-works, not to restrict the supply, yet to prevent waste.

The fact was referred to that the water supplied to cities was far in excess of the actual requirements of the inhabitants, and that the excess not only served no useful purpose, but was wasted and was prejudicial to the community. The waste was not intentional, but was, in a great measure, the result of an imperfect system of supply and of the irrational method of charging for water. It was alleged that improvement could only be effected by the abandonment of the present system of assessment of the charges for water for domestic purposes, and the adoption of the system of sale by measure. The sale, exclusively by meter, as in the case of gas, would effectually prevent waste, and would reduce to a minimum the difficulty with reference to the disposal of sewage.

The condition of Berlin in 1865, when the tariff charge for water was a percentage on the rental, was then described, and how that system gradually gave place to the sale exclusively by meter, the transition being finally completed in 1878, with equal advantage to the purchaser and to the seller of the water. The nature of the meter employed, the place and method of its instalment, and the system of control, as well as the peculiar character of the Berlin houses, were detailed. The regulations and tariff charges were explained, and the effect of the system on the consumption per head was illustrated by tabular statements based on the Census of 1880, referring to a large number of houses in each quarter of the city. The effects on the expenditure and revenue were also illustrated by tabular statements for the financial year 1889-90.

The objections urged against the sale of domestic water exclusively by meter were referred to, and it was shown that these were not valid as regards Berlin, and that as to how far they might be valid for other cities could only be determined in each case by a consideration of the circumstances to be met. That these objections, however, did not prevent the adoption of the system in many cases in Germany, was shown by an official statistical table of the water supplies of 7¾ millions, the inhabitants of seventy-seven German cities, in 26 per cent. of which the sale of water exclusively by meter and the control by meter of a considerable proportion of the remainder had been adopted.

It was conceded that the great stringency with which the various Governments enforced the laws for the protection of the streams against pollution had promoted the adoption of the system which was first introduced in Berlin.

Illustrations.

ST. PAUL'S CATHEDRAL.*

IN the illustration given this week of the celebrated London Cathedral, the object has been to select a point of view which would realise something of the soaring effect which the composition of the two campaniles and the dome presents to the eye when they are seen in conjunction on the approach from Ludgate-hill. In the flank view St. Paul's has too much the effect of a long box with a dome seated on the centre of it. Seen from the western position, where the campaniles group directly with the dome, the defect of this long level line is kept out of sight, and the whole assumes more the aspect of a spontaneously conceived architectural composition, with a unity of effect and conception which certainly does not strike one in the flank view of the building. In fact, the dome, which pre-supposes a wide central area perfectly different in character from the narrow "crossing" of a Mediæval cathedral with its central tower, is a feature much more fitted for the culmination of a plan of tolerably square proportions, a plan of the Greek cross type, than for a long narrow plan of the Mediæval type; it requires a pyramidal rather than a longitudinal composition; and there can be no doubt that Wren's architectural instinct was true in leading him to prefer his former plan for St. Paul's (the one worked out in the well-known model now in the Cathedral), in which a nearer approximation is made to the Greek cross type of plan, and the whole composition has more distinct reference to the dome as its central motive. The same principle is illustrated in the plan and design of St. Peter's, which must undoubtedly have presented a much finer external effect, as a composition, when in the dimensions left by Michelangelo, and before Carlo Maderno had added the lengthened nave which throws the dome back and prevents it from taking its proper place in the composition. St. Paul's is, in fact, a Mediæval plan treated as a Renaissance building, and the two elements do not harmonise.

A foreshortened view from the west realises this pyramidal effect of grouping which the dome seems to require, and affords an opportunity of throwing the more delicate and graceful treatment of the campaniles into contrast with the broad mass of the dome behind, the two features mutually assisting each other by contrast. There is no accessible point on the ground level, however, from which this combination could be shown in a drawing without distortion. There are photographs which give fine combinations of the dome and campaniles, but they are all taken from the roofs of houses, and even then the dome is in some cases either distorted or thrown too far back or too low in the composition, and loses its rightful predominance. We have therefore assumed a point of view sufficiently far back to allow the dome to be seen in its true proportions in combination with the campaniles. The assumed standpoint is distant from the building about two and a-half times its own length, and the proportions have been carefully worked out in perspective, from the plan and from Gladwin's careful engraving of the north elevation, made in 1828, a copy of which, in the possession of Mr. Penrose, he has very kindly lent to us for the purpose. Of this engraving we give with this number a zincograph reproduction, about two-thirds the size of the original, which may be of interest, as correct geometrical drawings of St. Paul's as a whole, and on a large scale, are not very plentiful or easy to come at;† and Gladwin's engraving, though in the formal mechanical style in vogue at the time it was made, has the merit of being an exceedingly correct representation of its kind, in every detail.*

The Queen Anne Monument, which should naturally have shown in the view, has been omitted intentionally, since it is no part of the building, and from this point of view it would have obtruded awkwarkly in front of the cathedral. The peculiar effect of the weathering on the building, which has divided its two stages almost precisely, over most of the building, into a light-coloured story above and a dark and smoke-blackened one below, it may be said is also an accidental effect having nothing to do with the architectural design of the building; but it is too characteristic and picturesque an effect, and too much blent with every one's recollection of the building, to be omitted. The sharp line of demarcation between the upper and lower stories almost suggests the idea that a different bed of stone had been employed in the upper portion; but the result is due, we believe, merely to the greater effect of rain on the more exposed upper portions, coupled with the fact that the cornice of the lower order affords a protection from rain to the parts immediately beneath it, and thus gives that marked separation between the blackened and the cleaner portions. The plinth stones are whitened again where the drip from the cornice has fallen on them, and the angle pilasters at the exposed south-west corner have also got their share of cleansing.

St. Paul's occupies a very different position from any of the cathedrals already illustrated in this series, and from nearly all those which will follow, in the fact that it was built in the post-mediæval period, and is the individual work of an architect whose name and history are well known. The building of St. Paul's followed, of course, upon the destruction of the Gothic cathedral in the great fire of London, but it is not popularly known, probably, that before that event the old Cathedral had been so much damaged by fire and neglect combined, that a complete scheme for its restoration had been formed, first entrusted to Inigo Jones, and latterly in the reign of Charles II. to Wren, who intended to add to the mediæval cathedral additions in the Italian style, "after a good Roman manner, instead of the Gothic rudeness of the old design." It was in the consideration of the method of doing this that Wren first suggested the idea of the central space with a dome over it, which was eventually to form part of his new design. In 1666 the estimates for the work had actually been ordered, when the great fire broke out and (perhaps fortunately) put an end to all idea of this patchwork of Gothic and Renaissance, by destroying the old church completely.

The first stone of the present Cathedral was laid on June 21 1675, and the top stone of the lantern laid in 1710. Before the existing design was finally adopted, there had been (besides stray sketches) two other designs made by Wren. One of these is the Greek cross design already referred to, of which the model was made, and another is one which received the formal approval of the King, but with leave to deviate from it, fortunately for us and for Wren's reputation, for this officially approved design is unquestionably the worst of the three. The central feature is a kind of melange of a dome with a minaret on it, and it is difficult to understand how an architect capable of designing the dome as we see it could have ever thought of erecting such a barbaric affair. In regard to the first design to which we have already referred, on the Greek cross type of plan, while there is no doubt that the plan was the finer and the general conception of the whole broader and more dignified than the present building regarded as a whole, we cannot share the wish sometimes expressed that the design shown in the model had been carried out in place of the present building. The type adopted is far better, but the details are much inferior, especially of the dome, which is far more refined, more graceful, and better proportioned than in the "model" design.

The plan of St. Paul's is changed in axis from that of the old cathedral, partly to get rid of the difficulty which would have been caused by building on the site of walls whose foundations could not be depended upon, and which it would nevertheless have been a work of great labour to entirely remove. As matters are, the oblique position toward Ludgate-hill which the Cathedral assumes is hardly a disadvantage to it, as it is so closely shut in by houses and so entirely devoid of anything like a grand approach that it seems better that it should have the element of irregular picturesqueness in its position, since that of stateliness is out of the question. It is greatly to have been desired that the surroundings of the Cathedral should have been laid out in a more stately and spacious manner while there was the opportunity afforded by the destruction of house property wrought by the fire; but in the natural eagerness of owners to repair their misfortune as soon as possible, the re-building of the adjoining houses had been commenced before anything was settled as to the plan of the Cathedral site, and Wren had to accept the position. As it stands, the Cathedral loses much of the dignity of effect it might have had on a better arranged site, and moreover there is no point whence it can be seen as a whole. On the other hand it perhaps gains a certain effect of sublimity,—what we have called its "soaring" effect,—from the very fact of rising out the confined mass of inferior buildings so closely surrounding it.

The two chapels eastward of the western towers were added to the plan much against the will of Wren, in order to be used as chapels to special saints in case the Romish ritual could be restored, as James II. secretly wished. Internally they are an addition to the architectural variety of the church, but externally they are an excrescence and a detriment to its effect, fitting awkwardly against the base of the towers, and shortening the apparant length of the nave when seen in perspective.

Architecturally speaking, the campaniles and the dome are the making of St. Paul's. The design of the substructure is very commonplace, consisting of a double order of applied pilasters repeated in an almost mechanical and formal manner all round the building; and the windows are of poor and ineffective design. The worst thing about it all, however, is the fact that the upper half of the wall is for the most part a mere empty sham with nothing behind it, and when once this is known it is impossible to forget it, or to have the same feeling towards the building which a spectator might have, despite its defects of detail, who believed its external visible mass to represent its interior arrangement and contents. The floral ornament above and about the windows is in the artificial taste of the day, and cannot be called ornament, being merely sets of festoons with no design whatever, though with a certain boldness and freedom of execution. The sculpture is respectable, and nothing more. The double-storied colonnade of the façade has however a fine effect, partly owing to the deep shadow from the recesses behind the columns; this in fact just shows what it is that the rest of the building wants; it is all too flat. All these faults of the substructure, however, are forgotten when the eye rises to the campaniles and the dome. The former are most graceful and original in design, and as full of play of surface and light and shade as the substructure (except the portico) is destitute of it. The dome, with its fine colonnade, with the original and truly constructive treatment of the solid bay at every fourth inter-columniation (marking the main points of support of the dome), and the deep recesses between and behind the columns, is a noble piece of architecture of its kind; and the actual dome, with its finely-curved outline, rises in a most effective and graceful manner above the main colonnade behind which it is recessed. The lantern also is a very graceful structure, though rather too heavy for its apparent situation; and here again we come on the drawback of want of architectural truth. The merest tyro in construction knows that the stone lantern could not stand on that timber dome; and the concealed cone to carry it (the line of which is partially discerned however, and not disagreeably, behind and between the main colonnade) only half reconciles us, by its ability and novelty as a constructive device, to the æsthetic sin which has been perpetrated. In a previous study for the dome Wren had adopted, like Brunelleschi, the device of a slightly-pointed masonry dome to carry the weight of the lantern, ingeniously counterweighting its exterior thrust at the base by a cove hung inwards. It is a pity that he did not adopt this completely logical constructive expedient, which would have made the exterior dome a reality instead of a sham.

With all these drawbacks, however, St. Paul's

* This series of Illustrations of the Cathedrals of England and Wales was begun in our issue of January 3, 1891. A list of those already illustrated, with particulars of future arrangements, will be found on page 20.

† The plan of St. Paul's given here is based on a large scale and very carefully-engraved plan in the possession of Mr. Somers Clarke, who was good enough to lend it to us as a basis of operations. It has been supplemented by measurements and observations on the building.

* The steps to the west entrance are not as shown in the engraving, but they have been altered since it was made.

dome remains one of the great things of architecture, which has produced few structures at once so grand and so graceful, and we do not say that the popular admiration of it is at all more than it justly claims.

We may call attention to one aspect of the colonnade which architects and artists will enjoy, though it cannot be shown on a drawing in consequence of the conditions of perspective drawing. Go on a bright day into the southern enclosure of the railed space, stand near the remains of the old cloister and carry the eye up the re-entering angle of nave and transept. Over where the two cornices meet curves the colonnade of the dome, three or four bays only visible, the whole depth and solidity of the construction emphasised by the manner in which we look up between the columns to the very back of the soffit over them, and realise the scale and the projection of the colonnade, crowned by the sweep of its cornice against the sky. The effect is quite sublime. H. H. S.

STAIRCASE, ST. PAUL'S CATHEDRAL.

This is a measured drawing by Mr. Stephen Ayling of the staircase in the south-west tower leading to the library. It serves to illustrate the style of the decorative detail within the building. The design of the ironwork is very good; the carved detail is in the usual style of the day. It may be a question, perhaps, whether Wren had very much to do with the design of these details; he was, in fact, an example of "that hybrid person, the Surveyor-Architect," of whom we have heard so much lately.

OLD ST. PAUL'S CATHEDRAL FROM THE NORTH-EAST.

As we have described Old St. Paul's Cathedral previously in a series of illustrated articles which have from time to time appeared in our columns, all we propose now to do is to say a few words about the drawing which we publish. In the first place, our readers will want to know what authorities exist for this "restoration." For this purpose the indications discovered by the excavations made under the direction of Mr. Penrose some years ago have been carefully studied. These show the form and the position of the east end of the church, the base of the respond at the south-east angle existing complete. It would appear from the foundations, which we have measured according to the indications marked out at the time the excavations were made, that the great east gable measured 36 ft. 6 in. between the buttresses; that the principal buttresses themselves were 7 ft. 2 in. wide; the aisles 15 ft. wide; and that the two buttresses at the angle of the aisle, which stood at right-angles to each other, measured together 14 ft.; that the great preaching-cross was 30 ft. distant from this point, and that, including steps and parapet, it was 36 ft. in diameter. The eastern wall of the church appears to have been 7 ft. 2 in. thick, but the aisle wall, on the north side, seems to have been as much as 10 ft. thick! This is corroborated by Hollar's drawings, because he shows wall passages in the aisles and none to the clearstory; several of his illustrations also show that the aisle walls were thick enough to admit of monuments being let into them without cutting through the wall arcade. The tombs of King Ethelred and King Seiba are cases in point.

Our view represents the church before the destruction of the spire in the year 1559. A drawing by Wyndgarde, the "Cowdray Picture," and a view by Hollar show the cathedral in this condition. The spire was of wood, and was, together with the parapet of the tower, erected in the year 1462, replacing one which was destroyed by lightning in 1444. Probably also at this time the flying buttresses at the base of the tower, were erected. They are shown by Hollar supported by plain, upright bars of stone, which look exceedingly ugly, but an earlier view by Vischer, 1616, shows these fillings-in as consisting of perpendicular mullions with ogee tracery heads between them. A very curious old picture of St. Paul's, from almost the same point of view as our illustration, is engraved in Wilkinson's "Londina Illustrata." It shows the preaching-cross, and King James I. attending a sermon preached therefrom. The gallery and Royal closet were then in existence; in fact, they probably remained until the year 1643, when the cross was pulled down by Lord Mayor Penington. The Consistory-court, together with its shrouds and cloisters, would seem to have been perverted to secular uses, because a number of chimneys are shown, with smoke rising out of them, over which is the following inscription:—

"Viewe, O! Kinge, howe my wall-creepers
Have made me worke for chimney-sweepers."

Another portion of the same painting is engraved in Nichol's "Royal Progresses of James I." This work is supposed to represent James I.'s visit to St. Paul's for the purpose of getting that monarch to restore the cathedral. There appears to have been some difficulty, however, about the matter, since, although the picture was painted representing the royal visit, James seems not to have gone until several years later, and, with his usual caution, appears to have suggested that so good a work should rather be the result of a "General Benevolence," than of a royal grant! The end of the whole proceeding is described by Dugdale as follows:—

"The collection of monies went so slowly forwards as that, though a good proportion of stone was brought in by the bishop, the prosecution of the work became wholly neglected, so that part of the said stone, lying useless, was after borrowed by the Duke of Buckingham for the building of the Watergate at York House, and there employed for that use." Of course this must not be confused with Laud's Restoration, which was not commenced until 1628.

The preaching cross was constructed of wood, and was rebuilt by Cardinal John Kemp. Dugdale appears to be wrong upon this point, as he attributes it to Thomas Kemp, Bishop of London. Kemp's arms were to be seen upon the leadwork of the roof. It was erected between 1422 and 1426. Sherrington's Chapel, Pardon-Church-Haugh, and the Charnel were pulled down by Protector Somerset, and their material used to erect Somerset House. The great campanile, called the clochier, is indicated in Wyndegarde and Vischer's views. Dugdale tells us that "within this clochier were four very great bells, called Jesus bells, in regard they specially belonged to Jesus Chapell, situate at the east end of the Undercroft of Paul's; and also, on the top of the spire, the image of Saint Paul, all standing till Sir Miles Partridge, Knight, temp. H. VIII., having won them from the King at one cast of the dice, pulled them down. Which Sir Miles afterwards, temp. E. VI., suffered death on Tower-hill for matters relating to the Duke of Somerset."

These isolated bell-towers seem to have been in frequent use in England during the Middle Ages, especially in the case of large and important churches. That of Chichester Cathedral still exists, and those of Salisbury, Westminster, and Worcester have only disappeared within the last two centuries. It is not quite known when the one belonging to St. Paul's Cathedral was finally destroyed; but, as it does not appear to be indicated in any view of a later date than Vischer's, and had entirely disappeared when Dugdale wrote in 1657, it is possible that, when the Duke of Buckingham "borrowed" the stone, brought for the restoration of the cathedral, he may have completed the destruction commenced by Sir Miles Partridge by "borrowing" the stone of which the tower was built also. H. W. B.

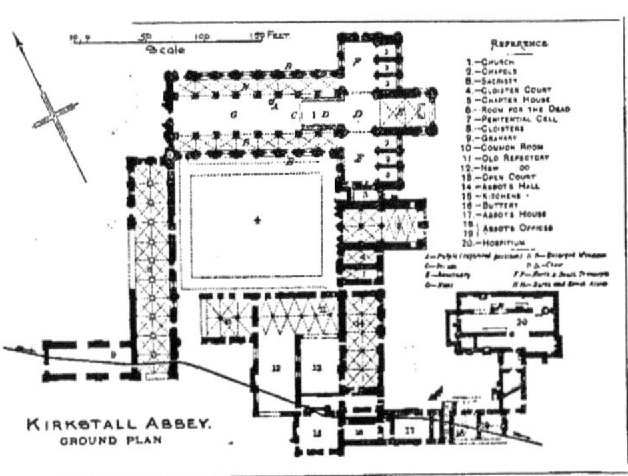

ST. PETER'S DOME, FROM THE PIAZZA DELLA SAGRESTIA.

This is a reproduction of a drawing by Mr. Fulleylove, whose reputation as an artist dealing with architectural subjects is well known to our readers. It gives a rather unusual and little known view of the dome from a terrace, "Piazza della Sagrestia," high above the ground level of the Cathedral, and shows the dome and the upper part of one of the transepts; the angle of the façade is seen beyond.

OLD ST. PETER'S, ROME.

Information as to this drawing will be found in Mr. Brewer's article on an earlier page.

NORTH TRANSEPT, WESTMINSTER ABBEY.

This is such an exceptionally fine example of what must be called restoration, so completely in the true spirit and feeling of Mediæval architecture, that we have wished to put it on record in a drawing worthy of its merits. Mr. Begg has taken special pains in the illustration of it, and as to the result we think there will be no difference of opinion.

THE KLINGEN THOR, ROTHENBURG, BAVARIA.

The fortifications of this interesting old town remain to-day in much the same condition as when they were completed and put in order for resisting the siege by Tilly in the thirty years' war. The town is of moderate size, completely encircled by walls, and each gate is guarded by an outer postern and tower; these are in each case intact. The Klingen or bell-tower is one of the largest and most interesting. The sketch shows the back of the tower towards the town, with the traces of the ancient clock-face. The galleries upon the walls are quite accessible as walks for visitors. The sketch shows the stairs to one section of them. Other views of Rothenburg have appeared in the *Builder*, by Mr. H. W. Brewer, and architectural artists in search of picturesque colour and old world scenes are to be recommended to try this quaint town, situated between Wurzburg and Nuremburg.

KIRKSTALL ABBEY.

The Cistercian community originally at Bernoldswic removed to the site of Kirkstall, near Leeds, in 1152, and the church was completed about thirty years afterwards. The building is one of the best known in Yorkshire, and is still a fine specimen of Norman transitional work. The central tower, the turrets flanking the gables, and also the tracery in some of the windows, are of Perpendicular date, the tower having probably been added by Abbot Marshall, 1509-1528. The situation of the Abbey must have been a very fine one. Its

St. Pierre, Coutances: Central Tower. *Secularised Church of St. Étienne, Caen: Central Tower.*

picturesqueness has now, however, largely disappeared, owing to the close proximity of Leeds and its outlying suburbs.

The photograph, an unusually good one, from which the illustration is reproduced, was taken by an amateur photographer, Mr. William Brown, of Leeds, and was sent to us, with permission to reproduce it, by Mr. G. Atkinson, of the same town. The publication of an illustration of Kirkstall has some special interest at present, inasmuch as there has been a great deal of dissatisfaction expressed of late at the removal of the ivy from the ruins, and a good deal of paper warfare has ensued on the subject; and it may be of interest to those who loved the old aspect of the Abbey to have a memorial of its aspect before the ivy was removed.

We should add, however, that while admitting that an ivy-clad ruin is far more picturesque than one of which the walls have been laid bare, we are not by any means blaming those who were responsible for removing the ivy from Kirkstall. The preservation of the remains of a great monument of Mediæval architecture is, after all, of more importance than the picturesque effect of the ivy; and there can be no doubt that the growth of ivy over remains of this kind hastens their destruction as architectural monuments.

"LE TEMPS PORTANT LA RENOMMEE."

"TIME bringing Fame" to Delacroix is the idea which M. Dalou has adopted for the monument to the eminent painter lately erected in the Luxembourg Gardens. Possibly the group may be criticised as being rather too full of movement for the true conditions of sculpture; but it has the great merits of boldness, spirit, and originality, and is one of the most striking works which French sculpture has recently produced.

Delacroix, who was born in 1799 and died in 1863, was one of the most remarkable of the distinguished French artists of the earlier part of the century, a painter of much originality of conception and great power as a colourist. His memory is celebrated in a monument worthy of his reputation.

TWO FRENCH TOWERS.

THESE illustrations of two characteristic French Mediæval towers are reproduced from sketches by Mr. R. A. Reid.

MEMORIAL STONE, KIRKINTILLOCH.—On the 19th ult. a memorial to the late Miss Beatrice Clugston was unveiled in the Old Aisle Cemetery, Kirkintilloch. The memorial, which is in the form of a red-stone monument of the English Gothic style, with a cast bronze panel inserted in the centre, stands at the head of the grave, and is 8 ft. broad at the base and 13 ft. high. The bronze panel is the work of Mr. Pittendrigh M'Gillivray, sculptor, Glasgow, and has in the lower part a group of figures representing charity, and above this a medallion portrait of Miss Clugston. The design of the monument was by Mr. W. F. Salmon, F.R.I.B.A., Glasgow, who superintended the work.

THE LONDON COUNTY COUNCIL.

AT the special adjourned meeting of this Council held on Wednesday, the 23rd ult., Sir John Lubbock, Chairman of the Council, presided.

The Bethnal-Green Slum Clearance.—The Housing of the Working Classes Committee reported as follows regarding this scheme:—

"The Council may desire to be informed of the progress being made in carrying the Boundary-street scheme into execution. The Provisional Order for the scheme was, after a local inquiry, confirmed by Parliament on July 3. The estimate of the cost of purchasing the lands and houses in the area, including trade and tenants' compensation, was 371,000*l.*; 129 claims have been received up to date, representing in the aggregate 414,856*l.* About forty-seven claims, it is calculated, remain to be received, the total amount of which will probably be about 90,000*l.* As regards the 129 claims received, negotiations are proceeding with respect to the greater number of them, and fifteen have been settled. The aggregate of the claims in these fifteen cases was 16,998*l.*, and the aggregate of the amounts at which they have been settled is 12,585*l.* Thirty claims have been referred to the Solicitor for submission to the Arbitrator, who will in due course be appointed, to decide the amount to be paid in all cases where agreements are not come to. There are in the area eleven licensed public-houses in respect of which claims have been received."

The Goldsmith-square Site.—The same Committee also reported with regard to the Goldsmith-square site in the following terms:—

"Before that portion of the Goldsmith-square site which is to be utilised for artisans' dwellings can be put up for sale it will be necessary to carry out the widening of Goldsmith-row. Your Committee have issued instructions for the demolition of the existing buildings, and have directed the Engineer to carry out the necessary paving works in connexion with the widening of Goldsmith-row, and also the paving works in connexion with the widening of that portion of Goldsmith-square which is required for the line of frontage of the artisans' dwellings proposed to be erected on the site. It is estimated that the cost of these works will amount to £600. An estimate for this amount will be submitted by the Finance Committee concurrently with this report. Your Committee recommend,—

'That the necessary paving works in connexion with the widening of Goldsmith-square and Goldsmith-row be carried out under the general contract at a cost not exceeding £600.'"

The recommendation was agreed to.

Rosebery-avenue.—The first paragraph of the Improvements Committee's report was as follows:—

"We have to report that the portion of the Rosebery-avenue improvement from Garnault-place to St. John-street-road, having been completed, was opened to the public by our Chairman, and the charge of the thoroughfare formally handed over to the local authority within whose district it is situated (the Vestry of Clerkenwell), on December 16. The Metropolitan Board obtained Parliamentary powers for this improvement in 1885. The contract for the works of the completed portion was entered into with Messrs. Mowlem & Co. in May, 1891."

Proposed Extension of the Chelsea Embankment.—The second paragraph of the same Committee's report ran thus:—

"On July 22, 1890, we reported to the Council in favour of continuing the river embankment from Battersea Bridge to Lots-road, Chelsea, on condition that the Vestry of Chelsea contributed one-half of the net cost of the work to be executed by the Council, such net cost being estimated at 62,000*l*. After considerable negotiation, the Vestry declined to contribute more than 3,000*l*., although it required to have possession, free of cost, of the whole land to be reclaimed from the river, about 3¾ acres. The Vestry has asked that the question may now be re-considered by the Council, but, having regard to the resolutions of the Council of October 6 last, which were to the effect that the Council would defer further street improvements until some portion of the cost could be thrown upon the owners of property, we propose to give instructions for the Vestry to be informed that the Council is not at present prepared to entertain the matter."

After some discussion, the report was agreed to.

A Palm-house for Battersea Park.—The Parks and Open Spaces Committee's report began with the following:—

"We have had our attention called to the desirableness of providing a palm-house in Battersea Park, not only for the accommodation of the palms which have outgrown the existing greenhouses, but also to be used as a winter garden and for the exhibition of chrysanthemums and other flowers. We submit a plan of the building, and propose that the central portion of it should be erected, leaving the wings to be added if necessary at some future time. We recommend,—

'That, subject to an estimate being submitted to it by the Finance Committee, as required by the statute, the Council do authorise the expenditure of 1,500*l*. on capital account, for the erection of a palm-house in Battersea Park, in accordance with the design submitted.'"

This recommendation led to a long discussion, but eventually it was carried.

Bethnal-green Poor's Land.—The seventeenth paragraph of the same Committee's report related to this much-fought-for piece of land, and was thus worded:—

"The Council will recollect that for some years the question of acquiring the land known as the Bethnal-green Poor's Land for the purpose of an open space has been before it, and the Council has already expressed its readiness to acquire the land, which is about 6½ acres in extent. According to a new scheme prepared this year by the Charity Commissioners, the trustees are to sell the land to the Council, and we consider that now is a fitting time for the Council to make an offer for the land. We therefore recommend,—

'That, subject to an estimate being submitted to it by the Finance Committee as required by the statute, the Council do make an offer of 5,000*l*. for the land known as the Bethnal-green Poor's Land, comprising approximately 6½ acres, in accordance with the terms of the new scheme prepared by the Charity Commissioners.'"

This recommendation was unanimously agreed to.

The Building Acts.—After a short discussion, the Council, on the recommendation of a special report of the Building Act Committee, printed by us last week,* agreed that the Council do express a general approval of the Committee's suggested amendments† to the Metropolitan Building and Local Management Acts, and authorise the Building Act Committee to lay them before the President of the Local Government Board, and to confer with him as to any other amendments which may appear desirable during the progress of the Bill, and report the result to the Council from time to time.

Having transacted other business, the Council adjourned until Tuesday, January 19.

NEW BLIND FITTINGS.

MR. W. HENRY THOMPSON, of 147, Queen Victoria-street (son of the well-known contractor, Mr. John Thompson, of Peterborough), has brought to our notice a very simple though at the same time very ingenious Venetian blind-cord-holder. Fig. 1 shows the new holder with the cord secured, and fig. 2 shows the same with the cord released. Among other advan-

Fig. 1. *Fig. 2.*

tages of this holder, which we have seen in action, we may mention the non-liability of the cord to kink, and the rapidity and facility with which the blind can be raised or lowered to any desired extent. The action is as rapid and as easy as that of a good spring roller blind. To raise or lower the blind the cord has to be held close to the window frame, and either pulled down or allowed to slide up, as the case may be. When the blind has attained the desired position, the cord is simply pulled away

Fig. 3.

from the window frame so as to raise the clutch, and the blind is instantaneously secured.

For roller blinds Mr. Thompson is also introducing a new and simple mechanical device for raising and lowering the blind, combined with a cord-holder. Amongst the small evils which householders have to bear, perhaps there is none more trying than the usual form of blind-cord-holder, which often either fails to hold at the proper moment, or wears out and cuts the cords prematurely. These defects appear to be entirely done away with in the cord-holder now under notice, which, as will be seen by the accompanying engraving, fig. 3, consists of two small arms, pivotted on different centres, the outer end of the upper arm passing through a slot in the lower one, the cord to be held passing through the same slot. The holding power is obtained through the differential movement of the arms, any upward movement of the arms tending to close them on the cord. The greater the strain the greater the grip, but the pressure on the cord is only just sufficient to hold the blind, automatically increasing or decreasing as the weight varies, thus preventing the fraying and cutting and wearing-out of the cords. As will be understood from the engraving, the revolution of the roller, when the blind is descending, winds the cord round the reel or drum; by pulling the cord down it winds off the reel or drum, turning the roller with it, and so raising the blind.

* See *Builder* for December 26, 1891, p. 487.

† We have received a copy of these amendments, but in the absence of the text of the Bill proposed to be introduced by Mr. Ritchie they are not very intelligible.

Mr. Thompson is also introducing a very handy and ingenious little tool, named the "Eureka" tack-driver. It is chiefly suited for domestic use, and consists of a brass socket, fitted with a magnetised plunger, worked by a coiled spring. The plunger picks up the tack, head-first, and recedes with it into the socket. A smart blow with the palm of the hand on the knob at the top of the plunger-rod or handle compresses the spring and protrudes the plunger, driving the tack into the desired position. No hammer is required.

COMPETITIONS.

SCHOOL BOARD OFFICES, KEIGHLEY.—The designs for new School Board Offices, Keighley, submitted in limited competition by Mr. Ledingham, architect, Bradford, have been selected.

SCHOOLS, CHADSMOOR.—The Cannock School Board have selected the designs of Mr. Geo. H. Cox, architect, Birmingham, for the proposed schools at Chadsmoor.

Books.

The Mechanical Engineer's Pocket-book. By D. K. CLARK, M.Inst.C.E. London: Crosby Lockwood & Son. 1892.

ANY attempt to bring to a focus the vast accumulation of knowledge with which it is desirable that an engineer should be acquainted, so that its practical value may at once be evident, will always be welcome to professional men. So much information has now been published in technical works, and is to be found scattered through the proceedings of the various scientific societies, that it is becoming more and more necessary to have it condensed for actual use; and no one is better able to undertake such a work than the author of this book. The amount of information that it is possible to compress into a work of the pocket-book class is, of course, somewhat limited, as a considerable portion has to be given up to such mathematical and other tables as are so often needed, but Mr. Clark has devoted the chief part of his work to such formulæ, rules, and data, as are required in the every-day practice of the mechanical engineer. In our opinion, the student who would study such a book as this in the same way as he would any other good technical work, and carefully read through it, committing to memory the more important formulæ and data that the author has taken so much care to select and arrange, would, in a short time, have ready for instant use an amount of information which has only been discovered after years of hard work by men who have devoted their lives to scientific investigation.

The Pre-Norman Date of the Design and some of the Stonework of Oxford Cathedral. By JAS. PARK HARRISON, M.A. With illustrations. London: Henry Frowde. Oxford: Clarendon Press. 1891.

THIS is only a pamphlet, a reprint of a paper read at a meeting in the Chapter-house at Oxford some little time since, but it is of more than passing interest, as in his treatment of the subject the author takes up the general question as to the correctness of the date assigned to some supposed transitional carving, and gives illustrations from Saxon missals to show that ornamental details exceedingly like those of many such capitals are actually found in Saxon illuminated missals. The question in regard to Oxford Cathedral partly rests on a study of the stonework in detail, and without making a special visit of inspection we could not undertake to pronounce on the validity of Mr. Harrison's views; but his paper is sufficient to show that the question is more open to discussion that has been generally supposed.

An Architectural Memoir of Old Basing Church, Hants. By the Rev. REGINALD A. CAYLEY, M.A. Basingstoke: C. J. Jacob. 1891.

THIS is a well-written description, in the form of a pamphlet, of a church which seems to have more points of archæological interest than it is generally credited with, and which rather goes to persuade the reader, as Mr. Cayley suggests, that those who are interested in old churches would find it worth while to break a journey at Basingstoke and visit the church (two miles from the railway). Mr. Jas. A. Salter, F.R.S., adds some details as to the monuments and their heraldry.

The "Law Almanack" for 1892, edited by Frederick Herbert (London: T. Scott & Co., 1, Warwick-court, Holborn), is a very useful and clearly-printed sheet for the office wall. ——Messrs. Shand, Mason, & Co., of Upper Ground-street, Blackfriars, send us a useful office-calendar, containing a spirited drawing, by Mr. Linley Sambourne, of firemen at work at the scene of a fire.——Messrs. John Ellis & Sons, of Leicester and Barrow-on-Soar, also send us a useful calendar, containing some very well-executed representations of fossils from the blue lias limestone at Barrow.

The General Manager of the Great Western Railway sends us a pamphlet entitled "Cornwall as a Winter Resort," which merits the attention of invalids and their friends. The pamphlet is published by Messrs. Waterlow Bros. & Layton, Ltd., Bitchin-lane. With it come two small guide-books, entitled "The Winter Resorts of Cornwall," and "A Holiday Trip Round the Pembroke Coast." Both these are published by F. E. Longley, 39, Warwick-lane, E.C.

RECENT TRADE CATALOGUES.

THE General Iron Foundry Company, Ltd., of Upper Thames-street, send us their new illustrated price-list (extending over more than 300 pages) of open, close, and self-setting ranges; tile and mantelpiece registers; overmantels; iron, marble, and wood chimney-pieces; rain-water pipes and gutters; socket-pipes, hot-water apparatus, baths, and sanitary ware; stable fittings, and general castings. The whole forms a very useful and comprehensive catalogue, and as it is well indexed, reference to any item in it is made easy.

Messrs. F. W. Reynolds & Co., of Southwark-street, send us a useful illustrated list of warming and cooking stoves and heating coils and radiators. The "Lucifer" slow combustion stoves, made in both square and round forms, and with large movable ashpans, appear to possess many good points. The same firm send us, from their other establishment, Acorn Works, Edward-street, Blackfriars-road, a sheet of very handy wood-working machines made by them. Both lists are well worth the attention of builders.

Woodhouse & Rawson United, Limited, Queen Victoria-street, send us two catalogues (List "B," Section 5, and List "B," Section 8) of electrical machinery and apparatus connected therewith, including engines, dynamos, accumulators, lamps, switches, fittings, instruments, &c. They are well worth attention, though the design of some of the electroliers and other fittings might be a great deal better than it is. Section 8 deals with steam and electric cranes, lathes, drilling-machines, tube-welders, &c.

Messrs. Taylor & Miller, of Argyle-street, Glasgow, send us an illustrated prospectus of "The Safety" Window, which presents many good points, though we have seen something very like it years ago. While retaining the ordinary sliding sash movement, both sashes can be opened into the room for cleaning, painting, or reglazing, without removing the parting-beads and without the jamming of weights. It is claimed that these windows are wind and water-tight.

BRITISH MUSEUM LECTURES.—Miss Millington-Lathbury is giving a series of four lectures on Greek Temples, Festivals, &c., at the British Museum, on January 28 and February 4, 11, and 18.

Correspondence.

To the Editor of THE BUILDER.

THE INSTITUTE AND ITS EXAMINATIONS.

SIR,—In your leading article of December 26, you refer to the passage in my letter, published in the same issue, where I speak of the surveyor-architect as "that hybrid personage of whom you think it unreasonable and impracticable that we [the memorialists] should want to get rid." Your reply is to the effect that when a man has been elected into the Institute as an architect it would be hard and un-Christian to turn him out because he earned an honest penny now and then, or habitually, by surveyor's work.

Very likely it would; but if I have rightly understood your reply, it does not meet my statement. When I said we wanted to get rid of the surveyor-architect, I did not mean to get rid of him out of the Institute. That is, of course, a matter of no concern to those who do not belong to that body. Our object is to get rid of the "surveyor-architect" altogether, and to get surveyors to stick to surveying, and architects to architecture. All we contend for is that the architect and the surveyor should stick each to his own last, and not be tempted by distracting, though possibly lucrative, invitations to follow two incongruous callings at once; because, if he does, it is certain that he will never make a good architect, and will probably make only an indifferent surveyor.

As regards the Institute, it may be, as you say, impossible for it to get rid of the surveyors within its ranks. I think it is. But at the same time this is a confession that, on its present lines, the Institute is not what it claims to be, a body of architects, and nothing but architects; and the five letters which denote membership, by this showing, only mean necessarily that he who owns them did at one time so far engage in architecture as to satisfy the very comprehensive conditions of the Charter. What then becomes of that protection which these five letters are supposed to afford to the confiding public?

T. G. JACKSON.

SIR,—In architecture, art and science are inseparable (as you very aptly illustrated in your reference to Peterborough last week). The two elements are so spun together into one thread that to remove either is to destroy the whole. Young men entering on a career may be materially helped by an organised system of teaching. Even the "little common sense" can be arranged and packed into the brain in a more accessible way with the aid of a teacher than without it; while the inherent art faculties of a youth, be they great or small, may be developed by good models and illustrations. It is true we cannot *make* a silkworm, but we can take care that the young grub is fed on mulberry-leaves as soon as it creeps out of the egg. It is perfectly idle to argue that a thorough system of education would prevent men of superior fibre from coming to the front. Occasionally, such a one may "ignore system" and survive, but to commend this example to the average youth is most pernicious teaching.

The Institute have thought fit to adopt an examination fence, which they are perfectly justified in doing, although, at the same time, examination without tuition is not a thing to be approved of in the abstract. Yet, the step is so decidedly in the right direction that it should be accepted frankly, and the next step at once demanded,—namely, tuition. The Association, with the characteristic youthfulness of that evergreen body, have rushed into the gap, and exhibit the most commendable zeal in so doing,—but the field is wide, and London is not the whole Kingdom.

It is obvious architecture demands better educational advantages than it now possesses,—that its equipments should be at least equal to those of the other professions,—and that it should be placed with them on an equal footing in the great University centres of the country. The University authorities have the means and the opportunity to do a great deal for architecture if properly directed, and the needs of the profession properly put before them. While the Institute is not qualified to become a teaching body, it is fully competent to direct the training of the younger members of the profession. It could, with the voice of authority, point out to the Universities what is required and the form it should take, and with their aid organise a general system of education for the whole country, and for the future exercise a supervising influence, seeing that the right materials were used in spinning the thread, otherwise it is possible the scientists may step in and try a new combination.

ARTHUR HILL,
Lecturer on Architecture.

Queen's College, Cork.

SIR,—As you were good enough to insert my letter last week, you will, I trust, allow me to finish my story.

I have told you of the benefits received from the Institute examination in the form of incentive and guidance. Let me tell you further of the tangible results. I commenced practice. I had no influence, no means. It would have been a hard struggle at first as an architect pure and simple in a provincial town, so I studied "quantities" and "surveying." These proved invaluable aids to myself, and of great service to my clients. When a client once found me out he stuck like a limpet to a rock. Financially, I prospered.

But what of architecture? I do not deny that, had I bestowed all my strength on the artistic side of my work, capacity as a designer would have been increased. Such capacity, however, was not in demand. I had a wife and family to support, and others looked to me for help. I had the instinct of an artist, and nothing could rob me of it. My little works, if simple, are truthful; others say, "they are well-proportioned, dignified, and pleasing." Add to this, that I knew about every quantity, could tell of every "extra" and every deduction; that adjustment of accounts was consequently easy, that my clients' interests were conserved, and strict justice meted out to my contractors.

My work may increase so as to prevent this careful management of every detail; of that I do not concern myself. I would almost rather it did not; but if it does, then I must drop my "crutches" and soar to higher flights. I am still young.

Now, I should not have troubled you with further writing, had it not been to say what follows. If "the memorialists" do not see their way to join the Institute, and to help by precept and example to purify and better it, it is a matter which concerns themselves. Nothing shall prevent me supporting it, or make me afraid to join with any man doing honourable work. I say with confidence, Prepare for this examination. It is the way to success. The youth without guidance wanders aimlessly on, gets befogged, and often turns aside from all earnest effort. The Institute has marked out the path, you know that your perseverance and energy are rightly directed, and, working along the way with vigour and intelligence, you are certain of prosperity. You will also find that the stimulus given will grow with what it feeds upon, and that you will acquire noble lessons by the wayside.

Do the work that comes ready to your hand with your whole strength and soul. The fittest survive. Leave the immutable laws of nature to set everything in its due place.

EPICTETUS.

December 28, 1891.

ALL SAINTS' CHURCH, HERTFORD.

SIR,—This, the last building in Hertford possessing any remains of antiquity, was burnt down on Monday, December 21, at five a.m. Two of the other five churches were pulled down in the sixteenth century, and St. John's about a century ago, and St. Andrew's was rebuilt gradually about 1870-75. The spires of the town could be seen distinctly from Finsbury-park, a distance of sixteen miles.

The original building consisted of a nave, chancel and transept, and west tower. There was no clearstory, and the nave was lighted by common domestic dormers.

The old portion appeared to have been built in the twelfth century, and had plain one-light lancet windows, and probably resembled Minster Church, near Margate. The tower formerly had a Decorated west window; the last remains of its tracery was removed in 1839 and restored in 1857. The south aisle was added about the time that the churches of St. Mary and St. Nicholas were pulled down. It is of unusual width, 32 ft., or nearly half as wide again as the nave. The north aisle was a stuccoed Gothic structure of the early part of the present century. The chancel aisle on the same side, built about 1875, was designed to match it in materials and style. The three lancet lights at the east end have been replaced quite recently by a three-light window. The east buttresses, the only part not concealed by stucco, contained a considerable quantity of Roman bricks. The leaded spire, about 40 ft. high, replaced one of double that height removed early in the present century. The churchyard is planted around all sides with a double row of large chestnut trees, as is the cemetery adjoining on the south side, which is simply an extension of the churchyard. These burial-grounds together make up about the finest churchyard in England.

WALTER SCARGILL.

Colchester, December 26.

ROOD-SCREENS.

SIR,—"W. S. B. H." will find the rood-screen of Cullompton, Devon, fully illustrated, in the third volume of "Transactions of Devon and Exeter Architectural Society." G. B. P.

Dec. 28, 1891.

SIR,—A correspondent in last week's *Builder* mentions the famous Caroline screen at Wiggenhall, St. Mary the Virgin. I fear it has been removed within the last five years. And it was doubly interesting, from its date, 1626, and also from its being erected just west of the mediæval screen, which had been cut down to the stall level, so common in Norfolk.

There has been a correspondence lately on vandalism at Totnes Grammar School. And there, too, the great rood-loft in St. Mary's Church has been destroyed within the last three years. This was some 14 ft. wide, covering the first bay of chancel, the staircase being at the north-east corner; and had a stone screen west, and an oak one east. Meantime a hideous north gallery remains.

Perhaps the vicars of Wiggenhall, St. Mary the Virgin, and Totnes would explain. VIATOR.

Oxford and Cambridge Club, December, 29, 1891.

*** We understand that photographs of the rood-screens of Devonshire and Cornwall can be obtained from J. B. Worth & Co., Cathedral-yard, Exeter. It may be a convenience to correspondents who are interested in the subject to know this.

The Student's Column.

WARMING BUILDINGS BY HOT WATER.

I.

INTRODUCTION.

THE purposes to which hot-water heating works may be put are both many and varied, but in dealing with methods, and the different forms of apparatus, it will be best to treat them under three distinct headings,—viz., horticultural works, building works, and works in which the heating is done by hot air alone. In the latter case the air is heated by pipes in a chamber specially provided, and differs from the two former methods by the absence of direct radiated heat.

From exposed pipes the heat is felt in two ways,—firstly, by direct radiation from the surface of the metal, that is, heat projected from the metal and being so transferred to surrounding objects; this warmth does not heat the air. Secondly, by the air being heated by contact with the pipes, which air instantly leaves the pipes and makes room for more air to come in contact and be heated, and so on. This is termed Convection,—*i.e.*, heat absorbed and conveyed by the circulatory action of air The difference between the two first and the third method mentioned is, therefore, that the former contribute heat by radiation and convection; the latter by convection only.

The object in treating these three purposes to which hot-water works are put separately, is that both the pipes and appliances generally differ to a considerable extent, and the actual phenomenon of circulation requires considering in different ways in each case. Before, however, proceeding with the description and examples of the work under discussion, it becomes necessary to say a word as to the manner in which heat operates.

Of course many readers may be conversant with the laws of heat, and, for the sake of those having this knowledge, we treat the subject as briefly as possible; but, on the other hand, so many following this calling have but imperfect ideas in this direction, that some description is really essential. No one erecting an apparatus can be certain as to the results it will give, unless the ways in which heat manifests itself are known to him. It is not sufficient that a man knows the principle of circulation of water only, as this deals with the action of the fluid by itself, and a hot-water apparatus, although it may be extensive, well constructed, and having a perfect circulation of hot water within it, is of no use whatever unless it freely parts with its heat and distributes it where required.

Heat.—Heat transmits or manifests itself to us in three different ways,—viz., by conduction, by radiation, and by convection. All these modes of action exist in connexion with every hot-water apparatus that is erected, and when once the principles are understood, it can be readily seen what description of apparatus is most suited for certain purposes and under certain conditions. There are other manifestations of heat, such as absorption, diffusivity, &c., which will be alluded to in due course. It is not proposed to deal with the theory of heat, as it does not come within the province of these papers; the action of heat, however, is all-important.

Conduction of Heat.—This is the way in which heat is transferred through or about a body. Every substance possesses this power of conduction to some degree, although there are many substances which are exceedingly slow in their action, and are frequently, though erroneously, termed non-conductors. It is in solids that we get the conductive power chiefly, metals in particular being mostly conductors of a very rapid character. In fluids, gases and liquids, the action is principally noticeable by its absence; but in these we get another more useful action, viz., convection, without which a hot-water apparatus, in its present form, would be a very useless contrivance.

It will be found in later papers that poor conductors of heat answer a very useful part in these works, when it is wanted to conserve the heat and prevent its loss. This happens when pipes have to be carried in very exposed places where the heat is not required, or wherever a waste of heat may occur.

For the purpose of these papers we have only to deal with the conductive properties of iron, this being, practically without exception, the only metal used in hot-water-heating work. If copper is ever used we may be content with the knowledge that it acts even better than iron. The following table shows the comparative conductive properties of various substances, and it will be noticed that iron, particularly that which is cast, stands high, and it possesses the important advantages of being inexpensive and durable. It has to be mentioned that there are several tables of conductivity compiled by different authors upon heat, and they vary considerably in the comparative powers of substances, but the materials in all the tables follow the same order as to precedence:—

COMPARATIVE CONDUCTIVE POWERS OF SUBSTANCES as given by M. Despretz:—

Substance	Power
Silver	97·30
Copper	89·82
Brass	75·20
Cast iron	56·90
Wrought iron	37·43
Lead	17·96
Marble	2·36
Firebrick	1·14
Water	0·90

We shall have to refer to silicate cotton presently, when speaking of its low conductive properties. This material stands very much lower than the lowest figure upon the above table.

Although water is such a poor conductor, it stands high as an absorbent of heat. This peculiar property has to be considered, as some substances seem positively averse to heat in every way, which is, fortunately for these works, not the case with water. Those substances which absorb heat readily, also part with it freely; this water does in a very satisfactory method, and it may therefore be looked upon as the medium by which the heat is collected and conveyed to the points required; collecting it rapidly and diffusing it just as quickly where it has opportunity. It seems a drawback that water should have to be confined in pipes, as under the best of circumstances some of its good qualities are thereby lessened, sometimes lost.

As just mentioned, conduction, in these papers, has only to be considered as regards iron, that is, the boiler-plates and the substance of the hot-water pipes or radiating media. It does not apply to the fire which is around the boiler nor the water that is within it, but only to the materials that separate the fire from the water, and the water from the air, respectively. There are, however, other necessary features to be observed, particularly the radiative power of the surface of the pipes, &c. For instance, if we had silver pipes, the conduction of the heat would be nearly twice as rapid as with iron, but, by referring to the table of radiating powers in the next paper, it will be found that although the heat is brought to be surface of the pipes, it would be very loath to dissipate, and the ultimate result might be worse than with iron pipe if precautions were not taken.

In concluding this brief explanation of "Conductivity," attention may be called to a peculiar property closely connected with the same subject, which has very correctly been termed "Diffusivity." Doubtless, all readers have seen "gilled" pipes, as figs. 1 and 2, and

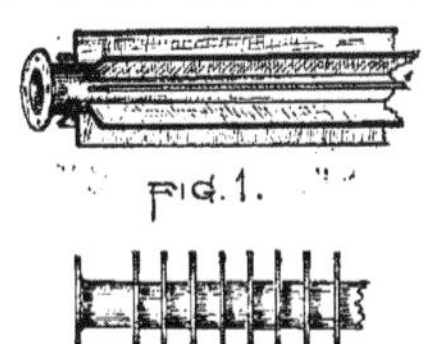

have also heard of or seen "Gill stoves," which are largely used, especially in public buildings. (The gills are a number of plates extending from the body of the stove, which is ribbed, so to speak.) It may not, however, be known to all what special use these gills fulfil. If we take a hot-water pipe and charge it with water at a temperature of say 200 degrees, the heat of the outer surface will bear a close relation to these figures. If, however, we add a number of gills to the pipe, as figs. 1 and 2, some of the heat will transport itself into these plates until the whole of the metal becomes of a fairly uniform heat, but it will be found that this heat no longer bears such a close relation to the 200 deg. In other words, we have the same quantity of heat distributed over a larger area, which reduces its quality, as we may say; a larger volume of heat at a lower temperature. We might almost liken the heat to an odour, which does not become lost, but weakened, as it spreads about. The utility of this heat-diffusion is that we get an equal value of heat at less temperature in greater volume. The aggregate is the same, but a more agreeable result is effected by the greater distribution of heat thus brought about by the increased radiating surface, and, instead of being insufferably hot near the coil and cooler elsewhere, we may look for a more equalised temperature all around.

With hot-water pipes this result is, however, not noticed to the extent, nor is such a gain effected, as when the gills are applied to stoves. They are, then, a decided advantage, and there is hardly a stove-maker who does not make use of them in one way or another. Stoves that are in exposed places, are thus rendered practically safe should any one lean against or come in contact with them.

Radiation of Heat.—This is the term used to express the way in which heat is projected or diffused from the surfaces of heated substances. Projected is a better word than diffused, as radiant heat travels in direct lines from the source of heat. Although just within a certain radius around the heated object the heat appears to be general and equal in all directions, we find that immediately a screen or anything is interposed between us and the source of heat, we at that same instant discover that radiant heat is not diffused in a literal sense. It is not diffused like an odour.

Radiant heat distributes itself in a measure, its area becoming enlarged as the distance from the heated body increases, in the same way as can be noticed with a projected beam of light; but for the warmth that we experience behind or upon the opposite side of objects that may be opposite a source of radiant heat we must look for a different cause. It is the re-radiation of heat and heated air that is accountable for this,—objects that have received heat redistributing it; and the air is heated by contact with these objects, and also by contact with the original radiating medium (assuming it is not an open fire). The air which is heated (that is, heated by contact with heated surfaces only) is distributed here, there, and everywhere by its property of convection, and screens and obstacles of a like character do not materially interfere with this means of heat distribution, as will be explained in the next paper.

A common example used to show that radiant heat does not heat the atmosphere, is to refer to the sun, which transmits heat to the earth by radiation, but leaving the outer or upper portion of the atmosphere, through which its heat has to pass before reaching the earth, in a state so devoid of heat as to cause death to æronauts unless the utmost precautions be taken. The sun may be shining brightly all the time, and the heat at the earth very great.

OBITUARY.

MR. WILLIAM SMITH.—The death is announced of Mr. William Smith, City Architect of Aberdeen. According to the *Times*, Mr. Smith was born in 1817, and was educated at Marischal College, Aberdeen, where he graduated M.A. After travelling in Greece and Italy for the purpose of perfecting himself in his profession, he returned to Aberdeen in 1842, and ten years later succeeded his father as City Architect, an appointment which he held until his death. He erected many of the churches and public buildings in Aberdeen. When her Majesty and the Prince Consort determined upon erecting a new castle in the Highlands, Mr. Smith was chosen to design the building and to superintend its erection, and Balmoral was the result. Mr. Smith erected many other private mansions, schools, hospitals, &c., in various parts of Scotland.

MR. JOHN SHILLITOE.—The death is announced of Mr. John Shillitoe, contractor, of Bury St. Edmunds, in his fifty-ninth year. The son of a builder, and descended, it is stated, from a line of builders which can be clearly traced back for a period of three hundred years, he was born at Campsall, near Doncaster, in 1833. In 1867 he commenced business at Campsall with his brother-in-law, the style of the firm being "Shillitoe & Morgan." After residing for a time at Birmingham, Norwood, and other places, he removed in 1885 to Bury St. Edmunds. In the previous year he had taken his only son, Mr. Thomas Shillitoe, into partnership, the style of the firm becoming "Shillitoe & Son." He built and restored a large number of churches, and erected Truro Cathedral, the new King's Weighhouse Congregational Chapel, Grosvenor-square, the additions to Westminster Hall, and many other important works. At the time of his death, amongst other works he had in hand is the new National Portrait Gallery in Charing-cross-road, adjoining the National Gallery. He was much respected by his employés, and was a Town Councillor of Bury St. Edmunds.

MR. WILLIAM WILKINSON. — We regret to announce the death of Mr. William Wilkinson, head of the firm of Messrs. B. Cooke & Co., of Phœnix Wharf, Battersea. The deceased was well known in the railway and contracting world. The early part of his career was spent on works in connexion with the Great Northern Railway, he having spent nine years as Resident Engineer on the Yorkshire district of that line. In 1872 he resigned this responsibility and joined the late Mr. Benjamin Cooke, and together they established the now well-known business at Battersea. The deceased was sixty-seven years of age, and will be interred at Wimbledon Cemetery this Saturday, January 2. He is succeeded in the business by his only son, who has been intimately connected with all contracts since 1875.

THE LATE MR. JOHN RÜNTZ.—We regret to record the death of Mr. John Rüntz, which took place at his residence, Linton Lodge, Stoke Newington, on the 19th ult., after]a short illness. Mr. Rüntz was for twenty-one years an energetic member of the Metropolitan Board of Works, and accomplished much useful work. He was mainly instrumental in introducing the sanitary clauses into the Metropolitan Building Amendment Act, having gained considerable experience as chairman of the Hackney Board of Guardians during the last cholera visitation. He was keenly alive to the necessity of improving the thoroughfares of London, and the minutes of the Metropolitan Board can testify to the knowledge and activity he brought to bear in the numerous committees upon which he served. One of his favourite schemes was a 100 ft. thoroughfare from Somerset House in a direct line to the British Museum, this scheme, somewhat modified, has recently been under the consideration of the London County Council. It was he who promoted the Bill for the Freedom of the Metropolitan Bridges over the Thames and Lea, in conjunction with Sir William McArthur, which Bill afterwards became law, the freedom sought being acquired with the revenue of the Coal and Wine Dues. Mr. Rüntz was, perhaps, best known for the active part he took in securing open spaces for the public,—Hackney Downs, Mill Hill Fields, Newington Green, Finsbury Park, and later, in conjunction with the late Mr. Joseph Beck, the acquisition of Clissold Park, by far the finest park in the north of London.

LONG-DISTANCE TELEPHONING.—The other Sunday a person at Cedersslund, in Northern Sweden, was enabled to converse with another at Lund, in the extreme south, a distance of nearly 800 miles. The words were perfectly clear.

GENERAL BUILDING NEWS.

BISHOPSGATE GIRLS' SCHOOL, CHAPEL, AND RESIDENCE. — These new buildings, situate in Spital-square, Bishopsgate-street, were recently opened by the Right Hon. G. J. Goschen. They have been erected on the south side of Spital-square, to replace the school buildings formerly situated in Skinner-street and Primrose-street, Bishopsgate, these premises having been acquired by the Great Eastern Railway Company for the widening of their line. The buildings, consisting of the schools, chapel, and curate's residence, are grouped more or less on three sides of the open playground, which is entered by wrought-iron gates, and has a tar-paved surface. The new school buildings have been designed to accommodate 550 pupils, and are planned to meet all the requirements of a modern middle-class girls' school. The school building is approached across the playground, being set back from Spital-square, thus giving more quiet for the work of the teachers. The school building contains three principal floors, as follows:—On the ground floor one enters a hall with a wide corridor running parallel to the length of the building, and off which are placed the class-rooms for the younger children, also the head and assistant mistresses' rooms and the committee-room, and running along the east side of the building is the large dining-hall, measuring 55 ft. by 25 ft., which is divided from the kitchen department by a serving-room. On the first floor are a series of class-rooms, varying in size, certain rooms being able to be thrown together, but all easily controlled and supervised by glazed pass-doors. On the second floor are the art and drawing class-rooms, the cookery kitchen, further general class-rooms; and in the east wing are a series of small and distinct music-rooms for practice, with a music library, &c. Each floor has ample cloak-room accommodation, with drinking fountains provided in the corridors. The double staircases of a fireproof character (without winders), so as to allow of the up and down traffic being kept separate, form a good feature in the plan. The kitchen department is severed by fireproof iron doors, and contains all the necessary offices for cooking and taking charge of the premises. Special care, we are informed, has been taken with the ventilation and the drainage of the buildings. The heating is by means of open stoves, which emit warm fresh air into the class-rooms, and these are aided in the corridors and larger rooms with a low-pressure hot-water system, so as to keep the building throughout at an even temperature in cold weather. The range of latrines is placed in the rear and outside the main building, having a direct access to the outer air. Externally the building has been erected in red bricks with buff terra-cotta dressings and enrichments, the style of architecture being based on collegiate buildings of the Jacobean period. Adjacent to the school, a chapel has been erected, with accommodation for upwards of 500 persons. This chapel, which is intended to be used for lectures, concerts, and other purposes, is 63 ft. long by 44 ft. broad and 34 ft. high, is largely lit by mullioned windows, and has a panelled wooden ceiling with coved sides, the main body of the building being divided from the aisle by polished granite columns. At the north end of the chapel a platform has been erected, and at the side the organ has been placed. The entrance is direct from Spital-square with a lobby, and there is also a further entrance from the schools at the rear. Adjoining the chapel and communicating therewith is a residence of three floors, with basement and attics in addition. Each of the principal floors contains a complete set of rooms, consisting of sitting, bed, and bath-rooms. The whole of the buildings have been designed by and carried out under the immediate supervision of the architects, Messrs. T. Chatfeild Clarke & Son, Messrs. Woodward & Co., of Wilson-street, Finsbury, being the contractors. The cost of the buildings has been about 18,000*l.*, which is exclusive of the value of the land.

RESTORATION OF WIMBORNE MINSTER.—On the 21st ult. an opening service was held in Wimborne Minster, which has just been restored. At a vestry meeting held in November, 1890, Mr. Pearson was appointed architect, and Mr. Fletcher was asked to act in conjunction with him in carrying out the work. The tender of Messrs. Merrick & Son, of Glastonbury, for the sum of 1,689*l.*, was accepted, and the work was commenced in May. Through the kindness of Mr. Walter Fletcher, who has been in charge of the work, we (*Dorset County Chronicle*) are able to give the following particulars of the principal work and the discoveries made:—The walls of the transepts have been raised about 2 ft., and thoroughly repaired. The dressed stone work, which was principally of Tisbury stone, and very much perished, has been renewed with Doulting stone from Shepton Mallet. The roofs have been entirely reconstructed with good English oak, and raised to the original height of the short transept roof, as they existed in the Norman period. On the removal of the roof and timbers of the north transepts the original line of the roof, as it was first constructed, was clearly to be seen where it abutted against the south side of the Norman staircase turret which in those days flanked the north-west angle of this transept. Why the fourteenth-century builders lowered the pitch of the transept roofs seems a mystery. Another peculiarity is that the angles of the water tables on the north side of the lantern-tower do not correspond with regard to their rake, that on the east side being 9 in. wider than that on the west. The length of wall between the lantern-tower and the Norman turret on the west side of the north transept was found to be nearly 10 in. less in thickness than the rest of the walls. This difficulty has been surmounted by keeping the wall-plate at a higher level, which also gives additional head to the gangway leading from the turret to the triforium. On removing the thick plaster from the walls of the north transepts it was clearly seen various alterations had taken place from time to time. The masonry was finished with a rather rough face, which had been whitewashed over. A very thin coat of plaster had been added at some subsequent date, and various coats of white and colour had been placed on this, then a thick coat of plaster or stucco, which was the finish when the restoration was commenced. This has now been entirely removed, and a very thin coat of plaster put on the walls. It was also proved that the outside faces of the walls in the Norman period were covered with rough-cast, as the wall on the north side of the Norman turret was not bonded in on every course when the new wall near the transept was lengthened in the fourteenth century, and the rough-cast had not been removed where it was not bonded. Another curious feature was that the stone string-course, which finished the wall, in the wall-plate was cut through at regular intervals about 11 in. apart and 4½ in. wide, as if the roof had been constructed with wall pieces coming below the string-course. These intervals had all been carefully filled up with stone-work. An altar recess has been discovered in the east wall of the north transept. The recess was originally 6 ft. 2 in. wide, and with a semi-circular Norman arch impost moulding on the north side corresponding in detail and situation with the impost moulding that remains in the north face of the north-west pier of the lantern-tower. When the archway between the north chancel aisle in the north transept was also enlarged, probably in the fourteenth century (late), this altar recess was found to be in the way. The recess appears to have been reduced on the south side as much as possible, so as not to interfere with the altar and the arch on that side. The wall at this place has for some years shown signs of considerable movement, which is not to be very much wondered at, for the pier which remained to take all the weight of the superstructure was only about 10 in. thick. Added to this, it appears that when the gallery in this transept was constructed, early in the present century, it was approached by a staircase from the chancel aisle, and in forming a doorway at the top of the staircase the builders cut right through the centre of the arch of this altar recess. On removing the rough stone wall with which the recess was filled some very interesting frescoes were discovered. There appear to have been no less than three subjects painted on the inside wall at various times. The uppermost one represented the Holy Rood. The cross springs from the base of the carved stone-work to form a bracket which has at one time formed part of a shrine, and a piece of the same stone-work is walled in a little to the north under the figure of the Virgin Mother to form a small bracket. Since the recess has been discovered the upper fresco has in places fallen off, disclosing the figure of a Saint, evidently of a much earlier date, and also an Agnus Dei over the head of St. John. The Holy Rood fresco must have been in its present position when the alterations in the archway between the chancel aisle and the transept were made, as they are not in the centre of the recess as it now exists. There are also indications of a third fresco, probably of a still earlier date, in several places. The stone altar has been restored, a line in the plaster showing its exact dimensions, and the defective pier rebuilt. The piscina, with corbel shelf over it, probably to take the figure which was found walled in the filling up of the recess, has now been placed on the north side, as there was not sufficient room, owing to the pier, to refix it in its original position on the south side. It might have belonged to another altar, as tradition assigns to this transept the site of Thomas de Brembre's chantry. The whole of the tracery of the west window of the transept has been restored, almost every vestige of it having been destroyed or removed. The wooden gallery, which rested on the tie-beams of the old roof, and formed the only means of access to the lantern-tower from the Norman turret, has been replaced with a handsome stone gangway, supported by a massive moulded arch, extending from turret to the lantern-tower, and finished with an iron railing. The north window is now being filled with stained-glass, the subject being the Te Deum. The window of the east side of the transept is a representation of the Nunc Dimittis. The window on the west side represents the Magnificat. The glass of these windows has been executed by Messrs. Clayton & Bell. The works in the south transept are somewhat similar to those in the north. The walls have been raised, and a new English oak roof of similar design restored to its original pitch and height. The remains of a single-light window were found in the east wall at the south end of this transept. The stone-work of this has been restored as far as possible, but as the vestry and library over it project beyond the line of the opening, it cannot be used for its original purpose. It appears to have at one time contained the stairs leading to the chamber over the vestry, now called the library, as it is purely circular on plan, and the remains of the steps were found. The altar recess, occupying a similar position to the one in the north transept, has also been restored. The arch had been cut through when the gallery was found as in the north transept. The south window is to be filled in with stained-glass by Messrs. Powell & Sons, to the memory of the late Mr. William Druitt. It is the gift of his children, to whose generosity the cost of the repairs in the south transept is due. The repairs still remaining to be done are the making good of the masonry of the walls of the main aisles. Besides these alterations the heating apparatus of the church has been renewed, and an oak screen placed to shelter the western door.

HOSPITAL EXTENSIONS, WOLVERHAMPTON.—Extensions to the Borough Infectious Hospital, Green-lane, Wolverhampton, comprising an entrance-lodge, additions to the administrative block, and a hospital pavilion, were opened on the 23rd ult. by Alderman J. C. Major (Chairman of the Sanitary Committee of the Town Council). The pavilion is designed to accommodate eighteen beds; and has two main wards, each for eight beds, a nurse's duty-room, and two single-bed wards, with bath-rooms for each ward, and other arrangements. The additions to the administrative block include doctors' or committee room, with dispensary and other conveniences, nurses' dining-room, eight bed-rooms, bath-room, and other apartments. The building has been carried out by Mr. A. Lovatt, his contract price being 3,604*l*. The designs for the buildings were drawn up by the Borough Surveyor (Mr. R. E. W. Berrington), with the assistance of the Medical Officer (Dr. Malet), and the suggestions of the Sanitary Committee and its Chairman.

NEW BATHS, SALISBURY.—These baths have just been completed for the Salisbury Swimming Baths, Ltd. The site chosen is in Rolleston-street, and the building is about 94 ft. long by 50 ft. wide, with slipper-baths adjoining. The roof consists of iron principals, with lantern ventilators, and is covered partly with slates and partly with glass. The bath itself is 80 ft. long by 34 ft. wide, lined with glazed bricks, and the water is procured from a well sunk on the premises, and warmed by steam injection to a temperature of 75° Fahr. A gallery runs along the two sides and one end of the building, under which the dressing-boxes are arranged, accommodation being provided for forty-one bathers. These dressing-boxes, as also the building, are warmed by steam-pipes. In connexion with the swimming-baths, and fronting on Church-street, a steam laundry has been erected, fitted with every modern improvement, and capable of turning out 60*l*. of work weekly. The hot water for baths and laundry is supplied by a 20-ft. Cornish boiler. The total cost of the laundry and baths, exclusive of the site, was about 4,500*l*. All machinery, pumps, laundry plant, &c., were supplied by Messrs. Thos. Bradford & Co., of London. The ironwork was supplied by the Redcliffe Crown Galvanised Iron Co., Bristol. The roofs were glazed by Messrs. Rendle & Co., of Westminster, on their patent "Acme" system. The contractor for the building was Mr. John Wort, of Salisbury; and the building was designed and carried out by Mr. Alfred C. Bothams, A.M. Inst. C.E., architect, of Salisbury.

FOREIGN AND COLONIAL.

BERLIN.—A competition has been opened for the design for an equestrian statue to the late Emperor Frederick III., to be placed on the battle-field of Woerth, in the Alsace, on which field he distinguished himself in the Franco-German war. Ten thousand pounds are at the disposal of the committee in charge of the erection. The statue is to be of cast bronze, and is to stand on a pediment of some 3 to 4 mètres high. The pediment is to receive decoration in the form of bronze figures representing the companionship in arms of North and South Germany against France. The designs (models of some size) are to be sent in by April next, and will be assessed by a jury of four sculptors and a painter. Four prizes (of 200*l*. each) are to be given.——The competition for the design of the equestrian statue of the late Emperor William I., to be placed in a central position on the memorial monument in course of erection on the Kyffhäuser, has been decided. The first prize has fallen to the sculptor, E. Hundriesser (Charlottenburg). The number of competitors was thirty-eight, and four prizes were awarded. The average quality of the designs sent in was poor, quite two-thirds of the number having no artistic value whatever. The selection of Herr Hundriesser's design for the first prize meets with the approval of those who have seen the work sent in. It will be remembered that the Kyffhauser monument is one of those large memorial piles in course of erection under the superintendence of the architect, Bruno Schmitz.——The competition for the large Government Travelling Studentship of Architecture by the Prussian Academy of Arts every two years has this time again been a farce, only three architects applying for it, and of these three (who had passed the preliminary examination required of them) only one of them entering for the competition proper. The studentship was given to this one candidate, although his work was not considered very satisfactory. His name is Hartmann (Stettin). The country he will be expected to travel in is Italy. The value of the studentship is 150*l*. a year for two years, together with 30*l*. extra for railway expenses.——Some activity apparently prevails in matters relating to the erection of some new buildings for the Prussian Upper and Lower Houses, referred to in a former number. The designs to be carried out are now settled: 10,000*l*. have been put at the disposal of the architect, "Baurath" F. Schulze, and the office at the works will be opened on the 15th inst. One of the two buildings will be commenced this year, but the other cannot be commenced for some years, the site on which it is to be placed being at present occupied by the premises of the Imperial Reichstag, which body will not vacate them until their new palace on the Koenigsplatz is complete.——The "programme" of the *salon*, to be held this year under the auspices of the Prussian Royal Academy of Arts, has been published, and from it we learn that there will at last be a stop put to artists exhibiting an unlimited number of works of art of the same class, as has been their wont on former occasions. Artists, as a rule, will not be permitted to exhibit more than three objects of the same class. Only a limited number of well-known men will be invited to exhibit more than three; and then, if possible, they are to exhibit a full collection of their best pieces of work, to be hung separately.——There is some talk of the Municipality of Berlin erecting a museum for modern sculpture, a bequest for this purpose having, apparently, been left to the city.——Some new regulations have been published relating to the erection of new buildings in the outer suburbs (independent villages as yet, lying outside the boundaries of the city). They are very stringent, and are causing much dissatisfaction.

MUNICH.—Herr Wilhelm Rettig has been elected to hold the post of City Architect, vacant since the death of Herr Zenetti. Herr Rettig, who will have the title of an "Ober-Baurath," made a name at the time of the great competition for the memorial monument to the deceased Emperor William I., at which he gained the first prize for a design made together with Herr Pfann. Since the year of this competition he has for some time been City Architect at Dresden, which post he had, however, to resign on account of a controversy with the authorities.

SWEDEN.—The Stockholm Building Association has just held its annual meeting, when all its officials were re-elected, the President being Herr C. A. Olsson, master builder, and the Secretary, Herr C. A. Flodguist, architect. A handsome building has just been completed at Gothenburg for the Gothenburg Bank of Commerce. The style is Florentine. The lower part of the façade is of roughly-hewn Swedish granite, whilst for the upper portion pressed Swedish cement has been employed. The architects are Messrs. K. Johansson & V. von Jegerfelt.——The Gothenburg and Bohus Län's Sparbank has been rebuilt by Herr Hj. Cornilsen, architect.——The agent of the Swedish Export Association writes from Argentina that the import of timber villas from Sweden has almost entirely ceased owing to the high premium on gold and the low prices of bricks and wages, houses of stone being therefore as cheap. Owing to the low value of the notes in which wages are paid labour is as cheap as in Sweden. Several planing and carpentering factories have stopped from want of work.

SANITARY AND ENGINEERING NEWS.

POOLE SEWERAGE SCHEME.—The Corporation of Poole, Dorset, have recently instructed their Borough Surveyor to proceed with the scheme of drainage designed by Mr. Lewis Angell in 1885, estimated to cost about 30,000*l*., and appointed Mr. Angell to act as consulting engineer therein; but in consequence of other official engagements, Mr. Angell has now been compelled to resign the position, at which the Council "express their regret," and have appointed Mr. James Lemon, C.E., Mayor of Southampton, in place of Mr. Angell.

SEWERAGE AND SEWAGE DISPOSAL OF KNARESBOROUGH (YORKSHIRE).—At a recent meeting of the Knaresborough Improvement Commissioners and Local Board of Health, Mr. D. Balfour, M.Inst.C.E., of Newcastle-on-Tyne, submitted report, estimate, and plans for a scheme of main sewerage and sewage disposal for the town, estimated to cost in execution 7,000*l*., the sewage being disposed of on land. After the scheme, with plans, &c., had been thoroughly gone into by the Board, it was agreed to adopt the scheme as submitted, in preference to any chemical process of disposal, there being ample suitable land in the district available. The engineer was instructed to submit the plans to the Local Government Board for sanction to obtain the necessary loan for the works. A Provisional Order has already been obtained for the land purchase.

MISCELLANEOUS.

CARPENTERS' COMPANY'S PRIZES, KING'S COLLEGE.—On the 17th ult., the prizes given by the Carpenters' Company to the students of technical classes at King's College were distributed by Mr. Henry Harben, L.C.C., the Master and many of the past-Masters of the Carpenters' Company, Dr. Henry Wace, the Principal of the College, and many of the Professors being present. There were many members of the British Institute of Wood-Carvers at work in the wood-carving room, and there were microscopes in Professor Groves's room showing specimens of wood and stone. Lime-light views of the various styles of architecture were given in the drawing-room, with explanatory notes by Prof. Banister Fletcher. A fine collection of wood-carvings belonging to Mr. Rogers, and diagrams and instruments, were explained in the new Electrical Laboratory. The students' drawings were hung on the walls, and photographs, &c., in the Reference Museum and Architectural Corridor. The following is the list of prizes awarded:—*Building Construction and Architecture: (Day Classes): Second Year*:—A. E. Mullins, prize of 5*l*. and silver medal; H. P. Fletcher, 3*l*. and bronze medal; H. G. Leslie, 2*l*.; J. Howard and T. H. Coad, Certificates of Approval. *First Year*:—H. T. Adlard, prize of 5*l*. and silver medal; A. T. Angell, 3*l*. and bronze medal; E. C. Monson, 2*l*.; T. A. Watson, Certificate of Distinction; H. Alberry, R. C. Master, and H. C. Trimnell, Certificates of Approval. *Evening Classes*:—J. Goddard, prize of 5*l*. and silver medal; C. M. Cobb, 3*l*. and bronze medal; E. C. Monson, 2*l*.; W. H. Lord, 2*l*.; J. Little, 1*l*.; J. Almond, 1*l*. 10s.; A. G. Hubble, 1*l*.; H. S. Cregeen, T. J. Barrett, A. S. Brighty, and F. H. Pearse, Certificates of Approval. *Architectural Drawing*:—W. H. Lord and T. J. Barrett, bracketted equal, prizes of 2*l*. each; W. G. Pritchard, prize of 1*l*.; C. M. Cobb and H. S. Cregeen, Certificates of Approval. *Wood Carving: Evening Classes*:—L. Aston, prize of 3*l*.; W. Watson, 3*l*.; C. M. Cobb, 1*l*. *Day Classes*:—C. G. Money, prize of 5*l*.; G. Stevens, 3*l*.; E. R. Hine, 3*l*.; F. Bevan, 1*l*.; and J. Wicks, 1*l*. *Ladies' Classes*:—L. Travers, prize of 2*l*.; and J. Stapleton, 1*l*.

THE MOVEMENT FOR NATIONAL REGISTRATION OF PLUMBERS.—A meeting of the Forfar, Perth, and Fife District Council of the National Registration of Plumbers was held on the 22nd ult. in the Burgh Court-room, Dundee. Lord Provost Mathewson presided, and there were present Dr. David Lennox, Dundee; Councillor Davidson, Perth; Councillor Smart, Perth; Mr. John Wood, Montrose; Mr. Thomas Kinnear, Dundee; Mr. P. Lorimer, Broughty Ferry; Mr. J. L. Warden, teacher of plumbing class, Montrose; Mr. J. J. Henderson, local secretary; Mr. W. Farquharson, local treasurer, &c. After the preliminary business, the Lord Provost said he felt that it was most important that every tradesman should have a scientific knowledge of the work to which he had devoted himself; but, above all, that plumbers should have a thorough scientific knowledge, so that they might, in every detail, understand their business. The plumbing trade affected not only the men employed, but the community at large to an extent that few trades did. In Dundee there was no excuse for any young man not having a proper scientific knowledge of his trade, for in the city there were the Technical Institute and the University College, both of which were splendidly equipped, and were doing excellent work. He thought he could say for the Police Commission that it was in favour of giving the 1,300*l*. grant to advance technical education. The Lord Provost then presented the prizes to the successful students during the year, the prizes consisting of volumes donated by the Worshipful Company of Plumbers. The prize-takers were (from Dundee) Messrs. Peter Edmonds (17 years of age), Thomas Kinnear (20), James Littlejohn (19), Alexdr. Young (19), and Alexander Ferguson (20). From Arbroath there were two prize-winners,—Mr. Thomas Grant (17) and Mr. James Carver (20).—Mr. Henderson submitted a letter to the meeting which the District Council had prepared to forward to the various Town and County Councils in the district. The letter set forth the claims of the plumbers, and asked that a portion of the residue grant in the hands of the Corporations approached should be devoted to the technical education of plumbers.—Dr. Lennox moved—"That this Council considers the technical education of plumbers a question of supreme importance, the provision of which is both difficult and costly, and approves of the proposed letter to the various health authorities in this district, recommending this question to their attention as one deserving substantial financial aid." He said it was perfectly obvious that the first requisite of technical education was to have efficient teaching, and good teaching, like good plumbing work, was a very costly matter. Plumbing was in reality a question for the community, and that trade, unlike others, specially affected the health and the well-being of the people in the town and district. Like the supply of water and other sanitary matters, it should be taken up by the sanitary authorities.—Mr. John Wood, Montrose, seconded the motion, which was carried.—Councillor Davidson, Perth, moved—"That this Council considers it

CONTRACTS AND PUBLIC APPOINTMENTS.

CONTRACTS.

Nature of Work or Materials.	By whom Required.	Architect, Surveyor, or Engineer.	Tenders to be delivered.
Stables and Sheds	Withington Loc. Bd.	A. H. Mountain	Jan. 5
*Station Improvements and Bridges over Railway and Stream, &c. Bridlington	North Eastern Rly.	H. Copperthwaite	Jan. 6
Road Materials	West Sussex C. C.	C. Adcock	do.
*Slaters' and Plumbers' Works	Parish of St. Leonard, Shoreditch	*Official*	do.
*Alarm Posts and Calls to Firemen, &c.	Chiswick Loc. Bd.	A. Ramsden	do.
*Carting Away Sweepings, &c.	St. Marylebone Vestry	*Official*	Jan. 7
*Foundations of Retort House	Boro' of Stockport Gas Committee	S. Meunier	do.
Flagging and Paving	Blaydon Loc. Bd.	*Official*	do.
*New Police Station, Romford	Essex C. C.	H. Stock	Jan. 8
*Sewerage Works	Lichfield U.S.A.	C. J. Corrie	do.
Piling and Concrete Foundation Work Electric Lighting Station	Bristol U.S.A.	H. Williams	do.
Engineer's Workshop, &c. near Kingston, Halifax	....	Jas. Farrar	Jan. 9
Additions to Bridge, Linwood, Renfrewshire	Committee	Caldwell, Muir, & Caldwell	Jan. 11
Villa, Rose-street, Elgin, N.B.	....	G. Sutherland	do.
12 Cottages, Ryton, Bar Moor, Newcastle-on-Tyne	Co-operative Society	....	do.
*Stoneware Pipe Sewer	Islington Vestry	J. P. Barber	do.
*Repair of Private Roads	Croydon Council	*Official*	Jan. 12
*Works and Materials	Wandsworth B. of W.	do.	do.
Subway (Contracts 2, 3, 12, and 13)	Glasgow Dist. Subway Co.	Simpson & Wilson	do.
Water Supply Works, Neilston	Renfrewshire C. C.	Niven & Haddin	do.
Waterworks	Ashton-under-Lyne, Stalybridge, & Dukinfield Waterworks Committee	G. H. Hill	Jan. 13
Waterworks, Innellan	Argyll County Council	Jas. Wilson	do.
*Erection of Pavilion on Pier Head	Brighton West Pier Co.	R. W. P. Birch	Jan. 14

CONTRACTS.—*Continued.*

Nature of Work or Materials.	By whom Required.	Architect, Surveyor or Engineer.	Tenders to be delivered.
Congregational Church and Schools, Chichester	....	E. J. Hamilton	Jan. 15
*Enlargement of Head Post Office, Brighton	H. M. Works	*Official*	do.
Private Railway Line, Hopetoun, near Winchburgh, N.B.	Young's Paraffin Light, &c. Co.	....	Jan. 16
Street Paving Works	Glasgow Police Com.	*Official*	Jan. 21
Lodge, Litford, Northampton	....	E. W. Collin	Feb. 1
*New Engine and Well House	Widnes Local Board	C. O. Ellison & Son	do.
*Erection of School Buildings	Hofmsey School Board	Chas. Bell	Feb. 2
*Iron Bridge over Railway, Hull	North Eastern Rly.	H. Copperthwaite	Feb. 8
*Alteration to Farmhouse, Carnford	....	....	No date.
Restoration of Church, Carlton, near Worksop	Committee	....	do.
Alterations, &c. St. Matthew's Parsonage, Crumlin-road, Belfast	....	J. Fraser & Son	do.
Residence, Longwall, Kirkandrews, Cumberland	J. N. Robinson	J. Graham	do.
Additions to "Whinfield," Headingley, Leeds	A. F. L. Hepton	T. Butler Wilson	do.

PUBLIC APPOINTMENTS.

Nature of Appointment.	By whom Advertised.	Salary.	Applications to be in.
*Architect and Surveyor	Worshipful Company of Cutlers	Not stated	Jan. 17
*Dublin District Surveyorships	Civil Service Commrs.	do.	Feb. 10
*Assistant Instructor in Geometrical Drawing	Royal Indian Engineering College	250*l*.	No date

Those marked with an Asterisk (*) are advertised in this Number. *Contracts, pp.* iv., vi., viii., & x. *Public Appointments, p.* xxxi.

desirable at the present opportune time to call the attention of every registered master in the district to the valuable assistance he may give to the registration movement by employing only such journeymen as are registered, and such apprentices as will attend classes in theoretical plumbing work if such be within their reach." Councillor Smart, Perth, seconded, Mr. Lorimer, Broughty Ferry, supported, and the motion was adopted.

TELEPHONES.—Messrs. Nussbaum have recently made a complete installation at the "Adelphi" Hotel, Liverpool. The installation comprises three floors, and on each floor a switch board for seventy directions is fitted. The total number of stations being 210. Each room is fitted with a call-box and double "Ader" instrument (magnetic transmitter), a separate call-bell and a three-contact pear push, which is suspended near the bed, so that the visitors can ring in the usual way or communicate through the telephone. The visitors are able to communicate through the telephone. The visitors can communicate with one another and with the staff of the hotel. This effects great saving of time both for visitors and staff.

THE PHOTOGRAPHIC LENS.—Messrs. R. & J. Beck, of Cornhill, send us a useful pamphlet they have issued, giving a simple description of the principles and method of application of the photographic lens, mainly with a view to assisting amateur photographers.

ENGINEERING EDUCATION IN THE BRITISH DOMINIONS.—Under this heading, a pamphlet of about seventy pages is issued by the Institution of Civil Engineers, giving a statistical statement as to the various educational institutions in the British Dominions where instruction is given bearing on the profession of civil engineering. The book also contains the regulations of the Council as to the admission of students, and a list of public examining bodies and examinations recognised by the Council.

PROPOSED RAILWAY THROUGH SIBERIA.—The Institution of Civil Engineers publishes in a pamphlet form the paper on this subject read before the Institution by Mr. W. M. Cuningham. The paper contains a consideration of the proposed routes, and a map containing special information from materials furnished by the author.

THE PUBLIC HEALTH (LONDON) ACT. — An abstract of clauses of this Act, reprinted from the "Metropolitan Local Government Journal," is issued by Messrs. S. Edgecumbe-Rogers. It is a useful guide to the Act in the shape of a small pamphlet summarising and classifying its provisions.

VENTILATION, MUNICIPAL BUILDINGS, ALLOA.—The Town Council of Alloa have entrusted the ventilating and heating of the municipal buildings of that town to Messrs. Baird, Thompson, & Co., of Glasgow. The County Council have also instructed this firm to examine and report upon the heating of the County Buildings, and to prepare plans.

CHRISTMAS FESTIVITY AT EXETER.—Mr. Harry Hems gave his twenty-third annual Christmas dinner to poor old people on Christmas day, when sixty *invités* sat down to table. On Monday last Mr. and Mrs. Hems entertained at tea seventy children from St. Martha's Orphanage and other places.

FAILURES IN THE BUILDING TRADE IN 1891.—The supplement to *Kemp's Mercantile Gazette* for December 30, in its statistical abstract of failures, &c., during the year 1891, states that the number of failures in the building and timber trades was 525, as compared with 564 in 1890, showing a decrease of thirty-nine.

THE "BRITISH ALMANACK."—In reference to our notice of this, we have received the following:—"Pardon my pointing out that the article on 'Engineering,' in the 'British Almanack' for 1892, was not written by Mr. J. S. Shedlock (who writes on 'Music'), but by your obedient servant, R. L. C. (the writer of the 'Architecture' article)."

VENICE AT "OLYMPIA."—We are informed that most of the houses forming modern Venice at Olympia were executed in fibrous plaster by the Plastic Decoration Company, Limited, Wellington-street, Strand, from photographs of buildings taken on the spot. The architectural features have, it is stated, been closely followed. The company have also carried out about 10,000 square yards of slab-plastering throughout the buildings to meet the requirements of the London County Council.

THE SANITARY INSTITUTE'S EXAMINATIONS FOR INSPECTORS OF NUISANCES.—At an examination for Inspectors of Nuisances, held at Manchester on December 18 and 19, fifty-three candidates presented themselves. Questions were set to be answered in writing on the 18th, and the candidates were examined *vivâ voce* on the 19th. Thirty-seven candidates were certified to be competent, as regards their sanitary knowledge, to discharge the duties of Inspector of Nuisances.

TERRA-COTTA AS A FIREPROOF MATERIAL.—The *Southampton Observer* of the 19th ult. contained an account of an experiment made two days before with the view of showing the value of terra-cotta as a fireproof material for the erection of houses and other buildings. The experiment took place at the works of Messrs. M. H. Blanchard & Co., successors to Coade's original Terra-Cotta Works, Lambeth (established 1769), and the scene for the experiment was at their works at Bishop's Waltham, Hants. The object of the experiment was to show that there need be no more burning floors, walls, staircases, or roofs if constructed of terra-cotta, even were ever so intense a fire to break out, that if the conflagration broke out in one room it could not possibly extend to the next apartment, nor could the means of escape from the upper to the lower part of the house be cut off through the burning of the staircase, which has been the occasion of many fatal disasters. This result is, it is claimed, ensured by using Mr. M. H. Blanchard's patent fireproof terra-cotta chambered blocks, slabs, and tiles, which are described as suitable for all building purposes, and artisans' dwellings, warehouses, residential flats, from the humblest dwelling to the palatial mansion. The experiment was made in a little building of the dimensions of one room of an ordinary house, with brick sides, and a terra-cotta floor above, the pieces being so dove-tailed as to render it almost hermetically sealed. This floor was reached by means of a wide staircase, with an ornamental balustrade resembling that of carved oak. In the room below faggots of wood were piled up to the ceiling. Round these at the bottom were placed tar barrels, with a layer of straw. The mass was set on fire, and the fire burnt with great intensity. While this was going on most of the visitors ascended the staircase, and stood on the floor, feeling the slabs from time to time to see if the heat was making any impression on them, but throughout the whole trial they maintained almost the same temperature, being quite cold. By-and-by the fierce flames lapped themselves round the staircase, cutting off retreat by that way, and had it been composed of wood short work would have been made of it. However, beyond being slightly blackened by smoke, it remained as impassive as the floor above. The room was one mass of white heat, resembling in colour molten lead. Had the floor fallen in at that time cremation would have been the fate of those on it. The party remained on the roof from half to three-quarters of an hour,—a sufficient period to put the experiment to the severest test,—and so little had they felt the heat below that many shivered with cold. Immediately the visitors descended, a large number of the workmen and boys ran up the stairs and jumped about on the floor, which apparently had not in any way been affected by the great heat, though the fire continued to burn for a considerable time afterwards.

SOCIETY OF ANTIQUARIES OF SCOTLAND.—The first monthly meeting of this Society for the present session was held in the Society's Library, Queen-street, Edinburgh, on the 14th ult., Sir Arthur Mitchell, K.C.B., in the chair. The first paper read was on trepanning the human skull in pre-historic times, by Dr. Munro, secretary.—The second paper was entitled "Notes on examples of old heraldic and other glass existing in or having connexion with Scotland, with special reference to the heraldic rondel preserved at Woodhouselee," by Mr. J. M. Gray, Curator of the National Portrait Gallery, F.S.A., Scot. The author showed the progress which had been made in our knowledge of the existence of examples of stained glass in Scotland since Mr. George Seton submitted a paper on the subject to the society in 1878, and he pointed out how the result of the recent Heraldic Exhibition had been to add considerably to the list then made up by Mr. Seton. Having referred to some fragments of stained glass from Dunfermline exhibited by Sir J. Noel Paton, and to the heraldic shields and other fragments in the windows of Stobhall, the fine rondel at Fyvie Castle, and the missing St. Bartholomew of the Magdalen Chapel, Mr. Gray exhibited a full-sized outline lithograph of a glass panel and border in the possession of Mr. Albert Hartshorne, F.S.A., the panel representing a traditionary event in the life of Sir Alexander Stewart, great grandson of Walter Stewart, Seneschal of Scotland, and the border including a Stewart family tree, the panel, however, being manifestly modern work, probably of the present century, although the border is, doubtless, of the date with which it was inscribed, viz., 1574. The rondel from Woodhouselee, it was explained, shows the Royal Arms of Scotland impaled with those of Anne of Denmark, Queen of James VI., with a decorative border of a conventional Renaissance arrangement of fruit and leafage.—The third paper was a notice of a submarine deposit of Sarnian ware from the Pan Rock, off the coast of Kent, by Mr. John T. Beer, F.S.A., Scot.

CHOIR STALLS, CHRIST CHURCH, CLIFTON.—The new choir stalls in Christ Church, Clifton, which have been placed there in memory of the late Rev. Edward Young, were used for the first time on the 20th ult. The stalls are of oak, in the Early English style of carving. The work has been carried out by Messrs. Cornish & Gaymer, of North Walsham, from the designs of Mr. Bassett Smith.

THE NEW GOTHENBURG WATERWORKS. — The water supply of Gothenburg having for some time proved insufficient, it has been decided to obtain an additional one from the Göta river. The works which are now being carried out will cost abou 70,000*l*.

TELEPHONE BETWEEN STOCKHOLM AND CHRISTIANIA.—The Parliaments of Sweden and Norwa have voted 3,600*l*. each towards establishing telephonic communication between the capitals of th two countries.

LIVERPOOL ENGINEERING SOCIETY.—The fifth ordinary meeting of the present session was held at the Royal Institution on the 23rd ult., Mr. George Farren, Assoc.M.Inst.C.E., in the chair. Mr. A. W. Brightmore, M.Sc., Assoc.M.Inst.C.E., read a paper entitled, "Methods of Collecting Water for Supply." The author divided his subject into three parts. 1. Interception of rain-water before reaching the earth, by collecting it directly in tanks or from the roofs of buildings. 2. Taking the water from streams or rivers directly, if the flow is sufficiently constant, or by equalising the supply by constructing a reservoir if the flow varies below the supply required. 3. Obtaining the water from the earth's crust by means of springs, shallow wells, intercepting tunnels or drains, or deep-seated wells. He then proceeded to discuss the probable state of purity of the water derived from each of these sources, and gave examples of towns and cities, either in Europe or America, supplied on each system. It was pointed out that the supply obtained by direct interception could only be very limited. With respect to the supply procured from streams or rivers, it was shown to be free from contaminating influences, if obtained near to the source of the streams, hence the advantage of a water-supply from an equalising reservoir. Referring to the third method, water collected from shallow depths by means of wells or intercepting drains was shown to be useful for supply when derived from sparsely populated districts. Water from deep-seated springs or wells, owing to its infiltration through the overlying strata, is often of great purity and valuable for supply. An interesting discussion followed.

"BLESSED COMPULSION" IN SANITARY MATTERS.—We are very glad to see that at some of the recent conferences of political parties sanitary questions have come very much to the fore. Sanitation of the village is to be already part of the work of the proposed parish councils, and the sanitation of London is likely to be prominent in the programme of parties in the County Council. We note with satisfaction a leading public journal speaking of that "blessed word compulsion" in this respect. It is all the more satisfactory because the blessings of such compulsion are lauded by an organ of the Liberal party. Hitherto it has been chiefly from Conservative statesmen that necessary compulsion in sanitary matters has been obtainable; and a good deal of the failure of the action of the Public Health Law and of Acts such as the Infant Life Protection Act has been due to the unwillingness of statesmen of the *doctrinaire* school of politics to accept the principle of compulsion, and their preference for the doctrine of education by painful local failure and voluntary repentance and enlightenment. Experience has, we hope, taught that a little "blessed compulsion,"—the word "must" instead of "may" in many Acts of Parliament,—would tend greatly to the public welfare.—*British Medical Journal.*

WELL-SINKING. — Mr. Richard D. Batchelor, artesian well engineer, of Chatham, has opened a London office and show-rooms at 73, Queen-Victoria-street.

ERRATUM.—In the article on "Architecture at the Scottish Academy" last week a printer's error, which escaped notice, transformed the "great fire-place" in the old Parliament Hall of Edinburgh Castle into the "Greek fireplace." Edinburgh has been called the "modern Athens," but had not quite come into the title at that date.

MEETINGS.

SATURDAY, JANUARY 2.

Sanitary Inspectors' Association.—The President, Dr. B. W. Richardson, will deliver a New-Year's Address. 6 p.m.

MONDAY, JANUARY 4.

Surveyors' Institution.—Adjourned Discussion on Mr. C. H. Bedells's paper on "Party and Party-Fence Walls." 8 p.m.

TUESDAY, JANUARY 5.

Glasgow Architectural Association.—Mr. C. R. M'Intosh on "An Italian Tour." 8 p.m.

WEDNESDAY, JANUARY 6.

British Archæological Association.—(1) Mr. Andreas E. Cockayne on "Archæology in Derbyshire." (2) Dr. Fryer on a "Find of Roman Remains at Caerleon." 8 p.m.

Civil and Mechanical Engineers' Society.—Mr. Reginald Bolton on "The Square Drilling Machine and its Uses." 7 p.m.

RECENT PATENTS:

ABSTRACTS OF SPECIFICATIONS.

16,497.—FIRE-PLACES AND RANGES: *S. Smith.*—The fret of the front bar in the fire-places and ranges described in this specification is cast with two pins or lugs, one at each end, and secured to the front and allowed to turn down. Two levers with toothed racks work on the frame and lift the bottom bar to the height required. Simplicity, and dispensing with false or loose bottoms, are the main points in the invention.

19,763.—CLOSET AND PIPE-FITTINGS: *Daniel Baker.*—The trap, arm, and junction are, according to this patent, cast in one piece, and will take any kind of pan or closet. A special joint is used, and lugs or ears are cast on the junction so as to form a drip, conducting the leakage or rain down the pipe and preventing its soiling the wall.

20,813.—BRICKMAKING MACHINERY: *A. Gibbs.*—According to this invention, rolls having rings provided with teeth or projections are so fixed and fitted that one revolves quicker than the other, the effect being that the grinding is facilitated, and the rolls are prevented wearing unevenly.

747.—FIRE-GRATES: *W. P. Redish.*—In the form of fire-grate, which is the subject of this patent, a stepped back advances from the bottom to the top. A pivotted ash carrier is fixed beneath, and grate bars are fixed at an angle to improve the combustion and facilitate the removal of the burnt fuel.

789.—WINDOW-SASHES AND FRAMES: *J. Gibson.*—To prevent draughts or the sashes becoming loose and shaking. The frames, which are the subject of this patent, have metal flanges or feathers, and grooves or guides of angle metal pieces which form the sliding arrangement.

917.—DECORATIVE MATERIAL: *E. S. Sears.*—This specification relates principally to embossed and decorative paper, wood pulp, cloth, leather, or similar materials which are simultaneously embossed, coloured, and tinted by improved machinery described in the specification.

5,988.—FLOOR AND STAIR-TREADS: *J. & J. Mason and Others.*—By this invention a hard metal plate is combined with a softer anti-slipping matetial. The main plate is prepared so as to give a back plate with raised ribs and openings. The ribs are made with a longitudinal V depression.

NEW APPLICATIONS FOR LETTERS PATENT.

December 14.—21,837, G. Toos, Fastening Device for Sky or Fanlight Windows, &c.—21,866, A. Taylor, Dressing and Levelling Flagstones, &c.

December 15.—F. Lynde, Joints of Drain and other Pipes.—21,909, W. Thornburn, Raising, Lowering, and Securing Sliding Sashes.—21,965, J. Bardsley, Door Springs and Checks.—21,967, G. Briggs, Bricks or Building Blocks.

December 16.—F. Hart, Measuring and Proportionally Describing Graphically Sections of Tunnels, &c., also Openings generally of Limited Height and width.—21,994, W. Hooks, Waste-water Preventing Flushing Cistern.—21,997, J. Thompson, Fire-resisting Brick and Material for Lining, Facing or Coating Fireplaces, &c.—22,031.—A. McKay, Extricating Damp from Walls, &c.—22,036, W. Tucker, Antidrip Sash Bar.

December 17.—22,048, R. Johns, Roofing, &c.—22,080, J. Grubb and W. Sturge, Roses for Ceilings and Wall-connectors for Electrical Purposes.—22,087, A. Mould, Fire-places and Mantel-pieces.—22,111, E. Nelson, Damp Course in Building Foundations.—22,121, L. Olmsted, Metal Handle for Saws.

December 18.—22,141, E. & O. Howl, Extracting Steam by Mechanical Arrangement from Hoffman and other Brick-kilns (other than by means of a Chimney or Stack).—22,171, T. Smith, Compounds or Cements.—22,172, J. Bordnave, Pipes, Tanks, and other Structures Composed of a Metal Framework Combined with Cement, &c.

December 19.—22,198, F. Willis and R. Astley, Fireproof Floor.—22,202, C. Henshaw, Shop-door and Casement-fasteners.—22,209, J. & A. Duckett, Water-closets.—22,212, E. Wilson, Machines for Carving or Shaping Wood.—22,215, E. Morrison & M. Ingram, Water-closets.—22,241, C. Lund, Window-sash Fasteners.—22,248, T. Bretherton, Iron-crete Pavement.—22,254, J. Lilly, Door-latches.—22,256, G. Couzens, Gully-traps.

PROVISIONAL SPECIFICATIONS ACCEPTED.

20,019, C. Watts, Pipes for Circulation of Hot Water in Heating Greenhouses, &c.—20,096, J. Wilson, Kilns for Drying and Burning Bricks, &c.—20,218, A. Boult, Devices for Protecting Window-curtains from Casement-windows.—20,290, Craven Dunnill & Co., Ltd., and F. Smith, Tiles, &c.—20,467, J. Kirkman, Waste Water-closets.—20,646, H. Parry, Kilns for Burning Lime.—20,725, W. Bloor, Door-latches.—20,772, H. Smart, Planes.—20,806, A. Illidge, Sash-fasteners.—20,998, A. Vincke, Window-frames and Fittings.—21,004, H. Cribb, Preparing, Fitting, and Laying Blocks for Floors, &c.

COMPLETE SPECIFICATIONS ACCEPTED.

(*Open to Opposition for Two Months.*)

1,885, H. Symons, Slate Slip, principally for Repairing Slated Roofs.—2,278, F. Smith, Bakers' Ovens.—2,536, J. Rae and J. Murdock, Chimney Tops, &c.—2,554, W. Ingram, Spirit Levels.—2,787, T. Hendry and J. Wilkinson, Ventilators or Ventilating Cowls.—3,161, C. Abel, Metal Framework for Portable Structures.—4,161, T. Kemp, Testing Drains.—14,776, L. Camus, Heating Apparatus.—14,820, C. Henderson, Warming, Ventilating, and Lighting Apartments.—19,661, J. Stevens and C. Major, Door Springs and Checks.—19,776, J. Fairfax, Doors and Windows.—19,962, A. Clark, Sash-fasteners.—19,966, H. Lake, Feeding Mechanism for Woodworking Machinery.—20,100, C. Harwood, Water-waste Preventing Cistern for Water-closets.

SOME RECENT SALES OF PROPERTY:

ESTATE EXCHANGE REPORT.

DECEMBER 17.—By *Wilkinson, Son, & Welch* (at Hastings): "Brunswick House," Marine-parade, Hastings, f., r. 150l., 2,400l.

DECEMBER 18.—By *Wilkinson, Son, & Welch* (at Brighton): 25, 23, and 27, Lower-rock-gardens, Brighton, f., r. 230l., 3,020l.; 1, Wyndham-st., f., r. 45l., 620l.; 38, Clarendon-villas, Hove, f., 700l.

DECEMBER 21.—By *Maddox & Son*: A moiety of the "Hope Tavern," in Tottenham-st.; and 41, Whitfield-st., Tottenham-court-rd., f., r. 212l. 10s., 2,250l.—By *J. E. Pinder*: 29, Albion-sq., Dalston, u.t. 48 yrs., no g.r., r. 40l., 455l.—By *B. Brown*: 155, Grundy-st., Poplar, f., 305l.; f.g.r. 10l., Canon-rd., Hornsey, with reversion in 84 yrs., 240l.; 22, Digby-rd., Homerton, f., r. 22l. 2s., 165l.—By *Jenkins & Sons* (at Deptford): 13 and 15, Walpole-st., New-cross, u.t. 61 yrs., g.r. 9l., r. 57l. 4s., 325l.; 193 and 195, Lewisham High-rd., u.t. 14 yrs., g.r. 70l., r. 195l., 1,000l.; 174, Lewisham High-rd., u.t. 59 yrs., g.r. 9l. 6s., r. 60l., 560l.; 55, Breakspeare-rd., u.t. 83 yrs., g.r. 11l. 15s., r. 68l., 600l.; 10, Bramblebury-rd., Plumstead, u.t. 53 yrs., g.r. 2l. 11s., r. 22l. 2s., 185l.

[*Contractions used in these lists.*—F.g.r. for freehold ground-rent; l.g.r. for leasehold ground-rent; i.g.r. for improved ground-rent; g.r. for ground-rent; r. for rent; f. for freehold; c. for copyhold; l. for leasehold; e.r. for estimated rental; u.t. for unexpired term; p.a. for per annum; yrs. for years; st. for street; rd. for road; sq. for square; pl. for place; ter. for terrace; cres. for crescent; yd. for yard, &c.]

PRICES CURRENT OF MATERIALS.

TIMBER.		
Greenheart, B.G. ton	9/0/0	0/0/0
Teak, E.I. .. load	9/10/0	15/0/0
Sequoia, U.S. ft. cu.	2/3	3/0
Ash, Canada load	2/10/0	4/0/0
Birch, do.	3/0/0	4/5/0
Elm, do.	3/10/0	4/15/0
Fir, Dantsic, &c.	2/0/0	3/10/0
Oak, do.	2/10/0	4/10/0
Canada	5/0/0	7/0/0
Pine, Canada red	2/10/0	3/10/0
Do. yellow	2/10/0	5/0/0
Lath, D'ntsic, fath	5/5/0	6/10/0
St. Petersburg	5/10/0	7/10/0
Deals, Finland, 2nd & 1st std 100	8/10/0	10/10/0
Do. 4th & 3rd ..	7/10/0	8/10/0
Do. Riga	6/10/0	8/0/0
St. Petersburg, 1st yellow ..	10/10/0	15/0/0
Do. 2nd yellow	8/10/0	10/0/0
Do. white	7/0/0	10/10/0
Swedish	7/15/0	16/0/0
White Sea	8/10/0	17/10/0
Canada, Pine 1st	19/10/0	25/10/0
Do. do. 2nd	14/10/0	16/10/0
Do. do. 3rd, &c.	6/10/0	10/10/0
Do. Spruce, 1st	8/10/0	11/0/0
Do. do. 3rd & 2nd	6/10/0	8/0/0
New Brunswick	7/0/0	7/10/0
Battens, all kinds	3/10/0	15/10/0
Flooring Boards, sq., 1 in. prep. 1st	0/8/6	0/14/6
Do. 2nd	0/7/6	0/11/6
Other qualities	0/5/3	0/8/0
Cedar, Cuba .. ft.	/3½	/4½
Honduras, &c.	/3½	/4½
Mahogany, Cuba	/4½	/6½
St. Domingo, cargo av	/4½	/6½
Mexican do. do	/4	/5
Tobasco do. do	/5½	/7
Honduras do. ..	/5½	/8½
Box, Turkey ton	4/0/0	13/0/0
Rose, Rio	10/0/0	20/0/0
Bahia	8/0/0	18/0/0
Satin, St. Domingo .. ft.	0/0/9	0/1/3

TIMBER (continued).		
Satin, Porto Rico	0/0/10	0/1/6
Walnut, Italian ..	0/0/3½	0/0/7

METALS.		
IRON—Pig, in Scotland .. ton	2/7/3	2/7/6
Bar, Welsh, in London	6/0/0	6/2/6
Do. do. at works in Wales	5/10/0	5/12/6
Do. Staffordshire, in London	6/10/0	6/15/0
COPPER—British, cake and ingot	48/0/0	49/10/0
Best selected ..	49/0/0	50/0/0
Sheets, strong ..	58/0/0	59/0/0
Chili, bars	45/0/0	45/7/6
YELLOW METAL lb.	0/0/5½	0/0/5½
LEAD—Pig, Spanish .... ton	11/5/0	11/6/3
English, com. brands	11/7/6	11/10/0
Sheet, English, 3 lbs. per sq. ft. and upwards ..	13/0/0	0/0/0
Pipe	13/10/0	0/0/0
ZINC—English sheet .... ton	26/0/0	0/0/0
Vieille Montagne	26/10/0	0/0/0
TIN—Straits	90/5/0	90/15/0
Australian	90/5/0	90/15/0
English ingots	94/0/0	95/0/0

OILS.		
Linseed .... ton	19/0/0	19/5/0
Cocoanut, Cochin	26/10/0	0/0/0
Do. Ceylon	23/10/0	0/0/0
Palm, Lagos	23/0/0	24/0/0
Rapeseed, English pale	20/10/0	0/0/0
Do. brown	27/15/0	0/0/0
Cottonseed ref. ..	18/10/0	0/0/0
Oleine	0/0/0	0/0/0
Lubricating, U.S.	4/10/0	5/10/0
Do. refined	6/0/0	11/0/0
TAR—Stockholm barrel	0/19/0	0/0/0
Archangel	0/12/6	0/0/0

TENDERS.

[Communications for insertion under this heading must reach us *not later than* 12 *noon on Thursdays.*]

CARDIFF.—For the erection of additional buildings, for the Cardiff Tin Stamping and Enamel Company, Limited, East Moors. Mr. W. I. Gyllis, architect, 37, St. Mary-street, Cardiff. Quantities by the architect:—

Jno. Strachan	£2,781	0	Thos. Gough	£2,369	10
Jas. Allan	2,572	3	John Hopkins	2,365	0
Edward T. Hatherly	2,557	0	John W. Roger	2,330	0
Johnson Bros.	2,507	0	Exors. of W. Gradwell	2,266	0
Powell & Mansfield	2,497	0	Thos. D. Ridley, Middlesbrough & Cardiff*	2,193	0
Williams & Thomas	2,490	0	E. Harvey	2,151	15
Thomas & James	2,477	0			

* Accepted.

CHISWICK.—For certain reparations to the fronts and basements of three houses, at Strand-on-the-Green. Mr. H. Hardwicke Langston, architect, 9, Great James-street, Bedford-row, London. Quantities not supplied:—

Vare Bros.	£278	Fagg*	£179
Patten	183		

* Accepted.

CLACTON-ON-SEA.—Accepted for building five pairs of Villa residences, for Mr. A. R. Chamberlain, in Station-road. Messrs. Homer & Ridler, architects, 35, Bucklersbury, E.C.:—

Ellis & Turner £6,218 0 0

DEVONPORT.—For the erection of farm buildings, at Inswork, Barton Millbrook, Cornwall, for the Right Hon. Baron Clinton. Mr. W. N. Richards, architect, 29, St. Aubyn-street, Devonport:—

Jenkin & Son	£3,561	10	W. Trevena	£2,593	5
A. Andrews	3,200	0	G. Smith & Son, Devonport*	2,479	15
G. Shellabear	2,940	0			
G. Glanville	2,900	0			

* Accepted.

ECCLESHILL (Yorks.)—Accepted for the erection of a cloth warehouse at The Old Mill, Eccleshill, for Messrs. Smith & Hutton. Messrs. Jowett Kendall & J. Barper Bakes, architects, Calverley-chambers, Victoria-square, Leeds. Quantities by the architects:—

Mason.—J. Thornton & Son, Idle	£289	0	0
Joiner.—Bakes & Overend, Eccleshill	146	0	0
Plumber and Painter.—Thos. Norton, Eccleshill	35	0	0
Plasterer.—Andrew Taylor, Eccleshill	15	0	0
Slater.—T. & A. Thornton, Eccleshill	23	18	6
Total amount	£508	18	6

GREAT YARMOUTH.—For the erection of a pair of semi-detached houses, Wellesley-road. Messrs. Bottle & Olley, architects, Great Yarmouth. Quantities by architects:—

J. F. W. Bray	£1,888	0	J. S. Cooper	£1,784	0
R. Darby	1,869	13	G. W. Beech	1,749	10
W. Cork	1,848	0	J. Batchelor	1,667	0
James Leggett	1,795	0	G. Beckett (accepted)	1,648	10

[All of Great Yarmouth.]

GREAT YARMOUTH.—For additions to Messrs. Arnold's premises, King-street. Messrs. Bottle & Olley, architects, Great Yarmouth. Quantities by architects:—

Rand & Cooper	£1,297	15	James Leggett	£1,250	0
C. Wiseman	1,284	16	G. T. Flaxman	1,242	10
G. W. Beech	1,282	0	J. S. Cooper	1,231	0
R. Eastoe	1,276	0	C. C. J. Cadey	1,230	0
R. Davy	1,259	17	Wm. Cork*	1,216	0
Grimble & Watts	1,258	0			

* Accepted.

[All of Great Yarmouth.]

LONDON.—For the erection of three factories in Kentish Town-road, N.W., for Mr. Thos. J. Brinsmead, and Mr. Chas. Goddard. Mr. Leonard V. Hunt, architect, 35, Queen Victoria-street, E.C. Quantities by Mr. Geo. Fleetwood:—

Holloway Bros.	£10,870	Pink, Pryer, & Co.	£10,143
W. Goodman	10,478	Macfarlane Bros.	9,770
J. Brown & Son	10,436	E. Toms	9,729
W. Scrivener & Co.	10,357	Matlock Bros.	9,660
Whitehead & Co.	10,250	Gould & Brand*	9,291
Harris & Wardrop	10,168		

* Accepted.

LONDON.—For alterations to "The Weavers' Arms" public-house, 1, Warley-street, Bethnal-green, E., for Mr. J. Russell. Mr. W. Seckham Witherington, architect, 79, Mark-lane, E.C.:—

Larke & Son	£1,384	Lascelles & Co.	£1,280
Kearley	1,366	Hood (accepted)	1,005

LONDON.—Accepted for sanitary works, additions, and decorations at 20, Albion-street, Hyde Park, W.:—

Benjamin & Robinson, 35, Cambridge-street, Hyde Park.... £288

LONDON.—Accepted for painting and repairs at the "Queen's Head" public-house, Wharf-road, City-road, for the Cannon Brewery Company. Messrs. F. Chambers & Son, architects:—

Snewin Bros. & Co., Clapton £105 0 0

LONDON.—For pulling down and rebuilding the "Langton Arms" public-house, Norman-street, St. Luke's. Mr. R. Roberts, architect:—

C. Cox	£2,464	W. Gladding	£2,377
Outhwaite & Son	2,447	Snewin Bros. & Co., Clapton (accepted)	2,293
Ashby & Horner	2,447		
F. & F. J. Wood	2,418		

LONDON.—Accepted for the erection of stables and other works in connexion therewith at Highgate Lodge, for Mr. H. Reguart. Mr. R. J. Beale, architect:—

Percival Hart, Station Works, West Green, N. .. £496 0 0

LONDON.—For alterations, new shop, and showroom, 164, Tottenham Court-road, for Messrs. T. W. Thompson & Co. Mr. Ernest H. Abbott, architect, 6, Warwick-court, W.C. Quantities by Mr. A. Johnson, 50, Imperial-buildings, Ludgate-circus:—

T. W. Smith & Son	£1,040 0	Hall, Beddall, & Co.	£802 0
A. J. & C. Hocking	845 5	Scrivener & Co.	780 0
F. & H. F. Higgs	837 6	Schurlen & Co.	730 0

LONDON.—For building new riding-school at Gloucester-gate, Regent's Park, for Mr. Parry. Mr. Horace Dove, architect, 4, Tokenhouse-buildings:—

Lowe	£2,663	Gould & Brand	£2,480
Scrivener & Co.	2611	Martin, Wells, & Co.	2,360
Williams	2,580		

RUGELEY.—For the erection of a new infants' school, Talbot-street, Rugeley. Mr. John Greenall, architect:—

J. T. Clark	£1,244	Bradney & Co.	£1,176
G. J. Muirhead	1,200	S. Wootton	1,113
C. Linford	1,192	Thomas Mason, Hednesford (accepted)	1,062
A. F. Whittome	1,179		

SOUTHAMPTON.—For alterations, additions, and improvements at the Eastern District Board School, for the Southampton School Board. Mr. J. H. Blizard, architect:—

Jackson	£2,830	Bolton	£2,296
J. Dyer	2,379	Rowland	2,199
Stevens & Co.	2,374	J. Crook & Son*	2,190
Roe & Co.	2,363	* Accepted.	

SUBSCRIBERS in LONDON and the SUBURBS, by prepaying at the Publishing Office, 19s. per annum (or 4s. 9d. per quarter), can ensure receiving "The Builder" by *Friday Morning's post.*

TO CORRESPONDENTS.

H. R. (should have sent amount).—J. J. D. (next week).—B. & J. B.—W. H. W.—G. C. H.—W. J. F.—H. S.—D. B.—"Free Lance" (no name or address enclosed).—G. A. N.—J. A. G. K.

All statements of facts, lists of tenders, &c., must be accompanied by the name and address of the sender, not necessarily for publication.

We are compelled to decline pointing out books and giving addresses.

NOTE.—The responsibility of signed articles, and papers read at public meetings, rests, of course, with the authors.

We cannot undertake to return rejected communications.

Letters or communications (beyond mere news-items) which have been duplicated for other journals, are NOT DESIRED.

All communications regarding literary and artistic matter should be addressed to THE EDITOR; all communications relating to advertisements and other exclusively business matters should be addressed to THE PUBLISHER, and *not* to the Editor.

The Builder Cathedral Series.

1891.

1. CANTERBURY	..	Jan. 3.	7. SALISBURY..	..	July 4.
2. LICHFIELD ..	..	Feb. 7.	8. BRISTOL ..	..	Aug. 1.
3. ST. ALBAN'S ..	..	Mar. 7.	9. NORWICH ..	..	Sept. 5.
4. PETERBOROUGH	..	April 4.	10. ROCHESTER	..	Oct. 3.
5. WELLS ..	..	May 2.	11. LINCOLN ..	..	Nov. 7.
6. EXETER ..	..	June 6.	12. GLOUCESTER	..	Dec. 5.

1892.

13. ST. PAUL'S ..	..	Jan. 2.	16. ELY ..	..	April 2.
14. HEREFORD ..	..	Feb. 6.	17. LLANDAFF ..	..	May 7.
15. CHICHESTER	..	Mar. 5.	18. OXFORD ..	..	June 4.

(Further arrangements will be duly announced.)

Price FOURPENCE each (by post 4½d.), except Nos. 1 and 2, which are *out of print*; but the VIEW, PLAN, AND DESCRIPTION of CANTERBURY and of LICHFIELD have been re-printed, and they can now be had, price ONE SHILLING each set; by post, 1s. 2d.

Portfolios, for Preserving the Plates unfolded, 2s. 6d.; by post, 3s.

TERMS OF SUBSCRIPTION.

"THE BUILDER" is supplied DIRECT from the Office to residents in any part of the United Kingdom at the rate of 19s. per annum PREPAID. To all parts of Europe, America, Australia, and New Zealand, 26s. per annum. To India, China, Ceylon, &c. 30s. per annum. Remittances payable to DOUGLAS FOURDRINIER, Publisher, No. 46, Catherine-street W.C.

Cathedrals of England and Wales.

No. 13. ST. PAUL'S. Drawn by The Editor.

St. Paul's Cathedral.

Ground Plan.

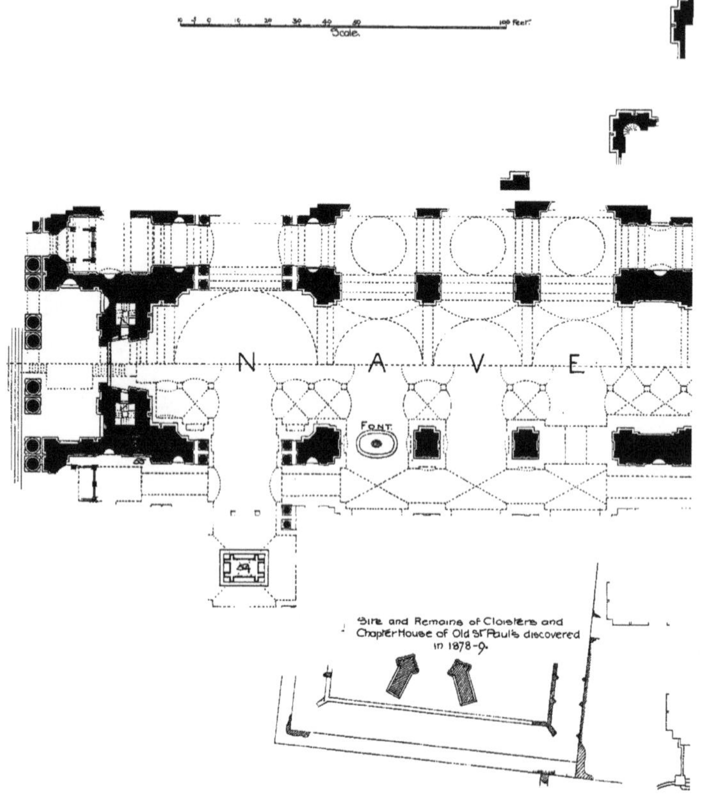

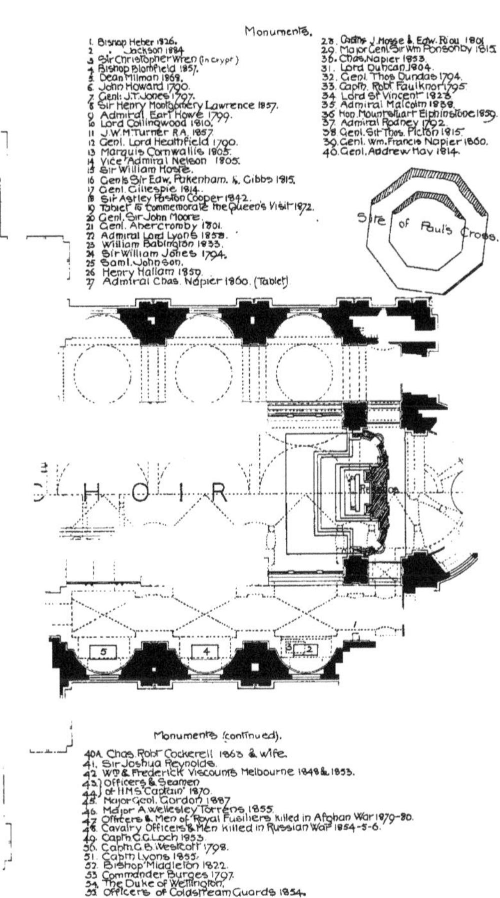
Monuments.
1. Bishop Heber 1826.
2 " Jackson 1884
3 Sir Christopher Wren (in crypt)
4 Bishop Blomfield 1857.
5. Dean Milman 1868.
6. John Howard 1790.
7. Genl: J.T. Jones 1797.
8 Sir Henry Montgomery Lawrence 1857.
9 Admiral Earl Howe 1799.
10 Lord Collingwood 1810.
11 J.W.M. Turner R.A. 1857.
12 Genl. Lord Heathfield 1790.
13 Marquis Cornwallis 1805.
14 Vice Admiral Nelson 1805.
15 Sir William Hoste.
16 Genls Sir Edw. Pakenham. & Gibbs 1815.
17 Genl. Gillespie 1814.
18 Sir Astley Paston Cooper 1842.
19 Tablet to commemorate the Queen's Visit 1872.
20 Genl. Sir John Moore.
21 Genl. Abercromby 1801.
22 Admiral Lord Lyons 1858.
23 William Babington 1833.
24 Sir William Jones 1794.
25 Saml. Johnson.
26 Henry Hallam 1859.
27 Admiral Chas. Napier 1860. (Tablet)
28. Captns J. Mosse & Edw. Riou 1801
29. Major Genl. Sir Wm Ponsonby 1815.
30. Chas. Napier 1853.
31. Lord Duncan 1804.
32. Genl. Thos Dundas 1794.
33. Captn. Robt Faulknor 1795.
34 Lord St Vincent 1823.
35. Admiral Malcolm 1838.
36 Hon. Mountstuart Elphinstone 1859.
37. Admiral Rodney 1792.
38 Genl. Sir Thos. Picton 1815.
39. Genl. Wm. Francis Napier 1860.
40. Genl. Andrew Hay 1814.
Site of Paul's Cross.
CHOIR
5
4
3
2
Monuments (continued).
40A. Chas. Robt Cockerell 1863 & wife.
41. Sir Joshua Reynolds.
42 Wm & Frederick Viscounts Melbourne 1848 & 1853.
43.} Officers & Seamen
44.} of H.M.S. 'Captain' 1870.
45. Major Genl. Gordon 1887
46. Major A. Wellesley Torrens 1855.
47 Officers & Men of Royal Fusiliers killed in Afghan War 1879-80.
48. Cavalry Officers & Men killed in Russian War 1854-5-6.
49. Captn. G.G. Loch 1853.
50. Captn. G.B. Westcott 1798.
51. Captn Lyons 1855.
52. Bishop Middleton 1822.
53 Commander Burges 1797.
54. The Duke of Wellington.
55. Officers of Coldstream Guards 1854.

St Pauls Cathedral

Staircase in S.W. Tower leading to Library.

Elevation of lower part of Stairs

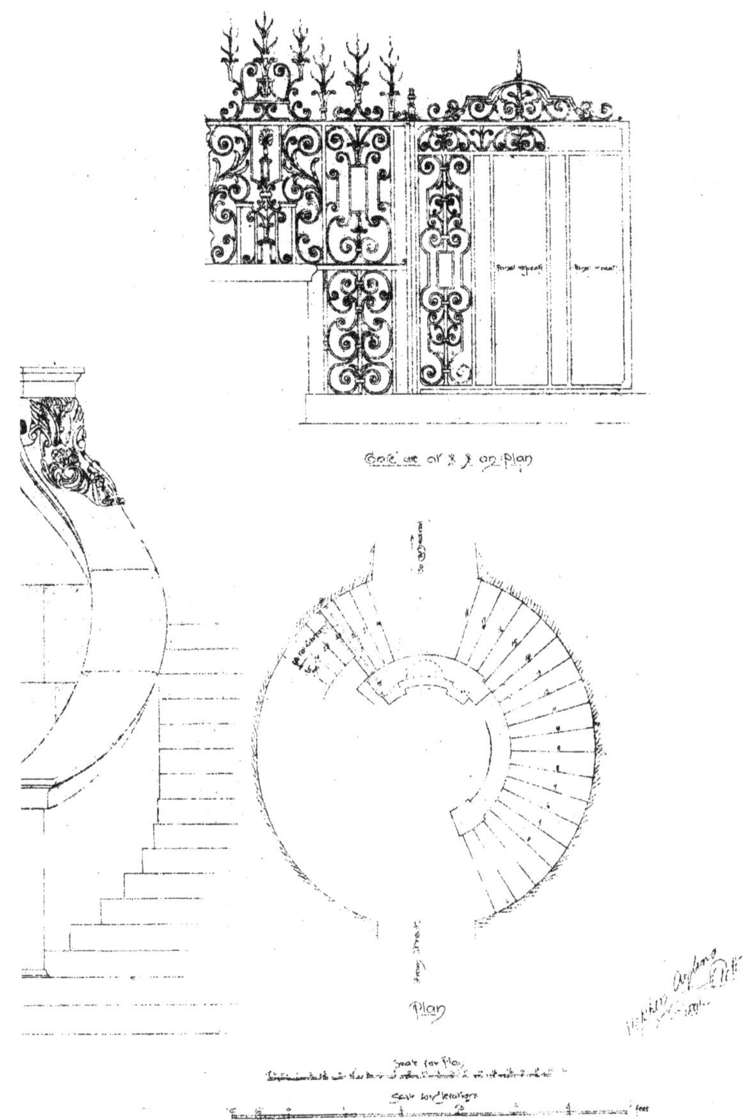

SAINT PAUL's
CATHEDRAL
Before the destruction of the Spire
Restored from Ancient Authorities
By H. W. Brewer. 1891
A
A

INDEX.
A The Clochier.
B. PAUL'S Cross.
C. The Kings Closet for attending the preaching at Paul's Cross.
D. The Shrowds.
E. The Consistory
F. Shiryngton's Chapel.
G. Shiryngtons Library.
H. Pardon Church Hawgh.
I. Bell-tower.
K. The Charnell.
C
D

ST. PETER'S DOME, FROM THE PIAZZA DELLA SAGRE

INK-PHOTO SPRAGUE & Co. 4 & 5, EAST HARDING STREET, FETTER LANE, E.C.

'ROM A WATER COLOUR DRAWING BY MR. JOHN FULLEYLOVE.

OLD·SAINT·PETERS·ROME.
ABOUT THE YEAR MCCCCL.
RESTORED FROM ANCIENT AUTHORITIES.
BY. H.W. BREWER 1891

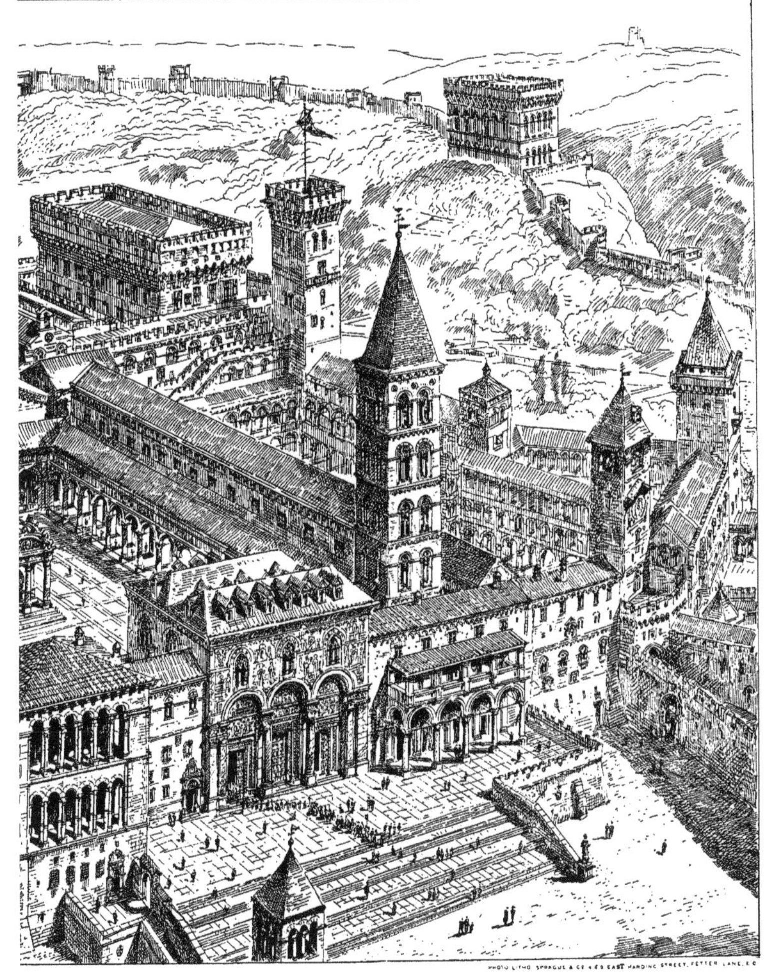

PHOTO LITHO SPRAGUE & Cº 4 & 5 EAST HARDING STREET, FETTER LANE, E.C.

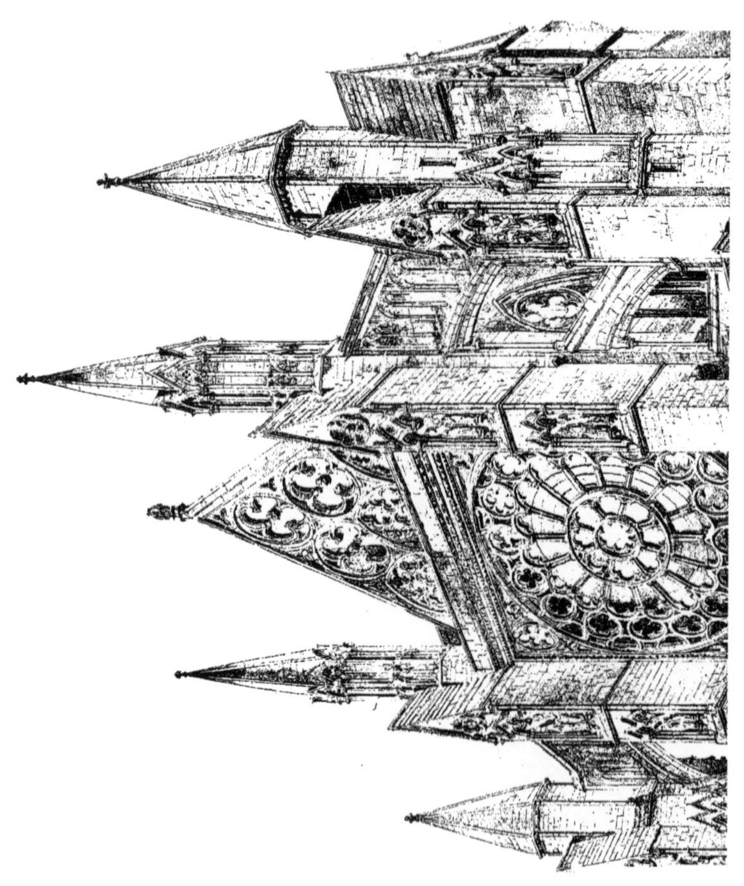

NORTH TRANSEPT, WESTMINSTER ABBEY: AS RESTORED BY MR. J. L. PEARSON, R.A.—DRAWN BY MR. JOHN BEGG.

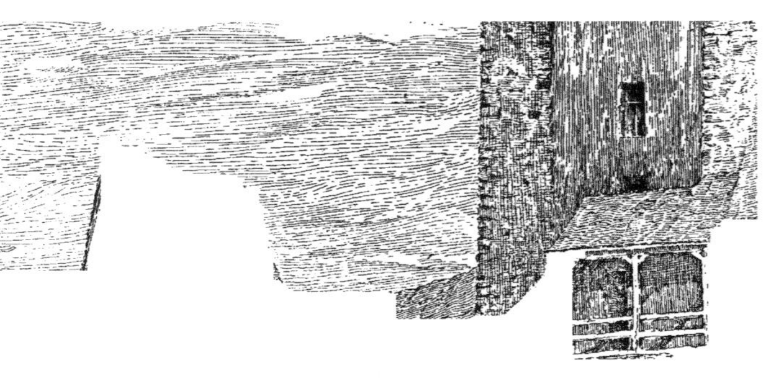

THE KLINGEN THOR, ROTHENBURG.—From a Drawing by Mr. A. Beresford Pite, A.R.I.B.A.

.EN BEFORE THE REMOVAL OF THE IVY.

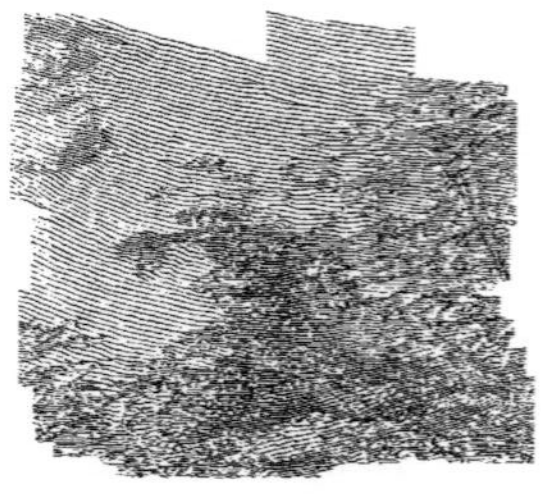

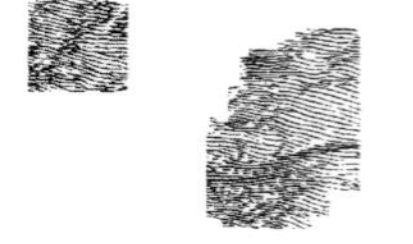

"LE TEMPS PORTANT LA RENOMMÉE.'

Monument to Delacroix in the Gardens of the Luxembourg, Paris. M. Dalou, Sculptor.

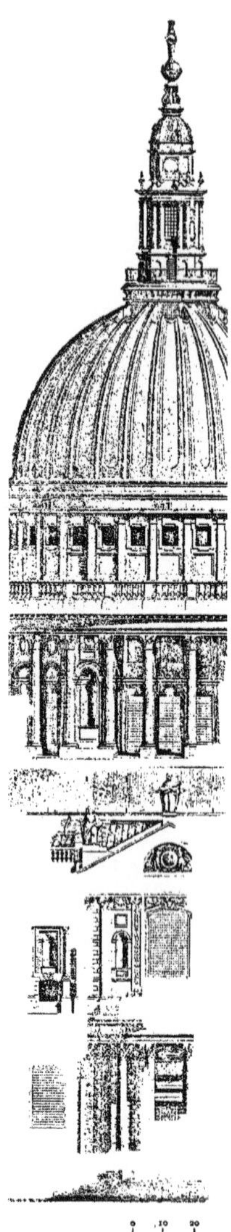

North Elevation of St. Paul's Cath

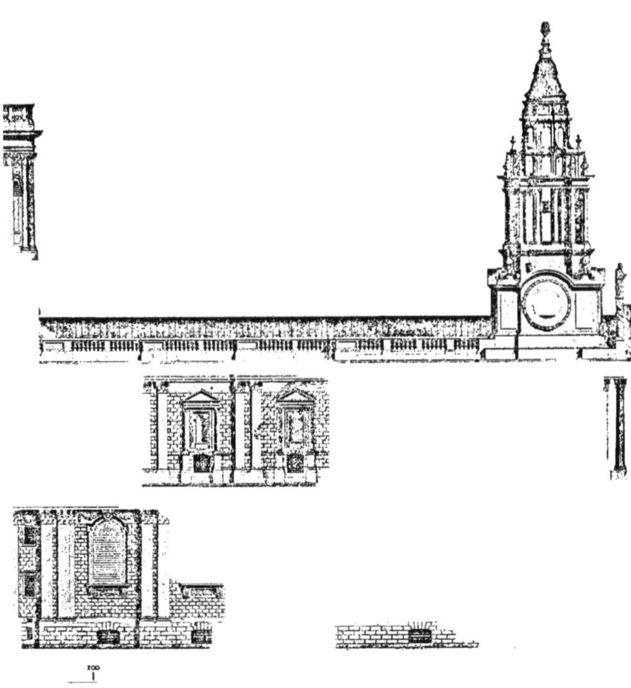

ing by Gladwin, published in 1828.

VOL. LXII. No. 2553. SATURDAY, JANUARY 9, 1892.

ILLUSTRATIONS.

Selected Design for Municipal Buildings, Bath.—Mr. J. M. Brydon, F.R.I.B.A., Architect .... *Extra Large Ink-Photo.*

Plans of New Municipal Buildings, Bath .... *Two Single-Page Photo-Litho's.*

Mosaics in St. Mark's, Venice.—From Drawings by Mr. Arthur C. Blomfield........ *Two Single-Page Ink-Photo's*

The Jew's House, Lincoln.—From a Drawing by Mr. A. H. Powell........ *Single-Page Ink-Photo.*

Design for "A Mountain Church."—Mr. George Ll. Morris, Architect .... *Single-Page Ink-Photo.*

Blocks in Text.

Plan of All Saints' Church, Hertford, destroyed by fire Dec. 21, 1891..........Page 31 | Diagrams in Student's Column: Heating by Hot Water .... Page 34

CONTENTS.

e Institute Suggestions for a Building Act 21

e Architecture of the Teutonic Order of Knights in Prussia .. 22

l Masters at Burlington House.......... 25

ily Life in the Ancient World ?.......... 26

tes 27

me Notes on the History of Enamelling 28

lected Design for the Municipal Buildings, Bath 30

saics in St. Mark's, Venice 30

e "Jew's House," Lincoln 30

"A Mountain Church".......... 30

Magazines and Reviews 30

Plan of All Saints' Church, Hertford.......... 31

Fixing Portable Ranges 31

The Sanitary Inspectors' Association.......... 32

The Polytechnic Institution 33

The Future Building Act for London.......... 33

Totnes Church.......... 33

Soft Tiles 33

Student's Column.—Warming Buildings by Hot Water, II....... 34

General Building News 35

Sanitary and Engineering News 35

Stained Glass and Decoration 36

Foreign and Colonial 36

Miscellaneous 36

Meetings.......... 37

Recent Patents 37

Prices Current of Materials 37

he Institute Suggestions for a Building Act.

HE Institute of Architects, as before noted, has issued a series of suggestions for a draft Bill for the codification and amendment of the Metropolitan Building ...cts. These suggestions were prepared in 890-91 by the Practice Standing Committee, nd were considered and adopted by the Council of the Institute on the 30th November, 891. The existing building regulations are rinted in one column and the proposed mendments or insertions in a parallel column, or more convenient reference and comparison.

In the course of some introductory remarks, it is suggested that the details of construction, which are subject to variation from me to time from different causes, but more specially on account of new inventions in uilding material or new methods of construction, should be omitted from the body of the .ct and placed in schedules as bye-laws which an be altered from time to time as may be lought desirable, without interfering with the eneral working of the Act or necessitating fresh gislation. This suggestion is so entirely in ccordance with common sense, and the necesty for such a provision has already been so ecisively shown in various instances, that we ay almost regard it as a foregone conclusion in nnexion with any fresh legislation on the ibject of building. Another general suggeson which is made, not in the introductory ntences, but in its place in the draft Bill, that the new Act should not be divided to parts—"The first part relating to the gulation and supervision of buildings; the cond part relating to dangerous structures" c. (Act of 1855), as such division "serves useful purpose." This we do not feel so re about. The more an Act for very multirious provisions is classified, the easier is it r those who have to obey it to find out hat is required of them in any special case, d that is certainly a "useful purpose."

Coming to the detailed suggestions of the aft, of which we only propose to notice a few of the most important, we are reminded on the second page of one of the curious oversights in our existing legislation, viz.: the absence of any direct or authoritative definition of a "building." "Building owners" are referred to, but with no definition of what it is that they own; "public buildings" are defined in reference to the qualifying adjective "public," but not in reference to the noun which it governs. The Institute of Architects therefore has the honour of attempting the first definition of a building for the purposes of legislation. This is the definition:—

"Building includes every erection comprising a cubical space defined by walls, piers, posts, or other structures, and a roof or other covering, whether such erection is wholly enclosed or not, and whether it is fixed on permanent foundations or not, and of whatever materials it is constructed, and for whatever purpose it is used or constructed or adapted (but so that this interpretation be not construed so as to exclude from the application of the term building as used in this Act any erection that would have been determined to be a building according to the true construction of this Act if this interpretation had not been inserted in this Act)."

The first part of the definition seems well worded and sufficiently comprehensive, and by the sentence "whether fixed on permanent foundations or not" any dispute about the nature of the foundation is no doubt barred. Still, as there is a distinct reference to "permanent foundations" and the reverse, we should have looked to find under the proper heading some definition of "permanent foundations," an expression which does not in itself convey a very distinct idea. But all we find under foundation is,

"Foundation shall mean that on which the walls piers and other supports of any building or other structure rest."

This is better than the sentence of 1878—"The term foundations shall mean the space immediately beneath the footings of a wall," which is very loose, inasmuch as a foundation is certainly not a "space." The word "other," however, is superfluous, because in the Draft Bill "structure" is already separately defined from "building" as follows:—

"Structure includes any wall or other erection and anything affixed to or projecting from any building wall or other erection."

It should have been "any building or structure," not "or other structure." That is only a detail of wording. Still, such inaccuracies of wording sometimes lead to disputes. And we should certainly wish to understand what a "permanent foundation" is, or rather what a "not permanent" one is.

But there is a more serious discrepancy between the above definition of a building and another clause in the draft; page 12, "Foundations and Sites of Buildings." We there read that

"Every building shall be enclosed with walls constructed of brick, stone, or other hard and incombustible substances, and the said walls shall rest on the solid ground, or upon a bressumer of fire-resisting material, or upon other solid substructure."

If every "building" shall be enclosed with walls constructed of brick, stone, &c., what becomes of the definition of a "building" as an erection "comprising a cubical space defined by walls piers posts or other structures, *whether such erection is wholly enclosed or not?*" The framers of the draft seem to have forgotten on page 12 what they had said on page 2. We presume what they meant to provide is that a building, *when it is enclosed*, should be enclosed "with walls constructed of stone, brick," &c; *i.e.*, it should not be enclosed with timber or lath and plaster walls. But as the wording stands the two sentences are contradictory.

What again is the value of that cunning-looking parenthesis appended to the clause defining a "building"? The clause aims at exactly defining a "building," and then follows a *caveat* that nothing should thereby escape being considered a building because it does not come under the terms of the definition. Then what is the use of the definition? Such cautionary clauses are only necessary when an Act is worded in loose and broad terms; but where there is an intention to define accurately, it is a confession of failure to fall back upon a vague expression about the "true construction of this Act." The definition is the "true construction" if it is a full precise definition. In this case we think it is; only some other clauses do not agree with it in terms.

To the original definition of "public building" the Draft adds some other classes (public bath-house, public gymnasium, &c.), but covers the whole, like the 1855 clause, with a general phase, "constructed or adapted to be used ordinarily or occasionally for any other public purpose." "Ordinarily or occasionally," it will be seen, is an important and indeed necessary addition.

"Sky-sign" is retained as at present in the definitions, but there appears a new definition of "wall sign," which will include the monstrous lettering often fixed upon buildings; and in a clause on page 15 we find it provided that no advertisement shall be set upon the face or in front of the external wall of any building in any street "except on frames or other construction of fire-resisting material," in "accordance with by-laws to be made by the Council in pursuance of this Act"; and the wholesome clause is added that "no such advertisement should be fixed to diminish the light from any habitable room." That would put an end to the late Mr. Barnum's compliment to us, that England was the only country he had been in where people were content to shut out the daylight from their dwellings for the sake of advertisement.

To return to the definitions, that of domestic building (a difficult expression to define) is well considered:—

"Domestic building shall mean (Class A) a building used, constructed, or adapted to be used wholly or principally for human habitation; (Class B) an outbuilding or stables appurtenant to a building of Class A or C whether attached thereto or not; and (Class C) a building used or constructed or adapted to be used wholly or principally for business offices or shops or any other building not being a public or a warehouse or domestic building of Classes A or B."

A "Habitable building" is a room in which a person passes the night, as distinct from a "Living room," "used for human occupation by day," which includes kitchen, scullery, and pantry (not larder). A separate definition of a "flat" is also given, and a definition of the often contested word "storey," which is full and satisfactory. The suggested definition of "site" is also better than that of 1878.

"Fire-resisting," in relation to material might perhaps have been relegated to a schedule. The definition includes concrete and allied materials, brick, terra-cotta and natural or artificial stone; iron, steel, or bronze, and "other material of similar character which the district surveyor may approve; and, for bressumers and posts, wood beams" of not "less depth and width in any part than 10 in." Should there not have been a difference made as to some kinds of woods? An oak post in this respect is a very different thing from a fir post, for instance. And it may be questioned whether stone should be included under "fire-resisting materials." It does not burn, it is true, but it is one of the first things to crack and become thereby useless for any purpose of upholding the structure.

In the list of buildings to be exempted from the operation of the Act one or two important modifications are suggested. The Bank of England is left exempt, but the exemption "shall not include any branch of such Bank erected in any other part of the metropolis." The Draft proposes the entire omission of the clause which exempts "the Inner Temple, the Middle Temple, Lincoln's Inn, Gray's Inn, Staple Inn, Furnival's Inn, or the close of the collegiate church of Saint Peter, Westminster."

The clause of 1855, which exempts any building "not exceeding in height 30 ft. . . . and distant at least eight from the nearest street or alley, and 30 ft. from the nearest buildings," has an important addition providing that no such building shall be exempt where it is erected on any estate laid out for building where it is intended to erect other buildings or to let or sell any ground "other than to the owner of such building" (not quite grammatical) "within the said distance of 30 ft." The exemption of greenhouses is proposed to be limited to those which do not exceed in area 300 ft., measured to the outside of the framing.

Another section of exemptions is to apply to the roofing over of open yards enclosed on one or more sides by buildings, and no yard so roofed over shall be deemed to be a building within the meaning of this Act. Then follows another clause which appears to clash with the definition of a "building" before referred to: "Sheds open on one or more sides may be erected if the roof be covered with fire-resisting material," &c. Now we look in vain for any definition of a "shed," and the words here used are equally applicable to a "building," considering that by the previous definition a building may be supported by "posts" and need not be enclosed at the sides to come under the definition. In that case what differentiates a "shed" from a "building"? Following this is a provision that external metal flue-pipes exceeding 10 ft. in length shall be inspected by the district surveyor every five years, and if in his opinion they are safe, a licence shall be granted for another five years.

A clause in regard to the alteration of buildings is suggested, providing that any exemption or privilege of building shall remain in force only so long as the building is retained for the special use on account of which or in respect of which it was exempted; and another important one follows in regard to the restoration of old buildings, which provides that when it is necessary to take down an ancient building and re-erect it in a more secure manner, then with the written consent of the Council such building may be re-erected as it was before, even if in contravention of the terms of the Act: it remains, in short, legally an ancient building, though newly erected; a provision which might certainly become necessary occasionally.

Clauses are suggested in modification of the existing clauses as to recesses in party walls, which define better what was probably intended but not properly expressed by the framers of the 1855 Act, stating distinctly not only that the backs of such recesses shall not be of less thickness than thirteen inches, but that "in no case shall the back of such recess be within four inches of the centre of the said wall." The loose wording of the old act in this respect has been the cause of much dispute and of much licence by builders who chose to construe it the way that suited their convenience. The clause as to chases in party walls is re-worded to a similar effect. Considerable additions are suggested to the clauses as to carrying up party walls above the roof; one dealing with a point hitherto overlooked, that where eaves or gutters not of fire-resisting material project beyond the face of the building, the party walls shall be corbelled out to an equal extent, and carried up to the height required by the Act as to other parts of the wall.

The most important additions after this are in regard to provision against danger from fires, one clause suggesting that the floors of every corridor, hall, or passage, as well as the stairs, in any building having a floor area exceeding three thousand six hundred square feet or containing more than fifty thousand cubic feet, shall be of fire-resisting material, which may however have wooden flooring on it "without an air space between." There follows on this an important clause on "egress from certain buildings," applicable to any building containing flats which has a greater floor area than five thousand feet, or where the greatest distance from the end of any corridor to a staircase in such building exceeds sixty feet, or wherever any warehouse contains any flat or other habitable rooms,—in all such cases the staircase shall be carried up to the roof and a portion of the roof, in no part less than 6 ft. wide, laid flat and with a railing for safety, to give access to another staircase of fire-resisting material; both such staircases to have communication with the street to afford means of egress in the event of fire. This is an important suggestion, and if carried out would make a great difference in the percentage of deaths from fires in inhabited buildings.

The portion of the Draft Bill now printed and circulated among Members of the Institute is that which deals with construction. The Practice Committee are still, we understand, at work on the subject, and in the further portions of the existing Acts many changes will be required "consequent on the foregoing revision of the first part as well as on the merits of the sections themselves." The "first part" means, we presume, the portions of the existing Acts which refer to the regulation and supervision of buildings, which formed the "First Part" of the Act of 1855: but it is not very clearly expressed. As far as the Institute revision has gone it appears to contain many excellent suggestions and to form a very good groundwork for a new Act, but like the existing Acts it fails sometimes from lack of clear definition in wording, which is a very important point in legislation dealing with a very complicated subject. The definition of a "building" certainly requires either revision or the modification of those clauses which at present clash with it. As the draft now stands there is room for a good deal of misunderstanding on the subject.

THE ARCHITECTURE OF THE TEUTONIC ORDER OF KNIGHTS IN PRUSSIA.

BY THE BARON DE GEYMÜLLER.

MEDIÆVAL castles, on the Continent at least, have been hitherto far less than other classes of monuments of the past the object of investigation by architects as well as by archæologists; no doubt, besides the ruined state to which wars and revolutions have generally reduced them, because, as dwellings and as fortifications many centuries old, they differ too much from the requirements of modern civilisation to be very suggestive to those who are in search of some inspiration for their own works.

But as documents for the history of architecture and civilisation, these habitations of a pre-eminent class of the nation are certainly important and worthy of consideration. It may, therefore, also interest some readers of the *Builder* to have their attention called to some recent German books treating of these subjects. An attentive examination of the two volumes published by Herr Steinbrecht,* a Prussian Government Architect, will soon show that even from their architectural merit, in the strict sense of the word, the buildings of the Teutonic Order offer not only considerable variety, but form an unexpected manifestation of Mediæval architecture, the importance of which, if I dare to judge from my own case, has not been suspected hitherto, even by the few who might have visited the celebrated Marienburg. The strict rules of a congregation and Power, at once military and religious, soon lead to a system and order which make their monuments differ considerably from the strongholds erected for the abode of feudal families.

The Teutonic Order was the third of the Christian Orders of Knights. Its origin was in 1190, during the siege of Acca, when citizens of Bremen and Lubeck, under the protection of Count Adolph, of Nassau, united with the brothers of the German hospital, which since 1128 existed at Jerusalem. Their object was twofold; the nursing of sick pilgrims and the defence of the Holy Land. Acca was the first home of the Order which received the same rights as the Templars and Knights of St. John. It had two classes of members; Knights and merciful brothers, later also priests. The Order under the fourth master, Hermann von Salza, the greatest statesman of the thirteenth century, became very powerful, had numerous possessions over Germany, Hungaria, Italy, and Sicily. Its help was then requested by the Duke Konrad of

* "Thorn im Mittelalter. Ein Beitrag zur Baukunst des deutschen Ritterordens." Berlin: Julius Springer, 1885. In folio, 45 pages of letterpress, with 39 illustrations and 14 plates on copper.

"Preussen zur Zeit der Landmeister, Beiträge zur Baukunst des Deutschen Ritterordens." Berlin. 1888. In folio, 128 of letterpress, and 184 illustrations.

assovia, against the heathen Prussians. ie Pope and the Emperor Frederic II., being vourable to this design, and the Culmer-
id having been assigned as the seat for the der, the Landmaster, Hermann Balk, was at (1230) with about ten Knights to begin e contest, which ended 1283 with the victory er the Prussians and their conversion.

If this undertaking did not, like those of e Orders in the East, meet with a resultless d, it is due to the merits of the Teutonic der, which completed the conquest, directed e colonisation of the country, founded wns and villages, and understood, for a long riod, how to direct and order wisely the inner d outer affairs of their dominion, which, at e time of its greatest power, extended from e Oder to the Gulf of Finland. To them so Prussia is indebted for the embankment the Vistula and Nogat.

Some buildings, it is true,—for instance, e celebrated Marienburg in Prussia, the ms of Königsberg and Frauenberg, the stle of Heilberg,—had been the object of ler as well as more recent publications. ie latter, due to Herr von Quast, had the erit of suppressing, by the minute examina- on of the Marienburg, the prevailing roneous opinions. One serious and im- rtant error continued, however, to mislead inion,—viz., that the principal architectural tivity of the Order was not anterior to the iddle of the fourteenth century. This idea mained at the bottom of all criticisms, and d to the belief that no remains of earlier ildings of any importance were to be found y more.

Professor Töppen, however, lately proved, r a series of documents concerning the stles of the Order, as well as those erected bishops, that if the Knights made a con- derable use of temporary constructions of ood and earth, wherever they had obtained solid footing, it was stone, and consequently onumental architecture, that they employed. lling the attention to an apparent contra- ction existing in the remarks of Herr von uast, according to which the oldest parts the Marienburg anterior, as generally mitted, to the year 1300, were far superior, hitecturally as well as technically, to the ts that had been added since by Dietrich Aldenburg (1335-41), he expresses the fident hope that a proper study of the herto neglected residences of the Order uld lead to the discovery of important ains of that earlier period, history ching that the oldest settlements of the ler are to be looked for on the border of intry on the right of the Vistula and on shore of the Haff, but, above all, in the lmerland and in the city of Thorn.

It must, therefore, be considered as a very ppy idea of the senate of the "Technische ochschule" at Berlin to propose in 1881, as eme for the Louis Boissonnet Prize, an tentive study of the buildings erected by e Teutonic Order in East and West Prussia, d principally those of the town of Thorn. ese countries have been hitherto little plored.

But before undertaking the minute study the monuments at Thorn, Herr Steinbrecht ought it advisable to visit throughout the intry the remains of the principal establish- nts of the Order, drawing their plans and ails, obtaining thus a precious source of truction.

These preliminary informations form part the first volume, whilst the second volume ntains a closer investigation and the exact wings of the more important of these numents erected during the period of vernment of the Landmasters. Among se, Culmsee has a Duomo of considerable ect, and a rich choir, partly of Romanesque le. Culm in its fortifications and by the im- rtance of its churches reminds us of Thorn; celebrated castle, the Althaus, distant one ur, was the first residence of the Land- sters, demolished in the last century.

Schwetz in the low country, accessible to e inundations of the Vistula, with a fine und angular tower and battlements.

Grandenz, from its elevated situation, was one of the strongest and most important castles; of this, one tower, the interesting Klimmek, alone remains.

From Grandenz, the three castles of Engelsburg, Rheden, and Roggenhausen are easily visited. The second of these, from its picturesque outline, its artistic value, its origin in the best period of the Order, and its never having been disfigured by later additions, is one of the principal places for the study of the architecture of the Order.

Riesenburg and Schöneberg are castles of the Bishop and the Chapter of the Duomo of Pomerania. Golub, situated very much out of the way, has changed little, offers numerous wood houses with low flat-arched arcades or loggie.

At Soldau begins the territory of the ancient Duchy of Prussia, and its buildings bear a different character. They belong to the later period of the Order, show a cheaper and more common art, have generally been transformed for modern use, and thus offer less interest to archæologists, but, on the other hand, by their often well-preserved general appearance, give an idea how grand an impression was produced in former days when the country, once possessed by the Order, was covered by many hundreds of such castles.

The Neidenburg, though erected for a mere bailiff, rises like a gigantic residence over the country. Heilsberg, in the heart of Ermland, is picturesque like a Thuringian place. Its castle, principal residence of the Bishop, has been sufficiently illustrated by one of H. von Quast's publications, and, though since then several changes have taken place, it is the castle in Prussia, which inside and outside, and by the preservation of the outer castle and surrounding parts, has best retained the noble and striking features of an "Ordensburg." The inner court has a beautiful Mediæval double-storied cloister.

The castle of Rastenburg is only small, but its St. George church rises like a citadel on the highest point of the town.

Batten, of considerable extent, well preserved in its general features, is of a late character, and from its chapel and other parts seems never to have been quite finished. More to the east one castle rises close to the other. Their transformation has seldom left more than the general plan, as is the case at Tapiau and at Tilsit, or some mere details or vaults, of archæological interest. Ragnit at least shows, besides its great extent, the energetic design of the façades.

In the border of land extending along the Frische Haff, once distinguished by a series of magnificent castles, such as those of Elbing, Brandenburg, Frauenburg, Balga, Königsberg, everything has been destroyed. At Lochsted alone a group of small rooms, elegantly vaulted, most likely the dwelling of its former lord, is left, likewise a chapel of extreme delicacy in design as well as care in execution; the terra-cotta ornaments of the old door can only be compared to those of the "golden gate" at Marienburg.

This exploration clearly proved that the castles of the south-east region belong, without exception, to the same and more recent epoch,—the second half of the fourteenth century. But in the oldest settlements, in the "Culmerland," along the Vistula and the Haff, differences of style corresponding to a period of about a hundred years backwards could be observed. Generally, it was not possible to fix the dates of the monuments in an isolated situation, on account of the want of documentary information. On returning to Thorn, a remedy was found for this latter deficiency. The monuments of this town units all the features observed separately in the castles of the places, and a rare abundance of documents given by the archives at the Town-hall enable one to fix the dates of building even unto the very details, and thus fixed points of comparison for dating the monuments all over the country were safely obtained, and an important step made concerning the historical as well as material knowledge of the architecture of the Teutonic Order.

In former times the valley of the Vistula was a broad, marshy, impracticable ground. In one single spot the higher banks approach on both sides of the river, an island rendering the passage easier. Here the Knights founded their castle, and the town of Thorn, as a base of operation for the conquest of the Culmerland. It was their first settlement beyond the Vistula.

From the very beginning the Order aimed at establishing a solid territorial dominion. For this German immigrants were necessary, the rights of the colonies settling under the protection of the castles were fixed 1233. Thorn and Culm, the two first towns, received the Magdeburgh municipal rights. Already (1264) the number of new colonists was so considerable that a new town (the "Neustadt") had to be founded outside the existing one, henceforth called the "Altstadt."

In the course of the fourteenth century Thorn became the first town of Prussia, the point of transit between Poland and the Baltic, and a member of the Hansa, and was called "The Queen of the Vistula." The old parish churches, the town-hall,—no more sufficient to satisfy the new circumstances,—had to be modified as well as amplified. After the defeat of the Order at Tannenberg (1410), and forty years of subsequent struggle, West Prussia was subsequently lost, and Thorn, after the so-called "war of the towns," renouncing its ties with the Order, became the chief head-quarters of the Prussian League, and put itself under the protection of the King of Poland. The peace of 1467 freed it from the hated yoke of the Order. From this period date the greater elevation given to the nave of St. John, and the building called "Junkerhof," erected on the place occupied until 1454 by the "Burg."

The return of Thorn to Prussia in our century has given new importance to this city, now the chief bulwark of the German Empire towards the east, a singular illustration as to the judicious choice made by the Teutonic Order of Thorn as a strategic situation.

The fortifications of Thorn are the oldest of the lower Baltic region, and are remarkable from the exceptional dimensions of their profile, gates, and towers. Herr Steinbrecht attributes this fact to the habits contracted by the Order in Syria. This opinion seems confirmed by another constant disposition in all the buildings of the Order. The ditch does not begin at the foot of the principal wall; it is separated from the latter by the "Parcham." This name is given, in the buildings of the Order, to a somewhat lower terrace all around the walls, protecting these against mining. Its battlements command the ditch and form a first line of defence. It comes from the προτειχισμα of the Byzantine engineers, which had been adopted in Frankish buildings in Syria. It was only by means of ancient views of the town that Herr Steinbrecht was able to restore the main features of this important castle. It rose on the right bank of the Vistula, at the upper end of the town, and outside its walls, beginning at the broad ditch of the Altstadt. Since the creation of the Neustadt, with its fortifications, the castle came to be partly situated between the two towns, preserving, however, an open space on the banks of the river, forming a new outer fortified precinct of considerable extent. The only parts of the castle actually existing are the "Dansker,"—a peculiar sort of tower, the explanation of which will be given further on,—and the building erected across the ditch containing the weir and all the contrivances for maintaining the water of the small river Bache in the ditch around the town and castle, when risen to the desired level. This castle contained seven outer courts or "Vorburgen," and, as Mr. Steinbrecht rightly observes, the Neustadt itself can be considered as a sort of outer "Burg." It was the first castle erected by the Order, begun in 1236, when the town of Thorn, founded five years before, was removed to its present site. When the war between the allied towns broke out, after a brave defence, it was

d

stormed by the citizens on February 7, 1454, and burnt down. This was the signal for the rising of the whole country.

The other buildings of Thorn which are the object of a complete description are the parochial church of St. John-in-the-Altstadt, its successive transformations being illustrated by four woodcuts, and St. Jacob-in-the-Neustadt, erected at the cost of the Order. In the former the three naves are equally high. A chromo-lithograph shows the effect of the green and yellow glazed ornaments of the choir of St. Jacob, with a frieze composed by an inscription with ornamental letters. St. Mary, the church of a Franciscan convent, shows original specimens of brick architecture.

The Town-hall (Rathaus) of the Altstadt, and several private houses, combine to give a very interesting idea of the buildings, which, like the whole town, owed their erection to the Teutonic Order, or to the impulse it had given.

In his second book, Mr. Steinbrecht describes twenty-two castles of the Order, in the districts of Culm, Pomerania, Natangen, and Samland. He deserves special credit for the clear and easy way in which he gives us, first, such historical and geographic informations as are necessary for the intelligence of the reader, the greater number of which are likely to feel otherwise strangers in the centres described.

The principal events of the history of the Order, before and since the conquest of Prussia; the state of the country before the arrival of the Knights; the history of the conquest, accompanied by two maps, are given in short, well-written chapters, and the volume finishes with two very interesting tables, the first giving the chronological succession of their foundation as strongholds of a temporary character, in earth and wood, and the dates of their transformation into permanent buildings of brick and stone. The second gives a comparative view of the composition of each castle, its superficial area, the dimensions of its most important elements, the character of its principal tower, and the position of the Dansker.

In some cases the outlines of the three castles, which generally composed the residences of the Knights, are preserved, or at least well recognisable, as is the case with Engelsburg and Balga. The outer castle, Vorburg, is the largest, then comes the middle castle (Mittlere Haus), finally the upper castle (Oberste Haus', Convents Haus).

The castles, according to their importance, were commanderies, district commanderies, and residences of the Landmeister, or governor of the whole dominion. Unfortunately, the palace of the latter, in the castle of Elbing, and since 1281 the principal of the Order, has totally disappeared. Since 1309 the "Hochmeister" of the Order established his residence in Prussia, instead of the Landmeister, and Marienburg became his abode. This celebrated castle is intended by M. Steinbrecht to form the subject of a separate monograph.

The strongholds which the Order erected in the conquered countries were destined, besides their strategical intent, to offer a shelter to the colonists. Under the protection of its walls, towns arise, the castle becomes the citadel of these cities, and it was the interest of the Knights to further order and prosperity of the new communities.

The flat configuration of the country certainly facilitated the development of the regular plans which are one of the striking features of these castles. Some are situated on the very shore of the sea, others on rivers or near lakes. When the position chosen for the castle offered an elevation of the ground, the outlines of the three different castles are quite irregular, following the lines of the ridge of the plateau. This is the case, for instance, at the Engelsburg, at Balga on the shore of the Frische Haff, and at Roggenhausen. In this latter case the area of the Schlossberg was sufficient to contain the second castle, and in it the upper house, which could receive a regular square plan; we see the same disposition at Mewe and Popau. This fact, combined with the circumstance that out of the twenty-two castles twelve show regular plans in the shape of a square, clearly illustrates that this disposition was considered by the Order as the best, whenever circumstances permitted its adoption. The square plan of Reden, preceded by two outer castles of less regular form, confirm this idea. At Lochsted, the upper and the middle castle each are on a square plan, separated by broad ditches from each other.

Generally inside the walls the four sides are surrounded by the different buildings, leaving a court-yard of regular form in the centre* buildings seem to have occupied only the two opposite sides of the square, being connected by lower galleries and the upper battlement.

In many cases the angles of the square are strengthened by four square towers, only slightly projecting, but rising to a moderate height above the battlement. Besides these towers sometimes a principal more important tower is added. At Reden it is octagonal and situated in one corner just behind one of the angular towers, which it commands by a far superior height. At Strasburg and at Mewe it takes the place of one of the four angular towers, whilst at Golub it was circular, and situated outside the square, in a diagonal position, quite close to one of the angular towers.

These hesitations as to the position of this tower, which may be considered as the doujon of the upper castle, in itself a sort of doujon, are worthy of notice. A very interesting example of such principal towers is that of Strasburg in the district of Culm. It is octagonal, of more than 10 mètres in diameter, 55 5 mètres high, with eleven stories inside, crowned by two terraces with battlements, the upper one of lesser diameter disposed around the conical roof. Strasburg shows another tower of an entirely different character erected over the Neumarker Gate in the town wall, showing above two storeys with windows one of those high gables frequent in Northern Germany, with several retreating storeys, separated by buttresses, ending in pinnacles, and dividing interspaces decorated like high and narrow windows. Roggenhausen exhibits another type of towers over a doorway. It is square, of imposing dimensions, of a simple but noble architecture. From what remains of the principal tower of Grandenz Castle, called "Der Klimek," it must have been interesting example of the round type.

Another disposition considered as belonging exclusively to the castles of the Teutonic Order is the so-called "Dansker," consisting in an isolated square tower, at a certain distance from the walls of the upper castle, situated on the slope of its eminence, or in the lowest part of the neighbourhood, opposite the side of the principal attack, and sometimes (as at Thorn) built on four piers, between which passes the running water coming from the water-mills. This tower is connected with the castle by a narrow corridor between battlements passing over lofty arches. For a considerable time the exact use of these "Danskers" seems not to have been fully understood. It was believed that they were intended to permit a final escape by the chimney-like descent they contain, or to attack from behind the enemy fighting near the foot of the castle-walls. But Mr. Steinbrecht tells us that their real use was much more prosaic, and that Professor Töppen † has proved them to have contained the privies destined for the numerous inhabitants, which the Knights were desirous of isolating as much as possible from the dwellings. Various examples of this disposition are those at Thorn, Lochstedt, Marienburg, &c.

In the second publication we notice, amongst the most interesting features, the plan of the town of Culm, showing all the streets at right-angles and equidistant, like many ultra-modern cities.

* As at Popau, Leipe, Schönsee, Golub, Reden, Strasburg, Elbing, Mewe, Brandenburg.

† Töppen, "Geschichte von Marienwerder," page 190, and Cohausen, "Bonner Jahrbücher," xviii., 22-25.

In considering the composition of the upper castle in the greater number of these strongholds, we feel that their architectural fundamental idea is similar to the peculiar character of their builders: warriors and monastic brothers at once. Unless admitting that the generally square form of the outer walls be some reminiscence of the Roman Castrum, it seems more natural to derive it from the square form of the cloister of the convent, around which are grouped chapel, chapter-room, refectories, dormitories, the dwelling of the commander, and so on. And consider the similitudes of composition existing between a great number of these castles, and forming, if we do not misunderstand the illustrations of Herr Steinbrecht's volume, a type of peculiar character, we feel inclined to ask whether the architects who built them did not belong themselves to the Order, following precise rules and principles of their own, and of experience far superior to what could be met with in the architects of Northern Germany.

The system of decoration of the monuments erected by the Teutonic Order is closely connected with the style adopted in the marches of Brandenburg, and illustrated many years ago by the publications of Professor F. Adler.* However, if we are not mistaken, the monuments of the Order, besides the special types of its castles, generally show a nobler and more powerful scale of proportions with greater elegance and signs of a more refined taste, which very likely are due to Southern and Arab influence which some way or other the Order contrived to preserve in the earlier period, at least, of its monumental creations. This seems to be also Mr. Steinbrecht's opinion, and he considers the examples of inscriptions with ornamental letters employed as decorations as a reminiscence of Arabian art hardly met with in Western Europe, except in the buildings of the Teutonic Order. (Vol. i., pl. ix., and Vol. ii., figs. 166 and 168).

The materials in which these monuments are erected, generally speaking, are bricks and terra-cotta. Popau, however, is built in random blocks of granite in layers from 50 centimètres to 1 mètre in height, with ornaments of hewn stone. In many cases the walls are decorated by various courses of glazed bricks,—Reden, Strasburg, Mewe, and, particularly, the Marienburg show examples of this system. The details of terra-cotta are generally obtained from moulds, and similar to those adopted in the marches of Brandenburg and northward, generally red alternating with green or yellow. Some of these forms, according to their disposition, permit of various patterns, for instance, in the village church at Balga. In other cases, according to Mr. Steinbrecht, the beautiful details of the Marienburg and some at Lochstedt have been obtained by a process described by him on a previous occasion,† consisting in artificial blocks of clay in which the ornaments are sculptured when dry and before being burnt.

These Italian and Arabian features can, I believe, nowise astonish if we reflect tha[t] the conquest of Prussia was begun unde[r] the Grand-Masterdom of Hermann von Salz[a]. This high-minded and noble statesman an[d] warrior was the friend and constant coun[-]sellor of the Emperor Frederic II. Both, it is well known, resided more in souther[n] Italy and Sicily than in Germany. Thei[r] constant intercourse with the East, an[d] Frederic's Body Guard of Saracens, suffic[e] to explain the source of such influences which may be supposed to have been eve[n] stronger in the earliest monuments, th[e] Althaus, Culm; and Elbing, the capital o[f] the New Dominion and the first Residence o[f] the Landmaster. Their total destructio[n] must be considered as an irreparable loss, th[e] more to be regretted since it becomes eviden[t]

* "Mittlalterliche Backstein-Bauwerke des Preu[s]sischen Staates," in fol. Berlin, 1860, and "Der Urspru[ng] des Backsteinbaues in den Baltischen Ländern," Berli[n] 1884; in 4to.

† "Centralblatt der Bauerwaltung," Berlin v[.] p. 391.

that, besides all the remarkable features alluded to, the superior qualities displayed in the composition of all the dispositions of the plan of these convent-castles are, perhaps, an unique phenomenon in the architecture of the Middle Ages, and, as such, may be considered as partly monuments of the genius of that extraordinary and unique Prince, Frederic II. of Hohenstaufen.

All these qualities, rarely found, I am inclined to believe, to such an extent in German monuments, seem united in the noblest way and with a superior degree of artistic skill in the north front of the Upper Castle at Marienburg.

It measures about 52 mètres length, and may be called majestic. Besides the tall corner towers, of Italian or Arab elegance, rising three stories above the battlements, with delicate tracery windows and arched friezes, the façade shows three unequal divisions in its length, corresponding to the chapel, the chapter-room, and the entrance. The latter, from its considerable height of above 14 mètres, reminds one somewhat of the imposing entrance-gates of Indian and Persian mosques. The large windows of the chapter-room, the still larger ones of the chapel, contrast beautifully with the broad surfaces of unbroken wall, the far smaller and rare windows of secondary rooms, and the regular openings of the crenelles (creneaux) of the battlement, decorated with shields. The monotony of the high brick-walls is cleverly avoided by a moderate use of glazed and coloured bricks, with dispositions reminding one in some places of oriental influence.

Herr Steinbrecht intends to close the exploration of these interesting buildings by a special monograph of this important residence, the restoration of which, if I am not mistaken, has been confided to him. By the way in which he has accomplished the task that was put into his hands, he has brought to our notice monuments of remarkable and, I dare say generally, unexpected qualities, well deserving the attention of those who, besides the mere architectural interest, are accustomed to read in the character of its monuments the reflection of the great deeds of history. He thus exhibits in a new light some of the characters of that once mighty Order, which, far weaker at its origin than the Templars and the Order of St. John, finally achieved results of a far more lasting and important nature, since, with the Margraves of Brandenburg, they are considered now as the founders of the Kingdom of Prussia.

H. VON GEYMÜLLER.

OLD MASTERS AT BURLINGTON HOUSE.

HE twenty-third loan exhibition of "Works by the old masters and by deceased masters of the British School," at Burlington House, is very unequal in interest, and betrays the difficulty which for the last few years has evidently been felt in keeping up these exhibitions to anything like their old level of interest, without repetitions. As we have before suggested, when the twenty-fifth exhibition has been held, and one generation may be said to have passed away, it is to be hoped that a new generation of owners will be asked and will consent to lend their greatest possessions in painting, already exhibited five and twenty years before, for the delight of a new generation of visitors who have had no experience of the glories of the earliest loan exhibitions of this series.

A good deal of the interest of the present exhibition resides in the landscapes, the comparison of which suggests besides some reflections as to the intellectual ends of landscape-painting, and the nature of the pleasure to be derived therefrom. Opposite to each other in the first room, for instance, hang a landscape of Müller's "Eel-bucks at Goring" (11), and one of F. Walker's, "Sunny Thames" (32). Are either of these two really like nature? And are they scenes on the same planet? We might allow an affirmative to the latter question, but certainly not to the former. Müller's picture (which at a first glance might be taken for a Constable) is a tremendous sketch of wonderful vigour, on the back of which we are told the painter has written "Left as a sketch for some fool to *finish* and ruin." Müller was right from his point of view; the picture is a most powerful piece of "impressionism," and the effect of it on the spectator arises in great measure from the sense it gives of the artist's power and freedom in recording his impression. As an actual representation of nature it is exaggerated in general effect and coarse in detail; it does not represent the scene, but the effect the scene produced on Müller's mind. Walker's painting is unlike nature in a totally opposite sense. Müller's scene is cold in tone and with a violent opposition of lights and shadows. Walker's is suffused by a warm quiet light in which the sky, the banks, and the stream are all harmonised. Walker never really saw bank and water and figures all in that suffused kind of pervading glow, but he saw them so in his sentiment, and the painting is the effect of the scene on his mind. So with Cotman's grand landscape (35), a poetic composition made up on the basis of an effect in nature. Bonington's "Coast Scene" (18) is far more like a real scene than any of these; it is managed nicely no doubt; the lights and shadows and half-tones are obsequiously in their places as regards the general composition; but still it is like an actual scene of the kind; it is real, not transcendental. Yet it must be admitted that it is a weak work in comparison with any of the three previously mentioned, and the pleasure it gives is weak also. There are more materials in the room for a "Philosophy of landscape-painting." Look at Richard Wilson's "Snowdon from Nantlle" (40), cut out of cardboard, as it were, and painted up like a theatre "flat." What a lesson on the debilitating effect of a constant course of "classical landscapes."

Both (48) and Hobbema (66, 67, 71) give their views of landscape also, the reduction of a landscape painting to a single recipe. Mr. Morrison's Paul Potter, "Carriage at a Roadside Inn" (89), is a nice little picture worth attention as a curiosity, being so unlike the typical Paul Potter, who is represented a few feet off by a very typical work, the "Young Bull" (94) from the Buckingham Palace collection. In the large room one of the places of honour is occupied by a landscape, Constable's "Opening of Waterloo Bridge" (137). As far as the foreground is concerned Constable, too, is here seen as an impressionist; he gives up the prosaic details of the sentinels and the caparisoned people in the barges, but raises the whole into a rich play of colour; and what a rich texture, too, in the architectural details of the foreground, and what a broad and airy light over the middle distance and the famous bridge. It is not like the real event probably, but it is worth a great deal more than any realistic transcript could have been. In the same room is a remarkably fine Turner, "The Lake of Geneva" (108), in his best period; his "Petworth House" (133) is one of the "pretty" Turner's, not to be despised in their way; his "Seapiece," (131) lent by Lord Leconfield, is another matter; "agitated sea" it is described in the catalogue, and so indeed it is—"agitated" in a way no sea ever was except in a picture of Turner's. One must not bow down blindly before even a great painter when he misrepresents nature in this way. As to the colour and texture of the waves, too, interrogations might be made; but we do not know how the present aspect of the canvas represents its original state.

Of the figure pictures the portraits are (as usual of late years) the strongest part, excepting the Earl of Dudley's Raphael, "The Crucifixion" (151) in Gallery IV. This is one of the pictures which makes one comprehend the feeling expressed by Ruskin and others as to the "Paganism" of Raphael. In this graceful composition we have the tragedy of the Crucifixion of Christ treated "in a decorative manner"; the Magdalene and St. Jerome kneel on each side in symmetrical pose, St. John and the Virgin stand behind in the same symmetrical manner, the cross in the centre; two small angels flutter in conventional attitudes beneath the arms of the cross, and their long fluttering ribands help to fill up otherwise empty space in the composition. In colour and grace of drawing the picture is a fine example of Raphael's work, but it is an extraordinary instance of the subordination of feeling and pathos to mere decorative effect. The painting by Lucas van Leyden opposite to it, "The Adoration of the Magi" (171) from the Buckingham Palace collection, is a fine and powerful work in its combination of gorgeously-clad figures with strange and abnormal piles of architecture in the background. Among the other works in Gallery IV., where as usual the older Italian paintings are collected, are to be noted Lucas Cranach's "Virgin and Child" (174) exquisite in the soft though formal beauty of the faces, which however have surely been freshened up to some extent; Da Vinci's "Virgin and Child" (165); and Sandro Botticelli's profile portrait of a girl in a red dress (144), a beautiful example of this type of art. Piero della Francesca's "Virgin and Child with Angels" (149) shows an interesting study of Renaissance architecture as a background.

Among the more modern pictures Reynolds's "Death of Dido" (105) occupies the centre position at the top of Gallery III.; a composition fine in colour and tragic in feeling, but undeniably theatrical. The curious decorative picture by Rubens and Snyder which hangs opposite to it, "Cupids, Fruit, and Flowers" (126), is a very fine work of its kind; the cupids by Rubens form an admirably painted group seated on the ground in the centre, Snyder's "swags" of fruit &c. hang across the upper part of the picture, and are painted with great force; the whole is a very fine piece of colour. Tintoretto is represented by two portraits of senators and by his "Apollo and Marsyas" (117), in which the figure of Apollo, with laurel branching round his head, and his right hand extended with the bow ready to commence playing his viol,* is a figure of remarkable beauty and a kind of godlike energy, which, indeed, seems to strike Marsyas, who is holding his own pipe away from his mouth, and anxiously awaiting Apollo's performance. Andrea del Sarto's "Virgin and Child" (121) is a charming example of that finish and balance of colour and composition which distinguished him who was called "the perfect painter." Mr. Beaumont's Giorgione, "The Adoration of the Shepherds" (112) is interesting more from the quaintness of the conception and the treatment of the landscape and buildings than from the qualities generally most characteristic of Giorgione.

Of the Dutch pictures, collected as usual in the second room, the finest is Teniers's "Man and Woman in a Cowhouse" (82), which is painted with great delicacy in every detail and is a fine specimen of Teniers in one of his "finishing" moods. The other Teniers near it, "Old Woman Consulting a Doctor" (87: lent, like the last-named, by Mr. Morrison), is admirable for the character of the two figures, especially in the scrutinising countenance of "The Doctor"; the picture is interesting also as illustrating an old superstition of the doctor's craft, mentioned in Shakspeare, but about which the catalogue is necessarily silent, and we must imitate its reticence. The picture by Maes, from the Buckingham Palace collection (85), is, like some others of the Dutch selection, a kind of second-best edition of what the painter has done better in other works; this part of the collection is not up to its usual level of interest. A Watteau in the same room, "L'Accordée du Village" (43) is curious for its resemblance

* Not "cithara," as stated in the catalogue. A cithara was played by snapping the strings with the fingers; "zither" is the modern form of the word. What Apollo is playing in the picture is the viol, an early form of the violin.

to the grouping and even the colour of Stothard (or Stothard's resemblance to it).

Among the portraits Gainsborough's "Mrs. Portman of Bryanston" (9) is a noble specimen of his powers: the lady is seated in an ample "white dress trimmed with lace," as the catalogue hath it, but in reality the very point of the matter is that there is no real white in it; Gainsborough knew better than that. The head is relieved against a crimson and flowered screen or curtain behind in half light; the "white" dress is just warmed sufficiently to harmonise and not clash with this; the whole has a grand unity about it. Raeburn's bust portrait of "Mrs. Smith of Jordanhill" (5) is a charming work; so also Romney's "Hon. Charlotte Clive" (36), in a pale yellow dress and reclined in a beautifully composed attitude. Romney's "Countess of Derby" (27), in a white dress and with a hand touching her chin, is still more delicate and graceful, though not so striking in colour as the former. Perhaps Romney's finest work here is "Mr. and Mrs. Lindow" (132), the husband seated and the wife standing by him, grouped so as to compose admirably without the slightest look of posing, and admirable also for the harmonious treatment of rather subdued colours in the two costumes; "a blue dress" Mrs. Lindow's is called in the catalogue, but it is something a great deal more subtle than that. Of a very different kind of power is Van Dyck's superb full-length of "The Earl of Portland" (123), one of the most remarkable impersonations of manly and aristocratic dignity ever realised even by Vandyck. A good Frank Hals is hung near this (124), and Rubens's remarkable portrait of the "Marchesa Isabella Grimaldi" (125) in her bridal dress; she married the Doge Doria, and her appearance and attire are worthy of so resplendent a match; the work is a superb example of what may be called the sumptuous or decorative order of family portrait.

The Water-colour Room and Black and White Room contain a fine series of water-colours, some of them well known (such as Cox's "Welsh Funeral"). There is a beautiful collection of William Hunt's works, especially fruit and flower subjects. A number of Turner's sketches and original drawings for vignettes and book illustrations are there, including the curious but certainly imaginative illustrations which he made for Egerton Brydges' edition of Milton; also a large number of sketches and studies by Cotman, which show him in the light of an architectural as well as a landscape artist. Turner's large and beautiful water-colour of "Fonthill" (19) is the culminating point of what is certainly not the least interesting section of the Old Masters Exhibition.

DAILY LIFE IN THE ANCIENT WORLD.

THE translator of Becker's "Gallus" says in his preface, "The idea of making an interesting story the basis of his exposition, and of thus 'strewing with flowers the path of dry antiquity,' is most judicious. We have here a flesh-and-blood picture of the Roman, as he lived and moved, thought and acted, worth more, a thousand times more, than the *disjecta membra*, the dry skeleton, to be found in such books as Adam's 'Roman Antiquities,' and others of the same nature, which, however erudite, are vastly uninviting." What Becker, with so much applause from his contemporaries, did for the daily life of ancient Greece and Rome, M. G. Maspéro, the distinguished Orientalist, and late Director of Archæology at Cairo, has essayed to do for the daily life of ancient Egypt and Assyria.* Whether the method of writing employed by the French, as well as by the German author, is the best which could be chosen for imparting knowledge, is a subject on which a word must be said later on, but if the method be accepted, much praise may be given to M. Maspéro for the able fulfilment of his task.

* "Life in Ancient Egypt and Assyria," from the French of G. Maspéro. London: Chapman & Hall. 1891.

We have here presented to us in one small volume the essence of a vast amount of widely-ranging investigation, including much original research, as well as comparison of the work of other labourers in the same field, and its publication ought to add considerably to popular acquaintance with two of the most remarkable nations of the ancient world. New and striking historical revelations are not, indeed, to be looked for here; the general aspect, both of Egyptian and of Assyrian society, is too well known for anyone to be able to astonish us by fresh accounts of their peculiarities, but any attempt to spread and render easier the acquisition of accurate knowledge of the ordinary conditions of life in former states of civilization is of great educational value. There are few phases of modern life, with which correspondences, often very instructive, may not be found in the pages before us, and without venturing into the deeper questions of religious and political organizations, a few matters of social interest may be noted, to give an idea of the variety of information which M. Maspéro has brought together.

Few subjects will have been so frequently in the minds of readers of this journal during the last few months as strikes of workmen, but neither the organisers nor the victims of our strikes need either flatter or bemoan themselves that they are better or worse off than were the citizens of Thebes three thousand years ago. We may read here,—

"Suddenly a great noise is heard at one end of the street, the crowd is violently opened, and about a hundred workmen, shouting, gesticulating, covered with clay and mortar, force their way through, dragging in the midst of them three or four frightened, piteous-looking scribes. These are the masons employed on the new buildings of the Temple of Mut, who have just gone on strike, and are now on their way to lay their grievances before Fearou, governor of the city, and general superintendent of the king's works. These small riots are not rare, they spring from misery and hunger. The greater portion of the wages consists of wheat, dhoura, oil, and rations of food, which the masters usually distribute on the first day of every month, and which ought to last until the first of the month following. The quantity allotted to each man would certainly suffice if it were economically used; but what is the use of preaching economy to people who reach home in a famished condition, after a day of hard work in which they have only eaten two cakes, seasoned with a little muddy water, about twelve o'clock? During the first days of the month, the family satisfy their hunger without sparing the provisions; towards the middle the portions diminish, and complaints begin; during the last week famine ensues, and the work suffers. If we consult the official registers of the scribes in the workyards, or simply the books of the overseers, we shall find notes in the end of each month of frequent idleness, and, at times, of strikes produced by the weakness and hunger of the workmen. Is their pay insufficient, or have they eaten their supplies unreasonably quickly? According to their own accounts, the scribes give them short measure, and enrich themselves by the robbery. On the other hand, the scribes accuse the poor fellows of improvidence, and assert that they squander their wages as soon as they receive them. No one could be astonished if both scribes and masons were found to be right."

It is often imagined that in ancient monarchies the occupations of soldier or priest were the only roads to riches and greatness, but in Egypt, at any rate, the "Civil Service" was highly esteemed, and its members often very prosperous; indeed, the attainments of an ordinary clerk might bring a man quite to the top of the social scale, as, after hearing of the education of a "scribe," we read:—

"His children will follow in the same path, and their children after them; there are whole dynasties of scribes, the members of one family having succeeded to the same posts for a century or more. Sometimes one of them, more intelligent or more ambitious than the others, makes an effort to rise above the usual mediocrity; his good writing, happy choice of words, activity, obligingness, and honesty,—perhaps, on the other hand, his prudent dishonesty,—attract the attention of his superiors and secure his advancement. Cases have been seen of the son of a peasant or of a poor citizen, commencing by booking the delivery of bread or vegetables in some provincial office, and ending, after a long and industrious career, by governing one-half of Egypt. The rooms of his barns overflow with corn; his storehouses are full of gold, valuable stuffs, and precious vases; his stable 'multiplies the backs' of his oxen, and the son of his first protector dare only approach him with his face bent to the ground, dragging himself upon his knees."

A curious parallel between the customs of modern London and ancient Thebes may be traced in the illustrations representing the royal chariot-horses, which have their heads as cruelly tied-in by tight bearing-reins as any unlucky horse to be seen now in a fashionable carriage; another, from which divers morals may be drawn, is shown by the statements that "beer-shops drove an excellent trade," and "beer has always been the favourite beverage of the people," in spite of "the moralists who cannot find words strong enough to express the danger of it."

Building, except in the case of temples, is described as being in Egypt a very simple and inexpensive operation. After an account of a disastrous hurricane, which has utterly wrecked every house in the district, we are told that:—

"Elsewhere such a catastrophe would entail utter ruin; here one or two weeks of labour suffice to repair it all. As soon as the rain has ceased, the whole population,—men, women, and children,—exert themselves, and hasten to draw from the rubbish the wood, provisions, and utensils that have resisted the inundation, then from the diluted mud of the old buildings they make new huts, which the sun quickly dries and cracks in all directions. Two days later no traces of the accident remain. A little more time and labour are required to rebuild the houses of the better classes. Two or three labourers go down to the nearest pool, and collect pailfuls of mud from the bottom, heap it upon the bank, knead it, mix it with gravel and finely-chopped straw, and press it into wooden moulds, which an assistant carries away and empties out into the sunshine. In a few hours the bricks are ready for use, and the building is commenced. No one thinks of clearing the ground or of digging foundations; the people are satisfied with levelling the rubbish, and placing the first bricks loosely upon the kind of bed they have thus prepared. A fortnight later the ground-floor is closed and roofed in, the family re-enter the dwelling with their cattle, and live in it whilst the upper story is being completed."

Turning to Assyria, we get some glimpses, in the second portion of the book, of the architecture of that country, from which it appears that private houses, just as in Egypt, were not built in a manner calculated for long endurance, and were also studiously devoid of any outward show. The art of building was evidently thought much of by the ruling orders of the Assyrians, for we read that "the bricks destined for public buildings are holy, and can be made only at certain seasons. They are prepared under the auspices of a particular god, Sivan, lord of foundations, and only during the month to which he gave his name;" and also that before beginning a new palace, the king, after sacrifices, and with great solemnity, prayed that "Sivan and his father, Bel, the architect of the universe, would consent to direct the works." But their architecture was almost entirely confined to palace-building, for their temples, unlike the great independent establishments of the Egyptian priesthood, were only what might be called chapels-royal, included in the general group of palace-buildings, and occupying a comparatively small corner of the inclosure; of which, however, they were often very conspicuous features, being built of tower-like form, and decorated with lavish wealth of ornament.

The Assyrian, or as it might more properly be called, the Chaldean, method of land transfer, is well known as having been brought to a system of elaborate completeness, and a specimen is given of a deed of conveyance of an arable field, though some other extant documents, relating to the purchase of town-property, are still more interesting, and show that surveying must have been an important profession amongst the inhabitants of the father-land of geometrical science. The plan adopted in these transfers for recording the particulars of sale and for guarding against subsequent attempts at fraud was extremely ingenious. The documents were inscribed on clay tablets, which, when sealed both with the seals of the contracting parties and the judge before whom all such transactions had to be performed, were placed in an oven and converted into almost indestructible bricks. But to prevent any tampering with them, besides taking the precaution of making three copies, the third of which was deposited with a royal notary, "the tablet, once sealed, was covered with a second layer of clay, upon which they traced an exact copy of the original deed. The latter thus became inaccessible to forgers, and if a dispute arose, and some alteration was suspected in the visible test, the enclosing tablet was broken before witnesses, and the deed was verified by the original writing preserved inside."

The translator's work (by Miss Norton) is very well done, and is not disfigured by those too literal interpretations of French phrases which make many translations look so awkward; but a few curious words, some of them probably only printer's errors, should be noted for correction, *e.g.*, "which *respond* to our cardinal points," "have faith in formulas and *talismen*;" "the head of a *cynophelus*;" "the Phœnician merchant-ships have at many points *stable* establishments;" "rising with bowed *spine* and drooping arms;" ("spine" is frequently used for "back") and "the experience acquired in navigation upon *soft* water, enables them to dispense with a long apprenticeship upon the sea," a most original use of the word "soft" as applied to water. The illustrations, though rather roughly executed, are all to the point, and greatly add to the interest of the book, which will probably achieve some success, although there already exist many others on the same subjects which might be thought better suited for English readers. It belongs to a peculiar, nondescript class of writings hitherto more popular in France than in this country, a good deal resembling the "architectural novelette" of Viollet-le-Duc, and, like that, being neither plain history nor an antiquarian treatise, nor yet a real story, but attempting to combine all three, having enough air of fiction to spoil the reality of the historical portion, and enough antiquarian detail to make it unreadable as a tale, and unconnected as a chronicle. The student of history or antiquities would probably prefer to enjoy his facts without the uncomfortable feeling of unreality which the method of presenting them gives him at every turn, while the ordinary reader, who cannot endure a book unless it contains a story, could not possibly be beguiled by such a thin film of narrative into wading through what is practically a dictionary of antiquities, heavy with the minutest erudition. We believe that the enthusiastic student will still prefer to go straight to the works of Wilkinson and Layard, which in popular editions are now easily accessible; while the more numerous class of readers who for a picture of Roman life would turn rather to the pages of "The Last Days of Pompeii," than to those of "Gallus," will still find their best realisation of the ancient world in such books as Ebers' "Uarda," or Whyte-Melville's still more romantic "Sarchedon."

NOTES.

WE regret to hear of the death of the venerable M. Bailly, Member of the Institut de France and President of the "Société des Artistes Français," and long an honoured name among contemporary French architects. He was eighty-two at the time of his death, and in spite of his great age, and of the illness which finally carried him off, and which two months ago prevented his attendance at the annual meeting of the Académie des Beaux-Arts, he pursued his studies almost to his last hour. Antoine Nicolas Bailly was born at Paris in 1810 and was a pupil of Debret and of Duban, and in 1834 was attached to the municipal administration as an Inspecteur. Ten years later he was appointed "Architecte du Gouvernement," and then diocesan architect at Bourges, Valence, and Dignes, and restored the churches in these ancient towns with great ability and erudition. He was subsequently appointed "Architecte-en-chef des travaux d'entretien" to the Paris municipality. At the close of the Empire he retired from this post with the title of "Inspecteur-Général Honoraire." Independently of the work which he carried out at the Hôtel de Ville under Godde and Lesueur, he also carried out the Mairie of the Fourth arrondissement, and the Lycée St. Louis at Paris, the Tribunal de Commerce, the restoration of the house of Jacques Cœur at Bourges, &c. He was a Commander of the Legion of Honour and received medals at various exhibitions. He replaced Labrouste as member of the Académie des Beaux-Arts. He took an active part in the foundation of the "Société des Artistes Français," where his zeal, impartiality, and amiability of character secured him general regard, and his loss is regretted by a large circle of friends.

IF ever a peerage is the fit reward for scientific eminence, never was that distinction better bestowed than on Sir William Thomson. The days are past when a man could say with Bacon, "I have taken all knowledge to be my province"; nor is it now possible even to so take all science, but Sir Wm. Thomson may justly claim to have taken all *physical* science as his province, and there are few who can rival him in any one branch of it. Go where you will, we find traces of his restless activity. Every telegraph office is stocked with instruments of his invention; a large part of London is lighted by dynamo machines which are modifications of one of his; and in the test-rooms of all the installations in the world the most accurate instruments are his also. We go to sea, and we find the means of taking soundings without stopping the ship, designed by Sir William Thomson; we arrive in port and find the height and time of the tides predicted by Sir William Thomson's tidal clock. Perhaps we are interested in questions of speculative science,—the age of the earth,—the constitution of matter, and the size of its ultimate molecules,—the origin of life on the earth and its probable duration,—none of these questions can be adequately discussed without mention of his name, and on some of them he is the only authority. In collaboration with Professor Tait he has written what is generally accepted as *the* text-book on Natural Philosophy, and some of the most brilliant mathematical investigations we have ever seen are due to him. When the history of science in the nineteenth century comes to be written, three names will stand out pre-eminent, those of Faraday, Darwin, and Sir William Thomson.

THE new volume of the *Transactions* of the Institute of Architects forms certainly one of the best practical answers which could be supplied to the charge brought against that body recently of being indifferent to the artistic side of architecture. With the exception of the paper, "A tour in the United States," by Mr. Cox (who, as holder of the Godwin Bousary, was under a special undertaking to direct his attention to practical construction), the whole volume, with its copious and in many cases beautiful illustrations, deals entirely with architecture in its artistic aspect. The volume includes Mr. Phené Spiers's copiously illustrated paper on "Sassanian Architecture"; Baron de Geymüller's essay on "The School of Bramante," one of the most valuable recent contributions to the study of the architecture of the Renaissance; Mr. Starkie Gardner's paper on "Wrought Ironwork" of the Mediæval period; Mr. Simonds's paper on "Some Aspects of Sculpture considered in relation to Architecture"; Mr. W. Simpson's paper on "Origin and Mutation in Indian and Eastern Architecture"; and papers by Mr. Brydon, Mr. W. B. Richmond, and Mr. Westlake, on "Decorative Painting." Mr. Somers Clarke's paper on the "Fall of a central Pillar at Seville Cathedral" may be said to partake both of archæological and structural interest, and is of value as coming from an architect who had special opportunities of studying the results of the catastrophe on the spot. Some of the authors are not members of the Institute, but that they should be invited to read papers on branches of art with which they were specially acquainted certainly does not argue indifference to the art of architecture on the part of those who invited them. The whole volume is one of the best and most interesting which the Institute has put forth, and the illustrations alone should give it a high value to all students of architecture.

IN the *Times* of the 6th Mr. Holman Hunt writes to call attention to a matter which may well make the whole artistic world feel a shiver of apprehension. Visiting the Campo Santo at Pisa the other day, Mr. Hunt saw an erection evidently raised for some painter's convenience, and on inquiry found it was not for the harmless exercise of copying the frescoes, but for an artist engaged in *repainting* the figures! Mr. Hunt adds—

"I was able to see that this meant the blackening of the celestial purity of colour, and the muddling of every delicate form in the innocent drawing of the figures. It is not disrespectful to the painter to say this, for surely no living master could trust his hand to improve a surface on which time, where he has been able to weaken, has had no power to unspiritualise the traits.

It is true that the work remaining has to risk peril of effacement, but this danger would surely be more wisely met, and it has been in other cases in this country, by covering the surfaces with sheets of glass, or even by glazing all the open spaces in the cloister. Should it be urged that the original strength of colour should be renewed, surely this might best be done on copies carried first to the existing pitch of strength and then enforced at discretion."

If there were no alternative, it would be better to take copies for preservation and let the originals die out, as in the long run they must. What is their value, artistically or historically, when "repainted"? It is one of the saddest and most hopeless pieces of news of the kind that we have heard of for some time back. Mr. Holman Hunt's letter, we may add, merits all the more attention because it is written calmly and judicially, and without that hysterical kind of exaggeration in which those who deplore restoration are too often wont to indulge, and which tends to defeat its own end.

THE various trading associations in Ireland are bestirring themselves, and have put in an appearance at the Board of Trade in opposition to the proposed rates for Irish lines. With a view of coming to some agreement whereby a protracted inquiry would be avoided, conferences have been arranged between the parties interested. At the first of these meetings, which was held last week, and which was well attended by representatives of the railway companies and the trading community, Mr. Courtnay Boyle presided; and on his recommendation an adjournment was made in order that figures might be obtained in support of the statements made as to the effect of the proposed changes. This, each party will doubtless be able to do to their own satisfaction; while the Board of Trade will probably, as before, steer between the two. Some of the English traders are still hoping to obtain amendments to the classification,—notably the timber merchants, who desire to have the term "timber" defined as embracing all rough and unmanufactured wood, whether round or squared. All are awaiting with some anxiety the appearance of the revised rates, and many supposed that alterations would be made on the 1st inst. As far as we can learn, however, the old rates generally remain in force; and, as has been previously intimated, it is very improbable that any important changes will be introduced until much later on in the year.

FOR the first time for many years the Railway Clearing House are not issuing a fresh edition of their Classification with the new year. It has always been the rule for a revised list to be published on January 1, incorporating the various additions and alterations which the previous year's experience has shown to be necessary; but on this occasion the revision is deferred pending the completion of the new rate-books, upon which the railway companies are still busily engaged. It is probable that a fresh edition will be published later in the year, remodelled on the lines of the Parliamentary classification settled last session, and possibly some of the provisions of the Act will be set forth.

THE agreement arrived at between the Great Northern Railway Company and the Manchester, Sheffield, and Lincolnshire Railway, by which the former company on certain terms has withdrawn its opposition to the extension to London of the latter, is likely materially to improve the chance of the passing of the Bill which was thrown out last Session. That the Bill will be modified in some form is pretty certain, but it is difficult to believe that the opposition of the inhabitants of St. John's Wood can prevent the passing of the Bill. That a new trunk line can be financially successful is, however, very improbable, but if the localities through which it passes desired, and there is no strong opposition, Parliament will hardly concern itself with the possibility that the shareholders may lose their money.

IN a "Note" on June 27 last we adverted to the Government scheme for an enlargement of the Record Office. Three weeks ago the materials of Nos. 6 to 20, on the eastern side of Chancery-lane, were sold at auction, and the fifteen houses are now being pulled down. The demolition includes the stone gateway, having a side footpath, which leads into Rolls-yard, and situated directly opposite to the chapel's western end. The old houses we speak of have for some years past been filled with Record Office stores, papers, &c., but being very unsuitable for that purpose will, as we understand, be replaced with a more commodious and fireproof structure.

BY their recent vote of 3,476*l.*, as half of the purchase-money, the London County Council secure the addition of 3½ acres, finely wooded, of the Bedford-hill estate, to Tooting Bec-common. This, and the adjoining Tooting-common,—being 207 acres in all, —their predecessors rescued from further encroachment and spoliation in 1875. The manors of Totinges, Estreham (Streatham), and Belgeham (Balham) are cited in Domesday survey; the former two as held of the Abbot of St. Mary de Bec. By an escheat of 8 Edward II., it appears that the priory of Okebourn, Wiltshire, an alien cell of Bec, held the two manors, by service of a knight's fee, of Gilbert de Clare, Earl of Gloucester, who fell at Bannockburn. At the seizure of alien priories, 2 Hen. V., the consolidated manor became vested in the Crown. In 1441 Henry VI. assigned it as part endowment to Eton College; but his successor, who resumed some of the grants to Eton, gave it to Lawrence, Bishop of Durham, for life. According to Rymer's "Fœdera," the priory or manor of Totyngbeke, as parcel of Okebourn, reverted, with the advowson of Streatham, to the King, who settled them upon John Tiptoft, Earl of Worcester, master, and the wardens of St. Mary's Guild, in All Hallows, Barking, Church. In 1599 it was bought by Sir Giles Howland, Knight, who is supposed to have built the manor-house at corner of Streatham-common, on the Croydon-road.* Elizabeth, heiress of John Howland brought the property in marriage to Wriothesley, second Duke of Bedford, who in 1695 was created Baron Howland, of Streatham. Their descendant Francis, fifth Duke, conveyed the house and grounds to Lord William Russell, and in June, 1816, John, sixth Duke, sold the manor, according to Brayley's "Surrey." Streatham Place, close to Tooting Bec-common, the home of the Thrales, has been quite dismantled. The house and its contents were sold in 1816; amongst the portraits being those, by Sir Joshua Reynolds, of Sir Robert Chambers (80 guineas), Goldsmith (127 guineas), Dr. Burney (80 guineas), Sir Joshua (122 guineas), Burke (240 guineas), and Dr. Johnson (360 guineas). A woodcut of the house is in the *Monthly Magazine* of July, 1823.

* The home of Lord William Russell, who was murdered by his valet Courvoisier (1840), and rebuilt by Lord Deerhurst, seventh Earl of Coventry.

THE usual correspondence in the papers about fogs and the wickedness of scientific men who do not stop fogs, has followed the recent fogs in London. We have the same thing every year, and indignant people write letters to the *Times* speaking as if the authorities of London had only to give the requisite orders to shut off fog at once, and that it is only through pure "cussedness" that they do not do so. One correspondent, "Lucifer," who unfortunately does not give his name, but who says that he is a chemist, seems to be possessed with a somewhat more reasonable spirit. He observes—

"What we need for the formation of an ordinary mist is a chilled vapour-charged atmosphere and minute, solid particles to serve as nuclei for the condensation of this vapour into the droplets of water of which mist is composed. This mist may be aggravated into a fog if from any cause it is made abnormally dense, and it happens that such conditions exist in towns. . . In towns these conditions are the existence in the air of an abnormally large supply of solid nuclei—which are quite independent of smoke—and the prevalence of sulphurous acid, which, likewise, is independent of smoke. This sulphurous acid comes from coal and, as you justly remark, will come from coal whenever and however that coal is burnt. The amount of this gas sent into the air of London in one day is prodigious, for it will weigh about one-fiftieth of the total coal consumed. That the intensity and pungency of town fogs are due to this is a view which has been confirmed by so high an authority as Helmholtz (the Sir William Thomson of Germany), and it is idle to talk of the reduction of fog to mist by the smokeless burning of coal. It is no doubt true that the dirtiness, flavour, and unpleasantness of fog are much increased by the admixture of smoke, and no effort should be spared, in fair weather or foul, to mitigate the smoke nuisance. It acts, too, as an intensifier of fog, as has been shown by Dr. Frankland, by retarding the evaporation of the droplets of water of which the fog is composed.

Scientific men are continually being called upon to invent some means of dissipating or preventing fog. Professor Oliver Lodge has shown that fogs may be dispersed by means of a continuous discharge of electricity into them; but he would, I feel sure, be the last person to anticipate that such a method could be applied outside Utopia to the smallest town in the kingdom."

We commend these remarks to the attention of those enthusiastic persons who are constantly urging that we can prevent London fog at will. "Lucifer" goes on to observe, truly, that the general adoption of gas for heating and electricity for lighting would be "a solution of the fog question"; but in saying that he himself goes too far. It would remove the excessive darkness and irritating character of the fogs; but would still leave them as white fogs. The recent fog of London extended over a considerable tract of country, only it had not the same character in the country as in London. And it would remain to be considered whether this change from a smoky brown fog to a white one would be a sufficient good to compensate for the permanent exchange of gas fires for the warm and cheerful coal fire. Some people would probably think otherwise; but of course the majority have the right to decide the point, and if coal fires are condemned the minority must give way. But we rather doubt it really coming to that. People may think so while a fog lasts, but when it is gone they will sigh over the loss of their comfortable fire.

THE fog correspondence has produced complaints also, as usual, from passengers by the railways. Some of these are perfectly reasonable, and some of the delays might have been prevented. At Euston it is extraordinary that the Board of the North-Western Railway have not introduced a more efficient system of lighting. In foggy weather the delays on that line are chiefly produced by the difficulty experienced in sending trains from the terminus. Strong lights will not altogether prevent difficulties from severe fogs, but they will do a good deal to alleviate the trouble.

SOME NOTES ON THE HISTORY OF ENAMELLING.

BY J. STARKIE GARDNER.

THE art of enamelling is very ancient, and consists of fusing a coating of glass upon metal. Metal, however, being tough and malleable, and in many other respects the opposite of glass, and the two bodies having different measures of expansion and contraction, skill and experience are needed to unite them. When the metal to be enamelled is thick its surface is divided into cells, in order that its expansion and contraction may not shiver the glassy skin; but when the metal is thin, it is usually coated all over by the enamel, which acts as an envelope and protects it uninjured by ordinary changes of temperature. This difficulty has probably gone far to determine the various forms of enamel known to art, and which may be grouped into cellular and glaze enamels. The cellular group is divided into those in which the metal surface is gouged out, called *champlevé*, and those in which cell walls are added to its surface,—*cloisonné*. Fusion in these was, and is usually, accomplished under the blow-pipe, while glazed enamels were fused in the muffle or closed oven.

The enamel is simply a more or less fusible glass which is transparent unless mixed with tin, when it becomes opaque. The colours used are of course only such as will stand heat, and practically are oxides of different metals,—copper, cobalt, iron, gold, manganese, &c. The range of colour is almost unlimited.

There is some difference of opinion as to whether the Egyptians ever fused the enamel paste they produced on to metal, or whether they merely used it as an inlay. There is none as to its very sparing use by the Greeks in jewellery. It seems to have been unknown to the Etruscans, Romans, or any other civilised nation previous to the Christian era.

It was, however, known to one barbarian nation, our own, in prehistoric times. It can never be known exactly, but as all British enamels are stanniferous, the discovery must have been due to some smelting of tin and bronze. Until the Roman colonisation, enamelling seems to have been confined to small trappings for man and horse, but later highly decorated vases and bowls were made and exported. The ivy was much used in their decoration, and the classic laurel-leaf border is often introduced. The Gallo-Romans seem to have practised the art to some limited extent, and the Italians appear to have produced a bastard enamel by inlaying the *millefiori* and other glasses in jewellery, and fusing them sufficiently to unite to the metal.

It is unlikely that this art was connected with enamelling as practised at Byzantium, many centuries later. On the other hand, there is sufficient evidence that it was never lost in the British Isles. A kind of *champ-levé* process had been handed down from time immemorial, the metal being cast, and the cells filled with yellow, red, green, white, and blue. Several vases of British manufacture have been found in France, Germany, and Denmark. In Ireland also, the art of enamelling was known in very remote times. The exquisitely beaten shields and helmet found in the Thames, and now in the British Museum, and the horns of the same workmanship in Dublin, are alike decorated with small blood-red enamels, and many of the Celtic brooches are set with enamels. The Ardagh chalice, which dates probably from the eighth century, is of peculiar interest, as being perhaps the earliest enamel in existence made for a sacred purpose, and as having served as a type on which others were fashioned. It is decorated with three kinds of enamel, all of them showing a marvellous amount of thought and skilful manipulation. The Irish enamels present indeed processes such as the inlay of one coloured enamel in another, and the pressing of the metal filigree into hot enamel, which are quite peculiar, and should enable us to recognise them wherever met with. While tin appears to have been a necessary ingredient in British enamels, it is not present in some of the oldest from Ireland, which are translucent; and the coarse British variety of *champ-levé* is abandoned for the more delicate *cloisonné*.

The next step in our history was a very important one, the introduction of pictorial representations in enamel, and this step also was taken in England. In the well-known Alfred jewel found in Athelney, and inscribed with the words, "Aelfred mec heht gevurtan," we have a most beautiful example of cloisonné on gold, bearing a portrait, and rich in translucent enamel of fine hue. No piece of cloisonné enamel, bearing such strong intrinsic evidence of its date, is to be met with which can compare with it in antiquity.

But it does not stand alone. An exquisitely worked brooch found on Dowgate-hill bears a delicate cloisonné portrait of a royal person, supposed to represent Alfred or his father. Like the Alfred jewel, it is rich in translucent green and blue, the flesh tints being opaque, with a golden-yellow crown, and with pearls and black enamel rosettes set in its filigree gold border. An equally beautiful brooch of the same workmanship reposes beside it in the British Museum, in the centre of which is a highly decorative cross in deep translucent blue and ruby. These superb specimens of cloisonné jewellery are linked to the older British enamels by a curious unfinished plâque, also in the British Museum, and found in London, enamelled in blue, red, yellow, and white, which has a somewhat Mediæval feeling; and still more so by the ring of King Æthelwulf, of blue and green champ-levé on gold, inscribed with his name and two eagles, or perhaps ravens. A ring of not dissimilar style, but filled with niello in place of enamel, is inscribed with the name Ahlstan, supposed to be the Bishop of Sherbon, 823-67.

These enamels have not hitherto been universally admitted to be of English manufacture, but the inscriptions on them, and their refined style and execution, are strong arguments in favour of their native production at the time when England occupied the leading position in the arts and sciences. We may admit, if necessary, that the introduction of portraiture may have been due to the journeys that Alfred and his father made to Rome. Those who find it difficult to admit an English origin for these enamels, regard them as of Byzantine origin, but there is no clear evidence of the production of enamels in Byzantium prior to the tenth century, and none exist which can be attributed with certainty to a date earlier than about its close. The pectoral crosses, of which there are two in the Kensington Museum, appear to be the oldest. The designs are fashioned in delicate gold filigree, and in colour and technique they are not dissimilar to our portrait enamels. The beautiful series of plâques discovered in a field, and now in the National Hungarian Museum, are typical Byzantine work, and their date is known to be between 1042 and 1054. They probably formed a crown like that of Charlemagne in form. The most famous Byzantine enamel in the world is the Pala D'Oro, the golden altar-piece of St. Mark's Cathedral, Venice. None of the enamels which enrich it are, in the opinion of Mr. Franks, older than the figures of the Empress Irene and the Doge Faliero, about 1105, while others are as recent as 1209. The equally remarkable golden altar at Milan, known as the Paliotto, is not believed to be Byzantine, and being executed by one Wolvinus, an unmistakably Saxon name, at a time, 835, when it cannot be shown conclusively that enamelling was practised except in England, there is some slight (*a priori*) ground for hoping that it may prove to be an English work. Small enamels, set as jewels, abound in works as old as this, such as in the crown of Monza, about 625; the reliquary of Sion, 720; that of Pepin, in the crown, sword, and gloves of Charlemagne; the A of Charlemagne and many other objects preserved in the Treasury of the Abbey of Conques, &c. Some of these may be English and Irish, and their origin may be as various as those of the gems which accompany them. The strongest evidence in favour of the antiquity of the art of enamelling in Byzantium is the fact that we find the art transported to Germany soon after the marriage of Otho with Princess Theophaine in 973. The enamels at Essen, inscribed with the names of Matilda, Abbess 974-1013, and Theophanie, Abbess 1014-1054, are generally regarded as the oldest of German origin. The former are of the finest work, being perhaps executed by Byzantine workmen. The Germans soon resorted to the champ-levé process on copper, very frequently combining it with gold cloisonné for the more delicate details. A few Byzantine enamels are known of this mixed kind, but in these the copper is beaten up to form the design, instead of being chased out as in the champlevé. The seat of the manufacture seems to have been at Cologne, and nearly all the large shrines and reliquaries preserved in Germany are of Rhenish production, and nearly thirty of them still exist in the diocese of Cologne. Among the most important is the shrine of the Magi at Cologne, of the Virgin at Aachen, Saint Servais at Mustricht. German enamels are characterised by somewhat rude drawing and the use of many colours, which are generally shaded and sometimes blended. As we have seen, cloisonné decoration was frequently, almost habitually, used for small details on the base of champlevé work. We possess in the Soltikoff reliquary at Kensington one of the finest specimens of early German enamel in existence.

In addition to the Rhenish production we have evidence of an important seat of the industry on the banks of the Meuse, in Lorraine, in the twelfth century, Abbot Suger having taken his workmen from thence to St. Denis in the years 1143-47. The splendid altar front of Klosterneubourg, consisting of fifty-one plates of champlevé enamel, was made by Nicolas of Verdun, 1181. Enamelling was also carried on at Maestricht in the thirteenth century, but the style of Limoges was followed.

The German and other enamels, about which little is really yet known, deserve most careful study, as many enamels are referred to a German origin, which in refinement of design, delicacy of detail, and general style, in no way resemble the ordinary expressions of German art. Still less do they resemble Byzantine or Limoges work. It is significant that most of these have been found in England, whilst much evidence can be brought forward to show that enamelling was an important art in England during the twelfth to the fourteenth centuries, when English enamels were prized on the Continent. Instances of this are the enamelled clasp in the Inventory of the Duke of Normandy, 1363, the enamelled gold goblet and ewer given by Henry IV. to Charles VI., the fine specimen taken as a souvenir of his visit to this country by Charles V., &c. We possess, moreover, a few acknowledged enamels of English production, such as the Lynn cup and Wykeham crozier, which are of fine workmanship; and, if we wish farther to gauge what English enamellers were likely to produce, we have only to look at the thirteenth-century glass remaining at Canterbury or York, to feel convinced that it would be of high quality, both in refinement of drawing and beauty of colour. It is interesting to notice that Richardin, an enameller from London, was one of the first of the craft established in Paris, 1292.

Among the most beautiful examples are those in which the surface is divided into small panels in the fashion of the contemporary stained glass. The dividing lines are generally ribbons bearing leonine verses remarkable for their erudition and thought. The compartments are round, lozenge shaped, or polygonal, and contain exquisitely-drawn groups of figures, either biblical or allegorical subjects. To this unfortunately rare group belong the Meyrick crozier, the Warwick bowl, the Bruce bowl, the Savernake horn, and the chalice of Wilten in Tyrol, and, perhaps, a curious enamelled flask in the Berlin Museum. That this panelled or diapered treatment was always a favourite one in England there is abundant evidence to show. We find it in all sorts of examples, such as the beautiful Fair Rosamond ring, the painted roof of Peterborough Cathedral, and many of the early cups belonging to colleges and corporations.

The triptych from Alton Towers, as pointed out by Mr. Franks, is not dissimilar in its style, being divided into nine compartments, with scriptural subjects and leonine verses. Another triptych, also in the Kensington Museum, which might be claimed as English, was found in Essex, formed part of the Arundel collection, and figured in the "Archæologia." It is remarkable for the fine drawing of the subjects in the eight compartments, and for its translucent enamels. A very similar specimen is in the Kensington Museum. The beautiful Lynn cup of the time of Richard II. is also divided into compartments, on which are small and delicately drawn figures on translucent enamel. Part of a very beautiful cup, 1276-1316, at All Souls' College, and the binding of the Bodleian Psalter, are also enamelled in brilliant translucent colours, and are undoubtedly English. The English origin of the Wykeham and the Limerick croziers and mitres, the latter inscribed by Thomas O'Carty, 1418, has never been questioned, and both are superb examples, not only of the goldsmith's, but of the enameller's art. When we remember that the goldsmith's and other artistic work produced at Ely, Glastonbury, Durham, York, Colchester, St. Albans, &c., was celebrated from the eleventh to the thirteenth centuries, and that vast treasuries of this work were frequently accumulated, it would, indeed, be matter for surprise if our country were as destitute of examples of its ancient art as is generally supposed.

When we can place the English origin of a few more enamels beyond doubt, the study of the rest will be greatly facilitated. They seem to have been much more varied than those of other countries, and hence require particular care in distinguishing them. Armorial bearings are enamelled on the shields to the tombs of Edward III. and Richard II., and on the shields and belt of the effigy of the Black Prince, while a sword of Edward III. has a handle enamelled with his arms. A few caskets, like that of De Valence in the Kensington Museum, a small shrine with St. George and the Dragon, with a few other objects, and the armorial bearings on the herse and tomb in the Beauchamp Chapel, belong to the same group. Of great interest, too, are the Garter plates at Windsor, beginning in 1368, and extending over a period of 500 years. The inventories of the jewels belonging to Edward II. and III. mention 200 distinct enamelled vessels.

The name of Limoges is first connected in a definite way with enamelling towards the third quarter of the twelfth century. The celebrated enamelled brass of Geoffrey Plantagenet, father of Henry II., is still preserved at Le Mans, and is especially interesting from its heraldry. This Prince died in 1151. The enamel, however, is very unlike any work of Limoges, and the proofs of its origin advanced are quite inconclusive. Among the earliest undoubtedly authentic works of Limoges are the two plaques from the Abbey of Grandmont in the Cluny Museum. One bears an inscription claimed to be in Limousin patois, and the date assigned them is prior to 1188. A still more characteristic specimen is the fine chasse of Mozac. Authentic twelfth century specimens of Limoges work are, however, extremely rare, the vast mass of Limoges enamels belonging to the thirteenth century. At this time they enjoyed an extraordinary popularity, and were exported far and near. One of the best known, and a signed work, is the pyx of Alpaïs in the Louvre. We possess an almost corresponding piece in the British Museum. The most important objects are the reliquaries in form of ecclesiastical edifices with high pitched roofs. Other objects are croziers, crosses, missal covers, pyxes, &c. These are nearly always decorated with figures representing the Adoration of the Magi, the Flight into Egypt, the Martyrdom of St. Catherine, St. Valerie, St. Thomas à Becket, &c. The figures on the reliquaries are stiff and without much movement, often badly drawn, and are either outlined on a gold ground on an enamelled field or enamelled on a gold field. The heads, or sometimes the whole figures, are often embossed in high relief. Gems and filigree are rarely used to enrich the effect. The tone of colour used is decidedly blue, and the effect brilliant. The ground is almost universally a deep ultramarine; but a darker blue, as well as turquoise and sky blue, are also used. Red, purple, light and dark green, white, yellow, and black are used sparingly. Ultramarine draperies are bordered with light blue or white, and green is bordered with yellow. There is great sameness about the work, which is often exceedingly coarse, as if the objects had been produced in quantities for export. Very highly finished Limoges work is rare, and the pedigree of several unusual examples claimed by French writers requires careful examination. It was, no doubt, partly owing to its inferior and monotonous execution that it fell into complete disfavour in the fifteenth century.

French writers claim that all the enamelled tombs and effigies, formerly abundant, but now excessively rare, were produced at Limoges, which held a monopoly of such work. A list of them is given in Ernest Rupin's "L'Œuvre de

Limoges." Many are only known from de Gaignière's drawings, and notes preserved in the Bodleian. The tombs of Blanche and Jean, children of St. Louis, who died in 1243 and 1248, are now in the Abbey of St. Denis, and the effigy of Blanche of Champagne, 1283, is in the Louvre. Other tombs, presumably of Limoges work, are preserved in Spain. That of William de Valence, made in 1296, is still in an extremely perfect condition as regards the effigy. It shows a pillow, belt, and shield, emblazoned all over in the richest way with the arms of Valence. The enamel is on plate copper, fixed to a rough wooden core. There is no record as to where it was made, and there is no other tomb resembling it in England; but an enamelled tomb was ordered from Limoges in 1277 for Walter de Merton, Bishop of Rochester. Enamelling was carried on in other parts of France, particularly in Paris, but hardly any pieces can be identified, and the study of Mediæval enamels, notwithstanding the books that have been written, is still in a very imperfect state. J. S. G.

Illustrations.

SELECTED DESIGN FOR THE MUNICIPAL BUILDINGS, BATH.

WE have already in a review of the Bath Municipal Buildings Competition (page 478 of our last volume) given a description of the main points of this design, by Mr. J. M. Brydon, which has been awarded the first premium and, we understand, accepted for execution. We give the principal elevation and the plans of the two principal floors.

We have nothing to add to the remarks we have already made on the plan and design; but the following summary, communicated to us by the architect, may be given as setting forth his view of the objects and treatment of the building:—

"In describing the general arrangements of the proposed new buildings, it will be noticed that the accommodation provided divides itself into two main sections.

1. The administration of justice, comprising the new Sessions Court and the rooms connected therewith. These are located on the ground floor.

2. The public service, comprising the new Council-chamber and the offices of the various departments for the business of the municipality. These are principally located on the first floor.

In working out the details of these two sections, the additions have been so arranged with reference to the present Guildhall that, though each is distinct in itself, together they form a complete scheme, in the consideration of which the old and new buildings may be taken as a whole. With this view the present entrance in High-street is allotted to the courts and the banquetting-hall, and a new entrance is provided at the Orange-grove corner for the Municipal offices. Spacious and amply-lighted corridors connect these two approaches, while a new municipal staircase is provided near the latter.

The new court is placed at the back of the building, away from the noise of the street traffic, and immediately around it are rooms for witnesses, jury, solicitors, barristers, and others connected with the business of the court, so arranged as to serve the purposes of both courts. The new Council-chamber is also placed in the rear, and over the court below. Near it are grouped the Mayor's parlour, the committee-rooms, Town Clerk's and Treasurer's offices, &c.

A special feature is made of the connexion between the old and new buildings on both floors,—on the ground floor by a new inner hall from which the court corridor opens; and on the first floor by a circular vestibule with a domed light, at the junction of the Council corridor and the present staircase. From this vestibule a new entrance is made into the banqueting-room, bringing it into suite with the Council-chamber, &c. Access for the public to the galleries of the court and Council-chamber is provided by a separate entrance and staircase from the proposed new market approach.

As will be seen from the view, the additions take the form of wings on each side of the Guildhall, with rounded corners at the return ends, marked by low flanking towers, and it is proposed to increase the importance of the centre block by crowning it with the low dome so characteristic of the style. Indeed, the whole question of style demanded the most special study and attention, it being considered of the first importance that the additions should so harmonise with the existing work that any impression of an after-thought should not only be avoided, but that the building, as a whole, should appear as if it had been so designed from the first, and, if possible, infuse the spirit of the old work into the new, while at the same time the importance and the dignity of the former should be increased rather than lessened as the central features of the whole composition.

The southern wing contains the new Municipal offices, and the northern wing the School of Science and Art, the sculpture in each rounded angle indicating the purposes to which they are devoted. The interior of the building will be carried out in harmony with the style of the exterior, and with the rooms of the existing Guildhall. It is, therefore, confidently hoped the result will be a work which, without any meretricious ornament, will, from the dignity of its treatment, proclaim itself essentially a public building not unworthy the architectural traditions or the civic home of such an historic city as Bath."

MOSAICS IN ST. MARK'S, VENICE.

THESE sketches represent St. Athanasius and St. John Chrysostom, two of the four Greek Fathers of the Church in the Baptistry of St. Mark's, at Venice. They were executed in mosaic by Greek artists of the twelfth and thirteenth centuries. In Mrs. Jameson's work on "Sacred and Legendary Art," she says:—"When they are introduced collectively as a part of the decoration of an ecclesiastical edifice, we may conclude in general that the work is Byzantine, and executed under the influence of Greek artists." They occupy the four spandrels of the vaulting, filling the same places here which are usually occupied by the four Latin Fathers in church decoration. Each has his name inscribed in Greek characters, and holds in his hand a scroll bearing some remarkable passage from his work in Greek. Thus St. Athanasius has "Often and anew do we flee to thee, O God," while St. John Chrysostom has, "God, our God, who hath given us for food the bread of life." St. Athanasius, the eldest of the Fathers, was born at Alexandria, A.D. 298, and died A.D. 372. St. John Chrysostom was born at Antioch, A.D. 344, and died A.D. 407. The tympana between the spandrels are filled with mosaic work depicting scenes in the life of John-the-Baptist. The sketches are by Mr. Arthur C. Blomfield, M.A., and the original drawings were exhibited at the Royal Academy Exhibition of 1891.

THE "JEW'S HOUSE," LINCOLN.

THE illustration of this well-known and interesting old house at Lincoln (why called the "Jew's House" no one seems to know) is from a drawing by Mr. A. H. Powell, which was included in the exhibits of the Architectural Room at the Royal Academy last year.

"A MOUNTAIN CHURCH."

THIS is a study for a church in a mountainous district; the fall of the ground towards the east suggests the position of the heating-chamber, the vestry being placed over, reached by an external staircase. The accommodation is for 300.

The drawing was exhibited in the Royal Academy of 1891. G. Ll. M.

MAGAZINES AND REVIEWS.

THE *Art Journal* commences with an article on "An Etcher of Architecture," by Mr. C. Lewis Hind, the etcher in question being Mr. A. W. Haig, who well merits a post of honour in any artistic journal. The article is illustrated by reductions from some of Mr. Haig's etchings. We learn from it that Mr. Haig commenced with shipbuilding or making designs for and drawings of ships, and subsequently was a designer of buildings in the usual way of architectural draughtsmanship, before he took to the career which has given him fame. Mr. Hind rightly notes the special quality of Mr. Haig's etchings of buildings as giving breadth of effect without overlooking accuracy and minuteness of detail. The first of a series of articles by Mr. Aymer Valance on "The Furnishing and Decoration of the House" deals with floors and ceilings. In regard to some very good (and well-known) ceiling papers which are illustrated, the author rightly points out that a ceiling decoration should have no tendency of line in one direction. "Sir Joshua Reynolds and his Models" is an interesting paper by Miss Frances A. Gerard. The first example of the promised stories, "The Sculptor's Mistake," is not very attractive *quâ* story; the illustrations are the best part of it.

In the *Magazine of Art* Mr. Reginald Blomfield starts what we presume is to be a series of articles on "Artistic Homes," illustrated by his own sketches of his friends' houses, and containing many good and pointed remarks as to house-designing. An article on "Book-edge Decoration," by Mr. S. T. Prideaux, touches a subject which has been rather overlooked, and gives several interesting illustrations from examples in the British Museum. We certainly cannot agree with him in thinking that landscapes painted on the edges of the pages form "the most attractive form of edge decoration;" on the contrary, nothing could be more out of place, in spite of old examples. An article on John Russell, "the Prince of crayon portrait-painters," is illustrated by a frontispiece from one of his works, a portrait of a lady. Russell was born in 1711; the article, by Mr. G. C. Williamson, is mainly biographical, and contains a good deal of interesting information. The whole number is a very good one.

Among things in *The Antiquary* which will interest our readers are "Latest Discoveries at Mycenæ" by Professor Halbherr; "Notes on the Lights of a Mediæval Church," by the Rev. F. W. Weaver, and "A List of the Inventories of Church Goods made temp. Edward VI," by Mr. W. Page.

The Architectural Review, of Boston, which is a successor to or expansion of *The Technology Architectural Review* to which we have several times referred, commences with an article on the late J. D. Sedding, by Mr. Ralph Adams Cram, which is sympathetic and enthusiastic, but errs in the way so common among a certain school of writers on architecture, of speaking with contempt of architects who are not, like Sedding, seekers after originality at all costs. Mr. Cram must be very ignorant of the subject to say that Barry was an architect of mere archæological exactness, and refer to his Parliament houses as therefore an anachronism. Has he never heard that the style of the building was imposed upon Barry by the Government? Barry was a very original architect, using Renaissance materials after his own fashion, and American critics had better learn something more about his works before they sneer at him. And we would also suggest to the editor to take the trouble of getting English architects' and artists' names correctly; we find references to "Mr. Bigg's" drawings of Lincoln in our pages, a design for a frieze by Mr. Arthur "Gwatke," and a "Beaford" grammar-school by Mr. E. C. "Robbins." Apparently the writer of the article cannot even read print correctly. He also describes an Academy drawing of Mr. Batley's as by Mr. "Bailey," and shows his perception by describing the panel, published in the *Builder* of November 21, as "a perfect orgy of design," "bad taste," &c., &c. The design, a pretty little unpretending relief in gesso, will be remembered by many visitors to the Architectural Room of the Royal Academy, who will probably be rather astonished to hear of its being an "orgy of design."

IN *Harper's Magazine* Mr. Besant's "London under Charles the Second" is the most interesting of these historical articles that we have seen. It is confined to the city and popular life, leaving on one side the manners of the Court, which Mr. Besant thinks had little effect on the general life of the middle classes. He has got hold of an old housekeeping account-book of a middle-class family from 1677 to 1679, from which most realistic details are obtained. Details as to the Plague and the Fire of course occupy a good deal of the article, which is also illustrated by some very pretty sketches of bits of the London of the period. An article in the same number by Mr. Julian Ralph, on "Our Exposition at Chicago" gives a good idea of the immense and ambitious scale on which this great show is being carried out. The manufactures' building itself is one-third of a mile long. The combination of water with the architecture will, no doubt, add much to the effect of the scene. According to the writer, the English section is to include a reproduction of some notable English mansion or manor-house.

Scribner devotes an interesting article to some "Correspondence of Washington Allston," the American artist of the early days of this century, whose name is probably little remembered among English lovers of art at present, but who was a man worthy to be had in remembrance on account of his general intellectual culture as well as the beauty of his design in figure subject; some of his sketches are given as illustrations; one, of the heads of angels from a picture of "Jacob's Dream," is notable for its Raffaellesque grace of outline.

· Elevation to the High Street ·

Feet.

Lin
Ga
the
chi
124
effi
Lo
wo
de
tre
It
all
Va
to
to
ton
ens
127
Fra
pie
Me
tha
per.

T

A

vol
poi
whi
and
We
of
V
hav
the
the
vie
bui

pro
acc
mai
1.
the
nee
floo
2.
cha
for
prit
I
the
to t
tinc
In
buil
vie
to t
ent
the
cor
mu
T
buil
and
jur
wit
ser
Cou
ove
Ma
file
A
bet
on t
the
a c
jun
stai
ma
snit
pub
cha
stai
A
the
wit
by
cre
ing
styl
mat
bei
add
wor
not
wh
fro
the
the

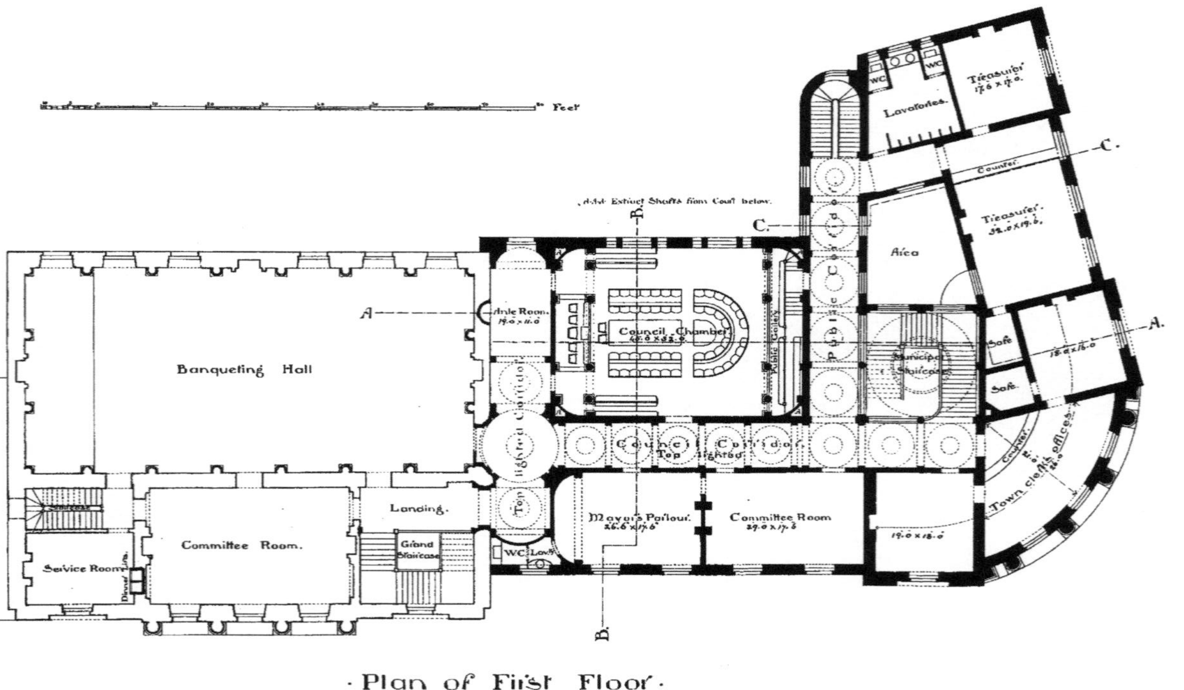

· Plan of First Floor ·

INK-PHOTO SPRAGUE & Cº 4 & 5 EAST HARDING STREET FETTER LANE, E.C.

MOSAIC IN ST. MARK'S, VENICE.—From a Drawing by Mr. Arthur C. Blomfield.

Royal Academy Exhibition, 1891.

INK-PHOTO, SPRAGUE & CO 4 & 5, EAST HARDING STREET, FETTER LANE, E.C.

MOSAIC IN ST. MARK'S, VENICE.—FROM A DRAWING BY MR. ARTHUR C. BLOMFIELD.

cademy Exhibition, 1891.

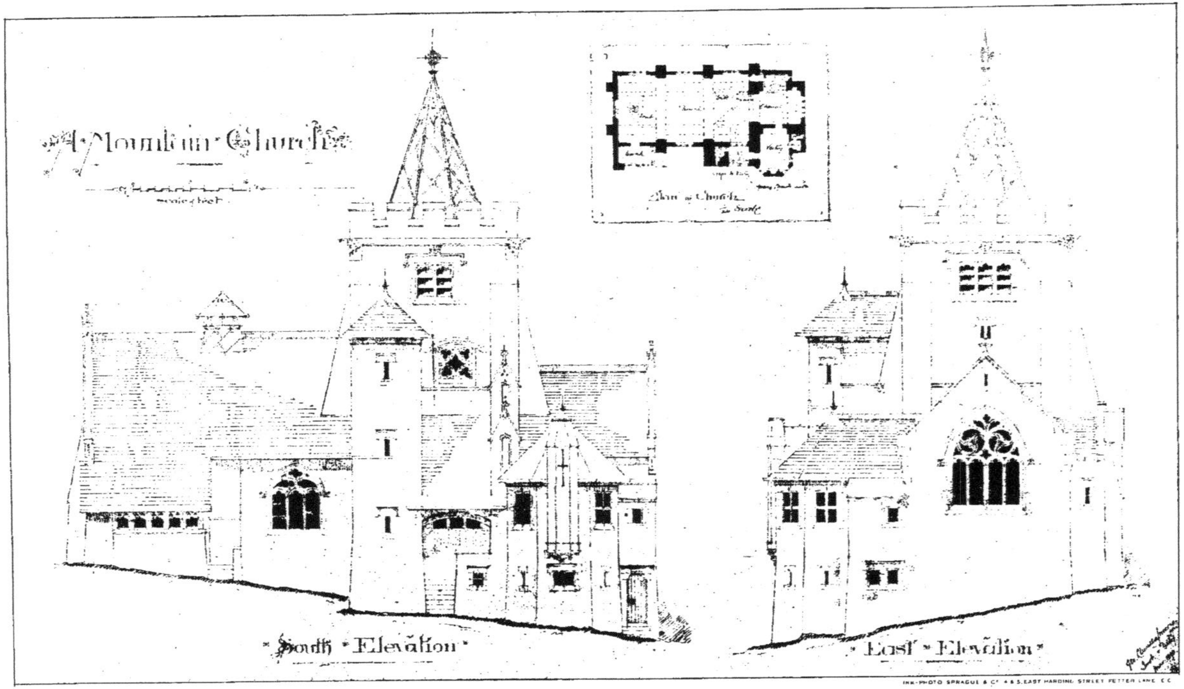

A MOUNTAIN CHURCH.—MR. GEORGE LL. MORRIS, ARCHITECT.

Royal Academy Exhibition, 1891.

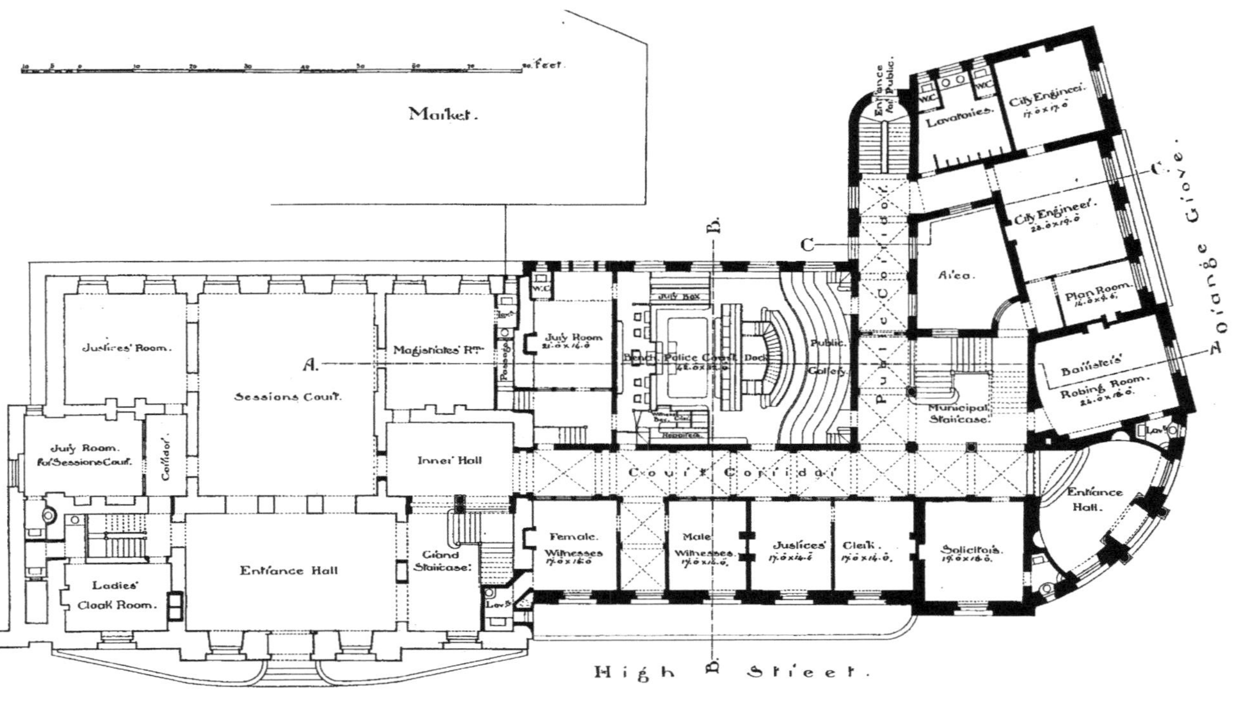

· Plan of Ground Floor ·

PHOTO-LITHO, SPRAGUE & CO 4 & 5 EAST HARDING STREET FETTER LANE E.C.

SELECTED DESIGN FOR MUNICIPAL BUILDINGS, BATH.—Mr. J. M. Brydon, F.R.I.B.A., Architect.

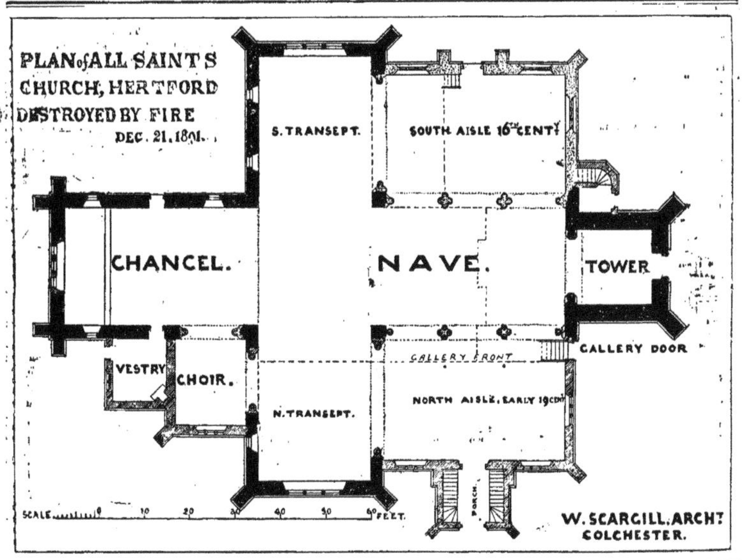

Allston visited and remained some time in England. His remarks on some English painters of the time are curious to read now, as instances of the different manner in which artists are seen by their contemporaries and by posterity. Northcote was a great painter then; and of Fuseli Allston observes that his picture of Hamlet and the Ghost was "alone sufficient to immortalise him." Haydon had a great admiration for that picture also: we know not where it is now.

The only paper in the *Century* dealing with art is Mr. Stillman's on Andrea del Sarto, in continuation of the series of articles on Italian old masters. The article is a short one, and gives a fair estimate of Andrea's powers and weaknesses. Mr. Stillman also reminds us that Andrea del Sarto was one of the artists who produced the model of the façade for the Duomo of Florence at the time of the visit of Leo X. It was produced conjointly with Sansovino, and one may naturally think that the latter had the most to do with it; Mr. Stillman observes however that "the masterly knowledge of perspective shown in some of his frescoes would suggest such a knowledge of architecture as most of the painters of the period possessed." The article is illustrated by engravings from two of Andrea del Sarto's works.

The *Nineteenth Century* of this month contains an interesting article on the "Electrical Transmission of Power," by the Earl of Albemarle, which repeats, quoting from M. Figurier, the pleasant fable that the reversibility of the dynamo was accidentally discovered. The article will give to the general reader a vivid idea of how a dynamo is a source of power, and when power can be transmitted electrically over a long distance. It is singularly free from technicalities, and is written in a powerful and graphic style. We feel particularly grateful to the Earl for the epigrammatic phrase, "vested interests and invested cash." Unfortunately the author resuscitates the notion disposed of by Mr. Swinburne two years ago, that a motor should have a relatively large armature. Small field magnets may be a necessary evil in motors for driving electric launches and tramcars, but the advantage in weight is gained at the cost of diminished electrical efficiency.

The Portfolio for this current month contains the first of a series of articles by the Reverend W. J. Loftie, upon a somewhat well-worn subject,—the Inns of Court. In reviewing Mr. Loftie's "History of London" a few years ago,* we had occasion to point out the absence of any logical principle of architectural thought or criticism from that work. In inveighing against the mischief which followed upon the first outbreak of the great Gothic revival, he would adopt,—

> A recent suggestion, namely, that in writing or speaking of modern, or mock, Gothic, as distinguished from the real thing, the term Vandal or Vandalic might be used.

He triumphantly asks what name can be more appropriate for Mr. Pearson's use of what he would persuade us is Gothic at Westminster? As he says that "even ordinary Gothic only exists in the Savoy and at Westminster," we infer that by "Westminster" he means the Abbey; in which case we are sorry for one who would stigmatise as Vandalism the recent work by that architect upon the exterior of the north transept. Possibly, however, he means to refer to the treatment of Westminster Hall, in which case we are with him. The "kind of garret," by the way, into which, as Mr. Loftie complains, some monuments have been removed at the Temple is, in fact, the triforium of the Round Church there. The article, however, is mainly concerned with topographical matters, in respect whereof Mr. Loftie treads upon surer ground. The complex story of Portpoole,—site of Gray's Inn,—is dismissed in thirty lines. It begins with a derivation for the name, thus:—

> But the "port" which means, in this connexion, rather an extra-mural market than a gate, may be found, perhaps, in the neighbouring Staple Inn . . . . . and the pool,—well, what can be more natural than that a horse-pond adjoined the market-place? (!!)

It ends by saying that the manor came to the crown at the Dissolution, but Henry VIII. renewed the lease,—which must now be taken as correct: and that "the Treasury still pays the rent to the Crown." It is quite clearly set out in Mr. W. Ralph Douthwaite's "Gray's Inn,"† that the society bought, in 1733, their fee farm rent (6*l.* 13*s.* 4*d.*) from parties deriving title from Sir Philip Matthews' co-heirs, and have held the property free from any rent or charge ever since.

* See the *Builder*, February 2, 1884.
† Reviewed in our columns on April 17, 1886.

The *Health Record* (Dublin) is a new Irish Journal of Sanitary Science, to which we wish success. The short articles on various sanitary subjects are written in a sensible spirit. We learn from it that the Corporation of Dublin have adopted the report of the Main Drainage Committee, and the *Health Record* recommends the Dublin authorities, to economise, if they like, in other matters, but to lose no time in carrying out a main drainage system for Dublin.

PLAN OF ALL SAINTS' CHURCH, HERTFORD.

WE are indebted to Mr. Scargill for the above plan of All Saints', Hertford, the destruction of which was referred to in our "Notes" and in Mr. Scargill's letter last week.

FIXING PORTABLE RANGES.

WE are here, speaking of kitchen ranges which have all the flues constructed in iron and made part of them, and which are sometimes called independent, or self-setting, or more commonly called "American" ranges. This style of range was introduced from that country, where it was found of the utmost service to pioneers and settlers, being independent of brickwork fixing, ready for use almost at a moment's notice, and being made of light metal they could be treated as an article of furniture. They are used in great quantities exactly in this manner at the present day.

In bringing this range into towns or cities, as was a matter of course when they were introduced into England, many new circumstances were encountered, the chief of these being the chimney opening and the brick chimney, and, strange as it may seem, these ranges which are so very simple to put up, and need so little labour in so doing, are as great sufferers as our brick-flue Leamington ranges in working badly through incompetent work in fixing.

Doubtless these portable ranges suffer through its being considered that they need no fixing, as the flues are already made. This is correct so far as the flues around the ovens and boilers are concerned, but unfortunately many workmen have a very imperfect notion as to what the "draught" is which impels the flame and heated gases through these flues in question; and, unless the range is in sound and proper communication with the chimney, the flues in the range will be of little use in assisting efficiency.

As every skilful range-fixer knows, the "draught" (without which every close fire-range would be utterly useless) is created in the chimney, and no range has ever been known to act correctly without a chimney of some sort, and they must be in proper connexion with each other.

To illustrate to what an extent carelessness enters into the fixing of these little ranges, it has been no uncommon thing to find one simply thrust into the chimney opening, with, say, two or three feet of flue-pipe placed on the nozzle, which is at the back of the hot-plate, and nothing else done except cementing the opening round to make it tidy. In such a case as this the range proves the worst of failures, as the up-current of air, the draught, all passes in the open mouth (or throat, as it is more commonly called) of the chimney, and none passes through the fire to carry the flames, smoke, &c., around the flues, and, in fact, it is found difficult to keep the fire alight.

There is one necessary feature in fixing any and every description of close fire-range. That the range must be fixed air-tight, so that every particle of air which passes into the chimney, and which constitutes the draught, must first pass through the fire; there must be no openings, crevices, other flues, or passages leading into the range chimney so that air can pass in without being heated by first passing through the fire. A copper flue running into the range chimney is permissible, provided it has a well-fitted damper in it, so that when the copper is out of use the damper can be closed; when the copper is in use no ill result occurs, as it is adding its proportion of hot air to keep up the draught.

The range just spoken of as an illustration failed for want of a covering-in-plate,—a plate extending across the top of the opening from side to side and front to back, a hole being cut in it to fit tightly round the flue-pipe, and a door being provided for the sweep to operate through and for ventilation or other purposes. The addition of this plate would have caused the pulling power (as it may be called in this instance) of the draught to exert itself wholly through the fire, and instead of the fuel being in a state of half combustion, it would burn fiercely as in a furnace, and the flame will be travelling through the flues at great speed with a roaring noise, which, however, can be instantly checked by the damper.

This is how every range should work if the conditions are normal, particularly iron-flue ranges which are expected to work a little more sharply, as there is no separation between parts and consequent leakage of air, as between the brick and iron work of brick-flue ranges. If a range does not work in this manner then there must be something wrong, but it does not follow that the range-maker is to blame, though no doubt some makes of ranges need a more complex method of fixing than others.

It is not very common for portable ranges to be fixed so that they will not work at all, as the majority of workmen know the need and use of the covering-in plate spoken of, but it is quite common for these ranges to be found working sluggishly, that is, taking an unnecessary long time to cook what is put in the oven, or on the hot-plate, the fire being rather dull, and the flues being quickly full of soot, which collects under the hot-plate in festoons, and the flues need sweeping almost daily instead of once a week. In a case like this it can with every confidence be stated that there is a leakage of air into the chimney somewhere, that is, the draught in the chimney is not wholly coming up through the fire.

If the range is newly fixed, it may be caused by the covering-up plate not fitting tightly round the edges, or the hole in it for the flue-pipe is badly cut, or it may be a copper or other flue running into the kitchen chimney, or a hole or aperture somewhere. It will undoubtedly be found that there is an opening at some point more or less easy to find that is causing the mischief. If the range has worked well, and then suddenly fails, it may be some of the soot-doors left out of place, the door in the covering-in plate left open, or some such oversight, unless some accident has occurred. The best way to discover leakages is with a lighted taper; by holding this to suspected places, the flame will be drawn in if there be an in-current of air. Sometimes a range will work well when a leakage is known to exist, but this only happens when the chimney is high and very efficient, and can work the range well with its draught somewhat reduced.

Frequently these ranges are fixed standing out in front of an existing range,—one of the old pattern open ranges most probably; in this case it is much the best plan to carry the flue pipe from the portable range through the chimney-breast above the mantelshelf, and have the original chimney opening stopped across the top with a covering-in plate, as described before; if, however, there is a positive objection to carrying the flue pipe through the breast, then it can be carried up through the covering-in plate; but, in any case, everything must be air-tight. This cannot be too strongly insisted on. The joints in the flue pipe, and the joint where the pipe fits on the hot-plate nozzle, must be made sound. Common glaziers' putty is the very best article for jointing purposes, but the surfaces should be painted or Brunswick-blacked before the putty is applied, to make it adhere. Putty hardens with heat, and makes a really successful joint for all purposes like this.

Sometimes the front of the old existing range and the opening is entirely covered over with a large iron sheet, and the flue-pipe is just carried through a hole in this. This is a very inefficient method, as it is next to impossible to make this large sheet tight-fitting round the edges, and then no provision can be well left for the sweep, except by moving the sheet, which the sweep will not trouble to replace as securely as it should be. If the front of the opening containing the old range must be covered, let a loose covering be used, but have a covering-in plate fitted inside as recommended.

If a portable range is fixed in front of an existing close-fire range or kitchener, there is a little feature which needs attention, and which may very readily be overlooked. This is the possible bad state of the brickwork flues behind the kitchener. If these are out of order, it is possible that the chimney will manage to draw air through this direction, to the prejudice of the small range, and it becomes very desirable to see that the range behind the portable one is air-tight everywhere before good results can be expected. In the same way, if a portable range is fixed in an opening from which a kitchener has been removed without pulling down the old brick flues at the back, these flues should be filled up solid with concrete or some such material.

In alluding to the frequency with which portable ranges may be found working sluggishly, let it be clearly understood that this is never, or hardly ever, connected with the height or build of the chimney. What has been spoken of is a sluggishness that is perpetual, no one day giving better results than another. If the range should work well sometimes and badly at others then the trouble cannot be overcome by any of the suggestions yet made; the fault will be most probably due to the chimney itself, which will be found to be subject to down-draught with more or less intensity at certain times when the wind blows from certain quarters. Of course, irregular results are oftentimes occasioned by irregular attention in cleaning the flues.

When a portable range is worked out in the open-air, as in military camps where there are no high surroundings, it is astonishing what a short length of pipe will act efficiently as a chimney. The writer saw some at Hounslow which were fitted with handles for convenience of removal from spot to spot, and these were working their very best with 10 ft. of 8-in. iron pipe for a chimney, but to do this it must be seen that all the joints in the range itself as well as in the pipe were well-made and sound.

Iron pipe flues for these ranges should be 7 in. for 30 and 36 in. size, 8 in. for 42 in. size, and 9 in. for 48 in. size or larger. Some may consider these sizes too large, for there is a strange notion prevalent that very small pipe flues will answer. These sizes are none too large, for the largest mentioned is smaller than a 9-in. square brick chimney, and no builder would think of building less than a 9-in. chimney for the smallest cottage range. Every joint in a pipe chimney must be made perfectly tight.

If desired two of these ranges can be worked into one 9-in. chimney, and will work perfectly, provided each has a well-fitting damper that can be tightly closed when either range is not in use.

THE SANITARY INSPECTORS' ASSOCIATION.

The annual presidential address to this Association was delivered on Saturday evening, the 2nd inst., at Carpenters' Hall, before a large audience, by Dr. Richardson, the main subject of the address being the change which during the past year has taken place in the constitution of the Association. The Association must be congratulated on having, at so early a period in its existence, become practically an incorporated society, or, to speak more exactly, a society limited by guarantee. Very rarely had any society so young been so greatly honoured. But the change brought with it increased responsibilities, and in carrying out the powers given to them in their articles he thought their first efforts should be to make a school—a thoroughly practical teaching school. Lecturers might be got and work commenced by next October. The President thought the programme of studies should include six subjects, but two of these were not of immediate necessity. The four necessary subjects were in order (1) Physiology; —not the teaching of the dissecting-room, though it should be of a serious, if popular, character; (2) Natural History, with microscopical studies; (3) Chemistry, with a well-fitted, if small, laboratory, where research would be practicable independently of the school programme; and (4) Hygiene, their own proper study, the laws of health. The two eventual subjects were "The Theory of Hygiene," which would present the philosophic side of the matter; and lastly, what had been called by Dr. Despéné, of Marseilles, "Moral Hygiene," for which they could at present probably get no teacher and no class, but which might in the end prove to be the most beneficial of all. It might, perhaps, enable them to go so far as to undertake the cleansing of the world from all uncleanliness. The lecture concluded with a retrospect,—a stocktaking of matters hygienic. English people often reproached the Continentals with neglect of practical sanitary measures, and we had now the French throwing back upon us the reproach, and retorting that we had done nothing to reduce the fatalities from disease, and had not touched epidemics. Whether the charge was true or not, could not be certainly known until we got the complete statistics of the last census, which would not be for another year. From an analysis of the statistics of the previous census, made by Sir E. Chadwick and himself (Dr. Richardson), it was found that in two classes of causes of death there had been not progress, but retrogression, although in the remaining classes improvement was shown. Taking each 100 deaths from 1847 to 1880, there were from zymotic diseases of all kinds 23·26 in the former year, and only 20·09 in the latter,—an important reduction. Deaths from consumption had also diminished from 12·67 per cent. in 1847, to 9·12 per cent. in 1880, and from diseases of the digestive organs, from 5·82 to 4·74. There was also a slight diminution in all other classes of causes of death, except the two already mentioned, viz., "brain and nervous diseases," and "respiratory diseases other than consumption." The latter, which stood at 12·14 per cent. in 1847, had risen in 1880 to 17·78 per cent., and the former had risen from 11·54 to 13·12. The reduction in the case of the spreading diseases was no doubt due to improved sanitation, drainage, and water supply, and the cases of consumption to the fact that people were better housed and better fed. Why there had been an increase in the case of the other respiratory diseases he could not tell, but that due to brain disorders was easily enough accounted for. Would there be an improvement for the decade 1880-1890? He would say Yes, with regard to consumption, not on account of improved methods of treatment, but because people were able to get better food and because they had better sense. The increased numbers of those who played lawn-tennis, and particularly of those who practised cycling, had been the most fruitful causes of progress; and the chief cause of the retrograde movement was, in his opinion, that *ignis fatuus*, the germic theory,—or rather the search for germs in all diseases. Good minds were led astray from seeing the paramount importance of cleanliness, from the principles established by the Board of Health, from the necessity of rapidly getting rid of excreta, of removing all obstacles from our streets, of systematising our methods of road-making to save man and horse, both great sufferers by finding here wood, there stone, and in other places macadamised roads, instead of one general system of pavement. It was possible that the retrogression might be found to have gone on during the last decade, and with regard to the unfavourable movement in other respiratory diseases, there was much room for doubt. Some people believed insanity to be on the increase; suicides certainly were, and it appeared that cancer was becoming more and more fatal. The greater activity in political and literary matters, the increase of ambition, and the race for wealth obviously introduced severer strains, and accounted for the retrogression in the class of nervous disorders. One respiratory disease,—influenza,—which was baffling all the doctors and sanitarians, might perhaps be due to cosmic causes. Here they must all bend low and look for more light. The members of that Association could be depended upon, in the meantime, to go where it was their duty to go, and do what they thought best to be done to check disease, and, in conclusion, he wished them every success in their important work.

A discussion followed on the proposal of a vote of thanks, in which Mr. Perry (Hon. Member), Mr. Coulson (Inspector, Chelsea), and Mr. Hugh Alexander (the Chairman of the Council) took part.

The vote of thanks was passed with warm acclamation, and Dr. Richardson briefly replied, explaining in doing so that he wished not to be misunderstood with regard to his remarks upon the germic theory. He did not deny the existence of germs nor their influence in one or two small classes of diseases, but he regretted that these discussions led to little practical result, while much practical good that might be done was neglected in theoretical discussions which absorbed energies that would be prolific in good results if devoted to the real battle against disease, and to improving our drainage and increasing public cleanliness.

During the proceedings, the death of Lady Chadwick (widow of the late President) and the cremation of the body at Woking were mentioned, and a resolution was carried asking the President to continue negotiations which were already in progress for a four days' visit to Paris at Whitsuntide, to hold the annual conference of the Association in that capital on the invitation of the most important Sanitary Association of France, namely, that presided over by the veteran sanitarian, Dr. Pietra Santa.

THE POLYTECHNIC INSTITUTION.

THE annual Industrial Exhibition of the Polytechnic Young Men's Christian Institute, which has been open since the first of the month at 309, Regent-street, and will remain open until the end of this week, admirably shows the wide extent of the work of this institution, under the guidance of Mr. Quintin Hogg, who generously devotes many thousands of pounds annually in furtherance of the objects of the Institute. The exhibition appears to show the work of the students in the various classes during the past year, and to this is added many specimens of the work of members who, though they may have been students once, are now more advanced. Though a distinction is made in the catalogue, it would have been more interesting if the arrangement of the exhibits had more distinctly marked this difference. Of the technical exhibits, the most interesting is undoubtedly the mechanical engineering work, and, considering that much of this has been done by students of eighteen or nineteen years of age, under the guidance of one technical instructor, Mr. Rogers, the result is an exceedingly good one. The exhibits include pumps, lathes, dynamos, engines, and tools of various descriptions. The lead-work shows the usual difficulties of bossing and soldering leadwork successfully overcome; and adjacent to this exhibit is an example of cut and rubbed brickwork, showing a niche head and various capitals carefully expected, though somewhat lacking in vigour of design.

The exhibits of bootmaking, tailoring, harness-making, and carriage-building are interesting, though they cannot here be alluded to in detail. The furniture is entirely by members, and not by students, and is an interesting collection, in which the workmanship far exceeds the design. On a screen in this room are some most interesting sketches by Messrs. Herbert Railton, J. Pennell, C. W. Wyllie, and lfred East, and others, which have been lent for exhibition by Messrs. Cassell & Co. The joiners' and carpenters' woodwork exhibited are the usual specimens of joints and hand-railing which are set as exercises for the students. There is a large collection of drawings prepared in the building construction classes, upon which an immense amount of care seems to have been bestowed, and the construction is clearly shown. One case, however, of a cornice-stone, shown in section, appears to be sadly lacking in "bed," and would inevitably over-balance itself were it constructed as it is shown. There are several sets of designs submitted in competition for the Spencer Chadwick prize, the subject being a block of flats; but there is a singular lack of artistic conception displayed throughout. Though the exhibition is mainly the work of students, and as such must not be judged from too high a standpoint, we would call attention to the fact that there seems a great deal of room for improvement in the designs displayed, especially in the architectural drawings and in the furniture, jewellery, and other articles where, with every advantage, beauty of form might be allied with precision of workmanship. It appears that at present more attention is given to the latter than to the former, and we would commend this point to the careful consideration of Mr. Quintin Hogg and his colleagues who are interested in the capital work which this Institute is no doubt doing. One of the most interesting portions of the exhibition is the collection of steel and iron work and goldsmiths' work, lent from the South Kensington Museum collection.

Correspondence.

To the Editor of THE BUILDER.

THE FUTURE BUILDING ACT FOR LONDON.

SIR,—It is understood that among the many and extensive modifications in the Building Acts suggested by the County Council, there is one which affects the vacant space to be left for the use of buildings for light and ventilation. As this is not simply a proposal for allotting more space, but also introduces a new system of determining that space, it ought to be very carefully considered by all interested in London buildings. Its results are sure to be to some extent a surprise, and it appears likely to be far-reaching in its operation.

The new principle is that an imaginary plane is to be drawn from the back of the site at an angle of 45 deg. to the horizon (our old friend the angle of forty-five having lost credit of late with lawyers, has found some one fresh to take it up), and this plane of 45 deg. is to form a limit which the building is not to pass. Circumstances have caused me to consider what the effect would be on a good class of property, —say houses approaching 100*l*. a year rent, and it appears that it is likely to excite an injurious influence directly by the alterations which would have to be introduced into the design, and indirectly by the changes that might be made inside to avoid the pressure of the enactment; and when I say an injurious influence, I mean an unsanitary one.

It will, of course, be remembered that by this rule no part of a building can be higher than its distance back from the starting point, —*e.g.*, 20 ft. back allows 20 ft. high, and no more. Now, *primâ facie*, it appears inconsistent that the same Act should allow the *fronts* of houses to be as high as they are distant from the points of opposite buildings, while the *backs* (supposing two rows of houses parallel and back to back) will have to be twice as far apart as they are high. Yet this would be the result.

Let us suppose a house of a basement and four stories planted, as many good houses are, so that the basement-floor is level with the back-yard or garden, the front road being on arches. If the house is 55 ft. high at the back, and the back land 45 ft. deep or less, the top rooms at the back would have to be entirely dispensed with, yet these would be the best-lighted and best-ventilated rooms in the whole house; but for sanitary reasons (!) they must go. If the room or rooms cannot be spared, they will have to be added above the back addition, with the result that they themselves will be less well ventilated and worse lighted; that they more or less must overshadow windows of other rooms at the back, making those rooms less healthy; and that they will turn a back staircased window into a door, darkening the staircase, and depriving the lungs of the house of part of their supply of air.

Supposing a "tight fit," the method to which a builder of such houses could have resort in order to get his building into his site, would be diminishing the height of his stories, sinking his house into the ground, diminishing the width of his front area, and keeping up the level of his back-yard or garden. Every one of these expedients would diminish the healthiness of the house. I hardly think the Building Act Committee of the County Council can have foreseen all this, which, however, follows naturally from this proposal.

A DISTRICT SURVEYOR.

TOTNES CHURCH.

SIR,—"Viator," in his reference to rood-screens in last week's *Builder*, through a want of accurate information as to the details of restoration of the above church, has conveyed an incorrect impression. He says: "The great rood-loft has been destroyed within the last three years"; makes mention also of an eastern screen of oak as though that had been demolished at same time; and adds, "Meantime a hideous north gallery remains."

An acquaintance of over thirty years with the church,—one of the handsomest in the west of England,—enables me to give reliable facts in this matter. The works of restoration, under the superintendance of Sir Gilbert Scott, and latterly of his son, which extended over a period of twenty-two years, were completed in 1888, nothing at all having been done to the fabric in *the last three years*. The beautiful rood-screen of stone is the most conspicuous feature of the interior, traversing its full width, an elaborate network of tracery, but lightly proportioned so as to present the least possible obstruction to the view of the chancel beyond. I well remember a gallery with high pews which, previous to 1870, bridged the church, topping this screen and resting on iron supports in the chancel; its floor *may* have been identical with the original rood-loft, but was quite a wreck after seventeenth-century "vandalism"; if an eastern screen of oak ever stood here it was at a period beyond the memory of any living inhabitant. This gallery shared the fate of the other galleries with which the building was encumbered; for all were removed in or soon after the year mentioned. The stair to the rood-loft still remains, though closed up with an ornate entrance; and to north and south there is a parclose of stone. A considerable sum was spent on the screen itself, the dilapidated stonework being repaired and re-instated, and the whole decorated in harmony with the old colouring which could still be seen. As to a "hideous gallery remaining," the only ground for such a mis-statement can be that in an outer north aisle, built at the time of the restoration, a small gallery was placed to provide needful accommodation; it is not in any sense prominent, and the front panelling, which corresponds with the architect's other designs, is quite the reverse of unsightly.

Your correspondent says, "Perhaps the Vicar of Totnes will explain." My reason for sending these few lines is that the late Rev. J. W. Burrough, who was the animating spirit throughout the very arduous undertaking of restoring so large a church, was well known to me. The fifty years during which he was vicar have indeed left their mark, and he will long be remembered as one who exhibited in himself a happy combination all too rare,—faithfulness in the discharge of parochial ministrations and unwavering loyalty to evangelical principles, with a zeal that could not allow neglect of the "earthy sanctuary," but by reverent care must make it worthy of its sacred purpose. It is fitting that his devotion to this object should thus be put on record in your journal, especially as his sympathies were ever with "conservative" restoration. He entered into rest in 1888, and the towering walls of his old church overshadow his grave.

DEVONIENSIS.

SOFT TILES.

SIR,—Can any reader tell me of a preparation to render the surface of soft paving-tiles hard and incapable of forming a fine dust, which finds its way from the kitchen throughout the house?

DUST-HATER.

THE ENGLISH IRON TRADE.—After the holidays, the English Iron market is naturally quiet, and the unfavourable character of the Scotch and Cleveland ironmasters' returns will retard any forward impetus. Prices, however, do not exhibit any material reduction. There is a better demand noticeable in the hematite iron trade of the north-west. Manufactured iron is still in moderately good inquiry; and in steel rails there is a slightly better tone, but the steel trade generally is quiet. Tin-plates show an improved tendency. Engineers and shipbuilders are fairly well engaged. The coal trade, on the whole, is moderately busy; and in South Wales fair shipments have been made, in spite of the stoppage of the pits which was threatened, the crisis, however, being fortunately averted.—*Iron*.

The Student's Column.

WARMING BUILDINGS BY HOT WATER.

II.

HEAT: RADIATION (*continued*).

THE following table shows the comparative radiating powers of substances. The absorbing and radiating powers of materials are equal, so that the table applies either way. The reflective powers of surfaces are in exact inverse ratio to the above; for instance, lampblack, which stands highest in radiating power, is practically devoid of reflecting power, as everyone knows. Polished metals, however, stand high as reflectors, but would give poor results as radiating media. A homely illustration is the copper kettle, which loses heat rapidly when dirty (the metal being an excellent conductor), but when polished the loss is reduced to a minimum.

Radiating and Absorbing Powers of Substances.

Lampblack	100
White Lead	100
Glass	90
Cast-iron, untouched	70
,, polished	32
Wrought-iron, polished	30
Lead, tarnished	45
,, clean	19
Zinc ,,	18
Brass, clean, rough	12
,, highly polished	7
Copper ,, ,,	7
Silver ,, ,,	3

Lampblack answering so well as a radiating material has led to the belief that colour affects the radiating power of substances, but this is not the case with dark rays of heat, such as we get with all hot-water works, and from all non-luminous bodies.

The radiating power of a body is not due to its substance, but to its extreme external surface, we may say, its skin. Lampblack, painted on, is very perfect as just mentioned. If this material composed the whole substance of the pipes, the effect would be bad, as being a poor conductor, the heat would not get through to its outer surface to be radiated. The high radiating efficiency of white lead points conclusively to paint being a very suitable material to apply to any exposed radiating surface which cannot be left untouched or coated with lampblack. All paints, particularly those whose colours consist of metallic oxides, answer exceedingly well, but they should be laid on thin, for the materials of paints are not all good heat conductors, and no barrier, however slight, should exist to prevent the free escape of heat where it is desired. Undoubtedly lampblack, applied as a water colour, gives the best results if appearance has not to be studied; an application of this material to the silver pipe referred to would overcome the trouble mentioned.

There is a fancy for bronzing pipes and radiators, especially the latter, but although the effect may be liked as regards appearance, the results in regard to radiation are bad. All bronze powders, also gold leaf, and metals electrically deposited, are practically bright metallic surfaces, which have been already pointed out as being bad radiators. They are less efficient than varnished or painted surfaces. If a radiator or coil which is in use be half-bronzed and half-painted black, the difference in heat radiation from the two different surfaces will be actually perceivable to the hand or face, if tested at about 12 in. distance. In making an experiment like this, however, it must be first ascertained that the actual temperature of the radiator is alike all over; this is not always the case.

From the table quoted it will be noticed that glass is a good radiator of heat; whatever heat it absorbs, it parts with readily. This by itself might bring glazed porcelain and Doulton ware radiators into use, and which would be exceedingly pretty; but there is another point to be considered in the fact that the material of the pipes and the glazed surface itself are all poor conductors of heat, and would, therefore, give but little chance for the outer surface to show its radiating efficiency. Probably something of the sort may be successfully brought into use some day. It would be worth doing, for radiators, although decided improvements upon coils, are capable of being improved upon also, and to a considerable extent. Stoves are made in earthenware, and have a very handsome appearance; but the higher temperature of fire heat can be more easily dealt with than that which we get from hot water. The former is retained, subdued, and tempered by the interposing poor conductor.

Detore quitting the subject of radiant heat, special attention must be drawn to its non-effect upon the air. The radiant rays, as before mentioned, pass through the air without raising its temperature, and they only have effect upon whatever they come in contact with and impinge upon. From these objects that they encounter, there proceeds a re-radiation of heat, which also goes on without heating the air. The particular advantage of this is that human beings, as also most living creatures, benefit, and are also made comfortable by their bodies being kept at a good warmth, but at the same time breathing a cool or cold air,—air at a much lower temperature than the body enjoys. The extremes that this can be carried to are very great; this can be judged by the pleasure experienced in breathing the cold air of a bitter winter day, the body at the time requiring to be thickly clothed and of a temperature that is registered quite at the other end of the thermometer. Radiant heat, which is the most natural heat, fulfils this requirement by affording warmth to the surroundings, but without affecting the air.

There is, however, another good feature connected with radiant heat which, as it does not alter the temperature of the air, does not interfere with its proper degree of moistness. The moistness or saturation of the atmosphere has always to be considered in warm or hot-air works, and it has often to be provided for in works with exposed pipes.

It has to be explained that the air with every difference in temperature has a different capacity for water. The cooler the air the less water it requires or can hold in suspension, but in direct proportion as it gains in heat, it will imbibe moisture. If air has not a sufficiency of moisture in it, it is, to say the least, disagreeable, sometimes injurious, especially affecting those with throat troubles (as an east wind does, which also lacks moisture). Air, when saturated, contains water vapour as follows:—

Temperature of the air (Fahrenheit) Degrees.	Quantity of vapour per cubic foot. Grains weight.
20	1·52
30	2·16
40	2·92
50	4·19
60	5·76
70	7·77
80	10·59
90	14·15
100	19·00

The capacity of air for water is about doubled by each increase of 27 deg. F.

As explained earlier, a hot-water apparatus with exposed pipes furnishes heat in two ways, viz., by radiation, and by heating the air which has contact with the pipes, &c., and not by radiation only, so that, properly speaking, some provision should always be made to add moisture to the air which is warmed. This, however, is seldom done, and as seldom needed, for with exposed pipes, the chief of the heat is radiated; the little increased heat to the air can readily supply itself with moisture from many sources. It is usually sufferers from bronchial affections who can instantly discover a dryness of the atmosphere. In this case moisture can be furnished by pans of water placed on the radiators; some radiators have the top castings capable of holding water which permits of the air helping itself, and the water itself also evaporates slightly with the warmth.

CONVECTION OF HEAT.—This is the way by which heat is conveyed (actually transported) by fluids. This action is almost of greater interest to the hot-water engineer than either of the others treated, as it really accounts for the existence of his calling. Water and gases—in fact, all fluids, are composed of elements existing in the form of minute molecules, grains, or particles. It is very necessary to understand that fluids are composed of atoms, to account for the action of convection. There is not the slightest friction or cohesive property existing among these particles—in fact, there is supposed to be a slightly repelling influence amongst them, for gases and water will spread great distances if unconfined and experiencing no restraining influence. It is to be assumed that the molecules of water are spherical to account for the very free motion amongst them; and a point to be impressed upon the reader is, that the utter absence of friction permits of an exceedingly rapid motion being attained. It is sometimes a little hard to grasp this theory, as there are no solid and visible substances that act with a freedom any way approaching this.

There is a simple means of experimenting to ascertain and become familiar with the process of convection. Take a medium-sized glass jar or a wide-shaped bottle, and nearly fill it with water; then place or suspend it over a lamp,—a spirit lamp gives the greatest heat, but the action is quite sufficient if the vessel is held over the glass chimney of an oil lamp. Before, however, any visible results can be obtained, we must put some substance in the water that will make the motion obvious. The best material to put in the water is amber, which must first be reduced to a dust, a fine powder. This should be stirred in. Amber most nearly approaches the gravity of water, and it will be found that a good proportion of the dust particles will remain suspended in the water without motion unless agitated. By watching the movements of these particles we may ascertain exactly what is happening with the water, for every movement is indicated by the amber.

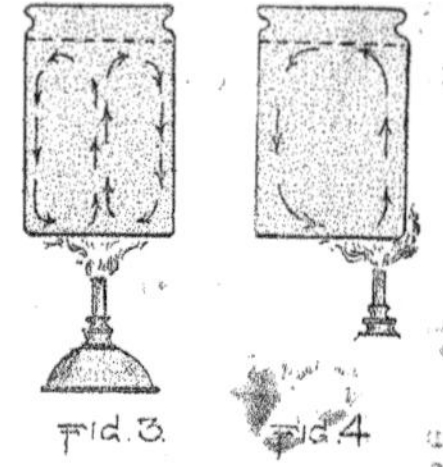

Fig. 3 shows the motion of the water, if the heat is applied to the centre of the bottom of the jar; if the heat is applied nearer the side the action is more as fig. 4. The exact cause of the action is as follows:—Before the heat is applied to the jar we may consider that the particles constituting the mass of water are stationary. Upon application of heat to the bottom we cause those particles which are in contact with the bottom surface to become warm, and as they absorb heat, they, like every other substance, to a greater or less extent, increase in size; that is, they expand when heated. When a material expands with heat it does not, of course, increase in weight, consequently it may be looked upon as a lighter substance while it is hot. This is the case with the molecules of water as they become heated; they increase in size but not in weight, and, consequently, are, bulk for bulk, lighter than their colder neighbours.

The result of this difference in weight is that the particles being so mobile and free from friction, the heavier ones instantly force their way below the lightened ones and cause them to rise. This is just the same action as takes place if we take a piece of wood or cork and plunge it into a vessel of water and release it at the bottom; it instantly ascends to the top, it being a lighter material than the water. Therefore, we may understand, and experiment will show, that immediately warmth is imparted to the water at the bottom, a circulatory action sets in, the warmed particles rising and cold particles taking their place, which also become warmed, and rising, give place to more, and so on. The circulatory action of water, and its application to hot-water pipes, will be dealt with in the next paper.

SOCIETY FOR THE ENCOURAGEMENT OF THE FINE ARTS.—The thirty-third annual report of this Society, for the year 1891, briefly chronicles the proceedings of the year, and appends the programme for the coming year. The *conversazioni* will continue to be held in the galleries of the Royal Institute of Painters in Water Colours, Piccadilly. It has been customary to hold the first *conversazione* in the month of January, but owing to the inclement weather which usually prevails at that time, the Council have decided to hold this *conversazione* at a later date.

BELLS, NORTHWOOD CHURCH, STAFFORDSHIRE.—Messrs. Charles Carr, of Smethwick, have secured the contract to recast and rehang the bell (weight, 22½ cwts.) at Northwood Church, near Bucknall, Staffordshire.

GENERAL BUILDING NEWS.

HORSHAM GRAMMAR SCHOOL.—The Governors of the Grammar School being about to erect new school buildings and residence, eight architects of repute were nominated, from whom they have selected Mr. Arthur Vernon, of London and High Wycombe, as their architect to carry out the new buildings, which are to be commenced in the spring.

SCIENCE AND ART SCHOOLS, HIGH WYCOMBE.—New science and art schools are about to be erected at High Wycombe, from the designs of Mr. Arthur Vernon.

NEW BUILDING ESTATE AT BIRMINGHAM.—The first portion of a large building estate, situated at Sparkhill, a suburb of Birmingham, has now been completed. The builders were Messrs. Hughes & Son, of Sparkhill. At Edgbaston, another large suburb of Birmingham, a number of villa residences of somewhat similar character to the preceding, but with wider frontages, have also been completed. The builder was Mr. Edward Airey, of Gillott-road, Birmingham. The architect of these was Mr. John Statham Davis, also of Birmingham.

RESTORATION OF WOODLEIGH CHURCH, DEVON.—For the past seven or eight months the Church of St. Mary, in the parish of Woodleigh, has undergone restoration, at a cost of 1,220*l.* The tower has been coped with granite, as it was found that the stones at the top were quite loose, and all the mortar was washed out. It has also been re-roofed, leaded, and pointed with cement. All the roofs of the building have been renewed, the inside showing oak boarding on a circular sweep, with oak purlin and ribs and bosses at the intersections. Inside the chancel roof has been treated the same way. The walls have been stuccoed with blue lias, these being previously covered with curious paintings in distemper. An attempt was made to preserve these, says the *Western Morning News*, but they have been so whitewashed over and over again that this was found to be impossible. Wood-framed windows have been replaced by granite, while those of stone have been renewed and pierced, the whole being filled with cathedral glass. What was known as the Hendham transept has been given up for use as a vestry and organ-chamber. The space underneath the tower, which formerly served for this purpose, is now converted into a baptistry. All the floors are tiled, and the pews, which have a flooring of Farr's patent wood blocks, are of red deal, stained and varnished. The chancel arch has been rebuilt, and quoined with granite. On the north wall of the chancel, a window, which has been walled up for years, has been opened, and the splays built with leaders and stretchers resting on granite sills. Within the chancel a rise is made by three steps of white Sicilian marble and encaustic tiles. In the north wall of the chancel there is an old eastern sepulchre, which has been preserved. Mr. G. H. Fellowes Prynne, London, was the architect; and Messrs. Farr & Sons, of West Alvington, were given the contract for the work.

COTTAGE HOSPITAL, HIGH WYCOMBE.—The High Wycombe Cottage Hospital has been recently enlarged and endowed with a sum of about 2,800*l.*, granted by the trustees of the Earl of Beaconsfield Memorial Fund from the surplus at their disposal. The new buildings consist of a large operation and convalescent room, bath-room, heated linen-chamber, and other conveniences, costing, with additional piece of land, about 800*l.* The new buildings were opened by Mr. Coningsby Disraeli, the heir of the late earl, on the 19th ult. Mr. Arthur Vernon was the architect, he having been the architect also of the new buildings which were erected in 1875; and Mr. H. Flint, of High Wycombe, was the contractor.

NEW BOARD SCHOOLS AT PERCY MAIN.—The formal opening of new schools, erected at Percy Main by the Tynemouth School Board, took place on the 30th ult. The site, purchased from the Duke of Northumberland, is in one of the most prominent thoroughfares of Percy Main, namely, in John-street, and containing 2,500 superficial yards, with a frontage of 134 ft. 6 in., and a depth of 158 ft. Provision is made for 172 children in Standards I. and II., and for 166 infants, with arrangements for future extension to accommodate 108 more children. The main school is 60 ft. long by 22 ft. wide, with a central recess 22 ft. by 16 ft., and class-rooms at each end 20 ft. by 18 ft. At the west end are two infant's-rooms, the larger one (fitted with desks) 27 ft. 6 in. by 22 ft., and the smaller one (with gallery) 22 ft. by 20 ft. Care has been taken to supply the largest amount of light and ventilation. The desks and fittings are all of oak. The playgrounds are cemented throughout, and the children will have the advantage of covered sheds for wet weather. The contractors for the whole of the works were Messrs. J. & W. Simpson, of North Shields and Blyth, and the buildings, which include a caretaker's house of four rooms, have been erected from the designs and under the superintendence of Mr. F. R. N. Haswell, F.R.I.B.A., of North Shields.

NEW COTTAGE HOSPITAL AT LEDBURY.—Mr. Michael Biddulph, M.P., has given to the town of Ledbury, in commemoration of the coming of age of his eldest son, Mr. John Biddulph, a cottage hospital, at a total cost of about 3,000*l.* The new building is erected in a most commanding position in the town, and immediately opposite a dwelling-house in which the Ledbury Cottage Hospital was opened nearly twenty years ago. The new building is of the Elizabethan style, and in addition to offering all the requirements of a cottage hospital, there is attached to it the residence for a town nurse. Mr. Hadrien, of Malvern, is the architect, and Mr. George Hill, of Ledbury, the builder.

THE BUILDING TRADE IN SCOTLAND IN 1891.—The *Aberdeen Free Press* reports that the building trade in that city during the past year has been "fully more prosperous" than during the preceding twelve months. "Fewer new buildings have been erected, but the operations have been all over, on a larger scale. This will be fully seen when it is mentioned that with an addition of about 170 new houses and cottages to the city, as against nearly 250 in 1890, there is an increase in the valuation of the town through the erection of these new buildings alone of 6,308*l.* 7s., as compared with 5,670*l.* for 1890. As a consequence, both the mason and joiner departments of the trade have been very fully employed. In the latter branch business was indeed exceptionally brisk during the summer months, and men were in great demand. This naturally led to a demand for a rise in pay. About the middle of May, therefore, and after the matter had been discussed by the trade 'Board of Arbitration,' the standard rate of pay was advanced from 6d. to 6½d. per hour, with 7d. and even 7½d. for very superior men. With the rise in wages, however, there was no corresponding rise in prices; competition has been tending, indeed, to become keener than ever, and as a result the profits of the employers continue to diminish. In fact, as one large employer in the city puts it, the masters begin to breathe an air of satisfaction when they find themselves clear on a job. The working day in the joiner trade, as among the masons, continues at the nine hours, and there appears to be no disposition towards a change on the part of either the masters or men. There is a feeling among the men, however, that another rise in wages might fairly be demanded about the beginning of the year; but it may be assumed that, before anything of the nature of strong measures are taken, the matter may be referred again, in the first instance, to the Joiner Arbitration Committee."——The *Dundee Courier* says that during the past year the building trade of Dundee has been exceptionally brisk, it being estimated that over 200,000*l.* has been expended in the erection of dwelling-houses and public buildings or on making additions to works in different parts of the city. From a public point of view, the principal undertaking has been the new Parochial Hospital in Mains Loan. The Old Asylum grounds, it may be mentioned, have been the centre of activity, some blocks of shops and dwelling-houses having been reared on the sites acquired from the Asylum Directors in Park-avenue, Morgan-street, Cardean-street, Albert-street, and Balmore-street.——The *Edinburgh Evening News* says that the year, on the whole, has been a satisfactory one from a labour standpoint. "Unskilled labour has been in fair demand, the works carried on in connexion with the Water of Leith Purification Scheme and railway extension having given regular employment to a large number of men, but our survey concerns workers of a superior grade, and it is gratifying to note that, in the main, the position of the artisan has rather improved than otherwise. With one of the most important classes, masons, a reduction of wage had recently to be endured, following, however, a previous increase. In the early autumn the standard wage was lowered from 8½d. to 8d., but, notwithstanding, the masons are financially better circumstanced than they were twelve months ago, and that things seem to have an upward tendency seems to be shown by the statement of one of the leading firms in the city that if they were asked to estimate for fresh contracts the possibility of increased expenditure in this department would be taken into account. The distinguishing feature of the past year from the builder's outlook has been the comparative absence of fluctuation, no congestion having occurred, in the first instance, because the openness of the weather at the beginning and end of the year has enabled the work to proceed unchecked. As has already been shown, speculative builders have not played so pronounced a part as in past years, and as private beneficence and commercial enterprise have alike provided, and will continue to provide, material for building operations, the year closes with the promise that in the succeeding twelvemonths matters will stand about their present level."

DISSOLUTION OF PARTNERSHIP.—We are informed that in consequence of the retirement of Mr. W. Frederick Simpson from the firm of W. B. Simpson & Sons, of 100, St. Martin's-lane, a dissolution of partnership takes effect from December 31 last. The business will be carried on by Mr. Edward Henry Simpson under the style of "W. B. Simpson & Sons," as heretofore.

PARTNERSHIP.—Mr. Charles H. Beloe, M.Inst.C.E., of Liverpool and Westminster, has taken into partnership Mr. Frank E. Priest, Assoc.M.Inst.C.E., a former pupil, and for several years past the manager of his Liverpool office.

SANITARY AND ENGINEERING NEWS.

SEWERAGE WORKS, HAYES (MIDDLESEX).—A Local Government Board inquiry was held on the 31st ultimo with respect to the application of the Uxbridge Union Rural Sanitary Authority for the sanction of the Local Government Board to their borrowing 10,500*l.* for the purposes of sewerage and sewage disposal for the Parish of Hayes. Details were given in connexion with the application, of which the Inspector, Col. Ducat, R.E., took notes, and promised to report thereon in due course to the Local Government Board. The engineer to the scheme is Mr. Frederick Beesley, M.Inst.C.E., of Westminster. The system proposed for dealing with the sewage is that known as the International Purification Company's process.

EAST BROOK AND DYNAS POWIS WATER-SUPPLY.—The Cardiff Rural Sanitary Authority have now, after a considerable amount of opposition, supplied these important and growing villages with an adequate supply of wholesome water. Dynas Powis was formerly supplied by springs from a catchment area, gravitating into a reservoir having a storage capacity of 100,000 gallons, thence the water, after passing through a filter, gravitated to the village of Dynas Powis by 3-in. cast-iron socket-pipes for a distance of half a mile, where lately, owing to the increase of population, the supply had to be worked on the intermittent system, which proved both wasteful and injurious to the health of the inhabitants. In the meantime East Brook was supplied with water from some fifty shallow wells sunk in the neighbourhood of cesspools and surrounded with highly-manured garden land, resulting, as might be expected, in causing a great deal of sickness, arising from the effects of polluted water. The Rural Sanitary Authority, after the consideration of several schemes for augmenting and improving their own existing supply, so as to extend the same to East Brook, eventually agreed with the Cardiff Corporation to extend their mains from Llandough, through East Brook, to Dynas Powis Bridge, levying their own water-rates at East Brook, and discharging a supplementary supply in bulk into the mains of the Rural Sanitary Authority at Dynas Powis Bridge. For this purpose the Cardiff Corporation have laid about 2,500 yards of cast-iron 4 in. socket-pipes, together with lead service-pipes laid to the external walls of each dwelling-house, and hydrants for fire-extinguishing purposes laid 100 yards apart on the 4 in. main, together with all necessary stopcocks, sluice and air valves complete. This work was effectually carried out under the superintendence of Mr. Priestly, Asso.M.Inst.C.E., Deputy Borough Water Engineer, Cardiff. The Rural Sanitary Authority have also extended their mains at Dynas Powis, having laid 1,000 yards 3-in. and 1,500 yards 2-in. cast-iron socket-pipes, with all necessary sluice and air valves, stopcocks, hydrants, and water-meters complete; also 300 yards ¾-in. and 200 yards ½-in. wrought-iron pipes, and 200 yards ¾-in. and 300 yards ½-in. lead pipes, with all necessary fittings complete. The excavation for this work was carried out almost entirely in rock by Mr. Edmund Lewis, contractor, Dynas Powis. The contract for the supply, laying and fixing all mains and fittings, was carried out by Messrs. Cross Bros., of Cardiff, and William Fraser, Asso.M.Inst.C.E., Surveyor to the Rural Sanitary Authority, was the engineer.

WATERWORKS AT AVINGTON PARK.—A new waterworks has recently been constructed for Avington House, the seat of Sir Charles Shelley, Bart., which not only supplies the domestic requirements of the mansion, but makes provision with a view of protection from fire, both at the house and at the stables. The supply is obtained from the Itchen at the waterfall in the Park, and close to the high road, the water being filtered through a small gravel filter bed before passing to the hydraulic rams constructed in a small building on the opposite side of the road. There are two 5-in. "Vulcan" high duty rams, each worked by a separate drive pipe, the effective working head being 7 ft. Each ram raises about 50 gallons of water per minute, and together they force upwards of 5,000 gallons per twenty-four hours to the reservoir, which is on a hill at a distance of 1,080 yards, and at an elevation of 126 ft. The rising main from the rams to the reservoir is of cast-iron socket-pipes, the spigots and sockets being turned and bored to ensure satisfactory joints, and is in two sections. The first section, from the rams to the mansion, distance 1,400 ft., is 8 in. internal diameter; the remainder, from the mansion to the reservoir, distance 1,840 ft., is 6 in. internal diameter. The rising main is let into the bottom of the reservoir, and is used both as an up-cast and down-cast, thereby obviating the necessity of two separate lines of pipes. The fire hydrants round the mansion are five in number, and are placed in the most advantageous positions to gain complete command of the entire building. The reservoir is situated on top of a hill in Chalkdale Field, the elevation, as stated above, being 126 ft. above the hydraulic rams. It is excavated out of the hill, and is divided into two compartments by a longitudinal wall, each compartment being 50 ft. long by 14 ft. 6 in. wide by 6 ft. 6 in. deep. The reservoir contains, when full, 60,000 gallons. It is constructed of brickwork laid

COMPETITION, CONTRACTS, AND PUBLIC APPOINTMENTS.

COMPETITION.

Nature of Work.	By whom Advertised.	Premium.	Designs to be delivered.
*Family Hotel, Clacton-on-Sea	J. Gilders	£100	No date.

CONTRACTS.

Nature of Work or Materials.	By whom Required.	Architect, Surveyor, or Engineer.	Tenders to be delivered.
Wards at Fever Hospital	Belfast Union	Yolinger & Mackenzie	Jan. 12
New Road, Culvert, &c.	Llandaff High. Bd.	Jas. Holden	do.
Well-sinking, Preston Brook	Manchester Ship Canal Co.	*Official*	do.
Water Supply Works, Neilston, N.B.	Renfrewshire C. C.	Niven & Haddin	do.
Sewerage Works	Armagh U.S.A.	J. F. Pedlie	Jan. 15
Water Supply Bore Hole	Rugeley Local Board	W. R. Radford	do.
Cemetery Extension Works	Llewe Town Council	G. Eaton-shore	Jan. 18
Jointing and Laying Cast-iron Pipes. Ynysybwl	Mountain Ash (Glam.) Local Board	J. Williams	do.
Brick Service, Reservoir	Belper R.S.A.	W. H. Radford	do.
Sanatorium, Repton, Derby	Governors of Sir J. Port's Charity	J. Shaw & Son	do.
*Broken Granite	Paddington Vestry	*Official*	do.
*Granite Kerb, York Paving, &c.	do.	do.	do.
*Roadmaking and Tar Paving Works	Lewisham Bd. of Wks.	do	Jan. 19
*Hosting Board's Offices	Hornsey Local Bd.	....	do.
Engines, Boilers, &c. Electric Light Station, Dickinson-street	Manchester Corp.	*Official*	Jan. 20
Iron Castings	Leeds Corporation	do.	do.
*Making-up and Paving Roads	Fulham Vestry	W. Sykes	do.

CONTRACTS.—*Continued.*

Nature of Work or Materials.	By whom Required.	Architect, Surveyor or Engineer.	Tenders to be delivered.
*Alterations to Gt. Stangerton Manor	....	Martin & Purchase	Jan. 22
Fireproof Floors, &c. at Public Library and Museum	Carlisle Corporation	W. Howard Smith	do.
Police Station, &c. Hurst-green	East Sussex C. C.	H. Card	Jan. 23
Working Men's Club, Methley, near Leeds	Earl of Maxborough	....	Jan. 25
*New Branch P.O. Manchester	Com. of H.M. Wks. &c.	*Official*	Jan. 26
*Public Convenience, &c.	London County Council	do.	do.
*Alterations to Sanitary Arrangements at Workhouse	Sevenoaks Union	Thomas Potter	do.
*Works and Repairs to Public Buildings, &c.	Com. of H. M. Wks. &c.	*Official*	Jan. 28
Waterworks	Widnes Local Board	G. O. Ellison & Son	Feb. 1
*New Engine and Well House	do.	do.	do.
*Erection of School Buildings	Hornsey School Board	Chas. Bell	Feb. 2
*Iron Bridge over Railway, Hull	North Eastern Rly.	H. Copperthwaite	Feb. 3
*Granite Setts, Curb, and Channelling	Hull Corporation	A. E. White	do.
Sewerage Works, &c. Birkdale, Southport	C. Weld-Blundell	C. A. Atkinson	No date.
Wesleyan Chapel, Talke-pits, Hanley	....	Elijah Jones	do.
*Two Pairs of Officers' Quarters, Devonport	War Department	*Official*	do.
*Wesleyan Chapel, Gipsy-lane, Upton-park	The Trustees	Elijah Jones	do.
*School at Chadsmoor	Cannock School Board	G. H. Cox	do.

PUBLIC APPOINTMENTS.

Nature of Appointment.	By whom Advertised.	Salary.	Applications to be in.
*Engineer's Assistant	Reigate Corporation	150*l.*	Jan. 23
*Dublin District Surveyorships	Civil Service Commrs.	....	Feb. 10

Those marked with an Asterisk (*) are advertised in this Number. *Competitions, p.* iv. *Contracts, pp.* iv., vi., & viii. *Public Appointments, p.* xviii. & xix.

in cement, the floor being of concrete, and the roof is formed of wrought-iron girders, placed at distances of 5 ft. apart, the spaces being filled with shallow arches of solid concrete levelled on the top. This portion of the work has been carried out by Mr. W. Shearman, builder, of Winchester. The hydraulic rams were manufactured by Mr. H. P. Vacher, of the Vulcan Ironworks, Worthy, near Winchester, who contracted for and carried out the entire installation.

STAINED GLASS AND DECORATION.

MEMORIAL WINDOW, ST. JAMES'S CONGREGATIONAL CHURCH, NEWCASTLE.—A stained-glass window has just been placed in St. James's Congregational Church, Newcastle, by Mrs. Scott, in memory of her late husband. The work has been executed by Messrs. Heaton, Butler, Bayne, & Co., of London, and represents the incident in the Gospels of the meeting of Our Lord and Nathaniel.

STAINED-GLASS WINDOW, PARISH CHURCH, IDLE.—A stained-glass window has just been unveiled in the Parish Church, Idle, in memory of the late Vicar of Idle (the Rev. Henry Harrison). The window, which is the work of Messrs. Kayll & Co., of Leeds, has been erected under the supervision of Messrs. Kendall & Bakes, architects, of Idle and Leeds. It is divided by the gallery into two equal parts. The upper portion is filled in with painted glass, geometric in design. The lower half of the window consists of a representation of the "Good Samaritan."

WINDOWS, GIGGLESWICK CHURCH, YORKSHIRE.—Mr. T. W. Camm, of Smethwick, has completed two windows for Giggleswick Church, Yorks. The east window contains the subjects of the Crucifixion and the Ascension, occupying the whole of the six lights, with their canopies and bases. The west window of the north aisle contains the subject of the Presentation in the Temple, in three lights. They are memorials to the Hartbury family.

FOREIGN AND COLONIAL.

DENMARK.—For a considerable time one of the leading questions in Copenhagen, as testified from time to time in our columns, has been the provision of better and safer accommodation for the valuable national museums,—viz., of Norse Archæology, the People's Museum, the Ethnographical Museum, the Numismatic Museum, &c., which are now located in the so-called Prince's Palace, and one plan was to erect a couple of large new buildings for the storage of these treasures between Gothersgade and Osterbro, where the new great Museum of Arts is in course of erection. But recently it has been considered whether, after all, the use of the Prince's Palace might not be continued by rebuilding it, and buying up certain properties around. An influential commission of *savants* and architects was appointed by the Government, and that body recommends that this plan should be carried out. It is proposed to buy up all adjoining properties, and by the making of a new street, to form a square complex of museums, isolated on all sides. The cost of this great undertaking is estimated at 87,000*l.*, the work occupying some five years. Professor Sterk has already prepared a preliminary design for the new building, which has been approved by the committee. The style naturally will be the same as that of the old building, viz., late Renaissance. It was built at the beginning of last century. The properties referred to around the Palace have already been acquired by the State.——In the neighbourhood of Vamdrup, in Southern Jutland, Dr. Henry Peterson, of the Museum of Northern Antiquities, has excavated some barrows from the Bronze Age, in which a large number of oaken coffins, made by hollowing out the trunks of trees, have been found, similar to those already found in Denmark, and being several thousand years of age. Some objects of bronze and wood were also found. Denmark is the only country possessing perfect costumes from the Bronze Age. Those of men are all alike, but not so those of women. Of female costumes only one has hitherto been found perfect in Denmark. The discovery is, therefore, of some interest in an archæological sense.

STUTTGART.—The new National Museum for Science and Art in course of erection is to have some mural frescoes and sculptural decoration in its central hall as a memorial to the late King of Würtemberg. 6,700*l.* have been set aside for this purpose, and a competition has been opened for designs. The very detailed programme of requirements published shows that eight prizes are to be given, having a total value of 500*l.*

VIENNA.—On the grounds of the so-called "Music and Theatre Exhibition" to be opened next summer a "model" theatre is in course of erection, at a cost of some 65,000 florins. There will be 1,500 seats, and standing-room for 500 visitors in the place. A large concert-hall is also being built on the grounds.

MISCELLANEOUS.

LECTURES ON ARCHITECTURE AT THE ROYAL ACADEMY.—Professor Aitchison, A.R.A., is announced to deliver six lectures at the Royal Academy on "Saracenic and Turkish Architecture." The dates are January 25 and 28, and February 1, 4, 8, and 11.

THE SLATE TRADE DURING 1891.—During the past year there has been a marked improvement in the demand for all sizes of slates, but more especially in one or two of the large sizes, orders coming in more briskly as the season advanced, so much so that the close of the year found the quarries with smaller stocks and better orders than they have had for the last fifteen years. The foreign and colonial trades have been very brisk, the home trade fairly so, but the present state of affairs is caused principally by the stoppage of over-production and the supply having been reduced so that it does not exceed the demand. When prices were low, quarries endeavoured to make up for diminished profits by increasing their make. This, in many cases, was forced to the utmost capacity of the quarry, and without any corresponding dead work being done, with the inevitable result that the make cannot now be kept up without considerable expenditure, and in some cases the quarries are nearly worked out. The process of the "survival of the fittest" has been going on, so that most of the weak quarries have been closed, and only three new slate quarry companies have been registered. All old quarries re-opened, as there is practically no undeveloped ground on the Bangor or Festiniog veins. There have been no strikes or labour troubles, and the men are earning fair wages.

THE HARD-WOOD TRADE.—Messrs. C. Leary & Co.'s annual circular, dated January 4, 1892, on ship-building, furniture, and other hard woods says:—"The total imports of timber and plank [during the past year] are $1\frac{1}{4}$ per cent. below those of 1890, whilst the deliveries show a reduction of 16 per cent., the stock standing at an increase of $14\frac{1}{2}$ per cent. There are 2,800 loads landing, as against 1,500 loads a year ago, the tonnage afloat is 9,086 tons, as compared with 18,826 tons, and that under charter but not yet loaded is 20,354 tons against 25,302 tons at the close of 1890. Timber.—The volume of business has been fairly satisfactory, but during the first half of the year prices steadily declined until very low figures were established. A decided improvement afterwards set in when it became evident that the supplies for the new shipping season would be light, in consequence of insufficient rains for floating operations. Prices have advanced about 20 per cent. from their lowest point, and the present position of the market is satisfactory. Although the prospective demand does not promise to be more than moderate, the tonnage engaged for loading during the year is very reasonable, and a steady and satisfactory market may be anticipated. Plank.—The import has been heavy, the largest, we believe, on record; the deliveries show a falling off of 10 per cent., and the stock is more than double that at the beginning of 1890. The market was favourable during the first quarter of the year, after which the constant arrivals began to tell, and prices quickly declined about 10 per cent. The demand has been languid during the last six months and prices remain depressed, but with moderation in the supplies we see no reason why there should not be a steady recovery to more satisfactory values."

RESULTS OF AUCTION SALES IN 1891.—According to "Extracts from late Exchange Registers," the total of sales reported from January 1, to December 31, 1891, amounted to 4,174,915*l.*; as compared with 4,447,840*l.* in 1888; 4,304,954*l.* in 1889; and 4,287,111*l.* in 1890. There has thus been a continued decline during the past four years.

A MAIN ROADS ARBITRATION.—A dispute between the Hampshire County Council and the Bournemouth Town Council respecting the cost of maintaining main roads through Bournemouth, was decided a few days ago. The length of road was three and a half miles. The Town Council originally claimed 1,868*l.*, which was refused by the County Council, on the ground that it was exorbitant. The County Council offered 1,400*l.* This was refused by the Town Council, on the advice of the Borough Surveyor, Mr. F. W. Lacey, by whom this claim was amended. The matter was ultimately referred to the arbitration of the Local Government Board, and in July last Mr. T. Codrington, M.I.C.E., attended at Bournemouth for that purpose. Besides Mr. F. W. Lacey, the Borough Surveyor, Mr. C. Jones, of Ealing, Mr. William Weaver, of Kensington, and Mr. J. Strachan, of Brentford, gave evidence for the Town Council, and Mr. Jas. Robinson, County Surveyor for Hampshire, Mr. Fletcher, County Surveyor of Dorsetshire, Mr. Thomas de Courcy Meade, of Hornsey, Mr. Robert Phillips, County Surveyor of Gloucestershire, and Mr. Charles Tomes, Borough Surveyor of Eastbourne, for the County Council. The award has now been settled at 2,608*l.*, nearly 800*l.* in excess of the original claim.

ENGINEERING TRADES' REPORT. — Messrs. Matheson & Grant, in their half-yearly report, dated January 1, 1892, on the engineering trades, say:—"The year just closed has been a prosperous one for manufacturers, and the prospects for 1892, though not brilliant, seem to promise a steady trade. The great activity of 1890 began to decline in the spring, and the sudden collapse in South American affairs gave rise to gloomy anticipations, which have not been realised. For while there has been a decrease in the total exports of the country, it is significant that in regard to engineering work the decrease has been much less than in the general average of trade returns. . . . . . The Bills in Parliament for the coming session exceed those of last year, capital being the more available because of the discredit which has fallen on so many foreign fields for investment. The Northern main lines still continue to widen and improve their roads. The East and West Coast Railway, already commenced, includes important tunnels and viaducts. The Manchester, Sheffield, and Lincolnshire railway to London, now being constructed to Nottingham will probably be authorised this year, the opposition of the Great Northern Railway having been satisfied. The contract is let for the tunnel under the Thames at Blackwall, though in the opinions of those best able to judge, a bridge would have supplied the necessities of the case better and more cheaply if only opportunities had been afforded for proffering designs. The Elevated Railway in Liverpool is nearly completed, and some portions of the Manchester Ship Canal will be at work during the year. Underground railways in London are almost certain to be authorised, now that the facilities and economies afforded by the clay strata for tunnelling are recognised. Abroad there are indications of progress in many directions which will benefit engineers here. In China, notwithstanding a general restrictive policy, the railways in the North are being extended; in Japan and Siam, where public works are encouraged, railways and bridges are being projected as far as means allow. In Australia there is a lull in railway enterprise, owing to the restriction of borrowing facilities here. In South America a revival will depend on the abundance of harvests and the amount of exports; in South Africa the railways already authorised will open out new fields for mining. As this country is able to find the means for well-devised schemes, as well as the machinery and plant, work may be anticipated with certainty."

THE VENTILATION OF THEATRES.—The *Lancet*, in a special report, protests that in England we have fallen behind Continental countries in respect to the ventilation of theatres. The time is ripe to take action in this matter. We have at last something approaching to a municipal government for London. On the other hand, new theatres are about to be built. Is it too much to ask that, by the intervention of the public authorities and of public opinion, we shall endeavour to secure for London at least one or two theatres worthy to be compared with those which exist not merely in large capitals such as Vienna, Brussels, Buda-Pesth, Rotterdam, and Geneva, but in smaller centres such as Gratz, Frankfort, Munich, and Nice? In London, with the best-paying public of at least this side of the Atlantic, we are content to continue breathing foul air in our theatres night after night, and suffer either from dangerous and violent draughts or from semi-suffocation. This is the more deplorable as, after all, the modern improvements realised on the Continent originated in the example given in ventilating the Houses of Parliament at Westminster. The *Lancet* then describes the campaign organised by M. Emile Trélat in Paris for the better ventilation of theatres, and the practical application of his theories at the Grand Opera of Vienna by Dr. Bohm. The Vienna Opera is large enough to contain 2,700 persons. The air is propelled into the building by a fan, and supplied at the rate of 1,059 cubic feet per head per hour. No less than three floors under the theatre are devoted to ventilating purposes. In the first or lower floor the fresh outer air accumulates. A portion is admitted into the second floor, where it is warmed by pipes containing steam. The upper floor receives the rest of the fresh air, which is there mixed with the warmed air, so as to attain just the degree of temperature required in the theatre. Under each seat, in the stalls, which are immediately above this mixing chamber, are openings. These are so numerous that there can be no sharp current of air. Separate shafts supply the other portions of the theatre. Telegraphic communications keep the chief ventilation-regulator informed as to the state of temperature in every part of the house. By nicely-adjusted valves, he can mix air to the desired temperature, increase or lessen the heat in any part of the building, and, without draughts, see that everyone is properly supplied with the amount of pure air and of warmth he requires. The methods employed with great success at Vienna have been imitated in the other towns mentioned, and their last application is to the great amphitheatre of the new Sorbonne at Paris. What has been done in Vienna and so many other places should surely, the *Lancet* thinks, be attempted in London.

MEETINGS.

MONDAY, JANUARY 11.

Clerks of Works' Association (Carpenters' Hall).—Monthly meeting. 8 p.m.

Liverpool Architectural Society.—Special Meeting. 7.30 p.m.

TUESDAY, JANUARY 12.

Institution of Civil Engineers.—Mr. Wilfrid Airy on "Weighing-Machines." 8 p.m.

Society of Biblical Archæology.—Anniversary Meeting. 8 p.m.

Sheffield Society of Architects and Surveyors.—8 p.m.

WEDNESDAY, JANUARY 13.

Liverpool Engineering Society.—Mr. A. J. Maginnis on "Transatlantic Lines and Steamships." 8 p.m.

THURSDAY, JANUARY 14.

Institution of Electrical Engineers.—The President, Prof. W. E. Ayrton, F.R.S., will deliver his Inaugural Address. 8 p.m.

Society of Antiquaries.—8.30 p.m.

Edinburgh Architectural Association.—Mr. Hippolyte J. Blanc on "Heriot's Hospital and Co-temporary Work." 8 p.m.

FRIDAY, JANUARY 15.

Architectural Association. — Professor Garnett on "The Design and Equipment of Technical Schools and Colleges." 7.30.

RECENT PATENTS:

ABSTRACTS OF SPECIFICATIONS.

1,095.—STOVES, &c.: *F. Jackson.*—This patent relates to improvements in or connected with stoves and other fireplaces for the better consumption of fuel.

6,915.—KNOBS AND DOOR-HANDLES: *W. E. Riley.*—In the construction of knobs or door-handles, and in adjusting and attaching them to spindles, the knob or handle is fixed to the spindle by a screw tapped into the end of spindle and passing through the trout of the knob.

10,645.—WINDOWS: *E. Keith.*—This specification refers to device for preventing windows from shaking. An indiarubber roller or wheel is attached to a suitable arm or bracket fastened to the frame of the window in such a position as to bring the roller or wheel in contact with one of the window-sashes, thus preventing the shaking of the windows.

10,948.—PARQUETRY-WORK: *H. Studte, jun.*—The specification describes improved machinery for the manufacture of parquetry or inlaid wood work. For manufacturing massive parquetry, especially of cross-grain wood.

17,768.—BRICKS AND TILES: *J. & A. Duckett.*—This refers to improvements in manufacture of bricks and tiles for paving roadways, streets, &c. To readily distinguish vitrified bricks or tiles used for paving from those not vitrified.

17,893.—STONE-CUTTING: *R. W. James.*—The subject of this invention is a stone saw to cut through stone with rapidity and ease, consisting essentially of a metal blade, with notches cut in such a manner that they will hold the chilled shot used in sawing stone as described.

NEW APPLICATIONS FOR LETTERS PATENT.

December 21.—22,268, T. Sterratt, Absolute Locking Brick.—22,288, D. Macrae, Locking Nuts on Bolts.—22,310, G. Wright, Inspection Eye or Plug for Sewer or Soil-pipes.—22,311, G. Doulsthorpe and T. Burrowes, Ventilating Rooms or Buildings, &c.—22,322, W. Jacques, Fire Exit Door Lock and Alarm.—22,336, A. Rowan, Cleansing Paint Brushes.

December 22.—22,359, G. Newman, Door Checks and Springs.

December 23.—22,424, G. Goldsmith and T. Stephen, Preventing Down Draught in Chimneys.—22,428, J. Jackson, Decorative Material for Walls, Ceilings, &c.—22,452, T. Twyford, Siphon-flushing Cisterns or Water-waste Preventers.—22,461, G. Hawke, Fastenings for Windows and Doors.

December 24.—22,492, J. Griffiths, Water-closets.—22,502, R. Harris, Foundations or Enclosures for Buildings, &c.—22,526, J. Pearson, Draught and Weather Excluders for Doors.—22,534, J. Radford, Siphon-flushing Apparatus.—22,547, A. Gray, Screw Nails.—22,548, F. Theissing, Construction of wooden Floorings.

December 28.—22,562, W. Horn, Brick-kiln.—22,577, J. Martin, Saws.—22,596, J. Pentland, Hinges.—22,610, A. & W. Gill, Paints and Lacquers.—22,629, G. Hughes, Sash-fasteners.

December 29.—22,662, T. Anderson, Gas-fittings.

December 30.—22,773.—C. Ennis, Electric-bells and Indicators.—22,790, P. Fowler, Fireplaces.

December 31.—22,809, M. Williams, Oil-paints and paint medium.

PROVISIONAL SPECIFICATIONS ACCEPTED.

18,871, R. Briggs, Bolts and Fastenings for Doors of Theatres and other public buildings.—20,493, F. Ashford, Heating Greenhouses, &c.—20,571, W. Nation, Erection of Buildings.—20,616, R. Taylor, Tunnelling in Soft and water-bearing Material.—20,821, H. Johnson, Valve Ventilators.—21,185, J. Reaney, Building and Materials for same.—21,201, W. Diprose, Sash-fasteners.—21,356, E. Edwards, Saws.—21,367, A. Smith, Securing Doors and windows from the Inside.—21,483, B. Peffard, Bricks to be used without Mortar.—21,613, P. Walker, Ventilators.—21,718, C. Major, Roofing-tiles.—21,754, L. Sutcliffe, Holding Devices for Sliding window-frames, &c.—21,779, E. Brook, Kilns.

COMPLETE SPECIFICATIONS ACCEPTED.

(*Open to Opposition for Two Months.*)

659, J. Stidder, Water-closets and Urinals, and in flushing, trapping, ventilating, and discharging same.—1,419, A. Ward, Fireproof Floors, &c. 2,740, F. Pescette, Flushing Apparatus.—3,166, J. Main, Roofing and other parts of buildings.—4,349, R. Mountain, Brick-making Machines.—18,487, R. Barker, Stone-cutting Machines.—30,437, W. Thompson, Manufacturing Plate-glass.

PRICES CURRENT OF MATERIALS.

TIMBER.

Greenheart, B.G. ton	6/0/0	0/0/0
Teak, E.I. load	9/10/0	15/0/0
Sequoia, U.S. ft. cu.	2/3	3/0
Ash, Canada load	3/10/0	4/0/0
Birch, do.	3 0/0	4/5/0
Elm, do.	3/10/0	4/15/0
Fir, Dantsic, &c.	2/0/0	3/10/0
Oak, do.	2/10/0	4/10/0
Canada	5/0/0	7/0/0
Pine, Canada red	2/10/0	3/10/0
Do. Yellow	2/10/0	5/0/0
Lath, Dantsic, fath	5/5/0	6/10/0
St. Petersburg	5/10/0	7/10/0
Deals, Finland, 2nd & 1st std 100	8/10/0	10/10/0
Do. 4th & 3rd	7/10/0	8/10/0
Do. Riga	6/10/0	8/0/0
St. Petersburg, 1st Yellow	10/10/0	15/0/0
Do. 2nd Yellow	8/10/0	10/0/0
Do. white	7/0/0	10/10/0
Swedish	7/15/0	16/0/0
White Sea	8/10/0	17/10/0
Canada, Pine 1st	10/10/0	25/10/0
Do. do. 2nd	14/10/0	16/10/0
Do. do. 3rd, &c.	6/10/0	10/10/0
Do. Spruce, 1st	8/10/0	11/0/0
Do. do. 3rd & 2nd	6/10/0	8/0/0
New Brunswick	7/0/0	7/10/0
Battens, all kinds	3/10/0	15/10/0
Flooring Boards, sq., 1 in. prep. 1st	0 8/6	0 14/6
Do. 2nd	0/7/6	0/11/4
Other qualities	0/5/3	0/8/0
Cedar, Cuba ft.	/3½	/4½
Honduras, &c.	/3½	/4½
Mahogany, Cuba	/4½	/6½
St. Domingo, cargo av	/4½	2 0
Mexican do. do	/4	/6
Tobasco do. do	/6½	/7
Honduras do.	/5½	/6½
Box, Turkey ton	4/0/0	13/0/0
Rose, Rio	10/0/0	20/0/0
Bahia	9/0/0	18/0/0
Satin, St. Domingo ft.	0/0/9	0/1/3

TIMBER (*continued*).

Satin, Porto Rico	0/0/10	0/1/6
Walnut, Italian	0/0/3½	0/0/7

METALS.

IRON—Pig, in Scotland ton	2/7/0	2/7/3
Bar, Welsh, in London	6/0/0	6/2/6
Do. do. at works in Wales	5/10/0	5/12/6
Do. Staffordshire, in London	6/10/0	6/15/0
COPPER—British, cake and ingot	49/0/0	50/0/0
Best selected	50/0/0	51/0/0
Sheets, strong	59/0/0	60/0/0
Chili, bars	46/12/6	47/0/0
YELLOW METAL lb.	0/0/5⅝	0/0/6⅛
LEAD—Pig, Spanish ton	11/3/0	11/6/3
English, com. brands	11/7/6	11/10/0
Sheet, English, 3 lbs. per sq. ft. and upwards	13/5/0	0/0/0
Pipe	13/15/0	0/0/0
ZINC—English sheet ton	25/0/0	23/10/0
Vieille Montagne	26/10/0	0/0/0
TIN—Straits	90/12/6	91/0/0
Australian	90/12/6	91/0/0
English Ingots	94/0/0	96/0/0

OILS.

Linseed ton	18 15/0	19/2/6
Cocoanut, Cochin	26 10/0	0/0/0
Do. Ceylon	23 10/0	0/0/0
Palm, Lagos	24/10/0	24/0/0
Rapeseed, English pale	28/15/0	0/0/0
Do. brown	27/5/0	0/0/0
Cottonseed ref.	18 10/0	0/0/0
Oleine	0 0/0	0/0/0
Lubricating, U.S.	4/10/0	5/10/0
Do. refined	6/0/0	11/0/0
TAR—Stockholm barrel	0/19/0	0 0/0
Archangel	0/12/6	0 0/0

TENDERS.

[Communications for Insertion under this heading must reach us *not later than 12 noon on Thursdays.*]

BRECON.—Accepted for the erection of new Board schools in Mount-street, for the Brecon School Board:—

B. Jenkins, Brecon £2 511 4 3

CHADWELL HEATH (Essex).—For the erection of a new Police-station at Chadwell Heath, for the Receiver for the Metropolitan Police District. Mr. John Butler, F.R.I.B.A., Architect. Quantities by Mr. W. H. Thurgood:—

Winter	£2,739	Hart Bros.	£2,379
Holloway	2,653	Scrivener	2,333
Ansell	2,521	Barnes	2,281
Garlick & Horton	2,397	Lathey	2,270
Morter	2,397	Willmott	2,161
J. Hammond	2,380		

CLACTON-ON-SEA.—For the erection of a pair of semi-detached houses on the Marine-parade, Clacton-on-sea, for Mr. John Jones. Mr. W. A. Finch, architect, 76, Finsbury-pavement, E.C.:—

J. Holland	£3,945	J. Brown	£3,300
J. Grimes	3,900	N. De Maid	3,390
Everett & Son	3,845	W. Sargeant, Clacton*	2,330
A. Porter	3,483		

* Accepted.

[Architect's estimate, £2,900.]

CROYDON.—For alterations to 13, High-street, for Messrs. R. Gould Wreford & Co. Mr. Alfred Broad, architect, 27, Dingwall-road, Croydon:—

Hanscombe & Smith	£614	E. P. Bulled	£579
Martin Taylor	597	E. J. Saunders (accepted)	568
W. Marriage	594		

[All of Croydon.]

CROYDON.—For the extension of dye works, South End, Croydon. Mr. Henry Gough, architect, Bank-chambers, North End, Croydon:—

Saunders	£609	Smith	£438
Bulled & Co.	494	D. W. Barker*	421
Bullock	474		

* Accepted.

HANWELL.—For erecting men's room and cart-shed, for the Hanwell Local Board. Mr. E. Herbert, surveyor. No quantities supplied:—

W. Blackburn	£547 0 0	Wm. Purner	£504 18 0
W. Brown	540 0 0	Ford & Son, Brentford	495 0 0
A. Jamieson	511 0 0	A. & B. Hanson	489 0 0
Terrill & Fish	509 10 4	T. Nye, Ealing*	453 0 0
Wallace Bettridge	509 0 0	C. J. Kiston	410 0 0

* Accepted.

LONDON.—For villa-residence at Blackheath, for Miss Pontifex. Mr. Thos. Dinwiddy, architect:—

Kennard (accepted) £900 0 0

LONDON.—For the erection of external iron balconies and staircases at the Infirmary, High-street, Homerton, E., for the Guardians of the Hackney Union. Mr. W. A. Finch, architect, 76, Finsbury-pavement, E.C.:—

T. W. Cole	£890 0	J. F. Clarke & Sons	£687 10
W. Harris	863 0	B. E. Nightingale	605 0
W. F. Codner & Co.	825 0	The St. Pancras Iron Work Co.*	582 0
J. Richmond & Co.	795 0		
The Constructional Iron Work Co.	785 0		

* Accepted.

[Architect's estimate, £620.]

LONDON.—For the construction of a road and sewer on the Raleigh House Estate, Brixton-hill. Messrs. F. & W. Stocker, surveyors, 90, Queen-street, Cheapside:—

	Road and Sewer.	Additional for Curbing.	Total.
Woodham & Fry	£2,175	£297 0	£2,470 0
J. Hoare & Son	1,984	288 0	2,272 0
W. Clarkson	1,720	360 0	2,080 0
Wood & Co.	1,695	353 15	2,048 15
Nowell & Robson	1,675	380 0	1,955 0
James Bowles	1,649	298 0	1,947 0
Neave & Co.	1,530	375 0	1,905 0
Mays	1,585	310 0	1,895 0
Killingback	1,595	285 0	1,880 0
Barlow & Roberts	1,470	300 0	1,770 0

LONDON.—For building warehouse in Mitre-street, E.C., for Mr. T. Roberts Watts. Mr. Frank W. M. King, architect, Billiter-square-buildings, E.C. Quantities by Messrs. Dunk & Bousfield:—

Perry & Co.	£5,187	Munday & Sons	£4,979
J. Morter	5,123	Ashby & Horner	4,877
J. T. Chappell	5,067	T. Rider & Son	4,740
Colls & Sons	4,988	E. Lawrance & Sons*	4,685

* Accepted.

LONDON.—Accepted for sanitary work and decorations at 61, Gloucester-place, W., for Miss Harrison:—

Greatorex & Co., Limited, 61, Stanhope-terrace, W. £380

LONDON.—Accepted for alterations and decorations and improvements to ventilation at 96, Inverness-terrace, W., for Messrs. McCulloch & Matthews:—

Greatorex & Co., Limited £319 0 0

LONDON.—Accepted for decorative works at No. 6, Upper Hamilton-terrace, N.W., for Mrs. Platau:—
Greatorex & Co., Limited £260

LONDON.—Accepted for alterations and sanitary Improvements and decorations at No. 8, Chester-place, W., for Miss Jones:—
Greatorex & Co., Limited £375 0 0

TWICKENHAM.—For sanitary and decorative repairs to "Chestlebank," Cambridge Park, for Dr. J. Compton Burnett, M.D. Mr. Alfred Brond, surveyor, 27, Dingwall-road, Croydon:—

R. Soper	£351	E. J. Saunders	£338
Hanscombe & Smith	340	E. P. Bulled, Croydon*	323

* Accepted.

WALLINGTON (Surrey).—For the reconstruction of small shop property, in Manor-road, Wallington. Mr. Henry Gough, architect, Bank-chambers, North End, Croydon:—

Stewart	£374 10	Owen	£224 0
Anderson	335 0	Burnand*	220 0
Clark	279 0		

* Accepted.

WIMBLEDON.—For paving work in the Hill-road and High-street widening, for the Wimbledon Local Board. Mr. C. H. Cooper, A.M.I.C.E., Engineer and Surveyor:—

	A. s.	A. d.	B. s.	B. d.
Patent Indurated Stone Company	3	1	4	8
Malcolm, Macleod & Co.	3	3	4	3
A. J. Phillips & Co.	3	4	0	0
Stuart's Granolithic Paving Company	3	8	5	6½
Haynes Bros.	3	9	4	3
W. B. Wilkinson & Co.	4	0	—	
Imperial Stone Company	4	0	—	
*Messrs. R. & W. Iles	4	0	—	
H. Coleman	4	2	—	
John T. Dove	4	8	—	
E. Parry	4	6	—	
Croft Granite Company	5	4	—	
†Patent Victoria Stone	—		—	
Jones Annealed Concrete Company	3	8	5	6
Bradford & Hancock	4	0	—	
Patent Paving and Construction Company	4	0	6	0
W. E. Constable & Co., 40, King William-street, E.C.	4	7	—	

A.—Price per yard super., laid in situ. B.—Ditto, laid in slabs.
* Imperial, 5s. 8d. † Indurated, 5s. 3½d. † Victoria, 6s. 2½d.
† Indurated, 5s. 5d. † Victoria, 6s.

SUBSCRIBERS in LONDON and the SUBURBS, by prepaying at the Publishing Office, 19s. per annum (or 4s. 9d. per quarter), can ensure receiving "The Builder" by *Friday Morning's* post.

TO CORRESPONDENTS.

E. S.—E. E. S.—D. T. & Co.—W. A. F.—F. W. L.

All statements of facts, lists of tenders, &c., must be accompanied by the name and address of the sender, not necessarily for publication.

We are compelled to decline pointing out books and giving addresses.

NOTE.—The responsibility of signed articles, and papers read at public meetings, rests, of course, with the authors.

We cannot undertake to return rejected communications.

Letters or communications (beyond mere news-items) which have been duplicated for other journals, are NOT DESIRED.

All communications regarding literary and artistic matter should be addressed to THE EDITOR; all communications relating to advertisements and other exclusively business matters should be addressed to THE PUBLISHER, and *not* to the Editor.

The Builder Cathedral Series.

1891.

1. CANTERBURY	Jan. 3.	7. SALISBURY	July 4.
2. LICHFIELD	Feb. 7.	8. BRISTOL	Aug. 1.
3. ST. ALBAN'S	Mar. 7.	9. NORWICH	Sept. 5.
4. PETERBOROUGH	April 4.	10. ROCHESTER	Oct. 3.
5. WELLS	May 2.	11. LINCOLN	Nov. 7.
6. EXETER	June 6.	12. GLOUCESTER	Dec. 5.

1892.

13. ST. PAUL'S	Jan. 2.	16. ELY	April 2.
14. HEREFORD	Feb. 6.	17. LLANDAFF	May 7.
15. CHICHESTER	Mar. 5.	18. OXFORD	June 4.

[Further arrangements will be duly announced.]

Price FOURPENCE each (by post 4½d.), except Nos. 1 and 2, which are *out of print*; but the VIEW, PLAN, AND DESCRIPTION of CANTERBURY and of LICHFIELD have been re-printed, and they can now be had, price ONE SHILLING each set; by post, 1s. 2d.

Portfolios, for Preserving the Plates unfolded, 2s. 6d.; by post, 3s.

TERMS OF SUBSCRIPTION.

"THE BUILDER" is supplied DIRECT from the Office to residents in any part of the United Kingdom at the rate of 19s. per annum PREPAID. To all parts of Europe, America, Australia, and New Zealand, 26s. per annum. To India, China, Ceylon, &c. 30s. per annum. Remittances payable to DOUGLAS FOURDRINIER, Publisher, No. 46, Catherine-street, W.C.

Now ready (86 plates), Price ONE GUINEA.

"THE BUILDER ALBUM"

OF ROYAL ACADEMY ARCHITECTURE.

1891.

Extract from the Preface.—"The accompanying set of plates comprises the drawings in the Architectural room of the Royal Academy Exhibition of this year, which have been lent by their authors for illustration in *The Builder*."

LONDON
Office of "The Builder," 46, Catherine-street, W.C.

HOWARD & SONS

25, 26, 27, BERNERS STREET, W.,

MANUFACTURERS AND CONTRACTORS

Deal Dadoes, from 1s. 2d. per ft. super.
Oak Dadoes " 1s. 8d. "
Walnut Dadoes " 1s. 11d. "
Oak, 1 inch Parquet Floors, laid and polished, from £7. 10s. a square.
Solid 1-inch Oak, straight boards, laid and polished, at £6. 18s. a square.
Solid ½-inch Oak Parquet for covering Deal floors, laid and polished, from £5 a square.
Oak Wood Tapestry Dadoes, from 1s. per foot super.
Walnut or Mahogany, from 1s. 3d. per foot super.
Ditto with Heavy Mouldings, 4d. ft. extra.
Ditto, ditto, with Carved or Painted Panels, prices according to sketches.

Prices given for all Interior Work, Doors, Architraves, Over-doors, Chimney-pieces, Stoves, and Hearths. Architects' and Surveyors' attention particularly called to the above Quotations for

BILLS OF QUANTITIES.

HOWARD & SONS
Tender for Contracts for any Joiners' work, or Ornamental Plaster. Painting, Plain or Decorative. Wrought-Iron Work. Stained Cathedral Glass, and any other Interior Work.

DEATH.

HADEN.—On January 3rd, at Hanefield, Trowbridge, GEORGE NELSON HADEN, aged 74 years.

THE BATH STONE FIRMS, LTD

BATH,
FOR ALL THE PROVED KINDS OF
BATH STONE.
FLUATE, for Hardening and Preserving Calcareous Stones and Marbles.

DOULTING FREESTONE.

THE CHELYNCH STONE. — The stone from these quarries is known as the "Weather Beds," and is of a very crystalline nature, and undoubtedly one of the most durable stones in England.

THE BRAMBLEDITCH STONE. — Is of the same crystalline nature as the Chelynch Stone, but finer in texture, and more suitable for fine moulded work.

Prices, and every information given, on application to CHARLES TRASK & SONS, Doulting, Shepton Mallet.
London Agent—Mr. E. A. WILLIAMS,
16, Craven-street, Strand, W.C. [ADVT.

HAM HILL STONE.

The attention of Architects is specially invited to the durability and beautiful COLOUR of this material. Quarries well opened. Quick despatch guaranteed. Stonework delivered and fixed complete. Samples and estimates free. Address, The Ham Hill Stone Co., Norton, Stoke-under-Ham, Somerset. London Agent: Mr. E. A. Williams, 16, Craven-st., Strand, W.C. [ADVT.

CRAIGLEITH STONE.

UNEQUALLED for Staircases, Steps, and Landings, especially for Public Buildings with great wear. VERY HARD, and NEVER WEARS SLIPPERY.
SOLE AGENTS for England,
J. & A. CREW, Cumberland Market, London, N.W.

Asphalte.—The Seyssel and Metallic Lava Asphalte Company (Mr. H. Glenn), Office, 42, Poultry, E.C.—The best and cheapest materials for damp courses, railway arches, warehouse floors, flat roofs, stables, cow-sheds, and milk-rooms, granaries, tun-rooms, and terraces. Asphalte Contractors to the Forth Bridge Co. [ADVT.

SPRAGUE & CO.,
PHOTOLITHOGRAPHERS,
4 & 5, East Harding-street,
Fetter-Lane, E.C. [ADVT.

QUANTITIES, &c., LITHOGRAPHED accurately and with despatch.
METCHIM & SON, 20, Parliament-st., S.W.
"QUANTITY SURVEYORS' TABLES AND DIARY." Revised and Enlarged for 1892 now ready, price 6d. post free 7d. [ADVT.

W. E. CONSTABLE & CO.

Granite and Limestone Quarry Owners,
TAR PAVING, ROAD, & GENERAL CONTRACTORS.
Are prepared to supply in any quantities, direct from their own Scotch Quarries, Kirkcudbrightshire, Granite Blocks up to 20 tons each, for Monumental work, &c.; also Setts or Kerbing, Channelling, &c. Lime and Limestone from their Matlock Bridge Quarries, Derbyshire.
Proprietors of the well-known Patent Limestone Tar Asphalt Paving.—Laid Complete or Materials supplied.
Offices: MONUMENT CHAMBERS, CITY.

The Reredos, St. Paul's Cathedral.

(Reprinted from "The Builder," Jan. 28th, 1888.)

Copies of this Plate (15½ in. × 11¼ in.) on stout paper, unfolded for framing, are on sale, Sixpence, by post, 8d.

London: Office of "The Builder," 46, Catherine-street, Covent Garden, W.C.

THE PORTLAND STONE QUARRYING AND WORKING COMPANY.

Stone of the Best Quality may be obtained in Blocks,

—— OR ESTIMATES FOR ——

EVERY DESCRIPTION of WORKED PORTLAND STONE DELIVERED or FIXED
UPON APPLICATION AT THE
COMPANY'S OFFICES, 54, OLD BROAD STREET, LONDON, E.C.

Vol. LXII. No. 2554. SATURDAY, JANUARY 16 1892.

ILLUSTRATIONS.

Architectural Study by Bramante: From an Engraving in the British Museum] .... *Double Page Ink-Photo.*
Seascale Church, Cumberland.—Mr. C. J. Ferguson, Architect .... *Double-Page Photo-Litho*
Hymers' College, Hull.—Messrs. Botterill, Son, & Bilson, Architects .... *Double-Page Ink-Photo.*
A Study for a Country House.—By Mr. J. H. Sellers .... *Double-Page Photo-Litho.*

Blocks in Text.

Sketches of Roman Remains discovered at Silchester	Page 41	Ossuary at St. Pol de Léon, Finistère	Page 46
Lanternes des Morts at Ciron and Pers, France	44	Ground-Plan, Hymers' College, Hull	47
Cemetery Crosses, St. Georges du Roc and Aiffres, France	45	Diagrams in Student's Column: Heating by Hot Water	50-51

CONTENTS.

Nature in Ornament		Books: Von Karl Masner's "K. K. Oesterreich Museum für Kunst und Industrie" (Wien: Gerold); B. C. Lodge's "Historic Towns" (London: Longmans & Co.); R. Grimshaw's "Practical Catechism" (New York: Wiley & Sons; London: Gay & Bird); J. Williams' "Sketches of Village Buildings" (London: Bentley & Son); "Sell's Dictionary of the World's Press, 1892" (London: Sell's Advertising Agency, Limited); "Sprague's Pocket Diary for 1892" (London: Sprague & Co.); Short Notices	48	Totnes Church	50
Silchester		Recent Trade Catalogues	49	The Old Watch-house at King's-cross	50
Notes		Building Act Amendment	49	Tar on Slates	50
Some Old French Cemetery Erections		Rood-Screens	50	Student's Column.—Warming Buildings by Hot Water, III	50
Architectural Societies				Surveyorships	51
Architectural Study by Bramante				General Building News	51
Seascale Church				Sanitary and Engineering News	51
Hymers' College, Hull				Foreign and Colonial	52
Study for a Country House				Miscellaneous	52
The Condition of Gloucester Cathedral	[illegible]			Meetings	53
British Archæological Association	[illegible]			Recent Patents	53
The Mersey Tunnel Railway	48			Prices Current of Materials	53

Nature in Ornament.

E fear that Mr. Day is not far wrong in his remark, in the introductory chapter to the book before us,* that "even in these days of supposed interest in things decorative, the Englishman generally speaking neither knows nor cares anything about the subject. e is in most cases absolutely out of sym-athy with it. . . . The forms of ornament most admires are those most nearly re-mbling something in nature, and it is cause of that resemblance he admires em: abstract ornament is quite outside his mpathies and beyond his understanding." . Day, indeed, thinks that the bias of the tural man is in the direction of nature; it only by thought that he arrives at the rception of the necessity for treating nature such a manner as to render its suggestion bservient to the true office of ornament. he reason why the Englishman, of all Euro-ans, is most out of touch with the art of nament, is probably that he has never been ustomed to regard it as a subject worth rious thought. If he could be got to give s mind to it, he is as intellectually capable comprehending it as most other people.

There are, however, many more people in ngland who understand the subject now an there were fifty, or even twenty years o, and it is at all events a satisfaction to onsider that there is sound teaching to be ad in this country for those who care to ok for it. Mr. Day's beautifully-illustrated ttle works on "The Planning of Ornament," The Anatomy of Pattern," and "The Appli-ation of Ornament," may be named among xt-books which are at once sound in prin-ples and attractive in style and manner, and hich may we hope have already exercised me influence. The present work, belonging the same series of "Text Books of Orna-ental Design," is naturally a larger work than its predecessors, for it deals with a much larger subject, the whole relation of natural forms to ornament; a subject which demands serious thought on the part of the artist himself, and on which a certain degree of difference of opinion may be expected and allowed for even among those who are entirely at one as to general principles in the design and application of ornament.

The subject of nature in ornament leaves on one side a whole division of the subject of ornament; all that kind, namely, which comes under the head of mere pattern-making, the arrangement of lines and squares and circles and other such geometric forms according to a certain order. The tendency to pattern-making of this kind is perhaps, after all, more inherent in the uncultivated mind of man than the tendency to the imitation of natural vegetation; at least we find it the predominant influence in most ornament of uncivilised peoples. In the earliest archaic Greek pottery, even, the ornament consists mostly of mere lines, marks, triangles, and other such forms, arranged in a more or less systematic manner. In a higher stage of culture these materials are refined into very effective forms of ornament, but the variety of designs to be made from geometric forms does not seem to be very great; at all events the actual variety developed and used in ornament has not been very great; they fall into a few well-known types, which have been used over and over again with little variety in the motive. The Japanese and Arabic puzzle-designs, as they may be called, look very intricate, and the Arabic forms have a good deal of variety in appearance, but an analysis of them rather reduces our respect for them; the method is simpler than appears at first sight, and the variation less. We cannot get very far in the elaboration of diaper ornament without introducing forms that are not geometric, and that bear some relation to physical nature, unless with the aid of colour. With that assistance the variety of permutations is no doubt much enlarged, as we can see in such a mere toy as the kaleidoscope, which has a practically endless range of patterns. But the production of patterns on that principle could perhaps hardly come under the category of design in the true sense; it is rather ingenuity.

But if geometric forms are rather limited in number, this cannot be said of the forms of physical nature, which are practically endless in variety; and it is, as Mr. Day remarks, somewhat curious to consider how few of these have really been used in ornamental design. Most schools of floral design have kept to a very few types or examples in nature. But in spite of this, even this small volume gives us evidence in its illustrations of an immense variety of ornament more or less directly connected with nature. And this variety, if we examine into it, we find arises to a great extent from variations of treatment suggested by the varieties of material or method of execution. Woven ornament on textiles is entirely different from carved ornament based on the same natural form; stencil ornament again is different from either; varieties of light and dark in treating the same type are endless. No one could even turn over Mr. Day's book without being struck by this immense variety in the illustrations; and this fact is certainly hopeful for the future. When we regard the variety of actually existing ornament, and the few natural types which have supplied it, and reflect what an amount of suggestion there is in nature which has never yet been pressed into our service in this way, we ought to feel that there is still a very large field open for the designer in ornament. If we have run in certain tracks, and repeated a great deal of what has been done before us, this is rather from want of enterprise, purpose, and thought, than from want of material supplied to us by nature.

"Material supplied to us by nature:" that is the true position in the relation of nature to ornament. However we may try to escape from this prison-house of the intellect, we are brought up, whichever way we turn, by the fact of the incapacity of man to absolutely originate form. Even if we regard such an ornament as the Greek "honeysuckle" as in reality "brush-work," and not imitation of floral form, we cannot help admitting that it is suggested and permeated by the recollection of floral form, unconsciously if not consciously. That is the true relation in which natural

* "Nature in Ornament." By Lewis F. Day. With 23 plates and 192 illustrations in the text. London: B. T. Batsford. 1892.

forms stand to ornament: they form the material on which to work by adaptation to the methods and materials employed.

And this consideration has something to do with the desire of the ornamentist for conventionalism. There is of course the fact to be taken into account, that we cannot, in the materials mostly used for ornament, really imitate and reproduce the infinite variety and delicacy of nature. If we could, there might be more excuse for naturalistic treatment. But naturalistic treatment really means flower-painting for its own sake, not the production of ornament suited to a special material and a special situation. The things which we ornament are in themselves artificial, and we have to suit the natural forms to their artificial position and employment,—to make them part and parcel of what they decorate. But beyond this is the desire to make them in a sense our own. We cannot originate form but we can originate treatment, and thereby render the form to that extent a new creation of our own. When we stop short of this, we have stopped short of inventing. "Nature" says Mr. Day, "is very ready to suggest, as the Pompeian bronze-worker realised when he went to the river side for a reed as 'motif' for the ornamentation of his candelabrum." But the fault of the candelabrum in question, as illustrated in cut 4 in the book, is that the Pompeian artist did not take it merely as a suggestion to work out his own idea from. The stalk of the candelabrum is too close an imitation of the original, too naturalistic; the artist contented himself with imitating, instead of working out his own treatment from the suggestion of nature. Hence this particular illustration is misleading, which cannot be said of many in the book.

The stalk is in fact one of the greatest difficulties in the adaptation of nature. Leaves and flowers mostly fall into forms which have more or less of the quality of artistic design in them; some of them require little conventionalising to fall into their place as ornament, others require a great deal; some are so deficient in grace and definiteness of form that they will hardly lend themselves to ornament in any recognisable form. This is the one drawback to the hopefulness of the prospect for the future, contained in the inexhaustible variety of nature. Not all the forms of natural foliage or flower will equally lend themselves to adaptation as ornament, and it cannot be denied that those already used (if not used up) are among the most suitable for this treatment. The instinct of men in past ages has led them to the best available forms. Still there are many left unused for us to try our hands upon.

But it is difficult to treat the stem conventionally except by conventionalising away most of its natural characteristics. Mr. Day remarks that the thickening of the twigs where they join on to the central stem is an incident which has been rather overlooked, and little or nothing been made of it. But it is rather difficult to see how it can be retained without retaining too much of the natural appearance. How often do we find, in wrought-iron work for instance, the stem the one blot on a design; the leaves sufficiently and finely conventionalised, the stalk half naturalistic, striking a false note in the combination. It would be an interesting subject of study to note the manner in which the generating stem of design founded on foliage has been treated in various styles of ornament. The Greek and the Hindu alike treat it in scrolls, with cleanly-defined artificial lines, and similar treatment is seen in the best periods of Gothic work. In some of the carved foliage of the Transition period it is partly naturalistic, and (what is worse) angular in its lines or crippled in its curves. In the later Decorated Gothic we meet with this vice of naturalism in the stalks again. In the Roman scroll there is no naturalism of detail, but there is too often the crippled curve which destroys the æsthetic balance of the design. How different from the Greek scroll, in which the central stem is an almost geometrically-designed curve, from which sprouts foliage having a closer alliance with natural form. That is the true treatment; the central portion from which the details spring should be the most highly-conventionalised; the nearer we get to extremities, to minuter details, the more freedom we may allow ourselves. The want of this perception is the one defect in the well-known and in some respects splendid piece of Indian perforated tree ornament of which a portion is given on Plate 77 in the book. The minor details are fully conventionalised, but the twisting stems from which they spring are too naturalistic, and bring us too close to the actual nature of a tree, which should only have been more distantly suggested.

Mr. Day commences with a chapter, after the introductory one, on "Ornament in Nature," notes on the ornamental character shown in natural objects, as a prelude to the reverse view of the subject, "nature in ornament." In the latter chapter the author emphasises somewhat the idea that apparently natural ornament may not always have been derived direct from the study of or from any desire to imitate nature; it may have been brush work with unconscious reminiscence of nature. He gives examples of the Greek and Roman acanthus leaf, and a classical scroll of his own, translated into brush work, but the illustrations will hardly be taken as supporting the view that the brush-work was the first form. They are interesting rather (the two forms of scroll especially) as examples of the entirely new effect which may be given to the same decorative idea, in a sense in fact the same design, by varied methods of execution. We then have two further chapters on contrasted subjects, "the simplification of natural forms," and "the elaboration of natural forms." Simplification is in a certain sense one form of conventionalising, generally adopted because certain details of the original object will not lend themselves to the process or material employed; sometimes because breadth and simplicity are gained by this means; but there is a danger in this simplification of losing the essential character and suggestiveness of the original; and indeed, as Mr. Day does not fail to point out, some of the distinctive character in natural foliage depends on such slight details that the simplification process may very easily result in destroying character and reducing several different types of nature to similarity. On the other hand, he gives an admirable example from a panel designed by G. E. Street, in which the thistle is simplified out of nearly all its smaller details and yet the character of it is fully preserved — it is a conventionalised thistle and nothing else. The elaboration of natural form, adding to it a greater multiplicity of detail than in the original, is a process which is justifiable or not chiefly in relation to the nature of the material in which the work is executed. To do it in carving would in most cases, perhaps in all, be the worst form of mistake. To do it in silk embroidery, where a highly enriched surface effect is desired, by filling in the surfaces of leaf forms with delicate ornamental work, is a perfectly suitable and even necessary kind of elaboration, without which embroidered design founded on natural forms would be but a poor and ineffective affair. In such a case the natural forms are the framework only of the design; in carved work they form the essential element. "Consistency in the modification of nature" forms the subject of the following chapter, a very important point which certainly receives more attention from designers now than it used to receive. That ornament which simulates or recalls growth should follow the natural laws of growth is now generally recognised. There are other forms of inconsistency however, not so obvious but equally important to avoid; such as inconsistency in character. Mr. Day gives two instructive examples of this in treatment of design derived from oak-leaves, with a delicacy and symmetrical character of the leading lines quite foreign to the character of oak growth. Such examples might be multiplied, no doubt; and another form of inconsistency, of which Renaissance ornament is full, is that of the combination in one design of details from plants which have no kind of relation to one another either botanically or in a decorative sense. "One of the most irritating things," as the author remarks, "is to see flowers like catherine-wheels, or other such prim rosettes, on stems suggesting growth, or to find naturalistic flowers springing from quite arbitrary and mechanical lines."

In two chapters on "Parallel renderings" the author gives a number of very interesting and instructive examples of the different rendering of the same plant in different styles and materials. A student of ornament would find it very good practice to extend these experiments, and see how many different treatments of the same flower, distinct in effect but each suitable to the circumstances, can be suggested by the various conditions of different materials.

"Animals in Ornament" forms the subject of a separate chapter, with some very good examples of conventionalised animals, and a warning against the rash employment of animal forms in too realistic a manner. We presume that the odious wall-paper with snails (Plate 98: German we are glad to say!) is a warning and not an example, though it does not appear to be condemned as heartily as it deserves. In regard to "The Element of the Grotesque" the author is apologetic, admitting that it has been much abused, but claiming that it has its rightful place in art provided that the designer can put so much of consistency, anatomical and otherwise, into his creation as to give a certain possibility of existence to it. Here we quite concur with him, though we cannot concur in thinking that even any half apology is possible for the monstrous panel by Sansovino given on plate 104. Such things are unpardonable under the shadow of whatever great name.

We may conclude with a very good paragraph, from the chapter on "Consistency," in regard to the general question of the manner in which the ornamentist should make use of his studies of nature:—

> "The designer can hardly make too many studies from nature, but he can easily make bad use of those he has made, and easily encumber himself with them. A man can design quite freely only when the burden of natural fact is so familiar that to him it ceases to be a burden. Refreshing as it may be to refer to his studies, or to nature herself, he cannot *design* with either in front of him. The actual thing is not malleable enough for his purpose, whereas an impression or a memory of it accommodates itself in the most surprising manner to the conditions of the case, and the necessary modification *occurs* as though it were matter of course."

SILCHESTER.

BY MR. G. E. FOX, F.S.A.

IT may be remembered that an account appeared in the *Builder* in January of last year of discoveties made in the course of the year 1890 at Silchester, near Reading, the site of the Roman city of Calleva Attrebatum.

The excavations on the site, undertaken in that year under the auspices of the Society of Antiquaries, were continued during 1891. Within the last fortnight, the antiquities then obtained have been exhibited to the public in the rooms of the Society at Burlington House, together with plans of such further portions of the city as were uncovered in the course of the last summer and autumn.

The discoveries of the second year of exploration do not yield in interest to the first, and our knowledge of the character and arrangement of the ancient Roman city has been considerably extended.

The examination of the remainder of the first Insula, a block, begun in 1890, formed part of the work last year, and two more of these blocks, formed by the intersection of the streets lying west of the basilica, were undertaken and thoroughly investigated. A

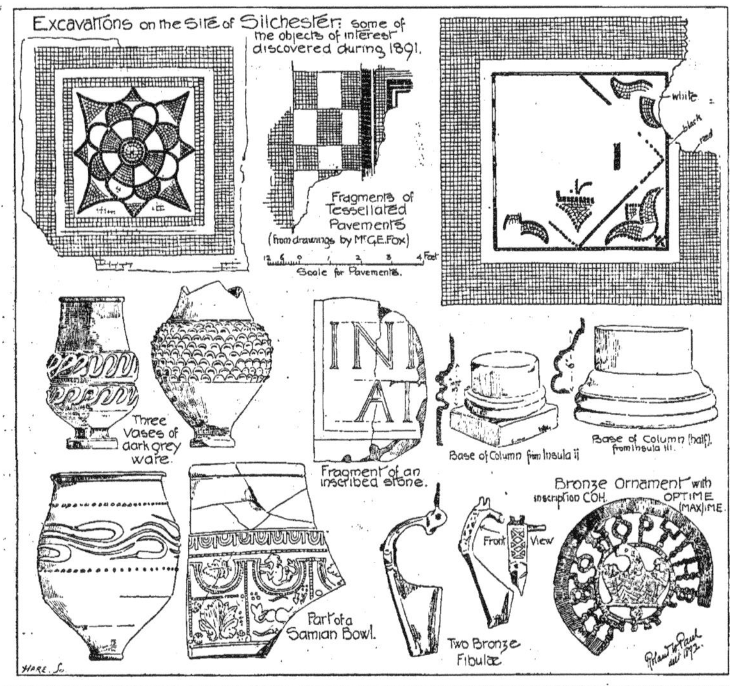

he south-west corner of Insula I. occurred races of a large house. From amongst the of the foundation was dug up the curious k of bronze here figured (see sketches). e inscription surrounding the eagle, its central ornament, has been read as COH. OPTIME. MAXIME, the missing letters being made out from another specimen, exactly similar, found in the station of Bremenium, beyond the Roman Wall. The use of the object has not yet been determined. Close by a drum of a column was dug out, and a fragment of a fine Corinthian capital which had once formed part of one of the olumns of the colonnade of the neighbouring basilica. A large piece of a wall-slab of foreign marble was also turned up near the same spot.

The examination of Insula II., to the west of the basilica, showed the former existence of a large house at its north-east angle, and along the east side an almost unbroken line of buildings. The mosaics here given came from a series of chambers. The centre of one floor was successfully raised, and was placed in the Society's exhibition this year. The mosaics formed the ornamentation of the rooms of a wing of the house just mentioned, and though of interest as revealing alterations made in the house at a late date, were but of simple character and design.

More fruitful, however, were the results obtained by the excavation of the south-west corner of this insula. There were found the foundations of a perfect house. The plan howed a small dwelling of four or five rooms, to which was attached a long line of shops and store-rooms. Access to these, from the house, was given by a long corridor at the back. Only one of the rooms of the house was warmed by a hypocaust, which was of a composite character,—*i.e.*, partly formed of pilæ of brick, partly of masses of masonry. A detached chamber, its use could not be determined, lay a few feet east of the house. It had a well-laid floor of brick tesseræ, and in one corner stood the little base, of which a drawing is given.

Insula III. showed as many traces of buildings as Insula II. did. It lay to the south of Insula II., and the houses in it had been much ruined. Traces of baths, or what may have been baths, were found in the south-east corner, and from among the foundations there came a fragment of the inscription cut in a slab of Purbeck marble, and figured here, and two bases of half columns also given. The plan of a small but very complete house could be made out in the centre of the south side, perhaps in some way connected with these baths.

The interior of both insulæ showed open ground dotted with rubbish-pits, but in both the houses were close together, and the open ground of smaller area than in Insula I., examined in 1890. Another fact worthy of notice was the presence of many hypocausts in the buildings, the house at the north-east corner of Insula II. having as many as five or six. Why this was is readily accounted for. The city stood on high ground, and was exposed to heavy gales from the south-west, bringing much rain, whilst the land to the north of it was open heath.

The rubbish-pits afforded a rich harvest of all kinds of objects, but mostly of pottery, specimens of which, illustrating leading divisions, are here given. The contrast between the strictly Classic ornamentation, as seen on the fragment of so-called Samian ware, No. 1, and the long, bean-shaped scrolls of thoroughly Celtic character on the pot-shaped vase, No. 2, is well worthy of remark.

The forms of the bronze *fibulæ* found were mostly those of the two illustrated, the front of one of which has been ornamented with enamel. These might afford to our jewellers some of the hints which they are so much in need of.

It would be quite possible to combine thin, graceful lines, full of character, with that display of the precious stones which seems to be the one thing sought after at the present day.

The exhibition at the rooms of the Society of Antiquaries closed on the 14th. The contents, like those of the former one, will be deposited in the museum at Reading, by the desire of the Duke of Wellington, to whom the site of the Roman city belongs. As the excavation of the site, under the auspices of the Society of Antiquaries, will be continued as long as public subscriptions are forthcoming for the purpose, as it is hoped they will be, the collection may become, in course of time, an exposition of the Romano-British period scarcely to be equalled in England.

G. E. F.

WESLEYAN CHAPEL, &c., HARROGATE.—We are asked to state that, in a limited competition for the Wesleyan chapel and schools, Harrogate, the design submitted by Messrs. Morley & Woodhouse, architects, of Bradford, has been accepted.

NOTES.

ALL our readers will concur with us in our expression of deep regret and sympathy in regard to the sad loss which has fallen upon the Royal family of this realm by the lamented death of the Duke of Clarence, an event so national in its interest that it must come home to all classes and professions. There would in any case have been a universal feeling of sympathy for the bereavement of the Prince and Princess of Wales, who have endeared themselves to the country by their general courtesy and kindness in public life, and who are known to be affectionate parents in private life; but in this case we have to deplore not only the loss of a son of the Prince of Wales but of a future heir to the English throne, while the event is rendered still more sad from the fact that the young Duke was in a few weeks to have entered into a marriage which had the good wishes of the whole nation, irrespective of creed or party.

THE Crystal Palace Electrical Exhibition was supposed to be open to the public last Saturday; those, however, who went there on that date in expectation of seeing the Exhibition were soon undeceived. The machine-room, generally the most interesting, was closed altogether, and the nave was redolent of paint and encumbered with ropes and ladders, while everywhere the sound of hammers was unceasing. Some few stalls, especially those at which light and portable articles were exhibited, were in a state approaching completion, while others were entirely empty, and in the galleries this latter state of things predominated. Special attention seems to have been paid to the question of electric fittings, and a good deal of taste and ingenuity is displayed in devising novel and artistic lamp supports and in pleasantly screening the light; but we regret to see that the heavy and ugly supports inherited from the gas decorators have too often survived. The exhibits of the General Post Office are nearly ready, but are not yet all numbered; most of them are very interesting historically, and, whether designedly or not, the earliest and roughest of these are in close proximity to cases containing highly-finished specimens of Sir William Thomson's latest instruments, as though to mark the advance in the science within less than sixty years' time. There is a catalogue moreover, "First edition under revision," as we are informed on the back. We trust the revision will be thorough: it is certainly required. If anyone wants to find a particular exhibit and chances to know the name of the exhibitor he may be able to find it; if he knows only the name of the instrument the index gives him no help; nor can one even walk conscientiously round, catalogue in hand, and trust to numerical order; the exhibits seem arranged in the catalogue quite at random. Thus we find on page 73 (we opened the book haphazard):—"No. 208 South Gallery, No. 76A Machine-room, No. 68 Machine-room" as consecutive entries. "The Court would be obliged to you, Mr. ——, if you would arrange your facts in some sort of order; chronological order is the best, but any order will do—alphabetical order," a witty judge once said to an embarrassed junior. The G.P.O. part of the catalogue adopts the judge's "best" chronological order, but this is unsuited to the rest of the exhibition, which is not historical, and we find on looking more closely that there the alternative is "alphabetical order." The exhibits are divided into sections lettered from A. to P., and in each section arranged according to the alphabetical order of the exhibitors' names. To each section there is an introduction, with a fair sprinkling of the usual blunders of popular science, but we must postpone further notice of the exhibition and its catalogue until the former is really open and the latter has been revised.

WE have to thank many correspondents who were exhibitors in the Architectural Room of the Royal Academy last year for their very cordial letters in regard to the "*Builder* Album of Royal Academy Architecture," which contains in a folio volume the illustrations published in this journal of drawings exhibited at the Royal Academy and lent by their authors, either before or after the exhibition, to be lithographed for our pages. Although some extra copies of the Album are available for those (non-contributors) who may wish to possess it (as will be seen from the publisher's announcement on another page), the main object in issuing it has been to present to the many architects who paid us the compliment of wishing their Academy drawings to be illustrated in the *Builder* a return for their courtesy in the shape of a collection of these drawings, which, besides being of interest for the moment, may in time have a certain historic value. The collection of a number of the Royal Academy exhibits in one volume in this manner may also have a value, as our contemporary the *Athenæum* has observed, in showing that the "Architectural Room" exhibits of the year "merited a great deal more attention than they had received." We refer to the subject here chiefly to point out that, as one of our correspondents says, "it will be the fault of architects themselves if the future volumes are not of equal interest to that now published." We desire to render these Albums a valuable series of permanent records of the Academy architecture of each year; but we can only hope to do so by the hearty co-operation of the exhibitors themselves.

THE Abbey Church of Notre Dame, at Fécamp, in Caux, totally destroyed by a fire which broke out in the liqueur distillery last Monday night, stands in the middle of the town on the river Fécamp. It had been founded in 666, by, as some say, St. Ouen, Dagobert's Chancellor, and Archbishop of Rouen, founder also of St. Wandrille, Jumiéges, Saint Saëns, and Fleury. William Longue-épée supplanted the nuns with some canons regular. His son, Richard I., Duke of Normandy, rebuilt and richly endowed the church, in honour of its relic of the Holy Blood, in 988; his grandson, Robert the Devil, the Conqueror's father, bestowed it upon a band of Benedictine monks from Dijon. To such wealth and extent did the monastery increase that when suppressed about 100 years ago, it covered 13 acres, including the gardens, and had a revenue of about 6,500*l.* per annum, with jurisdiction over 36 parishes, 11 priories, and 14 cells. The buildings, though unfinished until the sixteenth century, consisted mainly of fourteenth-century work: two round-arched apsidal chapels at the east end being earlier in date, the south side of the choir, and the Chapel of the Virgin, marked with its wolf and fox gargoyles, being later. By the Virgin chapel stood the tombs of Richard I., Sans-peur, and Richard II., le Bon, Dukes of Normandy. The nave, about 460 by 160 ft., had an arcade of ten piers carrying a smaller arcade, and above that a triforium. The tower (which has altogether fallen) at the crossing, and rising 210 ft., was of the eleventh century.* The monk Chardon's remarkable group of the death of the Virgin stood in the south transept; in the north transept the seventeenth-century big clock. Some of the abbey remains were adapted to purposes of the mairie, and the municipal library.

THE abolition of the second class on railways is slowly but steadily becoming more general, in spite of the protests raised by some of the Great Northern passengers who were "evicted" in consequence of the adoption of this policy by that company. The discussion which followed upon the Great Northern announcement proved that the main objection to the change was that it deprived a certain section of the travelling public of an "almost indispensable refuge" from the rough company sometimes, unhappily, encountered in third-class carriages,—a difficulty which, it will be remembered, was met on the Midland by reducing first-class fares to the figure charged on other lines to second-class passengers. Among the contributors to the discussion was the Chairman of the London and North-Western, who expressed a determination on the part of his company to continue their present policy, and not to throw their intermediate class overboard. Some surprise has, therefore, been expressed at the announcement that no second-class carriages would be run on the branch of the London and North-Western Railway opened this month between Mold and Coed Talon. Certainly this is a line upon which there cannot be many passengers of any class, seeing that it was made some time ago, but has been closed for passenger traffic for many years. Neither is it by any means a long branch, for the journey only occupies a quarter of an hour, and but two trains are run per day in each direction. Still, if the London and North-Western Company ever give way on this question, the little Flintshire line may be pointed to as the thin edge of the wedge.

THE tenth Building Exhibition is to be opened at the Agricultural Hall on March 14, and is to remain open a fortnight. It is two years since the last similar exhibition, and no doubt the discontinuance of the practice of holding the exhibition annually will render it more easy to make it worth holding, though we think an interval of three years would be even better than two. We are informed, however, that there is to be a considerable effort made to render this year's exhibition a successful one, and to give it some new interest, and among other things there is to be an "Art-work Branch" open to workmen, apprentices, or amateurs, for building and the allied trades. There will be eight groups in these exhibits viz.: Carpentry, Carving, Furniture, Painting and Decorating, Metal-work, Building Appliances and Materials, Building Facilitators, and Invention and Design. The last two are rather vague. One does not see very well how art is to come into "Building Facilitators" (as far as one can attach any definite meaning to the term), while "Invention and Design" is far too comprehensive a title.... What is meant, we presume is, drawings of work not executed otherwise than in the drawing stage: but it should have been more explicitly worded.

THE interim report of Mr. Rogers Field in regard to the sanitary arrangements of Wellington College is of too brief a character to require detailed notice at the present time. It states that there are defects of a grave character, but it does not state in detail what these defects are. Important sanitary work was done in 1883, that is, not ten years ago, and yet that work is now imperfect. The fact shows very strongly the necessity of periodical inspection of all buildings and drains which belong to colleges and schools. No other course gives real security, and it is in the long run the most economical system. Whether or not the diphtheritic epidemic at Wellington College was caused by these defects is by no means proved. On the contrary, it would appear to have been brought into the college from outside. It is probable, however, that even if this were so, the sanitary defects have made boys more liable to the disease than otherwise would have been the case. It is to be hoped that a thoroughly detailed report will in due time be issued by Mr. Field, for it would be of use as a warning to other schools and colleges,

* See the Encyclopédie Méthodique, 1782: Paris; Dictionnaire Général de Biographie et d'Histoire, 1889; and Larousse's Grand Dictionnaire Universel du XIXe Siècle, 1872.

and throw light on the defects of our public schools. Another point which cannot be passed over is the ascertained fact that the gas at the large school was very impure, and that there were many escapes. At the beginning of the winter we called attention to the negligence which apparently exists in regard to the lighting of many of our public and private schools. Here we have a glaring and clearly ascertained instance of the fact which we ventured to assert in a general form, though not without particular grounds. The authorities of every college and school in the country should without delay set this matter right.

IN the last issue of the *Transactions* of the American Society of Civil Engineers we observe that Mr. Latham Anderson, a member of the Society, is putting forth as a new idea what he calls "the single-trap system of house drainage," the principle of which consists in cutting off the outer drain from the house by a single trap, and using no other trap to any closet or waste-pipe, &c., in the house, but arranging an upcast ventilating pipe, with suction induced by a gas-jet or other means, to exercise a steady draw upon all the soil-pipes in the house and merely produce a constant suction of air from the interior of the house to the drain, rendering (as is supposed) traps to the water-closets unnecessary. This may be new in the United States: it is not new here; it was set forth and illustrated in our columns ten years ago at the instance of the late Sir Henry Cole, who was employing it in his own house, and a considerable correspondence on the subject followed. There is a beautiful simplicity about the system, provided one can always rely on the exhaust-shaft to act, and no doubt there are advantages in getting rid of traps to water-closets, the best flushed of which must collect deposit in the dip to some extent: but it does not appear that experience of the system has led to any great increase in its adoption in this country. It is an excellent system as long as it acts exactly as intended; but if anything gets out of order with the exhaust ventilator and its working power, people would very soon find that there was plenty of smell from the deposit on the sides of the pipes, even with the outer drain trapped off; and most people will feel safer from annoyance and danger to health by having the soil-pipes trapped off than by a system to prevent the air ever travelling up them. Still it is of interest to note that the system has been advocated in America, and we should like to hear what is the result, and whether it finds any favour there.

DYSART HOUSE, Fifeshire, together with the mansion-house portion (about 85 acres) of the estate, and lying along the shore of the Firth of Forth, is offered for sale by private bargain. The property to be sold includes Ravenscraig, or Ravensheugh, Castle, that stands upon a high promontory washed on three sides by the sea. This and Morton, Rait, and Tullyallan Castles are peculiar instances of a kind, since they present examples of a design and plan intermediate between those of the keep for refuge or defence, and of the castle with an inner quadrangle to serve as a residence. A work that we have recently reviewed* contains plans, sections, and views, with details, of Ravenscraig. Built by James II.'s widow, Mary of Guelders, and being, for most part, of one age, its leading features comprise a rounded keep towards the mainland, containing the principal private rooms, and joined by a curtain about 53 ft. long to a salient circular tower, 44 ft. in diameter, which stands on lower ground at the north-eastern angle,—the site is a rocky plateau, rising up 100 ft. above the water. The top story has been modernised, and the crow's-nest gables of the roof are regarded as a later addition. Shortly before the king's death, Walter Ramsay, and Janet his wife, vassals to the Earl of Fife, assigned Dysart to the queen for lands near to Linlithgow. Some accounts of Mary's lands and fermes, 1462-3, show payments of 600*l.* to Master David Boys, Master of Works, for directing the building, and of various sums for materials,—including 14 great timbers, "joists," from the woods by Allan-water: the payments cease with her death. Her son, James III., bestowed the castle and lands, 1470, upon William St. Clair, fourth Earl of Orkney, in exchange for his castle of Kirkwall and "his haill right to the earldom of Orkney." It subsequently passed to the Earls of Rosslyn, of Dysart House.

* "The Castellated and Domestic Architecture of Scotland, Twelfth to Eighteenth Centuries," by David Macgibbon and Thomas Ross, architects. See the *Builder*, December 25, 1886, and January 19, 1889.

THERE have been so much talking and writing about the desirability of making the national treasure-house of the British Museum better known to the public, and especially the working-classes, that we are glad to see something definite is about to be done. The trustees have given their consent to a course of evening lectures on "Greek Art and Life," as illustrated by the contents of the Museum, the first of which is to be given on January 19, at 8.30 p.m. The Keeper of Greek and Roman Antiquities will take the chair, so the movement has ample official countenance. The first five lectures are to deal with Greek sculpture in the fifth century B.C., and especially the Parthenon marbles, and are given by Miss Eugénie Sellers, who devotes part of her first lecture to the History of the Classical Collections in the Museum. There is an admirable paper on this subject by Sir Charles Newton in his Archæological Essays, but the spoken word will, we hope, reach many to whom the written word is a dead-letter. The originators of the scheme have wisely decided to divide the course between Greek art and Greek life, and this other branch of the subject is confided to Miss Millington Lathbury, our first *certificated* lady archæologist. She is to deal in five lectures with all those topics which to some minds come so much nearer home than any questions of art, *e.g.*, "Greek Festivals and Games," "Daily Life of Men and Women in Greece," "Greek Dress and Greek Armour Temple Services," and last, though not least, "Greek Grave-reliefs and Funeral Customs." The scheme has been set going by the two indefatigable honorary secretaries of the Chelsea and Whitechapel centres of the London Society for the Extension of University Teaching.

WE read in the *Times* that new premises for the Parcel-Post Service are to be erected in Paddington, and,—as in the case of Coldbath-fields,—upon the site of Tothill-fields Prison, Westminster. The latter prison was pulled down and the ground cleared in 1883-4.* Having latterly served as a female penitentiary, it was built, after Robert Abraham's designs, in 1830-4, for 800 prisoners, upon a plot of ground near to the then Palmer's village. The plan consisted of several wards, including 42 day and 348 night rooms, arranged round a garden; the governor's house, with chapel above, being in the front. The entrance, south-east, had a handsome elevation of granite with a portcullis, and the whole building was considered to form one of the finest pieces of brickwork in London. Ashley-gardens and Ambrosden-avenue now divide the site into two portions, whereof one is reserved for the proposed cathedral (R.C.): see the *Builder*, of March 8, 1884. The old Bridewell, first built in 1618, along the northern side of Green-coat School and Hospital, on Tothill-side, stood until 1836, when its gateway, with the keys, were removed, as relics, to the new position. The narrow stone portal, with its inscribed stone above, were afterwards set up against the north wall of the Sessions House, which is about to be enlarged at an estimated cost of 20,000*l.* The inscription stands thus:—

> Here are several Sorts of Work
> For the *Poor* of this *Parish* of St.
> *Margaret's Westminster*:
> As also the *County*, according to
> LAW, and for such as will Beg, and
> Live Idle in this City, and Liberty
> of *Westminster*. Anno 1655.

* The materials were sold at auction for 5,800*l.*, including, we were told, 2,300*l.* for 190 tons of lead.

IT is seldom that a freehold area of nearly one acre and three-quarters (75,000 feet superficial), with vacant possession, within the City of London, is offered for sale. Last April the Court of Common Council decided to sell the site and buildings of Farringdon Market, whereof certain existing rights are about to expire. Tenders were invited, for deposit on October 7 last. But it seems that none of these proved satisfactory, since the Corporation are now resolved to sell the property by auction early in the coming spring. The several frontages are to Shoe-lane, Farringdon-street, and Stonecutter-street, with a decline from west to east. We gave a brief account of the market and its site in a "Note" on July 2, 1887.

THE necessity for a public hall in Edinburgh, suitable to the requirements of the city, has long been felt and commented upon. The Music Hall, in George-street, the largest in the city, although admirable as regards situation, does not contain accommodation for an audience of 1,500; and, at this season of the year especially, complaints are continually cropping up as to the high prices charged for admittance to good concerts, oratorios, &c., as compared with those charged in cities where suitable provision is made for large audiences. The site occupied by the Music Hall is sufficient for a building adequate to accommodate at least 3,000 persons, without galleries, and, were they included in the plan, an additional 1,000 would find room. The present building contains, beside the Music Hall,—which is situated in the rear,—a suite of rooms appropriated to dancing assemblies, and on the ground-floor are two shops. The site is one which deserves to be occupied by a more attractive structure than the present building, which is of very little architectural merit.

WE have received a copy of a country newspaper, published not far from London, containing an advertisement which certainly exhibits "that hybrid personage the Surveyor-architect" in all his glory. It runs thus (omitting name and address):—

"Mr.——— ———
(*Associate Royal Institute British Architects*),
ARCHITECT, SURVEYOR AND SANITARY ENGINEER.
[here follows the address].

"In matters of Quantity Surveying, Arbitration, Settlement of Building Disputes, Compensations, Valuations, the General Sale or Transfer of Properties; also Drainage, Ventilation, &c., Mr. ——— can be consulted daily by appointment.
Preliminary Sketches, Plans, &c., prepared, and the approximate cost of proposed works ascertained free of charge."

The name of the person making this tradesman's advertisement is not in the list of members of the R.I.B.A. recently issued. If he has become a member since the issue of the last "Kalendar" of the Institute, he must have been admitted through the Examination, we presume; which would, at all events, show that the Examination is no protection against men getting into the Institute who have no sense of professional or artistic dignity, or of the self-respect proper to gentlemen. We have enclosed the original advertisement to the Secretary of the Institute of Architects, from whom the advertiser will probably hear, in one sense or another, according as he is, or is not, a member of that body.

THE *Scientific American* (Architects' and Builders' Edition) for December, 1891, we observe, gives two plates from drawings

"Lanterne des Morts," Ciron, Indre. " Lanterne des Morts," Cemetery at Pers (Deux-Sèvres).

by Mr. Alexander Graham of the Triumphal Arch at Tim-gad, Algeria, as existing, and restored. Reproductions of these drawings, from the originals lent to us for the purpose by Mr. Graham, were published by us as plates in the issue of the *Builder* for October 4, 1890. The illustrations in the *Scientific American* are obviously bad reproductions from our plates, reproduced without permission and without acknowledgment of the source from which they are taken. It is apparently useless, in the present state of literary law and literary morality in the United States, to expect common honesty in these matters from American journals; but they will at all events not be allowed to plunder from our pages without the fact being duly noted and made public.

SOME OLD FRENCH CEMETERY ERECTIONS.

The erections described and illustrated here are taken from old churchyards in Brittany, where especially there has been kept up what may be called the "cult des morts." Besides the stone cross which was a common object in Mediæval graveyards or cemeteries in connexion with a church, there is found frequently a small isolated tower, in the form of a hollow column and terminating in a kind of lantern. These erections, the use of which can be traced in France to a remote antiquity, have been called "Lanternes des Morts." Some of them have at their base a large stone, serving apparently as an altar; and a lighted lamp is said to have been placed every night in the "lanterne." It appears to have served the double object of indicating to strangers that they were in a burial-ground, and of keeping away, as was believed, evil spirits, vampires, "loup-garous," &c., which used to be a terror of the populations of the north and west of France.

In Brittany the little cemeteries surrounding the churches were quickly filled, and from time to time the good people exhumed their ancestors to make room for their descendants. But in place of re-interring the remains in a pit, the bones were piously preserved in ossuaries. Generally the ossuary formed a little chapel in a portion of the burial-ground, in close proximity to the church, with compartments arranged for the storing and exhibition of the remains. Often families, at the exhumation of the remains of their relatives or predecessors, would demand the skull as a memorial, and enclose it in a small box surmounted by a cross which was placed in the ossuary, or sometimes in some part of the church. Inscriptions, sometimes in French sometimes in Latin, were painted on the boxes; sometimes they are in the old Bretonne dialect, and in some villages are found constructions specially formed for the exhibition of these boxes.

As an example of these a sketch is given of the ossuary of St. Pol de Léon in the department of Finistère (see page 46); it is set against the wall of a cemetery, and divided into bays or niches to receive the boxes. This is one of the most curious and characteristic which I have met with.

I have thought also that it would interest English readers to see some representations of the old crosses and "Lanternes des Morts" which are still to be found in the cemeteries of the ancient provinces of the west of France. Sketches of four of these are given, two crosses and two of the characteristic "Lanternes."

Photographs of these and others are to be found among the fine collection of photographs of ancient remains made by M. Mieusement for the department of "Monuments Historiques."

Adolphe Guillon.

ARCHITECTURAL SOCIETIES.

The Architectural Association: Discussion Section.—The fourth meeting for the session 1891-92 was held at the rooms of the Association, on Wednesday, the 6th inst., when Mr. Cecil A. Sharp read a paper on "Workhouse Planning and Construction." The discussion which followed the reading of the paper was opened by Mr. A. W. Saxon Snell, F.R.I.B.A., and sustained by Messrs. Hall, Stockdale, Pywell, and the Vice-Chairman, Mr. S. Beale. Mr. T. Aldwinckle gave some excellent hints, and Mr. Gordon Smith's summing up was full of valuable information. The special Visitors for the evening were Mr. P. Gordon Smith, F.R.I.B.A., Architect to the Local Government Board, and Mr. Thomas Aldwinckle, F.R.I.B.A.

Carlisle Engineering, Architectural, and Surveying Association.—At the usual meeting of this Society, on December 29 last, a paper upon "Sewerage and Sewage Disposal,"

Cemetery Cross, St. Georges du Roc (Deux-Sèvres). *Cemetery Cross, Aiffres (Deux-Sèvres).*

was read by Mr. Arthur Turley, Civil Engineer, Carlisle. The most approved system of main sewer construction was described and illustrated, the lecturer explaining the mode of procedure for the preparation of a complete scheme of main drainage and sewage disposal for a district having a population of 20,000. The question of disposal of heavy rainfalls was dealt with, various forms of storm-water overflows being illustrated and described. The hydro-pneumatic system of sewerage was exhaustively dealt with, the lecturer having prepared explanatory plan, sections, and other details of that system as laid down at Henley-on-Thames. The ventilation of public sewers was fully gone into, and the use of factory chimneys to assist in this work was strongly advocated, wherever such facilities could be obtained. The various systems in vogue for the treatment of sewage were treated at great length, the cost and result of each being given. The systems dealt with were those of broad irrigation, intermittent downward earth filtration, various chemical processes, combinations of chemical precipitation and land filtration, and several patented processes, viz.: the Iron Process, the Ferrozone and Polarite Process, and others. The lecturer stated that these patented systems were worthy of careful consideration by those interested in the subject of sewage purification, and he thought it unfortunate that opposition to them should be offered by the Local Government Board by their insisting upon the purchase of land for the treatment of the effluents obtained from these systems, such supplementary process being, in his opinion, quite unnecessary.

LIVERPOOL ARCHITECTURAL SOCIETY.—A special meeting of this society was held at their Library on Monday last, under the presidency of T. Harnett Harrisson, F.R.I.B.A., when a paper was read on "Cement and Cement Testing," by J. A. Berrington, A.R.I.B.A., fully illustrated by practical tests of specially-prepared briquettes, by a Michele machine, and also by the use of Vicat's needle; and the methods of sifting, weighing, mixing, &c., in order to ascertain the quality of the cement, were fully gone into. All the briquettes tested yielded very good results,—as much as 1,000 lbs. tensile stress being registered on the area of 2¼ in., four days' old, dry mixed. Special attention was directed to the method of mixing in favour with manufacturers, *i.e.*, very dry mixing,—some of the tests being with briquettes mixed with 16 oz. of water to 48 of cement, and others with 10 oz. of water to 48 of cement,—the latter giving much better results; but it was pointed out that cement mixed so dry as the latter could only be used for such purposes as foundations for roadways, carefully rammed and consolidated (and the same method had to be adopted to fill the moulds for the tests). If used as mortar, or for other building purposes, 25 per cent. of water was as little as could practically be used, and this proportion was considered the legitimate test. The paper and the experiments were much appreciated by the members, as giving them a practical insight into the modes of testing and the best manner of judging of reliable cements, which are not always open to the investigation of architects.

SHEFFIELD SOCIETY OF ARCHITECTS AND SURVEYORS.—The monthly meeting of this society was held at the School of Art on Tuesday last. The departure from Sheffield of Mr. G. Alsing, C.E., for Glasgow, was considered, and the following resolution, moved by Mr. F. Fowler, seconded by Mr. E. M. Gibbs, was carried unanimously:—"That this meeting of the Sheffield Society of Architects and Surveyors desires to express to Gustave Alsing, Esq., C.E., on his leaving Sheffield, its high appreciation of his courtesy to the members of the society in carrying out his duties as Chief Engineer of the Sewerage and Rivers Department of the County Borough of Sheffield, and to assure him of the best wishes of the society for his future prosperity and happiness." Mr. F. R. Farrow, F.R.I.B.A., Vice-President of the London Architectural Association, then read an interesting and instructive paper on "The Ventilation of Public Buildings." He commenced by defining the principles on which ventilation depends, being the substitution of fresh air for foul air, which to be successful must be without draught. Foul air is air vitiated to a certain definite extent; fresh air, air in a normal state of purity. Draught is the unpleasant contact of moving air with the person, and air is a fluid and a gas, and therefore heated air is lighter than cold air of equal purity, and foul air is heavier than fresh air of equal temperature. In elaborating these points he gave figures as to and formula for the calculations of proper temperatures, speed of incoming air to avoid draught, size of flues, engines, &c., and described the proper means for effecting the purposes required, either by natural or artificial ventilation, showing the superiority of the latter over

Ossuary, St. Pol de Léon (Finistère). See page 44.

the former. He gave several examples of different forms of ventilating apparatus, and their application to different classes of buildings, including some of the large public buildings of Vienna, the Rathhaus, University, Bourse, and Grand Opera House, which are ventilated on elaborate systems. He showed what to avoid in planning-out systems, and the essential points to be provided. The lecture was well illustrated by drawings and diagrams.

Illustrations.

ARCHITECTURAL STUDY BY BRAMANTE.

THIS is a reproduction from an engraving by Bramante in the British Museum, of which only a very few copies are known to exist in Europe. It was specially alluded to by Baron de Geymüller in his paper on the School of Bramante read before the Institute of Architects last year, when a copy of it was exhibited. It is a striking example of the class of ideal architectural composition in which the leading architects of the Renaissance not unfrequently indulged. The treatment of the foreground arch in section is a characteristic feature, as also the introduction of the bust turned from the spectator, in the circular opening on the left. The figures are in the usual costume of the day, looking oddly out of keeping with the ideal design.

While on the subject we may refer to another composition "attributed to Bramante" and published in the *Builder* for March 21, 1891, about the authenticity of which Baron de Geymuller expressed himself, in the paper referred to, as somewhat sceptical. It may be of interest to note that we have recently heard from Baron de Geymüller that he has found reason to think that the design referred to is very probably an authentic design by Bramante.

SEASCALE CHURCH.

THE church at Seascale occupies a fine site on a little hillock above the rising seaside resort of Seascale in Cumberland; it is built of the local red sandstone from St. Bees' Head, an ancient quarry on the seaboard, from which Windsor Castle is recorded to have been repaired in the times of the Edwards. The church is from the designs of Mr. C. J. Ferguson, F.S.A., architect, of Westminster and Carlisle, and is so arranged that it may be added to if the increasing requirements of the place demand it. The drawing, by Mr. R. W. Paul, was exhibited in the Academy of 1890.

HYMERS' COLLEGE, HULL.

OUR illustration shows this building as it is now being carried out, some slight modifications having been made in the competition design, which was placed first by the assessor, Mr. E. C. Robins, F.S.A., and which we illustrated on June 28, 1890.

The building consists of sixteen class-rooms, eight on each floor, grouped around a central hall 92 ft. by 45 ft., in such a manner that every class-room is entered directly from the hall, or from the galleries which surround it on three sides. The Classical School, on the ground floor, consists of six class-rooms for thirty scholars each, and two for twenty-four each, the floor area being twenty superficial feet per scholar. The corresponding class-rooms in the Modern School (first floor) accommodate respectively forty and thirty-two, the floor area being fifteen superficial feet per scholar; the total accommodation thus being 532. Dados of cloak-lockers around the central hall, galleries, and corridors, provide accommodation for both schools, each scholar having a separate locker. The administrative offices are placed in the lower building along the principal front, beneath the large windows of the central hall. The principal entrance is in the centre, with the head-master's room and porter's room on either side. Beyond these are the secretary's room and the assistant-masters' common room, with lavatory and cloak-lobby. The principal staircase is directly opposite the main entrance, and communicates with a wide gallery behind the hall arcade, a narrow gallery at one end, and a wider gallery at the other end, with seats for the accommodation of some fifty persons. Two short and straight corridors lead from the central hall to the side entrances. The class-room doors will be glazed, and inspection windows provided. It will thus be seen that the whole building, with its entrances and exits, is brought directly under the supervision of the head-master and porter. It is intended to add, at some future time, Science and Art blocks at each end of the building, the corridors being extended for that purpose. Until these additions are carried out, class-rooms in the main building will be temporarily fitted for instruction in science and art. The latrines and lavatories are arranged in separate blocks on the east side of the main building. The external facing is of red brick, with Ancaster stone dressings, the central hall and corridors being finished in the same manner; the roofs will be covered with red tiles. The total cost of the main building, with the lavatories and latrines, will be about 12,900*l*. Messrs. Botterill, Son, & Bilson, of Hull, are the architects.

STUDY FOR A COUNTRY HOUSE.

THIS study, which speaks for itself, is by Mr. J. H. Sellers, and was exhibited in the Architectural Room of the Royal Academy last year. The plan is a peculiar one, with a flight of stairs direct from the entrance-porch, rather more suggestive of a club perhaps than of a country house. The kitchen presumably is on the lower level. The exterior design is treated with commendable simplicity.

THE CONDITION OF GLOUCESTER CATHEDRAL.

WE have received a copy of a recent report of Mr. F. S. Waller, the consulting architect to the Dean and Chapter of Gloucester, on the state of the building, which shows that an effort is necessary on the part of all who are interested in the Cathedral if it is to be kept in an adequate state of repair. It must be presumed that there is no "fabric fund" for the Cathedral, and it is stated in the circular accompanying the architect's report that twelve years ago the revenues of the Cathedral were more than double what they now are, and the Dean and Canons have, therefore, suffered a loss of more than 50 per cent. of their incomes. The Chapter have to the best of their ability laid out upon the fabric more than should rightly be spared from the maintenance of the services and the stipends of the staff. This expenditure on the fabric has been mainly in-

ARCHITECTURAL STUDY BY BRAMANTE FROM AN ENGRAVING IN THE BRITISH MUSEUM.

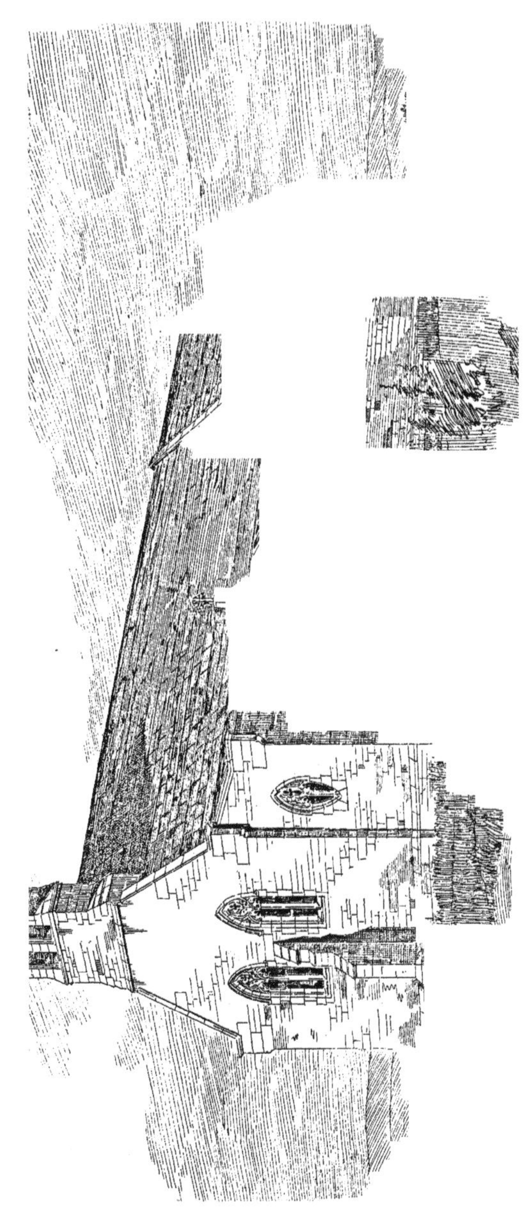

Royal Academy Exhibition, 1891

HYMERS' COLLEGE
·KINGSTON · UPON · HULL·
Botterill, Son & Bilson Archts

INK-PHOTO SPRAGUE & Co 4 & 5, EAST HARDING STREET, FETTER LANE, E.C.

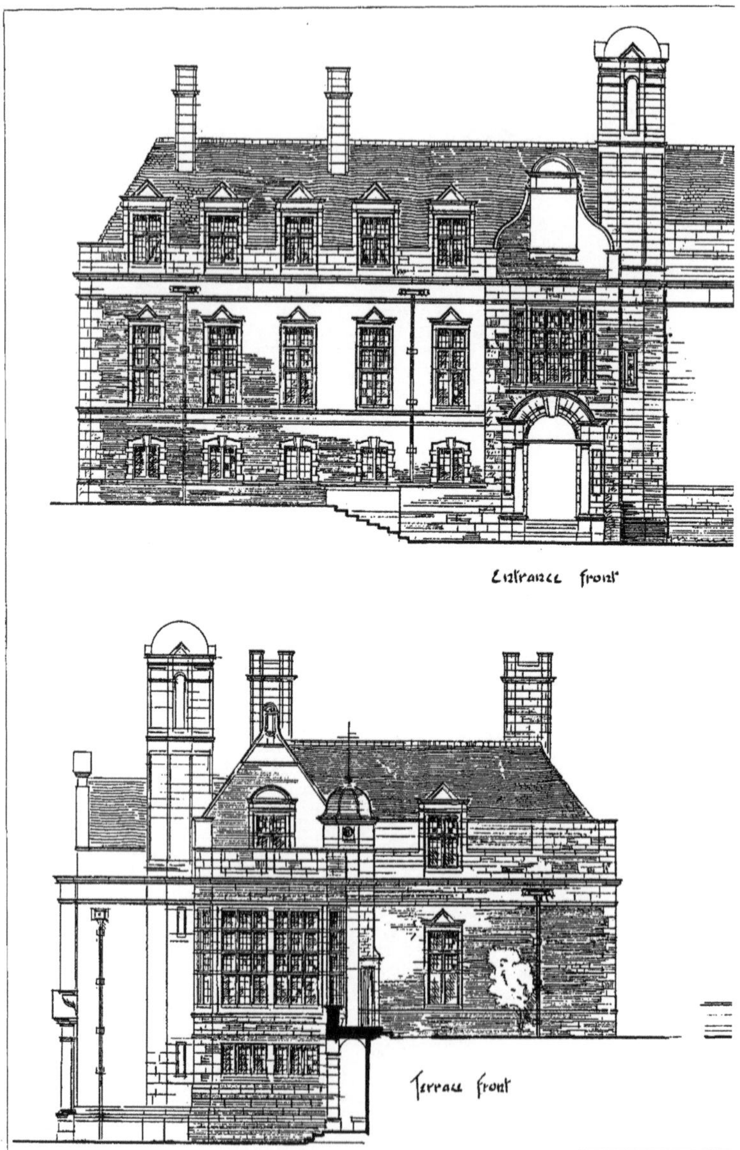

Royal Academy Exhibition, 1891.

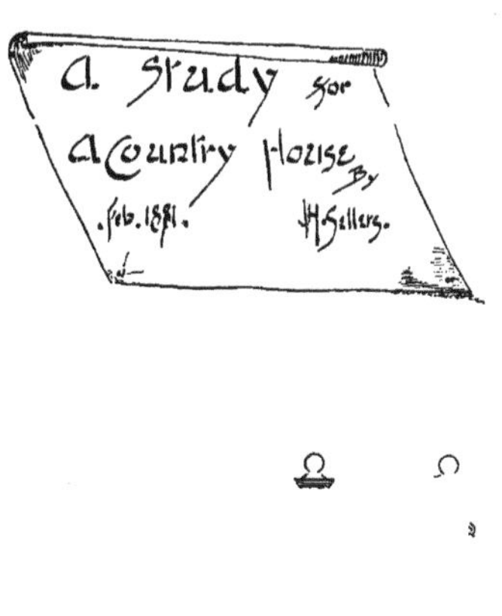

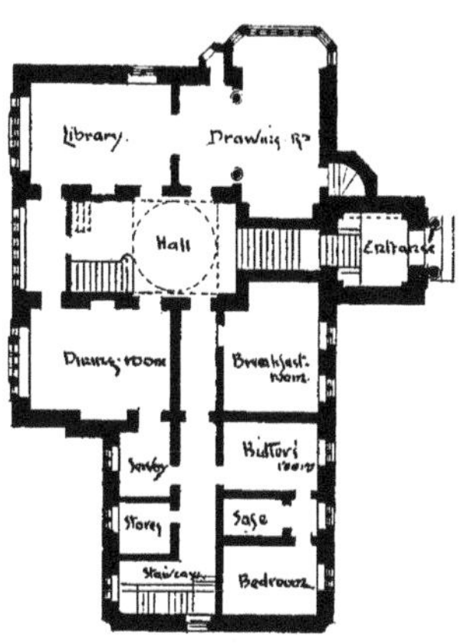

Plan.

Garden front.

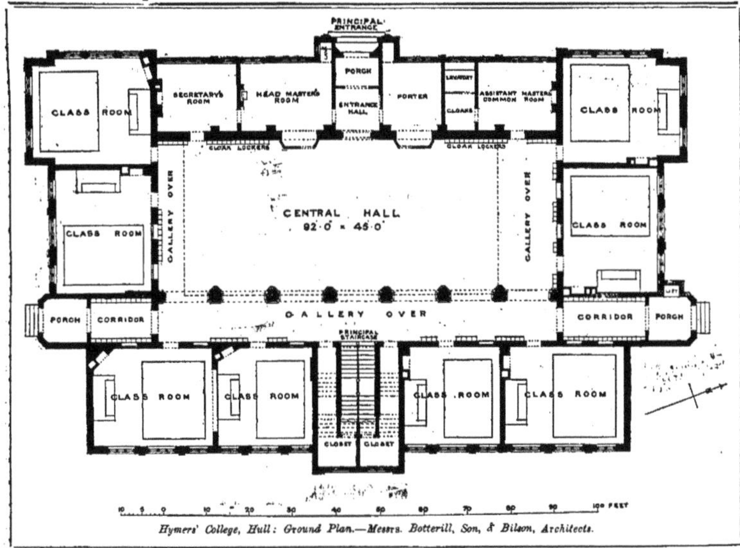

Hymers' College, Hull: Ground Plan.—Messrs. Botterill, Son, & Bilson, Architects.

curred in the constant employment of a body of skilled workmen, who, under the supervision of the architect, have executed such repairs as were from time to time absolutely necessary for the safety of the building. They are now, however, totally unable to exceed their present outlay upon the fabric (and it is a very inadequate outlay) without external aid. They have, already, during the last few months incurred a special expenditure of £124 on the reparation of one of the Norman turrets, and £50 on the reconstruction of the lightning conductors on the best modern system. These works could not be delayed, if positive disaster were to be averted.

They have also put forth an appeal for the Cathedral bells, which, owing to the state of the framework and partial wear of the metal, at present cannot be rung.

The following is Mr. Waller's report, which we give in full, as it must be of interest to many of our readers whom it would not otherwise reach :—

"Gloucester, December 1, 1891.

To the Very Rev. the Dean and Chapter of Gloucester.

Gentlemen :·I gladly avail myself of your instructions to report upon the present state of the Cathedral and on the buildings attached thereto, excluding of course the residentiary houses; and, as from conversations I have had with some of the members of your Chapter, I am led to believe that an appeal to the public is contemplated, to ask for assistance in doing works of repair which must, failing such help, remain entirely neglected, I may, perhaps, be allowed to preface this paper with a few explanatory facts, relating to the past, which are requisite to make the whole subject more readily understood, but which are not generally known.

Previous to the agricultural depression (now of many years duration), not only was there no difficulty experienced in finding the funds necessary for the ordinary repairs of all the Capitular buildings, but there was a considerable surplus for structural restorations; amongst the last and most important of which may be specially noted, the partial rebuilding of the north façade of the north transept, with its turrets, and also the entire reconstruction of the parapets and cornices, together with the four large pinnacles of the great central tower, the whole completed at a cost of several thousand pounds, derived solely from the Chapter funds.

These works were finished in 1879, since which time the depreciation in the value of landed property, then hoped to be only temporary, has continued to increase, resulting in a reduction of at least 50 per cent. in the Chapter revenues, whereby the funds for even the most ordinary annual repairs are necessarily reduced to a minimum, leaves absolutely nothing to arrest the great and steadily increasing structural dilapidations of the Cathedral and the interesting buildings by which it is surrounded.

To fairly understand your great liabilities as custodians of the Cathedral and the numerous buildings and grounds attached thereto, it will be necessary also to speak of these, which may be thus briefly described :—

BUILDINGS.	REMARKS.
The Cathedral, the Library, and Chapter-house, and minor rooms connected therewith, the great and little cloisters, the organist's house, and college school, and outbuildings attached thereto. The old gateways and Abbey walls, and other remains of the Monastery, the College-green, roads, and gardens, these latter now used as a public resort (for which one man is constantly employed), and the whole area of which occupies a space of about six acres.	These buildings consist of an immense pile of masonry, more or less ornamental, with buttresses, pinnacles, parapets, panelling, niches, copings, and other decorative and constructive work, constantly requiring attention and care, with the windows, doors, floors, drains, gutters, &c.; also a vast and costly extent of lead, stone tile, and slate roofs, nearly two acres by admeasurement, all the above requiring more or less annual repair, added to the everlasting contingent works pertaining to old buildings, to which must be added the serious dilapidations hereinafter detailed.

The foregoing list represents a formidable and grave charge for any public body, even if the buildings were in good repair, and under such circumstances the average annual outlay of several years past would be too small to keep them in sound and good condition; they are, however, very far from being *in good condition*,—indeed, in many parts they may be said to be in an *absolutely* ruinous state; a strong assertion, it is true, and one that to many people may appear almost incredible when taking into consideration the very large sums known to have been expended on the Cathedral during the last thirty years.

This, however, admits of easy explanation when we refer to the report made by the late Sir Gilbert Scott in 1866, and see how much of that which he then spoke of, as being necessary, has been *left entirely untouched*, remaining in the same condition, especially as regards the roofs and parapets, as when he inspected the Cathedral, excepting that the lapse of time has necessarily created still greater dilapidations.

Large sums have been expended on the choir and on internal fittings, and on windows for the reception of painted glass, and the external repairs have also been very considerable, including the north and south transepts, the south porch, the nave and choir, the pinnacles and parapets of the tower, and some other portions of the building; but many more remain to be done, as stated in the said report, and estimated therein to cost several thousand pounds.

In speaking of some of the most pressing of these works, I may mention especially the walls, windows, parapets, pinnacles, and roofs of the north and south aisles of the choir; the roof and gutters of the south aisle of the nave, and the condition of the great tower also, which, excepting the pinnacles, parapets, and chief cornice (which are in perfect condition), sadly requires pointing and general repair. Indeed, pointing alone would be the means of staying further decay, and of preserving the stonework for many years to come.

For these items alone and the repairs of the roofs a considerable immediate or annual outlay is now required, the present expenditure, as before stated, being wholly inadequate to stay the very serious dilapidations of which I have spoken, and which get decidedly worse year by year.

All of the foregoing are not only most important structural works, but they are absolutely essential for the preservation of the Cathedral; they are, in fact, simple repairs, due to the effects of old age. Unfortunately, when executed, they will be little seen, and therefore it is not probable that they will find favour with private individuals for memorial purposes, as is sometimes the case with the more conspicuous and ornamental parts of the building.

As regards the probable cost of the most pressing of these dilapidations, I am of opinion that 2,200*l*. will be sufficient to complete all that will be required for the walls, parapets, and roofs of the choir aisles and chapels, and the worst parts of the roof of the south aisle of the nave.

What may be required for the pointing and repair of the stonework of the Tower can only be known when the scaffolding is erected; the cost will vary on each face, and so much must depend upon the condition of the weather mouldings, and other dressed work, some of which appears to be very bad. I am quite sure the work must be attended with considerable outlay, probably not less than from 1,000*l*. to 1,500*l*. The other roofs spoken of by Sir Gilbert Scott are estimated by him to cost upwards of 2,250*l*. It will, therefore, be seen that between 5,000*l*. and 6,000*l*. is now required to simply repair and reinstate where necessary the most important of the dilapidations I have alluded to.—I beg to remain, gentlemen, yours very faithfully,

FREDK. S. WALLER.

P.S.—In this statement the subject of the restoration of the Lady-chapel has not been entertained, as it is altogether too grand a work to connect with the absolutely necessary repairs of the fabric, but as the windows are known to be in very bad condition, often admitting wind and rain from all quarters, and the mullions are in some parts so dangerously decayed that a ladder cannot with safety be placed against them, it would be very desirable to restore these as early as possible for the better preservation of the interior of the building, and so that the chapel may then be thrown open to the rest of the Cathedral and be properly warmed, which in its present state is impossible. The cost of this would be about 1,200*l.*, and one of the most expensive and important structural repairs of this chapel would than be completed, the decorative works remaining for future years."

It is not surprising that under these circumstances the Dean and Chapter have felt compelled to appeal to the public for assistance, and we hope that many unconnected with the Gloucester Diocese, but who feel that the cathedrals of England are a great national possession, will be willing to contribute towards the task of putting the fabric of Gloucester Cathedral into a satisfactory condition. Subscriptions to the amount of something over 2,000*l.* have already been promised, the Bishop, the Dean, Earl Ducie, the Archdeacon, and Mr. Dyer Edwards being among the largest subscribers. Subscriptions will be received either by the Dean, the Archdeacon (who is treasurer of the fund), or Canon Bowers, the secretary.

BRITISH ARCHÆOLOGICAL ASSOCIATION.

AT the meeting of this Association, held on Wednesday, January 6, Mr. C. H. Compton, V.P., in the chair, a large number of antiquities belonging to various members were exhibited, among which the following may be noted: Mr. B. Winstone, a very fine milk-white glass medallion of Sir Hans Sloane, Bart. Mr. Winstone also showed to the meeting one of the office books of the Commissioners of the River Stort, containing early minutes of proceedings. The Chairman described some interesting brasses in the Church of Ringwould, Kent, of which rubbings were submitted for inspection. Mr. J. M. Wood produced some hard Roman mortar from Colchester, and he also described some of the original lead piping used by Sir Hugh Myddelton at Sadler's Wells. The metal is ½ in. thick, formed of plates hammered into shape, and jointed in a remarkable manner without soldering. Mr. Watling showed drawings of curious Elizabethan paintings on the pillars of St. Clement's Church, Ipswich; and Mr. Earle Way, Roman and Mediæval remains, recently found at Southwark, including a large number of fine blue spherical Roman beads. A paper by Mr. Andreas E. Cockayne, on the "Antiquities of Derbyshire," was then read by Mr. W. de Gray Birch, in the author's absence. It treated for the most part of the evidences of the existence of man in pre-historic times, and the recent discoveries were passed in review. The Chairman read a note on the date of the foundation of Furness Abbey. The concluding paper was on a "Find of Roman Remains at Caerleon." These consist of the remains of former buildings. Roofing-tiles, stamped with the Legionary mark: "LEG II. AVG.," pottery, coins, &c. They have been found in excavating for a house for Mr. T. Parry, on the Common.

THE MERSEY TUNNEL RAILWAY.

ON Monday last the new station of the Mersey Tunnel Railway, at the bottom of Bold-street, Liverpool, was opened for traffic. The *Liverpool Daily Post* says that "probably as a feat of engineering the construction of the new station at Bold-street is not inferior to any part of the scheme advanced. Under very singular and perplexing difficulties it could only be proceeded with in its first stages from midnight until six o'clock the following morning, it being, of course, essential that the traffic at the Central Station should not be interfered with. During these hours, night after night, trenches were cut at intervals of 10 ft. across the roadway connecting the arrival platforms at the station, and into these were placed strong baulks of timber, across which planks were laid as a temporary roadway. Beneath these planks, which were taken up and put down as required, the rock was excavated to a depth of 9 ft., and the baulks supported upon stout props. Then from the driftway or rough boring beneath well-holes were bored to the upper excavation, and through them the strong upright iron pillars designed to support the roof of the new tunnel station were passed, bedded, and securely fixed in position. No sooner were they *in situ* than the most troublesome part of the task was entered upon, for the baulks had then to be removed in order to allow to be placed in position the girders running the length of the new station, and resting on the tops of the upright pillars. From these longitudinal girders cross-girders of great strength were Placed, and between these were built brick arches, packed above with concrete. This formed the roof of the new station. One portion of it passed under the rails in the station above, and had to be constructed without stoppage of the traffic. The rails had consequently to be supported on a temporary steel bridge of ingenious design, constructed by Mr. C. A. Rowlandson, the resident engineer and manager of the company, under whose personal supervision, as representing Sir Douglas Fox, the work has been carried out. With this device the men were enabled to go on in safety, although locomotives were passing immediately above their heads. After the completion of the roof the station below was excavated by what is technically called 'plug and feather' work,—that is to say, by drilling holes, into which powerful wedges are driven to split the rock.

Entering the new station by the convenient access under the Lyceum, the visitor proceeds through a wide vestibule on the street level to a spacious booking-hall lighted by windows. From this a short flight of steps, some 20 ft. in width, conducts to a broad corridor, which forms the entrance to a gallery overlooking the station. At the opposite end of this gallery are the steps leading to the booking-hall and entrance from the Central Station; and at one side, equally distant from either end, are some ten or twelve stairs leading down to the platform. The platform itself is an island 270 ft. long and 20 ft. broad; whilst the station is 50 ft. in width, and 27 ft. high. To avoid the shadows cast by the pillars supporting the roof and placed along the platforms at distances of 30 ft., Mr. Rowlandson has hung two rows of lamps, one over either side of the platform. The edges of the platform are thus thrown into relief, and passengers do not stand in their own light when entering the trains; while the effect of this double row of lights, and the entire absence of shadow, is remarkably pleasing. For the purpose of handling luggage, there has been erected on the platform a small lift leading to a hanging gantry, along which luggage can be passed to the Lyceum booking-hall on the street level. As to the important matter of ventilation, a fan, similar in design to those already in use, and 12 ft. in diameter, has been erected by Messrs. Walker Brothers, of Wigan, for the purpose of ventilating the station apart from the tunnel. The ventilation is, in consequence, excellent. The contractors for this work are Messrs. John Waddell & Sons, who have carried out the entire tunnel scheme at a cost of nearly 2,750,000*l.*"

Books.

K. K. Oesterreich Museum für Kunst und Industrie. Die Sammlung Antiker Vasen und Terra-cotten im K. K. Oesterreich Museum. Katalog und Historische Einleitung. VON KARL MASNER. Mit 10 Lichtdruck und 1 Steindrucktafel; 36 Abbildungen im Text. Wien: Gerold. 1892.

PRIMARILY a catalogue of the collection of vases and terra-cotta in the Vienna Museum, the book before us is incidentally much more. It is, in fact, in some respects a model that it would be well if the directors of all our public museums would imitate. Why, we are inclined to ask, is there for our collection of vases at the British Museum, a collection incomparably richer, no such book,—a book which, while it is a register of scientific facts for the specialist, is also so written and illustrated that for every educated art-lover it opens up a new field of delight? Of course, the answer is in part that the Vienna collection is a small one, and, therefore, can be dealt with succinctly without sacrifice of completeness,—this, with the large collections of our own Museum, of the Louvre, Berlin, Munich, and the Vatican would be impossible. Still, surely, a selection might be made, and some insight into the treasures of national storehouses facilitated to the general educated public. At present we have our large official catalogues,—too often quite unnecessarily bulky and out of date. We have, in some cases, a small popular "guide," both dull and superficial; but we have no book that stands between, scientific in basis, yet lucid and readable, and, above all, illustrated in the accurate fashion that modern processes permit.

What strikes us at the outset in the Vienna work is the due subordination of material. The writer has not, through long living in a museum, dimmed his sense of intellectual perspective. Every vase is registered, and with adequate completeness for identification; but an object which is scientifically unimportant, practically a duplicate, will be settled with in three lines, whereas a unique specimen, or one the subject of which is mythologically interesting or debateable, will get a column to itself. Then, further, two sorts of print are employed. The large print tells all that the ordinary visitor will need of explanation; the small print that follows is addressed to the specialist, and gives him not only a description that in the absence of the original is a substitute as adequate as possible, but also full reference to all the literature of the subject. The phototype plates (from photographs taken direct) give admirably what so often is neglected in illustrated books on vases,—the actual decorative effect, the massing of light and shade, and the spacing out of the subject in the vase itself; while, whenever this process shows the subject inadequately, and this is of interest and unpublished, the phototype plate is supplemented by a woodcut in the text. Many of the Vienna vases are, of course, already known through chance publications, but some will be new to most. One of the most noticeable (No. 321) is, we believe, in subject unique, and certainly most curious. Hermes holding his kerykeion, leads to an altar a large pig, obviously for sacrifice. On closer examination, the apparent pig is seen to be no pig at all, but a disguised dog. A dog is masquerading as a pig, and the paws that protrude below the pig's skin clearly betray the fraud. The Greeks were certainly not narrow in their conception of the character of their divinities if they can thus represent one Olympian god playing the fool at the expense, or, rather, for the amusement, of another. The detection of the concealed dog is due to the acuteness of Dr. Studniczka, who is going to publish a monograph on the subject.

The catalogue proper is preceded by a short and very useful "history of the collection." Anyone who knows how tiresome it is to be referred to *e.g.* "Coll. Scaramanga," and not to have the faintest idea where the "Coll. Scaramanga" has gone to, will appreciate the value of this. Nowadays most of the large private collections have gone piece-meal to the various public museums of Europe, and a tabular view of their present distribution would be a great boon. This is followed by a short, but much-to-the-point, history of Greek ceramics,—the best we know within a limited space. The account is, of course, mainly based on the specimens in the Vienna collection, but where this suffers from lacunæ they are filled up from other museums. The early local types, Trojan, Mycenæ (the author, be it noted, does not seem to be acquainted with Mr. Flinders Petrie's recent investigations as to the dating of Mycenæ art); Dipylon, &c. are well traced out, and everywhere common sense prevails. The student is told why the Dipylon and other vases are so called, with a few words of clear, straightforward explanation. The transition from black to red figured styles is particularly clearly made out, and the dominance of particular forms, *e.g.*, the cylix at particular times. Herr Karl Masner is a name new to us in archæology, but he must have been trained in a good school. Indeed, with Drs. Benndorf and Klein behind him at Vienna he could scarcely fail of a good tradition. Irresistibly the wish returns that our own Museum might furnish a book at once as practical and beautiful.

Historic Towns: Boston. By HENRY CABOT LODGE. London: Longmans & Co. 1891.

THIS, which is one of the "Historic Towns" series, is a well-written history of the rise and development of the United States city which may be said to be the most interesting to Englishmen, as the most English in feeling and the most closely connected in its rise and traditions with the old country. The history is almost entirely on political lines, and therefore out of our proper province; there is however useful map given in which the extent and configuration of old and new Boston are indicated by colouring, and there is a description of the aspect of the city about the middle of the last century, which we may quote:—

"As seen from the harbour, Boston was formed of an amphitheatre of houses, rising gradually one above the other from the water's edge. There were many wharves built out with much industry, and conspicuous among them was the Long Wharf, esteemed a prodigious work at the time, which was two thousand feet in length and covered with handsome warehouses. From Long Wharf ran King-street, then the principal business street, through the heart of the town; and at its head was the Town House, where the State Government in all its branches met, and beneath which the merchants held their exchange, and booksellers their stalls. The streets were sufficiently wide, but crooked and irregular, paved with cobble stones, with gutters in the middle, and side-walks marked off by a line of posts and chains. They were clean and well kept; and although not lighted with any sufficiency before the year 1773, were quiet and orderly . . . . There were also public buildings of no little pretence in size and appearance, and solidly built in the fashion of the eighteenth century. One of these was Faneuil Hall, which had been presented to the town by the rich merchant whose name it bore; another was the Town House, which still stands, like Faneuil Hall, practically unchanged; still another was the Province House, a handsome building where the Royal Governors lived, and there were besides not far short of twenty churches, the majority belonging to the Congregationalists, who were of course the prevailing sect. The harbour was always busy with shipping; and the Long Wharf, and its companions with their rows of warehouses, stretched far out into the water."

The Practical Catechism. By ROBERT GRIMSHAW, M.E., Ph.D. New York: John Wiley & Sons. London: Gay & Bird. 1891.

THE above little book is a collection of miscellaneous questions on technical subjects, each of which is followed by its answer. The work contains a large amount of information, and covers a very extensive field of inquiry. Mr. Grimshaw informs us in his preface that he is not responsible for the selection of the questions, but only for the replies, so that it is really not his fault if he is compelled on one page to give some useful remarks on the preparation of beef-tea, and on another a method of estimating approximately the weight of the earth. Between such limits as these what questions might not be asked? There is, however, an excellent index at the end of the book, so that even such a variety of information is reduced to order, and the clear and precise manner in which the answers are given make the little work a desirable one to keep in readiness for reference.

Sketches of Village Buildings. From designs by Jas. Williams, architect. With Notes. London: Richard Bentley & Son.

THIS small oblong volume is really a collection of reproductions from brush sketches of designs for village buildings by the author, without plans, however, and done solely for the sake of picturesque effect. The obvious aim, admitted indeed in the introductory essay, is to suggest the idea of imitating old cottages and villages more closely in building new ones. It might be better to do this, perhaps, than to build the mere brick cube with a blue-slate roof which is so often the new form of addition to the village architecture in these days; but in other respects we do not think the recommendation to copy old cottage buildings a wise one. Some of the sketches in the book are very pretty, though some are rather careless in perspective; but we do not see what object the book can well serve except to call attention to the author's facility for making old-fashioned cottages, or to furnish matter for "cribs" to those who prefer to make use of the sketches in that way without troubling the author. He has handicapped the amateur in this respect, certainly, by giving no plans.

Sell's Dictionary of the World's Press, 1892. London: Sell's Advertising Agency, Limited.

THIS bulky and in other respects notable volume now makes its twelfth annual appearance. It not only contains a directory of all the English, Welsh, Scotch, and Irish newspapers, periodicals, and magazines, and of the principal Indian, Colonial, and foreign newspapers and periodicals, but a fund of useful information which ought to prove interesting to all who read, write for, or advertise in, newspapers, and in the aggregate that is, of course, a very large class. Mr. H. R. Fox Bourne contributes an article on "The World's Press of to-day," tracing how, from very small beginnings, the newspaper press has become what it now is, and describing the organisation and division of labour which are brought into play in the production of a daily paper. We are glad to see that Mr. Fox Bourne deprecates the apparently increasing tendency to purvey personal gossip. If, as he says, much and perhaps most of this tittle-tattle is harmless, and though some of it may be even useful (which we are inclined to doubt), "there is nothing dignified in the pandering to idle curiosity, the indulgence in small spites or small flatteries, of which it gives evidence." A feature of this publication is the large number of well-executed portraits of prominent journalists which it contains. The work is well printed, but is not free from mistakes.

Sprague's Pocket Diary for 1892. London: Sprague & Co.

THE above consists of a nicely-made pocket-book of convenient size, containing a diary, in which, besides all the ordinary information generally given in almanacs, there is to be found much useful information on technical subjects. As the space that could be devoted to such matters is necessarily limited, great care has evidently been taken to select such rules and tables as are most frequently needed by those engaged in the architectural and engineering professions.

No. 5 of "The Local Government Handy Series" (London: S. Edgcumbe Rogers, Dorset House, Salisbury-square, E.C.) is devoted to an abstract of the clauses of the Public Health (London) Act, 1891, with an index. It has been reprinted from the *Metropolitan*, and is a very cheap and handy synopsis of a very important piece of sanitary legislation.

"Dutton's County Almanac and Essex Gazetteer" for 1892 (Chelmsford: John Dutton) is a very useful publication of nearly 200 pages, and is sold for the small sum of 2d. Besides a variety of information as to local institutions and organisations, it contains a very handy "County Gazetteer," originally compiled by Mr. Edward Smith, F.S.S., and now revised and considerably amplified by Mr. R. Burch. So far as we have tested it, the information given is correct and reliable. Probably nothing of a similar character has ever been issued before at so low a price for Essex or any other county. The undertaking deserves success, and is worthy of imitation in other counties.

Trade Diaries, &c.—Messrs. William Sugg & Co., Limited, of Vincent Works, Westminster, send us their very useful "Gas Engineer's Pocket Almanack and Lighting Table for the year 1892." It contains a great deal of information concerning gas-testing and other matters of interest to municipal and local authorities and their officers.——Messrs. Hayward Bros. & Eckstein, of Union-street, Borough, send us a useful diary, interleaved with blotting-paper, combined with a catalogue of their well-known specialties.——The Electrical Power Storage Company, 4, Great Winchester-street, E.C., have sent a blotting-pad and diary designed so as to keep the "E. P. S. System of Electrical Distribution" always in mind.

RECENT TRADE CATALOGUES.

Mr. W. G. Sutherland, of St. Ann-street, Manchester, sends us a "A Selection of Designs for Stained Glass Windows" executed by him at St. Peter's Works, Gaythorn, Manchester. Part I. includes designs for windows in houses, business premises, and secular public buildings, together with some heraldic and other special devices. Some of the designs are very suitable for their intended purpose. Part II. contains designs for church windows. The catalogue is worthy of the attention of architects.

Messrs. Charles Winn & Co., of St. Thomas' Works, Birmingham, send us the fifth edition of their catalogue of plumbers' goods. It fully describes and illustrates a great many practical appliances used in sanitary work in every-day practice, and is exceedingly convenient in arrangement; a plumber requiring one class of goods will find on adjacent pages the materials and appliances he will need for use therewith, and the various descriptions and qualities of any particular item are arranged in such a form that the buyer can see them all at a glance. The catalogue includes some excellent valve and other closets, urinals, sinks, baths and bath-fittings, traps, brasswork, and Messrs. Winn's now well-known and admirable "Acme" and "New River" flushing cisterns. The portable screwing-machines for wrought-iron bolts and tubing, illustrated and described at the end of the book, are well worth attention.

Messrs. Young & Co., of Victoria-street, Westminster, send us a useful catalogue of their iron fittings for stables and cow-houses, saddle and harness-room and coach-house fittings, &c. The catalogue, which is very comprehensive and well-illustrated, should be looked at by architects who may be called upon to carry out works of this character.

Correspondence.

To the Editor of THE BUILDER.

BUILDING ACT AMENDMENT.

SIR,—Might not the forthcoming Building Act provide as follows?

1. That no works shall be begun until the written authority of the District Surveyor has been obtained.

This would stop many irregular works *in limine*. The onus of justifying them would fall on the person proposing to do them, who could, of course, summon the District Surveyor in case of wrongful refusal. At present, the builder generally makes a start and the District Surveyor has to summon him.

2. That the person giving notice deposit with the notice the sum of, say, 5*l.* in the case of alteration works, or 10*l.* in the case of a new building. The difference between the authorised fee and the sum deposited to be returned to him when the District Surveyor has become entitled to payment.

No one who has not had (I have) to assist a District Surveyor in the management of his district can form any idea of the time lost in collecting the fees. And this time could be so well devoted to looking after the buildings, instead of running after the builders. I am sure that half my time went in fee-collecting.

I believe that the District Boards of Works insist on a deposit before any interference with public pavings. The amount to be deposited is fixed by their Surveyors, and the balance, if any, is returned when the Board has taken up and made good the footway or roadway.

The deposits which I suggest need not be made with the District Surveyor, or at Spring-gardens. Suburban banks are now very numerous, and would be glad enough to hold them.

January 7, 1892. L. C. R.

SIR,—As there is no definition of the word "building" in the present Act, on several occasions when proceeding against wrongdoers I have been asked to define a "building," and the following has been my definition:—"A structure or edifice for the purpose of trade, manufacture, occupation, use, or convenience." I think that a sufficiently inclusive drag-net.

I would suggest that "sheds," *i.e.*, slight buildings roofed in and supported on piers, or iron or wood posts, should be erected to the satisfaction of the District Surveyors. "Public building" should mean every building used for a public purpose, and should include banks, colleges, and schools. I had to contest the question of school construction, and lost the case because schools were not mentioned, yet the corridors and stairs were of wood, and numbers of boys in the school in question sleep on the premises. The Press took it up and commended me.

"Domestic building" should include every building, from a cottage to a palace, not otherwise described or defined.

"Warehouse" should include all buildings use for storage purposes, manufactories, breweries, distilleries.

Some years ago I had to contend with Mr. Dayman, police magistrate, who said that the ground floor was the floor next the ground. Finding he was about to decide against me, I applied for an adjournment for a fortnight that I might ask the world what it understood by the phrase "ground floor." I received some thirty replies, and some of the sketches were very ingenious, especially that by the late Mr. E. W. Godwin, who sketched a house next a hill and from it an entrance to each floor (the Yacht Club, Gravesend, is an illustration). Mr. Dayman was a little taken aback by it; however, he said he did not care what we all agreed on, the ground floor was the floor next the ground; but when I asked him to what floor cellars and underground rooms belonged, he said he couldn't say, and gave me my case.

I have a number of decided cases pasted in a copy of the 1855 Act, opposite to the section to which they apply. I will look them through and send on, as they may be instructive.

Let the definitions be as clear as may be, some omissions are sure to occur, and I would recommend that, in the absence of definition, the dictionary meaning should be adopted,—say, the "Imperial," "Walker," or "Webster." The judges have adopted this course. I give a case in point: "South African Bank *v.* Stokes." Stokes wanted to go down below the level of strong-room floor. The Bank, scared for the safety of its money-bags, resisted, on the plea that the Act gave only power to raise a party-wall, and that being so, Stokes could not underpin. Sir George Jessel, Master of the Rolls, tried the case, referred to the dictionary, and found to raise meant "to enlarge, to extend, to increase, to advance." He said that means making the wall deeper, higher, longer, and does not mean simply putting a piece on the top; Stokes can underpin. To underpin should be defined. T. E. KNIGHTLEY.

106, *Cannon-street, E.C.*,
January 13, 1892.

ROOD-SCREENS.

SIR,—I never said the stone screen or parcloses at Totnes had been removed. "Devoniensis" admits the rood-loft is gone; and that it was co-extensive with the original one is clear from the position of the staircase, one bay east of chancel-arch. This staircase now leads nowhere, though it may be "closed up with an ornate entrance." If the ugly north gallery is erected in a new aisle, there is still less excuse for it than I thought.

No doubt the late vicar was an excellent man; but his school are notoriously opposed to rood-screens. Your readers well know that during the last years of Archbishop Thomson, no new screens were permitted in his diocese, and many disappeared. That in Beverley St. Mary was stowed away over the vaulting of the north chapel. (The new one in the minster merely replaces another, and is rendered necessary by the returned stalls.) At Chesterton (Cambridge) the vicar swept away the fifteenth-century screen at the recent "restoration"; at North Repps, the squire (who has a Quaker name), during a vacancy of the living, removed the screen to a neighbouring barn. And similar instances will occur to many of your readers.

January 9, 1892. VIATOR.

TOTNES CHURCH.

SIR,—Will you allow me to correct an error in the letter of "Devoniensis" in your last week's number?

The repair of the stone staircase of the rood-loft and the new panelled and carved oak roofs throughout the church—which brought the work of restoration to a close—were carried out under the direction of Mr. C. R. Baker King, of London.

EDWIN G. S. LUSCOMBE.

Exeter, January 11, 1892.

THE OLD WATCH-HOUSE AT KING'S CROSS.

SIR,—In reference to your paragraph on page 7, *ante*, I well remember passing the old watch-house at King's-cross, when my then very infantine mind was delighted at seeing an individual conveying some fluid to a friend, who was incarcerated in the basement, by pouring it into the bowl of a tobacco-pipe, and so by the stem through an iron grating to the mouth of the recipient.

The foundation Just discovered only 2 ft. below the surface could not, therefore, I think, have served for this structure.

S. J. NICHOLL.

TAR ON SLATES.

SIR,—Can I learn from any of your readers how to remove tar from a roof of slates without displacing them? IGNORANCE.

ALTAR AND REREDOS, ST. KATHARINE'S, FELTON, SOMERSET.—The new altar and reredos given by the vicar (Rev. H. G. Phillips) and his sister, in memory of their father and mother, were dedicated on the 24th ult. in St. Katharine's Church, Felton. The altar and reredos were supplied by Messrs. Jones & Willis, and are of oak. The panels are filled in with paintings, the centre one in the reredos representing the Crucifixion, and the side ones the Virgin Mary and St. John. The centre panel in the front of the altar shows the Saviour in the act of blessing; and adoring angels are represented upon the side panels.

The Student's Column.

WARMING BUILDINGS BY HOT WATER.

III.

THE CIRCULATION OF WATER.

THE previous paper dealt with the convection currents of heated water, as they are manifested in an open vessel. This is not sufficient to illustrate how the motion is utilised for heating purposes in a system of pipes. If we take the glass jar mentioned in the last paper, and stop the mouth with a tightly-fitting cork, we can make use of it as a boiler in the following way. Get a few feet of ⅜ in. or ½ in. glass tube, which is easily obtainable at a glass-worker's or dealer's, and after cutting two holes in the cork of the bottle, fit up an apparatus something like fig. 5. This tube can be easily bent in the flame of a spirit lamp or over an ordinary gas-burner, and by marking it round with a small file it can be cleanly broken at any point. The tube is jointed where required by short pieces of rubber tube, a size smaller, and stretched on. Tee-pieces can be made from zinc or copper tube.

WATER LEVEL FILLING PIPE

FIG. 5

From a little apparatus like this very many useful results can be noted. Usually results are only attainable by feeling the pipes of an existing apparatus, and it is not always that any degree of certainty can be experienced in solving problems. With a glass model, filled with water containing amber dust, the causes of difficulties can be readily noted, and its simplicity of construction enables many things to be tested which might have to be guessed at otherwise. Sometimes, however, a certain allowance is necessary for the smallness of the apparatus.

The first and most important thing to be described as regards this little appliance is the reason for the different levels at which the pipes terminate in the boiler. It has been explained that immediately heat is transferred to the water the particles at the bottom ascend, and the cooler particles, those not yet affected by the heat, descend to take their place, and this brings about the circulatory motion or direction of the water. By having the opening of one pipe at the top of the boiler and the other at a lower point we can with certainty rely upon the heated water ascending the former and not the latter, and by this means the current is carried in the required direction. If, on the other hand, we terminated both pipes at the top of the boiler, we should still get as rapid and as efficient a circulation, but we should quite lose the feeling of certainty as to which pipe the heated water would pass up, or which would have the cold water descending it. In other words, we could place no reliance in one acting as the "flow" pipe and the other as the "return" regularly and unfailingly.

There is a commonly-accepted idea that if pipes were thus terminated, at exactly level and equal points in a boiler, no circulation would take place in the pipes; that is, the water in neither pipe would give to the other, and, consequently, both columns would remain stationary. This is incorrect; the little apparatus illustrated can be easily made to demonstrate how readily the circulation sets up, but with the pipes level it is impossible to say which will be the ascending column, the "flow," and which the reverse. Strange to say, the pipe which acts as the former one day may very likely take upon itself the duties of the latter the next day, although no interference with or alteration to the disposition of the pipes be made meanwhile. It is not, however, necessary to inquire further into this phenomenon, as it is never necessary, and never proper, to terminate the pipes at points level with one another, and if terminated at different heights irregularities of this kind cannot very well happen.

It will be now understood that the action which takes place when heat is transferred to water enables us to bring about a transference of the heated water from the boiler to any point we may require. There is no reasonable limit to the distance at which this can be effected, for the fluid is so free from friction amongst its particles, so exceedingly mobile, as to have a very rapid movement, and travel a considerable distance in a short space of time. This is supposing certain necessary features are observed in the construction of the apparatus.

In the first place, it will have been gathered that the point at which the heat is applied to the water, that is, the position of the boiler, must be the lowest of all, and from that point the pipes should be disposed so as to give the water every facility to proceed in the ascending direction the heat causes it to take. This would at the same time give the descending column of cold water (the "return") every opportunity to take its downward course towards the boiler and effect its downward pressure, which is an all-important feature, as will be described directly. In horticultural works, unfortunately, the ascending and descending pipes are very limited as to length, as from the top of the boiler to the highest point of the system of pipes is seldom more than a few feet, and this tends to minimise the desired effect. In building works, however, the reverse of this is usually the case, the height of the apparatus being everything that could be desired, and permitting of such an effective circulation as even to need the introduction of means to divert and check it. An apparatus extending in a horizontal direction, without height, has the least motive power; one that extends vertically and but little horizontally has the highest motive power. By motive power is meant speed of circulation, there being features which conduce to a free and high speed in the movement of the water.

In concluding the actual description of the circulation of water it has to be pointed out, as it was when describing the action of convection in an open vessel, that it is the weight of the cold water, in displacing the lighter warmer particles, that brings about the motion. It is decidedly essential that this be understood, for the prevailing notion that warm water has an inclination of its own to rise has led to very many strange conclusions in solving problems in these works. There can be no more peculiar idea than this, and a moment's reflection shows everyone that hot water does not rise of its own accord. If we put some heated water in a vessel it does not instantly rise up and flow over the sides, but if we put precisely equal quantities by measure of cold and very hot water in the opposite pans of an accurate pair of balances we should find the pan containing hot water would rise, not by any effort or will of its own, but because the cold water by its greater weight caused it to do so. The hot water in a system of pipes is quite a helpless element; the cold water by its superior gravity is the active force. It has been remarked:—"Were there no gravity there could be no convection. Were it not for gravity it would be of no consequence what part of a vessel we heated, the effect of the heating would be always the same."

It will be found, when examining the processes in a glass apparatus, that when a movement takes place it is instantly transmitted everywhere, or it would be better to say the movement takes place everywhere at the same instant. It might be supposed that when the lamp is first placed under the boiler that the circulation might set up in the boiler itself for a short period before affecting the water in the pipes. This is, however, not the case, for directly the faintest motion is observable in the boiler, the water in the pipes will be seen fulfilling its duties. This is due to the non-elasticity of water. We might almost compare it to the movement of a solid substance, if it be given a motion at one end we expect the opposite extremity to move at the same instant.

From all this we gather that the circulation of water in pipes is brought about by the different degrees of gravity of the water in the flow and return services,—that is, the ascending and descending columns of water; that, by increasing the vertical length of the pipes we increase the strength of circulation, or motive power, and that the water in horizontal pipes cannot aid circulation, but only go to retard its action, more or less, according as the length is great or little.

In horticultural works, as just mentioned, the vertical pipes are quite in the minority, for, as a rule, the services have to be carried horizontally, or very nearly so, almost immediately they leave the boiler; and to examine the action that takes place in this instance we should have to construct a little apparatus, as fig. 6. In this case we cannot very well use

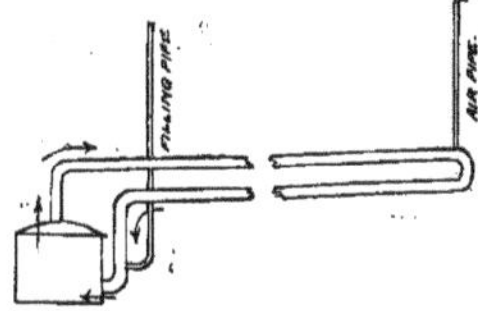

FIG. 6.

any glass vessel for the boiler, in consequence of the return-pipe having to enter its side as shown; but, as the other experiments with glass boilers give a very clear idea of what action takes place within them, we can get along very well with a zinc or copper one in this case. It is what takes place in the pipes that is of greater interest now.

It has now to be explained that when speaking of horizontal pipes in these works it must be understood that they are not perfectly horizontal, but have a slight ascent from the boiler to the furthest extremity or extremities. In all hot-water works for heating purposes a perfectly horizontal pipe is looked upon as a bad feature, and this applies with the greatest possible force to horticultural works, which have such a low motive-power at all times. The upward inclination of the pipes, however slight, aids the circulation, and there is rarely an instance in which a rise is not obtainable, even if only an inch in ten feet. Then there is another reason of fully equal importance why pipes should have a regular rise to their furthest extremities,—viz., to admit of the air escaping freely from within them, not only when first charging, but at all other times. Air-vents, pipes, or cocks are always situated at the extremities, these being the highest points, as stated. This subject will be fully dealt with in due course.

SURVEYORSHIPS.

BELFAST.—The Belfast Corporation have increased the salary of Mr. J. C. Bretland, M.Inst.C.E., City Surveyor, to 800*l.* per annum; that of Mr. Jas. Munce, Assoc.M.Inst.C.E., the Assistant City Surveyor, to 350*l.* per annum; and that of Mr. G. A. Boyd, third assistant and Superintendent of Buildings, to 150*l.* per annum.

DIOCESE OF LINCOLN.—On the 12th inst., at a meeting of the Archdeacons and Rural Deans at the Old Palace, Lincoln, the Bishop of Lincoln presiding, Mr. J. C. Traylen, architect, Stamford, was elected an ecclesiastical surveyor for the diocese of Lincoln.

GENERAL BUILDING NEWS.

NEW BOARD SCHOOLS AT BARKING, ESSEX.—The new schools in Gascoigne-road, erected by the Barking School Board, were opened on the 7th inst. The site is one and a half acres in extent, and each of the four frontages of the school faces a roadway 40 ft. in width. The schools provide accommodation for 1,409 children, viz., 545 infants on the ground floor, 432 boys on the first floor, and 432 girls on the second floor. The infants' department consists of one class-room for 110, and five class-rooms for sixty-four each, all fitted with Kindergarten dual desks on raised floors; and a abies' room for 115, also fitted for Kindergarten eaching,—the desks in this room being fixed on alleries. The boys' and girls' departments, on the rst and second floors respectively, have each two lass-rooms for eighty-six each, and five class-rooms or fifty-two each, all fitted with dual desks on aised floors. On each floor is a central hall, 64 ft. ong and 32 ft. wide, the seven class-rooms rom each department opening from the central halls, which will be used for assembling the children of each department at he commencement of school-hours, and for hysical drilling, examinations, singing, and other urposes. They will also serve as corridors for ccess from the various class-rooms to the staircases, entrances, &c. An entrance is provided at oth ends of each floor, so as to enable each department to empty at both ends at the same time, the rst and second floors having separate staircases eading from them for that purpose, thus obviating he inconvenience and danger of crowding a large umber of children at one part, as would be the ase if only one entrance for each floor were proided. The staircases have easy-going short flights of granolithic stone steps. Cap and cloak rooms for the use of the children are provided at both ends of each department, and the lavatories are placed in these rooms. A cookery class-room is provided on the second floor, and fitted with cooking-ranges, dresser, sink, and other appliances necessary for the purpose of teaching the girls plain cooking. A separate private room is provided for the head teachers and assistants for each department, and is fitted with an "Eagle" cooking-range, and furnished so that the teachers need not necessarily leave the building between morning and afternoon school. Separate and distinct cloak-rooms, latrines, and lavatory accommodation for the teachers are also provided within the building. The schools are well-lighted, and fifteen out of the twenty-two class-rooms have a direct north light. The whole of the class-rooms are warmed by open fireplaces fitted with fire-lump stoves, with wrought-iron fronts of a special character, the two large class-rooms on each floor having, in addition, a hot-water radiator. Each of the central halls is warmed by five hot-water radiators, three of which are made ventilating, the cold air being drawn in at the bottom from the outside, and discharged warmed on the inside at the top. Each of the cap and cloak rooms is warmed by hot-water pipes running round three sides of the same, for the purpose of drying the children's clothes when wet. The fronts of the cloak-rooms, being fitted with wire gratings, admit of the hot air escaping and warming the staircases and landings. The system of ventilation adopted is that of simple inlet and outlet, the whole of the windows throughout being of a special design, whereby, upon the lower sash being slightly raised, an upward current of air is admitted at the cill level and also at the meeting-bar level without causing draughts. A separate and distinct extraction shaft for carrying off the vitiated air is carried up in the chimney-stack from each class-room. The latrines, which are in two blocks, to suit the entrances, at each end of the buildings, are fitted with a range of closet-pans and flushing apparatus, specially designed by the architect. The walls are of yellow stock bricks faced externally, to a height of 4 ft. all round, with blue Staffordshire bricks, and above that height with malms, relieved with red brick pilasters and terra-cotta terminals, gauged red brick arches and aprons, and moulded red brick string courses. The internal face of the walls to all class-rooms, central halls, corridors, and cap and cloak rooms, to a height of 4 ft. from the floor, and the walls and newels of the staircases throughout, are faced with brown salt-glazed bricks. The locks, fastenings, and fanlight gearing throughout have been manufactured by Messrs. Hart, Son, Peard, & Co.; the sanitary fittings by Messrs. Tylor & Co.; the hot-water heating apparatus by Messrs. Wontner Smith, Gray, & Co.; the stoves by Mr. Thomas Elsley; and the wood-block flooring by the Westminster Patent Wood Block Flooring Company. The school furniture has been supplied by the Bennett Furnishing Company, of Glasgow. Four covered playsheds are provided for use in wet weather. The whole of the works have been carried out by Mr. F. T. Coxhead, of Leytonstone, Mr. Morley acting as the superintending foreman. The total cost of the buildings, including furniture, boundary-walls and fencing, latrines, play-sheds, drainage and paving of playgrounds, and architect's charges will not exceed 10*l.* per head. The schools have been erected from plans prepared by Mr. C. J. Dawson, F.R.I.B.A., Architect to the Board.

WESLEYAN METHODIST CHAPEL, FELTON (NORTHUMBERLAND).—This new building has just been opened. It is Gothic in style, built of local stone, and presents a high pitched gable towards the street. This gable is set back sufficiently to allow of two flights of steps; those on the north of the central entrance gates leading to the porch into the chapel, and those on the south side, to the path which leads to the schoolroom, which is placed across the western end of the building. The size of the chapel internally is 36 ft. in length by 24 ft. in breadth, and the schoolroom is 30 ft. by 15 ft., a part of the south end being screened off by revolving shutters to form a sewing-room, in case of tea-meetings, or at other times a minister's vestry. The architect is Mr. F. R. N. Haswell, F.R.I.B.A., of North Shields.

NEW BOARD SCHOOLS, HEELEY, SHEFFIELD.—On the 11th inst. the new schools erected by the Sheffield School Board in Gleadless-road, Heeley, were opened by the Ven. Archdeacon Blakeney. The schools, which have been built by Messrs. W. Ives and Co., contractors, of Shipley, are erected from the designs of Mr. C. J. Innocent, architect, Sheffield, and they are spoken of by the *Sheffield Daily Telegraph* as being the finest schools yet erected in Sheffield. In the school for boys and girls each department has a large room and five other rooms, which can be used for class teaching, with an arrangement by which a number of them can be thrown together for general purposes, and thus obtain a much larger room. There has been accommodation provided for 420 boys, 420 girls, and 360 infants. The infants occupy a separate building, and here the arrangements of the general school-rooms and class-rooms have been arranged on what the same journal says is an entirely new plan. The maximum of light has been secured all through the schools, and the rooms are exceptionally bright, well-warmed and ventilated. In each department there are two rooms set apart for the use of the teachers; and in every way the comfort of the staff and of the scholars has been studied. The cost of the site, which occupies 7,580 square yards, is 2,530*l.*; and the cost of the buildings, including the furnishing, is 11,170*l.*, making a total cost of 13,700*l.* As the accommodation is for 1,206 children, the cost per head for the site amounts to 2*l.* 2s., and for the building and furnishing 9*l.* 5s. 2d., the schools thus costing per head 11*l.* 7s. 2d. The amount of the contract, including the building of the caretaker's house, the raising of the extensive boundary walling, the playgrounds, and the sheds, was 10,200*l.* The heating apparatus has been fixed by Messrs. J. H. Pickup & Co. (Limited). Mr. Cartwright has acted as clerk of the works. The schools already opened by the Board provide school places for 29,626 children, and the opening of these additional schools will raise the total to 30,832. During the opening proceedings the architect was highly eulogised by more than one of the speakers.

SANITARY AND ENGINEERING NEWS.

NEW WATERWORKS, MARGAM, GLAMORGAN.—On the 17th ult. the new waterworks which have been provided to supply with water the Llettyhiri, Fenycai, and Gwaricaia districts were opened. The most populous part of this Local Board district is supplied from a reservoir at Llettypiod, which has a storage capacity of 1,700,000 gallons, but the hamlets named above have up to the present had a very inefficient supply. The springs which accumulate on the slopes of the Llettyhiri Mountain have been conducted down to the foot of the hill, where a storage reservoir of a capacity of 10,000 gallons has been constructed. From this pipes conduct the water to taps situate in convenient spots in the three villages. The contractor was Mr. John Davies, of Aberavon. The total cost was 1,000*l.*, which was defrayed by Miss Talbot.

SEWERAGE AND SEWAGE DISPOSAL SCHEMES, CHESTER-LE-STREET.—On the 18th ult. Mr. Arnold Taylor, Deputy-Chief Engineering Inspector of the Local Government Board, held a Government inquiry at the Board-room, Chester-le-Street, Durham, as to sanction to borrow the following amounts for schemes of main sewerage and sewage disposal for the following places, viz.:—Birtley, 5,000*l.*; Edmondsley, 2,000*l.*; Sacriston and Daisy Hill, 4,500*l.*; and Witton Gilbert, 2,300*l.* The schemes include main sewers, with ventilating and flushing arrangements, and land for sewage disposal by the process of intermittent land filtration. The plans, estimates, &c., were fully explained by the Engineer, Mr. D. Balfour, M.Inst.C.E., F.G.S., of Newcastle-on-Tyne; and after due consideration of the schemes, the Inspector expressed himself as fully satisfied with the proposed works as being the most efficient and economical in the circumstances. Provisional Orders for the compulsory purchase of the several lands had already been obtained, and the various sites visited and approved of by the Inspector.

WEST BRIDGEFORD WATERWORKS.—An influential water syndicate has been formed at West Bridgeford, and it has been decided to put down a deep boring into the Bunter sandstone to test the quality and quantity of the water. The West Bridgeford Local Board are now supplied by the Nottingham Corporation, but a large section of the ratepayers wish to have separate works. Mr. W. H. Radford is the engineer.

ORPHAN WORKING SCHOOL, HAVERSTOCK-HILL.—These schools, which usually have over 500 children in occupation, have had to be closed, and the children removed, owing to defects in the sanitary condition of the buildings, and the Estates Committee instructed their architect, Mr. Chas. Bell, to prepare plans and specification for putting matters in order. Mr. Bell prepared two schemes, one for improving the existing sanitary arrangements in their present positions, and another for building detached separate sanitary blocks. The Committee, under the advice of Mr. Edward Tidman, C.E., have adopted the system of separate detached blocks.

ESSEX COUNTY COUNCIL.—Mr. Edward Tidman, C.E., F.S.I., of Westminster, has just been appointed by the Technical Education Committee of the Essex County Council lecturer on "Hygiene," and will shortly commence a course of lectures under their auspices.

TIME MEASUREMENT FOR PHOTOGRAPHIC PLATES.—Messrs. Marion & Co., of Soho-square, send us a description of Hurter & Driffield's actinograph, by which the "speed" of a plate,—*i.e.* the necessary time of exposure for the best result,—is calculated for various times of the day and (approximately) for various states of the atmosphere in regard to light. It is proposed that manufacturers should test their plates according to the actinograph, and indicate their speed of production by a number, when reference to the actinograph index will give the exposure for the plate under various conditions of light. The subject may be of interest to some of our readers who make their own photographs of architecture.

CONTRACTS, AND PUBLIC APPOINTMENTS.

CONTRACTS.

Nature of Work or Materials.	By whom Required.	Architect, Surveyor or Engineer.	Tenders to be delivered.
Street Improvement Works	Barry & Cadoxton Loc. Bd.	J. C. Pardoe	Jan. 19
Excavation Work, Hambleton, Bolton Abbey	J. Green & Son	....	do.
*Superstructure of New Offices, Newcastle-on-Tyne	Prudential As. Co.	A. Waterhouse & Son	do.
*Roadmaking and Tar Paving Works	Lewisham Bd. of Wks.	*Official*	do.
Iron Castings, &c.	Leeds Corporation	do.	Jan. 20
Storage Shed, Newton Heath	Manchester Corp.	do.	do.
Shop and Cottages, Lofthouse	Leeds Indis. Co-op. Soc.	....	Jan. 21
Alteration and Additions, "Black Lion" Hotel, Cardiff	Wm. Evans	J. P. Jones	do.
*Alterations to Gt. Staughton Manor	....	Martin & Purchase	Jan. 22
Banking Premises, Ripon	Bradford Old Bank	H. E. & A. Bown	Jan. 23
Additions to Board School, Pontyrhyl	Bettws Sch. Bd.	*Official*	do.
Station-master's Houses	Belfast and County Down Ry. Co.	do	do.
Road-making, Wallsend, Newcastle-on-Tyne	Wallsend Sch. Bd.	Wm. Hope	Jan. 25
Drainage Works	Ayrshire C. C.	J. & A. Leslie & Reid	do.
*Repairs to Private Roads	Borough of Croydon	*Official*	Jan. 26
*Road-making and Paving Works	Willesden Loc. Bd.	O. Claude Robson	do.
*Broken Granite, &c., & Kerosene Oil	Bexley Local Board	E. R. Boulter	Jan. 27
*Warming and Ventilating Town Hall	Leeds Corporation	*Official*	do.
*Works and Materials	Chelsea Vestry	do.	Jan. 28
Brick Gasholder Tank	West Bromwich T. C.	do.	do.
*Works & Repairs to Public Buildings, &c.	Com. of H. M. Wks. &c.	do.	do.
School Buildings	Paisley School Board	T. L. Watson	Jan. 29
Cast Iron Standards, &c.	Sheffield United Gas Co.	F. W. Stevenson	Jan. 30
Timber Framing to Gasholder Tank	do.	do.	do.
Police Station, &c., Blyth	Northumberland C. C.	J. Cresswell	Feb. 1
*Making-up Roads	Finchley L. B.	*Official*	do.

CONTRACTS.—*Continued.*

Nature of Work or Materials.	By whom Required.	Architect, Surveyor, or Engineer.	Tenders to be delivered.
*New School, &c.—St. Mary Cray	Orpington Sch. Bd.	G. St. Pierre Harris	Feb. 1
Granite Setts, &c.	Hull Corporation	*Official*	Feb. 2
New Railway (Sherburn House and Durham Railway)	N. E. Railway Co.	C. A. Harrison	Feb. 3
*Two Infirmary Blocks, Melton	Suffolk County Asylum Com.	Giles, Gough, & Trollope	Feb. 5
*Broken Granite	Norfolk C. C.	T. H. B. Heslop	Feb. 6
*Additions, &c., to Ambulance Station, Fulham	Metro. Asylums Bd.	A. & C. Harston	Feb. 8
*Public Hall and Municipal Offices	West Ham Council	Lewis Angell	Feb. 9
*Erection of Workhouse	St. Giles, Camberwell, Guardians	Wilson, Son, & Aldwinckle	Feb. 15
*Sewerage Works	Guildford Corporation	C. N. Lailey	Feb. 16
*Two Pairs of Officers' Quarters, Devonport	War Department	*Official*	No date
*Pair of Semi-detached Villas, Ramsgate	....	Hill & Co.	do.
*First Portion of St. Mark's Church, Mansfield	....	T. N. Laslett	do.

PUBLIC APPOINTMENTS.

Nature of Appointment.	By whom Advertised.	Salary.	Applications to be in.
*Sanitary Inspector	Vestry of St. John's, Hampstead	110*l.*, &c.	Jan. 20
*Clerk of Works	Kingston-upon-Hull Sch. Bd.	3*l.* 3s.	Jan. 21
*Valuer and Surveyor	Vestry of Shoreditch	....	Feb. 5
*Dublin District Surveyorships	Civil Service Commrs.	....	Feb. 10

Those marked with an Asterisk (*) are advertised in this Number. *Contracts, pp. iv., vi., & viii.* *Public Appointments, p. xx.*

FOREIGN AND COLONIAL.

France.—Baron Alphonse de Rothschild has presented to the Louvre two remarkable Florentine bronzes of the sixteenth century. The museum has also received from Dr. Fouquet, of Cairo, some fine specimens of Mediæval Arabian art.——The Paris municipality intends to restore the fine frescoes in the Central Hall of the Palais de la Bourse, executed by Pujol.——A competition is to be opened shortly for the decoration of the Salle des Mariages of the Mairie of Montreuil-sous-Bois. The decoration will include four panels, and will cost about 20,000 francs.——M. Cargill, pupil of MM. Daumet and Girault, has obtained the Godebœuf prize at the Ecole des Beaux-Arts. The subject was "Un lustre électrique."——M. Dalou has been commissioned to execute, for the Conservatoire des Arts et Métiers, the statue of Boussingault, who is regarded as the founder of Agricultural Chemistry.——A committee has been formed with the object of raising at Colombes (Seine) a monument to Litolff, the musician, who died recently. M. Lucien Pallez is commissioned to execute it.——A fire has partially destroyed the fine Salle d'Audience at Grenoble. The fire has nearly ruined a splendid ceiling of historic interest, as well as some remarkable sculptures dating from the fourteenth and fifteenth centuries. The building was one of the ancient residences of the Dauphins of France.——The new railway line between Brienne-le-Chateau and Sorcy is shortly to be opened.——The French Government has issued a new postage-stamp for the colonies. The vignette is composed of two figures seated on the prow of a ship and symbolising Navigation and Commerce; they each hold the national flag with one hand.——M. Justin Rochet has been appointed architect to the general administration of "Assistance Publique" at Paris.——On the occasion of the new year M. Daumet, president of the Société Centrale des Architectes, has been promoted to be officer of the Legion of Honour. Among the architects MM. Leclerc, Mayeux, and Trélat have been created chevaliers.——The late M. Bailly has left a sum of 50,000 francs which will be converted into 3 per cent. rentes and will go to the foundation of an annual prize to the author of some work of architecture. He has left the Académie free to decide on what terms the prize should be awarded.——The bust of Jules Grévy by Carrier-Belleuse has been placed in the Palais de Justice at Paris, in the Advocate's Library.——The death is announced of the painter Charles Louis Muller, Member of the Institut, at the age of seventy-six. He was a pupil of Gros and Cogniet, obtained medals at the Exhibitions of 1838, 1846, and 1848, and a first-class medal at the Univeral Exhibition in 1855. Among his numerous works may be mentioned the "Assassinat d'Arthur de Bretagne par Jean Sans Terre" (Salon of 1839); "Jésus et le Démon sur La Montagne" (1840); "Combat des Centaures et des Lapithes (1843); "Entrée de Jésus à Jerusalem" (1844); "Primavera" (1846); "Lady Macbeth" (1849); "L'Appel des Derniers Victimes de la Terreur" (1850). This large picture, which till a few years back was to be seen at the Luxembourg, aroused great enthusiasm on its first exhibition. The works which followed it were little appreciated, and the artist was so much affected by their non-success that he retired almost altogether from society. He exhibited in 1857 a picture representing the arrival of Queen Victoria at the Palace of St. Cloud. He also decorated the "Salle des États" at the Louvre, and the cupola of the Pavillon Denon.——The fortieth Exhibition of the Société des Amis des Arts of Bordeaux will open on March 7.

Sweden and Norway.—The students of the Upsala University have decided to accelerate the work on their new assembly-hall, according to a new programme, by which the cost of the building will be reduced to one-half,—viz., 36,000*l.*——The budget of the city of Stockholm for the current year provides 55,500*l.* for the improvement of streets and open spaces.——We have previously referred to the competition for a new exhibition building at Bergen, in Norway, and we now learn from the *Teknisk Ugeblad*, the organ of Norwegian architects, that the first prize of 1,200 kr. has been awarded to Herr H. Bucher, and second prize or 800 kr. to Herr H. Bull. The Journal named again expresses great indignation with the competition, on the ground (1) that a second programme was substituted one month after the issue of the first, and (2) that on the first list of the jury the names of two prominent architects were entered without their consent, and when withdrawn the names of a contractor and a local architect of no standing were substituted. The architects whose time and labour have been wasted intend to claim damages.——At the last meeting of the Polytechnic Society of Christiania, Herr G. Stenberg, engineer, read a paper on the construction of iron bridges by native workmen, maintaining that native work was as good as foreign, as shown in the new bridge over the river Rena, the longest in Norway. He, with several other speakers, urged that the work of constructing the great bridges for the new railways about to be built should be given to the native engineering firms.——The secretary of the Royal Hunt Club in Madrid has requested Norwegian and Swedish manufacturers of timber villas to forward designs for a club house in Norse style at the El Pardo, near Madrid.——The first export of timber villas to India from Norway has been made by a firm in Throndhjem.

MISCELLANEOUS.

Messrs. Foy, Morgan & Co.'s Annual Wood Report, 1891, says:—"For London timber merchants there can be no doubt that the results of the past year's trading must be considered satisfactory, and to have gone some way to repair the disastrous losses incurred in 1890. It will be remembered that, although the close of 1890 was weighted by a heavy stock, the level of prices was such as to promise a good demand and general improvement in the market. That these expectations were falsified must be attributed to the heavy failures which took place early in January, and to the results entailed by the consequent shrinkage of credit. For these reasons the f.o.w. sales for London were restricted, and the necessity for consignments was avoided by the abnormal demand from France, caused by the desire of the merchants to forestall the proposed import duty. The coast ports absorbed a large quantity of goods for early summer shipment, and thus, when the London trade eventually came into the f.o.b. market, the smallness of the available stocks precluded the possibility of over speculation. The market began to show signs of mending about May, at first, however, almost imperceptibly, and it was not until the middle of September that the rise in prices attracted general attention. The last quarter of the year has been characterised by a certain expansion of the imports, due to the expectation on the part of merchants of higher prices, but also by a lessened demand arising from the unwillingness of consumers to pay enhanced prices. As soon as these opposing interests have been reconciled, and the market has settled down, a fair trade may be looked for. Among the Deal sizes the noteworthy features of the year have been, with respect to Redwood, the great scarcity of 11-in. widths, and the consequent widening of the difference between the values of 11-in. and 9-in. Redwood, of all qualities; it being probably many years since 11-in. Fourths have realised 20s. to 25s., and Mixed and Thirds 40s. to 60s. per standard more than 9-in. With respect to Whitewood the tendency has just been the other way, 11-in. having been seldom more plentiful than now, and 9-in. seldom scarcer. This is directly traceable to the early sales of Whitewood to the French market. In all qualities except Firsts there is practically very little difference in the present values of 9 and 11-in.; White Spruce 11-in., however, has always fetched 10s. more than 9-in. Batten sizes have generally tended to the reverse of the position occupied last autumn. Thus the glut of 2-in. battens, which occurred last fall, was found to consist mainly of the narrow widths, namely, 2 by 4, 2 by 5, and 2 by 6 in., the extreme depression in the prices of which consequently stood in marked contrast to the comparatively stable prices at which 2 by 7 and 8 in. were realised; whereas the close of this year discloses an inadequate supply of, and a rising market for, the former sizes, while 2 by 7 seems sufficient in stock, and exhibits no change in price. The lower qualities of 2½ and 3-in. battens have been in moderate supply throughout the year, and prices have shown only a slight fluctuation, with apparently very little immediate prospect of increasing."

The English Iron Trade.—The English iron trade remains practically unchanged, business, on the whole, being of but limited dimensions. The exports of iron and steel for the past year show a falling-off of no less than 760,395 tons as compared with 1890. During December they suffered a decline of 40,550 tons. In all the pig-iron centres trade is quiet, and only a moderate business is doing in manufactured iron. Tin-plates are inactive. The steel trade generally exhibits fair movement. The engineering trades are moderately active; but prospects are somewhat gloomy. Shipbuilders are busy. The coal trade is tolerably brisk, the demand being chiefly for household qualities.—*Iron.*

Westminster School of Art.—We are asked to mention that provision is made for a limited number of free students at this School of Art. Candidates must be workmen resident in the City of Westminster, or the sons of such workmen, and a preference is given to residents in the parishes of St. Margaret and St. John. They should have some aptitude for drawing, and candidates between the ages of fifteen and twenty-five are preferred. Applicants are invited to call on the Curator, at the Royal Architectural Museum, 18, Tufton-street, Dean's-yard, Westminster, on Monday, Wednesday, or Friday evening, between 7 and 8.30 p.m., and to bring with them a letter of recommendation from a clergyman, or some other person on whose testimony reliance can be placed.

Further Engineering Works at Antwerp.—Although the dock accommodation at Antwerp is constantly being improved, it is still found insufficient, and it has therefore been decided to construct another large dock, in order to establish direct connexion between the African Basin and the Scheldt. The project has been sanctioned by the Government.

SUGGESTED IMPROVEMENT OF COOKRIDGE-STREET, LEEDS.—The *Leeds Mercury* publishes the plan of a scheme suggested by Mr. Geo. Corson, architect, Leeds, for the extension of Park-row, recently submitted to the Streets and Sewerage Committee of the Leeds Corporation. The project is not included in the new Consolidation Bill which the Council are promoting, but it would, if carried out, obviously effect an important street improvement. It is proposed to construct a new thoroughfare, which, commencing at the top of Park-row, shall extend, with a graceful sweep near the Mechanics' Institute, to Woodhouse-lane, at the Girls' High School. It would, of course, involve the removal of St. Ann's Cathedral and the adjoining presbytery and buildings, but this apparently constitutes the most serious obstacle, for from that point to the Albert Hall the proposed line of new street passes, for the most part, over vacant land, and beyond there it would cut through a densely-populated and not too well-built neighbourhood to Woodhouse-lane. A spacious thoroughfare would thus be provided direct from the most important centre of the town, both as regards business, its contiguity to the railway-station and to Headingley, the most populous residential suburb.

ASSOCIATION OF BIRMINGHAM STUDENTS OF THE INSTITUTION OF CIVIL ENGINEERS.—An interesting and instructive paper on "Refuse Disposal" was read on the 7th inst. by Mr. Nowell Parr, of Walsall, at the Midland Institute, before the members of this Association. A lengthy discussion followed.

CORK PAVEMENT.—The Patent Cork Pavement Co. send us a specimen of their patent compressed cork pavement, for which they claim that it possesses extreme durability at very moderate cost, gives a reliable foothold for horses or pedestrians in any weather, and a safe kerb or edging for railway platforms, steps of carriages, and for all purposes where a compact uniform non-slippery surface is a desideratum. Of the durability one can only judge by the test of experience, but in other respects it seems to be a material worth attention for the purposes named, and likely to fulfil what is claimed for it.

PROPOSED NEW PARK FOR EDINBURGH.—It is understood that the Town Council of Edinburgh are negotiating with the proprietor of the estate of Roseburn for the purchase or lease of the unfeued portion of the estate, with the view of converting it into a public park. The lands, which comprise about twenty acres, are at present under irrigation, and are let on a long lease to a tenant, with a break in the immediate future. If the Corporation obtains possession of the estate the irrigation works would, of course, be demolished; and the question before the Council at present is whether they should purchase the land outright or lease it for a long period.

CLIMATOLOGY.—The Council of the Royal Meteorological Society have arranged to hold at 25, Great George-street, S.W. (by permission of the President and Council of the Institution of Civil Engineers), from March 15 to 18, an Exhibition of Instruments, Charts, Maps, and Photographs relating to Climatology. The Committee will also be glad to show any new meteorological instruments or apparatus invented or first constructed since last March, as well as photographs and drawings possessing meteorological interest. Communications relative to the Exhibition can be sent to Mr. William Marriott, the Assistant Secretary, at 22, Great George-street.

LECTERN, RANMOOR CHURCH, YORKSHIRE.—On the 25th ult. a brass lectern was brought into use for the first time in Ranmoor Church. The lectern is made of cast and wrought brass work, entirely polished. The stem is massive, with buttressed pedestal. At the termination of the four upright pillars of the flying buttresses there are the four archangels with their emblems,—St. Michael and the sword, St. Gabriel and the spray of lily, St. Raphael and the fish, and St. Ariel and the sun. The work above is enriched and above the foliated capital of the stem is the half-ball stand upon which are the seraphim, their wings supporting the Holy Gospels. The work is by Messrs. Hardman, Powell, & Co., of Birmingham.

NEW AUSTRIAN LAW RESPECTING ARTISANS' DWELLINGS.—The Austrian Chamber of Deputies has passed an important law aiming at facilitating the erection of cheap and wholesome artisans' dwellings, according to which corporations and companies founded for erecting labourers' and artisans' dwellings, as well as factory owners furnishing such for their own hands, will be exempted from tax on houses for a period of twenty-four years. There are, however, several conditions,—viz., there must be no underground dwellings in these houses, and the separate lodgings of a family must have an area of, at least, 15 square mètres, and at most 75 square mètres. The owners must not demand a higher rent than 1 florin 75 kreutzers per square mètre in Vienna, 1 florin 15 kreutzers in towns having more than 100,000 inhabitants, and 80 kreutzers in smaller towns. For instance, for a lodging in Vienna, consisting of a living room, a bedroom, and kitchen, the rent, according to this new law, would be 70 florins a year (about 7*l*.). A deputy, Herr Manthner, calculates that such a rent would yield interest at the rate of 3·9 per cent. on the capital invested. However, excellent as the new law may seem, several Austrian journals maintain that the law is unpractical, and will fail in its object. They are of opinion that a law like the English of 1885 would have been preferable, according to which the State advances, to communes and corporations desirous of furnishing such dwellings, money at 3½ per cent. interest.

THE IRON, STEEL, AND COAL PRODUCTION OF BELGIUM.—The production of pig-iron in Belgium last year amounted to 787,836 tons, as against 832,226 tons in 1889, or 44,390 tons less. The production of bar-iron was 514,311 tons, as against 577,204 tons in 1889, being a decrease of 62,893 tons. Of steel, 201,817 tons were produced, as against 214,561 tons in 1889. The output of coal was 20,500,000 tons, which yielded a profit of 59,000,000 francs.

MEETINGS.

SUNDAY, JANUARY 17.

Sunday Lecture Society.—Mr. Whitworth Wallis on "Ancient Egypt, its Temples, Pyramids, Monuments, and Mummies." 4 p.m.

MONDAY, JANUARY 18.

Royal Institute of British Architects.—Business Meeting (1) to elect Members and (2) to receive the deed of award of the prizes and studentships for 1891-2. Followed by a *Special General Meeting* to receive and consider a Paper of "Amended Suggestions for the Conduct of Architectural Competitions." 8 p.m.

Surveyors' Institution.—Paper by Mr. E. H. Morris on "The Four-course System, with Desirable Variations." 8 p.m.

Leeds and Yorkshire Architectural Society.—Mr. J. M. Brydon on "The English Renaissance." 7.30 p.m.

TUESDAY, JANUARY 19.

Institution of Civil Engineers.—Further Discussion on Mr. Wilfrid Airy's Paper on "Weighing-machines." 8 p.m.

London County Council.—3 p.m.

WEDNESDAY, JANUARY 20.

British Archæological Association.—(1) Mr. Thomas Blashill, on "Sutton in Holderness, and the Abbey of Meux." (2) Mr. Andreas E. Cockayne, on "Dorothy Manners (*née* Vernon of Haddon Hall)."—8 p.m.

Civil and Mechanical Engineers' Society.—Mr. H. Coward on "Forced Ventilation by Compressed Air." 7 p.m.

Society of Arts.—Prof. Vivian B. Lewes on "Spontaneous Ignition of Coal and its Prevention." 8 p.m.

THURSDAY, JANUARY 21.

Royal Institution.—Dr. A. S. Murray, on "Some Aspects of Greek Sculpture in Relief." 3 p.m.

Institution of Civil Engineers.—Students' Visit to inspect Electrically-driven Machinery at the works of Messrs. Willans & Robinson, Thames Ditton. Train from Waterloo at 1.50.

Society of Antiquaries.—8 p.m.

FRIDAY, JANUARY 22.

Royal Institution.—Lord Rayleigh on "The Composition of Water." 9 p.m.

SATURDAY, JANUARY 23.

Royal Institution.—Professor J. A. Fleming on "The Induction Coil and Alternate-current Transformer." 3 p.m.

RECENT PATENTS:

ABSTRACTS OF SPECIFICATIONS.

15,139.—BRICK KILNS: *W. Rennie.*—This inventor specifies improvements in the construction of brick kilns in order that the flame and smoke may be spread in the kiln, and the gases in the furnace completely consumed, the bricks being, it is claimed, properly burned, and no soft, pale, or overburned bricks being produced.

1,247.—LAVATORY BASINS: *J. Shanks.*—This specification refers to improvements in the form and construction of lavatories or wash-hand basins. The basin is made or combined with a rectangular table-like top. The contour of the basin resembles a triangle, the angles being rounded with the longest side in front. The discharge outlet is placed at the middle of the back of basin, where the remaining two sides of the triangle meet.

1,259.—CHIMNEY-TOPS: *H. Brasher.*—The object of this invention is to prevent wind blowing down chimney-tops or ventilating terminals, by locating above and near the top of the shaft or flue one or more hinged flaps, or a fixed or movable diaphragm, and placing over these a hood.

1,317.—CHIMNEY-TOPS: *W. Dalling.*—This specification refers to the construction of a top for ordinary chimneys to cause a uniform and steady upward draught in whatever wind or weather. This is effected by fixing a cover at a suitable distance from the top of the chimney to permit escape of the smoke. Below this are a series of circular outlets formed of conical pieces, and from the lowest part of the chimney-pot a number of tubes project in an inclined direction downwards.

1,852.—WATER-CLOSETS: *G. & J. Clarke.*—This patent refers to improvements in closets, and in flushing and cleansing the same by the use of waste water, which are effected by means of single automatic tippers, the top only of which comes into contact with stop-piece, also by the improved construction and form of wash-out basins, and an improved cover or guard placed over the tipper-box so arranged as to be readily removable.

18,364.—LOUVRE WINDOWS: *R. H. Leaker.*—This specification describes an improved method of hanging and operating the louvre boards, which are carried in brackets or shoes situated at each end of the boards, and pivotted in the window-frame. The brackets at one end are furnished with cranks, the pins of which are fitted into holes in a movable bar common to all the boards. The crank-piece of one of the boards is passed through a slot in the movable bar, the slot being cut at each side to receive the pin. The louvre boards are opened or closed by moving the bar downwards and inwards, or the reverse. They are kept open by a binding screw.

NEW APPLICATIONS FOR LETTERS PATENT.

January 1.—6, W. Smeaton, Water-closets, with traps and pedestal enclosures.—8, G. Harrington, Cowl and Shaft Arrangements for Ventilation.—20, J. Bennett, Ventilation of Sewers and Drains.—23, F. Collins, Bolts for Emergency Exit-doors, &c.—25, A. Milne, Bolts for Emergency Exit-doors, &c.—26, C. Stevenson, Tilting Lavatory Basin and similar utensils.—28, J. Bolding, Water-closets for use in Railway Carriages, &c.—46, R. York, Earthenware Pipes.—49, C. Kingzett, Scouring, Deodorising, and Disinfecting Rooms and other places.—51, E. Ward, Flush-cisterns.

January 2.—66, H. Simester, Ventilation.—71, W. Chesterton, Ventilator for Shop-window.—72, A. Davidson and R. Thom, Veneer Fabrics or Material for Decorative Purposes.

PROVISIONAL SPECIFICATIONS ACCEPTED.

18,954, F. Tyers and D. Barnsdale, Boilers for Kitchen Fireplaces or Ranges.—19,518, W. Kennett, Siphon Water-waste Preventive Cistern.—19,940, W. and E. Freeman, Flushing Apparatus for Sanitary purposes.—20,073, C. Heyworth, Taps or Cocks.—21,024, W. Wright, Window-sashes and Frames.—21,866, A. Taylor, Dressing and Levelling Flagstones, &c.—21,909, W. Thornburn, Raising, Lowering, and Securing Sliding Sashes.—22,031, A. McKay, Extracting Damp from Walls or other Structures.—22,048, R. Johns, Roofing.—22,080, J. Grubb and W. Sturge, Roses for Ceilings and Wall Connectors for Electrical Purposes.—22,111, E. Nelson, Material for use as a Damp Course in Building Foundations.—22,198, F. Willis and R. Astley, Fireproof Floor.

COMPLETE SPECIFICATIONS ACCEPTED.

(*Open to Opposition for Two Months.*)

3,457, W. and E. Bracewell, Flooring Cramp.—3,602, H. Denton and others, Bolts for Doors and Gates.—3,637, T. Brown, Ventilators for House Drains, &c.—20,978, O. White and J. Williams, Fastenings for Doors, &c.

PRICES CURRENT OF MATERIALS.

TIMBER.		
Greenheart, B.G. ton	9/0/8	0/0/9
Teak, E.I. .. load	9/10/0	15/0/0
Sequoia, U.S. ft. cu.	2/3	2/0
Ash, Canada load	2/10/0	4/0/0
Birch, do.	3/0/0	4/5/0
Elm, do.	3/10/0	4/15/0
Fir, Dantsic, &c.	2/0/0	3/10/0
Oak, do.	2/10/0	4/10/0
Canada	5/0/0	7/0/0
Pine, Canada red	2/10/0	3/10/0
Do. yellow	2/10/0	5/0/0
Lath, Dantsic, fathom	5/5/0	6/10/0
St. Petersburg	5/10/0	7/10/0
Deals, Finland, 2nd & 1st std 100	8/10/0	10/10/0
Do. 4th & 3rd	7/10/0	8/10/0
Do. Riga	6/10/0	8/0/0
St. Petersburg, 1st yellow	10/10/0	15/0/0
Do. 2nd yellow	8/10/0	10/0/0
Do. white	7/0/0	10/10/0
Swedish	7/15/0	16/0/0
White Sea	8/10/0	17/10/0
Canada, Pine 1st	19/10/0	25/10/0
Do. do. 2nd	14/10/0	16/10/0
Do. do. 3rd, &c.	6/10/0	10/10/0
Do. Spruce, 1st	8/10/0	11/0/0
Do. do. 3rd & 2nd	6/10/0	8/0/0
New Brunswick	7/0/0	7/10/0
Battens, all kinds	3/10/0	15/10/0
Flooring Boards, sq., 1 in. prep. 1st	0/8/6	0/14/6
Do. 2nd	0/7/6	0/11/6
Other qualities	0/5/0	0/8/0
Cedar, Cuba .. ft.	/3½	/4½
Honduras, &c.	/3½	/4½
Mahogany, Cuba	/4½	/6½
St. Domingo, cargo av.	/4½	2/0
Mexican do. do.	/4	/6
Tobasco do. do.	/3½	/7
Honduras do.	/3½	/5½
Box, Turkey ton	4/0/0	13/0/0
Rose, Rio	10/0/0	20/0/0
Bahia	9/0/0	18/0/0
Satin, St. Domingo .. ft.	0/0/9	0/1/3

TIMBER (*continued*).		
Satin, Porto Rico	0/0/10	0/1/6
Walnut, Italian	0/0/3½	0/0/7
METALS.		
Iron—Pig, in Scotland ton	2/7/0	2/7/3
Bar, Welsh, in London	6/0/0	6/2/6
Do. do. at works in Wales	5/10/0	5/12/6
Do. Staffordshire, in London	6/10/0	8/15/0
Copper—British, cake and ingot	49/10/0	50/10/0
Best selected	50/10/0	52/0/0
Sheets, strong	59/0/0	60/0/0
Chili, bars	46/2/6	46/7/6
Yellow Metal lb.	0/0/5⅜	0/0/5⅝
Lead—Pig, Spanish ton	11/2/6	11/6/3
English, com. brands	11/7/6	11/10/0
Sheet, English, 3 lbs. per sq. ft. and upwards	13/5/0	0/0/0
Pipe	13/15/0	0/0/0
Zinc—English sheet ton	25/0/0	25/10/0
Vieille Montagne	26/10/0	0/0/0
Tin—Straits	90/7/6	90/15/0
Australian	90/7/6	90/15/0
English Ingots	94/0/0	95/10/0
OILS.		
Linseed ton	18/15/0	19/2/6
Cocoanut, Cochin	26/10/0	0/0/0
Do. Ceylon	23/0/0	0/0/0
Palm, Lagos	22/0/0	22/10/0
Rapeseed, English pale	28/15/0	0/0/0
Do. brown	27/0/0	0/0/0
Cottonseed ref.	18/0/0	0/0/0
Oleine	0/0/0	0/0/0
Lubricating, U.S.	4/10/0	5/10/0
Do. refined	6/0/0	11/0/0
Tar—Stockholm barrel	0/19/0	20/0/0
Archangel	0/12/6	0/0/0

TENDERS.

[Communications for insertion under this heading must reach us *not later than* 12 *noon on Thursdays.*]

BOURN (Lincolnshire).—For the restoration of the Abbey Church, Bourn. Mr. J. C. Traylen, Diocesan Surveyor for Lincoln, architect:—

White & Wood	£1,550	0
S. F. Halliday	1,281	0
John Thompson	1,228	0
Roberts & Son	1,198	9
H. S. & W. Clowe	£1,160	0
Roberts Bros., Stamford*	1,139	0

* Accepted.

BRECON.—For the erection of new Board Schools. Mr. E. H. Lingen Barker, architect:—

J. D. Williams	£3,195	17	2
Stephens & Bastow	2,701	0	0
W. Dowland	2,692	0	0
Price & Deakins	£2,483	11	4
B. Jenkins, Brecon*	2,444	2	5

* Accepted.

BUSHEY (Herts).—Accepted for alterations and additional studios for the "Herkomer" Schools, Bushey, Herts. Mr. Edwin G. Salter, architect (Salter, Issott, & Salter), 13, Phœnix-street, N.W.:—

G. & J. Waterman, Watford £574 0 0

EASTBOURNE.—For the erection of six houses and shops, bakery, &c., in Seaside-road, Eastbourne, for Mr. David Gilbert. Mr. Oliver Mitchell, architect. Quantities supplied by the architect:—

J. W. Falkner	£7,395
Jas. Longley & Co.	6,795
M. Martin	6,750
Taylor Bros.	6,600
Eldridge & Cruttenden	£6,500
J. Muirland	6,465
Jas. Peerless, Eastbourne*	5,735

* Accepted.

ELGIN.—Accepted for the erection of a villa-residence in Reidhaven-street, Elgin. Mr. George Sutherland, architect, Elgin:—

Mason, Wm. Scott	Total cost, £1,000.
Carpenter, Jas. Macbeth	
Plasterer, Jas. Brodie	
Plumber, John Hunter	
Slater, John Wilson	
Painter, John James	

[All of Elgin.]

LONDON.—For alterations at the "Bow Bells," Bow-road, E., for Mr. J. W. Gibbs. Messrs. Fletcher & Migotti, architects, 73, Bow-road, E.:—

Lascelles & Co.	£782	Courtney & Fairbairn	£625
Salt	775	Sheffield Bros., Stoke Newington*	537
Walker Bros.	644		
Toole	625		

* Accepted.

LONDON.—For alterations and additions to the "Dolphin" public-house, Tonbridge-street, Euston-road, for Mr. A. Sheubert. Messrs. Kerslake & Mortimer, architects:—

Lidstone	£1,988 8 11	Picken	£1,885 0 0
Holloway Bros.	1,915 0 0	Higgs & Hill	1,825 0 0

LONDON.—Accepted for pulling down and rebuilding Nos. 49 and 51, Lisson-grove, Paddington. Messrs. Wylson & Long, architects, 15, King William-street, Strand:—

Williams & Richards, Clapham Junction £1,648 0 0

NANTWICH.—For draining, making-up, and metalling road at the hospital, for the Union Guardians. Mr. J. A. Davenport, surveyor, Heath-side, Nantwich:—

Henry Chesters	£175 0	John Thomas Gresty, Willaston*	£155 0
George Cox	168 10		
Thomas Jones	160 0		

* Accepted.

SOUTHAMPTON.—For sewage machinery, for the Corporation. Mr. W. B. G. Bennett, Borough Surveyor, Municipal Offices, Southampton:—

J. R. Hainsworth & Co.	£1,100 0 0	Manlove, Alliott, & Co.	£630 0 0
Hughes, Mann, & Gotto	860 0 0	Robey & Co.	627 0 0
Crossley Bros.	787 0 0	Bible, Hobson, & Co.	605 0 0
Leete, Edwards, & Norman	770 0 0	Fielding & Platt	584 0 0
Campbell Gas Engine Co.	725 0 0	W. Tasker & Sons	581 9 8
Jewell & Son	702 5 0	Wells Bros.	559 18 0
H. Prince	689 16 4	Noble, Robertson, & Co.	539 10 0
Pratchitt Bros.	678 0 0	Wyatt Bros.	520 0 0
		British Gas Engine Co.	487 5 0
		Dick, Kerr, & Co. London (accepted)	499 0 0

SOUTHAMPTON.—For laying certain stoneware pipe sewers and constructing manholes in connexion therewith, and for the erection of an engine-house and pump-well and other works incidental thereto, for the Bevois Valley Drainage, Southampton. Mr. W. B. G. Bennett, C.E., Borough Engineer:—

J. Crook & Son	£1,343	H. I. Sanders	£721
J. Crook	893	Roe & Co. (accepted)	675

[All of Southampton.]

UPTON PARK.—For alterations and additions to the Public Hall, Upton Park, E., for Mr. W. S. Hammerton. Mr. J. H. Carte, architect, Upton Park:—

Watson	£708 0 0	Chas. L. Cole*	£560 0 0
Wallis	707 15 0	Hammerton	550 0 0
Wyles	672 0 0		

* Accepted.

The Builder Cathedral Series.

1891.

1. CANTERBURY	Jan. 3.	7. SALISBURY	July 4.
2. LICHFIELD	Feb. 7.	8. BRISTOL	Aug. 1.
3. ST. ALBAN'S	Mar. 7.	9. NORWICH	Sept. 5.
4. PETERBOROUGH	April 4.	10. ROCHESTER	Oct. 3.
5. WELLS	May 2.	11. LINCOLN	Nov. 7.
6. EXETER	June 6.	12. GLOUCESTER	Dec. 5.

1892.

13. ST. PAUL'S	Jan. 2.	16. ELY	April 2.
14. HEREFORD	Feb. 6.	17. LLANDAFF	May 7.
15. CHICHESTER	Mar. 5.	18. OXFORD	June 4.

(Further arrangements will be duly announced.)

Price FOURPENCE each (by post 4½d.), except Nos. 1 and 2, which are out of print; but the VIEW, PLAN, AND DESCRIPTION of CANTERBURY and of LICHFIELD have been re-printed, and they can now be had, price ONE SHILLING each set; by post, 1s. 2d.

Portfolios, for preserving the Plates unfolded, 2s. 6d.; by post, 3s.

Now ready (86 plates). Price ONE GUINEA.

"THE BUILDER ALBUM"

OF ROYAL ACADEMY ARCHITECTURE.

1891.

Extract from the Preface.—"The accompanying set of plates comprises the drawings in the Architectural Room of the Royal Academy Exhibition of this year, which have been lent by their authors for illustration in *The Builder*."

LONDON
Office of "The Builder," 46, Catherine-street, W.C.

W. H. Lascelles & Co.

121, BUNHILL ROW, LONDON, E.C.

Telephone No. 270.

HIGH-CLASS JOINERY.

LASCELLES' CONCRETE.

Architects' Designs are carried out with the greatest care.

CONSERVATORIES
GREENHOUSES,
WOODEN BUILDINGS,

Bank, Office, & Shop Fittings

CHURCH BENCHES & PULPITS

ESTIMATES GIVEN ON APPLICATION.

SUBSCRIBERS in LONDON and the SUBURBS, by prepaying at the Publishing Office, 19s. per annum (or 4s. 9d. per quarter), can ensure receiving "The Builder" by *Friday Morning's* post.

TO CORRESPONDENTS.

W. & D. C. T. (hardly within our province).—F. J. N.—J. A.—F. S. W.—S. H. A.—A. L.—J. M.

All statements of facts, lists of tenders, &c., must be accompanied by the name and address of the sender, not necessarily for publication.

We are compelled to decline pointing out books and giving addresses.

NOTE.—The responsibility of signed articles, and papers read at public meetings, rests, of course, with the authors.

We cannot undertake to return rejected communications.

Letters or communications (beyond mere news-items) which have been duplicated for other journals, are NOT DESIRED.

All communications regarding literary and artistic matter should be addressed to THE EDITOR; all communications relating to advertisements and other exclusively business matters should be addressed to THE PUBLISHER, and *not* to the Editor.

TERMS OF SUBSCRIPTION.

"THE BUILDER" is supplied DIRECT from the Office to residents in any part of the United Kingdom at the rate of 19s. per annum PREPAID. To all parts of Europe, America, Australia, and New Zealand, 26s. per annum. To India, China, Ceylon, &c., 30s. per annum. Remittances payable to DOUGLAS FOURDRINIER, Publisher, No. 46, Catherine-street, W.C.

THE BATH STONE FIRMS, LTD.
BATH,
FOR ALL THE PROVED KINDS OF
BATH STONE.
FLUATE, for Hardening and Preserving Calcareous Stones and Marbles.

DOULTING FREESTONE.

THE CHELYNCH STONE. — The stone from these quarries is known as the "Weather Beds," and is of a very crystalline nature, and undoubtedly one of the most durable stones in England.

THE BRAMBLEDITCH STONE. — Is of the same crystalline nature as the Chelynch Stone, but finer in texture, and more suitable for fine moulded work.

Prices, and every information given, on application to CHARLES TRASK & SONS, Doulting, Shepton Mallet.

London Agent—Mr. E. A. WILLIAMS, 16, Craven-street, Strand, W.C. [ADVT.

HAM HILL STONE.

The attention of Architects is specially invited to the durability and beautiful colour of this material. Quarries well opened. Quick despatch guaranteed. Stonework delivered and fixed complete. Samples and estimates free. Address, The Ham Hill Stone Co., Norton, Stoke-under-Ham, Somerset. London Agent: Mr. E. A. Williams, 16, Craven-st., Strand, W.C. [ADVT.

Asphalte.—The Seyssel and Metallic Lava Asphalte Company (Mr. H. Glenn), Office, 42, Poultry, E.C.—The best and cheapest materials for damp courses, railway arches, warehouse floors, flat roofs, stables, cow-sheds, and milk-rooms, granaries, tun-rooms, and terraces. Asphalte Contractors to the Forth Bridge Co. [ADVT.

SPRAGUE & CO.,
LITHOGRAPHERS,
Employ a large and efficient Staff especially for Bills of Quantities, &c.
4 & 5, East Harding St. Fetter-lane, E.C. [ADVT.

The Reredos, St. Paul's Cathedral.

(Reprinted from "The Builder," Jan. 28th, 1888.)

Copies of this Plate (15 in. × 11½ in.) on stout paper, unfolded for framing, are on sale, Sixpence, by post, 8d.

London: Office of "The Builder," 46, Catherine-street, Covent Garden, W.C.

TWELVE GOLD AND SILVER MEDALS AWARDED.

IRON CISTERNS.

F. BRABY & CO.

VERY PROMPT SUPPLY.

LARGE STOCK READY.

Particulars on application. **CYLINDERS FOR HOT-WATER CIRCULATION**

LONDON:	LIVERPOOL:	GLASGOW:
352 to 362, Euston-road.	6 and 8, Hatton Garden.	47 and 49, St. Enoch-sq.

The Builder.

Vol. LXII. No. 2555. SATURDAY, JANUARY 23, 1892.

ILLUSTRATIONS.

Design for a Large Town Mansion : Perspective View of Front.—By Mr. A. H. Hart, A.R.I.B.A. .... *Double-Page Ink-Photo.*
Section and Plan of Mr. Hart's Design for a Large Town Mansion .... *Two Single-Page Photo-Litho's.*
House "Munstead Corner," Godalming.—Mr. E. L. Lutyens, Architect .... *Single-Page Ink-Photo.*
Design for a Proposed Church. East Elevation.—By Mr. J. E. Newberry, A.R.I.B.A. .... *Single-Page Ink-Photo.*
Wayside Notes in East Anglia : Sketches in Norwich, North Walsham, and Costessey.—By Mr. J. S. Corder .... *Double-Page Photo-Litho.*

Blocks in Text.

Bermondsey Public Library.—Mr. J. Johnson, F.R.I.B.A., Architect....... Page 60 | Diagrams in Student's Column : Heating by Hot Water .... Pages 66, 66

CONTENTS.

The Human Habitation	55	Design for a Proposed Church	62	Sanitary and Engineering News	67
Notes	57	Wayside Notes in East Anglia	62	Foreign and Colonial	67
Notes on Chalices and Patens	58	London County Council	64	Miscellaneous	67
Royal Institute of British Architects	59	The New Building By-laws for London	65	Legal	68
Architectural Societies	59	Flooring-Boards on Concrete	66	Meetings	69
Public Library, Bermondsey	60	Bolsover Colliery Competition	65	Recent Patents	69
The Architectural Association	61	Student's Column.—Warming Buildings by Hot Water, IV.	65	Some Recent Sales of Property	69
Design for a Large Town Mansion	62	Obituary	66	Prices Current of Materials	69
"Munstead Corner," Godalming	62	General Building News	66	Tenders	69

The Human Habitation.

LL who visited the Paris Exhibition of 1889 will remember the series of erections illustrating the history of the Habitation which were ranged along the Quai d'Orsay, and of which we gave at the time a description illustrated by sketches. The collection of models of dwellings, though it could hardly pass for a serious illustration of the vast subject of human habitations, was a remarkable *tour de force* in the way of archæological illustration, considering that it was got up gainst time, at short notice, and as a mere endant to the main body of the Exhibition. I. Chas. Garnier, under whose direction the ork was carried out, has not been content ith this extemporised scenic illustration, it has since then been occupied, in conunction with M. A. Ammann, in carrying it the illustration of the subject in a ore full and deliberate manner. The esult is before the world in a ponderous uarto of nearly 900 pages,* produced by a oint effort which is compared in the lively nd piquant preface (in which it is not difficult to trace the hand of M. Garnier) to the ld fable of the blind man and the paralytic: One of the authors is a historian who does ot see very clearly into matters of architecure; the other is an architect who hobbles ery much in the pathways of history." Iutually assisting each other, they have been ble to make a very long journey, "puisqu'il ure depuis plus de dix mille ans!"

The object of the book is rather to popurise the subject than to settle any disputed oints in archæology; in fact, it may readily e supposed that a book on so vast a subject roduced in three years' time could hardly y claim to occupying a position of exact iticism, since from that point of view the subject is too large for the lifetime of any one man. Contested points in regard to a subject of this kind can only be settled by those who devote themselves specially to one chapter of the history and follow it out in all its details. What the authors claim to have done, we may gather from the wording of their preface, is to have brought together and arranged in a systematic manner the best and most reliable information available from a collective treatment of their own researches and those of others who have treated special branches of architectural history.

The book is divided into five main heads, the first including the Pre-Historic period, the four others the Historic period, divided under the following sections—(1) Habitations prior to the Aryan invasions; (2) The Aryans and civilisations arising out of the Aryan invasions; (3) The great invasions and their consequences;* habitations of the Middle Ages and of modern times; (4) Habitations of people who have remained apart from the general movement of humanity. This latter heading includes the Chinese, the Japanese, the Cambodians, early American dwellings, &c., and makes (whether intentionally or not) a kind of connexion with or return to the opening subject, for it is in a considerable degree from the existing habitations of uncivilised tribes, where a kind of hereditary instinct rules, that we are able to conjecture the probable forms of pre-historic uncivilised habitations. It is in tacit recognition of this fact, we presume, that we find in connexion with the first chapter in the Pre-Historic section a view of the existing habitations of the tribe of Bongos, in the upper valley of the Nile: tent-like circular huts with thatched roofs and low walls of staves and wattles below.

The subject of pre-historic dwellings is fascinating enough in a speculative sense, and of course cannot be passed over in a general review of the history of the habitation, but it is an unsatisfactory element in a historical treatise, simply because it must for the most part be mere speculation. As in most cases, it leads the authors to those vague and general terms which we find in all such histories. Taking the habitations of the aboriginal Australian natives as known at the present day, and conveniently assuming Australia as "peut-être le plus ancienne terre de notre globe," it is "natural to admit" that this strange continent has maintained to our day the most ancient "documents" of the history of the race, and then "d'après ces données, nous pouvons aisément figurer quelle était l'existence des hommes vivant aux époques le plus reculées que vous puissions atteindre avec certitude." So we can in a general way; they were probably nomads, ignorant of the culture of the earth, chased by the large animals of those days, and having little to distinguish them from those animals except a certain faculty of arranging an artificial shelter from the weather where a natural one was not available, and of making some very rude cutting implements. All that can be imagined in a vague manner, with more or less realism according to the picturing power of each reader's mind. But it does not aid very much in tracing the history of the habitation. The authors, we observe, adopt the view that the formation of some kind of screen preceded the habitation in caves, and remark on it as a very important step in advance when men exchanged a temporary constructed shelter for a cave. We do not see why caves should be regarded as chronologically separate from the constructed shelter or *abri*. The use of caves for habitations would depend mainly on whether there were accessible caves in the locality; and in any case their use can hardly be considered a step in advance of the constructed shelter. Men living in natural caves have, so far, made no more progress in regard to a habitation than animals. The scooping-out of caves artificially is another matter, but the authors refer in the first instance to those "toutes préparées par la nature." A more important distinction between early classes of habitations is between those which were merely shelters from the elements, and those which were intended as defensible against human enemies. Between the shelter and the fortress is an immense step, and we should be disposed to say that it was the fear of other men, the tendency to fight and pillage, and therefore to form places of retreat and security, which was the more important factor in the development of the early habitations of mankind.

* "L'Habitation Humaine": par Chas. Garnier, embre de l'Institut, Architecte du Nouvel Opéra; A. Ammann, Agrégé de l'Université, Professeur au cée Louis-le-Grand. Ouvrage illustrée de 335 vignettes, contenant 24 cartes. Paris: Librairie Hachette et e

* This appears to refer to the historic invasions from the north to the south of Europe since the Christian era.

This desire for security against attack was of course the influence which developed the elaborate system of lake dwellings, our knowledge of which is only a matter of comparatively recent acquirement, and was at first even received with scepticism by those outside the world of archæologists. This dream of security, say the authors, had long haunted the brain of Troglodyte man, who probably first thought of some means of fortifying the entry of his cave, even as Robinson Crusoe did so elaborately in his island. Indeed, the whole description of the fortified cave in that wonderfully realistic narrative is a striking exemplification of the kind of work to which early mankind might have betaken themselves in the endeavour to get security from attack or at least from surprise; only the civilised brain of Crusoe (or Defoe) was equal to a systematic plan of fortification beyond what we may suppose the ingenuity of primitive man to have been equal to. Of such cave fortifications we have, however, no positive evidence, however probable the attempt may seem. If it was attempted, there seems to have come a time when it was recognised that it was a failure, or at all events that dwellings built out over the water were much easier to defend. For it is a primary object of all kinds of fortification to reduce as much as possible the length of barrier to be defended. Now in the case of a cave the fortification was almost necessarily a somewhat extended one, if it were to defend the approach to the cave; in a lake-built village the access to be defended could be reduced to a single narrow gangway, capable of being entirely cut off at pleasure. Our authors, as in the former chapter, give an illustration of the same kind of device from modern life. Living on trees seems an even more out-of-the-way and difficult kind of arrangement than living on lakes, yet villages in the Soudan, according to Dr. Nachtigall, are in the present day built in the boughs of trees, and the authors give, from his description, a sufficiently dramatic representation of an attack on a tree-village. The existence of such a method of building in the present day renders it probable that a similar resource occurred to peoples in the same stage of civilisation in early times: according to Henri Mürger, indeed, it is a natural resource of distressed persons in all stages of civilisation, and a needy literary man in the "Vie de Bohême" gives his address as "Boulevard So-and-So, third tree, fifth branch." The building of lake houses, however, was a step a good deal in advance of either cave-dwelling or tree-dwelling; the fixing of the supports for the platforms in the bed of the lake was a comparatively advanced piece of engineering, and the making of the platforms and houses thereon a piece of construction requiring care and skill. On the other hand we may presume that the development of the lake dwelling preceded the development of the boat, otherwise the security sought for would have been very largely discounted. Nowadays such lake villages as exist are found, as the authors show in illustrations, along with the use of canoes or other kind of boats; but it seems more probable that the earliest form of lake village was in a pre-boating period, and consisted of a peninsula of dwellings accessible by a narrow bridge, a portion of which was removable.

If we come to think of it, water has in later ages been a very important element in the defences of dwellings or fortifications. We have the moated châteaus of France as examples—practically lake dwellings of a more elaborate description; the moat for many centuries formed an indispensable girdle to castles and strongholds in various countries. And our own country is an example, in her past history, of the strength and security given by an insular situation, which is only the same thing on a larger scale.

When we first come within the Historic period we are still to a great extent in the Pre-Historic position in regard to the everyday habitation. The great buildings erected at the service of either religion or war, the temple and the tomb on the one hand and the fortress on the other, were monumental in character, and have endured so far as to leave us their main architectural elements complete, or open to intelligent study. But the everyday house was a more fragile and temporary structure, and has disappeared. Thus, in the book before us, the Egyptian habitation, the first on the list in what are called Historic times, is only decipherable from the data furnished by a few occasional conventional plans and representations, which leave us very far from arriving at a realistic conception of it. We know much more of the appearance and the social customs of the Egyptians themselves, from their pictured representations, than of the arrangement of the houses they inhabited. The authors go into a long description of the Egyptian house, but the only documents of any importance which they offer us are a "Plan of an Egyptian house" from a "peinture provenant d'un tombeau," and what they call a "maison égyptienne (d'après Champollion)," the latter a conventional kind of section with no unity of scale, and in which the figures alone convey the impression of being correct representations of fact; the house is capable of a very liberal interpretation. French writers are so fond of a complete theory that they are not easily deterred by a scarcity of data for it, and we can only regard the long description of the Egyptian house as an interesting but more or less imaginative document. It is characteristic of French archæological work of this class that no decisive information is given, in regard to the cuts, as to the precise place from which they are taken, or the presumable date of the representations. They furnish excuse for and illustration to a theory and a good deal of picturesque writing, but leave the less imaginative English reader unconvinced.

It is probable however that the authors are quite right in their dictum that the conditions of the climate as well as the social habits of the Egyptians led them to avoid confinement within the house as much as possible. The social habits in a great measure would arise out of the nature of the climate; they can hardly be considered entirely apart from it. There is however one point in regard to social philosophy, touched upon by the authors, which is entirely independent of climate. They remark on the fact that the position of women in Egypt was obviously that of a social equality with men; hence, they observe, we find "no *gynécée*, no harem, none of those domestic prisons in which Oriental civilisations have so often enclosed the women of the establishment." That this free position of women in ancient Egypt did exist is obvious enough from the Egyptian representation of social life, in which women are seen seated at entertainments and making calls much as they do in modern European society; though we doubt if this conclusion could have been arrived at from the dressing up of rather imaginary house plans out of the data furnished by the conventional representations on which these plans are professedly founded. All that can be said is that these representations of the arrangement of the house interior, so far as they are comprehensible, offer (as one might expect) no hint at variance with the social freedom of women as evidenced in the Egyptian representations of figures of contemporary life.

The social position of woman is however an extremely important factor in determining the arrangement of the house interior, either in a negative or positive sense, among all civilised peoples. The Oriental seclusion and comparative degradation of woman is an extreme instance. But in countries and times when woman took her place on a more or less social equality with man, there is even then the consideration, operating distinctly on the plan of the house, whether men and women were to live together habitually by daytime, or whether there was to be a separation of the sexes in their daily life, a "woman's quarter" separate from the rooms usually occupied by the men. This idea obtained, as we know, in Greece, where nevertheless women, even in the Homeric period, were in no condition analogous to that of Oriental harem life, though it could hardly be said that they enjoyed (or perhaps were fitted for) the modern position of intellectual and social equality of the sexes. The higher civilisation and culture advance, the more does this separation of the sexes disappear in family life and consequently in the family abode. In modern houses it may be said that the only survival of the old separation of the sexes in family life during waking hours is to be found in the existence of the smoking-room and the boudoir. And the provision for these, though they may be carefully arranged for a certain degree of seclusion, can hardly be said to affect the general character of the plan of the house; they can be worked into almost any type of plan. In fact, we have almost ceased to have a recognisable type of house-planning in modern Europe, unless we regard as one type that superposition of dwellings in the same block which is called "houses in flats." That is perhaps the most distinctively modern European type that can be named.

Viewing the subject at large, we may say that the most important influences in determining the type and arrangement of the dwelling-house have been (1) climate, (2) the social position of woman, (3) the habit of the society generally, whether hospitable and social or otherwise, (4) the degree of privacy thought necessary indoors, and (5) the state of police and government and the degree of security guaranteed to life and property. All these circumstances influence the arrangement and architectural treatment. The influence of climate is too obvious to need more than an allusion. In a hot and comparatively rainless climate the window openings diminish, and are covered with blinds or screens which may form an important decorative feature cornices project for shade; open loggias or verandahs abound for the same reason the roof is flat, partly because there is no need to make it otherwise, partly becaus it is a place for coolness when the sun i down. In the cold and rainy climate th loggia is rare, the windows expand and ar constructed to take in all the light they can the roof rises into a slope. The social posi tion of woman indicates whether the hous shall be divided into two distinct portions or b planned as a united whole. The habit of th society as to hospitality and free intercour will stamp itself to a certain extent on th dwelling, which will have its wide and orna entrance-door to invite access, or its narro wicket jealously guarded, according as it owner does or does not wish to entertai strangers; will present an external attractive ness and cheerfulness, or an exterior blan wall with all the amenities of the arch tecture turned within. The degree privacy rendered requisite by the manne of the day of course affects th type of the house most decidedly. In th simplicity of early Mediæval days, when a lived in the same room by day and all, nearly all, slept in the same room by nigh house-planning was a very simple problem as more refined manners demand great privacy the house divides itself up into sep rate rooms, and is even planned with co ridors and staircases for a separation of traffi An intermediate stage between the tw conditions is that in which one central livi room or hall suffices for all purposes, an sleeping rooms and other smaller rooms a divided off around it. We have a survival this in the central hall which is so common feature in large mansions of the modern er The introduction of this feature in small houses is an idea of the present day whic has been carried out occasionally, an which will probably receive more d velopment, though the liking for it m be said to depend more on architectural th on social motives. There is no better mea of giving dignity to a comparatively sm house than to give it a large central apa ment fit for partially living in; there is all t difference in the world between such a hou in point of effect and spaciousness of appearance, and one with the mere "entrance hall and staircase" of the average dwelling-house: but of course it is not economical. The fifth influence named, that of the state of government and of security to property, affects the house to some extent on the same lines as the third; an owner may be glad enough to see his friends, but if he has to provide against the forcible entrance of his enemies, or any who may choose for the moment to fancy themselves such, his house will have to be constructed accordingly: it must, if it be not principally a fortress, partake more or less of the character of one.

Large palaces, which are exceptional buildings, are not so interesting or instructive in connexion with the subject as ordinary dwelling-houses; and hence the plan of the Palace of Sargon, introduced as an illustration of the Assyrian house, seems rather beside the mark, and the illustration of the "Maison Assyrienne de l'Exposition de 1889" is beside the mark in the opposite direction; it all runs to height, a tall building on a small base, and seems rather like a piece cut out of a building than the whole building. This was a natural result of the necessity for keeping these model representations of houses within bounds as to size and cost, and it would have been better and more to the purpose if the authors had abstained from reproducing the imitation buildings of the Exhibition, confessedly imperfect and got up in a hurry, and had directed their efforts to making new drawings representing what we might really conceive the original buildings to have been. None of the models of the Quai d'Orsay, with the exception of some of the primitive dwellings and huts of savages, produced this impression; they showed characteristic details, but not complete buildings, and it would have been better to have forgotten them now, as temporary structures which had served their purpose, but which were not quite suitable for introduction into an important publication intended to be of permanent interest. We certainly cannot think that the "Maison Phénicienne," which is admitted by the authors to be "in part hypothetical," reproduces with any probability the civil architecture of the Phœnicians, or "may be considered as the type of one of their constructions." On the contrary, it strikes us as a remarkably Parisian piece of archæology. Nor is it by any means safe, as in the chapter on the habitations of the Etruscans, to take urns in the form of houses as models of the habitations themselves, which seems to have been the case with the Etruscan house of the Quai d'Orsay. In all ages such representations, like the representations of buildings on coins, have been mere reminiscences rather than copies of the actual building. They give hints as to some general features, but not more. There are coins representing the temple of Diana at Ephesus, which in certain respects confirm the descriptions and agree with the discovered remains of the building, yet how utterly unlike they are to what we now know the building must have been. Had we taken those as guides to a restoration of it, before Mr. Wood's discoveries, what a grotesque idea of it we should have evolved. Yet this seems to be very much what the authors of the work before us have been doing with some of their models.

We cannot help feeling a certain scepticism, also, about such illustrations as those of the peasants' houses on the borders of the Red Sea (page 362) which are intended to show the *origines* of the Greek columnar style. They seem too good to be true; they do not impress one as sketches taken on the spot so much as illustrations worked up to take their place satisfactorily as links in a chain of evidence which it is desired to establish. We are not told by whom, when, or where they were taken; a frequent defect, we may notice, in French works of this description. Such documents cannot be too precisely authenticated; but we get no authentication.

All that we mean to imply is that this is hardly a book to be taken *au pied de lettre* as a historical treatise. It is a remarkable work in its extent, its admirable and fascinating literary quality, its profusion of illustrations, and the immense amount of ground it covers; it is full of brilliant suggestion, and is a volume of such extent and elaboration that it is impossible to do justice to it, or even to give an adequate idea of its contents, within the limits to which such an article as this must be confined. But the very extent of the subject-matter is such as no one without superhuman faculties could have adequately dealt with in less than a lifetime, if indeed it is not more than enough for any one lifetime. It must be regarded rather as a remarkable and brilliant effort to convey in one volume a comprehensive sketch of a subject which is almost endless in its ramifications. As such it is well adapted to increase the interest of cultivated readers generally in the subject of architecture and architectural history. It can hardly take its place as a book to be relied on as an unimpeachable authority. But it must be read with interest, even with enthusiasm, by all who are interested in architecture.

NOTES.

THE exhibition of students' drawings at the Institute held during the past week in connexion with the annual awards of prizes and studentships cannot be considered a strong one. Although much solid and good work has been done amongst the old buildings, the designs are distinctly below the average. It is an exhibition, in short, rather of draughtsmanship than of design. Nine competed for the Soane Medallion—the subject being a chapter-house with an approach from a cloister—Mr. Rimmer being the successful one. His design consisted of an octagonal chapter-house of somewhat florid detail surrounded by an ambulatory, this latter taking the form of shallow semi-octagonal chapels between the angles. The perspective, showing the building perched on the edge of a cliff, though perhaps hardly the most likely position to be chosen, undoubtedly added some dignity to a design which was not in itself remarkable for originality or power. Mr. Begg's design, placed second, seemed to us distinctly more dignified, the plain wall space over the window-heads giving it repose; the window-jambs appear weak, however, and either a thickening of the buttresses or the carrying down of another order from the window-head would have given it more apparent strength. The others were not remarkable for their design; one or two were, however, for their draughtsmanship. The Tite prize, won by Mr. T. R. Kitsell, was for a church-steeple, and there were four competitors. Three competed for the Grissell medal—a stone railway-bridge—and two for the Masonry prize. At the further end of the room were exhibited Mr. Greenslade's sketches made during his Pugin tour last year—carefully pencilled drawings of Lincoln, Ely, and Norwich. One of the best was a measured drawing of a bay of the presbytery aisle at Lincoln. Mr. D. J. Blow has been elected Pugin student for the present year, and although we have seen the drawings submitted before, they promise well for the sketches and measured work to be done by him. Mr. Chas. A. Nicholson is placed second, and sends some careful pencil sketches and measured work. The absence of coloured work and measured drawings finished in ink, in competition for the Pugin, is noticeable in the majority of cases. The silver medal has been awarded to Mr. R. S. Balfour for a careful and valuable series illustrating Heriots Hospital at Edinburgh. A good set of drawings of Castor Church, Northants, was among those sent in, and there were also on the wall sets of drawings of the Salisbury Chantry at Christchurch, Hants, and the very beautiful Chapel at the Hospital of St. Mary, Chichester. We give a list of the prize-winners on another page.

FROM a memorial addressed by the Governors of the Manchester Royal Institution to the Mayor of Manchester, a copy of which has been forwarded to us, it appears that the Royal Institution Gallery, in which the autumn picture exhibitions at Manchester have been held hitherto, is now so far occupied by pictures bought for the permanent collection that it no longer affords adequate space for the annual exhibition, unless by the process of taking down and temporarily storing away all the pictures of the permanent collection to make room for the annual exhibition, which we agree with the memorialists is a most undesirable process, both in regard to the pictures and the public. The memorial therefore prays that the Corporation of Manchester would turn their attention to the provision of a new gallery for Manchester, suitable for the Autumn Art Exhibitions, and which might be useful for other purposes of exhibition at other times of the year. The memorial concludes,—

> "We feel very strongly that Manchester, so rich in its private collections, ought to maintain its position in relation to its public collections, and as an art centre generally, it should not be allowed to fall behind Liverpool, Birmingham, Edinburgh, or Glasgow. The latter city is, at this moment, maturing plans for a new art gallery, on a very large scale, and, as they have given great consideration and attention to the requirements of such galleries, we think it would be well to make inquiry as to the exact nature of the project."

We will add one recommendation. If a new Exhibition Gallery is built for Manchester, let it be planned from the first to provide rooms not only for painting and sculpture, but for architectural drawings and models and for decorative design, and thus set an example of breaking through the superstitution that "art" means only pictures and sculpture.

ON last Tuesday evening, in the Elgin Room, British Museum, Miss Eugénie Sellers gave the first of what promises to be a highly successful course of lectures upon Greek Art and Life, as promoted by the London Society for the Extension of University Teaching.* Miss Sellers's addresses have for their subject Greek Sculpture in the fifth century B.C., as illustrated by the Parthenon and its marbles. She invoked her audience to clear their minds of all pseudo-sentiment and unreasoning rapture, reminding them that the Athenians were as human as ourselves, and that their art, albeit beautiful and matchless, is in some points not absolutely perfect. This she illustrated for the moment by pointing out how even Pheidias in his Ionic frieze of the cella, or ναός, failed at the junction of the two ends of the ribbon, as it may be termed, which represents the Panathenaic procession. Miss Sellers glanced further at shortcomings in the direction of decorative arts as applied to their buildings, as contrasted with the Renaissance. She briefly compared the sculptures of the friezes of the Parthenon and of the Phigaleian temple to Apollo Epicurius, or the Deliverer, near to Bassæ, in Arcadia,—though of the same date. She referred to the labours of Wood and of Professor Cockerell in preserving sculptured remains of the Artemision at Ephesus, and Apollo's temple in Phigaleia; and gave an able description of the frigid reception that was accorded to the Elgin Marbles upon their arrival in England, when Haydon, the painter, stood almost alone in combating the supineness,—and, indeed, the hostility,—of the Committee who deliberated upon their purchase for the nation. The class was then taken into the Harpy-tomb, the Phigaleia, and Halicarnassus rooms, where some of the objects are being re-arranged so as to form, in a measure, a chronological exposition of Grecian sculpture.

FROM an advertisement in our columns it appears that engineers are liable to have the same liberal conditions extended to them in competitions which are frequently offered to architects. The Corporation of

* The latter five lectures upon the daily life and thought of the Greeks will be undertaken by Miss Millington-Lathbury.

Beaumaris offer a premium of ten guineas for the best design for a Promenade pier, to cost 3,000*l*.: a contemptible sum even as a premium. But they proceed to say that their decision as to the merits of the designs will be final, that the design for which they give the munificent sum of ten guineas is to remain their property, and that they do not bind themselves to carry out any design submitted. What class of engineers (or architects) do they suppose will respond to such an advertisement?

WE have received a circular from the "Artistic and Literary Association, Limited," which, we are told, is the designation of a new publishing company whose chief object is "to afford to those of its members who are artists or authors the unique advantage of sharing as publishers as well as originators in the profits accruing from their own works." We fear we fail to understand the exact meaning or object of the institution. We have always been under the impression that authors did participate in the profits of the sale of their works—at all events that they can make arrangements to do so unless they prefer to sell outright; and artists are not in the same position, inasmuch as a work of art is a single production, and not a thing to be multiplied in subsequent editions like a book.

THE exhibition of pictures by Mr. H. W. B. Davis at the Gallery of the Fine Art Society in Bond-street is one of the most satisfactory of these personal exhibitions which we have lately seen. Mr. Davis's "landscapes with cattle," as they may mostly be termed in the old crusted catalogue phrase, have the peculiar charm of combining realism and finish with poetic sentiment. There is no slurring over of detail, but the broad effects and the sentiment of nature are always present; and the animals introduced in the pictures, though finished and learned enough to hold their place as animal paintings alone, never seem to obtrude on the landscape; they take their part with it as a portion of the materials of the picture in a perfectly natural manner. Perhaps this result is partly due to Mr. Davis's method (as described in the prefatory notice to the catalogue by Mr. M. Phipps Jackson), of making a complete picture of the landscape first, and then introducing the groups of cattle. But Mr. Davis's landscapes do not depend on the cattle element for their interest; many of them are landscapes pure and simple, and very beautiful examples of landscape painting. Among those in this collection may be specially named "Now came still evening on" (7); "Sunny evening in April, Picardy" (20); No. 27, a study for No. 7, and in some respects finer in effect than the larger picture; "A break in a rainy sky" (32): "Conyhurst Hill, Surrey" (42). Some of the most powerful things are among the smaller studies, "Cloud and Sunshine" for instance (12), a grand little study of sky; and one cannot but remark on Mr. Davis's peculiar power of giving an effect of real light and radiance to the moon in his evening scenes; a point in which his works of this kind remind one much of Daubigny. One of the most remarkable things in the room is a sketch of moonlight effect (49) in a night sky covered with broken clouds whitened by the moonlight; the effect is remarkably true, the more so as Mr. Davis avoids the mistake of many painters of moonlight, that of showing too much detail. We should much have liked to have seen in this Exhibition a painting of Mr. Davis's earlier period, which was known to many in the collection of the late Mr. Pfeiffer of Putney; a painting of a down with sheep, showing one of the most remarkable studies of foreground vegetation we have ever seen. It is very different from the manner in which the artist paints now, but not the less excellent of its type. We know not what has become of the picture. The late owner wished it presented to the National Gallery; it was declined on the ground that it was the work of a living artist, though there are works by living artists (not the equals of Mr. Davis) already in the gallery.

A COLLECTION of Mr. Walter Severn's pictures and sketches in water colour is on view at the rooms of the Dudley Gallery Art Society, of which Mr. Severn is president. The result is not altogether satisfactory. Seen apart, many of these works would give the impression of considerable power over bright sunlight effect, and careful finish. Seen together, they give the impression of mannerism and repetition of rather superficial effects, especially in the treatment of water. Among those we like best are "Loch Gougha" (13), "Balloch Pier" (18), "Conway Castle" (22), "Netley Abbey" (30), "The South Stack, Anglesey" (31), and "Evening, Loch Lomond" (44). Mr. Severn paints architecture well and carefully, and we should have been glad therefore to have seen more architectural subjects in the collection: the view of Netley Abbey ruins is admirably like the place. But the landscapes hardly gain by being shown collectively.

IN reference to our "Note" last week as to an advertising architect who called himself "An Associate of the Institute of Architects," we are informed that the person in question is *not* a member of the Institute. He "ceased to be a member" some time since by a resolution of the Council in accordance with the provisions of one of the Bye-laws. The case is occupying the attention of the Institute authorities.

NOTES ON CHALICES AND PATENS.

THESE have been made of various materials in different ages of the Christian Church,—gold, silver, brass, tin, pewter, wood, stone, horn, glass, and in many Canons and Councils one sort would be ordered and another proscribed.

Becon says: "The cup wherein the Sacrament of Christ's blood was ministered, which we now commonly call the chalice, was in the time of the Apostles and of the Primitive Church made of wood. But Pope Zephyrynus commanded chalices of glass to be used in the year of our Lord 202. And afterwards Pope Urbanus ordained that the chalice should be made either of silver or of gold in the year 227." (Works 3, 262.)

This assertion probably only applies to certain countries, as six centuries later orders had to be made with regard to the material employed. St. Chrysostom, however, speaks of a "gold or jewelled chalice," Hom. 50 on St. Matt. St. Ambrose says, "Sacraments need not gold;" and sold his church plate to relieve captives. The Legatine Council of Cealcythe, A.D. 785, c. 10, forbids the chalice or paten to be made of horn; Elfric's Canons, A.D. 975 requires the sacred vessels to be made of wood; Edgar's Canons, a few years before, 960, require metal, and forbid wood. The Canons of Winchester, 1071, c. 11, forbid wax or wood. Richard's Canons, 1175, require gold or silver; the Council of Rheims, 630, allows tin, but not brass. Hubert Walter, 1195, c. 9, requires silver.

One ancient reason for discarding wooden chalices is because the wine soaked into the wood, as is shown in the following quaint passage in the Black Letter volume, "The Pageant of the Popes," date 1555:—

"Zephyrinus was a Romaine borne, a man, as writers do testifie, more addicted with all endeavour to the service of God than to the cure of any worldly affayres. Whereas before his time the wine in the celebrating the cõmuniõ was ministered in a cup of woode, he first did alter that, and in steade thereof brought in cuppes or chalices of glasse. And yet he did not this upon any supersticion, as thinking woode to be unlawefull, or glasse to be more holy for that use, but because the one is more comly and semely, as by experience it appeareth, than the other. And yet some wooden doultes do dreame that the wooden cuppes were chaunged by him because that part of the wine, or as they thought the royall bloud of Christe did soake into the woode, and so it cannot be in glasse. Surely soner may wine soake into any woode than any witte into those wiole heads that thus both deceive themselves, and slaunder this godly martyr who, in the yeare of our Lorde, 220, suffer
martyrdom under Aurelius."

Gold and silver chalices were probably in u
from the earliest Christian times, and wood ar
stone were most likely used in the poor
churches. The Council of Tribur, in 895, d
not ordain that chalices must be of the precio
metals, but only forbade their being of glass
wood.

In the ancient Irish churches stone chalic
were very usual.

Pre-Reformation chalices in England are ve
scarce; indeed, Mr. Cripps says he can find b
half-a-dozen. The finest of these are at Wiv
liscombe, in Somerset; Bishop Fox's chalice
Corpus Christi College, Oxford; and Sir Thom
Pope's chalice at Trinity College, Oxford.
the communion cup, with its cover (tem
Ed. VI.), there are still fewer examples than
the earlier ones. There is one of 1548-9 at S
Lawrence, Jewry, two at St. Margaret's, Wes
minster, of 1551-2; and others of the san
date at Hunstanton, Norfolk, and Totn
(Devon).

A beautiful specimen of an ancient paten is
Wyke, near Winchester. It is of silver, former
gilt, of which traces are very faintly to be see
The design consists of an Agnus Dei, in
sunk central circle, round which eight orn
mented foils are described, while round th
whole, on the rim, is the following inscri
tion:—

"✠ CUNTA (cuncta?) CREO: VIRTUTE
REGO: PIETATE: REFORMO."

In the Christy collection are two paten
which were found on St. Louis Hill, Carthag
with chalices, liturgical spoons, and seal
They are inscribed respectively, "Felicit
loquere," and "✠ DD. ICRESCONI CLARENT."

About 1854, a Cork jeweller bought a chali
from an Irish peasant, who had found it in
bog near Berehaven, in West Cork. It was
silver one, richly adorned with a foliage desig
enclosing a cross over a skull. Near the ri
in a small compartment, was a cock. The bul
beneath the cup, was chased in Norman sty
similar to the type on some silver pennies
the Conqueror; over this bulb was I.H.S. i
verted. It weighed 12 oz., and was richly gi
On the rim was the inscription, "Corneli
O. Sullivan Sacerdos Me Fieri Fecit 15
Dulcis Jesus Gloria Soli Deo Sa Ma O. P. N."

The same jeweller had another chalice,
octagon one, with scroll-work, and the followi
symbol: the Cross, on the left a ladder, a
on the right a spear; a heart transfixed wi
two arrows in saltier, and the letter H su
mounted with a Cross *patée fitchée*. The i
scription ran thus,—"ORATE PRO ANIMA
DANIELIS SWYNYE SACERDOTIS LISMORENS
DIŒCESIS QUI ME FIERI FECIT A° 1640."
weighed about 16 oz.

Another Irish chalice was inscribed,
"MAURICIUS COSTUN SACERDOS HANC CALIC
DD. ALTARI CAPELLÆ BEATÆ MARIÆ CLO
1607."

The next two inscriptions are on chalices
two churches (R.C.) in Cork:—

"DEO OPT MAXIMO ANO DNI 1598
DEDICABAT ALSONA MIAGHAE HUNC
CALICEM UT PRO ANIMÆ SUÆ
SALUTE JUGITER AD DEUM ORETUR."

And

"✠ Fr. Gulielmus irris Pro Conv^ts S^ti Fra
Corck Me Fecit Fieri 1611."

Both these run round the rim of the base.
Rheims Cathedral is a most splendid chalice
the eleventh century, gold, most beautifully
with diamonds, pearls, and rubies of pricel
value. It belonged in old times to the chu
of St. Remy, and is known as the chalice
St. Remy. On the band is deeply cut—

"✠ Quicumque hunc Calicem invadiaverit
ab Hac (hanc?) Ecclesia (Ecclesiam?) Reme
Aliquo Modo Alianaverit (alien averit?) A
thema sit Fiat Amen. ✠"

Inventories of the vessels existing in vari
English churches before the Reformation,
those taken at the time of the Reformati
show that the churches had gradually acqui
gold and silver and precious stones, in the fo
of shrines, images, reliquaries, vestments, sac
mental vessels, &c., to a great value.
Commissioners of Henry VIII. and Edward
visited all the monastic and collegiate church
to despoil them of all that was most valua
which was confiscated to the King's use.
seizure of the parish plate was not deci
upon till the last year of Edward VI., and p
bably then only partially carried out. La
on the accession of Elizabeth, inquiries w

made about the Church plate, and then it was found a great deal had disappeared, sold by churchwardens to save Church rates in some cases, or stolen by them, or their superiors.

Later, even in the present century, through ignorance, old Church plate has been exchanged for more admired and much less valuable modern plate, or some may have been simply stolen and sold to pawnbrokers and silversmiths. Other plate has been burnt with its church, or perhaps when housed in the vicarage. At Tawstock, in Devon, was a cup, dated 1576, which, with other very good Church plate, was stolen in 1841, and the thieves were never traced.

Hasted says of a Kentish church in his history: "When dressed up for the Sacrament, and covered with its costly and splendid service of rich plate, it has an appearance of grandeur and magnificence that blots from the mind as far as possible a regret for its having been bereaved of its former ornaments. All the plate (except the two great candlesticks) was new gilt, which altogether make a very handsome and splendid appearance."

Early in this century a silver chalice, dated 1387, was mentioned as being in Pakefield, near Lowestoft, but has long disappeared.

The inventories of Church plate taken in Edward VI.'s time are not all extant, but the following is taken from the MS. of the Cumberland inventory of 105 churches. "Of these churches eighty-seven had each but one silver chalice, fourteen had each two silver chalices, and four had each three. Eight had tin chalices, and two had none at all. Nothing else of silver was in any of the churches, except one broken cross and one pyx. There were but three other pyxes, one of which was of copper gilt, and another of latten; the description of the third is torn off. Only one church had cruets, and those of tin for the wine and water at the altar. Twenty churches had candlesticks of brass or latten. No paten or cover is mentioned. Nor is the weight of anything specified." This is a poor record of Church plate compared with that of many counties, but, however, all was fish that came to the king's net! Bishop Boniface has a quaint saying *re* wooden chalices: "When priests were gold, the chalice was of wood; now when the vessel is of gold, priests are wooden." He and St. Ambrose would have agreed in thinking against many contrary opinions of their times that Church plate can sometimes serve humanity better than by being kept sacred in the churches.

Two chalices, each with three bells hung around them, dated 1460 and 1530, were exhibited at Lisbon by the Royal College there. Possibly, they may have been ciboriums or pyxes; and, if so, the bells rung as they were carried along, and so would serve to give notice of the approach of the priest carrying the Blessed Sacrament.

Among the parochial payments of S. Andrew, Holborn, in 1558, is noted "Paide for the exchaunge of two chalices with the covers, weighing xxxii oz. halfe, for a communion cup waying xxx oz. and halfe, the exchaunge with the odd oz. at xiiijs. viijd."

Of old it was the custom to place a chalice and paten, symbolical of his office, upon the breast of a priest in his coffin. William of Bleys, 1229 A.D., ordered that a parish should, in addition to the usual sacred vessels, always keep an unconsecrated chalice, which might be of tin, for burial with the priest (see Wilkins, i. 623). Several examples of these mortuary chalices so buried have been found and preserved,—at Cheam, Surrey; Nettlecombe; and at Corpus Christi College, Oxford. The two latter have patens, silver, with a broad rim, the centre sunk in a sexfoil pattern, with an engraved head of our Lord in the middle.

The following notes from the List of Church Goods in Cornwall, Augmentation Office, 6th Edward VI., are interesting:—

"The p'ish of Delyn (St. Endellion), the sayde p'ishners have ij chalises p'cell gylt.

The Parishe of Egloshayle the sayde parishe hathe ij chalics of sylver."

In the Bodmin Corporation records, among the assignment of goods to the Church, in 1566, is "for ye commyon tabell ij polys, one of brasse, and a nother of yron. One comouyn cup of sylver and one other gylt, w[ch] hery cock vsed at weddynges." There may be others, but the document is so faded and worn as to be in many parts quite undecipherable.

At Blisland is an old chalice, still in use, but the cover is lost. It is thus noted in the Parish Register:—"Anno Dmi, 1604. At the Easter Anno pd. George Marrett did freely give and deliver one fayre silver cup wth a cover therevnto double gilted to remayne for a comunyon cupp for the parishe of Blisland, wth out any clayme." At Minster (also in Cornwall) are two "fayre sylver chalises" with covers, one very ancient.

C. F. Y.

ROYAL INSTITUTE OF BRITISH ARCHITECTS:

AWARD OF MEDALS AND PRIZES.

AT the business general meeting of the Royal Institute of British Architects, held on Monday evening last, the following report of the Council on the award of medals and prizes for the year 1891-92 was received and adopted:—

"Gentlemen,—In accordance with the provisions of By-law 66, the Council have the honour to report that they have examined the several essays and drawings submitted for the Silver Medals of the Royal Institute, the Soane Medallion, the Pugin Studentship, the Godwin Bursary, the Tite Prize, the Grissell Medal, and the Scientific Masonry Prizes.

The Essay Medal and Twenty-five Guineas.

Five Essays were submitted for the Silver Medal of the Royal Institute, the subject being 'The architectural treatment of the Fireplace and its accessories,' under the following mottoes:—i. Ignigenus. ii. Lincoln Green. iii. Pro aris et focis. iv. Terra del fuego. v. Veritas filia temporis.

The Council have awarded the Silver Medal and twenty-five guineas to the author of the essay bearing the motto (v) 'Veritas filia temporis,' as showing the best literary treatment of the subject, and as being adequately illustrated; and they desire to honourably mention the essay bearing the motto of (i) 'Ignigenus,' as possessing merit, principally in the illustrations.

The Measured Drawings Medal and Ten Guineas.

Three sets of measured drawings were received for the Silver Medal of the Royal Institute, under the following mottos:—i. Black spot,—Salisbury Chantry, Christchurch. ii. Nitor,—Heriot's Hospital, Edinburgh. iii. Pollux,—Castor Church, Peterborough.

The Council have awarded the Silver Medal and ten guineas to (ii) Nitor, for measured drawings of Heriot's Hospital, Edinburgh; and a Medal of Merit to (i) Black Spot, for measured drawings of the Salisbury Chantry at Christchurch, Hants.

The Soane Medallion.

For the Soane Medallion and, subject to the conditions laid down, £100 for foreign travel, nine designs for a Chapter-house were submitted, under the following mottoes:—i. Abbotsbury; ii. Anno 1891; iii. Byzantium; iv. Ex-cathedrâ; v. Griffin; vi. Red Cherub; vii. Sun; viii. Plume; ix. Volunteer.

The Council have awarded the Medallion, with the sum of 100*l.* for foreign travel as laid down in the conditions to the design bearing the motto (i) 'Abbotsbury;' and a medal of merit to the design bearing the device of a (vi) 'Red Cherub.'

Pugin Studentship.

For the Pugin Travelling Studentship applications, each with a select number of drawings and sketches, were received from the following gentlemen:—i. Mr. Detmat J. Blow; ii. Mr. Erskine S. Cumming; iii. Mr. Charles R. McIntosh; iv. Mr. Charles A. Nicholson; v. Mr. Percy D. Smith.

The Council have awarded the Studentship to (i) Mr. Detmar J. Blow, born in November, 1867, whose measured drawings of Beauvais Cathedral and of Barfreston Church have afforded him admirable training; and they desire to record that Mr. Blow received a medal of merit for drawings submitted for last year's studentship, and that he was honourably mentioned in 1890. The Council have also awarded a Medal of Merit to (iv) Mr. Charles A. Nicholson, born in April, 1867, for a fine set of drawings.

Godwin Bursary.

For the Godwin Bursary applications were received from the following gentlemen:—i. Mr. Owen Fleming, *Associate*. ii. Mr. Banister F. Fletcher, *Associate*. iii. Mr. Edwin O. Sachs. iv. Mr. T. Locke Worthington, *Associate*.

The Council have awarded the Bursary to Mr. T. Locke Worthington, *Associate*, who proposes to visit France, principally for the purpose of studying tenement buildings.

The Tite Prize.

For the Tite Prize—being a Certificate, and, under conditions, 30*l.* for travel in Italy—four designs for a Church Steeple were submitted, under the following mottoes:—i. Ashlar; ii. Quis; iii. Red Lion; iv. Design in a Circle.

The Council have awarded the Certificate and, subject to the conditions laid down, 40*l.* for travel in Italy, to the design (iii.) bearing the device of a Red Lion.

The Grissell Medal and Ten Guineas.

For the Grissell Gold Medal, for design and construction, three designs for a stone railway bridge were submitted, under the following mottoes:—i. Equilibrium. ii. Fundamentum forte opus sustinet. iii. Jacta est alea. The Council have awarded the Grissell Gold Medal and ten guineas to the design bearing the motto of (iii) 'Jacta est alea.'

The Scientific Masonry Prizes.

For the Scientific Masonry Prizes of six guineas and four guineas two designs have been submitted of the vaulting of an octagonal turret, under the following mottoes:—i. Saxum (with a model). ii. Voussoir.

The Council have awarded the prize of six guineas to the design bearing the motto (i.) 'Saxum'; and the second prize of four guineas to the design bearing the motto (ii.) 'Voussoir.'"

It was subsequently announced that the authors of the premiated or commended essays, designs, and drawings before referred to were as follow:—

"Veritas filia temporis," Mr. Charles E. Sayer, A.R.I.B.A. "Ignigenus," Mr. Richard Glazier, A.R.I.B.A.

"Nitor," Mr. R. Shekleton Balfour. "Black Spot," Mr. Percy D. Smith.

"Abbotsbury," Mr. Heber Rimmer. "Red Cherub," Mr. John Begg, A.R.I.B.A.

"Red Lion," Mr. T. Rogers Kitsell, A.R.I.B.A.

"Jacta Est Alea," Mr. Harold Harlock.

"Saxum," Mr. Herbert S. Wood, A.R.I.B.A. "Voussoir," Mr. Erskine S. Cummings.

ARCHITECTURAL SOCIETIES.

LEEDS AND YORKSHIRE ARCHITECTURAL SOCIETY (INCORPORATED).—A general meeting of this Society was held at the Rooms, Albion-place, Leeds, on Monday last, the President, Mr. W. H. Thorp, F.R.I.B.A., in the chair. Mr. J. M. Brydon, F.R.I.B.A., read a paper entitled "The English Renaissance." After briefly sketching the rise and development of Italian Renaissance, and showing the influence it had upon the English type, Mr. Brydon, taking such well-known typical examples of the English school as the contemplated palace at Whitehall, Ashburnham House, St. Paul's Cathedral, Blenheim, Somerset House, &c., dwelt upon the genius of their great designers, and the other masters of the craft of that period and later periods. Inigo Jones, who set on foot the English style, which in many respects possessed worthier features than its prototype, and which has left us in these days a precious heritage to study and maintain; Sir Christopher Wren, whose *magnum opus*, St. Paul's Cathedral, although marred by the architect having to follow the Cathedral form, and adapt the new style to the old Mediæval type of plan, instead of following his own bent, is, in Mr. Brydon's opinion, one of the greatest ecclesiastical structures of this style in the world. Mr. Brydon commented on the various distinctive features and characteristics, and drew from the examples lessons for the guidance of students of architecture of the present time.

LIVERPOOL ARCHITECTURAL SOCIETY.—This society has established a series of students' classes for the study of various subjects connected with architecture, building construction, and sanitation. Lectures are to be given by architects and engineers on the various subjects specified. Students' meetings are to be held weekly during the session.

MANCHESTER SOCIETY OF ARCHITECTS.—In a circular issued by the Education (in Architecture) Committee of this Society, it is stated that one of the leading objects of the re-construction of the Society was to afford facilities for the study of architecture, other than such as are found in ordinary office routine. This has now been to some extent accomplished by the formation of two classes for instruction in

Bermondsey Public Library. Mr. J. Johnson, F.R.I.B.A., Architect.

(1) History and Development of Architecture, and (2) Materials and Construction, which will be open to students, whether members of the Society or not. Mr. H. E. Stelfox, A.R.I.B.A. (Ashpitel Prizeman, 1888), has been appointed Lecturer, and the classes will be held weekly, at the Society's Rooms (Literary and Philosophical Society, 36, George-street), commencing from Monday, the 18th inst. Any further information may be obtained from the Hon. Sec. of the Education Committee, Mr. Ph. E. Barker, 24, Brazennose-street, Manchester.

DUNDEE INSTITUTE OF ARCHITECTURE.—On the 14th inst. Mr. R. C. Ritchie, of the Electric Construction Corporation, Limited, London, delivered a lecture to the members of the Dundee Institute of Architecture, Science, and Arts, on "Electric Light Supply." Mr. William Mackison, C.E., presided, and there was a good attendance. The chairman, in introducing the lecturer, made a few sympathetic remarks regarding the death of the Duke of Clarence. At the conclusion of the lecture several questions were put to Mr. Ritchie, who, in reply, said that electric light cost about 50 per cent. more than gas in London, and he predicted that in a short time they would be able to produce it at as cheap a rate. Regarding the propelling of tramway cars by electricity, he said that it was all a matter of traffic. If there was little traffic horses would be the cheapest, but where there was a large service, electricity would be preferable. On the motion of the chairman, Mr. Ritchie was accorded a vote of thanks for his lecture.

PUBLIC LIBRARY, BERMONDSEY.

THIS building was opened last Monday by Sir John Lubbock. It has been built from the designs and under the superintendence of Mr. J. Johnson, to whom we are indebted for the accompanying sketch of the building.

The principal entrance in the centre of the building, emphasised by an Ionic portico, leads to a hall and staircase, 15 ft. wide; on the right is the newspaper reading-room, 41 ft. by 33 ft. Immediately opposite the entrance is the lending library, 41 ft. square, fitted with cases for 20,000 volumes. "Cotgreave's" Indicators are used for ready reference. The librarian's-room and residence, with private access to lending department, adjoins the main entrance, thus giving complete control of the building. The stone stairs, with central and return flights, terminate in the large first-floor landing, paved with marble mosaic; the landing is arcaded at the sides, and has a large cove with lantern-light in the centre. The reference library is 41 ft. square, with a domical roof in the centre, supported by four Corinthian columns. It is lighted by the clearstory at the base of the dome, also by the windows in the side walls; the reading-tables are in the centre, the bookcases are arranged on the alcove plan around the sides. Next the landing is the magazine reading-room, 41 ft. by 24 ft.; adjoining is the ladies' reading-room, 20 ft. by 16 ft., with lavatory accommodation. On this floor is the commissioners' committee-room, with separate access from the exterior. The whole of the second floor is occupied by the librarian's apartments, forming a complete residence, with bath, larders, stores, coal-lift, and every residential convenience. In the basement are provided lavatories, &c., for the general readers; also a large space for additional book-store when required, a bookbinding-room, a general store-room, coal-cellar, and heating chamber. There is a side entrance for cases, &c., also a special staircase for the attendants, with a book-lift, so that every portion of the building can be conveniently reached without entering the principal staircase. Mr. Johnson's design was selected out of fifty-seven submitted in public competition. The builders are Messrs. F. & H. F. Higgs, of Loughborough Junction. The iron construction was executed by Mr. Dawnay; the warming (by radiators which keep a satisfactory temperature) was executed by Mr. J. Todd, of Wandsworth, who also provided bells and speaking-tubes; the marble mosaic by Messrs. Diespecker & Co.

The exterior is of Renaissance character, freely treated, executed in red Elham bricks, with dressings of Monks Park Bath stone; the carving has been executed by Mr. Baird, of Herne Hill, from the architect's designs; the central figures of "Literature" and "Science" are by Mr. Lawlor. The central turret was introduced to give height and dignity to the front, on account of the massive character of the adjoining Town-hall.

THE ARCHITECTURAL ASSOCIATION:

THE DESIGN OF TECHNICAL COLLEGES AND SCHOOLS.

THE first meeting of this Association since the Christmas vacation was held on Friday, the 15th inst.

Mr. Leonard Stokes, past President, was voted to the chair, in the unavoidable absence of the President, Mr. F. T. Baggallay (who was out of town) and of the two Vice-Presidents, Messrs. F. R. Farrow and E. W. Mountford, both of whom, it was stated, were, in common with Mr. E. S. Gale, senior honorary secretary, and many other members of the Association, suffering with the prevailing epidemic of influenza.

Messrs. J. Aldridge and J. E. van Abbott were elected members of the Association.

Mr. F. T. W. Goldsmith, honorary secretary, announced that Mr. T. M. Rickman had promised a donation of five guineas per annum to the Association's general fund, and that the Royal Institute of British Architects had promised to subscribe £100 per annum for three years. These announcements were received with much applause, and on the motion of the Chairman the secretaries were instructed to convey the hearty thanks of the Association to the donors.

The Chairman, in feeling terms, alluded to the lamented death of H.R.H. the Duke of Clarence, and proposed that a vote of condolence with the Prince and Princess of Wales be sent by the secretaries in the name of the Association. This was assented to in silence, all the members standing.

Professor Garnett then read the following paper on "The Design of Technical Schools and Colleges:—

Presuming the governing body of the school or college does not consist of educational specialists, it seems that the first step to be taken is to learn from some qualified person or persons what subjects should be taught in the institution, how they should be taught, and what accommodation and appliances will be required for teaching them. I have the honour of knowing some architects who are themselves educational experts, and if the governing body enjoys the advantage of having secured the services of one of these gentlemen it may proceed with safety without further preliminary; but men who can act in the double capacity of architect and educational expert are exceptional, and properly so, for although we may sometimes with advantage ask the advice of our solicitor not only on the form in which our bequests should be drawn up, but also on the manner in which we shall dispose of our belongings in our wills, it does not appear to me to be reasonable to expect the architect to tell us both what we want and how to secure it.

Hence it is generally desirable that the chief technical teacher, and sometimes two or three other members of the staff, should be appointed at the same time as the architect, though it will not generally be necessary to secure more than a very small portion of the services of the teachers until considerable progress has been made with the building. It should be the duty of the teacher, as soon as he is appointed, to advise the governing body with respect to the accommodation required in the several departments, the relations of these departments to one another, and the special appliances equired in each, particularly those for hich provision must be made in the ailding. Attention should be specially dicted to the relative positions of the rooms evoted to the several departments, so that hile each department forms by itself a comact whole, it should be contiguous to other epartments to which it is, in the character of s work, most nearly akin, that the applinces of each department may, as far as posible, be available to those students and eachers in other departments who are most kely to require their use. For example, a hotographic laboratory should be situated as ear as possible to the chemical laboratory on ne side and the art studios on the other. By ssociating the department of photography 'th that of chemistry it becomes unnecessary o reduplicate balances and other appliances for uantitative chemical analysis, while by making the art studios readily accessible to the students of photography the best possible facilities are afforded for camera practice and the study of grouping and light and shade. For similar reasons the metallurgical laboratory should, if possible, be placed between the departments of chemistry and of mechanical engineering, so that all facilities for chemical analysis may be readily accessible on the one side, and testing machines for the systematic examination of the mechanical properties of the metals and alloys may be equally available on the other. On the same principle, the department of electrical engineering should adjoin the engineering laboratory and workshops, for the double reason that steam-power may be available, and because every electrical engineer must be at the same time a mechanical engineer. Students of electrical engineering must also have ready access to the physical laboratory; but it is not desirable that the engine and dynamo-room should be geographically near to the physical laboratory, on account of the disturbance to all magnetic measurements which would be caused by the proximity of heavy moving machinery, of powerful electro magnets, and of strong electric currents.

But while it is desirable that the relative positions of the several departments should be carefully chosen, it is of paramount importance that each department should be compact in itself, so that its work may be conducted by the smallest number of superintendents. If the Professor of Chemistry has his students' laboratory at one end of the building, his lecture-room at the opposite end, his preparation-room somewhere near the middle, and his private room in some remote corner, the amount of assistance he will require will probably be doubled. His private room should be as near as possible to his students' laboratory; if it communicates directly therewith a further advantage will be gained; and his preparation-room should adjoin the laboratory on one side, and his lecture theatre on the other.

It very frequently happens that it is not possible to erect at first the whole of the buildings which it is intended ultimately to provide, and the question then arises whether a school or college complete in all its departments should be erected on a small scale, or whether plans should be made for the whole building, as though it were intended to erect the whole at once, and a selected position, representing certain departments only, should be built at first. There is, of course, some inconvenience attending the latter course pending the erection of the remaining portions of the building, but this inconvenience may be made comparatively small by a careful selection of the departments for which provision is at first to be made. If the former method is adopted, the institution will be complete in itself during the early years of its existence; but when the enlargement is carried out, several departments will be partly located in the old and partly in the new buildings, and the conduct of the work of each department will be rendered difficult and expensive. In selecting the departments for which provision should be made at first, it should be borne in mind that work which requires specially-constructed buildings cannot be satisfactorily conducted in ordinary lecture-rooms or class-rooms, while a class on mathematics or modern languages is not greatly inconvenienced if it is required to meet in a room provided with draught closets, or special supports for tables, or lighted as an art studio, or in some other way adapted for a purpose other than that for which the class is assembled; provided only that sufficient space is available for seats and desks, and the room is not one in which it is impossible for a lecture to be heard. Hence it is best to commence with the departments of chemistry, physics, applied mechanics, engineering, and fine art, erecting these departments as completely as the character of the plan for the whole building necessitates. Any rooms in these departments which are not at first fully occupied by the work of the department will be available for classes on mathematics, languages, and commercial subjects, while, at a push, a chemical laboratory will serve very well for biological work.

As regards the position of the several departments, it is desirable that in any institution in which popular lectures, university extension lectures, or any large evening classes form an important feature, there should be a large lecture theatre, as near as possible to the public entrance, and that it should be on the ground floor. This lecture-theatre may be common to several departments, but should be readily accessible from the physical department, as physical apparatus is likely to be very largely used in the theatre, and such apparatus is often very ponderous or very delicate. In this theatre as much length as possible should be given to the lecture-table. For a theatre capable of holding two or three hundred persons a lecture-table 30 ft. by 3 ft. is not too large, and 3 ft. is a convenient height. The table should be carried on its own foundations, the supports being entirely distinct from those which carry the floor, so that any movement of the audience may not disturb the most delicate apparatus on the table. It is generally best to carry brickwork for the support of the table up to within two or three inches of the floor level. The space beneath the table and within the brick wall should be accessible from the lecturer's side, as it may be usefully employed to accommodate resistance-coils and other accessories of the lecture-table. The floor should be carried on walls built a foot or more away from the wall which carries the lecture-table. In the Cavendish Laboratory at Cambridge the lecture-theatre is on the first floor, and the lecture-table is an oak slab carried on an 18-in. wall, which forms one wall of the gateway, the floor being carried on brick piers erected for the purpose, a few inches away from this wall, and this arrangement may be desirable when it is impossible to find accommodation for the lecture-theatre on the ground floor. As much space as possible should be left behind the lecture-table for such apparatus as cannot conveniently be placed upon the lecture-table itself, as well as to give a reasonable length for a beam of light reflected from the mirror of a galvanometer or other instrument on the lecture-table, and observed by the audience as it traverses a graduated scale on the wall behind the lecturer. Eight feet is not too much space to leave between the lecture-table and the wall. The gas or other lights in the room should be controlled by a valve or switch fixed underneath the lecturer's table, and readily accessible to the lecturer.

Another important adjunct to a lecture-theatre is a platform for the magic-lantern, which, like the lecture-table, is entirely independent of the floor of the room or of the gallery supports. For the exhibition of ordinary slides such an arrangement is, of course, unnecessary; but when it is desired to exhibit on the screen the motion of a magnet suspended by a silk fibre, or any other delicately-suspended body, the unconscious movements of the most attentive audience will be sufficient to completely spoil the experiment unless a special support for the lantern is provided. A hollow brick pier standing on its own foundation, and carried up through the gallery without coming in contact with the seats or floor, forms a very convenient support for the lantern. Gas, bottles, and other appliances may conveniently be stored within the pier, and, if an electric lantern be used, the conductors may be brought up from the basement and through the pier, and regulating resistance fixed within the space enclosed by the brick walls, which form an almost fire-proof structure. The windows should be arranged in order to throw the greatest possible amount of light upon the lecture-table, but the room should be capable of being darkened completely. If possible, openings should be made in the ceiling directly over the lecture-table, through which apparatus may be suspended at any height above the table from the floor above. A water-supply and sink should be within easy reach of the lecturer, and a large fume-closet with glass front should be fixed in a position in which the audience can readily see its interior. A chamber heated by a steam jacket, and provided with a glass front, is a very valuable accessory to a lecture-theatre, as it enables electrical and other apparatus to be kept warm and dry and in working order, whatever may be the state of the weather or the hygroscopic condition of the overcoats of the audience.

In the Physical Lecture-Theatre at Newcastle the seats have been so arranged that any person can see the front edge, and therefore the whole top, of the lecture-table over the head of a person who, when sitting down, is $2\frac{1}{2}$ inches taller than himself. This condition gives a slightly concave profile to the seats, but the steepness of the gallery is rapidly reduced if the distance between the lecture-table and the first row of seats is increased. It is only when the length available for the theatre is small and the seats have to be brought very near to the lecture-table that the gallery becomes inconveniently steep.

[*Continued on page* 62.

Illustrations.

DESIGN FOR A LARGE TOWN MANSION.

THE illustrations show the perspective view, section, and principal floor plan of the design to which the Royal Academy Gold Medal and Travelling Studentship of 200*l.* have been awarded this year. The author of the design is Mr. A. H. Hart, Associate of the Institute of Architects, who has given us the following brief notes as to the objects put before the competitors and the manner in which he has treated the problem:—

"The building required was a large town house, planned with a view to the proper placing and lighting of pictures, sculpture, and other works of art. The site was 180 ft. deep, with a frontage of 70 ft.

The problem, therefore, was to secure a symmetrical plan, such as a town mansion required, without in any way sacrificing convenience, and to provide proper accommodation for the display of pictures and sculpture, with efficient light both for the works of art and the house generally. To secure all these properties upon a deep site with no light obtainable on either side made the problem a difficult one.

The house is planned without a picture-gallery, the object being to display the pictures and sculpture in the rooms themselves, so that the inmates may enjoy them upon all occasions. An endeavour has been made to let the works of art form part of the architecture and contribute towards a harmonious whole, rather than to appear independent, as they generally do in a museum.

The first floor is devoted to the state apartments, in which stateliness and freedom of circulation have been aimed at, whereas the ground-floor contains the family living rooms, &c., where comfort is the first consideration.

The house is designed in the François I. style, and an attempt has been made to combine richness with dignity."

"MUNSTEAD CORNER," GODALMING.

THIS house, now approaching completion, is situated about one mile from Godalming. The walling generally is of Bargate stone, the upper story half timbered. The roofs are covered with red local tiles. The chimneys are of red brick.

Messrs. Mitchell Bros., of Shalford, are the contractors, and Mr. Edwin L. Lutyens is the architect.

The drawing of the house was exhibited at the Royal Academy last year.

DESIGN FOR A PROPOSED CHURCH.

THIS church has been designed for a large manufacturing town in the Midlands.

In plan it consists of nave and aisles, with transepts; the vestries are on the north side of the chancel, and the organ-chamber is above them, with openings into the chancel and north transept. The chapel is at the east end of the south transept, and will be vaulted. The chancel, also to be vaulted, has an ambulatory around it. The nave is 30 ft. wide, and has a lofty arcade and a flat-pitched roof of early character.

The church will accommodate 800 persons, and will cost about 10,000*l.* without the tower.

The drawing of the church was exhibited at the Royal Academy last year.

JOHN E. NEWBERRY.

WAYSIDE NOTES IN EAST ANGLIA.

DOORWAY, ST. ANDREW'S-HILL, NORWICH.

THIS doorway leads from St. Andrew's-hill to a passage in the rear of an old flint building known as the Old Bridewell.

It is fifteenth-century workmanship, and is constructed of English oak. The massive frame is moulded, and the four-centred head has carved spandrels, the door being hung on book-hinges to the frame, and being square headed. Above the arched head is a traceried transom light of open pierced work, but not glazed. Above the traceried panel is a cornice of battlemented moulding. It is a curiously unusual form, and very quaint.

OLD DOORWAY, GUILDHALL, NORWICH.

Though now forming part of the Guildhall, this doorway was not originally built in its present position. It was taken down from an old house formerly standing in London-street, Norwich, and was known as the Bassingham Gate. A drawing exists, published early in the nineteenth century, showing it *in situ* in 1815. The arch is elaborately moulded, the projecting moulds dying upon the caps of columns worked in the jambs on either side. The centre columns are interrupted, and canopied niches are placed in the jambs, the pedestal of the niche being supported by the column, which runs on to the base. The hood mould is crocketted, and, in place of the finial at top, a shield bearing the Royal Arms of England, with supporters, is carved.

In the left spandrel, looking at the doorway, is a filling-in of vine-leaf ornamentations, in the centre of which is a shield bearing the Norwich city arms; the corresponding right-hand spandrel is filled in with roses, and the shield with armorial bearings,—probably the quarterings of the original possessor.

NORTH WALSHAM CARVINGS.

In the pages of the *Builder*, August 24, 1889, there is a short description of North Walsham Church, and allusion is made to the elaborate woodwork and carving, and to the old screen, portions of which are still retained in the church.

I give a sketch of a piece of the screen now worked into the front of a bench, and also a fine poppy-head from one of the bench-ends. It may be mentioned that the church has no special chancel, and the western portion of the tower has collapsed, owing, it is said, to the imperfection of the round flint bonding.

A careful drawing of the Paston monument in the church appeared in the *Builder* of August 31, 1889.

STRANGERS' HALL, NORWICH.

The newel and baluster are from a building in St. Gregory's parish, now known as Strangers' Hall, though believed to be by most archæologists an old fourteenth-century city mansion. It was used at one time as a Guild Hall for the ancient guild of St. George, patron saint of England, and probably received the cognomen of Strangers' Hall from the fact of its having been lent to foreign refugees during the persecutions of the Huguenots. It has a beautifully-carved doorway to the street, and many points of interest inside.

COSTESSEY.

This picturesque locality lies about five miles out of Norwich, and is chiefly famous for its fine old Hall, one of the seats of the Staffords, though not at present occupied by the family. It was built by the Jerninghams in Queen Elizabeth's reign, and consists of a huge quadrangular building, principally in red brick, the details of which are highly ornate. The church does not exhibit any special features beyond a well-proportioned porch, and a picturesque little brick-capped tower, with spirelet of wood.

JOHN S. CORDER.

THE DESIGN OF TECHNICAL COLLEGES AND SCHOOLS.

(*Continued from page 61.*)

It is imperative that the principal laboratories in the physical department should be upon the ground floor, and that there should be no basement story below them. At least one room should be set apart for exact measurements in electricity and magnetism. The chief tables in this room should be of slate, carried on brick piers, which are built from their own foundations independently of the floor. Professor Ayrton has found it convenient to place slag wool between the brick piers, and slate slabs, instead of fixing the slate to the piers by cement, but the risk of vibration being communicated to the instruments depends greatly on the nature of the soil in which the foundations are placed and on the character of the traffic in the neighbourhood. Other things being equal, that side of the site which is most remote from the public thoroughfares, or traffic of any description, should be selected for the physical laboratory. Professor Herschel's laboratory at Newcastle was within a few feet of the North-Eastern Railway, and the approach of an engine was heralded by the disturbance of his magnets. The side tables throughout the physical department may be conveniently suspended from the walls. A plate of pine, 6 ft. or 7 ft. in height, 6 in. wide, and 2 in. thick, is fastened to the walls by ordinary engineers' bolts, made of Muntz metal, which screw into sockets made of brass or Muntz metal, and built into the walls. Except in the neighbourhood of the electrical-room, iron screws may be employed instead of brass, provided they are carefully protected from rust during the erection of the building by tar, or whitelead and tallow. The plates of pine terminate a little above the floor, and to them are mortised brackets suitable for carrying the slab of teak or ash which is to form the table. By this means we not only secure a table with supports independent of the floor, but for a height of 3 or 4 ft. above the table we have wooden plates, to which shelves or instruments can be attached without interfering with the walls, which in a physical laboratory may with advantage be of bare brick, provided its surface is smooth and hard. With the supports described, and with socket screws built into the walls in positions suitably chosen, it will generally be found unnecessary to make any other attachments to the walls whatever.

In the general physical laboratory gas and water should be provided, and, if possible, a fume-closet. If the building is heated by steam, a few T-pieces, by which flexible tubing can be connected to the heating pipes, will enable steam at a pressure of 3 lbs. or 4 lbs. per square inch to be available for experiments in calorimetry and other branches of physics.

When the physical laboratory is on the ground-floor, ordinary wooden tables may be conveniently carried on brick piers, 9 in. or 14 in. square, carrying stone caps only 6 in. square, which project through the floor without touching it, and form supports for the table legs. The brick piers carrying the tables should stand on foundations independent of those of the dwarf walls which carry the floor joists.

When the physical laboratory is on one of the upper floors, the table may be rendered to a certain extent independent of the floors by the contrivance adopted at the Cavendish Laboratory. Here corbels are fixed in the walls 1 ft. below the ceiling, and on these rest beams, upon which are fastened blocks, which project through the ceiling and floor to the floor-level of the room above. These blocks support the table-legs, which are thus carried from the walls of the building, but as the floors are carried from the same walls, it is obvious that the tables will not be free from vibrations which can be transmitted through a short length of wall. Tables mounted in this way are, however, immeasurably superior to tables simply resting on a wooden floor, and are sufficiently good for nearly all purposes, provided that the blocks on which the table-legs stand remain clear of the floor; but there is a great tendency for these blocks to twist and come in contact with the floor on one side, in which case the whole arrangement becomes practically worthless.

In the physical laboratory there should be at least one stone slab about 3 ft. square placed at the floor-level, but resting on a foundation of its own, so that a kathetometer or other instrument may be placed upon it and may be unaffected even by the movements of the observer himself. If it is possible to arrange trap-doors in the floors above the physical laboratory, so that wires or threads may be suspended freely from the roof of the building, such contrivances will frequently be found useful; but where this is not possible, supports should be arranged in accessible positions as high above the floor as may be, either by means of cantilevers fixed to the walls by socket-screws or otherwise, or else by beams carried across from wall to wall.

It is generally best to place the chemical laboratory on the uppermost floor, constructing it with an open roof, so as to give as much air space as possible. It is unnecessary here to enter into the details of the benches in the chemical laboratory, as full descriptions of many forms of benches have been published, notably by Mr. Robins, in his work on "Technical Schools and Colleges," which is, so far as I know, unique, and is certainly invaluable. There are, however, a few points in connexion with the fittings of the chemical laboratory to which attention may be directed, and in the first place it is desirable that the use of lead should be avoided as far as possible in the drainage of the benches. The benches themselves are best constructed about 5 ft. wide, and of length determined by the dimensions of the laboratory, but so arranged as to give not less than 3 ft. 6 in. to a junior student, and not more than 4 ft. 6 in. to a senior student. The depth of the cupboards and drawers from back to front is such as to leave a space in the centre of the bench running throughout its whole length of sufficient width for a man to pass through. This space serves to carry the gas and water pipes and the drainage trough. The

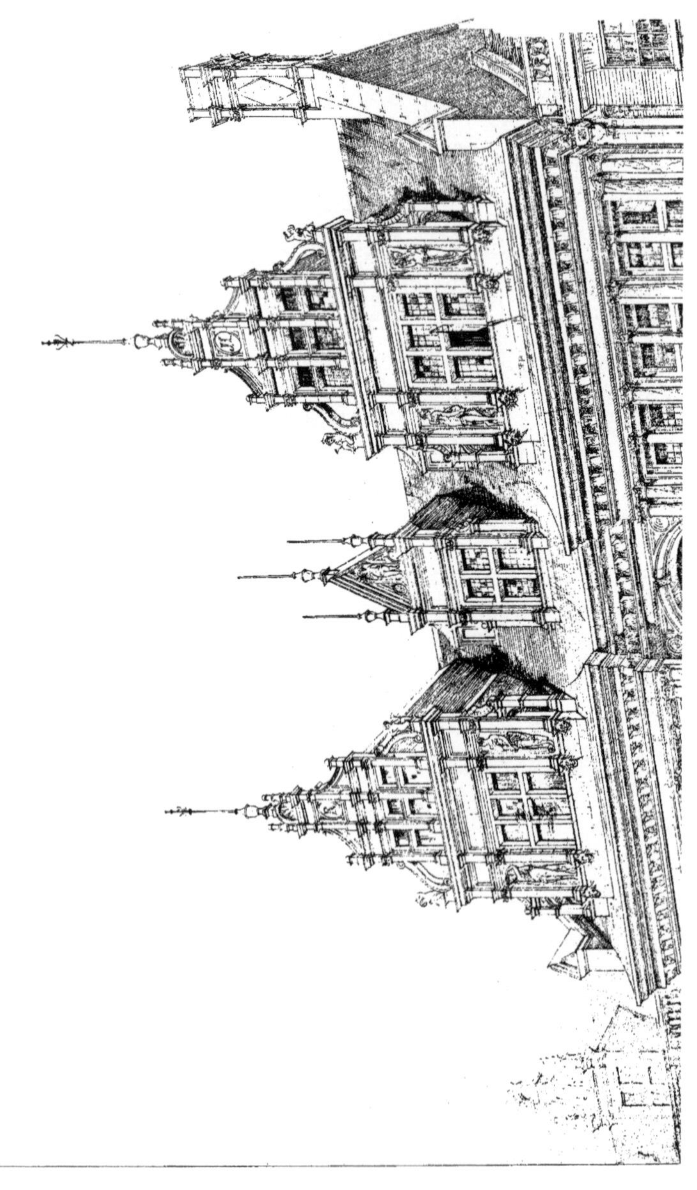

Royal Academy Gold Medal and Travelling Studentship, 1892.

DESIGN FOR A LARGE TOWN MANSION.—BY MR. A. H. HART, A.R.I.B.A.
PERSPECTIVE VIEW OF FRONT.

GROUND PLAN.

Wayside Notes in East Anglia

by

John Shewell Corder

PHOTO-LITHO SPRAGUE & Cº 4 & 5, EAST HARDING STREET, FETTER LANE, E.C.

SCALE OF FEET.

10 5 0 10 20 30 40 50.

BALL ROOM

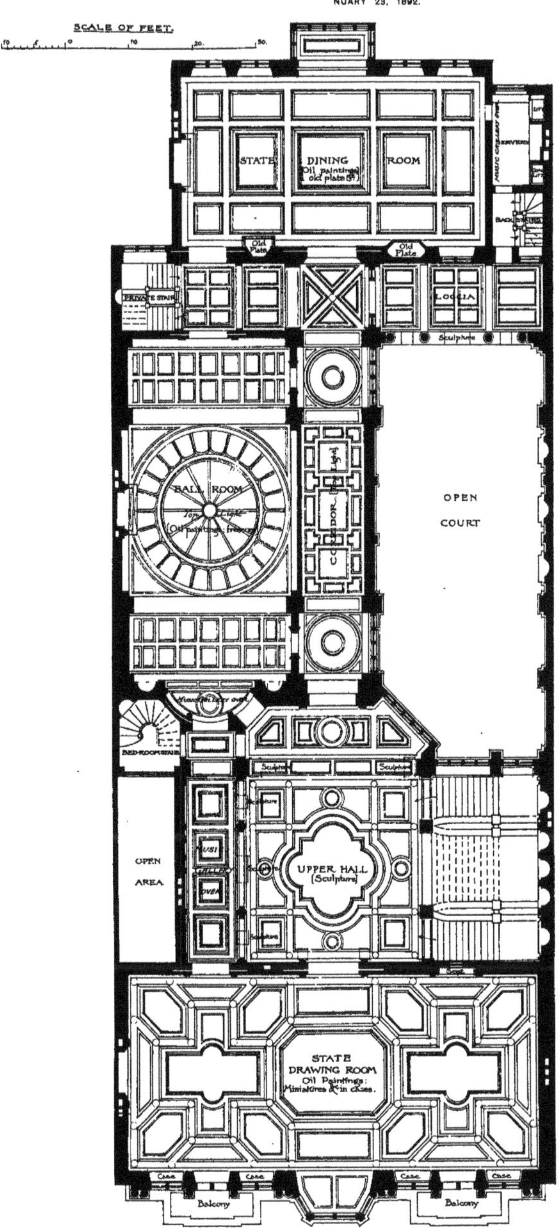

PHOTO-LITHO SPRAGUE & CO. 4 & 5, EAST HARDING STREET, FETTER LANE, E.C.

DESIGN FOR A LARGE TOWN MANSION.—By Mr. A. H. Hart, A.R.I.B.A.
FIRST FLOOR PLAN.

oyal Academy Gold Medal and Travelling Studentship, 1892.

DESIGN FOR A PROPOSED CHURCH: EAST ELEVATION.—By Mr. J. E. Newberry, A.R.I.B.A.

Royal Academy Exhibition, 1891.

latter may be made of 1 in. or 1½ in. red deal boards, jointed so as to form a V trough about 6 in. in depth. The trough is thoroughly caulked with a mixture of pitch and tar, put on hot, and this trough serves to collect the drainage from the sinks and deliver it into a sludge-box or small settling-tank, through an overflow on one side. The overflow from the sludge-box is delivered into a similar trough laid in a chase in the floor, which conveys it to the down-comer outside the wall. In place of V troughs, semi-circular troughs cut from the solid in red deal may be employed. These semi-circular troughs are largely used in chemical works, and avoid the joint of the V trough. For the down-comer best stoneware pipes, salt glazed, may be employed, but cast-iron pipes coated with preservative compound will last a very long time, and some experiments will probably be made shortly upon the suitability of enamelled cast-iron pipes for this purpose. Rectangular troughs have no advantage over V troughs, and only offer a much larger surface for the acid liquids to act upon. The chases in the floor, which may carry gas-pipes, water-pipes, pipes for distilled water, compressed air for the blowpipe, and vacuum for filtration purposes, in addition to the drainage troughs, should admit of being opened throughout their whole length for the purpose of inspection.

Fume-closets are generally more conveniently placed upon the walls than upon the working benches, and this arrangement simplifies the removal of the fumes without incommoding the laboratory with exhaust-pipes to the ventilating shafts. Special fume-closets should be provided in the walls for the conduct of evaporations which occupy much time, and in these closets both gas and steam should be available for heating purposes. The water-supply to the benches should be at a low pressure. Ten pounds on the square inch is more than sufficient, and ⅜ in. taps are quite large enough.

In many laboratories it is necessary that the same bench should be used by two different students at different times. In such cases the bottle-racks should be sufficiently large to accomodate two sets of re-agents, and each set should be provided with a locking-bar or frame, so as to be available to only one student, who will then be solely responsible for their purity. When three or more students are obliged to use the same bench, personal responsibility fot the purity of the re-agents must be sacrificed.

The balance-room is an essential appendage to the chemical laboratory, and, while readily accessible therefrom, care should be taken that it does not communicate directly therewith. The chemical laboratory and the balance-room will generally be on the first or second floor, and in that case the balances should be carried on the walls by brackets. If a separate sulphuretted hydrogen chamber is provided, it should be as far as possible from the balance-room.

A separate room should, if practicable, be set apart for gas analysis and for other operations which require the use of considerable quantities of mercury. The floor of this room should be of asphalte, in which a shallow channel of circular or other convenient form is made for the purpose of collecting any mercury which may be spilled and conveying it to an iron receptacle, whence it is collected and redistilled for future use. When mercury is spilled on a wooden floor, unless the joints are exceptionally close, a very large portion is lost and accumulates between floors and ceilings.

It will generally happen that the same lecture-room will have to be used by several departments, but it is very desirable that separate lecture-rooms should be provided for the departments of physics and chemistry, though each of these rooms may be used for lectures on any other subjects. For lectures on chemistry and physics a large amount of apparatus is frequently required, and sometimes it is desirable that the same apparatus should remain properly adjusted on the lecture able for several lectures in succession. This notably the case with galvanometers and ectrometers, some of which require much me for their adjustment. Such apparatus ould not have to be disturbed in order to ake provision for a lecture on a purely erary subject or one which required only the agic-lantern or diagrams for its illustration or ly a comparatively small amount of lecture-ble apparatus. But if the same lecture-room s to be used both for chemistry and physics a eat and wasteful expenditure of labour will be incurred in removing the apparatus after each lecture.

The engineering laboratory and the principal workshops must be on the ground, and, when land is available, they are best placed in a one-story building, with a "ridge and furrow" roof, separate from the main building, but communicating directly with it. When it is necessary to place the engineering laboratory and workshops on the ground floor of the principal building, the floor above should be of concrete, and the principal shafting should be carried on A frames, or other supports independent of the structure of the building.

The engineers' drawing office should be readily accessible from the workshops, so that the superintendent of the department may be easily able to supervise both, as it will not generally be possible, or even desirable, to employ separate staffs of teachers for the drawing office and workshops, though in commercial works the drawing office staff is clearly differentiated from the shop foremen and managers.

The biological department may with advantage be located on the highest floor, so as to command the best possible light and ventilation. A good range of windows on the north side coming within 3 ft. of the ground is, perhaps, the chief desideratum in a biological laboratory. Sinks, a good water-supply, and tables which are strong enough not to yield to the pressure of the hand, because perfect steadiness is required for microscope work, with gas connexions for table-lamps on every table, are also important desiderata.

The uppermost story is also specially fitted to meet the requirements of the department of fine art, but of these requirements it is unnecessary for me to speak, inasmuch as every architect is necessarily thoroughly conversant with them. I will only point out that an open Mansard roof constructed with steel principals, which are stiffened by gusset stays so as to avoid the necessity for tie-bars, which might throw a shadow on a cart, seem most suitable for roof construction in this department.

Lastly, with regard to the general arrangements of the building:—

A corridor of ample width should be carried on the ground floor throughout the whole length of the building, but in many cases through corridors will not be necessary on all the floors, provided that there are sufficient staircases to allow ready access to each department. It is difficult to carry corridors through a building on every floor without interfering with the access of light to the rooms, and in order to permit of the lighting of the rooms from both sides it is sometimes worth while to dispense with the through communication. In the College at Newcastle the first and second floor corridors extend for only one-quarter of the length of the building, so that the chemical laboratory and adjoining rooms, the physical lecture theatre, the apparatus rooms, the first-floor physical laboratory, and the optical laboratory occupy the whole width of the building, while the through corridor on the ground floor is built like the side aisle of a church as an annexe to the main building, but the roof being a lead flat and the corridor only 9 ft. high, while the ground-floor rooms are 16 ft. 6 in. high, it has been possible to construct windows above the roof of the corridor to afford a cross light to the ground-floor rooms.

Where steam power is required in the workshops or laboratories, it is most economical to employ low-pressure steam for the heating of the building, and to adopt engines which admit of efficient working with a back pressure of four or five pounds per square inch on the exhaust, so as to enable the heating-pipes of the building to be employed as a surface condenser. If the building is lighted by electricity, the utilisation of the exhaust steam becomes an important consideration, as when the whole of the building is lighted, the exhaust steam from the electric light engines is about sufficient for the heating on a very cold day. For example, a room of a floor area of 1,200 square ft., and 16 ft. in height, may be very brilliantly lighted with high efficiency lamps, by the expenditure of two electrical horse-power. To develop this amount of power by non-condensing engines of twenty or thirty horse-power, and of moderate efficiency, will require about 75 lbs. of steam per hour. A much greater efficiency may, of course, be obtained with larger engines, or with high-speed engines coupled directly to the dynamos, and specially constructed for electric lighting. Now, 75 lbs. of exhaust steam in condensing and cooling in the pipes will give about 40,000 pound-centigrade units of heat, and this will raise about 10,000 lbs. of air through 16 deg. C. This quantity of air is equivalent to 130,000 cubic feet, and the capacity of the room being only 19,200 cubic feet, the air might be changed about seven times in an hour, which is more than twice the frequency required for class purposes. The ordinary allowance of electric light is one 60-watt lamp for 64 square feet of floor, reducing the quantity of steam for the room mentioned to rather less than 60 lbs. per hour. As the corridors and some other parts of the building do not require to be illuminated as brilliantly as the class-rooms, and as the ventilation will be continued in many of the rooms when the lights are not burning, it will be found that if boilers are laid down for the supply of the electric lighting engines they will suffice and not be much too large for the heating of the building in cold weather. When the engines are not running, the heating coils will, of course, be supplied directly from the boilers through a reducing value.

If it is necessary that any section of the building should be heated by a low pressure hot water system, and if steam boilers are provided for the electric lighting and steam heating of the remainder of the building, it seems undesirable that a special boiler fire should be kept up for the one section, especially if that section of the building to be heated by hot water is remote from the boiler-room. In this case the hot water circulation may be maintained by a coil of steam-pipe carried through a tank to which the hot water circulating pipes are connected, the tank being placed, like a circulating boiler, at the lowest level available, and the steam supplied from the main boilers and drained back to the hot well.

For the conduct of steam-pipes, return hot-water pipes, gas-pipes, cold-water pipes, electrical conductors, and, with some systems of ventilation, of the exhaust air-shaft, it is desirable that a subway, or basement corridor, should be constructed throughout the length of the building. From this corridor access may be obtained to the space beneath the floors of all ground-floor rooms whose floors are boarded in the ordinary way.

The question of ventilation has already been alluded to in relation to the heating, as the two subjects are inseparably connected. It has been pointed out by Professor O. J. Lodge, and it is a matter of common experience, that when the air is warmer than the walls or other objects in the room there is a tendency for the dust in the air to be deposited on the colder surfaces, and this is generally associated with an unpleasant feeling of "stuffiness." Hence heating by heated air is a dirty method unless steps are taken to cleanse the air before it enters the rooms. This may be done to some extent by causing it to pass through a sheet of water produced by a "spreader," but the method is somewhat expensive. Any attempt at filtering the air through wool or other material introduces an amount of resistance to the current which is practically fatal. On the other hand, if the incoming air is cold, and the room heated only by radiation from the steam-pipes, it is very difficult to avoid currents of cold air, with the practical certainty that the inlets will be closed by the persons occupying the rooms. A compromise between the two methods leads in some cases to satisfactory results. By boxing-in one-half of the steam-pipes with wooden casing, and allowing air to enter through the walls beneath the windows, and to pass over the hot pipes, and thence diffuse through the room, the whole of the entering air may be suitably warmed, while one-half of the steam-pipes remains for the heating of the walls and furniture by radiation.

If radiators, instead of steam-pipes, are used in the best rooms, care should be taken in selecting the type of radiator to see that the castings, if such be employed, are so designed that it is impossible for unequal heating to cause strains of such a nature as to produce fracture of the casting. If two terminals are connected by three or more tubes forming one casting, it is possible to arrange such a distribution of temperature as to necessitate the fracture of at least one of the tubes. If the castings are held together by light wrought-iron ties which are external to the steam-tubes, so that their temperature is raised very slowly. the ties are liable to be strained beyond their elastic limits during the rapid heating of the castings, and to require frequent screwing-up in order to keep the radiators steam-tight. There are types of radiators in the market which avoid all these difficulties.

With regard to the removal of the exhaust-air, there is little doubt that mechanical ventilation is most effective, and air-propellers of the Blackman type, driven by a gas-engine or electric motor, have proved very successful, even when the air has had to be drawn through a couple of hundred feet of tubes. The propeller may be inserted in a wall at the top of the principal staircase, or in some other convenient position, and the corridors may be used as air-ways, the air entering the rooms as above described, and passing through the opposite walls into the corridor. The system, perhaps, offers the least resistance to the air-currents, and a large propeller driven at a comparatively slow speed will do its work without noise or vibration. An electric motor may be directly coupled with the fan, whatever its position, or the fan may, itself, be wound as a motor, but if a gas-engine is employed, the power should be transmitted by a belt outside the building. It is clear, however, that the chemical laboratory, or any other rooms in which noxious fumes are produced, must be cut off from this general system of ventilation, and be treated specially. If it can be arranged to erect the boiler-chimney-shaft within a few feet of the chemical laboratory, the exhaust from the fume-closets, as well as the general ventilation of the laboratory, may be carried into the shaft, at the cost of somewhat reducing the steaming power of the boilers. It is very undesirable that any attempt should be made to carry the whole exhaust from the building into the boiler-shaft. If the chimney-shaft is not available for the chemical laboratory, it is best to provide a special fan for the exhaust of the fume closets and the laboratory generally, conducting the air to the fan along a system of carefully-constructed tubes. In small laboratories the general ventilation may be effected by ventilators in the roof, and the exhaust of the fume closets may be carried out by ordinary chimney-flues, in which an upward current is maintained by a gas-burner; but when it can be employed the fan gives by much the best results.

It should always be borne in mind that any system of air conduits will serve also as tubes for the transmission of sound, so that rooms, like workshops, in which noisy operations are carried on, should be provided with separate ventilation. It must also be noticed that when a fan is driven at sufficient speed to exhaust through a great length of narrow tubes, it will necessarily be noisy, and the sound will be carried to every room which communicates with the ventilating system.

Where rooms of different capacity communicate through independent tubes of different lengths, with the same exhaust chamber, the diameter of the tubes should be proportional to the fifth root of the square of the quantity of air to be removed per hour, and to the fifth root of the length of the tube.

The great expense incident to efficient ventilation lies in the heat required to raise the temperature of the entering air in very cold weather. For example, suppose a building to contain 1,000,000 cubic feet of air, and this is to be renewed only once an hour on the average of the whole building, and that the entering air must be heated through 27 deg. F., or 15 deg. C. The weight of 1,000,000 cubic feet of air will be about 77,000 lbs., and its specific heat being ·24, the number of heat units required to raise this quantity of air through 15 deg. C. is 277,200 lbs.,—centigrade units. This will involve the condensation of 504 lbs. of dry steam, and the combustion of about 60 lbs. of coal; but this allows nothing for the cooling of the air within the building, which in a brick or stone building takes place mainly through the windows.

If we adopt the usually-accepted principle that the amount of carbon di-oxide in the air should not be allowed to exceed ·06 per cent., and that the supply of fresh air should, therefore, be at the rate of about 3,000 cubic feet per hour for each individual, and three times that amount for each ordinary gas-burner (but nothing for electric lights), we find that for 1,000 persons in a building lighted by 333 gas-burners 6,000,000 cubic feet of air per hour will be required, necessitating the combustion on a very cold day of 360 lbs. of coal per hour. If electric light were substituted, current for 333 sixteen-candle lamps would require only 120 lbs. of coal per hour for its production, but if the gas-burners are so arranged that the products of combustion escape immediately, there can be no need for the double supply of air, and if the products of combustion mix with the air they will supply more than half the heat required to warm it.

In the above sketch, arrangements have been suggested suitable for a building of considerable size, possessing, for instance, a capacity of 1,000,000 cubic feet. In the case of small schools, the same guiding principles may be adopted, though it will be impossible to attain the same degree of specialisation in the appropriation of the rooms. At the Royal Grammar School, Newcastle-upon-Tyne (Mr. R. J. Leeson, of Newcastle, architect), a stone building which had formerly been used as an elementary school became available for the departments of chemistry and physics. The principal school-room measured internally 50 ft. by 30 ft., and the infants' school-room 30 ft. by 20 ft. In addition to these rooms there was a small master's room. When a matchboard ceiling was removed there was an open roof with the ridge about 30 ft. from the floor, and a large lantern with louvres for ventilation. Skylights were inserted on the north side of the roof, and plate glass windows were substituted for the wooden frames, and small diamond panes which had previously done their best, by accumulating dust, to obstruct the light. The floor was about 2 ft. above the level of the ground outside, and there was a clear space beneath the floor about 4 ft. in height. In the large room there were two fireplaces with open chimneys, and one in the small room. The open fires were replaced by "tortoise" stoves, and the open chimney-breasts closed by sheet iron. The chimneys then served both for the stoves and for the fume-closets.

The infants' room was made to serve the double purpose of balance room and physical laboratory. Around three sides of the room an ash table was suspended from the walls on brackets similar to those previously described, while a large and heavy table, measuring 10 ft. by 5 ft., was placed in the centre of the room, and carried on brick piers, whose stone caps were finished off level with the floor. The large room was divided into two by a pitch-pine partition. The smaller portion, measuring 30 ft. by 22 ft., was fitted up as a lecture room, capable of accommodating sixty boys; the larger, measuring 34 ft. by 30 ft., was fitted as a chemical laboratory. Two benches, each 28 ft. in length, occupied the centre portion of the laboratory, and afforded accommodation for thirty-two boys working at one time, while tables were provided along the side walls to supplement the accommodation afforded by the benches. The sinks drained directly into a V trough, coated with pitch, and suspended by iron ties from the joists beneath each bench. One of the two troughs was continued under the floor of the lecture room to take the drainage from the lecture table. The two troughs discharged into a third trough, which crossed their ends at right-angles, and carried the drainage through a hole in the front wall and discharged it over an open gulley of glazed stoneware. A number of Tobin's pipes, 1 ft. square and 8 ft. in height, served for the access of fresh air.

Where the students are mostly adults, 3 ft. is a convenient height for laboratory benches and tables, and 2 ft. 9 in. or 2 ft. 10 in. in the case of school laboratories.

It is impossible in a paper of this description to enter into the arrangements which must be made in order to provide for the teaching of special local industries. Where such teaching is necessary, the first thing to be done is to acquaint oneself with the machinery and methods employed in the factories or workshops where the particular trade is practised, and then to learn precisely the extent to which these appliances should be introduced into the technical school. When spinning and weaving are taught, the technical school is to a very great extent simply a model factory or weaving-shed; but in most cases, it is the function of the technical school to provide those facilities for instruction and experimental investigation which are not to be found in the workshop; and it is comparatively seldom that the equipment of the factory requires to be reduplicated in the technical school.

In teaching purely technological subjects, the classes for which consist wholly of members of one particular trade, it is most important that the instruction should be under the general direction of a committee consisting wholly of members of that trade—masters, foremen, and operatives being all duly represented. Such a committee will do more to inspire confidence among apprentices and workmen in the practical character of the teaching than the most distinguished governing body; and there is no danger that under such direction the teaching will sink to pure empiricism if the teachers on the permanent staff of the institution are men of the right stamp.

[The paper was illustrated by working drawings and tracings of the existing and some of the proposed buildings of the Durham College of Science, prepared by Mr. R. J. Johnson and Mr. F. W. Rich, the architects, to whom the author tendered his acknowledgments.]

A brief discussion ensued as to various matters of detail, the members taking part in the discussion being Mr. Paul Waterhouse, Mr. C. H. Brodie, Mr. W. J. H. Leverton, Mr. W. H. White, and Mr. E. Sim. Professor Garnett having replied to several questions which were asked, the proceedings terminated.

THE LONDON COUNTY COUNCIL.

THE first meeting of this Council since the Christmas vacation was held on Tuesday afternoon last, the Chairman, Sir John Lubbock, presiding, but, for the reason hereafter mentioned, its sitting was a short one.

Vote of Condolence with the Royal Family—On the motion of the Chairman, a vote of condolence with the Royal Family on the death of the Duke of Clarence was agreed to unanimously, and it was further resolved to take only non-contentious business, and to adjourn early.

The London Water Question.—The Chairman announced that he had received the following important letter from the President of the Local Government Board:—

"Local Government Board, Whitehall, S.W., Jan. 13.

SIR,—Referring to the correspondence which has taken place between the London County Council and her Majesty's Government, I have to intimate to you for the information of the Council that her Majesty's Government have resolved to advise the appointment of a Royal Commission to inquire,—'Whether, taking into consideration the growth in the population of the metropolis, and the districts within the limits of the metropolitan water companies, and also the needs of the localities not supplied by any metropolitan company, but within the watersheds of the Thames and the Lea, the present sources of supply of these companies are adequate in quantity and quality, and, if inadequate, whether such supply as may be required can be obtained within the watersheds referred to, having due regard to the claims of the districts outside the metropolis, but within these watersheds, or will have to be obtained outside the watersheds of the Thames and the Lea.'

I remain, Sir, your obedient servant,
CHARLES T. RITCHIE.

To the Right Hon. Sir John Lubbock, Bart., M.P., Chairman, London County Council."

The proposal contained in the letter, said Sir John Lubbock, was substantially in accordance with the suggestion made to the Government by the Council, and he was sure that the decision of the Government must be satisfactory to them all.

The letter was ordered to be recorded on the minutes, and was referred to the Special Committee on Water Supply.

Date of the First Meeting of the New Council.—The General Purposes Committee reported as follows:—

"In our report to the Council of the 1st of December we pointed out that by the County Council Elections Act, 1891, the Council may fix the day and hour for the statutory meeting at which the Chairman and Aldermen of the new Council are to be elected.* Having considered the matter, we have come to the conclusion that Tuesday, the 15th day of March, will be the earliest convenient day for the meeting. We recommend:—

'That Tuesday, the 15th day of March next, at 3 o'clock, be fixed as the day and hour for the statutory meeting at which the Chairman and Aldermen of the new Council are to be elected.'"

This was unanimously agreed to.

Tenders: Return of Deposits of Money.—The General Purposes Committee's Report also con-

* As we have already announced, the date of the election of the new Council itself has been fixed to take place on Saturday, March 5.

tained the following paragraph and recommendation, which were agreed to:—

"The Main Drainage Committee has represented to us that it would be desirable that some general order should be made with reference to the return of the deposits of money made by persons applying for specifications and drawings of an advertised work. In many cases the money deposited is returned to persons who subsequently send in *bonâ-fide* tenders, but in some case of large works, in connection with which great expense has been incurred in the preparation of drawings, it has been the practice to retain the amounts deposited. We think that this variation in practice should not continue, and that in all cases money so deposited should be returned to persons who send in *bonâ-fide* tenders. We accordingly recommend—

"That the following be a standing order of the Council,—The money deposited with the Council by persons who apply for specifications and drawings of an advertised work shall afterwards be returned to those who shall have sent in *bonâ-fide* tenders.'"

Emanuel Hospital, Westminster.—The Corporate Property, Charities, and Endowments Committee presented the following report on the proposed removal of this building:—

"This foundation has recently been the subject of a special inquiry held by Mr. Clabon, on behalf of the Attorney-General, with a view to ascertain the wishes of the inhabitants on the question which has been raised whether the site of the hospital should or should not be sold; and, at our request, a gentleman from the Solicitor's department attended the inquiry to watch the proceedings on behalf of the ratepayers.

The charity was founded in the time of Queen Elizabeth, and the hospital buildings erected shortly after its foundation are still standing, and are still used as almshouses. It appears, however, that the income of the endowment has largely fallen off, and is not likely to recover itself. The present annual income of 620*l.* is all that is applicable to the hospital (as distinguished from the schools, with which we do not now concern ourselves), and this is found insufficient to carry on the work of the charity; several of the rooms are in consequence unoccupied, and the property is in a state of dilapidation. The site, however, is situate in close proximity to Victoria-street, and is now a very valuable one, and if it were sold a large sum might be expected to be applicable, either for the establishment of the hospital elsewhere, or for some alternative scheme.

We are of opinion that the site of the hospital should be sold, and that the proceeds should be devoted to out-pensions for the aged instead of the hospital being erected elsewhere. We think that the views of the Council should be submitted to Mr. Clabon, with a view to his transmitting them with his report to the Attorney-General, and he has indicated his willingness to do this.

We therefore recommend:—

'That the Council do approve of the proposal to sell the site of the hospital, and that the Clerk be instructed to inform the Attorney-General (through Mr. Clabon) and the Charity Commissioners to that effect, and also to intimate that in the opinion of the Council the proceeds of such sale should be devoted to out-pensions for the aged instead of re-erecting the hospital elsewhere.'"

On the motion that this recommendation be agreed to, Mr. Acworth said he should oppose the proposal strongly, as its adoption would have the effect, without doubt, of covering what was now for a great part virtually an open-space, surrounded by low buildings, with lofty blocks of flats or other buildings.

As the recommendation was thus opposed, its consideration stood adjourned.

After transacting some other business, the Council adjourned at 10 minutes to 4 o'clock.

DECORATIVE WORK.—In the little R.C. Church of St. Joseph, at Christchurch, in Hampshire, two designs, executed in the "Curvo Arras" method, were unveiled for the first time on Christmas Day. The panels (each 100 in. by 34 in.) are adapted to their position on either side of the chancel arch, with lines that harmonise with the building. The subject is the Annunciation. A ray of light crosses from the upper left-hand corner of one to the lower right-hand corner of the other. In this ray, on the left panel, the Archangel Gabriel is kneeling, in a dalmatica of primrose hue with apparels and orphreys of blue embroidered on silver. He bears a lily sceptre set with sapphires. On the other panel, the Virgin sits on a throne. On the footstool beneath her feet is brocaded the dragon crushed and dead. Behind her, bearing aloft a crown of fleur de lys above her head, the Archangels Michael and Raphael float in the air. The whole design is encrusted with gems, and silver, and gold, like the initials of an antique missal.

LIVERPOOL ENGINEERING SOCIETY.—The sixth ordinary meeting of the present session was held at the Royal Institution, on Wednesday evening, January 13, Mr. F. Hudleston, Assoc. M. Inst. C.E., occupying the chair. Mr. A. J. Maginnis, M. Inst. N. A., read a paper entitled "Transatlantic Lines and Steamships, No. 2."

Correspondence.

To the Editor of THE BUILDER.

THE NEW BUILDING BY-LAWS FOR LONDON.

SIR,—It would be well that the new By-laws should be carefully read by everyone who has to do with building works in the county of London. It sometimes seems as if some people do not read their *Builder*, as they should properly, from first page to last every week, and people of that sort may remain ignorant of the new things in the By-laws for a long time, and give to themselves and to others very much trouble in consequence.

I would suggest that the London County Council should make a special effort to bring the By-laws well under people's attention. A letter might be sent, pointing out the novelties, copies of the By-laws being enclosed with the letter. If every architect, surveyor, house agent, master bricklayer, carpenter, and plasterer in London was reached in that way, a good beginning would be made. The expenditure would be very small, and the saving to the community, probably, a thousandfold at least.

Contractors should supply foremen, sub-contractors, &c., with copies of the By-laws. The R.I.B.A. might lay in a small store, and supply copies to members at, say, a shilling for twelve, for distribution to clerks of works, hanging-up in offices, &c.

A DISTRICT SURVEYOR.

FLOORING-BOARDS ON CONCRETE.

SIR,—In some workmen's dwellings, I am anxious to lay ordinary deal flooring tongued, directly on concrete, composed of coke breeze and Portland cement, to which the flooring would be nailed.

Will any of your readers kindly state their experience of floors so laid? Are the boards liable to "cockle" or to decay more rapidly than if laid on joists? If they are, what is the best means of getting over these objections? Block flooring would be too expensive.

SURVEYOR.

11, *Leinster-street, Dublin.*

BOLSOVER COLLIERY COMPETITION.

SIR,—I wrote for the particulars of the above competition, and duly received a copy of the same from a Mr. Houfton.

It may interest your readers to know that, on perusing the requirements, I found that a sum of 40*l.* was offered for the best set of plans for seven private houses, schools for 600 children, a workmen's club, a hospital, and a co-operative stores.

I need hardly say that I returned Mr. Houfton his particulars, and at the same time expressed a hope that no one in the profession would find it worth while to undertake this exceptional amount and charming variety of work, for the ridiculous sum offered as first prize by the Bolsover Colliery Company.

H. G.

The Student's Column.

WARMING BUILDINGS BY HOT WATER.

IV.

DISPOSITION OF PIPES IN AND NEAR BOILER.

IT will be found that in describing different phenomena, reference may be made more often to horticultural than to building works. The reason for this is that minor points and features of no great moment do not need the consideration in the latter that they do in the former undertakings, with the low power of circulation that is the prominent feature; consequently, unless the question touched upon is of some importance, it may probably be spoken of as applying to horticultural works only. Of course, all methods and works will be treated as fully as possible; but the two descriptions of works now being spoken of cannot well be treated together, on account of the vast difference the speed of circulation in each makes. In speaking of air dislodgment, and some appliances, &c., the two subjects need no separation, but otherwise than this, they will be dealt with distinctly, and horticultural works had better be taken first.

The preceding papers have shown the necessity of terminating the two different services,—that is, the flow and the return,—at different levels in the boiler: the flow the highest, and acting as an outlet for the heated water; the return at the lowest point, being an inlet for the cold or cooler water. The most desirable point for the flow-pipe to be connected is at the crown of the boiler, the very highest point on the top, this being conducive to the free and unimpeded escape of the outgoing water, and also permitting of the free exit of air. Fig. 7 shows in front elevation the flow-pipe situated upon the apex of a saddle-boiler,—its correct position.

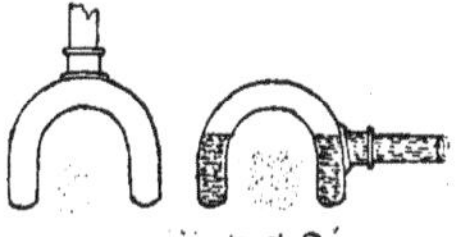

FIG. 7. FIG. 8.

If we carried the flow-pipe from the side of a boiler, the fact of its starting in a horizontal direction would not suffice to destroy the circulation (provided the return-pipe entered at a still lower point, and other features were correct), but it would leave no means for the air to escape from the upper part of the boiler, as fig. 8. This would cause not only inefficient results, but the destruction of the boiler by the action of the fire on the unprotected boiler-plate. The inflow of water when the apparatus was charged would not expel the air, as might possibly be supposed; and even if it did, there is the perpetual absorption and expulsion of air by water, in the cooling and heating processes, to be guarded against. When the flow-pipe starts from the side of a boiler, as is most usually the case with small boilers, and also with the Loughborough pattern boiler, it has of necessity to be taken from the extreme highest point to avoid this trouble. A collection of air at any point in an apparatus will nearly always ruin its efficiency.

If there were two or more flow-pipes proceeding from a boiler, as is usually the case with the larger sizes, it would not matter if any were connected at lower points, provided one started from the top. One pipe would quite overcome the air-collection difficulty, but it is better for general purposes to take all flow-pipes from the top if anyway possible, more especially in large works. However favourable general conditions may be to an effective circulation, it is not well to do anything opposed to efficiency if it can be avoided.

In ordering boilers, the desired number, sizes, and positions of the pipe connexions are usually indicated, and so furnished and fitted by the maker. In this case no fear need be experienced of the connexions being wrongly made; and, as a rule, the fittings for connecting cast-iron pipes to boilers cannot very well be wrongly attached. If, however, it is proposed to use wrought-iron pipes, as is nearly always the case in building works, the most the maker generally does, unless otherwise instructed, is to drill and tap (screw) holes in the boiler of a suitable size for the pipe in question. If this be so, there is the possibility of the fitter screwing his flow-pipes right through the substance of the boiler, so that it projects inside.

If this projection occurs, it becomes impossible to fill the boiler quite full, as the water cannot rise above the end of this pipe, as fig. 9. This would be rather evidence of bad work than otherwise, and if there be the least likelihood of its occurring, it is better to have a flange affixed for the flow-pipe to be connected into. With a flange we may screw the pipe in about ½ in. without causing the trouble referred to.

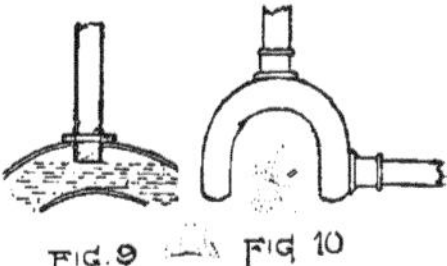

FIG. 9. FIG. 10.

With the return-pipe we have practically none of the details to consider that are so important with the flow. The chief point is to give it the lowest possible position, and, when convenient, as far removed from the flow as possible. The return can rarely ever be brought vertically into the boiler, as the present forms of boilers, almost without exception, necessitate its entering at the side. With the saddle-boiler it would enter as fig. 10, but where circumstances and the size of the apparatus are favourable, it is a good plan to have a return entering on each side (there are commonly two returns and one flow connected to the boiler, as will be seen later). When the boiler has but one return, as illustrated, it causes, by the action of the water, the greatest deposit to accumulate in the bottom of the boiler on the opposite side, instead of being more equally distributed. This leads to an early fracture of the boiler at this point, unless it is cleaned out with regularity. If there be two returns, one on each side, the deposit does not so readily collect at one point, and this tends to lengthen the life of the boiler.

There is no question of air dispersion, or of freedom in the action of convection currents, to be considered in the connexion of the return pipe to the boiler. It is sufficient that it should be properly connected, and cause no obstruction to the regular passage of water through it.

It is usual when carrying out these works to arrange for the flow-pipe or pipes to be carried above the returns; that is, the two pipes are run one above the other, the flow uppermost, and the return beneath. This applies whether there be but two pipes or a number, and it also applies whether the pipes be mains or branch services. The regularity of this practice induces many people to think that the arrangement is necessary to effect the proper circulation of the water. This, however, is not the case,—it is merely a practice, and nothing more, but, of course, it is based upon getting the best results, and being a method that prevents doubt and confusion when erecting new or re-arranging old works.

If it would prove a convenience there is not the slightest objection to carrying the flow and return side by side, and this is usually done when two pipes are run in a channel (with grating over), this arrangement permitting of the channel being shallow, and both pipes are effective in distributing heat. They would not be so effective if one pipe was below the other in a trench, as the lower would be interfered with by the confinement. If, also, it ever became necessary to reverse the usual position of the pipes, and carry the flow beneath the return, it would not destroy efficiency, provided the connexions at the boiler were correct; as fig. 11 for instance. The customary arrangement is as fig. 12.

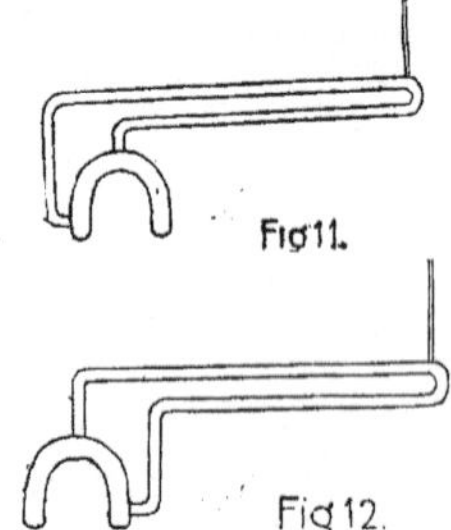

Fig 11.

Fig 12.

The object in showing this is to do away with the general idea that the least departure from the ordinary state of things will ruin the undertaking. In conducting experiments with the little glass apparatus already referred to, there will be found a real difficulty in preventing the water circulating, however oddly the pipes may be carried, provided there is free escape for the air. It will be found that an accumulation of air at some point is the commonest difficulty to overcome, and, if this can be avoided, then a circulatory motion is sure to set up in the water. In experimenting with unusual arrangements of the pipes, the chief difficulties, after the air question is settled, will be the liability of a reversed circulation, or perhaps a circulation in the right direction, but too sluggish to be of service if the works be extensive. As a rule, however, for ordinary requitements, it can be arranged for the pipes to be carried according to the usual method.

OBITUARY.

MR. ALFRED PORTER, F.R.I.B.A.—We regret to hear of the death, on the 14th inst., of Mr. Alfred Porter, F.R.I.B.A., aged fifty-five. He became an Associate of the Institute in 1856, and a Fellow in 1860.

MR. THOMAS MORGAN, F.S.A., died on the 13th inst. at his residence, Hillside-house, Streatham, Surrey, at the age of seventy-two. For a considerable time he was a Vice-president of the British Archæological Association, and for fifteen years was their honorary treasurer. During his connexion with the Association he contributed, as the *Times* says, "many scholarly and learned papers, chiefly relating to his favourite subject, Roman archæology. In 1886 he published his 'Romano-British Mosaic Pavements,' which contained a history of their discovery and a record and interpretation of their designs, and which is now a standard work on the subject. Up to a few days before his death he was busily engaged completing another work on a kindred subject." All who knew him and had accompanied him on archæological excursions will remember his amiability and the ardour with which he entered into his favourite pursuit.

GENERAL BUILDING NEWS.

NORWICH CATHEDRAL.—The Dean of Norwich, preaching in the cathedral on Sunday morning, the 10th inst., gave notice that on and after Monday, the 11th, all the services would be held in the nave, the reason being the restoration of the three great columns, which, with the fourth, recently repaired, support the tower. The three columns, now at last to be dealt with, have been in a state of dilapidation for some fifty years, if not more. From inquiries which have been made (says the *Norfolk Chronicle*), it is encouraging to learn that the stone to be used in the work is already cut. A large staff of masons have been busily engaged, under the direction of the cathedral architect, and this portion of the cathedral restoration will proceed as rapidly as is consistent with security, and with due regard to the preservation of that regularity which so strongly characterises Norman work. The Ethelbert-gate is now complete. This structure has been restored under the direction of Mr. Ewan Christian. The restoration of the cathedral is to be reported upon by Mr. Pearson.

NEW CHURCH AT SHALDON, TEIGNMOUTH.—The river Teign divides Teignmouth and the pretty villages of Shaldon and Ringmore, the latter place having one of the most interesting and complete little thirteenth-century churches that the large county of Devon can boast of, with an east window that commands the admiration of all who see it. It has been found necessary to build a separate church for the larger place, Shaldon, for which Mr. Edmund Sedding, of Plymouth, has been asked to prepare plans.

YORK CITY AND COUNTY BANK, LEEDS.—New premises for the York City and County Bank are now being erected at the junction of Park-row and Bond-street, Leeds. The exterior of the building is being carried out in Bradford stone. The ground-floor is treated externally with rusticated quoined courses, the windows being circular-headed, and the entrance to the bank is placed at the angle of the building, the frieze and pediment being carried by polished red granite columns. Extending upwards over the height of the first and second floors are eight pairs of coupled Corinthian columns, and the whole is crowned by an elaborate frieze and cornice. The interior arrangements will, according to the *Leeds Mercury*, both in design and finish and completeness of equipment, be carried out in a style consistent with the external appearance of the building. The basement contains porter's house, strong-rooms, heating and dynamo rooms. On the ground-floor, and facing Park-row, is the bank-room, lighted at the back by a lantern light, and opening out of the public-room are the manager's and waiting rooms, strong-room, &c. The walls of the bank will be lined internally with Burmantofts faïence. All the counters, desks, &c., will be in half-polished oak, having brass fittings of special design. There will be a fine suite of offices on the ground floor, with separate entrance from Park-row. The first and second floors, which will be entered from Bond-street, will also be fitted up as offices, having strong-rooms on each floor. The works are being carried out by Messrs. W. Nicholson & Son, of Hunslet, from the designs and under the superintendence of Messrs. Smith & Tweedale, architects, Leeds. Mr. Appleyard, of Leeds, has been entrusted with the execution of the carved work.

HOSPITAL FOR INFECTIOUS DISEASES, BRENTFORD.—The new hospital erected by the Brentford Local Board for the reception and treatment of cases of infectious diseases was opened on the 14th inst. The building has been constructed by Messrs. Allen Sons, of Kilburn, from plans by Mr. J. H. Strachan, the Surveyor to the Board. It has aspects to the west and east, and is built on a piece of land contiguous to the Board's sewage works in the Ealing-road. It has a main approach from Clayponds-lane, in addition to one from the Brentford sewage works. In shape it is oblong, with a wing at either end, and it consists of one story throughout, raised 8 ft. on concrete to the level of the road. It is built of stock bricks, with facings of Lawrence's red bricks. Its extreme length is 125 ft., and the widest part, exclusive of the wards, is 20 ft. across. The basement will be used only as cellarage. Forty-eight feet away from the main building, and adjoining the main entrance in Clayponds-lane, is situated the administrative cottage, containing a sitting-room, kitchen, surgery, four bedrooms for the use of the nurses, and a bath-room, all spacious and conveniently adapted for the purposes for which they are required. In another direction, 40 ft. away from the main building and 40 ft. from the nearest fence, is the mortuary, laundry, and disinfecting house, each of which is fitted with its necessary furniture. The hospital itself is 80 ft. from Clayponds-lane, and 55 ft. from the boundary fence of the sewage works. The wings are occupied solely as wards, and their dimensions are 36 ft. by 18 ft., and 13 ft. high, the latter figure representing the height of all the rooms in the building. The smaller wards measure 24 ft. by 18 ft. by 13 ft. high; and the two nurses' duty rooms, which adjoin the wards, are 16 ft. by 14 ft. by 13 ft. high. The whole of the interior walls have been finished in Parian cement, painted and varnished to a high gloss. All the interior and exterior angles in the wards and nurses' duty rooms have been rounded, and the skirting and cornices have been designed with a view of preventing the harbouring of germs, &c. Attached to each ward are verandahs fitted with necessary conveniences for the use of the patients who become convalescent. The building is constructed for the accommodation of ten cases of an infectious nature only at a time, and it is designed so as to permit of the admission of two kinds of diseases, and further, the wards are so arranged that a person cannot get from one block to another without having to walk a distance in the open air of 56 yds. The sanitary arrangements are of the ordinary kind, and lighting is by means of gas brackets. The heating is by fire-places, which also act as ventilators, "hit and miss" ventilators being inserted in the skirting, and the windows having fanlights opening in the wards near the ceiling, so arranged that a through current of air is ensured in each ward. The contract price for the erection of the building was 3,630*l.*, and it was stated by Mr. Strachan during the proceedings that the building had been erected absolutely without "extras."

NEW BUILDINGS IN BIRMINGHAM.—Mr. F. W. Lloyd, the City Buildings Surveyor of Birmingham, has supplied us with a return of new buildings, &c., for which plans were approved during the year 1891, together with a summary of the three previous years. The total for 1891 was 1,541, as compared with 1,708 in 1890, 1,530 in 1889, and 2,587 in 1888. About 1,000 houses are erected each year in the city. During the year 645 notices were forwarded to property owners and others as to dangerous buildings, projecting signs, emblems, &c., and a quantity of land, amounting to 176½ yds. super, has been conceded to the Corporation by owners of property setting back projecting windows, steps, &c.

NEW SWEDENBORGIAN CHURCH, SALFORD.—A new Swedenborgian church was formally dedicated on the 15th inst. It is situate at the corner of Walness and Lower Broughton-road. The new structure is of Gothic design, and has been erected by Mr. J. Ramsbottom from designs by Mr. Thomas Browne, architect, Manchester, at a cost of 4,300*l.* The church consists of chancel, minister's and choir vestries, and a ladies' retiring-room. There is also a school-room under the church, giving accommodation for 350 scholars. The church will seat about 300 worshippers. It has been built to replace the church known as "The Temple," the site of which was recently acquired by the Lancashire and Yorkshire Railway Company.

NEW BANKING PREMISES AT ADLINGTON, LANCASHIRE.—On Monday last new premises for Messrs. Williams Deacon & Co. and the Manchester and Salford Bank were opened for business. The new building, which occupies a prominent corner site in Church-street, have been erected from the designs of Messrs. Jolly & Buckley, architects, Chorley. It is constructed of Yorkshire stone parpoints, with polished stone dressings. The style is Classic. The contractors were: Excavator and masons' work, Mr. W. Fairclough; carpenter and joiners' work, Mr. Robert Brownley; slater, plasterer, and flagger, Mr. W. Hampson; plumber, glazier, and painter, Mr. T. Sharples. The work has been carried out at a cost of about 2,500*l.*

LOCAL BOARD OFFICES, FELIXSTOWE.—The foundation-stone of the new offices for the Felixstowe Local Board was laid on the 14th inst. The site was given to the Board by Captain E. G. Pretyman. The new offices will front Undercliff-road at a point just beyond the road leading up to the cliff near the Convalescent Home. The new building, which is to be "Early English" in character (according to the *Suffolk Chronicle*), will occupy a frontage of some 62 ft. to Undercliff-road, its extreme depth being 32 ft., and its mean depth about 26 ft. This will still leave room for the erection of a further building 40 ft. by 25 ft., should it be thought desirable to add to the offices at some future time a reading-room and library, or, as the population increases, a building to which the name of Town Hall might be given. The front elevation will be of plain red brick on a plinth of blue bricks, with tiled roof, relieved by a gable at the east end. The architect is Mr. G. S. Horton, the Board's Surveyor, and the contract, for 1,670*l.* has been entered into by Mr. H. Runnacles, Halstead.

NEW CHURCH AT STAINES.—The Solicitor-General and Lady Clarke have generously undertaken the cost of a new church at Staines, at a cost of not less than 5,000*l.* A site has been secured facing the river, and the building is to be designed by Mr. G. H. Fellowes Prynne, whose fine church at West Dulwich, which we illustrated in the *Builder* October 18, 1890, has attracted so much admiration.

SANITARY AND ENGINEERING NEWS.

SEWERAGE WORKS, &C., AT ACCRINGTON.—On the 14th inst. a Local Government inquiry was held at Accrington, by Colonel W. M. Ducat, R.E., into an application made by the Council for the borrowing of 12,740*l.* for works of sewerage, street improvement, public lighting, and the erection of stables. The Town Clerk said the first item on the application was for the improvement of Willows-lane, for which they asked 1,610*l.*, and for sewering to same 1,000*l.* The period for which they asked the loan, as under the Public Health Act, was for a term not exceeding sixty years. In regard to the Dyke Nook sewerage scheme, the Town Clerk said this was to prevent the pollution of the Altham stream, which ran through the borough from the adjoining township of Altham, within the Rural Sanitary District of the Burnley Union, and from that authority they had received now, for a period extending over four or five years, written intimations that unless they took their sewerage out of the stream they would take proceedings against them. The amount asked for under that head was 4,913*l.* For the sewering of Burnley-road the Council asked 1,494*l.* For part of this district there was practically no system of sewerage. The cost of similar work in Whalley-road and adjacent streets was included under the head of the Dyke Nook schemes. For the Corporation stables they asked for the "extras," which, on an estimate of 15,000*l.*, only amounted to 180*l.* The last item of the application was for 2,022*l.* for street lamps and their erection. The town was rapidly increasing, and that sum would provide them with lamps for eight or ten years. The Inspector subsequently visited the various places referred to in the application.

CASTLE DONINGTON SEWERAGE.—The Shardlow Rural Sanitary Authority have applied to the Local Government Board for a loan of 4,000*l.* for the sewerage and sewage disposal of Castle Donington. The sewage will be purified by irrigation on land. Mr. W. H. Radford is the engineer.

SEWAGE PURIFICATION AT BIRKDALE. — Major-General C. Phipps Carey, R.E., of the Local Government Board, recently held a public inquiry at the Town-hall, Birkdale, about the disposal of the Birkdale sewage. The lime treatment of the sewage having produced bad results, the Southport Corporation obtained an injunction against the Birkdale Local Board for polluting a brook. To remove this injunction, the Birkdale Board proposed to continue treating their sewage with lime, but carrying their effluent therefrom through a pipe-sewer into the sea. This was opposed by the Corporation of Southport and by neighbouring landowners. Dr. E. Frankland, F.R.S., of the Rivers Pollution Commission, and Mr. Mansergh, M.Inst.C.E., gave evidence for the Southport Corporation against lime treatment of the sewage. These eminent authorities recommended the Ferozone and Polarite process of the International Company, as in their opinion it would produce the most satisfactory results, and would be less costly than the method proposed. After hearing this evidence, the representatives of the Birkdale Local Board withdrew, and, after a short deliberation, announced their willingness to give an undertaking to adopt the international process, whereupon the opposition of the Southport Corporation and the other opponents was withdrawn. The Birkdale Board have accordingly instructed Mr. Charles H. Beloe, M.Inst.C.E., of Liverpool, the Consulting Engineer to the International Water and Sewage Purification Company, Westminster, to prepare the scheme in conjunction with Mr. J. H. Fairbairn, the Surveyor to the Board.

UNIVERSITY EXTENSION LECTURES.—The following are the remaining lectures of the course which are being delivered by Mr. T. Locke Worthington at Hampton Court, before alluded to in our columns:—January 15, "Basilican Romanesque," "Diocletian Romanesque," "Primitive Romanesque" (so-called), "Mature Romanesque" (so-called); January 22, "The Primitive and Mature Romanesque of England"; January 29, "The Periods of Pointed Gothic in England"; February 5, "The Later Periods of Pure Gothic in England"; February 12, "The Movement and Styles of the Renaissance"; February 19, "Modern Architecture in London," "New Style of Architecture and Modern Developments." The above course, reduced to ten lectures, will be repeated at Finchley and at Sutton (Surrey).

FOREIGN AND COLONIAL.

FRANCE.—M. Bonnat has been elected President of the Société des Artistes Français, in place of M. Bailly, and M. Dutert has succeeded M. Bailly as member of the Conseil Supérieur of the Ecole des Beaux-Arts.——The Champ-de-Mars Salon is to open on May 7.——M. Edouard Garnier has been appointed Conservateur of the ceramic museum at Sèvres, in place of M. Baumgart.——The architectural department under the Municipality of Paris has prepared plans for the restoration of the tower of the Ducs de Bourgogne, known as the "Tour Jean Sans Peur."——The Municipal Council has under consideration a proposal to erect statues of Racine and Corneille in the Place du Theâtre Français.——The impressionist painters have made a curious attempt at practical architecture; a house is being built in the Quartier des Invalides, from the designs of M. Besnard, the painter. The decorative paintings are being executed by M. Luce, and the sculpture by MM. Berthet and Léon Gausson.——M. François Lafon is to execute, for the foyer of the Théâtre du Chatelet, two decorative panels symbolising "Dancing" and "Music"; these are to replace the portraits of Napoléon III. and the Empress Eugénie which formerly decorated the two fireplaces of the foyer.——There is to be an art exhibition at Amiens from June 5 to July 14.——At Châtillon-sur-Loire there have just been discovered the remains of three aqueducts, in the course of the works for the formation of a canal. The largest of these is not less than 1,500 mètres in length. Knives, pottery, and ancient arms have been found during the excavations. As a statue of Venus and some Gallo-Roman coins were found in the same place some years ago, it is supposed that there was an important Roman station here.——A statue to Montesquieu is to be erected at Brede, near Bordeaux.——A statue to the painter Ribot is to be erected at Breteuil.——The "Union Artistique du Nord" is to open shortly, at Lille, an exhibition of art industries applied to the habitation.——Parliament has passed an additional vote of a million francs towards the construction of the Ecole des Arts et Métiers at Lille, which will be shortly completed.——The monument to be erected at Mée (Seine-et-Marne) to the memory of Chapu is to be carried out under the direction of MM. Daumet and Vaudremer. The sculptural portion is to be entrusted to M. Antonin Mercié. The monument will be composed of three steles in marble; the centre one will be surmounted by a reproduction of Chapu's fine figure of Immortality, from the tomb of Jean Reynaud. The two other steles will be adorned with medallions of the sculptor's father and mother.——In the course of road works at Gloughia, in Tunisia, the Government contractor has discovered two fine and well-preserved Roman statues, which have been placed in the Museum at Bardo.——The Louvre is to receive shortly several archæological curiosities discovered last year at Lambessa (Algeria), especially a fine sarcophagus of early Christian date.——The death at Paris is announced of M. Pierre Chabat, architect, at the age of sixty-five. He was a pupil of Garrez, and had filled the position of a Professor at the Conservatoire des Arts et Métiers and at the École Spéciale d'Architecture. He carried out the abattoirs at Pontoise, Biarritz, and Montereau. He was well known by numerous publications, among others his Dictionary of "Termes de la Construction," a very useful and complete work.——M. Conil-Lacoste, "architecte-réviseur" of the City of Paris, has died at the age of seventy-four. His son, also an architect, took part in the work of construction for the 1889 Exhibition.——We have to record also the death of M. Riffaud, contractor, who has had a share in many of the larger works in Paris and its environs, especially the new Louvre, the Comptoir d'Escompte, the Crédit Lyonnais, the Château of Chantilly, the Hôtel de Ville, the Pavilion Marsan, and the Church of the Sacré Cœur; he also carried out the new portions of the Faubourg St. Honoré, and the alterations in the neighbourhood of the Arc de Triomphe. He began life as a simple stonemason.

MISCELLANEOUS.

FREE LECTURES AT CARPENTERS' HALL ON MATTERS CONNECTED WITH BUILDING.—Under the auspices of the Worshipful Company of Carpenters, in conjunction with the Sanitary Institute, the usual course of free lectures to artisans and others on matters connected with building has just commenced. The first lecture of the series was announced to be given on Wednesday evening last, by Sir Douglas Galton, on "Ventilation, Warming, and Lighting." The remaining lectures of the course are as follow:—January 27, Mr. P. Gordon Smith on "Building Acts and By-laws adapted to various Localities." February 3, Professor H. Robinson on "Drainage of Buildings and Building of Sewers." February 10, Professor W. H. Corfield on "Water Supply and the Pollution of Water." February 17, Professor Banister Fletcher on "Sanitary Building Construction." February 24, Professor A. Wynter Blyth on "Sanitary Appliances." March 2, Professor T. Roger Smith on "Sanitary Construction of Public Buildings."

PROGRESS AT WEST HARTLEPOOL.—This town, judging from recent proceedings of the Council, appears to be fully alive to the duties devolving upon it in view of the very rapid increase in its population. A large outfall sewer for the Northern District has recently been completed. A new cemetery, twenty acres in extent, with boundary wall and specially-designed drainage, is now in progress, and is expected to be completed shortly. New abattoirs are to be erected as soon as a suitable site can be obtained. A large central depôt and stable yard has been completed, with stabling for all the Corporation horses, cart-sheds for forty carts, steam-roller house, and special machinery for cutting chaff and grinding corn for horses. Besides the new station for the fire brigade, with special drying tower for the hose pipes, a new façade to the Public Market, composed of six large three-story shops and offices, is to be built at once; the designs and plans were approved at the last Council meeting. Two new intercepting sewers of large dimensions are to be proceeded with at an early date, one along the Burn Valley, as an outlet for the Park district (which is rapidly developing), and the other as an outlet for the entire western section of the borough. New streets at an estimated cost of many thousands of pounds are also in hand. A large scale-plan of the borough has been made, and a survey of the whole of the sewers in the borough is in progress, which will give the position, direction of flow, size, kind, depth, and condition, together with the manholes, ventilators, and gullies. Mr. J. W. Brown, A.M.Inst.C.E., F.G.S., the Borough Engineer, who has designed and carried or is carrying out the whole of the above works, would appear to have plenty of work on hand at present.

THE COPPER TRADE IN 1891.—Messrs. Stedman, Crowther, & Co.'s "Metal Report for 1891" says that the copper trade was very active during the year for both consumption and speculation. Supplies from the United States increased 14,000 tons; those from Chili were 5,000 tons less than in 1890, a result arising in large measure from the civil war in that country. The imports from other sources altered but little, but deliveries so far exceeded supplies that the stock was reduced 8,000 tons during the twelvemonth, and to a smaller figure than it had touched for four years. The exports of manufactured copper showed considerable increases over those of 1890, especially to Brazil, the Levant, and the East Indies; shipments to India, however, were yet a long way below those of the years 1884 to 1887, periods of low values. In the Warrant market G.M.B. copper fell during the first three months from 53*l.* to 51*l.*, notwithstanding decreases in stock and irregular supplies from Chili. In March an upward movement began which was helped by the news of the closing of the Anaconda Mine in America. The rise continued till June, when G.M.B. touched 56*l.* 10s., the highest point during the year. In July, large forward sales caused a relapse to 51*l.* 10s., followed by a recovery to 53*l.* The prompts of this copper, when they fell due in October, were met by a supply of warrants that had been held off the market for some considerable time, and the oversupply of cash copper brought about a decline of 5*l.* per ton. In November the market was further depressed, partly by the re-opening of the Anaconda Mine, and partly by the fear that part of the large stock of copper held by the Société des Métaux in France would be thrown on the market when the works were put up to auction by the liquidator of the company. This sale was successfully concluded on December 2, when there followed a strong reaction, and G.M.B. advanced from 44*l.* 10s. to 47*l.* 5s. The rise held but a short time, as a desire to realise, and lower quotations from America, brought back the market to 44*l.* 10s. Good buying the last week of the year sent the price up again to 46*l.* 12s. 6d. cash.

LECTURES AT YORKSHIRE COLLEGE.—Mr. W. Spinks, Lecturer in the Sanitary Engineering Department of Yorkshire College, Leeds, is delivering a series of Thursday afternoon lectures at the College on Sanitary Science as applied to Towns; The Public Health Acts, 1875 and 1890; The Rivers Pollution Prevention Act, 1876; and The Sewering of Towns. The latter subject includes the selection of lines and routes; sewage and rainfall; sizes, inclinations, flow, and discharges of sewers; construction and materials; ventilation and cleansing; and sewage disposal works.

INSTITUTION OF MECHANICAL ENGINEERS.—The annual general meeting of this Institution will be held on February 4 and 5, in the hall of the Institution of Civil Engineers, Great George-street. The papers to be read and discussed (after the adoption of the annual report, the election of officers, &c.) will be (1) "Notes on Mechanical Features of the Liverpool Waterworks, and on the supply of Power by pressure from the public mains, and by other means," by Mr. Joseph Parry, Water Engineer, Liverpool; and (2) "On the Disposal and Utilisation of Blast Furnace Slag," by Mr. William Hawdon, of Middlesbrough.

BOROUGH SURVEYORSHIP, LUTON.—Mr. T. Ridyard Roscoe, C.E., Assistant Surveyor, Islington Vestry, N., has been appointed Borough Engineer and Surveyor of Luton, in succession to Mr. E. J. Lovegrove, A.M.Inst.C.E., who was recently appointed Borough Surveyor of Richmond.

COMPETITIONS, CONTRACTS, AND PUBLIC APPOINTM

COMPETITIONS.

Nature of Work.	By whom Advertised.	Premium.	Designs to be delivered.
Wesleyan Chapel & Schools, Blaina, Mon.	Rev. Joseph Wells....	....	Feb. 2
*Iron Swing Bridge	Sandwich Corporation	15l.	Feb. 17
*Promenade Pier	Beaumaris Corp.	10l. 10s.	Mar. 1

CONTRACTS.

Nature of Work or Materials.	By whom Required.	Architect, Surveyor or Engineer.	Tenders to be delivered.
*Drainage Works	Richmond (Surrey) Town Council	J. Lemon	Jan. 25
*Restoration of Windows	Camberwell Bur. Bd.	E. R. W. Whellock	do.
Fire Clay Retorts	Sowerby Bridge L. B.	J. Marsland	Jan. 26
*Road-making and Paving Works	Willesden Loc. Bd.	O. Claude Robson	do.
*Works and Materials	Hammersmith Vestry	Official	Jan. 27
*Granite Kerb	Worthing Corp.	do.	do.
Street Works	Cardiff Corporation	do.	do.
*Warming and Ventilating Town Hall	Leeds Corporation	do.	do.
*Removal of House Refuse, &c.	St. Pancras Vestry	do.	do.
*Works and Materials	Chelsea Vestry	do.	Jan. 28
Re-roofing Corn Market, Wakefield	Corn Exchange Co.	W. Watson	do.
Pipe Drain and Brick Tunnel	Gateshead Town Improvement Com.	J. Bower	do.
Widening Waver Bridge, Wigton	Cumberland C. C.	C. J. Ferguson	Jan. 29
Fifty Workmen's Houses, Southmoor, Chester-le-Street	....	J. W. Rounthwaite	do.
*Making-up Roads, &c.	Walthamstow Loc Bd.	G. W. Holmes	do.
Sewerage Works	Cardiff U.R.S.A.	T. Waring & Son	Jan. 30
New Road, near Blackwood	Mynyddislwyn H. B.	Official	do.
*Repairs to St. Margaret's Churchyard	Burial Bd. of St. Margaret's, Westminster	do	do.
Training Home Buildings, Sheffield	....	H. W. Lockwood	do.
Gasholder Tank, Grimesthorpe Station	Sheffield Gas Co.	F. W. Stevenson	do.
Alterations, &c School, East Hetton	Coxhoe (Durham) Bd. School	Official	Feb. 1
*Three Snow Ploughs	Islington Vestry	do.	do.
Porter's Lodge, Waiting Room, Laundry, Fences, &c. Lodge Moor	Sheffield Town Coun.	Flockton & Gibbs	do.
Additions, &c. "Bush Inn," Aberdare	....	C. H. Elford	do.
*Cast-iron Pipes	Standish-with-Langtree Local Board	Heaton & Ralph	do.
*Making-up Roads	Finchley L. B.	Official	do.
*Waterworks	Buckingham U.S.A.	B. Latham	Feb. 2
*Pipe Sewers	Tottenham Loc. Bd.	J. E. Worth	do.

CONTRACTS.—Contin

Nature of Work or Materials.	By whom Required.	Architect, Surveyor, or Engineer.	Tenders to be delivered
Four Shops and Houses, Taffstreet, Pontypridd	D. R. Evans	A. O. Evans	Feb. 2
*Making-good Roads	Southend Loc. Bd.	Peter Dodd	do.
Business Premises, High-street, Southampton	Edward Cox	W. Burrough Hill	Feb. 3
Two Dwelling-houses, Dufftown, N.B.	P. M'William	....	do.
*Footbridges	Gt. Western Ry.	Official	do.
*Engine House, Pumping Station, &c.	Maidstone Wtrwks Co.	E. Easton & Co.	do.
Additions, &c. Schools, Williamstown, Penygraig	Llantrisant Board Sch	J. J. Evans	Feb. 4
Sewerage Works	Ystradyfodwg L. B.	J. W. Jones	do.
Private Road Improvement Works	do.	do.	do.
*Broken Granite	Norfolk C. C.	T. H. B. Heslop	Feb. 6
*Additions, &c., to Ambulance Station, Fulham	Metro. Asylums Bd.	A. & C. Harston	Feb. 8
*Road Materials	H. M. Works	Official	do.
*School and Cookery Kitchen	Northfleet Sch. Bd.	Walford & Legg	do.
*Public Hall and Municipal Offices	West Ham Council	Lewis Angell	Feb. 9
*Removal of Dirt, Dust, &c.	Crown Estate Paving Commissioners	Official	Feb. 10
*Drainage Works	West Ham Union	J. M. Knight	do.
Bridge and Covering over Water	Bristol Corporation	F. Fox	Feb. 12
*Erection of Workhouse	St. Giles, Camberwell, Guardians	Wilson, Son, & Aldwinckle	Feb. 15
*Sewerage Works	Guildford Corporation	C. N. Lailey	Feb. 16
*Public Baths	Shrewsbury Corp.	J. Johnson	Feb. 22
*Superstructure of Mill	Atherton Cotton Spinning Co.	Bradshaw & Gass	No date
*Carriage Factory, Tunbridge Wells	....	H. H. & E. Cronk	do.
Additions to Barracks, Lichfield	War Department	Official	do.
Banking Premises, Bridlington, Yorks	York Union Bank Ltd	Smith & Brodrick	do.
Twelve Through Houses, Leicesterplace, Leeds	....	W. A. Hobson	do.
*Pair of Semi-detached Villas	Ramsgate Corp.	Hill & Co.	do.
*Library Buildings, Southampton	The Committee	Official	do.

PUBLIC APPOINTMENTS.

Nature of Appointment.	By whom Advertised.	Salary.	Applications to be in.
*Sanitary Inspector	Islington Vestry	104l.	Feb. 3
*Valuer and Surveyor	Vestry of Shoreditch	....	Feb. 5
*Inspector of Nuisances	Norwich T. C.	175l.	Feb. 6
*Surveyor and Inspector of Nuisances	Ashford L. B.	150l.	Feb. 16

Those marked with an Asterisk (*) are advertised in this Number. *Competitions, p.* iv. *Contracts, pp.* iv., vi., viii, & ix. *Public Appointments, p.* xx. & xxi.

THE SLADE PROFESSORSHIP OF FINE ARTS AT CAMBRIDGE.—The Vice-Chancellor gives notice that the Professorship of Fine Art in the University of Cambridge, on the Foundation of Felix Slade, Esq., will become vacant on February 22, and that the election of a new Professor will take place on Tuesday, February 23. The Professor will receive by way of stipend the dividends of a sum of 12,186*l.* 12s. 7d. New Two and Three-quarters per Cent. Consolidated Annuities. He is not required to reside at the University. Candidates are requested to send their names to the Vice-Chancellor on or before Tuesday, February 16.—*Cambridge Chronicle.*

THE ENGLISH IRON TRADE.—The English iron market continues very quiet, and there are no indications of an immediate revival. Very little change is exhibited in any of the branches of the trade, and prices remain practically unaltered. Pig-iron is still dull at most of the centres; but a slightly better tone has been manifested in the Cleveland market. Manufactured iron is only in moderate request, and in the steel trade business generally is not too brisk, except in shipbuilding material, which, however, in the North-west is in lessened demand. The tinplate trade is still quiet, but better times are anticipated. Shipbuilders and engineers are, on the whole, moderately busy. The coal trade exhibits fair activity.—*Iron.*

THE SANITARY INSPECTORS' ASSOCIATION.—In consequence of the death of the Duke of Clarence, the annual dinner of this Association has been postponed from February 6 to March 12.

SETTING CIRCULAR SAWS.—Messrs. A. Ransome & Co. send us the description and illustration of an apparatus for setting the teeth of circular saws with rapidity and a certainty of the right set. The saw is mounted horizontally on a travelling pivot, to suit any circumference of saw; the periphery of the saw rests on an anvil with a bevel on the edge. The saw is turned round and a blow of a hammer on each alternate tooth gives it the angle of the bevel, all the teeth being necessarily set at the same angle. The saw is then reversed and the remaining alternate teeth set in the same way. The bevel is eccentric, and the anvil can be turned on its axis so as to give any required angle of setting.

THE NORTHERN OF SWEDEN TRUNK RAILWAY.—Work on the Northern of Sweden Trunk Railway, a line running right through the whole of Northern Sweden, and which is to be continued to the Russian frontier, is actively progressing. The other day a further section, 30 kilomètres in length, was opened, making its total length from Stockholm 858 kilomètres, and by 1894 it is expected that the distance to Boden will have been covered, 300 kilomètres. Thereby this railway and those of the rest of Sweden will have joined the Lulea-Gellivara Railway. The distance hence to the Finnish frontier is estimated at some 500 kilomètres. On the other hand, the Northern of Finland Railway now terminates at Uleåborg, about 150 kilomètres from the same.

UNSEASONABLE STREET SCAVENGING.—Travellers in Holland know that there is in general use there a method of street scavenging which consists in thoroughly washing the surface with water from a hose, followed by a good brushing. Dwellers in London will have noticed that in certain parishes an attempt has been made to adapt this cleanly Dutch custom to English ways, but with a difference; for, whereas in Holland the washing is done at cock-crow, and the man with the hose is closely followed up by an army of sweepers, the time chosen in London appears to be from nine to noon, and the street,—and often the pavement also,—is allowed to remain for long covered by a mixture of mud and water, with which the two or three languid sweepers are unable to cope. The consequence is that thousands who have trusted to the absence of rain to take them to shops or offices dry shod, find themselves quickly suffering from the miseries and dangers of wet feet. Probably in no other city in the world would such a piece of blundering bumbledom be allowed to continue for a week.—*British Medical Journal.*

TRADES HALL FOR EDINBURGH.—It was briefly announced at the meeting of the Edinburgh Trades Council on the 5th inst. that a gentleman in Edinburgh had made the offer of a sum of money for the purchase of premises to be used as a centre for trade organisation in the city. The sum which he has offered amounts, it is said, to 4,000*l.*, and he is willing to increase the amount if necessary. The offer has been made through the officials of the Trades Council, and already the project has been so far advanced that the building known as the Trades Hall in the High-street has been purchased. The Trades Hall, originally a bank, afterwards used as a Free Church, then purchased by the Good Templar organisation, is a commodious building, having a large upper and smaller lower hall, a number of committee rooms, a range of vaults, keeper's house, and other accessories, and is at present largely used by the trades as a meeting-place. It will require an extensive overhaul, but as the purchase price of the building is understood to be 2,700*l.*, that leaves a balance of 1,300*l.* for renovation. The premises will be under the management of a Trades Committee, and will be used as a centre of labour propagandism, which will be pushed by means of lectures, by the formation of a library, and in other ways. It is probable that such terms will be offered to trade unions as will induce them to make the hall their meeting-place, instead of meeting, as at present, in different places in the town.—*Scotsman.*

LEGAL.

CASE UNDER THE METROPOLIS LOCAL MANAGEMENT ACT:

WANDSWORTH DISTRICT BOARD OF WORKS *v.* LOWER.

THIS case came before Mr. Denman, at the Wandsworth Police-court, on the 13th inst. The defendant, a local builder, was summoned under section 76, Metropolis Local Management Act, for a breach of the Regulations for the Construction of New House-drains, adopted some time since by the Wandsworth District Board of Works, in respect of two new houses, Rectory Grove, Clapham. Mr. W. W. Young, Solicitor to the Board, supported the summons.

Mr. S. Fairchild, Sanitary Inspector for the Parish of Clapham, stated that the stoneware traps of the waterclosets were not connected to the soil-pipes by means of sound and suitable joints, as required by the Regulations, but that the joints were made by simply inserting the outgo of the traps into the branch piece of the soil-pipes and stopping it round with red-lead. And, also, that the waste-pipes from the sinks were fixed without syphon-traps intervening between the sinks and the discharging ends, the Regulations requiring that waste-pipes from lavatories, baths, and sinks shall be trapped at the outgo of the receptacles and made to discharge outside over the seal of syphon gulley trap. Inspector Fairchild produced models and drawings, and explained how the work should be executed so as to ensure the sanitary condition of new houses.

The defendant took several exceptions to the regulations, and finally contended that the Board of Works had not the power to make drainage regulations under the Metropolis Local Management Acts.

Mr. Denman, the magistrate, in giving his decision, said that the Board had the power under section 76 to make regulations, and he must decide against Mr. Lower.

Mr. Young did not press for a penalty, this being the first case in respect to these regulations, and he would be satisfied if the defendant undertook to make the necessary alterations within a month.

The learned magistrate advised Mr. Lower to adopt this course, and he consented to do so.

EMPLOYERS' LIABILITY:

PATMORE *v.* KENNERLEY.

IN the City of London Court last week, before Mr. Julian Robins (Deputy Judge), the case of Patmore *v.* Kennerley & Shiefer was heard, in which the plaintiff, John Patmore, bricklayer, sought to recover 50*l.* damages for personal injuries sustained in an accident caused by the alleged negligence of the men in the employment of the defendants, Messrs. Kennerley & Shiefer, builders, 31, Lombard-street, E.C.

Mr. Walters, counsel for the plaintiff, said the accident happened on October 2 last, at the New English Homes, Holloway-road, which were being built by the defendants, the plaintiff at the time being a bricklayer in the service of the defendants. The building was being erected without any scaffolding at all. As the building progressed, the beams of each floor were put in, and a structure called a Yankee jib was put up at the top, which was used for the purpose of raising materials.

The Deputy Judge: It is a sort of crane?

Mr. Lynch (for the defendant): It is a derrick.

Mr. Walters, continuing, said as each floor was raised, the defendants built up the next floor upon tresties, the beams were then put in on the floor above, and the jib was raised to the next floor, and so on. The sole access to the top of the building was by means of a ladder which was placed in such a position that when the crane was being worked it caused it to become very dangerous. Bricks and mortar were constantly dropping on to the heads of those who had to use the ladder, and the plaintiff had on several occasions complained to the defendants' foreman about the unsafety of the place. He was only laughed at. While the plaintiff was descending from the ladder when about half way down a quantity of bricks and masonry work fell from the top, and this would have struck the plaintiff on the head, the consequences being very serious. Seeing the great danger the plaintiff was in, several people shouted to him to jump to the ground. Knowing the chances he ran if he stayed on the ladder, the plaintiff jumped to the ground, a distance of 25 ft. He was seriously injured as it was; but had the plaintiff not jumped, the bricks would have fallen on his head. He was immediately removed to the Great Northern Hospital, where he was detained for eight days, and afterwards attended the hospital for ten weeks as an out-patient. This claim for damages was now raised under the provisions of the Employers' Liability Act, because of the defect in the non-protection of the space above the ladder—the only means of access.

For the defence, Mr. Jubal Kennerley, one of the defendants, stated that he was present when the unfortunate accident happened to the plaintiff. The plaintiff should have used a different ladder to the one he came down by on the day in question. Witness never knew that the ladder the plaintiff did use was dangerous. He had gone up and down it himself. The accident was brought about by the man in charge of the derrick pulling it in too early, when several bricks fell out. There was no need for the plaintiff to have jumped as he did. The truth was, the plaintiff became frightened, and hearing men calling out, being a nervous man, he jumped to the ground. In cross-examination, he said the structure used for raising the building was much in vogue in America. No security was provided by boarding in the place, because it was not necessary.

The defendant's foreman denied that any complaints were ever made to him about the defective condition of the works.

The Deputy Judge, having regard to the importance of the case, said he would take time to consider his judgment. Two days later he delivered judgment at great length, finding for the plaintiff for 45*l.* and costs.

MEETINGS.

SATURDAY, JANUARY 23.

Royal Institution.—Professor J. A. Fleming on "The Induction Coil and Alternate-Current Transformer." I. 3 p.m.

MONDAY, JANUARY 25.

Royal Institute of British Architects.—Address to Students by the President, Mr. J. Macvicar Anderson, who will present the Prizes and Studentships for the year 1891-92. 8 p.m.

Royal Academy of Arts.—Professor Aitchison, A.R.A., on "Saracenic and Turkish Architecture." I. 8 p.m.

Society of Arts (Cantor Lectures).—Professor George Forbes on "Developments of Electrical Distribution." I. 8 p.m.

Liverpool Architectural Society.—The Rev. F. F. Grensted on "The Rise of Civilisation in Babylonia." 7 p.m.

TUESDAY, JANUARY 26.

Society of Arts (Applied Art Section).—Mr. William Morris on "The Woodcuts of Gothic Books." (Illustrated by Lantern Slides). 8. p.m.

Institution of Civil Engineers.—(1) Further Discussion on Mr. Wilfrid Airy's Paper on "Weighing-machines." 8 p.m. (2) Reception by the President and Council in the Library. 9 p.m.

Glasgow Architectural Association.—Mr. James Lindsay, A.R.I.B.A., on "Approximate Estimating." 8 p.m.

Liverpool Engineering Society.—Adjourned Discussion on Mr. A. J. Maginnis's paper on "Transatlantic Lines and Steamships." 8 p.m.

WEDNESDAY, JANUARY 27.

Carpenters' Hall, London Wall.—Mr. P. Gordon Smith, F.R.I.B.A., on "Building Acts and By-Laws for Controlling the Construction of Buildings, adapted to Various localities. 8 p.m. (*Admission Free*).

Royal Meteorological Society.—Annual General Meeting. Address by the President (Mr. Baldwin Latham, M.Inst.C.E.) on "Evaporation and Condensation." 7.15 p.m. (Postponed from the 20th inst. in consequence of the death of the Duke of Clarence.)

Society of Arts.—Mr. F. W. Edridge-Green on "The Scientific Value of Lovibond's Tintometer." 8 p.m.

St. Paul's Ecclesiological Society.—Mr. T. A. Martin on "Some Religious Subjects on Misericordes." .30 p.m.

THURSDAY, JANUARY 28.

Royal Academy of Arts.—Professor Aitchison, A.R.A., on "Saracenic and Turkish Architecture." II. 8 p.m.

Royal Institution.—Dr. A. S. Murray, on "Some Aspects of Greek Sculpture in Relief." II. 3 p.m.

British Museum.—Miss Millington-Lathbury on Greek Temples, and leading motives of Greek Religion," as illustrated by the monuments in the Museum. 45 p.m.

Institution of Electrical Engineers.—Inaugural Address by the President, Professor W. E. Ayrton, F.R.S. 8 p.m. (Adjourned from the 14th inst. in consequence of the death of the Duke of Clarence.)

Society of Antiquaries.—8 p.m.

Edinburgh Architectural Association.—8 p.m.

FRIDAY, JANUARY 29.

Architectural Association.—Mr. N. H. J. Westlake on "Fashion in Architecture and its kindred Arts." 7.30 p.m.

Institution of Civil Engineers.—Students' meeting. 7.30 p.m.

Liverpool Engineering Society.—Annual Dinner.

SATURDAY, JANUARY 30.

Royal Institution.—Professor J. A. Fleming on "The Induction Coil and Alternate-Current Transformer," II. 3 p.m.

RECENT PATENTS:

ABSTRACTS OF SPECIFICATIONS.

20,215.—WINDOWS: *W. Hooker.*—This patent relates to an improved system of hanging sliding windows to be opened from the inside, for cleaning, &c., by detachable hinges, the wings of which are attached to plates on sash-frames and sashes, the plates being slotted and dovetailed to receive the wings. The lower wings of hinges are connected to the plate on the frame and the upper wing in a similar manner to the style of sash.

2,534.—SCAFFOLDING: *W. Parsey.*—Instead of the usual mode of timber scaffolding, scaffolds of iron or steel bars are constructed of suitable shapes, such as angles, tees, &c., all the parts of which are interchangeable in their relative positions, and have holes drilled or punched in them at some uniform pitch throughout, or are provided or formed with equivalents, so that they can be put together by bolts and nuts, cotters, or drifts, or the like to form pillars, girders, or other forms, with the distance and diagonal bracing bars to form perfectly rigid structures of various dimensions. The scaffolding may be taken down and used over and over again.

3,056.—METALLIC CHIMNEYS: *T. P. Lomas.*—This specification relates to improvements in the manufacture of metallic chimneys and flues. Sheet-metal, copper, tin, or other metallic plates are cut approximately to the required sizes. These pieces are sheared, stamped, pressed, corrugated, buckled, and flanged to fit them to form portions of the chimneys. In some cases the whole of the plate is corrugated and buckled except the flanged edges, the plate being made in portions of cylinders or of a frustrum of a cone. In other cases the plates are stamped out plain and rectangular with flanges all round, and sometimes tapered at one end, and when riveted, grooved, or soldered together they form polygonic structures for various purposes.

11,812.—DOORS AND GATES: *R. H. Dawe.*—This patent relates to an appliance for fastening and securing doors and gates, and facilitating opening and closing of same. This is effected by means of a stay with a knuckle-joint or hinge in or near the middle, each end of the stay being provided with a plate, bracket, or staple attached, the one end to the door, and the other to a post, wall, or other suitable place.

17,389.—CHANDELIERS, &C.: *R. Roderick.*—This relates to a method of supporting and retaining in position gasaliers, chandeliers, and the like, by using a circular, oblong, or other shaped collar of metal, which forms the balance weight, instead of the separate weights now used. To the metal collar, which extends round the tube of the gasalier, &c., the usual chains are connected, and the gasalier can be raised or lowered in the usual way.

19,131.—SASH-CORDS: *E. J. Jeyes & C. J. E. Kinslow.*—By this invention it is proposed to remedy the defects in the usual method of attaching sash-cords to window-sashes. These defects are stated to be the liability of the cords to be broken away from the sash, and the expense of fitting. The improvement is effected by means of a metal bush or ring with a cut away part, perforations, and bevelled or sharpened lower edges, the whole being sunk into the window-sash. The end of the cord is passed through the cut away part and knotted.

NEW APPLICATIONS FOR LETTERS PATENT.

January 4.—155, H. Schmidt, Iron Retaining wall.

January 5.—165, T. Hunt, Glazing Earthenware Pipes, Tiles, &c.—166, A. Cannon, Chimney-pots.—174, G. Deacon, Glazing Roofs, &c.—187, G. Skinner & J. Hill, Attaching Door-knobs or Handles to their Spindles.—190, S. Dix, Water-closets.—215, A. Boult, Fire-grates.

January 6.—251, H. Cribb, Preparing, Fitting, and Laying Blocks for Floors, &c.—258, J. Costick, Chimney-pots for preventing downward Draught.—285, R. Barker, Sewer-pipe and Drain-tile Machines.—288, R. Barker, Sewer-pipe and Drain-tile Machines.—308, W. Sykes, Jointing Earthenware Pipes, &c.

January 7.—323, A. Whittome, Wood-block Floors.—337, T. Helliwell, Glazing Buildings.—364, H. Conolly, Water-closets.

January 8.—G. Parkinson, Guarding Circular or other Saws.—432, A. Ford, Bolts for Doors, Windows, &c.—446, A. Haworth, Pipes for Sinks.

January 9.—488, T. Wilkinson, Joints for Sewer and other Pipes.—490, H. Warrington, Kilns or Ovens for Bricks, &c.—497, F. Lorch and others, Construction of Hinge-joints.—507, G. Martin, Screw-drivers.

PROVISIONAL SPECIFICATIONS ACCEPTED.

17,854, J. Green and G. Meecle, Window Sash-fasteners.—20,323, A. Fiddes and others, Hot-water Apparatus for Heating Horticultural Buildings, &c.—20,549, S. Kirk and W. McYougal, Lock and Hanging Window-frame and Sash.—20,643, R. Rankin, Marking the Styles and Rails of Doors and Sashes and other Joiners' Work for Mortising while on Slide of Tenoning-machine or otherwise.—20,798, M. Reed, Slow Combustion Stoves.—20,816, H. Dent and J. South, Furnaces and Domestic Fireplaces.—20,853, E. Heydenreich, Tool-holder.—21,142, W. Adams, Ceiling Roses for Electrical Fittings.—21,148, J. M. Hardy and W. Garland, Upright Sawing-machines.—21,520, T. Harries, Artificial Stone.—21,763, J. Saunders, Opening and Closing Fanlights, Casements, &c.—22,202, C. Henshaw, Shop Door and Casement-fasteners.—22,212, E. Wilson, Machines for Curving or Shaping Wood.—22,562, W. Horn, Brick Kiln.

COMPLETE SPECIFICATIONS ACCEPTED.

(Open to Opposition for Two Months.)

3,877, C. Green, Window Ventilation of Dwelling-houses and other Buildings.—16,518, W. Thompson, Blocks or Stones for Use in the Sinking of Wells or Shafts and in the process of placing the same in position.—20,210, R. McMillen, Window-sash Balance.—21,423, P. Jensen, Heating Buildings by means of Steam or Hot-Water.

SOME RECENT SALES OF PROPERTY:

ESTATE EXCHANGE REPORT.

JANUARY 12.—By *G. F. Francis*: 11, 13, and 15, Page-st., Westminster, u.t. 8½ yrs., g.r. 60*l.*, r. 150*l.*, 200*l.*—*Rogers, Chapman, & Co.*: "Cumberland Lodge," Streatham Hill, u.t. 43 yrs., g.r. 23*l.*, 990*l.*

JANUARY 13.—By *Tobin & Sons*: 49 and 50, Greenfield-st., Whitechapel, f., r. 76*l.* 14s., 680*l.*—By *H. & A. Harris*: 15, Lambton-rd., Hornsey, f., r. 32*l.*, 446*l.*; 74, Shaftesbury-rd., u.t. 83 yrs., g.r. 7*l.*, r. 36*l.*, 340*l.*—By *Elgood & Fuller*: 18, York-ter., Regent's-park, u.t. 29½ yrs., g.r. 8*l.*, r. 212*l.* 11s., 2,060*l.*, 41, Devonshire-st., Portland-place, u.t. 18½ yrs., g.r. 68*l.*, r. 160*l.*, 780*l.*

JANUARY 14.—By *W. W. Jenkinson*: 152, Queen's-rd., Peckham, f., r. 40*l.*, 520*l.*—By *Newbon & Co.*: 14 and 15, Upper North-st., Caledonian-rd., u.t. 53 yrs., g.r. 10*l.*, r. 54*l.*, 435*l.*; 102, Walton-st., Chelsea, u.t. 50 yrs., g.r. 2*l.*, r. 45*l.*, 660*l.*; 40, First-st., u.t. 53 yrs., g.r. 5*l.*, r. 42*l.*, 460*l.*; 35, 37, and 39, Hungerford-rd., Holloway, u.t. 60 yrs., g.r. 14*l.*, r. 127*l.*, 1,145*l.*; 59, 61, 63, and 71, Hungerford-rd., u.t. 69 yrs., g.r. 16*l.* 6s. 8d., 1,620*l.*; 2 and 4, Isledon-rd., u.t. 51 yrs., g.r. 10*l.* 10s., r. 60*l.*, 645*l.*

JANUARY 15.—By *Baker & Sons*: F.g.r. of 38*l.*, Regent's-sq., with reversion in 13 yrs., 2,075*l.*; f.g.r. of 24*l.*, Sidmouth-st., with reversion in 10 yrs., 1,305*l.*; f.g.r. of 21*l.* 10s., Pembridge Villas, Bayswater, with reversion in 51 yrs., 615*l.* By *R. W. Scobell*: No. 41, Fitzroy-sq., f.r. 225*l.*, 2,020*l.*; l.g.r. of 22*l.*, Albany-st., &c., Regent's Park, u.t. 32 yrs., g.r. 10*l.*, 165*l.*; l.g.r. of 22*l.*, Albany-st., u.t. 32 yrs., with reversion for 24 yrs., 305*l.*; i.g.r. of 103*l.* 4s., Albany-st., u.t. 32 yrs., with reversion for 7½ yrs., 2,550*l.*; improved rental, Brewer-st., Pimlico, u.t. 31 yrs., g.r. 11*l.*, r. 84*l.*, 960*l.*

[*Contractions used in these lists.*—F.g.r. for freehold ground-rent; l.g.r. for leasehold ground-rent; i.g.r. for improved ground-rent; g.r. for ground-rent; r. for rent; f. for freehold; c. for copyhold; l. for leasehold; e.r. for estimated rental; u.t. for unexpired term; p.a. for per annum; yrs. for years; st. for street; rd. for road; sq. for square; pl. for place; ter. for terrace; cres. for crescent; yd. for yard, &c.

PRICES CURRENT OF MATERIALS.

TIMBER.		
Greenheart, B.G. ton	9/0/0	0/0/0
Teak, E.I. load	9/10/0	15/0/0
Sequoia, U.S. ft. cu.	2/3	3/0
Ash, Canada load	2/10/0	4/0/0
Birch, do.	3/0/0	4/5/0
Elm, do.	3/10/0	4/15/0
Fir, Dantsic, &c.	2/0/0	3/10/0
Oak, do.	2/10/0	4/10/0
Canada	5/0/0	7/0/0
Pine, Canada red	2/10/0	3/10/0
Do. yellow	2/10/0	5/0/0
Lath, D'ntsic, fath	5/5/0	6/10/0
St. Petersburg	5/10/0	7/10/0
Deals, Finland, 2nd & 1st std 100	8/10/0	10/10/0
Do. 4th & 3rd	7/10/0	8/10/0
Do. Riga	6/10/0	8/0/0
St. Petersburg, 1st yellow	10/10/0	15/0/0
Do. 2nd yellow	8/10/0	10/0/0
Do. white	7/0/0	10/10/0
Swedish	7/15/0	16/0/0
White Sea	8/10/0	17/10/0
Canada, Pine 1st	19/10/0	25/10/0
Do. do. 2nd	14/10/0	16/10/0
Do. do. 3rd, &c.	8/10/0	10/10/0
Do. Spruce, 1st	8/10/0	11/0/0
Do. do. 3rd & 2nd	6/10/0	8/0/0
New Brunswick	7/0/0	7/10/0
Battens, all kinds	3/10/0	15/10/0
Flooring Boards, sq., 1 in. prep. 1st	0/8/6	0/14/6
Do. 2nd	0/7/6	0/11/6
Other qualities	0/6/3	0/8/0
Cedar, Cuba ft.	/3½	/4½
Honduras, &c.	/3½	/4½
Mahogany, Cuba	/4½	/6½
St. Domingo, cargo av	/4½	2/0
Mexican do. do	/4	/5
Tobasco do. do	/5½	/7
Honduras do.	/5½	/6½
Box, Turkey ton	4/0/0	12/0/0
Rose, Rio	10/0/0	20/0/0
Bahia	9/0/0	16/0/0
Satin, St. Domingo ft.	0/0/9	0/1/3

TIMBER (continued).		
Satin, Porto Rico	0/0/10	0/1/6
Walnut, Italian	0/0/3½	0/0/7
METALS.		
IRON—Pig, in Scotland ton	2/7/0	2/7/3
Bar, Welsh, in London	6/0/0	6/2/6
Do. do. at works in Wales	5/10/0	5/12/6
Do. Staffordshire, in London	6/10/0	6/15/0
COPPER—British, cake and ingot	48/0/0	50/10/0
Best selected	51/0/0	51/10/0
Sheets, strong	59/0/0	60/0/0
Chili, bars	45/10/0	45/17/6
YELLOW METAL lb.	0/0/5½	0/0/6¼
LEAD—Pig, Spanish ton	11/3/9	11/8/3
English, com. brands	11/7/6	11/10/0
Sheet, English, 3 lbs. per sq. ft. and upwards	13/5/0	0/0/0
Pipe	13/15/0	0/0/0
ZINC—English sheet ton	25/0/0	25/10/0
Vieille Montagne	26/10/0	0/0/0
TIN—Straits	90/0/0	90/10/0
Australian	90/0/0	90/10/0
English Ingots	94/10/0	95/10/0
OILS.		
Linseed ton	18/15/0	19/2/6
Cocoanut, Cochin	26/10/0	0/0/0
Do. Ceylon	23/0/0	0/0/0
Palm, Lagos	23/0/0	23/10/0
Rapeseed, English pale	28/15/0	0/0/0
Do. brown	27/0/0	0/0/0
Cottonseed ref.	18/0/0	0/0/0
Oleine	0/0/0	0/0/0
Lubricating, U.S.	4/10/0	5/10/0
Do. refined	6/0/0	11/0/0
TAR—Stockholm barrel	0/19/0	1/0/0
Archangel	0/12/6	0/0/0

TENDERS.

[Communications for Insertion under this heading must reach us *not later than* 12 *noon on Thursdays.*]

BECKENHAM.—For private improvement works in Lucas-road, for the Beckenham Local Board. Mr. Geo. B. Carlton, C.E., Engineer and Surveyor:—

Wondham & Fry	£526	Mid-Kent Building and Contracting Co.	£417
E. & W. Iles	506	John Mowlem & Co.*	395
R. Mayo	436		

* Accepted.

BERKHAMSTEAD.—For the erection of a police-station, lock-up and residence, at Great Berkhamstead, for the Standing Joint Committee of the Quarter Sessions and the County Council for Herts. Mr. Urban Smith, C.E., County Surveyor, architect. Quantities by Mr. Alfred Burr:—

Stephens, Bastow, & Co.	£4,444	G. & J. Waterman	£3,827
John A. Hunt	4,176	J. Honor & Son	3,690
Jas. Payne	4,070	E. Smith & Son	3,650
S. Grist	3,888	F. Dupont, Colchester*	3,637

* Accepted.

LICHFIELD.—For the erection of a new Infirmary, for the Lichfield Board of Guardians. Mr. W. H. Woodroffe, architect, 214, Great Dover-street, London, S.E. :—

F. N. Stephens	£12,058	Parnell & Sons	£8,935
H. Dorse & Son	10,500	Hodges	8,790
Chas. Gray Hill	10,190	R. Willcock	8,576
G. Parker	10,150	H. Vickers	8,500
Jackson Bros.	9,350	Thos. Lowe & Sons, Burton-on-Trent*	8,400
B. Whitehouse	8,981		
G. F. Smith & Sons	8,950	* Modified and accepted at £8,000.	

LONDON.—For erecting new Infirmary, High-street, Lewisham, for the Guardians of the Lewisham Union. Messrs. A. & C. Harston, architects, 15, Leadenhall-street, E.C. Quantities by Messrs. Franklin & Andrews, 25, Ludgate-hill, E.C. :—

Allen & Sons	£62,870	A. Kellett	£52,674
Shillitoe & Son	58,923	Higgs & Hill	51,974
G. Wall	54,675	J. O. Richardson	51,450
C. Miskin	54,394	W. Johnson & Co., Wandsworth-common*	51,000
Leslie & Co.	54,250		
J. & M. Patrick	53,780	W. Brooks	50,850

* Accepted.

LONDON.—For the erection of an Administrative Block and Three Ward Pavilions at the Infirmary, Marloes-road, for the Guardians of the Parish of Saint Mary Abbotts, Kensington, W. Mr. Thos. W. Aldwinckle, architect. Quantities prepared by Mr. W. T. Farthing :—

Garlick & Horton	£56,650	Brass & Son	£42,300
J. O. Richardson	44,210	Leslie & Co.	41,355
J. Mears	43,067	Scharien & Co.	40,750
J. J. Robson	42,984	A. Kellett	40,580
J. P. Plew	42,709	G. Wall	39,241
Kirk & Randall	42,633	W. Johnson & Co.*	35,500

* Accepted.

LONDON.—For new shed, in Market-street, Bermondsey, for Messrs. P. Margetson & Co. Messrs. Elkington & Son, architects :—

S. Kipps	£1,442	A. Stephens	£1,148
W. Higgs	1,285	B. Wells	1,116
W. Castle	1,179		

LONDON.—For hot-water supply apparatus to blocks D, E, & F. of the new Workhouse at St. Pancras. Messrs. A. & C. Harston, architects :—

C. P. Kinnell & Co.	£690 0	J. & F. May	£545 0
J. Fraser & Sons	571 10	Wenham & Waters, Croydon (accepted)	455 0
Clements, Jeakes, & Co.	563 0		

LONDON.—For alterations at the "White Hart," High-street, Shadwell :—

R. L. Williamson	£409 12	Geo. Lane	£368 0
Edwards & Medway	385 0	James Cox*	365 0
Ellis & Turner	370 0	* Accepted.	

LONDON.—Accepted for the erection of residence at Blackheath, S.E., for Mr. J. H. Robinson. Mr. Ebenezer Saunders, architect :—
Kennard Bros., Lewisham Bridge £1,020 0 0
[No competition.]

LONDON.—Accepted for alterations and decorating to "Dartmouth House," Blackheath, for the Bishop of Southwark :—
Kennard Bros., Lewisham £587 10 0

The Builder Cathedral Series.

I. Canterbury	Drawn by	*The Editor*	Jan. 3	1891.
II. Lichfield	"	*W. H. Bidlake*	Feb. 7.	
III. St. Alban's	"	*H. W. Brewer*	Mar. 7.	
IV. Peterborough	"	*A. Mitchell*	April 4	
V. Wells	"	*R. W. Paul*	May 2.	
VI. Exeter	"	*A. N. Wilson*	June 6.	
VII. Salisbury	"	*The Editor*	July 4.	
VIII. Bristol	"	*R. W. Paul*	Aug. 1.	
IX. Norwich	"	*R. K. Greenslade*	Sept. 5.	
X. Rochester	"	*H. W. Brewer*	Oct. 3.	
XI. Lincoln	"	*John Bryn*	Nov. 7.	
XII. Gloucester	"	*C. E. Mallows*	Dec. 5.	
XIII. St. Paul's	"	*The Editor*	Jan. 2.	1892.
XIV. Hereford	"	*J. Johnson*	Feb. 6.	
XV. Chichester	"	*A. B. Pite*	Mar. 5.	
XVI. Ely	"	*Gerald Horsley*	April 2.	
XVII. Llandaff	"	*C. E. Mallows*	May 7.	
XVIII. Oxford	"	*R. W. Paul*	June 4.	

[Further arrangements will be duly announced.]

Price FOURPENCE each (by post 4½d.), except Nos I. and II. which are *out of print*; but the VIEW, PLAN, AND DESCRIPTION of CANTERBURY and of LICHFIELD have been re-printed, and they can now be had, price ONE SHILLING each set; by post, 1s. 2d.

THE REREDOS, ST. PAUL'S.
Reprinted from "The Builder," January 28, 1888 (15 in. by 11½ in.), on stout paper, unfolded, for framing, 6d.; by post, 8d.

PORTFOLIOS,
for Preserving the Plates unfolded, 2s. 6d.; by post, 3s.

London: Office of "The Builder," 46, *Catherine-street, W.C.*

Now ready (66 plates). Price ONE GUINEA.

"THE BUILDER ALBUM" OF ROYAL ACADEMY ARCHITECTURE.

1891.

Extract from the Preface.—"The accompanying set of plates comprises the drawings in the Architectural Room of the Royal Academy Exhibition of this year, which have been lent by their authors for illustration in *The Builder*."

LONDON
Office of "The Builder," 46, Catherine-street, W.C.

SUBSCRIBERS in LONDON and the SUBURBS, by prepaying at the Publishing Office, 19s. per annum (or 4s. 9d. per quarter), can ensure receiving "The Builder" by *Friday Morning's* post.

TERMS OF SUBSCRIPTION.

"THE BUILDER" is supplied DIRECT from the Office to residents in any part of the United Kingdom at the rate of 19s. per annum PREPAID. To all parts of Europe, America, Australia, and New Zealand, 26s. per annum. To India, China, Ceylon, &c., 30s. per annum. Remittances payable to DOUGLAS FOURDRINIER, Publisher, No. 46, Catherine-street, W.C.

TO CORRESPONDENTS.

S. F.—J. & B.—W. H. B. (shall have attention).—C. Bros.—A. T. W. H. W.—"A Constant Reader" (we cannot answer questions [of] that kind).—A. M. (should have sent amount).

All statements of facts, lists of tenders, &c., must be accompanied by the name and address of the sender, not necessarily for publication.

We are compelled to decline pointing out books and giving addresses.

NOTE.—The responsibility of signed articles, and papers read [at] public meetings, rests, of course, with the authors.

We cannot undertake to return rejected communications.

Letters or communications (beyond mere news-items) which have been duplicated for other journals, are NOT DESIRED.

All communications regarding literary and artistic matter should be addressed to THE EDITOR; all communications relating to advertisements and other exclusively business matters should [be] addressed to THE PUBLISHER, and not to the Editor.

The Builder.

VOL. LXII. No. 2556. SATURDAY, JANUARY 30, 1892.

ILLUSTRATIONS.

Sparrowe's House, Ipswich.—Drawn by Mr. John S. Corder .... Double-Page Photo-Litho.
St. Cuthbert's College, Worksop.—Messrs. Carpenter & Ingelow, Architects .... Double-Page Ink-Photo.
Mission Church and Hall, Old Kent-road, for Corpus Christi College, Cambridge.—Mr. R. J. Lovell, Architect .... Double Page Ink-Photo.
Messrs. Schweppe & Co.'s Factory, Malvern.—Messrs. Truefitt & Truefitt, Architects .... Double-Page Photo-Litho

Blocks in Text.

Plan of the Temple of Mecca .... Page 76 | Painted Tile Panel representing the Kaaba at Mecca .... Page 77
Diagrams in Student's Column: Heating by Hot Water .... Pages 85, 86

CONTENTS.

Examples of Mosaic Paving 71
Ancient Sculptures from Central America in the South Kensington Museum 72
Notes 73
Saracenic Architecture 75
Royal Institute of British Architects 78
Old House, Ipswich 80
St. Cuthbert's College, Worksop 80
Mission Church and Hall, Canterbury-road, S.E. 80
New Mineral Water Works at Colwall 80
Architectural Societies 83
London County Council 83
Competitions 84
Nottingham Master Builders' Association 84
Books: S. Hellyer's "Principles and Practice of Plumbing" (London: G. Bell & Sons); F. O. Ferguson's "Architectural Perspective" (London: Crosby Lockwood & Son); "Notes on Building Construction" (London: Longmans, Green, & Co.); "The Essex Review" (London: T. F. Unwin, Chelmsford; E. Durrant & Co.): Short Notices 84
Adjoining Buildings 85
Flooring-Boards on Concrete 85
Bolsover Colliery Competition 85
Student's Column.—Warming Buildings by Hot Water. V 85
Surveyorships 86
Obituary 86
General Building News 86
Foreign and Colonial 87
Miscellaneous 87
Legal 88
Meetings 89
Recent Patents 89
Some Recent Sales of Property 89

Examples of Mosaic Paving.

IN the large thin folio volume brought out under this title,* Mr. Bolton has undoubtedly initiated a new and valuable method in the illustration of ancient examples of mosaic paving. Published illustrations of such examples have hitherto consisted in general of small drawings in which the pattern or design was delineated with as much truth as could be achieved on a small scale, and the ground of the drawings covered with lines to represent the jointings of the mosaic cubes and convey a general idea of mosaic surface, with little attempt at any precise reproduction of the actual facts of the work in detail. As, however, in ancient buildings much of the character depends on the arrangement of the masonry, so in ancient mosaic much of the character depends on the size, shape, and arrangement of the small cubes which form the design. In measuring old buildings enthusiasts have not infrequently measured and plotted all the jointings of the masonry. A similar process is practically impossible with mosaic, but the jointings of a fair-sized portion can be reproduced the actual size by rubbing, and photographed down to a convenient scale for publication. In this instance the examples are reduced to only one-half the original size, which for purposes of study and comparison is nearly as good as the full-size.

The author is undoubtedly quite right in his remark that "the secret of the art of mosaic paving consists in the due recognition of its cube formation." It is this which gives to the surface that peculiar rich and varied texture which is the special attribute of mosaic. An attempt to carry out the work so carefully and with so much finish as to hide the joints is only taking a great deal of trouble to do what could be done much more completely and with less trouble and cost by intarsia work with large pieces of material cut to the required shapes. Wall decorations in mosaic, especially where the subjects approach a pictorial character (which must always, however, be in subordination to a severe conventionalism), may be carried further in refinement of finish than pavements, but even here the toothed surface must not be refined away; part of the effect of the decoration depends on it. In the case of pavements this rule holds good in a more decisive manner. For mosaic in such a situation is really a form of pebble paving; it has actually been carried out in one or two known instances with natural pebbles, and the roughly-squared cubes of ancient pavements in *opus tesselatum* still preserve something of this character. The surface formed has the practical advantage of being a remarkably good one for foothold; the artistic interest consists in the arrangement of the pebbles so as to form a design. To lose this pebbly character is to lose the whole characteristic of this method of forming a floor. Hence, however the finer methods of *opus vermiculatum* may be applicable to wall and ceiling decoration, it is unsuitable to transfer this method to floors.

It must be admitted, however, that the recognition of this pebble character as suitable to mosaic pavement carries with it a great deal of restriction as to the class of subject and the style of ornament which can properly be treated in a mosaic floor of this type. And in this respect it appears to us that Mr. Bolton's natural enthusiasm for the style of work which he has so well and carefully illustrated has rather misled him. We can see nothing for admiration in the clumsily-designed figures executed in large irregular tesseræ, of which he has given one example full size in Plate iii., a figure representing (so he says) a man swimming. We doubt the interpretation even; the position of the arms might represent the action of "hand-over-hand" swimming, but there is no corresponding action of the legs, and the delineation of the hands and feet is ludicrous in its coarseness. The size of the tesseræ in comparison with the scale of the figure renders it in fact quite impossible to give any satisfactory representation of the figure, and we should be disposed to apply to it the same criticism which Professor Middleton applies to the larger mosaics of Caracalla's Baths: "The floors were mostly of mosaic, with coarse figures of athletes, gladiators fighting with beasts, or tritons and dolphins, all rudely executed with large tesseræ, and usually drawn in the most clumsy and inartistic way possible." Generally speaking, in fact, Roman pavement mosaics, however they may claim the merit of frank recognition of the character of the material, are in an artistic sense bad and coarse in execution and mistaken in taste; they represent subjects which cannot adequately be represented in mosaic of this class, and are far too naturalistic in their aim and conception. A fine exception is the notable pavement from Cirencester (not given in this book) of Orpheus taming the beasts, where Orpheus is in the centre of a circle formed by a conventional wreath or garland, while the beasts and birds, treated in profile, walk round the circle in a regular and symmetrical order; an example of true conventional treatment of a legend, suitable to the material and the situation. But anything nearly approaching naturalistic treatment on a mosaic floor is entirely out of place, both in regard to the method of execution and the position in which the work is placed. Naturally-treated figures are out of place even in a mural mosaic, with small tesseræ; they are doubly out of place on a floor, which is a thing to walk over, and more so than ever when made with large tesseræ, with which anything like correct representation even of silhouette figures is an impossibility. The famous Pompeian boar, given in Plate vi., is equally out of place as far as design is concerned, but it is a very remarkable example of spirited and to a great extent truthful representation, or rather indication in work of this kind; the manner in which the cloven hoofs are indicated is especially masterly; but this is work executed in much smaller tesseræ. This figure furnishes Mr. Bolton with matter, however, for a very true bit of criticism, as to the importance of preserving the relation between the ground and the design; and he points out quite rightly the artistic importance of the indication of the ribs of the animal, light against the mass of the rest of the body, thus bringing a portion of the tone of the ground

* "Examples of Mosaic Pavings; from Remains of ...rs at Pompeii and Venice, with Additional Patterns ...n Palermo and Rome." By Arthur Bolton, ...I.B.A. London: B. T. Batsford. 1891.

into the figure. Without these the boar would be a dark mass, distinguishable by outline merely. But this boar is obviously, in every respect, the work of a very clever artist, and deserves all the author claims for it, which certainly cannot be said of the "swimming" man before referred to.

It may be questioned whether the best application of mosaic is not found in geometric patterns rather than in designs from life. At all events, where the latter are introduced, they should be of a very conventional type, and treated rather as centre points in a scheme of geometric design than as the main factors of the design. The kind of things that are frequently found in Roman mosaic are really not design at all; merely attempts at realistic representation introduced at random. In geometric patterns for mosaic the Romans were often exceedingly successful, and have indeed produced some of the best pattern designs that have ever been seen: designs which have passed into what may be called "proverbial" use, forming common elements of mosaic design just as proverbs come to form part of common conversation. It was by the use of intercepted circles or segments that some of the best of these diaper designs were produced; one or two examples of this class are given in Mr. Bolton's book, though not among the very best of them. A remarkable piece of pattern-work is given on Plate viii., the pavement of the "House of Sallust;" this is an exceedingly ingenious piece of design as far as its lines are concerned, but one requires something more than line in a mosaic diaper, it should be rather an arrangement of contrasted surfaces than of mere lines. It would be quite possible to work out such a design on the lines of the "House of Sallust" pattern. The employment of a design formed mainly in lines is suitable for scrolls and conventional foliage; but a diaper pattern in lines only has a thin and hard effect. One absolute rule may be laid down, viz.; that nothing in mosaic pavement should be designed so as to give the effect of relief of surface. The Romans were well-known sinners in this respect, and seemed to enjoy the use of shading so as to produce the effect of solid cubes with sinkings between them. It would be impossible to misuse the material or the art of design (so-called) more utterly, and it does not appear that Mr. Bolton has quite the holy horror of this kind of work which we should have expected him to express.

One or two chromo-lithographs are given, showing examples of colour in mosaic. One of these, Plate x., from the house of Holconius at Pompeii, is about as poor a piece of work of the kind as could well be seen, and, both in colour and design, looks like a very commonplace piece of worsted-work for a cheap cushion or footstool. The peacock from the pavement of the Church of San Donato, Murano, is a fine piece of conventionalism in its way; the treatment of the bird, within the limits of mosaic, is excellent, and the colour effect rich and harmonious, but the large irregular pieces of coloured enamel in the tail of the bird, put in in one piece, have not the best effect, and the introduction of large single pieces in this manner, among the smaller cubes of the rest of the work, is quite out of keeping with the proper principle of mosaic, as the author indeed points out in the course of his introductory remarks, though he seems to have passed it over here.

As an illustration of ancient mosaic this book is a new departure which the author might very well follow up on a larger scale in future. He tells us that the book was not planned till after his return from Italy, or some examples would have been included which have now been unavoidably omitted. The method of production enables one to study the character of the ancient mosaic work depicted, almost as well as from the originals; and the plates serve to remind one of what is often forgotten in modern mosaic, that too great symmetry and rigidity in laying the tesseræ is not to be desired, and in fact detracts from the proper character of the work, giving it a hard mechanical appearance. Mosaic pavement is a pavement of blocks on a small scale, and should preserve this character whatever design it is worked into; care being taken however that there should be some fit relation of scale between the size of the blocks and the scale of the design. The Roman tendency was to introduce designs too small to be properly defined by the tesseræ, or to use tesseræ too large for the design, whichever way we take it. For a pavement this is a better mistake than using the tesseræ too small; but it is still a mistake, and some of the plates in this book illustrate the fact, though in general they serve to exemplify the true and proper use of mosaic in pavements.

ANCIENT SCULPTURES FROM CENTRAL AMERICA IN THE SOUTH KENSINGTON MUSEUM.

WITHIN the past four years some interesting additions have from time to time been made to the exhibits in the Architectural Court of the South Kensington Museum, in the shape of casts of obelisks, altars, and, in some cases, originals of pieces of sculptured stones from certain of the ruined "cities" or pueblos of Central America. The originals, or the moulds, as the case may be, were brought to this country by Mr. A. P. Maudslay, who has devoted so much time to the research and systematic exploration of the sites of these ancient Indian towns. Most of the objects represented were found at Copan, in Honduras, and there is a large model of the mounds and ruined terraces of that place, clearly showing the enormous extent of the excavations and surveys made and indicating the sites whereon the obelisks, &c., were discovered. Excellent descriptions of the works at Copan have been published by Mr. Maudslay, notably in the "Proceedings of the Royal Geographical Society," Vol. viii., n. s. 1886, pp. 568 *et seq.*, and "Biologia Centrali Americana" *Archæology*, pt. i., 1889. The former also contains descriptions of the remains at Quirigua, whilst the text of the latter work, illustrated by photogravures, is accompanied by a large atlas, with photographs reproduced by the autotype process, and the manner in which the whole has been "got up" is certainly worthy of the important discoveries to which they refer.

Other travellers, and especially Messrs. Stephens & Catherwood, have also written of the Copan ruins, and all agree that the most interesting are the sculptured obelisks or monoliths, of which five are represented by plaster casts in the Museum. Three of these are elaborately carved, and each bears on its front a long-robed human figure, standing full-faced in a stiff and conventional attitude, with profuse head-gear; the sides and back of the monuments being covered with tables of hieroglyphics. The fourth has a human figure both back and front, with beads represented on its sides, whilst the fifth is covered with hieroglyphics on all sides. The human figures alluded to have been described as priests in pontifical robes; but evidence is not wanting to show that they represent gods; some which were found certainly look like idols. Nobody has yet succeeded in unravelling the meaning of the hieroglyphics, which are found not only on the monoliths, but on the altars and some of the tablets. Mr. Maudslay says* that the "tables of hieroglyphs should be read in double columns from left to right and from top to bottom. . . . . One of the most interesting points which I have noticed is that all the inscriptions which I have reason to believe are complete from the commencement are headed by what I shall call an initial scroll (the type of which is permanent throughout many variations), and begin with the same formula, usually extending through six squares of hieroglyphic writing, the sixth square, or sometimes the latter half of the sixth square, being a human face, usually in profile, enc
in a frame or cartouche."

* "Proc. Roy. Geog. Soc.," *op. cit.* p. 593.

Four blocks from Copan, which are bel
to be altars, are exhibited in the Mu
The carvings on the sides of one of
represent men in an Eastern-looking
dress, the majority of whom are sitting
legged on small tablets of hieroglyp
position which, to judge from similar car
in the other stonework, seems to ha
peculiar significance. In this connexio
may call attention to the face of a step f
in a temple, the original of which is also
in the Museum. It may be noted that
of the seated figures are exactly in the
posture, some have one foot on the gr
holding a scroll or other object in one
and having the arm raised in the a
resting by the side, and each figure poss
different details on the head-gear so
the monotony of the whole is some
relieved.

The plaster cast of a seat, the orig
sculptures of several heads, the body
"singing girl," and a foot showing th
passing between two of the toes and faste
round the ankle by a buckle, all of w
were found amongst the ruins, are
exhibited.

Before the survey of Copan was c
menced, the whole site was covered with fo
trees or an almost impenetrable scrub, an
was found necessary to clear a great par
this growth away before any idea of the p
could be obtained. The monuments had
to be cleaned down, the superfluous moss
vegetation having to be removed before c
could be taken. Without going much i
details, it may be mentioned that the st
tures met with during the course of the ex
vations were composed of a rubble of sto
and earth, faced with well-laid masonry.
was shown that the pyramidal structu
were almost in every case the raised foun
tions which supported roofed buildings
probably temples,—which were approac
by steep flights of steps; the bui
ings were most profusely ornamen
with sculpture. To give some idea of
character of this work, Mr. Maudslay il
trates an elaborate doorway leading to
inner chamber of a temple, and also sun
fragments and figures from other positi
which are highly instructive. Speaking
the doorway he says that there are in
design good examples of two marked cha
teristics of all American sculpture, nam
the inability of the artist to leave plain
faces alone, and the love of introducing
tesque faces or scroll-work derived from t
into the ornamentation of details.

The smaller mounds shown on the m
referred to in the Museum are the rem
of what were probably dwelling-houses.
were stone-roofed, and the "system of roo
here used (as in almost all ancient Ameri
buildings) was what may be called the h
zontal arch." The age of these buildin
extremely doubtful. Certain authors a
opinion that they were erected and use
the Indians at the time of the Spanish
covery and conquest of the country, b
seems that there is very little to support
view. The doings of the Spanish conque
are fairly well known through the writ
of Cortez, Bernal Dias, and others,
either mentioned or described impor
places. No mention is made of
important city at or near Copan, and
Indians in the vicinity were not adva
enough in the arts of civilisation to
executed such works. We think there
be no doubt that the civilisations which
duced the buildings and sculptures at Co
and in all similar ancient pueblos in Gu
mala, Honduras, and Yucatan, had p
away long prior to the Spanish conquest
they were in a flourishing condition in
time of Cortez, he would certainly have
tioned them, as he gives such good acco
of his different journeys.

The largest obelisk represented in the
lection at the South Kensington Mus
comes from Quirigua, and does not mater
differ from those described from Co

ring the conventional erect human figures, on both back and front, the sides of the nument being covered with hieroglyphs. large, rudely-carved tablet, showing a ted human figure holding a bowl with an mal's head in it, comes from the same ce.

There are also some tablets, carved in relief, excellent condition, from ruins on the bank the Usumacinta river, Mexico, which ms the boundary of the province of basco and the Republic of Guatemala. ne of these represent a serpent with a man head rising out of a bowl and leaning r a man crouched or sitting on his anches. The serpent plays a conspicuous rt in many of these ancient Central nerican works, and by means of such symbols, gether with the numerous picture writings d strings and tables of more or less turesque hieroglyphs, we may some day be le to learn more concerning the remarkable ople who made them. The indefatigable nner in which Mr. Maudslay has photo-phed and had plaster casts made of all the st-preserved or striking hieroglyphs on the ot, in spite of the many dangers he has countered, is deserving of the highest aise. We may mention that he has also sented a series of the plaster casts to the chæological Museum at Cambridge.

NOTES.

THE Royal Academy, we are glad to see, has recognised Architecture in its last election of Associates, and added an able and cultivated ntleman to its numbers in the election of r. T. G. Jackson. That Mr. Jackson should the next choice whenever a new Architect sociate was elected must have been con-ered for some time past a foregone conclu-n, and we have only wondered that the nour should not have been offered earlier an architect whose claims to it were so lisputable. The other Associates elected Mr. Stanhope Forbes and Mr. Harry tes, and both of these elections will also, think, meet with general approval. Mr. nhope Forbes may be considered to be *ile princeps* among the younger school of nters of *genre*, to use a hackneyed term ich seems, however, hardly adequate to icate a class of paintings which combine much admirable delineation of character h so much of moral feeling and purpose. Harry Bates, on the other hand, is an artist e and simple, who uses sculpture as a form oetic expression, sometimes in telling again antique legend, sometimes in the mere ression of energy and grandeur of line modelling, as in his powerful group of ounds in leash."* There can be no ques-of his claim to the honour; but we ret that in doing justice to some of the nger sculptors of the day the Academy so persistently passed over an older mant, Mr. G. A. Lawson, whose works e exhibited qualities both of design and ception which have not received the recog-on they merit.

N article in the current number of the *Quarterly Review*, on "The Water ply of London," is obviously written in interests of the Water Companies. The ct is to show that the Thames can be d on for everything; that the objection he use of the Thames on the ground of ution of the water is without foundation, that the water supply of London can be er provided by private enterprise than by public body. That the complaints some-s made as to the character of the water at ent supplied to London have often been ly exaggerated is perfectly true, and it is ally true that the Companies have improved supply very much in the course of their tence, and have in fact done their best for public in regard to the quality of the ply, whatever may be thought as to their tactics in regard to their commercial dealings with their customers. To maintain, however, the advisability of trusting to open rivers for water-supply is to ignore the increasingly pronounced opinion of the medical profession generally; while in considering the capacity of the Thames to maintain an adequate supply for London the *Quarterly Review* quietly ignores altogether the fact that the river, *quâ* river, is in process of being ruined by even the present amount of abstraction from its stream; let alone what further raids may be made upon it by a constantly-increasing demand. The *Quarterly Review* refers com-placently to the testimony of the late Mr. John Harrison in regard to "other ad-ditions that might be obtained, if necessary, within the locality." If the writer of the article had been present at the meetings of the Institution of Civil Engineers a few months ago, when Mr. Harrison's proposi-tions were discussed, he would perhaps scarcely have had the hardihood to cite an authority whose proposals and arguments were so completely and almost contemp-tuously disposed of as were Mr. Harrison's on that occasion. The scheme for storage reservoirs in connexion with the upper por-tions of the Thames is advanced again as a solution of the difficulty, with a convenient forgetfulness of the fact that reservoirs in such a position (the only possible position if they are to supply by gravitation) must allow the great bulk of flood water to escape, while they must utterly ruin the upper portion of the Thames as a river. The bias of the whole article, in supporting the water companies through thick and thin, and ignoring every scheme that might be supposed to be in opposition to their interests, is so obvious as to be almost ludicrous; but such an article may do a great deal of harm in influencing the large majority of readers who know nothing of the subject, and who fondly imagine that a paper of this kind in a review of long standing is to be taken as an impartial discussion of the sub-ject. Probably the editor of the *Quarterly Review* is no better informed on the subject than the bulk of his readers; but the ap-pearance of an article in this style of mani-fest advocacy, on a subject which especially demands, in the public interest, a purely impartial and scientific treatment, is not creditable to a review of the standing and position of the *Quarterly*.

* Illustrated in the *Builder* for June 6, 1891.

THE present epidemic of influenza draws attention to the great desirability of every house in the country, and every large house in town, having a large room or rooms isolated as far as possible, and capable of being used as a sanatorium. In every large family there is always liability to infectious diseases, and if there is a part of the building which can be used with success as a sana-torium, it is, undoubtedly, a safeguard against the spread of disease, and a great convenience to all concerned. In small houses this kind of isolation is practically impossible; but this fact again compels attention to the want in London of hospitals for the use of those who can pay for them,—not in cases of accident, but in cases of disease, especially of an infectious character. There is an idea that a hospital of such a kind is a danger to the community; on the contrary, by concentrating sick persons in a proper building, and removing them from private houses, much of the risk of the spread of disease is removed. We are thus brought face to face with another consideration, viz., whether such hospitals should be erected and managed by the governing bodies of localities? Some day they will certainly form one of the types of buildings necessary in any well-organised social community.

IT is curious how long a monument of first-rate importance may lie *perdu* in an archæological collection of long standing, apparently just because the collection itself is so well known that the novelty hunter passes it lightly by. A terra-cotta relief, just published in the last issue of the Roman section of the *Mittheilungen* of the German Archæological Institute (vi. 3), well illus-trates this point. Dr. Studniczka has dis-covered in the well-known Santangelo collec-tion of the Naples Museum, hidden in a mass of terra-cotta lamps of Græco-Roman date, an archaic relief, curious and important, both for subject and treatment. The relief, of which about a fourth at either end is unfor-tunately broken off, represents a female *Xoanon* of the most archaic type. The figure is standing erect, with hands stiffly depend-ent at each side. The right hand held some uncertain attribute; but the remarkable point about the figure is the elaborate decoration of the formal, foldless robe. It is divided into three parallel friezes. In the topmost of these is depicted, in the well-known type, Ajax carrying the body of Achilles. In the second frieze a *choros* of women are dancing hand-in-hand; in the third a similar *choros* of men. Clearly we have here the copy of a cultus image wearing a ceremonial robe, just such a robe as was woven for the Pan-athenaic Athene. Dr. Studniczka's paper should be read by all those interested in archaic art. In the same number of the *Mittheilungen* is published a charming little bronze, which its owner, a dealer in Rome, lent to Dr. Petersen for the purpose. The bronze represents a boy, stooping, with a hand firmly planted on each knee and his feet somewhat widely apart. The meaning is made clear by a vase in the British Museum (recently published by Mr. A. H. Smith, in the "Journal of Hellenic Studies," 1890, plate xii., p. 279). Here a family of Satyrs are playing a sort of modi-fied form of leap-frog—the leaper, instead of clearing the Satyr who is "giving him a back," descends on his shoulders, and there remains. Examined by the light of this vase, the outline of the bronze becomes clear, and to make things yet more satisfactory, traces of a figure now broken off are ob-servable on the boy's shoulders. It is an interesting instance of the light thrown by vase-paintings on sculptural art, as well as a pleasant glimpse into the boy-life of antiquity. The boy who carried the other was called, we learn from Pollux, the "donkey," and he was sometimes made to fill the post by way of "forfeit."

ADVERTING to two of our "Notes" of the 16th and 23rd instant, we are sorry to find that an attack of influenza incapa-citates Miss Sellers from continuing, for the present, her class at the British Museum. Last Tuesday Miss Millington-Lathbury, upon very short notice, took her colleague's place, and gave her opening lecture upon the daily life and thought of the Greeks, dealing, from an archæological standpoint chiefly, with their temples, ritual, and religious cult. Showing, firstly, how the king-priest, as priest-king, had his counterpart in the head of even the smallest or meanest household, the lecturer dwelt upon the political solidity which grew out of the religious ceremonies of the Greeks, and explained how these,—which, however simple or complex, they always exactly observed,—expressed con-ceptions of a deity whom they at first saw in every natural thing, and went on to set up as a god, humanwise, of something—a god to be propitiated and dreaded, and on occasion, as we know, to be cajoled. Thus they passed from animism to an at once elevated and debased anthropomorphism. The temple of such a deity was not, Eleusis excepted, a resort for worshippers or suppliants: it was his secluded dwelling-place and treasury; the altar, whether there or at their own homes, formed the point around which the cult con-centrated, and on the altar they made sacri-fices of expiation or appeasement, with an underlying idea that the deity should partake of their cheer, hospitably offered. Then, with the aid of plans, Miss Millington-Lathbury traced the temple's growth. The pristine wooden hut yielded to one of brick or clay, and that to the stone-built cella, though it seems that wood was never quite discarded; yet with its successive accretions of portico, πρόναος and ὀπισθόδομος, until they attained to the dipteral Olympieium itself, the whole ἱερόν was but a fort or stronghold for the cella (ναός, or σηκός), wherein the god abode. And here it occurred to us that the difference between the old religion and the new might be briefly illustrated by contrasting the templum, or τέμενος, or hedged-in enclosure, wherefrom, save in a few instances, the dead, and many of the living, were excluded, with our church, or τὸ κυριακόν, the Lord's house, in which all alike gather for praise and prayer. We may add that in regard to the lighting of Grecian temples the lecturer expressed accord with Dr. Dörpfeld's opinion, on which we recently commented.

THE restoration,—or, rather, re-erection,—of the monument of Queen Eleanor in Lincoln Minster, unveiled recently, is noteworthy as being the munificent gift of a leading Nonconformist to the cathedral of the city of his adoption. The monument takes the place of that erected by Edward I. over the portions of his consort's body removed in the process of embalming, which, though on a somewhat smaller scale, was in all essential features a *replica* of that placed over her grave in Westminster Abbey. The priceless "Hatton MS." belonging to Lord Winchilsea, and deposited temporarily by him at the rooms of the Society of Antiquaries for inspection, among the many drawings of sepulchral memorials in our cathedrals and great churches, taken under the direction of Sir W. Dugdale before the outbreak of the Great Rebellion, contains a careful representation of this monument, which, aided by the Westminster tomb, has served as a guide to Mr. Pearson and Mr. Nicholls in their restoration of the tomb and effigy. The effigy of the Queen, which was cast by Mr. Singer, of Frome, is executed in gilt bronze; the altar tomb, on which the effigy reposes, of dove-coloured Hopton-Wood stone, contrasts well with the subdued brilliancy of the effigy. The sides of the tomb are decorated, as at Westminster, with shallow canopied recesses containing shields with the armorial bearings of England, Castile and Leon, and Ponthieu, dependent from bunches of natural foliage,—oak, vine, and maple. The carving of these, as well as of the crockets of the canopies and the other decorative work, is admirable. Mr. Pearson may be congratulated on the success, from one point of view, of a somewhat difficult undertaking. Whether this re-making of approximate copies of lost monuments is a process altogether worth the pains and cost expended on it, may however be a question.

A COMMITTEE of those interested in architecture and the various artistic crafts, such as decorative painting, wood and stone carving, metal working, &c., has been formed in Edinburgh. Dr. Rowand Anderson, President of the Committee, in an address to the Edinburgh Trades' Council on the subject last week, said:—The kind of technical education they proposed was the teaching of the eye and the hand to work in harmony and sympathy with one another, and of the judgment and imagination to invest all handicraft work with intelligence, purpose, and grace. For this purpose they would require 2,000*l*., and 1,567*l*. had already been received or promised. Funds would also be required for travelling and other scholarships. The sanction of the Secretary for Scotland had been obtained for the use of the rooms in the Royal Institution formerly occupied as an antiquarian museum. It was intended that the classes should be managed by a representative Committee and a Committee of the Board of Manufactures, and that they should be conducted by men of eminence. At present, work requiring an artist had too often to be left out of consideration, or when art was required, workmen had too often to be brought from elsewhere, or the work sent out of the country. There was, he argued, no reason why Edinburgh should not be a centre of art.

THE Official Examiners have passed the Bill for enabling the trustees to borrow 100,000*l*. for an enlargement, with improvements, of the Borough Market, one of the oldest in London. In 1290 a number of stalls were cleared away from London Bridge; and for a long period, as we gather from Dr. Rendle's communication to *Notes and Queries* of December 17, 1887, the market was carried on within the precincts of (old) St. Thomas's Hospital, or at St. Margaret's Church-gate, and then in Long Southwark, as they called the main street between the church (its site being that of Town Hall-chambers), near the Tabard Inn, and the bridge-foot. In its midst stood a cage and pillory, with whipping-posts near at hand. Booths and stalls, too, seem to have been placed in the churchyard. In Stow's time they sold leather on St. Margaret's-hill, and the church, "being put down," served for a compter, or jail, as well as for courts of assize and the Admiralty. Under an Act of 1756 the Local Authorities suppressed the traffic; a subsequent enactment set up the market again, in the Triangle at the back of Three Crown-court, and near to Foul-lane and Rochester-yard: a site anciently known as Grimes Croft, which William, second Earl Warren, had granted to the monks of Rochester. There stood Rochester House, an "inn" of the Bishops of that See, and pulled down in 1604. Fifty years ago they extended the market area by demolishing St. Saviour's Grammar School, which Thomas Cure, Queen's saddler, and a great benefactor to the parish, had, with others, founded in 1562, and to which Queen Elizabeth gave a charter of incorporation. The old school buildings, on the site of the prior's house, south of St. Mary Overie's, were rebuilt after the great fire, which devastated this part of Southwark in May, 1676;* the new buildings were erected, 1838, after the designs of Mr. Christopher Edmonds, architect, on land given by Dr. Sumner, Bishop of Winchester, in the street bearing his name. In 1885 Mr. McIntyre North, architect, prepared plans for a proposed increase of this market, by taking in more ground between Borough High-street and Messrs. Barclay & Perkins' brewery, Park-street, at an estimated cost of about 65,000*l*. The annual profit, arising from the sale of mostly fruit and vegetables, was then assessed at nearly 7,000*l*. Rebuilt in 1686, the Town Hall was pulled down in 1793, and its statue of King Charles II. re-erected in Three Crown-court, where—as at King's Cross—the pedestal served for a watch-house and lock-up.

THE great height of buildings in America is beginning to make the fire insurance companies uneasy. It appears that the Chicago Fire Underwriters' Association, which includes all American and foreign companies doing insurance business in America, with one exception, has decided that all office buildings of non-combustible description should be limited in height to not more than one and a-half times the width of the street. It further appears that this important association regards many of the so-called non-combustible buildings as practically unsafe from their great height. There is no doubt that high buildings are one of the dangers of modern city life,—a danger which will probably increase rather than decrease. The United States would have to pass a general Act of Congress on this point if they wish to have uniformity and safety; but the subject is one of those which by the constitution is essentially one which must be dealt with by each State according to its own views.

IN a letter in the *Times* of the 26th, in regard to the ventilation of the House of Commons, Sir Douglas Galton gives a description of the "wet screen" in use at the Victoria Infirmary at Glasgow for the removal of dirt and fog from the air previously

* See the woodcut in the *Mirror*, April 18, 1840. Here Dr. Heberden, and John Harvard, founder of Harvard, U.S.A., are believed to have been educated.

eness of the water, but through the king of the pipes. Large volumes of air :e pumped in, and the water was also :ed with purer water from Lake Tegel. the light of further experiment, it was cluded that by throwing the water in a ies of cascades, and afterwards filtering, difficulty could be got over. In the :lin waterworks, Mr. Oesten, the Engineer, devised an apparatus by which the water nade to pass in fine streams through a tance of about 6 ft., and it is then passed ough a filter. It is said that with this cess of aëration, filtration can safely be formed at three times the speed of ordinary er-beds used for purifying surface-water.

---

a paper read before the Dresden Society of Engineers and Architects, some parlars have been given of the regulations in e with regard to the hygienic conditions railway carriages on the Prussian State ways. The amount of air-space in the partments required per passenger is 68, and 30 cubic feet for first-class, second-ss, and third-class carriages respectively. e average percentage of passengers being y 24·6 per cent. of the available seats, the ount of air-space actually provided is proximately four times as great as that ve stated. The amount of ventilation uired, in order to limit the percentage of bonic acid in the air of a railway compartnt to one-tenth per cent., varies between) and 1,360 cubic feet per hour per pasger. Herr Pfuelzner, the author of the er referred to, considers it hardly possible obtain so vigorous a ventilation without ducing draughts. In England it would m as if we had solved the paradox of pro-ing draught without any ventilation at so draughty to the legs and feet, and so ffy may be the upper part of a carriage; ugh in rolling-stock fitted with "torpes" there is a great improvement in this pect. The author of the paper objects to oves for heating as being dangerous, prerring steam-pipes under the seats, but below e level of the floor. Carriages with iron or eel under-frames, he states, are more noisy an those with under-frames of wood. On e other hand, spoke-wheels are less noisy an solid disc wheels, but the former produce ore dust.

THE Electrical Exhibition at the Crystal Palace is still far from complete, though has now been opened for nearly three eeks. In the South Gallery most of the alls are still empty, and some elaborately-rnished rooms are lighted by a line of gas-ts a few feet from the floor. The catalogue s reached a second edition, though still ated to be "under revision." The plans of e Exhibition in this edition are on a larger ale, but the general arrangement of the ok is unaltered, and it still tells us that the oard of Trade unit is 1,000 watts per hour, : watt-hours, as though the expressions ere equivalent. The machine-room is open, d the exhibits in it fairly complete, as also e most of those in the nave. Amongst ese latter, some of the most generally teresting are the portable lamps and e apparatus for heating and cooking by ectricity. In the Gallery, Mr. Harness llects a crowd to receive shocks from a rson on an insulated stand, who is charged r means of a large influence machine—a me-worn experiment that seems never to se its charm.

THE Committee of the Whitworth Institute have taken a very unusual course in lation to the competition for designs for the oposed building (the result of which is iefly noticed in our "Competitions" column), admitting competitors only to the exhibion of the drawings, and refusing to admit e representative of an architectural journal, : (we presume) of any paper, to inspect and iticise the designs. The matter is of no nsequence to us, but we do not think the rangement will be satisfactory to competitors, who wish an award in an important competition to be open to public criticism; and the reasons given for it appear to indicate that the committee are under a misapprehension as to the nature of the interest which architectural journals and their readers take in a matter of this kind. The committee are apparently committed to some change of policy in the matter, and do not wish any public clue to be given as to what they have intended or now intend. We care nothing whatever about their policy; the matter to our readers is simply a consideration of the manner in which a given architectural problem has been treated in regard to plan and design, with the further interest to competitors that they may wish to have the award independently criticised, if there should be anything open to criticism in connexion with it. We may point out also to the Committee that it would of course be perfectly easy, for any journal which chose to adopt such a method, to get a competitor to write an account of the designs. We expect to find that this has been done, and in that case all the committee will have got by their scrupulous adherence to official privacy will be the publication of descriptions written by interested persons, instead of by perfectly independent critics who have no interest of their own to serve.

SARACENIC ARCHITECTURE.*

BY PROFESSOR AITCHISON, A.R.A.

IF the saying of Sir Joshua Reynolds be true "that it is by being conversant with the inventions of others that we learn to invent," I want no further excuse for speaking of Saracenic architecture.

The vulgar reproach addressed to architects is that they do not invent a new style, while the Saracens certainly did, which, in its developed form, no one can mistake. Those who reproach architects with not inventing a new style forget that hundreds of years are required to evolve one, and that one of the conditions of its evolution is that the people should appreciate and admire the new grafts on the old stock.

The architects of the early Saracen monuments were probably Byzantine, or if not they were natives of the countries the Saracens conquered. When the Saracens began to have a style it would be interesting to know on what former style it was founded, and of what nationality the architects were who made the first steps forward. It would, however, be a hopeless task to trace their genealogy, as polygamy then prevailed, even if we knew their names, and few of their names are known, so we must be content to call that architecture Saracenic that flourished in countries under the rule of the Caliphs, unless we know to the contrary.

I was curious to learn what architectural art the Saracens brought with them from their native land, but if they had any, it seems impossible to ascertain what it was. Mecca is said to have been built with stone cut from the granite mountains that surround it, but I had never seen even a photograph of it, until Mr. Carpenter lent me these a few days ago. The Kaaba, or great Temple of the Arabs, supposed to have been built by Abraham, existed in Mohammed's time, and was rebuilt when he was a man of thirty-five, after being ruined by a flood. We know that its walls were then taken down to the footings, and rebuilt to a height of 4 ft. or 5 ft. with pieces of grey granite from the adjoining mountains, and that at this point the black stone was carried to it in Mohammed's Cloak by a man holding each corner, and that each of the men belonged to one of the four divisions or tribes of Mecca. It was fixed in the south-east angle by Mohammed himself. What the upper part of the Kaaba was made of we do not know. A Greek or a Byzantine ship had been wrecked at the time of the rebuilding, on the neighbouring shore of the Red Sea. The Koreish bought the timber of the vessel, and employed the captain, named Bacûm, who was skilled in architecture, to assist in the rebuilding of the Kaaba, and it was roofed with sixteen rafters or joists, resting on six central pillars. The Kaaba was originally covered with cloth that hung like a curtain on all sides, and was its only roof, *i.e.*, it was an hypæthral temple, until this wooden roof was made by Bacûm; it was subsequently enlarged by the Caliphs Omar, Othman, Ibn-Zobeir, and Abd-al-Melik, afterwards by the Sultans of Egypt, and its present form dates from the work of the Sultan of Turkey, Amurath III., in 1576, in our Queen Elizabeth's reign. On the east side, about 6 ft. from the corner of the black stone, was a door 6 ft. or 7 ft. from the ground, and entrance could only be got by a set of steps on wheels being rolled up to it.

It is not quite clear whether the idol Hobal, of red agate, was inside the Kaaba or outside. The Kaaba must, I fancy, have been mainly of wood, as it is said to have been burnt down in Yezid I. and Abd-al-Melik's time, but it may have been that the curtains caught fire and burnt the roof, the curtains or coverings in Omar's time were of linen, and afterwards of silk and cotton brocade, attached to the walls, and till the time of the Abbassides the new coverings were put over the old ones. There was a celebrated temple in Arabia, mentioned by Diodorus Siculus about 8 B.C. (Lib. 3, cap. 3):—"The people that inhabit these parts are called Bizomenians, and live upon wild beasts taken in hunting. Here's a sacred temple in high veneration among all the Arabians;" but whether it was the Kaaba or not I am unable to say, though it is believed to have been, as there was no other celebrated temple in Arabia. The Kaaba is now said to be an irregular oblong in plan, about 50 ft. by 40 ft.

It is stated that in Mohammed's time, an aqueduct was tried to be built from Mount Arafat, but without success, so the Saracens of his day were evidently not great builders; although there were Christians, Jews, Abyssinians, and Persians among them. Mohammed, it is true, had a mosque built at Medina when he settled there, but it is believed to have been mainly of wood, with wooden columns; his wives' houses, that formed the east side of the enclosure of the mosque, were of unburnt bricks, with partitions of wattle and dab. Mohammed had no house of his own, but lived with his wives in turn; he, however, speaks of columns and arched vaults in the Koran (cap. 104); and a splendid tomb, with a cupola, is said to have been built over his grave, but of what material we know not. His tomb was built in Ayesha's house, at the spot where he died, and the tombs of the two succeeding Caliphs were also erected there.

The Saracens were of three sorts,—(1) Wandering tribes of herdsmen or nomads, who, as Aristotle says ("Politics," Lib. I., cap. 8), combined brigandage with it for convenience; (2) those who lived in towns and tilled the land, as the people of Medina; but husbandmen were looked down on by the wandering and by the trading people; and (3) those who were carriers and merchants, like the people of Mecca, all of them seem to have found it convenient to add brigandage to their other occupations; one of the principal quarrels between the people of Mecca and Medina, after Mohammed settled there, was the marauding expeditions he ordered against their caravans.

The Meccans looked upon themselves as the people of most capitals do, and the tribe whose head men had the care of the Kaaba, and the well of Zem-Zem, the Koreish, considered themselves as by far the most important tribe, looked down on the rest, and held the wandering Arabs in contempt; but, unfortunately for the continuance of Saracen sway, the wandering Arabs equally despised husbandmen and merchants. After their first foreign conquests, the leading families of this tribe of Mecca were called the Princes of the Koreish, and Mohammed was of this tribe. The east coast of Arabia was a convenient landing-place for the products of Persia, India, and the far East, as well as for those of the east and south coasts of Africa; while the ports on the Red Sea were possibly used for the exchange of the products of the East with those of Europe, Asia Minor, Syria, and the North Coast of Africa; though in old times all the main trade routes were land routes, and the whole Saracen Nation was at one time engaged in carrying. This business was greatly interfered with by the Romans discovering the passage to the East by the Red Sea, through the Straits of Bab-el-Mandeb, "The Gate of Tears," and was the probable cause of the large migration of Arabs to the

* Being the first Royal Academy Lecture on Architecture this session. Delivered on Monday evening, January 25.

North of Syria, but caravans still went to Palestine and Syria, as Mohammed accompanied his uncle Abu Talib there, and it is said that one caravan in Mohammed's time went to the Court of Cosroes, the King of Persia. Even as late as the first three Caliphs, there was great reluctance shown by them to let their people trust to the dangers of the sea. Arabia itself is said to produce frankincense and other gums, —gum-arabic, for instance,—manna, and odoriferous herbs, we have all heard of "the perfumes of Arabia." It also contained precious stones, the onyx, the ruby, and the Mocha stone, and pearls were found in the Persian Gulf. Coffee was not then discovered, and it is doubtful if the lead mines were worked; silver and gold were said to be found there, but as Arabia was an emporium, it is only from modern travellers that we can judge of what it produces, as the old writers spoke of all the things that came from Arabia as native products, hence its ancient reputation for wealth.

Although architecture has perhaps no direct connexion with any form of belief, still temples have mostly been the greatest works that architects have created, and each particular belief has greatly influenced the adornments bound up with the architecture; so I think it necessary to say something of the new religion of the Saracens, for it welded for a time a set of hostile tribes into a nation, and sent them forth to conquer all the countries of the ancient world; it thus caused the creation of mosques, and probably the modification of the plans of other buildings, and of ornament, the latter through the exclusion of animal life.

Before Mohammed published the Korân, and declared himself the last prophet of God, the Arabs were mostly idolators, though some had embraced Judaism or Christianity; the idolators mostly worshipped the host of Heaven, or some particular gods or goddesses, and did not believe in another life; this time of idolatry was afterwards called by them,—"the days of ignorance."

The Kaaba at Mecca was the great temple of Arabia, to which all the tribes came once, and sometimes twice, a-year to worship and to sacrifice, and these were called the greater and less pilgrimages. The four months kept sacred from war were devoted to the time occupied in making the pilgrimages, the sacrifices, and the religious exercises.

In the enclosures round the Kaaba were 360 idols, including the black stone, probably a meteorolite, said by modern travellers to be roughly hemispherical, about 6 in. high and 8 in. in diameter, and of a reddish-black colour.

During the time of the pilgrimage a fair was held at Mecca; Mecca itself was in a barren valley that produced nothing, so that two caravans a year had to bring the Meccans the staple articles of food, besides what they got from the environs. The pilgrimage of people from all parts of Arabia to the Kaaba, and this fair greatly enriched the inhabitants.

The condition and habits of the Arabs in the days of ignorance were thus described by a new convert to Islâm:—"The men who had clothes had generally a garment of camel's hair, besides the turban; fed on fruits, parched grain, broiled snakes and lizards, and drank brackish water, killed anyone they could who was worth robbing, and buried alive all their superfluous female children. Their courage, ferocity, and bloodthirstiness were probably unparalleled, until the turn of the Tartars came; they were probably not more inhuman and perfidious than other savages, and, as Cetywayo said of the negroes, could only be governed by killing large numbers of them. Hajjaj, the governor of Cufa and the East, is said to have put 120,000 persons to death, besides those slain in battle, by the time of his death, 95 A.H., 713 A.D. The Saracens were insubordinate, quarrelsome, vindictive, and revengeful to the last degree, and so fond of fighting that Kalid, their great general, called by Mohammed 'the Sword of God,' told the Persians that 'his men were as fond of death as they were of life,' and afterwards the Caliph Omar said:—'My people are as fond of fighting as the Christians are of eating swines' flesh and drinking wine.'"

The Arabs valued themselves on their eloquence and poetry, on their skill in horsemanship, and the use of arms; on their hospitality, and the number of their sons. Like all conquering nations, they were probably the strongest, most vigorous, and best-educated people then in the world, though few of them could read or write; they were frugal, mainly

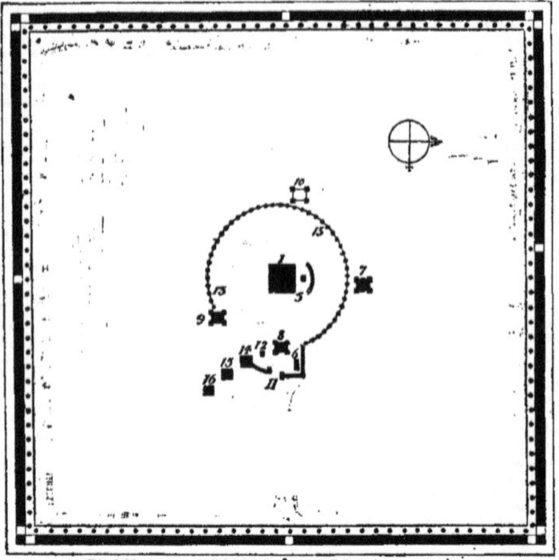

PLAN OF THE TEMPLE OF MECCA. SALE.

References.

1. Al Kaaba.
5. Sepulchre of Ishmael.
6. The pulpit.
7. The station of the Hanifites.
8. The place of Abraham and the Shafeites.
9. Station of the Hanbalites.
10. Station of the Malekites.
11. The old gate.
12. The steps on wheels to mount up to door of Kaaba
13. The inner enclosure.
14. The building over the well Zem-Zem.
15. The treasury.
16. The cupola of Al Abbas.

no doubt from necessity, hardy from constant exercise, and exposure, accustomed to endure the extremities of cold and heat, of hunger and thirst, and the terrors of solitude in a country infested with beasts of prey, keenly observant of the stars, and of every slight natural indication that would enable them to find their way over trackless deserts and pathless mountains, or to discover underground springs, and they had to practise every art and every device to preserve their lives amid hostile tribes, beasts of prey, and sand-storms. They were adepts in every ruse of savage warfare and were a constant terror to their neighbours from their incursions and robberies, but the reason they were not a menace to the adjoining potentates was that they had no cohesion, and were always quarrelling and fighting with one another, consequently, outside their own country, they never made any permanent head against the armies of the Kings of Persia, or the Byzantine Emperors, until after their conversion to Islâm.

It would be interesting to know what industrial arts they possessed in Mohammed's time: he said, there were five iron things that came down from heaven, the anvil, the tongs, the great and little hammer, and the needle. We know he cobbled his own shoes, that one of his wives tanned leather, that there were sword cutlers, that there was striped stuff called the cloth of Yemen, that they arched his grave over with unburnt bricks, and that the men possessed the art of dying their hair red.

Mohammed was the illiterate prophet who could neither read nor write, and propagated his faith without the aid of miracles. He believed that the Angel Gabriel repeated to him certain passages from an inscription by the throne of the Almighty, which, when complered, formed the Korân, but it must be observed that both at home and in his travels he had heard much of religions from Jews, Romish, and Orthodox monks, the Christians of Arabia and Abyssinia, from the Magians of Persia and possibly from the Buddhists, and he admittedly borrowed many of the stories in the Korân from the Old Testament, the Talmud, and the Apocryphal Gospels; he had been much struck by the preaching of Coss, Bishop of Najrân, had visited synagogues, Christia[n] churches and shrines, and had observed th[e] sacred pictures in the churches and abhorre[d] them, so that he afterwards had the pictures i[n] the Kaaba erased. I presume idolatry was [so] ingrained in the people that it was difficult t[o] eradicate, for though he allowed chess playin[g] he looked with an evil eye on chessmen carve[d] into figures.

The inspirations furnished him with a pu[re] monotheistic creed, with a resurrection, a da[y] of judgment, and an eternity of pleasure [or] pain, forbade idolatry and infanticide, an[d] contained a few stories, a few moral, admin[is]trative, and ritual observances, and inculcate[d] an ascetic life of prayer, fasting, and alm[s]giving. The inspirations also informed hi[m] that all martyrs went straight to paradise, an[d] that those killed in battle against unbelieve[rs] were martyrs, and declared that he was th[e] last prophet.—Adam, Noah, Abraham, Mose[s] and Jesus Christ being his precursors,—th[at] their doctrines were superseded by his, an[d] that there should be no priests or Monk[s]. The short creed of Islâm is,—"There is no G[od] but God, and Mohammed is his apostle." T[he] Moslems call a prophet who is the author of [a] book an apostle. At first his inspirations we[re] rather Christian in spirit, and his Kibla, [or] the line of prayer, was to the Temple [of] Jerusalem. After his first revelations [he] converted his elderly wife and his slav[e], afterwards a few relations and others, bu[t] as he insisted on publicly preaching again[st] idolatry, on the unity of the Creat[or], and that he was the prophet, he incurred t[he] enmity of the people; he and his converts we[re] persecuted, and, after escaping assassination [on] several occasions, his converts eventually fl[ed] to Medina, and were followed there by him a[nd] Abu Becker, the father of his wife, Ayesh[a]; this was called the Hegira, or flight, a[nd] became, in the days of Omar, the Moslem e[ra]. It happened on June 20 or July 15 or 16, 6[22] A.D., and those who fled were called Mohajeri[ns], or the flyers, and those who received him [at] Medina, the Ansars, or helpers. Some [of] his first inspirations were altered, and so[me] were reversed at Medina, his Kibla w[as] there changed to the Kaaba at Mecc[a]

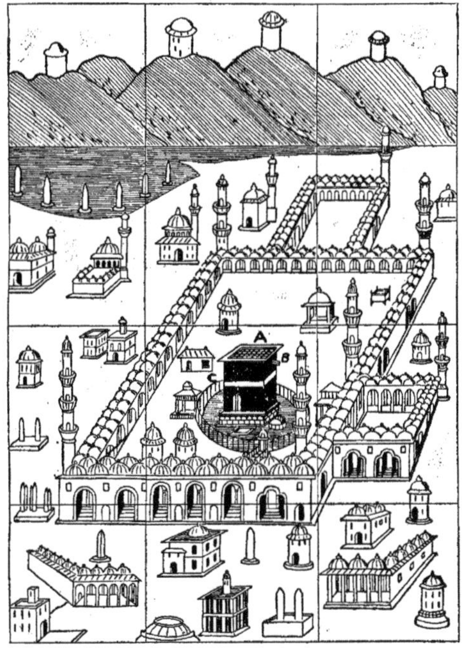

Painted tile panel representing the Kaaba at Mecca (Palace at Esbekieh, Sixteenth Century).

A. The Kaaba. B. Golden Spout. C. Golden Band.

nd the idolators, including his enemies, were ıot merely left for punishment in the next world, but were to profess Islâm or be extirpated in this; Jews and Christians, however, were to be tolerated on the payment of a ribute. One-fifth of all plunder taken by the believers was to go to the prophet for the support of the faith and for alms to the faithful, ınd there was also a tithe on all Moslems for he same purpose. I should say that, besides prohibiting infanticide, the Korân greatly improved the condition of women and orphans as regards their property and their treatment, hough some say that the restriction of the reedom women enjoyed in the days of ignorance was not counterbalanced by the advantages they gained under the Korân.

The peculiar veneration that Mohammed's converts had for him went so far that they aved the water he washed in as something holy, and cherished as relics and talismans the airs that fell from him. Sidi-Sahab, one of the companions," was presented by Mohammed with three hairs from his beard when he was eing shaved. These Sidi cherished, and after he "Apostle's" death he accompanied Ocba to Kairouan, where he died, and his instructions were that one of these hairs should be placed ın his tongue, and one on each eye when he was buried, which was done. Mohammed's ollowers were also delighted by his consecrating the wells of drinking water by spitting into hem. The alterations in the faith and ritual, he command to bring in the whole world to Islâm by the sword, together with his successful marauding expeditions, brought in many converts. A few battles with his enemies the Meccans, the destruction of the neighbouring Jews, and the apportioning their land among the refugees, brought in more, so that after a few years he summoned the Byzantine Emperor, the King of Abyssinia, the King of Persia, and the Jewish, Christians, and idolatrous tribes out of Arabia to be converted to Islam. On account of the murder of one of his messengers by Sharahbil, the chief of an independent tribe, he despatched an army against him, but the Saracens were nearly cut to pieces at Muta by a Byzantine army, led by the brother of the Byzantine Emperor Heraclius, aided by the forces of Sharahbil. The same year of the Hegira, in spite of this defeat, he was enabled to take Mecca, practically without resistance, though there was some slaughter in one quarter of the city, and to make the whole of the idolatrous inhabitants embrace Islâm, by that most cogent of all reasonings,—the sword; he then had all the idols in the Kaaba and its courts destroyed. It was then necessary to convert the rest of his idolatrous countrymen, and make them pay the tithe for the support of the faith, those that objected were butchered to the last man, and all the women and children sold for slaves.

In spite of Mohammed having become the prophet and absolute prince of the most warlike people in the world, he still kept to his frugal fare, his poor dress, and lived with his wives in their mean houses at Medina; he claimed nothing of his people beyond his share of the plunder, the tithe, and tribute, but absolute obedience, and an extra allowance of wives; the army being paid by the plunder they took.

On Mohammed's death at Medina in 11 A.H., 632 A.D., the converts outside Mecca and Medina mostly relapsed into idolatry, partly from habit and partly from their objecting to political subjection and to paying the tithe, but all the backsliders and recusants were either converted to Islâm or butchered in the reign of his successor, the Caliph Abu-Beker. When the whole of the natives were nominal believers, the Saracens were launched on Chaldæa and Syria, and in little more than a century they had not only conquered Persia, Khorasan, Afghanistan, Bokhara, Scind, and the Punjab, from the Indus to the feet of the Himalayas, and had penetrated to Samarcand and Kasgar, but they had also subjugated Mesopotamia, Syria, and Palestine, Egypt, and the north coast of Africa to the Atlantic, the greater part of Spain, the south-east of France, and had ravaged Asia Minor and the main islands of the Mediterranean, and besieged Constantinople.

Mohammed's immediate successors, the Caliphs Abu-Beker and Omar, imitated his frugality, simplicity of dress and living; but, as in Omar's day, the fifth of the plunder, the tithe and the tribute became enormous, he paid large stipends out of it to the early believers, thus creating a sort of superior nobility above those of the Koreish, which afterwards brought trouble, though he kept nothing for himself, but distributed daily the Caliph's share. At his death only one piece of gold was found in the treasury, which had been overlooked in a dark corner. The third Caliph, Othman of the Omeyya family, had other views, became enormously rich, built himself a palace at Medina, with marble columns, and walls covered with costly stucco, and gave all the principal employments to his relations. All the nobles of the Koreish, and the governors of cities or countries, built themselves palaces in many places; some of them had revenues of a thousand gold pieces a day. This caused a great scandal to the ascetic Moslems, just as splendid private buildings had scandalised the Romans of the Republic, and, of course, the poor were furious with envy; from this time forward there were constant riots, rebellions, and revolutions; and the old tribal feuds broke out again. After the first three Caliphs, the Caliphate became a vulgar despotism of the ordinary type, only with religious despotism superadded.

Even in the first few years of the second Caliphate, these half-starved barbarians, the Saracens, had obtained the main treasures of the Persian Empire, and the rich plunder of Syria; private troopers had got 500*l.* or 600*l.* a-piece as their share in one expedition, equal to at least ten times that amount now; the imperial carpets of Persia, embroidered with gold and precious stones, were cut up and sold by auction at Medina. The army took to drinking wine, and exchanged their camel's-hair garments for silk robes, while their generals bathed in wine, for which they were all bastinadoed by Omar's orders. Great Arab settlements, Kufa and Mosul, were at once made on the Euphrates and Tigris, and these as well as all the other settlements must have had mosques built. In some places, as at Damascus, the cathedral was shared between the Moslems and Christians. We know of the Mosque of Amru being built at Cairo, and Omar's mosque at Jerusalem, but whether this was the dome of the rock or the Mosque El Aksah, I must leave the learned to decide, the best authorities believe it to have been a little wooden mosque: these monuments, when not of wood, were doubtless constructed with materials plundered from ancient edifices, and were designed by Byzantine, Syrian, Persian, or Koptic architects.

If Byzantine architecture is chaotic as regards dates, what can be said of Saracenic architecture, of whose early work we know nothing, nor of the Indian, or Koptic architecture, from which or from the Byzantine all their new architecture must have been taken, and we know very little of Persian architecture. Even before a conquered world lay at the feet of the Saracens, fierce conflicts were waged between the rival Caliphs and claimants of the Caliphate; religious seditions were rife and tribal feuds, so that between them everything was destroyed; the holy Medina, the scene of much of the prophet's life, inspirations, and preaching, and the site of his tomb, was given up to pillage by Yezid I.; horses were stabled in Mohammed's mosque, and the very Kaaba of Mecca was burnt down; and besides all the plundering, burning, and destruction in the days of the Omiades, in the first days of the Abbassides, 132 A.H., the empire began to break up. Spain never acknowledged their sway, and all North Africa, except Egypt, had to be re-conquered, and still greater destruction took place at the end of the Abbasside dynasty, when the private disputes of Turks and Tartars were added to those about the religion, the predominance of tribes, and rival dynastic claims. After the Arabian Caliphate was at an end, and the rulers were mainly Turks, the part under their sway was like the East after Alexander the Great's death, the kingdoms were constantly being overrun and re-conquered, and then there was the destruction by the Crusaders. Subsequently a fresh tide of destruction overwhelmed the greater part of Asia when Tamerlane and his savage hordes swept over it.

I think it most probable that while the Conquests were being made, the Saracens, who were little better than banditti, loosely held together by a common faith, and the love of bloodshed and plunder, were not very likely to settle down to study the fine arts, even if pure Arabs ever did, and this is, to some extent, borne out by the fact that Welid I., 86 to 96 A.H. (705 to 715 A.D.), although he built much, and encouraged manufacture and design, accepted 60,000*l.* in gold, camel-loads of mosaic, and one hundred Byzantine masons from Justinian II., Philip Bardanes, or Anastasius II., for the construction of new mosques and the repair of old ones; it is also said that, in a treaty between him and the Byzantine Emperor, the latter was to furnish the mosaic for his new mosque at Damascus.

As late as Abd-al-Rahmán I., the last of the Omiades, who became Caliph of Spain, and reigned from 138 A.H. (754-787 A.D.), architects and skilled workmen are said to have been sent him by the Byzantine Emperors to build the mosque at Cordova, and all the monarchs of Europe sent him columns plundered from ancient edifices for the same purpose. Ab-al-Rahmán I. is said to have founded universities in Spain.

We do not read of much study of philosophy and the arts till the days of Harun-el-Rashid and his son Mamun, 169-188 A.H. (785-813 A.D.).

Haroun was the son of the Calif Mehdy, and Kheizran, the daughter of the Governor of Herat. His famous Vizier, Jafar, the barmecide, so well known to us from the "Arabian Nights," a patron of learning and the arts, was descended from a great family of Balkh. He is said to have been the greatest instance of the vicissitudes of fortune, for in Harun's "Book of Accounts" 400,000 pieces of gold are entered as the price of a dress of honour for him, and a few days afterwards ten karats (5*s.*) for reeds and naphtha to burn Jafar's body. Mamun was also the son of a Persian Princess, and for some time held his Court at Merve. I merely mention this to account for the encouragement given by them to Turks, Persians, and Indians. Mamun is said to have founded colleges and libraries, and to have commanded Mohammed Ben Musa to publish a book on quadratic equations, called "Al Jebre al Mokabala" (restoration and reduction), from which comes our word Algebra. The substance of the work appears to have been derived from Hindoo sources. Subsequently, the works of the Greek physicians, philosophers, arithmeticians, and geometers were translated, and physic and mathematics became favourite studies of the Saracens. The Abbassides had great influence in Persia, Khorasan, Afghanistan, and Bokara. They were descended from El Abbas, the time-serving uncle of the prophet, and, not like the Omiades, descended from his enemies. They seem, however, to have been less noble and less liberal, and even more bloodthirsty and perfidious than the Omiades, yet their reigns are held to be the golden age of the Caliphate: they introduced Turks for their fighting men, and Greeks and Persians for posts where intellect was wanted, commonly called officers of the sword and of the pen. After their extinction, Turks mostly filled their places; the Arab race having lost its religious enthusiasm, fell gradually into a lower grade.

In some respects the Moslem world,—as far as architecture was concerned,—was in much the same position as Europe is now; it had become enormously wealthy, new buildings were made on an unprecedented scale, and the main architecture of the world lay before it for study, but there was no Saracenic style; the buildings were in the style of the country or town in which they were erected, or in the style used by architects who designed them. I say this, however, with some diffidence, for the mosque at Cordova, San Cristo dela Luz, at Toledo, and Sta. Maria de la Blanca, are unlike anything else I know. The attractions of living styles are greater than we could imagine, if we had no such frequent examples before our eyes.

English architects of all degrees of excellence and talent go to our dependency, India, and whether they affect Classic, Gothic, or Renaissance architecture here, they at once take up with the native style of that part of the country they inhabit, or paraphrase the Moslem buildings they find there; and it is the same in Egypt. The last hotel built by an English architect, close to the Pyramids, has its architecture borrowed from the mosques, even to the niche. It is admitted that the Saracens brought no style with them from Arabia, but adopted features that pleased them from the countries they conquered, the most characteristic feature being the minaret, and this is said to have been Persian; the dome was taken from the Byzantines or Persians, the niche (mehrab) from the apse of Christian churches, floral ornament that was not Byzantine probably from Afghanistan or India. Fergusson remarks on the similarity of the ornaments on the tomb of Mahmúd of Ghuzni to those used in the mosque of Ahmed-Ibn-Tulun at Cairo, only this would suppose that it was not indigenous, unless indeed it was not done till Lagin's time, for Ahmed-Ibn-Tulun died in 883 A.D., and Mahmúd of Ghuzni was not born till 967 A.D. Architects in the Arabian Nights are mostly called mathematicians or geometers, and when they were thoroughly imbued with geometry, they made great advances on the geometrical patterns of the Byzantines, on which it was based, so as to completely transform them. One of the most striking peculiarities of Saracen art is the stalactites. There is an ingenious and plausible theory that may turn out to be the true one, that the stalactites or honeycomb work sprang from the brick niches in the domes or steeples of the tombs of Ezekiel and of Zobeida, Er-Rashid's head wife, both near Baghdad. These spires strongly remind us of jelly-moulds. If it came from these niches the Moslems developed them to a degree that bears no resemblance to the originals, for who would trace from this the stalactite domes of the Alhambra? These are certainly some of the most wonderful achievements of man, in fact, they suggest the work of enchanters, or of being sent down from another world. At first sight their maddening complexity and their apparent want of support makes it impossible for us to conceive that mere human beings could ever have invented or produced them; one would be led to believe that the Spanish ones were suggested to some genius by his seeing some pieces of wood of unequal length, whose ends had been shaped, put together for mosaic, like Tunbridge ware, for every wood corbel or capital I examined in Spain was made up of separate squares, oblongs, and triangles. The Saracens also invented a system of ornament, in which one pattern was laid over another in low relief, and perfected by colour and gilding; this is magical in effect, for each change of position brings out a new pattern and a new predominating colour. To them, too, we owe the perfection of mnemonic ornament, formed by overlaying a floral ground with Kufic or other writing, which is as distinctly Moslem as their maddening geometrical ornament on stalactite work. The ancient Egyptians, Persians, Greeks, Romans, and Byzantines produced works infinitely grander and more dignified; and the Greeks works infinitely more beautiful, and of a higher style of beauty, but no people have ever produced anything so magical or so sumptuous in colour. The human figure and the representation of any living thing was forbidden by their religion, though Mesopotamians and Persians did even try their hand at this form of art. By the Moslems every handicraft was carried to a perfection before unknown in the world; from the temper of a sword-blade to the weaving of a robe or a carpet; even now their enamelled glass and pottery, their damascened work, their wooden lattices, cabinet-work, carpets, and illuminations, are, in some respects, unsurpassed, and fine specimens fetch their weight in gold. And so superior were their works to those of European manufacture, that when the Christians began to imitate their costly stuffs, chased brass, or damascened work, it was a common practice to put Arabic letters on them, to ensure a market, in the form of texts from the Korán, but meaning nothing. As late as the Porta della Carta of the Ducal Palace at Venice, Arabic letters in imitation of an inscription were put on the dress of one of the figures, the solution of which was long an enigma to scholars.

It is quite possible that the real Saracens had no capacity of invention nor for the fine arts. At any rate, scarcely any buildings of great artistic merit have survived them, for, with t exception of the Mosque at Cordova, re Saracenic buildings are of the eleven and twelfth centuries. But, supposing th had neither taste nor invention, they wou none the less claim our admiration a gratitude. They expunged the worn-o civilisations of the world, and imparted to t survivors their own resistless energy, th simple faith, and a lavish generosity, so th their successors, perhaps blessed with high capacities, overspread the world with elega and sumptuous monuments from Spain to t Indus, and from the Red Sea to t Atlantic. Every country beneath their sw flourished like a garden. Stock was increase and the breed of horses greatly improve Every town was a hive of industry, fro which issued the most splendid arms a armour, glass, metal, and woodwork, enamell earthenware, velvet, satin, silk, and clo of gold, of splendid patterns and gorgeo colours; from them lawns, crapes, a delicate muslins were spread over the eart arts and literature, science and speculati philosophy found their homes amongst the and spread light among the surrounding dar ness; the inventions of the East were commun cated to the West, not the least of which we the Arab arithmetic, algebra, and the mariner compass, until they may be said to have be smothered by the wealth and plenty the industry had created. The splendid mosque tombs, towers of victory, hospitals, khans, a palaces with which the Moslem conquerors e riched India alone, probably exceed in numb and magnificence all the monuments of Euro since the Renaissance; not to speak of th bridges, aqueducts, and tanks, new phases architecture, and new systems of illuminati and ornament were invented, and in the lat Crusades the manners and morals of t Moslems were held up as patterns to t Christians by their priests.

It seems a pity that most of their monumen are perishing by decay, or by more want destruction, and when they are gone we sh have but indifferent records of their glory.

We are now in Egypt and in India: in bo these countries we have done much for t natives, and nothing for ourselves. It humiliating to remember that the great Nap leon, though he only held Egypt for a sho time, began that work on Egypt that the su ceeding French Governments continued an completed in thirty-seven volumes of "Atlas folio. There is very much admirable Saraceni work to be deciphered and delineated, and w also hold Scind and the Punjab, that we the extreme confines of Saracen sway, not t speak of the Mohammedan art of India th was created under the Mogul rulers.

From our friendship with the monarchs Afghanistan and Persia, their monuments migh be drawn and published, which would probab give us the clue to the development of Saracen art. Unhappily our Government is not onl quite unmindful of such duties, but does i best to prevent private enterprise. In Fran an expensive work of the sort would be patr nised by the Government, and even if it did n contribute directly to it, many copies of t work would be purchased and distributed i libraries and art schools; but here, on the co trary, the unfortunate author would be plu dered by the Government; and yet we wond that so few magnificent architectural works a published in England.

ROYAL INSTITUTE OF BRITISH ARCHITECTS:

THE PRESIDENT'S ADDRESS TO STUDENTS.

THE sixth ordinary meeting of this Institu for the present session was held on Mond evening last, at 9, Conduit-street, Mr. Macvicar Anderson, President, in the chair.

Mr. W. H. White, Secretary, said announced with regret the decease of M Alfred Porter (Fellow) and Mr. H. C. Elworth (Associate).

Mr. Aston Webb, Hon. Secretary, read a co of a letter from the Council of the Institute the Architectural Association, notifying to t latter body the determination of the Institu to grant 300*l.* in support of the Association educational scheme, such sum to be paid three annual instalments. A letter from t Secretary of the Architectural Association, co veying a special vote of thanks to the Roy Institute for its promised donation, was al read by Mr. Webb.

The President then delivered the following ddress to students:—

If it be true that one of the chief difficulties at attend the study of architecture is to be und in the number and variety of subjects ith which it is essential to be more or less amiliar, it is no less true that the comprehen-ive nature of the pursuit constitutes one of its reatest attractions, for it opens up a field of nquiry over which the mind may roam with ver-increasing vigour and interest. Absorption n one particular subject of study may produce assitude, but no amount of devotion to a study o varied as that of architecture should ever onduce to such a result, for mental refresh-ent is to be found—not in cessation—but in variety of thought, and the student of architecture need never experience difficulty in finding mental repose by turning from one to another of the many fields of research that lie before him. For example, in History he will find the phases depicted through which the art has passed in by-gone ages; in Literature he will become familiar with the opinions of great masters which imparted individuality to the art of different epochs; in Nature he will gather, from the development of the mineral and vegetable creations, the properties of the materials in which his designs will have to find expression; in Science he will learn what is the strength and formation of such materials, and how to adapt them to his requirements without doing violence to their material characteristics; in observation of the executed works of others, whether ancient or modern, he will, from sketching and measurement, discern how successful results have been attained, or artistic effects produced; while in Design he will apply the varied knowledge he has thus acquired from History, Literature, Nature, Science, and observation, and, by the artistic and scientific treatment of the materials at his command, he will impress his ideas and personality on the architecture of his day.

For the successful pursuit of a study so varied and so fascinating many qualifications are desirable, but three are essential: Natural aptitude, Application, Imagination. Without the first, the student will do well to abandon the career, even though he may have spent time in discovering his want of affinity with it. Many illustrations from real life might be quoted of men who had devoted years to the preliminary study of a profession only to find that they had no aptitude for it, and have with good sense left it for a more congenial career, in which they have earned reputation and renown. If the heart, as well as the intellect, is not engaged in the work of life, you may possibly, in favouring circumstances, attain to respectable mediocrity, but you will never achieve real success. Be sure, therefore, at the outset, that you possess that earnestness of purpose and heart-love for your work which spring from natural affinity and cannot exist without it. It is needless to insist on the importance of Application. Original genius or natural endowments cannot be acquired or imparted, but it is marvellous to what an extent application compensates for the lack of such gifts. Was it genius that led George Stephenson to perfect the invention of the locomotive steam-engine,—probably the greatest promoter of civilisation that the world has ever seen,—or was it simple indefatigable application? Read his life, if you have not done so, full of lessons for all, and judge for yourselves. Or, again, look at a life but recently terminated; admittedly unendowed with genius, but possessed of good sense, honesty of purpose, and earnest application, how startling the success, how remarkable the position, which was achieved by the late First Lord of the Treasury! If you have application, you possess one of the most powerful levers with which to remove and triumph over difficulties. But it is obvious that natural aptitude and application, invaluable as they are, are not sufficient to qualify you for the career on which you are entering. Far away the most important work of your lives as architects will be that of design, and if you are devoid of the mental endowment of imagination,—by means of which alone can there be design,—you will be like a ship without compass or rudder, your lives will be aimless, and you will miss the prize of your calling. Possessed of all knowledge, your works, without imagination, will be but imitations and reproductions, not designs. Equipped with learning, but devoid of creative power, you would not be artists, and, therefore, could not be architects.

I have glanced at the varied nature of your engagements as students of architecture; it would be manifesty impossible within the brief compass of this Address to discourse on all, or even a few, of these with any prospect of a beneficial result. I propose, therefore, to confine my remarks to one branch of them only, and to ask your attention to a few suggestions respecting it. The subject which I have selected is what I do not hesitate to refer to as "The Art of Planning." No doubt there are those who will regard such a designation as a contradiction in terms, for it is to be feared that there are not a few who consider planning as, at the best, a very prosaic part of an architect's work, and to whose poetic fancies the idea of elevating it to the dignity of an art may appear to be a sort of architectural blasphemy. There are others who, without going so far as this, do not hesitate to relegate planning to an inferior and subordinate place, not worthy of the exercise of the higher and artistic faculties of the designer,—a constructive skeleton, as it were, admirable it may be in its mechanism, but which the architect must clothe with grace before it can be admitted to the sacred courts of art. Now I do not hesitate to declare that such views of planning are thoroughly fallacious and injurious to the best interests of architecture, because derogating to a commonplace utilitarianism what is really an integral and inseparable part of the art, the root from which grow the loftiest conceptions, the suggestive source from which springs all that follows.

Thus viewed, you will see at once that it is impossible to exaggerate or over-estimate the importance of the study of planning. It may indeed be safely asserted that there is no study in which the human mind can engage, on the results of which the comfort, convenience, and happiness of society so much depend. This, I admit, is claiming a good deal, but no more than the study properly demands. It is not my purpose at present to emphasise utilitarianism, but do not forget that every building is designed for use; to say so is not to derogate from art, because the highest art is displayed when a building is so designed as most successfully to fulfil its purpose by combining fitness with beauty. Thus the primary field for the exhibition of the architect's art is planning. This does not appear to admit of doubt. Let me demonstrate it. What is architecture? Is it the mere clothing of the structure? or is it the artistic design of the structure itself? Unquestionably the latter, and if so, how can the study of planning be other than artistic work, the primary stirring of the dry bones out of chaos, and the life inspiration which creates out of them the useful and the beautiful? for planning is not the mere casual throwing together of so many forms; the chance disposition of so many lines representing walls, enclosing so many haphazard spaces representing rooms; it involves the exercise of imagination. The design of the plan is the medium for educing this quality, just as much as the design of the elevation; it is customary, no doubt, to hear the word design applied to the latter much more than to the former, but the one is really just as much design as the other; consequently the plan affords the opportunity for the display of artistic power just as much as the elevation. Not only so, but a true artist, while studying and elaborating his plan, has a mental drawing-board by his side, on which he rears in his mind's eye forms and proportions suggested by it and emanating from it; he disposes the arrangement so as not only to meet the requirements but also so as to produce a happy result in point of effect; in short, the two things go together, they are mentally indivisible, and must be elaborated, not without reference to one another, but in unity. Hence experience demonstrates that a good plan will generally be found to produce a good elevation; they are integral parts of a whole; the one having been artistically studied with a view to the other, the result will be harmonious; if the tree is good, so will the fruit be.

Did time permit, it might be interesting to divide the subject, and classify it under separate heads, treating each in turn, as for example:—The plan ecclesiastical, the plan collegiate, the plan palatial, the plan municipal, the plan judicial, the plan official, and the plan domestic; and a moment's reflection will show you how easily we could find in the elaboration of the characteristics and requirements of each, much that might profitably engage our attention. I must, however, content myself with a more general treatment, touching briefly what may be called principles, leaving the application of them to your own imagination.

None but those who have made a real study of planning, have any conception of the infinite breadth and variety of the field of design which it creates; they only know experimentally the charm of puzzling over difficulties; of revising, re-arranging, and re-disposing, in order to overcome them; thereby probably creating other difficulties, which in their turn have to be surmounted by a further similar process, and so on, until, after many disappointments, many failures, and many inventions, a satisfactory result is at length reached. It is now many years since I resolved never to let a plan leave my hands until I felt satisfied that it was right; and in battling with the difficulties thereby created until they have been successfully obviated, I have found some of the most engaging studies of professional life. The question with you should never be, whether a plan is good enough,—that is an unworthy standard,—but rather, is it the best that I can design? the former, the "it-will-do-well-enough" standard prevails far too commonly, the latter is the only standard really worth working for, because the only one which will lead to attainments beyond mediocrity. Never, then, rest content with a plan until you are satisfied that it meets and fulfils all the requirements of the case, in the best and most complete manner that you can think of; the plan is the foundation of the whole design, and I need not say to architectural students that if the foundation is faulty, there is not much hope for the superstructure.

It may seem like insisting on an elementary truism to say that the plan of a building must necessarily be adapted to, and governed by, the exigencies of the site, but the not infrequent violation, or rather neglect, of so obvious a principle, justifies me in emphasising its importance. The peculiarities of a site in respect to levels and aspect frequently constitute difficulties that at first sight appear insurmountable, but out of which emanate in skilful hands the happiest results, which otherwise might not have been thought of, or attained. Herein is displayed the skill of the artist, to lay hold on all such adventitious circumstances and hindrances, and conform them to his will, translating obstacles into mediums for achieving success. The neglect of such opportunities is unpardonable, and betrays the bungler.

Prospect, again, constitutes an important factor in planning. When the right aspect presents the best views, the case is simple, but this is often not the case, and few conditions call for more ingenuity that when the proper aspect is at variance with the prospect that it is desirable to secure. In towns, indeed, aspect and prospect must necessarily, and to a great extent, be subordinated to immovable conditions, but in the country it is different. While, therefore, striving for comfort, convenience, and grace within, never neglect an opportunity of securing the inestimable attraction of a higher than any art loveliness, the prospect of nature and creation. In connexion with prospect let me in passing condemn a practice too much in vogue, the glazing of the upper portions of windows with tinted stained or painted glass, sometimes uglier than anything it is intended to obscure from view. Situated as we are in London, the expedient is, no doubt, attended with advantages, shutting out hideous objects which one's neighbours are so fond of obtruding, or excluding the impertinent gaze of the too curious; but in the country, where it is frequently adopted, what possible justification can be urged? Is it possible that anything can compensate for the light of the sun, the beauties of nature, or the marvels of the heavens? Never, then, attempt to obscure the contemplation of God's universe by the commonplaces of humanity.

I would say, further, that a plan to be good must be simple. No doubt the arrangement of some buildings is necessarily more elaborate than that of others; but you may take it as an unerring guide, that when you find a plan becoming complicated and confused, you are on the wrong tack. I have seen an artist, after hours of work, wipe from his canvas all he had painted, and then make a fresh start with manifest advantage and no real loss of time; so when your planning results in complication, your best course is ruthlessly to obliterate what you have done, and begin *de novo*. Nothing will compensate for the absence of simplicity in a plan. This is a golden test which I have never hesitated to apply, and I speak from no inconsiderable experience.

[*Continued on page* 80.

Illustrations.

OLD HOUSE, IPSWICH.

THIS house, which is known in the town as "the Ancient House," is one of those buildings which has passed through many hands, and has received great care from its various owners, who were all presumably wealthy men. Erected in Tudor times, it was added to and beautified in Elizabeth's reign, still further decorated in the Jacobean era, and shortly after the accession of Charles II. the magnificent pargetted front was added, and, finally, in Queen Anne's reign the front rooms on the ground floor were all redecorated in the prevailing style of the time.

The principal front is towards the Butter Market, but it has also a return elevation to St. Stephen's-lane. The first floor consists of four large oriel windows to the Butter Market, and one on the return elevation to St. Stephen's-lane. These oriels sustain a wide projecting cornice, and between them are massive pilasters, all in plasterwork. Above the oriels, set back to wall line, are four dormer windows breaking out of the main roof.

Many years ago in one of the attics there was a portion of the roof space that had not been carefully investigated for a long space of time. It chanced, in 1801, that this was broken into, and the result was that a beautiful little single hammer-beam roof was revealed with carved arches and angels on the ends of the hammer-beams. On examination this proved to be the roof of a chapel or ball ceiled and floored over at the plate level, the main body being absorbed in the room below. The space covered by this roof was 23 ft. long by 15 ft. 7 in. wide, and the principals were three in number. This ancient relic gives us a clue to the probable age of the original structure, which was probably the residence of a wealthy man in the fifteenth century. The next addition seems to have been made in 1567, as in that year a certain George Copping and Elizabeth, his wife, caused a room on the ground-floor to be panelled out and inserted the date and their monograms in the mantel-piece. An open corridor with rooms over it, forming the wing before alluded to, in St. Stephen's-lane, was also added about this time.

In 1603 a room on the ground floor, away from the street, was panelled in oak whole height of the room, the beams were encased in panelling, and a gorgeous mantel-piece was put up, covering the end of the room entirely with the exception of two small doorways. This is, presumably, the work of a man called John Sparrowe, who owned the house at this time, and from whose family it derives the name of "Sparrowe's House." The initials J. W. S. and the Sparrowe arms, together with the date 1603, all appear on the mantel, and a representation of the arms is also repeated in the glass in the window, though this is evidently not in its original setting.

The treatment of the design is as follows:—On a brick base, some 4 ft. high, is placed an oak sill, into which are framed elaborately carved pilasters, 7 ft. 4 in. high, with Ionic caps, from which spring highly ornamental carved brackets carrying the overhang, the corner-post being similar in design to the pilasters, but on a larger scale, and placed anglewise. The overhang, which is very great, is still further emphasised by the projection of four oriel windows to the Butter Market and one to St. Stephen's-lane. Above the oriels runs a bold Classic cornice in wood, and over each oriel to the front is a dormer window lighting the attics, also enriched with pargetting. On the front faces of the oriels to Butter Market the four quarters of the globe are represented in high relief in parget, and the return oriel to the lane has Atlas supporting the world on its similar face. The curved sides of the oriels are decorated in scroll work and other devices. Under the upper cornice are swags composed severally of flowers, fruit, birds, fishes, and musical instruments. Between the two centre oriels is a panel containing the Royal Arms, with supporters and crest, and the letters C. II. R. (Charles II, Rex.). In the gablets above are various Classic scenes and characters, and on the end gable St. George slaying the dragon, and Phillida and Corydon below. The modelling is coarse, but the general effect is bold and striking. In the centre of the house is a courtyard, with some rich parget work depicting a triumphal procession on a gable face. Inside are several panelled rooms and some highly ornate ceilings. The building is minutely described in Glyde's "Old Ipswich."

JOHN S. CORDER.

ST. CUTHBERT'S COLLEGE, WORKSOP.

THE drawings show the southern front of the quadrangle and the southern side of the dining-hall of the buildings now in course of erection for a lower middle-class school in connection with Lancing and Denstone Colleges, corresponding with the schools at Ardingly and Ellesmere.

The college is founded by the Provost and Fellows of Denstone College as a public school for 500 boys, to be boarded and educated at a cost of less than twenty guineas a-year, and the buildings are being erected under the College Architects, Mr. R. Herbert Carpenter and Mr. B. Ingelow, of London. The site, of ninety-three acres, given by the Duke of Newcastle, commands the Clumber Woods on the south, and the Priory Church and town of Worksop to the north-west, with the Yorkshire hills beyond. In addition to his gift, the Duke has formed and planted the roads and grounds.

Excepting the chapel and dining-hall with its offices, the buildings are arranged round a quadrangle, 170 ft. square, of which the school-room and class-rooms occupy the north side; and dormitories, day-rooms, masters' rooms, &c., for 200 boys on each of the side wings, with dormitories, associates' rooms, &c., in the southern front building, the head-master's house being at the south-west angle. The chapel is to the north-east, and the dining-hall (and offices, laundry, &c.) to the north-west of the great quadrangle. The chapel, exclusive of the ante-chapel, will be 140 ft. long by 40 ft. wide; the hall, 120 ft. by 36 ft.; the school-room, 100 ft. by 36 ft.

The buildings are faced with Nottingham bricks, which are also used for mouldings. The dressings are of Kiveton Park (Anstone) stone. The principal rooms and the cloister, which is on the inner side of the quadrangle, are faced with similar bricks, while Lincoln bricks are used for the inner walls.

The contract for a great part of the superstructure is taken (in divisions) by Mr. Vickers, of Nottingham, the foundations having been put in by Mr. Bentley, of Waltham Abbey. The architects' clerk of the works is Mr. F. E. Smith.

The elevations are from drawings exhibited at the Royal Academy of 1891.

MISSION CHURCH AND HALL, CANTERBURY-ROAD, S.E.

THIS building, the drawing of which was in last year's Academy, has been erected for the Mission at Camberwell in connexion with Corpus Christi College, Cambridge. It is a building of two floors, having on the ground floor a large hall with glazed brick dado, 5 ft. high all round, and a platform at one end, kitchen, heating-chamber, &c., and a distinct entrance to the hall from the street. On the first floor, approached by two wide stone staircases, with separate entrances to the church, capable of seating about 400 people, with chancel, organ-chamber, and vestries. The exterior is faced with red brick, and has stone dressings with traceried windows to the chancel of the church. All floors are fireproof, and the heating has been carried out on Grundy's Hot-air System. The cost of the buildings was nearly 5,000*l*. The architect is Mr. Richard J. Lovell, of London, who was also the architect of Holy Trinity Church and buildings, Old Nichol-street, Shoreditch, completed some little time ago, and originally built in connexion with Magdalene College, Oxford Mission, but now used and consecrated for a parish church.

NEW MINERAL-WATER WORKS AT COLWALL, NEAR MALVERN, FOR J. SCHWEPPE & CO., LIMITED.

THIS building, which is now nearing completion, is being erected for the Directors of J. Schweppe & Co., Limited, for the manufacture of their mineral waters.

It is placed at the foot of the Malvern hills, close to the Great Western line, and adjoins Colwall station, in the midst of some of the most beautiful scenery of the west of England, and considerable trouble has been taken to make the building harmonise with its beautiful setting, the usually more or less hideous "factory" features having been so toned down and metamorphosed as to be quite unobjectionable.

The building, which forms the nucleus merely of a much larger establishment proposed in the future, consists of a manufactory, with packing, unpacking rooms, store-rooms, carpenters' shop, engine-room, boiler-house, &c., and is of red local bricks, with Bath stone dressings, roofed with Brosely tiles; the internal paving is being carried out by Stuart's Granolithic Company; the ornamental ironwork by Messrs. Braun, of Birmingham; the cranes and hoists by Mr. Stannah; and the boilers, engine, &c., by the Riley Manufacturing Company, of Lambeth. The contractors for the whole are Messrs. Josh. Wood & Son, of Worcester. The architects are Messrs. Truefitt & Truefitt, of London.

ROYAL INSTITUTE OF BRITISH ARCHITECTS.

(*Continued from page 79.*)

Again, a plan is only good when it is the embodiment of thrift. Much has been said, and more has been written, on the moral aspect of thrift, and it would be easy to enlarge on the advantages of its application, not merely to the life, but also to the artistic work of the student of architecture. I must, however, be content for the present to deal with it in its relation to my subject, and to show that without thrift, both of space and material, a plan cannot properly fulfil its purpose. Thrift is not parsimony, any more than liberality is waste. Each space in a plan, be it room, hall, stair, or passage, should be just the size that is necessary for its purpose; if it be less, there is parsimony, for what is inadequate will have to be enlarged hereafter at much more than what would have been the original cost; if it be more, there is waste, for it has involved the expenditure of more capital than was required, and will incur needless labour and consequent cost in maintenance. Take, as an illustration, a room which has been designed on a scale beyond the necessities of its occupants; it is obvious that it has cost more to build and furnish than it should have done, and involves a perpetual cost for maintenance and service, which should have been avoided; hence the happy medium is to be found in thrift. So in respect to materials; walls should be of sufficient thickness, floors and roofs of sufficient strength for their respective functions, not much more, and not much less; else there will ensue, either waste in the first instance, or parsimony, which will involve waste in the long-run. There are, however, cases in which materials should not be too sparingly employed; in a mansion, for example, intended to be a family home, and to pass from generation to generation, it would be unwise, and out of keeping with its purpose, to apply too literally such a condition as this; for nothing imparts more dignity and a greater idea of the enduring purpose for which such an edifice is designed than massive walls, thicker no doubt than may be actually required for sound construction, but not more than is called for in order to be in harmony with the traditions and associations that the structure will represent. This, however, is but one of those exceptions that prove the rule of thrift which I have enforced. I am, of course, not unprepared for the inevitable protest of the art-student, who in a burst of æsthetic enthusiasm will denounce the suggestion that so prosaic a quality as thrift should dare to enter the hallowed sanctuary of the art studio; but while entertaining much sympathy with the enthusiasm of youth, and by no means desiring to curb it, and while respecting opinions which I doubt not are perfectly genuine, I venture to think that it would be easy to demonstrate that it would be in the true interest of art, were her portals more frequently and more hospitably thrown open for the admission and entertainment of the prosaic maiden I have introduced to your notice. How often, for instance, might she, with manifest advantage, restrain the artist hand in scattering with inartistic profusion ornament which is misplaced and therefore ineffective? But to enter on such matters would be to deal with other branches of the architect's studies, and be foreign to my present purpose.

I need not detain you by enumerating conditions, more or less obvious, each one of which contributes in its place to the merit of a plan. Apart from considerations of aspect, prospect and dimensions, each place should be—not only

View from S. Stephens Lane.

HOUSE, IPSWICH.—Drawn by Mr. John Shewell Corder.

TH

ST CUTHBERT'S COLLEGE, WO

Royal Academy Exhibition, 1891

INK-PHOTO SPRAGUE & Cº 4 & 5, EAST HARDING STREET, FETTER LANE, E.C.

MISSION CHURCH AND HALL: FOR CORPUS CHRISTI COLLEGE CAMBRIDGE.

CANTERBURY ROAD. S.E.

Royal Academy Exhibition, 1891

INK-PHOTO, SPRAGUE & Cº 4 & 5, EAST HARDING STREET, FETTER LANE, E.C.

MESSRS SCHWEPPE & CO'S FACTORY, M

PHOTO-LITHO SPRAGUE & Cº 4 & 5 EAST HARDING STREET, FETTER LANE, E.C.

MESSRS. TRUEFITT & TRUEFITT, ARCHITECTS

convenient in itself—but should be in its proper position in relation to other places; the work of an establishment, as well as the cost, may be materially diminished or increased, according as this condition is observed or neglected; doors, windows, fireplaces, should be arranged so as at once to promote comfort and convenience without needlessly destroying wall-space, or incurring draughts; the amount of window-space should be regulated according to the aspect; and many other considerations of a similar nature should be duly thought of; in short, the perfect plan is, and can only be, the result of the thoughtful study of each principle and every detail: none are too minute to be overlooked: as little things sweeten life, so attention to little details makes a plan complete.

I have written to little purpose if I have not convinced you that planning is one of the most important, difficult, and artistic studies of the architect.

Now let me inquire why it is that plans are so frequently bad. I am aware that there are men in the profession who are adepts in planning, and whose productions in this respect we admire. But are they the majority? Rather, I fear, will they be found to be the small minority. Rarely do I examine published plans without detecting faults which are obviously not the necessary outcome of the circumstances. Why is this? In the majority of cases it does not, I belive, arise from lack of ability on the part of the author, but from the neglect to apply the ability he possesses to the working out of a good plan. Where plans are bad, they are so from two causes. 1. It is impossible to produce a satisfactory result without practical knowledge of the requirements; in the case of a gentleman's house, for example, how can we expect to succeed without being familiar with the nature and working of the establishment? 2. Plans are bad because they are not studied as they should be; I am satisfied that there are many practising architects who have never realised the true nobility of planning, who have never experienced the fascination of the almost exhaustless field it presents for the display of imaginative artistic skill, and who consequently have concentrated their artistic powers in the design of the elevation. Need I guard myself from possible misconception by adding that not one word I have written is intended to militate against the importance of artistic design as applied to the elevation? My subject is Planning, and my remarks naturally apply specially to it. Moreover, architects are not likely to regard the design of the elevation as the least artistic portion of their work, and it is because I entertain the conviction, judging from results, that they do far too much regard the design of the plan in that light, that I have emphasised its artistic character.

The architecture of the future will derive its character, and find its development, from the students of to-day; hence I have been tempted to embrace this opportunity to bring specially before you the subject of planning, believing that those who undervalue it do so because they have not studied it and tasted its fascination, and in the conviction that there is no more useful as well as artistic study in which you can engage. Remember that the subject vitally affects you who are devoting your lives to the study of architecture, and that your treatment of it will still more vitally affect those for whom, by and by, you will be called on to design; nothing will so certainly secure for you their grateful blessing as to promote the comfort, convenience, and beauty of their homes, for on nothing does the daily happiness of civilised society so greatly depend. If I have succeeded in elevating the study and lifting it out of the prosaic level from which it is too generally regarded; if I have inspired in any of you, whom it is my privilege to address, the determination to throw yourselves into it with an enthusiasm which you may not hitherto have displayed; if I have thus, through influencing you, sowed seed which will fructify for the benefit of succeeding generations; if I have demonstrated that in this study is to be found one of the most interesting, fascinating, and artistic pursuits, the time will not have been misspent which we have this evening devoted to the consideration of the Art of Planning.

On the conclusion of his address, the President stated that he had originally intended to embody in it some critical observations of the prize drawings; but in consequence of illness he had been unable to do so. Mr. Aston Webb, however, had been kind enough to prepare some critical remarks with regard to the drawings, which he would now call upon him to read.

A REVIEW OF THE STUDENTS' WORK.

Mr. Aston Webb, before reading his criticism of the various drawings which had been submitted, said that he was sure they must all feel delighted to have their President back in his accustomed place that evening. He was sorry that, under the circumstances, it had fallen to him (the speaker) to read the notes instead of the President. He continued as follows:—It has been usual year by year for the Institute to publish in its *Proceedings* a more or less critical notice of the designs submitted for the various medals and prizes annually offered in competition by this Institute, and it has been thought that it might interest our students if I were to put down, as your Honorary Secretary, a few notes on the designs and drawings submitted this year. In doing so, I shall address myself to the students, and especially to those who are intending to compete in future years, and if what I say has been often said before, this is my excuse for it. The prizes which are offered by the Institute are for,—1. Original architectural designs. 2 Designs in which construction is the principal problem. 3. Drawings of old work on given subjects and written essays.

Pugin Studentship and Institute Silver Medal.—I will take the drawings of old work first, for which are offered the Pugin Studentship and Institute Silver Medal, and before noticing the drawings sent I should like to say a word on the sketching of old work generally. This sketching may be of the greatest use to you hereafter, or it may be absolutely useless; you must sketch with your head as well as your hand, as Mr. Waterhouse said in one of his addresses; do not lay by too many pretty sketches to be shown to admiring relations and friends, for if they are of such general interest you may be pretty sure they are of no practical value. I believe you learn far more by measuring thoroughly a well-designed, moderate-sized church, a single bay of a cathedral, or a complete portion of any other good building plan, elevation, section, and details, and by trying to understand what were the difficulties of the designer and how they were met, than by any number of sketches of pretty bits. Not that I mean for a moment to underrate the importance of detail,—it is, of course, the essence of design; but many of the sketches one sees are valueless without some figured data of the position in which they occur. When you sketch an arcade, make a plan, however rough, with figured dimensions of the width of nave and aisle, and heights of both; if you sketch carving, note the height from ground and the scale of the work around; above all things, learn to appreciate scale and dimensions,—a difficult thing to do, no doubt. In sketching a roof, make a note of the main scantlings and a window, the size of mullions, widths of lights, thickness of wall, height from ground of the sill, and so on; this seems a mere truism, yet it is often absent, even in the drawings here. It is not necessary that all your drawings should be geometrical ones, but do not be afraid of disfiguring your sketches with a few main dimensions: it will add to their value. The late Mr. Street's sketches were models in this respect, as in so many others. Try and realise the scale and dimensions of things, how they were designed for their respective positions; and so, when the time comes to turn your own ideas into stone, you may be able to realise your own ideas, and know beforehand what will be the result of the work you will produce so sanguinely at your drawing-board. If you do not do this, disappointment and discouragement only await you. Remember most can appreciate the effect of work when executed; it is for an architect to appreciate its effect in an earlier stage when it is on paper only. But to turn to the drawings.

For the "Pugin" this year five sets of drawings have been submitted, the Studentship being awarded to Detmar J. Blow, his principal contribution being plans, sections to ½-in. scale, and full-size details of the choir aisle of Beauvais Cathedral, a case in point of what I have just said, for I am sure Mr. Blow would tell you how much benefit he has gained by this sound and solid work. Perhaps more time than necessary has been spent in shading and tinting these geometrical drawings, though one is unwilling even to suggest an objection to the means employed in obtaining so excellent a result.

The portions of Barfreston Church are also most thorough and careful; while the coloured sketches show much appreciation of tone and colour, and make us look forward with interest to the result of Mr. Blow's tour next summer.

Another beautiful set of drawings for the same prize are those by Charles A. Nicholson. He sends a particularly able set of interiors, drawn firmly in pencil and well selected; particularly one may mention the Lady-chapel of Long Melford, a perfect little building, and the church at Tilney All Saints; but how much a rough figured section would add to the value of these. The stalls of the choir of Lincoln is another interesting sketch, and the two roofs of St. Stephen's, Norwich, and Wymondham Church, are as well sketched as could be. From these sketches there can be no doubt we shall hear of Mr. Nicholson again.

In quite a different manner are the drawings submitted by Mr. C. R. McIntosh; particularly admirable being his pencil-drawings of Italian Renaissance work,—holy water stoups, torch-holders, &c. The coloured sketches of the Certosa of Pavia are also very delicate and full of feeling, though their effect, I venture to think, is rather interfered with by the exaggerated blue of the shadows. I am also a little doubtful whether the manner of mounting has been the best for drawings of such delicacy.

E. S. Cummings sends another good set. The drawings are wonderfully neat and clean specimens of pencil-work, though I would suggest to Mr. Cummings not to carry the dot-and-spot manner too far; it is very effective as shown in his drawings, and it is pleasant enough to play with, I know, but it is dangerous, and I am afraid leads nowhere. Mr. Cummings, I think, has carried it as far as it ought to go, if not a little farther. The shaded details of carving in the Lady-chapel at Ely are charming, and in quite another manner, though perhaps a trifle overworked.

Percy D. Smith sends some interesting bits, but largely taken from work somewhat later in character than is intended for the study by competitors for the "Pugin," which they should do well to remember was founded for the study of that Gothic architecture which was so much admired and understood by the man in whose memory this studentship was founded.

After the "Pugin" drawings we come to those submitted as the result of his Pugin tour by S. K. Greenslade, the Pugin Student of last year. These are all good, and should be very satisfactory to those who took part in founding this studentship, many of whom are still amongst us. Here is a carefully-measured bay of the Presbytery of Lincoln, plan, section, internal and external elevation. Mr. Greenslade not only knows how to draw, but knows how to select the subjects to be drawn. There is a capital sketch of St. Peter Mancroft, east front, which I missed when I was there. There is a view across the nave at Lincoln showing the Lady Chapel, in which, however, one misses a plan, and many others equally good. Mr. Greenslade appears a giant for work, and has attacked no less than four cathedrals,—Ely, Lincoln, Norwich, and Exeter,—in this single tour, to say nothing of smaller churches such as St. Peter Mancroft and others; dimensions are abundantly sprinkled over these drawings, and add greatly to the value of them.

The other competition for drawings of old work is the Institute Silver Medal, which has been obtained by R. S. Balfour for a very complete set of drawings of Heriot's Hospital, Edinburgh, shown by plans, elevations, sections, perspective internal details, and mouldings to a large scale.

Percy D. Smith obtains a Medal of Merit for a careful, if rather hard, set of drawings of the magnificent Salisbury Chantry at Christchurch, erected at that interesting period when the Gothic architect was yielding to the blandishments of the Italian Renaissance. A chapel of St. Mary, Chichester, appears a most interesting building, though, again, one misses a plan; a sketch of the slightest character would have been welcome.

"Pollux" sends a thoroughly careful and complete set of drawings of Castor Church, Peterborough.

The next set of prizes are those offered for original design, and while in the previous sets of drawings we find the power of draughtsmanship fully developed, the power of design is of slower growth and not developed to the same extent. Remember in these competitions it becomes a matter of far more importance what you show than how you show it, and though draughtsmanship may greatly help a design, it cannot convert a bad into a good one. A carefully thought-out design will stand a better chance of success than one less considered, however elaborately worked up, and it may be useful to remind intending competitors of the clause in the conditions, "the geometrical drawings must be in outline, with the openings and sectional parts alone tinted in monochrome or hatched." This is intended to exclude shading or etching, but not of course stone-jointing.

The Essay Medal.—Five essays were received, the prize being awarded to "Veritas filia temporis" (Chas. E. Sayer). I have not read these myself, but the judges have done so most carefully, and I believe had no difficulty in coming to the decision they did.

The Essay Ignigenus (Richard Glazier) is very beautifully illustrated, but I understand the judges consider these essays show a tendency to become too much a mere catalogue of the illustrations, whereas literary power and merit is what is primarily intended to be rewarded in this prize.

The Soane Medallion.—This prize is now the most valuable one offered by the Institute, and open to all British subjects under thirty years of age. The amount has this year been increased from 50*l.* to 100*l.*, and the subject given was a severe one. A chapter-house to a cathedral, plans, section, and elevation to quarter scale, with full-size details, and an exterior perspective. The labour this entailed was considerable, and I have known of more than one who relinquished the task. Eight, however, have sent in designs which show a great deal of honest hard study and work. Two were so equal that the judges had considerable difficulty in placing one first, but, as you are aware, they finally placed "Abbotsbury" (Heber Rimmer) first, and "Red Cherub" (John Begg) second.

In considering the designs for a chapter-house one naturally turns to those in our own cathedral establishments, where we find the general form is octagonal, though by no means necessarily so. Canterbury and Ely and Norwich (before it was destroyed) had chapter-houses, parallelograms on plan, while that at Lichfield is an irregular octagon. The groining of most is supported by a central column and as a rule they are level, or nearly so, with the cloister, though Westminster Abbey and Wells are well-known exceptions.

Of the eight designs submitted four are octagonal, three are hexagonal, and one is more or less of a parallelogram. Several provide an ambulatory round the outside between the buttresses, which appears to have no particular use beyond extending the cloisters, and adding, as it undoubtedly does, to the picturesqueness of the exterior.

The design marked "Abbotsbury," to which the Soane Medallion has been awarded, is shown in an admirably worked-out set designed in a Late Decorated style. An octagonal building is raised some 8 ft. above the cloister level, is surrounded by an ambulatory at the cloister level, out of which open recesses which in any other position would have been chapels. The appearance of the exterior as seen in elevation is almost that of the apse of a great church. It is placed on the summit of a rocky eminence, which makes me regret that it does not grow out of its foundation more as the buildings do at Mont St. Michel; for instance, the perspective as shown could only have been taken from a similar rocky eminence adjoining, and the building hardly has the appearance of being designed for an unusual site such as this. The interior is vaulted without the aid of a central column, but a pendentive common in fan-vaulting is suspended from the centre, which I venture to think would have been better omitted, as it seems to suggest a central column which was afterwards thought better of.

Though the chapter-house is raised, no crypt is shown under, and which crypt, owing to the ambulatory, would have been in perfect darkness. The entrance to the chapter-house is very dignified and noble, and the whole design shows a good knowledge of the capabilities and treatment of Gothic work, and is most conscientiously worked out, though the detail hardly comes up to the small-scale drawings.

The design marked "Red Cherub" (John Begg), to whom a Medal of Merit has been awarded, is hexagonal on plan, with a central shaft, the style being a Late Perpendicular. A narrow passage here runs round outside the chapter-house, which appears to me useless, though it makes a very picturesque feature in the view, with its square little windows between the buttresses. The perspective is very well drawn, and cleanly washed in in monotone. A feature in the exterior has been made of the disposal of the water from the roof through and down the face of the buttresses, finally being discharged into the open by gargoyles,—a method which, if I am right in understanding it, would not be very dignified, nor, I think, an advisable way of disposing of the water from the roof. I am aware flying buttresses over aisle roofs were used in this way, but this is hardly a case in point. The great vault of the chapter-house is elliptical, and does not reach within 8 ft. of the tie-beams of the roof over; this space is, therefore, wasted, and would have better been thrown into the chapter-house. An elaborate timber roof is shown over, which might well have derived some support from the stone roof below. The sections of the entrance from the cloister are admirably drawn, and show much knowledge of Gothic,—as, indeed, does the whole design. As I am criticising, I should doubt the good effect of the hexagonal form, and wish the tracery and mullions were thicker and the horizontal division of the lights different; in the perspective the lights in the windows nearest the buttress in high light are in each case darkened, apparently for the purpose of throwing up the buttress, but the effect cannot, I take it, be natural, or therefore proper.

Another very interesting design is submitted under the motto "Sun"; this, again, is hexagonal on plan and treated in a later manner. The centre space is covered with a cupola, the centres of support to which are shifted from the angles of the hexagon to the centres of the sides, the small spandrel spaces thus formed outside the cupola being stone-vaulted in the usual manner, the cupola itself being left perfectly plain, no doubt for decoration. This is an ingenious arrangement, and would, I think, look well, the objection being that the weight of the cupola is thrown off the angle buttresses, which would probably be strong enough, to the intermediate ones, which would not. This cupola forms the actual roof of the building, with no other external covering. Had the author heard Mr. Somers Clarke's paper on Seville Cathedral, which was treated somewhat in this way, he would probably have thought better of this. In this country a further difficulty would arise, inasmuch that when the building was heated the condensation would make it practically uninhabitable. On the exterior the want of a roof is much missed. The arrangement of entrance and steps is charming, though it hardly grows out of the requirements; but the whole design shows great originality and power of treatment, and we shall look forward to further work from the same hand with interest and expectation.

"Volunteer" sends a Renaissance design octagonal on plan, surrounded by buildings some 20 ft. wide, used partly as a library, and which would cut off far more of the chapter-house than shown on the perspective; the lighting is deficient, the central eye with a cupola over it being of little use for this purpose. I think also if the author had considerably increased the height of this chapter-house he would have added much to its effect in the interior and exterior.

"Byzantium" sends a clever design, but from the colour of the sky in the perspective it is presumably not to be erected in England. The author could, I think, hardly have expected to carry off the prize with this design; it undoubtedly has good points in its particular style, and the perspective is well and powerfully coloured, but the immense labour spent in etching up the sections and plan, which is contrary to the rules as I read them, might certainly have been better employed.

"Blue Griffin in Circle." A clever Renaissance design, octagonal on plan, covered internally with a plain vault, with suggested decoration most admirably shown. A very well-tinted perspective shows the exterior, but the parapet and niches externally are, perhaps, rather restless, and the detail hardly comes up to the rest of the work.

"Ex Cathedrâ" has not been afraid of plenty of wall-space—a good feature—but the decorative portions might have been more studied. A very good internal feature, as it seemed to me, is a gallery running round, which would be very effective, and might be useful on occasions.

"Plume," another hexagonal plan, has a cleverly-treated exterior, shown in a powerfully-drawn perspective. The triangular buttresses, with their arch moulds dying upon them, might be made a very effective feature, and the parapet without a cornice below it is a novelty. The detail shows profiles only.

"Anno 1891." A very good design, admitably worked out; and, with some of the labour spent on the design which has been spent on the perspective, it might have become one of the best in the room. I don't feel equal to say anything about the perspective. It is clever, no doubt, but that sort of thing has been done before. If the author contemplates another such, and would take my advice, I should certainly say "Don't." The motto of "Anno 1891" on such a drawing is out of place; it is at least 500 years before that.

The Tite Prize.—A design "For a Church Steeple," according to the principles of Bramante, Palladio, or Sir William Chambers. Four designs were sent in for this, and the prize has been awarded to "Red Lion" (T. R. Kitsell) for a very good design after the manner of Wren or Chambers, Bow Church in Cheapside, apparently, being the model. The perspective hardly does justice to this design. The detail is strongly drawn, and with great feeling. The section is careful and interesting, but hardly satisfactory constructionally. There are no less than four complete stone cupolas to carry the various stages, and these in many cases are heavily weighted, while I do not see any ties to take the thrust. I took the opportunity, through the kindness of the architect, Mr. Innes, to go up the Bow Tower the other day, and I should strongly recommend Mr. Kitsell and all students to take the opportunity of an Association visit to inspect it. This spire, as all know, is constructed on a single elongated cone most securely tied to the springing. The whole is a splendid piece of work, composed entirely of Wren's favourite materials, Portland stone and English oak, easy of access throughout, and perfectly sound.

"Ashlar" is another Wren or Chambers design. The circular spire is very small, increasing the difficulty of construction, and requiring stronger terminals than are shown at the angles.

"Quis" is a carefully-drawn design, but the subject is rather beyond the candidate's power. He requires a greater knowledge of detail, and will no doubt do better another time.

"Design in a Circle" is a capital Renaissance design, reminding one somewhat of St. Mark's, Venice, presumably after Bramante, and shown in a well and firmly-drawn perspective. The figure drawing is first-rate throughout. The detail is disappointing, probably through want of time. For the safety of the structure I should say the bells are hung too high.

The Grissell Gold Medal.—Three sets of drawings were submitted for a "Stone Railway Bridge," the prize being gained by "Jacta est alea" (Harold Harlock) for a design admirable in its simplicity, as such a structure should be. The calculations are carefully gone into, and the judges had no difficulty in awarding the prize

"Equilibrium" is another simple and very good design; but in order to maintain its motto, the foundations even if on rock should surely go down below the river bed.

"Fundamentum forte opus sustinet" is a good design spoilt by unnecessary abutments at the springings of the arch, which could be no use and interfere with the continuous intrados of the arch, which should be naturally the most effective feature of the design.

The Masonry Prize.—The judge here had no hesitation in awarding the prize to "Saxum" for his drawing and model, which he states are admirable, and show a perfect knowledge of the subject; "Voussoir" is also very carefully worked out.

The Godwin Bursary.—Four applications for this were received, Mr. T. Locke Worthington being successful. I may give students a hint that, in applying for this, they would do well beforehand to consider carefully the subject they propose to take up if successful, and then to show that they have prepared themselves by preliminary study to take advantage of what they may see abroad in connexion with the subject; foreign travel without preliminary study is of little worth.

I have now been through (very imperfectly, I am afraid) all the work submitted this year. I think the Institute may be proud of it, and probably those who have not got prizes would be the first to admit they have got much benefit by the work. It would have been a more congenial task to me to have pointed out only the merits of these drawings, but I suppose a critic's duty is to criticise. I have spent a good deal of time among these drawings, and am much impressed with the ability shown in practically all of them.

In a short time the competitors will be competing in a still more important sphere, and either encumbering or beautifying the face of this fair world of ours with their buildings. If the promise of their draughtsmanship of to-day is fulfilled in their buildings of to-morrow, we may be very hopeful of the architecture which is yet to come.

The President said they would all agree with him in thanking Mr. Webb for the admirably exhaustive and critical notes which he had made upon the competition drawings. Those criticisms would be particularly useful because they referred not only to the drawings submitted by prize winners, but to the other drawings submitted. He had listened with great interest to the remarks made by Mr. Webb, and he would recommend the students to take them to heart. Friendly criticism was always valuable, especially when coming from one so competent to offer it.

Mr. John Slater, in proposing a vote of thanks to the President for his address, said that while they must all agree with the remarks made by the President concerning Mr. Webb's criticisms of the drawings, they must also acknowledge the merit of the President's own address. He was sure that they must all have been impressed by what the President had said as to the art of planning, and if those who were present that evening were to take to heart what he had said, it would be to their advantage in the future.

Mr. Charles Barry, in seconding the vote of thanks, said that the President's address was made to students, but he thought it contained some excellent advice which would appeal to those who, perhaps, like himself, no longer thought they were students, although, in point of fact, there was no time in the life and practice of an architect at which a man was not a student. In that sense the address would be of value to them all. He had been interested in hearing the catalogue of subjects which the President had given them, the study of which was to give them relief in their occupations; but the President had omitted one subject which was of great interest, viz., the study of the characters of clients, both single and corporate. He would strongly recommend them not to neglect that form of diversion. Diversion of that kind was frequently very necessary. The President had, he was sure, every reason to believe that planning was an art, for it was well known to most of them that the plans which had emanated from his hand, as well as from the hand of his old master Mr. Burn, were models of the most careful study of adaptability to the purposes concerned. He thought they must all feel the force of the President's observation that no man could make a good plan without picturing in his mind what the elevation would be and what the character would be, and without regarding its adaptability to the purpose for which it is intended.

Mr. Slater then put the vote of thanks, which was unanimously agreed to.

The President, in acknowledging the vote, said, in reference to Mr. Barry's remark about the study of character, important and interesting as that study was, and although some part of an architect's success depended upon the tact which was displayed in dealing with clients, still it was hardly a matter which formed part of the subject of planning. If he had lifted the idea of planning out of the too prosaic level in which it was too generally placed, and if he had led any of them to regard it as an artistic study, he was much more than rewarded for the time which he had devoted to his address.

The President then proceeded to present the prizes for 1892, a list of which appeared in the *Builder* last week, page 59.

The meeting then terminated.

LIFT AT THE METROPOLITAN TABERNACLE.—A hydraulic lift is to be fitted up at the Metropolitan Tabernacle to take Mr. Spurgeon from the yard up into his Vestry or down into the Lecture Hall. Messrs. Easton & Anderson, Ltd., are constructing the lift, which, it is stated, will be the first lift ever erected in a place of worship, at any rate in this country.

ARCHITECTURAL SOCIETIES.

BIRMINGHAM ARCHITECTURAL ASSOCIATION. On the 19th inst., a paper entitled "Four Suffolk Churches" was read before this Association by Mr. Paul Waterhouse, A.R.I.B.A. The churches dealt with by the lecturer were those of Southwold, Blythburgh, Covehithe, and Walberswick, of which the two latter are for the greater part in ruins. Mr. Waterhouse detailed something of the history, characteristics, and present state of these churches, and dwelt on the marked peculiarities which emphasise the church work of the particular period and locality represented by them. The lecture was illustrated by photographs, and by sketches, mostly the work of the author, though some were by Mrs. Paul Waterhouse. In explanation of the building methods of the early fifteenth-century, quotations were made from Gardner's "Dunwich" (published in 1735), which preserved, among other miscellaneous information on the buildings of the neighbourhood, a *verbatim* copy of the contract for building Walberswick Church, bearing date "the fourthe yeere of King Henry the Sexte." The lecturer pointed out as two prominent features of the procedure of the time, the absence of an architect and the explicit directions that the various details of the design were to be imitated from such points as were most admired in the then existing churches of the neighbourhood. Mr. Waterhouse dwelt on the terrible architectural results of the Cromwellian iconoclastic fury, which was particularly savage in the Eastern Counties, and concluded his paper with an imaginary picture of the glories which must have existed before the destruction of those days.—In proposing a vote of thanks to Mr. Waterhouse for his able paper, Mr. W. H. Bidlake said that the county in which the churches described lay was one which, from its historical associations and from the fact that it was a county which had, from being the seat of a wealthy commerce, become the scene of agricultural pursuits, appealed strongly to the imagination. The severe outlines of the churches of the Eastern Counties appeared to him particularly impressive, standing, as they did, in the wide, flat lands of the district, and the churches had great apparent stability, notwithstanding the weakness caused in appearance by the almost continuous clearstory windows. The vote of thanks was seconded by Mr. Doubleday, and supported by Mr. F. Barry Peacock (Vice-president), Mr. W. Hawley Lloyd, and others, and was unanimously passed.

CARLISLE ASSOCIATION OF ARCHITECTS, ENGINEERS, AND SURVEYORS.—The usual fortnightly meeting of this Association was held on January 12, when Mr. J. Rush Dixon, C.E., of the City Surveyor's Department, read a paper on "Road and Street Formation." The laying out and various modes of formation of streets, with their footways, kerbs, channels, and carriageways were fully described. The lecturer also gave a specification of the materials and formation of footways of gravel, tar, asphalte, cement, brick, and flagging, and of carriageways by macadam, tar-paving, asphalte, concrete, and stone-pitched pavements. The advantages, durability, cost, and disadvantage in each system were given, and the various thickness of material illustrated by drawings.

GLASGOW ARCHITECTURAL ASSOCIATION.—The usual monthly meeting of this Society was held on the 19th inst., when a paper on "Electric Lighting" was read by Mr. Alexander, electrical engineer. After an introductory notice of the extraordinary development within the last few years of the practical application of electricity to lighting, a short history of the first discoveries by Davis and Faraday was given. From laboratory to workshop he passed, and described the varieties of dynamos. The measurement of the force transmitted from producer to consumer was of the greatest commercial importance; this was described, and also the safeguard against fire or dangerous shock afforded by means of fuses that readily melt and at once cut off connexion upon any dangerous increase of electrical power. The three-wire system, by which the public will be supplied from the Corporation central stations, was described. Finally, a specification was given of the requirements in appliances of a private house having 100 lights, with the approximate cost. Throughout the lecture experiments were made, apparatus and specially-prepared diagrams being shown; and at its close a hearty vote of thanks was awarded to Mr. Alexander.—The following resolution anent the proposed Buildings Regulation Bill was then submitted as the outcome of a special meeting held last month, and revised by committee:—"The Glasgow Architectural Association, having considered the draft of the Glasgow Buildings Bill, while approving of its general purpose, believe that many of its provisions are inimical to the interests of architecture in Glasgow, and consider that a number of the by-laws in the schedule annexed to the Bill are most unpractical and unscientific in their relation to building construction; also, that it is very undesirable to promote any new Building Act which maintains the unskilled character and empirical procedure of the Dean of Guild Court, and does not provide for some form of control by qualified District Surveyors or otherwise, and for appeal in certain matters to a skilled and competent tribunal." The resolution, having been duly moved and seconded, was unanimously carried."

LIVERPOOL ARCHITECTURAL SOCIETY.—On the 25th inst., at the meeting of the Liverpool Architectural Society, in the Royal Institution, the Rev. F. F. Grensted delivered the third lecture of his series on "Egypt, the Home of the Early Arts," and dealt with the rise of civilisation in Babylonia, showing by some interesting photographs of sculptural remains that the great characteristics of the people were pride, war, and field sports.

NORTHERN ARCHITECTURAL ASSOCIATION STUDENTS' SKETCHING CLUB.—The second annual social gathering and exhibition of sketches of this club, was held on Monday evening last, when eighty or ninety members and friends were present. The exhibition included the work done by members at the fortnightly excursions, and Mr. C. Spooner kindly lent his Royal Academy Studentship drawings, which were greatly admired by those present. The President, Mr. W. S. Hicks, in opening the proceedings, congratulated the members on their work during the past year and his compliments were endorsed by Mr. Archibald Dunn. A programme of vocal and instrumental music was given by the members and their friends.

THE ARCHITECTURAL ASSOCIATION (DISCUSSION SECTION).—The last meeting of this section was held on the 20th inst., when Mr. A. H. Clark read a paper on "English Spires," dealing principally with their various forms and æsthetic qualities. The special Visitor for the evening was Mr. Philip J. Marvin, who, having had unusual facilities for studying the actual erection of spires, was able to give some most useful information. The paper was well illustrated by Mr. Clark's own sketches, principally from that county of spires—Northamptonshire.

THE LONDON COUNTY COUNCIL.

THE usual weekly meeting of this Council was held on Tuesday afternoon last, the Chairman, Sir John Lubbock, presiding.

Mode of Repayment for Local Loans.—The greater part of the meeting was occupied in the discussion of the following report of the General Purposes Committee as to the mode of repayment for local loans:—

"We have had under consideration the question as to the mode in which loans advanced by the Council to local bodies should be repaid. The Council is aware that as a rule the loans advanced by the late Board and the Council to Vestries and District Boards are repayable by equal annual instalments of principal, and the interest quarterly on the amount outstanding. The loans vary in period of repayment from 5 to 15 years for paving, 20 to 30 for works and buildings, and 60 years, or approaching thereto, for land and improvements to streets and bridges. This mode of repayment provides that in cases where there is the least outlay for repair and maintenance (*i.e.*, at the commencement of the loan), the work having but just been completed, there shall be the largest payment of principal and interest together, and the smallest at the end of the term, when the cost for repair and maintenance is necessarily increased, the two thus fairly balancing each other. In addition however to this, the payment of the interest quarterly provides the means to meet the quarterly payment of dividends on the Council's stock, which, when not thus provided, have to be obtained temporarily from other sources.

As regards loans to Guardians, whose power to borrow does not extend beyond 30 years, the case is different. The Metropolitan Board was first authorised to advance these loans by the Loans Act of 1875, and in 1876 the Local Government Board was requested by the Guardians of St. Marylebone to obtain the sanction of Parliament to an extension of the period for loans to Guardians. The Local Government Board did not deem this course expedient, but desired the late Board to meet the case by allowing Guardians borrowing them to repay their loans by way of annuity. To this the Board assented, and the loans for new workhouses or new additions have been made repayable by the annuity system, when sanctioned by the Local Government Board, ever since.

Having regard to the near dissolution of the Council, we do not think it desirable that the course hitherto followed should be altered, nor that it should be the rule to make loans, for whatever period of currency, repayable on the annuity principle; but that they should be repaid on the lines previously stated. We think also that it would be well to settle the question, and we therefore recommend the Council to pass the following resolution—

'That the terms as to repayment on which loans were made prior to December 15 shall remain unchanged during the remainder of the Council's term of office.'"

Mr. Campbell moved, as an amendment,

"That the Council, under the circumstances, holds it inadvisable to pass any general resolution on the subject, and is of opinion that each application for a loan should be considered and decided on its own merits."

After a long discussion, the amendment was rejected by 44 votes against to 39 for it,—a majority of 5 votes against.

Mr. J. Williams Benn moved, as a further amendment,

"That the consideration of the subject be adjourned until after March 5."*

This amendment was seconded by Mr. Dickinson, and carried by the narrow majority of 1,—43 for to 42 against.

Site for the Proposed New Offices for the Council.—The Offices Committee presented the following report:—

"The Council, on January 28, 1890, passed the following resolution:—

'That it be an instruction to the Council Chamber and Offices Committee to consider and report as to acquiring a suitable site for a Council Chamber and offices, having also regard to any site which already has erected upon it buildings of a character likely to be available for the purpose.'

We have from time to time given careful attention to the matter, and we now report for the information of the Council that we have under consideration three sites, either of which, subject to price, would be suitable for the erection thereon of new offices for the Council. We are, however, unable to proceed further until the Council gives us authority to enter into negotiations. We accordingly recommend—

'That we be authorised to enter in negotiations with regard to the sites referred to, and to report the result to the Council.'"

The recommendation was agreed to without discussion, and after transacting other business the Council adjourned.

* That is to say, until after the election of the new Council, which is fixed for that date.

COMPETITIONS.

WHITWORTH INSTITUTE, MANCHESTER.—In the first competition for the Whitworth Institute at Manchester, the assessor, Mr. A. Waterhouse, R.A., has recommended the following three designs for premiums, in the order named: "Terra-cotta (No. 2)," by Messrs. T. W. and R. F. Beaumont; "Floreat Mancunium," by Mr. Archibald Neill; and "Three Sisters," by Mr. Geo. Freeth Roper. From what we hear, it seems doubtful whether anything further will be done on the lines of this competition, as circumstances have occurred to alter the views of the promoters, and the scheme, if carried out, will probably be much modified.

NOTTINGHAM MASTER BUILDERS' ASSOCIATION.

THE annual meeting of the Nottingham Master Builders' Association was held on the 22nd inst. at the Mechanics' Institute, Mr. J. W. Woods. end presiding over a large attendance, in the absence of Councillor Wright (President). The following are the objects of the Association:—The consideration and discussion of all questions affecting the building trades; the promotion of excellence in the construction of buildings, and just and honourable practices in the conduct of business; the adoption of equitable forms of contract and encouragement of settling disputes by arbitration; the providing of facilities for social intercourse between the members of the Association and their friends, &c.

After the general business had been disposed of, and the officers elected for the ensuing year, notices from the Bricklayers' and Labourers' Societies asking for an advance of wages and code of working rules were read and discussed.

It was the unanimous opinion of the members that the present state of the building trade in Nottingham did not justify any advance on the present rate of wages.

Books.

Principles and Practice of Plumbing. By S. STEVENS HELLYER. London: Geo. Bell & Sons. 1891.

MR. HELLYER is so well known as a writer on matters connected with the plumber's craft that it is not suspriaing to find that he is the author of the volume on that subject in the series of technological handbooks edited by Sir H. Trueman Wood, and the choice is sufficiently justified by the extensive and thorough knowledge which Mr. Hellyer possesses of all kinds of plumbing work.

We regret, however, to find in this, as in other books written by Mr. Hellyer, that he is too much addicted to attempts at humour, which savour somewhat of vulgarity without being amusing. We can excuse Mr. Hellyer for his very natural expression of his opinion that his own manufactures are superior to those of his competitors in trade, but we should very much more enjoy the useful information which he gives us if he would not try to be funny.

Mr. Hellyer commences with a description, or rather illustrations, of the tools employed by the plumber, and then proceeds to tell us something of the history and manufacture of lead. In connexion with this he gives a very useful table, for which we have searched in vain in many other works on plumbing, of the weight of different lead pipes according to their substance. Some particulars about tin and its connexion with plumbing are also interesting and useful, as is also the description of soldering and lead-burning apparatus. The author then proceeds with a very excellent account of the execution of the various parts of the plumber's work applied to roofs, which will be of very great service as an addition to the practical experience of young plumbers, and also furnish for their employers many useful hints amongst which is a table of the different thicknesses of lead to be employed on the different parts of a roof. The description of bossing is very well treated, and the chapter on roof cess-pools is particularly minute and careful. We are specially glad to note the emphasis the writer lays on the importance of avoiding solder as much as possible in roof work, and also his advocacy of overflow-pipes from cess-pools. In the description of hips and ridges there is an omission which might be well supplied in any future edition. The author assumes that lead hips and ridges are universally formed over wood rolls, and omits to make any mention of the devices so frequently employed in our days for constructing hips with the lead work covered by close-cut slates. In speaking of rolls we notice that Mr. Hellyer advocates the keying of lead into the acute angles by the diminished roll rather than the right-angle junction employed by some practical men.

Very helpful to those readers, whose minds are not of a high mathematical order, will be the explanation of the manner of calculating the number of soakers for any particular piece of roofing. Another example of careful attention to minute detail is the description of a good method of constructing a torus moulding to a lead flat, a matter which is often not so skilfully arranged as it should be.

Leaving the subject of external plumbing, the author then proceeds to internal work, commencing with a full account of the various joints and the methods of making them. Mr. Hellyer defends the use of copper-bit and blow-pipe joints, though he is rightly careful to limit their application to special circumstances only; we should like to see also considerable emphasis laid upon the necessity for the workmanship of these joints being very accurate and careful, even in the limited number of cases where they may be used. Following the subject of joints comes that of bends, and we are glad to see that the author rightly condemns the use of mitre joints instead of bends. Any plumber who values his reputation as a craftsman should never make a joint where a bend serves the purpose. Apart from the question of skill, it will be within the experience of some of our readers that plumbers occasionally make joints for the mere purpose of charging for them, even, as we have sometimes known, if they have to cut a pipe in a half to do it.

Mr. Hellyer then once more gives us his views on the subject of traps, many of which, as he frankly says, have already appeared in other of his writings.

The chapter on lining cisterns and sinks with lead is well and carefully teated; and Mr. Hellyer then proceeds to treat in detail the plumbing work connected with soil-pipes, water-closets, sinks, baths, and lavatories, his views and practice as to which are well known to most of our readers.

The work finally concludes with some chapters on house drains, which do not, of course, profess to treat the subject so fully as Mr. Hellyer has done in other of his works.

Architectural Perspective. By F. O. FERGUSON. London: Crosby Lockwood & Son. 1891.

IT is a great advantage for young architectural draughtsmen to have placed before them a clear and straightforward description of the way in which they may prepare architectural perspectives without going through the large amount of needless drudgery usually entailed by attending any school of art class on perspective after the South Kensington fashion.

Decidedly the best way for a young architect to learn so much of perspective as is necessary for him, is to get an expert draughtsman to give him two or three hours personal instruction; then, if he has a clear head of his own and a reasonable amount of artistic ability, he will be quite free of books and teachers for the remainder of his days.

For those who are unable to get this personal instruction, Mr. Ferguson's book will do something and enable them to make a fairly decent perspective without an undue amount of labour, but there are some points upon which the author would do well to obtain a few more wrinkles before he issues a new edition.

The best positions for the point of sight, picture plane, and consequently the measuring line, are not sufficiently explained. Mr. Ferguson's method of making the measuring line on the nearest angle of the building with his picture plane touching the same angle is not calculated to produce the best grouping. Further, the rule which the author gives, that the point of sight should be distant about three times the height of the building, is only one of the points that an expert takes into consideration, as will be seen from the large extent of the angle of vision which the author uses.

The most serious blemish in the book, however, is fig. 24 in Part I., where we have what is evidently intended to be an example of isometrical projection, but clearly showing that the author does not understand correctly what isometrical projection is, nor its advantages when properly used. We quite agree with the author's opinion that the diagram he shows "is extremely ugly"; this ugliness would vanish to a very considerable extent if the diagram were correct.

The plate which Mr. Ferguson shows of his finished drawing will hardly commend itself to embryo draughtsmen, who have the advantage of frequently seeing much better specimens of pen-and-ink drawing. Mr. Ferguson would do well to obtain the collaboration of some of our well-known experts in draughtsmanship to give an illustration of what is understood in our days as the artistic treatment of light and shade in architectural drawing.

Notes on Building Construction. Part I. New edition. London: Longmans, Green, & Co. 1891.

IN our review of the new edition of Part II. of this well-known students' manual, we called attention to the omission of certain chapters which had appeared in the first edition of Part II. We are glad to find that in the new edition of Part I., which has now reached us, these matters have been included, so that the important subjects of riveting, centreing, and the building up of timber beams, are now no longer omitted, as would appear from an examination of the new edition of Part II. only. The chapters on these subjects are practically the same as before with some few modifications and additions which have been judiciously made, and increase the value of the work.

The chapter on iron roofs has been practically re-written, and although the volume is intended for elementary students only, it virtually contains information, well and clearly expressed, sufficient for the practice of certainly the majority of architects.

The inclusion of a so clear and thorough description of the construction of iron roofs in what is now the standard handbook for architectural students, cannot fail to render the use of iron for this purpose more general amongst the rising generation, who will no longer be led to look upon ironwork as something which is beyond their capabilities, and only to be employed with the extraneous assistance of a civil engineer.

The remainder of the work is almost the same as before. Some few additions, chiefly an increase in the number of illustrations, have been made, and will enable the "Notes on Building Construction" to maintain the high position it has reached as a manual for architectural students.

The Essex Review. Vol. I., No. 1, January, 1892. London: T. Fisher Unwin; Chelmsford: Edmund Durrant & Co.

THIS is the first number of a quarterly publication, the object of which is "to gather up into one publication all matters of permanent interest relating to the prosperity, history, and literature of the county." The idea is an excellent one, and the first number promises well for the future. It contains "Notes of the Quarter" in regard to a variety of subjects, including new churches and church restoration. The Rev. Thomas Rogers, Mus.Doc., furnishes well-written notes on what has been done in music in the county during the past quarter, and Mr. F. Chancellor contributes the first of a series of articles on "Essex Churches," a description (with an illustration) of St. Augustine's, Birdbrook. The housing of the agricultural labourer in Essex is the subject of another article, and various notes and queries, and notices of new books, are added. The *Essex Review* ought to be a publication of much interest to the inhabitants of the county, and certainly, if it goes on as it has begun, deserves their support.

"The Advertiser's A.B.C. and Press Directory" (London: T. B. Browne, 163, Queen Victoria-street), is a well-arranged and admirably printed directory of English, Colonial, and Foreign newspapers, which are well indexed. In some respects, however, the lists of foreign papers need revision. For example, there is more than one newspaper published at Dunkerque, and the one mentioned in the book, the *Phare de Dunkerque*, is a daily and not a weekly journal. The ordinary directory matter is prefaced by some interesting articles concerning the production and distribution of newspapers. Particularly interesting are the articles on "Special Newspaper Trains," "The Old Journalism and the New," "Lobby Men and Lobby Manners," and "The Gallery of the House of Commons."

Our trade contemporary *Timber* issued last week an interesting illustrated number entitled "Timber and Woodworking Machinery." It contains a great deal of information about timber, its production, conversion, and conveyance, and is very fully illustrated.

The Manufacturers' Engineering and Export Journal is the title of a new monthly journal the first number of which has been sent to us. It is published at 22, Paternoster-row.

We have received Messrs. Line & Sons' illustrated catalogue of wall-papers, glazing, &c. The illustrations of wall-papers show some good designs by Mr. Brophy, Mr. A. Silver, and others. There is also mention of an embossed wall-covering consisting of wood fibre embossed in hollow relief, "as lasting as the wall itself," and which may have an excellent effect in suitable regions; we do not approve of these relief papers for London houses: they collect and hold dirt. The particular design illustrated of this material is rather like "Japanese run mad," but no doubt it would have its admirers. The examples of combed wall surfaces in "Alabastine" suggest a good many possibilities of diaper surface decoration of a simple kind.

THE FIRST SUSPENSION BRIDGE IN ICELAND.—After twenty years of agitation, the first suspension bridge in Iceland has been finished. It spans the Olves river, is made of iron and steel wires, and is 360 ft. long and 6 ft. wide, the height above the river being 60 ft. The cost of the bridge is 3,500*l*. It has been made in England by Messrs. Vaughan & Dymond, Newcastle, and placed in position by English engineers.

Correspondence.

To the Editor of THE BUILDER.

ADJOINING BUILDINGS.

SIR,—One cannot pass along any thoroughfare in London without being struck by the careless way in which architects, in designing their own buildings, treat adjoining ones. No attention is paid to the horizontal lines of floors, openings, or cornices on either side. The elevation is worked out in the office, without any reference to their neighbour's design, with the result that strings and cornices are either ruthlessly cut off and left unreturned, or jumbled into their own elevation, and thus spoil both buildings. The County Council, District, and parish Surveyors should all insist upon some definite rule to govern such cases, and then see it properly enforced. I cannot conceive anything easier for an architect to carry into execution.

A somewhat similar matter is the treatment of adjoining chimnies. Mr. Edis's successful building for the Junior Constitutional Club in Piccadilly is a case in point. Here the chimnies of houses on east and west sides are carried up, no doubt at the expense of the owners of the Club, in different material and design to the club, and effectually destroy the otherwise satisfactory appearance of the gables and chimnies of the club. Truly in this case to have so treated the adjoining chimneys both in design and material to accord with the club, would neither have been a difficult or an expensive work, and could not have been objected to by adjoining owners. R. J. W.

*** The problem is not quite such an easy one as our correspondent seems to think, though no doubt more attention might be paid to it in many cases.

FLOORING-BOARDS ON CONCRETE.

SIR,—If "Surveyor" lays a tongued floor directly on concrete, I think he will have trouble from dry rot. I have heard of ordinary floors, not tongued, being so laid, but how they have behaved I know not.

Let me caution "Surveyor" against carrying his coke-breeze concrete into the fireplaces. It is a very perfect conductor of heat. The heat will accumulate in it sufficiently to char any wooden skirtings or other combustible work, at quite a respectable distance from the fireplace. This I know from ocular demonstration.

I am not sure that coke breeze is a safe material to place even near flues. The mere admixture of cement with it does not entirely deprive the coke of its very combustible properties.

Another hint as to coke-breeze concrete. It is apt to scale off from below the flanges of any iron joists which may be embedded in it. I should, therefore, hesitate about plastering directly on to the concrete. Of course, the soffit can be battered and lathed. Possibly the same scaling-off may sometimes occur with other concretes. Possibly, too, a liberal use of cement may get over this difficulty.

The concrete, whatever the "aggregate" used, must have plenty of time to dry,—not always an easy matter when a building has to be rushed. The floor-boards may be cut and laid in place, and nailed later on.

Coke-breeze concrete has, of course, the advantage of being light, and of taking nails kindly. The disadvantages are, I think, those which I have cited, and also that, like all concretes made with porous material, it lets water through too freely; so the extinction of even a small fire may do a good deal of mischief. ANOTHER SURVEYOR.

January 25, 1892.

BOLSOVER COLLIERY COMPETITION.

SIR,—I am glad to see that your correspondent "H. G." has brought to light the conditions of the above-named competition; but he has, I think, missed one of the most beautiful points, for the whole seven houses, schools for 600, workmen's club, hospital, and co-operative stores are to be carried out for 3,000*l*.! I did not return my particulars, but have kept them as a sad memento of what our profession has fallen to, and whenever I feel unduly elated by success I shall get them out and read them through. J. H. H.

THE ENGLISH IRON TRADE.—The most important feature in the English iron market has been the drop of 4s. in the price of Scotch warrants. The result has been the disorganisation of the small amount of legitimate business being transacted, buyers holding back until the market becomes again settled. Heavy sales of Cleveland and hematite warrants took place on Monday, on the reduction in the price of Scotch warrants being published. There is less doing in manufactured iron and common bars, and black sheets are 2s. 6d. and 5s. lower respectively. Tinplates are quiet; but the improved tone continues. There is very little change in the steel trade. Shipbuilders are still busy, and engineers maintain fair activity. The coal trade is somewhat quieter.—*Iron.*

The Student's Column.

WARMING BUILDINGS BY HOT WATER.

V.

ARRANGEMENT OF PIPES. AIR IN PIPES. (HORTICULTURAL WORK.)

IT is sometimes questioned as to where the vertical portion of the return-pipe should be situated, and likewise, upon the same grounds, where the vertical portion of the flow should be. As a rule, both are near to, or directly in, the boiler, this being convenient, and it is also the correct position, although the majority of workmen would be quite at a loss to explain why.

It has been shown that the circulation is wholly dependent upon the difference of gravity or weight between the water in the flow-pipe and that in the return (the vertical portions of the pipe, not the horizontal, which have no assisting effect), and the greater this difference the more effective or strong the circulatory movement will be. There are two ways of increasing this difference in weight in the two vertical columns, viz., by increasing their height, as will be understood (a means not available in the low-lying horticultural works), and by increasing the difference in temperature of the two columns of water, for we have shown that a variation in temperature is a certain variation in gravity or weight. The former method applies to buildings, in which the pipes commonly extend up great heights, and at all times higher than in greenhouse work. The latter method will explain why the vertical portions of the pipes in a horticultural apparatus should be near the boiler in the following way.

If an apparatus is erected as fig. 13, which is the approved way (the extent of pipes and

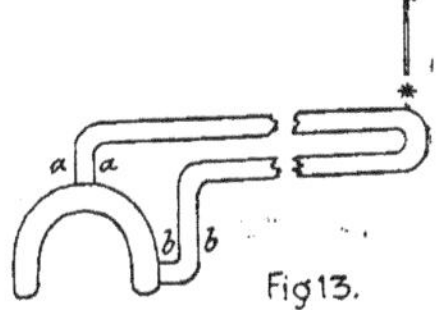

Fig 13.

branches do not affect this explanation), we shall get the hottest water as it leaves the boiler, in the vertical portion of the flow pipe, *a*. As this water travels on and along the horizontal pipe, it loses heat (as it is intended to do), and becomes of an increased weight, until, as it is upon the point of entering the boiler again by the pipe *b*, it is of its greatest density, and differs the most from the water in the pipe *a* in temperature, and consequently weight. Therefore, if it is the difference in weight of the water, and this is only effective in vertical pipes, then near the boiler is the most effective position for them, for here, both in the flow and the return, we get the two extremes of temperature.

Sometimes it is argued that the vertical portion of the return should be at the opposite end to the boiler, as fig. 14, the supposed favourable

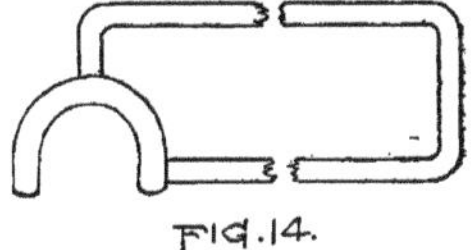
FIG. 14.

feature being that the fall, *i.e.*, the descent of the heavier water, occurs before it has to pass along the lower horizontal pipe; and, as a horizontal pipe is opposed to the circulation, by offering a certain resistance by friction, the descent occurring first aids in getting the water towards the boiler. But the least investigation shows that a loss is experienced in the fact that when the water falls at the further extremity of the apparatus, as fig. 14, it cannot be so cool as it would be near the boiler, as fig. 13. As (it will bear repetition) the circulation is dependent upon the water in this return pipe being heavier than the water in the flow-pipe from the top of the boiler, it must be better to let its effective vertical part be where the water will be coolest and heaviest, that is, near the boiler, than for it to be away where the water has not lost so much heat.

In brief, the water is hottest in the pipe which leaves the top of the boiler and coolest in the pipe that enters the bottom of the boiler. By keeping the vertical (*i.e.*, the effective) parts of the pipes near these two points, we get the greatest possible difference in temperature, consequently weight and motive power.

Another argument to be heard occasionally, and worth mentioning, is that, by carrying the flow-pipe in the ordinary manner, but sloping the return all the way to the boiler, as fig. 15,

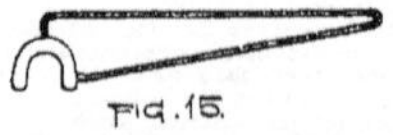

FIG. 15.

advantageous results are obtained by reason of the fall of water being free through the whole length of the return and no part horizontal. (It must be noticed by the way that this arrangement would be useless in a large apparatus, as it would not admit of branch services being connected very easily.)

This suggestion sounds very feasible, but it is nearly as valueless as the last. The fact of the return pipe being given this descent its whole length does not increase the aggregate distance it falls; that is, if the distance between flow and return pipes at the boiler be as in figs. 13 and 15, the actual fall given to the return pipes cannot exceed that distance in either case. Sloping the return all the way, as fig. 15, is a disadvantage from the fact that the descending force of water commences a long way from the boiler where the water has only lost a part of the heat it will lose before it re-enters the boiler. In other words, the actual result is as near as possible like giving an abrupt descent to the return, half way between boiler and extremity of apparatus, as fig. 16.

Another arrangement sometimes suggested is to make the pipes wholly returns, as fig. 17.

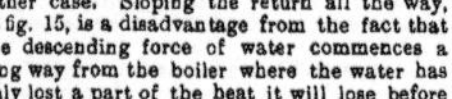

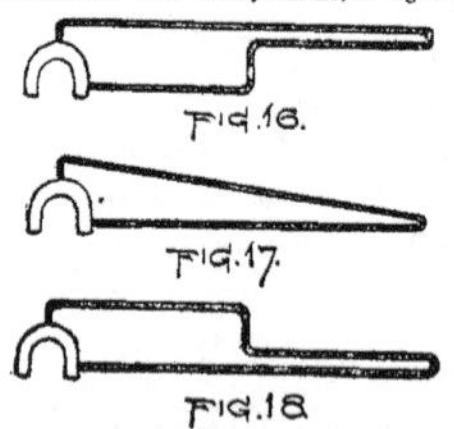

FIG. 16.

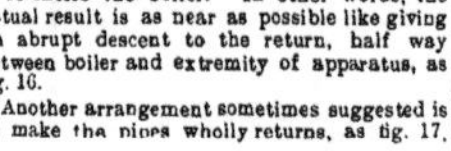

FIG. 17.

FIG. 18

From the information given, it will be seen that this is a worse arrangement than ever. In this case it is giving the water the fall or descent immediately it leaves the boiler when it is hottest, and it would give a worse circulation than any example yet given. It would practically amount to arranging the pipes as fig. 18.

These different suggestions, although some of them are next to impracticable, are given so that the reader may know what lines of argument are occasionally taken when discussing these works, and become familiar with the different phenomena that go to aid efficiency or otherwise. It will now be understood that the correct practice is to put all vertical pipe of the flow immediately on the top of the boiler, and all the vertical pipe of the return as near the boiler as it can be got. This arrangement is subject to conditions being favourable, and in any case allowance must be made for all pipes run in a horizontal direction having a regular rise from beginning to end.

AIR IN PIPES.

This, as before referred to, is a subject needing every consideration, for it frequently introduces real difficulties. Following the suggestion offered, we shall only now deal with the question as regards horticultural work. Its application to buildings will be treated in its place later. There is but little resemblance between the two, even as regards this subject, air tubes being used in one case, and air cocks in the other; and there are other differences.

In the first place, let it be understood that under any circumstances an air pipe must exist at the highest extremity, which is the furthest point from the boiler, marked * on fig. 13. This would suffice for a simple little apparatus like that one. If the works be such that branch services exist, which are carried in various directions, then each furthest extremity requires an air outlet; these extremities, it is understood, being the highest points in these different directions. It is hardly necessary to explain that air, being so much lighter than water, always seeks the highest position it can occupy, and there it will persistently stay. If, however, an air pipe be at that point, then there is no question of the air remaining, for it will instantly make its exit as the water fills the apparatus.

As an example, let us suppose a simple apparatus of two straight pipes which have the customary rise from the boiler, but in which the air-pipe has incorrectly been placed near the boiler, as shown in fig. 19. The proper

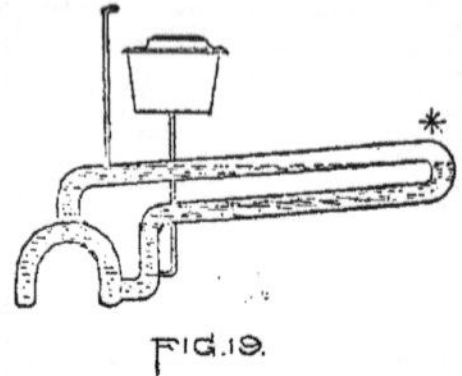

FIG. 19.

position for it would be where marked *. In this case, when first filling the apparatus, the water passing in from the small cistern shown, the pipes would gradually fill up until the lower aperture of the air-tube was covered, and then it would cease. This would leave the flow-pipe from the air-tube to * more or less charged with air, and it would require some rather strenuous efforts before it could be dislodged. Assuming it could be dislodged, the trouble would only be temporarily obviated, for water varying in temperature absorbs and expels air, and an accumulation would soon be formed again. If the air-pipe be shifted to *, the remedy would be complete; but until then the apparatus would be a failure. No circulation could be effected while this air was imprisoned.

If the accumulation of air was less, and did not wholly fill the extremity of the pipe, then the water would circulate, and if the apparatus was small, probably no particular ill results would be noticeable, but, if the apparatus be extensive, this fault would prove a check to the circulation until discovered. Air vents must be on the highest points, the points that the air seeks when the inflowing water begins to disturb it. We shall show in a later paper how this question often requires a good deal of consideration when pipes are dipped or run in irregular ways. It is quite useless imagining the air will find its way out if left alone, or that the water will manage in any way to displace the air, or occupy its place by some other means. When air is thus imprisoned (this word correctly expresses the state of things) there is no chance of matters remedying themselves without assistance.

SURVEYORSHIPS.

PARISH OF ST. PANCRAS.—The Vestry of St. Pancras, London, have appointed Mr. W. N. Blair, Assoc. M. Inst. C.E., the Borough Surveyor of Bootle, to the post of Chief Surveyor to their Vestry at a salary of 600*l.* per annum. There were originally seventy-three candidates for the position, and from these the Highways and Works Committee selected twenty-two for personal interview, after which they recommended for the consideration of the full Vestry the following six in the order of selection given: Mr. W. N. Blair, Borough Surveyor, Bootle; Mr. J. P. Norrington, Vestry Surveyor, Fulham; Mr. W. Howard-Smith, City Surveyor, Carlisle; Mr. J. P. Barber, Vestry Surveyor, Islington; Mr. G. J. C. Broom, Borough Surveyor, St. Helen's; Mr. H. Monson, Vestry Surveyor, St. James's, Westminster. These gentlemen accordingly had an interview with the full Vestry, who proceeded to select two of the number for final consideration, these two being Messrs. Blair and Howard-Smith, and after a discussion lasting over some hours, a ballot was taken, when Mr. Blair was found to have received the greater number of votes, and was, accordingly, appointed.

OBITUARY.

DR. ALFRED CARPENTER.—We regret to hear of the death, at Ventnor, on Wednesday last, of Dr. Alfred Carpenter, the well-known sanitarian, of Croydon. According to the *Times*, he was born in 1825, and was a native of Northamptonshire. He was educated at Moulton Grammar School, Lincolnshire, and studied medicine first at Northampton Infirmary, and afterwards at St. Thomas's Hospital, where, besides gaining the first scholarship ever given at that institution, he took the Treasurer's Gold Medal at the end of his course. Dr. Carpenter had long been known as an advocate of sanitary reform. In 1859 he became a member of the Croydon Board of Health, and he was Examiner in Public Health to the Universities of London and Cambridge. In 1891 he was appointed to serve on the Royal Commission which inquired into the condition of the London hospitals for smallpox and fever cases and into the means of preventing the spread of infection. Among his many works on sanitary subjects are "Hints on House Drainage," "The First Principles of Sanitary Works," and the "Physiological and Mechanical Aspect of Sewage Irrigation." We may add that many contributions from his pen on sanitary matters have appeared in the pages of the *Builder*.

MR. WILLIAM BASEVI SANDERS, late Assistant Keeper of the Records, died of bronchitis last week. When the Record Office decided, in 1861, to take advantage of the discovery of photo-zincography and to publish a series of facsimiles of the national manuscripts, Mr. Sanders was selected to take charge of the manuscripts, to see that the facsimiles made by the Ordnance Survey Department were correct, and to translate such documents as required translation. The facsimiles of Domesday Book; of the National manuscripts of England (4 vols.); of Scotland (3 vols.); of Ireland (3 vols.), of the Anglo-Saxon Charters (3 vols.); and of the Black Letter Prayer-book of 1636, with the translations and explanatory notes attached to them, are the result of his labours.—*Times*.

MR. W. FOGGIN.—On the 20th inst. the death took place of Mr. William Foggin, builder, of Newcastle. Deceased was sixty-nine years of age. Mr. Foggin was a native of Corbridge, but in early life he came to Newcastle. He had a large building connexion, says the *Newcastle Chronicle*. He built the Catholic Church of St. Andrew's, in Worswick-street, and also the Catholic schools at the Manors, the convent schools in Villa-place, the presbytery at St. Mary's Cathedral, the Freemasons' Hall in Maple-street, the Catholic Church dedicated to Our Lady and St. Oswin at Tynemouth, and a number of other public buildings in Newcastle and the district.

GENERAL BUILDING NEWS.

LONDON BUILDING LEGISLATION.—At the next meeting of the Royal Institute of British Architects, to be held on Monday, February 8, Mr. Edwin T. Hall is to read a paper on "London Building Legislation." The paper will be descriptive of the Suggestions of the Practice Standing Committee, adopted by the Council of the Institute, for the proposed Codification and Amendment of the Metropolitan Building Acts. The main lines of such suggestions are:—1. It is suggested that the details of construction, which are subject to variation from time to time by reason of, *inter alia*, new inventions, new materials, or modes of construction, &c., should be omitted from the body of the new Act, and be placed in schedules attached thereto, power being given by the Act to the County Council and to the Commissioners of Sewers, as the case may be (subject to provisions corresponding to those of Part II. of the Metropolitan Management and Building Acts Amendment Act, 1878), to vary these as occasion shall require, the object being to allow of changes in details of construction without the necessity of going to Parliament. 2. It is suggested that the new Act should be confined to and extend to everything within and enclosing the curtilage of a building, including any vaults under a public way; it is also suggested that it should include sanitation (*i.e.*, drainage, air spaces, ventilation, plumbing, &c.) and regulations respecting lines of frontage of buildings. 3. The construction of roads, sewers, and bridges, and of everything in the nature of public thoroughfares for use in common by the public, to be excluded. 4. Rights of light and air to be excluded, as they are in the nature of private property. 5. Restrictions on design, which are questions of taste, to be excluded. 6. Erections which are not buildings should be subject to control or supervision of district surveyors. Under this head would come: glass covers to yards, private bridges between buildings in one occupation, telephone and telegraph posts on buildings, wall signs, towl-houses, and similar domestic structures, metal pipes for flues, &c.

NEW CHURCH, WESTCOMBE PARK, BLACKHEATH.—On the 23rd inst. the Church of St. George, Westcombe Park, was consecrated by the Lord Bishop of Rochester. The church is in the Early French style, and when completed, with chancel, tower, and spire, will cost 10,000l. The interior and exterior are faced with red bricks, relieved by Bath stone dressings and strings, and the roof open timbered. The floors are fireproof, and covered with wood-block flooring. The church has been erected from the designs of Messrs. Newman & Newman, architects, Tooley-street. by Messrs. Balaam Bros., of Shenton-street, Old Kent-road. The pulpit was executed in oak from the designs of the architects by Mr. A. Robinson, of Broad-street, Bloomsbury. The gasfittings are by Messrs. Gardener, of Bristol; and the heating arrangements by Mr. John Grundy, of City-road. The church is built upon the slope of a hill facing the river, and, when completed, will form a prominent feature in the neighbourhood.

SUNDAY-SCHOOL BUILDINGS, SKIPTON:—On the 12th inst. the new Congregational Sunday-schools erected in Otley-street, Skipton, were opened by Alderman J. Hopkinson, of Manchester. The foundation-stones were laid in August, 1890, and the premises have been built upon modern lines. The assembly-room, on the ground floor, contains a platform, and on each side there are six class-rooms, and there is a large room which will be used as a day-school for the infants. The assembly-room is encircled by a gallery, and on each side there are also four class-rooms. The building has been erected at a cost of about 3,000l. Messrs. Healey & Son, of Bradford, were the architects; Mr. B. Kirk, of Skipton, was the contractor for the stone-work; Mr. Smith, of Keighley, the joinery; and Mr. G. H. Mason, of Skipton, the plumbing and painting.

HOSPITAL EXTENSION, MIDDLESBROUGH.—On the 5th inst. a new wing, which has been added to the North Ormesby Cottage Hospital, Middlesbrough, was opened by Viscountess Falkland. On the ground floor of the new building there is a large room for out-patients, with a dispensary, doctors'-room, and a dressing-room. The second floor contains the nurses', day, and bed rooms, bath-room, and other conveniences. Mr. Thos. Dickinson, of Middlesbrough, has executed the work from designs of Mr. J. M. Bottomley, of that town. The cost has been 2,006l.

PUBLIC HALL, CWMAMAN, GLAMORGAN.—The new public hall at Cwmaman was opened by Lord Aberdare on the 25th inst. The building, which is constructed of stone, has been erected at a cost of 1,500l. Besides the hall, which is capable of seating 700 persons, there is a library, two reading-rooms, a room for games, and a billiard-room. The architect is Mr. T. Roderick, of Aberdare, and the builders Messrs. Powell & Mansfield, of Cardiff.

ALTERATIONS TO WYCLIFFE CHAPEL, DEVONPORT.—Wycliffe Congregational Chapel, Devonport, was re-opened on the 24th inst., after extensive alterations and repairs. The whole of the roof and a large portion of the western wall has been taken down. The roof has been lowered 10 ft., and the roofs over the aisles have also been altered so that their appearance might correspond with that of the main roof. The interior has been coloured and re-varnished. Mr. H. J. Snell was the architect, and the builder was Mr. J. Williams, of Stonehouse.

CO-OPERATIVE PREMISES, BROOMHILL, NORTHUMBERLAND. — On the 2nd inst. new business premises for the Broomhill Co-operative Society were opened by Mr. Albert Grey. The building, which has cost about 2,600l., has been designed by Messrs. Oliver & Leeson, architects, Newcastle, the contractor being Mr. D. M. Spence, of Amble. On the ground floor there are shops, and on the first floor there is a hall for public meetings, committee-rooms, secretary's office, &c.

GYMNASIUM BUILDING, HULME.—On the 6th inst. the Procter Gymnasium, which has been built on land in Silver-street, off Chester-road, Manchester, the gift of the Corporation, was opened for use by Lord Egerton of Tatton. The building has frontages into Silver-street, Pryme-street, and Southam-street, Chester-road, with two main entrances from Silver-street, one for members and the other for the public. The accommodation for members consists of a room, 100 ft. long by 50 ft. in width, lighted by a lantern light in roof and side windows. There are dressing-rooms and lavatories with slipper and shower baths, &c.; also three large fives courts leading out of the large room. A gallery is formed across one end of the large room and down one side to accommodate the public. Two reading-rooms, committee-room, and instructor's office are also provided, with kitchen and store-rooms in the basement. The building has been fitted with gymnastic apparatus by Mr. Renshaw. All the work has been carried out by Messrs. Wilson & Toft, contractors, from the designs and under the superintendence of Messrs. W. & G. Higginbottom, architects, of Manchester.

CANAL PROJECT IN FINLAND.—The Finnish Government has decided upon the canalisation and regulation of the rivers between Pielavesi and Jisvesi at an estimated cost of 28,000l., a large expenditure in that country. The depth of new waterway will be 6 ft. The work will occupy three years.

FOREIGN AND COLONIAL.

FRANCE.—The posthumous exhibition of the works of Ribot will be opened at the Ecole des Beaux-Arts in May. The monument to the painter, to be erected at Paris, has been entrusted to M. Rodin, sculptor.——In consequence of the extension to the Luxembourg of the Sceaux railway, the statue of Marshal Ney on the Boulevard St. Michel will have to be moved. This, which was the work of Rude, stands on the place where Ney was shot. It will be re-erected at the angle of Rue Notre Dame des Champs and Boulevard Montmartre.——M. Gustave Moreau, painter, has been appointed to the post of "Professeur Chef d'Atelier," formerly held by Delaunay.——A bust of the sculptor Aimé Millet has been erected at Père la Chaise. It was modelled by one of his pupils, M. Emile Guillaume.——A statue of Chevreuil, the celebrated chemist, is to be placed in the galleries of the Conservatoire des Arts et Métiers at Paris; it will be executed by M. Fayal.——M. Marius Vachon has been appointed Director of the exhibition of "Arts de la Femme" which is to be organised in August at the Palais d'Industrie, under the direction of the Union Centrale des Arts Décoratifs. Mdme. Rosa Bonheur will preside over the Fine-Art Section.——It is stated positively that the Minister of Public Works is at last about to submit to Parliament the long-delayed Metropolitan Railway scheme. The project will include, it is said, the completion of the Rue Réaumur, which is to connect the Rue du Temple with the Place de l'Opéra.—There is talk of the purchase by the Government of the site of the old Théâtre Italien (Place Ventadour) to instal there the Opéra-Comique. The building is at present occupied by a large financial establishment.——The Committee for the decoration of the Hôtel de Ville have commissioned M. Puvis de Chavannes to execute the decoration of the ceiling of the grand staircase, formerly given to Delaunay.——The death is announced of M. Guivogne, of Lyons, who was specially charged with the services of the Beaux-Arts and Architecture of that town.——At Biarritz a competition has been opened for a sea-bathing establishment on the beach, to cost about 600,000 francs.——In a field near Degoin (Saône-et-Loire) there has been discovered an interesting Roman burying-place, in which M. Veillerot, the antiquary, has found Gallo-Roman pottery, bronze bracelets, arms, and coins with the heads of Augustus, Nero, Vespasian, and Antoninus.——By a decree of the Conseil d'Etat, the town of Montpellier is condemned to pay to the architect of the Municipal Theatre, M. Cassier Bernard, the amount of his fees calculated at four per cent., with interest at five per cent. from May, 1888.——It is announced from Cairo that M. Grébaut, Director of Excavations at Tel-el-Amoma, has discovered a royal tomb of the eighteenth dynasty of Egypt. This tomb includes a gallery 50 mètres long terminating in a large rectangular apartment in which are found traces of painting of which the colour has faded.——M. Ernest Christophe, sculptor, has died at Paris, at the age of sixty-five. His principal works were "La Douleur," a marble statue now in the Tuileries Gardens; "La Fortune," in the Luxembourg Museum; and a sketch for a monument to his master, Rude, now in the Museum of Dijon.——The death is also announced, at the age of eighty-one, of Comte Emile de Nieuwerkerke, formerly "Super-intendant des Beaux-Arts" under the Second Empire. He was a sculptor of merit, and had acquired a great many friendships by his amiability as well as his enlightened taste in matters of art.——One of the masters of French engraving, Louis Pierre Henrique Dupont, has just died at Paris, at the age of 94. We will refer more at length in our next "Letter from Paris" to the career of this eminent artist, only remarking now that he was, since 1849, a member of the Académie des Beaux-Arts, and commander of the Legion of Honour since 1878. He was, since 1863, Professor of Engraving at the Ecole Nationale des Beaux-Arts.

SYDNEY.—The tender for the erection of the Newcastle Cathedral, from the foundation already completed to the roof (which will be a separate contract), has been accepted. The architect is Mr. T. Horbury Hunt.

MISCELLANEOUS.

ELECTION OF THREE ASSOCIATES OF THE ROYAL ACADEMY.—At a general assembly of Royal Academicians and Associates, held on Wednesday evening last, Mr. Stanhope A. Forbes, painter, Mr. Harry Bates, sculptor, and Mr. T. G. Jackson, architect, were elected Associates.

RAWLINGS' EMERGENCY STAIRCASE.—This is a form of folding staircase intended especially to provide a means of exit from the upper floors of factories or other such buildings. A light folding staircase is connected with a trap-door in such a manner that when the trap-door is raised the stair is by the same action let down to the floor below. A handrail unfolds with it, extending sufficiently far down the stair or ladder to afford safety to children in descending. It is proposed that the trap-doors should be formed one over the other in each floor, at the farthest point from the permanent staircase, so as to afford an uninterrupted way down. Of course in a case where one floor or story was filled with flames and smoke it would not be of much use, as it would not pass the point of danger: an outside exit is the thing really wanted. In many cases, however, it would afford an available exit, and its comparative cheapness and the readiness with which it could be fitted to existing buildings recommend it to attention.

THE SANITARY INSTITUTE.—A list of lectures has been arranged by the Sanitary Institute for the special instruction of those desirous of obtaining knowledge of the duties of Sanitary Officers. The various subjects will be dealt with in the course of seventeen lectures, given by well-known authorities, and will be illustrated with diagrams, drawings, and models. These lectures are a continuation of the courses previously held by the Parkes Museum, and it is proposed to repeat the course in London twice each year, to suit the requirements of persons preparing for the examinations of the Institute. The lectures will comprise the subjects scheduled for these examinations, and will be given on Tuesdays and Fridays, commencing Friday, January 29. Students and others desirous of attending the lectures are requested to send in their names at once to the Secretary of the Institute, 74A, Margaret-street, W.

THE SORBONNE, PARIS.—An illustrated history of this famous College is in preparation by Mr. John A. Randolph, to be published by subscription. It will be completed in six monthly parts.

DESIGNS FOR FLOORCLOTH.—Messrs. M. Nairn & Co., of Kirkcaldy, are offering a number of prizes for the best designs for floorcloth and linoleum. The judges are to be Mr. M. B. Nairn and Mr. John Nairn, assisted by one of the examiners of the South Kensington School of Art. Designers on the staff of the firm are excluded from the competition.

SOCIETY OF ARTS.—In consequence of the illness of Prof. W. C. Unwin, F.R.S., the Howard Lectures on "The Development and Transmission of Power from Central Stations," which he was announced to deliver on February 5 and five following Friday evenings, have been postponed.

CHICAGO EXHIBITION.—The first meeting of the Electricity Committee was held on Tuesday afternoon, 26th inst. Present:—W. H. Preece, F.R.S., in the chair; Sir Frederick Abel, K.C.B., D.C.L., F.R.S., Colonel R. T. Armstrong, C.B., R.E., R. E. B. Crompton, Prof. James Dewar, M.A., F.R.S., Major-General E. R. Festing, F.R.S., Prof. George Forbes, M.A., F.R.S., Prof. G. Carey Foster, F.R.S., Edward Graves, Prof. D. E. Hughes, F.R.S., Gisbert Kapp, J. C. Lamb, C.M.G., W. M. Mordey, J. Fletcher Moulton, M.A., Q.C., F.R.S., Prof. John Perry, D.Sc., F.R.S., Alexander Siemens, Prof. Silvanus P. Thompson, D.Sc., F.R.S., with Sir Henry T. Wood, Secretary of the Royal Commission.

PRESSED-STEEL WINDOW-FRAMES.—The National Telegraph Works Company send us a description and illustration of these frames, for which they claim the advantage over cast-iron frames that they are produced at less cost, are less than one-quarter the weight, and do not require careful packing to ensure them against damage in carriage by rail and sea. Of the statistics as to weight and cost we can say nothing, merely giving the patentees' statement, but they are certainly likely to be stronger than cast-iron frames, and if all that is claimed for them is realised they certainly demand attention.

THE NINETEENTH CENTURY ART SOCIETY.—Saturday, February 6, has been appointed for the private view of the Spring Exhibition (the twenty-sixth) of the Nineteenth Century Art Society, at the Conduit-street Galleries, and the exhibition will open to the public on Monday, February 8.

THE RATING OF MACHINERY. — A conference, under the auspices of the National Society for the Exemption of Machinery from Rating, was held on Tuesday, at the rooms of the Manchester Chamber of Commerce. Sir W. H. Houldsworth, M.P., presided, and gentlemen attended from all parts of the country. The Chairman said at present the law was applied differently in different localities, and the decisions of the Judges had only made confusion worse confounded. Mr. W. Mather, M.P., said he thought it would be futile to re-introduce the old Bill into Parliament, and he was rather in favour of going in for seven-eighths of what they wanted by supporting their No. 2 Bill, drafted by the Society, eliminating words so as to prevent rating of any machine which does not require any special foundation or special adaptation of the hereditament in connexion with the use of their particular machine. He moved an amendment accordingly, and Mr. H. D. Marshall (Gainsborough) seconded. Mr. Hughes (Sheffield), Mr. Bonser (Nottingham), and Mr. Tomlinson, M.P., supported the amendment. Mr. D. Rhodes said he thought the amendment would satisfy the Lancashire Poor-Law Guardians, of whom he was one. The amendment was carried by a large majority. The Bill to be promoted in accordance with their decision provides that machinery which is not fixed, or is only fixed to the hereditament for purposes of steadying it, and which, with the foundation thereof, can be removed without permanent injury to the hereditaments or itself, shall not be rated. Machinery for producing motive power, however, is excluded, and it is not proposed to apply the Bill to Scotland or Ireland.

COMPETITIONS, CONTRACTS, AND PUBLIC APPOINTMENTS.

COMPETITIONS.

Nature of Work.	By whom Advertised.	Premium.	Designs to be delivered.
*Technical School Building	Heywood Corp.	20l. 10l. and 5l.	Feb. 15
*Floorcloths and Linoleum Designs	M. Nairn & Co.	15 amounting to 200l.	No date

CONTRACTS.

Nature of Work or Materials.	By whom Required.	Architect, Surveyor or Engineer.	Tenders to be delivered.
*Waterworks	Buckingham U.S.A.	B. Latham	Feb. 2
*Pipe Sewers	Tottenham Loc. Bd.	J. R. Worth	do.
Four Shops and Houses, Pontypridd	D. R. Evans	A. O. Evans	do.
*Making-wood Roads	Southend Loc. Bd.	Peter Dodd	do.
House and Six Cottages, Arthington	N. E. R. Co.	Wm. Bell	Feb. 3
*Purchase and Pulling-down Building Materials	School Bd. for London	Official	do.
Two Dwelling-houses, Dufftown, N.B.	P. M'William	....	do.
Footbridges	G. W. R. Co.	Official	do.
Sewerage and Road Works, Canton, Cardiff	....	Veall & Sant	do.
*Engine House, Pumping Station, &c.	Maidstone Wtrwks Co.	E. Easton & Co.	do.
*Works and Materials	St. John's Vestry, Hampstead	Official	Feb. 4
Joinery Fittings, Municipal Buildings	Plymouth Corp.	G. D. Bellamy	do.
*Goods' Sheds at Ilkeston, Beckford, and Redditch, &c. &c.	M. R. Co.	Official	Feb. 5
Additions and Alterations to Premises	Blaenavon (Mon.) Co-op. Soc. Lim.	....	do.
*Broken Granite	Norfolk C. C.	T. H. R. Heslop	Feb. 6
Sewerage Works (Contract No. 1)	Idle Local Board	Woodhead & Son	Feb. 8
*Road Materials	H. M. Works	Official	do.
Bank and Residence, Chesterfield	Crompton & Evans' Union Bank	Rollinson & Son	Feb. 9
*Public Hall and Municipal Offices	Boro' of West Ham	L. Angell	do.
*Iron Gangway and Railings	Richmond Main Sewerage Board	J. C. Mellise	do.
*Works and Materials	Willesden Loc. Bd.	O. Claude Robson	do.
*Pipe Sewer, Drain, &c.	do.	do.	do.
*Works and Materials	Kingston Highway Bd.	A. J. Henderson	Feb. 10
*Removal of Dirt, Dust, &c.	Crown Estate Paving Commissioners	Official	do.

CONTRACTS.—*Continued.*

Nature of Work or Materials.	By whom Required.	Architect, Surveyor, or Engineer.	Tenders to be delivered.
*Drainage Works	West Ham Union	J. M. Knight	Feb. 10
*Block of Buildings, Merthyr Tydfil	T. J. Masters, Esq.	T. C. Wakeling	Feb. 11
*Additions to Engine House	West London School District	Official	Feb. 12
Public Baths, Woodside, Haley Hill	Halifax Corporation	Horsfall & Williams	Feb. 13
*Erection of Workhouse	St. Giles, Camberwell, Guardians	Wilson, Son, & Aldwinckle	Feb. 15
Asphalting at Cemetery	Batley Burial Board	Official	Feb. 16
*Fire Brigade Station, East Dulwich	London County Council	do.	do.
*Works and Materials	Vestry of St. Margarets, &c. Westminster	G. R. W. Wheeler	Feb. 16, 17 & 18
*Public Baths	Shrewsbury Corp.	J. Johnson	Feb. 22
*Free Library	West Ham Council	Lewis Angell	Feb. 23
*Superstructure of Mill	Atherton Cotton Spinning Co.	Bradshaw & Gass	No date
Alterations to "Earl Grey" Inn, Newcastle-on-Tyne	....	B. F. Simpson	do.
Offices, Newcastle-on-Tyne	Prudential As. Co.	A. Waterhouse & Son	do.
Miners' Hall, Reading-rooms, &c. Silksworth, Sunderland	Wm. Palmer	H. Grieves	do.
Alterations and Additions to Netherall, Maryport	H. P. Genhouse	C. J. Ferguson	do.
*School Furniture	Sch. Bd. for London	Official	do.
*Public Library, Southampton	The Committee	do.	do.
*System of Drainage, Beverley Barracks	War Department	do.	do.
*Pair of Semi-detached Villas	Ramsgate Corp.	Hill & Co.	do.

PUBLIC APPOINTMENTS.

Nature of Appointment.	By whom Advertised.	Salary.	Applications to be in.
*Sanitary Inspector	St. Pancras Vestry	100l.	Feb. 4
*Inspector of Nuisances	Norwich Town Council	175l. &c.	Feb. 6
*Clerk of Works	Hove Sch. Bd.	3l. weekly	Feb. 8
*Cemetery Superintendent	St. Mary Islington Burial Board	150l. & residence	do.
*Surveyor and Inspector of Nuisances	Ashford L. B.	150l.	Feb. 16
*Sanitary Inspector	Vestry of St. Margarets, &c. Westminster	130l. &c.	Feb. 22

Those marked with an Asterisk (*) are advertised in this Number. *Competitions*, p. iv. *Contracts*, pp. iv., vi., viii. & ix. *Public Appointments*, p. xx. & xxi.

ROYAL CAMBRIAN ACADEMY OF ART.—At the annual meeting of the Royal Cambrian Academy of Art, held last week, Mr. Arthur Baker, F.R.I.B.A., author of "Plas Mawr," and architect to the Academy, was elected an Associate.

DISINFECTING APPARATUS.—The State Sanitary Department of Berlin has certain regulations as to disinfection of clothing, bedding, &c., and in order to meet these Messrs. Oscar Schimmel & Co., Chemnitz, have devised a disinfecting apparatus, which is described in a German contemporary. There are two forms, one having a chamber of rectangular section, and the other one of cylindrical form. A frame, to receive the things to be treated, is arranged to run in and out of the disinfecting-chamber on rails. The chamber is then closed, and the clothing is heated by steam, which is introduced by means of two copper coils. There is a separator by which all water is taken from the steam, and the chamber and its contents are heated to 70 degs. centigrade before free steam is allowed to be blown in. By means of valves the air is forced out of the clothing into the chimney, and the admission of air can be regulated. The clothing is then subjected to a temperature of 105 degs. centigrade during the space of one hour, by which time the heat has penetrated to the middle of even large bundles of clothing.

ROYAL METEOROLOGICAL SOCIETY.—The annual general meeting of this Society was held on Wednesday evening, the 27th inst., at the Institution of Civil Engineers, 25, Great George-street, S.W.; Dr. W. Marcet, F.R.S., Vice-President, in the chair. The report of the Council for the past year showed the Society to be in a very satisfactory position. In May the library and offices were removed to more commodious premises at 22, Great George-street. After defraying the cost of fitting up the new offices and the increased rental, there still remained a balance in hand of 224l. Thirty-four new Fellows were elected during the year, the total number on the roll of the Society now being 552. Owing to the absence of the President, Mr. Baldwin Latham, M.Inst.C.E., through an attack of influenza, his address on "Evaporation and Condensation" was read by the Secretary. The question of evaporation, the author said, is as of great importance as the study of the precipitation of water on the face of the earth, as the available water supplies of the country entirely depend upon the differences between these two sets of observations. The earth receives moisture by means of rain, dew, hoar frost, and by direct condensation. It loses its moisture very rapidly by evaporation. Although evaporation mainly depends upon the difference between the tensional force of vapour due to the temperature of the evaporating surface, and the tensional force of the vapour already in the atmosphere, yet it is largely influenced by the movement of the air and by its dryness, or the difference between the dew point and the actual air temperature. Evaporation goes on at night so long as the water surface is warmer than the dew point. With sea-water the evaporation is about 4½ per cent. less than with rain-water, while with water saturated with common salt the evaporation is 15 per cent. less than with rain-water. Mr. Latham next described some percolation experiments which were carried out by Mr. C. Greaves at Old Ford, by Messrs. Dickinson & Evans at Hemel Hempstead, and by Sir J. B. Lawes and Dr. Gilbert at Rothamsted. He then detailed the results of his own experiments, and also the gaugings of the underground waters in the drainage areas of the rivers Wandle and Graveney. He further stated that in the course of his observations on the flow of underground water he had observed that at certain particular seasons of the year it was possible to indicate the direction and volume of the flow of underground streams, even when they were at a considerable depth, owing to the formation of peculiar lines of fog. Dr. C. Theodore Williams was elected President for the ensuing year.

THE PROPOSED NEW STREET FROM HOLBORN TO THE STRAND.—A meeting was held on Tuesday night at the Holborn Town-hall in order "to urge the London County Council to facilitate a necessary and direct route from north to south of London through the very centre of the metropolis." Mr. T. W. Maule, L.C.C., presided, and said the London County Council had favoured a scheme through Little Queen-street and Drury-lane, but all the proposals for improvements had been interrupted by the betterment question. In connexion with the proposed new street, however, two committees were sitting, and there were proposals to utilise Lincoln's Inn-fields. The latter proposition, he maintained, would mean a saving of half a million of money, and would result in the formation of a very beautiful street. Such a route would open up King's College Hospital to the public view, and would mean a very near cut from Holborn to the Law Courts. The route he advocated was *via* Vernon-place, Bloomsbury, Kingsgate-street, Holborn, Lincoln's Inn-fields, and Clare Market. Dr. Maybury supported the route detailed by the Chairman, and contended that it was the cheapest and the best in every way. Mr. A. H. Hoare, L.C.C., said that the Improvement Committee of the County Council decided in favour of the Drury-lane scheme. Mr. J. C. Dear estimated that the new street would cost 600,000l., while the Drury-lane route would cost 933,000l. He moved a resolution cordially supporting the efforts of the Holborn Extension Committee to obtain a new street from Holborn to the Strand through Lincoln's Inn-fields, and expressing the hope that the London County Council would take early steps to carry out such a much-needed improvement. The motion having been seconded by Mr. Theobald, Mr. Fusedale moved a resolution in favour of the alternative route approved by the London County Council, and this was seconded and adopted by a large majority.

LEGAL.

CASE UNDER THE METROPOLIS MANAGEMENT AMENDMENT ACT, 1890: WANDSWORTH DISTRICT BOARD *v.* BIRD.

In the Queen's Bench Division on Wednesday last, judgment was given in this case, which was heard on the 14th inst., and in which the Court had taken time for consideration. The case raised the question whether under the Metropolis Management Amendment Act of 1890 the District Board can absolutely refuse to the owner of land laid out or intended to be laid out in a street permission to excavate and remove sand, gravel, or subsoil under such land, or can only impose conditions on such removal. The statute (53 and 54 Vict., c. 66, s. 6) provides that it shall not be lawful to form or lay out any street from which the gravel, &c., has been excavated, until the subsoil has been made good and levelled, &c., and that it shall not be lawful to remove or take away sand, gravel, &c., from any land on which any street or road is laid out or intended to be laid out except on such conditions as to the making good the same as the Board may think fit. And if the Board shall refuse to give their assent or impose any conditions, &c., the owner, if dissatisfied, may appeal to the London County Council. In the present case the owner of a piece of land near the Wandsworth station of the Brighton Railway had proposed and intended to lay out a street or road, to be called Braybrooke-avenue, and had applied to the Board for power to make sewers, &c., and had proposed to excavate along the whole length for gravel, sand, &c., to be removed. He had on April 18 last applied to them to know what conditions as to levelling or making good, &c., the Board might desire to impose. On May 8 the Board Clerk wrote a letter in reply, that the Board had resolved to refuse their consent to the excavation of any part of the land for the purpose of removal of any subsoil, sand, or gravel. The owner, nevertheless, proceeded to excavate and remove a large quantity of gravel from the land. The Board took out a summons against him for excavating and removing subsoil without their consent in writing, but the magistrate (Mr. Haden Corser) refused to convict, and stated a case which raised the question.

The case was argued by Mr. Channell, Q.C., and Mr. Earl for the Board; and by Mr. R. Bray for the owner.

The Court had taken time to consider their judgment, which was now delivered in favour of the owner and upholding the view taken by the magistrate.

Mr. Justice Hawkins delivered judgment at some length to that effect. The Board, he said, had complained that the owner had removed subsoil in disregard of their refusal to allow it, and he contended that their consent was not required, and that they had no power to refuse to allow it. The real question is whether their consent was required and they had power absolutely to refuse it, or whether they could only impose conditions as to making good or levelling the soil. And, on the best consideration they could give to the Act, it appeared to them that the contention of the respondent, the owner, was good, and that no power was given to the Board absolutely to refuse to allow any subsoil to be excavated and removed, but only to impose conditions as to levelling and making good the soil. The learned Judge went fully into the provisions of the Act to support this view as to its construction, and arrived at the conclusion that the magistrate was right in not convicting, and the appeal must be dismissed.

Mr. Justice Wills concurred.

Appeal accordingly dismissed.—*Times.*

MEETINGS.

SATURDAY, JANUARY 30.

Royal Institution.—Professor J. A. Fleming on "The Induction Coil and Alternate-Current Transformer." II. 3 p.m.

St. Paul's Ecclesiological Society.—Annual Meeting. 2.30 p.m.

MONDAY, FEBRUARY 1.

Royal Academy of Arts.—Professor Aitchison, A.R.A., on "Saracenic and Turkish Architecture." III. 8 p.m.

Surveyors' Institution.—Adjourned Discussion on Mr. R. H. Morris's paper on "The Four-Course System." 8 p.m.

Society of Arts (Cantor Lectures).—Professor George Forbes on "Developments of Electrical Distribution." II. 8 p.m.

Society of Engineers.—(1) Presentation of Premiums. (2) Inaugural Address by the President, Mr. J. W. Wilson, Jun. 7.30 p.m.

Royal Institution.—General Monthly Meeting. 5 p.m.

Victoria Institute.—8 p.m.

Leeds and Yorkshire Architectural Society.—Mr. F. W. Bedford on "Spanish Architecture." 7.30 p.m.

TUESDAY, FEBRUARY 2.

Institution of Civil Engineers.—Mr. Alfred Harper Curtis on "Gold Quartz Reduction." 8 p.m.

Sanitary Institute (Lectures for Sanitary Officers).—Mr. H. Law on "Principles of Calculating Areas, Cubic Space, &c.; Interpretation of Plans and Sections to Scale." 8 p.m.

Glasgow Architectural Association.—Demonstration on "The Architecture of the Human Figure, and its Application," by Mr. F. H. Newbery. 8 p.m.

WEDNESDAY, FEBRUARY 3.

Royal Archæological Institute.—(1) The Rev. Precentor Venables on "The Roman Colonnade Discovered at Lincoln last Spring." (2) Mr. J. Park Harrison on "A Pre-Norman Clearstory window, and other Early Work in Oxford Cathedral." 4 p.m.

British Archæological Association.—(1) Mr. Thomas Blashill on "Sutton-in-Holderness and the Abbey of Meaux." (2) Mr. Andreas E. Cockayne on "Dorothy Manners (*née* Vernon of Haddon Hall)." 8 p.m.

Carpenters' Hall, London Wall.—Professor H. Robinson on "Drainage of Buildings and Construction of Sewers." 8 p.m. (*Admission Free*)

Civil and Mechanical Engineers' Society.—Mr. J. F. Reade on "Main Drainage Extension in Towns." 7 p.m.

Institution of Electrical Engineers (At the Royal Institution).—"Experiments with Alternate Currents of High Potential and High Frequency," by Mr. Nikola Tesla. 8 p.m.

Society of Arts.—Mr. T. Pridgin Teale, M.A., on "Dust, and How to Shut it Out." 8 p.m.

THURSDAY, FEBRUARY 4.

Royal Academy of Arts.—Professor Aitchison, A.R.A., on "Saracenic and Turkish Architecture." IV. 8 p.m.

Royal Institution.—Dr. A. S. Murray, on "Some Aspects of Greek Sculpture in Relief." III. 3 p.m.

British Museum.—Miss Millington-Lathbury on "Greek Sacrifices and Priests," as illustrated by the monuments in the Museum. 2.45 p.m.

Institution of Mechanical Engineers.—Annual General Meeting, when two papers will be read. (1) Mr. J. Parry on "Mechanical Features of the Liverpool Water works, and on the Supply of Power by Pressure from the Public Mains, and by other means." (2) Mr. W. Hawdon on "The Disposal and Utilisation of Blast-Furnace Slag." 7.30 p.m.

Society of Antiquaries.—8.30 p.m.

FRIDAY, FEBRUARY 5.

Sanitary Institute (Lectures for Sanitary Officers).—Mr. Louis Parkes on "Water Supply, Drinking Water, Pollution of water." 8 p.m.

Institution of Mechanical Engineers.—Annual General Meeting (continued). 7.30 p.m.

Royal Institution.—Professor Roberts-Austen on "Metals of High Temperatures." 9 p.m.

SATURDAY, FEBRUARY 6.

Royal Institution.—Professor J. A. Fleming on "The Induction Coil and Alternate-Current Transformer." III. 3 p.m.

RECENT PATENTS:

ABSTRACTS OF SPECIFICATIONS.

1,885.—ROOFS: *H. M. Symons.*—This invention refers to an improved method of repairing slated roofs by the employment of metal slips, made smaller on underside, to partly fit the bevelled edges of the under-slates, and thereby leaving a thicker substance of metal without raising the new slate more than ordinary. At the underneath side of one end of the slip a spike projects forming a nail. Nail and slip are thus in one piece, and a saving of time is effected in fixing.

2,153.—WATER-CLOSETS: *J. Smith.*—This specification relates to an improvement in the inlet or distributing water orifices of water-closet basins for the better distribution of the water for flushing and cleaning the basin. The novelty claimed consists in introducing the water to the upper part of the basin by three inlet openings instead of only by one as usual.

2,536.—CHIMNEY-TOPS: J. *Rae* and J. *Murdoch.*—To prevent back-smoke and back-draughts the chimney-can which is the subject of this atent has around its circumference, near the base, a series of openings so arranged that from whatever point the wind strikes the can, it enters through the openings, and is carried upwards towards the mouth of the can, thus causing a draught or suction in the chimney. About the middle of the can a similar series of openings is provided, causing a further draught in the chimney.

2,745.—WATER PIPES: *H. J. Minsharp.*—In a combination fitting, constructed with a stop-cock in the centre and two outlet sockets, either draw-off, taps or plugs are inserted. The fitting is fixed to the service-pipe near the main, and is used to prevent the bursting of water-supply or service-pipes.

461.—DRAIN-TESTING: *T. Kemp.*—This patent refers to an improved apparatus for drain-testing, passing a chemical of strong odour into the drain without the aid of a machine. It consists of a small glass tube containing the chemical, fitted with a coil spring on the outside, and an india-rubber cap firmly held on the top of the tube by a paper tape passing over and attached to the spring which seals up the contents. On the tester being passed into a closet trap, the tape becomes wet in passing through the water, and is broken by the force of the spring, and the contents of the tube are discharged.

19,076.—WATER-CLOSETS: *T. Crapper.*—This refers to an improvement in the soil pipe connexions of water-closets. The inventor connects the earthenware trap of a closet basin with the soil pipe by means of a pipe passing down the interior of the trap, and terminating at a point below the level of the water seal in the trap. Any escape of sewer gas is impossible.

NEW APPLICATIONS FOR LETTERS PATENT.

January 11.—530, J. Wilkinson, Preventing Down-draughts in Chimneys.—534, W. & E Freeman, Shave-hook for Plumbers' use.—536, J. Robson, Burglar-proof Sash-fastener.

January 12.—574, A. & T. Sabine, Machinery for forming the Sockets of Sanitary-pipes, Chimney-pots, &c.—587, R Thwaites, Preventing Water and Gas-pipes from Freezing.—590, J. Phillips, Method to prevent Pipes Bursting during Frost.—591, W. White & H. Harry, Coverings for Walls, &c.—600, H. Rhodes & R. Holland, Domestic Hearths.—608, R. Spring, Preventing waste of water in or from Cisterns.—620, J. Shannon, Wood-graining Machines.

January 13.—651, H. Sayle, New Automatic Noiseless Flushing-valve for Water-closets and Urinals.—663, L. Dove, Automatic Disinfecting Apparatus for attaching to Flushing-cisterns.—680, F. Nour, Head-service Piping.—691, C. Coe, Preventing waste of water.—698, A. Boult, Glue.—715, G. Couzens, Gully-traps.—727, J. Rainey, Tool-holding Attachment for Grindstones.

January 14.—C. Griffiths, Stoves.—756, D. Nainby, Preventing Smoky Chimneys.—757, J. Brown, Lock and Latch Furniture.—804, W. Byers, Sliding-bolts for Securing Doors, &c.—805, F. Smythies, Sash-fasteners.

January 15.—814, J. Faulds, Masons' Tools.—827, W. Orr, Metallic Girders.—828, O. Hutchinson, Bakers' Ovens.—854, E. Cooper and E. Turrall, Door Springs and Checks.—861 A. Boult, Carving-machines.—869, G. Dunell, Metallic Flooring or Decking for Bridges, &c.

January 16.—901, A. Wilson and C. Johnson, Joints for Metal Pipes.—905, T. Lane and A. May, Chimney-tops or Cowls.—907, C. Johnson and A. Wilson, Joints for Pipes constructed of Stoneware, &c.

PROVISIONAL SPECIFICATIONS ACCEPTED.

15,471, J. Barlow, Window and other Frames.—17,715, W. Kenney, Butt Joints or Hinges.—20,797, J. Hughes and E. Jones, Screws and Screw-drivers.—20,803, J. Dewhurst, Disinfecting water-closets, Drains, &c.—21,237, F. Webster and A. Thorman, Fire Stoves, &c.—22,030, W. Tucker, Anti-drip Sash-bar.—22,171, T. Smith, Compounds or Cements.—22,243, T. Bretherton, Paving Roads, &c.—22,428, J. Jackson, Decorative Materials for Walls, Ceilings, &c.—22,546, J. Pearson, Draught and Weather Excluders for Doors.—22,577, J. Martin, Saws.—174, G. Deacon, Glazing Roofs, &c.

COMPLETE SPECIFICATIONS ACCEPTED.

(*Open to Opposition for Two Months.*)

3,070, G. Lawford, Water waste-preventing Cistern.—3,555, W. Thompson, Concrete-mixing Machines.—4,287, T. Panario, Supplying Disinfectants to the Flushing Pipes of Urinals, &c.—4,484, J. Townshend, Folding or Collapsible Seats.—17,160, W. Donslin, Mortice Locks.—17,375, W. Errington, Stone-cutting and Stone-dressing Machinery.—21,965, J. Bardsley, Door Springs and Checks.

SOME RECENT SALES OF PROPERTY:

ESTATE EXCHANGE REPORT.

JANUARY 14.—By *C. C. & T. Moore* (on the premises): No. 40, Oxford-st., the lease and goodwill, u.t. 20 yrs., r. 240*l.*, 310*l.*

JANUARY 19.—By *Dowsett & Co.*: 79, Ringford-rd., Wandsworth, f., r. 28*l.*, 350*l.*; 12, Southfield-rd., f., r. 23*l.* 8s., 230*l.*—By *Slade & Butler*: 7 to 16, Alma-cottages, Harrow, f., r. 104*l.*, 525*l.*; 17 to 21, Alma-cottages, f., r. 66*l.*, 400*l.*—By *Sherrin & Cullman*: 46, Brooksby's-walk, Homerton, f., r. 55*l.*, 905*l.*; 104 to 116 (even), Glenthorne-rd., Hammersmith, u.t. 90 yrs., g.r. 25*l.*, r. 132*l.*, 705*l.*

JANUARY 20.—By *Kelf & Son*: an enclosure of f. land, 7a. 3r. 21p., Folly-lane, Walthamstow, 1,300*l.*; 43, Calabria-rd., Highbury, u.t. 95 yrs., g.r. 8*l.* 15s., r. 42*l.*, 315*l.*

JANUARY 21.—By *Beadel & Co.*: "Thames Wharf," f., area 3,600 ft., Limehouse, 1,200*l.* By *F. Varley*: 27, Oakfield-rd., Stroud Green, u.t. 85 yrs., g.r. 8*l.* 10s., r. 55*l.*, 575*l.*; 101, Wilberforce-rd., Finsbury-pk., u.t. 75 yrs., g.r. 8*l.*, r. 45*l.* 470*l.* By *H. J. Bliss & Sons*: 2, 3, 4 and 5, Frying Pan-alley; and 1 and 2, Sandy-row, Bishopsgate-st., u.t. 10 yrs., g.r. 11*l.*, r. 174*l.* 4s., 435*l.*; 179, Hanbury-st., Mile End, u.t. 10 yrs., g.r. 5*l.*, r. 29*l.* 18s., 75*l.*; 21 and 23 Newark-st., Whitechapel, u.t. 14 yrs., g.r. 4*l.* 2s. 6d., r. 66*l.*, 250*l.*; 25 and 27, Nelson-st., u.t. 15 yrs., g.r. 4*l.* r. 52*l.* 4s., 235*l.*; 44 and 46, Jane-st., Commercial-rd., u.t. 8 yrs., g.r. 4*l.* 15s., r. 57*l.* 4s., 135*l.* By *Newbon & Co.*: 33, Half Moon-cres., Barnsbury, u.t. 20 yrs., g.r. 5*l.* 5s., 200*l.*; 91, Winston-rd., Stoke Newington, u.t. 68 yrs., g.r. 5*l.* 290*l.*

JANUARY 22.—By *Ball, Norris, & Hadley*: I.g.r. of 60*l.*, Kentish Town, u.t. 48 yrs., g.r. 6*l.*, 910*l.*; I.g.r. of 65*l.*, u.t. 48 yrs., g.r. 2*l.*, 1,030*l.*; 414 and 416, Coldharbour-lane, Brixton, f., r. 25*l.* 10s., 1,210*l.*

[*Contractions used in these lists.*—F.g.r. for freehold ground-rent; l.g.r. for leasehold ground-rent; I.g.r. for improved ground-rent; g.r. for ground-rent; r. for rent; f. for freehold; c. for copyhold; l. for leasehold; e.r. for estimated rental; u.t. for unexpired term; p.a. for per annum; yrs. for years; st. for street; rd. for road; sq. for square; pl. for place; ter. for terrace; cres. for crescent; yd. for yard, &c.

PRICES CURRENT OF MATERIALS.

TIMBER.		
Greenheart, B.G. ton	9/0/0	0/0/0
Teak, E.I. ... load	9/10/0	15/0/0
Sequoia, U.S. ft.cu.	2/8	3/0
Ash, Canada load	2/10/0	4/0/0
Birch, do.	3/0/0	4/5/0
Elm, do.	3/10/0	4/15/0
Fir, Dantsic, &c.	2/0/0	3/10/0
Oak, do.	3/10/0	4/10/0
Canada	5/0/0	7/0/0
Pine, Canada red	2/10/0	3/10/0
Do. Yellow	2/10/0	5/0/0
Lath, D'ntsic, fath	5/5/0	6/10/0
St. Petersburg	5/10/0	7/10/0
Deals, Finland, 2nd & 1st std 100	8/10/0	10/10/0
Do. 4th & 3rd ..	7/10/0	8/10/0
Do. Riga	6/10/0	8/0/0
St. Petersburg, 1st yellow ..	10/10/0	15/0/0
Do. 2nd yellow	8/10/0	10/0/0
Do. white	7/0/0	10/10/0
Swedish	7/15/0	16/0/0
White Sea	8/10/0	17/10/0
Canada, Pine 1st	19/10/0	25/10/0
Do. do. 2nd	14/10/0	16/10/0
Do. do. 3rd, &c.	6/10/0	10/10/0
Do. Spruce, 1st	8/10/0	11/0/0
Do. do. 3rd & 2nd	6/10/0	8/0/0
New Brunswick	7/0/0	7/10/0
Battens, all kinds	3/10/0	15/10/0
Flooring Boards, sq., 1 in. prep. 1st	0/8/6	0/14/6
Do. 2nd	0/7/6	0/11/6
Other qualities	0/5/3	0/8/0
Cedar, Cuba .. ft.	/3½	/4½
Honduras, &c.	/3½	/4½
Mahogany, Cuba	/4½	/6½
St. Domingo, cargo av	/4½	2/0
Mexican do. do	/4	/8
Tobasco do. do	/5½	/7
Honduras do..	/5½	/6½
Box, Turkey ton	4/0/0	12/0/0
Rose, Rio	10/0/0	20/0/0
Bahia	9/0/0	18/0/0
Satin, St. Domingo ..... ft.	0/0/9	0/1/3
TIMBER (*continued*).		
Satin, Porto Rico	0/0/10	0/1/6
Walnut, Italian..	0/0/3½	0/0/7
METALS.		
IRON—Pig, in Scotland .... ton	2/7/0	2/7/1½
Bar, Welsh, in London	6/0/0	6/10/0
Do. do. at works in Wales	5/10/0	6/0/0
Do. Staffordshire, in London	6/5/0	6/15/0
COPPER—British, cake and ingot	46/0/0	49/0/0
Best selected ..	49/0/0	49/10/0
Sheets, strong..	58/0/0	59/0/0
Chili, bars	44/13/9	45/1/3
YELLOW METAL lb.	0/0/5⅝	0/0/5¾
LEAD—Pig, Spanish .... ton	10/15/0	10/17/6
English, com. brands	11/2/6	11/5/0
Sheet, English, 3 lbs. per sq. ft. and upwards ..	12/0/0	0/0/0
Pipe	13/10/0	0/0/0
ZINC—English sheet ...... ton	25/0/0	25/10/0
Vieille Montagne	26/10/0	0/0/0
TIN—Straits	89/17/6	90/7/6
Australian	90/0/0	90/10/0
English Ingots	93/5/0	93/10/0
OILS.		
Linseed ...... ton	18/15/0	19/2/6
Cocoanut, Cochin	26/5/0	26/10/0
Do. Ceylon	23/0/0	0/0/0
Palm, Lagos	23/0/0	23/10/0
Rapeseed, English pale	28/15/0	0/0/0
Do. brown	27/0/0	0/0/0
Cottonseed ref...	18/0/0	0/0/0
Oleine	0/0/0	0/0/0
Lubricating, U.S.	4/10/0	5/10/0
Do. refined	6/0/0	11/0/0
TAR—Stockholm barrel	0/19/0	1/0/0
Archangel	0/12/6	0/0/0

TENDERS.

[Communications for Insertion under this heading must reach us *not later than* 12 *noon on Thursdays.*]

BILSTON.—For market hall fittings, shops, stalls, offices, &c., and engine and boiler-house for electric light installation, for the Bilston Township Commissioners. Mr. C. L. N. Wilson, C.E., architect:—

Geo. Ball	£2,356	Jas. Light	£1,875
H. Dorse & Son	2,000	Morrell Bros., Bilston*	1,780

* Accepted.

[Architect's estimate, £1,887. 12s. 6d.]

BRISTOL.—For erecting and constructing a sixteen-chamber brick kiln (Searcombe's patent), with flues and 80 ft. Chimney-shaft, for the Netham Brick and Tile Works Company. Mr. Herbert J. Jones, surveyor, Bristol:—

A. Krauss	£2,930	R. Wilkins & Sons	£2,645
W. Galbraith	2,789	Eastabrook & Sons	2,497
G. H. Wilkins	2,750	H. Humphreys	2,374
Cowlin & Son	2,743	J. Perrott, Bristol*	2,340

* Accepted.

CHESHAM (Bucks).—For the construction of a new road, curbing, channelling, and sewering, &c., New Town, Chesham, Bucks, for Mr. D. G. Patterson. Mr. Geo. R. Green, surveyor, Chesham:—

Capper	£771	Hill	£567
Mead	650	Morecroft, Acton (accepted)	570

GREAT YARMOUTH.—For the erection of grand-stand at the Recreation Ground, for the Great Yarmouth Town Council. Mr. J. W. Cockrill, A.R.I.B.A., Borough surveyor. Quantities by the Borough Surveyor:—

H. Beckett	£1,237 10 0	Eastoe	£1,055 12 5
J. Leggett	1,176 0 0	Beech	1,033 0 0
Rand & Cooper	1,171 0 0	Stevens	1,028 0 0
Cork	1,150 0 0	Flaxman	1,021 0 0
M. Barnard	1,096 13 8½	Grimble & Watts	1,020 0 0
J. F. W. Bray	1,088 0 0	Bond, Yarmouth (accepted)	1,015 0 0
W. Bracey	1,056 6 0		

HADLEIGH (Essex).—For erection of various buildings at the Salvation Army Farm Colony. Mr. Alexander Gordon, architect:—

Dairy Buildings.

Neil	£564 10	Morgan	£350 0
Coxhead	549 0	Good	348 10
G. H. Martin & Co.	431 0	Ansell	341 19
Inwood	409 0		

Bakery Buildings.

Coxhead	£321 15	French & Ellwood	£250 0
Good	318 15	Alderton	240 0
Neil	299 0	G. H. Martin & Co.	231 0
Potter	265 10	Inwood	227 0

Covered Cow Yard.

Neil	£3,368	French & Ellwood	£2,098
Coxhead	2,906	Good	1,990
Potter	2,237	Inwood	1,367
G. H. Martin & Co.	2,183		

Slaughter House.

Barlow & Roberts	£311	G. H. Martin & Co.	£335 0
Neil	478	Baxter	314 0
Ansell	396	French & Ellwood	288 0
Inwood	330	E. Good	227 17

Piggery Buildings.

Neil	£828	French & Ellwood	£750
Coxhead	797	Good	743
G. H. Martin & Co.	793	Potter*	688
Ansell	789		

* Accepted.

HASTINGS.—Accepted for the erection of five blocks of artisans' dwellings, in Castle-road. Mr. Mark J. Lansdell, architect:—

Excavations.—G. Davis	£531 5 0
Underpinning.—G. Davis	43 10 0
Patent Stone Steps, Landing, &c.—Elliott & Co.'s	113 15 0
General Buildings.—Moon & Garner	4,330 0 0

LONDON.—Accepted for alterations, decorations, repairs, and sanitary works, at No. 36, Gloucester-place, Hyde-park, for Miss Ponsford. Mr. T. H. Watson, architect, 9, Nottingham-place, W.:—

Greatorex & Co., Limited, 11, Stanhope-terrace, W. .. . £535

LONDON.—For erecting new sanitary blocks, laying new drains, and supplying new sanitary fittings and other works at the Orphan Working School, Haverstock-hill, N. Mr. Charles Bell, F.R.I.B.A., architect, Mr. Edward Tidman, C.E., F.S.I., consulting engineer:—

Clarke & Bracey	£4,388	Irwin Wallis	£3,580
Holliday & Greenwood	4,139	Allen & Sons	3,550
Burford & Sons	3,884	Geo. Bryan & Sons	3,508
Wall	3,647	Geo. Sharp	3,380

LONDON.—For cleaning down stone-facings and painting all woodwork, 101, 103, and 105, Queen Victoria-street, E.C. Mr. A. Gordon, architect:—

Coxhead	£158	G. H. Martin & Co.	£109
Good	112	Toutt (accepted)	100

LONDON.—For erecting cookery and laundry centres and schoolkeeper's house on the Charing Cross-road site, Soho, for the School Board for London. Mr. T. J. Bailey, Architect:—

J. T. Chappell	£4,583	T. Boyce	£3,759
R. & W. Pattinson	4,591	E. Lawrance & Sons	3,461
H. Lovatt	4,295	M. Marsland	3,458
W. M. Dabbs	4,185	C. Cox*	3,306
Treasure & Son	3,923		

* Recommended by the Works Committee for acceptance.

LONDON.—For providing and fixing heating apparatus on the low pressure hot-water system for the Deaf and Dumb School which is now in course of erection on the Hugh Myddelton site, Clerkenwell, for the School Board for London. Mr. T. J. Bailey, Architect:—

Rosser & Russell, Limited	£233 10	J. Fraser & Son	£193 17
J. & F. May	230 0	J. Wontner Smith, Gray, & Co.	188 0
G. Davis	229 10		
W. G. Cannon	210 0	Purcell & Nobbs*	164 0

* Recommended by the Works Committee for acceptance.

LONDON.—For building a shed for manual training purposes in the boys' playground of the Medburn-street School, St. Pancras, for the School Board for London. Mr. T. J. Bailey, Architect:—

H. C. Clifton	£244	G. Ball	£213
Kirby & Chase	236	Norris & Luke*	194
J. Pestle	226		

* Recommended by the Works Committee for acceptance.

ROMFORD.—For alterations and additions in forming Refrigerator and Wort Receiver Rooms, and alterations in Cooler Room, at the Brewery, Romford, for Messrs. Ind, Coope, & Co. Messrs. Inskipp & Mackenzie, architects, No. 5, Bedford-row, W.C. Quantities by Messrs. R. L. Curtis & Sons:—

Dowsing	£1,190	Kirk & Randall	£1,102
Morter	1,172	Watson*	1,098
Hammond	1,149		

* Accepted.

ST. HELEN'S.—For the erection of shop, show-rooms, warehouses, and workshops, for Mr. John Jones. Mr. W. Wallace-Gandy, architect, St. Helen's:—

G. Waiston & Son	£1,892 0 0	S. Beckett	£1,820 0 0
F. Clarke	1,854 4 0	R. Ellison*	1,810 0 0
R. H. Davis	1,839 0 0		
W. Molyneux	1,829 0 0		

* Accepted.
[All of St. Helen's.]

WOOD GREEN.—For the erection of mission-hall. Mr. J. Williams Dunford, architect, 100c, Queen Victoria-street:—

Baker	£900	French & Ellwood	£675
Good	657	Say	512
G. H. Martin & Co.	628	A. Martin	506
Coxhead	627		

Kensington Infirmary.—The amount of the accepted tender of Messrs. W. Johnson & Co., Limited, for this work should be £39,560, and not £35,560, as misprinted in our last number.

SUBSCRIBERS in LONDON and the SUBURBS, by prepaying at the Publishing Office, 19s. per annum (or 4s. 9d. per quarter), can ensure receiving "The Builder" by *Friday Morning's* post.

TERMS OF SUBSCRIPTION.

"THE BUILDER" is supplied DIRECT from the Office to residents in any part of the United Kingdom at the rate of 19s. per annum PREPAID. To all parts of Europe, America, Australia, and New Zealand, 26s. per annum. To India, China, Ceylon, &c., 30s. per annum. Remittances payable to DOUGLAS FOURDRINIER, Publisher, No. 46, Catherine-street, W.C.

The Builder Cathedral Series.

1891.

1. Canterbury	Jan. 3.	7. Salisbury	July 4.
2. Lichfield	Feb. 7.	8. Bristol	Aug. 1.
3. St. Alban's	Mar. 7.	9. Norwich	Sept. 5.
4. Peterborough	April 4.	10. Rochester	Oct. 3.
5. Wells	May 2.	11. Lincoln	Nov. 7.
6. Exeter	June 6.	12. Gloucester	Dec. 5.

1892.

13. St. Paul's	Jan. 2.	16. Ely	April 2.
14. Hereford	Feb. 6.	17. Llandaff	May 7.
15. Chichester	Mar. 5.	18. Oxford	June 4.

(Further arrangements will be duly announced.)

Price FOURPENCE each (by post 4½d.), except Nos. 1 and 2, which are *out of print*; but the VIEW, PLAN, AND DESCRIPTION of CANTERBURY and of LICHFIELD have been re-printed, and they can now be had, price ONE SHILLING each set; by post, 1s. 2d.

THE REREDOS, ST. PAUL'S.
Reprinted from "The Builder," January 26, 1888 (15 in. by 11½ in.), on stout paper, unfolded, for framing, 6d.; by post, 8d.

PORTFOLIOS,
for Preserving the Plates Unfolded, 2s. 6d.; by post, 3s.

London: Office of "THE BUILDER," 46, *Catherine-street, W.C.*

Now Ready (86 plates). Price ONE GUINEA.

"THE BUILDER ALBUM" OF ROYAL ACADEMY ARCHITECTURE. 1891.

SOME PRESS NOTICES.

"In numerous well-drawn and well-printed plates of plans, elevations, and sections of buildings, this comely folio illustrates the latest Royal Academy Exhibition of Architectural designs, and effectually proves how much greater attention that room in Burlington House deserved than it received."—*Athenæum.*

"A handsome folio volume."—*Guardian.*

"A large and extremely handsome volume."—*Newcastle Daily Chronicle.*

"While the collection has a special value for Architects, it has an interest for all, and it forms a very handsome book."—*Glasgow Herald.*

"To Architects who were unable to visit the Academy will be very welcome."—*Western Morning News.*

"A handsome series of eighty-six reproductions of drawings exhibited in the Architecture room . . . executed in the best possible style."—*Scotsman.*

"A collection of the best and most important drawings hung in the Architectural room of the Royal Academy Exhibition . . . . A most valuable record of the year's Architectural work . . . . A useful addition to any library, as well as a first-class work of reference to the student and busy professional man."—*Leeds Mercury.*

LONDON
Office of "The Builder," 46, Catherine-street, W.C.

W. H. Lascelles & Co.

121, BUNHILL ROW, LONDON, E.C.

Telephone No. 270.

HIGH-CLASS JOINERY.
LASCELLES' CONCRETE.
Architects' Designs are carried out with the greatest care.
CONSERVATORIES
GREENHOUSES,
WOODEN BUILDINGS,
Bank, Office, & Shop Fittings
CHURCH BENCHES & PULPITS
ESTIMATES GIVEN ON APPLICATION.

TO CORRESPONDENTS.

M. T. A.—G. F. R.—O. & Co.—W. H. B.—J. P.

All statements of facts, lists of tenders, &c., must be accompani by the name and address of the sender, not necessarily for publicati

We are compelled to decline pointing out books and givi addresses.

NOTE.—The responsibility of signed articles, and papers read public meetings, rests, of course, with the authors.

We cannot undertake to return rejected communications.

Letters or communications (beyond mere news-items) which ha been duplicated for other journals, are NOT DESIRED.

All communications regarding literary and artistic matter shou be addressed to THE EDITOR; all communications relating advertisements and other exclusively business matters should addressed to THE PUBLISHER, and *not* to the Editor.

THE BATH STONE FIRMS, Lt
BATH,
FOR ALL THE PROVED KINDS OF
BATH STONE.
FLUATE, for Hardening and Preserving Calcareous Stones and Marbles.

DOULTING FREESTONE.

THE CHELYNCH STONE. — The stone from these quarr is known as the "West Beds," and is of a v crystalline nature, and doubtedly one of the mo durable stones in England.

THE BRAMBLEDITCH STONE. — Is of the same crystalli nature as the Chelynch Ston but finer in texture, and mo suitable for finemoulded wo

Prices, and every information given, application to CHARLES TRASK & SON Doulting, Shepton Mallet.
London Agent—Mr. E. A. WILLIAMS, 16, Craven-street, Strand, W.C. [Ad

HAM HILL STONE.
The attention of Architects is special invited to the durability and beautiful colo of this material. Quarries well opened. Qui despatch guaranteed. Stonework delivere and fixed complete. Samples and estimates free Address, The Ham Hill Stone Co., Norton, Stok under-Ham, Somerset. London Agent: Mr. E. Williams, 16, Craven-st., Strand, W.C. [Advt

Asphalte.—The Seyssel and Metallic La Asphalte Company (Mr. H. Glenn), Office, Poultry, E.C.—The best and cheapest materials fo damp courses, railway arches, warehouse floors flat roofs, stables, cow-sheds, and milk-rooms granaries, tun-rooms, and terraces. Asphalt Contractors to the Forth Bridge Co. [Advt

SPRAGUE & CO.,
STATIONERS, &c.,
Keep a Special Stock of Sundries for Professional Offices.
4 & 5, East Harding St. Fetter-lane, E.C. [Advi

MICHELMORE & REAP
Manufacturers of
CHARLES COLLINGE'S PATENT.
COLLINGE'S PATENT HINGES
LEVER, SCREW, & BARREL BOLTS,
Self-Acting "FALL DOWN" GATE STOPS,
and IMPROVED GATE FITTINGS of every descriptio
36A, BOROUGH ROAD, LONDON, S.
PRICES REDUCED. LIST SENT ON APPLICATION.

TWELVE GOLD AND SILVER MEDALS AWARDED.

ZINC AND COPPER ROOFING.

F. BRABY & CO.

LONDON. ++ LIVERPOOL. ++ GLASGOW.

352 to 362, Euston-road. 6 and 8, Hatton Garden. 47 and 49, St. Enoch-square.

VIEILLE MONTAGNE SOLE MANUFACTURING AGENTS.

NO SOLDER. NO EXTERNAL FASTENINGS

Particulars on Application. Chief Offices:—Fitzroy Works, EUSTON ROAD, LONDON, N.W.

The Builder.

Vol. LXII. No 2557. SATURDAY, FEBRUARY 6 1892.

ILLUSTRATIONS.

Cathedrals of England and Wales: XIV., Hereford.—Drawn by Mr. J. J. Johnson, A.R.I.B.A. .... *Double Page Ink-Photo.*
Plan of Hereford Cathedral.—Drawn by Mr. Roland W. Paul .... *Double-Page Photo-Litho.*
Illustrations of Old Chester: I., Fireplace in Bishop Lloyd's Palace.—Drawn by Mr. T. P. Ivison .... *Double-Page Ink-Photo.*
House, South Hill Park, Bromley, Kent.—Messrs. Williams & Hopton, Architects .... *Single-Page Photo-Litho.*
House and Shop, Fore-street, Redruth.—Mr. Hubert A. Gregg, Architect .... *Single-Page Photo-Litho.*

Blocks in Text.

Diagram illustrating Drainage at the Foundling Hospital .... Page 93
Mosque of Amru, Cairo: Plan 96
Mosque of Sultan Hasan, Cairo: Plan 97
Doorway from Cloisters to Chapter House, Hereford Cathedral 102
Tomb of Bishop Thomas Charlton, Hereford Cathedral 103
Tomb of Sir Richard Pembridge, Hereford Cathedral .... Page 103
Font, Hereford Cathedral 103
Arms of the See of Hereford, from Bishop Stanbury's Tomb 104
Plan of House, South-hill Park, Bromley, Kent 104
Diagrams in Student's Column: Heating by Hot Water 107-108

CONTENTS.

The Science of Construction 91
Notes 92
Letter from Paris 95
Saracenic Architecture 95
Fashions in Architecture and its Kindred Arts 99
Hereford Cathedral 102
Illustrations of Old Chester 104
Villa, South-hill Park, Bromley, Kent 104
House, No. 79, Fore-street, Redruth, Cornwall 104
Competitions 104
Architectural Societies 104
Society of Engineers 105
London County Council 105
Archæological Societies 105
Books: T. Codrington's "Maintenance of Macadamised Roads" London: Spon); D. Denning's "Art and Craft of Cabinet-making" (London: Whittaker & Co); T. M. Maguire's "London Householder's Chart" (London: Simpkin Marshall & Co.); "The Metropolitan and Provincial Local Government Annual and Diary" (London: S. Edgcumbe-Rogers) 106
The Jew's House, Lincoln 106
Concrete for Artisans' Dwellings 107
Flooring-Boards on Concrete 107
Monuments to Architects 107
Berlin Waterworks 107
Student's Column.—Warming Buildings by Hot Water, VI 107
Obituary 108
General Building News 108
Sanitary and Engineering News 109
Foreign and Colonial 109
Miscellaneous 109
Legal 110
Meetings 111
Recent Patents 111
Some Recent Sales of Property 111
Prices Current of Materials 111

The Science of Construction.

HATEVER differences of opinion may be held as to the use or desirability of examination for architectural students, we imagine there would be practical unanimity among all classes of architects as to the importance of education, and the strongest advocate of the architect's position as an artist would be constrained to admit the necessity of a certain amount of scientific training for those who, whatever their genius may be for artistic designing, are constrained by the very nature of their calling to be constructors. The constructive problems which have to be faced and worked out even in a small building are of a far more complicated nature than is apparent at first sight, and although a few years' experience will enable a man to gain such an amount of practical acquaintance with the materials which he uses that he will avoid gross blunders, yet without scientific training he will never be able to explain even to himself the reason for preferring one form to another, nor will he understand why under certain conditions materials behave in a very different manner from that which characterises them under other conditions. The "rule of thumb," which is the watchword of the severely practical man, is generally safe, but eminently unscientific, because it is useless to meet new conditions, and when these arise the practical man adopts another rule, which he defines as "being on the safe side," the result of which is generally safety at the cost of wastefulness. The evils of theoretical knowledge alone, unchecked by practical experience, are, of course, obvious, and would be far more likely to have dangerous effects, particularly with those who have to carry out designs; but in the case of the architect, who must be the designer not only of beautiful forms and harmonious arrangements, but also of strong and stable structures, we hold that he cannot afford to neglect the theory any more than the practice of his art. The accurate determination of the conditions upon which depend the strength and the stability of structures requires, in many cases, a knowledge of advanced mathematics which is probably never possessed by ninety-five per cent. of students of architecture; and a generation or so ago, no attempt had been made to approach the elucidation of such problems from any but the mathematical side. As a consequence, the whole of this portion of his educational equipment was practically a sealed book to the architectural student, who was compelled to take on trust a number of formulæ and tables without the slightest knowledge of the principles on which they were based. Whatever else the institution of examinations by various bodies may have done or not done, it has undoubtedly created a demand for science text-books on building construction suited to the comprehension of those who are unacquainted with advanced mathematics. Among the best of these are the "Notes on Building Construction," the first three parts of which were originally published by Messrs. Rivingtons, and have been noticed by us on more than one occasion. The fourth part of this work is now before us.*

We cannot recall a case where a work of this importance has been published anonymously, and we regret to notice from the preface that the author has been compelled by ill-health to depute a considerable portion of his work to an anonymous friend. Although he modestly states that by this arrangement "he feels he has conferred a great benefit on his readers," we cannot help feeling that in parts the work shows signs of negligence, and we shall be compelled to note some instances where the want of careful revision is sadly manifest. We consider the scheme of the book altogether admirable, the object being not only to give the various formulæ for calculating the dimensions of beams, girders, &c., but to explain fully the reasons for the use of these formulæ, and to show how graphic methods can be used for their solution with much less chance of error than abstruse mathematical calculations. The detailed manner in which the various problems are worked out, and the number of examples given, abundantly justify the publication of this portion of the work as a separate volume, for it is quite evident that it could not have been incorporated with the volume on materials without rendering it altogether too bulky.

The first chapter explains the terms in general use, such as live and dead load, breaking load, &c., the various stresses which act upon bodies, the strains in the bodies set up by these stresses, and the modes of fracture, and such expressions as the "modulus of elasticity," which is the quotient obtained by dividing the stress per unit of area by the strain, being generally expressed in pounds per square inch; or, in other words, it is the weight that would be required to stretch a rod of one square inch sectional area to double its length, supposing it did not break. The subject of equilibrium is next treated; the diagrams explaining how the re-actions at the points of support are ascertained as soon as the position of the load is known with reference to the supports are very clear, and a student carefully reading these remarks cannot fail to gain a clear insight into the subject. The determination of the external forces acting upon a structure and their re-action is generally simple enough, and the real difficulty of understanding the theory of the resisting power of materials comes in when the equilibration of the bending moment with the moment of resistance at any section of a beam is investigated; in other words, when the internal stresses produced by the action of the external forces are considered, and the way in which the fibres of the material resist these stresses. We are inclined to the opinion that the thorough elucidation of these problems can only be attained by the use of the Calculus, but after a very careful perusal of this portion of the book we are convinced that this is the clearest and most successful attempt that has been made to fully explain them in a simple manner that can be understood by the ordinary student. The terms in use, such as "neutral axis," "modulus of rupture," "shearing stress," and others, are

* "Notes on Building Construction." Arranged to meet the requirements of the Syllabus of the Science and Art Department of the Committee of Council on Education, South Kensington. Part IV. Calculations for Building Structures. Course for Honours. London: Longmans, Green, & Co. 1891

explained, graphic representations being always given alongside the ordinary figures, showing the varying position and distribution of loads on a simple beam. The student will easily learn how to delineate the figures, and he will, moreover, see for himself the reason why,—to take one example only,—a distributed load over a beam exerts only half the effect on it that the same load concentrated does. The difference between *strength* and *stiffness* is clearly described, and the formulæ for deflection are investigated as thoroughly as is necessary. The authors in this portion of the book have been compelled to touch the fringe of advanced mathematics, and as they are obliged to use the term, "moment of inertia," we think it would have been well to attempt some explanation of it, or the student will be hopelessly perplexed when he meets it. If a body be imagined as composed of an infinite number of minute particles, each of these particles is at a certain distance from the neutral axis of the body; if the weight of each particle be denoted by w, and its distance from the neutral axis by d_1 d_2 d_3, &c., then $wd_1^2 + wd_2^2 + wd_3^2 + \ldots . wd_n^2$, *i.e.*, the sum of the products of the weight of each particle by the square of its distance from the neutral axis is the "moment of inertia" of the body about that axis. It may possibly be objected that this explanation would not be of much value to the ordinary student; but even if this be so, we cannot think it right to introduce, without any attempt at elucidation, a term which by no means carries its meaning on the face of it. The effect of fixing the ends of beams, instead of merely supporting them, is excellently shown by diagrams, in which the points of contra-flexure are very clearly indicated, and a careful study of these diagrams will be of the greatest possible use to the student; in fact, we are not aware of any other attempt to explain graphically the great difference in the curve of deflection of a beam caused by preventing its ends from tilting up. The diagrams to which we particularly refer are figs. 111 to 119. The next chapter is upon wrought-iron rolled beams, and the method of finding the moment of resistance of an I beam is fully and clearly shown. Cast-iron girders are next treated, but as the use of these has almost died out, and as the author himself observes that "the material of which they are made is so treacherous and uncertain that it is always necessary to use a large factor of safety," this chapter is not of very material use or interest.

The chapter on tension and compression bars is well written, and the reason why the calculation of the resistance of a compression bar is a much less simple problem than in the case of a tension bar is clearly shown, and it is easy to understand from the considerations here laid down what an important element in the strength of columns or struts a slight inequality of load constitutes, producing as it does irregularity of pressure, so that the stress never presses absolutely through the centre line. In this connexion we think the author should have made some reference to the experiments of Weyrauch, Bauschinger, and others, on the effect of variations in load, as formulæ of comparative simplicity have been deduced giving a means of obtaining from the quiescent stress what is called the vibration safe strength,—*i.e.*, the strength of pieces when subjected to alternate tension and compression. It is true that early in the book Wöhler's tests are barely alluded to, but the whole question is of so much interest and importance that it should have been treated at greater length. The element of uncertainty with regard to columns and struts has evidently sorely tried those investigators who have endeavoured to make one formula apply to all cases, for in an example worked out on page 115 from the various formulæ which are given, the results vary to the extent of 500 per cent., and it is not surprising that one of the most recent experimenters, Prof. Fidler, C.E., has come to the conclusion "that the strength of columns cannot be defined by any hard-and-fast line." Rivetted and other joints, both in wood and in iron, are explained, and we are glad to find that pin joints have received adequate attention, for the increasing use of iron roofs renders it very desirable that this form of connexion should be clearly understood; and the calculations for a large plate-girder are very fully worked out, with graphic delineations of the bending moments. Ample attention is given to framed and braced structures such as roofs, and the method of drawing the stress diagrams suggested by Professor Clerk-Maxwell is explained. We should have been glad to find here a more detailed reference to and explanation of Bow's system of notation, which is so excellently adapted to all structures, whether simple or complex, and, when once mastered, simplifies calculations immensely. This is only shortly noticed in one of the appendices. Numerous examples are worked out in a large number of diagrams, some of which are in plates at the end of the work, but these have been generally so arranged that they can be unfolded and read simultaneously with the letterpress referring to them. This is a matter of no small importance. The conditions of stability of brickwork and masonry structures are investigated, such as chimney-stacks, retaining walls and arches, the diagrams illustrating the latter being to a large scale and very clearly drawn; and the last chapter treats of the motion of fluids in pipes. We should have been glad to see a few pages devoted to the motion of gases and the calculations of the sizes of pipes required for gas supply, as these are not readily attainable.

At the end of the book are a series of useful appendices, of which No. 11 seems particularly valuable; but we are not quite sure whether the last—No. 21—is not somewhat dangerous. For ourselves, we should prefer to keep in the memory the various formulæ in the forms in which they are generally used; for if one sometimes uses a formula for the strength of beams, for example, in which the length is taken in inches, and the result comes out in pounds; and at other times the same formula, altered so that the length is in feet and the result in hundredweights, the chances of error are increased. A number of most useful tables are given, which appear, as far as we have tested them, carefully drawn up; but has not the author given much too high figures for the moduli of rupture of various woods in Table I.? Certainly, if the experiments carried out by Mr. Lanza in the United States are correct, these figures should be reduced. We must also say that, practically, we should scarcely be satisfied with the dimensions given on p. 340 for the tie-beams and principals of wooden roofs, even though they carried no ceiling.

We have already stated that the author has wisely given a number of examples in which the application of the rules of formulæ is illustrated by working out the calculations in detail, and there is nothing more useful to the student than studying such examples, as without their help he would be likely to flounder hopelessly. In such a work as this the greatest possible care is required to ensure accuracy, as there is nothing in the context to suggest the rectification of errors, and we regret to notice some serious inaccuracies which are evidently due to carelessness, and which will mightily perplex the conscientious student. We do not profess to have checked a tenth part of the calculations; but we feel compelled to call attention to the fact that in a future edition,—which we have little doubt will soon be called for,—the whole of these examples must be carefully revised. For example, the use of the sign of addition instead of that of multiplication occurs far too often, the position of the decimal point is wrong in some cases, and many other small errors will be found; but on page 79 there occurs an accumulation of blunders that is quite inexplicable. We refer to example 6, where 20 ft. is said to equal 120 in.; 1,100 lbs. is put down as the modulus of rupture, instead of 11,000; the safe load is calculated at "about 3 tons," whereas, if the figures actually put down are worked out, the result is 11 tons 16 cwt., while the correct answer is 5 tons 18 cwt.!!

Again, on pages 84 and 85, the introduction of the letter *n* into the description of the stress area (shown graphically) of the flange only of a rolled-iron joist, makes it quite wrong, and would puzzle a student very much. On page 91, example 10, in calculating the deflection of a beam by the formula $\Delta = \frac{n\,W\,l^3}{E\,I}$ when W is the *total* load on the beam, the serious error is made of putting for W the load per inch-run. In several cases we notice that the scale of the diagrams is stated to be $\frac{1}{8}$ in. = 1 ft., when it is really $\frac{1}{8}$ full size. Seriously, these errors—and we have not exhausted the list—ought not to have occurred, and it is because the book, as a whole, is so good, that we have called attention to them, in the hope that they will soon be rectified.

NOTES.

ANOTHER great labour dispute has broken out in the North, originating in the apportionment of work between two branches of the engineering trades. The number actually on strike is variously stated at from 6,000 to 8,000, but only a small proportion of the strikers are really concerned with the matter in dispute. It is understood that the same question has previously been referred to arbitration, but the struggle has recommenced in consequence of dissatisfaction with the arbitrator's decision on the part of some of those affected. There is still much friction at the shipbuilding yards with regard to the old-standing question of overtime, and, although the dispute as to distribution of work seems to have been the pretext for all the strikes which have taken place during this last week, there is every probability that the former question will also be forced into prominence before work is resumed. It would be well for the strikers to consider the arguments put forward by Earl Ravensworth at the annual meeting of the North of England Steamship Owners' Association last week. There is no doubt that the present position and outlook of our trade points to a shrinkage in wages; and the maintenance of harmonious relations between capital and labour is one of the principal safeguards against this state of things becoming still more serious. The ostensible cause of the present dispute is eminently one for arbitration, and the strike is a great mistake,—especially on the part of those who are participating without any grievance of their own. The trades unions are apparently very sensitive and imaginative, one society having passed a resolution on Saturday approving of the strike on the ground that "we believe the employers are anxious to deal a blow at the organisation which dares to do battle for our trade." The "sympathy" of affiliated industries which would be highly commendable under some circumstances is now leading them to the unreasonable length of driving work out of their own yards, without any regard to the relations existing between themselves and their employers. Ill-feeling will inevitably ensue, as the consequences are sure to be disastrous to some employers with whom there is no ground for quarrel. A reckless disregard is shown for the prosperity of the district as a whole, for the coal trade and the carrying and other industries will necessarily be seriously affected by the stoppage, and it is, indeed, difficult to say where the mischief may end. Strong condemnation of strikes and lock-outs at the present time has been expressed at mass meetings in Newcastle, the men themselves being anything but unanimous as to coming out.

THE recently-issued "Second Annual Report of the Geological Survey of Texas," 1891, contains some exhaustive particulars of the different kinds of building itone found in the State. Granites, used for ɔuilding, occur in two areas,—the Central Mineral Region, and in the extreme west, or Trans-Pecos Texas. The best-known granite n the first-mentioned area is red to dark ·eddish-grey, varying from fine to rather coarse grain in structure, and susceptible of a high polish; it was used in the construction of the Capitol building. The outcrop of the granite, which can be quarried to any desired dimensions, covers an area of more than 100 square miles. In the northern part of Gillespie county there is a brownish granite of very fine grain, and others varying in colour from light to dark grey, well adapted for building purposes. The granites of Trans-Pecos Texas lack the variety of colour which is found in those of the central region. They are all near good railway accommodation, however. Porphyries of almost every shade and colour abound also in the western portions of the State. Amongst the marbles, that known as Austin is the most noteworthy; it is quarried from the Cretaceous formation. The body of the stone when polished is of a light yellow colour, and the tracings of the contained fossil shells in pure calcite imparts to it a very pleasing effect. The Carboniferous limestones of the northern part of the State also produce good marbles; and those known as "Burnet," from the Silurian are pink, white, buff, blue, and grey in tint. Abundant marble, destined some day to become the basis of a great commercial industry, is found in the Carrizos and Quitman mountains; it is banded or striped and clouded, as well as pure white. "Some of them," says the State geologist, "when polished will rival the Aragonite or Mexican Onyx in delicacy of colouring." The limestones of Texas suitable for building purposes are abundant and widespread in their occurrence; the best Cretaceous limestone is that from the Fredericksburg and Washita divisions, which varies from white to yellow. The area of the central coalfield produces excellent building sandstone, which is extensively utilised; and the Central Mineral district furnishes good slate for roofing purposes. As a test for durability,—f building stone it is stated that, if in the eld, a bed of stone under examination is ntirely hidden from observation by the aterial of its own destruction, it will rove to be a stone that will suffer greatly ı exposure; but if it stands out in bold scarpments whilst the other part of the rata are decomposed, it shows that it as a strong power to resist atmospheric influences. This may be very ell as a rough-and-ready rule, but it ertainly does not always apply. The method dopted in describing the building stones in he work alluded to might very well serve as pattern to geological surveyors on this side f the Atlantic. The majority of the Geological Surveys of the United States, recognising he fact that they have been constituted to ollect geological information of commercial alue, carry out their work in that spirit; let s hope that the Geological Surveys of Great Britain, now that they have given us good eological maps and philosophic descriptions f the strata, &c., will shortly turn their ttention also to the practical aspect of their ience. There is a wide field open before em, and the public might then get some lequate return for the large sums of money nually disbursed for the purpose, from hich but little result has hitherto accrued.

THE lecture on "Dust" delivered by Dr. Pridgin Teale at the Society of Arts on Wednesday evening was intended evidently the first suggestion of a new sanitary mpaign against the admission of dust into ır houses. The lecture consisted mainly of ı exposition of the means which have been lopted by Dr. Teale for some time past to gulate the movement and settling of dust. e pointed out in the first place that the cess of dust into receptacles, such as cupards and closets, arose from the constant anges of temperature and barometrical pressure in the atmosphere, which caused frequent currents of the air in and out through crevices and the interstices of doorways, carrying the dust with them and depositing it as the air settled. Shortly stated, Dr. Teale's principle is to stop out the air from all access to a closet or box save through one aperture, of an area in proportion to the internal space to be protected, and filling that aperture with a dust-filter, cotton-wool being the most efficient of various materials experimented on. To carry out the method requires very good workmanship and fitting of doors, and the application of air-excluding strips of soft material at the sides of doors and windows. The application of the method to keep dust out of drawers, boxes, and closets is proposed to be further extended to keep it out of houses, by similar treatment of the windows. The sash window must be given up, as not sufficiently controllable in regard to access of air, and windows formed with the greater portion fixed, and only a tall narrow sash hinged to open as a casement, and protected in the same way as closet-doors and boxes. This, of course, presupposes a special admission of air through ventilators, which are also to be protected by dust-filters. As far as concerns the exclusion of dust from closets and drawers where papers may have to remain a long time undisturbed, the suggestions are perfectly practical, and the demonstration of the results of the method incontestable. The exclusion of dust from the whole house is another matter. Some of the dust is created within the house, by decay and other causes; Dr. Teale affirms that most of the dust in towns is connected with smoke, but we think he attributes too large a proportion to this cause; and it is obviously of no use to have elaborate methods for keeping out dust if any considerable part of it arises within. The adoption of his principle for the whole house would mean an amount of delicate and costly work which cannot generally be afforded; a degree of care and supervision which would only be given by those who had an anti-dust "fad"; and, last but not least, a practical stoppage of direct fresh air through open windows. This latter, from a sanitary point of view, would be a worse evil than the dust, and we will never listen to any suggestion which is to interfere with the free opening of windows to the outer air. For the exclusion of dust from the house, therefore, we think Dr. Teale's method can hardly be regarded as "within the region of practical politics." For the exclusion of dust from store-closets, boxes and drawers it is perfectly practicable and may be very valuable, and the thanks of the community are due to Dr. Teale, in this as in so many other cases, for his investigations as well as for his clear and lucid exposition of the results.

A REPORT on the recent outbreak of enteric fever at the Foundling Hospital, by Dr. Sykes, the Medical Officer to the St. Pancras Vestry, gives an instructive account of the search made throughout the premises for any probable cause of disease, and the unexpected cause to which it was ultimately traced. The annexed plan, copied from one of the diagrams published with the report, explains the circumstances from which the disease originated. The grease-trap shown on

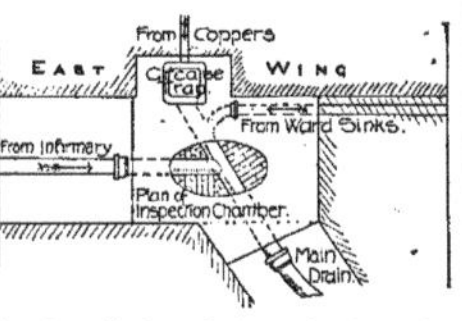

the plan discharged into the inspection-chamber through a pipe with the end dipped into the grease-trap to form a seal. Excreta were found in the grease-trap, and it was discovered that the periodical discharge of an automatic flush-tank down the infirmary drain caused a backwash into the grease-trap, the flush of water coming faster into the inspection-chamber than it could get away, and some of the contents of the drain were thus washed over into the grease-trap. The grease-trap took the discharge from the coppers in the kitchen, and on filling it with a charge of ammonia and peppermint it was found that the smell in a few minutes rose from the coppers and thence permeated a great part of the building. Dr. Sykes observes,

"This grease-trap was even a better incubation-chamber than the suspected water-cistern in the warm lumber-room. The warmth from the hot-copper water, the restricted and confined air supply, the nutritive material discharged into the trap, the access of infected fæcal matter, the fermentation set up, and the rush of the warm expanded air and vapour through the copper pipes and copper into the kitchen, the offices, and the staircases, are all factors favourable to the cultivation of infective matter, and to its diffusion by vapours covered by the odour of cookery."

It may be added that the pipe from the ward sinks (see plan) which also acted as a ventilating pipe to the inspection-chamber, was connected into the drain and untrapped, and may thus have assisted in leading up effluvia through the sinks; but the main evil was the close connexion of the grease-trap with the inspection-chamber on one side and with the interior of the kitchen on the other side.

THE Borough of Nottingham has issued an excellent coloured chart illustrating the relation of the number of deaths from various causes to the principal meteorological conditions on each day of the year 1891. The chart and tables of rainfall are very well got up, and the example here set might be followed with advantage by other Corporations and County Councils. The study of the results in detail is of course rather a matter for a medical journal than for our columns.

WE opened the *Fortnightly* this month with some curiosity on finding that it contained an article by Professor William Crookes, F.R.S., on "Some Possibilities of Electricity." The learned Professor had somewhat astonished the electrical world last November, in an after-dinner speech, by saying that "it has been computed that in every single cubic foot of ether there are locked up 10,000 foot-tons of energy which has hitherto escaped notice;" and we naturally expected that we might find in his article in the *Fortnightly* some explanation of this hard saying. We were, however, disappointed. The article covers much the same ground as the speech, though, of course, addressed to a larger audience. It deals with Professors Lodge and Hertz's investigations of electrical vibrations of ether, and anticipates the time when they may be made use of to telegraph without posts or wires. It alludes to Tesla's experiments with rapidly alternating currents, and points out the great possible gain in obtaining light, with far less heat, and, therefore, with far less expenditure of energy. There is also some Utopian talk of dissipation of fogs, controlling the weather, &c., and with it the very practical remark that the electro-static machine can no longer be regarded as a toy. But the 10,000 foot-tons have disappeared with the ether whence they came. Professor Crookes supplies us instead with another riddle; he tells us that the total *vis-viva* of sunlight per acre amounts to 800,000 horse-power per year, of which 3,200 horse-power are used by the crops. If Professor Crookes would only condescend to use words in their ordinary sense, we might make out what he means by this; at present it is much as though he were to tell us that the rainfall is equal to the speed of an express train. The article is pleasantly and easily written, and we find in it occasional gleams of transatlantic humour. Perhaps more of it than we suppose is intended to be taken humorously, which would account for much. The Professor's interest in psychical theories is well known, consequently we are not astonished to find thought-transference and brain-waves cropping up again, this time with the suggestion that the brain-waves are electrical.

IN a recent correspondence with the County Council, the St. Saviour's (Southwark) Board of Works have moved for a removal of the bars and gates which of late years have obstructed traffic through Montague-close. A way formerly led north of the church to Pepper stairs, High-street, and (old) London Bridge. Like the Mint, and the neighbouring Deadman's-place (now Park-street) and Clink, the close has been a sanctuary, privileged, it is said, from the circumstance that Lord Monteagle lived there when he received the letter that betrayed Guy Fawkes. But the facts, as set forth in the *Archæologia*, vol. xii. 200-11, by no means support the tradition*; and confusion has arisen between the names of Montague and Monteagle. At the suppression the priory, with the close, the church of St. Mary Magdalen, and appurtenances, its income being valued at 624*l.* 6s. 6d., was granted to Sir Anthony Browne, Henry VIII.'s Master of the Horse, whose son was elevated Viscount Montague. This family were staunch Catholics, and the close became to be known as "Little Rome." In the "Gentleman's Magazine," September, 1808, is a view of the house they built in the close; taken down in November, 1828. It stood close against the church's north side, for in the parish books for 1596 is an entry for making a new door in the church wall entering into my Lord Montacute's house. John Carter carefully inspected the remains of the conventual buildings in 1797 and 1808. Allen, twenty years later, describes the then state of a crypt standing north and south, measuring 100 ft. by 25 ft., with two aisles, and a groined roof supported by octangular columns. Over this extended a spacious room, which retained traces of an open timber roof. Some exterior corbels carried fragments of groin-springing, probably of the cloister.† But all above ground remains, together with the two quaint rows of Alice Overman's almshouses, gave place before the large warehouses and the Bridge House Hotel, planned and designed, 1838, by George Allen, architect. The Guildhall Library contains several good views of portions of the close, with Montague House, and the main gateway at the western end of St. Saviour's.

A CORRESPONDENT writes:—"In regard to the proposed new clock for St. Paul's, we read that 'the old clock strikes the hours on the old "Phelps" bell, but the new one will strike upon "Great Paul," which is nearly 17 tons weight, with a hammer weighing 680 lbs.' Is it wise to run the risk of damaging the best and soundest bell in the British Empire by smashing a 680 lbs. hammer upon it every hour? I should like to see in print a certificate from Mr. Taylor, of Loughborough, the designer and successful founder, that he desires 'Great Paul' to be thus rudely treated; so that, when the bell gets cracked, the blame can be apportioned in the right quarter."

FROM some correspondence which has taken place in the *Manchester Guardian* it is evident that our remarks concerning the Whitworth Institute competition and the policy of privacy in regard to it are entirely in accordance with local feeling on the subject. One correspondent comments on the fact that only twenty-three designs were sent in, although the scale and importance of the building as proposed were such that it should have been one of the great competitions of the day. In reply to this, Mr. E. Salomons, the President of the Manchester Society of Architects, writes that the conditions imposed upon competitors were such that he for one felt quite unable, consistently with professional self-respect, to send in designs, and that he presumed others had the same feeling. It appears that, now that the designs are sent in on the scheme issued to competitors, the committee have changed their ideas, and that consequently the plans now sent in are useless. In that case the competing architects have certainly very strong right to complain. Competitions under the best circumstances involve an immense amount of wasted labour on the part of the architectural profession, and those who call upon architects for competing designs should at least make up their minds first what they are going to do, otherwise they are merely amusing themselves at the expense of the architects. If this present competition is really to be entirely abandoned, after the issue of an elaborate scheme of instructions, the committee ought to feel that it is incumbent on them, in common fairness (we might almost say in common honesty) to give some pecuniary compensation to the architects who have been tempted into wasting their time and labour to no purpose.

TO the February number of *A. A. Notes* Mr. W. B. Richmond contributes an excellent little paper on "Architecture from the painter's and sculptor's points of view," in which, so far from repeating a favourite theory of the moment, that architecture is nothing without sculpture, he emphasises the idea that architecture is *building*; that the business of the building is to be effective and impressive in itself without any aid from other arts; and that these can do little to redeem it if it is not in itself noble building. It is to be hoped that some of the architects who are so anxious to be sculptors, and to look down on unadorned building as uninformed with art, will duly consider this counsel from an artist who is not an architect, but who sees more art in architecture pure and simple than some architects seem able to find in it. "Give us," he says to the architects, "works of art as builders. And when you have done that, then we sculptors and painters will try in our way to help, not mar your work, which, if it is very good indeed, will need neither sculpture nor painting to make it perfect art."

MISS EUGÉNIE SELLERS is to give six afternoon lectures on Greek sculpture at the British Museum on Wednesday, February 10, and the five succeeding Wednesdays. The lectures will deal with the development of sculpture and relief, and its technique, and Miss Sellers, we perceive from the prospectus, proposes to uphold the position that the Greeks "were masters of rhythm and symmetry but not of decoration." We certainly have been under the impression that the Parthenon frieze was the finest decorative bas-relief in existence, though it is in the wrong place in some respects. An extra lecture is to be given on March 23, on the horses and other animals of the Parthenon frieze, by Mrs. N. Cohen, who has made a special study of the subject.

THE exhibition of Mr. Wyllie's "Holiday Drawings in France and Italy," at the Fine Art Society's Gallery, is a remarkable example of the varied interest which a true artist may get out of a single scene in all its different aspects. The French sketches, sixty-one in number, are the most important part of the collection, and are all at the fishing town and watering place of Berck. They are nearly all scenes on the beach, under varying aspects of weather, and with varied sketches of fisher-folk, visitors, and boats, but there is no sense of monotony in the sketches, almost everyone of which has its special interest. Two which are especially good are 15, an evening effect, and 18, the breakers on a breezy morning. A pleasant interest is given to the catalogue by a new method of presenting the subjects; instead of a series of dry titles, there is a picturesque account of the expedition and the place, signed "Marian A. Wyllie," and the number of the drawing which illustrates each sentence or allusion is given in the margin.

A COLLECTION of small oil paintings by Mr. Wimperis, "Rustic and Riverside Pictures" is on view at Messrs. Dowdeswell's Gallery. It consists principally of pictures of river and meadow scenery, and shows the breadth of treatment and the fine aërial effect which have always characterised this artist's work, but to those who have known Mr. Wimperis best by his water-colours it also suggests that he is best known so; his broad free style is essentially a water-colour style, and when transferred to oil it seems a little toneless and hard, the technique which brings out the best effects of water-colours not being equally applicable to the other vehicle. In the same gallery is a collection of "Pictures of London street life," by Mr. Chas. P. Sainton (the son of the late eminent violinist of that name), which, amid a good deal of *chic*, contains studies of street children which are natural and piquant, especially "A Siesta in Covent Garden" (9), "Street Arabs" (21), and "A Picnic in the heart of London" (27). In "Au revoir" (25), a study of a young lady stepping into a hansom, the artist has made a pretty little *genre* picture out of an everyday London incident.

THE case of "Morris *v.* Brinsmead and another" throws an interesting light, for the outside public, on the manner in which laudatory paragraphs in newspapers are managed in these days. Part of the plaintiff's claim against the defendants was for commission for getting paragraphs inserted in newspapers about their pianos. This is only one instance of what is continually going on in the Press in these days, in the way of notices of inventions, and a most discreditable thing it is to the English Press of to-day, which however is probably not worse and possibly much better in this respect than the Press of some other countries. The charge is not that papers will insert such puff paragraphs for direct payment,—few of them descend to that, though many of them will bargain for an advertisement in exchange for a "notice"; but inventors and patentees can get notices (written by themselves) into a journal by paying a man who is not officially on the staff of the paper, but who has credit with them and whose contributions are accepted without any troublesome questions being asked. They are people who are useful to the paper, in short, and are favoured accordingly. In the leading daily papers of the day there are constantly to be seen descriptions and recommendations of new inventions, which are in fact written by those who are commercially interested in them, and then appear to the confiding public as independent expressions of opinion on the part of the journal in which they are printed. "Puffs" of this kind are sent to us constantly by persons interested in building inventions; paragraphs describing the excellence and advantages of their own patents, and intended for insertion as "notices." It seems almost incredible sometimes that people should suppose that any editor would accept such barefaced puffs and give currency to them; but they are accepted in many quarters, either directly, or through being smuggled in by some one who has credit with the paper; and readers may take it for granted that not one in a hundred of the paragraphs on new inventions which "go the round of the papers" are the independent opinion of an independent person; they are the statements of persons commercially interested in the matter. The cause of this, in the case of the higher class of papers, is apparently sheer carelessness and an absence of the proper sense of responsibility. The

* The letter, inscribed to "The lord Mow'teagle," was delivered to his footman "as he passed in the streets towards night"; the conspirators agreed to preserve Lord Montague and others, with, at Percy's request, the Earl of Northumberland and Lord Monteagle.

† See also Concanen and Morgan's book, 1795; the account by Carlos in the "Gentleman's Magazine," June, 1835; and "Old Southwark and its People," by Mr. Wm. Rendle, F.R.C.S., 1878.

plain rule ought to be that no one is allowed to write anonymously in a paper upon anything in which his own interests are concerned. Until that becomes a generally accepted principle, the readers of newspapers will do well to distrust all paragraphs recommending this or that invention.

LETTER FROM PARIS.

THE two grand balls, given every winter at the Hôtel de Ville by the Municipality of Paris, have had the attraction of an artistic novelty this year, as the public can now see, by the numerous electric lights, the Salle des Fêtes with its ornamental decorations; though the ceiling paintings of Benjamin Constant, Aimé Morot, and the other artists engaged, are still wanting. At the death of Lavastre, the ornamental work was undertaken by MM. Carpezat and Guifart, who have in fact only followed the scheme sketched out by their predecessor. The effect is very sumptuous, though it will look somewhat crude until the gold has toned down a little. At present, the eye finds no repose amid the crowding of bas-reliefs, medallions, statues, many-coloured emblems and escutcheons encumbering the too massive frames of the panels. This plethora of decoration makes one regret the more the Salle des Fêtes of the old Hôtel de Ville, as it used to appear at Imperial receptions, with its elegant decoration in pure Renaissance style. The ceiling was soberly treated in coffers and garlands, and the compositions with which Henri Lehmann had decorated the pendentives and the spaces of the vault formed an admirable frame to the paintings by Horace Vernet, Léon Cogniet, Ingres and Delacroix. Instead of these we have now the commonplace figures of M. Milliet, the uninteresting compositions of M. Aubiet, and the ceiling by M. Gervex symbolising Music, the foreground occupied by an imaginary proscenium of a theatre, where the eye rests first on the realistic black dresses, lorgnettes, and bald heads of the occupants of a realistic orchestra.

"Fin de Siècle" is the expression that sums up the character of this decoration; nor can one admire more unreservedly the blue and red eccentricities of M. Besnard or the contorted torsos of M. Carrière, which are supposed to combine the drawing of Michelangelo with the chiaroscuro effect of Rembrandt. In the whole assemblage of work there is nothing really decorative except the large composition by M. Puvis de Chavannes, though it is to be hoped that the artist will modify the heavy effect of the mass of trees in the middle distance which seems to crush the figures. If he does away with this one fault his work will remain the dominant one in this curious collection of decorations, which impresses one somewhat like an orchestra in which each player is performing an independent part, with no reference to the others.

It is, therefore, gratifying to find that the Municipal Council have chosen this eminent artist to succeed Elie Delaunay in decorating the vault of the grand staircase; though M. Puvis de Chavannes has never before painted a ceiling, and his dislike to the task was with difficulty overcome. It will be interesting to see the result, and there is no doubt at all events that in this case the decorative painting will be subordinated to the lines of the architecture, both in design and colour.

The Paris municipality have been making a curious experiment, in giving a commission to M. Jules Cheret to design some cartoons for tapestry for the decoration of a room in the Hôtel de Ville. M. Cheret is well known for his designs of posters, with which he has covered many walls as well in Paris as in provincial towns. These very original works make quite a popular museum of art, and have almost revolutionised the art of the placard. The object of the commission is to obtain some tapestry designs with little delay, as it is useless to appeal to the majestic inertia of the Gobelins manufactory.

The "Cercle Artistique et Littéraire" of the Rue Volney has been first this year in the usual series of small winter exhibitions, and the collection is on the whole superior to its predecessors. Among the exhibits is a fine portrait of M. Henner by M. Carolus Duran, two beautiful portraits by M. Jules Lefebvre, other portraits by Rixens, Weerts, and E. Sani, landscapes by MM. Yon, Busson, Nozal, Félix Boucher, and a highly-coloured representation of the Ducal Palace at Venice by M. Benjamin-Constant. There is also M. Henner with his eternal blond figures, ivory on a black background; M. A. Maignan has painted a "Cigale" shivering in the snow, and M. Olivier Merson exhibits a set of important sketches for windows intended for the Church of Saint Adresse.

The Salon of Water-colour Artists has just opened its doors, we may find space on another occasion for a few words about it. We may just notice in passing a small but charming exhibition of landscape-paintings by a young artist, M. Paul Liot, collected at the Hôtel Bellevue, Avenue de l'Opéra, views in Normandy and sea-pieces. M. Pissaro, the impressionist artist, has also opened an exhibition of his works in the Durand Ruel gallery, which for some years past has rather made a specialty of artistic eccentricities.

We have mentioned already that in consequence of dissensions among the representatives of the late M. Meissonier the exhibition of his works has been given up. The quarrel is in fact about to come before a legal tribunal. On the one hand the widow of the painter wishes the paintings, sketches, and statuettes to be sold by public auction, while the children of the first marriage demand that the works of their father should be divided among the inheritors instead of being sold. Such seems to be the opinion of the magistrates, who consider that such a division was much more in accordance with the painter's wishes than a sale. The decision is, however, still pending. It is somewhat pitiful to see these wretched squabbles among the relatives of the great painter almost at the very moment when the anniversary of his death, according to Parisian custom, is being celebrated solemnly at the Madeleine.

A decree of the Minister of Instruction has regulated the mode of appointment of the architects of the Service des Monuments Historiques, who henceforth will be appointed by competition. The same decree announces that in future the Inspecteurs-Généraux in this service cannot be charged with the works carried on in a classified monument. An exception is made in favour of those who are actually carrying on such works at present on a commission dated prior to this decree. Another Ministerial decree provides for the creation, at the École Nationale des Beaux-Arts, of a course of history of French architecture in the Middle Ages and the Renaissance; a decision which will fill a deficiency long felt in the scheme of architectural education. We may add that the Minister of Instruction will shortly have to appoint a successor to Henriquel Dupont, who was professor of engraving in the École des Beaux-Arts.

A few particulars may be added as to the work of the École. On January 21 a committee, presided over by M. Ginain, gave the award in the competition entitled "Prix de Reconnaissance des Architectes Américains." The subject of the competition was "a mansion in a considerable number of storeys, similar to those in New York, Chicago, Boston, &c." After having examined nine designs submitted, the Committee awarded the prize to M. Deperthes (pupil of MM. Deperthes and Ginain). In the "Enseignement Simultané des Trois Arts" M. Binet, pupil of M. Laloux, has obtained a third medal for decorative design. In the competition in History a third medal has been awarded to MM. Goupy and Kohn, pupils of M. Reclou.

The Government some time ago commissioned four marble statues for the principal entry of the National Library, Rue de Richelieu. One of these statues has been recently erected, and gives a good promise for the decorative effect of the whole group when completed. It is the work of M. Hugues, and symbolises "La Gravure." The others, which are to complete the group, will represent "L'Imprimerie," "Les Médailles," and "Les Manuscrits."

The Louvre has acquired recently an interesting collection of sketches, among which is a study by Pierre Guérin, "Dido and Æneas," a splendid sketch by Ingres, and three masterly drawings by Géricault.

We have seen recently, at the atelier of M. Rodin, the clay model for the monument to Balzac to be placed in the Palais Royal. The author of the "Comédie Humaine" is represented standing, draped in a kind of monkish robe which he was accustomed to wear in his study, the arms crossed, the head raised and with an expression at once energetic and meditative. Not far from this statue will be placed those of Corneille and Racine, at the right and left of the entry to the Avenue de l'Opéra. The modern generation having, among so many statues, forgotten these two glories of French literature, the Municipal Council headed a public subscription for funds to arrange a competition for the execution of these two monuments.

The death is announced, at Paris, of a Swedish artist, Mdlle. Christine Lundberg, who came every winter to pursue her studies under M. Courtois and M. Raphael Collin. She had exhibited, in the Salons of 1888, 1889 and 1890, portraits and *genre* subjects; and a picture of hers, "La Toilette," was in the Swedish section of the 1889 great Exhibition.

In the last issue of the *Builder* allusion was made to the death of Dupont, the celebrated engraver. Louis Pierre Henriquel Dupont was born in Paris in 1797, and has died therefore at the age of ninety-four. He studied painting first under the painter Pierre Guérin, and engraving under Bervie. At the age of twenty he had already obtained sufficient reputation to open an atelier which had an immediate success. He gave promise already of the qualities which have been predominant in his work; a rare correctness and a remarkable purity of style. He engraved most of the portraits painted by Ingres. He had some great successes with the works of Delaroche, and finally engraved his chef-d'œuvre, the "Hémicycle des Beaux-Arts," and subsequently "The Entombment of Christ," by the same painter. He also engraved various works by Ary Scheffer, Hersent, and Lehmann, and among his engravings from the old masters may be mentioned the "St. Catharine," after Correggio, and the "Walk to Emmaus," after Veronese. Among modern works which he interpreted may be mentioned also the portrait of the Baron de Rothschild by Hippolyte Flandrin, the "École Turque" after Decamp, and "Entry of Henri IV. into Paris," after Gérard.

Since 1849, Dupont was member of the Académie des Beaux-Arts, and had a multitude of medals at various exhibitions, and the cross of commander of the Legion of Honour. In 1863 he was appointed professor of engraving at the École des Beaux-Arts.

It is a long engraver's career of which the first plate dates from 1815. According to his express wish no discourse was pronounced over his tomb, nor any flowers or wreaths placed on it. But he remains honoured in memory as the last representative of that remarkable group of French artists of the earlier part of the century which included such names as those of Delaroche, Ingres, and Delacroix.

SARACENIC ARCHITECTURE.*

BY PROFESSOR AITCHISON, A.R.A.

I WILL begin at the beginning with the Kaaba. We heard in the last lecture that it is now about 40 ft. by 50 ft. on plan, of trapezoid shape, and it may have been kept to its original foundation to the last. You will also recollect that in the early part of Mohammed's life it was hypæthral, the roof being formed by the cloth curtains that shrouded it, and that it was roofed with wood when he was thirty-five. I fancy the walls must have been pretty thick.

If we take 3 ft. for the walls, we get joists 17 ft. long, and the longitudinal girders could only have had a bearing of about 6 ft. 3 in. from centre to centre if there were six columns.

One is apt to think ancient ships, with the timbers of which the Kaaba was roofed, were small. I am by no means sure that the large merchantmen werel not of considerable tonnage; at any rate, the ancients could and did build very large ships. The pontoon that carried an obelisk from Egypt to Rome, was big enough to form the caisson for the foundation of one side of the dock at Ostia, that the Emperor Claudius had built; and Ptolemy Philopater (222 B C) built a vessel 420 ft. long, 57 ft. wide, and 72 ft. from the water to the gunwale. This, it is true, was not so great as our *Great Eastern*, but it showed that the ancients could build vessels that were not in the category of fishing-smacks, so we may suppose the timbers of Bacûm's vessel were big enough to roof the Kaaba.

If there was any ornamental art displayed in the interior, it must have been in carving on

* Being the second Royal Academy Lecture on Architecture this session. Delivered on Thursday evening, January 28.

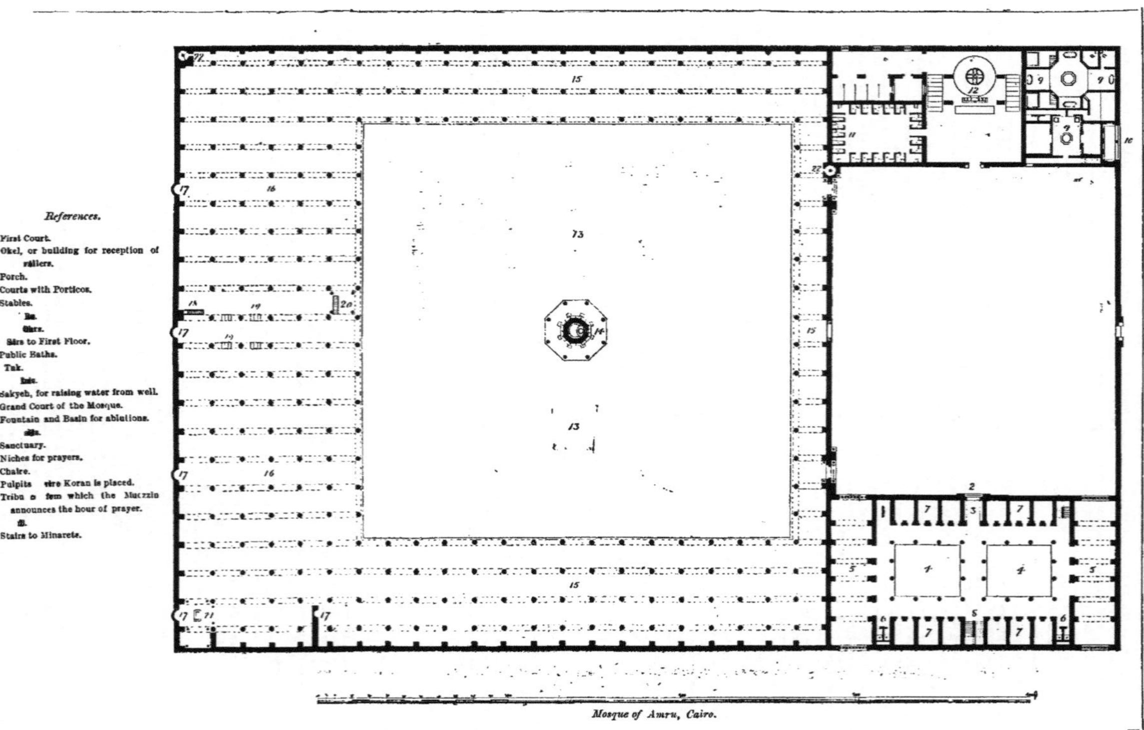

Mosque of Amru, Cairo.

References.

1. First Court.
2. Okel, or building for reception of [illegible]allers.
3. Porch.
4. Courts with Porticos.
5. Stables.
6. [illegible]
7. [illegible]
8. [illegible] to First Floor.
9. Public Baths.
10. T[illegible]k.
11. [illegible]
12. Sakyeh, for raising water from well.
13. Grand Court of the Mosque.
14. Fountain and Basin for ablutions.
15. [illegible]
16. Sanctuary.
17. Niches for prayers.
18. Chairs.
19. Pulpits [illegible] Koran is placed.
20. Tribu[illegible] [illegible] which the Muezzin announces the hour of prayer.
21. [illegible]
22. Stairs to Minarets.

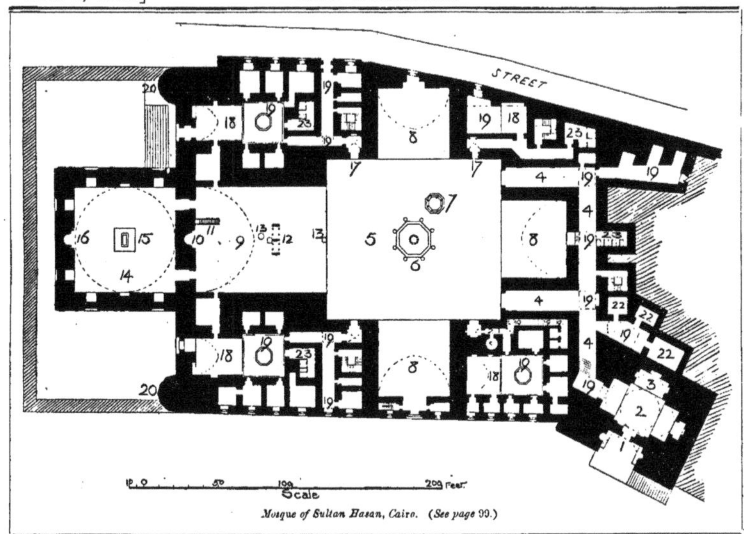

Mosque of Sultan Hasan, Cairo. (*See page* 99.)

the beams, or in the capitals of the columns; but Bacûm, the architect, was either a Greek or a Byzantine, so this art, if it existed, cannot be put down to the credit of the Saracens, and as little can the wall-paintings of Abraham and the Angels be attributed to them; these were the pictures Mohammed had erased when the idols were destroyed.

The Kaaba had a golden spout, and its doors are said to have been plated with gold; it was covered with cloth outside. It is no use speaking now of the black silk damask with which it was covered by the Abbassides, with a gold band, and a Cufic inscription.

The next religious building we know of was Mohammed's Mosque at Medina; this, no doubt was greatly bigger than the Kaaba, as Mohammed's followers had become numerous. It is by no means certain that at the pilgrimages many were admitted into the Kaaba; at any rate, Mohammed most distinctly stated that entering the Kaaba was not necessary for the due performance of them, and regretted that he had gone into it at the taking of Mecca (8 A.H.—630 A.D.).

This mosque at Medina was probably like the Kaaba internally, only with many rows of wood pillars, probably with the girders parallel to the long side; there appear to have been buildings or porticoes for shelter on both sides of the court,—viz., one for men and one for women,—but this court seems to have been divided from the Mosque by a street. We also know that its kibla was changed from Jerusalem to Mecca,—*i.e.*, from north to south, so the Mosque was possibly walled in; it had no mehrab, or niche, for that was only adopted in 53 A.H., and was probably copied from the apse of a Christian church, but this mosque was rebuilt, and the houses of Mohammed's wives destroyed and taken into it by Welid I., between (86 and 96 A.H.) 705 and 715 A.D.

The next mosque we know of was that of Omar, at Jerusalem. Omar visited Jerusalem in 15 A.H., and it was built after he left. Some believe it was the dome of the rock.

Fergusson gives a small building about 90ft. by 30 ft. over all, in the mosque of El Aksah, as Omar's mosque, which he says is 80 ft. by 18 ft. inside, but the latest authorities believe it was a small wooden mosque since destroyed.

The next considerable one was built at Old Cairo by Amru-Ibn-al-Aás, the conqueror of Egypt, in 20 or 21 A.H., some ten years after Mohammed's death; it was built for the use of the army, and was only about 75 ft. by 45 ft., and without a mehrab. It was enlarged by Moawia, and again by Abd-al-Aziz, the son of Merwan I., then governor of Egypt, who raised the roof.

In the days of Mamun (193-198 A.H.) the mosque was 435 ft. by 225 ft.; in 275 A.H. the mosque was burnt, and the green table destroyed, and was restored by Ahmed-Ibn-Tulun's son, who expended about 4,080*l.* on it, and the architect's name was El-Adjifi; a new portico was added 357 A.H., and it was restored by Saladin between 567-589 A.H. = 1172-1193 A.D., and afterwards repaired by Beybars and Kalaun 658-689 A.H. It can only be hoped that from its being the first mosque built in Egypt, so soon after the prophet's death, that the peculiar sanctity, which in the eyes of devout believers still adheres to it, occasioned the restoration to be as much as possible on the original lines. All that can be safely said is that it conforms in plan to the early mosques.

The town of Kairouan was founded by Ocba, three days' journey to the south of Tunis, in 50 or 55 A.H., and the mosque was probably built shortly afterwards. Welid I.'s mosque at Damascus was probably built about 86 A.H., and the mosque and Cordova 170 A.H. = 786 A.D. The year of our era may always be got approximately by adding 622 to the year of the Hegira, but it is not exact as the Moslem year is lunar.

The original idea of a mosque for Islám was a wall at right angles to the meridian cr kibla of some holy place; first, the Temple of Jerusalem, and then of the Kaaba at Mecca, with a shelter to shade the worshippers from the sun. As the prophet got old he introduced a pulpit, with three steps and a seat, so as to be heard better, and to rest when he was tired. Subsequently the exact line of the kibla was defined by the niche or mehrab, and the pulpit (mimbar) became a fixture, mostly on the right side of the niche, as you face it. Nearly in face of this was the tribune (dikka), from which the Korân is recited, and the prayers intoned by the imam. A courtyard, with a tank or fountain, was wanted for the legal purifications before praying.

It is most embarrassing to know which of the early mosques should be chosen as the type, as they were all altered. I have spoken of the Kaaba, Mohammed's mosque, and the Mosque of Omar; the mosque at Kairouan, founded in 50 or 55 A.H., is said to have been wholly rebuilt by Hassan in 84 A.H., except the mehrab, and altered subsequently up to the date of Mamun A.H. 212, so probably that at Damascus will be the best to begin with. It is about 460 ft. by 316 ft., with a small projection to the right and left, looking at the niche; the sanctuary itself is about 130 ft. deep by 460 ft. long, the rest being a courtyard, with a single portico or cloister round three sides of it; the wall with the niches is nearly due south; the sanctuary itself consists of three aisles, with the arcades parallel to the niche, or south wall, an unusual arrangement in later mosques; there are twenty-three arches, the centre one, opposite the niche, is as wide as three ordinary arcades; in the middle aisle, in front of the niche, is a dome supported on four massive piers. The sanctuary is described by an eye-witness as having pointed arches, resting on marble columns, and over them clearstory windows, the north ones are traceried and filled with beautiful stained-glass; the lower part of the walls are lined with marble, and remains of mosaic are found in the upper part of the central space fronting the niche.

The Mosque of Amru, at Old Cairo, is about 361 ft. wide by 548 ft. long, but this includes an outer court, with a khan on one side and baths on the other; the mosque proper, with its court, is about 384 ft. long by 361 ft. wide, and the sanctuary 361 ft. long by 111 ft. deep. The mosque has one single cloister to the entrance wall and a cloister on each side: looking to the niche, the right-hand cloister has three aisles, and that to the left four,—in both cases the aisles next the walls are very narrow. The mosque itself has six arches in depth, with the arcading at right angles to the niche wall, and twenty-two aisles in all,—those next the end walls are narrow, being continuations of the cloisters. The arcades have slightly-pointed horseshoe arches, supported on Classical or Byzantine columns of marble, with carved capitals; a pier of three courses rises from the cap, and then there is a slight projection formed by the heels of the horseshoe arches. The voussoirs are of two differently coloured stones alternating, or the alternate ones are painted red; the columns are tied both ways with wooden ties, after the fashion of Byzantine work. In 1866 this mosque was the Government "refuge for the destitute," and young ragamuffins were playing at buttons with the carved ivory panels they had knocked out of the pulpit.

The next is that of Kairouan, called El-Kebir. This mosque is not rectangular, nor are its sides parallel; it is about 407 ft. deep by

245 ft. wide. There is a double cloister at the north, or entrance, end, with a minaret in the middle of its length, embracing both aisles, and with similar double cloisters on each side. The sanctuary itself, which is about 156 ft. deep and 242 ft. long, has seventeen aisles at right angles to the niche wall, the middle one, in which are two domes, being as wide as two of the ordinary aisles, and with double columns, and is mainly arched the same way, though there are three lines of arcading parallel with the niche wall, which carry the domes. It has ten arches, with a wide one next the niche wall, carried on coupled columns. There is a dome in front of the Mehrab, and one over the first two arcades, both in the centre aisle. The arcades have slightly horseshoed arches, supported on marble columns with Corinthian, Composite, or Byzantine capitals. The columns are tied above the caps both ways with wooden ties. The niche is covered with inlays of lapis lazuli, mosaic, and white marble, and is flanked with two porphyry columns, said to have then been worth their weight in gold, with white marble Byzantine capitals. The pulpit is of wood, elaborately carved, and pierced, with the divisions of the balustrade vertical,—a rare occurrence in Moslem work. One point of interest attached to this mosque is its having served as the model for that of Cordova, and was doubtless endeared to Abd-al-Rahman when he was skulking about in Numidia. He landed in Spain 138 A.H., 755 A.D., and was shortly after proclaimed Kaliph in Spain, in the days when the Abbasside Mansur was Kaliph at Baghdad.

The mosque at Cordova is said to have been begun in 786 A.D., the year before he died, and consisted of eleven aisles, twenty-one bays deep, and was continued by his son Hisham, and completed by him or his son El-Hakim, who added the court. El-Hakim II. (961-70 A.D.) extended these eleven aisles southwards by twelve bays, and built the niche and some chambers. El-Mansour (981-1000 A.D.) is believed to have added the eight aisles to the east, thirty-five bays deep, and probably the remainder of the court.

The total enclosure of the mosque is 580 ft. by 435 ft., and the sanctuary 435 ft. by 390 ft.; there must have been at least 650 arcade columns, besides others for enclosures. The court-yards had cloisters round three sides, and were planted with orange-trees, in continuation of the columns of the open aisles.

The arcades of the mosque are at right angles to the niche wall, and consist of horseshoe arches on the capitals of antique marble columns; above these are semi-circular arches carrying the walls, which support the trusses and gutters of the roof. The voussoirs of the arches are alternately stone and cut red bricks. There was an enclosure in front of the Mehrab (the Maksura), and an enclosure or pew for the Kaliph in front of that, now called La Villa Viciosa.

The arches forming the Maksura are cusped, and each span is equal to the space between three columns, as arches below spring from each side of each column they intersect.

On corbelled projections, on each deep abacus, stand small shafts bearing horseshoe arches above the upper interpenetrating cusped arches.

In the Emir's pew, the lower cusped arches are not intersected, but have a cornice carried on colonettes; from the colonettes horseshoe arches are turned, and from the centre of each cusped arch below there is an upper cusped arch, which cuts the horseshoe arches, and fills up the spandrel. In my opinion, the architecture is more curious than beautiful.

An illustration is given of the arcading of the Villa Viciosa, and some of the ornament of the arch of the Mehrab.

Even now, with a great Christian church dropped into the middle of it, the effect of this forest of columns is wonderful, the diagonal vistas being unique. These congregational mosques of Egypt, Syria, Tunisia, and Spain are grouped together, because they seem to show the early idea of a congregational mosque; for, though some of them are not early, the early idea seems to have been kept up. The mosque at Cordova was co-eval with the first break-up of the Kaliphate, and though the next, the Mosque of Ahmed-Ibn-Tulun was not the end, still it was one more step towards the general breaking up, when each country had an independent ruler,—Sultan, if not a Kaliph,—of its own. The independent rulers and Sultans sometimes owned the spiritual supremacy of the one a Baghdad, and sometimes did not. Saladin was the first Sultan of Egypt (567 A.H., 1172 A.D.). Selim I. the Ottoman Sultan of Constantinople took with him from Egypt Mutawakkil the last Abbasside Kaliph in 1517, who transferred the Kaliphate to Solyman the Magnificent, about 1520 A.D., so that now the Sultan of Turkey is the spiritual head of Islâm. Ahmed-Ibn-Tulun was a Turk from beyond the Oxus, brought up in the Court of Mamun, and in the School of Samira, and was the cause of the murder of the Kaliph Mustain, who had promoted him to a post of honour. He was afterwards made Deputy Governor of Egypt, 254 A.H., and gradually assumed independent power, and made a good ruler; he died 270 A.H., 883 A.D. As all the tithe and the tribute that formerly went to the Kaliphs remained in Egypt, Tulun was enabled to spend it in improvements and buildings. He built the celebrated mosque at Cairo, which Fergusson has taken as the starting point of the Saracenic style; but I should say this was at least two centuries too early; it was finished in 265 A.H., 878 A.D.; it is said to have been designed by a Coptic architect; the Copts are the native Christians of Egypt, and are said to have been very skilful in the arts, and, until we know more about Coptic and Byzantine ornament, nothing can be safely advanced on the origin of Saracenic work. Tulun had sense enough to object to any material being used but brick, as he said it was the only thing that would resist fire and water, his architect disagreeing with him, he put him in prison, but the architect managed to bribe his gaoler to deliver a letter to Tulun,* in which he offered to build a brick mosque, and, being summoned, he drew out his design on a skin of parchment; this was approved; he was furnished with money and materials, and completed the mosque in two,—some say three,—years, and was presented with ten thousand pieces of gold by Tulun, and a pension for life. The dome in front of the niche, and the wooden stalactites beneath it, are supposed to be of the time of the Sultan Lagin (696 A.H., 1296, A.D.), who repaired the mosque and put up the pulpit, now at the South Kensington Museum: whether he put up the dome over the fountain in the court is not known, but it is said to be at least a century later than Tulun, and may be looked on as one of the first domes we know that was carried on stalactites. The mosque is surrounded by a wall and a space on three sides to keep it quiet; in the space between the outer and inner walls of the mosque, opposite the niche, there is the minaret, with a corkscrew staircase outside, and the water-wheel, and,—as I read it,—the rest of the space was devoted to students, who studied theology. The outer walls are about 513 ft. square over all, inside are the walls of the mosque and its court, about 390 ft. wide by 450 ft. deep. The sanctuary is 301 ft. long by 100 ft. deep. A double cloister runs round three sides of the court, and the sanctuary itself has five aisles parallel with the niche wall, and an arcade of 13 arches; the piers are wholly formed of plastered brick, with engaged brick columns at each angle, with ornamented capitals and no bases: the piers are about 8 ft. wide, the arches form 17 bays at tight angles to the niche wall, two at each end, being railed off. The arches are pointed and slightly horseshoed; over the abacus is a guilloche, which runs round the inner edge of the arch and along the bottom of the impost, and the archivolt and impost are enriched with a wide plaster ornament, both of the same pattern; this ornament consists of the "raie de cœur" on a gigantic scale, each leaf is filled in with ornament, after the manner of late Roman work. I have never observed that this has been noticed,—and some of the soffits are ornamentally plastered, with a large square guilloche, the large squares and angles are filled with ornament, and the small squares with rosettes.

On the external wall, in each arcade, are arched recesses with an ornamental archivolt and impost on engaged brick columns, the shafts of which are about the height of capitals; inside the first arch is another, with a Cofic inscription round it, and the windows are filled with pierced stone lattices that much resemble the geometric patterns of the fifth century, shown in De Vogües Central Syria, not copies, but even more ingenious. In the spandrel of each pier, a little above the impost, is a narrow opening with a stilted arch. The plaster ornament is very like Indian work. Below the wooden ceiling is a board with a carved Cufic inscription.

* This ruler's name was Ahmed, the son of Tulun, but the mosque is best known by the father's name.

The principal mosques that still exist at Cairo are those of* :—

A. H.	A. D.	
20	640	Amru.
265	878	Tûlûn.
361	971	El-Azhar, repeatedly restored down to 1753 A.D.
380-403	990-1012	El-Hâkim, restored down to 1423 A.D.
608	1211	Esh-Shâfi'y, a mausoleum, also restored to 1516 A.D.
647	1249	Es-Salih, a mausoleum, restored by En Nasir.
667	1268	Edh-Dhâhir (Beybars I.).
683	1284	Kalaun (Maristan, or mad-house), minaret rebuilt.
687	1288	Kalaun (Kubba, tomb mosque).
698	1298	En-Nasir.
706	1306	Beybars II., Gasbenkir.
718	1318	En Nâsir, in the Citadel.
723	1323	Sengar, El-Gâwaly, and Salâr, joined.
739	1338	El-Mâridâny (architect, El-Mu'allim Es-Suyûfy).
748	1347	Aksunkur, restored 1652 A.D.
756	1355	Sheykhû.
757	1356	Suyurghatmish.
760	1358	Sultan Hasan.
770	1368	Umm-Sha'ban.
786	1384	Barkuk (architect, Cherkis el-Haranbuly).
808-813	1405-1410	Barkûk, in the Karâfa, built by 'Abd-el'-Aziz and Farag, sons of Barkûk: architect, Lagin Tarabay(?).
823	1420	El-Muayyad; in process of restoration.
827	1423	El-Ashraf Bars Bey; also mausoleum in the Karâfa.
860	1456	El-Ashraf Inal, in the Karafa.
877	1472	Kâit Bey, in the Karâfa; also mosque within Cairo.
886	1481	Kigmâs, Amir Akhor.
905	1499	Ezbek.
909	1503	El-Ghory (two); restored 1883.

El-Azhar, the brilliant mosque, founded in 361 A.H., 971 A.D., is a congregational mosque (Djami), with oratories, and is used as a university for the study of theology and Jurisprudence by students from all parts of the Mohammedan world. The mosque is, roughly, an oblong, 280 ft. deep by 295 ft. long; outside this are three mosques, a court, and some chambers, and a fountain. The sanctuary is 282 ft. long by 126 ft. deep, and has in addition an open portico beyond it. One noticeable peculiarity is that the gate of Upper Egypt, which goes into the sanctuary, is composed of two doorways that have all the appearance of Early Gothic doorways, with trefoil cusps under the semi-circular arches that stand on the capitals of three slender shafts, undoubtedly done by some European architect of the Gothic school.

As regards the plan, it has a single cloister on the four sides of the court; on the right and left are aisles of three bays, with two columns on either side of the central aisle, all used for class-rooms. The sanctuary itself has nineteen bays at right angles to the niche wall, and at its deepest is nine aisles deep, the arcades being parallel to the niche wall. The centre bay opposite the main niche has three columns on each side, which support a high pavilion.

It is useless to speak of its decoration which may date from the middle of the eighteenth-century. If it was not burnt down, the 380 marble columns it is said to contain, are probably Classic and Byzantine, plundered from the temples and churches of Upper Egypt. The Mosque of Beybars I., called Edh-Dhahir (667 A.H., 1268 A.D.) looks like a congregational mosque. It is 351 ft. deep by 345 ft. wide, with flat projecting towers at the angles, and projecting gateways on three sides. The sanctuary is 345 ft. long by 125 ft. deep. The court is surrounded by an arcade on piers, these enclose two aisles each, in the middle the supports are columns. The sanctuary is divided longitudinally in the centre by a line of arcades, parallel to the niche wall, supported on small piers. There are six aisles in depth, with the arcades of the rest supported on columns, the three centre bays next the niche are formed by arcades on piers, the square so formed in front of the niche is covered by a dome, about 39 ft. in diameter, whose angles are supported by stalactites. There are nineteen bays in the sanctuary.

The oratories or mosques of Kalaun are attached to a mad-house (Maristan), and to the

* Extracted from "The Art of the Saracens in Egypt." By S. Lane-Poole. 8vo. London; 1886.

right of the entrance is the tomb oratory or mosque (Kubba) 683-7 A.H., 1284-8 A.D.

As land got more scarce in Cairo, the old form of mosque, with its forest of columns, was given up, and a form much like the domed palaces of Persia was adopted. The mosque of Sultan Hasan is a brilliant example of this sort of mosque without piers or columns; it was built in 760 A.H., 1358 A.D. It is built on an irregular-shaped piece of ground, and though his tomb and the minarets face an open space, the main entrance is in a narrow street. At the end of the vestibule here, Sultan Hasan used to sit to administer justice. Some narrow tortuous passages from this entrance lead into an open oblong court about 115 ft. by 104 ft., with a fountain in the middle, shaded by an open octagon shelter, with a dome over it,—the dome has a band round it with the signs of the Zodiac; on each of the four sides are the arms of a Latin cross, —three are about 46 ft. wide, and the same depth, and one, forming the sanctuary of the mosque, 67 ft. wide, and 89 ft. deep, behind which is the domed tomb, also 67 ft. square. Each arm of the cross is vaulted, with a pointed vault, having an arch on each face about 92 ft. high to the crown from the pavement of the court; nothing grander can be conceived, as each of the archways open on to the court without any screen. The vault, besides the soffit of the arch, has four flush ribs with red and white voussoirs. At the niche end the sanctuary is panelled with marble up to the frieze from which the vault springs; at the end there are two doors into the tomb and the pulpit; above these doorways are two-light pointed windows, with a bull's-eye over the centre. The frieze which runs round it is ornamented with a Cufic inscription on a floral ground, with a cresting above, the whole carved in low relief. The frieze is of the exact proportion required, and is in such flat relief that the ornament in no wise interferes with the general effect; the sublimity of this vast plain vault suggests Greek art.

There is a charming little mosque and tomb of Kait Bey 877 A.H., 1472 A.D., this is also without columns, and instead of an open court has a covered one, with a latticed lantern.

In the earlier mosques, the exterior has no architectural display, as they are mostly merely walls with battlements pierced in fantastic shapes, or with the regular stepped battlements called "bearded," and it is not until domes and minarets make their appearance that there are any very striking external features.

I omit the mosque of El-Azhar, as the date is quite uncertain.

It seems most probable that the wooden stalactites in the dome in front of the niche at the Mosque of Tulun were put up by Lagin 696-8 A.H., 1296-9 A.D., and that, therefore, at that time they were fashionable, though unknown in the time of Tulun 270 A.H., 883 A.D.; we may be pretty sure there was not much building in Egypt and Syria between 1099 and 1249 A.D., considering the Crusades and the disputes between the Fatemite Caliphs, the Kurd Dynasty, and the Turks or Mamluk Sultans.

One of the most striking peculiarities of the religious architecture of Cairo is this, that many of the mosques were built with courses of red and white stone, or occasionally with white and black, or they were coloured to imitate them. The black and white courses, though not so common as the red and white, are in this respect like the Cathedral at Genoa and the churches at Florence and elsewhere in Italy. The external appearance of a mosque is that of a two-storied building, the lower windows being mostly square-headed; the lintels and the arches over them mostly had the junctions of the voussoirs of the most fantastic outline, and of two differently-coloured stones or marbles; if these outlines were worked through the stones it implied incredible labour and superhuman accuracy. The upper windows are mostly plain pointed, or doublets with a bull's-eye over the centre spandrel, surrounded by a trefoiled frame. Here and there wide flat piers were brought out with stalactites between them at the top to make the cornice and battlement in one line. Sometimes there was a cornice above, consisting of tiers of stalactites, and sometimes no cornice beyond a moulding, but as a rule battlements crowned the whole. A most original feature occurs in many of the later mosques; a flat recess was made where a door occurs, which was carried up the whole height of the two stories, and finished at the top with a trefoiled arch, mostly filled in with stalactites, while between the head of the door and the bottom of the stalactites are windows or ornamental panels. As far as we can now see, there was no general system, but each architect had genius enough to make a picturesque whole, in spite of the openings being arranged only for the plan. The architects as often as not drew away attention from the want of symmetry in the main building by curious and elaborate ornament and the sharp shadows of the stalactites, while minarets and domes broke up the outline. The front of the tomb of Sultan Hasan is symmetrical, the centre is crowned by the dome, and the whole front is flanked by two minarets. The domes mostly have a drum, and this is generally pierced; only the domes that are plain externally are usually four-centred; the later ones are three-centred, and are covered with flutes, reeds, or chevrons; while some have elaborate geometrical ornaments carved on them, and some have counterchanging ornamental patterns; some are covered with an elaborate floral ornament, and then diapered over. Domes are usually constructed over square chambers, especially if they are sepulchral. The domes have no pendentives, but are supported by corbelling at the angles, the corbelling being cut into stalactites. The edges of these mark out the external truncated gables. The angles of the square base of the dome were mostly chamfered off, and ornamented with triangular stops, or deeply moulded, while the truncated gable is most commonly filled with a triplet window, with three circles or bull's-eyes over it, enclosed in a cinquefoil border; the centre part of the gable is sometimes formed into a square, with two triangles on each side; these are commonly filled with circular ornamental panels. The pointed tops of the domes are mostly finished with a finial of bronze crowned by a crescent.

It was a favourite plan to make the bottom of the tall minarets solid up to the roof of the mosque, but it is by no means always the case; it is the case, however, at the mosque of Sultan Hasan, where the large minaret, to the top of the masonry finial, is about 330 ft. high; a great many of the smaller minarets are from 150 to 160 ft. high from the ground; they form the most striking architectural feature in Saracen mosques, and are often most elegant in shape and proportion. Sometimes they spring from above the cresting or battlements of the mosque, and sometimes their bases form projections from the main wall. As they are used instead of belfries, the cryer calling the hour of prayer five times a day from them, they are mostly formed in stages, the balconies or the stages being carried by a deep stalactite cornice, the balustrades being of pierced stonework, or more commonly of wooden rails. The minarets are mostly crowned by a stone pear-shaped finial like an Indian cup and ball; the finials frequently look as if pierced with arrows, these are, however, slight wooden gallows, for holding lamps. The minaret of Sultan Hasan's mosque being the highest, a slight description of it may be given. Its solid base is polygonal, and gathers into a circle beneath the deep stalactite cornice of the mosque, which once had a flower-de-luce battlements; the minaret above the cornice is about 26 ft. square, and runs up vertical to a height of little more than its width, in alternate courses of red and white, it is then chamfered off into an octagon, just above that the stage is marked by a stalactite balcony, on each of the four square faces, the chamfered ones are ornamented in the flat with a square set anglewise in a square frame in each of the eight faces above it one long window-shaped recess with red and white courses, the stilted arch stands on slender engaged colonettes, the circular heads have half-domes in them, a deep stalactite cornice forms the next stage, with a pierced stone balustrade, and a slightly smaller octagon goes up to the next story, and here the stalactites are grouped at the angles, this also has a pierced stone balustrade, above is a circular open lantern with cusped arches on columns, this has a stalactite cornice and a stone balustrade, out of this springs the cup and ball in masonry, and above this there is a finial with a crescent, and round the pear-shaped finial are a cluster of little gallows, for supporting the lamps; in its ruined state the first stage is not marked enough by the corbelled balconies. That of the mosque of Kait Bey is one of the most elegant, but like that of Sultan Hasan, since the battlements have gone, is a trifle thin at the base above the mosque. The treatment is very similar to that of Sultan Hasan's, but better proportioned, and the third division is circular, and covered with a geometrical pattern, with a central star on each face. Most of the mosques are roofed internally with wood, with the exception of those of Sultan Hasan and Barkuk. The latter has piers instead of columns, and the aisles of the sanctuary are domed with domes, whose pendentives are of the same radius as the flat domes, and not marked by a different curvature. Some of the wooden-ceiled mosques are panelled, but the most striking ones are those with circular timbers, bracketted into a square next the walls, the junction between the square and the circle being effected by means of stalactites. When the whole of the beams and the ceilings are painted and gilt the effect is very gorgeous, and unlike anything else one has seen elsewhere, for almost all the Venetian ceilings so treated have rectangular beams. The lattice work, inlaid wood and marble work, chased and damascened brass work, some of the mosaic where mother-o'-pearl is used for white, and the stained-glass windows, are models of elaborate and excellent work, and the stained-glass windows are lovely. What the effect must have been in the palmy days, when everything was in perfection, and all the accessories were to match, we can scarcely picture to ourselves. The descriptions in the "Arabian Nights" of all this work, which in our youth we fancied were wholly imaginative, are merely descriptions of what met the writer's eyes every day. The "Arabian Nights" are believed to have been put into the form in which we read them, just after the Ottoman conquest of Egypt, and represent the palmy days of Saracen art, at the time of the later Mamluk Sultans, though the stories and adventures are said to have occurred in the days of Harun al Rashid or earlier.

FASHIONS IN ARCHITECTURE AND ITS KINDRED ARTS:

THE ARCHITECTURAL ASSOCIATION.

THE ordinary fortnightly meeting of this Association was held on Friday, the 29th ult., Mr. F. T. Baggallay, President, in the chair

The following gentlemen were elected members of the Association:—Messrs. C. H. Thewlis, W. Hearn, G. B. Gosling, F. G. Hunt, R. V. Hunt, and W. J. Langley.

Mr. F. T. W. Goldsmith, Honorary Secretary, announced that Mr. Arthur Bolton had presented to the Library his book on "Examples of Mosaic Paving," and that the Editor of the *Builder* had presented "The *Builder* Album of Royal Academy Architecture, 1891." Thanks were voted to the donors.

Mr. Goldsmith also announced that a visit would be made on February 6 to Mr. Aston Webb's new assurance building* in Moorgate-street, and also to the tower and spire of Bow Church, by kind permission of Mr. Innes. And on February 20 a visit would be made to the Imperial Institute, by permission of the architect, Mr. T. E. Collcutt.

The President said that he regretted to say that Mr. N. J. W. Westlake, who was to read the paper of the evening on "Fashions in Architecture and its Kindred Arts," was unable to be present, but Mr. Goldsmith had very kindly consented to read the paper for him.

Mr. Westlake's paper was as follows:—

I have selected as the subject of my paper "Fashions in Architecture and its Kindred Arts," and, for the purpose of illustrating this, have made a short *résumé* of some of the various changes that have taken place during the present century.

It will be at once evident that any observations on the ancient and recognised styles can only, in this slight essay, be dealt with in a summary way.

In commencing, it is my intention to epitomise some of the differences of style that fashion, from time to time, has adopted during the present century. I shall then put certain propositions before you as the cause or causes of the rapidity of these changes in recent years, and conclude by attempting to show how all this may be worked to a good purpose.

We are all of us continually told by those who claim to be men of "light and leading"

* Illustrated in the *Builder* for May 17, 1890.

what is *the* thing, especially in the way of style. Notwithstanding this, we have seen sometimes the same leader change, from a dogmatic adherence in preaching the imitation of some ancient style,—because of some supposed or real subjective value that its characteristics enshrine,—and, altering his opinion, use the same arguments in favour of another, and, finally, perhaps boldly relinquishing his line of argument, opinions and all, in favour of this, advocate something entirely different. The cause of this is difficult to explain. Often it is because some architect or artist having made a success and a reputation in another style to that formerly in vogue, has attracted many followers, thus forcing a change of fashion, and your man of "light and leading" is fashionable in his opinions, or nothing.

We can all of us, however, if we will, observe motives and note their spring, and giving them as much value as we think they deserve, arrive at our own conclusions and practices accordingly, not placing any value on the mere customs or tastes of a day. We are, however, forced to ask ourselves this question: Why, during the last century the changes in architecture and the kindred arts have become rather those of fashion than of style, and why we now have no distinctive style proper to this great period—no style which embodies a real religious or national character, and why for a certain short period we design in any adaptation of either of the old styles and then discard it for another?

For me to attempt to answer this, here, would be going a little too much in advance of my introduction, and I must first give you, as far as I can recollect the succession in which some styles have been fashionable, for where a style is fashionable, the less informed in learned circles will see no merit in building or design out of it.

We may ask ourselves, could any method of enshrining a beautiful idea in architecture or art be more inviting than that of the Adelphi Adams, and the period of Reynolds, of Flaxman, of the Wedgewoods, and all the eminent men of that time whom I have no space to catalogue. Can you on looking back see any reason why such a fashion ceased, and that shown in the Houses of Parliament for a time arise, and Pugin,* Sir C. Barry, and kindred artists be in vogue? We all know Pugin's arguments in favour of the Gothic revival, and if my memory rightly serves me, one of the most celebrated art thinkers and writers that ever arose, whilst in some respects following the same line of thought as Mr. Pugin, said hard things about him and the "houses." Of course, you know I allude to Mr. Ruskin, who has been a power in the influence that at one time changed the mode of thought and fashion in art. The action of the Royal Academy during the century has been rather that of a body with an unsettled purpose. In its early days composition, design, and the more intellectual branches of the art were represented. Amongst its roll of members we often find the names of eminent composer-artists such as Flaxman, Maclise, and Dyce. The main object of the majority seems to have been simply to encourage mechanical and technical excellence until quite recently, under the present President, who with some few others has encouraged the study of the architectonic arts. The Academy has not, however (notwithstanding the recent advances in the architectural school), as yet during the present century shown us even the elements of a school of national artist-composers, great as some of its individuals are in separate branches of art. About half a century ago there arose the school of design at South Kensington, but I cannot think the influence of that expensive machine has been other than dangerous at times.† It has given us cheap drawing schools, but is national design, as national design, developed at all in proportion to the influence of the great and expensive machinery? My own impression is that nearly all modern developments and improvements are from minds that were outside its influence. I cannot, therefore, consider it a large factor in the changes that have taken place.

Many of us can recollect the influence that the Lille competition and the publication of Viollet le Duc's dictionary had for a period on our fashions. The Early French style adopted by Burges and Clutton,—the successful competitors for Lille Cathedral,—began to dominate, and I think you can find that adaptations of this style became so prevalent that nearly every architect practised it more or less.

We all know of work in that style by Clutton, by Burges (who never entirely deserted it), by Street, and by a host of followers, with a result that, personally, I sometimes think, was lamentable; for the host of followers seem to have delighted in the eccentricities, rather than the merits, of the style, and many of the arts were involved in its study and practice for a considerable period.

Later on, the competition for the Law Courts perhaps did much to produce a change in this, and we saw many of the competitors working from English models, although the successful architect never completely escaped from his French "convictions."

The youngest of us have seen through the change, from Decorated to Perpendicular, the devotion to the so-called Jacobean and Queen Anne, and our present rising fancy, if there is one dominant, for a mixed Renaissance of a very indefinite character.

It would be superfluous before the present audience to go into greater details, you all know the names of the leading men of this century, and their changes of style, and many of you can perhaps give a reason for these changes as well as the architect or artist himself.

This brings me to the second part of my subject. Why have these changes taken place? Why, if one of the antique styles did for centuries, and one of the Mediæval styles for one hundred years, and was consequent and consonant to its predecessor, must we have now twenty or thirty different, and often incongruous, styles adopted in the same period?

What is the cause, not the accidental,—but the essential,—cause of this? Is it that there is no dominant national or religious character to enshrine, no dominant thought requiring a dominant idiom, no great and leading poetical aspiration in us, no really important idea for us as a nation to represent? So that we have fallen from the regions of the ideal, and are become more professional men and few poets! For I take it that architecture and art in their perfection are but concrete renderings of the author's finer imaginings.

The language, the idiom in which he spoke in ancient days, embodied an idea of which he was a part,—it was almost a "chironomia,"—and we even now, when gazing at times on these ancient works, seem to feel the author's emotions, and to be inspired by the same sublime ideas.

We appreciate at evening the grand outlines of their buildings as they appear like dreams, their masses showing dimly against the setting sun, and in the daylight we dwell on the sweet intentions or bold determination of their details or mouldings. We read their language, but have little occasion to speak it as they spoke it, and too great a love of various knowledge to limit ourselves as they were limited,—to the perfect expression of a few ideas; we forget that in this limitation of action there is an increase of power.

My argument may thus be condensed,—the higher architecture is an art, and like the other arts is a language* for the expression of thought; in this it distinguishes itself entirely from the science of building; perhaps to many my definition would be more acceptable if I were to say that it is a language combining science and art. In ancient times it expressed the ideas of the period in the idiom of the period.

In these times what is its position, what expression of living national or local idea is there in the Houses of Parliament, the Law Courts, the Meat Market, in the various new Board schools or workhouses? You may answer, little; but tell me to look to the railways and their stations, the City warehouses and those real expressions of living national architecture, the ships, but for my own part in these last only do I find what I desiderate. If, then, there is neither dominant idea nor dominant idiom, what is the architect to do? and the most rational answer to this, in my own mind, is that he must either express his own ideas, embody his own fancies, or represent the ideas of some living energy to which his mind is affiliated.

When I said that we were now more professional men than poets, it was not my intention to imply that there are no poets left,—no architects whose works speak of their nobility of aspiration or intelligence. Far from it. There are some few. It would be invidious to choose examples amongst the living, but I may mention the names of two who have not long passed away, and with whom I was intimate; and so far as I had opportunities of forming an opinion, I think they had minds so full of sympathy and intelligence that they would have been marked men, no matter in what method they expressed themselves. I allude to Burges and Sedding, and I would take them as exponents of the two ideas I have mentioned,—Burges of the first, and Sedding of the second. Burges imbued his sensitive and poetical mind in Mediæval lore; he was almost at home in its ideas when an accident led him to study early French architecture, and he learnt to speak in an idiom of his own formed upon that basis. He cared not to speak much in any other way; if he did, he did it with that difficulty with which one speaks a foreign tongue, and you all know at sight Burges' works, and from them Burges' ideas; they are not, as far as I can appreciate anything, more than an individual expression, but they expressed the man, his intelligence, his great information, his power of adapting that information, and his poetical disposition.

Sedding affords us a complete contrast; intelligent, fairly learned, of a refined and poetical mind, he rather represented an idea than himself. He did not work long enough in any style to form for his own use a distinct idiom, although he managed by his ability and sympathy to express himself in many ways; his individuality was never so apparent in his work as was that of Burges.

This, then, I suppose is the highest point in which the architectural arts can now aspire as national arts. What might be done by the nation, or even by the City of London, or the various large parishes, is one thing,—what might be done had they unity and honesty of purpose is magnificent to think of; but what is done amounts, I fear, to little more than a series of jobs in which those capable of intrigue have had far greater chances of success than men of reflective, conscientious, and poetical dispositions.

Look at the majority of public buildings, the workhouses, and the Board-schools, and tell me do they represent in any way the best or the second-best architectural genius of their period. You, who can form a fair opinion, tell me,—am I right or wrong.

Returning, then, to my subject, I fear this change of fashion, then, is unavoidable, we shall not have a nineteenth-century style. The era will pass without any distinct architectural expression like the period of a nation, if such a society can be so-called, of mixed languages. But what are the advantages of this disadvantageous position, as we are soon to enter a new era,—the twentieth century? History never repeats itself, yet its life and ideas are the products of its predecessors. I will return to this point presently.

I daresay most of you will agree with me now in the statement that this is the first century in the history of the world's civilisation unmarked by any dominant architectural style.

If the history of a country is written in its monuments, what will the historians of future centuries say of this? Will they be right in saying that it was a century of "Fashion,' of vacillating thought and of changing or unsettled purpose, in which everything was tried and nothing stuck to? One cannot tell, but this we know, that if as a nation, as a people, we have made no great and distinct monumental mark, as individuals we may still have character and purpose.

Perhaps, then, as a necessity of the position in which we live, if we differ in our characters and purposes, the great knowledge of the various styles which have been diffused by the successive study of them will be of some use to us and to coming men, from which each mind can adopt that best suited to its bent. Wren and Inigo Jones did this as Burges and as Pugin did. Moreover, this knowledge of the character and the details of each style enables us by comparison to form a clear and intelligent knowledge of the capacities of each, as though we could speak many languages and choose that which best expresses our thoughts, even if we lacked a mother tongue. Of course, a mind allied to very firm convictions and of a strong character may out of this knowledge evolve a style which may embrace the thoughts

---

* Probably the Oxford movement assisted this, but was not the cause.—N. H. J. W.

† One instance alone shows a mischievous tendency, the establishment of a school of design at Bombay, which did something to injure the previous Indian tradition.—N. H. J. W.

* Of course, it is not a language, but like it, in being a method of expression.—N. H. J. W.

of an age, and become that of a coming era, but I think, as yet, we are looking for this mind. At any rate, when such an one arises there is a vast store of knowledge in the Art literature of this century, so collected and ordered that he will not require mental food. He will have this advantage over those who have preceded him, in any period, for never has there been so vast a store-house, nor so much accumulated store, so readily obtainable, and to this cyclopædic accumulated store of Art knowledge the Architectural Association has been no small contributor.

Mr. Owen Fleming, in proposing a vote of thanks to Mr. Westlake for his somewhat philosophic paper, and to Mr. Goldsmith for reading it, said that the paper was rather difficult to discuss; in fact, he did not think there were very many points in the paper which one could discuss in any detail. There was the large question as to whether the architects of the nineteenth century were inventing a new style; and as to that question he was getting tired of hearing the public talking so much about "a new style." In the *Standard* the other day there was a leading article commenting upon the election of Mr. Jackson to the honourable position of Associate of the Royal Academy. He was sure they were all glad that Mr. Jackson had obtained that position, which he ought to have obtained long ago. The *Standard* said that architects did not appeal very much to the general public unless they invented a new style. That statement seemed to him to show an entire misconception of architecture as a whole. Architects never had invented, and, he ventured to say, never would invent, a style. To talk of *inventing* a style of architecture was to show a complete ignorance of the subject. To his mind, a style was that which grew out of the natural necessities of building, and out of the position that a people held in the civilisation of the world. It was frequently urged against architects that this nineteenth century was an age of individualism and eclecticism. That was so, no doubt, to an extent; but he thought that we English of the present day were not competent judges whether we had a definite style or not. Four or five centuries hence the historian who wrote the history of the nineteenth century would be able to find out the prevailing characteristics of nineteenth-century architecture, just as we had discovered the characteristics of the architecture of the Greeks or Venetians, or of that of the thirteenth or seventeenth century. Each century had its own individual style, but he did not think that any of the persons who created that style were aware of what they were doing; they acted just as they felt prompted to act, without any consciousness of "inventing."

Mr. Paul Waterhouse, M.A., in seconding the vote of thanks, said the subject which had been touched upon in the paper and commented upon by the last speaker was a very deep one, and one which exercised the minds of architects a great deal; still more did it exercise the minds of those who, without being architects, took a great interest in architecture. Architects were perhaps, as a rule, too busy to theorise about their art. The remarks made by Mr. Fleming as to the possibility of a future historian recognising in the architecture of the present day chronological characteristics which we of the present time could not see, contained, he thought, the germ of a very great truth. All the original styles of the world had been the outcome of national characteristics and geographical conditions. As the original styles were exhausted, or, perhaps, not exhausted, but rather fulfilled, in their original form, the world had been obliged to modify them, and very little good architecture, perhaps, had been produced since the year 1400 (or, say, 1500), in which there had not been a more or less conscious imitation of the styles of the past. But if they were to consider, for instance, the stream of revival which first began in Italy about the year 1425, they would see that that stream flowed in certain countries in Europe, more or less continuously, down to the beginning of the present century, perhaps even longer. He supposed there had been no break in the string of those who had been following in the wake of the Renaissance movement, first started in Italy, and carried on in Italy, France, and other countries for four centuries. And yet an expert in architecture could, by studying the buildings of those countries during that period, pick out the half or quarter of a century to which a building belonged. He thought we made a great mistake in comparing the conditions of to-day with those of the past. Those who cried out for a new style asked whether the world was so played out that it could not bring a new style into existence? But the conditions had altered; and why? If they looked at the architecture of those countries where the means of communication were good, a similarity of architecture was to be seen. In England, for instance, there was a distinct architecture of districts, due to the fact of easy communication within those districts. As communication in the world increased, of course the natural result followed that similarity of architecture took place. That was due not merely to the fact that architects were necessarily plagiarists, but to the more important fact that association played so great a part in our satisfaction with architectural design. They could not get away from the feeling of association. There was something absolutely repugnant in the idea of novelty for novelty's sake in architecture, except in the matter of grouping and the modification of detail; and thus it was that when communication became more or less universal, architects were universally imbued with the associations of surrounding architecture, and leaned upon them; and their critics leaned upon them too.

Mr. C. H. Brodie said he would like to refer back to Mr. Westlake the question whether he, as an artist, would be satisfied with the effect produced by buildings which so entirely spoke their purpose as some of our railway-stations, for instance, and some of our ships?

Mr. Leonard Stokes said he was not quite sure that he gathered what Mr. Waterhouse intended to say; but if he meant that communication governed architecture, or, rather, if he meant that because it was easy to get from one place to another, therefore the architecture of all districts should be the same in character, he (the speaker) could not agree with him. If they happened to be in a stone district, and were, by means of a railway or a canal, able to bring bricks into the district from a brick district, he thought it would be wrong, from an architectural point of view, to import bricks into the stone district, and build a red-brick mansion, for instance, with terra-cotta dressings. He thought the proper thing to do was to build in stone, provided it was good stone, if they were in a stone district. No doubt Mr. Waterhouse agreed with him, and would not wish to see architecture too much alike all the world over. For his own part, he hoped that such a thing would never be brought about. He felt that one great charm of architecture was that it did adapt itself so admirably to local facts and difficulties: in flint districts they had flint churches, in brick districts brick churches, and in stone districts stone churches. The old architects made good use of their materials, whatever they were, and he thought it would be a great pity if the day arrived when, because one might happen to like terra-cotta, which he (the speaker) did not, that therefore it should be used everywhere, regardless of local circumstances and traditions.

Mr. Waterhouse said he respectfully disagreed with the deductions which Mr. Stokes had drawn from his remarks.

Mr. F. T. W. Goldsmith said he took it to be Mr. Brodie's wish that the question he had put should be conveyed to Mr. Westlake; but as he (the speaker) was in some sort Mr. Westlake's champion in his absence, he wished to say that he did not think that the question quite embodied the idea which Mr. Westlake meant to convey by his paper. He did not think Mr. Westlake meant that they were to design their buildings with an entire absence of decorative detail, but rather that they were to design them in such a way as to indicate clearly their different purposes and the period when they were built. Mr. Stokes had remarked that he would be sorry to see architecture alike all the world over, but the tendency was in that direction. Old customs and influences, which they clung to with affection owing to their associations, were gradually being swept away in the face of what was called modern civilisation. He did not think it was a thing to be regretted if they took it in the proper spirit,—in the spirit which animated the architects of the Renaissance,—for we found that during that period, in France and Italy particularly, many almost identical designs were carried out, executed, however, with different materials and with details differing according to the idiosyncrasies of the architect. He thought that it would be well for them if they were to attempt to carry out the ideas suggested by Mr. Westlake with singleness of purpose, and he must say that he had a great admiration for a building which was built "up to date." A modern city warehouse, for instance, in which economy of space and suitability of plan had been studied, and in which everything, such as matters of lighting, &c., had been carefully thought out, was capable of being made, in a degree, as good and true a piece of architecture as a Gothic cathedral or Renaissance palace. He did not wish to institute comparisons, but he thought that if modern problems were approached in the same consistent spirit that the old men would have approached them, whether in Gothic or Renaissance times, whether in the manner of Pugin or of Sedding, the result could not but be satisfactory. He thought Mr. Westlake was quite right in contending for absolute honesty of purpose in building, and that every new building should be erected, not in the spirit of the thirteenth or any other century, but in the spirit of 1892.

Mr. E. Woodthorpe, M.A., said he quite agreed with Mr. Waterhouse's remarks. In the present age of steam and railways, we were so easily brought into contact with other countries,—facilities for travel were so great,—that they got ideas from all countries in the world, and a great many of them imbibed different ideas, some from the Renaissance, and some from the Gothic. The ancients of the earlier centuries had more or less copied one another. He himself did not believe in originality in architecture at all. He had never seen anything that was quite original,—not even in the work of Sir Christopher Wren, for nearly all the detail of Wren's work was to be found in Italy; as far as he could see, that great man and very successful architect had all the details at his fingers'-ends and in his head, and had been able to put them together in a different way. To take a modern building, he had been to the Law Courts a great many times, but he had not seen any single bit of detail that was absolutely original; and nearly all our finest buildings were more or less imitations of other buildings. He thought that the Victorian age would some centuries hence be recognised as the greatest age of architecture that ever had been. He liked to see the individuality of thought which was shown by our buildings in the streets of the City and in other parts of London. If, however, we went to Paris, we saw very beautiful public buildings, because the Government spent a great deal of money on them, while the Government of this country would not spend money on art of any kind, and had no Department of Architecture. In Paris the Government took the public improvements in hand, and they also helped to educate the architects. The streets of Paris were very much more uniform, and the public places much better laid out, but the streets of Paris were not nearly so pretty or picturesque, and did not possess so much individuality, as the streets of London. He thought the English architecture of the present day was *par excellence* that of the country-house style, initiated by Mr. Norman Shaw. In France, however, the architects did not seem to have any idea of any style adapted to a small country house.

The President, in putting the vote of thanks, said he took it that Mr. Westlake's paper was not meant to have any very distinct end in view. Mr. Westlake had not set himself to teach any very definite lesson. It was, however, a very philosophical consideration of fashion in architecture. One of the influences which guided design in architecture at the present time was fashion, whether they liked to admit it or not; and none of them could escape from fashion. He supposed not even the strongest designer in architecture could get away from the fashion of the moment, although he might guide it and mould it, to a certain extent, to his own ideas. In former ages tradition exercised a much greater influence on design, but since that was dropped, and we began to copy previous styles, more or less, that influence had been lost. Besides the influence of fashion, there now only remained to them the primary influences of materials and situation, and the circumstances generally with which architects had to comply. Mr. Westlake's paper was intended to deal exclusively with the question of fashion in architecture. A good deal of discussion had turned upon some remarks made by Mr. Waterhouse as to the influence of facilities of inter-communication on architecture. He did not understand Mr. Waterhouse to say that such facilities ought not to influence architecture, but that they were bound to influence it, as they influenced language and even the character of men. Mr. Woodthorpe had spoken of the question of originality in architecture. He did not think that Mr. Woodthorpe meant to say that he altogether disliked originality in architecture. He (the speaker) took it that he only meant the originality which was forced and for its own sake.

Mr. Woodthorpe said what he said was that he did not believe that there was anything in architecture perfectly original.

The vote of thanks having been passed, the meeting terminated.

Illustrations.

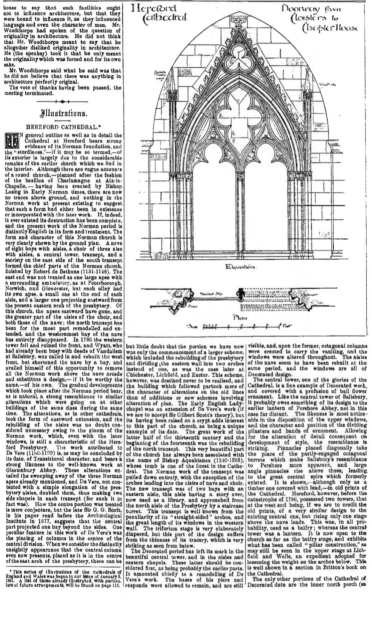

HEREFORD CATHEDRAL.*

IN general outline as well as in detail the Cathedral at Hereford bears strong evidence of its Norman foundation, and the "sturdiness,"—if it may be so termed,—of its exterior is largely due to the considerable remains of the earlier church which we find in the interior. Although there are vague accounts of a round church,—planned after the fashion of the basilica of Charlamagne at Aix-la-Chapelle,—having been erected by Bishop Losing in Early Norman times, there are now no traces above ground, and nothing in the Norman work at present existing to suggest that such a form had either been in existence or incorporated with the later work. If, indeed, it ever existed its destruction has been complete, and the present work of the Norman period is distinctly English in its form and treatment. The form and character of this Norman church is very clearly shown by the ground plan. A nave of eight bays with aisles, a choir of three also with aisles, a central tower, transept, and a sacristy on the east side of the south transept formed the chief parts of the Norman church, finished by Robert de Bethune (1131-1148). The east end was not treated as one large apse with a surrounding ambulatory, as at Peterborough, Norwich, and Gloucester, but each alley had its own apse, a small one at the end of each aisle, and a larger one projecting eastward from the present eastern arch of the presbytery. Of this church, the apses eastward have gone, and the greater part of the aisles of the choir, and both those of the nave; the north transept has been for the most part remodelled and extended, and the westernmost bay of the nave has entirely disappeared. In 1786 the western tower fell and ruined the front, and Wyatt, who had already been busy with deeds of Vandalism at Salisbury, was called in and rebuilt the west front, but shortened the nave by a bay, and availed himself of this opportunity to remove all the Norman work above the nave arcade and substitute a design,—if it be worthy the name,—of his own. The gradual developments which took place after the Norman period bear, as is natural, a strong resemblance to similar alterations which were going on at other buildings of the same class during the same time. The alterations, as in other cathedrals, took the form of eastward extension, and the rebuilding of the aisles was no doubt considered necessary owing to the gloom of the Norman work, which, even with the later windows, is still a characteristic of the Hereford Presbytery. The work attributed to De Vere (1186-1199) is, as may be concluded by its date, of Transitional character, and bears a strong likeness to the well-known work at Glastonbury Abbey. These alterations entailed the sweeping away of the three Norman apses already mentioned, and De Vere, not contented with a simple elongation of the presbytery aisles, doubled them, thus making two side chapels in each transept (for such it in fact was). How the centre portion was treated is mere conjecture, but the late Sir G. G. Scott, in his paper read before the Archæological Institute in 1877, suggests that the central part projected one bay beyond the sides. One peculiar feature in this work of De Vere's was the placing of columns in the centre of the central division. When we consider the distinctly unsightly appearance that the central column even now presents, placed as it is in the centre of the east arch of the presbytery, there can be but little doubt that the portion we have now was only the commencement of a larger scheme, which included the rebuilding of the presbytery and dividing the eastern wall into two arches instead of one, as was the case later at Chichester, Lichfield, and Exeter. This scheme, however, was destined never to be realised, and the building which followed partook more of the character of alterations on the old lines than of additions or new schemes involving alteration of plan. The Early English Lady-chapel was an extension of De Vere's work (if we are to accept Sir Gilbert Scott's theory), but its having been raised on a crypt adds interest to this part of the church, as being a unique example of its date. The great work of the latter half of the thirteenth century and the beginning of the fourteenth was the rebuilding of the north transept. This very beautiful part of the church has always been associated with the name of Bishop Aquablanca (1240-1268), whose tomb is one of the finest in the Cathedral. The Norman work of the transept was pulled down entirely, with the exception of the arches leading into the aisles of nave and choir. The new transept was of two bays with an eastern aisle, this aisle having a story over, now used as a library, and approached from the north aisle of the Presbytery by a staircase turret. This transept is well known from the peculiarity of its "straight-sided" arches, and the great length of its windows in the western wall. The triforium stage is very elaborately diapered, but this part of the design suffers from the thinness of its tracery, which is very striking as seen from below.

The Decorated period has left its mark in the beautiful central tower, and in the aisles and eastern chapels. These latter should be considered first, as being probably the earlier parts. It amounted chiefly to a remodelling of De Vere's work. The bases of his piers and responds were allowed to remain, and are still visible, and, upon the former, octagonal columns were erected to carry the vaulting, and the windows were altered throughout. The aisles of the nave seem to have been rebuilt at the same period, and the windows are all of Decorated design.

The central tower, one of the glories of the Cathedral, is a fine example of Decorated work, and covered with a profusion of ball flower ornament. Like the central tower of Salisbury, it probably owes something of its design to the earlier lantern of Pershore Abbey, not in this case far distant. The likeness is most noticeable in the disposition of the upper windows, and the character and position of the dividing pilasters and bands of ornament. Allowing for the alteration of detail consequent on development of style, the resemblance is striking. Pinnacles placed diagonally take the place of the partly-engaged octagonal turrets which make Salisbury's resemblance to Pershore more apparent, and large angle pinnacles rise above these, leading to the great central spire which formerly existed. It is shown,—although only as a timber one covered with lead,—in old prints of the Cathedral. Hereford, however, before the catastrophe of 1786, possessed two towers, that at the west end being, if we are to credit the old prints, of a very similar design to the existing central one, but rising only one stage above the nave leads. This was, in all probability, used as a belfry; whereas the central tower was a lantern. It is now open to the church as far as the belfry stage, and exhibits what has been called "pillar construction," as may still be seen in the upper stage at Lichfield and Wells, an expedient adopted for lessening the weight on the arches below. This is well shown in a section in Britton's book on the Cathedral.

The only other portions of the Cathedral of Decorated date are the inner north porch (as

* This series of illustrations of the Cathedrals of England and Wales was begun in our issue of January 3, 1891. A list of those already illustrated, with particulars of future arrangements, will be found on page 112.

Cathedrals o

No. 14. HEREFORD,

and Wales.

J. Johnson, A.R.I.B.A

PHOTOLITHO SPRAGUE & Cº 4 & 5 EAST HARDING STREET, FETTER LANE, E.C.

HEREFORD CATHEDRAL
GROUND PLAN.

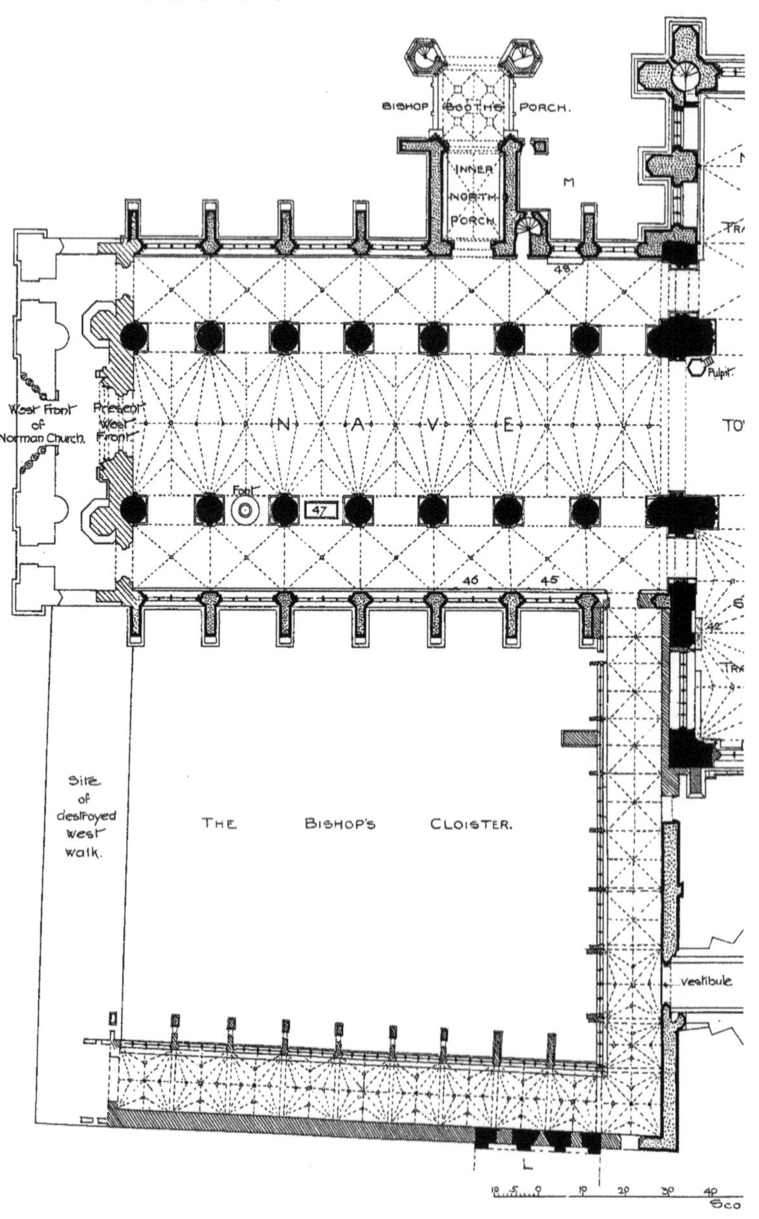

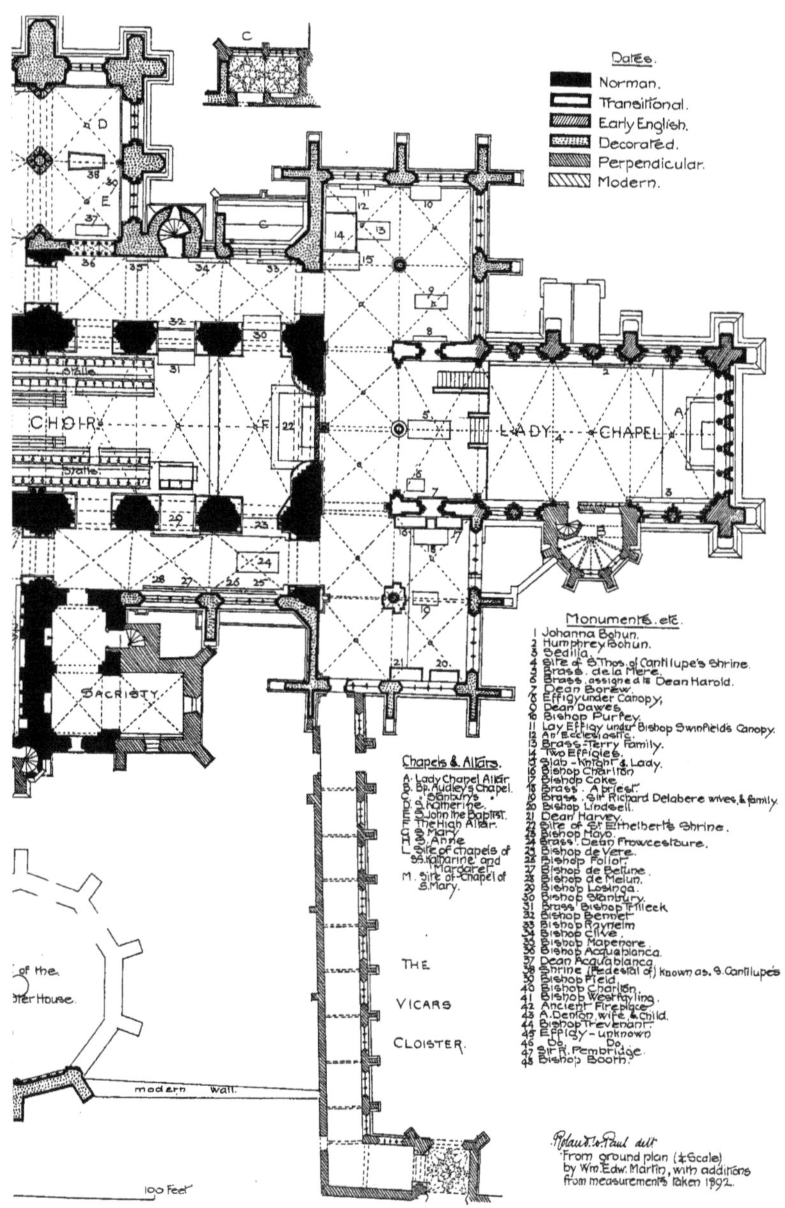
Dates.
Norman.
Transitional.
Early English.
Decorated.
Perpendicular.
Modern.
CHOIR.
Stalls.
LADY CHAPEL
SACRISTY.
Monuments. etc.
1 Johanna Bohun.
2 Humphrey Bohun.
3 Sedilia.
4 Site of S. Thos. of Cantilupe's Shrine.
5 Brass. de la Mere.
6 Brass. assigned to Dean Harold.
7 Dean Borew.
8 Effigy under Canopy.
9 Dean Dawes.
10 Bishop Purfey.
11 Lay Effigy under Bishop Swinfield's Canopy.
12 An Ecclesiastic.
13 Brass - Terry Family.
14 Two Effigies.
15 Slab - Knight & Lady.
16 Bishop Charlton
17 Bishop Coke.
18 Brass. A priest.
19 Brass. Sir Richard Delabere wives & family.
20 Bishop Lindsell.
21 Dean Harvey.
22 Site of St. Ethelbert's Shrine.
23 Bishop Mayo.
24 Brass. Dean Frowcestoure.
25 Bishop de Vere.
26 Bishop Foliot.
27 Bishop de Betune.
28 Bishop de Melun.
29 Bishop Losinga.
30 Bishop Stanbury.
31 Brass. Bishop Trilleck
32 Bishop Bennet
33 Bishop Rayneim
34 Bishop Clive.
35 Bishop Mapenore.
36 Bishop Acquablanca.
37 Dean Acquablanca
38 Shrine (Pedestal of) known as S. Cantilupe's
39 Bishop Field
40 Bishop Charlton.
41 Bishop Westfayling.
42 Ancient Fireplace
43 A. Denton, wife & Child.
44 Bishop Trevenant.
45 Effigy - unknown
46 Do. Do.
47 Sir R. Pembridge.
48 Bishop Booth.
Chapels & Altars.
A. Lady Chapel Altar
B. Bp. Audley's Chapel.
C. " Stanbury's "
D. S. Katherine.
E. S. John the Baptist.
F. The High Altar.
G. S. Mary
H. S. Anne
L. Site of chapels of SS. Katharine and Margaret.
M. Site of Chapel of S. Mary.
THE VICARS CLOISTER.
modern wall.
of the
pter House.
100 Feet
Roland W. Paul delt
From ground plan (¼ Scale) by Wm. Edw. Martin, with additions from measurements taken 1892.
THE VICARS' COLLEGE.

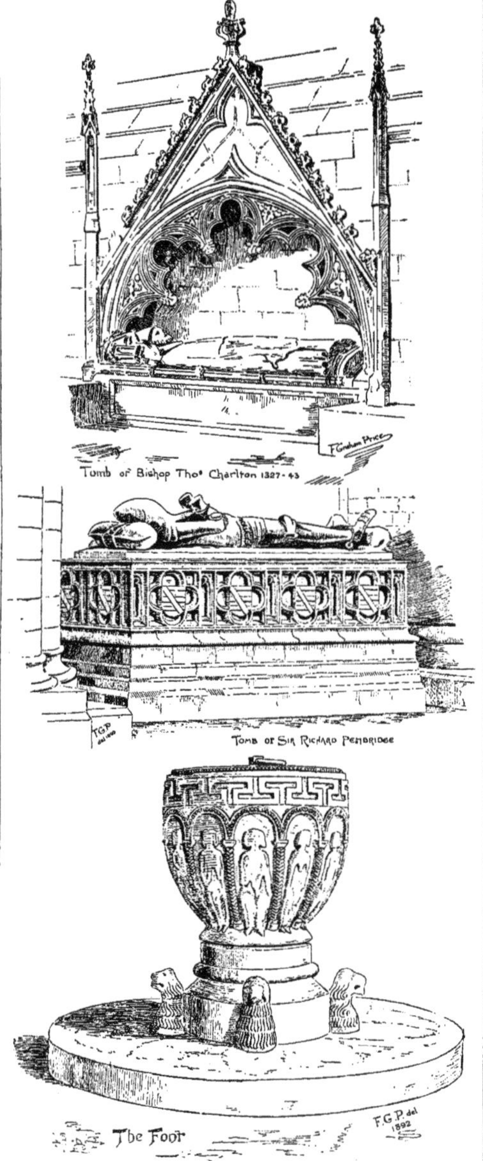

Tomb of Bishop Thos Charlton 1327-43

Tomb of Sir Richard Pembridge

The Font

distinct from Bishop Booth's addition) and what remains of the chapter-house. The north porch, especially in the doorways, has some very delicate detail, and what remains of the chapter-house shows it to have been a very beautiful piece of design. We here give an elevation of the entrance to it from the cloister, from a drawing by Mr. H. D. Walton. The chapter-house itself was, as will be seen by the plan, a decagon, each side (except the one occupied by the entrance) being sub-divided into five panels or seats. Remains of three sides only are left, and even these only as far as the window-sills, and in a very ruined state.

The remaining portions of the Cathedral are additions made in the fifteenth and sixteenth centuries. The Chantry-chapel of Bishop Andley (1492-1525) is placed on the south side of the Lady-chapel, and is in the form of a semi-octagon, two stories in height, with an elaborately panelled screen towards the Lady-chapel. Bishop Booth (1516-1535) lengthened the great north porch, and his design, although later in date, somewhat resembles the porch in the centre of the west front at Peterborough Cathedral. It is a very bold piece of Perpendicular work, the outer arch having richly-panelled spandrels and a large five-light window over. Octagonal turrets flank the entrance on either side, and contain staircases which lead to the room over the porch. An earlier addition of the Perpendicular period is the chapel of Bishop Stanbury (1453-1474), approached from the north aisle of the presbytery, and richly panelled and vaulted. Some additions were made to the Norman sacristy, on the east side of the south transept, in Tudor times, lengthening it a bay eastward, and placing a turret in the angle leading to an upper story. It was used for some time as a chapter-house, but is now a vestry.

The cloisters are on the south side of the nave, and of three walks, two,—the east and south,—remain, and are of late Perpendicular date. Against the south wall, towards its east end, are some remains of two Norman chapels dedicated to SS. Katherine and Margaret. A second cloister, known as the Vicar's Cloister, connects the Vicar's College with the south-east transept. The arrangement here is interesting to compare with Chichester, as showing the probable arrangement there before the destruction of the south walk, and its connection with the cloister of the Vicar's Choral.

It now only remains to notice the objects of interest in the Cathedral. A very large and interesting series of episcopal and military effigies exist here. Amongst the former, the beautiful tomb of Bishop Aquablanca, in the north aisle of the choir, stands first, with its delicate detail and simplicity of design. Near it is the base of the shrine known as the Cantilupe shrine, but thought by some to be the remains of the shrine of St. Ethelbert. It consists of two stages, the lower having a series of cinquefoiled niches and fourteen figures of Templars in chain armour, and the upper an open arcade, the slab inside still bearing the matrix of the brass of an episcopal figure having traces of the arms of the See (those of Cantilupe), and another space formerly occupied by a brass figure of St. Ethelbert, now in the sacristy east of the south transept. The traces of where the shrine fitted in on the top are still visible. The material is a fine sandstone.

Amongst the other monuments worth particular notice are those of Bishop Charlton in the north transept (here illustrated),* and Bishop Stanbury's tomb on the north side of the Presbytery opposite his chapel, with some good heraldic work, one of which bears the arms of the See.

Another good monument is that of Sir Richard Pembridge in the nave,* formerly at the Greyfriar's Monastery, but removed here at the Suppression. He was a Knight of the Garter in the time of Edward III., and died 1375. Hard by is the Norman font,* a circular bowl ornamented with mutilated figures of the twelve Apostles. On the opposite side of the church, near the porch to which he added, is the tomb and effigy of Bishop Booth.

On the north side of the Lady-Chapel is a fine monument hitherto ascribed to Humphrey de Bohun, and so called in the reference on the plan, but said in the guide to the Cathedral, by Rev. Francis T. Havergal, to be the monument of Peter Baron de Grandisson' who died 1358. There is a very fine recumbent effigy, and, on the canopy, statuary representing

* These three illustrations are from drawings by Mr. F. Graham Price.

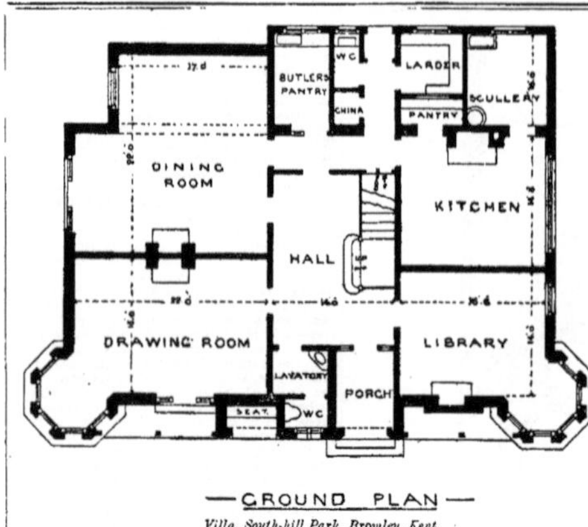

—GROUND PLAN—

Villa, South-hill Park, Bromley, Kent.

the crowning of the Virgin in the centre, with figures of King Ethelbert and St. John the Baptist on one side, and St. Thomas à Beckett and Bishop Thomas de Cantilupe on the other.

The choir-stalls are largely ancient, with good canopy work and quaint misereres. The screen and reredos are, however, modern, the former of metal, from the design of the late Sir G. G. Scott, and the latter one of the additions made during the restoration by the late Mr. Cottingham. Immediately north of the altar is placed the ancient bishop's chair, attributed to the twelfth century. Scattered about the eastern end of the Cathedral are several fragments of stained glass, some of the best, apparently of

Hereford Cathedral - The Arms of the See from Bp: Stanbury's Tomb.

early fourteenth century date, being in one of the lancets on the south side of the Lady-Chapel, west of the Audley Chapel, having a Majesty and the font evangelistic symbols, besides other fragments of interest. There are also some figures of saints in the windows of the eastern transepts, but not of a very high order of merit, although apparently of fourteenth-century date.

The ground-plan of the Cathedral which we publish to-day has been reduced from a very carefully plotted quarter-scale plan by Mr. William E. Martin, and kindly placed at our disposal by Mr. Kempson, of Hereford. To this have been added the cloisters and chapter-house, as they exist at the present time. We have to acknowledge also much help and valuable information received from Mr. St. John Hope and Mr. Gordon Hills. A paper by the latter in the Archæological Association "Proceedings" of 1871 is a very valuable and exhaustive account of the building.

ILLUSTRATIONS OF OLD CHESTER.

I.—FIREPLACE IN BISHOP LLOYD'S PALACE.

This fine apartment, originally forming one of a suite in Bishop Lloyd's Palace, has evidently been approached by a handsome staircase and hall, now removed, except the large window and ornamental plaster ceiling. The room is about 32 ft. by 17 ft. by 13 ft. 6 in. high to the ceiling. The floor is of oak. The panelling is deal painted, which appears to have been general throughout the street. It extends along the side occupied by the fireplace, and about half the opposite side.

In the north wall are three windows, which, being rather small, do not light the room sufficiently; between the windows are panels. The south wall, with the entrance doorway, has been brought forward into the room, reducing its length about 6 ft., and is perfectly plain. The fireplace is entirely of red sandstone, and is surmounted by a broken pediment and phœnix, and is carried above the line of ceiling, which is coved to receive it. The cove is enriched. The plaster ceiling is delicately treated, but has been much injured by repeated coatings of distemper, otherwise the room is in very good preservation.

The adjoining room, with which this communicated, will form the subject of another illustration in the series. T. P. Ivison.

VILLA, SOUTH-HILL PARK, BROMLEY, KENT.

This villa, built as a private residence at Bromley, is faced with red bricks up to first floor, and rough-cast and half-timber work above same. The position is a high one, and the oriels and turrets command good views of the adjoining country. The cost was about 2,200*l*., Messrs. W. A. Williams & Hopton, of Bromley and London, being the architects.

The contractors are Messrs. Baxter, Payne, & Lepper, of Bromley.

HOUSE, No. 79, FORE-STREET, REDRUTH, CORNWALL.

The rebuilding of these premises has recently been completed, local stone being used for the walling, with Portland stone dressings, cornices, strings, &c. The works have been carried out by Mr. Arthur Carkeek, of Redruth, from the designs and under the supervision of Mr. Hubert A. Gregg, A.R.I.B.A., of London.

The City Architectship, Aberdeen.—Baillie Rust will, it is understood, at once intimate his resignation as a member of the Town Council in order to become a candidate for the City Architectship. Messrs. Matthews & Mackenzie, architects, are also candidates for the office.—*Aberdeen Free Press.*

COMPETITIONS.

Truants' Schools, Lichfield.—In t competition for the Midland Truants' Schoo to be erected at Lichfield, the plans sent in Mr. R. Stevenson, Burton-on-Trent, under mot of "Adaptability with Economy," have be accepted, and he has been appointed to ca out the work. Mr. E. R. Robson was the assess in the competition.

Chacewater Church Restoration.—T *Cornwall Gazette* says that plans for t restoration of Chacewater Church have be submitted by six architects. These are n under the consideration of Prebenda Hingeston-Randolph, who has kindly und taken to act as assessor. Should his opini confirm the selection made by the committ it is hoped that the work will at once be op to tender, and the building in a contracto hands in the early spring. So far 1,100*l.* h been contributed, but it is to be hoped that t additional sum required will be subscrib before the completion of the work.

ARCHITECTURAL SOCIETIES.

Edinburgh Architectural Associatio —A meeting of this Association was held the 28th ult., Mr. John Kinross, the President, the chair. A letter was read from the Fi Commissioner of Works regarding the conditi of Linlithgow Palace, and notice was given the following motion, to be submitted to t next meeting of the Association:—"That th Association, in acknowledging the commu cation from the First Commissioner of H Majesty's Works of date December 29 las intimating that he had caused a sum of 25 to be provided in the estimate of the Depa ment for the ensuing year 'in order to adm of the more urgent and special repairs of t Palace of Linlithgow being carried out an early date,' begs to thank the Fi Commissioner for having taken action in t matter, and to express its satisfaction that t immediate necessity for certain repairs has th been recognised; but, looking to the exception importance of the Palace in regard both to t history and architecture of Scotland, the As ciation feels that the thorough repair of t entire fabric is the only proper course, and b respectfully to represent that such thoron repair can only be properly carried out by placing the burnt timbers and flooring, reglazi the windows, and covering the whole with a ro so that the walls may be firmly tied togeth and the whole rendered wind and water tigh The meeting then proceeded to consider the f lowing motion, moved by Mr. G. S. Aitken "That this Association, in view of the rec architectural changes made in the appro to the Register House, is of opinion that Wellington statue in front thereof should removed, and that for the following reaso viz.:—(1) It is an obstruction to the thoron fare; (2) it is out of scale with Adam's building; (3) it is incongruous with its s roundings; (4) its merits as a work of art not advantageously displayed in its pres position." After some discussion, the mat was remitted to the Council of the Associat for further consideration.—Mr. Hippolyte Blanc then read an interesting paper "Heriot's Hospital and Cotemporary Work."

Glasgow Architectural Association The fifth lecture of the session was delive by Mr. James Lindsay, A.R.I.B.A., on the 2 ult., his subject being "Approximate E mating." The President, Mr. Wm. J. Anders occupied the chair. The lecturer's endeav was to give some helpful hints to archite called on to approximately state the cost some building without awaiting contract exact estimates. The capabilities of the cub system were discussed. If from some exist building of a similar character to the one posed is obtained its price per cubic foot, t applied to the bulk, as found from plans of other contemplated, ought to approxim pretty nearly to its cost. The difficulty was find the nearest precedent, and even w found error was made when simple contract of bulk was expected proportionately to red the expense. The features in which lie chief expense must be reduced rather than mere walling, roofing, and flooring. Anot system,—superficial measurement,—was scribed, with illustrations on the blackbo At the close of the lecture a discussion lowed, and the customary thanks were vote Mr. Lindsay.

LEEDS AND YORKSHIRE ARCHITECTURAL SOCIETY.—At a meeting of the Leeds and Yorkshire Architectural Society on Monday night, Mr. F. W. Bedford read a paper entitled "Some Account of the Arts in Southern Italy and Sicily." Mr. W. H. Thorp, President of the Society, introduced Mr. Bedford, who, he explained, had spent a considerable time studying the architecture of Spain, Southern Italy, and Sicily. Mr. Bedford illustrated his lecture with photographic views thrown upon a screen, and the audience were much interested, especially in the very complete Pompeiian series which the lecturer possesses.

THE SOCIETY OF ENGINEERS.

THE first ordinary meeting of the Society of Engineers for the present year was held on Monday evening last, at the Town Hall, Westminster. Mr. W. N. Colam, the President for 1891, first occupied the chair, and presented the premiums of books awarded for papers read during his year of office, viz.:—The "President's Premium" to Mr. G. M. Lawford for his paper on "The Drainage of Town Houses." The "Bessemer Premium" to Mr. J. H. Paul for his paper on "Corrosion in Steam-Boilers." A "Society's Premium" to Mr. John Kerr for his paper on "Portable and Pioneer Railways."

Mr. Colam introduced the President for the present year, Mr. Joseph William Wilson, jun., to the meeting, and retired from the chair, receiving a hearty and unanimous vote of thanks for his services during the past year.

Mr. Wilson then took the chair, and upon his proposition, seconded by Mr. Colam, a vote of condolence with the Queen and the Prince and Princess of Wales in their recent bereavement was agreed to.

Mr. Wilson then proceeded to deliver his inaugural address. After returning thanks to the members for electing him as their President, and calling upon them for their cooperation in advancing the growing prosperity of the Society, he reviewed the work done under its auspices during the past year, during which time the number of members of all classes had increased more than 9 per cent.; Sir George Barclay Bruce, Past President of the Institute of Civil Engineers, having been elected to the vacancy in the roll of Honorary Members occasioned by the lamented death of Earl Granville. The chief points of interest in the papers read and discussed during the year were then touched upon, and reference was made to the professional visits undertaken during the summer, which included those to the Ice Works of the Linde British Refrigeration Company, at Shadwell; the City and South London Electric Railway Company's Stockwell Depôt; the Royal Engineers School of Military Engineering, at Chatham; the Shortlands and Nunhead Railway Works; and the Crystal Palace Gas Company's Works at Lower Sydenham. The President then referred to the growth of the population of the world and the corresponding development of engineering enterprise; and to the present unsatisfactory condition of the London sewage question, in reference to which he had received from Sir Robert Rawlinson an epitome of his solution of the sewage disposal as being "Out of the River Thames and into the Sea over Maplin Sands." The work of the recent International Congress of Hygiene and Demography, especially in reference to the section of "Engineering in relation to Hygiene" was touched upon, and it was felt that, although much had been done, much still remained to be accomplished in relation to not only sewerage disposal, but also the adequate supply of water to, and the prevention of smoke in, London. The President then enumerated the proposed railways in and around London; and, pointing out the great need that existed for these and other methods of relieving the overgrown street traffic, urged the necessity for a conference of competent authorities in order to decide upon some definite scheme of gradual re-organisation for existing London, with a due regard to its systematic outward development. He then dealt with increasing railway speeds and the connexion of the question with the recent Norwood Bridge accident, and the consequent re-construction of many railway bridges on the lines throughout the country; and he advocated a more general adoption of the plan utilised on the Forth Bridge of laying the rails in iron troughs so as to avoid the lamentable accidents at present produced by a train leaving the metals when crossing a bridge and immediately crashing through the floor. The rapid increase in third-class passengers, and the gradual disappearance of second-class carriages, and the approaching abandonment of the remainder of the broad-gauge system were touched upon, and Mr. Wilson proceeded to consider the important engineering development of subaqueous tunnelling. Tunnels had already been successfully carried beneath the St. Clair River in America, and the Severn and Mersey Rivers in England, and the Blackwall Tunnel beneath the Thames was about to be commenced; besides which there were many such works proposed in various parts of the world; the most important schemes being for tunnels beneath the sea, of which that designed by Sir Douglas Fox for connecting Prince Edward's Island with New Brunswick was likely to be the first actually constructed; and he proceeded to give particulars of this, with approximate estimates for the various diameters designed for alternative conditions of traffic. Extracts from the latest reports of Sir John Fowler and Sir Benjamin Baker upon the maintenance and present satisfactory condition of the Forth Bridge were given, and allusion was made to the approaching completion of the Manchester Ship Canal, the Tower Bridge, and the Liverpool Overhead Railway, and the commencement of the Dover Harbour Completion Works, and the Harbour and Improvement Works at Ramsgate; and, after referring to the Crystal Palace Electrical Exhibition, which promised to outshine all previous Exhibitions, and where the development of electrical machinery was so prominent a feature, the President concluded by dealing with the question of engineering education, with which he had been intimately associated during the last twenty years; emphasising the fact that the true solution of the question is to be found only in a judicious and simultaneous blending of theory and practice, under the highest *personal* supervision; and that success would be ensured to the engineer if he would but "deserve it" by an honest and unwearied application of all his energies of mind and body to the requirements of his great profession throughout his career.

THE LONDON COUNTY COUNCIL.

THE usual weekly meeting of the London County Council was held on Tuesday last, the Chairman, Sir John Lubbock, presiding. The greater part of the sitting was taken up by a discussion on the incidence of local taxation.

Appointment of an Assistant Medical Officer of Health.—On the recommendation of the General Purposes Committee, Dr. W. H. Hamer was appointed Assistant Medical Officer of Health, at the commencing salary of 500*l*. a year, rising to 600*l*.

The Valuation of Land.—The Special Committee on the Valuation of Land presented a report recommending the appointment of a central assessment committee under the direction of the County Council, to have the same powers as the surveyor of taxes under the Act of 1869, together with other powers giving them authority to secure through the local assessment committees uniformity of assessment throughout the metropolis, and the separate assessment of all land in the county, irrespective of buildings and improvements, and authorised to appoint an assessment clerk to act as their agent. The Committee believed that even under existing Acts all land ought to be rated on its value, and recognised the fact that land not yet built upon had not in practice been rated according to its value, and they proposed that legal advice should be taken as to whether such practices were legal, and could only be altered by new legislation. In the event of counsel advising that such legislation was required, the Committee recommended that application should be made to Parliament to obtain powers authorising rating authorities and assessment committees to calculate for rating purposes, not only the annual rent, but also the capital value of land, and to assess the property either on the rent "which a tenant might reasonably be expected to pay," or on a statutory percentage of the capital value. The Committee further recommended that this report should be referred to the Parliamentary Committee with instructions to take measures for obtaining from Parliament during the present Session such powers as might be required to carry out the foregoing recommendations.

The recommendations were adopted.

Enlargement of Banstead Asylum.—On the recommendation of the Asylums Committee, it was resolved to provide further infirmary accommodation at Banstead Asylum, at an estimated cost of 14,000*l*., from plans prepared by Mr. G. T. Hine, the architect of the Claybury Asylum, now building.

Regulations for Ensuring the Public Safety in Theatres.—The Theatres and Music-halls Committee brought up a series of regulations for ensuring the safety of visitors to theatres, music-halls, &c. The consideration of the subject was postponed for a week, and,

After transacting other business, the Council adjourned.

ARCHÆOLOGICAL SOCIETIES.

LANCASHIRE AND CHESHIRE ANTIQUARIAN SOCIETY.—The annual meeting of the Lancashire and Cheshire Antiquarian Society was held on the 29th ult. in Chetham's College, Manchester, presided over by W. E. A. Axon. Mr. W. Harrison (in the absence of the hon. secretary, Mr. G. C. Yates, F.S.A.) read the annual report, which stated that the steady growth in the number of members maintained until last year had been arrested, but in other respects the success which had attended previous years had continued. The total number of members now was 337—283 ordinary, 49 life, and 5 honorary members. The Duke of Devonshire was unanimously elected President of the Society, and Mr. T. Letherbrow and Mr. G. C. Yates were re-elected treasurer and secretary respectively.

LEICESTER ARCHITECTURAL AND ARCHÆOLOGICAL SOCIETY.—The annual meeting of this Society was held on the 25th ult. Mr. W. J. Freer, hon. sec., read the thirty-seventh annual report, which mentioned the fact that seventeen new members had been elected.

Books.

The Maintenance of Macadamised Roads. THOMAS CODRINGTON. Second Edition. London: Spon, 125, Strand.

AS a reliable handbook Mr. Codrington's "Maintenance of Macadamised Roads" has been universally recognised since its publication twelve years ago. The exhaustion of that edition has consequently produced a second, for which we have been waiting with some degree of expectation. In the meantime Mr. Codrington, as one of the Engineering Inspectors of the Local Government Board, made a "Report on Road Maintenance" to that Board, which was published "By Authority," and sold to the public in the form of a pamphlet at the time of the birth of the first County Councils. This second edition incorporates in some measure the contents of that pamphlet, which brought road-matters a little more up to date, but incorporates little else. What the cause for this may be we know not, but it cannot be otherwise than a regrettable circumstance that the issue of a new edition of this deservedly popular work was not made the occasion for introducing much that would have added to it value.

It may be interesting to know that the cantonniers,—the men who are charged with the manual labour connected with the maintenance of the roads in the cantons of France,—wear blue jackets and leather hats, "round which shall be a band of copper, 0·28 in. long and 0·555 in. broad;" that their punishment for a first offence of absence is the loss of three-days' pay; for the second similar offence, a loss of six days' pay, and for the third offence dismissal; that from May 1 to September 1 they *begin work at 5 a.m. and cease at 7 p.m.*; and that they have to plant a staff on the roadside within a short distance of where they are working, so that a man can be found in case he has gone for a doze into a shady and adjacent wood. All this, and more, is included in the "Regulations for Cantonniers," which forms Appendix I. of the volume under notice. A perusal of those "Regulations" may afford some faint guide for a frame on which to weave a code of laws for roadmen; but what it chiefly does is to furnish grounds for doubt whether such stringent semi-military regulations would be acceptable to, or accepted by, the class of man who it is understood is to be the future model roadman of this country. Nevertheless, there is something to note in them, and it was well to append them to the work. The magnitude of the subject, from a financial point of view may be appreciated from the following statement:—

"The annual taxation returns now show a total expenditure in England and Wales of upwards of 5,500,000*l.* a year on highways, street improvements, and turnpike roads. Of this amount, 2,000,000*l.* is expended by highway authorities in rural districts, almost entirely on macadamised roads. The other 3,500,000*l.* is expended in the metropolis and by urban sanitary authorities."

A very sensible proportion of this three-and-a-quarter millions is, of course, also expended on macadamised streets in the towns and cities of the country. Why, in treating of the value of a binding material, a quotation from Mr. Deacon's paper in the Proceedings of the Institute of Civil Engineers has been placed under the head of rolling instead of under that of binding, it is not easy to discern, nor why it is there alluded to as a *blinding* instead of a binding for macadam.

We are glad to see a little,—though a very little,—more information about the machine tests adopted in France by the road authorities, and hope that the time may not be far distant when the Local Government Board, or the County Councils' Association, or some large Municipal or County Council, whose expenditure on these matters is very considerable, will take up this branch of the subject, purchase or construct machines, either on the French or any other suitable designs, and carry out tests, which are bound to be of very great assistance to them.

To this part of the work a little more care in the revision of proof would have prevented the publication of such peculiar formulæ as:—"Grammes of detritus : 20 = 20 : coefficient, and 3,000 : crushing weight per square centimètre = 20 : coefficient."

The author ought to have been aware that the stone of Mount Sorrel is not a hard trap. An error of this kind is important, as it much disturbs the value of the subsequent information relating to the cost of crushing by machinery, the details of cost given being naturally assumed by a reader to be those for breaking a hard trap, which is not the case. We are aware that quarry owners might reasonably object to furnishing for publication the details of cost of the operations which go on in their respective quarries, but the way in which this branch of chapter iii., viz., "Stone-breaking by Machinery," has been treated by the author is altogether inadequate to its importance; in a great measure it is a piece of ancient history.

The fact of the "Cost of Road Material" having been condensed into a page and a half, as in the first edition, will also give a correct notion of the adequacy of treatment of that part of the subject.

There are some useful observations on the merits of the artificial application of water to roads, and as this matter is one on which the author has on several occasions had to adjudicate as an arbitrator, it is well to know his published opinion, as follows:—

"For the sake of the road itself, a road, except one of a silicious nature, seldom requires watering in this country." The contention of urban surveyors on this point of dispute between them and county surveyors would not, therefore, be deemed by him to be of great weight.

A small amount of additional information is given respecting the cost of road maintenance in the metropolis, and a good deal more about the cost of roads elsewhere, and this chapter is on the whole more complete and better revised than most other portions.

The section which relates especially to road management,—*i.e.*, the *systems* of road management,—has also received beneficial additions, and we fully endorse the strictures passed on contracting for road management. With a good surveyor,—*i.e.*, a man who knows and does his work and is honest,—no contract for maintenance can be necessary, nor can a contract in such a case be other than a discreditable extravagance.

In spite of the deficiencies and blemishes to which we have been compelled to draw attention, this is a work far ahead of any other of its kind. It will still probably hold its own as the best handbook on the subject.

The Art and Craft of Cabinet-making. By David Denning. London: Whittaker & Co.

This useful work forms one of Messrs. Whittaker's series of practical manuals on the arts, sciences, manufactures, and industries, and the author states in his preface that his intention has been to supply "amateurs and young professional cabinet-makers with a reliable guide to the construction of cabinet-making." This the author may be said to have done in a very clear and concise manner, and the chapters dealing with the craftsmanship of his subject may be praised without reservation. The title is a taking one, as at the present time the connexion between artists and craftsmen is receiving the attention of the former in the attempt to make the crafts fine arts. This book may be confidently recommended to the furniture-building architects of the day. The descriptions of the use of tools, the materials, and the methods of workshop practice are admirably explained, and the knowledge of these principles of handicraft cannot fail to assist these architects in their ardent wooing of the craftsman. It cannot be claimed, however, that Mr. Denning's book will throw much light upon the methods of designing really (not so-called) artistic furniture; for the promise which the title of the book holds out is not redeemed in the text. The book contains many illustrations of articles of furniture, most of which seem to be reminiscences of Tottenham-court-road. The principles of good design do not appear to have been grasped by the author, and many of his remarks in this direction might easily be misleading. The perusal of Mr. Denning's book emphasises the gulf existing now-a-days between the designer and the craftsman who executes the work, each failing at times to comprehend the difficulties arising in the province of the other, and the question naturally arises as to whether it is possible, with our existing institutions and their developments, that the good old days shall return, and the craftsman be an artist who is equally alive to beauty of form and colour, and the precision of craftmanship necessary for its execution.

The London Householder's Chart: Public Health Act, 1891. By T. Miller Maguire, LL.D., Barrister-at-Law. London: Simpkin Marshall & Co.

This is little more than a pamphlet in size, but may be a very useful one to many householders. It contains a brief statement as to the working of the Public Health Act as it will affect householders, directing them what to do and to whom to apply in specified cases, and to whom and to what extent they are liable for infringements of the Act &c. There is a list also of the districts in which the Vestry is the Sanitary Authority, and those in which the District Board is the Sanitary Authority; an existing irregularity of administration which is a puzzle to many. It will be found a very useful little manual of facts put into a small compass.

The Metropolitan and Provincial Local Government Annual and Diary, 1892. London: S. Edgcumbe-Rogers, Dorset House, Salisbury-square, E.C.

This is the first appearance of what is likely to prove an exceedingly useful and convenient publication. The object of the editor, Mr. Edgcumbe-Rogers, as he tells us in the preface, has been to give within the two covers of this book (the price of which is 1s. 6d.) information "which previously could only be obtained by buying some four or five different volumes ranging in price from 2s. to 15s., at a total cost of £2." The first in order of the many useful features of this diary is "The Local Government Remembrancer," which sets forth the duties to be discharged by public bodies and officials in each month of the year. Then follows a list of the chief officials of the Local Government Board, and this, in turn, is succeeded by lists of the members and chief officers of the London County Council, the Metropolitan Asylums Board, the School Board for London, and the Corporation of London; then comes a list of the various District Boards of Works and Vestries, with the names of their officers, and a variety of other information. The country section is commenced by a list of associations connected with local government, with their chief officers. Then follow the Municipal Corporations, with the names of the new Mayors, the Town Clerks, and Surveyors. The County Councils, with the names and addresses of the Clerks and Surveyors, and the country Unions, with the names and addresses of Clerks and the Masters, are given in a clear form. Everything appears to be up to date. Among the forty-one distinct features of the book are to be found information about the City Companies, the District Surveyors, burial boards, cemeteries, coroners, sick asylums, county-courts, police-courts, baths and washhouses, public libraries, gas, water, and electric light companies; public parks, and port sanitary authorities. The book, which includes a diary of three days to the page, may be strongly commended to the attention of all who are engaged in the work of local government, and will be especially useful to the intelligent ratepayer.

Correspondence.

To the Editor of The Builder.

THE JEW'S HOUSE, LINCOLN.

Sir,—The reason why the "Jew's House" at Lincoln, of which you have recently given an illustration from Mr. Powell's drawing (January 9), is so called, is simply because it was the house of a Jew. Lincoln has two such houses, of nearly the same date, *i.e.*, about the middle of the twelfth century. That represented in Mr. Powell's drawing is the more perfect, but the other is the more historically interesting. It was the home of "Aaron the Jew," the prototype of the Isaac of York of Sir Walter Scott's "Ivanhoe," one of the chief, if not the very chief, of the money-lenders of Henry II.'s time, whose name is of very frequent occurrence in the legal documents of the period. The other house (that of your drawing) which stands some way further down the almost precipitous "Steep-hill," on the opposite side of the way, though built a hundred years before her time, was in the latter part of the thirteenth century the property of a Jewess named Belaset [Belle assez?], of Wallingford. This lady in 1271, betrothed her daughter Judith to Aaron, the son of Benjamin, endowing the young pair with twenty marks sterling, and a copy of the Hebrew Bible, written on calf-skin. The marriage took place four years later, in 1275, and the wedding-feast, of which we have a record, may probably have been held in this very house. Fifteen years later, in 1290, the same year in which the Jews were expelled from England, Belaset was hanged on the charge of clipping the King's coin. Belaset's messuage having escheated to the crown, was granted to Walter le Fevre of Folletby, from whom it passed by gift to Canon William de Thornton, Prebendary of Stow Longa, and was presented by him to the Dean and Chapter. On the surrender of the Chapter Estates to the Ecclesiastical Commissioners, the Jew's House became the property of that body. Applications have been recently made to the Commissioners to redress some of the damage caused by the neglect and wanton mischief of former years, and maintain so precious a relic of the Domestic Architecture of our forefathers in its integrity, but they have obtained little attention. The house is thus described by Mr. Hudson Turner ("Domestic Architecture in England," vol. i., p. 7):—"A building at Lincoln, known as the Jew's House, is a fine specimen of the period. The principal dwelling-room is on the first floor, where there is a fireplace on the side towards the street. The chimney is corbelled out over the door, the lower part with the corbels forming an arched canopy over the doorway, which is richly ornamented." He adds: "There is another house in the same street," that known as the house of Aaron the Jew, "of equal antiquity, but in a less perfect state." Both houses are described more fully on pp. 41, 42. Mr. H. Turner writes of Belaset's House, "it is small, and seems to have consisted of two rooms only, one on the ground floor, and one above" (not quite accurate: there was a back room as well as front room). "These may, however, have been originally divided by partitions." His concluding remark that "the interior has entirely lost all original character," I am happy to say, is not strictly accurate. In the northern division of the house, now occupied as a butcher's shop, in both stories a perfectly plain round-headed Norman archway, tall for its width, forms the communication between the front and back rooms, and in the north wall of the lower room is a broad, shallow Norman recess. From all of these the wall-paper and plaster by which they were obscured was stripped off, and the stonework cleaned and left bare on a recent change of tenant. Of Aaron's House Mr. Turner says:—"The same arrangement of the arch of the doorway carrying the fireplace is found here also. The Norman ornamented string, on a level with the floor, may be traced along two sides of this house, which stands at a corner, and some windows" (only one now) "may be distinguished, but less perfect than those of the first house." I may add that a blacklead pencil drawing of this house by Mr. J. C. Buckler, executed in the exquisitely-delicate style in vogue seventy or eighty years back,—now, to my regret, quite out of fashion,—is to be found in the collections of the British Museum, in a volume containing drawings of the monumental slabs ejected from Lincoln Minster at the time of the disastrous repaving at the close of the last century and placed in the cloisters. This drawing, which in undated, depicts the house in a much more perfect state than now, with two of its Transition Norman windows on the south front in a perfect state. At a repair of the house in 1878 a similar window was discovered on the west face, and carefully restored by the Minster masons under the direction of the clerk of the works.

It is noticeable that the few examples of town houses of the twelfth century remaining in this country are almost without exception traditionally assigned to members of the Jewish community. Besides the two at Lincoln there is a very remarkable Jew's house at Bury St. Edmund's, known as "Moyses' (the Vulgate spelling of Moses) Hall," of statelier character than its fellows. The reason is that when houses in towns were, as a rule, constructed of wood and plaster, the Jews built theirs of stone as a security for their persons and their property, especially their bags and chests of coin, from the assaults and plunder to which they were continually exposed. "It is certain," writes Mr. Turner, "that in all early deeds relative to the transfer of tenements once held by Jews, those tenements are usually described as built of stone" (p. 47). "Examples, these," says Mr. Freeman, "of the stately houses of these favoured chattels of the King to which men pointed with envy as rivalling the King's own palaces" ("Towns and Districts," p. 215).

EDMUND VENABLES.

The Precentory, Lincoln,
January 26, 1892.

CONCRETE FOR ARTISANS' DWELLINGS.

SIR,—I am very much obliged by your insertion of my inquiry as to laying flooring on concrete, and to those who gave the valuable suggestions in reply.

The great importance at the present time of the question of housing the labouring classes in cities will, I trust, be a sufficient excuse for troubling you with a question or two more, which may elicit from some of your readers their experiences for the benefit of those who, like the writer, are endeavouring to solve the question of economical, and yet substantial, labourers' tenements in their own localities.

It is proposed to replace joists on upper stories by slabs of coke breeze concrete, the walls being levelled off for each story at underside of floor concrete, which would be then laid on the walls through their full thickness, and the walls of next story carried up from top surfaces of the slabs. On these slabs the flooring would be nailed.

1st. Should the breeze be used just as it is got from the gas-works, or is it necessary to remove any of the very fine part of it, or to add any other material to it, and in what proportions should it be mixed with Portland cement for this particular purpose?

2nd. What is the largest size of floor that is shown by *practical* experience to be safe without any support, except on the walls as above described, and using slabs of 5 in. or 6 in. thick?

3rd. If breeze is used for the walls, which would vary from 5 in. to 9 in. thick, would it be necessary to add any other material? and what proportion of cement should be used for wall work?

SURVEYOR.

FLOORING-BOARDS ON CONCRETE.

SIR,—I had some 1 in. yellow deal flooring nailed to 2 in. of coke breeze concrete, on a bed of brick rubbish and Portland cement concrete (6 to 1) five years ago. The whole of the concrete was left for a month to get thoroughly dry before the floor boards were nailed down. I saw this flooring about a month ago. It has stood perfectly, and is as solid to walk upon as on the day it was laid. The boards were not, and ought not to be, tongued.

C. F. M.

SIR,—I would advise "Surveyor" not to lay tongued-wood floor direct on to flat surface, either of breeze or other concrete, for the following reasons: If nailed to the concrete without intervening air space, dry-rot is almost sure to follow; and if nailed to fillets embedded in the ordinary ballast concrete without intervening space, the same result will ensue.

Providing "Surveyor" wishes to do without wood fillets, sleepers can be formed of breeze concrete, keeping the surface not less than 1 in. above the general surface of concrete floor, and making provision for the admission and circulation of air.

In no case should floor-boards be "cut down" directly the concrete-floors are laid, and nailed down later on, as suggested by "Another Surveyor," as the boards will become saturated on the underside by the moisture emitted from the concrete during the process of drying, and when nailed down considerable shrinkage will ensue.

The most satisfactory results will be gained by allowing the concrete to dry thoroughly, or as much as possible, before the boards are laid.

"Another Surveyor" suggests that he is not sure "that coke-breeze is a safe material to place even near flues, that it is a very perfect conductor of heat, and that the heat will accumulate in it sufficiently to char any wooden skirting," which appears to me to be entirely contrary to facts.

I have used breeze concrete most extensively for years, and have put it to the severest tests in every way, and found it both a non-conductor and non-absorbent of heat, and most fire-resisting and incombustible,—in fact, much more so than ordinary ballast concrete, as if heat is applied to the latter the "aggregate" will immediately crack and fly to pieces.

I have no doubt "Another Surveyor" is cognisant of the use of "Wright's" fireproof bricks for fixing wood skirtings, &c., round fire-flues and similar situations, which have had the test of at least ten years without causing any catastrophe, and from the facts mentioned above there is no possibility of any heat from the grates or stoves being communicated to the concrete if carried into the fireplaces sufficiently to char any woodwork placed in juxtaposition.

It is admitted that breeze concrete is lighter than ballast concrete by about 25 per cent., but there is no ordinary concrete made that is water-tight, or will prevent the percolation of water through it.

The experience of "Another Surveyor" in regard to coke-breeze concrete scaling off from below the flanges of the iron joists is unfortunate, and I would suggest that, instead of using coke as an aggregate, he should use coke-breeze mixed with the usual proportion of Portland cement, and keep the soffit of the concrete at least an inch below soffit of joist; he will then find the soffit of the concrete throughout perfectly sound, which can be plastered on direct, and be thorough good work without the needless expense of battens and lathing.

I have encased girders up to 26 in. wide in a similar way with same satisfactory results.

"EXPERIENCE."

*** "Experience" is a correspondent who has a right to the signature, but we may point out that the "experience" of others is tending to show that boards may be laid on concrete with proper care, without dry-rot supervening (see as one example the letter of "C. F. M." above); and the plan of laying the boards with a space between them and the concrete, supposed to be necessary, keeps up that system of inaccessible hollows in house-building, which it is desirable on sanitary grounds to get rid of entirely.—ED.

MONUMENTS TO ARCHITECTS.

SIR,—May I, with your kind indulgence, ask through your columns whether any of your readers are aware of the names of any English architects, besides Sir Charles Barry, G. E. Street, and Professor Cockerell, who have had statues or sculptured memorials, funerary or otherwise, erected in their honour?

O. F.

BERLIN WATERWORKS.

SIR,—I venture to bring to your notice an error in your last week's "Notes." You refer to Herr Oesten as "the engineer" of the Berlin waterworks. The engineer, who has held this position ever since the waterworks were built, is Mr. Henry Gill, M.Inst.C.E., an account of whose paper on "Water-meters," read at the Institution of Civil Engineers, a few weeks ago, was published in your columns. Herr Oesten only holds the position of chief assistant-engineer. I trust you will see your way to correcting your slip of last week.

GEORGE H. GILL.

OLD TOBACCO-PIPES.—In digging ground for the foundations of the Patent Office extension buildings, an unusually large number of seventeenth-century tobacco-pipes have been found. They lay, all together, about 14 ft. deep in what had been the garden of a house in Took's-court, and close to the southern wall of the Staple Inn block, which was re-built in 1699, as the date over its doorway testifies. They are made of fine white clay, with straight stems, in some cases 12 in. long; a few are glazed, and have initial letters on the wide foot under the bowl. Whilst after the customary type of a thick stem and a deep bowl, not much larger than the stem, the pipes have bowls of varying outline, many of them, indeed, showing well-moulded shapes. Out of those we have seen a good collection could be made of these humble specimens of plastic art. In the basement of the house in Took's-court was found the ornamented leaden cistern, bearing date "1675," to which we recently referred (see the *Builder*, vol. lxi., fol. 161).

The Student's Column.

WARMING BUILDINGS BY HOT WATER.

VI.

AIR IN PIPES (*concluded*). WATER SUPPLY. (HORTICULTURAL WORKS)

AIR tubes can be made of almost any material; copper tube, composition tube, or iron pipe. The former is very usually adopted when convenient, as it does not perish readily, and its rigid nature prevents injury by blows, which the compo pipe could not withstand. Composition pipe is, however, used to a considerable extent, owing to its cheapness, the easier way in which it can be worked (bent, &c.), and it can be more easily obtained if the material for the air-tube has to be purchased in the country. Iron pipe is sometimes used, but it entails more labour, cutting and screwing, is more clumsy looking, and no more effective than copper.

The size for the tube is small, varying from ¼ in. to ½ in., according to the engineer's ideas or requirements. A very small pipe is sufficient, in fact, a pin-hole would permit of the air escaping, but a very small hole or tube bears a risk of becoming stopped. There is one essential feature to be observed when putting up air-tubes, which is that they must not on any account be dipped anywhere in their course. That is, from the point where they are connected to the hot-water pipe upwards, they must be carried in an ascending direction. If it is necessary to carry the pipe horizontally, then it is permissible, although it would be better if it could be given an ascending direction, however slight, but on no account must the pipe descend anywhere, or its purpose will not be fulfilled.

Supposing an air-pipe was erected, as fig. 21. This would have a dip or descent in the pipe

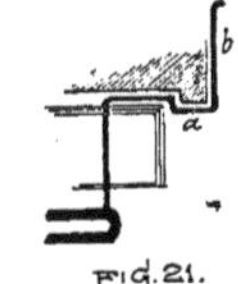

FIG. 21.

where marked *a*. Now, this dip would not be found objectionable when first charging and testing the apparatus, but when the fire had been alight some time the little vapour that escapes by this pipe would cause a collection of water to occur at *a*, with no means of removing it. This collection of water, when once formed, would afterwards prevent the escape of air that is perpetually being given off by the water as it changes temperature, and the result would be the volume of air collected becoming great enough to stop circulation by locating itself in the extremity of the water-pipes where the air-tube is connected. The common term expressing this state of affairs is to describe the pipes as being "air-locked," and this is really the case, as the collection of water at *a* will quite prevent the air passing out from *b* unless the water was heated to boiling-point, when the steam would, doubtless (depending upon the depth of the dip), effect relief. We could not, however, depend upon raising the water to boiling temperature for this purpose, and it must somehow be arranged to carry the pipe in an ascending direction and not dip it anywhere. This is always possible, the pipe being so small as to permit of its being placed anywhere without being unsightly or objectionable in any way.

This pipe is always connected to the water-pipe by a union-joint; this admits of its being simply disconnected and removed if required. It frequently happens that these pipes have to be taken down, as insects, fine leaf débris, and other substances, find a collecting-point there, sufficient to quite stop the pipe up sometimes, and this has to be removed and the pipe cleared. The air-pipes are usually terminated inside the house if convenient, they are then less liable to stoppage. If they terminate outside, care should be exercised to see that no part of the pipe containing water be placed out of the house, or the first severe frost may freeze the water within it, and be an objection in several ways.

The upper extremities of these pipes are

usually turned over, as shown at fig. 21; this assists in preventing falling matter lodging within the pipes, and so bringing about a stoppage. When two branch services of hot-water pipes terminate near one another, the air-tubes can be joined, if a saving of pipe can be so effected, but both before and after the junction the same care must be used to see that the pipes rise more or less throughout their whole extent.

WATER-SUPPLY.

It is, of course, necessary to provide some convenient means of, not only filling the apparatus when it is newly erected, but (more important) of regularly replenishing and making good the loss of water by evaporation. Sometimes a draw-off tap is inserted in the apparatus, which the gardener resorts to when warm or tepid water is required for watering purposes, but this arrangement necessitates some special provisions, and the loss by evaporation only will be spoken of first.

It is, of course, understood that an apparatus, such as which we are speaking of, with open pipes at the extremities, loses water by evaporation very freely when it is in use; the evaporation being brought about by the heating of the water, as every one is aware. If it were not for this, a simple hole at some point would suffice for the first filling, but as the subsequent loss referred to necessitates moderately frequent attention (varying with the size of the apparatus, the power of the boiler, and other circumstances), a provision must be made for convenient replenishment, and at the same time it should be arranged so that the gardener or attendant can see at a glance when water is needed.

This is all fulfilled by an ordinary supply cistern,—a square cast-iron cistern of somewhat small size, placed in any convenient spot just above the highest point of the circulating pipes. No gain,—rather the reverse,—is effected by placing it higher. By keeping it low it is easily looked into, and the want of water seen in a moment. By keeping the bottom of the supply-cistern above the highest circulating pipe, we know that the pipes are full while there is water in the cistern, however little it may be, assuming nothing is amiss with the apparatus in other respects. With a cistern placed in this manner, the water is added, as required, by simply pouring it in from a can.

The important feature in connexion with the supply-cistern is that it should bear some relation to the size of the apparatus. The reason for this is, that when the apparatus is charged, it is, of course, filled with cold water. Now water, as explained in the earlier papers, expands to a most noticeable extent when heated, and the exact extent of this expansive or swelling property is one in twenty-four when heated from freezing to boiling temperature. This amounts to an increase of bulk, so that a quantity of very cold water occupying 24 cubic inches would be found to fill the vessel to 25 cubic inches when heated to 212 deg. In the works under discussion, we do not get such extremes of temperature, and a difference of about 130 deg., viz., from 50 deg. to 180 deg., is about the maximum, and the increase in bulk in this case would be only about one in thirty-six.

The object in dwelling upon this question is to point out that if a supply-cistern be put to the apparatus, and the apparatus then charged and the fire lighted, we shall get an overflow of water when it becomes heated and expanded, unless the cistern be of sufficient capacity to allow for this increase of bulk. The proper calculation to settle the size of the cistern is to use one capable of holding one-thirtieth of the whole contents of the apparatus. (Allow a trifle over half-a-gallon for every foot length of 4-in. pipe; 10 ft. of 4-in. pipe will hold 5·433 gallons.) When the apparatus is first filled, the cold water should not reach higher than about ½ in. above the bottom of the cistern; the cistern will then nearly fill as the water reaches its highest temperature.

Some gardeners (and some engineers) do not trouble about this variation in bulk, and the allowance it necessitates; they use a small cistern, and when charging fill it up. As the water heats they let it overflow, until the expansion ceases, and the water level then remains fairly constant, unless the water cools down again. If the apparatus is one that has regular and skilled attention it may be taken for granted that the water will not cool down again until the fires are drawn in the warm weather, and not even then, if there is a tropical house being heated. It will be seen that the variation in the bulk of water is in ratio with its heating and cooling, and if the boiler fire is kept going night and day, and the water thus always kept hot, the bulk will not vary to any important extent. The expanded water will not contract so long as heat is imparted to it from the fire, which, as just stated, is not allowed to go out all the winter months, under any circumstances.

The supply cistern should always have a lid to prevent dirt, insects, and leaves from falling in and stopping the supply pipe. Dirt is very usually a conspicuous feature in these works when they have had a little use; the causes just named contribute some, but the bulk (and the quantity is large sometimes) is due to the supply water being furnished from ditches or some such rather impure source. In towns the water used is generally from a company's mains, or, at any rate, clean water is abundant, but in country places it is not so conveniently accessible for the gardener's use, and resource is had to rain or surface water. This water answers excellently, but has generally some suspended matter in it which collects at all available points in the apparatus. It is this matter when deposited in the boiler that requires removing periodically.

The supply pipe from the cistern to the radiating pipes is usually ¾ in., sometimes ½ in. but considering the short length generally required, the former size might be used in every instance. It is less likely to get stopped. This pipe should have a dip, or syphon (inverted) in it, the object of this being to prevent the heated water finding its way into the supply cistern.

In the first papers it was explained that the circulation of water by convection currents was due to the heated particles of water taking an ascending motion by the superior descending force exerted by the colder particles. Now, this action will take place in a single pipe ftom a boiler; the heated particles going up the centre and the cold particles descending close to the inner surface of the pipe. This action is very free, and, although of no use for practical purposes, it is quite sufficient to admit of the rapid transference of hot water from the pipes into the supply cistern, if the pipe was carried in a straight line from one to the other without the dip just referred to.

This dip as shown in fig. 22 is merely the supply pipe carried down about 6 in. or 8 in.

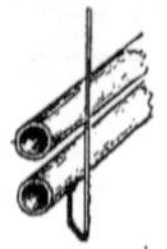

FIG. 22.

below the circulating pipes and then it ascends, entering the return pipe below as illustrated. By this arrangement, the heated water to find its way into the supply cistern would have to first take a descending and downward direction, and this it will not do; and although the supply pipe is open and clear right through, no hot water will enter it so long as the dip exists.

OBITUARY.

Mr. Philip C. Hardwick, F.S.A., F.R.I.B.A.—We regret to learn from the *Times* that Mr. Philip C. Hardwick died after a long and painful illness on the 27th ult. He was born in 1822, and, after having been trained under Mr. Edward Blore, he joined his father in architectural work in 1842. Among the many useful works to which he devoted himself mention may be made of the Artists' Benevolent Institution, of which he was the honorary treasurer, and to which he rendered invaluable service. He was architect to the Bank of England, to St. Bartholomew's Hospital, to the Goldsmiths' Company, to the Merchant Taylors' Company, to Greenwich Hospital, and to the Charterhouse, and was surveyor to the Portman Estate. Among his principal works are the central hall of Euston Station, added to his father's building; the Great Western Hotel at Paddington Station; the Ship Hotel, Greenwich; Adair-house; Madresfield-court; Addington-manor; and the New Charterhouse School buildings at Godalming. Besides these he designed a very large number of banks and office buildings in the City and elsewhere. He was one of the competitors selected to send in designs for the Albert Memorial, and he was also invited to compete for the Law Courts, but declined. In 1884, when the designs for the rebuilding of the War Office were under consideration, he, together with Mr. Ewan Christian, was appointed to the committee of selection as a professional adviser.

Mr. John E. Price, F.S.A.—As the *City Press* remarks, London archæologists have sustained a grievous loss by the decease, which occurred a few days ago, of Mr. John Edward Price, F.S.A., of Harvey-road, Leytonstone. Mr. Price, who was in his fifty-second year, had been in failing health for some months. He had long been a keen student of archæology, taking in this respect after his father, whom he invariably accompanied on his visits to spots where Roman and other remains had been discovered. For a long while Mr. Price was in business, but, the study of archæology proving more attractive to him, he severed his partnership, thenceforward devoting the whole of his time and attention to his literary labours. In the world of archæology he was regarded as a high authority on Roman relics in London. Mr. Price was the author of innumerable pamphlets and works bearing directly or indirectly on the hobby of his life. Possibly the work by which he will be chiefly remembered in time to come is the one he wrote nearly six years ago for the Library Committee of the Corporation, the title being "An Account of the Guildhall." The deceased for a number of years had rendered substantial assistance to the Library Committee in connexion with the acquisition and arrangement of articles now on view at the Museum at Guildhall, a museum that now contains not a few of the relics which Mr. Price in the course of his life had succeeded in collecting. Some years ago Mr. Price held the post of secretary of the London and Middlesex Archæological Society.

Dr. G. G. Zerffi.—The death, in his seventy-second year, from pneumonia following on influenza, of Dr. G. G. Zerffi occurred on the 28th ult. at Chiswick. Dr. Zerffi was for upwards of twenty-four years Lecturer on Historic Ornament at the Science and Art Department, South Kensington, and was expected to have resumed his lectures from week to week since his illness. He wrote, amongst other works, "A Manual of the Historical Development of Art," "Spiritualism and Animal Magnetism," and "Studies in the Science of General History," and was a well-known lecturer on historical subjects. He was a member of the Councils of the Royal Society of Literature and of the Royal Historical Society. According to the *Times*, Dr. Zerffi was a Hungarian by birth, and took part in the Hungarian Revolution of 1848, serving as a captain in the 2nd Corps of the revolutionary army. He also edited the *Ungar*, published at Pesth. He became naturalised soon after taking up his residence in this country some forty years ago.

GENERAL BUILDING NEWS.

Restoration of Peterborough Cathedral.—This work, which has been in progress for the Past ten years, is, says the *Leeds Mercury*, now rapidly approaching completion. The workmen have finished off the first set of stalls on the south side of the choir, and so much progress has been made that service will be resumed beneath the lantern in about a week or a fortnight. The altar will be placed as far back as the new pavement will permit, and the workmen will continue their work behind it. The new marble mosaic pavement, too, which is a gift by Dean Argles, is rapidly approaching completion. The designers,—Italian artists,—are now engaged on the second elevation eastward. The development of the pattern as it progresses shows a magnificent conception of design and colouring.

Lecture-Hall, Salisbury.—On the 27th ult. a lecture-hall was opened at the rear of the Congregational Church, Fisherton, Salisbury. The dimensions of the hall are 45 ft. by 25 ft. On either side are two class-rooms, 15 ft. by 15 ft. These class-rooms are shut off from the hall by movable partitions, and when these are taken away the room is capable of seating 450 persons. The hall itself will accommodate about 250. It is also intended to erect three other class-rooms and a kitchen at the farther end of the hall. The material used was red brick and stone work for the windows, with a wood-block floor and rough rolled cathedral glass. Mr. E. Witt was the builder, and the architect was Mr. Stevens, of Bournemouth.

Church and Schools, Brighton.—In a limited competition for a church and schools, Florence-road, Brighton, the designs submitted by Mr. George Baines, architect, were adopted. The church will seat 524, and 154 more in a future end gallery; total, 678. The school will seat 250. There are also seven other vestries and class-rooms. The style is Late Gothic, and the walls are faced with flints, with red brick and terra-cotta dressings. The front gable of the church will be flanked by two turrets, one 85 ft. high.

Proposed Reconstruction of the Free East Church, Aberdeen.—According to the *Aberdeen Free Press*, there is a proposal at present under the consideration of the congregation of the Free East

Church for the purchase of the buildings of the Free South Church, soon to be vacated by the congregation therein assembling, and by whom the church at the lower end of the Rosemount Viaduct has been erected from designs by Mr. Mackenzie, architect. It is proposed to make certain structural alterations in the Free East Church, and to convert the structure of the South Church, divided into two floors, into class-rooms, session-house, upper hall, &c. In the words of the report prepared by Mr. William Kelly, architect, who has been consulted on the subject: "The present session-houses of both churches and the vestry of the Free South Church would be removed. Within the East Church the present entrance lobby and the staircases to the gallery would be cleared out, and the area added to the church. The main entrance to the East Church buildings, as altered, would be by a porch in the centre of the north gable of the South Church, leading by a vestibule 9 ft. 6 in. wide to an inner vestibule or hall, lighted principally from the roof. Direct access from this vestibule would be had to the church and to the various halls and rooms on the ground floor. In the centre of the vestibule would be placed the staircases to the first or gallery floor, landing upon a passage 6 ft. wide, which would be carried round the vestibule at the present gallery floor level. From the passage just mentioned there would be direct access to the gallery of the church, to the large hall, and to a couple of cloak-rooms on the first floor. The structural alterations within the East Church include the formation of windows under the side galleries, the building up of the doors in the north and south walls, and the formation of a porch door at the north-east corner, corresponding with the present porch door at the vestry entrance. These alterations would greatly increase the light under the galleries, and would remove the draughts caused by the opening of the present entrance and exit doors. On the gallery floor the only structural alterations proposed are the formation of two new doorways for access, and the connexion of the church gallery passages with those of the vestibule. It is proposed to improve the whole of the seating. The number of sittings in the church would remain as at present, but the pews in the area would be widened. It is proposed to divide the remainder of the space within the South Church into two floors. The lower floor would contain office-bearers'-room, cloak-room, small hall (or session house), 28 ft. by 21 ft., and two large class-rooms, besides storage accommodation. On the upper floor would be the church hall (43 ft. square and having a height of about 20 ft.), capable of seating an audience of 350 to 400." The cost of the work is estimated to be about 2,350*l.*

SCHOOLS, WIGAN.—A new infants' school and class-rooms are to be built to the present Church Schools of St. Catherine, Whelley, Wigan. The architects are Messrs. Heaton & Ralph, of Wigan. —The Church Schools of St. Paul's, Goose-green, Wigan, are also to be largely added to and altered, under the direction of the same architects.

SCHOOLS, NORTHFLEET. — The present Board Schools being inadequate for the number of children attending, a new school is about to be erected in the High-street for 500 boys. The *Gravesend Journal* says that the Board have selected the plans of Messrs. Walford & Legg, architects, submitted in competition.

HOSPITAL, TORBAY.—The Governors of Torbay Hospital held their annual meeting on the 28th ult., and decided to accept the sum of £7,000 bequeathed to the hospital under the will of the late Miss L. A. Warrington. It has long been desired, says the *Western Morning News*, to rebuild the hospital. This will now be possible, the chief condition of the legacy being that the work shall be done after the plans and under the supervision of Messrs. Habershon & Fawckner, architects, and that one of the wards in the new building shall be named "The Lavinia A. Warrington Ward."

ANITARY AND ENGINEERING NEWS.

CRANLEIGH SEWAGE PURIFICATION.—A Local Government Board Inquiry was held on 14th ult. before Mr. T. Codrington, C.E., to consider the application of the Hambledon R.S.A. for a loan to carry out works of sewage disposal for the parish of Cranleigh, the treatment of the sewage on land having proved an expensive failure. Mr. C. Nicholson Lailey, C.E., of 16, Great George-street, Westminster, who had prepared the scheme, explained that the method of disposing of the sewage was that known as the International system, by which the sewage was first treated in tanks and then passed through polarite filter-beds.

SEWAGE PURIFICATION WORKS AT SALE.—An inquiry was held at Sale, near Manchester, on the 1st ult., by Mr. R. G. Walton, C.E., who has recently been appointed one of the inspectors of the Local Government Board. The application was from the Sale Local Board for power to purchase additional land and erect a pumping-station and large sewage purification works for the treatment of the sewage of Sale by the polarite and ferozone process of the International Water and Sewage Purification Company, Limited. The works will be of very considerable extent, and will include 2,300 square yards of polarite filter-beds. The plans have been prepared by Mr. McBeath, the Surveyor to the Local Board. Mr. Charles H. Beloe, the Consulting Engineer of the International Company, gave evidence to the effect that the plans were well adapted to carry out the process of the company.

SEWERAGE AT LLANDAFF YARD.—At a special meeting of the Cardiff Rural Sanitary Authority on the 30th ult., the tender of Mr. J. Straghan, contractor, Cardiff, was accepted for the sewering of Llandaff Yard and Maindy, for the sum of 2,743*l.* 12s. The building by-laws, as amended under the Public Health Acts Amendment Act, 1890, so as to apply to the whole of the district of the Authority, were also considered.

CLONMEL WATERWORKS.—A Local Government Board inquiry was held on the 20th ult. to consider objections from persons interested against the execution of works outside the district. The Clonmel Corporation are about to carry out waterworks at an estimated cost of 14,437*l.* The Government Arbitrator sat on Tuesday, February 2, to decide the value of the various lands required for the works. Tenders have been received for the iron pipes and valves, and the tender of the Stanton Iron Works Company, Limited, for 4,848*l.* 14s. has been accepted. The works will commence immediately. The engineer to the scheme is Mr. W. H. Radford, of Nottingham.

FOREIGN AND COLONIAL.

FRANCE.—At Pantin, near Paris, an excavation has been discovered, lined with marble slabs, in which have been found jewels, arms, a helmet surmounted by a Roman eagle, an alabaster vase, and various other objects apparently connected with the Roman occupation of Gaul.——M. Fagel, the sculptor, has just completed the monument in commemoration of the battle of Wattignies, the plans of which were prepared by M. Dutert. The monument will be inaugurated shortly.——A serious fire has destroyed the fine château belonging to M. Guishot de Lagarde, near Toulouse. The château contained a valuable library, and a rich collection of furniture and works of art.——There has been found, in the district of Chalons-sur-Marne, a sepulchre of the neolithic age, containing skeletons, flint hatchets, necklaces formed of wolves' teeth, and fossil shells of the Tertiary epoch, arrows and other weapons. ——A monument at Vannes, to Le Sage, the author of "Gil Blas," is to be inaugurated in May.——On April 3 next the Minister of Public Works is to go to the department of La Manche to open the new line of railway between Vère and Saint Lot.——It is announced that part of the ancient church of Val-les-Bains (Ardeche) has fallen.——M. Auguste Génin has been commissioned by the Minister of Public Instruction to make a journey to Mexico with the object of carrying on further researches into its archæology and ethnography.——For some days past dealers in works of art have been offering for sale pictures and studies by M. Puvis de Chavannes. These, executed about twenty years ago, have been stolen from his studio, and the artist has begged the Parisian press to put the public on their guard against purchasing such works. He intends to have all such works seized by the police as soon as information is obtained of any of them being offered for sale.——The death is announced of M. Emile Allard, a retired Inspecteur-Général des Ponts et Chaussées. —— We learn also of the decease of M. Foulhoux, architect-in-chief on the Indo-Chinese station, to whom we owe most of the work done at Saigon. He had published some interesting studies on Annamite architecture.——In the Palais de Justice at Lyons has been placed a portrait of M. Devienne, formerly first President of the Cour de Cassation. He was born at Lyons in 1802.—— The Académie des Beaux-Arts has appointed MM. Daumet and Gruzer on the committee to judge the competition opened by the town of Nantes for the construction of a museum of painting in that town. ——The committee charged to prepare a list of candidates for the chair left vacant by the death of M. Alphand has put forward, as candidate in the first rank, M. Georges Lafenestre, in the second rank M. Georges Berger, in the third M. Michel, in the fourth M. Corroyer, and in the fifth rank M. Charles Yriarte. The names follow of M. Phillippe Gilles and M. Roger Ballu. The election will have been made by the time these lines appear.

DENMARK AND NORWAY.—The new Church of Jesus in Copenhagen, to which we recently referred, has just been consecrated with great ceremony, the Danish Royal family being present, although, as yet, the exterior is not quite finished, and it will take some three years to complete the tower. It is the gift of the well-known Mecænas and philanthropist, Herr Carl Jacobsen, the Copenhagen brewer; the cost, when completed, is estimated at 50,000*l.* In front of the entrance stands a bronze cast of Michelangelo's "Moses," whilst the façade is ornamented with statues of Christ and four Evangelists. It is stated that the church, when finished, although comparatively small, will be the finest structure of its kind in Scandinavia. ——A monumental building to be used for military offices will shortly be completed in Copenhagen. It is three storeys in height, the materials used in the construction being red bricks, sandstone, and granite.——A new cement company, the Danish Portland Cement Company, Limited, has been constituted, in order to work a deposit of cement near Aalborg.——At the last meeting of the Danish Old Norse Record Society, Dr. Müller, the distinguished archæologist, presented his new work on the Bronze Age in Denmark, being an important link in Danish historical culture.——The large new Masonic Hall in Christiania is now approaching completion. Work is now carried on with the new Customs House to be built in Christiania, but with some difficulty, owing to the entrance of sea-water. ——A large market building, with fifty-six shops, has just been opened in Christiania, constructed of iron and glass. It is lighted by electricity.

MISCELLANEOUS.

LECTURES TO ROYAL ACADEMY STUDENTS ON SCULPTURE.—The following lectures have been arranged for:—Three lectures on "Archaic compared with Archaistic Sculpture," by Dr. A. S. Murray, of the British Museum, to be delivered on February 15, February 18, and February 22; and three lectures on "Michael Angelo" (continued from last year), by Professor J. H. Middleton, to be delivered on February 26, March 4, and March 7.

THE SURVEYORS' INSTITUTION.—Of the candidates who presented themselves at the Students' Preliminary Examination of the Institution, held concurrently in London and Manchester on the 26th and 27th ult., the following satisfied the Examiners: —Messrs. G. J. F. Adams, H. C. Adams, A. Arnold, P. C. Beasley, G. Beken, jun., H. O. Bell, F. R. Betenson, R. Bonella, A. Bruce, C. V. Cable, S. G. Carnell, A. S. Cartwright, J. A. Chubb, J. W. Clayton, R. W. Clutterbuck, H. L. Cowell, W. S. Cowper, H. H. Crawford, S. J. Cribb, D. B. Davies, W. J. Davies, G. P. Desley, E. A. Deer, C. R. Finch, H. E. Folkes, J. S. Garner, H. A. Glover, C. H. Godfrey, W. Harris, W. H. Hicks, W. H. Hull, W. Jarmain,* D. H. Jeboult, W. T. Lamprill, W. B. Leane, S. B. Lee, F. P. Lightfoot, E. C. Lyons, F. C. T. Mann, A. J. Martin, T. C. Nevett, H. A. Newbrouner, S. H. Page, W. H. Pain, W. Parks, J. W. Paul, J. A. Peppercorn, F. J. Phillips, F. F. Rootham, C. S. Sandford, A. S. E. Sedgwick, H. E. B. Sewell, A. P. Skeat, A. C. Skingle, A. G. Smith, R. W. Smith, A. C. Stauden, C. W. Stupart, W. S. Walker, H. J. Watson, H. B. Whitby, and S. A. Wilde.

PROPERTIES FOR SALE.—In course of the Spring, at the Mart, will be offered for sale (by Messrs. E. & H. Lumley) Killeen Castle, with its demesne of 1,000 acres, in county Meath. This stone-built castle was erected, according to Lewis's Topographical Dictionary of Ireland, in 1180, by Hugh de Lacy, who built also those of Clonard, Delvin, and, as some maintain, Trim, in this county. The castle, being now in good repair, was enlarged by Johnston to meet more modern requirements. King John is known to have been for a while in Meath, and at Killeen Castle they show "King John's tower" which he is said to have occupied in the year 1210. The estate, for the most part, there being no tenantry, is let at from 3*l.* to 4*l.* per acre annually for the rearing and fattening of stock. The church of St. Mary, rebuilt by Sir Christopher Plunkett (died 1445), contains ruins of ancient tombs, with figures clad in episcopal robes: Tegharne was of opinion that Killeen is identical with Colgan, famous for the burial therein of seven bishops. St. Endeus founded an abbey here, and a nunnery for his sister, St. Fanchea (Carecha), its first abbess. Joan, only daughter and heir of Sir Lucas Cusac, brought the barony of Killeen in marriage, 1403, to Sir Christopher Plunkett, whose descendant Lucas, tenth lord baron Killeen, was elevated Earl of Fingall in 1628.——By direction of Mr. Whitehead, who has established a new torpedo factory at Weymouth, his Sussex estate at Paddockhurst, in Balcombe, Worth, and Ardingley parishes. This property, valued in all at 250,000*l.*, consists of 3,000 acres, whereof one-third is under separate cultivation. The house, since enlarged, was built thirty years ago, with stone quarried on the land. A homestead, known as New House, is of Elizabeth's day, and is conjectured to have been designed by the architect of Wakehurst Place, in the neighbourhood, in Surrey.—— And on 26th inst., at the Mart, the block lately erected along the southern side of Coventry-street, Haymarket, having a frontage of 81 ft. between Arundel-place and Oxendon-street. The block includes Piccadilly-chambers on the four floors over the four shops: it is held from the freeholder for a term of which 92½ years are unexpired, at an annual ground-rent of 800*l.* The premises are severally let for an aggregate rental of 2,270*l.* per annum. This side of the street,—so named after Henry, son of the Lord Keeper, Coventry,—was pulled down in 1881-2, and with it No. 21, whereat David Wishart established himself as a tobacco and snuff dealer, by sign of the Highlander, Thistle, and Crown, in 1720. The Civil Service Stores, Haymarket, stand on the site of Coventry House. Next northwards, occupying the whole south side of Coventry-

* Passed at head of list.

COMPETITIONS, CONTRACTS, AND PUBLIC APPOINTMENTS.

COMPETITIONS.

Nature of Work.	By whom Advertised.	Premium.	Designs to be delivered.
*Technical School Building	Heywood Corp.	20l. 10l. and 5l.	Feb. 15
*Pavilion to accommodate 10,000 persons	Royal Nat. Eisteddfod of 1892	Not stated	No date

CONTRACTS.

Nature of Work or Materials.	By whom Required.	Architect, Surveyor or Engineer.	Tenders to be delivered.
Sewerage Works	Maidstone U.S.A.	W. G. Scoones	Feb. 9
*Works and Materials	Willesden Loc. Bd.	O. Claude Robson	do.
*Pipe Sewer, Drain, &c.	do.	do.	do.
Outfall Pipe Sewer	Chester-le-Street U.R.S.A.	D. Balfour	Feb. 10
New Cemetery, Penymaes	Rhyl Impt. Codmrs.	R. Hughes	Feb. 11
Block of Buildings, Market-square, Merthyr Tydfil	....	T. C. Wakeling	do.
Distillery, Glenspey, Rothes, N.B.	Proprietors	....	Feb. 12
Road and Two Entrance Lodges	F. T. Treeby	R. H. Harbottle	do.
Culverts, Draining, and Roadmaking near Mountain Ash, Glam.	....	T. Roderick	do.
Public Baths, Woodside, Haley Hill	Halifax Corporation	Horsfall & Williams	Feb. 13
House and Shop, Bodmin	E. & H. G. Liddell	W. T. H. Mear	do.
Road Works	Wallsend Local Board	Official	Feb. 14
*Widening Railway between Spring's Branch and Wigan, &c.	L. & N. W. Ry. Co.	do.	Feb. 16
*Roadmaking and Paving Works	Bromley Local Board	do.	do.
*Pipe Sewers, &c.	Southend Local Board	P. Dodd	do.
Additions to Church, Cromdale, Inverness, N.B.	....	Ross & Macbeth	do.
Farmhouse, Blairvie Castle, Turriff, N.B.	....	Jas. Duncan	do.
*Brick Sewer, &c. Hackney Wick	London County Council	Official	do.
Street Improvement Works	Barton-upon-Irwell R.S.A.	C. C. Hooley	do.
*Works and Materials	Vestry of St. Margarets, &c. Westminster	G. R. W. Wheeler	Feb 16, 17 & 18

CONTRACTS.—*Continued.*

Nature of Work or Materials.	By whom Required.	Architect, Surveyor, or Engineer.	Tenders to be delivered.
*12,000 Tons Stone for Macadamising	Hull Corporation	Official	Feb. 17
*Roadmaking and Paving Works	Fulham Vestry	W. Sykes	do.
*Removal of House Refuse for One Year	St. Pancras Vestry	Official	do.
Road Works	Willington Quay Loc. Bd.	Official	Feb. 19
*Fever Hospital, Langfield, Yorks	....	J. Sutcliffe	do.
*Enlargement of P.O. Dudley	Commissioners of H.M. Works, &c.	Official	do.
*Public Baths	Shrewsbury Corp.	J. Johnson	Feb. 22
*Free Library	West Ham Council	Lewis Angell	Feb. 23
Electrical Conductors and Culverts	Manchester Corp.	Official	do.
*Palm House, Battersea Park	London County Council	do.	do.
*Erection of Schools, near Romford	Hornchurch Sch. Bd.	C. Allam	Feb. 24
*Warming and Ventilating Town Hall	Leeds Corporation	Official	Feb. 27
*Works and Materials for One Year	St. Pancras Vestry	W. N. Blair	Feb. 29
Enlargement of Vestry, Camborne	....	J. P. St. Aubyn	Mar. 1
*Wesleyan Chapel, Brentwood	The Committee	F. Boreham	No date
Six Cottages, Dawlish	Miss Empson	C. Cole	do.
Farmhouse, Penllyne, Glam.	D. Rees	....	do.
Roads, Canton, Cardiff	....	Veall & Sant	do.
Warehouse, Woodhouse, Leeds	George Lax	....	do.
Printing Works, Cookridge-street, Leeds	F. R. Spark & Sons	Harry May	do.
Six Terrace Houses, Cross Green, Otley, Leeds	W. E. Turner	A. Marshall	do.
Co-operative Stores, Low Wortley, Leeds	Co-op. Soc. Lim.	C. F. Wilkinson	do.

PUBLIC APPOINTMENTS.

Nature of Appointment.	By whom Advertised.	Salary.	Applications to be in.
*Surveyor	Wrotham Loc. Bd.	90l. &c.	Feb. 17
*Assistant Surveyor	Islington Vestry	200l.	Feb. 20
*Sanitary Inspector	Vestry of St. Margarets, &c. Westminster	130l. &c.	Feb. 22

Those marked with an Asterisk (*) are advertised in this Number. *Competitions, p. iv. Contracts, pp. iv., vi., & viii. Public Appointments, p. xxi.*

street (*prius* Piccadilly), and over against Piccadilly Hall, was Shaver's Hall, erected *circa* 1620, which, with its bowling-alleys, orchards, courts, &c., covered about 3½ acres, according to a survey made in 1650. The tennis-court cited in the survey is, perhaps, that in James-street; to which we adverted in a "Note" on July 30, 1887; nearly opposite to the doorway of "Hickford's" auction-rooms, *temp.* George I., for the Shaver's Hall ground is set out as "abutting on the Earl of Suffolk's brick wall south." Henry, fifth Lord Arundell of Wardour (*ob.* 1726), married a daughter of Colonel Thomas Panton, the gamester (*ob.* 1681) and last proprietor of Piccadilly Hall.

Concrete-mixing Machine.—Concrete machines are frequently a part of a builder's plant used in house-building in Paris. They are usually of the vertical type, but Messrs. Coster, Rikkers, & Co., of Saint Denis, have recently introduced a horizontal machine which, it is claimed, will supply large quantities of concrete of good quality. It consists of an inclined wrought-iron cylinder supported by rollers held in the framing. The cylinder is caused to revolve by geared wheels driven by a belting from a counter-shaft. There are forty paddles inside the cylinder to cause the concrete to become more thoroughly mixed. The materials are introduced through a hopper at the upper end, and there is a suitable receptacle for the concrete at the lower end. The capacity of this machine is 654 cubic yards of concrete per day, and it is driven by a 10-horse-power portable engine. The cylinder revolves ten times per minute. The stones and cement are brought to the machine in trucks, and are shot in from a platform provided. As the trucks hold a definite quantity, no further measurement is required. The water is measured by a suitable valve.

The Land Sales of 1891.—The *Estates Gazette* contains a review of the land sales effected in 1891, from which it appears that in England there has been a great falling off in the returns of sales in 1891, more noticeable in several of the home counties than elsewhere, although the average price per acre is only 2l. short of that of 1890; but in Scotland and Wales there was a most decided improvement in the number of properties sold, although the average prices are very low, in the former country especially, due principally to the sale of two very large estates, one of which of some 72,000 acres in Ross-shire only realising about 1l. 10s. per acre, which, of course, materially had the effect of lowering the averages in the other counties. The following is a statement of areas of land sold and the price realised per acre:—In England, 49,592a. 3r. 29p. sold for a total of 2,106,683l., which is an average of 43l. per acre. In Scotland, 98,457a. 0r. 14p. fetched 425,062l., or at the rate of 4l. an acre. In Wales, 8,663a. 2r. 15p. realised 163,337l., equal to 19l. per acre.

The "Cross-Bones" Burial-ground, Southwark.—In a "Note" on July 27, 1885, we directed attention to this burial-ground in Union-street (corner of Red Cross-street) Borough. A few months afterwards, Sir James Bacon, who was then Vice-Chancellor, dismissed with costs a summons under the Vendor and Purchaser Act, 1874, *in re* Trustees of St. Saviour's Rectory, Southwark, to Messrs. Oyler. The purchasers had bought of the rectory trustees, for 2,300l., what was described in the particulars of sale as "valuable freehold building-land in Union-street, Borough, occupying the large area of about 13,000 ft., adapted for a builder, contractor, timber-yard, &c." An Act of 1833, to abolish church-rates in St. Saviour's parish transferred this land from the parish "wardens" to the trustees, and empowered the latter to sell it, or grant building leases in respect thereof. Section 5 of the Act of 1884 for the prevention of building on such grounds, contains an exception of any burial-ground disposed of under any Act of Parliament; and this section was cited in the conditions of sale. The purchasers, stating they had intended to buy for building purposes, declined, on their side, to complete the sale. A summons taken out by the vendors was adjourned into court, with the result stated. Meantime the ground has been occupied by three persons, who for some while past have there carried on a sort of fair, with all latest "improvements" in shape of steam-organs and roundabouts, shooting-galleries, &c., which proved, as alleged, a source of great disturbance and annoyance to the neighbourhood. Arraigned on indictment, the defendants were found guilty at the London County Sessions, on Friday last week, fined in sums of 25l. and 40s., and bound over to keep the peace. The area we speak of may possibly have taken its name from a carving on the stone that formerly stood over its entrance,—see the interleaved copy of Manning and Bray's "Surrey," in the Guildhall Library. It formed a place of interment for the inmates of the licensed houses, or bordellos, on Bankside, in the liberty of the Clink, and belonged to the estate of the see of Winchester. A large number were buried here at the time of the Plague; as many as, it is said, 600 in one week. *Circa* 1708, the bishop gave a lease for three lives to the parish. A subsequent lease for three lives and sixty-one years (June 9, 1820) was enfranchised by the wardens for 3,338l. On October 31, 1853, two burials (the last) took place, with the prescribed service and payment of fees as in the case of consecrated ground. On November 8, 1854, the wardens granted a twenty-six and a half years' lease, at 50l. rent, the Vestry consenting. In 1791 were rebuilt on the southern side, the parochial schools, established, at first, in Montague-close, and then removed for a while to Angel-court.

A Monster Building.—Chicago journals state that the Society of Oddfellows in that city has plans prepared for a building to be erected on a site in the central part of the town, 177 ft. by 120 ft. in area, and having ten stories. The central portion, moreover, will have ten additional stories, crowned with a tower, making the number here twenty-two in all. The tower portion will contain 132 offices, situated above the lower part of the building. There are to be eighteen lifts and four grand staircases. The summit of the tower, 70 ft. square, will be situated 450 ft. above the street. The two first stories will be arranged for offices. The architects who have prepared the plans of the building are Messrs. Adler & Sullivan, and its cost is estimated at 1,222,000l.

The English Iron Trade.—The disorganisation in trade produced by the fall in warrants continues to become more pronounced. Although Scotch warrants remain stationary, both Cleveland and hematite warrants have suffered considerable reduction. Scotch makers' iron is more active, but quotations generally are lower. The North of England pig-iron trade is practically at a standstill, and in all the other crude iron centres a depressed tone is observable. Tin-plates are still quiet, and manufactured iron is only in moderate request. In the steel trade matters are a trifle brighter, and a better demand is noticeable for rails. Shipbuilders are less active, and engineers are not so busy. The coal trade generally is quieter.—*Iron.*

Liverpool Engineering Society.—The seventh ordinary meeting of this Society for the present session was held at the Royal Institution, Colquitt-street, on the 27th ult., Mr. John T. Wood, President, in the chair. The principal portion of the evening was devoted to an adjourned discussion upon a paper entitled "Transatlantic Lines and Steamships," read by Mr. A. J. Maginnis, M.Inst. N.A., at the previous meeting. The discussion, which was a very interesting one, dealt principally with the various improvements in the design and construction of Atlantic liners and their machinery during the last few years. The speakers included the President, Messrs. F. Hudleston, Henry H. West, T. L. Miller, Jennings Campbell, and others. Mr. Maginnis, having replied on the points raised during the discussion, a vote of thanks was accorded to him by acclamation for his paper.

The Telford Park Estate.—Messrs. E. E. Croucher & Co. announce in our advertisement columns the sale of a portion of the well-known Telford Park estate, which is freehold, and extends from Streatham Hill to Tooting Bec Common.

LEGAL.

CASE UNDER THE EMPLOYERS' LIABILITY ACT:

WILLETTS *v.* WATT AND CO.

This was an appeal from the County Court of Stafford, holden at West Bromwich, and was heard in the Queen's Bench Division on the 22nd ult., before Mr. Justice Hawkins and Mr. Justice Wills. It raised a question as to what was the meaning of the word "way" in the first section of the Employers' Liability Act. It appeared that the defendants had large works, and that there was a yard in them 50 yards by 50 ft. The surface of the yard was covered more or less with machinery and tanks, which were not always lying in the same place. In the yard there was a well which had not been uncovered for seven years, but on the day of the accident, some water being required for testing an iron cylinder, it was uncovered and left so. Half an hour later the plaintiff, while going across the yard between the bits of machinery, for the purpose of seeing whether more steam was wanted, fell into the well, which was in his direct line of way, and injured his arm and head. For these injuries he brought this action, and in the particulars, claimed damages by reason of a defect in the "ways." The jury awarded him 150l.

Against this judgment Mr. Hugo Young, for the defendants, appealed, and argued that no defect in the way had been shown. "Way" meant a passage marked out in a particular direction, and there was no special or usual passage across this yard—"M'Griffin v. Palmer's Shipbuilding Company" (10 Q.B.D., 1), "M'Shaen v. Baxter" (The *Times* Law Reports, Nov. 12, 1890).

Mr. Disturnal, for the plaintiff, argued that if the word "way" meant any defined way, then the passage traversed by the plaintiff was defined by the machinery and other obstacles he had to pass. But the word did not mean a defined way.

Mr. Justice Hawkins, in giving Judgment, said—Judgment ought to be entered for the defendants on the ground that it is not a way within the section. I think, if it can be considered a way within the section, it was, under the circumstances, defective. The question is—Is it a "way connected with and used in the business of the employer?" I take Mr. Justice Field's definition in M'Griffin v. Palmer's Shipbuilding Company. The learned Judge, after stating the facts, continued:—In my opinion the question is, was it a way which was habitually used, or pointed out, or intended to be used as a way from one part of the works to another? "Way" does not mean every piece of ground that may be used for passage.

Mr. Justice Wills.—The word "way" does not stand alone in the Act; it is coupled with the words "connected with and used in the business of the employer." This shows the word "way" means a line of passage more or less habitually used. Under some circumstances, no doubt, a way, even though used for the first time, may come within the description in the Act. If the plaintiff's contention is correct, every line from one part of the works to another where the workmen passed would be a way. There was no evidence that this line of passage was habitually used as a way. The fact that obstacles were placed there temporarily does not define the passage as a way.—*Times*.

MEETINGS.

SATURDAY, FEBRUARY 6.

Architectural Association.—Visit to the new Metropolitan Life Assurance building in Moorgate-street, and to the tower and spire of Bow Church.

Sanitary Inspectors' Association (*Carpenters' Hall*).—Address to be delivered by Dr. Geo. Reid. 6 p.m.

Royal Institution.—Professor J. A. Fleming on "The Induction Coil and Alternate-Current Transformer." III. 3 p.m.

MONDAY, FEBRUARY 8.

Royal Institute of British Architects.—(1) To receive the announcement of the name of the person the Council propose to submit to her Majesty the Queen as the recipient of the Royal Gold Medal. (2) Mr. Edwin T. Hall on "London Building Legislation." 8 p.m.

Royal Academy of Arts.—Professor Aitchison, A.R.A., on "Saracenic and Turkish Architecture." V. 8 p.m.

Society of Arts (*Cantor Lectures*).—Professor George Forbes on "Developments of Electrical Distribution." III. 8 p.m.

Clerks of Works' Association (*Carpenters' Hall*).—Paper by Mr. G. Calvert. 8 p.m.

Liverpool Architectural Society.—The Rev. F. F. Grensted on "Babylonia and Assyria as a Home of Early Literature and Science." IV. 6.30 p.m.

TUESDAY, FEBRUARY 9.

Institution of Civil Engineers.—Discussion on Mr. A. H. Curtis's paper on "Gold-Quartz Reduction." 8 p.m.

Sanitary Institute (*Lectures for Sanitary Officers*).—Professor H. Robinson on "House Drainage." 8 p.m.

Sheffield Society of Architects and Surveyors.—Mr. W. Randolph on "Town Churches." 8 p.m.

WEDNESDAY, FEBRUARY 10.

British Museum.—Miss Eugénie Sellers on "Greek Sculpture: 'Æginetan' Work." I. 2.30 p.m.

Carpenters' Hall, London Wall.—Professor W. H. Corfield on "Water Supply, Drinking Water, and Pollution of Water." 8 p.m. (*Admission Free.*)

Sanitary Institute.—Papers on "Refuse Disposal" by Mr. Charles Jones and Mr. James Russell. 8 p.m.

Society of Arts.—Mr. E. Price Edwards on "Burning Oil for Lighthouses and Lightships." 8 p.m.

Liverpool Engineering Society.—Mr. Thomas Morris on "Engineers' Tests of Iron and Steel." 8 p.m.

THURSDAY, FEBRUARY 11.

Royal Academy of Arts.—Professor Aitchison, A.R.A., on "Saracenic and Turkish Architecture." VI. 8 p.m.

British Museum.—Miss Millington-Lathbury on "Mysteries and Oracles" as illustrated by the Greek Monuments in the Museum. 2.45 p.m.

Society of Antiquaries.—8.30 p.m.

Institution of Electrical Engineers.—(1) Mr. Alexander Siemens on "Some Experimental Investigations of Alternate Currents." (2) Mr. W. H. Preece on "Insulated Conductors for Electric Lighting and other purposes." 8 p.m.

Society of Arts (*Indian Section*).—Lord Lamington on "Recent Travels in Indo-China." 4.30 p.m.

Edinburgh Architectural Association.—Mr. Æneas J. G. Mackay on "The Architecture of Scottish Towns, illustrating Scottish History." 8 p.m.

Dundee Institute of Architecture.—Mr. John Honeyman on "Glasgow Cathedral." 8 p.m.

FRIDAY, FEBRUARY 12.

Sanitary Institute (*Lectures for Sanitary Officers*).—Professor H. Robinson on "Sewage Disposal." 8 p.m.

Institution of Civil Engineers (*Students' Meeting*).—Mr. H. B. Ransom on "Fly-wheels and Governors." 7.30 p.m.

Royal Institution.—Mr. G. J. Symons on "Rain, Snow, and Hail." 9 p.m.

RECENT PATENTS:

ABSTRACTS OF SPECIFICATIONS.

21,191.—PORTABLE BUILDINGS: *E. E. Allen.*—This patent relates chiefly to portable buildings. Sheets 8 ft. to 12 ft. long, and 2 ft. 6 in. to 3 ft. 6 in. wide, composed of three thicknesses of thin wood, are formed for the lining of the buildings, the grain of the central layer being arranged at right angles to the other two layers, thus making large and very strong sheets not liable to split. With the above sheets are combined sheets of galvanised corrugated iron, placing between them inodorous felt or silicate cotton, and rivetting or otherwise attaching them by turning over edges of the iron, or enclosing them in a light wooden frame. Similar sections or sheets are formed with slight modifications for the roofs and floors of the building. Compound standards are constructed as set out in the specification and are used for the purpose of securing the sections together. The inventor claims the saving of bulk and weight for transport, and time and labour in erecting the building.

3,166.—ROOFING: *J. A. Main.*—This claim is for an improved method of supporting "purlin" bars on the rafters of roofs, though the invention is also applicable to other parts of the building.

4,349.—BRICK-MAKING MACHINES: *R. Mountain.*—This is an invention referring to machines where the moulds for the bricks are made in revolving barrels. The barrel is preferably provided with several moulds, uniformly distributed over the circumference of the barrel. At one side of the barrel is provided a mixer or pug mill, into which the clay is fed, and thence pushed forward to enter and fill the moulds as they successively come opposite the mill or mixer. The bottom of the moulds are formed as moveable rectangular pistons. By means of mechanism described these pistons are moved radially in the moulds. without the barrel a die or top piston is provided moveable within radially placed guides for the purpose of pressing the brick in the mould; and at a suitable position past this die there is a delivery table on to which the formed bricks are delivered. Mechanism for locking the barrel truly in position is also described.

12,429.—BUILDING CEMENTS: *F. J. Reynolds and J. Brown.*—This invention claims the preparation of a cement more efficient, harder, and more durable than those in ordinary use. Lime, well calcined, is incorporated with carbonate of potash and reduced to powder in the form of a hydrate, and when required for use is treated with a combined saccharine and metallic solution such as iron, copper, or other metal as described. The inventor states that mortars made of the above with any kind of hard gritty substance will harden under water.

19,754.—BRACE-BITS: *T. O. Smith.*—This patent refers to an improved adjustable attachment to brace-bits provided with an adjustable counter-sinking blade, the whole device being fixed to the bit by means of screw pins as described. The specification also describes a hole-boring and counter-sinking device for attachment to brace-bits, consisting of an adjustable block provided with a mutilated conically-shaped cutting head for counter sinking, the block being provided with a screw adjustable stop to regulate the depth of counter-sinking required.

NEW APPLICATIONS FOR PATENTS.

January 18.—939, A. Baxter, Connecting Earthenware Sanitary Appliances, &c., to Metal Pipes.—954. A. Young and R. Chesney, Lock.

January 19.—1,023, S. Middleton, Operating window-sashes.—1,024, J. Evans, Apparatus for Utilising waste Heat for Heating Buildings.—1,039, G. and C. Rollason, Joint for Hot-water Pipes.—1,041, S. Rollason, Generating Electricity for Buildings.—1,062, J. Chappell, Parquet and Block Flooring.—1,058, J. Schneider, Chimney-cowl.—1,062, J. Barber, Device for Curing Smoky Chimneys.—1,092, T. Brown, Chimney-pots and Tall-boys for Chimneys.—1,095, G. Williamson, Kitchen-ranges.

January 20.—H. Hansen and Others, Hoods or Cowls for Ventilating or other Shafts.—1,114, W. Copping, Bolts or Fastenings for Emergency Doors of Public Buildings.—1,121, W. Turner, Glue-pot.—1,129 A. Fowler, Automatically-flushed water-closets.—1,132, D. Shaw, Gulley-pipes.

January 21.—1,154, W. Riley, Construction of Knobs or Door-handles, and Adjusting and Holding them upon the Spindles.—1,170, J. Leech and J. Lewis, Fastening of Sash Windows.—1,195, A. Willard, Artificial Stone, 1,196, J. Banks, Flush and other Bolts.—1,206 R. Frost, A Joint for Pipes or Tubes in Stoneware or Metal.—1,238, J. Smeaton, Water-closets.

January 22.—1,281, H. Dowty, Hot-water Pipes and Connections.—1,292, R. Browne, Fire-grates.—1,294, E. Brookes, Safety Fastener for Sash Windows, when open or closed.—1,323, A. Ransome, Felling and Cutting Timber.

January 23.—1,336, R. Mooney, Earthenware Gulley-traps.—1,342, E. Hunt, Gasaliers and Chandeliers.—1,346, J. Hunt, Automatic Ventilator and Foul-air Exhauster.—1,357, H. Wethered, Ventilation of Closet-basins and Water-closets.

PROVISIONAL SPECIFICATIONS ACCEPTED.

17,105, J. Walley, Fastening of Stable-doors.—21,088 R. Roberts, Accessories for water-closets.—21,503, G. Johnson, Drain-pipe Junctions.—21,904, W. Hooks, Water-waste Preventing Siphon-flushing Cistern.—22,209, J. & A. Duckett, Water-closets.—22,268, T. Sterratt Farnworth, Bricks.—22,464, S. Hawke, Fastenings for Windows and Doors.—22,402, J. Griffiths Water-closets.—22,534, J. Radford, Siphon-flushing Apparatus.—22,610, A. & W. Gill, Paints and Lacquers.—22,773, C. Ennis, Electric Bells and Indicators.—22,793, P. Fowler, Fireplaces.—22,800, M. Williams, Oil Paints and Paint Medium.—71. W. Chesterton, Ventilator for Shop Window.—72, A. Davidson, and R. Thorn, Veneer, Fabrics or Materials for Decorative Purposes.—190, S. Dix Water-closets.—337, T. Helliwell, Glazing Buildings.—364, H. Conolly, Water-closets.

COMPLETE SPECIFICATIONS ACCEPTED.

(*Open to Opposition for Two Months.*)

4,361, W. Munns, Shutter-fastening Device.—4,750, The Society Anonyme des Ardoisieres, De Deville and V. Heyden, Material suitable for Building, &c., from Waste Pieces or Débris of Slate.—4,779, T. James, Glazed Panels for Furniture and Interior Decorative work.—5,068, F. Quéry, Kilns for Use in the Manufacture of Pottery, &c., and other Similar Goods.—5,203, W. Hughes, Opening and Closing of windows.

SOME RECENT SALES OF PROPERTY:

ESTATE EXCHANGE REPORT.

JANUARY 25.—By *Surridge & Son*: 6 to 9, Curlew-st., Horsleydown, u.t. 12 yrs., g.r. 9*l*., r. 101*l*., 350*l*.

JANUARY 26.—By *A. Robertson*: 48 to 60 (even), Holland-st., Kennington, u.t. 7 yrs., no g.r., r. 208*l*., 710*l*.; 27 and 28A, Richmond-st., u.t. 25 yrs., g.r. 6*l*., r. 46*l*. 16s., 170*l*.—By *Messrs. Aldridge*: 9 and 11, New-road, Selhurst, u.t. 74 yrs., g.r. 8*l*., 05*l*.—By *T. G. Wharton*: F.g.r. of 34*l*., with reversion in 36 yrs., Bromley-by-Bow, 860*l*.—By *Arber, Rutter, & Waghorn*: 16, Wilton-cres., Belgravia, u.t. 32 yrs., g.r. 1*l*., r. 315*l*., 4,100*l*.—By *Orgill, Swann, & Orgill*: "The Farmer's Arms," Amlwch, Anglesea, u.t. 12 yrs., g.r. 20*l*., 50*l*.; "The Clarendon Arms," Beer House, Birmingham, u.t 6 yrs., at 50*l*., 110*l*.; "The Junction Inn," and 40 to 45, Cromwell-st., f., Dudley, Worcester, 950*l*.; "The Bridge Inn," Swindon, u.t. 2 yrs., at 30*l*., 30*l*.; 81 and 82, Heath-st., and "The Forge Hammer" Beer House, f., Wolverhampton, 520*l*.

JANUARY 27.—By *J. A. & W. Tharp*: 1 to 9, Beaconsfield-ter., Leytonstone, f., r. 226*l*., 2,365*l*.; 9 to 12, Barclay-ter., f., r. 119*l*., 1,335*l*.; 1, 2, 9, and 10, Denmark-ter., f., r. 125*l*., 1,290*l*.; 2 to 7, Layspring-ter., f., r. 183*l*., 2,000*l*.

JANUARY 28.—By *Henry & Latchford*: 28, Harrington-gardens, Kensington, u.t. 90 yrs., g.r. 2*l*., 3,010*l*.—By *C. C. & T. Moore*: 90, Red Lion-st., Wapping, f., 300*l*.—By *Newbon & Co.*: 41, Colebrooke-row, Islington, f., 800*l*.; 3, Highbury-grange, Highbury, u.t. 26 yrs., no g.r., 550*l*.; 52, Highbury-pk., u.t. 27 yrs., g.r. 20*l*., r. 90*l*., 510*l*.; 19, Lupton-st., Kentish Town, u.t. 75 yrs., g.r. 7*l*. 7s., r. 42*l*., 360*l*.; 18, Almington-st., Hornsey-rise, u.t. 78 yrs., g.r. 6*l*. 15s., r. 33*l*., 300*l*.—By *Stimson & Sons*: No. 23, Clapham-common, u.t. 21 yrs., g.r. 2*l*. 5s., r. 100*l*., 690*l*.; 4, Southborough-rd., Hackney, u.t. 50 yrs., g.r. 5*l*., r. 28*l*., 275*l*.; 6 and 8, Southborough-road, u.t. 50 yrs., g.r. 2*l*., r. 56*l*., 650*l*.; 1 and 2, Rosemary-cottages; and 18, 20, and 22, Diamond-st., Camberwell, u.t. 56 yrs., g.r. 18*l*. 10s., r. 93*l*. 12s., 455*l*.; 137, Avondale-sq., Old Kent-rd., u.t. 63 yrs., g.r. 5*l*., 370*l*.; 6, Wansey-st., Walworth, u.t. 50 yrs., g.r. 5*l*. 5s., 350*l*.; 52 and 54, Knowles Hill-cres., Lewisham, u.t. 81 yrs., g.r. 11*l*., 220*l*.; 4 and 6, Edith-villas, Lower Tooting, u.t. 80 yrs., g.r. 12*l*., 160*l*.

JANUARY 29.—By *Jones, Lang, & Co.*: No. 77, Bishopsgate-street Without, f., r. 100*l*., 1,230*l*.—By *F. J. Bisley*: 16, Hadland-st., Rotherhithe, u.t. 64 yrs., g.r. 2*l*. 5s., r. 24*l*. 14s., 240*l*.; 5, Adam-st., f., r. 15*l*. 12s., 150*l*.

[*Contractions used in these lists.*—F.g.r. for freehold ground-rent; l.g.r. for leasehold ground-rent; i.g.r. for improved ground-rent; g.r. for ground-rent; r. for rent; f. for freehold; c. for copyhold; l. for leasehold; e.r. for estimated rental; u.t. for unexpired term; p.a. for per annum; yrs. for years; st. for street; rd. for road; sq. for square; pl. for place; ter. for terrace; cres. for crescent; yd. for yard, &c.

PRICES CURRENT OF MATERIALS.

TIMBER.		
Greenheart, B.G. ton	9/0/6	0/0/0
Teak, E.I. load	9/10/0	15/0/0
Sequoia, U.S. ft. cu.	2/3	2/0
Ash, Canada load	2/10/0	4/0/0
Birch, do.	3/0/0	4/5/0
Elm, do.	3/10/0	4/15/0
Fir, Dantsic, &c.	2/0/0	3/10/0
Oak, do.	3/10/0	4/10/0
Canada	5/0/0	7/0/0
Pine, Canada red	2/10/0	3/10/0
Do. yellow	2/10/0	5/0/0
Lath, D'ntsic, fath	5/5/0	6/10/0
St. Petersburg	5/10/0	7/10/0
Deals, Finland, 2nd & 1st std 100	8/10/0	10/10/0
Do. 4th & 3rd	7/10/0	8/10/0
Do. Riga	6/10/0	8/0/0
St. Petersburg, 1st yellow	10/10/0	15/0/0
Do. 2nd yellow	8/10/0	10/0/0
Do. white	7/0/0	10/10/0
Swedish	7/15/0	16/0/0
White Sea	8/10/0	17/10/0
Canada, Pine 1st	19/10/0	25/10/0
Do. do. 2nd	14/10/0	16/10/0
Do. do. 3rd, &c.	6/10/0	10/10/0
Do. Spruce, 1st	8/10/0	11/0/0
Do. do. 3rd & 2nd	6/10/0	8/0/0
New Brunswick	7/0/0	7/10/0
Battens, all kinds	3/10/0	15/10/0
Flooring Boards, sq., 1 in. prep. 1st	0/8/6	0/14/6
Do. 2nd	0/7/6	0/11/4
Other qualities	0/5/3	0/8/0
Cedar, Cuba ..ft.	/3½	/4½
Honduras, &c.	/3½	/4½
Mahogany, Cuba	/4½	/6½
St. Domingo, cargo av.	/4½	2/0
Mexican do. do	/4	/5
Tobasco do. do	/5½	/7
Honduras do.	/5½	/8½
Box, Turkey ton	4/0/0	13/0/0
Rose, Rio	10/0/0	20/0/0
Bahia	8/0/0	18/0/0
Satin, St. Domingo ...ft.	0/0/9	0/1/9

TIMBER (continued).		
Satin, Porto Rico	0/0/10	0/1/6
Walnut, Italian	0/0/3½	0/0/7
METALS.		
Iron—Pig in Scotland ...ton	2/3/0	2/3/3
Bar, Welsh, in London	6/0/0	6/10/0
Do. do. at works in Wales	5/10/0	6/0/0
Do. Staffordshire, in London	6/5/0	6/15/0
Copper—British, cake and ingot	47/10/0	48/0/0
Best selected	48/10/0	49/0/0
Sheets, strong	57/0/0	58/0/0
Chili, bars	44/5/0	44/16/3
Yellow Metal lb.	0/0/5¼	0/0/5½
Lead—Pig, Spanish ...ton	10/12/6	10/15/0
English, com. brands	10/17/6	11/0/0
Sheet, English, 3 lbs. per sq. ft. and upwards	12/10/0	0/0/0
Pipe	13/0/0	0/0/0
Zinc—English Sheet ...ton	25/10/0	0/0/0
Vieille Montagne	26/0/0	0/0/0
Tin—Straits	90/10/0	91/7/6
Australian	91/12/6	92/2/6
English Ingots	93/5/0	93/10/0
OILS.		
Linseed ...ton	19/0/0	19/15/0
Cocoanut, Cochin	28/5/0	0/0/0
Do. Ceylon	23/0/0	0/0/0
Palm, Lagos	23/10/0	0/0/0
Rapeseed, English pale	28/15/0	0/0/0
Do. brown	27/0/0	0/0/0
Cottonseed ref.	18/5/0	0/0/0
Oleine	0/0/0	0/0/0
Lubricating, U.S.	4/10/0	5/10/0
Do. refined	6/0/0	11/0/0
Tar—Stockholm barrel	0/19/0	1/0/0
Archangel	0/12/6	0/0/0

TENDERS.

[Communications for insertion under this heading must reach us *not later than* 12 noon on *Thursdays*.]

ANERLEY.—For decorative repairs to 14, Anerley-park, for Mr. F. A. Bell:—

T. W. Jones, Beckenham £120 0 0

[No competition.]

CHELSFIELD (Kent).—For re-building shop, house, and premises, after fire, at Pratt's Bottom, Chelsfield, Kent, for Mr. O. Osgood. Mr. St. Pierre Harris, architect and surveyor, 1, Basinghall-street, E.C.:—

T. Knight	£979 0	R. A. Lowe	£953 0
F. Wood	960 0	W. Owen, Farnborough*	798 10

* Accepted.

CRICKLEWOOD.—For the erection of new Congregational schools, Cricklewood, for the Committee. Messrs. Spalding & Cross, architects and surveyors, 15, Queen-street, Cheapside, E.C.:—

Balaam Bros.	£2,021	E. Toms	£1,741
W. & H. Castle	1,873	J. Allen & Sons	1,710
Elthwaite & Son	1,827	Gould & Brand	1,707
Aitchison	1,793	Neave & Neave	1,680
Lorden & Son	1,787	Rowe Bros., Camden-town	1,700

GREAT YARMOUTH.—For additions to Cobholm Island Boys' School, for the Great Yarmouth School Board. Messrs. Bottle & Olley, architects, Great Yarmouth:—

M. Barnard	£1,339 0 0	R. Davy	£1,241 15 6
R. Easter	1,319 8 0	Brand & Cooper	1,211 0 0
G. T. Flaxman	1,410 0 0	Grimble & Watts	1,200 0 0
T. Howes	1,267 9 0	G. W. Beech	1,198 0 0
J. H. Howes	1,251 0 0	J. F. Cooper	1,197 15 0
W. H. Larkins	1,245 5 0	J. Leggett, Great Yarmouth (accepted)	1,162 0 0
G. Beckett	1,243 0 0		

LONDON.—For alterations and additions to "Lynmouth," Tulse-hill, for Mr. J. Fitter. Mr. E. Crosse, architect, 32, Bermondsey-square, S.E.:—

T. W. Jones, Beckenham £287 0 0

[No competition.]

NORTHALLERTON.—Accepted for the construction of two reservoirs, &c., in Oak Dale, and a service reservoir at the Northallerton Waterworks for the Local Board. Mr. A. M. Fowler, engineer, 1, St. Peter's-square, Manchester:—

Contract No. 1: Cast-Iron Pipes.

The Clay Cross Company, Clay Cross £3,367 0 0

Contract No. 2: Pipelaying.

Joseph Goldsbrough, Chester-le-Street, Durham £1,493 5 7

ORPINGTON (Kent).—For the erection of a shop and house and three cottages at the "Chislehurst-road," Orpington, Kent, for Mr. James Cox. Mr. St. Pierre Harris, architect and surveyor, 1, Basinghall-street:—

W. Owen	£918	T. Knight	£815
F. Wood	848	Somerford & Son, Clapham and Orpington (accepted)	697
C. Stebbings	843		

ORPINGTON (Kent).—For additions and alterations to the Wellington-road School, Orpington, Kent, for the Orpington School Board. Mr. St. Pierre Harris, architect, 1, Basinghall-street, E.C. Quantities by Messrs. C. Stanger & Sons:—

R. A. Lowe	£2,683 0	Holt & Son	£2,492 0
Grubb	2,673 0	Stebbings	2,481 0
Laurence & Son	2,625 0	Mid-Kent Building Co.	2,232 0
Staines & Son	2,504 0	Gratty	2,259 0
Smith & Son	2,559 0	Rick	2,228 0
White & Son	2,705 4	Martin & Co.	2,229 0
W. Willis	2,596 13	Somerford & Son	2,216 0
Duthoit	2,083 0		

SUBSCRIBERS in LONDON and the SUBURBS, by prepaying at the Publishing Office, 10s. per annum (or 4s. 9d. per quarter), can ensure receiving "The Builder" by *Friday Morning's* post.

The Builder Cathedral Series.

1891.

1. CANTERBURY	Jan. 3.	7. SALISBURY	July 4.
2. LICHFIELD	Feb. 7.	8. BRISTOL	Aug. 1.
3. ST. ALBAN'S	Mar. 7.	9. NORWICH	Sept. 5.
4. PETERBOROUGH	April 4.	10. ROCHESTER	Oct. 3.
5. WELLS	May 2.	11. LINCOLN	Nov. 7.
6. EXETER	June 6	12. GLOUCESTER	Dec. 5.

1892.

13. ST. PAUL'S	Jan. 2.	16. ELY	April 2.
14. HEREFORD	Feb. 6.	17. LLANDAFF	May 7.
15. CHICHESTER	Mar. 5	18. OXFORD	June 4.

[Further arrangements will be duly announced.]

Price FOURPENCE each (by post 4½d.), except Nos. 1 and 2, which are *out of print*, but the VIEW, PLAN, AND DESCRIPTION of CANTERBURY and of LICHFIELD have been re-printed, and they can now be had, price ONE SHILLING each set; by post, 1s. 2d.

THE REREDOS, ST. PAUL'S.

Reprinted from "THE BUILDER" January 28, 1888 (15 in. by 11½ in.), on Stout paper, unfolded, for framing, 6d.; by post, 8d.

PORTFOLIOS,

for Preserving the Plates unfolded, 2s. 6d.; by post, 3s.

London: Office of "THE BUILDER," 46, Catherine-street, W.C.

Now ready (86 plates), Price ONE GUINEA.

"THE BUILDER ALBUM" OF ROYAL ACADEMY ARCHITECTURE.

1891.

SOME PRESS NOTICES.

"In numerous well-drawn and well-printed plates of plans, elevations, and sections of buildings, this comely folio illustrates the latest Royal Academy Exhibition of Architectural designs, and effectually proves how much greater attention that room in Burlington House deserved than it received."—*Athenæum.*

"A handsome folio Volume."—*Guardian.*

"A large and extremely handsome volume."—*Newcastle Daily Chronicle.*

"While the collection has a special value for Architects, it has an interest for all, and it forms a very handsome book."—*Glasgow Herald.*

"To Architects who were unable to visit the Academy will be very welcome."—*Western Morning News.*

"A handsome series of eighty six reproductions of drawings exhibited in the Architecture room . . . executed in the best possible style."—*Scotsman.*

"A collection of the best and most important drawings hung in the Architectural room of the Royal Academy Exhibition . . . A most valuable record of the year's Architectural work . . . A useful addition to any library, as well as a first-class work of reference to the student and busy professional man."—*Leeds Mercury.*

LONDON

Office of "The Builder," 46, Catherine-street, W.C.

TERMS OF SUBSCRIPTION.

"THE BUILDER" is supplied DIRECT from the Office to residents in any part of the United Kingdom at the rate of 19s. per annum PREPAID. To all parts of Europe, America, Australia, and New Zealand, 26s. per annum. To India, China, Ceylon, &c., 30s. per annum. Remittances payable to DOUGLAS FOURDRINIER, Publisher, No. 46, Catherine-street, W.C.

TO CORRESPONDENTS.

R. R. R.—F. L. (We could only publish such a suggestion if backed by the opinion of an eminent river and harbour engineer as to its feasibility).—H. S.—K. B. (should send amount).

All statements of facts, lists of tenders, &c., must be accompanied by the name and address of the sender, not necessarily for publication.

We are compelled to decline pointing out books and giving addresses.

NOTE.—The responsibility of signed articles, and papers read at public meetings, rests, of course, with the authors.

We cannot undertake to return rejected communications.

Letters or communications (beyond mere news-items) which have been duplicated for other journals, are NOT DESIRED.

All communications regarding literary and artistic matter should be addressed to THE EDITOR; all communications relating to advertisements and other exclusively business matters should be addressed to THE PUBLISHER, and *not* to the Editor.

The Builder.

Vol. LXII. No. 2558. | Saturday, February 13, 1892.

ILLUSTRATIONS.

Houses, 190 and 191, Queen's Gate, South Kensington.—Mr. F. O. Knight, Architect .... *Double-Page Photo-Litho.*
East Window, Leigh Church, near Manchester.—Executed by Messrs. Shrigley & Hunt .... *Double-Page Ink-Photo.*
Design for a Free Library for a County Town.—By Mr. Arthur Bartlett .... *Double-Page Ink-Photo*
House at Wokingham.—Mr. Ernest Newton, Architect .... *Single-Page Photo-Litho.*
Design for a Painter's House and Studio, by Mr. F. M. Simpson, Architect .... *Single-Page Photo-Litho.*

Blocks in Text.

Plan of Djûma Mosque, Ispahan .... Page 117
Ruined Tower at Rei, Persia 119
Plans of House, Queen's Gate .... Page 12[illegible]
Diagrams in Student's Column: Heating by Hot Water .... 12[illegible]

CONTENTS.

The Electrical Exhibition at Sydenham 113
Notes 114
Saracenic Architecture 116
Magazines and Reviews 119
Royal Institute of British Architects 120
Houses, Queen's Gate 122
East Window, S. Mary's Church, Leigh, Lancashire 122
Design for a Public Library for a County Town 122
House at Wokingham 122
A Painter's House and Studio 122
Competitions 122
The Architectural Association Spring Visits 123
Sheffield Society of Architects and Surveyors 123
National Association of Master Builders of Great Britain 123
The Institute of Builders 124
London County Council 124
Dr. Teale on "Dust" 125
Concrete for Artisans' Dwellings 125
Match-boarding on New Brick Walls and Oakblock Flooring on Concrete 126
Student's Column.—Warming Buildings by Hot Water, VII 126
Obituary 127
General Building News 127
Sanitary and Engineering News 127
Foreign and Colonial 127
Miscellaneous 128
Meetings 129
Recent Patents 129
Some Recent Sales of Property 129
Prices Current of Materials 129

The Electrical Exhibition at Sydenham.

ON Saturday last the Lord Mayor and Lady Mayoress visited the Crystal Palace. This second opening of the Exhibition has had the effect of stimulating the efforts of exhibitors, and many of the stalls which have hitherto remained almost empty since the first opening in January are now fairly complete. In exhibitions of this class the readiness of manufacturers to advertise their wares is made use of to instruct the public, and with this latter aim the catalogue has been drawn up.

The exhibits are divided into sections,—"Phenomena and Laws of Electricity," "Electrical Measurements," "Batteries," "Motors," &c.,—seventeen sections in all; with two or three pages of what, after revision, may be accurate popular explanation, as a preface to each section. The idea is a good one could the Exhibition be arranged on the same plan, but that is obviously impossible; no exhibitor could be expected to distribute his goods over a dozen stalls, where they would be mixed with those of some fifty other firms; consequently, to follow out the catalogue plan, one would have to go through the Exhibition seventeen times,—an appalling prospect.

From this general scheme the Government exhibits of telegraphic instruments is exempted. Here we have chronologically-arranged specimens of the principal apparatus used from 1837, down to the present day.

Amongst them is a delightful placard of 1837, announcing the opening of the first telegraphic office, and engaging to send messages "with most confiding secrecy" at a shilling each. From this placard it appears that people were willing then to pay a shilling to see the telegraph in operation (as we should now to see, or hear, a phonograph).

Those were the ages of faith. No one then doubted the material existence of electricity, and the very rate at which the "fluid" travels is given.

The Postal Telegraph Department, moreover, not only arranges the exhibits well, but gives a concise but intelligible account of what Clerk Maxwell, as a boy, used to call the "go of it" in the majority of cases.

Leaving the Government stall we come at once to Mr. James White's exhibit of Sir William Thomson's measuring instruments, including current meters which will measure any current from the hundredth of an ampere to a thousand amperes, watt meters, an improved rheostat, and the exquisitely delicate siphon recorder for submarine telegraphy.

On the right is an interesting exhibit of the Maquay Electric Light Syndicate of portable lamps, driven by primary batteries, in which the tiny filament is raised to a very high degree of incandescence.

One of these lamps is burning under water, showing that it may be used as a diver's lamp; with this we may contrast the Mining and General Electric Lamp Company's hand-lamps on the opposite side of the Nave, which are driven by lithanode cells and have a switch connected with resistances so that the brightness of the light may be varied.

A recess between the Mediæval and Renaissance Courts has been appropriately fitted up by Messrs. Benham & Froud as the chancel of a church electrically lighted. The advantages of the electric light in church are as obvious as in the theatre, but we fear it will make its way there slowly; wax candles on the altar are likely to survive for reasons of ritual long after they cease to be used elsewhere, as a *stone* sacrificial knife existed long after the Stone Age.

The stand of the Consolidated Telephone Company, No. 7, and No. 104, that of the National Telephone Company, will be attractive to all who are interested,—and who is not?—in this marvellous application of electricity to the service of man. Here will be found numerous compact and beautifully-finished instruments, receivers, and transmitters, including the pretty little watch receiver. The National Telephone Company also exhibits a multiple switchboard, so that visitors can form an idea of what takes place daily in a Central Exchange. Its instruments are in communication with London, Manchester, Liverpool, and other towns, not only illustrating the great advance of late in long-distance telephoning, but giving its customers an opportunity in the Music-room, No. 191, of, in effect, attending various London and provincial theatres.

For those who live far from a Central Lighting Station, who prefer additional cost of up-keep to heavy initial expense, and who consider that the constant re-charging of primary cells is less troublesome than the occasional attention required by a gas or petroleum engine, the Weymersch Battery Syndicate, Stand 113, provide primary batteries which claim a high degree of constancy for many hours.

Messrs. Rashleigh, Phipps, & Dawson have a prettily-arranged stall in the North Nave, with all the latest improvements in electric fittings, and some quaint and fanciful allegorical designs; they also light and contribute part of the decorations to some rooms in the South Gallery, artistically furnished by Messrs. Godfrey Giles & Co.; they use, with good results, translucent plates of ivory to soften the light, or bead ray-diffusers to distribute it effectually over a room. The electrical effects introduced into the Pantomime are also arranged by this firm.

In the south nave the most conspicuous object is an electric crane shown by Messrs. Crompton & Co., and near it the search light exhibited by the same firm flashes its rays on the fountain which is playing close by. They also exhibit a four-pole machine capable of supplying over 8,000 lamps, besides other dynamos, some specially designed to give heavy currents for electric plating or for the new process of electric welding. A completely-furnished municipal testing laboratory for testing meters and for faults in insulation should attract the attention of County Councillors, actual or potential, as also should their model of the system of mains; while builders and architects will be interested in the ornamental mouldings, picture-rails, cornices, &c., designed for carrying and concealing the house wires. Of more technical interest are their twisted armature bars to reduce Foucault currents, their cut-outs and heavy discharge switches.

The beautifully-furnished show-rooms in the Western Gallery, decorated by Messrs. Wallace & Co., are also lighted by Messrs. Crompton & Co.

d

Messrs. Swinburne & Co.'s stand will be one of the most remarkable in the Exhibition when their transformer, giving 0·2 ampère and 100,000 volts, can be seen regularly in action. It has been working for some time at Teddington, where it sparks a distance of 6 in. in air, establishing an arc which can be drawn out to almost any length, and sends a current through substances hitherto regarded as amongst the best insulators, heating them as currents of ordinary voltage do conductors. There is, of course, a display of "hedgehog" transformers, with their accompanying condensers, so valuable in conjunction with open circuit converters.

Considerable interest will be taken in the General Electric Company's (No. 7, south nave) exhibition of apparatus for heating and cooking by electricity. Though it is admitted that the production of heat by electrical means is expensive, yet for some purposes this disadvantage is more than compensated for by the economy in its use, the heat being obtained exactly where, and only while, it is wanted. In most of these appliances the resistances which can be heated by an electric current are embedded in enamel. The electric cigar lighter has a platinum wire coil embedded in asbestos, which is raised to incandescence by the current, and would certainly be useful in a house where reliance on the electric light has made people careless in the supply of matches. The lady, too, whose dismay at finding her room lighted by electricity and warmed by hot-water pipes Mr. Du Maurier has lately depicted in *Punch*, should present her hostess with a pair of electric hair curlers, so should modern science remedy the "disadvantages of modern science." We question, however, whether electrically-heated foot-warmers have any future before them. The expense here is a fatal objection; one does not want a foot-warmer for five seconds or for five minutes only. At this stall also may be seen an improved automatic cut-out, and ampère-meters and voltmeters on Donnison's system.

The most remarkable of Messrs. Woodhouse & Rawson's exhibits is the "Kingdon" alternator, in which, as in a transformer, the coils of both field-magnets and armature are stationary; the current is produced by the revolution of inductor blocks, which thus vary the induction in the armature. The mechanical advantages of having the moving parts of iron only are obvious, and the clearance can be made very small.

Messrs. Siemens Brothers contribute, besides the usual measuring instruments, batteries, &c., a carbon contact switch for heavy currents, a model of the cable steamer *Faraday*, and an apparatus for illustrating the curves formed by the vibrations of the diaphragm of a telephone. Their most sensational exhibit, however, is the 52,000 volt-transformer; but this will have to take a second place when Messrs. Swinburne & Co.'s 100,000 volter is at work.

The Brush Electrical Engineering Company exhibit an electrical tramcar which is so placed that it is impossible to see anything of the motor which should drive it,—tramcars can be seen without visiting Sydenham. They have also a number of the well-known Brush machines of various sizes, several of which are of the old discarded pattern with channelled instead of laminated armature cores. Two or three Mordey alternators are also shown, one of which is apparently taken to pieces the better to show the construction: we say *apparently*, for the parts of this machine never were, or could be, put together,—the armature belongs to a much smaller machine than the field magnets; we find from the catalogue that this is not due to an oversight, as we at first imagined, but that the firm have deliberately chosen to exhibit different parts of two machines, the out-put of one being half as much again as the other; but the purpose of this arrangement remains a mystery.

For the system of concentric wiring shown by Messrs. Andrews & Co., Stand No. 162, it is claimed that the leads and house wires occupy less space, that wood casing is unnecessary, and that joints can be made with less skilled labour than on the ordinary plan. On the other hand, it seems that a fault is more difficult to find, or, when found, to remedy. The advantage of a short circuit, and fuses going, whenever there is the slightest fault, will hardly be so clear to others as it is to Messrs. Andrews, but the saving of space is a real gain, and if the wires can be run, and bent round corners, without bringing the inner wire into contact with the outer, there may be some field for this system.

The specialty of Messrs. Frank Suter & Co., No. 154, North Nave, is their appliance for picture lighting by means of reflectors, so that the direct glare of the lamps may not dazzle the eyes of the spectator; but their prettiest exhibit is a little glow-lamp of frosted glass shaped like the flame of a candle and mounted on a candle-like support; at a short distance these lamps may easily be mistaken for very bright and steady candles.

In the machine-room, where the dynamos are at work, the great improvement in dynamo design since the exhibition of 1881, or even since the South Kensington Exhibition of 1885, strikes even a casual observer.

The modern machine is much more compact, makes less noise, and has a far greater output; the sparking at the brushes is imperceptible (except in one Brush, and, of course, the Thomson-Houston machines); many of the machines are direct-driven, saving the waste of space and energy implied by the older belt and pulley method. The number of gas-engines used is also a prominent feature of this exhibition, and it is noteworthy that here they work almost in silence, which they can seldom be persuaded to do in any private installation. The absence of belts and shafting noticeable throughout the Palace, and not merely in the machine-room, is a striking illustration of the advance made in the electrical transmission of power; nearly all the machinery in motion which is not driven directly by an engine being actuated by an electric motor.

Visitors to the Frankfort Exhibition were attracted to the Thomson-Houston machine by the blaze of the commutator sparking, due to the spherical armature being wound in three sections only, and the curious crackling noise as it is blown out by the air blast. The makers apparently do not care for this sort of advertisement, for in the present exhibition the commutator is turned away from the spectators and the noise lost in the general hum of the machinery.

The South Gallery is chiefly given up to examples of domestic lighting to which we have already referred, and to medical batteries and belts, of which the less said the better. The Consolidated Telephone Company have here a supplementary stand, but at several of the stalls the exhibits are only indirectly electrical, as No. 221 N., Cash & Co.'s exhibit of bleached shellac varnishes, &c.; Wake & Sanders's mica exhibition at 206 A.; and (No. 227) Britannia Rubber and Kamptulicon Company.

The exhibit of Messrs. Johnson & Phillips, though conspicuous, is not at first sight obviously connected with electricity. The prominent objects on their stand, No. 10, South Gallery, are some large buoys and grapnels, which are used in laying and picking up cables. Less easily seen are a set of linesman's tools, and specimens of switches, resistances, &c. They also show D.P. accumulator cells designed to bear a high rate of discharge without injury to the plates.

In the Machine Room, No. 60, this firm also exhibits a number of Mr. Kapp's dynamos, both direct and alternating, including a large eight-pole dynamo of 130 kilowatts output, coupled with a Davey-Paxman triple expansion engine. Mr. Kapp, who in the earlier days of electrical engineering had much to do with the designing of Messrs. Crompton's dynamos, claims for his own a very high efficiency, due to the care with which the proportions have been worked out beforehand.

The steam and gas engines in the machine-room, though indispensable for the production of the electric light, can scarcely be regarded as themselves part of an "electrical" exhibition, and we may be pardoned if we pass them by with a mere nod of recognition. Even less claim to the title of electrical has the stand of Messrs. Chubb & Son, where safes and locks are shown on the strength of the addition of an electrical alarm. Similarly a diver's dress is displayed by Mr. Applegarth, with the addition of an electric lamp in the helmet; but all these have a better claim than the Homacoustic Speaking Tube Company, who introduce their speaking tubes, by adding to them an electric bell call.

To sum up, the general effect of the exhibition, especially at night, is very good. The blaze of light from the stands, softened and freed from glare by every kind of shade and screen, contrasts well with the harsher white light of the arc lamps, which, burning with a steadiness unhoped for ten years back, and hung too high to clash with the milder glow lamps, illuminate the rest of the Palace. There is every reason, in spite of the absence of many important firms, to expect the exhibition to be a success. The Palace Company and the exhibitors mutually assist each other, the former supplying a roof and appropriate surroundings, and a certain number of habitual visitors; the latter decorating and beautifying the Palace, and attracting many visitors who would otherwise never think of going down to Sydenham.

Amongst the firms who do not seem to appreciate the advantages offered them may be mentioned Messrs. Mather & Platt, Paterson & Cooper, Latimer, Clark, Muirhead, & Co., Goolden, Parsons, and Ferranti & Co., but we understand on good authority that the last-named firm has, though late, repented of its determination, and we may expect to find it in the next edition of the catalogue.

NOTES.

REFERENCE has been made once or twice in our columns to the large and highly-finished model of the Parthenon, constructed in Paris a year or two ago under the direction of M. Chipiez, and which has since been purchased for and erected in an Art Muesum in New York. The model itself we have not had the opportunity of seeing, but from the fine set of photographs of it which have been taken in New York we fear that the American institution which has purchased it has obtained a representation or restoration of the celebrated temple which is in some important points very far from accuracy. In the first place, M. Chipiez has chosen to insert seated winged sphinxes at the bases of the pediment, and a very large acroterion, flanked by winged genii, at the apex. The sphinxes, or something of the kind, may be probable, though there is no authority for them; the acroterion and its figures in some sort also, but the genii are represented as apparently silver figures, or burnished metal of some kind, and in this respect and in their attitude have a somewhat tinsel and Parisian appearance. A more important point, which is demonstrably wrong, is that the entasis of the columns is greatly exaggerated. The actual deflection from the straight line in the columns amounts roughly to about ½ in. in a height of over 31 ft. It is not visible to the eye even on the building, except to those who know it is there and fancy they see it. Yet it is so exaggerated in the model that it is distinctly visible in a photograph which reduces the columns to about 3½ in. in height, and must represent a deflection from the straight line of 4 in. or 5 in. But the most extraordinary blunder is that the metope sculptures are in their wrong places. Beneath the pediment sculpture of the east front are shown the metope sculptures which belong to the west front, and *vice-versâ!* This is a curious example of the light-hearted indifference of French archæologists to accuracy in matters of this kind. All the information as to the real positions which were occupied by the metope sculptures is easily accessible at the British Museum, but we presume it could not be supposed possible that a French *savant* could learn anything from English sources. It is a pleasant consideration for the New York people, who have probably paid a large sum for a model of the Parthenon containing, besides minor inaccuracies, a serious blunder which the most ordinary care and investigation might have prevented.

THE promoters and framers of the new proposed Glasgow Building Regulations Bill seem rather to have laid themselves open to opposition by the sweeping nature of their clauses and the rather high-handed manner in which it seems intended to carry them out. The measure is no doubt a very well-intended one, but it has obviously been framed in the first instance without sufficient regard to what is fairly practicable under present circumstances. A good many modifications have been made in the direction of a more moderate policy; but we agree with some of the critics of the measure in thinking that one of the first points to be considered in connexion with such a Bill should have been the provision of a better-constituted authority for the administration of building legislation. It is perfectly evident from what is stated (and not contradicted) in the Glasgow press, that the Dean of Guild Court, with its constant change of direct personal authority owing to the system of election of a new Dean of Guild every two years or so, is on this if not on other accounts a most unfit authority to deal with permanent building legislation. On the other hand it is perfectly evident that a good deal of the opposition comes from landlords and others who are concerned for their own pockets more than for the public good. A proposed By-law that no building should exceed the height of the street on which it abutted has provoked violent opposition, and is characterised in a leader in the *Glasgow Herald* as 'absurd," while a memorial from the Glasgow Institute of Architects speaks of it as injurious and uncalled-for, and one which would lower the value of some of the most important sites in the city. Such a By-law certainly should not be passed without the reservation of a dispensing power in special cases; but in the main a restriction of height of buildings in proportion to width of streets is in accordance with the best sanitary opinions of the day, and the Glasgow Institute of Architects must be rather behind the age if they are not aware of this. Such legislation is distinctly for the good of the city community generally, as promoting both the health and the pleasant aspect of a city, and the fact that it will prevent some owners of sites from making as much out of them as they otherwise would is an entirely secondary matter in relation to wider public interests. The clause has, it appears, been entirely removed in deference to what we should call one-sided and rather ignorant criticism. For our part, we hope the principle will not be lost sight of, and that it will be retained in some form or other in the final arrangement of the new regulations.

THE strike of engineers on the Tyne, &c., still continues, and a good deal is being made of the fact that in some cases the notices were given by the employers, the dispute being generally referred to at meetings of the men as a "lock-out." Sir C. Palmer,—at whose establishment the dispute practically commenced,—protests against this as being altogether misleading, and states that the whole trouble might have been avoided had the fitters agreed to have the questions at issue submitted to arbitration. The effect of these unlooked-for stoppages in the shipbuilding industry is to increase the difficulty of estimating the cost of and probable time occupied in constructing vessels. This was demonstrated by the managing director of the Thames Ironworks Company (and also by the First Lord of the Admiralty and the Director of Naval Construction), on the occasion of the launching of the cruiser *Grafton*. During the construction of this vessel, the gates of the builders' yard were picketed for eighteen months, so that the men employed were unable to go to and from their work without running considerable risks. Again, at the Newcastle Chamber of Commerce last week, Sir B. C. Browne, a large employer of labour in the disaffected district, stated that when the dispute occurred between the carpenters and joiners a year or two ago, an order for a steamer went to Scandinavia which would have been given to his firm but for the stoppage. The question then at issue was very similar to that which has brought about the present deadlock, and the recurrence of strikes of this nature must produce hesitation as to the acceptance of large contracts,—possibly to the permanent injury of the whole district. It seems strange that the men cannot recognise this, and make an effort to adjust their differences amicably. Certainly ship-building proper is not so much affected at present, but what has been said of ship-building applies equally to ship-engineering.

THE correspondence which has recently taken place in the *Times* on the subject of professional persons taking commissions without the knowledge of their principals, has done no more than again call attention in a public manner to what is well known to nine out of every ten men of business. But until agents are prohibited by law from taking commissions without the knowledge of their principals, this practice will flourish. The competition of the present day is so keen that men will do anything to gain business. It must be admitted also that in some respects the giving and taking of commissions behind the back of the principals is not so injurious to their interests as might at first be supposed. Thus, if an estate-agent gives back part of the commission on the sale of an estate to the solicitor who has introduced the business, the principal does not suffer, since if this part of the commission which he has paid did not go into the solicitor's pocket it would have remained in that of the estate-agent. We do not defend the practice, for its indirect results are often bad; but, on the other hand, it is desirable that the public should not be under the impression that they will get much direct advantage by its legal abolition.

THE destruction by fire of the Hotel Royal at New York directs attention to the dangerous character of these large buildings,—a subject to which we referred in a recent "Note" in regard to the action of certain insurance companies in Chicago. Such a building as a large hotel of great height is not safe without a watchman constantly on guard throughout the night, and it is essential also that means of escape should be easy and numerous. We are aware that it is easier to give the latter advice than it is to carry it out, and those who erect these buildings will certainly try if possible to avoid everything which does not tend to profit. It has been pretty well demonstrated, indeed, that enormous buildings of a public kind, such as hotels, will have to be periodically inspected by the public authorities under legislative directions, if there is to be real security for the members of the community by whom they are used. We have fortunately been free in this country from such calamities as that which has just occurred at New York, but it may well serve as a warning to us to be on our guard.

IT was gravely announced in an evening paper a few days ago that the Midland Railway Company contemplate introducing dining and sleeping cars on their long-distance trains. This information would appear to be some years behind-hand, but the words "third-class" had probably escaped either the scissors or the paste-brush, as we understand that this enterprising company are about to try the experiment of running third-class sleeping-cars on some of their trains. The rapid advance in the matter of accommodation is one of the most remarkable features of railway development in this country, and to the Midland Company much of the credit for this must be given. That their policy of making things as comfortable as possible for their patrons is a wise one, is evident from the increasing prosperity of the line, as measured by the gross receipts; although the expenditure it entails apparently tends to keep down the amount available for dividend. The past half-year has been one of the most successful in the history of the company, which has now reached a position second only to the London and North-Western as regards traffic receipts. But in spite of the increase in gross earnings, the dividend declared is at the same rate as that for the corresponding period last year, with a smaller balance to be carried forward. The announcement to which we have alluded may, therefore, be received with some disfavour by shareholders who have an eye to economy; but the travelling public are too quick to appreciate any additional comforts that are offered them for there to be much room for distrusting the action of the directors,—especially in view of the increasing competition for the passenger traffic to and from the north. Another effect of this announcement will be to make the less-favoured third-class travellers on some of the southern lines devoutly wish that similar incentives were at work on their side of the Thames. The contrast in accommodation is striking enough already.

DR. A. KÖRTE, in a letter to the *Berliner Philologische Wochenschrift* (February 6), suggests an addition to the list of the supposed hypæthral temples of antiquity. The temple of Apollo at Delphi was not included in the instances cited by Dr. Dörpfeld in his recent article on the subject ("Athen. Mitteil.," xvi., pp. 334-344). The reason given by Dr. Körte for supposing the temple to be hypæthral is curious and ingenious. In a passage in Diodorus (xvi., 27),—a passage which, by the by, seems so far to have escaped the attention of the warmest supporters of the theory,—there occurs the following statement:—"An omen occurred to him (*i.e.*, Philomenus), also in the Sanctuary of Apollo, — an eagle that was hovering over the temple of the god swooped down to the earth in pursuit of the doves that were reared in the sanctuary and caught some of them from the very altars." Dr. Körte thinks that, if the eagle came down straight, as birds of prey usually do, he must have descended through a hypæthral opening. The passage is certainly worth noting, but it does not seem to us absolutely conclusive. An eagle might appear to be hovering over the actual temple (ὑπερπετόμενος τὸν νεων) to one standing outside it, and yet come down straight enough and alight on an altar *outside* the temple but within the sanctuary (ἐν τῷ ἱερῷ).

SINCE the publication of Mr. J. G. Frazer's "Golden Bough," the Temple of Diana at Nemi has become a reality to many to whom it was before a bare name, if so much. Probably, however, there are still some who are not aware that the antiquities discovered there by Lord Savile, in his recent excavations, are now lodged in the Art Museum of Nottingham Castle. If sufficient subscribers are forthcoming (200 is the minimum) Mr. Wallis, the Director of the Museum, proposes to publish a descriptive catalogue of these antiquities in quarto size, with illustrations and views. Lord Savile is to contribute an account of the discovery of the temple, of which there will be a ground-plan, and all the principal objects found will be reproduced in photo-mezzotype. These objects range in date from B.C. 300 to B.C. 80. The coins are an unusually complete sequence, beginning from the "aes rude," and containing fine examples of every type and fraction of the Roman "as." There are few sculptures, but one portrait bust and stele, inscribed (of Fundelia C. F. Rufa), to judge from the specimen illustration, is certainly a very fine piece of work. There are also a multitude of terra-cottas, personal ornaments, sacrificial utensils, and many architectural details. Among the bronzes are many statuettes of nymphs and priestesses of Diana, and a remarkable sacrificial ladle inscribed Diana in archaic characters.

WHEN, at the beginning of this century, iron pipes were placed down the face of the Castle rock of Edinburgh, to carry off the sewage, it was thought to be a great improvement upon the state of matters which previously existed. The advance of civilisation is conducive to fastidiousness, and now the exposed pipes cannot be tolerated, and are in course of being removed. The sewage will then be carried off by hidden conduits.

THE space in the Scottish National Gallery is now too restricted to allow of a proper display of the existing art treasures. No room can be found for some recent bequests, and works offered by the Royal Scottish Academy have been refused,—works which are, undoubtedly, superior in art-work and public interest to many of those now in the Gallery. The Government have given a grant of 1,000*l.* a year for the purchase of pictures, and it is obvious that more extended premises are required, so that the new works acquired from the grant and those gifted to the nation may be made available for public delectation and instruction. Two courses are open,—either (1) that the Royal Scottish Academy shall be required to vacate the portion of the premises allotted to them, and be provided for elsewhere, whereby the National Gallery would be doubled in space capacity; or (2) that the present building be given up entirely to the Academy, and a new National Gallery erected. In the event of the latter course being resolved upon, it is suggested that the National Monument on the Calton Hill should be completed and made available for the display of the national art treasures. To finish the National Monument according to the original conception would require a larger sum of money than it is probable would be forthcoming, but a modification of the too ambitious design might be carried out at a moderate cost, and a building produced worthy of the site and suitable for the purposes of an art gallery. Indeed, such a design was prepared, and exhibited, by the late Mr. Dick Peddie, and in that design he made use of the existing pillars which form a conspicuous feature in the Scottish capital. Mr. Dick Peddie did not carry the rows of Doric columns along the flanks of the building, and the eastern portico was much simplified. When it is kept in view that, through the munificence of Mr. Findlay, Scotland has been supplied with a National Portrait Gallery (in which, by the way, are placed several portraits which formerly occupied space in the National Gallery), it would not to be too much to expect that Government should provide funds for the proper housing of the present collection, and of future additions thereto. Were this done we have reason to believe that donations of works would flow in which are now withheld.

IN one of the cellars of the British Museum there are now being put together some fragments of a very interesting terra-cotta cornice of probably the sixth century B.C., found at Civita Lavinia by Lord Savile. The corona of the cornice is faced with thin plaques of terra-cotta with low relief ornament and with many traces of colour. The peculiar point about it is that the terra-cotta veneer forms at its lower edge a serrated ornament or fringe which is visible both at front and back, and in fact reminds one not a little of the facias formed of boarding, with the ends cut into ornamental shapes, which are often seen in railway-station verandahs and other such erections: another instance that there is nothing new under the sun. This terra-cotta fringe is painted and ornamented both on the back and front. Above the cornice are disproportionately large antefixæ formed of heads with a large open-work ornament making a kind of nimbus round them.

SARACENIC ARCHITECTURE.*

BY PROFESSOR AITCHISON, A.R.A.

I MUST now transport you to Persia, not because the Persian buildings we have delineated are in regular sequence to those described in the last lecture, nor are even of antecedent date, but merely to show the peculiar forms that Moslem art took in that country, which was the first they conquered. The peculiar form of arch was, in all probability, first adopted to save centreing; the springing of the arch was probably carried to the slipping-point, and then continued in a nearly straight line until it touched the centre line. It much resembles the four-centred Tudor arch, and is now said to be struck by a reel of string, the marking-point being held in the hand, and moved as the string unrolls until it reaches the centre line, the reel being held by a pin running through its middle and placed in the centre of the small radius. We know more about the modern method of building in Persia than about any other contemporaneous work in the East, through the sagacity and perseverance of Mr. C. Purdon Clarke. He saw much work done in Persia, had some done under him, secured a large number of the architects' pattern-books, and discovered some of the rules by which the architects work; and these rules are understood by the builders and workmen. Probably something of the same sort prevailed in Mediæval times in Europe.

In Persia the only drawings required are plans, with details for stalactites, inscriptions, and other ornaments. The drawings are made on squared paper mounted on boards and varnished, the solid parts or walls are shown by tinting the whole or portions of the squares with Indian ink. Every room and opening has its height proportioned to its width by a fixed rule, and a similar rule is observed as regards the formation of stalactites, so that, given the plan of the stalactites, the builder can lay down the lines, and the plasterers can properly finish them. I think all the architectural students will be interested in knowing how these mysterious creations of the Saracens' mind are now formed. A stalactite dome or ceiling is done thus,—the floor of the chamber to be thus ornamented is levelled and strewn with ashes and then struck with a rule; on this a coating of plaster of Paris is laid and floated; the builder then sets out the full-size plan from the architect's drawing on the plaster floor, making the lines with a blackened cord, as our carpenters do with a chalked line; his men then cut a V-shaped groove in the plaster with the black line for its centre, and when the plaster cuttings are swept off the whole is saturated with hot melted suet, to prevent the castings from it sticking to the mould; the first or lowest plan of the stalactite ceiling is then run, taken up and cut into the shapes marked by the projecting V ridge; each piece is then fixed in its place by plaster on the wall and supported by ties made of bits of stick or reeds secured to the wall and the plaster slabs by dabs of plaster. The plasterer then works down the stalactites to their proper shape, which he knows by heart, and then another line of plan is cast and put up in the same way, the great pendant stalactites being supported by iron cable chains made rigid with plaster. I went over to Paris early in 1878 to see this work done by the Shah's men in a little pavilion he had erected in the grounds of the Exhibition, but when I got there all the stalactites were just done.

I look on the discovery of the Persian architects' pattern-books as the most curious and important discovery, to us, that has been made in this century, as regards the habits and practices of the past, as it is quite within the range of possibility that this practice has descended from Saracen times. As far as I understand the matter, the pattern-books contained plans of buildings t[h]
architects had designed, and possibly other
and all the well-known domes and stalactite
so that the employer had only to choose h[is]
plan, or to state what additions he required
it, or on what scale he wanted his mansion
palace built, and to choose the pattern of th[e]
stalactites, domes, wood, and plaster-wor[k].
Occasionally the architect had original desig[ns]
of his own for new arrangements of dome[s,]
stalactites, plaster-work, doors, sashes, an[d]
wood-work, and we may be sure that a wealth[y]
and tasteful employer would require large[r]
reception-rooms than ordinary, magnificentl[y]
enriched, and would prefer having the la[test]
fashion, or a new one, for his mansion an[d]
rooms.

Besides the peculiar forms of the arches an[d]
domes, and the stalactite enrichments, there a[re]
two striking features about Moslem art [in]
Persia, one architectural and one decorativ[e].
The architectural peculiarity is this: That fro[n]-
tispieces of oblong shape are erected to ma[in]
entrances; in these are large four-centred arche[s]
with recesses at the back, mostly covered wit[h]
half-domes, carried on squinches, and frequentl[y]
enriched with stalactites. These frontispiece[s]
are also found in the centres of each front [of]
the courts of mosques, and greatly resemble th[e]
ancient Roman exedræ. The only modern instance of a similar feature that I know [in]
Europe is the triclinium of Pope Leo III., clo[se]
by the Scala Santa, in the Lateran Piazz[a].
Whether you like this feature or not, it mu[st]
be admitted that it is a striking one.

Ispahan, from which most of the illustratio[ns]
are taken, is situated midway between the hea[d]
of the Persian Gulf and the Caspian, a little [to]
the eastward of the head of the Persian Gulf, an[d]
is in that division of Persia called Irak-ajem.
The air is said to be so dry there that iron do[es]
not rust. A mosque seems to have been bu[ilt]
there in the Kaliph Mansur's time, which ha[s]
been replaced by the Mesdjid-i-Djuma, thoug[h]
a crypt of Mansur's time is said to be under i[t].
The reason that nothing earlier than the si[x]-
teenth century remains is possibly due t[o]
Ispahan being taken by the troops of the destroyer Gengbis-Khan, and subsequently to i[ts]
being stormed by that scourge of God, Tame[r]-
lane. He admitted the town to capitulation an[d]
tribute, but, from the excesses of his collector[s]
a riot took place, in which most of his peopl[e]
were killed, and the Persians then defende[d]
the town, and it was taken by storm. Afte[r]-
wards, in cold blood, Tamerlane sent his me[n]
to butcher 70,000 of the people, whose head[s]
were formed into a pyramid on the plain [in]
front of the town. He seems to have been [in]
an amiable humour, as on like occasions he wa[s]
wont to build towers, whose walls were composed of living persons laid in mud. Thoug[h]
the Saracens occasionally ground the corn f[or]
their army with rivers reddened with the[ir]
conquered enemies' blood, there are no accoun[ts]
of atrocities quite equal to those of th[e]
Monguls.

The great frontispiece in front of the ves[ti]-
bule of the sanctuary, at the mosque [of]
Mesdjid-i-Shah at Ispahan, is oblong, 75 [ft.]
wide, and 108 ft. high. The arch within it [is]
about 57 ft. wide, and 79 ft. high to the crow[n].
The frontispiece is flanked by two cylindric[al]
minarets, and has a dome behind it, whi[ch]
towers above the frontispiece. The do[me]
covers the space in front of the niche.

The decorative peculiarity is the use [of]
brilliantly-coloured enamelled bricks or ti[les]
for facing, ornamented with scrolls. Almo[st]
all important external work is so finishe[d,]
including domes. The patterns on domes a[re]
made by inlaying or by cutting plain-colour[ed]
tiles into the required patterns. In the t[ile]
work at the Alhambra the texts are inlaid. T[he]
effect of a whole building executed [in]
brilliantly-coloured pottery must be ve[ry]
splendid. There is a great opportunity [in]
London and in all manufacturing towns for t[he]
use of this material, which would have t[he]
advantage of substituting for the dingy brick [or]
stone a beautifully-coloured front; it wou[ld]
greatly add to the brightness of the streets a[nd]
could be easily cleaned by a hose.

When the western part of Persia, with [its]
capital Medain, fell into the hands of t[he]
Saracens (in 15 or 16 A.H., 636 A.D.) in [the]
second year of the reign of the Kaliph Om[ar,]
and about two years after the great battle [of]
Cadesiya, the Saracens had no architecture [of]
their own, and had come upon the architect[ure]
of a civilised people. Here was the palace [of]
Chosroes with its white pavilion; one of

* Being the third Royal Academy Lecture on Architecture this session. Delivered on Monday evening, February 1.

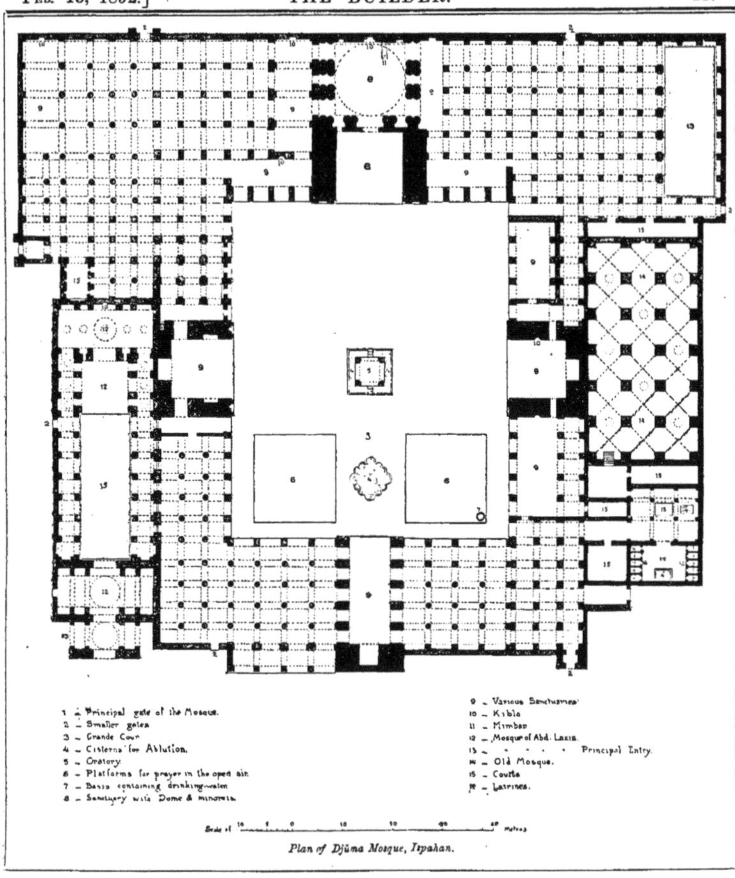

Plan of Djūma Mosque, Ispahan.

grand halls was used by the conquerors for a mosque. The whole of Persia was conquered in Omar's time, about 643 A.D. The Persian Empire, however, extended to the Oxus and the Indus, and this part was not conquered till the reign of Moawia.

About fifteen miles above Medain the second Abbasside Kaliph Mansur founded Baghdad in 145 A.H., 762 A.D., and Medain was destroyed, at least as far as the Saracens could destroy it, to supply materials for the new city of Baghdad. An arch near the Tigris resisted all their efforts, and was to be seen from the Tigris some forty years ago, but has, I believe, since fallen. (Photograph, taken about forty years ago, exhibited.)

The great congregational, or Friday, mosque at Ispahan, Mesdjid-i-Djūma, also called the old mosque, is said to have been originally built by the Kaliph Mansur, though it has been altered and added to since, if not rebuilt. It is situate not far from the north gate Tokhtchi, in that part of the town that is to the north of the river Zendehroud, some 2,228 yards above the mosque of Mesdjid-i-Shah. The mosque is about 462 ft. long by 406 ft. wide over all; but it is not a perfect oblong square, but is slightly T-shaped, and seems to be a collection of at least ten mosques, though it is in many respects like the early congregational mosques that were described in the last lecture. That which looks like the original mosque is of a more strongly-marked T shape, the sanctuaries on the Kibla wall forming the head of the T; there is a large oblong courtyard with triple aisles to the right and left, and with five aisles on the side opposite to the main sanctuary forming the upright of the T. It looks as if the external mosques had been subsequently added, a covered one on the right with courts, and an open one on the left of the side cloisters. The court itself is an oblong square, about 213 ft. by 180 ft., with a basin of water in the middle, with an oratory over it, with two paved spaces about one step high, and a basin, with a jet of water. This court looks on plan as if it had been laid over the centre of a Latin cross, allowing the ends of the four arms to project beyond it; the bulk of the supports of the mosque are piers, but there are some columns, twenty-nine in the left sanctuary, and eight in the right, and there are forty-three in the left hand and back cloisters. The court itself may also have been used as an open-air mosque, as the two raised spaces, about a step high, may have been used instead of Dikkas, or tribunes.

In Egyptian mosques, the niche is invariably semi-circular, although you will recollect that it was not introduced until the year 53 of the Hegira, and the use of this semi-circular niche is confined to mosques, and is carefully avoided in lay buildings; but in Persia, a square recess or half of a stepped square is used indifferently with the semi-circle; to take the niche wall, beginning at the left, there is a narrow sanctuary and niche, then there are the nine aisles, only these are arched both ways, then another narrow sanctuary touching the vast piers of the main one, which is domed; to the right another narrow sanctuary, then ten more aisles, and an open court, equal in width to three aisles; the left side goes into the flank, up to the arm of the cross, and is twelve bays deep from the niche wall,—the left side is only eight bays deep. Behind the piers that form the sanctuary-side of the court are two spaces right and left of the recess; that to the left is a sanctuary with a niche; on the right flank of the court are two small mosques; both arms of the cross have prayer niches. The two outside mosques have been mentioned before. The vaulted mosque on the extreme right is groined, and has immense piers, about 6 ft. 8 in. square, though the span of the arches is but about 16 ft. 6 in.; possibly these piers are very high. There is only one pulpit, at the right side of the niche in the central sanctuary. The court looking to the sanctuary consists of a central frontispiece, containing a four-centred arch, about 43 ft. span, with an archivolt running down to the plinth; beyond are wide piers, panelled, with arches and square panels alternating, and the whole is framed by a wide border, on which are inscriptions; behind are two cylindrical minarets, like Egyptian columns, with stalactite cornices, and with their thinner cylinders above partly ruined. At the back is a pointed bulbous dome, with an inscribed band. The recess is domed on a series of large arched semi-domes. This side of the court is made up by arcades of four arches, two stories high, on each side, that rise to about half the height of the frontispiece; each arch is framed by vertical and horizontal bands. The left side of the court has also a frontispiece in the middle, and two-story arcades on either side of six arches each, only the pieces enclosing the single arcades, next the frontispiece, are higher, so as to make a sort of stepped frontispiece; the half dome of this is carried on Persian stalactites. The front of the frontispiece seems to be of plain brick, but the spandrels are in patterns, while all the rest is faced with enamelled brickwork on a marble plinth. The central basin, with the oratory over it, is formed of four piers, with slender columns between on the long sides, carried by four-centred arches over the water, and is reached by steps. The flat roof has projecting eaves, carried by cantilevers. The whole of the court is paved. The interior of the mosque is mainly stuccoed.

The external arrangement of the architecture of the court is precisely similar to that used in all comparatively recent Persian buildings, whether they be khans, colleges, palaces, or mosques,—*viz.* two-storied arcaded buildings, with four centered arches, with a frontispiece in the middle.

Nearly in the centre of that part of Ispahan that is on the north side of the river Zendehroud is a group of buildings, consisting of the palaces of the Shah, the bazaars, and the horse-course, set out nearly due north and south; this block is connected with the southern part of the town by a grand cloistered avenue, in the middle of which is the bridge over the river; on the east side of this avenue the grounds of the palaces abut. At the south end of the group is the great mosque Mesjid-i-Shah, whose kibla is nearly south-west. The entrance to the mosque is in the middle of the south end of the bazaar, which surrounds the horse-course, and to get the entrance to the court of the mosque in the middle, too, the north angle of the mosque is cut off. It was built by the great Shah Abbas I., who took Baghdad. He was born in 1557 A.D., and died in 1628 A.D.

This mosque is like the later ones at Cairo, almost without columns, and has a central court with four arms, like the mosque of Sultan Hasan at Cairo, only in that case the arms take up a larger proportion of the sides of the court, while in this mosque the widths of the openings of the arms are about a quarter of the length of the side. The arm forming the mosque at Sultan Hasan's is 68 ft. 6 in. wide, while here it is but 56 ft., and is divided from the sanctuary by a wall, the main entrance to Mesjid-i-Shah being in the centre of the horse-course, and the exit being in the centre of the court. The two axes of the doorways make an angle. The same device was used here that Sir John Soane used in the passage to the Rotunda at the Bank of England. The mosque is very nearly an oblong square, with the north corner cut off, and is 341 ft. deep and 423 ft. wide; the supports are wholly walls and piers, except six octagonal columns that divide the side sanctuaries into two aisles each. At the niche end there are two open-air mosques, one to the right and one to the left, with basins of water for ablution. These two open mosques have two half-round niches to each; the domed sanctuaries on either side of the central one have rectangular niches, and the centre sanctuary has a stepped half-square for its mehrab, and is almost cut off from the side sanctuaries by the huge piers that support the great dome. There are certainly five separate mosques, if not nine, four with half-round niches and five with square ones.

The Persians were mostly Shiyas,—*i.e.*, of the main heretical sect,—and the Shiya creed is now the national faith. The Shiyas believe the first three Kaliphs,—Abu Bekr, Omar, and Othman,—were wrongly elected, and, therefore, do not acknowledge them; they say the Kaliphate could only descend through the family of the Apostle, and consequently by Ali, who married Mohammed's daughter, Fatima, and that Hasan and Hosein, the Apostle's grandsons, were the legal successors; to show their contempt for the first three Kaliphs they tattoo A and O on their heels. By this means Harun, in the "Arabian Nights," knew that the corpse was not that of Aladdin Abushshamat, who was supposed to have been hanged. There may be peculiarities about these Shiya mosques. A graphic description of the sort of mystery play of the death of Hosein now performed in Persia was given in a magazine a year or two ago. The mosque has two minarets flanking the frontispiece of the main entrance in the horse-course, and the court of the mosque has in the centre of each of its four sides a frontispiece; between each side frontispiece are triple arcades, two storeys high, and each flank of the entrance side has five arcades. The entrance to the sanctuary has a frontispiece flanked by two cylindrical minarets, and beyond them rises a bulbous dome on a drum pierced by windows filled with lattices. The spaces between this frontispiece and the flanks are filled with arcaded walls faced with enamelled bricks, divided into two unequal compartments; the division is marked by ornamental panels on a white ground, all the rest of the court having a blue ground. In each of the spaces are arches; those next the frontispiece are about 34 ft. 6 in. wide and 36 ft. high. Within this is another parallel arch, recessed, leaving a margin of 5 ft. all round; the outer arches go up to the crowning band, or flat cornice, and are, therefore, in one height. The arches at the end are in two storeys, and are simple combinations of the arcades of the flanks.

The real dome is about 71 ft. in diameter inside, carried on squinches, and 124 ft. from the pavement to the crown; this carries a timber roof, which, with the masonry filling up the lower part of the bulbs, support the bulbous dome; this is about 90 ft. in diameter externally at its widest part, and 164 ft. to its apex from the pavement; beneath it is a circular drum, pierced with eight windows, with lattices, and stands on an octagonal platform, the face of which is arcaded. The angles of the recesses are brought into the half-circle by means of squinches, and the present one in the horse-course is carried in the same way, only the form is hidden by its stalactite decoration. The decoration of the mosque is superb; above the marble or alabaster plinth, which is about 7 ft. high, the whole of the facing is of enamelled pottery; the ornament mainly consists of coloured scrolls on an azure ground; the minarets have a green ground, covered with a large pattern of crosses set anglewise; the crosses have a line of dull red as an outline, while at a little distance inside the form is repeated by black dots, and inside this again with white ones; the capital or gallery is of a golden yellow with an inscribed band, with the letters in black and the panels above, and those of the stalactites have blue panels with white flowers in the centres; the outside of the dome is enamelled and diapered in colours, with a flower in the middle of each diaper; below the dome is a band of blue, with an inscription, and below this inscription the whole drum is of enamelled bricks down to the octagonal platform; the walls, arches, and semi-domes of the frontispiece have an azure ground, enriched with coloured patterns, and the top of the semi-domes is of golden-yellow, with slight coloured patterns. The view on entering the court must be magnificent, with this splendour of colour, and the vast archway over 60 ft. wide, and nearly 100 ft. high, facing you with its grandeur enhanced by the low buildings on the flanks, while through the two-fold gloom of the recess, and the sanctuary, the light of heaven is seen through the piercings of the lattice over the mehrab. It may not be quite equal in monumental grandeur of colour to the superb friezes of Darius' Palace at Susa, now in the Louvre, with the green-bearded troops of the White Nile, but it still keeps up the traditional glory of the enamelled ware of Mesopotamia. The inside is also covered with enamelled pottery, except the plinth, which is of some marble like agate, and when lit up with thousands of lamps must have the appearance of fairyland. I did not see the tiled mosque of Ahmed at Constantinople lit up.

It must be remembered that this Mosque of Mesdjid-i-Shah was built late in the sixteenth century, and has remarkably few stalactites; these are mainly confined to the cornices of the minarets and that part of the entrance that abuts on the horse-course. Almost all the other domes and semi-domes have intersecting arches. The brick stalactites of the half dome of the recess fronting the horse-course are cut in the elongated voussoirs of the inner shell of the half dome. The thrust of the great half dome of the sanctuary must be very great, for though it has a radius of nearly 100 ft., with a centre nearly 40 ft. below the springing, the top abutment is nearly 11 ft. thick, besides being weighted with the parapet, while the bottom abutment is 13 ft. thick, though it is loaded with the weight of the drum and dome in addition. The proportions are not quite to one's taste, the bulk of the openings being squat; the best piece is the frontispiece of the sanctuary, but though the height of this is not more than an additional fifth of its width, the opening of the grand archway itself is about three-fifths of its height. The minarets, which are, to all intents, columns on tall square pedestals, are about 5½ diameters high, but the wooden balustrade and roof increase this to about 6½; the finials are but small cylindrical shafts, with flat bulbous domes, and contrast very unfavourably with the elegant minarets of Cairo. The four-centred arches of the openings are not agreeable, but the most probable cause of the shape was to get rid of centreing; the whole of modern Persian architecture has an air of being done by rule, and no very good rule either, and lacks altogether the apparent spontaneousness and artistic invention of the architecture of Cairo. The grand exedræ, too, lose much by being nearly alike on all the four sides of the court. Still, in spite of all adverse criticism, the effect of these magnificent exedræ must surpass anything else in the world. The same style was pursued, and is, to some extent, pursued to this day in every building, though it became duller and more mechanical the later it was in date, and the taste in colour diminished till quite modern work is garish and vulgar when seen in the light of this country.

A few monuments, however, that have been delineated deserve mention. The principal one is the blue or orthodox mosque of the Sunnis at Tabriz, the ancient Tauris, in Azerbijan, midway between the west side of the Caspian and Lake Van. This mosque was ruined by an earthquake in 1721; it was built by Djehan Shah, one of the Mongol Princes of the dynasty of the black sheep, in the fifteenth century; it was called the blue mosque from the prevalence of blue in its enamelled brick decoration. Its plan has a strong family resemblance to that of Sta. Sophia at Salonica, only its sanctuary is rectangular, with a small, half-round niche in a rectangular recess. The narthex goes round three sides, as at Sta. Sophia; the main dome, which has fallen, was about 54 ft., internal diameter; the front was flanked by two minarets at the extreme angles; the frontispiece to the central entrance, which still remains, has its half-dome carried on squinches; the internal plinth is said to have been of a sort of agate. Sultaniah, in the north-east corner of Irak-Ajemi, was built by Argoun Khan in 1290 A.D., one of the descendants of Genghis Khan; his brother and successor, Oldjaïtou Mohammed Khoda-Bendeh, carried on the works with great vigour. In 1305 A.D., the town was called Sultaniah in honour of the birth of his son, and Khoda-Bendeh then built his own tomb-mosque, which consists of an octagonal chamber, with a dome, and the tomb-chamber behind it. This has a half-octagon niche, and a small dome over the tomb. The building is a square of about 120 ft., with the back angles cut off; above, the front angles are cut off, too, making an octagonal base for the dome. The main dome is about 79 ft., internal diameter, with a total external height of 177 ft.

The exterior has a stalactite cornice with a triple arcade below it on each face of the octagon; the arcade consists of one wide central arch with a narrow one on each side; this arcade forms an ambulatory, with a balustrade for protection; the entrance-front is square, with staircases and recesses in each of the square angles, lit by two narrow pointed windows at two levels. In the middle of each of the square sides there is a small doorway enclosed in a frontispiece, with an arch over it

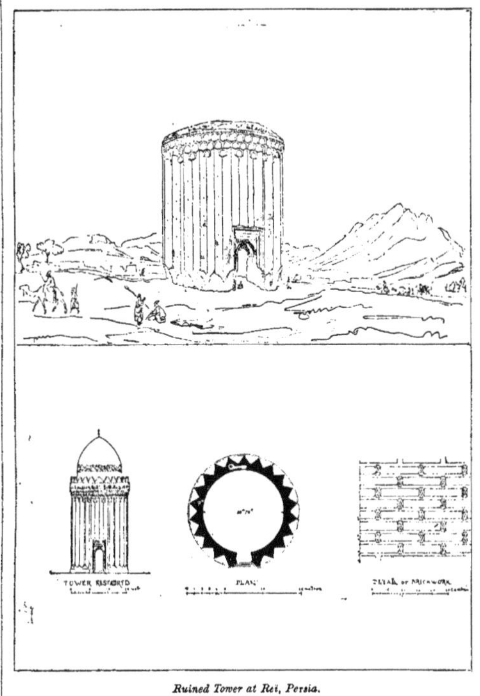

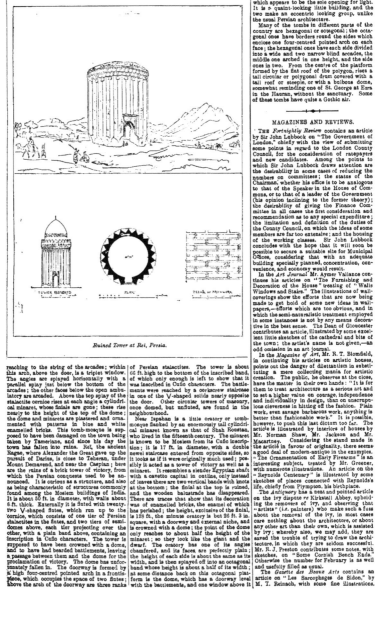

Ruined Tower at Rei, Persia.

reaching to the string of the arcades; within this arch, above the door, is a triplet window. The angles are splayed horizontally with a parallel splay just below the bottom of the arcades; the other faces below the open ambulatory are arcaded. Above the top splay of the stalactite cornice rises at each angle a cylindrical minaret, whose finials are gone; these rise nearly to the height of the top of the dome; the dome and minarets are plastered and ornamented with patterns in blue and white enamelled bricks. This tomb-mosque is supposed to have been damaged on the town being taken by Tamerlane, and since his day the town has fallen into ruins. Reï, the ancient Ragae, where Alexander the Great gave up the pursuit of Darius, is close to Teheran, under Mount Demavend, and near the Caspian; here are the ruins of a brick tower of victory, from which the Persian conquests used to be announced. It is curious as a structure, and also as being characteristic of structures commonly found among the Moslem buildings of India. It is about 50 ft. in diameter, with walls about 6 ft. thick. Externally it is fluted with twenty-two V-shaped flutes, which run up to the cornice, which consists of one tier of Persian stalactites in the flutes, and two tiers of semi-domes above, each tier projecting over the other, with a plain band above, containing an inscription in Cufic characters. The tower is supposed to have been crowned with a dome, and to have had bearded battlements, leaving a passage between them and the dome for the proclamation of victory. The dome has unfortunately fallen in. The doorway is formed by a high four-centred pointed arch in a frontispiece, which occupies the space of two flutes; above the arch of the doorway are three ranks of Persian stalactites. The tower is about 66 ft. high to the bottom of the inscribed band, of which only enough is left to show that it was inscribed in Cufic characters. The battlements were reached by a corkscrew staircase in one of the V-shaped solids nearly opposite the door. Other circular towers of masonry, once domed, but unfluted, are found in the neighbourhood.

Near Ispahan is a little oratory or tomb-mosque flanked by an enormously tall cylindrical minaret known as that of Shah Roustan, who lived in the fifteenth century. The minaret is known to be Moslem from its Cufic inscription; it is 17 ft. in diameter, with a double newel staircase entered from opposite sides, so it looks as if it were originally much used; possibly it acted as a tower of victory as well as a minaret. It resembles a slender Egyptian shaft with a cavetto capital in outline, only instead of leaves there are two vertical bands with knots at the bottom; the finial at the top is ruined, and the wooden balustrade has disappeared. There are traces that show that its decoration was of enamelled bricks, the enamel of which has perished; the height, exclusive of the finial, is 128 ft., the minute oratory is but 26 ft. 3 in. square, with a doorway and external niche, and is crowned with a dome; the point of the dome only reaches to about half the height of the minaret; so they look like the giant and the dwarf. The oratory has one of its angles chamfered, and its faces are perfectly plain; the height of each side is about the same as its width, and is then splayed off into an octagonal band whose height is about a half of its width; at some distance back on this octagonal platform is the dome, which has a doorway level with the battlements, and one window above it which appears to be the sole opening for light. It is a quaint-looking little building, and the two make an eccentric looking group, unlike the usual Persian architecture.

Many of the tombs in different parts of the country are hexagonal or octagonal; the octagonal ones have borders round the sides which enclose one four-centred pointed arch on each face; the hexagonal ones have each side divided into a wide and two narrow blind arcades, the middle one arched in one height, and the side ones in two. From the centre of the platform formed by the flat roof of the polygon, rises a tall circular or polygonal drum covered with a tall roof or steeple, or with a bulbous dome, somewhat reminding one of St. George at Ezra in the Hauran, without the sanctuary. Some of these tombs have quite a Gothic air.

MAGAZINES AND REVIEWS.

THE *Fortnightly Review* contains an article by Sir John Lubbock on "The Government of London," chiefly with the view of submitting some points in regard to the London County Council, for the consideration of ratepayers and new candidates. Among the points to which Sir John Lubbock draws attention are the desirability in some cases of reducing the numbers on committees; the status of the Chairman; whether his office is to be analogous to that of the Speaker in the House of Commons, or to that of a leader of the Government (his opinion inclining to the former theory); the desirability of giving the Finance Committee in all cases the first consideration and recommendation as to any special expenditure; the limitation and definition of the duties of the County Council, on which the ideas of some members are far too extensive; and the housing of the working classes. Sir John Lubbock concludes with the hope that it will soon be possible to secure a suitable site for Municipal Offices, considering that with an adequate building specially planned, concentration, convenience, and economy would result.

In the *Art Journal* Mr. Aymer Vallance continues his articles on "The Furnishing and Decoration of the House" treating of "Walls Windows and Stairs." The illustrations of wall-coverings show the efforts that are now being made to get hold of some new ideas in wall-papers,—efforts which are too obvious, and in which the semi-naturalistic treatment employed in some instances is not by any means decorative in the best sense. The Dean of Gloucester contributes an article, illustrated by some excellent little sketches of the cathedral and bits of the town; the artist's name is not given,—an odd omission in an art journal.

In the *Magazine of Art*, Mr. R. T. Blomfield, in continuing his articles on artistic houses, points out the danger of dilettantism in substituting a mere collecting mania for artistic creation. The public, he observes at the close, have the matter in their own hands: "It is for them to treat architecture as a serious art and to set a higher value on courage, independence and individuality in design, than on unscrupulous cleverness in hitting off the fashion. Plain work, even savage barbarous work, anything is better than fashionable work." It is possible, however, to push this last dictum too far. The article is illustrated by interiors of houses by Mr. Norman Shaw, Mr. Jackson and Mr. Macartney. Considering the stand made in the article in favour of originality, there seems a good deal of modern-antique in the examples. "The Ornamentation of Early Firearms" is an interesting subject, treated by Mr. Greener, with numerous illustrations. An article on the "Reynolds Centenary" is illustrated by some sketches of places connected with Reynolds's life, chiefly from Plympton, his birthplace.

The *Antiquary* has a neat and pointed article on the ivy dispute *re* Kirkstall Abbey, upholding the removers of ivy, and observing that "artists" (*i.e.* painters) who make such a fuss about the removal of the ivy, in most cases care nothing about the architecture, or about any other art than their own, which is assisted by ivy; whereby also, we may add, they are saved the trouble of trying to draw the architecture, in which they are seldom successful. Mr. R. J. Preston contributes some notes, with sketches, on "Some Cornish Bench Ends." Otherwise the number for February is as well and usefully filled as usual.

The *Gazette des Beaux Arts* contains an article on "Les Sarcophages de Sidon," by M. T. Reinach, with some fine illustrations.

There is an article of rather special interest on "Hugues Sambin," a little-known architect and sculptor in wood of the latter part of the sixteenth century. An illustration is given of his design for the façade of the Palais de Justice at Besançon.

The *Contemporary Review* contains an article of some importance on the "Unhealthiness of Cities," by Sir Francis Peek and Mr. Edwin T. Hall, to which (from internal evidence) we shall probably not be wrong in concluding that the last-named gentleman is the larger contributor. It deals first with "sewer-gas," suggesting the principle of having inlets of fresh air at the highest point of a sewer system, and exhaust shafts at the lowest point, in order to draw the air in the same direction with the sewage flow and get the assistance of the latter. Against this must be put the fact that the air in sewers naturally tends to ascend, and it would require rather a quicker current than usual to counterbalance this tendency. However, the suggestion is worth consideration; the main object being to ensure that inlets shall always be inlets, and not inlets or outlets at various times. Other subjects dealt with in the article are "London Fog," "Poisonous Ground Air," "Jerry Building," and "Sanitary House Planning and Construction." In this latter portion of the article we observe the caution that "all cisterns should be well covered" to exclude vermin, dust, &c. To this should have been added the caution that such cover should be easily removable and the cistern easily accessible so as to be readily inspected. In another paragraph, we are glad to see, the authors call attention to the importance of doing away with unventilated hollow spaces hidden from light, as a matter important to the sanitary condition of a house.

In the *Nineteenth Century* the "London Water Supply" is the subject of a paper by Sir John Lubbock, whose main conclusions are "that the question is one of vital and pressing importance; that the population of the Thames Valley is rapidly increasing, and the limits of the present water supply nearly reached; that it will shortly be necessary to go elsewhere for a fresh supply; and, last but not least, that unless we do so soon we may find that the available areas have been appropriated by other cities, and that we are too late;" which is what we urged in nearly the same words a good many months ago. Sir John Lubbock is opposed to the idea of buying up the water companies, but suggests additional supply either by the companies with the aid of the Council, or by the Council by arrangement with the companies; and that an agreement should be made with the companies for dividing future profits equitably between them and the ratepayers. The article is a sensible and judicious one in general, and deserves attention.

In the *Century* Mr. Stillman continues "The Italian old masters" with an article on "Titian," very short and slight for so great a subject, and giving the impression of having been merely written to accompany three engravings from Titian's works. An article on "Pioneer Days in San Francisco," by Mr. J. W. Farmer, is illustrated by sketches of the original streets, the first hotel, &c, which throw an interesting light on the local colouring of Bret Harte's stories of towns in a similar embryo stage, and seem made to illustrate the scenes in "Red Dog" or "Tuttleville."

Harper's Magazine has an article by Mr. Julian Ralph on Chicago as "the main exhibit" of the 1893 exhibition. The article is not calculated to tempt European visitors. The position and the marvellous prosperity of Chicago within so short a time are picturesquely set forth; but we are given also the picture of Chicago as a place of absolute turmoil of money-making, where no one has time to be civil; where if you ask the way you must run by the side of your man to get his answer, for no one has time to stop in the street in Chicago; where to ask a necessary question of a ticket-taker or tram conductor is to expose yourself to gratuitous insolence; and where an average of six hundred people are annually killed by railways on level street crossings. This is not the testimony of a prejudiced "Britisher," but of an American writer in an American magazine; and judging from his account we should imagine that to cultivated Europeans Chicago must prove the most detestable of all the large cities of the world.

The *Atlantic Monthly* has an interesting sketch of "A Venetian printer and publisher of the sixteenth century," one Gabriele Giolito to wit, derived from recent investigations by Signor Salvatore Brongi.

In the *New Review* Mr. Spielman suggests the founding of the proposed National Gallery of British Art in the rear of *the* National Gallery, on the site of the barracks, and with a new street opened to westward of the block. We doubt whether the site can be acquired, otherwise its contiguity to the National Gallery would in itself be an advantage rather than the reverse; but then the question would arise whether the works by English painters now in the National Gallery are or are not to be considered part of the "National Gallery of British Art." The trustees of the National Gallery would probably demur, and there would be dissensions.

The *Quarterly Statement* of the Palestine Exploration Fund contains an article by Mr. Flinders Petrie on the "Tomb-cutters' Cubits at Jerusalem," an attempt to investigate the length of the cubit by a comparison of the measurements of different sides of the tombs where it may be expected that exact multiples of the "foot-rule" of the period would be found. This practically enforces a suggestion we have already made, that the exact proportion in length and breadth of some ancient structures may merely have arisen from the natural use of so many lengths of a measuring rule in each direction, and not from any theory of proportion.

In *Temple Bar* is an article on Benjamin Robert Haydon, chiefly in relation to Tom Taylor's biography, which may serve to recall the name of a painter who is little heard of by the younger generation, and who, whether in regard to his talents or his tragic career, should not be forgotten. The article in *Macmillan* on "The Beautiful and the True" seems rather high-sounding than valuable or pointed; one has had enough of "the beautiful" with the definite article. The *English Illustrated Magazine* includes an interesting article on "The London and North-Western Locomotive Works at Crewe," by Mr. C. J. Bowen Cooke (Assistant Running Superintendent); an article on Brahan Castle by the Marchioness of Tweeddale, with illustrations by Mr. T. Riley, and one on "The Mosques of Tlemcen," written and illustrated by Mr. Edgar Barclay, but the illustrations (as might perhaps be expected) are of pictorial rather than architectural interest. The *Ludgate Monthly* gives a short article on Malling Abbey, with some sketches (not very first-rate), and *All the Year Round* makes a concession to the increasing popularity of archæology by an article on "A Dead City of Etruria," which is, however, picturesque and chatty rather than archæological.

ROYAL INSTITUTE OF BRITISH ARCHITECTS:

LONDON BUILDING LEGISLATION.

The seventh general meeting of this Institute for the present session was held on Monday evening last, the President, Mr. J. Macvicar Anderson, in the chair.

Obituary.

The minutes of the previous meeting having been read and confirmed,

The President said:—Since our last meeting, an architect whose name was well-known has passed away. I do not think we should be content with a mere official or formal notification of his death, and therefore I refer to it specially. Mr. Philip Hardwick was a man whose works were important and numerous, and he occupied a distinguished position. It is with grief that we have heard that his latter days were embittered by a painful illness. He was a man who, while in practice,—for it is now some years since he retired,—was looked upon as an able architect and an honourable man, and it is with great regret that I have to announce his decease.

Nomination of the Recipient of the Royal Gold Medal for 1892.

The Secretary, Mr. William H. White, having read By-law 64, regarding the award of the Royal Gold Medal,

The President said:—I beg to announce that the Council propose to submit to her Majesty the Queen the name of M. César Daly, Hon. Corr. Member, Paris, for his writings in connexion with architecture. I cannot refrain from reading an extract from a letter I have received from M. Daly this morning. He writes:—

"The Secretaries of the Institute have officially informed me of the Council's very flattering decision of presenting my name before her Majesty the Queen, as a worthy recipient for the Royal Medal to be given in 1892. . . . . . . I beg you to receive my most grateful acknowledgment for this kindness and honour. You know already the strong ties which bind my youngest memories with England and Englishmen; but the favourable vote of the Council binds my old age to the old country by a new tie that no strain will ever weaken. By their generous and large feeling in favour of architectural progress through the whole world, and their decision of seeking the worthy amongst all nations, the English Institute has created a sort of architectural senate, of which every architect must be highly flattered to become a member."

It is some satisfaction, gentlemen, to find that those abroad who are nominated for the reception of this honour from her Majesty so highly and thoroughly appreciate the honour.

London Building Legislation.

Mr. Edwin T. Hall, Fellow, then read a paper on "London Building Legislation." In his opening remarks he referred to the great importance of the subject, especially as the codification and amendment of the Metropolitan Building Acts was now occupying the attention of the Government and the London County Council. He desired to expound the views of the Practice Standing Committee, who for the past two years had had the matter before them, and whose suggestions for a Draft Bill had been approved by the Council of the Institute. The Committee had throughout realised that the question must be approached in a public spirit, with the endeavour to ensure safe and sanitary building with as few restrictions as possible on artistic design. The main lines of the suggestions had been issued with the notice convening the meeting; and, having drawn attention to the importance of excluding the construction of roads, sewers and bridges, &c., from a Building Act, Mr. Hall proceeded to treat with the details of the draft. Great attention had been given to definitions. Many subjects defined by the committee were not defined in the existing Acts, while new definitions had been given to many others; among the former were,—building, structure, wall-sign, warehouse, domestic building, living-room, flat, business offices, story, topmost story, floor area, superficies, cubic contents, and fire-resisting; and the latter included public building, site, base of the wall, foundation, builder, street (instead of roadway), and centre of street.

Several of the existing exemptions to the Act, he pointed out, were manifestly opposed to the public interest, and therefore recommended to be removed or limited in scope, while new exemptions of very small buildings from the general rules of the Act were suggested, but placed under the control of the District Surveyor. An important addition to the Act was the section dealing with the "alteration in purpose or character of a building," and a new section also provided for the restoration of buildings of architectural, archæological, or historical interest; while the section for "rebuilding old buildings" was varied. With reference to foundations and sites, several alterations were suggested. The existing rule as to the thickness of concrete under a wall was inadequate: the suggested section said the thickness of good concrete shall vary according to the height and class of building, and allowed of the omission of concrete, with the approval of the District Surveyor, where the site was "a natural bed of solid gravel or chalk of not less than 3 ft. in thickness." The subject of recesses and openings in external walls had received careful attention, and it was proposed to modify the law by enacting that the recesses and openings *in any story* shall not "exceed one-half of the superficies of the wall of such story in which they are made;" this limit not to apply to that portion of an external wall between its base and 30 ft. above the level of the public footway immediately in front of the centre of the façade, or, where there is no such footway, then above the actual level of the ground before excavation. Turning to party-walls, a principle had been adopted for fire prevention and stability which, it was hoped, would commend itself to all; the theory of ownership in the existing Acts was not interfered with, but the new principle of construction was that there shall be in the centre of the new party-wall a continuous backbone of brickwork, the thickness of which neither owner shall diminish. On its own side only of this backbone could the flues of any building be placed. Applying the principle, it was proposed that in no case shall the back of a recess be within 4 in. of the centre of the wall. As to the formation and superficial limits of recesses in party-walls, the new section provided that the recesses shall be arched or corbelled over in the height of the story in which they are made, and that their extent shall be measured by width, not area, and that the "width shall not exceed one-half the whole length of the wall of the story in which they are made." As to the section governing uniting buildings, a discretion to the County Council was suggested to consent to the uniting of buildings which were not wholly in the same occupation. In the case of floors of fire-resisting materials such uniting might, he thought, within limits be permitted with perfect propriety. The new section forbade openings in "any party-wall or any two external walls dividing buildings," and further provided that "no opening in such wall or walls on any one floor" shall be "nearer than 25 ft. to any other opening on the same floor;" and the existing section, requiring openings in party or dividing walls to be stopped up, had been made much stronger. Under the heading of "Miscellaneous," an effort had been made to get rid of the public danger arising from advertisements on combustible hoardings "on the face or in front of the external wall of any finished building." Mr. Hall next dealt with "Timber in external walls," bressumers, the height of party-walls above roofs,—treating the last-mentioned at considerable length,—and then turned to the payment of the cost of party-walls and the question of stories in the roof. A new section for "Chimney-shafts from furnaces" incorporated the essentials of the existing rules which the County Council adopted in sanctioning such shafts, while in the rules as to other chimneys and flues many variations in detail had been made. Considerable alterations had also been made as to the construction of habitable rooms, the minimum height, except in the roof, being increased from 7 ft. to 8 ft., and minimum areas of windows, of dormers, lantern-lights, &c., had been fixed. The Draft next embraced all the building regulations of the Public Health Act for underground rooms let as separate dwellings, and added regulations for other underground rooms not so let; and he considered it a matter of congratulation for the Institute that the Government in framing that Act had adopted so many improvements suggested by the Institute. Projections beyond the general line of building had also received careful attention. The sections had been drawn anew, and it was affirmed that cornices of shops might to a specified extent overhang the public way, but no other part of a shop front encroach on it. Permission for bay windows and similar projections over building-owner's own land was given, thus legalising what was a pretty general practice; while adjoining owners were protected by the condition that no such projection shall come within 2 ft. of the centre of a party-wall, nor shall it extend outside a line drawn at an angle of 30 deg. from the point in the front of the building where it touches the centre line of the division of the properties. It was a pleasure to note that the County Council, too, in their amendments, had a section with the object to concede greater freedom of design to architects, or rather building-owners; this section allowed, under restrictions, projecting oriel windows or turrets not only over the building owner's land, but 12 in. over the public way. The County Council had apparently considered overhanging constructions only in relation to the public way, for, though right and proper so considered, the limit for oriels and turrets not to be lower than a certain height above the level of the footway was unnecessary and undesirable where they were over the building-owner's own land. The author then dealt with a sub-section designed to ensure the construction of party-walls in buildings subsequently converted into two or more buildings, and a section to secure fire-resisting construction in a building erected or converted into two or more divisions, intended for or adapted to be used as flats, or as warehouses, or which is let or occupied in two or more such divisions, with reference to which an incidental change of great importance was made. The old sub-section said: "Sets of chambers or rooms tenanted by different persons shall in certain buildings be deemed to be separate buildings." The new section assumed a building to be that which it was popularly understood to be, viz., a cube resting on the ground and covered by a roof. Having described the suggested regulations as to "egress from certain buildings" referred to, and the incorporation of section 29 of the London County Council (General Powers) Act, Mr. Hall proceeded to treat of those to govern lift-shafts. Lifts, in the suggestions of the Committee, were divided into three classes,—(1) those which were inside a building with fire-resisting floors containing flats or business offices; (2) those outside the external wall; and (3) those inside warehouses which pass through fire-resisting floors, and where it is not the practice to enclose the lifts with walls. In the first class it was suggested that the lift be separated from flats or offices by brick walls, and all openings into the shafts from within the entrance doors of flats must have an iron door in addition to a wooden one. In the second class the enclosures to the shafts or for cylinders, balance weights, or gearing, were to be either of brickwork, ironwork, or other fire-resisting material approved by the District Surveyor; if the floors of the building are required by the Act to be of fire-resisting construction, then any openings into the shafts from within the entrance doors of the flats, or from any warehouse or business offices, are required to have an iron door as above. In the third class all openings in the floors must have a horizontal door, hatchway, or other cover of iron or other fire-resisting material as specified. With reference to the present maximum of heights of buildings in the 1890 Act, that maximum was proposed to be reduced to 75 ft., and the height of two stories in the roof limited to 20 ft. The provision for open spaces at the rear and sides of dwelling-houses was next dealt with; and, having referred to the many points of view from which this question had to be considered, and the dangers of insufficient space, Mr. Hall said the London County Council were now going to an extreme in proposing to require an open space at the rear, not only of domestic, but of all buildings, which space between the opposite backs of two buildings would be practically double the width required between the opposite fronts of buildings. Proceeding to analyse the working of the proposed section, he assumed there were three buildings which were parallelograms,—*i.e.*, with no back additions. Two faced each other: their front walls were 75 ft. high, and they were separated by a street 70 ft. wide; the third was behind, and backed on to the second; between the second and the third was also a road 70 ft. wide. By the operation of the section there must be above the ground-floor of the building 90 ft. between the backs of the blocks, and the external walls forming the backs cannot be more than 45 ft. high, while the front walls, 70 ft. apart, may be 75 ft. high. Could there, asked Mr. Hall, be any justification whatever for such a consequence? The section would afford room for much litigation and its ultimate abrogation by evasion. Which was the front of a building? Or, given two good roads, why should a building have a back at all? Moreover, if the case were bad when there was a back street, it was worse when there was none; for if the depth of a site be 55 ft., the building might then be 45 ft. deep; but the application of the County Council's rule would only permit the rear wall to be 10 ft. high, and the front wall to be 50 ft. high, and that with a sky-line of dull and dreary monotony in a street 70 ft. wide. The varied problems of open spaces had all received careful attention, and he thought upon further consideration the County Council would agree that the necessities of the case were met by the suggestions in the Institute Draft. Mr. Hall then referred to a new section dealing with drains and sanitary apparatus, &c., which left all details to by-laws; and he gave an epitome of matters relating to the construction of public buildings, concluding his paper by alluding to questions which had been settled in principle, but not yet formulated by the committee,—among others the making of by-laws, the machinery for settling disputes by the award of the Surveyors, the Tribunal of Appeal, and the duties and remuneration of District Surveyors.

The President, in inviting discussion, said that Mr. Hall had given them a lucid explanation of a very voluminous document. As he saw present several gentlemen who were practically acquainted with all the intricacies of the subject, he trusted that they would have an interesting discussion.

Mr. H. H. Collins said that at that advanced period of the evening he felt he could do little more than propose a hearty vote of thanks to Mr. Hall for his admirable paper. Most of the suggestions made in the draft Bill of the Institute had occupied the attention of various other bodies; but he was very glad that the Practice Standing Committee of the Institute had considered the matter, not with the view of framing a new Bill, but with the view to the codification and amendment of the existing law. In a large number of bodies with which they were all more or less connected, it seemed to have been the idea that a new Bill should be proposed, and he was fearful when he came into the room that evening that he should hear an exposition of new ideas, new notions, and new provisions embodied in Mr. Hall's paper. He was glad that was not so, for he was sure that an Act which had borne the hard test of thirty-six years' wear, and which had not been found wanting in its main principles, was one which deserved to be retained. He did not think it was desirable to have over-legislation in building matters. They did not want to go to school again. Architects, builders, and clerks of works had their minds now pretty well saturated with existing legislation, and he thought that, with some amendment of the existing laws, they would be able to jog on again very comfortably for another thirty-six years. The way in which Mr. Hall had treated his subject had disarmed criticism. In reading a book entitled "Called Back" a short time ago, various criticisms of the proposals therein set forth by the author arose to his mind on almost every page; but on succeeding pages the very objections which had occurred to the reader had been anticipated and met by the author. That was very much what had occurred with Mr. Hall's paper. As it proceeded he (the speaker) saw objections to what was proposed; but when Mr. Hall got a little further those objections were met. With regard to the point about the extension of the footings of party-walls upon each side, the thing was absolutely impossible to carry out in practice, and if it were carried out it would have the effect of leaving an unsanitary space at the side of each house. He was very glad that Mr. Hall had criticised the curious proposal of the County Council as to space at the rear of buildings. If that requirement were worked out to its logical conclusion, it would involve nothing less than confiscation, and it should not be entertained for one moment. He did not think that the House of Commons would be at all likely to agree to any such legislation. He therefore warned all who were promoting this legislation not to overload their ship, or they would be in danger of getting on the rocks and going to pieces. That was so in 1884, when the Bill then introduced contained many of the present amendments. One after another these were eliminated, until at last the Metropolitan Board of Works found that their measure was so emasculated that they preferred to abandon it altogether. He was glad to see that in the new Bill they were seeking to ensure not only safety in case of fire, but the health of the people who might have to live in the buildings erected. He had much pleasure in proposing a vote of thanks to Mr. Hall for his able paper.

Mr. Arthur Baker said he regretted to have heard very little in the proposals before the meeting as to fireproof construction. At Kensington there was just now in course of construction an enormous brick and stone building standing entirely upon iron legs. He hoped that when they got a new Building Act such a structure as that would be impossible. Such buildings were most dangerous, and ought to be prohibited.

Mr. Alexander Payne said that whatever might be their views on the provisions of the proposed new Bill, they would all agree that Mr. Hall was deserving of their very hearty thanks, and he therefore had much pleasure in seconding the proposal made by Mr. Collins. The amount of work which Mr. Hall had done was very great, and the amount of detail which he had gone into was appalling. From his (the speaker's) own experience as one of those who had to assist in the administration of the existing Act and its amending Acts, he knew what a very difficult thing it was, in the first place to know what the Act meant, and in the second place to know how the lawyers would interpret it, and it would be no easy task to clear up all existing difficulties by the proposed new Act.

Mr. Ralph Nevill said he had heard with very great satisfaction that very strict rules were to be laid down in the proposed Bill with regard to the thickness of the walls of the flues of kitcheners. But the remarks which had been made as to the necessity of thick walls behind flues were applicable not only to kitcheners, but to many of the new-fashioned grates, which were almost equally dangerous when placed against thin walls. As to projecting windows, he rather gathered that Mr. Hall saw no objection to projecting windows being brought out over a building-owner's own land beyond the line of frontage, not only at a height above the pavement, but down to the ground; but that seemed to be very objectionable. If a bow-window might be brought out down to the ground beyond the line of frontage, why might not the whole building be brought out? He did not know whether the Institute Committee had yet taken into consideration the schedules of the old Act, but they were certainly open to amendment. He had had a good deal of experience in concrete building, and he had always been very much annoyed by the very foolish provision for stepping concrete foundations. Such a provision might have been applicable to lime concrete, but it was wholly unnecessary in the case of concrete made of selenitic or Portland cement, which rapidly became as hard as stone.

Mr. Edmund Woodthorpe said he should be glad to support the vote of thanks to Mr. Hall, knowing the immense amount of labour that he had spent on the subject during the last two years. With regard to the question of lifts, or rather lift openings, he thought that some special attention should be given to the subject, with a view to the prevention of fire. The need of every possible precaution in regard to them had been shown by the disastrous fire in the hotel at New York. Another point needing attention was that where, as was frequently the case in the City, the lower floors were used for the storage of inflammable goods, and the upper floor as a residence for the housekeepers or caretakers, special means should be taken to make that part of the building fireproof, and it should be reached by a fireproof staircase entirely cut off from the warehouse buildings, so as to allow a means of escape in case of fire.

Mr. Arthur Cawston said that when a modern half-timbered building originally erected when there were no other buildings near it needed restoration or rebuilding, it would, perhaps, be desirable only to sanction its rebuilding when there were no other buildings erected close up to it. As to the fronts of warehouse buildings having a certain proportion of brickwork or stone to window openings, why should not such fronts, if necessary, be entirely of iron and glass? He thought that the proposal that no external wall should be used as a party-wall, except under the conditions specified in the Institute's suggestions, rather a hard one on the owner of the wall. A great incentive to the spread of fire in warehouse and factory buildings was the use of match-board lining to the walls, with the irevitable hollow spaces behind it. Such walls should always be plastered, or left with the brickwork face.

Mr. Bernard Dicksee suggested that with regard to wooden bay-windows, the County Council might be relieved of a large amount of labour if such windows were allowed to be erected on certain conditions, as, for instance, if they did not come nearer than 10 ft. to the adjoining property, or project more than 3 ft. or 4 ft. Another point that he thought might be introduced into the new Act was that District Surveyors should be given full control over the house drainage, and that it should not be left in the hands of the Vestry Surveyors. Very often the latter knew nothing of drains at all: they were mostly road men.

Mr. Hall explained that in the proposed new Act the drainage, and everything within the curtilage of the house, would be under the control of the District Surveyor.

Mr. Dicksee, continuing, said he thought that the definition of a building in the proposed new Bill was a little too all-inclusive. It seemed to him that it would include everything, from a pill-box to a cathedral. He thought it would include a tent, but he thought that the definition of a building should not cover things of that kind.

Mr. H. H. Statham said he also had some objection to offer to the definition of the term "building," but it was not the same objection as that of the last speaker. He thought that in the "suggestions" of the Institute there e was some confusion between the terms "building" and "shed." A "building" was defined as including every erection comprising a cubical space defined by walls, piers, posts, or other structures, and a roof or other covering, whether such erection was wholly enclosed or not; and then, later on, it was proposed that "sheds" which were not enclosed, but which were open on one or more sides, might be erected if the roofs were covered with fire-resisting material. What was the differentiation here between "shed" and "building"? And was a "shed" only one of the varieties included under the general term "building"? As to back-to-back houses, which had been incidentally spoken of with favour by one of the speakers, he hoped they would hear no more advocacy of them in that assembly. As to fire-proof construction, he thought a little further definition was required, especially with regard to the mention of stone as a fire-proof material, for although stone would not burn, it would crack and fly. It was also worth consideration whether the use of "oak" beams might not be specified in certain positions, not merely "wooden" beams, for, on the testimony of Captain Shaw, an oak post or beam took a long time to burn through, and although it might get charred on the outside, it would not be consumed, or materially weakened under the action of fire for a long time.

Mr. J. Douglass Mathews said that, with regard to By-laws, there was great danger that they would embody various whims or fancies not at all to be desired in the interests of the public. Mr. Hall had flattered the District Surveyors by proposing to give them a great deal of discretionary power, but they (the District Surveyors) wished to be vested with as little discretionary power as possible.

Mr. Thomas Blashill said that with regard to the proportion of openings to solids in front of buildings, fronts entirely of iron and glass were prohibited because of the danger of the spread of fire. He defended the proposals of the County Council as to space in the rear of buildings, and contended that Mr. Hall's unfavourable illustration was that of an extreme case. Of course the provision of increased space was made primarily in the interests of health. With regard to the definition of the term "building," he did not see why it should not include a tent, because tradesmen and others frequently rigged up tents at the back of their premises, and used them for the storage or exhibition of goods.

Mr. John Slater said it was gratifying to him to find that many suggestions which he had made in a paper he read before the Institute two years ago had been embodied in the Institute's draft Bill. But he agreed with Mr. Statham's criticisms, especially as to fireproof construction, and deprecated the use of iron without fire-resisting casing; and he was convinced that the schedules and definitions would need much more careful consideration.

Mr. T. M. Rickman and the President having made a few remarks, Mr. Hall replied to some points raised in the discussion, and the meeting terminated.

Illustrations.

HOUSES, QUEEN'S-GATE.

THIS is an illustration showing the work that has been carried out in refronting two houses at Queen's-gate, South Kensington, after removing the stucco, cement cornices, and enrichments on the existing front. One has been recased with red brick and terra-cotta enrichments, and the other with red brick and Portland stone dressings.

Considerable structural alterations have also been made in the interior of the building. Bath-rooms, lifts, and other modern requirements have been added, and a considerable portion of the old building has been removed from the rear to give direct light into the hall and principal staircase. The stone stairs immediately in front of the entrance-door have been removed, and the hall considerably widened, with a new oak staircase approached through an oak colonnade. The hall and dining-room have been lined with a high wainscot dado. The ceilings to the principal rooms have been enriched with ribs in geometrical forms, supported by deep modelled friezes.

The kitchen has been removed from the body of the building and placed at the rear, with offices adjoining; and a large billiard-room placed in the basement, having a separate staircase from the hall.

The work has been carried out by Mr. J. Douglas, under the superintendence of Mr. Fred G. Knight, architect.

EAST WINDOW, S. MARY'S CHURCH, LEIGH, LANCASHIRE.

In the principal lights are standing figures under canopies, with small subjects in the bases. A figure of Our Lord in Majesty occupies the centre light, and in the side lights are the four Archangels. The small subjects or scenes below bear reference to the figures above them. Thus, in the centre light is the Resurrection; below the figure of Raphael, "Tobit drawing the fish from the water at the angel's command"; below S. Gabriel, "The Annunciation to the B. Virgin"; under S. Michael is depicted his combat with the dragon; and in the fourth light S. Uriel explains to Esdras his vision. The row of traceries immediately above these lights represent the nine orders of angels, supplemented by virgins. The remaining pieces of tracery are filled with figures of prophets and angels.

The work is broadly treated, as demanded by the scale of the building and the size of the window (the principal lights being over 2 ft. in width), with large masses of silvery-white glass and simple colour. It may be noted that the wings of the Archangels, which come out so darkly in reproduction, are in a pale golden stain.* The artists are Messrs. Shrigley & Hunt, of Lancaster and London, and the drawing was exhibited in the Royal Academy last year.

DESIGN FOR A PUBLIC LIBRARY FOR A COUNTY TOWN.

In this design, the elevations of which were hung in last year's Academy exhibition, the designer sought to get interest and effect out of the necessary features of the building rather than introduce unnecessary ones. The material was to have been red brick and Bath stone, with green slates, finished with a stone ridge. The angle turret at the corner was crowned with an oak and shingle flèche covered with copper. This turret contained the librarian's private stair, which gave him access from his flat on the top floor to the reading-rooms and reference-library on the first floor, to the lending-library on the ground floor, to the caretaker's rooms in the basement, and also into the street. The site was a corner one, with light only on two sides; the back was, therefore, lighted by a long well, and the windows in the front made as large as possible without being unsightly, and glazed with iron casement frames.

A. Bartlett.

HOUSE AT WOKINGHAM.

This is one of three houses being built at Wokingham. Messrs. Bottrill & Son, of Reading, are the builders, and the architect is Mr. Ernest Newton. The house is built with local red bricks and tiles.

A PAINTER'S HOUSE AND STUDIO.

This is a design for a small house and studio; the house to contain dining-room, drawing-room, hall, offices, &c., and on the first floor, four bedrooms, bath-room, &c. There is no room over the studio. From the verandah there are doors to both studio and drawing-room, so that there should be free circulation at receptions. The approximate cost was 1,500*l.*

Fred. M. Simpson.

COMPETITIONS.

Chacewater Church, Cornwall.—The competition for rebuilding the Parish Church, Chacewater, Cornwall, has resulted in the selection of the designs sent in by Mr. Edmund Sedding, of Plymouth. There were six sets of plans sent in for it, and various were the ways suggested for treating the hideous building, which was erected early in the present century, with accommodation for 1,500 persons. The church has for some time been closed as unfit for public worship, the roof and other parts being in a bad state, so it is intended to commence the work in March.

* All colours tending to yellow or gold are liable to come out dark in photographing.

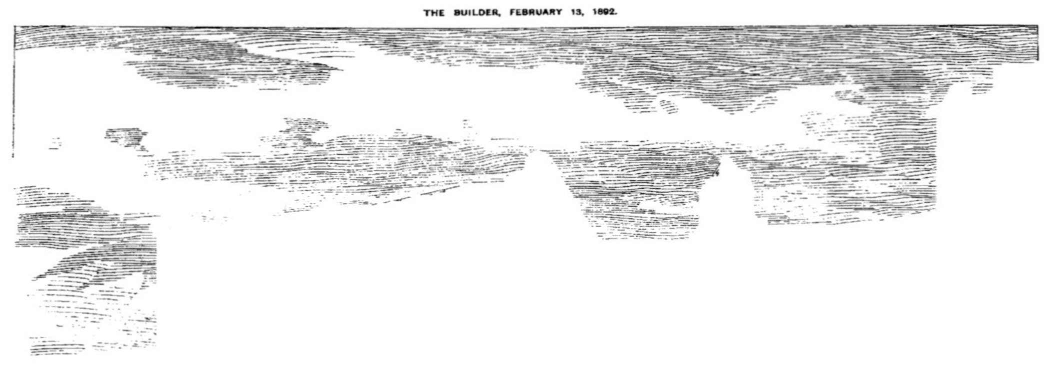

190-191 Queens Gate
South Kensington.
Fred G. Knight - Archt

PHOTO HO SPRAGUE & C

Leigh Church
Nr. Manchester
East Window

Shrigley & Hunt

INK-PHOTO SPRAGUE & Co 4 & 5 EAST HARDING STREET, FETTER LANE, E.C.

Royal Academy Exhibition, 1891.

Drawing Rm
Hall
Dining Room
Library
Pantry
Kitchen
Scullery
Coal
Yard
feet
House
at
Wokingham
Ernest Newton Archt
14 Hart St. Bloomsbury
William D. Gravell Delt

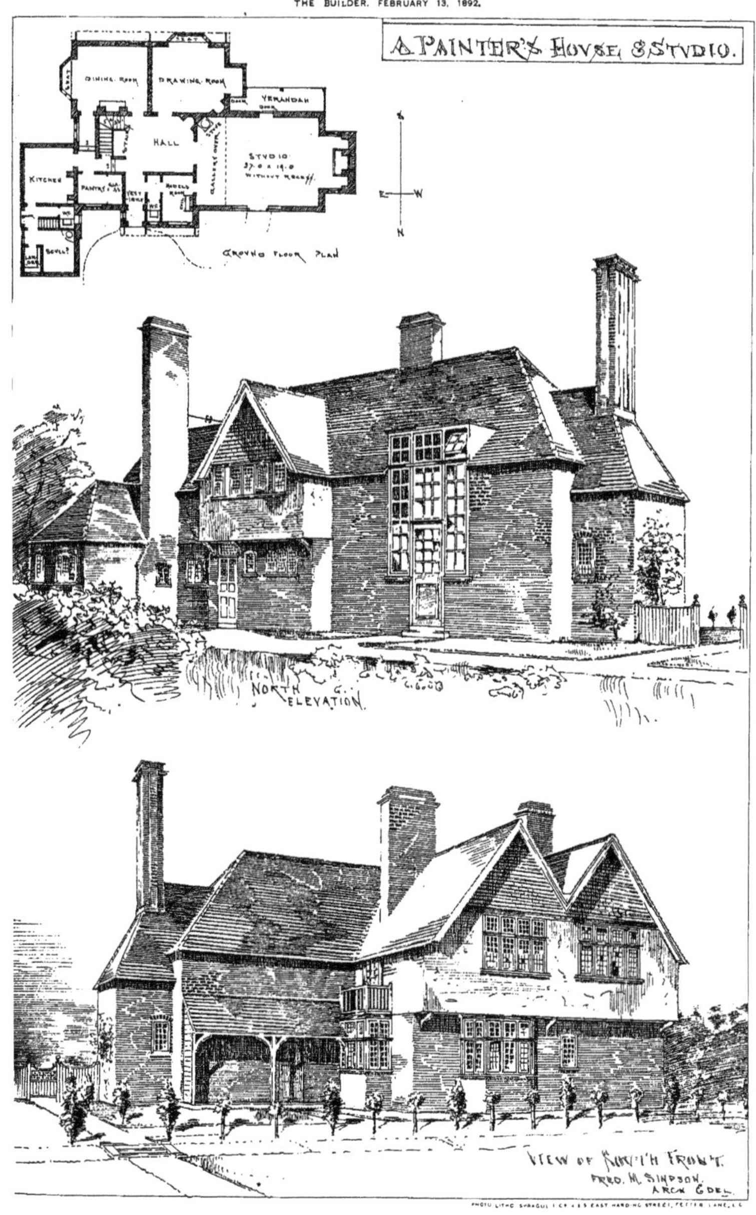
A PAINTER'S HOUSE & STUDIO.
DINING ROOM
DRAWING ROOM
VERANDAH
HALL
STUDIO 37.0 x 19.0 WITHOUT RECESS
KITCHEN
PANTRY
GROUND FLOOR PLAN
NORTH ELEVATION
VIEW OF SOUTH FRONT
FRED. M. SIMPSON. ARCH. & DEL.

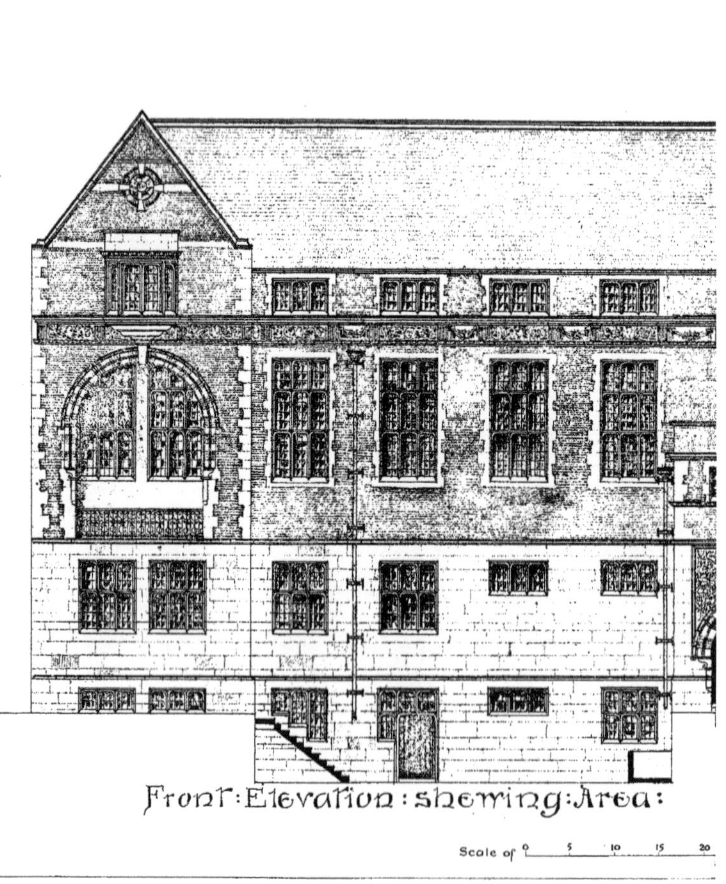

DESIGN FOR A FREE LIBRARY F(

Royal Academy Exhibition, 1891.

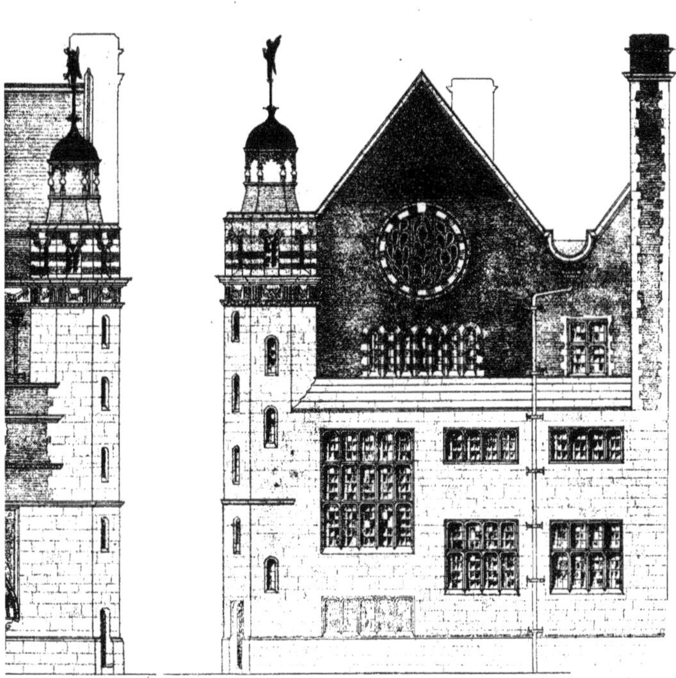

Ink-Photo, Sprague & Co. 4 & 5 East Harding Street, Fetter Lane, E.C.

TOWN.—By Mr. Arthur Bartlett.

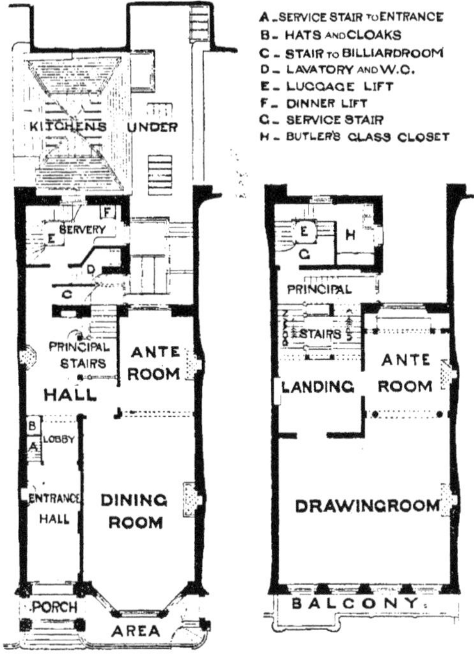

House in Queen's Gate.

THE ARCHITECTURAL ASSOCIATION SPRING VISITS:

THE METROPOLITAN LIFE ASSURANCE BUILDINGS.

THE block of buildings in Moorgate-street ich has been erected for the Metropolitan Life surance Society, from the designs of Messrs. ton Webb and Ingress Bell, was visited on turday afternoon by a large party of members the Architectural Association, under the idance of the Junior Honorary Secretary, :. F. T. W. Goldsmith, the occasion being the st spring visit of the present session. In the avoidable absence of the architects, the ildings were carefully described by the Clerk the Works, Mr. Warburton. These two build-s now occupy the site of three houses which ve been removed. The offices of the Society :upy the basement, ground, and first floors of corner building,* and the rest of the mises is devoted to offices, access to the oer portion over the insurance office ng gained from Coleman-street, at the :k. The principal point of interest the rooms of the Society, which are ed throughout with Spanish mahogany, graceful design of which is materially en-:ced by the high character of the workman-p. The chief office occupies the whole of front of the corner building with corner entrances, a smaller room for committees, and two rooms for the actuary and assistant actuary, occupy the remainder of the ground floor. The first floor contains a large board room facing Moorgate-street, with doctor's and dressing-rooms, a small room, and a luncheon-room adjacent. The board-room has a low mahogany dado, and the upper portion of the wall is divided into panels by light moulded plaster ribs, and these panels are to be covered with embossed Japanese paper, which will doubtless give a rich effect. The ceiling is executed in Jackson's fibrous plaster, and the same material has been used in the vallances of the windows, of exceedingly delicate design, though the use of the material in this position is somewhat open to question. It is to be hoped that the dummy door on the left-hand side of the entrance is not really intended, and that the balance of the decoration will be maintained without resort to this old-fashioned architectural sham. The barrel-vault shaped ceiling of the staircase, gracefully modelled *in situ* received much attention. The façades of the building have been executed in Portland stone, with polished Cornish granite base, and the elaborate detail of the windows is emphasised by the deep bands of plain surface between them. The treatment effectually disguises the fact of the existence of two buildings. The dreary monotony of Moorgate-street is now broken by this interesting addition to city architecture, and it is to be hoped that this building may be followed by many more of an equally pleasing design. The general contract has been carried out by Messrs. Cubitt & Co.

A visit was then made to the tower and St. Mary-le-Bow, which is now undergoing restoration under the superintendence of Messrs. Tress & Innes. The opportunity of investigating this interesting work of Wren's was much appreciated.

* For view of the corner building see *Builder* for y 17, 1890

SHEFFIELD SOCIETY OF ARCHITECTS AND SURVEYORS.

THE monthly meeting of this Society was held at the School of Art on Tuesday evening last, Mr. Innocent, the President, in the chair.

Mr. W. Randolph read a paper on "Town Churches, Ancient and Modern." He referred to the absence of a matured type of Town Church in Mediæval England. Our country churches were adopted fifty years ago as models for the orthodox church of the Gothic Revival. Exceptions in favour of a broader treatment were instanced in the works of Pugin and a few other architects, but no general movement was apparent till about 1850, when both the art and the literature of the Revival began to witness to the influence of foreign studies. After dealing with the brickwork and church furniture of North Germany and the Netherlands, the lecturer passed on to English precedents. The last portion of the paper was devoted to showing how the character of church work since the middle of the century had been widened under such influences as had been reviewed.

The lecture was illustrated by photos, diagrams, and sketches.

NATIONAL ASSOCIATION OF MASTER BUILDERS OF GREAT BRITAIN.

THIS Association held its twenty-eighth half-yearly meeting, in the rooms of the Central Association of Master Builders of London, on Tuesday, the 26th ult.

Mr. J. C. White, of Liverpool, the President, presided, and representatives from London, Liverpool, Manchester, Birmingham, Bristol, Hull, the Potteries, Cambridge, and Preston were present.

The report and accounts for the past half-year were read and adopted.

The following Officers and Council were appointed for the ensuing year:—President, Mr. J. C. White, Liverpool; Vice-Presidents, Messrs. Robt. Dennett, Nottingham, and John Bowen, Birmingham. Hon. Vice-Presidents, Messrs. Stanley G. Bird, London; Robt. Neill, jun., Manchester; and Mr. J. Howard Colls, London. Hon. Treasurer, Mr. Jos. Stevenson Jones, Liverpool. Hon. Auditor, Mr. C. W. Green, Liverpool. Council: Birmingham, Messrs. C. H. Barnsley and W. Sapcote; Bolton, Mr. Jos. Hy. Marsden; Bradford, Messrs. William Moulson and William Holdsworth; Bristol, Mr. A. Krauss; Cambridge, Mr. A. G. Bell; Derby, Mr. John Walker; Edinburgh, Mr. Thomas Bonnar; Glasgow, Mr. R. Bennett; Hull, Mr. R. Beevers; Leeds, Mr. C. Tomlinson; Lincoln, Mr. Wm. Hy. Close; Liverpool, Messrs. A. G. White and J. B. Johnson; London, Mr. Thos. F. Rider; Manchester, Mr. Wm. Southern and Alderman Wm Brown; Northampton, Mr. W. H. Smith; Potteries, Mr. Jas. Bowden; Wigan, Mr. Chas. B. Holmes; and Wolverhampton, Mr. J. Bradney. The Presidents of the Local Associations are also Members of the Council, *ex-officio*.

Several matters of great interest and importance to the building trades were discussed, and the meeting was brought to a close by a vote of thanks to the President.

It was decided to hold the next half-yearly meeting at Newcastle-on-Tyne.

THE ENGLISH IRON TRADE.—The English iron market, although practically unchanged, exhibits a slightly improved tone. The Glasgow warrant-market is dull; but more movement is noticeable in Scotch makers' iron, with most brands showing considerable reductions. In the Cleveland market prices are stronger. The hematite pig-iron trade remains depressed. The tin-plate market is dull. Manufactured iron is only in limited inquiry. The steel trade shows little alteration; the demand for heavy sections of rails is a little fuller. Ship-builders, with the exception of west-coast yards, are quiet. Engineers are only moderately employed; the strike on the Tyne exhibits no sign of conclusion. The coal trade is rather quiet; the Durham miners are preparing to resist the proposed 10 per cent. reduction.—*Iron.*

THE INSTITUTE OF BUILDERS.

The eighth annual general meeting of the Institute of Builders was held at the offices, 31 and 32, Bedford-street, Strand, W.C., on Tuesday last., the President, Mr. H. T. Ashby, being in the chair.

The Secretary, Mr. Richard S. Henshaw, read the following report, which was adopted unanimously:—

"1.—The Council have the pleasure to present their Eighth Annual Report, and in so doing regret having to record the death of one of the Members of the Institute, Mr. William Henry Cowlin, of Bristol, late President of the National Association of Master Builders of Great Britain, and a Director of the Builders' Accident Insurance, Limited.

2. The building trade of the year was seriously interfered with by the prolonged strike and lock-out of the carpenters and joiners, lasting as it did for nearly six months.

3. The Council in their last Report, stated that they had appointed a Committee to consider the draft 'General Conditions of Contract,' proposed by the Royal Institute of British Architects to take the place of those formally agreed between the Royal Institute and the 'Builders' Society.' The Committee devoted much time to the consideration of the proposed Conditions, and after fourteen sittings reported to the Council, who adopted the report, and forwarded the revised Conditions to the Royal Institute. The Council are now awaiting further communications on the subject.

4. The Council appointed a Committee to consider the Building By-laws proposed by the London County Council. The Committee formulated their objections to the By-laws and in due course presented them to the Home Secretary.

5. The London Building Law (Consolidation) Bill, prepared by the Government, is now being carefully considered by the Parliamentary Committee, who will comply with the request of the Secretary of the Local Government Board to report to him the views of the Institute upon the Bill.

6. The Council have the pleasure to present the audited accounts of the Institute, and the Library and Benevolent Funds for the year 1891.

7. In accordance with the Articles of Association, the President, Mr. H. T. Ashby; one of the Vice-Presidents, Mr. Robert Neill, Junior; the Treasurer, Mr. G. Plucknett; one of the Auditors, Mr. H. J. Sanders; and four members of the Council,—Mr. John T. Chappell, Mr. W. H. Clarke, Mr. Basil P. Ellis, and Mr. Woodman Hill,—retire, but are eligible for re-election."

Mr. Herbert Henry Bartlett was elected President; Mr. R. Neill, jun., and Mr. John M. Burt were respectively re-elected and elected Vice-Presidents; Mr. George Plucknett and Mr. H. J. Sanders were re-elected Treasurer and Auditor respectively; and Mr. J. T. Chappell and Mr. Woodman Hill were re-elected, and Mr. Benjamin Hannen, jun., Mr. William Scrivener and Mr. G. Williams were elected, members of the Council.

A vote of thanks to the President for his services during the past year concluded the proceedings.

THE LONDON COUNTY COUNCIL:

NEW THEATRE REGULATIONS.

The usual weekly meeting of the London County Council was held on Tuesday afternoon last, the Chairman, Sir John Lubbock, presiding.

Regulations for Ensuring the Public Safety in Theatres.—The Theatres and Music-halls Committee reported that, in the interest of the public safety, they had, after much consideration, drawn up a set of regulations for theatres and music-halls in lieu of those now in existence. These regulations have been framed under the Metropolis Management and Building Acts Amendment Act, 1878, with respect to the requirements for the protection from fire of theatres, houses, rooms, and other places of public resort within the administrative county of London, and are divided into three parts, viz., Part I., relating to Structural Matters; Part II., General; and Part III., Electric Lighting. It is provided that "these regulations shall, unless otherwise specified, apply to all theatres, houses, rooms, or other places of public resort within the administrative county of London, to be kept open for the public performance of stage-plays, and to all houses, rooms, or other places of public resort within the said county, to be kept open for public dancing, music, or other public entertainment of the like kind, under the authority of letters patent from her Majesty the Queen, her heirs or successors, or of licences by the Lord Chamberlain of her Majesty's household, or by the London County Council, other than letters patent, or licences which may have been granted for the first time before the passing of the above-mentioned Act." The following are the regulations relating to structural matters, in the form in which they were amended and finally agreed to, *seriatim*, after some discussion:—

"1. *Applications and Drawings.*—Every person who for the first time after the making of these regulations shall be desirous of obtaining authority to open any such premises* within the said County, shall first make an application in writing to the Clerk of the Council for a certificate under the above Act.

Such application shall contain a statement as to the nature and extent of the interest of such person in such premises, and the character of the entertainment for which such premises are proposed to be used, and be accompanied by complete plans, elevations and sections, drawn on tracing linen, to a scale of one-eighth of an inch to a foot; and by a block plan showing the position of such premises in relation to any adjacent premises, and to the public thoroughfares upon which the site of such premises abuts, drawn to a scale of not less than $\frac{1}{16}$th of an inch to a foot.

Such drawings shall be coloured to distinguish the materials employed in the construction of the building; the width of all staircases, corridors, gangways, and doorways, together with the heights of the tiers, and other parts of the building.

The thicknesses of the walls, and scantlings of the various materials, shall be clearly shown by figured dimensions; and the cardinal points shall be marked upon each plan.

Such drawings shall be accompanied by a specification of the works to be executed, describing the materials to be employed and the mode of construction to be adopted, together with such other particulars as may be necessary to enable the Council to judge whether the requirements of these regulations will, when such premises have been completed, have been complied with.

Such drawings shall also show the respective numbers of persons to be accommodated in the various parts of such premises, and the area to be assigned to each person, which shall not be less than 1 ft. 8 in. by 1 ft. 0 in. in the gallery, and not less than 2 ft. 4 in. by 1 ft. 8 in. in other parts of such premises.

2. *Site.*—One-half at least of the total length of the boundaries of the site of any such premises which consist of an entire building, and in case of a room or other such premises not consisting of an entire building, one-half at least of the total length of the boundaries of the site of the building of which such room or other such premises form part, shall abut upon public thoroughfares, of which one thoroughfare at least shall be not less than 40 ft. wide, and of the remainder none shall be less than 30 ft. wide if a carriageway, or 20 ft. wide if a footway.

If, in compliance with Regulation No. 10, an additional passage or way should be necessary, it may be provided by means of a private passage or way.

Such passage or way shall not be less than 10 ft. in width, and under the complete control of the owner of such premises, and no doors, windows, or other openings of the adjoining premises shall communicate therewith, or overlook any portion of such passage or way.

3. *Windows overlooking site.*—No such premises shall be erected upon a site within 20 ft. of any windows or other openings belonging to any other premises overlooking the site.

4. *Walls.*—All such premises shall be enclosed with proper external or party-walls of brick or stone.

The thickness of such walls shall not be less than the thickness prescribed by the Metropolitan Building Act, 1855, for walls of similar height and length in buildings of the warehouse class.

5. *Dressing-rooms.*—Dressing-rooms shall be arranged in a separate block of buildings, or divided from the place of public resort by party-walls, with only such means of communication therewith as may be approved by the Council.

All such dressing-rooms shall be constructed of fire-resisting materials, and connected with an independent exit leading directly into a thoroughfare or way.

All such dressing-rooms shall be ventilated to the outer air by windows in the external walls.

The walls of all such dressing-rooms shall be hung, for decorative purposes, only with materials completely adhering to the surface of such walls.

No such dressing-rooms shall be situated more than one story below the street level.

Sufficient and separate w.c. and urinal accommodation, properly ventilated to the outer air, shall be provided for the use of the male and female artistes.

6. *No theatre under or over any other building.*—No theatre shall be constructed underneath, or on the top of, any part of any other building.

7. *Number of tiers.*—No such premises shall have more than three tiers or horizontal divisions, including the gallery, above the level of the pit.

Where the front seats of the gallery are separated from the gallery by a partition, such seats shall not count as a separate tier.

8. *Height of tiers.*—Where the first tier or balcony extends over the pit, stalls, or area, the height between the floor of the pit and the first tier shall not be at any part less than 10 ft., and the height between the floor of the highest part of the gallery and the lowest part of the ceiling over the same shall not be less than 12 ft.

9. *Floor of pit.*—In all such premises the floor of the highest part of the pit, or of the stalls where there is no pit, shall not be more than 6 in. above the level of the street adjoining the principal entrance to the pit, and the lowest part of the floor of the pit or stalls shall not be more than 15 ft. below such level.

10. *Entrances and exits.*—Two separate exits, not leading into the same thoroughfare or way, shall be provided to every tier or floor of such premises.

If any tier or floor shall be divided into two parts, two separate exits, not leading into the same thoroughfare or way, shall be provided to each of such parts.

Such exits shall be arranged so as to afford a ready means of egress from both sides of each tier or floor, and shall lead directly into a thoroughfare or way.

11. *Vestibules.*—Where vestibules are provided, not more than three tiers or floors (or where such tiers or floors are divided into two or more parts, such parts of tiers or floors) shall communicate with one vestibule.

The width of each vestibule shall be at least one-third greater than the united width of all the doorways or passages that lead thereto.

The united widths of all the doorways or passages that lead from a vestibule towards a thoroughfare or way shall be at least of the same width as such vestibule.

Not more than one exit from each separate part of a tier or floor shall be used as an entrance.

12. *Proscenium-wall.*—In all such premises where a stage with a proscenium shall be erected, such stage shall be separated from the auditorium by a brick proscenium-wall not less than 13 in. in thickness, and such wall shall be carried up the full thickness to a height of at least 3 ft. above the roof, such height being measured at right angles to the slope of the roof, and shall be carried down below the stage to a solid foundation.

Not more than three openings shall be formed in the proscenium-wall, exclusive of the proscenium opening.

No such openings shall exceed 3 ft. in width and 6 ft. 6 in. in height, and each of such openings shall be closed by a wrought-iron door not less than $\frac{1}{4}$ in. in thickness in the panel, hung in a wrought-iron frame, so as to close of itself without a spring.

No openings formed in the proscenium-wall shall, at the lowest part, be at a higher level than the floor of the stage.

All the decorations around the proscenium shall be constructed of fire-resisting materials.

13. *Proscenium opening.*—The proscenium opening shall be provided with a fire-resisting screen to be used as a drop-curtain, of such pattern, construction, and gearing, and with such arrangements for pouring water upon the surface of the screen which is towards the stage, as may be approved by the Council.

14. *Roof over stage.*—The height of the wall-plate carrying the rafters of the roof over the stage shall not be less than twice the height of the proscenium opening, such height being measured from the level of the stage at the curtain line.

An opening shall be formed in the roof near the back of the stage, of a superficial area at the base of at least $\frac{1}{10}$th of the superficial area of the stage. Such opening shall be covered with a lantern light, glazed on the top and sides, and be fitted with suitable exhaust cowls.

15. *Corridors, passages, and staircases.*—Every staircase, landing, lobby, corridor, or passage intended for the use of not more than 400 persons of the audience shall be formed of fire-resisting materials and shall not be less than 4 ft. 6 in. wide; but if communicating with any portion of the house intended for the accommodation of a larger number of the audience than 400 persons, it shall be increased in width by 6 in. for every additional 100 persons until a maximum width of 9 ft. be obtained.

16. *Staircases.*—Every staircase for the use of the audience shall have solid square (as distinguished from spandrel) steps of York or other stone or fire-resisting materials, to be approved by the Council, with treads not less than 11 in. wide and with risers not more than 6 in. high, without winders, in flights of not more than twelve or less than three steps each.

The treads of each flight of steps shall be of uniform width, and be pinned into brick walls at both ends.

The several flights of such steps shall be supported and enclosed upon all sides by brick walls not less than 9 in. thick, to be carried down to the level of the footways.

No staircase shall have more than two flights of twelve steps each without a turn.

All landings shall be 6 in. thick, be square upon plan and have brick arches 9 in. deep turned under them in the middle of such landings.

Every staircase shall have a roof of fire-resisting materials to be approved by the Council.

A continuous handrail shall be fixed on both sides of all steps and landings, supported by strong metal brackets built into the wall.

Such handrails shall be chased into the walls, where the thickness of the walls will permit, but in all cases where the flights of steps re-turn, the newel wall shall be chased so as to allow the handrail to turn without projecting on the landing.

17. *Gangways.*—A clear passage or gangway not less than 3 ft. wide shall be formed at the sides and in the rear of the seating in every part of such premises.

Such passages or gangways shall at all times be kept entirely free from chairs, flap-seats, or other obstructions, whether permanent or temporary.

18. *Ironwork.*—All constructional ironwork in such premises shall be embedded in fire-resisting material in a manner to be approved by the Council.

19. *Workshops, &c.*—All workshops, store-rooms, wardrobe or painting rooms, in connexion with such premises, shall be separated from such premises by brick walls not less than 9 in. thick.

All openings in such walls shall be closed with self-closing wrought-iron doors hung in a wrought-iron frame.

All such doors, if consisting of a single fold, shall be made to overlap, when closed, the door frame at least 3 in.; and, if made in two folds, such folds shall overlap each other, when closed, at least 3 in. on each side.

All floors and ceilings of such rooms shall be formed of fire-resisting materials.

All such rooms shall be ventilated by windows in the outer walls.

20. *Limelight tanks, boilers, and dynamos.*—All limelight tanks, boilers with engines, and dynamos with engines shall be each placed in a ventilated chamber or building of fire-proof construction.

Such chambers or buildings shall be separated from such premises, and from each other, by brick walls and fireproof floors without openings, and shall be enclo[sed] upon one or more sides by external walls.

21. *Scene Dock.*—All scene docks or stores and property rooms in connexion with such premises shall be enclosed by brick walls not less than 9 in. thick, and shall have floors and ceilings of fire-resisting materials.

All openings from such docks, stores, or rooms to such premises shall be closed by self-closing wrought-iron doors, hung in wrought-iron frames.

All such doors, if consisting of a single fold, shall b[e]

* In these regulations the expression "such premises" means a theatre, house, room, or other place of public resort to be kept open for any of the purposes aforesaid.

ıde to overlap, when closed, the door-frame at least n.; and, if made in two folds, such folds shall overlap ch other, when closed, at least 3 in. on each side.

22. *Enclosures.*—No enclosure shall be provided upon y such premises where the public can assemble for y other purpose than to view the performance, except far as the Council shall consider necessary for the ovision of refreshment-bars, or, in the case of a eatre, for the provision of a *foyer*, or smoking-room.

23. *Skylights.*—All skylights, and the sloping sides of ntern lights, shall be protected by galvanised iron-ire guards, securely fixed on the outside of such ylights or lantern lights.

24. *Gas.*—All such premises when lighted by gas shall ave separate and distinct gas services and meters as llows:—(*a*) To the stage; (*b*) To the auditorium; (*c*) o the staircases, corridors, and exits.

Such meters shall be placed in properly ventilated hambers of fireproof construction.

All gas-brackets shall be fixed without joints; and all urners within reach of the audience shall be fitted ith secret taps, and be efficiently protected by glass or ire globes.

All gas-burners within 3 ft. of the ceiling shall have anging shades of uninflammable material to distribute he heat.

All gas-pipes shall be made of iron or brass.

Where there is a stage or wings with scenery, the ootlights or floats shall be protected by fixed iron-wire uards, and the burners shall be provided with glass himneys.

The rows and lines, and gas-burners in the wings which must commence 4 ft. at least from the level of he stage) shall be protected by fixed iron-wire guards.

All battens shall be hung by at least three wire ropes, nd be protected at the back by a solid metal guard, nd wire fixed to a stiff iron frame, at such a distance rom the gas-jets that no part of the scenery or decora-ion can become heated.

All movable lights shall be fitted with flexible tubes, nd the gas in every case shall be turned off by the tap n the stage as well as by that on the flexible tube.

All flexible tubes shall be of sufficient strength to esist pressure from without.

An indicating gas-plate shall be provided at a con-enient place at the side of the stage.

25. *Doors and fastenings.*—All doorways used by the ublic shall be at least 4 ft. 6 in. wide in the clear, with loors hung in two folds made to open outwards towards he thoroughfare or way.

All internal doors shall be so hung as not to obstruct, when open, any gangway, passage, staircase, or landing.

No door shall open immediately upon a flight of steps, ut a square landing at least the width of the doorway hall be provided between such steps and such doorway.

All exit doors having fastenings shall be fastened by utomatic bolts only, of a pattern to be approved by the Council; but where such doors are also to be used by the public for entrances, they shall be fastened with spagnolette or lever bolts only, of a pattern to be ap-proved in each case by the Council, and fitted with lever andles at a height of 3 ft. 6 in. from the floor.

All doors used for entrances, and all gates, shall be ade to open both ways, and shall, when opened in-ards, be locked back against the wall in such a manner to require a key to release them.

All barriers and internal doors shall be made to open utwards, with no other fastenings than automatic olts.

No locks, monkey-tail, flush, or barrel bolts, or lock-ng bars, or other obstructions to exit, shall be used on ny doors, gates, or barriers.

26. *Ventilation.*—All parts of such premises shall be roperly and sufficiently ventilated in a manner to be pproved by the Council.

All openings for ventilation shall be shown on the lans, and described in the specification, which shall be ubmitted to the Council for its approval.

27. *Warming.*—No fireplace shall be formed in any ortion of the auditorium or stage of such premises.

All open fireplaces or stoves in any other part of such remises shall be protected by strong fixed iron-wire uards and fenders, part of which may be made to open or all necessary purposes.

All heating apparatus shall be placed in a position to e approved by the Council, and enclosed upon all sides y brick walls not less than 9 in. thick, and shall be roperly ventilated.

All hot-water pipes or coils shall, where necessary, be ecessed in the walls, or otherwise arranged so as not to iminish the clear width of the gangway.

Where such premises are heated by artificial means, he high-pressure hot-water system with sealed pipes vill be inadmissible, and either hot-air or the low-ressure hot-water circulation system shall be adopted, aving an open cold-water supply cistern, and the pipes hroughout the system shall be of galvanised wrought-ron, with the exception of those in immediate contact ith the boiler, which may be either of galvanised rought iron or copper.

The boiler shall be made of wrought iron, copper, or olid steel, and shall be provided with a dead weight or ther approved safety-valve, which must be attached to he boiler by an independent galvanised wrought iron r copper pipe, and must not under any circumstances e fixed to the circulating-pipes, and must be placed in uch a position as will ensure protection from soot and irt.

The term low pressure shall be understood to mean he pressure due to the vertical head of water between he boiler and the supply cistern.

28. *Water supply.*—All such premises containing a uperficial area for the accommodation of the public of 000 ft. and upwards shall be provided with a sufficient umber of hydrants, each of a diameter of not less than ½ in., to be connected by a 3-in. main with a water ompany's high pressure street main.

Each of such hydrants shall be provided with at least 30-ft. length of hose, with fittings of the Metropolitan ire Brigade pattern.

In all such premises, where there is no constant upply of water, there shall be provided on the top of e proscenium wall, or at some other place to be ap-roved by the Council, two cisterns, to be kept always lled with water.

Such cisterns shall be each capable of containing at ast 250 gallons of water for every 100 persons of the udience to be accommodated in the building.

Such cisterns shall be properly protected from all danger from frost.

Fire-mains shall be connected with such cisterns to hydrants to be fixed in such places and manner as may be approved by the Council.

29. *Addition or Alteration to Premises.*—Notice shall be given to the Clerk of the Council of any intended structural addition to, or alteration of, any such premises, in respect of which the Council may have granted a certificate under the said Act of 1878, to the effect that such premises were, on their original completion, in accordance with the Council's regulations.

Such notice shall be accompanied by plans, elevations and sections, block plan, and specification of the works to be executed similar to those required in the case of premises to be certified for the first time by the Council, and showing such intended addition or alteration.

The Council will, if necessary, cause a fresh survey of such premises to be made.

No doors, bolts or other fastenings, obstructions to the means of egress, flap seats, or other means of diminishing or stopping up the gangways, shall be put, nor shall any alterations of a like nature be made to such premises without the previous consent of the Council being obtained thereto."

Railway and other Schemes.—On the recommendation of the Parliamentary Committee, it was decided to petition against various railway and other schemes affecting the Metropolis, including the Manchester, Sheffield, and Lincolnshire Company's proposed new trunk-line to London.

Gower-street.—Amongst other recommendations of the Improvements Committee which were agreed to was one approving of an arrangement for removing the bar at the top of Gower-street, so as to open up another direct line of communication between Euston-road and Holborn. The land occupied by the roadway between University College and University College Hospital is, it seems, the property of the Hospital authorities, who are willing to sell it for 15,000*l*. The Council propose to contribute 10,000*l*. towards the cost, the Vestry contributing the remaining 5,000*l*.

After transacting other business, the Council adjourned.

Correspondence.

To the Editor of THE BUILDER.

DR. TEALE ON "DUST."

SIR,—In your article of February 6 upon my lecture at the Society of Arts upon "Dust and Fresh Air," you throw doubts upon some of the points I contended for. Upon these kindly permit me to make some comments.

1. "The windows to be formed with the greater portion fixed, and only a tall, narrow sash hinged to open as a casement, and protected in the same way as closet-doors and boxes." My proposal is,—that, in an ordinary window, one half should be fixed, the other half should open as a casement inwards, but that in the case of a wide window the two outer thirds should be fixed, and the centre third should open on hinges. The casement should not open in one tall piece, but in two portions, or even in the case of very tall windows in three portions, in order to avoid the clumsiness and inaccuracy of the ordinary fittings of French windows. This hinged window is not protected against ingress of wind and soot after the manner of drawers and closets, but by very *accurate fittings against a "double rebated frame,"* after the manner of a jeweller's case.

2. "The adoption of this principle would mean a practical stoppage of direct fresh air through open windows." Not at all. The windows can be opened whenever it is wished to have extra fresh air; as in summer, when few fires are burning, and there is but little soot in the atmosphere. But no one in London would have a window open night and day, because of the dirt and dust; whereas with the "Hardy diffuser" and screen we have virtually an open window, with most of the dirt screened off,—day in and day out, year in and year out.

3. "For the exclusion of dust from the house we think Mr. Teale's method can hardly be regarded as 'within the region of practical politics.'" Well, I can only say that I have had the system practically at work in my consulting rooms and in my lodgings for patients for several years, and that I am quite satisfied as to its value, practicability, and effectiveness. Neither is it very costly.

Let me repeat, what I said at the end of my lecture, my conviction, from long observation, that by far the most serious part of the dirt in a house consists of soot drawn in through the windows. T. PRIDGIN TEALE.

⁂ Dr. Teale's letter at all events confirms our opinion that his system of complete dust exclusion applied to closets and boxes cannot be applied to houses in the same complete manner. Dr. Teale does not live in London; every architect and architectural draughtsman who works in London knows that when the drawing-office windows are opened in summer for air and coolness, there has to be a constant dusting of the drawing-board to keep it clean. Nor do we speak of summer only; windows ought to be frequently opened in winter, and then what becomes of straining the dust out? You cannot treat a dwelling-house like a cupboard or a chest.—ED.

CONCRETE FOR ARTISANS' DWELLINGS.

SIR,—Breeze from gasworks is very far from being the best material for concrete floors, especially of large span, its use being confined chiefly to short spans, with a free use of iron or steel girders. Breeze is improved,—so far as strength goes,—by washing, but it is even then too sandy and deficient in strength to make good concrete. It requires a greater proportion of Portland cement than many other aggregates to make, in comparison, concrete capable of withstanding moderate tensile and compressive strains. Where the materials are of a suitable nature, floors of 12 ft. to 20 ft. span may be constructed in one slab, but a judicious use of iron or steel girders, and spans of 10 ft. or thereabouts,—if the floors are quite flat on the under side,—are the best to adopt in a general way.

Breeze is not a good aggregate for walls, and assuming it was obtainable for nothing, would, if measured by strength, be probably the most costly of any in use.

As there appear to be conflicting opinions with regard to the susceptibility of deal floors laid on concrete to dry-rot, I have sent you a piece of deal, half an inch in thickness, which formed part of a cottage floor nailed down to concrete nearly eight years ago, and which is as sound now as on the day it was fixed. The advantage of nailing floor-boards to the concrete, beside that of no intervening space for mice and other house pests, is, that much thinner flooring is required, for it is well-known that if supported on joists 12 in. apart, a floor is unsafe when it is worn to about half an inch in thickness, but if laid on solid concrete, the whole thickness is available for wear. The great point is for the concrete to be thoroughly dry before the boards are nailed thereto, but it takes a long while,—months, indeed,—to arrive at a fit condition to case with wood.

My own experience points to forming the mass of concrete at the earliest opportunity, leaving about 1½ in. or 2 in. in thickness of coke breeze (or fine crushed or broken soft brick débris, screened through a half-inch sieve, is quite equal thereto when breeze is unavailable), to be laid down at last and carefully levelled. Even this should have a month allowed it to dry, and be exposed to all the wind and air possible, not covered up, as "Another Surveyor" suggests, which not only retards the concrete from drying, but saturates the wood flooring. THOMAS POTTER.

Alresford.

SIR,—I cannot see how the 1-in. space, which "Experience" recommends between the floor-boards and the concrete, is to be properly ventilated on the upper floors of an ordinary building. The imperfect jointing of the floor-boards is, of course, what would actually ventilate this space in many cases; but we have no right to trust to this. A few years ago I saw dry rot break out on the upper floors of a building where something like a 6-in. space had been left. The upholsterer had bordered the rooms with linoleum, and the margins went wrong in about three months.

I do see, and have felt for many years, that a layer of either one or more inches of what must be very dirty air is a nasty dangerous thing to live over. You, Sir, dealt with this most trenchantly in your paper at the Health Congress last year, and my heart went out to you for exposing one of my pet horrors; a horror from which hardly any house is free. Our noses are all night long within about 2 ft. of the abomination. Supposing it possible to ventilate the space, it still remains a "run" for vermin and a home for microbes of every sort.

"C. F. M." seems to have gone nearer than anyone else to ridding us of this danger. His 2-in. screed of coke breeze and cement seems to me excellent. Nails can be driven everywhere into it, ordinary inch floor-boards can be used instead of 1½-in. wood blocks (which, spite of all efforts to the contrary, give trouble from shrinkage and absence of nails), and the dirty, stagnant, stratum of air disappears.

I wish the London School Board would give "C. F. M.'s" plan a trial in a few of their buildings. A five-years' test in an isolated case is not entirely sufficient.

Of the combustible character of coke-breeze concrete, I have had, as I stated, ocular evidence. The layer of coke breeze and cement had been carried into the fireplaces, and became almost red hot from the heat of an ordinary fire. The heat travelled *viâ* the coke breeze through a 9-in. brick back, and made havoc with the decorations in the adjoining room, the paint becoming completely frizzled. Luckily, the skirtings were of cement. So hot was the concrete that, after taking out the stove, nothing could be done for several hours; the concrete would not cool down! It seems to me a farce to call coke and cement fireproof.

"Experience" says that ballast concrete is not fireproof,—and that it is even less so than is the coke mixture. But can he quote any instance in which the latter has been put to the test of a big fire? And is it not well known that the former was so tested at a serious fire in the Borough some few years ago, and that it gave admirable results?

I know Wright's fireproof fixing blocks, having introduced them into quite a dozen buildings. They are much better than wood bricks; they do not shrink; and will, of course, resist fire for a very long time where the wood bricks would not. Did "Experience" ever try how one of these fireproof blocks behaves in a fire? A friend of mine, who received a sample block, had the curiosity,—cruelty, I had almost said,—to put it in the fire, and thus made both fuel and fun of it. Nevertheless, I think them very good things indeed in the right place,—not in the fireplace.

Of course I did not advise that the floor-boards be "cut down" until the concrete was practically dry. What I meant was, that they should be cut down at that stage, and nailed down as late as possible.

"Experience" advises coke breeze instead of coke for the "aggregate." The scaling off, about which I wrote, occurred where coke breeze had been so used.

"Experience" suggests keeping the layer 1 in. down to prevent such scaling. But this means either adding 1 in. to the layer of stagnant air above the concrete, or of making the concrete 1 in. thicker than is actually necessary for strength.

I do not like battening the soffit, but for a good job,—a richer job than artisans' dwellings, —I should always batten and lath, whatever the concrete; in no other way that I have seen can a fireproof building hope to be at all sound proof. I am afraid, Sir, that when the absolutely solid floor comes into general use our clients will still not be happy, but will say that they preferred the risk of their old condition to living in a sort of drum, upon which every passing footstep overhead beats a tattoo. "ANOTHER SURVEYOR."

February 8, 1892.

MATCH-BOARDING ON NEW BRICK WALLS, AND OAK-BLOCK FLOORING ON CONCRETE.

SIR,—I should be much obliged if any reader would tell me, through the medium of your columns, how long a time should be allowed to elapse before putting match-board lining on new brick walls built in the winter months. The match-boarding is to be kept 1 in. from the brickwork, with perforations to admit air.

Also, how long a time is required for a bed of Portland cement concrete, 6 in. thick and laid on the ground, to become thoroughly dry and fit to receive oak-block flooring? INQUIRER.

The Student's Column.

WARMING BUILDINGS BY HOT WATER. VII.

WATER SUPPLY (*concluded*). DIRT IN BOILERS AND PIPES. (HORTICULTURAL WORKS.)

THE necessity for a dip or siphon in the cold-supply pipe was pointed out in the last paper, and it was shown how it was effected by merely carrying the service down a few inches below the circulating pipes and then ascending into the under side of the return. This is the most simple way, but does not give very easy access to the dipped part of the pipe if it gets stopped with dirt, as it is likely to do. Some, therefore, prefer to set the pipe as fig. 23; this answers the same purpose and just as effectively, and it is frequently suggested that a plug be put at the point marked *, so that any deposited matter may be easily removed without disconnection of the pipe. This is especially desirable for those works which are fed with surface water.

Occasionally the two methods of dipping the pipe are resorted to as fig. 24. There is, however, but rarely occasion for this.

A very useful appliance for small apparatus is an expansion box end, as fig. 25. This is put at the extremity of the pipes furthest from the boiler, the flow and return being connected at the points shown. This article fulfils the duties of a supply cistern, a siphon (the connecting-piece which unites the flow and return at their furthest extremities) and a substantial support for the pipes. These expansion boxes are now made in a variety of sizes and styles, but the one here shown, by the enlargement at the top, admits of a ball-valve being fitted within it, if needed. It should have been mentioned that this appliance also does away with the necessity of an air-pipe that would be otherwise required at that point.

The point at which the cold-supply pipe (from a cistern) is connected into the apparatus is generally near the boiler into the return service. It does not matter much where it is situated, if the apparatus is heating a conservatory or any glass-house without divisions; but

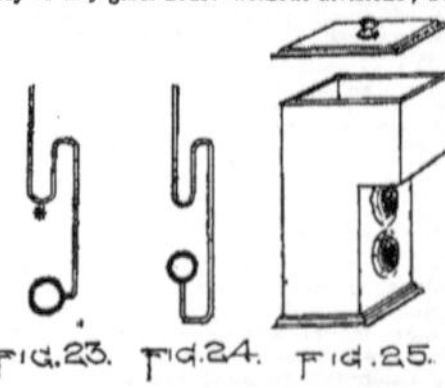

FIG. 23. FIG. 24. FIG. 25.

when there are two or several houses heated from one boiler, the cold supply must be kept near the boiler, as otherwise, in shutting off the circulation from one or more of the houses, we should possibly shut off the water-supply as well, and this would not do.

When means are provided for drawing warm water from the apparatus for watering purposes there must also be some arrangement for automatic self-filling, as it would cause a great deal of trouble to replenish by hand every time the tap was applied to. No doubt this is done sometimes, but the more usual practice is to introduce a ball-valve into the supply cistern, assuming there is a storage cistern somewhere that will furnish the required quantity. If surface water is used, dipped from a pond or ditch, then the ball-valve and automatic replenishment will probably not be feasible. Of course, warm water for watering purposes need not necessarily be drawn from the apparatus, and there are a number of gardeners, if not the majority, who are averse to it. In drawing water it naturally follows that the pipes are cooled down somewhat by the bulk of cold water that is introduced, and this is an objectionable feature, although care may be used only to draw water in the warmest hours of the day (winter day). A common means of providing warm water is to carry one or two pipes through a tank, and so heat its contents. There is no objection to this method, for although the water in the tank may take a good while to heat, and have a cooling influence upon the apparatus in the first instance, there is but little expenditure of heat when once it is all heated.

It is necessary to notice one particular feature that is manifested when water is regularly withdrawn (which means the frequent changing of the water in the apparatus), and this is the accumulation of incrusted lime deposit that occurs when hard water is used. In the usual way it is soft water, rain-water, collected in tubs or in ponds or ditches, that is supplied to the apparatus, particularly in country places; but in towns, and also when a ball-valve is used, the water supply is generally from a water company's mains. In the southern half of England the water furnished from this source is almost invariably what is known as "hard," that is, having lime in solution. The lime thus held in a dissolved state within it is, as a rule, due to the water having originally come from or through chalk strata, and, far from being noticeable, the water is usually conspicuous by its clearness and crystal-like appearance.

This lime or chalk matter (calcic bicarbonate), so soluble in water, is, as before mentioned, quite invisible and unnoticeable to the eye, but when the water is heated, a change in the state of the lime is effected, and instead of being in the fluid or gaseous state just referred to, it, by losing carbonic acid, is at once converted into a visible, hard, and solid substance (calcic carbonate), a sort of limestone. The amount of this substance obtained by heating one charge of water in the apparatus would be scarcely perceptible, and the heating and re-heating of the same water would never result in giving us more; but if the water is changed, —that is, new water introduced,—we get another precipitation of lime deposit when it is heated. By the time the water has been changed a great number of times the accumulated matter will have become, perhaps, ¼ in. or ½ in. in thickness, and unless it be soon removed a fracture will occur in the boiler-plate. The fracture is brought about by the deposit, which is generally very dense and hard, keeping the water away from the iron, and the boiler-plate perishes by the action of the fire. The action of the fire has no ill-effect while water is directly in contact with the opposite side of the boiler-plate; but it has, as every one knows, a rapidly destructive effect upon iron-plate that is unprotected.

It is necessary to speak of this peculiar result with hard water, when water is drawn from an apparatus causing the contents to be frequently changed, for the deposit must one day become of sufficient thickness to do harm if not removed. When it is known that water is going to be drawn from an apparatus, it is usual to order manlids of a proper size and number for the removal of this hard scale, for it may need a tool to be inserted to loosen it, even if an anti-incrustation fluid be used when cleaning it out.

In the worst of cases, however, the hard deposit trouble never assumes the state in these works that it does in domestic supply boilers, for when using these in hard water districs, we get a ½-in. deposit of "fur" in three to six months; and frequently a boiler will crack, from this cause, within a year, if it is not cleaned out. In horticultural works,—and, in fact, all heating works,—it is best to do without drawing water from the apparatus (except for the periodical emptying and cleaning) if anyway possible.

In concluding the subject of water supply, it remains to be explained that with an apparatus from which no boiler is drawn it is not generally recommended to use a ball-valve to the supply cistern with the view of automatically replenishing the loss of water by evaporation. The quantity of water lost this way is really very small (unless the apparatus happens to be a rather extensive one), and consequently the services of the ball-valve are in very little request. This usually results in it becoming stuck or out of gear by mere want of use,—a weakness that these articles are subject to. Of course, a ball-valve can be used, if looked to now and again, but it must not be implicitly relied upon.

It will be gathered from the information given that the use of surface water, whatever care be used, introduces a deal of dirt matter into the apparatus, and this must be removed periodically. Its removal from the boiler is very necessary, as when in sufficient quantity it will bring about the destruction of the boiler-plate, in almost the same way as the hard deposit just referred to.

In a saddle-boiler, which has but one return-pipe entering it at the side, there will always be found a collection of dirt at the bottom, on the side opposite to that which the return-pipe enters. This, it will be understood, is due to the rapid movement of the water keeping the dirt clear at the point where it flows into the boiler, but it thus causes the collection to settle and form on the opposite side, where the action of the water is less strong. When a saddle-boiler has but one return and is fed with water from impure sources, the fracture, when it takes place, will almost always be at the point just explained, and that part of the boiler will be found choked up with dirt.

The dirt will also settle in pipes that are run horizontally; the more horizontal they are the easier for the dirt to rest within them; and the lowest pipes may be expected to have the larger share. This dirt is removed by a periodical flushing of the apparatus, and this suffices for all general purposes, as it is not so inclined to cake and become hard in the pipes as it does in the boiler with the fire acting upon it. Provision is made for this flushing when setting the boilers; pipes being connected into low points of the boiler, which not only admit of the issue of the water flushed through, but also admit of a cane or other instrument being passed in to disturb any sedimentary matter in the boiler that may not yield to the flushing process.

BIRMINGHAM ENGINEERING STUDENTS.—A meeting of the Association of Birmingham Students of the Institution of Civil Engineers was held on the 4th inst. at the Midland Institute, the President, Mr. J. Edward Willcox, A.M.Inst.C.E., being in the chair. A paper was read by Mr. T. Rooke, Student Inst.C.E., "On the Design and Construction of Dynamos," which was followed by an interesting discussion.

OBITUARY.

MR. M. H. BLANCHARD.—We regret to hear that Mr. M. H. Blanchard, formerly of 74, Blackfriars-road, London, terra-cotta manufacturer, died on the 1st inst., at his residence, Bishop's Waltham, Hants, after three days' illness, of influenza. He was one of the earliest revivalists of terra-cotta, and obtained the prize medal of the 1851 Exhibition for material and workmanship in terra-cotta. He carried out some of the most extensive terra-cotta works throughout the country, including, we believe, the South Kensington Museum and the Horticultural Gardens. His latest novelty was a terra-cotta staircase and floor, which were tested by fire on December 17 last, with satisfactory results, under the circumstances detailed in the *Builder* for January 2 last, p. 18. Mr. Blanchard was born November 9, 1816. His remains were interred on the 5th inst. at Norwood Cemetery.

GENERAL BUILDING NEWS.

PROPOSED RESTORATION OF LICHFIELD CATHEDRAL.—On the 3rd inst. a public meeting, convened by the Dean and Chapter, was held in the School of Art at Lichfield to consider the subject of the needful restoration of Lichfield Cathedral. The Dean and Chapter a short time ago issued an appeal asking for nearly 20,000*l.* for this purpose. About 80,000*l.* has, in past years, been expended on the renovation of the Cathedral, but other repairs remain to be taken in hand, and that without delay, says the *Lichfield Diocesan Calendar*, if the fabric is to be maintained, in some places with safety, in others in its integrity. These are as follows, and they are stated in the order of the urgency with which they are required to be executed:—(*a*) Structural repair in central tower and spire, parts of which are in such a state as to threaten their stability. (*b*) Resetting of glass in two windows, with new mullions, and repair of buttresses in Lady Chapel. (*c*) Restoration to original design of buttresses in south transept, with repairs urgently needed. (*d*) Renovation of north transept, with fresh windows as originally constructed. (*e*) Repairs of parapets and clearstory in the choir and Lady Chapel. (*f*) Repair of north aisle of nave, and other like work elsewhere. Besides these repairs, which press for attention at the very earliest opportunity, the raising of the roofs to the original pitch has been urged by the architect, Mr. J. O. Scott. This alteration, which would not in the least degree, it is stated, interfere with the beautiful groining as seen from the inside, would involve probably a further outlay of about 5,000*l.* But besides these external reparations, some outlay in the interior is almost a necessity. A reredos of lasting material, probably of mosaic, ought to be placed in the Lady Chapel; the two western windows in which require to be filled with stained glass in some degree corresponding to the beauty of the other seven. The present doors, fixed inside the three main entrances for keeping out draughts, are hardly such as befit the dignity of a cathedral. Proper fittings are required for the prebendaries' vestry and sacristy; and the present muniment-room would amply repay the cost of opening out its fair proportions. The nave also ought to be seated throughout with oak benches, of the same character as those which are already provided in the front. The Rev. Canon Lonsdale having entered into a detailed explanation of the work required to be done, Colonel T. J. Levett proposed:—"That this meeting having had brought before it the present condition of the fabric of Lichfield Cathedral, and the urgent necessity of undertaking its repair, desires to express its earnest hope that the appeal issued by the Dean and Chapter for this purpose may be liberally met throughout the diocese and elsewhere, and pledges itself to do the utmost to support the effort about to be made." The resolution, having been seconded, was carried unanimously. Over 1,000*l.* was subscribed in the room.

NEW SCHOOLS, COLLEGE OF SURGEONS, DUBLIN.—On the 1st inst., the new schools which have been built in connexion with the Royal College of Surgeons, Stephen's-green, Dublin, were opened by the President of the College, Dr. Croly. The schools constitute a new wing at the rear of the College, and include a dissecting-room, a smaller dissecting-room for lady students, a chemical laboratory, and a lecture theatre. The architects were Sir Thomas Deane & Son, and the work was executed by Messrs. H. & J. Martin. The principal dissecting-room is 74 ft. in length by 64 ft. wide and about 22 ft. in height. The roof, of which the central portion is higher and is glazed, is supported by metal columns and beams; it is composed of asphalted concrete, and is fireproof. The floor is of concrete asphalted, and is also fireproof. The ladies' dissecting-room is about 30 ft. square. The chemical laboratory is 64 ft. by 28 ft. All the rooms are provided with electric lamps supplied by the Electric Engineering Company of Ireland, and are heated by hot-water pipes supplied by Messrs. Musgrave, of Belfast. There is also a bone-room, in which specimens of human bones are preserved for purposes of study, and a lift extends through the rooms by means of which the dead subjects are raised from a cellar below.

NEW FREE CHURCH, NEAR EDINBURGH.—A new church, to be called the Restalrig Free Church, has just been erected at Parson's-green, on a triangular gusset of ground between the Portobello and Willowbrae-roads. The church has been designed by Messrs. Sydney Mitchell & Wilson, and is in the Early Gothic style. Its length is 100 ft., its breadth 25 ft., and the axis is placed east and west. There being a rapid fall of the ground to the east, advantage has been taken thereof to construct a hall under the main building capable of holding 300 people. The church consists of a nave and aisles, transepts, and chancel. Externally, at the north-east angle, is an oblong tower, with corbelled parapet, over which rises a hexagonal spire. The entrance is placed in a narthex, at the west end of the building, and above it is a six-light window, with pointed lancets and cusped circles. In the transepts the windows consist of five simple lancets grouped under an arch; the aisle windows are small with square heads; and the clearstory range consists of two-light windows arranged in pairs. The chancel is lighted from the south side by a window of the clearstory order. The church is built of red Corsehill stone, and the columns of the nave bays and the sides of the windows are of the same material. The internal walls are plastered and painted,—the upper part of yellowish-green and the under a dull red. The roof is of timber, practically of open construction; the pews are of pine. The aisles, separated from the nave by four bays, are not seated, being used solely as passages. There are no galleries. The chancel is separated from the nave by a carved wooden screen. The lower walls of the chancel are draped with deep blue hangings; on the upper portion the mural decorations are in the same tints as the rest of the church. The pulpit, an octagon of carved wood, is placed at the south angle of the chancel. The church is seated for about 600 people. The heating is accomplished by means of high-pressure hot-water pipes; and the artificial lighting by wrought-iron gas coronæ hung from the centre of the nave-roof. In the transepts and chancel there are wrought-iron wall brackets. The bust of the late Mr. Smith, who left funds to defray the cost of the building, has been executed in marble, by Mr. D. W. Stevenson, sculptor. The church has cost about 5,700*l.*

MISSION CHURCH, WESTBURY-PARK, BRISTOL.—On the 6th inst., the Dean of Bristol (Dr. Pigou) laid the foundation-stone of a new mission church at Westbury-park. The proposed building will consist of a nave 32 ft. wide and four bays in length, and will provide accommodation for 250 people. The style is to be fourteenth-century Gothic, and the principal feature will be the east window, which will be traceried. The building will be of brown Pennant with freestone dressing, and Broseley tiles will be used for the roof. The side walls will be low, so as to have a high-pitched roof. The church will be heated with hot-water pipes. Provision is made for an extension of the building by the addition of three more bays, and when this is done accommodation will be provided for 500 persons. There will also be a timber porch and a bell-cot added when the extension takes place. The architects are Messrs. Crisp & Oatley, of Bristol.

UNITED METHODIST CHAPEL, ILLOGAN, CORNWALL.—The new United Methodist Free Church which has been recently erected at Paynter's Lane-end, Redruth, and which was opened on the 3rd inst., stands on a site at the junction of roads leading from Redruth, Pool, Illogan, and Tehidy. The site is the gift of Lord Robartes. The building is in the Romanesque style. The outside measurements are 40 ft. in width by 62 ft. in length, and 27 ft. in height from the floor to the crown of the semi-circular ceiling. The front is of Plymouth limestone, with granite dressing, and the principal features in the design are three deeply-recessed arches supported on pilasters. Under the centre arch there is a bold geometrical window of granite, and the entrance-doors, with circular windows over, are in the other recesses; the pilasters and arches are also continued around the sides of the building. The seats are arranged in amphitheatre form, and accommodation is provided at the orchestra end for a large choir and also for an organ, and on either side are vestries for minister and choir. The orchestra is spanned by a moulded segmental arch supported on Corinthian pilasters, the mouldings and pilasters being continued the whole width of the end. The orchestra end is lit by two circular-headed windows, and a quatre-foil. The ceiling is segmental, springing from a cornice and frieze moulded into panels. The pews are of red deal framing and pitch-pine standard ends and panelling. The rostrum and orchestra front are of pitch-pine and mahogany. The main entrances open into lobbies, with tiled floors and pitch-pine screens. The cost of the work is about 1,000*l.*, and it has been designed and superintended by Mr. Sampson Hill, architect, of Redruth. The contractors are Mr. W. H. Moyle, of Chacewater, for carpentry and joinery, and Mr. W. H. Gray, of Illogan, for the masonry. The windows of front and orchestra are of cathedral glass, in lead lights, made by Messrs. Solomon & Co., of Truro.

SANITARY AND ENGINEERING NEWS.

SANITARY ASSURANCE ASSOCIATION. — The eleventh annual meeting of this Association was held on the 8th inst., at the offices, 5, Argyll-place, W., the President, Surgeon-General Cornish, C.I.E., in the chair. Mr. Joseph Hadley, secretary, read the annual report, from which we quote the following:—"The properties inspected and certified during the year have as usual been of the most varied character, and the Council has again to report that in no case of first inspection has the sanitary condition been such as could be certified without alteration, though there is evidence on every hand of continued improvement, and with newly-built property fewer alterations have to be insisted on before granting sanitary certificates." The balance-sheet showed that the income of the year had been 464*l.* 3s. 8d., and after meeting all liabilities a balance was carried forward.—On the motion of the President, seconded by Mr. Andrew Stirling, the report was unanimously adopted.—Surgeon-General Cornish and Mr. Henry Rutherfurd, barrister-at-law, were re-elected members of the Executive Council. The President was re-elected, and Sir Joseph Fayrer, K.C.S.I., M.D., F.R.S., and Professor Roger Smith were re-elected vice-Presidents.

RAWDON SEWERAGE. — A Local Government Board inquiry was held by Colonel Ducat, R.E., on the 27th ult., into the application of the Rawdon Local Board for the issue of a provisional order to take land compulsorily for sewage disposal purposes. There was opposition from the owners of the land. It is proposed to sewer the whole district of the Rawdon Local Board, and purify the sewage by chemical precipitation, followed by filtration through land. The area of land required to be taken is 16½ acres. The cost of the works is estimated at from 8,500*l.* to 10,000*l.* Mr. W. H. Radford, of Nottingham, is the engineer of the scheme.

FOREIGN AND COLONIAL.

FRANCE.—Messrs. Dutert, Raulin, Boitte, Formigé, Nénot, and Ancelet have been appointed by the Académie des Beaux-Arts as jurors for the Prix de Rome competition of this year.——M. Hardy, Diocesan architect at Cambrai and Nancy, has been appointed Diocesan architect at Limoges in place of the late M. Bailly.——The Société Centrale des Architectes has appointed five members as a Committee of research to study the best lines on which to require a diploma for persons practising architecture.——It is announced as almost certain that the Opéra Comique will shortly be rebuilt on the former site of the Salle Favart, burned a few years ago. The scheme will be submitted to Parliament, and can be commenced in two months if approved.——The scheme for the Metropolitan Railway is to be submitted to the Chamber of Deputies early in March.——The death is announced of M. Alfred Arago, son of the celebrated naturalist, at the age of seventy-seven. He was a pupil of Paul Delaroche, and from 1841 to 1852 exhibited various historical paintings. In the latter year he was attached to the Government as "Inspecteur Général des Beaux-Arts," and became a "Chef de Division des Beaux-Arts" in 1870.——The Civil Tribunal of the Seine has given its judgment in regard to the Meissonier dispute, and has pronounced for the division of his works among the inheritors, and against their sale.——The new Hôtel des Telephones at Guttenberg is shortly to be opened. The building is entirely constructed of brick and iron.——The well-known pavilion at Saint Adresse, near Havre, successively inhabited by Alphonse Karr, Alexandre Dumas, and Victor Hugo, is in course of demolition.——M. Lambert, the sculptor of the Voltaire statue at Ferney, has offered to execute gratuitously a bust of Louis Favre, the engineer of the St. Gothard Tunnel works. It will be erected at Geneva, opposite the post-office.——A dispute arose last year between the Bishops of Verdun and Saint Dié, about the Joan of Arc monument. The former wished the heroine to be glorified at Vaucouleurs, which is in his diocese, while the latter wished it to be at Domrémy, in his diocese. They have come to an agreement at last on the understanding that there should be a Joan of Arc monument in each town.——The Académie des Beaux-Arts proceeded to the election of a successor to M. Alphand. M. Lafenestre was elected by 20 votes out of 38, M. Michel had 9, M. Georges Berger 6, M. Corroyer 2, and M. Philippe Gille 1.——A competition is to be opened for the pictorial decoration of two new rooms in the Hôtel de Ville at Paris, adjoining the Galerie des Fêtes.

SWEDEN.—The funds accumulated for the building of the new Swedish Houses of Parliament now amount to 300,000*l.*——An aquarium is to be built in Stockholm at a cost of 2,000*l.*——The designs for the new Opera House to be built in Stockholm have been approved by the Crown authorities, some slight alterations having been made in the plans for reasons of greater safety.——Arrangements are being made for the building of a new theatre at Carlstad, at a cost of about 5,000*l.*——A German

COMPETITIONS, CONTRACTS, AND PUBLIC APPOINTMENTS.

COMPETITIONS.

Nature of Work.	By whom Advertised.	Premium.	Designs to be delivered.
Public Hall and Offices, and Enlarging Market, Abertillery, S. Wales	Mr. Baker	25 guineas	Feb. 17
*Cemetery Buildings	Northfleet Loc. Bd.	15l. 15s.	Mar. 2
School Buildings	Goole Sch. Bd.	50l. ; 20l.	Mar. 7

CONTRACTS.

Nature of Work or Materials.	By whom Required.	Architect, Surveyor or Engineer.	Tenders to be delivered.
Water Supply Works	Belper R.S.A.	Robert Argile	Feb. 16
Sewerage Works	Walker Local Board	T. W. Laycock	do.
Additions to "Pump House" Hotel, Llangammarch Wells, South Wales	....	T. P. Martin	do.
Dule Room, Asquith Bottom Works, Sowerby Bridge	....	S. Wilkinson	do.
Sewerage Works, Dearne Valley	Barnsley Twn Council	J. M. Taylor	do.
*Roadmaking and Paving Works	Bromley Local Board	Official	do.
Road Materials	Tynemouth R.S.A.	John Waters	Feb. 17
Repairing Bridges and Road Works	Elgin County Council	H. J. Mackenzie	do.
Additions to Coxlodge School	South Gosforth (Newcastle-on-Tyne) Sch. B.	W. Lister Newcombe	do.
*Removal of House Refuse	St. Pancras Vestry	Official	do.
*Works and Materials	St. Marylebone Vestry	do.	Feb. 18
*Broken Stone, Kerbs, &c.	do.	do.	do.
*Collection, &c. of Dust, Ashes, &c.	St. George-in-the-East Vestry	do.	do.
Two Cabmen's Shelters	Cardiff Corporation	do.	do.
Boarding House	Falmouth Hotel Co. Lim.	Silvanus Trevail	do.
Farmhouse, Wester Elchies, N.B.	Cameron & Allan	....	do.
Iron Castings	Halifax Corporation	T. Holgate	do.
*Painting Schools, Banstead	Kensington & Chelsea Sch. Dist. Managers	Official	Feb. 19
Additions to Memorial School, Hedley, near Chester-le-Street	....	J. W. Rounthwaite	do.
Heating Apparatus	Longton Town Council	J. W. Wardle	Feb. 20
Pair Double Cottages, Albert-street, Dufftown, N.B.	....	D. McKay	do.
*Union Offices, Board-room, &c.	Croydon Union	F. West	Feb. 22
Villa, Grantown, Elgin, N.B.	Capt. Grant	Geo. Sutherland	do.
New Road, Keynsham, Bristol	Keynsham Union	John Mackay	do.
*Paving New Street	Camberwell Vestry	Official	do.
*Supply of Road Materials	do.	do.	do.
*Works and Materials	do.	do.	do.
*Works to Sewers and Drains, &c.	do.	do.	Feb. 23
*Free Library	West Ham Council	Lewis Angell	do.
*20,000 tons Lime	London County Council	Official	do.
*Roadmaking and Paving Works	Willesden Loc. Bd.	O. Claude Robson	do.

CONTRACTS.—*Continued.*

Nature of Work or Materials.	By whom Required.	Architect, Surveyor, or Engineer.	Tenders to be delivered.
Sewerage Works	Maidstone U.S.A.	W. O. Scoones	Feb. 23
Sewerage Works, Brislington	Keynsham R.S.A.	Francis Fox	do.
*School Buildings	Kingston-upon-Hull School Board	W. Botterill	Feb. 24
*Repairing, &c. Police Stations	Receiver for Metropolitan Police	Official	do.
Paving and Road Works	Cardiff C. C.	W. Harpur	do.
*Erection of Schools, near Romford	Hornchurch Sch. Bd.	C. Allam	do.
*Alterations, &c. to Board's Offices	Mile-End Old Town Guardians	C. F. Burden	Feb. 25
*Works and Materials	Vestry of St. Mary, Islington	Official	do.
*Public Elementary Schools	Brighton, &c. (U.D.) Sch. Bd.	T. Simpson	do.
*Making-up Roads, &c.	Walthamstow L. B.	G. W. Holmes	Feb. 26
*New Parochial Offices	Battersea Vestry	E. W. Mountford	do.
Widening Finkle-street	Carlisle Corporation	W. Howard Smith	Feb. 27
*Works and Materials	Mortlake Dist. Highway Board	H. Richards	Feb. 29
*Works and Repairs to Foot and Carriage-ways	Limehouse B. of W.	Official	do.
*Works, Materials, &c.	Kensington Vestry	do.	do.
*Wagon and Carts	Vestry of St. Mary, Islington	do.	do.
*Hose, Stand-pipes, Tools, Hand-carts, &c.	Toxteth-park L. B.	John Price	do.
*Asphalte Works	Edmonton Loc. Bd.	Official	Mar. 8
*Wrought-iron Fencing	Boro' of West Ham	do.	do.
*Completing Stores, Dwelling-house, &c.	....	C. Dunch	do.
Convalescent Home, Penzance	T. B. Bolitho	O. Caldwell	Mar. 9
*Cemetery Chapel, Lodge, &c.	Tring Local Board	W. Huckvale	Mar. 21
*Making-up Roads	Chiswick Loc. Bd	Official	do.
*Alterations, Repairs, &c. to Schools	London Sch. Bd.	do.	No date
Congregational Sunday School, Lightcliffe, Bradford	....	T. Barker	do.
Vicarage, St. Thomas, Swansea	Rev. Wm. Evans	J. B. Wilson and G. Moxham	do.
*Three Houses and Shops, Lee Green	....	....	do.

PUBLIC APPOINTMENTS.

Nature of Appointment.	By whom Advertised.	Salary.	Applications to be in.
Surveyor	Banbury & Bloxham Highway Board	150l.	Feb. 17
*Assistant in Boro' Surveyor's Office	Colchester U S.A.	Not stated	Feb. 19
*Clerk of Works	London Sch. Bd.	150l. rising to 250l.	do.
*Engineering Assistant	Toxteth Park L. B.	2l. 10s.	do.
*Assistant Surveyor	Kettering L. B.	100l.	Feb. 23

Those marked with an Asterisk (*) are advertised in this Number. *Competition, p.* iv. *Contracts, pp.* iv., vi., viii., & ix. *Public Appointments, p.* xx.

architect, Herr F. Seeselberg, of Veersen, has obtained official sanction to prepare plans, &c., of the Cathedral of Lund, and of two other old churches in the province of Scania. —— A monumental chapel is to be erected at Filipstad over the remains of John Ericsson, the famous inventor, the Swedish Riksdag having voted 1,100l. for the purpose.—— The Stockholm Building Board has elected Colonel A. M. Lindgren its chairman for the current year. The board is most active in enforcing its new regulations. The other day a builder was prohibited, through a report of the Sanitary Board, from letting a house that had not been dried for the stipulated time. ——The board of the Academy of Arts to be built in Stockholm has submitted the designs for the building prepared by Professors Dahl and Grundström, and Messrs. C. Möller and E. Lallerstedt, to the Government for approval. The principal façade shows a lofty, imposing, central structure, with two lower wings, rising from a terrace approached by a monumental flight of steps. As regards the interior, the chief consideration has been the exhibition-rooms and the hall for teaching. On leaving the flight of steps referred to, a gallery is entered running right through the transverse section of the building, intended for the exhibition of sculpture, behind which is a smaller one for the same purpose, covered with a glass roof. On both sides of this hall are situated open courts, upon which abut other exhibition rooms, ateliers, and the hall for teaching. There are in all fourteen exhibition rooms, whereas in the old building there are only two. The great festival hall will be situated on the second floor.——Some more stringent regulations than the present are to be added to the Stockholm Building Regulations, with the object of affording greater protection to men at work on the roofs of houses. Larger and stronger footboards are to be provided, as well as a solid wire rope running along the middle of the roof.——New waterworks are to be constructed in the town of Östersund at a cost of about £5,000l.——A Royal Commission has recommended the painting of three huge wall frescoes in the National Museum, one by Baron G. Cederstrom and two by Herr C. Larsson, but the subjects have not yet been decided.——Of late there has been considerable agitation in the Swedish press against the paving of the streets of Stockholm with granite, making that city "the noisiest in Europe." Wood-paving is recommended (London being cited as an example) for its noiselessness, durability, and cleanliness.* Wood, too, would, of course, be very cheap in Sweden.——The laying down of asphalte on the Vasa Bridge has been a complete failure, the company having the work in hand having adopted a new method as regards the foundation, which has proved worthless. The whole work has to be done over again.

* This last seems an extraordinary recommendation. The one serious objection to wood-pavement in cities is its insanitary and dirt-holding character.

MISCELLANEOUS.

Sim's Improved Casement Window.—This is a form of casement invented by Mr. Sim, architect, of Montrose, which contains an improvement of some importance. Mr. Sim's casement is hung to open inwards, but the bottom rail of the window, when closed, descends below the rebate of the sill in the same way as a lifting-sash window. To open the window it is raised by a handle fixed on the bottom rail, the hinges being specially constructed to allow of lifting, and the sash can then be swung inwards, the weight being taken by a gun-metal plate beneath the bottom corner of the sash, which is also shod with gun-metal. The fastening of the window is also new, effective, and simple; it consists of a gun-metal wedge fixed on the upper part of the vertical rail, which slips behind a spring fixed vertically on the window frame, the wedge driving the spring out a little and being thus securely held between it and the frame. The action of dropping the sash into its place when closed automatically fastens it by this spring arrangement. We have examined only a model on a small scale, and of course the method is open to the objection that the lifting would be inconvenient in the case of a heavy sash of large size; but the objection is not important in regard to house-windows of average size.

A Workmen's Sanitary Congress.—The French labour party have determined that their Ninth Annual and National Congress shall be devoted to the discussion of one single subject. It was, of course, somewhat embarrassing to decide which question should thus be considered, to the exclusion of all others; but it was ultimately resolved to give the preference to hygiene in its relations to the working classes. The debates of the Congress will be divided into three different phases of this great subject. First will be taken the problem of food-supply, especially in reference to the laws of March 27, 1851, and May 5, 1855. The workers will demand that the quality of the bread they eat shall be as carefully guaranteed by the State as the quality of the gold of which the current coinage is made. The second question relates to the sanitation of the worker's home, when the futility of the Commission on Unwholesome Dwellings will be dwelt on. The last subject is the sanitation of the workshop and factory, when the decree of 1810 will be denounced in no measured terms. According to this law the public are protected against dangerous industries, but not the workers. Thus, lead works are put in the second category, because they do not give rise to injurious emanations, and are only injurious to the workmen themselves. Such will be the general scope of the Congress; but before the delegates of the trade unions and the workmen's societies who form the labour party discuss these problems they will invite the best-known scientific authorities on hygiene to deliver addresses to the Congress so as to enlighten the delegates as to the technicalities at issue. This precautionary measure is at once as wise as it is modest, and denotes considerable discretion and tact on the part of the workmen. They will find a scientific basis for their demands and make their wants known to men of science.—*Lancet.*

Automatic "In-and-out" Turnstile.—Mr. G. Williamson, of Hunslet, Leeds, sends us particulars of a four-armed turnstile so contrived that one arm acts as a coin-freed ingress and the other arm as an outlet, thus requiring only one turnstile instead of two. The ingress arm is locked till the insertion of a coin in a slot, when it opens sufficiently to allow one person to pass, and automatically adjusts itself to the locked position again. According to the description, the other arm can be pushed for an outlet without the necessity to unlock the ingress arm, and sets itself automatically again to the locked position. We do not see from the description what is to prevent one person inside from opening the turnstile for another outside without the ceremony of putting in the coin, but we have not seen the machine at work; this may be provided for.

Glasgow Buildings Regulation Bill.—A sort of small civil war has sprung up in Glasgow over the Town Council's Buildings Regulation Bill. Drastic in its proposals, that measure has seriously alarmed a great number of persons interested in the property of the city, and various public bodies have actively taken part in the fray. The Measurers and the master plumbers, for instance, are for the Council, while arrayed against it are the Landlords' Association, the Institute of Architects, and the Procurators' Committee. So strong, in fact, has been the opposition that the Buildings Regulation Committee have had to yield on a number of points, such as the re-erection of burned buildings, hollow squares, the making of by-laws, the height of buildings, compensation for property taken down, and so on. It is to be hoped that in making the needful concessions to those whose pockets will be affected, care will be taken not to obliterate the good features of the Bill. A measure that will check the jerry-builder and secure proper sanitation should have the support of every loyal and sensible citizen.—*Scottish Leader.*

London and County Banking Company.—The directors of this Company, in submitting the balance-sheet for the half-year ending December 31 last, report that the net profits of the half-year amounted to 217,239l. 10s. 7d. They recommend a dividend at the rate of 11 per cent. for the half-year, making a total dividend of 22 per cent. for the year. The balance-sheet, which will be found in our advertising columns, was adopted at the annual general meeting of the Bank, held on the 4th inst.

Safety of Railway Bridges in America.—According to the *Engineering Record* of New York (January 23, 1892), the subject of railway bridge legislation, although somewhat in advance of that relating to highway bridges, is, nevertheless, in a backward condition in the United States, as compared with other nations. The Railroad Commissions of the several States, when there are any, exercise more or less supervision over the railway bridges. Massachusetts has had such a Commission since 1869, and until 1883, one of the members was a civil engineer, although there have been none since then. In New York a Board of Railroad Commissioners was established in 1883, and within a year three important bridge failures occurred. During the investigation of these failures it became apparent that there was a pressing need of more efficient supervision of bridge construction and maintenance. Accordingly the Commission sent out circulars in January, 1884, requesting every railway company to forward strain sheets of each bridge on its lines. These were carefully analysed by Charles F. Stowell, M.Am.Soc.C.E., and the data thus collected was published last June in a volume of nearly 2,000 octavo pages. The publicity thus drawn to defective structures has had a good effect on the management of all the roads, many being in actual ignorance of weak places on some of their bridges, which were immediately repaired when discovered. Other States exercise more or less defective supervision of the bridges within their boundaries, but nothing so rigid as in the two States above mentioned.

MEETINGS.

MONDAY, FEBRUARY 15.

Royal Academy of Arts.—Dr. A. S. Murray on "Archaic Compared with Archaistic Sculpture." I. 8 p.m.

Surveyors' Institution.—Paper by Mr. J. W. Grover, C.E., entitled "An Explanation of the London Water Question." 8 p.m.

Clerks of Works' Association of Great Britain.—Ninth Annual Dinner, Mr. Aston Webb, F.R.I.B.A., in the chair. Holborn Restaurant. 6.30 p.m.

Society of Arts (Cantor Lectures).—Professor George Forbes on "Developments of Electrical Distribution." IV. 8 p.m.

Victoria Institute.—8 p.m.

Leeds and Yorkshire Architectural Society.—Exhibition of Sketches by Mr. H. V. Lanchester and others. 7.30 p.m.

TUESDAY, FEBRUARY 16.

Institution of Civil Engineers.—Resumed Discussion on Mr. A. H. Curtis's paper on "Gold-Quartz Reduction Machinery." 8 p.m.

Sanitary Institute (Lectures for Sanitary Officers).—Mr. P. Gordon Smith, F.R.I.B.A., on "Sanitary Building Construction." 8 p.m.

Society of Arts (Foreign and Colonial Section).—Mr. Lewis Atkinson on "The Forthcoming Exhibition at Kimberley, South Africa." 8 p.m.

Glasgow Architectural Association.—Annual Supper, Exhibition of Studentship Drawings, Sketches, &c. 8 p.m.

WEDNESDAY, FEBRUARY 17.

Carpenters' Hall, London Wall.—Professor Banister Fletcher on "Sanitary Building Construction." 8 p.m. (*Admission free.*)

British Museum.—Miss Eugénie Sellers on "Greek Sculpture: The Parthenon Frieze." II. 2.30 p.m.

British Archæological Association.—Dr. Alfred Fryer on "The Church of Perranzabuloe." 8 p.m.

Civil and Mechanical Engineers' Society. — Mr. R. Booth on "Gas Producers." 7 p.m.

St. Paul's Ecclesiological Society.—Mr. T. A. Martin on "Some Religious Subjects on Misericordes." 7.30 p.m.

Royal Meteorological Society.—Four papers to be read. 7 p.m.

THURSDAY, FEBRUARY 18.

Royal Academy of Arts.—Dr. A. S. Murray on "Archaic compared with Archaistic Sculpture." II. 8 p.m.

Institution of Civil Engineers.—Students' visit to the works of the Chelsea and Lambeth Water Companies, at Molesey, and subsequently to those of the Grand Junction, Southwark and Vauxhall, and West Middlesex Water Companies at Hampton. Train leaves Waterloo (South station) at 12 noon.

British Museum.—Miss Millington-Lathbury on "The Chief Greek Festivals and Agonistic Gatherings," as illustrated by the monuments in the Museum. 2.45 p.m.

Society of Antiquaries.—8.30 p.m.

FRIDAY, FEBRUARY 19.

Architectural Association. — Mr. Max. Clarke on "Domestic Electric Lighting." 7.30 p.m.

Sanitary Institute (Lectures for Sanitary Officers).—Professor W. H. Corfield, M.A., on "Sanitary Appliances." 8 p.m.

Royal Institution.—Professor P. F. Frankland on "Micro-Organisms in their Relation to Chemical Change." 9 p.m.

SATURDAY, FEBRUARY 20.

Architectural Association.—Visit to the Imperial Institute, South Kensington, by permission of the architect, Mr. T. E. Collcutt. 3 p.m.

RECENT PATENTS:

ABSTRACTS OF SPECIFICATIONS.

2,591.—METAL SCREWS: *J. T. Steen.*—This invention relates to nails, hooks, fasteners, and the like that may be threaded for screwing, and to screws of all kinds; and the special novelty claimed is the making of metal screws oval instead of round, or with flat or nearly flat sides slightly oblong, and with threads for screwing cut only on the surfaces of longer radii, so that the screw when driven home, or part of the way home, may be firmly held on being turned a quarter round by the threads embedding themselves in the sides of the hole that have the shorter radii.

2,700.—WASTE-PREVENTING CISTERNS: *W. D. Scott-Moncrieff.*—This invention claims an improvement in the mechanism of waste-preventing cisterns, enabling them to be more simply made, and at a reduced cost. An ordinary drop-valve, provided with a suitable washer fitting upon a proper seating, is used, the raising of which starts a syphon; but instead of an ordinary spindle fixed to the pull-up attachment, the spindle is carried up and terminated with a disc or piston, and over this is slipped a loosely-fitting cylinder open at the bottom, but with a cover on the top which is attached to the pull-up mechanism. The cylinder cover is provided with a very small air-hole. When the pull apparatus is released the loose cylinder drops down by its own gravity until it rests upon the disc on the valve-spindle, but when the cylinder is raised by the pull-lever a partial vacuum is formed between the disc and the upper part of the cylinder sufficient to lift the valve and start the syphon which empties the cistern; but as the level of the water falls the vacuum between the disc and the top of the loose cylinder is destroyed, and the pull-up mechanism only moves the loose cylinder up and down without moving the drop-valve, which must remain closed until the cistern is refilled, when a pull-up of the loose cylinder will again lift the drop-valve by means of the partial vacuum.

3,457.—FLOORING CRAMP: *W. & E. Bracewell.*—The inventors claim a screw flooring-cramp with several details of novelty in the mechanism.

3,637.—DRAIN VENTILATION: *T. Brown.*—This invention relates to improved apparatus for ventilating drain-pipes, and is principally applicable to dwelling-houses. It consists in surmounting the top of the ventilating-pipe with a square box or chamber open on the side exposed to the atmosphere. To the upper and inner edge of this opening is hinged a door or "flap-valve" of mica or other light and durable substance, which will readily yield to permit the air to enter the pipe, and, closing by its own weight, prevents any return draught. Around the exposed sides of the above chamber is fixed a series of deflecting plates on the louvre principle consisting of short truncated cones fixed one within the other and leaving air-passages so that currents striking the plates laterally or upwards or downwards are deflected towards the face of the chamber, and thus is secured a constant admission of air.

20,535.—DOORS AND SWINGING SHUTTERS: *H. H. Leigh.*—This invention relates to improvements in the mechanism for closing doors and swinging-shutters of either single or double leaves, and has for its object to render them absolutely safe from being burglariously entered. The leaf or leaves are when closed made practically one with the frame and inseparable from it, excepting in the special way described.

NEW APPLICATIONS FOR PATENTS.

January 25.—1,415, F. Edwards, Concrete and Iron Beams, or Beams composed of similar materials.—1,421, F. Gsron, Screwless Knob for Fastening Knobs to Spindles of Door-handles.—1,431, S. Bastow, Sliding Windows.—1,449, G. Mumford, Drain-traps.

January 26.—1,514, W. Thompson, Grinding Tools.—1,551, C. Blunch, Pavement or Covering for Roads, Pathways, Floors, Steps, &c.—1,560, H. Lake, Wood-working Machinery.—1,577, J. Ottaway, Window-sashes.

January 27.—1,603, J. Merry, Syphon Flushing Apparatus for Water-closets and Other Cisterns.—1,621, W. Gwinnett, Machinery for making Wood Screws.—1,624, J. Linley & J. Bennett, Preventing Shop Windows from being Steamed.—1,628, S. Gratrix and Others, Gas-chandeliers.—1,650, P. Fowler, Fire-places.

January 28.—1,663, A. Morris, Blow-pipes.—1,687, H. Brooke, Fittings for Shop-windows, &c.—1,693, E. Harvey, Water-closets.—1,707, J. Snelling, Trap to Prevent Stoppage of Drains, made in Portland Cement.—1,708, C. Francione and J. Baconnet, Sanitation of Buildings.—1,736, W. Beddows, Triple-pitched Cutter Side Plane.—1,742, J. Hudson, Low-water Alarms for Kitchen or Domestic Boilers.

January 29.—1,760, W. Bracewell and R. Holden, Handrail for Steps and Ladders.

January 30.—1,821, R. Ardagh, Wooden Paving or Flooring Blocks.—1,827, W. Brown, Jointing Concrete Paving.—1,839, G. Paley, Water-closet Cisterns.—1,845, W. and A. Anty, Sink-traps.—1,857, O. Hawkes, Joints for Fanlights, Ventilators, &c.—1,861, A. Campion, Hydraulic Cement and Concrete.—1,869, W. Francis, Surveying Instruments.

PROVISIONAL SPECIFICATIONS ACCEPTED.

22,000, P. Beer, Chimney-pots.—22,288, D. Macrae, Locking Nuts on Bolts.—22,629, G. Hughes, Sash-fasteners.—6, W. Smeaton, Water-closets, with traps and pedestal enclosures.—26, C. Stevenson, Tilting Lavatory Basin and similar utensils.—49, C. Kingzett, Scenting, Deodorising, and Disinfecting Rooms, &c.—51, E. Ward, Flush Cisterns.—587, R. Thwaites, Preventing Water and Gas-pipes from Freezing.—589, J. Phillips, Preventing Pipes Bursting during Frost.—698, A. Boult, Glue.—727, J. Rainey, Tool-holding Attachment for Grindstones.—828, O. Hutchinson, Bakers' Ovens.

COMPLETE SPECIFICATIONS ACCEPTED.

(*Open to Opposition for Two Months.*)

3,550, W. Barns and J. Cockburn, Wheelbarrows.—5,424, J. Pulham, Fireproof Staircases, Floors, and the like.—15,673, J. M'Creery, Heating and Ventilation for Buildings, &c.

SOME RECENT SALES OF PROPERTY:

ESTATE EXCHANGE REPORT.

FEBRUARY 2.—By *Joshua Baker & Son*: 18, Canterbury-ter., Maida-vale, u.t. 48 yrs., g.r. 2*l.*, r. 100*l.*, 1,110*l.*—By *Rutley, Son, & Vine*: No. 67, Regent's-pk.-rd., f., 730*l.*; "Launcelot Cottage," West-end, Hampstead, c., r. 24*l.*, 300*l.*

FEBRUARY 3.—*Charles & Tubbs*: The residence, "Elm Lawn," Woodberry-down, u.t. 72 yrs., g.r. 26*l.*, 1,600*l.*; 9, Beech-st., Barbican, f., r. 69*l.* 10s., 1,220*l.*; 10, Beech-st., f., r. 60*l.*, 1,160.

FEBRUARY 4.—By *T. B. Westacott*: 130, Sandwich-st., Burton-crescent, u.t. 16 yrs., g.r. 8*l.* 8s., r. 40*l.*, 140*l.*; 32, Sandwich-st., u.t. 15 yrs., g.r., 8*l.* 8s., r. 40*l.*, 140*l.*; 173, Gray's Inn-rd., u.t. 18 yrs., no g.r., r. 23*l.* 6s., 170*l.*

(*Contractions used in these lists.*—F.g.r. for freehold ground-rent; l.g.r. for leasehold ground-rent; i.g.r. for improved ground-rent; g.r. for ground-rent; r. for rent; f. for freehold; c. for copyhold; l. for leasehold; e.r. for estimated rental; u.t. for unexpired term; p.a. for per annum; yrs. for years; st. for street; rd. for road; sq. for square; pl. for place; ter. for terrace; cres. for crescent; yd. for yard, &c.

PRICES CURRENT OF MATERIALS.

TIMBER.		
Greenheart, B.G. ton	9/0/0	0/0/0
Teak, E.I. ... load	9/10/0	15/0/0
Sequoia, U.S. ft. cu.	2/3	3/0
Ash, Canada load	2/10/0	4/0/0
Birch, do.	3/5/0	4/10/0
Elm, do.	3/10/0	4/15/0
Fir, Dantzic, &c.	2/0/0	3/10/0
Oak, do.	3/0/0	5/0/0
Canada........	5/0/0	7/0/0
Pine, Canada red	2/10/0	3/10/0
Do. yellow	2/10/0	5/0/0
Lath, D'ntsic, fath	5/5/0	6/10/0
St. Petersburg	5/10/0	7/10/0
Deals, Finland, 2nd & 1st std 100	8/10/0	10/10/0
Do. 4th & 3rd ..	7/10/0	8/10/0
Do. Riga	6/10/0	8/0/0
St. Petersburg, 1st yellow ..	11/0/0	15/0/0
Do. 2nd yellow	8/10/0	10/10/0
Do. white	7/10/0	10/10/0
Swedish	7/15/0	16/0/0
White Sea	8/10/0	18/0/0
Canada, Pine 1st	20/0/0	26/0/0
Do. do. 2nd	14/10/0	16/10/0
Do. do. 3rd, &c.	8 5/0	10/10/0
Do. Spruce, 1st	8/10/0	11/0/0
Do. do. 3rd & 2nd.........	6/15/0	8/0/0
New Brunswick	7/0/0	7/10/0
Battens, all kinds	3/10/0	15/10/0
Flooring Boards, sq., 1 in. prep. 1st	0/8/6	0/14/6
Do. 2nd	0/7/6	0/11/6
Other qualities	0/5/0	0/8/0
Cedar, Cuba .. ft.	/3½	/4½
Honduras, &c.	/3	/4
Mahogany, Cuba	/4½	/6½
St. Domingo, cargo av	/4½	2/0
Mexican do. do	/4	/6
Tobacco do. do	/5½	/7
Honduras do..	/5½	/6½
Box, Turkey ton	4/0/0	15/0/0
Rose, Rio	10/0/0	20/0/0
Bahia	9/0/0	18/0/0
Satin, St. Domingo ..... ft.	0/0/8	0/1/3

TIMBER (*continued*).		
Satin, Porto Rico	0/0/8	0/1/6
Walnut, Italian ..	0/0/3½	0/0/7
METALS.		
IRON—Pig, in Scotland .... ton	2/2/0	2/3/1½
Bar, Welsh, in London	6/0/0	6/10/0
Do. do. at works in Wales	5/10/0	6/0/0
Do. Staffordshire, in London	6/5/0	6/15/0
COPPER—British, cake and ingot	47/0/0	48/0/0
Best selected ..	49/0/0	49/10/0
Sheets, strong ..	57/0/0	58/0/0
Chili, bars	43/13/9	44/1/3
YELLOW METAL lb.	0/0/5½	0/0/5¾
LEAD—Pig, Spanish .... ton	10/10/0	10/12/6
English, com. brands	10/13/9	11/5/0
Sheet, English, 3 lbs. per sq. ft. and upwards ..	12/10/0	0/0/0
Pipe	13/0/0	0/0/0
ZINC—English sheet ...... ton	25/10/0	0/0/0
Vieille Montagne.........	26/0/0	0/0/0
TIN—Straits	80/7/6	81/10/0
Australian	84/10/0	81/12/6
English Ingots	93/0/0	93/15/0
OILS.		
Linseed ...... ton	18/17/6	19/2/6
Cocoanut, Cochin	26/0/0	0/0/0
Do. Ceylon	23/0/0	0/0/0
Palm, Lagos	25/0/0	0/0/0
Rapeseed, English pale	26/10/0	0/0/0
Do. brown	25/0/0	0/0/0
Cottonseed ref...	17/15/0	0/0/0
Oleine	0/0/0	0/0/0
Lubricating, U.S.	4/10/0	5/10/0
Do. refined	5/0/0	10/0/0
TAR—Stockholm barrel	0/19/0	1/0/0
Archangel	0/12/6	0/0/0

TENDERS.

[Communications for insertion under this heading must reach us *not later than* 12 *noon on Thursdays.*]

BRIGHTON.—For Repairs, &c., to No. 68, Lansdowne-place, Hove, Brighton, for the Misses Barbord. Mr. Walter J. Ebbetts, F.R.I.B.A., architect, Savoy House, 115, Strand, W.C.:—

H. Baylis	£160	W. & A. Elliott	£140

BURGESS-HILL (Sussex).—For new manse in connexion with Congregational Church, Burgess-hill, Sussex. Mr. E. J. Hamilton, architect, Brighton. No quantities:—

Wm. Downer	£921	Wm. Briant*	£735
Simeon Norman	862	(All of Burgess-hill.)	
Oram	757	* Accepted subject to reductions.	

CHICHESTER.—For new Congregational Church Schools, &c., Chichester, Sussex. Mr. E. J. Hamilton, architect, Brighton. Quantities by the architect:—

Stephens, Bastow, & Co.	£3,400	Thos. P. Hall	£2,658 0
Holloway Bros.	3,138	Joseph Potter	2,545 0
W. H. G. Curtis	3,107	J. C. Budden, Chichester*	2,535 0
Arthur Burrell	3,100	P. Peters	2,460 0
Walter Wallis	2,794	Stallard	2,450 0
W. R. Sight & Co.	2,757	Alfred Jones	2,350 0
J. O. Holt	2,730	Fred. Stevens	2,329 0
Snewin Bros.	2,687	W. Winslade	2,120 15
John Croad	2,670		

* Accepted subject to reduction for omissions.

LEEK.—For erecting two houses at Wall Grange, Leek, for Mr. W. Challinor. Messrs. W. Sugden & Son, architects, Leek:—

W. Knowles & Joseph Stubbs (accepted) £415 13 0

LEYTON.—For constructing teachers' rooms, and other alterations to the Harrow-green Schools, for the Leyton School Board. Messrs. J. T. Newman & Jacques, Architects to the Board, 2, Fen-court, E.C.:—

Wood	£423	Gregar	£368
Reed	413	Coxhead	349
Scott	397	Holland*	344
Catley	380	* Accepted.	

LINCOLN.—For the formation and completion of a new road along the west side of the Lincoln County Hospital, from Greetwell-road to Hill-top-road, including sewering and channelling. Mr. Wm. Watkins, surveyor:—

Wright & Sons	£655 0 0	Howson (accepted)	£584 17 4
Otter & Co.	631 5 9	Bradley	574 1 9

LLANTRISSANT.—For alterations, additions, &c., of Williamstown Schools, Penygraig, for the School Board. Mr. J. J. Evans, C.E., architect, Penarth:—

T. Morgan	£597 0	B. Cole & Son, Williamstown*	£432 13
Lemuel Evans	595 0	* Accepted.	
Chedzy & Thomas	580 0		

(Architect's estimate, £578.)

LONDON.—For alterations and additions to "Poley House," Hampstead Heath, for Mr. Edward Gotto, J.P. Mr. E. Burgess, architect. Quantities by Mr. W. Thornicraft:—

Dove Brothers	£2,735	Scrivener & Co.	£2,422
Lawrence & Sons	2,488	Pearce & Ellis	2,381

LONDON.—For the erection of a warehouse in rear of No. 6, Upper Thames-street, E.C., for Messrs. Hilton, Anderson, & Co. Messrs. Hudson & Booth, architects. Quantities by Mr. Henry Lovegrove:—

Thomas Rider & Son	£1,698	W. Scrivener & Co.	£1,611
E. Lawrence & Son	1,647	B. E. Nightingale	1,525
Hall, Beddall, & Co.	1,620	John Greenwood	1,499

LONDON.—For additions and alterations to the Orphan Working School, Haverstock-hill, N.W. Mr. Charles Bell, architect. Quantities by Mr. Henry Lovegrove:—

Bryan & Sons (accepted) £3,508 0 0

[For full list see *Builder* for Jan. 30, p. 89.]

LONDON.—For the construction of a new class-room for babies, and other works, at the Denmark-street schools, Plaistow, for the West Ham School Board. Messrs. J. T. Newman & Jacques, Architects to the Board, 2, Fen-court, E.C.:—

Vigor	£617 0	Goodchild	£549 0
Morter	605 0	Sharpe	530 0
Maddison	595 0	Catley	529 0
Reed & Son	593 0	Hosking	527 0
Hearle & Farrow	589 0	Norton & Son	489 0
Good	569 10	Allen & Cleminson*	460 0

* Accepted.

LONDON.—For the erection of a furniture store adjoining the Stock-street Schools, Plaistow, E., for the West Ham School Board. Messrs. J. T. Newman & Jacques, Architects to the Board, 2, Fen-court. Quantities by Messrs. R. L. Curtis & Son:—

Vigor	£3,138	Catley	£2,470
Good	2,995	Morter	2,455
Hearle & Farrow	2,579	Goodchild	2,447
Allen & Cleminson	2,530	Maddison	2,387
Norton & Son	2,515	Sharpe	2,300
Hosking	2,485	Reed & Son (accepted)	2,278

LONDON.—For alterations and additions to the Hallsville Schools, Canning Town, for the West Ham School Board. Messrs. J. T. Newman & Jacques, Architects to the Board, 2, Fen-court, E.C.:—

Maddison	£3,391	Sharpe*	£2,060
Hearle & Farrow	2,246	* Accepted.	

LONDON.—For alterations and repairs to No. 152, Fleet-street, E.C., for Mr. S. Ahlerton. Mr. Walter J. Ebbetts, F.R.I.B.A., architect, Savoy House, 115, Strand, W.C.:—

		Extra.
Drew & Cadman	£630	£28
C. Spreckley	922	53
W. Smith	798	47

LONDON.—For repairs, &c., to No. 1, Rosslyn-gardens, Belsize-lane, Hampstead, for Messrs. Clarke & Calkin. Mr. Walter J. Ebbetts, F.R.I.B.A., architect, Savoy House, 115, Strand, W.C.:—

R. A. Yerbury	£270	H. Bayliss	£185
Manktelow & Co.	227	W. Steel	198

LONDON.—For providing and fixing heating apparatus on the low pressure hot-water system for the new school which is now in course of erection on the Lauriston-road site, Victoria-park, South Hackney, for the School Board for London. Mr. T. J. Bailey, Architect:—

W. G. Cannon	£498 15	Jones & Attwood	£430 0
R. Crane	494 0	Russell & Co.*	433 0
Purcell & Nobbs	444 0		

* Recommended by the Works Committee for acceptance.

LONDON.—For providing and fixing heating apparatus on the low pressure hot-water system for the new school in course of erection in Sayer-street, Walworth, for the School Board for London. Mr. T. J. Bailey, Architect:—

Wenham & Waters, Lim.	£580 0	Jones & Attwood	£490 0
W. G. Cannon	528 0	J. Wontner Smith, Gray, & Co.	454 15
Russell & Co.	516 0	J. Fraser & Son*	443 10
Messenger & Co.	510 10		

* Recommended by the Works Committee for acceptance.

LONDON.—For the erection of school buildings, water-closets, playgrounds, boundary walls and gates, school-keeper's house, &c., at Gayhurst-road, in the Hackney Division for the School Board for London. Mr. T. J. Bailey, Architect. Quantities by Mr. Henry Lovegrove:—

J. Mowlem & Co.	£17,880	E. Lawrence & Sons	£16,348
T. Boyce	17,740	C. Cox	16,264
G. S. S. Williams & Son	17,494	Kilby & Gayford	15,018
Hart Bros.	16,873	W. M. Dabbs*	15,097

* Recommended by the Works Committee for acceptance.

LONDON.—For building new warehouse at Stevens-street, Lisson-grove, Paddington. Messrs. Wylson & Long, architects, 15, King William-street, Strand:—

Summerfield	£1,708	R. Wright	£1,590
Kearley	1,684	Williams & Richards, Chipham Junction (accepted)	1,373
Marks	1,665		

ORPINGTON (Kent).—For Poor Law Schools, Orpington, Kent. Mr. Frederick A. Walters, architect, 4, Great Queen-street, Westminster. Quantities by Mr. John B. Lofting, 4, Great Queen-street, S.W.:—

Stimpson & Co.	£14,480	H. Sanders	£13,285
Holloway Bros.	14,019	F. & H. Higgs	13,080
Patman & Fotheringham	13,975	J. Smith & Sons	13,065
Silver & Sons	13,768	J. Longley & Co.	12,925
W. Smith	13,674	T. Gregory & Co.	12,797
Bottrill & Sons	13,600		

PONTYPRIDD.—For the erection of four shops and dwelling-houses, Taff-street, for Mr. D. R. Evans. Mr. A. O. Evans, architect, Pontypridd. Quantities by architect:—

W. Thomas & Co.	£3,924 0	W. Julian	£3,624 0 0
E. Turner & Sons	3,888 0	D. C. Jones & Co.	3,548 0 0
O. Griffiths	3,636 17	Howell Powell	3,570 13 9

WIMBLEDON.—For the erection of a new boiler-shed and new lavatory, at the Wimbledon Steam Laundry, Cranbrook-road, Wimbledon. Mr. Walter J. Ebbetts, F.R.I.B.A., architect, Savoy House, 115, Strand, W.C.:—

H. Harmer £154 14 0

TO CORRESPONDENTS.

A. G. (we cannot enter into a discussion on the point).—W. P. B.—G. B. M.—"Foghorn" (next week).—G. J. C. (see permanent answer to your question below, in regard to books).—R. J. B. (we must ask for an authoritative statement from the Committee or the Assessor).

All statements of facts, lists of tenders, &c., must be accompanied by the name and address of the sender, not necessarily for publication.

We are compelled to decline pointing out books and giving addresses.

Note.—The responsibility of signed articles, and papers read at public meetings, rests, of course, with the authors.

We cannot undertake to return rejected communications.

Letters or communications (beyond mere news-items) which have been duplicated for other journals, are NOT DESIRED.

All communications regarding literary and artistic matter should be addressed to THE EDITOR; all communications relating to advertisements and other exclusively business matters should be addressed to THE PUBLISHER, and not to the Editor.

SUBSCRIBERS in LONDON and the SUBURBS, by prepaying at the Publishing Office, 19s. per annum (or 4s. 9d. per quarter), can ensure receiving "The Builder" by *Friday Morning's* post.

PUBLISHER'S NOTICES.

Registered Telegraphic Address, 'THE BUILDER,' LONDON.

CHARGES FOR ADVERTISEMENTS.

SITUATIONS VACANT, PARTNERSHIPS, APPRENTICESHIPS TRADE, AND GENERAL ADVERTISEMENTS.

Six lines (about fifty words) or under .... 4s. 6d.
Each additional line (about ten words) .... 0s. 6d.

Terms for Series of Trade Advertisements, also for Special Advertisements on front page, Competitions, Contracts, Sales by Auction, &c. may be obtained on application to the Publisher.

SITUATIONS WANTED.

FOUR Lines (about thirty words) or under .... 2s. 6d.
Each additional line (about ten words) .... 0s. 6d.

PREPAYMENT IS ABSOLUTELY NECESSARY.

** Stamps *must not* be sent, but all small sums should be remitted by Cash in Registered Letter or by Money Order, payable at the Post-office, Covent-garden, W.C. to

DOUGLAS FOURDRINIER, Publisher,
Addressed to No. 46, Catherine-street, W.C.

Advertisements for the current week's issue must reach the Office before THREE o'clock p.m. on THURSDAY, but those intended for the front Page should be in by TWELVE noon on WEDNESDAY.

SPECIAL.—ALTERATIONS IN STANDING ADVERTISEMENTS or ORDERS TO DISCONTINUE same must reach the Office before TEN o'clock on WEDNESDAY mornings.

The Publisher cannot be responsible for DRAWINGS, TESTIMONIALS, &c. left at the Office in reply to Advertisements, and strongly recommends that of the latter COPIES ONLY should be sent.

PERSONS Advertising in "The Builder" may have *Replies addressed to the Office,* 46, Catherine-street, Covent Garden, W.C. *free of charge.* Letters will be forwarded if addressed envelopes are sent, together with sufficient stamps to cover the postage.

AN EDITION Printed on THIN PAPER, for FOREIGN and COLONIAL CIRCULATION, is issued every week.

Now ready.
READING CASES. { NINEPENCE EACH. By Post (carefully packed), 1s.

TERMS OF SUBSCRIPTION.

"THE BUILDER" is supplied DIRECT from the Office to residents in any part of the United Kingdom at the rate of 19s. per annum PREPAID. To all parts of Europe, America, Australia, and New Zealand, 26s. per annum. To India, China, Ceylon, &c., 30s. per annum. Remittances payable to DOUGLAS FOURDRINIER, Publisher, No. 46, Catherine-street, W.C.

The Builder Cathedral Series.

A SERIES of Illustrations of all the English and Welsh Cathedrals is now being published in "The Builder," and will be continued, in the first issue of every month, until completed.

The Illustrations in each case include an exterior view, reproduced from a drawing specially prepared for the purpose; and a ground plan, to a large scale, shaded to indicate the date and style of the several parts.

There is also a short descriptive article, having reference to the Church and its surroundings, with sketches of some of the details, &c.

No trouble or expense is being spared to make this series in every sense *artistic and trustworthy,* and as such it is confidently offered to all lovers of Ecclesiastical Architecture.

1891.

1. Canterbury	Jan. 3.	7. Salisbury	July 4.
2. Lichfield	Feb. 7.	8. Bristol	Aug. 1.
3. St. Alban's	Mar. 7.	9. Norwich	Sept. 5.
4. Peterborough	April 4.	10. Rochester	Oct. 3.
5. Wells	May 2.	11. Lincoln	Nov. 7.
6. Exeter	June 6.	12. Gloucester	Dec. 5.

1892.

13. St. Paul's	Jan. 2.	16. Ely	April 2.
14. Hereford	Feb. 6.	17. Llandaff	May 7.
15. Chichester	Mar. 5.	18. Oxford	June 4.

[Further arrangements will be duly announced.]

Price FOURPENCE each (by post 4½d.), except Nos. 1 and 2, which are *out of print;* but the VIEW, PLAN, AND DESCRIPTION of CANTERBURY and of LICHFIELD have been re-printed, and they can now be had, price ONE SHILLING each set; by post, 1s. 2d.

THE REREDOS, ST. PAUL'S.
Reprinted from "The Builder," January 28, 1888 (15 in. by 11½ in.), on stout paper, unfolded, for framing, 6d.; by post, 8d.

PORTFOLIOS,
for Preserving the Plates unfolded, 2s. 6d.; by post, 3s.

London: Office of "The Builder," 46, Catherine-street, W.C.

VOL. LXII. No. 2559. SATURDAY, FEBRUARY 20, 1892.

ILLUSTRATIONS.

Staircase, Renishaw Hall, Derbyshire.—Mr. F. M. Simpson, A.R.I.B.A., Architect .... *Double-Page Ink-Photo.*
Mosque of Shah Abbas, Ispahan: Plan and Section .... *Double-Page Ink-Photo*
Hanover Schools, Gilbert-street, Grosvenor-square.—Mr. W. D. Caröe, Architect .... *Double-Page Photo-Litho.*
Church, Proposed, at Long Clawson, Leicestershire.—Mr. John Howitt, Architect .... *Double-Page Photo-Litho.*

Blocks in Text.

Plan of Old Buildings at Venice .... Page 133
Cordova Cathedral: Capilla de Villa Viciosa 136
Mosque at Cordova: Sections 137
The Alhambra, Granada: Section 138
Plan of the Alhambra, Granada .... Page 139
Early Celtic Monastery, Skellig Michael: Plan 140
Remains, Skellig Michael 141, 142
Diagrams in Student's Column: Heating by Hot Water 145

CONTENTS.

ower Distribution from Central Stations 131
The Original Ducal Palace at Venice 132
otes 134
aracenic Architecture 136
taircase, Renishaw Hall 140
osque of Shah Abbas, Ispahan 140
anover Schools, Gilbert-street, Grosvenor-square 140
ew Church, Long Clawson, Leicestershire 140
kellig Michael 141
Demonstrations on Greek Sculpture at the British Museum 141
Architectural Societies 142
Competitions 143
London County Council 143
The Sanitary Inspectors' Association 143
Clerks of Works' Association: Annual Dinner 144
Coke Breeze Concrete 144
Air-Bound Pipes 144
Student's Column.—Warming Buildings by Hot Water, VIII 145
Obituary 146
General Building News 146
Foreign and Colonial 146
Miscellaneous 147
Legal 147
Meetings 147
Recent Patents 148
Some Recent Sales of Property 149
Prices Current of Materials 149

Power Distribution from Central Stations.

T the annual meeting of the Institution of Mechanical Engineers, just held, Mr. Joseph Parry, the Water Engineer to the Corporation of Liverpool, gave some interesting particulars of the recent endeavour of that Corporation to extend the area of operations of the water service by introducing a system of low-pressure power supply. Although the information given by Mr. Parry might have been cast into better shape, it is nevertheless valuable as giving authentic data on ordinary commercial working; which is a very different thing from trial-trip results. It may be stated that the average rate of water supply per head per day, for all purposes, is, in Liverpool, twenty-four and a quarter gallons.

The distribution of power from central stations is the coming engineering problem, for until we extend the "factory system,"—the great modern illustration of the fable of the bundle of sticks,—to the production of power, our civilisation will have lagged behind in one important particular. Efforts are being made in this direction, but on a small and unimportant scale compared with the importance of the subject. Perhaps, however, these tentative methods are the best; certainly they are the safest. No one knows yet which is the best vehicle for power: steam, gas, water, air, or electricity. The New York installation is the most notorious effort made to use the former. Great things were expected of this, but it is a fact that about eighteen months ago there was something very like a howl of public indignation, ascending from the press and elsewhere, against this company; and that the way along the streets was frequently blocked by earth disturbances, which had every appearance of being due to boiling springs, but were in reality, we were informed, simply caused by the disrupted pipes of the steam-supply company's mains. Expansion and contraction of the mains through variations in temperature is a most fruitful source of trouble in steam distribution; condensation is another. The steam motor, too, gives off heat, and is ill-smelling. On the other hand, when steam has to be the prime source of power there is at least one conversion the less. Steam distribution from a central station does not, however, appear likely at present to be extended in this country.

Gas is, of course, at present the chief agent in the distribution of power from central stations. The great economy of the gas-engine has led to its introduction of late in many situations where a few years back it would have been looked upon as out of the question, even by the most staunch of its supporters for smaller uses. As an instance we may mention that one of the new machine shops at Armstrong's enormous works at Elswick is being run, or, at any rate, was to be run, entirely by gas-engines, and there are gas-engines at work of 170 indicated h.-p., the fuel consumption, it being claimed, being equal to 1 lb. of coal per hour per indicated h.-p. This, of course, is far ahead of anything yet done by the steam-engine. But these latter cases, after all, do not come under the category of "power distribution," for the engines are mostly supplied with Dowson gas, which, as is well known, is made in separate producers, just as, in the ordinary way, steam for engines is generated from separate boilers. Nevertheless, even when using the expensive illuminating gas of the companies, the gas-engine fairly holds its own in many positions. If the demand ever lead to the distribution of purely power or heating gas, then we may expect to see the gas-engine almost make a clean sweep (and, indeed, many other clean sweeps will be made if that time ever arrive); unless, of course, corresponding advances are made in other quarters. The gas-engine, however, is hot and malodorous, like its brother the steam-motor. It also makes a most irritating noise, and is difficult to start, but improvements have been made in the latter respect of late.

Distribution of power by hydraulic means has been successfully installed, notably in London; but the applications have been chiefly in passenger-lifts and the hoisting of goods. The great thing to be desired in the application of water power is a means by which the quantity of water used may be apportioned to the load. At present we know of no satisfactory device for compassing this end, or, we hasten to add,—with a wholesome dread of expostulation from the many inventors at work in this field,—we know of no satisfactory device the merits of which have been adequately recognised. A great struggle has been made lately by the advocates of the compressed-air system, and that struggle has ended in their defeat. Birmingham offers, perhaps, a more favourable field for the application of a power-distribution scheme than any other town or city in the kingdom, inasmuch as there are more small industries, using small motors, there than in any other equal area. In Paris, the Popp compressed-air system, first started for simply working clocks, has been a success. One chief point against compressed air is that in compression heat is given off, and in expansion heat has to be replaced. This, of course, represents a loss of efficiency, and, in some cases, much inconvenience through ice forming in the engine. In the Birmingham scheme an effort was made to get over this difficulty by heating the air before using by means of stoves which were fed by waste heat. This does not appear to have been very successful, and there were also serious troubles, owing to leakage in mains, due to expansion and contraction. It is but fair to compressed air, however, to say that those connected with the scheme complain that their hands were fettered by official restrictions. Whatever may be the merits of the case in this respect, the Birmingham failure cannot but be a serious discouragement to the advocates of this means of power distribution.

Electricity comes next on our list. Perhaps the safest thing to say about it at present is that it is too dear; but that is largely due to commercial or financial rather than physical causes. The Liverpool Electric Supply Company offer power at the rate of 5d. per indicated horse-power per hour. Such a price puts electricity out of the running, excepting for very small applications such as those of dentistry, sewing-machines, or other light and delicate applications. It may be said in favour of electricity that there is more hope for improvement than in any other of the methods of distributing power above enumerated. We can see nearer to the end with water, steam, air, and gas,—we have named them in what we consider the order of precedence in this respect,—than we can with electricity. There is a vast undiscovered country round which thousands of able explorers are ever wandering, watchful and eager to obtain entrance. Let but one lucky individual, a Thompson, a Crookes, or a Tesla, find the pass, and the armies of applied science will flock in to conquer the domain for the occupation of industrial enterprise. As it stands, however, electricity offers an admirable means of power distribution. So much attention has been directed to its adaptation for lighting purposes, that its perhaps more important function has been neglected. The efficiency of the electric motor is very high, and it is a pity that even such knowledge as we have does not receive more frequent application.

To return to Mr. Parry's paper, which deals with Liverpool in particular, we find that in that city, steam, water, gas, and electricity have all been utilised, to a greater or less extent, for the distribution of power; but, up to the present, only water and gas have found any fairly extended practical application. The figures Mr. Parry quotes were obtained in the course of an investigation he made about two years ago for the purpose of reporting to the Corporation of Liverpool on a proposal of the Hydraulic Power Company to extend their mains outside of an area within which they had been allowed to supply power. Liverpool offers a favourable field for the application of the central station system, more especially in the working of cranes and lifts. The weight of goods handled in one year exceeds 14 million tons, and the work required for this is of an intermittent character.

The number of hydraulic machines now worked by direct pressure from the Corporations mains is 102. The Mersey Dock and Harbour Board have, of course, a system of their own. The majority of these motors are for lifting goods, but organ-blowers stand second on the list, so it will be seen that many of the installations are small; indeed, the total consumption of water per annum does not exceed 125,600,000 gallons, of which 118,000,000 gallons are used for lifts and elevators. The pressure varies from 50 lb. to 80 lb. per square inch. The great bulk of the loading and unloading is still done by steam; but gas-engines are coming into use, and are in some cases taking the place of steam. There are 650 now in use in Liverpool, of which city we are at present alone speaking.

The average amount paid per annum for working a goods hoist from the Corporation mains is 13*l*., or 10d. per hoist per working day. With an available pressure of 60 lb. per square inch, properly utilised, and at the present rate of 7d. per 1,000 gallons, the cost of lifting is 1d. per 50 foot-tons. In cases where the waste water can be used there is an important saving in this respect; for instance, at the Exchange Station, the Lancashire and Yorkshire Railway Company work elevators and fill the boilers of their locomotives with the exhaust water. In a table Mr. Parry gives some figures which would be more valuable were there a little further explanation of the working conditions. We are told, however, that in the lifts instanced in this table counterbalance weights are not used, so that the weight of ram and platform has to be added in order to arrive at the gross weight lifted: also that none of the hydraulic machines are fitted with devices for varying the expenditure of water. Proceeding at once to the vital question of money expenditure, we find that, in three cases taken, the cost in lift A is 1·79d. per 50 foot-tons, in lift B is 5·95d. per 50 foot-tons, and in C is 3·05d. per 50 foot-tons. It would have been of value had the author of the paper helped us by some explanation of the vast difference between, say, 1½d. and 6d. spent for the same total work done. In the absence of positive information, we can only conjecture that the more economical lift was working up to or near its full capacity, whilst the wasteful one was very lightly loaded. Thus, if in both cases the lifts were of one ton capacity, and A was taking only one 6 or 7 cwt. bale at each journey, while B was carrying a ton each time, it would approximately account for the difference in economy, for it takes practically as much water to send a hydraulic lift up empty or lightly loaded as when full. That is the chief point to remember in connexion with hydraulic lifts. Of course the discrepancy may have been due to cut leathers, a scored ram, or leaky valves. In that case the waste should be set down to negligence of the user; but when it occurs through light loads it will be inherent in the system, until someone introduces a cheap and practically effective method of apportioning the water used to the useful work done.

Turning to another of Mr. Party's tables we find the cost given of working warehouse hoists by steam, gas, and compressed air. Here again we have wide variations in charges with the use of the same description of power, any explanation of which we have not been able to find in the paper. A 12 nominal h.p. engine works at the rate of 0·62d. per indicated h.p. per hour. An 8 nominal h.p., at 1d. per i.h.p. per hour. Here is a very wide difference, not to be accounted for by any of the details given. The cost appears to include coal, stores, water, wages, and repairs. It is a great pity, too, that Mr. Parry did not adhere to his original unit of work of 50 foot-tons, instead of complicating the matter by indicated horse-power, in which there are so many uncertain factors, including that totally unknown quantity, the friction of the machine, to be added. The foot-ton is a simple and certain quantity. Two gas-engines are instanced. These cost, respectively, ·33d. and ·52d. per i.h.p. per hour. Two compressed air-lifts cost 1·00d. and 0·40d. per 1 h.p. per hour, respectively. We quote the above figures, because they are the unbiassed results of actual commercial working, and will prove useful if taken as rough guides.

There is in the paper another table, in which further information is given of two other gas-engines working hoists. These engines were started in the morning and kept running all day, whether the lifts were in use or not. They were probably engines of the older pattern. The results of five trials are given, and cost for gas varied between 0·385d. per fifty foot-tons and 1·460d. per fifty foot-tons. The economy varied inversely as the total work done, nearly, and we should judge by the figures that by far the greater part of the excess of 50 per cent. of cost (in the latter case over the former) would be done away with if the gas-engine had been stopped and started as the work was required. It would therefore seem that for intermittent work care should be taken to provide a modern, easily-started gas-engine.

Further results of trials made by Mr. Parry have been published as an appendix to his paper. From this we see that in the case of three steam-hoists the best average result was a cost of 0·0689d. per foot-ton; whilst on a gas-engine the equivalent cost was 0·0542d. Here, however, fuller details are required to make an exact comparison.

Finally, Mr. Parry compares high and low pressure water-service for power purposes. Low-pressure (50 to 80 lbs.) water from the Liverpool public mains is charged at the uniform rate of 7d. per 1,000 gallons, whilst the Hydraulic Power Company charge a varying rate for their high-pressure (700 lbs.) water, according to the quantity used; thus, for 4,000 gallons the rate would be 10s. per 1,000, which equals 2*l*. for the total quantity. Equivalent power from the Corporation's mains would cost 1*l*. 7s. 2d. For a total of 10,000 gallons (7s. per 1,000) used, the total cost would be about equal as between high and low pressure; but above that, the high-pressure water is cheaper. When we come to 300,000 gallons, the rate of high-pressure water is 2s. 10d. per 1,000. For that total (300,000 gallons) the cost would be 42*l*. 10s. for high-pressure water, whilst the Corporation would charge 102*l*. 1s. 8d. for the same power supplied. Mr. Parry's comment on this part of the question may be quoted. "It is obvious that ordinary water-mains laid for domestic and manufacturing services can be utilised only to a very limited extent for power purposes, and that the relatively low pressure they carry cannot be economically applied as a motive power for driving large machinery. With a pressure of 700 lb. per square inch a main 6 in. diameter will carry about 100-h.p. To obtain the same power from a main conveying water at the pressure ordinarily available for town supplies the diameter of the pipe required would be 21 in. Pressure from the mains of corporations and water companies cannot compete with high-pressure water from mains specially laid for hydraulic purposes when the power water is sold at rates not exceeding 5s. per thousand gallons."

THE ORIGINAL DUCAL PALACE AT VENICE.

FROM AN ITALIAN CORRESPONDENT.

THE recent restorations carried on under the guidance of Signor Forcellini, architect, have contributed to spread a considerable amount of new information with reference to the construction and the history of the Ducal Palace in Venice, and have likewise aided Signor Galli in discovering whether, previous to the existence of the present Ducal Palace as it now stands, there was not another in existence, and also what was its form and its site.

The study of Signor Galli is very interesting, and the results which he has obtained are calculated to awaken the curiosity of the archæological and architectural world.

As is well known, the construction of the Ducal Palace at Venice may be regarded as distributed over five epochs: from the time of Angelo Partecipazio (814) to Sebastiano Ziani (1173), from Sebastiano Ziani to Bartolomeo Gradenigo (1340), from Bartolomeo Gradenigo to Francesco Foscari (1425), from Francesco Foscari to Giovanni Morcenigo (1484), and from Giovanni Morcenigo down to our own time.

During the successive Governments of all these doges, therefore, the Ducal Palace continued to undergo a gradual transformation. Hence the question: How much is there left of the Palace such as it was in the first period? Filiosi, Cicognara, Daru, Selvatico, Zanotto, Lorenzi, Fulin, and all who have written on the subject, held that of the Ducal Palace erected by Partecipazio not a single stone was left, nor can anything about it be discovered.

But now recent observations have completely upset this theory. The façade of the basilica is on the west side of the Piazza San Marco, and further back on the Piazzetta are the "Gran Porta della Carta" and the western front of the Palace. In the rear on the south side of the basilica, between this and the Porta della Carta, extending for a few mètres, are two walls forming a right-angle. In the angle, after being converted into a room, was placed some centuries ago the treasury of the church; but there is nothing in the interior to show that that portion of the building was erected to contain it. By careful observation we discover that the wall is thickened in order to make the room square; therefore an old wall existed previously which was not built for the treasury-room. Let us bear this in mind. From the exterior we gather other elements which give us ground for belief in the pre-existence of a construction which differed from the present one. The decorated cornices which surround the angle are as ancient as those of the vestibule of the basilica, but their projection shows that they were not placed there before this portion of the building in the eleventh and twelfth centuries (as well as the church) was veneered with marble. Hence the most superficial examination is enough to convince one that this brickwork angle was not originally annexed to the church,—that is to say, not connected in any organic way with its structure.

We must now trace in the mind's eye the lines of this angle; the walls become delineated, the buildings reassume their shape, and we can imagine that previous to the eleventh century, when the church was in the shape of a basilica, that church was detached from the Palace; detached from the south side, which ran in a straight line; detached from the two chapels (Zen and

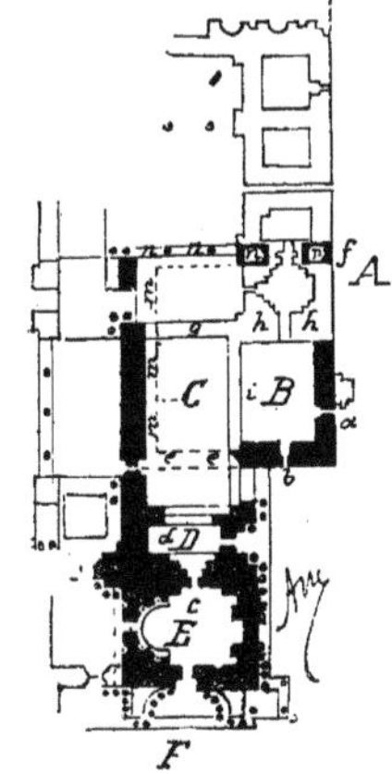

References.

Angle of the basilica of St. Mark.
Black shows the buildings of the ninth century.
The others are additions of the tenth, eleventh, and twelfth centuries.
A. The Ducal Palace.
B. The Treasury.
C. The Baptistry.
D. The Putti Chapel.
E. The Zen Chapel.
F. Principal façade of St. Mark.

Putti), which stood on the angle on that side. And is it possible that that angle (*a b*), projecting from the Palace with an immensely thick wall, would have been erected in so much isolation, standing solitary in space, without rhyme or reason? Then, as Signor Galli justly observed, a story told of Candiano IV. flying from the burning Palace, and saved by taking shelter in the court of the church, would be unintelligible; nor would the older chronicles be intelligible, especially the one discovered by Signor Galli as contemporaneous with the foundation of the basilica, which describes it as "Juxta Palatium;" nor other more recent ones,—one, for instance, about Dandolo, in which the basilica is stated to have stood in an angle of the Palace: "in angolo ducalis palatii condita est."

But Professor F. A. Gfrörer, who, referring to the subjection of Venice to the Byzantines, takes as the starting-point of this subjection the translation (or removal) of the body of St. Mark. on the basis of a statement of Deacon Giovanni considers that the first church of the Evangelist was not a separate building but a part of the Palace, namely, a chapel standing in an angle of the ducal palace. In that case it is certain that the Zen Chapel originally had nothing to do with the present basilica of St. Mark; and it is further certain that originally, not only when the church was enlarged in the shape of a Greek cross, but when built in brick, the site of the present baptistry was either left vacant or contained no buildings annexed to the church. The baptistry owes its origin to the Doge Dandolo (fourteenth century), who must have built the wall between the new chapel and the angle which was subsequently used for the treasury. Probably it was he who pulled down the thick wall (*ee*) which started from the ducal palace, and stretched straight in front of the original chapel of St. Mark, as far as the basilica. Let us bear in mind the length of this wall (*e e*); this same length carried to the wall of the basilica in an eastern direction, gives another side (*m m*), which terminates at the pilaster of the inside southern dome, and previous to the eleventh century formed a part of the wall of the brick basilica. This length, if carried parallel to the first side (*n n*) will meet the thick wall which we saw rising from the sanctuary of the relics, and is a sufficient explanation of it. The remaining side is constructed from the wall (*f a*), which even now enclosed the Palace, and turns at that angle from which we took our starting-point. We thus proceed from the fixed and ancient points, and we have a square. This is the discovery of one of the first portions of the Ducal Palace, and of one of its defences.

Signor Galli says that it clearly follows that the northern wall of the Palace (814) ran precisely on the line which bounds it even now, and leads to the large gate called the Porta della Carta, having joined which it extended to the west, forming a tower. When the church was built (829), dangers from without still existed, internal animosities were still kept up: therefore the defences of the communal palace could not have been diminished. If they were anxious to erect the basilica to the patron saint, "juxta Palatium," how could it be placed up against the wall of the latter? Would not the projecting tower have been an obstacle in the front? It would have been necessary to find some other means; it would have been necessary to place the basilica not along the wall of the Palace, but along the wall of the most prominent part, that is the portion on the northern side of the tower. This explains the line of the whole basilica at a distance from the Palace; here is [where the northern side of the tower stood. The result of the researches in the interior is that the tower must have been rectangular with sides of about 14 mètres and an area of over 200 square mètres. As to the façade of the Palace,—the one on the Piazzetta,—this appears to have been constructed in two different epochs. The portion from the angle on the quay to the eighth column was built between 1340 and 1370. The portion from the eighth column to the great entrance-gate, or, rather, to the supposed tower, was built by decree of 1422, hence we read, "On March 27, 1424, they commenced to pull down the old palace in order to re-erect it," this being under the Government of Francesco Foscari. Almost sixty years therefore passed, from 1370 to 1424, during which the first portion of the new palace, as it is now seen, and the last portion of the old one, had stood together on the western side.

Let us now glance at the Porta della Carta; its history may be suggestive. Sansovino speaks of this celebrated gate as erected by the Buonos in 1438, but previous to that time did there exist a *great* palace gate? And what was its position? In order to discover it, excavations were undertaken. These excavations were carried 2 or 3 mètres along the front of the column which marked the division between the "new" and the "old" palace, and at a depth of 40 centimètres a pavement was discovered. Signor Galli followed its traces, and succeeded in discovering that that pavement led to a wall the height of which was 2 mètres. This is a very important point, and worthy of notice. From the line of the present columns it was 1·70 mètres distant. It was a buttress of oblique wall, consisting of masses of stone taken from the Euganean hills, placed roughly, but regularly, so that it appeared as though intended to serve as a parapet, and to be in sight. It ran towards the north. In front of the fifteenth column (always reckoning from the angle of the quay), the wall turned and crossed the Piazzetta in an oblique line* towards the Piazza; but after a few mètres it continued on the original line, along the pillars of the portico, passing along the front of the Porta della Carta, and ending at the projection of the angle which now forms a portion of the treasury of St. Mark, namely, the southern side of the ancient tower. In front of the Palace then there was a canal (this canal no longer exists) and the entrance-gate which, according to the most careful observations, must in ancient times have occupied the same position as the present Porta della Carta, and have been provided with a drawbridge.

All this renders it obvious that the arrangement of the Palace must have been originally different from what it is now. As a matter of fact, the researches which have been made to discover the truth of such a supposition have shown that the ancient palace did not possess any projecting portico. A large stone wall was discovered on its outer surface, and filled in roughly, the extremity of which was behind the seventh column, where a much wider pilaster than any other is to be found, and where the above-mentioned canal commenced. The limit of the gate and the height of the wall clearly indicate that before the erection of any gallery or portico that line constituted one of the extremities of the Palace.

To resume, the main dates stand thus:—

814. Angelo Partecipazio builds the Palace.

946. Partially burned under Candiano IV., it was not restored until the time of Pietro Orseolo I. This is the original one restored.

1,000. Deacon Giovanni, speaking of Angelo Partecipazio, says "qui palatii manentis fuerat fabricator," therefore Partecipazio's Palace in its general formation was still in existence.

1,105. The Palace partially burned was restored by Ordelaffo Falieri. The restoration refers, therefore, to the ancient remnant.

1,172. Zinni, according to one of the chronicles, renovates and enlarges the Palace, in such a way, adds another chronicle of older date, as to be regarded as the founder; "et fuit tempore sui principatus inchoatum palatium Venetiarum." Therefore, the old palace was preserved down to the time of Ziani, together with the projecting tower, the gate attached to the drawbridge and the surrounding wall, and it was opened to the boats by means of a 7-mètre canal (the measurement has been taken from a series of observations which I cannot offer in a brief survey like the present).

Other researches have brought to light that in the space comprised by the transverse foundations,—or, in other words, from the thick seventh column as far as the quay,—there was no palace existing previous to 1173. The older palace ended here; the great stone wall was one of its extremities, as I have observed, and the tower abovenamed standing within the angle raised on high its castellated walls. The importance of Professor Galli's studies is confirmed (if it needed confirmation) by a manuscript existing at Oxford, and written by three monks of the fourteenth century (English, perhaps), who went from Venice to the East, and on their return home wrote their account of the journey, "qui parole de la graund Armente de Persie et des Tartares et d'Ynde et de graund merveilles qui p. tout le mond sont." In this account they described the Church of St. Mark, the Ducal Palace and the Piazzetta, nor did they forget to put the date, 1360. This manuscript belongs to an epoch too distant from the original Ducal Palace, but in some points it may be considered as precious since it confirms the studies and researches made on the angle wall containing the Treasury, it shows the existence of the tower and a castellated wall, viz., the same one that enclosed the ancient palace of 814. The general external appearance of the original Ducal Palace was that of a very strong castle; nor need we be astonished at this, as in Venice many of the most important buildings had the same

* Our readers should refer to the plan of the Piazza of St. Mark, but most of them will doubtless remember it.

appearance, from Ca Foscari and Ca d'Oro of the sixteenth century back to Ca Loredan Da Mosto and Pisaro (later on converted into the Fondaco dei Turchi) of the twelfth century. A. M.

NOTES.

IT seems to be a recognised function of the House of Lords to utter from time to time a note of wailing on the subject of London smoke and fog, coupled with the suggestion of heroic remedies the adoption of which is to be pressed upon the legislature as a public duty, without much consideration either of the scientific possibilities of the course recommended, or of the practical working of the legislation to be set in operation. Viscount Midleton's speech on Friday the 12th was in the traditional style of utterances of this kind in the Upper House. A Royal Commission was to be appointed (which after many months would probably tell us only what we know already), and the inhabitants of London were to be subjected to a system of house-to-house visitation on the part of officials who were to see that they burned only one kind of coal and used only an approved pattern of grate. Lord Salisbury's comment on the speech was a model of common sense. After drawing attention once more to the fact (which anti-fog agitators apparently wilfully keep out of sight) that the fogs to which London and its neighbourhood is liable arise in the main from natural causes which we cannot contend with, he proceeded to say that—

"He quite agreed with his noble friend that there were certain remedies which might be adopted if they were willing to carry out a particularly drastic line of legislation. By far the most effective remedy they had heard of was that everybody should be forbidden to use any fuel except anthracite coal. The result, however, of such a prohibition would naturally be to increase enormously the price of that class of coal, and likewise to condemn the population to give up the use of open grates. In his opinion, it was very doubtful whether the people of London would condemn themselves and their children to sit by a flameless fire. Such were the difficulties which attached to remedies of this character. He believed that as far as scientific investigation had gone there was not much to ascertain either as to the nature of the London fog or as to the remedies to be applied to it. The main difficulty was political, because they would be requiring from the owners of the million and a half chimneys in London a sacrifice which they could not expect from the people of a free country. Moreover, such a remedy would require the establishment of a gigantic system of inspection. Was it possible to conceive a state of things in which inspectors should be going into every house in London to see whether the grates were properly made or whether proper fuel were being burnt in them? The burden thus entailed upon the inhabitants of the metropolis would be worse than the results from any London fog."

That is the plain common sense of the matter. People are naturally liable, when under the infliction of a London fog impregnated with smoke, to curse their existence for the moment and to feel that "somebody ought to be hanged for this." But if the whole population of London were condemned to sit by black and cheerless fires, under the penalty of an inspector demanding entrance to their Penates at any moment to report them for a fine, we should soon have a more dire outcry on the other side. One course, however, we will suggest, which it may be possible to carry out, which need not involve discomfort or serious expense, and for which it might be practicable to legislate. This would be, to enforce, within the boundaries of London, the use of gas for cooking. A considerable proportion of what may be called "private smoke" arises from kitchen fires, even in winter, and in summer of course they form the principal source of it. The adoption of gas would relieve us from this proportion of smoke, and though it would entail a certain expense in the installation, it is in the long run cheaper than coal cooking, besides having many other advantages in point of convenience. Lord Salisbury would be willing to assent to the appointment of a Committee of the House to consider the question; and if such a Committee is formed, we commend to their attention the possibility of enforcing cooking by gas, as one practicable method of lessening the amount of London smoke.

SUCH disputes as the London Coal Porters' strike touch the general community more nearly than some labour disputes of far greater magnitude. When supplies of food or fuel are stopped,—as in this case or in that of the great dock strike,—public interest is strongly aroused, and much gratification is felt when the dispute is settled. It is very fortunate that the coal strike terminated so speedily, or the hardships of many in the metropolis would have been considerably aggravated by the return of winter this week, had the strike been prolonged. The work of the railway companies, too, would soon have been seriously hampered by their sidings being blocked with coal. The question at issue seems to have been the now oft-recurring one of whether masters are to have the power to employ free labour or not. No fewer than fifty-nine strikes last year had their origin in the refusal of trades unionists to work with non-unionists, although, of this number, 57·6 per cent. were unsuccessful. The Secretary of the Society of Coal Merchants, in his statement of the causes of the dispute, said that the Committee had always set their faces against any discrimination between unionists and non-unionists; but a clause in a circular issued by him in the name of the Society last week, requesting merchants not to engage anyone unless he could produce a satisfactory reference from his last employer, was regarded by the unionists as a breach of this rule. In fact, peace was only restored on the Society passing a resolution recommending its members to fill up vacancies from the best men who applied, whether they had been on strike or not. A considerable section of the strikers have since been roundly abusing their officers for their efforts in the cause of peace, and for some time they refused to return to work. Of course, the resolution just quoted did not bind the masters to immediately re-instate every man who had left his employment, but this is what the malcontents among the unionists seem to have expected their President to have demanded. The order of the Council for a general resumption of work is being obeyed with such very bad grace that it may be that we are not yet out of the wood in this matter.

THE National Association for the Promotion of Technical and Secondary Education has issued an address to the electors for the new County Council for London. This address points out that the only two counties which are doing nothing for technical education are Middlesex and London, and that the amount of money available for this purpose in London is 163,000*l.* a year. The appeal is well timed, and it is very desirable that candidates should declare their views on this question. It may be doubted whether the money is quite wisely spent by some County Councils: there is a good deal of groping in the dark. But in London the need for technical education is so clear, and it could so easily be carried out, that there can be no doubt that the new Council should at once take up this subject. This object will be much surer of attainment if electors will consider the matter and obtain pledges from candidates. No new rates are required,—the money is ready, and its use for the purpose for which it was intended will conduce to the welfare of London and of its trade. Lord Lingen has, in a letter to the *Times*, endeavoured to excuse the London County Council on the plea that the use of this money for the purposes of technical education was permissive only, and that it was reasonable to throw it into the general funds of the Council. There is no doubt, however, that the Government did intend that this sum should be used for technical education, though they wisely left the matter very much at large, so as in no way to fetter the action of local authorities. Lord Cranbrook's answer in the House of Lords on Monday last to Lord Cowper's inquiry as to the permanence of this grant indicates plainly that the Government will still continue to make this grant for the purposes of technical education. Under these circumstances it is clear that not only should London follow the example of other local bodies in regard to technical education, but that in those parts of the country where the grant is considered as temporary only, it should be looked on as permanent, and be used accordingly.

THE excavations now in progress on the site of the Athenian Agora seem likely to be productive of unusual practical gain to the community. Dr. Dörpfeld has long had his eye on the ancient aqueduct of Peisistratos, by which water was brought from the Ilissus to the Agora, the supply being rendered available at the so-called Enneakrunos fountain. Four years ago Dr. Dörpfeld pointed out to us *in situ* what,—from somewhat complex *a priori* reasoning, and certain marks of boring in the rocks near the Pnyx,—marks noticeable only to the trained eye,—he believed to be the course of the aqueduct. This belief is now (we learn from the *Athenæum*, February 13), conviction. During the last fortnight, in digging near the Areopagos, the excavators have come upon a substantial bank of polygonal stonework, which supported the north side of the great Panathenaic road. Close to this wall a reservoir has been found, and two or three paces away remains of the ancient aqueduct are to be seen. The modern Athenian has already utilised the water-course of Hadrian, and he hopes to do the like with the ancient aqueduct of Peisistratos. Be that as it may, the discovery both of the lie of the Panathenaic road and the position of the Enneakrunos is of the first importance to Athenian topography. Everyone who has mentally, or in print, drawn a plan of the Athenian Agora will have to look to his imaginings by the cold light of fact, and it is not too much to hope that this same cold light may lay for ever the ghost of the "Enneakrunos Episode," which has so long troubled the dreams of archæologists.

NOT less interesting is the news that Dr Waldstein has obtained for the American School of Classical Studies at Athens permission from the Greek Government to excavate during a term of seven years the site of Sparta, with Amyclæ and other adjacent Laconian places. If America has lost Delphi, Sparta is a good second in interest. We owe to the neighbourhood of Sparta the unique collection of archaic grave-reliefs, now for the most part housed in the local museum there. Vaphio, near Amyclæ, has yielded the gold cups which have taught us so much that was unexpected as to pre-Dorian art. Popular expectation will look to Sparta for statues of Helen and Menelaus, Leda and the Dioscuri; science will look for the ground-plans of some of the countless buildings, civic and religious, mentioned by Pausanias; also for inscriptions, for votive offerings that will throw some light on ancient pre-historic cults that may tell us of Amyclæ before the Dorians destroyed it, of Hyakinthos who came before Apollo, of Alexandra before she became Cassandra. English and Germans, as well as Americans, will congratulate Dr. Waldstein on his good fortune, and will eagerly look to see where he first puts in his spade.

TUESDAY next is the one-hundredth anniversary of the death, at 47, Leicester-square, of Sir Joshua Reynolds. Most of the houses he occupied in London can yet be traced. After his father's death, in 1746, he settled in London. Returning from Italy at the end of 1752 (see Northcote's "Life" *),

* Mrs. Thrale records that Johnson's essay upon Procrastination, in "The Rambler," was hurriedly written in Sir Joshua's parlour. The essay appeared on Saturday, June 29, 1751.

he, by advice of his early friend and patron, the first Lord Edgecumbe, came to town, and lived in a house by St. Peter's-court, on the western side of St. Martin's-lane, over against May's-buildings. Thence he removed to No. 5, Great Newport-street, northern side, originally the central portion of a house since sub-divided into Nos. 4, 5, and 6. The then garden has been covered by a picture-gallery. Here Reynolds raised his charges to twenty-five, fifty, and one hundred guineas for a head, a half-length, and a whole-length respectively. In 1761 he bought a house in Leicester-square, now occupied by Messrs. Puttick & Simpson, the auctioneers. On July 20, 1762, Dr. Johnson writes to Baretti at Milan: "Mr. Reynolds gets six thousands a year. . . ." Six years later he is knighted, and elected first President of the Royal Academy. The large sale-room at the back of No. 47, Leicester-square, is commonly taken for his painting-room there. But we are authoritatively informed that that apartment was built about fifty years ago, for purposes of the Western Literary and Scientific Institution. Reynolds's studio was a back room, beyond the present lobby, octagonal in shape, and about 15 ft. high. The railings of the main staircase are, we understand, of the painter's time; they are curved out at the foot, to afford more space for the ladies' hooped dresses. This house was afterwards inhabited by the fifth Earl of Inchiquin and first Marquess of Thomond, who, in 1762, had married, for his second wife, Mary, daughter of John Palmer, of Torrington, a niece of Sir Joshua. Reynolds first met Dr. Johnson at the house, in what was then Castle-street, Oxford Market, of the Misses Cotterell, and attracted the attention of Johnson (who lived in Castle-street) by replying to the ladies that the death of a friend to whom they owed obligations had, at any rate, relieved them of a burden of gratitude.

THE proposed Berlin Cathedral is again being talked about in the German capital, the interest in the subject having been revived by the Emperor, who has expressed a wish to inaugurate the "Dom" on his first birthday in the new century. Professor J. Raschdorff has, apparently, during the months he has been in oblivion, had some steady work done in the reduction of his last design to a less extensive and cheaper one, and we hear that a very complete set of drawings of this "reduced" scheme will be put before the Prussian Houses of Parliament, when the vote for the first 15,000*l.*, of an estimated total of 500,000*l.* will be asked for by the Government. Of the 30,000*l.* voted some years back for the preliminary office work, some 20,000*l.* yet remains unspent, but this sum is to be applied for the erection of a provisionary wooden or iron church, for the use of the Court whilst the cathedral is in course of erection on the site of the present church. The 15,000*l.* referred to above is intended for the preliminary foundation work which the Emperor and his architect would like to see commenced this summer. We, however, scarcely believe that the money will have more chance of being granted this session than in the one of last year in which it was refused. The old objections relating to site, architect, plan, and architecture, are making Raschdorff's Cathedral scheme more unpopular every year, and the provincial representatives in the House are not much in favour of their constituents having to pay for what they regard as an unnecessary luxury in the capital. If the Landtag will not vote the money, and the Emperor wishes to stick to site and architect, he can however still have recourse to his privy purse, or to his power of granting a public lottery.

THE Sandwich Corporation have invited tenders for the construction of an iron swing-bridge,—in place of the present wooden one,—across the river Wansum or Stour. The existing bridge, being opposite to the Davis, or David's, Gate, stands midway between the ancient ferryway at Key or Fisher Gate (east), and the site of St. Mary Gate (west). The first bridge at this spot was build in pursuance of an Act passed in 1754, and consisted of two arches with a lift-bridge between them. An illustration of it will be found in W. Boy's "History of Sandwich" (1792). In Hasted's "Kent" (1799) the bridge is described as having been "lately rebuilt with great improvements." On crossing the bridge one is in Stonar, the supposed Lapis Tituli of the Roman occupation in Thanet, and sees stretching before him into the distance northwards the straight level road to Ebbesflete, and so on to Ramsgate. The Canterbury Gate in the walls of Sandwich was pulled down in 1784, and three others shortly afterwards, so that there now remain only the Fisher Gate and the David's Gate with its two conically-roofed turrets,—the one the Barbican, the other the Custom House, a favourite "bit" of old Sandwich.

ON March 21 last we adverted, in a "Note," to the impending demolition of the Skinners' Company's Almshouses (as rebuilt in 1729), founded by Sir Andrew Judd, Knight, in Great St. Helen's. In that same place a fine specimen of our old merchants' houses will soon, in all likelihood, be destroyed; for its site is about to be put up at auction on a building-lease for a term of eighty years, and the materials are included in the letting. The house, marked by its handsome elevation, of red brick, is numbered 8 and 9, in Great St. Helen's, and is that which Sir John Lawrence built in 1646, employing, it is said, Inigo Jones as his architect. The pilasters have stone capitals, the second floor window-sills project boldly beyond the deep voussoirs beneath; on the front are L , A I 1646. In No. 9, are a good mantelpiece, and a handsome Jacobean staircase. Lawrence was elected Lord Mayor in 1664. He erected a white marble altar tomb to his wife Abigail (1682) in St. Helen's Church; where Judd was buried (1558); and there, against a pillar in the chancel, was set up, over his seat, a carving of his coat-arms. The Crace collection contains a copy of Prattent's small print, 1796, and a drawing, 1856, by T. Hosmer Shepherd, of this house. An adjoining house, No. 10, was, reputedly, a home of Anne Boleyn's father, and is believed to have been one of the oldest private residences of its kind in London. We also find that the lease, for about fifty-two years unexpired, of No. 18, St. James's-square, corner of King-street, was announced for sale by auction at the Mart on Thursday last. Here Lord Castlereagh resided for a while, and on more occasions than one was made to feel his unpopularity with the mob. Converted into residential chambers, at rents amounting to 1,270*l.* per annum, it is now held at a ground-rent of 100*l.* a year.

WE are very glad to see that (as we report in another column) the London County Council propose to acquire power for the decent preservation and protection of York Water Gate, at the bottom of Buckingham-street, Strand, on the edge of the Embankment garden. The neglected condition of this monument has long been a reproach to those who own it or claim to be its owners. There is, it is stated, no "beneficial ownership" in the gate, and this, perhaps, accounts not only for the neglect which it has suffered, but for the fact that it has come down to the present day at all. If the Council acquire the powers they seek, as we hope they will, we trust that their professional advisers will be conservative in their treatment of the monument. From the fact that it is at present partly situated in a hollow, owing to the formation of the Embankment and its garden, it has been proposed to lift the whole thing bodily, but objections more or less weighty have been urged against this course being taken. Without altering the level of the gateway, it might perhaps be utilised as an entrance to the garden from Buckingham-street. The gateway is generally (and we believe rightly) attributed to Inigo Jones, although it has been ascribed to Nicholas Stone, who was probably only the executive master mason. On this point we may refer our readers to an article in the *Builder* for June 21, 1879, p. 677.

IN his last four weeks' report on the sanitary condition of Kensington, Dr. Orme Dudfield, the Medical Officer of Health for that district, makes some strong remarks, in the spirit of which we entirely concur, in regard to the power still left to the Water Companies, though under certain salutary restrictions, of cutting off the water supply from premises in default of payment of water-rent. Commenting on the clause in section 48 of the new Act, which rules that "an occupied house without a proper and sufficient supply of water shall be a nuisance liable to be dealt with summarily under this Act," Dr. Dudfield observes that,—

> "It does seem absurd in these days of sanitary progress, that the Companies should have the power to cut off the supply, and so create a nuisance 'liable to be dealt with summarily under this Act.' The position of the Sanitary Authority, moreover, it being their duty to take proceedings for the abatement of the nuisance thus created,—a duty which in effect makes them the agents of the Company to secure payment of the rate,—is undignified, not to say ridiculous. Surely it is time that steps were taken to correct such an anomalous state of affairs, affecting, as it does, a question of prime importance from the public health point of view."

THE water-supply of Chicago was cut off on two occasions last January, by what is known in America as "anchor ice," which appears to be similar to the "ground ice" of this country. The ice lodged round the intakes in the lake, and in one case the flow of water was stopped until a fire float had cleared the gates by means of sinking hose to the spot and pumping through it. At another intake an arrangement had been specially provided for the purpose. This consisted of a perforated pipe, which surrounded the intake, and by means of which compressed air was forced into the water to prevent ice accumulating. This apparatus is said to have been ineffective, but it is questionable whether the obstruction was not caused by ice piling up round the gates, the water having been very low at the time. In that case the compressed air would naturally have been insufficient.

WE hear that Sir John Coode, the eminent engineer and past President of the Institution of Civil Engineers, has been elected a member of the Athenæum Club under the special rule which empowers the Committee to elect from time to time such eminent persons as they may select for that honour.

THE *Transactions* of the Edinburgh Architectural Association, Part IV. of the first volume, contains a great deal of information about Scotch castles and mansions visited by the Association at different times during the past three or four years, a paper on each being read by the member who conducted the visit. The buildings treated of include the Parliament House and Argyle Tower, Edinburgh Castle; Kinross House, Tullibole House, Drum House, Dirleton Castle, Linlithgow Palace, Norham Castle, Bonhard House, and others.

A NEW monthly review, under the title *Natural Science*, and devoted more especially to biology and geology, is to be issued by Messrs. Macmillan next month.

THERE is to be an International Exhibition this year in the Isle of Man, of all places. The site is at Belle Vue, near Douglas, and the Exhibition is to include industrial and fine art exhibits, with a special division for "women's industries."

A CORRESPONDENT writes to us complaining very strongly of the absence of attendants at the stalls of the Crystal Palace Electrical Exhibition from whom any information can be got, and the difficulty of persuading the few who are there to give any information as to the exhibits of their firms. The managers of the Exhibition of course cannot exercise any control over exhibitors in this respect. We can only appeal to the exhibitors themselves, in their own interests, to assist the visitors as far as possible by giving information as to the machines they exhibit.

WE wish to call the attention of patentees and inventors who may send us descriptions and illustrations of their inventions for criticism, to the importance of sending technical diagrams (if only sketches) showing the method of working and of construction, especially in the case of patents involving mechanical action. Descriptions of such things are frequently sent to us accompanied merely by pictorial representations, which may do very well to catch the public eye in an advertisement, but which are totally useless in the way of conveying any real information upon which an opinion as to the value of the invention can be formed.

SARACENIC ARCHITECTURE.*

BY PROFESSOR AITCHISON, A.R.A.

THE Saracen architecture of Spain has a double, if not a triple, claim on our attention; it includes the finest early mosque in Europe, whose interior is at once the most striking and unique of modern buildings. This mosque, too, affords us some hints of how, and from what, some of the peculiarities of Saracen art were developed, while the Alhambra shows one branch of Saracen art carried to its ultimate conclusion. We may be proud of that splendid monograph that saw the light through the patriotism of our countryman, Owen Jones, in spite of the discouragement of Government,—I mean "the Alhambra," by him and Jules Goury, though we must not forget the gratitude we owe to Murphy for his work on the Arabian antiquities of Spain.

It is necessary, I think, to say a few words on such parts of Spanish and Saracen history as may enable you to comprehend some of the causes that produced these results, one of which was the falling of Spain under the sway of such patrons of the fine arts as the Omiades.

Those portions of Spain that were held by Carthage fell into the hands of the Romans during and shortly after the third Punic war, and all Spain and Portugal fell into their hands about the time of Augustus, and became a portion of the Roman Empire. Roman towns, with their temples, were built, as well as magnificent villas. Cordoba on the Baetis, now Cordova on the Guadalquiver, was called the "Patrician colony," as it was peopled by decayed Roman patricians.

On the conversion of the Roman Empire to Christianity, cathedrals, churches, and monasteries were built there as elsewhere. Spain was afterwards overrun by the Huns, the Swedes, the Vandals, and the Visigoths, the Vandals having left their name in Andalusia. These savages were also converted to Christianity, so there were Roman, Byzantine, and Romanesque buildings, and not to speak of the use made of the columns of these buildings by the Saracens, their ornament and some of their architectural features had great influence on Saracenic buildings. Musa-Ibn-Nuseyr, who is said to have been a descendant of a Christian student of a Nestorian seminary on the Euphrates, and who is well known to us as the principal actor in the story of the "City of Brass," had conquered Barbary, and was invited into Spain in Welid I.'s reign; he deputed his freedman Taric with a handful of troops to reconnoitre it. Taric landed in July, 710 A.D., at Calpe, now called Gibraltar, from Taric (Jebel-Taric, the hill of Taric), and successfully plundered the neighbourhood. Reinforcements were sent him, and he defeated the Gothic army on the River Guadalete. Malaga and Granada were taken, Cordova besieged, and Taric proceeded

Cordova Cathedral: Capilla de Villa Viciosa.

to Toledo, then the capital of Spain, which was deserted by all but the Jews, who fraternised with the invaders. In some of the expeditions to the hills the "Table of Solomon" was taken, set with pearls, rubies, and all sorts of jewels, and with 360 feet. Musa landed in 712 A.D., and, with Taric, proceeded to conquer the remainder of the country; and practically all Spain and Portugal were conquered, except the Crags of the Asturias. Subsequently the Saracens passed the Pyrenees, and took the south part of France, until an Abd-al-Rahman was conquered by Charles Martell (732 A.D.) at the battle of Tours; and subsequently Charles Martell wrested Avignon from the Saracens, and they were driven back to Narbonne. This took place about 737 A.D., in the reign of the Kaliph Hisham I.; subsequently Spain almost fell into anarchy. The Berbers, who came over in large numbers with the Saracens, were looked down on, and so were the new converts, and the old tribal feuds broke out again. Tyranny was producing its baneful effects throughout the Moslem dominions. An indulgence in luxury, indolence, and dissipation were unfitting the leading families for rule; while able Generals and Governors were murdered, imprisoned, or grossly insulted and degraded by the Kaliphs. The consequences were soon felt; able men were driven into opposition,—a new claimant for the Kaliphate was found in Abul Abbas, "the bloodthirsty," a descendant of the Prophet's uncle, El Abbas, who after the defeat and death of Merwan II. (750 A.D.) became the first Abbasside Kaliph. It was difficult to destroy the main descendants of the Omiades, so an amnesty was proclaimed, and about ninety of them were invited to a banquet and there butchered. The uncle of the Kaliph, the originator of this piece of treachery, with his followers, had a carpet spread over the slaughtered victims, and finished their banquet. This reminds one of Cæsar Borgia's banquet at

* Being the fourth Royal Academy Lecture on Architecture this session. Delivered on Thursday evening, February 4.

Mosque at Cordova.

Sinigalia, only he did not use his slaughtered victims as a table for his own banquet. Afterwards those that had escaped were hunted down.

The Omiade Abd-al-Rahman, an ambitious youth, and a grandson of the Kaliph Hisham, made his escape by swimming the Euphrates, and got safely into Africa, where he passed some five years, always intriguing for sway when he had a chance, but without success; he was eventually invited to Spain by the followers of the Omiades there, and landed in 755 A.D., and after two successful battles he became the first Kaliph of Spain. His bitterest enemy, the Kaliph Mansur pronounced the highest eulogy on him. On Mansur asking his courtiers, "Who was the greatest man of Islâm?" they naturally said "he was," but he replied "No, Abd-al-Rahman is. He was a penniless refugee, without friends or an army, and he is now the ruler of Spain, with the largest revenue of any potentate in the world."

I make a few extracts from an article on the mosque at Cordova by Professor Middleton, in which he gives from Arab sources the eloquent speech Abd-al-Rahman made to his Court, when he was about commencing the splendid mosque at Cordova (786 A.D.). This was to surpass anything before built, and was to be the rival of the Kaaba, and thus save the pilgrims of Spain and Barbary from the tedious and dangerous journey to Mecca. Abd-al-Rahman, after extolling the charms and advantages of Islâm over the wretchedness and corruption of Christianity, spoke thus of his proposed mosque:—"We will raise at Ala a shrine only equalled by the holy building at Jerusalem. . . . Let us raise the Kaaba of the West on the very site of a Christian church, which we must needs destroy in order that the Cross may fall amid ruins, and El-Islâm may rise up all radiant. Let its plan be like that of the Basilicas of the Crucified, that the house of God may crush the house of idols. Let it have an atrium, a portico, aisles, and sanctuary, all within an enclosure of four angles, and four sides, like the Holy House of Mecca." The Arab historians say that Abd-al-Rahman took the most enthusiastic interest in his new mosque, visited the works every day, and drew out a great part of the ornamentation with his own hands, and undoubtedly supplied the ancient columns and marbles.

The building of the mosque was carried on by his son Hisham, who devoted his fifth of the plunder of Narbonne and Carcassonne to the work; it was completed in 796 A.D., Hisham dying in the June of that year, so it is not certain that it was opened by him or by his son Al-Hakem I. It is said to have cost a million and a half sterling of our money. In it was the Korân, written by the Kaliph Othman, who was reading it when he was assassinated, so that it got stained with his blood; this was torn up by the Christian soldiers, when Cordova was given up to Alfonso in 1146 A.D. This mosque, called Aljama de Medina Andalus, was subsequently enlarged southwards by El-Hakem II. (961-76 A.D.), who built the Mehrab and the Maksurah, the enclosed sanctuary. The mosque was finished, with its nineteen aisles, thirty-six bays deep, by Mohammed-al-Mansur, the Vizier of Hisham II., though practically the Kaliph, and called Mohammed I., between 976 and 1001 A.D. Supposing Abd-al-Rahman I. was a draughtsman and designer, and did design some of the ornament of his original mosque, I doubt if any of it remains; all the capitals appear to be Roman, Byzantine, or Romanesque; all the ornamentation of the enclosure to the sanctuary and the Mehrab are strongly Byzantine in character, though slightly marked by some foreign influence; and there is a tradition that the Mehrab and its mosaics were done by Byzantine workmen sent from Constantinople. The peculiar cusped arches of the sanctuary, and the Emir's pews (La Villa Viciosa), one tier riding on those below, are possibly original.

San Cristo de la Luz, at Toledo, originally a mosque, has much the same character, with peculiar ribbed domical vaults, like that of the Mehrab at Cordova. The ribs of this last form in plan a Solomon's Seal. The south part of the mosque, with the Mehrab, Maksurah, and the back chambers, are supposed to have been built between 961-76 A.D., nearly a century after Tûlûn's mosque at Cairo (878 A.D.). These cusped arches of the Maksurah and the Villa Viciosa, however, had an important effect on the subsequent Moslem architecture of Spain, for to the last cusping was a favourite device. The ceilings of the mosque were originally of wood, arched, panelled, and enriched with inlay and gilding.

We heard before how the Kaliph Othman built himself a splendid palace at Medina, and every succeeding Kaliph did the same. Moawia's was at Damascus, and that of the Abbassides at Baghdad, and there is little doubt that the Viceroys had splendid palaces at their seats of Government. We know that Mamun held his court at Merv, but probably there is nothing left of any of these palaces. The Spanish Kaliphs were not behind-hand, and the description left us would make us believe that the Spanish one near Cordova was not inferior to the others.

A palace usually included a fortress, round which a town was sure to spring up. This one, called Medinet Azahra, was on the banks of the Guadalquiver, five or six miles below Cordova, was finished in 936 A.D., for Abd-al-Rahman III., and is said to have contained, besides the barracks and a mosque, a mint; coins with this mint mark upon them alone attest its reality. The palace is said to have been 4,000 ft. in length, by 2,000 ft. in width, and naturally consisted mainly of gardens; but 4,300 columns of precious marbles are said to have supported the roofs of its halls; 1,013 came from Africa, 19 from Rome, and 140 were presented by the Byzantine Emperor. The halls were lined and paved with marbles; the roofs were of cedar, ornamented with interlaced work and gilding, but without a trace or an illustration to judge by,—it is mere talk.

The Omiad Kaliphate of the West ended with Hisham III. (1031 A.D.). After that their kingdom was split into pieces, and ruled by independent rulers, was then successively overrun by the Almoravides and Almohades, religious sects almost wholly composed of Berber tribes. Their dominion was, however, brief, from 1073 to 1228 A.D., when Mohammed-ibn-Yusuf-ibn-Hud, descended from the Kings of Saragossa, overcame the Almohades, and ruled for a time over the best part of Murcia, Andalusia, and a bit of Alicante, but the Spaniards were fast narrowing the dominions under Moslem sway.

The first Royal Palace of the Alhambra is supposed to have been built between 1232 and 1272 A.D., by Mohammed Ibn-Yusuf called Ibn-al-Ahmar, who reigned as Mohammed I. of Granada; he was a descendant of Sa'd-Ibn-Obâda, one of the companions of the Prophet; he began to reign after the power of the Almohades was broken, and the greater part of Spain had been wrested from the Moslems by the Spaniards, and was a vassal of Ferdinand III. of Castile. His son, Abdallah, Mohammed II., added to the palace built by his father, and is said to have lavished treasures on the artists who decorated its gilded saloons; he died in 1302 A.D., and successive sovereigns enlarged and decorated the palace. I think that it is only necessary to add that Granada was ceded to Ferdinand and Isabella in 1492. If we could learn the studies pursued by the Saracen or Moorish architects, masons, plasterers, and decorators of that day, it would be useful and interesting, but as we cannot we must try and pick up what we can from the buildings themselves.

The hill on which stands the fortress of the Alhambra is now reached by steep but excellent roads, deliciously shaded by overhanging trees, whose foliage is sometimes so dense that the sun does not pierce it, and sometimes sufficiently open to make a spangled pattern on the road, with channels of clear running water on either side. If its fortress be

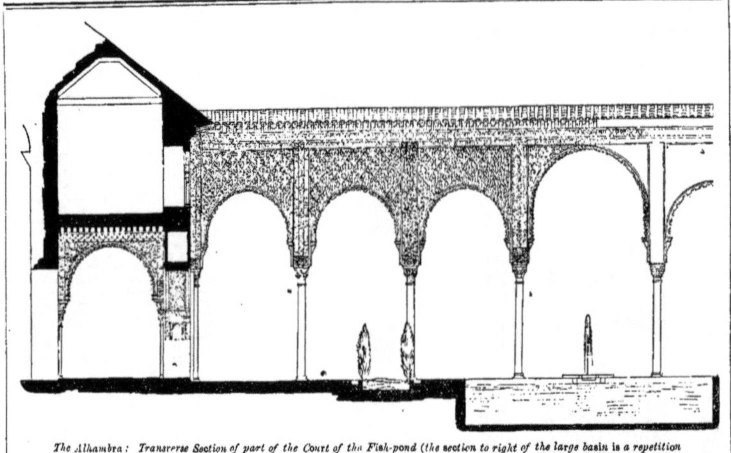

The Alhambra: Transverse Section of part of the Court of the Fish-pond (the section to right of the large basin is a repetition of that on the left.

entered by the Gate of Justice, you come on to the unfinished Renaissance palace of Charles the V., with its circular open court or bull-ring, the north side of which touches the Saracen palace. The palace of the Alhambra has the appearance of having been added to at various times; the centre is about 168 ft. north and south, and 107 ft. wide; it mainly consists of a large open court, with a piece of water in the middle, called the Court of the Fish-pond, with cloisters at each end; beyond the north cloister is the Hall of the Bark, a narrow hall like the narthex of a Christian church; this Court of the Fish-pond has no cloisters on its sides, but only suites of narrow chambers; at the back of the Hall of the Bark is a large building, nearly square, 59 ft. long, north and south, 55 ft. wide, forming internally a single chamber, about 36 ft. square, called the Hall of the Ambassadors. To the left of the Court of the Fish-pond is a building about 62 ft. wide, east and west, and 130 ft. long, containing the mosque and its court, and chambers, probably for the Mollahs; there is a niche near the mosque, not shown on the plan; the mosque itself probably had one, but it may possibly have been obliterated by the Christian sovereigns. To the right of the Hall of the Fish-poud, northwards, are the baths and a pavilion for music; and on the same side, southwards, is the Court of the Lions, so called from a fountain supported on the backs of marble lions; this court at the Crystal Palace is about half the size of the original; the court, with its dependencies, is about 103 ft. from north to south, 165 ft. from east to west; to the north of the centre is a projecting building about 63 ft. by 40 ft., containing the Hall of the Two Sisters; opposite in the part already mentioned is the Hall of the Abenserrages.

Ayesha and Zoraya, two of the wives of Muley Ali Abul Hasan, the King or Sultan of Granada, who reigned between 1470 and 1483, quarrelled, and had their partisans; the tribe of the Beni Serraj (the Abenserrages) supported Zoraya, and their head men were said to have been butchered in this hall. The total area of the part of the palace now existing, exclusive of the parts restored or rebuilt by the Catholic kings, contains but 52,625 superficial feet, including the open courts.

We must bear in mind that all the decoration of this palace is in plaster, once painted and gilt, except the enamelled tiles of the dados and floors. It would be very interesting to know what the costly stucco of Othman's Palace at Medina was like, and it is not impossible that, if the Arabs were to allow excavations to be made at Medina, some fragments of it might be found; however, we may be sure that it bore very little resemblance to that at the Alhambra. The Saracens made great strides in geometry when they began to study it, and may be called the inventors of æsthetic geometry.

Welid I. (705-715 A.D.) is said to have founded universities, and Cordova was, from the days of Abd-al-Rahman I, one of the greatest, if not the greatest, university in the world. The main subjects taught, besides Moslem theology and jurisprudence, were medicine and mathematics. Between 808 and 818 A.D. Musa's treatise on quadratic equations was published, and, we may be sure, gave a great impetus to the study of mathematics. Architects are mentioned in the "Arabian Nights," but they are mostly called mathematicians and geometers.

To speak of the architecture of the Alhambra fitst, although most of us know very little of the requirements of an Oriental palace, we can form some judgment of the skill exhibited in the planning, for when the arrangement is characterised by simplicity, it is the marked attribute of a good plan. The Court of the Fish-pond is adapted to be lined by troops, so as to impress ambassadors, and the narrow vestibule to be passed through would enhance the effect of the hall; while the Court of the Lions, at the end of which the Sultan sat to administer justice, is surrounded by cloisters to afford shelter to the suitors. The narrow passages in front of the other two halls were convenient for their service. There were many reasons for the exteriors of buildings being plain and almost repellant; among so turbulent a people every large building might be wanted as a place of safety in a riot,—it might even have to be used as a temporary fortress; while in the case of the Sultan's palace, the chances of its being wanted for such purposes were at least doubled. But besides this there was a desire not to provoke envy; the effects of the evil eye were greatly dreaded by every Moslem, so we can only expect to get architectural fronts in courtyards, and these are generally well, and sometimes elegantly, proportioned. The front of the cloister at the north end of the Court of the Fishpond is particularly graceful. There are the six slender white marble columns, and the two half ones carrying elegant arches only just pointed enough to prevent their looking flattened, delicately cusped and gracefully corbelled out beyond the piers on the capitals, and with a most gracefully-proportioned archevolt with vertical panels from the columns, held together by a horizontal band below the frieze; the spandrels and upper part above the arches are diapered; while the centre arch is wider and stilted, runs right up to the horizontal band, and has floral spandrels of much smaller pattern than the diapers, but overlaid by a very large scroll. There is very little architecture in the world that would take the palm from this, merely looked on as a piece of proportion.

The proportions of halls are to our eyes rather excessive in height; but we not only have to consider the need of air in a hot climate, but the passion the natives had for a "mighty contiguity of shade." In the Hall of the Ambassadors, however, the width is but three-fifths of the height. The horseshoe arch, supposed to be an invention of the Eastern Christians, but said to be found in the Pantheon at Rome, is mostly abandoned, or is so slight as to be imperceptible except in the case of the niche, where it is possibly kept from religious conservation or from a cherished recollection of the great one at Cordova, then in the hands of the Christians. The capitals of the columns are original and graceful inventions,—not equal, I admit, to good floral capitals of the Greek, Roman, or Renaissance artists, but superior to most, if not to all, Gothic ones. The capitals are mostly cushion-shaped, but the stalactite ones are an original creation of the Saracens, which are not so interesting, but have a better outline. I must confess that the stalactite arches and domes with their vague outlines do not excite my admiration, and though I am astonished at the domes, I hate their maddening complexity, and their trick of looking without support. Gothic stone pendents are certainly not more agreeable to look at, but they have the merit of being really constructive. Doubtless, the vagueness of outline in the stalactite arches and domes, and their complexity and mystery, had a charm for the Oriental mind. The Western Mediævals were certainly saturated with Saracen thought, work, methods, and manufactures, and they loved complexity, and had learned, most probably from the Saracens, that marvellous effects could be got by the ordered repetition of simple parts. The Saracens were never masters of profiling, and the Spanish ones never admired a firm outline. We see as early as the great mosque at Cordova how fond they were of ugly cusped arches,—cusped, too, on the intrados and extrados, and intersecting one another. At the Alhambra, this passion is carried to excess. The outlines, it is true, are not so ugly as those at Cordova, but they lack the barbaric vigour, and sometimes are almost as imbecile as the ornamented mouldings that are put in modern pianos.

It is impossible to speak of Saracen decoration without considering its colour, for it was made for the colour, and without it is but poor stuff. I will fitst speak of the tile dadoes:

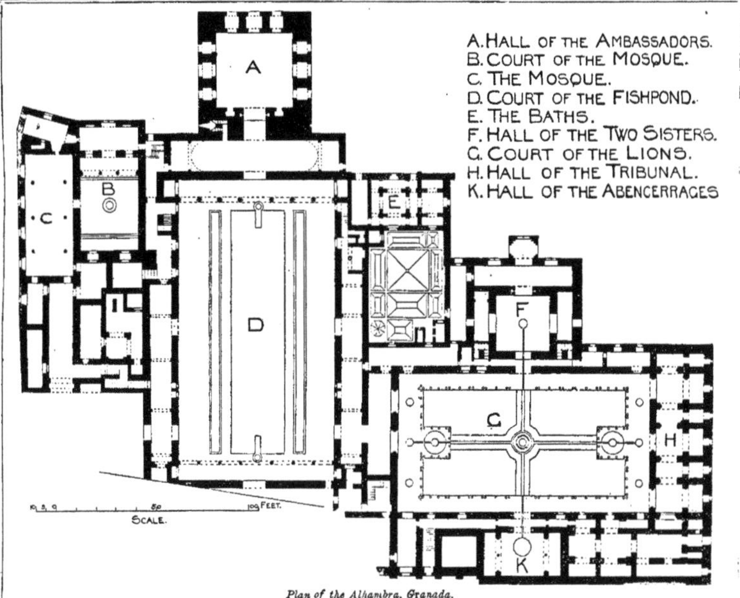

Plan of the Alhambra, Granada.

these are mostly bad; they have all the faults of oddness or complexity of pattern, without being redeemed by the colour, though there are a few almost wholly made up of blues, greens, and white, with a touch of yellow, which fall just short of being delightful; and there are a few pieces of tolerably agreeable colour, with quaint patterns that are certainly striking. One of these patterns is made up of a sort of rough sketch of a swallow flying, seen from underneath, and this unit is used in pairs, kissing; one pair is green and one black, or dark blue, on a white ground; one pair has the lines of the wings horizontal and the other has them vertical. Admirable borders are made of black bearded battlements on a white ground, and there are some very pretty ones made of texts from the Koran, cut in black tile and inlaid on a white ground.

The ornamental plaster-work is made up of checkers and curious Saracen geometrical forms, sometimes over scrolls and sometimes merely filled up with flowers and leaves in low relief, with diapers superposed, sometimes many deep; by the apposite juxtaposition of blue, red, and gold, the two former tempered with white, the whole mass at a certain distance forms a warm grey, a blue grey, or a red grey, and when you are slightly closer the least change of position brings out a new pattern of a different colour, in a way that is absolutely magical. On a sunshiny day I could watch the changes of pattern and tint at the Alhambra Court of the Crystal Palace by the hour.

The main ideas that underlie Saracen decoration seem to me to have been two-fold—what may be called a poetical passion for flowers, and an intellectual interest in the creation of new geometric forms, too often of maddening intricacy. It seems natural that people who came from sandy deserts should passionately admire flowers, and even if the decorators themselves had never seen a desert, their constant perusal of the Korân would suggest it; for besides the black-eyed houris of paradise, there is a constant reference to gardens with rivers flowing beneath them, to shady trees, to flowers, and fruit. Where the flowers, plants, and fruit they chose to copy or conventionalise came from, I know not, but the bulk of them are like nothing else one has seen, and no travelled botanist seems ever to have attempted a solution. It is only natural that the Saracens, who had made great advances in geometry, should have delighted in their own geometrical puzzles, for though they cultivated their intellect at the expense of their taste, they had an excellent excuse. No mosque could have in it the representation of any living thing, and no pious Moslem could tolerate such representations in the decoration of his house, furniture, or utensils, so architects and decorators must have been hard put to it to gratify their employers' taste for richness and magnificence. They might, it is true, have elaborated a new system of floral decoration, though hitherto that has been dull when not associated with animals or man, but they took up with studies that were rather intellectual than artistic. They found the solution of these problems in æsthetic geometry, and this, to some extent, supplied the want of the human figure, for the beholder, when tired of the mere gorgeousness, could endeavour to solve the geometric puzzle. When once the Saracens had started on this line, there was the pride of the inventor on the one side, and the pride of the possessor in having a new invention of his own race, on the other. If these geometric ornaments had been much uglier than they are, the Saracens could have made Touchstone's boast,—"An ill-favoured thing, Sir, but mine own,"—just as some people in England admire the engine-turning of a watch, and think it is artistic ornament. Their ornament seems to me, as a rule, to treat floral forms in a coarse and commonplace way; there is none of the style and preciousness of nature in them.

The best Greek, Roman, and Renaissance sculptors and decorators extracted, as it were, the essence of floral beauty, while I have never seen a single piece of floral ornament from the Alhambra,—except, perhaps, the capitals,—that I should care to possess. It must, however, not be forgotten that the object was to make a superb mass of coloured decoration, so that if we merely look at the ornament as means to an end, elegance of floral form was of secondary importance. As a mass, however, these forms occasionally have a very bad fault,—they look as if they were crawling, which is as agreeable to look at as a pan of live eels. Some of their patterns, however, are superb, both in composition and colour. I may instance that on the panels of the Hall of the Ambassadors, composed of two similar meanders reversed, touching one another and interlacing; the pointed ovals formed by the meanders have heart-shaped pieces at the bottom from which spring two of those Saracen twin leaves, the upper leaves having scrolls; a single leaf springs from each of these, crosses the meander and goes into the adjoining heart; in the space of the oval thus left is a reversed shield covered with floral ornament on a small scale; the bands of the meander have wide edges, and the centre is filled in with a text in cursive characters; the whole ground is red; the grounds of the meanders, shields, and leaves are blue; the leaves are ribbed, and all the inscriptions, ribs, and patterns on the shield and edges of the meanders are gold. The branching leaves bind each alternate oval together and break up the monotony of the meander, and the whole is a broken surface of gold and blue, with a few bits of red as jewels; while the hearts, the top of the oval, and a piece of the shield are of massive gold. Naturally, imitation has had a great deal to do with the emergence of their style of ornament; the strongly-ribbed leaves of Byzantine carving seem to have taken the fancy of the Saracens; almost all underlying leaves are so treated, and some look as if these were meant for the edges of leaves not yet quite unfolded; these edges or ribs are blue if the leaf is white, but if the leaf be red or blue the ribs are gilt, thus texture is got, and also those broken bits of colour which are very valuable as contrasts to larger masses of pure colour and gold.

The Byzantines seem to have taken a good many interlaced patterns from the ropes and wickerwork of the Northern nations, besides those they had from Greece and Rome; these were greatly adopted by the Saracens, and were made more intricate.

I mentioned that in the great mosque at Cordova the arches were mostly rusticated by

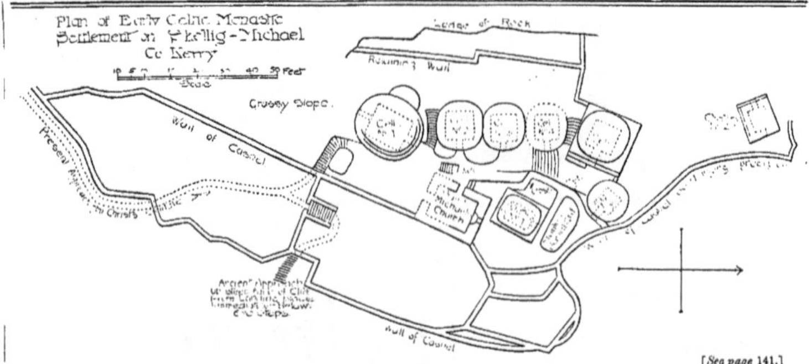

[*See page* 141.]

projecting stone voussoirs alternating with red brick, the ornament being confined to the stone rustications. This characteristic method of decoration is continued at the Alhambra, only the ornament is pure Saracenic and is applied to every voussoir, as may be seen in the flat arches of the court of the mosque. The horseshoe arch of the niche has every voussoir carved, and their circular heads form the cusping of the extrados of the arch, the intrados being ornamented with crockets, and the whole was painted and gilt.

The later Saracens of Spain had no feeling for plainness, nor did they appreciate its value in heightening the effect of the ornamented parts, as the Greeks did; for every square inch is covered with ornament, except the marble shafts of columns, which were gilt; but they understood the value of gradation better than any other people have done.

Considering that by their religion the Saracens were debarred from using human or animal forms, we must admire the consummate art with which they covered the whole of their interiors with arabesques, and yet varied the patterns and relief so that the patterns fulfilled the duties of separation and prevented the eye from being satiated and disgusted with their monotony.

Little as I admire their stalactites, it must be admitted that by these they were enabled to accentuate certain parts, and thus redeem the whole from distressing uniformity of relief. Hate Saracen ornament as you may, every judge of decoration must admit that the Saracens knew every trick of the trade,—large surfaces of flat ornament are redeemed from dulness by projecting shields or panels, whose ornament is large enough to give a marked preponderance of accent. I believe they were the inventors of superposed ornament, which was used with such effect in inscriptions, and you may note with what art they used the different sorts of writing. A band of the stiff and monumental Cufic is often followed by another in the African or in cursive letters. I should only weary you if I attempted to describe the thousand devices by which they secured the desired effect. One phase of the subject has particularly struck me,—the enormous variety of patterns and ornament. It seems unlikely, if not impossible, that any body of men could be gifted with so much off-hand invention. We may be sure that these fighting despots, whose power and life were held by the slightest tenure, were not to be put off by the architect, mason, plasterer, or decorator saying he had to design the building, the construction, the carving, the plastering, or the painted ornament. The Sultan, or ruler, or captain probably sent for the architect at his sitting in the morning, gave him a sheet of parchment, and told him to make his design then and there, and if it was approved, a sum of money was handed to him, and he was told to hire men, and to begin at once: probably to carry on the work night and day. I imagine that the palaces built in one night by Jins, Ons, and Marids were suggested by this practice. The same thing possibly happened to the plasterer, the painter, and the goldsmith who did the gilding, only the employer probably did not have a design, but merely mentioned the sort of effect he wanted. Yet the decoration of each hall must have been under the guidance of one master mind; it could not have been done in pieces haphazard. The whole of each hall is so designed as to be properly effective as a whole, with certain parts more accentuated than others; I therefore come to the conclusion that the decoration of halls like those of the Alhambra, though probably on a smaller scale, was common; that the master plasterer had one or more designs for halls of a certain size and character, and that he had a staff of men who knew the exact relief required for each part, and that he worked in conjunction with a master painter and goldsmith, who also had staffs who knew exactly what ornament, and what colours, and what gilding to use to this particular plaster pattern. Some of the patterns of the plaster-work may have been kept in stock, but this cannot always have been the case, for some were evidently carved. We see the slabs put up, with the main lines of the patterns only marked on them, in the Court of the Lions and elsewhere.

The late Mr. Lundgren, the artist, told a curious story about plastering. He went to India after the Mutiny to make sketches of the natives, and while in the Punjab with his interpreter, they went into an unfinished tomb for shelter from a storm; the ceiling appeared to be just plastered, and there was an old tub in the tomb; a man with three laths came in and measured the length and breadth of the tomb, he then got on the tub, broke the ends of the laths into different shaped points, and set out some triangles on the ceiling; he then began at one end and modelled with the laths a most elaborate floral pattern in the wet plaster. Lundgren stayed there till the plasterer left, and told his interpreter that this plasterer was the cleverest man he ever met with; the interpreter said, on the contrary, "He is an idiot." Lundgren replied, "I have been a painter for forty years, and I could not do such a thing straight off." The interpreter said, "His father was a clever man,—he could do five patterns; he had three sons,—one could do three patterns, one two, and this idiot could only learn to do one." On this, Lundgren said, "Oh! if he has been all his life doing this one pattern it is not so extraordinary as I supposed."

Illustrations.

STAIRCASE, RENISHAW HALL.

RENISHAW HALL, Derbyshire, originally built in Elizabeth's reign (about 1600), was largely added to at the beginning and end of the eighteenth century. It has always belonged to the Sitwells, the present owner being Sir Geo. R. Sitwell, Bart. The new staircase is erected in the room to the left of the hall, which was originally, probably, the buttery, the staircase being formerly where the drawing-room corridor is now. The walls of this corridor and the ground-floor walls of staircase hall, Jambs of arches, &c., are panelled in deal painted white. The staircase itself, including the panelling up the stairs, and on the first floor, &c., is of oak. The door (existing) seen through the arch on the first floor, has new pediment, &c.; it leads to the private drawing-room over the library. The hall is paved with 14 in. squares of black and white marble; the hearth and between the arches being small diamonds of the same materials.

The deal panelling was made by Mr. Geo. Stevenson, of Eckington; the staircase, &c. by Mr. Franklin, of Deddington, Oxon, the "badges" round the tops of the newels being carved by Mr. J. E. Knox, of Kennington. The architect was Mr. Fred. M. Simpson, of Westminster, S.W. The library (part of the old house) has a fine Elizabethan plaster ceiling and frieze.

MOSQUE OF SHAH ABBAS, ISPAHAN.

THE plan and section of this mosque, given here, formed two of the diagrams to Professor Aitchison's third Royal Academy lecture, printed in full in our last issue. His description of the building will be found on page 118 *ante*.*

The section, as will be seen, is taken righ through the centre or backbone of the plan the turn or angle formed in the back portion o the plan being laid out in one plane on th section.

HANOVER SCHOOLS, GILBERT-STREET GROSVENOR-SQUARE.

THE new Hanover Schools were erected ir 1889 for the Hanover parish in conjunctio with the parish of St. George's, Hanover-square to take the place of the old schools in Soutl Molton-street, which had become inadequate.

The site was a free gift in perpetuo to th parish by the Duke of Westminster.

The drawing from which we illustrate th building was hung in the Royal Academy i 1889.

The contract was carried out by Messr Turtle & Appleton, of Wandsworth, from d signs by Mr. W. D. Caröe.

Accommodation is provided for 110 boy 110 girls, 150 infants, with master and mi tress's residences.

NEW CHURCH, LONG CLAWSON, LEICESTERSHIRE.

THE existing Church of St. Remigius, Lon Clawson, being in a dilapidated condition, an devoid of any architectural or archæologic detail, it has been decided to pull down the o church and erect a new one, as shown in o illustration. The old church has had north a south transepts, as well as nave and chan abutting up to its central tower; and in d signing the new church the architect has a hered to the original architectural outline a grouping.

The cost of the new church will be abc 5,500*l*., exclusive of taking down and re-hangi the five bells, which is being done by Mess Taylor & Sons, of Loughborough.

Mr. John Howitt, F.R.I.B.A., of Nottingha is the architect.

* The drawings being in use for the Professo lectures, we were not able to give the illustration la week.

STAIRCASE RENISHAW HALL, DERB

Royal Academy Exhibition, 1890

M. Simpson, A.R.I.B.A., Architect

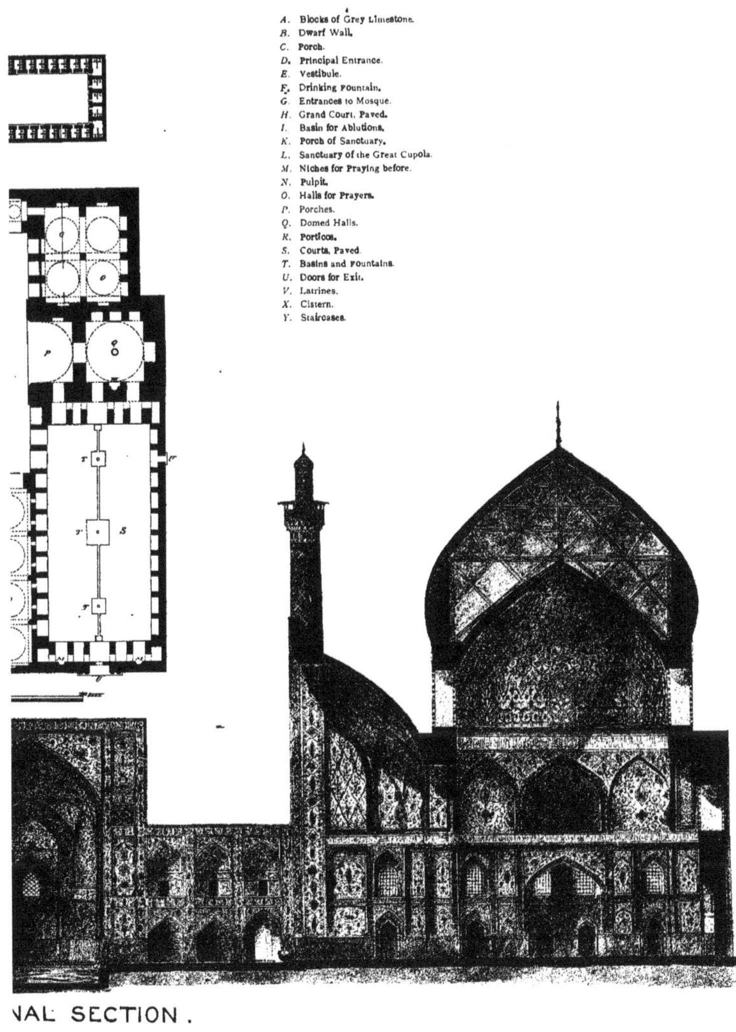
A. Blocks of Grey Limestone.
B. Dwarf Wall.
C. Porch.
D. Principal Entrance.
E. Vestibule.
F. Drinking Fountain.
G. Entrances to Mosque.
H. Grand Court, Paved.
I. Basin for Ablutions.
K. Porch of Sanctuary.
L. Sanctuary of the Great Cupola.
M. Niches for Praying before.
N. Pulpit.
O. Halls for Prayers.
P. Porches.
Q. Domed Halls.
R. Porticos.
S. Courts, Paved.
T. Basins and Fountains.
U. Doors for Exit.
V. Latrines.
X. Cistern.
Y. Staircases.
NAL SECTION.
FEET.

. ISPAHAN.

yal Academy lectures.)

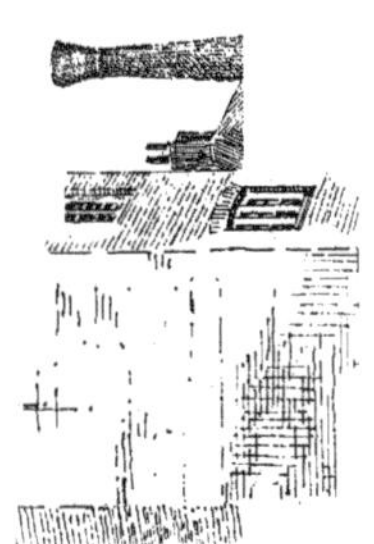

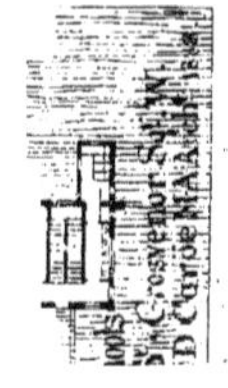

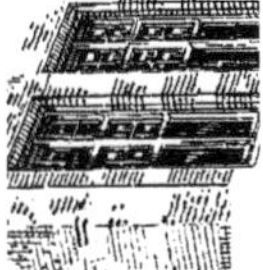

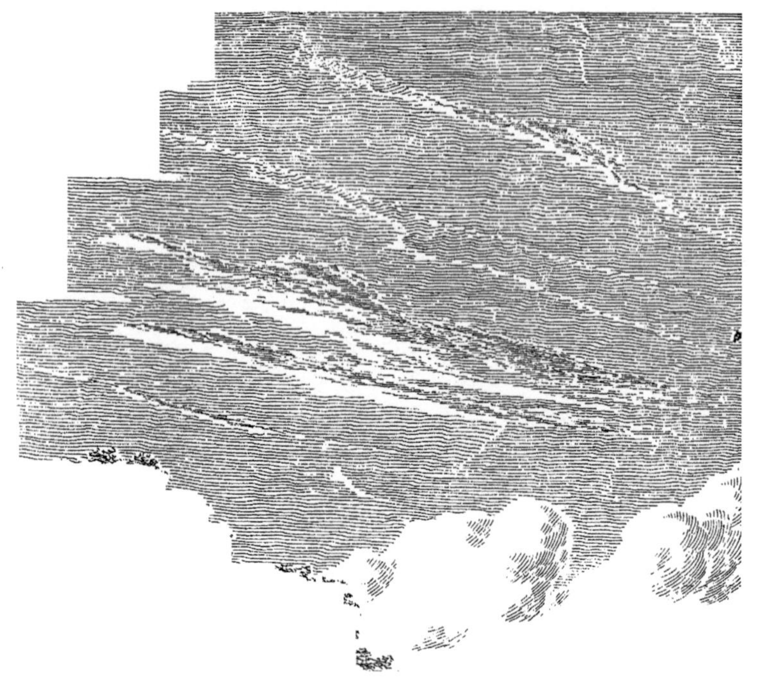

SKELLIG MICHAEL.

AN account was given in the *Builder* for Sept. 12, 1891, of the visit paid last summer to the ancient Celtic monastery on Skellig Michael by the Royal Society of Antiquaries of Ireland and the Cambrian Archæological Association. We now illustrate the very interesting remains at this place by a plan of the monastic buildings, two views, and a measured drawing of one of the oratories. The main outline of the plan is taken from the one in Lord Dunraven's "Notes on Irish Architecture," and the additions were sketched in on the spot last August. The views are reproduced from photographs done by Dr. Norman, of Bath, who has kindly given permission to use them.*

The Great Skellig, or Skellig Michael, is a rocky island in the Atlantic, off the west coast of Kerry, 8½ miles from Bolus Head, which is the nearest point on the mainland. The 6-in. ordnance-map shows the size and shape of the rock, and the position of all the buildings upon it. The island has an area of a little over 44 acres, and consists of two conical peaks rising, respectively, to heights of 714 ft. and 611 ft. above the sea, and joined together at their bases. Between the two peaks is a grassy valley, 422 ft. above the sea, called, on account of its peculiar shape, "Christ's Saddle." There are two lighthouses at the southern end of the island, which are approached from the landing-place at the northern end of the island by a zig-zag road along the edge of the cliff. The monastic buildings are situated just below the summit of the lower of the two peaks, on its eastern side, at a height of 545 ft. above the sea, advantage having been taken of the only piece of ground which is sufficiently level for the purpose.

The present path up to the monastery is through the valley called "Christ's Saddle," which is reached by pursuing the road from the landing-place to the lighthouses for a short distance southwards, and then turning off to the west. The old route was straight up the almost perpendicular face of the cliff from the landing-place, but the lower part has now been cut away in order to make the road to the lighthouse.

At the back the monastic settlement is protected by a retaining wall and the rounded ledge of rock which rises up behind it to the westwards. Beyond this ledge of rock, further west, is a sheer precipice down to the sea. In front, where the slope is less steep, the settlement is surrounded by a dry-built stone wall, forming a sufficiently strong defence in case of attack.

The whole area enclosed measures about 300 ft. long by 100 ft. wide, and the buildings within occupy a space of 150 ft. by 50 ft. The earlier remains consist of six beehive cells, two oratories, two wells, five ancient burial-grounds, and several rude crosses. The church of St. Michael is of later date, and is built with mortar, whereas all the other structures are of dry rubble. The ground, which is highest next the retaining wall at the back, and slopes down towards the east, has been artificially levelled up in a series of steps, so as to form a more suitable foundation for the different buildings. The raised ground is in each case faced with low retaining walls, and rude flights of stairs lead from one level to the next. The photographic view in which the cross appears is taken from a point between cell No. 2 and St. Michael's Church looking northwards, and shows the flight of nine steps leading from the space in front of cells Nos. 1 to 4 to that in front of cell No. 5.

The other view shows the interior of the ruined church of St. Michael, with the Lemon Rock and the coast of Kerry in the distance. It will be noticed that the side wall of the church is built directly over the wall of the cashel or fortress, on the edge of the cliff, and there is an uninterrupted view of the sea below.

Whatever may be the actual date of the remains on Skellig Michael (and it can hardly be later than the eighth century), the type of Christian structure here found is the earliest of which we have any knowledge in Great Britain, exhibiting as it does transitional features between the Pagan and subsequent methods of building, and showing the evolution of the stone-roofed church from the pre-Christian beehive cell. The most primitive form of the clochaun, or bee-hive cell, is probably that which is circular in plan both inside and out. The cells on Skellig Michael are an advance upon this in being rectangular inside, although still retaining the rounded shape outside, but in the oratories an entirely new departure is taken in the adoption of the square corners altogether. The drawing of oratory No. 2 shows the Irish stone-roofed church in this its first stage of development, after emancipating itself from the Pagan traditional methods of building, an advance in style which was eventually to culminate in the design of Cormac's Chapel at Cashel. The oratory is in such a position that it requires a steady nerve to stand beside it and look over the edge of the retaining wall at the sea, hundreds of feet below. One is lost in admiration for the skill and daring of the monkish builders who, with their lives in their hands, could construct a wall actually sloping outwards over empty space, like one side of the Leaning Tower of Pisa. The character of the masonry of this wall is almost identical with that of the celebrated Staigue Fort, co. Kerry. Another resemblance to the Staigue Fort that will not escape the notice of the keen observer is in the ingenious contrivance for relieving the weight on the horizontal lintel of the doorway of cell No. 1, by placing a second lintel above with a small intervening space. Yet, whilst we are struck by constructive features that the Skellig Michael remains possess in common with the Pagan fortresses, the Christian character of the buildings is rendered sufficiently obvious by the crosses over the doorways formed of quartz pebbles, showing up white against a background of dark coloured slate.

* Copies of all the views taken by Dr. Norman during the Kerry excursions can be obtained from Mr. W. Middleton Ashman, 12a, Old Bond-street, Bath.

View on Skellig Michael, showing the Cross and some of the Cells.

Skellig Michael: Remains of the Church.

DEMONSTRATIONS ON GREEK SCULPTURE AT THE BRITISH MUSEUM.

MISS EUGÉNIE SELLERS gave on the 10th inst. the first of a course of six demonstration lectures on Greek sculpture in relief.

Miss Sellers said that Greek sculpture begins with intense realism, which is in itself hostile to decorative schemes. For example, in the little pediment of poros stone at Athens which represents Herakles slaying the Hydra, there is no centre-figure; while the chariot of Herakles, with complete disregard for decorative effect, is turned away from the centre ready for the homeward journey when the contest is over. Again, in the Harpy Tomb in the British Museum, there is no adequate centre, and the Harpies that should frame in the composition, fly away from the centre, realistically pourtraying the idea of souls passing away in death.

Passing to the consideration of the sculptures of the Temple of Ægina, Miss Sellers incidentally claimed these for Attica, basing her claim on the close resemblance between them and the bronze helmeted head in the Akropolis museum and the beautiful archaic head of a youth, now at Copenhagen, which was found at Athens; and further bearing in mind the fact that Pausanias, — to whom we owe the term "Æginetan art," — had seen scarcely any archaic art, all the statues that recent excavations on the Akropolis have reclaimed being in his day buried under the walls built by Kimon and Perikles. But Ægina still had its archaic sculptures; hence the term *Æginetan* came to be synonymous with *archaic*.

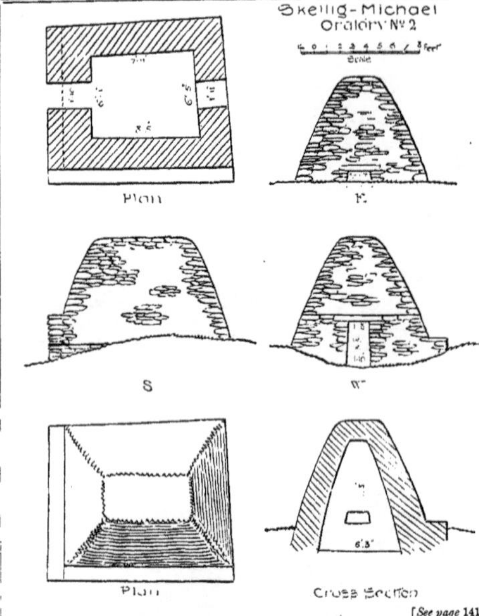

[*See page* 141.]

In the pediments of Ægina the sculptor began to feel the need of a centre, and we find him balancing his figures one against the other with perfect symmetry, but with the unsatisfactory result that they have somewhat the air of ornaments neatly arranged upon a shelf.

In the second lecture, last Wednesday, it was shown that the same principle applies to the pediment sculpture of the Temple of Zeus at Olympia. Again we have the central figure with figures symmetrically arranged on either side; but, for all the beauty of the individual figures, the whole lacks harmony and fusion. As in the old poros stone pediment, chariots form part of the scheme; but this time they are turned inwards, without regard to realism, and stand stiffly on either side of the centre.

In the Parthenon, the central composition of the western pediment shows a great advance. This time, the chariot horses that frame the centre are represented in active movement. But the angles still have that obtrusive symmetry which deprives the grouping of any charm. It is, however, in the eastern pediment where we have figures combined in groups which are themselves subordinate to the central group, that the Greeks approached most nearly to that combination of living forms into patterns which characterises, for example, the work of Donatello in his famous gallery of singing boys.

Miss Sellers here discussed at some length the various interpretations which have been given from time to time of the figures of the East pediment. She would revert to the old interpretation of Nux for the figure commonly called Selene; for in vase paintings it is Nux that drives while Selene rides.* The group often called "the Fates,"—which have been interpreted by Dr. Waldstein as Hestia, Gaia, and Thalassa, she unhesitatingly calls "the Charites," thus obtaining a group of three whose attributes as well as whose attitudes would be closely symmetrical with the figures on the other side if interpreted as the Horai and Dionysus (rather than Olympos)—a combination that appears in the representation of the marriage of Peleus and Thetis in the François vase.

* The head of the "Selene" horse quite allows of the supposition of a rider instead of a driver.—Ed.

Finally, in the Parthenon frieze,—for all the flow and movement of the sides,—the centre is certainly weak. Mr. Murray suggests that the gods and goddesses are to be conceived as sitting in a semi-circle in a different plane from the procession, which advances in front of them from both sides,—an explanation, by the way, which Miss Sellers applies to the interpretation of the west side of the Harpy Tomb, where, as here, the artist has tried to represent two sides of one scene at the same time,—but no archæological knowledge gets rid of the fact that the eye, in travelling rapidly on with the procession, is checked by the disagreeable impression of those five inadequate vertical figures, on whom the gods are turning their backs.

ARCHITECTURAL SOCIETIES

Leeds and Yorkshire Architectural Society.—A social gathering of the members of this Society was held on the 15th instant, in the Law Institute, Albion-place, Leeds. A collection of drawings and sketches of architectural subjects was hung on the walls. Mr. Frank Bedford showed the collection of sketches of Italian and Spanish architecture he had executed while on a tour of study on the Continent, and Mr. H. V. Lancaster, who has also studied and sketched abroad, exhibited some drawings. Other sketches were also shown by Mr. W. J. Mettam and Mr. Carby Hall (secretary). Specimens of wood and ivory turning, by Mr. H. B. Buckley, were also exhibited.

Edinburgh Architectural Association.—On the 11th inst. the Edinburgh Architectural Society met in the hall, 42, George-street, Edinburgh, under the chairmanship of Mr. John Kinross. Mr. James Bruce, W.S., Edinburgh, moved that the Association, in acknowledging the communication from the First Commissioner of Her Majesty's Board of Works, intimating that he had caused a sum of 250*l.* to be provided for the "urgent and special repair of the Palace of Linlithgow," thanked him for having taken action in the matter, but felt that the thorough repair of the entire fabric was the only proper course, and begged to represent "that such thorough repair could only be carried out by replacing the burn timbers and flooring, re-glazing the window and covering the whole with a roof, so that th walls might be firmly tied together, and th whole rendered wind and water tight." H said that the sum of 250*l.* was utterly in adequate for the purpose they aimed at, an they, as Scotsmen, should insist upon tha palace being put into proper order.—Mr. Ros seconded the motion, which was supported b several members, and agreed to.—The Counc of the Association, under remit from the las meeting on Mr. G. S. Aitken's motion regardin the removal of the Wellington statue, recom mended that the Association should take n further steps in the matter. This recommenda tion was unanimously adopted.—Sheriff Macka then read a paper on "The Architecture o Scottish Towns as illustrating Scottish History. Taking the four periods of Scottish history—th Celtic-Roman, the Celtic-Saxon, the Scottish Norman or Feudal, and the British or Modern —he described the known architectural charac teristic of each. The Celts, he said, had n architecture prior to the Roman invasion, and it was not until after that event that ther occurred the transition from the Scottis manner of building with wood to the Roman manner of building with stone. The Roman influence, however, upon town architecture wa nil. The Celtic-Saxon period was the era o the origin of the earliest Scottish towns,— their sites being fixed near castles, rive mouths, and (at a later date) cathedrals o churches,—but scarcely a vestige of their styl of architecture remained. The third perio was contemporaneous with the form of Gothi or Norman architecture prevailing from the tim of David I. to the Reformation, which put a end to the feudal character of the Church, and to the Revolution, which put an end to feudalism in the State. The signs of advance in architecture were seen in churches, colleges, palaces and private houses. In the last or modern period the Revolution settlement, and the Union in 1707, led to the development o Scottish burghs. After the Rebellion of 174 the feudal burghs burst their bonds, new town and new architecture afterwards arose, and, as time went on, a higher standard of comfort, produced by increased wealth, preceded a higher standard of art.

Glasgow Architectural Association.—The usual monthly meeting of this society was held on the 9th inst., the Honorary President, Mr. W. Forrest-Salmon, in the chair, when a demonstration was given by Mr. Francis H. Newbery upon "The Architecture of the Human Figure, and its Application." He referred tc the besetting weakness of architects' undue regard for precedent, exemplified chiefly, perhaps, in their reproduction of the Classic orders by means of a unit of measurement,—the module —found in the half-diameter of the column For encouragement he instanced the modern development of sculpture and figure-painting. At one time the human form was studied in th same exact but, withal, mechanical way. I had been discovered than in Egyptian re presentations of the figure the unit was th middle finger. In Greece the principle wa further elaborated, and the palm, and then th head, taken as the multiple for all the propor tions of the body. Leonarda da Vinci, a grea artist, did not scorn the aid given by a know ledge of the normal proportions of the body a codified, but he went further, and to acquaint ance with antique canon added the study o nature at first hand. Mr. Newbery's "applica tion" was that, beyond the precise analysis o past styles, the architect must appreciate th human figure, Nature's supreme example in pro portion, symmetry, and beauty of line, if hi architecture is to advance from academic cor rectness to the artistic realisation of Nature' principle in its proportion. The demonstratio was given on the blackboard.—Mr. Keppi opened the discussion which followed, and a its close a hearty vote of thanks was awarde Mr. Newbery.

Chicago Exhibition.—We are officially informe that the British railways have undertaken to carr goods for British exhibitors at the Chicago Exhib tion, to and from the port of shipment, at ha rates. The American railways will charge the usual rates to Chicago, but will bring back th goods free at the close of the Exhibition. Man of the principal steamship companies have reduc their rates considerably, and will take freight f the Exhibition at 11s. per ton. Many of them ha also consented to adopt a reduced passenger tar for exhibitors and their *employés*, certified as su under the authority of the Royal Commission.

COMPETITIONS.

THE COXLODGE ASYLUM EXTENSION.—On Wednesday afternoon, at a meeting of the Coxlodge Asylum Committee of the Corporation of Newcastle, it was announced that the professional assessor, Mr. G. T. Hine, had reported that eighteen sets,—with four alternative plans, making twenty-two in all,—had been sent in. The successful competitors were, in his opinion, to be placed in the following order:—1. Motto, "Norstan," Mr. J. W. Dyson, Grainger-street. 2. "Compact," Messrs. Montgomery and Carr, Grainger-street. 3. "Order," Mr. W. L. Newcombe, Pilgrim-street. 4. "Northumbria" (second plan), Messrs. R. Knill Freeman and S. R. Robins, Grainger-street. The committee are to meet again shortly to consider the report of Mr. Hine. The cost of the extension is expected to range from 70,000*l.* to 80,000*l.* The competition was confined to Newcastle architects.

BOROUGH LUNATIC ASYLUM, SUNDERLAND.—At the meeting of the Sunderland Town Council on the 10th inst., the Visiting Committee of the Borough Lunatic Asylum recommended:—"That the common corporate seal be affixed to agreement for purchase of land at Ryhope as the site for the Borough Lunatic Asylum. That the Town Clerk take all necessary steps for obtaining the approval of a Secretary of State to such agreement. That Mr. C. H. Howell, architect to the Commissioners in Lunacy, the assessor, having reported that, after a careful examination of the drawings submitted for the proposed Borough Lunatic Asylum, he is of opinion that the designs marked as follows should be awarded the prizes in the undermentioned order:—1st, Scio; 2nd, Turpi Secernis Honestum; 3rd, X. The Committee have so awarded them, and they recommend that No. 1 plan, "Scio," be adopted for the asylum and forwarded to the Commissioners in Lunacy, subject to an arrangement being previously made with the author thereof as to the architect's commission, &c."—Ald. Shadforth moved the adoption of the report, and proposed that the first should be adopted as the plan for the asylum.—Mr. Bruce seconded the motion.—Ald. Swan moved that the matter be adjourned for a fortnight, so that the members of the Council should have an opportunity of seeing the plans.—Mr. W. Sanderson seconded the amendment, which was put and lost.—Ald. Swan then moved that the Council ought not to be asked to approve of anything which they knew nothing about, and under the circumstances he suggested that a special meeting of the Council be held on Wednesday, the 17th, to consider the matter. This was agreed to.

THE LONDON COUNTY COUNCIL.

THE usual weekly meeting of the London County Council was held on Tuesday afternoon last at Spring-gardens, the Chairman, Sir John Lubbock, presiding.

Tenders.—Tenders were received for the construction of the Hackney-wick, &c., relief sewer, and for the erection of a new Fire Brigade Station at East Dulwich. The lists will be found on another page.

Proposed Appointment of a Parks Superintendent.—The General Purposes Committee presented the following report:—

"Under the resolution of the Council of November 3 last*, an advertisement was issued inviting applications for the post of Superintendent of the Council's parks and open spaces, at a salary of 700*l.* a year. The applications were in the first instance considered by the Parks Committee, who at our request submitted to us the names of the three candidates whom they considered the most suitable for the appointment. The three candidates selected by the Parks Committee were Lieut.-Colonel F. Bailey, Colonel I. C. Walker, and Mr. C. J. Ponsonby. Having seen the three selected candidates, and weighed their respective merits and qualifications, we recommend—

'That Colonel Inches Campbell Walker be appointed Superintendent of Parks and Open Spaces, at a salary of 700*l.* a year, upon the following conditions—That he do hold his office during the pleasure of the Council; that he be required to give his whole time to the duties of his office, and be not allowed to take any private business; that any fees received by him either as a witness or in any other capacity be paid to the Council; and further, that he do accept the condition that on retirement he shall not be entitled and shall not make any claim to any superannuation or pension, and that he will submit to any general scheme which the Council may adopt with respect to insurance for pensions or superannuation.'"

* See *Builder* for October 31, and November 7, 1891.

Mr. Corbett moved, as an amendment,

"That, as it was stated in the advertisement for a Parks Superintendent that the age of candidates must not in any case exceed fifty years, and as two of the selected candidates exceed that age, the question be referred back to the Committee for further consideration."

In the course of the long and somewhat acrimonious discussion which ensued, the Parks Committee was criticised by some of the members for not having stated in their report that two of the candidates, Col. Walker and Lieut.-Col. Bailey, were beyond the prescribed age. Whether the strict limitation of age was desirable or not, it was contended that to adopt the recommendation of the Committee would be to break faith with other applicants for the appointment. Apart from this irregularity, however, many members objected to any such appointment,—to the creation of any such office. They urged that the existing Park Superintendents having charge of individual parks had shown themselves to be men fully competent for their posts. This was not denied by the Committee and its supporters, but it was urged that admirably as the individual Park Superintendents fulfilled their duties, the proposed new officer was much wanted in the interest of efficiency, economy, and uniformity of administration. To this it was replied that Messrs. Sexby and Nairn, two officers in the employment of the Council,—one in the Architect's department and one in the Clerk's department,—had managed the work of supervision very well. On behalf of the Committee it was rejoined that the existing state of things had only been made passably satisfactory through the untiring vigilance and unremitting supervision of members of the Committee. Some of the members of the Council who were not on the Committee advocated the appointment of a general superintendent of parks and open spaces, on the ground that there had been great mistakes made in the laying-out of the new park at Dulwich,—mistakes which they feared would be repeated in Waterlow and other parks. On being put to the vote, Mr. Corbett's amendment was carried by a large majority over the recommendation of the Committee. On being put as a substantive motion, several new amendments were proposed and lost. One of these amendments was to the effect that Mr. Ponsonby, who, it was said, fulfilled all the required conditions, should be appointed to the post. It was stated that, while possessing all the knowledge of forestry possessed by the other two candidates named, he was under fifty years of age, and had a knowledge of horticulture and landscape-gardening. This amendment was lost by a large majority, and ultimately Mr. Corbett's amendment was adopted as a substantive motion. The question was therefore referred back.

Appeal by the School Board against an Order of the Shoreditch Vestry.—The Report of the General Purposes Committee also contained the following paragraph:—

"We have to report that, acting as the Statutory Appeal Committee appointed under Section 212 of the Metropolis Management Act, 1855, we have heard an appeal by the School Board for London against an order of the Vestry of Shoreditch, requiring certain water-closets proposed to be erected at the Board schools in Shap-street, Kingsland-road, to be separately drained with a separate trap, pan, and water supply for each water-closet. Having heard the parties for and against, we came to the conclusion that the order of the Vestry should be varied, and we accordingly passed the following resolution:—

'That the order be varied by allowing the construction of the water-closets as proposed by the School Board, provided that the Board construct the water-closets so that the flushing of the troughs shall take place automatically at intervals of every half-hour during the day, commencing with school hours, and ending half an hour after.'"

The Bar at the Top of Gower-street.—The Improvements Committee again brought up their report on this subject, which was not adopted at last week's meeting, as we inadvertently stated on p. 125, *ante*. The following is the text of the report, which we did not print last week:—

"We have received a letter from the Vestry of St. Pancras stating that the authorities of University College and Hospital are willing to give up for the sum of 15,000*l.* the land in front of the Hospital, with a view to the opening up of the line of communication north and south through Gower-street, and asking the Council to contribute 10,000*l.* towards the cost. The land referred to has an area of 1 rood 4 poles 27 yards, is situated between Gratton-street and University-street, and divides University Hospital from University College. The Hospital authorities claim the ownership to the land, and though they permit it to be used by foot passengers (save on one day in the year) they can at any time close it to traffic, and utilise the land for building purposes. Indeed, at the present time the Hospital authorities are anxious to reconstruct their Hospital, and in the event of their so doing it is open to them to use the land which they now offer to sell, and thus prevent the opening up of Gower-street. We have satisfied ourselves that the authorities possess the freehold of the land to the exclusion of any public right of way across it, and we are, therefore, of opinion that the present opportunity for acquiring it should be seized. The Vestry has agreed, in the event of the Council contributing the 10,000*l.*, to undertake all further expenditure, including the cost of making the roads and footways over the land. The price asked for the land may, from one point of view, appear somewhat excessive, but we would point out that in the event of the Hospital authorities acquiring the property on the west side instead of this area, they would certainly have to expend a larger sum than 15,000*l.* The removal of the bar in Gower-street and the opening up of a direct line of communication between New Oxford-street and Euston-road would be a great public advantage, and in harmony with the avowed policy of the Council respecting the removal of gates and bars. We can confidently advise the Council to accede to the request of the Vestry, particularly as if this opportunity be suffered to pass, it may never occur again. We recommend,—

'That, subject to an estimate being submitted to the Council by the Finance Committee, as required by the statute, the Council do contribute 10,000*l.* towards the cost of opening up the line of communication north and south through Gower-street, such contribution to be made on the usual conditions with regard to contributions to improvements undertaken by local authorities.'"

The recommendation was now agreed to without discussion.

York Water-gate.—The second report of the Parks and Open Spaces Committee contained the following paragraph:—

"We have had our attention called to the partially dilapidated condition of the York Water-gate at the bottom of Buckingham-street and adjoining the Victoria-embankment-gardens, and also to the untidy condition of the ground around it. There is no beneficial ownership in the gate, and the persons who are, or claim to be, in possession of it consequently take no steps to keep it in proper order. We have no desire to alter the ownership of the gate, but having regard to its position as a monument of the past and an object of public and architectural interest, we think that the Council would be quite justified, as it forms a feature of the Victoria-embankment-gardens, in undertaking its future maintenance. We therefore recommend,—

'That the Council do direct the Parliamentary Committee to insert a clause in the next General Powers Bill to enable it to maintain the York Water-gate next the Victoria-embankment-gardens.'"

The recommendation was adopted *nem. con.*

The Inhabited House Duty.—Mr. Beachcroft moved:—

"That, in the opinion of the Council, the Inhabited House Duty should cease to be an Imperial tax, and should be substituted for the share of the Probate Duty grant now carried to the local taxation account, so that the amount actually leviable in respect of house duty in the County of London may be appropriated to the County Fund, and that a representation to this effect be made to the Chancellor of the Exchequer."

After some discussion, the motion was referred to the Local Government and Taxation Committee, and the Council adjourned shortly after six o'clock, having got through its business an hour earlier than usual.

THE SANITARY INSPECTORS' ASSOCIATION.

THE ordinary monthly meeting of this Association was held on the 6th inst. at Carpenters' Hall, London-wall, when an address was delivered by the Medical Officer of Health of the Staffordshire County Council, Dr. Geo. Reid, D.P.H., an hon. member of the Association. Mr. Hugh Alexander, Chairman of the Council, presided, and there was a good attendance of members.

The lecturer selected for his subject "Infection and Disinfection," and, in his treatment of it, he limited himself almost exclusively to two salient points,—(1) the nature of contagion and its phenomena, and (2) methods of prevention by disinfectants. We had long passed, he said, the epoch of curious hypotheses as to the causes of infection, and we now knew that certain kinds of disease were propagated by low forms of animal life, which were known as germs. The existence and the various shapes and forms of these organisms, though mostly so minute as to be invisible to the naked eye, had been in various ways demonstrated. These organisms, or their spores, which were more difficult to kill than mature germs, often clung for a long time to clothing, remaining perhaps for a considerable period in a state of suspended animation for want of proper food. It was still a moot question whether such germs had a spontaneous origin or were only to be found after an antecedent case of sporadic disease, and as there were facts to support both theories of origin, it might be possible that they had a double development. Whatever might be the truth as to their origin there was no doubt that an atmosphere of dirt, moisture, and a certain temperature were necessary conditions of their existence. As fish could not live in water without air, so these morbific germs could not live in the air without filth; and ozone, as their distinguished President so often maintained, was fatal to them. Armed with that knowledge, and knowing also where to look for the conditions of filth, the inspector would be in a position to fight the evil and to conquer it. An infected person was a centre of contagion, and from him, by means of the breath, emanations of the skin, secretions, contact with clothing or through water, milk, food, or air, it might be communicated indefinitely from person to person. The different ways in which the same or different diseases had been communicated in observed cases were illustrated by diagrams. Disease in animals played an important part in the spread of epidemics, particularly tuberculosis, diphtheria, and scarlet-fever. Entering upon the second portion of the subject, the lecturer explained by means of a table the effects of dry and moist heat at different degrees of temperature upon the bacilli, and stated the various times required to destroy life in them under the different conditions. Moist heat at 212 degs. Fahrenheit effectually destroyed germs after five minutes exposure, which would require from one to four hours with an exposure up to 220 degs. in dry heat; the former was therefore to be preferred to the latter. It was fortunate that they now knew enough of the habits of the enemy to follow him to his haunts and combat him successfully, but they were heavily handicapped in the fight by the ignorance of the public and the apathy of local authorities.

On the conclusion of the lecture, a vote of thanks was proposed by Mr. F. G. Bell (Epping), and a discussion took place in which the Chairman, Mr. West (Walthamstow), Mr. Dee (Westminster), and other members took part. The motion having been carried by acclamation Dr. Reid briefly replied in acknowledgment.

CLERKS OF WORKS' ASSOCIATION:

ANNUAL DINNER.

THE ninth annual dinner of the Clerks of Works' Association of Great Britain was held on Monday evening last in the Venetian Saloon of the Holborn Restaurant, Mr. Aston Webb, F.R.I.B.A., in the chair, supported by Mr. F. T. Baggallay, F.R.I.B.A., President of the Architectural Association; Mr. Wyatt Papworth, F.R.I.B.A.; Mr. T. H. Watson, F.R.I.B.A.; Mr. C. Stanley Peach, F.R.I.B.A.; Mr. Thomas F. Rider (Rider & Sons), Mr. Joseph Randall, Mr. Edwin Brooks, Mr. J. Merifield, Mr. J. Brady, Mr. F. Dashwood, and many other gentlemen.

The Chairman, in proposing "The Queen and Royal Family," feelingly alluded to their recent bereavement. It was sometimes said, he continued, that the Victorian Age would not be remembered much as an age of art, but that its chief claim to remembrance would be its scientific and engineering achievements. Without wishing to decry the latter, he thought that there was something to be said on behalf of architecture, for an age which had produced the Houses of Parliament and other prominent public buildings, and which had produced architects such as Sir Charles Barry, Sir Gilbert Scott, George Edmund Street, Alfred Waterhouse, Norman Shaw, and many others whom he might name, could not be said to be undistinguished in architecture.

The Chairman next proposed "The Army, Navy, and Reserve Forces," coupled with the name of Sergeant J. M. Jefferson, who briefly responded.

Mr. G. Dalton, in a humorous speech, proposed "The Architects and Surveyors," coupled with the names of Mr. C. Stanley Peach, F.R.I.B.A., and Mr. Stanley Clarke, both of whom, in replying, spoke of the indebtedness of professional men to clerks of works.

The Chairman, in proposing the principal toast of the evening, "The Clerks of Works' Association," said that he was glad to find that the position of the Association was a most favourable one. He understood that it now numbered 130 members, and that it had been established ten years. The members had gradually increased, and during the past year there had been an increase of ten. The Association appeared to be in the happy position of having an income slightly in excess of its expenditure, and to be able to place to reserve something every year, although there was no absolute necessity for them to do so. The advantages of the Association were thoroughly known and appreciated by the members of the architectural profession. The register of competent clerks of works which the Association kept was one which was now pretty well known and resorted to by most architects in search of capable clerks of works. The Association was to be congratulated on the publication of its useful little *Journal*, which contained a great deal of valuable practical information. Another advantage which had been gained by the establishment of the Association was the opportunities which it afforded of enabling the members to make each other's personal acquaintance and to exchange opinions and experiences. He did not know whether the Association had in connexion with it any benefit society or club, for mutual assistance in case of illness, accident, or other misfortune, but if they had not, they had possibly already given attention to the subject. He was very glad to notice, in reading their *Journal*, that they were fully alive to the importance of technical education, and that they were co-operating with Prof. Banister Fletcher and the Carpenters' Company, in that desirable work. He would impress upon them all, and especially upon their younger members, the great importance, and, indeed, the absolute necessity, of keeping abreast of the times. Every decade of the present century had brought forth some invention, some improvement, some important progress, and it therefore behoved clerks of works, as well as architects and builders, to make themselves conversant with every new thing, as far as they possibly could do so. He had been asked to say something on the question of salary, but that was a rather delicate matter. He was not one who thought that the salaries of clerks of works were always adequate, but he did not think it would be possible, with advantage to themselves, to fix a uniform salary which all should receive. As he apprehended, the Association had no such object in view; it was not, in fact, a trade union. He believed that a thoroughly capable and experienced clerk of works would generally be able to obtain employment at such a salary as his merits entitled him to receive. He thought there were indications that the position of clerks of works would before many years be much better than it was at the present time, for it was probable, and even possible, that their functions would be greatly extended. There were growing signs of the tendency to divide the work of erecting a building into the several trades, and the general contractor seemed to be on the wane. If that were so the probabilities were that the clerk of works would become more and more in request, and he would have greater and greater responsibilities thrown upon him. With the toast he had much pleasure in coupling the name of Mr. J. Brady, the President of the Association.

Mr. Brady, in responding, said that with regard to the subject of a benefit club or society, they had considered that matter at first, and determined to exclude it from their programme, wishing to make membership of the Association independent of all pecuniary considerations, save, of course, the payment of the annual subscription. But they did not in the least wish to disparage other societies which adopted a different course on that matter.

Mr. F. Dashwood, secretary, in a humorous speech proposed "The Worshipful Company of Carpenters," coupled with the name of Professor Banister Fletcher, who, in replying, referred to some criticisms which had appeared in the Association's *Journal* concerning the examinations at Carpenters' Hall.

Other toasts followed, including "The Hon. Treasurer" (Mr. J. Oldrid Scott, who was, we regret to learn, unable to be present through illness); "The Press" (coupled with the name of our representative); "The Visitors" (coupled with the name of Mr. F. T. Baggallay, President of the Architectural Association); and "The Chairman" (proposed by Mr. R. Wheeler).

BRETT'S AUTOMATIC REVERSIBLE SASH.—This sash, the invention of Mr. A. Cutting, is a form of reversible sash-action which has the merit of being exceedingly simple in its working, containing nothing that is liable to get out of order. In place of the rebate at the edge, there is a loosely-fitted lath of brass or other metal working in a slot in the side of the sash, and when the sash is closed, fitting loosely into another slot in the frame. A small bar on this lath projects through the frame at each side, and by a knob or handle can be raised and by the same action drawn inwards obliquely towards the centre of the window, when the lath leaves the window-frame slot, and the sash is free to swing round on centre bearings. On returning the sash to its place the metal lath drops automatically downward and outward, by its own weight, into its place, being guided outward by the oblique line of the slits in which the bars carrying the handles work. The make of the sash is very inexpensive.

Correspondence.

To the Editor of THE BUILDER.

COKE BREEZE CONCRETE.

SIR,—I am much surprised at the opinion expressed by Mr. Potter in your last issue as to the suitability of coke breeze for concrete, and as to the strength of concrete made with it. The use of breeze for concrete is not known in my neighbourhood, though there is plenty of breeze to be had, hence my wish to get practical opinions about it. I proposed to use it for the floor-slabs and walls of artisans' dwellings in consequence of seeing in one of the papers of the Royal Engineers a report of experiments on concrete beams from which it appeared that a beam made with "gasworks breeze" was much stronger than one made with "gravel screened to 1 in. and washed," the proportion of cement being the same in each case,—perhaps some other experiences of the use of breeze for concrete will be given. I regret that my inquiry as to the sizes of rooms that can be spanned by flat slabs of concrete without iron joists, and with practical safety, has not received other replies than that kindly given by Mr. Potter, as this is a point upon which definite practical experience would be of great value, and especially so as it may now, I think, be taken as experimentally proved that durable floors can be formed by nailing deal flooring direct on such concrete slabs, without leaving air-spaces, and so doing away with timber joists entirely. If, as Mr. Potter states, breeze is a bad material for making a strong concrete, his suggestion of forming the lower portion of the floor-slabs of an aggregate that would make a stronger concrete, and putting a layer of 1½ in. of breeze concrete over it to nail into, is good, but I cannot see the use of postponing the laying of this layer until after the lower portion is dry; on the contrary, it seems to me, that it would be very much better to lay, say, 4½ in. of the strong concrete, roughly levelled, and at once to lay on it the breeze concrete, properly levelled off to receive the boards, so that the two layers would be practically incorporated into one mass, and the whole would dry out together. In the records of some experiments on concrete floor-slabs, it is stated that they were wetted daily for a week after they were laid. Is this an advantageous thing to do? Perhaps some further and more definite practical experiences may be given by your readers on this important subject. In the particular case in which I am interested the rooms are 13 ft. by 14 ft., surrounded by 8 in. walls.

1. Can such such rooms be safely spanned by 6 in. slabs of coke breeze concrete, gauged, say, 5 to 1 of best Portland cement,—on which the flooring would be nailed?

2. If not, would the necessary strength be secured by using broken brick or other material, instead of breeze, for, say, 4½ in. thick of the slabs, as suggested above?

SURVEYOR.

AIR-BOUND PIPES.

SIR,—Can any of your readers instruct me how to cure above? The cold main outside my house is only a three-eighth pipe, whilst my service from it up to cistern is ½ in., with branches half-way up to lavatories, &c. The hot-water pipes from cylinder to bath, &c., have no after circulation. When the hot-water taps are turned, lowering the water in cylinder and cistern, a terrible noise, like a fog-horn, sets up, and continues till it is relieved by turning the cold on also, and letting it run for some time; the cold pipe vibrating violently.

What is the cause, and what is the simplest cure?

FOGHORN.

*** From the above letter we gather that the service of water to "Foghorn's" residence is constant and not intermittent; what is generally known as "constant supply." This being the case, the cause of the noise is not far to seek, although it is due to something that might not in the general way be readily thought of. The noise and the vibration engendered proceeds from the ball-valve in the cold-water cistern.

This peculiar trouble is not very frequently experienced, and it does not follow that it proceeds from the same cause in every instance, but on the few occasions it has come to our notice it has in each case proceeded from the ball-valve, and has been easily remedied.

If "Foghorn" opens one of the hot-water taps and then (while the noise and vibration are proceeding) places his ear as near as he conveniently can to the ball-valve in the cold-water cistern, he will doubtless come to the conclusion that this is the seat of the trouble. He rightly likens it to a foghorn, for the noise is due to a similar cause,—viz., the passage of a fluid through a narrow aperture at high pressure. If there is any doubt, let him either lift the ball of the valve to close it or press it down to fully open it, and the noise will cease if the trouble proceeds from the cause that our experience has shown us.

The remedy is to change the ball-valve for one of a different pattern, or to check the pressure of the water before it arrives at the ball-valve. This latter could be done by inserting a stop-cock and partially closing it, or choking the pipe in some way, or reducing the passage way in the tail part (not the outlet) of the ball-valve; but in adopting a remedy every consideration must be given as to what "Foghorn's" water company will be agreeable to.

It will be plainly seen that the opening of a cold-water tap must relieve the pressure at the ball-valve, for the cold-water taps are all in direct connexion with the supply-pipe, and take the water at a lower point. This relief, as "Foghorn" states, proves sufficient to cause a cessation of the noise. It is, of course, understood that this trouble is due to the water flowing in from the main the instant water is drawn from the cold-water cistern. This scarcely ever permits of the ball-valve opening to its full extent; if it did, then there would be no troublesome noises (assuming the ball-valve was of sufficient size)—no more than happens when the cistern is filled once or twice a day upon the intermittent system. This, it must be repeated, is the probable cause, to the best of our experience, but it does not follow that it is the correct solution in every case.

The Student's Column.

WARMING BUILDINGS BY HOT WATER. VIII.

EXAMPLE WORKS (HORTICULTURAL.)

IT must be clearly understood that these examples do not represent copies from which other works can be carried out, as in the first place the sketches are merely imaginary requirements. But in explaining these, the principle and general idea of the work can be correctly described, and this is all that is needed. When an apparatus has to be put up it is best when, or after, viewing the place to plan the arrangement of pipes, their disposition and quantity, without reference to any suggested examples, as in no two cases are the requirements exactly alike. This may sound as if the examples about to be given would convey no useful information, but this is not the case, for without dealing with a few complete works it is hard to convey to the inexperienced mind the connexion between the different separate subjects treated.

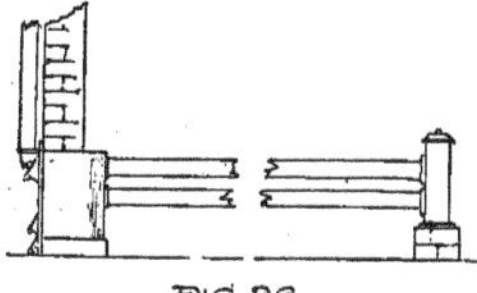

FIG 26.

The first example, fig. 26, shows about the most simple apparatus we have with a boiler in which coke or coal fuel is used. This does not represent the smallest style of boiler by any means, but the whole erection is simplicity itself. This simple structure is due in a great measure to the boiler, which is of the "Loughborough" pattern. This boiler, which has now been in use some little time (and will be referred to more fully presently), is of a shape which permits its being built in the substance of one of the walls of the greenhouse or conservatory. By this method of fixing the front of the boiler, with its feeding and stoking doors, and the smoke-nozzle, are outside the building, while the back of the boiler, with the connexions, show inside, so that the whole of the pipes can be used for radiating purposes. Ordinarily, a certain amount of pipe has to exist between the boiler and the house, and which has to be carefully covered or it will cause a waste of heat. It will be noticed that the design of the boiler is such that, although some part of it is within the house, yet all attention, stoking, &c., is done outside.

From the back of the boiler are carried flow and return pipes having a slight rise towards the further extremity, where they terminate in expansion box, as referred to in the last rticle. The pipes in a small apparatus like his would probably not exceed 3 in. diameter. he usual size for all medium and large-sized orks is 4 in. This is an apparatus that is conidered sufficiently simple for an amateur to rect himself, the pipe joints being made with ndiarubber rings. (These will be spoken of ater.) It can be just as easily carried round aree sides of a house as along one side only, if he necessary quantity of pipe and bends are rovided. No air-pipe would be needed if the expansion box is used and the pipes have a rise all the way. If more than two pipes be needed, the connexions can be effected, as will be shown presently.

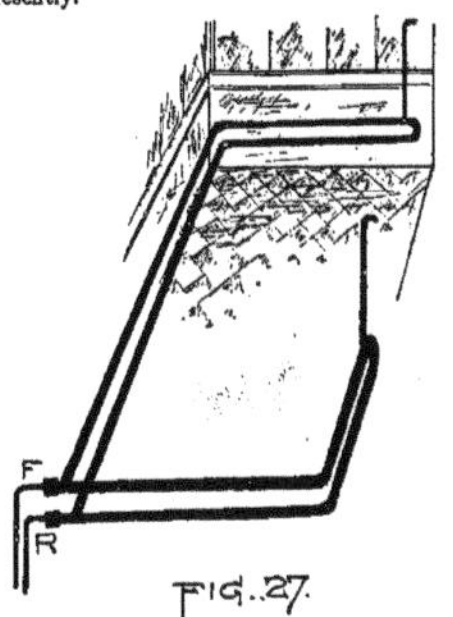

FIG. 27.

The next example, fig. 27, shows an apparatus to heat a small glass-house, the boiler situated outside the house somewhere; but we may assume it is not far away. It would also probably be somewhere below the house level. If this were a conservatory attached to a residence, the boiler might be in a cellar or basement-room near. In this case, the boiler would be of the independent kind, with the flow-pipe leaving the top (or the side, near the top) and the return entering at a low point, as fig. 28.

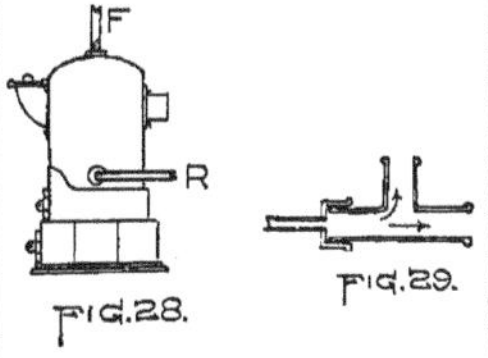

FIG. 28. FIG. 29.

The difference, however, between these pipes in this case, and that last explained, is that they should not be of full size,—viz., 3 in. or 4 in., until they enter the place to be heated.

Between the boiler and the radiating pipes in an apparatus like this the pipes would not require to be larger than 1½ in. Probably 1 in. would do, if the boiler was below, and the radiating pipes were not extensive, say not more than 40 ft. in all. This effects a saving in cost, and a deal of heat would be lost from these pipes, if large, and not carefully covered. Pipes which are not required for radiating purposes should always be covered with a poor heat conducting material, and, of course, it costs more to cover large pipes than small, and the large pipes answer no good purpose in a small apparatus like this.

The pipes now referred to, between boiler and radiating pipes, as they are small, would be of wrought iron, and in ordering the boiler, and also the cast pipe connexions, this must be remembered and prepared for, as otherwise no provision will be made for pipes that are to be screwed in. Both boiler and pipe makers will arrange for this if instructed. These pipes are run in the same manner as already described, that is, ascending everywhere.

The illustration shows the connecting pipes from the boiler entering the house at such a point that the radiating pipes have to branch off in different directions. Of course, if the connecting pipes can be brought in and connected to either extremity of the radiating pipes it would be better, but this example is given to show how branched services should be treated when needed.

There is nothing complex in connecting the branch services, especially in a small work like this. If a tee-piece be put at the angle where the connecting-pipes come, instead of the usual bend, a cap or socket drilled and tapped and fitted to the projecting end of the tee is all that is needed for the reception of the wrought-pipe. This practically leaves the two branches of the radiating pipes open for the water to circulate which way it chooses, as fig. 29. If the branches are of about equal lengths and working under the same conditions, the circulation may be expected to be fairly equal each way. If, however, as here shown, the branches are of unequal length, we may probably get unequal results, the shortest most likely "taking the lead," as it is termed, to the prejudice of the longer service, which will appear to be acting very sluggishly. In a larger apparatus any irregularity in the working of the different branches is controlled by stop-valves which have to be provided; but in this we can get sufficiently equal results by giving a little greater rise to the long branch than to the short one.

Air-tubes would have to be connected at each extremity as shown, these extending two or three feet above the level of the supply-cistern; ½ in.-tube would be quite large enough. The water-supply would be furnished by a small cistern placed in the most convenient position just above the level of the radiating-pipes. It is usually arranged for this cistern to be placed out of sight, behind rockery or plant staging. Of course, an expansion-box at each extremity would be very suitable, and dispense with the air-tubes, and supply-cistern, and provide the end supports, as already explained.

Sometimes it is desired to have three or four pipes on one side of the house, but only two on the other. The greater number of pipes would be upon the exposed side, the lesser number on the wall side, but this quantity is not usually required for greenhouses or conservatories, unless they are very wide or roomy. If three pipes are required, it is usually the flow that has the extra pipe, the return being single. The extra pipe is connected by a branch pipe, as

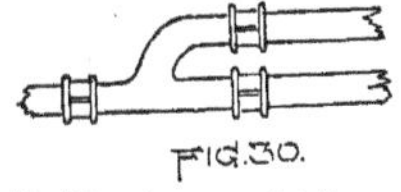

FIG. 30.

fig. 30. If four pipes are needed, they are not placed one above the other, as three pipes very commonly are; they are generally placed two and two, and they then consist of two flows and two returns, the flows on top, the returns below.

In fixing the boiler of this example apparatus, it is to be supposed that if placed in a cellar or basement-room, it can be connected with one of the residence chimneys by a pipe. The size of this pipe will be governed by the size of the smoke nozzle on the boiler; the makers putting that size which is most suitable. If the apparatus is to be a permanent affair the smoke-pipe should be of cast-iron, and although coke may be the usual fuel it is best to provide soot-doors in all the elbows used. This gives access for sweeping should it ever be needed, or should access be required for any other purpose. Wrought-iron smoke-pipe answers very well in dry situations, and if the fire is not let out all the warm weather. If the conditions are different to this, it will soon fail even if it be galvanised.

To effect the proper working of the furnace, the pipe joints and the connexion of the smoke-pipe with the chimney should be air-tight, so that we may consider that all the air entering the chimney has to first pass through the fire. Most boilers will, however, work without such precautions as this; but if it is possible to fix the boiler in this air-tight manner, it is best to do so. In fitting up the flue-pipe a damper must be put close down by the boiler, where it can be conveniently used. The fire-doors of the boiler are usually provided with a sort of hit-and-miss ventilator to fulfil the purpose of a damper; but an additional damper in the flue-pipe should be provided, and it should be a well-fitting one, if the boiler is to be regulated with any degree of nicety.

It will have been noticed that the boiler shown is of the upright variety, which, like the "Loughborough," is capable of taking a charge of fuel to last through the night without attention. This is an essential feature if the green-house has anything else but hardy plants in it. If the conservatory is heated for the sake of the plants, the night is the time when the boiler should do its best. If, on the other hand, heat is only needed to make the conservatory comfortable for occupation during the day, the night cold is not so much thought of; of course, in this latter case, only evergreen shrubs, &c., would be placed in it.

OBITUARY.

Mr. John Chesser.—The death is announced at Dorlin, Corstorphine, of Mr. John Chesser, architect, late Superintendent of Works to George Heriot's Trust. Born at Dalmeny, the deceased, on acquiring a knowledge of the joiner trade, crossed the Border, and while yet a young man held the post of master of works during the erection of some public buildings in Lincolnshire. On the death of his father he returned to Dalmeny, and succeeded him as Superintendent of Works on the estate of the late Earl of Rosebery. In 1858 Mr. Chesser was appointed Superintendent of Works to the Governors of Heriot's Hospital, in room of the late Mr. Alexander Black, and he continued to act in that capacity until about three years ago, when, on account of failing health, he resigned, and was granted a retiring allowance. During Mr. Chesser's term of office a large amount of Heriot Hospital ground had been feued, and in this connexion the late Superintendent of Works rendered valuable service, not only in connexion with the feuing of the land, but in preparing the ground and elevation plans. He also drew the plans for a number of the more recent Heriot Schools, the reorganisation of the Hospital School, and the reconstruction and extension of the Heriot-Watt College. The deceased, who is survived by a widow and grown-up family, was in his 73rd year.—*Scotsman.*

GENERAL BUILDING NEWS.

Willis's Rooms, St. James's.—This historical building (originally "Almack's") is now in course of alteration, and before many weeks are over will have been completely changed. The block of buildings has been acquired by Messrs. Robinson & Fisher, the auctioneers, of Old Bond-street, whose present premises are not sufficient for their business. The ground-floor is being converted into shops with mezzanines over, and the old ball-rooms will become sale-rooms for pictures and works of art. It is thought that this alteration in King-street, which is generally recognised as a centre for dealers in works of art, will help to further centralise the trade. A considerable portion of the block, at the end nearest St. James's-street, is being altered to form suitable premises for a first-class restaurant or a dining-club. The front to King-street will be refaced, and will have a more architectural treatment than heretofore. The alterations, of which we hope shortly to illustrate the plans and elevations, are being carried out by Messrs. W. Johnson & Co., from the designs and under the direction of Messrs. J. T. Wimperis & Arber, architects.

Restoration of Bonnx Abbey.—The ancient Abbey at Bourn is to be immediately restored. The work will be carried out in sections. Some months ago a committee was formed, having as its secretary Mr. R. M. Mills, who is a munificent subscriber to the cost. It is now announced that the response to the appeal made has been sufficient to justify the committee in giving instructions for the work to be immediately commenced.—*Leeds Mercury.*

New Bank, Leeds.—A branch of the London and Midland bank was opened in Kirkgate a few years ago, and in 1890 designs were prepared by Mr. William Bakewell, architect, of Leeds, for a new bank, which was opened at the commencement of this year, on a site opposite the market. The façade is executed in stone from the quarries at Idle and Morley. The building is Classical in character, with Corinthian columns and pilasters. The pediment over the entrance is surmounted by a statue of "Midas," and the tympanum of the pediment is enriched with carving; the arms of London and Leeds are carved in the sunk panels on each pedestal. The interior of the banking room has a dado, 5 ft. high, executed in walnut; the walls above are lined with Italian marble. The floor of the bank is laid with mosaic pavement. The banking-room is warmed by hot-water coils; the fresh air is admitted and passed through the coils of hot-water pipes. The vitiated air is extracted by a shaft prepared for the purpose. The strong-rooms are placed in the basement; and a hydraulic elevator is provided for the service of the bank. The contractors for the work are Messrs. Nicholson & Son, Barrand Bros., Moore, Heavyside, Emley, De Grelle Houdret, Appleyard, Shroeder, Nutt, Paylor, Oldroyd, Churton, Barratt & Russell, Ratcliff & Horner, Chatwood, and Elgood. Mr. Charles Goulden has acted as clerk of the works.

New Chancel, Parish Church, Emsworth, Hants.—On the 6th inst. the consecration took place of the new chancel just added to St. James's Parish Church, Emsworth. In November, 1890, the plans of Sir Arthur Blomfield, A.R.A., the Diocesan Architect, for the extension of the church at the east end, were approved, and on July 8 last the foundation-stone of the chancel was laid. The total cost of the work has been about 2,500*l.* The addition of the chancel has restored the church to something of its original form. When first built, about fifty years since, its ground-plan was cruciform, but the extension of the aisles to the outer walls of the transepts made it almost square. The new extension converts the church to the form of a Greek cross, and increases the sitting accommodation to just over 500. The style of the building is Late Norman, and the external walls are of flint with Bath stone dressings. Three bold arches have been cut in the old east wall communicating with the chancel, organ-chamber (on the north), and vestry (on the south), while between those three sections other arches have been constructed. The new chancel is 31 ft. in length and 25 ft. in width, and the vestry and organ-chamber are each 22 ft. by 17 ft. The former is approached from the nave by three steps, and separated from it by a low wall of stone. The altar is raised three steps above the choir level, and above the carved-oak table the east wall is pierced by three narrow windows filled with stained glass, the subjects of which are the "Crucifixion," the "Virgin Mother," and "St. James." A tesselated pavement has been provided in this part of the church. On the south side of the altar a sedilia, piscina, and credence table have been cut. The choir stalls and clergy seats are of pitch-pine, and accommodation is given for twenty-two choristers. Adjoining the northern pillar of the chancel arch is a pulpit, carved in alabaster, coloured marbles, and Bath stone. The body of the church has been repaved with wood blocks, and the old pews have given place to pitch-pine seats. The organ has been removed from the western end of the south aisle to the new organ-chamber, where room has been left for its extension. The windows have been filled with cathedral tinted glass, and the stained-glass window which formerly occupied the east end has been placed in another part of the church. A new heating system has been introduced.

Town Hall, Cleckheaton.—On the 10th inst. Cleckheaton Town Hall, which has been erected in the centre of the town, was formally opened. The building is in the Queen Anne style, and has been built from the designs of Messrs. Mawson & Hudson, architects, of Bradford. The interior arrangements of the building include a large hall, which is planned to accommodate 1,000 persons and 100 more in the orchestra, the latter having ample retiring-rooms. The Board-room is on the same floor. The Local Board offices are all situated on the ground floor underneath the large hall, and provision has been made for their enlargement at any future time if necessary. The basement is devoted to workshops for the gas and water departments of the Board, kitchen, &c., from which there is a lift in connexion with the large hall, and the entire building is lighted by electricity. The principal features of the façade are a massive tower, rising to a height of nearly 100 ft., and capped by a turret, a projecting oriel window which lights the principal room in the suite allotted to the Local Board, and a gable at the south corner with bay windows. The contractors for the work were:—Masons, Messrs. Holdsworth Bros., Cleckheaton; joiner and carpenter, Mr. W. Isherwood; plumber, Mr. T. W. Cragg, Cleckheaton; plasterers, Messrs. Metcalfe & Lockwood, Staincliffe; ironfounder, Mr. Robert Hird; painter and decorator, Mr. Squire Nutter, Cleckheaton; slaters, Messrs. Albert Hill & Son; electric lighting, Messrs. J. H. Holmes & Co., Newcastle-on-Tyne.

Proposed Restoration of St. Margaret's Church, Wetton.—It is proposed to restore the Church of St. Margaret, Wetton, Staffordshire, by the provision of new roof and ceiling, which are at present dilapidated and unsafe; new floor, the old being damp and rotten; the removal of an end gallery and partition, so opening up the Mediæval tower arch at present buried thereby; a new heating apparatus; the entire reseating of the church in lieu of the old deal pews; rebuilding of the organ; and making safe the interior of the tower, which contains bells of the dates 1690, 1703, and 1815. Plans have been submitted by Messrs. W. Sugden & Son, architects, Leek, and adopted.

Church of St. Anne, Ambergate, Derbyshire.—The new Church of St. Anne, at Ambergate, was opened on the 13th inst. by the Bishop of Southwell. The structure will accommodate 250 worshippers, and there is a schoolroom below. Mr. A. Coke Hill, of Derby, was the architect, and Mr. J. Glossop, of Ambergate, the contractor. The church is in the Early English style, with nave, chancel, organ-chamber, choir vestry, and clergy vestry, with bell-turret. The roof is covered with red tiles, while the walls are of Ambergate stone, lined with red brick.

Bishopthorpe Palace.—Alterations are being made at the Archbishop of York's Palace at Bishopthorpe. The old wooden floor in the chapel has been taken out, and a fireproof one substituted. Messrs. Mark Fawcett & Co. have been entrusted with the work. Mr. Ewan Christian is the architect.

FOREIGN AND COLONIAL.

France.—The Jury of Architecture of the Ecole des Beaux-Arts has given judgment on the competion opened for "Un Hôtel Général d'Association des Etudiants," awarding a medal to M. Lajoie, pupil of M. Laloux.——It is announced that the City of Paris is about to purchase, at the price of a million francs, the celebrated hôtel of the Archbishops of Sens, which will become a kind of dependency of the Carnavalet Museum.——The Louvre has acquired the original model executed by Rude for the bronze statue erected at Fixin (Côte d'Or) to the memory of Napoleon.——On April 21 a new art exhibition organised by the "Union Libérale des Artistes Français" is to be opened in the Palais des Arts Libéraux. It will remain open till June 20.——The fine collection of faience of the late M. Maillet du Boulay, formerly curator of antiquities at Rouen, has been acquired for the Louvre.——The "Nord" Railway Company proposes to commence shortly the arrangements for penetrating further into Paris with auxiliary lines serving the Halles Centrales and the Paris Opéra.——A fire which might have had serious consequences broke out last Saturday at the Sèvres Manufactory. The collections escaped, however, and the injury was only to *matériel* of the value of 50,000f. or thereabouts.——The work of dismantling the fortifications of Arras has been stopped by a general strike of the workmen engaged.——An international exhibition is to be opened at Bordeaux during this year.——At Tours there is to be an exhibition in May, chiefly connected with public instruction, hygiene &c. It will be open till August.——An industrial and artistic exhibition is to be held at Cannes in the months of March and April, and at Reims there is to be an art exhibition in the autumn, opening October 1.——M. Gerôme, the painter, has just finished a bust of Philippe Rousseau, to be set up in the garden of the Museum at Evreux.——M. André, the architect, has been commissioned by the Municipality of Lyons to design the monument to be erected there to the memory of the lyric poet Dupont.——The Minister of Public Instruction has appointed M. Degré Professor of Architecture at the Ecole Nationale des Beaux-Arts at Dijon.——The jury of architecture of the Ecole des Beaux-Arts has awarded the Edmond Labarre prize to M. Bardey, pupil of M. Guadet.——M. Maggesi, Honorary Director of the School of Sculpture at Bordeaux, has just died in that city. He was born at Carrara in 1807, and exhibited in the *Salons* of 1838, 1841, 1845, and 1857, and settled at Bordeaux in 1862. Among his numerous works are the marble statues of Montaigne and Montesquieu in the Place des Quinconces at Bordeaux; and eight busts or statues in the Museum at Bordeaux, especially "Jupiter Olympius" and "Giotto." In the Cathedral of St. André is to be seen the fine tomb which he executed for Cardinal de Cheverus. He also executed some of the colossal statues placed on the Palais de Justice, and the fine bust of the architect Louis which decorates the foyer of the theatre at Bordeaux.——The Minister of Public Instruction has granted a credit of 40,000 francs for the restoration of the ancient theatre at Orange. M. Formigé is the architect entrusted with the work.

Berlin.—The members of the Prussian Royal Academy had a special meeting to celebrate the Emperor's birthday. Herr Professor Otzen (Hon. Corresponding Member of the R.I.B.A.) was the orator for the day. In a lengthy harangue he treated of matters pertaining to the gradual development of church-building in Berlin. It may be noted that no less than twenty-five Protestant churches have been built or commenced within the city and suburbs of Berlin since the day on which Emperor William II. ascended the throne.——Anton von Werner will for the coming year 1892-3 again hold the president's chair in the "Verein Berliner Kuenstler." There was a close contest with a second candidate, Herr Karl Becker, President of the Prussian Royal Academy, who obtained 108 votes to Anton von Werner's 109. If Herr Becker had been elected the unpleasant relations between the Society and the Academy would probably have now seen an end, especially as the "Academy party" in the "Verein" is gradually but surely getting stronger.——During a business meeting of the "Verein Berliner Kuenstler" a large participation at the Chicago show was decided on. Berlin will be well represented as regards to quantity if not quality of work. Munich will send only a small collection of South German works of art, but it is to be a very select one.——The "Vereinigung Berliner Architekten" intends exhibiting at Chicago as a body, and will send a fairly representative collection of architectural work done in the city by its members. Each member of the Society has been invited to prepare drawings of work he has carried out during the last decade, special conditions as regards the scale of the drawings, and the different sizes of sheets, being added. The drawings are to become the property of the "Vereinigung," who will (on their return from the Chicago show) use them as a basis for a larger collection of members' work planned some time back. This latter collection of members' work, which will be kept up to date by the regular contributions of drawings of all the more important buildings erected year after year, will some day be a valuable one for the historians of the future.——Herr Kayser, at a meeting of the "Vereinigung Berliner Architekten," reported on the progress made by the special committee of members of the society occupied with framing a new code of building regulations intended to replace the very unpopular one at present in force. When ready the different paragraphs of the new code are to be put before the authorities in the form of propositions, and it is hoped that they will be passed with but few alterations as early as 1893.——The proposal to erect a so-called "Provincial Museum" in Berlin, which has been before the municipal authorities for some time, has found favour. The financial part of the question has been solved, and a site for the new museum selected in the city proper. A competition for a suitable design for the building (which is to cover some 2,000 square mètres of ground) is to be opened at once; three premiums (125*l.*, 75*l.*, and 50*l.*) are to be awarded.——The two Court playhouses, the opera-house and the theatre, will be subjected to some extensive alterations in accordance with the requirements of the Prussian police regulations relating to the protection of human life in theatres. In the budget put before the Prussian Parliament a vote of 25,000*l.* is asked for this purpose, and will have to be granted, as the houses would otherwise have to be closed. The regulations require the alterations to be complete by October, 1893.——The large building of the Imperial Bank of Germany (the "Reichsbank"), generally considered to be one of the finest in the city, is to be extended. The foundations for a new wing are to be taken in hand at once, and the new rooms are to be occupied in 1894.——At the "Kunstgewerbe Museum" a special exhibition of Japanese work has been opened for a charitable purpose (relief works in Japan). Some sixty private collectors, among them a number of the members of the Royal Family, headed by the Emperor, have lent objects of interest.——Messrs. Hennicke & v. d. Hude, a firm of architects of old standing and repute, have dissolved partnership. Among the work done by the firm we note the Lessing Theatre and Central Hotel, both in Berlin.——An exceedingly popular member of the profession, Herr Giesenberg, the manager and junior partner of Messrs. Ende & Boeckmann, died last month after a tedious illness of some duration. He had been senior assistant to the late Professor Lucae at the time of the erection of the Frankfort Opera House, and had, after the death of his chief,—which occurred during the time of the erection,—the completion and entire interior decoration of this building in his hands. In 1884 he was one of the four winners classed equal in the great competition for the so-called "Museum Island" design.

MISCELLANEOUS.

NATIONAL REGISTRATION OF PLUMBERS.—A meeting of the local district council was held at the Guildhall (by kind permission of the Mayor) on the 8th inst., under the presidency of Mr. T. J. Pope, architect. There was a good attendance of representatives, and the following, amongst other resolutions, was adopted:—"That this council, recognising the close connexion between the public health and the plumber, and thus the necessity in the public interest for members of the craft of plumbing to be properly acquainted with the laws of sanitation, expresses its warm approval of the efforts being made by the Worshipful Company of Plumbers to obtain the sanction of Parliament to a Bill for the registration of plumbers and for the efficient examination of all entering the trade, and desires that local members of Parliament be requested to support the same." It was also resolved to form a local committee, composed of five members and a secretary, the public and master operative plumbers being equally represented, at Bath, Cheltenham, and Gloucester.

ROYAL METEOROLOGICAL SOCIETY.—The usual monthly meeting of this Society was held on Wednesday evening last, at the Institution of Civil Engineers, 25, Great George-street, Westminster, Dr. C. Theodore Williams, President, in the chair. Four papers were read, the first one being on "The Untenability of an Atmospheric Hypothesis of Epidemics," by the Hon. Rollo Russell, M.A., F.R.Met.Soc. The author is of opinion that no kind of epidemic or plague is conveyed by the general atmosphere, but that all epidemics are caused by human conditions and communications capable of control. In this paper he investigates the manner of the propagation of influenza, and gives the dates of the outbreaks in 1890 at a large number of islands and other places in various parts of the world. Mr. Russell says that there is no definite or known atmospheric quality or movement on which the hypothesis of atmospheric conveyance can rest, and when closely approached it is found to be no more available than a phantom. Neither lower nor upper currents have ever taken a year to cross Europe from east to west, or adjusted their progress to the varying rate of human intercourse. Like other maladies of high infective capacity, influenza has spread most easily, other things being equal, in cold, calm weather, when ventilation in houses and railway-cars is at a minimum, and when perhaps the breathing organs are most open to attack. But large and rapid communications seem to be of much more importance than mere climatic conditions. Across frozen and snow-covered countries and tropical regions it is conveyed at a speed corresponding, not with the movements of the atmosphere, but with the movements of population and merchandise. Its indifference to soil and air, apart from human habits depending on these, seems to eliminate all considerations of outside natural surroundings, and to leave only personal infectiveness, with all which this implies of subtle transmission, to account for its propagation. In the second paper, on "The Origin of Influenza Epidemics," by Mr. H. Harries, F.R.Met.Soc., another theory was propounded. The author has made an investigation into the facts connected with the great eruption of Krakatoa in 1883, and the atmospheric phenomena which were the direct outcome of that catastrophe. He has come to the conclusion that the dust derived from the interior of the earth may be considered the principal factor concerned in the propagation of the recent influenza epidemics, and that, as this volcanic dust invaded the lower levels of the atmosphere, so a peculiar form of sickness assailed man and beast. The third paper was a "Report on the Phonological Observations for 1891," by Mr. E. Mawley, F.R.Met.Soc.; and the fourth a "Note on a Lightning Discharge at Thornbury, Gloucestershire, on July 22, 1891," by Dr. E. H. Cook.

"L'AIR FROID" SYSTEM.—We have received a description and illustrations of what is called "L'Air Froid System of Ventilation," the main object of which is to prevent the condensation of moisture on the internal surface of shop-windows, by which they are often obscured. The device consists simply of fresh-air inlets arranged below the window and foul-air outlets above it, and would doubtless achieve the end principally aimed at by the author, Mr. G. C. Vernon Inkpen. The system, as a means of ventilation, would have but small effect, as the action would be confined almost entirely to the portion of the shop atmosphere immediately contiguous to the window. A patent has been granted for this invention, but, as in England, such a grant is no evidence of validity, we do not hesitate to express our doubt as to the invention possessing sufficient novelty to maintain the patent.

AUTOMATIC "IN-AND-OUT" TURNSTILE.—Mr. G. Williamson, the patentee of this turnstile, which we noticed briefly last week, sends us a sketch diagram of the mechanism, from which we see that we misunderstood the description formerly sent, and did not do justice to the ingenuity and usefulness of the turnstile. The ingress and egress are through the same opening, the space occupied by the opposite arm being permanently blocked in the usual manner for egress turnstiles, the motion being capable of reversal for ingress on the insertion of the coin. The method by which the turnstile sets itself, after the insertion of the coin has allowed it to pass a quarter revolution, is ingenious and simple, the only weak point being the dependence on the action of a spring, which is always an undesirable element in mechanism, though it cannot always be dispensed with.

LIVERPOOL ENGINEERING SOCIETY.—The eighth ordinary meeting of this Society for the present session was held on February 10, at the Royal Institution. Mr. Thomas Morris, F.G.S., read a paper entitled "Engineers' Tests for Iron considered, and Suggestions for Standard uniform Tests." The author showed by tables of numerous engineers' tests how engineers would ask for different tensile strains for the same class of work, adding that the iron must be equal to some known "brand," as though the iron produced in the localities named was uniform in quality. He paid a high tribute to the reduction of area test, as being one that gave more consolation to the engineer in case of work coming to grief than any other test specified. The elongation test, which he said was only another form of test for ductility, was not to be depended upon with the same ease and comfort as contraction of area, and the manner in which the former test was specified by nearly all engineers was anything but creditable. He treated the "limit of elasticity test" with disfavour almost amounting to ridicule. His suggestions for "standard uniform tests and conditions" were put in the simplest form, and were thoroughly explained to those present. The discussion was adjourned to the next meeting.

CIVIL AND MECHANICAL ENGINEERS' SOCIETY.—At the meeting of this Society on Wednesday evening last, a paper on "Gas Producers" was read by Mr. R. Booth, M.I.M.E. The author first of all dealt with the increased attention which has lately been given to the economical use of fuel, and the possibilities which lay ready to hand for avoiding smoke and mitigating the fog nuisance by means of the use of gaseous fuel. He pointed out that it had been satisfactorily proved that the discharge of black smoke from factory chimneys could be entirely obviated by using gas instead of solid fuel, but the application of gas to domestic purposes did not come within the scope of his paper. He then proceeded to compare the chemical and physical problems presented by the two systems of burning coal from a broad point of view, pointing out that the process of combustion was by no means a simple one,—that while, considered as a process of oxidation, the amount of heat was invariable, the intensity varied with the rate at which the oxidation took place.

A PERFECT SCREW.—What is claimed to be a perfect screw has recently been made by Professor Rowlands, of the Johns Hopkins University, in the United States. This screw forms part of a dividing machine of wonderful accuracy which the Professor has devised. It is 17 in. long, 1¼ in. in diameter, and has twenty threads to the inch. It is described as being made of "Jessop tool steel," from which we gather that the material has been sent from Sheffield. It was cut in a lathe and then ground with fine emery for three weeks in oil and water kept at a constant temperature. The dividing machine will rule 100,000 lines to the inch on highly polished speculum metal; and it is said a 1,000,000 lines to the inch can be ruled if required; 110,000 lines to the inch have been done. The cutting part is a diamond.

THE ENGLISH IRON TRADE.—The English iron market remains in a quiescent state. There is still great want of animation on the Scotch warrant market, and in the Cleveland district there is a lessened demand for crude material. The hematite pig-iron trade is still depressed. Manufactured iron is in limited inquiry, and Welsh bars are slightly lower than last week. The tin-plate market remains dull. In steel there is an increased call for heavy sections, which have again been advanced, but other descriptions exhibit little alteration. Shipbuilding is tolerably active, except on the north-east coast. Engineers are only moderately employed; the strike on the Tyne still shows no signs of termination. The coal trade is quiet.—*Iron.*

THE BROOKLYN BRIDGE has long been insufficient for the traffic between Manhattan and Long Island, and a Bill is now being brought forward in the New York State Legislature by which the East River Bridge Company and the Union Elevated Railway Company seek power to build two bridges across the strait which is called by New Yorkers the East River. Twenty-five million dollars is the capital set apart for the undertaking.

LEGAL.

CASE UNDER METROPOLIS MANAGEMENT ACT, 1878.

HOUSE FRONTING MORE THAN ONE STREET: CROWN LANDS.

MR. JAMES POLLOCK, builder, Mottingham, was summoned at the Woolwich Police-court, on the 5th instant, by the London County Council, for not setting back the external fence of the forecourt or other space in front of a house on the east side of a footway leading from Chislehurst Park to Lee.

Mr. Chilvers, from the Solicitor's department, supported the summons, and called a surveyor, who proved the erection of the fence at less than the prescribed distance from the centre of the footway.

The witness on cross-examination admitted the house fronted Chislehurst Park, and only had a flank wall abutting on the footway.

Mr. Sampson, solicitor for the defence, submitted that sections 6 and 8 of the above-named Act applied only to the forecourt or other space in front of a house, and not to a piece of land at the side; and, further, that as the land on which the fence was erected was Crown property, the Council could not proceed without the consent of her Majesty's Commissioners of Woods and Forests, as provided by section 27 of the Act.

Mr. Chilvers contended that that section did not apply to a Crown lessee, and that the summons was in respect of the fence and not the land; also that in the lease held by defendant it was provided that the powers of the late Metropolitan Board of Works should be complied with.

The magistrate, Mr. Marsham, held that a house could front three or four roads, and that a Crown lessee was not exempt; and he ordered the fence to be set back in a month, and allowed 2*l.* 2*s.* for costs; but, on application, he granted a special case.

MEETINGS.

SATURDAY, FEBRUARY 20.

Architectural Association.—Visit to the Imperial Institute, South Kensington, by permission of the architect, Mr. T. E. Collcutt. 8 p.m.

MONDAY, FEBRUARY 22.

Royal Institute of British Architects.—Messrs. R. Herbert Carpenter, F.S.A., James Powell, N. H. J. Westlake, F.S.A., and Clement Heaton on "Painted and Stained Glass." 8 p.m.

Royal Academy of Arts.—Dr. A. S. Murray on "Archaic Compared with Archaistic Sculpture." III. 8 p.m.

Liverpool Architectural Society.—Mr. James Dod on "Light and Air."

COMPETITIONS, CONTRACTS, AND PUBLIC APPOINTMENTS.

COMPETITIONS.

Nature of Work.	By whom Advertised.	Premium.	Designs to be delivered.
Intermediate School, Bridgend	Committee	20l. 10s.	Mar. 9
*Two Swimming Baths, &c. Frederick-st.	Rotherham T. C.	Not stated	Mar. 16
*Laying-out Public Park	Corp. of Newport, Mon.	52l. 10s. and 21l.	Mar. 25
*Construction of Bridge over Canal	Corp. of Bootle	100l. and 52l. 10s.	June 1

CONTRACTS.

Nature of Work or Materials.	By whom Required.	Architect, Surveyor or Engineer.	Tenders to be delivered.
*Roadmaking and Paving Works	Willesden Loc. Bd.	O. Claude Robson	Feb. 23
Flint Road Metal	Southampton Corp.	W. B. G. Bennett	do.
Mission Church, Calder Grove, near Wakefield	....	W. S. Barber	do.
Junior Schools, Caretaker's House, Willington Quay	Wallsend School Board	Wm. Hope	do.
Drainage, Workhouse, Ponteland, Newcastle-on-Tyne	Castle Ward Union	W. Lister Newcombe	do.
Stables and Depot at Horfield	Bristol Tramway and Carriage Co. Lim.	Official	do.
*Removal of House Refuse, &c.	St. Pancras Vestry	do.	do.
Supply of Timber	G. W. R. Co.	do.	Feb. 24
Jetty Extension, &c.	Stonehouse Pool Impt. Commrs.	....	do.
Cast-iron Water Mains, Treval, near Torpoint	St. Germans U.R.S.A.	S. P. Hosking	do.
Drainage Works	Newcastle-u-Lyme T.C.	Jas. Pattison	do.
Station Buildings and Goods' Yard, Ribbleton	Lancs. & Yorks. Ry.	Official	Feb. 25
*Supply of Gas Fittings	Vestry of St. Mary, Islington	do.	do.
*Iron Staircase at Workhouse	Birmingham Guardns	do.	do.
*Repairs at Workhouse, Borough	St. Saviour's Union	Jarvis & Son	do.
Wood Paving	Gateshead Impt. Comrs.	J. Bower	do.
Cast-iron Pipes (400 tons)	Thurlstone (near Sheffield) Local Board	G. & O. H. Crowther	do.
New Schools, Still House-lane, Bedminster	Bristol School Board	W. V. Gough	Feb. 26
*New Parochial Offices	Battersea Vestry	E. W. Mountford	do.
Schools and appurtenances at Methodist Church, Blackhill, co. Durham	Rev. J. Elliott	Joseph Shields	Feb. 27
*Works and Materials	Mortlake Dist. Highway Board	H. Richards	Feb. 29
*Works and Repairs to Foot and Carriage-ways	Limehouse B. of W.	Official	do.
*Public Baths	Borough of Shrewsbury	do.	do.
*Purchase and Pulling-down building Materials	School Bd. for London	do.	do.
Street Work	Chertsey R.S.A.	do.	do.
*Wood Paving Blocks	Paddington Vestry	do.	do.
*Thames Ballast, Sand, and Cement	do.	do.	do.
Thirteen Houses, Theresa-street, Blaydon-on-Tyne	Blaydon Co-op. Soc.	do.	do.
*Works and Materials	Hendon Local Board	S. S. Grimley	do.
Re-building Church, Chacewater	....	E. Sedding	do.
*Supplying and Laying Victoria Stone and Kerbing	Farnham Local Board	R. F. Hankins	do.
Thirteen Houses and Completion of thirty-three others, The Graig, Pontypridd	....	T. R. Phillips	Mar. 1
Granite Road Metal, &c.	Lower Strafforth and Tickhill High. Bd.	Official	do.
*Works and Materials	Lewisham Bd. of Wks.	do.	do.
Landing Stage, Promenade Pier, Teignmouth, Devon	Devon Steamship Co.	J. C. Inglis	do.

CONTRACTS.—*Continued.*

Nature of Work or Materials.	By whom Required.	Architect, Surveyor, or Engineer.	Tenders to be delivered.
Road-metal, Flagging, Kerbs, &c.	Plymouth Corp.	G. D. Bellamy	Mar. 1
Road Works	Wigton Highway Bd.	J. Sibson	do.
*Pipe Sewers, &c.	Southend Loc. Bd.	F. Dodd	do.
New Schools, Ogmore Valley, near Bridgend	Llangeinor Sch. Bd.	G. F. Lambert	Mar. 2
Private Street Improvement Works	Halifax Corp.	R. S. Escott	do.
Six Through Dwelling-houses, Halifax	....	C. F. L. Horsfall & Son	do.
*Pipe Sewer, &c.	Fulham Vestry	J. P. Norrington	do.
*Making-up and Paving Roads	do.	W. Sykes	do.
*30,000 Paving Bricks	Bognor Loc. Bd.	Official	Mar. 3
*Circular Gasholder-tank	Rugby Gas Co.	do.	Mar. 4
*Oak Fencing	Southgate Local Board	C. G. Lawson	do.
*Maintenance and Repairs to Roads	Kent County Council	Official	Mar. 5
Oblique Bridge, Blackpool-gate, Bewcastle	Longtown (Cumberland) Highway Bd.	R. Maxwell	do.
Concrete and Brick Gasholder Tank (No. 2)	Sheffield Gas Co.	F. W. Stevenson	do.
Wrought-iron Roof, Kirkgate Market	Leeds Corp.	T. Hewson	do.
*Works and Materials	St. Giles B. of W.	Official	Mar. 7
*Making-up Roads	Rotherhithe Vestry	do.	Mar. 8
*Wrought-iron Fencing	Boro' of West Ham	do.	do.
*Completing Stores, Dwelling-house, &c.	....	C. Dunch	do.
*Works and Materials	Battersea Vestry	J. T. Pilditch	do.
*Supplies, Collection of House Refuse, &c.	West Ham Council	Lewis Angell	do.
*Asphalte Works	Edmonton Loc. Bd.	Official	do.
*Works and Materials	Sheffield Town Coun.	C. F. Wike	Mar. 9
*Making-up Roads	Hornsey Loc. Bd.	T. de Courcy Meade	Mar. 11
*Sewerage Works	do.	do.	do.
*Two Cottages	do.	do.	do.
*Works and Materials	do.	do.	do.
*Iron Fencing, with Gates	do.	do.	do.
Extension of Schools, Tylorstown, and other work	Ystradyfodwg Sch. Bd.	J. Rees	Mar. 12
*Sewerage Works	Corp. of Durban, Natal	W. H. Radford	Mar. 15
*Road Materials and Tools	Bedfordshire C. C.	Official	Mar. 17
*Church, Millbrook, Cornwall	....	G. H. Fellowes Prynne	No date
*Supply of School Furniture	Smethwick Sch. Bd.	Official	do.
Doctor's House, Morpeth	Ashington Med. Soc.	W. J. Charlton	do.
Convalescent Home, Hexham	....	Johnson & Hick	do.
New Buildings, Harrogate	Harlow Manor Hydropathic Co. Lim.	H. A. Cheers	do.
Two Cottages, Willbrighton, Newport, Salop	Sir T. F. Boughey	W. B. Wedge	do.
Girls' School, Castle Eden Colliery, near Newcastle-on-Tyne	Rev. J. Burdon	....	do.
Road Work, near Cadoxton, Cardiff	S. Rooney	....	do.
House and Workshop, Stainford-street, Leeds	W. Watson	....	do.
Eight Houses, Dolly-lane, Leeds	....	C. F. Wilkinson	do.

PUBLIC APPOINTMENTS.

Nature of Appointment.	By whom Advertised.	Salary.	Applications to be in.
*Assistant Surveyor	Kettering L. B.	100l.	Feb. 23
*Clerk of Works	Hornsey Sch. Bd.	3l. 3s.	do.
*Extra Assistant City Engineer	Cape Town Corp.	275l.	Feb. 24
*Clerk of Works	Canterbury U.S.A.	....	Feb. 27
*Inspector of Nuisances	Brentford Loc. Bd.	100l.	Feb. 29
*Second Assistant Surveyor	Croydon County Boro'	100l.	Mar. 1
*Sanitary Inspector	Hanley County Boro'	104l.	Mar. 8

Those marked with an Asterisk (*) are advertised in this Number. *Competitions*, p. iv. *Contracts*, pp. iv., vi., viii., ix. & xxiii. *Public Appointments*, p. xx.

TUESDAY, FEBRUARY 23.

Institution of Civil Engineers. — (1) Mr. W. T. Douglass on "The Bishop Rock Lighthouses." (2) Mr. David C. Salmond on "The Illumination by Gas of Tory Island Lighthouse, Co. Donegal." 8 p.m. The meeting will be adjourned at 9 p.m., when the President and Council will hold a reception in the libraries.

Society of Arts (Applied Art Section). — Mr. J. William Tonks on "Artistic Treatment of Jewellery: Jewel and Address Caskets." 8 p.m.

Builders' Clerks' Benevolent Institution.—Twenty-fifth Annual General Meeting of Donors and Subscribers. 7.30 p.m.

Sanitary Institute (Lectures for Sanitary Officers).—Mr. J. Wright Clarke on "Details of Plumbers' Work." 8 p.m.

WEDNESDAY, FEBRUARY 24.

Carpenters' Hall, London Wall.—Professor A. Wynter Blyth on "Sanitary Appliances." 8 p.m. (*Admission free.*)

British Museum.—Miss Eugénie Sellers on "Greek Sculpture: Sculptures from Bassae." III. 2.30 p.m.

Society of Arts.—Mr. Ernest Hart on "Ancient and Modern Art Pottery of Japan." 8 p.m.

Liverpool Engineering Society.—Adjourned Discussion on Mr. Thomas Morris's paper on "Engineers' Tests for Iron considered, and Suggestions for Standard Uniform Tests." 8 p.m.

THURSDAY, FEBRUARY 25.

Society of Antiquaries.—8.30 p.m.

Institution of Electrical Engineers.—8 p.m.

FRIDAY, FEBRUARY 26.

Royal Academy of Arts.—Professor J. H. Middleton on "Michael Angelo." I. 8 p.m.

Institution of Civil Engineers (Students' Meeting).—Mr. G. H. Sheffield on "The Construction and Efficiency of Locomotive Boilers." 7.30 p.m.

Sanitary Institute (Lectures for Sanitary Officers).—Mr. Charles Jones on "Scavenging, Disposal of Refuse." 8 p.m.

Institute of Certified Carpenters.—7.30 p.m.

SATURDAY, FEBRUARY 27.

Builders' Foremen and Clerks of Works Institution.—Annual Dinner, Holborn Restaurant. 6 p.m.

Edinburgh Architectural Association.—Visit to St. Nicholas Church, Dalkeith and to Newbattle Abbey.

RECENT PATENTS:

ABSTRACTS OF SPECIFICATIONS.

3,797.—Cement: *G. H. Skelsey.*—This patent refers to a process of manufacturing Portland cement from chalk to be found in large quantities near Hull and other places. An ordinary wash-mill in combination with an edge-runner mill, made with specially-constructed heavy runners, is employed. The chalk is weighed into the required quantities before it is passed to the edge-runner mill, where it is mixed with a proportion of water and ground into a thin paste of the required gravity, and then is passed to a wash-mill, in which it is mixed with a certain proportion of clay. The manufacture is then proceeded with in the ordinary manner. The inventor claims that cement made in this way can be produced at much less than the usual cost.

3,877.—Window Ventilation: *C. R. Green.*—This patent refers to an improved method of window ventilation effected by means of a series of holes bored in the sash-frame where the top sash shuts against it when closed. Further arrangements for carrying out the invention are fully described in the specification.

3,908.—Fireplaces: *J. W. Lewis.*—This invention relates to the construction and arrangement of the back parts of domestic fireplaces so that the fireclay or like back block may be made separately from, and if desired much thicker than, the baffle block. Means are described for connecting the same together and to the firebox.

4,424.—Ventilators: *A. W. Kershaw.*—The inventor claims that an improved ventilator for the admission of fresh air is made by combining two forms of inlet ventilation, the one part after the form of the Sheringham or box inlet, and the other part the application to the same of the inventor's patent diffusers. The said inlet ventilator consists of a frame for building or fixing in wall, of a face-plate with sides hinged at foot, or sliding in and out of frame, for opening and closing, and of the above patent diffusers.

14,570.—Glazing Bars: *J. Jeffreys.*—This refers to an improvement in glazing bars for fixing glass on roofs, &c., to form a water-tight covering, and consists of the combination of two separate bars to form a channelled sash bar, the insertion of an elastic packing between the two bars to equalise the pressure, and an arrangement for securing an even line when seen from below.

18,757.—Fireplaces: *A. C. Freemant.*—This specification relates to what is described as an improved method of inducing and increasing up-draught and preventing down-draught in fireplaces. This is effected by providing a front cover or screen of sheet-metal (iron-plate) as described. Above the same is a bar or rod which may be elongated by a screwed socket-fitting or by a slide arrangement for the purpose of adjusting the height between the screen itself and the mantel-piece, to which a screw clamp or like fitting may be applied in connexion with the adjustable rod.

NEW APPLICATIONS FOR LETTERS PATENTS.

February 1.—1,929, H. Stewart, Ventilating Sewers, &c., and Disinfecting or Deodorising the Gases therefrom.—1,942, S. Renschel, Fastening Devices for Handles of Furniture, &c.—1,945, A. Smith and J. Emery, Centre Revolving Ball in Taps.

February 2.—1,961, W. Dransfield, Water and Gas Pipe Hooks.—1,966, R. Hunter and J. Turnbull, Cooking Ranges.—1,978, J. Shubrook and W. Belemore, Fire-grates or Stoves.—2,003, R. Esplin, Hinges.—2,009, J. Brook, Chimney-cowls.—2,011, K. Dieterich, Wainscoting.—2,018, W. Day and E. Eden, Safety Ladder Hook.—2,033, C. Baker and Others, composition Material forming Boards, Slabs, Linings, &c., in Substitution for Wood, &c.—2,047, J. Price, jun., Pipe-joints.

February 3.—2,085, A. Bremner, Wood Screws.—2,058, H. Penn, Socket-bolts for Doors, &c.—2,091, W. Blackhand and H. Charles, Door-nobs, &c.—2,094, J. Bolding, Automatic or Self-acting Valve and Index, constructed in such a manner as to cause the siphon of a flushing-tank or cistern to discharge its contents, and simultaneously to register such discharge.—2,110, J. Harrison, Sash-fasteners.

February 4.—2,131, F. Stokes, continuous treatment of cement, &c., and in the lining of kilns and furnaces for burning materials of a basic character.—2,123, C. Kaye and J. Whitehead, increasing and regulating the draught in ordinary Fireplaces.—2,134, C. Horton, Water-closets.—2,137, C. Crompton and G. Taylor, Window-catch.—2,161, A. Kershaw, Ventilators.—2,201, R. Clark, Varnish.

February 5. — 2,224, G. Spencer, Window Sash-fastener.—2,232, G. Haskins, Spring Hinges for automatically returning movable parts of structural detail to normal position.—2,239, G. Cartwright, Plane Iron-fastener.—2,248, E. Weber, Hardening Tools.—2,250, T. White, Burning of Bricks and Cements.—2,291, F. Martin, Door Furniture.

February 6.—2,322, S. Cooper, Hoists or Elevators.—2,325, W. Pitt, Folding-gates.—2,333, F. Kress, Devices for holding centres in making masonry vaults.—2,344, R. Batey, Door-locks.

PROVISIONAL SPECIFICATIONS ACCEPTED.

20,332, A. Spaulding, Flexible Doors.—21,074, F. Hart, Measuring and proportionally describing graphically Sections of Tunnels, Arches, and Bridges; also Openings generally of limited height and width.—22,141, E. and C. Howl, Brick-kilns, &c.—22,330, A. Rowan, Cleansing Paint Brushes.—22,424, G. Goldsmith and J. Stephen, preventing Down Draughts in Chimneys.—22,754, W. Hoyte, Lock Nuts.—23, F. Collins, Bolts for Emergency Exit Doors, &c.—25, A. Milne, Bolts for Emergency Exit Doors, &c.—187, G. Skinner and J. Hill, attaching Door-knobs or Handles to their Spindles.—432, A. Ford, Bolts for Windows, &c.—530, J. Wilkinson, Down Draughts in Chimneys.—608, R. Spring, preventing Waste of Water in or from Cisterns.—663, L. Dove, Automatic Disinfecting Apparatus for attaching to Flushing Cisterns, &c.—732, C. Griffiths, Stoves.—762, S. Bearder, Stops for Joiners' and like Benches.—804, W. Byers, Sliding Bolts for securing Doors, Windows, &c. 805, F. Smythies, Sash-fasteners.—814, J. Faulds, Masons' Tools.—827, W. Orr, Metallic Girders.—869, G. Dunell, construction of Metallic Flooring or Decking for Bridges, Viaducts, or Buildings.—1,024, J. Evans, utilising Waste Heat for Heating Buildings.—1,195, A. Willard, Artificial Stone.

COMPLETE SPECIFICATIONS ACCEPTED.

(Open to Opposition for Two Months.)

1,050, H. Lake, Fire-grates.—2,882, G. Scollay, Paint or Paint-stocks. — 2,819, J. Nicholls, Window-sash

Holder.—5,772, C. Huelser, Clay Presses, for making tiles, &c.—12,760, J. Pullan and others, Brick-pressing Machines.—17,891, A. Emery, Automatic Locking Sash-fastener.—19,910, C. Knapp, Automatic Sash-lift and Lock.

SOME RECENT SALES OF PROPERTY:

ESTATE EXCHANGE REPORT.

FEBRUARY 4.—By *Worsfold & Hayward*: "Holly Lodge," near Dover, f., 570*l.*; a plot of freehold land, St. Margaret's Bay, 125*l.*

FEBRUARY 9.—By *Thurgood & Martin*: F.g.r. of 13*l.*, Lordship-villas, Wood-green, with reversion in 71 yrs., 260*l.*; f.g.r. of 18*l.*, with reversion in 71 yrs., Acacia-villas, 360*l.*; f.g.r. of 16*l.*, with reversion in 71 yrs., William-ter., 320*l.*; f.g.r. of 143*l.*, with reversion in 83 yrs., Alfred-ter., &c., 2,692*l.*; f.g.r. of 173*l.* 5s., with reversion in 71 yrs., Harriet-villas, &c., 3,577*l.*; f.g.r. of 9*l.*, with reversion in 72 yrs., Clifton-ter., &c., 180*l.*; f.g.r. of 21*l.*, with reversion in 73 yrs., Clifton-ter., 445*l.*—By *C. P. Whiteley*: 26, Ingersoll-rd., Shepherd's-bush, u.t. 89 yrs., g.r. 6*l.* 6s., 320*l.*

FEBRUARY 10.—By *A. Richards*: F.g.r. of 45*l.*, with reversion in 76 yrs., Crown-st., Camberwell, 900*l.*; f.g.r. of 40*l.*, with reversion in 76 yrs., Millgrove-st., Battersea, 580*l.*; f.g.r. of 12*l.*, with reversion in 75 yrs., Chatham-st., 250*l.*; f.g.r. of 30*l.*, with reversion in 76 yrs., Blucher-st., Walworth, 560*l.*—By *A. & A. Field*: 30 and 34, Spital-st., Mile-end, f., r. 83*l.* 4s., 810*l.*; 28 and 29, Dorset-st., Spitalfields, u.t. 27 yrs., 100*l.*—By *A. Barton*: 5 and 6, Fassett-sq., Dalston, u.t. 60 yrs., g.r. 10*l.*, r. 63*l.*, 625*l.*—By *D. L. Gooch*: F.g.r. of 15*l.* 10s., Upper Cheyne-row, Chelsea, 365*l.*; f.g.r. of 28*l.* 1s., with reversion in 98 yrs., Holland-villas, Lewisham, 665*l.*; f.g.r. of 27*l.* 10s., with reversion in 98 yrs., Pk. View-villas, 635*l.*

FEBRUARY 11.—By *C. C. & T. Moore*: 89 to 95 odd, Cable-st., St. George's-in-East, f., r. 72*l.*, 1,000*l.*; 30 and 32, Grove-st., Commercial-rd., E., u.t. 9 yrs., g.r. 6*l.*, 75*l.*—By *Newbon & Co.*: 40 and 41, Poet's-rd., Canonbury, u.t. 57 yrs., g.r. 14*l.*, r. 102*l.*, 865*l.*; 41, St. Paul's-rd., Camden-rd., u.t. 53 yrs., g.r. 7*l.*, 440*l.*; 10, Kenmore-rd., Hackney, u.t. 84 yrs., g.r. 6*l.* 10s., r. 36*l.*, 225*l.*; 54, Buckland-st., Hoxton, u.t. 43 yrs., g.r. 5*l.*, r. 36*l.*, 350*l.*; 86 and 88, Marlborough-rd., Holloway, u.t. 55 yrs., g.r. 12*l.* 12s., r. 58*l.*, 510*l.*—By *W. & F. Houghton*: 61, Down's-rd., Clapton, f., 1,500*l.*; 64, Grosvenor-pk.-rd., Walthamstow, f., 300*l.*; freehold residence, Church-hill, 1,100*l.*; a plot of freehold land, 105*l.*—By *Stimson & Sons*: 38, Spa-rd., Bermondsey, r. 24*l.* 14s.; and l.g.r. of 42*l.*, u.t. 24 yrs., 300*l.*; 127 to 133 odd, Spa-rd., u.t. 26 yrs., g.r. 15*l.* 4s., r. 135*l.*, 510*l.*; 24, Frean-st., u.t. 22 yrs., no g.r., r. 26*l.*, 105*l.*; 40 and 41, Frean-st., u.t. 23 yrs., g.r. 5*l.* 5s., 220*l.*; 53 and 54, Frean-st., u.t. 24 yrs., g.r. 6*l.*, 210*l.*; 7, Willow-walk, u.t. 24 yrs., g.r. 4*l.*, 205*l.*; 243 and 245, Fort-rd., u.t. 44 yrs., g.r. 9*l.*, 390*l.*; 18, Beatrice-rd., u.t. 43 yrs., g.r. 5*l.*, 200*l.*; 49 to 59 odd, Beatrice-rd., u.t. 41 yrs., g.r. 21*l.*, 1,440*l.*; 50 and 52, Anchor-st., u.t. 46 yrs., g.r. 6*l.*, 390*l.*; 317, Lynton-rd., u.t. 46 yrs., g.r. 3*l.*, 220*l.*; 171 and 177, Weston-st., u.t. 13 yrs., g.r. 7*l.* 10s., 105*l.*; 191, Weston-st., u.t. 17 yrs., g.r. 2*l.* 15s., 38*l.*; 20, Kinglake-st., Old Kent-rd., u.t. 15 yrs., g.r. 3*l.*, 65*l.*; 1 to 7 odd, Bagshot-st., u.t. 15 yrs., g.r. 9*l.* 5s., 255*l.*; 27, Mina-rd., u.t. 19 yrs., g.r. 3*l.* 16s., 130*l.*; 105 and 107, Coburg-rd., u.t. 15 yrs., g.r. 9*l.* 2s., 225*l.*; 219 to 229 odd, St. George's-rd., Peckham, u.t. 60 yrs., g.r. 17*l.* 10s., 1,250*l.*; 57, Cator-st., u.t. 70 yrs., g.r. 4*l.* 4s., 130*l.*; 71, 73, and 75, Cator-st., u.t. 70 yrs., g.r. 12*l.*, 370*l.*; 76, Clayton-rd., u.t. 82 yrs., g.r. 5*l.*, 275*l.*; 102 to 106, New Church-st., Bermondsey, u.t. 6 yrs., g.r. 3*l.*, 245*l.*; "The Chestnuts," Grove-hill, Dulwich, f., 1,200*l.*

[*Contractions used in these lists.*—F.g.r. for freehold ground-rent; l.g.r. for leasehold ground-rent; i.g.r. for improved ground-rent; g.r. for ground-rent; r. for rent; f. for freehold; c. for copyhold; l. for leasehold; e.r. for estimated rental; u.t. for unexpired term; p.a. for per annum; yrs. for years; st. for street; rd. for road; sq. for square; pl. for place; ter. for terrace; cres. for crescent; yd. for yard, &c.]

PRICES CURRENT OF MATERIALS.

TIMBER.		
Greenheart, B.G. ton	9/0/0	0/0/0
Teak, E.I. ... load	9/10/0	15/0/0
Sequoia, U.S. ft. cu.	2/3	3/0
Ash, Canada load	2/10/0	4/0/0
Birch, do.	3/5/0	4/10/0
Elm, do.	3/10/0	4/15/0
Fir, Dantsic, &c.	2/0/0	3/10/0
Oak, do.	3/0/0	5/0/0
Canada	5/0/0	7/0/0
Pine, Canada red	2/10/0	3/10/0
Do. yellow	2/10/0	6/0/0
Lath, Dantsic, fath	5/5/0	6/10/0
St. Petersburg	5/10/0	7/10/0
Deals, Finland, 2nd & 1st std 100	8/10/0	10/10/0
Do. 4th & 3rd ..	7/10/0	8/10/0
Do. Riga	6/10/0	8/0/0
St. Petersburg, 1st yellow ..	11/0/0	15/0/0
Do. 2nd yellow	8/10/0	10/10/0
Do. white	7/10/0	10/10/0
Swedish	7/15/0	16/0/0
White Sea	8/10/0	18/0/0
Canada, Pine 1st	20/0/0	30/0/0
Do. do. 2nd	14/10/0	16/10/0
Do. do. 3rd, &c.	8/5/0	10/10/0
Do. Spruce, 1st	8/10/0	11/0/0
Do. do. 3rd & 2nd	6/15/0	8/0/0
New Brunswick	7/0/0	7/10/0
Battens, all kinds	3/10/0	15/10/0
Flooring Boards, sq., 1 in. prep. 1st	0/8/6	0/14/6
Do. 2nd	0/7/6	0/11/1
Other qualities	0/5/0	0/8/0
Cedar, Cuba .. ft.	/3½	/4½
Honduras, &c.	/2½	/4
Mahogany, Cuba.	/4½	/6½
St. Domingo, cargo av	/4½	2/0
Mexican do. do	/4	/6
Tobasco do. do	/5½	/7
Honduras do. ..	/5½	/6½
Box, Turkey ton	4/0/0	15/0/0
Rose, Rio	10/0/0	20/0/0
Bahia	9/0/0	18/0/0
Satin, St. Domingo .... ft.	0/0/8	0/1/3

TIMBER (continued).		
Satin, Porto Rico	0/0/8	0/1/6
Walnut, Italian ..	0/0/3½	0/0/7
METALS.		
Iron—Pig, in Scotland .... ton	2/3/0	2/3/1½
Bar, Welsh, in London	6/0/0	6/10/0
Do. do. at works in Wales	5/10/0	6/0/0
Do. Staffordshire, in London	6/5/0	6/15/0
Copper—British, cake and ingot	47/0/0	47/10/0
Best selected ..	48/0/0	49/0/0
Sheets, strong ..	57/0/0	58/0/0
Chili, bars	44/0/3	44/13/9
Yellow Metal lb.	0/0/5¼	0/0/5½
Lead — Pig, Spanish .... ton	10/12/6	0/0/0
English, com. brands	10/15/0	10/17/6
Sheet, English, 3 lbs. per sq. ft. and upwards ..	12/15/0	0/0/0
Pipe	13/5/0	0/0/0
Zinc — English sheet ...... ton	25/5/0	0/0/0
Vieille Montagne	25/15/0	0/0/0
Tin—Straits	88/17/6	84/0/0
Australian	89/0/0	89/2/6
English Ingots	92/10/0	92/15/0
OILS.		
Linseed ...... ton	18/17/6	19/2/6
Cocoanut, Cochin	25/15/0	26/0/0
Do. Ceylon	23/0/0	0/0/0
Palm, Lagos	23/0/0	0/0/0
Rapeseed, English pale	26/10/0	0/0/0
Do. brown	24/15/0	0/0/0
Cottonseed ref. ..	17/15/0	18/0/0
Oleine	0/0/0	0/0/0
Lubricating, U.S.	4/10/0	5/10/0
Do. refined	6/0/0	10/0/0
Tar — Stockholm barrel	0/19/0	1/0/0
Archangel	0/12/6	0/0/0

TENDERS.

[Communications for insertion under this heading must reach us *not later than 12 noon on Thursdays.*]

BELPER.—Accepted for the construction of a brick-service reservoir, laying water mains, &c., at Duffield, for the Rural Sanitary Authority. Mr. W. H. Radford, C.E., Angel-row, Nottingham. Quantities by Mr. W. H. Radford:—
Iron Pipes—Stanton Iron Works Company, Limited, near Nottingham £1,395 6 0
General Contract—G. F. Todd, Derby 1,268 0 0

BLACKWOOD (Mon.).—For the construction of a new road at Rhiw-sir-David, for the Mynyddislwyn Highway Board. Mr. Seth Phillips, Surveyor, Pantycelyn, Pontllanfraith, Mon.:—

Goldsworthy £197 0 0	James Thomas	£132 10 6
Rees Morgan 150 5 6	Wm. Lewis, Bargoed*	125 0 0

* Accepted.

BRIGHTON.—For alterations to Chatfield's Hotel, West-street, Brighton. Messrs. Dorey & Carden, architects:—

Patching & Sons	£430 0	Wilson	£410 0
Taylor	420 0	V. P. Freeman	396 6
J. J. G. Saunders	419 10	C. & F. Cheesman*	393 0

* Accepted.

BRISTOL.—For the erection of the "White Swan" hotel, Bristol. Mr. W. P. Glascodine(?), architect, Bristol. Quantities by Mr. A. Barratt, Bristol:—

H. A. Forse	£3,475	Robertson	£3,126
Neale Bros.	3,330	Stephens, Bastow, & Co. ...	3,018
Veals	3,320	G. Humphreys	3,050
E. Walters	3,300	E. Love	2,985
Easterbrook & Son	3,280	R. Wilkins & Son	2,944
Cowlin & Son	3,143	T. R. Brown	2,725
E. T. Hatherly	3,137	J. Perkins (accepted)	2,665

[All of Bristol.]

CARDIFF.—For the construction of a sewer and formation of new roads, Romilly-crescent, Canton, for the Canton Land Syndicate. Messrs. Veall & Sant, architects, 6, Arcade-chambers, High-street, Cardiff. Quantities by the architects:—

H. & F. Osmond	£343 8 6	Wm. Symonds	£290 0 0
T. Jones Davies	292 14 2	Thos. Rees (accepted) ..	275 8 3

[All of Cardiff.]

DURHAM.—For the alteration and enlargement of East Hetton Board School, for the Coxhoe School Board. Mr. John Henry, architect, 11, North Bailey, Durham. Quantities by the architect:—

Lodge & Sons	£630 0 0	M. R. Draper	£553 2 0
W. Grainger	604 6 0	J. Heslop	519 7 0
J. Shepherd	545 0 0	Bell & Sanderson, Coxhoe (accepted) ..	500 0 0
Elliott & Lazenby	544 19 0		

HATCHAM (Surrey).—For the erection of St. Catherine's Church, Hatcham. Messrs. Stock, Page, & Stock, Architects, 9, Denman-street, London Bridge, S.E. Messrs. Widnell & Trollope, surveyors, Westminster:—

Petw Bros.	£23,170	H. L. Holloway	£21,680
Stimpson	23,050	Dove Bros.	21,455
Stephens, Bastow, & Co. ..	22,999	B. E. Nightingale	21,380
W. Downs	22,820	Brown, Son, & Blomfield	20,850
S. & W. Pattinson	22,334	Goddard & Son	20,833
T. Rider & Son	21,928	Rudd & Son	20,400
Collins	21,780	Higgs & Hill	19,984
S. J. Jerrard	21,779		

HORNSEY.—For new schools, &c., at Frobisher-road, Hornsey, for the Hornsey School Board. Mr. Chas. Bell, architect. Quantities by Mr. Hy. Lovegrove:—

	Total.		
Ansley	£23,027	*£151	†£1,965
Payne & Son	22,926	100	463
Bryan & Son	22,813	725	1,383
Rowe Bros.	22,788	300	1,400
Lawrence & Sons	22,012	153	2,195
J. W. Dixon	21,860	80	1,775
B. E. Nightingale	21,776	162	1,720
S. G. Bailey	21,691	110	1,375
Maddox Bros.	21,649	150	2,100
Allen & Son	21,250	173	1,800
C. Dearing & Son	21,220	430	2,000
Holliday & Greenwood	21,137	—	1,977
Tenbure	21,076	183	1,564
Hepsell	19,300	165	1,450
Coxhead	19,229	243	1,130
C. Wall, Chelsea (accepted) ..	18,883	165	1,411
F. Stevens	17,308	183	993

* Less for York stone instead of granite.
† Extra for cream coloured glazed bricks over stock brick.

LEEDS.—Accepted for the erection of a butcher's shop and two cottages, at Lofthouse, for the Leeds Industrial Co-operative Society, Limited. Mr. W. A. Hobson, architect, 82, Albion-street, Leeds:—
Brick and Mason.—John Bloks, Outwood £315 0 0
Joiner.—Wm. Holmes, Lake Lock 106 10 0
Plasterer.—Ed. Heslop, Armley 18 19 0
Plumber.—G. Wilson, Rothwell 15 15 0
Slaters.—J. Atkinson & Son, Leeds 22 0 0
Painter.—E. Watkin, Rothwell 7 0 0
£485 4 6

LEWES.—For the erection of a police station and petty sessional room at Hurst Green, for the East Sussex County Council. Mr. Henry Card, County Surveyor, Lewes:—

J. & V. Daniels	£2,046 2 0	Taylor Bros.	£1,843 0 0
F. Piper	1,969 10 0	H. Knock	1,730 0 0
A. Comport	1,960 0 0	P. Peters, Horsham*	1,680 0 0
A. W. Nunn	1,919 0 0	* Accepted.	

LONDON.—For a workhouse for 1,000 aged and infirm inmates at East Dulwich, for the Guardians of the Poor of the parish of Saint Giles, Camberwell. Messrs. Wilson, Son, & Aldwinckle, architects, 1, Victoria-street, S.W. Quantities supplied by Mr. R. C. Gleed, 5, Adelaide-place, London Bridge, E.C.:—

Garlick & Horton	£77,640	H. Kellett	£66,457
Reed, Blight, & Co.	72,777	H. L. Holloway	66,215
W. Brooks	72,079	J. Allen & Sons	65,888
Balaam Bros.	71,806	Leslie & Co.	65,264
J. T. Chappell	69,420	Braide & Co.	65,000
Lawrance & Son	68,040	Kirk & Randall	61,928
R. Ballard	67,600	F. & H. F. Higgs*	61,000

* Accepted.

LONDON.—For the erection of business premises and printing works at Tower-hill, E.C., for Messrs. Chas. Skipper & East. Messrs. Beazley & Burrows, Architects, 17, Victoria-street, S.W. Quantities by Messrs. Pryce, Cuxson, & Leigh:—

Higgs & Hill	£36,980	Lovatt	£35,209
Patman & Sons	36,368	Mowlem	34,877
Bywaters	35,902	Morter*	34,232
Ashby & Horner	35,761	Patman & Fotheringham*	33,900
Holloway Bros.	35,286	Grover & Sons	33,291
Nightingale	35,282	Boyce	32,400

* Too late.

LONDON.—For the erection of a Public Library, Church-street, Stoke Newington, for the Library Commissioners. Messrs. H. H. Bridgman & Goss, architects, 42, Poultry, E.C.:—

Clark & Bracey	£3,262	Ashby Bros.	£2,790
J. Stapleton	3,218	Neave & Neave	2,770
Josolyne & Young	2,963	Wm. Shurmur	2,745
T. Emmett	2,847	S. H. Lamble	2,729
Harris & Wardrop	2,836	Godfrey & Son	2,697
E. Toms	2,790	Wm. Dabbs (accepted)	2,648

LONDON.—Accepted for alterations to stables, and building loose-box, coach-house, and open shed, at Balham, for Mr. Cooke:—
W. Lang, Grove-road £140 0 0

LONDON.—Accepted for rebuilding the "Prince William Henry" public-house, Blackfriars-road, S.E. (exclusive of sundry fittings), for Mr. W. H. Burney. Mr. W. M. Brutton, architect, 171, Queen Victoria-street, E.C.:—
Romaine & Co. £2,500 0 0

LONDON.—For alterations to the "Rose and Crown" public-house, Collingwood-road, S.E., for Mr. J. Hall. Mr. W. M. Brutton, architect, 171, Queen Victoria-street, E.C.:—

J. Mills	£469	Pritchard & Renwick	£342
C. Ansell	449	Whitehead & Co. (accepted)	340

LONDON.—For alterations to the "Pilgrim" public-house, Upper Kennington-lane, S.E., for Messrs. Grimes & Co. Mr. W. M. Brutton, architect, 171, Queen Victoria-street, E.C.:—

Burman & Sons	£345	Pritchard & Renwick*	£284
Edwards & Medway	335	* Accepted.	

LONDON.—For the erection of a warehouse, Gold Hawk-road, Shepherd's-bush, W. Mr. J. H. Richardson, architect. Quantities by Mr. Henry Lovegrove:—

Brass & Son	£3,188	Adamson & Son	£2,675
Swan	3,163	Chamberlen Bros.*	2,672
Kirk & Randall	2,723	Tennant & Co.	2,646
Marks	2,690	* Accepted.	

LONDON.—For the erection of Pope's Laundry, Shepherd's-bush. Mr. J. H. Richardson, architect. Quantities by Mr. H. Lovegrove:—

Chamberlen Bros.	£615	Lyford	£520
Heyward	582	Mauder	509
Towse	568		

LONDON.—For alterations and additions to "Foulden Lodge," Clapton, for Dr. Frederick Wallace. Mr. W. A. Finch, architect, 78, Finsbury-pavement, E.C.:—

Thomerson & Son	£598 10	A. Porter	£496 0
Godfrey & Son	514 0	J. Hicks, Stamford-hill, N. (Accepted)	478 0
Jarvis & Son	499 10		

LONDON.—For alterations, &c., to the "Adelphi Stores," 75, Strand, W.C., for the Brewery Assets Corporation, Limited. Mr. H. I. Newton, architect, 49, Victoria-street, Westminster, S.W.:—

F. Mark	£1,089	R. Plummer	£865
Edwards & Medway	1,072	Charles Dearing & Son, Islington (accepted)	860
Patman & Fotheringham	1,054		

LONDON.—Accepted for alterations, &c., to the "Prince's Head," Buckingham-street, Strand, W.C., for the Brewery Assets Corporation, Limited. Mr. H. I. Newton, architect, 49, Victoria-street, Westminster, S.W.:—
Edwards & Medway, Kennington-cross £670

LONDON.—Accepted for alterations, &c., to the "Moorgate," Moorgate-street, E.C., for the Brewery Assets Corporation, Limited. Mr. H. I. Newton, architect, 49, Victoria-street, Westminster, S.W.:—
R. Plummer, City £724

LONDON.—Accepted for alterations, &c., to the "Cannon," Cannon-street, for the Brewery Assets Corporation, Limited. Mr. H. I. Newton, architect, 49, Victoria-street, Westminster, S.W.:—
R. Plummer, City £350

LONDON.—Accepted for alterations, &c., to the "Opera" Haymarket, S.W., for Miss Farmer. Mr. H. I. Newton, architect, 49, Victoria-street, Westminster, S.W.:—
Edwards & Medway, Kennington-cross £977

LONDON.—Accepted for re-building No. 6, Old Jewry. Mr. Delissa Joseph, architect, 17, Basinghall-street:—
G. H. & A. Bywaters £10,680 0 0

LONDON.—Accepted for building the Hampstead Synagogue. Mr. Delissa Joseph, architect, 17, Basinghall-street:—
John Allen & Sons £9,162 10 0

LONDON.—For decorative, sanitary, and structural works at the Chief Rabbi's residence, 22, Finsbury-square. Mr. Delissa Joseph, architect, 17, Basinghall-street:—
Clarke & Mannooch .... £625 | C. F. Kearley (accepted) £617

* LONDON.—For building a studio at the rear of No. 2, Hanover-terrace, Regent's Park, and for decorative, sanitary, and structural work to No. 2, Hanover-terrace. Mr. Delissa Joseph, architect, No. 17, Basinghall-street:—

Studio.

A. W. Hammond	£277	Prestige*	£248
Watson	257	* Accepted.	

Decorative Work.
Hackforth (accepted) £122 0 0

Sanitary and Structural.
Clarke & Mannooch (accepted) £286 0 0

LONDON.—For the construction of the Hackney-wick, &c., relief sewer, for the London County Council. Mr. A. R. Binnie, Engineer:—

J. Mowlem & Co. ..	£53,221 0 6	G. Pauling	£37,105 7 9
T. Adams	45,484 5 6	E. & W. Iles	36,600 0 0
J. Dickson	41,640 8 6	F. D. Bentley	31,046 14 0

LONDON.—For the erection of a Fire Brigade Station at East Dulwich, for the London County Council. Mr. Thomas Blashill, Architect:—

J. Garrett & Son	£14,080	Scharien & Co.	£11,427
Stimpson & Co.	11,540	G. Munday & Son	10,480

LONDON.—For the erection of a caretaker's lodge in St. Pancras-gardens, for the Works Committee of the Vestry:—

Vernall & Griffith	£1,093 0	Steed	£786 0
Toms	888 0	Scrivener & Co.	771 0
Bangs	870 0	Wall & Co.	750 15
Gould & Brand	814 0	Rowe Bros., Camden Town (accepted)	697 0
Drew	719 0		

NORTH CRAY (Kent).—For repairs to "Baxley" farm-house, North Cray, Kent. Mr. St. Pierre Harris, architect and surveyor, 1, Basinghall-street, E.C.:—

R. A. Lowe	£311 15	H. Marchant	£220 0
Somerford & Son	259 0	C. F. Stebbings, Sidcup*	189 0
T. Knight	241 0	* Accepted.	

NOTTINGHAM.—For the completion of Industrial Art Gallery, &c., at Nottingham Castle. Mr. Herbert Walker, C.E., architect, Nottingham:—

Hodson & Sons	£1,984 10	F. Evans	£1,927 0
Bell & Sons	1,932 0	J. Hutchinson	1,900 0
W. Woodsend	1,919 10	T. Fish & Sons	1,894 0
H. Vickers	1,930 0	J. G. Thomas (accepted)	1,833 0

[All of Nottingham.]

ORPINGTON.—For decorative repairs and re-instatements to private residence at Chislehurst-road, Orpington, Kent. Mr. St. Pierre Harris, architect and surveyor, 1, Basinghall-street, E.C.:—

F. Wood	£247	D. Payne	£169
R. A. Lowe	200	Somerford & Son, Orpington*	159
Stubbings & Pannett	192		
W. R. Taylor	170	* Accepted.	

READING.—For alterations to the Corn Exchange and Market Passage, for the Corporation of Reading. Mr. Arthur E. Collins, Borough Engineer and Surveyor:—

Botterill & Son	£2,798	Winter & Pitt	£2,592
G. H. Tucker	2,788	T. H. Kingerlee, Oxford* ..	2,517

* Accepted.

READING.—For warming the Corn Exchange by hot water. Mr. Arthur E. Collins, Borough Engineer and Surveyor:—

Jones & Attwood	£385 0 0	Hart & Sons	£312 12 4
Williams & Sons	373 10 0	E. Margrett	294 10 0
J. G. Spencer	335 17 0	G. H. Tucker, Reading*	287 7 0

* Accepted.

READING.—For laying wood block floor in the Corn Exchange. Mr. Arthur E. Collins, Borough Engineer and Surveyor:—
Wood Block Flooring Co. (accepted) £160 0 0

RHYL.—Accepted for the construction of a new public cemetery at Penymaes, for the Improvement Commissioners. Mr. Robt. Hughes, Town Surveyor, Rhyl:—
Excavating for Roads, &c.—Jones & Roberts, Rhyl £177 2 0
Lodge, Entrance Gates, Front Walls, &c.—Jones & Roberts, Rhyl 661 10 0
Wrought-iron Unclimbable Railings and Fixing.—Economic Fencing Co., Billiter House, E.C. ... 111 10 0
Drainage.—Isaac Hughes, Rhyl 240 7 3

SOUTHAMPTON.—For rebuilding shop and premises, No. 23, Above Bar, Southampton, for Messrs. G. A. Permain & Co. Mr. William Burrough Hill, architect, Southampton:—

Wright & Son	£2,578 3	Stevens & Co.	£2,077 0
Udall & Co.	2,220 0	Hinton	2,050 0
Sanders	2,198 0	Crook & Son	1,983 0
J. Bull, Sons, & Co., Ltd.	2,130 0	Cawte*	1,922 0
Morgan, Isted, & Morgan	2,098 0		

* Accepted. [All of Southampton.]

SOUTHAMPTON.—For rebuilding shop and premises, No. 82, High-street, for Mr. Edward Cox. Mr. William Burrough Hill, architect, Southampton:—

Sanders	£774 0	Rowland & Son	£690 12
Morgan, Isted, & Morgan	750 0	Crook & Son	648 10
H. Stevens & Co.	725 0	Witt*	547 10
Hinton	720 0		

* Accepted. [All of Southampton.]

SOUTH SHIELDS.—For the erection of a dwelling-house, for Mr. Bendry, Baring-street, South Shields. Mr. Henry Grieves, architect, Albany-chambers, South Shields:—

Goodwin & Son	£491 0 0	J. W. Robertson	£470 0 0
S. Sheriff	575 0 0	Wm. Scott	464 10 0
Wm. Winter	562 0 0	J. Ross (accepted)	453 19 6

[All of South Shields.]

WEST HARTON (South Shields).—For the erection of the Victoria Hotel, West Harton, for Mr. Matthew Wood. Quantities by Messrs. Debenham & Morton, Sunderland. Mr. Henry Grieves, architect, Albany-chambers, South Shields:—

S. Sheriff	£2,072 16 5	R. Summerbell, Tyne Dock*	£1,783 0 0
R. Allison	2,046 13 1	Wm. Scott	1,768 3 6
Stirzar & Son	1,978 0 0		
Jas. Young	1,900 8 0		

* Accepted.

SUBSCRIBERS in LONDON and the SUBURBS, by prepaying at the Publishing Office, 19s. per annum (or 4s. 9d. per quarter), can ensure receiving "The Builder" by *Friday Morning's post.*

The Builder Cathedral Series.

A SERIES of Illustrations of all the English and Welsh Cathedrals is now being published in "The Builder," and will be continued, in the first issue of every month, until completed.

The Illustrations in each case include an exterior view, reproduced from a drawing specially prepared for the purpose; and a ground plan, to a large scale, shaded to indicate the date and style of the several parts.

There is also a short descriptive article, having reference to the Church and its surroundings, with sketches of some of the details, &c.

No trouble or expense is being spared to make this series in every sense *artistic and trustworthy*, and as such it is confidently offered to all lovers of Ecclesiastical Architecture.

1891.

1. Canterbury	Jan. 3.	7. Salisbury	July 4.
2. Lichfield	Feb. 7.	8. Bristol	Aug. 1.
3. St. Alban's	Mar. 7.	9. Norwich	Sept. 5.
4. Peterborough	April 4.	10. Rochester	Oct. 3.
5. Wells	May 2.	11. Lincoln	Nov. 7.
6. Exeter	June 6.	12. Gloucester	Dec. 5.

1892.

13. St. Paul's	Jan. 2.	16. Ely	April 2.
14. Hereford	Feb. 6.	17. Llandaff	May 7.
15. Chichester	Mar. 5.	18. Oxford	June 4.

(Further arrangements will be duly Announced.)

Price FOURPENCE each (by post 4½d.), except Nos. 1 and 2, which are *out of print*; but the VIEW, PLAN, AND DESCRIPTION of CANTERBURY and of LICHFIELD have been re-printed, and they can now be had, price ONE SHILLING each set; by post, 1s. 2d.

THE REREDOS, ST. PAUL'S.
Reprinted from "The Builder," January 26, 1889 (15 in. by 11½ in.), on stout paper, unfolded, for framing, 6d.; by post, 8d.

PORTFOLIOS,
for Preserving the Plates unfolded, 2s. 6d.; by post, 3s.

London: Office of "The Builder," 46, Catherine-street, W.C.

PUBLISHER'S NOTICES.

Registered Telegraphic Address, 'The Builder,' London.

CHARGES FOR ADVERTISEMENTS.

SITUATIONS VACANT, PARTNERSHIPS, APPRENTICESHIPS TRADE, AND GENERAL ADVERTISEMENTS.
Six lines (about fifty words) or under .... 4s. 6d.
Each additional line (about ten words) .... 0s. 6d.

Terms for Series of Trade Advertisements, also for Special Advertisements on front page, Competitions, Contracts, Sales by Auction, &c. may be obtained on application to the Publisher.

SITUATIONS WANTED.
FOUR Lines (About thirty words) or under .... 2s. 6d.
Each additional line (about ten words) .... 0s. 6d.

PREPAYMENT IS ABSOLUTELY NECESSARY.

*** Stamps must not be sent, but all small sums should be remitted by Cash in Registered Letter or by Money Order, payable at the Post-office, Covent-garden, W.C. to

DOUGLAS FOURDRINIER, Publisher,
Addressed to No. 46, Catherine-street, W.C.

Advertisements for the current week's issue must reach the Office before THREE o'clock p.m. on THURSDAY, but those intended for the front Page should be in by TWELVE noon on WEDNESDAY.

SPECIAL.—ALTERATIONS IN STANDING ADVERTISEMENTS or ORDERS TO DISCONTINUE same must reach the Office before TEN o'clock on WEDNESDAY mornings.

The Publisher cannot be responsible for DRAWINGS, TESTIMONIALS, &c. left at the Office in reply to Advertisements, and strongly recommends that of the latter COPIES ONLY should be sent.

PERSONS Advertising in "The Builder" may have *Replies addressed to the Office*, 46, Catherine-street, Covent Garden, W.C. *free of charge*. Letters will be forwarded if addressed envelopes are sent, together with sufficient stamps to cover the postage.

AN EDITION Printed on THIN PAPER, for FOREIGN and COLONIAL CIRCULATION, is issued every week.

READING CASES, { Now ready. NINEPENCE EACH. By Post (carefully packed), 1s.

TERMS OF SUBSCRIPTION.

"THE BUILDER" is supplied direct from the Office to residents in any part of the United Kingdom at the rate of 19s. per annum Prepaid. To all parts of Europe, America, Australia, and New Zealand, 26s. per annum. To India, China, Ceylon, &c., 30s. per annum. Remittances payable to DOUGLAS FOURDRINIER, Publisher, No. 46, Catherine-street, W.C.

TO CORRESPONDENTS.

M. & Co.—T. D. M'C. (the question is a legal one, and must depend mainly on the terms of the lease).—"Architect" (no name enclosed, and we have reason for doubting whether the writer has a claim to that signature).—R. H. R.—F. R. F. (thanks).

All statements of facts, lists of tenders, &c., must be accompanied by the name and address of the sender, not necessarily for publication.

We are compelled to decline pointing out books and giving addresses.

Note.—The responsibility of signed articles, and papers read at public meetings, rests, of course, with the authors.

We cannot undertake to return rejected communications.

Letters or communications (beyond mere news-items) which have been duplicated for other journals, are NOT DESIRED.

All communications regarding literary and artistic matter should be addressed to THE EDITOR; all communications relating to advertisements and other exclusively business matters should be addressed to THE PUBLISHER, and not to the Editor.

The Builder.

VOL. LXII. No 2560. SATURDAY, FEBRUARY 27, 1892.

ILLUSTRATIONS.

Illustrations of Old Chester : II., Watergate-street.—Drawn by Mr. T. P. Ivison .... *Double-Page Ink-Photo.*
Stanford Hall, Nottinghamshire.—Mr. Westley H. Fletcher, Architect .... *Double-Page Photo-Litho.*
Examples of Saracenic Architecture, in illustration of Professor Aitchison's Royal Academy Lectures :—
Entrance of the Fountain Kaid-Bey, Cairo ; Dome of Tomb, Karateh ; Shop at Tantah, Egypt .... *Double-Page Ink-Photo*
Examples of Saracenic Ornament :—
Mosaics from Mosque at Cordova ; Wall-diaper, Hall of the Ambassadors, Alhambra .... *Double-Page Ink-Photo.*

Blocks in Text.

Sundial, Wrest, Bedfordshire .... Page 152
Garden-gate, Tissington, Derby 152
Gatepiers, Canons Ashby, Northants 153
Lead Figure of Cupid, Melbourne, Derby .... Page 154
Mosque of Sultan Hassan, Cairo : Section 157
Plan of a Cairo House 158
Diagrams in Student's Column : Heating by Hot Water 166-167

CONTENTS.

Formal Gardens 151
Notes 154
Saracenic Architecture 156
Royal Institute of British Architects 159
Old Chester.—II. Watergate-street 162
Stanford Hall, Nottinghamshire 162
Examples of Saracenic Architecture and Ornament 162
The Architectural Association : Domestic Electric Lighting 163
Demonstrations on Greek Sculpture at the British Museum 164
The Architectural Association's Spring Visits 165
British Archæological Association 165
London County Council 165
Competitions 165
Builders' Clerks' Benevolent Institution 165
Concrete for Artisans' Dwellings 166
Liverpool Motive Power 166
The Extinguishing of Fires 166
Student's Column.—Warming Buildings by Hot Water, IX. 166
Surveyorships 167
General Building News 167
Stained Glass and Decoration 168
Sanitary and Engineering News 168
Foreign and Colonial 168
Miscellaneous 169
Meetings 170
Recent Patents 170
Some Recent Sales of Property 171

Formal Gardens.

THE appearance of another book on gardens by an architect* is a further instance of the interest now taken in this subject by the members of the "art or profession" of architecture, and of a growing determination on their part to have the design of the garden, so far as it is connected with a building, in their own hands. Mr. Blomfield's book, however, though a small one in size, is not to be considered quite on the same platform as the late J. D. Sedding's "Garden-craft," which we noticed a short time since. Sedding's work, charming and suggestive as it is, is more a rhapsody than a treatise from which any principle or aim can be deduced; it was obviously written quickly and easily, and, as we observed at the time, though delightful reading, there is not much to be learned from it. Mr. Blomfield's book, begun we believe a good while before the other, is closely reasoned and gives evidence of a considerable amount of study of the older literary works on the subject. The illustrations, reproduced from sketches by Mr. F. Inigo Thomas, are very pretty examples of book-illustration on a small scale. Four of them, by the kindness of the publishers, are reproduced with this article.

The main object of the book is to recommend the treatment of the garden in connexion with a residence as a piece of design, on more or less architectural principles, and to discredit the principles and practice of the landscape-gardener. This latter personage is doing penance, and is likely to do penance for some time to come, in all treatment of the subject by artists. He has had, it must be admitted, a very long innings, has imposed himself on society in a triumphant style, and has little right to complain that it is his turn to be shunted. Nor need landscape gardeners, as a race, altogether despair of the resuscitation of their mystery, though not in the present generation. Many have been the changes in fashion in regard to gardens, followed dutifully by wealthy planters of parks, without any too curious inquiry into the philosophy of the matter; and what has happened before may happen again. Nor is it certain that landscape gardeners have deserved all the abuse they now get, or that formality may not be carried too far. But for the present it is clear that the landscape gardener will have to stand aside; society having (as they say of an officer dismissed from the army) "no further occasion for his services."

The main sins of the landscape gardener are twofold. First, that he deliberately adopts the principle of the false or imitative picturesque; secondly, that he ignores the architecture of the house, and designs his garden quite irrespective of it. The first is the more heinous offence of the two, as involving a broad principle of falsity. Because Nature in her irregularity of woodland and glade is charming, we are to make artificially a similar irregularity in the garden. Paths are to wind about as if in accidental meandering, and clumps of trees or bushes are to be carefully, but as if carelessly, placed here and there to give colour to the windings of the walks, as if they were compelled to bend from their course to avoid obstacles which have been purposely contrived beforehand. There is not the slightest difference in principle between this process and the now exploded one of making artificial ruins, which was current in the last century. Because the ruined remains of part of an old abbey are picturesque and suggest poetic association with the past, therefore, if there are no genuine ruins about, we may deliberately create some. The common-sense of the present day revolts at this; but it is only the same principle carried further. The only real difference lies in the fact that the sham ruin is a palpable imposture built up of artificial materials, while the sham landscape is created of materials which are in themselves the work of nature, though artificially disposed, and the imposture is less easily seen through. Once seen through, its charm, if not gone, is at least largely discounted. Besides, there is nothing of a professional mystery in it, after all. Anyone can do it who chooses to exercise himself in that way. Any one can plant his garden irregularly, and say, here I will have a clump of trees, here a winding walk, here a piece of pond which shall be arranged to look like the end of a large lake of which the remainder is hidden by the trees. Of course the amateur will not do it quite according to the devices of the professional landscape gardener; but then those devices are worth nothing except to the landscape gardener. They are his creed, but not ours, unless we tamely allow him to impose them on us. As we had occasion to remark when reviewing a landscape-gardening book some little time since, we are told certain trees must be placed in a certain way, &c.; but *why* must they? Simply that it is the landscape gardener's notion, which has nothing to do with either nature or art, but is a kind of hybrid concoction in obedience to arbitrary rules. It is his way of doing the trick; but if we do not want the trick at all, what then?

There may no doubt be such a thing as judiciously clearing out or planting up a park for certain ends of effect; but a park is not a garden. The essential error in treating a garden in this mock-natural manner, as stated by Mr. Blomfield, is of two kinds; in reference to what is outside and what is inside the garden; the landscape without and the habitation within (for we are considering the garden specially as an appanage of the habitation). As regards what is without, it is no business of the garden to imitate or blend with that; the garden is an enclosed space or "paradise," separated from the wildness of natural landscape, and intended as a place of retirement for man, in which he may follow the bent of his own devices and make a design after his own pleasure. Now a design which pretends not to be a design merely stultifies itself. As Mr. Blomfield observes "Any one who loves natural scenery will want the real thing; he will hardly be content to sit in his rockery and suppose himself to be among the mountains." A garden is an artificial enclosure, and what we look for in it is an artificial design and not an attempt to make it look like nature. And this argument has double force when we consider that the garden is

* "The Formal Garden in England." By Reginald Blomfield and F. Inigo Thomas. London: Macmillan & Co. 1892.

d

SUNDIAL: WREST: BEDFORDSHIRE

GARDEN GATE: TISSINGTON: DERBY.

immediately connected with the architecture of the house, which is necessarily an artificial design. A house growing out of a "wilderness" is a thing out of place, coming abruptly out of the ground, with nothing to lead up to or form a base to it. The laying-out and planning of the garden should have a direct reference to the style and to the laying-out of the house. It is a pendant to the architecture. In the mock-natural landscape garden it is impossible this ean be the case, for the characteristic of this type of garden is a studied irregularity: the clumps of trees must be disposed as if to persuade the eye that they naturally grew there; the walks must take all kinds of apparently accidental curves and windings. There is something absolutely repelling to the architectural eye in the plan of one of these gardens, with its walks deliberately laid out in broken-backed curves.

There are certain points, no doubt, in the book before us, which are pressed a little too far, both in the direction of formality and in the condemnation of informality. It may be questioned (as indeed Mr. Blomfield hints) whether the title "The Formal Garden" is altogether the best one, the word "formal" having an acquired secondary sense which is the reverse of complimentary; though we are not prepared to suggest a better title for the present purpose. But tho tendency of some of the examples and of some of the remarks is a little too much in favour of a degree of artificiality in the garden design which some may think deserving of the worser meaning of the word "formal." Mr. Blomfield condemns indeed the sheer pattern-making of the Dutch system, observing that the votaries of this style seem to have forgotten that, after all, a garden was a thing compounded of natural growths, of herbage and flowers. But he appears to defend the artificial clipping of trees rather further than we should be disposed to follow him. It is quite true, as Mr. Blomfield says, that it is really no more unnatural to clip trees than to clip grass; but to clip them into imitative shapes is another matter, and though the author admits that this was carried to excess under William and Mary, he seems to have a kindness for it which we cannot feel. It is interesting and pleasant in the garden of an old house, where it belongs to and recalls the taste of the period to which the house belongs, and has an association of old times about it; but we should be very sorry to see it revived in modern gardens. It is an artificiality precisely the opposite to that of the landscape gardener, and (to our thinking) equally false in taste. We doubt whether even the cutting of shrubs or small trees into purely geometrical shapes. such as cones and obelisks, is not over formal. At all events it is certain that a garden treated with this extreme degree of symmetry requires fine weather and warm sunshine to look at home; it is a melancholy spectacle in winter. Then again we are disposed to think that some place may be found for landscape-gardening, on a small scale and without an actual pretence of naturalness, in gardens which have no connexion with architecture; those which form a secluded portion of a park for instance. Mr. Blomfield is sarcastic over Battersea Park, which we always thought rather a wilderness of a place; but the enclosed quasi-garden portions of Birkenhead Patk, which have no relation to any architecture, but are merely secluded portions railed off from the open park for special treatment, realise a very charming effect with their plantations and small glades and water, which can hardly be said to pretend to pass for natural, though irregular in their lines; and we doubt whether a treatment of the whole as a single formal garden open to the eye at all parts would have given as much pleasure or beauty, on the whole, within such a confined space of ground. The vice of twisting the water about so as to carry it out of sight from every point of view is a piece of trickery, certainly, that cannot be defended, nor the use of a bridge where one could as easily walk round the end of the pond; but (in spite of principles) it is a very pretty spot. Then we think also that the author rather fails to recognise the real merits of Repton, who lived in a bad day and practised in a bad style, but who may be called a genius in his way, and was at least far above his immediate predecessors and followers in power and perception in dealing with estates according to the method then in vogue. Mr. Blomfield talks of Repton having ruined this and that place; but we do not feel quite sosure about this; and in regard to his sins in cutting down avenues, it should be remembered that it is one thing to admire one fine avenue, and another to go, as Repton did, all over the country from one "seat" to another, and find everywhere the eternal avenue, as if nothing could be done without it. At all events, we do not think Repton was a man to be dismissed with a sneer. A man may be a genius, though working in a bad style. There is no doubt Bernini's style was execrable; Adam's was formal and tame; Street's Gothic Law Courts are a mistake; but Bernini, Adam, and Street were all remarkable men in their way, and so we take it was Repton.

To return to the book before us, the second and third chapters give an interesting historical sketch of "The Formal Garden in England," in which a great deal of curious antiquarian information, illustrated from various old prints, is compressed into a small space, followed by a chapter on "the end" of that institution, accompanied by the sarcasms of Pope and the mild fatuities of Addison. It is perhaps hardly correct to say that Milton of all men loved the formal garden. His "trim gardens" suggests the idea, but in his later great poem he makes it one of the beauties of Paradise that the scene had nothing to do with "nice art" but with "nature boon,"—

> Wild without rule or art, enormous bliss."

"Enormous" is no doubt used in a quasi-Latin sense, the absence of *norma* or rule. The succeeding chapter deals with "Courts, Terraces, and Walks" in a fashion partly historical, partly critical. Concerning the critical portion we entirely concur in the importance of a terrace near the house, as a base for it to rise from, and in the fine effect of a "fore-court," now too often represented only by the carriage "sweep" and the oval of green grass in the centre of it. The charm of the fore-court of Ham House we alluded to not long since. Fully do we agree also in the recommendation of a liberal breadth for walks. Nothing more tends to give meanness even to an otherwise stately garden than cramped and narrow proportions in the walks. A charming specimen of the fine effect of the fore-court in a comparatively small and unpretending mansion is given in the view of Ambrosden (fig. 25).

In the following chapter on "Knots, Parterres, and Grass-work," we hope that we are not intended to admire the examples from Markham, with the apparent interlacing of the borders, as bad in garden design as German "interpenetration" in architecture: but we do not notice any protest against it. In regard to grass-work it is suggested that the lawn-tennis court presents some opportunities,—

> "that is, if the scale given by the dimensions of the court itself are" [query—"is?"] "sufficiently adhered to, and the features introduced are kept sufficiently large and simple. To make the court a really valuable part of the garden it is not enough to lay out a sufficient expanse of grass, which loses itself at the earliest opportunity in shrubs and flower-beds. The court should be taken as a definite problem, and designed as an integral part of the garden. And this applies to all grass-work. The mistake of the landscapist is that he considers grass only as a background, not as a very beautiful thing in itself. Grass-work ought to be designed with reference to its own particular beauty. The turf of an English garden is probably the most perfect in the world, certainly it is far more beautiful than any to be found on the Continent, and even the French admitted this two hundred years ago. It is wilfully throwing away a most valuable means of delight to treat grass-work as a mere affair of haphazard convenience."

In the chapter on "Fish-ponds, Pleaching, arbours, Hedges" &c. the author refers to the decline of the old fish-pond under the influence of Le Nôtre, to make way for the vast sheets of water which formed an essential feature in his system. "Great canals and basins took its place, and the transition from this to the artificial lakes of the landscape-gardener was easy." The long canal form of ornamental water is however to our thinking a very fine incident in a garden; it has this advantage over a broad sheet of water, that it gives distance and perspective of water-reflections without interfering with the sense of repose, enclosure, and privacy in a garden. The view given of the canal-like fish-pond at Wrest, with its parallel lines of thick hedge on each side, forms a charming example of this. "Pleaching," a revived old English word, signifies, according to the author, "the trimming of the small boughs and foliage of trees or bushes to bring them to a regular shape"; but we doubt if this is the old meaning. Walker's dictionary gives "to bend, to interweave," with the note "obsolete"; but Lord Tennyson (who, though not a dictionary-maker, is one of the first authorities on the true use of old English words) revived it in a well-known passage which confirms Walker's reading—

> "Round thee grow, self-pleached deep,
> Bramble-roses, faint and pale,
> And long purples of the dale."

Mr. Blomfield distinguishes it from "plash," 'which refers to the half-cutting of the larger branches and bending them down to form a hedge." We rather think it will be found that "pleach" and "plash" are two forms of the same word. The illustrations, from Markham's "Country Farm," of hedges cut into elaborate ornamental outlines at the top, are curious, but we should have liked to have seen them condemned; the weak garden-owner may take them as models, to the astonishment and alarm of his visitors.

Chapter viii. is devoted to the interesting and fruitful subject of "Garden Architecture," on which a book might be written; books have indeed been written on it, and bulky ones, but no good one that we know of; they are mostly advertisements of designs for lodges and entrance-gates. Many remains of old garden architecture are delightful in their combined dignity and simplicity. "Rustic bridges" were unknown in those better times. The two great stumbling-blocks are rusticity on the one hand, which is quite out of place in the formal garden,—it is the landscape gardener's pet "fad"; and "classic" pretension on the other hand; gardener's lodges in the shape of Greek temples, &c. These are not out of keeping with the garden so much as with the purpose to which they are put, making them cottage-homes inside and temples outside. Gate-piers in the seventeenth century are well worth study; the same general idea runs through many of them, but constantly varied in little details, though without any attempt at strange or sensational treatment. Canons Ashby, of which we give an illustration, is a good example; notice the admirable effect of the consoles at the back of the piers, breaking the harsh angle between them and the wall. Tissington gate is a characteristic specimen, but to our thinking owes its picturesqueness rather to age and association than to the actual merit of the design: it would look rather bald and heavy if executed as a new work in freshly-hewn stone. The gate from Pitmidden, Aberdeenshire, of which an illustration is given in the book, with its double returned flight of steps and the fountain-niche in the centre of the inner retaining wall, and the gate-piers flanked by a short length of balustrade on each side, is one of the pleasantest examples of the combination of simplicity, dignity, and picturesque character in this kind of work. The sundial is one of the most beautiful and suggestive features that can be introduced in a garden; we give the illustration of the one from Wrest. In regard to statuary, we think Mr. Blomfield is right in condemning marble for this country; it is only suited to a bright southern climate, and gets stained and looks unhappy and starved in a rainy climate. Portland stone is preferable, but the author especially recommends the revival of the old use of lead for such garden statuary, which weathers into a silvery grey, rather improving than deteriorating with time, as far at least as appearance goes. We give the example of the little leaden cupid from Melbourne. Statuary is a beautiful addition to a garden; but let it be good statuary. Nothing is more easy or more fatal than to put up commonplace reproductions of well-worn works.

GATE PIERS: CANONS ASHBY: NORTHANTS

In the concluding chapter are some remarks on the treatment of gardens in London squares which deserve special consideration. A London square, the author observes, is an entirely artificial affair, bounded by rectangular blocks of buildings.

> "In Bloomsbury, till within the last few years, there existed a good old-fashioned square garden, laid out in four simple grass plots, with a lime walk and a border of flowers running round the sides. It was restful and pleasant to look at. The grass plots were good for lawn-tennis and the lime walks kindly to the citizen; but the landscape gardener appeared on the scene and speedily put all this to rights. He cut up the grass plots and destroyed two sides of the lime walk, and heaped up some mounds, and made the most curiously unreasonable paths; and then charged a handsome sum for having destroyed one of the few Square gardens in London with any pretence to design."

We think we know the garden, and sympathise. The present treatment, with its feeble "mounds," is puerile. But there is something to be said on both sides, where a wealth of tree foliage exists. Has Mr. Blomfield ever noticed the effect of the mass of foliage in Brunswick-square gardens on a bright day in spring or early summer? We doubt whether any parterre would compensate for that.

In regard to one point touched on in the general criticism of landscape-gardening in the earlier part of the book, we do not quite agree with the author in condemning the idea (carried out, as he observes, by Barry in his well-known scheme at Trentham) of treating the park immediately outside the garden enclosure in a partially formal manner, so as to lead out by stages to the informality of natural landscape. It may be carried out so as to appear too pedantic and contrived, but there is something in the idea. Hampton Court is an example. Outside the semicircular fence enclosing the formal garden we have only trees, meadows, and water, but trees and water laid out in formal avenues and canals. The contrast with the formal garden within the fence is quite sufficient to mark off the garden as the more artificialised portion, and we should certainly lose a fine palatial effect in the loss of the formal arrangement of the avenues and canals.

LEAD FIGURE OF CUPID MELBOURNE: DERBY.

One other criticism we have to make. Had Dante lived in the age of printing, he would certainly have had a place in one of the circles of his "Inferno" reserved for authors who issue books without an index, who would probably have been condemned for ever to search for references which they could not find. By his prudence in living after Dante, Mr. Blomfield has escaped this inconvenience; but we hope an index will be added in the next edition.

NOTES.

AT the meeting of the Hellenic Society on Monday last an interesting paper was read by Professor Percy Gardner, on "the Chariot Group of the Mausoleum," the object of which was to suggest that the two nearly perfect statues discovered by Sir Charles Newton among the other remains on the mausoleum site did not form part of the quadriga group on the top of the pyramid. That the statues do in all probability represent (according to their accepted nomenclature) Mausolus and Artemisia, Professor Gardner admits, but denies that they were placed in the chariot. The following are his principal arguments: Pliny describes the chariot but makes no mention of portrait-statues; such statues would probably not be placed at such a height that the portraiture would be lost, and even the figures themselves hidden behind the group of horses; the attitudes of the figures do not suggest the driving or controlling of horses, nor is the dress of the man such as would be worn in a chariot; and (which seems the most important argument) the figures are too small in scale for the wheel and the horses. The wheel of a chariot in Greek sculpture is usually about half the height of a man, and when figures are combined with horses, the figure is almost always, if not always, about the same height as the complete height of the horse, up to the top of the horse's head. These conditions of proportion would have required the figures to be about 14 ft. high, whereas in fact they are respectively 9 ft. 10 in. and 8 ft. 8 in. Mr. A. S. Murray, who is now engaged in setting up the remains of the quadriga and the figures in relation to one another (which was perhaps the reason the paper was read), replied in favour of his view, his most important arguments being that the stratification of the marble was similar in all the fragments, showing that they had come from the same locality in the quarry and presumably had been worked together; and that there is a break in the side of the statue of Mausolus just about the height where the chariot rail might be supposed to come. There is, of course, also the fact that the statues and the quadriga fragments were found close together on the site, but Professor Gardner replied that this, as is known in other instances, is no certain criterion as to their relative situations on the building. A glance at the remains, since the meeting, convinces us at least that Professor Gardner's argument about proportions is valid. The statues are decidedly too small in scale for the fragments of the horses; they would be thought so even in modern art, still more in Greek art, where the horse is always smaller in comparison with the human figure than in modern art. Mr. Murray's arguments must not be overlooked, but if the figures did belong to the quadriga they were out of scale to a degree of which we believe there is no other example in Greek art. If, however, these dignified and highly-finished statues were not in the place which has been supposed, there appears to be no fitting site for them in Pullan's restoration of the Mausoleum, so that the question affects the architectural as well as the sculptural restoration of the monument. We may take the opportunity of observing that two things are much wanted at the Hellenic Society's meetings, viz., ventilation and punctuality. Of the former there is none; and as to the latter, the meeting is always kept waiting from ten minutes to a quarter of an hour after the stated time, before the chair is taken.

THE subject of "Stained Glass" drew a large meeting at the Institute on Monday evening, and the large collection of diagrams of stained-glass designs exhibited was an element of considerable interest; but nothing very new was said about stained glass either in the papers or in the discussion, in spite of a return to the old and (we thought) exploded system of "calling on" selected speakers by name. This system certainly has the one advantage that it stops the mouths of certain irrepressible gentlemen who are always wanting to hear the sound of their own voices, but otherwise it is a principle rather at variance with freedom of discussion, and its advantage was not very obvious on Monday night, when one artist admitted that he had nothing to say, and another appeared to think the chief object of the meeting was to hear him speak, and had eventually to be stopped by the Chairman. Among points which might have been noticed in discussion and were not, we may call attention to the unfortunate suggestion made in one paper, that for the treatment of the extremities of the figure in stained glass we should study Botticelli, *i.e.*, conventionalise some one else's convention. Certainly the wiser course would be to begin at Nature and do our own conventionalising so far as it is necessary. Among the remarks made on iron work not a word was said about a point that has excited a good deal of controversy in some quarters lately, whether the heavy supporting iron work should not rightly be *outside* the window and not in, and be so treated as to be a decorative feature externally; a view of the matter on which there is a good deal to be said. There are, we believe, Mediæval examples of this. Another matter which requires criticising, and to which not the slightest reference was made, is the perpetual repetition in stained glass of details imitated from stonework; the eternal "canopy" which seems to sum up the idea of so many designers for filling up the head of a window, and which is not only uninteresting but is entirely unfitted for glass work. Now and then we see a window in which there has been some attempt at the design of an ornamental filling specially suitable for glass, but in the majority of cases it is just the same recipe, the figure of a saint in coloured robes below, and the imitation architectural canopy above. Stained glass should have its own forms of ornament, which are essentially distinct from those of architectural masonry. Speaking of the coloured robes reminds us, too, how little attempt has been made, and how much might be made, to adapt the idealised or conventionalised nude figure to treatment in glass, in combination with decorative detail. All these matters might have raised points for really new discussion, in place of some of the rather worn-out enthusiasm about "jewelled effects," &c., of which we have heard often enough by this time.

A FACULTY has been obtained (as recorded on another page) for the removal of human remains from St. Helen's, Bishopsgate, with which it is impossible to deal otherwise, with proper regard to sanitary precaution. This course will probably have to be adopted in other city churches from time to time. It is natural that descendants of those who have been interred in a church and to whom monuments have been erected in it should feel grieved at the necessity, but there are cases in which it is a necessity, and sentiment must give way to sanitation. We hope the same course will be taken with the remains under St. Mary Woolnoth, instead of adopting the insane project of pulling down this, one of the most characteristic buildings in London, which has been mooted in some quarters. The absurdity is the greater inasmuch as, even if the church were destroyed, the mass of human remains would have to be removed all the same, for the safety of the city.

IT has long been held that section 157 of the Public Health Act, 1875, which authorises Local Sanitary Authorities to make By-laws with respect to certain structural arrangements of new buildings, does not authorise the making of a By-law with respect to the height of rooms, and, accordingly, in the Public Health Acts Amendment Act, 1890, a section (No. 23) has been introduced extending the powers under the Act of 1875 so as to enable any Sanitary Authority, after having formally adopted the Act, to make By-laws with respect to, *inter alia*, the height of rooms intended for human habitation. In many old codes of building By-laws a clause has been introduced with this object; but, owing to its having been declared by the Law Officers to the Crown to be *ultra vires*, it has been used only with the greatest caution. Such clause has usually prescribed a minimum height for any habitable room, and has then prescribed a further minimum height for any habitable room situated either wholly or partly in the roof. There is obviously much inconsistency in determining, for purposes of health, a minimum height for any room intended for human habitation and immediately afterwards fixing a smaller minimum height for another room intended for the same purpose but happening to be in the roof of the building. If a certain minimum height,—say, 8 ft.,—is requisite in order to secure adequate breathing-space in a room having a rectangular section, it is clear that a similar height throughout only half the area of the room when situated in the roof must be inadequate, and yet this is what has commonly been demanded. Now that the Legislature has specially authorised the making of by-laws for regulating the height of habitable rooms, the subject has received the consideration of the advisers of the Local Government Board, and a memorandum signed by Dr. George Buchanan, F.R.S., the Medical Officer of the Board, and Mr. Gordon Smith, their architect, has recently been prepared for the guidance of those sanitary authorities who may contemplate making such a By-law. It is recommended in this mem. that the minimum height for a habitable room should be 9 ft., though 8 ft. 6 in. is regarded as permissible, and even 8 ft. would not be refused; but it is suggested that no By-law proposing less than 8 ft. of height should be submitted for the Board's approval. For rooms in the roof it is pointed out that no part of any room should be less than 5 ft. in height, thus doing away with the unsatisfactory arrangement of having part of the floor so circumstanced that the sloping ceiling under the rafters comes down to meet the floor at an acute angle; there must be, in attic rooms intended for human habitation, vertical sides at least 5 ft. high. For the rest the room must be of such a height as will give a mean height over the whole floor-area of not less than 8 ft., or whatever greater height may be determined upon. There can be no doubt that more decisive legislation on this subject is called for, and it is to be hoped that the point will receive attention in framing the new Metropolitan Building Act.

THE action of the Amalgamated Society of Engineers, in regard to the strike in the North, has been condemned in outspoken fashion by some of the affiliated societies. Although the dispute is now affecting some 18,000 men,—the majority of whom are idle against their will,—the engineers stubbornly refused to submit the question at issue to arbitration, until unusual pressure was brought to bear upon them by the Federation of Engineering and Shipbuilding Trades of the United Kingdom. This body urged them to show more willingness to come to a peaceful settlement, and, although they were at first told that their advice was "a scandal to trades unionism," it eventually received more reasonable consideration. Happily, the Unions are not all so averse to conciliatory measures. The following passage occurs in the last "Monthly Report of the United Society of Boiler-makers and Iron Shipbuilders":—"Let us always, if possible, adjust our differences by peaceful means; and this is possible in ninety-nine cases out of every hundred if there is a desire to do so." The desires of the disputants in this case have inclined in quite an opposite direction, and the interests of their employers have been so entirely ignored, that the latter have been goaded into adopting a rather uncompromising attitude. Messrs. Palmer & Co.—at whose yard the dispute arose,—have had to send work away from Jarrow to Glasgow for H.M.S. *Revenge*, and other work is in like manner being lost to the district. In accepting a proposal from the societies interested for a conference, the employers have stipulated that the discussion must take cognisance of the original dispute; whereas the engineers characteristically desired it to be confined, in the first instance, to the lock-out, which was really the inevitable outcome of that dispute.

THE case of Hart *v.* The Monarch Land Company, Limited, tried this week before Mr. Justice Mathew and a special jury, shows the difficulty in which owners of property are placed when they have to rely solely on the opinion of experts. The action was brought to recover damages for injuries done to the Star Music Hall by the erection of some model dwellings which abutted on the east wall of the hall, and which, by placing too great weight on this wall, caused the front wall to crack. On the one hand, various architects and surveyors state that in their opinion the cracks were caused by the defendants' buildings. On the other hand, an equally numerous body of experts asserted that in their opinion the causes of the damage were certain defects and weaknesses in the wall itself. Each of these adverse opinions was, no doubt, put forward quite honestly; the mistake which professional witnesses make is in adhering too confidently to matters of opinion as if they were matters of fact. It is this which brings professional witnesses into disrepute. In the present case, the jury agreed with the plaintiff's witnesses, or it may be they gave him the benefit of the conflict of evidence. When in doubt, find for the plaintiff, is a maxim dear to the juryman's heart. But such a dispute as this ought to have been kept out of the law courts: a competent architect with a judicial mind might surely have settled the matter after an examination of the buildings.

THE London School-Board have again been in litigation against one of the builders of their schools, on the ground of fraud and wilful deviation from the contract. The result was a verdict for the defendant. Nothing could be more ill-advised than to claim damages on such a serious ground as this without very complete proof. Mere carelessness, however reprehensible, is entirely different from fraud. The contract in question made the builder liable for four years if fraud and wilful deviation could be proved. It is businesslike for a public body to have a clause making the builder liable for bad workmanship and materials for a stated period after the end of the contract, for the deviation from the contract is not always ascertainable. But it is thoroughly unbusinesslike to bring actions for fraud unless there is proof positive; to do so in an uncertain manner is simply to throw good money after bad.

WE have repeatedly expressed our opinion that London, in considering its future water-supply, ought to aim at finally abandoning direct supply from the Thames; and in support of this opinion from the medical point of view we may draw the attention of our readers to the following remarks in the last issue of the *Lancet*:—

"While recognising to the utmost the value of modern improvements, we find ourselves unable to abandon our old belief that the Thames affords a most unsatisfactory water-supply. The Thames drains a large and highly populous area, and pollutions of all kinds pass inevitably into it. Every storm of rain carries down in muddy streams the washings of towns, villages, manured fields, and pigstyes. In spite of all care human sewage certainly finds its way into the stream even at distances not far above the intakes of the great companies. At the mouth of the Wey, close to Shepperton, a cluster of houses with cesspools certainly pollute the water, for the cesspools fill during flood time and empty as the water recedes. Such at least was the state of things at the time of our last inspection, and we have no reason to suppose that any change has been effected. This, at all times unpleasant, might evidently become a source of urgent danger if a single case of cholera or choleraic diarrhœa occurred in one of the cottages. In the same way barges and even house-boats, in spite of the prohibitions of the Thames Conservancy, might evidently and at any time communicate some deadly pollution to the water-supply. London would then be protected only by the filters, and surely nobody would drink with comfort water which, having received the cholera virus, had been purified solely by passage through sand. As to other pollutions, we have ourselves seen the putrid bodies of dead dogs floating in the river within half a mile above the intakes of the companies."

PROFESSOR HAMMER has been making an investigation of the different slide rules in the Stuttgart Technical School, and has published the results of his inquiry in the German surveyors' organ, *Zeitschrift für Vermessungswesen*. For simple multiplications or with multiplications with three factors, the 25 centimètre slide rule gives an approximation of within about 0·1 to 0·2 per cent. of accuracy. Professor Hammer tested a number of German celluloid slide rules, and found the mean error in simple multiplication to be $\frac{1}{800}$ with rapid reading. The less portable office slide rules in use in Germany are the 50 centimètre slide rule, giving an accuracy of 0·08 per cent. with rapid reading; others of various dimensions, such as the Landsberg 723 m.m. long; and Beyerlens calculating circle, which represents a length of 754 m.m., and with which the accuracy is 0·07 to 0·05 per cent. The Fuller and Thacher rules are used in England and the United States respectively. Mr. Hammer made careful tests with the former, with the result that it was found to give a mean error of 0·008 per cent., which showed that the accuracy claimed by the makers, — *i.e.*, $\frac{1}{10000}$ is not too much. Still, more nearly accurate results were obtained with the Thacher rule, the mean error with careful adjustment being 0·0031 per cent., or approximately $\frac{1}{32000}$ with careful reading.

THE Middlesex County Council intend to enlarge, at an estimated cost of 20,000*l.*, the Council Chamber and Sessions House at the Westminster Guildhall. The present octagonal building, of brick with a stone Doric portico, was erected in 1804-5, after C. P. Cockerell's designs. The site is that of a meat market, built in the Sanctuary in 1751, and which had been established, as we read, as early as 1568. It appears, too, that the market stood over part of the foundations of the Sanctuary church, whose remains, supposed to be of Edward the Confessor's time, were drawn and described by Dr. Stukely,—see *Archæologia*, Vol. I.* Maitland (1756) gives an account of "a prodigious strong stone building . . . . 72½ ft. the length of each side, and the walls in thickness no less than 25 ft.," and identifies a portion of it with the bell-tower which Edward III. built here for the use, it appears, of the Minster.. This is "the strong clochard of stone and timber, covered with lead," mentioned by Stow as having been erected in Little Sanctuary by that sovereign. For the bell-tower they removed the outer staircase at the church's south-eastern angle, and built another on the eastern side, as shown in the drawing and plans made by Stukely. Part of the fabric was afterwards converted into the "Three Tuns" tavern; all above ground had disappeared by the year 1760. The original "Quaker" tavern gave place to an extension of the market area.

AT a sitting of the Consistory Court, in St. Paul's, on the 18th inst., Dr. Tristram, Q.C., Chancellor of the Diocese, granted faculties in respect of certain London churches. The works for restoring St. Helen's, by Mr. Pearson, R.A., reveal the existence of a large amount of human remains beneath the floor, which we gather is to be replaced with another and levelled. It was stated that of 4,335 interments during the period 1652-1883 one-third were made inside of the church. In view of Dr. Sedgwick Saunders' evidence, and the opinion of the medical adviser to the Home Office, the Court agreed to issue a faculty for a removal, generally, of the remains to the City of London Cemetery at Ilford, or elsewhere, as may in particular instances be desired, but with exception for non-interference with the McDougal (1835), Robinson and wife (1599, 1592), and Sir Julius Cæsar (1636) vaults, upon representations by the respective relatives and descendants. The exception extends also to the Sir John Spencer (1609), Sir William Pickering and his son (1542-74), Sir Thomas Gresham (1579), Sir John Lawrence (Dame Abigail, 1682), Sir John Crosby, and Sir Francis Bancroft (above ground, 1723: he died 1726) vaults and tombs.* Towards the cost of the repairs, calculated at about 7,000*l.*, the Merchant Taylors, as patrons, contribute, we believe, 2,000*l.*, and the Charity Commissioners 4,092*l.* out of the common fund set up under the City of London Parochial Charities Act, 1883. Another faculty, following that of August 18 last, for laying out and planting the churchyard of St. Botolph-without-Aldgate, provides for the non-disturbance of the Sidney family monument (1801), and for the levelling and filling of the John Gibbon vault (1765) at the north end, with the removal of the memorial slabs to against the church wall. In the case of Christ Church, Spitalfields, Dr. Tristram said he would grant a faculty—its conditions to be based upon a visit he would make to the ground—for converting the graveyard into an open space, in pursuance of a resolution of the Vestry, passed last December, to profit by the Metropolitan Open Spaces Act. It was stated in Court that the Metropolitan Public Gardens Association are prepared to expend 450*l.* upon the work.

THE Dudley Gallery Water-Colour Exhibition is not a very interesting one as a whole, but contains some works of marked character. Among these are Mr. G. Marks's very beautiful little landscape studies, which give the idea of large paintings reduced to a small scale (Nos. 192, 193, 197, 200, 201); "Lengthening Shadows" (201) the smallest of all, an evening view in a harvest field, is particularly fine. Among larger works Mr. J. Carlisle has a fine landscape, "Until the Evening" (21), a cold spring sunset with a ploughed field in the foreground; "Allington Gorse" (42) is another good work by the same hand. Mr. Sidney Evans exhibits two small drawings of Eton (81 and 87) of very artistic quality; Mr. Henry Bailey's "A Rich Harvest" (92) is fine in sentiment and composition, though rather weak in handling; Miss Skidmore's "The Glow of Eventide" (136) is fine in feeling, and Mr. Fulwood's "Whispers of Gloaming" (150) is noticeable for colour. Mr. Harry Goodwin is rather palpably imitating the style of his brother in some of his views of special localities, such as "Winter Sunset, Hastings" (341), in which however he is not much behind Mr. A. Goodwin, and his "Lucerne Twilight" (162), more in a style of his own, is one of the most striking pieces of colour in the room. We rather quarrel with Mr. F. G. Coleridge, in his various sketches about Salisbury, for not doing more justice to the cathedral; in the "Canon's Garden, Salisbury" (172), the building, which occupies a considerable part of the middle distance, is incorrectly and very weakly treated, becoming a mere wash of brown, and there is no indication (otherwise) of any mistiness in the atmosphere to excuse

* His view, with plans, of the upper and lower churches are reproduced in Allen's "London." 1828.

* The dates are those of the deaths of the persons named. For an account, with illustrations, of their monuments, and of the church, see the *Builder*, March 15, 1884, and June 29, 1889.

this silhouette kind of treatment. Signor Giampietri, as usual, treats ancient architecture admirably, especially in his "Roman Forum, Remains of Fourth Century" (110), which is perfect as a representation of antique remains of this class. Mr. Barnett Stuart has some interesting representations of ancient architectural remains in various parts of the world,—"Temple Gateway, Kioto" (129), the "Sanchi Tope" (186), the "Caves of Ellora" (224), and the strange scene of the "Approach to Ming Tombs, Pekin" (343), with its elephants and other creatures rudely carved on either side of the road, like a burlesque on the Egyptian avenues of Sphinxes. Mr. T. A. de Moleyns has some "colour notions" in his slight sketches of foreign town scenes, but the best, the "Rath-Haus, Basle" (137) is spoiled by the buildings being out of perpendicular. Mr. W. Tyndale gives a good architectural picture in "Pont Flamand, Bruges" (138); Mr. L. Block's studies of old books (158, 163) are admirable bits of still life; and the studies of shipping by Miss Nora Davison—especially "A Farewell Visit" (69) and "From the Far North" (90),—show great truth of perception, and a very original style of handling. We have not too many good painters of shipping (as distinct from sea), and Miss Davison seems to have a style and handling of her own in this class of subject.

WHILE Londoners grumble (often in a very exaggerated strain) at the inaction of municipal authorities in clearing away snow, it appears that the Parisians have had an opposite reason for complaint. According to a sarcastic paragraph in *La Semaine des Constructeurs*, the energy of the "Ponts et Chaussées" in washing away snow by the application of jets of water has threatened to render Paris a kind of Venice:—

"On a canalisé le boulevard Saint-Germain, la rue de Rivoli, l'avenue de l'Opéra, toutes les grandes artères où commencement déjà à circuler des bateaux . . . . d'ailleurs à fonds plats; le service de navigation est chargé de l'entretien de ces voies. On ajoute que les phoques du Jardin d'Acclimatation vont être dressés sous la haute surveillance du sympathique directeur de cet établissement, M. Geoffroy St. Hilaire. On les destine à trainer la gondole du Président de la République. L'administration compte sur un effet saisissant."

THERE appears to have been a very odd kind of critical objection raised in Glasgow on the passing by the Town Council of the draft Building Regulations Bill in its final form. The complaint is that the Bill will raise the cost of house building. Of course it will: who ever heard of a Building Regulation Bill that did not, if it were worth anything, raise the cost of house building? The necessity for such Bills arises from the tendency of speculating builders to build as cheaply and as badly as possible, and it is to prevent them doing so for the future. The champions of the existing state of things in Glasgow speak with sympathy for the poor builders, who wish to build houses that will pay. No doubt they do, but they are not to indulge this desire at the expense of the public health. The public pays in the long run, not the builders; and the Glasgow public, if it has any common sense, will be willing to pay higher for better and more sanitary building.

CANTERBURY CATHEDRAL.—The Dean of Canterbury writes to the *Times* (Wednesday) in regard to what is being done at the Cathedral:—"The north and south walls of the nave of Canterbury Cathedral have for a century and more been out of the perpendicular, each leaning slightly outside, from the pressure of the roof. When a new roof was put upon the nave, forty or fifty years ago, much was done to correct the pressure, but some months ago we asked Mr. Christian, the architect of the Ecclesiastical Commissioners, carefully to examine these walls and see if they had moved at all. He reported that they were perfectly safe and had not moved, but that it might be as well to brace them together for more perfect security. He gave us drawings for the braces, which are now being put in position, and will tie the two walls together. What we are doing is thus simply a matter of precaution."

SARACENIC ARCHITECTURE.*

BY PROFESSOR AITCHISON, A.R.A.

IT will now, I think, be opportune to give a general review of Saracenic architecture. When I proposed to take up this subject, I intended to include Ottoman architecture, but I felt that in one sense Ottoman architecture should not be included, for though certain Saracenic forms and ornament were retained, it was in fact a branch of Byzantine architecture. Most of the early mosque builders at Constantinople, after the Ottoman conquest, were Byzantines, and when they were not, the main problem the architects had to solve was to improve on the methods adopted at Sta. Sophia; so that in reality it would be extraneous to the main purpose of these lectures.

The research into the origin of Saracenic architecture has been the cause of a certain satisfaction to me in respect to our art,—I use the word art in its most comprehensive sense, just as we speak of the art of the goldsmith and the potter. The Saracens in a century could conquer more of the world than ever belonged to the Egyptians, Chaldeans, the Persians, the Greeks, or the Romans, but with all their resistless energy, and with most of the architecture of the world before them, they could not for four or five hundred years elaborate a Saracenic style; in spite, too, of an influx of wealth, and of a demand for buildings, that was unprecedented. I do not think they were great constructors. At least there seems to be nothing that they built which could vie with the domes and vaults of Rome, or the dome of Byzantium. And in point of durability their works seem to have fallen short of those of Greece, Rome, and Persia. They do not appear either to have originated any great novelty or advancement in what I may call constructive planning. They added a few distinguished picturesque features, and they perfected,—we may almost say invented,—a new scheme of decoration. We know nothing of the causes that produce architects, or poets, or astronomers, but we fancy that certain conditions will produce architecture, and all, or almost all, these conditions were found in the Saracens. They were more magnificently generous than any people of whom we have any knowledge,—in fact, to be called generous was, in their eyes, the summing up of all the virtues. At first they were ascetics, but at a very early period, after their emergence from Arabia, they gave up asceticism, and were more celebrated for the gorgeous magnificence of their buildings, dress, houses, and furniture, than Persian kings or Byzantine emperors. Founding mosques, hospitals, khans, and fountains, were looked on as claims to paradise, and, when the rulers were Turks, they were great tomb builders. Free education was as great a programme with them as it is with us, and the meanest freedman, or the poorest beggar, was admitted to the Society of Kaliphs and Emits, if he was a Hadji, a holy man, or was distinguished in the arts or sciences. Many of Kaliphs cultivated the arts and sciences with success, while music and poetry excited the most passionate enthusiasm in all the Saracens. There was, too, in the mind of every Moslem a strong belief in the marvellous and the weird, in all sorts of spiritual beings, good, bad, and indifferent; in astrology, in incantation, and in amulets and talismans. Hidden treasures of fabulous values must have been common, when a wealthy world had been conquered in less than a century, so a shrewd man might easily get a reputation for his divining rod, talisman, or incantation; and with what wonders had this simple people been confronted; many of them had seen the deserted or buried temples of Egypt, the deserted palaces in Persia, the sculptured caves in India, and fountains of fire. The strange beasts, birds, and fishes of many countries had met their eyes, and they were familiar with the learning of Greece, Rome, Egypt, and India, not to speak of glimpses of the Chinese.

Bactria which they conquered was a Greek Kingdom, and even to this day, it is said, that half the words of the Afghan tribes are ancient Greek. Many of the Saracens had visited Ceylon, Sumatra, Java, Borneo, and probably the islands of Japan, if not Australia itself. Homer had been read, for we find the cannibal of Sumatra, called Fenioun; evidently the shot of a Saracen at Polyphemus. Early people can no more copy than children can; certain strong characteristics strike both savages and children, and both only portray, as well as they can, the salient features that have struck them. This trait appears to me to be very characteristic of the Saracen style, and we must allow something for national characteristics and personal proclivities. Striking features they had seen in the architecture of the countries they had conquered were used in a new way, and where the Moorish element was largely mingled with the Saracen, as in Spain, a passion for vague outline is a marked characteristic, and all else was derived from the profound study and love of geometry; this, however, seems to me to have been chiefly confined to ornament; they seem to me never to have worked out a logical style irrespective of ornament. One part of Kalaun's mosque is almost purely Romanesque, another small piece is Gothic; the later mosques, if you exclude the ornament, are two-storied warehouses or mansions with lines of recessed windows; and this seems to me the most persistent type. When they made a grand success, as at the mosque of Sultan Hasan, they did not make continued efforts to perfect it. I admit that this would have been difficult to improve on; as it is, it looks like the isolated effect of one genius.

We learnt from Abd-al-Rahman himself that the aisles of Christian basilicas had struck him, and he evidently thought he could not have too many aisles, nor could they be too long. He made in his mosque eleven aisles, more than 200 ft. deep, and his successors increased the number to nineteen and the depth to 350 ft.; but take the 200 ft., there was an effect produced that is unrivalled, an effect like that of a pine-tree forest, at once suggesting an infinity of number and boundless space; for the limits are shrouded in mist and gloom.

Doubtless Abd-al-Rahman I. had seen Acba's mosque at Kairouan, but we must be all the more thankful to him for appreciating what was fine, and seeking to perpetuate it. Two hundred years later on, we have the arches of Maksurah and the Villa Viciosa cusped on the intrados and extrados, which in some form or other persisted in Spain and Barbary till the end of the Moslem sway. Similar features are found at San Cristo de la Luz, and Sta. Maria della Bianca, at Toledo, yet we know not where these cusped arches came from. They may have been a pure invention of the Saracens.

We next come to those two curious monuments near Baghdad, the tombs of Ezekiel and Zobeida. Zobeida was alive in 833 A.D., and at Mamun's wedding; therefore, if it was her tomb it was after that date. As to the domes, they are not confined to Saracen architecture, though they are one of its most characteristic features, for they abounded in Persian and Byzantine times, not to speak of Rome itself.

If M. Choisy is wrong, and the Persian domes were not of the days of Achæmenides, where did Agrippa's architect get his idea of the dome of the Pantheon from? for this was erected in 27 B.C., and the Sasanian dynasty did not begin till the third century A.D. Where the minarets came from I do not know, but they might have been suggested, and probably were, by Byzantine watch-towers, for if they were suggested by the isolated columns of Persepolis, they took an entirely different shape, except in Persia and very late in Cairo, but they are at once the most striking, original, and well-designed features of Saracen architecture. I am equally ignorant of when they were first used; the one at the mosque of Amru is, I should fancy, early, and so is the one at the mosque of Tûlûn.

The most striking ornament is the stalactite. The author of the theory I mentioned in my first lecture is of opinion that they had their origin in Persia. In the Cavetto of the crowning member of doorways in the days of Archæmenides there is an ornament consisting of three ranges of leaves, and each leaf has a semi-circular top. When seen in a drawing to a small scale, this ornament is not to be distinguished from the Saracen stalactites over door-heads; and a great part of Saracen stalactites in Persia are merely niches superposed. I believe the dome over the fountain in the mosque of Tûlûn contains the first example of stalactites, but all we know of its date is a remark in Mr. Poole's "Art of the Saracens in Egypt," where he says it was at least a century after Tûlûn's death in 883, or in 983, but, as a rule, those peculiarities that made the true Saracen style are not observed till about the twelfth century.

The main peculiarity to be noticed is the founding of all ornament on elaborate geo-

* Being the fifth Royal Academy Lecture on Architecture this session. Delivered on Monday evening, February 8.

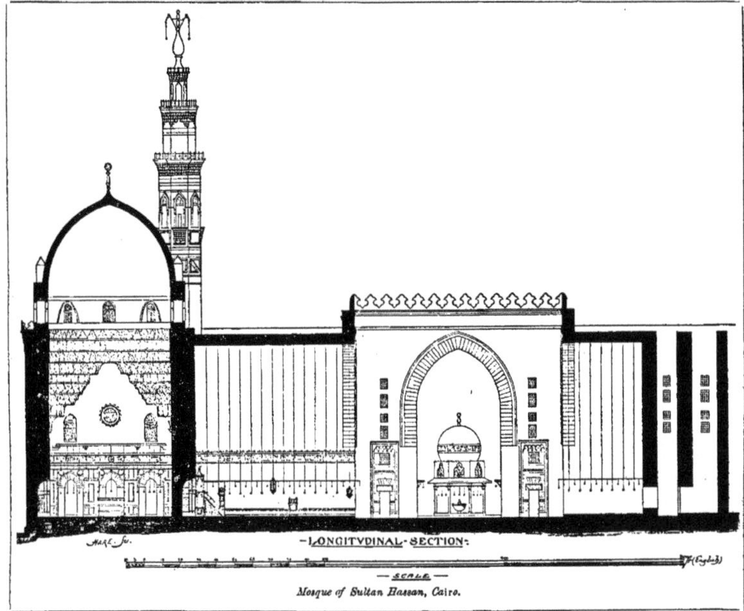

Mosque of Sultan Hassan, Cairo.

metrical framework, and as often as not the geometrical framework was the only ornament. It is not flattering to one's national vanity to find that every book on Saracen architecture is a French one, except Murphy's and Owen Jones's on the Saracen work of Spain, and Mr. Poole's on "The Art of the Saracens in Egypt." Pascal Coste is our sheet-anchor, and Girault de Prangez and Prisse d'Avennes, the bowers. M. Jules Bourgoin has published a charming book called "Les Arts Arabes," to show the different patterns founded on geometrical figures that are to be found in Egypt and Syria. In the book there is an essay on the methods of design employed, which he calls "æsthetic geometry." He is, however, a man of few words, and so imbued with this æsthetic geometry that he treats it much as Sir Isaac Newton did Euclid, when, after reading the statement at the head of each proportion, he said it was ridiculous to attempt to prove what was self-evident. M. Bourgoin gives a few examples worked out with the most concise descriptions, which leave us like the Irishman, who was described as "a mark of interrogation standing prostrate." He also gives what he considers to be the key to each example.

As geometry is the foundation of architecture, the students may be safely advised not only to make themselves acquainted with the æsthetic geometry of the Saracens, but to work out every example he gives in the plates, seeing that it has been the foundation of a new style of ornament. I may add that any one who would publish a book giving the geometrical solution of all the patterns would do a good work and earn the gratitude of those who desire to fathom this subject; he might, too, be the founder of a new style of ornament; as it is not likely that the Saracens exhausted all the capacities of geometry.

I will now speak of some of the architecture which has merits of its own, unconnected with this very elaborate æsthetic geometry. You may see in the plans of the Persian mosques, though their date is late, that they bear a strong resemblance, as far as their court and transepts go, to the mosque of Sultan Hassan; and this is not surprising, as the idea is supposed to have been taken from some of the Persian palaces, but I do not think that this diminishes the credit we must award it. In the Pantheon at Rome we have without doubt the Roman rendering of some foreign colossal dome. The eye which lights it, and which is the main cause of its sublime effect, was due to an accident, that is, to its being built as the laconicum of Agrippa's baths, but to seize on a happy accident is one of the characteristics of genius. A witty architect* once said, "All the finest things in the world originated in accident, and such accidents happen to every one, but the man of genius alone knows how to make use of them." Every one has seen a hungry dog gnawing a bone and an old tailor trying to thread his needle, but Dante alone has made these into immortal similes.

The sublime effect of the mosque of Sultan Hasan is solely due to its plan, its proportion, and its method of lighting. After passing through a dark, narrow, and tortuous passage, one emerges into the brilliant sunshine of the central court, and sees in the middle of each of the four sides a vaulted nave or transept, the faces of which come sheer down to the pavement, without a screen. The pointed arches of three of them are nearly twice their width up to the soffit of the crown. Some small doors and tiers of windows doubtless help to give scale. The sanctuary of the mosque has the same sort of pointed arch, whose height is but a third more than its width, and this vaulted sanctuary has for its only ornament a deep band of Cufic writing. The sanctuary is nearly as deep as it is high, and standing at the niche end you look out of the gloom into the blinding sunlight of the court; so you see that vastness, simplicity of form, and lighting are the main causes of the sublime in architecture. The main features of the design are doubtless taken from the old Persian palaces; almost all of them had a vaulted vestibule, that at Feruz Abad has a very deep one, and there is one there in the centre of each end of the courtyard; at the same place there is a fire temple, whose plan is precisely similar to that of the mosque of Sultan Hasan. The arched recesses of the courtyard of the Persian mosques are the same feature, and the frontispieces suggested by the doorways of the Achæmenid palaces give them greater dignity. It is only to be deplored that the hideous, four-centred arch has taken the place of some more dignified form.

The grand frontispieces were doubtless suggested by the vast doorways at Persepolis, and these were evidently taken from Egyptian doorways. The Persian minarets were, I think, imitations of the isolated columns of the palaces at Persepolis and elsewhere, and though the splendid enamelled pottery, with which Saracen buildings of Persia are covered, took its rise from that of Babylonia and Assyria, it became Persian, and was not only much affected by the Saracens of Egypt, but was used by the Ottomans at Brusa and Constantinople.

The mosque of Edh-Dhahir Beybars outside the walls of Cairo, built about 1268 A.D., looks like a fortress; its front is about 354 ft. long, the walls are nearly 50 ft. high, crowned with bearded battlements; this sort of battlement, by the bye, was taken from the Persians; this front of Edh-Dhahir has a central projecting gate-tower, and two flat towers at the ends, the gateway having a pointed arch supported on columns, and its front is ornamented with two tiers of niches and some panels; the gate-tower is slightly higher than the walls, has bearded battlements, and a square tower over it, with square battlements; below the cornice of the wall are eight slightly-pointed windows on each side of the gate-tower, about 18 ft. from the ground to the sills; at the back of the gate-tower, at the other end of the mosque, is the dome over the bay in front of the niche.

The mosque of Sultan Barkuk, built about 1384 A.D., has his and his family's tomb at each end of the sanctuary. As far as its external features are concerned, it is a good type of a Cairene mosque, as many of the features persisted to the last, but, like that of Beybars I., it is not striped outside. The niche wall is about 236 ft. long, and 53 ft. high. The battlements

* The late W. W. Deane.

have disappeared, but were doubtless of the flower-de-luce pattern. In the centre of the wall there is a wide pier, with a square projection in the middle of it for the niche; over this is a little dome, that covers the bay in front of the niche. The dome is reeded, and on a pierced drum. The wall on either side of the central pier has three recesses, two stories high, in which are the windows. The upper windows are single, and slightly pointed; below are square-headed windows, with segmental discharging arches. The recesses for the windows are brought out flush with the piers by stalactites below the cornice. The walls which enclose the tombs at each end have a wide central pier, and two recesses with windows and stalactites like those in the other walls; above the cornice are truncated gables, the angles being moulded into grand toruses and cavettos, so as to bring the angles into an octagon for the dome to spring from. Each gable contains a triplet window, with three bulls'-eyes over it, but is not framed. The domes, which are about 50 ft. diameter externally, have a short drum pierced with windows, the external domes are chevronned. On the entrance side are two minarets about 150 ft. high; these are towers about 12 ft. 6 in. square, starting from the cornice of the building, and from this to the top of the first cornice of the minaret is about 34 ft.; its cornice is a stalactite one, and resembles machicolations, and is crowned with a stone balustrade, in this stage are windows with balconies on stalactites, above the minaret is circular, with a deep stalactite cornice and a stone balustrade, the circular shaft is enriched with an interlaced rope ornament, leaving only plain narrow bands between it, the cornice, and the balustrade. Above the circular part is an open octagon turret on columns with trefoiled arches, crowned with a stalactite cornice, and above is the stone cup and ball, with a bronze finial and crescent. The tombs of the Mamluk Sultans are mostly domed, and are very picturesque, the domes being covered with every variety of ornament,—reeds, flutes, chevrons, geometric and floral patterns, the latter mostly overlaid with diapers,—and in the clear air and dry climate of Egypt these are not only delightful to look at, but answer the purpose of keeping the domes dry; here the ornament would perish by the wet and frost, and would, too, be wholly clogged up with soot and dust.

The university mosque of El Azhar can only be described as far as its courtyard goes, which is about 160 ft. by 124 ft.; it was founded in 971 A.D., but has been so altered and restored up to the middle of the last century that little of the original building remains. The court is surrounded with an arcade of Persian arches on marble columns; over this is another storey ornamented with niches, and very small windows with bulls'-eyes beneath them; it has a geometric frieze and pierced bearded battlements; over its entrance is a graceful minaret, and at the end of the same front another; originally the wall seems to have been striped and subsequently plastered over.

I must not omit the charming little mosque of Kaït Bey, 1472 A.D. Its flank is not straight, but one end projects considerably, and its entrance is at the narrow return end. The walls are striped and mainly ornamented with windows in recesses, their tops brought out flush with stalactites, and the whole building is crowned with flower-de-luce battlements; on the flank by the entrance-angle, the first-floor has a triple arcade to an open belvedere, and this has a double arcade on the entrance front; but this is over the fountain which externally forms part of the mosque. Beyond is the high recess for the doorway, Persian fashion, that looks as if it had been built separately, as the courses do not match. Just beyond the door recess, the minaret springs from behind the battlements. Over the projecting flank is the dome covered with a geometric star ornament, filled in with foliage (a beautiful water-colour drawing of it by Mr. Spiers is on the table); except for its minaret and dome, you would never take it for a mosque, but all the ornamented parts have a quaint kind of elegance.

The mosque of Sidi Amar Abada, at Kairouan, shown in Mr. Alexander Graham's book on Tunisia, forms a picturesque group, with its five domes, three of which are on stepped square bases.

The Persian mosques must have been very striking; at that of Shah Abbas you come into a court 170 ft. deep and 223 ft. wide, with low sides, not more than 42 ft. high, in the centre, opposite you, the vast frontispiece, 95 ft. wide, towers up to a height of 105 ft., and is flanked by the cylindrical minarets, with the top of the dome just peering over the frontispiece; the deep shadow of the recess, when the sun is high, must greatly add to its impressiveness, and when we picture to ourselves that the whole courtyard is faced with enamelled bricks in gorgeous colours, it must surpass anything we have seen in magnificence.

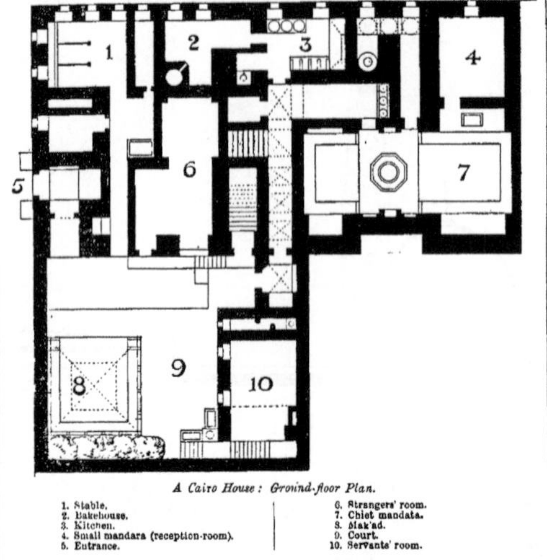

A Cairo House: Ground-floor Plan.

1. Stable.
2. Bakehouse.
3. Kitchen.
4. Small mandara (reception-room).
5. Entrance.
6. Strangers' room.
7. Chief mandata.
8. Mak'ad.
9. Court.
10. Servants' room.

I am painfully aware of the dulness of descriptions, but to fully illustrate all I have to say would take years to do; I will not, however, trespass on your patience much longer. I did mention the trefoiled-headed recesses that are often used to mark doorways. Their effect is both striking and unusual to our eyes, and I think with a little study, might be introduced here, and would greatly relieve the dull monotony of fronts. There are a few small architectural exhibits in Egypt that are marked by extreme care, delicacy, and originality of proportion, that are well worth profound study. Our best architects are very careful and painstaking about some of their smaller works, and often introduce delicious little bits. The study of these Saracenic motives would, I think, greatly aid them. The Saracen architects were not nearly so much fettered by rules of proportion as we are, and rightly thought that the object was to please the tasteful; I think that the late Professor de Morgan's dictum, which he applied to mathematics, is quite as applicable to architecture, "that rules are excellent things for those who can do without them." There is a doorway at Cairo in M. Bourgoin's book that illustrates in its details what I have been saying, and I may remark that the Saracen notion of marking the entrance by a grand feature was a happy one. A narrow band, consisting of two beads and fillets with a space between them, forming a guilloche at intervals, is used as a dado, leaving wide jambs to the doorway; it then rises up so as to form an oblong enclosure, high enough to frame in a small mezzanine window; the door jambs are quite plain, but the course at the top of the door is made into two delicate corbels, one on each side; above this is a deep enriched lintel, nearly as deep as the Jambs are wide; the frame runs out on either side below the lintel, till it is in a line with the jambs of the door; and from this the frame runs up again on both sides, and across over the lintel, and again over the discharging arch, thus making two panels of unequal heights. The parts below the segment of the discharging arch is recessed and ornamented. The arch has voussoirs of the wildest shape, in two kinds of marble; above it, in the centre, is the little half-story window, the moulded band, that frames the doorway, going round it, leaving a square panel on either side. A little above the framing of the door is a square panel, not so wide as the frame of the doorway, with a large circular panel in it, which, with the spandrels, are ornamented. The rectilinear patterns are of the most recondite Saracen geometry, and are intermingled with floral patterns; but an equivalent in colour or texture would answer the same purpose, at any rate, if the shape of the voussoirs were kept. There is also a little wooden shop-front at Tantah that is replete with exquisite grace. It consists of the square framework of a doorway, and two windows, grouped with the door; the height of the doorway is about two and two-thirds of its width, and the windows are about two and a-half times their width. Some woodwork is fitted into the doorway and windows to make the openings "rastremati," as the Italians say,—*i.e.*, narrower at the top; the heads are flat ellipses, and at the springings there are peculiar hooked corbels; round the frame of the door is a narrow piece of lattice. Two pieces of panelled woodwork go from the windows to the fronts of the adjoining houses; above, under the bressumer, is a broad band of intricate panelling in the centre, with the ends filled with lattices. I should say that the bottoms of the windows are filled in with turned balusters. You may think the upper lattices, from their position, more quaint than beautiful; but the exquisiteness of the lower part is certainly due, and due only, to a certain originality and a most refined and cultivated taste.

I have mainly confined myself to mosques, except in the case of the Alhambra, not because there are no other Saracen buildings, but because I thought that these more completely show the peculiarities of the style, but there are khans (the Xenodochia of the Byzantines), colleges, fountains, palaces, baths, houses, &c. The khans are curious, but are hardly of much use to us in England; they are fortified places where merchants, with strings of camels, mules, and horses, can put them up, lock up their goods, and have a small living-room for themselves; the palaces are mostly those adapted to a burning climate, and to Oriental potentates; it is curious that some features are precisely the same as in the days of the Achæmenides,—*i.e.*, the structure consists of a roof, supported on slender columns, open between, the enclosures being made by curtains or hangings.

The arrangements of a good house are always more or less interesting, and there are two or three requirements to be noted in Moslem houses. Well-to-do people mostly keep a horse, a mule, or a donkey to ride on; the donkey is not the dull, slow animal in a hot climate that it is here, but, if of a good breed, it goes like the "blinding lightning." Well-to-do people bake their own bread, and, from keeping their women separate, may enjoy the society of whom they please. The Viceroy of Egypt would probably admit to his saloon and table a beggar who was a Hadji, he certainly would if he were an agreeable person as well; a Hadji being one who has performed the pilgrimage to Mecca, run seven times round the Kaaba, and kissed the black stone, and run up to the top of Mount Arafat, and had his head shaved. When I was in Cairo I visited a house, then desetted, that was said to have belonged to the Sheykh-el-Islâm, the chief mufti, or doctor of the law, a title that was first conferred by Mohammed II., when he took Constantinople. There is generally a stone seat for the porter outside the door, called a mastaba, the entrance-passage makes a sharp turn, so that no one can see inside, and the entrance is generally into the court, in which is an open pavilion, raised above the ground, a sort of summer-house or belvedere; there is often another on the first-floor of the house. The floor of the grand reception-room is on two levels, mostly paved with marble, with mosaic borders; in the middle is a plashing fountain, rising from the middle of a basin, mostly octagonal, often with little ones at the angles, with jets falling into the middle basin, like the font in the Baptistery at Florence. Over it, above the roof, is a latticed dome, and just beyond the fountain is the step up to the carpeted dais; you leave your shoes on the lower level. On either side of this dais, and sometimes at the end, are slightly raised seats covered with cushions that form the divans. The walls are lined with marble, sometimes inlaid, sometimes bordered with mosaic, and sometimes they are covered with enamelled tiles, and this is finished by a wood shelf, on which the fine crockery is put, so that if any of the pieces fall, they may fall on the cushions. There are, too, cupboards for keeping the cushions, &c.; these are closed by doors, but some have fantastically-pierced openings for bottles and vases. In the lower part of the saloon are often stepped fountains in the middle of each side, down which water trickles. Above the shelf there were, in this house, hunting-scenes on the walls; on one side of the daïs there is often a projecting lattice, or bow-window, in which the porous water-bottles stand, commonly called meshrebiyas, or drinking places; the saloon is mostly very lofty, and, whenever there is a recess or a break, the woodwork comes down in long stalactites; the ceiling is mostly flat, and the beams round and not far apart, the ends of the beams are brought into the square next the walls by stalactites; between the bearers the ceiling is panelled, and the whole covered with elaborate patterns, coloured and gilt; if one side looks into the garden, the lower window is often a plain lead light with circular panes of clear glass; above are the windows of pierced plaster, filled with stained glass that look like jewels. We know these saloons well from the pictures of the late John Lewis and Mr. Dillon. All architecture and decoration is, as a rule, confined to the inside; the house is mostly of stone to the top of the ground story, above of lath and plaster on a bressummer, carried on heavy stone corbels, often peculiarly moulded, looking as if folding-wedges had been driven in between the mouldings, and this part has windows filled with flat lattices, generally with one latticed bay-window; the eaves of this are decorated with pierced woodwork like our railway stations, often in two or three ranges, the bottoms coming below one another; the eaves generally project considerably for shade, and are carried on slight framed gallows pieces, with the double or triple rows of delicate pierced lear-boards. These, of course, cast long, sharp, fantastic shadows. Some of these pierced lear-boards [t]o the schools over the fountains are peculiarly [g]raceful and effective. Here and there, how[e]ver, there are houses whose fronts have archi[t]ectural pretensions, but I think mostly to the [g]ardens or courtyards. Sometimes the archi[t]ectural effect is confined to the ground story, [a]nd frequently to one feature. Sometimes a [t]all recess with an architrave runs up above the bressummer, and has a lintel of its own, carried by short puncheons on the corbels. The door is in this recess, with a half-story window over it, and with ornamental panels at the sides; the top is enriched with stalactites, and on either side of the architrave and beyond it there are sometimes panels of flat ornament; but when there is a mak'ad or belvedere on the first-floor the whole front may be architecturally disposed. A low door mostly forms the entrance to the ground-floor magazine, which has as well plain segmental or square-headed windows, with iron gratings. Above the belvedere is open, the upper part being supported by arches standing on a central column, with enriched spraudrels, and projecting eaves on corbels. The house door is reached by a flight of outside steps, and is enclosed in a recess running above the arches of the belvedere, with a trefoiled head filled with stalactites like those to some of the mosques; the recess has often two tiers of windows. Above the door and in the spaces between the door and window and between the two windows are filled with ornamental panels.

In one of the streets in Cairo, called Khot-el-Mokharbelyn, is a little oratory, called the Oratory of Abd-el-Rahman, who was lieutenant of the Janissaries from 1743 to 1754 A.D. The ground-floor is now used for shops, but from there being a semicircular niche in the back wall, it is most probable that it was originally an oratory; the present oratory is on the first-floor; the entrance doorway has a slightly pointed arch on columns; the lower fascia of the archivolt is godrooned, the upper fascia is ornamented, and is carried up square as well, and connected at the top by a guilloche, so as to frame the doorway; above is an ornamental pierced stone balcony, carried on stalactites, in front of an opening used by the cryer to call the hour of prayer; the rest of the front is separated from this by a frame. The ground-floor has three square-headed windows; over them is a triple arcade, carried on columns with peculiarly cusped arches; the arcade contains three square-headed windows filled with iron gratings; above the framework of this is a deep oblong frame, rather within the one below, and is formed into three square panels over the centres of the arches, with blank spaces between; in each is a bull's-eye, with a frame round the circle, connected on the four centres with the outer frame, and with ornamental spandrels; there is no cornice above this, but the whole wall is finished with flower-de-luce battlements, bulbed below the flower. It was, as you have heard, designed for ecclesiastical purposes, and has only been turned, by decay of piety, into domestic use.

ROYAL INSTITUTE OF BRITISH ARCHITECTS:

STAINED AND PAINTED GLASS.

THE eighth ordinary general meeting of this Institute for the present session was held on Monday evening last, the President, Mr. J. Macvicar Anderson, in the chair.

The minutes of the previous meeting having been confirmed,

The Chairman announced that letters had been received from the Home Secretary and Sir Francis Knollys on behalf of Her Majesty and the Prince and Princess of Wales in reply to the votes of condolence which had been sent by the Institute on the occasion of the lamented death of the Duke of Clarence.

The Honorary Secretary, Mr. Aston Webb, then read a long list of candidates recommended for admission as members of the Institute,—22 as Fellows, and 24 as Associates.

Two or three members attending for the first time since their election were formally introduced to the President; among them was the Bishop of Ely, Lord Alwyne Compton, of whom the President said that he was competent to form and express correct opinions on subjects of art and architecture.

Painted Glass.

The Chairman said that as they had four papers to be read, he would not detain them with any preliminary remarks, but would at once call upon Mr. Herbert Carpenter to read the first paper, of which the following is an abstract:—

Although the architect should be responsible for the whole internal effect of his design, it was not, in the author's opinion, necessary to determine exactly how far the stained-glass decoration should be under his control. He should, however, be able, without vexatious interference, so to direct those working with him that the painted glass should in style and treatment harmonise with the architectural design of the building and with its decorative treatment. As an example of the satisfactory result of the co-operation of the architect and the artist in glass-painting, he referred to the case of Truro Cathedral, in which Mr. Pearson and Mr. Clayton had together produced a very beautiful and harmonious interior. Through successive centuries the relationship between architecture and glass-painting had been very intimate. In early Christian times the intense eastern sunlight, streaming through small window-openings filled with gem-like glass, afforded a striking and brilliant contrast to the large wall-spaces. As architecture travelled westwards and northwards into less sunny regions, in the eleventh and twelfth centuties, windows necessarily became larger but the "mosaic" glass, with its Byzantine ornamentation, was still used, the gorgeous and jewel-like effect of colour being emphasised and intensified by lines and points of white glass, and the bold, black geometrical forms of the frame-work. In the thirteenth century not only the gem-like glass, but silvery and brilliant pattern-glass, of white with a bluish tinge in it, was used, together with rich bands of pictorial figure-subjects, on a white ground. In the fourteenth century the mosaic glass, as such, went out of use in the great mullioned windows, but its rich colours were retained, in combination with a lemon-yellow strain. The window tracery of this period was designed to frame the translucent pictures, though as time went on, and the masonry became more studied in design, the glass had to adapt itself to the masonry, rather than the masonry to the glass. As large windows multiplied, a large proportion of white or greenish-white or quarry-glass was employed. By very gradual changes the most characteristic English glass, that of the fifteenth and the early part of the sixteenth centuries, grew up, acquiring greater breadth than the gorgeously-tinted earlier glass, and infinite delicacy of drawing and tone, and combining with it especially painting on white glass with enamel colours and stains. At this time one mind and one idea inspired the designers both of the buildings and of their glass. After animadverting on Professor Moore's statement that nowhere, save in France, was there in glass-painting an actual spirit of original invention, the author spoke of the crude and incongruous designs or imitations of Mediæval work in memorial windows erected in the last half century, as compared with those described to have existed in Long Melford Church or in the Grey Friars Church, London. It appeared to him that the principle of the memorial window was of inestimable value, not only artistically and historically, but as a link of the present with the past. Symbolism in stained glass he considered should be neither too patent nor yet too recondite. With reference to modern painted glass he laid down the following postulates:—1. That the glass be brilliant, translucent, and jewel-like. 2. That the colours be, to a great extent, of pot-metal, of unequal tone and thickness. 3. That in each building its due proportion of white glass be fixed and adhered to throughout. 4. That the ironwork designed by the architect should be carefully considered in designing the glass, and that no sound ancient ironwork should be removed. 5. That the leading be an essential part of the design, to be shown on the glass-painter's sketch drawings. 6. That each window should form part of a complete scheme previously determined by the architect with the authorities of the church. 7. That the representation of sacred subjects should not be pictorial, nor realistic, nor sentimental, but should be treated in an architecturesque and conventional manner. 8. That a carefully-thought-out system of symbolism should be adopted. 9. That pictorial subjects extending over more than one light should only be selected when they lent themselves to arrangement in divisions. 10. That the series of figures or subjects be selected in proper doctrinal and historical gradation from west to east of the church. 11. That in memorial windows the kneeling figure should be introduced in the "predella" with a legible inscription. 12. That heraldry should be an essential part of the design, especially in memorial windows. 13. That in ancient churches, with windows of varying date, the glass should be assimilated in each case to the designs of the masonry. In conclusion, he urged that, as in architecture, so in the art of painted glass, history and archæology should not be disregarded, and that there should be no spasmodic attempts at originality.

Some Details and Technicalities of the Glass-Painter's Art.

This was the subject of the second paper read by Mr. James Powell. The following is an abstract:—

In making a painted window, the first process is to prepare a small coloured sketch of the design, usually to a scale of one inch to a foot. On this drawing should be shown the ironwork, which should be so arranged as to assist and not interfere with the design of the glass.

The sketch having been approved, full-sized cartoons are prepared. For these, studies from the life are required, the hands and feet especially needing careful study. White subjects surrounded by colour should be drawn smaller that when against a white background. On these cartoons the ironwork and lead lines should be definitely shown, and upon the latter great pains should be bestowed, the lead lines being more conspicuous than the folds of the drapery. From the finished cartoon a tracing, called the "cutline," is made on calico of all the lead lines, and from this the cutter cuts the glass in corresponding lines. Great discrimination is required in the choice of the glass, so that its varying thicknesses shall coincide with the light and shade of the figures. When the glass is cut, it is taken to the painting-room, and all the leading lines of the cartoon, and also the ornamental patterns of draperies or diapers of backgrounds are shown with enamel pigment. The glass, after having been fired in the kiln, is then fixed with wax to a framed piece of plate-glass, so that it can be placed against the light on an easel. The paint (water-colour process) is then applied to the glass with a large flat brush, and worked flat or rough, according to the requirements of the design. The high lights are then removed with scrubs, or short hog hair brushes, and in the half-tones the pigment is reduced in density, and the shadows deepened by laying on another mat of colour. The glass is then again fired, and the above process repeated until the required strength is obtained, great care being taken to keep the shadows luminous. When the paint is finished, the silver stain is added, where required, to such parts as hair, embroidery of draperies, or foliage. The glass is next laid on its "cutline" on the glazier's bench, and the leading is put in. Mr. Powell himself prefers flat lead, as being stronger than the round, and better for the cementing. The lead should be from ¼ in. to ⅜ in. in width. After the window is soldered on both sides the leads are raised, and a cement of oil, lead, &c., is rubbed well in on both sides. The copper ties are then soldered on, and after a few days the cement has hardened and all is ready for fixing. As to materials used. Coloured glass is obtained by melting certain metallic oxides with the raw material or base. A good workman can so handle the melted glass as to produce variations of thickness, from which of course result varied tints of the same colour in one sheet. In some recent experiments the traditional charcoal yellow had been hit upon, and it had been found to be almost identical with the straw-yellow of the thirteenth century. Glasses made as above described are known as pot-metal colours. Flashed or cased glass, is used chiefly for ruby glass, the colouring matter of which is so dense that it is blown on a base of white glass; beautiful shades are also procured by casing the ruby with a blue or yellow glass. One great advantage of the cased glass is that you can with hydric fluoride remove parts of the coloured film and expose the base colour underneath. This is especially useful in heraldic designs or the patterning of robes. The enamel used by the glass-painter for shading and outlines is a fusible glass containing a sufficient quantity of an infusible powder to produce the effect of opacity. The window may be painted entirely in water-colour, or it may be traced in oil-colour and matted in water-colour. The lead is first cast in short lengths, and then elongated by mechanical pressure. The leads used in old windows were usually very narrow, and were cast in their full length. A great deal of the old work had been re-leaded with wider lead than that originally used. The leading of the thirteenth and fourteenth centuries was mostly designed in diagonal lines, and this diamond form gave a perfect drain for the water. For a window designed in a strong key of colour as much lead as possible should be used; in the whiter windows less lead is required. To the ironwork the artist should pay special attention. Saddle-bars should not be more than 12 in. apart. The most useful arrangement for modern work, except in very narrow windows, is to have a double stanchion, with saddle-bars at distances varying from 10 in. to 12 in., according to the width of the light. If the architect wishes for outside iron as well the glass-painter need not grumble, for it enhances his work. Wire-guards are an abomination to the glass-painter and a detriment to the architect, and sheets of plate-glass outside look worse still. A lead across a broken pane is preferable to a wire-guard. The glass-painter should remember that a window is made to admit light, and white glass should predominate, though an east window requires more colour than a side window. On these points the architect should advise. Too many different colours should not be used in one window. The best decorative effects are produced with a simple scheme of colour. There should be harmony between the glass and its frame. This harmony is never wanting in the old work of the best periods, and hence it may be supposed that the architect must have had considerable supervision of the glass. The design of the glass should be in relation to that of the stone. Windows should not be crowded with too many figures. A better decorative effect might be produced by using more ornament and fewer figures. The scale of the figures used requires careful study, and as to this the architect should assist. Arms and legs should not be thrown behind mullion; large compositions of figures and canopies running across several lights should also be avoided. Lastly, a scheme should be carefully prepared for the subject of the window; and the glass-painter should work in harmony with the architect.

The Painted Windows at Fairford, Winchester, and King's College, Cambridge, as Models for Modern Work.

The third paper, by Mr. N. H. J. Westlake, F.S.A., was on the windows mentioned above.

After suggesting a few of the many questions which arise from a study of the ancient examples of painted glass, the author pointed out that the considerations in studying old work were, (1) The appropriateness of glass to the church so far as light is concerned. (2) The scale of the details in proportion to the building. (3) The composition and colour value. He intentionally omitted the theological *schema* and iconography, because those ought to be settled beforehand by the theological and art authorities with the architect. The first consideration, he said, involved the questions of the size of the building, the size of the windows, the position and locality of the church, the amount of carving, painting, and other decorations, and the comfort of the congregation. At Fairford and at King's College, although the edifices were completely filled with painted glass, there was plenty of light. At Winchester the treatment was very similar to that at Fairford. At Fairford the openings were moderately large and plentiful, the glass fairly but not densely covered, and there was a great area of white in the canopies and draperies. At King's College the openings were larger and more numerous, there was less white, and the paintings were more dense. Chartres, he said, was an instance of a dark church,—the darkness not resulting from the amount of shadowing pigment on the glass, but from the smallness of the details, which involved so much lead and iron that a great area was rendered opaque. The architect could not dictate how much colour should be used until he knew whether all the windows were to be done. The proper character and quality of the painting on the glass, the quantity of pigment to be used, the amount of obscurity in painting on white and on colour, had been but slowly learnt by the artists in different countries. The earliest work was similar wherever found, but in the early years of the sixteenth century the northern countries used less pigment than the southern. English work of the best periods was as delicate and translucent as any: compare Fairford, King's College, and Winchester with the German and Flemish glass of St. Mary's, Shrewsbury, and Lichfield Cathedral. Between French and English work there was no great difference of tone. In the nave aisles of Cologne the covering of the glass was moderate; at Milan the covering was increased; at Florence, Bologna, Arezzo, and SS. Giovanni è Paolo, Venice, the glass was all more or less heavily painted. The painting at Fairford was often unequal in tone, the inequality being in most instances intentional; *e.g.*, the east window had more pigment than the aisle windows; but the diversity in covering the glass at Fairford was not so apparent or so necessary as in a large edifice like Winchester Cathedral. The windows from Winchester College (now at South Kensington) were a good example of the amount and character of the painting used in a chapel with plenty of large openings. In King's College the difference between the chapel glass and that in the large windows afforded an excellent comparison by which to acquire a knowledge of the painting of the glass under different conditions. Many of these windows, however, had been badly over-painted in restoration.

The Renaissance Period and the Use of Enamel.

The fourth and last paper was by Mr. Clement Heaton, who treated of the above-named subject. He said glass-painting originated from enamelled metal work, and in its early form was an assemblage of small pieces of glass, heavy in texture and strong in colour. As years went on it became lighter and lighter in general tone, the glass itself becoming thinner in substance and the colour less intense, while in all ways there was a progression towards lightness. A style of work was arrived at late in the fifteenth century containing principles which could not be departed from without loss of effect, and which he considered was in England more successful than in France. Admirable as this work was, it was not the highest development of glass painting. There was a limitation of design and conception, power of colour and drawing, compared with both earlier and later work. The earliest glass was geometrical in character, and the later Gothic purely architectural. The canopy work based on architectural models was monotonous through its endless repetition. In the sixteenth century, when new ideas came into France from Flanders and Italy, glass painting was thriving as regards technique, and the "Renaissance" was really in design alone; *motifs* of ornament from Flemish and Italian Renaissance were adapted and expressed in Gothic *technique*. In Rouen examples remained showing the transition; and the earliest of them exhibited this use of Renaissance detail, treated technically in the same manner as the Gothic canopies. In King's College Chapel, Cambridge, was a similar series of English examples, in which, however, the Italian influence appeared less direct. This was not surprising, as Leonardo da Vinci, Andrea del Sarto, Benvenuto Cellini, Rosso, and Primatice, and many other less-known Italian craftsmen, worked in France for a time. The art of glass painting was the more influenced because the line of separation between architect, sculptor, painter, and glass-painter was little marked. Jean Cousin was at once architect, sculptor, a prominent painter, glass-painter, and engraver, while he possessed enough knowledge of anatomy and geometry to write treatises thereon. It was to the breadth of study then in vogue that Mr. Heaton attributed the power of the work done from 1520 to 1550. The works of the Middle Renaissance showed a wondrous combination; the true principles of glass painting,—glorious colour, refinement, grace and power of drawing, vigour of design, and individuality of conception,—all might be found united in the same work, and that work such as only artists who knew all the *technique* of glass painting could produce. After 1550 the glass painter aimed less at producing a beautiful glass painting than a picture full of strong contrasts in light and shade; the *technique* was interfered with to obtain such contrasts, and so the grace and the silveriness of the glass was lost and the colouration sacrificed. There were therefore three distinct phases of work to consider:—(1) Where sound principles and traditions were worked upon, but with limited artistic power; (2) where these same principles were used combined with great artistic power; and (3) where this power was misdirected and crippled by the abandonment of the true principles. Study of the second phase,—the most notable,—showed that certain principles must be adhered to, and that mere use of them, without individuality of conception and personal care, would only lead to monotony. The personal care of the artist must not stop at the design, but must be carried through every step of the work. The breadth of study among the artists of the Renaissance was well worthy of attention. M. Lucien Magne, who had closely studied sixteenth-century glass, had written: "The first cause of the inferiority of modern work as compared with the old appears to me to be in the isolated instruction of the arts." Mr. Heaton then proceeded to mention the introductions in *technique* of the Renaissance. The pot-metal colours had been much extended in range, which was due to the system of plating; the silver stain was made to produce not only yellows, but orange and red; the brown painting colour was supplemented by a red; and finally transparent enamels were introduced about 1540. This last he made special mention of as being so influential and so specially a Renaissance feature. In the MS. of Theophilus,—twelfth to thirteenth century,—instructions were given for "placing gems on glass," and a description was added of how small pieces of glass were to be cut out, put on the white glass, and melted on to it. Various examples of this process were known, but the method was unsatisfactory; the use of fluoric acid had done away with the necessity of grinding the glass, but the use of transparent enamels best got over the difficulty of which all glass painters had been sensible. It was probable that the application of transparent enamels arose through the use of enamel in goldsmith's work, as was indicated by a recipe in Mrs. Merrifield's translation of the Bolognese MS. of the fifteenth century. Whether the idea came direct from Italy, or the French themselves adapted the enamel to glass from the enamelled jewellery and pottery, it was difficult to say. At Rouen there were several examples of the use of enamel in conjunction with pot metal glass; and enamel colour alone was used in the sixteenth century for panels and medallions, specimens of which could be seen in Rouen Museum, and some of a later date at South Kensington. It was also used by Giovanni da Udini in Florence about 1560, and in England in the time of Elizabeth. Although so extensively used it had sometimes been urged that its use was illegitimate, which was probably in consequence of its misuse and of ignorance in working it. Properly worked it was very reliable, as was proved by the fact that enamels done in 1540 were sound at the present day. As to the artistic use of enamel, any attempt to use enamel colour in large quantities and in rivalry to pot metal glass the author condemned. It was, so used, an inferior result obtained in a roundabout way; but in conjunction with pot metal glass he considered it might be of great value if used with proper artistic discretion. For domestic use it could be a means of rendering colour in a fine way in harmony with modern interiors, which leaded colour was certainly not. It was an additional power, and as such required additional judgment in its use, while without artistic judgment and the restraint of good taste it would be more than likely to lead to very objectionable results.

The President, in inviting discussion, said they had with them so many distinguished artists who could speak with authority on the subject which was before them, that he proposed at once to call upon them to do so. He would ask their good friend and distinguished colleague, Mr. Alma Tadema, to move a vote of thanks to the authors of the papers.

Mr. Alma Tadema, R.A., said he felt honoured in being asked to move a vote of thanks to the readers of the papers. He had been very much interested in hearing so many artistic and technical views on a subject which had had so much influence on art and architecture. They would remember how Violiet-le-Duc was led to the pursuit of art by seeing the stained-glass windows of Notre Dame at Paris. He was quite convinced that the development of the art feeling of the people in France was greatly due to the people going in and out of the churches and seeing such wonderful windows, full of rich colour, and illustrating subjects which could not fail to influence them. It was therefore quite natural that the majority of the papers were devoted to the religious expression of stained glass. Perhaps the question of the use of stained-glass windows in domestic architecture had not been touched upon so much, though in modern times the architect must often have been asked for such windows. In towns, for instance, where one had a window opposite an ugly blank wall, it was a great advantage to have a stained-glass window. Of course, figures of saints and other things strictly belonging to religious art were a little out of place, and, therefore, a purely decorative scheme of treating the glass would be preferable. Mr. Lafarge, in America, had applied himself to work of that kind with a very great deal of success, and he (the speaker) was the happy possessor of one of the finest specimens of his work. As they knew, he admired the old Romans very much, and he rather believed that they had stained glass, though not in our sense of the term. He knew that there was in Pompeii, in a little house, a piece of sheet-glass of a beautiful purple colour, built in the wall. In conclusion, he said he was quite sure he expressed the views of the meeting in proposing a hearty vote of thanks to the authors of the four most interesting papers which had been read that evening, and to whom they could not be grateful enough.

The Chairman said he hoped that the Bishop of Ely, out of the profundity of his knowledge, would be kind enough to second the vote of thanks.

The Bishop of Ely said he should have pleasure in seconding the vote of thanks to the authors of the papers, but he feared that it would be out of the shallowness of his knowledge, rather than out of its profundity. He had been exceedingly interested in hearing the four papers read; they were most instructive, and contained many most valuable hints. He was delighted to hear Mr. Powell denounce the practice of putting wires outside painted windows. That was a thing he had been fighting against for many years. An occasional crack would be far better than having the effect of the window always spoilt by the wires. There would be some reason in putting up the wires to protect an ancient window, but why should they put such wires in front of modern windows? He had seen many modern windows which he should be very glad to see broken. There was one point which was very often forgotten: that it was necessary that they should have light on certain parts of the interior of a building. Very often in the east end of a church painted glass was put in, and gradually worked in towards the west. The result, as a rule, was that the east end was perfectly dark, while the nave was so light that when standing in it the chancel appeared to be a dark hole. He thought that was a great mistake. He thought it was possible to use a good deal of white glass in the eastern end of the building. He was not very fond himself of glass which was all white. He quite agreed with what Mr. Carpenter and Mr. Powell said, for he thought that the one effect proper to painted glass was colour, and the very white-toned windows were unsatisfactory in that respect. Of course, he did not mean to depreciate good form and beauty of drawing, but he thought they might have that in combination with colour. As to the Romans making use of coloured glass, there was a passage in one of the old authors directing one how to make blue glass, and the reader was directed to take and grind down "sapphires." He thought that the "sapphires" in question must have been Roman blue glass; for, of course, they would not grind down gem sapphires. He had very great pleasure in seconding most heartily the vote of thanks to the four gentlemen who had so kindly favoured them with such interesting papers.

The President said he should next call upon one of their professional brethren,—one whom they were very glad to see with them that evening,—and who, he hoped, would allow them that opportunity of publicly congratulating him upon the honour which had been recently most deservedly conferred upon him. Of course, he referred to Mr. T. G. Jackson, who had recently been elected an Associate of the Royal Academy.

Mr. T. G. Jackson, A.R.A., who was heartily received, said that in the first place he must thank them very sincerely for the kind way in which they had received his name in connexion with the reference which the President had made to his recent election to the Academy. He was glad to have the opportunity of accepting their invitation to hear such admirable papers as those which had been read that evening. Benefit was always to be derived from such meetings, and he thought that the more opportunities artists of all kinds had of meeting together and discussing their different crafts, the more they were likely to advance art. The art of glass painting seemed to possess an unusual share of the perils which had assailed the art of architecture, one of the greatest of which was the danger of lapsing from art into archæology. Glass painting was, of course, exclusively a Mediæval art, and could be best studied in the buildings of the Middle Ages; but in designing or considering the subject of stained glass, one of the difficulties that they had was, out of the mass of material, to select what was best suitable for their adoption and development. In England and France, having discovered, as they did very early, the means of making extremely rich and brilliant coloured glass, they seemed to have gone to the very extreme, and to have thought that they could not make the colours rich and heavy enough; but while one was impressed by the charm of such glass as that at Canterbury and Chartres, it would be impossible for us in the present day to attempt anything of the kind. It used to be said that we could not get the glass of the right quality; but he thought they might dismiss that altogether, because the production of any kind of glass was now quite within the power of modern chemistry. But something besides the glass was wanted, viz., the habit of mind which enabled the artists of old times to produce such designs as they did. We in the present day could not work in the simple, naïve manner which to them was natural, for in us it would be mere affectation; and without following their manner it would be impossible to produce glass like theirs. The most useful stained glass for our study was, he thought, the later glass, in which one got more perfect designs and a higher form of art, although, perhaps, not in the same gorgeous and transient effects of colour as in the early glass. For our modern purposes, he thought, the lighter glass was most useful. Many interiors owed a great deal of their charm to the pure light, or even the dusky light, which came in through windows glazed with ordinary glass. Nothing that had been done of late in Westminster Abbey in the way of filling the clearstory with painted glass compensated to his mind for the loss of the old wonderful light which used to steal in by the clearstory windows through the dusky and somewhat murky atmosphere that filled the Abbey, producing the most exquisite effects. That was now lost, and what had been done was, in his opinion, loss rather than gain. In town churches there might, perhaps, be good reason for using stained glass more extensively, but in country churches stained glass must be very good indeed if it was to compensate for the loss of the blue sky and the green trees seen through the windows. He might, perhaps, mention one or two old examples where stained glass had been used in combination with ordinary glass with very happy effect. In both the great churches of Nuremberg, the Sebaldskirche and the Lorenzkirche, he thought there were windows which, in the lower part, were filled with richly-coloured stained glass, but which was not carried right up to the head, but finished some part of the way up with a sort of canopy,—he forgot exactly how, but, at all events, there was a definite finishing, showing that it was never intended to go any higher,—the remainder of the window being filled in with ordinary white glass; the effect was admirable. Another instance, with which he was more familiar, was in one of the chapels at Oxford. In Wadham College Chapel there were on each side of the choir five transomed windows. The lower part below the transomes was filled with painted glass and the upper part was filled with ordinary window glass, which was the original arrangement, and the effect seemed to him to be extremely pleasant. It dated from the year 1622. The chapel was perfectly light, and, at the same time, a very rich effect of colour was obtained by the amount of painted glass in the lower parts of the windows. Of course, if glass in such a position as that were painted very heavily, it would look dirty, but at Wadham College Chapel, to his mind, it was treated with great success.

Mr. Henry Holiday said he was glad to perceive the distinct advance which artistic opinion had made on the subject since it was before the Institute some years ago. It was now generally recognised that archæology was not art, although it might greatly aid them in its study. They ought all to be ready to learn from the study of the past, but the duty of artists was not to imitate the work of the past. No great artist had ever succeeded in doing anything good by imitating that which had been done before him. Art was growth, and each artist at any of the old periods when great work was produced had done what he did, not as an imitator, but as a producer. Of course it did not follow that every development was an improvement, but he thought that any artist worthy of the name would rather make a few technical errors in his art than produce lifeless work, for mere imitation must always be absolutely lifeless. All good artistic work must express the ideas of the artist and the ideas of his time. Thirteenth-century work was modern; so were Giotto and Michelangelo, and so must be every great artist. One great question which came home to the artist in dealing with the decorative arts was: How far could realism be united with true architectonic principles? There was a certain confusion of ideas often to be met with in discussing that subject with outsiders, who often seemed to think that if a piece of decorative art was not archaic in character it must be an imitation of an oil-painting. They all knew that what was known as the "Munich school" had wholly failed, by attempting to make stained-glass windows imitations of oil-paintings. They failed in the way that the Gobelins tapestries failed,—in endeavouring to make one material imitate the effects of another material; they failed to get the effects of the other material, and they sacrificed all the beauty of the material with which they were dealing. The question, then, as he had said, arose, How far could an artist be realistic without failing in architectonic qualities? In his opinion, that was a question which would settle itself for each artist if he remembered that he had to consider his material, his situations, that he was working for a window and not painting on a wall, that he was working in transparent glass joined by leads and not with oil-paints. If he kept those things clearly in mind, then would he never fail by attempting to secure all the interest that could be obtained by imitating beautiful forms in outline and even beautiful forms in modelling. He would ask any one who had examined the frieze of the Parthenon whether he thought that the splendid decorative qualities of that frieze had been in the slightest degree sacrificed by its most beautiful imitation of the forms of horses and of human beings? In the thirteenth century, as well as at the present day, some of the greatest beauties of art had been obtained by what was to the artists of that day realism. If we compared the stained glass of that period with the miniature painting of that period we found precisely the same qualities in both. It was clear that they imitated to the best of their power. The fact that they could not imitate as accurately as we could detracted to some extent from the perfection of their forms; but, on the other hand, it left them a little freer to consider the mere technical qualities of the material, the jewelled beauty of the glass. But was there anything in the delicate play of tone about such figures as those of Mr. Burne-Jones, in the drawings exhibited, which would not add to rather than detract from the beauty of the glass for which they were prepared?

Mr. C. W. Whall said that an experimental practice which he himself adopted, and which he had not seen used elsewhere, was that of designing a window in glass itself. He made a sketch of the window in glass, cutting the pieces out on a small scale to an inch scale tracing.

Mr. Lewis F. Day said there was a suggestion that anything like originality must necessarily be spasmodic, and that if we were to do good work we ought to copy something old; but Mr. Holiday had practically answered that. With regard to the influence of style upon design in stained glass, he thought people in general, and perhaps architects in particular, were a little too much inclined to insist, for a church or whatever it might be, upon precisely the style in which the glass-workers of that particular period worked. Of course, every artist who designed stained glass, if he were an artist at all, did instinctively consider the style of his architecture, and he must do so; but that was quite a different thing from insisting that he should work in the style in which the glass-workers of that particular period worked. His own idea was that the artist in stained glass (as in anything else) should study the course of stained glass, and be perfect master of all that had been done in stained glass in every period. He should also study the styles of architecture. Being conversant with those two things, he should do the best he could with the glass, bearing in mind its surroundings. He did not think that necessarily meant that he was to do what was done by the glass-painters of that period. It was possible that the men in the thirteenth century did not know so much about stained glass as the men in the fifteenth, and so on. We found that men insisted upon having Renaissance work, for instance, after the manner of artists who knew very little about glass. In the Renaissance there were stained glass artists who did glass that was almost as "mosaic" as thirteenth-century work.

The President, in putting the motion for a vote of thanks to the authors of the papers, said they owed a debt of gratitude to the Art Standing Committee, and more particularly to their Vice-Chairman, Mr. Carpenter, and one of their Honorary Secretaries, Mr. Caröe, for the great trouble they had taken to arrange that meeting.

The vote was passed by acclamation, and Mr. R. Herbert Carpenter, on behalf of the readers of papers, briefly returned thanks, and the meeting terminated, with the announcement that the next business meeting of the Institute would be held on March 7, followed by a special general meeting to elect the Royal Gold Medallist for 1892 and to consider the amended paper of "Suggestions for the Conduct of Architectural Competitions."

Illustrations.

ILLUSTRATIONS OF OLD CHESTER.*

II.—WATERGATE-STREET.

IN the sixteenth century, Watergate-street was of great commercial importance. Each side yet possesses immense bonded warehouses. When Chester was a thriving port, it was the principal street in the city, and contained several interesting mansions; in fact, it is the most picturesque and characteristic street in Old Chester. The Rows are especially interesting, although the purpose for which they were designed is doubtful. They form galleries or piazzas, one story above the street, to which they run parallel, and are approached by flights of steps at various places. At the Cross their elevation is about 10 ft. In front the Rows are generally open, and have a low railing. In the Rows are ranged the principal shops, and between these shops and the railings is the main thoroughfare of the citizens. Over all are dwellings, so the thoroughfare forms an agreeable promenade in all weathers. Underneath the Rows are other shops entered from the street. Various and contradictory are the theories of the origin of the Rows. The most rational contention appears to be that they were used as covered entrances to the residences of eminent Roman citizens, as, in the rear, remnants of extensive gardens are traceable. The Row, on the north side of Watergate-street, is a good example of the Rows as they existed in the last century; the south side possesses the greatest number of interesting buildings. Near the Cross is "God's Providence House" (restored). Two hundred years ago this was the residence of a family of distinction, evident from the armorial bearings carved on one of the beams. According to tradition this was the only house in the city which escaped the plague in the seventeenth century, and in gratitude for that deliverance the owner had carved on the front "God's Providence is mine Inheritance, 1652." Lower down on the same side,—under the Row,—is the old crypt, said to date from 1180, and adjoining this the remains of the town residence of Leach of Carden, a very fine example of old woodwork; the high hall and pendant still remain, and there is a noble fireplace of great height. At the back of this tenement is the "Lady's Bower."

Continuing downwards we reach "Bishop Lloyd's Palace," which is, without exception, the most remarkable house in Chester, and, perhaps, has no equal in Great Britain. The origin of this house is not known. Bishop Lloyd died here about 1650. The date carved in one of the front panels and certain armorial bearings have an analogy to the bearings of his family. The centre gable of the three, seen to the right of the illustration, exhibits a profusion of grotesque ornament carved in oak. Under the windows are eight panels. The first contains "Adam and Eve in Paradise," and "Cain slaying Abel," next "Abraham offering Isaac"; the seventh has a curious representation of the Immaculate Conception; the eighth symbolises the completion of the sacrifice in Simeon's prophecy, "Yea, a sword shall pierce thine own heart also." The centre panel contains the arms of James I., the supposed arms and quarterings of Bishop Lloyd, and a Latin inscription with the date 1615. The supports in the row are profusely carved with indescribable forms of men and beasts, the three windows to the left belong to the room in which is placed the fireplace, already illustrated, the panels in this gable, which are now quite plain, are supposed originally to have been decorated similar to the last. A little lower down is a passage or entry called "Puppet Show Entry," chiefly memorable as the scene of a terrible explosion, which took place on December 5, 1772. Opposite formerly stood a fine old mansion of wood and plaster, the city residence of the Mainwarings, a notable Chester family.

Continuing on the south side is the Yacht Inn, at the corner of Nicholas-street, of no architectural importance. At one time this was the first hotel in the city, and here Dean Swift lodged on one of his journeys into Ireland, and invited the dignitaries of the cathedral to a supper; but, to his great mortification, not one of them appeared. Disgusted, he scratched on one of the windows,—

"Rotten without and mouldering within,
The place and its clergy are both near akin."

Lower down, and up a narrow and inconvenient passage is "Stanley Palace," formerly the residence of the Earls of Derby. This is an elaborately-carved three-gabled house, and is, perhaps, the oldest unmutilated specimen of a timbered house in Chester. The date of its erection, 1591, is carved in front. Near to this is the Water-gate and the Roodee. Returning on the opposite side is Stanley-place, the Old Linen Hall, and opposite the Yacht Inn is Trinity Church. Little, if any, of the original remains. In the entrance lies the defaced effigy of a knight in mail armour, Sir John Whitmore, of Thurstaston, in the reign of Edward III. The legend runs:

"Hic jacet Joannis de Whitmore, qui obiit
3 kal. Octob. A.D. 1374."

In Trinity-street, adjoining, stands the dissenting chapel, erected by Mathew Henry and his friends in 1700. Continuing east we enter the North Row, in which is situated the new Liberal Club, formerly the County Court-buildings. Two doors higher, 24, Watergate-row, contains an effective hall and staircase, on a small scale, the subject of one of our illustrations; and in the next Row (near St. Peter's Church) the Deva Tavern, in which there is a handsome oak mantelpiece, and below, on the same premises, is a curious chamber, entered from the street.

T. P. Ivison.

* The first of this series of views was given in the *Builder* for February 6 last.

STANFORD HALL, NOTTINGHAMSHIRE.*

This is the north view of Stanford Hall, the seat of R. Ratcliff, Esq., to which considerable alterations and additions have recently been made.

The centre square block and the circular wing walls are the only portions of the old Hall. New offices entirely have been added on the east end, also fine oak stairs, conservatory, and reception rooms facing the south, and an addition to the drawing-room. On the west, the library has been enlarged, and new smoke-room, billiard-room, garden entrance, gun-room, lavatory, &c.

Messrs. Walker & Slater, of Derby, are the builders who carried out the works. The decorations and upholstery were executed by Messrs. Trollope & Sons. Mr. Westley H. Fletcher is the architect for the whole of the works.

EXAMPLES OF SARACENIC ARCHITECTURE AND ORNAMENT.

The two plates showing portions of Saracenic architectural detail, and of mosaic and wall ornament, formed a portion of the illustrations to Professor Aitchison's fifth Royal Academy lecture on Architecture, and are referred to in that lecture, which will be found in full on other pages.

London County Council.—Under the title "Three Years' Work of the London County Council" the *Metropolitan* issues a small separate pamphlet giving a summary of the work of the Council from 1889 to 1892. It may be useful to electors at the present moment.

* This is correct, and not Leicestershire, as stated on the plate, which the architect tells us was a mistake on the original drawing.

ILLUSTRATIONS OF OLD CHESTER.—Drawn by Mr. T. P Ivison
No. 2. WATERGATE STREET

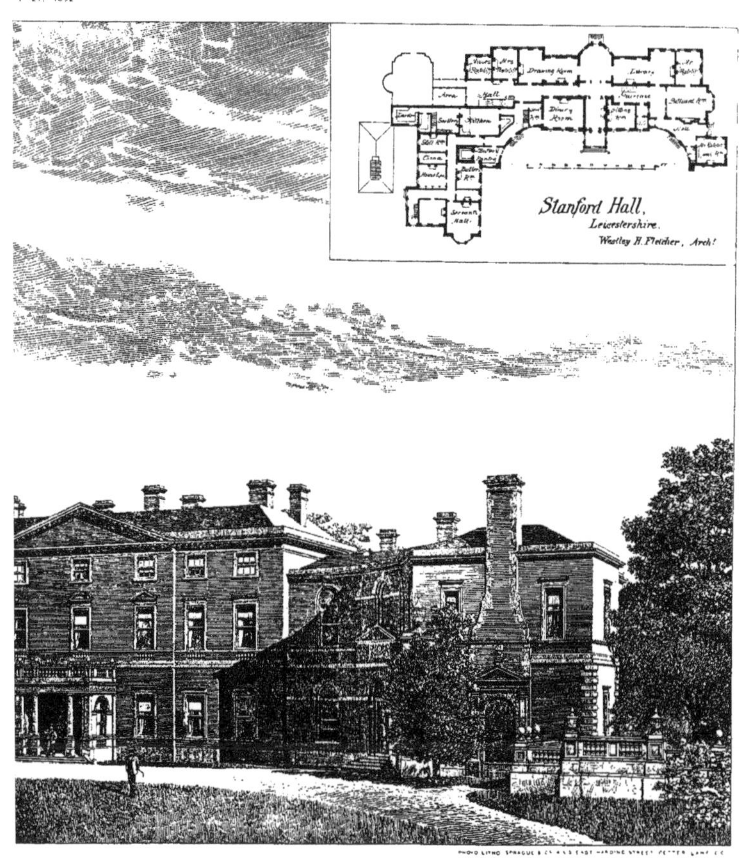

PHOTO LITHO SPRAGUE & Co 4 & 5 EAST HARDING STREET FETTER LANE E.C.

ENTRANCE OF THE FOUNTAIN
KAÏD-BEY CAIRO.

DOME OF TOMB KARAFEH.

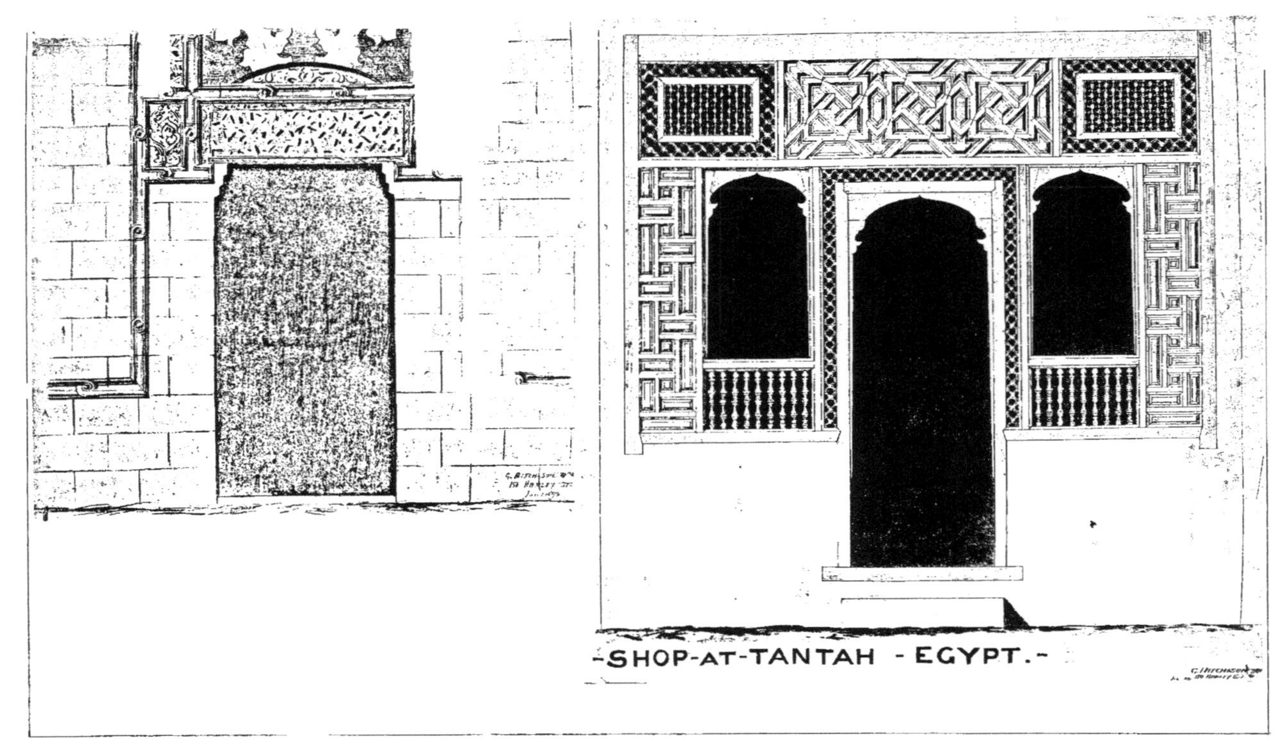

-SHOP-AT-TANTAH - EGYPT.-

MOSAIC FROM
MOSQUE AT CORDOVA
(ENTRANCE TO MIHRAB.)

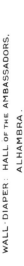

WALL-DIAPER: HALL OF THE AMBASSADORS, ALHAMBRA.

MOSAIC FROM MOSQUE AT CORDOVA.

EXAMPLES OF SARACENIC ORNAMENT

THE ARCHITECTURAL ASSOCIATION:

DOMESTIC ELECTRIC LIGHTING.

THE ordinary meeting of this Association was held on the 19th inst. in the Meeting-room of the Royal Institute of British Architects, 9, Conduit-street, the President, Mr. F. T. Baggallay, in the chair.

Mr. E. S. Gale, senior honorary secretary, read a letter which had been received from Sir Francis Knollys, on behalf of the Prince and Princess of Wales, thanking the members of the Association for their expression of sorrow at the recent death of the Duke of Clarence and Avondale.

Messrs. F. R. Betenson and E. F. Ware were then elected members of the Association.

Mr. Gale announced a donation to the Studio, by Mr. F. R. Farrow, of a set of plates on building construction. A vote of thanks was awarded to the donor.

Mr. Gale also announced that a member of the Association, who wished his name to remain unknown, had generously offered an annual prize of 5*l*. 5*s*. for measured drawings made under certain conditions.

The President proposed a vote of thanks to the anonymous donor, which was carried by acclamation.

Mr. Max Clarke then read a paper on "Domestic Electric Lighting." The following is an abstract of the paper:—

After some preliminary remarks, the lecturer said that the question naturally arose, "What had architects to do with electric lighting beyond seeing that there was light, and that it was properly disposed about the various apartments to be dealt with, and that the fittings or apparatus by which the light was brought to view were of what might be termed an "artistic" character? By some, the answer to that question would be, "Nothing whatever. When the building is sufficiently advanced, send for the electric light engineer; he will see to all that." And such was, no doubt, the course often adopted with regard to special branches of work. But while, perhaps, few architects went into the question of the size of the gas-pipes in which gas was laid on, or whether the pipes were run in the best way, it was desirable that they should know something about the capacity of electric-light wires, for although too high a pressure of gas in a gas-pipe would only have the effect of giving a bad and wasteful light, too strong a current of electricity in a wire might cause a building to be set on fire.

He took it for granted that everyone would admit that lighting by electricity was the light *par excellence* of the present age. No light was in any way to be compared to it, whether for public or domestic purposes,—for galleries where there were valuable pictures, for museums where there were art treasures, and for the fire-side. For all, the incandescent electric light possessed every advantage, without any of the drawbacks of any of the other illuminants in use. He proposed to confine his remarks to incandescent lamps, and to saying nothing of the arc lamps used for lighting streets and railway termini.

The plant necessary for a domestic installation of electric lighting might be summed up as (1) the power,—water, steam, gas, or petroleum engines; (2) the generators, or dynamo-electric machines; (3) the accumulators, or storage batteries; (4) the wires or conductors; and (5) the lamps, which produce the light.

1. *The Power.*—A great deal of the cost of an installation hinged on the power. Sometimes water-power was to be had at a very low cost, while in factories and the like, as well as in many mansions and private houses, spare steam power was often available. In towns or anywhere where there was gas, the gas-engine was always available where steam could not be used, and for small installations the gas-engine was perhaps the best, as it was not very expensive in itself, required little attention, and could be put up in a small space. The great point to be borne in mind was to have the engine, of whatever sort or type it might be, well up to its work. An engine which was always worked much above its nominal power was more or less distressed, did not go so regularly, did not last so long, and needed more repairs than one well up to its work.

2. *The Generator*, or dynamo electric machine, briefly described, consisted, in its simplest form, of a large magnet or of a number of magnets between the poles of which a number of coils of wire, usually of copper, wound upon an iron core, were made to revolve. Each coil had its terminals connected to a separate strip of copper, these strips being arranged near one end round the shaft upon which the whole revolves, the coils and core so arranged being called the "armature," while the copper strips at the end were called the "commutator." Copper strips or brushes were held against the commutator, and as the current or electricity was generated in the coils of wire it was conveyed or driven into (Mr. Clarke said he hardly knew which) the commutator, collected by the brushes, and transmitted either to accumulators or direct to the lamps, the supposition being that the current flowed away through one brush and returned through the other. There were so many dynamos, all, no doubt, possessing merits of their own, that it was impossible to give within the limits of a short paper anything more than a general idea. As a rule, the magnets were made magnetic by being excited; in their normal state they were only bars of soft iron. The soft iron had a certain amount of what might be called latent electricity or magnetism in it, and when the armature was made to revolve a very slight current was produced; the current passed through the coils surrounding the soft iron bars, and the result was that the bars became electro-magnetic, gradually getting stronger, and when it could take up no more from the armature the full current was conducted along the cables for use. There were also machines producing what were called alternating currents, which at the present time were largely used. Professor Thomson's definition of a dynamo-electric machine was that it was "a machine for converting energy in the form of electric currects, or *vice versâ*, by the operation of setting conductors (usually in the form of coils of copper wire) to rotate in a magnetic field." For the purposes of the present paper, then, the dynamo-electric machine might be taken as a machine for the manufacture of electricity. As before mentioned, there were many varieties of such machines. Those "wound in series" were best adapted for arc lamps; those wound "compound self-regulating" were best for incandescent lamps driven direct; and "shunt-wound" were best for charging accumulators.

3. *The Accumulators, or Secondary Batteries.* The accumulators, which were to electric lighting what gasometers were to gas-lighting, had an important part to play. By their use a serious drawback,—the liability of instantaneous failure of the light by the breakdown of some part of the machinery,—was got over, and they also rendered the light absolutely steady, which was not the case, as a rule, when the lamps were fed with the current direct from the dynamo,—at any rate not in small installations. The accumulators, the action of which was discovered by MM. Faure and Plante in 1860, though they were not brought into a practical form until within the last ten years, consist of plates of metal placed in boxes made of glass or wood,—usually the former,—the glass boxes or "cells" being filled with liquid. They were chemical batteries, in fact, but batteries possessing peculiar properties. The name, "secondary batteries," explained somewhat the difference between them and the ordinary battery. The secondary could not generate a current on its own account, but could only hold or retain one with which it had been supplied. Another difference was that there was no consumption of its elements during its work of charging and discharging, although there was an actual deterioration which might perhaps be lessened by future improvements. The accumulators manufactured by the Electric Power Storage Company, Millwall, under various patents, were, the author understood, made in the following way:—Plates of prepared lead were perforated or indented all over, and the holes or indentations were filled with a composition consisting substantially of red lead for the positive or peroxide plates, and with litharge for the negative plates. The plates were then "formed" by means of the electric current, and then placed in the glass cells, so many positive and so many negative, all the positive being connected together and also all the negative. The cells were then connected up together, the positive plates of one cell to the negative of the next cell, and so on. The cells were then filled with a solution of sulphuric acid and water, in the proportion, roughly, of 1 of acid to 7 of water. The ends or terminals of the cells were attached to the wires from the dynamo, the action being that when the armature of the dynamo was rotated, the current driven into the plates caused a chemical action to take place, the result of which we saw in the fact that when the dynamo was stopped, a current could be obtained from the cells sufficient to light the lamps without the intervention of the dynamo at all. The great advantage of the secondary battery was that the light could be used at any hour of the day or night, and the light was the very best that could be produced. But, as in every form of transformation of energy, there was a loss in using storage batteries, and they of course added to the cost of an installation. Completeness, however, must always be paid for, and private house lighting could never be thoroughly satisfactory without the use of accumulators. The loss entailed by their use amounted to about 20 per cent. of the energy stored. With regard to the maintenance of storage batteries, they could be kept in working order for from 11 to 15 per cent. per annum on their first cost. Accumulators should not be allowed to run down; they lasted longer when used regularly than when used and left uncharged intermittently. They should always be kept well charged, and when not in use charged, say, once a fortnight, until the bubbles rose to the surface of the liquid, which should always cover the surface of the plates, the evaporation being made up for by adding water. The cells should be kept in a cool place, not above 65 deg. Fah., and never in the hot engine-room. Ample provision should be made for the ventilation of the accumulator-room, so as to get rid of the disagreeable fumes of the acid solution. The number of cells required in an installation depends upon the description of lamp used,—how many volts it was made for. The size of the cells depended upon the number of lamps required to be in use at the same time. In an ordinary house, as a rule, less than twenty cells would be of no use, as the electro-motive-force of each cell never exceeds about two volts.

4. *Wiring.*—The work of "wiring," or putting in the mains to distribute the electricity to the various points where the light was required was the first item in which the cost of labour formed a consideration. What was required was the most perfect conductor, *i.e.*, a conductor capable of conveying the current with the least possible loss, for there was always some loss. The metals which were good conductors were silver, copper, gold, zinc, platinum, iron, &c. Copper was usually used, it being comparatively cheap, very pliable, and lasting. Iron would do very well, but an iron wire to convey the same amount of current would have to be about six times the sectional area of a copper conductor. Therefore iron was not used except in some special instances. The copper conductor did not consist of one wire, but of a number of fine wires twisted together, which not only made the conductor more pliable, but gave a much greater surface-area, which was a *desideratum*, for electricity was said to affect surface. Upon the purity and gauge of the copper wire, and the amount and quality of the insulating material, depended the good or bad results obtained in wiring a house, and upon them depended also very largely the question of cost. In many instances the estimate for wiring was based upon the number of lights. The cost of wiring varied from 17*s*. 3*d*. to 40*s*. per light. Either these figures did not represent work of the same quality, or the higher estimates must include more than a fair working profit. It was most important that the wires should be large enough to carry the requisite current, and, in the case of a private house or public building, to carry such additional current as might at any future time be added. People who had electric lighting in their houses were too fond of adding extra lights, until the wires were so hard-worked that they became hot, set the house on fire, and acquired a bad character. The Phœnix Fire Insurance Company had issued a set of regulations which were looked upon as a sort of standard; and the London County Council had just issued new regulations for lighting theatres and music-halls by the electric light, but he did not think that a single theatre in London complied with the standard in every particular. Great care must be taken with the joints in the wire: bad joints were a frequent source of danger. He was under the impression that wires well twisted together, and then carefully soldered, made a good joint, but the County Council's regulations (last item in clause 3) said that "joints in conductors shall be avoided" (there was a charming simplicity about that), "but

where unavoidable they shall be electrically and mechanically perfect. Soldering fluids shall not be used in making such joints." Did "soldering-fluids" mean the solder itself or the fluid put on as a flux? There was some ambiguity about the regulations. Wires should never be fixed behind plaster or in the thickness of the plaster, but they should be in wood casings, made with grooves to receive the wires. The London County Council regulation said that such casings should be of "hard wood." Such casings should always be screwed together; nails should not be allowed, as they were liable to damage the insulation or even the wires. It was absolutely necessary that the wires should be kept dry. Water was an admirable conductor, and if it got to the wires the current would go to earth. If the wires were fixed in inaccessible positions and damp got at them so as to cause a leak, the only way to get out of the difficulty was to cut off the wires and run new ones. In Messrs. Andrews's system of concentric wiring there was a copper conductor or wire, insulated, and then, wound round the insulating material was a series of iron wires forming the return, the latter not being covered in any way. It was said that that system did away with the necessity for casings, and had other advantages. The difficulty heretofore existing with the system had been as to making the branch joints, but Mr. Andrews claimed to have got over all trouble in that way now. There were several methods of arranging the wires between the dynamo or accumulators and the lamps. The most usual way, perhaps, was that known as "in parallel" Another plan was the "series" system, in which the lamps were arranged one after the other on the same wire, but that plan was more usual for arc lighting. Another method was that known as "the three-wire system" which had been adopted by the Parish of St. Pancras in their public supply installation, and by other companies. Switches were in electric lighting work what gascocks were in gasfitting work,—they were simply a means of turning the light on or off. The best switches were those known as the "quick-make, quick-break" switches, for it was of great importance and essential to safety that connexion should be made and broken instantly. The "cut-out" or safety fuse was a great safeguard in electric lighting,—in fact, the safeguard,—but in some cases it was much abused. In such cases, instead of being a trusted servant it was an insincere friend, lulling its users into a sense of false security, and then setting the house on fire. The idea was that each wire was intended to carry a certain amount of current in excess of what normally passed through it. When a too powerful current passed it heated the wire, sometimes melting it and causing a fire. To avoid that, at certain points short lengths of soft metal are fixed in suitable enclosures, and when the current became too strong, usually by accident, the soft metal melted, broke the connexion, and everything was right, except, of course, that all the lamps on that circuit went out. A new length of soft wire could easily be put in. The danger was when the soft metal was too large and would carry too much current: then it ceased to be a safety fuse, and became an element of danger. Every "cut-out" or safety fuse should be made exactly to suit its intended position, and should not be left to the discretion of the men who did the wiring, who often knew nothing about electric lighting. The "cut-outs" should be real ones, not shams, and had better be fixed on the switch-board or in some other accessible place, instead of on ceilings or high up on the walls, where they were difficult of access.

5. *Lamps*—The lecturer next described the incandescent lamps, the cost of which he stated to be about 3s. 6d. each at present, though after the date of the expiry of the Edison-Swan patent, in December next, the price would perhaps be reduced to 2s., or less. The average life of an incandescent lamp was usually stated to be 1,000 hours; what was meant was probably that at their best they lasted as long as that. But sometimes the filament of carbon broke before they had been in use ten or twelve hours, though that was not usual if the current were steady, and did not vary its electro-motive force. Jars or shocks would, of course, break the filaments, so that the lamps should not be hung on door-frames where the doors were likely to be banged or slammed. As an incandescent lamp became old it gave less light, and the glass became black inside, owing to the deposit of minute pieces of the carbon filament. With regard to the design of fittings, much remained to be done by architects.

In conclusion, the lecturer referred to several practical points in some detail. Referring to some specimens exhibited, he said that the wooden casings for wires made by Mr. Fawkes, of Chelmsford, embodied an admirable idea. But where these casings were screwed up, the screws should be oiled before being driven, and not driven in too tight. After dealing with the question of the measurement of electricity, he entered into calculations of the cost of a 50-light installation, each light being equal to 16 candles. His estimate was as follows:—Engine, 138*l.*; dynamo, 30*l.*; accumulators, 126*l.*; fitting of engine, dynamo, &c., 20*l.*; wiring and switches, 30*l.*; fittings, 20*l.*; total, 364*l.* In planning the engine-room, it should be remembered that the longer the driving-belt the better, as it would run looser, last longer, and give less trouble. It should be at least 14 ft. long. No trouble should be spared in bedding the engine and dynamo so that they might be perfectly firm, and the dynamo must be completely insulated. Entering into figures, the lecturer calculated that the cost of working such an installation as he had described would be about 67*l* 10*s*. per annum. For that sum they would get 20,857 hours' light of the very best sort, the cost per hour (*i.e.*, the cost per hour for every hour that one 16-candle lamp was alight) being a trifle over ⅔d., including depreciation of plant. The cost of an argand gas-burner would be about ¼d. per hour. Time did not permit the lecturer to go into the cost of the light produced by any of the primary batteries before the public, which were generally, in his opinion, unsatisfactory for lighting purposes.

Mr. R. Langton Cole proposed a vote of thanks to Mr. Clarke for his interesting paper. It happened that he (the speaker) had been obliged to know a good deal about electric lighting, and he could therefore bear witness to the care and trouble the lecturer must have taken in bringing such a mass of detail before them. He thought the temperature of that apartment (the Institute meeting-room) was an eloquent testimony to the sanitary value of the electric light, for though he had never felt cold in it before, he wished that he had not taken off his overcoat. As to the difficulty in securing good insulated wire, his advice was to get the "Silvertown" list,—and no doubt other makers issued similar lists. That list gave the sizes and class of insulation of all wires made, and the architect could specify the wire he wanted, and obtain samples direct from the makers to compare with those supplied by the contractor. Then there was the Electrical Standardizing Institution, which, for a small fee, would test wires or instruments submitted to them, and he saw no reason why architects' specifications should not contain a clause like that usually found in reference to Portland cement, thus:—"The wires shall be tested at the expense of the contractor." He thought Mr. Fawkes's moulded casings excellent, but it was curious that the covers were all screwed in the centre, although he quoted, in his preface, the Phœnix rule, that all covers should be screwed at the sides. A small point about switches was that it was good to have a luminous tablet over them like those used on match-boxes; examples could be seen at the Crystal Palace Exhibition; and, as to cut-outs, it was just as well not to replace a burnt-out fuse without finding why it failed, as its failure was meant to be an indication that something was wrong. He quite agreed that every architect should design the fittings he required, but there were several points which must be attended to to ensure success.

Mr. C. Stanley Peach, in seconding the motion, said there could be no doubt that it was very desirable that architects in the present day should devote some attention to the study of electric lighting. He believed that electricity was at present merely in its infancy, and that there were many important developments before it.

Mr. Beresford Pite, in supporting the motion, said they were very much obliged to Mr. Clark for his paper, and to Mr. Langton Cole for his supplementary remarks. The profession was much indebted also to Mr. Cole for his writings in the "British Almanac and Companion." In the course of his remarks Mr. Pite strongly criticised the way in which some details of the electric-light fittings of the Institute meeting room had been carried out, to the disfigurement, as he thought, of the architectural details. He thought that some of these details might have been made far less obtrusive under proper direction.

Mr. A. H. Clark and another member having made a few remarks,

The President put the vote of thanks to the meeting, and, Mr. Max Clarke having replied to several points raised in the course of the discussion, the meeting terminated.

Discussion Section.—The seventh meeting of the Discussion Section of the Association was held on the 17th inst., when Mr. W. Pywell, A.R.I.B.A., read a paper on "Flues and Fire-places." The Special Visitor for the evening was Mr. E. Prioleau Warren. There was a good attendance, and an excellent discussion followed the reading of the paper, in which Messrs. A. H. Clark, T. E. Pryce, H. A. Satchell, and F. T. W. Goldsmith (chairman) joined. Mr. Warren then dealt with the subject very fully, and his practical and suggestive remarks were much appreciated. The paper was well illustrated, a capital collection of sketches and photographs being exhibited.

DEMONSTRATIONS ON GREEK SCULPTURE AT THE BRITISH MUSEUM.

In her third lecture,* Miss Eugénie Sellers dealt with the sculptures of the Temple of Apollo Epikourios at Bassae, near Phigaleia. It has been generally held that this temple was built in gratitude to Apollo for the escape of the inhabitants from the great plague of 430; but, as Attic artists were employed upon it, it seems more likely that it was connected with a plague in the year 420, of which we have scantier notice, by which time the scene of the Peloponnesian War had shifted from the Peloponnesus.

The plan of this temple is peculiar, for it has an inner cella, lying north and south, which is open to the sky, while it has been shown by Dr. Dörpfeld that it was usual for temples to be wholly closed and lighted only by the central door in front. But behind this cella is a small chamber, lying east and west, which is completely closed, save for a door in the eastern side. This must have been the original temple, containing the statue of Apollo, to which the cella served as a sort of courtyard. On the inner side of the cella are buttresses terminating in columns that have their origin in rough buttresses like those which prop the walls on the inner side of the court of the so-called palace of Priam at Hissarlik, and which were retained when later such a court formed the plan of a temple of a god.

The frieze, which is very high relief, runs round the inner side of the cella, where it would be seen in the full daylight. On two sides are represented the battle of the Centaurs and the Lapithæ, and on two that of the Greeks and the Amazons. The arrangement of the slabs is somewhat difficult. According to Mr. Murray, the group of Apollo in his chariot would form a centre-piece; but possibly its function is rather to form a link between the two subjects.

As a composition it is very successful. The subject lends itself to the formation of small groups, with interlacing lines—a scheme of decoration which suits the ribbon-like space of a frieze better than the rapid flow of the Parthenon frieze, with its somewhat inadequate centre. The figures are full of life and power, though the workmanship is often rude and coarse. The passion of the Centaurs, contrasting with the comparative lifelessness of the Centaurs of the Parthenon metopes and the pathos of some of the Amazon slabs, are very remarkable. Here, too, we find perspective being applied to sculpture, and we notice a development of the pictorial element in the evident dislike to empty spaces and the devices framed to get rid of them. In conclusion, Miss Sellers referred the popularity of these two subjects with Greek sculptors to the variety of treatment of form offered by the contrast of male figures with those of women and of Centaurs.

Birmingham Association of Students of the Institution of Civil Engineers.—A meeting of this Association was held on the 18th inst. at the Midland Institute, the President, Mr. J. Edward Willcox, A.M.I.C.E., being in the chair. A paper was read by Mr. H. W. Butler, Student Inst.C.E., on "The Maintenance of Roads," which was followed by an interesting discussion.

---

* For brief notes of previous lectures see p. 142, *ante*.

THE ARCHITECTURAL ASSOCIATION'S SPRING VISITS:

THE IMPERIAL INSTITUTE.

THE Imperial Institute at South Kensington as usual attracted a large number of members of the Association on Saturday afternoon last, when, by the kindness of the architect, Mr. T. E. Collcutt, an excellent opportunity was afforded of carefully inspecting this interesting building. Considerable progress has been made since the visit of the Association last year; and, though glimpses of the finished work of the interior can now be obtained, the plant and scaffolding stand somewhat in the way of a definite opinion upon the finished aspect of the work. The building is expected to be opened sometime in June, and by then more than three-fourths of the proposed buildings will be nearly completed. The long gallery at the back of the building is in an advanced state, and the portions that will remain incomplete for a time are a wing at each end, the continuation of the central hall opposite the entrance, and the grand staircase. The scaffolding of the front elevation is gradually being removed, and gives a better opportunity of judging of the exterior. This is chiefly marked by the extreme delicacy of the detail, and, though it is generally most graceful, it is to be feared that the fineness of much of the detail will be materially obliterated by the sooty weathering which so soon overtakes every stone building of this murky metropolis. To the same cause must be ascribed the dead colour of the copper, which is largely used on the numerous cupolas. The prevailing fineness of detail is in the interior of the building seen to much greater advantage, and appears in this position to be much more suitably employed. The Hopton Wood stone lining to the corridors is distinctly pleasing in its effect, and the capital light provided throughout shows to the best advantage the care that has been provided upon the detail.

Messrs. Mowlem are the general contractors, and some excellent specimens of their work were seen. Mr. Wallace, the clerk of the works, conducted the party over the works. It may be mentioned that some of the corridors are laid with glass mosaic. This would have doubtless received more attention had the representative of the firm who laid it not been so conspicuously present.

BRITISH ARCHÆOLOGICAL ASSOCIATION.

AT the meeting of this Association on the 17th inst., Mr. J. W. Grover, F.S.A., in the chair, Mr. Macmichael read some notes on hair-curlers of the seventeenth century, used for the preparation of the long ringlets or "heart breakers" worn by ladies, and the wigs worn by men, a large collection of the clay curlers being exhibited. Some notes on the ancient signs of London were also read. Mr. Marriage exhibited a fine example of Egyptian bronze. The Rev. W. S. Sykes exhibited a remarkable prehistoric hatchet, 14 in. long, formed of calliard, a white slate-stone of the locality. It has recently been found at the Crow's Nest Farm, Lawkland, Settle. The Rev. Carus V. Collier reported the opening of a barrow at Bradwell, Derbyshire. Three skeletons have already been found within it, two being on their sides with the knees bent up to the chins. They were surrounded by a low wall or cist of flat stones on their edges. Many bones visible in the part not excavated appear to be from older interments. A paper was then read by Dr. A. Fryer on the present condition of the ancient church of Perranzabuloe, Cornwall, which was excavated from beneath a great drift of sand. The ruins are very greatly reduced in height. The paper was illustrated by photographs. In the discussion which ensued, Mr. Loftus Brock, F.S.A., and others took part, and Mr. Langdon described the process by which a large portion of the locality has been invaded and covered by sand slowly blown from the sea-shore. Mr. Park Harrison then reported his recent discovery of traces of the old Saxon church, now Oxford Cathedral. Some of the shafts of what was believed to be a triforium of Norman date in the south transept are found to be grooved for the frames of windows, the grooves being continued through the bases and in some of the arches, but not in the capitals, which are probably Norman insertions in what appear to have been some of the ealier Saxon windows of the older church. Several drawings were exhibited. The Chairman described some objects of antiquarian interest noted in his recent journey to the Azores and America.

THE LONDON COUNTY COUNCIL.

PRIOR to the commencement of the proceedings of the meeting of the London County Council on Tuesday last, the Chairman, Sir John Lubbock, unveiled a bust of the late Mr. J. F. B. Firth, the first Deputy Chairman of the Council. The bust, which is by Mr. Verheyden, stands in a corner of the Council Chamber.

The London Water Question.—The Chairman said that on Friday in last week it came to his knowledge that the Birmingham Corporation had put down their Water Bill for second reading on Monday last. The Council had passed a resolution to petition against the Bill, but he was not quite sure whether the Council desired to oppose the second reading. At the same time, having regard to the importance of the question, he thought he ought not to allow the second reading to pass unquestioned. He conferred, therefore, with the member in charge of the Bill, who consented most courteously to defer the second reading until next Monday. He (the Chairman) then asked the metropolitan members of Parliament, with some members of the Home Counties County Councils, to come to a conference in that chamber. They had a rather large meeting thereon Monday, and considerable discussion took place on the question. He thought they all felt that if they were to proceed as against the Birmingham Bill it was desirable that they should do so with the support of the metropolitan members, or allow them to co-operate in the matter. Eventually the conference appointed a committee, comprising several members of the Council,—Mr. Lawson, M.P., Lord Compton, M.P., and Mr. Dickinson,—to confer with the Birmingham representatives, and it was hoped that some amicable agreement would be come to. While they did not wish to oppose any Bill which was promoted by Birmingham, they felt that, having regard to the recommendations of the Committee of the House of Commons on the London Water Question, they could not allow the present Bill to pass unquestioned.

Sewage Precipitation Operations during 1891.—The Main Drainage Committee's report contained the following:—

"We submit for the information of the Council a statement as to the results of the operations at the sewage precipitation works at Barking and Crossness during the year ended December 31, 1891.

At the Northern outfall at Barking Creek 30,172 millions of gallons of sewage have been treated by means of 8,516 tons of lime and 1,563 tons of sulphate of iron, which operation resulted in the production of 536,000 tons of sludge, which were sent to sea by means of the two steamers. During the summer 500 tons of manganate of soda, and 347 tons of sulphuric acid were employed in deodorising mainly that portion of sewage which was untreated by precipitation.

At the Southern outfall at Crossness 2,228 millions of gallons of sewage were only partially treated with 407 tons of lime an d 113 tons of sulphate of iron, which yielded 46,873 tons of sludge. If the ships had been available for carrying to sea a larger quantity of sludge than the above it could readily have been obtained at this station, but in consequence of the whole of the vessels' carrying capacity being required at the Northern outfall, precipitation operations at Crossness were entirely suspended on August 5. The untreated sewage discharged at Crossness during the summer was deodorised by means of 923 tons of manganate of soda and 532 tons of sulphuric acid.

In consequence of the better system of working at the Northern outfall during the latter portion of the year the percentage quantity of sludge (corrected to 90 per cent. moisture) obtained from the sewage rose from 0·28 per cent. in 1890 to 0·36 per cent. in 1891 for the whole year, which is in itself evidence of the better working of the system, as the theoretical quantity obtainable on the assumption that 30 grains per gallon are precipitated, is 0·43 per cent. In addition to the sludge at the Northern outfall, 2,691 tons of filth have been removed by means of the filth hoist and gratings and entirely consumed by means of the destructor; 5,106 tons of sand were also removed from the precipitating channels.

The cost for lime used at both outfalls during 1891 was about 8,146*l.*, and that for sulphate of iron about 3,184*l.*, as against 7,034*l.* for lime and 2,692*l.* 10s. for iron in 1890.

The cost of manganate of soda and sulphuric acid used at the outfalls and storm overflows was 27,525*l.*, the great bulk of which will be saved as soon as the precipitation operations are in full working order. The cost for the year 1890 was 24,560*l.*

The following is a comparative statement of the quantities of the materials used in the years 1890 and 1891:—

Northern Outfall:—

	1890.	1891.
Quantity of sewage treated	35,093 mil. gals.	30,172 mil. gals.
Sludge obtained	449,500 tons.	536,000 tons.
Filth destroyed	—	2,691 ,,
Sand removed..	—	5,106 ,,
Lime used........	8,638 ,,	8,516 ,,
Iron used	1,362 ,,	1,563 ,,
Manganate of soda..	427 ,,	500 ,,
Sulphuric acid......	311 ,,	347 ,,

NOTE.—The works were in an incomplete condition during 1890, the improvements in methods for collection of sludge at the Northern outfall having been brought into action in August, 1891.

Southern Outfall:—

Quantity of sewage treated	3,370 mil. gals.	2,228 mil. gals.
Sludge obtained	61,735 tons.	46,873 tons.
Lime used	924 ,,	407 ,,
Iron used	158 ,,	113 ,,
Manganate of soda..	1,054 ,,	923 ,,
Sulphuric acid......	379 ,,	532 ,,

The report was agreed to, and after transacting other business, the Council adjourned.

COMPETITIONS.

DARWEN TECHNICAL SCHOOLS.—In reply to the advertisement for competitive plans, twenty-five sets were received. Mr. Murgatroyd, F.R.I.B.A., was called in by the Committee to make the selections. The design placed first is that of Mr. J. Lane Fox, of Dewsbury. The design placed second is by Messrs. Morley & Woodhouse, Bradford. The design placed third is by Messrs. Dunn & Watson, of London.

NEW POLICE-STATION, SHREWSBURY.—At a special meeting of the Shrewsbury Town Council, on the 22nd inst., Major-General Herbert moved that the plans of the new police-station, sent in by Mr. Johnson, of Westminster, and selected by the Watch Committee as the best, be adopted, and that Mr. Johnson be appointed the architect for the work, the cost of which will be about 3,000*l.*—Alderman Crump seconded the proposition, which was ultimately agreed to.

BUILDERS' CLERKS' BENEVOLENT INSTITUTION.

THE twenty-fifth annual general meeting of the donors and subscribers of this Institution was held on Tuesday evening last at the offices, 21, New Bridge-street, Blackfriars, the President-elect, Mr. Colin Grant Patrick, in the chair, supported by Messrs. E. Brooks (Treasurer), E. B. Gammon, W. D. Gilbert, E. W. Holland, F. S. Oldham, H. W. Parker, E. S. Rider, J. A. Robson, E. C. Roo, C. K. Turpin, T. H. Winny, and other gentlemen.

The retiring President, Mr. Benjamin Hannen, jun., was accorded a hearty vote of thanks by the Committee, at their meeting held just prior to the general meeting, and in vacating the chair he expressed his acknowledgements to the officers and Committee for the methodical, businesslike, and economical manner in which the work of the Institution is carried on.

The Secretary, Mr. H. J. Wheatley, having read the advertisement convening the meeting, the minutes of the last annual general meeting, and of a subsequent general meeting, were read and confirmed.

Mr. Wheatley next read the annual report of the Committee, which stated that the income for the past year amounted to 806*l.* 0s. 9d., the largest total which it had yet been able to record. That amount was made up of 293*l.* 4s. in annual subscriptions, 406*l.* 18s. 6d. in donations, 103*l.* 16s. 1d. in dividends, and 2*l.* 2s. 2d. interest on deposit account. The sum expended was 455*l.* 0s. 1d., including 340*l.* paid to pensioners and 15*l.* given in grants for temporary relief. During the year one of the pensioners (Mrs. Olver) was removed by death, and another (Mrs. Hadrill) resigned, having re-married. The number of pensioners now on the books was sixteen, but the total number elected since the foundation of the Institution was 32; of these, 9 had died, while 7 had retired owing either to re-marriage or to improved circumstances in other respects. With reference to the orphan presentations (three in number) held by the Institution, the Committee report that the vacancy caused by the expiration of the school-term of Edith Friend was filled up during the year by the election of Cyril Ludford, who was now in the school. There was still a vacancy for another child, and the Committee were prepared to receive applications on behalf of orphans whose friends might wish to place them in nomination for the vacancy.* The Committee were also prepared to receive applications for two vacant pensions, the amounts granted being 25*l.* per annum to builders' clerks who might be eligible, and 20*l.* per annum to

.* It may be as well to mention that only orphans of builders' clerks are eligible.

their widows. One applicant was already before the Committee. The thirteenth annual dinner of the Institution was held on April 6 last, under the presidency of Mr. Benjamin Hannen, jun., whose earnest appeal on behalf of the Institution was most heartily responded to, the sum of 433*l*. 16s. 6d. being obtained. The amount of 200*l*. placed on deposit in 1890 was last year brought into current account, and a further purchase of 500*l*. 2¾ per cent. Consolidated Stock was effected, bringing up the total Stock now held by the Institution to 4,150*l*. The Committee expressed their hearty thanks to the retiring President for the very practical help rendered by him to the Institution during his year of office, and announced that Mr. Colin Grant Patrick had kindly consented to accept office as President of the Institution for the ensuing year. According to the Rules, one-third of the Committee retired, but were eligible for re-election. In conclusion, the Committee acknowledged the help so steadily afforded to the Institution by the builders, architects, and merchants connected with the building trade, and expressed the hope that their support of so useful a charity would be continued.

The Chairman, in moving the adoption of the report, said he had accepted the position of President of the Institution with great pleasure, and would do all he possibly could to further its interests during his year of office. The Institution was one which was particularly worthy of support, and he trusted that it would continue to prosper.

Mr. E. C. Roe, in seconding the motion, said he thought it was a matter of great satisfaction that the Institution was able to fund money from time to time. They were very desirous, indeed, of increasing their funded property, so that in times of depression the interest of their funds might enable them to meet their liabilities and carry on the work of the Institution without relying upon current donations or subscriptions.

The report was unanimously adopted.

The new President having been elected, the other officers and the retiring members of the Committee were re-elected; and Messrs. S. J. Thacker and Thomas Stirling were re-elected auditors. Mr. Ernest S. Rider being also elected as an auditor in succession to his father, Mr. Thomas F. Rider, who has become one of the trustees of the Institution.

Hearty votes of thanks were accorded to the retiring President and other officers for their services during the past year, and it was announced that the annual dinner of the Association would be held on March 30.

Correspondence.

To the Editor of The Builder.

CONCETE FOR ARTISANS' DWELLINGS.

Sir,—I have no recollection of seeing any statement as to experiments made with concrete beams where it was definitely proved that coke-breeze concrete was superior to gravel; nor would such experiments be very conclusive evidence unless the quality and fitness of the gravel employed were known. Some descriptions of gravel used for concrete prove totally unfit for the purpose, although apparently otherwise. If "Surveyor" refers to Colonel Seddon's experiments some years ago, I believe he will find the results went to prove that broken bricks or brick ballast made the best concrete for large span floors, and that one experiment therewith, a floor 17 ft. 6 in. by 9 ft. 9 in. between supports, and 6 in. thick, carried a load of 3 cwt. per foot superficial before it collapsed. But there is another difficulty with concrete floors formed of huge monolithic slabs,—viz., their tendency to develop cracks or fissures on their under sides, and which it seems impossible to entirely prevent; and although it is assumed these do not lessen the strength of the floor, it is a doubtful point.

The objects of postponing the layer of coke breeze are:—1. The mass of concrete when first deposited in place is in a quaggy condition and not in a fit state for depositing thereon the finer layer and accurately levelling it ready for nailing boards thereto; some portions might get disturbed and disarrange the accuracy required. 2. It would cause delay in performing the straightening portion of the work; men would of necessity be moving about thereon, and the initial set of the cement would be protracted; concrete should be allowed to rest as quickly as possible after being deposited in place. 3. The surface should be true, smooth, and free from defects when the boards are nailed thereon; this is not likely to be the case if workmen have been tramping on the floors soon after completion, and for a considerable time longer, as would be the case if the floors were finished when the walls were the right height to receive them, let them be covered up ever so carefully.

"Surveyor" asks if floors should be wetted directly after they are finished; it is desirable to do so, and keep them wet for several days, as the slower cement sets, in reason, the better; but not, on the other hand, to deluge the concrete with water before it has obtained its initial set and disturb the particles of cement.

Colonel Seddon and others have proved that it is quite practicable to make floors of 14-ft. span or more; but the point "Surveyor" appears to wish to ascertain is whether, in a general way, it is advisable. I think not; but I hope to see what others have to say relative thereto. I have made floors 12 feet by 10 feet clear of supports, and resting on walls on three sides only, without a failure.

With regard to coke breeze as an aggregate, it should be borne in mind that the good quality of concrete depends not only upon the affinity of the cement for the aggregate, but the inherent strength of the latter, and coke breeze does not stand high in this respect. If concrete made of one part of cement to seven parts of crushed bricks is broken asunder, it will be found that the fracture is a clean one,—*i.e.*, the particles are not disturbed, but the brick aggregate is divided wherever the line of fracture occurs,—and this points, I suggest, to the desirability of balancing, where possible, the tensile strength of the aggregate and the adhesive strength of the matrix. Coke breeze, as a rule, contains a great deal of dirty matter,—the products of combustion possibly,—and to fit it for concrete this should all be washed out, incurring much labour; being very small, too, in size, it needs more cement than a larger aggregate to secure as good results. These two drawbacks explain my former assertion, that "measured by strength, it is, perhaps, the dearest of any." Thomas Potter.

Alresford.

LIVERPOOL MOTIVE POWER.

Sir,—When I revise, for publication in the "Proceedings" of the Mechanical Engineers, the paper on which you commented last week, I hope to explain some of the apparent inconsistencies and omissions to which you (writing upon a proof printed for the meeting) have called attention. It would have been much more satisfactory to me, and probably to everyone interested in the subject, if I had been able to reduce all the costs of work done to a common unit, and also to discuss the bearing of the facts upon the general question of distribution from a central station. But, if I had waited to do this, the paper would not have been written, and a promise would have been broken.

Some day, if other engagements will permit, I hope to deal more fully and comprehensively with this important and interesting topic; and, meanwhile, you have exactly appreciated my object in publishing "authentic data" for the use and benefit of professional men, who generally experience great difficulty in getting anything but "trial-trip results." J. Parry.

THE EXTINGUISHING OF FIRES.

Sir,—The use of mineral-oil lamps being so very general, the following incident may be suggestive to some of your readers:—

Last night, a large suspended oil-lamp fell in our library. The room was instantly a "sea of fire." Some members of the staff showed much presence of mind, and rushed for "hand-grenades," the use of ten or twelve of which extinguished the fire in five minutes, confining the damage to the room in question, although the flames had reached from floor to ceiling.

The points to which I think attention might be invited are:—

1. The lamp should have "extinguished itself" in falling. It failed to do so.

2. The "finest water-white oil" (the quality used) is supposed only to ignite at a very high temperature (we won't dispute about a few degrees). This took fire at once.

3. The hand-grenades (which have been rather depreciated, and which may or may not be of value in the open air, when the gas generated is promptly dispersed) certainly acted with magical effect within the compass of a large room.

Your readers will draw their own conclusions.

Robert Johnson.

The Colonial College, Hollesley Bay, Suffolk,
February 19, 1892.

Board School, Greenheys, Lancashire.—On the 18th inst., the Dean of Manchester (Dr. Maclure) laid the memorial stone of a new board school to take the place of three school buildings which have been condemned as unsuitable in the neighbourhood of Greenheys. The principal front of the new buildings is to Webster-street, Greenheys. The walls externally are faced with Ruabon stock bricks, being relieved with stone strings, heads, cornices, mullions, &c. An imposing feature is the central gable, and to the right and left dormers are placed, giving light to the covered portion of an upper playground. The main block of the building is placed in the centre of the site. Right and left are playgrounds for girls and infants, with entrances from Webster-street and Leaf-street. A cookery school-room and scullery will be provided. The whole of the space over the girls' department is utilised for a playground for the girls, a considerable portion at each end being covered. Accommodation is provided for 1,116 children. The works are being carried out by Messrs. William Southern & Sons, contractors, of Salford, from the designs and under the supervision of Messrs. Royle & Bennett, architects, Manchester.

The Student's Column.

WARMING BUILDINGS BY HOT WATER
IX.

EXAMPLE WORKS (HORTICULTURAL)
(continued).

THIS next example, fig. 31, shows an apparatus heating two glass-houses, or what may more probably be the case

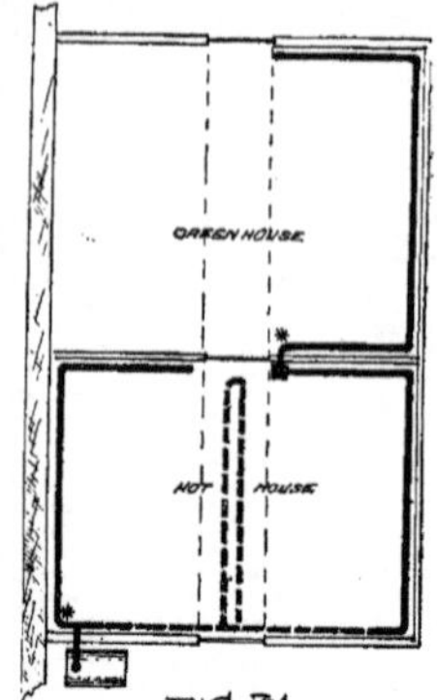

FIG. 31.

one glass-house with a division in it. The two parts of the house are used for different purposes, one as a hot-house for tropical productions, &c., and the other as a greenhouse, for more hardy plants that perhaps only require warmth at night or in winter. The boiler would, in this case, be brick-set, and situated in a pit sunk below the greenhouse level. There is no objection to an independent boiler, but when a pit has to be sunk, it is less expensive to use the other kind, and there is less risk of loss of heat. We are supposing this glass-house is not against a residence, but is of the lean-to character, and placed out in the garden. Even if against a residence it is doubtful if the boiler could be conveniently placed in a cellar, as this apparatus would need the regular attention of a gardener. Boilers in cellars or basement rooms are generally attached to less important works, and are attended to by a page-boy or female servant.

It was just mentioned that this example is of an apparatus heating a greenhouse of the lean-to shape, bounded on one side by a wall, as fig. 32. This lessens the quantity of pipe re-

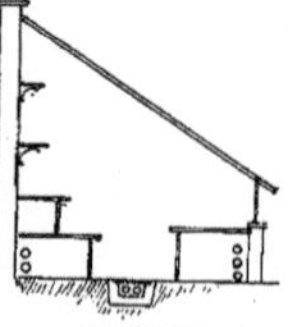

FIG. 32.

quired, for on the wall side no actual loss of heat occurs, and by this arrangement a deal of protection is gained by having the wall facing north or north-east if any way possible.

In the first house the pipes (only the topmost flow-pipe is shown on fig. 31) enter at the point shown on the left-hand side, but it would be arranged for them to come in below the level of the path or floor. By this means the branch required for the front of the house (the side opposite the wall) can be first carried along the end below the floor-level without dipping down anywhere, and so miss the doorway, which is sure to exist, as shown in the illustration. The pipes which are carried below the floor-level ar shown broken or dotted; those above the floor-level, solid.

As the first house is devoted to plants requiring a high temperature, we may consider that pipes along the front only would hardly suffice; so a branch along the back, *i.e.*, the wall, is shown. This being the side requiring the least heat, two pipes will, probably, suffice (as shown at fig. 31). This would be one flow and one return. Along the front three pipes (perhaps four may be needed) are carried, but the portion below the floor-level along the end, need only be but two pipes, branched into three or four as soon as they rise above the floor-level.

The two pipes up the centre of the house are a flow and return, also carried beneath the floor-level.

All pipes beneath the floor-level are, as a rule, carried in brick channels, with a grating at top. By this means the pipes, although not exposed, contribute to the aggregate results, although not in proportion to pipes that are exposed, as the rule that is to be given will show. The gratings which cover these channel pipes must be easily removable, so that the pipes can be brushed and kept clean. A dirty pipe, even with a little dust, loses in efficiency, as dirt and dust, of whatever nature, are nearly always composed of poor conducting materials, and go far towards preventing the pipes losing their heat. If only 2 ft. or 3 ft. of pipes were carried below the floor-level, then they could be covered over entirely, as no great gain would be effected by placing such a small quantity in a channel. If pipes are covered entirely, then it must be with some poor conducting material, sand or dry earth will do.

It is desirable to point out that showing a certain number of pipes, and pipes in certain positions, does not indicate that the work should be always carried out in this manner. The illustration is merely to describe possible ways of doing the work, if such ways are considered the best to meet the conditions. But in the majority of cases it is not for the hot-water engineer to arrange the disposition of the pipes at all; he may settle the quantity, but the gardener is the person who settles general questions, and he will decide where the pipes may be run and where not, In works of fair size the engineer's first business should be to confer with the gardener. The pipes and their disposition can then be arranged to meet all requirements to suit the purposes to which the houses are to be put, also as to avoiding vine-roots, trees, &c., should such exist or be likely to exist. Many gardeners are very skilled in planning these works; it is, to all intents, part of their business, and usually forms part of their training.

Both the front and back services in the hot-house are extended around and along the division, as far as the doorway. This may not always be necessary, although, as a rule, a tropical house wants a deal of pipe, and few

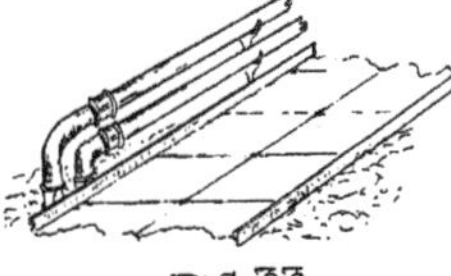

FIG. 33.

spaces are left empty. It is on this account a service is shown below the floor-level, up the pathway, although it is more often the inability to place the pipes against the walls, owing to

FIG. 34.

roots existing, that makes this plan necessary. Sometimes, if pipes cannot be carried close to the walls, they are run along the edge of the pathway, as fig. 33, or along the edge of a raised bed, as fig. 34.

The second house will probably be heated sufficiently by two pipes carried along the front, and extending to the division doorway and the end doorway as shown. These pipes are simply continuations of those along the front of the first house. To avoid ugly work just where the pipes pass through the division, there being three pipes in the first house and but two in the second, a box-end, as fig. 35, will be found very

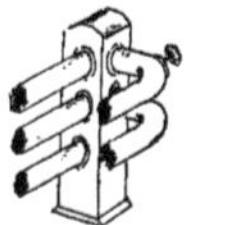

FIG. 35.

useful. The illustration shows exactly how the connexion is made; the whole of the box is in the first house.

As illustrated, it is customary to have the tropical house nearest the boiler, as it requires the greatest heat; the houses (if there are more than two) succeeding this are then placed in order of precedence as to the heat required. This is the usual plan, although, like all other rules, it has exceptions. When there are two or more houses, however, it becomes necessary to introduce stop-valves to regulate the heat in any particular spot,—that is, to check or retard the circulation as required. This regulation is needed, as the most careful measurement and calculations will not result in a quantity of pipe that will do the work exactly, neither too little nor too much. Then, again, as the weather changes, and as the growth of the plants or fruit proceeds, regulation of the heat is needful, and at various other times. With one house only the regulation is effected by checking or urging the fire, but this does not do with several houses, as it is certain that the heat of all houses will not require regulating at the same time or to the same extent.

In the apparatus under discussion a stop-valve would be needed in the flow-pipe just inside the second house, where marked * on fig. 31, and as shown in the last illustration. This would provide a means of checking the second house without interfering with the heat of the first; this will suffice, as the reverse of this would never be required with an apparatus of this character. It might also be desirable to put a stop-valve in the service against the back wall in the first house, where marked *, to prevent this short and direct service from "leading" the circulation, to the detriment of the longer services in the other direction. This valve might, however, be dispensed with if the service was kept nearly flat and a good rise given to the other branch.

In the whole of this apparatus 4 in. pipe would be used. No gain would be effected by using a smaller pipe between the boiler and the circulating pipes, the distance being so short. Smaller pipes,—say, 2 in.,—would be permissible if the distance was greater and the houses not very large. There is no need, however, for the stop-valves to be 4 in., they can be 2 in., the pipes being reduced to this size just where the valves come. This effects economy, as the valves are rather expensive. In larger works than this, it would be necessary not to use smaller pipes or valves than 4 in. anywhere, for, as explained in an earlier paper, the strength of the circulation, the motive-power, is very weak in horticultural works which are so deficient in vertical pipes, that is, of such little height. Air-tubes would be needed at each extremity and one on top of the box junction, fig. 35.

SURVEYORSHIPS.

Leicester.—The Leicester Corporation has, almost unanimously, increased the salary of Mr. E. G. Mawbey, the Borough Engineer, from 700*l.* to 1,000*l.* a year. Mr. Mawbey succeeded the late Mr. Joseph Gordon at Leicester about two years and a half ago, when that gentleman was appointed Chief Engineer to the London County Council.

The Cutlers' Company.—Mr. Alex. R. Stenning, F.R.I.B.A., F.S.I., has been elected Surveyor to the Worshipful Company of Cutlers.

Pulpit, Bridestone.—An oak pulpit has been placed in Bridestone Church, Devon, made by Messrs. Luscombe, of Exeter, from the design of Messrs. Tait & Harvey, The Close, Exeter.

GENERAL BUILDING NEWS.

Proposed Reconstruction of Glasgow Court-house.—At a general meeting of the Glasgow Court-house Commissioners, held on the 18th inst., it was decided to adopt the plan prepared by Mr. Bell, of Messrs. Clarke & Bell, for the reconstruction of the Court-house and the provision of additional accommodation for the conduct of the business of the court. The plan deals with the premises at present occupied by the sheriffs, as well as those vacated by the Corporation, and involves the complete reconstruction of the building, at an estimated cost of 48,000*l.* The basement floor will be occupied mainly with fire-proof record rooms in connexion with the departments of the Sheriff-Clerk and the Justice of Peace Clerk. In addition it will contain a witness-room for the Justice of Peace Court, and there will be sixteen cells for the temporary detention of prisoners. In the Ingram street end of the ground floor accommodation will be provided for the Justice of Peace Court; and there will be rooms for the J.P. Clerk and Fiscal, as well as retiring-rooms for the justices. The Sheriff-Clerk's department will occupy the remainder of this floor, and here also will be refreshment-rooms and retiring-rooms for the agents. On the first floor there will be five courts for the Sheriffs-Substitute. Attached to each will be a retiring-room. Three spare court-rooms will be provided, in the view of the ultimate appointment of an additional Sheriff; in the meantime these would be available for other business. On this floor also will be placed the Sheriff-Principal's reception-room, the Ordinary Court, the Appeal Court, and the Jury Court rooms, with retiring-rooms for the judges in connexion with each. The Jury Court, where the criminal trials will take place, will have a gallery fitted up, to which independent access will be had by the general public. The Sheriff Small-Debt Court will continue to occupy its present position on the second floor, but the main entrance will be from Hutcheson-street, and improved communication with other parts of the building will be provided. The Sheriffs-Fiscal's department will likewise be located on this floor, and eighteen large rooms will be set apart for the conduct of business; while, for the reception of prisoners awaiting examination, six cells will be provided. The remainder of the floor will be occupied with agents' retiring-rooms, witnesses' rooms, and the offices of the auditor. The attic floor will probably be occupied by the house of the caretaker, with additional retiring-rooms, lavatories, &c. There will be entrances in the centre, both from Wilson-street and Ingram-street, which will be connected by staircases with corridors running round the building on each floor, with access to the various departments. There will, in addition, be elevators at both ends, running to the top of the building.

Business Premises, Cardiff.—Some new business premises for the Atlas Furnishing Company have just been erected in the Hayes, Cardiff. The frontage of the premises is over 100 ft., and the extreme depth measures 160 ft. The building contains a basement, ground, and four floors. The front elevation is worked in white brick, with carved Bath stone facings, with polished granite pillars. The new premises have a basement extending 150 ft. back, and above this is a glass-fronted shop. There are also suitable offices and waiting-rooms, and on either side is a doorway,—on the left leading to the warehouses, workshops, packing-rooms, and stables; and on the right to an area in which lavatories, &c., are placed. The staircase gives access to the show-rooms above and also to the basement warehouse. Iron pillars form a central support to each succeeding floor. Behind the show-rooms are the warehouses and workshops, stables, and coach-house. The former measures 60 ft. by 40 ft., the workshops being comprised in the two upper stories. The front building is supplied with a lift, and the workshops with hoists. The premises were designed by Mr. J. P. Jones, of Cardiff.

Congregational Church, near St. Helens.—The new Congregational church and schools at Blackbrook, St. Helens, which were commenced in August, 1890, have just been completed. The architectural design is Late Gothic in character, the plan of the church being cruciform, having chancel and transept. The outside of the building is composed of Monk & Newell's Ruabon brick, with red sandstone facings, and the inside is of white Cefn stone. There are several entrances, the main one being in the front, and two on the sides. There are also rear entrances for the choir, &c. Internally, the clearstory is carried upon moulded arches, supported on octagon pillars having moulded caps and bases. On one side of the rostrum is the organ-chamber, and on the other side the vestry, with cloak-room in the rear. The internal woodwork is of pitch-pine toned and varnished, and the rostrum is constructed of selected pitch-pine. The traceried windows are filled with tinted leadlights. The church stands back from the main road, and has a tower and spire 120 ft. high. A drinking-fountain is let into the boundary wall. The Sunday school building adjoining consists of an assembly-room with accommodation for over 300 children, and boys' and girls' and infants' class-rooms. The architect has been Mr. Thomas W. Cubbon, of Birkenhead, and the contractors Messrs. Hughes & Stirling, of Bootle. The work has been carried on under the supervision of Mr. A. Halsall.

WESLEYAN CHAPEL, BEVERLEY.—On the 10th inst. the new Wesleyan Chapel in Tollgavel, Beverley, erected on the site of the superintendent minister's house, and backing up to the old building in Walkergate, was formally opened. The building is from the design of Messrs. Morley & Woodhouse, of Bradford, and is in the Italian style. The chapel is designed to accommodate 100 more than the old building. A minister's vestry, inquiry-room, and kitchen are provided in the rear. The front entrance vestibule is reached by three doors, and has a tiled floor. The organ recess has pilasters with enriched capitals and trusses supporting an elliptical arch and pediment with enriched panels and cornices. The front gable windows are filled in with leaded glass. An open portico, with polished granite columns and circular arches, projects beyond the main line of frontage; the floor is laid with mosaic tiles, and the walls inside lined with glazed bricks. The total cost has been about 4,000*l.*

BATHS, STOCKTON.—The new baths of the Stockton Corporation were opened on the 19th inst. They have been erected on the site of the old baths in Portrack-lane, by Mr. Campbell, the Borough Surveyor. The building is of brick and stone, with wrought-iron roofing. There are two entrances, respectively for women and men, divided by the ticket or pay office. Above this is a series of first-class slipper baths for gentlemen, and also a vapour and a shower bath. Beyond these apartments is the new swimming or plunge bath. The height of this hall is 36 ft., and the width 33 ft. The length of the swimming bath is 75 ft., and its width 27 ft. It is 6 ft. 6 in. deep at the deepest, and 4 ft. at the shallow end, and holds 60,000 gallons of water, kept at an even and warm temperature, and also cleared of surface impurities by an arrangement of water sprays. The building contractor was Mr. W. C. Atkinson. The contract for the building and machinery was 6,448*l.*

RESTORATION OF MICKLEHAM CHURCH, DORKING.—On the 15th inst. the Church of St. Michael, at Mickleham, near Dorking, was opened by the Bishop of Winchester, after undergoing alterations and additions. New Norman arcades have been erected, and the north aisle has been enlarged. The galleries, which previously existed in the aisles, have been removed, and a lighter gallery placed in the tower above the chief entrance. The old-fashioned "box" pews have been demolished, to give place to seats of a more modern construction, and the arcades, which formerly stood in the nave on brick piers, have been taken away, and Norman pillars and caps substituted. New screens have been erected for the north aisle and the tower. The tower has also been renovated externally, the stucco having been taken off and the flint work brought out. The turret has been shingled and put in good order. A stained window, containing three lights, has been erected in one of the aisles in memory of the late Mrs. Gordon Clark. The work of restoration has been carried out by Mr. Shillitoe, contractor, of Bury St. Edmunds, the plans having been prepared by Mr. Ewan Christian, architect to the Ecclesiastical Commissioners, the cost being about 3,900*l.*

PROPOSED ARTISANS' DWELLINGS, DUBLIN.—On the 19th inst. Mr. C. P. Cotton, C.E., Local Government Board Inspector, held an inquiry at the City Hall, Dublin, in reference to the proposal of the Corporation to borrow a sum of 13,000*l.* to erect dwellings suitable to the working classes at Blackhall-street, Blackhall-place, and North King-street. Mr. Harty, C.E., Borough Surveyor, was examined, and stated that the place was suitable for the erection of artisans' dwellings, and there were large numbers of working people employed in that locality. He proposed to take down the old houses there, which were in a terrible state. There were various classes of houses to be built. Fronting Blackball-street there would be shops, and there would be ninety-one tenements included in the scheme. The annual profit on the scheme, after paying for all outgoings, would be 56*l.* a year. Mr. Moore, on behalf of the Governors of the King's Hospital, Blackball-street, objected to the scheme as regards the houses proposed to be erected at the rear of Blackhall-street, and also to the conversion of the houses in Blackhall-place. If the scheme were passed it would have the effect of depreciating the property of the Hospital, which was originally given by the Corporation. Other evidence having been given, the proceedings terminated.

METHODIST CHAPEL, WITHINGTON, LANCASHIRE.—A new Primitive Methodist Chapel was opened at Withington on the 14th inst. The building is of Gothic design, and consists of a chapel, Sunday-school, minister's vestry, and two class-rooms. The building faces Burton-road and Ashford-road. The walls are built of local bricks, faced with pressed Ruabon stools and bricks, relieved with terra-cotta dressings. The principal entrance to the chapel consists of an outer porch and a vestibule. The north and south aisles are approached from the vestibule. The chapel is capable of seating 300. The school-room, which communicates therewith, will accommodate 140, exclusive of the two class-rooms and minister's vestry. The walls of the chapel are wainscotted in pitch pine for some distance above the pew backs, and the pews and the flooring of the chapel are finished in selected varnished pitch pine. The roof principals, and the exposed portions of the roof timbers, are of stained pitch pine. The pulpit has been treated to imitate walnut, and is relieved with figured pitch pine panels. The windows of the chapel and school are fitted with leaded lights, glazed with tinted cathedral glass. The buildings are heated with hot water on the low-pressure system. The contract for the building was 1,600*l.*, and has been executed by Messrs. Burgess & Galt, of Manchester, in accordance with the designs and under the supervision of Mr. Joseph Swarbrick, of Manchester.

METHODIST CHURCH, RAMSEY, ISLE OF MAN.—On the 18th inst., memorial-stones of a Primitive Methodist church and schools were laid at Ramsey, Isle of Man. The church has been designed to seat 400 people, and the estimated cost is 1,700*l.* The architecture is Early English. On the basement there will be a schoolroom and three classrooms. There will be two aisles in the church, and the rostrum will be placed opposite the entrance. The ministers' and stewards' vestries will be behind the transepts, and the organ-loft and choir-gallery are to be placed immediately behind. The inside fittings will be of pitch-pine, and open-timbered roof. The architect is Mr. Thos. Howdill, of Leeds, and the builder is Mr. W. C. Southward, of Ramsey.

STAINED GLASS AND DECORATION.

WINDOW, PARISH CHURCH, GREAT HALLINGBURY.—A stained-glass window, which has been put in the east end of the Parish Church, Great Hallingbury, Essex, by Mrs. Houblon, to the memory of her husband, has just been dedicated. The window, which has been erected by Messrs. Clayton & Bell, of London, consists of three lights. In the centre is a representation of the Crucifixion, while on the right of it are depicted the three Marys, and on the left St. John, Joseph of Arimathea, and the Centurion. Above the centre light is represented Michael the Archangel.

WINDOWS, ST. JOHN'S CHURCH, RADCLIFFE.—A number of Munich stained-glass windows have recently been placed in St. John's Church, Radcliffe, in memory of the late vicar, the Rev. W. D. Carter, M.A. The subjects are "The Good Shepherd," "Christ's Charge to Peter," "The Pool of Siloam," and "Feeding the Multitude." Another memorial window has been placed in the same church in remembrance of the Rev. J. W. Taylor, who was the first curate-in-charge of the parish. The window has been presented by his only son, Mr. Alfred Kaye Taylor, Liverpool, and the subject is "The Good Samaritan." The windows, six in number, were supplied by Messrs. Mayer & Co., of Munich and London.

SANITARY AND ENGINEERING NEWS.

SEWERAGE WORKS, SWANSEA.—A Local Government Board inquiry was held at the Town Hall, Swansea, on the 10th inst., by Mr. Smith, Local Government Board Inspector, into the proposal of the Swansea Corporation to borrow 87,760*l.* for sewerage and other improvements in the borough. The Town Clerk explained the proposed works, which consisted of drainage works in the added area, a new main sewer and outfall at the western boundary of the borough, to carry off the sewage matter and storm-water for the St. Helen's district, &c.—Mr. Wyrill, Borough Engineer, explained the proposed works at Morriston, Pentrepoth, Brynhyfryd, Cwmbwrla, &c., and produced plans showing their outfalls into the Tawe or the existing sewers. With regard to the proposed western sewer, the Town Clerk explained that at Brynmill the proposed sewer was not carried to low-water mark, and that it would not be necessary to extend it so far. If it was insisted upon it would result in the total expense amounting to nearly 100,000*l.* Other evidence having been given, the inquiry closed.

COUNTY BRIDGE, WRITTLE.—The bridge which has been built over the river Wid, at Writtle, by the County Council, to replace the brick structure washed away by the flood of 1888, was thrown open for public traffic on the 15th inst. The bridge has been constructed from the designs, and under the superintendence of the Engineer to the Council, Mr. Percy J. Sheldon, Assoc.M.Inst.C.E. It consists of two steel girders, and a steel plate flooring, filled in solid with concrete. The parapets are of cast-iron of an ornamental design. The contractor was Mr. G. Watson, of Ilford, the steel and iron work having been supplied and fixed by Messrs. Westwood & Bailey, of London. The total cost is estimated at 3,000*l.*

ELECTRIC LIGHT IN AUSTRALIA.—Mr. E. R. Dymond has just contributed to the *Proceedings* of the Institution of Civil Engineers a paper in which he gives a description of the electric lighting at Tamworth, New South Wales. Although Tamworth has only a population of 4,000, and a rateable value not exceeding 33,700*l.*, its streets have been lit by electricity since the year 1888; and was, indeed, the first place in Australia to adopt the new system. The plant is in duplicate, and was sent out from England. There are 13½ miles of streets now lighted, the distance of the furthest lamp from the station being 2,100 yards. The average loss of pressure is stated to be not more than 5 per cent. In the main street there are four arc-lamps of 3,000 nominal candle-power each, which are worked in series off a separate cable. The other lights are glow-lamps. In the most important positions near the station, each lantern has three 75-volt lamps in series. As the distance increases, two 110-volt, and, lastly, two 105-volt lamps are used. All glow-lamps are 16 candle-power. There are 185 glow-lamps contained in eighty-six lanterns. The number does not seem great for the area covered, but in a modern town such as this the engineer can place his lights to much greater advantage, as the streets are straight and run at right-angles to each other, and, moreover, are spaced regularly, the rectangular blocks of houses being of uniform shape and size. The previous cost per mile of street lighted by gas equal to 94 candle-power was 56*l.* 19s. 10d.; whilst with electricity it is 51*l.* 2s. 8d., the light being equal to a standard of 219 candles. These figures will not, of course, afford any basis of comparison for English practice, where gas is so much cheaper, and where Board of Trade rules must be observed; but the author puts them forward as a fair example of country town lighting in Australia.

FOREIGN AND COLONIAL.

FRANCE.—The statue of Theophrastus Renaudot, said to be the founder of French journalism, will probably be placed on the open in space in front of the Marché aux Fleurs, near the Tribunal de Commerce.——The statue of Balzac, on which M. Rodin is now at work, is to be erected on the Place du Palais Royal, on the axis of the Cour d'Horloge.——The Société des Artistes Français has decided that the next Salon is to include a section of Decorative Art.——The Government is having two casts made from Rude's celebrated bas-relief, the "Chant du Départ," on the Arc de Triomphe de l'Etoile. One of these is to go to the Society of Arts of New York, the other the Trocadéro Museum.——The "Société Française d'Hygiene" will open this year another competition on various subjects connected with town and country dwellings. The competition is to be closed on July 1.——The Ministry of Public Instruction is preparing an inventory of works which are in the stores of the Louvre and for which no exhibition space is available. There are 146 of these hidden treasures.——Important restoration works are shortly to be commenced at the Palace of Fontainebleau. The Pavilion Serlio will be taken in hand first, and from thence the work will proceed in the Cour de Cheval Blanc, the pavement of which, worn by the carriages of all the generations since Louis XIV., has never been repaired.——The creation of a commercial and industrial museum has just been decided on at Toulouse, which will form a permanent exhibition of raw materials and their application to manufactures.——The competition for a museum at Bayonne has been a failure; one "second prix" was given to M. Planckaert, but nothing further has resulted from it.——The director of the Museum of Lyons has asked for the restitution of the panel painted by Perugino which decorates the central window of the nave of St. Gervais at Paris. The painting, representing the Lord surrounded by angels, formed once the crowning portion of a grand composition of which the remainder is in the Lyons Museum. In exchange, the Lyons Museum offers four very interesting views of Paris of the fourteenth century.——The Government is going to erect at Luneville a fort in béton constructed after the type of fortification made use of by the Belgian General, Brialmont, for the defence of the Meuse. The work will have two armoured cupolas.——The Government has allotted a credit of 3,250,000 f. for the expenses of the French representation at the Chicago Exhibition.——Mdme. Cogniet, widow of the celebrated painter, has died at the age of seventy-nine. She was herself a painter and exhibited in the Salons of 1835 and 1853 some *genre* pictures, under the name of "Caroline Thévenin." She obtained a medal in the Salon of 1843.——The death is announced also of M. Jacques Alfred Brielman, landscape-painter; a pupil of Laveille. He received a medal in the Salon of 1882. The last Salon contained two of his works.——It is proposed to organise this year an international exhibition of "Black and White"; a special section being devoted to a historical collection of engravings etchings and lithographs of the French, Italian, English, Dutch, German and Spanish schools.——It is proposed to construct a new Lyric Theatre at Paris on the site now occupied by the Eden Theatre, which will be pulled down.

BERLIN.—The Emperor has given some further attention to the "National Monument" question, and Herr Ziller has made some proposals relative to the position of the monument on the very difficult site in front of the royal castle. The Emperor entered into a lengthy discussion of the merits of the different proposals.——The sarcophagus of Emperor Frederick III. has been placed in its position in the new mausoleum near Potsdam. Reinhold Begas was the sculptor, and his work is considered to be a great success by those who have seen it. The mausoleum is to be open to public inspection next month.——The older of the two architectural societies, the "Architektenverein zu Berlin," has elected Baurath Hinckeldeyn as president for the coming session.——The "Allgemeine Elektricitaets Gesellschaft" (who are now remodelling their design of the proposed underground metropolitan railway in accordance with requirements made by a special committee) intends constructing a specimen piece of tunnelling for the purpose of demonstrating that no technical difficulties oppose the carrying out of their electric railroad scheme under the main thoroughfares of the city.——In one of the suburbs of the city a batch of villas and cottages is being put up in Norse style. A Swedish builder sends the logs and fittings for each residence ready for putting together, and supplies the artisans necessary for the work from his own country.

VIENNA.—The Ferdinand Bridge over the Danube Canal, which will have to be replaced by a new crossing (bearing the same name), is to have a row of shops on either side of it, and its footways covered in with arcades. The reasons for erecting the shops are purely financial, as the rents to be obtained are to cover the expense of the reconstruction of the thoroughfare. The design for the new bridge is by "Baurath" von Wiekmannsand, engineer. Vienna, which city since December last calls itself "Gross Wien," and, after having acquired the whole or part of the ground of some sixty neighbouring parishes, can boast of a superficial area of 177 square kilomètres (*i.e.*, 120 more than it had before), and a population of 1,300,000 (instead of 800,000), will now undergo some important changes as regards sanitation, canal regulations, and local railway intercommunication. The alteration and extension of the sewage system, which includes the construction of two main sewers on either side of the Danube canal, will cost over eleven million florins, and will have to be ready by 1895. The Danube canal, a channel of some 15 kilomètres length, is to have new embankments, and is to be used as a harbour for the river shipping. The proposed new railway intercommunication will be brought about partly by constructing several minor lines between the terminal stations of the different great railroads which run into the city, and partly by the construction of some secondary, purely local roads. Up to but a few years back Vienna took a most prominent position in the erection of public buildings, architectural monuments of the largest scale, grouped together in an imposing way. This period of activity in architecture having come to an end, another, in which the civil engineer will play the leading part, is apparently about to commence, and, from all appearances, promises to be a most important one for "Gross Wien's" development.

NORWAY.—The Corporation of Christiania, not wishing the city to be disfigured by the usual tall, ugly chimney-stacks of electrical stations, has offered three prizes for designs for the chimney-stack of the new municipal central station now in course of construction, the jury having been named by the Association of Engineers and Architects of Christiania.——The Norwegian production of bricks last year was about the same as in the preceding one—viz., about forty millions; and the out-turn of calcined roof tiles about one million, against about 800,000 in 1890. The demand for bricks was brisk during summer and autumn in Christiania, where the principal kilns are found, owing to considerable building operations. In consequence, stocks are now small. The price of bricks remained steadily throughout the year at 24 kr. (27s.) per thousand, a price leaving a good profit. For red calcined roof tiles the price varied between 40 kr. and 44 kr. per thousand (55s. and 59s. 6d.), being about the same as in 1890. Wages rose further still last year, although a steady rise has taken place during recent years. However, during the last few months of 1891 and up to the present the demand for bricks and tiles has fallen off, owing to the monetary crisis prevailing. There were imported into Christiania in 1891 about 11,000,000 bricks from other parts, about 800.000 fireproof bricks from abroad, and about 150,000 roof tiles. The Norwegian stone industry flourished fairly well in 1891, the demand for granite of various colours from this and other countries being good.——From the report for 1890 of the Society for the Preservation of Norwegian Ancient Memorials it appears that fourteen old churches were examined and partly restored, and thirty-eight barrows excavated, but the finds were of little value. The excavations of Lyse Cloister were continued, and the ruins enclosed. The Society attempted in vain to purchase for the Christiania Museum a remarkable reliquary preserved in the Hedal Chapel, upon which is represented in relief the murder of Thomas à Becket, but it was permitted to take three casts of it for the museums of Christiania, Bergen, and Throndhjem.

CONSTANTINOPLE.—The idea of bridging over the Bosphorus for railway traffic has often been spoken of. There is now some chance of it being done if the financial arrangement can be managed.——Messrs. Giano and Gourrée, two engineers resident in the city, have designed a railway-bridge which is to cross the straits from Stamboul to Scutari. This design has been put before the Government for approval. The length of the bridge, including viaducts at either end, is 2,000 mètres; the central span measures 1,400 mètres. The floor of the bridge will have a width of 15 mètres, and its altitude over average water-level will be 40 mètres.—*Deutsche Bauzeitung.*

NEW SOUTH WALES.—The Minister for Works has appointed Mr. Horbury Hunt (President of the Institute of Architects of New South Wales) to act with Mr. Vernon (Government Architect) and Dr. Manning (President of the Board of Health) to report on the competitive designs for the Rossiville Asylum buildings at Goulburn; and Mr. Wardell to act with Mr. Darley (Engineer-in-Chief for Harbours and Rivers) and Mr. Hixson (Engineer-in-Chief for Roads and Bridges) to report upon the designs for the new Pyrmont Bridge.

MUNICH.—The arrangements for the "International" Art Exhibition to be opened here next summer are most elaborate, and promise well. Of the countries invited to exhibit, Austria has already accepted, and its Government has voted 5,000 florins towards the expenses of fitting up the hall of its section. Japan is to have a section, and a great novelty, in form of a room devoted entirely to architecture, is proposed. We hope that there will be some English work to be seen in the exhibition.

MISCELLANEOUS.

SALES OF PRINTS, ENGRAVINGS, &C.—Last week (Feb. 18-19) Messrs. Sotheby, Wilkinson, & Hodge sold the remarkable collection, formed by Dr. Joly, of Dublin, of the works of Hogarth, and books in connexion therewith. One lot, bought by Mr. Quaritch for 500*l.*, consisted of twenty-five volumes, atlas folio size, containing about 158 drawings and 6,097 prints, being nearly the whole of Hogarth's engravings, and after his designs, with no two prints (plate impressions excepted), in exactly the same state included. Vols. i. and ii. were compiled for Lord Charlemont (Hogarth's patron) by R. Livesay; vol. iii. is the Kingsbury Collection,—86 prints. Similar folios, of the same size, by T. Cook, J. Nichols, J. and J. Boydell, with others, were also sold. Of the books we may mention,—Allen's "Lambeth," 1827, 5s.; "Apuleius; or, The New Metamorphosis," 1708, 1*l.*; J. Ashton's "The Fleet: its River, Prison, and Marriages," 1888, with M. Jackson's "History of the Pictorial Press," 1885, 16s.; A. W. Tuer's "Bartolozzi and his Works," parchment, 1885, 7s.; three copies, fol. size (two with faults), of G. Bickham's "Musical Entertainer," 8*l.* 11s.; Butler's "Hudibras," on large paper, sixty portraits by R. Cooper, India proofs, fol., 1821, 5*l.* 12s. 6d.; "Calliope, or English Harmony," with 2 vols. of G. and R. Cruikshank's "Universal Songster," 1828, 3*l.* 3s.; "Clio and Euterpe," a collection of songs and cantatas, 3 vols, 1762, 3*l.* 10s.; T. H. Ward's "English Art in the London Public Galleries," 15 parts, fol. 1888, 2*l.* 14s.; J. Forbes-Robertson's "Great Painters of Christendom, 4to., 10s.; J. Forster's "Life of Goldsmith," original edition, 1848, 12s.; C. Knight's "Gallery of Portraits," 7 vol., 1833-7, 2*l.*; Mrs. S. C. Hall's "Pilgrimages to English Shrines," illustrated by Fairholt, 2 vol., 10s.; J. Grego's "History of Elections and Electioneering in the Old Days," large paper, 4to, 1886, 13s.; and A. J. C. Hare's "Walks in London," 1878, with J. Timbs's "London and Westminster," 1868, 4 vols., 1*l.* 5s. In the same week Messrs. Puttick & Simpson disposed of a good collection of engravings in illustration of British topography, with some scarce early views of London and Westminster. The principal lots comprised:—F. Jukes's aquatint, after E. Dayes, by R. Pollard, of "Warren Hastings' Trial, 1789," 18s.; "Election of Members for Westminster, 1818," and "George IV.'s Coronation Procession," etched by G. Scharf, engraved by R. Havell, in colours, 2*l.* 2s.; Gosselin's "Promenade at Carlisle House" (Soho-square), in mezzo, 17s.; "Queen-square" (Holborn), and "Grosvenor-square," by R. Pollard, after E. Dayes, 2*l.* 7s.; "The Masons' Procession" (with view of Denmark [Somerset] House, Strand), on April 27, 1742, 13s.; Werner's "London and the Thames," 15s.; "Lord Lovat's Trial in Westminster Hall, 1747," by J. Freeman, 2*l.* 4s.; Alix's (old) "Westminster Bridge," showing the houses at either end, 10s.; W. Daniell's large coloured aquatints of the West India Docks, Isle of Dogs, 1800–2, and of the East India Docks, Blackwall, built by John Perry in 1803, 9s.; and two of the views, by R. Dodd, of the port of London, in mezzo, Greenwich, and Limehouse with one of the windmills upon the shore, 1793, 15s.; C. Bowles's "Peep into the Court of King's Bench," coloured, 1785, 12s.; and "Deptford Dockyard," with plan, engraved by Woollett, after R. Paton, 1775, 5s. The engraved copper plate, with the entire remaining stock of about 400 impressions, of J. S. Copley's painting (now in the National Collection) of the "Death of Major Pierson" (at St. Helier, in Jersey, on January 6, 1781, all the figures being portraits) was bought for 20*l.*

"L'AIR FROID" SYSTEM.—The patentee of this system, Mr. Inkpen, in reference to our comment on page 147 *ante*, writes to say that he makes no claim in his patent for any improvement in ventilating as such, but only for a system of distributing cold air over plate-glass window surfaces.

STREET HYGIENE.—At a recent meeting of the German Public Health Society, Dr. Theodor Weyl spoke on the street hygiene of Paris and London, and recommended the adoption in Berlin of many of the arrangements in vogue at those places. The gist of his remarks was as follows:—Wooden pavement has been in use in London and Paris for many years past, and has proved a great success, even in the most frequented streets. The fact that it has been less successful in Berlin may be due to faults of construction and treatment. In Paris and London there are no rails in streets paved with wood. The pavement is copiously watered. Drains and pipes are not laid under it, but under the side-walks. The main thing, however, is good construction. In London and Paris sweeping is always preceded by watering, which is not the case here, to the serious detriment of the public health. The public closets in Paris are not worthy of imitation, because hygienic considerations are to a large extent subordinated to advertising purposes, but those of London are exemplary. The depositing of rubbish within or even in the immediate vicinity of cities is altogether to be condemned. The removal of snow costs Berlin about 19,000*l.* a year, because it is not thrown into the river or sewers as in London and Paris, but carted out of the city. In conclusion, Dr. Weyl warmly recommended the London plan of regulating traffic by placing the lamp-posts in the middle of the street.—*Lancet.*

AMERICAN STANDARD FOR SEWER-PIPES.—Messrs. Blackmer & Post, of St. Louis, are large makers of vitrified sewer-pipes. Having been led to suppose that a change in dimensions of these articles would be advantageous, they took the step of sending out a circular to the city engineers, sewer commissioners, civil engineers, and others in the United States interested in sanitary matters, asking their opinions upon the subject. It was proposed to make the sewer-pipes in 2½-ft. lengths, instead of the usual 2-ft. lengths. Over 800 replies were received, and 95 per cent. of these were in favour of the change. This has led the firm to change its standard of length, and other makers, says *Engineering News*, from which journal we take these particulars, will doubtless follow to meet this well-expressed demand for longer sewer-pipes. T and Y junctions, however, are to remain 2 ft. long as before. Another change in the American sewer-pipe is the alteration of the socket, which was formerly 1¾ in. deep, and is now increased to 3 in.

A STRONG PAVING-BRICK.—Mr. W. N. Williams, in a letter to an American technical paper, gives particulars of tests made with a paving-brick, which would seem to possess very remarkable properties. The tests were made by the Mechanical Superintendent of the Union Pacific Railway shops at Omaha. The brick is known as the "Wade Paving-brick," and is the subject of a United States patent. One specimen, 7 square inches in area, was subjected to crushing stress of 28,000 lbs. to the square inch, and then gave way by simply cracking in two. A piece of Sioux Falls granite, 4 in. square, tested at the same time to afford a basis of comparison, crushed when subjected to 23,300 lbs. to the square inch. The brick is said to be made of fire-clay, but in this case, we are told, the great strength of the material is due to a peculiar earth found in the neighbourhood of Omaha. It is not stated how much of the "peculiar earth" is required, but, if the quantity is not excessive, one would think it would pay to import it and make these bricks in this country.

ELECTRICITY *v.* GAS IN BERLIN.—To what extent illumination by means of electricity is becoming popular in Berlin can be seen by the figures contained in the 1890-91 report of the municipal gas-works of that city. Instead of having had to supply the inhabitants with an extra five million cubic mètres of gas, as in the preceding year, only two and a-half million cubic mètres extra were required, and this in spite of an extraordinary increase in the number of new tenements and new streets. In the city proper the amount of gas required during the year 1890-91 was 7·9 per cent. less than the amount supplied in 1889-90.

NEW CLOCK, SCALBY PARISH CHURCH, NEAR SCARBOROUGH.—Scalby, so well known to visitors to Scarborough, has had an important addition to its old parish church in the shape of a public clock, with two large external dials, one facing eastward, over the body of the church, towards the village of Scalby, the other on the west, towards the residence of the donor, Mr. J. E. Ellis, M.P., Wrea Head, Scalby, and the schools and cottages adjoining. The clock strikes the hours upon the large or tenor bell. The work has been executed by Messrs. William Potts & Sons, Leeds.

BRUSSELS A SEAPORT.—An advance has been made with the scheme for making Brussels a seaport, as, according to official statements, the cost of enlarging the existing canal to the sea is estimated at 830,000*l.*, the cost of the harbour works and dry dock at Brussels at 500,000*l.*, and the enclosing of the river Sermette, at 83,000*l.* Negotiations are now in progress as to the division of the cost between the State and the provinces.

DEATH OF MR. THOMAS BEATY, CARLISLE.—We regret to announce the death, at the early age of forty-seven years, of Mr. Thomas Beaty, of the firm of Beaty Bros., builders, of Carlisle, which occurred on the 17th inst.

COMPETITION, CONTRACTS, AND PUBLIC APPOINTMENTS.

COMPETITION.

Nature of Work.	By whom Advertised.	Premium.	Designs to be delivered.
*Construction of Bridge over Canal	Corp. of Bootle	105l. and 52l. 10s.	June 1

CONTRACTS.

Nature of Work or Materials.	By whom Required.	Architect, Surveyor, or Engineer.	Tenders to be delivered.
*Works and Materials	Hendon Local Board	S. S. Grimley	Feb. 29
*Supplying and Laying Victoria Stone and Kerbing	Farnham Local Board	R. P. Hankins	do.
Bridge, Warehouse, &c. Hebden Bridge	....	Utley & Gray	Mar. 1
Sewerage, &c. Works, Northwich	Salt Union, Lim.	....	do.
House, Lazonby, Carlisle	Isaac Longrigg	....	do.
*Pipe Sewers, &c.	Southend Loc. Bd.	P. Dodd	do.
*Works and Materials	Lewisham Bd. of Wks.	*Official*	do.
*Sweeping and Cleaning Streets	St Saviour's Board of Works	do.	Mar. 2
*Removing Concrete Bed, R.N.E.	Royal Hospital, Chelsea	do.	do.
Road Metal (10,000 tons)	Hardingstone High. B.	do.	do.
*School Extension, Penrhiwceiber	Llanwonno School Bd.	A. O. Evans	do.
Cottage, Glenlivet Distillery, Elgin, N.B.	....	C. C. Doig	Mar. 3
Two Houses and Shops, Lightcliffe, Leeds	....	Harry Pyrah	Mar. 4
*Erection of Institute, Derby	Midland Railway	*Official*	do.
*Maintenance and Repairs to Roads	Kent County Council	do.	Mar. 5
Improvement Works	Neath U.S.A.	do.	do.
Sunday School and Premises, Runcorn	Trustees	John Wilson	do.
*Removal of Street Sweepings, &c.	St. Giles' Board of Works	*Official*	do. Mar. 7
*Sewerage Works	Richmond (Surrey) Town Council	do.	do.
*Works and Materials	Romford Local Board	do.	do.
*Purchase and Pulling-down Property	Sch. Bd. for London	do.	do.
*Construction of Portion of Canal	Manchester Ship Canal Co.	do.	Mar. 8
*Repair of Private Roads	Borough of Croydon	do.	do.
*Works and Materials	Rotherhithe Vestry	do.	do.
*Wrought-iron Fencing	Boro' of West Ham	do.	do.
*Completing Stores, Dwelling-house, &c.	....	C. Dunch	do.
*Works and Materials	Battersea Vestry	J. T. Pilditch	do.
*Supplies, Collection of House Refuse, &c.	West Ham Council	Lewis Angell	do.
*Supply of Materials	Colchester Town Coun.	*Official*	Mar. 9
*Oak Fencing	West Ham Union	do.	do.
*Brick Sewer, &c.	Battersea Vestry	J. T. Pilditch	do.
*Works and Materials	Chiswick L. B.	A. Ramsden	do.
*Widening, Deepening, &c. Hockley Brook	Aston Manor Loc. Bd.	W. A. Davies	Mar. 10
*Brick and Concrete, and Pipe Sewers, &c.	Twickenham L. B.	O. B. Laffan	do.
*Making-up Roads	Hornsey Loc. Bd.	T. de Courcy Meade	Mar. 11
*Sewerage Works	do.	do.	do.

CONTRACTS.—*Continued.*

Nature of Work or Materials.	By whom Required.	Architect, Surveyor or Engineer.	Tenders to be delivered.
*Two Cottages	Hornsey Loc. Bd.	T. de Courcy Meade	Mar. 11
*Works and Materials	do.	do.	do.
*Iron Fencing, with Gates	do.	do.	do.
*Supply of Materials	do.	do.	do.
*Wood Paving Blocks	St. Pancras Vestry	W. N. Blair	Mar. 14
*Works and Materials	Fulham Vestry	*Official*	Mar. 15
*Supply of Materials	Borough of St. Helens	do.	do.
*Works and Materials	Wimbledon Local Bd.	do.	do.
*Works and Materials	Tottenham Loc. Bd.	do.	do.
*Sewerage Works	Corp. of Durban, Natal	W. H. Radford	do.
School Building, Quaker's-yard, Glam.	South Wales and Monmouth Trustees' Sch.	W. H. D. Caple	Mar. 16
Flags, Paving Stones, &c.	Carlisle Corporation	W. H. Smith	do.
*Making Roads, &c. at Infirmary	St. Olave's Union	Newman & Newman	Mar. 17
*Fire Escape Staircases	do.	do	do.
*Cast-iron Mains, &c. for Water Supply	Shardlow Union	G. Hodson	Mar. 19
*Repairs, &c. to Chimney Shaft	Commrs. for P. B. & W. St. Giles, &c.	J. Waldram	Mar. 23
*Iron Staircases	London C. C. Asylum Committee	*Official*	Mar. 26
*Public Baths	Corp. of Coventry	do.	April 4
*Police Buildings	Guildford T. C.	W. G. Lower	No date
Residence, Bramley, Leeds	....	E. P. Peterson	do.
House and Stabling, Pontefract	....	S. J. Holliday	do.
Pair of Villas, Lightcliffe, Leeds	....	Rhodes Calvert	do.
Additions to Wedgwood Institute, Burslem	....	Ford & Slater	do.
Iron Footway, Oundle	Northampton C. C.	*Official*	do.
Two Cottages, Siddal, Leeds	....	Jackson & Fox	do.
Mountsorrell, &c. Granite	Towcester High. Bd.	R. W. Rolfe	do.
Branch Bank, Atherton, Warrington	Williams, Deacon, & Manchester & Salford Bank	Bradshaw & Gass	do.
Church, Millbrook, Cornwall	....	G. H. F. Prynne	do.

PUBLIC APPOINTMENTS.

Nature of Appointment.	By whom Advertised.	Salary.	Applications to be in.
*Borough Surveyor	Bootle Corp	300l.	Mar. 3
*Clerk of Works	Camberwell Guar.	4l. per week	do.
*Extra Assistant City Engineer	Cape Town Corp.	275l.	Mar. 5
*Assistant Engineering Surveyor	Birkenhead Corp.	120l. &c.	Mar. 8
*Sanitary Inspector	Hanley County Boro'	104l.	do.
*Surveyor and Inspector of Nuisances	Braintree Loc. Bd.	100l. &c.	Mar. 9
*District Surveyor	Everley and Pewsey Highway Board	160l.	Mar. 10
*Road Surveyor	Norfolk C. C.	2l. &c.	Mar. 12

Those marked with an Asterisk (*) are advertised in this Number. Competition, p. iv. Contracts, pp. iv., vi., viii., ix. & xxiii. Public Appointments, p. xx. & xxi.

THE ENGLISH IRON TRADE.—Consequent upon the break in Scotch warrants reported last week, the English iron market has been very irregular; in most districts depression is the prevailing characteristic. The present state of inaction in the Glasgow warrant market will, it is expected, continue for some time. Scotch warrants have been as low as 40s. cash and 39s. 10½d. one month fixed. The Cleveland market has been disorganised, but closes more cheerful and stronger. The hematite pig-iron trade remains dull. Manufactured iron is quieter. Tinplates continue unchanged. In the steel trade, rails are tolerably brisk, but other descriptions exhibit no alteration. Shipbuilding yards, except on the Tyne and Wear, are fairly well employed. Engineers and ironfounders are rather slacker. There appears a possibility of the strike on the Tyne approaching settlement. The coal trade is steady.—*Iron.*

A LARGE WIRE ROPE.—What is said to be the heaviest colliery wire-rope ever made in Sunderland has been produced by the Hendon Patent Ropery. It is six miles in length, and weighs twenty-four tons. It was carried through Sunderland on two heavy wagons drawn by twenty horses.

GLASGOW AND WEST OF SCOTLAND TECHNICAL COLLEGE.—On the 20th inst. the students of this College attending the honours and advanced stages in building construction visited the City Saw-mills, Port Dundas. Beginning at the log pond, they were conducted through the saw-mills, workshops, &c., finally through the creosoting work, at which a hearty vote of thanks was, on the motion of Mr. Gourlay, the lecturer, accorded Mr. Robb, manager, for his guidance, and the large amount of instruction he so kindly gave.

ELECTRICAL EXHIBITION IN MOSCOW.—It is officially announced that an international Electrical Exhibition will be held in Moscow between April 14 and October 14 next. The Exhibition will be divided into eight sections, Section VII embracing new apparatus in all branches of electrical science.

PORTRAIT BUST OF THE LATE MR. W. H. SMITH, M.P.—At a meeting of the Court of Common Council, held last week at the Guildhall, the model (in a competition of six) submitted by Mr. Joseph Whitehead, of Westminster, was selected to be executed in marble, the sum voted for its execution being 200 guineas. The successful competitor is a son of the senior member of Messrs. J. Whitehead & Sons, The Granite Works, Aberdeen.

THE FIRST TELEPHONE IN BULGARIA.—The first telephone in Bulgaria has just been opened between Sophia and Philippopolis, a distance of 160 kilomètres.

ARTISANS', LABOURERS', AND GENERAL DWELLINGS COMPANY.—The twenty-fifth annual report of this Company states that the principal work of the year has been the completing of the blocks of buildings at Rosoman-street; the pressing forward of the blocks at Skinners'-street and Crawford-street; and the elaboration of a detailed scheme for the development of the Leigham-court estate. The plans in connexion with Leigham-court have received careful consideration and study in order to meet the various requirements of the London County Council, and of the Local Authorities; and the assent of these Authorities has now been given to their proposals. A statement appended shows that between 1871 and 1891 the capital of the Company has increased from 18,580l. to 1,902,100l.

MEETINGS.

SATURDAY, FEBRUARY 27.

Builders' Foremen and Clerks of Works' Institution.—Annual Dinner, Holborn Restaurant. 6 p.m.

Edinburgh Architectural Association.—Visit to St. Nicholas Church, Dalkeith and to Newbattle Abbey.

MONDAY, FEBRUARY 29.

Surveyors' Institution.—Adjourned Discussion on Mr. J. W. Grover's paper entitled "An Explanation of the London water Question." 8 p.m.

Society of Arts (Cantor Lectures).—Professor William Robinson on "The Uses of Petroleum in Prime Movers." I. 8 p.m.

Leeds and Yorkshire Architectural Society.—Mr. A. Beresford Pite on "The Architecture of Michael Angelo." 7.30.

TUESDAY, MARCH 1.

Institution of Civil Engineers.—Discussion on the following papers:—(1) "The Bishop Rock Lighthouses." by Mr. W. T. Douglass. (2) "The Illumination by Gas of Tory Island Lighthouse, Co. Donegal," by Mr. David C. Salmond. 8 p.m.

Sanitary Institute (Lectures for Sanitary Officers).—Professor A. Wynter Blyth on "Diseases of Animals in relation to Meat Supply; Characteristics of Vegetables, Fish, &c., Unfit for Food." 8 p.m.

Society of Biblical Archæology.—8 p.m.

Glasgow Architectural Association.—Annual Business Meeting. 8 p.m.

WEDNESDAY, MARCH 2.

Carpenters' Hall, London Wall.—Professor T. Roger Smith on "Sanitary Construction of Public Buildings." 8 p.m. (*Admission free.*)

Royal Archæological Institute.—(1) Mr. A. Heneage Cocks on "Scandinavian Prim-Stav Calendars." (2) The Rev. Greville I. Chester on "Archaic Engravings on Rocks near Gebel Silsileh in Upper Egypt." 4 p.m.

British Archæological Association.—(1) Mr. E. P. Loftus Brock, F.S.A., on "Waddington Church, Lincoln." (2) Dr. F. R. Fairbank, F.S.A., on "Roman Pottery found at Doncaster." 8 p.m.

British Museum.—Miss Eugénie Sellers on "Greek Sculpture: Sculptures from Halikarnassos and from Temple of Priene." IV. 2.30 p.m.

Civil and Mechanical Engineers' Society.—Paper by Mr. R. J. Friswell, entitled "Some Practical Notes on the water-supply of Boilers." 7 p.m.

Society of Arts.—Professor Vivian B. Lewes on "Spontaneous Ignition of Coal, and its Prevention." 8 p.m.

THURSDAY, MARCH 3.

Society of Arts (Indian Section).—Surgeon-General Sir William James Moore on "Indian Sanitation and the International Congress of Hygiene." 4.30 p.m.

Society of Antiquaries.—8.30 p.m.

FRIDAY, MARCH 4.

Architectural Association.—Mr. J. Alfred Gotch o "How they Built in Shakespeare's Time," with lantern illustrations. 7.30 p.m.

Royal Academy of Arts.—Professor J. H. Middleton on "Michael Angelo." II. 8 p.m.

Sanitary Institute (Lectures for Sanitary Officers).—Mr. Shirley F. Murphy on "Infectious Diseases an Methods of Disinfection." 8 p.m.

SATURDAY, MARCH 5.

Institution of Civil Engineers.—Students' visit to the Oil-gas works of the Great Northern Railway at Holloway. 3 p.m.

RECENT PATENTS:

ABSTRACTS OF SPECIFICATIONS.

1,767.—SASH-FASTENER: *J. Trick.*—This patent refers to what is described as an improved ventilating sash-fastener, whereby the window or sashes may be partially opened at top or bottom for ventilation, and may be fastened in that position from the inside, and so secured from burglars or from being shaken by the wind. It consists of a plate containing lock-holes attached to the upper sash, in combination with a cylinder mounted on the meeting-rail of the lower sash and carrying a spirally slotted pin, the point of which is designed to be placed in the above lock-holes.

2,791.—BRIDGE-FLOORING, &c.: *J. V. Boyd-Wilson.*—The object of this invention is to provide more ready and effective means for the formation of bridge-floors or decking, fire-resisting flooring, and similar constructions. For this purpose it is proposed to use a channel-beam or girder of a peculiar section as described, the section being an arch springing from the upper portions of two right angles facing each other inwardly. In combination with the above a special concrete of "Kieselguhr," alone or with Portland or other cement, in the formulæ described, is used.

3,070.—CISTERNS: *G. M. Lawford.*—This specification refers to an improved form of water-waste preventing cistern, dispensing with all unsightly external arms and levers, and producing an entirely self-contained ornamental cistern. A form of cistern is used with a slotted lug cast on each side, at the centre in which a spindle works. The spindle is held in place by a split pin at each end. The cover rests on a continuous external bead, and, when in place, conceals the lugs. On the spindle is fixed a lever, one end of which is attached to a syphon valve. The lever is worked by a chain passing through the cistern inside a tube held in place by two nuts.

4,565.—CHIMNEYS: *E. R. Salwey.*—This patent refers to an invention for the purification of smoke from chimneys specially applicable to dwelling and other houses. It may, however, be applied to the chimneys of factories and works of a similar character. The smoke passes through a lightly-packed mass of asbestos, talc, or other non-inflammable suitable substance, which retains the sooty particles. This mass is contained in a wire cage fitted with a door and inserted in the chimney through a side aperture, preferably near the top of the chimney. The cage and its contents, constituting a trap for the impurities in the smoke, are supported in place upon narrow shelves fixed in the masonry, and may be withdrawn for the purpose of removing the deposited impurities.

4,768.—UNDERGROUND CHANNELS: *G. Lawson.*—This specification describes a method of excavating underground channels for building the walls of subways and other purposes by employing longitudinal moving shield walls, composed of a series of longitudinal sections, built vertically, to slide horizontally forward over each other, as described and illustrated. There is also described the combination and use of a series of horizontal moving sectional cutting and earth-removing frames, and of sectional excavating side frames, working horizontally over each other.

NEW APPLICATIONS FOR LETTERS PATENTS.

February 8.—2,348, M. Syer, Disinfecting Apparatus for attachment to Flushing Cisterns, Pipes, &c.—2,349, M. Syer, Syphon Flushing Tank.—2,358, C. Baker, Safety Gates.—2,364, G. Thompson, Nails.—2,375, Sir A. Hickman, Refractory and Basic Bricks and Tuyeres.—2,385, M. Hallam, Fasteners for the Cords of Window-Blinds.—2,392, W. and E. Freeman, Flushing Tanks or Water Waste Preventers.

February 9.—2,543, H. Sutcliffe, Water-closet Basins, and in Means of Ventilating the Soil-pipes of same.—2,547, H. Whiteley, Automatic Safety Apparatus for Opening and Closing the Doors of Hoists.—2,496, F. Phelps and H. O'Brien, Carpenters' Planes, also applicable to Levels.—2,547, H. Baxter, Windows.

February 10.—2,566, W. Andrews, Door-spring.—2,568, R. Kirlew, Chimney and Ventilating Shafts.—2,577, A. Milne, Double-action Bolts for Doors, French Windows, &c.—2,585, W. Mounsey, Flushing and Ventilating Apparatus for water-closets.—2,602, W. Sterling and T. Swann, Sanitary and other Pipes and an Improved Method of Constructing Sewers and Drains.—2,614, W. Bly, Flushing Apparatus for Closets, &c.

February 11.—2,642, W. Shaddock, Protection of Wood, Granite, or other Pavement in Roadways and Tramways.—2,651, R. Somers, Fireplaces.—2,683, W. Wardle, Ventilating-fans.—2,687, B. Faux, Stops or Checks for Doors, &c.—2,691, J. Green, Unions and Pipes for Drainage Purposes and Soil-pipes.—2,711, F. Humpherson, Automatic or Intermittent Syphon-flushing Apparatus.—2,713, T. McCulloch, Window Sash-fastener.—2,716, E. Parr, Screws.

February 13.—2,813, W. McKinlay, Automatic Sash-fastening and Lock.—2,814, J. Hullinghorst, Roofing Shingle.—2,872, H. Alexander, Chimney-tops to prevent Down-draughts, &c.—2,894, J. Golding, Arches or Girders for Flooring.

PROVISIONAL SPECIFICATIONS ACCEPTED.

21,083, W. Whitehead, Recording and Checking workmen's Time, and for other similar purposes.—22,310, E. Wright, Improved Inspection Eye or Plug for Sewer-pipes or Soil-pipes.—22,682, T. Anderson, Gasfittings.—8, G. Harrington, Cowl and Shaft Arrangements for Ventilation.—20, J. Bennett, Ventilation of Sewers and Drains.—28, J. Bolding, Construction of Water-closets for use in Railway Carriages, &c.—46, R. Yorke, Earthenware Pipes.—T. Hunt, Glazing of Earthenware Pipes, and analogous Articles.—379, G. Parkinson, Guarding Circular or other Saws.—591, W. White and H. Harry, Coverings for Walls, &c.—651, H. Sayle, New Automatic Noiseless Flushing Valve for water-closets and Urinals.—905, T. Lane and A. May, Chimney-tops or Cowls.—1,058, J. Schneider, Chimney Cowl.—1,101, H. Hansen and others, Hoods or Cowls for Ventilating or other Shafts.—1,323, A. Ransome, Machinery for Felling and Cutting Timber.—1,560, H. Lake, Wood-working Machinery.—1,561, R. Schram, Rock Drills.—1,577, J. Ottaway, Window-sashes.—1,821, R. Ardagh, Wooden Paving or Flooring Blocks.

COMPLETE SPECIFICATIONS ACCEPTED.

(*Open to Opposition for Two Months.*)

3,971, J. Piocaver, Fastener for Doors, &c.—6,041, J. Craven, Kilns for Drying and Burning Bricks or other articles or materials.—6,274, J. Lee, Window-fastener.—6,321, R. Pye, Moistening, Heating, Cooling, and Ventilating Factories, and other Buildings.—620, J. Shannon, Wood Graining Machines.—715, G. Couzens, Traps.

SOME RECENT SALES OF PROPERTY:

ESTATE EXCHANGE REPORT.

FEBRUARY 16.—By *A. J. F. Gibbons*: 26, Tabley-rd., Tufnell-pk., u.t. 90 yrs., g.r. 7*l*., r. 40*l*., 371*l*.—By *Stokes & Pinder*: 20, Dorset-st., Portman-sq., u.t. 22 yrs., g.r. 40*l*., 420*l*.

FEBRUARY 17.—By *Brodie, Timbr, & Baker*: 67 and 69, Nightingale-rd., Wood-green, f., 260*l*.

FEBRUARY 18.—By *Nokes & Nokes*: 77, 79, and 81, Bride-st., Islington, f., r. 122*l*., 1,610*l*.; 10, Westbourne-rd., Barnsbury, and house adjoining, f., r. 89*l*., 1,195*l*.; 105 and 107, Benwell-rd., Holloway, u.t. 42 yrs., g.r. 12*l*., 350*l*.—By *D. Watney & Sons*: F.g.r. of 600*l*., with reversion in 41 yrs., Cannon-st., E.C., 18,250*l*.; 1 to 6, Stafford-cottages, Beddington, f., 850*l*.—By *Messrs. Trollope*: No. 18, St. James's-sq., u.t. 52 yrs., g.r. 100*l*., r. 1,270*l*., 10,000*l*.—By *H. J. Bliss & Sons*: F.g.r. of 20*l*., with reversion in 18 yrs., Ellwood-st., &c., Islington, 680*l*.; 222, Green-st., Bethnal Green, f.r. 30*l*., 415*l*.; 73, Moss-st., f., r. 28*l*. 12s., 280*l*.; 185, Green-st., f., r. 32*l*., 650*l*.; 10A, Hersee-pl., f., 250*l*.—By *Gilders Bros.*: 110, Murray-st., Hoxton, u.t. 50 yrs., g.r. 4*l*. 4s., r. 55*l*., 535*l*.; 66 and 67, Ashburton-grove, Holloway, u.t. 48 yrs., g.r. 8*l*. 8s., r. 56*l*., 460*l*.; 43, Exmouth-st., Clerkenwell, u.t. 24 yrs., g.r. 7*l*., 380*l*.; 97, Rosoman-st., u.t. 24 yrs., g.r. 8*l*. 10s., r. 38*l*., 240*l*.; "The Two Brewers," Warner-st., f.r. 32*l*., 610*l*.; 4, 24, 26, and 30, Great Bath-st., 4 and 5, Bath-ct., and 43, Warner-st., u.t. 14 yrs., g.r. 190*l*., r. 436*l*., 200*l*.; 28 and 29, Great Bath-st., u.t. 14 yrs., g.r. 80*l*., r. 206*l*., 150*l*.; 11, Albemarle-st., u.t. 66 yrs., g.r. 26*l*., r. 100*l*., 800*l*.; 89, Battersea Pk.-rd., and 2, Savonia-pl., Battersea, u.t. 52 yrs., g.r. 17*l*., r. 66*l*. 10s., 330*l*.; 1 to 7, Bartholomew-sq., St. Luke's, u.t. 6 yrs., g.r. 175*l*., r. 321*l*., 65*l*.; 7, King-st., u.t. 12½ yrs., g.r. 24*l*., 35*l*.; 22 and 23, King-st., u.t. 14 yrs., g.r. 48*l*., 35*l*.; 70 and 72, Mildmay-grove, Mildmay Pk., u.t. 64 yrs., g.r. 14*l*., r. 80*l*., 675*l*.; 8 and 10, Lamont-rd., Chelsea, u.t. 53 yrs., g.r. 28*l*., r. 95*l*. 18s., 790*l*.

FEBRUARY 19.—By *Ventom, Bull, & Cooper*: 22 and 24, Flodden-rd., Camberwell, u.t. 87 yrs., g.r. 24*l*., 1,500*l*. By *Wells & Read*: 31, Defoe-rd., Stoke Newington, u.t. 78 yrs., g.r. 6*l*., r. 28*l*., 225*l*.

[*Contractions used in these lists.*—F.g.r. for freehold ground-rent; l.g.r. for leasehold ground-rent; i.g.r. for improved ground-rent; g.r. for ground-rent; r. for rent; f. for freehold; c. for copyhold; l. for leasehold; e.r. for estimated rental; u.t. for unexpired term; p.a. for per annum; yrs. for years; st. for street; rd. for road; sq. for square; pl. for place; ter. for terrace; cres. for crescent; yd. for yard, &c.]

PRICES CURRENT OF MATERIALS.

TIMBER.		
Greenheart, B.G. ton	9/0/0	0/0/0
Teak, E.I. ... load	9/10/0	15/0/0
Sequoia, U.S. ft. cu.	2/3	3/0
Ash, Canada load	2/10/0	4/0/0
Birch, do.	3/5/0	4/10/0
Elm, do.	3/10/0	4/15/0
Fir, Dantsic, &c.	2/0/0	3/10/0
Oak, do.	3/0/0	5/0/0
Canada	5/0/0	7/0/0
Pine, Canada red	2/10/0	3/10/0
Do. yellow	2/10/0	5/0/0
Lath, D'ntsic, fath	5/5/0	5/10/0
St. Petersburg	5/10/0	7/10/0
Deals, Finland, 2nd & 1st std 100	8/10/0	10/10/0
Do. 4th & 3rd	7/10/0	8/10/0
Do. Riga	6/10/0	8/0/0
St. Petersburg, 1st yellow	11/0/0	15/0/0
Do. 2nd yellow	8/10/0	10/10/0
Do. white	7/10/0	10/10/0
Swedish	7/15/0	16/0/0
White Sea	8/10/0	18/0/0
Canada, Pine 1st	20/0/0	26/0/0
Do. do. 2nd	14/10/0	16/10/0
Do. do. 3rd, &c.	8/5/0	10/10/0
Do. Spruce, 1st	8/10/0	11/0/0
Do. do. 3rd & 2nd	6/15/0	8/0/0
New Brunswick	7/0/0	7/10/0
Battens, all kinds	3/10/0	15/10/0
Flooring Boards, sq., 1 in. prep. 1st	0/8/6	0/14/6
Do. 2nd	0/7/6	0/11/6
Other qualities	0/5/0	0/8/0
Cedar, Cuba ... ft.	/3½	/4½
Honduras, &c.	/2½	/4
Mahogany, Cuba	/4½	/6½
St. Domingo, cargo av.	/4½	[illegible]
Mexican do. do	/4	/6
Tobasco do. do	/5½	/7
Honduras do.	/5½	/8½
Box, Turkey ton	4/0/0	15/0/0
Rose, Rio	10/0/0	20/0/0
Bahia	9/0/0	18/0/0
Satin, St. Domingo ... ft.	0/0/6	0/1/3

TIMBER (*continued*).		
Satin, Porto Rico	0/0/8	0/1/6
Walnut, Italian	0/0/3½	0/0/7
METALS.		
Iron—Pig, in Scotland ... ton	2/0/6	2/0/7½
Bar, Welsh, in London	6/0/0	6/10/0
Do. do. at works in Wales	5/10/0	6/0/0
Do. Staffordshire, in London	6/5/0	6/15/0
Copper—British, cake and ingot	47/0/0	47/10/0
Best selected	48/0/0	49/0/0
Sheets, strong	57/0/0	58/0/0
Chili, bars	43/12/6	43/15/0
Yellow Metal lb.	0/0/5½	0/0/5¾
Lead—Pig, Spanish ... ton	10/17/6	11/0/0
English, com. brands	11/0/0	11/5/0
Sheet, English, 3 lbs. per sq. ft. and upwards	13/0/0	0/0/0
Pipe	13/10/0	0/0/0
Zinc—English sheet ... ton	23/5/0	0/0/0
Vieille Montagne	23/15/0	0/0/0
Tin—Straits	89/7/6	89/10/0
Australian	84/10/0	84/15/0
English Ingots	92/10/0	92/15/0
OILS.		
Linseed ... ton	18/17/6	0/0/0
Cocoanut, Cochin	25/15/0	26/0/0
Do. Ceylon	23/0/0	0/0/0
Palm, Lagos	23/0/0	0/0/0
Rapeseed, English pale	26/5/0	0/0/0
Do. brown	24/10/0	0/0/0
Cottonseed ref.	17/15/0	18/0/0
Oleine	0/0/0	0/0/0
Lubricating, U.S.	4/10/0	5/10/0
Do. refined	5/0/0	10/0/0
Tar—Stockholm barrel	0/19/0	1/0/0
Archangel	0/12/6	0/0/0

TENDERS.

[Communications for Insertion under this heading must reach us *not later than 12 noon on Thursdays*.]

BEXHILL-ON-SEA.—For the erection of new Premises for Lloyd's Bank, Limited. Mr. Arthur Wells, architect, Hastings:—

S. Bukef	£3,472	P. Jenkins, St. Leonards*	£3,075
C. Thomas	3,289		

* Accepted.

BROMLEY (Kent).—For kerbing, paving, &c., in High-street, for the Bromley Local Board. Mr. Hugh S. Cregeen, surveyor:—

T. Lansbury	£511 16 0	W. H. Wheeler	£416 6 1
E. Pelli & Sons	507 5 4	Woodham & Fry	411 18 4
B. Glenny	434 12 6	John Mowlem & Co.*	371 10 2

* Accepted.

BROXBOURNE.—Accepted for residence at Broxbourne, for Mr. J. Kirkaldy. Messrs. Newman & Newman, architects, 31, Tooley-street, London Bridge:—

J. A. Hunt £4,000 0 0

[No competition.]

CANNING TOWN (Essex).—For the erection of Public Hall, Canning Town, West Ham. Mr. Lewis Angell, Borough Engineer, architect:—

Reed, Blight, & Co.	£20,941	J. F. Coxhead	£19,299
J. Robson	19,985	Perry & Co.	19,159
W. Gregar	19,930	Allen & Sons	18,825
J. Holland	19,860	Kirk & Randall	18,718
W. J. Maddison	19,850	A. Kellett, Willesden*	17,984

* Accepted.

CRANFORD.—For alterations to dwelling-house at the Park Farm, for the Right Honourable Lord Fitzhardinge. Mr. B. H. Bansford, surveyor:—

Simmonds	£690	Briant	£570
A. Martin	685	Hanson	565
Gibson	600	Brown	520
G. H. Martin & Co.	579	Foord & Son	499

CROYDON.—For the erection of Union offices, boardroom, and out-relief station, for the Guardians of the Croydon Union. Mr. Frederick West, architect, Croydon. Quantities by Mr. R. Peters, 72, Wool-exchange, E.C.:—

D. W. Barker	£7,959	Akers & Co.	£7,140
A. H. Howe	7,947	Smith & Sons	7,079
Lorden & Son	7,900	P. Peters	6,950
W. Smith	7,800	J. O. Richardson	6,758
Bryan & Son	7,523	M. Taylor	6,700
E. J. Saunders	7,440	Martin & Co.	6,683
T. W. Jones	7,400	A. Bullock, Croydon*	6,193
Bulled & Co.	7,277		

* Accepted.

FOOTSCRAY.—For pulling down and re-building grocer's shop, alter &c. Mr. J. Drake, architect, Rochester:—

Otway	£822 0	Multon & Wallis, Gravesend*	£740 0
Knight	787 10		
Brightling	764 0		

* Accepted subject to modifications.

FOOTSCRAY.—For building new show-rooms for Mr. Clarke, coachbuilder. Mr. J. Drake, architect, Rochester:—

Otway	£297	Multon & Wallis, Gravesend*	£189
Knight	265		
Brightling	235		

* Accepted.

HARROGATE.—Accepted for alterations and additions to Craven Lodge, Harrogate, for Mr. Cooper Eddison. Mr. T. Butler Wilson, architect, Central-chambers, Harrogate:—

Mason—Isaac Dickinson, Harrogate	£176 0 0
Joiner—Wm. Wilcock, Harrogate	72 10 0
Plumber—Geo. Lazenby, Leeds	34 0 0
Plasterer—Chas. Fortune, Harrogate	48 7 1
Slater—Joseph Shepherd, Harrogate	19 17 3
Decorator—George Dent, Harrogate	61 0 0

HARROW (Middlesex).—For works required to be done in erecting and completely finishing a house in Maxwell-road, Northwood, near Harrow, Middlesex, for Mr. J. C. Wilbee. Mr. W. Gillbee Scott and Mr. George F. R. Scott, architects, 25, Bedford-row, W.C.:—

	House.	Drainage.	Time.
Faulkner	£3,500 0 0	£108 0 0	..
Molly	3,380 0 0	140 0 0	..
Hearn & Bigood	3,213 0 0	85 0 0	6 months.
Lee & Co.	3,200 0 0	110 0 0	8 "
Lawrence & Son	3,150 0 0	95 0 0	6 "
W. Johnson	3,096 0 0	96 0 0	10 "
Godfrey & Son	3,035 0 0	78 0 0	7 "
Harris & Wardrop	3,023 0 0	76 0 0	7 "
Chaton & Co.	2,998 0 0	75 0 0	7 "
Jones & Co.	2,875 0 0	76 10 0	6 "
Turk & Appleton	2,815 0 0	76 0 0	9 "
French & Co.	2,530 0 0	68 0 0	7 "

HEADINGLEY (Yorks).—Accepted for additions to Whinfield, Headingley, for Mr. Arthur F. L. Hepton. Mr. T. Butler Wilson, architect, 12, East-parade, Leeds:—

Mason—Matthew Wilson, Headingley	£810 0 0
Joiner—J. Hanson Firth, Leeds	270 0 0
Slaters—J. Atkinson & Son, Leeds	13 14 0
Plumber—Thos. Story, Leeds	99 10 0
Plasterer—R. Branton, Leeds	41 9 0

HORFIELD (near Bristol).—For laying sewer at Ashley Down, Horfield, near Bristol. Mr. A. P. I. Cotterell, Surveyor, Bristol:—

G. Heard	£290 5 5	Wm. Rogers*	£178 5 5
W. Merewether	288 0 0		

* Accepted.

[Surveyor's estimate, £287. 1s. 6d.]

LEEDS.—Accepted for the erection of six terrace houses, Cross-green, Otley, for Mr. W. E. Turner. Mr. Alfred Marshall, architect, Bank-chambers, Otley, Leeds:—

Masons' Work.—Fred. Cawood, Otley	£1,124 0 0
Joiners' Work.—Peter Patrick, Otley	560 0 0
Plasterers' Work.—John Laycock, Otley	140 0 0
Plumbers' Work.—Jas. Suttle & Son, Otley	115 0 0
Slaters' Work.—John Baynes, Ripon	86 0 0
Total	£2,025 0 0

LONDON.—For the erection of a palm-house in Battersea Park, for the London County Council. Mr. Thomas Blashill, Architect:—

W. H. Lascelles & Co., £3,965 and £4,170.

Clarke & Co., £3,675 and £2,799.

M. Marsland, £3,617 and £2,965.

G. Munday & Son, £3,417, less £211 if own system of glazing adopted, and £2,680, less £120 if own system of glazing adopted.

W. Parham, £3,317, less £600 if own system of glazing adopted, and £2,358, less £400 if own system of glazing adopted.

E. Coles & Son, £3,255 and £2,845.

[Referred to Parks and Open Spaces Committee.]

LONDON.—For the erection of public conveniences on Parliament-hill, Hampstead, for the London County Council. Mr. Thomas Blashill, Architect:—

Heatley & Annan	£911 10	A. Wallis	£767 0
J. Garrett & Son	800 0	Jackson Bros.	688 0
Peattie & Axtell	738 0	H. Fowler	675 18
W. Wells	720 0		

[Referred to the Parks and Open Spaces Committee.]

LONDON.—For the supply of 20,000 tons of lime, for the London County Council (Main Drainage Department). Mr. A. R. Binnie, Engineer:—C. Christopherson & Co., 5,000 tons at 13s. 6d. per ton, 5,000 at 14s. 3d., and 2,000 at 16s. 6d.; Youlng & Son, 2,000 tons at 16s. per ton; W. Lee, Son, & Co., 20,000 tons at 16s. 6d. per ton; T. Fisher & Co., 5,000 tons (grey lime) at 17s. 3d. per ton; Hall & Co., 10,000 tons at 17s. 6d. per ton, 3,000 tons at 17s. 7d., 7,000 tons at 18s. 5d., 5,000 tons at 19s. 6d., and 5,000 tons at 20s. 3d.; P. Champion, 10,000 or 20,000 tons at 18s. per ton; Buxton Lime Firms Co., Limited, 20,000 tons at 18s. 6d. per ton; J. S. Peters, 5,000 tons at 19s. 6d. per ton; Hilton, Anderson, & Co., 13,000 tons at 19s. 6d. per ton; Formby's Cement Works Co., Limited, 5,000 tons at 19s. 10d. per ton; and the Minerva Lime Company, 20,000 tons at 22s. per ton.

[Referred to the Main Drainage Committee.]

LONDON.—For alterations and additions to the Western Ambulance Station, Seagrave-road, for the Managers of the Metropolitan Asylums Board. Messrs. A. & C. Harston, architects, 15, Leadenhall-street. Quantities by Mr. W. T. Farthing, 46, Strand:—

Courtney & Fairbairn	£4,900 0 0	A. Kellett	£4,072 15 10
J. J. Richards	4,398 0 0	C. Miskin	3,987 0 0
J. & M. Patrick	4,364 0 0	B. E. Nightingale	3,970 0 0
Johnson & Co., Ltd.	4,250 0 0	Leslie & Co.	3,750 0 0
W. Wells	4,200 0 0	F. G. Minter*	3,480 0 0

* Accepted.

LONDON.—For fitting-up hot-water supply apparatus in Blocks D, E, and F of the new workhouse, Pancras-road, for the Guardians of the Parish of St. Pancras. Messrs. A. & C. Harston, architects, 15, Leadenhall-street:—

C. P. Kinnell	£590 0	J. & F. May	£545 0
J. Fraser & Son	579 10	Wenham & Waters, Paragon Works, Croydon*	455 0
Clements, Jeakes, & Co.	563 0		

* Accepted.

LONDON.—For providing and fixing heating apparatus on the low pressure hot-water system, for the Deaf and Dumb School now in course of erection on the Hugh Myddelton site, Clerkenwell, for the School Board for London. Mr. T. J. Bailey, Architect:—

Rosser & Russell, Ltd.	£235 10 0	T. Fraser & Son	£193 17 0
J. & F. May	230 0 0	T. Wontner Smith, Gray, & Co.	188 0 0
G. Davis	229 10 0	Purcell & Nobbs*	164 0 0
W. G. Cannon	210 0 0		

* Accepted.

LONDON.—For providing and fixing heating apparatus on the low-pressure hot-water system, at the school now in course of erection in Glyn-road, Homerton, for the School Board for London. Mr. T. J. Bailey, Architect:—

J. & F. May	£465 0	Comyn, Ching, & Co.	£448 70
J. Fraser & Son	483 15	J. Smeaton, Son, & Co., 56, Gt. Queen-st., W.C.*	364 0
G. Davis	450 0		

* Accepted by the Works Committee.

LONDON.—For providing and fixing heating apparatus on the low-pressure hot-water system, at the school now in course of erection in Ancona-road, Plumstead, for the School Board for London. Mr. T. J. Bailey, Architect:—

Rosser & Russell, Lim.	£501 0	T. Potter & Sons	£418 0
W. G. Cannon	535 0	J. Smeaton, Son, & Co., 56, Great Queen-street, W.C.*	369 0
Purcell & Nobbs	487 0		
R. Crane	455 0		
J. Wontner Smith, Gray, & Co.	447 5		

* Accepted by the Works Committee.

LONDON.—For providing and fixing heating apparatus on the low-pressure hot-water system, at the school now in course of erection in Childeric-road, New Cross, for the School Board for London. Mr. T. J. Bailey, Architect:—

Wenham & Waters, Limited	£470 0	J. Wontner Smith, Gray, & Co.	£396 0
J. & F. May	445 0	Russell & Co.	384 0
J. Fraser & Son	440 15	R. Crane, 6, Binfield-road, Clapham*	382 0
T. Potter & Sons	398 0		
Purcell & Nobbs	396 0		

* Accepted by the Works Committee.

LONDON.—For providing and fixing heating apparatus on the low-pressure hot-water system, at the school now in course of erection in Munster-lane, Fulham, for the School Board for London. Mr. T. J. Bailey, Architect:—

Rosser & Russell, Limited	£549 0 0	R. Crane	£476 0 0
W. G. Cannon	545 0 0	J. Fraser & Son	454 17 6
Wenham & Waters, Limited	510 0 0	J. Wontner Smith, Gray, & Co., 81, Finsbury-pavement*	450 0 0
Russell & Co.	488 0 0	Jones & Attwood	449 0 0

* Accepted by the Works Committee.

LONDON.—For providing and fixing heating apparatus on the low-pressure hot-water system, for the new school now in course of erection in Lillie-road, Fulham, for the School Board for London. Mr. T. J. Bailey, Architect:—

W. G. Cannon	£515	Purcell & Nobbs, 87 and 89, Cleveland-street, Fitzroy-square*	£482
Wenham & Waters, Limited	510		
G. Davis	496		

* Accepted by the Works Committee.

LONDON.—For new public library, Lambeth. Messrs. E. H. Burnell and J. E. Trollope, architects. Quantities by Mr. Charles [illegible] Goode:—

Brass & Son	£7,384	Pete Bros.	£6,887
Castle Bros.	7,381	Holloway Bros.	6,850
Candler & Son	7,320	Holliday & Greenwood	6,777
F. & H. F. Higgs	7,270	Nightingale	6,648
Hall, Beddall, & Co.	7,200	Perry & Co.	6,497
Higgs & Hill	7,180	Jerrard	6,363
Chappell	7,066		

LONDON.—For new bar fittings and alterations to "The Royal" public-house, Holborn. Mr. Hy. Ward, architect:—

Foster	£1,473	Taylor Bros.	£1,198
W. H. Lascelles & Co.	1,247	Drew & Cadman	1,198
Nightingale	1,238	Lester & Co.	1,180
Gregory	1,220		

LONDON.—For fitting up shop, No. 446, Holloway-road, for Messrs. Rabbits & Sons, Limited. Mr. A. G. Hennell, architect :—

Mark	£1,031	Kearley	£380
Holloway Bros.	880	Lascelles & Co.	827
Johnson	843	Burman	810

LONDON.—For fitting shop at Seven Sisters'-road, for the United Kingdom Tea Co. Mr. A. G. Hennell, architect :—

Mark	£1,070	Burman & Son	£797
Holloway Bros.	885	Lascelles & Co.	779
Johnson	861	Kearley	718

LONDON.—For alterations to the "Prince of Wales" public-house, Fulham. Messrs. Bird & Walters, architects :—

Mark	£1,980	Goodall	1,889
Burman	1,980	Todd	1,846
Williams & Son	1,947	W. H. Lascelles & Co.	1,739
Gould & Brand	1,924		

LONDON.—For new premises in Stephen-street, Lisson-grove. Mr. F. W. Hunt, architect :—

Bywaters	£2,792	Lathey Bros.	£2,650
Holloway Bros.	2,762	W. Johnson & Co.	2,595
Pearce	2,698	Charteris	2,895

LONDON.—For new premises in Charles-street, Lisson-grove. Mr. F. W. Hunt, architect :—

Holloway Bros.	£2,928	Pearce	£2,802
Bywaters	2,972	Lathey Bros.	2,797
Charteris	2,863	W. Johnson & Co.	2,780

LONDON.—For the construction of three sewers and roads on the Cotton Estate, Fulham. Messrs. P. D. Tuckett & Co., surveyors, 2, Basinghall-street, E.C. :—

Wilson	£1,575	Mears	£1,498
Nowell & Robson	1,549	Killingback & Co.	1,481
R. Ballard	1,525	Rogers*	1,430
W. H. Watts	1,519	* Accepted.	

LONDON.—For erecting lodge cottage on Dartford Heath, for Mr Gibson. Mr. W. Leonard Grant, architect :—

Brightling	£375	Miller	£267
H. Thomas	357		

LONDON.—Accepted for the erection of residence in Lyford-road, Wandsworth Common, for Mrs. Arthur Dickses. Mr. Bernard Dicksee, architect :—

Frank Kirk £1,550 0 0

LONDON.—For works at the "Prince of Wales," St. James's-road, N. Messrs. Bird & Walters, architects, 64, Seymour-place, Bryanston-square, W. :—

Burman	£1,628 0	Evans	£1,483 15
Marks	1,573 0	Lascelles	1,483 0
Todd	1,529 0	Edwards & Medway, Kennington*	1,451 0
Goodall	1,488 0		

* Accepted.

LONDON.—Accepted for work at the "Queen's Arms," Spa-road, Bermondsey. Mr. J. Brooker, architect, 13, Railway Approach, London Bridge :—

Edwards & Medway, Kennington' £480 0 0

LONDON.—Accepted for the restoration of the tower and spire of St. Giles's Church, Camberwell. Messrs. Newman & Newman, architects, 31, Tooley-street, London Bridge :—

Colls & Son, Camberwell £3,500 0 0

[No competition.]

LONDON.—Accepted for building stables in Long-lane, Bermondsey, for Mr Samuel Taylor. Messrs. Newman & Newman, architects, 31, Tooley-street, London Bridge :—

W. & H. Castle £3,700 0 0

[No competition.]

LONDON.—Accepted for work at "The Union," King's Cross-road, Mr. J. Brooker, architect, 13, Railway Approach, London Bridge :—

Edwards & Medway, Kennington £674 0 0

ST. LEONARDS-ON-SEA.—For alterations, repairs, and new bar front at the "Prince of Wales" Hotel, for Messrs. Ballard & Co. Mr. Arthur Wells, architect, Hastings :—

W. F. Villier	£264 12 9	S. Smith, St. Leonards*	£254 11 0
T. Salter	305 0 0	* Accepted.	

SOUTHSEA.—For the erection of business premises in Palmerston-road, Southsea, for Messrs. W. & H. Stevenson. Mr. George Judge, architect, London. Quantities by Mr. Chas. W. Bevis :—

W. R. & C. Light	£3,033 0 0	Scammell & Dowdell	£2,610 0 0
J. Crockerell	2,846 9 8	E. & A. Spalgings*	2,510 0 0
H. Jones	2,778 0 0	* Accepted.	

(All of Portsmouth and Southsea.)

TO CORRESPONDENTS.

O. M. M. (There are unfortunately a good many instances of this kind of procedure now, but it is mostly only the resort of obscure members of the profession).—"General Foreman" (no name or address enclosed).—J. H. P.—G. B. C (shall have attention).—S. W. (should have sent amounts).—J. F. W. (ditto).—C. J. K. (too late).

All statements of facts, lists of tenders, &c., must be accompanied by the name and address of the sender, not necessarily for publication.

We are compelled to decline pointing out books and giving addresses.

NOTE.—The responsibility of signed articles, and papers read at public meetings, rests, of course, with the authors.

We cannot undertake to return rejected communications.

Letters or communications (beyond mere news-items) which have been duplicated for other journals, are NOT DESIRED.

All communications regarding literary and artistic matter should be addressed to THE EDITOR; all communications relating to advertisements and other exclusively business matters should be addressed to THE PUBLISHER, and not to the Editor.

SUBSCRIBERS in LONDON and the SUBURBS, by prepaying at the Publishing Office, 19s. per annum (or 4s. 9d. per quarter), can ensure receiving "The Builder" by *Friday Morning's* post.

PUBLISHER'S NOTICES.

Registered Telegraphic Address, 'THE BUILDER,' LONDON.

CHARGES FOR ADVERTISEMENTS.

SITUATIONS VACANT, PARTNERSHIPS, APPRENTICESHIPS TRADE, AND GENERAL ADVERTISEMENTS.

Six lines (about fifty words) or under .... 4s. 6d.
Each additional line (about ten words) .... 0s. 6d.

Terms for Series of Trade Advertisements, also for Special Advertisements on front page, Competitions, Contracts, Sales by Auction, &c. may be obtained on application to the Publisher.

SITUATIONS WANTED.

FOUR Lines (about thirty words) or under .... 2s. 6d.
Each additional line (about ten words) .... 0s. 6d.

PREPAYMENT IS ABSOLUTELY NECESSARY.

⁂ Stamps must not be sent, but all small sums should be remitted by Cash in Registered Letter or by Money Order, payable at the Post-office, Covent-garden, W.C. to

DOUGLAS FOURDRINIER, Publisher,
Addressed to No. 46, Catherine-street, W.C.

Advertisements for the current week's issue must reach the Office before THREE o'clock p.m. on THURSDAY, but those intended for the front Page should be in by TWELVE noon on WEDNESDAY.

SPECIAL.—ALTERATIONS IN STANDING ADVERTISEMENTS or ORDERS TO DISCONTINUE same must reach the Office before TEN o'clock on WEDNESDAY mornings.

The Publisher cannot be responsible for DRAWINGS, TESTIMONIALS, &c. left at the Office in reply to Advertisements, and strongly recommends that of the latter COPIES ONLY should be sent.

PERSONS Advertising in "The Builder" may have *Replies addressed to the Office*, 46, Catherine-street, Covent Garden, W.C. *free of charge*. Letters will be forwarded if addressed envelopes are sent, together with sufficient stamps to cover the postage.

AN EDITION Printed on THIN PAPER, for FOREIGN and COLONIAL CIRCULATION, is issued every week.

READING CASES. { Now ready. NINEPENCE EACH. By Post (carefully packed), 1s.

The Builder Cathedral Serie

1891.

1. CANTERBURY .. Jan. 3.	7. SALISBURY .. .. July
2. LICHFIELD .. .. Feb. 7.	8. BRISTOL .. .. .. Aug.
3. ST. ALBAN'S .. .. Mar. 7.	9. NORWICH .. .. Sept.
4. PETERBOROUGH .. April 4.	10. ROCHESTER .. .. Oct.
5. WELLS .. .. .. May 2.	11. LINCOLN .. .. .. Nov.
6. EXETER .. .. .. June 6.	12. GLOUCESTER .. .. Dec.

1892.

13. ST. PAUL'S .. .. Jan. 2.	16. ELY .. .. April 2
14. HEREFORD .. .. Feb. 6.	17. LLANDAFF .. .. May 7
15. CHICHESTER .. .. Mar. 5.	18. OXFORD .. .. .. June 4

(Further arrangements will be duly announced.)

Post-free FOURPENCE HALFPENNY each except Nos. 1 and which are *out of print*; but the VIEW, PLAN, AND DESCRIPTION CANTERBURY and of LICHFIELD have been re-printed, and the can now be had, price ONE SHILLING each set; by post, 1s. 2d.

THE REREDOS, ST. PAUL'S.
Reprinted from "THE BUILDER," January 28, 1888 (15 in. 11½ in.), on stout paper, unfolded, for framing, 6d.; by post, 8d.

PORTFOLIOS,
for Preserving the Plates unfolded, 2s. 6d.; by post, 3s.

London: Office of "THE BUILDER," 46, *Catherine-street, W.C.*

TERMS OF SUB

"THE BUILDER" is supplied direc in any part of the United Kingdom PREPAID. To all parts of Europe, Au Zealand, 26s. per annum. To India, annum. Remittances payable to Publisher, No. 46, Catherine-street, W

Vol. LXII. No. 2561. SATURDAY, MARCH 5, 1892.

ILLUSTRATIONS.

Cathedrals of England and Wales: XV., Chichester.—Drawn by Mr. Beresford Pite .... *Double-Page Ink-Photo.*
Plan of Chichester Cathedral, Revised to date .... *Double-Page Photo-Litho.*
Chichester Cathedral: Interior View across Nave.—Drawn by Mr. R. W. Paul .... *Single-Page Ink-Photo.*
Tomb of Bishop Sherborne, Chichester Cathedral: Drawn by Mr. R. W. Paul .... *Single-Page Ink-Photo.*
Details of Saracenic Ornament (in illustration of Professor Aitchison's Royal Academy Lectures) .... *Double-Page Ink-Photo.*

Blocks in Text.

End Wall of a Drawing-room, by the Brothers Adam .... Page 174
Design for a Chimney-piece, by the Brothers Adam 175
Trellis, Cairo 180
Trellis-work at Rosetta, Egypt 181
Brick Door-head 182
Tomb of Bishop Langton, Chichester Cathedral 186
The Bell-Tower, Chichester Cathedral 187
Pier and Column in Presbytery, Chichester Cathedral .... Page 188
Plan of Ancient Rood-screen, Chichester Cathedral 189
Organ-case and Stalls, Chichester Cathedral, before the fall of the Tower. Sketched by Mr. A. B. Pite, from an old Drawing 189
Monumental Slab, North Aisle of Presbytery, Chichester 189
Inscription on Tomb of Bishop Sherborne, Chichester 189
Diagrams in Student's Column: Heating by Hot Water 190, 191

CONTENTS.

The London County Council Election 173
Robert Adam 174
Notes 176
Letter from Paris 179
Saracenic Architecture 179
Competitions 183
Architectural Societies 183
London County Council 183
Demonstrations on Greek Sculpture in the British Museum 184
The Royal Commission on Labour 184
The "Builder" Album of Royal Academy Drawings 186
Chichester Cathedral 186
View Across the Nave, Chichester Cathedral 189
Bishop Sherborne's Tomb, Chichester Cathedral 189
Details of Saracenic Ornament 189
Provident Institute of Builders' Foremen and Clerks of Works 190
Concrete for Artisans' Dwellings 190
"Insula" 190
Architectural Casings for Electric Wires 190
The Late Strike still Smouldering 190
Student's Column.—Warming Buildings by Hot Water, X. 190
Obituary 191
General Building News 191
Sanitary and Engineering News 192
Foreign and Colonial 192
Miscellaneous 193
Legal 194
Meetings 194
Recent Patents 195
Some Recent Sales of Property 195

The London County Council Election.

AS this number of the *Builder* reaches the hands of its readers, most of those who have their business house or place of residence in London will, no doubt, be turning over in their mind the manner in which their vote shall be given at the County Council Election. We assume that no person who takes sufficient interest in municipal affairs, or in professional matters, as to be a reader of the *Builder*, will fail to vote at this election. The true way in which to assure the prosperity of the Metropolis, and to safeguard a prudent progress, is for each citizen to exercise his franchise. But it must be confessed that householders may well be in doubt what course to pursue at this election. Most men who look at things in a business-like and calm manner must regret that political influences have come so largely into this election, and that the political machinery of the Metropolis has been imported into the present struggle. It is difficult for men to realise the enormous material and social interests which the County Council has to serve. The work connected with a seat on this municipal council would tax the ability and the tact of the most capable of our men of business; and no one with a knowledge of current affairs will deny that in our large mercantile centres are to be found men of higher ability and greater practical capacity than any, except two or three, of our leading statesmen. It is such persons that we wish to see members of the London County Council,—men versed in business, well acquainted with practical work, accustomed to the management of large concerns; merchants, architects, engineers, and those who have served their country in important official places beyond the seas. The struggling journalist, the pushing barrister, the doctrinaire with a fad to air, inexperienced and without a capacity for business, these are the persons we do not wish to see on the County Council. We do not deny that a considerable amount of useful work has been done by the late Council, but we assert emphatically that a great deal of valuable time has been wasted by useless talk, and by mere academic discussion. We hope to see this remedied in the new Council, but it will not be cured unless the majority are composed of men of business, having a central object in view. This object is the good administration of London as it is. There is work enough and to spare, without entering on new ventures. Take for example the purchase and the working of tramways. This is a standing example of ill-considered zeal. The Council have enough to do with those matters under their control, yet they rush into new schemes when those matters over which they already have control are not satisfactorily managed. Again, take for example the resolution which was passed on April 11, 1889, that the Council should have control of the police. This was done by a body which had been barely three months in existence, which could not possibly appreciate the extent and difficulty of its existing work, and which had yet to obtain the confidence of its constituents. This act showed not only a spirit of overweening self-confidence, but a want of appreciation of the true administrative functions of the Council. It is this spirit which we desire to see banished from the new Council, and replaced by one of modest but anxious solicitude for economy and good administration.

The practical question for the voter to answer is how is he to do something by his vote towards this object. As we have already stated, we look at the election absolutely without party bias. Regarding the two parties, the Progressives and the Moderates, from this point of view, we cannot but note that the Progressives are the party which in principle asks for larger powers, and desires new principles of administration; while the Moderates desire to administer the affairs of London as they are and in an economical spirit. Therefore, without going into personal questions, a Moderate candidate is primarily more worthy of support than a Progressive candidate. In certain instances, however, the Progressive candidate may be a man of greater business capacity than his Moderate opponent. Under such circumstances it may be desirable to support a Progressive candidate. But such a step should be taken with caution, and only when the personal capacity and character of the candidate are thoroughly known.

On the other hand, some of the Moderate candidates seem to be possessed mainly by the spirit of opposition, and to be ready to frame their programme not according to any consideration of what should be the proper scope and powers of the future County Council, but on the mere principle of opposing anything and everything that is suggested by the "Progressives." Such a candidate, for instance, will announce his intention to oppose the placing of the Water Supply of London in the hands of the Council (obviously the most fitting body to deal with the supply of a necessary of life which ought not to be made a vehicle for money-making), on no other apparent ground but because taking over the water supply is part of the Progressive platform. This kind of thing is simply puerile, and only shows that the Moderates themselves, or some of them, are just as guilty of importing party politics into the County Council as any of the Progressives. The essence, or the essential evil, of party politics, consists in the pursuance of a course of action merely to thwart the opposite party, and not because it appears in itself the best course for the general good. The spread and increase of this spirit of mere party opposition is one of the great curses of public life in the present day, and it can nowhere be more out of place than in a body the primary duty of which is the carrying out of the works necessary for the material management and well-being of such an immense city as London.

As we have said, the question must in many instances be one difficult for the voter who wishes to do his best for the Metropolis to decide. In some instances in America independent citizens have combined to place men on municipal councils who are free from political influences and belong to no party. If the result of the present election is unsatisfactory, there can be no question that before another election comes round some such movement must be begun in London. For the moment, however, the duty of every voter appears to be to vote for practical

End Wall of a Drawing-room. From "Works in Architecture, by Robert and James Adam."

men, and also to bear in mind that the Progressive party have had the upper hand on the late Council, and that the spirit of their programme is theoretical rather than practical.

Willesden.—A new cottage hospital is about to be built from the designs of Messrs. Newman & Newman, architects. The accommodation to be at first provided is for nine beds, with the necessary offices; but the plans provide for the future extension of the building to accommodate eight male and eight female patients, with a separation ward.

ROBERT ADAM.

THE 3rd of March will have recalled to memory the name of a man well known in the history of architecture, and, indeed, of art generally, for on that day exactly a hundred years ago died Robert Adam, whose inventive genius wrought a considerable change in the architectural style of his day, and whose taste and compositions,—although the one has been denounced as "vicious" and the other as "depraved,"—have established his fame as an independent artist and a man who has left his mark on the architectural history of this country.

Robert Adam was born in 1728 at Kirkcaldy, in Fifeshire (the birthplace also of Adam Smith), and was the second and, we may add, the most noted of four brothers, sons of William Adam of Maryburgh, himself an architect of some distinction, having designed Hopetoun House and the Royal Infirmary at Edinburgh, and holding also the appointment of

Design for Chimney-piece. From "Works in Architecture, by Robert and James Adam."

King's Mason at Edinburgh. He was educated at Edinburgh University, where he formed friendships with such men as Hume, Robertson the historian, Adam Smith (author of "The Wealth of Nations"), and Adam Fergusson. In later life, too, he enjoyed the friendship and society of Archibald, Duke of Argyll, the Earl of Mansfield, and many other notabilities of his day.

In order to improve his knowledge of his art, the young architect visited Italy in 1754 in company with a clever French draughtsman named Clérisseau, and remained there until 1757, in which year he sailed from Venice to Spalatro (as it was then called). There he was busily engaged for some time studying and making careful drawings of the ruins of Diocletian's palace for the purpose of obtaining some idea of the residential architecture of the ancients, the knowledge of Classical architecture in England being at that time almost entirely confined to public buildings. During his absence from England he was elected a Fellow of the Royal Society, and also of the Society of Antiquaries, and, after his return, was appointed architect to the King. In 1768, however, he was elected Member of Parliament for the county of Kinross, and had consequently to resign that position.

In the following year, in conjunction with his brother James, he began the large block of buildings on the banks of the Thames with which their names are associated. The shore was raised by means of a succession of arches, upon which were built three fine streets, and a terrace facing the river, the locality being called the Adelphi (ἀδελφοι, brothers), in memory of himself and his brothers. Before the scheme could be carried out, it was necessary to reclaim a portion of land from the Thames, a proceeding which was strongly opposed by the Corporation, who claimed the ground beneath the river as their property. The brothers, however, obtained a Bill in 1771 enabling them to effect their purpose. As a commercial speculation, this undertaking proved a failure, and in 1774 another Bill was obtained, sanctioning the disposal of it by lottery.

Robert Adam's more important works were the *façade* of the Admiralty, which was built to hide the inelegant portico designed by Thomas Ripley; Luton House, Beds; Lansdowne House, Berkeley-square; Caen Wood House, near Hampstead; Osterley House, near Brentford; Sion House; Keddleston, Derbyshire; Compton Verney, Warwickshire; and the General Register House, Edinburgh.

The brothers Adam are generally credited with introducing the method of building several houses together, so as to represent, when completed, one building of imposing dimensions, instances of which may be seen in Portland and Hamilton Places, and elsewhere. They appear, also, to have introduced the practice of facing brick houses with stucco. In 1764 Robert published the results of his visit to Diocletian's Palace at Spalato, and in 1773, with the co-operation of his brother James, commenced the publication of "The Works in Architecture of R. and J. Adam," which was not completed until 1822, after the death of both authors.

The great merit of the Adams, says Fergusson, "is that they stamped their works with a certain amount of originality, which, had it been of a better quality, might have done something to emancipate art from its trammels. The principal characteristic of their style was the introduction of very large windows, generally without dressings. These they frequently attempted to group three or more together, by a great glazed arch over them, so as to try and make the whole side of a house look like one room." Fergusson's rather bald criticism, however scarcely does justice to Robert Adam (whom we may take to have been the real mind of the "firm"), as he omits to take into account one of his greatest merits, namely that of refinement of detail, and the fact that, while, basing his work on Classic models, Adam put a good deal of his own spirit and treatment into the details, and to some extent invented what may be called a sub-style of Renaissance of his own. He was especially good in his design for the internal decorative treatment of his buildings, and much of his design for furniture detail and the decorations of doors and windows is very good. His style in this kind of work is no doubt open to the charge of being too "pretty" and sometimes verging on flimsiness; but in spite of these defects his work was never vulgar. We give reproductions of two designs showing his treatment of this class of work. The first of these, the section of one end of the "second drawing-room" in the Earl of Derby's house in Grosvenor-square (as given in his "Works in Architecture") is a typical example of his manner of treating the side of a room, and partly illustrates the device on which Fergusson lays rather too much stress, of grouping two openings under one arch, the tympanum over the doors being in this case filled with a graceful ornamental design of somewhat Pompeiian character, only that it is in relief instead of being painted. The other illustration shows a design for a chimneypiece and looking-glass frame or overmantel in the same house. The floating wreaths, cut out so as to hang free of the main design, are certainly not in very pure taste, and we should not wish to see such a feature imitated in decorative work now; but the remainder of the details are exceedingly refined and graceful in their way.

In his exterior architecture there is no doubt that Adam's style was very deficient in architectural incident, force, and generally in picturesqueness (though there are exceptions in this latter respect), but it had also the merit of refinement, and it must be said also that his buildings look better in execution than they do in the highly-finished but tame and mechanically-shaded elevations in which he illustrated them. Yet even these drawings are of interest in their way, as showing how completely the architectural taste of one age is opposed to that of another. In the present day there is always an endeavour, even in elevation drawing, to secure a certain degree of picturesque surface texture. Yet a century and a half ago the ablest and most successful English architect of his day lavished the greatest care in engraving and the most sumptuous pages, both in regard to size and quality of paper, on drawings from which all that we call picturesque was carefully excluded. It is useful to bear this in mind, and to consider whether possibly our present picturesque method of drawing architecture may not seem as much beside the mark to our descendants a century hence.

The book to which we have referred, "Works in Architecture of Robert and James Adam, Esquires" (not "architects," please to note) is in itself a remarkable relic of architectural illustration of a former day. It is in two mighty folios, printed on thick paper, and the text in broad parallel columns of English and French. The fact that it was thought necessary to have this dual language is an indirect testimony to the fact, which we know otherwise, that Adam's reputation was not only English but European. There is an anecdote we remember to have read (but cannot give the source of it) of Robert Adam's reply to the agent of some nobleman who was very much offended because the architect would not waste time in waiting two or three days to have an interview with him about a building: "Does he expect that I, who have been presented to nearly all the crowned heads in Europe, am to lose my time waiting on his pleasure?"

Robert Adam continued to display his vigorous talent almost up to the day he died, for in the year preceding his death he designed no less than eight public buildings and twenty-five private houses. His talent, however, was not confined to the limits of his own profession, for he gained no little distinction as a designer of ornamental furniture, and also as a landscape painter. He was also a man of high social qualities, a good singer and evidently admired for his accomplishment in this respect; we quoted some time since the enthusiastic reference to him made by Fanny Burney in the diary of her younger days, where she (who was well qualified to judge) mentions his singing with admiration, and his conversation with even more enthusiasm, and evidently thought him one of the most pleasant companions for an evening that she had ever met.

It is a curious circumstance that two different branches of art,—painting and architecture,—should have been deprived almost simultaneously of their respective leaders, for only a week previously to the death of Adam, Sir Joshua Reynolds was carried to his last resting-place in St. Paul's Cathedral. The eminent architect died at his house in Albemarle-street, and was interred on March 10 in the south aisle of Westminster Abbey,—a sufficient proof of the estimation, both socially and professionally, in which he was held. The pall was supported by the Duke of Buccleuch, the Earl of Coventry, the Earl of Lauderdale, Lord Viscount Stormont, Lord Frederick Campbell, and Mr. Pulteney.

NOTES.

WHATEVER may be the ultimate result of the forthcoming stoppage in the coal trade, there seems but little doubt that merchants and agents will fare best at the outset. The general public,—especially those whose circumstances compel them to adopt a "hand-to-mouth" system with regard to coal,—are finding already that it will be a somewhat expensive experiment, as far as they are concerned. For the action of the miners in forcing a stoppage is regarded on all hands as an experiment, and one the effect of which it is very difficult to forecast. The officials of the Miners' Federation are careful to state that they have no wish to raise the price of coal to the consumers; but it is difficult to see what else they could expect. Mr. Pickard, M.P., who may be said to have built up the Federation, justifies the stoppage in the following terms:—"(1) Because there is no lessened demand for coal. 2. The general public do not and will not gain any benefit if coal is lowered. 3. Because the lowering of the price of contract coal will do three things: (*a*) Lessen coal owners' profits; (*b*) lower miners' wages if allowed; (*c*) transfer or put into dividend-hunters' pockets the money coal owners and miners should have put into theirs. There is no depression in the coal trade," says Mr. Pickard, "and we are setting political economy at defiance, as we did in 1888. We were condemned then, as we are now, and as we expect to be condemned." It will be seen that the position of manufacturers (who are urgently pressing for relief in price of coal and coke) is passed over without any consideration, and yet our manufacturers,—especially in the iron and steel trades,—are losing much of their old supremacy in foreign markets, mainly as a natural consequence of the higher wages obtained by this boasted policy of defiance. This is exemplified by the statistics recently published by the Board of Trade with respect to contracts for railway material for Egypt. Before the year 1889, we are told, English manufacturers almost invariably secured the orders for rolling-stock, &c., no Continental firms being able to quote so cheaply. Since that year, however,—*i.e.*, following upon the general rise in wages so triumphantly referred to,—we have gradually had to give place to our foreign competitors, who have been enabled to offer prices we could not touch. Our quotations appear to have continued to advance, and last year, in an open contract for truck work, the lowest British tender was considerably higher than four separate Belgian and French quotations. When will the labour leaders recognise that it is a fallacy for them to regard these things as being no concern of theirs?

MR. A. S. MURRAY, in an interesting letter on the subject of the mausoleum controversy, offers us some figures in controversion of our opinion (page 154 *ante*) that Professor Gardner was in the right in judging that the statues of the mausoleum room at the British Museum are out of scale with the horses. "Science is measurement" (as Mr. Marks suggested in one of his cleverest pictures), and Mr. Murray's figures are important as far as they go. He compares the measurements of the heads of man and horse. He finds that the head of Mausolus in the statue is 15 in. in length, and that of the mausoleum horse 41 in., a proportion of 1 to 2[illegible]. The head of the Theseus in the Parthenon pediment is 12 in. high, that of the horse of Helios 31½ in., giving a proportion of 1 to 2[illegible]. He has measured an ordinary man's head and an ordinary horse's head, and finds them respectively 9 in. and 24 in., giving a proportion of 1 to 2[illegible]. This is pretty close certainly, as far as details are concerned; but there is no doubt the horse as a whole is larger in comparison with the figures than the Greeks generally represented them in sculpture (their horse being perhaps a small breed); and there is a general appearance about the mausoleum horses of breadth and simplicity of style, as if intended for a position far from the eye, while the figures are much more minute in detail. If they were in the chariot, they must have looked mere dolls at the height at which they were put. The scale is only one-fourth larger than that of the Parthenon pediment figures, and the height (if they were in the chariot) nearly three times as great. We do not (and did not) regard Professor Gardner's position as proved, but those statues do not look like works to be placed at such a height, or as running parallel with the horses in regard to mode of execution for the position. If they were placed in the quadriga, they must have entirely failed in their effect as portrait statues, and have looked rather awkwardly placed, standing up in a chariot with no action connecting them with the horses. They appear to us as figures which would have have had a closer decorative connexion with the architectural design of the structure.

IF we are correctly informed by an auditor, Miss Sellers, in the first of a course of evening lectures at the British Museum, delivered on Tuesday last, in dealing with the architecture of the Parthenon, told her audience that the architectural design of the Parthenon resided in the *cella*, not in the external order, and that in place of the triglyphs representing the ends of beams and the metopes the spaces between them, the real explanation was that the triglyphs represented spaces to put the ends of the beams in, and the metopes the wall between. In regard to the latter statement the lecturer cited Vitruvius, who however does not precisely say that, but that the triglyphs were an ornamental covering over the ends of the beams. Anyone however who is acquainted with the forms of the quasi-timber rock-cut designs of Asia Minor (of which Vitruvius knew nothing) can have no doubt whatever as to what the triglyphs really represented; and it was exactly because they represented solid constructive portions that the Greek architects shifted the last triglyph to the angle of the building, instead of leaving it over the centre of the column as the Romans did; the Roman method aptly representing, no doubt, the false theory of Vitruvius. And in regard to the metopes, is Miss Sellers aware that in the Parthenon itself the metope slabs are thin facing-blocks which could carry no weight, and which are entirely separated from the wall structure? And that Mr. Tadema has found representations (we think at Pompeii) of metope slabs represented as turning on a pivot, an arrangement which he reproduced in one of his pictures? In regard to the main architecture of the building, no doubt the *cella* is the constructive *raison d'être* of the temple, but nearly all which makes the exterior architecture of the Parthenon expressive in detail resides in the column and entablature. We have no wish to say unkind things, but this kind of architectural criticism, addressed to those who come to sit at the feet of a lecturer and learn wisdom, cannot be allowed to pass without comment. Such teaching confirms us in a belief we have long held, that woman is generically incapable of understanding construction and constructional expression in architecture, just as she is generically incapable of drawing buildings upright (a weakness which she shares, no doubt, with some painters of the other sex). It is amusing also to notice the emphasis laid on Vitruvius when he can be cited to support an eccentric theory of architecture, compared with the indifference with which he is dismissed with costs when (as in the matter of the Greek theatre) his statements do not fit in with the theories of Dr. Dörpfeld, the idol of the Hellenic lady students of the day.

IN Berlin, one may say throughout Prussia, a proposed reform in all matters relating to the education of the lower classes is causing intense excitement. The Prussian Government wishes to pass a piece of legislation which will cause an entire change in the administration, the curriculum, &c., of the Board Schools (a change which must have a most marked effect on the coming generation of the labouring classes) and their new Bill has been placed before the Diet. It is well to note that in framing their long list of proposals (worded in about two hundred paragraphs) the question of the housing of the school children during the hours of their education has had attention. Whilst, according to section 21 of the proposals, the civil governors of the provinces will have the right of making special general regulations for the erection of school buildings in their districts, the Government in section 22 distinctly wishes to see the following points taken into consideration throughout the country:—1. Every school is to have its own school-building, no part of which is to be used for any purpose liable to injure educational interests. 2. Every school class is to have a class-room for its own sole use. 3. In the selection of the site for a school-building sanitary requirements are to be taken into account, and in the planning of the building the amount of air and light to be given to each pupil, the mode of heating and ventilating to be adopted, the source of and the manner of distributing drinking-water, and the arrangement of the lavatories, are to have careful attention. 4. In each school-house there are to be residential quarters for at least one teacher. According to sec. 24, it will also be compulsory throughout the country to have an open space, "on which gymnastics can be exercised," and "on which the children can inhale fresh air during the pauses between each class hours," attached to, or in close proximity to, each school-building.

THE poor accommodation provided for third-class passengers on certain southern lines, to which we incidentally alluded a week or two ago, was last week the subject of an action at the Westminster County-court. The London Chatham and Dover Company sued a Mr. Addison for the difference between second and third-class fares between London and Birchington. The defendant admitted that on more than one occasion he had travelled in a second-class carriage with a third-class ticket, but stated that it was in consequence of the third-class carriages being so bad, and that he defended the action on public grounds. The Judge gave his verdict for the plaintiffs, but refused to allow costs, a decision which was received with loud applause,—renewed outside the court in the shape of approving newspaper comments. Now at the risk of being accused of condoning the short-comings of railway companies, we must say that this creates a very awkward precedent. A decision of this kind, when it does not carry costs, is really punitive as regards the plaintiff; and the Judge, in refusing the application for costs with indignation, evidently intended it as a punishment. Singularly enough the President of the Board of Trade was interrogated in the House of Commons the following day, as to how railway companies could be prevented from allowing passengers holding third-class tickets to travel in carriages of a higher class. Sir Michael Hicks Beach could only reply that the evil complained of would be extremely difficult to prevent. Hitherto, the first and second-class carriages have been invaded by third-class passengers mainly in consequence of insufficient accommodation. After Judge Scott's decision, however, railway companies may plead that passengers appear to be encouraged in this proceeding whenever they choose to regard the accommodation provided as being unsatisfactory. Certainly they are not allowed to escape paying the difference in the fare in the event of being discovered, but they have only to force the companies to put the matter into Court to make the latter lose more than the amount of the fare in recovering it. It may be urged that the need for improvement is so great that this discovery of a practical way of bringing pressure to bear upon the delinquents is a public gain. But where is the line to be drawn? Who is to decide whether the accommodation provided is or is not worth a penny a mile? It is, after all, only a matter of comparison. The carriages complained of would perhaps have been regarded as almost luxurious on one of the early Parliamentary trains, although, compared with the general run of modern rolling-stock, they are wretchedly uncomfortable.

THE passing of the second reading of the Bill for constructing a tramway line across Westminster Bridge must not be taken as assuring its ultimate success, for, in Committee, the Bill may be so altered as to make it useless for it to be carried out. It is clear, however, that the House of Commons was right in sanctioning the principle of the Bill. There is ample room for a tramway line on the Embankment, and it will interfere with no "amenities." Whether, however, there is any real public demand sufficient to make this extension a financial success is doubtful. There are no places of business along the route, and the District Railway, with low fares, is in competition. We should therefore be in no way surprised if the project is never realised.

TO the catalogue of the Electrical Exhibition at the Crystal Palace, now no longer "under revision," has been added a guide to the exhibits in the form of "a personally-conducted tour by the Editor." We are glad to see that "watts per hour," to which we lately called attention, has been removed from the last edition. Had we hoped for this result we would have quoted the errors more nearly in bulk, instead of giving a sample only. Since a fourth edition cannot be expected, it is now too late, and we will only give one further instance:—"A joule is the heat generated by a current of one ampère flowing with the force of one volt through a resistance of one ohm. In other words, one watt per second will produce an amount of electrical heat called a joule." Here we have two definitions, the second only of which is approximately right—we say approximately, because the joule is also a measure of energy in forms other than heat; the first is not merely incorrect through admitting the time factor, but is also redundant. Will Mr. Dowsing tell us how a current of one ampère can flow through a resistance of one ohm, under any other pressure than that of one volt?

THE interest taken in electricity and physical science, stimulated doubtless by the Exhibition now being held at Sydenham, is naturally reflected in current literature. No less than three leading London periodicals contain articles on these subjects in their March issue. First in importance and interest is Lord Kelvin's contribution to the *Fortnightly Review* on the "Dissipation of Energy," a subject which he made his own, or, rather, which he originated just forty years ago, when he was plain Mr. Thomson. The *Nineteenth Century* has an article by J. E. H. Gordon, on the "Latest Electrical Discovery," and the *Contemporary Review* one by Mrs. Faithfull, on the "Electrical Cure for Cancer." We content ourselves for the present with simply noting the simultaneous appearance of these three articles, and reserve comment till next week.

THE February number of the *Journal of the Franklin Institute* contains the first instalment of Mr. Wm. S. Aldrich's papers on Electro-magnetic Machinery. Mr. Aldrich has evidently been struck by the beauty and simplicity of M. Reuleaux's analysis and classification of mechanisms in his classical work on the "Kinematics of Machinery"; and in these papers he aims at extending these modes of classification to dynamos, motors, &c., which could not be included in the original work, because they were not then invented. He is met at the outset by the difficulty of finding anything analogous to a kinematic chain in the transmission along a cable, but he boldly cuts the knot by assuming (provisionally) Dr. Oliver Lodge's somewhat fanciful scheme of the "gear-wheel" construction of the ether. This once granted, the writer shows by considering several practical applications of the motor-generators, or combinations of motors and generators, what electro-magnetic equivalents can be devised for belts, spur-gearing, and like means of transfer of rotation from one shaft to another, whether parallel or inclined at an angle. He then gives some ideal examples of what he calls the Electro-Kinematic Chain, which it is hopeless to attempt to make clear without the aid of a figure. The intention seems to be, by clamping the axis of a motor armature to cause the field to rotate and to carry with it the dynamo which supplies current to the motor, and which is rigidly connected with the rotary field of the latter. Returning from the imaginary to the real, the writer describes two electric drills, calling special attention to the "mechanical equivalents" of the electro-magnetic mechanisms. He promises in a later paper to give a "diagram of the electro-magnetic mechanism of the Van Depoele machine," which is the latter of the two drilling machines described.

SOME old London house-signs have been recently added to the Guildhall Museum. They consist of an ostrich, carved in stone; the two leather bottles purchased on the demolition, — for rebuilding, — of "The Leather Bottle" public-house at the corner of Leather-lane and Charles-street, Hatton-garden; a stone carving (one head restored) of a two-headed spread eagle, with date 1669, and initials E. (or L.) R. M., presented by Mr. M. Pope, F.S.A. Whence this sign came is not known; the spread eagle formed a common device. The famed "Spread Eagle" tavern in Gracechurch-street, whose predecessor is cited by Taylor, the Water Poet, in his "Carrier's Cosmographie," 1637, was pulled down in October, 1865. A fine specimen, and well preserved, is that of the "Cock and Bottle," in blue and white tiles. It belonged to a tavern on the southern side of Cannon-street, which was removed for an improvement of the thoroughfare in 1853-4. This sign was set up there about thirty years after the Great Fire. The house has been rebuilt, being now Nos. 94-6, and known by the same sign. A collection has been deposited in the Museum to illustrate the various shapes of the seventeenth century tobacco-pipes, whose discovery we announced in our issue of 6th ultimo. They were found in a bricked-in space beneath a vaulted cellar, on a spot that was latterly a garden, but where, according to Ogilby's survey of 1677, had stood a building of some kind. In clearing the ground two old walls, 62 ft. apart, reaching southwards from against Staple-inn towards Took's-court, have been laid bare to a considerable depth. A few of the pipes bear, on the heel, the name of a maker,—"JOHN HUNT." The Tobacco-pipe Makers' Company, ranking seventy-eighth in precedence out of eighty-nine, were first incorporated in 17 James I.; they obtained fresh charters in 10 Charles I. and 15 Charles II., with jurisdiction throughout England and Wales. References to them and to losses sustained by the grant of monopolies to certain persons, will be found in the Calendars of State Papers (domestic) for the period 1641-1667. A report (1834) of the Commissioners appointed to inquire into municipal and trade corporations shows that at that time the Company comprised 316 members, all engaged in the trade, with an income of about 100*l.* yearly, derived for the most part from quarterage paid by non-freemen. A petition by pipe-makers, of London and Westminster, made to Parliament in December, 1643, against the duty on their wares avers that "nearly 1,000 poor persons" lived by that industry.

IT seems likely that the projected preservation of Hilly Fields, Lewisham, as an open space, will be accomplished. The purchase-money for the 41 acres is stated to be 42,000*l.* Towards this the London County Council agreed, last week, to contribute, conditionally, not more than 22,000*l.*; the Greenwich District Board have promised 7,000*l.*; and other subscriptions amount to about 8,000*l.* The fee of 17¾ acres out of the area belongs to the Bridge House Estates: in respect of that portion, the Court of Common Council have decided to offer no opposition in the event of an application being made to Parliament for a Bill to enable the Corporation to sell the same. The Kyrle and the Commons Preservation Societies are co-operating with the Metropolitan Public Gardens Association to secure the ends in view.

AT Messrs. Dowdeswell's Galleries are exhibited a series of forcible though rather slightly-executed sketches of "Native life in and around Tangier," by Mr. Aubrey Hunt, some drawings of Venice by MM. Vizzotto and Mainella, and a set (second series) of water-colour drawings of London churches, by Mr. C. H. Herne. These last are of considerable interest, and as far as artistic effect and colour are concerned they are drawings of a high order, and form a valuable series of illustrations of London topography. Unfortunately several of them are marred by bad drawing. In "St. Peter's, Cranley Gardens" (15) the spire is crooked; the tower of St. Mary-le-Strand (22) is out of drawing, the different stages not being set properly over each other; in "St. Margaret's Westminster" (24) the sketch of the clock-tower in the background is absurd; but the worst of all is the largest, a drawing of "St. Paul's at Daybreak" (20), very fine in effect and colour, but the dome is completely out of drawing, and looks as if it had been squeezed out of shape. It is extraordinary how few painters can draw a circular building in perspective. The two points constantly overlooked are, that the central portion of a horizontal cornice in this position is always a comparatively flat curve, dropping quickly into a sharper curve at the receding sides; and secondly, that the vanishing curves at each side must necessarily be exactly the same. In this drawing we have a sharply convex curve at one side and a nearly straight incline at the other. It might have been thought that any one undertaking a series of drawings of architecture would recognise that correct perspective was the necessary foundation for such work. Mr. Herne, it must be added, is by no means an exceptional sinner in regard to defects of this kind, which we have frequently seen in the works of artists of much greater reputation.

OUR Berlin correspondent writes that it will only be doing justice to the Berlin workmen to positively contradict all the statements that have appeared in the daily press charging them with participation in the tumults which occurred on Thursday and Friday last week in the streets of the Prussian capital. It is true that there is a great deal of distress and discontent in the city this month, owing to the artisans and labourers of the building trades, who are out of employment in the winter, not having their usual occupation with snow clearance; and it is also true that these unemployed, after having held a meeting in one of the suburbs, marched (some 3,000 strong) to the Town-hall to ask for relief works, and sent a deputation to the "Ober Buergermeister," who did not go to the trouble of even receiving them; but these men dispersed as quietly as they had come after they had found that they could not obtain a hearing. It was an entirely different crowd that took advantage of the apparent state of dissatisfaction among the workmen, a crowd made up of the scum of the populace,—roughs and idlers of the worst and most cowardly type. At present quiet reigns again as regards the roughs, and, as to those who really require help and whose discontent was unintentionally the indirect cause of the outbreak, we hear that the municipal authorities will vote some of the sums to be spent on works to be carried out according to next year's Budget, and that these works, which are then to be commenced at once, will give employment to several thousand men. The *bonâ-fide* workmen are exceedingly vexed about last week's occurrences, which have done much injury to their cause.

WE are glad to learn from a letter which appeared in the *Standard* last Friday, that a circular has been sent to many candidates for the London County Council, putting before them definitely as an object the suppression of the London organ-grinding nuisance, a matter which is not included, as far as we are aware, in any of the extensive promises of London reform and improvement put forth by many candidates. The following is the first portion of the circular referred to:—

"Sir,—It is earnestly requested that, if elected, you will endeavour to suppress the nuisance of organ-grinding. It may be seen, from a return presented to Parliament last year (Miscellaneous, No. 2, 1891, moved for by Mr. Jacoby), that this nuisance has been practically suppressed in all but English-speaking countries. Our law, however, amounts to a legislation of the nuisance, and puts difficulties in the way of those who want to protect themselves. No one has the right to complain at all, even at any hour of the night, unless on the ground of illness or occupation interfered with, and then you can only move them on, and they can come again as often as they please. If you will not suppress it, pray, at least, pass such regulations as will enable any one annoyed to promptly and effectually stop and prevent the recurrence of the nuisance within his hearing."

We have, we must confess, little hope of it, but we do earnestly wish that the next County Council would turn their thoughts towards eradicating once for all this intolerable nuisance of London life; a nuisance which is a source of continual misery and irritation to thousands; for which there is no sort of excuse; which affords opportunity to a host of idle vagabonds to avoid honest work and to prey upon and harass the community. There is nothing like it, in extent, we believe, in any other capital in the world; its existence is a disgrace to the Government of London, and the County Council ought to put it down with a strong hand.

THE LAND ON THE VICTORIA EMBANKMENT.—The *City Press* says that there is no truth in the rumour that the Corporation has at last received a satisfactory bid for the vacant land on the Victoria Embankment. There are several offers besides that of the Salvation Army before the City Lands Committee, but neither of them is considered satisfactory, being far below the value of the land fixed by the Corporation's Surveyor.

LETTER FROM PARIS.

LAST month saw a perfect avalanche of snow in Paris, which for three days pretty nearly stopped all street traffic. This event, not so very extraordinary at this time of year, has been the occasion of a storm of exaggerated accusations against the Direction des Travaux, even extending to personal invective against M. Huet, who three months ago succeeded M. Alphand as Inspecteur Général du Ponts et Chaussées, coupled with lamentations over the death of the latter, who it was said would never have left the Parisians thus stuck in an ocean of snow and mud. As a matter of fact however the same reproaches were uttered twenty years ago under the same circumstances, and on December 15, 1871, the Municipal Council of Paris demanded the immediate dismissal of M. Alphand, who was accused of carelessness in having taken no sufficient measures for removing the snow. It is amusing to note that among the signatures to this demand was that of M. Lockroy, who, when he became Minister of Commerce, appointed Alphand to the post of Director of the Works for the 1889 Exhibition.

The recent criticisms against the engineers of the Paris Municipality are certainly unjust and exaggerated, and the fact is that the corps of the Ponts et Chaussées department has shown a great deal of activity, but there seems to be a want of unity and of a fixed system of direction since the death of Alphand, who was a man of prompt decision and an admirable organiser of labour. In this respect the municipal services require improvement and re-arrangement, and if any scheme of reorganisation is carried out it may be hoped that architects, who have been rather left out lately, will be given their old place in the service, instead of everything being left to the engineers.

At the Gallery of the Water-colour Society the celebrated water-colour by Meissonier, "1807," has been on view, taking the place of honour in the Galérie Petit; the work will probably be remembered by many in England, having been already exhibited both in London and at the 1889 Exhibition at Paris. The exhibition of the "Aquarellistes," after fourteen years of existence, is as prosperous as ever. M. Detaille, in his "Charge de Cavalerie," rivals Meissonier himself, and in minuteness of detail the picture almost suggests a coloured photograph. M. Besnard, in his fantasies, seems to be amusing himself by puzzling the good public. It is absolutely impossible to understand the meaning of his gigantic "Éléphants du Roi Baskir" tossing about women in their trunks at the edge of a cascade; M. Besnard seems in this case to have succeeded in even burlesquing himself. Among other exhibits is a fine collection of landscapes by M Harpignies, powerfully treated though a little dry. A new comer, M. Paul Lecomte, sends some beautiful works, which at once give him a high rank among the landscape painters of the day. There are also some fine landscapes by M. Zuber, and some pretty Venetian scenes by the Baronne de Rothschild.

The President of the "Aquarellistes," M. Vibert, not only continues to inflict on us every year his eternal figures of cardinals, but these carefully-painted ecclesiastics meet us again at the "Cercle de l'Union Artistique," which has also opened its doors. This exhibition holds a good place among the smaller annual collections, and contains this year seven or eight works of great interest by such artists as Bonnat, Carolus Duran, Dagnan-Bouveret, Gervex, and Cormon; compared with which the remainder of the works impress one as rather mediocre and amateurish.

At the Palais de l'Industrie the new exhibition of "Femmes Peintres et Sculpteurs" has opened. It is the eleventh of the series, and it must be confessed that it is as mediocre in character as any of its predecessors. Two or three more such exhibitions will probably succeed in finally wearying the public of this attempt at feminine emancipation in art. The only exceptions to the general level of poverty are the sea pieces by Mdme. Elodie La Villette, the cats of that able animal painter Mdme. Ronner, and the studies by Mdme. Berria Blanc.

Among the minor exhibitions are to be noted the "exhibitions particuliers" of MM. Iwill, Huas, Gagliardini, and Pissaro. M. Iwill is an artist who excels in cloud effects and in autumn mists. His pictures, collected at the "Galerie des Artistes, Modernes," Rue de la Paix, are landscapes of great charm and variety.

M. Huas and M. Gagliardini exhibit at the Galerie Petit. The former has made a specialty of portraits of infants and young girls, which he treats with a skilled hand and which show close observation of nature. The latter, who, in spite of his Italian name, is a native of Alsace, is a painter of the sunny landscapes, white houses, dusty roads and blue sky of Provence.

M. Pissaro, the acknowledged chief of the Impressionists, exhibits at the Galerie Durand Ruel seventy-two works in oil, which form a kind of *résumé* of the extremely odd and curious studies of a long and (in its way) conscientious artistic life. There is a decided relation between his work and that of M. Besnard, only that M. Pissaro is an Impressionist by temperament and M. Besnard by convention.

There has been talk lately of the formation of a syndicate of artists who are to look after the material interests of painters, to undertake their defence in case of litigation, and even to intervene between them and the Government to obtain official commissions. The scheme emanates from the "Société Libre des Artistes Français" presided over by M. Bartholdi. Many objections are raised against it, and it has not much chance of success; and in fact the "Société des Artistes Français" presided over by M. Bonnat constitutes a real professional syndicate quite sufficient for all the purposes which the proposed body could carry out. In connexion with this latter society it is proposed to introduce this year at the Salon of the Palais de l'Industrie an innovation already suggested at the Champ de Mars Salon, viz. the exhibition of products of industrial art. The idea however has raised a great deal of opposition, and acrimonious discussions which have led at present to no result. If the decision is in the negative, this will probably tend further to the success of the opposition exhibition of the Champ de Mars.*

At the Ecole des Beaux-Arts the Government has nominated occupants for the two vacant professional chairs. M. Jules Jacquet, President of the "Société des Graveurs au Burin," has been appointed Professor of Engraving in place of M. Henriquel Dupont. He is an artist of ability who has engraved various important works by Lefebvre, Cabanel, Meissonier, &c. Instruction in the history of French architecture is to be confided to M. Paul Boeswillwald, an architect reared in the traditions of Viollet-le-Duc, and who seems eminently fitted for the post.

We announced recently the intended purchase by the Municipality of Paris of the celebrated Hôtel de Sens. Though nothing is absolutely settled, it is hoped that the purchase will be carried out and this interesting building saved from demolition. The "Société des Amis des Monuments Parisiens" has interfered in its defence, and there is little doubt that the Municipal Council, always anxious to preserve remnants of old Paris, will vote the necessary funds. The Hôtel would be admirably suited for the arrangement of the historic collections now very much crowded in the Hôtel Carnavalet. It is a building with many curious historical associations, and though it has suffered much injury from decay and rough treatment, it still remains a fine monument of French architecture of its period. It will require a good deal of reparation, but if preserved it will be a building almost equal in interest to the Hôtel de Cluny, and it is important to preserve at least all we can of the architectural history of old Paris.

* We may add, however, that the much-talked-of introduction of industrial art-work at this exhibition last year did not amount to anything worth speaking of, and the result was somewhat disappointing.—ED.

INSTITUTION OF CIVIL ENGINEERS.—Mr. Berkley, President of the Institution, entertained at dinner, at the Grand Hotel, on Thursday in last week, the following officers and past-officers of the Institution:—Sir Frederick Abel, K.C.B., hon. member; Mr. Abernethy, Sir Frederick Bramwell, Bart., F.R.S.; Mr. Woods and Sir George Bruce, Past-presidents; Mr. Alfred Giles, M.P., Sir Robert Rawlinson, K.C.B., and Sir B. Baker, K.C.M.G., F.R.S., Vice-presidents; Mr. G. F. Lyster, Mr. E. A. Cowper, Sir Jas. N. Douglass, F.R.S., Mr. J. W. Barry, Sir Douglas Fox, Mr. W. H. Preece, F.R.S., Dr. W. Anderson, F.R.S., Mr. Charles Hawksley, Mr. W. Shelford, Mr. J. C. Hawkshaw, Sir Bradford Leslie, K.C.I.E., and Sir Guildford Molesworth, K.C.I.E., Members of Council; Mr. Shand, Mr. Burt, Mr. H. Graham Harris, Mr. W. Matthews, Mr. F. S. Courtney, Mr. Berkley, jun., and Mr. James Forrest, the secretary.

SARACENIC ARCHITECTURE.*

BY PROFESSOR AITCHISON, A.R.A.

ANY description of Saracenic architecture would be incomplete without a sketch of its ornament and colour.

It might not be impossible to pronounce the style of a late building to be Saracenic, even if it were stripped of its ornament; but I think that, unless its date were known, the question of its style might be open to controversy, and some might affirm that it was of a local Byzantine or Romanesque school; but if its ornamentation were given the only controversy that could arise would be as to whether it were purely Saracen or built under Saracen influences. The stalactites alone would settle the question.

That much of the Saracenic ornament that consists of purely geometrical arrangement was founded on the Byzantine does not, I think, admit of a doubt; some of the Saracenic geometrical patterns, and much of their ornament, is undoubtedly Byzantine; there are patterns shown in books on Saracenic art that may be found in the Byzantine ruins of Central Syria. What Saracenic architecture got from Chaldæa, from the Greek kingdom of Bactria, and from India, we know not; from Persian architecture it got something, but not much. Though Persia in Chosroes' time had shrunk to the Euphrates, it contained Assyria and Babylonia, and I believe still reached to the Indus, so I was technically right in saying that they borrowed their bearded battlements from the Persians, but these were probably of Chaldæan origin, and no doubt the Saracens got something from the Westerns during the days of the Crusades, and they probably got much from the Copts in Egypt. They were greatly troubled as to their ornament by the exigencies of the faith, for not only did a pious Moslem refuse to make the likeness of any living thing, but he was troubled for his *post-mortem* interests by even sitting with them in his own room. The President has got a curious illustration of this. Some Persian fire-worshipping potter, who pretended to be a Moslem, or some infidel Cufan, had painted tile panels of a park, with men fishing, in which were swans, peacocks, falcons taking game, and cheetahs seizing antelopes; a pious, but tasteful Moslem subsequently inhabited the house, and tried to make the best of both worlds: so he cut the throats of all the living things, and thus enjoyed their portraiture with a clear conscience. Some of the Fatemite Kaliphs and Turkish rulers of Egypt were not so strait-laced, and, not to speak of carpets and embroidery with wild-beast patterns on them, had animals painted on their shields, carved on the walls of their buildings, and engraved on their plate. The griffin of Pisa is an instance, and we do read of Saracen statues; the Pisan griffin had plaques on its forelegs, one engraved with a lion, the other with an eagle; it is said to have been made by the order of El Hakem, the Fatemite Kaliph of Egypt, between 996 and 1020, and to have been captured by the Crusaders. On the citadel of Cairo, built by order of our old friend Saladin, is a double-headed eagle, supposed to be his crest, and thought by some to be a piece of ancient Egyptian sculpture; but his eunuch who ordered and looked after the building was called "The Black Eagle," so it was possibly a rebus of his name. In Kalaun's mad-house are carved friezes of wood, with hunting martichores, antelopes, falcons, peacocks, and figures of men drinking or playing musical instruments; these are introduced in medallions or amid foliage. The martichore is an animal which Mahomet saw in Paradise; it had the feet of an antelope, the tail of a tiger, and the head of a woman; it is this martichore that is in the mad-house of Kalaun. Some such beast, however, called by the same name, was said to have been hunted by Apollonius of Tyana in India. His beast had the head of a man and the body of a lion. Apollonius lived in Nero's and Vespasian's time, but martichores are said to have been spoken of by Ctesias 400 years before.

Apollonius, too, was a prophet, and a statue of him was in the hall or chapel where Severus Alexander had statues of illustrious persons and prophets, among whom were Alexander the Great, Moses, and our Saviour. Many of the

* Being the sixth and last Royal Academy Lecture on Architecture this session. Delivered on Thursday evening, February 11.

hand-mirrors of Saracen manufacture had martichores, animals, and hunting scenes on their backs. The ivory coffer of Bayeux has its hinges and angle and face clamps of silver, beaten up and chased into peacocks and flowers, enamelled in blue and parcel-gilt; it is supposed by some antiquaries to be Saracen work of the twelfth century, on account of the style of the Arabic writing which forms an inscription round the lock; it was deciphered by Petis de La Croix, in 1714. The legend is the common one found on hand-mirrors and such-like objects. "In the name of God, the merciful, the compassionate, perfect blessing and complete happiness," to my possessor being understood. It is supposed to have been part of the plunder brought by St. Louis from the Crusades. Some antiquaries, however, attribute it to the days of that Abd-al-Rahman who was killed at the battle of Tours, 732 A.D., and say it was then found in the Saracen camp; it certainly has not got the geometrical forms that were prevalent at the later date, but one requires to be acquainted with the Saracen plate to give a definite opinion.

Some of Kalaun's and other Sultans' plate, candlesticks, plates, water-buckets, flambeau stands, vases, and ink-horns, are ornamented with animals or figures; one candlestick has a medallion with birds round the edge; a plate has a medallion with fish nibbling at a bit of bread, with their tails curved like the flower of the cyclamen; the bottom of a water-bucket is damascened with a shoal of silver fish; a flambeau stand is damascened with gold and silver on a *niello* ground, and has bands of hounds, stags, elephants, and winged horses, as well as figures of men and hunting scenes.

When we get into the thirteenth century, the Easterns and Westerns had got mutually acquainted by a century of fighting, and whether this taste for animals and figures was aroused in the Saracen by the Crusaders, or was merely dependent on the tastes of the rulers, or whether the Muftis had agreed that the portraitures of men and animals was not sinful, but was only forbidden in mosques, I know not, but Saracen books of the thirteenth century are to be found illustrated with pictures of men and animals, no longer confined to scrolls and medallions, but forming whole page illustrations. These may be seen in an illuminated MSS. of the sittings of Hariry, a book of anecdotes of an adventurer: it was written in pure Arabic by a believing Moslem who was a poet, the author being a native of Saroudj, a small town in Mesopotamia, but the illustrations are supposed to be by Yahia-el-Wassety, a Persian artist, and to have been done in Cairo in 1236 A.D.; the borders have scrolls with cheetahs, stags, hares, and foxes, and in the spandrels of one page are winged figures with the nimbus.

The writing-masters, too, formed texts from the Koran into ducks, eagles, lions, and men on horseback. The Fatemy Kaliphs and the Mamluk Sultans and their followers had a passion for silk; the Moslems, who had still before their eyes the Prophet's objection to silk, evaded it by using cotton with the silk. The curtains of the Kaaba were woven at Cairo of cotton and silk dyed black, the colour of the Abbassides. It was Mehdy, the father of Harun al Rashid, who first stripped off the old coverings. As soon as silk came into vogue, the royal patterns of Byzantium, Persia, and Egypt seem to have been adopted by the Saracens, and many of them had figures or animals woven in them with inscriptions in Arabic, mostly in Cufic characters. Pliny speaks of the embroidered work of the Parthians and Babylonians as well as the "Attalicæ vestes," and, without doubt, the wild beast patterns of India were known at an early date. Plautus speaks of "the purple carpets of Alexandria" with "wild beast patterns" (Pseudolus 1, 2, 14). Quintus Curtius speaks of the robes of the Persian satraps, ornamented with golden falcons which rush at one another like the beaks of ships, and, not to speak of the band of figures on Minerva's robe, we all know the imperial purple robe of Theodora in San Vitale, with the Adoration of the Magi on it. The Copts seem to have been the designers and weavers of the Egyptian stuffs with figures, which included wild beast patterns.

Persian and Byzantine artists and workmen designed and wove other stuffs ornamented with animals and human figures. Under a Turkish Governor, Iconium in Lycaonia, the Rûm of the Saracens, seems to have been a great centre of manufacture; one of the patterns preserved in the Lyons Museum is of the first half of the thirteenth century, was produced at Iconium, and consists of two lions back to back in gold on a crimson ground; it has rather a Chinese air about it, the claws being like those of the Chinese dragon: and the Saracens had intercourse with China. The manufacture was also carried on by the Saracens when they were masters of Sicily, and was continued by Saracen artists and workmen when it fell under Christian sway. The fabrics of the Saracens were so celebrated that many materials bear their name to this day: "Damask" from Damascus, though I believe this got the name before Saracen days; "Sarcenet" from Saracenicum,—Shakespeare speaks of "a green sarcenet flap for a sore eye;" "Muslin" from Mosul, "Dimity" from Damietta, and "Tabby" from a quarter of Baghdad, called so after Prince Attab, a great grandson of Omeyya; "Mohair," from the Arabic name for stuff of goats' hair, now called "Moire," which is watered silk.

Trellis, Cairo.

> "And when she sees her friend in deep despair,
> Observes how much a chintz exceeds mohair."
>
> *Pope.*

Saracen artists and workmen were also employed by the Christians at Lucca, Venice, and elsewhere, just as the oriental carpets of Poland in the seventeenth century were made by Persians. When the art was learnt, the manufacture was often carried on by Christians, who not unfrequently made a mess of the inscriptions. Whether we have any remains of the stuffs that were actually worked by Moslem hands in Moslem countries seems doubtful, but we have plenty of copies or imitations, mostly to be found in the treasures of churches or in textile museums. Nearly all the thirteenth and fourteenth-century textile fabrics of Europe were based on Saracen designs. We know that the Renaissance book-bindings, as late as Grolier, often retained the Saracen patterns.

The Saracens followed the Byzantine habits, and royal stuffs were not to be had for love or money.

In Byzantine times the mere possession of a mantle of imperial purple was enough to found a charge of high treason on, and to subject the possessor to torture and probably to death. At Tinnis there was a factory for royal robes. Amongst other articles it manufactured was an iridescent stuff called "Chameleon"; the cost of a piece of this for a turban was fifty pieces of gold. It is said that a king of Fars offered 20,000 pieces of gold for a royal robe of Tinnis stuff, and sent an agent to get it, who, after trying for several years, gave it up in despair. The price of some of the more precious stuffs was fabulous, but I presume that the robe that cost 400,000 pieces of gold, which Harun-al-Rashid cajoled Jafar with, before he cut his head off, was embroidered with precious stones like Chosroes' carpets, that the Saracens sold by auction at Medina. Embroidery was largely employed on dresses of honour, as well as on the coverings of tents. In the inventory of the Fatemite Kaliph El Mustansir, in 1035-95 A.D., tents are described, made of cloth of gold, velvet, satin, damask, and silk; some plain, some embroidered with men, elephants, lions, peacocks, and horses, and lined with velvet, satin, or silk shot with gold. Some of these tents would contain 150 horsemen, had poles 65 cubits high, nearly 100 ft., and took seventy-two camels to carry them, each camel load being 1,000 lbs. The "Arabian Nights," which represents the manners and customs prevalent amongst the last Mamluk Sultans, is full of descriptions of embroidery. You must not suppose that this was an original Saracen art; the Romans employed it largely, and it is more than suspected that some of the large chambers in Diocletian's palace were workshops for it. In the story of Seyf-el-Molook, he sees on the tunic sent to his father by King Solomon, "the portrait of a damsel delineated in gold," and this was so well done that he incontinently fell in love with her, travelled into barbarous countries, and endured all sorts of hardships and horrors to find her. In the City of Brass "the party entered a passage paved with marble, upon the sides of which were curtains, whereon were figured various wild beasts and birds, all these being worked with red, gold, and white silver, and their eyes were of pearls and jacinths; whoever beheld them was confounded." In the story of Alee Shír and Zumurrud, the professional embroideress, she said to him, "Buy for us a piece of silk, as much as will suffice for a curtain, and buy gold and silver thread, and silk thread of seven different colours. . . . . The damsel took the curtain and embroidered it with coloured silks, and ornamented it with gold and silver thread. She worked a border to it with figures of birds, and represented around it the figures of wild beasts, and there was not a beast in the world that she omitted to portray upon it."

I have gone rather far afield before coming

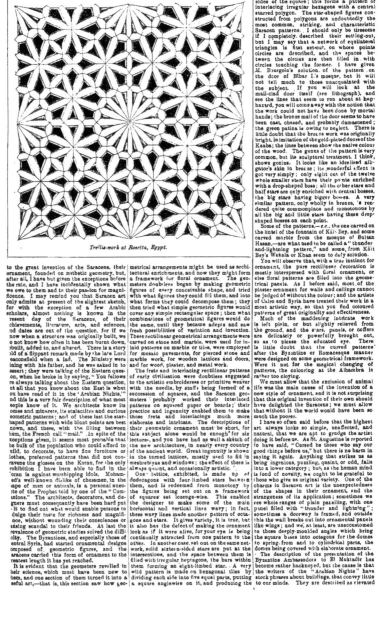

Trellis-work at Rosetta, Egypt.

to the great invention of the Saracens, their ornament, founded on æsthetic geometry, but, after all, I have but given the exceptions before the rule, and I have incidentally shown what we owe to them and to their passion for magnificence. I may remind you that Saracen art only admits at present of the slightest sketch, for with the exception of a few Arabic scholars, almost nothing is known in the resent day of the Saracens, of their chievements, literature, arts, and sciences, nd dates are out of the question, for if we now when a structure was originally built, we o not know how often it has been burnt down, ebuilt, added to, and altered. There is a story old of a flippant remark made by the late Lord eaconsfield when a lad. The Ministry were ining with his father, and he was asked in to essert; they were talking of the Eastern ques-on, when he broke in by saying, "You fellows re always talking about the Eastern question, ut all that you know about the East is what ou have read of it in the 'Arabian Nights,'" nd this is a very fair description of what most eople know of it. We architects know its omes and minarets, its stalactites and curious eometric patterns; and of these last the star-haped patterns with wide blunt points are best nown, and these, with the filling between hem, the French call "mail." In spite of the xceptions given, it seems most probable that he bulk of the population who could afford to uild, to decorate, to have fine furniture or lothes, preferred patterns that did not con-ravene the glosses on the Koran, for the only rohibition I have been able to find in the oran is against worshipping idols. Moham-ed's well-known dislike of chessmen, in the ape of men or animals, is a personal anec-ote of the Prophet told by one of the "Com-anions." The architects, decorators, and de-gners must consequently have been hard put it to find out what would enable persons to dulge their taste for richness and magnifi-nce, without wounding their consciences or ausing scandal to their friends. At last the revalence of geometric studies solved the diffi-ulty. The Byzantines, and especially those of entral Syria, had started ornamental designs omposed of geometric figures, and the aracens carried this form of ornament to the reatest length it has yet reached.

It is evident that the geometers revelled in heir science, which must have been new to hem, and one section of them turned it into a seful art,—that is, this section saw how geometrical arrangements might be used as architectural enrichments, and how they might form a framework for floral ornament. The geometers doubtless began by making geometric figures of every conceivable shape, and tried with what figures they could fill them, and into what forms they could decompose them; they then tried what simple geometric figures would cover any simple rectangular space; then what combinations of geometrical figures would do the same, until they became adepts and saw fresh possibilities of variation and invention. These rectilinear geometrical arrangements were carved on stone and marble, were used for inlaid patterns on marble or tiles, were employed for mosaic pavements, for pierced stone and marble work, for wooden lattices and doors, and for wood, plaster, and metal work.

The frets and interlacing rectilinear patterns of early civilisation were doubtless suggested to the artistic embroideress or primitive weaver with the needle, by stuffs being formed of a succession of squares, and the Saracen geometers probably worked their interlaced patterns on squared paper or boards; their practice and ingenuity enabled them to make those frets and interlacings much more elaborate and intricate. The descriptions of their geometric ornament must be short, for this subject alone would be enough for six lectures, and you have had as well a sketch of the new architecture, in nearly every country of the ancient world. Great ingenuity is shown in the turned lattices, mostly used to fill in meshrebiyas and windows; the effect of these is always quaint, and occasionally artistic.

One lattice, exhibited, is made up of dodecagons with four-limbed stars between them, and is redeemed from monotony by the figures being set out on a framework of squares set lozenge-wise. This enabled the designer to make some of the main horizontal and vertical lines wavy; in fact, these wavy lines made another pattern of octagons and stars. It gives variety, it is true, but it also has the defect of making the ornament look as if it were alive, for your eye is being continually attracted from one pattern to the other. In another case, set out on the same network, solid sixteen-sided stars are put at the intersections, and the space between them is filled with irregular heptagons, the bars within them forming an eight-limbed star. A very wild pattern is made on hexagonal tiles by dividing each side into five equal parts, putting a square anglewise on it, and producing the sides of the square; this forms a pattern of interlacing irregular hexagons with a central starred polygon. The star-shaped figures constructed from polygons are undoubtedly the most common, striking, and characteristic Saracen patterns. I should only be tiresome if I completely described their setting-out, but I may say that a network of equilateral triangles is first set-out, on whose points circles are described, and the spaces between the circles are then filled in with circles touching the former. I have given M. Bourgoin's solution of the pattern on the door of Bibar I.'s mosque, but it will not tell much to those unacquainted with the subject. If you will look at the mail-clad door itself (see lithograph), and see the lines that seem to run about at haphazard, you will come away with the notion that the work could not have been done by mortal hands; the bronze mail of the door seems to have been cast, chased, and probably damascened; the green patina is owing to neglect. There is little doubt that the bronze work was originally bright, in imitation of the gold-plated doors of the Kaaba; the lines between show the native colour of the wood. The genus of the pattern is very common, but its sculptural treatment, I think, shows genius. It looks like an idealised alligator's skin in bronze; its wonderful effect is got very simply; only eight out of the twelve whole smaller stars have their points enriched with a drop-shaped boss; all the other stars and half stars are only enriched with central bosses, the big stars having bigger bosses. A very similar pattern, only wholly in bronze, is rendered quite commonplace and monotonous by all the big and little stars having these drop-shaped bosses on each point.

Some of the patterns,—*e.g.*, the one carved on the lintel of the fountain of Käït Bey, and some carved marble from the mosque of Sultan Hasan,—are what used to be called a "thunder and-lightning pattern," and some, from Käït Bey's Wekala or Khan seem to defy solution.

You will observe that, with a true instinct for ornament, the pure rectilinear decoration is mostly interspersed with floral ornament, or else floral patterns are filled into the geometrical panels. As I before said, most of the plaster ornament for walls and ceilings cannot be judged of without the colour; and the artists of Cairo and Syria have treated their work in a most artistic way, so that you find coloured patterns of great originality and effectiveness.

Much of the maddening intricate work is left plain, or but slightly relieved from the ground, and the stars, panels, or coffers are delicately or powerfully brought out, so as to please the educated eye. There is little doubt that the curved patterns after the Byzantine or Romanesque manner were designed on some geometrical framework. Were it not for the magical changing of patterns, the colouring at the Alhambra is rather too cloying.

We must allow that the exclusion of animal life was the main cause of the invention of a new style of ornament, and it is not surprising that this original invention of their own should have delighted the Saracens; we must allow that without it the world would have been so much the poorer.

I have so often said before that the highest art always looks so simple, unaffected, and natural, that we are apt to grudge the artist doing it before us. As St. Augustine is reported to have said, "Cursed be those who say our good things before us," but there is no harm in saying it again. Anything that strikes us as being ingenious, puzzling, quaint, or odd, falls into a lower category; but, as the human mind is fond of novelty, we ought to be grateful to those who give us original variety. One of the charms in Saracen art is the unexpectedness of the shapes in their ornament, and the strangeness of its application; sometimes we see whole ranges of plain panelling, with one panel filled with "thunder and lightning"; sometimes a doorway is framed, and outside this the wall breaks out into ornamental panels like wings; and we, at least, are unaccustomed to those deeply-moulded angles which bring the square bases into octagons for the domes to spring from and to cylindrical parts, the domes being covered with elaborate ornament.

The description of the presentation of the Byzantine Ambassadors to El Muktadir has become rather hackneyed, but the cause is that the writers of the "Arabian Nights" have stock phrases about buildings, that convey little to our minds. They are described as elevated pavilions, containing lofty chambers; or palaces are described as magnificent buildings with lofty angles. The great hall of the palace in the City of Brass is described as "a saloon constructed of polished marble, adorned with jewels. The beholder imagined that upon its floor was running water. . . . . They found in it a great dome, constructed of stones, gilded with red gold . . . . and in the midst of that dome was a great dome-crowned structure of alabaster, around which were lattice-windows, decorated and adorned with oblong emeralds, such as none of the kings could procure. In it was a pavilion of brocade, raised upon columns of red gold. Within this were birds, the feet of which were of emeralds. Beneath each bird was a net of brilliant pearls, spread over a fountain; and by the brink of the fountain was placed a couch, adorned with pearls and jacinths, whereon was a damsel resembling the shining sun."

The decoration is briefly described as interlaced work, painted with vermilion, ultramarine, and gold. The bearers of stories were evidently satisfied with a slight description that implied grandeur and magnificent colour, but they were more curious about costly silks, satins, and embroidery, jewels and gold.

Whatever may be said against the sumptuousness and magnificence of clothes, personal adornments, furniture, and the architecture and decoration of private houses, I have always found them to exist when there was admirable architecture in public monuments.

In the golden age of Rome, Julius Cæsar wore shoes enriched with engraved gems; and we know from Petronius and Martial, in the silver age of Roman architecture, the splendid shawls and dresses, and the Babylonian embroideries with which the couches of the dining-rooms were covered: even as early as Plautus we hear of the carpets of Egypt with wild beast patterns, and the choice colours of ladies' dresses. I think there are many reasons for this. In the first place, there could hardly be sufficient employment in public monuments alone, to give the due reward and the necessary practice in the arts, nor could there be a sufficient taste created in those who ordered public buildings nor in those who admired them, if there were nothing but plain white robes, plain houses, and whitewash. I think, too, Hume's argument may be reversed, for where there are not excellent carpenters, weavers, stonemasons, and the like, we can hardly expect the master arts to flourish,—and architecture is one of the master arts. Be this as it may, I think it is evident that what are now called the sumptuary arts kept pace with architectural art, or architectural art kept pace with the sumptuary arts. The finest mosques,—viz., from the twelfth to the fifteenth century,—were contemporary with the most gorgeous stuffs, the finest cabinet, metal, glass, and enamelled work,—in fact, much of it was used for the decoration and furnishing of the mosques.

We fortunately have an inventory of the plate, jewels, stuffs, and furniture of the Fatemite Kaliph Mustansir that were sold by auction. He reigned from 1035 to 1094, just before the Crusades. I will give you a list of the most striking things. Besides bushels of uncut emeralds and necklaces, each bushel being worth 300,000 pieces of gold, there were 1,200 gold and silver rings, ornamented with gems which had cost 600,000 pieces of gold,—these surely must have been bangles: beer-jugs of the finest carved crystal; 18,000 crystal vases, amongst which were an enormous water-bottle and bowl, perfectly clear, and of the most exquisite workmanship; dishes of gold, some enamelled in patterns; 9,000 caskets of precious woods, enriched with gold, and lined with silk; a hundred cups of bezoar stone, on the greater part of which was engraved the name of the Kaliph Harun-al-Rashid,—the Arab word bezoar means an antidote to poison; inkhorns of different shapes, of gold, silver, sandal, aloe, and every other sort of wood, and of ivory, enriched with gems, gold, or silver, and remarkable for the excellence of the workmanship. The gold marriage-mat of Mamun, with his name on it; twenty-eight enamelled dishes enriched with gold, that had been presented to the Kaliph Aziz by the Byzantine Emperor, each of the value of 3,000 pieces of gold; chests full of hand-mirrors of steel, porcelain, and glass, enriched with filigree work of gold and silver, some bordered with jewels and with handles of cornelian or fine stones,—one had its handle covered with emeralds,—and there mirrors were in cases of silk, velvet, or beautiful woods, with gold or silver locks; a thousand articles enriched with gold, remarkable for their fine workmanship; a prodigious number of pieces of silk for playing chess and draughts on, embroidered with gold, with the men of ebony, ivory, silver, gold, and precious stones; 6,000 gold flower-pots for narcissus bulbs or violets; 36,000 pieces of crystal, and an enormous box of the same, sculptured; knives of the value of 36,000 pieces of gold; 22,000 large pieces of amber; a turban, embroidered with jewels of the value of 130,000 pieces of gold; a gold peacock, with eyes of rubies, enamelled in colours after nature; a gold cock, with a crest of rubies, and the body covered with pearls, and a gold gazelle, also ornamented with jewels; a dining-table, of sardonyx, with legs of the same, big enough for several persons to dine at; a garden of silver gilt, with silver trees, whose fruits were of jewels; and a palm-tree of gold, enriched with pearls, with the growing dates represented by jewels in every degree of maturity, in a golden box. Among a multitude of carpets woven with gold thread, were a thousand representing the different dynasties, with portraits of the kings and celebrated men, inscribed with their names, dates, and principal works. There was a map of the world woven in blue and gold tissue, with the names of the seas, rivers, countries, mountains, and towns; besides these were tons of camphor, moulded into cups, fruits, &c., and sacks of musk; there were specimens of the fine porcelain of Persia and China; arms, armour, and standards; and the tents were extraordinary both for size and the splendour of their stuffs.

One tent, called the great rotunda, was supported by a single upright, 97 ft. 6 in. high, and said to be nearly 10 ft. diameter. It was a column presented by the Byzantine Emperor. The tent was about 250 ft. diameter. It took 100 camels to carry it, *i.e.*, the column, the cords, and the vessels for the Sultan's use. The hangings of the tent were adorned with the figures of animals, and as part of its fittings it had a vast sea of silver. It is said to have taken 150 workmen for three years to make, and to have cost 30,000 pieces of gold. Some of the tents were supported by silver pillars, and the hangings were of cloth of gold, velvet, damask, and silk of every colour embroidered with men and animals often in gold embroidery. One tent was called the "Crusher," because a man was always crushed in pitching it. One may be sure that all the appointments were on a corresponding scale of splendour. When the Sultan reviewed his troops or held a durbar, there were gold or silver lavers, gold plate enriched with jewels or enamelled, candlesticks, swinging censers of the precious metals, enamelled or enriched with precious stones; the tables made of more common materials were of exquisite workmanship, the goblets and cups of crystal, gold, jasper, or agate, enriched with gems. Most of us have seen the precious cups, ewers, and centre-pieces in the Louvre, but it is their artistic merits we most admire; but at Madrid there are cups of gold as big as sugar-basins, rough with carving, and large masses of turquoise; these, the most gorgeous-looking things I have ever seen, are said to be presents from the East. Golden ewers and basins with their silk towels embroidered at the ends, and whenever they drank they had vases of flowers and dishes of fruit. A pageant of this sort must have exceeded anything we can imagine, the Sultan sitting on his throne, as often as not plainly dressed, surrounded by his Viziers and officers of the pen, all clothed in gorgeously-coloured dresses embroidered with gold and precious stones, and behind them black eunuchs and handsome page-boys, and environed by his guards, in sumptuous damascened or burnished armour; while the cavalry, on high-bred horses, pranced and curvetted in front of the tent, with their armour damascened, or clad in gilded mail, their sword and dagger hilts and scabbards jewelled, their baldricks stiff with many gems, and necklaces of jewels, with their horse cloths of cut velvet, embroidered satin or cloth of gold. On great festivals, when the army formed itself into a procession through the principal streets, the roads were strewn with green leaves and flowers, and the houses were all hung with costly carpets, velvets, and embroidered silks, the standards flying, and the people deafened by the tramp of horses, the clang of armour, and the blare of trumpets, as they escorted the Sultan to a great mosque, through the crowds of people. Most of the poor were barefooted, with blue gowns and white turbans, the girls with their long blue or white face-veils, with beads and coins dangling on their foreheads, and the whole ceremony finishing by a public banquet in the horse course, in which the banquet was spread. The huge dishes towered to a man's height above the table, filled with baked sheep, fowls, and small birds, filled between with dry sweetmeats, and the table covered with flowers. In spite of all this magnificence, "uneasy lies the head that wears a crown." One of the sleepless Sultans had a pond of quicksilver made in his garden, and here he tried to woo sleep on an air bed.

I have now given you a slight sketch of the Saracens from "the days of ignorance" to their acceptance of Islâm; of their emergence from their native land and of their conquests of the principal countries of the ancient world; of their early mosques in Europe, Asia, and Africa: of some of the leading characteristics of the style in Egypt, Persia, Barbary, and Spain. I have, too, pointed out the chief characteristics of the style when it became purely Saracenic. I have given you some hints of how the geometric ornament, which is most characteristic of the perfected style, was produced, and some account of Saracen manufactures, so that nothing remains for me to say but to draw an architectural moral. Nothing is to be despaired of in our art, so long as we have virtue, energy, industry, and perseverance; accompanied by a desire to improve it, to give it the character of our age, and of our own personality. In the Byzantine lectures of last year,* I showed you that even when a nation had sunk very low, and was engaged in a death struggle with savages, there was still hope, if the architects would only keep pace with the advance of knowledge, throw off self-imposed fetters, and work out truthfully and boldly the problems they had to solve; that, even then, a style might gradually be evolved, which would charm its contemporaries and elicit the admiration of succeeding ages; an example of the truth of this may be seen in Sta. Sophia of Constantinople.

In the Saracenic style you see that a race composed of barbarians and savages, almost destitute of the commonest arts of life, but fraught with courage, energy, and enthusiasm, could gradually acquire the architectural skill that had preceded it, and carry architecture, in certain directions, to a height it had never reached before; for nothing more fantastic and magical has ever been produced. This was mainly due to an ardent pursuit of geometry, and geometry is the foundation of all architecture.

Brick Door-head.

We, like them, have most of the architecture of the world before us, at least in engravings and photographs, and since the Crusades there has never been so much travelling. During my lifetime never has such energy been displayed by young architects and students, and never have the means of acquiring a knowledge of the principles of architecture been so near the hand of students. Shall we, then, "who rift the hills and roll the waters, flash the lightnings, weigh the sun," abandon ourselves to despair, and think we are not able to surpass our predecessors? No. We must, however, remember that man's power is limited, and a new style is neither to be created in a day nor in a lifetime; all we can do is to learn the elements of architecture,—a tremendous task, I must allow,—not copy, and understand that all that an architect can do to show his skill, taste, and the mighty thoughts within him, is by building. When we have mastered the grand fundamental

* Published in the *Builder* at the time.

principles of this almost infinite art, we can only do our best with those powers with which we are endowed; but depend upon it that when you have mastered the art, and have something beautiful or great to express, you will impress those with whom you mix, and they will entrust you with their work.

I fear, however, that the rising architects are too open to the ungallant remark of Swift about the young ladies of his day, that they were busy in making nets rather than cages. Showy draughtsmanship may get the most work, but when you can plan conveniently and construct soundly, fine composition, subtle proportion, and elegant profiling will ensure the most lasting fame.

COMPETITIONS.

BOROUGH LUNATIC ASYLUM, SUNDERLAND.—In the recent competition for the new Sunderland Lunatic Asylum, in which Mr. Howell, of London, acted as assessor, the first premium has been awarded to "Scio," Mr. George T. Hine, London, the architect for the Claybury Asylum; the second to Messrs. Hine & Odgers, Plymouth, whose motto was "Turpi secernis honestum"; the third to Messrs. Giles & Gough, London.

PROPOSED TECHNICAL SCHOOL, ASTON MANOR, BIRMINGHAM.—At a meeting of the General Committee, held on the 29th ult., the designs under *nom de plume* "Science and Art" were accepted, and the author of them, Mr. Geo. H. Cox, of Birmingham, was appointed architect for the new buildings.

BLACKBURN COUNTY BOROUGH ASYLUM.—We understand that the plans for this competition, confined to architects practising in Blackburn, were sent in on February 29. The assessors appointed are Messrs. Hine & Odgers, architects, Plymouth.

ARCHITECTURAL SOCIETIES.

CARLISLE ARCHITECTURAL, ENGINEERING, AND SURVEYING ASSOCIATION.—The usual fortnightly meeting of this Association was held on Tuesday last in the Town Hall, when a paper on "Trigonometrical Surveying" was read by Mr. A. Turley, C.E. The most approved methods of surveying and mapping large areas was fully described. A system of traversing and planning without the use of the protractor, ensuring most accurate results, was fully dealt with.

EDINBURGH ARCHITECTURAL ASSOCIATION.—On the 27th ult. the Edinburgh Architectural Association visited St. Nicholas' Church, Dalkeith. Mr. Hippolyte J. Blanc, who conducted the party, described the building as one of the collegiate churches, so many of which were founded in Scotland during the fifteenth century. A few were erected at the end of the fourteenth century, of which he noted that at Dalkeith as one. Mr. Blanc traced the various changes which the fabric had undergone, explaining in detail the characteristic features in the door, windows, and buttresses. He also illustrated his exposition by a series of drawings prepared from measurements of several other collegiate churches built during the fifteenth century, and which bear all the characteristic detail found at St. Nicholas'. Mr. Blanc was thanked for his lecture, and for the manner in which he had exhausted all the points of interest in his subject. The party thereafter proceeded to Newbattle Abbey, which, through the courtesy of Lord Lothian, they were enabled to visit, Mr. Archibald Macpherson acting as leader. The Abbey stands on the site of a Cistercian monastery, founded by David, the "sair sanct for the Croon," in the twelfth century—1140. The excavations made by the directions of Lord Lothian several years ago exposed the foundations of the church and some remains of the walls of the conventual residence. The church, which measured 239 ft. long and 57 ft. broad, consisted of nave with aisles, short transepts, and square-headed apse. The examinations of the remains fully bore out the theory that Newbattle shared the fate of other churches and abbeys when Richard II. of England and John of Gaunt made their expedition across the Border, burning and destroying the religious edifices on their way. It is supposed that it was restored in the fourteenth century. The party thereafter were shown through the Mansion-house. At the close of the proceedings, a hearty vote of thanks was accorded Lord Lothian for his kindness, and to Mr. Macpherson for his paper.

GLASGOW ARCHITECTURAL ASSOCIATION.—The annual supper of this Association was held on the 23rd ult., in the Grand Hotel, Glasgow. The honorary president, Mr. William Forrest Salmon, F.R.I.B.A., occupied the chair, and there was an attendance of about forty members and guests. The chairman, in speaking to the toast of "The Association," congratulated the members on its continued prosperity. He also announced that the Travelling Studentship had been gained by Mr. Eric A. Sutherland, Kelvinside, for his designs for an Art Gallery and Museum, submitted in competition with five others.

LEEDS AND YORKSHIRE ARCHITECTURAL SOCIETY.—At a meeting of this Society held on Monday night in the Law Institute, Leeds, Mr. Beresford Pite (London) read a paper on "The Architecture of Michelangelo." After describing the early life and training of the great architect, sculptor, and painter, the lecturer said Michelangelo did not undertake architecture until he was forty years of age. He was born in 1474, and died in 1563, at the age of ninety years, having spent seventy years in working. He was the contemporary of Raphael, Bramante, and St. Gallo, who all died before he had begun his work at St. Peter's. Bramante began St. Peter's in 1502, and Michelangelo followed him in 1540. The church was not completed till the next century. His work was characterised by great originality, breadth of treatment, majestic form, and vast scale.

THE LONDON COUNTY COUNCIL.

THE last meeting of the first London County Council was held at Spring gardens on Tuesday afternoon last, Sir John Lubbock, Chairman, presiding.

The Water Question.—The Chairman said:—Since our last meeting, the Committee appointed by the metropolitan and home county members of Parliament have conferred with the representatives of Birmingham. We were assured that an additional supply for Birmingham was a necessity. Mr. Chamberlain said that to obtain it would require at least eight years, and as prudent men they must look ahead. They would, however, gladly meet us on points of detail. They urged strongly that in the opinion of their engineer there would be a sufficient supply left for London. They courteously, however, consented to postpone the second reading till next Tuesday. I may add that we are informed there is considerable opposition to the Bill in Birmingham itself. The result of this interview was communicated yesterday to a second conference of metropolitan and home county members. Much regret was expressed that any further appropriation of water-bearing areas should be agreed to until the Royal Commission has reported. At the same time, though no resolution was arrived at, there was a general feeling that, if the needs of Birmingham are so urgent, which, of course, would have to be proved to the satisfaction of the Committee on the Bill, and subject to some agreement on details, it would not be reasonable to oppose the second reading. It was hoped, however, that the Bill would not be passed by the Committee unless the urgency was clearly proved. If the Council approve, I should propose to take this course on the second reading.

At a later stage of the sitting of the Council, the Water Committee submitted a special report with the following recommendation:—

"That this Council trusts that Parliament will not pass the Birmingham Corporation Water Bill before the water consumers of the metropolitan area have had an opportunity of putting their own case before the Royal Commission, except on the clearest possible evidence that the urgency of the matter in the case of Birmingham is so great that it must be pushed forward immediately without regard to the requirements of the population of the Thames basin; and the Council hope that, should the Birmingham Bill be referred to a Select Committee, an instruction will be given to the Committee in this sense."

Mr. Lloyd moved, as an amendment,

"That this Council will take every step to prevent the Birmingham Water Bill being passed until the Royal Commission has reported."

After some discussion the amendment was negatived, and the resolution of the Water Committee adopted.

Lauderdale House, Highgate.—The Parks and Open Spaces Committee reported as follows:—

"The Council on the 7th July, 1891, decided to remove the old building in Waterlow Park known as Lauderdale House, but as its removal would to a certain extent spoil the effect of the old terrace and gardens adjacent, we have had prepared a plan showing how the house could be restored, at a cost of 2,250*l.* It is proposed to divide the upper part into sets of rooms to be occupied by the Council's *employés* in the park at a rental of 65*l.*, and to let some of the lower rooms for refreshment purposes at a possible rental of 65*l.*, retaining others for conveniences for both sexes. We submit the plan referred to, and recommend:—

'That, subject to an estimate being submitted to it by the Finance Committee, as required by the statute, the Council do authorise the Committee to incur an expenditure of 2,250*l.* in the restoration and alteration of Lauderdale-house, Waterlow-park, to suit it for the purposes of a refreshment house, conveniences, and residences for workmen employed in the park.'"

This was agreed to without discussion.

The Hackney-Wick and Isle of Dogs Relief Sewer.—The Main Drainage Committee reported that they had considered the tenders referred to them on the 16th ult., for the construction of the Hackney-Wick and Isle of Dogs Relief Sewer. The tenders varied from 31,046*l.* 14s. to 53,221*l.*, the lowest being that of Messrs. S. & E. Bentley*. The Committee had made inquiries relative to Messrs. Bentley, and as these were satisfactory, they recommended that their tender, amounting to 31,046*l.* 14s., be accepted. But the Chairman of the Committee, Mr. Howell Williams, added that since the report and recommendation were printed, Messrs. Bentley had written withdrawing their tender, owing to a serious error made by them, and the Committee therefore recommended that the next lowest tender, that of Messrs. E. & W. Iles, amounting to 36,600*l.*, be accepted.

This proposition led to considerable discussion, in the course of which it was suggested by Mr. Acworth and Mr. Beresford Hope that the contractors tendering were collusive. It was explained by Mr. Howell Williams and another member of the Committee, Mr. MacDougall, that there was no ground for such an assertion. The error arose in pricing a large quantity of excavators' work. An amendment was moved to refer the matter back to the Committee, with instructions to re-advertise the works. It was urged against the amendment that the relief sewer in question was urgently needed, and that the tender of Messrs. Iles was well below the amount of the Engineer's estimate for the work. The amendment was defeated by 34 votes against to 15 for it, and the recommendation of the Committee was then agreed to.

The Labourers on the Blackwall Tunnel Works.—On the motion of Mr. Leon, it was resolved:—

"That the Council refuses to consider a lower payment than 6d. an hour as a fair rate of wages to be paid to labourers by the contractors for the works of the Blackwall Tunnel, and as complying with the declaration made in their tender that they pay the rate of wages generally accepted as fair in the trade."

Vote of Thanks to the Chairman.—On the motion of Mr. Fardell, seconded by Mr. J. Williams Benn, and supported by Mr. G. W. E. Russell and Mr. Thornton, it was resolved "That the best thanks of the Council be accorded to the Right Hon. Sir John Lubbock, M.P., for his able, courteous, and impartial conduct in the chair."

Sir John Lubbock, in reply, said:—I am, I assure you, very grateful to you for the kind resolution which you have just passed. But I have even more to thank you for the generous and constant support which you have always given me in the chair. I shall leave the Council, in many respects, with much regret and many pleasant memories. We are just now the subject of a good deal of criticism, especially as regards our expenditure; but when the time has come for a calm and impartial judgment, I think it will be said that if we have raised the rate a halfpenny in comparison with that of our predecessors, we have a good deal to show for it. I may refer, not as more important than the heavy, unostentatious, and ever-increasing work of our other committees, but in justification for the rise, to the fact that, in addition to other heavy items, we have completed Rosebery-avenue, begun the Blackwall Tunnel, finished the Northern main drainage works at Barking, and our successors will be able in a few weeks to open those at Crossness. This will do much to purify the Thames. We have also increased the precautions against fire, and we have enlarged and beautified the parks. Three years ago we met with feelings of some suspicion and antagonism, but, while we still differ in opinion, we have

* For full list of tenders see *Builder* for February 20, page 149.

learnt more and more to respect and appreciate one another. We began as opponents, we end as friends; and the reason has been that, however much we may differ about the means, we have been united by our desire to promote the prosperity of London, and the comfort, health, and happiness of our fellow-citizens in this great metropolis.

Vote of Thanks to the Staff.—On the motion of Mr. Æneas Smith, it was resolved as follows:—"That the Council desires to place upon record its high appreciation of the services rendered during its term of office by the entire staff of officers, clerks, and workmen, and that this resolution be communicated to the officers at the asylums and out-stations."

A vote of thanks was also passed to Messrs. Beachcroft and Osborn for the assistance they had given to the Chairman since the death of the second Deputy-Chairman of the Council, Mr. Haggis.

The Council then terminated. The election of the new Council, as our readers know, is to take place this Saturday, March 5, and the first meeting of the new Council is fixed for Tuesday, March 15. Some ten or twelve of the old members of the Council have already been re-elected without a contest at the polls; and nine of the Aldermen, who were elected three years ago for six years, will retain their seats on the new Council. The nine Aldermen referred to are Mr. Arthur Arnold, Mr. Frank Debenham, Sir Thomas Farrer, Mr. Frederic Harrison, Lord Hobhouse, Mr. Quintin Hogg, Lord Lingen, Mr. Edmund Routledge, and Mr. G. W. E. Russell.

DEMONSTRATIONS ON GREEK SCULPTURE IN THE BRITISH MUSEUM.

Miss Eugénie Sellers considered, in her fourth lecture,* the sculptures of the Mausoleum and of the Nereid monument. Greek funeral monuments consisted of single slabs, with the figure of the dead man or woman represented as engaged in some ordinary occupation; but in Asia Minor the funeral monument of a rich prince took the form of an elaborate building, which was in effect a kind of temple, in which stood the statue of the dead man, who was worshipped there with divine honours. Such was the Mausoleum, the funeral monument of Mausolus, of Halikarnassos, which was built at the beginning of the fourth century. Miss Sellers discussed various theories with regard to its restoration, but said that in the absence of any blocks of the stylobate giving the intercolumniation no final conclusion could be arrived at.

The figure of Mausolus is interesting as being one of the earliest specimens of portraiture. The sculptures of the friezes are interesting. We know from Pliny that Greek masters worked on them. The chariot race is specially remarkable for the flatness of the planes of the relief, and for the excellence of the work, in part of which we can trace the hand of Skopas. Yet for all the beauty of individual slabs, the general effect is decoratively not quite satisfactory, missing as it does both the flow of the Parthenon and the balanced groups of the Phigaleian frieze.

The Nereid monument from Xanthos, also a funeral monument, shows Asiatic work under Greek influences. Of the friezes, that representing a fight, probably of barbarians against barbarians, is the most Greek. The besieged city of the second frieze, with its fortresses, is eminently pictorial, and not at all Greek in character. Another gives us faithful renderings of scenes of daily life.

The composition of the pediments is quite elementary, that representing a battle-scene, which is the more advanced of the two, recalling the symmetrical arrangement of the figures on the pediments of the temple at Ægina.

Miss Sellers ended her lecture by a reference to the far finer work of the frieze of the temple of Niké.

Art Union of London.—The Art Union are issuing to their subscribers Mr. Wyllie's powerful etching of the escape of "H.M.S. *Calliope*," a work well worth popularising. The alternative etching, after a picture by Mr. Dendy Sadler, was not worth doing on the large scale on which it is executed: a constant mistake of the Art Union, which encourages the ignorant to think that half the merit of an engraving consists in its size.

* For brief notes of the previous lectures see *Builder* pp. 141, 164, *ante*.

THE ROYAL COMMISSION ON LABOUR:

BUILDING TRADES EVIDENCE.

Section C. of the Royal Commission on Labour which embraces textile and miscellaneous trades proceeded to receive evidence concerning the building trades on the 25th and 26th ult. The Right Hon. A. J. Mundella, M.P., Chairman of the Section, presided, the other Commissioners present being the Duke of Devonshire, Sir F. Pollock, Mr. L. Courtney, M.P., Mr. Bolton, M.P., Mr. Burt, M.P., Mr. Tait, Mr. Austin, Mr. Tunstill, and Mr. Livesey. The witnesses were representative men coming from the three kingdoms, and those from Ireland were the first called.

Mr. John Simmonds, Secretary of the Dublin Trades Council, although speaking for trades generally, alluded specifically to a strike in the building trade last June, arising from the refusal of unionists to work with non-unionists; and in reply to very pointed questions he defended this action, on the ground that workmen had a right to join a union if they chose, and to object to non-unionists reaping the benefits obtained by efforts in which they had not assisted. In this instance the union used no unusual means; they first requested the employer to induce the non-unionists to join the organisation, and on his declining to interfere, they gave a month's notice. They informed the employer that they could not work with the other men, whereupon he sent a circular to other employers urging them not to employ unionists. In another instance a dispute in the carpentering trade was amicably settled after a month's duration, and in the bricklaying and building trades a six weeks' dispute was terminated by the intervention of the architects of Dublin and some other gentlemen. As a rule, strikes were few in Dublin, and his Council were strongly in favour of the creation of a Board of Conciliation. Dealing with other points, this witness stated that some members of his Council were also in favour of taxing labour-saving machinery, seeing that the introduction of machinery had greatly injured manual labour, and had driven men into the workhouse. He did not say that in his own trade planks ought to be sawn with the old saws in a pit, but at the same time there was more employment under that system than there now was. He did not wish to convey that machinery ought to be abolished.

The Chairman: But you suggest the taxation of it, which is worse.

Witness: Humanity is taxed, and what takes the place of humanity ought to bear a portion of the taxation.

The Chairman: It assists humanity; it does not tax them.

Mr. P. Lynskey, representating the Amalgamated Carpenters' and Joiners' Society of Dublin, which contained about 1,100 members, said that at present there was a good understanding between employers and employed, but he agreed with the previous witness as to the right of unionists to object to non-unionists. At the same time he also approved of having a Board of Conciliation. In the instance given by Mr. Simmonds, the Society first approached the other men, who then said they would join the Union, but they failed to do so, and that caused the Union men to strike.

The Chairman: Do you think that a proper thing to do?

Witness: I do. The unionists are the men who fight, and who obtain all the reforms; and the non-unionists, who take no part whatever in the struggle, receive all the advantages which the unionists have gained. Witness added that in this case the employer got men over from Scotland, and then issued a black-list to prevent the men who had struck from earning their living in Dublin. The non-unionists were not driven to starvation because they were struck against, because there were certain "jerry-shops" in Dublin where they could get work, at rates lower than the standard rate. He did not think that that course was injuring the trade, for in Dublin the first-class shops all employed unionists, and the best men were unionists. The inferior shops never got a fair class of workmen. Prior to 1890 the working hours were 60½ per week, but they were now 54, and he believed the carpenters were satisfied with that period. But he advocated the legislative abolition, to some extent, of overtime, and with regard to the eight-hours' question, he thought that such a system should be international, so that English workmen should not suffer from the competition of other countries where the hours were unrestricted. The introduction of machinery had displaced about 10 per cent. of the men in his Society. A great many carpenters had left Dublin during the last few years through the adoption of machinery worked by men who were not carpenters. In moulding they would do in ten minutes what men would require two days for to do by hand. He would, therefore, tax that machinery, to pay for the up-keep of the men displaced. He also advocated greater facilities for giving technical and manual instruction.

Mr. R. S. MacNamara, Chairman of the United Building Trades Society of Cork, which includes carpenters, masons, stone-cutters, and plasterers, and numbers about 1,000 men and boys, explained that there were something like 1,500 hands in those four trades, of whom 600 were unionists, 150 non-unionists, 200 apprentices, and 500 unskilled labourers. The general minimum rate of wages was 5s. a day of ten hours, the working hours being sixty a week. The relations between the masters and the men were, on the whole, amicable, and the present rate of wages and working hours had been in operation for twenty years; but the trades had given notice for a reduction of an hour a day from May 1. Personally, he should favour a Board of Conciliation for the building trades, but not for all general industries. When work was abundant the unionists had no objection to non-unionists working with them, but otherwise they did object, and, in fact, they had struck against non-unionists. Mentioning that the Government paid a lower rate of wages than private firms, the witness recommended the appointment of a responsible Minister who should acquire information on all subjects upon which disputes were likely to arise between capital and labour, and that if possible a State Board of Arbitration should be formed, of which such a Minister would have charge. As to machinery, its introduction would, of course, at first displace a considerable number of men, but ultimately it would, he thought, benefit the workmen. This witness also considered that overtime should be abolished, and with respect to the suggestion of an international agreement as to working hours, such agreement would have to be made, not only by all foreign nations, but by the United States and some of our colonies.

Mr. J. H. Jolly, representing the Trades' Council of Cork, having also been examined, the Irish evidence was for the time closed. English evidence was opened by the examination of

Mr. Arthur Otley, General Secretary of the National Association of British Plasterers, who, in the course of his testimony, said his trade had had a great many disputes in recent years, and the chief cause had been the system of sub-contracts. Upon this theme he entered at some length, and not without warmth. Under this system builders sublet their work to "piece-masters" or "task-masters," who contracted for labour only. They were men who had no reputation to lose. They took the work at a low figure, but, as the builders knew, they could not properly carry it out. In illustration of this subject, he mentioned an instance which occurred at the Birmingham Post-office, where the whole of the plastering work was sublet in this way, and as no other work gave such opportunities for inferior material and for adulteration, in this case there was adulteration to the extent of 50 per cent. Again, a similar case took place in connexion with the Imperial Institute, a contract being sublet to a man who was well known as one of the greatest "scampers" in London. Against this man the members of the Association struck, knowing that the work was not being done as it ought to be done, and as the result of a deputation to the Committee the Association were ultimately assured that for the future the work should not be sublet. When they found that work which should take two days was being done in one day, they considered it their business to see about it.

The Chairman observing, "You struck work because the work was not lasting long enough?" witness replied that that was not their reason. They struck against the method, because the system was injuring the trade. The men were working at the usual rate of pay and of hours. The point being put to him whether this was not a matter for the clerk of the works, Mr. Otley asserted that the work was being "scamped," and on the question whether there was not the architect to redress their grievance, he replied that when he considered how architects were sometimes connected with building he felt that it was quite impossible to get any redress from them. He explained this by reference to cases where architects and surveyors had started building, and observed that under these circumstances it was useless to appeal to them. The strike lasted eight weeks, and in the end the contractors put in a fair foreman, and the work had been better done. A similar experience occurred in connexion with the "New Scotland Yard" buildings, and the man complained of was dismissed after representations had been made to the Home Secretary. The witness next described certain strikes which had taken place in regard to wages, and expressed himself as strongly in favour of a Board of Conciliation.

Mr. George Dew, Secretary of the London Building Trades Committee, was the next witness, and he strongly confirmed the views of the preceding witness respecting sub-letting. Being asked to explain this, he said the practice meant that the same amount of work was squeezed out of four men which in the ordinary way would require five men. In order to do that a man must adopt various methods of slovenly work. The work was pushed on in such an inferior manner that it was not only bad for the men but for the people for whom the work was being done. This applied to every class of building,—the evil prevailed in all the branches. The Council endeavoured to deal with the evil by inducing public authorities to insert in their contracts a clause prohibiting this practice. For this purpose they had appointed a special Committee, and the first body with whom

Cathedrals of England and Wales.

No. 15. CHICHESTER. Drawn by Mr. Beresford Pite A.R.I.B.A.

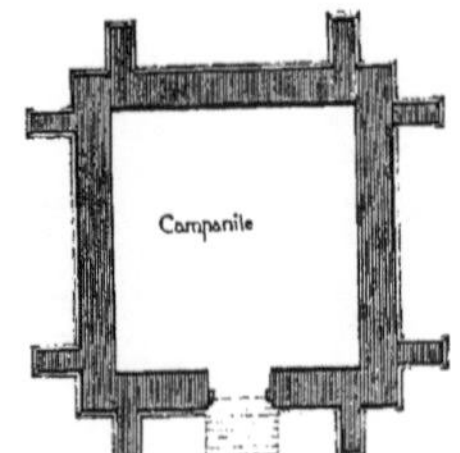

·THE·CATHEDRAL·CHURCH·

·CHICHESTER

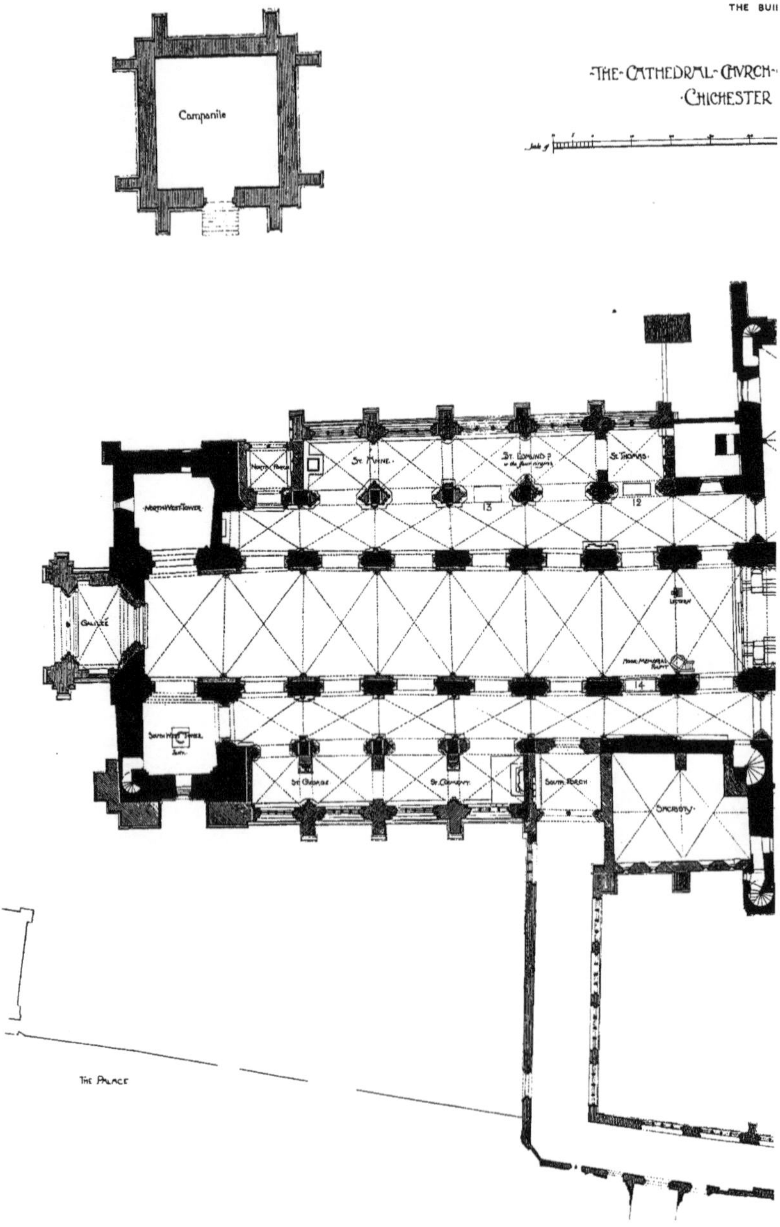

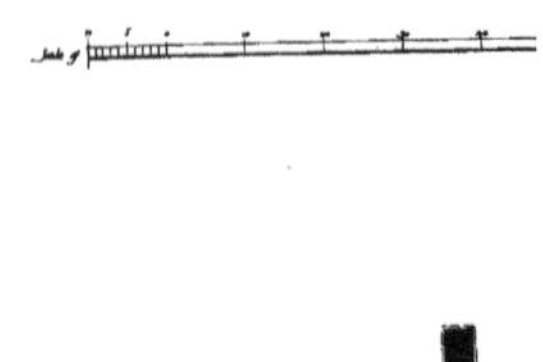

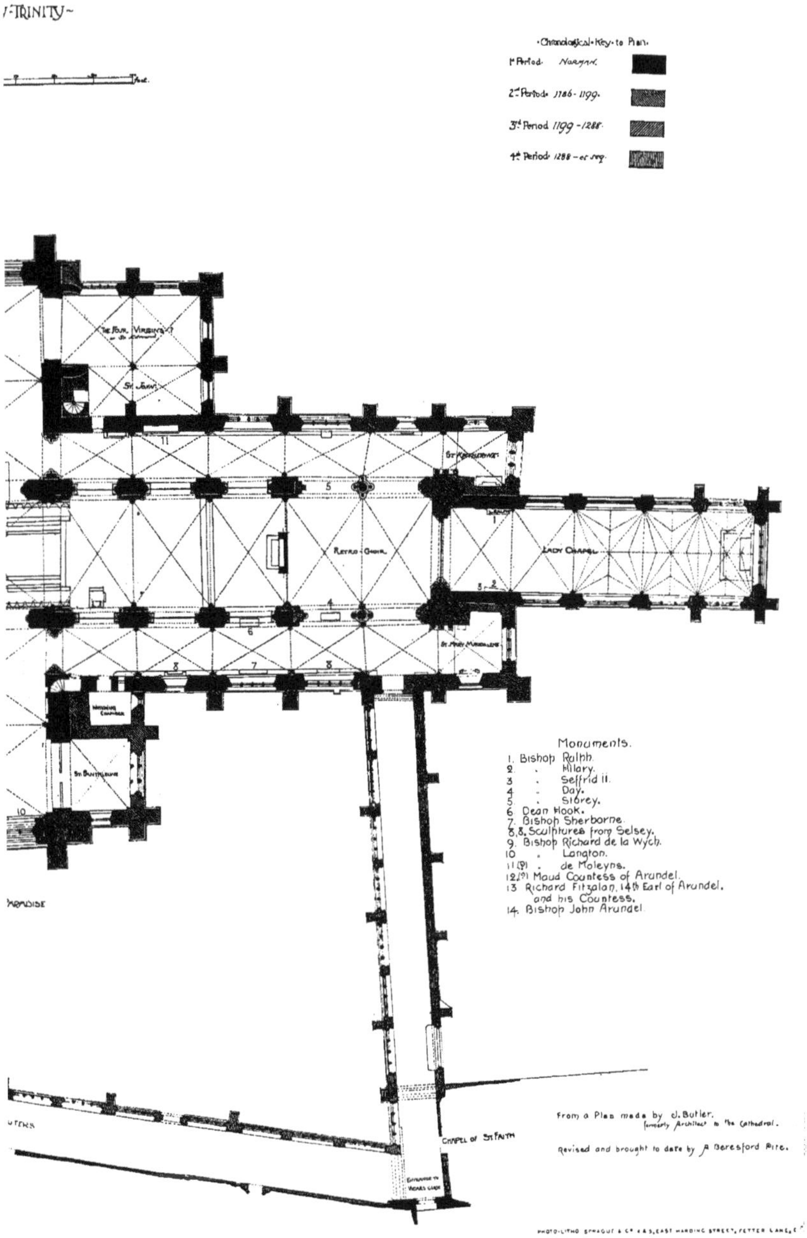

-TRINITY-
Chronological Key to Plan.
1st Period. Norman.
2nd Period. 1186-1199.
3rd Period 1199-1288.
4th Period. 1288 - et seq.
The Four Virgins
St. John
St. Katherine
Retro-Choir
Lady Chapel
St. Mary Magdalene
Watching Chamber
St. Pantaleone
Paradise
Chapel of St. Faith
Entrance to Vicars Close
Monuments.
1. Bishop Ralph.
2. " Hilary.
3. " Seffrid ii.
4. " Day.
5. " Storey.
6. Dean Hook.
7. Bishop Sherborne.
8, 8. Sculptures from Selsey.
9. Bishop Richard de la Wych.
10. " Langton.
11 (?) " de Moleyns.
12 (?) Maud Countess of Arundel.
13 Richard Fitzalan, 14th Earl of Arundel, and his Countess.
14. Bishop John Arundel.
From a Plan made by J. Butler, formerly Architect to the Cathedral.
Revised and brought to date by A. Beresford Pite.

PHOTO-LITHO SPRAGUE & Co 4 & 5, EAST HARDING STREET, FETTER LANE, E.C.

CHICHESTER CATHEDRAL: VIEW ACROSS NAVE.

CHICHESTER CATHEDRAL: BISHOP SHERBORNE'S TOMB.

PAINTED TILES.

¼ DOOR OF MOSQUE SULTAN DAAHIR BIBARS, CAIRO.

MOSQUE OF TOULOUN, CAIRO
(DETAIL OF PLASTER CARVING.)

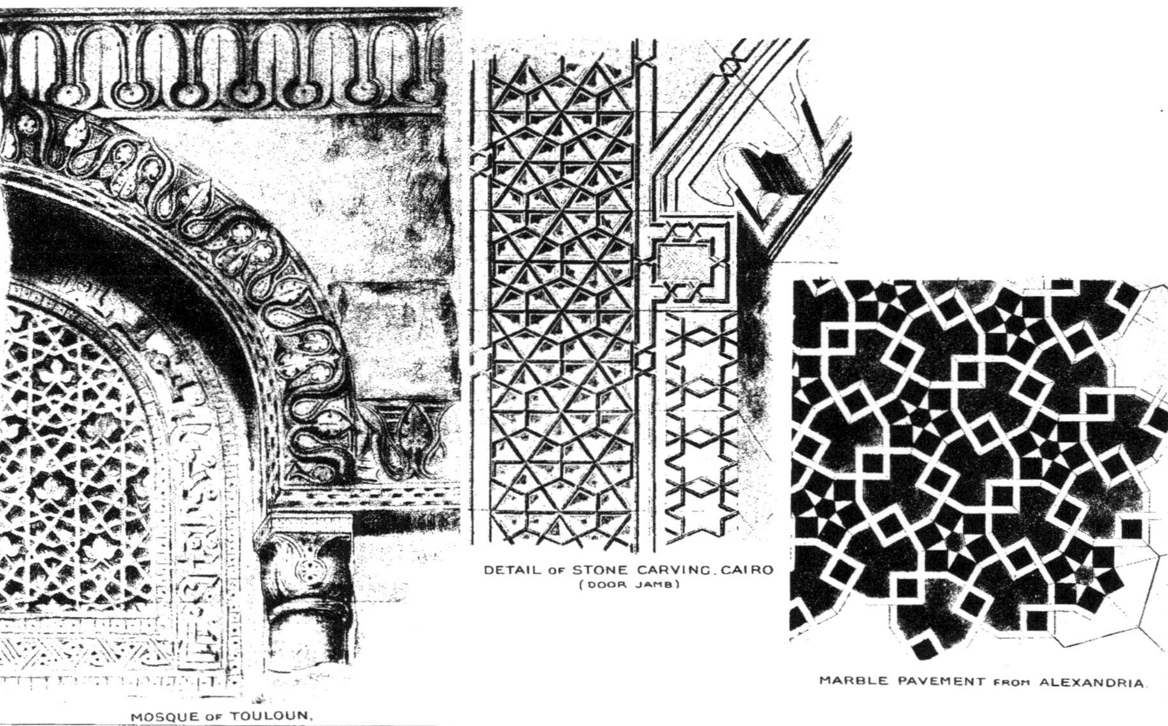

MOSQUE OF TOULOUN.
DETAIL OF STONE CARVING, CAIRO
(DOOR JAMB)
MARBLE PAVEMENT FROM ALEXANDRIA.

DETAILS OF SARACENIC ORNAMENT.

(In illustration of Professor Aitchison's Royal Academy lectures.)

they were successful was the London School Board. It was well known that some of the schools were falling to pieces, and in consequence costing the Board a large sum of money. This kind of work had become unbearable, and at last the workmen, who were being prejudiced by being hurried and forced, determined to submit to the system no longer. Accordingly, in 1888, the Council convened a conference of the various branches to consider what could be done, and the first result was a deputation to the First Commissioner of Works to induce him to insert a prohibitory clause in the Government contracts to prevent subletting, and to ensure the payment of the wages recognised in the trade. They adopted the same plan with the School Board, and had succeeded in securing a clause, not only forbidding this sub-letting, and providing for the payment of the recognised wages, but that the rates to be paid shall be attached to the contract. Moreover, they had gone a little further with the London County Council in this matter, and had secured the insertion of a clause providing for the rate of wages and also for the working hours, and also a penalty of 500*l*. for sub letting a contract. So far the penalty had not been enforced. With the Government they had not succeeded quite so well. Three years ago the contract for repairs and maintenance of all public buildings in the metropolis was in the hands of Messrs. Brass & Son, at a low rate of wages, viz., 1½d. per hour less than the trade-union rate. By this all union men were shut out from Government work. The contract was, in fact, let on distinctly sweating lines. The Government simply issued a schedule asking contractors for their tender of rates. The rate in the schedule would be 9½d. an hour; and the contractors would be asked what rebate they would make and how much they would return as discount. This schedule was issued every three years, and each time the contract was retaken there was, generally, a larger amount of discount, and this became so bad that when, three years ago, Messrs. Brass took it, 16½ per cent. was struck off. Therefore they could only pay 7½d. per hour when they ought to have paid 9d. Under these circumstances the Building Trades Committee made a representation to the Government, and ultimately got a resolution proposed in the House of Commons on February 13, 1891, on the subject. They first proposed, through Mr. Sydney Buxton, that in all Government contracts a clause should be inserted "requiring that the contractor shall, under penalty, observe the recognised customs and conditions as to rates of wages and working hours that prevail in each particular trade; and that the contractor should, under penalty, be prohibited from sub-letting any portion of his contract, except where the department concerned specially allows the sub-letting of such special portions of the work as would not be produced or carried out by the contractor in the ordinary course of his business." Mr. Plunket, First Commissioner of Works, after considerable debate on the motion, stated that be Government were in favour of the proposal, but key were not able to accept the wording of the esolution, and proposed instead the following:—

"That, in the opinion of this House, it is the duty of he Government in all Government contracts to make rovision against the evils recently disclosed before the weating Committee, to insert such conditions as may revent the abuse arising from sub-letting, and to make very effort to secure the payment of such wages as are enerally accepted as current in each trade for competent workmen."

That was agreed to by the House unanimously, ut it was not all they wanted. The question of ours was not included in the resolution, but if that ere done they would be satisfied. They did not ant the Government to fix the hours, but simply recognise in their contracts the hours agreed to etween employers and employed. Good as that esolution was, and determined as the House eemed to be to make the condition of the men etter, still the Government had broken faith with hem. In a schedule of wages presented to him y Mr. Plunket as to the rate to be paid in London, arpenters were to have 9d. an hour, and men of xtra skill 1d. more. Masons and painters, and ther men, were to have the same, but soon after ie contract was signed the rate for painters was ut at 8½d. to 9d. But after that rate had been ccepted by Messrs. Holland & Hannen, to whom e contract was let, they reduced the rate to 7½d. long correspondence had been going on between Trade Committee and the Office of Works, and compromise had now been effected, under which other ½d. was to be given, and the minimum was ed at 8d. On the question of hours, Mr. Dew pressed himself as in favour of eight hours; that is to say, that the Government should legislate for general eight hours, but that it should then by trade option, because some trades might int it and others not. If the Government uld only insert the hours clause in their conicts, that would have a great and good effect on e workmen throughout the country. Their olution was, in fact, as much in favour of contractors as of the men, or even more so, cause it would tend to put a stop to the present -throat system. Mr. Dew's next point was that, the building trade was carried on at great risk, ncipally from scaffolds falling, the Employers' ability Act ought to be amended. At present a contractor was allowed to insure himself out of his liability for accidents. A great deal of plant was used by builders, and it should be of the very best quality; but, if an employer could make an arrangement with an insurance company, it would be cheaper to do that than to spend more money on good plant. That was dangerous to the men, and the practice was ruining the trade, for the contractor, knowing he was insured whatever happened, did not care. Therefore, he wanted the Act altered to make the employer personally responsible.

The Duke of Devonshire: How can you prevent him from insuring?

Witness: Well, you might make it a penal offence.

The Chairman: You might say you would prevent a shipowner from insuring his ships?

Witness: Yes; I think it would be a good thing for the sailors, for I believe a great many lives are lost through insuring. The witness further urged that there should be a better system of inspecting builders' works,—not the premises being built, but the shops where the materials were being prepared. A large amount of machinery was employed, and accidents frequently occurred, for proper precautions were not taken to fence round the machinery,—the sawing machinery, for instance. Persons of all ages were employed on the machinery, and, in fact, two-thirds of the men and boys so employed had lost fingers. He had never seen an inspector going through these shops, and he knew no one who had; but he considered that as much care should be taken in those shops as in factories. Reverting to the strike at the Imperial Institute, he stated that all means possible were taken to settle it. In fact, they always tried to settle disputes amicably with the employers, by conference and conciliation, and it was never the fault of the workmen if they did not succeed. In this case they first asked the Commissioners of the Institute to interfere with the contractor, and to hold an investigation. They replied that they had no right to interfere between the contractor and his workmen, and refused to do so. The Committee, after the strike had lasted some time, again asked them to do so, but without success; and then, as a last resource, he got a petition signed by all the workmen and presented it to the Prince of Wales, asking him to intervene. How it came about he did not know, but the men were then successful, for the obnoxious man was removed, and the foreman was put back in his place. Stating, in answer to the Chairman, that he was not at present prepared to reply to questions respecting strikes in his trade in the last six months, and that that had better be left for another occasion, Mr. Dew gave some examples of discount being allowed to the Government. He observed that the *status* and character of the workmen were better maintained when they dealt directly with the contractor, and insisted that the middleman ought to be abolished, for the middleman caused scamped work, and that cast reflections on the men themselves. Speaking again with regard to hours, he said he would regulate that according to districts and towns. He would let London decide for itself, and then let every other large town do the same. He was not in favour of a universal eight hours, but of the proposal in the "Fabian Bill," which provided that, while an eight-hours' Bill should be passed by the Legislature, then any trade might by a two-thirds majority of votes come within the provisions of the Act. With that the masters had nothing to do; for, if the eight-hours' limit was adopted all round alike in each town or district, it would not matter to them. He again urged that if employers knew they had no insurance to fall back upon, they would be more careful, and there would be fewer accidents; but on this point he admitted that there might be a strong case for allowing mine-owners to insure, though he would allow no other exception. Finally, he mentioned that the wages under the Government three years' contracts had been raised by from 25 to 30 per cent., and that had made a great difference as to the character and efficiency of the men employed. The best class of men did not work under the old system, because the union would not allow them to do so.

Mr. G. J. Davies, of Manchester, formerly Chairman of the Amalgamated Society of Carpenters and Joiners, and Mr. F. Chandler, General Secretary of the same body, were examined together. The latter stated that the Society was formed in 1860, and that in that year there were 680 members, with an income of 321*l*.; but in 1870 the number had risen to 10,178, and their assets to 17,568*l*. In 1880 there were 17,764 members, with assets 46,395*l*.; and in 1890 there were 30,693 ordinary members and 803 trade sections, with assets 66,359*l*. Having described the objects of the Society, he said the wages varied in different localities. In London the rate was 9d. an hour; in Manchester, Liverpool, and Birmingham it was 8½d.; in Leeds, Sheffield, Leicester, and Derby it was 8d. Speaking generally, the rate in the North and in the Midlands was 8½d.; it was somewhat lower in the South of England, and lower again in the West. The working hours in London were 51½ in the summer and 47 in the winter; and in Manchester they were 52 in summer and 47 in winter. Referring to the strike in London, he stated that it lasted seven months. The strike was for increased pay and reduced hours, and in the end, as the result of arbitration, the men resumed work on the old scale of pay,—9d. an hour, but with a slight reduction in the hours per week. Thus practically the men in London had got fifty hours a week and 9d. an hour. The joint committees of masters and men had worked together excellently. Mentioning that the branches of the Society extended not only throughout the United Kingdom, but to some of our colonies, and to the United States, he said a great many members went to America, where they joined existing, or opened new, lodges; but owing to the relative cheapness of living in this country he thought the men were quite as well off at home as those who went to the States. With respect to the question of insurance, he admitted that the Employers' Liability Act was fairly effective, but he considered that employers ought to be made personally responsible. Insurance took away any motive for protecting the men; if employers were able to shift their responsibility on to the insurance companies, then the whole object and spirit of the Act would be defeated. Therefore, he would alter the Act so as to bring them under the common law. Mr. Davies took a similar view on this question, and held that insurance by employers ought to be abolished, for it made them careless as to their plant and as to the safety of the men. With better organisation the conditions of trade had greatly improved, and the relations between masters and men had likewise improved. The Society's working rules had always provided for masters and men meeting (six on each side) to arrange disputes, and they had generally come to an amicable understanding without having to resort to arbitration. Alluding to the Labour Bureau of the Board of Trade, he acknowledged that the information it had supplied on trade questions had been very valuable, so far as it went, but he wished to see the organisation improved, in order that the workmen should have as much information about the employers as the latter had respecting the employed.

Mr. W. Knox, Secretary of the National Association of Master Builders, Liverpool, described the existing state of affairs in the building trades in that city. Correcting Mr. Chandler by stating that the wages in Liverpool were 8d., and not 8½d. an hour, he stated that the relations between the masters and the men were amicable, and experience showed that good organisation on both sides led to good feeling. They found the best workmen among the unionists, but when engaging men they did not ask them whether they were unionists or not, and they kept no black lists. Extra pay was given for overtime, and compensation was given for accidents. Labour-saving machinery was introduced whenever and wherever practicable. He was of opinion that sub-contracting worked well and harmlessly, and he denied that insurance against risks made the employers careless as to the men's safety. There had long been a system of arbitration in Liverpool in case of disputes, and it had never failed but once, viz., in 1890, when the men refused to abide by the decision of the arbitrator. A strike ensued, and lasted six months, when the matter was again referred to arbitration, and the men accepted what the employers had at first offered them. The masters had a system of mutual insurance, but they wished to see a system established jointly between the masters and the men, for they found that more money was often spent in litigation than was eventually paid as compensation. The London strike had lost the men 200,000*l*. in wages, and, after all, they had to accept the masters' original offer; but if there had been a Board of Arbitration in London, such as there was in Liverpool, he believed the dispute would have been settled without a strike.

Scotch evidence being next taken,

Mr. J. Beveridge, of Glasgow, Secretary of the Associated Carpenters and Joiners of Scotland, stated that the Society was established in 1861, and in that year the members numbered only about 500, but it now had a membership of 5,795, out of a total of 7,000 unionists in these trades. The witness having mentioned that the Society had fifteen branches in England and two in Ireland, he was invited to account for the singular circumstance, as it appeared to the Commissioners, that an essentially Scotch association had English and Irish offshoots, especially as there was a very strong Amalgamated Society of Carpenters and Joiners in England. This he did by explaining that they were instituted mainly for the convenience of members who left Scotland in search of work. The English branches were mainly composed of Scotchmen, but still there was a fair number of English members, while the two Irish branches, in Belfast and Londonderry, were composed chiefly of Irishmen. In the next place he stated that wages varied in Scotland according to locality. In Glasgow the rate was 8½d. an hour, but in Aberdeen and Inverness it was 6½d., and he partly accounted for this extent of variation by the fact that wages were generally highest where the trades were well organised. Aberdeen, he said, was very much behind Glasgow and other large towns in regard to wages. But while there was that inequality in wages, they had equality in working hours in Scotland, and employment was fairly regular, except in the winter. A good deal of machinery was used, and there was no hostility to it on the part of the men. The trade unions were generally recognised by the employers, and the unions claimed the right to refuse to work with non-unionists. Upon this point the witness was somewhat closely pressed by the Commissioners.

The Chairman: Do you think that a wise and sound policy?

Witness: We think it is only through the unions that a number of advantages have been derived, and the non-unionists would reap the same benefits. They would get the same wages.

Do you think that is consistent with perfect freedom and individual liberty?

Witness: The employers have the same right as ourselves.

Then you think there is nothing wrong in the employers making black lists?

No.

Then you think employers are perfectly justified in putting a mark against certain men and circulating their names through the trade to prevent their obtaining employment, because they may be leading members of a trades union?

I maintain that the employers have the same right as the workmen have. We have no black list.

If you say it is a sound policy that a non-unionist may be struck against wherever he goes, how can you complain of employers for doing the same?

We do not complain. Non-unionists are sometimes as good as unionists.

Is it not hard for them to have to contend against the unionists?

It is equally hard for the unionists to have to contend against them. The contention is the other way: if a man is not connected with us in a dispute he is against us.

The witness further said that the relations between the employers and the employed were generally amicable, and there were very few strikes in Scotland. Some of their branches had Boards of Conciliation, and generally he was in favour of that method. In Glasgow there was a sub-committee of the men appointed to meet a sub-committee of masters, who only met on special occasions. Regular fixed meetings would, he thought, be better, and would tend to the disappearance of disputes. During the last ten years the Society had spent 4,109*l.*; but as the organisation had improved, the relations with the employers had been better and the strikes fewer. They were anxious to settle disputes peacefully.

Mr. J. Brough, secretary of the Glasgow Branch of the Operative Masons' Society, followed, and after giving details respecting the membership, he mentioned that the wages in 1860 were 4½d. an hour, but they rose gradually until 1877, when they stood as high as 10d. In the following year, however, they fell away to as low as 6d., and this he attributed mainly to the failure of the Glasgow Bank, which put a stop to the building trade. By last year, however, the rate had risen to 8d. He described the relations between masters and men as good, and expressed himself in favour of an eight hours legal day, but admitted that it might not be right for him to insist upon other trades only working a certain time because he chose to do so, and said he had no objection to the use of machinery, if it was not employed longer than the manual labour.

This Section has now adjourned for a fortnight. When it meets again further building trade witnesses will be called.

"THE BUILDER" ALBUM OF ROYAL ACADEMY DRAWINGS.

WE hope that those architects who are sending drawings to the Royal Academy will assist us to keep up this collection of illustrations of Royal Academy Architecture annually, in the same manner in which it was commenced in 1891, by lending us for publication whatever drawings they have for exhibition for this year's Royal Academy.

Every contributor of a drawing which is exhibited at the Royal Academy is presented with a copy of the Album, containing all the Royal Academy drawings of the year that have been published in this journal.

Architectural drawings have to be delivered at the Academy on March 25, 26, and 28. All drawings sent to the office of the *Builder* for illustration will be duly delivered at the Royal Academy by the publisher of the *Builder*, and removed and returned to their owners at the close of the Exhibition. It is, of course, understood that such drawings should not appear in any other publication.

We must also especially draw attention to the necessity for sending all such drawings duly provided with the descriptive labels required by the Royal Academy. We cannot undertake the responsibility of writing and affixing the required labels, which must rest with the owners of the drawings.

Chichester Cathdl. Canopied Tomb of Bishop Langton etc. in South Transept.

Illustrations.

CHICHESTER CATHEDRAL.*

"CHICHESTER has received a heavy blow, and England a warning," are the words with which this journal announced the fall of the central tower and spire of the Cathedral in the *Builder* of March 2, 1861, and the most instructive record of the great collapse is told in full by an eye-witness in the ensuing article. To the visitor of to-day, whether architect or layman, the chief interest of the place lies in the story of the fall, and a thrilling and almost tragical tone, quite unusual in the literature of Cathedral buildings, pervades the description referred to. In spite of the advice of eminent architects in consultation, aided by an experienced civil engineer and three contractors, with all the forces that they could bring to bear, the beautiful tower and spire that had stood for 600 years, with slow deliberation akin to stateliness, descended into the body of the church, and laid itself in a conical heap. The mystery is not yet solved how it came to pass that what had stood for so many centuries, in the year 1861, after some months of warning and preparation, collapsed, in defiance of all that modern skill could effect.

The history of most English Cathedrals is interspersed with fires and falls; but they are mostly remote from our time, and do not come home to our minds with any vividness; but one cannot avoid the remark that such catastrophes in the Middle Ages were made the occasions of greater elaboration and beauty in the re-erected structure, as we shall see was the case at Chichester in the twelfth century, while in our time the greatest architectural authorities that could be brought to bear upon such a situation only considered the opportunity as one for imitating with accuracy all that had been done in the earlier ages, and in one modern work have reproduced the rough-backed stonework of the Norman imposts and shafts and the delicate traceries of Decorated diapering. Surely the fall and reconstruction of Chichester tower and spire should have tragic reflections for architects in this age of light and progress!

Following the method adopted by the late Professor Willis in his "Architectural History of Chichester Cathedral," the plan that is now published indicates four periods of its constructive history. Generally speaking, the Cathedral was as complete when first erected in Norman times as it is to-day, and the work of the subsequent builders was confined to rebuilding portions of the Norman church on differing lines, and in throwing out a series of chapels from each aisle of the nave, and in extending the Lady Chapel. The four periods are: 1. Norman. 2. Works consequent on the fire of 1186. 3. Addition of chapels on the south side of the nave. 4. Similar additions on the north side, and some other works. These divisions correspond roughly with the eleventh to the twelfth, the twelfth to the thirteenth, thirteenth and early fourteenth, and fourteenth and fifteenth centuries respectively. The building internally is a Norman frame, clothed with an early thirteenth-century dress, with more fully-developed accessories.

* This series of illustrations of the Cathedrals of England and Wales was begun in our issue of January 3, 1891. A list of those already illustrated, with particulars of future arrangements, will be found on page xxii.

and throughout there is no breach or want of harmony in the Mediæval work. The See of the South Saxons was founded at Selsey ("Seals Island"), a few miles distant, by St. Wilfrid, and removed to Chichester after the Conquest, in 1082, in accordance with the Conqueror's decree, that the Bishops were to be located in the larger towns by Stigand, who was William's chaplain. Two curious carved slabs fo Our Lord raising Lazarus and of His meeting with Mary and Martha, now in the choir, of Saxon workmanship, are said to have been brought from Selsey. Gosfried succeeded Stigand, and of his penance for some unknown default, and absolution by the Pope, a small leaden sepulchral cross, preserved in the Cathedral, tells; and he was followed by Radulph, 1091-1123, the founder of the Cathedral building. Under this Bishop the whole of the Norman work which we now see was executed.

His plan was cruciform with the four great Norman arches of the crossing, whose *fac-similes* exist, carrying a low Norman tower, the presbytery eastwards terminating in a large apse and ambulatory; two circular chapels and a prolonged square Lady-chapel opened from the ambulatory. The foundation of the apse exists below the paving of the present presbytery, and the commencement of the radiating wall can be clearly seen in the masonry of the easternmost bay of the choir aisle from the cloister garden. The position of the Norman external triforium window, not over the centre of the square wall below, but to the westward at this point, also clearly points to the diminishing bays which radiated around the apse. Three of the five bays of the Lady-chapel are of Norman walling, and it will be, therefore, seen that the original Cathedral of Radulph extended nearly as far east as the present one. The transepts were without aisles, but each had an apsidal chapel on its eastern side of the diameter of the arches now existing in the transepts. That on the north side can be traced in the springing of circular masonry from the wall in the chamber over the now altered chapel below. The nave consisted, as now, of eight bays, four consistent in style with the work of the choir and the four western bays differing slightly in detail and dimensions (see lithograph "View across Nave"). These may not have been erected until after a fire which occurred in 1114, during the same episcopate, of which we are informed by Malmesbury, who states that Henry I. principally assisted in repairing the damage. This difference in the dates of the nave shows that the eastern portion of the church was built first. The ground story, triforium, and clearstory of the Norman church remain, altered only on the face presented to the nave. The triforium is large, and lighted by small windows in the external walls. The side aisles are similarly intact, the outer wall and windows only having been altered. These were vaulted, though vaulting was not contemplated for the nave, which, undoubtedly, had the usual ceiling and low wooden roof. Two western towers and a connecting front completed the church, though there is no evidence that this work was finished. The two lower stories of the existing southern tower are Norman.

This completes the account of Bishop Radulph's work,—a singularly great achievement, as his building, unlike most others, remains of sufficient dignity and elasticity to serve the purposes of subsequent ages. His character and work were as remarkable as his church. He withstood William Rufus manfully in Anselm's defence, and distributed the whole of his estate to the poor. The tomb in the Lady Chapel in the western bay of the north wall, marked "Radulfus Epi," has a special interest as probably being the modest resting-place of one of the group of great building Bishops of the Norman epoch, who created so many of our English Cathedrals.

The second period of architectural activity does not open until after the great fire of 1186, in the episcopate of Siegfried, formerly Dean of the Cathedral, who was Bishop from 1180 till 1204, and fourth after Radulph. This fire involved the greater part of the city as well as the church, and the Bishop energetically divided his rebuilding benefactions equally between both. The roofs and fittings of the Cathedral were completely destroyed, and the walls consequently damaged in the upper ground stories by the burning and falling timbers. The mischief, however, to the walls was only superficial, and the Norman construction, perhaps with the exception of the apse, remained intact. Siegfried refaced the lower story below the imposts of the piers throughout the nave with Caen stone, and rebuilt the inner face and arcade of the clearstory. The new Early English spirit in architecture was now beginning to glow throughout the land. St. Hugh of Lincoln came to his see in the year of the Chichester fire. Thomas à Becket had been martyred at Canterbury twelve years before, and four years before Chichester suffered the Cathedral of Canterbury was destroyed by fire, and already was beginning to arise from its ruins as the most beautiful shrine in England, rich with the offerings of pilgrims to the martyr's tomb. But Chichester and Siegfried had no wonder-working saint. St. Richard of Chichester was scarcely born, as he was not consecrated Bishop until 1245 (he died 1253 and was canonised 1261), and no very extensive or costly alterations could be made to suit the new taste. But the skill of the Bishop's architect enclosed the Norman arches with a face of delicate English moulding in place of the large rude roll, and carried it upon slender Purbeck shafts with gracefully-carved capitals instead of upon the heavy semi-round Norman ones. To the side aisles these earlier and ruder features remain now for comparison.

Moulded Purbeck strings were inserted above and below the triforium throughout, and the new clearstory arcade had shafts and caps of similar material. The whole Cathedral, nave and aisles, was then re-roofed with a simple and elegant quadripartite vault supported on delicate triple shafts with foliaged capitals carved in Purbeck.

The pointed arch first appears in the new vault in juxtaposition with the Norman work, Siegfried having retained in his reserved outer arches of the ground story the older form. The whole of this work was most carefully bonded into the walls, and its present condition testifies to the constructive as well as artistic skill of its architect. Limited as the Bishop evidently was in means, his simple economy in the body of the church enabled him to accomplish notable work in the retro-choir, which he built upon the site of Radulph's embryo chevet. Whether the arches and columns of the apse became unsafe on losing the support of the abutting roofs during the fire, or whether they were purposely removed, does not appear, but probably the former supposition is correct. Siegfried, being in sympathy with the new national life that was being expressed in buildings throughout the country, departs from the French type, and plans a square-ended choir with two square chapels to take the place of Radulph's circular ones, but preserves the Norman square lady-chapel beyond. Thus the area of the Cathedral was not extended, but its character altered by a bold stroke from Norman to English, and though, even in the new work, Siegfried retained the circular form for the enclosing arches, which mark his work as, after all, transitional it is the product, not of the Norman conquerors or their descendants, but of a fresh spring of art in the life of the new English people. The retro-choir or presbyery is a work of singular beauty of design and detail; the proportions, though low, are suited to the circular arches employed, and there is a

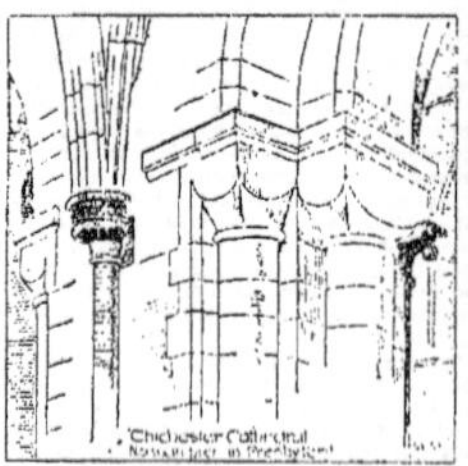

breadth of treatment and display of wall-surface, especially in the design of the east wall, that most satisfactorily closes the Cathedral vista, and yet opens it into the lady-chapel without the weakness of result or awkwardness of expedient that exists to mind in so many

other cases. The general height and spacing of the adjoining earlier work was retained, but the strings above and below the triforium were stepped up to provide increased height for the wider arches and mouldings of the ground story. The piers are of singular and beautiful design, each member of the Purbeck cluster of shafts manifestly doing its own work around the central column, which is also of marble. The capitals are fully carved with rich trefoil leafage, and are proportioned in depth to the varying diameter of their shafts. The abacuses are varied, some round and some square, in each story. The triforium of the east wall is very fully decorated with the best type of Early carving,—strong, virile, small figures,—Our Lord in majesty in the centre spandrel, with angels on each side in the tympanums of the adjoining arches, with clusters and bands of interesting foliage, clear and simple in form, and so justly recessed that it is far more effective from the floor of the church than from any nearer position. The arches of the clear-story arcade are all pointed; in the nave only the centre one was pointed, the supporting side arches being round. The vault is continuous with the new one to the nave and choir. The work of this period includes the rebuilding of the transept chapels, thus removing the remaining apsidal terminations from the plan. Adjoining the north transept a large double chapel was built, elegantly vaulted from a central marble-shaft. After doing duty for centuries as a parish church, these chapels are now used as the chapter library, a circular stair gives access to a large upper chamber, in the wall of which are to be seen the springing stones of the former Norman apse. In this room now repose extensive remains of the fifteenth-century wooden reredos. The chapel in the south transept was simply re-designed by Siegfried, and a chamber, either for watching friars or some subsidiary purpose, fitted into the space between it and the aisle wall. The double Norman window from the aisle exists into this room, the only one of its kind left. The south porch of the nave, now opening into the later cloisters, is of this period; a double arch with centre shaft, above which is a quatrefoil niche for a figure, forms the porch. The sacristy, which adjoins the porch and the south transept, though of the same style, must have been built after the porch, as the wall of the latter, though obviously lengthened and used, and is of a greater thickness. This is a fine apartment, and is vaulted. This room would have served the purposes of a chapter-house, but it is believed that though the site is lost, there was a detached building for the purpose. A porch on the north side of the nave, with a double arch and centre column supporting a tympanum with a trefoil niche, and the necessary addition of buttresses everywhere for the new vaults, complete the records of the Second Period. Excepting the sacristy, there seems to be no doubt that all these works were carried out by Siegfried, and the rebuilt Cathedral was dedicated in 1199 to the Holy Trinity. It was in this year that Bishop Siegfried assisted at the coronation of King John. A special chronological interest is thus given to the Early-English work at Chichester included in this description, as the date of the fire, 1086, and that of the dedication are recorded, and within the comparatively narrow period of thirteen years we are able to observe the genuinely national style springing into power, and as yet treating the pointed arch not as a matter of necessity, or the round arch as something to be avoided.

With the Cathedral so far completed, the scope of the two remaining periods is narrowed, and it can easily be imagined that if no local saint had attracted pilgrims and canonisation to his remains there would have been no need for further extension of the plan. The Third Period, however, embracing the thirteenth and the opening of the fourteenth centuries, witnessed the erection of two chapels adjoining the south aisle of the nave, each occupying two bays in length, and filling up the unoccupied space between the south porch and the south-west tower. They are divided from each other by a cross-wall, which has been removed in post-Reformation times. The eastern of these two chapels was dedicated to St. Clement, and the western to St. George. The south aisle wall was pierced by four wide arches of the period, and a width and effect gained in the Cathedral nave that was soon to be emulated on the other side. Large windows were provided with gables over them, and the ridge of the vault was tilted up in order to include a larger window area. The similarity and the slight development of the style shows that no great period had elapsed since the last link had been added to the architectural chain. A small chapel in the easternmost available bay of the north aisle was built at this period, and dedicated to St. Thomas; it contains a very beautiful and perfect stone reredos arcade and adjuncts. There are traces in the southern chapels of such reredoses, but in its present condition the northern one is quite unique.

To this period we must assign the central tower that lasted until thirty years ago; the spire to the succeeding period; the battlements and turrets are not original. The rose window in the east gable of the choir, which is of graceful geometrical design, belongs to the Third Period; also the upper story of the south-west tower. The earliest works of the Fourth period are the two remaining chapels of the north aisle, which very exactly correspond with the earlier ones on the south side. They were, however, only separated from each other by a screen-wall. These two groups of chapels give, with the nave and aisles, such width to Chichester, that it is difficult to realise that it is second only to York among English Cathedrals, the former being 90 ft. and the latter a little over 100 ft. across the nave. Very picturesque and sombre effects of light and shade and of grouped arches give interest to what is quite a small interior in general appearance The Lady-chapel was lengthened by the addition of two bays, and the same character given to the three Norman bays. This was executed by Bishop Gilbert de Sancto Leofardo, 1288—1304. For purity and beauty of detail this work can be considered as one of the best examples of the early fourteenth century. The western Galilee porch of the nave is of about the same period, but the date of its erection cannot be fixed by contemporaneous facts; its contains a founder's tomb on its south wall, which may be that of Bishop Berghestede, the predecessor of Gilbert, who died in 1287, and was buried after a pilgrimage to Rome to be absolved from excommunication, and whose authority was obtained for the works. The design of the porch is simple and large, the mouldings and piers marking the steady development of the Geometrical into the Decorated style. The very fine Decorated window in the south transept, with the adjoining wall, buttresses, gable, and rose window, are the work of Bishop John de Langton, and recorded as given by him in 1308. The great window occupies the whole southern wall, and immediately below its south-east corner is the canopied tomb of Langton (see illustration, page 186); he was Chancellor of England, as was also his successor, Robert Stratford.

The parapets to the nave are Decorated in period. The unusually crooked character of the building, in spite of its homogeneity of design, made their treatment a matter for the exercise of considerable skill. The difficulties have been overcome by the use of two corbel tables, one over the other, the varying projection of the corbels making the parapet straight without drawing attention to the way in which it is effected. The spire, with its solid dormers and octagonal pinnacles, was added to the central tower in the fifteenth century; the proportions are distinctly elegant, and the ornament refined and well concentrated. The traceried bands around the spire emphasise the satisfactory diminution of the spire, which is of a somewhat wide angle of 13 deg. Fergusson remarks that this is similar to Lichfield, and with it differs from Salisbury, Norwich, and Louth, which are only 10 deg., and far too slender.

Passing on to Early Perpendicular work, a large window was inserted in the north transept to emulate Langton's on the south, but was much more clumsily carried out, a great flying buttress being necessary to save the upper portion of the north wall from falling. The settlements caused by this window are apparent now. An upper story was added to the sacristy with two buttresses. This room was used as a consistory court, and from it access is obtained to a vaulted treasury over the south porch by a secret door in the panelling.

The episcopate of Sherborne of New College, Oxford, 1508-1536, was a time of much gain to the Cathedral. There existed until a short time previous to the fall of the central tower in 1861 a very beautiful stone rood-screen, known as the Arundel Shrine, containing two shrines within a graceful and richly-vaulted arcade of Early Perpendicular work, behind the eastern wall of which were staircases giving access to the rood, and in later times to the organ, as shown in the sketch. Most of the decorative details of this screen are preserved in the north-west tower. Within the choir Sherborne erected a complete range of simple but beautiful stalls under a canopy arcade returning at the back of the rood-screen. A fine reredos and similar screen work was also erected by him, and he provided some most interesting painted decorations, by employing an Italian, named Theodore Bernardi, some of which remain on the vaulting of the Lady Chapel, and in the screens of kings and bishops portraits that lined the south transept walls. A drawing of Bishop Sherborne's tomb, by Mr. R. W. Paul, will be found among the lithographs in the present number.

The cloisters, which lie around the south transept as a centre, instead of against the south aisle of the nave, as more usual, are Perpendicular, with a simple arched wooden rafter roof; the detail is interesting, and the enclosing wall of the three sides is probably of very varying dates, and its irregular shape indicates that it formed the boundaries of buildings to which the cloisters lead, rather than that it was laid out on the usual plan. In the south-east corner the cloister passes under the west end of St. Faith's Chapel, the gable of which stands upon the angle and adjoining bay of the east walk. An archway at this point opens into an interesting Vicar's close, one side of which only remains, with the ancient hall adjoining St. Faith's. The Bishop's Palace occupies the corresponding angle of the precinct. The massive detached campanile to the north-west of the Cathedral is of Late Perpendicular style (see sketch, page 187), and appears by its breadth and low proportions to have been designed for the purpose of emphasis-

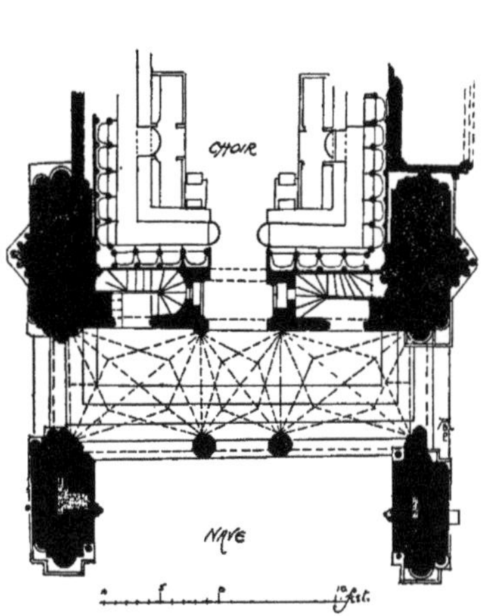

Plan of Ancient Rood Screen at Chichester Cathedral, between the tower piers, called the "Arundel Shrine," and the return stalls of the choir. Drawn by Mr. Beresford Pite.

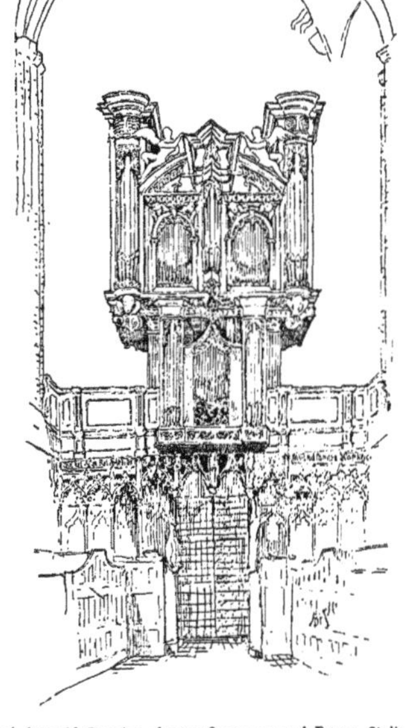

Sketch from old Drawing, showing Organ-case and Return Stalls, Chichester Cathedral, before the fall of the tower. Drawn by Mr. Beresford Pite.

; the gracefulness of the ancient central ire. There is a Renaissance monument to shop Sherborne in the south choir aisle, intained by his former college. In the

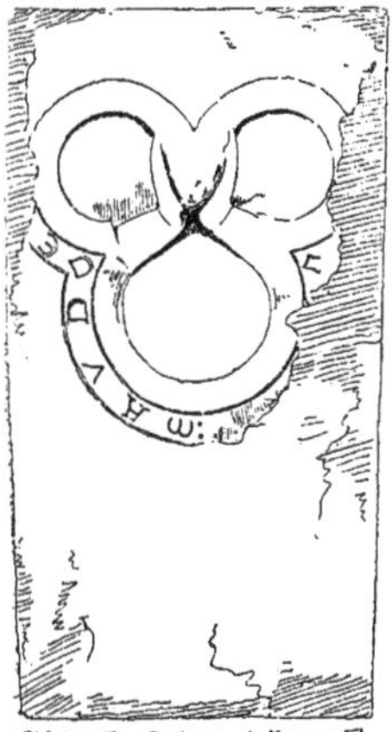

Chichester Cathedral - Monumental slab now in N. Aisle of Presbytery.

rliamentary wars Chichester was stormed by aller, whose men damaged the monuments d organ. Sir Christopher Wren rebuilt the per portion of the central spire, and devised a heavy pendulum within it of timber to preserve its centre of gravity under wind pressure. Nothing, however, since the completion in the thirteenth century can be compared in importance to the works preceding the fall of the tower in our time. The stonework walls of the Arundel Shrine, with the return stalls and handsome organ, were removed to throw open the nave for services with the choir, and shortly after the fall took place, destroying shrine, stalls, and organ, though the damage resulting to the rest of the building was comparatively slight. Sir Gilbert Scott rebuilt the tower, with its supports, and added 6 ft. to its height. Old prints exist, and a view was published in the *Builder* of March 2, 1861, showing the old proportions, which were, perhaps, not improved upon. A very large masonry reredos was erected in the presbytery by the late Mr. Slater, and Messrs. Bodley and Garner have recently finished a large and delicate oak choir-screen. The comfortable proportions and effect of the old choir will not, however, be regained until Bishop Sherborne's oak reredos and the return stalls are restored to connect what are now but two detached ranges of stalls and canopies, and complete the interest of a very satisfactory interior.

A. B. P.

VIEW ACROSS THE NAVE, CHICHESTER CATHEDRAL.

THE view has been taken from the south aisle looking north-east, showing a portion of the chapels beyond, which were thrown out in Decorated times. The large mass of the nave piers, however, makes a good view of the whole width of the church difficult to obtain.

R. W. PAUL.

BISHOP SHERBORNE'S TOMB, CHICHESTER CATHEDRAL.

THIS is the best-preserved tomb in the Cathedral, and the most elaborate in design. It is of alabaster, with a good deal of colour. This and the head of the effigy have been restored, and the monument is kept in repair by New College, Oxford. The heraldic charges on the shields of the tomb itself have been painted in a very indifferent manner. Those on the shield at the back of the tomb are better, and are carved in relief. A curious part of the design is the raking of the jambs of the canopy, the little turrets which flank it being, however, upright. On the front of the tomb is the following marginal inscription:—

NON INTRES
IN IVDICIVM
CVM SERVO
TVO DOMINE
Robert Shurburne

The tomb was made during the Bishop's lifetime, and is an effective piece of work, bearing strong evidence of Renaissance feeling. Sherborne's stalls still exist, and the remains of painted screens are in the transept. The fragments of his reredos, of wood, are lying at present in the room over the library.

R. W. PAUL.

DETAILS OF SARACENIC ORNAMENT.

THESE formed some of the diagrams illustrating Professor Aitchison's sixth and last Royal Academy Lecture on Saracenic Architecture, printed in full in this number. They are chiefly illustrations of the geometric ornament of the Saracens, to which is added an example of floral ornament executed in tiles.

PROVIDENT INSTITUTION OF BUILDERS' FOREMEN AND CLERKS OF WORKS:

ANNUAL DINNER.

THE annual dinner of the donors, subscribers, members, and friends of this old-established Institution (which has just attained its Jubilee, having been established January 31, 1842) was held in the Venetian Saloon of the Holborn Restaurant on Saturday, Feb. 27, Mr. J. Howard Colls (of the firm of Colls & Sons) in the chair, supported by a very large number of the members and friends of the Institution,—so large, indeed, that some of the friends had to dine in adjacent rooms.

The Chairman, in proposing the principal toast of the evening, "Prosperity to the Institution," said that when he was asked to accept the position of President of the Institution he accepted it at once, without any hesitation, having previously made himself acquainted with the good work that it had done and was continuing to do year by year. No one could read the annual reports of the Institution without being convinced of its value and importance to a large section of the building trade. Before entering upon his position as President he had spoken about it to the respected Governor of the Institution, Mr. George Plucknett, whom he was very glad to see present with them that evening, and Mr. Plucknett said: "I have been connected with the Institution for thirty years, and I feel sure that it is doing and has done a great work." Higher testimony than that he could not have. As they all knew very well, builders' foremen and clerks of works were very often associated together,—not always quite so happily as on the present occasion,—and they were all the better for the opportunities of intercourse which they had through the medium of that Institution. The importance and responsibility of the duties which they fulfilled in their respective callings could not be over-estimated by architects or builders. The architects and builders, as well as their clients, owed a very great deal to the foremen and clerks of works, who were to be commended for combining together in an effort for mutual help and providence. But he confessed that it was a great mystery to him why the Institution possessed, comparatively speaking, so few members. Here was an Institution, excellent in its aims and objects, admirably managed, and possessed of considerable funded property, and yet it did not number nearly so many members on its roll as it ought to have, considering the number of men there must be who were fully qualified to join the Institution. The advantages of the Institution to those whom it was designed to benefit could not be questioned. To quote a few words from the annual report for 1891, "the advantages of the Institution begin to show our colleagues the advisability of joining and putting their shoulders to the wheel while young to help to build up a provision for themselves, their widows, and orphans. Eighteen new members have joined during the year, being the largest number for several years. This is very gratifying to the Directors; but, at the same time, they would urge on all our members the necessity of caution in introducing new candidates, so that everyone that joins may be a credit to the Institution." Those were admirable words, and he trusted that one result of that gathering would be a substantial accession of new and worthy members. With the toast he proposed, he had very great pleasure in coupling the name of Mr. Bedford, one of the secretaries.

The toast was heartily received, and Mr. Bedford, in reply, expressed his gratification at the fact that no fewer than 363 friends of the Institution were present to testify to their interest in it.

Mr. G. Groome, in an amusing speech, proposed "The Governor, Trustees, Donors, Subscribers, and Visitors," coupled with the name of the Governor, Mr. George Plucknett. This toast was also very heartily received.

Mr. Plucknett, in replying, reviewed the work of the Institution, but expressed regret that it had only eighty-eight members, while there ought to be hundreds, if not thousands.

Mr. J. Mowlem Burt, in proposing "The Architects, Engineers, and Surveyors," coupled with the name of Mr. H. Percy Monckton, F.R.I.B.A., referred to the responsibilities which devolved upon architects, engineers, and builders in the carrying out of buildings. They could not afford to work for only eight hours a day, or even for only ten hours; their responsibilities and anxieties could not be dropped in a moment, as they could be by the workman when he "downed tools."

Mr. Monckton replied, and referred in highly appreciative terms to the work of a good foreman and a good clerk of works.

Mr. J. Adams proposed "The Builders," coupled with the name of Mr. John Mowlem Burt, who, in reply, again referred to the anxieties of builders, especially with regard to accidents and the Employers' Liability Act. Builders found that, do what they might in the way of providing proper plant, appliances, scaffolding, &c., many workmen appeared to have no thought whatever for their own lives and limbs, nor any care for those of their fellow workmen. The result was that accidents were of frequent occurrence, and these led to vexatious actions for damages against the employers,—actions too frequently prompted by unprincipled lawyers.

The remaining toasts were "The Chairman" (proposed by Mr. J. W. H. Bedford), and "The Press" (proposed by the Chairman, and coupled with the name of the representative of the *Builder*).

During the evening, subscriptions and donations to the amount of about 110*l.* were announced by the secretary.

Correspondence.

To the Editor of THE BUILDER.

CONCRETE FOR ARTISANS' DWELLINGS.

SIR,—I cannot see why "Surveyor" should be so anxious to avoid iron joists, for they are cheap enough. I am writing far from price-lists and formulæ, but I think that two rolled-iron joists, 10in. in depth, dividing each room into three moderate sized bays, would cost about 5*l.* for the two. Against this "extra" there would be, of course, an "omission" of concrete, by reason of the layer having to span, say, 4 ft. instead of 12 ft.

The iron joists would tie the walls together,—a very necessary precaution, if there be none of wood,—and the centreing for the concrete could be hung from them instead of being strutted. They would also help to form a scaffolding until the floors are put in,—an operation which should not be undertaken until the roof is on.

ANOTHER SURVEYOR.

P.S.—Why does not "Surveyor" make an experiment or two with different spans and thicknesses of whatever concrete he proposes to use? It would be a very simple matter, and, spite of all printed testimony, "seeing is believing."

"INSULA."

SIR,—In the articles referring to the excavations in process at Silchester, which appeared recently in the *Builder*, I noticed frequent reference to the various "insulæ" that had been laid bare in the course of the excavations. I understand that the term "insula" applies to the square blocks of ground, bounded by roads or streets on all four sides, and covered by houses and shops and their courtyards and gardens. Perhaps some of your archæological correspondents will oblige by informing me if the term "insula" so applied was used by the Roman dwellers in Silchester and other Romano-British cities; or if, on the contrary, "insula" is only a term used by modern archæologists to describe these separate blocks of buildings.

My reason for asking the question is as follows:—In Ayr we have a narrow street or lane bounded on both sides by the oldest buildings in the town, and this lane, while its official or directory title is "Hope-street," has been known from time immemorial, and is colloquially spoken of to-day by most of the inhabitants as "The Back o' the Isle." This lane lies at the back of a square block (insula?) in the very centre of the town, lying like an island in the middle of the High-street. The High-street passes on the east front of this island block, and is 50 ft. wide. The "Back o' the Isle" is on the west front of the island block, and averages 15 ft. in width.

Now, supposing the term "insula" was an old Romano-British term for such a building stance,* would it be too liberal a deduction from the facts to argue that this present island block in the High-street of Ayr occupies the site of an "insula" of the old Roman township, which probably existed on the site in old Roman occupation times, and that the local "phrase-title" is a reminiscence of the old Roman days, although its origin had been long ago forgotten and lost sight of! I should perhaps have mentioned that the Roman road through the western lowlands of Scotland passed through Ayr.

If, on the other hand, the term "insula" is nothing more than a modern archæological term, it is at least interesting that the same term, or a variation of it, should have been in use in Ayr for very many years past.

JAS. KENNEDY HUNTER.

Ayr, February, 1892.

ARCHITECTURAL CASINGS FOR ELECTRIC WIRES.

SIR,—I notice in your report of the discussion upon Mr. Max. Clarke's paper at the Architectural Association, that Mr. R. Langton Cole considered my moulded casings excellent, but thought it curious that the covers were all screwed in the centre, although I quoted, in the preface of my book, the "Phœnix" rule that all covers should be screwed at the sides. Will you kindly allow me to explain to architects that neither the Phœnix, nor any other company, makes it a *sine quâ non* that the covers shall be screwed at the sides; but simply recommends that this should be done where possible. In point of fact, so far as the majority of small-sized casings are concerned, there wou[ld] be a considerably greater risk of the scre[ws] damaging the insulation of the electric wires, [if] such screws were inserted at the sides than if th[ey] were driven in the centre of the covers. In m[y] book, where the width of the casing allows, [I] invariably indicate screws at the sides. I think a[n] architect will see at a glance that the fillet betwe[en] the grooves in all my designs is sufficiently wide t[o] minimise any risk attending the insertion of scre[ws] in the centre.

F. A. FAWKES.

Chelmsford, February 27.

* "Stance," we are informed, is a Scottish term for a building lot.—ED.

THE LATE STRIKE STILL SMOULDERIN[G]

SIR,—The carpenters and joiners do not appe[ar] to have got over the autumn's strike. Last wee[k] upwards of one hundred men had a shop meetin[g] in one of the best-known firms in London (four me[n] out of five had attained to grey hairs and "specs.", presumably in their service), and passed a res[o]lution requesting the firm to discharge two "blac[k]legs" forthwith, because they acted differently [to] them in an important crisis. The reply virtuall[y] was, that the petitioners were quite as black [as] their two mates; that they would not be paid o[ff] at their dictation, even if all of them left their em[]ployment. I trust you will record this to the cred[it] of the firm and Master Builders' Association, who[se] ordinary course in similar cases is to discharge me[n].

This occurred in my experience when I was sh[op] foreman of joiners. I then kept for my own sati[s]faction the prime cost of the work of each ma[n]. After the men's requests were acceded to, I foun[d] the output of work of each man declined on th[e] average three shillings per week. When firms a[re] confronted in such emergencies, let them compu[te] on this average for profit and loss.

BENCH.

The Student's Column.

WARMING BUILDINGS BY HOT WATE[R].

X.

EXAMPLE WORKS (HORTICULTURAL) (*continued*).

THIS next example, fig. 36, introduces [a] new feature, viz., the "main" pipe[s] which are nearly always necessa[ry] when the houses exceed two. These mai[ns] fulfil the purpose of conveying the heated wat[er] to the different branches, and returning th[e] cooler water to the boiler after it has done i[ts]

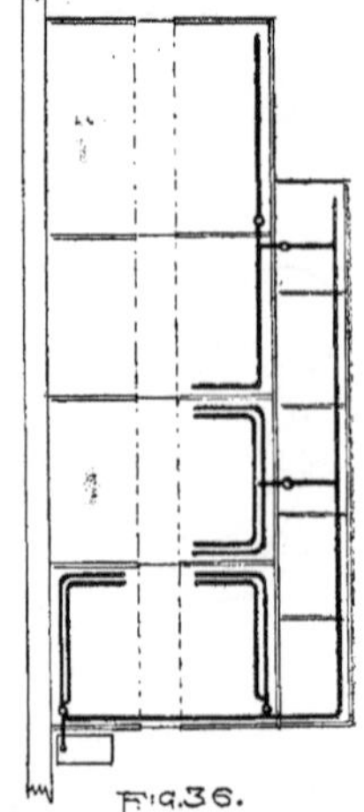

FIG. 36.

work, so to speak. In some cases the mains [do] nothing but this; that is to say, the pipes [are] not used for radiating purposes, but are entir[ely] covered up. In the example now treated t[he] mains are made use of for radiating purpo[ses] as well, for it will be seen that after comi[ng] along the end of the first house they proce[ed] direct along in front, passing through a ra[nge] of melon pits which are heated by this mea[ns]

(These pits are commonly used for melons hence the name; other things are often grown in them, of course.)

These pits are generally kept at a little lower level than the houses, and this enables the proper rise to be given to the branches as they pass into the houses. In this case, the mains would be kept below the ground-level where they pass along the side of the first house. They could be run in a channel with grating over, or be quite covered up.

It will be noticed that the particular value and need of the main flow and return is to permit of the simple yet exact regulation of the heat in the different houses independently of one another. In the illustration it will be seen that every branch from the main has a stop-cock at the point indicated by a small circle, and it will be equally obvious that by this arrangement the circulation can be adjusted to any house with the greatest ease, and almost instantaneously. This means of independent regulation, as explained in the last paper, is very necessary, for not only may there be too much pipe in a house, but sometimes, for reasons often hard to account for, one branch will work more freely than another and to the detriment of others, and has to be checked. If these four houses were heated by continuing the pipes from one to another, as in the example given last week, regulation would be next to impossible. If we attempted to check the circulation in, say, the second house, we could not do so without seriously affecting the third and fourth houses. It might be mentioned that another reason for having a stop-valve in each branch of the example being treated (fig. 36) is that it is no uncommon occurrence for one branch to work to almost the entire exclusion of the others, to "short-circuit," we may say. There are various reasons for this, and the subject will be touched upon in later papers.

When an apparatus extends a good distance in one direction, it is particularly desirable to get the boiler as low as possible so as to give a fair rise to the mains the whole of their length. The mains would only consist of two pipes, one flow and one return. To obtain this rise necessitates rather a deep boiler-pit, and this is arranged for if it is possible. In many situations when digging a pit, water is met with inconveniently near the surface, and for the pit to be taken down below this point means expense in the first place, and the risk of its being but a poor success afterwards. There are now many boilers made expressly for "shallow drainage," as the difficulty is called, and if by using these dwarfed boilers there is no occasion to go below the water-level, then it is best to adopt this course. Instead of there being the risk of water finding its way into the pit, there should always be a drainage to the pit itself. If the "shallow drainage" difficulty is known to exist, there are many remedies that can be, and are, resorted to, when building the houses. The person who erects horticultural buildings knows, of course, that they have to be heated, and should make all proper and possible preparation.

Again, referring to the "mains," it is sometimes thought best to carry them up the centre of the houses in a channel or trench. The houses then get the benefit of the heat from these as well as the branches, and allowance has to be made accordingly when calculating the quantity of pipe required. It will, however, be found that pipes in channels are not of such value in heat-giving as exposed pipes. When mains are carried in this way through he houses the rise they require necessitates heir being started rather low down, and the hannel would need to be deep at the commencement if all the houses were on a level. If he houses are on slightly rising ground it roves very satisfactory in many ways, supposing the boiler can be placed at the lowest nd.

Carrying the pipes in this latter manner within an open channel, probably with grating over, not considered so satisfactory as covering hem. In the first place, exposed mains enerally result in the end houses of a long run eing poorly supplied with heat; then the xpense is a little greater if gratings are used. f we cover up the mains in a satisfactory anner no loss of heat occurs, the branches are ell supplied, and there is not the trouble of eeping the channels clean. In this case it is nderstood that the main pipes do not enter nto the calculations as to the quantity of adiating pipe required. They take no active art beyond supplying the branches.

In carrying the mains beneath the ground in covered channels, they can either pass under the houses or beneath the ground just outside them. In either case it is customary to make a brick trench, allowing the proper rise required, and the pipes are laid in this. It will not do, though, to leave the pipes without filling in the trench around them, and the best material for this purpose is sand. When the pipes are thus surrounded with this poor heat-conducting material the channel is covered with bricks or slates and the earth filled in. If desired fillets of wood can be placed beneath the pipes to lift them a little, and so allow the sand to completely envelope them. Fig. 37 shows in cross

FIG. 37.

section the pipes as they lie in this covered trench. If the channel was unfilled and there was any possible chance of air entering it, we should get an action resembling in some ways the draught in a chimney, that is to say, the air near the pipes would become heated and would rise; at the same moment cold air would flow in, a continuous current would result, and the in-flowing cold air would rob the apparatus of heat at a very rapid rate and to no good purpose whatever.

Sand is the best material to surround these pipes with to prevent loss of heat. Sawdust or hair would answer well, except that it would not withstand moisture so well as tightly-packed sand, and moisture may be expected with tolerable certainty if the channel is not beneath the house. Silicate cotton is also an excellent material, but for this purpose it would be unnecessarily expensive, and give but little, if any, better results than sand.

The last question to be discussed respecting the main services is as to their size. There used to be a prevailing idea that the mains should be of a sectional area equal to the area of all the branches. When there were many branches this led to really enormous pipes being used, the bulk of water they contained necessitating some extra power at the boiler. They occupied much room, and the cost was a very disagreeable element.

This plan soon fell into disuse when it was discovered that there was no necessity for such relative areas. Theoretically it carried weight, but in practice results proved it to be unnecessary. For the example under discussion, 4-in. mains will do very well. It is found that this size is quite enough to permit of the water circulating freely, and if we get a moderately-rapid circulation to carry the heated water to the branches, and convey the cooled water back to the boiler, it will be found sufficient. A very rapid circulation is not so much needed, as the water does not lose its heat from the pipes instantaneously, and in this apparatus, although there are four houses, the distance is not great. In a larger apparatus than this, having a greater number of branches, or in instances where the branches are more extensive but the mains limited in length, it may be considered best to use 6-in. pipes for the mains. This is one of the points it is difficult to decide except by actual experience, but it may be assumed that the necessity for 6-in. mains is not very common.

LIVERPOOL ENGINEERING SOCIETY.—The ninth ordinary meeting of this Society for the present session was held at the Royal Institution, Colquitt-street, on the 24th ult., Mr. John T. Wood, President, in the chair. The evening was devoted to the adjourned discussion upon a paper read by Mr. Thomas Morris, F.G.S., at the previous meeting, entitled "Engineers' Tests of Iron Considered, and Suggestions for Standard Uniform Tests." Mr. Thomas L. Miller, Assoc.M.Inst.C.E. opened the discussion at some length, and dealt principally with the contraction of area test. Messrs. Joseph Price, J. J. Potts, Robert E. Johnston, C. H. Darbishire, Prof. H. S. Hele-Shaw, and others, took part in the discussion, upon the conclusion of which Mr. Morris replied. A vote of thanks was accorded by acclamation to Mr. Morris for his interesting and practical paper.

OBITUARY.

SIR JOHN COODE.—The *Times* announces the death of the eminent engineer, Sir John Coode, K.C.M.G., which took place on Wednesday, at Brighton, after a long illness. Sir John, who was born in 1816, was a son of the late Mr. Charles Coode, of Bodmin. He was educated at the Grammar School of his native town, and early in life chose the profession of civil engineer, in which he soon distinguished himself. He began his career under the eminent engineer Rendel, and for a short time was employed on the Great Western Railway. As early as 1847 he was appointed resident engineer at Portland harbour and breakwater, and, on the death of Rendel, engineer-in-chief in 1856. He continued in charge until the completion of this great work in 1872, when he was knighted. He was for many years consulted by the Board of Trade and other Government departments on matters connected with harbours, docks, rivers, and drainage. Many important works were carried out from his designs, including the great breakwater and docks at Cape Town, the breakwater at Colombo, the improvement of the river Bar, in Ireland, the harbours of the Isle of Man, and similar works elsewhere. He was a member of the Royal Commission on Harbours of Refuge in 1858-59, and of the Royal Commission on Metropolitan Sewage Discharge, 1882-83. The harbour of refuge now in progress at Peterhead, and the new harbour works at Dover, for which the Act was obtained last session, are from the designs of himself and his firm. He was President of the Institution of Civil Engineers in the years 1889 and 1890.

GENERAL BUILDING NEWS.

BOARD SCHOOLS, WEST HARTLEPOOL.—The School Board have decided to build upper grade schools, adjoining the Oxford-street schools, which were built two or three years ago for 630 children. They have accordingly instructed the architect,—Mr. J. P. Pritchett, of Darlington,—to prepare a design and carry out the erection of an upper grade school for about 500 children on land adjoining.

WESLEYAN CHAPEL, WEST AUCKLAND.—On the 24th ult., Mr. Joseph Albert Pease, of Snow Hall, Darlington, laid the memorial-stone of the West Auckland Wesleyan chapel, schools, and vestries. These comprise a chapel to seat 250 adults, Sunday-school for 350 children, infant-school, minister's vestry, large class-room, &c. The new buildings are to be constructed of stone, in the Early English style of Gothic architecture, with internal fittings in pitch-pine. The entrance doors of chapel and school are arranged to swing both ways in case of a panic arising. The work will be carried out from designs and under the superintendence of the architect, Mr. J. W. Taylor, Newcastle.

RE-OPENING OF NORMACOT CHURCH, STAFFORDSHIRE.—On the 25th ult., the Bishop of Lichfield re-opened, after restoration, the Church of the Holy Evangelists, Normacot, Longton, and dedicated the new aisle and vestry. Nearly twelve months ago, instructions were given to Mr. John Lewis, architect, of Newcastle-under-Lyme, to form a north aisle to the church. The various works in connexion with this were entrusted to Messrs. H. & R. Inskip, of Longton. According to the *Birmingham Gazette*, the initial design of the church is by the late Sir Gilbert Scott, the building being constructed of red sandstone. The new portion, although not exactly similar, is in unison with the south aisle, and is constructed of Alton stone. The principal rafters are of deal, the plaster work between being executed in adamant. The columns are of brown Wall Grange stone to match the existing ones. The floor of the porch is laid with Hopton Wood polished stone. The aisle floors are laid with tiles from the Campbell Tile Company. The heating arrangements have been carried out by Messrs. Hartley, of Macclesfield. The total cost will be about 1,600*l*.

NEW CHURCH, WEST BROMWICH.—On the 1st inst. the foundation-stone of a new church, which is being erected in the Beeches-road, West Bromwich, was laid by Alderman Farley. The church is to accommodate 350 people. It will be built in the Gothic style, and will consist of nave (52 ft. by 25 ft.), and a chancel with a transept on one side and a vestry on the other. It is intended at some future time to erect a permanent church in front of this, which will then be converted into a parochial room. Messrs. Henry Smith & Son, of West Bromwich, are the builders, and Messrs. Wood & Kendrick the architects.

SESSIONS COURT, GREAT WITLEY, WORCESTER.—On the 24th ult. the new police-court at Great Witley, which has been erected by direction of the Worcestershire County Council, was opened for public purposes. The building is of red brick with Bath stone dressings. The Sessions Court is 33 ft. long by 20 ft. wide, and there are three entrances, one from the magistrates' retiring-room, one for officials, and a larger door for the general public. A room is placed near the public entrance as a witnesses' waiting-room, and there are other conveniences, a porch being erected over the main entrance. The floor of the court-room is of wood blocks. The ceiling is partly open, and panelled, the frame-work being of pitch-pine, stained and varnished. Tobin's shafts have been introduced, with extra ventilators in the roof. The court is heated with hot-water apparatus supplied by Messrs. Ward & Sons, Worcester. The architect was Mr. Rowe and the contractor was Mr. T. Vale, of Stourport.

NEW POST-OFFICE, GOOLE.—On the 27th ult., the new arcade and Post-office, which occupies a position at the juncture of Aire-street and North-street, Goole, was opened. The arcade connects those thoroughfares with Victoria-street. The main front consists of rooms for the accommodation of the Post-office officials. The arcade, with light iron roof covered with glass, contains sixteen shops on the ground floor, varying in size from 27 ft. by 15 ft. to 17 ft. by 15 ft. An illuminated turret striking clock has been fixed near the Victoria-street entrance, and is the work of Messrs. Wm. Potts & Sons, of Leeds. Mr. H. B. Thorp, of Goole, was the architect.

PROPOSED NEW HOTEL, BELFAST.—According to the *Belfast News Letter*, the Belfast Central Hotel Company intend to erect a new hotel in Belfast. On the ground floor there will be a dining-hall, capable of dining over 200 persons; also billiard-room, smoking-room, and all other necessary accommodation. On the first floor there will be dining, drawing, music, writing, and ladies' coffee rooms, and a number of private sitting apartments. The hotel will contain between 200 and 300 bedrooms. There will be a large number of rooms of various sizes, which will be specially designed for stock-rooms. It is at present intended that the entire building will be lighted with electric light, and it will be fitted up with lifts for passengers and luggage. Mr. Samuel Stevenson, C.E., is the architect.

RE-OPENING OF EPISCOPAL CHURCH, PORTOBELLO.—On the 27th ult. St. Mark's Episcopal Church, Portobello, near Edinburgh, was re-opened after undergoing alterations and additions. The principal change which has been effected in the building is the erection of a chancel, but the whole interior has been altered, the side galleries having been removed and the sittings re-arranged. The ceiling has been panelled, and the church has been painted and decorated. The new chancel is 25 ft. long and 27 ft. wide, with an organ-chamber beyond, shut off by an oak screen. The floor is laid in marble and tiles, and rises in five marble steps to the sacrarium. The altar-table, of carved oak, stands on a marble footpiece a step higher. The credence table is of polished alabaster. Carved stone corbels support the springing of chancel arch. A parapet of dressed stone, with polished brass rail, marks off the chancel. The architects are Messrs. Hay & Henderson, Edinburgh.

BANK BUILDINGS, OLDHAM.—New bank buildings have just been erected in Union-street, Oldham, for the Oldham Joint-Stock Bank, Limited. Entrance is gained from Union-street through two vestibules. The banking-room,—50 ft. square by 26 ft. high,—is lined with faïence tiling, with mosaic floor. The general rooms for management of the bank are placed up to Union-street. The basement has been utilised for bullion and strong rooms, connected with the banking-room by a hydraulic lift. The upper portion of the site facing Queen-street has been utilised as chambers, which have a separate entrance. The building throughout is fireproof. The exterior of the block is faced with ashlar and moulded stonework. The following firms have been engaged upon the building:—Messrs. C. Spencer Bros., Oldham, excavating; Mr. Whitworth Whittaker, Oldham, brickwork; Mr. Thomas Dunkerly, Oldham, masonry; executors of Mr. E. Whittaker, Oldham, general joiners' work; Messrs. S. Ashton & Sons; Oldham, slating, plumbing, and glazing; Mr. James Hall, Oldham, plastering; Burmantofts Works, Leeds, faïence work and fireplaces; Messrs. Pattison, Manchester, granite base and steps and mosaic floors; Messrs. Homan & Rodgers, Manchester, fireproof floors and ceilings; Messrs. Pearson & Brown, Manchester, fittings to banking-room and wood-block flooring; Mr. Hand, Oldham, decorating and painting; Mr. Davenport, Oldham, wrought ironwork; Mr. Schofield, Oldham, ventilator; Messrs. Kaye & Sons, Leeds, locks; Mr. R. Middleton, Leeds, hydraulic lift; Messrs. Guthrie & Co., Glasgow, lead lights; Messrs. Standring & Co., Manchester, gas-fittings, &c. The whole has been designed and carried out under the superintendence of Mr. Thomas Taylor, architect, Oldham.

NEW GOODS-RECEIVING OFFICE FOR MESSRS. PICKFORD & CO.—Messrs. Pickford & Co. are about to open an extensive new goods-receiving and forwarding office at No. 34, Queen-street, Cheapside. It is entered by a lofty gateway which occupies the greater portion of the lower part of the frontage of a new block of offices and warehouses erected by Messrs. Pink, Fryer, & Co., of Bloomburg-street, Westminster, Mr. Robert J. Worley, of Cannon-street, being the architect. The goods depôt is large, light, and spacious, and from it an easily stepped incline, paved with granite setts, leads down to a stable for thirteen horses. Although this stable is below the ground level, it is light and well-ventilated. The floor of the stable is paved with Claridge's patent asphalte laid on a solid bed of concrete 1 ft. thick. The asphalte surface is 1¾ in. thick, except where the groovings for foothold occur. These groovings are V-shaped in section and cross each other at right angles, forming small squares. There is no stable-drain, except the one to catch the waste from the water-trough. It is intended to use peat or other similar litter for the horses, and this will absorb the urine from the horses and will be frequently removed, so that no drainage will be required other than that mentioned, so we were told by Mr. Bowles, the foreman of the works.

NEW OLYMPIA CIRCUS, EDGE HILL, LANCASHIRE.—The new Olympia Circus in Overton-street, Edge Hill, capable of accommodating over 2,500 spectators, was opened on the 29th ult. It has been designed by Mr. J. Havelock Sutton, architect, of Liverpool. The building is of brick, covering a large site. An entrance through a hall, paved with tiles and finished with light and dark oak adorned with bevelled glass, gives access to two staircases, one on either side, leading to the stalls, side, and private boxes, &c. The interior has been finished and decorated by an Italian artist, Signor Dondy, and assistants. Over a tier of private boxes is a device of the Royal arms, draped with the flags of all nations, relieved by medallions of crimson leather. Attached to the circus are stables.

HIGHWEEK CHURCH, NEWTON ABBOT.—This church was reopened on the 1st inst., having been closed some months for alterations and additions. The chancel and south aisle have been extended, and the organ, which stood in a tower gallery, has been placed at the east end of this aisle, the gallery being removed, and the tower opened up. The work has been carried out from the designs of Messrs. Tait & Harvey, of Exeter, by Messrs. Parker Bros., of Newton Abbot, the new oak choir stalls and west screen being executed by Messrs. Luscombe, Exeter.

EXTENSION OF PREMISES, CO-OPERATIVE STORES, LEEDS.—The Leeds industrial Co-operative Society is about to make an addition to its central stores in Albion-street. A frontage of 80 ft. on the west side of Albion-street, with a depth back of 104 ft. to Upper Mill-hill, has been acquired. The area of the site to be covered by the new structure is 1,000 yards. The basement floor, having an area of 560 yards, will be utilised for the storage of furniture. In addition, provision will be made for a gas-engine, for electric light, for heating and ventilation apparatus, and other purposes. The ground floor will be divided, with a two-thirds frontage to Albion-street for drapery, and one-third for furniture. Each department will be approached through the large central entrance, and purchasers will be able to pass from one department to the other without going outside. In addition, provision will be made for the loading and unloading of goods. Parcel-rooms, store-rooms, and lavatories will also be provided. The first floor will be divided similarly to the ground floor. The second floor will contain rooms for fur goods, for reserve stock, for the mantle and millinery department, and also dining-rooms, kitchen, lavatories, &c. The third floor will be devoted to workrooms and stockrooms. The elevation to Albion-street will be of local stone, and the other elevations will in all probability be faced with white glazed bricks. The rooms will be carried on iron girders and iron columns, and will be made fireproof. The designs have been prepared by Mr. W. S. Braithwaite, architect, of Leeds, who will superintend and carry out the works.

SANITARY AND ENGINEERING NEWS.

THE SANITARY INSPECTORS' ASSOCIATION.—The ninth annual dinner of this Association will be held on Saturday, March 12, Dr. B. W. Richardson, President, in the chair.—A movement is on foot amongst the members for a visit to Paris for a few days. It is proposed that the party shall leave London on Thursday, June 2, returning from Paris on Monday, June 6. At the sitting of the Society of Hygiene of France, on January 8, Dr. Pietra Santa made a communication which he had received from Dr. Richardson, F.R.S., of London, President of the Sanitary Inspectors' Association, respecting the proposed visit. Upon the proposition of the Secretary-General, the Society of Hygiene decided, by acclamation, that it would do all in its power to receive heartily the sanitary inspectors of Great Britain. All necessary steps would be taken with the Municipal Council and public bodies of Paris to facilitate the visits to the fields of irrigation of Gennevilliers and other establishments which are likely to be of interest. A banquet will also be given to the visitors. A committee of twelve members, consisting of MM. Cacheux, Féret, Joltrain, Dr. E. Monin, Joseph de Pietra Santa, Nicholson, Michaels, Ch. Clifort, Bruhat, Rogers, and Dr. Paul Chevandier, with power to add the names of other members who may wish to show their goodwill towards the visitors, was immediately nominated to carry out the details of the reception.

TESTIMONIAL TO A SANITARY ENGINEER.—On the 23rd ult., at the Cutlers' Hall, Sheffield, Mr. Gustav Alsing, formerly Engineer of the sewage works at Blackburn Meadows, was presented with a testimonial in recognition of his services to the town. The testimonial consisted of a cabinet of cutlery and a travelling-bag. An ornamental plate bore the following inscription:—"Presented to Mr. G. Alsing, A.M.I.C.E., on the termination of his engagement as Engineer to the Sewerage and Rivers Department of the Sheffield Corporation, in acknowledgment of the valuable services rendered by him to the town, and his uniform courtesy in the fulfilment of his duties." The chair was taken by Mr. T. J. Flockton, and among those present were Aldermen William Smith and H. Bramley, Councillors W. E. Clegg and J. R. Lockwood, Mr. John Merrill, Mr. Frederick Fowler, Mr. J. D. Webster, and Mr. Charles Hadfield (representing the Sheffield Society of Architects and Surveyors). A letter was read from Mr. C. J. Innocent (President of the Sheffield Society of Architects and Surveyors) regretting his inability to be present.

THE MAIN DRAINAGE OF BOURNEMOUTH: THE EXTENSION SCHEMES.—Last week a Local Government inquiry was held in the Board-room, Town-hall Buildings, Bournemouth, by Col. J. O. Hasted, R.E., respecting the application made by the Bournemouth Town Council to borrow 24,000*l.* for works of sewerage. The Borough Surveyor, Mr. F. W. Lacey, A.M.I.C.E., gave details as to the proposed schemes. From these it appeared that the No. 1 scheme comprised an enlargement of and additions to the existing central sewer, including an additional 3 ft. outfall 2,150 ft. long, to be laid east of the pier. A large iron sewer in connexion with this outfall will run through the gardens. This scheme will cost 12,000*l.* The second scheme comprises an enlargement of and additions to the existing eastern sewers, with a new 3 ft. outfall of 1,400 ft. in length, east of the Boscombe Pier. This will cost 11,000*l.* The third scheme deals with a re-arrangement of the Wimborne-road sewer, and is to cost 1,000*l.*

PROPOSED BRIDGE, &C., STOCKPORT.—It is proposed to construct a new bridge and road to connect Chestergate with Heaton-lane, at Stockport, on the low level. This improvement will consist not only of the new bridge and road, but also the appropriation of a large area of land known as the Mersey Mill site up to Wellington-road, which will form an open space. The levels of the streets adjoining this land vary considerably, the open space at Wellington Bridge being a considerable depth below the Wellington-road. The scheme will provide for making this land comparatively level with Wellington-road between the river and Heaton-lane. The approaches to the bridge on the Chestergate side, along Chestergate itself, will vary from 1 in 30 to 1 in 40. The bridge is to be of a lattice tubular form, and will be of steel, having a span across the river of 80 ft. The width inside between the parapets will be 54 ft. The question of the construction of the bridge and the utilisation of the land has been the subject of a Local Government Board inquiry, by which authority it has been approved. The work has been entrusted to Mr. A. M. Fowler, M.Inst.C.E., of Stockport and Manchester.

FOREIGN AND COLONIAL.

FRANCE.—M. Courtois-Suffit, architect, has been commissioned to design the monument to be erected in Paris to the memory of Théodore de Banville. The poet's bust will be modelled by M. Roulleau. ——MM. Falguière and Mercié have completed the monument to Alfred de Musset, which is to be erected on the Place d'Augustin at Paris. The poet is represented seated, his eyes fixed on a lyre. Before him passes an allegorical figure of the Muse, scattering roses.——M. E. de Joly has been delegated by the Société Centrale des Architectes to take a place on the jury which is to decide the competition for the Museum of Sculpture and Painting at Nantes.——At Molière there has been discovered a subterranean habitation composed of seven grottoes with pointed roofs separated by a central gallery. A great number of bones have been found, and it is supposed the grottoes served as a refuge for the inmates of a neighbouring convent during the religious wars.——A serious accident has happened at the building in progress for the International Exhibition at Tours: a whole pavilion, 40 mètres long, fell at once, injuring many of the workmen in its fall.——It is announced that the inhabitants of Hyères are about to erect two triumphal arches in honour of the Queen of England, one at the railway station and the other at the Place de la Rade.——At the Museum of Montpellier a new gallery has been opened specially for the designs and drawings of Alexandre Cabanel. In the middle of the gallery will be placed a bust of the celebrated painter, by M. Paul Dubois. Near it will be placed his palette, his brushes, and the numerous decorations which he had received. ——The old houses at Rouen, so characteristic in their plans and in their half-timber work, are beginning to give way to the attacks of time. A fortnight since, a house in the Rue Martainville fell down; last week there followed another equally curious example, No. 21, Rue du Bac. If the Municipality do not take some steps to preserve them, there will soon be no more left of these interesting structures.——Dr. Cosse, who died recently at Paris, has left his fine collection of works of art to the museum at Nantes.——The Municipal Council at Nantes has voted 65,000 francs for the erection of the fine fountain by Bartholdi which, in the Exhibition of 1889, stood in the central gallery leading to the Galerie des Machines.

BERLIN.—The memorial church to the late Emperor William I., which is in course of erection in one of the suburbs, is to be inaugurated on March 22, 1895. This statement sounds strange when one hears that of the 1,800,000 marks necessary to complete the building only 950,000 are forthcoming. By order of the Emperor, a collection is to be held throughout the country for the purpose of raising the funds, but how much will be obtained is very questionable.——Professor Raschdorff's latest design for the proposed Berlin Cathedral was put before a Commission of high State officials last week, prior to its publication for the members of the Prussian Parliament. It seems absolutely impossible to ascertain if a reliable estimate of the cost of the cathedral has been worked out; one only hears of the total sum of ten millions.——The Imperial Government has voted a sum of 75,000 marks (some 3,750*l.*) towards expenses to be incurred by artists and craftsmen exhibiting at the Chicago Show.——Some fifty architects and engineers from all parts of Germany assembled on the 24th ult. to hear some proposals of the German Special Commissioner relative to the two professions being well and practically represented at the Chicago Exhibition. Although the professional men of the different countries or cities of the Empire intend exhibiting separately or in small groups, there is to be some unity in their groups in the German section; and for this purpose, after much debating, a central committee, with its headquarters at Berlin, has been elected. It is interesting to note that architects are advised to send designs of practical work and not of ideal schemes.——The Emperor will attend the ceremony of laying the foundation-stone of the Kyffhäuser Monument in memory of the late Emperor William. The date selected is May 10.——The great Opera ball took place on the 24th ult., and, as usual, the complicated transformation of the auditorium and stage into a ball-room was cleverly done. This time, combinations of evergreens and water (small fountains and cascades) were used for the decoration of the stage, with good effect.——"Geh. Oberbaurath" Wiebe, a civil engineer and Government official of repute, died last week in his eighty-eighth year, and was buried with great ceremony. He played a most important part at the time when Berlin received its new sewage system, and has of late years done much good work throughout the country as technical adviser to sanitary boards.

VIENNA.—The proposed international "Musical and Theatrical Exhibition," before alluded to, is exciting interest among the educated classes of the capital, and we hear that a very fair show is expected as far as German, Italian, Swiss, and home exhibits are concerned. From England and France little is apparently expected, although a well-represented section from each of these countries would be absolutely necessary before the word "international" could be justified, and the Austrians would only be too glad to be able to rightly affix this word to their show. Preparations are being made with energy, and the large halls of the Prater Exhibition Building are nearly ready for the reception of exhibits, due next month. As before observed, a temporary "model theatre" is being run up, in which dramatic or operatic companies from all parts of the Continent are to play in turns. This building is now roofed, and promises to be an object of interest for architects both as regards to plan, interior arrangements, and stage-fittings. Messrs. Fellner & Helmer, the Austrian theatre specialists, have designed it to hold an audience of 1,500, of which a thousand are placed on the sloping floor of the auditorium, and the rest on a balcony; the stage has a total depth of 26 mètres and a proscenium opening 13·50 mètres wide; measurements large enough to permit the rendering of any play. The material used for the erection is mainly timber, which has been painted over with one of the so-called fire-proof washes; coatings of asbestos have been used on the main partition wall and the curtain to the stage opening. The exits have been so arranged as to permit a clearance of the house within three minutes. Electric lighting has been adopted throughout the building, a system of ventilation which will permit an influx of 60,000 cubic mètres of fresh air every hour is to be carried out, and the compulsory high-pressure water distribution laid on.

SWITZERLAND.—Last year a new theatre was completed at Zurich. Now another large place of amusement is to be erected in this city. A competition has been opened for the design of a block, containing some assembly-rooms, two concert halls, restaurant, &c. One of the concert halls is to hold an audience of 1,400. The cost of the building is not to exceed 1,200,000 francs.

OLDENBURG.—In place of the Court Theatre, which was destroyed by fire shortly before Christmas, a provisional one, with a seating capacity for an audience numbering 840, has been erected. In spite of a severe spell of cold weather, it only took seven weeks to put up this building, the construction of which shows points of interest, as various patent fabrications, such as plaster-boards, cement and wire combinations, have been used for the vertical surfaces, the necessary support being given by a timber framework.

HEIDELBERG.—The Government of the Duchy of Baden has voted some 12,500*l.* towards works on the historical Heidelberg Schloss. The works to be taken in hand include a thorough drainage of the very damp site on which the castle stands, some alterations in the old castle-yard, and the taking of plaster-casts of the more valuable pieces of sculpture and "relief" work on the façades of the castle proper.

SWEDEN.—Herr Carl Moller, a prominent Swedish architect, has been commissioned to restore the ancient Church of St. Christina in Falun. It contains a large quantity of beautiful old wood carving, partly still in its place, and partly stored away in a loft. All will be carefully placed in the original position.——In order to raise further funds for an Artists' Club, in Stockholm, an exhibition of paintings with lottery is to be held, to which Prince Eugen, Prof. Kronberg, and other leading artists are contributing paintings.——A large quantity of the interior artistic fittings and decorations in the Old Opera House in Stockholm, just closed in order to make room for a new one, and dating from about 1600, is to be removed to the Northern Museum of Antiquities.——It is intended to build a new lunatic asylum in Stockholm, at a cost of 12,000*l.*——In order to afford greater safety for men at work on the roofs of houses, the City Board has adopted some further regulations. In addition to iron handrails or chains, the workman is to have a rope and lifebelt attached to the former, whilst chimneys of more than 1·2 mètre in height are to be fitted with iron ladders, and having at least, on three sides, handrails.——An electrical central station has been opened at Helsingborg, constructed by Messrs. Siemens & Halske, of Berlin. It is intended for feeding 1,000 lamps.

ELECTRIC LIGHTING IN SOUTH AFRICA.—The progress of electric lighting in South Africa is indicated by the list of works carried out or projected in Pretoria by Messrs. Woodhouse & Rawson during the past year. These consist of the preparation of plans and specifications for the electric lighting of Pretoria; the supply and erection of plant for lighting the works, both above and below ground, of the City and Suburban Gold Mining Company and the Metropolitan Gold Mining Company; the lighting of the Battery House of the Van Ryn Gold Mining Company; the lighting of the Globe Theatre, Pretoria; and the preparation of the plans and specifications for transmission of power by means of electricity, for Moodies Gold Mining and Exploration Company.

MISCELLANEOUS.

WINCHESTER CATHEDRAL BELLS.—We are informed that Mr. John Colson, F.R.I.B.A., the architect to Winchester Cathedral, has suggested that the bells at present hanging in the tower should be taken down and re-hung with the two hoped-for new ones in a temporary structure until a proper campanile can be built for them. By doing away with the two floors and removing the vaulting to a position in which the defects of its construction would be less obvious and its beauty of design better displayed, the rich interior of a most magnificent Norman lantern, hidden now save to those who can climb a close winding stair, would be open to the view of all, and the bells, at present muffled by walls never meant to enclose them, could speak their message far and wide.

GLASGOW AND WEST OF SCOTLAND TECHNICAL COLLEGE.—On Saturday afternoon the students attending the Greenock Class in Plumbers' Work paid a visit to the meter department of the gas-works in Crawfurd-street. The different sections of the works, the construction, management and care of wet and dry meters, photometers, gas-testing, meter-testing, &c., were very ably described by Messrs. Maitland, Fordyce, McCubbun, and Wright.

FOG.—In no case can it be supposed that scientific measures will prevent the inevitable formation of mist; but if London fog can be stripped of its colour which is coincident with its irritating character, and which is due to the presence of carbon particles, tarry matter, and sulphur, then a vast improvement will have been accomplished, and a giant stride onward in hygienic science achieved. As we have pointed out more than once, even when coal is perfectly burnt or consumed, we still have to deal with the products of combustion of sulphur, which element occurs to the extent of from 1 to 2 per cent. in most kinds of coal. Carbon, hydrogen, sulphur, and nitrogen in coal, when completely burnt in air, produce carbonic acid (CO_2), watery vapour (H_2O), sulphurous and sulphuric acids (SO_2 and SO_3), and a trifling quantity of free nitrogen. Given, therefore, the complete consumption of the coal,—that is to say, that no smoke or unburnt carbon is produced,—what is to be done with the combustion products of sulphur? and how will these products (SO_2 and SO_3) alter the character of the fog? We suggested in a leading article some time ago that probably lime or any of the alkalies placed at some point in the chimney could be used to absorb these acids, and those who claim to have secured the perfect combustion of coal by the adoption of a particularly constructed stove should be induced to put this simple suggestion into practice.—*The Lancet.*

CIVIL AND MECHANICAL ENGINEERS' SOCIETY.—On Wednesday a paper on "Some Practical Notes on the Water-supply of Boilers, and its Treatment," was read by Mr. R. J. Friswell, F.I.C., F.C.S., &c., in which a number of patents taken out between 1882 and 1891 were described, and comments made on them. The true cause of boiler incrustation was considered, and its origin traced to the enormous solvent powers of water and the character of the earth's surface. The probable cause of the presence of other than the strictly insoluble constituents of boiler deposits was indicated, and attention called to some unusual kinds of river water. Methods of treatment were then taken in hand, and it was argued that treatment previous to use is best; Clark's process was described, and modern improvements of it glanced at. Mr. Spence's introduction of soda ash was described, and also its mode of action. Caustic soda was shown to be efficient but dangerous, and silicate of soda as useful but quite safe.

INVENTORS' INSTITUTE.—At the last meeting of this Institute, Dr. Glover Lyon in the chair, Mr. Walter Smartt (Member) read a paper "On Improvements in Burning Bricks, Soft-core, and other matters, without causing nuisance." The author has patented special means of roofing-over clamps, and treating the gaseous emanations therefrom for the purpose of removing the nuisances which cause so much complaint, and in many cases give rise to serious litigation against the manufacturers of bricks and tiles. A few of the advantages expected are:—Enabling the bricks to be made and burned in places where there are superior materials and conveniences, but where hitherto there has been too strong objection; the protection of the bricks when in clamp from storms and rains and the consequent depreciation of the goods produced; rendering unnecessary the expense of placing extra layers of bricks over the clamp; and expediting the burning of the bricks with the use of less fuel. Associated also with this system would be important results for Sanitary and other local authorities, and the improvement of the value of the surrounding land and of the brickfield when exhausted. In regard to the waste of prepared materials through litigation set up against brickmakers, an instance was given at Hammersmith, where recently, through an injunction, prepared earth to the extent of 3,000,000 of bricks remained unused. And, as to the necessity for more uniform conditions of burning than under the present exposure to all the changes and inclemencies of weather, it was stated that, with a rainfall of 3 in. per month, a large clamp from first to last would receive as much as fifty-six tons of water, the detriment to the bricks being very serious. The paper was closely criticised in the discussion which followed, in which, amongst others, Mr. Picking, of New Southgate; Messrs. Broad, Mead, and Clayton, of Paddington; Mr. Bird and Mr. Williams, of Shepherd's-bush; Mr. Eastwood, of Lambeth; and Mr. Craven, of Wakefield, took part. Mr. Smartt replied to various questions, and stated that it was intended shortly to give a demonstration on a practical scale in one of the brickfields near London.

THE WIND AND ELECTRICITY.—The midst of London is not a promising site for windmills; nevertheless Messrs. Williams, of Great Eastern-street, have erected two such motors,—one on their own premises, and the other on those of Messrs. Carwardine, in the City-road. Like sky-signs, they constitute of themselves conspicuous advertisements. But the sky-signs can be turned to no other useful purpose. The windmill can: and both the firms referred to have for some time made them do intermittent duties. We say intermittent, because of the fluctuating nature of the wind, which is on no two days alike, nor hardly ever without variations of strength from one minute to another. To say nothing of calms, the ordinary fluctuations leave the wind the most uncertain of all the natural sources of power. Windmills, like almost every other machine, have, however, gone through much improvement, and the Halladay type has certain special features which fit it for doing more advanced work than the old mills could possibly be put to. Under these circumstances, the application of the wind to the generation of electricity has really more chance of success than at first sight would appear. For, with a mill-wheel which adapts itself to the blast of the storm or to the gentlest zephyr, working in conjunction with a battery of storage-cells, irregularities of all kinds can be merged into a common tranquil reservoir from which electric current can be drawn off as required with perfect uniformity of pressure. The Halladay mill has a wheel divided into flexible sections, and thus differs essentially from the old rigid wheels upon which the gusts acted with brutal roughness. Each of the Halla-

COMPETITION, CONTRACTS, AND PUBLIC APPOINTMENTS.

COMPETITION.

Nature of Work.	By whom Advertised.	Premium.	Designs to be delivered.
*Artisans' and Labourers' Dwellings	Halifax Corp.	Not stated	April 4

CONTRACTS.

Nature of Work or Materials.	By whom Required.	Architect, Surveyor, or Engineer.	Tenders to be delivered.
Additions and Alterations to Church, Selside, Kendal	....	C. J. Ferguson	Mar. 8
Six Cottages, Queen's-road, Snodland	Rochester Land & Gen. Invest. Co. Lim.	J. W. Nash	do.
Bridge, 50-ft. span, Marshaw Cragg, Yorks	....	Sam Shaw	do.
*Road Materials	St. Saviour's B. of W.	*Official*	do.
Drainage, Torpoint	St. Germans R.S.A.	do.	Mar. 9
Earthenware Pipes, &c.	Northwich Loc. Bd.	do.	do.
*Supply of Materials	Colchester Town Coun.	do	do.
*Oak Fencing	West Ham Union	do.	do.
*Road Making and Paving Works	Hammersmith Vestry	H. Mair	do.
School Buildings	W. Hartlepool Sch. Bd.	J. M. Bottomley	do.
Making-up Land, St. Deny's, Southampton	Hants Land & Building Soc.	W. B. Hill	do.
Two Semi-detached Cottages, Farm-buildings, &c. Elgin, N.B.	....	Geo. Sutherland	Mar. 10
Two Filter Beds, Trench Cutting, &c.	Thurlstone Loc. Bd.	H. & G. B. Crowther	do.
*Brick and Concrete, and Pipe Sewers, &c.	Twickenham L. B.	G. B. Laffan	do.
*Making-up Roads	Hornsey Loc. Bd.	T. de Courcy Meade	Mar. 11
*Sewerage Works	do.	do.	do.
*Two Cottages	do.	do.	do.
*Works and Materials	do.	do.	do.
*Iron Fencing, with Gates	do.	do.	do.
*Supply of Materials	do.	do.	do.
Two Houses and shops, Lightcliffe, Halifax	....	H. Pyrah	Mar. 12
Alterations and Additions to School	Lytchett Minster Sch. Bd.	H. F. J. Barnes	do.
Waterworks (Contract No. 1) and Tunnel	Pembroke T. C.	Mr. McAlpin	do.
*Maintenance and Repair of Main Road	Middlesex C. C.	F. H. Pownall	Mar. 14
*Broken Blue Guernsey Granite	do.	do.	do.
Infirmary Block and Workshops, Asylum, near Bridgend	....	Giles, Gough, & Trollope	do.
Alterations to Town Hall, Blaenavon, (Mon.)	Westlake's Brewery (Ltd.)	E. A. Lansdown	do.
Alterations and Additions to Premises Academy-street, Elgin, N.B.	....	Jas. Jamieson	do.
Road Metal, Flagging, &c.	Plymouth Corporation	G. D. Bellamy	do.
School Building	Norton (Sheffield) Sch. Bd.	T. H. Wilson	do.
*Supply of Road Materials, &c.	St. Mary, Newington, Vestry	*Official*	do.
Iron Screw Pile Lighthouse, near Newport Mon.	Trinity House Corp.	do.	do.

CONTRACTS.—*Continued.*

Nature of Work or Materials.	By whom Required.	Architect, Surveyor or Engineer.	Tenders to be delivered.
*Works and Materials	Finchley Local Board	*Official*	Mar. 14
*Works and Materials	Tottenham Loc. Bd.	do.	do.
*Widening Railway between Euxton and Standish	L. and N. W. Railway	do.	Mar. 15
Two Shops, Commercial-street, Halifax	....	Utley & Gray	do.
*Roadmaking and Tar-paving Works	Lewisham Bd. of W.	*Official*	do.
*Roadmaking and Paving Works	Fulham Vestry	W. Sykes	Mar. 16
*Central Library, Peckham-road	Camberwell Commrs.	R. P. Whellock	do.
*Bridge over River Mersey	County Borough of Stockport	A. M. Fowler	do.
Sewerage Works	I. of Wight R.S.A.	W. Lidstone	do.
*Constructing Roadway	Wandsworth and Clapham Union	T. W. Aldwinckle	Mar. 17
*Cast-iron Mains, &c. for Water Supply	Shardlow Union	G. Hodson	Mar. 19
Wrought-iron Roof, Kirkgate Market, Leeds	Leeds Corporation	T. Hewson	do.
Alterations to Hotel Premises, High-street, Elgin, N.B.	....	C. C. Doig	do.
*Additions, &c. to Claybury Hall	Asylums Com. L.C.C.	G. T. Hine	Mar. 21
Dwellinghouse, Grantown-on-Spey, N.B.	....	Brown & Watt	do.
*Painting, &c. Coroner's Court	St. Luke's Vestry, Middlesex	*Official*	Mar. 21
*Repairs, &c. to Chimney Shaft	Commrs. for F. B. & W. St. Giles, &c.	J. Waldram	Mar. 23
*Infirmary, &c.	Parc Gwyllt Asylum, near Bridgend	Giles, Gough, & Trollope	April 4
*Public Baths	Corp. of Coventry	*Official*	do.
Entrance Lodge, Allt-y-ferin, Carmarthenshire	R. H. Bath	Wilson & Moxham	No date
Stables and Clock Tower, do.	do.	do.	do.
*Married Soldiers' Quarters, Eastbourne	War Department	*Official*	do.
Re-building "Globe Hotel," &c. Abertillery, Mon.	Mrs. Edwards	Alfred Swash	do.
Railway Embankment and Siding, Pontypridd	Brown, Lennox, & Co.	....	do.
Widening Bridge, Upleatham, Yorks	....	Walker Stead	do.
New Wing, Aske Hall, Richmond, Yorks	....	Clark & Moscrop	do.

PUBLIC APPOINTMENTS.

Nature of Appointment.	By whom Advertised.	Salary.	Applications to be in.
*Assistant Engineering Surveyor	Birkenhead Corp.	120*l.* &c.	Mar. 8
*Engineer	Commrs. of Public Baths, &c. Chelsea	2*l.* 10*s.*	Mar. 9
*District Surveyor	Everley and Pewsey Highway Board	180*l.*	Mar. 10
*Clerk of the Works	Guildford T. C.	3*l.* per week	Mar. 15

Those marked with an Asterisk (*) are advertised in this Number. *Competition, p. iv. Contracts, pp. iv., vi., & viii. Public Appointments, p. xxiii.*

day sections is connected to a counterpoise, and the balance is so nicely adjusted that the wind turns the sections back to angles greater or less according to its own force, thus tending to maintain uniformity of power in the wheel from winds of all strength,—the vane always acting as a rudder to keep the face of the mill towards the wind. The mill thus constantly settles to its work, and is in no danger of being wrecked. As the current for lighting is only required for a few hours periodically, and the mill and the dynamo have all day to generate and store, there ought to be an easily ascertainable amount of storage to suffice for the occasional occurrences of calms. The windmill must not be allowed to race the dynamo; and the mill can in large degree govern itself. The dynamo's number of revolutions per minute will depend on the speed of the mill, but the electric generator must not be allowed to send too strong a current to the storage cells. By putting an ordinary governor on the spindle of the dynamo it can be made, as the governor moves swifter or slower, to put on more or less resistance coils, and so maintain a uniform charging current of the capacity required. The overcharge of the battery being provided for, any inopportune discharge from it is guarded against by a contact-maker, which fundamentally cuts out the generated current when too weak for charging the cells, but automatically applies itself to pass the current when of the requisite capacity. The little installation at Messrs. Carwardine's, which has been carried out by the Wenham Company, Ltd., runs two arc lights of nominal 1,500 candle-power and a few incandescents. A year's experience of its working will afford useful data for the extension of wind-power to the generation of electricity.

County Council Elections. — Mr. Silvanus Trevail, architect, Truro, has just been returned unopposed as the representative for the Eastern electoral division of that city in the Cornwall County Council. Mr. Trevail's return for the same division in the first County Council was also unopposed.

The Surveyors' and Auctioneers' Clerks' Provident Association.—The annual report of this Association, which was submitted at the annual meeting of members, held at the Auction Mart, Tokenhouse-yard, on Wednesday last, states that the number of members in the respective divisions of the Association is as follows,—viz.: Sick allowance fund, 43; life assurance fund, 28; superannuation fund, 8; and benevolent fund, 6. The sick allowance for the year has amounted to about the normal expectation, and exhibits a pleasing contrast to the heavy demand made in the previous year, owing to the epidemic of influenza. A small grant from the benevolent fund has been made in one case. The total grants from this fund up to the present time amount to 28*l.* No claim has yet been made upon the life assurance fund. The whole of the outlay of the Association for the year has been met out of the income received from investments. A further sum of 200*l.* has been invested, making the satisfactory total of 2,503*l.* The Committee thank the honorary subscribers for their continued support; also the directors of the Auction Mart for the use of a room for meetings. The report was adopted.

The English Iron Trade.—The approaching stoppage in the coal trade has had the effect of further restricting business. As the supply of fuel is likely to be extremely limited, many ironmasters have taken the precaution of issuing notices to their men for the period during which the stoppage will apply. The statistics issued by the British Iron Trade Association show that the total production of pig-iron during the year 1891 was 7,228,496 tons; of Bessemer steel, 1,642,005 tons; and of open-hearth steel, 1,514,538 tons, exhibiting decreases, as compared with 1890, of 616,634, 372,838, and 49,662 tons respectively. Pig-iron prices generally are tolerably firm, with little business passing. Scotch makers' iron is very quiet, with quotations lower. Finished iron is in but moderate demand, and no further change has taken place in the position of tin plates. The steel trade generally is quiet. Shipbuilding shows fair activity, so far as launches are concerned, but new orders are scarce. The engineering and allied trades are slack. The coal trade exhibits great activity with the approach of the stop-week, which will be almost general.—*Iron.*

Partnership.—Messrs. Ashbee & Sons, timber and slate importers, Gloucester, inform us that they have taken into partnership Mr. C. W. Estcourt, and that the business will in future be carried on under the style of "Ashbee, Sons, & Co."

LEGAL.

SURVEYOR'S FEE FOR NEGOTIATING PURCHASE.

LOVEGROVE *v.* TRUMAN, HANBURY, & CO.

This was an action in the Mayor's Court, Guildhall, brought by Mr. Henry Lovegrove, of 26, Budge-row, City, against Messrs. Truman, Hanbury, & Co., the well-known brewers.

Mr. Lewis Glyn (in the unavoidable absence of Mr. Edward Boyle), instructed by Messrs. Auyone & Bromwich, appeared for the plaintiff; and Mr. Paul Taylor, instructed by Messrs. Hanbury, Hutton, & Whitting, appeared for the defendants.

Mr. Lovegrove stated that in the autumn of 1889 he was acting for the defendants' lessees in Fetter-lane, and when at the brewery on a day in November of that year the acquirement of an adjoining slip of land was discussed, and Mr. Fraser requested the plaintiff to try to purchase the property. After this, for some weeks, the plaintiff was in communication with the vendors, and eventually purchased the land conditionally on giving up some rights of light.

The defendants' evidence proved that such an interview took place, but they considered that plaintiff was acting on behalf of their tenant. The judge, in summing up, pointed out that the land was conveyed to the defendants, and afterwards sold by them, and it was evident that the plaintiff, and nobody else, had arranged the matter.

The jury gave a verdict for the plaintiff for the amount claimed and costs.

MEETINGS.

Saturday, March 5.

Architectural Association.—Visit to St. Saviour's, Southwark, by permission of Sir Arthur W. Blomfield, A.R.A. 3 p.m.

Institution of Civil Engineers.—Students' visit to the Oil-gas works of the Great Northern Railway at Holloway. 3 p.m.

Monday, March 7.

Royal Institute of British Architects.—(1) General Business Meeting to ballot for candidates. (2) Special General Meeting (*a*) to elect the Royal Gold Medallist for the current year (*b*), to receive and consider an amended paper of "Suggestions for the Conduct of Architectural Competitions," recommended for adoption by the Council. 8 p.m.

Royal Academy of Arts.—Professor J. H. Middleton on "Michael Angelo." III. 8 p.m.

Society of Arts (Cantor Lectures).—Professor William Robinson on "The Uses of Petroleum in Prime Movers." II. 8 p.m.

Society of Engineers.—Mr. Stephen Sellon on "Electrical Traction and its Financial Aspect." 7.30 p.m.

Liverpool Architectural Society.—Mr. D. Harrison on "Pre-historic Rome." 6.30 p.m.

Tuesday, March 8.

Institution of Civil Engineers.—Professor W. C. Unwin on "Petroleum Engines." 8 p.m.

Sanitary Institute (Lectures for Sanitary Officers). Mr. J. F. J. Sykes on "General Powers and Duties of Inspectors of Nuisances." 8 p.m.

Sheffield Society of Architects and Surveyors.—Mr. J. A. Gotch on "How they Built in Shakespeare's Time," illustrated with lantern slides.

Wednesday, March 9.

Architects' Benevolent Society.—Annual General Meeting of subscribers and donors, the President, Mr. J. Macvicar Anderson, in the chair. 5 p.m.

Society of Arts.—Mr. A. P. Laurie on "Experiments on the Durability of Modern Pigments." 8 p.m.

British Museum.—Miss Eugénie Sellers on "Greek Sculpture: Sculptures from the Temple of Artemis (Diana) at Ephesus." V. 2.30 p.m.

Sanitary Institute.—Dr. Louis Parkes on "The Air and Water of London: Are they Deteriorating?" 8 p.m.

THURSDAY, MARCH 10.

Society of Antiquaries.—8.30 p.m.

Edinburgh Architectural Association.—Mr. J. Balfour Paul on "Heraldry in Relation to Architecture." 8 p.m.

Dundee Institute of Architecture.—Mr. T. Claxton Fidler on "The Evidences of Scientific Knowledge and Constructive Skill in the Remains of Ancient Architecture and Engineering." 8 p.m.

FRIDAY, MARCH 11.

Institution of Civil Engineers (Students' Meeting).—Mr. James B. Ball on "The Manufacture of Oil Gas at the Holloway works of the Great Northern Railway Company." 7.30 p.m.

Sanitary Institute (Lectures for Sanitary Officers).—Mr. J. F. J. Sykes on "Objects and Methods of Inspection." 8 p.m.

Bradford Historical and Antiquarian Society.—Mr. Butler Wood on "Some Old Bradford Artists." 8 p.m.

SATURDAY, MARCH 12.

Sanitary Inspectors' Association. — Ninth Annual Dinner, First Avenue Hotel, Holborn. Dr. B. W. Richardson, President, in the chair. 6 p.m.

Edinburgh Architectural Association.—Visit to Roslin Chapel and Roslin Castle.

RECENT PATENTS:

ABSTRACTS OF SPECIFICATIONS.

5,203.—WINDOWS: *W. Hughes.*—This specification refers to a new sash spring-coil and axle-pulley. A spring made of thin steel is inserted in a hollow groove of the wheel of an axle pulley, the pulley being fixed to either casement or solid frame window. The spiral spring is wound up tight and held in position by means of pins, which run through it and connect it with the axle of the pulley; the spring coil runs outside the wheel, to which it is also fastened. When the window is opened the spring coil pays out. When closed, it winds up, being set in action and governed by the spring inside the pulley wheel. No cords or other appliances are required, and the pulley, made of cast-iron, is simply let in flush with the woodwork and inside of sash. Two must be attached to the window, one on each side.

14,157.—DOORS: *C. Scriven.*—This patent refers to an improvement on an application dated July 17, 1891, in respect of an apparatus for closing doors, and, if necessary, holding them open in any desired position. This is effected by means of twisted indiarubber or other elastic material, arranged as set out in specification.

14,184.—FIREPLACES: *J. Shaw.*—The inventor claims that by means of the arrangement described below, the effect is to contract the draught space of the chimney, to secure effective combustion of fuel, and to prevent the creation of smoke. A metal pin about 6 in. long is constructed with a spring clip near its centre, for the purpose of fixing on the top of a register or other plate in an open fireplace. The pin is placed horizontally with its shorter end projecting against the inside front of the grate-plate or chimney, the back end projecting towards the chimney-wall, and so maintaining the register in a forward position.

4,981.—DRAINAGE: *H. Clark.*—This invention relates to drains only, and has for its objects the prevention of the passage of sewer-gas, &c., from one part of a system of drainage to another, and the absolute prevention of sewer-gas, &c., rising and accumulating at the higher levels, the provision of sufficient outlets for stench and inlets for fresh air, and to render the use of gullies, syphons, or other traps with a water-seal unnecessary. The invention is carried out by arranging the pipes, and the use of the apparatus as described and illustrated in the specification.

NEW APPLICATIONS FOR LETTERS PATENTS.

February 15.—2,899, T. Potter, Building Monolithic Concrete Walls.—2,912, H. Jenning, T-square Drawing-easel for the use of Architects, Engineers, and Surveyors.—2,932, J. Salomon, Pottery-ware Domestic Stoves for Heating Purposes.—2,951, C. Logan, Wire Nails.—2,964, M. Kann, Apparatus for use in working Stone.—2,967, H. Woodhouse, Firegrates or Stoves.

February 16.—3,007, R. Wylde, Chimney-pots.—3,015, H. Haddan, Manufacturing Screws.—3,016, G. Lawford, Closet Connexions.—3,021, A. Frisby, Construction of Machinery for Carving Wood and other Compressible Materials.

February 17.—3,083, R. Walker, Machine for Grinding Portland Cement.—3,093, J. Carr, Mortising Chisel.—3,101, W. Jackson, Chimney-pot.—3,125, J. Bridson, Brick for Building Purposes.

February 18.—3,201, D. Halpin, Treads for Stairs.—3,215, C. Pryce, Kilns.

February 19.—3,220, F. & J. Butterfield & Co., Limited, and W. Pearson, Mechanism for Operating Band-saws.—3,266, J. Jones, Drainage Appliances.—3,286, J. Caldecourt, Sockets or Joints of Rain-water Pipes.—3,290, J. Leighton, Chimney Cap or Cowl.—3,302, W. Jones, Water-waste Preventer.—3,304, F. Pateman and J. Ashman, Chimney-top, Pot, Cowl, or Ventilator.

February 20.—3,356, R. Bell, Apparatus for Heating Dwelling-houses, Hotels, and other Buildings.

PROVISIONAL SPECIFICATIONS ACCEPTED.

21,589, W. Dawkes, Valves for Flushing Cisterns, superseding separate air-pipe and affording an after flush.—22,322, W. Jacques, Fire-exit Door, Lock, and Alarm.—85, R. Barker, Sewer-pipe and Drain-tile Machines.—86, R. Barker, Sewer-pipe and Drain-tile Machines.—408, William Sykes, Jointing Earthenware, Concrete, and other like Pipes.—488, T. Wilkinson, Joints for Sewer and other Pipes.—600, R. Rhodes and R. Holland, Domestic Hearths.—680, F. Noar, Lead Service Piping.—707, C. Johnson and A. Wilson, Joints for Pipes, constructed of stoneware, earthenware, concrete, &c.—939, . Baxter, Connecting Earthenware Sanitary Appliances.—1,039, G. & C. Rollason, Joints for Hot-water Pipes.—1,041, S. Rollason, Generating Electricity for Buildings.—1,114, W. Copping, Bolts or Fastenings for Emergency Doors of Public Buildings.—1,154, W. Riley, Knobs of Door-handles and in adjusting and holding them upon the spindles.—1,196, J. Banks, Flush and other Bolts.—1,238, J. Smeaton, Water-closets.—1,281, H. Dowty, Hot-water Pipes and Connexions.—1,330, P. Mooney, Earthenware Gully Traps.—1,342, E. Hunt, Gasaliers and Chandeliers.—1,357, H. Wethered, Ventilation of Closet, Basins, and Water-closets.—1,514, W. Thompson, Grinding Tools.—1,603, J. Merry, Syphon-flushing Apparatus for Water-closets.—1,628, S. Gratrix and others, Gas Chandeliers.—1,687, H. Brooke, Fittings for Shop-windows, &c.—1,742, J. Hudson, Low-water Alarms for Kitchen or Domestic Boilers.—1,857, O. Hawkes, Joints for Fanlights, &c.—1,869, W. Francis, Surveying Instruments.—2,161, A. Kershaw, Ventilators.

COMPLETE SPECIFICATIONS ACCEPTED.

(Open to Opposition for Two Months.)

3,299, J. Prentice and others, Door-handles.—6,830, J. Fairbank, Gas-fittings.—6,922, A. Damp, Water-closet Cisterns.—18,247, W. Thompson, Nail-driving Tool.—21,997, J. Thompson, Fire-resisting Brick and Material for Lining, Facing, or Coating Fire-places, Fire-boxes, &c.—954, A. Young and R. Chesney, a Lock.—1,052, J. Chappell, Parquet and Block Flooring.—1,062, J. Barber, Device for Curing Smoky Chimneys.

SOME RECENT SALES OF PROPERTY:

ESTATE EXCHANGE REPORT.

FEBRUARY 22.—By *R. A. Notley*: Freehold premises, Maltby-st., Bermondsey, area 18,743 ft., 4,500*l.*—By *A. Richards*: F.g.r. of 30*l.*, with reversion in 70 yrs., Elsa-st., Limehouse, 575*l.*—By *Messrs. Willmott*: 26 to 32 even, Vespan-rd., Shepherd's-bush, u.t. 82 yrs., g.r. 25*l.* 4s., 450*l.*—By *Prickett, Venables, & Co.*: 44, Florence-rd., Stroud-green, u.t. 86 yrs., g.r. 7*l.* 10s., r. 40*l.*, 400*l.*; a plot of freehold land, Cecile-pk., Crouch-hill, 1,360*l.*; a plot of freehold land, Gladwell-rd., 1,100*l.*

FEBRUARY 23.—By *Toplis & Roberts*: 44, Hethpool-st., Edgware-rd., u.t. 46 yrs., g.r. 7*l.* 7s., r. 93*l.* 12s., 510*l.*; 85, Park-st., Camden Town, u.t. 28 yrs., g.r. 5*l.*, r. 52*l.*, 400*l.*—By *Debenham, Tewson, & Co.*: "The Oxford Arms" beerhouse, Brushfield-st., Spitalfields, f., r. 50*l.*, 900*l.*; 64 and 66, Brushfield-st., f., r. 125*l.*, 2,000*l.*; freehold premises in Little Paternoster-row, r. 60*l.*, 800*l.*; 31 and 33, Gascony-av., Kilburn, u.t. 88 yrs., g.r. 21*l.*, r. 90*l.*, 510*l.*; 28, 30, and 31, Napier-st., Deptford, u.t. 53 yrs., g.r. 5*l.* 8s., r. 66*l.* 6s., 415*l.*—By *Dowsett & Co.*: A plot of freehold land, Wellington-st., Slough, 1r. 10p., 250*l.*; a plot of freehold land, ditto, 80*l.*; 84 and 86, Sebert-rd., West Ham, f., r. 70*l.* 4s., 675*l.*; 28, Taniwha-ter., f., r. 29*l.* 18s., 300*l.*; "Windsor Cottage," Windsor-rd., Upton-pk., f., r. 26*l.*, 265*l.*; "Chesterton Cottage" and plot of land, Western-rd., Plaistow, 180*l.*; the lease of 95, Woodgrange-rd., Forest-gate, u.t. 12 yrs., 20*l.*—By *A. Young*: The letting of a plot of land, Cheyne-walk, Chelsea, area 7,033 ft., 80 yrs. at 65*l.* per annum; 49, Mount Pleasant, Clerkenwell, f., 650*l.*; three plots of freehold land, Cable-st., Shadwell, 100*l.*; 40, Battersea-bridge-rd., Battersea, f., 425*l.*; 46 to 68 even, Battersea-bridge-rd., f., 4,230*l.*

FEBRUARY 24.—By *W. H. Hilton*: 37, Clifden-rd., Clapton, u.t. 76 yrs., g.r. 5*l.*, r. 26*l.*, 235*l.*—By *D. Young*: 16, Hadley-rd., Barnet, f., 145*l.*; 41, Poplar Walk-rd., Herne Hill, u.t. 75 yrs., g.r. 3*l.* 10s., 240*l.*; 18, Burnley-rd., Stockwell, u.t. 70 yrs., g.r. 6*l.* 10s., 400*l.*; 31 and 35, Dalyell-road, u.t. 72 yrs., g.r. 13*l.* 15s., 430*l.*—By *R. Tidey & Son*: 79, Felton-st., Hoxton, u.t. 26 yrs., g.r. 3*l.*, 105*l.*; 40, Hertford-rd., Kingsland, u.t. 27 yrs., g.r. 5*l.*, 135*l.*; 71 and 73, Hertford-rd., u.t. 26 yrs., g.r. 14*l.*, 275*l.*; 128, De Beauvoir-rd., u.t. 29 yrs., g.r. 4*l.* 5s., 300*l.*; 105, Kingsland-road and goodwill, u.t. 77 yrs., g.r. 20*l.*, 160*l.*; 107, Kingsland-rd., u.t. 30 yrs., g.r. 25*l.*, r. 43*l.*, 60*l.*; 37 and 39, Ash-grove, Hackney, u.t. 34 yrs., g.r. 9*l.*, r. 62*l.*, 400*l.*; 9 and 11, How's-st., Kingsland, u.t. 26 yrs., g.r. 15*l.* 8s., r. 72*l.* 16s.; and a l.g.r. of 7*l.* 14s. (same term), 205*l.*; 3, William-st., Islington, u.t. 53 yrs., g.r. 4*l.*, 300*l.*

FEBRUARY 25.—By *B. Brown*: 157, High-st., Poplar, f., r. 24*l.*, 205*l.*; 30 and 31, Ellerthorpe-st., u.t. 51 yrs., g.r. 6*l.* 6s., r. 50*l.* 14s., 310*l.*; 4 and 6, Bedford-st., u.t. 14 yrs., g.r. 4*l.* 10s., r. 41*l.* 12s., 100*l.*; 37, Stainsby-rd., u.t. 25 yrs., g.r. 4*l.* 10s., r. 32*l.*, 210*l.*; 147 and 149 Grundy-st., Bromley-by-Bow, f., r. 46*l.* 16s., 550*l.*—By *W. W. Jenkinson*: 19, Almida-st., Islington, u.t. 30 yrs., g.r. 8*l.*, 410*l.*; 12, Spa-rd., Bermondsey, f., r. 42*l.*, 495*l.*—By *Debenham, Tewson, & Co.*: "The Rising Sun" beerhouse, Newburn-st., Lambeth, f., r. 65*l.*, 1,000*l.*—By *Walters & Lovejoy*: The Residence, "Dalkeith," Cambridge-rd., Leytonstone, f., r. 35*l.*, 505*l.*; No. 25, Clapham-common, f., r. 50*l.*, 745*l.*—By *Newbon & Co.*: 33 and 35, Frederick-st., Islington, u.t. 59 yrs., g.r. 11*l.*, r. 61*l.*, 500*l.*; 5, Charlesworth-st., Caledonian-rd., u.t. 60 yrs., g.r. 6*l.*, r. 30*l.*, 275*l.*; 70, Bride-st., u.t. 69 yrs., g.r. 7*l.* 10s., r. 40*l.*, 380*l.*; 7, 8, and 9, Providence-row, King's-cross, u.t. 99 yrs., g.r. 1*l.* 10s., 285*l.*—By *Stimson & Sons*: 3, East Chapel-st., Mayfair, u.t. 847 yrs., g.r. 2*l.*, r. 80*l.*, 1,700*l.*; 59, 61, 67, and 69, Dunstan's-rd., Dulwich, u.t. 86 yrs., g.r. 10*l.* 10s., 690*l.*; 33, 35, and 37, Lettsom-rd., Camberwell, u.t. 377 yrs., no g.r., r. 91*l.*, 860*l.*; 90, Portland-pl. North, Clapham, u.t. 10 yrs., g.r. 4*l.*, r. 31*l.* 4s., 87*l.*; 72 to 78 even, Wilcox-rd., Lambeth, u.t. 63 yrs., g.r. 12*l.*, 1,080*l.*; l.g.r. of 30*l.*, Wandsworth-rd., u.t. 17 yrs., g.r. 10*l.*; and 39, Pascal-st., 160*l.*

FEBRUARY 26.—By *L. Farmer*: 122, Maida-vale, f., 1,425*l.*—By *Harman Bros.*: "The Lions," Mount Pleasant-lane, Clapton, u.t. 10 yrs., g.r. 9*l.* 10s., 190*l.*; 5 and 6, High-rd., u.t. 14 yrs., g.r. 20*l.*, r. 90*l.*, 305*l.*—By *Hards & Bradly*: 12 and 14, Eustace-rd., Fulham, u.t. 80 yrs., g.r. 10*l.*, r. 72*l.* 16s., 580*l.*; 1, Lacon-rd., Dulwich, u.t. 82 yrs., g.r. 7*l.*, r. 83*l.* 16s., 150*l.*; 2 and 4, Turner-rd., Lee, u.t. 38 yrs., g.r. 4*l.* 10s., r. 62*l.*, 490*l.*—By *R. Reid*: 8, Fouberts-pl., Regent-st., f., r. 70*l.*, 1,340*l.*; 82, Berwick-st., f., r. 75*l.*, 1,330*l.*; the lease of 14, Fouberts-pl., u.t. 6 yrs., 50*l.*—By *Field & Sons*: F.g.r. of 15*l.*, with reversion in 18 yrs., Peckham, 475*l.*; f.g.r. of 8*l.*, with reversion in 39 yrs., Clayton-rd., 120*l.*; 20 and 22, Rye-lane, f., 2,720*l.*; f.g.r. of 10*l.*, with reversion in 8 yrs., Tottenham-court-rd., 550*l.*; 79, Drury-lane, f., r. 30*l.*, 575*l.*; 41, Great Ormond-st., Bloomsbury, f., r. 50*l.*, 1,200*l.*; 10, Winslade-rd., Brixton, u.t. 75 yrs., g.r. 7*l.* 10s., r. 36*l.*, 300*l.*

[*Contractions used in these lists.*—F.g.r. for freehold ground-rent; l.g.r. for leasehold ground-rent; i.g.r. for improved ground-rent; g.r. for ground-rent; r. for rent; f. for freehold; c. for copyhold; l. for leasehold; e.r. for estimated rental; u.t. for unexpired term; p.a. for per annum; yrs. for years; st. for street; rd. for road; sq. for square; pl. for place; ter. for terrace; cres. for crescent; yd. for yard, &c.]

PRICES CURRENT OF MATERIALS.

TIMBER.		
Greenheart, B.G. ...ton	9/0/0	0/0/0
Teak, E.I. ... load	9/10/0	16/0/0
Sequoia, U.S. ft. cu.	2/3	3/0
Ash, Canada load	2/10/0	4/0/0
Birch, do.	3/5/0	4/10/0
Elm, do.	3/10/0	4/15/0
Fir, Dantsic, &c.	2/0/0	3/10/0
Oak, do.	3/0/0	5/0/0
Canada	5/0/0	7/0/0
Pine, Canada red	2/10/0	3/10/0
Do. yellow	2/10/0	5/0/0
Lath, D'ntsic, fath	5/0/0	6/10/0
St. Petersburg	5/10/0	7/10/0
Deals, Finland, 2nd & 1st std 100	8/10/0	10/10/0
Do. 4th & 3rd ..	7/10/0	8/10/0
Do. Riga	6/10/0	8/0/0
St. Petersburg, 1st yellow ..	11/0/0	15/0/0
Do. 2nd yellow	8/10/0	10/10/0
Do. white	7/10/0	10/10/0
Swedish	7/15/0	16/0/0
White Sea	8/10/0	18/0/0
Canada, Pine 1st	20/0/0	26/0/0
Do. do. 2nd	14/10/0	16/10/0
Do. do. 3rd, &c.	8 5/0	10/10/0
Do. Spruce, 1st	8/10/0	11/0/0
Do. do. 3rd & 2nd	6/15/0	8/0/0
New Brunswick	7/0/0	7/10/0
Battens, all kinds	3/10/0	18/10/0
Flooring Boards, sq., 1 in. prep. 1st	0/8/6	0/14/6
Do. 2nd	0/7/6	0/11/6
Other qualities	0/5/0	0/8/0
Cedar, Cuba .. ft.	/3½	/4½
Honduras, &c.	/3½	/4
Mahogany, Cuba	/4½	/6½
St. Domingo, cargo av	/4½	2 0
Mexican do. do	/4	/6
Tobacco do. do	/5½	/7
Honduras do. ..	/5½	/8½
Box, Turkey ton	4/0/0	15/0/0
Rose, Rio	10/0/0	20/0/0
Bahia	9/0/0	18/0/0
Satin, St. Domingo .... ft.	0 0 8	0/1/8

TIMBER (continued).		
Satin, Porto Rico	0/0/8	0/1/6
Walnut, Italian ..	0/0/3½	0/0/7
METALS.		
IRON—Pig, in Scotland ...... ton	2/0/3	2/0/4
Bar, Welsh, in London	5/0/0	6/10/0
Do. do. at works in Wales	5/10/0	6/0/0
Do. Staffordshire, in London	6/5/0	6/15/0
COPPER—British, cake and ingot	46/0/0	47/0/0
Best selected ..	48/0/0	48 10/0
Sheets, strong ..	57/0/0	58/0/0
Chili, bars	44/2 6	44/10/0
YELLOW METAL lb.	0 0/5½	0/0/6½
LEAD—Pig, Spanish .... ton	10/15 0	10/17/6
English, com. brands	11/0/0	11.2 6
Sheet, English, 3 lbs. per sq. ft. and upwards ..	13 0 0	0/0/0
Pipe	13/10/0	0/0/0
ZINC—English sheet ...... ton	20/5 0	0/0/0
Vieille Montagne	15/15 0	0/0/0
TIN—Straits	89/7/6	89 15/0
Australian	89/10/0	89/15/0
English Ingots	92/10/0	93/15/0
OILS.		
Linseed ...... ton	18/15 0	18 17/6
Cocoanut, Cochin	25/0/0	25/10/0
Do. Ceylon	22/15/0	0/0/0
Palm, Lagos	23/10/0	0/0/0
Rapeseed, English pale	26/0/0	26 5/0
Do. brown	24/5/0	24 10/0
Cottonseed ref. ..	18/5/0	0/0/0
Oleine	21/10/0	22 10/0
Lubricating, U.S.	4/10/0	6/10/0
Do. refined	5/0 0	10/0/0
TAR—Stockholm barrel	0/19/0	1/0/0
Archangel	0/12/6	0/0/0

TENDERS.

[Communications for insertion under this heading must reach us *not later than 12 noon on Thursdays.*]

ABERDARE.—For alterations and additions to the "Bush" Inn, Aberdare, for the Ely Brewery Company, Limited. Mr. C. H. Elford, architect, 15, Cardiff-street, Aberdare:—

John Jones	£355	William Thomas	£330
Michael Thomas (mislaid) ..	..	A. E. Thomas	305
John Morgan, Monk-street, Aberdare*	370		

* Accepted.

BRISTOL.—For new road and approaches to the Keynsham Union, near Bristol. Mr. John Macker, architect and surveyor, Kingswood, Bristol:—

Wm. Thomas	£299	15	7	A. Kendall	£225	0	
R. R. Facey	282	14	0	W. Merryweather ...	216	0	0
Fred. Martin	278	12	0	J. Carpenter	186	0	0
Jas. Wiltshire	265	0	0	H. West, Bath*	165	10	0
A. Webb	241	14	9				

* Accepted.

CHISWICK.—For building a pair of villa residences in Chiswick for Mr. W. Boughton, Hammersmith. Mr. J. Boone, architect and surveyor, Chiswick. Quantities supplied:—

S. Hunt	£1,185	Adamson & Son	£1,09[illegible]
Chamberlen Bros.	1,110	— Nye, Ealing (accepted) ..	59[illegible]

DAWLISH (Devon).—For the erection of six cottages, for Miss Empson. Mr. Chas. Cole, architect, 50, High-street, Exeter. Quantities by the architect:—

Tree & Bailey	£2,187	0	0	Cundy & Stoyle	£1,935	8	8
F. Friend	2,095	0	0	J. H. Lemacraft	1,941	0	0
Ham & Passmore	2,000	0	0	J. Wescott	1,909	6	4
Friend & Cundy, Dawlish*	1,976	3	10	C. Hawking	1,780	0	0
				H. Ferris	1,576	11	

* Accepted.

HASTINGS.—For the construction of roads on the St. Helen's Park Estate, Hastings. Mr. P. H. Humphreys, surveyor, Hastings:—

	Estimate No. 1.			Estimate No. 2.	
W. J. Boite Ill	£974	0	0	£998	0
A. Cohen	790	0	0	860	0
W. H. Wheeler	636	0	0	742	0
Barlow & Roberts	642	0	0	662	0
P. Jenkins	517	0	0	596	8
K. Gutsell	481	17	0	549	14
Piper & Son	456	7	2	493	12

HOUNSLOW.—For rebuilding shops, Nos. 161 and 163, High-street, Hounslow, for Mr. H. Perks. Messrs. J. H. & H. B. Jones, architects, 9, Moorgate-street, E.C. Quantities by the architects:—

W. Hogbin	£2,534	8	W. H. Lascelles & Co. ..	£2,236	0
G. Daniels	2,300	0	T. Hiscock, Hounslow* .	2,224	0

* Accepted.

HULL.—For the erection of the proposed new Catholic schools on the Beverley-road Boulevard, Hull. Messrs. Smith & Brodrick, and A. Lowther, joint architects:—

John Drury	£2,287	1	M. Harper	£2,087	2
Geo. Houlton	2,271	0	H. Vickers	2,030	8
Hockney & Liggins	2,125	0	G. Jackson & Sons	1,979	0
F. Blackburn	2,094	19	Colley & Levitt*	1,946	15

* Accepted.

LONDON.—For alterations to 227, Strand, W.C., for Mr. F. Pake. Messrs. Saville & Martin, architects, Dacre-house, Arundel-street, Strand, W.C. Quantities supplied:—

H. B. Oldrey	£2,511	Gould & Brand	£2,325
S. Goodall	2,349	S. Toms	2,248
C. Dearing & Son	2,343		

Fitter's Work.

Sage & Co.	£332	Drew & Cadman	£223
S. Yardley & Sons	253		

LONDON.—For pulling-down and re-building the "Horse Shoe" public-house, Tottenham Court-road. Mr. J. M. Knight, architect:—

Mowlem & Co.	£12,057	W. Brass	£10,140
Stimpson & Son	11,164	Kirk	10,190
J. Bywaters	10,480	Ashby Bros.	9,975
W. Shurmur	10,449	Patman & Fotheringham	9,853
Colls & Son	10,250	Allen & Son	9,665

LONDON.—For new addition, shop-front, fixtures, &c., at Nos. 462 and 444, Holloway-road, N., for Messrs. Isaac Walton & Co.:—

John Wynne, 62, Newington-causeway, S.E. £2,360 0

[No competition.]

LONDON.—For alterations and additions to the "Burlington" Restaurant, Regent-street, W., for the London Catering Company. Messrs. Saville & Martin, architects, Dacre-house, Arundel-street, Strand, W.C. Quantities supplied by Messrs. Woodward & Argent, 8, Duke-street, Adelphi:—

Thos. Gregory & Co.	£2,962	Colls & Sons	£2,795
F. L. Green	2,982	Higgs & Hill	2,770
Ashby Bros.	2,893	G. H. & A. Bywaters*	2,719

Pewterer's Work.

S. Heath	£151	Sanders & Sons	£109
W. Helling	130	J. Edwards*	105

* Accepted.

LONDON.—For alterations and additions to the "Royal Oak" public house, St. John's-road, Holloway, N., for Messrs. G. Soole & Son. Messrs. Saville & Martin, architects, Dacre House, Arundel-street, Strand, W.C. Quantities supplied:—

E. Toms	£2,867	W. Scrivener & Co.	£2,795
S. Goodall	2,848	Dearing & Son	2,715
Ward & Lambie	2,822	Gould & Brand (accepted)	2,607

Pewterer's work.

S. Heath	£200 0	J. C. Edwards	£161 5
W. Helling	186 10	Sanders & Sons (accepted)	159 0

Gasfitter's work.

Vaughan & Brown	£187 0	E. Morris	£169 9
J. Biggs	178 0	E. Pragnell (accepted)	144 0

LONDON.—For pulling down the "Rising Horse" public-house, Oxford-street, W., and premises adjoining in Buzter's-court, for Messrs. H. & R. Baker. Messrs. Saville & Martin, architects, Dacre House, Arundel-street, Strand, W.C.:—

Kirk & Randall	£545	J. Allen & Sons	£195
Ashby Bros.	406	Colls & Sons	192
G. H. & A. Bywaters	241	T. L. Green (accepted)	187

LONDON.—For alterations to the London and South-Western Bank, West Norwood Branch. Messrs. Tolley & Sons, architects, 66, Cannon-street:—

Bristow	£1,947	Pullen & Co.	£1,698
Mitchell	1,943	Marriage	1,697
Smith & Sons	1,826	Lyon & Sons	1,671
Bowyer	1,789	Carmichael	1,676

LONDON.—For erecting warehouse, Tottenham-road, Kingsland. Mr. J. Hamilton, architect:—

S. Hayworth	£1,676	G. Beale	£1,397
Gould & Brand	1,647	W. Shurmur	1,395
B. E. Nightingale	1,600	S. Goodall	1,390

LONDON.—For the erection of a new public-house, to be known as the "White Hart" Hotel, Gipsy-lane, Upton Park, E., for Mr. J. Davies. Mr. Fred. A. Ashton, architect, 8, Crooked-lane, E.C.:—

Cousell Bros	£3,443	W. Watson	£3,217
Harris & Farrow	3,398	W. Shurmur*	3,195
F. Voller	3,369		

* Accepted.

LONDON.—For erecting new warehouse at 86, Kingsland-road. Mr. T. N. Laslett, architect:—

				Time for completion.
Holloway Bros.	£3,800	0	0	10 weeks.
Martin Wells	3,400	0	0	18 "
T. Boyce	3,300	0	0	12 "
Higgs & Hill	3,280	0	0	— "
Staines & Son	3,150	0	0	14 "
E. Garner	3,075	0	0	13 "
Paramore	3,060	0	0	16 "
W. Dabbs	2,980	0	0	15 "
B. Cromwell	2,972	0	0	20 "
King & Co.	2,950	0	0	14 "
W. Shurmur	2,889	0	0	12 "
J. Marter	2,870	0	0	14 "
Jarvis & Son	2,800	0	0	16 "
Adlard	2,685	0	0	8 "

LONDON.—For painting and repairs at the Fire Brigade Station, Islington, for the London County Council. Mr. Thomas Blashill, Architect:—

Davis Bros.	£335 0	A. D. Smith & Sons	£196 0
J. R. Powditch & Co.	227 0	W. Wills	173 10
J. Knight	207 0	G. & S. Williams & Son*	154 0

* Accepted conditionally.

MERTHYR TYDFIL.—For building a block of buildings, Market-square, Merthyr Tydfil, South Wales, for Mr. T. J. Masters, Cardiff. Mr. S. C. Wakeling, architect, Merthyr Tydfil:—

Burton & Co.	£11,875	Cowlin & Sons	£9,920
Hy. Welsh	11,000	T. Jones	9,700
S. Watkins & Co.	10,893	D. C. Jones & Co.	9,582
T. Noss	10,175	Stephens, Bastow, & Co.	8,980
S. D. Williams	10,145	Bowers & Co.,* Hereford	8,100

* Accepted.

NEWPORT (Mon.).—For rebuilding 168, Commercial-street, for Mr. W. Allen. Messrs. William Graham, Son, & Hitchcox, architects:—

Morgan & Roberts	£2,099 0	George Wilkins	£2,016 0
John Linton	2,045 10	William Blackburn*	1,997 0

* Accepted.

SHEFFIELD.—For the construction and erection of police-station, constables' dwellings, &c., at Millhouses, Sheffield. Plans, specifications and quantities prepared by Mr. C. F. Wike, C.E., Borough Surveyor:—

Jas. Richerby	£3,?00 14 6	Walker & Slater, Derby*	£2,130 0 0
G. J. Helliwell	2,866 9 8	J. H. Hurst†	1,901 19 3
J. Fish & Son	2,740 12 0		
R. Hunt	2,733 19 11		

* Accepted. † Withdrawn.

SUNDERLAND.—For the erection of a new Infirmary, Stockton-road, for the Committee of the Sunderland and North Durham Eye Infirmary. Mr. J. W. Donald, A.R.I.B.A., architect, Russell-chambers, King-street, South Shields. Quantities by the architects:—

R. Goodwin & Son	£4,989 10 0	Walter Scott & Son	£4,621 0 0
W. B. Cooper	4,853 0 0	Joseph Howe	4,611 0 0
T. P. Shaftoe	4,833 0 0	D. & J. Ranken, Sunderland*	4,463 0 0
W. J. Robertson	4,736 18 3	M. Howarth	4,397 18 0
H. Brown & Co.	4,718 18 4		
J. Huntley	4,655 0 0		

* Accepted.

WARRINGTON.—For alterations to baths and construction of new swimming-bath, for the Town Council. Mr. Thos. Longdin, Borough Surveyor, Warrington:—

W. Gibson & Son, Warrington £3,716 0 0

WATERFORD.—For new Training College, for the Brothers of the Christian Schools, Newtown, Waterford, Ireland. Mr. Wm. H. Byrne, architect, 20, Suffolk-street, Dublin:—

Collin Bros.	£20,810	G. Nolan, Waterford*	£20,700
T. Hearne	20,364	M. Hunt	17,647

* Accepted subject to modifications.

New Premises, Charles-street and Stephen-street, Lisson-grove.—Regarding the lists of tenders for these works published in our last (p. 172), the architect, Mr. F. W. Hunt, asks us to say that they are inaccurate, but he declines to tell us in what respect. Whatever errors there are, they are not ours.

SUBSCRIBERS in LONDON and the SUBURBS, by prepaying at the Publishing Office, 19s. per annum (or 4s. 9d. per quarter), can ensure receiving "The Builder" by *Friday Morning's post*.

TO CORRESPONDENTS.

W. B. D.—H. E.—J. W. T.—C. P. P.—W. H. M. (thanks; not required).—V. L. (we can see no special cause for your appeal at this moment).—J. P.

All statements of facts, lists of tenders, &c., must be accompanied by the name and address of the sender, not necessarily for publication.

We are compelled to decline pointing out books and giving addresses.

NOTE.—The responsibility of signed articles, and papers read at public meetings, rests, of course, with the authors.

We cannot undertake to return rejected communications.

Letters or communications (beyond mere news-items) which have been duplicated for other journals, are NOT DESIRED.

All communications regarding literary and artistic matter should be addressed to THE EDITOR; all communications relating to advertisements and other exclusively business matters should be addressed to THE PUBLISHER, and not to the Editor.

TERMS OF SUBSCRIPTION.

"THE BUILDER" is supplied DIRECT from the Office to residents in any part of the United Kingdom at the rate of 19s. per annum PREPAID. To all parts of Europe, America, Australia, and New Zealand, 26s. per annum. To India, China, Ceylon, &c., 30s. per annum. Remittances payable to DOUGLAS FOURDRINIER, Publisher, No. 46, Catherine-street, W.C.

The Builder.

Vol. LXII. No. 2562. SATURDAY, MARCH 12, 1892.

ILLUSTRATIONS.

Illustrations of Old Chester: III., Ancient Crypt in Watergate-street.—Drawn by Mr. T. P. Ivison .... *Double-Page Ink-Photo.*
Grandtully Castle, showing proposed Additions.—Messrs. Williams, West, & Slade, Architects .... *Double-Page Ink-Photo.*
Indian Decorative Balustrades (From the "Jeypore Portfolio of Architectural Details") .... *Double-Page Photo-Litho.*
Hall of the Broderers' Company.—Mr. H. Huntly-Gordon, Architect .... *Single-Page Photo-Litho.*
Additions to St. Stephen's Church Schools, Canonbury.—Mr. A. Ardron, Architect .... *Single-Page Photo-Litho.*

Blocks in Text.

Plan of St. Stephen's Schools, Canonbury .... Page 206 | Diagrams in Student's Column: Heating by Hot Water .... Pages 211, 212

CONTENTS.

Asylums for the Insane 197
Indian Architectural Details 199
Notes 199
How they Built in Shakespeare's Time 202
Magazines and Reviews 205
Illustrations of Old Chester 206
Grandtully Castle, Perthshire 206
Indian Decorative Detail 206
The Hall of the Worshipful Company of Broderers 206
St. Stephen's Church Schools, Canonbury 206
Architectural Societies 206
The Architectural Association Spring Visits 207
Demonstrations on Greek Sculpture in the British Museum 207
British Archæological Association 207
Competitions 207
Architects' Benevolent Society: Annual Meeting 207
Books: Murray's Handbook for India and Ceylon (London: J. Murray); Prof. Jervis' "I Tesori Sotterranei dell' Italia" (Turin: E. Loescher); E. Naville's "Two Hieroglyphic Papyri from Tanis" and "The Mound of the Jew and the City of Onias"; F. Ll. Griffith's "Antiquities of Tell-el-Yahûdîyeh"; E. Naville's "Bubastis": A. Dumont's "Mélanges d'Archéologie et d'Epigraphie" (Paris: E. Thorin); P. N. Hasluck's "Milling-machines and Processes" (London: Crosby Lockwood & Son); "Wilson W. Phipson" (London: G. Chard); M. B. Huish's "Year's Art, 1892" (London: Virtue & Co.); "The Clifton and Bristol Pictorial" (Bristol: W. F. Mack) 208
Coke-breeze Concrete 210
Valuation 210
Brickwork 210
Halifax Artisans' Dwellings Competition 210
"The Late Strike Still Smouldering" 211
Student's Column.—Warming Buildings by Hot Water, XI. 211
Obituary 212
General Building News 212
Foreign and Colonial 213
Miscellaneous 213
Meetings 214
Recent Patents 215
Some Recent Sales of Property 215
Prices Current of Materials 215
Tenders 215

*Asylums for the Insane.**

FROM any of the great main lines of railway which run through the shires, a traveller will be sure to spy, in some comparatively secluded position, a great group of buildings, which by heir modern air and their tall chimney tacks, and possibly their bulky water-tower, eem to belong rather to the busy town than o country seclusion. If he inquires, he will probably learn that this is the County Lunatic Asylum; for throughout England, is, indeed, throughout Europe, vast structures are now established, and are being added to almost every year, in which those mentally afflicted are to be lodged and medically cared or. To give an account of such asylums in every part of the world is the ambitious programme which Mr. Burdett set before himself when he undertook the preparation of the two bulky volumes now before us, and which are really only an instalment, though complete in themselves, as they are to be followed by two others on the hospitals of the world. Very great industry has been brought to bear upon the task, and a very large amount of information on the subject of asylums has been collected and will be found in this book, hough it will be nothing but the truth if we add that the very extent of the work will tand in the way of its being as popularly useful as a smaller book containing only carefully selected and condensed information might have been.

Mr. Burdett divides asylums into four groups, separated from one another by radical differences of arrangement, for in so extensive a structure as an asylum for 500 up to 2,000 patients, the disposition of the plan becomes a matter of vital importance. His first group is the Agglomerate, or irregular in type. These asylums are buildings that are thrown together upon no very definite system, and in many cases have reached their present extent by successive and often make-shift additions, or by the use of buildings designed for some other purpose. No new asylum of any importance would now be erected on this system; at the same time, and especially among private asylums, there are not a few buildings of this sort which, though occasioning a certain amount of inconvenience, are practically very serviceable, and are made use of at the present day, and will not soon be abandoned.

The next group is what may be termed Corridor asylums. Here the patients are, for the most part, housed in a kind of compound structure not in use in other classes of building. The day-room is a very wide corridor,—elsewhere in this volume called a gallery,—having fireplaces, and, usually, a large bay-window, or two such; while on the side opposite the windows is a series of doors opening into the bedrooms of patients and nurses. These form the units which can be grouped together to provide for a classification more or less minute, as circumstances may dictate; and, of course, with an administration block for a central feature. There are also in buildings of this class corridors proper,—*i.e.*, passages used only for the purpose of access from one part of the building to another, and not available as living-rooms. Rather more than fifty English examples of this class are more or less briefly described, and a plan and description of one English and one American specimen are given; a plan of another English example, of which we have failed to find a description, is also given. It would, in our opinion, have added very much to the value of the book, if under this and other heads more plans had been included, notwithstanding Mr. Burdett's assertion that "it was quite unnecessary to publish more plans," and that "in effect it would almost amount to the reproduction of almost identical plans." If so, we ask, why praise some designs as better than others? If plans could not be published, at least, in the case of such of these buildings as have been illustrated in our own pages or elsewhere, it would have been easy and very useful to add some indication of the fact, and some reference to the actual volume and page, at the end of the description in the text. Perhaps, too, we may be excused if we suggest that if Mr. Burdett had given the name of the architect of each asylum it would have been no more than an act of proper recognition. This information, however, has been left out in the very great majority of cases.

The third group are Pavilion asylums. These are asylums which resemble modern hospitals, in consisting of a series of pavilions, each two or three stories high, and connected together by corridors of communication, usually of one story only. This group includes, among others, the Asylum for Idiots at Darenth, to which our author pays the compliment of saying that it is "incomparably the best-planned idiot asylum in England." No plan, however, is given of this Asylum, but plans of the second Gloucester County Asylum are included. This is a building in which the blocks project from a V-shaped corridor,—an arrangement here designated as the broad-arrow form, and which Mr. Burdett does not approve. Only a small number of asylums are described under this head, but they include the gigantic ones at Coulsdon and Leavesden, each providing for about 2,000 patients.

The fourth group, the one to which our author gives the preference, consists of buildings of what he calls the Corridor-Pavilion type; and he describes this as a combination of the second and third types. Four English examples are described, but no plan is given of any one of them, though they include the Lancashire County Asylum, praised as "one of the finest specimens of asylum architecture in England," with the very remarkable addition that "its leading features show at once that it was designed by a medical superintendent. It consists of twelve blocks arranged in horse-shoe form." We are, however, furnished with two model plans, which are intended to illustrate the general idea of this group of designs, but do not show a complete mastery of the difficult art of disposing the parts of a great building. The plan of the Gretlock Asylum for the Glasgow District Board, which is included and nearly corresponds to the description of the corridor-pavilion type of hospital, on the other hand, strikes us as most satisfactory as well as economical, and well deserves study. Asylum construction in Scotland forms the subject,

* "Hospitals and Asylums of the World." By Henry C. Burdett, in four volumes and portfolio. Vols. 1 and 2. London: Churchill. 1891.

we may add, of a short, pithy, well-written chapter, to which the plan we allude to is appended, and which we are disposed to consider the best bit of writing and to contain the most valuable, certainly the most condensed, practical information in the whole book. In addition to the descriptions and plans above enumerated, a large number of brief references to asylums existing in different parts of the world and belonging to the above-mentioned four types of asylum is furnished, so that Continental and American examples of each type may be readily recognised. To these notes references are in some cases added, giving indications of where published plans and detailed descriptions may be found, such as we should have liked to see incorporated with the accounts of English asylums.

Two systematic chapters on asylum construction in France and in Germany give compactly the salient features, and even many of the details of the buildings established in those countries for the care of the insane, and these chapters close the original matter of the volume which we have been considering. There remains a bulky appendix, but, before we refer to its contents, it may be desirable to add a few observations as to general principles which are treated of near the beginning of the volume. The all but invariable scheme of an asylum is to divide it into a men's and a women's side and to place the administration block in the centre. That being taken for granted, Mr. Burdett lays down certain rules which he considers should always be borne in mind. Of these there are six which are considered by him as essential:—1. Some modification of the block principle. 2. Not more than two stories. 3. Each floor of each block to contain dormitory space sufficient for those patients who occupy its day-rooms. 4. Passages between main blocks (*i.e.*, corridors of communication) to be two stories high and fireproof, and main staircases to be incorporated in such passages. 5. A disposition making it possible to reach any ward without passing through any other ward. 6. Single bedrooms for at least one-fourth of the patients, each containing at least 800 cubic feet, and with at least 80 ft. of floor area. In the infirm ward these should open direct from the day-room. Five other principles are laid down as "highly desirable":—7. A minimum day and night space of 600 cubic feet per patient, with floor space of 60; but the day-space may be 500, when separate dining-rooms and a recreation-hall are available. 8. Each ward to have its own dining-room. 9. Minimum width of corridors to be 8 ft. No corridors to run under the window-sills of the single rooms. 10. The whole of the ground floor to be on one level. 11. In order to ensure abundance of light and air three walls of all day-rooms and dormitories should be free.

These principles and much detailed advice are supposed to be embodied in the model plan already alluded to; but the plan, whatever its excellences, is open to serious objections. Take, for example, the administration block; the text contains a careful description of what such a block should contain, and in what order the departments should come, but the plan in important respects departs from this description; and the account of it also, of course, differs, and that not merely in minor points. Which of the two is correct? or is it intended to convey the idea that the programme is not of much importance? For example, the programme very properly prescribes a porter's-room and a waiting-room. The plan omits the waiting-room. The programme provides a chaplain's-room, a dispensary, and a dining-hall. Not one of these appears on the model plan, and, though the absence of the dining-hall is accounted for by a provision of separate dining-rooms, one to each block, it does not seem easy to do without the dispensary. We think also a better provision might have been made on the plan for the surgery than to light it with south windows looking into a court less than 15 ft. wide. All the dormitories and sleeping-rooms of the proposed buildings for the inmates are lighted and ventilated from internal quadrangles, and though the length of corridors of communication, 8 ft. wide, does not on our computation actually reach a mile, it approaches that considerable dimension very closely. While admitting the desirability of means of separate access to every ward, we cannot but think that a more skilled designer could have secured this desirable end without burdening an asylum for 750 patients with a feature so expensive to build, so monotonous to traverse, and so costly to keep clean and sweet as this enormous development of corridor,—from our measurement of which we exclude all those corridors (or galleries) used as day-rooms.

Our author's views on plans, planning, and architects, put forward with an air of great authority, are on a par with the specimen of his skill which he has furnished us. The County Surveyor, he says, should never be employed as the architect of the County Asylum, for it is "giving one man a small fortune merely because he happens to be a County Surveyor, and is holding a fairly well-paid permanent appointment." It is forgotten that if the County Surveyor has secured and kept such an appointment, it is because he is competent and trustworthy. An unlimited competition among architects must always, he advises, be adopted, and not even a limited competition among half a dozen architects of experience in asylum work will please him, "for it is notorious that, with scarcely an exception, the second or third attempts of asylum architects are not improvements on their earlier attempts." A more absurd or improbable statement was never published; and, if experience is to go for nothing, might not Mr. Burdett's boasted experience in hospital matters (see the title-page of his book) disqualify him for writing upon them with the success which as a younger and untried man he might have secured?

The appendix to the volume under notice contains, besides a good index and an asylum bibliography, papers of great value; bearing, perhaps, rather on the medical aspect of the treatment of insanity than on hospital construction. The third of these, a paper by Dr. J. P. Bancroft, an American specialist, contains some valuable suggestions to which we gladly direct attention. He desires to see simple, less formal, and more subdivided structures. In his opinion, "buildings should be provided for the noisy classes separate from others," and out of hearing. An essential feature would be, according to him, detached houses, of various sizes and styles, "not in rigid rows and uniform, but dropped down here and there in the grounds in pleasing variety and homelikeness, while convenient for administration." "The old, long, monotonous ward style should be entirely discarded," even in such situations as call for larger buildings. Such outward forms and internal divisions should be chosen as will multiply and diversify situations and give the greatest possible diversity of personal groupings, and thus afford the physician the greatest possible control over individual relations and contacts. By adopting "a broken and irregular style of architecture, a competent artist should be able to produce all these desirable conditions, adding at once immensely to utility and grace without materially larger cost than that of the traditional homely and monotonous block style." With these opinions many thoughtful men will be disposed to agree. Only if Dr. Bancroft is right, are not the hundreds of asylums described in these volumes all more or less wrong? We are glad to see that in the preface Mr. Burdett specially directs attention to Dr. Bancroft's views, and endorses them with the weight of his own authority.

What we have hitherto been considering is contained in the second of the two volumes now issued. The first volume has probably a value for persons specially responsible for the care of the insane, which it hardly can have for the majority of our readers; and it will not detain us long, notwithstanding that it i the more bulky of the two. History an Administration form the subjects, and (wit indices, &c.) the printed matter extends t 700 pages, yet that portion of it which goe back more than a few years is but scanty and is much of it at once depressing and sad

It is pointed out that traces, in fact definite accounts, of the existence of lunac and of the treatment of lunatics are to b found in ancient writings, and that there wa among the Greeks and Romans "a fair knowledge of mental diseases from the earlies time, and that their methods of treatment were not infrequently wise and prudent." There seems little or no ground for saying th same of the highly-civilised Egyptians, no can the references to insanity in the Old Testament, several of which are enumerated be said to throw much much light upon th existence of any general custom among th Jews with regard to the treatment of th mentally afflicted. The case of David playing before Saul on the harp seems to show tha soothing measures were recognised a desirable.

In the earlier ages of Christendom i appears as though some pains were taken t care for those afflicted in mind, but from th end of the sixth century to the middle o the eighteenth (from A.D. 600 to A.D. 1750) was a time in which unfortunate lunatics were treated in a manner dictated by wild and barbaric superstition. The belief in demoniacal possession was strong, that in witchcraft was equally strong, and much cruelty was inflicted on the unhappy persons who were deemed to be possessed or bewitched, or to be themselves witches. It is stated that in 100 years 20,000 lunatics were burnt in France, and in double that number of years 30,000 persons were condemned to death and executed for witchcraft in England. Some places for the care of the insane were, however, established in various parts of Europe, and among the very early instances is that of our own Bethlehem Hospital, founded in the reign of Edward III. When, however, asylums had begun to be usual it is distressin to read of the treatment to which patient were subjected in them during the time whic our author correctly terms that of bruta suppression and ill-treatment; a time whic as is shown convincingly by the statements i these volumes, extended far on into the nineteenth century. Under this treatment th case of a patient once removed to the hospital was practically hopeless, and the person in whose charge he was behaved as if thi were an established fact, and treated him lik a savage beast rather than an unfortunat human being.

Almost within our own day, a revolutio of the most complete kind has been effecte —humanity, kindness, forbearance, and intelligent care have rendered the lot of patient in an asylum not only immeasurabl more endurable, but more hopeful. Th physician who deals with mental disease no endeavours, and not infrequently with succes to effect a cure; and if this be unhappil out of the question, he soothes instead terrifying, and influences his patient by mor means instead of a strait-waistcoat and padded room. Those who wish to pursu this history in some detail will find the fact clearly stated in Mr. Burdett's book, an will rise from the perusal of the chapte where they are narrated with a conviction tha in the treatment of mental diseases we a now at last on a track which ought to lea to good results, and which, certainly, i creditable alike to the humanity and th intelligence of the medical scientists an "alienists" of the present day.

A great deal of information is contained i the chapters devoted to Great Britain an Ireland, and in the statement of the law o this subject, which it will be of advantage t County Magistrates, County Councillors, an others responsible for the care of the insan to have in an accessible form: but we cann help suggesting that a more frequent additio of references to the authorities for statement made by the writer would have added to th value of the book. The field gone over is so extensive that, even in this bulky volume, much has been condensed, and a reader interested in a particular locality would have been grateful for some foot-notes directing him to the sources of information where he could pursue his studies further. While making this remark we do not desire to undervalue the carefully-prepared enumeration of books given under the title of "Asylum Bibliography," the preparation of which must have been a work of great labour. The two volumes are separately and very elaborately indexed, and the printing and style of getting-up generally are all that could be wished in a work which aspires to be the standard book on this subject, and will, no doubt, remain so for many years.

We shall look forward with expectation to the volumes in course of preparation which are to deal with the hospitals of the world, and are to include plans of all the hospitals of London in the Jubilee Year of Queen Victoria's reign. We trust that from this interesting series of plans the names of the architects to whose skill they will owe their value will not be omitted, and we trust also that small sanatoria and cottage hospitals will not be overlooked. The absence of much reference to private asylums of moderate size for the insane, and of any plans for such (except a so-called model plan capable of being altered to receive 200 private patients) seems to us a deficiency in the volumes now before us, and in hospital-building practice small institutions are far more numerous than in asylum-building. We therefore hope that while the great hospitals of this and other countries are fully described, an adequate space will be given to the smaller ones, which furnish types that are constantly required in order to meet the needs of small towns, or even of rural districts. Meantime, we cannot but congratulate the author on the thoroughness with which he has carried out this first portion of what must for years be one of the most comprehensive books of reference on the subject of asylums and hospitals.

INDIAN ARCHITECTURAL DETAILS.

E publish among our lithographic illustrations this week some examples of decorative treatment of balustrades from various build- ıgs in India, which are reduced from lates in Part VI. of the "Jeypore Port- olio of Architectural Details,"* a remark- bly sumptuous collection of plates of de- ail from Indian architectural monuments, arried out under the patronage of an ndian Prince, and entirely drawn by ative draughtsmen in the employ of he Public Works Department of India, nd under the immediate direction of olonel Jacob, Engineer to the Jeypore tate. The drawings are in a somewhat hard ad mechanical style, which however is robably due not so much to the natural ten- encies of Indian draughtsmen as to the fact f the work being done under the very ngineering influence of the Public Works epartment. In every other respect they re admirable, and show the most conscien- ous care and finish.

The buildings from which the details are ıken are mostly of the sixteenth, seventeenth, ıd eighteenth centuries, though some xamples are of considerably earlier date. he first Portfolio illustrates copings and linths, to a rather larger scale than is at all ecessary with much of the very simple detail own. Many of the examples of coping naments are however, very charming and teresting, and illustrate the principle of re- tition of dual contrasting forms on exactly e same principle as in Greek ornament, but ith the adoption of more free and sometimes rtially realistic forms of flower and leaf. ɔis is not in itself an improvement on the more abstract and severe forms of the Classic types of ornament, but is interesting as a contrast and as suggesting new treatment of this class of decorative detail; and it may be observed that a good deal of the treatment shown would be specially suitable for terra-cotta, the use of which has so largely increased in England of late years.

The second Portfolio illustrates pillars, caps, and bases; and here Indian art does not show to so much advantage. The pillars are too much encrusted with ornament and sculpture, the latter of somewhat barbaric type; the lack of reticence and severity of form is much felt in the more elaborate examples. Some of the simpler ones may afford new suggestions for balusters. What strikes one especially is the entire absence of the sense of proportion of parts and refinement of profile in mouldings: the mouldings are coarse in outline, the caps out of all proportion to the pillars, heavy and clumsy in effect; the distinction commonly found between Eastern and Western architectural detail. The sense of refinement of profile in mouldings, in fact, as has often been pointed out, is above all other things the measure of high culture in architecture.

In the third Portfolio, illustrating doors, the most notable work is in the inlaid heads and doorposts, many of which are beautiful work, and very well shown in the coloured plates. It is in this application of coloured ornament on a flat surface that the Eastern artist, in his turn, excels the Western. Some of the carved doorposts and panels are also of beautiful design, for in this kind of work the exuberance of detail, which seems out of place in the more monumental portions of a building, is quite suitably applied. There is a curiously Renaissance look about some of the ornaments applied in the panels of doors, mingled with touches half-Hindu, half-Saracenic; and the ubiquitous bead-and-reel ornament of course is not absent here.

The fourth Portfolio is devoted to brackets, a feature over which the Indian architect was apt to run somewhat wild. Heads of elephants and of creatures distantly resembling horses are worked into brackets in a style more grotesque than effective; and in the more sober foliated forms of bracket it is characteristic of Indian taste, to which decoration is always a more prominent object than construction, that the appearance of constructive power and tenacity, the true object of the bracket as a support, seems too often to be lost sight of, and the bracket seems as much hung to the superstructure as supporting it. There are exceptions to this no doubt, and there are many ideas contained in these illustrations which are worth the attention of architectural designers who are finding the possible variations on Classic forms of bracket nearly exhausted. Too great exuberance of detail, and want of severity and precision of line both in the design of the bracket itself and in its decorative treatment, are the common faults of this class of Indian detail. The well-known serpentine form of bracket, however, strengthened by a straight-lined filling within the curves, at once ornamental and constructive in appearance, will always retain its place as one of the most picturesque and suitable details ever designed for timber construction. One or two examples of this form are included among the plates.

The forms given under the heading "Arches," in the fifth Portfolio, are such as seem very familiar to the eye, and run all on the same idea of a many-cusped arch with carving in the spandrels,—at least as far as the examples in relief are concerned. In the examples showing inlaid colour on a flat surface the arches are mostly not foliated, and the colour ornament, it may be added, has a good deal of sameness and is not of a very interesting character.

The illustrations in our plate (see lithograph in this number) are taken from the sixth Portfolio, and represent two balustrades in sandstone and three in marble: the stone being worked in solid forms, the marble in that pierced ornament so dear to Oriental fancy. The two marble examples in which foliage is employed are characteristic both of the strength and weakness of Indian decorative art in the employment of foliage forms. In the balustrade from the Madrasa, Delhi, at the lower right-hand corner of the plate, while the general lines of the design are satisfactory and well balanced, and the modelling of detail very refined, it will seen on close inspection that the junction of one element in the design with another is clumsily and illogically managed; a heavy stalk butts out at right angles from the curling end of a leaf, in a manner totally at variance with any law of growth, whether as to flow of line or balance of weight. Such design would never have satisfied either a Greek or a Gothic artist.

Further Portfolios are in hand illustrating Tracery, String Courses, Wall Decorations, Cornice and Ceiling Decorations, Parapets, Projecting Eaves, and Finials, which will be issued as they are completed. The collected set will make a splendid addition to a library of illustrative architectural work, but it is almost a pity that the scale on which the work is brought out must put it out of the reach of a majority of those who would have been interested in the possession of such a collection of drawings of Indian detail.

* Jeypore Portfolio of Architectural Details. Parts I. VI. Prepared under the supervision of Colonel S. S. cob, C.I.E. Issued under the patronage of His High- ss Maharaja Sawai Madhu Sing, G.C.S.I., of Jeypore. ndon: Bernard Quaritch.

NOTES.

NEXT week will probably find many thousands of our coal-miners voluntarily enrolled in the great army of "the unemployed," while this week some of them are working eleven hours a day. They will, perhaps, be willing to make up for lost time in a similar manner when they have taken a sufficiently long holiday,—if the demand for coal is not met from elsewhere in the meantime. The panic-price offered during the last week or two has naturally attracted attention on the Continent, and it is understood that at least one large contract has been completed for delivery of coal from Belgium. It remains to be seen how far the strikers will be successful in preventing the importation of foreign coal; for it may be taken for granted that they will forbid the unloading of vessels by Union men. It would hardly appear probable that they will receive much support outside their own industry, as the movement is such a purely selfish one. In fact, it is not even calculated to do otherwise than embarrass or positively injure nearly all other branches of trade, more or less directly. The advantages to be gained by the miners themselves by means of the stoppage are, to say the least, exceedingly problematical; and even if their "defiant" experiment (as Mr. Pickard terms it) should prove a success from the miners' point of view, the loss to the country at large will probably far outweigh any benefits that they may appear to secure. Impartial observers, however, fail to see that the miners can expect any ultimate advantage at all.

THE result of the London County Council elections has been so sufficiently commented upon by the Press generally, that it is unnecessary to notice it at any length in these columns. The elections appear to indicate that the great mass of ratepayers have not yet sufficiently appreciated the need of taking part in municipal elections. This is not surprising, for London has been without the collective local life which distinguishes provincial towns. It is at any rate satisfactory that among the dominant party on the Council are to found some men of individual power who, we hope, though Progressive in their general views, have yet sufficient strength of character to resist impracticable proposals.

THE debate on the Birmingham Waterworks Bill shows pretty clearly that the introduction of the Bill is really, what it has before been said to be, a kind of race for a water-area, to get in before London to what seems a promising gathering-ground. Though the Bill has passed the second reading, there can be little doubt that this aspect of the matter will be duly considered in Committee, as also the interests of Wales as far as possible. But unless the growth of large towns is to be checked, there can be no doubt that the time has arrived when the necessity, on mere sanitary grounds, of furnishing them with a liberal supply of water, will have to take precedence of smaller local interests.

NO one can feel surprised that Mr. Tate has withdrawn his munificent offer to present the nation with a gallery of British Art, when the nation, through its constituted authorities, gives him no better thanks than to haggle about a site. The incident is only too characteristic of this country. The loss of such an offer is a national misfortune, or would be thought so in France, but in England no one cares. Mr. Goschen's objection that the building would have been overshadowed if placed on the site adjoining the Imperial Institute, and would have been too low for its surroundings, is a valid one; but it will certainly be regarded as extraordinary, by other nations, that such an offer should have been made and that London can find no adequate site for the building.

THE deputation from the National Union of Elementary Teachers, which interviewed the Vice-President of the Council on Saturday last, had a hopeless task to perform. The deputation urged that drawing should be made an optional instead of an obligatory subject in elementary schools. Sir William Hart-Dyke showed in his reply that drawing had now been practically taken up throughout the country, and that it would be impossible to go back upon the steps which had been taken. To have acceded to the request of the deputation would have been a most retrograde step. Most persons will find with satisfaction that an educational advance of great importance has been accomplished with so little friction. Drawing throughout the country has in a short time been accepted as a necessary part of the national elementary education, and this first step accomplished, we may fairly hope that a basis has been laid for a larger extension of technical education. The deputation was ill-advised to endeavour to stop the reform which has been accomplished, but it has done some service by enabling the Education Department to show how satisfactorily the recent change has been accomplished.

USERS of the electric light must have read with alarm the account of a sad accident which occurred at Chatham on Monday. The *Pall Mall Gazette* published on Tuesday evening a sensational report, which has also appeared in other papers, according to which a tailor's cutter, named Jay, lost his life, and a foreman of the local Electric Light Company, named Readwin, was so severely injured as to necessitate the ultimate amputation of a hand and a foot. Both men are alleged to have received their injuries by coming in contact with the high tension mains of the Chatham, Rochester, and District Electric Lighting Company connected to a transformer which had been placed in a damp cellar. Having reason to doubt the accuracy of the report, we have taken some trouble to find out the real facts of the case. Messrs. J. W. Taylor & Co., on whose premises the accident occurred, being unable to get any light, complained to the Supply Company, who sent Readwin to see what was the matter. During his investigation he caught hold of one of the leads coming from a high tension fuse. One of his feet was on the wet floor of the cellar, and he had omitted to put on his insulating gloves; the covering of the wire was moist, and sufficient current passed through his body to give him a severe shock, and cause him to fall to the ground. In doing so he jammed the wire between the fuse-box and the cellar wall. Readwin has blistered his hand and foot, but he appears to have received no serious injury. The leakage from the wire to the wet wall was great enough to make the insulation smoke. Jay heard of this, became wildly excited, and rushed to the cellar with an iron rod, intending to beat out the supposed fire. He was followed by a companion, into whose arms he fell senseless while still several feet from the apparatus, dying a few minutes afterwards. Readwin deserves as much sympathy as a gasfitter who, called upon to stop a gas leak, takes a naked light into a room filled with an explosive mixture of air and gas. The verdict of death by electricity through misadventure, returned by the coroner's jury, is not to be wondered at; but in view of the facts that Jay was several feet from the apparatus when he fell insensible, that his body showed no marks of any burn, and that the doctors who gave evidence were not familiar with the signs of death by electricity, we shall be strongly of opinion, until further evidence is produced, that his death was caused solely by excitement.

THERE is no doubt that the custom of appointing a professional assessor to advise the promoters or committees of competitions, though rendered futile at times by the bad faith or unreasonableness of committees, as well as from other causes, has in the main been beneficial both to architects and to the public, guiding the latter to the selection of the best buildings and guarding the former from some portion at least of the injustice which they have so frequently suffered from either favouritism or incompetency in the adjudication of competitions. There is however one weakness which seems to be inherent in the system, and which, unless subjected to some check, is likely rather to increase than diminish, viz.: the tendency to choose the same architect as assessor over and over again for one competition after another. This is not desirable, because, however competent and however honourable is the man who is selected, he is one man and has one man's special ideas on planning, &c., and the result is naturally that whatever competitions he adjudicates upon are decided in favour of certain tendencies in plan and design which seem to him the best. And the more often any one architect is engaged as an assessor, the more often is he likely to be, as a committee are thus saved the trouble and responsibility of casting about for an assessor: they go to a man whose name they have already heard of in that capacity. We have before us, furnished by a correspondent, a list of five hospital competitions in which the same architect was assessor, and in which the same competitors were in each case placed either first or second; not through any favouritism,—that is not suggested in the least,—but because their ideas of treatment accorded with those of the assessor. In a competition of the same class, where another and equally good man was the assessor, the premiums went another way, and the architects who were first in the other competitions were not placed. This fact speaks volumes, and shows that it is well that corporations and committees should be exhorted to look for variety of professional advice in these matters, and not run it all in one groove.

WE may call attention to the letter of "A Non-Competitor" on another page in regard to the "Halifax Artisans' Dwellings Competition," as a specimen of what is demanded from architects by the promoters of competitions. The quotation given by our correspondent from the "Conditions of Competition" deserves the attention of the Institute of Architects, and we hope will receive it. In the meantime we may point out to the promoters of the competition that by their conditions they have effectually deprived themselves of the chance of obtaining the services of any high-class architect in the profession.

THE case of Phillips *v.* Low reported in a recent number of the Law Reports decides an interesting point in connexion with the law of light. It is remarkable, indeed, that it has never been settled before, since it would have been thought that it must have previously arisen. The point cannot be put more clearly than it is by Mr. Justice Chitty in the beginning of his judgment. "The question then," he says, "may be stated in this simple form: a man being in possession of a house with windows and of an adjoining field over which the light required for the windows passes, devises, by will, the house to one and the field to another,—does the right to the light over the field pass to the devisee of the house, or is the devisee of the field entitled to block up the windows?" It is settled law that if the owner of a house and field grants by deed the house but retains the field, or grants house and field contemporaneously, the right to the light over the field still belongs to the house, on the principle that a man cannot derogate from his own grant. The question which Mr. Justice Chitty put to himself he answered by his judgment, namely, that the right to the light passes by will just as much as by grant. The decision is in accord with settled principles, though the point is new so far as regards judicial decisions. To have decided otherwise would have caused inconvenience and confusion, and it is a matter for congratulation that the principles of law have been worked out so as to be in harmony with the existing state of matters.

SOME twenty photo-lithographs of the drawings of Raschdorff's latest design for Berlin Cathedral have been published. As regards general style, the design now published differs but little from the preceding one. It is, as it was generally expected to be by those who knew the author and his mode of work, simply a "reduced" design, in the full meaning of the word. As the Berlin critics put it, "everywhere the same items have been copied from good publications of Renaissance work as before; the scale to the drawings has only been changed, and hence the encyclopedia of Renaissance ideas and details has simply been condensed." The public was not satisfied with the last design, and it is scarcely to be expected that the reduced one will tend to make the Parliamentary representatives more willing to vote money towards the erection in this session than in the last. Twenty million marks was the estimate for the former design; the present one the author would erect for ten, although no architect can see where so grea a reduction in the cost comes in.

THE case of Giddy *v.* Ross, which was re ported this week in the *Times*, show that persons should very carefully peruse th conditions which surveyors and house agent place before them for signature when the put business in their hands. Messrs. Gidd & Giddy's conditions contained the followin paragraph:—"Should a tenant eventuall purchase, the commission on sale will b charged less the amount previously receive on the letting." The learned Judge, wh tried the case, expressed his opinion that an person who came to do business with th surveyors should put his pen through th clause. We agree with him. This claus would apparently cause an unguarded perso to pay commission on a sale which might b effected several years after the tenancy begar and without any service on the part of th auctioneers. A claim was made by Messr Giddy under this clause, but the jury foun against them. They came to the conclusior as we read the report, that the property wa not sold through Messrs. Giddy's introductior and that it was not the same in all respect as that which they were instructed to let, an that they were not instructed to sell. It i clear their instructions were to let, and tha the tenancy fell through. It was, therefore equally clear that only by the meres technicality could Messrs. Giddy recover commission. Messrs. Giddy & Giddy some little time ago broke into a correspondence in the *Times* with a view of purifying the legal profession in regard to the taking of commissions. The lawyers may now ask that auctioneers should look to the character of the conditions under which they do business.

FOR a few years past the London County Council have used the gatehouse of Horsemonger-lane Gaol as their office for the verifying and stamping of weights and measures. Their new premises for that purpose, planned and designed by Mr. T. Blashill, architect, are nearly ready for occupation. They stand upon part of the prison ground next north-westward of the gatehouse. This, being the County Gaol, was erected in 1798-9, for 300 prisoners, to replace the White Lion Prison, originally an inn, mentioned by Stow and his contemporary, John Taylor, the Water Poet. It is noteworthy as having been due to John Howard's philanthropic labours. In 1791 the county justices bought for 1,350*l.* a plot of about 3½ acres in some market gardens, belonging to St. Thomas's Hospital, on the southern side of the lane now re-named Union-road. The prison, mainly of brick, and the adjoining Sessions House, pulled down thirty years ago, and rebuilt, cost 39,682*l.* They were designed by George Gwilt the elder, Surveyor to the Surrey Commissioners of Sewers, and architect, also, of Great Suffolk-street Bridewell. The gateway contained the office, gatekeeper's room, and a staircase leading to an upper floor, where they kept the scaffold, which, when required for use, was set up on the roof above. Within stood the ten wards, and the governor's house, flanked with two wings for county-court and sheriffs' debtors. An apartment in the gate-house has been pointed out to us as that wherein Leigh Hunt, despite the advocacy of his counsel, Lord Brougham, passed a part of his two years' confinement * for the libel, in the *Examiner* of March 22, 1812, in reply to a fulsome panegyric upon the Prince of Wales, printed by the *Morning Post*, in relation to the banquet on St. Patrick's Day. Here he wrote his Descent of Liberty, Story of Rimini, and Feast of Poets, was visited by Moore, Cyrus Redding, Horace Smith, Shelley, with others, and made acquaintance with Byron. The prison was finally closed on August 31, 1878; two years later the inner area was cleared, and in January, 1884, a portion, about 1¼ acre, was opened by Mrs. Gladstone as a children's playground *à curis* St. Mary, Newington vestry. The playground, we understand, is about to be enlarged, and the remains of the prison demolished. The Sessions House interior has been remodelled under the directions of Mr. Howell, County Surveyor. The hall, the two courts, and the Magistrates' room are fine, spacious apartments, and the accommodation is much improved.

AS will have been seen by our "Tender" list of February 27, the tower and spire of St. Giles's Church, Camberwell, are about to be restored, under the direction of Messrs. Newman & Newman, architects. This (the parish) church was built in 1842-4, at a total cost of 20,000*l.*, after the designs of Sir G. Gilbert Scott and his then partner, Mr. W. B. Moffatt; Messrs. Webb, contractors. Being cruciform on plan, and built of Kentish rag, faced with hammer-dressed Yorkshire stone, and having Caen stone dressings, it is in the Transition style, and takes rank amongst the largest churches of its kind in England. Some considered that its predecessor, destroyed by fire in 1841, retained portions of the original fabric,—cited in Domesday Survey,—as reinstated *temp.* Stephen, and subsequently enlarged. Lysons thought it was entirely rebuilt *circa* 1510; yet the north, St. Nicholas, aisle and eastern semi-octagonal apse were of an earlier date. In 1154 the advowson and church were given to Bermondsey Abbey by William de Melhent, Earl of Gloucester. The register of Bishop Edington, at Winchester, records the issue of a commission, 1346, "for reconciling Camberwell Church, which had been polluted by bloodshed." In Charles I.'s reign the rectory had passed to Sir E. Bowyer, Knight, and here were buried many members of that family, as well as of the Scotts, Smiths, and Windhams. Bartholomew Scott's second wife was Margaret, widow of Cranmer. The monument of Sir Peter Scott, Knight, *ob.* 1622, recorded that "hee married Elizabeth eldest daughter of Edmund Kedarmister, Esq., one of the Sixs Clarkes of Chancery,"—one of the very few instances which remind us that the Six Clerks' office was for a short period called Kedarmister's Inn. Sir George Buc says:—

"These clearkes live and lodge and common together in one house in Chancery-lane, purchased and accommodated for them by Maister John Kedermister, Esquire. . . . . Their house was in auncient time the Inne of the Abbot of Norton, in Lincolnshire, and was since the house of one Herfleet, and of him it was called Herfleete's Inne. But now it is, or ought to be, called the Six Clearkes Inne, or Kedermister's Inne, of the aforesaid founder thereof."

* This must have been his second and better lodging here. See the *Examiner* of February 7 and 14, 1813 "I have obtained, as an indulgence, the society of my wife and infants. . . . I am cut off from all others, and locked up at six."

A COMMITTEE of the Edinburgh County Council, which met on the 3rd inst., had before them a report and plans prepared by Dr. Rowand Anderson, for the extension and internal re-arrangement of the County Buildings. This involves the entire reconstruction of the west elevation of the buildings facing George IV. Bridge, which was exposed to view when the new thoroughfare was opened up, presenting a very unsightly aspect towards that important thoroughfare. Dr. Rowand Anderson explained that the designing of the west front presented considerable difficulties of an artistic nature, as it was impossible to reproduce the Temple Greek of the east and north elevations, owing to the difference in the number of floors and distribution of the fenestration. He had, therefore, adopted a style, the details of which were borrowed from that phase of Italian architecture which acquired a distinctly British feeling in the hands of Robert Adam and the earlier architects of the period of Inigo Jones. That style, he said, formed the easiest transition from an unyielding style of architecture to one applicable to modern wants. An open balustrade will take the place of the present rough retaining wall, and a new entrance will be formed at the south-west end of the line of building. The estimated cost of these alterations, internal and external, is 20,000*l.*

THE tenth exhibition of the "Royal Society of Painter-Etchers" (the new style of the Society) contains a great quantity of interesting work in true etching style, and less than in previous years of the elaborate attempts to make etching resemble engraving, which we hold to be a mistaken direction of the art. Mr. David Law's two etchings, "Arundel Castle" (69) and "Goring-on-Thames" (135), which are in a style that is popular no doubt, and looks very finished and elaborate, contain no effect which could not be obtained by drawing with a fine pen in slightly-tinted ink, and are absolutely without the special quality and power of etching. Mr. Strang's peculiar works are there in great (too great) numbers, no less than seventeen of his ugly and eccentric creations being hung; these are true etchings in regard to method, and have a remarkable force and originality together with an apparently deliberate and defiant preference for what is ugly and repulsive—"Fleurs du Mal" in etching. The finest is perhaps "The Nymph" (292), which is remarkable for its quality of design. In "The Fish-Stall" (39), the intended effect of light is not a success, and in both this and "The Violoncello Player" and "Socialists" there is apparent a heartless enjoyment in exhibiting the ugliness and unhappiness of the lowest types of modern humanity in an even exaggerated form. It is fortunate that there is not much of this unhealthy type of art to be found in the room; on the contrary, one of the pleasures one finds in going round the Painter-Etchers' collection is the variety of pleasant and picturesque fancy and suggestion that we obtain often even from works which are slight in their material execution. Among those which are more highly finished, architects will be interested in the various fine plates by Mr. A. H. Haig, of which an "Old Castilian City" (235), showing the town of Segovia rising dark against the sky, is perhaps the finest of all, in sentiment if not in execution. Among other architectural subjects of interest are the late Mr. Luxmore's exquisite little etchings of Canterbury (83, 92), in both of which the tower is treated with the most remarkable union of breadth of effect with delicacy in the indication of detail. Mr. Slocombe has some good architectural bits, "Old Houses on the Wear, Durham" (130) and "A Canal at Amsterdam" (147) and others, and Mr. Niven contributes a sketch of "Timber Houses at Exeter" (307) now destroyed. M. Helleu's slight line etchings of girls' heads are among the things with a style of their own, especially clever is the right-hand one of the three heads in No. 21, looking down and foreshortened. Among works remarkable for special power are Mr. Slocombe's dry-point study of two nude figures (44); Mr. Percy Robertson's beautiful and poetic little idyl, "But One" (59), and Mr. Herkomer's remarkable expression of wind and storm in dry-point line work, "Wild Weather" (183). The exhibition of a collection of portrait etchings by Vandyck, mostly in more than one state, form a special attraction of the exhibition.

AT a meeting of the Royal Scottish Academy held in Edinburgh last week, it was resolved that on the 30th inst., twelve artists should be elected to the position of Associates. The members were unanimous in recommending that of these four should be architects, two sculptors, and six painters.

THE water-colour drawings of "Vales and Dales in Derbyshire and Yorkshire," by Mr. Sutton Palmer, now on view at the Fine Art Society's Galleries, give us a somewhat regretful feeling, inasmuch as it appears to us that the artist has deliberately deserted a powerful, broad, and truly artistic style, as shown in a minority of the drawings, for a more popular but essentially false and pretty style. Many of what appear to be the more recent drawings really look more like work painted for theatre scenes, full of strong effects of light and glitter, than like the transcripts of an artist from nature. What Mr. Palmer can do if he likes is shown in such drawings as "Moorland above the Tees Valley" (23) "Barnard Castle" (20), "Between the Showers, Cotherstone, Teesdale" (58) and one or two others. These, however, are but a small part of the show, and with the test we could feel no kind of sympathy.

WE have received a copy of a circular issued by the Dean of Lincoln calling a meeting at 2.15 p.m. to-day (Saturday March 12) at the Chapter-house, to consider a scheme set forth in the following paragraph of the circular:—

"It has probably come to your knowledge that Mr. Shuttleworth has made some very acceptable proposals to the Dean and Chapter. He wishes to effect a long-desired public improvement on the north-east of the Minster Green by removal of the eight houses now standing thereon, and the keeping for the future, as an open space, almost all the ground so cleared. These proposals include also, by request of the Dean and Chapter, another, which seems to them a not less important, improvement, viz., the removal of Sir Christopher Wren's Library and its re-building, as near as possible stone for stone, upon the Western boundary of the ground cleared, together with the re-building of the ancient North Walk of the Cloisters—destroyed after the Civil War. Mr. Shuttleworth, however, makes it a condition of the assistance which he offers to give that the Library be removed and re-built without any delay."

The circular is dated February 23, but was only sent to us on Wednesday last, otherwise we should have taken an opportunity of re-visiting the site before expressing an opinion on the project. But until we know of some better reason than appears in the circular for meddling with Wren's Library, we can only say that it appears to us a very questionable proceeding, and we hope that the meeting will not come to any hasty decision to carry out or support such a scheme. The proposal to remove the houses and retain the open space is probably a desirable public improvement; about that we are not specially concerned: but the removal of Wren's Library from the place where Wren built it, to substitute a cloister in a modern imitation of Gothic, is to substitute, for what in its own way is an architectural reality, an architectural pretence; and an old building, even in a Renaissance style, standing where it was built, will be far more in harmony with the whole surroundings than a brand-new imitation-Gothic cloister. Such a proposal would no doubt have been generally popular thirty or forty years ago, when probably Wren's building would have been pulled down without it being thought necessary to provide for rebuilding it anywhere else. But of late there has been a much clearer perception as to the value of Renaissance buildings and of the picturesque harmony of old architecture in mingled styles, and the Dean of Lincoln is rather behind the age in this respect if he thinks he is going to do anything for the picturesque character of the cloister enclosure by removing an old piece of Renaissance architecture and building a new Gothic cloister.

HOW THEY BUILT IN SHAKSPEARE'S TIME:

THE ARCHITECTURAL ASSOCIATION.

The usual fortnightly meeting of this Association was held on the 4th inst., in the meeting room of the Royal Institute of British Architects, 9, Conduit-street, the President, Mr. F. T. Baggallay, in the chair.

The minutes of the last meeting having been read and confirmed,

Mr. W. Percival was elected as a member of the Association.

Mr. F. T. W. Goldsmith, honorary secretary, then proposed a vote of thanks to Mr. Aston Webb, for allowing the members to visit the new Metropolitan Life Assurance buildings, in Moorgate-street; to Mr. Innes, for permitting them to visit the tower and spire of the Church of St. Mary-le-Bow, Cheapside; and to Mr. T. E. Collcutt, for allowing them to visit the Imperial Institute. The vote of thanks was carried unanimously.

Mr. Goldsmith also stated that although the matter had not been definitely arranged, yet he believed that a visit would be arranged for the 19th inst. to the Tower Bridge by permission of Mr. Wolfe Barry, the engineer.

The Chairman said he had very great pleasure in calling upon their old friend and colleague, Mr. J. A. Gotch, to read them a paper entitled, "How They Built in Shakspeare's Time." The paper* was as follows:—

When Falstaff paid his second visit to Justice Shallow, in Gloucestershire, and was taken by his host to see the orchard, he could not help exclaiming, as he looked back upon the house, "'Fore God you have here a goodly dwelling and a rich." Now, although Falstaff is supposed to have lived about the beginning of the fifteenth century, he was, in reality, drawn from contemporaries of Shakspeare; and, similarly, all the incidental touches which give so much local colour to the poet's pictures of life were suggested by the persons and things which he saw from day to day. So the goodly dwelling of Justice Shallow was, doubtless, such an one as might have been seen within a short distance of Stratford, and it is no great assumption to suppose that as the Justice had his prototype in Squire Lucy, of Charlcote, so a remembrance of Charlcote itself may have been floating in Shakspeare's mind, when he put these words into Falstaff's mouth.

It may afford us some interest to inquire what were the processes by which these rich and goodly dwellings came into existence. Whom have we to thank for these stately homes, which the public never tire of seeing on the pages of the magazines, and which present inexhaustible mines of detail whence we architects may fill our many sketch-books?

We know whom to thank for such things in the present day. It is the architect. He holds himself responsible for every scrap of design, from the plinth to the chimney-cap; he fathers every article mentioned in the specification, from the trade of the excavator to that of the bell-hanger; and not content with that, when the specification is exhausted, he betakes himself to the wall-papers, the curtains, and the furniture. Or, if he doesn't, there are many who say he ought to.

One consequence of this is that a good deal of the work that is springing up around us has a very self-conscious air; it has clearly been designed, and often evidently at a great deal of pains. The same impression is hardly conveyed by most of the old work; that seems to have much more of spontaneous growth about it, though, indeed, there are a few examples of Early-Renaissance work in which the striving and the straining of the designer is amusingly evident. Possibly this difference may result from the different processes employed.

But what happened when anyone in Shakspeare's time set about building? Let Shakspeare himself answer. "When we mean to build," says Lord Bardolph, in the "Second Part of King Henry IV.,"—

> "When we mean to build,
> We first survey the plot, then draw the model;
> And when we see the figure of the house,
> Then must we rate the cost of the erection."

The necessity of "surveying the plot" might be irksome to some who occasionally find a voice in *A. A. Notes*, perhaps, but by "surveying" Shakspeare probably meant examining. However, it is clear that it was thought desirable to know something of the site before the house was designed. To "draw the model" was to prepare the drawings,—hardly to construct an actual model, though we hear of such a course being taken in one or two instances, and even of a model being brought from Italy. The drawings prepared, the next matter was to calculate the cost, and of this process we have various records and examples left to us. One I will quote in parts as a specimen. It begins:—

> "Yt maye please yo^u to understand an Estymate of certayne newe buyldinges to be erected and sett upp at Woollwiche by Mr. Allen the Queens Maties Marchante as hereafter ffolloweth etc. 1572."

I will only give one or two of the items, thus:—

"Imp'mis a Seller of xx^ti ffoote wyde and xxx^ti ffoote in lengthe to be broughte up wth bricke Rounde abowte viij fote high tow bricke in thicknes will take xxiiij^m brike The storrye upon the said sellor etc. . . . will take xxij^m of brike in all—xlvj^m at x^s the thowsande	xxiij^li
Itm to the Brycklayer for the layinge of iiij^xx xv^m of bricke at iij^s iiij^d the thowsande laying	xv^li xvj^s viij^d
More to the Carpenter for the makinge and Settinge up of a newe frame of tymb^r for the tarrehouse Conteyninge in Lengthe lxxx ffoote and in wydth xx^ti foote at vj^s viij^d the ffoote he fynding all mane^r of tymbr sawinge fframinge and ffull fynnyshinge of al the worke belonging to the Carpente^r"	xxvj^li xiij^s iij^d

Then follows the roofing. So many thousand tiles at 10s. the thousand, so many bushels of tile-pins, so much lime and sand, so many loads of lath, and so much for laying at 2s. 6d. the thousand. Similarly with the plasterer; the materials so much and the "lathinge and layinge of all the wales and sellinges," so much. The whole estimate amounting to 750*l.* 19s., and occupying only three and a-half sheets of foolscap. How many pages would a modern bill of uan i ies for work to the like amount run to ?q t t

But Lord Bardolph had more to say that is of interest to us:—

> "Then must we rate the cost of the erection;
> Which if we find outweighs ability,
> What do we then but draw anew the model
> In fewer offices; or at least, desist
> To build at all? Much more, in this great work
> (Which is, almost, to pluck a kingdom down
> And set another up), should we survey
> The plot of situation, and the model;
> Consent upon a sure foundation;
> Question surveyors; know our own estate,
> How able such a work to undergo,
> To weigh against his opposite; or else,
> We fortify in paper, and in figures,
> Using the names of men, instead of men;
> Like one that draws the model of a house
> Beyond his power to build it; who, half through,
> Gives o'er, and leaves his part-created cost
> A naked subject to the weeping clouds,
> And waste for churlish winter's tyranny."

Not a word here about an architect. A good deal of drawing a model, and of surveyors and surveying, but nothing of an architect. Indeed, although the word was in use then, it does not seem to have been in general use, but rather as an academical term. Marcus, in the play of "Titus Andronicus," calls Aaron, the Moor, "chief architect and plotter of these woes"; but I have not come across another instance of its use by Shakespeare. John Shute, in his book on the "First and Chiefe Groundes of Architecture," published in 1563, uses the term freely, but he invests it with an air of complete unreality by the remarks he makes in connexion with it. His definition is the old one, derived from Classic times, of "chief-workman"; and indeed, for the next century the same definition was used, for in a dictionary of 1656, "architect" is defined as "the master-builder, the chief workman in architecture, the first inventer." Another instance of the use of the term is to be found in the epitaph of Robert Smithson, in Wollaton Church, dated 1614. He is therein described as "Architector and Survayor unto the most worthy house of Wollaton, with diverse others of great account," which is probably the first recorded instance of that conjunction of the two words which appears to give so much offence just now.

We are accustomed to look upon the well-known John Thorpe as an architect; and no doubt he was in so far as providing plans and elevations of many large houses constitutes an architect. But he is never called so. He is always designated a surveyor: in all the references to him that occur in the State papers his functions are those of a surveyor. Among the State papers of March, 1609, there is a "list, signed by Robert Earl of Salisbury, of the Commissioners for surveying the Duchess of Suffolkes Land, viz.: for the King, William Hill, John Thorpe, and John Woodward." On April 4, 1609, "Notes of Repairs necessary to be done about Westbury Lodge with request from John Thorpe to — Wingfield to move the Lord Treasurer that they may be done." And again on September 26, 1611, there is a "Warrant to pay various sums amounting to 52*l.* 3s. to John Thorpe, surveyor, for repairs of the posts, pales, and rails of Richmond Park carried away by the flood in the last winter." But although he is called a surveyor, and did the work of a surveyor, there can be no doubt that he designed architecture, and that to him we owe the general arrangement and appearance of some of the richest and goodliest dwellings of Shakespeare's time.

But my aim is not so much to show that the combined architect and surveyor flourished during that brilliant period, as to point out how widely different were the processes then employed from those in vogue at the present day. The course of procedure seems to have been somewhat as follows:—

"We first survey the plot." In the building of Hatfield House we have the Earl of Salisbury's own account of this part of the work in a letter written to Sir Thomas Lake on April 15, 1607. "I must confess unto you," he says,

> "That I have borrowed one daye's retraict from London, whither now I am returning this morning, having looked upon Hattfield also, where it pleased my L. Chamberlaine, my L. of Worcester, and my L. of Southampton to be contented to take the payne to view upon what part of ground I should place my habitation, where I doubt not ere it be long, to have the honor to see my Master. This I write because you may knowe that yor l̃r̃s (letters) of yesterday will find me in my pilgrimadge at my little lodge, wth a fayre sight of read deere before mine eies."

"Then draw the model." This, so far as can be gathered, constituted one of the chief duties of the architect of those days: the other being to survey the works during their progress. Drawing the model was the work of such a man as John Thorpe, and the way in which he did it may be seen in his book at the Soane Museum.

Plans and elevations were all that the architect provided in the way of drawings, as a rule, though he sometimes appears to have furnished a few details,—as we shall presently see.

Still adhering to our text, we have already

* The same paper was read by Mr. Gotch before the Sheffield Society of Architects and Surveyors on Tuesday evening last, as elsewhere mentioned.

seen how they "rated the cost of the erection;" and as to the process of "drawing anew the model in fewer offices" when the cost was too great, John Thorpe's book furnishes us with an example of this also; for he has two sets of plans for Sir Walter Covert's house at Slangham, in Sussex, the one adopted being somewhat the smaller.

These architects or surveyors, who provided the drawings, were well versed in their art, and in the fashions of the day. Some of them went to Italy, as John Shute did, "being," he says, in the Dedication of his *First and Chief Groundes*,—

"Servant unto the Right honorable Duke of Northũberlãd 1550. It pleased his grace for my further knowledg to mãitaine me in Itallie ther to cöler wt the doiges of ye skillul maisters in architectur, and also to view such aũciẽt Monumentes hereof as are yet extant. Wher upon at my retourne presenting his grace with the fruites of my trauailes, it pleased the same to shewe them unto that noble King Edward the VI. your maiestie's most deare brother of famous memorie, whose delectation and pleasure was to se it, and suche like. And having the sayde trickes and deuises of sculture and painting as also of Architecture, yet in my keping I thought it good at this time to set fourth some part of the same for the profit of others, especially touching Architecture: wherein I do followe not onelye the writinges of learned men, but also do ground my selfe on my own experience and practise, gathered by the sight of ye Monumentes in Italie."

Thus writes the first travelling student of whom we have any record.

Those who either could not, or did not, go direct to the fountain-head, in the manner of John Shute, studied the books published on architecture, of which there were a good number. There is very clear evidence that John Thorpe, for instance, did this, since he has copies among his drawings of some of the illustrations of books then recently published. The "models" of houses, therefore, were drawn by experts who had imbibed great draughts of foreign influence, and who, with minds full of what they had seen abroad, and fingers itching to draw Classic columns and pediments, nevertheless had the good sense to remember that their clients were Englishmen, and lived in England. The result of these opposing forces is to be seen in the beautiful houses which covered the land from one end to the other.

But the model drawn and its extent definitely fixed, there came the process of executing it. With the amplification of his small scale drawings, the architect of those days seems to have had little to do. Of detail drawings, except a few full-size sections of strings, mullions, and handrails, John Thorpe has absolutely none. I only know of one detail drawing of that time, and that is preserved in the State Papers, and is endorsed in Lord Burghley's own hand "Henryck's Platt (or plan) of my baye Wynd." It is drawn to a scale of about one inch to the foot, and shows a plan and elevation, but whether it is the plan of a window already built, or is the drawing from which it was to be built, can only be conjectured.

The probability is that the general small-scale drawings were handed over to a local agent or foreman, or clerk of the works, who hired labour on behalf of the building proprietor, overlooked the men for him, made bargains with them for doing the work, and paid them from time to time. All the correspondence that has been found relating to building in those days, points to this conclusion. At Burghley we have Peter Kemp; at Cobham, Richard Williams; and at Hatfield, Robert Liminge,—each one writing to his master for instructions, and reporting progress, but always referring points that required settling to the decision of the employer, not of an architect.

The various workmen, or the chief of them, were engaged for their skill in their particular work, not only as workmen, but also apparently as designers. That is to say, the stonemason would have to carry out the work from the small scale drawings, and would supply all the details himself; and, accordingly as he was skilful or the reverse, the details were good or bad. This seems to be borne out by much of the work of that time, which looks well at a distance, but loses by a close inspection. The architects or the surveyors did undoubtedly themselves study the details of such things as cornices and columns, since Shute's book is little else than a display of the Five Orders, and Thorpe has one or two pages wholly devoted to technical drawings of the same kind; but there is no evidence that they supplied to the masons full-sized sections of any of the numerous entablatures that were executed. The masons, it is true, did not work away entirely on their own responsibility; they kept in touch with their employer to a certain extent. We know that the mason at Burghley, one Roger Warde, got into rather a fog, as may be seen from the following letter addressed:—

"To the Ryght worshypfull Syr Wyllam Cecille Knyght at the canan rowe in Westmynyster gyve thys wythe speyde at London."

"RYGHT worshypfull my dewty Remẽberyd thys shalbe to advertyse yow that I dowe understand youre plesewre ys to have iij lukon wyndows for youre inercowrt but I cãnot understand by Johne nores after what sort yow wolde have them but as I dowe understand by hys talkeyng yow dowe intend to have them after the same molds that the beye wyndowe ys mayd by, but whether yow dowe thynke to have them of the same wyde that byt ys or not I cane nott tell, therfote I shall dyssyer yowe to drawe yowre menynge how and after what facyon yowe Wolde have them to be made in all poynte bothe the wyde of the lyght and allsoe the heght of the same, wythe the fassyon of all the molde that dowthe belonge there vnto and in what plaice ye wolde have them to stande, and yower plessewre knowne I shall dowe the best yt lyethe in me to dowe I Wold be verye glade to knowe yowre plessewre for yore stera forthe of yowre basse kowrt up to the tares and for the proporcion of them and allso for the gatte att the ende of ye tares wythe the proporcion of the same bothe for the heght and wydthe that yow wolde have theme of I woldegladlye understande youre mynde after what facion yow wolde have the gabyll-ende over the lucan wyndow therefore I shar dyssyer yowe to drawe a tryke of the upryght for youre lucan wyndowe and the gabylle end over hytt that I ma the better understande yowre plessewre in all thynge yt ye wolde that I shulde dowe. I thynge yowre owne stone ys to soft for to make any stere of hytt the best stone yt I dow knowe for stepe or stere ys att clypsame. the lyvynge god kepe yowe ever more frome all evyll & my goode Ladye wt all ye rest of yowre worshypfull howse.

frome burlaye the xiij of June. By yowre at all tyme to cõmande ROGER WARDE mason."*

It is not impossible that, in consequence of this urgent appeal of Roger Warde, Lo'd Burghley got Henryck to make the plan of his bay window already mentioned.

The carved stonework was not always executed on the spot. The most important features no doubt were; but there seems to have been no objection to having the carved strings, where the pattern repeats, done away from the work in large quantities and then fitted into the spaces that required filling. This is very evident at Kirby Hall, where, in many cases, the carved group of flowers or fruit is ruthlessly cut in two, so as to fit up to one of the large projecting pilasters. Such an expedient is hardly excusable, even in a terra-cotta building like Sutton Court, near Guildford, where, no doubt, they sent some distance for their moulded work; but in a stone building, with masons on the spot, it is a distinct blemish, and exhibits a neglect of that good finish which marks the conscientious and careful workman.

But as the mason provided his details, so did the plasterer provide his, and the joiner, most likely, his. Richard Williams, the foreman at Cobham, has something of interest to say upon this. Writing to his master, "the right Honorable Lord the L. Cobham L. Warden of the five ports" he says,—

"I have thought it mete that the Joyner shall begin to worke upon moundaie com seavenight next at the furthest, and to goe in hand first with those 2 chambres wch yor L. meanes, and afterwarde wth the 2 newe Chambres, and those upr Lodginge, and then yf the time of the yeate will permitt the same wth the floaring of the parlour, and to thend it maie be prepared and made readie for his worke, the plasterer would be sent for to come to bring to yor Lo. modells or paternes of the maner of the sealing that yor L. maie make yor choice of that kind of work that shall best like you, and some care would be had that he be a good workman and the price reasonable, wherof this bearer the Joyner and Simondson can better judge than I am hable."

The spectacle of the plasterer submitting his models to his lordship, and a joint council of his lordship, the joiner, and Simondson passing judgment upon them, is interesting.

The same Richard Williams has also something to say about another artificer: "Yor Lo. must resolve," he writes in 1601, "what and how much you are pleased to have doen by Giles de Whitt either upon some newe chymney peece or uppon my Lo. yor father's tombe, that the poore [man] maie have some worcke to get wherwth all to maintaine and susteyne himself." It is evident that Giles de Whitt, apparently a Fleming, was ready to do any fine stone carving, and it is evident that he was to work from his own design, and not from that of another man. This was not the first time that Williams had written about the foreigner. Some months before he had said, "We have bargained with Giles de Whitt for making two chimney pieces for the two chambers next to your new chapel. He demands £65 for both: I will not give above £50 and he will accept it in the end rather than fail." Here is a characteristic picture! The needy foreigner stranded at Cobham, hoping to get work "wherewithall to maintain and sustain himself"; too poor to move to more likely quarters, preferring rather "to bear those ills he had than fly to others that he knew not of." No wonder he was willing to abate his terms 25 per cent. "in the end, rather than fail."

Yet one more extract from this same Richard Williams in the same year of 1601. It is from "A pticuler of Buildinge thought necessary to be dōen this yeare at yr L. house at Cobham, together with an estimate of the charges thereof as well for materialls to be bought as for the workmanship of the same." There are nine items, of which we need only quote four:—

1. "First the building of the foureth turrett according to the modell agreed upon by yr Lo: alreadie."

3. "A newe doorecase to be made and sett up in the newe plot."

5. "The plastering of the same parlour over hed wth suche kinde of worke as it shall please yr Lo. to sett downe."

8. "Joyners worck to be doen in the Great Chambre and the Lodging adioyning to the Queen's Chambre."

All these particulars, it must be remembered, are sent to Lord Cobham by his own foreman or agent, who not only looked after his buildings, but mixed up reports on building matters with the information that he had "spoken to ye drap to make provision of cloth for Liveries." Not one word of a controlling architect. We see the plasterer submitting his own models, we easily infer that the foreign mason supplied his own designs, and it is not straining probability to believe that the joiner, who was artist good enough to judge of the plasterer's work, would be able to work also from his own designs. How differently matters are managed to-day may be seen from the account in the last number of *A. A. Notes* of the Association's visit to Mr. Aston Webb's new insurance offices in Moorgate-street, where, in criticising the plaster work, it is Mr. Webb's sections and Mr. Webb's patterns that are praised.

I have troubled you with a good many extracts from ancient letters, but my aim is to throw the light of contemporary evidence upon the subject, and in furtherance of this object I must inflict one or two more quotations upon you.

We have seen how the workmen were regarded; and now, to supplement that picture, let us see what was the position of the surveyor. One part of Lord Bardolph's advice was to "question surveyors." As a matter of fact, in the building of Burghley House, Sir William Cecil did question several. We have learnt how he employed Henryck to make a plan of his bay window. We find that at different times he sent at least two other surveyors to report upon the progress of the works. One Edmund Hall writes thus on August 30, 1564,—and it is evident from his letter that he was a man accustomed to criticise the effect of architectural features, and to advise his employers upon technicalities much in the same way as an architect would in the present day. He writes:—

"It may please youe to vnderstande that accordinge to yor requeste I have bene at Burley and have conferred wth Kempe & Norris accordinge to yor pleasure to me declared: I assure youe I take yor determinacon for the staires to alter into the Chappell shall do verie well, wch alter will not be past ij foote di. in the nether ende of the Chappell, by occasion whereof I doubte not but youe will like the proportion of yor chamber much the better, to passe cleane thorough to the maine wall of the hall, and a Portall to rise before the dore: To leave a half pase betwene the hall and the Chamber of iiijr foote di. it wolde be to litle purpose, and yet it wolde be a great blemishe to yor chamber to take so much in length. ffor thoughe the portall risinge in the midest of yor chamber, takinge at the least iiijor foote di yet notwthstandinge it will bewtifie yor chamber beinge well wrought and the romes on both the sides will serve for good purposes. But if the Portall might be placed in the side corner of the Chamber, it Wold stande much more apter then in the midest: on the East side of yor chamber it can not stande, because the dore wold spoile the side of the hall, where the longe borde shoulde stande, and on the West side of it, it will take half the windowe in the chamber, wch may be borne, but the dore standinge against the end of the high table in the hall, will pester yor dore, except youe do apoint the shorter table to serve that place. Youe may consider of it as to youe shall seme best, and so to be followed accordingly, youe shall finde that the breadth of the Chamber will beare the whole length very well. And accordinge to yor minde Kempe will provide as many Masons as he canne gett, so as the south side of yor house may be perfected before winter, wch is a great pece of worke to cutte out of yor harde stone so shortlie."*

* State Papers, Domestic, Mary, Vol. ix. No. 4.

* State Papers, Domestic, Elizabeth, vol. xxxiv. No. 51.

The rest of the letter I need not read*; it deals with the disposition of the terraces and garden, but at least it goes to show that the surveyor (or architect) of that time had his say about the garden as well as the house. The letter concludes:—

"Thus beinge bolde to write to youe my minde wch as I thinke shal be as well a beutifying to yor orcharde to geve it an even head before yor house, as to the beutifying of the growndes, next adjoyninge to the principall side of yor house to be even and levell, howesoever it shall please youe to use it. Further herein at this tyme I have not to say; but from tyme to tyme as occasion shall serve, I shal be glad to do my dever to the uttermost of my power to do youe & yors any pleasure or service I shal be able.

Written from Greatforde the xxxth day of August 1584,
Yours to cömaund
EDMUND HALL

[Addressed] To the honourable Sir Willm Cecill Knyghte."

The other surveyor was a Richard Shute,—not John, the author,—and he writes to report progress on July 30, 1578.

Leaving Burghley for another great palace of the time, Holdenby, we get an interesting glimpse of that great house in course of its erection. In the year 1579 it was approaching completion, and Lord Burghley, being in the neighbourhood, and being himself a great builder, writes to Secretary Walsingham to tell Sir Christopher Hatton that on his way to Northampton he and the Chancellor "mean to survey his house at Holdenby, and when we have done to fill our bellies with his meat and sleep also, as the proverb is, our bellies-full all Monday at night, and on Tuesday in the morning, we will be at Northampton." Sir Christopher was then at Greenwich, so he wrote to Lord Burghley to welcome him and make him free of Holdenby. In the course of his letter he says:—

"I fear me that as your Lordship shall find my house unbuilt and very far from good order, so through the newness you shall find it dampish and full of evil air . . . . I humbly beseech you, my honourable Lord, for your opinion to the surveyor of such lacks and faults as shall appear to you in this rude building, for as the same is done hitherto in direct observation of your house and plot at Tyball's [Theobalds] so I earnestly pray your Lordship that by your good corrections at this time it may prove as like to the same as it hath ever been meant to be."

So the surveyor (or architect),—perhaps John Thorpe himself,—attended, we may suppose; while the Lord Treasurer, in company with Sir Walter Mildmay and a great multitude of gentlemen and servants, made a tour of critical inspection. How far Sir Christopher was prepared to accept Lord Burghley's suggestions, how far the soul of the architect or surveyor (if souls surveyors are allowed to have) was to be wrung with the necessity of altering his design at the bidding of his client's grand friend, we are spared the necessity of inquiring, for his Lordship was mightily pleased with the house, and he wrote next day to his host to say so. He says:—

"But approaching to the house, being led by a long straight fair way, I found a great magnificence in the front or front pieces of the house, and so every part answerable to other, to allure liking. I found no one thing of greater grace than your stately ascent from your hall to your great chamber; and your chambers answerable with largeness and lightsomeness, that truly a Momus could find no fault. I visited all your rooms, high and low, and only the contentation of mine eyes made me forget the infirmity of my legs. And where you were wont to say it was a young Theobalds, truly Theobalds I like as my own; but I confess it is not so good as a model to a work, less than a pattern, and no otherwise worthy in any comparison than a foil."

Thus Lord Burghley. Yet, still, there is no acknowledgement of an architect, as we interpret the word. The praise is all given to the promoter. Such, indeed, is the custom now. If you take up any newspaper account of the opening of a new building, do you ever find the name of the architect mentioned? And yet to him above all is the abiding interest of the whole affair due. Indeed, the neglect of the nineteenth century reporter is a greater injustice than that of Shakspeare's contemporary, the Lord Treasurer, for whatever beauty the building of to-day possesses is mainly owing to one man, whereas, in Shakspeare's time, the credit was divided between a dozen or more.

But now, having learned incidentally, as it were, what the public of those times thought of architects,—or rather, perhaps, having learned that they did not think of them at all,—let us see what architects thought of themselves. This we gather from the already-quoted book of John Shute. Amid a wonderful deal of tedious verbosity and long-winded pedantry, we find a few things that are worth remembering. Among all studies he considers the most profitable to be—

"That by the Grekes named Architectonica and of the latines Architectura (I think not altogether unfite nor unaptlie by me termed in Englishe, the arte and trade to rayse up and make excellent edifices and buildinges)."

There the wearisome John is not far wrong. Then he proceeds to dilate upon the wide reach that architecture has, the number of allied studies that its pursuits necessitates,—

"So that without a neare acquaintance or understanding in them, neyther paynters, massons, gold smythes, enbroderers, carvers, joynars, glassyers, gravers in all maner of metalles and divers others more can obtayne anye worthy praise at all. Nowe all these being braunches of that forsayd foundation, stocke or science shall bring forthe the frutes of it to their great profites."

So that he, too, regarded the artificers named as sharing almost equally with the architect in the burden and heat of design. His most interesting chapter is on "What the office and Duetie is of him that wyll be a Perfecte Architecte or Mayster of buijldings." Yet this is merely an echo of Vitruvius. His rules and exhortations are those of Italy in the early years of the Christian era, not those of England in Shakspeare's time. Of course, they are somewhat to the point, but their interest is general and not particular, and one cannot help feeling that in laying down rules for the guidance of architects John Shute was addressing a body of men *in posse* not *in esse*. For the architect of Shakspeare's time was still a surveyor, who shared with the mason, and the plasterer, and the joiner, the glory of producing "the goodly dwellings and the rich" that Falstaff admired and that are at once the envy and admiration of us in the present day. And it will do us no harm to remember that it was not to one brain, but to many, that we owe those beautiful places. Nor will it be amiss if we try to bring about such a state of things that once again the mason and the plasterer and the joiner may be able to help us in design as well as execution. And it may also be worth while to remember that the English architect of Shakspeare's time was not the great artist whom princes loved to court, but the unknown surveyor, who divided his time between designing the body of palaces like Holdenby or Burghley or Wollaton, and "repairing the posts, pales, and rails of Richmond Park carried away by the flood."

Mr. A. H. Clark said he had much pleasure in proposing a hearty vote of thanks to Mr. Gotch for the very interesting paper which he had read to them. He (the speaker) had had a great many opportunities of examining some of the old buildings in Northamptonshire, and although he had, perhaps, devoted more time to the study of ecclesiastical remains,—which were quite as noticeable in Northamptonshire as in other districts,—than to the study of domestic work, still, what domestic work he had seen in that county had been so charming that he thought the impression it made would always remain in his mind. He thought that Mr. Gotch had conferred upon them a great kindness by so admirably illustrating his paper by lantern views. Quite apart from the high literary merit which the paper possessed, its value was doubled by being illustrated by lantern views. He felt sure that if they could improve the illustrations to some of the papers which were read in that room, and endeavour to bring them up to the very high level which had been maintained during the present session, there would be no more scanty attendances at their fortnightly meetings.

Mr. C. H. Brodie, in seconding the motion, said that if the Discussion Section of the Association, in which he was rather interested, continued to produce speakers like Mr. Clark, then the Association would owe that Section much gratitude.

Mr. F. T. W. Goldsmith, in supporting the motion, said the paper had been an excellent one. He was sure they were all glad to hear Mr. Brodie speak up for the Discussion Section of the Association, and to hear that Mr. Clark was a member of that Section. Mr. Gotch had dealt so particularly and clearly with the functions of the surveyors and craftsmen who erected the buildings about which he had been speaking, and which were admired so much by everybody, that it would be absolutely impossible to supply any information to the meeting which Mr. Gotch had not already given; but he should like to draw one or two inferences from what had been said. First of all, it seemed to him that the modern idea that the architect of the period under discussion was a great person was altogether an erroneous idea. The architect, from what Mr. Gotch had said, was a man who was not afraid of hard work, and was not above descending to minute details, which were put together so as to produce buildings which of their kind, he supposed, had no rivals. It was amusing to hear that the architect was as much concerned in the "repairing of fences washed away by the flood" as he was in the design of "my lord's chamber" or "my lord's bay window." Evidently Mr. Gotch was of opinion that the architect of that period was more identified with the craftsmen and with the practical side of his art than he seemed to be at the present day. The excellent paper which they had heard from Mr. Gotch was what they expected from him, and the illustrations which he had shown were fully worthy of it.

Mr. Bernard Dicksee said that Mr. Gotch had stated that architects in the time of Shakspeare did not supply any detail drawings. He (the speaker) would like to know whether that was the invariable rule, and, if so, when that rule was broken through? because he believed there was a letter in existence from Sir Christopher Wren apologising for supplying so many details. He would like to know when that custom came in.

Mr. J. C. Stockdale said a similar question had occurred to him when Mr. Gotch referred to the architects of those days only supplying small scale details. The full-size mouldings and the sections of cornices, as executed, displayed considerable knowledge of Italian work, which could scarcely have been possessed by the ordinary masons of those days. Did the architects supply them with full-size profiles? The existence of foreign workmen in this country might account for some of the mantelpieces and features of that kind, but could scarcely account for the cornices and plinths; and he thought our masons could not have had that knowledge unless they had had full-size models to work from.

Mr. A. O. Collard said it was interesting to look into the domestic life of the architects of past days, and he should therefore like to know the method of life of Thorpe, Shute, and others, and the estimation in which they were held by people,—not by Lord Burleigh and other notabilities of the period, but by those among whom they lived. Did they live in comfort or misery? And did they spring from a sort of clerk of works' existence, or were they properly educated? Did they travel about much for the purpose of collecting information? Or did only those few mentioned by Mr. Gotch act in that way for their clients? Another point upon which he should like to obtain information was as to how the architects of those days were remunerated. Mr. Gotch had quoted an instance in reference to palings and things of that sort, but could he give them no other information on the question of remuneration,—whether they were well paid, and whether they were paid just so much for their time? It was certain that the present five per cent. system was not in use at that time. Any information on that point would be of interest, for it might, perhaps, be found that a return to the practice adopted in those days would be better in some respects than that in vogue at the present time.

The President, in putting the vote of thanks to the meeting, said the real and deep interest of the paper which they had heard read that evening consisted in the contemporary evidence of the way in which work was carried on in the period under discussion. It was most interesting to hear that a system of quantities was in use then, not exactly in our sense of the word, but for the purpose of ascertaining the number

---

* We reprint it here, however. It continues: "I have advised Kempe to make a prufe of v foote square, what the chardges wilbe, to take ye grounde out of yor garden to the loones of the flower in yor lower gallerie, so as you may have an estimate of the rest for that yor tarresses be alredie set forth and the stoone work of a great part of them done thei will take litle more earth then alreadie is bestowed of them. But for ye bestowinge of yor earth, if it shall seme to youe so good, I thincke the angell of yor orcharde, wch lieth of the west side of yor garden, & on the south side of yor base courte, wch grownde hath a great desent, wch dessent beginneth about xxxte foote from the wall of the base courte, to the end of the wall of the garden. My mind is for to spend the earth that shall come out of yor garden I Wolde have a wall to goe from the rounde mounte of the south west corner of yor garden. Westwarde to the water, to be even with the height of the grounde adjoyninge upon the wall of yor base courte and so to make all that Angell levell, to use as to youe shall seme good. And if the earth that cometh out of the garden will not suffise to make the lower parte equall to the higher, as it is at this present the higher parte maye be cast downe to the lower wch is no great chardge, and so it will awnswere the better wth the flower of yor garden."

bricks, &c., which were used, and in regard matters of that sort; and no doubt the timate which Mr. Gotch had quoted had ade them wish that they could get work done the same rate in the present day. With gard to the question of architects supplying tail drawings, he was very often sorry, when looked at some of the old buildings, that the chitects had evidently not supplied them, and good many of the old buildings would have oked better had their architects done so. As r. Gotch had said, the detail of almost any ilding of the period was of the coarsest scription, and to anyone who liked really ood detail it was sometimes rather trying to e such coarseness. The very widely-spaced lasters on the top of Wollaton was an instance.

The vote of thanks was then put to the meeting and carried with acclamation.

Mr. Gotch, in reply, said it always gave him reat pleasure to read a paper before the Association. With regard to the views which he ad shown, many of them would be recognised s old friends, and some of them as having been ublished in his book. With regard to the uestions which had been asked, he was afraid hat he could not give much information, for hey happened to be just the questions about which he had vainly endeavoured to satisfy imself. As to when the custom of supplying etail drawings began, he had no information o give. He should be very glad to know when he custom did begin. The evidence which ould be obtained was somewhat fragmentary, nd was really negative evidence. That was to ay, he could not find any record of an architect having supplied full-size details in the time about which they were speaking, but he should think that the full-size details and profiles were made by the working masons themselves, who were then, he took it, better artists than they were now, for now they could only work from another man's details. In those days, he supposed, they had schools among themselves, and profiles were passed from one to the other. Where some profiles came from would be an exceedingly interesting matter to decide. For instance, the profiles of the cornices of Lyveden New Building were exceedingly refined: they could not have been supplied by an English mason. He thought they must have been imported in some way, possibly by the builder or employer. It was quite possible, although it was only a suggestion, that Sir Thomas Tresham, who was a Roman Catholic, might have had correspondents in Italy, and one of them might have supplied him with a full-size cornice in detail. Something of the kind must have happened, for the work was exceedingly pure. He thought that they ought not to regard the masons of those days as being like the masons of the present day, but as men who belonged to schools, and who were better versed in the art of their business than the masons of the present day. As to the rank of life of architects in the period under review, he could not say very much. The Robert Smithson from whose epitaph he had quoted was described as "Robert Smithson, gent.," and in those days, he thought, a man would not be called gentleman unless he had had gentle nurture; Robert Smithson was therefore probably of good family, and had been brought up in a good manner; that was to say, he had not risen absolutely from the position of a workman. As to John Thorpe, there was no information as to his birth; but he was a man of some education, because to be able to write as he did implied that. He wrote and spelled in quite a different manner from some of the workmen whose letters he (Mr. Gotch) had referred to,—Roger Warde, for instance. The architects of those days must have been educated to some extent, and he should think that a good many of them, like John Shute, did go abroad, and did do a good deal of sketching. Of course, the first architect who took the position of architect, as understood at the present day, was Inigo Jones, who came over to England in the train of a foreign princess. He must have come of a good family or he would not have been attached to the Court. How the architects of those days were remunerated he had no idea, except that he thought they were not particularly well remunerated, and he doubted whether the system of payment in vogue at that time would be better than the present five per cent. system. He agreed with the President that it would have been better if the work of the period under discussion had been more homogeneous,—if there had been one controlling mind that would have regulated general matters of design, even if it did not regulate detail. Had that been the case, the work would have been more even in merit than that shown in many of the buildings of the period.

The meeting then terminated.

MAGAZINES AND REVIEWS.

THE *Gazette des Beaux-Arts* starts with a sympathetic article on Henriquel Dupont, the late eminent engraver, by M. Alfred de Lostalet, with impressions from some of his engravings. "Rembrandt et l'Art Italien" is the subject of an article by M. Eugène Müntz, in which the writer endeavours to trace the influence on Rembrandt's style of the collection of Italian engravings which he is known to have possessed. A significant comparison is made between an engraving of a dead Christ by Mantegna and that of the corpse in Rembrandt's "Lesson in Anatomy by Dr. Deymann," in each of which the dead body is foreshortened in the same position, with the feet towards the spectator. Facsimiles are given of a sketch by Rembrandt after Da Vinci's "Last Supper" and of a study (an etching) by him after Correggio's "Antiope." "Coysevox et le Grand Condé" is the subject of an article by M. Germain Bapst, illustrated by an engraving of a bust of Condé by the sculptor.

In the *Art Journal* Mr. Aymer Vallance's third article on the "Furnishing and Decoration of the House" deals with "the Fireplace," and the illustrations, as examples of what may be done in fireplace furnishing in a moderate way, are all pleasing and in good taste. For the treatment of the fireplace in summer the writer suggests a brass or copper repoussé shutter made to fit the opening, as better than anything that has hitherto been tried. An article on "Paris Pleasure Resorts—the Marne" is illustrated by sketches which tend to make one resolve to go for a row on the Marne next time one goes to Paris. Mr. Wilfrid Meynell contributes an article on Mr. Stanhope Forbes, with engravings from some of his pictures.

In the *Magazine of Art* Mr. Lewis F. Day contributes the article on "Artistic Homes," dealing with wall-papers, and illustrated by some good designs, of which the "Wethenden" pattern, by Mr. A. B. Pite, is one of the best and most powerful. Some engravings are given of the Old Masters recently at the Royal Academy, and Part I. of an article on "The Art Treasures of the Comédie Française," by Mr. Theodore Child, is illustrated by two engravings of interiors in the celebrated house. The frontispiece to the number is an etching by M. Chauvel from a picture of Troyon's.

The *Revue des Deux Mondes* contains a long and well-written article by M. Gaston Deschamps, entitled "Un Séjour à Athènes." His description of the first blank disappointment on arrival at the station amid a collection of huts is feelingly told, as also his full satisfaction with the Parthenon remains when he attained to them. This paragraph, an eloquent tribute to the beauty of the famous temple, we may quote:—

"Si ruiné, si délabré, si émietté, qu'il soit, malgré ses trous béans, l'énorme lézarde qu'il fendu en deux et qui a jeté à terre, dans un pêle-mêle des décombres, les colonnes écroulées et les chapiteaux brisés, le Parthénon reste la plus belle demeure que les hommes aient construite, pour y abriter l'effigie visible de Dieu. Il est l'idéal de la perfection logique. Jamais peut-être l'esprit humain n'a remporté sur le désordre des choses une plus belle victoire, que le jour où il a conçu cet équilibre stable où il a atteint la beauté non par un furtif éclair d'imagination et de fantaisie, mais par l'effort de la pensée, la précision du calcul, par la splendeur de cette harmonie supérieure que les Grecs appelaient, d'un si beau mot, *l'eurythmie*. . . . Aucune gravure, aucun tableau, ne peuvent donner l'idée de cette merveille. Il faut admirer les temples de l'Acropole, dans le clair décor où ils ont fleuri, sous le chaud soleil qui a doré leurs marbres, sous le ciel en fête, qui baigne d'azur impalpable leurs colonnes et leurs frontons. Vers la fin du jour, les rayons oblique dorent de lueurs fauves la façade sévère du Parthenon; le Temple d'Erechthée profile sur l'horison vermeil ses hautes et minces colonnes ioniques, qui ressemblent à des tiges de fleur. Le Temple de la Victoire-sans-Ailes, si petit qu'on le prendrait presque pour une chapelle, brille comme une châsse, tout au bout de la terrasse et si près du bord, qu'on a peur de la voir croula dans les précipices. Peu à peu le soleil descend dans le ciel enflammé, étoilant d'étincelles les maisons de Phalère et du Pirée, et posant sur les eaux du golfe Salonique de larges et aveuglantes splendeurs. Salamine, toute violette, flotte dans le pourpre et l'or."

The *Revue Générale* (Brussels) includes the eighth and apparently the last of the series of "Lettres du Floride" by M. Victor Watteyne, which are written with a great deal of spirit and give an interesting glimpse into a part of the United States not yet very much known in England.

In the English magazines there are naturally various papers in relation to the County Council. The *Contemporary* contains an optimist article by Lord Hobhouse, who is an out-and-out "Progressive," and declares that in fact the Progressives want real municipal government and the Moderates merely want a repetition of the Board of Works. To this it may be replied that the Board of Works at all events did more practical work in the way of London improvements than the L.C.C. has yet done. This article may be compared with that in the *Nineteenth Century* by Mr. John Burns, who openly professes that he considers his duty as a County Councillor to be to improve the wages and shorten the hours of labour of the working-classes, and that he is paid a salary by a representative body of his fellow-workmen to enable him to maintain his place in the Council and look after their interests; and that is Mr. Burns's notion of the objects of the County Council. Mr. Prothero makes a reply to the article in the same number, which might have been made a good deal more effective in certain points than it is; but then the writer was under restrictions as to good taste and reasonableness which do not affect Mr. John Burns. In the *New Review* "the impeachment" of the L.C.C. is written by Mr. T. G. Fardell and "the defence" by Mr. C. Harrison. The former maintains that economy has only been realised by the last Council because it has neglected to carry out public works which were called for. Mr. Harrison retorts that there is no improvement asked for which has not been carried out. (What about the Strand and Holborn?) Mr. Fardell asserts that the Blackwall Tunnel was only wrung from the Council, and that as a set-off they refused to contribute to the southern approach to the Tower Bridge, without which it must be all but useless. Mr. Harrison's best point is his praise of the arduous work done by the committees, in which he is probably justified.

Lord Kelvin's article in the *Fortnightly* seems to have been suggested by Mr. Crookes's article of last month, in that it opens by a reference to the vitality of "the perpetual motion" in "the scientific imagination." It should be read as a corrective by those who are inclined to be thrown off their mental balance by the sensational and striking experiments of Mr. Tesla. While there is little that is new in the article there is much that is true, and its modest and temperate tone is particularly refreshing. Lord Kelvin gives some interesting anecdotes of Sadi Carnot, and mentions,—what is not generally known,—that from some of his posthumous papers it appears that he had thought out for himself the principle of the conservation of energy, and discovered the identity of heat and work. At the close of the article is re-iterated the conclusion that "within a finite period of time past the earth must have been, and within a finite period of time to come, must again be unfit for the habitation of man as at present constituted, unless operations have been, and are to be, performed which are impossible under the laws governing the known operations going on at present in the material world."

Mr. J. E. H. Gordon runs some risk of being taken seriously when he hoaxes the *Nineteenth Century* with what is very like a promise of perpetual motion. To the initiated, the confusion he deliberately makes between force, energy, and power will supply a clue to his intention, but it is to be feared that the majority of his readers will no more notice it than Mark Twain's readers in a similar case observed the peculiar and suggestive arrangement of the hands of the "petrified man." Moreover, Mr. Gordon hardly keeps up the joke throughout, but drifts into giving a serious account of Mr. Tesla's remarkable experiments. The conclusion is, however, an excellent parody of the bathos of newspaper science:—"Few who attended Mr. Tesla's lecture will forget the possibilities which seemed to open to their minds when they saw a living man standing in the midst of an electric storm, receiving unharmed in his hands flashes of veritable light-

e

ning, and waving above his head a tube, through which the very life blood of creation pulsed, in waves of purple fire"

Macmillans publishes an article by the Rev. Harry Jones on "Hours of Labour," which seems rather worded with the view of conveying the writer's sympathy with the working man's desire for shorter hours, without committing himself to any definite expression of opinion.

In *Longmans* is a short charming article by poor Richard Jefferies, on the lions in Trafalgar-square, which struck him as the one outdoor work of art worth getting enthusiastic about in London. This is a little overstating it, perhaps, but he draws an eloquent contrast between the hurry and bustle of London life constantly streaming past, "and in the midst the calm lions, dusky, unmoved, full always of the one grand idea that was infused into them." The article is at least such a one as only an original and fervid mind could have produced.

The *English Illustrated Magazine* contains an article on "The Queen's Riviera Residence," with illustrative sketches of scenery which are not, however, of very special interest or excellence. An article on "The Royal Mews" conveys some information upon a historic London establishment, with illustrations of two or three of the State carriages, of which it may be said that the "semi-State" coach, built by Hutton, who was Lord Mayor of Dublin at the time of the Queen and Prince Consort's visit in 1852, is a much better piece of design in a general way than the State coach, though the latter was designed by no less a person than Sir William Chambers. State coaches, like other State articles, seldom escape the reproach of being gewgaw, and this is no exception. The panels were painted by Cipriani. Mr. H. M. Cundall contributes a brief article on The Speaker's Mace, with illustrations of that and two other maces, now in Jamaica.

In the *Gentleman's Magazine* is a very able article by Mr. Hume Nisbet on "Illustrative Art, Past and Present," to which we have not space to refer further, but which is well worth reading by any who are interested in the subject.

The *Cornhill Magazine* devotes a short and useful article to an account of "How the Egyptian Monuments were read," meaning we presume the inscriptions on the monuments. The *Antiquary* continues various serial articles before noticed, and contains one on "The Tombs of the Kings of England" and one on "Prehistoric Rome" by Canon Isaac Taylor." "Lettering on the Helmets of Effigies" is the subject of another article.

The *Century* opens with a very well-written and very enthusiastic article on "St. Paul's," which should be read by Englishmen with sympathy and admiration. It is signed by M. G. van Rensselaer, and illustrated by Mr. Joseph Pennell. The article is partly historical and partly critical, and the criticism is very able and discriminating. The writer thoroughly appreciates Wren's greatness, without being blind to the defects of his famous building The writer considers the outer dome Wren's great triumph.

> "The merits of the exterior far outweigh its defects, for though we may object to certain features and arrangements, the church as a whole never fails to impress in the profoundest way both the eye and the imagination. It is a magnificent building, and we cannot always say as much of buildings in which we discover fewer special faults. People who have no eye for the picturesque sometimes complain of its colour, or rather of the way in which smoke and soot have altered its colour. But fresh in the first whiteness of its Portland stone, it could hardly have been as imposing as today, when great streaks and patches of inky black accentuate the pallor of more sheltered portions."

The interior views by Mr. Pennell are particularly admirable specimens of illustration. In the same magazine Mr. Stillman's series of articles on "Italian Old Masters" deals this month with Giorgione, and is accompanied by two engravings, the "Knight of Malta" and "St. Liberalis." Two articles on the great pianist Paderewski, the one biographical and the other critical, with two portraits, will interest some of our readers.

In *Scribner's Magazine* Mr. W. A. Coffin concludes his series of three papers on "American Illustrations of To-day," with engravings illustrating the work of various American artists. Other articles of special interest are "The Water-route from Chicago to the Ocean," by Lieut. C. C. Rogers; "Small Country Places" by Mr. Samuel Parsons, jun.; "Paris Theatres and Concerts" by Mr. W. F. Apthorp; and "Speed in Locomotives," three very interesting papers under one heading, giving the results of special inquiry and experiment on the subject, and leading to the conclusion that we are not likely to get higher, on the whole, than the highest speeds now habitually run.

In *Harper* is an interesting and picturesquely-written article on "The Capitals of the North-West," describing some towns whose very names are as yet unfamiliar to Englishmen, and a well-illustrated article by Mr. Walter Besant on "The London of George II.," a continuation of the series of historical articles on London which he has been contributing to *Harper*, and which will make a valuable book if published collectively.

Illustrations.

ILLUSTRATIONS OF OLD CHESTER.*

III.—THE CRYPT IN WATERGATE-STREET.

THIS remarkable double crypt is supposed to have been built by Ranulph de Blondville, sixth Norman Earl of Chester, about the year 1180; it runs under a substantial modern house, which was for many years the residence of Mr. Pattison Ellames, who was Mayor of Chester in 1770, and is situated between the well known "God's Providence House," and the family mansion of the Leches of Carden. Its direction is north and south; it had one entrance at the north-west angle, and a door at the opposite extremity seen in the illustration, which apparently at one time communicated with a crypt in Bridge-street, this last was cleared of rubbish in 1839. In the walls are three aumbreys, one in the south, seen behind the figures, which is smaller than the others, and in it one of the hinges remains *in situ*, the others are on the east side, and all are in very good preservation. The dimensions of the crypt are as follows:—Length, 44 ft.; breadth, 22 ft.; and height to the groining, 11 ft. The crypt was used as the Customs' bonded cellar, No. 5, from the time that the Bonding Act came into operation, until the month of February, 1864. It is now occupied by Messrs. Quellyn, Roberts, & Co., wine merchants.

A few doors lower down Watergate-street, there is a small single crypt, of similar construction, also forming part of Messrs. Roberts & Co.'s premises. THOMAS P. IVISON.

* For preceding views of this series, see *Builder* for Feb. 6 and Feb. 27 last.

GRANDTULLY CASTLE, PERTHSHIRE.

THE drawing shows the proposed additions delineated at the request of Mr. Walter Fotheringham, "of that ilk" and of Forfar, N.B., to whom the castle has recently reverted through a very ancient entail.

The castle is intended as the future residence of Lady Stewart, widow of the late owner. It is a very ancient structure, and is believed to be the original of the old castle (Tully-Veolan) referred to by Sir Walter Scott in "Waverley." The tower portion is the old part. The plan, the architects write, "is uninstructive and uninteresting, and merely worked out to conform with the slopes of the ground"; that is their answer to our request for a plan.

INDIAN DECORATIVE DETAIL.

THESE examples of balustrades from Indian buildings are reproduced from the "Jeypore Portfolio of Architectural Details," and are referred to in an article on that publication on another page.

THE HALL OF THE WORSHIPFUL COMPANY OF BRODERERS.

THE original building of the Broderers' Company dates back to the tenth century, when it formed part of a monastery; and during the excavations in forming the basement traces of Roman work were found, also pottery and glass of that period, whilst several loads of human bones were removed.

The increased value of land in the City is remarkably shown by the fact that in the year 1291 the site upon which the new Hall stands was bought by a certain William de Herlake and Agnes his wife, in fee simple, for 10 marks. It is now, in all probability, worth 20,000*l.*

The front of the building is of Portland stone and, with the exception of the ground floor story, has been kept plain on account of the narrowness of the street and the height of the building. The lower portion, however, forming the entrance, has been enriched with the arms of the Company, and also of the master and wardens. The lobby is richly treated with Roman mosaic and a moulded frieze with figures representing the ancient art or mystery of embroidery. In the upper part of the building is a large dining-hall capable of accommodating 100 persons, and the necessary offices in connexion therewith. Inasmuch as the Company have now but little use for a hall, the premises have been erected to suit the requirements of Messrs. Morley, the well-known Manchester warehousemen.

The hall was rebuilt from the designs and under the superintendence of the architect of the Company, Mr. H. Huntly-Gordon. The contractor was Mr. D. Charteris, of Westminster. The carving, and also the plaster frieze, were excellently carried out by Mr. Gilbert Seale, and the mosaic by Messrs. Simpson, of St. Martin's-lane.

The drawing from which the illustration has been taken was exhibited in the Royal Academy of 1890.

ST. STEPHEN'S CHURCH SCHOOLS, CANONBURY.

THIS view shows an addition to the old schools attached to St. Stephen's Church, Canonbury.

The new building is planned so that it might be used in conjunction with the old rooms for concerts, entertainments, and for other parochial purposes.

The work throughout is of a plain and simple character. Stock bricks for facing walls have been used both internally and externally. The

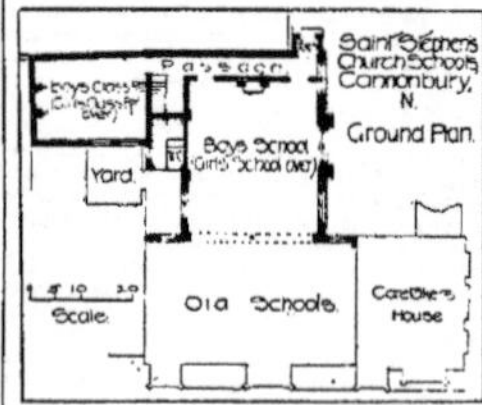

interior joinery is stained and varnished. Shorland's ventilating stoves are used for warming purposes.

The freehold site was a gift from the Marquess of Northampton.

The Bishop of Bedford opened the building last year, and expressed his approval of the arrangements generally.

Messrs. McCormick & Sons, of Canonbury were the builders, and Mr. Arthur Ardron of London, is the architect.

ARCHITECTURAL SOCIETIES.

BIRMINGHAM ARCHITECTURAL ASSOCIATION—At a meeting of this Association on the 1st inst., a paper was read by Mr. T. W. F. Newton on "Architectural Poetry." In his opening remark Mr. Newton said that his object was to draw attention to the aid afforded to an architect by the study of the imaginative descriptions of architecture and the kindred arts to be found in English verse, and he wished to point out that the ideas therein contained would often prove of great value to the man who was conversant with the facts and necessities of the works under his control, and could combine the poetry with the practice. Mr. Newton then gave a large number of quotations showing from what widely different points of view the poets have regarded the art of architecture.

GLASGOW ARCHITECTURAL ASSOCIATION.—The annual business meeting of this Association was held on the 1st inst., the President, Mr. William J. Anderson, in the chair. The Committee's report on the past session's work shows that the affairs of the Association are in a satisfactory condition. There is a membership of eighty-nine; the syllabus of essays,

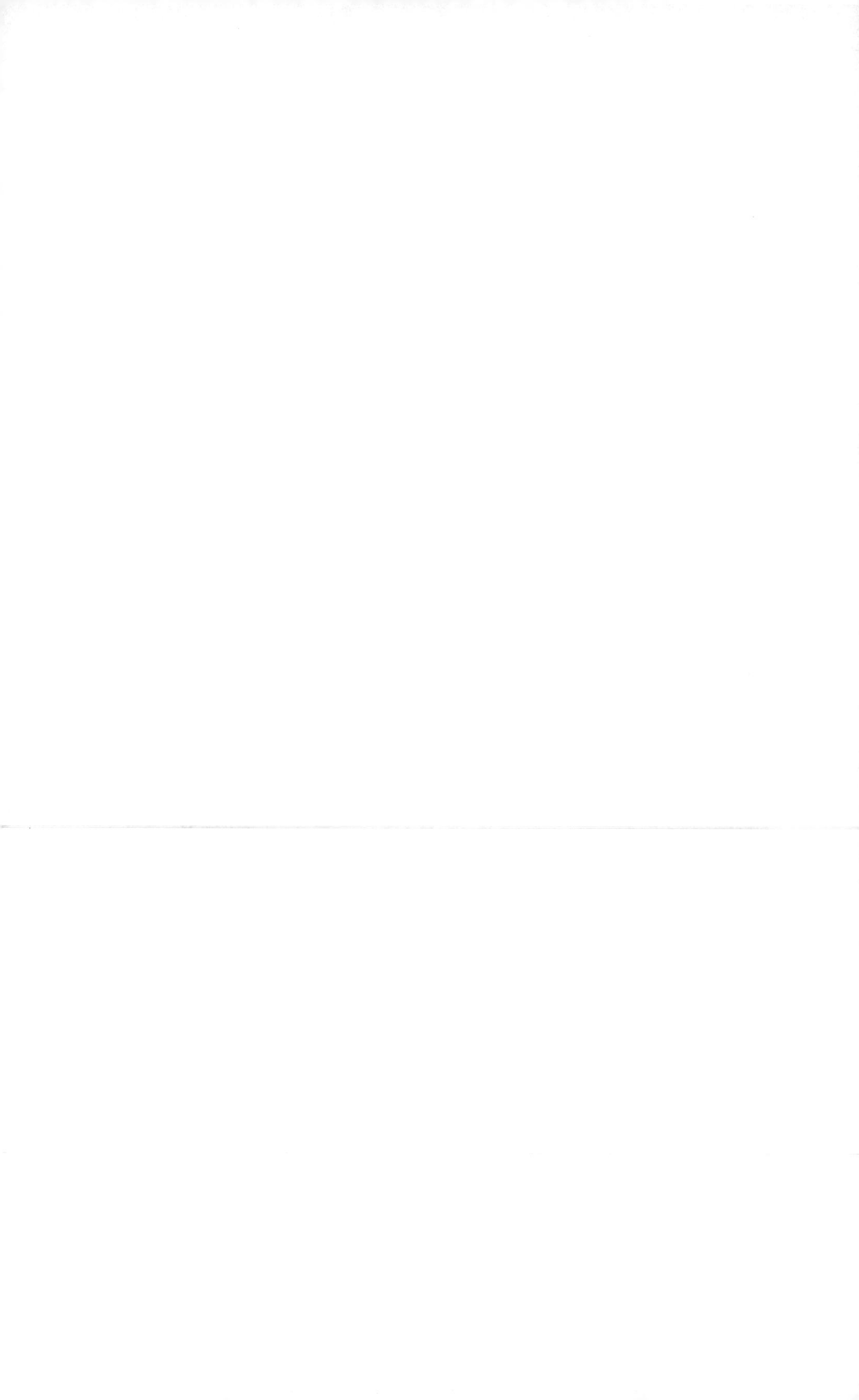

ILLUSTRATIONS OF OLD CHESTER.—Drawn by Mr. T. P. Ivison.
No. III. ANCIENT CRYPT IN WATERGATE STREET.

GRANDTULLY CASTLE: SHEWING PROPOSED

—Messrs. Williams, West & Slade, Architects.

HALL OF THE WORSHIPFUL COMPANY OF BRODERERS, REBUILT 1889.
MR. H. HUNTLY-GORDON, A.R.I.B.A., ARCHITECT.

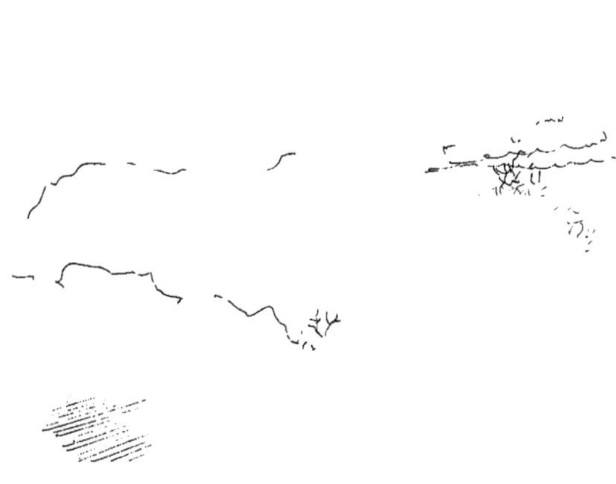

STEPHEN'S CHURCH SCHOOLS, CANONBURY, N.—Mr. A. Ardron, F.R.I.B.A., Architect

JAGAT SARWAN TEMPLE, AMBAIR.

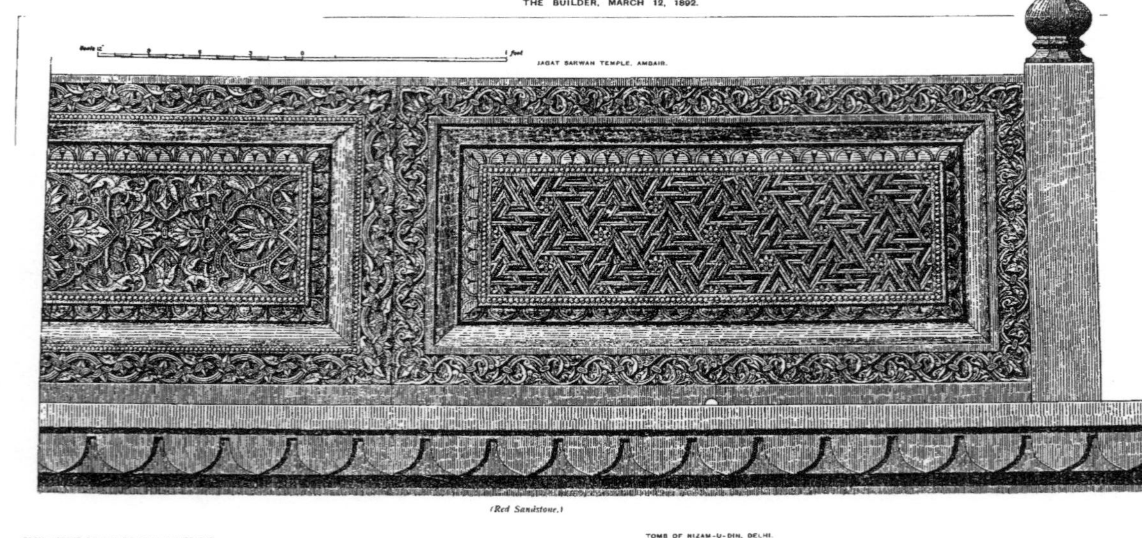

(Red Sandstone.)

FROM MOSQUE OF MAHAFIZ KHAN, AHMEDABAD.

TOMB OF NIZAM-U-DIN, DELHI.

PHOTO-LITHO. SPRAGUE & CO. 4 & 5 EAST HARDING STREET, FETTER LANE, E.C.

INDIAN DECORATIVE DETAIL: BALUSTRADES.
(From the "Jeypore Portfolio of Architectural Details.")

lectures, and visits were carried out with almost no variation; and notwithstanding heavy expenditure in improvements in the rooms, there still remains a balance in hand. The following gentlemen were elected as the office-bearers for the coming session:—Honorary President, Mr. William Forrest Salmon, F.R.I.B.A.; President, Mr. Alexander M'Gibbon; Vice-president, Mr. Alexander N. Paterson, M.A.; Secretaries, Mr. L. Douglas Penman and Mr. John White; Treasurer, Mr. Andrew Muirhead; Librarian, Mr. George S. Hill; Committee, Mr. William J. Anderson, Mr. Robert J. Gildard, Mr. Andrew Robertson, and Mr. William Watson.

LIVERPOOL ARCHITECTURAL SOCIETY.—At a meeting of this Society held on the 7th inst., in the Royal Institution, Colquitt-street, a paper was read by Mr. Damer Harrisson, F.R.C.S., on "Prehistoric Rome." His remarks were illustrated by lantern views, showing the rude artistic efforts of the early Romans. The intelligent interpretation of these, and of the names of places and things, seemed to elucidate much of the early history of the Romans in a way that was novel and attractive.

SHEFFIELD SOCIETY OF ARCHITECTS AND SURVEYORS.—The monthly meeting of this Society was held at the School of Art on Tuesday night. Mr. J. B. Mitchell-Withers presided, in the absence of the President, Mr. Innocent, and Mr. J. A. Gotch, of Kettering, read a paper entitled, "How they Built in Shakspeare's Time." This paper was read before the Architectural Association of London on the 4th inst., and is fully reported on another page.

THE ARCHITECTURAL ASSOCIATION SPRING VISITS:

ST. SAVIOUR'S CHURCH, SOUTHWARK.

THE third spring visit of the Association was held on Saturday afternoon, March 5, when, by the kindness of Sir Arthur Blomfield, the works in connexion with the new nave to St. Saviour's, Southwark, and the old building were visited by a large party of members, under the guidance of Mr. F. T. W. Goldsmith, jun., honorary secretary. The removal of the old nave which had disgraced this church for a period of fifty years has been welcomed by all architects, and its place will be taken by a nave of six bays, with side aisles and a south entrance. A small portion of the walls and foundations of the Early English nave has been discovered and carefully incorporated in the new work. The walls are faced on the exterior with flints, and the stone used is Bath, Weldon, and Ancaster. The nave walls and arcade are hardly above the caps of the columns, and consequently little can be seen of the work at present, and comment must, therefore, be reserved. It is to be hoped that the contemplated restoration of the north transept will be proceeded with; the walls are in very bad structural repair, and the interest of the old building does not lie in this quarter. The careful examination of the old choir is always interesting, with its altar-screen erected by Fox, Bishop of Winchester, and its tombs, most notable of which is that of Gower, the poet, who died in 1402. Some interesting burials have taken place in this church. Amongst them Edmund Shakspeare, 1607, brother of the poet; John Fletcher, 1625, who collaborated with Beaumont; and Philip Hemlow, 1615.

*** It has been represented to us on the part of the Architectural Association that critical remarks in some of these reports of visits of the Association have given offence to the owners or architects of buildings, who have supposed them to emanate from the Association, which has been accused of getting permission to visit a building, and then criticising it. To prevent any such misconception, we beg to say that the reports of these visits are made at our request by a contributor who is responsible only to the Editor of this journal, and that the Architectural Association officially has no concern whatever with them.—ED.

LINLITHGOW PALACE.—A meeting of the Linlithgow Town Council was held on Tuesday night, when, on the motion of Bailie M'Alpine, it was agreed that the whole Council act as a committee to co-operate with the Edinburgh Architectural Society, and any other parties interested in the matter, with the view of inducing the Government to augment the sum which had been voted for the repairs on the Linlithgow Palace.—*Scotsman.*

DEMONSTRATIONS ON GREEK SCULPTURE IN THE BRITISH MUSEUM.

IN her fifth lecture,* Miss Eugénie Sellers dealt mainly with the two temples of Artemis at Ephesus. The older temple dates from the sixth century, and was itself no doubt built about some still older shrine, where Artemis was worshipped in her distinctively Asiatic character as a nature goddess. Herodotus says that some of the columns were dedicated to the goddess by Crœsus, the truth of which statement has now been proved by the fragments of an inscription to this effect discovered on the moulding at the foot of one of the drums. The drums were separated from the plinth by a deep double moulding, and were surmounted by Ionic columns. It is now clear that the drums were sculptured, for fragments of figures, recalling the type of the figures of the Harpy Tomb, have been found, rough at the back, and moreover convex. This proves the antiquity of this custom; yet, before excavations had established this, Pliny's statement that Skopas sculptured one of the drums of the later temple at Ephesus was discredited on the ground that such a practice belonged to a debased style of art. Numerous fragments have been found of the sculptures of the cornice, which has been wonderfully restored by Mr. Murray. In these Asiatic temples, which were, however, the work of Greek artists, the sculptures are far more lavishly disposed than in Greek temples, being found, as here, on the cornice and the drums, and as on the Nereid monument, and elsewhere on the architrave. This may possibly be due to the greater abundance of means in Asia Minor rather than to any difference of taste.

The second temple at Ephesus was built in the fourth century, on the destruction of the first by fire. Here, again, excavations have brought to light fragments of sculptured drums, in the figures of which, as in the figures of the Mausoleum frieze, we can recognise the characteristics, at any rate, of the style of Skopas. Miss Sellers discussed the subjects of these sculptures, and also, as usual, dealt somewhat fully with the question of technique.

In conclusion, she spoke of the sculptured frieze of the Temple of Athena at Priene, which represents a combat between Greeks and giants. This is the last development of Greek sculptures in relief, and in the rounded figures, and in their excessive activity, we find an affinity with the work of the Pergamene school.

BRITISH ARCHÆOLOGICAL ASSOCIATION.

AT the meeting of this Association on the 2nd inst., Mr. J. W. Grover, F.S.A., in the chair, several curious brooches of bronze recently found in the City, in deep excavations, were exhibited by Mr. Macmichael. Mr. T. Blashill described a remarkable mould for casting leaden figures of St. Thomas-à-Becket, discovered beneath the foundations of a building at Hull, by Mr. J. Simons, who, at Mr. Blashill's suggestion, has presented it to the British Museum. Facsimile casts were produced. Mr. Earle Way communicated a notice of the discovery of portions of the palace erected by the Duke of Suffolk in Southwark, to receive his wife, the sister of Henry VIII., and the widow of King Louis. Several fragments of elaborately-moulded terra-cotta have been met with, some of which were produced. A number of crucibles, apparently for making money, have also been found close to the palace in the Mint. A portion of carving, supposed to be from the Church of St. Margaret, Southwark, demolished in the sixteenth century, has also been found on another site. Mr. Oliver exhibited a crucifix in cast-iron, which led to a discussion and the enumeration of the oldest-known examples in this material. The Chairman referred to several fire-backs which were made in the Weald of Sussex early in the seventeenth century for exportation to the Low Countries. A paper was then read by Dr. Fairbank, F.S.A., descriptive of some Roman pottery which was found at Doncaster in 1885, on the erection of the Yorkshire Bank. Among several examples of usual type, a curious grey pottery has been found with peculiar frillings of raised slip laid on to the surface, which has seldom been noticed elsewhere. The second paper, on Bracebridge Church, Lincoln, was by Mr. Loftus Brock, F.S.A., who passed in review some objections that have been made to his assertion that the two well-known Lincoln churches of St. Peters-at-Gowts, and St. Mary-le-Wigford are of Saxon date. At Bracebridge an Early Norman tower occurs added to an Early Saxon church, and he pointed out various technical details common to Norman work which appear in this tower, and which would equally have appeared in the other two were they of Norman date. The comparison of the three churches appears conclusively to confirm the Saxon age of the two first, as well as that of the body of the latter, there being a general resemblance of workmanship.

* For brief notes of the previous lectures, see *Builder*, pp. 141, 164, 184, *ante*.

COMPETITIONS.

THE INSTITUTE "SUGGESTIONS FOR THE CONDUCT OF ARCHITECTURAL COMPETITIONS."—At a special general meeting of the Royal Institute of British Architects on Monday evening last, the amended paper of "Suggestions" having been taken as read, it was resolved "That the principle of the amended Paper of 'Suggestions for the Conduct of Architectural Competitions' be adopted; and that it be left to the Council to issue the same as an Institute Paper, after due consideration of the suggestions made at that Meeting."

NEW GENERAL HOSPITAL, BIRMINGHAM.—A meeting of the General Committee for the new General Hospital, Birmingham, was held on the 8th inst., in the Reception Room of the Council House, Birmingham, to receive the adjudication of the Building Committee and their assessor, Mr. Alfred Waterhouse, R.A., on the competitive designs sent in for the new hospital. The Building Committee recommended that the first premium of 150*l.* should be awarded to the architect of the plans numbered "1," the second premium of 100*l.* to the architect of plans "No. 2," and the third premium of 50*l.* to the architect of plans "No 6 B." The recommendation having been moved and seconded, was agreed to. The envelopes containing the names of the three prize winners were then opened, and it transpired that the first premiated design was by Mr. W. Henman, of Birmingham; the second design that of Messrs. Worthington & Elgood, of Manchester; and the third design that of Mr. F. Barlow Osborn, of Birmingham.

NORTHFLEET CEMETERY CHAPELS.—Fourteen designs were received by the Local Board for these buildings, and at a meeting on Tuesday last the plans of Mr. J. T. Walford were accepted.

ARCHITECTS' BENEVOLENT SOCIETY:

ANNUAL MEETING.

THE annual meeting of this Society was held in the Council-Room of the Royal Institute of British Architects, Conduit-street, on Tuesday afternoon last, Mr. J. Macvicar Anderson, President, in the chair.

The minutes of the last annual meeting having been read and confirmed,

Mr. H. B. Verity, the Assistant-Secretary, then read the annual report, which was as follows:—

"Gentlemen,—Your Council are gratified at being able to again congratulate you upon the satisfactory condition of the Society. As in the previous year, the invested capital has been increased during the year 1891, although your Council regret to state that the subscribers have not increased in the number which might have been anticipated. Fortunately, the demands upon the funds have not been so great, the number of applicants being less than that in the two previous years. It cannot be expected, however, that the demands on the funds will in future years diminish, and substantial and continuous additions to the list of subscribers is most desirable. The 'Red Book' is sent to every new member of the Institute, and it is to be hoped that as the members of that body increase in number the subscribers to the Society may increase in at the least a like ratio.

During the past twelve months seven meetings have been held by your Council; three pensions of 20*l.* each have been paid; and 339*l.* have been distributed among twenty-two persons. The number of persons who have received grants is less than in some previous years, but the benefit afforded has not decreased. In several instances permanent good has been effected by timely and substantial grants to architects and architects' assistants; and thus the hope expressed by your Council in the last Annual Report, 'to be the better able to assist those to whom aid will be of permanent service, and to more effectually relieve temporary embarrassment,' has been fulfilled. It is, therefore, hoped that members of the profession not subscribers will, realising the good done by the Society, show recognition of it in a practical form.

The subscriptions received in 1891 amounted to 313*l.* 17s., as against 317*l.* received in 1890; while the donations show an increase of 27*l.*, being 57*l.*, as against 30*l.* received during the previous year. Among the contributors of donations were:—Mr. William Emerson, Mr. W. Milford Teulon (Leamington), Mr. H. C. Boyes, Mr. Robert Sawyer, Mr. R. Reynolds Rowe (Cambridge), and the Leicester and Leicestershire Society of Architects. The Worshipful Company of Carpenters have become subscribers of twenty guineas, while the Architectural Association and the Royal Institute of the Architects of Ireland continue their subscriptions of ten guineas and three guineas respectively.

With reference to the capital of the Society, your Council have the satisfaction to state that they were enabled in December last to invest 320*l.* 12s. 6d. in the purchase of Caledonian Railway 4 per cent. Debenture Stock, making the total capital of the Society 8,212*l.* 6s., namely, invested in Stocks (at cost price), 8,199*l.* 2s. 4d., and cash 13*l.* 3s. 8d.

The Income Account and Balance-sheet for the year ended December 31, 1891, duly audited by Mr. Fred. W. Hunt and Mr. George Judge, are herewith submitted.

Your Council regret to have to record the deaths of Mr. Thomas Verity, a Member of the Council, who had been a generous subscriber since 1881; Mr. T. Scarancke Archer; Mr. P. C. Hardwick, F.S.A., a subscriber since 1871; and Mr. Harry Oliver, a contributor to the Society for forty-one years, who served on the Council from 1874 to 1877.

Professor T. Hayter Lewis, F.S.A., who held office as Hon. Treasurer from 1885 to 1889, resigns his seat on the Council, to the regret of his colleagues, and the following gentlemen retire by rotation,—namely, Mr. Samuel Hill, Mr. Reginald St. A. Roumieu, Mr. George Scamell, F.G.S., and Mr. Lewis Solomon. To fill these vacancies and that caused by the decease of Mr. Thomas Verity, your Council have the pleasure to nominate Mr. H. H. Collins, Mr. Thomas Harris, Mr. W. Hilton Nash, Mr. J. G. Finch Noyes, Mr. Andrew Oliver, Mr. C. J. Shoppee, all of whom have consented to serve if elected.

Your Council cannot conclude without again urging the claims of the Society upon the profession generally, and in particular upon the members of the Institute,—to all of whom, whether contributors or not, the 'Red Book' containing this Report, the By-laws, and list of contributors, &c., will be forwarded as soon as practicable."

The income account and balance-sheet, audited by Mr. George Judge and Mr. F. W. Hunt, were also read. From these we learn that during the year ended December 31 last, 60*l.* was paid to three pensioners, and 339*l.* was expended in grants to applicants for help. The expenses of management, including printing, advertising, Assistant Secretary's salary, &c., amounted to 52*l.* 9s. 6d., 200*l.* had been transferred to capital account, and a balance of 46*l.* 6s. 11d. was carried forward to the current year's account. The receipts for the year, including 138*l.* 9s. 9d. brought forward from last account, amounted to 697*l.* 16s. 5d., including 245*l.* 9s. 8d. dividends on stock, and 313*l.* 17s. for subscriptions.

The Chairman, in moving the adoption of the report and balance-sheet, said things were so far satisfactory that they had been able to add to their capital account to a certain extent, but he regretted to say that that was not due to any increase in receipts, but to the fact that no great demand had been made upon the funds during the past year. He thought it was a very unsatisfactory reflection that there were so few subscribers,—only about 225. The Institute itself numbered between 1,300 and 1,400 members; and then there were the architects unhappily outside the Institute, who might fairly be expected to subscribe, seeing that the benefits of the Society were not restricted to those who were members of the Institute. He thought that the limited number of subscribers to the Society was discreditable to the profession as a body.

Mr. George Scamell seconded the motion, which was agreed to.

Mr. Wyatt Papworth moved a vote of thanks to the outgoing members of the Council, and expressed regret at the retirement of Professor Hayter Lewis, owing to ill-health.

The motion was seconded by Mr. John Hebb, and agreed to.

On the motion of the President, seconded by Mr. Scamell, Messrs. H. H. Collins, Thomas Harris, W. Hilton Nash, J. G. Finch Noyes, Andrew Oliver, and C. J. Shoppee were elected to supply the six vacancies on the Council.

Mr. Arthur Cates was re-elected Treasurer, Messrs. Percival Currey and John Hebb were elected Auditors, and Mr. William H. White was re-elected Hon. Sec. During the proceedings, the Treasurer and one of the auditors spoke highly of the way in which the accounts were kept by the Assistant Secretary, Mr. Verity.

Votes of thanks were given to the retiring Auditors, to the Institute for the use of its rooms, and to the Chairman, and the meeting terminated.

Books.

Murray's Handbook for India and Ceylon. London: John Murray. 1891.

AS early as 1859 Murray began to extend the sway of his handbooks over the Land of Ind. In that year two volumes appeared,—one for Madras and the other for Bombay. These were followed by two more, for Bengal and the Punjab; making four volumes in all for India. The handbook just published is an effort to produce a guide-book for the whole of India and Ceylon in one volume. To accomplish this the work has been re-written, and the four volumes condensed into the size of one of the previous four handbooks. The author's name is given in the early edition as Edward B. Eastwick; and although no name appears in the new edition, it is understood to be the work of the same writer, who is a high authority on the languages and literature of India. He has evidently bestowed great care in producing the present handbook, and he acknowledges the assistance he has received from men qualified to give information, including Dr. Burgess, who has had ample means of making himself acquainted with the architecture of India; to this it may be added that all the proofs have passed through the hands of Professor Forrest, of Calcutta.

In compressing four volumes into one, it need scarcely be stated that much had to be left out; but we have the peculiar fact to record that the references to architectural remains have undergone the least curtailment, and in many cases extensive additions to these have been made. This results from the accumulation of knowledge since the early edition appeared. In 1859 the Archæological Survey Department did not exist. It was only in 1871 that the first volume of "Reports" was published, and under Sir Alexander Cunningham's direction twenty-two volumes have been given forth. There are also the reports of the work of Dr. Burgess in the Bombay Presidency; while Madras has also something to show regarding the archæology of that Presidency. The valuable material of all these labours has been freely used in compiling this new handbook, and this will account for the great accuracy it shows in treating of the various periods and styles of architecture to be found in Hindostan. This merit, unfortunately for the critic, leaves him but a limited opportunity for exhibiting what he may suppose to be his superior knowledge.

The new handbook would have rejoiced the heart of Mr. Fergusson, had he been living now to see it. His constant grumble was that so few persons cared for Indian architecture; he often said that "there are not above half-a-dozen persons in England who know anything about it, or who take the slightest interest in the subject." The early edition gives a very long list of books,—"to be perused by the traveller before starting"; but there is not an architectural one among them. The new handbook says that to enjoy the journey through India in an intelligent manner, books of reference are necessary—and the first among those recommended is Fergusson's "History of Indian and Eastern Architecture"; this is followed by Burgess's "Archæological Survey of Western India." Here, a great change is manifest. The large numbers who now go every winter to India, prepared for the journey with such books in their portmanteaus, will have the architecture of India forced on their notice: and it may be presumed that many will be attracted and led to study the subject.

In the introductory information there is a list of useful words, with their meaning and etymology; here again the architectural tendency is also apparent in some of the words given, as many of them are necessary in the study of ancient remains. The author frequently, in reference to Indian temples, uses the word "pagoda." This appears quaint and old-fashioned in the present day to those accustomed to the modern literature of Indian archæology. Although not a Chinese term, it is still applied to the peculiar towers of China. The explanation of this term given in the list of words is from the Persian, *but-kadah*, "an idol temple." This explanation has been usually accepted, but Sir Henry Yule, in his "Glossary of Anglo-Indian Words and Phrases,"—one of the books recommended in the handbook,—gives a long notice of this word, but he inclines to a derivation from *bhagavat*, or *bhagavati*. Dagoba is given as derived from *deh*, "the body," and *gup*, "to hide." The usual form of the last syllable has been understood as from *garbha*, a "matrix," or "receptacle," for containing a relic. A Chaitya is the same as a Dagoba, only that in some cases the first was commemorative, and did not at all times contain a relic. The handbook defines this word as "a hall of assembly," which is very wide of the sense given to it by archæological writers. The Buddhist rock-cut temples that have a Chaitya in them, have been at times described as "halls of assembly"; but this is doubtful, as it would imply a congregational worship; while the plan of these caves would lead to the supposition that the worshippers walked along the left-hand aisle, went round the Chaitya at the end, and passed out again by the other aisle,—thus making a *pradakshina*, or circumambulation, of the Chaitya, as if it were the altar of the Temple.

As the architectural remains of India seem now to be among the principal attractions of the traveller, the introductory information would become much more useful if it contained a section, even a short one, giving a list of the principal styles, with approximate dates. A description of the parts of a temple would also be useful; such distinctive features as those which belong to the northern and southern styles, or the Buddhist and Brahminical, would be valuable for a traveller to understand, and it would tend to increase his interest in the subject.

In former times Central India and Rajputana were out of the route of travellers; now the railway has opened them up. There is a station at Bhilsa, from which the Sanchi Stupa can be easily visited. There is also a station at Chitor, which used to be known as "Chittoregarh,"—a place no one interested in Indian architecture should fail to see. The old Jain Tower of Sri Allat would itself repay a visit to that city of ruins. The account given,—considering the space at the author's disposal,—of the Mohammedan architecture of Delhi and Agra will be found to be a very good guide to these two localities. As might be expected, the Taj Mahal at Agra is praised far beyond its real merits, and here the handbook fails in being up to the latest knowledge by expressing a doubt as to who was the principal architect of this monument. Judge Keene has brought forward the authority of a work published in Rome in 1653, written by an Eremite monk, named P. Maestro Fra Sebastian Manrique, who was in Agra before the Taj was finished,—that was in 1640,—and this author states that the architect "was a Venetian named Geronimo Verroneo, who came to India with the ships of the Portuguese, and who died in the city of Lahore a little before my arrival." Manrique gives some details about his will, and the "various models of very fine architecture" which he produced for Shah Jehan to select from, and that the Emperor was,—"according to his barbarous and arrogant pride,"—dissatisfied with the "modesty" of the estimates. Shah Jehan ordered three krors of rupees to be spent, and when this "wonderful sum" was finished the architect was to ask for more. Three krors would be equal to three millions sterling; but the handbook, while giving one estimate close on this sum, quotes another account which gives 18,465,186 rs.,—or little more than the half of the first. The handbook states that 30 lakhs, or 300,000*l.* was paid to the masons. The piercing of the marble, and fitting in of the precious stones which form the ornament, must have been a work of much time, but unless the Emperor's magnificence, described above as his "arrogant pride," had been imposed upon, it would be natural to suppose that these reputed sums have been largely exaggerated.

I Tesori Sotterranei dell' Italia: Parte Quarta. Prof. Guglielmo Jervis. Turin: Ermanno Loescher.

THE fourth and concluding part of this painstaking work certainly deserves its second title: "a repertory of useful information." It deals with the economical geology of Italy, and forms a goodly volume, crammed with statistics of Italian quarries, marbles, and building-stones, with introductions, indices and tables that (with one exception) are substantially complete. The whole of Italy and its islands is included, and is systematically noticed by provinces and districts. Much information of interest and value is incidentally gathered in accessible form,—particularly as regards the materials used for both ancient and modern buildings and works of art; many of these are illustrated. Prof. Jervis, who, if we mistake not, is of English extraction, is Curator of the Royal Industrial Museum at Turin. An accomplished geologist, he is evidently well qualified for the task, on which, we learn, he has laboured over five and thirty years. The work is well done. Its literary style is simple and direct; there is a commendable absence of "fine writing," though this lurks in foot-notes, and fairly breaks out in the introduction. The printing is excellent; the abundant illustrations are generally good, —sometimes very good indeed. On the whole, the book is welcome, with a welcome that is partly relief; one cannot be too thankful when laborious years of compiling and condensing are found congenial by someone else.

The bulk of the volume is naturally somewhat of a catalogue. The notices of more special places, however, amount to brief but valuable monographs. Thus, to Massa and Carrara nearly thirty pages are devoted, between sixty and seventy different quarries being mentioned by name, with statistics as to the different marbles, their density, weathering qualities, &c. There are woodcuts illustrative of the district and of famous works of art in Carrara marble, from a Roman bas-relief and altar to the Moses of Michelangelo, and the modern monument dedicated to Cavour at Turin. There are geological notices of the Apuan Alps and the Carrara marble-beds, and historical notices of the quarrying in ancient and modern times. There is thus much interesting reading besides the dry bones of statistics. The geology is quite modern and up to date, the labours of Gerlach and Gastaldi being the basis of the author's notes. Prof. Jervis, with quite excusable complacency, points out that he has not hesitated to revise his own published opinions as to the origin of the crystalline metamorphic rocks. At the same time the revision is too sweeping. No geologist now will hesitate to accept the Apuan marbles as "stratified sedimentary rock of marine origin, a compact limestone metamorphosed"; but it is an unnecessary revulsion against the ultra-plutonism of former geologists to attribute the metamorphosis solely to "simple but extremely slow chemical action under enormous pressure." Heat, also, must have been a potent factor, for the limestone is practically cooked. Instances all over the world are numerous, and we need not go further than Scotland to find marbles of precisely similar derivation. The author is also not quite correct in his note on the origin of serpentine. Dr. Sterry Hunt is probably alone in maintaining it to be an original, but not an eruptive rock; the consensus of opinion is practically unanimous that it is a metamorphic product [of an olivine-bearing eruptive rock]. One reads, too, with surprise that the bad weathering of some of the white crystalline marbles is due to carbonate of magnesia. The reverse is the accepted belief; but Prof. Jervis considers the carbonate of magnesia to be isomorphic only, not isodynamic with the carbonate of lime, and tending, therefore, to separate out.

To architects and archæologists the frequent references to actual buildings and works of art, both ancient, mediæval, and modern, will be a most interesting feature of the work. It is of great importance to have an authoritative statement as to the materials used for these and their origin, such as Prof. Jervis is able frequently to give. These notes are full of varied interest. Under "Carrara," for instance, we are taken to the ancient walls of the Etruscan Luna, and are reminded of Michelangelo's personal visits to the quarries for the blocks out of which he created the David, the Moses, and the Tombs of the Medici. On another side, the author's remark is to be noted that the price of marble might be reduced one-third, and the output increased tenfold, were the industry not practically a monopoly. One learns, too, that "Sicilian marble" is the singular name given in England to the products of two Carrara quarries. The whole book is full of these most interesting notes, of which a single further specimen must suffice. Under "Verona" we find a paragraph on the famous amphitheatre (a building second only to the Colosseum), which affords very striking evidence of the fate of these grand remains during many centuries. A disastrous earthquake, felt through most of Europe, shattered the external arcading in 793, and from the dislocated stones was derived the material not only for the walls of the city, but for many private dwellings. Still worse was the fate of the theatre, which fell in part in 895, killing forty persons. Thereupon, yielding to the prayers of the bishop and clergy and people (for once in harmony), the King Berengarius ordained its destruction. His quaint decree is given in extract, and is a very striking commentary on Mediæval respect for antiquity. By it any one who presumed to interfere in any way whatever with the "undertaking" was to be mulcted in twenty pounds of gold, refined and pure, so that every man might wreak his own sweet will upon the ruins, and without let or hindrance conduct to end the work he had begun. Truly, history has no need of either Goth or Vandal; time and again it seems the bridges of Verona have been rebuilt out of these two Roman works

The whole of this side of the book is so interesting and useful that it might be with advantage extended and made much more complete. It is disappointing to have no single building in Venice thus identified with its original materials. The task, with collaboration, is possible, and would result in a standard work for the archæologist and architect. In any case, the want of an index to such buildings as are mentioned is greatly felt. It is the one serious omission to be noted, and should certainly be rectified when a new edition of the book is called for.

It is a pity that its Introduction should mar this useful book. Not only are we harassed by "fine writing" and much architectural nonsense; we are launched, without profit, into controversy which is absurdly out of place. The author's sweeping division of architectural history into three periods of 1,000 years each corresponds to nothing substantially true in either nature or art. The Temple of Jerusalem was *not* one of the "seven wonders of the world" of antiquity, though scarcely two writers agreed as to what these seven (?) wonders were. To discuss with conviction the bricks of which the Tower of Babel was built is fatuous; as well might we canvass the building stones of the Palace of Priam. Two pages after the Tower of Babel we are bewildered by a heated attack upon evolution, in which modern pathology is cited in refutation of Darwin. There is no need to follow Professor Jervis into this; but most readers will learn with surprise that the Darwinian theory is "hasty, grotesque, ill-founded," and "dishonouring to man"; also that, "once admitted, it robs palæontological studies utterly of all their worth." The reason of it all is not apparent, but the "Index Expurgatorius" still exists at the Vatican; and from references, dragged in, to Holy Writ, one is tempted to ascribe it to the exigencies, not of science, but of creed. The learned Professor may or may not be in a position to consign the Darwinian theory to the limbo of unscientific extravagance, but in any case he should attempt the task elsewhere.

---

(1) *Two Hieroglyphic Papyri from Tanis;* (2) *The Mound of the Jew and the City of Onias, &c.*, by E. NAVILLE; and *The Antiquities of Tell-el-Yahûdiyeh*, by F. Ll. GRIFFITH; (3) *Bubastis*, by EDOUARD NAVILLE; being an Extra and the Seventh and Eighth Memoirs of the Egypt Exploration Fund. London: 1889, 1890, 1891.

THE publication from time to time of these excellent memoirs is in itself ample justification for the existence and support of the Egypt Exploration Fund. With plans, sections, photographic reproductions, and numerous plates of objects and hieroglyphic and other texts, it is possible to follow closely the results of the excavations, and to consider at leisure the many problems they suggest. Since, also, many important objects found during the excavations have been sent to this country and deposited in the British Museum, the study of them is greatly facilitated.

The first of the volumes under notice, an extra memoir issued for 1889, treats of two hieroglyphic papyri, found by Mr. Petrie at Tanis. One of these, a sign papyrus, described by Mr. F. Ll. Griffith, is the first native list of hieroglyphics that has come down to us from ancient times, and, though disappointing in some respects, is of great interest as being "the only document bearing upon the system by which the Egyptians arranged and taught their huge syllabary." It appears to be of Roman date. The other papyrus is a sort of religious Gazetteer or Kalendar.

The seventh memoir issued by the Fund gives an account by M. Naville and Mr. Griffith of the discoveries at Tell-el-Yahûdiyeh. This place is already well known from the enamelled tiles, &c., found there by Brugsch Bey in 1870, believed to be the wall ornaments of a beautiful chamber built for Rameses III. The re-examination of Tell-el-Yahûdiyeh was undertaken by M. Naville in the hope of finding proof of its identity with Heliopolis, but in this he was disappointed. From other evidence M. Naville concludes that the place was known in the time of Rameses III. as "the house of Ra on the north of On," but its civil name has not yet been recovered. It subsequently became a Jewish settlement called Onion, or the City of Onias, and under the Romans was called in official documents *Scenæ Veteranorum.* The varied and numerous antiquities found are carefully described by Mr. Griffith, who prefaces his notice with some carefully-considered and useful remarks on antiquarian research in Egypt generally. This memoir also contains brief notices of some other sites visited by M. Naville and Mr. Griffith, and is illustrated by a carefully-drawn series of plates.

The Eighth Memoir of the Fund deals solely with the important excavations made by M. Naville in 1887-89 at Bubastis. Of the famous sanctuary on this site described by Herodotus all that now remains is an enormous number of granite blocks (for all the limestone has been carried away), strewn in the most hopeless fashion over an area about 500 ft. long and nearly 200 ft. wide. These represent the ruins of a great temple, comprising: (1) an entrance hall, 80 ft. long and 160 ft. wide; (2) the great "festival hall," 80 ft. long and 130 ft. wide; (3) a magnificent colonnade or hypostyle hall, 190 ft. long, and perhaps nearly 80 ft. wide, that led to (4) the great hall of Nekhthoreb, 160 ft. square. All is now so completely destroyed that the explorers found it difficult even to reconstruct the plan from what is left. The oldest temple at Bubastis is believed, from inscriptions bearing their names, to have been built by two kings of the fourth dynasty, Cheops and Chefren, the constructors of the two great pyramids. This early temple M. Naville thinks remained unaltered until the time of Usertesen III., of the twelfth dynasty (whose architraves bore inscriptions with signs over 2 ft. high), to whom is ascribed the addition of the great hypostyle hall to the west of the two first halls of Cheops and Chefren. The great hall beyond this was not built until the thirtieth dynasty by Nekhthoreb. Of the repeated alterations, &c., made by successive kings and dynasties, disclosed by the erased and usurped inscriptions, and re-use of older buildings, it is not necessary to write here. Nor can we discuss M. Naville's conclusions, which are not generally accepted by experts, as to the relative dates of many of the more important monuments found. Among other discoveries, we note with interest that of the remains of painting on statues, even when carved in black granite, and the finding of a carved head-dress that must have belonged to a colossal figure, made seemingly in separate pieces, and over 20 ft. high. The memoir is profusely illustrated by more than fifty fine plates, mostly photographic reproductions of sculptured fragments and hieroglyphics. These are, however, not always as valuable as they might be, owing to the absence of a scale. There is nothing to show, for instance, whether the fine head in the frontispiece (now in the British Museum) is there given full-size or reduced, and even the rough ground-plan on plate iii. is utterly devoid of a scale. The simple expedient of setting up a rod, divided according to some standard English or French measure, by the side of the object while being photographed, would give an approximate scale sufficient for all general purposes.

Mélanges d'Archéologie et d'Epigraphie. Par ALBERT DUMONT. *Réunis par* TH. HOMOLLE *et précédés d'une notice sur Albert Dumont, Par* L. HENZEY, *avec xvii planches, &c.* Paris: Ernest Thorin. 1892.

THIS book is frankly a memorial volume, and, as such, addresses itself primarily to M. Dumont's large circle of archæological friends. Most of the papers, and, if our memory serves us, all the plates have appeared before—mainly in the *Bulletin de Correspondance Hellénique*, to which M. Dumont so largely contributed. It is, however, convenient to have these monographs united in one volume. They are very various, both in subject and merit. The largest and every way most important is that in the "monuments and inscriptions of Thrace," which embodies the observations made personally by M. Dumont in a tour made through Thrace in 1868. This, together with No. xxiv., contains not only a catalogue of existing monuments, but a very complete discussion of their value in relation to ethnology, history, mythology, and art. It seems a pity to print along side with these valuable and original papers early essays on archæology like that on the "Banquet Funèbre," which is now completely out of date, simply because, "l'auteur l'aimait comme son premier travail archéologique."

Milling-machines and Processes; a Practical Treatise on Shaping Metals by Rotary Cutters. By PAUL N. HASLUCK. London: Crosby Lockwood & Son.

THIS is a large book to be written on a single description of machine tool, and, to an engineer out of touch with the recent development of workshop practice, it might reasonably seem altogether too voluminous for the importance of its subject. Those, however, who are acquainted with the working of the best-managed metal-working establishments in the country will recognise that Mr. Hasluck has chosen for his theme the most important development in engineering machinery which has taken place since the planing-machine reduced so greatly the laborious, uncertain, and costly processes of chipping and filing. The lathe will still hold its own as the chief machine tool, but its supremacy will be, perhaps, to some extent, due to precedence of invention; for were the two tools now to be for the first time invented simultaneously, the supporters of the milling-machine would have a strong case. A universal milling-machine can do the work of the planing-machine, shaping-machine, or slotting-machine, and can often be used with advantage in place of the lathe itself. Its chief drawback is its want of range, especially in surfacing long parts. In order to meet this, milling-machines have been devised of the same general design as the ordinary planer. It would, perhaps, be fairer to call these planing-machines, having a milling-cutter,—for we do not see why a tool which produces a plane surface should not be called a planing-machine, even though it work with a rotary cutter. It is true popular usage is opposed to this view, "planing" generally being understood to mean a ploughing or scraping action.

Mr. Hasluck with great industry has collected the particulars of a large number of milling-machines of various types. The book is profusely illustrated; the majority of the blocks, to judge by their appearance, being taken from the most authentic and cheapest source, *i.e.*, the manufacturers' catalogue. The plan has its drawbacks. The author exclaims against the weak construction of milling-machines, and rightly attributes to this fault the idea, that was for a long time prevalent, that milling was only suitable for light cutting. Probably this view was chiefly due to the fact that our milling practice largely came to us from America. In the United States many designers are terribly afraid of putting plenty of metal in machine standards and framing. They exclaim against the clumsy appearance of British machinery, and pride themselves on their own lighter constructions, made possible by the superior cast-iron which they use. There is no doubt that American iron foundry practice is very good, in some respects in advance of that of this country, but there is something required beyond strength of material to give the great necessary virtue of a machine tool,—steadiness. No doubt ill-disposed masses of metal may detract from, rather than add to, steadiness, and in this respect some of the older designs of British machinery were often very faulty. Again, it is useless to make the foundations and framing rigid if the cutter and the work are not well held and supported; and here again there has been great improvement of late years in this country, more especially in the design of milling-machines. British engineers owe much to the example of United States manufacturers, but it is well they have not followed the American craze for extreme lightness, which alike offends the eye and detracts from efficiency. It is satisfactory to note that the best designs of both countries are now very similar in essential particulars; and doubtless engineers on both sides of the Atlantic have profited by an interchange of ideas.

The author's remarks which touch on the craze for universality in milling-machines are good. The milling-machine shows to greatest advantage in special repeat work, where a large number of similar parts have to be turned out.

The chapter which is devoted to examples of milling work is of interest, and well illustrated by useful sketches. After this we come to the section in which the various types of milling-machines are shown. We begin with examples of treadle-machines, a class of tool for which, we should imagine, there is but little demand. After other examples of small machines we come to some of the large universal machines. In the chapter on attachments for milling-machines various kinds of chucks, vices, slides, &c., are illustrated and described. Another chapter is devoted to cutter-grinders, and the final chapter has the suggestive heading of "speed, feed, stiffness, and chatter." On the whole the book is a useful production, and should prove of benefit to those seeking information on the subject.

Wilson W. Phipson: A Memoir. London: G. Chard. 1892.

THIS is a short memoir of the distinguished heating and ventilating engineer whom we recently lost, chiefly interesting from the sketch it gives of the genial personal character of Mr. Phipson, who had far more accomplishments, social and artistic, than were suspected by many who only knew him in his professional capacity.

The Year's Art, 1892. Compiled by MARCUS B. HUISH, LL.B. London: Virtue & Co. 1892.

THIS useful annual epitome of matters relating to art and exhibitions is continued with its usual completeness. Among the new matter added is a list of pictures purchased under the Chantrey bequest since its foundation; instructions to artists under the new American Copyright Law, and information respecting the Art Department of the Chicago Exhibition. The volume contains, as usual, a series of small reproductions from leading pictures of the year; and there is also a complete series of portraits of the members of the Royal Institute of Painters in Water-Colours.

The Clifton and Bristol Pictorial. Bristol: W. F. Mack.

THIS is an illustrated account of the principal views and buildings about Clifton and Bristol, in which the illustrations, reproduced from photographs, are very well done, and superior to those of most guide-books of the kind.

Correspondence.

To the Editor of THE BUILDER.

COKE-BREEZE CONCRETE.

SIR,—In reference to the recent correspondence in your columns, I can confirm Mr. Potter's opinion as to the suitability of coke-breeze for concrete,—of course, for certain purposes.

I have used it for the last twenty-four years. The object in using it principally is on account of its lightness; for landings, stairs, floors, balconies on cantilevers, and for many other things too numerous to mention, it is invaluable. I have known shingle concrete to be gauged precisely the same as coke-breeze, and placed in a similar position, to crack, while the coke-breeze has stood without the slightest indication of failure. The shaking of a building, the deflection of a girder, or the slight settling of a wall, in many cases have proved fatal to a shingle concrete. Coke-breeze is more elastic, therefore it has a better chance of holding its own.

I should advise "Surveyor" to have the concrete for ground floors as follows:—6 parts of coke-breeze to 1 of Portland cement; be careful that it is thoroughly incorporated, and be sure not to use too much water; 2½ in. in thickness is sufficient. Let the concrete have a chance to dry on the surface, or your boards will swell. All concrete exposed to the sun should be kept damp for a few days; when under cover it is a mistake.

Do not trust the covering over of 14 ft. by 13 ft. with 5 in. or 6 in. of concrete of any description. Introduce a 5-in. rolled-iron joist the 14 ft. way, and then two smaller ones at equal distances on each side, all thoroughly secured into the walls. Use five parts coke-breeze and one of Portland cement for the concrete. There should always be a recess left in the walls, if only 1 in. deep, for the concrete to rest on.

The great secret is in gently tapping the concrete with a broad-bottomed wood punner till the whole is brought up to a level surface.

I have just completed a theatre under an eminent London architect. All the landings and stairs are of coke-breeze concrete, and although only completed eight or nine days before the opening, and with a tremendous rush, of course, the stairs and landings were loaded, but not the slightest sign of any defect is to be seen. CONTRACTOR.

VALUATION.

SIR,—Would any of your readers kindly state if an appraiser's licence is required by any one who values property for a building society? The valuation would be to secure the society from advancing money to a greater extent than the property would be worth.

I am informed by a trading London auctioneer that any one who makes a valuation of any sort, for which he is to be paid, ought to have an appraiser's licence; that many architects are in the habit of making valuations for mortgage and other purposes without a licence, and that if the authorities could only detect them, they would prosecute, and the parties would be fined.

I understand that if a valuation is made for the information of one party only, the valuation need not be stamped.

I should feel grateful for any information on this subject. ARCHITECT.

BRICKWORK.

SIR,—Why do London architects in their quantities reduce the item of brick walls to the rod of 272¼ superficial feet of a brick and a-half thick, whereas in the Northern counties the same item is reduced to superficial yards of a brick length thick?

If a builder in those parts receives London quantities, he reduces the rods of a brick and a-half into yards of a brick thick, because it is comparatively easy to ascertain the number of bricks in a yard, and the price of the same, to a rod. In the first place, all the separate items of walls, in taking out the quantities, are brought into superficial feet of one brick and then added up, which, divided by nine, gives the number of yards, and the thing is done, instead of the loss of time entailed in bringing the same into the standard rod. Surely, in these days of technical instruction and smartening up of Trades Guilds this antiquated standard will go the way of the unfittest.

To ascertain the number of bricks in a superficial yard there are several ways; perhaps the better way, if a builder has built work with the same kind of bricks as those proposed to be used, is to measure four bricks long and ten courses high as set (which, of course, would contain eighty bricks), and compare the proportion of space they occupy with a superficial yard. Or go to the brickyard and lay down four bricks long with joint-space between, and measure the length, then pile them up and measure the height, and allow 1 in. for joints. Suppose the above thirty-two bricks measure 38 in. long by 13 in. high, equals 494 in., a superficial yard contains 1,296 in., it then becomes a simple rule-of-three sum, multiply 1,296 by 32, and divide by 494, gives, say, 84 bricks to the yard. Or it may be that only one brick is sent as a sample to calculate by. Say it measures 9½ in. by 3¼ in., allowing for one joint and bed, which equals 31 in. as nearly as possible, then 1,296 divided by 31 equals 42 nearly for half-brick, or 84 for one brick thick.

To ascertain the price of the bricks in a yard of one brick thick is again a simple rule-of-three (depending always, of course, on the size and price of the bricks). Supposing the bricks are 25s. per thousand, and 84 in the yard super., then 25s. multiplied by 84 and divided by 1,000, equals 2s. 1¼d. per yard for the bricks.

Warrington. ROBERT JONES.

HALIFAX ARTISANS' DWELLINGS COMPETITION.

SIR,—As a matter of interest to the profession in general, as showing the value put upon architects' services by the Sanitary Committee of the Borough of Halifax, I beg to draw the attention of your readers to the conditions of this competition, just advertised.

The competition is for *two* large blocks of artisans' dwellings, one on a site about 190 ft. by 100 ft., and the other on an irregularly-shaped piece of ground of 2,960 yards superficial area, and averaging about 240 ft. by 130 ft.

The following extracts from the printed conditions will, I think, speak for themselves, and need no comment:—

"*Clause* 3. The designs of competitors must be exhibited by plans, elevations, and sections drawn *to a scale of 8 ft. to an inch** (except the block plan), and consist of the following drawings:—

Block plan (16 ft. to an inch), showing system of drainage, with all gullies, traps, inspection holes, sewer ventilation, &c., indicated by brown lines thereon.

* The italics throughout are our own.—ED.

Cellar plan, ground plan, roof plan, and plans of each floor where more than one is intended.

Elevations of every frontage.

Sections as may be necessary, and on such lines as may best show the general internal arrangements.

Clause 6.—All the drawings must be made upon sheets of plain white drawing-paper, without borders, and mounted on plain white stretchers of one uniform size of 4 ft. by 3 ft. As many drawings as conveniently possible to be placed on each stretcher. No framed or glazed drawing will be received.

10.—The Committee reserve to themselves the right to reject the whole or any of the designs, should they be considered unsuitable. The selected designs will only be accepted subject to a *bonâ-fide* tender from a reliable contractor or contractors being obtained for carrying out the work within the estimated sum so arrived at by the author thereof.

11. The Committee offer two premiums of 30*l*. and 20*l*. respectively, which will be paid to the authors of the design, which, fully complying with all the conditions and instructions herein set forth, shall in their opinion be considered as first and second in order of merit. *The two premiated designs will remain the exclusive property of the Committee, who will make their own arrangements as to carrying out the erection of the building.*"

The stipulation in Clause 6 as to "no framed and glazed drawing" being received is distinctly amusing, and indicates a grim sense of humour in certain members of the Committee.

It would be interesting to know how many members of the profession intend to make a bold bid for fame and fortune by submitting designs.

A NON-COMPETITOR.

"THE LATE STRIKE STILL SMOULDERING."

SIR,—The two "blacklegs" your correspondent, "Bench," refers to have a perfect right to work where they can. The men also have a right to object to work with them. The employers equally have the right to employ anyone they choose.

There you have three opposing interests,—first, individual selfishness; secondly, combination, sinking selfishness for the advancement of all; thirdly, capitalism, whose object is to encourage the former at the expense of the latter. These varying interests are inevitable under the present system of production.

As Adam Smith observes in his "Wealth of Nations":—

"Masters are always and everywhere in a sort of tacit but constant and uniform combination not to raise wages above the actual rate. To violate this combination is everywhere a most unpopular action, and a sort of reproach to a master among his neighbours and equals."

That being so, and modern events show it is as true to-day as it was when first written, more than a century since, your correspondent must therefore admit that the action taken by the men in the firm he refers to is merely a combination to protect their own interests; and to allow any attempt to pass unnoticed that threatens such interests would be detrimental to that combination. Consequently, when individuals choose to work against the well-being of their fellows, they will have to put up with the obloquy and reproach attached to such action.

His reference to "grey hairs and specs." is in very bad taste, and quite in accordance with the mental capacity of a man who could write such nonsense, especially the latter portion of his letter.

JOINER.

The Student's Column.

WARMING BUILDINGS BY HOT WATER. XI.

EXAMPLE WORKS (HORTICULTURAL) (*continued*).

WITH the example commenced in the last paper, the space did not permit of dealing with more than the main services, their uses, and the different methods of laying them in. We can now proceed to deal with the branch services; but to make the explanation and reference clear, fig. 36 is repeated here.

If the mains were brought along at the side of the end house and then carried up the front to melon pits, as shown, that part from the boiler to the front would be beneath the ground level. If the boiler pit be deep then they would not lie in an open trench very well, but would probably be covered up. In this latter case it would not matter very much whether they were beneath the house, as shown, or outside. The former would in most cases be given preference.

In the first house, for tropical plants, branch services are carried along each side and around at the ends as far as the doorway. The number of pipes would be either four or six (result of calculation), half flows and half returns. Before, however, the single pipe from the main was branched into two or three, as the case may be, the stop-valves should be inserted as shown. The small circular marks on the illustration represent these. Of course only the top pipes of the apparatus can be shown in this plan drawing.

In the second house, which we may suppose is reserved for grapes, and, perhaps, also for strawberries, so great a quantity of pipe as the

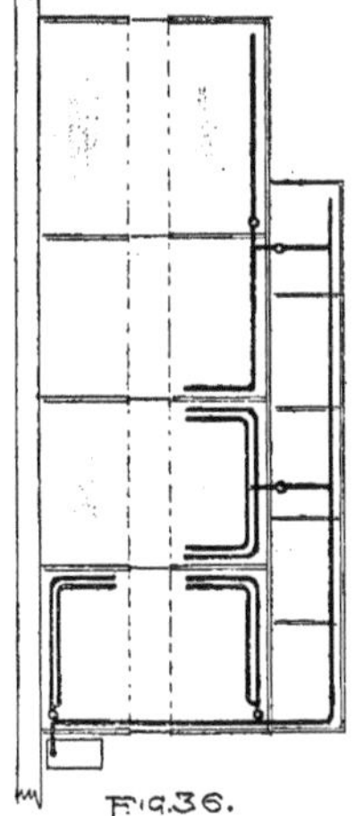

FIG. 36.

last is not needed. The pipes are shown extending across the front (the coldest part) and also along the sides as far as the doorways. There would probably need to be four pipes, viz., two flows and two returns to keep up a temperature sufficient for this house. The stop-valve is shown in the melon pit; this is a convenient place for it, but it can be placed in the house, if desired. The quantity of pipe will be governed by calculation, but the actual temperature required will be, in every case, settled by the gardener. Grape-houses require different heats according to the particular kind of grape being grown.

In the third house, which may be used as a greenhouse, for plants, sub-tropical productions, &c., a less quantity of pipe than the last is needed. The quantity of pipe, however, will be governed entirely by what the gardener intends stocking the house with. In this example the pipes are shown extending across the front and up the left side as far as the doorway. Three pipes, perhaps two, will be found sufficient. The stop-valve is shown situated as with the second house.

The end, which may be termed a cool house, is shown with two pipes only, a flow and return, across the front. This will probably be sufficient, as the house may only be used for semi-hardy trees and shrubs, apricots, tomatoes, &c., which have to be preserved from frost, or have to be kept under glass until the cold nights of spring have ceased. For this purpose it is not necessary to have a distinct branch service; a continuation from the third house will do; but this, again, is a question for the gardener to decide. If the service is carried out as illustrated, there should be a means of checking the heat in this last house without interfering with the heat of the one preceding it, and it would probably be found that an H-piece with valves, inserted in the flow and

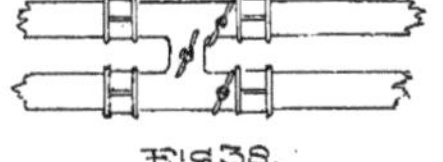

FIG. 38.

return as fig. 38, would best effect this. By the use of these valves the circulation could be stopped in the last house if desired, yet by opening the middle valve the water will have a clear way to flow up and down the pipes in the third house normally.

The pits in front of the houses are heated by the two main pipes, but there cannot be any means of checking the heat of the water, as to do so would interfere with the other and most important parts of the apparatus. If the mains prove a little too hot for these pits, their heat can be lessened by shifting their lights or covers a little.

The extremities or farthest points of all the services, both main and branch, must have air-pipes. The stop-valves may be in the flow-pipes only, or in both flows and returns; this is another question the gardener will usually settle. Generally, the stop-valves used in this work are of the throttle pattern, being something like a short length of pipe, with a circular disc in it, which is operated by a handle. (Full description will be given in a later paper.) This disc does not fit tightly in consequence of its having to revolve freely in the pipe. Therefore, although it is well suited for checking and regulating the motion of the water, it will not entirely prevent circulation if the valve exists in one pipe only.

It can be readily seen that if a small aperture exists through the valve in the flow-pipe, and the return-pipe is quite open, a circulation will take place, and, should it be desired to keep heat from the house, this can only be done imperfectly. But by putting a stop-valve into the return-pipe as well, the circulation becomes stopped sufficiently for all practical purposes. In grape-houses the valve question is given a good deal of consideration, as the gardener can only regulate the budding of his vines by regulating his heat. If grapes are required either early or late, it is due to the stop-valves chiefly that this arrangement can be carried into effect either way. The "throttle" is not the only imperfectly-fitting valve, but, on the other hand, there are now made throttle-valves that are perfectly fitting.

It should have been mentioned when describing the arrangement of pipes in the second house, that, if it is to be used for grapes, the gardener requires to be consulted as to where the roots or trunks of the vines will be situated. Sometimes the vine is rooted inside, but it is just as commonly outside. The famous vine at Kew is rooted outside its house, the trunk passing through to the inside just as it leaves the ground. Many growers adopt this practice, considering it the most successful method.

When an apparatus has of necessity to extend in different directions from the boiler, say as in fig. 39, it becomes necessary to intro-

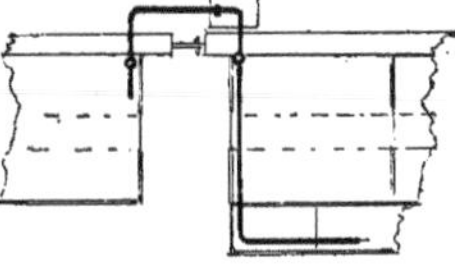

FIG. 39

duce stop-valves in the mains. This is to enable the gardener to regulate the heat to his requirements, for should an apparatus branch in two or more directions it may be taken for granted that usually a more effective circulation will set in one way than the others, and it will be necessary to check one to make them work at all equally.

In this illustration the boiler is shown placed between the houses, but notwithstanding this arrangement, in works of moderate size there need be but one flow-pipe from the top of the boiler, but branched as in fig. 40. It might be advisable in this case to have the short vertical portion immediately on the top of the boiler, a size larger than the mains which proceed to the right and left. The returns of the mains need not however enter the boiler by one pipe; with these it is better to bring them in one on each side as shown in the last illustration. By this means an undue accumulation of dirt does not occur on one side of the boiler should surface water be used. This was more fully alluded to in an earlier paper.

The insertion of stop-valves in these branch mains needs a little care. They must be of the full size of the pipes (so should all the cocks in an apparatus of fair size) and probably throttle-valves would be best to use as they have a straight way or passage through them of the full size of the pipe, or very nearly so. Any valve that has a smaller or irregular passage through it, should be omitted from the mains

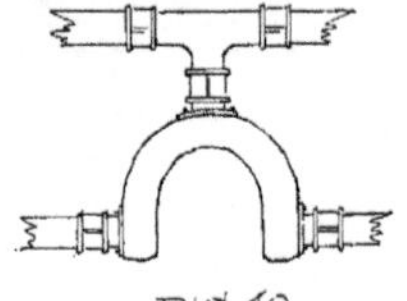

Fig. 40.

of a horticultural apparatus as a rule. There need be no valve put in the returns if regulation is all that is required. If the circulation has to be quite stopped or very carefully adjusted, then valves are required in both flow and return-pipes.

The previous examples have dealt wholly with glasshouses of the lean-to shape, and the other style, termed "span" houses, have not been dwelt upon. This latter shape, usually like fig. 41 (cross section), requires different

Fig. 41.

treatment to the others in heating, as we may suppose all sides are equally exposed, and no shelter exists on one side, as is effected with the brick wall of the lean-to house. Span houses always require more pipe than a lean-to house of the same area; and owing to the greater loss of heat they are not generally used as tropical houses. The illustration shows four pipes under the staging each side and four pipes in a trench up the centre. A trench is usually required for the centre pipes, as it is a common practice to occasionally alter the position and re-arrange the middle staging, and it would not do in this case to have the pipes above ground. Of course the pipes are less effective in a trench, and if they can be arranged otherwise it is best. Fig. 42 shows in plan how the pipes in this

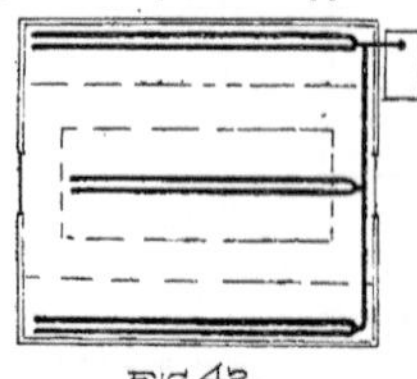

Fig. 42.

house would be connected up. The pipes along the right side of the house would be below ground, so as to take the pipes in the trench up the centre, and also to miss the doorway that would doubtless exist there.

SURVEYORSHIPS.

Islington. — Mr. George Green, Assoc. Mem. Inst. C.E., of the Borough Engineer's Department, Nottingham, was on the 4th inst. appointed,—out of a large number of applicants,—Assistant Surveyor to the Northern district of Islington, N., in succession to Mr. T. R. Roscoe, the recently appointed Surveyor of Luton. Islington is one of the largest London parishes, and had a population of 319,259 in 1891.

The Civil and Mechanical Engineers' Society: Change of Address.—The address of this Society will in future be 12, Delahay-street, Westminster, S.W.

OBITUARY.

Mr. Isaac Barradale, F.R.I.B.A.—We regret to announce the death of Mr. Isaac Barradale, which took place at his residence at Stoneygate, Leicester, on the 19th ult., after a short illness. The deceased gentleman was born at Leicester in 1845, and was articled to Messrs. Flint & Shenton, of that town. He commenced practice in 1870, and his works, which are mostly in Leicester and the neighbourhood, are of good repute. Several of them have been exhibited at the Royal Academy, and illustrated in this journal. Mr. Barradale was elected a Fellow of the Institute in 1879.

Mr. William Hudson.—We record with regret the decease, on the 2nd inst., of Mr. William Hudson, architect and surveyor, formerly of Bennet's-hill, Doctors' Commons (now renamed Godliman-street). Mr. Hudson was well known throughout the City, and during his professional career held several appointments. He was, for about half a century, surveyor in London to the West of England Fire-office, at one time Assessment Surveyor to the Commissioners of Sewers, and, until his recent retirement from practice, Surveyor to the Saddlers' Company, and for many years a Fellow of the Surveyors' Institution and also of the Surveyors' Club. As an architect he erected many warehouses and City premises, and his design was selected in a limited competition for the City of London Union offices in Bartholomew-close. Mr. Hudson partially relinquished active work in the year 1880, when he was joined in partnership by his son, Mr. Arthur B. Hudson, F.S.I., and Mr. A. C. Bulmer Booth, A.R.I.B.A., under the style of William Hudson, Son, & Booth." He retired entirely in 1889, when the style of the firm was altered to "Hudson & Booth." Mr. Hudson was in his eightieth year, and was throughout a long and busy life much respected, both in his profession and out of it. He leaves a widow, and, of a numerous family, five sons and four daughters survive; his eldest son, Mr. Wm. H. H. Hudson, M.A., is Professor of Mathematics at King's College, London. The interment took place on Saturday last at Brompton Cemetery.

Mr. Henry Poole.—Mr. Henry Poole, who died on the 25th ult., aged eighty-eight years, had held the office of "Master-Mason" of Westminster Abbey since the year 1856. He largely assisted the late Sir Gilbert Scott in his researches,—researches which led to the production of the well-known paper entitled "Gleanings from Westminster Abbey," read by Scott before the Institute in 1859.—*R.I.B.A. Journal*, March 10.

GENERAL BUILDING NEWS.

Proposed Extension of the Bath Pump-room.—A meeting of the Bath Town Council was held on the 8th inst., when Mr. Radway, as Chairman of the Baths Committee, presented the report dealing with the proposed extension of the Pump-room at an estimated cost of 45,000*l*. The committee state that the subject has pressed itself upon them from three considerations, viz.:—1. The necessity of protecting the Roman Bath from injury by exposure to the weather. 2. The necessity of undertaking such works as would render the surroundings of the Roman Bath more presentable than they are now. 3. The crowded state of the Pump-room during the performance of the daily concerts. "With respect to the Roman Bath, which has now been uncovered for several years, it is obvious, from the most cursory examination of the remains, that unless something is done to protect them from the effects of the weather, a large and interesting portion will within a very short time have ceased to exist. With respect to providing additional accommodation in connexion with the Pump-room, it may be observed that, although it is generally admitted that the bathing establishments are unrivalled, the qualification is invariaby added that Bath is sadly deficient in the accommodation offered to visitors in connexion with the Pump-room. . . . . Your committee are of opinion that the present Pump-room should be devoted exclusively to the drinkers, with provision for readers. Your committee are of opinion that the new buildings should comprise on the same floor with the present Pump-room a good entrance corridor and vestibule, a cloak-room for ladies and another for gentlemen, complete sanitary arrangements, and ticket-collector's office. A concert-room, not more than half as large again as the present Pump-room, should be the first consideration in the plan; but this room must be so contrived as to permit of a corridor of sufficient length and width for the use of invalids to walk up and down in. A conversation-room and a similar room for chamber music, and, if possible, another room for smoking, should also be provided on the same floor. Connected with these rooms should be an arrangement for providing light refreshment. The Roman Bath should be roofed in and enclosed, as well as the King's Bath. The roof of the Roman Bath should be sufficiently lofty to admit of the erection of a side balcony all round it on a level with the floor of the Pump-room, or nearly so. Easy access should be provided by a staircase to the lower level of the *scholæ* of the bath, to which the general public should be admitted by a separate entrance. The area beneath these additions to the Pump-room should be excavated to the level of the Roman Bath, and, if anything should be found of antiquarian interest, it should be left accessible, as are the present Roman remains. If, in addition to this, a portion of the basement, well lighted, could be set aside for a museum for all the Roman antiquities belonging to the Corporation, and more especially those that have been or may hereafter be discovered on the site of the Baths, it would be a very desirable addition. Your committee hope that in connexion with this contemplated work some arrangement may be made for storing the water, which now runs to waste during the night and on Sundays. It is proposed to acquire the whole block of property lying between the Pump-room and the Abbey. This would give an area of 88 ft. by 88 ft., or 7,74[illegible] square ft. If to this is added the area of the Roman Bath, 96 ft. by 72 ft., or 6,912 square ft., the total amounts to 14,656 square ft., or nearly three times the space occupied by the present buildings of the Pump-room . . . . Your committee recommend that the provisional contracts for the purchase of No. 3 and 4, Abbey-churchyard, be forthwith completed, that an application be made to the Local Government Board to sanction a loan sufficient to pay the purchase moneys, and that as soon as the whole of the property is in the hands of the Corporation it be pulled down and excavated to the level of the floor of the Roman Bath, in order that the arrangement of the suggested buildings may be planned with a full and precise knowledge of the foundations and the existence of any Roman work, which it shall be the imperative instruction to the committee to preserve. After the excavations are completed your committee will in due time bring up a full and detailed report." He moved the adoption of the report. Mr. Jolly seconded the proposal. Alderman Gibbs proposed an amendment to the effect that a minor part of the scheme should be adopted, and the rest reconsidered. Ald. Chaffin seconded, believing that the scheme was far too comprehensive. Ultimately the consideration of the question was adjourned.

Board Schools, Hastings.—On the 26th ult. Councillor Stubbs opened the new board school at Clive Vale, Hastings. The school is built in the "Queen Anne" style. The external walls are of local red brick and Bath stone dressings, and the interior is lined with white Suffolk bricks. The floors are of fireproof construction by Messrs. Homan & Rodgers, of London, upon which is laid wood block flooring, by Mr. Roger Lowe, of Farnworth. The heating and ventilation is by Messrs. Wenham & Waters, of Croydon. Open fireplaces have also been provided with terra cotta flues. Advantage has been taken of the rapid fall of the ground from front to back to provide a covered playground for both boys and girls. The building contains on the ground floor, or girls' school, an assembly-hall, 65 ft. 6 in. long by 30 ft. wide, with a supplementary door and stone passage in addition to the regular entrance, which can be used for rapid exit in case of panic. Opening from this hall are six class-rooms. A cloak-room and lavatory, fitted with Adams' patent wash-basins, have been provided. On the first floor is the boys' department, similar in arrangement to the girls'. A teachers' room is provided for each department. The staircases, landings, and passages are of Elliott's patent stone, and fireproof, while the walls by the side of staircases are faced with white glazed bricks. The building was designed and carried out by Messrs. Elworthy & Son, architects, St. Leonards; the foundations and brickwork up to the ground floor were built by Mr. T. Taylor, of Hastings; and the remainder completed by Mr. T. Salter, of St. Leonards. The class-rooms provide accommodation for 534 boys and girls. The total cost of the building is about 7,050*l*.

Proposed Artisans' Dwellings, Manchester.—An inquiry instituted by the Local Government Board was held on the 1st and 2nd inst. at the Manchester Town-hall by Mr. S. J. Smith, C.E., one of the inspectors of the Board, for the purpose of inquiring into an application by the Manchester Corporation as the local authority under the Housing of the Working Classes Act, for permission to borrow the necessary funds for carrying out the erection of labourers' dwellings on what are defined as the Oldham-road and Pollard-street areas, and for other purposes. Mr. Thomas Hudson (Deputy Town Clerk) appeared for the Corporation, and supported the application, which was unopposed. He stated there were four points to which the inquiry would be directed, firstly, for the sanction of the Local Government Board to a proposal that the Corporation should themselves erect the dwellings; secondly, that a restriction should be removed imposed upon the Corporation with respect to the scheme that the houses should not be razed from the second block of property in area No. [illegible] until the completion of the new buildings on the first plot; thirdly, for borrowing powers to enable the Corporation to perform the work; and, fourthly, to the provision which the Corporation were under obligation to make for persons of the labouring class displaced by the carrying out of the scheme. Mr. Hudson further stated that the intention of the Corporation had always been to construct the new buildings themselves, as had been stated at a former inquiry, and had been approved by the Lo[illegible]

Government Board. Evidence would be given showing that the Corporation had greatly considered the question of providing the best class of dwellings. Designs had furthermore been obtained in competition, and those of Messrs. Spalding & Cross, of London, were adjudged by the Sanitary Committee the most suitable for the purpose. They had been modified to some extent by the Committee and the responsible advisers of the Corporation, and it was now considered that if buildings were erected upon the principles in the designs they would form a model of their class.—Mr. Councillor McDougall, the Deputy-Chairman of the Sanitary Committee, stated that it was desirable the Corporation should have power to erect the buildings themselves, which they desired to make model buildings of their class. It had always been contemplated that the work should be performed by themselves, and he knew of no one who would execute the work if the Corporation did not.—The City Surveyor (Mr. John Allison) stated that the plans chosen provided ventilation to both sides of the houses in a manner and to an extent which was quite satisfactory.—Evidence having been given by the architects in explanation of the plans, and by Mr. Andrew T. Rook, the Superintendent of the Sanitary Department of the Corporation, in confirmation of the unhealthy condition of the area, the inspector stated that he would report to the Local Government Board in due course.

ADDITIONS TO CHAPEL, BARNSTAPLE.—On the 2nd inst. a chapel, which was built in Barnstaple fifteen years ago in memory of Rev. James Thorne, was re-opened after being altered and enlarged. About 20 ft. has been added to the length of the chapel, with an organ-chamber beyond that. Side galleries have been provided at the expense of the stone arcades. These galleries contain four rows of seats, and are supported by cast-iron pillars, of terra-cotta tint, picked out in colours. The front panelling of the gallery is of pierced iron-work, bronzed. The seating accommodation of the chapel has been doubled. In addition to this work, the scheme included a tower. This tower, rising 77 ft., contains the main staircase to the galleries, a strong-room, and also a large class-room. It is built of Muddiford stone, with Bath stone dressings. The total cost of these alterations and enlargements will be about 1,800*l*. Messrs. Barwick & Sillifant were the contractors, Mr. John Chapple did the plumbing, and Mr. M. Croot the decoration. The architect was Mr. W. C. Oliver.

CO-OPERATIVE STORE BUILDINGS, PELAW, DURHAM.—On the 5th inst., the new branch stores of the Boldon Industrial Co-operative Society were opened at Pelaw by Mr. A. Bell. The new building is situated close to Pelaw Railway-station. The building, which has cost about 2,000*l*., contains a large shop on the ground floor, with warehouse, committee-room, office, &c., upstairs; a house for the manager being attached to the premises. The architect was Mr. Morton, of South Shields, and the builder Mr. R. Allison, Whitburn.

MISSION CHURCH, PLYMOUTH.—A new mission church, which has just been erected in connexion with St. Matthias parish, Plymouth, at the corner of Amity-place and Armada-street, was opened on the 24th ult. It is built of red brick with Portland stone dressings, from designs by Mr. G. D. Bellamy, the builders being Messrs. A. R. Lethbridge & Sons, Mr. W. J. Egford having been clerk of the works. It is 60 ft. long by about 45 ft. wide, and has attached to it a class-room and vestry. The roof is panelled. The stained glass and general glazing work has been carried out by Mr. Horsman, and the plumbing work by Mr. Bannerman. A chancel-screen is in process of erection. The total cost of the building has been about 1,400*l*.

RE-OPENING OF SAUNDBY CHURCH, NOTTINGHAMSHIRE.—On the 26th ult. the church of St. Martin, Saundby, was re-opened after restoration, by the Bishop of Southwell (Dr. Ridding). The chancel was restored in 1885 by a former Vicar of the parish (the Rev. T. Hudson), who has also furnished the tower, re-hung the bells, and his latest act of munificence has been the re-roofing of the nave, the addition of another aisle lighted by four stained-glass windows, by Kempe, of London; the provision of a new west screen of oak, the opening of the arches between the nave and the new aisle, and the re-seating of the church in oak. The architects were Messrs. Weatherly & Jones, of London. The contractors were Mr. Henry Clipsham, Newark (masonry), and Messrs. T. & J. Hawley, Penistone (plumbing, glazing, slating, &c.). The church is heated by hot-air pipes.

VICARAGE, ST. MARK'S CHURCH, ST. HELENS.—The work of erecting a vicarage for St. Mark's Church, St. Helens, has just been commenced. The design is in Gothic, and from the plans of Messrs. J. and W. Gandy, architects. The site is close to the church on the south side, and the total cost will be about 1,650*l*. Messrs. Rothwall & Sons are the contractors.

ST. MARK'S CHURCH, TORQUAY.—Various alterations and improvements in this church have been completed. These consist in some structural alterations and the addition of bishop's throne, sedilia, and new altar; a reredos, altar, credence, &c., in the morning chapel, which has been refloored in oak and teak, and a west lobby screen. All this work is in oak, and has been executed by Mr. Hems, of Exeter. New gas pendants, clusters, and brackets, wrought in iron and copper, have been made by Messrs. Hardman & Powell, Birmingham. The new coloured windows have been added by Messrs. Burlison & Grylls and Mr. Kempe respectively. The designs for the work have been made by Messrs. Tait & Harvey, architects, of Exeter, and carried out under their direction.

FOREIGN AND COLONIAL.

FRANCE.—The Académie des Beaux-Arts has elected M. Ancelet in place of the late M. Bailly. He obtained in the final *scrutin* seventeen votes against ten for M. Sedille and five for M. Guadet. ——M. Deperthes has obtained the Prix Rongevin at the École des Beaux-Arts.——At the Montparnasse Cemetery there has just been inaugurated a monument to Mdlle. Nancy Fleury, who invented or first used the method of teaching now employed in girls' schools in France.——The new Minister of Public Works, M. Viette, is to inaugurate next Sunday one of the new docks at Fécamp.——The twelfth water-colour exhibition of the Society, mostly architects, organised under the name of "Amants de la Nature," has just been opened. It is a small collection of seventy-eight water-colour sketches—"croquis de voyage." Those which may be selected as the best are the work of M. Paul Wallon, M. Deslignières, and M. Robert de Massey, the last-named of whom died only a few weeks ago.——The new Palais des Beaux-Arts at Lille, said to be a remarkable building, has just been opened.——The municipality of Fougères has acquired the château overlooking the town, one of the finest feudal remains in Brittany. M. Juste Lisch, Inspecteur-Général des Monuments Historiques, is commissioned to oversee the restoration of this fine monument, which has thirteen towers, and dates from the twelfth century.——At Vouziers (Ardennes), on the territory of Belval-Bois-des-Dames, a stone statue of a Roman soldier with a lance has been discovered, along with two sculptured stones representing combats of animals. The excavations going on in the same neighbourhood have also revealed an ancient Roman road and numerous pieces of Roman money with the effigy of Marcus Aurelius.——The Direction des Beaux-Arts has authorised the municipality of Toulouse to restore the "Salle des Illustrés" in the Palais du Capitol, so called because it contains the busts of the forty-four most illustrious natives of Languedoc. MM. Esquié and Pujol, architects, are to be commissioned to direct this important work, with the assistance of a certain number of artists of Toulouse. M. Jean Paul Laurens will decorate another gallery close to this; M. Benjamin Constant will execute a ceiling and a panel; M. Henri Martin, two panels; M. Debat-Ponsan, a ceiling and a panel; M. Rixens, a ceiling; and MM. Gervais, Destrem, Yarz, and Rachon will complete the work. The sculptural portion of the work is reserved for MM. Falguière, Mercié, Marqueste, Barthélemy, and Labatut. The total expense is estimated at half a million francs.——The death is announced of the curator of the Luxembourg, M. Etienne Arago, at the age of ninety. He was a son of the eminent astronomer François Arago, and uncle of M. Benjamin Constant the painter. He had been mayor of Paris in 1870, and since his youth had been mixed up with the Republican party. His portrait figures in the large picture by Schuetz at the Hotel de Ville, which represents the capture of the building by the rioters in the Revolution of 1830.

BERLIN.—At a State Council held last week, the Emperor, after having previously conferred with his Chancellor in private, made some propositions relating to the present and future finding of work for unemployed artisans and labourers. The propositions are said to have been received favourably, and the Ministries concerned are busy working them out into practical form. According to the official *Gazette*, the Emperor has received a number of addresses from workmen in which they express their confidence in him and the different measures he has already enforced for their benefit during his reign. At a Socialist meeting held last week, the 2,000 workmen present unanimously passed a resolution in which they strongly protested against the misrepresentation in certain organs of the press about their participation in the riots, and in which they ordered all fellow-workmen to do their best to oppose such proceedings.——A well-attended meeting of those interested in the success of the "Vienna Musical and Theatrical Exhibition" has been held at the Opera House, the "Intendant" of the Court Theatres taking the chair. The German participation at the Vienna show promises well, in spite of the petty controversies between the representatives of the minor states of the Empire on matters relating to precedence and system. All divisions are to be well represented, but special attention is to be given to "history." The Emperor wishes this part of the German group to be perfect, and has ordered the custodians of his private collections and the Government Institutions to put at the disposal of the managing committee all objects of interest at present in their charge.——Until of late the numerous interesting archæological remains in Prussia were taken care of by only one custodian, Herr "Ober-Regierungsrath" Persius. Now each province is to have its own sub-curator, who will be responsible to the chief-resident at Berlin, and each province is to pay its own expenses.——Entrance to the Royal Technical Colleges of the country has been facilitated. The Emperor has had the statutes altered so that the amount of schooling and class of education necessary for entrance is such as can be obtained at "Ober Realschulen" establishments of lower standing than the "Gymnasiums" and "Real Gymnasiums."——The so-called Louis Boissonnet Studentship (100*l*.) is to be given to a civil engineer this year. The successful candidate will have to do some extensive work in Norway, consisting of reports and illustrated essays.——A well-attended general meeting of persons interested in the Portland cement trade was held last week. It was decided to send a collective exhibition case of German samples to the Chicago Show. After the business had been gone through a number of interesting papers were read.

MISCELLANEOUS.

THE ROYAL GOLD MEDAL FOR ARCHITECTURE, 1892.—At the special general meeting of the Royal Institute of British Architects, held on Monday evening last, it was resolved, subject to the sanction of the Queen, to present this year's Royal Gold Medal to Monsieur César Daly, of Paris, "for his works as a man of letters in connexion with architecture."

THE MOVEMENT FOR THE REGISTRATION OF PLUMBERS.—An important step in this movement was the second reading of the Plumbers' Bill, on the 3rd inst. The Bill is claimed by its promoters as supplying the missing link in sanitary legislation, for they say that hitherto the numerous enactments about plumbers' work have entirely omitted any provision for the efficiency of the men who have to carry it out. Numerous petitions in favour of the Bill have been presented to Parliament from the plumbers and sanitary authorities.

THE PEABODY FUND.—The twenty-seventh annual report of the trustees of the Peabody Donation Fund states that the net gain of the year, from rents and interest, has been 29,659*l*. 4s. 7d., as shown by the accounts. The sum given by Mr. Peabody was, in 1862, 150,000*l*.; in 1866, 100,000*l*.; in 1868, 100,000*l*.; and received by bequest from him in 1873, 150,000*l*.; making a total of 500,000*l*.; to which has been added money received for rent and interest, 553,105*l*. 6s. 6d., making the total fund on December 31 last 1,053,105*l*. 6s. 6d. Of the 390,000*l*. borrowed of the Public Works Loan Commissioners and others, mentioned in previous reports, the trustees have paid off 206,833*l*. 6s. 8d., leaving a balance unpaid of 183,166*l*. 13s. 4d., the amount repaid during the year being 29,166*l*. 13s. 4d. The capital expenditure on land and buildings to the end of the year was 1,233,904*l*. 13s. 9d., the whole of the repairs for the year amounting to 8,332*l*. 11s. 1d., being charged to income as in previous reports. Up to the end of the year, the trustees have provided for the artisan and labouring poor of London 11,273 rooms, besides bath-rooms, laundries, and wash-houses, occupied by 20,269 persons. These rooms comprise 5,070 separate dwellings, viz., 75 of four rooms, 1,788 of three rooms, 2,402 of two rooms, and 805 of one room.

APPOINTMENT OF CITY ARCHITECT, ABERDEEN.—The Aberdeen Town Council, at its monthly meeting on the 7th inst., proceeded, in terms of a previous resolution, to fill the vacancy in the post of City Architect, caused by the death of Mr. William Smith. Bailie Lyon proposed that the appointment be deferred, to permit of the advisability of terminating the office and transferring the duties to the City Surveyor being considered, but this proposal was negatived by 14 votes to 11. Mr. John Rust, jun., till recently one of the Bailies (and who resigned to become a candidate for the post), and Mr. G. M. Mackenzie (of Messrs. Matthews & Mackenzie, architects), were nominated; and Mr. Rust was elected by 19 votes to 4 for Mr. Mackenzie.

THE INCORPORATED ASSOCIATION OF MUNICIPAL AND COUNTY ENGINEERS.—A Home Counties district Metropolitan meeting of this Association is to be held at Kensington this Saturday, March 12, at 11 a.m. The members will meet in the Council-chamber, Town-hall, Kensington, when Mr. Weaver will call attention to certain provisions of the Public Health (London) Act, 1891, and will move a resolution thereon. Mr. William Weaver, M.Inst.C.E., Chief Surveyor of Kensington, will then read a paper on "Kensington, its progress and work." After this has been discussed, the members will partake of luncheon, kindly provided by the Kensington Vestry, and they will proceed in breaks to view the Recreation Ground, Notting Dale; Kensal Wharf; the Warwick-road and Pembroke-road depôts; electric lighting station, West Brompton (House-to-House Electric Light Supply Company, Limited); Salopian Wharf, Chelsea, Refuse Disposal Company's Works; Wharf, Lot's-road, Chelsea; and Kensington-court Electric Lighting Station (Kensington and Knightsbridge Electric Lighting Company, Limited). In the evening the members will dine together at the Holborn Restaurant.

COMPETITION, CONTRACTS, AND PUBLIC APPOINTMENTS.

COMPETITION.

Nature of Work.	By whom Advertised.	Premiums.	Designs to be delivered.
*Cemetery Chapel and Caretaker's Lodge..	Ripon Corporation ..	20l. & 5l.	April 4

CONTRACTS.

Nature of Work or Materials.	By whom Required.	Architect, Surveyor, or Engineer.	Tenders to be delivered.
*Road Making and Paving Works	Lewisham Bd. of W..	Official	Mar. 15
*Paving Works	Brentford Loc. Bd..	do.	do.
Wesleyan Chapel, Shadwell, near Leeds	....	Geo. F. Danby	do.
Water Supply Works	Newark Corporation	H. Rofe	do.
*Bridge over River Mersey	County Borough of Stockport	A. M. Fowler	do.
Caretaker's House, West Vale Board School, Halifax	....	Jas. Farrah	Mar. 16
*Relief Station and Residence	Wandsworth & Clapham Union	T. W. Aldwinckle	Mar. 17
*Additions, &c. to Two Houses, Commercial-road, E.	Mr. W. Harries	R. B. Coe	do.
Mission Hall and Cottage, Tomnavoulin, Glenlivet, N.B.	Rev. D. Robertson	....	Mar. 18
Thirty-one Houses, Cemetery-road, Wombwell	Barnsley British Co-op. Soc.	Jno. Robinson	do.
Alterations to Hotel, High-street, Elgin, N.B.	....	C. C. Doig	Mar. 19
Alterations, &c. Central Hall, Blyth	John Robinson	Gilson Pyle	do.
*Guernsey Granite	Bournemouth T. C.	F. W. Lacey	Mar. 21
*Erection of New Works	Edward Cockey Co. Lim.	Official	do.
*25,000 yards Wood Pavement	Vestry of St. George's Hanover-square	do.	do.
*Supply of Materials	Mortlake Dist. Highway Bd.	do.	do.
*Taking-down, &c. Building	R. T. Wragg	....	do.
Dwelling-house, Grantown-on-Spey, N.B.	....	Brown & Watt	do.
New Wing, Blocks, &c. at Workhouse	Newcastle-under-Lyme Union Guar.	John Blood	do.
Granite Macadam, Kerbs, &c.	Reading Corporation	Arthur E. Collins	do.
*500 tons Broken Granite	Chelmsford Twn Coun.	Official	Mar. 22
Road Diversion and Girder Bridge, Brynna	Glamorgan C. C.	do.	do.
Diversion of Road, &c. Cilfynydd	do.	do.	do.
*General Paving Works	West Ham Council	Lewis Angell	do.
*Works and Materials	Southgate Local Board	C. G. Lawson	Mar. 23
Fire Brigade Station, Market-street	Carlisle Corporation	W. Howard Smith	do.

CONTRACTS.—*Continued.*

Nature of Work or Materials.	By whom Required.	Architect, Surveyor, or Engineer.	Tenders to be delivered.
New Church, Pennar, Pembroke Dock	....	Nicholson & Son	Mar. 2.
Boundary Walls, &c. near Warrington	Burtonwood Sch. Bd.	Pierpoint & Frazer	Mar. 2.
Enlargement of St. Michael's Home, Treforest, S. Wales	Very Rev. Mons. Williams	....	Mar. 2.
Large Additions, &c. to Altyre House, near Forres, N.B.	....	A. & W. Reid	do.
*New Sorting Office, Tothill Fields, S.W.	Com. of H. M. Works	Official	Mar. 2.
*Post Office, Dover	H. M. Works	Official	Mar. 2.
*Infirmary, &c.	Pare Gwyllt Asylum, near Bridgend	Giles, Gough, & Trollope	April
*Sewerage Works	Oldbury Local Board	H. B. Nichol	April
Alterations, &c. Castle Inn, Treforest, S. Wales	Forest Estate Office	....	No date
*Cottage Sanatorium, Reading	Friends Public School Co.	A. Waterhouse & Son	do.
Additions to Warehouse, Shed, &c. Halifax	....	Petty & Ives	do.
Alterations and Additions to Residence, Framlington-place, Newcastle-on-Tyne	....	J. W. Taylor	do.
Wesleyan Chapel and Schools, Consett, co. Durham	....	Lamb, Armstrong, & Knowles	do.
Alterations to "Hotspur" Hotel, &c. Haymarket, Newcastle-on-Tyne	W. J. Sanderson	Oliver & Leeson	do.
Alterations, &c. Board School, Gowerton, Loughor, S. Wales	....	T. P. Martin	do.
Farmhouse, Penybank, Llangadock, Carmarthenshire	....	J. W. Jones	do.
Wesleyan Schools, Grove-road, Harrogate	....	Morley & Woodhouse	do.
Vicarage, Woodlesford, Leeds	....	R. J. Smith	do.
New Church, Cudworth, Hull	....	Smith & Brodrick	do.
*Married Soldiers' Quarters, Eastbourne	War Department	Official	do.
*Rectory House, Great Carlton	....	C. Kirk & Sons	do.
*Erection of Chimney Shaft	London Tramways Co. Limited	....	do.
*Wooden Pier and Pavilion with Iron Roof, Southend-on-Sea	Mimius Sailing Club	....	do.

PUBLIC APPOINTMENTS.

Nature of Appointment.	By whom Advertised.	Salary.	Applications to be in
*Clerk of the Works	Guildford T. C.	3l. per week	Mar. 1
*Road Surveyor	Ilford Local Board	150l. &c.	Mar. 1
*Foreman	Ilkeston Corporation	Not stated	Mar. 1
*Road Inspector	Bournemouth T. C.	2l. 5s.	Mar. 1

Those marked with an Asterisk (*) are advertised in this Number. *Competition, p. iv. Contracts, pp. iv., vi., & viii. Public Appointments, p. xx.*

English Fire Engines in Australia.—The Sydney *Daily Telegraph* contains an account of the casting of a new steam fire engine of the "equilibrium" pattern sent out by Messrs. Shand, Mason, & Co. of London, which appears to be regarded as an extremely satisfactory addition to fire-extinguishing plant in Sydney. The engine is the largest portable one turned out of London, and can deliver 900 gallons per minute at a water pressure of 200 lbs. to the square inch. It has three steam cylinders working direct to the treble set of double-acting pumps. On the trial it threw a jet of water 250 ft. perpendicularly and 180 ft. horizontally. The cost was 1,328l. Steel is largely used in the construction.

Stanford Hall.—In reference to our illustration of this house in our issue of February 29, Messrs. John Smeaton & Son ask us to mention that they carried out all the work of water-supply, pumping-engines, drainage, and sanitary work generally, under the supervision of the architect, at a cost of about 11,000l.

Metropolitan Drawing-classes.—Lord Cranbrook has accepted the invitation of Mr. Busbridge to deliver the "Queen's Prizes" to the students of the Metropolitan Drawing-classes. The ceremony will take place in the Carpenters' Hall on Friday, March 18. The chair will be taken at eight o'clock by the Archbishop of Canterbury.

Debt Recovery and Water-Supply.—A case was decided last Saturday at the Westminster Police-court, which clearly shows the great inconvenience and injury which threaten the ratepayer who may from any mischance be unable to discharge his account with a London water company. The defendant, who seems to have been overcharged, refused to pay for water which he had not used. The company, not seeing the matter in this light, proceeded to enforce payment by cutting off his household supply, and for seven days,—that is, until the hearing of the case in court,—persisted in this course. Their attitude in the matter, though entirely legal, was severely criticised by the presiding magistrate, who regretted that none of the various Acts as at present constituted allowed consumers any guarantee against such a high-handed mode of procedure. He was strongly of opinion that the water-supply to any house should under no circumstances be terminable at the will of a company. Debt recovery should rather be arranged, as in the case of parish rates, by taking proceedings in a court of summary jurisdiction. In this opinion we concur. Whatever may be said of the commercial principle involved, it is indeed astonishing that no legal check should be placed upon the application of a process which prohibits the use of an absolute necessity of life and health. Water certainly can under no circumstances be dispensed with, and it is no mitigation to say that the sufferer by an adverse verdict may borrow sufficient for his temporary needs. It is not clear to our mind how he can even do this. Yet his necessities, his health and cleanliness, are intimately connected with the well-being of his neighbours, and the case is one in which, if he suffer, others suffer by and with him. Some amendment of the existing law such as that above suggested is, therefore, evidently needful as a mere matter of sanitary requirement.—*The Lancet.*

Electric Lighting at the Mansion House.—On Monday last the Mansion House was thrown open for a private view of the electrical installation which has been carried out there by the Planet Electrical Engineering Company, of 4, Victoria Mansions, Westminster, and 80, Coleman-street, E.C., under the direction of Mr. A. Slatter, the manager. The proceedings commenced at six o'clock by a presentation to the Lady Mayoress on behalf of the Company of a silver and ebony battery set and portable lamp, with the arms of the Lord Mayor and Lady Mayoress on one side, and an inscription recording the occasion of the presentation on the other. A basket of flowers illuminated by an electric lamp in the midst was also presented at the same time to the Lady Mayoress. Mr. James Salmon, Chairman of the General Purposes Committee of the Company, was spokesman on the occasion, and, after a graceful acknowledgment by the Lord Mayor, those present dispersed to view the installation. This consists of 825 lamps, mostly of sixteen-candle power, fitted over the whole of the Mansion House. The fittings are chiefly in handsome brass-work, and the lamps are for the most part hung so high that shadows are avoided, and shading is unnecessary. In the drawing-room the lamps are mounted in imitation of candles, and the old spangled fittings have been adapted to them. In the billiard-room and saloon also the gas-fittings have been utilised, with the result, in the former case, that the corners of the billiard-table are imperfectly illuminated. The lamps in the dining-room and the Lady Mayoress's boudoir are enveloped in coloured leaf-shape shades, the light is thereby much softened, and the effect is pleasing, but we doubt if the sacrifice of illuminating power is not carried too far. The switch-boards in the basement are mounted on marbled slate, and (a somewhat unusual arrangement) the main fuses are copper strips. The current is direct, and is supplied by the City of London Lighting Company. The band of the Coldstream Guards played a selection during the evening in the saloon, where also was an exhibition of electrical apparatus.

Discovery of Metopes at Selinus.—Of the three metopes found on February 10 at ancient Selinus during the excavations now in progress amongst the fortifications to the north of the acropolis on the east side, one is irretrievably broken, but the other two are of the highest artistic value, both as regards technique and colouring. The first is 0·84 mètre high by 0·69 wide, and represents Europa seated on a bull, with long thick tail waving over its head in the air. The treatment is altogether archaic. The second, measuring 0·84 m. by 0·68, has quite an Egypto-Assyrian character, and represents a winged sphinx in the usual heraldic pose. Both metopes are ascribed to the seventh century B.C. Strange to say, neither of them corresponds in measurement with the dimensions of any of the know[n] temples at Selinunte. The excavations will there[-]fore be continued in search of some other building [to] which they may have belonged. Photogravures an[d] a descriptive account of these important landmark[s] in the history of art will appear as soon as possib[le] in the *Monumenti Antichi* of the Roman Lincei.—[*The*] *Athenæum.*

Manchester Cathedral.—A new footpace h[as] been made for the high altar at the Manchest[er] Cathedral. The steps are of richly figured marble[,] the lower of Vert des Alpes, and the upper [of] Levento marble, moulded on the edges and high[ly] polished. The footpace is executed in mosaic, wit[h] a guilloche border, enclosing emblems of th[e] Trinity and the Virgin, also the Alpha and Omeg[a] and a floriated cross with Central Sun of Righteou[s]ness, worked in various coloured marbles an[d] gold and blue Venetian glass. The work is fro[m] the designs of Mr. J. S. Crowther, architect, an[d] has been executed by Messrs. J. & H. Patteso[n] of Manchester.

Hints to Taxpayers.—We have received [a] handy and practical little book, entitled "Hints [to] Taxpayers; or, How to Appeal against Income T[ax] Assessments, with Illustrative Cases," by G. [ ] Mitchell, which is published by the author at [ ] Victoria-street, Wolverhampton. It is just one [of] those cheap and useful works which are handy f[or] everyday reference, and, being without any preten[-]sions, are frequently of greater value than work[s] which make a greater show.

The English Iron Trade.—Very little chang[e] has taken place in the English iron market durin[g] the past week. Business is restricted to hand-t[o-]mouth requirements, and on every side notices [to] close works on account of the miners' stoppage a[re] being exhibited. The Cleveland market remains [in] an unsettled condition, with prices exceeding[ly] irregular, and in all the other pig-iron centres trad[e] is very quiet. Manufactured iron is in limit[ed] inquiry, and tinplates remain dull. The steel trad[e] shows little alteration. The rail branch is neglecte[d.] The Board of Trade Returns just issued exhibit [a] deplorable falling-off in the quantity of railwa[y] material exported, which amounted to only 18,4[ ] tons, a decrease on February, 1891, of 37,350 ton[s.] Shipbuilding shows no change since our last repor[t.] Engineers are getting slacker. The coal trade i[s] still active prior to the suspension of work.—*Iron*

MEETINGS.

SATURDAY, *March* 12.

Incorporated Association of Municipal and Coun[ty] Engineers.—Home Counties District Metropolit[an] Meeting, Kensington Town Hall. 11 a.m.—Dinner[,] Holborn Restaurant. 6.30 p.m.

Sanitary Inspectors' Association.—Ninth Annu[al] Dinner, First Avenue Hotel, Holborn. Dr. B. [W.] Richardson, President, in the chair. 6 p.m.

Edinburgh Architectural Association.—Visit to Ros[lin] Chapel and Roslin Castle.

MONDAY, MARCH 14.

Surveyors' Institution.—Discussion, to be opened by Mr. J. F. L. Rolleston, on the "Small Agricultural Holdings Bill." 8 p.m.

Society of Arts (Cantor Lectures).—Professor W. Robinson on "The Uses of Petroleum in Prime Movers." III. 8 p.m.

Clerks of Works' Association (Carpenters' Hall).—Paper by Mr. George Calvert. 8 p.m.

Leeds and Yorkshire Architectural Society.—Lecture by Professor Goodman. 7.30 p.m.

TUESDAY, MARCH 15.

Institution of Civil Engineers.—Further discussion on Professor W. C. Unwin's paper on "Petroleum Engines." 8 p.m.

Sanitary Institute (Lectures for Sanitary Officers).—Mr. J. F. J. Sykes on "Nature of Nuisances, including Nuisances the Abatement of which is Difficult." 8 p.m.

Society of Arts (Foreign and Colonial Section).—Mr. F. A. Pezet on "Peru: its Commerce and Resources." 8 p.m.

WEDNESDAY, MARCH 16.

British Museum.—Miss Eugénie Sellers on "Greek Sculpture: Echoes of Greek Master-pieces in Græco-Roman work." VI. 2.30 p.m.

Civil and Mechanical Engineers' Society.—Mr. A. Fairlie Bruce on "Water Works Fittings." 7 p.m.

Surrey Archæological Society.—Annual General Meeting (8, Danes' Inn). 4 p.m.

Society of Arts.—Mr. Tempest Anderson on "Iceland." 8 p.m.

Builders' Foremen and Clerks of Works' Institution.—8.30 p.m.

THURSDAY, MARCH 17.

Society of Antiquaries.—8.30 p.m.

FRIDAY, MARCH 18.

Architectural Association.—Mr. E. A. E. Woodrow on "The Planning of Theatres." 7.30 p.m.

Institution of Civil Engineers.—Students' visit to the Salopian Wharf, Lot's-road, Chelsea, to inspect the works of the "Refuse Disposal Company"; and subsequently to the "Destructor" Works of the Ealing Local Board. 1.30 p.m.

Royal Institution.—Mr. George Du Maurier on "Modern Satire in Black and White." 9 p.m.

Sanitary Institute (Lectures for Sanitary Officers).—Professor A. Bostock Hill on "Trade Nuisances." 8 p.m.

SATURDAY, MARCH 19.

Architectural Association.—Visit to the Tower Bridge Works, by permission of Mr. J. Wolfe Barry. 8 p.m.

Glasgow Architectural Association.—Visit to Kilbirnie Church.

RECENT PATENTS:

ABSTRACTS OF SPECIFICATIONS.

5,100.—DRAIN PLUG: *T. Pratt, jun.*—This patent refers to what is described as an improved combination drain plug and testing apparatus. A length of metal tube, having one end thickened, is taken as a foundation. In the interior of the thickened end, a screw thread is cut and a solid plug of metal or other material is fitted in it. On the exterior of this pipe, a screw is cut from its open end nearly to the enlarged portion, and a loose, tapered flange slipped on till it engages on the enlargement, forming a watertight joint. A second tapered flange, corresponding to the other, is also placed on the tube, and between these two flanges a ring of rubber or other flexible material. A ring thumb-screw is then screwed on to tighten the whole. On inserting the apparatus into the mouth of the drain, the ring thumb-screw is screwed down, forcing the two flanges together and squeezing the rubber against the sides of the pipe until an air-tight joint is obtained. By the insertion or removal of the solid-screwed plug before fixing the apparatus in the pipe, it can either be used as a plug or stopper, or for testing the drain.

4,872.—SINKS: *S. S. Hellyer.*—This specification refers to an improvement in sinks, more especially intended for use in hospitals, as a slop sink, and for washing or cleansing bed-pans or similar articles.

5,424.—FIREPROOF STAIRCASES AND FLOORS: *J. Fulham.*—This inventor seeks to provide means for preventing the collapse of staircases, floors, and the like, composed of terra-cotta, fire-clay, or concrete, by reason of the expansion of the metal girders, joists, and pillars supporting the same. The metal girders or joists are enclosed or embedded in the stair treads of staircases, and between suitable mouldings in the case of joists; a packing of slag-wool, asbestos, or other non-conducting material being placed around the girders or joists. The landings of staircases may be constructed in the same way as floors, and the spaces between the mouldings covering the girders are closed in by a series of sections of fire-clay, terra-cotta, or the like, which, when placed together, form arches, the tops being covered with concrete or other suitable fire-proof material.

22,256.—GULLY-TRAPS: *G. Couzens.*—According to this inventor, an improved gully-trap for the prevention of the back-flow of water from drains, constructed with a copper-ball arranged to be floated up against a rubber-ring for additionally closing the connexion to the drain, the ball being capable of supporting a quantity of liquid, making an additional water-seal.

22,469.—EARTHENWARE-PIPES: *H. Greening.*—The object of this invention is to provide a secure joint for earthenware pipes, traps, bends, and the like, especially sanitary drain-pipes. Each pipe is constructed with a screw thread around the exterior of the spigot-end to correspond and engage with a screw-thread around the interior of the socket of the adjacent pipe. The screwed portion may be single or double-threaded, and one or more turns of the screw may be employed, or two half-threads springing from opposite points in the circumference of the pipes in the case of a double-threaded screw.

NEW APPLICATIONS FOR LETTERS PATENTS.

February 22.—3,401, J. Sainty, Covering Roofs and Gutters for Houses and other Buildings.—3,403, W. Bates, Water-closets.—3,411, C. Formby, Paint Brushes.—3,429, S. Allin, Check Springs for Doors.—3,446, K. Friedrich, wood-working Tools.—3,448, E. Parr, Screws.—3,465, D. Andrew, Drain, Sewer, and like Pipes.

February 23.—3,483, J. Brecknell, Gravity Syphon for Returning and finally Entrapping Smoke from any nature of Stack or Chimney.—3,531, G. Hayes, Metallic Lathing.—3,539, H. Brunson and E. Gillett, Building or Paving Blocks.—3,576, J. Trier, Stone-dressing Machines.

February 24.—3,586, C. Armstrong, Kilns or Ovens for Burning and Glazing Sanitary ware, &c.—3,608, F. Grew, Appliance to be Attached to Doors.—3,609, U. Bairstow, Securing Door-knob to their Spindles.—3,642, W. and E. Freeman, water-waste Preventers or Flushing Cisterns.—3,645, W. Sanderson, Soldering-irons.

February 25.—3,656, C. Preston, Brick.—3,658, F. Brown, Gully-trap and Grate.—3,664, R. Tootall, Ventilating Fans.—3,671, M. Piper, Door or other Fastenings.—3,686, J. Lodge, Brick Kilns.—3,690, P. Morgan, Safety Sash-fastening.

February 26.—3,739, H. Stockman, Tools and their Handles.—3,749, F. Fitton, Ventilation.—3,771, H. Cottrell and G. Pauling, Device for Preventing the Smoke Nuisance.—3,778, J. Asten, Clip for Roofing Slates or Tiles.—3,801, L. and W. Winnall, Electric Bells.

February 27.—3,845, J. Buchanan, Brick-making Machinery, &c.—3,862, S. and S. Parr, Fireproof Slabs for Floors, &c.

PROVISIONAL SPECIFICATIONS ACCEPTED.

253, J. Cosstick, Chimney-pots for preventing down-draughts.—440, A. Haworth, Pipes for Sinks.—1,132, D. Shaw, Gully-traps.—1,294, F. Brookes, Safety-fastener for Sash-windows when open or closed.—1,621, W. Gwinnett, Machinery for making Wood-screws.—1,663, A. Morris, Blow-pipes.—1,839, G. Paley, water-closet Cisterns.—1,845, W. and A. Auty, Sink-traps.—1,929, H. Stewart, Ventilating Sewers, &c.—2,003, R. Esplin, Hinges.—2,009, J. Brooke, Chimney-cowls.—2,085, A. Bremner, Wood-screws.—2,201, R. Clark, Varnish.—2,239, G. Cartwright, Plane-iron Fastener.—2,314, R. Batey, Door-locks.—3,125, J. Bridson, Brick for Building Purposes.

COMPLETE SPECIFICATIONS ACCEPTED.

(Open to Opposition for Two Months.)

7,133, E. Wehrlis, Facings or Covering-plates, Plates or Slabs for architectural purposes.—15,628, A. Fowler, water-closets.—215, A. Boult, Fire-grates.—323, A. Whittome, wood-block Floors.—2,382, Scollay, Paints.—2,819, Nicholls, Window-sash Holder.—5,601, Smith & Elmore, White Lead.—7,883, Southall, Flushing Cisterns.—12,760, Pullan and others, Brick-pressing Machines.—19,010, Knapp, Sash Lifts and Lock.—20,274, Londer, Paint.—21,240, Boyle, Ventilators.

SOME RECENT SALES OF PROPERTY:

ESTATE EXCHANGE REPORT.

FEBRUARY 24.—By *Dennant & Co* (At Deptford): 83 and 85, Cranfield-road, Brockley, u.t. 75 yrs., g.r. 10*l.*, 620*l.*

FEBRUARY 29.—By *Broad & Wiltshire*: 124 and 126, Goldhawk-rd., Shepherd's-bush, u.t. 61 yrs., g.r. 12*l.*, r. 100*l.*, 800*l.*; 130 and 132, Goldhawk-rd., u.t. 61 yrs., g.r. 12*l.*, r. 100*l.*, 950*l.*; Stable and Coach House, u.t. 61 yrs., g.r. 2*l.*, r. 25*l.*, 230*l.*; 85, Disraeli-rd., Putney, f., r. 30*l.*, 340*l.*

MARCH 1.—By *J. McLachlan & Sons*: 22, Leathwaite-rd., Clapham-common, u.t. 89 yrs., g.r. 1*l.*, 295*l.*; Nos. 24 and 26, Leathwaite-rd., u.t. 89 yrs., g.r. 16*l.*, 610*l.*—By *Furber, Price, & Furber*: A freehold perpetual rent-charge of 100*l.* a year, Rotherhithe, 2,000*l.*; 20 and 22, Lewes-rd, Camberwell, f., 435*l.*; 3 and 4, Padfield-st., f., r. 67*l.* 12s., 560*l.*; "Astor House," Dalmain-rd., Forest-hill, f., r. 31*l.* 4s., 300*l.*; a plot of freehold land, 55*l.*—By *H. Haines & Son*: I.g.r. of 39*l.*, Kentish Town, u.t. 43 yrs., at a peppercorn, 720*l.*—By *Ellgood & Fuller*: 47 and 49, High-st., Hornsey, c., r. 65*l.*, 505*l.*—By *Sherrin & Coltman*: 17 and 19, Faunce-st., Kennington, u.t. 72 yrs., g.r. 12*l.*, r. 72*l.*, 650*l.*—By *E. E Croucher & Co.*: 31, Albion-st., Broadstairs, f., r. 60*l.*, 790*l.*; a f.g.r. of 10*l.* a year, Chandos-rd., 165*l.*—By *Debenham, Tewson, & Co.*: 1 to 9, Alexandra-ter., Carshalton, u.t. 95 yrs., g.r. 63*l.*, 220*l.*; the residence, "Enmore," the Grove, Clapham-rd., u.t. 16 yrs., g.r. 48*l.*, 195*l.*; 87, 89, and 89A, Stroud-green-rd, Finsbury-pk., u.t. 40 yrs., g.r. 80*l.*, 1,000*l.*; 91, Stroud-green-rd, u.t. 40 yrs., g.r. 50*l.*, r. 110*l.*, 500*l.*; 99 and 101, Stroud-green-rd., u.t. 40 yrs., g.r. 80*l.*, r. 156*l.*, 650*l.*; 108, Stroud-green-rd., u.t. 86 yrs., g.r. 28*l.*, r. 105*l.*, 1,140*l.*; 149, Queen Victoria-st., City, u.t. 62 yrs., g.r. 405*l.*, r. 1,000*l.*, 7,800*l.*; 44, Milton-rd., Mildmay-pk., f., r. 26*l.*, 300*l.*; 81, Forest-rd., Dalston, u.t. 23 yrs., g.r. 3*l.* 10s., r. 30*l.*, 165*l.*

MARCH 2.—By *Fuller & Fuller*: 35, Pond-st., Hampstead, f., r. 60*l.*, 940*l.*; 187, St. John's-hill, Wandsworth, f., r. 35*l.*, 580*l.*; 6 and 7, Eagle Wharf-rd., Hoxton, u.t. 9 yrs., g.r. 6*l.* 12s., 150*l.*; No. 192, Dalston-lane, u.t. 9 yrs., g.r. 7*l.* 10s., 85*l.*—By *Bray, Young, & Co.*: F.g.r. of 19*l.* 10s., with reversion in 88 yrs., Red-lane, Enfield, 425*l.*; two houses, cottage, and garden, Southgate, u.t. 95 yrs., g.r. 115*l.*, r. 225*l.*, 100*l.*—By *Rutley, Son, & Vine*: 128, Stanhope-st., Hampstead-rd., u.t. 33 yrs., g.r. 6*l.*, r. 52*l.*, 510*l.*

MARCH 3.—By *A. J. Sheffield*: 18 and 19, James-pl., Poplar, f., 250*l.*; 136, Abbott-rd., Bromley, E., u.t. 81 yrs., g.r. 5*l.*, 245*l.*—By *Newbon & Co.*: 14, Ennis-rd., Finsbury-pk., u.t. 75 yrs., g.r. 6*l.* 6s., r. 32*l.*, 305*l.*; 5 to 9, South-st., Ponder's-end, u.t. 69 yrs., g.r. 10*l.*, r. 104*l.*, 630*l.*

MARCH 4.—By *Maddox & Son*: No. 12, Long-acre, f., r. 260*l.*, 4,000*l.*; 274 and 276, Pentonville-rd., King's-cross, u.t. 12 yrs., g.r. 30*l.*, r. 135*l.*, 1,030*l.*; "The Scottish Stores," Caledonian-rd., u.t. 12 yrs., g.r. 20*l.*, r. 74*l.*, 420*l.*; 6 and 8, Caledonian-rd., u.t. 12 yrs., g.r. 25*l.*, r. 97*l.* 15s., 480*l.*; 22, St. Bartholomew-rd., Camden-rd., u.t. 27 yrs., g.r. 4*l.* 12s. 6d., 490*l.*; a plot of freehold land, Greyhound-rd., Fulham, 760*l.*; f.g.r. of 15*l.*, with reversion in 94 yrs., 415*l.*

[*Contractions used in these lists.*—F.g.r. for freehold ground-rent; l.g.r. for leasehold ground-rent; i.g.r. for improved ground-rent; g.r. for ground-rent; r. for rent; f. for freehold; c. for copyhold; l. for leasehold; e.r. for estimated rental; u.t. for unexpired term; p.a. for per annum; yrs. for years; st. for street; rd. for road; sq. for square; pl. for place; ter. for terrace; cres. for crescent; yd. for yard, &c.]

PRICES CURRENT OF MATERIALS.

TIMBER.		
Greenheart, B.G. ton	9/0/0	0/0/0
Teak, E.I. ... load	9/10/0	15/0/0
Sequoia, U.S. ft. cu.	2/3	3/0
Ash, Canada load	2/10/0	4/0/0
Birch, do.	3/5/0	4/10/0
Elm, do.	3/10/0	4/15/0
Fir, Dantsic, &c.	2/0/0	3/10/0
Oak, do.	3/0/0	5/0/0
Canada	6/0/0	7/0/0
Pine, Canada red	2/10/0	3/10/0
Do. Yellow	2/10/0	5/0/0
Lath, Dantsic, fath	5/0/0	6/10/0
St. Petersburg	5/10/0	7/10/0
Deals, Finland, 2nd & 1st std 100	8/10/0	10/10/0
Do. 4th & 3rd	7/10/0	8/10/0
Do. Riga	6/10/0	8/0/0
St. Petersburg, 1st yellow	11/0/0	18/0/0
Do. 2nd yellow	8/10/0	10/10/0
Do. white	7/10/0	10/10/0
Swedish	7/15/0	16/0/0
White Sea	8/10/0	18/0/0
Canada, Pine 1st	20/0/0	28/0/0
Do. do. 2nd	14/10/0	16/10/0
Do. do. 3rd, &c.	8/5/0	10/10/0
Do. Spruce, 1st	8/10/0	11/0/0
Do. do. 3rd & 2nd	6/15/0	8/0/0
New Brunswick	7/0/0	7/10/0
Battens, all kinds	3/10/0	15/10/0
Flooring Boards, sq., 1 in. prep. 1st	0/8/6	0/14/6
Do. 2nd	0/7/6	0/11/6
Other qualities	0/5/0	0/8/0
Cedar, Cuba ft.	/3¼	/4½
Honduras, &c.	/2¾	/4
Mahogany, Cuba	/4¼	/6¼
St. Domingo, cargo av	/4¼	2/0
Mexican do. do	/4	/5
Tobasco do. do	/5¼	/7
Honduras do.	/5¼	/6¼
Box, Turkey ton	4/0/0	15/0/0
Rose, Rio	10/0/0	20/0/0
Bahia	8/0/0	18/0/0
Satin, St. Domingo ft.	0/0/8	0/1/8

TIMBER (continued).		
Satin, Porto Rico	0/0/8	0/1/6
Walnut, Italian	0/0/3½	0/0/7
METALS.		
Iron—Pig, in Scotland ton	2/1/0	2/1/3
Bar, Welsh, in London	6/0/0	6/10/0
Do. do. at works in Wales	5/10/0	6/0/0
Do. Staffordshire, in London	6/5/0	6/15/0
Copper—British, cake and ingot	48/0/0	48/10/0
Best selected	49/0/0	49/10/0
Sheets, strong	58/0/0	0/0/0
Chili, bars	45/15/0	46/2/6
Yellow Metal lb.	0/0/5¼	0/0/5½
Lead—Pig, Spanish ton	10/12/9	10/16/3
English, com. brands	10/17/6	11/0/0
Sheet, English, 3 lbs. per sq. ft. and upwards	13/0/0	0/0/0
Pipe	13/10/0	0/0/0
Zinc—English sheet ton	25/5/0	0/0/0
Vieille Montagne	25/15/0	0/0/0
Tin—Straits	89/5/0	89/15/0
Australian	89/7/6	89/17/6
English Ingots	92/10/0	99/15/0
OILS.		
Linseed ton	18/15/0	19/0/0
Cocoanut, Cochin	25/0/0	25/10/0
Do. Ceylon	22/15/0	0/0/0
Palm, Lagos	23/10/0	0/0/0
Rapeseed, English pale	25/10/0	26/0/0
Do. brown	24/0/0	0/0/0
Cottonseed ref.	19/5/0	0/0/0
Oleine	21/10/0	22/10/0
Lubricating, U.S.	4/10/0	5/10/0
Do. refined	5/0/0	10/0/0
Tar—Stockholm barrel	0/19/0	1/0/0
Archangel	0/12/6	0/0/0

TENDERS.

[Communications for Insertion under this heading should be addressed to "The Editor," and must reach us *not later than 12 noon on Thursdays.*]

BEDFORD.—For erecting stores, stabling, coach-house, &c., and chimney-shaft at Horne Lane Brewery, Bedford. Messrs. Usher & Anthony, architects, Bedford:—

T. Spencer	£2,595	S. Foster	£2,344
S. Freshwater & Sons	2,446	W. Hayles (accepted)	2,285

[All of Bedford.]

BRISTOL.—For erecting stables and depot at Horfield, Bristol, for the Bristol Tramways and Carriage Company, Ltd. Mr. Joseph Kincaid, engineer, 11, Great George-street, Westminster, London. Messrs. Corderoy & Selby, surveyors, 19, Queen Anne's Gate, Westminster:—

E. Walters	£6,750	Love & Wait	£5,419
G. H. Wilkins	6,620	Reed, Blight, & Co.	5,136
R. Wilkins & Son	6,490	Cowlin & Son	5,083
Stephens, Bastow, & Co.	5,749	A. Krauss (accepted)	4,700
A. J. Beaven	5,420		

BROMLEY.—For additions to Rose Cottage, for the Rev. H. A. Soames:—

T. W. Jones, [Be]ckenham (accepted) £296 0 0

COLCHESTER.—For the erection of a "Friends' Meeting House." Mr. Brightwen Binyon, architect, Ipswich. Quantities by Mr. W. Thornicraft, 6, South-square, Gray's-Inn:—

Runnacles	£2,015	Dobson	£1,788
Orfeur	1,893	Dupont	1,744
Grimwood	1,835		

CROYDON.—For the erection of brass and iron foundry in the Cromwell-road, Croydon, for Mr. R. W. Gillett. Mr. Henry Gough, architect, Bank-chambers, North-end, Croydon:—

M. Taylor	£1,249	A. Bullock	£999
D. W. Barker	1,233	E. P. Bulled & Co.*	995
E. J. Saunders	1,200		

* Accepted.

DERBY.—For cast-iron pipes, laying pipe-mains, &c., Lea and Holloway Water supply, for the Rural Sanitary Authority. Mr. Robert Argile, engineer, Ripley, Derby. Quantities by the engineer:—

Contract No. 3.—Supply of Pipes, Valves, &c.

Jas. Oakes & Co.	£691	6	8
Hughes, Mann, & Gotto	688	18	10
Butterley Company	635	0	0
Stanton Iron Co.	602	2	6
Clay Cross Company, Clay Cross (accepted)	559	0	5

Contract No. 4.—Laying Mains, &c.

T. Crump & Co.	827	12	2
Hughes, Mann, & Gotto	737	17	5
Jno. Taylor	654	0	0
J. W. Pearson, Holloway (accepted)	547	18	0

FELIXSTOWE.—For alterations and additions to "Anchorage." Mr. Brightwen Binyon, architect, Ipswich. Quantities by Mr. W. Thorncraft, 6, South-square, Gray's-Inn:—

Runnacles	£919	Thos. Ward	£899
Grimwood & Sons	918		

LONDON.—For the erection of cider-stores, dwelling-house, and boundary-walls, &c., situate in Butcher-row and White Horse, Ratcliffe, London, E., for Mr. Henry Symons. Mr. Charles Dunch, architect, St. Clement's House, Clement's-lane, E.C. Mr. James F. Westry, surveyor, 294, Romford-road, Forest-gate:—

Jefford	£7,180	E. Triggs	£5,524
Nightingale	6,490	G. H. Martin & Co.	5,383
Stephens, Bastow, & Co.	6,149	Perry & Co.	5,374
Jerrard	5,985	Harris & Wardrop	5,344
Munday & Sons	5,803	Trappitt & Batley	5,030
Calnan & Co.	5,625	Norman Phillips	4,889
Scharien & Co.	5,643	J. H. Johnston	4,646

LONDON.—For new sewer in Filmer-road, Fulham, for the Vestry of the Parish of Fulham. Mr. James P. Norrington, C.E., Surveyor:—

Tomes & Wimpey	£245	R. Mullett	£219
S. Saunders	230	E. Parry	218

LONDON.—For rebuilding the "Gosset Arms," Bethnal Green. Messrs. T. & W. Stone, architects:—

R. Edwards	£2,230	Jarvis & Sons	£1,884
Higgs	2,184	Thomerson & Son	1,884
Wire	1,943	Hughes	1,705
Beale	1,888	Young	1,549

LONDON.—Accepted for alterations and additions to No. 3, Ennismore-gardens, S.W., for Mr. S. Bennett:—

Greatorex & Co., Ltd., 11, Stanhope-terrace, W. .. £598 0 0

LONDON.—For rebuilding premises, Nos. 216 and 217, Upper-street, Islington, N., for Mr. T. R. Roberts. Mr. J. Kingwell Cole, architect. Quantities by Mr. Edward S. Mansergh:—

W. Brass & Son	£2,495	Dove Bros.	£2,345
J. Grover & Son	2,468	Drew & Cadman	2,337
Harris & Wardrop	2,370	B. E. Nightingale	2,298
G. S. S. Williams & Son	2,367	G. Neal	2,153
S. Chafen	2,356		

LONDON.—For making certain alterations to Mr. R. Sefer's premises, High-road, Kilburn. Mr. Reginald O. Wills, architect and surveyor, 51, Willesden-lane, N.W. :—

S. Barnet	£880 0	T. Pessell	£567 11
F. Colwill	840 0	W. H. Pryor	550 0
C. Shire	690 15		

LONDON.—For alterations and additions to the Guardians' Offices, Bancroft-road, Mile-end, under the superintendence of Mr C. F. Burden :—

C. B. Fenton & Co.	£750	R. Crow & Son	£455
Peirce & Co.	650	G. H. Martin & Co.	447
White & Son	635	A. S. Judd & Son	440
Hall & Co.	591	A. Martin*	405
J. H. Johnson	542	* Accepted.	

LONDON.—For erecting stables, "Bramington," Streatham. Mr. William Hunt architect, 5, York-buildings, Duke-street, Adelphi, W.C. :—

Charles Wall	£1,155	B. Nightingale	£1,076
H. L. Holloway	1,147	Holliday & Greenwood	1,047
Bovis & Co.	1,113	William Downs	1,022
Marten Wells & Co.	1,112	Somerford & Sons	998
Hill Brothers	1,110	Sydney Knight	998
Turtle & Appleton	1,085	Smith & Sons	983
Johnson & Co.	1,080	K. P. Bulled & Co.*	967

* Accepted.

LONDON.—For erecting additional office accommodation for the Infants' Department of the Earl-street School, Plumstead, and also for refitting the existing infants' water-closets, for the School Board for London. Mr. T. J. Bailey, Architect :—

J. B. Gerrans	£195	J. H. Hodgin, 66, Sandy-hill,	
W. H. Lorden & Son	155	Plumstead*	£127

* Recommended by the Works Committee for acceptance.

LONDON.—For fittings and machinery to public wash-house and laundry, Hornsey-road, N. Mr. A. Hessell Tiltman, F.R.I.B.A., architect :—

	Contract No. 1.	No. 2.	Total.
Clements, Jeakes, & Co.	£2,556 10 0	£946 0 0	£3,502 10 0
J. Fraser & Co.	1,872 0 0	796 12 0	2,668 12 0
Z. Berry & Son	1,807 0 0	748 10 0	2,555 10 0
J. & F. May	1,717 0 0	710 5 0	2,427 5 0
Thomas & Taylor	1,620 8 0	669 13 8	2,290 1 6
T. Bradford & Co.*	1,540 15 0	656 6 6	2,196 1 6

* Accepted.

Contract No. 1 includes washing-box' metals, drying-closet, and supplies. Contract No. 2 includes machinery.

LONDON.—For the erection of Providence Baptist Chapel, Hainborough-road, Streatham. Mr. Harold Griffin, architect :—

Hammond	£529 0	Barlow & Roberts	£475 0
Jenkins	497 0		

LONDON.—For new jeweller's shop window, at 72, Westbourne-grove for Mr. B. K. Smart :—
Spreckley (accepted) £300 0 0

LONDON.—For fitting up new premises at 225, Regent-street, W., for the Crown Boot Company :—
Charles Spreckley, President-street, Goswell-road* £715 17 0
* Accepted.

LONDON.—For alterations and additions, for Mr. George Wright, Brandon Lodge, Clapham park :—
T. Potterton, Walham (accepted) £450 0 0

MAIDSTONE.—For sewerage work, at Boxley-road, for the Urban Sanitary Authority. Mr. W. G. Scoones, C.E., Borough Engineer, Maidstone :—

J. Neave	£269 0	G. Candler	£146 0
C. J. Slade	243 0	J. C. Trueman	140 0
J. Farrow	190 10	J. H. Bridge, Maidstone*	129 0
W. Coker	169 10	* Accepted.	

MAIDSTONE.—For the construction of sewers, &c., at Fant-lane, for the Urban Sanitary Authority. Mr. W. G. Scoones, C.E., Borough Engineer, Maidstone :—

C. J. Slade	£545 0	G. Candler	£316 0
J. Neave	450 0	J. C. Trueman	303 0
Hope & Freeman	379 7	Springett & Son, Maidstone*	275 10
J. Farrow	360 0		
W. Coker	333 0	* Accepted.	

PAIGNTON.—For new lodge, alterations of chapels, &c., at cemetery. Mr. W. J. Wyatt, surveyor :—

R. Harris	£512	Rabbich & Blown	£458
Webber & Maunder	473		

REDRUTH.—For alterations and additions to the "Commercial Hotel," Camborne, for the Redruth Brewery Company, Limited. Mr. Jas. Hicks, F.S.A., architect, Redruth :—

Jas. Julyan	£1,370	W. H. Stevens, Penzance*	£1,200
Pooley	1,207	* Accepted.	

ROCHESTER.—For the erection of six cottages, Queen's-road, Snodland, for the City of Rochester Land and General Investment Company, Limited. Mr. J. W. Nash, architect, 7, Medway-terrace, Rochester :—

J. Lee	£1,213	M. C. Fenton	£927
R. Langridge	1,112	E. G. Brown	189
E. Norman	1,030	J. Wilford, Snodland*	900
W. F. Bishop	1,017	* Accepted.	

ROMFORD.—For the erection of new School, for the Hornchurch School Board. Mr. B. C. Allain, architect, Dashwood House, New Broad-street, E.C. :—

A. Brown	£3,965	Treppitt & Batley	£3,333
J. Baxter	3,972	J. Webb	3,247
A. Kellett	3,886	T. Henty	3,295
H. Booth	3,785	G. Grimwood & Sons	3,244
French & Ethelwood	3,683	Martin & Co.	3,253
Hitchin	3,497	H. J. Carter	3,157
W. Watson	3,481	J. H. Johnson	3,127
W. Wallis	3,397	Hammond & Sons*	2,785

* Accepted.

SWANLEY.—For the erection of villa residence and stabling, for Mr. F. Annoots :—
T. W. Jones, Beckenham (accepted) £1,050 0 0
[No competition.]

TRING.—For erecting chapel in cemetery and boundary walls, for the Tring Local Board. Mr. W. Huckvale, architect :—

Richardson	£3,197	Payne	£2,247
French & Co.	2,827	Pincher	2,080
Fawy	2,789	Smith & Son	2,080
G. H. Martin & Co.	2,593	Honour & Son*	1,961
Webster & Cannon	2,390	* Accepted.	

WEST HAM.—For 8,500 yards of wrought-iron fencing on the top of the Metropolitan Northern Outfall sewer, West Ham. Mr. Lewis Angell, Borough Engineer :—

J. G. B. Marshall	£4,610 0 0	H. Pynegar	£3,667 10 0
Jukes, Coulson, & Co.	4,520 10 0	D. Rowell & Co.	3,602 6 0
Metal Supply Co., Limited	4,500 0 0	G. B. Smith & Co.	3,584 1 10
W. Brettell	4,210 0 0	W. Bain & Co.	3,535 4 0
Murdock & Cameron	4,171 0 0	A. & J. Main & Co.	3,515 1 5
J. Turner	4,139 0 0	Johnson Bros. & Co.	3,420 0 0
Brownlie & Murray	4,041 0 0	J. Davies	3,403 8 4
Morton & Co. Lim.	4,023 10 0	W. Hayward & Sons	3,240 0 0
Economic Fencing Co.	3,867 15 0	Bayliss, Jones, & Bayliss	3,191 11 1
E. C. & J. Keay	3,881 8 4	W. Longbottom	3,155 5 0
M. McVey	3,760 0 0	Hill & Smith, London (accepted)	3,068 16 0
J. Priest & Son, Limited	3,703 15 0		

WEST HAM.—For erecting Free Libraries, Canning Town, West Ham. Mr. Lewis Angell, Borough Engineer, architect :—

Reed, Blight, & Co.	£9,989	Kirk & Randall	£8,874
J. Holland	9,483	Perry & Co.	8,843
A. Kellett	9,121	Gregar & Son, Stratford*	8,787
Allen & Sons	8,938	F. J. Coxhead	8,733

* Accepted.

WINCHMORE HILL (Middlesex).—For rebuilding the "Green Dragon" Hotel, with stables, coach-house &c., for Mrs. Parkin. Messrs. George J. Skipper & F. W. Skipper, architects, Opie-street, Norwich :—

Holliday & Greenwood	£3,063 0 0	Patman	£2,647 0 0
Walker Bros.	2,893 0 0	Whyman	2,622 19 9
Shurmur	2,887 0 0	Ivory	2,573 10 0
Anley	2,808 0 0	Todd	2,494 0 0
Cornish & Gaymer	2,783 0 0	Hood	2,306 0 0
Youngs & Son	2,675 14 6	Goodall (accepted)	2,281 0 0

London and South-Western Bank, West Norwood.—Messrs. G. E. Bryan & Son, of High-street, South Norwood, write to say that in the list of tenders for this job on p. 196 of our last number, there were two mistakes. Firstly, their name was erroneously given as "Lyon & Sons"; and secondly the amount of Mr. Carmichael's tender was 1,475*l.*, not 1,575*l.*

SUBSCRIBERS in LONDON and the SUBURBS, by prepaying at the Publishing Office, 19s. per annum (or 4s. 9d. per quarter), can ensure receiving "The Builder" by *Friday Morning's* post.

TO CORRESPONDENTS.

Y. & M.—A. J. G.—R. J.—M. & Co.—"Gainsborough" (we cannot go out of our way to find answers to such question).—R. J. T. (thanks; not desired).—C. H.

All statements of facts, lists of tenders, &c., must be accompanied by the name and address of the sender, not necessarily for publication.

We are compelled to decline pointing out books and giving addresses.

NOTE.—The responsibility of signed articles, and papers read at public meetings, rests, of course, with the authors.

We cannot undertake to return rejected communications.

Letters or communications (beyond mere news-items) which have been duplicated for other journals, are NOT DESIRED.

All communications regarding literary and artistic matter should be addressed to THE EDITOR; all communications relating to advertisements and other exclusively business matters should be addressed to THE PUBLISHER, and *not* to the Editor.

TERMS OF SUBSCRIPTION.

"THE BUILDER" is supplied DIRECT from the Office to residents in any part of the United Kingdom at the rate of 19s. per annum PREPAID. To all parts of Europe, America, Australia, and New Zealand, 26s. per annum. To India, China, Ceylon, &c., 30s. per annum. Remittances payable to DOUGLAS FOURDRINIER, Publisher, No. 46, Catherine-street, W.C.

The Builder.

Vol. LXII. No. [illegible] — Saturday, March 19, 1892.

ILLUSTRATIONS.

Design for Proposed Gallery of British Art.—Mr. Sidney R. J. Smith, Architect .... *Double-Page Ink-Photo.*
Staircase, 191, Queen's-gate, South Kensington.—Mr. F. G. Knight, Architect........ *Double-Page Ink-Photo.*
Brasses in Sussex: William Fienles, Knt., Hurstmonceaux: William de Etchingham, Etchingham.—From rubbings by Dr. Fairbank, F.S.A. .... *Double-Page Photo-Litho.*
House on Stanmore Park Estate: Messrs. Goddard, Paget, & Goddard, Architects .... *Single-Page Photo-Litho.*
House, "Mountfield," Chislehurst, Kent.—Mr. W. Harber, Architect .... *Single-Page Photo-Litho*

Blocks in Text.

Comparative Outlines of Proposed British Gallery and Some Existing Buildings Page 226
Sedan-Chair.—Designed by Robert Adam 127
Proposed Thoroughfare, Strand to Holborn: Plan by Mr. F. M. Simpson ....Page 229
Diagrams in Student's Column: Heating by Hot Water 231

CONTENTS.

he Competition for the Birmingham New General Hospital .. 217
eam-Rolling on Main Roads........ 218
otes 219
rchaic Compared with Archaistic Sculpture 222
gypt Exploration Fund 224
emonstrations on Greek Sculpture at the British Museum.... 225
rchitectural Societies 225
urrey Archæological Society 225
roposed British Gallery 226
nterior of House, Queen's-gate........ 226
wo Sussex Brasses........ 226
ouse, Stanmore Park Estate........ 226
Mountfield, Chislehurst, Kent 226
Design for Sedan-Chair........ 226
London County Council........ 228
Building Exhibition at Islington 228
Sanitary Inspectors' Association 228
"Proposed Thoroughfare—Strand to Holborn" 229
M. Chipiez's Model of the Parthenon 230
Coke-Breeze Concrete 230
The Royal Commission on Labour 230
Payments on Contract 230
Halifax Model Dwellings Competition 231
Varnish 231
Student's Column.—Warming Buildings by Hot Water. XII. .. 231
Surveyorships 231
Obituary 231
General Building News 232
Stained Glass and Decoration........ 233
Foreign and Colonial 233
Miscellaneous........ 233
Meetings 234
Recent Patents 234
Some Recent Sales of Property 235
Prices Current of Materials........ 235
Tenders........ 235

he Competition for the Birmingham New General Hospital.

HE insanitary nature of the surroundings of the existing General Hospital at Birmingham has been generally acknowledged, and the removal of the establishment to a more convenient and central site, and t the same time to one that would be ore healthy, has occupied the atten- on of the Hospital authorities for some e. A generous bequest by the late Miss lands, of the sum of 25,000*l.*, upon the ndition that within five years of her cease proper and permanent accommo- tion for the whole of the in-patients the Hospital shall have been provided a new site, and the liberal dona- ns of the people of Birmingham, have abled the Committee to take immediate ps to provide the stipulated wards prior to e expiration of the five years, some time in 94, at an estimated cost for the building of out 80,000*l.* The acquisition of a site at would be suitable for a Hospital, d at the same time central, was no sy task, but it is a matter of congra- lation that such a good one has been tained. The new site lies at the back of e Victoria Law Courts, and is bounded on e south-east by Steelhouse-lane, and on the er sides by Whittall-street, Weaman's- v, and Loveday-street; its shape approaches it of a square, and it has an inclination m south-west to north-west, producing a nsiderable gradient. A fine open space unds the site on the north-west. A portion the site at the corner of Steelhouse-lane d Whittall-street has not yet been acquired, d this has affected the disposition of the ildings. At the present time workshops d small dwellings occupy nearly the whole ce, and the removal of these will shortly commenced.

The engagement of Mr. Alfred Water- e, R.A., as consulting architect and essor insured that the conditions would be complete and explicit as possible, and that the award would be satisfactory, and one that would be generally endorsed. The accommodation required in the new buildings as scheduled may be briefly summarised thus:—Total number of in-patients 304, of whom 117 will be in two male and two female medical wards of twenty-four beds, and two separation wards to each, and a half-sized twelve-bed ward, and one separate ward to accommodate thirteen children; 156 patients will be provided for in three male and two female surgical wards of twenty-four beds, and two separation wards, each with a half-sized twelve-bed ward, and the separation ward to accommodate thirteen children. In addition to these, eight patients must be provided for in a half-sized ward for six gynæcological cases, with two single-bed separation wards. A half-sized ward for severe burns, to contain twelve beds, and a separation ward, will accommodate thirteen patients, whilst a small ward for septic and delirious cases will accommodate ten more patients, making up the total of 304.

It is stated that seventeen invitations to compete were issued, and that complete sets of designs were received from the following twelve architects:—Mr. W. Henman, Messrs. Worthington & Elgood, Mr. F. B. Osborn, Mr. Brightwen Binyon, Messrs. Dempster & Heaton, Messrs. Dunn & Hipkiss, Messrs. Cossins & Peacock, Mr. W. Doubleday, Mr. William Hale, Messrs. Bateman & Bateman, Mr. Ewen Harper, and Mr. W. H. Bidlake. The report of Mr. Waterhouse was made on Tuesday, March 8, and awarded the first place to Mr. Henman, and the second and third to Messrs. Worthington & Elgood and Mr. F. B. Osborn respectively. The drawings of the whole of the competitors were privately exhibited in one of the reception-rooms of the Council House on Wednesday, Thursday, and Friday of last week. A considerable diversity of opinion appears to have existed in the minds of the competitors as to the proper position for the principal entrance and frontage, and each frontage has found favour with some one or more of the competitors. There are points in favour of each, but we are inclined to think that Mr. Henman has chosen the right position in placing the main entrance in Steelhouse-lane at a point where the roadway is fairly level, and a slight angle occurs in the boundary. Here Mr. Henman has placed his entrance-gates and porter's-lodge leading into a quadrangle, with buildings upon three sides. The end of the administrative block faces the street, and on the left is the building, which contains on the ground floor the board and committee-rooms, and wards above. A covered cloister connects this building and the one on the opposite side, and crosses the front of the administrative block. It was required that one entrance should serve both in and out-patients; that out-patients should have access to the dispensary and thence to the street, and that a separate corridor should allow the in-patients to reach the hospital. This entrance for patients Mr. Henman places on the right-hand side of the entrance quadtangle. The block of buildings at the angle of Steelhouse-lane and Loveday-street accommodates the out-patients' waiting-hall, &c. To briefly explain the disposition of the blocks, it may be stated that a main corridor runs through the centre of each, from south-west to north-east, parallel with Weaman's-row; the nurses' home occupies a separate block facing Whittall-street. The lecture-theatre is at the east-end of the corridor facing Loveday-street. The main corridor passes through the administrative block, and the rest of the wards lead right and left, as will be further explained. The laundry and pathological department occupies a separate building facing Weaman's-row, immediately at the back of the administrative block, and this block has wards on each side of it. A septic ward block also faces Weaman's-row, and is at the end of the gynæcological ward, which will be further described.

The patients' entrance from quadrangle shows a vestibule, with space for splints and ambulance and porter's box on one side, with a consulting-room on the other, to which badly-mutilated cases can be carried without exposure to the gaze of patients in the waiting-hall.

The waiting-hall, which it is intended shall be also occasionally used as a recreation-room, is lighted from a clearstory, and is surrounded by a ring of top-lighted retiring-rooms in connexion with an outer ring of top and side lighted consulting-rooms, with lavatory accommodation. At the west corner of the hall an exit leads into the quadrangle, and an adjacent door opens into a waiting-room to the dispensary, which occupies a position between this and the administrative block, and is chiefly top-lighted. A separate exit gives out-patients egress into the quadrangle, after calling at the dispensary. A short corridor connects the main corridor and the north end of the hall, and here are placed two wards for noisy patients. This corridor will be used for in-patients, and access to the wards on each floor will be gained by the lift in the administrative block adjacent to the main corridor. The lecture theatre at this end of the corridor has been mentioned. On the opposite side to the waiting-room a corridor leads to a twenty-four-bed male surgical ward block, which overlooks, and is parallel to, Loveday-street. This ward is rectangular in shape, with canted corners. Thirteen beds are placed on each side, with a window on each side of every bed. Angle turrets at the north end, separated from the ward by cross-ventilated lobbies, contain the patients' baths and water-closets, and the turrets are connected on the exterior by a balcony with a north-west aspect. A kitchen and two single-bed wards are placed at the other end of the ward. Continuing down the main corridor, a bath-room and water-closet are found on the right, and then the administrative block is reached. On the north of the corridor dining-rooms for the nurses, servants, and medical officers are placed in close proximity to the lift-room, communicating with the third floor of this block, where the kitchens for the whole establishment are placed. Mr. Henman has made a point of providing only two lifts, side by side, for goods and for patients, in this central position, and has also enclosed these in a service room, which prevents accidents to, and interference from, those using the adjacent corridor. It may be mentioned here that the entrance for goods is in Weaman's-row, and that carts will unload at the basement level of the administrative block, and stores will then be in a convenient position for immediate hoisting by the lift to the third floor kitchen. The upper floors of this administrative block are devoted to the medical officers' quarters in front, and the servants' and matron's quarters at the back. The third floor has the kitchen in front, and the carving and service rooms behind. Following the corridor the central block is reached; the front portion, or that to the south, accommodates board and committee rooms and general offices; these are reached by an entrance from the corridor to the quadrangle, which has been already mentioned, and here a waiting-room for patients' friends is provided adjacent. Above this portion, on the first and second floors, twenty-four-bed female medical wards are placed, with two single-bed wards, and patients' day-rooms at the north end. On the ground floor of this block, to the north of the corridor, two six-bed burn wards are placed, with corridor on the east side, and kitchen and a single-bed ward at the main corridor end; above these wards on the hrst and second floors are twenty-four-bed female surgical wards, each with two single-bed wards and a secretion-room. On the ground-floor corridor adjacent to this block, a sewing-room, linen and bedding stores are placed, and above this, on the hrst floor, the patients' chapel appears, with a small vestry. Only one block now remains between the nurses' house and that last mentioned; this has on the south two circular children's wards for twelve beds each, and to the north a six-bed gynæcological ward, with a small, carefully-devised, north-lighted, small operating-room. The main corridor then leads on to the house; but before reaching it, it is widened out into a spacious conservatory, which will serve as a pleasant oasis for the refreshment of nurses who are off duty, and convalescent patients. The main corridor is provided with through ventilation in several positions between the blocks, and, in addition, air space is provided at intervals by arching the wall over the roof of the corridor below. The staircases in this corridor are treated as separate chambers, cut off as much as possible, to prevent unnecessary draught. Two of the staircases have been carried up above the roof, and treated as water-towers. With regard to Mr. Henman's elevations we refrain from naming the style, though we may mention they have been described as free Classic, conceived in a Gothic spirit. They will harmonise well with their near neighbour, the Victoria Law Courts, and a certain impression is somehow conveyed by the design that the work of Mr. Waterhouse has received a certain amount of study. The elevations, however, are distinctly pleasing in their treatment, and there is every reason to expect that they will also look well in execution. The materials intended to be used are red brick and terra-cotta, and green slates.

Messrs. Worthington & Elgood, who have been awarded the second premium of 100*l*., have adopted a different disposition of their blocks of buildings. Though they have placed the main entrance in Steelhouse-lane, the frontage of the building has been brought out to the street line. A covered carriage-entrance leads to a vestibule, with a short corridor running right and left. On the right the waiting-hall is reached, and around this are arranged the medical and other consulting and retiring rooms. The dispensary occupies a somewhat inconvenient position away from the rest of the building, and the patients who are to be admitted to the hospital from the consulting-rooms will have to retrace their steps against the stream of the incoming patients. On the left of the entrance a corridor runs at right-angles to Steelhouse-lane, and joins the main east and west corridor. The principal staircase is centrally placed at the junction of these two corridors, and communicates with the upper floors of the administrative block, which are arranged as officers' quarters and nurses' home. The kitchens are placed on the third floor. The arrangement of the nurses' home, incorporated with the officers' quarters and the other compartments of the administrative block, does not appear to be a good one. The gynæcological ward is placed in the block which runs back to the centre of Weaman's-row, and on each side are placed smaller blocks containing children's medical wards and wards for severe burns. The surgical and medical wards are placed parallel to, and facing, Loveday-street, and are separated by the main corridor, which terminates in a staircase at each end. The laundry has been placed on the south-west of, but distinct from, the main corridor, and abuts upon the block of old buildings. The number of lifts appears to be excessive. The elevations are treated in a Renaissance style, both Late and Free, and are kept studiously plain. The position of the tower, placed at an angle of the frontage to Steelhouse-lane, does not appear to be a happy one.

The design of Mr. F. B. Osborn, which has gained the third premium of 50*l*. value, differs in many respects from the others. A main corridor runs direct north-west and south-east from the centre of Steelhouse-lane to Weaman's-row. At the corner of the lane and Loveday-street the out-patients' block is placed. This block has a top-lighted waiting-room, surrounded by top-lighted consulting-rooms and retiring-rooms, some of which will necessarily be poorly lighted, owing to the position of the ward above. From this waiting-room a passage on the west leads to a second waiting-room adjoining the dispensary. For the removal of bad cases, a somewhat circuitous corridor leads into the main corridor, and is joined by a shorter corridor from the north side of the waiting-room for out-patients. Once the main corridor is reached, the wards are easily gained by the staircase in the centre or by the lift immediately adjacent thereto. On the south-west of the main corridor facing Steelhouse-lane, the administrative block is placed, and immediately behind this another block accommodates the dining-rooms and the kitchens above. The first and second floors of the administrative block accommodate the quarters of the officers and nurses on duty, and the third floor is devoted to maids' quarters and housekeepers' rooms. On the first floor on the south-east of the main corridor two femal[e] surgical wards of twenty-four beds are fol[-]lowed by the gynæcological wards, and th[e] children's ward at the corner of Weaman's[-]row and Loveday-street. Two female medica[l] wards of twenty-four beds each occupy th[e] north-west, with male medical wards abov[e] each. The lecture theatre is placed on th[e] main corridor, opposite the main stairs, an[d] the operating theatre above it. The nurses[']house occupies the west corner of the site, an[d] overlooks Weaman's-row and the open spac[e] beyond, but this gives a north-west aspect[.] The elevations show a Renaissance treatmen[t] of rather a severe aspect.

Of the remaining designs space prevent[s] any adequate mention, but it may be note[d] that design No. 4 has the entrance in th[e] centre of Weaman's-row frontage, which i[s] the least accessible to the city. Design No. [?] also favours Weaman's-row for the mai[n] entrance, and provides a quadrangle. Desig[n] No. 5 places the main entrance in Whittall street.

The award of the first place to Mr. Hen[-]man can be entirely endorsed, though w[e] fail to see sufficient reason for the award o[f] the second premium.

STEAM-ROLLING ON MAIN ROADS.

WE referred some time since* t[o] a report which had been com[-]piled for the County Surveyor[s'] Society by Mr. Heslop, the Count[y] Surveyor of Norfolk, and hoped that thi[s] might be an annual publication. We ar[e] therefore, pleased to see that this is, to som[e] extent, the case.† But it is only to a certai[n] extent, for the number of County Surveyor[s] who have, in 1891, supplied answers to th[e] questions circulated to them is considerabl[y] less than in the previous year,—*e.g.*, in 189[0] replies were received from forty-eight countie[s] against thirty-five in 1891. As there a[re] sixty-three County Council counties [in] England and Wales, it will, therefore, b[e] seen that Mr. Heslop's report relates to ve[ry] little more than one-half of this part of th[e] kingdom.

Nevertheless, there is very much in [it] which is most worthy of careful perusal, [as,] so far as it goes, it is an indicator, and t[he] only one, of the progress, or the want of [it,] which is being made in this important bran[ch] of public work. Not the least interesting a[re] the replies to the question, "Have you an[y] further information to offer as to cost an[d] desirability of road-rolling by steam or oth[er]wise?" Many of the County Surveyors ha[ve] either given no reply, or not one of any valu[e,] but it appears from the remainder that (*a*) [in] eleven counties the main roads are now stea[m-]rolled, and that the adoption of this meth[od] in those counties meets with general approv[al;] (*b*) in three counties steam-rolling is not y[et] practised, but is recommended; whilst (*c*), [on] the other hand, three County Surveyors a[re] doubtful of its advantage, or disapprove [of] it. These are as follows:—1. Hertford.—[I] still think that too much is expected from t[he] use of a steam-roller, and frequently roa[ds] made by its use are less able to bear hea[vy] traffic than roads formed without a rolle[r."] It is apparent, however, from what t[his] gentleman subsequently adds—"I am, how[-]ever, going to try the use of steam-rolle[rs] and horse-rollers on some of our main road[s"] —that his opinion is not based on any exp[e-]rience with respect to the main roads [in] Hertfordshire, and that he still proposes [to] experiment with that which has been una[ni-]mously condemned, viz., horse-rolling. [We] beg leave to doubt the value of the eviden[ce] on which this opinion about the comparati[ve] inability of steam-rolled roads to bear hea[vy] traffic may have been formed.

We will pass on to the report from t[he] North Riding of York. The County S[ur-]veyor here says, "I find that steam-roll[ed] roads wear to a very uneven surface, lum[py]

* The *Builder*, May 30, 1891, p. 423.

† Particulars of "Management of Main Roads [in] England and Wales." 1891.

.nd full of potholes." The experience of this .urveyor is not exceptional, but is generally lue, not to the use of the steam-roller, but to :arelessness or ignorance in the best mode of pplying it; in the arrangement of the metal which has to be so treated, in the want of udgment of the nature and treatment of the ubsoil, and in the quantity of water and inding material necessary. Where these oints have received the considerable attenion which is necessary, the defects above nentioned have disappeared. It is a business which requires to be learned, like all others, nd is successful if well done, but not therwise.

The third case of objection is that of Northamptonshire, whose Surveyor is very lecided, as follows: "Nothing further than his, that I will do my best to prevent steam r other rollers being used in my county. Abundant use of the rake, &c., is far better, nd considerably more economical, than any oller."

It will be as well before making any further omments on this matter, to quote one or two pinions from other counties, in diametrical pposition to those proceeding from the three ounties above named.

Kent.—"Experience proves beyond doubt hat the lengths of roads which were rolled ast season in those districts where the roller ad not been previously used, bear the traffic etter than the remainder not so treated, and he general public highly approve of the hange."

Westmoreland.—"I am a strong advocate or rolling by steam-power, and think it is in he long run a great saving of cost. In one ase, on a heavy-trafficked road, which reuired metalling every second year, it has tood five years."

Norfolk.—"The two 10-ton rollers worked y me have given every satisfaction, and have ffected a considerable saving in labour and aterials."

York (West Riding).—"All roads should be olled by steam-rollers. Horse-rollers are orthless. Having the supervision of 1,000 niles, I am decidedly of this opinion."

The actual cost of steam-rolling is not given n many cases, but is stated to be as ollows:—

heshire ...	1*l*. per day per roller.
hropshire.	18s. 8d. " "
ssex	1d. per yd. super.
orfolk ...	9d. to 1s. 1d. per yd. cube for granite.
ent	1s. per yd. cube for flint and limestone.
	1s. 3d. per yd. cube for granite.

There is no doubt that though there are rtain limits above and below which the st of steam-rolling never runs, it is not ery easy to generalise.

One of the most complete reports recently ade of the cost of steam-rolling has been at made by Mr. Allan Greenwell (the Surryor of Frome Highway Board) to his Board Somersetshire. The stone used, 6,000 bic yards, was nearly all mountain limeone, and the cost was 8·8d., or nearly 9d. r cube yard, or about ½d. per square yard. ach cubic yard sufficed for 17 superficial rds of road. Part of this work was on ain and part on district roads, and the work as carried on in the spring and summer. e roller used was 10 ton, with a width of ft. 3 in. He says:—"I believe that at least per cent. of material is saved as compared th stone worked in by the traffic; and, as gards labour, all after-raking is avoided, d scraping is reduced to a minimum. Exordinary instances in favour of steamlling have been furnished by the late severe nter. Materials which were laid in the tumn of 1890, but not rolled, were still consolidated in the spring of 1891, and the ste caused by the trituration under the ffic upon the frozen roads was so great as necessitate a further coating in that year. this coating had been rolled, it should have ted three years."

In connexion with this matter the imrtance of the use of a binding material is o very often overlooked, and it is well to recall the experiences of Mr. Deacon* at Liverpool:—

No. 1. 1,200 superficial yards trap rock took twenty-seven hours to roll and consolidate without any binding.

No. 2. 1,200 superficial yards ditto took eighteen hours to consolidate with trap rock chips from a stone-breaker.

No. 3. 1,200 superficial yards ditto took nine hours to consolidate with a binding composed of one-fourth macadam sweepings, obtained in wet weather, mixed with silicious gravel, from ⅜ in. to pin's-head size.

And he reported that No. 3 wore better than No. 2, and No. 2 better than No. 1, whilst the time taken for No. 3 was *one-third* that for No. 1. This points very clearly to the fact that it is an economy, as practised in Monmouthshire and some other parts of the country, to transport binding material as well as metalling on to the roads; and more especially is this the case where inferior metal, such as Kentish rag, is used.

But the point of all others which is to counties the most vital is the establishment of a correct system of management, and, therefore, we have perused with considerable interest the replies which this report supplies to the question, "Do you contract for the entire maintenance of any of your roads?" In analysing these replies, we find that after two years of County Council control, six different methods are at the present time being practised in these thirty-five counties, as follows:—

4 counties, viz., Leicester, Hereford, Northampton, and the North Riding of Yorkshire, contract with Highway Boards.

4 counties, viz., Hants, Oxford, Huntingdon, and the West Riding of Yorkshire work on agreed estimates between Highway Boards and County authorities, the actual cost of the work being paid in some, and perhaps in all, of these cases to the Highway Boards.

2 counties, viz., Salop and Wilts, contract for a portion of the roads with Highway Boards, and place the remainder under the direct control of the County Surveyor.

1 county, viz., Gloucester, contracts for labour only.

1 county, viz., Kent, contracts for the whole, partly with Highway Boards and partly with private contractors.

20 counties are under the direct management of the County Surveyor and his staff, and

3 gave vague or no replies.

—
35

It will be seen, therefore, how large a proportion have decided to adopt the policy which has on several occasions been advocated in our columns, viz.: the direct control and management of the main roads for the County Councils by an experienced professional man of satisfactory status, in preference to any form of general contract for maintenance.

The systems of Gloucester and Kent are in each case peculiar. In the former the contracts are confined *to labour only*, a method which meets with the decided disapproval of the County Surveyor. The County Surveyor of Kent, on the other hand, says that "the result has been very satisfactory." There seems to be something in connexion with contracts in that county which we do not understand, but it is certainly remarkable for roads to cost over 100*l*. per mile throughout a whole county, even for one in metropolitan proximity, and it must not merely be questionable whether the system in that county is an economical one, but whether the great satisfaction is real or imaginary.

Next to the system of direct control, that of agreement to repay Highway Boards the whole cost of the main roads seems the most sensible one, where those Boards have authority over large areas, or considerable lengths of main roads; but there are these strong objections to it,—firstly, that the Highway Board's surveyor, who executes the work under the County surveyor's specifications, has two masters,—his Highway Board and the County Council,—and, secondly, that one part of his work is paid for out of local rates, whilst the cost of the remainder is covered almost entirely by general taxation. We have treated this branch of the subject at greater length than we should otherwise have done, because we are satisfied that much public money is being wasted or misdirected in those counties where the *direct* system of control of main roads is not in force. There are other matters in Mr. Heslop's Report, especially those connected with footpath responsibility, and the working time of roadmen, which merit perusal, and we trust that he will receive general support in the compilation of complete returns from every part of the Kingdom, for the preparation of these annual reports, from which everyone should derive much benefit.

* "Proceedings Inst. C.E.," vol. lviii. p. 18.

NOTES.

WE print in another column a letter which Mr. W. H. White has been commissioned by M. Chipiez to write in answer to our remarks (pp. 114-115 *ante*) in regard to the inaccuracies of the Parthenon model made under his direction. M. Chipiez does not apparently attempt to question our statement as to the inaccuracy of the position of the metope sculptures, but asserts that the Americans must have made a mistake in putting together the model, which was sent over in pieces. As far as the metopes alone are concerned the succession of subjects is arranged, as he says, in accordance with Michaelis; but the series commences at the wrong end of the building; the series is right in itself, but wrong in relation to the pediment sculptures. Whether they were correct in the model as erected at the 1889 Paris Exhibition we cannot say, because though we visited that Exhibition two or three times, the model was not on view there till a late period of the Exhibition, subsequently to our visits. In regard to the entasis of the columns, M. Chipiez states that they were worked according to a photograph which showed fully that degree of entasis. This appears to amount to an admission both that the model was not made from measurements, and that M. Chipiez did, as we said, neglect English data which would have prevented this mistake. Owing to the partial decay of the upper parts of many of the columns, a photograph of the remains does at first sight produce the effect on the eye of a considerable entasis; but we have examined the line of the better preserved columns in a photograph which gives them about 6 in. height, and found the lines absolutely straight with a straight-edge, while a photograph of M. Chipiez' model, making the columns 3¾ in. high, shows a most decided and measurable curve. The actual curve is about half an inch in 31½ ft., which of course could not possibly show on that scale.* M. Chipiez is indignant with us for accusing him of indifference to British sources of information. We may ask him whether it ever occurred to him to test his work by the minute measurements given in Mr. Penrose's book on the Parthenon? If he had availed himself of that source of information as to the actual facts of the Parthenon design, instead of trusting to the general impression conveyed in a photograph, he would have saved himself from a palpable mistake (which he cannot in this case put off on the Americans), and would have been able to say that he had gone to the best source of information within reach, which he has obviously not done.

REPORTS had reached us that the Corporation of Manchester intended to alter the interior of Barry's building, the Royal Institution, in order to obtain more hanging

* We may add that the entasis is equally exaggerated in the model in the British Museum, but that is confessedly a much rougher piece of work.

room for the annual picture exhibitions, but it is only within the last few days that we received the information that the Corporation propose to do this by deliberately destroying the most original and characteristic feature of Barry's interior, viz.: the two colonnaded corridors leading from each side of the gallery of the central hall. It seems almost incredible that such a piece of stupidity should be seriously contemplated, and that too in the name of Art. Barry is our greatest architect since Wren, and his work should in any case be respected; but in this case the feature it is proposed to destroy is one of special elegance and originality. The two small galleries were designed for the exhibition of sculpture, for which they are admirably adapted, while the effect of the vista through them is a charming one, worth in itself a visit to the building. The additional space obtainable for hanging pictures by this piece of architectural destructiveness will be very small, but the important point to be noted is that the Manchester Corporation or their advisers seem totally blind to the fact that architecture is an art as well as painting; that art does not mean pictures (which is the popular idea of the matter) but all forms of artistic expression; that architecture is the monumental and central art on which all the others depend and around which they are grouped, and that to destroy the most artistic feature in the building in order to find more room to hang pictures is the most ludicrously illogical proceeding that can be conceived, and is opposed to common sense as much as to artistic perception. The proposed alteration will rob the building of an area for light and air which is very much wanted, will add very little to the picture-hanging space, and destroy the best feature of the architecture. If it is carried out, it will be a lasting discredit to the Manchester Corporation authorities, in regard to any claims to æsthetic perception, that they should have deliberately spoiled the work of a great architect on such illogical and inadequate grounds. No one has more interest in pictorial art than we have, but the idea that painting is the only art, and that everything else is to give way to hanging pictures, and architecture to be cut up or destroyed at pleasure with this object, is the idea only of people who are ignorant of what art really means.

THE meeting in the Chapter-house at Lincoln last Saturday, to which we referred last week, appears to have resolved on the demolition of Wren's Library without a dissentient voice. The scornful remark of one speaker that "in one case they had a specimen of the most beautiful period of Gothic architecture, and in the other they had a Palladian structure," is like going back to the days of the *Ecclesiologist*. Cathedral cities are usually about fifty years behind the rest of the world in their ideas, and Lincoln seems to be no exception to the rule.

THE great "stoppage" experiment in the coal trade is now being tried, and a great amount of unanimity prevails among the many thousand miners of this country on the subject. A very small proportion remain at work this week, and great pressure has been brought to bear upon the few who have not come out. Several collieries in North Wales at which the men had not given in their notices were visited by Federation agents last Saturday with the view of persuading the men to cease work. The attempt was only partially successful, and those who still persisted in remaining at work were threatened with expulsion from the Federation. Certainly many worse things might befall them, and perhaps some of the more far-seeing among their English brethren would be rather glad if they were likely to be punished in a similar manner. There is no disputing the fact, however, that the majority of the miners look upon the step they have taken as being a wise one; and consider that they will be able to resume work next week free from any apprehensions of a reduction in wages. They are exhibiting an utter disregard for anyone but themselves, and appear to think that they are now in a position to dictate what shall be done in regard to production, hours of labour, &c., independently of masters, or of any other interest whatever. The spasmodic inflation of prices, combined with the reduced output, will doubtless produce great temporary activity; but it cannot be long before things will find their own level again, and the loss sustained by the country in the meantime will intensify the demand for a reduction in the cost of fuel. The effects of the struggle will be keenly felt on the Tyneside, where much distress exists already in consequence of the protracted strike of engineers, which is still unsettled. There will doubtless be distress in many other districts, and certainly a great amount of inconvenience in all directions; but it is to be hoped that the fact that the greatest hardships are already falling upon the poorest classes, will have its due influence in bringing about a speedy termination of the dispute.

THE following are the members of the Royal Commission appointed to consider the question of metropolitan water supply: Lord Balfour of Burleigh (chairman), Sir George Barclay Bruce, C.E., Professor James Dewar, F.R.S., Sir Archibald Geikie, Mr. George Henry Hill, C.E., Mr. James Mansergh, C.E., and Dr. William Ogle, M.D., F.R.C.P. This is a very good and representative Commission, but the terms of the reference are not satisfactory. The Commission is only to consider—

"Whether, taking into consideration the growth of the population of the metropolis, and the districts within the limits of the metropolitan water companies, and also the needs of the localities not supplied by any metropolitan company, but within the watersheds of the Thames and the Lea, the present sources of supply of these companies are adequate in quantity and quality, and, if inadequate, whether such supply as may be required can be obtained within the watersheds referred to, having due regard to the claims of the districts outside the metropolis, but within those watersheds, or will have to be obtained outside the watersheds of the Thames and the Lea."

Thus apparently the most important question, viz. *where* London is to go for water if the supply has to be obtained outside the watersheds of the Thames and Lea, is outside the power of the Commission; so at least the wording of the reference would lead one to infer.

THOSE who are interested in the maintenance of open spaces and the prevention of the further overcrowding of buildings in London should turn their attention to the proceedings on the Bedford Estate, where there seems to be a fixed intention to turn every available corner of ground into money, at the expense of sanitary conditions. Lately some small houses facing Caroline and Charlotte streets, just south of Bedford-square, have been pulled down, and the longitudinal space between them, parallel with the south side of Bedford-square, is offered as a building lot, for the formation of a new street of houses between Caroline and Charlotte-streets. Not only will such a street crowd up the houses very much, and deprive the district of some much-required breathing space, but the operation must necessitate the cutting down of a good many trees now standing on the ground. To deprive the centre of London of any trees still remaining, unless under absolute necessity, is a piece of mischief which cannot be too strongly deprecated, and the policy of the Bedford Estate in these matters is both selfish and shortsighted, as it is not only spoiling the amenity and healthfulness of the neighbourhood, but reducing the value of the property in the effort to grasp every penny that can be made out of it. Surely some higher authority ought to have power to check this insanitary crowding up of London spaces by grasping ground landlords.

BY a clever *coup* the Prussian Governme obtained from the Budget Committee the Diet a resolution which recommends t House to vote ten million marks (sor 500,000*l.*) towards the expense of erecting cathedral at Berlin, and, as such recor mendations are mostly followed, Profess Raschdorff now has some chance of seei his design for the new "Dom" carried ou According to a report on the discussion th took place on the matter in the Budget Cor mittee, the Emperor will erect the cathedr and not the nation as such. The nation w only vote the money towards the erectio the Emperor's private Board of Works w manage all matters relating to the buildir and will also bear all responsibilities. T Government stated that on no account wou they at a future date ask the taxpayers f more money than the ten millions, and must hence assume that the Emperor w raise such extra funds as may be necessa For the German public the cathedral questi no longer exists,—the matter has becor distinctly distasteful to them. In art circl the feeling is not so much against the cath dral scheme, as such, as against the despo selection of the architect (a Court favouri and the adoption of a poor design on unpopular site.

FROM Berlin we hear also that the distrib tion of the Schinkel Medal and Travelli Studentships which took place on Sund last has, for once, after an interval of seve years, been a most satisfactory affair, and t in spite of the small number of candidat Architectural competitors were required send in a design for a "people's theatre," engineers were to send in designs for a bri over the Rhine between Cologne and Deu In both cases only two sets of drawi were submitted, but in both cases each pi of work was considered to be so satisfact that the assessors decided to give four med of equal value. The names of the two arc tects are O. Spalding and H. Heutrich. T medals were, as usual, given at the spe meeting which the Berlin Architekten-Ver regularly holds on Schinkel's birthday, this time the Minister of Public Works sented them in person instead of sendin representative.

IT was recently announced that the "Je salem" Exchange would be removed Tuesday last from Cowper's-court, Cornh to fresh quarters in Billiter-buildings. T is severed an old association, in resp of locality, with its quondam neighbo "Robin's," "Jonathan's," and "Garrawa in Change-alley, and the "Jamaica," in Michael's-alley. The last-named was reb from the designs of Mr. Banister Fletc architect, in 1885.* The "Jerusalem," wh is stated to have been established in 1 became a well-known coffee-house some y later, when coffee had been first made and in St. Michael's-alley; Aubrey says by Bowman, or, according to other accounts Pasqua Rosee, a Greek, "at the sign," his handbill, "of his own head." Unlike others, it retains its pristine character, hav for long formed a meeting-place for merch and shipowners connected with our So African, East Indian, and Australasian c merce. The subscription-rooms, and Jer lem-chambers, Cowper's-court, were buil 1879, after the late E. Bassett Keeling's desi A fire which broke out in the powder closet of Eldridge, wig-maker, in Exchan alley, on March 24, 1748, destroyed all coffee-houses we mention: "Tom's," "Rainbow," and the "Three Tuns," in C hill; with several others between Corn and Lombard-street, including the "Ge and Vulture," the "Pennsylvania," "Marine," the "Fleece," the "Swan," also the house in which Gray the poet born, and the London Insurance Office appears from a plan made by Thomas Jef in that year.

* See our "Illustrations" of September 19, 188

AT the Mart, on May 30 next, will be offered for sale the Rothley Temple estate, lying on the high road between Loughborough and Leicester, by a branch of the Soar, and near Charnwood Forest. It consists of 900 acres, with a total rent-roll exceeding 2,000*l*., that of the house included. In the house, which is built of stone, and was at that time the seat of his uncle, Thomas Babington, was born Lord Macaulay (of Rothley) on October 25, 1800. Adjoining it stands a small chapel, reputedly of the thirteenth century, a relic of the Templars' Commandery or Preceptory at Rothley. In 1086 the manor of Rosle or Rodolie, was held by the King. In 1230 Henry III. granted the manor and church together with Croxton Abbey to the Knights Templars, who had another settlement at Swinford, in the same county. On their suppression these possessions passed, 17 Edward II., to the Knights Hospitaller of St. John. At the Dissolution the preceptory was valued at 87*l*. 13s. 4d. in the MS. *Valor*, but Dugdale's assessment of Rothwell, Heather, and Dalby-on-the-Wolds preceptories (Leicestershire) amounts to 231*l*. 7s. 10d. nett.* In 35 Henry VIII. Henry Cartwright had a grant of the manor and advowson: he sold the former to Humphrey Babington, who, in 1567, bought the latter of Sir Ambrose Cave. Some exceptional jurisdiction, in both civil and ecclesiastical affairs, prevails throughout the Soke, as derived under Henry III.'s grant to the Templars, and which passed with the conveyance to Babington. In 1722 a Roman pavement, and some foundations of a wall, were discovered at Rothley.

SOME extensive re-building is about to be carried out at and near the southern end of Tottenham-court-road. The Association for Promoting the General Welfare of the Blind, founded in 1856 by the late Miss Gilbert, have cleared a large space for their new premises and workshops by the north-eastern corner of Tavistock-street, the ground butting on Morwell-street in the rear. The Horse Shoe" tavern and dining-rooms are be re-built after the designs of Mr. J. M. night, architect; the "Oxford" Music-hall, one of the earliest of the kind in London, d standing on the site of the old "Boar d Castle" posting-house,—is to be re-nstructed at a cost, we hear, of 27,500*l*.; d the "Flying Horse," together with me adjoining premises in Bozier's-court, to be demolished (Messrs. Saville & artin, architects). Our readers will perhaps member that the last-named quarter was arked for demolition under the first London ounty Council's scheme for widening this id of Tottenham-court-road, at a cost of ,900*l*. A committee recommended that the wners of houses on the western side of ozier's-court, which would then acquire ontages to the road, should contribute one-alf of the increased annual rental value for limited period, but their recommendation as rejected—see the *Builder* of October 10 st. The beneficial leasehold interest in the Oxford," together with the "Boar and astle," and Nos. 18 and 20, Oxford-street, as sold at auction in October, 1890, for 7,100*l*., the lease having then twenty years o run, and the ground rents amounting to 25*l*. per annum.

A GENEROUS offer, made by Sir John Lennard, Bart., lord of the manor, to ell his interest in West Wickham Common or 2,000*l*., considerably lightens the labours of the Bromley and District Commons and Footpaths Preservation Society. That Society, we gather, proposed to contest a threatened nclosure of the land. The area consists of 25 acres, whose value is tentatively computed as between 700*l*. and 800*l*. per acre, lying between Hayes Common and Coney Hall Farm, and not far distant from Croydon, Bromley, and Beckenham. It includes some finely-wooded hilly ground, together with some ancient earth-works. In response to an application for a scheme to secure the land for public enjoyment, the Board of Agriculture undertook to hold a preliminary inquiry to decide whether it falls within purview of the Metropolitan Commons Acts. The Board have now postponed such inquiry *sine die*, and it is to be hoped that the efforts promoted by Miss Octavia Hill, Mr. S. B. Bevington, Mr. Shaw-Lefevre, M.P., Mr. Israel Davies, and others to raise the necessary purchase-moneys will prove successful.

* See vol. vi., part 2, of the 1830 fol. edition. In W. Burton's "Leicestershire," 1777, will be found full details of the three rentals, as scheduled 46 Edward III.

WE may call attention to the useful work unobtrusively carried out by the "Society for Preserving Memorials of the Dead," one of whose recent meetings is briefly noticed in another column. The Society takes on itself the task of promoting the repair and preservation of memorials which seem in danger of being forgotten, neglected, or injured, and in so doing is carrying out (in accordance with its motto, "Patribus et Posteris") a work of reverence towards past generations and of usefulness, in a historical sense, for future generations.*

A CORRESPONDENT sends us the following extract from the *Kentish Gazette* of July 4, 1787, which, in connexion with the subject of strikes and combinations of working men, is worth reprinting as a curious illustration of the way in which these things were regarded a century ago, and of the progress of Liberal ideas since then:—

"TO JOURNEYMEN CARPENTERS.

NOTICE.

The Commissioners of the Canterbury Pavement, having taken into consideration the late combination among the journeymen carpenters for advance of wages, by which the public improvements intended to be made in this city, are very much impeded, do hereby give notice, that they are determined, at the next General Sessions of the Peace to be holden for this city, on Monday next, the 9th inst., to indict such of the said journeymen carpenters as do not in the meantime return to their work, all such combinations being contrary to law, and every person having entered therein by subscription or otherwise, is liable to be punished by fine or imprisonment, or both, at the discretion of the Court.

By order of the Commissioners,
JOHN HODGES, Clerk.

Guildhall, Canterbury,
July 4, 1787."

THE rage for architectural competitions seems in Australia to be passing all bounds of reasonableness. A Sydney building journal mentions the case of a man who has been advertising for competition plans and designs for "a mountain residence," not even offering a premium or binding himself to accept any design or employ any one of the competing architects. We have not quite got to that in England yet, though we seem on the high road to it.

THE exhibition of the Institute of Water-colours cannot be said to rank very high this season. There is the usual amount of commonplace and less than the usual amount of noteworthy work to redeem it. We may remark however in the first place that there is rather a large proportion of drawings in which architecture takes a principal part. Mr. Yeend King's small works, "Salisbury Spire" and "On the Bath Road" (20, 22) are very clear little pictures full of light; Mr. Alfred East in "Wet Weather" (30) gives the prominent place to a curious little roadside church; Mr. S. Graham Petrie has painted "Clivus Capitolinus, Rome" (57); Mr. Jules Lessore sends a large view of the "St. Mark's, Venice" (120) and the Piazza, broadly treated but dull in colour; Miss Louise Rayner sends what we call a topographical drawing of "High-street, Oxford" (130), correct but ineffective: Miss Walker's "Tomb of Richard II., Westminster Abbey" (131*) has the same kind of merit; Mr. Walter Tyndale gives a pleasant study of a quiet old building, "The Beguinage at Bruges" (133); Mr. C. E. Herne makes a fine study, on a large scale, but again somewhat prosaic, of the west towers of Westminster Abbey (168); Mr. Macquoid paints effectively "An Old Cloister, S. Pablo, Barcelona" (248); Mr. Yeend King again greets us with a brightly-treated little view of "Norwich" (388); Mr. Graham Petrie contributes a fine study of part of the Roman forum remains, one of the best things of the kind in the exhibition; Miss E. Rynd gives a carefully-worked but rather loaded view of the "Courtyard of the Palazzo Vecchio, Florence" (443); Mr. H. Pilleau the entrance to the Ducal Palace (447), a pretty but hard drawing; Mr. H. G. Hine a clever and real effect of "Ludgate Hill in Fog" (472); Mr. Lessore has a study of houses bordering "Tutton Pool, Plymouth" (504), and Mr. Macquoid a view of "Stokesay Castle" (709). Among works of special interest in a larger field may be mentioned Sir James Linton's one contribution, "Ah me, when shall I marry me" (407), a figure of a country girl, with more of character and less of decorative effect than is usual with this artist; "Harvest Time" by Mr. Leopold Rivers (121); "Arab Trophies" (255), a good bit of still-life, by Mr. S. B. G. Watkin; "Ammonites" (283), a study of the same class by Miss Kate Whitley; "His ain fireside" (284), a capital little painting of an interior with a Renaissance mantelpiece, by Mr. Fulleylove; "Carting sand, Hambledon Common" (19) by Mr. Jas. Orrock, a large landscape in a fine pure water-colour style, a little dead in colour; "On the Downs" (416) by Mr. E. M. Wimperis; "Pilgrims to Holy Island" (459), a characteristic scene by Mr. F. G. Cotman; "Evening Glow" (487) by Mr. J. M. Bromley, a large powerfully-treated landscape rather startling at first in its strong colour, but which is really a very truthful representation of a landscape under a rather unusual effect of evening light; and "On the River Arun, Sussex" (596), a fine landscape by Mr. C. E. Johnson.

* The Secretary is Mr. William Vincent, to whom communications can be addressed at the rooms of the Royal Archæological Institute, 17 Oxford-mansion, Oxford-street.

THE views of "The Tidal Seine" by Mr. W. H. Bartlett, now at the gallery of the Society of Fine Arts, form an interesting collection of views of the lower Seine, executed in a slight but broad and thoroughly artistic style. Some of the best are not on the Seine (visibly) but in field-nooks on its banks. The artist has in two of the drawings endeavoured to give a realisation of the remarkable feature of the river, the formidable "bore" that rushes up it at spring tides, a phenomenon so striking and unusual that any picture of it must be interesting, though we cannot feel that the effect is very powerfully given here. The quieter scenes are more successful; "Among the Willows, Vieuxport," which has a beautiful effect of sunlight; "A Lavoir on the Gertrude," with the village on the opposite bank framed in the opening of the washing hut; "On the Villequier Road;" "The Quarries, Yainville;" "A Silver Summer Morning," &c. The collection is well worth a visit both for its artistic and topographical interest.

AN interesting and clever Friday evening discourse was given at the Royal Institution last week, by Mr. F. T. Piggott, whose articles on Japanese decorative art in our columns a little while since, under the signature "F. T. P.," will be remembered by our readers. Mr. Piggott took for the title of his lecture "Japanesque," the word expressing the character of some of the English work done when Japanese art first began to attract attention here, and when it was thought that any kind of irregular throwing of sprigs on a plate or other object gave it Japanese character; an idea which perhaps is not quite extinct now in some quarters. Some of the illustrations of "Japanesque" of this kind were very amusing, and fully justified Mr. Piggott's criticisms. His claim for true Japanese art is that it shows a clear regard for proportion and contrast in the placing of decorative design, and a perception of the value of untouched spaces; that Japanese sprigs are not tossed anyhow on a surface, but exhibit a definite system of growth and design, which is of course perfectly true, and was illustrated in the examples shown. Some other conclusions of the lecturer we cannot so readily accept. He denies that the Japanese misuse landscape as decoration, maintaining that they only paint a landscape upon a plate instead of on a piece of canvas, and that it is "landscape" and not "decoration." The result to the eye, however, is the same, and we are still of opinion that landscape-painting is out of place on plates and trays. Mr. Piggott also pointed out that in decorating door-panels the Japanese do *not*, like their English quasi-imitators, begin a branch of tree on one panel and continue it on the next as if it had passed under the stile; they paint a picture the size of the two panels, and cut it in two, placing half in each panel, and the line of a tree or a hill commences on the second panel where it left off on the first, and is not continued by an imaginary line under the stile. This was illustrated by a picture of the eternal Fusiyama, treated in this way. The method is constructively logical, no doubt, but that does not prevent it from being pictorially clumsy. Some of the illustrations of Japanese design shown on the screen, however, were charming, and the library was filled with interesting pieces of Japanese work which formed a centre of attraction after the lecture. The subject of Japanese figure-drawing was wisely avoided, and the lecture was a complete success in the way of interesting an audience and giving them something to think of; but we fear it did not convert us to a belief that all the mystery of decorative art resides in Japan, and there only.

ARCHAIC COMPARED WITH ARCHAISTIC SCULPTURE:

ROYAL ACADEMY LECTURES.

Dr. A. S. Murray, F.S.A., Keeper of the Greek and Roman Antiquities in the British Museum, delivered the first of a series of three lectures on sculpture to the students of the Royal Academy on the 13th ult. He commenced by observing that the archaic age of Greek sculpture lasted, roughly speaking, from 600 B.C. to 500 B.C. There was no doubt much sculpture before 600 B.C., but it inclined rather to the primitive order. After the year 500 B.C. there was a period of perhaps fifty years in which many traces of archaism lingered on, but, broadly, it was between 600 and 500 B.C. that Greek sculpture passed through the stages commonly called archaic. Considering the archaic sculptors, with their love of minute observation in every kind of detail, and the graciousness with which their laborious accuracy was generally set forth, one was struck by the amazing contrast which they presented to the great age which immediately followed,—which, in fact, followed so quickly that the men who were greatest in the great age had been as youths trained in the archaic school. It was matter of conjecture whether the great age of Greek sculpture would ever have been but for the long period of elaborate painstaking which had gone before. But we failed to trace the transition, so suddenly did the new age burst forth in all the glory of Pheidias. The archaic sculptors were as men leading the way to a Promised Land which they must not enter. One or other of them might have had a precognition of what was to come, but as a rule the scope of all their thought and labour was the attainment of perfection within the particular manner and method in which they had been trained. When that perfection of manner and method was achieved, it was for a fresh generation to break new ground, and so it happened that in archaic sculpture we had a clear and distinct set of phenomena which might be studied apart, without reference to the subsequent age. They had to make a comparison between archaic sculpture on the one hand, and between a series of sculptures which at first sight seemed not to be different. The latter were called "archaistic," and perhaps the very slight difference in the form of the two words "archaic" and "archaistic" was not a bad indication of what they had to expect. Yet there was in the meaning of the two words a strong contrast. The Greek in which the New Testament was written was called "Hellenistic" because the writers were not Hellenes; but, not to cite further instances, the distinction was that "archaic" meant truly "old" while "archaistic" meant an "affectation of being old," the termination "istic" always implying imitation or affectation. They might demand to have some proof that there was such a thing as archaistic sculpture, however ready they might be to accept a stage of sculpture of that kind as a perfectly natural result of civilisation of Greece in later times. The lecturer pointed to a cast of a marble relief found in Athens, and representing the side view of a temple, in front of which, separated by a wall, were two figures, recognisable as Leto with her sceptre and Artemis with her torch. On the extreme left, behind Leto, is a pillar surmounted by a tripod; and when they compared that fragmentary relief with other reliefs of the same subject (there were several in existence) they found that the missing portion on the right had contained a group of Apollo Citharoedos receiving a libation from Victory: just such a group, in fact, as they saw in another marble relief in the British Museum, where Apollo Citharoedos was receiving a libation from Victory beside a temple. From the presence of a tripod on the fragmentary relief it was supposed that all these reliefs had been sculptured at the instance of men who had gained prizes in musical contests and who wished to commemorate their own success under the guise of a victory of Apollo. That would be consistent with the reverential feelings of the Greeks. But a special point in these reliefs was that the capitals of the temples were always Corinthian. It was plainly impossible that the sculpture could be archaic, since the Corinthian capital was not known until long after the archaic age. One of the earliest examples of the Corinthian order was the monument of Lysicrates at Athens,—the "Lantern of Demosthenes," as it used to be called,—and it was erected to commemorate a musical victory in the year 335-4 B.C. Between then and Roman times was the flourishing period of that order, and somewhere in that period the two reliefs mentioned would fall. If for no other reason than the architecture they could not be archaic, but they affected to be archaic, and, therefore, they must be called "archaistic." Incidentally, the lecturer pointed to the curious device of the sculptor in placing a high wall between the figures and the temple; what he wanted was, of course, a background for the figures, and nothing could be better than a wall. Most temples were enclosed by walls, and figures outside the walls would revive a familiar association of ideas. In a similar manner the sculptor of a well-known relief in the Museum, called the "Apotheosis of Homer," had chosen to hang a curtain in front of the columns of his temple. So, also, in another very interesting relief in the Museum, representing the visit of Dionysos to Icarios in Attica, there was a curtain stretched to form a background to the figures, and so far concealing the architecture behind. What the sculptor required in all these instances was a background. What the facts of the case required was a view of the interior of a temple or a house within which the scene was believed to be taking place. If we took the sculptor literally, the scene was quite outside the temple,—even outside the enclosing-wall. But he meant the temple to be taken as a sign or symbol of a locality where there was a temple within which such scenes were conceived to be enacted. In the case of these musical reliefs the Temple of Delphi seemed to be indicated by the presence of an omphalos and of a great plane tree in another of these reliefs. The lecturer next directed attention to a cast from a relief in granite which represented Hermes holding his caduceus and a lyre,—not that he was a musical god like Apollo, but he was inventive, and it was he who invented the lyre. He had thus a right to carry the instrument as a symbol. The relief in question was found at Canopus in Egypt, on the site of a temple erected there by King Ptolemy Energetes I. It could not therefore be olde[r] than the date of that king,—the second centur[y] B.C., and might be considerably later. Yet a[t] first sight it seemed a piece of archaic sculpture. The lowness of the relief, the way i[n] which the mantle was folded and pressed flat[,] the attitude of the figure, the shape of the head, the manner of rendering the hair, these were all points suggestive of archaic art. But that was only at first sight. Looking closer, we saw that the long piece of drapery was absurd and that the whole figure was decidedly imitative. These instances, selected from many would be sufficient to show that there did exist in the later age of Greece an actual school of archaistic sculpture. But how did that curious taste arise? We had to remember that in that later age Greek art was in the condition of having exhausted its creative faculties. It had expended them in the grandest fashion: still it had exhausted them. Its technical skill was unabated. Demands for new sculptures came thick and fast from the Roman conquerors, and perhaps those Romans might have spared some of the older sculptures of Greece if the contemporary Greek artists could have supplied them with works equally suitable to their taste. No one could justly say that the Greeks after the Roman conquest never made an effort to do something great,—to lash their jaded imagination, and to create a new school. The sculptures of Pergamon would be a contradiction. But the general fact remained, that after the Roman conquest the imaginative power of the Greeks was gone, while their technical skill and training were great. Artists in that condition would naturally have a keen sympathy for archaic sculpture. It[s] mannerism and methods were all within narrow limits. They could easily be appreciated. The trick could be acquired of imitating them with the same facility as contemporary poets showed in imitating Homer, and what added to the success of the new movement was that the Roman conquerors and patrons had a particular passion for archaic Greek sculpture. But it was only fair to the Greeks to bear in mind also that though the spirit which had pervaded archaic art was swept out of existence in the early part of the fifth century B.C. by the great wave of freedom which produced works like the sculptures of the Parthenon, yet a very considerable portion of those archaic sculptures remained in Greece to be seen of all men even down to the time of Pausanias. Under these circumstances the appreciation of works o[f] archaic sculpture would never wholly die ou[t]. Mr. Murray concluded his first lecture b[y] appealing at some length and in great minuteness to the evidence afforded on the subject b[y] painted vases and coins.

Mr. Murray delivered his second lecture o[n] the 18th ult. He said it would not take lon[g] to run over the various points which, accordin[g] to his light, distinguished the archaic from th[e] archaistic among the sculptures of which h[e] exhibited casts or drawings. Among the cas[ts] were two figures from the outside of a marb[le] cylinder which appeared to have been used a[s] a well-head or puteal, forming a sort of barri[er] round the mouth of the well. For its purpo[se] there was an obvious convenience in the lo[w] flat relief. If the work were archaic, the lownes[s] of the relief would be a simple matter of necessity, for nothing else was then known. B[ut] let them see whether the work was n[ot] archaistic. The marble puteal in question wa[s] found at Corinth and brought to this countr[y] by Lord Guilford in the early part of the prese[nt] century. It was placed in his house in [St.] James's-square, and was there seen frequent[ly] by persons interested in ancient art. A ca[st] was made and presented to the then Lord Abe[r]deen,—"The travell'd Thane, Athenian Abe[r]deen." From him the cast came to the Briti[sh] Museum. But meanwhile the original marb[le] had disappeared. What had come of it no o[ne] knew. The time came when Lord Guilford['s] house was sold. The new owner set to work [to] alter it greatly, but it did not appear to [be] quite certain whether he had acquired a rig[ht] to the sculptures in the house as well as t[he] house itself. There were other sculptures besid[es] the puteal. At all events the house seem[ed] to have been pulled to pieces a good deal, a[nd] the sculptures were no more heard of, with o[ne] exception. A few years ago the lecturer w[as] asked to look at an interesting Greek bas-reli[ef] in a house in Connaught-square. It turn[ed] out to be one of Lord Guilford's marbles, a[nd] was at once presented to the Museum. But t[he] puteal was still missing, notwithstanding creditable attempt which was made by the Hellenic Society some years ago to hear of it by circulating engravings which they had made from the casts. For the immediate purpose of the lectures this Corinthian puteal was a sort of test. The Hellenic Society, in publishing the engravings referred to, printed at the same time an article by Prof. Michaelis, of Strassburg, to whom they had sent photographs. Speaking of one of the figures known as Alcmena, he said (*Hellenic Journal*, vi., p. 48):—"The character of real archaism is still more apparent in the figure of Alkmena, the hard archaic treatment of whose drapery is scarcely to be recognised in the engravings. It strongly recalls some figures in the Thasos relief in the Louvre. On the whole, the photographs strongly corroborate the view of those scholars who would like to ascribe the marble, not to some late period of imitated archaism, but to an earlier epoch in which true archaic feeling began to be blended partly with a certain dawn of freedom, partly with a slight exaggeration of traditional habits." It would thus be gathered that there had already been a good deal of dispute about this Corinthian puteal. The subject, which extended around the whole surface, represented the gods going to the marriage of Heracles, the principal feature being a line of deities following one after the other, each carefully marked out by some special attribute, and each at a fair distance from the other, as would be seen in the casts exhibited. There was a suggestion of fear lest the deities might not be all recognisable unless their familiar attributes were clearly put forward: that did not look archaic by any means. Then we were struck by the amount of vacant space between and around the individual deities, which gave the design an air of parade—not to mention that it saved the sculptor from difficulties of composition, which a closer grouping of his figures would have caused. Further, there existed a number of reliefs on marble, which represented very similar subjects, and in a strikingly similar manner. These reliefs had been found in Rome; they occurred on bases or altars which from their shape belonged as clearly to the Roman age as anything that could be conceived; there never had been the least question about it. On these also the figures were wide-spread, eminding us of a line of columns; the relief vas low and flat; there was hardly such a hing as artistic composition in them; whatver composition there was was more of an rchitectural kind. There was a manifest inention to imitate archaic sculpture in details, ut an equally evident regardlessness of its pirit of design. What was true of these oman altars and bases seemed to be true also f the Corinthian puteal, and the lecturer ierefore considered it quite natural that any archæologists had considered the ulpture to be an archaistic work of oman times. If others, like Professor ichaelis, had thought otherwise, it was ecause they assumed that the true archaic age ad in its last days exhibited an "exaggeration f traditional habits," and because they left o wide a margin for these exaggerations. rof. Michaelis had compared these casts with e archaic reliefs from Thasos, in the Louvre. ut on examination the widest differences would e found. For example, to take the figure of ermes, with wings on his heels. Archaic sculprs knew that these wings were attached to andals, and did not grow out from the heels of ermes; they would never have allowed themlves to represent those wings in such a manner. he sculptor of the figure must also have nown that the wings ought to be attached o sandals; but he was probably afraid to put andals on the feet, lest by so doing he might ake away from what some would call the urism of his figure, but which we should call e affectation. Besides, the archaic curl of he wings told more instantaneously when not ttached to sandals, and the desire of the culptor was to get an instantaneous effect of chaicness. So, also, the drapery which fell ver the arms of Hermes had been planned and etched simply and solely for a pretty effect. he female figure, taken by itself, and ot, as it stood on the marble, in he middle of a line of ten figures, ad not much that was easily detected s archaistic. It was a much simpler matter o catch the archaic manner in a draped emale figure like that. But even then, how ifferent was the beautiful freshness and signiicance of every part of the Thasos reliefs. One could never see the originals in Paris without the deepest admiration, so sweet was the conception of each individual figure, and so true to that conception was the careful, assiduous, affectionate working-out of the details of drapery and form. Of the ten figures in the Corinthian puteal, three were male, the Hermes already referred to, then Apollo and Heracles. The lyre of Apollo was very conspicuous, as was to be expected; but when we came to Heracles, the sculptor had made quite sure of the recognition of the figure. A club or lion's skin would have been enough: he had given us club, lion's skin, bow, and quiver. The lecturer next proceeded to speak of another and unquestioned archaistic example,—a marble relief in the British Museum representing a female figure offering an oblation or sacrifice before a warrior, behind whom was his horse and attendant. On the top of the slab was a late Greek inscription commemorating certain men who had fallen in some battle. The battle was not specified, nor was the name of any particular man mentioned in the inscription. The writing was clearly very late, and it was equally clear that the monument was not the monument of one man, but a memorial tablet for a certain group of men who had fallen. The warrior with his horse and attendant was a type of those who had fought and perished. The slab being undoubtedly of a late date, it followed that the sculpture, so far as it professed to be archaic, must really be archaistic. It professed very much to be archaic. To consider the figure of the warrior, and to take just one point,—the way in which the lower part of his cuirass was rendered. Compared with fact or with true archaic art, it was an absurdity, a gross exaggeration; and yet, with its preciseness, and its truthfulness to the actual shape of a cuirass apart from its adaptability to the man who wore it, the cuirass might be archaic. The aim of the sculptor was first to get his cuirass exact, whatever happened to the man; and, secondly, by that and similar means to imitate archaic art, which he knew was always faithful in details. The horse was a great difficulty, and the sculptor was, perhaps, wise in his generation to show us only a part of the animal. Anything more wooden it was impossible to conceive. Horses and animals generally did not suit the archaistic sculptor, for they were the same, or nearly so, in all ages. They had no pronounced habits or peculiarities which could be caught up and made conspicuous, like the armour of men or the costume of women. In the costume of men and women in the archaic age there were certain points which were easily recognised. For instance, there was a love of long ends of drapery falling in characteristic folds of a zig-zag outline. Having dwelt upon the treatment of drapery in archaic sculpture, Dr. Murray concluded his second lecture by referring to the influence of the conquering Romans in promoting the production of archaistic Greek sculpture. We could not but feel, he said, that the imitation of archaic work must always have appeared more or less insincere to the Greek artists, however little able they might have been to produce anything original. The Romans had no such ideas. They had known archaic Greek work in its own day, and their hereditary love for it caused them to seek imitations of it. When the great ages of Pheidias, Praxiteles, and Lysippos were passing in Greece, the Romans were busy with their own affairs. When the archaistic revival occurred in Greece, it must have appealed strongly to the Romans, who, as fate would have it, just then acquired dominion over Greece.

Dr. Murray delivered the third and concluding lecture of this series on the 22nd ult. In the latter portion of it he returned to the archaistic manner of representing animals. In one relief they had already seen the fore-hand of a very feeble horse. But there was in the British Museum another sculpture which represented, in very low, flat relief, and with an obvious pretence of being archaic, a group of Castor holding back his horse; behind him was a dog. He might say "Beware of the dog!" but, bad as it was, it was not much worse than most of the dogs of true archaic art, and therefore its badness could not be cited alone as a proof that the work was archaistic, but only as being perfectly consistent with that being the case. Even in so fine an archaic work as the Harpy Tomb, there was a dog which, so far as he was visible at all, was little better than the one on the Castor relief.. But it was the painted vases which furnished the best examples of the feebleness of the archaic Greeks in the representation of dogs. Indeed, the Greeks never appear to have succeeded perfectly in their dogs,—a strange thing, considering how unsurpassed they were in most other animals. The dogs of modern Greece were very ferocious and unfriendly; they might have been so in antiquity also, and that might have led to negligence in the study of them. But even pet dogs, like that of the poet Anacreon, as we saw it on several of our painted vases, were rendered with an amount of feebleness which was unintelligible, side by side with the strong, confident drawing of the figure of Anacreon. Returning to the relief, it would be a fair inference to say that the sculptor could have made a much better dog if he had not been following a poor archaic model, making bad worse. The tail of the horse was a failure as a reproduction of the archaic manner. His mane was more like a frill than a true bogged mane, such as was seen in the Parthenon frieze. But here there was some excuse, because the bogged mane was rare in archaic work; a long, flowing mane was what was liked, as we saw in abundance on the painted vases. What struck one as curious in this relief was that a sculptor who was obviously desiring to produce an archaic effect should have taken the conception of his group from the Parthenon frieze, which had nothing to do with the archaic spirit. The figure holding back a horse was a conception which was first immortalised in the Parthenon frieze. But while retaining the Parthenonic element in the horse, the sculptor had added an archaic element in the figure of Castor. The design as a whole suggested a comparison with a slab of the west frieze of the Parthenon, where we saw a horseman on foot holding back a horse which reared with impatience to join the cavalcade in front. In that slab the horseman was standing at the off-side of the horse, and was thus partly concealed from view; but we could compare the manner in which the drapery flowed across his left shoulder with what was seen in the Castor relief. It would be observed that the mantle of Castor was represented in very low artificial folds, intended to look archaic, and that at the point where they had to cross from the shoulder to the background the sculptor had made them sink down immediately to the background, as if he had been afraid lest an appearance of thickness in the drapery just there would have been injurious to the effect of very low flat-relief which he desired to produce. It was a complete disregard of the true and natural movement of drapery in such an attitude. How different it was on the slab of the Parthenon. There, the left arm was extended in the same way; and the mantle, in a perfectly natural manner, was thrown backwards by the movement, and then rushed out into one of the most magnificent realisations that could be imagined of the thick folds of a mantle as affected by rapid movement. It was true enough that the Greeks, even in the good times, did not always pay due regard to the obvious effects of movement in such matters. In the Phigaleian frieze, for instance, there were many examples of drapery which, instead of following the movement of the figure, was made openly to adapt itself to a certain space which had to be occupied, even in defiance of the action of the figure. The lecturer next called attention to another cast from a marble relief in the British Museum, representing Heracles overpowering the Keryneian stag. The subject was common in antiquity, and as to this particular version of it, it had been disputed whether it was truly archaic, or only archaistic. Suspicions were aroused at first by the fact of its being placed within a frame obviously designed for some casual decorative purpose, and from its being altogether wanting in those true architectural mouldings which we should expect in earlier work. Some parts of the relief were modern restorations. But among other parts the neck and shoulders of the deer were ancient; and yet, could anything be more absurd than the rendering of them? It was the merest feebleness and imbecility. The body and head of Heracles were more carefully studied from earlier models; but if they were examined in detail it would be seen that they also were little better than a parody of true archaic art. Yet the whole composition and execution had passed for a time, among otherwise good judges, as "probably archaic," with just a slight reservation of doubt. In conclusion, Dr. Murray said that in these lectures he had tried to point out the differences that existed between archaic and archaistic sculpture. In most cases those differences were obvious enough. In regard to others, a certain amount of controversy still existed. He had thought it would be interesting if we could in some measure trace the origin of the archaistic movement in Greece in the third and second centuries B.C., and the reasons why the Romans, when they became masters of Greece, gave so liberal an encouragement to that movement. These inquiries bad often led them away from the actual works of sculpture to the consideration of such matters as the conditions of national life, or the characteristics of national literature in the two periods in question, in the hope of deriving some light from those quarters. He could only hope that those inquiries might not have been altogether unprofitable.

EGYPT EXPLORATION FUND.

THE fifth ordinary general meeting of the members of this Fund was held on the 11th inst. in the hall of the Zoological Society, Hanover-square. Sir John Fowler, the President, occupied the chair.

Mr. H. Grueber, the hon. treasurer, read his report, which stated that the balance-sheet would be found to compare very favourably with its predecessors, and even with that of last year. The favourable state of affairs was again due to the indefatigable labours and splendid organisation of the hon. secretary and vice-president, Miss Amelia B. Edwards; to the continued valuable and unremitting labours of the hon. treasurer for America, the Rev. W. C. Winslow; and to many individual members of the Fund. The total expenditure for 1890-91 was 2,547*l*. 15s. 4d. The total receipts for the same period were 3,092*l*. 18s. 8d., including subscriptions and donations amounting to 2,694*l*., 1,050*l*. being sent through the Rev. W. C. Winslow; and 100*l*. from the University of Philadelphia. He wished to draw attention to the fact that the Fund was now freely launched into a double undertaking,—viz., into that of survey as well as excavation. How successful the latter had been it was unnecessary for him to say, but he might add that the survey promised well to follow in its footsteps.

Mr. Mackrell, in moving the adoption of the report, said that it was not creditable that England should be almost outdone in its support of the work by America.

Mr. A. J. Woodhouse seconded the motion, which was adopted.

The President said that the first word he had to address to them was to express his and their deep sorrow and regret at the absence of Miss Edwards, and especially at the cause of her absence. Miss Edwards had been for many weeks dangerously ill, and he was sure they all hoped that she might be soon restored to health and strength. They had suffered great losses in the deaths of Sir William Gregory and the Hon. Russell Lowell. Proceeding to mention some of the work which their explorers had done in Egypt last season, he said that M. Naville had excavated the Temple of the Egyptian Hercules at Abnas, which he surveyed the previous year. He had found six granite columns, about 17 ft. in length, with palm-tree capitals. One of these, quite perfect, was now in the British Museum, and having personally seen and admired it, he (the President) could strongly recommend them all to pay it a visit, for it appeared to him to be one of the most perfect and remarkable Egyptian works he had ever seen. This column bears the names of Ramesis II. and his son Menaphtheb, the Pharaoh of the Exodus. The other five columns had been distributed amongst various museums. M. Naville had also found a granite colossal statue of Ramesis II., sent to the United States, also a large lion couchant, which had been sent to the Watt Institution, Greenock, and a red granite bust of Ramesis, sent to the Charterhouse, besides many valuable small objects which had been distributed. The Rock Temples of Beni Hassan and Elbesteh had been surveyed, the inscriptions copied, and the best of the wall-paintings reproduced. This important work had been performed by Mr. Newberry, Mr. Fraser, and Mr. Blackden. The whole of their united work would be brought out in two parts during the present year, and would undoubtedly be one of the most interesting and valuable publications of the Fund. In conclusion, the Chairman mentioned that Mr. Blackden, the artist (an Academy Student), had given his services gratuitously to the Fund.

A report by Miss Paterson, on behalf of Miss Edwards, having been read, a resolution was passed recognising the valuable services of Miss Edwards and Miss Paterson.

Mr. Percy E. Newberry then read a paper on the work of himself and his colleagues at Beni Hasan and El Bersheh, in the course of which he said:—I have been asked by the Committee to lay before you the report of the work done by the officers of the Archæological Survey of Egypt since it was started eighteen months ago, and to report to you that the great work which you have undertaken now rests on a solid basis. The general object of the survey was explained to you at the last general meeting in a paper by Mr. Griffith, the originator of the idea and the honorary superintendent of the work. The object was briefly this,—to catalogue, measure, and copy all the monuments which exist above ground in Egypt. The scheme was suggested by Mr. Griffith in 1889, approved of and referred to the Committee at the general meeting in 1890. The Committee considered the matter, and, in August, 1890, a sum of money was voted in order to enable me to study under Mr. Griffith and work out with him the details of the scheme. The details having been duly prepared, I started for Egypt early in November, 1890, and, on my arrival in Cairo, I was joined by Mr. Fraser, who had meanwhile been appointed engineer to the survey. On the 25th of the same month we left Minieh, and arrived the following day at Beni Hasan, the site agreed upon for our first season's work. The report of that work has already been published by me. . . . Mr. Fraser, Mr. Blackden (the artist who Joined the expedition in February, 1891), and I remained at work in the tombs of Beni Hasan until the early summer, when we returned to England. During the summer Mr. Fraser was engaged in drawing in ink the plans of the tombs at Beni Hasan; I meanwhile preparing for the photographer some 10,000 square feet of tracings which I had outlined in pencil at Beni Hasan. At the same time I also worked through the MSS. of Burton, Hay, and Wilkinson, preserved in the British Museum. Early in October Mr. Fraser left England for Beni Hasan, where he arrived on October 30, to complete his sketch survey of the tombs there, and on the 15th of the same month I followed, taking Paris on my way, to examine the MSS. of Champollion and Nestor de l'Hote. After making copious excerpts from these, I immediately proceeded to Egypt, and was joined at Alexandria by Mr. Howard Carter, a young artist whom the Society had engaged to assist me in tracing. We then proceeded together to Beni Hasan, and within three weeks Mr. Carter and I finished our work there, having traced some 2,000 square feet of painting. We then moved on to El Bersheh, and encamped in the ravine behind the Coptic village of Dêr en Nakhleh. At El Bersheh, curiously enough, only two inscribed tombs were previously known to Egyptologists. These were: the well-known tomb of Tahutihotep, containing the paintings of a colossal statue on a sledge being drawn by 172 men; and the tomb of Abanekht, inscriptions from which had been published by Professor Sayce in the *Recueil* about two years ago. Within a quarter of an hour of my arrival at El Bersheh, however, I had the good luck to discover ten more inscribed tombs, all of about the twelfth dynasty, and containing many lines of inscriptions. It is simply extraordinary that these should never have been noted before, as they all lay within 100 yards of the tomb of Tahutihotep, and six of them were actually on the same level. They had most of them suffered from the effects of an earthquake, which must have taken place before Coptic times, as on many of the fractures of the stones are painted Coptic crosses and inscriptions, which date from an early period. Several of the walls of the tombs here have fallen in, and been fractured into hundreds of pieces,—some weighing about a ton, others no bigger than a walnut-shell. The bigger blocks had to be carefully moved, and then I had, with Mr. Carter's assistance, to fit the smaller pieces on to the bigger blocks and then trace them. By this means I was enabled to restore many a picture and several important things. In one case I fitted together about thirty fragments, and restored a block about 1 ft. square, taking nearly half a day to do it. But I was well repaid for my trouble, as I found that the name of one of Tahutihotep's daughters was inscribed upon it, and, moreover, the name of one of the daughters we did not know of previously. By fitting up an innumerable quantity of fragments, and by the help of the inscriptions and paintings still intact upon the walls, we have been able to glean a goodly harvest from the El Bershed tombs, and withal a harvest which shows the importance of the scheme which the Society has undertaken. It is only by the most patient examination and study of the inscriptions and paintings that one can attain any really satisfactory result. . . . . The chief result of the past two seasons' work is, of course, that we have now not only plans of the tombs, and water-colour *fac-similes* of many of the most interesting scenes, but copies of the inscriptions and outline tracings of all the wall-paintings in the tombs at Beni Hasan and El Bersheh. The entire work of the past two seasons up to three weeks ago (with the exception of four of Mr. Blackden's drawings) is now before you. There are, as you will see, water-colour drawings by Mr. Blackden, plans by Mr. Fraser, photographs by Mr. Fraser and myself, as well as these rolls of tracings. The majority of these I pencilled in on the walls during my first season's work; and I reckon that there are here upwards of 14,000 square feet of tracing-paper covered with pencil outlines, 12,000 ft. of which at least I have done with my own hand. . . . Before concluding this part of my report, I ought to add that the sketch survey of the tombs and hill at El Bersheh is now being done by Messrs. Blackden and Fraser, and that it is hoped that it will be completed before the hot weather sets in. It is much to be regretted that we have not more water-colour drawings this season (we have only about an eighth part of what were done last year), but this is owing to the fact that Mr. Blackden has had to superintend the work of excavating and the sketch survey of the tombs. . . . . Making copies of the paintings and inscriptions at Beni Hasan and El Bersheh is not, however, all that I have done for you this season in Egypt. I have also explored the Nile Valley from Minieh to Kusîyeh, on the left bank, and from Zawyet el Mayyitin to Hawâta, on the right bank, and have noted all the mounds, place-names, and objects of archæological interest within that district,—a district abou forty miles long. No records of exploration o the left bank have been made since the begin ning of the century. Going down the Nile a far as Nezala Ganub, I struck to the wes through the town of Kusîyeh to a Copti village named Mûr. To the west of this villag is the Bahr Yusef, then a stretch of cultivate land. To the west of this, again, is a wide ex panse of sandy desert, traversing which on reaches the hills of the Libyan chain. Excavate in these hills due east of Mêr are tombs of th sixth, twelfth, and twenty-sixth dynasties. A few miles further to the north is the village o 'Awûga. To the west of this are tombs in th hills, and a very large cemetery at the edge o the desert,—a cemetery which extends north ward nearly as far as Bawit. North-west o Bawit are two uninscribed limestone quarries From Bawit to Minieh the hills are all sand choked, with the exception of a few cliffs eas of Derwa and Tuneh. At Gebel Tuneh is one of the boundary stelæ of Chuenaten, dated in the eighth year of that monarch's reign; Having explored the Libyan hills from Mêr to Minieh I then took a horse and explored the villages and mounds of the cultivated land At Daschlût, Hour, Derut en Nakhleh, and a few other villages are small mounds. The village of Gilga is built on an enormous mound one of the highest that I have seen in Egypt The mounds at Eshmunên, which mark the site of the Greek Hermopolis, are being dug away for sebâkh, and in a few years' time all traces of them will be as completely obliterated as the extensive mounds which are said to have existed opposite Beni Hasan. On the east bank of the river are remains of sixth dynasty tombs a Zawyet el Mayyitin and at Shekh Said; eleventh and twelfth dynasty tombs at Beni Hasan and El Bersheh; eighteenth dynasty tombs and monuments in the ravine behind the modern village of Beni Hasan, at El Bersheh, and further south at Tel el Amarna. Behind Dêr abu Hannes and Der en Nakhleh are enor mous limestone quarries in the hills, containing hundreds of Demotic graffiti of the time o Nectanebo, as well as many Coptic graffiti and paintings. In the *débris* below th tombs at El Bersheh and Shekh Said I also found a large number of stone chisel similar to those I discovered last year. It is probable that these boulder-chisels were used very generally in Egypt, but none have been recorded from other sites than those already mentioned. On December 21 I left camp early in the morning with Mr. Carter to visit Mr. Petrie at Haggi Qandil—a village situated about twelve miles south of El Bersheh. Returning along the hills the same evening, we fell in with a party of Bedawin. I had previously been making inquiries among the natives as to whether any tombs existed in the ravines some distance from the river. These Bedawin had heard of this, and their Shekh volunteered the information that he knew of a tourba, or tomb, some distance back and in the desert immediately east of Haggi Quandil. On my offering him a little bakhshish he promised to take me to the place. I then bargained with him to supply the necessary camels, and asked him to stay the night at our camp, so that he might not have the chance of giving us the slip, as Arabs often try to do. He stayed with me; and next morning, at sunrise, Mr. Carter and I, together with the Bedawee Shekh and four of his men, armed with guns and spears, started off into the desert for this "tourba." At four o'clock the same afternoon, after a hot day's desert ride, we sighted large masses of limestone and alabaster chips, and in less than half-an-hour were inside what proved to be, not a tomb, but the famous alabaster quarry of Hat-Nub,—the quarry to which Una went to cut the alabaster altar for his sovereign more than 5,500 years ago. This quarry was the most famous one of the ancient kingdom, and in it I found cartouches of Chufu, Mer-en-ra Pepi, and Nefer-Ka-Ra, as well as several short inscriptions.

The paper was illustrated by a number of water-colour drawings by Mr. M. W. Blackden, an Academy student, and tracings and genealogical tables by Mr. Newberry.

The President, in proposing a vote of thanks to Mr. Newberry, said that his paper was a clear indication of the immense value of the publication which would shortly be issued.

Mr. Stanley Lane Poole, in seconding, alluded to the patience and assiduity which Mr. Newberry had bestowed on the work, and to the exceedingly valuable records which he had rescued.

A vote of thanks to the President brought the proceedings to a close.

DEMONSTRATIONS ON GREEK SCULPTURE AT THE BRITISH MUSEUM.

MISS EUGÉNIE SELLERS began her sixth lecture,* which was the last of the series, by shortly summing-up the subject-matter of the preceding lectures, in which she has traced the development of Greek sculpture in relief from its beginnings in extremely realistic work, such as we find on the Harpy Tomb, through its later stages, in which increasing concessions are made to the principles of decoration, down to the sculptures of Priene, the last examples of pure Greek art, which ceased to exist before the combination of living forms into pattern was perfected.

The rest of the lecture was occupied with the examination of various sculptures in the Græco-Roman rooms, in many of which we have copies, or at least distant echoes, of the works of great masters. Such are the figures of a youth binding a tænia upon his head, which recalls Polykleitus, whose statues were made to conform to his canon of proportions; the disc-thrower, after the famous bronze statue of Myron, who is in the very act of swinging back his arm preparatory to the throw,—a momentary action, the representation of which was Myron's individual contribution to the art of his age, of which the frequent copies attest its popularity in later years; the slim figures of athletes which are echoes of the work of Lysippus, who aimed rather at the representation of Nature as it appeared to him than at the accurate reproduction of the anatomy of the human form; and, lastly, of the class of *genre* subjects, the figure of a boy pulling a thorn out of his foot, long thought to be Italian work, but now considered to be a copy of an early statue, to which parallels may be found in the homely scenes on the pediments of Olympia, pointing, perhaps, to a Peloponnesian school that affected *genre* subjects.

* For brief notes of the previous lectures, see *Builder*, pp. 141, 164, 184, 207, *ante*.

ARCHITECTURAL SOCIETIES.

DEVON AND EXETER ARCHITECTURAL SOCIETY.—The annual meeting of the Devon and Exeter Architectural Society, which is in alliance with the Royal Institute of British Architects, was held at the College Hall, South-street, Exeter, on Monday last. The President (Mr. E. H. Harbottle) occupied the chair, and, in the course of his address, observed that in the Associate section no names were yet enrolled, but seeing there was no lack of assistants and pupils possessing the necessary qualifications, no doubt this would soon be altered, especially if the society was enabled to offer some inducements to them. The forthcoming lectures should form an attractive commencement. He referred to the projected excursions by members for the purpose of visiting, as a body, architectural works of interest, and called their attention to a communication received from the Secretary of the Royal Institute of British Architects, on the subject of "Education in Non-Metropolitan Centres," in which reference was made to the efforts of the Sheffield Society to inaugurate a scheme of education in that centre. He fully concurred with the Secretary in the importance of the movement, and hoped that some such scheme might be inaugurated, with Exeter as a centre, for the south-west. Unfortunately, Exeter had not the educational advantages possessed by Sheffield, where, in addition to the School of Art, there was the Firth College, as well as a Technical School. In that town it was proposed to establish a studio affiliated to those institutions, and conducted by an efficient paid teacher or superintendent. In Exeter they must be content, for the present, at least, with a much lesser scheme by expanding as far as possible the combination of office instruction with that which might be gained at the Science and Art Schools.

EDINBURGH ARCHITECTURAL ASSOCIATION.—On the 10th inst. a meeting of this Association was held in the Architectural Hall, 42, George-street, Edinburgh. Mr. J. Balfour Paul (Lyon King of Arms) gave a paper on "Heraldry in Relation to Architecture," and, after referring to the views of Mr. Ruskin on the subject, he went on to state that the tomb of the so-called Earl of Essex in the Temple Church was the most frequently mentioned instance of early heraldry in Britain. He pointed out that it was perhaps not heraldic at all, and that the practice of bearing arms did not generally prevail in this country till the thirteenth century. In Scotland they found shields adapted to the purpose of mural decoration in the walls of Dundonald Castle, which dated from the fourteenth century, but it was not till considerably later that heraldic decoration became general. He exhibited examples of armorial lintels from Woodhouselee, Caxton Tower, Balconie Castle, Ancrum, and other houses. After describing the heraldic carvings of churches, he exhibited a fine series of armorial battlements from Harpley Church, in Norfolk, and also an interesting coat-of-arms from the Bridge of Dee at Aberdeen. Having specified the form of heraldic decoration in the interior of houses, he concluded his paper with some observations on the use and the beauty of heraldry as applied to architecture, and gave some practical hints to architects on the treatment of heraldic details. The paper was illustrated by lantern views, and at the close Mr. Paul was heartily thanked.—The Secretary read the following letter he had received regarding the proposed restoration of Linlithgow Palace:—"Her Majesty's Office of Works, 12, Whitehall-place, S.W., March 8, 1892. Sir,—I am directed by the First Commissioner of her Majesty's Works, &c., to acquaint you that the resolution of the Edinburgh Architectural Association, copy of which was forwarded with your letter of 16th ultimo, has been laid before the Board. As, however, the estimates for the ensuing financial year were closed before the resolution was received, it was too late to consider the matter further in connexion with the services of that year.—I am, sir, your obedient servant (signed), H. W. PRIMROSE." There was also read a letter from the Town Clerk of Linlithgow, expressing the desire of the Town Council to co-operate with the Association in approaching the Board of Works to have the amount proposed to be expended on the works increased.

LEEDS AND YORKSHIRE ARCHITECTURAL ASSOCIATION. — On Monday, Dr. Waite, of Wortley, delivered a lecture on "Some English Ecclesiastical Buildings." Mr. W. H. Thorpe (president) occupied the chair. Dr. Waite treated his subject chiefly from an historical and antiquarian point of view, but additional interest was imparted to the lecture by the exhibition of views of the principal cathedrals, abbeys, and priories of England, which were thrown upon a canvas through the medium of a lantern.

YORK ARCHITECTURAL ASSOCIATION.—At a meeting of the York Architectural Association, held at the Church Institute, on the 10th inst., Mr. W. G. Fenty, F.R.I.B.A., past-President, delivered the first part of a lecture on "Technical Education in Relation to Architecture and Building." Mr. A. Pollard, President, presided. A discussion subsequently ensued, and Mr. Fenty was heartily thanked for his excellent lecture.

SURREY ARCHÆOLOGICAL SOCIETY.

THE annual general meeting of this Society was held on Wednesday afternoon, at the offices, 8, Danes'-Inn, Strand, the President, Lord Midleton, in the chair.

Mr. Mill Stephenson, F.S.A., one of the honorary secretaries, read the thirty-seventh annual report, which, after referring to the meetings of the year, said that Part II., Vol. X., completing the volume of "Proceedings" was issued in August last. It contained several highly interesting papers, that on the "Early History of Battersea" being an important addition to local history. The first instalment of the "Catalogue of the Church Plate of the County" also appeared, and the catalogue would be continued in the succeeding parts. In carrying out this laborious task the Society was to be congratulated upon having such an energetic worker as the Rev. T. S. Cooper, one of the honorary secretaries. To those working at genealogy the extracts from the "Surrey Wills", and the continuation of the "Visitation" would be found of value. The volume for 1892 was well in hand, and would be issued in due course. An offer of a manuscript "Calendar of the Feet of Fines for the County of Surrey from Richard I. to Henry VII." had been made to the Council, on condition that it be published in a single volume complete. In order to enable the Council to publish that important contribution towards the history of the county, it was proposed to ask for authority to borrow from the reserve fund a sum not to exceed 80*l.*, the same to be repaid by yearly instalments of not less than 10*l.* per annum. It was proposed to issue the calendar free to all members whose subscriptions were paid up to date, the Council being of opinion that some recompense was due to the members for shortcomings in the past. The Council regretted the loss of a valued and active Member by the death of Mr. C. Vade Walpole, C.B. Mr. F. A. Crisp was elected to fill the vacancy. The following eight Members of Council retired by rotation, but were eligible for re-election, viz.: Hon. G. C. Brodrick, D.C.L.; Mr. J. W. Butterworth, F.S.A.; Mr. G. E. Cokayne, M.A., F.S.A.; Lieut.-Col. Davis, F.S.A.; Mr. E. Freshfield, LL.D., F.S.A.; Major Heales, F.S.A.; Mr. W. M. Molyneux; and Mr. Ralph Nevill, F.S.A. The number of Members is 317, viz.: Annual, 218; Life, 95; Honorary, 4. During the year 23 Members had been elected, viz.: 19 Annual and 4 Life. By death, the Society had lost 7 Members, viz.: 3 Annual and 4 Life; by resignation 12 members. Gain over loss, 4. The Society was again represented at the Third Conference of Societies in Union with the Society of Antiquaries of London, held at Burlington House, on Thursday, July 23. A summary of the proceedings will be found in the next part.

The report and balance-sheet having been adopted, and the President and Officers and Council having been re-elected, the meeting was made special for the discussion of the following resolutions, which were unanimously agreed to:—

I.—"That this Society undertake the publication of a Calendar of the Feet of Fines for the County of Surrey, from Ric. I. to Hen. VII., the MS. having been placed at the Society's disposal by one of its members, on condition that it is printed and published in a single volume."

II.—"That, in order to carry out this work, the Council be empowered to borrow a sum not exceeding 80*l.* from the reserve fund, the same to be repaid by annual instalments of not less than 10*l.* per annum."

A vote of thanks to the Chairman concluded the proceedings.

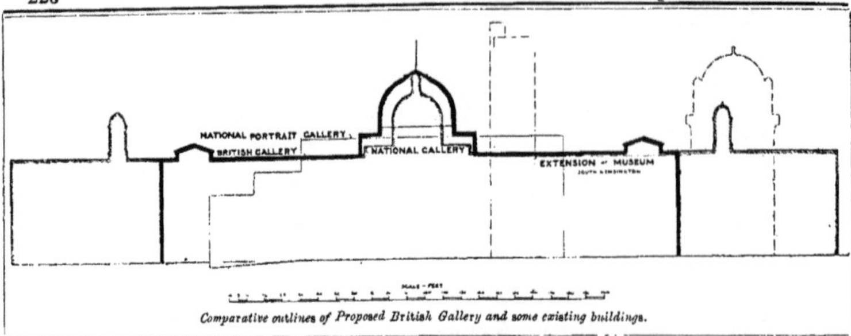

Comparative outlines of Proposed British Gallery and some existing buildings.

Illustrations.

PROPOSED BRITISH GALLERY.

THE view and plan published in this number illustrate the Art Gallery as proposed to be built by Mr. Henry Tate for a gift to the nation, together with his valuable collection of modern paintings, which offer (owing to the Government being unable to find a site) has been withdrawn.

All pictures would be brought in at the back of the building and under the large gallery, for which purpose a good receiving-room is provided, as also cleaning and store-rooms, lifts being in accessible positions to convey the pictures and sculpture to the principal floor; a tramway is also formed to convey the heavy works from one side of the building to the other, and to the lifts. There are also the private and public staircases; the latter continue up to the principal floor, and also to the first and second floors and gallery round Hall, and have at the sides lavatories for men and women: these are externally placed, and can be thoroughly well ventilated; corridors also on either side of staircases lead to special rooms.

The entrance to the principal floor is by a broad flight of steps, having figures on each side (which would be emblematic of Painting and Sculpture), into a large vestibule with offices on either side for the sale of catalogues, and umbrella counter; immediately adjoining this vestibule are covered corridors, in which seats could be placed.

The general entrance to the galleries is (after passing the vestibule) into a large arcaded hall, and with a gallery round. The roof over the hall would be a cupola glazed with ground and figured plate-glass, all the columns, walls, &c., being in British marbles; the floor in centre in large marble slabs, and the parts under the gallery in marble mosaic, and in the centre of the hall a basin and fountain. The hall and adjuncts would be exclusively devoted to sculpture, while the galleries round could be used for the exhibition of miniatures and other pictures.

Not more than two (or at the most three) varieties of marbles, with gold introduced into some of the principal positions, would form the decoration.

The picture-galleries themselves would not be much ornamented, but would simply be in decorative painting in the Pompeian style, and with a good warm colour for background of pictures. The wall-space for pictures (from floor to cove) is on an average 24 ft. high, and the skylights single (blinds being provided to regulate the light).

The floors of galleries would be of concrete, with iron girders, and the top surface finished with oak parquet, while the roofs would be of iron, and fireproof doors at places shown on plan to divide galleries into sections.

The number of galleries is as follows:—

Two 75 ft. by 40 ft.
Two 70 ft. by 35 ft.
Two 50 ft. by 35 ft.
Two 40 ft. by 40 ft.
Two 30 ft. by 35 ft. { These could be used as special rooms.
One grand gallery 130 ft. by 40 ft.

On the first floor is provided the gallery round the large hall, approached from two staircases, and with two galleries for pictures. On the first floor also is a council-room, secretary's office, cloak-room, lavatories, &c., while above would be two rooms for clerks.

As to the style of the building: Necessarily a picture-gallery must be top-lighted and practically on one floor; the only suitable style is Classic; refined mouldings with Greek feeling and ornament sparingly introduced, the chief study being to get good sky outline, proper massing, good proportion, and well-broken front, and carving and figures of the best character. Panels for suitable inscriptions are introduced, and the crowning feature (at the base of the cupola) is a bronze group of figures which would be illustrative of British art.

The building would have been faced with stone in two colours, with polished granite columns to the principal entrance.

A diagram is given showing the size of the building as compared with the National Gallery, National Portrait Gallery, and South Kensington Museum new proposed additions.

SYDNEY R. J. SMITH.

INTERIOR OF HOUSE, QUEEN'S GATE.

THIS is the hall and staircase of one of the two houses in Queen's Gate, illustrated in our issue of February 13th, which have been altered under the direction of Mr. F. G. Knight. A description of the work was given when the elevations were published.

TWO SUSSEX BRASSES.

THE two brasses of which we give representations are very fine specimens, and they have also an interest apart from their beauty.

BRASS OF WM. DE ETCHINGHAM.

Etchingham Church is of much interest to the archæologist. Mr. Sharpe, addressing the Archæological Institute at the Chichester meeting (Chichester Volume, 1856) said:—

". . . . The two finest examples of entire churches in Sussex (*of the Curvilinear period*, 1315-1360) are undoubtedly those at Etchingham and Alfriston; they belong both to the latter part of the period, but differ from one another considerably in their general design. Etchingham has nave with aisles, central tower, but no transepts and chancel; its windows have all their original tracery, of good but peculiar form; the chancel retains its original woodwork and wood screen,—its sedilia and piscina, all of considerable interest, as well as two fine founder's brasses. . . . ." The screen is now gone.

The two brasses Mr. Sharpe refers to lie in the centre of the chancel; one of them is the brass now represented. It lies immediately in front of the steps of the sacrarium. It is perfect with the exception of the head, which has been wrenched away, the hilt of the sword, and the canopy, which is all gone except one base. There is an inscription on a quadrangular plate below, and another, a semicircular one, over his head, which latter sets forth that: — "This William caused this church to be entirely,—*de novo*,—rebuilt in honour of God, and of the Assumption of Blessed Mary, and of St. Nicholas. The said William was the son of James de Etchingham, Knt." The inscription below states that he died about midnight,—*entour my noet*, —January 18, 1388. This inscription is useful in arriving at the date of the building.

THE BRASS OF WILLIAM FFIENLES, CHEVALER.

This is an extremely fine brass, and it has a perfect canopy. It lies in the floor of the chancel of Hurstmonceaux Church, immediately in front of the steps of the sacrarium. The inscription is peculiar in setting forth a promise of six score days' pardon for all who shall say a "Pater Noster" and an "Ave" for the soul of the deceased. The inscription is imperfect; the name and date only are given in the illustration.

The proof of age of this William Ffienles was taken at Worthing, December 6, 1378. Among the witnesses who remembered his birth, one knew the day because it was written in the Missal of the parish church,—an early form of "registration." Another because in that year,—1357,—Giles Parker struck an arrow through his leg in the churchyard of Hurstmonceaux. Another, because the father of the said William Ffienles, then lord of Hurstmonceaux, came to his house and wished to beat him.

There is also in the chancel of this church a fine canopied monument to a descendant of this Wm. Ffienles and his son. They were the lords Dacre "of the South." F. R. F.

HOUSE, STANMORE PARK ESTATE.

THIS is the second of a series of houses lately designed by Messrs. Goddard, Paget, and Goddard, of Leicester, for Mr. Frederick Gordon, Chairman of the Gordon Hotels Company. They are situated upon the Stanmore Park Estate, a new residential district in the neighbourhood of London. Five houses of varying dimensions and a pair of cottages have already been built upon the estate from the designs of the architects above named. On Dec. 12, 1891, the *Builder* published a drawing of "Montrose," the largest of these villas. "Evian House," the subject now illustrated, is of a smaller type; but the most has been made of the space at command.

Leicestershire bricks have been used throughout; those for the facing being wire-cuts from Heather. The tiles for the roof and wall hangings are from Messrs. Lewis's Works, at Cannock Chase. Mr. John Bentley, of Leicester, was the contractor, and Mr. Rees, the estate surveyor, has acted as clerk of the works.

MOUNTFIELD, CHISLEHURST, KENT.

THE above house is composed of red bricks with portions half-timbered. The dressing to windows, porch, &c., is Portland stone; parts are tile-hung, and the roof covered with red Broseley tiles.

The hall is oak-panelled and the ceilings to the reception-rooms are ribbed; casements and other windows are painted white.

The kitchen is placed in front, owing to the situation of the house, which faces nearly north.

The work was carried out by Mr. W. Willett, of Camden-park, from the designs and under the supervision of the architect, Mr. W. Harber.

DESIGN FOR SEDAN-CHAIR.

THIS very graceful design was made by Robert Adam for a sedan-chair "for the Queen": it is not apparent which Queen, as we have not the date of the design. It is engraved in "Works of Architecture, by Robert and James Adam," and we give it as a pendant to the notice and illustrations of Robert Adam's works published in our issue for March 5.

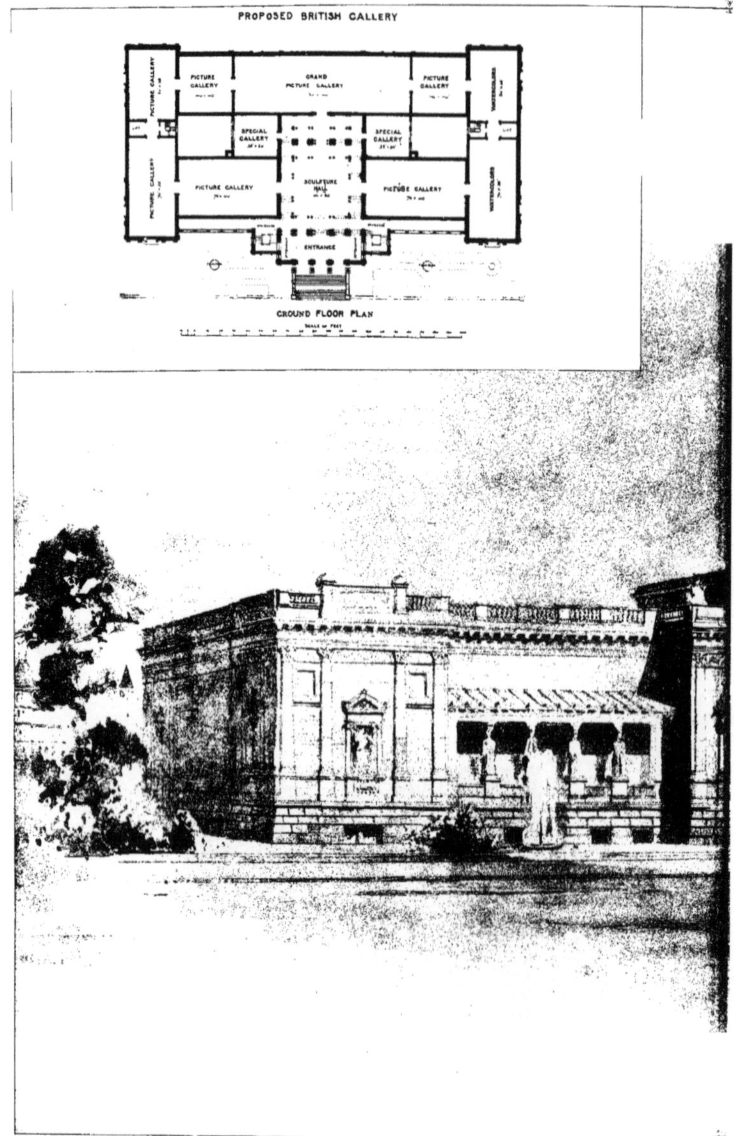

DESIGN FOR PROPOSED GALLERY OF BRI

-Mr. Sidney R. J. Smith, A.R.I.B.A., Architect.

House Yard
Kitchen
Scullery
Morning Room
Hall
Dining Room
Drawing Room
Ground Plan
Scale of feet

Scale
Pantry
Dining Room
Drawing Rm
Scullery
Kitchen
Bedroom
Bedroom
Bedroom
Bedroom
Dressing Rm
Bedroom
Balcony
"MOUNTFIELD."
CHISLEHURST, KENT.
Wm Harber Archt

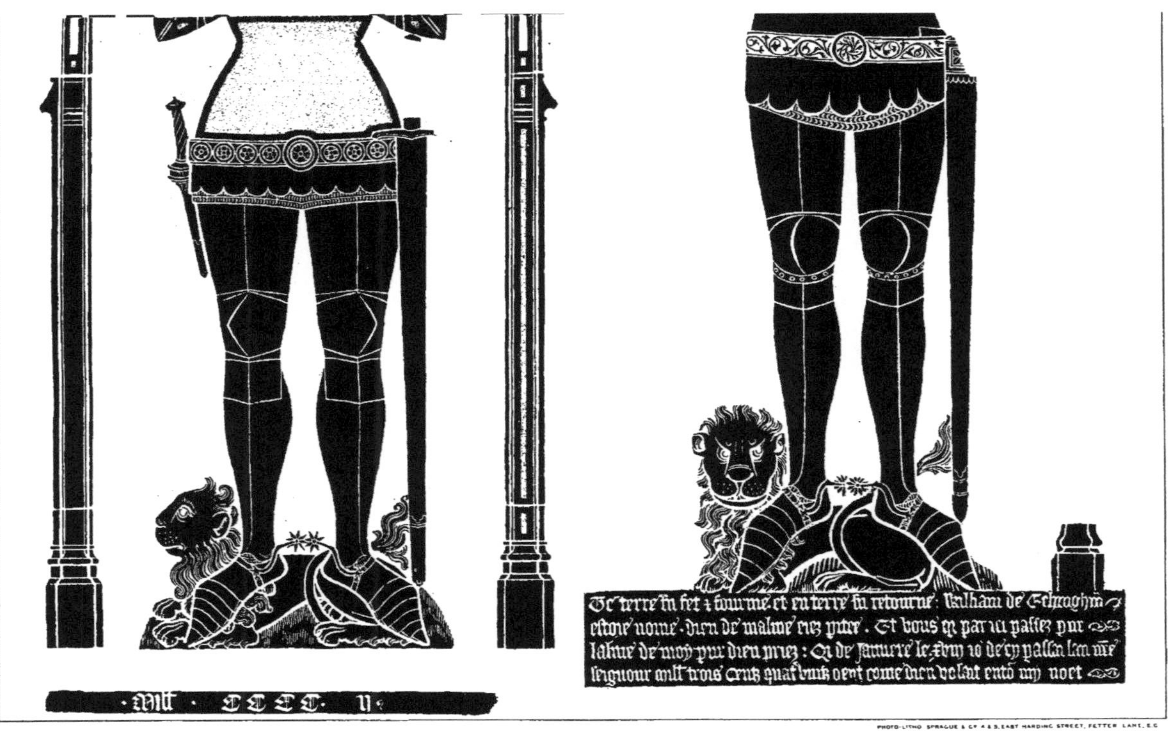

PHOTO-LITHO SPRAGUE & Cº 4 & 5, EAST HARDING STREET, FETTER LANE, E.C.

THE BRASS OF WILLIAM FFIENLES, KNT.,
HURSTMONCEAUX, SUSSEX.
One of the "Pardon" Brasses.

THE BRASS OF WILLIAM DE ETCHINGHAM,
ETCHINGHAM, SUSSEX.
Re-builder of the Church.

FROM RUBBINGS BY F. R. FAIRBANK, M.D., F.S.A., NOVEMBER, 1891.

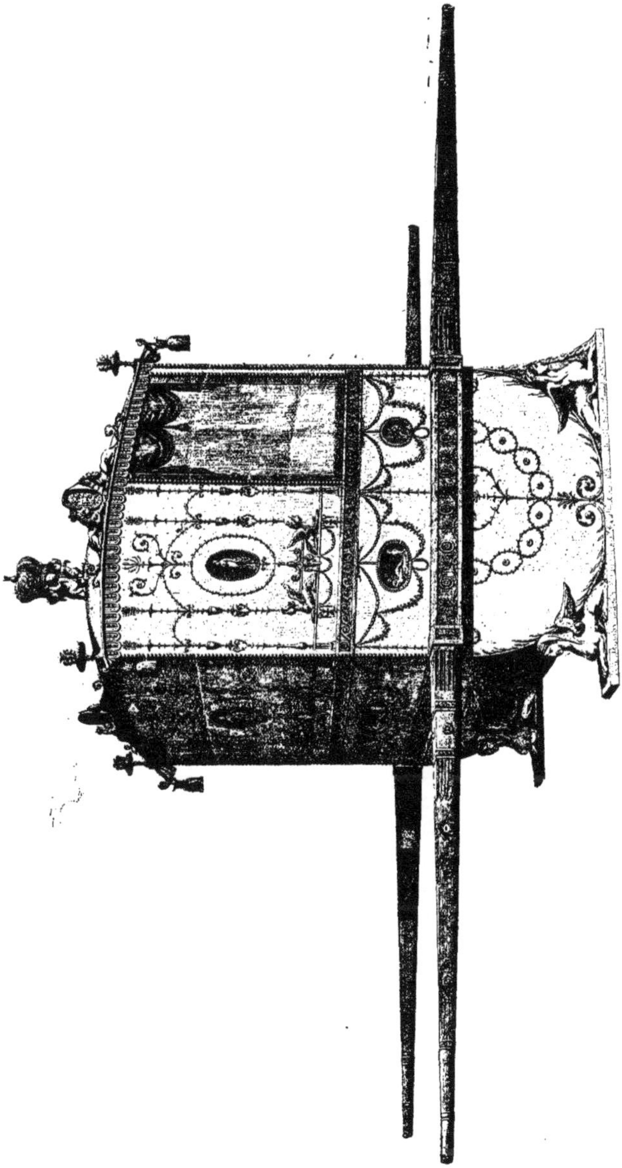

Sedan-Chair.—Designed by Robert Adam.

THE LONDON COUNTY COUNCIL.

THE first meeting of the newly-elected Council was held on Tuesday last, when Lord Rosebery was elected Chairman (although he only promised to hold the position for a few weeks); Mr. John Hutton (Chairman of the Building Act Committee in the last Council) Vice-Chairman; and Mr. W. H. Dickinson Deputy-Chairman, at a salary of 1,500*l.* a year, although notice was given by some of the members of their intention to move that the salary to be attached to this post in future shall be reduced to 1,000*l.* per annum. Mr. Dickinson, as Chairman of the Parks and Open Spaces Committee on the last Council, and in other ways, did good work.

The ten aldermanic vacancies were filled up, Sir John Lubbock and Mr. Beachcroft receiving the highest number of votes. Mr. Beachcroft is a "Moderate," but his work on the Housing of the Working Classes Committee, and on the Parks and Open Spaces Committee during the last Council made him an acceptable candidate to the "Progressives."

The remainder of the sitting was devoted to the consideration of the appointment of committees.

Now that the new Council is complete, it may be interesting to mention that it includes one architect (Mr. Walter Emden), five builders (Messrs. Holmes, Keylock, Marsland, Roberts, and Stevens), five engineers, and six doctors. The lawyers are, however, much stronger numerically than either of the professions we have named.

BUILDING EXHIBITION AT ISLINGTON.

WHAT is described by the promoters as "The Tenth Annual Building Exhibition" was opened, in the half-ready and confused state which seems a chronic weakness of such enterprises, on Monday morning last, but even on Wednesday evening it was not completely ready. The tenth exhibition of the kind held in the same building it may be; but it is not the "tenth annual" exhibition in the sense that such an exhibition has been held for ten consecutive years past. As we said on the occasion of the last two or three exhibitions,—which were egregious failures so far as they claimed to be properly representative of the building trades and allied industries,—the idea that such frequent exhibitions can supply any deeply-felt or widely-spread want seems to be played out. Such exhibitions, as we have before said, may be useful, and even desirable, occasionally,—at intervals of sufficient length to enable progress to be marked. But to be really useful they should be promoted on other grounds than are involved in the pecuniary benefit of the promoters. There should be a responsible and qualified Committee of selection, who would certainly not admit some of the things shown in the present exhibition. For example, there are two or three large stands taken up with broughams, Hansom cabs, and carriages of all kinds. Again, there are several stands occupied with furniture, which might have been more usefully replaced by exhibits of sanitary appliances, which are very meagrely represented. The present exhibition is undoubtedly a better one than the last two or three which were held, but it is not by any means up to the standard which it might attain under such conditions as those we have indicated. Not that there are not here and there a few novelties to be met with, but they need looking for. The great bulk of the exhibits are things which have been shown over and over again. The Exhibition does not by any means completely cover the ground floor, and it would have been far better and more convenient if the exhibits of the Polytechnic and People's Palace Technical classes, &c., had been placed in the vacant space available downstairs, instead of being relegated to the dreary desolation of the otherwise empty galleries.

It is not necessary for us to do more than to give a brief summary of the contents of the Exhibition, which we will for convenience group together according to their kind, without any reference to the numbering of the stands, which is incomplete, and therefore somewhat difficult to follow.

Messrs. Mark Fawcett & Co. show, at the end of the hall nearest the Islington Green entrance, a couple of sections, built up *in situ* full size, of their now well-known method of fireproof floor construction, the merits of which we were amongst the first to recognise. A recent improvement consists in ribbing or fluting the haunches of the tubular lintels, which are shown made in fireclay (in which material they are being used in the New National Portrait Gallery) as well as in ordinary clay.

The Patent Adamant Stone Company show specimens of their material in its varied applications. In the *Builder* for November 28 last we described this material, and detailed some experiments which were made with it at that time, so that we need not now say more about it. Messrs. A. C. W. Hobman & Co. show specimens of their "Clifton stone" mosaic paving, which has many useful applications, and has been laid in some of the London Board schools, for corridors, &c. Messrs. Fambrini & Daniels show what they call their "Excelsior Art" concrete. Whatever may be the excellence of the material, we will not pledge ourselves as to the "artistic" treatment of some of the specimens exhibited. Mr. E. Jarrett, as agent for Mr. Erik A. Gude, exhibits some columns of Norwegian granites, syenites, and labradorites, which are worth attention.

In the department of bricks, tiles, &c., Messrs. F. Rosher & Co. have a large display of Suffolk and other facing bricks, moulded bricks, copings, string-courses, tiles, ridges, garden vases, balustrades, &c. Messrs. Ellis, Partridge, & Co., have also a good display of "Redbank" pressed bricks and "Woodville" sandstocks, together with Broseley roofing tiles and Welsh slates. Messrs. Geo. Skey & Co., Messrs. P. & S. Wood, Messrs. Carter & Co., and the Lane End Works, Ltd., are exhibitors of decorative wall and encaustic tiles, &c.

Sanitary pottery is well represented by Messrs. Thomas Smith & Co., and by Messrs. Broad & Co. The exhibits of both these firms include a great variety of stoneware pipes, traps, inspection channels, &c., too numerous to mention in detail.

Architectural joinery and decorative woodwork is represented by Mr. F. A. Fawkes, who shows a pediment-headed door, a dado, and a chimney-piece and over-mantel; by Mr. S. Elliott, who exhibits some admirably clean mouldings; by Mr. Henry Bassant, who has a good display of parquetry; and by Turpin's Parquetry Company, who show, besides parquetry, a large carved oak chimney-piece and over-mantel. The Hand-Carved Wood Company exhibit a large collection of stock patterns of various carved features.

Plaster-work is represented by the Adamant Company, Limited, who show a small erection decorated externally and internally with their "Adamant" plaster; by Messrs. S. Wright & Co., who show their fibrous slabs, with cornices and other enrichments; and by Messrs. Robinson & Co., of Carlisle. As a key for plastering we may mention the production of the British Metal Expansion Company; and as a fireproof and sound-deadening material for packing the hollows of partitions there is exhibited the silicate-cotton or slag-wool exhibited by Messrs. Frederick Jones & Co.

Ventilators are well represented by Messrs. Baird, Thompson, & Co.; Messrs. C. Kite & Co.; the British Ventilating Company; Messrs. J. D. & W. Fryer (at Messrs. Walter Monnery & Co.'s stand); and Messrs. H. W. Cooper & Co.; the last-named firm exhibit glass louvre and hit-and-miss disc ventilators. As mechanical ventilators, we may mention the Blackman and the Wing disc fans, which are shown in motion.

Machinery in motion is exhibited by Messrs. Tangye, of Birmingham; by Messrs. M. Powis Bale & Co.; by Mr. E. S. Hindley; by Messrs. Thomas Middleton & Co. (who exhibit Murray's patent brick-making machine); and by Mr. S. Eddington (who shows brick-moulding machinery). One of the machines at work which attracts a great deal of attention is Moore's "Universal Carving Machine," which performs its work by means of a small reciprocating cutter revolving at a very high speed. The results attainable with this machine appear to depend upon the operator, but the effect is somewhat flat and tame, as there is no undercutting.

Glazing is shown in two or three varieties Those we noticed were Mellowes & Co.'s "Eclipse" glazing and Mr. S. Deards's "Victoria glazing."

Safety window-sashes and casements are shown in a variety of forms; among them we may name the "Brilloo," Denbeigh's, and Hough's; they all effect the same end by means differing in detail but not essentially in principle, and there is nothing very new about any of them that we saw. Sash-fasteners are too numerous to particularise.

Amongst miscellaneous exhibits we may mention Kemp's "Unique" water-closet, which is a very good form of the improved hopper closet, with direct flushing, the pan and trap being made in one piece. As far as we observed, Mr. Kemp is the only exhibitor of water-closets in the whole exhibition. Messrs. Durrans & Co. show their patent double-pointed nails, and their man-hole covers, &c. Messrs. E. H. Bayley & Co. show a very good tip-up dustmen's or scavenger's waggon, with top-covers arranged in a better way than any we have hitherto seen. Mason's stair-treads, excellent for their durability; Aspinall's enamel, always useful; Hamilton's brushes; Tilghman's sand-blast apparatus, shown in action engraving glass, granite, or other materials; and a large trophy of tools of all kinds shown by Mr. Nurse, are among other miscellaneous exhibits which we can do no more than mention.

The Harrison Patents Company show self-sustaining gear for hoists and lifts. Harper's new portable elevator or safety scaffolding, consists of a movable platform geared by toothed wheels into the sustaining angle-posts, and capable of being raised or lowered by a man on the platform working a winch handle. The apparatus appears to have a variety of uses, especially for internal decorative work, &c., as well as serving as a lift from floor to floor. It should certainly be seen by visitors to the exhibition.

The "Homacoustic" speaking-tube, shown by the company bearing its name, is certainly a marked improvement on the old-fashioned speaking-tube, with its faulty mouth-piece and whistle, always getting out of order, and its many other objectionable features. This invention should be seen and examined by visitors to the Exhibition.

We must not bring our notes of the Exhibition to a close without mentioning that Mr. W. H. Thompson exhibits, amongst other things, a patent appliance in the shape of a safety hold-fast for the jibs of cranes. Every one is now familiar with the huge Scotch cranes now used on every large building job, and numerous have been the serious accidents caused by the chain which holds up the jib suddenly breaking. The method which Mr. Thompson adopts consists of having an automatic pawl and ratchet arrangement at the head of the jib, which comes into play when the sustaining chain breaks, causing the load-bearing chain to become locked in the head of the jib, and thus holding it up. One of these safety jibs is now at work on the building for the Royal College of Music at Kensington, for which the exhibitor's father (the well-known "Thompson of Peterborough") is the contractor. This invention is certainly well worth the attention of builders and contractors; it has only just been made public.

The Exhibition will remain open until Saturday, March 26.

SANITARY INSPECTORS' ASSOCIATION:

ANNUAL DINNER.

THE ninth annual dinner of this Association (the first since its incorporation) was held on the 12th inst. at the First Avenue Hotel, Holborn. The President (Dr. B. W. Richardson, F.R.S.) occupied the chair, the vice-chair being occupied by Mr. Hugh Alexander, Chairman of the Council. Among the principal guests were Earl Fortescue, Professor Banister Fletcher, F.R.I.B.A., Mr. Thomas Woolner, R.A., Mr. J. Robbins, Mr. F. O. Crump, Q.C., Dr. Edmunds, Dr. Louis Parkes, Dr. George Reid (Stafford County Council), Dr. Lyon, Mr. Lewis Thomas, Mr. Bonthron, Mr. Macmillan, Mr. F. W. Lyon (L.C.C.), and other well-known sanitarians. In succession to the loyal toasts given by the President, that of "The Houses of Parliament" was proposed by Mr. Crump, and responded to by Earl Fortescue for both Houses, in the absence of Mr. J. J. Colman, who had been put down to respond for the Lower House. Lord Fortescue congratulated the Association on attaining to the dignity of an incorporated society, and on the fact that they appeared so well to comprehend and to apply the motto "Union is strength." He regretted to know that harmony did not always prevail among authorities charged with the care of the public health, and when members of local bodies,—either through ignorance, prejudice, or other motives,—set themselves against the reforming suggestions of the sanitary inspectors, they would have reason to feel glad that they had become an incorporated body.

The President, in subsequently proposing the toast of the evening, "Success to the Sanitary Inspectors' Association," commenced by referring to the question asked by the Prince of Wales in opening the Congress of Hygiene, "If these diseases are preventible, why are they not prevented?" That question had by some been thought childish, but it was one that demanded an answer, though it was found difficult to answer by those who made these matters their special study. Many diseases were preventible, but there were some which were beyond their control altogether. It was not surprising that it should be so, for the planet on which we lived, in its flight through space, was influenced by causes out of human control, and certain diseases were produced by causes that man would never know. On the other hand, there were diseases caused by famine, war, bad sanitation, bad social customs, and want of cleanliness; and no better argument could be advanced in favour of the toast than the fact that the Association whose success they pledged was formed for the purpose of controlling preventible diseases. It would interest some of those present to know that it was not only in this but in other countries that the importance of the work of that Association was meeting with due appreciation. A great French Association, the Society of Hygiene, had invited the Association to visit Paris next June, where the Municipal Council and other public bodies would co-operate with the Sanitary Society, and would entertain them at a banquet after showing the members everything that was best worth seeing by men of their profession. He had given reasons to show that a great amount of success had been already achieved, but they must not rest there. They had obtained by the charter the status of a teaching body, and they must both learn and teach. They must have a school, and that school they should have a real, scientific, and not a *dilettante* school. They must have a home, and some person would some day be generous enough to give them one, or would help them to get it. The toast was then drunk amidst cheering.

The toast of "The President" was proposed by Mr. Macmillan, who said that on first making the acquaintance of the Association at the previous annual banquet, he had been much impressed with the importance of the work of the Association, and what he had since learned of it deepened that impression.

Dr. Richardson replied to the toast. He said that whatever might be his own opinion as to the eulogies bestowed upon himself by his friend Mr. Macmillan, he had no hesitation in declaring his agreement with the high estimate he put upon the work in which they were all engaged. Quoting two lines of his own, founded on a Classic text, the President said:—

> "Men never nearer to the gods attained
> Than in the task of giving health to men."

He subsequently proposed "Science and Art," coupling with the toast the names of Dr. Louis Parkes (instead of that of Sir J. Crichton Browne, absent through illness) and Mr. Woolner, R.A.

In replying for "Science," Dr. Parkes said he had a due sense of the honourable nature of the task, and he was personally grateful for the generous words of their President in encouraging him to hope to worthily succeed a famous father. The greatest *desideratum* of the time was that a closer spirit of unity should exist between the two branches of the sanitary service. Between the Medical Officers of Health, charged with the task of curing the sick, and the Sanitary Inspectors, charged with the task of preserving the health of those who were well, there ought to be the most complete *entente cordiale*.

Mr. Woolner, R.A., said he could perceive the beneficial influence of work such as that of the Sanitary Inspectors' Association upon art and upon the community in general. There could be no question that when persons were healthy they were larger and better shaped, and their faces were more comely. People now were less in sympathy with the poetical idea which was once accepted as a characteristic of beauty—that the face should be "sicklied o'er with the pale cast of thought," than with that of our greatest living poet when he spoke of "Daughters of the plough, blowzed with health." If their labours did not yet produce the splendour of colouring of the old Venetian paintings, their tendency was in that direction, for the paintings of our day were more ruddy and splendid in colour than in the days of his youth. Coming suddenly to a practical point, Mr. Woolner said he wished they would help the community to do away with dust-holes. When they went to Paris they would find no trace of the unclean thing. There the dust was brought from the houses by ten o'clock every morning, and by eleven o'clock it had disappeared. He thought one little ounce of practice was worth a good deal of theory.

Among other toasts were "The Executive," proposed by Professor Banister Fletcher, and responded to by Mr. Hugh Alexander; and "Local Government," proposed by Mr. E. Lewis Thomas, and responded to by Dr. Geo. Reid and Mr. J. Bonthron.

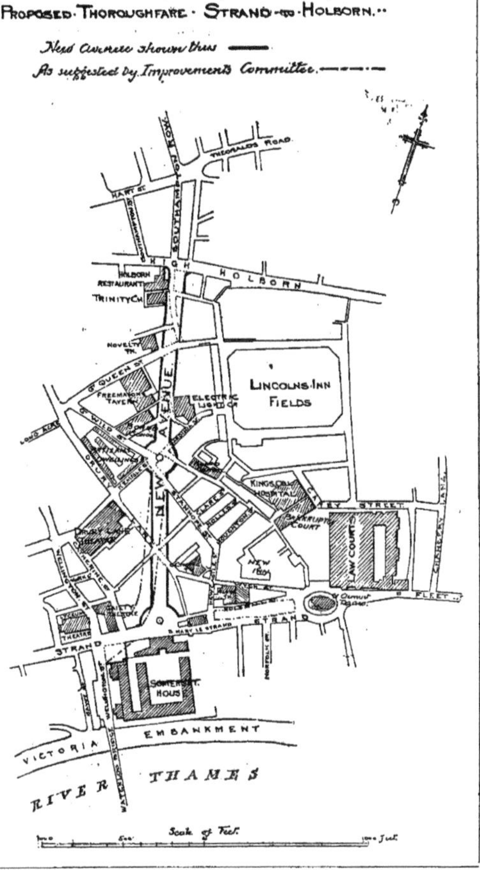

Correspondence.

To the Editor of THE BUILDER.

"PROPOSED THOROUGHFARE—STRAND TO HOLBORN."

SIR,—Any proposed alterations affecting London streets must be of interest to architects and lovers of London alike. I hope, therefore, that you will allow me to draw attention to what I consider to be a great fault in the scheme suggested by the "Improvements Committee of the London County Council" for the "Proposed new thoroughfare from Strand to Holborn."* I am aware that the project has been abandoned for a time, but as it is probable that something of the sort will be done before very long, I trust you will be able to find space in your journal for this letter and the accompanying plan.

Of all the large new thoroughfares which have been formed in London during the last few years, there is not one which has a decent beginning or a decent ending. If this new street is to be "gently curved," as suggested, half into the Strand, and half into Catherine-street facing a portion of the side of the Gaiety Theatre, it can only result, I feel certain, in one more architectural failure.

"The object of bending the street in this direction is to obtain an easy gradient" (I quote from the report), a laudable object, and one to be considered, no doubt, but not, I venture to think, the *only* one when planning a new and important thoroughfare like the one suggested. Its effect architecturally surely ought to receive some consideration. This portion of the scheme is to be condemned not only because it would result in another of those shapeless spaces to which the eyes of Londoners are, unfortunately, becoming so accustomed, but also because, by slightly altering the direction of the street, a noble and dignified termination can be obtained, and without, I believe, any great difference in the gradient.

Somerset House is one of the few fine public buildings that London possesses; unfortunately

* Published in the *Builder*, October 19, 1889.

the Strand front is so hemmed in at present that it is impossible to see it properly. Any scheme, therefore, which touches that part of the Strand and does not take into consideration the possibility of improving the view obtainable of that fine building carries its own condemnation. But this scheme goes further. If carried out it would utterly prevent any attempt at improvement in this respect being made in the future; in fact, it ignores Somerset House altogether. This is, I think, the great mistake its authors make. They take trouble to plan an ugly, inartistic ending to their street, when a grand artistic one can be obtained without any trouble at all. If this new thoroughfare, instead of curving to the west, were brought a little to the east,—barely its own width at the widest point,—it can then, as you will see by the accompanying plan, be carried in a straight line (from Great Wild-street) into the Strand, exactly central with Somerset House. The result will be a fine ending, worthy of a fine thoroughfare. The vista down the new street and under the entrance vestibule of Somerset House into the courtyard beyond ought to be particularly pleasing, and one will then too be able to see Sir William Chambers' design as it deserves to be seen; to greater advantage probably than has been possible since the days it was built.

It may be urged that this plan necessitates a bend in the street higher up. This must be so, I am afraid, in order to avoid interfering with large existing buildings, but I do not think the drawback a really great one. The most pleasing parts of the principal Boulevards of Paris are where they curve, following the lines of the old fortifications, and in this new avenue there would still be a straight vista of nearly 400 yards, which is far enough to be effective, especially considering our existing atmospheric conditions.

To turn to the difficulty in the gradient, I should propose that a half circus be formed at the end of the new street, so that the traffic would not have to go up at right angles to the Strand. This, I believe, would bring the gradient pretty much the same as in the plan suggested by the Committee. Even if such were not the case, even if the gradient were a little steeper, better that surely than an ending which it would be impossible to treat satisfactorily. A large open space would consequently be formed here,—the Strand is already wider opposite Somerset House than it is at the end of Catherine-street,—and this space, with the Strand and the new avenue branching out on two of its sides, and Somerset House and St. Mary-le-Strand on the other two, ought to have a really fine effect.

I am told that if proposed alterations interfere with existing public-houses they have to be abandoned. Is London, then, so poor, and are Londoners so indifferent to all artistic considerations affecting their great city, that they will allow a public-house or two to block the way of manifest, artistic improvements? I hope not, sincerely.

One other point I will merely touch upon, and that is the way it is proposed to cut a "slice" off the houses at the end of Wellington-street, to assist the traffic over Waterloo Bridge. That something must be done here is evident; that this is not the way to do it is, I trust, still more evident. If possible, the whole block of houses east of Wellington-street ought to be swept away, and Somerset House allowed to stand free; if that be impossible, at all events some arrangement better than the one "recommended" can surely be managed.

FRED. M. SIMPSON.

18, *Cowley-street, Westminster.*

M. CHIPIEZ'S MODEL OF THE PARTHENON.

SIR,—A "Note" published in the *Builder* on the 13th ult.,—an extract from which appeared in the R.I.B.A. *Journal* on the 10th inst.,—referred to a model of the Parthenon, which is now at New York, but which was executed in Paris, two or three years ago, under the direction of M. Chipiez; and the writer based his remarks upon it from a set of photographs received from America. Having stated that the model appeared to be (1) far from accurate, he criticised (2) the sculptural additions introduced by the restorer, described (3) the entasis of the columns as greatly exaggerated, and stated (4) that the sculptured metopes were in their wrong places, adding (5) that the model was a curious example of French lightheartedness in matters of the kind, as a French *savant* could not be supposed to learn anything from English sources.

From a written statement by M. Chipiez, which he has forwarded to me, I have learnt:—

1. The Committee in New York, by whose instructions the model was made, appointed a sculptor to prepare a reproduction of the existing portions of the Parthenon according to Mr. Penrose's measurements, and this sculptor employed an architect, unknown to M. Chipiez, to make the necessary drawings. The only drawings supplied by M. Chipiez for the model were of the destroyed parts of the Parthenon.

2. Many of the restorations thus made were "creations." The entire system of roofing was restored, and so were the doors of the Naos and the Opisthodomus. In France, where innumerable restorations of the Parthenon have been and are being made, it is usual to say, "so many architects, so many different restorations," the best of which can only be described as likely to be possible. The declared object of the munificent American donor of the model was to obtain, not a scientific study of archæological restoration, but a general idea of the complete Parthenon as a work of architecture.

3. The model was exhibited in the Paris International Exhibition of 1889, and the photographs then taken of it, compared with photographs, to the same scale, of the actual monument in Athens, show,—M. Chipiez states,—an entasis of column almost identical. If in the American photographs the entasis appears exaggerated, it is due to circumstances beyond his control.

4. The sculptor referred to appears to have arranged the metopes after Michaelis, whose book is thought to be an authority on the subject. The metopes, when fixed in Paris, were numbered in the order followed by the German archæologist. The model was despatched to New York, not in one piece but in a hundred pieces, and put together again after its reception in that city; for the results of which M. Chipiez is not responsible.

5. Both M. Perrot (who has also written to me) and M. Chipiez express themselves much hurt at the assumption that they could not be supposed to learn anything from English sources; and they point to the five volumes of which they are joint authors, and which are well known in England, as direct evidence to the contrary.

I feel sure, from your habitual courtesy and sense of fair play, that you will allow this letter, which is written with the authority and at the request of M. Chipiez, to appear in an early issue of the *Builder*. Permit me, at the same time, to add that a slight acquaintance during many years with distinguished French architects, and with the text of their literary works, has convinced me that their respect for British Classical learning is almost deferential, and that they attach an exceptional value to the collections of the British Museum.

WILLIAM H. WHITE.

9, *Conduit-street, Hanover-square, W.*
March 16, 1892.

*** See "Note" with reference to this letter, p. 219.

COKE-BREEZE CONCRETE.

SIR,—The apparent uncertainty of some of your correspondents on the subject of concrete induces me to repeat what I have formerly said thereon in your columns.

Several years ago I put up, in some large blocks in London, about sixty floors of coke-breeze concrete, without joists and with a bearing (in the majority) of between 12 ft. and 14 ft. the narrow way of the rooms. The concrete was laid 7 in. thick, and had 2½ in. by ⅓ in. iron bars buried 18 in. apart on edge an inch above its soffit, the ends being threaded on continuous iron rods, built into the walls. Each floor was made as the walls reached the required level. A cement ceiling and floor surface afterwards increased the thickness to 9 in. For a plaster ceiling and wood floor I would have made the concrete itself 9 in. thick. These floors set so as to form single slabs, and a heavy weight, accidentally dropped on one of them from a great height during the building, merely cut a clean hole, and did no other damage. The roofs were similar, but asphalted on top. Their only fault is that they allow the rooms next under them to get unusually cold in winter, on account of the rapid radiation of heat through the single solid slab; and if I were repeating them now, I should make them double, putting a second skin of concrete 3 in. or 4 in. thick on rough boards, on fillets resting on the main slab. These boards would have to be left there, as they could not be got out.

I have also made a concrete floor and roof, ea 60 ft. by 20 ft. between the walls, without joists girders. The bars were only a foot apart, b rather smaller, and the aggregate was main broken brick (new hard bats). I would never tru so heavy and brittle a material as river ballast shingle for floors and roofs.

I think it is best to put up the floors along wi the walls, in order that the bars and the rods which they are threaded may be securely built i The bearing of the concrete itself is of no co sequence, as, even if it merely abuts against t walls, it becomes absolutely one with them so so as it has set.

The walls of the former building were mainly concrete made of Thames ballast, and, on o occasion, when the British workman, with his usu thoughtfulness, had made a large fire in a stovele chimney-opening, the ballast concrete was damage and some woodwork on the other side of the parti wall got charred. But I never heard of any troub with our coke-breeze hearths. I remember to ha been told by an experienced concreter that, wh one wished to make floors especially proof again fire-effects, it could be done by mixing flowers sulphur with the cement. I think the proporti named was one measure of sulphur to twenty cement. This might be worth trying for hearth if there is any difficulty.

It is strange to me that we go on making shrin ing, rotting, combustible floors and roofs of forei materials, for which we have to pay away ha cash, whereas we have at home all the means making such as will neither shrink, rot, nor bur and that cost scarcely more than the others. Chinese pigsties one could account for it as do with a view to cheap roast-pork, but we do not our roast humanity.

WILLIAM SIMMONS

Rosebank, Enfield.

* SIR,—Your correspondent, "Contractor," sa (page 210) "be sure not to use too much wate Some of your readers might, from this remark, to the other extreme and not use enough. should be borne in mind that coke-breeze in its absorbs a great quantity of water, and that, the fore, more water is required, in fact that it shou be more sloppy than would be right for shin concrete.

There seems to be some doubt as to the ca bility of coke-breeze concrete to resist fire. I ha no experience in this respect myself; but a buil told me the other day that he once set a stove w coke-breeze concrete, made, however, with lime, Portland cement, and it had to be taken out reset with brickwork, because the coke-breeze c crete got red hot and set the skirting on fire.

C. F. M

THE ROYAL COMMISSION ON LABOU

SIR,—To avoid mistakes cropping up, I beg say most emphatically that my clear and disti contention in to-day's evidence before the Labo Commission — ("Building Trades of Englan Section)—was as to the vicious system of "gen contracting" for works of magnitude. I explai that a superintending architect could "let o each branch of the works to a master workm or, better still, price the work by surveyor's val ation and hold the master workman responsible quality of materials and workmanship.

By this means the skilled workman of ene and enterprise and with a small capital could e the field as a master workman in his proper bra of trade.

I know of more than one architect of emine who began by being a skilled workman first. T 9d. or 10d. per hour rule of payment for one all is deadening in its effects upon workmen. most skilful and industrious are discouraged w their pecuniary reward is no greater than t received by the rawest, slowest, and most inco petent of their fellow workmen.

In Italy and the United States of America "master workman" is well-known and appreciat and I venture to say that it will be a happy day England when we return to that grand old cus of trade under which our noble old abbeys, ca drals, palaces, and castles were erected, and ren to us standing evidences of beauty and strengt construction.

F. A. MOOR

March, 15, 1892.

PAYMENTS ON CONTRACT.

SIR,—May I, in your columns, ask a questio some importance?

A contract is signed and sealed between a Sc Board and a builder to carry out certain w (with clause as to extra works, &c.,) "to the sa faction of the architect."

Payment is to be made in the usual man during progress, leaving 20 per cent. (say) t paid "two months after completion."

The architect gives his "final certificate," cluding his assessment of extras on complet The builder thereupon claims payment of same.

Question: Is he entitled to payment before two months have elapsed, as some allege, but fail to understand? If so, it seems to me that certificate does more than that great friend to architects, Louis XIV., who changed the gender of a noun, for it abolishes an appreciable portion of time!

I send you my name, but for this purpose initials will suffice. D. Y. B.

HALIFAX MODEL DWELLINGS COMPETITION.

SIR,—I was interested to read the letter in your issue of last week relative to this competition, more especially as four days before I had written to the Institute for their "Suggestions" on competitions, and forwarded these at once to the Corporation, clearly stating that unless the conditions were materially altered I should be unable to send in a design. If all who have applied for the "Conditions" did likewise, whilst under the stimulating influence of their disgust at the clauses, it would be well for the profession.

LOCKE WORTHINGTON.

VARNISH.

SIR,—I should be much obliged if any of your numerous readers would be good enough to advise me, through your columns, as to the best varnish to use over delicate and artistic internal paint work; a clear and transparent varnish, that will not in any way change or dull the finishing tints, but, at the same time, one that is hard and durable, and easily applied.

Copal varnish or French oil varnish make a marked difference in the tone of the light tints, so much used at the present time. INQUIRER.

The Student's Column.

WARMING BUILDINGS BY HOT WATER. XII.

FORCING-PITS OR BEDS (HORTICULTURAL WORKS).

IN every horticultural work of any pretension there will be required a pit, or bed, with pipes beneath it, for forcing purposes, or for the growth of pine-apples, &c. The term "pit" is not intended to convey the idea that it is a place dug in the ground, as this is rarely, if ever, the case. Fig. 43 shows

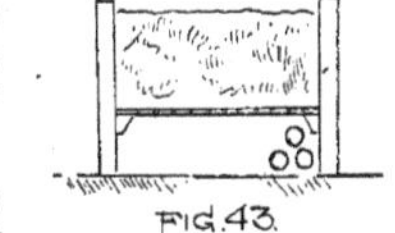

FIG. 43.

the thing in question. This represents a structure of wood, with a false bottom supporting about 18 in. of earth. The bottom is perforated. The heat is applied to this by three or four pipes run underneath as shown, or should the bed be standing alone, away from the general run of pipes, a branch might be carried to and under it, as fig. 44 (plan). The

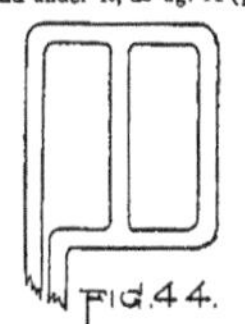

FIG. 44.

object of this bed is the cultivation of those things which require a bottom heat, that is a heat to the earth in which the roots exist, as well as a warm atmosphere to the parts above ground. It is the same result as we obtain by putting manure at the bottom of a bed, except that in the latter case the heat is not so regular and uniform, nor can it be regulated when required.

Sometimes a gardener will signify a preference for the pipes being carried through the material of the bed itself. When this is required the pipes are run at the bottom, and first well covered with clinker and rough material, as fig. 45. If the pipes were a distinct branch, an air tube would require to be carried up through the earth from the highest extremity as shown.

When these beds are arranged for cucumbers, &c., they usually extend along the side of the house, as fig. 46; this permits of the proper training of the vines. In a span house the side will be governed by the gardener's wishes, but in a lean-to it would in nearly every case be

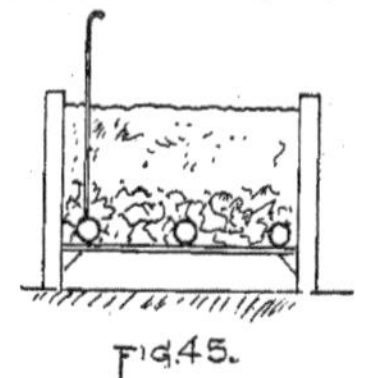

FIG. 45.

along the front furthest from the wall. If the pipes are simply carried underneath, as shown in the last illustration, they contribute heat to the bottom of the bed, and also to the atmosphere generally. This is not so effective for

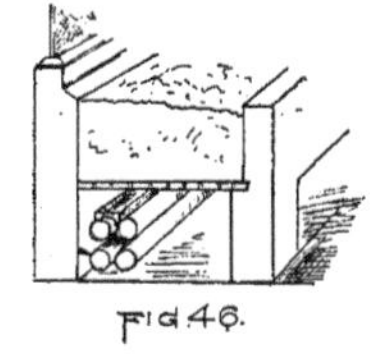

FIG. 46.

the beds as when the exit of heat from beneath is less free. Messrs. Messenger & Co., specialists in this work, have an ingenious plan of affording bottom heat to pits, yet afterwards utilising the air for top heat. Fig. 47 illustrates the

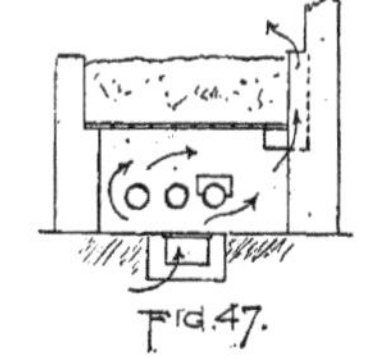

FIG. 47.

method, and it will be seen that the heat does not so readily pass up from the bottom as to prejudice the heating of the bed.

When expense is not of primary importance, it is often arranged for pipes to run under the beds for bottom heat, and additional pipes run round the edge of the bed for top heat, or heat to the atmosphere.

For the growth of many things it is the practice to have a tank of water beneath the pit or bed, as fig. 48, the object being to afford abund-

FIG. 48.

ance of moisture of a warm temperature, or, in other words, a warm atmosphere fully saturated with moisture. To effect this, pipes have to be run beneath the surface of the water as shown, and should they be a branch by themselves, an air-pipe must be carried up through the bed. In the construction of this bed conveniences for adding water to the cistern as it evaporates, &c., have to be provided.

Means to impart a sufficient moistness to the atmosphere have always to be provided in these works in conjunction with the hot-water apparatus. It requires to be explained that as air is raised in temperature it has an increased capacity for water in equal ratio with its increased heat. In fact, it has not only greater capacity but a positive need of water, for if no means are provided by which moisture be added in sufficient quantity, the air will help itself from the surroundings. This proves that the air actually requires the moisture, and it would never do to have it furnished from the earth and the very plants which are in particular need of it themselves.

Now it is not only necessary to provide for what we may term the normal saturation of the air as it increases in temperature, but it is necessary to furnish a superabundance of this moisture, particularly in fern-houses, as an instance, which usually require an atmosphere heavily laden with water. Provision should be made in every house for this purpose, although it is not always required. In some instances, with grapes for example, moisture is required at certain times but not at others.

The provision for saturating the air is usually in the form of a trough fixed on one of the hot-

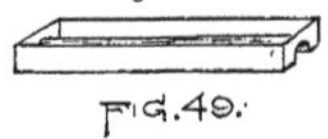

FIG. 49.

water pipes. It can be a trough to lie on the pipe as fig. 49, or the pipe can be procured with the trough cast on it as fig. 50. The latter is generally used; the former being more in request when the amount of ordinary trough pipe is afterwards found insufficient. If a

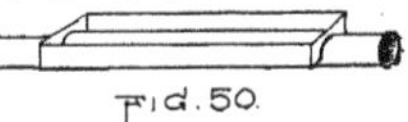

FIG. 50.

gardener cannot conveniently get a cast-iron trough of this description to lay on his pipes, a local whitesmith can make one in zinc which will prove just as effective.

There is a trough or channel-pipe, made as fig. 51, but this is not in common request, as it

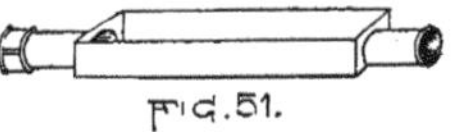

FIG. 51.

can only be placed at the highest point in an apparatus (level with the supply-cistern), otherwise the water would overflow or escape from it. It will be noticed that this trough differs from the others by being practically an open top pipe, the water flowing from the pipe at one end into and through the trough, making its exit at the other end. A pipe like this has sometimes been placed at a high point, and used as a supply-cistern.

It should have been mentioned that the tank beneath the bed, fig. 48, has very frequently a tap in it, which the gardener applies to for the warm water needed in watering his beds and delicate plants. If this be so, a little extra pipe would be needed, so as to more quickly heat up the fresh water that is introduced.

SURVEYORSHIPS.

SOUTHAMPTON. — Major W. B. G. Bennett, Borough Engineer of Southampton, who met with an accident three months ago, has now so far recovered as to able to resume his duties, which have been carried out during his absence by the Assistant Borough Engineer, Mr. A. D. Greatorex. The Borough Surveyor of Southampton has been instructed by the Hartley Council to prepare plans for the erection of an engineering laboratory in connexion with the Hartley Institution.

DORSET.—Mr. C. E. Ponting, F.S.A., Lockeridge, Marlborough, who holds a similar appointment for the Archdeaconries of Wilts and Bristol, has been elected Surveyor for the Archdeaconry of Dorset.

OBITUARY.

PROFESSOR FREEMAN.—The *Times* of Thursday announces that Professor E. A. Freeman died at Alicante, in Spain, on Wednesday morning, from small-pox. In addition to his work as a historian, he will be well known to many of our readers for his writings on architectural subjects. He was approaching his seventieth year.

GENERAL BUILDING NEWS.

NEW COLLEGE, GLASGOW.—St. Peter's College, New Kilpatrick, the gift of Archbishop Eyre to the Catholics of the arch-diocese of Glasgow, has just been completed. The new college occupies a situation at the junction of the Dumbarton and Stirling roads. The building, which is four stories in height, is in the domestic Gothic style. The principal front, including the two wings, measures 190 ft.; to the copestone the height is about 70 ft.; and from the centre rises a flèche, 142 ft., to the top of the vane. The main entrance leads into a hall, open to the top of the central tower. To the right and left runs a corridor, repeated on the several floors, which are reached by stone staircases at either end of the building. On the ground floor, in the central block, are waiting-rooms, reception-rooms, and four class-rooms. The west wing, which measures 78 ft. in length by 36 ft. in width, is meantime set apart as a dining-hall, kitchen, and servants' apartments; while the east wing, measuring 90 ft. by 36 ft., will be fitted up as a temporary chapel. The scheme includes a chapel to be erected to the east of the main building, and a refectory, kitchen, and servants' rooms at the rear to the north; but the construction of this section of the work is meanwhile delayed. On the first floor of the college is a suite of rooms for the Archbishop, and adjoining are rooms for the rector. In the back portion of the main block are four class-rooms. The western wing is occupied chiefly for library purposes, and the eastern is fitted up as students' rooms. The professors' rooms are in the front portion of the main building, and on this floor are four class-rooms, the remainder of the space being devoted to rooms for the students. On the third floor the chemistry class-room and laboratories are placed, and here also is the billiard and recreation-room. The entire cost is estimated at about 25,000*l*. The contractors for the work were Messrs. John Devlin & Son, and Mr. Thomas Geggie represented the architects, Messrs. Pugin & Pugin. We gave an illustration of the building in the *Builder* for September 21, 1889.

PROPOSED RECONSTRUCTION OF MARKET HALL, ABERTILLERY, MON.—The present market hall being found very inadequate for the growing requirements of this district, a company has been formed to acquire and reconstruct it. It is proposed to considerably extend the market, erect shops and offices, and to build a hall to accommodate 1,500 people. Plans are being prepared by Mr. Alfred Swash, architect, of Newport, Mon.

SCHOOLS, BEARPARK, CO. DURHAM.—The Board schools here are shortly to be altered and enlarged for the Elvet St. Oswald School Board by Mr. H. T. Gradon, architect, Durham.

PUBLIC BATHS, SOUTHAMPTON.—On the 10th inst. the new Corporation Baths on the Western-shore, Southampton, were opened by the Mayor, Mr. J. Lemon. We gave a description of the new buildings in the *Builder* for March 21, 1891. The contractors are:—For the sea-wall round the baths, Messrs. Roe & Co.; for the buildings, Messrs. Morgan, Isted, & Morgan; for the iron roofs, Messrs. Roe & Co.; and for heating apparatus, Messrs. Bradford & Co., of London and Manchester. The ornamental ironwork has been supplied by Messrs. Macfarlane & Co., the electric bells by Messrs. Sauby & Co., the fittings and furniture by Mrs. Horseman, Mr. Freeley, Messrs. Hart & Co., the Provincial Furnishing Company, and Messrs. Permain & Co., of Southampton. The buildings have been designed and erected under the superintendence of the Borough Surveyor, Mr. W. B. G. Bennett, C.E., assisted by the Assistant Borough Surveyor, Mr. A. D. Greatorex. The open-air swimming-bath has been made ready for use, and new dressing-boxes have been provided by Messrs. Roe & Co., and a boundary-wall is being erected.

PRESBYTERIAN CHURCH, NEWTONBREDA, NEAR BELFAST.—The opening services in connexion with the Newtonbreda new Presbyterian Church took place on the 13th inst. The new building has been designed by Mr. Vincent Craig, of Belfast, and erected under his direction by Mr. Robert Corry, contractor, of Donegall Pass. The style of the building, which has been constructed of Scrabo stone, with red cut stone dressings, is Gothic, of the Early English period. Its width at the transept is 78 ft., and its length 92 ft., while the chancel is 13 ft. long and 17 ft. wide. Situated at the north-east corner is the spire, which when completed will be 150 ft. in height. Accommodation has been provided for 600 sittings. In the front there are two entrances facing Ormeau-road, and on the north side a third entrance is provided from Knockbreda-road. The buildings at the rear include a session-room, vestry, space for organ-bellows and motor, a ladies'-room, lavatory, and heating apparatus accommodation. In the interior the columns are of cut stone, with moulded caps, and spring arcade arches dividing the nave and side aisles. The transept and chancel arches are of the same materials. Above the level of the side aisles runs a row of clearstory windows. The woodwork in these windows is of polished pitch-pine. The same has been used in sheeting the ceiling, which has the constructional timbers exposed to view. The heating is by Musgrave's high-pressure system. Two ornamental windows have been supplied by Messrs. Carlisle & Wilson, while the plumbing and gas-fitting have been done by Mr. John Dowling, both of Belfast.

CONSECRATION OF CHURCH, TOTTINGTON, LANCASHIRE.—On the 10th inst. the new Church of St. Mary, at Hawkshaw-lane, Tottington, was consecrated by the Bishop of Manchester. The new building is in the thirteenth-century style of Early English Gothic, from plans by Messrs. Maxwell & Tuke, of Manchester, which have been carried out by Messrs. Thompson & Brierley, builders, of Bury. Yorkshire stone has been employed, backed by rubble, with facings from the Holcombe quarries. A nave 65 ft. and a chancel 17 ft. long give a total length of 82 ft. A tower is to be erected at the north-west corner. At present the tower is carried only to the eaves and surmounted by a bell turret. The church is entered through the tower, and a large western door has been placed in the building to be used for exit on special occasions. The side windows are filled in with cathedral glass. An open timbered roof in one span covering the nave is of varnished pitch-pine, and the benches for the worshippers are of the same material. The pulpit and font are of Caen stone and alabaster. On the north side of the chancel is the organ chamber, and the vestry is reached through an arch at the south-east corner of the nave. Choir stalls have been presented by the girls' Sunday school. Accommodation is provided for 364 worshippers. The cost of the church is about 3,500*l*.

COMPLETION OF ST. CATHERINE'S CHURCH, CARDIFF.—On the 9th inst. the corner stone of St. Catherine's Church, King's-road, was laid by Mrs. Vaughan, of Llandaff. Up to the present time, only a portion of the nave has been completed, but funds being now forthcoming, it has been decided to complete the chancel and east end, with vestries, organ-chamber, and side chapel. The style is Early English, and the plans from which the work will be executed have been prepared by Messrs. Kempson & Fowler, architects, of Llandaff, the total cost of the added portion of the building being about 2,000*l*. The existing building is composed of three bays out of a total of five, which will form the completed church. The chancel will be 40 ft. in length by 24 ft. in width, and opening from it through arcade arches will be a south chancel aisle or mourning chapel, 20 ft. long by 16 ft. wide; an organ-chamber and vestry 24 ft. by 20 ft. in all. The design provides for the chancel being rectangular in form, with a three-light eastern window and a two-light window in the east end of the chancel aisle. The floor will be finished in tiles. The outer walls will be of Treforest stone with Bath stone dressings and mullions. The contract has been let to Mr. Councillor W. Symonds, of Canton. When finished, the church will provide sitting accommodation for about 836.

THE PROPOSED EXTENSION OF THE BATH PUMP-ROOM.—A meeting of the Bath Town Council was held on the 15th inst., the Mayor (Mr. J. S. Turner) in the chair, when the debate was resumed on the report from the Baths Committee recommending the addition to the pump-room and the covering in of the Roman remains, estimated to cost 45,000*l*., as mentioned in last week's *Builder*, p. 212. After a long discussion, the amendment moved by Alderman Gibbs was put. Thirteen voted for and 35 against. The adoption of the report was then carried by 31 votes to 15.

ADDITIONS TO THE "MORNING POST" OFFICES.—Considerable additions are being made to the offices of the *Morning Post*, and a new block of buildings is to be added at the corner of Wellington-street and the Strand. Mr. H. O. Cresswell is the architect. The whole of the floors and both staircases are to be fireproof, on "The Fawcett" system. Messrs. Mark Fawcett & Co. are also doing the constructional ironwork.

NEW INFIRMARY BUILDINGS, LEEDS.—On the 12th inst., on the invitation of Mr. George Corson, the architect, the members of the Leeds and Yorkshire Architectural Society were shown over the new buildings which have been erected in connexion with the General Infirmary. The cost of the building, which, it is said, will in a few weeks be opened for the reception of patients, will be about 35,000*l*. Mr. Corson explained all points of interest, and at the close of the inspection, a cordial vote of thanks to that gentleman was passed on the motion of Mr. Thorp, and seconded by Mr. Watson. The new buildings consist of four separate blocks,—namely, the ward pavilion, the out-patients' department, the pathological department, and the isolation wards. The new ward pavilion follows, externally, the design of the original building, and is connected with it by a screen of four open arches, of brick and stone, supported on polished granite pillars. The internal arrangement differs from the original wards. Instead of one large ward on each floor, with staircase at the end, the staircase is placed in the middle, dividing the wards. There are on each floor one ward, 65 ft. long by 27 ft. 6 in. wide, arranged for sixteen beds; and another 37 ft. long by 27 ft. 6 in. wide, for ten beds. These wards are in height, from floor to ceiling, 18 ft. on the ground floor, 17 ft. on the first floor, and on the top floor, which has an arched ceiling rising into the roof, there is an averag[e] height of 22 ft. There are also on each of these floors a special ward for one patient, and a nurse's room. Bath-rooms and water-closets are also pro[-]vided, the baths being of earthenware, white glaze[d] out and in, without casing, and standing free i[n] the middle of the room. These were made by th[e] Farnby Company. The water-closets were sup[-]plied by Doulton, of Lambeth. Over the nurse[s'] room and small wards, &c., an entresol is arranged one in each story, containing a small special war[d] and a room for patients' clothing; and a water[-]closet. Altogether there is provision for eighty[-]four beds. An hydraulic lift, provided by Rober[t] Middleton, of Sheepscar Foundry, gives access t[o] all the floors. The floors throughout are constructe[d] with iron joists and concrete, upon which, in th[e] wards, a solid oak block floor has been laid i[n] pattern and polished by Mr. J. F. Ebner, [of] London; and in the corridors, stairs, baths, an[d] water-closets there is a marble terazzo floor, lai[d] by Messrs. J. and H. Patteson, of Manchester. O[n] the ground floor the new building is connected t[o] the old by a corridor, and on the first floo[r] to the out-patient corridor by a bridge. Th[e] wards are heated by steam pipes, and also b[y] open stoves, by Shorland, of Manchester, place[d] in the middle of the wards, with down draught flue[s]. The out-patients' department consists of a waitin[g] hall, surrounded by the consulting, examinatio[n,] operating-rooms, &c., of the various departments. The hall is 126 ft. long by 45 ft. wide, with tw[o] aisles, each 74 ft. by 12 ft., divided from the ma[in] area by arches and granite pillars. The roof [is] semi-circular, and the height from floor to ceili[ng] is 42 ft. The hall is lighted by a series of clearsto[ry] windows on all sides, and at night by gas pendan[ts] and brackets. The floor is on a level with the fir[st] floor of the Infirmary, and the department is con[-]nected with the original building by an extensi[on] of the north and south corridors. The entrance [is] by a carriage porch, and an entrance-hall (23 ft. [by] 17 ft.), from the New-street, and a separate exit f[or] patients are also provided. The Dispensary, whi[ch] is 58 ft. by 15 ft., is at the west end of the ha[ll,] and has in connexion with it rooms for the d[is]penser. Two staircases are provided in recesses fro[m] the corridor, for access from lower stories. Bat[hs] for men and women are arranged below the surgic[al] department, and on the south side, owing to t[he] fall of the ground, two stories of rooms are obtaine[d,] the upper intended as bedrooms for domestics, t[he] lower for stores. The pathological department [is] placed on the north side, and is connected by [a] corridor from the main north corridor. It co[n]tains a post-mortem-room, a mortuary, a laborato[ry] with retiring-room, and a waiting-room, [for] relatives. The isolation wards are placed upon t[he] site on the north of the New-street, and are reach[ed] from the Infirmary by a tunnel under the stre[et] from the basement floor level. These war[ds] will consist of one story only, with sta[irs] from the tunnel and a lift from that le[vel] to the ground floor. There will be two war[ds] (15 ft. by 16 ft.), with kitchen, pantry, and sto[re-]room. The out-patients' department is to [be] heated by steam radiators, from the present boile[rs,] and Messrs. Ashwell & Co., of Leicester a[nd] London, have the contract for this work. T[he] principal contractors and sub-contractors are [:] Messrs. Gould & Stevenson, for brick, stone, a[nd] wood; Watson & Worsnop, for slating; [...] Lindley, for plumbing and glazing; A. & [...] Wheater (Calverley), plasterers; Stephen Macf[ar]lane, concreter; Bateman, painter; Leon[ard] Cooper, steel and iron beams, joists, and [...] ribs; Macdonald (Aberdeen), granite pillar[s;] Verity Bros., gearing for windows; C. Smith [&] Son (Birmingham), locks and boundary railin[gs;] J. & H. Patteson (Manchester), "terazzo" flo[ors;] and J. F. Ebner (London), oak floors in war[ds.] Mr. J. T. Brown is the clerk of works.

NEW CHURCH, BRIDGETON, LANARKSHIRE.—[A] new church has just been erected in Muslin-stre[et,] Bridgeton, on the site of the old church. T[he] architect is Mr. John C. M'Kellar, I.A., Glasg[ow.] The walls are of red stone. The church will [be] seated for 900 persons; and in the rear of [the] building, on the same level, there is a large hall [for] 350, a small hall for 100, a vestry, and a few oth[er] rooms. The estimated cost is 4,500*l*.

BATHS, ASTON, BIRMINGHAM.—At the pub[lic] baths, now in course of erection, the first and seco[nd] swimming-baths are roofed in and the baths a[re] lined. The electricity for lighting both the ba[ths] and the public offices will be generated with [the] baths' pumping engine. A refuse-destructor [is] being erected, and will commence work in [the] course of six or eight weeks.

PROPOSED PUBLIC OFFICES, &C., BARK[ING,] ESSEX.—On the 10th inst. a Local Governm[ent] Board Inquiry was held by Major-General Phi[lip] Carey, R.E., respecting the application by [the] Barking Town Local Board for a loan of 17,30[0l.] for the erection of public offices, free library, f[ire-]engine station, mortuary, stables and cart-she[ds,] and works of street improvements, as designed [by] Mr. C. J. Dawson, F.R.I.B.A., Surveyor to [the] Board. The buildings are proposed to be erec[ted] on two acres of land in East-street, sufficient sp[ace] being reserved for future extension of public off[ices] and the erection of public baths.

STAINED GLASS AND DECORATION.

MEMORIAL WINDOW, ST. MARK'S CHURCH, SHEFFIELD.—A new window has just been added to St. Mark's Church, Broomfield, Sheffield. Mr. W. F. Dixon, of London, the artist, has devoted the space to the subject of "The wise men and shepherds travelling from the East to the birthplace of the Saviour." The window contains six large lights with considerable tracery.

ST. JOHN'S CHURCH, BRADFORD.—A large rose window of Munich stained glass, representing Christ in twelve distinctive characters, such as the Good Shepherd, the Light of the World, &c., has recently been presented to St. John's Church, Bradford, by Mr. C. Briggs, in memory of his late parents. The window was designed and executed by Messrs. Mayer & Co.

MEMORIAL WINDOW, PARISH CHURCH, POWERSTOCK.—On the 12th inst., at the parish church, Powerstock, Dorset, a window in memory of the late Archdeacon Sanctuary was unveiled. The window is placed above the west door, and was supplied by Messrs. Hardman & Co., Birmingham, who also supplied the windows in the chancel. The representations are,—the central figure, Christ as the Good Shepherd, with a crown of thorns; on the right is St. John the Baptist; while on the left is St. Paul. A brass plate is to be placed underneath the window with an inscription.

PAINTED WINDOW, SOUTH DARLEY CHURCH, DERBYSHIRE.—The east window of South Darley Church has, says the *Manchester Courier*, just been filled with painted glass by Messrs. Morris & Co., of Merton Abbey, Surrey. The design and drawings were prepared by Mr. Burne Jones, A.R.A., while the colouring is the composition of Mr. William Morris. The window consists of three separate lights, the architecture of the church being an imitation of the Norman style. One of the side lights is filled with the figure of St. Mary. The other side light is occupied with the figure of St. John. The centre light is taken up with a representation of the Crucifixion.

MEMORIAL WINDOW, LANGTREE PARISH CHURCH, DEVON.—A three-light stained glass window has recently been dedicated to the memory of the late Archdeacon Barnes in Langtree Parish Church. In the centre light of the window is depicted Our Lord as the Good Shepherd under a canopy, of the Perpendicular period, of white and gold upon a quarry ground. In the two side lights are sacred monograms of I H S and X P C. The quarry treatment, as groundwork, is maintained in these two side lights also, as well as in the centre. The window is situated on the south side of the chancel. The work has been executed by Messrs. Ward & Hughes, of London.

WINDOW, ST. MARY'S CHURCH, WEST WORLINGTON.—On the 13th inst., a stained glass window, the gift of Mr. J. G. S. Troake, was unveiled in the Church of St. Mary, West Worlington, Devon. The window stands on the north side of the chancel immediately over the choir stalls, and consists of two lights, filled respectively with figures of King David and St. Mary the Virgin. The work was designed and executed by Messrs. Fouracre & Son, of Stonehouse.

FOREIGN AND COLONIAL.

PARIS.—On the 15th inst. the general annual meeting of the "Société Française des Habitations à Bon Marché" was held, under the presidency of M. Jules Simon. M. Siegfried read a history of the movement, and the Society's first prize, 1,500 francs and three silver medals, was awarded to MM. Teissier, Muller, and Guinard, of Marseilles; the second, 1,000 francs and a silver medal, to M. Chas. Robin, of Poissy; the third prize, 500 francs and a silver medal, to M. Léon David, of Havre.

BERLIN.—The election of new members of the Prussian Royal Academy, which took place last January, has been officially recognised by the Government. The number of vacancies to fill up was a large one, so that no less than twelve painters, three sculptors, two etchers, and an architect were nominated. The architect is Herr "Stadtbaudirector" Hugo Licht, the city architect of Leipsic. Among the painters we notice Mr. Walter W. Ouless, of London, two Spaniards, an Italian, and a Frenchman; of the three sculptors one is Professor Unger, of Vienna.——The municipal authorities have received a petition signed by the majority of junior artists resident in Berlin, requesting that a certain sum of money be annually voted for the purchase of works of art either for the decoration of municipal buildings, or for one of their city collections. The municipality has done little or nothing in the acquisition of works of art for several years. We hear that the petition was favourably received.——The number of *bonâ-fide* unemployed has increased this week. The Municipality is unfortunately not keeping its promise relating to the quick commencement of relief works. Several persons who could find work for over one thousand men, cannot do so on account of official delay in granting the so-called "building permission."——The municipal authorities have at last decided on the adoption of some suitable means of facilitating the reading of names of streets and house numbers at night. The regulation white lettering on blue enamel in use has given much satisfaction in daylight, but is difficult to distinguish after dark.——The railway tickets on the metropolitan railway are henceforward to be distributed by automatic machines. There will be no booking-offices at the stations, but change-offices instead.——The Imperial Bank (Reichsbank) has had to pay 4,750,000 marks (or over 235,000*l.*) for a site adjoining their present block, which is required for the new wing to be erected this year.——Herr Louis Schwartzkopff, an engineer of great repute, whose iron castings and machines are used all over the Continent, died on March 7, in his 66th year. He was a member of the Emperor's Special State Council and of the Academy of Public Works.

MUNICH.—The Bavarian Government has voted 5,000*l.* towards the acquisition of works of art for the Munich Pinakothek, and 2,000*l.* for the purchase of works of art for the decoration of Government property.

MISCELLANEOUS.

CLOCK-TOWER AND SANITARY CONVENIENCES NEAR VICTORIA STATION.—On Monday morning last the Vestry of St. George's, Hanover-square, threw open to public use some very admirably-arranged underground conveniences, situate below the "refuge" at the junction of Vauxhall Bridge-road with Victoria-street. The conveniences, which have been constructed by Messrs. Doulton & Co., of Lambeth, include five water-closets of the "Simplicitas" wash-out pedestal type; and thirteen urinals, semi-circular on plan, the backs being formed of enamelled fire-clay, and the divisions being of marble. The urinals are automatically flushed at intervals. The whole of the interior is well-lighted from the top by means of prismatic pavement lights, and there is a convenient recess for the attendant close to the entrance steps. This work has been carried out from the plans and under the direction of Mr. C. Livingstone, the Surveyor to the Vestry. The whole is surmounted by an iron clock-tower 25 ft. high, containing a clock by Messrs. Gillett & Co., of Croydon. The clock is illuminated at night.

SOCIETY FOR PRESERVING MEMORIALS OF THE DEAD.—At the second general meeting of this Society for the Session 1891-92, held in the rooms of the Royal Archæological Institute, 17, Oxford Mansion (Regent-circus), London, W., on Monday, February 15, a paper on "Dore Abbey, Herefordshire: an Outline of the Principal Facts and Features," by the Rev. Alfred Phillips, rector, was read by Mr. Arthur E. Griffiths, supplemented by some valuable and interesting remarks from Miss E. Bayley. A discussion on this comparatively unknown, half-ruined Cistercian abbey in the Golden Valley of Herefordshire took place, and in which the President, Messrs. C. E. Keyser, F.S.A., F. Chancellor, Herbert Jones, and the Rev. Prebendary Salmon joined. For thb tenth annual meeting, the second or third week in June was suggested, and combined with it two days' excursion to some interesting churches, where great good may result from the Society's visit. Bishops Stortford was considered a suitable place for head-quarters; one day to be given to Essex churches, and the second to Hertfordshire churches. At the next general meeting on Tuesday, April 5, a fully detailed plan will be submitted for approval.

PHŒNIX PHILANTHROPIC SOCIETY OF HOUSE PAINTERS.—The annual meeting of this, which, we are told, is the oldest benefit society in the trade, was held on the 12th inst. at the Society-house, 28, London-street, Fitzroy-square. First established in 1823 as a "Chapter of Communication," this Society has had an interesting history. According to a correspondent, it has paid over 20,000*l.* in sick and funeral benefits. Some years ago it nearly collapsed from the payment of a too liberal scale of benefits. For the usual weekly subscription, it endeavoured to assure to its members not only the customary sick benefits, but a superannuation pension more than double that proposed by Mr. Chamberlain's scheme. In ten years 2,500*l.* was paid by way of superannuation. A reconstruction of the rules placed the Society on a sounder financial basis, and the balance-sheet for the past year shows that for the sixth time consecutively a satisfactory increase has been made in the capital of the Society. The funds are entirely applied to the relief of sickness, and the assurance of a small sum on the death of a member. There is, however, a winter fund for the relief of members out of employment. None but duly-qualified painters can become members, and for many years it has numbered among its members most of the foremen and leading workmen of the first West-end firms.

NEW USE FOR WASTE SLATE.—M. Victor van Heyden, a Belgian engineer, has devised a method of treating waste slate-chippings as the constituent of an artificial material which he calls "ardoisine." The waste slate is, in the first place, reduced by the steam-hammer to fragments of a size suitable for being treated in the crushing-mill, which comminutes them into small nuts. These nuts, taken up by a bucket-chain, are disposed on a grinding-machine of very ingenious construction, which, in addition to its work of pulverising, acts simultaneously as a separator, the powder being placed on one side, while the chippings or scales are carried elsewhere. These are the two substances which, united with certain agglomerants, form the principal ingredients of "ardoisine." The powder and the chippings, in calculated proportions, are carried, by means of a channel furnished with an interior agitator or mixer, into a mill-hopper with a movable bottom, which constitutes the orifice of a kneader of special construction, which is heated by gas, in order to regulate more exactly the degree of heat. In this kneader are automatically cast in exact proportions the above-mentioned agglomerating substances, which, in their totality, constitute 9 per cent. of the product. When it leaves the kneader, it is run into a mould; a portable wagon receives it, and conveys it under a press of the power of 150 tons. It then forms a material capable of use for paving and other similar objects, or of high polish as slabs, and it is claimed that it resists a very high crushing pressure. Unfortunately, we are not told what are the "agglomerants" which form a large part of the material, and till we know that we cannot form much opinion as to its durability.

SITE FOR NEW PATENT OFFICE.—A portion of the property which the Government have taken for the Patent Office extension buildings consists of two houses in Took's-court, occupied by Mr. John C. Francis, in succession to his father, the late Mr. John Francis, for the printing and publishing departments of our contemporaries,—*Notes and Queries* and the *Athenæum*. For those papers new premises will shortly be ready, at the corner of Church-passage, Bream's-buildings, Chancery-lane, built by Mr. B. E. Nightingale, contractor, after the designs of, we are informed, Mr. W. C. Street, architect. They stand next westwards of the *Field*, *Queen*, and *Law Times* offices, designed by Messrs. Satchell & Edwards, architects, of which we gave a description on May 31, 1890. *Notes and Queries*, as established in 1849, was at first issued by Mr. George Bell, from No. 186, Fleet-street; in 1872 its ownership passed to the proprietor of the *Athenæum*, and the two journals were thenceforward issued from No. 20, Wellington-street, the *Athenæum* having been meanwhile removed from No. 5 Catherine-street. The two publishing departments were subsequently transferred to Took's-court, where the latter has been printed for more than sixty years past. Mr. Nightingale is building the first block of the Patent Office extension, next southwards of Staple Inn, after designs by Mr. Taylor, architect to the Office of Works. The block will be about 55 ft. high, with a front of Portland stone towards Took's-court, and is to contain one large room, rising through two stories, for the purposes of consultation and the adjustment of matters wherein counsel and patent-agents are employed on behalf of their clients' interests.

NEW SOUTH WALES.—According to the Sydney *Building and Engineering Journal* (February 6), satisfactory progress is being made with the work of judging the designs sent forward for the Rossiville Asylum, to be erected near Goulburn, New South Wales. There are thirty-nine competitors for this work, whose plans number 350 sheets of drawings. Mr. Vernon, the Government Architect, and Mr. Horbury Hunt, have inspected the site, and Dr. Manning and these gentlemen have paid a visit of inspection to the two principal asylums in that colony, for the purpose of ascertaining the nature of the best arrangements connected with these institutions. It is expected that several weeks hence Dr. Manning, Mr. Vernon, and Mr. Horbury Hunt, as an advice board, will forward a recommendation to the Minister for Works concerning the designs under examination, and all inquiries made. A few days ago, Mr. Lyne personally inspected the plans now on view in the Museum. In the opinion of the Minister, the competitive drawings are so excellent in quality as to be superior to any yet submitted for works connected with the public service.

REGISTRATION OF PLUMBERS: SHEFFIELD MEETING.—The annual meeting of the Sheffield Centre of the Association for the National Registration of Plumbers (connected with the Worshipful Company of Plumbers, London) was held on the 9th inst., at the Firth College. The chair was occupied by Mr. J. B. Mitchell-Withers, Vice-President of the Sheffield centre. The Chairman, in opening the proceedings, referred to work done in connexion with the Sheffield branch during the past year. He said the importance of such a society was being more thoroughly appreciated, and public bodies were beginning to see the importance of the necessity that none should be allowed to do drainage and other such plumbing work unless they were registered as thoroughly qualified men. The Chairman next distributed the certificates granted by the Worshipful Company of Plumbers to those plumbers who had qualified themselves for the same. Mr. Thompson, C.E., next gave an address on "Modern Sanitary Improvements." Professor Hicks proposed a vote of thanks to Mr. Thompson, and this was seconded by Professor Ripper, and carried with applause. A vote of thanks to the Chairman concluded the proceedings.

NEW ADDRESSES.—Messrs. W. & G. Shearburn, architects and surveyors, of Dorking, have opened a London office at Effingham House, Arundel-street, Strand.—Mr. T. E. Collcutt informs us that he is removing his offices from 5, Lancaster-place, Strand, to 36, Bloomsbury-square.

COMPETITIONS.

Nature of Work.	By whom Advertised.	Premium.	Designs to be delivered.
*Cemetery Chapel and Caretaker's Lodge..	Ripon Corporation ..	20*l*. & 5*l*.	April 4
*New County Council Buildings	Staffordshire C. C.	150*l*. 100*l*. & 50*l*.	May 27

CONTRACTS.

Nature of Work or Materials.	By whom Required.	Architect, Surveyor, or Engineer.	Tenders to be delivered.
*25,000 yards Wood Pavement	Vestry of St. George's Hanover-square	*Official*	Mar. 21
*Supply of Materials	Mortlake Dist. Highway Bd.	do.	do.
Farmhouse, &c. Lochs, Urquhart, N.B. ..	....	A. & W. Reid	Mar. 22
*General Paving Works	West Ham Council ..	Lewis Angell	do.
Repairs to School Buildings...............	Plymouth Sch. Bd. ..	*Official*	do.
Granite Road Metal.......................	Irthlingboro High. Bd.	do.	do.
*Footbridges over Railway	Great Western Railway	do.	Mar. 23
*Girder Work for Bridges	do.	do	do.
Cottage, Elgin, N.B.	....	A. & W. Reid	do.
Paving Setts, Kerbs, Road Metal, &c.	South Shields U.S.A.	Matthew Hall	do.
Lunatic Wards at Workhouse............	Hunslet (Leeds) Union Guardians	R. J. Smith	do.
*Roadmaking and Paving Works..........	Hammersmith Vestry	H. Mair	do.
*Laying down Wood Blocks	do.	do.	do.
Fever Hospital, Asylum, Wadsley, near Sheffield	West Riding C. C.....	J. Vickers-Edwards ..	Mar. 24
New Buildings, Truro......................	Roswin Training Sch.	W. Swift	do.
Outfall Sewer, &c..........................	Chester-le-Street U R S A	D. Balfour............	do.
Stores and Cottage, Garforth	Leeds Indus. Co-op.Soc.	....	do.
Additions to Mansion House, Deluabo, Elgin, N.B	....	C. C. Doig........ ..	do.
Farmhouse, Garlickhill, Kinstary, N.B.	....	Ranald Macdonald ..	do.
Three Cottages, Cogenhoe, Northampton	....	H. H. Dyer	Mar. 25
Sewerage Works (31,256 yards)............	Pontypridd Loc. Bd...	Edwd. Rees	do.
Gasholder Tank............................	Normanton Gas Co. ..	*Official*	do.
Laying Water Pipes (10,440 yards), &c. ..	Nantwich U.R.S.A. ..	J. A. Davenport......	do.
Road Metal	Durham County Coun.	Wm. Crozier...........	Mar. 26
Granite and Slag	King's Cliffe High. Bd.	*Official*	do.
Improvement of Robert-st. Ynysybwl	Mountain Ash L. B...	J. Williams	Mar. 28
Calvinistic Methodist Chapel, Taibach, Port Talbot, S. Wales	W. Griffith	....	do.
Work at Burghead and Hopeman station	Highland Ry. Co.	Alex. Shand	do.
Additions to School, East Barry, Glam. ..	Barry United Dist. Sch. Bd.	Seward & Thomas	do.
Additions and Alterations, East-end School, Elgin, N.B.	....	A. & W. Reid	do.
*Purchase and Pulling-down Building Mat.	Sch. Bd. for London..	*Official*	do.

CONTRACTS.—*Co*

Nature of Work or Materials.	By whom Required.	Architect, Surveyor or Engineer.	Tend[ers] to b[e] delive[red.]
*Making-up and Paving Road	Lewisham Bd. of W...	*Official*	Mar.
*Making-up and Paving Road	Bromley Loc. Bd. .. .	do.	do.
*New Sorting Office, Tothill Fields, S.W...	Com. of H. M. Works	do.	do.
*Post Office, Dover........................	H. M. Works	do.	Mar.
Timber	G. W. R. Co...........	do.	do.
Square Bridge, 50ft. span, Dovecote, near Brampton, Cumberland	Brampton High. Bd...	do.	do.
Stores, Offices, and other Buildings, Albion-square, Pembroke Dock........	Pembroke Dock Co-op. Soc.	H. C. Reid............	do.
*Roadmaking and Paving Works.........	Fulham Vestry	W. Sykes	do.
Levelling, Paving, and Channelling Work	Gateshead Imp. Com.	J. Bower	Mar.
*Enlargement, &c. of Workhouse	Northwich Union	Mr. Joseph Cawley ..	do
*Laying New Sewer	do.	*Official*	do.
*Reconstructing Roadway at Infirmary ..	Wandsworth & Clapham Union..........	T. W. Aldwinckle	do.
*Relief Station and Residence	do.	do.	do
Board Sch. Work, Bedwas, Newport, Mon.	Bedwas Sch. Bd.......	*Official*	Apri[l]
*Sewerage Works	Oldbury Local Board..	H. B. Nichol	Apri[l]
*Supply of Cast-Iron Pipes...............	Brighton T. C.........	*Official*	Apri[l]
*Alterations, &c. to Workshops, Leavesden Asylum	Met. Asylum Board ..	A. & C. Harston	Apri[l]
Methodist Church, Gateshead, and other Work	....	Davidson & Bendle '..	No d[ate]
Three Houses, Armley-road, Leeds	....	Swale & Mitchell	do
Alterations and Additions to St. Michael's Schools, Meanwood-road, Leeds......	....	Richd. Wood	do
Additions and Alterations to Hotel, Gosforth, Newcastle-on-Tyne.............	....	B. F. Simpson........	do
Re-building "Westoe" Tavern, South Shields....................................	R. Henderson	Fred. Renneldson	do
Wesleyan Chapel and Schools, Consett, co. Durham	....	Lamb, Armstrong, & Knowles	do
Cottages, Upper Whiston, nr. Rotherham	....	Fowler & Marshall...	do.
*New Offices, Leicester....................	Prudential Assur. Co.	A. Waterhouse & Son	do.
*Rectory House, Great Carlton...........	....	C. Kirk & Sons,.......	do

PUBLIC APPOINTMENTS.

Nature of Appointment.	By whom Advertised.	Salary.	Appli[ca]tions [to] be [in].
*Assistant Street Inspector and Inspector of Nuisances	St. Giles B. of W.	100*l*. 4s. &c.	Mar.
*Surveyor and Inspector of Nuisances	Hanwell Loc. Bd.	150*l*.	Mar.
*Road Foreman	City of Birmingham ..	2*l*.	Mar.
*Clerk	St. Olave's Gram. Sch.	300*l*.	Mar.
*Clerk of Works and Collector	do.	100*l*. &c.	do
*Draughtsman, Admiralty Outports	Civil Service Com.....	....	Apri[l]
*Assistant Examiner in Patent Office.....	do.	....	do

RAILWAY ACCIDENTS IN INDIA.—The statistics furnished by the Public Works Department of the railway accidents in India tend to show that if railway trains do not run with such speed in this country as they do in others, they are at least worked with more than average immunity from accident. The New York Central Railway Company claims recently to have eclipsed all the fast runs of the world, and asserts that it has run 436½ miles in 425¾ minutes, exclusive of stoppages. It will be many years, says a Bombay contemporary, before India can even hope to do this, but it may be assumed that the New York Central would be glad to show so clean a record per thousand miles and per thousand passengers in the way of casualties involving loss of life or personal injury. English railway managers, we imagine, will not willingly admit that they have been surpassed as regards speed, for the American train was an experimental one specially run; the record speeds in England have been made by every-day express trains in ordinary competition. But in England out of seven hundred officials one was killed and almost one in every hundred injured during the last year; 1,076 lives were lost and 4,721 injured; 118 of the killed and 1,361 injured being passengers. Of course, this is but a small total compared with the enormous number of passengers carried; but it is greater than is the case in India, and we doubt if any country can boast so few accidents. The returns are not so prepared as to make any minute comparison between the railways of the world possible. Indian returns are furnished half-yearly, and details are given which are not readily available on other lines. But a total of twenty-three killed and eighty-four wounded in accidents to trains over almost five millions of miles run is surely not a bad average. This is the return for the half-year ending June last. More than half the fatal accidents occurred to trespassers, or were due to want of caution or misconduct; of the injuries exactly half were due to want of caution by servants and others, 118 to carelessness on the part of passengers. —*Indian Engineer.*

BIRMINGHAM ENGINEER STUDENTS.—A meeting of the Birmingham Association of Students of the Institution of Civil Engineers was held on the 3rd inst. at the Midland Institute, the President, Mr. J. Edward Willcox, A.M.I.C.E., being in the chair. A paper was read by Mr. H. Shoosmith, A.M.I.C.E., on "Stability of Walls," which was followed by a discussion.

NEW BUSINESS PREMISES AT STRATFORD.—Messrs. Young & Marten, of Caledonian Works, Stratford, London, E., wholesale purveyors for the building trade, have recently made extensive alterations and additions to their already large establishment in the Broadway, Stratford. In it are the show-rooms for chimney-pieces, mantels, and over-mantels, tile-grates, stoves, and tile-hearths, &c., &c.

THE ENGLISH IRON TRADE.—Great irregularity prevails in the iron trade, owing to the miners' "play-period." Most of the large ironworks are suffering from the scarcity of fuel, and in many instances have ceased work altogether. Prices are rather firmer on account of the limited production; but business in both crude and manufactured iron is only of a hand-to-mouth character. The steel trade exhibits little alteration, but heavy rails are a trifle weaker. The tin-plate trade shows a slight improvement. Shipbuilding is quiet and the engineering branches are in an unsatisfactory condition. The coal trade is somewhat easier.—*Iron.*

MEETINGS.

SATURDAY, MARCH 19.

Architectural Association.—Visit to the Tower Bridge Works, by permission of Mr. J. Wolfe Barry. 3 p.m.

Glasgow Architectural Association.—Visit to Kilbirnie Church.

MONDAY, MARCH 21.

Royal Institute of British Architects.—Professor Aitchison, A.R.A., on "Byzantine Art." 8 p.m.

Society of Arts (Cantor Lectures).—Professor W. Robinson on "The Uses of Petroleum in Prime Movers."—IV. 8. p.m.

Victoria Institute—8 p.m.

Liverpool Architectural Society.—Special meeting. Paper by Mr. H. Hartley.

TUESDAY, MARCH 22.

Institution of Civil Engineers.—Mr. A. R. Binnie on "Mean or Average Annual Rainfall, and the Fluctuations to which it is Subject." 8 p.m.

Sanitary Institute (Lectures for Sanitary Officers).—Professor A. Wynter Blyth on "Sanitary Law, English, Scotch, and Irish; General Enactments; Public Health Act, 1875; Model Bye-Laws, &c." 8 p.m.

Photographic Society of Great Britain.—(1) Mr. Dallmeyer will show his Telephotographic lens. (2) Mr. Chapman Jones on "Copying Inclined Pictures." 8 p.m.

WEDNESDAY, MARCH 23.

Society of Arts.—Mr. Gilbert R. Redgrave on "Manufacture and Industrial Application of Flexible Tubing." 8 p.m.

THURSDAY, MARCH 24.

Society of Antiquaries.—8.30 p.m.

Edinburgh Architectural Association.—Mr. J. J. Burnet on "The Relative Position of the Architect and the Craftsman." 8 p.m.

FRIDAY, MARCH 25.

Institution of Civil Engineers (Students' Meeting).—Mr. G. Lambert Gibson on "The Seafield Dock and the Kirkcaldy and District Railway." 7.30 p.m.

Sanitary Institute (Lectures for Sanitary Officers).—Professor A. Wynter Blyth on "Sanitary Laws and Regulations governing the Metropolis." 8 p.m.

Institute of Certified Carpenters.—7.30 p.m.

SATURDAY, MARCH 26.

Edinburgh Architectural Association.—Visit to Roman Wall at Cboy.

RECENT PATENTS:

ABSTRACTS OF SPECIFICATIONS.

2,819.—WINDOW-SASHES: *J. T. Nicholls.*—This patent relates to additions in the construction of the improved window-sash holder patented November 10, 1886.

5,501.—WHITE-LEAD: *W. Smith and W. Elmore.*—This invention consists of improvements in the production of white-lead from galena or from suitable residual products or substances containing sulphide of lead. [The] process is fully set out in the specification.

7,883.—FLUSHING CISTERNS: *J. Southall.*—T[his] refers to an improvement in flushing cisterns. The [in]ventor uses by preference a cistern having a well cas[t in] a suitable position in its bottom. In this well is m[ade] an outlet pipe, terminating at its upper end in a val[ve] seat, the top standing somewhat above the bottom [of] the well. On this seat works a valve, which can [be] raised at will in the usual manner by means of a le[ver] worked by a rod or chain outside the cistern, the le[ver] being attached to a link connected loosely to the valv[e]. This link works through a hole in a piece of metal bri[dg]ing the top of the well, the lever of the ball-cock work[ing] up and down between its two sides for a certain d[is]tance, the sides being connected by two cross-piec[es] of metal, one at the top forming a jaw, and anot[her] lower down at such a point as to be under [the] ball-cock lever, so that when the link is raised [it] lifts the ball-cock lever up with it, closing the b[all-] cock, and when the valve is on its seat permitting [the] ball-cock lever to fall just low enough to allow a g[ood] flow of water to come in at the cock. The link has a[lso] a projecting part near the lower end forming a cat[ch] which holds the valve up off its seat whilst [the] cistern empties as it slips over, and rests on [the] bridge piece, as described below, when the link [is] raised. On the bridge piece of metal near to one s[ide] of the hole in which the link works are two lugs, [on] which a lever is pivoted, the lever having a float at [one] end, the other end nearest the link having a slot in [it], the slotted part working between the sides of the li[nk] on which it operates by means of a pin passing thro[ugh] the slot. The pin is fastened at its end into the si[des] of the link. The action of the above arrangemen[t is] fully described in the specification.

12,760.—BRICK-PRESSING MACHINES: *J. S. Pul[...] and Others.*—This is an invention to provide an au[to]matic stop motion on brick-pressing machines, [by] which, after the brick is pressed, and the plunge[r] raised to the top, the machine automatically stops [for] the removal and insertion of the bricks. It has also [for] its object the making the bricks of one uniform thi[ck]ness outwardly. For this purpose a catch or proj[ec]tion is employed, preferably operated by, and c[on]nected with, the crosshead of the machine. This ca[tch] comes in contact with the handle of the clutch-le[ver] and automatically stops the machine at the top a[s] the plunger is raised. A following-up spring retu[rns] the handle. The clutch consists of a pin passing thro[ugh] the clutch-boss, and having an angular projecting h[ead] in the groove of the boss of the clutch. A sim[ilar] angular projection is formed on the clutch-lever.

NEW APPLICATIONS FOR LETTERS PATENT.

February 29.—3,896, W. Fox, Mitre-cutter or Trimm[er]—3,905, J. Roots, Suspending, raising, or lowering G[a]liers, &c.—3,908, S. Jacobs, Fire-grate.—3,939, C. Luth[...] Wood Flooring.

March 1.—3,991, G. Nunn, Electrical-call and Indic[at]ing Apparatus.—4,037, T. Hawkesley, Dry-earth Clos[et] —4,048, J. Ottoway, Window-sashes and Frames.—4,[...] J. Thomas and G. Kitchen, Work Bench.—4,052, P. M[...]cheron, Fire-grates.

March 2.—4,061, G. Williamson, Kitchen Range[s] 4,062, C. & C. Kite, Ventilators.—4,083, G. Leicht, C[on]necting or fastening together building stones or s[...] for the formation of Walls.—4,131, J. Knowles, a [Pro]cess for the treatment of raw materials to be used in [the] production of Portland Cement.—4,149, W. Charleswo[rth] Slurry Drying Structures used in the manufactur[e of] Cement.—4,159, H. Austie, Sash-fasteners.—4,162, [...] Carr, Screw Nail.

March 3.—4,188, W. Waite, Window-sash Fastene[r]—4,213, H. Cheesman, Ladders.

March 4.—4,269, F. Fitton, A Safety Stair-step and Street Grate-tread, applicable to Lighting, Ventilation, &c.—4,274, F. Tolchard, Shuttles, used in connexion with the Seats of Water-closets for flushing purposes.—4,280, R. Hocking, Water-closets.—4,281, W. Shears, Tools employed in Working Wood, such as Planes, Spokeshaves, &c.—4,286, E. Fulcher, Machine for Moulding Slabs, Building, Ornamental, and other Blocks and Bricks.—4,295, J. Ardin and J. Brown, Construction of Blocks or Bricks for Street Pavements.—4,301, A. Illidge, Sash-fasteners.—4,332, C. Abernethy, Device for the Prevention of Draughts through Doors.

March 5.—4,373, T. Walford and J. Hodgkins, Caps or Terminals for Chimneys.—4,379, J. Shanks, Fittings for Baths, &c.—4,389, A. Emley and J. Symington, Bends for Water-pipes, &c.—4,405, S. Morrell, Sash-fasteners.—4,408, C. Dobbs, Scoria or Slag Blocks for Paving, &c.—4,424, M. Brophy, Door-locks or Latches.—4,426, M. Brophy, Door-knobs and Spindles.

PROVISIONAL SPECIFICATIONS ACCEPTED.

691, C. Cobham, Water-taps.—1,292, R. Browne, Fire-tables.—2,134, Water-closets.—2,322, S. Cooper, Hoists for Elevators.—2,566, W. Andrews, Door-springs—2,568, Kirlew, Chimney and Ventilating Shafts.—2,577, A. Milne, Double-action Bolts for Doors, French-windows, &c.—2,585, W. Mounsey, Flushing Apparatus for Water-closets, &c.—2,711, F. Humpherson, Automatic or Intermittent Syphon Flushing Apparatus.—2,716, E. Parr, Screws.—2,813 W. McKinley, Automatic Sash-fastening and Lock.—3,083, R. Walker, Machine for Grinding Portland Cement.—3,220, F. & J. Butterfield & Co., Limited, and W. Pearson, Mechanism for Operating Hand Saws.—3,356, R. Bell, Heating Dwelling-houses, Hotels, and other Buildings.

COMPLETE SPECIFICATIONS ACCEPTED.

(*Open to Opposition for Two Months.*)

7,850, J. Merrill, Syphon Flushing Cisterns.—7,431, J. Pole, Window-fastenings.—7,432, E. Breething, Machinery for moulding Bricks.—10,137, H. Lake, Construction of Floors.—1,827, W. Brown, Jointing Concrete Paving.

SOME RECENT SALES OF PROPERTY:

ESTATE EXCHANGE REPORT.

MARCH 7.—By *T. G. Wharton*: Three plots of freehold land, Hazel-rd., Kensal-green, 186*l.*; six plots of freehold land, St. Margaret's-rd., 360*l.*; twenty plots of freehold land, ditto, 1,152*l.*; 6 and 8, Princess-rd., Finsbury-pk., u.t. 71 yrs., g.r. 23*l.* 17s., r. 105*l.*, 845*l.*—By *J. Slee & Son*: 44, Sutherland-sq., Walworth, u.t. 20 yrs., g.r. 5*l.* 7s., 190*l.*; 17, Cross-st., Holborn, f. r. 90*l.*, 1,180*l.*; 127 and 129, High-st., Homerton, c., r. 27*l.* 6s., 240*l.*—By *Wagstaff & Warman*: 79, Gopsall-st., Hoxton, u.t. 4 yrs., g.r. 6*l.* 6s., r. 32*l.*, 225*l.*—By *Weatherall & Green*: 94, Walton-st., Chelsea, u.t. 50 yrs., g.r. 6*l.*, 80*l.*; 82 and 84, the Grove, Hammersmith, f., r. 115*l.*, 1,820*l.*; 98, Dalling-rd., u.t. 76 yrs., g.r. 6*l.* 10s., r. 40*l.*, 400*l.*; 12, 14, 16, 22 to 30 (even), Wharf-rd., Notting-hill, u.t. 74 yrs., g.r. 48*l.*, 660*l.*; i.g.r. of 100*l.*, Manchester-st., u.t. 74 yrs., g.r. 35*l.*, 850*l.*; 1, 11 to 17 (odd), Lockton-st., u.t. 74 yrs., g.r. 36*l.* 6s., 460*l.*; 4, 6, 12, and 14, Lockton-st., u.t. 74 yrs., g.r. 26*l.*, 270*l.*; 23 and 24, Manchester-st., u.t. 74 yrs., g.r. 12*l.* 12s., 160*l.*; 411, Latimer-rd., u.t. 83 yrs., g.r. 5*l.*, 130*l.*

MARCH 8.—By *Debenham, Tewson, & Co*: 51 to 59 (odd), White-st., Bethnal-green, f., r. 162*l.* 10s., 1,580*l.*; 28, Hersee-pl., f., r. 23*l.* 8s., 260*l.*; 7, Seven Star-alley, St. George's-in-East, f., r. 16*l.* 18s., 100*l.*; 12 to 15, Brunswick-pl., Commercial-rd., E., f., r. 62*l.* 8s., 405*l.*; 5, Mona-rd., Peckham, f., r. 22*l.* 2s., 305*l.*; "Neal's House," Woodhouse-rd., Leytonstone, f., r. 22*l.* 2s., 175*l.*; three plots of freehold land, Forest Hill, 130*l.*; a plot of freehold land, Hadleigh-rd., Southend, 60*l.*; 16 to 32 (even), Love-lane, Ratcliff, u.t. 68 yrs., g.r. 27*l.* 10s., r. 204*l.* 2s., 990*l.*; 40 to 48 (even), Love-lane, and 1, 2, and 3, Love Lane-sq., u.t. 64 yrs., g.r. 70*l.*, 100*l.*; 50 to 58 (even), Love-lane, u.t. 68 yrs., g.r. 60*l.*, r. 239*l.*, 860*l.*; 2 to 20 (even), Brook-st., u.t. 68 yrs., g.r. 40*l.*, r. 221*l.*, 740*l.*; 28 and 30, Brook-st., u.t. 8 yrs., g.r. 21*l.*, r. 54*l.* 12s., 15*l.*; 32, Brook-st., u.t. 68 yrs., g.r. 13*l.*, r. 39*l.*, 75*l.*; 4, Apsley-st., Stepney, u.t. 32 yrs., g.r. 1*l.*, 75*l.*; 63 and 65, Kender-st., Peckham, u.t. 59 yrs., g.r. 2*l.*, r. 53*l.* 6s., 415*l.*; 194 and 196, Edward-st., Deptford, u.t. 52 yrs., g.r. 4*l.* 2s., r. 52*l.*, 405*l.*; 54, Margery-pk.-rd., Stratford, u.t. 79 yrs., g.r. 5*l.*, r. 28*l.*, 240*l.*—By *C. W. Davies*: 25 and 26, New Charles-st., City-rd., u.t. 51 yrs., g.r. 9*l.*, 630*l.*; 29 and 31, Frome-st., Islington, u.t. 54 yrs., g.r. 8*l.*, 485*l.*; 27 and 28, Matilda-st., u.t. 53 yrs., g.r. 10*l.*, 565*l.*; 96, Southampton-st., King's-cross, u.t. 32 yrs., g.r. 5*l.* 5s., r. 38*l.*, 255*l.*; 19, Wyndford-rd., u.t. 15 yrs., g.r. 5*l.* 5s., r. 28*l.*, 125*l.*; 68 and 70, Cumming-st., Pentonville, u.t. 27 yrs., g.r. 9*l.* 5s., r. 43*l.* 10s., 235.—By *H. Oughton & Son*: 103 and 105 Walton-st., Chelsea, f., r. 80*l.*, 1,100*l.*; the residence called "Bancroft," Parson's-green, u.t. 89 yrs. g.r. 10*l.*, 610*l.*; 88, Shorrold's-road, Walham-green, u.t. 93 yrs., g.r. 5*l.* 5s., r. 30*l.*, 260*l.*

MARCH 9.—By *Briant & Son*: 32, Hanover-rd., Plumstead, u.t. 41 yrs., g.r. 2*l.* 10s., r. 24*l.*, 290*l.*; 38, Hanover-rd., u.t. 38 yrs., g.r. 3*l.*, r. 24*l.*, 285*l.*; 261 and 263, Lynton-rd., Bermondsey, u.t. 51 yrs., g.r. 10*l.*, 500*l.*; 38 to 41, Kinross-st., u.t. 23 yrs., g.r. 12*l.*, 375*l.*—By *Walker & Runtz*: 27 and 28, Wyvil-rd., Lambeth, u.t. 54 yrs., g.r. 10*l.* 14s., r. 78*l.*, 660*l.*—By *Hobson, Richards, & Co.*: "Talbot Lodge," Muswell-hill, f., 620*l.*; 11 and 12, Peter's-lane, Smithfield, u.t. 91 yrs., g.r. 70*l.*, 215*l.*—By *Ellis Morris & Co.*: "The Surly Hall Hotel," near Windsor, f., 4,500*l.*; 15, Elgin-mews South, Maida-vale, u.t. 68 yrs., g.r. 6*l.*, r. 55*l.*, 310*l.*—By *Orgill, Swann, & Orgill*: F.g.r. of 80*l.*, with reversion in 39 yrs., Notting-hill, 1,930*l.*; an i.g.r. of 80*l.*, Alexandra-rd., St. John's-wood, u.t. 65 yrs., g.r. 20*l.*, 1,190*l.*; 61 and 62, Chester-mews, Regent's-pk., u.t. 26 yrs., g.r. 20*l.*, r. 45*l.*, 150*l.*; 51, Marine-st., and 30, Frederick-st., and "The Britannia" public-house, Bermondsey, u.t. 33 yrs., g.r. 6*l.*, r. 85*l.*, 1,010*l.*; "The Manor House Tavern," Finsbury-pk., u.t. 38 yrs., g.r. 15*l.*, r. 200*l.*, 3,010*l.*; "The Shovel Tavern," Cable-st., St. George's-in-East, f.g.r. 80*l.*, reversion in 7 yrs., 1,200*l.*; "The Rose and Crown," St. George's-st., Ratcliff, f.g.r. 40*l.*, reversion in 21 yrs., 900*l.*; "The Silver Tavern," Burdett-rd., Limehouse, f.g.r. of 75*l.*, reversion in 48 yrs., 1,570*l.*

MARCH 10.—By *Herring, Son, & Daw*: Two freehold houses and shops, Streatham Common, 1,100*l.*—By *Chesterton & Sons*: 1, Gliddon-st., Kensington, u.t. 94 yrs., g.r. 30*l.*, 1,820*l.*; 92, Gloucester-mews West, Hyde-pk., u.t. 50 yrs., g.r. 2*l.*, 210*l.*—By *E. Evans*: 90, Merton-rd., Wimbledon, f., r. 28*l.*, 330*l.*; 9 and 10, Spring-gardens, u.t. 88 yrs., g.r. 14*l.*, 290*l.*; 10, Lessar-av., Clapham, u.t. 92 yrs., g.r. 13*l.* 10s., r. 50*l.*, 390*l.*; No. 305, Wandsworth-rd., u.t. 15 yrs., g.r. 8*l.*, r. 42*l.*, 190*l.*; 13 and 29, Belle Vue-gardens, Earlsfield, u.t. 96 yrs., g.r. 10*l.*, 310*l.*—By *Stimson & Sons*: A plot of freehold land, Friern-rd., Dulwich, 150*l.*; 26 to 36 (even), Landell's-rd., u.t. 86 yrs., g.r. 27*l.*, 690*l.*; 10, Chesterton-rd., Notting Hill, u.t. 75 yrs., g.r. 8*l.*, r. 40*l.*, 390*l.*; 15, Nelson-sq., Peckham, u.t. 48 yrs., g.r. 10*l.*, 80*l.*; 19 and 22, Nelson-sq., u.t. 38 yrs., g.r. 12*l.* 12s., 250*l.*; The Residence, "Reefton," Tooting-pk.-rd., f., r. 26*l.*, 300*l.*; f.g.r. of 14*l.* 17s., with reversion in 91 yrs., 315*l.*; two c. cottages, Bricketwood Green, St. Albans, r. 10*l.* 14s., 150*l.*; 16, Solesbridge-lane, Chorley Wood, f., r. 5*l.* 8s., 200*l.*—By *C. C. & T. Moore*: 143, Rendlesham-rd., Clapton, f., r. 34*l.*, 450*l.*; 15, Bromley-st., Commercial-rd., E., u.t. 27 yrs., g.r. 3*l.*, r. 32*l.*, 265*l.*; 10, Portland-st., u.t. 27 yrs., g.r. 3*l.*, r. 32*l.*, 260*l.*; 44, West India Dock-rd., Shadwell, f., r. 24*l.*, 280*l.*; 23, George-st., Commercial-rd., f., 230*l.*; 25 to 31 (odd), Love-lane, Shadwell, u.t. 19 yrs., g.r. 12*l.* 10s., 340*l.*; 22 to 26, King David-lane, u.t. 12 yrs., g.r. 22*l.*, 255*l.*; stabling and store, Pope's Hill, u.t. 8 yrs., no g.r., r. 30*l.*, 65*l.*; 70 to 73, Bridge-rd., Stratford, u.t. 78 yrs., g.r. 10*l.*, 475*l.*; 123, Ball's Pond-rd., Islington, u.t. 12 yrs., g.r. 6*l.*, r. 38*l.*, 110*l.*; 16 and 17, Tysoe-st., Clerkenwell, u.t. 23 yrs., g.r. 8*l.*, r. 120*l.*, 940*l.*; 114, 116, and 118, Copenhagen-st., Islington, u.t. 53 yrs., g.r. 36*l.*, 680*l.*—By *Newbon & Co.*: 1 to 7, Nelson-sq., Islington, u.t. 39 yrs., g.r. 50*l.*, 765*l.*; 93 to 105 (odd), Tower Hamlets-rd., Forest Gate, u.t. 84 yrs., g.r. 14*l.*, 620*l.*; 42 and 44, Hargrave-pk., Holloway, u.t. 60 yrs., g.r. 21*l.*, r. 124*l.* 10s., 880*l.*

MARCH 11.—By *Baker & Sons*: 1 and 3, Clifton-ter.; and 1 to 6, Meadow Cottages, Clayton, Sussex, f., r. 72*l.* 19s.,—ex mortgage, 250*l.*—By *Wood & Kirby*: 9 and 10, Jerusalem-passage, Clerkenwell, f., r. 85*l.*, 1,020*l.*; 53 and 55, Outram-st., Caledonian-rd., u.t. 66 yrs., g.r. 12*l.*, 705*l.*—By *E. Christian*: 2, Cayley-st., Stepney, u.t. 17 yrs., g.r. 2*l.* 2s., 85*l.*; 104, Whitehorse-st., u.t. 17 yrs., g.r. 5*l.* 6s., 80*l.*; 108, Whitehorse-st., u.t. 17 yrs., g.r. 7*l.* 7s., 150*l.*

[*Contractions used in these lists.*—F.g.r. for freehold ground-rent; l.g.r. for leasehold ground-rent; i.g.r. for improved ground-rent; g.r. for ground-rent; r. for rent; f. for freehold; c. for copyhold; l. for leasehold; e.r. for estimated rental; u.t. for unexpired term; p.a. for per annum; yrs. for years; st. for street; rd. for road; sq. for square; pl. for place; ter. for terrace; cres. for crescent; yd. for yard, &c.]

PRICES CURRENT OF MATERIALS.

TIMBER.		
Greenheart, B.G. ton	9/0/0	0/0/0
Teak, E.I. ... load	10/10/0	15/0/0
Sequoia, U.S. ft. cu.	2/3	3/0
Ash, Canada load	2/10/0	4/0/0
Birch, do.	3/5/0	4/10/0
Elm, do.	3/10/0	4/15/0
Fir, Dantsic, &c.	2/0/0	3/10/0
Oak, do.	3/0/0	5/5/0
Canada	5/10/0	7/0/0
Pine, Canada red	2/10/0	3/10/0
Do. yellow	2/10/0	5/0/0
Lath, D'ntsic, fath	5/0/0	6/0/0
St. Petersburg	5/0/0	7/0/0
Deals, Finland, 2nd & 1st std 100	8/10/0	10/10/0
Do. 4th & 3rd ..	7/10/0	8/10/0
Do. Riga	6/10/0	8/0/0
St. Petersburg, 1st yellow ..	11/0/0	15/0/0
Do. 2nd yellow	8/10/0	10/0/0
Do. white	7/10/0	10/10/0
Swedish	7/15/0	16/0/0
White Sea	8/10/0	18/0/0
Canada, Pine 1st	20/0/0	26/0/0
Do. do. 2nd	14/10/0	16/0/0
Do. do. 3rd, &c.	8/0/0	10/3/0
Do. Spruce, 1st	8/10/0	11/0/0
Do. do. 3rd & 2nd	6/15/0	8/0/0
New Brunswick	7/0/0	7/10/0
Battens, all kinds	3/10/0	15/10/0
Flooring Boards, sq., 1 in. prep. 1st	0/8/3	0/14/6
Do. 2nd	0/7/6	0/11/6
Other qualities	0/4/6	0/6/0
Cedar, Cuba .. ft.	/3¼	/4¼
Honduras, &c.	/2¾	/4
Mahogany, Cuba.	/4½	/6¼
St. Domingo, cargo av	/4¼	2/0
Mexican do. do	/4	/5
Tobasco do. do	/5¼	/7
Honduras do. ..	/5¼	/6¼
Box, Turkey ton	4/0/0	13/0/0
Rose, Rio	10/0/0	20/0/0
Bahia	9/0/0	16/0/0
Satin, St. Domingo ..... ft.	0/0/8	0/1/3

TIMBER (continued).		
Satin, Porto Rico	0/0/8	0/1/6
Walnut, Italian ..	0/0/3½	0/0/7
METALS.		
IRON—Pig, in Scotland .... ton	2/0/4	2/0/7
Bar, Welsh, in London	6/0/0	6/10/0
Do. do. at works in Wales	5/10/0	6/0/0
Do. Staffordshire, in London	6/5/0	8/15/0
COPPER—British, cake and ingot	40/0/0	49/10/0
Best selected ..	50/0/0	51/0/0
Sheets, strong ..	60/0/0	0/0/0
Chili, bars	46/5/0	46/12/6
YELLOW METAL lb.	0/0/5	0/0/6¼
LEAD—Pig, Spanish .... ton	10/17/6	11/0/0
English, com. brands	11/2/6	11/5/0
Sheet, English, 3 lbs. per sq. ft. and upwards ..	13/0/0	0/0/0
Pipe	13/10/0	0/0/0
ZINC—English sheet ...... ton	20/5/0	0/0/0
Vieille Montagne	25/15/0	0/0/0
TIN—Straits	89/5/0	89/15/0
Australian	89/7/6	89/15/0
English Ingots	92/10/0	92/15/0
OILS.		
Linseed ...... ton	18/12/6	19/0/0
Cocoanut, Cochin	25/0/0	25/10/0
Do. Ceylon	22/5/0	0/0/0
Palm, Lagos	23/0/0	23/10/0
Rapeseed, English pale	25/10/0	26/0/0
Do. brown	24/0/0	0/0/0
Cottonseed ref. ..	18/15/0	0/0/0
Oleine	21/10/0	22/10/0
Lubricating, U.S.	4/10/0	5/10/0
Do. refined	5/0/0	10/0/0
TAR—Stockholm barrel	0/19/0	1/0/0
Archangel	0/12/6	0/0/0

TENDERS.

[Communications for Insertion under this heading should be addressed to "The Editor," and must reach us *not later than* 12 *noon on Thursdays.*]

ABERTILLERY (Mon.).—For rebuilding the "Globe" Hotel, and adjoining Shop, for Mrs. Edwards. Mr. Alfred Swash, architect, 3, Friars-chambers, Newport, Mon. Quantities by the architect:—

Thomas Webb	£1,447	Dyson Parfitt	£1,285
R. Williams & Son	1,418	Thos. Foster	1,240
Wm. Price	1,400	A. P. Williams, Abertillery*	1,200
W. Jones & Son	1,397	John Jenkins	1,065

* Accepted.

ASTON MANOR (Birmingham).—For the complete electric installation of the baths and public offices, for the Local Board. Mr. W. Augustus Davies, Engineer to the Board:—

Verity & Sons	£1,661 7 6
Fowler, Lancaster, & Co.	1,594 0 0

ASTON MANOR (Birmingham).—For the erection of two cabmen's shelters, at Aston, from designs by Mr. W. Augustus Davies, Surveyor to the Board:—

S. Garratt & Son	£275	F. N. Stephens	£149
J. Simons	165	J. E. Moorhouse, Birmingham (accepted)	138
Clarke & Co.	150		

ASTON MANOR (Birmingham).—Accepted at schedule of prices, for widening, deepening, and improving the Hockley Brook Course, for the Aston Manor Local Board and the Birmingham City Council. Mr. W. Augustus Davies, Engineer:—

Currall & Lewis, Birmingham.

ASTON MANOR (Birmingham).—For the construction of a new road, Aston Manor. Mr. W. Augustus Davies, Surveyor to the Board:—

Jones & Fitzmaurice	£446	J. Biggs, Birmingham*	£385
Currall & Lewis	409	* Accepted.	

BARNET (Herts).—For the erection of two shops, High-street, Barnet, for Mr. C. Mees. Mr. A. E. Smith, architect, Luton:—

Pearson	£1,458	Curzon	£1,280
Ashton	1,429	J. Baughan, Barnet*	1,250
Bateley	1,397	* Accepted.	

BOUNDS-GREEN, N.—For additions and decoration to Magdala House, Brownlow-road, for Mr. George Wagner. Mr. Chas. W. Latter, architect, 1, Oak-lane, Bounds-green, N. Quantities by the architect:—

F. Voller	£397 10 0
S. Yardley & Son, Wood-green (accepted)	393 15 0

BRISTOL.—For erecting St. Philip's Branch Bank, West-street, Bristol, for the Bristol and West of England Banking Company. Mr. Henry Williams, architect, 28, Clare-street, Bristol. Quantities by Mr. A. Baffatt, Somerset-chambers, Corn-street, Bristol:—

E. T. Hatherley	£3,873	Cowlin & Son	£3,473
Eastabrook & Son	3,800	E. & G. Howell	3,415
R. James	3,799	C. A. Hayes	3,399
Jas. Wilkins	3,760	G. Humphreys	3,379
Wm. Veals	3,725	R. Love	3,350
E. Walters	3,700	H. E. Forse	3,300
S. E. Davies	3,642	G. H. Wilkins	3,280
Stephens, Bastow, & Co.	3,549	R. Wilkins & Son	3,274
Wm. Church	3,547	[All of Bristol.]	

None accepted. Estimate to be revised.

CARDIFF.—For the supply of 323 cast-iron columns for new biscuit factory and warehouses, Cardiff, for Messrs. Spillers & Bakers, Limited. Messrs. Veall & Sant, architects, Cardiff. (Twenty-two different patterns):—

	Totals. Cast Horizontal.	Totals. Cast Vertical.	Per Ton. Horizontal.	Per Ton. Vertical.
T. Spittle, Limited	£1,164 2 9	—	£7 0 0	—
J. Allan, sen., & Sons	1,100 0 0	—	6 15 0	—
E. Wood	1,057 4 0	£1,216 0 0	6 10 0	£7 10 0
A. Handyside & Co., Limited	—	1,215 0 0	—	7 12 6
Laidlaw & Son	—	1,162 0 0	—	7 10 0
C. Jordan & Sons	996 0 0	—	6 0 0	—
J. Williams & Sons, Cardiff	*957 6 9	1,079 6 9	5 18 0	6 18 0

* Accepted.

CARDIFF.—For pitching, paving, and channelling streets, for the Corporation. Mr. W. Harpur, C.E., Borough Engineer, Town-hall, Cardiff. Quantities by the Borough Engineer:—

J. Allan	£3,881 18 6	Ellis & Davies	£3,080 8 6
R. Smith	3,826 17 6	T. Williams	3,030 3 11
J. C. Pearson	3,738 14 9	J. Rich (accepted)	2,950 5 2
T. Harries	3,443 6 1	[All of Cardiff.]	

CARLISLE.—Accepted for the erection of a one-arch oblique bridge, Blackpool-gate, Bewcastle. Mr. Richard Maxwell, Surveyor, Longtown, Cumberland:—

George Kyle, Newcastleton, N.B. £728 10 0

CHACEWATER (Cornwall).—For rebuilding the parish church, for the Building Committee. Mr. E. Sedding, architect, 7, Buckland-terrace, Plymouth:—

John Borlase	£1,467	W. Moyle, Chacewater*	£1,425
Farr Bros.	1,450	* Accepted for first contract.	

CHERTSEY.—Accepted for levelling, metalling, channelling, &c., Mills-road and North-road, Hersham, for the Rural Sanitary Authority. *Mr. W. Durrant*, Surveyor:—

G. A. Franks, Guildford £135 8 0

DORCHESTER.—For additions to the brewery at Dorchester, for Messrs. Eldridge, Pope, & Co. Messrs. Crickmay & Sons, architects, No. 17, Parliament-street, Westminster. Quantities by Messrs. H. Raven & Harry W. Crickmay, 12, Dartmouth-street, Westminster:—

Builders' Work.

R. Davis & Son	£2,198 10 0	A. H. Green*	£1,912 0 0
J. Guy & Son	1,961 0 0	* Accepted.	
J. T. Whettam	1,940 0 0		

Iron Work.

A. H. Green	£1,380 0 0	W. H. Lindsay, Neal, & Co.	£1,130 0 0
S. Griffith	1,365 9 0	Foster, Lott, & Co.*	1,053 18 6
Matthew T. Shaw & Co.	1,192 0 0	J. T. Whettam	995 0 0
Thornewill & Warham	1,180 0 0	* Accepted.	

Builders' Work and Iron Work.

W. Gibson	£3,798 0 0	J. A. Bartlett	3,527 14 0

FARNHAM.—For alterations at Seaforth Heath End Hall, Farnham, for Major R. Dixon. Mr. A. J. Sturges, architect and Surveyor, Guildford:—

Stanley Ellis	£850	Diamodal & Sons	£754
T. H. Kingerlee	845	Patrick, Farnham*	725
P. C. May	829	* Accepted.	

GUILDFORD.—For alterations, Guildown Cottage, Guildford, for Mr. J. W. Bentley. Mr. A. J. Sturges, architect and surveyor, Guildford:—

May	£506	Stanley Ellis, Guildford*	£467
Riglett & Hammond	484	* Accepted.	

HARROGATE.—Accepted for the erection of new buildings, for the Harlow Manor Hydropathic Co., Limited. Mr. Henry A. Cheers, architect, Twickenham:—

Gould & Stevenson, Leeds £11,500 0 0

(Full list of tenders too long for publication.)

HEXHAM.—For the erection of a convalescent home. Messrs. Johnson & Crawford Hick, architects, Arcade, Newcastle-on-Tyne:—

Martinson & Wilton	£3,283 11 8	E. Snowball	£2,743 4 0
Middlemiss Bros.	3,000 0 0	W. & J. Darlington	2,721 10 0
Hutchinson	2,800 17 4	H. Brown & Co.	2,651 14 6
Rutherford & Armstrong	2,798 0 0	C. Hope	2,587 0 0
G. Gradon & Son	2,793 14 0	J. Herdman & Son, Hexham*	2,466 4 2
J. Ewell	2,709 11 2	* Accepted.	
R. Darlington	2,747 3 9		

HORNSEY.—For new roads, sewers, surface-water drains, &c., for the British Land Company, Limited, on their estate at Harringay-park, Middlesex. Mr. Henry B. Michell, surveyor:—

Nowell & Son	£9,127	Rogers & Co.	£6,610
Killingback & Co.	8,035	Pettit & Son	6,220
Bloomfield	7,808	Wilson	5,934
Pizzey	7,519	Jackson, Leyton*	5,678
Dunmore	7,318	* Accepted.	

LANGFIELD.—Accepted for the erection of a fever hospital, for Mr. John Ashton Fielden. Mr. J. Sutcliffe, architect, 8, Roomfield-buildings, Todmorden, Lancashire. Quantities by the architect:—

Mason and Bricklayer—Thos. Mitchell, Warley, Halifax
Carpenter and Joiner—James Haigh, Hebden Bridge
Plumbers' and Glaziers' work—Jonas Alderson & Sons, Luddenden Foot
Slaters and Plasterers—Thos. Wrigley & Son, Hebden Bridge
Blacksmith—John Horsfield, Luddenden Foot
Concrete—Geo. Greenwood & Sons, Halifax
Ventilators—Hill & Hey, Halifax
£5,729 10 3

LIVERPOOL.—Accepted for erecting Public Offices for the Huyton-cum-Roby Local Board, near Liverpool. Mr. Henry A. Cheers, architect, Twickenham:—

C. Burt £3,374 0 0

LONDON.—For the erection of shop addition to Norfolk Villa, 185, Larkhall-lane, Clapham, for Miss Mannering. Mr. Richard Price, Surveyor, 25, Park-road:—

Dent	£145 10	Ford (accepted)	£128 0

LONDON.—For gas-fitting work and lamps at the "Abbey" Tavern, Kentish Town-road, for Mr. A. T. Cowling. Mr. John T. Alexander, architect, 40, Great James-street, Bedford-row:—

Vaughan & Brown	£300 0	Morris	£231 10
Steadman	262 0	Biggs, Boro'-road, S.E.	218 0

LONDON.—For re-building warehouse, No. 10, Osborn-street, Whitechapel, for the Victoria Wine Co. Mr. George Waymouth, architect, 23, Moorgate-street, E.C. Quantities supplied by Mr. Alan Paull, 6, Quality-court, Chancery-lane:—

F. & F. J. Wood	£6,510	W. Morter	£5,839
Perry & Co.	5,990	Richardson Bros.	5,638
W. Gladding	5,960	J. Sparks (accepted)	5,275

LONDON.—For the erection of new warehouse in Bream's-buildings, Fetter-lane, E.C., for Messrs. Sampson Low, Marston, & Co., Limited. Mr. W. Seckham Witherington, architect, 79, Mark-lane, E.C.:—

Foster & Dicksee	£8,333	O. Cromwell	£7,365
W. H. Lascelles	7,860	B. Nightingale	7,187
J. Grover & Son	7,635	W. Shurmur	6,993
W. G. Larke & Son	7,565	H. King & Sons	6,482
C. F. Kearley	7,546		

LONDON.—For alterations and additions to the "Black Lion" Public-house, High-street, East Ham, E., for Mrs. C. Keep. Mr. Fred A. Ashton, architect, 3, Crooked-lane, E.C.:—

W. Shurmur	£2,943	W. Watson	£2,390
Hearle & Farrow	2,695	Coulsell Bros.	2,383
Walker Bros.	2,677	F. Voller (accepted)	2,379

LONDON.—For three steel Cornish boilers, for ink factory, Finsbury-park, N., for Mr. H. C. Stephens, M.P. Messrs. Crickmay & Sons, architects, 17, Parliament-street, Westminster:—

J. Foster & Sons	£1,000	Fraser & Fraser	£942
Oldham Boiler Works Co.	1,000	E. Heason & Son, Manchester*	846

* Accepted.

LUTON.—For the erection of warehouses, Bute-street, Luton. Mr. A. E. Smith, architect, Luton:—

Wright	£1,978	Neville	£1,760
Saunders	1,944	Partins	1,639
Smart	1,780	Pryer (accepted)	1,597

[All of Luton.]

LUTON.—For the erection of saw-mill, Bedford-road, Luton, for Messrs. Arnold & Co. Mr. A. E. Smith, architect, Luton:—

Kimham	£813 0	Pryer	£794 0
Neville	775 0	Saunders	713 0
Long	774 10	Parkins*	627 10
Smart	729 0		

* Accepted.

[All of Luton.]

MORPETH.—For the erection of a doctor's-house, for the Ashington Medical Society. Mr. W. J. Charlton, engineer, Ashington Colliery, Morpeth:—

Waterson	£550	Douglass Bros., Blyth*	£520

* Accepted.

NEWCASTLE-UNDER-LYME.—For the execution of certain drainage works for the Town Council. Mr. Jas. Pattison, Borough Surveyor, Newcastle-under-Lyme:—

J. Horobin	£1,612 10	Smith & Taylor	£1,373 10
F. Barke	1,552 13	(Surveyor's estimate, £1,370.)	

PLYMOUTH.—For building new parish room and School, All Saints, Plymouth. Mr. Edmund Sedding, architect, Plymouth:—

John Finch	£1,330 0 0
F. Blowey, Plymouth (accepted)	1,150 0 0

SEVERN TUNNEL JUNCTION (Mon.).—For the erection of ten cottages at Severn Tunnel Junction, for Messrs. Parnall. Mr. Alfred Swash, architect, 3, Friars-chambers, Newport, Mon. Quantities by architect:—

Morgan & Roberts	£2,690	Jno. Linton	£2,350
Wm. Price	2,685	Executors of W. Gradwell	2,330
Thos. Webb	2,680	Geo. Wilkins	2,327

TOOTING.—For the erection of chapels, lodges, and boundary walls, for the Streatham Burial Board. Mr. W. Newton Dunn, A.R.I.B.A., architect, 1 and 2, Bucklersbury, E.C. Quantities by Messrs. Evans & Deacon:—

	Chapels. £ s. d.	Lodges. £ s. d.	Boundary Wall. £ s. d.	Totals. £ s. d.
Hill Bros.	4,787 0 0	2,471 0 0	3,629 0 0	10,887 0 0
Carmichael	4,920 0 0	2,420 0 0	3,450 0 0	10,790 0 0
Candler & Sons	4,750 0 0	2,550 0 0	3,400 0 0	10,700 0 0
Higgs & Hill	4,644 0 0	2,500 0 0	3,540 0 0	10,684 0 0
Dove Bros.	4,875 0 0	2,375 0 0	3,425 0 0	10,675 0 0
Peacock Bros.	4,268 0 0	2,194 18 11	3,246 18 10	9,709 18 1
Smith & Sons	4,297 0 0	2,160 0 0	3,137 0 0	9,594 0 0
A. M. Deacon	4,195 6 10	2,090 6 10	3,141 6 4	9,427 0 0
F. & H. Higgs	4,288 0 0	2,264 0 0	2,813 0 0	9,365 0 0
Lorden & Sons	4,083 0 0	2,172 0 0	2,694 0 0	8,949 0 0

Drainage and Roads.

C. T. Newman	£3,542 10	Neave & Son	£3,065 0
Pelll & Sons	2,396 0		

Wrought-Iron Railing and Gates.

Baylis, Jones, & Baylis	£319 7 6	Main & Co.	£208 0 0
E. L. Cooper	275 0 0	Hill & Smith	183 0 0
Stevens Bros.	270 0 0	Letheram (Cheltenham)	152 5 10

SHEFFIELD.—For the erection of a School, Derbyshire-lane, Norton, for the Norton School Board. Mr. T. H. Wilson, architect, 63, Norfolk-street, Sheffield:—

	School.	Walls.
Thos. Lowe & Sons	£1,725 0 0	£400 0 0
Thos. Astling	1,686 0 0	368 0 0
Jno. Morton	1,617 0 0	365 0 0
J. H. Hurst	1,579 0 0	311 0 0
J. Bee & Sons	1,502 10 0	328 0 0
Abraham Gibson	—	259 0 0
Thos. Roper	1,647 0 0	—
Cecil Skelton	1,690 0 0	—
Hy. Harrison, Greenhill, Derbyshire*	1,465 8 0	263 3 4

* Accepted.

N.B.—Separate tender required for boundary walls.

WALTHAMSTOW.—For alterations at the "Lorne Arms" public-house, Queen's-road, Walthamstow, E., for Mr. C. A. Nicoll. Mr. Fred. A. Ashton, architect, 3, Crooked-lane, E.C.:—

W. Shurmur	£396	Hearle & Farrow	£296
Coulsell Bros.	323	F. Voller (accepted)	284
W. Watson	312	F. Linzell	265

WATERHOUSES (co. Durham).—For alterations and additions to property for Mr. Jonathan Hall. Mr. H. T. Gradon, architect, Durham:—

Wm. Ayton & Sons	£403 18 0	James White	£340 0 0
Thos. Walton	395 18 0	M. R. Draper & Sons, West Rainton*	328 1 10
James D. Carr	380 0 0		
James Robson	380 0 0		

* Accepted.

WEST BROMWICH.—For the construction of a brick gas-holder tank, 124 ft. diameter, at Albion, for the Town Council:—
Jno. Aird & Sons, London. (Accepted on a schedule of prices.)

SUBSCRIBERS in LONDON and the SUBURBS, by prepaying at the Publishing Office, 19s. per annum (or 4s. 9d. per quarter), can ensure receiving "The Builder," by *Friday Morning's Post.*

TO CORRESPONDENTS.

J. P. M. W.—T. L. W.—W. L.—T. S. (shall have attention).—V. & S. (we cannot conveniently insert the information in the tenders column).—E. G. W.—W. A. D.—"A Non-Gambler" (we have not space for your letter).—H. J. N. (ineligible, amount not being sent).

All statements of facts, lists of tenders, &c., must be accompanied by the name and address of the sender, not necessarily for publication.

We are compelled to decline pointing out books and giving addresses.

NOTE.—The responsibility of signed articles, and papers read at public meetings, rests, of course, with the authors.

We cannot undertake to return rejected communications.

Letters or communications (beyond mere news-items) which have been duplicated for other journals, are NOT DESIRED.

All communications regarding literary and artistic matter should be addressed to THE EDITOR; all communications relating to advertisements and other exclusively business matters should be addressed to THE PUBLISHER, and not to the Editor.

TERMS OF SUBSCRIPTION.

"THE BUILDER" is supplied DIRECT from the Office to resi[dents] in any part of the United Kingdom at the rate of 19s. per a[nnum] PREPAID. To all parts of Europe, America, Australia, and [New] Zealand, 26s. per annum. To India, China, Ceylon, &c. [30s. per] annum. Remittances payable to DOUGLAS FOURDRIN[IER,] Publisher, No. 46, Catherine-street, W.C.

The Builder.

Vol. LXII. No. 2564. Saturday, March 26, 1892.

ILLUSTRATIONS.

Sculpture for New Church at Domrémy: "Jeanne d'Arc entend ses voix."—M. André Allar, Sculptor .... *Double-Page Ink-Photo.*
Business Premises, Copthall Avenue.—Mr. T. Barnes-Williams, Architect .... *Double-Page Photo-Litho.*
Selected Design for Birmingham General Hospital: Mr. W. Henman, Architect:—
Elevation towards Steelhouse-lane, and Section .... *Single-Page Photo-Litho.*
Detail of South Pavilion .... *Single-Page Ink-Photo.*
Plans .... *Two Single-Page Photo-Litho's.*

CONTENTS.

The Building Sandstones of Ireland 237
Notes 238
Royal Institute of British Architects 240
Some Recent Developments in Theatre-Planning 242
The London County Council 244
The Architectural Association Spring Visits 244
The Labour Commission 244
Sculpture: "Jeanne d'Arc" 246
"Token House," Copthall-avenue 246
Birmingham General Hospital 246
Competitions 247
Manchester Royal Institution 247
"Restoration" at Lincoln Cathedral 247
Crypt in Watergate-street, Chester 248
Miss Sellers's Lectures 248
Steam-Rolling on Main Roads 248
Measuring 249
Student's Column.—Warming Buildings by Hot Water, XIII. 249
General Building News 250
Sanitary and Engineering News 250
Foreign and Colonial 250
Miscellaneous 250
Legal 251
Meetings 251
Recent Patents 252
Some Recent Sales of Property 252
Prices Current of Materials 253

The Building Sandstones of Ireland.

VERY little attention has hitherto been paid in this country to the various building stones of the sister island, yet there is a more complete literature on the subject than we possess respecting the building stones of England. Wilkinson,[*] Kane,[†] Hull,[‡] Houghton,[§] Griffith,[||] Kinahan,[¶] and others, have produced many excellent treatises on Irish building stones, and all these works are remarkable for their philosophic inception and characteristic thoroughness. We would call particular attention to the recent papers by Mr. Kinahan, last referred to, which, if little accessible in their original form, are decidedly the most complete of them all. The subject is a large one, and we can do no more than dissect a part of it. On the present occasion we shall restrict our observations mainly to the consideration of the sandstones of Ireland which, in remote times, have been, or are at present, used for building purposes. We shall also briefly glance at the deposits of sandstone hitherto untouched by the quarryman, and which could easily be made accessible to the builder with the expenditure of but little capital.

We know that sandstones were favourite building materials with the early inhabitants of Ireland, in spite of the fact that softer and much easier worked stone was frequently nearer at hand. When we reflect on the primitive tools with which the refractory material was wrought into shape, it speaks not a little for the perseverance of these ancient builders, who evidently thoroughly appreciated the enduring qualities of the sandstones, and were careful in the selection of what they used. Whether they intended that their work should stand as monuments to their ability in the remote future, we know not, but certain it is that much of it will remain for centuries to come when the flimsy productions of the modern "competitive contractor" will have decayed into dust—despised and then forgotten.

Slate rocks were called into requisition in those districts where they existed when mortar first began to be used in the country; eventually the sandstones were largely superseded by limestones, which were capable of being worked with greater facility, and lent themselves more readily to delicate mouldings. The bias of the workmen, however, frequently led them to employ stones brought from a distance, even in those districts where equally good stone could have been raised; and this peculiarity is by no means extinct at the present day. Thus, we learn from the researches of Mr. Kinahan, that when the Scotch workmen were building at Muckross Abbey, Killarney, about forty years since, they ignored the excellent limestone of the neighbourhood, and imported sandstone from Chester, that being the nearest place where they could get sandstone similar to that which they were accustomed to work. The engineers of the Ballast Board, when building lighthouses, brought Dublin granite to various localities where stone well suited to the purpose already existed.

Good examples, showing the durability of the sandstones, may be seen in the old doorway of Maghera Church, co. Derry; a doorway at Killeshin, co. Carlow; St. John's-gate, Drogheda; at Boyle Abbey, co. Roscommon; and some dressed work at Mellifont. The last mentioned also shows that the prevalence of mica materially influences the weathering of certain parts of the stone.

Irish sandstones are found in nearly all the geological formations of the island. The most ancient come from rocks of Silurian and Devonian age, but they are not much worked at the present time, by reason of their extreme hardness and the proximity (in some instances) of good limestones. Many of the early structures were made of it, however, and the stone has proved very durable. The Old Red Sandstone, met with about Castlebar, and extending from Newport to Lough Conn, in Mayo, is a reddish-brown sandstone and conglomerate. In the central tracts of Ireland red sandstone occurs in the elevated parts of Slieve Bloom, the Inchiquin, Berungh, Keeper, and Galtee Mountains. Other areas of the same class of stone occur in the promontory of Dingle, the vicinity of Killarney and Bantry, Kenmare River, Bantry Bay, and in Muntervary, Mizen Head, and Cape Clear promontories. The Old Red Sandstone in co. Cork is, at least, 5,000 ft. in thickness; but the largest area is that which surrounds Cork, Youghal, Dungarvan, and Waterford. The beds in the last-mentioned districts have much analogy with strata of the same geologic age in Pembrokeshire, and, like them, are traversed by slaty cleavage, the angle of inclination of the cleavage to the plane of the strata often varying from bed to bed. In Ireland, the Upper Old Red Sandstone consists of a lower thick series of green, purple, and red grits and slates; and an upper and thinner group of yellowish, or grey, flagstones, frequently suitable for paving purposes. These divisions have also been partly classified with the Lower Carboniferous.

Carboniferous rocks occupy more than half the area of Ireland, but they are largely composed of limestones. Here and there on definite horizons, however, sandstones occur; in the southern part of Ulster and the adjoining part of Connaught a pure arenaceous rock is found in the limestone, or as independent beds. This arenaceous rock is called the "Calp" sandstone, and furnishes the stones now held in the highest esteem by Irish architects and builders. The Coal Measures, as usual, contain sandstones, but, with the exception of those of the Fermanagh series, are not in much repute.

Mr. Kinahan states that in the West Munster coal-fields the sandstones are almost invariably hard, and although they can be dressed on the face of the beds, they cannot be worked across, as they chip and fly at the edges. In places, they produce excellent flags, but to give good joints their edges generally require to be sawn, as they chip on the face if dressed. In the East Munster (Tipperary) and Leinster coal-fields

[*] G. Wilkinson, "Practical Geology and Ancient Architecture of Ireland." 1845.

[†] Sir R. Kane, "Industrial Resources of Ireland." 1844.

[‡] Professor Hull, "Building and Ornamental Stones." 1872.

[§] Rev. Dr. Haughton, "Quart. Journ. Geological Soc.," vol. xviii., and other papers.

[||] Sir R. Griffith, "British Assoc. Report," 1863.

[¶] G. H. Kinahan, "Journ. Royal Geological Soc. of Ireland," vol. xviii. 1886-88.

good stones suitable for dressed work are found. In Monaghan and Fermanagh are the well-known Lisnaskea stones; and good flags were formerly sent extensively to the market from the Connaught coal-field.

Sandstones in Ireland of later age than the Carboniferous do not seem to bear a very good character, with the exception of some, of the Triassic period, coming from North Devon, Scrabo, and Dundonald, which are much sought after. Other Triassic sandstones are abundant enough, but they are not of a very durable nature.

We will now briefly describe the chief building sandstones as they occur in the various counties, adopting the classification of Mr. Kinahan, but omitting many geological details, and arranging the counties in alphabetical order.

Antrim.—The Geological Survey Memoir states that the fine beds at Cave House were at one time largely quarried, and shipped to Belfast for building purposes. At Ballyory quarry, near Ballycastle, the stone is very fine-grained and friable, largely made up of grains of quartz, slightly micaceous, and with a few iron spots; it works with facility, but, of course, the blocks containing the iron spots should be rejected. It is light yellow and pink in tint. Certain varieties have been used for bridge-work and in several buildings in the North of Ireland, and have proved to be very durable, but the stone requires to be carefully selected. It is remarkable that in Ballymena, the nearest large town to the quarry, Ballyory stone is not much used, it having been beaten out of the market by the Scotch and Dungannon stones, which are cheaper. Several quarries in red stone, of Triassic age, known as "Red Free," exist in the valley of the Lugan, and near Larne.

Armagh.—Many sandstones occur in this county, but they have not been quarried to any great extent. A fine-grained stone of Carboniferous age is raised at Grange, and was employed in the restoration of Armagh cathedral in 1835; and a conglomeratic bed, near the county town, was formerly used for building.

Carlow.—The Lower Coal Measures in West Carlow contain many fine sandstones, which might be raised for architectural purposes but only one quarry, worthy the name, now exists — namely at Killeshin. The material is of a brownish-grey colour.

Cavan.—Quarries in the "yellow sandstone" formation near the county town have been much drawn from for local purposes; and good building stones exist in the north-western part of the county, but they are not worked to an appreciable extent.

Clare.—At Ballyheigue, near Scariff, a yellowish, ferruginous sandstone is found which was largely employed in the Shannon improvement works at Killaloe. A dark grey stone is raised at Ennistimon, and at Crag and Money Point good flags occur, which have been largely exported to different places along the coast in times gone by. Rather more than thirty-five years since there was a large industry at Killaloe manufacturing these flagstones into chimney-pieces, but the business has long since disappeared. This is another instance similar to those which, on previous occasions, have been pointed out in these columns of the decay of the stone industry of Ireland. The causes of the closing-up of the "Killaloe Marble Works" are not very apparent. As Mr. Kinahan very truly remarks,* "Killaloe is most favourably situated, having command of the greatest water power in Ireland, and ought to be one of the great centres of industry; but for some reason all this great water-power is allowed to remain idle. Prior to 1850 the Killaloe works were a great source of employment, not only in the town, but in the flag quarries on the Lower Shannon, and in various marble quarries, principally in counties Tipperary and Limerick. All these quarries seem to have failed when the Killaloe works ceased."

Cork.—This county has many sandstones of excellent quality, and several quarries exist, but the industry is not as important as it should be. The greyish-green stone from Sherkin Island, off Baltimore Harbour, has been extensively employed in Skibbereen, and is said to be very durable. The greenish stone of Drumcona is also in good repute, and so is the brown freestone of Horse Island. Other good sandstones are found at Glandore, Rahan, and Quarry mountains, near Mallow, Knightfield, Whitechurch, and Youghal. In rocks of Carboniferous age quarries occur, amongst other places, at Coolcoming, Belleview, Shippool, and Ballymartel, the two last-mentioned localities being situated near Kinsale. Speaking of the stones raised on the river Lee, north of Cork, Mr. Wilkinson says that some are yellowish-white, close, having compact quartzose grains, with felspathic cement, and semi-vitreous; whilst others are green, siliceous, close, and dense, but with numerous fissures and bedded portions, the latter causing the stone to fail.

Donegal.—Quarries near Mount Charles produce durable stone of much repute. That from Drumkeelan has recently been used in building the museum and library at Leinster House, Dublin; it is a yellowish-grey material, felspathic, slightly micaceous, with a siliceous, ferruginous matrix or cement. There seems to have been some difficulty in getting an adequate supply, judging from experience in building a bank at Ballyshannon. The greyish-yellow sandstone of Altito, near Donegal, was used as ashlar in Lough Eske Castle. Other stones of a somewhat similar nature are found at Beauwin, Kildoney, near Ballyshannon, and at Dog's mountain.

Down.—The Triassic beds along the valley of the Lagan yield a dark red stone which has been considerably worked for local requirements. The different quarries at Scrabo Hill, near Newtownards produce some of the best-known sandstones in Ireland. The variety is very good, and, as is usual in such cases, the material is variable in quality. The predominant colours are grey, yellow, and red. It has been much employed in the neighbourhood of the workings, and in Belfast; examples in that city are afforded by the Albert Memorial, St. Enoch, Fortwilliam, Sinclair's Elmwood, and Donegal-street churches. The red stone from Dundonald is also used in Belfast and in Dublin; it is very similar to Scotch Annan stone in appearance.

Dublin.—In the city of Dublin, sandstone is largely displayed in the public buildings, but Mr. Kinahan states that none of the cut stone appears to have been obtained in the county, whilst most of it, especially in the buildings erected during the last century, and in the beginning of the present, is English stone. Arenaceous rocks, belonging to the Carboniferous system, have yielded good flagstones, especially in the "Windmill" quarry, Rathgar; whilst local stone is obtained from the lower Coal Measures in the north of Co. Dublin.

Fermanagh. — Near Lisnaskea several quarries of note occur, which produce a cream, yellow, or greyish free-working stone. That from Slush Hill has been used in several buildings in Enniskillen, Clones, and Irvinestown, but the quarry is now closed. The "Geological Survey Memoir" for the district states that good hard siliceous stones may be procured in the Derrygonnell "Calp" area, to the west of Lower Lough Earne—as in the neighbourhood of Church Hill. About Monea they are, in general, massive, with subordinate flaggy beds. Other sandstones are found in the west of the county, where there are several small quarries.

Galway.—Although fine stones occur in co. Galway they are not, at present, much worked. A thin laminated flag, known as "Dunmore slate," was formerly raised at Slieve Dart for roofing purposes.

Kerry.—The Devonian and Coal Measure sandstones were much used in the early Norman architecture in the county; but the numerous small quarries open at the present time merely provide material for local pur-

* "Journal Royal Geological Society of Ireland," vol. xviii. (1887), p. 238.

ɔut of the bed of a river or stream seems to have been not uncommon with the early builders, as in different places holes are pointed out so situated, which tradition states were quarries where the stones were procured for adjoining structures." A good example of such a quarry, he adds, may be seen at Kilmacrenan, co. Donegal; not long since this hole was pumped out, and a rude set of steps to the floor of the old working was discovered. Near Castlerea good sandstones have been raised, and also in Slieve Baun, near Roscommon, and other places.

Sligo.—Although this county is by no means deficient in fine sandstones, they are not much drawn upon by reason of the preference given to limestone for building. West of Ballysodare Bay, and in Dromore West, freestone quarries occur.

Tipperary.—Sandstones were largely raised in this county in ancient times, but, although of good quality, they are not much sought after at the present time. Quarries exist in the Devonian rocks at Knockmeeldown and Mount Anglesey; and in Carboniferous at Dundrum, Tinnakilly, Drumbane, and near Roscrea.

Tyrone.—This county produces the best sandstones in Ireland, and they are largely quarried. The majority are of Carboniferous age. The "Calp," especially, yields some beautiful stones; the workings in the vicinity of Cookstown show a cream or blue tint stone, slightly micaceous, open-grained, and having a calcareo-siliceous cement. North of Dungannon, at Bloom Hill, cream and red stones are raised; and the quarries of Gortnagluck and Carlan have provided much building stone for Ballymena, Londonderry, &c. Ranfurly or Mullaghana stone is yellowish, fine-grained, and does not tool easily. It was used, amongst other places, in the Post-office and Northern Bank, Belfast. These materials are known generically as "Dungannon stone."

Waterford.—The Devonian and Lower Carboniferous sandstones are very generally used throughout the county; they are usually brown, yellow, or greenish. Quarries occur ear Dungarvan, Lismore, Clonmel, and at ther places.

Westmeath, Wexford, and *Wickow.*—The t-mentioned county, being almost entirely mposed of Carboniferous limestone, conins no sandstone of any note. In the cinity of Wexford Harbour shaly sandones have been wrought, and also at places Forth and Burgy. The only sandstone orth mentioning in Wicklow is quarried at lencormick, north of the Great Sugarloaf. is cream-coloured, fine-grained, and has en much used at Bray, and in the surroundg district.

From the foregoing it will be observed at Ireland is rich in arenaceous rocks, d many of them are of excellent ality. With increased prosperity, and the troduction of a little more capital, the Irish ndstone industry would doubtless be reived. It is a deplorable but significant fact hat, whilst suitable building material is ound in abundance in the island, a considerble quantity is imported. Surely such a tate of things will not exist much longer!

NOTES.

HE coal-miners have had their holiday, and the merchants their harvest at the expense of the public, and now we may look for e reaction. It set in, indeed, some days fore the men resumed work, prices dropng (almost as rapidly as they had risen) en while there was hardly a ton of coal ing raised in any part of the country. ich, however, had been the activity during e week preceding the stoppage,—particurly in regard to household coal,—that there as actually more coal in the London depôts the beginning of this week than there was fore the stoppage. The resumption of work delayed in some instances owing to the ines getting out of order in consequence of he refusal of the Federation to allow work f any kind to be proceeded with during the stoppage. With regard to the scheme for working five days a week, it is not anticipated that the masters generally will offer much opposition to its adoption, as the demand for fuel has now fallen to such an extent that there would, in many cases, be some difficulty in finding work enough to occupy the men full time. Probably, if the suggestion had come from the masters there would have been a great outcry; indeed, some difficulty will doubtless be experienced as it is, for this continued voluntary sacrifice of wages is not altogether approved of by some of the men. From Derbyshire, for instance, where there are 33,000 miners, it is reported that many of the men complain of loss of wages, and opposition may develop to the five-days week resolution. The present outlook is most serious in Durham, where the strikers will receive the support of the Federation men in their efforts to resist a reduction of wages, and where some bad feeling is already being displayed.

THE hearing of the Bill of the Manchester, Sheffield, and Lincolnshire Railway Company, for the extension of their line to London, has commenced. It is clear that so far as the extension is concerned it is practically an unopposed Bill. The real fight is over the question of the London terminus. The company proposes to swallow up squares and streets in a very wholesale fashion. When all the facts and plans have been clearly stated, it is really a question for the House of Commons to decide. As the matter is in a sense *sub judice* it would be undesirable to enter into details, but the absorption of a large part of a district of London is a subject not only of vital importance in itself, but is also a matter which must be regarded as likely to become a precedent. For some day, perhaps, the South-Western Railway might wish to locate themselves in the midst of South Kensington. Then, again, there is in close connexion with the terminus, the question of street approaches. A large terminal station must obviously have an influence on the vehicular traffic for a considerable distance. The points will be found probably to resolve themselves into conditions upon which the Bill should be passed; but these conditions seem to be of a character which require discussion from a larger assembly than a handful of members in a committee-room.

THE demolition of the block of buildings near the Rolls Chapel, at the south-east side of Chancery-lane and opposite Carey-street, will, it is to be hoped, result in the widening at this part of the "Lane." This main communication between Holborn and Fleet-street is too narrow for the traffic, and the ground which has lately been cleared should not be allowed to be built over to the same extent as before the destruction of the old buildings. We must also again call attention to the fact that though the new Bankruptcy Court and offices are completed, the access to them for carriages and cabs is very inadequate. There must be a direct approach made from Holborn if persons who have to attend at these buildings are not to be delayed and inconvenienced, since both the Chancery-lane and the Little Queen-street routes are constantly blocked.

RAILWAY passengers are decidedly getting the best of it just now in regard to the overcrowding question. The latest decision in their favour was given at the Birmingham County-court last week, when the Midland Company were sued by a first-class passenger for having inflicted some third-class company upon him against his will. It was decided that the company had no right either to put more than six passengers into a first-class carriage, or to put third-class passengers into carriages of a higher class, without the consent of the occupants; and the complainant was awarded forty shillings damages for the inconvenience and discomfort to which he had been subjected. This gentleman seems to have frequently been the victim of overcrowding, for it appeared from his evidence that on two occasions he had to take refuge in the guard's van in consequence of insufficient accommodation. It was argued, however, that entering the guard's van was his own act, and the Judge held that no case had been made out in this instance. There may have been, perhaps, some difficulty in deciding whether such an act, under such circumstances, should be described as voluntary or not, although it is certain that it would go very much against the grain; but it would be some satisfaction to the plaintiff to succeed on the other portion of his case. The Midland will evidently have to look to their accommodation for this section of their line, while other defaulters in this respect will do well to take warning.

MR. CECIL TORR'S article in the last number of the *Classical Review* (March, 1892) is sure to be the beginning of a smart controversy on a point of importance to all Hellenists. The occasion for the article in question is the appearance of Mr. Flinders Pettie's "Illahun, Kahun, and Gurob," but Mr. Torr directs his polemics mainly against what he is pleased to call Mr. Petrie's "sensational article" in the *Hellenic Journal* for October, 1890. To this article and its great importance we drew attention at the time. Mr. Torr, in his dogmatic fashion, says: "Nobody could take such an article very seriously; but nobody could fairly criticise it at the time, for Mr. Petrie merely stated his results and reserved most of his evidence for publication in his work on Illahun." By an odd coincidence in this very same number of the *Cassical Review* we have evidence that one Homeric archæologist of notably sound judgment does take Mr. Petrie very seriously. In reviewing the English edition of Schuchardt's book on the Schliemann excavations, Dr. Walter Leaf writes:—"It is pure ill-luck that it (*i.e.*, second German edition) should come out just too soon to take advantage of Mr. Petrie's paper in the 'Journal of Hellenic Studies,' which must form the foundation of all the chronology of the Mykenaean period." The lists are set for a tournament of no common interest, and we hope to see Dr. Leaf, as well as Mr. Petrie, break a lance.

THE Prussian Diet has granted the ten million marks asked for by the Government towards the cost of a new Berlin Cathedral, and the House has made a start by voting the hrst 300,000 marks necessary for the preliminary works on the proposed site. The grant of the ten millions has been made on condition that no extra sums shall at any future date be asked for, that the money be voted in smaller sums, according to the requirements, and that a Board of Works standing under the sole control of the Emperor's Master of the Royal Household Affairs carry out the building, and bear all responsibility in relation to it. As to who will have the future responsibility of keeping the building in condition when it is in use, nothing has been decided. In the course of the discussion that took place before the voting, Herr Richter, the Leader of the German Liberals, opposed the grant. He considered the financial state of the country too bad at present to permit of such luxuries as cathedrals, whilst urgent necessities were being crossed out in the General Purposes Budget; he also reminded the Government that the number of places of worship in the country was considered to be far too small in comparison to the population, and that the sum asked for would cover the expense of erecting a number of these buildings. He then went on to question the House as to who was to guarantee that such money as they were asked to vote would not be used for the erection of a public eyesore, and that the Emperor's despotic *sic volo sic jubeo* would not also be used in this matter. If the House was going to acquiesce in the Government's demand, the right of having a band in the selection of architect and design should, at all events, be reserved. He finished by pointing out that the means of the reigning Hohenzollerns were not so small as not to permit the Emperor to build a cathedral on his own account, if he thought fit, without making the taxpayers' burden a heavier one than it was already. Another member observed that the discussion would not have taken so disagreeable a turn if it had not been for the selection of the unpopular design and architect. The end of the matter was as above stated, that the country will have to pay its money towards the cost of an erection, the design of which is decidedly unpopular, without any power of interference on the part of their representatives.

THE Church of St. Gervais, some of whose fine old windows, and images in the baptistry, narrowly escaped total destruction by an explosion with felonious intent upon the Lobau barracks, is one of the most noteworthy in Paris. Conspicuous for its range of flying buttresses, it stands behind the Hotel de Ville* and the (former) Caserne Napoléon. The fabric was completed in 1420; a Classic façade by Salomon de Brosse was added in 1616. The windows, originally filled in by Pinaigrier and Cousin, had already suffered much. One, in a chapel on the south side of the choir, representing the "Judgment by Solomon," was set up in 1531. The older glass in the Lady Chapel, restored in 1845, is ascribed to Pinaigrier. Here were buried Scarron, after whom the Chapelle Scarron, with late seventeenth century decoration, is named; P. de Champagne, painter; the Chancellor Letellier; and Madame de Maintenon's husband. The grotesque carvings of the choir stalls are of the sixteenth century. St. Gervais is clearly depicted in Mr. H. W. Brewer's "View of Paris in Francis I.'s Time," published by us on January 5, 1889.

SOME repairs, undertaken by the Burial Board of St. Margaret's and St. John's, Westminster, to the churchyard of the former parish, supplement the more extensive alterations that were made ten years ago. The present turf and Eureka-paved pathways are a great improvement upon the unsightly area of cracked and sunken tomb-stones. The latter were re-laid some feet below the surface, and the only stone now visible is one opposite to the church's new western porch, which is inscribed "T II." St. Margaret's grave-yard is crowded to excess. The Report by the General Board of Health upon a scheme for Extramural Sepulture (1850) contains some forcible strictures by Dr. Reid on its insanitary condition. In the churchyard were buried Hollar, in a grave, says Aubrey, near the north-western corner of the tower (1677), and Dr. Hickes, author of the "Thesaurus" (1715). After the Restoration, they dug a pit for the remains, taken out from the Abbey, of Admiral Blake; his bust, by Baily, was put in the Shire-hall of Taunton, his native county town, about thirty years since. Since the date (August 29, 1885) of our illustrated article upon the artistic features of this church, which in antiquity of foundation ranks next to St. Paul's and the Abbey, two coloured windows have been set up. One was presented by Mr. G. W. Childs, of Philadelphia, in memory of Milton's marriage to, and the burial of, his second wife, in the church.† Another, of three lights, by subscription, in honour of Blake, designed by Mr. Edward Frampton. At the ceremony of unveiling the latter, on December 18, 1888, Archdeacon Farrar is reported to have said it formed the thirteenth window placed in the church to the memory of great men since he became rector. The lines on the Caxton, Milton, and Blake windows are by Lord Tennyson, Browning, and Mr. Lewis Morris respectively. The original organ, by "Father" Smith, was sold soon after his death. In 1882, the then organ was rebuilt and enlarged by Messrs. W. Hill & Son, and enclosed in an oaken case designed by Mr. A. G. Hill, F.S.A. It is now proposed to set up here a stained-glass window to the late Mr. W. H. Smith's memory.

* For description, with illustration, of the old Hotel de Ville see the *Builder* of January 26, 1889.

† Buried on February 10, 1658: a gift to the poor by the poet's daughter is cited in Mr. Wm. Bardwell's "Brief Historical Narrative of the Royal Church and Parish of St. Margaret the Martyr," circa 1878. The marriage took place on November 3, 1656.

AT the sale by auction on the 18th inst. of the Farringdon-market site (for 68,100*l.*) the question was raised whether portion of the area covers a disused burial-ground. There seems to be but little doubt that this is so. For the market buildings, between Shoe-lane and Farringdon-street, was cleared a space whereon stood (reckoning southwards from Plum Tree-court) Mellin's-rents; St. Andrew's, Holborn, Workhouse, in the lane, and just opposite to Robin Hood-court; Brew House-yard; Cross-alley; George-alley; the "Rose and Crown"; and Love-court. A graveyard belonged to, and lay behind, the Workhouse, and is that wherein Chatterton found a pauper's burial. Close by, southwards, between Stonecutter-street and Harp-alley, stands another disused graveyard, which belongs to the parish of St. Bride.

THE collection of paintings by Mr. Whistler, at the Goupil Gallery, consists mainly of works which have been exhibited before in London, and seems to have been intended as a kind of demonstration in honour of the fact that his portrait of his mother has recently been acquired for the Luxembourg Gallery. Mr. Whistler is always amusing on these occasions, and in his catalogue he quotes after each picture some of the contemptuous remarks which have been made about it by various critics, and winds up with a quotation from the *Chronique des Beaux-Arts* in praise of the Luxembourg purchase as "destinée à l'éternité des admirations," with the object of showing what imbeciles are the English critics who have scoffed at Mr. Whistler's productions. We fear the argument will not bear much examination. In the first place the Luxembourg picture is one of the very best Mr. Whistler ever painted, and has been recognised as such by many who would not stand his nocturnes and other vagaries; and in the second place the work exactly hits the most recent French taste in painting, and therefore naturally gets rather extravagant praise from a French critic. This will not prove that all the things in the Goupil Gallery are worth the same praise. In regard to the portrait of Miss Alexander (23) Mr. Whistler is kind enough to put on record our own criticism, "There is character in it, but it is unpleasant character. Of anything like real flesh tones the painting is quite innocent." We are obliged to him for giving prominence to a criticism which we believe the majority of people who know anything about painting will admit to be a completely fair and just estimate of it. Among works exhibited are some that we can admire more unreservedly, especially the "Dame au brodequin Jaune" (why this affectation of French in an English exhibition?), a full-length portrait of a lady just in act to walk away from the spectator, showing her profile over her shoulder, which we have before remarked on for the admirable indication of figure and movement given in it. The exhibition as a whole is half amusing, half vexatious,—the work of one who might have done great things in his art if he could have troubled himself to take it seriously.

CARLISLE ARCHITECTURAL AND ENGINEERING ASSOCIATION.—The usual fortnightly meeting of this Association was held in the Town Hall on Tuesday last, when a paper was read by Mr. J. W. Smith, the Sanitary Inspector for the city, on "The Sanitary Arrangements of Public and Private Buildings." The paper contained some good, practical information as to matters of house drainage.

ROYAL INSTITUTE OF BRITISH ARCHITECTS: BYZANTINE ARCHITECTURE.

THE tenth general meeting of this Institute
the present session was held on Monday ev
ing last, Mr. J. Macvicar Anderson, Presid
in the chair.

The late Professor E. A. Freeman.

The President: Gentlemen, I am sure
will all mourn with me the loss of a dis
guished man, Dr. Freeman, Professor of Mod
History at the University of Oxford. Dr. F
man was, as you are aware, an Honorary Fel
of this Institute, and has been so for m
years. Whatever may be the exact posi
which posterity may assign to him as a
torian and as a prolific writer of the Eng
language, we at all events will all agree
deploring the removal from our roll
members of so eminent and distingui
a man. As architects we are more
ticularly interested in his loss from the circ
stance that, prolific as were his writings,
first work that he published, in 1849, wa
"History of Architecture," followed, in 1
by his "Essay on Window Tracery," and
1851 by his pamphlet on "Llandaff Cathedr
I am sure, gentlemen, you will all mourn w
me the loss of our distinguished Hono
Fellow.

The Examinations.

The President next made what he called
interim report on the Institute Examinati
He said that eighty applications had b
received to be admitted to the Prelimin
Examinations, seventy-four of which were
applications, six being applications from ca
dates who had been relegated to their stu
on previous occasions. Of the total of eig
twenty-nine were exempted, in accordance w
the rule, and were admitted as Probationers
the remainder, thirty-six had been exami
in London and fourteen in Manchester.
results of this Examination were not yet kno
the number of papers to be dealt with by
Examiners being so large. An Intermed
examination had also been held, at wh
twenty-two Probationers presented themsel
out of twenty-five who applied; of t
thirteen had passed, the remainder b
relegated to their studies for a period.
Examiners reported that "the testimonie
study" submitted in this Examination
been of high merit, particularly those of
non-metropolitan candidates. The names of
successful candidates in this Examination w
in order of merit, as follow:—Crompton
E. V., Bradford; Coussens, H. W., Hasti
Stratton, A. J., East Sheen; Vercoe, A.
London; Phillips, J. St. J., Belfast; C
J. P., London; Marchant, R., Sutton-at-H
Kent; Davis, E. R. O., Leicester; W
E. A., London; Gordon, T. W., Not
ham; Parkinson, F. J., Blackburn; Co
P. P., London; and Kendall, F. K., Lon
These gentlemen were now qualified for r
tration as Students of the Institute, a
subscribing class of members now numb
forty-one. For the Examination in Architec
which would commence on Monday next, M
28, there had been seventy-one new applica
received from candidates,—a larger nu
than had ever before applied at one time
addition, twenty-one candidates who had
relegated to their studies on previous occa
had also applied to be admitted to the exa
tion, making a total of ninety-two; but, th
plications of eleven of the new candid
having been disallowed, by reason of their
bationary work not being equal to the req
ments of the Board of Examiners, the
number of candidates to be examined
eighty-one,—sixty-six of whom would b
amined in the Institute Rooms, and fift
Liverpool. He ventured to think that
figures he had quoted were eminently
factory.

A New Theatre at Amsterdam.

Mr. J. M. Brydon said he had been asked b
Jan Springer, a well-known architect at Am
dam, to offer, for the acceptance of the
tute, a complete set of the working pla
the new theatre now being erected in that
He thought they would be found very
and interesting. The theatre itself was a
important structure, costing about 100,
and was built entirely on piles. The who
the construction was shown in the most m
way, and he though that the drawings w
be found very well worth study.

The President said he was quite sure the meeting would give its thanks by acclamation to Mr. Jan Springer.

Byzantine Architecture.

The President, in calling upon Professor Aitchison to read his paper on Byzantine Architecture, said it was with great gratification that they all welcomed their old friend and colleague, Professor Aitchison. It was particularly kind of him to undertake to give them a paper so soon after the arduous labours of his course of lectures at the Royal Academy.

Professor Aitchison then read his paper, of which the following is an abstract:—In the author's introductory remarks he said architects were now interrogating every architectural monument to discover how building had been converted into architecture in every country in the world, so that they might make the step forward towards a style characteristic of modern civilisation. In Byzantine architecture was to be seen the gradual adaptation of the plans of antique buildings to the ritual of a new faith; the universal adoption of the dome; the successive devices by which the equilibrium of the dome was at last attained; and the new æsthetic problems solved. In studying Byzantine architecture, two difficulties were encountered: the date of its beginning and its chronological sequence. He had taken the dedication of Constantinople (330 A.D.) as the first, although the buildings erected then were of Roman architecture, and probably designed by Roman architects. Having referred to the buildings erected in the time of Constantine, the author said the greatest benefit the Emperor had conferred on architecture, beyond his buildings, was to enact that all persons in North Africa and Italy should be freed from taxes if they allowed their sons of eighteen years of age and of liberal education to be brought up as architects. As to the sequence in date of Byzantine buildings little could be traced from Constantine's death to the days of Justinian, because the study of Byzantine architecture had been neglected; but if masterpieces were again to be erected old ones must be studied, and one masterpiece of the world was the Sta. Sophia of Constantinople. From a description, by Eusebius of Cæsarea, of an early Christian church, it would be seen that the churches originally faced east and the priest faced the congregation; the right and left sides of the altar were the priests' right and left, the right or south aisle being for men, and the left or north for women. In the fifth century the orientation was reversed, the priest standing with his back to the congregation and facing east, although the sides of the altar remained as before. The pure basilica type, in the form of a circus, did not, however, find favour except in Italy and the West. When domes on pendentives were first used was not known; M. Dieulafoy and others had discovered that the ancient Persians used egg-shaped domes over square chambers, carried by a pendentive pierced by a squinch; and M. Choisy was of opinion that those found at Serbistan, Firouzabad, and Ferachbad were of the days of the Achæmenides (about 800 B.C.). A pendentive, not quite regular in form, was found at Caracalla's Baths (211 A.D.), and mentioned by Ware in his tract on vaults in 1822. It was generally agreed, however, that the first great dome on four pendentives was that of the great Sta. Sophia; and next to Sta. Sophia the most important building, for its influence, was the Church of the Apostles at Constantinople, eventually destroyed by Mohammed II. for his mosque, but said to have served as the model for St. Mark's at Venice and St. Front at Périgueux. The earlier buildings of Central Syria seemed to have had considerable influence on Byzantine architecture. After the building of the great Sta. Sophia, the constructive problem to be solved was making domes on pendentives safe. The original dome of Sta. Sophia had fallen twice, and, though rebuilt with a higher rise, was not absolutely secure. The weakness of the abutments to the dome and pendentives was mainly on the north and south sides. No other big dome was to be found in Byzantine work; in minor and later examples barrel-vaults took the place of the arches. M. Choisy had pointed out that the dome of Sta. Sophia at Salonica was abutted by vaults one-third the diameter of the dome, but that the church was probably two centuries later than its prototype. The church to the Virgin at Salonica, called by Texier and Pullan St. Bardias, has been looked on as an early specimen of a dome on a drum, but the date of its dedication was 1028 A.D., and its arrangement also pointed to a late date, for the plan showed three apses at the east end, with a large central dome supported on columns and surrounded by four small domes. A similar arrangement of five domes was found at St. Nicholas at Myra, which was nearly identical in plan with St. Theodore at Constantinople. In Greece the squinch or conch seemed to have been preferred to the pendentive. Most of the peculiarities in churches after the building of the great Sta. Sophia were structural ones to prevent the spread of domes on pendentives, and the use of drums added to the weight; they showed, however, that the Byzantines had learnt to build domes securely. The æsthetic devices of early Byzantine work were not easy to describe, for most of the columns came from temples. The slips of entablature over the columns in the groined halls of the Roman baths were roughly imitated by a block put over the capitals; these blocks were universal up to a certain period. It was also possible that the treatment of the arcade over the Porta Aurea at Diocletian's Palace was a common practice. Besides the cup, cushion-shaped, or cubical capitals, the turning of the apophyges of the columns into bands was worthy of note. Æsthetically, the outsides of the buildings appeared to have received little attention, although some fronts were ornamented with blind arches or open arcades, and in later work bricks in zigzags, or rude imitation of the Greek fret, were used. The profiles of Byzantine work were tame and commonplace, with no proper æsthetic sequence in the mouldings. The interiors were splendidly decorated after the Roman manner, which the author described. The five Imperial palaces at Constantinople all joined together were as curious in construction as they were splendid in internal decoration. As the Byzantine Empire shrank away, the position of these palaces was found to be too exposed to attack from the Bosphorus, and another was built at Blachernæ, on the Golden Horn. The great tank called the Cistern of Pholoxenus, believed to be of Constantine's time, was interesting as exhibiting how the Byzantines built for pure utility. The peculiarities of Byzantine construction were given in M. Choisy's work, *L'Art de bâtir chez les Byzantins*, and was most original and interesting. The vastness of the interior of Sta. Sophia, the author considered, was most striking, and was greatly aided by one having to go down the narrow narthex, through the Imperial door into the main edifice. In the course of his description of the interior, Professor Aitchison drew special attention to the lighting, as matter he deemed not sufficiently thought of in modern buildings. There were forty windows round the base of the dome; the aisles on both floors were flooded with light, and there were many windows in the north and south clearstories. The decoration also was splendid; the lower part of the walls panelled with precious marbles, the sprandrels of the upper arcades and friezes inlaid with magnificent patterns on black and white marble, superb monolithic columns of porphyry and verde-antique and gold mosaic combined to produce a dignified and superb magnificence. The Professor concluded his paper with a reference to the present age, perhaps the most marvellous the world had seen, and said architecture had made great strides, and architects were bestirring themselves to make greater. What seemed, however, to be overlooked was that architecture was a structural art, and that all that architects could tell was by building; yet very few seemed to thoroughly acquire the art of construction. As a nation, the English could not pose like the Greeks as lovers of the beautiful; but they were not so far removed from the Roman character that they need despair of producing the grand and the dignified. Success was only to be achieved by the united and continuous efforts of many for generations. Noble architecture could not be looked for until there was a passionate desire for it among the people, devotion in the architects, and the opportunity of acquiring perfection by a long series of monuments to one noble purpose.

The President, in inviting discussion, said that not only did the valuable paper to which they had listened bristle with information interesting to architects, but it was occasionally enlivened by characteristic touches of what he would venture to call that Aitchisonian humour so familiar to them all. The Professor was also particularly deserving of their thanks for the very complete way in which he had illustrated the paper by means of drawings and plans.

Mr. R. Phené Spiers, in moving a vote of thanks to Professor Aitchison, said he had had the advantage of visiting Constantinople and of seeing Sta. Sophia; there was no building in the world which gave an internal effect equal to that which one obtained on entering that great church. Professor Aitchison had brought before them the various features of the interesting style of which he had spoken, and he had also drawn a moral. He was glad to say that the advice contained in his moral was carried out to a certain extent in the French school, where, according to his recollection when he was a student at Paris, the Mosque of Sta. Sophia, as illustrated in Salzenberg and in Reynaud' *Traité de l'Architecture*, was frequently referred to by them. In fact, the new Greek style in France was based much more upon Byzantine than upon Greek elements. He therefore cordially endorsed the Professor's remarks, as he did not know that there was any style which it would be of greater advantage for a student to begin to cut his teeth upon, if he might so express it, because of the great simplicity of its masses and the exquisite beauty, as he thought, of its detail. He confessed that he should have liked to see a little longer duration given to the Byzantine style. The Professor had fixed the period at 1123 years—from the time of the removal of the Empire to Constantinople to probably its being taken by the Turks; but he thought it would be well to direct the attention of students to the fact that the elements of Byzantine art existed for centuries before that, in Central Africa and elsewhere, and that we might go back another couple of centuries to find some of its earliest features. As a matter of fact, curious as it might seem, by bringing all his Roman architects to Constantinople, Constantine really retarded the development of the Byzantine style for probably half a century. It was a singular and peculiar judgment on him that of all the works which he erected at Constantinople by the hands of Roman workmen, not a single one remained, and it was only in the cistern of the 1,001 columns, and in the Yerebatan Serai, both of them executed by Byzantine workmen, that we found two examples of his work existing at the present day. Constantine would have done better if, instead of being in such a hurry, he had trusted to those Eastern workmen who were the builders of that magnificent system of vaulting which the Professor had brought before them. The Neo-Byzantine style was continued in Russia till nearly the end of the seventeenth century, so that instead of 1123 years about fifteen centuries would be more correct. In a paper which he (Mr. Spiers) read before the Institute some months ago, he attempted to prove that the theory of M. Dieulafoy as regards the Palaces of Serbistan and Firouzabad in Persia was illusory, but the Professor was of a different opinion.

Mr. Alexander Payne seconded the motion, and said it always seemed to him that the period of Byzantine architecture was perhaps one of the most original periods of architecture that we had in the whole list; and when one came to consider why it was so original, he thought the reason was not far to seek—which was that the whole needs of Christendom then were quite different from the needs that had gone before. The old Roman Empire had fallen, and the architects had to work out a new problem altogether. Hence we had that extraordinarily interesting period of architecture. It always seemed to him that the real birth of the style was in Syria. In the Marquis de Vogüé's book,—a book not well known except amongst architects,—one saw almost all the types of the churches that were to be found in Constantinople; and when one came to Constantinople one came to perhaps absolutely the most interesting architecture one could find. There was a great deal more to be found out in Constantinople than was known.

Professor Kerr and Mr. Loftus Brock having supported the vote of thanks, the President put it to the meeting, and it was heartily carried.

Professor Aitchison having replied, and Mr. E. Wyndham Tarn having made a few supplementary remarks, the meeting terminated with the announcement that the next meeting of the Institute would be held on Monday, April 4, when Mr. Starkie Gardner would read a paper on "Wrought-Ironwork of the Renaissance Period."

SOME RECENT DEVELOPMENTS IN THEATRE-PLANNING:

ARCHITECTURAL ASSOCIATION.

THE ordinary fortnightly meeting of this Association was held on the 18th inst., in the Meeting Room of the Royal Institute of British Architects, 9, Conduit-street, Mr. F. T. Baggallay, the President, in the chair.

Mr. F. T. W. Goldsmith, junior honorary secretary, announced a change in the date of the *soirée*, which is now fixed to be held on May 6, and not on the date mentioned in the "Brown Book."

Mr. Goldsmith further announced that the next Visit would be made on April 2, to the new South London Ophthalmic Hospital, St. George's-circus, by permission of Mr. Keith D. Young, the architect.

Mr. Goldsmith also proposed a hearty vote of thanks to Sir Arthur Blomfield for allowing the Association to visit the Church of St. Saviour's, Southwark, on the 5th inst. The vote of thanks was carried by acclamation.

The President then called upon Mr. E. A. E. Woodrow to read the following paper on "Some Recent Developments of Theatre-Planning":—

When the Committee of the Association honoured me with the request to read a paper on theatres to-night, I was asked if I consented to send the title of the paper to the secretary by return of post, as the Brown Book was ready to go to the printer's. In my haste to obey and anxiety not to delay so important a publication as our Brown Book, I pitched upon the title of "The Planning of Theatres," thinking that wide enough to cover any ground; but when I seriously sat down to prepare for this evening, I found I had committed myself to a task quite impossible to fulfil within the limit of time allowed. In fact, if I had attempted to speak at all fully on theatre-planning, it is probable that I should have been left here till midnight reading my paper to empty benches. The feelings I experience on finding out this may, perhaps, have been also felt by some of you who have had similar commands from our committee. On wondering how I was to overcome this dilemma, it occurred to me that I had better confine myself to recent developments and improvements in theatre-planning, but I fear I can only touch upon the fringe of even this section of my subject. Through the kindness of several gentlemen, I am enabled to-night to bring before your notice several drawings of theatres that have been erected in London during the past few years. It will be my endeavour to trace from these drawings some of the recent developments in theatre-planning. I think it will be of more practical use to us, as members of the Association, to spend the evening studying the plans of buildings built, or being built, than to deal with any ideas for theatre-constructing that exist only on paper, and have not undergone practical test. The great difficulty the student in theatre-planning has to surmount is to learn all that is wanted in and about a theatre; and unless he has had the advantages of seeing the nightly working of the front of the house, as well as of the stage, it is quite impossible for him to design a theatre that will meet the requirements of a London manager. Theatres have to be built to pay. It is a notorious fact that the same play may be a great success in one house and a perfect failure if produced in another. The theatre must be chiefly designed for the particular and special business that the manager intends carrying on therein, although, with changes of fashion and fortune, there *must* be some slight changes of the class of entertainment. I cannot quote a better example to illustrate my meaning than the special arrangements made by Mr. Phipps when he reconstructed the Haymarket to meet the demands of the class of performance given at this house and the class of people frequenting it. Large sums of money are required to mount a Haymarket piece; Mr. Bancroft, therefore, decided to abolish the pit, and fill the whole of the ground-floor of the house with high-priced seats. On the first night the experiment looked like failing, as loud cries of disappointment came from the exalted pit circle; but experience has proved that architect and manager were right in arranging the auditorium as they did. The same arrangement of seats would, however, be fatal to such a house as the Grand Theatre, Islington, the Olympic, or the Adelphi, where the large pit is looked upon as the mainstay of the house. The President of the Royal Institute of British Architects, in his excellent address this year to students, said that "a perfect plan is, and can only be, the result of the thoughtful study of every principle and every detail." It is necessary to find out all that is wanted, and to provide for such wants. To again quote Mr. Macvicar Anderson:—"It is impossible to produce a satisfactory result without practical knowledge of the requirements." . . . . "A plan to be good must be simple."

Site.—The first point which we should consider is, what is a desirable site for a theatre? and in endeavouring to answer the question we shall do well to ascertain what are the regulations enforced in other countries with regard to sites for places of public entertainment. In Austria, theatres holding more than 600 people must be perfectly isolated; those with a seating capacity for less than that number may have the back wall abutting on other houses. In St. Petersburg, there must be an open space on every side, with doors and windows upon all four sides. In Brussels, every theatre must be separated from adjoining premises by an open space or by brick walls. In Italy, perfect isolation is insisted upon; and in Paris, theatres that are detached must have a clear space of at least 9 ft. 10 in. to divide the theatre from neighbouring houses; where they are attached, there must be an independent wall within the theatre 9 in. thick, to protect the party-wall. From this it will be seen that on the Continent isolated sites are required. Such a site is undoubtedly the most desirable, but there is one serious drawback,—the cost. It must be remembered that on the Continent there is "State aid" to assist theatrical enterprise, but that in England it has to be carried on entirely as a private speculation. The New York regulation is a good one: the front must be on the public way, and open spaces at least 8 ft. wide must be left on both sides, from the line of the proscenium wall, the full length of the auditorium. It is seldom in a city like London that the chance offers itself for an isolated site; indeed, it is only when there are important street improvements that theatres such as the Royal English Opera House can be built within the given radius in which the theatres can be made to pay. There are a few cases where houses have been successful outside the centre of the Strand and Haymarket; for instance, the old Prince of Wales in Tottenham-street, made famous under Mrs. Bancroft's management; but there are few managers who would to-day care to risk such an experiment and start a theatre beyond the fashion-bound limits of the West-end. By the aid of street improvement an isolated site was obtained for the Shaftesbury Theatre, but the Savoy site was formed by pulling down a whole block of buildings. The insurmountable difficulties in acquiring perfect isolation in London renders it necessary to make the best of what can be got. How this difficulty has been overcome in some of the new theatres now in course of construction will be seen from the plans of the new theatre in Cranbourne-street, where two sides and part of a third are on public ways, and the new theatre in St. Martin's-lane, where Mr. Emden has so designed the theatre that above the ground level there is an open area or passage-way left all round the building. The drawback to perfect isolation is the prohibitive cost of the land; but a theatre must of necessity be a costly building; a cheap theatre is sure to be a dangerous one. The advantages of isolation are that the risks from fire and panic are greatly reduced. There is not the same danger from surrounding property; the exit passages, staircases, and corridors can be made shorter; and deliver into four different streets. The old-fashioned plan of buying a house in the main thoroughfare, and a plot of vacant land some distance in the rear on which to build a back-yard theatre, reached by a tunnel, is no longer permissible. Theatres on cramped sites hemmed in on all sides, with a narrow frontage to the principal street, sufficient only to carry a flaming gas device, are things of the past. Nearly all the plans before us show that a site of oblong shape is best adapted to a theatre. The Lyric, however, is an example of what can be done on an irregularly-shaped plot of ground. A very clever arrangement of the auditorium is displayed by Mr. Phipps in the planning of the Gaiety, on a site of most irregular formation, but with exits into four different streets. We have before us examples of one of the greatest modern improvements and economy of space if we look at the drawings of the Savoy, Lyric, the Garrick, Cranbourne-street, and St. Martin's-lane theatres In all these cases it will be observed that a limit to the height of the building is obtained by sinking the pit below the level of the pavement, thus placing the back of the dress-circle on a level with the street. The many advantages of this arrangement do not, perhaps assert themselves at first sight. The distance to be travelled by the various sections of the audience are equalised; the gallery and upper circle have shorter staircases; the dress-circl is on the street level; and the pit and stall have but a few steps to the exits. In the cas of the Savoy, the sloping site is taken advan tage of. It has been argued that a pit belo the ground level must be dangerous, but surel people are less likely to fall ascending tha descending a staircase. There is another grea advantage in reducing the height of the build ing above the ground. It tends to facilitat the extinction of fire by the brigade, an renders the fire-escapes of greater value in the work of rescue. The pit of a theatre, not below, should be on the ground leve I do not think any room or hall whe large numbers of people congregate shoul be built over and above other premise as it only augments the dangers of fire, an needlessly adds to the height. It is certainl unwise to rob the space which is most valuab for exits by building shops or cafés as part the scheme, on the ground floor of a theatre. theatre should be a theatre pure and simpl Even with every precaution enforced that known to man, there must and will be dang from fire and panic; and dangers arising fro other sources should not be added thereto. Th passage of smoke to the theatre from a fire such a shop or restaurant, would be sufficient cause a panic. There is undoubtedly a gre temptation in making the largest return for th outlay on the building, and the rents from sho in the vicinity of popular playhouses assist swell the profits.

Exits.—It is clearly the duty of the archite to design his building so as to reduce th chances of panic to a minimum, and one the chief provisions to this end is short an unobstructed exits. Everything in and abo a theatre should tend to make the audien have confidence in their own security, and gi them a feeling that, should anything happe they would be able to help themselves witho causing injury to others. Where people feel think they are safe, the chances of danger a small. As better sites have been acquire better designs have naturally followed. Si plicity in the plan, and uniformity in the tw sides of the house tend towards the solution the difficulty, as seen by the plans of t Shaftesbury Theatre designed by Mr. Phip Thus, where there is a pit entrance the one side, a pit exit will now be fou on the other; where there is a gallery sta case on the right, a gallery staircase is the left, and so on for each tier or divisi of the audience. Every such division is pr vided with two separate exits leading direct into the street. Such is the London theatre to-day. People, as a rule, naturally desire leave a building by the door by which th enter, and it seems it is only by making t two sides of a theatre alike that the pub will find the exits provided. The audien should be taught the way out of a theatre habit; to speak of "alarm exit," "fire exi "exit in case of need," is only to encour nervousness. The suggestions of danger shou never be breathed in a building where hum beings are packed. I believe that printing key-plan on the programmes would grea assist many visitors to theatres in acquiri confidence and self-possession, and learni the way out. The use of automatic panic bo on exit doors is undoubtedly a great boon, it renders them always available to the public

Entrances.—There is a great deal to be s with regard to the manner in which the pit a gallery of a theatre are entered, and there much to learn from our Continental neig hours, both as to the arrangement of t entrances and the way in which to enter the Mr. D'Oyly Carte was, I believe, the first introduce the *queue* system to a London pit, example which has been followed at the Ly Shaftesbury, and Royal English Opera Hou and within the last month, I believe, at t Gaiety. At the Shaftesbury you enter by narrow passage which discharges into the m corridor after you pass the pay-box. A simil rangement is contemplated at the new Cranbourne-street Theatre. This allows the whole width of the main passage to remain free for exit at all times, as no obstructing barrier or paybox is needed. The arrangement shown on the above-mentioned drawings obviates the necessity for barriers, and allows the public to stand in *queue* to await admission one by one, and prevents the scrimmages seen nightly at most pit and gallery doors,—a state of affairs that prohibits a visit to the play to many an one who cannot afford more than 2s. 6d. for admission, and who has not the courage to face the fighting mob which assails the houses where popular plays are running. Were it possible to adopt the *queue* at all theatres, those who desire to follow the example of the lady who took up her stand, or rather her camp-stool, at the Lyceum pit-door at ten in the morning for admission to the first night of "Henry VIII.," could spend the day with just a degree more comfort than that lady could have done with the pressure of a pit crowd behind her. The wonder is she survived to tell the tale. I think that much of the excitement created by the struggle to enter a theatre is retained during the whole evening, making the audience highly sensitive to alarm.

Staircases.—One feature of the old theatre seems to have completely disappeared in the theatre of to-day. I refer to the grand staircase, such staircases as are found at Drury-lane, Covent Garden, and Her Majesty's. The principal staircase at the Royal English Opera House is the only attempt in theatres of the last few years to create such a special feature in the interior. One has not far to seek to find the reasons for the change. With the pit sunk below the ground, and the dress-circle on the ground level, there is no demand for such a luxury. Much space is therefore saved, for a staircase of ordinary proportions, as a rule, leads to the upper-circle and saloon on the first floor level. From an architect's point of view one cannot help regretting the loss of this grand staircase, with the spacious vestibule and crush-rooms; but the demands of to-day are for small theatres not requiring such adjuncts. As to the width generally allowed for the ordinary staircase, it has been found that ft. 6 in. is sufficient for 400 persons, with an additional 6 in. in width for every additional 0 persons to be accommodated. There should, wever, be a limit to the width, as a staircase wide is as bad as one too narrow. yond a certain width those occupying the ntre obtain no support either directly from e handrails, or indirectly by holding on to ose who grasp the handrails. Six feet wide sufficient to allow four persons abreast to up or down, and should the numbers accommodated in the house require it, a third stairse should be provided in lieu of a greater dth. Every division of the audience should ve at least two staircases leading to the eet. For economy of space two staircases e frequently constructed within the same ntaining walls, as the new upper circle and llery exit staircases at the Gaiety. Long, raight flights of steps are bad, as they do not ford the rest on landings required in ascendg or descending. Too few steps in a flight e as bad as too many, there should not be ore than twelve or less than three. Single eps, or steps at half landings are certain umbling blocks. Of course there should be winders, and the steps should be supported both ends upon brick walls carried up to the of. The risers and treads must be uniform roughout. No exit staircase should serve o tiers, or have pass doors leading from tier below, through which any stream of ople would be likely to enter and impede the ogress of those at a higher level. With gard to landings, they should never be less in ngth than the width of the staircase. The ore rest they afford the better.

The Auditorium.—Returning once more to e drawings of the several new theatres, which have had lent us to-night, we find that by e recent development of planning and conuction the audience have been relieved of e numerous columns, which were ever a cause annoyance and an obstruction to the view of e stage from several seats in each tier. It as the constant cry for the abolition of these stacles that first gave birth to the cantilever nstruction now almost universally adopted in eatre-building. I believe I am correct in ying that the Alhambra was the first house nstructed in this manner, and I am able to ring to your notice the details of this construction, as well as the general plans of the excellent auditorium of this house and its rival, the Empire. Those members of the Association who took advantage of the visit to the Royal English Opera House during its construction will remember that these cantilevers were tied into the back walls of the theatre; projecting from these walls, they were connected by girders, making a perfect cobweb of steelwork upon which to build up the fireproof construction of the tiers. The drawings of the ironwork of the Royal English Opera House, kindly lent me by the Horseley Company, and of the Garrick Theatre, and the diagrams of fireproof construction, lent us by Mr. Emden, will convey more to your minds of the manner of construction than anything I can say in the short time I must of necessity give to this branch of our subject. Doing away with the supporting columns of the galleries has done far more than remove the annoyance from the audience of obstructing the view of the stage: it has also tended towards perfecting the fireproof qualities of the structure. Theatres that were built with supporting columns had the tiers and roof, as a rule, entirely constructed of wood. With the cantilevers the tiers are made of concrete or firebrick on steel girders imbedded in concrete, and the roofs are made fireproof. Where a theatre is constructed entirely of fireproof materials, and the audience know it, and there are good exits, the chances of panic are small. The knowledge that the building is fireproof will do as much to reduce panic as good exits—in fact, even more, as it will destroy the nervousness which generates a stampede. There has been a recent improvement in the auditorium, first introduced, I believe, by Mr. Emden in Terry's Theatre, whereby every row of the tiers have direct access to the side corridors by a doorway. By this means much inconvenience is overcome in gaining the seats, and the exit from the circles is greatly facilitated. Theatres of the past were, as a rule, dark holes into which daylight never entered; the consequence was they became dirty, dusty, and unhealthy, besides being much more dangerous than a building which is flooded with daylight. The cleaners in a theatre are, like most human beings, liable to scamp their work and leave little heaps of dust and rubbish in out-of-the-way corners. The recent disaster at Gateshead to a certain extent teaches us that there is danger in the accumulation of dirt in a theatre, for we hear by some of the accounts that a lighted match fell on some paper and sawdust, which produced the smoke that filled the gallery, and caused the stampede. In Austria there is a special regulation enforced, insisting upon the daily removal of all rubbish and trade refuse, and advocating cleanliness in all parts of the house as a special duty. Where an auditorium is provided with daylight, the use and cost of artificial light during the day-time is saved, cleaners and careless attendants have not to go about their work with lamps or candles, and there is no excuse for striking matches in the building. Another and still more important demand for windows, quite apart from their use for ventilation, is the means of escape they provide in case of fire, especially where they lead to outside balconies. Hundreds of lives could have been saved if windows, external balconies, and escape ladders had been provided not only in theatres, but in all buildings where large numbers congregate. I, for one, shall be glad to see the day when external balconies and staircases are adopted in this class of buildings, as seen in the drawings of Mr. Jan Springer's Municipal Theatre, Amsterdam, which he has specially sent for our use. Iron bars before windows should never be allowed, as they prevent the firemen entering a building by the windows, or the occupants to use the fire-escape. It was not my intention to enter into the smaller details of the arrangements of the auditorium, or to speak of sight lines, the curves of balcony fronts, or the seating of the house; but I must refer for one moment to the gangways. Much diversity of opinion appears to exist as to the number of the seats that should be placed between intersecting gangways. Managers complain that certain portions of the audience will stand in the centre gangways and create a disturbance. On the other hand, long rows of seats without intersecting gangways, make it difficult for the people to get out, especially where the seats have backs. I expected to have had a model here to-night of an automatic seat, a German patent, the back of which falls, and the seat rises when the occupant gets up, thus leaving gangways at right-angles to the curtain line, as well as parallel to it. In the rules enforced in Continental cities, the question of intermediate gangways is rigidly dealt with. For instance, in Austria gangways must divide every six seats, and be in a line with an exit door; in Brussels there must be at least two lateral gangways to the rows of seats, and a central gangway may be required. In St. Petersburg not more than twelve seats may be in a row between the gangways, and the middle passage must not be less than 4 ft. 8 in. wide; but in Paris the authorities appear to be satisfied with two side gangways, each 3 ft. 3¼ in. wide, or in lieu thereof with a single centre gangway 4 ft. 3 in. wide. I cannot now enter into the questions of acoustics, ventilation, heating, lighting, or fire protection of the auditorium. I therefore propose to pass rapidly over a few details with regard to the improvements behind the curtain.

Stage.—I think we all know that modern theatre-construction demands the division of the stage from the auditorium by a brick proscenium wall passing up through the roof above the stage, and down below and across the underside of the stage to divide the orchestra from the mezzanine. This, of course, leaves the large or proscenium opening unprotected. Common-sense at once tells us that a proscenium wall without a proscenium fire or smoke resisting curtain is but a half-measure for retarding the spread of smoke or fire from stage to auditorium. I am fortunate to-night in being able to ask my friend, Mr. Max Clarke, to speak to us on this subject; as you know, he has made a special study of this very important detail of theatre-construction, and it would be presumption on my part to dwell further on the point, when I hope we shall have his views laid before us at the conclusion of this paper. From the various sectional drawings and models of the theatres it will be seen that there are two floors below the level of the stage; the mezzanine floor, on which is placed all the machinery for working the traps and sliders below the stage, and the cellar or well into which the scenes and sets are lowered. Above the stage are galleries on either side known as the "flies," from whence the ropes governing the cloths and scenes are manipulated, and over the whole of the stage in the roof, or at level of the wall-plate, is the gridiron, an open or skeleton flooring, so-called on account of its likeness to that domestic utensil. From the gridiron hang all the cloths, sky-borders, gas-borders, &c. Over the gridiron, modern requirements demand a large exhaust ventilator to carry off the fumes of the many gaslights on the stage, and the smoke in case of fire. The next point we have to consider, after the division of the auditorium and stage, is the size of the stage. Everything is governed by the size of the proscenium opening; 30 ft. is about the average width of the proscenium opening in the medium-sized theatres, so I will take that width as an illustration. Supposing the opening to be 30 ft. square, the width of the stage from side wall to side wall should be at least 60 ft., or twice the width of the proscenium opening, to allow the removal of the scenes to right and left; passage-way is necessary in addition to this. The height from stage-floor to gridiron should be 60 ft., or twice the height of the opening, to allow the scenes to be lifted up to the gridiron without rolling or folding. Where this can be done the scenery lasts much longer, and money is therefore saved in wear and tear of material; there is also less danger of gas battens coming in contact with the canvas. I do not propose dwelling upon the much-debated question of turning the stage into a furnace or tall chimney by carrying up the walls to a great height above the auditorium, and placing huge ventilators in the roof, or making the stage-roof entirely of wood, that it may burn away and create a tall shaft. There are doubtless some present who will give us their views on this matter. All I have to say is that ample ventilation, both inlet and outlet, should be given to the stage, and, unless there are inlets at a low level, the outlets in the roof will make a down-draught. With regard to the dressing-rooms, the plans of the Garrick and the new theatre in St. Martin's-lane show an excellent arrangement, whereby the dressing-rooms are erected in a separate block or building connected with the theatre by one opening only, and with a separate exit into the open air from such block. By this means the whole of the fire-risk in the dressing-rooms is taken away from the theatre. As so much of the scene-painters' and carpenters' work which used to be done in the theatre is now done by the scene-painter in his own painting-room, and by the carpenter in his own workshops away from the theatre, it has been found unnecessary to provide rooms for these purposes in our modern play-houses on such a scale as was necessary in the past, and the risks arising from the various trades have been removed. Many of the larger theatres still have their workshops in use, but the day has gone by when the space over the auditorium ceiling, commonly called the "dome," was used for a carpenter's shop or a store for any old lumber and scenery. This space in old theatres was divided from the audience by only a canvas ceiling and wooden floor, with the sunlight flue passing through the midst of the shavings and inflammable material. Where workshops are needed they should be built, like the dressing-rooms at the Garrick, in a separate block of buildings. Another improvement in theatrical matters is that nowadays a large stock of scenery is never kept on the premises. In the West-end theatres pieces are played which are intended for, even if they do not have, long runs. In the outlying theatres travelling companies fill the bill, and bring with them their own scenery. The consequence is that large scene-docks and stores are not wanted. The valuable space can be used by the architect to better advantage, and the manager avails himself of an outside store. So the risk of large stores, like the risk of workshops, is taken away from the theatre. Scene-docks on the stage level are, of course, needed to shift the scenery into, which is in nightly use. You will see many examples on the plans. The introduction of electric light into theatres has induced managers in many houses to provide the wherewithal to generate their own light. Engine-rooms, boiler-houses, and heating-furnaces should be placed away from the theatre, or divided from it by brick walls and fireproof floors and ceilings. In no case should an opening from the engine-room be permitted into any part of the theatre; access should be either directly from the street or from an open area. There is one part of the play-house which does not seem to have gone ahead like the rest of the building. I refer to the stage machinery. The model upon which the stage of to-day is built is the same as used years ago. This, I believe, is the case in America as well as here. No one has appeared to think it worth while to seriously study the requirements of stage machinery, and endeavour to improve the present state of things. It is looked upon purely as a stage carpenter's job, and when a theatre is built, it is left for the stage carpenter to put in his stage to please himself. When the Royal English Opera House was first started, I remember hearing of the great improvements that were to be made in stage machinery, and that nearly everything but the boards of the stage was to be in iron. True, there are some minor improvements in the details, but the broad principles on which this stage is built is the same as used generations ago. There is certainly an opening for the architect to use his power of design towards the perfection of the stage. Mr. Emden, in a paper read before the Society of Arts in 1888, described at great length the stage of the Buda-Pesth Opera House, where the stage floor could be raised in sections, or as a whole by hydraulic pressure. I believe hydraulic power is used in some of our theatres to raise the larger traps called the "bridges," but the "sliders" are still taken off in the old-fashioned way. I cannot enter into the details of stage lighting, or the advantages gained by the use of the electric light; this, like many other points I have not touched upon, I think comes beyond the scope of my paper; but, before concluding, I wish very briefly to draw the attention of the members of the Association to the great improvement in the materials now used in the construction. We have already noticed how the cantilever system brought about the use of the concrete tiers in lieu of the wooden balconies. In the new theatre in St. Martin's-lane these tiers are constructed of patent metallic stone, 2½ in. to 3 in. thick, composed of granite chips, iron slag, and Portland cement. Fawcett's fire-proof floor was used in some recent alterations at the Lyceum. The roofs, ceilings, and staircases are now constructed of concrete, in place of wood and stone, and where ironwork is used it is always protected. In providing fireproof construction, so necessary for the safety of the public, one may depend upon materials which, either by nature or the aid of man, have passed through the ordeal of fire, being safe units of fireproof construction. To-day, in place of the theatre on a bad site, constructed of wood, with match-boarded partitions, no proscenium wall, exits, and staircases out of proportion to the number who had to use them, ill-lit, ill-ventilated, with no regard to sanitation, and everything that was most unsatisfactory, we have rising in London playhouses on good sites, built entirely with fireproof materials, with good exits and staircases, and every precaution taken to prevent fire and panic. Nothing I can say to you will illustrate this more, or make a greater impression upon you, than these drawings, and I am deeply indebted to the gentlemen who have so willingly lent me the many plans I have been able to bring here to-night. They tell their own tale, and I wish to take this opportunity of thanking Mr. Phipps, who has specially prepared these plans for our use, Mr. Emden, Mr. Chadwick, Mr. Jan Springer, Messrs. Perry & Reed, Mr. Verity, Messrs. Crewe & Sprague, Mr. Max Clarke, Mr. Holloway, and the manager of the Horseley Company, for the valuable aid they have rendered me in endeavouring to explain to you some recent developments in theatre planning. Many thanks are also due to Mr. Baker and Messrs. Kaye for the models of automatic panic-bolts, and Mr. Nolting for the automatic theatre-seat.

[For want of space we defer our report of the discussion until next week].

THE LONDON COUNTY COUNCIL.

The second meeting of the newly-elected County Council was held on Tuesday afternoon last, the Chairman, Lord Rosebery, presiding.

Tenders.—Tenders were received for alterations at the Cane Hill Asylum. The list will be found under the heading "Tenders."

Proposed Reorganisation of Internal Administrative Work.—The Chairman made a speech of some length as to the internal conduct of the work of the Council, which, as it has been fully reported in the daily papers, we need not give here; and he moved

"That it be referred to a special committee of twenty-four members, with the Chairman, Vice-Chairman, and Deputy-Chairman as *ex-officio* members, to examine into the present organisation of the Council's business, and the method of conducting it, and to report whether any and, if so, what changes are expedient and practicable."

Mr. J. W. Benn seconded the motion, which was unanimously agreed to.

The Committee was then constituted as follows:—Messrs. Arnold, Beachcroft, Benn, Burns, Boulnois, M.P., Clarke, and Fardell, Sir Thomas Farrer, Mr. C. Harrison, Lord Hobhouse, Captain James, Sir John Lubbock, M.P., Mr. Martineau, Lord Carrington, Lord Monkswell, the Duke of Norfolk, Messrs. Pickersgill, M.P., Russell, Saunders, Æneas Smith, Strong, Spicer, Stuart, M.P., and Howell Williams.

The Council then proceeded to elect its standing committees.

The Building Act Committee is constituted as follows:—Messrs. Fletcher, Ford, Harvey, Holmes, Longstaff, Marsland, Ranyard, Roberts, Stevens, Strong, H. R. Taylor, and Yates.

The "Betterment" Proposal Again.—The Parliamentary Committee reported, as to the General Powers Bill of the Council, now before Parliament, that the second reading of the Bill had been postponed by the House of Commons in order to afford the new Council an opportunity of considering its provisions. Mr. Baumann had given notice of his intention to move the omission of clause 7, relating to the improvement rate proposed by the Bill to be levied for the purposes of the Cromwell-road Bridge improvement. The Committee thought it advisable that the new Council should definitely state its opinion upon the provisions of the Bill, more especially with regard to the question raised by Mr. Baumann's opposition, and they therefore recommended that the approval of the Bill by the Council on December 10 last be confirmed.

Mr. Charles Harrison said that the proposed improvement involved the principle of betterment, and that it would greatly strengthen the hands of the Committee in promoting the Bill if they were able to state that the new Council had endorsed the policy of the old Council on that question. He, therefore, asked that a division might be taken, so that there might be a record of the opinion of the Council.

The result of the division was that the recommendation of the Committee was approved by 82 votes to 7.

After transacting some other business, the Council adjourned.

THE ARCHITECTURAL ASSOCIATION SPRING VISITS:

THE TOWER BRIDGE.

THE fourth visit of the session, on the afternoon of Saturday, March 19, was attended by a large number of members of the Association, Mr. J. Wolfe Barry, the engineer, having courteously granted permission for the inspection of the works of the Tower Bridge. The party was met by Mr. Crutwell, the resident engineer, who gave an interesting description of the works. Considerable progress has been made since the Association last visited the bridge. The centre towers have been carried up to the full height as far as the steelwork is concerned, and the cantilevers, which are being built out from each tower, without scaffolding, have made considerable way across the centre-span. These cantilevers will become two bridges for foot passengers when the centre-span of the lower bridge is open for the passage of vessels. Portions of the balance girders for the centre span, and the steel cables which will connect the upper and lower towers, were to be seen, though in an incomplete state at present. There is as yet little to be seen of the architectural casing which will conceal the elaborate steelwork of the frames of the towers, though some portion of this casing appears in the gateway on the north shore. Messrs. Arrol & Co. are the contractors for the steelwork, and Messrs. Perry & Co. for the builders' work.

THE LABOUR COMMISSION.

FURTHER BUILDING TRADE EVIDENCE.

DURING the last sittings of that section of the Royal Commission on Labour, over which Mr. Mundella, M.P., presides, further evidence* was taken with respect to building trades.

Mr. D. B. MacGregor, Secretary of the Glasgow Master Masons' Association, which embraces forty-three firms, employing 3,000 men, explained that in 1884 a joint committee of masters and men was appointed, which met once a year to discuss matters relating to work and wages. At that annual meeting the hours and the wages were settled for the year, and the system had worked very well. If any master or workman violated the regulations thus laid down, he would be brought before a standing committee, by whom the matter was arranged. They had not, however, been able to apply that method to masons' labourers, because the Masons' Labourers' Union comprised all the labourers in Glasgow, whether they served the masons or were engaged in other industries. Mr. MacGregor further stated that the standard wages were 8d. an hour for operative masons and 5½d. an hour for masons' labourers. The ordinary working hours were 51 a week—that was nine hours a day for five days and six on Saturday. During the five days the men worked from six a.m. to nine; from ten to one, and from six to nine p.m. The employers insured with the Accident Insurance Company for all their men, and this was found to be also a very good plan. He also explained that the Association did not at all object to operatives being members of the trades union, and, as a matter of fact, the masters would be very glad if all the operative masons and the masons' labourers were members of the Union. Finally, he said he was in favour of boards of conciliation and arbitration for the settlement of trade disputes.

Mr. F. Moore, a London carpenter, speaking on behalf only of himself, complained very strongly of the system of overtime, which he described as one of the deadly evils of the building trade, mentioning that he had known men to be kept at work from six in the morning to nine and ten, and even twelve, at night, when they returned home completely exhausted. This evil had existed in the building trade in London generally until recently, when trade had become less brisk, and there was consequently less overtime. The men were, no doubt, paid for overtime, but he felt that the system ought to be abolished, because it was detrimental to the welfare of the men. Mr. Moore also complained of the sweating and driving which prevailed in the building trade, employers sometimes engaging a foreman, not because of his superior knowledge of the trade, but solely because of his capacity for driving and bullying, and getting the utmost

* For previous report of Building Trades evidence see *Builder* for March 5, p. 184.

amount of work out of the men, irrespective of the quality. The result of this was that work was scamped, especially in the busy season. Further, the witness complained of the insanitary condition of many of the shops, and the total absence of proper inspection. Then again, he considered the position of skilled workmen very unsatisfactory. For instance, the cleverest man was on exactly the same level as to pay as the most inefficient man in the shop; there was a dead level of mediocrity, because the sharp workman was not encouraged to make the most of his abilities. He admitted that to a certain extent the action of the trades unions had tended to improve the position of the men and to ameliorate the conditions under which they worked, but still there were isolated shops where these abuses existed unchecked. He also admitted that, although he was himself a non-unionist, the evils he had described would have now been more prevalent, and that the workmen's position was far better in these days than it was, owing to the better education which youths entering the trade had received at the elementary schools. The introduction of machinery, too, had done good by relieving the men of much of the heaviest and most laborious work. Citing other evils existing in the building trades, Mr. Moore stated that it was notorious that at one time foremen often received bribes from workmen to keep them on, but that was now a matter of rare occurrence, owing to exposures. To some extent, no doubt, the association of the men was a protection against that practice, but the inferior shops, where it might still exist, were largely isolated. But for the trades unions these evils would have run riot. But there were certain evils in the unions. One was the equality of wages to which he had previously referred. He considered that the men in London were in a better position than men in the country, for they had a wider field of observation and work, and thus had a better chance of getting on. Speaking generally, the workmen now were well educated, and there was a great desire for improvement. The higher they rose the higher became their standard of living, and general refinement increased. In many cases architects' and surveyors' sons entered the trade, and served time both in the shops and in the office, in order to acquire a perfect mastery of the trade. The rising young men, having received technical instruction, were better fitted for constructive work than their predecessors were; while the introduction of machinery tended to make the men more intelligent and serviceable. This, no doubt, cheapened production, but it was better for the men in the end. Reverting to the trades unions, Mr. Moore, while allowing for all the good they had done, advanced as a strong ground of objection to them the fact that the meetings of branches were so often held in public-houses. He was not a sworn teetotaller, but an abstemious man, and he knew that a great many men who were staunch unionists strongly objected to this system, as opposed to the moral welfare of the men, and he urged that the public-house as a place of meeting ought to be done away with. He next advised that more encouragement should be given to individual merit among the men, and that there should be a better understanding between employers and employed, for, with the master on a pinnacle at one end and the men at the other end, there could be no common ground of good relations. He was anxious to see some system of settlement of difficulties in London such as that described by Mr. MacGregor, and in reply to the inquiry whether with arbitration and conciliation the men must be in a union, and bound by the decision, he replied that in the last strike in London a number of men who were not unionists had a great deal to do with the settlement, many non-unionists being put forward to speak upon the question. As to the reasons which prevented many men from joining the union, he thought the necessity of continually giving a shilling a week for problematical benefits was a strong deterrent. The men did not derive benefit corresponding with the subscription, and they did not care to keep up such a subscription. It seemed to him that the time had come for us to readjust our views as to the status of skilled workmen. He objected to a common term of description being applied to skilled workmen; and he urged that the general status of the men ought to be still further improved in the future. He allowed that the workman was socially more respected and honoured for any virtues he possessed than he formerly was, but even that was not so much the case in England as in America. He believed that the men of the best ability and education did not come to the front in the trade union agitations, but remained quiescent in the background. The agitation was left largely to the official representatives. The superior class of men were steadily increasing, especially among the younger men, who benefited by the easy access to free libraries, by cheap literature, and by the facilities for attending social meetings and educational classes. With respect to hours, Mr. Moore did not advise legislative regulation, because many difficulties might arise, but he would have legislative action to prevent overtime, to which employers so readily resorted. This might be done by the insertion of clauses in the Metropolitan Building Acts, prohibiting work being carried on beyond a certain hour by the same body of men. If the work was really necessary, day and night shifts could be provided. This might be accomplished by the trades unions demanding and obtaining regulations, each trade accommodating itself to the circumstances of the case, if they could; but in the recent strike the masters had been able to coerce the men. The best mode of settling disputes would be a standing board, with a referee, but the referee must be a practical man, and not the architect, whose whole interests were bound up with those of the employer.

Replying to questions from the general members of the Commission present, Mr. Moore complained that there was too much equality of pay, and he objected to piece-work, although in America it acted well. He would discriminate between the different abilities of the men, and have a varying scale of wages. He would not, however, say a joiner, for example, should be called second class or third class, but would use his own discretion and see that his foreman carried that out, in order to encourage the best workmen. If the foreman was incapable of discriminating as to the qualities of the men, he would not be capable of carrying on the work. Every man should have a minimum pay, and increased pay according to abilities. The inferior workman was the loudest, and the first to complain; the slower and more inferior his work the louder was his grievance. Witness had not paid attention to a discussion in the engineering trade as to introducing a gradual classification, but no doubt in general terms the question was much the same as he had raised.

Professor Marshall: Do you think it would be worth while to have for each district various minimum rates for class A, B, and C, and so on?

Mr. Moore replied that that might be possible, but if it led to hard and fast lines it would not work. Such arrangements must be simple to be effective,—there must not be too much hard and fast classification. There should be direct dealings between the masters and the men, with a view to sympathetic action. In the next place, Mr. Moore condemned the preset system of giving contracts for public works. The acceptance of the lowest tender was a serious evil, for the contractor had then to rely upon sweating and driving and inferior material. The Law Courts were carried out under the lowest, or nearly the lowest, tender, and the result was bankruptcy of the builder and very inferior workmanship. He knew of buildings which within two or three years had to be shored up, and those had been erected on the lowest tender, driving, and sweating system. The reasonable method would be to receive a good number of tenders and to select the middle tender. The witness finally advocated the establishment of trade halls as valuable and useful, and the provision of technical libraries.

Mr. George Sunley, Secretary of the National Amalgamated Society of House and Ship Painters, having described the constitution, membership, and financial arrangements of that body, explained that they had a system which they called "working rules," which were mutually agreed upon by masters and men, and signed by both. They had also arrangements for providing an arbitrator to decide disputes, and, although they had had several small strikes since 1887, they had generally been settled by arbitration. There was a strike at Hartlepool. It was not about wages, but with respect to the legality of a notice by the men. The employers locked the men out for a fortnight, and the matter was settled by arbitration, the decision being that the notice of the men was illegal. His experience led him to the belief that unionist men were superior as workmen to non-unionists. In many cases the branches of his Society met in public-houses, and he did not agree with the last witness on this point. He had often heard the meeting at public-houses given as an excuse for not joining, but it was not a reasonable excuse. He did not say that public-houses were the best meeting places, but many of the branches were respectably conducted in public-houses, and no drink was allowed in the room while the business was proceeding. The Branch paid for the use of the room. In Chester their meetings were held in the Court House, and in Huddersfield in the Trade Hall; and he was very much in favour of that system as to meetings. Being invited to make suggestions, the witness urged an amendment of the Employers' Liability Act, so that employers should not be able to shift the responsibility for accidents on to the shoulders of insurance companies. To illustrate this, he mentioned the case of a man who recently sustained a serious accident through insufficient scaffolding, and he had to have one leg amputated. The man had taken action in the County-court, and the employer, on receiving notice of claim, simply sent it on to the insurance society. That was not likely to lead the employer to improve his scaffolding, and he had heard of several complaints by men in the same employment respecting insufficient scaffolding. He was not prepared to say that in consequence the insurance society would require the employer to erect safe scaffolding, or would charge a higher premium; but he knew of many employers in Manchester who were in insurance societies, and he had never seen an insurance inspector examining the scaffolding. At the same time, he admitted that there had been in some directions more care and better material employed in scaffolding. It might be difficult for some of the small and comparatively poor employers to provide compensation if they were not allowed to insure, but as a rule the larger employers were the more negligent as to the safety of their men, owing to the system of insurance.

Mr. W. Phillips, speaking as a representative of the London and Counties House-Painters' Society, informed the Committee that his trade had established a rate of wages, and this had been done through the agency of this Society and men who were not organised. In 1872 an agreement was entered into between the masters and the men with the result that the rate of wages was 8½d. an hour. Less was, however, paid in some cases, which was due to the action of employers in employing inferior workmen, putting in scamped work, and refusing to concede the full rate. The recognised rate was paid by the most respectable of the masters; if any paid less, then that was a matter for the union to deal with. The subscription was 2d. a week, but that included nothing beyond the membership of the union. The normal working hours were 52½ per week. Considerable overtime was in operation, which was a matter of serious grievance, especially with respect to night shifts. That work ought to be paid for according to the schedule of the agreement of 1872, but it was not, and he thought the masters ought to be made to observe that agreement. Scamped work, and the employment of unskilled labour, were causing serious injury to the trade, and he suggested that employers should be required to employ only skilled labour and skilled supervision of the work. That, perhaps, was one of the objects of his Society, but at the same time he thought the Legislature should exercise some control and supervision in the matter. In the same way, he believed that if the Legislature adopted some means by which the qualifications of workmen were inquired into, that would remedy a great many of the existing evils. Being asked how this was to be accomplished, Mr. Phillips replied that opportunity might be given to the public in regard to work done, to call in a properly-qualified inspector to see that the work was properly carried out. That would be better for workers and the trade and the community generally. In fact, it should be open to the people interested to have the work examined just as they could have a pound of butter analysed, and he suggested the appointment of some skilled person in every town and district for this purpose. With a view to disputes, he also suggested the appointment of a committee consisting of an equal number of representatives of masters and men, to whom any issue should be submitted prior to a strike taking place. He believed that would effectively do away with strikes. The committee would take care that no strike or lock-out took place without serious grounds and close investigation. In his trade, witness further stated, there was a small amount of co-operation, and there had been some attempt at profit-sharing, but the experiments, so far, had been too limited for him to deal with the question at present. Turning to other points, Mr. Phillips urged the amendment of the law as to the relations between employers and men. For instance, it ought to be made a penal offence for an employer to apply any power against a workman for joining a trades union; any man should be at liberty to do so, and any attempt to black-list or boycott him should be a penal offence. That being so, he would accept the converse, viz., that the boycotting of non-union men by unionists should also be made illegal. With respect to the regulation of hours, he considered that legislative restriction was the most effective method. He would have the Legislature fix a maximum rate as to hours, and make it punishable to employ men beyond that period. A statute should be passed enforcing a maximum of eight hours a day, but with permission to work beyond on sufficient evidence of necessity being shown,—provided also that men who were idle should be taken on, and that under no circumstances should extra hours be imposed on those already employed, unless there were no idlers. This should be decided by a joint committee of masters and men. Many serious difficulties which now arose with reference to season work could in that way be removed. A great deal of the work could be done in the winter which was now done in the summer, and he advised that Government work and municipal work should be held over in order that men should be able to fill up time at a later period, believing that the community would prefer to see a useful worker properly employed than to have to support a pauper and his family. Public work, in short, should be done either in the winter or during the slack season. In many cases external work could be as well done in the winter as in the summer, and in some cases internal work could be better done in the winter; and in the winter there was not so much temptation to the men to "play" at the work. Local authorities should do all they could to employ men when they were not generally engaged in private houses. Making a black-list was the refusal of an employer to employ a man because he belonged to a trades union and took part in a strike, not only during the strike, but even afterwards, so that a man might starve. He did not know of any specific cases during the last nine years; but the practice might crop up again, and unless there were some means of dealing with them the evils would increase.

Mr. J. Anderton, President of the Operative Plumbers' Association of Great Britain and Ireland, stated that up to the end of 1891 the Association had 5,500 members, and there had been some subsequent increase. There was another Plumbers' Association in Scotland, but it was an open institution only, and his Association had a number of lodges in Scotland. The subscription had advanced in time from 6d. a week to 8d., and now it was 9d. Having explained the system of relief and benefits, the witness said the trade had had eleven disputes between 1889 and the end of 1891, but they had arbitration rules whereby a board of conciliation and arbitrators were appointed by employers and employed, and all these disputes,—in Birmingham, Newcastle, Liverpool, and elsewhere,—had been settled in that manner. Since 1865 they had spent 13,180*l.* on trade strikes and disputes, but during the last two years only 132*l.*, for they found they could arrive at the same results without strikes. They had, indeed, spent a great deal more in sick-relief and other benefits than on all the strikes and disputes; and he admitted that they would now be very glad to have in hand all they had spent on strikes. In this trade there was very little friction between masters and men, for the fact was that most of the masters had been workers themselves. They knew the workmen's ways and weak points, and stubbornness, and the workmen knew their ways, and thus there was mutual respect and sympathy. They did not want the Legislature to settle disputes and hours and wages, preferring to do all that themselves, but they were very much in favour of boards of conciliation all over the country,—voluntary boards. They also desired voluntary registration, and not registration enforced by the Legislature. The registration measure now before Parliament aimed at elevating the men, doing away with slop work and jerry work; and it was to the interest of the public that every plumber should be registered. He further advocated an examination and test, and suggested the appointment of a registration committee when a new district was opened.

Mr. Albert Emmett, Secretary of the Operative Bricklayers' Society, Ashton-under-Lyne and District, explained that his union, which numbered some 300 members, decided for itself all questions respecting pay, hours, and so on; and, although the men might strike if they chose, they would do so at their own risk, and would receive no strike pay. The weekly subscription was 6d. For this the men received no sick pay, but if they met with an accident they received 12s. a week for three months, and 9s. a week for a further three months. In the event of total disablement an allowance gradually falling to 5s. a week was made. He was in favour of the establishment of a standing committee of masters and workmen for settling all disputes and avoiding strikes, but no attempt has as yet been made in that direction; but he was not in favour of legislative regulation of hours.

Mr. J. Stirk, Secretary of the Leeds and District Operative Stonemasons' Society, stated that although that Society only numbered about 400 members, and there were about the same number of non-union masons, there were in the district something like 3,000 men altogether concerned in the building trade. The Society had no means of settling disputes, and, therefore, if any difficulty arose they must fight it out with the masters as best they could. But as six months' notice had to be given on either side, they thought that allowed sufficient time for arriving at a conclusion, and for making up their minds. They did, however, settle the wages and hours themselves, subject to the consent of the executive. There was no feeling in the trade against settlement by arbitration, and the feeling between the employers and the men was very good. Mentioning that at the present time there was a notice out which was given last October for a rise of wages, which notice would expire in May next, the witness said the present rate of wages was lower than it was ten years ago. During thirty-six weeks they worked fifty hours a week, and during the remaining sixteen weeks, forty-three hours. They were paid overtime, and double for work on Sundays, Good Friday, and Christmas Day; but their work was very irregular, and they suffered a good deal from that. He thought they would get on better if all the masters were associated as well as the men, and when they had any difficulty with a non-associated employer, they tried to induce him to become associated. They got on "first-class" with the employers; but they objected to work with non-unionist men when the unionists were in a majority, otherwise they worked all together. They did not directly refuse to work with non-unionists; but if the latter were in a minority they had to join the union, or the unionists would leave. They did, in fact, boycott the non-unionists when they could,—the latter could not boycott them,—and they had a black-list on which they placed a man for six years, unless he joined the union before that time elapsed. He admitted that it would be fair for the non-unionists to "black-list" the unionists, if they chose; and, as the union had got fully half of the men in the trade with them, he thought they had done very well. The trade had no piecework, for they objected to it; and there was no sub-contracting. He thought the Employers' Liability Act operated fairly, but no case had yet arisen in his district. And, in fact, since the Act was passed there had been a great improvement in regard to scaffolding and other matters, which he attributed to the enactment of that measure.

Mr. H. Hamm, Secretary of the London branch of the Alliance Cabinet Makers' Association, next gave the Commission some striking information respecting his trade. In the whole country, he said, there would be about 70,000 or 80,000 cabinet makers; of these London had from 20,000 to 25,000, and his Association had 6,500 members. He calculated that only about 15 per cent. of the total were union men, and this he attributed to apathy. In fact, he rather thought the trade was deteriorating, partly because the older firms mostly bought their furniture, instead of making it as they formerly did, and partly because the men were not allowed sufficient time, and had to hurry over their work. A further reason was that the trade was now very much split up into departments, so that men had less chance of becoming good all-round workers. Some men worked by the day, some on piecework, and some on the "lump." On the "lump" work the employer paid so much for the whole article; on the piece system, so much for each portion of the article. In the provinces the rate for piecework was from 7d. to 8½d. an hour; in London it was 9d., but some men took less. The hours in London were fifty-four a week, but the sanitary condition of the workshops was in some cases very bad. To illustrate his views as to the decline of the cabinet-making trade, Mr. Hamm said not only was furniture frequently displayed and described as "our own manufacture" when it was not so, but had been bought in, but very often a piece of furniture marked "solid brown oak" was likely enough only white oak, browned or veneered. It was the same with regard to articles marked "solid walnut,"—it would be white oak overlaid. It was supposed that there was a law to deal with such deception, and they meant at some future time to test that point. The Merchandise Marks Act might make such a trick punishable, but 99 out of 100 purchasers would not detect the fraud. Another trick was for a master, on being offered a new design by a workman, to detain it on the pretext of considering the offer, to get an imitation of it made up, and then to return the original, as not wanted, to the designer. A further evil was that apprentices were taken in and allowed to play about in the shops without being properly instructed, and the result was that very few ever became highly skilful workers. Mr. Hamm further stated that his Association managed to maintain, and to some extent to improve, the rate of wages without resorting to strikes, and he expressed himself favourable to the establishment of an eight hours' day.

Mr. Whitley, Secretary of the Leeds Branch of the Alliance Association, described the prejudicial effect of the employment of Jews, who worked at a low rate for long hours, and turned out inferior articles; he denounced the system of inspection as inadequate, and stated that there was a diversity of opinion in his district as to the eight hours' question.

The remainder of the evidence taken by this section related to coach-building, cooperiog, chemical, and copper works.

The Commission have decided to present to Parliament an *interim* report, comprising the evidence taken up to Christmas, and to adjourn all the sections from the close of this week to May 3.

Illustrations.

SCULPTURE: "JEANNE D'ARC."

THIS group, entitled "Jeanne d'Arc entend ses voix," represents Joan of Arc in the act of listening to the "voices" which inspired her to arise and save her country. The figures above represent St. Michael, St. Catherine, and St. Marguerite.

The group, which is by M. André Allar, was commissioned for the new church in course of erection at Domrémy to the memory of Joan of Arc, and is to be placed over the porch. The group formed a conspicuous object among the sculpture exhibits at the Salon of 1891. The figures are of life-size.

"TOKEN HOUSE," COPTHALL-AVENUE.

THIS building is situated in what was formerly known as Little Bell-alley, but which has now been improved by the Commissioners of Sewers into Copthall-avenue, and has been recently erected for Messrs. Fred. C. Mathieson & Sons, printers and financial publishers.

In the façade an attempt has been made to gain a somewhat greater effect of repose and solidity than is sometimes found in elevations, which are required, as in this instance, to comprise the greatest aggregate area of openings allowed by law. The horizontal divisions between the ground and first and the second and third floors respectively have with this view been almost obliterated, so as to leave greater masses of wall-space available for the pavilions at either end of the building.

The materials of which the front is built are Cornish granite from the Colcerrow quarries for the lower portion, the plinth and base being rough and the piers polished, and Portland Whitbed stone for the remainder.

The ground and first-floors have been arranged for letting as offices; the basement being used by Messrs. Mathieson for their heavy machinery, the second and third floors as composing-rooms, and for reference books and papers, and the upper floors for binding and work in connexion therewith. A hydraulic and other lifts connect these floors.

The work has been carried out from the designs and under the superintendence of Mr. T. Barnes-Williams, F.R.I.B.A., and the contractors were Messrs. Higgs & Hill.

BIRMINGHAM GENERAL HOSPITAL.

WE give this week the plans and principal elevations and sections of the designs for this important hospital by Mr. Henman, of Birmingham, which have been selected in the recent competition. We gave such a full description of the general arrangement of the plan in our leading article of the 19th (to which the reader is referred), that it is only necessary here to give a few further details from the architect's report, in regard to some special points.

In regard to the subject of lifts, staircases, and water towers the report says:—

"*Lifts.*—Two in number, worked by hydraulic power,—viz., one suitable as a bed-lift, and a smaller one for stores, &c., are advisedly placed in a service-room holding a central position just off the main corridor.

In most of the hospitals visited I noticed that the lifts open direct from the main corridor; and as an evidence that they have been abused or the cause of accident, printed notices are posted near them giving warning that they are not to be used without the presence of an attendant. In some hospitals two or more lifts are provided in different parts of the buildings. This is proved to be unnecessary, for I found in such cases only one in general use. It must be evident, that such appliances, when constantly used, are more likely to be kept in perfect working order,—available at a moment's notice,—and, requiring the attendance of a person experienced in manipulating same, should be in the most central position. The use of light stretchers on wheels, so greatly facilitating the transference of patients from one part to another on the level, obviates the necessity of distributing lifts throughout the buildings; and when the kitchen is on the top story, the frequent traffic up and down warrants the employment of an attendant being *constantly* in charge of the lifts.

Staircases.—With lift accommodation such as is proposed, the staircases become of secondary importance, but must be well distributed for the use of the staff, and of fireproof construction as a precaution in the event of fire or alarm (more than ever necessary since the recent deplorable catastrophe in America). In many hospitals the staircases appear to have been designed rather with a view to architectural effect than to utility, and being entirely open to the corridors on the several floors, convey the air from the lower to the upper wards. This it is proposed to obviate by screening them off on each story, and separately warming and ventilating them.

Water Towers.—Above the two principal staircases the buildings are carried up as towers, in which large cisterns, for the storage of water, will be placed.

Although Birmingham is fortunate in having a constant water-supply, there are occasions when, for repairs to mains or other causes, the supply is cut off for a time. Even such a temporary stoppage might be attended by serious, and even disastrous, results, in case of fire, unless there were on the premises ample storage capacity at a high level. Hence, what at first sight may appear simply ornamental features added for architectural effect, are in reality, when used as proposed, supplemented by suitable mains and properly-distributed hydrants, of the utmost importance for the well-being and safety of the establishment."

The following remarks may be quoted in reference to the sanitary arrangements, heating, ventilation, &c.:—

"The utmost care has been exercised in planning the several sanitary requirements so that they shall be convenient, inoffensive, simple, and effective.

To all the principal wards they are situate in octagonal turrets at the ends furthest from the main corridors, cut off from the wards by intercepting lobbies provided with cross-ventilation,—intentionally of moderate size,—so that they can only

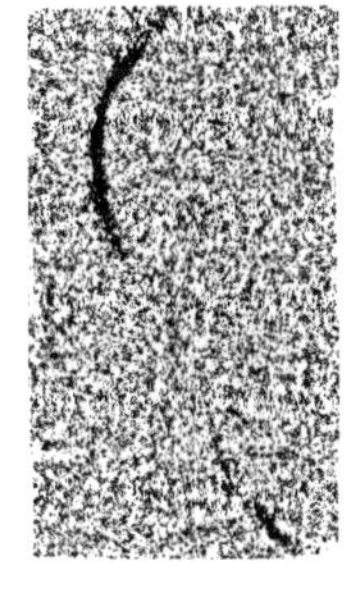

INK-PHOTO SPRAGUE & Co 4 & 5 EAST HARDING STREET FE[illegible]ER LANE E.C.

"JEANNE D'ARC ENTEND SES VOIX": SCULPTURE GROUP FOR THE NEW CHURCH AT DOMRÉMY.—M. ANDRÉ ALLAR, SCULPTOR.

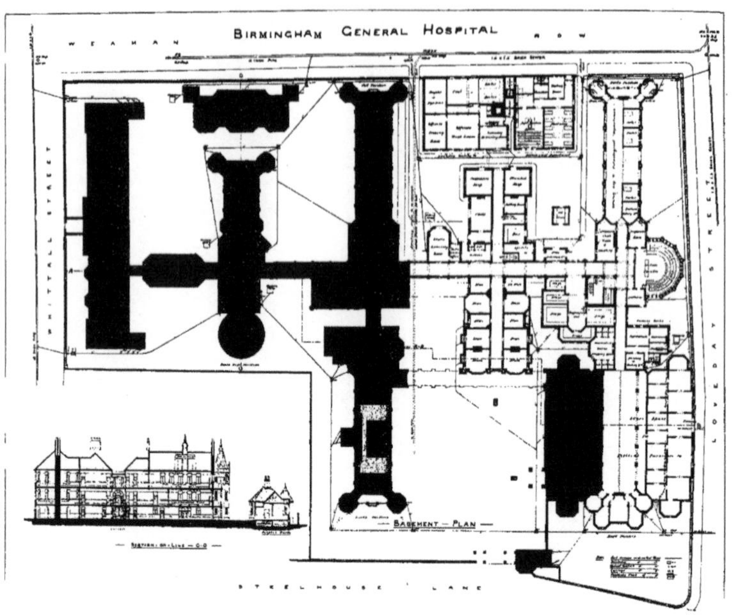

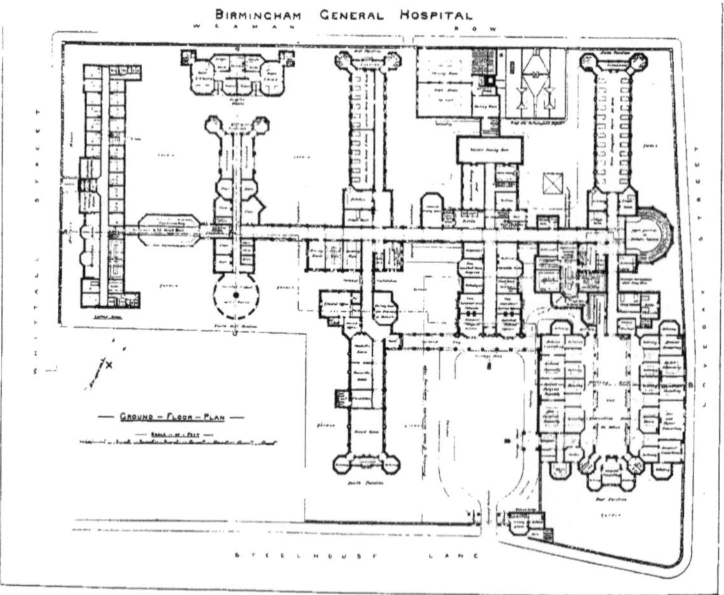

SELECTED DESIGN FOR BIRMINGHAM GENERAL HOSPITAL.—Mr. W. Henman, A.R.I.B.A., Architect.

PHOTO-LITHO. SPRAGUE & C° 4 & 5 EAST HARDING STREET, FETTER LA

NEW PREMISES, COPTHALL AVENUE.—Mr. T. Barnes Williams, Architect.

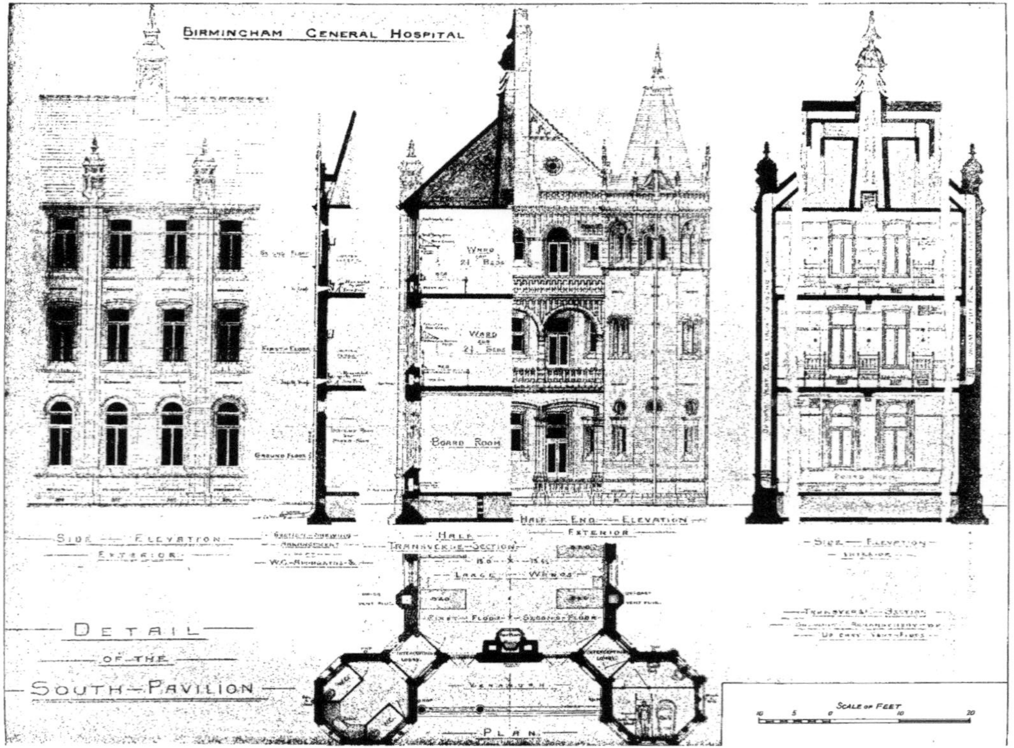

Birmingham General Hospital

Second Floor

First Floor

Ground Floor

Ward for 21 Beds

Ward for 21 Beds

Board Room

Side Elevation — Exterior

Section showing Arrangement of W.C. Annexes &

Half Transverse Section

Half End Elevation — Exterior

Side Elevation — Interior

Large Wards

First Floor & Second Floor

Transverse Section

Up Cast Vent Flues

Verandah

Plan

Scale of Feet

10 5 0 10 20

Detail of the South Pavilion

Chapel
Female
Medical & Surgical Wards
Board & Committee Room
Corridors
Administrative Department
Corridors
Male
Medical & Surgical Wards
Outpatients' Waiting Hall, Casualty & Consulting Rooms

ELEVATION — TOWARDS — STEELHOUSE — LANE

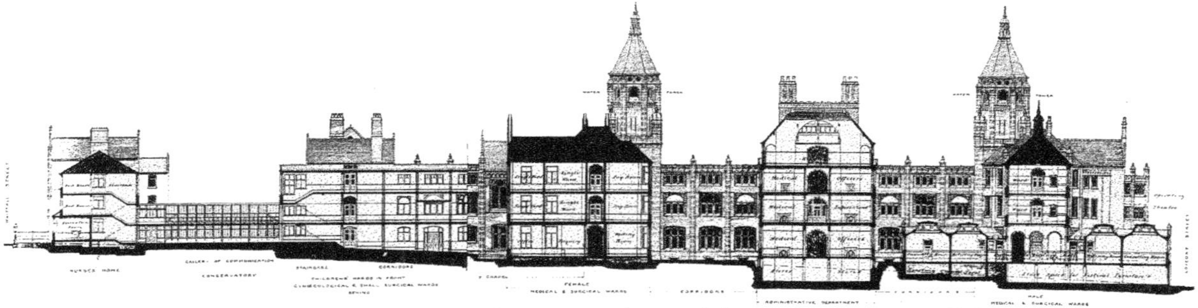

Nurses' Home
Gallery of Communication
Conservatory
Staircase
Corridors
Children's Wards in Front
Gynaecological & Small Surgical Wards
Behind
Chapel
Female
Medical & Surgical Wards
Corridors
Administrative Department
Male
Medical & Surgical Wards
Casualty Rooms & Outpatients Department

SECTION — ON — LINE — A-B

SELECTED DESIGN FOR BIRMINGHAM GENERAL HOSPITAL.—MR. W. HENMAN, A.R.I.B.A., ARCHITECT

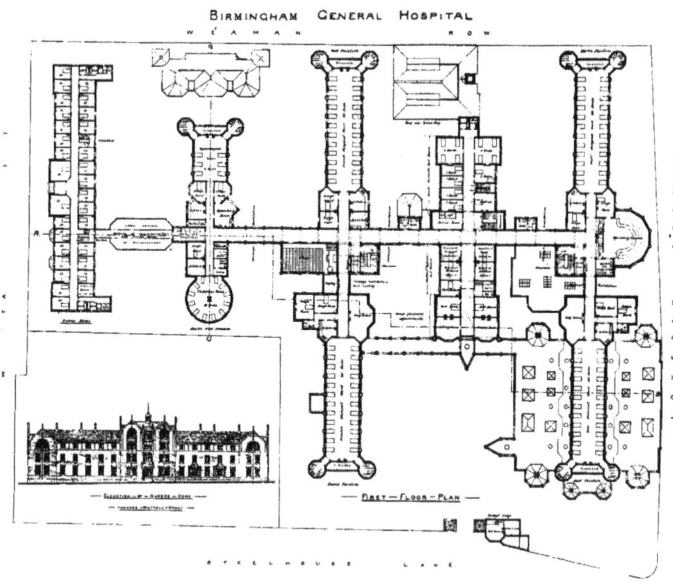

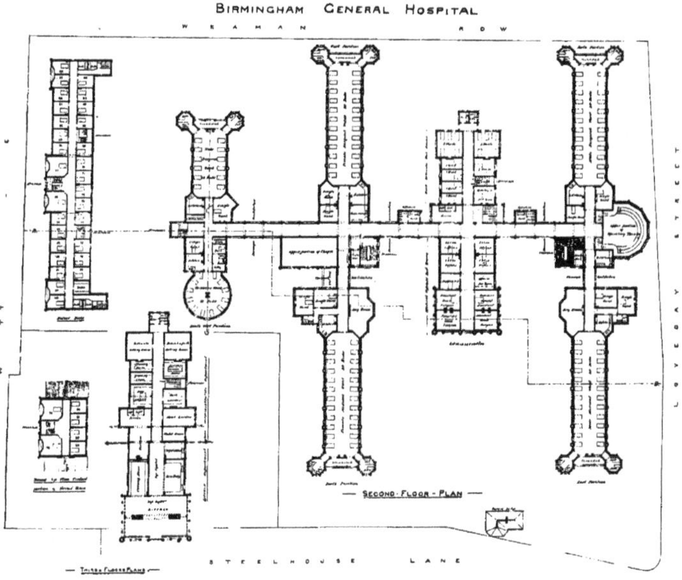

PHOTO-LITHO, SPRAGUE & CO

SELECTED DESIGN FOR BIRMINGHAM GENERAL HOSPITAL.—MR. W. HENMAN, A.R.I.B.A., ARCHITECT.

e used as passage-ways, because where of large imensions they are often improperly supplied with ash-up sinks, and used for storing articles which ould be better further removed from the wards.

The octagonal turrets will not obstruct light and r so much as if they were square on plan.

On one side are two w.c.'s and a wash-up sink; 1 the other, lavatories and a bath, with crane rangement above for bathing helpless patients.

The w.c. apparatus throughout will be of the destal-hopper form, with trap and funnel-shaped itlet (which prevents syphonage, and does not low the lodgment of sewer-gas in any part), taken rectly through the wall to the soil-pipe and upcast ntilator (see detail drawing).

An attempt has been made to incorporate these il and vent pipes in the architectural composition ithout detriment to their sanitary usefulness; for, though they must necessarily become prominent atures, there is no reason why they should appear all their crude ugliness. The wastes from baths d lavatories are treated in a similar manner . . . .

I propose to rely upon what is popularly known natural ventilation. Steam-pipes will be emoyed for the general heating of the wards. Cheerlness is secured by the open fireplaces at the ds. Along the side walls, between the windows, cast ventilating flues are provided,—*separate* for ch ward,—carried up to the very apex of the roof, e draught being accelerated by means of steam ils, and down-draughts prevented by oiled silk flaps. esh air will be admitted by the windows and by ecial openings direct from the outside, arranged that in cold weather the incoming air will be armed by impinging upon the steam-pipes, prosion being made for filtering the incoming air rough cotton-wool, &c. The ventilating openings d heat can thus be regulated in each room by elf.

To each of the principal wards there will be six -cast flues, each 18 in. by 18 in., in addition to e flue from fireplace, or a total superficial area of ½ ft. super, so that if the upward movement in em is at the rate of only one foot per second, e whole air of the ward will be changed every lf-hour, whereas it is generally accepted as adetate if provision be made for the air to be newed once every hour, travelling at the te of two feet per second in the flues. In rtain states of the atmosphere, however, th so limited a flue area, difficulty is in practice perienced to secure a sufficiently rapid change of in hospital wards. I therefore advise that the at flues be large and numerous,—for they can dily be reduced in power of extraction, when cessary, by closing valves, but can only be inased hereafter at heavy cost, and probably by disfigurement of the buildings.

or use in summer weather, means of propelling into the wards may be advisable. In such case uggest that it should be applied direct, the ive-power being from the Corporation highssure hydraulic mains, the apparatus being ched to each ward to be supplied with air. The antage of using water as the motive-power is t as its force is spent it may, in the same apatus, be employed for cleansing the incoming . . . .

ross Venilation to Corridors.—With a view to isolation of any ward, in case of need, pors of the corridors are of less height than the ainder, entirely open above to encourage circuon of air around the buildings. Generally, rs across the corridors would be objectionable inconvenient, but, when necessary, temporary eens could easily be provided at these points.

Vindows.—As boxings and linings of all kinds objectionable in a hospital, solid frames will be ployed throughout, the lower portions of the dows formed as casements, and the upper pors hung at bottom, all opening inwards. By means the patients are best protected from ughts when the windows have to be opened, and n necessary to thoroughly air the wards, the le area of each window will be capable of being ned to its full extent,—a feature of considerable ortance, yet very rarely attained. To prevent idents to patients, light iron guards are provided side.

he Electric Light is suggested for use at night e, so that the air of the wards may not be ated by the fumes from burnt gas. A movable cket would be provided to each bed, so as to be ilable for close inspection of the patient."

n regard to the question of cost, the architect isiders it preferable to prepare as complete 1 perfect a building as possible, and state ich portion could be erected for the proposed lay. He estimates that by omitting such tions of the building as are not detailed in requirements, viz., the two towers (leaving the staircases, &c.), the conservatory, the kish and medicated baths, the porter's lodge, septic wards as a separate building, a portion the nurses' home, and reducing the laundry the course now adopted be continued of ding the bulk of the washing to be done ay), the remainder may be carried out for the n of 80,000*l.*, and, as funds permit, the design ild be completed.

COMPETITIONS.

THE COXLODGE ASYLUM EXTENSIONS.—A meeting of the Visiting Justices was held at Coxlodge Asylum on the 16th inst., under the chairmanship of Alderman W. H. Stephenson. After the ordinary business had been transacted, it was resolved that the recommendation of Mr. Hine, the architectural assessor, with respect to the premiated designs for the extension of the Asylum should be adopted. That recommendation, as mentioned in the *Builder* for February 20, places the plans of Mr. J. W. Dyson 1st, those of Messrs. Carr and Montgomery 2nd, those of Mr. W. L. Newcombe 3rd, and those of Messrs. Knill Freeman and S. R. Robins 4th. Mr. Dyson will consequently be appointed official architect of the extension, and premiums of 150*l.*, 100*l.*, and 50*l.* will be proportioned in the order named to the other successful architects. This decision requires the confirmation of the Newcastle City Council to be carried into effect.

NEW BOARD SCHOOL FOR GOOLE.—A special meeting of the Goole School Board was held on the 18th inst. for the purpose of deciding the best and second best of the fifteen sets of plans sent in to the Board for competition in respect of the new school premises proposed to be erected in Bookferry-road. Premiums of 50*l.* and 20*l.* had been offered for the first and second best designs. The plans of Mr. W. Watson, of Wakefield, were accepted, and that gentleman was appointed Architect to the Board. The second premium was awarded to Mr. A. Williamson, Goole and Bradford.

Correspondence.

To the Editor of THE BUILDER.

MANCHESTER ROYAL INSTITUTION.

SIR,—May I be allowed to express my warm sympathy with you in your remarks as to the contemplated destruction of the beautiful interior of this unique example of happy adaptation of Classical forms and character to modern uses?

From the first time of my acquaintance with it, now nearly half a century ago, I never lost an opportunity when in Manchester of looking into the building, were it only for a possible minute, to enjoy the charming architectural picture you so well describe, and it is really almost inconceivable that a municipality possessed of such a gem of art should be so insensible of its value, or so utterly without sound advice in the treatment of their buildings, as to propose branding their community with vandalism to such a degree. It is hard to express the feelings of astonishment, and, indeed, shame, which such a project inspires, and one would fain hope that a timely protest might yet avail to prevent what would be almost a national disgrace; and in a day when so much is urged as to the need of general instruction in art to enable us to keep our place in the ranks of European civilisation. AN OLD ARCHITECT.

March 22, 1892.

"RESTORATION" AT LINCOLN CATHEDRAL.

SIR,—It now seems but too certain that the Dean and Chapter of Lincoln are preparing to destroy a part of that most majestic and historical building entrusted to their care. The building bears on its face the evidences of its growth through many centuries. It is left to the nineteenth century fully to discover that this is not as it should be. It is left to us to forge, to tell archæological lies, to try and falsify history under the name of restoration,

We are told that the page of architectural history written out for us in this church by Sir Christopher Wren (who, it must be remembered, did not himself pull down, but, finding a void, filled it up in the style current in his time, just as his predecessors had done before him) is out of keeping. Of course, we all knew this, but a genuine work of any style is better than a piece of sham. You have, however, in the *Builder*, so well stated the case against the absurdity of setting up a sham Gothic side to the cloister that on this head no more need be written.

We cannot doubt that Dean Butler and most of his colleagues have visited Salisbury. No doubt they have, as the fashion is, condemned the barbarities of Wyatt. Wyatt pulled down the Hungerford and Beauchamp Chapels, because they were intrusions and not in style with the rest of the cathedral. The Dean and Chapter of Lincoln wish to do the same by their cloisters. Wyatt pulled down the bell tower because it spoiled the view. These gentlemen do the same by their close, removing, amongst others, one mediæval house of great interest; and if it be true that they propose to set up Wren's Library where they have pulled down the houses, such a course seems but the adding of folly to folly. But, Sir, are we quite right in throwing all the blame on the Dean and Chapter of Lincoln? Does not the evil begin in our own profession? If the architect had been more anxious to preserve and honestly repair, rather than to "restore" and build up sham antiques, would our churches be the cold, lifeless, unhistoric edifices most of them have become? It is to be feared that our profession is chiefly answerable for raising the monster of destructive restoration, and it is only as yet amongst a few that the hopeless folly of trying to turn back the wheel of Time is realised. The clergy have learnt the lesson of restoration but too well. When their churches have been "thoroughly restored" they look brand new, and that is what is really liked.

We may excuse the ardour of the budding Gothic revivalist. Nothing, however, can make up for the destruction he has wrought; and still less can be forgiven deliberate falsifications by those who in the fulness of time and ripeness of knowledge go on in the stupid rut in which they first began.

It seems clear that in the present instance Mr. Pearson is responsible for the useless destruction now recommended to the Chapter. This unfortunate cloister has already suffered at his hands. The open walls toward the garth had soon after their erection swung over a little. They had been supported by small intermediate buttresses, examples of the skill with which our forefathers could make even a prop an object not unpleasing to look upon. Mr. Pearson has "restored" the cloister and restored away the intermediate buttress so that this page of history is carefully removed. Then to reveal the outside of the doorway to the Chapter-house which was altered by the builders of the cloister, the cloister itself has been cut about and its eastern walk falsified. To crown the work we are now to have a sham north walk. A good building is to go and a thing which can have no real interest for any intelligent man is to be set up.

Are we told that Wren's building is to be set up somewhere else? Our answer is that it is impossible. Wren's work was often somewhat dull, but he was always careful of his proportions and that the building he designed should suit its place and purpose.

The library, following these rules, stands on an arcade, which forms the north walk of the cloister. When the building is set up elsewhere, what reason will there be for the open cloister below it? The east end of the library, with the stairs, is engaged in the east walk of the cloister, the west end is similarly engaged. Here is a nice opportunity to "complete" Wren's design and add that to his building which he never thought of.

Would any man of cultivation venture to treat a manuscript in the way in which a restoring architect treats an ancient building? Would he tear out a damaged page and trust to put in a new one so that no one should know? or would he daub his fanciful restorations over the old but damaged page?

The worst feature of an architectural restoration is that the old evidence is destroyed in setting up the new work. If the restorer would confine himself to paper it would not matter.

I venture to believe that we ought not so much to blame the cathedral dignitaries, and find them fifty years behind their time, as we should blame their advisers. Who now thinks about the Chapter of Salisbury who followed the advice of Wyatt? It is Wyatt himself who is held up to reprobation. So is Scott blamed for many a so-called "restoration," and not the Chapters under which he worked. So will be Mr. Pearson, as the historic spirit grows and the restorer fades away. Perhaps one niche in this temple of fame may be reserved for Lord Grimthorpe; but, fortunately, his practice is limited, and his attempts at architectural restoration so clumsy that the youngest tyro would hardly be deceived. SOMERS CLARKE.

Dean's-yard, Westminster Abbey,
March 21, 1892.

CRYPT IN WATERGATE-STREET, CHESTER.

SIR,—Every architect must feel grateful to Mr. T. P. Ivison for his beautiful illustrations of Old Chester which you have so admirably reproduced. The view in Watergate-street which you published in your number of 27th ult. is a masterpiece. Both Mr. Ivison and yourself will, however, be glad of two corrections:—

1. The date of the erection of this crypt is given in your text as about A.D. 1180.* From the sketch, however, it is clear that the work is of the reign of Edward I., 1272-1307. The writer states that it is believed to have been erected by the sixth Earl of Chester of the Norman line, which shows that the date given for Earl Ranulph de Blonville (query Fairton) is correct, as this allows an average of nineteen years to each tenant of the title.

2. Mr. Ivison has introduced an altar. This is right enough, but he has placed the altar against the *south* wall, instead of toward the east. No Catholic altar *can* be placed, *according to the rubrics*, as that the celebrating priest shall face in any other direction than *eastward*, following, of course, the arrangement both of the Jewish Tabernacle and Temple, and of the Pagan temples also, as mentioned by Vitruvius.

I may here state that there exists a very similar crypt,—known as that of the Grey, or Franciscan Friars,—in Middlegate-street, Great Yarmouth. GEORGE GILBERT SCOTT.

London, March 14, 1892.

P.S.—The Jewish Holy of Holies was toward the *west* (cf. Exodus, cap. 26), and the Petrine Basilicas followed this occidentation. The Pauline Basilicas, however, have their sanctuaries toward the east, in this following the Orientation of the Pagan temples. But in all cases the celebrating priest faces eastward (cf. my "Essay on the History of English Church Architecture," cap. 1. and 2).

MISS SELLERS'S LECTURES.

SIR,—I have only just had my attention called to a paragraph in your issue of March 5, criticising portions of my lecture on the development of the Greek temple. I would ask permission to state what I actually did say, as the writer of the paragraph obviously laboured under the disadvantage of having to criticise statements which he had only heard at second-hand. The attack being chiefly directed against my explanation of a passage in Vitruvius (lib. iv., cap. ii. 4), it will be simplest to begin by quoting the passage in full. "Non enim, quemadmodum nonnulli errantes dixerunt fenestrarum imagines esse triglyphos, ita potest esse; *quod in angulis contraque tetrantes columnarum triglyphi constituuntur; quibus in locis omnino non patitur res fenestras fieri. Dissolvuntur enim angulorum in ædificiis iuncturæ, si in his fuerint fenestrarum lumina relicta*; etiamque ubi nunc triglyphi constituuntur, si ibi luminum spatia fuisse indicabuntur, iisdem rationibus denticuli in Ionicis fenestrarum occupauisse loca uidebuntur. Utraque enim, et inter denticulos, et *inter triglyphos, quæ sunt intervalla metopæ nominantur*; ὀπὰς enim Græci tignorum cubilia et asserum appellant, uti nostri ea caua columbaria: ita quod inter duas opas est intertignium, id metopa est apud eos nominatum." The first passage I have italicised shows sufficiently that Vitruvius is speaking of buildings where the triglyph occupied precisely the position which the writer in the *Builder* claims for it in Greek buildings, where "it was shifted to the angle of the building," and not left "over the centre of the column, as the Romans did." My words are most unfortunately misstated in the *Builder*. To say that "the triglyphs represented spaces" would be a mere repetition of the nonsense which even Vitruvius had to refute (". . . . . . nonnulli errantes dixerunt," &c.); what I did say was that I believed the architrave represented the binding-beam of the old mixed clay-brick and wood construction, and then,—following Vitruvius,—that the triglyph represented the end of the beam that was laid in the *ope*, *i.e.*, the *cubile*, or "bed," made or left to receive the beam in the strip of wall above the architrave, while the metope (a space between two *opai*) represented the solid piece of wall left standing between the *opai*. I think this may be allowed to be a rational explanation. As to the *metope* representing a space originally left open (the explanation given in any architectural primer), this is by no means proved by the fact that the *metopai* of the Parthenon are thin facing slabs. Because at some given date an architectural member had become merely ornamental, and was, therefore (probably for economy), built as slightly as possible, there is no need to deny its constructive origin. Nor does the pivot metope help the matter. A more striking instance, which I am astonished not to have had quoted against me, is afforded by the well-known passage;—

ὅρα δὲ γ'εἴσω (or γεῖσα?) τριγλύφων ὅποι κενὸν δέμας καθεῖναι.—Eurip. "Iphig. Taur.," 113.

Quite so, but starting with the solid wall,—a portion of it could be removed to make one or more windows, in the same way as portions had been removed for the ὀπαί.

Bötticher has been a great authority in his day, but the difficulties he created for himself and his readers from his attempt to preserve the *metope* as the open space between two triglyphs, instead of the closed space between two ὀπαί are quite amusing. He tries to show that *ope* and *metope* are the same! ("Tektonik der Hellenen," p. 205). He gets enraged with Vitruvius, calls him "unklar und verworren"; further, does not hesitate to correct him on the passage "quod inter duas ὀπάς est intertignium." Not so, he says, "Sondern es hätte heissen sollen *quod inter duos tignos est intertignium.*" And yet Vitruvius had read Silenus on the Doric orders, and Iktinos on the Parthenon! (Lib. vii. Præf). The great Semper thought the whole *triglyphon* merely ornamental in its purpose. It would be pure pedantry to go on quoting. A glance at the list of contradictory opinions collected by Joseph Durm (p. 83 of "Baukunst der Hellenen") affords perhaps sufficient excuse for the bewildered student who deserts these latter-day authorities, and finds that Vitruvius's statements become absolutely luminous when he is read in the light of the *facts* of Greek architecture, without the help of his commentators.

Further, the connexion of Doric architecture with the "quasi-timber rock-cut designs" of Asia-Minor is by no means so well proven as the writer in the *Builder* implies. It is not a point I feel competent to discuss, yet I may quote the following passage from so able an architect as M. Charles Chipiez: "Dans la charpente asiatique on ne rencontre pas de triglyphes—on ne voit pas de mutules; on reconnait simplement le principe des modillons." ("Hist. Critique des Arts et de la Formation des Ordres Grecs," p. 207, seq.) Surely it is in the clay-brick construction, with its binding-beams and stone sub-structure—such as the excavations of Hissarlik, Tiryns, Mycenæ, and, above all, the Heraion at Olympia, have revealed it to us—rather than in the lignite constructions of Asia-Minor, that we must seek for an explanation of Doric forms.

With regard to one other point. I am criticised for starting architectural examination from the *cella* instead of from the *order*, though my critic owns that "in regard to the main architecture of the building, no doubt the cella is the constructive *raison d'être* of the temple." Without entering into the large question of the *generic* incapacities of woman, I can yet honestly state, as an *individual*, that I was fully aware of how unpopular my attempt at arguing from the essential to the ornamental would be with a public trained amid those productions of English architecture where the *raison d'être* is so often left for a possible afterthought. EUGÉNIE SELLERS.

March 19, 1892.

P.S.—May I take this opportunity of answering one other stricture made upon my lectures, and which had escaped my memory till now? In a note to the report of my second afternoon lecture at the British Museum (*Builder*, February 20), when I had interpreted the so-called Selene of the eastern pediment as a figure of Nux, *because she drives*, it is stated that "the head of the 'Selene' horse quite allows of the supposition of a rider." Possibly, so long as we only had one horse to deal with. Bruno Sauer's admirable investigation of the actual Parthenon pediments (See "Athen. Mittheil.," Heft I., 1891) has fortunately settled the whole question, as in addition to the one horse in London, two remain *in situ* on the temple, leaving us to infer a fourth. Short of being a circus-rider, the charming little figure must henceforth be looked upon as a charioteer. In speaking to a class of students I had not thought it necessary to revert to the Sauer discoveries. I had discussed them at great length last term.—E. S.

*** Miss Sellers's clever letter certainly shows that she has given more attention to the subject than we had supposed, but it does not convince us that Vitruvius knew much of the real origin of the triglyph, and it does not alter the fact that, to any architect, the triglyphs are the piers or supporting parts of the upper structure (just as the columns are below), and the spaces between of less constructive importance; hence their peculiar suitability for sculptural treatment. On the subject of the original open-space character of the metopes we may call Miss Sellers's attention to Fergusson's foot-note and sketch in the "History of Architecture," Vol. I., page 24[illegible] (second edition), which is much more to the point than the remarks of Vitruvius. Miss Sellers's sarcasm at the close about the productions of English architecture where "the *raison d'être* is left as an afterthought" is neat enough, but has nothing to do with our criticism. What we pointed out was that in regard to architectural design and expression the Greek exterior columnar order is the great fact of Greek architecture. It has influenced the architectural design of the whole civilised world for two thousand years, which certainly cannot be said of the *cella* of the temple, however important that was at the time.—ED.

STEAM-ROLLING ON MAIN ROADS.

SIR,—I have read with much pleasure your article upon "Steam Road Rolling" in your issue of the 19th inst. My report upon the subject to the Frome Highway Board, to which you so kindly refer, was written mainly for the use of the County Works Committee of the Somerset County Council, and was made the basis of a resolution offering the various contracting Highway Authorities in the county the sum of 10d. per cubic yard for all stone rolled in by the steam-roller, subject to the quality of the stone being approved by the County Surveyor. It is almost impossible to obtain an accurate comparison of the actual cost of steam road rolling in different districts, owing to the variety of opinion as to the particular items which should be included in that cost. In some statements only the wages of the driver and cost of coal, oil, and waste are included; whilst, on the other hand, some surveyors include the cost of the stone. In the report above referred to, I have included all the *extra* items of expense which would not have occurred had the stone been left to consolidate by the traffic, and these items only. They consist of driver's and sweeper's wages; horse hire for hauling water; coal, oil, waste, brushes, &c.

The principal item is the horse hire, and this must depend upon the distance from which the water has to be hauled. I find, however, that by using a water-barrel containing 175 gallons I can generally manage with one horse, making the cost about 2½d. per cubic yard.

The steam-roller and water-carts are the property of the authority, and, in a further report to my board, I have estimated that the depreciation and repairs would be about 1½d. per cubic yard consolidated.

Including these last-mentioned items, I find that I can satisfactorily consolidate Black Rock (Mountain Limestone) at a cost of 9d. per cubic yard.

With regard to "binding," I always use a small quantity (about 5 per cent.) of well-weathered road-scrapings, applied when the materials are nearly consolidated.

I have all stone broken to a 2½ in. gauge.

ALLAN GREENWELL, A.M.I.C.E.,
Surveyor to the Frome Highway Authority.

Surveyor's Office, Frome, March 22, 1892.

SIR,—Kindly allow me to correct a few errors in the article on the above.

Gloucestershire does not contract for manual labour. We employ day labour, except in one district of 54 miles, where the system of letting the labour on stated lengths of road (we found in existence when we took over the roads) is continued.

It does not commend itself to me in any way and encourages a low form of sweating. My own experience of road contracting is that it does very well for five years, then the roads go to pieces, and you have to spend all your previous savings to put them to rights.

Steam-rolling cannot be defended on economy of cost, but it can as a saving to the user of the road.

Ten years' careful watching their cost in this county show they add 53*l*. per mile to the annual cost, that rolling alone costs 24*l*. per mile.

It saves by consolidation without abrasion or trituration one-eighth of the metal.

There are three distinct operations,—rolling, watering, brushing,—not required for wheel-rolled roads, and I have hitherto failed to find the surveyor that can do this for nothing.

The cost of breaking-up the surface to refuse is also considerable. Notwithstanding this, I am so convinced that they are necessities of civilisation that I am asking my council to buy four more, making eight in all, and I could find work for thirty on the 1,060 miles of road we maintain.

It must be a thicker coating to make steam-rolling economical, and we find that a cubic yard only covers 8 yards superficial, and not 17 yards as at Frome.

The use of blindage requires great judgment, and for that reason I discourage it. Town experience such as Mr. Deacon's is useless for rural roads, where the roads are wet and unsheltered; and a road blinded as we see done in towns would be like a ploughed field after a frost. But there is a time,—when the stones have begun to interlock and are settled in

* Mr. Ivison, who signed the article, is responsible for its contents. We felt some doubt about his date.—ED.

ce,—when blindage is invaluable, and this is ecially necessary in finishing steam-rolled roads. to horse-rolls, the blows of the horses' hoofs do what the roller does.

ROBERT PHILLIPS,
County Surveyor for Gloucestershire.

MEASURING.

SIR,—The letter of Mr. Robert Jones, in your ue of March 12, raises a question which ought t to be let drop. He asks why London architects luce brick walls to rods a brick and a half thick? d suggests the adoption of the Northern (and dland) "use" of yards one brick thick. Why do her? A new building is planned,—an old one measured,—in feet. Why, then, should not all antities be taken in feet also? For surfaces ere a larger unit is wanted, we have already (in ne trades) the "square" of 100 ft. sup., which ght well be made general. Then all measure- nts taken straight from the plan or building by le or rule could be put into quantities at once. d the yard relegated entirely to the linen-drapers. ny generations may, indeed, have gone on com- tably in the old way, but will any architect say at he likes, when looking out or receiving prices, have some in rods, others in feet, some in yards, hers in squares, and that he would not prefer to ve them comparable at a glance, without any ocess of reduction?

With the much longer list of materials, and the ich finer cutting of their prices, that we have now deal with, the simplification of our needlessly undabout methods of measuring would surely be reform worth making? Could not the "Practice mmittee" of the Institute take it up?

A. S. FLOWER.

The Student's Column.

ARMING BUILDINGS BY HOT WATER.
XIII.

QUANTITIES FOR HORTICULTURAL WORKS.

HOOD, in his standard work upon hot-water engineering, published a rule for arriving at the quantity of pipe quired to raise and keep the temperature of a ilding to whatever heat was needed. Owing, wever, to the complexity of the calculations eded this rule has been little thought of, not- thstanding the very correct result it gave.

The rule in question ran as follows:—"Mul- ly 125 by the difference between the tempe- ure at which the room is purposed to be pt, when at its maximum, and the temperature the external air, and divide this product by difference between the temperature of the es and the proposed temperature of the room; en the quotient thus obtained, when multi- ed by the number of cubic feet of air to be rmed per minute and this product by 222, ll give the number of feet in length of pipe, n. in diameter which will produce the desired ect."

This rule is based upon the fact that every perficial foot of glass which constitutes the s-house will cool 1¼ cubit of warmed air per ute down to the temperature of the external . The result arrived at by this rule gives the antity of 4-in. pipe that is required containing ater at about 180 deg. to make good this loss heat. In calculating in this manner, only e glass has to be considered, wood, brick, and one work being practically inactive in the ansference and loss of heat. The rule is thus od for any shape of house, whether high or w, lean-to or span, and in this respect it is ch better in results than the rapid calculat- tables that will be spoken of directly. ese latter are based upon cubical area, or ntents, and consequently a house bounded on e side by a wall would be given the same antity of pipe as a house having glass on all des, unless a certain allowance is made.

The working out of Hood's rule would be as llows:—Supposing a grape-house, having 000 superficial feet of glass, was required to heated to 60 deg.; this temperature to be tainable during the coldest midwinter nights. or this purpose it would be necessary to calcu- te upon the external air being as low as deg. Fahr. Multiply 125 by 50 (difference tween the external and the required internal mperatures) = 6,250, divided by 120 (the fference between heat of pipes, 180 deg., and e internal temperature, 60 deg.) = 52, multi- ied by 1,250 (cubic feet of air cooled by 000 superficial feet of glass per minute) = ,000, divided by 222 = 293 ft. of 4-in. pipe, to keep up a heat of 60 deg. in the house, when the outer temperature is 10 deg.

All calculations are usually based upon using 4-in. pipe, as 1 ft. length of this is almost exactly a superficial foot, and should any irregular-shaped radiating media be used, then by ascertaining its superficial measurement in feet, its value can be instantly seen. 3-in. pipe is three-fourths of a superficial foot per foot-run, and 2-in. pipe half a superficial foot per foot-run. In other words, if 100 ft. of 4-in. pipe was required to give a certain temperature, it would require 133 ft. of 3 in., or 200 ft. of 2-in. pipe, to attain the same result.

In arriving at the quantity of glass in a glass-house the material of the frames are included, but if they be wood about one-eighth total area can be deducted. If the frames be metal, no allowance can be made, as they reduce the temperature as quickly as glass. In the same way, if corrugated sheet-iron should ever enter into calculation, it can be treated as glass.

As just mentioned, Hood's rule, although possessing accuracy, is rarely, if ever, used. It is hardly suited for the understanding of many who undertake these works. Even those capable of using it give preference to some more expeditious mode of arriving at results, and this has led to the almost universal use of tables based upon cubical contents.

The particular objection to these tables has been pointed out,—viz., that we get a certain quantity of pipe to a given area, quite irrespective of the quantity of glass. This is a great weakness, as it is the glass wholly, and nothing else (except open ventilators), that goes to reduce the temperature. In span and lean-to houses it is sometimes possible to get nearly double the quantity of glass in the former than in the latter, with the same cubical contents; under such circumstances as these, the tables referred to give erratic results, to say the least. It is usual to apply the tables to lean-to houses, and allow a certain additional percentage for span houses, &c.

An example of rapid calculating tables is as follows:—If we have a glass-house, 30 ft. by 10 ft. by 10 ft., we can easily find its cubical capacity or contents is 3,000 ft. If we require a temperature of 60 deg. (Fahr.) when the thermometer registers 10 deg. outside, we must allow 50 ft. of 4-in. pipe to each 1,000 ft. capacity, which would amount to 150 ft. of 4-in. pipe for the house in question.

The following table shows the length of 4-in. pipe needed to keep up a given temperature to every 1,000 cubic feet capacity in a glass horticultural building, the pipes being at about 180 deg., and the outer air at 10 deg. or higher:—

Temperature Required (Kahr.) Deg.	Quantity of Pipe to each 1,000 cubic feet capacity. Ft.
90	80
85	75
80	70
75	65
70	60
65	55
60	50
55	45
50	40
45	37
40	35

The above table requires allowances, &c, as follows:—

For span-houses add one-fifth or one-fourth to the above quantities. About the same allowance should be made for any house that has glass on all four sides and top.

The position of the house should be considered. They are invariably placed in a sheltered position when it is possible, but if impossible, then it is desirable to put a little more pipe.

Pipes carried in trenches must be calculated as being one-fourth less effective than those that are exposed; therefore one-third must be added to the quantities given for pipes carried in channels with gratings over. Channels should be as roomy as possible, or the pipes will be still less effective. At least a width equal to the diameter of the pipe used (say, 4 in.) should exist between the pipes and the sides of the channel.

If the boiler is attended to by a gardener or man having some skill in stoking, very different results will be obtained to what will be effected if the reverse is the case. It might almost be taken for granted that a horticultural apparatus will have the best attention, but it is not always the case. If such a thing has to be provided against, then a little extra pipe will meet the trouble, as it only means that the water will not be kept at a regular high temperature, as it should be. This trouble is of common occurrence in residence and buildings works, as the boiler is then very generally attended to by a page-boy or odd man, whose chief idea is to economise the time spent in stoking.

The quantities given in this table, although sufficient and correct for all ordinary purposes, can be increased with decided advantage if cost is not of chief importance. It is quite recognised that a benefit is derived by putting a more than necessary quantity of pipe, in the same way that a fully-large boiler (beyond the size arrived at by calculation) gives better, more reliable, and economical results. In the first place, it is an advantage to have an apparatus that will respond rapidly to whatever attention is devoted to the fire. Then, with an apparatus that would be considered overpowerful in the ordinary way, we can afford to keep low fires, with little attention, and the fires when banked for the night will, without fear of failure, keep up an efficient heat during the night, when they have the least, or perhaps no, attention whatever.

This is a question that should always be prominent in the engineer's mind, viz., that during the daytime, when attention can be and is given to the boiler, and the best results can be easily effected, the natural temperature is higher than at night, and assists matters materially. At night, when the fire is banked and left to smoulder and do the best it can by itself, the temperature registers its lowest point, and if the boiler and apparatus are not fully capable, mischief will be done—sufficient, perhaps, to destroy the work of the season. With all calculations of quantities, heating surfaces, &c., the coldest winter temperature has to be guarded against, with a fire that is left, perhaps, all the night through without attention.

It has been mentioned how uncertain the results must be with a table based upon cubical contents, especially when comparing lean-to and span-houses in which the quantity of glass varies to such a great extent. This variation, however, can be met by a fixed allowance as just shown, but the quantity of glass varies in other ways. Supposing we have two glass-houses of exactly the same height and width, but one measuring 15 ft. and the other 30 ft. in length, here we get exactly double cubical capacity, but not double the quantity of glass (the glass being the sole cause of heat-loss as explained). In this case no harm would ensue, as by calculation we should give the smaller house sufficient pipe and the larger house too much. The only objection would be, that assuming the job to be one in which cost was of primary importance, we should be spending money on pipe unnecessarily in the larger house. It will be understood that the difference in quantity of glass occurs by the fact that the 30 ft. house has but two glazed ends, whereas two 15 ft. houses would have four glazed ends.

Another example may be illustrated in a high-domed conservatory or a palm-house. With these we get double the cubic contents (or more) of a low glass-house, but not double the glass area. In this case, if we get a more than exact quantity of pipe, certainly no harm ensues, for in high houses we require a full sufficiency of pipe, as the heat, or, rather, heated air, rises, and gets out of the way at the top more quickly than is desirable.

Hood plainly saw the fault that the complexity of his rule gave rise to, and compiled a table of figures which greatly simplified matters, although it still remained based upon the glass-area, and not cubic contents. A cubic contents table was also given by Hood, but not willingly, as it was opposed to the exactitude of his general information. Although errors crept in here and there, his work has been practically beyond criticism, and has only fallen behind by reason of its age, which made it somewhat unsuited to modern practices and requirements. An excellent new edition of this work has, however, now been published.

When an apparatus is first tested, some idea of its efficiency can be gained by the time it takes to heat up the previously cold and possibly damp interior. Of course, accuracy is rather out of the question, as results will vary with the normal temperature of the air. If an apparatus be erected in the summer time, it is difficult to judge its efficiency except by feeling the temperature of the pipes, and having confidence that the quantity of pipe is sufficient. If, on the other hand, the first trial of the apparatus be made in cold weather, the time occupied in getting the interior of the house to its required heat should be about as follows:—

Width 4-in. pipe	...	4 hours.
" 3 " "	...	$3\frac{1}{4}$ "
" 2 " "	...	$2\frac{1}{2}$ "

A perfectly dry house would be heated in less time than this, for with moisture (water) we have a substance that possesses a great affinity for heat. Moisture is a very necessary feature in all glass-houses, and its presence materially delays the heating up of the air. When the apparatus is first getting warm, it is the air and moisture alone that takes up the heat; after the air becomes somewhat warm, the glass begins to transfer the heat from the air in contact with it to the outer air which is in need of it. A familiar example of this is the cold downward current of air that always exists near windows, this down current being air robbed of its heat by contact with the glass, and being thus rendered heavier than the general air of the room. It is much like the circulating action of hot water, but reversed as to the cause.

GENERAL BUILDING NEWS.

PROPOSED TECHNICAL SCHOOL FOR SALFORD.—Mr. Arnold Taylor, an inspector of the Local Government Board, held an inquiry at the Salford Town Hall, in respect of an application by the Salford Corporation for sanction to borrow 55,000*l.*, under the provisions of the Municipal Corporations Act and the Technical Instruction Act, 1889, for the provision of a school of technical instruction in the borough. Plans of the proposed new school were exhibited on the walls of the committee-room where the inquiry was held, and the details were explained to the inspector by the architect, Mr. Henry Lord.—The Town Clerk, in supporting the application of the Corporation, said the purchase of the land was put at 1,833*l.*, and the cost of the erection of the school buildings at 43,500*l.* The subjects proposed to be taught in the school included chemistry, building construction, machine construction and drawing, magnetism and electricity, mechanical engineering, and theoretical mechanics. After the inquiry closed the inspector visited the site of the proposed school.

NEW CLUB, LINCOLN.—On the 9th inst. a Liberal Club building was opened at Lincoln. The building is situated between St. Swithin's-square and Water-side. The approach to the building, which is of red brick with stone dressings, is from the first-named street. A vestibule leads into a large central hall. On the left of the vestibule is a reading-room, 26 ft. by 22 ft., and on the right is a corridor leading to two offices. At the back of this corridor, on the west side of the building, there is a lecture-hall, capable of seating 500 persons. It is 60 ft. by 30 ft., and has at the end two cloak-rooms and the usual offices. On the left of the central hall is a refreshment bar, and beyond, on the east side, is a smoke-room, 32 ft. by 22 ft. The first-floor is reached by a staircase from the central hall. The billiard-room, 62 ft. by 26 ft., occupies the entire front of the building on the first-floor, and two French windows in it give access to a verandah, 22 ft. long, over the main entrance. A room, 24 ft. by 22 ft., is set apart for games, and there is also a lock-up library, 15 ft. by 10 ft., on the first floor. Adjoining it is the directors' room, 16 ft. by 14 ft. The caretaker's rooms are also situated here. In the basement there is a cellar, 76 ft. by 28 ft., a club kitchen, two hot and cold water baths, and the apparatus for heating the club. The architects were Messrs. Sington & Brameld, of Manchester; and the contractors Messrs. Lansdown & Son, of Lincoln.

CO-OPERATIVE STORES, SEATON BURN.—On the 19th inst. new branch stores at Seaton Burn, belonging to the Cramlington Co-operative Society, Limited, were formally opened. The buildings comprise upon the ground floor dry goods and flour warehouses, with large cellar underneath, grocery and drapery, boot and shoe, and hardware departments, greengrocery and vegetable store, butcher's shop, slaughter and hanger-houses, oil store, and the usual conveniences. Upon the first floor is a large hall 65 ft. by 36 ft., capable of holding 500 adults, and two ante-rooms. The ventilation is by means of Messrs. Boyle's air-pump ventilator; the heating by hot-water pipes, the apparatus having been fixed by Messrs. Henry Walker & Son, engineers, Gallowgate, Newcastle; the seating by the North of England School Furnishing Company, Darlington; and patent roller shutters by Messrs. Francis & Co., London. The architect for the buildings is Mr. J. G. Crone, 50, Granger-street, Newcastle-upon-Tyne, and the contractor was Mr. Amos Gray, of North Gosforth, while the clerk of works was Mr. Amos Gray, jun., Wide-open. The internal fittings are carried out in pitch-pine, also the cleading of walls and ceilings, and the cost of the buildings has been 2,250*l.*

FORESTERS' HALL, PLYMOUTH.—On the 19th inst. a new Foresters' Hall, which has been erected at the Octagon, Plymouth, was opened. The building is three stories high, and is built of local stone with Portland stone dressing and stucco front. On the ground floor, on the left of the entrance lobby, is an apartment intended as the district secretary's office, and approached through a small waiting-room. Behind it is court-room No. 1. The large hall is approached through a passage leading from the Octagon entrance to a circular porch, which opens through swing doors into the hall. The latter is 66 ft. long by 28 ft. 6 in. wide, and lighted from the top by a double sky-light, the framework being formed of steel, filled with Helliwell's patent glazing. At the upper end a platform will be erected, and seating accommodation will be provided for 500 persons. Behind the hall is a kitchen, and over it a retiring-room for ladies. Emergency exits open out into Bath-lane. On the second floor of the main building are two additional court-rooms; overhead are the caretaker's apartments. All the court-rooms are fitted with mica flap ventilators, the window being filled with cathedral stained-glass. There are also cloak-rooms and lavatories, fitted with Sicilian marble ware, for both ladies and gentlemen. The premises have been erected by Mr. S. Harvey, Plymouth, from the designs of Mr. H. J. Snell, architect. Mr. G. H. Julian has been clerk of works.

BAPTIST CHAPEL, LAUNCESTON.—On the 17th inst. the foundation-stone was laid of a Baptist Chapel, which is to be erected in the Western-road, Launceston. The building, designed by Mr. Otho B. Peter, architect, Launceston, will be of Gothic style. A gable end and porch of cut and dressed stone will face the Western-road. Seating accommodation will be provided for 120 persons, the seats and sittings being of pitch pine. Underneath the chapel will be a school-room. The building is to be heated throughout by hot-water pipes. Mr. G. H. Strike is the contractor.

SANITARY AND ENGINEERING NEWS.

HEMSWORTH WATERWORKS.—On Wednesday, March 9, a Local Government Inquiry was commenced at Wakefield relative to an application of the Hemsworth Rural Sanitary Authority for a provisional order to acquire lands and easements otherwise than by agreement. Major-General Crozier presided. There was no opposition on the part of the landowners concerned, but the project, which is to supply water to no less than nine townships, was opposed by ratepayers in some of the contributory places, and the inquiry was adjourned to Monday, the 14th inst., and again to March 29. The scheme is to supply an ultimate population estimated at 25,000, with 350,000 gallons of water to be purchased from the joint Boards of Dewsbury and Heckmondwike, with whom a provisional agreement has been completed. The water is derived from the moorlands at the head waters of the River Don. The works are estimated to cost about 28,000*l.* The supply will be by gravitation. Mr. M. Paterson, M.Inst.C.E., gave evidence, and stated that he had investigated the existing supply, which consists of surface wells and springs, more or less polluted, and entirely inadequate to the needs of the district; that he had failed to find a sufficient local supply, and that this was the best and cheapest scheme for a combined supply. He also stated that it had been agreed to supply the high levels of two townships on the line of pipes, and also the township of High Hoyland. The chairman (Col. Ramsden), Dr. Coleman (medical officer), and others gave evidence.

FOREIGN AND COLONIAL.

FRANCE.—A committee has been formed to raise a monument at Paris to M. Alphand.——M. Achille Jacquet has been elected a member of the Institute, in place of the late Henriquel Dupont.——On the recommendation of M. Daumet, the ten pupils who have entered in competition for the Prix de Rome in architecture have been given as a subject "Un Musée d'Artillerie."——The "Société des Amis des Arts" at Dijon is to open its seventh exhibition of painting, sculpture, and architecture on June 1. The exhibition is to be open till July 5.——The "Société Académique d'Architecture" of Lyons proposes to architects (French and foreign), for the subject of the competition of 1892, "Une École de Commune," to be erected on a site at Lyons. The first prize will be a gold medal and a sum of 200 francs; the second a silver medal, and the third a bronze medal. The designs must be sent, carriage paid, to the Palais des Beaux-Arts at Lyons, addressed to the Secretary of the Society, before December 1 of this year.——Six French architects have sent in competition designs for a cathedral for Tunis, but no decision has yet been arrived at.——A monument to the painter Angevin Bruneau is to be erected in the cemetery at Rueil (Seine-et-Oise).——The sculptors Desca, Escoula, and Mathet are commissioned to make the model for a monumental fountain for the town of Tarbes (Hautes-Pyrénées).——The Société des Amis des Arts at Cognac is organising an art-exhibition in that town, to open on June 1.——M. Manceau, a former pupil of Cabanel, has been appointed professor of drawing at the College of Beauvais.——The death is announced of Madame Jenny Gaupillat, sculptor, author of a fine bust of Mdlle. Marie Bashkirtseff exhibited in the Salon of 1886.——M. Gabriel Emanuel Faraill, a talented sculptor, has died suddenly at the age of fifty-four. He was a pupil of Oliva and Farochon. From 1886 to 1891 he exhibited at the Salon various statues and busts remarkable for their conscientious execution. Among his works may be mentioned a figure of a young girl which gained a third medal in the Salon of 1886, and a large bronze statue of the painter Rigaud which stands in one of the public squares at Perpignan, after having figured in the Salon of 1889.——A fine paining by Mantegna, representing the martyrdom of St. Sebastian, in the parish church of the small town of Aigueperse (Puy-de-Dôme), has been seriously damaged by some person unknown.

BERLIN.—The proposed metropolitan overhead railroad scheme is apparently to be carried out without much delay. The electrical engineers, Messrs. Siemens & Halske, have altered their route in accordance with the wishes of a special committee which had criticised their scheme for the authorities when first mooted. The altered plans have been put before the Police President for approval, and he has sent them to the Minister of the Interior with his recommendation. If the Minister's approval be obtained at once, the preliminary works are to be commenced this summer, and, if this be the case, the new line can be opened in 1894.——The Emperor wishes to have some of the old houses in the vicinity of his "Schloss" pulled down. This proposed extension of the "Schlossfreiheit" will require a large sum of money. For the purpose of raising the necessary funds, the Emperor wishes again to have recourse to his favourite "lottery" system. The Privy Counsellor in whose department the matter would have to be settled has apparently refused to help the Emperor this time. He has asked for his dismissal from his unpleasant post, and will receive it.——According to the annual report there is a decrease in the number of members in the older of the two architectural societies, "Der Architekten Verein zu Berlin." The number is 1,849 this year; it was 1,887 last year. This is probably due to the popularity of the new "Vereinigung." The library has 11,786 volumes.——A third society has been founded; its name is "Skitze," and it will have a large number of juniors on its roll.——The money for the Berlin Cathedral being forthcoming, the old "Dom" is now to be pulled down and an iron church put up for the use of the parish during the years in which the new building is to be erected. 20,000*l.* are at the disposal of Professor Raschdorff for this purpose.——The total cost of the eight covered markets lately erected is 829,900*l.*

MUNICH.—The *Deutsche Bauzeitung* states that the preparations for the Munich International Art Exhibition this summer have progressed wonderfully well. Besides a good show of Bavarian and North German work there is to be a good representation of Spanish art. Hungary is expected to send a large collection of paintings, and it is hoped that Scotland will be fairly represented. A member of the managing committee has gone over to America to bring over a collection of paintings from the United States. As to the architectural group, we hear that there are to be some specimens of von Hansen's, von Ferstel's, and the late Semper's drawings on view in separate rooms.

SWITZERLAND.—Nineteen designs were sent in for the proposed concert-halls and assembly-rooms to be erected at Zurich. The competition for this imposing block has been won by Herr Bruno Schmitz, the "memorial monument specialist" at Berlin. He had also won the preliminary competition some time back.

MISCELLANEOUS.

WREN'S LIBRARY AT LINCOLN.—At a numerously-attended meeting of the Society of Antiquaries, on Thursday, March 17, Dr. John Evans, F.R.S., President, in the chair, the following resolution was unanimously adopted:—"That the Society of Antiquaries of London hears with much regret that the Dean and Chapter of Lincoln have avowed an intention to pull down the north walk of the cloisters of their church, and the library over it, in order to build on the same site an imitation of the other three sides of the cloister, which are of the fourteenth century; against this proposal the Society desires to protest as strongly as it can, and at the same time to point out that the existing building, which is the work of Sir Christopher Wren, is a good piece of architecture, well fitted to its place, and convenient for the uses for which it was intended, whilst the substitution of new work in its place will be a falsification of history, and there will be little compensation for the loss of Wren's building, even if the ornamental parts of it should be worked up, as has been proposed, into

ther building on another site." On the pro-
al of Sir H. B. Bacon, Bart., seconded by Mr.
I. Ferguson, it was unanimously resolved "That
opy of the resolution be forwarded to the Dean
Chapter of Lincoln."

ENTENARY OF "THE BATH HERALD."—We
e received from the proprietors of the *Bath*
ald an interesting account of the history of
t journal, which has lately celebrated its
tenary. We have also received a *fac-simile* copy
the first number of the *Herald*, which bears
s March 3, 1792. It is admirably printed in
-style type supplied by Messrs. Caslon & Son.
contents of the number include news of the
th of Sir Joshua Reynolds, of whom it speaks as
ows:—

THURSDAY, FEB. 23, Died, much lamented by his
erous friends, in the 69th year of his age, Sir
HUA REYNOLDS, Knight, President of the Royal
demy.—Genius was his, not confined merely to his
peculiar art, for his talents were truly various.
was the first of Painters, because he chose to be so:
might have stood with BURKE in Oratory, or
LONE in Criticism and elegant Literature, if either
been his subject.
is compositions, chiefly discourses on the art he
essed, are marked by an attic elegance of expres-
, clearly the result of the harmony of his mind.
KESPERE owes to him some very beautiful elucida-
s, and his country, her school of painting.—Virtue,
ever, bestows the best praise. He was a firm
nd, a benevolent and honourable man.
is talents of every kind, powerful from nature, and
meanly cultivated by letters, his social virtues in
the relations, and all the habitudes of life, rendered
the centre of a very great and unparallelled variety
agreeable societies. He had too much merit not
xcite some jealousy, but too much innocence to
voke any enmity. The loss of no man of his time
be felt with a more sincere, general, and unmixed
ow."

quote this as an interesting contemporary testi-
y to the talents and character of Sir Joshua.
Herald also contains some lines to his memory
mencing—

Reynolds, 'twas thine with magic skill to trace
The perfect semblance of exterior grace."

proprietors have in their possession a file of the
ald complete for the whole of the century, and
y say that permission can always be obtained to
rch the file for any legitimate purpose. We
gratulate them on the centenary of their excel-
journal.

PPOINTMENT OF COUNTY ARCHITECT FOR CUM-
LAND.—Mr. Geo. D. Oliver, F.R.I.B.A., of
lisle, was elected County Architect at the last
ting of the Cumberland County Council.

SLE OF MAN INTERNATIONAL EXHIBITION, 1892.
Ir. George North, M.I.M.E., of 90, Queen-
et, London, E.C., has been appointed represen-
ve for London and the South of England for the
e Exhibition, which will be opened on July 4
. Intending exhibitors can obtain all informa-
on application to Mr. North.

IE "GRAVITA" WATER-METER.—This is a new
r-meter which appears to ensure accuracy of
urement. It possesses great simplicity of con-
ction, and consists, essentially, of a box divided
two measuring chambers of equal capacity, but
rranged that the narrow end of one chamber is
llel with the wide end of the other. The box
g pivoted on centres, it tilts by gravity first to one
and then to the other. The act of tilting trans-
the incoming supply from one chamber to the
r, and at the same time discharges the contents
e full chamber, and the operation is repeated
matically as long as the water comes in. We
seen something like this meter before, but
embodies some very marked improvements.
easily adaptable to all existing fittings, and is
ble for use with any pressure of water, and
constant or intermittent supply. It is also
ble of being used either in substitution for, or
ombination with, existing water cisterns.

UST-COLLECTING.—The Vestry of St. Pancras
organised a system of dust collection from
e to house and street to street, by which the
will be removed from every house in the parish
a week. The streets and other places in each
ct are arranged on a consecutive route list, in
order that each street is followed by the
est adjoining street. The dust-carts being
bered, and the dustmen being compelled to
each house, every ratepayer is enabled to see
the system is administered to all fairly, and
to secure regularity and efficiency by promptly
plaining to the Health Department in case of
ect or irregularity. The dustmen are under
uctions to report every case of refusal to allow
lust to be removed, and in the case of repeated
persistent refusal the Health Department will
such action as may be deemed necessary for
protection of health.

IE LARGEST LOG-SAW.—Messrs. A. Ransome &
have produced the largest machine-saw for
er-cutting as yet designed. It is intended for
ania, where it will have to do with huge logs
ue-gum and other hard woods. The design
s a main standard of a hollow box casting of
strong section, the lower end splayed to a wide
for bolting down to the foundations. The saw
ys are very large, and adapted to work band-
up to 9 in. in width. They are accurately turned, and balanced to run perfectly true and steady at a speed of 300 revolutions a minute. The top pulley is constructed of forged steel, the rim being lagged with well-seasoned wood, overlaid with india-rubber cloth, which gives a slightly elastic surface for the saw to bed upon. The bottom pulley is similarly constructed, but is much heavier, to prevent the saw over-running when entering the cut. The pulley-shafts are also of forged steel, and are supported in very long self-lubricating bearings fitted with self-adjusting swivel blocks. There are provided also various means of adjustment of the saw blade to its proper position: for giving its proper tension, and for varying the tension according to the requirements of the sectional areas of the different sizes employed. The feed motion ranges from 6 ft. to 60 ft. per minute, and can be varied by a friction disc whilst the saw is in cut. The log is borne on a separate timber-carriage running on rails. The band-saws of this type now in use will cut at the rate of 80 superficial feet per minute in soft wood, or 50 ft. in oak. The large machine, which a number of visitors inspected on the 17th instant, will accomplish much more than the above result. The huge vertical post or standard is 16 ft. in height, with pulleys 8 ft. in diameter, making the total elevation 21 ft. over all, and the jaws between the pulleys will deal with logs of 7 ft. diameter,—the actual cut being 6 ft. 4 in. The effective running speed of the saw-edge is 7,000 ft. per minute. Any intelligent sawyer can readily be trained to work the saw, but, doubtless, the instructions must be strictly followed. Two men are required at the cutting,—the sawyer who remains by his saw, and another man who rides on the timber-carriage. This carriage is an important portion of the arrangements, and is constructed with a strongly-bolted wood framing furnished with iron-clips for rapidly fixing the log. Other devices enable the log when laid on the carriage to be gripped by the operation of one lever and dealt with by the man who rides on the carriage. The same man can also work another lever which sets the log clear of the saw when running back. The movements of the log-carriage are so rapid that the loss of time when a log of 30 ft. is being sawn is only a few seconds. Special tools are provided for automatically sharpening the saw, for slightly stretching when the back or front edge has varied in tension by reason of being heated in working, and the band-saw itself, if broken, can be brazed together and re-adjusted to its working duty.

BUILDING TRADE WAGES IN HAVRE.—According to a recent report of the United States Consul at Havre on wages and food prices in that locality, the rates paid in the building trade are:—Blacksmiths, per day of ten hours, 5s. 2½d.; bricklayers, per day of ten hours, 5s. 2½d.; labourers, per day of twelve hours, 2s.—2s. 4½d.; cabinet-makers, per day of ten hours, 4s. 10d.; carpenters, per day of ten hours, 4s. 0½d.; gas-works' employés, per day of ten hours, 2s. 10d.—4s. 10d.; painters, per day of ten hours, 4s. 10½d.; paper-hangers and decorators, piece-work, rate not fixed; plasterers, per day of ten hours, 6s. 5d.; plumbers, per day of ten hours, 5s. 7½d.; apprentices, per day of ten hours, 1s. 8½d.; stone-cutters, per day of ten hours, 5s. 2½d.; teamsters, per day of twelve hours, 3s. 4½d.; water-works' employés: fountain men, per year and after, 72*l.* 7s. 6d.; twenty-five years' service pensioned on half-pay; labourers excavating canals, per day of ten hours, 2s. 4½d.—2s. 10d.; labourers, street, per day of ten hours, 1s. 7½d.

ROYAL INSTITUTION.—The lecture arrangements after Easter include the following:—Professor T. G. Bonney, two lectures on "The Sculpturing of Britain—its later Stages" (the Tyndall Lectures); Mr. Frederick E. Ives, two lectures on "Photography in the Colours of Nature"; Professor Dewar, four lectures on "The Chemistry of Gases"; and Professor H. Marshall Ward, three lectures on "Some Modern Discoveries in Agricultural and Forest Botany" (illustrated by lantern).

THE ENGLISH IRON TRADE.—With the return to work of the federated colliers, the English iron market has become more settled, but the Durham miners' strike has caused a state of stagnation in the Cleveland district. The troubles with the men have somewhat strengthened pig-iron prices, but very little is doing in either crude or manufactured iron. In the tinplate market the tone is still dull. The steel trade shows little alteration, but prices of heavy rails have recovered from last week's decline. Blooms, on the other hand, have receded. Shipbuilding-yards are in a depressed state generally, and engineers, on the whole, are slack. The coal trade is quieter.—*Iron.*

BRITISH ARCHÆOLOGICAL ASSOCIATION.—At the meeting of this Association, on the 16th inst., Mr. C. H. Compton in the chair, it was announced that an invitation had been received from the Town Council of Cardiff to hold the forty-ninth Congress of the Association in that town in August, and that the invitation had been accepted. The Marquis of Bute will read a paper, and has accepted the office of patron. Mr. Earle Way exhibited some interesting pieces of Roman pottery and others of later date, which had formed part of the Gwilt collection of objects found in Southwark. Mr. W. de Gray Birch, F.S.A., read some notes on a series of seals, mostly unpublished, of the Abbots of Rievaulx. A cast of a curious seal of Hyde Abbey was also exhibited, showing the head of St. Valentine, which had been purchased by a Royal donor at great cost. Mr. Macmichael exhibited a large collection of yellow glazed ware, of fifteenth-century date, found in excavations near Charing-cross. He also read some notes on some of the signs of the old trading firms of London and its vicinity, and produced numerous old engravings and sketches of the various signs referred to. A paper was then read by Mr. R. Lloyd on the history of the Guelph family.

A PIPE BENDER.—Messrs. C. Winn & Co., of Birmingham, send an illustration of Billing's patent device for bending lead pipes without flattening the pipe. It consists of a long spiral spring, tapered at one end and with a loop at the other end to pull it out. The coil is inserted in the pipe before bending, and preserves its circular section; after the operation it is drawn out by the loop referred to.

CLOCK, HUDDERSFIELD CORPORATION SEWAGE WORKS.—The Huddersfield Corporation having selected the firm of Messrs. Potts & Sons, of Leeds, to supply the new bell and make the new clock for the new sewage works at Deighton, the work has been put in hand by them from instructions received from Mr. R. S. Dugdale, the Borough Surveyor, and is now nearly completed. The time is shown upon four large external skeleton cast-iron dials, filled in with white opal glass for illumination. The hours are struck upon a large bell of bell-metal.

THE "BELVOIR" STOVE.—Amongst the exhibits of Messrs. Walter Monnery & Co., at the Building Exhibition, is the "Belvoir" tiled register stove, which possesses some points meriting attention. The back of the stove is entirely of firebrick, and slopes forward towards the top. This arrangement promotes perfect combustion, and makes the heating-power of the stove much greater than that of a stove with a vertical back. The bars are of ½ in. iron, and are arranged vertically, 1 in. apart. The bottom grate consists of a fine mesh. It is claimed that this stove combines the advantages of an open fire with those of the slow combustion stove designed by Mr. Pridgin Teale. The canopy is movable. Messrs. Monnery & Co. also exhibit their well-known wall-ties, kitcheners, the "Larbert" self-setting ranges, and general builders' ironmongery.

LEGAL.

CASE UNDER THE METROPOLITAN BUILDING ACT.—FEE FOR IRREGULAR BUILDING REMOVED.

FLETCHER *v.* LEWIS.

THIS summons was heard at the Lambeth Police-court, on the 15th inst., by Mr. Hopkins, the presiding magistrate, which had been taken out by Mr. Banister Fletcher, the District Surveyor for West Newington and part of Lambeth, against Mr. Lewis, of No. 56, Penton-place, Walworth, for refusing to pay the fee for surveying a shed used as a store for paraffin, &c., in the rear of 56, Penton-place, Walworth.

It appears that the District Surveyor discovered the shed had been erected, and, after surveying it, gave notice to the defendant, who was his own builder, to amend the irregular work, as required by the Act, by enclosing the shed with brickwork, &c.; but, instead of doing this, the building was taken down, after which the District Surveyor demanded his fee in respect of the building, which, being refused, the present summons was taken out.

The defendant argued to the effect that no fee could be claimed unless there was a permanent building, built in conformity with the Act, and that if the building were taken down, the District Surveyor had no claim.

Mr. Banister Fletcher claimed that under clauses 49 and 51, taken with schedule 2, a fee is assigned for every new building surveyed by the District Surveyor, and that such fee accrues immediately on the covering in of the roof, and is payable one month thereafter, and argued that the removal could not affect the question.

The magistrate decided that the District Surveyor was entitled to his fee of 15s., and made an order for payment of the same, with the amount of costs asked for (12s. 6d.).

MEETINGS.

SATURDAY, MARCH 26.

Edinburgh Architectural Association.—Visit to the Antonine Wall near Kilsyth.

MONDAY, MARCH 28.

Surveyors' Institution.—Professor E. Kinch on "The Valuation of Feeding Stuffs and Foods." 8 p.m.

Society of Arts (Cantor Lectures).—Mr. Bennett H. Brough on "Mine Surveying." I. 8 p.m.

Leeds and Yorkshire Architectural Society.—(1) Lecture by Mr. G. Corson. (2) Nomination of Officers. 7.30 p.m.

COMPETITION, CONTRACTS, AND PUBLIC APPOINTMENTS.

COMPETITION.

Nature of Work.	By whom Advertised.	Premium.	Designs to be delivered.
*New County Council Buildings	Staffordshire C. C.	150l. 100l. & 50l.	May 27

CONTRACTS.

Nature of Work or Materials.	By whom Required.	Architect, Surveyor, or Engineer.	Tenders to be delivered.
*Making-up and Paving Road	Lewisham Bd. of W.	*Official*	Mar. 29
*Making-up and Paving Road	Bromley Loc. Bd.	do.	do.
Retorts, Fire-bricks, &c.	Cleckheaton Loc. Bd.	do.	do.
Macadam and Paving Setts	Sale Loc. Bd.	A. G. McBeath	do.
Flagging, &c.	Plymouth Corp.	G. D. Bellamy	do.
Restoration of Farndon Church, near Newark	....	C. Hodson Fowler	Mar. 30
Two Semi-detached Houses, Stanningley, Leeds	Joseph Brooks	W. D. Gill	do.
Market Buildings	Plymouth Corp.	*Official*	do.
Four Houses, Low Wincobank, Rotherham	J. Tantum	J. Platts	Mar. 31
Additions to Property, Bramley-lane, Lightcliffe, Halifax	....	Sharp & Waller	do.
Granite Road Metal	Pontefract Corp.	Jas. Hesseltine	do.
Kerbing, Flagging, &c.	York Corp.	A. Creer	do.
Thirteen Artisans' Dwellings and Three Shops, Hipperholme, Halifax	....	Jos. F. Walsh	do.
*Painting Works	Midland Railway	*Official*	April 1
Gasholder Tank	Normanton Gas Co.	do.	do.
Alterations and Additions, Police Station, Pontypridd	Glamorgan C. C.	do.	do.
*Supply of Materials	Walthamstow L. B.	G. W. Holmes	do.
Improvement of Claypdane, &c.	Ovenden Loc. Bd.	Utley & Gray	April 2
Timber, Wire Rope, &c.	Lanc. & Yorks. Ry.	*Official*	April 4
Pumping Engines and other Machinery	Horbury Local Board	S. Shaw	do.
Sewage Works	do.	do.	do.
*Sewers and Road Work, &c.	Bolling Estate, Windsor	Thomas & Taylor	do.
Alterations, Ruskin Museum	Sheffield Corp.	C. F. Wike	April 5
*Sewerage Works	Leyton Local Board	W. Dawson	do.

CONTRACTS.—*Continued.*

Nature of Work or Materials.	By whom Required.	Architect, Surveyor or Engineer.	Tenders to be delivered.
*Construction of Portion of Canal	Manchester Ship Canal Co.	*Official*	April 5
*Sewerage Works	Oldbury Local Board	H. B. Nichol	do.
Eighteen Houses, Consett, Durham	Consett Indus. and Prov. Soc.	W. S. Shell	April 11
*Making-up Roads	Southgate Local Board	C. G. Lawson	do.
*Roadmaking Works	Bournemouth T. C.	F. W. Lacey	do.
*Paving Works	West Ham Council	Lewis Angell	April [illegible]
*Making-up Road	do.	do.	do.
*Circular Iron Urinal	do.	do	do.
Stone Arched Bridge, Brook Mould	Abergavenny High Bd.	John Gill	do.
Widening Roads, Bassaleg	Newport (Mon.) High Board	*Official*	do.
*New Market, Arcades, and Shops	Borough of Halifax	Leeming & Leeming	do.
*Cleansing and Painting Works, S. W. Fever Hospital	Met. Asylums Board	T. W. Aldwinckle	April [illegible]
*Forty New Arches, &c. &c.	Brighton Town Coun.	F. J. C. May	do.
Technical School	Halifax Corporation	Jackson & Fox	April [illegible]
Houses, Broomfield-terrace, Headingly, Leeds	W. B. Pearson	....	No date
Four Cottages, Beeston-hill, Leeds	....	T. E. Farmery	do.
Mission Rooms at St. John-the-Baptist Church, Newtown	....	Arch. Neill	do.
Alterations and Additions to St. Michael's Schools, Leeds	....	Richd Wood	do.
Shop and Warehouse, Land's-lane, Leeds	....	Ambler & Bowman	do.
New Roofs on Nave and Chancel, Bishops Norton Church, Lincoln	....	Goddard & Son	do.
*Offices, Warehouses, Stables, &c. Southampton	....	A. W. Galbraith	do.

PUBLIC APPOINTMENTS.

Nature of Appointment.	By whom Advertised.	Salary.	Applications to be in.
*Road Foreman	City of Birmingham	2l.	Mar. [illegible]
*Clerk of Works	Teddington Loc. Bd.	Not stated	April [illegible]

Those marked with an Asterisk (*) are advertised in this Number. *Competitions, p. iv. Contracts, pp. iv., vi., & viii. Public Appointments, p. xx.*

TUESDAY, MARCH 29.

Institution of Civil Engineers.—Further discussion on Mr. A. R. Binnie's paper on "Mean or Average Annual Rainfall, and the Fluctuations to which it is Subject." 8 p.m.

Society of Arts (Applied Art Section).—Mr. E. Roscoe Mullins on "The Decorative Uses of Sculpture." 8 p.m.

WEDNESDAY, MARCH 30.

Builders' Clerks' Benevolent Institution.—Fourteenth Annual Dinner, Holborn Restaurant. 6 p.m.

Institution of Civil Engineers.—Students' Visit to the works of Messrs. W. H. Allen & Co., York-street, Lambeth, S.E. 2 p.m.

Civil and Mechanical Engineers' Society.—Mr. A. Wollheim on "Modern Sewage Precipitation Works." 7 p.m.

Builders' Foremen and Clerks of Works' Institution.—Quarterly meeting of the Directors. 8 p.m.

THURSDAY, MARCH 31.

Society of Antiquaries.—8.30 p.m.

Royal Institution.—Dr. B. A. Whitelegge on "Epidemic Waves." 3 p.m.

FRIDAY, APRIL 1.

Architectural Association.—Mr. Horace Townsend on "Literature and Architecture." 7.30 p.m.

Royal Institution.—Professor Oliver Lodge on "The Motion of the Ether near the Earth." 9 p.m.

SATURDAY, APRIL 2.

Architectural Association.—Visits to (1) the Newington Weights and Measures Offices, Union-road, Blackman-street, S.E., by permission of Mr. Thomas Bleshill. 3 p.m. (2) the Royal Ophthalmic Hospital, St. George's-circus, S.E., by permission of Mr. Keith D. Young. 4 p.m.

RECENT PATENTS:

ABSTRACTS OF SPECIFICATIONS.

3,971.—SASH-FASTENER: *J. A. Piccaver.*—This invention refers to an economical, effective, and simple fastener of window-sashes and the like. On the meeting-rail or bar of one window-sash is secured a metal plate carrying a staple through which has been passed a link of oval shape, the link being free to work in the staple, but otherwise firmly secured therein. On the opposite meeting-rail is secured a corresponding metallic plate, carrying in place of the staple and link a pin or pivot with a flat curved head or thumb-piece over which the link may be passed. The head is then turned and the link secured.

[The invention was illustrated and described in the *Builder* for December 12, 1891, p. 448.]

6,041.—BRICK-KILNS: *J. Craven.*—This refers to an invention for providing means whereby the heat from the chambers of kilns in which bricks or other articles have been burnt can be introduced to the chambers in which green goods are contained, so that the heat from the first-named chambers is utilised in drying the green goods. A metal main-pipe is led in proximity to each chamber of the kiln, and from each chamber a branch pipe leads into the said main pipe, which has in connexion with it an air drawing and forcing device. The branch pipes are each provided with valves or dampers, by which their communication with the main pipe can be closed. The branch pipes communicate with the openings in the crown of each chamber. When it is desired to pass the air from a chamber from which the charge is being drawn into a chamber containing green goods, the valves or dampers are operated so that the communication between the two chambers is established, and the air-forcing and drawing device being set in operation, the hot air is drawn from the chambers from which the charge is being drawn, and delivered into the chamber containing the green goods at the lower part, which may be done by means of descending pipes introduced into the openings in the arch, with which the branch pipes communicate.

6,142.—PIPE-JOINTS: *T. R. Murray.*—This patent refers to an improved joint for wrought-iron, steel, or other metallic pipes, so as to remain quite tight when subjected to very high pressure. Each pipe-end is made with a thickened collar, and the joint face of one pipe-end of a pair is made with an annular projecting rib, the joint face of the other pipe-end of a pair being made with an annular recess or rebate, into which the projection enters when the two pipe-ends are brought together. Lead or other suitable slightly-compressible material is put into the annular recess to make the joint tight. The pipe-ends are fixed together by means of screw-bolts, which connect rings fitting, or nearly fitting, on the pipes, and bearing against the inner sides of the collars on the pipe-ends; or lugs may be formed on the collars to receive the screw-bolts, by means of which the pipe-ends are fixed together.

6,257.—KILNS: *W. C. Gibson.*—This invention relates to kilns for biscuiting and burning clay goods which are to be glazed or enamelled, and has for its object to so construct such kilns that the waste heat from the burning or glazing muffle is utilised for heating the biscuiting kiln, a great saving in fuel being thereby effected. The inventor constructs a kiln for glazing or enamelling the clay goods. The kiln is a muffle kiln, as the burning chamber must, of course, be free from smoke or other impurities. Beside, near to, or as a part of this kiln is constructed a second kiln or chamber for biscuiting the ware. This kiln is also preferably a muffle. By means of one or more vents the waste heat is conducted into the biscuiting kiln to heat it up. By means of dampers these vents may be closed, or partially closed, at any time. A flue with damper door may be arranged in connexion with each kiln. When the twin kilns are working simultaneously, the flue of the glazing kiln may be closed, so that the waste gases may pass to and heat up the biscuiting kiln. When the biscuiting kiln is not used the dampers in the connecting vents may be closed, and the flue of the glazing kiln opened.

1,052.—PARQUET FLOORING: *J. T. Chappell.*—This invention relates to the preparation of pieces of wood used for parquet or block-flooring, and to the joining and laying of the same to ensure their firm fixing and junction. Each piece of wood is made with an ogee moulding at its lower edge, and with a groove to receive metal dowels.

NEW APPLICATIONS FOR LETTERS PATENT.

March 7.—4,445, G. Fawson, Securing Knobs to Brass Mountings of Door and other Furniture.—4,448, T. Jackson, Grates and Fireplaces.—4,496, J. Holliday, Artificial Stones.

March 8.—4,511, S. Turner, Fireproof Floor.—4,518, A. Carey, Hydraulic Lifts.—4,525, H. Fitzpatrick, Glass Bricks.—4,531, C. Horrell, Sash-fasteners for Windows.—4,534, T. Shurmer, Bricks.—4,535, I. Irlam, Bricks.—4,540, G. Graham, Building or Paving Blocks.—4,553, J. Knights, Burning Portland Cement.—4,572, W. Macnamara, Stops for Gates.—4,573, T. Whale, Valves in Water-closet Cisterns.—4,590, A. Thrower, Girders.—4,593, C. Adams, Machines for Sanding Brick Moulds.—4,624, J. Cohn, Water-closets, &c.

March 9.—4,650, R. Harrison, trading as Loach & Clarke, Devices for Opening, Closing, and Adjusting Windows, &c.

March 10.—4,751, A. Bromley, Open Firegrates.

March 11.—4,790, T. Robinson, Self-acting Cross-cut Saw-benches.—4,791, T. Bradbear, Closet Fittings.—4,826, P. Pierpoint, Smoke or Ceiling Protectors for Chandeliers, &c.—4,842, T. Johnson, Garden Tile or Ridge.

March 12.—4,871, T. Robinson, Connecting Metal Pipes to the Basins or Traps of Water-closets, &c.—4,913, E. Peters, Chimney-tops or Terminals.

PROVISIONAL SPECIFICATIONS ACCEPTED.

536, J. Robson, Sash-fasteners.—1,023, S. Middleto[n] Operating Window-sashes.—1,129, A. Fowler, Automa[ti]cally Flushed Water-closets.—1,170, J. Leach & [?] Lewis, Fastening Window-sashes.—1,693, E. Harvey, Water-closets.—1,942, S. Renschel, Handles for Furniture-drawers, &c.—1,945, A. Smith and J. Emery, Ce[ntre] Revolving-ball in Taps.—2,018, W. Day and E. Edge, Safety-ladder Hook.—2,091, W. Blackband and [?] Charles, Door-knobs, &c.—2,131, F. Stokes, Continuous treatment of Lime, Cement, &c., and in the Lining of Kilns and Furnaces for Burning Cement, &c.—2,35[?], C. Baker, Gates.—2,385, M. Hallam, Rack-pulleys for the Cords of Window-blinds.—2,392, W. & E. Freeman, Flushing-tanks of Water-waste Preventers.—2,453, B. Sutcliffe, Water-closet Basins, and in means for Ventilating the Soil-pipes of same.—2,951, C. Logan, Wi[re] Nails.—2,964, M. Kann, Working-stone.—2,967, H. Wood[-]house, Fire-grates or Stoves.—3,016, G. Lawford, Close[t] Connections.—3,093, J. Carr, Mortising Chisel.—3,20[?], D. Halpin, Treads for Stairs.—3,266, J. Jones, Drains Appliances.—3,302, W. Jones, Water-waste Preventer[s].—3,608, F. Grew, Doors.

COMPLETE SPECIFICATIONS ACCEPTED.

(Open to Opposition for Two Months.)

1,154, W. Riley, Knobs or Door-handles, and adjus[t]ing and holding them upon their Spindles.—2,713, [?] McCulloch, Window-sash Fastener.

SOME RECENT SALES OF PROPERTY:

ESTATE EXCHANGE REPORT.

MARCH 10.—By *Worsfold & Hayward* (at Dover): 4, [?] and 7, Chapel-st., Dover, f., r. 36l., 605l.; 21 and 2[?] Biggin-st., Dover, f., r. 80l., 1,430l.; 20, Biggin-st. a[nd] Malthouse, f., r. 40l., 900l.; 28, Pencester-rd., f., r. 36[l.], 620l.; 57, Folkestone-rd., f., 570l.; 20, Military-rd., [?] 225l.; 12, Worthington-lane, f., 220l.; 51, Dour-st., u.[t.] 67 yrs., g.r. 2l. 5s., r. 17l., 245l.; 7 and 8, Palmersto[n] Cottages, Charlton, f., 245l.

MARCH 14.—By *Hinee & Lewis*: 19, Morton-r[d.], Islington, u.t. 61 yrs., g.r. 5l. 10s., r. 34l., 300l.—[By] *Phillips, Lea, & Davies*: f g.r. of 15l., with reversion [in] 79 yrs., Norman-rd., Bow, 330l.; 1 and 4, Merton-r[d.], Wandsworth, u.t. 91 yrs., g r. 10l., 640l.—By *S. A. Lock*: 80A, 82 to 86 (even), Boundary-st., Bethnal-green, [?] 945l.—By *T. P. Rider*: 77 and 79, Bramley-rd., Notting-hill, u.t. 70 yrs., g.r. 18l., 600l.; 6, 8, and 10, Rigele[y]-rd., Kensal-green, u.t. 87 yrs., g r. 15l. 15s., 390l.—By *Rouch & Parkhouse*: 20, Victoria-rd., Stroud-gree[n], u.t. 81 yrs., g.r. 6l. 10s., r. 40l., 400l.; 45, Drummon[d]-st., Euston-sq., u.t. 18 yrs., g.r. 18l. 18s., r. 80l. 525l.—By *A. G. Windsor*: 38, Almorah-rd., Islington, u.t. [?] yrs., g.r. 6l., r. 40l., 315l.; 29 to 37 odd, South-st., u.[t.] 35 yrs., g.r. 31l. 10s., 850l.; 2, 4, and 6, Nailour-st., u.[t.] 59 yrs., g.r. 16l. 10s., 450l.; 30 and 32, Hyde-rd., Hoxto[n], u.t. 44 yrs., g.r. 12l. 12s., 1,120l.; 144 and 146, Shepherdess-walk; and 1, Foraton-st., u.t. 7½ yrs., g.r. 9l. [?] 2l., 185l.; 148, Shepherdess-walk, u.t. 6½ yrs., g.r. 5l., 30l., 85l.; 39, 40, and 41, Eagle Wharf-rd., u.t. 16½ yr[s.], g.r. 15l. 15s., 330l.

MARCH 15.—By *Debenham, Tewson, & Co.*: The letti[ng] of 8 and 9, Great St. Helens, City of London, a[rea] 3,077 ft., term 80 yrs., at 930l. a year; 83, Tooley-st., a[nd] 13, Bull-ct., Southwark, f., r. 120l., 2,200l.—By *Dri[ver] & Co.*: Nos. 49A and 50, and 10, 11, and 12, York-p[lace], Strand, f., area 2,880 ft., 16,000l.—By *Rogers, Chapman, & Thomas*: 29, Redcliffe-gardens, Kensington, u.[t.] 56 yrs., g.r. 20l., r. 120l., 1,000l.

MARCH 16.—By *Inman & Co.*: F.g.r. of 42l., wi[th] reversion in 13 yrs., Barnsbury, 1,160l.; 59, Lana[rk]-villas, Maida Vale, u.t. 58 yrs., g r. 10l., r. 60l., 450[l.]; 8 and 9, Goldsmith's-pl., Kilburn, u.t. 52 yrs., g.r. [?] 405l.—By *C. P. Whiteley*: 7, Spencer-rd., Kentish Tow[n], f., 300l.; 8, Spencer-rd., u.t. 65 yrs., g.r. 4l., 205l.; [?] Spencer-rd., u.t. 66 yrs., g.r. 6l. 6s., 185l.—By *A. Bart[?]*: 70, New North-rd., Hoxton, u.t. 24 yrs., g r. 30l., 150l.

H. Donaldson: 7 and 8, Tilley-st., Spitalfields, f., r. l. 4s., 1,440l.; freehold site area 2,000 ft., Widegate-, 1,550l.; profit rental of 60l., 18 and 19, Artillery-ne, u.t. 15 yrs., 175l.

MARCH 17.—By Glasier & Sons: f.g.r. of 60l. 15s., th reversion in 89 yrs., Uxbridge-rd., Shepherd's-bush, 95l.; f.g.r. of 63l., with reversion in 89 yrs., Arminger-, 1,560l.—By Newbon & Co.: 2, Beresford-rd., Canon-ry, u.t. 58 yrs., g.r. 8l., 445l.; 6, Annette-rd., Hol-way, u.t. 72 yrs., g.r. 6l. 6s., 265l.; 54 and 56, Mintern-, Hoxton, u.t. 17 yrs., g.r. 7l., r. 62l., 850l.; 6, Rheidol-, Islington, u.t. 24 yrs., g.r. 5l., r. 40l., 290l.; 21, 23, d 29, Northampton-st., u.t. 26 yrs., g.r. 12l., 290l.; De Beauvoir-crescent, Kingsland, u.t. 37 yrs., g.r. 4l.; d a g.r. of 12l. (same term), 260l.—By H. J. Bliss & ns: 1 to 7 (odd), Baker-st., Bethnal-green, u.t. 33 yrs., . 8l., 385l.; 60 and 62, Warley-st., u.t. 14 yrs., g.r. 6s., 70l.; 19 and 20, Lessada-st., u.t. 40 yrs. g.r. 6l. 6s., l.; 25, Sale-st., u.t. 33 yrs., g.r. 4l. 3s. 4d., r. 25l., l.

MARCH 18.—By Dolman & Pearce: 1, Modbury-st., ntish-town, u.t. 57 yrs., g.r. 7l., 295l.—By Weatherall Green: The site of Farringdon-market, E.C., area 000 ft., 98,100l.—By D. J. Chattell: 8 and 9, Dicken-n-rd., Crouch-hill, u.t. 89 yrs., g.r. 12l. 12s., r. 72l., 590l. By Rushworth & Stevens: 16 and 16A, Sandwich-st., rton-crescent, u.t. 15 yrs., g.r. 50l. 8s., r. 75l., 100l.; a ofit rental of 40l., u.t. 15 yrs., on same houses, 300l.; and 5, Wakefield-st., Regent's-sq., u.t. 10 yrs., g.r. , r. 84l., 370l.; 36 and 37, Margaret-st., Clerkenwell, . 24 yrs., g.r. 40l., r. 64l., 125l.—By H. V. Chew: 1, ayton-ter., Leytonstone, u.t. 85 yrs., g.r. 5l., 625l.

Contractions used in these lists.—F.g.r. for freehold ound-rent; l.g.r. for leasehold ground-rent; i.g.r. for proved ground-rent; g.r. for ground-rent; r. for rent; for freehold; c. for copyhold; l. for leasehold; e.r. estimated rental; u.t. for unexpired term; p.a. for annum; yrs. for years; st. for street; rd. for road; for square; pl. for place; ter. for terrace; cres. for scent; yd. for yard, &c.]

PRICES CURRENT OF MATERIALS.

TIMBER.

nheart, B.G. ton	9/0/0	0/0/0
, E.I. ... load	10/10/0	15/0/0
oia, U.S. ft. cu.	2/3	3/0
, Canada load	2/10/0	4/0/0
h, do.	3/5/0	4/10/0
, do.	3/10/0	4/15/0
Dantsic, &c.	2/0/0	3/10/0
do.	3/0/0	5/5/0
nada	5/10/0	7/0/0
, Canada red	2/10/0	3/10/0
, yellow	2/10/0	5/0/0
, D'ntsic, fath	5/0/0	6/0/0
Petersburg	5/0/0	7/0/0
s, Finland, 2nd & 1st std 100	8/10/0	10/10/0
4th & 3rd ..	7/10/0	8/10/0
Riga	6/10/0	8/0/0
. Petersburg, 1st yellow ..	11/0/0	15/0/0
o, 2nd yellow	8/10/0	10/0/0
o. white	7/10/0	10/10/0
wedish	7/15/0	16/0/0
White Sea	8/10/0	18/0/0
anada, Pine 1st	20/0/0	26/0/0
o. do. 2nd	14/10/0	16/0/0
o. do. 3rd, &c.	8/0/0	10/5/0
o. Spruce, 1st	8/10/0	11/0/0
o. do. 3rd & 2nd	6/15/0	8/0/0
New Brunswick	7/0/0	7/10/0
tens, all kinds	3/10/0	15/10/0
oring Boards, , 1 in. prep. 1st	0/8/6	0/14/6
o. 2nd	0/7/6	0/11/6
ther qualities	0/4/6	0/8/0
ar, Cuba .. ft.	/3½	/4½
Honduras, &c.	/2½	/4
hogany, Cuba.	/4½	/6½
t. Domingo, cargo av	/4½	2/0
Mexican do. do	/4	/5
Tobasco do. do	/5½	/7
Honduras do..	/5½	/6½
, Turkey ton	4/0/0	15/0/0
, Rio	10/0/0	20/0/0
ahia	9/0/0	16/0/0
in, St. Domingo .... ft.	0/0/8	0/1/3

TIMBER (continued).

Satin, Porto Rico	0/0/8	0/1/6
Walnut, Italian ..	0/0/3½	0/0/7

METALS.

IRON—Pig, in Scotland ...... ton	2/0/11	2/1/6
Bar, Welsh, in London	6/0/0	6/10/0
Do. do. at works in Wales	5/10/0	6/0/0
Do. Staffordshire, in London	6/5/0	6/15/0
COPPER—British, cake and ingot	50/0/0	50/10/0
Best selected ..	51/0/0	51/10/0
Sheets, strong ..	60/0/0	0/0/0
Chili, bars	47/7/6	47/15/0
YELLOW METAL lb.	0/0/5	0/0/5¼
LEAD—Pig, Spanish .... ton	10/17/6	11/0/0
English, com. brands	11/2/6	11/5/0
Sheet, English, 3 lbs. per sq. ft. and upwards ..	13/0/0	0/0/0
Pipe	13/10/0	0/0/0
ZINC—English sheet ...... ton	25/5/0	0/0/0
Vieille Montagne	25/15/0	0/0/0
TIN—Straits	89/2/6	89/5/0
Australian	89/5/0	89/7/6
English Ingots	92/10/0	92/15/0

OILS.

Linseed ...... ton	18/17/6	19/0/0
Cocoanut, Cochin	25/0/0	0/0/0
Do. Ceylon	22/10/0	22/15/0
Palm, Lagos	23/0/0	0/0/0
Rapeseed, English pale	25/10/0	26/0/0
Do. brown	23/15/0	0/0/0
Cottonseed ref. ..	18/15/0	0/0/0
Oleine	21/10/0	22/10/0
Lubricating, U.S.	4/0/0	6/0/0
Do. refined	5/0/0	10/0/0
TAR—Stockholm barrel	0/19/0	1/0/0
Archangel	0/12/6	0/0/0

TENDERS.

[Communications for insertion under this heading should be addressed to "The Editor," and must reach not later than 12 noon on Thursdays.]

BISHOPS STORTFORD.—For additions to a cottage, Grange-d, for Mr. G. Speechly. Mr. Alfred Brett, architect:—
Glasscock & Son ...... £600 | Martin & Fuller* £529 10
* Accepted.

BISHOPS STORTFORD.—For erecting house in Thornfields-road, Mr. J. O. Sell. Mr. Alfred Brett, architect, South-street, Bishops Stortford:—
J. & A. Handscomb £344 0 0
[No competition.]

BISHOPS STORTFORD.—For proposed alterations to a dwelling-house. Mr. Alfred Brett, architect:—
Champness ...... £815 0 | Glasscock & Son (too late) £750 0
Martin & Fuller ...... 769 10 | [Architect's estimate, £879.]

BOSCOMBE (Hants).—For the superstructure of the Hotel Burlington, Boscombe, Hants. Mr. Thomas E. Collcutt, architect, 36, Bloomsbury-square, London, W.C. Quantities by Mr. James Candy, Essex-street, Strand:—

	To be completed by Oct., 1892.	If given till	
...gary & Co.	£30,300	Sept., 1893	£27,650
Williams	29,800	,, ,,	27,150
Holloway Bros.	27,550	March ,,	25,450
...nders	26,700	,, ,,	26,400
...kins	26,495	,, ,,	25,436
Hoare	—	June ,,	27,880
...phens, Bastow, & Co.	26,446	April ,,	24,080
...d, Bligh, & Co.	24,635	,, ,,	23,400
... Chappell	24,588	June ,,	22,988

BOSTON (Lincolnshire).—Accepted for the erection of a ...men's Institute at Boston. Mr. James Rowell, architect, Boston:—
W. & H. Hinds, Boston £425 0 0

BRADFORD (Yorks).—Accepted for the erection of a congregational school at Lightcliffe. Mr. Thomas Barker, C.E., architect, 5, Bond-street, Bradford, Yorks. Quantities by the architect:—
Mason.—T. Dawson, Lightcliffe, near Halifax .. £1,600 0 0
Carpenter and Joiner.—Michael Woodhead, Lightcliffe, near Halifax 620 0 0
Plumber and Glazier.—George C. Calvert, Lightcliffe, near Halifax 215 0 0
Slater.—James Smithies, Great Horton, Bradford 190 10 0
Plasterer.—John Marshall, Hipperholme, near Halifax 111 0 0
Painter.—Hincliffe & Hainsworth, Northowram, near Halifax 28 0

BRENTWOOD.—Accepted for the erection of small Wesleyan chapel, for the building committee. Mr. Frederick Boreham, architect, 75, Finsbury-pavement:—
G. H. Martin & Co., West Croydon £927 0 0

CANE HILL (Surrey).—For alterations at the Cane Hill Asylum, Surrey, for the London County Council. Mr. G. T. Hine, Architect:—
Potter ...... £9,962 | Reed, Blight, & Co. £8,998
Faulkner ...... 9,789 | Peters 8,697
Doyley & Co. ...... 9,162 |

COLWALL (near Malvern).—For alterations and additions to Stretton Lodge, for Mr. R. Cave Browne-Cave. Mr. C. H. Godsel, architect:—
J. Lloyd ...... £657 | W. P. Lewis & Co. (accepted) £600
[All of Hereford.]

GUILDFORD.—For the main drainage of the Borough of Guildford, and also works of sewage disposal. Mr. C. Nicholson Lailey, engineer, Westminster:—
W. Cunliffe, Kingston-on-Thames (accepted) .. £27,325 0 0

HEREFORD.—For pulling-down and rebuilding the "Wellington Hotel," for Mr. Thos. Tapp. Mr. C. H. Godsell, architect:—
Jas. Lloyd ...... £1,090 | L. Bowers & Co. £1,075
Thos. Lewis ...... 1,090 | W. P. Lewis & Co. (accepted) 1,035
[All of Hereford.]

HORNSEY.—For new sewers, for the Hornsey Local Board. Mr. T. de Courcy Meade, Engineer:—

Archway-road to Hampstead-lane.
John Neave ...... £14,236 | James Dickson £10,053
Leonard Foster ...... 11,117 | T. G. Dunmore 9,823
Thomas Adams ...... 10,936 | J. Bentley 8,993
Killingback & Co. ...... 10,724 | B. Cooke & Co., Battersea* 7,959
* Accepted.

Glebe Estate.
John Neave ...... £3,166 | J. Bentley £2,273
Leonard Foster ...... 2,876 | B. Cooke & Co. 2,068
Thomas Adams ...... 2,709 | T. G. Dunmore, Crouch
James Dickson ...... 2,500 | End (accepted) 1,930

Crouch-hill Estate.
John Neave ...... £898 | John Bentley £602
Thos. Adams ...... 767 | B. Cooke & Co. 602
Leonard Foster ...... 767 | T. G. Dunmore, Crouch End* 497
Jas. Dickson ...... 752 | * Accepted.

HORNSEY.—For various improvement works, for the Hornsey Local Board. Mr. T. de Courcy Meade, Engineer:—

Brittles-hill, Muswell Hill-road.
J. Mowlem & Co. ...... £2,434 | Thos. Adams £2,235
Sidney Hudson ...... 2,294 | B. Cooke & Co., Battersea* 1,762
* Accepted.

Colney Hatch-lane.
Thos. Adams ...... £970 | Sidney Hudson 867
John Mowlem & Co. ...... 955 | B. Cooke & Co., Battersea* 798
* Accepted.

Crouch-hill.
Thos. Adams ...... £783 | J. Mowlem & Co. £706
Sidney Hudson ...... 763 | B. Cooke & Co., Battersea* 668
* Accepted.

Muswell Hill-road (near Woodlane).
Sidney Hudson ...... £705 | J. Mowlem & Co. £610
Thos. Adams ...... 670 | B. Cooke & Co., Battersea* 514
* Accepted.

Park House-road.
Sidney Hudson ...... £638 | J. Mowlem & Co. £599
T. Adams ...... 607 | B. Cooke & Co., Battersea* .. 477
* Accepted.

Tottenham-lane.
Sidney Hudson ...... £432 | T. Adams £406
J. Mowlem & Co. ...... 414 | B. Cooke & Co., Battersea* .. 341
* Accepted.

HORNSEY.—For sewering and making up new streets. Mr. T. de Courcy Meade, M.Inst.C.E., Engineer:—

Roads.	J. Mowlem & Co., Westminster.	Thos. Adams, Wood-green.	B. Cooke & Co., Battersea.	John Neave, Forest-hill, E.	Sidney Hudson, West Dulwich.
	£	£	£	£	£
Coleridge-road (2nd section)	2,553	2,475	2,142*	2,445	—
Bryanstone-road (1st section)	1,150	1,061	985*	1,100	—
Berkeley-road (2nd section)	1,085	1,021	893*	1,010	—
Birchington-road (2nd section)	1,740	1,630	1,442*	1,627	—
Glasslyn-road (1st section)	891	857	750*	870	—
Edison-road (2nd section)	594	563	490*	572	592
Onslow-gardens (1st section)	2,524	2,451	2,143*	2,488	—
Stanhope-road (1st section)	3,674	3,793	3,303*	3,825	3,400
North-grove	1,040	1,076	919*	1,110	—
Wightman-road (6th section)	97	90*	114	104	—
Barrington-road (1st section)	1,030	1,010	917*	1,030	982
Nelson-road (1st section)	2,150	1,976	1,898*	2,014	—
Harold-road (2nd section)	995	968	836*	950	882
Glebe-road (1st section)	366	323	314*	344	316
Dickenson-road (2nd section)	1,079	1,036	916*	1,008	—
Haringey-passage (2nd section)	115*	172	147	194	—

* Accepted.

HORNSEY.—For erecting gardener's cottage, Middle-lane, and park-keeper's cottage, Barrington-road, for the Hornsey Local Board. Mr. T. de Courcy Meade, M. Inst. C.E., Engineer:—

	Gardener's Cottage.	Park-Keeper's Cottage.
J. Willmott & Son	£906	£761
Marchant & Hirst	719	670
E. Kerry & Son	700	660
Pearce & Co.	700	650
Seath & Harris	680	617
Geo. J. Hosking	666	617
Gardner & Hazell	631	606
John Groves	631	645
Hy. Faulkner, jun.	625	589
Edward Hughes, Stroud Green	518*	564*

* Accepted.

LONDON.—For road-making and paving works, for the Vestry of the Parish of Fulham. Mr. W. Sykes, New Streets Surveyor:—

—	Parry.	Rogers & Co.	Nowell & Robson.	Mowlem & Co.	Tomes & Wimpey.	Imperial Stone Co.	Greenham.	T. Adams.	Victoria Stone Co.
Princes Mews:—	£.	£.	£.	£.	£.	£.	£.	£.	£.
Road and Footway	435	—	377	349	264	—	—	—	—
Mornington Avenue:—									
Roadway	610	543	540	515	525	—	497	695	—
York stone	—	206	200	225	199	—	—	—	—
Victoria stone	—	—	—	218	—	—	—	—	180
Imperial stone	—	—	—	197	—	—	—	—	—
Patent adamant stone .	—	—	—	207	—	—	—	—	—
Stuart's Granolithic stone	—	—	—	207	—	—	—	—	—
Kinnoul-road:—									
Roadway	580	560	642	578	534	—	535	696	—
York stone	—	297	296	314	282	—	—	—	—
Victoria stone	—	—	—	269	—	—	—	—	253
Imperial stone	—	—	—	270	—	224	—	—	—
Patent adamant stone ..	—	—	—	284	—	—	—	—	—
Stuart's Granolithic stone	—	—	—	284	—	—	—	—	—
Wandsworth-bridge-road, Sec. V.:—									
Roadway	—	—	1189	1240	1220	—	—	1494	—
York stone	—	—	743	745	725	—	—	—	—
Victoria stone	—	—	—	708	—	—	—	—	628
Imperial stone	—	—	—	634	—	565	—	—	—
Patent adamant stone ..	—	—	—	671	—	—	—	—	—
Stuart's Granolithic stone	—	—	—	671	—	—	—	—	—

LONDON.—For alterations and additions to bank premises, High-road, Tottenham, N., for the London & Provincial Banking Company. Mr. A. R. Barker, architect, 11, Buckingham-street, Strand, W.C. Quantities by Messrs. Young & Brown:—
A. Monk ...... £2,100 | P. Hart £1,744
Wheeler ...... 1,869 | J. Giles 1,721
A. Porter ...... 1,799 | H. Knight & Son 1,716
M. A. Humphreys ...... 1,746 | J. Groves 1,567

LONDON.—For building fourteen villas in Rosenthal-road, Rushey Green, Catford. Mr. Albert L. Guy, architect, 78, High-street, Lewisham:—
Kennard, Lewisham (accepted) £6,300 0 3

LONDON.—For pulling down and rebuilding "The Castle" public-house, High-street, Lewisham, S.E., for Mr. T. W. Watts. Mr. Albert L. Guy, architect, 78, High-street, Lewisham:—
Kennard ...... £3,200 | Knight £2,750
J. O. Richardson ...... 2,979 | S. J. Jerrard, Lewisham* 2,809
Holloway ...... 2,870 | * Accepted.

For Fittings.
Sanders & Sons, High Holborn (accepted) £812 0 0

LONDON.—For erecting stabling, &c., in rear of Nos. 321-327, Walworth-road, S.E., for Messrs. Claridge & Lidle. Mr. Albert L. Guy, architect, 78, High-street, Lewisham:—
Kennard, Lewisham (accepted) £525 0 0

LONDON.—For carrying out certain alterations and additions to the "Hare and Billet" public-house, Blackheath, for Mr. Coppinger. Mr. Albert L. Guy, architect, 78, High-street, Lewisham:—
Kennard ...... £815 | Roblon £750
S. J. Jerrard ...... 790 | Knight, Sidcup (accepted) .. 729

LONDON.—For rebuilding Nos. 151 and 152, Upper-street, Islington, for Mr. Thompson. Messrs. Puller & Fuller, architects, 70, Queen-street, Cheapside, E.C.:—
Austin ...... £3,400 | E. Houghton & Son £2,577
Mollett ...... 2,895 | King 2,109

LONDON.—For structural alterations (A) and internal fittings (B) at No. 1, Giltspur-street, E.C., for Messrs. Arnold & Sons. Mr. E. Haslehurst, architect, 7A, Laurence Pountney-hill, E.C.:—

	A.	B.
Young & Lonsdale	£336 0 0	£436 0 0
Drew & Cadman	—	420 0 0
Yardley & Sons	317 0 0	413 0 0
Lidstone & Son (accepted) ..	343 0 0	295 0 0

LONDON.—For re-building the "Cross Keys" public-house, Brick... for Messrs. Truman, Hanbury, Buxton, & Co. Mr. Bruce J. Capell, architect, 70, Whitechapel-road, E.:—
H. L. Holloway ...... £2,889 | Jerrard* £2,393
Young & Lonsdale ...... 2,397 | * Accepted.

LONDON.—For the erection of warehouse and offices at Narrow-street, Limehouse. Mr. M. N. Inman, architect:—
H. Izor ...... £6,651 | J. Grover & Son £5,794
T. Boyce ...... 6,540 | Patman & Fotheringham 5,773
Holloway Bros. ...... 6,078 | J. Simpson & Son 5,750
J. Chessum & Sons ...... 5,995 | W. Shurmur 5,697
Clark & Bracey ...... 5,894 | Brown, Son, & Blomfield .. 5,650
Pink, Flower, & Co. ...... 5,845 | J. H. Johnson 5,430

LONDON.—For building stables at Mile End, for Messrs. Carter, Paterson, & Co. Mr. W. Eve, architect:—
Godfrey & Son ...... £847 | W. Shurmur £794
Chafen ...... 826 | T. Salt 792
J. Chessum ...... 795 | Harris & Wardrop 783

LONDON.—For the erection of stabling and depot at Fulham, S.W., for the London Parcels Delivery Co., Limited. Mr. Henry Poston, F.S.I., architect, 39, Lombard-street, E.C.:—
T. Rider & Son ...... £3,336 | J. Mears £3,070
J. Morter ...... 3,198 | B. E. Nightingale 2,974
M. Patrick & Son ...... 3,137 | Woodward & Co. 2,925
W. E. French & Co. ...... 3,130 | W. Shurmur (accepted) .. 2,920
[Architect's estimate, £2,906.]

LONDON.—For the construction of tunnel at Roll's-buildings, Fetter-lane, E.C., for the London Parcels Delivery Company, Ltd. Mr. Henry Poston, F.S.I., architect, 39, Lombard-street, E.C.:—
W. Shurmur.—Accepted on schedule of prices.

LONDON.—For re-instating warehouse at Tottenham-road, Kingsland-road, after fire. Mr. J. Hamilton, architect:—
S. Goodall ...... £1,313 | W. Shurmur (accepted) £1,289

LONDON.—Accepted for alterations and additions to Wesleyan chapel, New North-road, E.C. Mr. Frederick Boreham, architect, 76, Finsbury-pavement:—
G. H. Martin & Co., West Croydon £1,149 0 0

LONDON.—For alterations and fittings at the "Mall Coach," Farringdon-street, E.C., for Mr. Coyle. Mr. O. Hardy, surveyor:—

Tibbetts & Co.	£323	Pringle	£219
Lawrence	241	H. & F. Pearman	191
Todd	220	Silk (accepted)	189

LONDON.—For alterations to No. 416, Harrow-road, for the London and South-Western Bank, Limited. Messrs. Truefitt, architects, 5, Bloomsbury-square, London. Quantities by Messrs. H. Evans & Son:—

Pryor	£1,890	J. Hunt	£1,645
Tennant	1,822	Scharien	1,541
G. Stuart	1,764	G. Bryan & Son (accepted)	1,547

MILLBROOK (Cornwall).—For proposed new church at Millbrook, Cornwall. Mr. Geo. H. Fellowes Prynne, architect, 6, Queen Anne's-gate, London. Quantities by Mr. R. Henry Hale, 6, Duke-street, Adelphi:—

Luscombe & Son	£5,480	0	0	Reed, Blight, & Co.	£4,300	0	
F. Merrick & Sons	5,214	14	0	Ambrose Andrews	4,250	0	0
James Julian	4,614	0	0	Isaac Rosekilly	4,192	7	10
Toser & Sons	4,594	0	0	Lapthorne & Goad	4,000	0	1
Stephens, Bastow, & Co	4,432	0	0				0

NEW TREDEGAR.—For building new church at New Tredegar, for the Rev. Thos. Theophilus. Messrs. Seddon & Carter and Messrs. James & Morgan, joint architects, Cardiff:—

Bowers	£3,298	H. Welsh	£3,000
Haines	3,025	Stephens, Bastow, & Co.	2,946
Osborne & Co.	3,011	Williams & Son	2,636

POTTERS BAR (Middlesex).—For erection of dwelling-house, at Potters Bar, for the Rev. F. W. Poland. Messrs. Marshall & Vickers, architects:—

Voller	£2,718	Meskin	£2,586
W. Shurmur	2,643	Bell & Son	2,564

SUNNINGDALE.—For the erection of a rectory for St. Alban's Church, for Mr. C. D. Kemp Welch. Messrs. Truefitt, architects, 5, Bloomsbury-square, London:—

Walker	£925	0	0
J. Norris & Sons (accepted)	890	0	0

TOTLAND BAY (Isle of Wight).—For the construction of a sewerage system, for the Isle of Wight Rural Sanitary Authority. Mr. W. Lidstone, engineer, 12, Victoria-street, Westminster, London, S.W.:—

James Dickson	£7,054	0	James Ball & Son, Cowes, Isle of Wight*	£3,182	0
W. Fortescue	5,615	10			

* Accepted provisionally.

WELWYN (Herts).—For erecting villa residence at Welwyn, Herts, for Mr. Thomas B. Blows. Mr. Ellis Reves, architect, Welwyn:—

Wm. Lawrence & Sons	£790	0	Wilmott	£615	0
Janes	678	0	Johnson	587	0
Foster	633	0	Russell	487	15

[Architect's estimate, £600.]

WELWYN (Herts).—For erecting residence at Welwyn, Herts, for Mr. Wm. Hitchcock. Mr. Ellis Reves, architect, Welwyn:—

Lawrence & Sons	£681	Foster	£585
James	645	Wilmott	580
Johnson	597	Russell	490

[Architect's estimate, £500.]

WEST GREEN (Middlesex).—For erecting new parish room, West Green. Mr. Geo. H. Fellowes Prynne, architect, 6, Queen Anne's-gate, Westminster. Quantities by Mr. R. Henry Hale, 6, Duke-street, Adelphi:—

J. Carmichael	£3,100	0	0	G. L. Wilson & Co.	£2,045	0	0
G. Gray	2,404	0	0	H. Knight & Son	2,030	0	0
J. Stewart	2,285	0	0	P. Hart, West Green*	1,990	0	0
J. & C. Bowyer	2,224	0	0	C. C. Brown	1,963	10	11

* Conditionally accepted.

SUBSCRIBERS in LONDON and the SUBURBS, by prepaying at the Publishing Office, 19s. per annum (or 4s. 9d. per quarter), can ensure receiving "The Builder," by *Friday Morning's Post*.

TO CORRESPONDENTS.

C. J.—P. G. P.—J. B. (sent too late).—S. & G. (should have sent amounts).—J. P. L. (we cannot print your letter).

All statements of facts, lists of tenders, &c., must be accompanied by the name and address of the sender, not necessarily for publication.

We are compelled to decline pointing out books and giving addresses.

NOTE.—The responsibility of signed articles, and papers read at public meetings, rests, of course, with the authors.

We cannot undertake to return rejected communications.

Letters or communications (beyond mere news-items) which have been duplicated for other journals, are NOT DESIRED.

All communications regarding literary and artistic matter should be addressed to THE EDITOR; all communications relating to advertisements and other exclusively business matters should be addressed to THE PUBLISHER, and *not* to the Editor.

Now ready (86 plates), Price ONE GUINEA.

"THE BUILDER ALBUM" OF ROYAL ACADEMY ARCHITECTURE. 1891.

SOME PRESS NOTICES.

"In numerous well-drawn and well-printed plates of plans, elevations, and sections of buildings, this comely folio illustrates the latest Royal Academy Exhibition of Architectural designs, and effectually proves how much greater attention that room in Burlington House deserved than it received."—*Athenæum.*

"A handsome folio volume."—*Guardian.*

"Various attempts have been made to collect in a convenient form the best architectural work of the year, but the 'Builder Album' ... is by far the best effort of its kind that we have seen..... Very well arranged and printed."—*A. A. Notes.*

"Should be in great request among architects and students."—*Pal Mall Gazette.*

LONDON

Office of "The Builder," 46, Catherine-street, W.C.

TERMS OF SUBSCRIPTION.

"THE BUILDER" is supplied DIRECT from the Office to residents in any part of the United Kingdom at the rate of 19s. per annum PREPAID. To all parts of Europe, America, Australia, and New Zealand, 26s. per annum. To India, China, Ceylon, &c., 30s. per annum. Remittances payable to DOUGLAS FOURDRINIER, Publisher, No. 46, Catherine-street, W.C.

W. H. Lascelles & Co.

121, BUNHILL ROW, LONDON, E.C.

Telephone No. 270.

HIGH-CLASS JOINERY.

LASCELLES' CONCRETE.

Architects' Designs are carried out with the greatest care.

CONSERVATORIES

GREENHOUSES,

WOODEN BUILDINGS,

Bank, Office, & Shop Fittings

CHURCH BENCHES & PULPITS

ESTIMATES GIVEN ON APPLICATION.

The Builder Cathedral Serie

1891.

1. CANTERBURY	Jan. 3.	7. SALISBURY	July
2. LICHFIELD	Feb. 7.	8. BRISTOL	Aug.
3. ST. ALBAN'S	Mar. 7.	9. NORWICH	Sept.
4. PETERBOROUGH	April 4.	10. ROCHESTER	Oct.
5. WELLS	May 2.	11. LINCOLN	Nov.
6. EXETER	June 6.	12. GLOUCESTER	Dec.

1892.

13. ST. PAUL'S .. .. Jan. 2.

14. HEREFORD	Feb. 6.	20. WORCESTER	Aug.
15. CHICHESTER	Mar. 5.	21. BANGOR	Sept.
16. ELY	April 2.	22. ST. ASAPH	Sept.
17. LLANDAFF	May 7.	23. WINCHESTER	Oct.
18. OXFORD	June 4.	24. TRURO	Nov.
19. SOUTHWELL	July 2.	25. ST. DAVID'S	Dec.

(Further arrangements will be duly announced.)

Post-free FOURPENCE HALFPENNY each, except Nos. 1 and which are *out of print*; but the VIEW, PLAN, AND DESCRIPTION CANTERBURY and of LICHFIELD have been re-printed, and th can now be had, price ONE SHILLING each set; by post, 1s. 2d.

THE REREDOS, ST. PAUL'S.
Reprinted from "THE BUILDER," January 28, 1888 (15 in. 11½ in.), on stout paper, unfolded, for framing, 6d.; by post, 8d.

PORTFOLIOS,
for Preserving the Plates unfolded, 2s. 6d.; by post, 3s.

London: Office of "THE BUILDER," 46, Catherine-street, W.C.

THE BATH STONE FIRMS, Lt
BATH,
FOR ALL THE PROVED KINDS OF
BATH STONE.
FLUATE, for Hardening and Preserving Calcareous Stones and Marbles.

DOULTING FREESTONE.

THE CHELYNCH STONE. — The stone from these q[uarries] is known as the "W[eather] Beds," and is of a crystalline nature, an[d un]doubtedly one of th[e most] durable stones in Engla[nd].

THE BRAMBLEDITCH STONE. — Is of the same crys[talline] nature as the Chelynch Sto[ne] but finer in texture, and m[ore] suitable for fine moulded w[ork].

Prices, and every information given, [on] application to CHARLES TRASK & SON[S], Doulting, Shepton Mallet.

London Agent—Mr. E. A. WILLIAMS, 16, Craven-street, Strand, W.C. [AD[VT.]

HAM HILL STONE.

The attention of Architects is speciall[y] invited to the durability and beautiful colou[r] of this material. Quarries well opened. Quic[k] despatch guaranteed. Stonework delivere[d] and fixed complete. Samples and estimates free. Address, The Ham Hill Stone Co., Norton, Stoke-under-Ham, Somerset. London Agent: Mr. E. A. Williams, 16, Craven-st., Strand, W.C. [ADVT.

Asphalte.—The Seyssel and Metallic Lav[a] Asphalte Company (Mr. H. Glenn), Office, 42, Poultry, E.C.—The best and cheapest materials for damp courses, railway arches, warehouse floors, flat roofs, stables, cow-sheds, and milk-rooms, granaries, tun-rooms, and terraces. Asphalt Contractors to the Forth Bridge Co. [ADVT.

SPRAGUE & CO.,
LITHOGRAPHERS AND PRINTERS,
Estate Plans and Particulars of Sale promptly executed.
4 & 5, East Harding St. Fetter-lane, E.C. [ADVT.

TWELVE GOLD AND SILVER MEDALS AWARDED.

ZINC AND COPPER ROOFING.

F. BRABY & CO.

LONDON. ++ LIVERPOOL. ++ GLASGOW

352 to 362, Euston-road. — 6 and 8, Hatton Garden. — 47 and 49, St. Enoch-square.

VIEILLE MONTAGNE SOLE MANUFACTURING AGENTS.

NO SOLDER. NO EXTERNAL FASTENINGS

Particulars on Application. Chief Offices:—Fitzroy Works, EUSTON ROAD, LONDON, N.W.

Vol. LXII. No. 2565. SATURDAY, APRIL 2, 1892.

ILLUSTRATIONS.

Cathedrals of England and Wales: XVI., Ely.—Drawn by Mr. Gerald C. Horsley .... *Double-Page Ink-Photo.*
Plan of Ely Cathedral.—Measured and Drawn by Mr. Roland W. Paul .... *Double-Page Photo-Litho.*
Wrought-Iron Gate to Bishop West's Chapel, Ely Cathedral.—Drawn by Mr. S. K. Greenslade .... *Single-Page Ink-Photo.*
A Bay of Arcading, West Porch, Ely Cathedral.—Drawn by Mr. S. K. Greenslade .... *Single-Page Ink-Photo.*
Sketches near Peterborough.—By Mr. Arnold B. Mitchell .... *Two Single-Page Ink-Photo's.*

Blocks in Text.

Wren's Library, Lincoln Cloister.—Drawn by Mr. W. G. Watkins .... Page 260
Door and End Wall, Wren's Library, Lincoln 261
One of the Tables, Wren's Library, Lincoln 262
Casement, Wren's Library, Lincoln 263
Ely Cathedral: Plan of Foundations of Norman Apse .... Page 265
Prior's Door in the Cloisters, Ely Cathedral 268
Heraldic and other Details, Ely Cathedral 268
Diagrams in Student's Column: Heating by Hot Water 272

CONTENTS.

he Remains of Ancient Rome 255
iscoveries in the Athenian Agora 257
otes 257
ir Christopher Wren's Library at Lincoln Cathedral 259
etter from Paris 263
ome Recent Developments in Theatre-Planning 264
he Atmosphere of Railway Tunnels 265
ly Cathedral 266
ketches near Peterborough 268
Architectural Societies 268
The London County Council 269
Builders' Clerks' Benevolent Institution 269
Works of Reference 270
The Lincoln Library Question 270
Building-Stones in Ireland 270
Ripon Cemetery Competition 271
Japanese Art 271
Varnish 271
Students' Column.—Warming Buildings by Hot Water. XIV. 271
General Building News 273
Sanitary and Engineering News 273
Foreign and Colonial 273
Miscellaneous 273
Meetings 274
Recent Patents 274
Some Recent Sales of Property 275
Prices Current of Materials 275

The Remains of Ancient Rome.

LITTLE more than six years ago we had the pleasure of noticing at some length* Professor Middleton's single volume on "Ancient Rome in 1885," a book which, though a mall one for so great a subject, had the ecial value that it combined the observa- n of the practical architect with that of e archæologist, and brought to notice many oints in regard to the construction of ancient Roman buildings which had been overlooked, nd probably not understood, by the many rchæological writers who have described nd illustrated the topography of Rome. In he meantime Professor Middleton has not een idle, and he now produces what is to a eat extent a new book,† though founded on e former one. The two volumes of "The emains of Ancient Rome" contain most of e matter which was to be found in "An- ent Rome in 1885," but rearranged and rgely added to both in regard to literary atter and illustrations.

Professor Middleton's book is one to be commended to those who take their Rome riously. It is not a handbook for the neral sightseer, who would no doubt be uch the better for studying and endeavour- g to understand it, but is hardly likely to so; he will find the practical descriptions interesting to him and the diagrams of nstruction unintelligible, and will probably turn contentedly to his "Murray" for food ore convenient for him. But to those who ish for real knowledge about the ancient uildings of Rome, and especially to archi- ctural students, this is a most valuable ook, the more so in containing so much in- ormation in such small and convenient olumes. Professor Middleton appears to possess an unusual faculty of noting little things in ancient remains, indications which are slight in themselves, but which furnish the data for very important conclusions as to the structure and structural history of a building. He seems in many cases to have looked into the actual indications of construction in a manner which has hardly been done before, and though he has not given us sumptuous drawings of the remains of ancient Rome, he gives us a number of diagrams of facts of construction, from observation at first hand, which are of permanent value.

In the present form of the book we commence with a chapter on the general question of the site of Rome, followed by one giving a general description of Roman methods of construction. In the Introduction we have also a useful list of existing books on the topography and antiquities of Rome, and of the most important existing inscriptions, coin collections, and other sources of information ancient and modern. In the sketch of the history of the site of Rome we are reminded of some of the early history of London; "the Forum Romanum, the velabrum, the great Campus Martius (now the most crowded part of modern Rome), and other valleys, were once almost impassable marshes and pools of water." There seems to be a tendency in the history of great cities to this crowding important quarters on to low marshy sites. London has her Westminster and Lambeth, and Paris her "Marais." The history of the contour of the site of Rome, in the author's rapid generalisation, is the history of a progress from accentuating the natural inequalities of level to reducing them as far as possible: a common history in the progress from an uncivilised to a highly civilised stage. At an early period, as Professor Middleton observes, when each hill was crowned by a separate village fort, it was an object of the rival inhabitants "to increase the natural steepness of the cliffs, and so render access more difficult and defence easier." As the various parts of the site became united under one Government, the object naturally became to get rid of the disjoining effects of this variation of contour, and in Imperial times especially great works were carried out in order to get rid to some extent of the inconvenience of hills and vallies. The same history is repeated constantly in large cities on uneven sites, as we see in the case of Holborn Viaduct; Union-street, Aberdeen; and the bridges which connect the Old and New Towns of Edinburgh. The two Scottish towns, however, have not obliterated the naturally picturesque character of their sites, and the passenger along Holborn Viaduct has still the evidence before him that there was once a Holborn valley. But under modern municipal regulations Rome is being, as far as possible, reduced to a condition of entire oblivion of her old title as the city of seven hills; the effort being not so much to connect the high levels by bridges and viaducts as to gradually obliterate the differences of level altogether and bring the town to the condition of an elevated plain half way between its ancient higher and lower levels. Along with this effort goes the constant formation of new and uninteresting modern streets intruding upon and shouldering out the reverend vestiges of the ancient city. In our review of the former book in 1886, we referred with gratification to the map of modern Rome appended to it, as showing that the contemplated improvements and extensions, the new quarters, seemed at all events to be kept pretty well out of the range of the most valuable portions of the ancient city. But alas! since then the march of enlightenment has gone on with giant strides. In his former preface the author could refer, without any expression of dissatisfaction, to the important discoveries of early tombs and houses "brought to light by the extensive excavations made in laying out a new quarter of modern Rome." But now it seems to be not so much a question of laying out new quarters as of laying out ancient Rome over again. It is melancholy to read in the preface to the new book of what Professor Middleton has noted since the publication of the earlier volume; the Ludovisi gardens built over with "villas," the demolition of the picturesque old houses on the Tiber banks to make way for a stone embankment. "No words," he says, "can adequately express the disgust which must be experienced both by the antiquary and by the lover of beauty in any form who now visits

* *Builder*, January 2, 1886.

† "The Remains of Ancient Rome." By J. Henry iddleton, Slade Professor of Fine Art, Director of the itzwilliam Museum, and Fellow of King's College, ambridge. London & Edinburgh: Adam & Charles lack; 1892.

d

this unhappy city. The injury done in former periods of destruction was but superficial compared to the ruin which is being wrought by the present scheme of *piano regolatore*, which aims at and is partly succeeding in levelling the seven hills and filling up the intermediate valleys; changing the very face of nature, and utterly destroying the character of the former capital of the world." The author is reasonable enough, however, to remember that since Rome has become the capital of Italy, it would be hardly fair to blame the admininistration of a modern city for doing what every other modern municipality is doing, improving roadways and approaches. It is the case of Venice over again. As we observed some time since, in connexion with the much-dreaded Venice "improvements," we can hardly demand that the modern Venetians, who have their own way to make in the world, should keep ancient Venice as a picturesque sight for the rest of the world, if it is not to their own interest or convenience to do so. To modern Romans, as to modern Venetians, the ancient buildings, seen by them every day, have apparently none of the poetic interest which they have in the eyes of the visitor; they are only obstacles in the way of modern improvement. The great monuments of Rome are indeed of such exceptional and world-wide importance and interest that they have so far escaped any threat of demolition, though we should not be surprised to find that there were those among the modern Italians who would be willing, if public opinion permitted it, to clear the Colosseum and Forum sites and lay them out for new building-lots. The great monument of all, however, is Rome itself, the most wondrous and enthralling remnant of the central life of the antique world, which is now in process of being gradually wiped out. The poetry, the glamour, of this great relic of a great past will ere long be only recognisable in the verse of Byron, and the next generation will be left to wonder what it was which inspired his nobly-expressed enthusiasm. It is a melancholy consideration that all these links with the past are being little by little stamped out and effaced: but apparently the only remedy for it, before long, will be for Europe to buy up some of the great sites of ancient splendour and preserve them as a possession for the educated world. Whether that is a possible alternative we do not venture to suggest; but it appears likely that it will prove the only one.

To return to Professor Middleton's book: in his second chapter, on Roman methods of construction and decoration, he warns the reader that no subject has been treated in so misleading a manner, partly because it has been largely treated by archæologists who had no practical knowledge of building, partly because "the real methods of construction in ancient Rome are frequently hidden behind very deceptive modes of surface decoration." The author notes that the purpose of mortar, which was only introduced at a late period in Roman building, was apparently not to bind the blocks together but merely to give the joints and beds smooth-fitting surfaces. In still later times, towards the close of the Republic and under the Empire, even this thin bed of mortar disappears, and the stones are apparently fitted as in the Greek columns, by rubbing them on one another. He mentions a remarkable example in the recently-exposed angle of the temple of Faustina, where the masonry has been well preserved at the lower part under accumulations of earth, and where he remarks that the beds and joints are so close as to be imperceptible except with the closest examination. This is the perfection of masonry building, but a perfection not to be obtained, of course, under a contract system of building against time. The Romans were bad artists (as Professor Middleton fully admits), but there is something worthy of the highest respect in this kind of perfection of building work; on which we might learn a lesson from them, if we could first unlearn our own modern lesson of building as quickly as possible rather than as well as possible.*

The most singular feature in Roman construction is perhaps the constant employment of superficial brick arches, surface arches, too shallow to be of any use constructively, and not intended for appearance, as they were used on walls intended to be stuccoed. The so-called relieving arches in the wall of the Pantheon are of this class, the wall being solid concrete behind them. Professor Middleton offers no explanation of this curious custom, though he comments on it in several places; nor does it seem possible to give any reasonable explanation. It seems as if it were a survival from some earlier manner of building; it is certainly oddly at variance with the otherwise practical character of Roman building, that they should have persistently used a piece of sham construction of this kind for which no practical object can be assigned. But the author arraigns the whole apparent brick construction of the Romans as a mere sham, a face to concrete walls, but a face which was to be covered up again either with stucco or (in special cases) with marble veneer. He gives a sketch showing the exterior facing and the section of a wall of this kind, the entire mass composed of concrete except a facing of thin bricks, triangular on plan, with the points inwards. As the author observes, this brick facing could not possibly be meant as a matrix for the concrete, for it obviously would not have withstood the pressure of the latter while in a wet state. It must have been necessary to support this and the concrete with an external timber framing in the same way as for unfaced concrete; and the author evidently set himself to look for the signs of such timber framing, which ordinarily would not show on the brick-work, and thinks he has found it in the remains of the Golden House of Nero, under the Thermæ of Titus, where he says "the channels formed by the upright posts are clearly visible. These upright grooves on the face of the wall are about 6 in. wide by 4 in. deep, and they were afterwards filled up by the insertion of little rectangular bricks so as to make a smooth unbroken surface for the plastering." We cannot suggest any other meaning for the upright grooves as described, but the explanation seems rather problematical. If the object were to support the brick skin along with the concrete, why place the supports within the line of wall-surface? They would have been more effective for their purpose outside of it, and left no spaces to fill in afterwards. In regard to the concrete itself, Professor Middleton notes that the larger pieces of the aggregate in the concrete, which are not close together, are so evenly spaced apart as to lead to the conclusion that they must have been put in by hand, piece by piece: a hint perhaps for our concrete builders. But that again would not do for building carried out against time and at prices cut down to the lowest margin by competition.

Of the boldness of the Romans in using their splendidly-made concrete for roofs and vaults Professor Middleton points out some significant examples besides the now well-known one of the Pantheon; we say "now" well-known, because it has been described and even drawn by various writers as essentially a brick dome, being in fact a vast inverted cup of concrete standing in its place like a single solid mass. Professor Middleton mentions a striking instance in the Thermæ of Caracalla, at a point where a brick-faced concrete wall originally rested on a marble entablature supported by two granite columns. "In the sixteenth century the columns and the marble architrave above them were removed for use in other buildings,† and yet the wall above remains, hanging like a curtain from the concrete vault overhead." The vaulting and dome system of the Romans, indeed, may be said to have been the use of the arch form with the statics of the beam, the cohesion of the material supplying the place of the buttress in preventing the spreading of the walls, the vault having practically no thrust at all. Brunel practically adopted this system on one occasion, when a railway bridge fell just after building; instead of altering the design of the bridge, he simply rebuilt it in cement. The Roman method cannot be called unscientific as the Romans used it, for the science, instead of going into the constructive problem, went into the composition and making of the concrete; thought was saved in construction by thought bestowed on material. There must, as the author observes, have been very elaborate construction of centreing for these great thick concrete vaults. He gives, as an ascertained fact, a common late method of avoiding the necessity of building the centreing from the ground, by setting the springing of the arch back from the face of the pier, so as to leave a ledge from which the centreing was built, the line of the pier being afterwards carried up till it met the intrados of the arch, thus filling the lower part of the arch and leaving it the segmental one. This is a very ingenious surmise on existing evidence, very likely to be correct, but ought it, with the diagram of the centreing, to be given as an ascertained fact?

The third chapter of the book deals with the half-legendary subject of the prehistoric period, which has left only the remains of the wall of Roma Quadrata as hard fact, and the regal period, in regard to which the author brings together the record of all remains, known or imputed, of this period. Further chapters in the first volume deal with the Palatine Hill (to which two chapters are devoted), the Forum Romanum, also occupying two chapters, the Capitoline Hill, and a chapter on "The Architectural Growth of Rome." The description of the remains on the Palatine is very full and detailed and of great interest. In speaking of the Flavia palace Professor Middleton remarks in rega to the porphyry statues with which the stat room is known to have been decorated, th the Romans probably acquired from Egyp both the taste for statues in this har material and the tools with which to wor it; and in a note on another page h observes that the circular markings o the side of drilled holes in this materi "show by the rapidity of their spirals that th drills must have sunk into the hard granit with wonderful speed;" a passage which w quote as showing the minuteness of observa tion which the author has brought to bear o his subject. In speaking of the rostra i the Forum also, he has not failed to notic the positions of the holes drilled, and th remains of metal pegs, for securing th rostra (beaks of ships) which gave the nam to the erection, and by which it is possible t fix their position and number, as shown o a restored elevation of the front of th platform. A restored plan of the Forum printed in colours to show the differen materials and the distinction betwee restored and existing work, is given in pocket in the cover of the volume, and form one of the most valuable items in the book it should be studied by all who intend t visit this famous site. A similar coloure plan was given with the author's forme book, but has been revised and brought up t date for the present publication.

The second volume treats of the Imperi Fora of Rome, the Circi, Theatres, Baths Tombs and Honorary Monuments, and tw chapters are devoted to the water-supply o Rome, and the Roads and Bridges. Thes latter are not the least interesting portions o the book. The author reckons the amount o water brought into Rome by the aqueduct as probably 340 million gallons per day. C course the extensive and constant use of bath necessitated a quantity far in excess of wha would be considered liberal for a city of th same size in the present day; but though w

* We are not, however, the worst sinners in this respect among modern nations. To judge from accounts which we have printed not long since of American methods of bricklaying, it should seem that the United States is quite ahead of us in the art of rushing through walling in the quickest way in which a tolerable show can be made on the surface, bond or no bond.

† What is the evidence of this, and of the date of removal? It is not given.

ll not see the Roman passion for bathing ived in our day and in this climate, it is l to remember, in connexion with the stion of water-supply, that the increasing of bath-water by all classes is a now con- ntly-increasing factor in the estimate to made for the water-supply of a modern glish city.

We have been able but to indicate a few of items of interest in this book, which for size is one of the most complete treatises the kind ever produced, and is full of in- mation on every page, and can hardly be l to contain a superfluous line. The author erves the best thanks of all who are in- sted in the history and monuments of this atest and most important of ancient cities hin our knowledge, for the conscientious e and acute observation with which he has ated the subject, and which render his k unquestionably the standard English rk on ancient Rome.

ISCOVERIES IN THE ATHENIAN AGORA.

WE drew attention in a recent number to the discovery by the German Archæological Institute, in their excavations during the winter, of ces of the Panathenaic-road and of the educt of Peisistratos, both of the first portance for deciding certain moot points the topography of Athens, points left pelessly uncertain by the account of usanias. Since then a fuller report of se excavations has been issued in the last mber of the Athenian *Mittheilungen*, a nmary of which may be of use to our ders.

The German Institute began its work at end of January, with the avowed in- tion of throwing light on the arrange- nt of the buildings known to exist in the henian Agora. The idea was to begin a le to the east of the so-called Theseion, rth of the new railway line, just at the ce where, according to Pausanias, the Stoa ileios (Paus. I, iii., 1) must have stood. tacles, however, at once arose; negotia- s could not for the present be concluded h the owner of that particular piece of und, so the excavators, though hoping return to that point later, have l to renounce the natural sequence their work, and begin to the south, ween the Areopagos and the Pnyx. y one walking along the modern road e can see, to the right as he comes from "Theseion," traces of an old water-course ried through the Pnyx rock, the purpose which was obviously to carry water to the ient market-place. These traces were sen as the starting point for excavation; problem was to find the continuation of aqueduct,—whence the water came, and what point in the Agora it was directed. one fountain in the Agora, and one only, mentioned by Pausanias, — *i.e.*, the eakrunos (I, xiv., 1), there is, of course, ge presumption,—nay, almost certainty,— if the goal of the water-course be dis- ered, that goal is the Enneakrunos.

he first part of the problem is already ed, and to it we have recently drawn ntion, and have only now to add a few ticulars. To the left side of the modern l the continuation of the rock channel ady visible has been discovered and cleared . It consists of a watercourse constructed arge limestone blocks, and covered in with same sort of masonry About its direction re is no doubt. It ran, as Dr. Dörpfeld predicted, from the Ilissos Valley along south slope of the Acropolis. It can connected unquestionably with the rocky nnel described in detail by E. Ziller hen. *Mittheil.*, II., p. 112), which runs er the palace garden, and which is now l as a water-course. The character of the onry of the portion of this water-course ch has just now been laid bare shows rly that it was Greek, not Roman work. size further makes it certain that in Greek times it was the source of the chief water-supply of the ancient city.

The excavations have now been finished northward, beyond the point where the traces were visible in the rock. So far it is a little disappointing that no evidence of the continuation of the watercourse has come to light. Continuation, of course, there must have been, as the watercourse could not have ended abruptly in the Pnyx rock. The excavators, however, have found what is almost better, *i.e.*, a substantial ancient road, resting on a supporting wall, built of large stones. This led in a gentle curve through the market to the Acropolis. Its inclination is just of the gradual nature required for such a road. Near this road, a little north of it, there was found a structure of Roman or Byzantine date, which proved to be a cistern with a clay pipe. Beneath this a late Greek or Roman building, with a mosaic pavement; close at hand three marble heads, of Roman date, and a statuette of Hekate came to light.

The excavation of the ground between the ancient road and the end of the rock channel is as yet unfinished. From the elevation of the ground at that point, the fountain may quite well have stood there; the hope of finding the Enneakrunos may still be cherished. Even, however, if it has altogether been destroyed, to make room for subsequent structures, or if it lay too far north of west for the present excavations, the discovery of the aqueduct and of the ancient road is a substantial contribution to Athenian topography, and one for which we have to thank Dr. Dörpfeld, who predicted the lie of both lines before the excavation was begun. This may plainly be seen by the plan of the agora issued in a recent work on Athens ("Mythology and Monuments of Ancient Athens," p. 3), based on Dr. Dörpfeld's conjectures. The Panathenaic road followed by Pausanias is here made to pass round the west of the Areopagos, whereas in every previous plan it was made to pass east; the western position is now conclusively proved.

We have elsewhere given from the Athenian *Mittheilungen* some detailed account of the excavations in the Agora at Athens. Since writing this account, we learn from a note in the *Athenæum* of March 26 that the hope there expressed of the discovery of the site of the Enneakrunos has been practically fulfilled. The excavations have been pushed a little further north and west, and Dr. Dörpfeld has come across three terminal stelæ, inscribed, ὅρος λέσχης,—one of them in archaic letters of at latest the early fifth century, the others about the beginning of the fourth. Close at hand is a small building in the form of a Π, and in front of it an altar. This must have been a small temple-like building in some relation to the Enneakrunos. That the Enneakrunos really was here is clearly shown by the fact that all about the building are water-conduits leading in various directions, and their masonry shows them to have dated before the Persian wars. The small original building seems to have been superseded by another structure, which served as a lesche,—a very natural appendage to a large public fountain.

NOTES.

THE clearest exposition that has been given of the effect of the new maximum railway rates,—so far as they are at present settled,—is to be found in the report of the Mansion House Association on Railway and Canal Traffic, which has recently been issued. Numerous comparative tables are given, a complete copy of the new classification, and all necessary information as to the charging powers of the companies; together with a summary of the advantages and disadvantages of the new Acts as compared with the old. The conclusion is that, so far as the general conditions are concerned, they are, on the whole, favourable to the traders; while, with respect to classification and the maximum rates and charges for all classes of traffic, the decisions of the Joint Committee are regarded as equivalent to an emphatic condemnation of the railway companies' proposals. It is remarked that this goes to prove that the opposition of the traders has found ample justification; and to this it might be added that the energetic body presided over by Sir James Whitehead may be congratulated upon their share of the work. In spite of the oft-repeated declarations of the railway companies that they had no intention of disturbing their rates where they were found to be within their statutory powers, we believe that on most lines a completely new set of rates will be put into operation as soon as practicable after the date fixed by Parliament; and that, in respect of some classes of traffic, the system of charging will be entirely different from that now in force. In view of this probability, the information given in the report referred to will be of great value to members of the Association, as the powers of the companies are defined in a manner at once clear and concise. The Bills of the North-Eastern and some twenty or thirty other lines are now under the consideration of a Joint Select Committee of both Houses of Parliament, and will probably be disposed of this Session.

WE are very glad to see that the London County Council, at its meeting on Tuesday last (reported in another column), resolved to make application to the Railway Commissioners for an order calling upon the London, Chatham, and Dover Railway Company to carry out such works at the Walworth-road Station as will render it adequate to its great traffic, and will put it into a safe and sanitary condition. The state of this station has been a scandal for twenty years; repeated remonstrances of passengers have received little attention until lately, when the Company condescended to erect some 60 ft. or so of cover over No. 1 platform. The staircases are steep and dangerous, and, from the multitudes who are forced to descend them, the station was long ago not inappropriately nicknamed "the Shoot." If the County Council can succeed in compelling the London, Chatham & Dover Railway Company to improve Walworth-road Station, there are other stations on the metropolitan extension of the line that may also be taken in hand.

IN reference to the proposed destruction of Wren's Library at Lincoln, the following letter was read by the chairman, Dr. John Evans, at the meeting of the Society of Antiquaries last week, being the reply of the Dean of Lincoln to a protest from the Society against the removal of Wren's building:—

The Deanery, Lincoln,
March 19, 1892.

The Dean of Lincoln begs to acknowledge receipt of Mr. Milman's letter and enclosure.

The Dean and Chapter are acting under the strongly-expressed opinion of their highly-competent architect, Mr. Pearson, and they have no doubt that his judgment is right in the matter.

The Library will not be destroyed, but re-erected in a far better situation and made more available for its purpose, which is to hold books and encourage study. They have reason to believe that for lack of proper accommodation they have already lost a most valuable legacy of books.

It is, moreover, to be remembered that the cloister existed for 400 years before the library, and there is ample evidence in the other three walks for the restoration of the fourth, of which, indeed, traces still remain.

H. S. Milman, Esq.,
The Society of Antiquaries of London,
Burlington House, Piccadilly, W.

Thereupon it was moved by Mr. Higgins, seconded by Sir J. Charles Robinson, and carried unanimously:—

"That the Society of Antiquaries of London, having heard the Dean of Lincoln's reply to the Resolution passed by the Society at its meeting of March 17, desires to point out that the competency of Mr. Pearson as an architect, which the Society does not question, affects in no way the point at issue, viz.: whether it is proper to demolish a piece of architecture of undoubted historic interest and of considerable beauty to make way for a presumed reproduction of a building which has long since disappeared, and thus to destroy a portion of the history of an important national monument;

That it is quite clear from an inspection of the plans of the cloister and adjacent buildings that ample room might be found for the extension of the library without interfering with the present buildings;

That this is the only example of a cathedral cloister of post-Reformation date in England;

And that for these reasons the Society views with the greatest possible concern the proposal to remove and thus practically to destroy this interesting example of the work of Sir Christopher Wren."

THE case of Nickalls *v.* Briscoe, which came before Lord Penzance, the Dean of Arches, on appeal from the Chancellor of the Diocese of Rochester, is one of more than merely ecclesiastical interest. A gentleman desired at his own expense to place a new stained-glass window in Watfield Church. The "faculty" allowing him to do so was issued by the Chancellor of the Diocese, though it was opposed by the majority of parishioners, not on any tangible grounds, but because the donor was suspected of a leaning towards Ritualism. The window was characterised by Lord Penzance as being "handsome and artistic, of appropriate design and good taste." It was also, in his opinion, an improvement to the church. It was therefore clear that the faculty was properly granted, unless the fact that the majority of parishioners were adverse to the change was a valid reason against it. But, said Lord Penzance, "if a majority of parishioners is to settle the question, what becomes of the discretion,"—that is, of the Bishop? Clearly the mere wish of the majority could not prevail unless supported by valid reasons. That it is doubtful policy to force, so to say, a gift on an unwilling parish may be granted, but it is well that parishioners who object without real grounds to changes in their church should understand that a mere negative unsupported by reasons is not sufficient.

YET one more "overcrowding" case is entitled to a passing allusion, in fairness to the railway companies. Last week, at Wolverhampton, a passenger was fined 10s. and costs for travelling in a second-class carriage with a third-class ticket. The defendant in this case was a season-ticket holder, —one of the class of whom it was said at one of the recent half-yearly meetings with somewhat severe sarcasm,—that "in consequence of paying in advance they consider themselves sole proprietors of the company's rolling-stock." The action was brought by the London and North-Western Company, and the defendant did not contend that there was not sufficient third-class accommodation, but that all the third-class smoking-compartments were full, and that he consequently got into a second-class smoking. This places the matter on a different footing from the other cases to which we have recently alluded, and the conviction scores one to the railway companies. Season-ticket holders are looking after themselves just now, and it seems that the companies are looking after them, too.

THE Staffordshire County Council have set a good example in the conditions for the competition for their proposed new County Council buildings. They have not only offered the liberal scale of premiums of 150*l.*, 100*l.*, and 50*l*, for a building which is only to cost 18,000*l.* but they also state that the architect who receives the first premium will be employed as architect to the building, and that his commission on the usual scale will be paid in addition to the premium, instead of the too common practice of deducting the amount of the premium from it. This is really the only fair way to treat the architect in such a case, as the premium in almost all competitions affords no more than the barest return for the time employed, and it is inevitable that fresh drawings have to be made for the actual working out of the building.

IN the last issue of the Athenian *Mittheilungen* (xvi. 4, 1891), which has just appeared, Dr. Paul Wolters publishes some fragments of a "Loutrophoros" which, besides the importance of their subject, have a melancholy interest as having been the chief "find" in the very last excavations conducted by Dr. Schliemann in a piece of ground close to the new buildings of the German Archæological Institute—ground, it will not be forgotten, that belonged to the great excavator himself. The Loutrophoros, or, to give it its nearest English equivalent, "holy-water carrier," in question is one of the well-known shape, with the long, slender neck and high handles. On it is represented a stile, standing on two steps, on one of which is lying a broken lekythos. Close at hand, on a low basis, is a youth riding a horse. The fact that the horse stands on a basis is painted white instead of being the natural colour, shows that the horse is a monument and the rider the dead man. Three other youths are grouped about representing living visitors to the tomb. Dr. Wolters takes occasion to discuss the whole class of loukophoroi. They are of great interest, as we know from a passage in Demosthenes (c. Leoch. § 18), that they were placed only on the grave of the unmarried—the orator uses it as *proof* that a certain man (Archiades by name) died unmarried, that a loutrophoros stood on his tomb. They were used in marriage ceremonies for carrying water, and hence placed on the grave of the unmarried by way of compensation, perhaps, for the blessing missed. The actual terra-cotta vase was temporarily set up and later replaced by a stone copy.

THE many old-fashioned almshouses built along the Mile-end-road, and by Stepney-green, are being gradually removed. The Drapers' (John Pemel foundation) has disappeared from what was known as the Stone Bridge, Bancroft's has given place to the "People's Palace," and now the Skinners' Company invite tenders for the purchase of their freehold building-site on the northern side of Mile-end-road, in St. Dunstan, Stepney, parish. The ground, having a 51-ft. frontage to the road, covers 10,850 ft. superficial. The twelve one-storied cottages are built in two rows, with a chapel and garden at the further end. Over the gate are a carving of the Company's arms and two little figures of cripples,—these, together with the cistern, door-knockers, the pulpit and woodwork in the chapel, the two inscription stones, and other similar objects, the Company wish to retain. A modern painting of these almshouses is at Skinners' Hall: they make a pretty picture. One of the inscriptions sets forth that they were built in 1688, in the mastership of Benjamin Alexander; the other stands thus:—

The GIFT of
Mr. Lewis Newbury
BUILT By
Thomas Glover, Esq.
his Executor committed
to the Management of the
COMPANY of SKINNERS
LONDON.

On March 21, last year, we called attention, in a "Note," to the proposed pulling down of this Company's almshouses, founded by Sir Andrew Judd, in Great St. Helen's. Next, eastwards of their almshouses in Mile End-road, stands a handsomer and larger property. "This Almeshouse / wherein 28 decay'd Masters & / Comanders of Ships, or yᵉ Widows / of such are maintain'd was built / by yᵉ Corpᵒ of Trinity House / An. 1695." On the grass-plots are statues of two benefactors, — Captains Robert Sandes (1721) and R. Maples (1680). The older buildings, of red brick, and two stories high, are very little changed from what they were in the time of S. Gribelin's print; but an extensive addition has been made behind the chapel, upon the removal, in 1875-6, of the hospital at Deptford. The buildings are richly ornamented with carved work, coats-of-arms, the models of four ships, &c. Then again, a few yards further east, are the Vintners' almshouses, originally founded in Vintry Ward in 1357, erected here in 1676, and re-built, with extended benefits, under the will of Benjamin Kenton, citizen and Vintner, in 1802. Close by stood another set, which, with one at Hoxton, was established under the will (1592) of Judge Fuller, of Stepney parish. The Mercers' almshouses, on Dame Mico's foundation, were built in 1691, near to St. Dunstan's Church.

CONSEQUENT upon the death of Sir J. Pope Hennessy, M.P., a historical property is about to be sold. It is the house at Youghal, county Cork, which Sir Walter Raleigh built for himself in 1587-8, and is known as Myrtle Grove. The grounds, about five acres in extent, have long been famed for their plantations of yew, bay, myrtle, and arbutus trees. It was on a hill behind the town that Raleigh is said to have first planted the potato. The greater part of his estates here passed to the Boyle family, some of whom, together with Richard, first Baron Boyle, of Youghal, Earl of Cork, who migrated hither from Hereford, *temp.* Elizabeth were buried in Our Saviour's Chapel of St Mary's Collegiate Church, founded for Dominicans by Thomas Fitzgerald, *circa* 1270 Here, too, they set up monuments to Sir Edward Villiers, Viscount Grandison (1626) the popular governor of Munster province, half-brother of George, first Duke of Buckingham, and grandfather of Barbara, Duchess of Cleveland; and to Roger Boyle, the Lord Broghill of Cromwell's day. King John gave a charter of incorporation to Youghal in 1209; a few years later Lord-Justice Maurice Fitzgerald established a religious house of Franciscans, the oldest, it is said, of the order in Ireland. Raleigh's house is a good example of the Domestic Elizabethan style and, whilst containing some modern windows is well preserved.

THE volume of the *Transactions of the American Society of Civil Engineers* for last November contains a paper written by Mr. Ward Baldwin on the stresses on "Railway Bridges on Curves." The author gives several general formulæ, from which the effect of the side-pressure on such structures can at once be calculated. This side-pressure due to centrifugal force, is considerable, and produces a very appreciable effect. As an example of this we may take the case of a train passing over a bridge of 100 ft. span and at the same time round a curve of 1,000 ft. radius. With a speed of 40 miles per hour there will be a uniformly distributed horizontal pressure developed along the bridge of 16 tons. The same volume also contains an interesting paper by Mr. William L. Saunders on "Dimension Stone Quarrying." The Knox system of blasting is only a recent invention, but it is rapidly growing in America and is being much adopted. Its purpose is to release dimension stone from its place in the bed by so directing an explosive force that it is made to cleave the rock in a prescribed line and without injury.

ON the 12th instant will be offered for sale at the Mart, a freehold building-site of some 51,800 ft. superficial, until lately occupied by the Artillery Brewery, Westminster. That property, including the "King's Arms" has frontages to Victoria-street and Strutton-ground. The sale will extend to an adjoining plot, of about 4,000 square ft., held until Michaelmas, 1904, at a reserved rent of [illegible] per annum. Thus long has been preserved memory of the time when the men of St. Margaret's would sally forth to practise at the butts set up there by the parish in compliance with Queen Elizabeth's ordinance. The vestry accounts for the sixteenth and seventeenth centuries contain many entries of divers sums paid for cleaning "pairs of harness," daggers, and bills; to men "for wearing the same harness" on muster-days, for powder and shot, and so on. John Lock mentions (1679) shooting with the long-bow d stob-ball, in Tothill-fields; and Steele, in e "Tatler" says:—

"You shall have a fellow of a desperate fortune, the gain of one half-crown go through all dangers of Tothill-fields, or the artillery-ound . . . .

1720 this artillery-ground covered a space about 300 ft. east to west, and 400 ft. rth to south. The northern portion, which y against Palmer's Alms-houses,—removed even years since to Rochester-row,—is w traversed by Victoria-street. According some old maps, encroachments appear to ve been begun towards the end of last ntury, but some of the field, westwards of rutton-ground, is yet shown as open in Horwood's supplemental map, fourth ition, of 1819. Strutton-ground com-mmorates Stourton House, a home there of Lords Dacre of the South. Artillery-urt, Chiswell-street, Artillery lane and street, italfields, and Artillery-street, Horsely-wn, still remain elsewhere in evidence of r fellow citizens' bygone military exercises. e site in part of Palmer's Village, close that under review, has been taken for ad-quarters in James-street of the Queen's estminster and of the "London Scottish" lunteers, those for the latter being planned d designed (1885) by Mr. John Macvicar derson.

TWO vacant houses on the eastern side of Panyer-alley, Newgate-street, with their es, upon an eighty years' building lease, offered for sale. Their removal will erfere with the position of the old sign, rved in stone, representing a naked boy ted upon a pannier or basket, and holding at is commonly taken for a bunch of apes, together with his foot, in one hand. neath is an inscription which says that re is the highest ground in the City; lowed by the date August 27, 1688. The n, once vulgarly known as "Pick-my-toe," nds on the pavement level; half of it is bedded in the wall of one of the two uses. This property appertains to an owment formerly known as the parish ate of St. Michael-le-Querne.

SOME years ago the Mortuary Chapel of the Sick Children's Hospital in inburgh was decorated as a labour of love Mrs. Traquair. The same artist has now pleted a much more important work of al decoration at the Cathedral Song ool, on which she has been engaged since 3. The Mortuary Chapel, a tiny room ch has been spared in the recent olition of the hospital, is an essay full of aise, with much suggestive treatment, iderable imagination, and, on the whole, edingly good colour. It is very pleasant ote that this former promise has been well lled, the later, and much more ambitious k showing advance in every way. The r School is a sober Gothic building by Rowand Anderson, a somewhat common-e adjunct to Sir Gilbert Scott's prosaic edral. The whole of the interior from to wall-head has now been decorated in by Mrs. Traquair, who has taken as her ne the canticle "Benedicite Omnia ra." The work is thus of considerable nitude and importance, on a wholly erent scale of effort from the diminutive pel. Yet of the two it is the more essful; both intention and execution w marked advance; the indefinable sense s being amateur work is greatly lessened; colour is stronger and richer; faults drawing are less obtrusive; and the orative imagination is both fuller and more tain. In these qualities of decorative sense l appropriate imagination, Mrs. Traquair els; the rendering of her theme is fresh l modern, quite free from the stock-in-de symbolism of well-worn types at so ch the square yard; the whole has dently been a labour of love and ntaneity, and the procession of praise bodying the works of the Lord, praising and magnifying Him for ever, is full of interest and charm. Especially note-worthy is this modern spirit in the groups representing the "Powers of the Lord," the "Servants of the Lord," and the "Spirits and Souls of the Righteous," in which are introduced portrait heads of the great men of to-day, from Browning, Carlyle, and Watts, to Cardinal Newman, Father Damien, and General Gordon; the cathedral clergy and the choir are gracefully intro-duced, as also the workmen engaged upon the building. Faults, of course, there are, particularly in drawing. Mrs. Traquair is much stronger at ideal heads than at sugges-tive portraiture, and she is rarely successful with the "beasts of the field"; she lacks architectural and constructional knowledge, her architecture being more suggestive of missal-illumination than of structure. But, taken as a whole, the St. Mary's Long School is a remarkable piece of work, of great merit and much charm. It is an addition to the art-possessions of the city, and may be looked to with confidence to exercise strong influence for good on local decorative work.

THE thirty-ninth Exhibition at the French Gallery in Pall Mall, which was opened to the public on Monday, contains a remark-able work by Professor Von Uhde, who, as our readers will remember, has devoted him-self a good deal to the treatment of subjects of New Testament history in a realistic spirit. It is called "Der Heilige Abend," (43) and represents a desolate snow scene on a winter's evening; in the fore-ground stands a poorly-clad young woman, the mother of the Christ who is to be born, leaning against a fence, while in the distance Joseph, a labouring man, is seen going off to the village to look for lodgings. Strange as is the contrast to the usual method of treat-ing such subjects pictorially, it is impossible to deny that Von Uhde comes nearer to the simplicity of the New Testament narrative than most of the more conventionally "reli-gious" painters. There is a true pathos in the picture, and the pictorial effect of the scene is fine and true. Fauvel's large landscape, "Les Fonds de Beaurepaire" (60), is out of place in so small a gallery, and cannot be fairly judged of except as to the fine draw-ing of the landscape; his smaller work, "Sheep Pastures, Brittany," can be appre-ciated better, and though the texture of the landscape is somewhat peculiar and crude, nothing can exceed the care and truth with which the effect of the light and shadows on the hills is rendered. The exhibition includes a small number of works by deceased artists, — Dupré, Daubigny, Corot, Millet, Rousseau, and Troyon. The larger of the three Corots, "Le Clocher de St. Nicholas, près Arras" (15) is an exquisite work, one of the most beautiful in sentiment and balance that we have seen; it is a woodland scene really, the tower only coming in in the dis-tance and serving to give a distinctive name to the picture. Rousseau's real genius is best shown on a large scale, his small works here do not do justice to him. There is a fine little work by Georges Michel, "Outskirts of Fontainebleau" (7). Millet's "L'Amour Vainqueur" (25), which we have seen before (unless this is a repetition) shows a quality of design and composition which the painter did not often display. Among other noticeable works are Professor Seiler's "A Critical Move" (34), admirable both in the painting of costumes and accessories and in the expression of the figures; Joanowich's "Servian War Dance" (39), spirited enough in action; Poetzelberger's "The Well-known Footstep" (52), a beautifully painted interior with a figure looking through the window; C. Probst's highly-finished little scene "A Hard Bar-gain" (69), and Professor Firle's large painting, "A Rehearsal" (71) a very clever work in which a young woman is singing to the accompaniment of another who is seated at a piano facing the spectator. The intense and rather puzzled expres-sion of the player, who apparently finds the music difficult, is admirable, and the whole scene pictorially effective, except that the piano forms rather an awkward mass of dark on the right of the foreground. This and other paintings here, however, are some-what large for the scale of the room; the ex-hibition was originally supposed to be *par excellence* an exhibition of cabinet pictures, and had better be kept to that.

IT is difficult to believe we live in the nineteenth century when we read that the Committee of Visitors of the Northampton-shire County Asylum recently gravely marched after one Mr. John Mullins, who calls himself "Water Discoverer by means of the Divining Rod," whilst this individual walked about the grounds to see where his twig would point to the presence of water. If some inmates of the asylum had amused themselves in this manner we should not have been surprised. Curiously enough, this divining-rod nonsense is still believed in by some worthy persons who ought to know better, though it is exceedingly difficult to understand the character of such persons' minds, or of what, as the late Lord Westbury would have said, they are pleased to call their minds. But that a body of presumably com-petent business men should go through this comedy would not have been believed, were it not apparently, according to the reports of the newspapers, actually a fact.

WE must enter a protest against a system which has come into favour in daily journals, of quoting passages from publica-tions possessing special information, with only an ambiguous reference to the paper from which the paragraph is taken, leaving the reader to infer that the bulk of the matter is original and not quoted. We have just been favoured with an attention of this kind on the part of the *Globe*, which a few days ago quoted a long paragraph from an article in the *Builder* of March 19 on "Steam rolling on Main Roads," merely introducing towards the end of the paragraph a paren-thesis, "as *The Builder* points out," leaving the reader to infer that the rest of the para-graph was original matter. It must be obvious that the intention of this disingenuous system of quotation (?) is to produce this confusion of *meum* and *tuum* in regard to literary matter, and that it has that effect is proved by the fact that the paragraph in question has actually been quoted in a country paper as an extract from the *Globe*, though every word of the matter is from our columns. We prefer not to say all we think about this system of "quotation," which is not a creditable feature of modern journalism, but we may observe that publications which indulge in it at our expense will be likely to hear more about it.

SIR CHRISTOPHER WREN'S LIBRARY AT LINCOLN CATHEDRAL.

THE attention recently directed to Wren's Library at Lincoln Cathedral by the scheme proposed for taking it down and re-erecting it on another site, according to a plan of Mr. Pearson's, on which some criticisms were passed in the *Builder* for March 12 (p. 202), will, we think, render some account of the building in-teresting at the present time. We are fortunate enough to be able to give a copy of the articles drawn up in 1674 between the Dean, Dr. Michael Honywood, who not only supplied the funds for the erection of the library, but pro-vided it with books, and the builder he employed, which, from the extreme rarity of documents of the kind of so early a date, possesses no little value.

The library of Lincoln Cathedral is almost coeval with the Cathedral itself. But it was a library in the sense of a collection of books, not of a room for housing them. For the safe keeping of the small collection of MSS. volumes which formed a Cathedral library in its earlier years, a strong, iron-bound chest, under lock and key in a closet (*armarium*, Fr. *armoire*) was quite sufficient. The chest or cupboard would

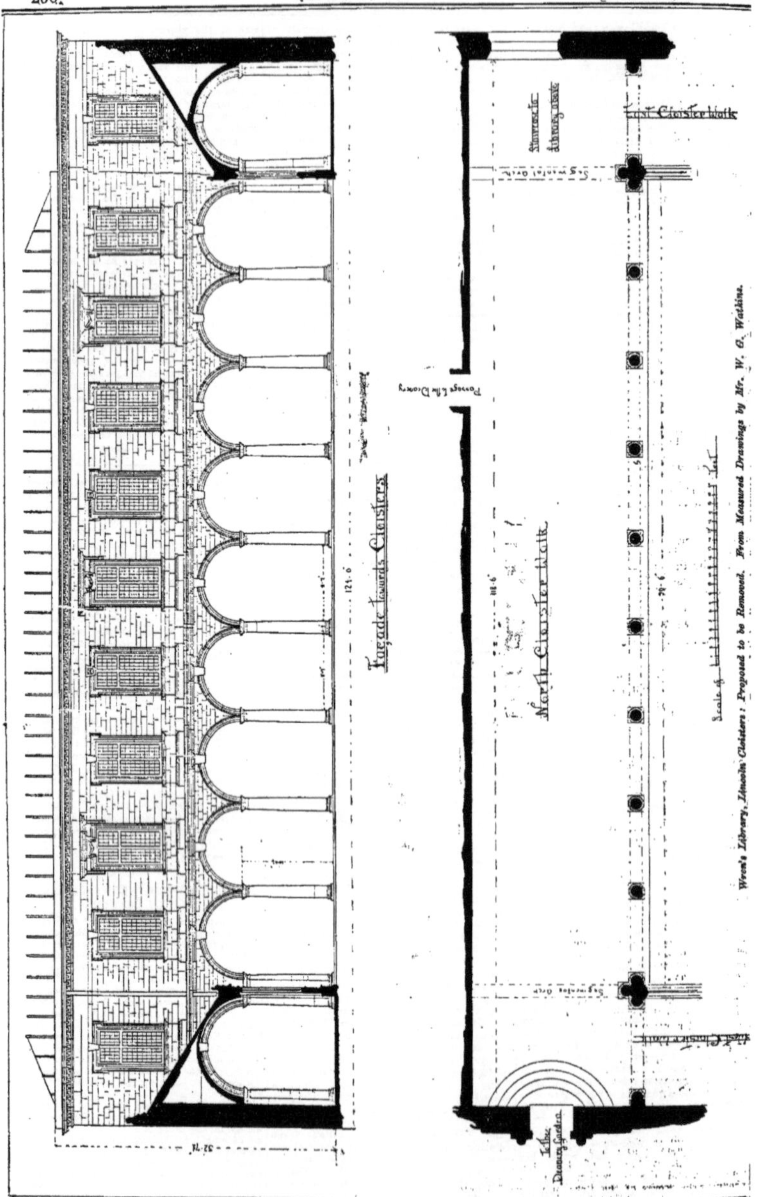

Wren's Library, Lincoln Cloisters: Proposed to be Removed. From Measured Drawings by Mr. W. G. Watkins.

Elevation of Door and End wall, Wren's Library, Lincoln. From a Measured Drawing by Mr. W. G. Watkins.

nd in the treasury, or in some other strong ce where it would be secure against theft or . A long course of years usually passed ore the books outgrew these narrow bounds l required a separate chamber for their lodgnt. The earliest catalogue of the Lincoln ary, dating from the middle of the twelfth tury, speaks of the books, not more than y in all, being kept in a cupboard "in o," under the charge of the Chancellor, literary officer of the chapter.* The nucleus, elsewhere, was a copy of the Holy Scriptures ording to the Vulgate translation. It was two volumes, and, as a contemporaneous ry at the head of the first page testifies, it s the gift of Nicholas, the first Archcon of Huntingdon, who was appointed Remigus, the earliest bishop of coln, and died about 1109. The name under ich it is entered in the catalogue, written on first fly-leaf of the volume, is not "Biblia," the earlier title, found in the writings of ome, describing its composite character, ibliotheca," "the Divine Library,"—not one k, but many. Of the two volumes, the ond has, unhappily, been lost for several turies. The first is still in the place it has upied for nearly eight centuries, a huge folio vellum, recently rebound in strong oaken rds in the workshops of the British Museum, l preserved with all the care due to so pre- as a relic of antiquity, the germ from which present library, with its thousands of lumes, has sprung. Some twelve of the forty lumes in the twelfth century catalogue are ll on the shelves of the library. All belonged patristic or canonical literature, with the ception of Virgil, Eutropius, Vegentius, and iscian. There was also a "Mappa Mundi," ich it would have been interesting to comre with that still existing at Hereford. But is gone. The catalogue also particularises the gifts of later donors. Bishop Alexander, "the magnificent," Bishop Chesney (five of whose books are still in the library), and others, including Giraldus Cambrensis' "Topography of Ireland," given by himself.*

Where the books were kept after they outgrew the limits of the original "armarium" is not known. Towards the middle of the second decade of the fifteenth century, c. 1420, we find notices of a new library, "nova libraria," being built. Bishop Repyndon, after his resignation of the See in 1419, gave a book, "Petrus de Aureolis"—which, subsequently, somehow found its way into the Royal Library, and thence to the British Museum,—"to the new library to be built within the Church of Lincoln." Thomas Duffield, formerly Chancellor, who died in 1426, bequeathed another book, "Novæ Librariæ ejusdem Ecclesiæ." We may, therefore, safely place the erection of this "new library" between 1420 and 1426, a date with which the portion still remaining, forming the vestibule to Wren's Library at the east end, perfectly agrees. It was a long, low room, built, as at Wells and Salisbury, over the eastern walk of the cloister, running north and south, and approached by a newel staircase from the vestibule of the Chapter House. The existing fragment is a very good plain work of the period, with a timber-framed roof, having tie-beams slightly arched and struts, the intersections of the rafters being ornamented with boldly-carved bosses of angels and foliage. At a later period,—tradition fixes it in 1609,—the library suffered from fire, of which the charred remnants of some of the MSS. are as evidence. What was the extent of the damage done to the building and its contents we have no certain knowledge. Few books, however, seem to have perished, as the greater part of those enumerated in the second extant catalogue, c. 1450, which were, of course, exclusively MSS., are still in the collection. From a view taken by Lumby, the cathedral surveyor, in 1784*, supplemented by the Chapter accounts,† the damage would appear to have been made good in a mean and inexpensive fashion with timber and plaster and small casement windows, continued southwards over the east walk of the cloisters up to the Chapter House. This poor, patched-up building served as the Cathedral library till the latter part of the seventeenth century, when, on the Restoration of the Monarchy, Bishops and Deans, almost universally, set about vigorously redressing the havoc made in their cathedrals by the Puritan fanatics. The Chapter of Lincoln was then presided over by Dr. Michael Honywood, appointed Dean Oct. 12, 1660. He had been a Fellow of Christ's College, Cambridge, while Milton was a student there, and Henry King ("Lycidas") a brother Fellow. At the beginning of the Parliamentary Wars, Honywood retired to the Low Countries, where he resided, chiefly at Utrecht, during the Protectorate, devoting himself to the collection of books, of which he amassed a huge store, amounting to between 4,000 and 5,000 volumes. The whole of these Dean Honywood presented to his Cathedral, and there being no adequate place to receive so large a collection, he determined, at his own expense, to erect a building to receive them.‡ The place selected for the new building

* This catalogue, written on the first page of the lgate, which was the first book of the library, begins as:—"Quando Hamoni cancellario cancellaria data t, et librorum cura commissa, hos in armario invenit ros." Hamon was Chancellor from 1150 to 1183.

* This, which is one of the earliest known catalogues of a Mediæval Library, is printed in the Rolls edition of "Giraldus Cambrensis," vol. vii., pp. 165-171, with notes by the late Prebendary Dimock. It will be found of great interest.

* Now in the possession of Alderman P. P. Dickinson, of Lincoln.

† The Cathedral accounts give the following estimate: 1789, "Taking down ye old library, i.e., the Timber side and end, Board Floor, Joist, and Roof, £2. 6s.; making good the roof up to the Front of the Library Wall, same pitch as the Cloister Roof, £4. 5s.; taking down the old Stairs, strings, and Banisters, 14s.: two shed partitions, £2. 10s.; two new window-frames, £1. 16s.; Roofing and ceiling joists, £5. 12s. 6d.; Putting up old Stairs, £6. 10s.

‡ Honywood's epitaph on the mural monument now at the east end of the south aisle of the nave contains these words, "Monumentum sibi cum libris duraturum posuit, utpote qui claustri hujus ecclesiæ dilapso in latere exstructo prius, sumptibus suis non exiguis, Bibliothecam eam postea libris nec parcis nec vulgaribus locupletaverit."

was the north alley of the cloisters, originally erected under Bishop Oliver Sutton, in 1296, which, through faulty construction, had fallen down, and had lain in ruins for a long period. For the erection of the new library, he called in the services of the great architect of the age, Sir Christopher Wren, who, naturally, we may almost say, necessarily, designed it in the Classical style, which was then in possession of the field. Wren's library, which comprises the whole north side of the cloister, as the accompanying illustration shows, consists of an arcade of nine semi-circular arches, with uncarved keystones, supported on eight Roman Doric single columns, with a clustered pier at each end, where the arcade joins the walls of the other sides of the cloister. The upper story, or library proper, has eleven windows of the Classical type, rising from a slightly-projecting plinth, set in moulded window-cases, that in the centre of the range, and two of those on either side, being further decorated by a cornice supported on consoles, and having a wreath of flowers over the centre window, and drapery of a corresponding form over those on each side. The keystones of the windows right and left of the central window bear the arms of Dean Honywood, a chevron between three cocks' heads, erased. The windows are casements, with the customary upright and horizontal wooden divisions. The design is finished with a bold entablature, ornamented with acanthus leaves. The bay at the north end (where a break in the masonry is indicated) represents the remaining fragment of the fifteenth century library, refaced to correspond with the other portions. This refacing appears to have been done nearly a century later, when the old library over the east cloister was taken down. A different stone was employed, and, as the elevation shows, the blocking-course was omitted. The old library being so much lower than the new, the upper part of this bay is a mere screen wall, and the upper part of the window is blocked, sham Gothic casements being framed within. On the outside of the west end of the cloisters, opening towards the Deanery, is a portal, under a compass pediment, supported on Roman Ionic columns, the capitals much mutilated. Above is a window of the same character as the others, but of larger dimensions and more richly ornamented, bearing Dean Honywood's arms.

Within, the library forms a long, narrow apartment, 104 ft. long, by 17 ft. 6 in. broad, and 14 ft. high. The ceiling is flat, springing from a hollow cove, and perfectly plain. The room is lighted by ten windows in the south wall, and one larger one at the west end. The entrance is by a richly-ornamented portal at the east end, the jambs of the door case carved with acanthus leaves, and surmounted by a compass pediment supported on Corinthian columns with gilt capitals. In the centre of the pediment is a shield bearing the arms of the founder. The same stately design is repeated at the west end, a window occupying the place of the door. According to Wren's plan the shelves for books occupied the whole of the north wall, the other walls and window jambs being wainscotted. This arrangement afforded sufficient accommodation for the books given by Honywood, but with no room for subsequent additions. To receive these, shelves corresponding in form and arrangement to Wren's have been set up between the windows along the south wall. This must be acknowledged to be a very inconvenient position, as no light falls on the backs of the books, and, the eyes being dazzled by the bright light coming through the windows, it is by no means easy to read the titles. In the libraries of earlier date, the books universally occupied cases running into the room, at right-angles to the walls, between the windows. The windows being on both sides, this plan afforded sufficient light for every shelf, but the cases being usually low, the accommodation for books was not large. Wren appears to have been the first to adopt the arrangement which has, since his time, been almost universally followed of shelves along the side-walls. It is commonly said that the library of Trinity College, Cambridge, was the first in which this new arrangement was introduced. But as that was not begun till 1676, nor completed till 1689, the Lincoln library, which was commenced in 1674, affords an earlier example. The bookcases rise the whole height of the wall from a plinth 3 ft. 2 in. high, which may have originally contained cupboards, but which now is filled up with shelves. They are

One of the Tables

set in compartments, wider and narrower, of two and three divisions alternately, the whole being finished with a bold entablature running all round the room, decorated with acanthus leaves and the egg-and-dart moulding, broken in the middle of each compartment with a gilt bracket bearing a grotesque mask, below which is a tablet on which are inscribed the languages to which it was intended that the compartment should be devoted. Of these two were for manuscripts, two for Greek books, nine for Latin, one for Latin and English, five for English, one for English, French, Spanish, and Italian, one for Italian, German, Flemish, Dutch, one for Saxon, Irish, Welsh, Russian, &c. These titles indicate the breadth of Honywood's book-collecting avidity and the varied riches of his collection, which it is stated on a tablet over the doors, amounted to 4,451 volumes. The furniture of the room in the main is of Wren's time, and was probably designed by him, as that at Trinity College Library certainly was. It consists of sturdy oak tables, with moulded legs, strongly braced at the bottom, of different sizes and heights, and provided with drawers with quaint bronze handles. The sitting accommodation consists of high-backed armchairs, which can hardly claim Wren as their designer. The table, of which a drawing is given, is earlier than Wren, being an example of Jacobean work. The most noteworthy objects in the library are the magnificent oak desks, which evidently belonged to the old library, and which afford an excellent example of the ancient arrangement for chaining books in mediæval libraries. Unhappily, these have lost their chains, and a wooden rod has been substituted for the iron rod to which they were attached, while only cavities in the wood show the position of the hasps and locks which fastened the rod in its place. They are described by Mr. J. W. Clark, in his "Architectural History of Cambridge," as "provided with two shelves, a broad one below and a narrow one above the sloping portion,"—or desk,—"on either of which the books could be laid when not in use. The bar passes through the standards,"—which are of considerable height, and resemble the poppyheads of church stalls,—"at about six inches above the top of the desk." The arrangements for opening and shutting the casements and securing them open are very interesting. But they will be better understood from Mr. Watkins's sketch than from any description.

The erection of the library having been undertaken by Dean Honywood entirely at his own expense and under his own direction, the building accounts do not appear in the capitular records, nor, strange to say, is there any allusion to this noble gift in the chapter acts.

The following document, already referred to, which gives the terms of the contract between the Dean and the builder employed by him, is taken from a transcript made by the well-known Lincoln antiquary, Mr. E. J. Willson, recently purchased by the Dean and Chapter. Mr. Willson does not state whence he derived it, and the original has been searched for in vain among the muniments.

"Articles agreed upon and made between Dr. Michael Honywood Deane of the Cathedral Church of Lincoln of the one part and William Evison of the City of Lincoln of the other part, Jan. 2, A.D. 1674.

Imprimis the above-named William Evison doth for himself covenant and promise that he will before the feast of St. Martin Bp. next ensuing [Nov. 11] raise up and build a range of buildings designed for a Library and cover it with timber and lead, which will take up the whole length of the north side of the Cloyster adjoining to the said Cathedral which North side is now ruined, and that this building shall contain eighteen foot breadth within according to Sir Christopher Wren's directions and Mr. Tompsons modell, which it shall agree with and equall in all things therein specified; having one upright stone wall of the same height and consisting of the same number of stone pillars and arches and which pillars shall not have less (*sic*) than in the same modell contained and that the whole building shall be made according to the same modell and directions in all things, except what shall be in these articles hereafter excepted or thereunto in these articles added.

2. He doth also covenant and promise that he will bear all the charges of glazing as well lead and glass and all the charges of Iron with Iron barrs for the Windows, and whatsoever other Iron work the building shall be judged to require.

3. And that he will make the lead wherewith the roof is covered of the better & softer sort of lead and of substance enough to weigh seven pounds in each square foot.

4. That he converts to his own use in this building now (*sic*) of the stone of that ruined wall that is to be pulled down but only that which is not carved nor moulded & so employ what is allowed for his own use nowhere but in that building; and that he may have that parcell of lead that remains of the roof of the North Cloyster and joins to the old Library, about a yard breadth more or less.

5. That he will use no firre in this work but for the floor and stairs and boards under the lead which should be at least an inch thick, and the two board doores, and that all the rest of the wood and timber shall be Oak and that of the better sort and well seasoned.

Sketch of Casement shewing Opening Gear

W. G. Watkins del.

6. That he will make spouts and conveyances for ne water to go clear off the roof, the spouts to be ad near the ground.

7. That he will make large two-leaved doores out f the new into the old Library with railes and anisters to the steps there and also large two-leaved oores above the same stairs at the West end at the ntrance into the new Library with railes and anisters at the head of those stairs.

8. That he will draw the inside walls where there re to be no shelves and both ceilings with lime and air.

9. That he will make the timber which bears the aden covering to rise above the plain, three foot nd a halfe.

10. He doth also covenant and promise to and ith the said Doctor Honywood, that he will mainaine the stone wall with Arches and Pillars upright nd good for Ten Years; that is against such efects as may proceed from ill workmanship or ad materials, and no other.

11. That he will also provide Casements as well s Ironwork as glasse for every second window.

12. That he will carry off all the rubbish of the round and leave the said North Cloyster when the ork is finished fitt for pavement.

13. That he will take down the Coping of the North Wall where it is too high, & where it is on he upper part too thin, take it down and make it f sufficient thickness for such a building.

14. And the above named Dr. Michael Honywood doth for himself covenant and promise to and ith the said William Evison, that he will pay to he said William Evison for the work above mentioned the summe of seven hundred and eighty pounds [£780] of lawfull current money of England n the proportion and at the times following,—that s to say, two hundred and fifty pounds in hand, and on July 1 one hundred pounds! on Augt 1 one hundred pounds more, and on Septembr 1 one hundred pounds more, and on October 1 fifty pounds more, and on Novr 1 eighty pounds, and when the work is finished, so that he takes of his workmen, one hundred pounds more.

15. And he doth also grant that the said William Evison may have the use of any pulleys, ladders, and ropes that belong to the Church, when they are not about the Church otherwise employed and that he may his lime out of the Church limekiln at the same rate as the Church payeth.

16. And the above named Dr. Michael Honywood and William Evison joyntly covenant each with other and agree that all such matters that by their part are forgotten and about which there (*sic*) any difference hereafter shall be referred to the decision and arbitration of two indifferent persons, each party then making choice of one and in case those arbitrators so chosen cannot agree in their award, that then the difference be referred to one single person chosen by those two arbitrators, and that from him there shall be no appeale.

And it is also agreed between both parties that when the Chapter Clark cames home, these articles without adding or diminishing any materiall thing shall be put into a more legall form if it be thought fit by either party, and then, this paper being cancelled, sealed, and in witness whereof both these parties above mentioned have interchangeably sett to their hands and Seales. June, A. Dom. 1674.

Sealed and Signed in the presence of
William Wyat [Precentor].
Jam. Gardiner [Sub-Dean]. William Evison."

AN ELECTRIC SAW-MILL.—An installation of woodworking machinery for Lord Rothschild has just been erected at Tring Park. The plant comprises band-saw and circular-saw machines for converting logs, deals, &c., as also planing, moulding, mortising, and tenoning machines, the whole of which are driven by electric motive force. The machinery has been supplied by Messrs. A. Ransome & Co., of Chelsea, and erected under the superintendence of the resident engineer, Mr. C. Burman Callow.

LETTER FROM PARIS.

IT is fortunately very rare to find a genuine artist becoming the principal actor in a sanguinary drama, and quitting the pursuit of art to sit in the criminal's seat in the assize courts. Some years ago, however, the sculptor Baffier stabbed a Republican deputy who did not realise his political ideal, and now another sculptor, Lecreux, who under the pseudonym of Jacques Frame had obtained a certain notoriety, has made a murderous attempt on the life of an arbitrator of the Tribunal of Commerce. He is a typical specimen of the Bohemian class, who in 1878, in conjunction with one of his friends, Charles Gauthier (recently deceased), produced a bust of "La République" which he wished to have accepted as the official type of this head imposed by the Government on all its documents. The work had no artistic value, and could not be compared with the bust by Gautherin, the least bad production of the kind so far. From the time when he failed in this attempt he seems to have given himself up to dissipation and intrigues, terminating in a crime which seems to have been the result of an utterly disordered intellect. It is not the first time that a sculptor has had the idea of getting a bust accepted as the official type of the Republic. The Municipality of Paris even instituted a competition in 1880, in which many artists took part, with the object of securing a satisfactory and typical official bust; but the result was a failure, none of these symbolic works rising above utter commonplace.

Symbolism of another kind seems to have occupied the minds of a group of artists who have opened at the Durand Ruel Gallery an exhibition under the title of the "Rose Croix." Among the painters in this group are MM. Dereux, Aman Jean, Maurice Chabas, Henri Mertin, Durasse, Léon, and others; among the sculptors the better known names of Charpentier and Pézieux; and a Swiss architect, M. Vrachsel. The exhibition is a curious kind of reaction against realism, not without interest, but with a good deal of charlatanism mingled with it, especially in the architectural conceptions which M. Vrachsel calls "visions plastiques de l'Art," things without rhyme or reason, the nature of which may be partially guessed by their titles, "Palais des Extases," "Le Palais de l'Effroi," "Scherzo," "Le Temple du Silence" &c. After this kind of thing one quite looks forward to the annual architectural exhibits of the Salon, with their severe and sober restoration studies of Classic work!

The exhibition of the "Independants" is another artistic eccentricity which has become an annual institution and made itself a certain name. It is enlarging its borders, and on this occasion the exhibition includes no less than 1,230 works. It is held in the Ville de Paris Pavilion. The quality of the exhibition however does not progress in the same ratio with the quantity, and, as usual, its real interest is centred around a small group of names, and the remainder of the works are more or less absurd.

After the Independants the Pastellites, and after these the Engravers, have successively opened their exhibitions. In the meantime the jury of the Salon has been pursuing its labours, having commenced eight days since on the paintings. The admission for works in architecture commences to-day (April 2) and will last till the 5th. No architect can send more than two works.*

It is to be hoped that there will be seen at the Salon the monumental fountain for Tarbes, by the sculptors Desca, Escoula, and Mathet, which has already been referred to in the *Builder*. This work is 14 mètres in height, and includes a circular basin from the centre of which rises a group of figures surmounted by a statue of Aurora. The lower statues personify the principal rivers and torrents of the Pyrenees, and around the lower basin are groups symbolising the principal valleys of the country.

We may mention in the same connexion, that M. Cain, the well-known animal sculptor, has offered to the city of Paris a monumental fountain with a design representing eagles and vultures fighting over the body of a bear. It is proposed to erect the fountain in the Square Montholon.

It is proposed also to adorn presently some other public places in Paris. The statue of

* That is, two designs; each design may be illustrated by several drawings, if necessary.—ED.

Claude Chappe, an inventor in telegraphy, will be placed on the Boulevard St. Germain, opposite the Ministry of War; that of Renaudot, the earliest French journalist, will be erected at the Marché aux Fleurs; and M. Mercié has just completed his model of the Meissonier monument intended for the "Jardin de l'Infante" at the Louvre. As will be seen, the public ways are more and more invaded by the homages rendered to departed merit.

The Commission des Bâtiments Civils has given its approval to various important works to be carried out at the Louvre and the Tuileries. These works have been the subject of a voluminous report drawn up by M. Bardoux, formerly Minister of Fine Arts, who has divided them into three categories; *travaux urgents*, requiring an expenditure of 480,000 francs; *travaux nécessaires*, for which 1,238,000 francs are required; and *travaux d'avenir*, estimated at 1,168,000. Among the "travaux urgents" is included the completion of the Jardin du Carrousel and that of the mosaics of the Escalier Daru, so much abused in Parliament by M. Antonin Proust. M. Bardoux, on the other hand, strenuously defends this experiment in the Italian style of decoration, and insists especially on the completion of the various cupolas and of the lower parts of the staircase, the marble steps of which have been hid in the cellars of the Louvre for twenty-five years back.

The "Travaux nécessaires" refer to the work necessary for keeping the buildings in repair. The "Travaux d'Avenir" concern the enlargement of the museum by the addition to it of the Salle des Etats and the Pavillon de Flore, still occupied by the Prefect of the Seine. The Louvre galleries would then occupy the whole side parallel to the Seine, and would suffice for all demands for some time to come. Although the cost is considerable, there is no doubt that Parliament will vote the money to make the Louvre worthy of and adequate to the great national collection of works of art.

At the Luxembourg, M. Bénédite has been appointed curator in the place of the late M. Etienne Arago.

At the Gobelins Museum a gallery has been opened to be exclusively dedicated to the drawings of Van der Meulen, which have been at the manufactory since the time of Louis XIV. This curious collection comprises views of the royal châteaux of the seventeenth century, the military displays of that epoch, and the sieges at which the "Roi-Soleil" was present.

Dynamite has been a good deal talked of for some time in Paris, and after having attacked private property, it is putting in peril our public monuments. The last attempt in this way has been to blow up the Caserne Napoléon, behind the Hôtel de Ville, and the explosion has seriously damaged two old windows in the church of St. Gervais. These windows with figure designs, which represented a value of at least 30,000 francs, were painted by Robert Pinaigrier, and were two splendid specimens of the art of the fifteenth century. The church of St. Gervais being at once a property of the Municipality and a "historic monument," it is probable that the Administration will take the necessary measures to secure it for the future, and save the remainder of the windows. Some reaction is required against the carelessness of the authorities in regard to the religious edifices under their care.

This carelessness is shown, not only in the religious buildings, but also in the most frequented cemeteries, where the tombs of eminent persons are at times in a terribly dilapidated condition. A rich foreigner, of whose good taste we have several times had occasion to speak, M. Osiris, and to whom we owe the monument to Alfred de Musset, now in course of construction, has generously offered to restore a certain number of monuments. It will be curious to see if this private offer will be accepted in place of administrative protection.

We have to announce two new competitions, which will shortly be opened, one for the Hôpital Boucicaut which is to be erected in the Quartier de Vaugirard. The money has been left by the widow of the late proprietor of the "Bon Marché." The second is for the decoration of the Hôtel de Ville and includes the painting of the ceilings and walls of the large Salle des Fêtes. We may mention that the public may have an opportunity of seeing in the Salon this spring the designs executed for this Salle by MM. Benjamin Constant, Gabriel Ferrier, and Aimé Motot.

M. Benjamin Constant has painted in a masterly manner great allegorical figures against a background of dark-blue sky. M. Ferrier has represented in a charming manner flowers and perfumes, and M. Motot, who had to symbolise the dance, has copied M. Gervex's design for music, which is already in its place. Whatever may be the merit of these paintings taken separately, it is to be feared they will not be satisfactory from a decorative point of view, when in place. On the other hand, the Salon du Champ de Mars will contain a magnificent work of Puvis de Chavannes, entitled "L'Hiver," and which will worthily complete the decorative *ensemble* which has been commissioned for the Hôtel de Ville. The artist will also at once set to work on the ceiling of the grand staircase which has been entrusted to him, which was before given in turn to Baudry and Delaunay. M. Dalou has been commissioned to produce a statue in marble, for the Salle des Banquets, symbolising "Le Chanson," a former commission to Chapu.

The celebrated founder Barbédienne has just died at Paris, at the age of 81. He founded in 1888 the establishment on the Boulevard Montmartre. His success grew rapidly under the Second Empire, and in 1867 he was created Officer of the Legion of Honour, and was promoted to be Commander in 1878, after the Vienna Exhibition. For more than sixty years, besides its reproduction of antiques, the firm of Barbedienne has reproduced the greater portion of the works of our modern artists. He leaves an important collection of works of art, among which the bronzes of Barye hold a prominent place.

We have to record also the death of the painter Jean Baptiste Auguste Leloir, who has died at the age of eighty-two. He studied in the atelier of Picot, and obtained a Third Medal in the *Salon* of 1839, and a Second in that of 1841. He was especially a painter of religious subjects, and among his most important works are the decoration of the chapel of St. Louis in the Church of St. Severin, the cartoons for the windows of the Church of La Trinité, and the moral paintings in the Church of St. Jean Baptiste at Belleville. Auguste Leloir was the father of the painters Louis and Maurice Leloir, of whom he was the first instructor. The former, of whom much was expected, unhappily died some years ago.

SOME RECENT DEVELOPMENTS IN THEATRE-PLANNING:

ARCHITECTURAL ASSOCIATION.

In the discussion which followed the reading of Mr. E. A. E. Woodrow's paper on this subject, read before the Architectural Association on the 18th ult., and printed *in extenso* in our last number,

Mr. E. Woodthorpe proposed a hearty vote of thanks to Mr. Woodrow for the very exhaustive paper which he had read to them, and also for the trouble he had taken in bringing together such a large collection of plans. The paper had, he was sure, been of great interest to them all. With what had been said by Mr. Woodrow about the advantage of getting rid of the pit in the Haymarket Theatre he could not agree. He thought it a very great mistake to remove the pit from the place which it had occupied ever since theatres had been established,—at any rate, in this country. Our English theatres did not compare at all favourably with a great many theatres in Paris and abroad, because here no support was given to them by the State; and people who built theatres found that if they spent too much money on the architecture and the site, and if they gave up much room to lounges and staircases, their theatres did not pay. Mr. Woodrow had said that he did not attempt to touch upon a great many subjects connected with theatre construction, and doubtless for that reason he had not mentioned the value of iron curtains. The first iron curtain that was put up in England was erected by Mr. Phipps in the Prince of Wales's Theatre, but its use in stopping fire had not been practically shown, and he was glad to say that there had not been a great theatre-fire in London in recent years. Mr. Woodrow had not gone into the large subject of heating and ventilation, as to which he (the speaker) was astounded by some remarks made by Mr. Phipps at a recent meeting of the Institute, to the effect that in London there was not a theatre which was thoroughly well ventilated and heated, because the owners could not afford to spend enough money on such a matter.

Mr. Bernard Dicksee, in seconding the vot
of thanks, said there was one point that w
not sufficiently attended to in the planning
theatres, and that was the proper width of th
exits. It was even worse to have the exits t
wide than too narrow. The regulations of th
London County Council made provision th
the width of the exits should depend upon th
number of people who would have to pa
through, but he thought that was a mistake
provision. He did not think that any ex
should be more than 5 ft. wide at the outside-
4 ft. 6 in. would be better. There should als
be a handrail for every person to place his hand
upon, and the exits should therefore only b
wide enough to allow two people to pass o
side by side. There should be a greater numb
of exits rather than a few of large width. Th
reason why grand staircases had almost entirel
gone out of use was their great danger. The
in Her Majesty's Theatre was particularl
dangerous. He thought it should be mad
compulsory that on the backs of programm
the plan of the theatre should be shown, an
that the exits should be clearly indicated. I
reference to the remarks made by Mr. Woodro
with regard to hydraulic arrangements for th
stage, he (the speaker) remembered that M
Phipps had said that at the Lyric Theatre h
had provided hydraulic power for working th
stage, but that it had never been used.

Mr. Max Clarke said that Mr. Woodrow ha
gone so fully into the subject under discussio
that what he could say would be very largel
a reiteration of what had already been sai
The first thing that they had to do in designin
a theatre in London was to get the new regula
tions to work to, for it would be possible t
select six or more of the plans exhibited, whic
were twenty years in advance of the Count
Council's regulations as in force at the prese
time. With regard to the exits, the Count
Council regulations stated that the staircas
must be 4 ft. 6 in. wide for a building whic
would accommodate 400 people. If th
arrangement were carried out, there would b
eighty-eight persons coming out of the door
a theatre per foot wide of opening. At th
Shaftesbury Theatre, which was the fir
modern symmetrical theatre built in Londo
and which was, indeed, the most symmetric
theatre built up to the present time, there w
a series of openings to the street, which totalle
up to 75 ft. Supposing that the Shaftesbu
Theatre held 2,000 people, there would be
provision for exit of 1 ft. for twenty-s
people, so that at the Shaftesbury they we
about sixty people ahead of the regul
tions. The regulations only asked for 1 ft.
exit for eighty-eight persons, and the exits
the Shaftesbury provided 1 ft. for twenty-s
people. At the present time, according to th
regulations, it was not compulsory to build
theatre of fireproof material. The new regula
tions stated that the dressing-rooms were to b
of fire-resisting materials, but not a word w
said about the auditorium; and so far as th
regulations were concerned, they might constru
the tiers and line the walls completely with woo
but it was a question whether the County Coun
would pass the plans for such a theatr
probably they would not, for although the
was no written law against the erection of
wooden theatre, there was an unwritten la
With regard to theatre-building in London, the
was a growing desire on the part of successf
actors to be complete masters of buildings
their own, and the consequence was that the
were many small theatres. In the designs
the new theatre at Amsterdam, which Mr. J
Springer had sent for exhibition that evenin
the Continental idea of theatre-building w
exemplified. There was a large *foyer* or vest
bule, right underneath the pit, and very wi
entrances, which were divided by bars. T
staircases were very wide; but supposing the
were a sufficient number of handrails down
wide staircase, the difficulty which had bee
mentioned would be obviated. Mr. Woodrow h
spoken about the balconies for the Amsterda
theatre, but he had forgotten to say that t
Shaftesbury Theatre was provided wi
balconies on three sides to the dressing-roo
portion. In New York it was possible to run
iron staircase right down to the street, and th
would have been done at the Shaftesbu
Theatre had it been permitted. At the Théât
Flamand at Brussels there was a series
balconies round the theatre, so close togeth
that a person could jump from one to the oth
Eventually the balconies finished at so small
height from the ground that a person could dr

nto the street without difficulty. With regard to he cost of management of large theatres, the akings at the Grand Opera House in Paris in 884 were 57,167*l*., and yet there was a dead oss on the whole year of 650*l*. Mr. D'Oyly Jarte also found that he could not keep his arge theatre open without entailing a loss. Vithout disagreeing entirely with what Mr. Voodrow said about the absence of columns in heatres, he would call his attention to the Alhambra, where there were columns all round. Ir. Woodrow's remarks on this point might ot have been understood by all of them, but hat he had meant was that in small theatres ike those they were speaking about, although here were no columns, the cantilevers were nsignificant. But in the new Opera House nd the Alhambra and the Empire Theatres the antilevers became increasingly larger, having n the first-named building a projection of bout 20 ft.; but in small theatres it was not nore than 12 ft. or 14 ft. Mr. Emden's, Terry's," "Court," and "Garrick" theatres vere constructed upon a similar principle, ut it was at the English Opera House that here was the greatest amount of cantilevering, vhich had been very successfully carried out by he Horseley Iron Company. In remarking pon the development of theatre-planning, ome notice ought to be taken of the fact that lthough Mr. D'Oyly Carte's theatre (the new pera House) showed a perfectly symmetrical rrangement according to the partial plan exibited, it was very different when the whole of he plan was seen. The entrances and exits ere certainly not symmetrical, and as the heatre was built upon a fairly symmetrical site nd was isolated, it seemed a failure as far as he arrangement of the exits was concerned. Ie did not know whether Mr. Woodrow had ientioned the matter, but in New York the uthorities objected to more than six seats being rranged without a gangway. In the Royal nglish Opera House first tier, although the doors ere at the side, there was what he considered n objectionable feature, and that was that the ery best position in the house for a seat,—viz., he centre,—was given up to a gangway. In the yric Theatre, although there were only four oors, there were two good gangways, and here were only two rows of seats between any f the doors. It was the same at the Shaftesury Theatre, where there were six doorways ound the sides. With regard to fireproof curains, a fireproof curtain was put up in Edinurgh many years ago, which was made of ome material like twisted iron wire, but it was complete failure. But where his own curtain ad been put up, and there had been a fire, the urtain had been found to answer. The only hing against which one had to guard in a proerly-planned fireproof theatre was smoke. An rchitect had told him that a piece of cloth fixed etween the auditorium and the stage was quite ufficient to keep back the smoke, and so long s this was done they did not require anything ore. It was questionable whether this was the ase. The owner of the Garrick Theatre had aid that a fireproof curtain was perfectly useess, and so did the owner of the Royal English pera House; but at the back of the gallery of he last-named building, right at the top, there as an air-propeller, which extracted the hot r, and it seemed to him (the speaker) that if fire occurred in that building the extractor ould draw the smoke up into the gallery. ention had been made of the fact that Mr. hipps had put up an iron curtain at the Prince Wales's Theatre and he (the speaker) supposed that more of those curtains would have een erected had he not thought of something hich was less costly and less in weight, and ot so liable to damage when a fire did occur; nd the County Council had backed up his efforts y making similar provisions in their new regulaons. His own curtains had been put up in ondon, Liverpool, and in two or three other aces, before any regulations of the kind were ade by the L.C.C. With regard to staircases, he grand staircases at the Lyceum Theatre, hich had not been referred to, were, though on a nall scale, as successful as any. The Lyceum nd Drury Lane Theatres were built by the same an, Mr. Beazeley, and he had the same ideas arried out in both theatres, which were perectly symmetrical. At Her Majesty's Theatre he staircases were not very symmetrical, nor ere they very grand. One must not forget at a theatre had to be built for a particular urpose, and in Her Majesty's Theatre there ere many private boxes, and the tiers were ery close together. Mr. D'Oyly Carte's theatre had been built with a small number of tiers, no boxes, and the tiers wide apart, something like the arrangement at the Cranbourne-street theatre. Mr. Woodrow had said that they should not make their staircases with more than twelve steps or less than four steps in each flight. But suppose that an extra staircase could not be put in without eighteen or nineteen steps in one flight, would it not be better to have the extra staircase than not? It was important that the tops of the staircases should be covered with separate concrete ceilings of their own. That was a very important matter, because if a theatre had a wooden roof which went right over the exit staircase, it would be bad for the people in the staircase if the roof caught fire, while if the staircase had a concrete ceiling of its own, the people passing out stood a good chance of getting out without damage. He did not think that Mr. Woodrow's interpretation of the word "pass-door" was quite right. A pass-door was one which was put in the theatre merely for the use of the management, and for no other purpose, and, if it was used by the audience, then it was the duty of the County Council to interfere. If an iron door was used,—although generally he did not believe in iron doors or iron shutters,—or some fire-resisting material, they obtained all that they required without any objectionable features. The question of sites was a very important one, but he could not make head nor tail of the County Council regulations respecting them. If they had a theatre with a passage-way round it, 8 or 10 ft. wide to the open air, that passage-way would contain all the people that the theatre would hold without any difficulty whatever. Why one street should be 40 ft. wide and why another should be 20 ft. wide was very difficult to understand. He supposed that unless they had one street 40 ft. wide on the site they could not build a theatre there at all. Again coming to the regulations, why should not the pit be more than 15 ft. below the ground? Mr. Buckle, who had published a book on theatres, had shown a design for a theatre entirely below the ground level, and it seemed to him (the speaker) that it would have been perfectly safe to have built it. Such a theatre would take a large area of ground, but why it should not be safe he did not know. There was a small point in the planning of theatres which had not been sufficiently touched upon, he thought. Most people knew that at the Exeter Theatre fire a great many people were burnt to death, and those people were burnt because a man at the top of the gallery staircase had a wooden ticket box, which was knocked down, and the first person who left that part of the theatre tumbled over the fallen box. The box had no business to be there. He thought the Lyric Theatre was the only theatre where the ticket-boxes were built into the wall. The ticket-man, too, had no business to have a chair at the top of the stairs; that should be absolutely prohibited. The Gateshead Theatre accident occurred, it was said, owing to a lighted match falling through a crack in the wooden floor and setting light to an accumulation of rubbish. It was enough to say that there should be no floors in theatres with such cavities. It was unnecessary to have the floor of granite concrete, as suggested. The best material was broken-up brick, and there was no reason why that should not be used. Granite was difficult to fix to, and the only benefit to be derived from its use was the hard wear that it would take. With regard to the ventilation of the stage, if the regulations were followed, it would be found difficult to prevent a great down-draught, as there would be, he feared, at the Cranbourne-street Theatre, where a large ventilator was to be used. He suggested as a means of curing that difficulty that a sort of velarium should be stretched over the opening, and the air would go round the curtain without producing the down-draught.

The President, in putting the vote of thanks, said that as most of them were no doubt anxious to look at the drawings, he would not detain them by any words of his own. He thought they ought to include Mr. Max Clarke in the vote of thanks for the valuable information which he had given them. They were particularly indebted to Mr. Woodrow for bringing together such a large collection of diagrams and models, and for all the trouble which he had taken.

The vote of thanks was then put to the meeting and carried unanimously.

Mr. E. S. Gale said that Mr. Woodrow had expressed his own thanks to the architects who had lent him drawings, but he (the speaker) wished to move a vote of thanks to those gentlemen from the Association.

This being agreed to, Mr. Woodrow briefly replied, and the meeting terminated.

Discussion Section.—The ninth meeting of the Discussion Section for the present session was held on the 16th ult., when Mr. E. Greenop, A.R.I.B.A., read a paper on "The Public Health (London) Act, 1891." The Special Visitor for the evening was Mr. Charles Mason, A.M.I.C.E., A.R.I.B.A., Surveyor to the Vestry of St. Martin-in-the-Fields. Mr. Greenop dealt with his subject in a short, pithy manner, and pointed out that the chief sections affecting architects were those relating to underground-rooms, drainage, and water supply; and the Special Visitor added some valuable hints in the discussion which followed the paper.

THE ATMOSPHERE OF RAILWAY TUNNELS.

No one who has travelled much by the Metropolitan Railway will be inclined to deny consideration to any feasible scheme that may be proposed for preventing the fouling of the atmosphere, which now renders such a journey a most disagreeable penance; and we are therefore glad to notice a scheme which has been proposed for the prevention of the fouling of the atmosphere of the London Underground Railways by the products of combustion.

On Saturday last this scheme was practically illustrated to a large number of gentlemen representing the engineering and other societies, and the inventor, Mr. Anderson, gave an explanatory account of the way in which the scheme is proposed to be worked.

The invention consists, briefly, of a cast-iron trunk, or foul-air duct, laid between the metals, through which the products of combustion from the engines are drawn off by means of powerful fans placed in suitable positions. Coming to the detailed method in which this is carried out, we have first of all the cast-iron duct 2 ft. 9 in. wide by 6 in. deep internally, which is put together in sections connected by indiarubber flanged joints. Ou the top surface of the cast-iron duct are valves 16 ft. apart, which are opened by a slider suspended beneath the locomotive as it passes over them. When the slider has opened a valve, it forms a connexion between that valve and the smoke-box, so that this latter is in direct communication with the duct as long as the slider is in coutact with any particular valve. The valves are so arranged with reference to the length of the slides that at least one valve is always in contact, and at the moment of passing from one valve to the next the slider is in contact with both, hence for a moment two valves are connected with the fire-box, thus it will be seen that the fire-box is always in connexion with the cast-iron duct.

This is the great point of Mr. Anderson's invention, as it is at once obvious that if the smoke-box of a moving engine can be always brought in connexion with a fixed duct, the products of combustion may be readily taken away from the smoke-box, through the duct, by the application of a sufficiently powerful exhausting apparatus, instead of passing into the external air by the chimney in the ordinary way.

The inventor proposes to place his exhaust stations about two miles apart, and, by means of powerful fans, to exhaust one mile of duct each side of the station.

At the demonstration on Saturday, Mr. Anderson gave some particulars as to the cost of his scheme, and taking the thirteen miles of the Metropolitan and Metropolitan District Railways as a basis, he told the visitors that the complete installation of his arrangements for that distance would cost 130,000*l*., that is at the rate of 10,000*l*. per mile. Allowing 5 per cent. interest on this sum, and the cost of working expenses, depreciation, and other outgoings, the inventor estimates the annual expenditure for the same installation at 28,000*l*. These figures are, of course, at first sight very considerable; but turning to the other side of the account Mr. Anderson considers himself justified in assuming that if the tunnels of the Metropolitan and Metropolitan District Railways were free from mephitic vapour the increased receipts from passenger traffic would amount to 5 per cent. on the present takings of this company; this amounts to 52,000*l.* a year, hence the inventor is sanguine as to the financial aspect of his scheme. It was urged, moreover, that a considerable space of ground which is now devoted to openings for the tunnels and stations of the company might, if Mr. Anderson's scheme were adopted, be covered and built over at a very considerable profit.

At the demonstration which took place on Saturday, a light engine belonging to the Metropolitan Company was run backwards and forwards over a length of about half a mile of the duct, and, as care had been taken to feed the engine with a coal producing large volumes of smoke, the utility and efficiency of Mr. Anderson's invention was clearly demonstrated, and the contrast between the dense volumes of smoke which poured from the chimney of the locomotive while it was off the duct and the perfect absence of that smoke when the same engine was over the duct was very striking, emphasised as it was by the appearance of the smoke from the chimney over the exhaust station half a mile away.

The inventor stated that the cost of altering this engine for the purpose of fitting his invention was about 60*l.*, but intimated that in building new engines this expense would be avoided.

Certainly the very serious drawback to the health and comfort of Londoners which the tunnels of the underground railways now present would alone be sufficient to induce the directors of the railway companies to adopt some such scheme as that now proposed if they had not the fear of shareholders and dividends before their eyes; but as the inventor appears to have a good case from a financial point of view, the question ought to be considered as practically settled if Mr. Anderson is able to make good his financial statements.

We certainly think that he is within the mark in assuming that a clear atmosphere in the tunnels would increase the traffic of the Metropolitan Railway, if not of the Metropolitan District, by the 5 per cent. which he assumes. Increased traffic would, however, not be wholly profit, and Mr. Anderson certainly did not on Saturday last take any account of the increased cost to a railway company of carrying this increased traffic of 5 per cent.

It would be interesting also to know what would be the probable annual cost in repairs to keep the valves in order. Taking a double line of rails of thirteen miles in length, we have about 8,680 valves in constant process of being opened and closed by violent and sudden action every two or three minutes during about seventeen out of the twenty-four hours. How long will the system remain in working order under those conditions?

Illustrations.

ELY CATHEDRAL.*

ELY has not got what is called a picturesque Cathedral. Its great church does not occupy such a commanding position as Durham does, dominating over the city at its feet; its half-ruined west front is disappointing, after those of Lincoln and Peterborough; the reckless destruction of the monastic buildings, the cloisters, and gatehouses, gives a bareness to the precincts which contrasts painfully with the surroundings of Canterbury or Wells; and, finally, the loss of the chantry on the Green, and of the gallery or ancient connexion between the Bishop's palace and the west transept, has destroyed the continuity of structure which probably once formed an entrance-court similar to that which has been spared to its sister Cathedral at Peterborough. But, in spite of the ravages of age and neglect, the Cathedral has, for an architectural student, interests of the highest order; it has specimens of the rudest and of the richest Norman masonry; of Early English, almost coeval with that of Hugh the Burgundian at Lincoln; and it possesses examples of the work of the fourteenth century, which it is difficult to rival.

The foundress and first abbess of the monastery was Etheldreda, daughter of Anna, the ruler of East Anglia, and she is said to have been born in the year 630, at the little village of Exning, in Suffolk. When she was two-and-twenty years of age she married Joubert, an ealdorman, or prince, of the South Girvii, and the Isle of Ely was settled on her as a marriage-dower. Joubert did not live long; but died A.D. 655. The isle became her separate estate, and she settled herself in her little kingdom, and spent four years in strict retirement. At the end of this seclusion, when she must have been thirty-two years old, she married Ecgfrith, or Egfrid, of Northumbria, then a mere youth, but, after being his wife for twelve years, she became a nun in the monastery of Coldingham, where Ecgfrith's aunt was abbess. Her husband wished to carry her off from his aunt's custody, but she escaped, was miraculously saved from apprehension by his agents, and, after toilsome wanderings, reached Ely with two of her women, and in the year 673 she began to build a church, which she endowed with her estate.

The events connected with Etheldreda's second marriage maintained their hold on East Anglian sentiment, and some six hundred years after her death became the subjects of the eight pieces of sculpture which are the bases of the tabernacles which decorate the lantern piers, built by Alan de Walsingham in the time of Edward III., viz.:—

Her marriage with Ecgfrith.

Her taking the veil at Coldingham.

Her escape from Ecgfrith by means of a miraculous flood.

Her staff budding while she slept,—a repetition of the prodigy which converted the javelin of Romulus into the cornel tree of the Palatine.

Her election as Abbess of Ely.

Her death and burial.

Her translation.

A representation of a miracle wrought by her merits after she had been canonized.

In 870 the Danes destroyed Ely, but a college of seculars established themselves there, and remained undisturbed till the pacification of England by Edgar and the revival of a stricter monarchism by Dunstan, the inspirer of Edgar's wise policy. Ethelwold, Bishop of Winchester, and friend of Dunstan, repaired the monastery, settled in it a body of monks, and appointed an East Anglian, Brithnoth, as the first abbot.

In the year 1081 William I. appointed two of his connexions, Walkelin and Simeon, respectively to the See of Winchester and Abbacy of Ely. Simeon was an old man of eighty-seven, but nevertheless he laid the foundation of the church which now exists. Shortly after his brother began a similar undertaking at Winchester, and it is instructive to remark the similarity in the plans of the two structures. If any part of Ely Cathedral can be attributed to the Abbot, it is the basement storey of the eastern transept, which was originally built with continuous aisles, like the corresponding part of his brother's church.

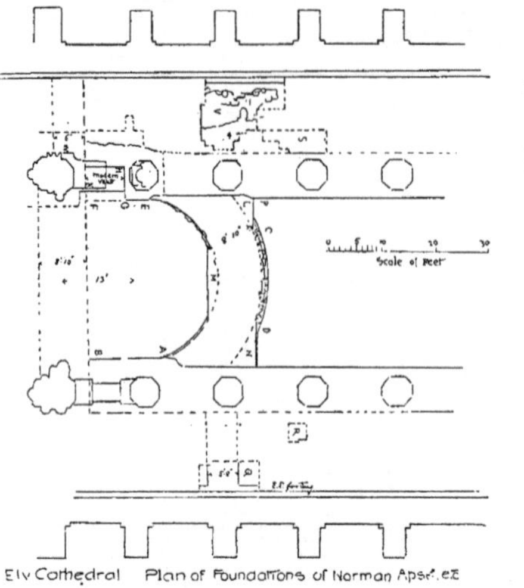

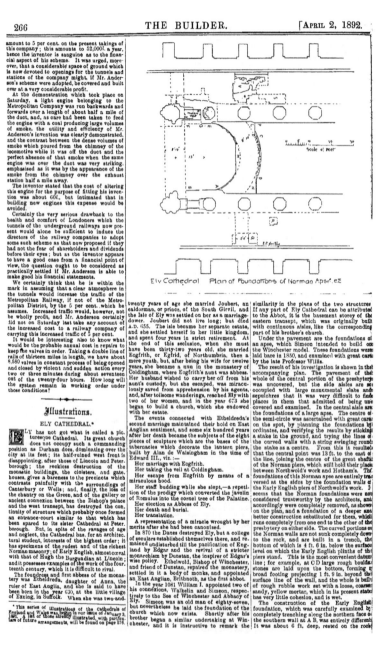

Ely Cathedral Plan of Foundations of Norman Apse, &c.

Under the pavement are the foundations of an apse, which Simeon intended to build on the Winchester model. These foundations were laid bare in 1850, and examined with great care by the late Professor Willis.

The result of his investigation is shown in the accompanying plan. The pavement of the whole of the central portion of the presbytery was uncovered, but the side aisles are so occupied with large monumental slabs and sepulchres that it was very difficult to find places in them that admitted of being uncovered and examined. In the central aisle are the foundations of a large apse. The centre of the semi-circle was ascertained with great care on the spot, by planning the foundations by ordinates, and verifying the results by sticking a stake in the ground, and trying the lines of the curved walls with a string swinging round the stake as a centre. From this it resulted that the central point was 13 ft. to the east of the line, joining the centre of the great shafts of the Norman piers, which still hold their place between Northwold's work and Hotham's. The foundations of this Norman apse are entirely traversed at the sides by the foundation walls of the Early English piers of Northwold's work. It seems that the Norman foundations were not considered trustworthy by the architects, and accordingly were completely removed, as shown on the plan, and a foundation of a deeper and better construction substituted for them, which runs completely from one end to the other of the presbytery on either side. The curved portions of the Norman walls are not sunk completely down to the rock, and are built in a trench, the bottom of which is 4 ft. 6 in. below the surface level on which the Early English plinths of the piers stand. This is the most convenient datum line; for example, at C D large rough boulder stones are laid upon the bottom, forming a broad footing projecting 1 ft. 9 in. beyond the surface line of the wall, and the whole is built of rough rubble work set with a loose, coarse, sandy, yellow mortar, which in its present state has very little cohesion, and is wet.

The construction of the Early English foundation, which was carefully examined by completely trenching along the northern face of the southern wall at A B, was entirely different. It was about 6 ft. deep, rested on the rock

* This series of illustrations of the Cathedrals of England and Wales was begun in our issue of January 3, 1891. A list of those already illustrated, with particulars of future arrangements, will be found on page 276.

Cathedrals of

No. 16. ELY.—Dr

h and Wales.

-RALD C. HORSLEY.

SKETCHES NEAR PETERBOROUGH.—By Mr. Arnold Mitchell, A.R.I.B.A.

ELY CATHEDRAL

GROUND PLAN

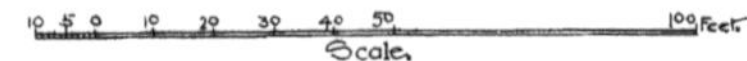

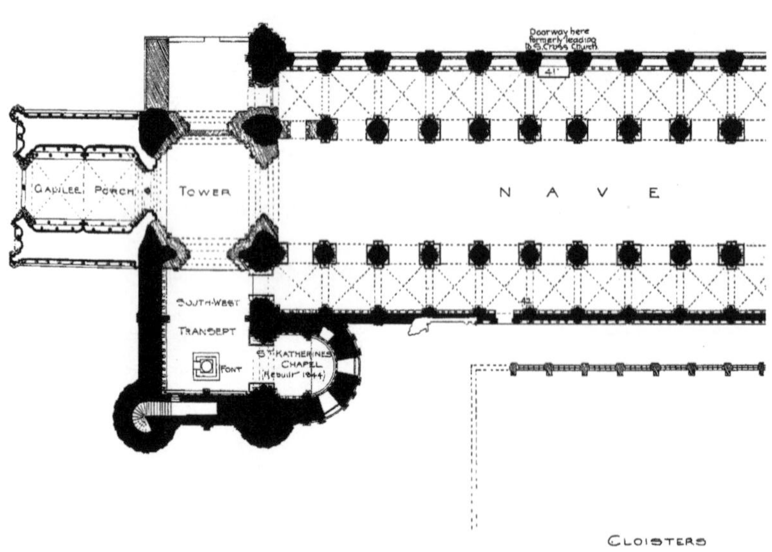

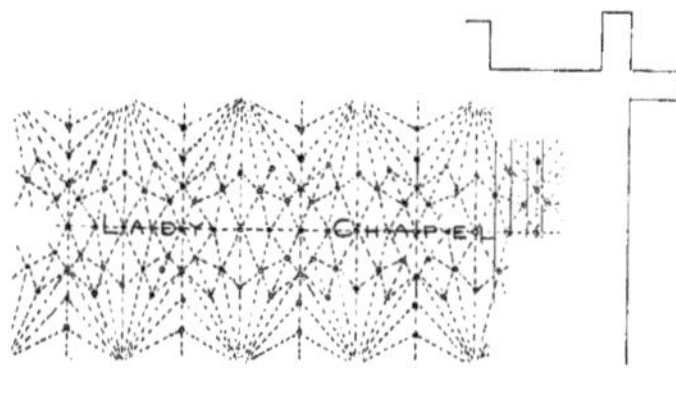

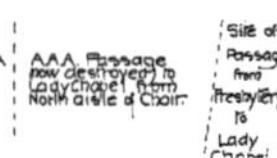

B.B. Foundations of Norman Apse.

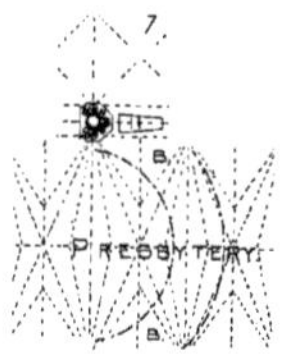

Monuments, etc.

1. Bishop Alcock.
2. " Laney.
3. Sir William Thorpe (?).
4. Part of Episcopal Chair.
5. Bishop Mawson.
6. " Simon Patrick.
7. Effigy.
8. Bishop Grey.
9. " Northwold.
10. S. Etheldreda's Shrine.
11. Bishop Wm of Kilkenny.
12. " Redman.
13. Chas. Fleetwood.
14. Bishop Fleetwood.
15. " Hotham. (slab).
16. Prior Crauden.
17. Bishop Moore.
18. " Butts.
19. " Greene.
20. " Allen.
21. Sir Mark Steward.
22. Sir Robert Steward.
23. Brass of Bishop Tyndall.
24. " " " Goodrick.
25. Bishop Heton.
26. " Wm de Luda.
27. " Barnet.
28. Lord Tiptoft & two wives.
29. Dean Steward (last Prior).
30. Bishop Gunning.
31. Bishop Hotham.
32. Canon Selwyn.
33. Norman stone from S. Mary's church.
34. Dr. Mill.
35. Bishop Allen.
36. Cardinal Luxemburg (Archbp. of Rouen).
37. Bishop Westo.
38. " Sparke.
39. Double Piscina.
40. Dean Caesar.
41. Bishop Woodford.
42. Ovin's Cross.
43. Matrix of brass of Alan de Walsingham.

Roland W. Paul mens. et delt. 1892.

PHOTO LITHO SPRAGUE & Cº 4 & 5 EAST HARDING STREET, FETTER LANE, E.C.

II

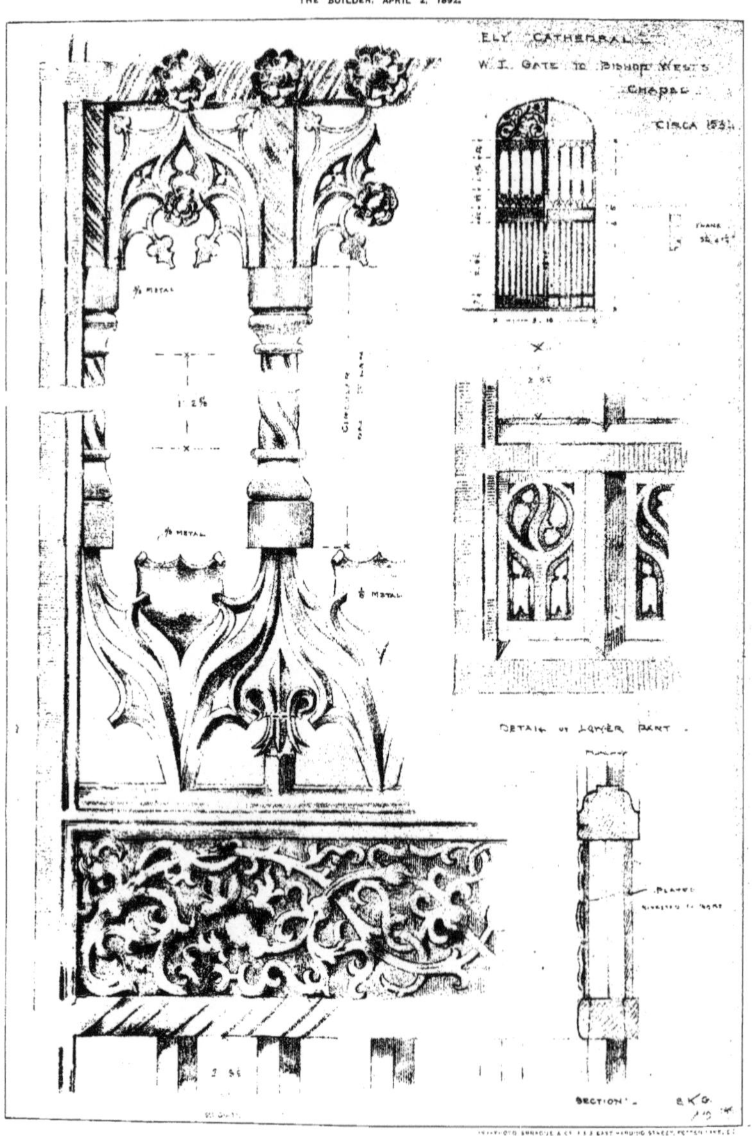

DRAWN BY MR. S. K. GREENSLADE.

DRAWN BY MR. S. K. GREENSLADE.

SKETCHES NEAR PETERBOROUGH.—By Mr. Arnold Mitchell, A.R.I.B.A.

was formed of a kind of concrete, and the face exposed slightly overhung its base. The southern face of this Early English wall in the side aisle was not accessible, because the pavement was wholly occupied by large monumental slabs. The corresponding wall at E F on the opposite side of the Presbytery was almost entirely destroyed by a vault which had been excavated in this foundation under Bishop Redman's monument for the reception of some unknown person, apparently in the seventeenth century. The extent of this rashly-constructed and injurious chamber is marked on the plan G H K. The outer corner of the semi-circular apse and the middle of its internal curvature were filled up by portions of foundation work as shown on the plan at L, M, N, so as to convert the whole into the foundation of a straight wall of the same thickness as the circular wall.

These outside portions were certainly constructed before the Early English foundation. A very careful examination of the junction of the two walls at the northern angle P, showed that these portions had been cut through to allow of the passage of the Early English work, and that they had not been subsequently applied against its face. The first, and most natural, conjecture was that these triangular pieces had been put in to form a foundation for some transverse steps or works required for the decoration of the Presbytery. But this, for other reasons, was very improbable, even if the nature of these foundations had not shown that they were subsequent additions to the Norman work, and previous to the Early English.

These portions were built with more care than the Norman already described, and with a somewhat deeper foundation; their faces also, when exposed, appeared nearly vertical.

A sub-wall of the same thickness as that just described, namely, 8 ft. 10 in., crossed the presbytery. Connecting the great Norman piers from F to B, as shown in the plan, the centre of the wall coinciding, as nearly as possible, with the centre of the existing prominent Norman shafts. No foundations of a wall forming a semi-circular aisle surrounding the apse as at Norwich and Gloucester could be found. For the purpose of verifying the existence of this aisle and laying it down with precision, search was made in the side aisles at the places indicated in the plan at Q R S and T (the only ones practicable), and the ground in the presbytery to the east of the apse was carefully sounded. No foundations, however, of such an external aisle wall could be discovered. The whole of the central space, with the exception of a few vaults, proved to be soft ground.

In the south-side aisle at Q, instead of a curved wall, a transverse wall, 5 ft. 8 in. in thickness appeared, as shown in the plan, nearly opposite to one of the Early English piers. The mortar and construction of this was similar to the added portions of foundation L, M, N, and its want of symmetrical position with the Early English piers also shows that it was not a bond wall connected with them. The ground at R was completely soft.

In the north-side aisle the removal of the pavement disclosed soft ground at S, in the track of the supposed side-aisle wall, and at T, an irregular mass of stones V, about 1 ft. below the pavement, that would not have belonged to any foundation, but might have been the remains of a causeway, or a mere undisturbed collection of rubbish. There was clearly no transverse wall here to correspond with that discovered on the south side at Q; but a transverse wall was found in this north aisle at W, opposite to, and in continuation of, the Norman bond wall of the great piers.

This foundation was 6 ft. in thickness and its eastern face coincided with the eastern face of the central wall, as shown in the plan. It was impossible to ascertain whether a similar wall had existed in the corresponding position in the south aisle, for the whole space there was occupied by gravestones.

The interpretation of these remains appears, on the whole, to be that the original plan of the great Norman apse was circular, that it had no aisle round its eastern extremity, and that before it was completed it was resolved to convert it into a square-ended presbytery, such as we now see at Oxford Cathedral and St. Cross.

Simeon's brother, Walkelin, raised his church at Winchester on a crypt; at Ely the rock was too near the surface, and it was not advisable to have such a sub-structure in a marsh country. With this exception, the plan adopted by the two brothers was very much the same.

The presbytery at Winchester was terminated by an apse with a circumscribing aisle. The great bond wall which connects the two existing Norman piers shows that a lofty arch was erected there, probably carrying an eastern gable, from which the circular apse would have projected; and in a similar manner the square-ended presbytery, which served as the Feretory of Etheldreda and her three relations, did actually project. The change of form was probably because this square form better suited the quadruple group of shrines than the semi-circular plan would have done. The great arch must have been flanked and buttressed by walls crossing the aisles, and hence the foundation W discovered in the north aisle, to which must have corresponded a similar one in the south aisle. Peterborough, Hereford, Norwich, and many other churches exhibit this construction. These side aisle walls are sometimes pierced with arches which give access to lateral apses, or to eastern aisles when they exist. In the present case no apse was traceable on the north side, and on the south the transverse wall to the east of the one under discussion seems to show that a chapel stood there in continuation of the south aisle. This was probably the lady chapel still kept on the south side of the church."

Simeon died November 20, 1093, and for seven years the temporalities of the Abbey were appropriated by William Rufus; but on August 5, 1100, Henry I. appointed Richard, a Norman monk, Abbot, who carried on the work begun by his predecessor, and had so far finished the church that on October 17, 1106, the second translation of the remains of Etheldreda and her sisters took place. The eastern part of the church must have then been complete, and, as the Norman choir included two compartments of the nave, a good deal of the western limb must have been built. Richard may, of course, have left behind him a completed structure, but, even if he did, the present west transept and tower belong to a later school of Norman architecture, and are the work of unknown builders, except in their upper ranges, which were added between 1174 and 1189 by the third Bishop, Ridel. Hervey, who succeeded Abbot Richard, became the fitst Bishop of Ely, and discharged himself and his successors from any obligation to support or repair the fabric of the church. Bishop Nigel, who came next, was a member of an able family, in whose hands the financial business of the kingdom had been for thirty years; he was one of the Barons of the Exchequer under Henry II., while his son sat in the same court as Treasurer; he was a politician exclusively rather than a builder of churches, so that the history of Ely's west transept must remain a problem till some new documentary evidence solves the puzzle.

Bishop Ridel's magnificent additions to the fabric of the Cathedral are characterised by the introduction of the pointed arch, and it would be difficult to find more graceful open arcades than those erected under his direction,—forerunners, it may be, of the complete Early English style adopted by Bishop Eustace in the west porch which he added between 1197 and 1220, during the reigns of Richard I., John, and Henry III. Bishop Ridel seems to have contributed to the fabric of the infirmary, which is now imbedded in the canons' dwelling-houses, for the details of its north door are nearly identical with those of his transept windows, and the style of the opening in the central cross wall represents the Transitional Romanesque or Norman style prevalent in his day. The only known representation of the stone reredos of the Norman Cathedral is a very rude diagram made by the late Mr. Essex in the last century, and it represents the central opening as a doorway with a segmental arch and ornamental tympanum, possessing a family likeness to the features of the north door of the infirmary.

The west porch is now only a fragment of a much loftier structure built by Bishop Eustace at the beginning of the thirteenth century on the foundations of an earlier one, which may have been an original entrance to the Norman church, and it has been brought into its present condition by neglect, and by repairs of which no detailed accounts exist, which might have supplied a clue to the Bishop's whole design.

In 1757 Mr. Essex reported this porch and the west transept to be so ruinous that they were not worth the cost of repair, and advised the Chapter to take them down and "apply the materials to the use of the other parts of the church." This recommendation was rejected, and the porch must have been repaired to some extent, because in 1796 Mr. James Wyatt stated that its restoration "will neither be difficult nor expensive," and he proposed to make good all defects with "composition stucco," to plaster the vault, and wash the whole with a stone-colour wash. He "restored" the west front, but seems to have left the north and south walls pretty much in the state in which he found them. The remains of the Bishop's work have a special historical value, because they must have been built very shortly after Hugh the Burgundian laid the foundation of his cathedral at Lincoln, and the works of the two Bishops are possibly the earliest examples we have of that new style which the Rev. G. Miller so happily named Early English in 1805. Bishop Hugh is said to have become Bishop of Lincoln in 1186, to have laid the foundation of the Cathedral in 1192, and to have died in 1200; and the main characteristic feature of the portion of the church he is believed to have left complete at his death is the double-wall arcade of the east transept, which consists of a range of trefoil arches, combined with an inner range of pointed ones, both being carried by shafts of equal height rising from the same bench-table. The same design is found in the Ely porch, but with such differences or extensions as unusually thick walls afford to the resources of a skilful architect. The vault is planned in two compartments, and the face of the wall below the wall rib of each takes the form of two tiers of arcades, separated by a flat vault. The upper tier has a single range of arches, but the lower is composed of two, and represents the Lincoln feature. At Lincoln, however, the two ranges are combined, and carried by slender columns rising from the same level, while at Ely they are set apart as far as the thickness of the wall allows, and carried by shafts, whose bases are disposed at two different levels. At Ely the front range consists of three trefoil arches in each compartment, rising from a bench or ground table, while the pointed arches behind them have bases set on a high broad plinth.

If Bishop Hugh laid the foundations of Lincoln Cathedral in 1192, Bishop Eustace must have begun his work at Ely at least five years later, since his episcopate was limited to the period 1197-1220; but whether he thought out for himself an independent design for his porch, or adopted the suggestions of the Lincoln choir, he proved himself to be a consummate artist, and everyone interested in the development of English art must regret that we can now see and study nothing but the wreck of the Bishop's conception of a fitting entrance to a Norman church.

Nine years after the death of Eustace, *i.e.*, in 1229, Hugh Northwold became Bishop of Ely, and built an Early English presbytery in continuation of the Norman one, an extension of the east arm of the building, which is one of the many examples we have of churches lengthened to ennoble the shrines of founders and benefactors. Although the cost of this new work was borne mainly by the Bishop, general contributions were sought in aid of the expenses entailed by it, and the sacrists' accounts show the amount of annual subscriptions paid to them from 1234 to 1250, inclusive.

As the new building was a continuation of an old one, the Bishop placed its architectural members within and without at the same levels as in the corresponding parts of Abbot Richard's Church, and so maintained the low outer wall of the triforium, and one compartment of this Early English triforium still remains on the south side of the church.

The new building was consecrated in 1252, and the whole fabric remained without important changes till 1322, when the old Norman tower in the middle of the church tumbled down and ruined the choir beneath it.

The catastrophe was not unexpected; but the Sacrist of the Monastery and the Bishop of the Diocese happened to possess unusual architectural taste, and, as they were prepared for the disaster, Alan de Walsingham at once began the construction of the lantern, and John Hotham, the Bishop, undertook to build the three compartments which still join it to Bishop Northwold's work.

In replacing the ruined Norman choir, Bishop Hotham preserved the interior levels of the great members of the composition; but the outer wall of his triforium is high, and furnished with lofty windows filled with the tracery of

Ely Cathedral The 'Prior's Door' at the NE. angle of Cloisters.

his period, and this seems to be the first introduction of the high outer triforium wall into this Cathedral. The open tracery of the high inner triforium is singularly delicate; but the symmetry of the whole design, and to some extent of Northwold's work also, is disturbed by the intrusion of a modern organ-case. In Hotham's day the floor of the Cathedral was not level, but rose gradually from the west end; the choir occupied two compartments of the nave; its stone rood-loft was in existence; and the floor of the presbytery was raised by two steps, which crossed the central aisle between the two eastern piers of the lantern.

In the south aisle of the Early English presbytery the Lady Chapel was standing over the fragmentary foundations noted in the plan of the abandoned Norman apse; but it was superseded by the magnificent structure which Bishop Montacute completed, A.D. 1373-4, and became the chapel of John Typtoft, Earl of Worcester.

Ely has fragments of the tombs of several of the bishops who helped to build the church, we can see and admire; and the chapels of West and Alcock are tolerably perfect. The tomb of Bishop De Ludd stands at the entrance of the old Lady Chapel, and belongs to that class which may be treated as open Ciboriæ, and of which Westminster Abbey possesses valuable specimens on the north side of the presbytery.

D. J. STEWART.*

In addition to the ground-plan and a general view of the Cathedral as far as the lantern from the south-east, showing the west tower and central lantern, we give illustrations of a bay of the interior of the west porch, and the ironwork,—very good of its kind,—from the late chapel of Bishop West, which terminates the south aisle of the presbytery eastward (see lithographs). For these we are indebted to Mr. S. K. Greenslade.† The doorway to the cloisters from the south aisle of the nave, known as the Prior's door, is a rich piece of Late Norman, and traces of another of similar character remain blocked near it, formerly communicating with the west aisle of the south transept. In the north aisle of the presbytery are remains of a stone chair, said to have been brought by Bishop Northwold from the Abbey of Bury St. Edmunds. A lion is represented holding the head of St. Edmund, and a sculptured panel at the foot of Northwold's effigy, hard by, gives the scene of the martyrdom. Amongst a good deal of florid detail, the arms and rebus of Bishop Alcock, on his chapel, are good examples of a mode of decoration common in Perpendicular times.

Ely Cathedral. Arms & Rebus of Bishop Alcock from his chapel at east end of N aisle of Presbytery

* Mr. Stewart wishes us to mention that the portion of his article giving the description of the old foundations is taken from his book "On the Architectural History of Ely Cathedral."

† We will give next week a drawing of the east end of the choir (exterior) by Mr. Greenslade, which we are not able to give in the present number.

SKETCHES NEAR PETERBOROUGH.

THESE two charming sheets of sketches by Mr. Arnold Mitchell, from churches and houses in the Peterborough neighbourhood, we give along with our illustrations of Ely Cathedral, as they are from nearly the same part of the country, and will be of interest to many of those who are also specially interested in Ely.

The subjects speak for themselves. As examples of refined and artistic architectural sketching our readers will agree that the drawings can hardly be too highly praised.

ARCHITECTURAL SOCIETIES.

EDINBURGH ARCHITECTURAL ASSOCIATION.—On the 24th ult., Mr. John James Burnet, of Glasgow, read a paper on "The Relative Position of the Architect and the Craftsman," to the members of the Edinburgh Architectural Association, in the Hall, 42, George-street. Mr. Burnet said he was of opinion that there never had been an age when the life of the individual was more governed by the practical necessities of the day, nor the demand upon him more clearly defined; and therefore never before was the architect's problem, if varied, more easy of enunciation. Defining what an architect of the present day was, he said he was first a master builder, having a thorough knowledge of the science of building and of the crafts engaged in building, keenly appreciative of the possibilities of each, and ingenious in their application to the needs of his fellow-men, and he was also the poet of modern necessity. If they accepted that definition then they might easily permit, or even recommend, the registration of master-builders, as, while all of them could not be architects, all architects worthy of the name would be proud to call themselves master-builders, and would be pleased that while on the one hand the public might be pro tected against the device of incompetent pro fessional men, the profession would also b protected against the degrading results of thei incompetency. Describing the function of a architect, he believed the most importan factor was that he should have the confiden of his clients, and that harmonious working o the craftsmen without which it was impossibl that the work could be satisfactorily accom plished. The modern architect must be pre pared to act, if his work was to have any of th grandeur and nobler qualities of master-build ing with the keenest and most detaile appreciation of the crafts, his particular wor being in their co-relation and the co-relation o the contributory arts. If the work was to b true architecture it must not only be suitable f its purpose, but it must be the work of one ma executed by craftsmen and artists each free to th development of his own art or craft, with th individual liberty of thought and action without which art in any form was impossible, leavin it only to the hand that guided him to his wor to restrain him in its execution. Passing o he said that they would agree with him th the handing of schedules to tradesmen, advertising for tenders indiscriminately was o of the greatest weaknesses of the present co tract system; and he concluded by throwin out a few suggestions, in the course of whic addressing himself first to the architects, said that they should dread no advance science, whether in economic production or form of demand; and that they should pe suade their clients against an indiscrimina issue of schedules, which made the skill craftsmen's work appear costly by contra with that of his less skilled brother. He a vised the craftsmen to study their craft a the theories which underlie its practice, that they might not fail to see its applicati to the work to be executed.—Mr. Burnet w accorded a hearty vote of thanks at the clo of his paper.

LEEDS ARCHITECTURAL SOCIETY: STE APPLIED TO CONSTRUCTION.—At their meeti in the Law Institute, Leeds, on the 28th ul members of the Leeds Architectural Socie listened to an interesting and practical lectu on "Steel as Applied to Construction," deliver by Professor Goodman, of the Engineering D partment of the Yorkshire College. Mr. W. Thorp presided. The lecturer gave a comparis between timber and cast-iron, wrought iron a steel, pointing out the irregularities and defec of cast-iron, and its low tensile strengt Wrought-iron, he showed, was considerab stronger, but very inferior to the b qualities of mild steel. By using iron and st any structure could put in much bigger spa and take up less head room. Steel, un recently made by the Siemens process, was n very largely made by the Basic process, a

:st-rate material was turned out by the various eel works in Leeds. The strength of each ıried from 30 to 32 tons per square inch, ıd stretched 25 per cent. before breaking. A uch stronger steel could be made, but it was :ittle, and not so reliable for structural purposes. Steel was liable to hidden defects, hich could only be detected by testing. It :quired more careful handling than wrought on, otherwise it might be very seriously amaged. Although from 30 to 50 per cent. tronger than iron, it was only about 10 to 12 er cent. stiffer, consequently steel girders leflected more in proportion than iron. The ollowing officers were elected for the ensuing ear:—President, Mr. G. B. Bulmer; vice-residents, Mr. H. B. Buckley and Mr. J. H. Greaves, and the past presidents of the society; ıon. treasurer, Mr. W. A. Hobson; hon. ibrariarn, Mr. J. Mettam; hon. secretary, Mr. W. Carley Hall; Council, Messrs. W. Watson,). H. Thornton, A. Neill, E. J. Dodgshun, Beevers, and Marshall; auditors, Messrs. F. Rusto and F. W. Bedford.

THE LONDON COUNTY COUNCIL.

The usual meeting of this Council was held n Tuesday afternoon last at Spring-gardens, he Chairman, Lord Rosebery, presiding.

Tenders were received for alterations, &c., at he Southwark Gas-meter Testing Station. They will be found amongst our lists of enders.

Finance.—The Finance Committee reported hat they estimated that it would be necesary to borrow the sum of 5,761,748*l.* during e present year, including 2,215,000*l.* to be nt to other bodies, the amount required for e Council's own purposes being 3,546,748*l.* he estimate was referred to the Parliamentary ommittee in connexion with the preparation f the Council's Money Bill, which will this ear be introduced as a private Bill, and not nder the auspices of the Government, as has itherto been the case. Some discussion arose ut of some proposals for loans to local odies, on the vexed question of the relative dvantages of the annuity and the instalment ystems of repayment; and complaint was nade of the action of the Treasury in vetoing a oan proposed to be made to the Shoreditch Library Commissioners, at the desire of the Commissioners and with the sanction of the Local Government Board, on the annuity principle of repayment. The Commissioners esired that system of repayment, it was tated, because, if the loan were repaid on the nstalment principle, it would leave them no noney wherewith to purchase books during ne next few years. As the Treasury had efused to sanction the loan being granted by ne County Council on the annuity principle, ne Library Commissioners had arranged to orrow the money from an insurance company. Eventually it was decided to raise the question t a future meeting of the Council.

The Easter Holidays.—On the motion of Mr. enn, it was resolved that the Council should djourn for the Easter Recess on Tuesday, April 12, and meet again on Tuesday, May 3.

Mr. Tate's Offer.—On the motion for the doption of the Corporate Property Committee, Mr. Evan Spicer moved

"That it be referred to the Corporate Property ommittee to report whether there is any land on the hames Embankments, or elsewhere, belonging to the ouncil which would be suitable to offer to the Government for the purpose of building the picture gallery ffered by Mr. Tate."

He reminded the Council that Mr. Tate had ffered pictures to the value of about 80,000*l.*, s well as a sum of 80,000*l.* for the erection of a uilding, if a site were provided. The Government had not been able to find a site, but he hought it was very important that London hould not lose the benefit of that munificent ffer. In answer to a question from the Chairman, it was understood that Mr. Spicer proosed that the Council should give a site for he proposed gallery.

Bars and Gates.—The Highways Committee resented a report relating to a reference made o the Committee during the last Council as to ne controlling authority of the gates in Harley-treet and Portland-place. It appears that the ates are under the control of the Commissioners f Her Majesty's Works, and the Committee eported that in their opinion no effective steps ould be taken for the removal of the gates until the Council should see fit to promote a Bill for the removal of all such obstructions in the streets of the metropolis. The Committee added that in due course they intended to submit a recommendation upon the subject.

Walworth-road Railway Station.—The same Committee's report also contained the following paragraph:—

"We have had before us a report by the Architect (ordered by the Sanitary and Special Purposes Committee before the transfer to us of the reference under this Act), as to the state of the Walworth-road Railway-station, and what steps had been taken by the company to remedy certain defects at the station. In July last the company was furnished with a statement of the Council's grounds of complaint and the relief or remedy to be claimed, and at the same time the company was asked what measures it would take to remedy the matters complained of. To this the company replied, in September, that plans would be prepared for the improvement of the station, and that the works would shortly be proceeded with. The Architect now reports that certain alterations which have been carried out, although improvements, do not in any way remedy the defects which he had previously reported, namely, amongst others (1) bad arrangement of ticket-office and absence of waiting-room in connection therewith; (2) bad arrangement and ventilation of urinals; (3) want of protection to the skylight over the passage-way from anything falling upon it from the railway, and (4) steepness of staircases. We are of opinion that measures should be taken for effecting improvements in these matters; and we therefore recommend—

'That an application under the Railway and Canal Traffic Acts be made to the Railway Commissioners for an order enjoining the London, Chatham, and Dover Railway Company to carry out such works at the Walworth-road station as will remedy the detective arrangements there.'"

The recommendation was agreed to without discussion.

Toole's Theatre.—The Theatres and Music Halls Committee's report contained the following paragraph and recommendation:—

"On July 23 last a draft notice was transmitted to the owner of Toole's Theatre, King William-street, Strand, containing certain requirements which were, in the opinion of the Council, necessary in order to render the premises safe for the reception of the public. We have since conferred with Mr. Toole's architect, and it appears that it would be quite impossible to carry out the principal requisitions within the limits of the present site, and further, that the Council of Charing-cross Hospital, who are the landlords, have passed a resolution to the effect that they had no premises they could lease to Mr. Tools for the extension of his theatre. Mr. Toole's lease has only three and a-half years more to run, with the option on either side of its being renewed for another seven years. We are of opinion that all the requirements mentioned in the draft notice are absolutely necessary, but it appears to be impossible to carry them out. The minor requisitions which could be done would, in our opinion, remedy matters but very little. Having fully considered the case in all its bearings, we recommend—

'That Mr. Toole be informed that, though the Council considers the present condition of the theatre unsatisfactory, it recognises that the conditions cannot be adequately altered, except by practical rebuilding, and the Council is, therefore, willing not to proceed with the requisitions contained in the draft notice, if Mr. Toole will give an assurance that neither he nor any assignee of his will renew the lease of the theatre when it terminates in 3½ years' time.'"

This led to some discussion, in the course of which Mr. E. Bowen Rowlands moved that the report be referred back. He said he thought the recommendation made by the Committee was most inconsistent and weak. Either the theatre was dangerous or it was not: if dangerous, it ought to be closed or pulled down. The Rev. Fleming Williams having seconded the amendment, Mr. Routledge, Mr. Russell, and Mr. Emden defended the Committee's report and recommendation as embodying the only course that could be taken without inflicting great hardship on Mr. Toole. Mr. Stockbridge supported the amendment, which was, however, lost, only 9 members voting for it.

The London Water Question.—Sir Thomas Farrer, upon the presentation of a report, with correspondence, dealing with the London Water (No. 1) Bill, stated that the constituents of the present Council had entirely approved the policy of the late Council on this subject. In proof of that he would quote from the *Economist* the statement that there had been a great fall in the price of the shares of the water companies. Between the date of the elections and March 19 the fall in the price of the shares had ranged from 2½ per cent. to 17½ per cent., and on the whole the average fall was from 8 per cent. to 10 per cent. That fall had been, as he thought, rightly attributed to the consciousness on the part of the companies of the fact that the population of London,—the voters of London,—approved of the Council's policy on the water question, and intended to follow it out. Still, the realisation of that policy was no easy matter, although they were in accordance with the views of their constituents. There was a great deal to be done, and one of the most important questions to be decided was—What were to be the future sources of supply? Upon that question the Special Committee of the Council were preparing evidence to lay before the Parliamentary Commission. He asked to be allowed to move a resolution to the effect that the Council adopted the policy of the late Council in regard to the water question, and approved of the London Water Bill.

The Chairman said he did not think he could take so large a resolution without having received previous notice of it; but, on the motion of Mr. C. Harrison, the report was received, and it was resolved to proceed with the Bill.

The Salary of the Deputy Chairman.—Mr. Elliott proposed, "That the resolution of November 7, 1889, fixing the salary of the Deputy-Chairman at 1,500*l.* a year, be rescinded." Mr. Fletcher seconded the motion.

Dr. Longstaff moved, as an amendment, "That as the Council has recently appointed a Committee to consider the organisation of the Council's business, it be referred to that Committee to consider and report as to the duties and emoluments (if any) of the Deputy-Chairman." Mr. Westacott seconded the amendment, which was lost by a large majority.

Mr. Thornton then moved a further amendment to the effect that the amount of the salary be £1,000 per annum in the future. Mr. Hubbard seconded the amendment, which was also lost by a majority of 16,—by 59 to 43.

The original resolution of Mr. Elliott was then submitted, and a division was taken, with the result that there were for the motion, 49; against, 53; majority against, 4.

After transacting other business, the Council adjourned.

BUILDERS' CLERKS' BENEVOLENT INSTITUTION:

FOURTEENTH ANNUAL DINNER.

The fourteenth annual dinner of this Institution was held on Wednesday evening last in the Venetian Saloon of the Holborn Restaurant, Mr. Colin G. Patrick, President, in the chair, supported by members and friends of the Institution to the number of 254, including Messrs. W. R. Freeman (John Mowlem & Co.), B. E. Nightingale, W. A. Colls (Colls & Sons), B. Hannen, jun. and E. C. Hannen (Holland & Hannen), Joseph Randall (Kirk & Randall), J. W. Hobbs, J.P. (J. W. Hobbs & Co., Ltd.), E. S. Rider (Rider & Son), H. D. White, Geo. Pearson, and J. G. Drower. The usual loyal and patriotic toasts having been honoured, Captain Ros responding for the "Army, Navy, and Auxiliary Forces,"

The Chairman proposed the toast of the evening, "The Builders' Clerks' Benevolent Institution." The Institution, as they were aware, was founded for the relief and the granting of temporary pensions to decayed builders' clerks, and for granting pensions to the widows of builders' clerks who might be left unprovided for. In addition, the Institution had within the last few years started an orphan fund, which had been found very useful in giving a start in life to the orphan children of builders' clerks. In order to make the charity as far-reaching as possible, the amount that could be paid to any one pensioner was limited. The Institution had now a sum of between 4,000*l.* and 5,000*l.* invested in Consols. Although he was glad to see that they had a most influential list of subscribers to the funds of the Institution, including not only builders, but merchants and others intimately connected with the building trade, he was sorry to find that there were a great many names absent from the list which ought to be there, and names of repute too. He believed that there were between 3,000 and 4,000 master builders in the London district. Now if they could only get a subscription of one guinea from each of those firms, what a splendid position the Institution would be in! He was speaking only of the builders, not of the merchants. Why, the little blue-book of the Institution ought to be as thick as "Laxton," and it ought to contain as many figures. It certainly could not be said that the building trade was overridden with charities. The master builders had their own excellent Builders' Benevolent Institution for those of their number who had been unfortunate; then there were the Provident Institution of Builders' Foremen and Clerks of Works, and their own Institution, so that he did not think it could be said that the building trade, as a trade, was overdone with charitable institutions. At any rate, he was quite sure that there was no society connected with the building trade which had greater claims to their support than the Builders' Clerks' Benevolent Institution. It was greatly to be wished, however, that a greater number of builders' clerks would interest themselves in the Institution. There were probably 10,000 builders' clerks in the London district, and, if they would each give but a small annual subscription, the Institution would not only be able to meet all demands upon it, but would probably have no further occasion to appeal for outside aid. In conclusion, he asked the company to drink with him "Prosperity and Success to the Builders' Clerks' Benevolent Institution."

The toast was very heartily received.

Mr. W. A. Colls next proposed "The Architects and Surveyors." The architects, he said, sometimes grumbled at the builders, and the surveyors did not always give them the prices they desired; nevertheless, the builders were very frequently much indebted to those gentlemen. With the toast he coupled the name of Mr. George Pearson, who briefly replied.

Mr. J. E. Drower proposed "The Builders," saying that as a surveyor he was able to bear testimony as to the excellent manner in which the principal builders of London carried out their contracts, turning out the best work they could for the money they got. But, greatly as he respected the builders, whenever he came to think of builders' clerks he always felt inclined to take off his hat and make a deep obeisance to them, because they were the gentlemen who were responsible for those remarkable documents called "Prime Cost Accounts," according to which any builder must infallibly go to ruin if he did not get 15*l*. per rod for brickwork; and yet the same gentlemen would price-out any number of rods at 12*l*. 10s.! How that came about was a problem which he regarded as insoluble. With the toast he had much pleasure in coupling the name of Mr. Joseph Randall, of the well-known firm of Kirk and Randall.

Mr. Randall, in responding, expressed his acknowledgments of the appreciative words which had been uttered by Mr. Drower regarding the London builders.

Mr. W. R. Freeman proposed "The Merchants, to whom, he said, the Institution was much indebted for generous support. He paid a high tribute to the good qualities of builders' merchants, observing that, no matter how sorely those gentlemen were tried, they were always amiable and obliging and ready to do the best for their customers. He thought that in many cases difficulties could be smoothed over if the merchants and dealers in specialties could more often be brought in direct contact with the architects. At present the builder had not always an enviable position between architect and merchant. With the toast he had great pleasure in coupling the name of Mr. J. Nicholls, of the firm of Nicholls & Clarke.

Mr. Nicholls briefly replied.

The other toasts were "The Past Presidents" (proposed by Mr. Edwin Brooks, Treasurer of the Institution, and coupled with the name of Mr. Benjamin Hannen, jun., who was President last year); "The President" (proposed by Mr. J. W. Hobbs): and "The Visitors" (proposed by Mr. B. E. Nightingale, and responded to by Mr. F. Dashwood, Secretary of the Clerks of Works' Association).

During the evening, subscriptions and donations to the amount of 314*l*. 9s. 6d. were announced by the Secretary (Mr. H. J. Wheatley). This sum included 26*l*. 5s. given by the President, and 10*l*. 10s. given by the Worshipful Company of Carpenters, the total of the President's list alone being 211*l*.

WORKS OF REFERENCE.

"The City of London Directory for 1892" (London: W. H. & L. Collingridge, *City Press* office), presents, in this its twenty-second annual issue, all its old excellent features and many new ones, and we can speak from experience as to the reliability and exactness of its information relating to the City and City institutions. An excellent coloured map of the City, to a large scale, accompanies the volume, but, as we have said before, the usefulness of this map would be enhanced if it were mounted on linen in the same manner as the map in the "Post Office London Directory."

"The Newspaper Press Directory" for 1892 (London: C. Mitchell & Co., Red Lion-court, Fleet-street) is the forty-seventh issue of what is the oldest book of reference of its kind. Though it has now many competitors, it more than holds its own, and the present issue contains many useful features. Besides a revised alphabetical list of the newspapers, periodicals, and magazines of the United Kingdom, there is a supplement relating to the press of Australasia, South Africa, and India, while particulars are given of the principal journals of all foreign countries. The notes of recent cases as to the law relating to the press, by Mr. W. F. Finlason, chief of the law reporting department of the *Times*, will be found very useful. A new feature of some interest is occupied with portraits and memoirs of deceased pressmen of distinction.

"Willing's (late May's) British and Irish Press Guide" (London: Willing & Co., 162, Piccadilly) is the nineteenth annual issue of a very compact and well-arranged handbook and directory for advertisers and readers.

"Shelley & Co.'s Complete Press Directory for 1892" (London: Shelley & Co., 38, Gracechurch-street) is the sixth appearance of the work, a useful feature of which is the summary of leading newspaper law cases for the year 1891.

"The Garden Oracle and Illustrated Floricultural Year-book, 1892" (London: *Gardeners' Magazine* office, 4, Ave Maria-lane) appears this year in a new dress, and has been considerably enlarged. The "Oracle" was ably and successfully conducted for thirty-three years by the late Mr. Shirley Hibberd, the Editor of the *Gardeners' Magazine*, and the present issue has been compiled by Mr. Hibberd's successor in the editorial chair. It is full of useful information, and among the new features is a section devoted to the enumeration and brief description of the public parks and gardens of the country, but this is by no means complete. Glancing at it haphazard, we find, for example, Exeter and Southampton absent from the list of towns having public parks and gardens. This section will no doubt be made more complete in future issues of the work.

Correspondence.

To the Editor of THE BUILDER.

THE LINCOLN LIBRARY QUESTION.

SIR,—I have just read with painful interest Mr. Somers Clarke's letter about the "restoration" proposed at Lincoln. As an outsider, being a clergyman, unconnected with the S. P. A. B., or, in fact, any society of the kind, I venture to ask your leave to endorse every word of his letter. It is more than lamentable,—it is monstrous, that some semi-public, semi-private bodies, like the chapters of Lincoln and Westminster, the governing fellows of Pembroke College, Cambridge, the vicar and churchwardens of St. Helen's or St. Stephen's, should have the power to do what they have done, or contemplate doing. We want a law like that of France as to "national monuments."

March 26, 1892. W. J. LOFTIE.

SIR,—I venture to think that in Mr. Somers Clarke's excellent letter of last week he has not done full justice to the late Sir Gilbert Scott. I have it in my mind that when Sir Gilbert Scott was engaged in the restoration of Ripon Cathedral some thirty years or so ago, he was called on to take down the Lady-loft, now the Library, an addition of the fourteenth century to the early apsidal chapel, which forms the Chapter-house and sacristry on the south side of the choir, in order that this chapel might be restored to its supposed original condition.

This, Sir Gilbert Scott, to his great honour and credit, declined to do, and we may, therefore, reasonably assume that Sir Gilbert Scott would have acted at Lincoln as he did at Ripon, and would have been on the side of preservation.

CHARLES J. FERGUSON.

BUILDING-STONES IN IRELAND.

SIR,—The article on this subject in the *Builder* of March 26 gives some condensed information that it may be worth some man's while to pigeon-hole as a geological memorandum, but for practical or commercial considerations it is of little value to anyone. The game of seeking most of the stones set out in the list is not worth the candle, and never will be. As to the kindly bit of sentiment that winds up the article, we almost inevitably look when Ireland or Irish industries are brought up for a little poetic touch about "long-faded glories," &c., and "decay of arts and industries" and their "revival," which practical people, who are not professional patriots or poets, in Ireland know had never any existence to be decayed from. "Surely," says the sanguine writer, "such a state of things in importation of stone will not exist much longer."

It has so existed from very early times, and is likely to exist. The hewn stone in the vas majority of the Mediæval buildings in Irelan is an English oolite, and we know the distric of its source from records of cargoes occa sionally impounded at Bristol, and it is un mistakeably the same species of stone as i found at Glastonbury and Montacute. It i nearly universal in Ireland wherever ston could be water-borne, and there are not many places that could not be reached by water carriage from the sea-board *viâ* rivers, lakes and creeks. It is the ancient stone of th Dublin Cathedrals and Castle, and of suc ancient churches as there are remains of. I is the stone of Tintern Abbey, in the extrem south-east, in Wexford; of Altrassel Abbey, in Tipperary (close to abundant granite and lime stone); of the French Abbey of Mellifont mentioned in the article, lying beside th Drogheda limestone quarries, in the midlan county of Louth; and is found far north at Gre Abbey, lying close by those sandstone quarrie of Scrabob, county Down, commended by th article, and in hundreds of the ancient building that lie between these places. The facilities o water-carriage, or the familiarity of Englis builders with English stone, does not accoun altogether for this nearly universal employmen of a Somerset oolite.

People who write magnificently about th development of Irish mines and minerals a apt to leave out of sight the peculiarly con torted and fire-affected geological system o Ireland, and form their notions on the business like and well-behaved strata, reliable to b found in their proper place when looked for, i England. As to your Irish stone,—you a rarely sure where you can get at it, or whe found how you will get it out of the quarry, what it will be like to work when you get it or how at any reasonable cost you can get to your building. In a great number of th localities indicated in the *Builder* article, industry of stone raising ever did exist or eve will be started. Here and there, in century, a quarry has been opened get a few quoin-stones and window-sil for the big plain house the Irish countr gentleman used to build. Now, the countr gentleman of Ireland builds no house, an local demand for the local stone there neve will be. But lately I was architect of a cu stone mansion for an Irish country squire, about the last of his race likely to build a Irish mansion,—and we proceeded hopefully t build that house from a quarry of promisin sandstone three miles from the house. It one indicated in the *Builder* article. It w not long until, to my disappointment, it w proved that Portland stone shipped to Dubli trans-shipped across that city, carried rail 87 miles, and carted 5 miles w much more economical! Flagstones referred to as near this same district, a also at Carlow and elsewhere. So th are plenty of flagstones, but who wants the or is ever likely to want them, now? T Avigna quarries in the Leitrim coal-fields, instance, will find you big flags,—cheap flags,—say for a yard super., 2s. 3d.; carriage to Dublin and cartage, say 2s. more, and you have it laid in Dublin certainly not less than 6s. per superficial ya You have then a rough kind of floor at be Who is likely to want such flags, when beautiful granolithic cement floor can be l for 2s. 6d. or 3s. per yard? Carlow flags spoken of as worth consideration. W Carlow flags of old Dublin houses are one the horrors of the basements of that c black, moist, and unsanitary, and they being rooted out everywhere, to be replaced concrete or dry tiles. In fact, with the devel ment of the cement industry, the day of f stones is over. For no useful purpose tha can see will flags be ever quarried in Irel again.

Take, again, as an example, under head "*Dublin*," a stone described approvingly as the "arenacious rocks belonging to the c boniferous system such as found in the Wi mill Quarry, Rathgar." This once prevail stone, locally known as "the Calk," has b the curse of Dublin, and chief cause of ruinous condition century after century. now utterly discredited and unmarketable, cept to mend roads with, for which purpose about the very worst stone to be found in British Isles. It is a hard, indurated d which softens and reverts to its ancient co tion of mud if it gets water enough. It to be universally used for foundations. S e Vartry water supply came into Dublin, and l lower Dublin became water-logged from dis- e of its thousands of pumps, the Calk foun- ations have universally softened and rotted, d the houses have settled and cracked, and any totter towards their doom. It is a vile one in walls, as it "sweats" in Irish climate. oncrete is universal in new foundations; new alls are never built of this Calk stone, and as "industry" it will never be heard of again.

Where is the chance of any practical develop- ent of Irish sandstone industries by people in eir senses?—of, say, such folly as bringing om the interior of the country by expensive ilway carriage hard, unworkable, uncertain ones at great cost, while at most places in ach of the seaboard excellent Dumfries stone, hich stands the Irish climate well, can be laid own at 2s. per cubic foot?

There are exceptions, but they are very few, d should be distinguished as alone worth the hile of practical people to catalogue them. It annot be said that I have a preference person- lly for "foreign" stone. Some of the buildings oted in the *Builder* are works of mine where prevailed in forcing in the native stone. I lieve I was the first person thirty years ago to ggest the trial of Irish limestone in an impor- nt front in a Dublin street. It would, of course, ave developed in time without my patronage, at limestone is now *the* building-stone of ublin—in my opinion the first of all building- ones in the British Islands. What it is pable of is witnessed in the last important at stone building of Dublin, the Ulster Bank, College-green. There is, if you will, a stone orth cataloguing and developing, but there is o fear of its being an industry wanting foster- g care. It can take care of itself. Granites re good stones, but they are not neglected ther, and require no sentiment wasted on em. The sandstone of Mount Charles uarries is worth attention. Sir Thomas Deane to be credited with forcing this stone into otice. Mount Charles quarries are on the sea- oard of Donegal. Magnificent specimens of one are being now raised and shipped. This one has, probably, a future before it, both in eland and other parts of the world.

But there remains a strange stone with a ture, I think, which lies unknown and un- uarried and utterly neglected, the Steatite of onegal, not alluded to in the *Builder* notice. was lately my experience to find this curious ne, in the course of a restoration, as being inly used in the out-of-way ancient Cathedral St. Adamnan, Raphoe. It is a thirteenth ntury building, and its cut stone remains as arp as if it were cut yesterday or cast in onze, and yet you may cut it with a car- nter's hand-saw or carve it with your pocket- ife. It is fire-proof, and called by the tives, Cam stones, and only used by them in dern times when they want to line a lime- n. Then they strip the top of a quarry and ke out what is wanted and cover it up again. ey cut it with a carpenter's axe. It is ad- irably adapted for lining furnaces, fire-grates, tchen ranges, &c. You select a "seasoned" one, cut it with your hand-saw to any size d shape, and "there you are." The dust om the saw, like French chalk, seems adapted make an asbestos paint with silicate. bestos is found in layers in the quarry. Soft it is, the stone can be polished, and thus sembles Lizard Serpentine.

I am glad to say I believe I have aroused ough spirit to have these quarrels re-opened supply the store required for the restoration the small cathedral. Its locality—but five iles from railway carriage—makes its develop- ent not hopeless. I believe, with the excep- ons I have noted, the laments of the *Builder's* ndly reviewer over the long list of neglected ish stones are thrown away.

A specimen of the limestone, which I do not ink I unfairly vaunt, may be seen in a great onolithic cross at Lee Church, Blackheath.

THOMAS DREW, F.R.I.B.A.

*** Mr. Drew has apparently forgotten the bject of the article in our columns alluded to. e expressly wrote on the "Building *Sand- ones* of Ireland," and not on Irish building- ones generally, as our correspondent's tter seems to imply. Moreover, we dis- nctly stated that the article treated not ly of the sandstones at present raised, but of ose of historic interest and of deposits as yet touched. If we had alluded merely to the ish sandstones at present quarried, the list ven would have been considerably curtailed. e are perfectly aware of the fact that English and Scotch stone is largely used in Ireland, and have more than once written on the subject in these columns; indeed, the article under notice stated as much, and that is one of the reasons why we said that, with such an abundance of good stone at hand, it was remarkable that so much was imported. That the Irish sandstone industry has declined in importance is evident *inter alia* from the quarries at present abandoned. Mr. Drew's observations on Irish mines and minerals and steatite, like many of the other remarks in his letter, are irrelevant to the subject of the article.—ED.

SIR,—With reference to the very interesting article upon the above in the *Builder* of this date (perhaps the more interesting to those of us who are either Irishmen or directly connected or concerned with the Emerald Isle), I may add that, not only did the Scotch workmen, when building Muchross Abbey, Killarney, about forty years since, according to Mr. Kinahan, ignore the excellent stone of the neighbourhood, and import sandstone from Leicester, but I noticed when visiting the Nunnery at Kenmare (not far from Killarney) a few years since, the dressings of that establishment were constructed from Bath stone, notwithstanding the fact that they have, according to Mr. Kinahan, a very excellent stone close at hand. It was not as though there was any apparent benefit in thus importing stone from practically the heart of England to the far West of Ireland, but it was rather a case of going farther and faring worse, as the stone has already begun to decay considerably.

Their reason for doing this was, probably, the immediate saving in the cost of manipulation, but, as I should imagine they would have now to restore these decayed portions, instead of their submitting themselves to the first and only expense, the expenses will now be continuous.

I. of Portland, SEMI-HIBERNIAN.
March 26, 1892.

RIPON CEMETERY COMPETITION.

SIR,—The frame of mind in which promoters of competitons sit down to draw up their instructions to architects is difficult to realise. Apparently, if they have any common-sense to start with, they cast it all to the winds. The Corporation of the city of Ripon have, perhaps, "beaten the record" in this respect. They made up their minds to have a new cemetery,—of course they did not make up their minds themselves, the Government did that for them,—and, according to a wise law, all Burial Board works must be put up to public competition. I was induced by an advertisement in your paper to invest ten shillings in the purchase of their instructions for the same, and received for my money a plan of the ground and two sheets of (restrictions rather than) instructions, all printed on splendid paper, in very good style, but the purport of the documents failed to fulfil the augury of their presentment.

In the first place, the ground, about 4½ acres, is to be laid out, at a cost of not more than 200*l.*, which sum is to pay for all roads and footpaths, levelling, planting, and the superintendence of these works. For such a design, provided the Corporation obtain a tender to do the work for a sum not exceeding the specified amount, including the commission, they offer a premium of 10*l.* (the secondary premiums need not be considered); they do not bind themselves to accept any design, or to employ the designer; but, if the last-named event result, he is to prepare "all sketches for approval," to write "full and complete specifications," to make "working and detail drawings and estimates," to "superintend the works as landscape gardener," and give "all attendances on the Corporation." As 5 per cent. on 200*l.* comes to 10*l.*, and the premium "merges" into the commission, it is not clear that the "successful" man gets anything for doing the long list of work enumerated; apparently, he had better leave it alone severely, and yield himself to the delight of spending the premium only, or he will find that, by a wonderful bit of prestidigitation, somewhat resembling the three-card trick, the same sum covers both—in the right hand it is a premium; in the left hand it is a commission. The Corporation will employ an assessor (at what fee?), but they do not undertake to abide by his report: they put the pot on the fire, but they take care that it shall never boil. For this lovely 10*l.* they will not allow any one to send in more than "one alternative scheme"—that is, two designs in all! To deprive the designer of all hope of other remuneration, the Corporation announce that they will themselves make the drains and boundary walls—that is to say, the easy and remunerative work is to be given perhaps to a salaried official, or to some other favoured individual—anything, in short, rather than pay the designer for his work. But, they have one trait of munificence: any one may inspect the site, free of charge.

In the second place, they offer a premium of 20*l.* for designs for a chapel, a lodge, front boundary wall (length indefinite) and entrance gates, to cost collectively 1,670*l.* The usual commission on this stupendous amount must form in the eyes of the Corporation, a veritable Golconda—so rigorously is it guarded in the instructions. The stretchers are to be 30 in. by 20 in.,—no other size will do,—surely an unnecessary annoyance to would-be competitors if they have others in stock! No framed or glazed drawings; all drawings are to be black and white. (Why has it come to be the rule that *plans* may not be coloured in competitions? The reasons against colouring elevations and sections are cogent enough; but colour is necessary to help unpractised eyes to read plans.) You may send perspectives. All the restrictions and limitations described for the laying-out designs are repeated in this.

Is this the way that an enlightened community expects to get good service? Architects must either be too wealthy to need any payment for work done, or so poor that they must accept any dole that is offered. Where is the commonsense of the Corporation of Ripon? IPSISSIMA.
March 28, 1892.

JAPANESE ART.

SIR,—I think Mr. Piggott's discourse on Japanese art, referred to in your number of March 19, is, in one particular, not absolutely correct.

I have a Japanese cabinet in which the landscape on the door panels *is* obviously continued from one panel to the other, as if it had passed under the stiles.

The cabinet was brought from Japan for my father, in one of his own ships, about twenty-five years ago, and there is no doubt as to its being genuine Japanese. NORMAN WIGHT.
Santa Catalina, Boscombe Park, Bournemouth,
March 26, 1892.

VARNISH.

SIR,—In reply to the letter of "Inquirer" (page 231 *ante*), No reliable varnish for the purpose he requires is made. The best method is to get up the work in enamel—*i.e.*, varnish colour—and Blundell, Spence, & Co., Hull, I believe, supply the best ready-made article; but painters usually make their own enamels. L.

The Student's Column.

WARMING BUILDINGS BY HOT WATER.
XIV.

BOILERS.

WE have now practically come to an end of those subjects which exclusively apply to horticultural works. With boilers, the subject of this paper, and appliances which follow, no distinction can or need be made, as, even with the ordinary description of hot-water pipe that is so regularly seen in glass-houses, there is a large demand for identically the same article in heating buildings, particularly church work, warehouses, &c. If there is a distinction at all in boilers, then it is that the somewhat recent pattern upright cylindrical boiler is better suited than some of the other patterns, the saddle for instance, for withstanding the great strain or pressure that exists when an apparatus extends up several floors of a high building. It is generally understood that the saddle and similar shapes are likely to bulge if subjected to heavy pressure. This pressure, and its attendant features, will be fully referred to presently.

Within the scope of these articles it will be impossible to do more than treat the subject briefly, as will be understood. The first question is as to what constitutes a good boiler. To judge by the great number of patterns already introduced and the regular and frequent advent of new designs, it might be thought that the question had never been satisfactorily settled. Of course the primary object sought to be attained is to get the greatest possible effect from a given quantity of fuel, but in doing this there are other features that must not be wholly sacrificed. The heating surfaces of a boiler are divided into two kinds, viz., direct and indirect, which are really those surfaces which are directly against and opposite the fire, and those that are not, but are in flues. Direct heating surface is the most useful in about the proportion of three to one, that is to say, one foot of direct heating surface will heat the water as effectively as 3 ft. of flue surface. This is the rule usually laid down in books relating to this subject; but either it is intended only to apply to what we may term primary flues,—that is, the flues that receive the flame or heated products immediately they leave the furnace,—or the figures were arrived at before the more complex forms of boilers were introduced. The flue-heating surfaces that receive the heat directly it leaves the fire-box doubtless bear the value just attributed to them; but second and third flues do not. Third flues are now quite common (as fig. 53),

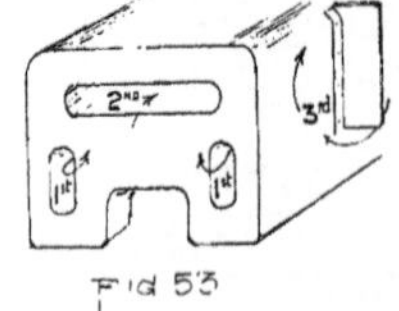

FIG 53

if the chimney draught is sufficient, and the works require a powerful boiler occupying small space. It would be somewhat exceptional for a boiler of this description to be used in private horticultural works, as the chimneys are usually very short, and the draught proportionately poor. This does not apply, however, to professional growers, who do not study whether a high chimney is unsightly or not, so long as they gain efficiency.

It is somewhat evident that the old pattern saddle-boiler, fig. 54, has fulfilled the require-

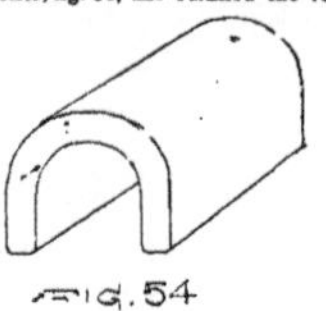

FIG. 54

ments that are at present considered necessary in a good boiler, so far as our knowledge of the subject extends at present, for, notwithstanding its age, it is still in great demand, and the majority of new patterns follow it in some way or another, as a glance at any maker's list will show.

The particular feature to be aimed at in a boiler is, as just stated, to benefit to the utmost extent by the direct heat from the glowing fuel. If the fire is in an incandescent state we have the effect of the glowing fuel lying against the boiler plates, and which we might say are absorbing the heat; and we have radiated heat acting against all those surfaces which are opposite to, or face the fire so to speak. This is best effected by making the boiler to envelope the fire, to encompass it, and a boiler made many years ago, much resembling a large inverted basin, was very effective in this way, although leaving much to be desired in other directions. The "terminal end" saddle boiler has the advantage referred to, without the disadvantages. It will be seen how much less effective a boiler can be made by unskilled stoking, by the fact that unless the fuel be kept bright at top, that is to say the fire not too heavily fed, we lose the effect of radiant heat, which cannot pass through the mass of black coal or coke that overlays the bright fuel, and a considerable lessening of results must ensue. Those forms of boilers that have top feeders are apt to induce careless stoking, if the ttendant is so inclined.

With the direct heating surfaces of boilers we may consider that those parts over the source of heat are more effective than those that come at the side of a source of heat, in the same way that we should expect a kettle to boil more quickly if placed over a fire than if placed at the side of the fire. This difference in the value of heating surfaces is balanced, however, by the fact that the top and most effective surface of the fuel is not always as bright and active as the rest, owing to each fresh charge deadening it for the time being.

With flue surfaces we have quite a different action so far as the application of heat is concerned, by the fact that we have neither radiant heat nor the contact of glowing fuel to rely upon, and the absence of these two sources of intense heat goes far to make the effectiveness of these surfaces much less. In addition to this, we seldom have top-flue surfaces, that is a flue bounded on the top by a heating surface (having, of course, water on the other side of it). We do not get this with the saddle or any, what we may call common, form of boiler, only when a flue is carried through the boiler itself, as fig. 55. From this it will be seen that

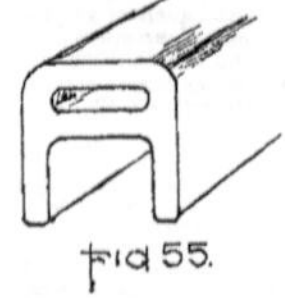

FIG 55.

flue surfaces are at a special disadvantage in not experiencing any of the direct results of the fire heat, and then only having side or vertical surfaces to be acted upon or surfaces which come *beneath* the source of heat, and which are, as a rule, practically useless. By surfaces beneath the source of heat is meant those like the top of a saddle-boiler, which generally has a flue-way made over it. A surface beneath flame or heated gases will always be found nearly, if not quite, valueless for practical purposes, and in addition to this it so readily gets a coat of dust or fine ash upon it, that, by its poor heat-conductive properties, quite completes its uselessness. In the majority of modern boilers, especially (strange to say) those that are held to be very powerful, the illustrations show the brickwork brought right tight on to the boiler-top, and this surface in question is made no use of whatever except to carry building material.

We now have to consider the actual value of heating surfaces. Of course, a hot-water engineer does not measure up and by calculation determine the size of the boiler by allowing so much heating surface to so much pipe. The usual plan is to study a boilermaker's list, where the dimensions of boilers are given, and their capability to deal with certain quantities of pipe under normal conditions plainly stated. Notwithstanding this, however, the question of heating-surface values ought to be treated, as no papers on these works are considered complete otherwise, and, further than this, the writer has to point out one or two things that are both important and interesting.

The first thing to be observed is that the values of boilers given in nearly all makers' lists are theoretical and not practical values, and if an engineer buys a boiler listed as being capable of heating, say, 500 ft. of pipe, and puts it to heat this quantity, or even 450 ft. of pipe, he will experience a disappointment, to say the least. It must not be thought that this is a deception on the makers' part, but they are a little to blame. It came about in this way:—Hood, who we have referred to, and whose rule the majority of boiler-makers have followed in compiling their lists, settled that one square foot of direct heating surface was capable of heating 50 ft. of 4-in. pipe, and for flue surface three times the area should be allowed (that is, 3 square feet of flue surface to 50 ft. of 4-in. pipe). By means of a rule like this, it was easy enough to arrive at the heating power of certair sized boilers. By measuring the surface tha bounded the fire-box, and measuring the cute: surface which would have heat conducted to i by flues, the quantity of pipe this boiler woulc heat was known in a few minutes.

This method of calculating the power of boiler was, we may assume, only applicable t the saddle and older forms of boilers, and th method had a very desirable degree of cer tainty attending it. The fault, however, wa that Hood, notwithstanding every care an allowance he could think of, put too high value upon the heating surfaces in questio and although a boiler constructed upon thes lines will actually heat the quantity of pir given, it will only do so by forced firing, an great care in stoking and attention. For ord nary practical purposes it has been settled th the allowance is insufficient, and conducive ill results.

This was not discovered until most of tl boiler-makers had compiled their lists upon and the remedy adopted is to issue a little sl or notice in each catalogue, which general runs as follows:—"The heating powers given

GENERAL BUILDING NEWS.

A PROPOSED CATTLE MART FOR WIGAN. — The itreets Committee of the Wigan Corporation had efore them on the 23rd ult. the details of a scheme or a proposed cattle mart for the town and district. The author of the scheme is Mr. Thomas Johnson, ngineer, Wigan, who has had plans prepared by Messrs. Maxwell & Tuke, architects, Manchester. The site for the mart, which will be situated in Prescott-street, has a frontage of 140 yards, and overs an area of 15,000 yards. Rising from Prescott-street there will be buildings for the accommodation of sheep, cattle, and pigs. The principal ntrance by road will be from Prescott-street, and t the gate there will be an hotel, which will occupy ne side of the entrance passage, the other side eing occupied by various other places. At the end f the passage there is a toll office, beyond which is he parade ground, coming direct from the railway wharf. Beyond the parade ground are more ouses for the storage of animals, while nearer he railway are stores for meat, and two laughter-houses. The slaughter-houses will be o constructed that 200 cattle and 600 sheep an be slaughtered a day, and by means of verhead rails the carcases can be sent from the tores to the railway trucks. There are also four ale rings, and provision is made for the conducting f a branch banking business on the spot. The ccommodation for storing and keeping cattle rovides for the housing of 800 cattle and 5,000 heep and smaller animals. All the internal fittings re to be of iron, and the draining has, it is said, een carefully considered. The floors of the various uildings will be of concrete, and the inside walls vill be lined with enamel bricks. The whole place vill be lighted by a continuous line of skylights aised so as to provide ventilation. The mart will e connected with the Lancashire and Yorkshire Railway and the North-Western Railway. At the ancashire and Yorkshire it is proposed to construct siding and railway wharf.

HIGHER GRADE SCHOOL, PORTSMOUTH. — The Higher Grade School for boys, Portsmouth, which as frontages of about 200 ft. and 100 ft. respectively in Victoria and Fawcett-roads, is rapidly pproaching completion. The main building is onstructed of brick, from the Rowland's Castle rick works, with Portland stone string courses, ills, &c. The east front, some 200 ft. from Fawcett-road, has a central tower, carrying a short runcated spire, which is surmounted by a stone urret. At the base of the tower is the entrance to he school, leading to a wide corridor or small entral hall, and surrounded on three sides with lass-rooms, while on the fourth side are the cloakrooms and lavatory. On the upper floor is another orridor, at one end of which is the lecture-room. At the other end is the laboratory, and the remaining space on the floor is appropriated to another lass-room, a preparation room, teachers' rooms, tore, and other rooms. The heating arrangements have been carried out by hot water n the low-pressure system. The vitiated ir from the building is carried through a haft in the tower, into which the waste eat from the boiler-furnace induces a rapid p-draught. In the rear of the main block stands range of buildings for workshops, and the caretaker's lodge. The erection of the school is being arried out by Mr. W. Learmouth, contractor, of Portsmouth, from plans prepared by Mr. C. W. Bevis, architect, of Southsea. Mr. Henry Lawence is clerk of works. The hot-water and ventilating arrangements have been left to Messrs. Haden & Sons, the wood-block flooring has been upplied by Messrs. Duffy & Co., London, and the arving has been executed by Mr. S. Horsman, ondon.

CHURCH OF ST. MARGARET'S, HARROW-GREEN, LEYTONSTONE.—On the 19th ult., the Marchioness f Salisbury laid the foundation-stone of the new Church of St. Margaret's, Harrow-green, Leytonstone. The site upon which the church is being rected is situated at the corner of the Woodhouse nd Cobbolds-roads, near Leytonstone High-road. The designs are by Messrs. J. T. Newman & Jacques, f London, and the work has been entrusted to Mr. S. J. Scott, builder, of Walthamstow. The hurch will be of the thirteenth-century style, and vill be constructed of brick. Seating accommodaion will be provided for 821, exclusive of the choir.

CLUB BUILDINGS, NEWMARKET.—On the 18th ult. the foundation-stone of the Newmarket Workngmen's Conservative Club was laid by Lord Chelsea. The site of the club is at the corner of Exeter-road. It will be built of red bricks, with Bath stone facings. There will be an entrance hall, n assembly-room, 60 ft. by 29 ft., a billiard-room, ard and committee rooms, bar, lavatory, &c., on he ground floor, and rooms for the caretaker on he first floor. The roof will be covered with Broseley tiles. The estimated cost of the building s 1,010*l*. The architects are Messrs. Holland & on, and the builders Messrs. Hunt & Blyth, of Newmarket.

NEW CHURCH, GREENOCK.—On the 24th ult., he new Congregational Church in St. Lawrencetreet, Greenock, was opened. The new buildings measure 120 ft. along St. Lawrence-street, the hurch occupying the east or higher portion of the ground, and the hall buildings the west end. There is sitting accommodation in the church for 550. The pulpit is an open platform, with a lower platform in front for the choir; and behind is a recess for an organ. The church longitudinally is divided into five bays, three of them having single lancet windows. The gable to the street is flanked by a turret spire 67 ft. in height. The hall buildings comprise a Sabbath-school hall, with two classrooms, a vestry, and deacons' room; and there is a kitchen under the basement at the west end of the church. English Gothic is the style of architecture. The cost is about 2,000*l*. Mr. D. B. Stewart, Greenock, was architect.

RESTORATION OF PARISH CHURCH, WINTERBORNE STICKLAND, DORSET.—The parish church at Winterborne Stickland, Dorset, was opened on the 29th ult. after restoration. To the tower a new roof and vane have been provided, and the walls, as well as those of the main structure, have been repointed and defective stones replaced. On measuring a portion of the chancel roof for repair, portions of an old oak waggon-headed roof were discovered. This has been carefully restored and made good. Portions of an old oak carved screen were also found behind the wooden lining of the doorway, between the chancel and the chapel. This also has been restored, and left in the position in which it was discovered. A discovery was also made in the porch of a rude sculpture of the Holy Rood. The sculpture was found bedded with the faced side hidden in the east wall of the porch. The walls, which were probably rebuilt in 1716, says the *Dorset County Chronicle*, have all been underpinned with concrete, as the foundations were found to be very defective. The roof of the porch has been taken off and repaired where necessary. A new heating chamber has been built at the north side of the tower for heating the church with hot air, the apparatus being supplied by Messrs. Haden & Sons, of Trowbridge. The "Skinner" mausoleum has also had its roof repaired. In the interior, the old gallery and organ have been removed; the tower has been thrown open and the west window is plainly seen; the arch from the nave to the tower has been cleaned and repaired; and the old high-backed pews have been replaced by modern pitch-pine seats. The floor within the Communion rails is of tiles of various colours, laid in pattern. The entrance to the mausoleum is ornamented with oak carving. The floor of the body of the church is formed of wood blocks laid on cement. The windows are glazed with cathedral glass with a coloured design in the centre of each light. The walls are coloured grey. Mr. W. J. Fletcher, of Wimborne, was the architect; Mr. George, of Milton Abbas, the contractor; Mr. Gillingham executed the plumbing, glazing, and painting; and Messrs. Meyrick & Son, of Glastonbury, undertook the renovation of the old oak roof.

SANITARY AND ENGINEERING NEWS.

LOUGHBOROUGH SEWAGE DISPOSAL. — The Borough Surveyor of Loughborough, Mr. A. W. Cross, has prepared a scheme for the sewage disposal of Loughborough. The population of Loughborough is about 18,000. A provisional agreement has been signed for the purchase of 33 acres of land. It is proposed to pump the sewage and treat it by chemical precipitation in tanks, followed by filtration through land. There will be three precipitation tanks, of a total capacity of 600,000 gallons. There will be a storage tank for night-sewage, and buildings for pumping and mixing-machinery. The dry ash refuse from the town will be carted to the works and utilised in "forced draught" destructors for the production of steam for pumping the sewage. About half the land will be laid out with carriers and under-drainage for land filtration. The sewage will be brought to the site through 21-in. and 24-in. iron intercepting outfalls, the sewers being laid about 8 ft. below subsoil water-level. The Town Council have decided to borrow 20,000*l*. The Council have engaged Mr. W. H. Radford, C.E., of Nottingham, to act as Consulting Engineer throughout the preparation of the plans and the execution of the work, and various amendments and alterations suggested by him have been incorporated in the scheme.

DRAINAGE AND SEWAGE WORKS, STONE. — The Stone (Staffordshire) Local Board a few months ago invited engineers to submit designs for the drainage of the town and for the disposal of the sewage, and a premium of 100 guineas was offered for the most suitable. Twelve schemes were submitted. A special committee, having carefully considered these, have now reported in favour of the scheme prepared by Mr. Theo. S. McCallum, C.E., of Manchester; and at a meeting of the Board on March 24 the committee's recommendation was adopted. Every street in the town will require a new sewer. About nine-tenths of the sewage will reach the purification works by gravitation; the remainder will have to be pumped. The sewage will be purified by the "International" process—precipitation by "Ferozone" and filtration through "Polarite." The sludge will be pressed. A large proportion of the sewage of Stone consists of brewery refuse.

FOREIGN AND COLONIAL.

FRANCE.—A bust of Dr. Damaschino, the work of Alfred Bouche, sculptor, has just been erected in the Hall of the Faculty of Medicine, Paris.——The sculptor Michel Malherbe has been commissioned to execute a monument to the poet Ephraim Mikhaël, which is to be paid for by a subscription committee.——The Department of Fine Arts has Just presented to the Faculty of Literature in Paris (for the decoration of one of their amphitheatres) a Gobelins tapestry representing the deification of Homer. It has been executed about fifteen years after a copy of Balze and Dumas, which forms a ceiling in one of the halls in the Louvre.——The Fécamp Museum has just received an addition in the shape of a very fine drawing by Ulysse Butin, one of a collection belonging to Louis Lelois.——June 2 is the day fixed for the inauguration of the Monument at Agen to the memory of the leaders of Lot and Garonne.——The French Alpine Club is going to hold an exhibition of pictures at Grenoble, which is to consist entirely of Alpine scenery. This exhibition will last from July 16 till August 31.——The statue of Admiral Bruat at Colmar has been defaced by some unknown persons. The Municipality has offered a reward for the discovery of the authors of this act of vandalism.——The new Lycée of Argenteuil at Mantes is to be opened on May 29 instead of April 25.——The death of M. John Flornoy, artist, is announced from Nantes. In the recent exhibition in that town he had some fine landscapes.——We have also to record the death of M. Audru, who had a very fine collection of works of arts at Tours, and one which was much appreciated by connoisseurs.

MISCELLANEOUS.

EXHIBITION OF WORKS IN WOOD.—It is announced that the Worshipful Company of Carpenters and the Worshipful Company of Joiners will hold an exhibition of works in wood and wood-carving in May next. All particulars as to prizes, &c., may be obtained at Carpenters Hall, London Wall, where the Exhibition will be held.

THE NEW FRENCH EMBASSY IN ST. PETERSBURG.—According to the *Grashdanin*, the new French ambassadorial hotel is now ready. It is a palace situated on the Neva. On the ground floor are the official rooms of the Ambassador. The walls are hung with real Gobelins tapestries, and the entire furniture is of historic and artistic value. The colours used throughout the building are purple and olive-green. On the first-floor are situated the fête rooms, and in the grand reception-room, the colour prevailing being red, the walls are hung throughout their entire length with costly Gobelins tapestries. Next to this room is situated a smaller chamber, in olive-green, ornamented with valuable paintings and huge mirrors, and next to this again is a card-room, in red. On the same floor are situated the grand banqueting-hall and a smaller dining-room for the *personnel* of the Embassy. In the former is mounted a statuary group in marble, representing Lully, in the dress of a kitchen boy, playing the violin before the Duc de Montpensier. Between the two latter chambers is situated the concert-hall,—a chamber with rich stucco gold ornamentations. From this hall huge portals open upon a balcony, affording a fine view of the Neva. The French hotel is one of the finest buildings in St. Petersburg. The Gobelins tapestries therein alone are valued at several million francs.

AN ARTIFICIAL STONE.—The *Moniteur de la Céramique et de la Verrerie* gives a formula for an artificial stone:—Forty parts of granite, fifteen parts of flint, and five parts of feldspar are mixed as a fine powder with four parts of plastic clay and slightly moistened. The compound is then powerfully compressed, dried, and burnt at a high temperature in a porcelain-oven. The stone thus obtained is stated to be capable of withstanding great pressure, and is impervious to water.

THE ENGLISH IRON TRADE.—Depression still characterises the English iron trade. Business in both crude and manufactured iron is extremely limited; few changes in quotations, however, are recorded. For tin-plates the demand continues quiet, and in the steel trade rail mills and works engaged in manufacturing shipbuilding material are those best employed, although only to a moderate extent. In the shipbuilding and engineering trades a quiet tone is manifested. The coal trade is rather inactive.—*Iron*.

THE RAILWAYS OF THE WORLD.—According to the *Eisenbahn Zeitung*, the railways of Europe increased from 214,328 kilomètres in 1888, to 220,261 kilomètres in 1889, or by 12·6 per cent. The largest increase, 119·2 per cent., is shown by Greece, Roumania coming next with 51·2 per cent. The increase in Great Britain and Ireland was 4·0 per cent. In the United States the increase was 52,179 kilomètres, or 25·1 per cent. In British India the increase was 6,180 kilomètres, or 32·0 per cent.; in the Cape Colony, 80 kilomètres, or 2·9 per cent.; and in Natal 190 kilomètres, 102·1 per cent. In Australia the increase was 4,975 kilomètres, or 38·3 per cent. The increase for the entire world was 108,600 kilomètres, or 22·3 per cent.

COMPETITIONS, CONTRACTS, AND PUBLIC APPOINTMENTS.

COMPETITIONS.

Nature of Work.	By whom Advertised.	Premium.	Designs to be delivered.
*Improving Open Space called "The Maes"	Criccieth Loc. Bd.	6l. 6s.	May 27
School Buildings	St. George (Bristol) Sch. Bd.	Not stated	No date.

CONTRACTS.

Nature of Work or Materials.	By whom Required.	Architect, Surveyor, or Engineer.	Tenders to be delivered.
Road Works	Dynas Powis High. Bd.	S. R. Lewis	April 5
Granite Road-metal	Thrapston High. Bd.	Geo. Siddons	do.
Pipe Sewers, Manholes, Pumping Station, &c. Kegworth, Derby	Shardlow R.S.A.	W. H. Radford	April 6
House, Caerphilly	....	Phillips & Holdgate	do.
*Iron and Glass Porch	Hackney Union	Official	do.
*Alteration, Goods Shed, Pengam	Gt. Western Ry.	do.	April 7
Service Reservoir, Panteg	Pontypool Gas and Water Co.	do.	do.
*Wooden Doors to Lifts at Infirmary	St. Saviour's Union, Surrey	do.	do.
*Repairs at St. George's Workhouse	do.	Jarvis & Son	do.
Three Houses, Upper Range, Northowram, Halifax	....	G. Buckley & Son	do.
Alterations to Premises, Westgate-road, Newcastle-on-Tyne	J. W. Parker	Philip Spicer	do.
School Premises, Aberllon	Merthyr Tydfil Sch. Bd.	J. Williams	do.
Forty-two Houses, Ystrad Rhondda, S. Wales	J. C. Rees	....	April 8
Alterations to Gray's Hospital, Elgin, N.B.	....	A. & W. Reid	do.
*Purchase and Clearing away Building Materials	Sch. Bd. for London	Official	do.
School, Ripley, Derby	....	R. Argile	April 9
Steam Laundry Block, Sedgefield Asylum	Durham County Lunatic Asy. Com.	W. Crozier	do.
Additions, &c. Altyre House, near Forres, N.B.	....	A. & W. Reid	do.
Distillery, Warehouses, &c. Parkmore, near Dufftown, N.B.	....	Gordon & McBey	do.
130 Houses, Aberdare Junction	Ynysmeurig Club	A. O. Evans	do.
Additions, &c. Crow Beacon, Linney Head, Milford Haven	Trinity House Corp.	Official	April 11
*Pit Sand	Com. of H. M. Works	do.	do.
*New Sewers	St. Giles Bd. of Works	do.	do.
Work, Llandaff Cathedral	Llandaff Highway Bd.	G. Wallace	do.
Road Works	do.	J. Holden	do.
Street Making, and Eighteen Houses, Consett, Durham	Indus. and Prov. Soc. Lim.	do. / W. S. Snell	do. / do.
*Sewerage Works	Hambledon R.S.A.	W. N. Lailey	April 12
*New Room at Girls' School	Walthamstow Sch. Bd.	W. A. Longmore	do.

CONTRACTS.—*Continued.*

Nature of Work or Materials.	By whom Required.	Architect, Surveyor or Engineer.	Tenders to be delivered.
*Paving Works	West Ham Council	Lewis Angell	April 12
*Making-up Road	do.	do.	do.
*Circular Iron Urinal	do.	do.	do.
*New Market, Arcades, and Shops	Borough of Halifax	Leeming & Leeming	do.
*Kerbing and Channelling	Hackney Bd. of Wks.	Official	April 13
*Gullys, Grates, Manhole Covers, &c.	do.	do.	do.
*Asphalte Works	do	do.	do.
*Sewerage Works	Petersfield R.S.A.	W. N. Lailey	do.
*Making-up and Paving Roads	Fulham Vestry	W. Sykes	do.
*Repair of Laundry Drying Horses	Lambeth Guardians	Official	do.
*Blue Guernsey Granite Spalls	West Ham Union	do.	do.
Widening Bridge, &c. Chesford, Kenilworth	Warwickshire C. C.	do.	April 16
Large Hall and Two Shops, Woodfield-street, Morriston, S. Wales	Morriston Public Hall Co. Lim.	....	do.
*Oak Fencing	Harrow Loc. Bd.	Cowell & Gray	April 19
Cooperative, Blackfriars-road, Elgin, N.B.	G. Gorrod	....	April 21
*Sewage Works	Horsham U.S.A.	B. Latham	do.
*Drainage of Christchurch Workhouse	St. Saviour's Union, Surrey	Jarvis & Son	do.
Cast-iron Water Mains, &c.	Lower Brixham Local Board	Ed. Ellis	April 23
*Tarpaving Works	London County Council	Official	April 26
*Completion of New Workhouse	St. Pancras Guardians	A. & C. Harston	April 27
*Building, &c. Gymnasium	London County Council	Official	April 29
Dredging, Newport, Mon.	Harbour Commrs.	L. F. Vernon Harcourt	April 30
*Electric Lighting	Chiswick Loc. Bd.	A. Ramsden	May 4
*R. C. Church, Shelfield, near Walsall	The Building Com.	S. Loxton	No date
*Alterations, Sea Lion Hotel, Hanley	The Proprietors	do.	do.
*Erection of New Premises, &c., Walsall	do.	do.	do.
*Erection of Nine Villas, Walsall	do.	do.	do.
*Works at St. Paul's Church Inst., Burton-on-Trent	....	R. Churchill	do.
*Erection of Church, Dulwich	....	Oliver & Leeson	do.
*Additions, &c. Holmesburst, Sussex	....	R. J. & J. Goodacre	do.
*Alterations, &c. Torbay Hospital	The Commrs.	Habershon & Fawckner	do.
Alterations to Premises, Shields-road, Newcastle-on-Tyne	Wm. Thompson	J. W. Thompson	do.
Shop and Dwelling-house, Haydock, Wigan	Mr. Pilling	....	do.
Enlargement of Schools, Goose Green, Wigan	....	Heaton & Ralph	do.
Mill, Westbury-street, Elland	W. Iredale & Co.	....	do.

PUBLIC APPOINTMENTS.

Nature of Appointment.	By whom Advertised.	Salary.	Applications to be in.
*Draughtsman, Hydrographical Dept. of Admiralty	Civil Service Commrs.	....	April 6
*Clerk of the Works	Northallerton L. B.	2l. 2s. per week	April 7
*Superintendent (Cleansing & Dusting, &c.)	Commrs. of Sewers	400l.	April 19

Those marked with an Asterisk (*) are advertised in this Number. *Competition*, p. iv. *Contracts*, pp. iv., vi., & viii. *Public Appointments*, pp. viii. & xx.

A Warning to Builders.—At the North London Police-court, on March 25, Messrs. Parsons & Co., contractors, were summoned for executing work at the Lead Works, Southgate-road, Islington, without having previously given notice to the District Surveyor. Mr. Henry Lovegrove, District Surveyor of South Islington, proved the case, and Mr. Haden Corser fined the defendants 20s., with 12s. costs.

Walls of Insufficient Thickness. — Mr. Pereira, a builder, was summoned by Mr. C. Fowler, District Surveyor of Shoreditch, for erecting a building with walls of a thickness less than as prescribed by the Building Act. Mr. H. Lovegrove, Deputy District Surveyor, proved the case, and stated that the defendant had been repeatedly warned. Mr. Mead ordered the work to be amended, and the costs, 22s., to be paid.

Portland Cement Tests.—Mr. V. de Michele, the inventor of the well-known testing machine which goes under his name, sends us his suggestion for a specification for cement under his test, which he considers may be relied on to ensure good sound Portland cement. The conditions are as follows:—"Pats ½-in. thick in water, absolutely sound at seven days. Tensile strength, 400 lbs. per square inch at seven days. Fineness, 10 per cent, residue on a 50 sieve. The pats to be gauged on glass, immersed in water immediately, and left there for the whole period. One pat to each three bricks. The test bricks to be gauged by a skilled man, with any quantity of water, in any way he likes. The average of three to be taken, which shall represent about 100 tons or less. The strain to be applied as quickly as possible. The sieve to have 2,500 holes per square inch, and to be of wire $\frac{1}{100}$th of an inch in diameter. Shaking to be continued until nothing ground in the mill passes."

Removal.—Messrs. Prickett & Ellis inform us that they have removed from No. 60, Chancery-lane, to No. 57, the adjoining building.

"Fire and Water."—This little periodical for April gives as a supplement a sheet of illustrations, to a small scale, of some new English fire-brigade stations. It also contains much interesting information relating to fire extinction, including a description of a system of fire-recording adopted by the Chief of the Chicago Fire Brigade. Each record of a fire consists of a report, accompanied by a plan or map, showing adjacent properties, fire-plugs used, positions taken up by the engines, disposition of the lines of hose, direction of the jets brought to bear on the fire, and other details.

The Water Tunnel under the Mersey.—A comparatively small but nevertheless essential part of the great scheme for bringing water from the Vyrnwy valley to Liverpool,—it might be more fitly described as the last link in the gigantic chain,—has been brought to a successful termination. At eight o'clock on the morning of the 22nd ult., the long tunnel bore under the Mersey at Fidler's Ferry was completed.

Stained Glass Window, Arbroath.—A Munich stained glass window has just been erected in the St. Mary's Episcopal Church, Arbroath, N.B. The scene represented is the Angel at the Tomb in the centre light, and the figures of Mary Magdalen, Mary, the mother of James, and Salome, in the two side lights. The window was designed and executed by Messrs. Mayer & Co., of Munich and London.

MEETINGS.

SATURDAY, APRIL 2.

Architectural Association.—Visits to (1) the Newington Weights and Measures Offices, Union-road, Blackman-street, S.E., by permission of Mr. Thomas Blashill. 3 p.m. (2) the Royal Ophthalmic Hospital, St. George's-circus, S.E., by permission of Mr. Keith D. Young. 4 p.m.

Institution of Civil Engineers.—Annual Dinner of the members, in the Town Hall, St. Martin's-in-the-Fields, Charing Cross-road. 6.30 p.m.

Sanitary Inspectors' Association.—Mr. J. Davenport on "The Sanitary Inspector: His High Calling." 6 p.m.

MONDAY, APRIL 4.

Royal Institute of British Architects.—(1) Paper by Signor Luca Beltrami on "The Construction of the Central Pillars of Milan Cathedral." (2) Mr. J. Starkie Gardner on "Wrought-Ironwork: the Renaissance Period." 8 p.m.

Society of Arts (Cantor Lectures).—Mr. Bennett H. Brough on "Mine Surveying." II. 8 p.m.

Society of Engineers.—(1) Adjourned discussion on Mr. S. Sellon's paper on "Electrical Traction and its Financial Aspect." (2) Mr. Reginald Bolton on "The Application of Electricity to Hoisting Machinery." 7.30 p.m.

Liverpool Architectural Society.—Paper by Mr. T. Mellard Reade.

TUESDAY, APRIL 5.

Institution of Civil Engineers. — Mr. H. Alfred Roechling on "The Sewage-Farms of Berlin." 8 p.m.

Society of Arts (Foreign and Colonial Section).—8 p.m.

Glasgow Architectural Association.—Mr. C. E. Whitelaw on "The Parish Churches of Scotland." 8 p.m.

WEDNESDAY, APRIL 6.

Royal Archæological Institute.—(1) Mr. A. L. Lewis on "The Stone Circles of Britain." (2) Mr. J. L. André on "Widows and Vowesses." 4 p.m.

St. Paul's Ecclesiological Society.—Mr. F. J. Beckley on "The Round Towers and Romanesque of Ireland." 7.30 p.m.

Society of Arts.—Mr. R. McCormick on "The Future Trade Relations of Great Britain and the United States." 8 p.m.

Builders' Foremen and Clerks of Works' Institution.—8.30 p.m.

THURSDAY, APRIL 7.

Society of Arts (Indian Section).—4.30 p.m.

Society for the Encouragement of the Fine Arts.—8 p.m.

Society of Antiquaries.—8.30 p.m.

Institution of Electrical Engineers.—Discussion of Mr. A. Reckenzaun's paper on "Electric Tramways and the Cost of Electric Traction." 8 p.m.

Royal Institution.—Dr. B. A. Whitelegge on "Epidemic Waves." II. 3 p.m.

Edinburgh Architectural Association. — Mr. A. H. Millar on "The Hie Gait and Sautmercat of Glasgow in the Olden Time." 8 p.m.

FRIDAY, APRIL 8.

Institution of Civil Engineers (Students' Meeting).—Mr. R. J. Durley on "Some Forms of Petroleum Engines." 7.30 p.m.

Royal Institution. — Professor W. E. Ayrton on "Electric Meters, Motors, and Money Matters." 9 p.m.

Bradford Historical and Antiquarian Society.—Mr. W. Claridge on "Bradford Grammar School." 8 p.m.

Dundee Institute of Architecture.—Mr. W. D. M'Kay on "The Art of the Low Countries." 8 p.m.

SATURDAY, APRIL 9.

Edinburgh Architectural Association.—Visit to Yester House and Old Castle, and Nunraw.

RECENT PATENTS:

ABSTRACTS OF SPECIFICATIONS.

18,755.—Saws: *W. Junge.*—This relates to an invention to provide saws with teeth presenting sharp knife-edges for cutting the material, and having clearance spaces for the waste, applicable to saws having their teeth made in one piece with the blade, and also to those provided with inserted or exchangeable teeth. The inventor provides the teeth of saws alternately on their right and left hand side at or near the top with a narrow recess or groove of any suitable depth or shape, from the front to the rear, in such a manner that extremely sharp knife-edges for cutting the two sides of the kerf are produced. Along the top of the teeth is preferably formed a thin ridge constituting a sharp knife-edge for cutting the base of the kerf. In this improved saw the dust or waste produced by one tooth passes through the aforesaid groove in the same into the throat space in front of the following tooth, by which it is removed from the kerf. The inventor claims that by his improvements very smooth surfaces and clean edges are produced, so that little or no finishing is required, and a considerable saving of material, labour, and motive power effected.

5,520.—Bricks: *S. G. Phillips.*—This refers to an invention for drying bricks after they have been moulded from the wet clay, preparatory to burning. The material is traversed slowly through a long building carried in open-work tiers on cars moved either continuously or intermittently, and is subjected to lateral currents of air artificially warmed. Heat is economised, and uniform and just sufficiently rapid drying induced by causing the warm air, loaded with moisture, to impart its heat as it goes out to the incoming cold bricks, and causing the warm bricks as they go out to impart their heat to the incoming cold air.

6,545.—Ventilators: *J. W. M. Peyton and O. Y. Rhodes.*—This specification relates to a new form of apparatus specially designed for ventilating or removing foul air from rooms, railway-carriages, drains, soil-pipes, and the like. The apparatus consists of a vertical pipe or tube having around its periphery a series of openings carried up vertically in the form of small tubes, and terminating within the central tube some distance from its top. These openings are larger at the inlet than the outlet, so that as air enters them and passes up through the contracted parts in small tubes it will be compressed and thus acquire velocity in ascending the several tubes, so that on the air entering the central tube it will create an up-draught therein, the suction of which draws the air upward from the room or other place to which it is applied. In some cases a revolving cap or cowl may also be used advantageously.

6,839.—Gas Fittings: *J. Fairbank.*—This relates to an invention to prevent waste of gas while alight, and the escape of gas while not burning. The inventor constructs a spring of brass, steel, or other suitable material, having notches, stops, or grooves at one end formed by stamping up the metal into suitable shapes, and a clipping apparatus at the other end for securing it to the gas-pipe. This spring presses upon the tap and holds it firmly in the position in which it is placed, and is claimed to answer in all ways the purposes indicated above.

19,515.—Cowls: *W. E. T. Bennett.*—This refers to an invention designed to prevent gusts of wind blowing down chimneys, and so causing them to smoke, and to utilise such down-blasts to improve the up-draught in the chimney. To the top of the chimney-pot is attached a truncated cone, to the base of which is secured an upwardly projecting inclined flange. In the gutter thus formed are punched a few holes for the escape of any rain that may collect. Above the chimney, and supported by stays, is fixed a hollow conical cover, the diameter of the base being about the same as that of the base of the truncated cone. By this arrangement the cover prevents the down-blasts from entering the chimney, whilst the inclined flange catches a part of the downward current, and deflects it on to the side of the truncated cone, which, in turn, deflects it on to the opposite side of the hollow cover, whence the current passes away by the annular open space, increasing as it goes the up-draught in the chimney.

21,997.—FIRE-RESISTING BRICKS, &C.: *J. K. Thompson.*—This invention consists of a special mixture of fire-resisting material, composed of fireclay, plumbago, graphite, and cement, in the proportions set out in the specification. This material may be made into bricks, under hydraulic or other pressure, and baked in the usual manner, or, diluted, it may be applied in a liquid state as a wash or coating for fireplaces, fireboxes, furnaces, ovens, or kilns.

NEW APPLICATIONS FOR LETTERS PATENT.

March 14.—4,969, H. Thorpe, Gas-brackets.—5,010, J. Grundy, Ventilator and Chimney-cowl.

March 15.—5,053, A. Ransome, Band-sawing Machines.—5,054, A. Ransome, Band-sawing Machines.—5,063, T. Robinson, Window-fastenings.—5,067, H. Anglee, Imitation Faience Tiles, &c.—5,094, R. Crompton, Linings or Coverings for Walls, Ceilings, &c.

March 16.—5,147, C. Harwood, Combined Non-corrosive and Water-waste Preventing Cistern for Water-closets.—5,156, P. Field, Sash-fastening for Windows and doors.—5,180, J. Johnstone, Screw-drivers.—5,221, W. and R. Smith, Chimney-pot, Cowl, or Ventilator.

March 17.—5,254, A. Lamplough, Sash-fasteners.—5,291, W. Morton, Ornamental Materials for Decorating Walls, &c.—5,292, W. Morton, Construction of Walls, Partitions, and Ceilings.

March 18.—5,346, M. Martin, Rule and Plumb level.—5,353, E. Stoefler and F. Alexandre, Smoothing-iron with Removable Handle.—5,365, Munro's Electrical Manufacturing Company, Ltd., and J. McFarlane, Joints for Electric-light Fittings.—5,390, J. Hamblet, Paving Bricks.—5,401, L. Jenkins, Paint and other Brushes.

March 19.—5,437, C. Wallworth, Wooden Flooring-blocks.—5,446, T. Barrow, Stoves, 5,471, E. Louap, Stoves.

PROVISIONAL SPECIFICATIONS ACCEPTED.

854, E. Cooper and E. Turrall, Door-springs and Checks.—2,232, G. Haskins, Spring Hinges.—2,325, W. Pitt, Folding Gates.—2,364, G. Thompson, Nails.—2,872, E. Alexander, Chimney-tops to prevent Down-draughts, &c.—2,894, J. Golding, Metal-covered Truss-work for Carrying Concrete Floors and Ceilings.—3,286, J. Caldecourt, Sockets or Joints of Rain-water pipes.—3,448, E. Carr, Screws.—3,465, D. Andrew, Drain, Sewer, and like Pipes.—3,466, D. Andrew, Laying Sewer-drain, &c., also for testing the same.—3,845, J. Buchanan, Brick-making Machinery or Apparatus.—4,048, J. Ottaway, Window-sashes and Frames.—4,062, C. and C. Kite, Ventilators.—4,149, W. Charlesworth, Slurry Drying Structures, used in making Cement.—4,424, M. Brophy, Door-locks or Latches.—4,426, M. Brophy, Door-knobs and Spindles.

COMPLETE SPECIFICATIONS ACCEPTED.

(*Open to Opposition for Two Months.*)

8,234, E. Davis and T. Baldwin, Joints for Coupling Pipes and other articles.—8,508, A. Lamplough, Sash-fasteners.—20,743, J. Abell, Paving.—21,669, H. Woodcock, Flushing Cisterns for Water-closets.—536, J. Robson, Burglar-proof Sash-fastener.—1,092, J. Brown, Chimney-pots and Tall Boys, Cowls, &c.

SOME RECENT SALES OF PROPERTY:

ESTATE EXCHANGE REPORT.

MARCH 21.—By *R. A. Notley*: 10 and 12, Tooley-st., Southwark, f., area 2,550 ft., 6,050*l*. By *Wagstaff & Warman*: 17 and 19, Northampton-st., Islington, u.t. 26 yrs., g.r. 10*l*. 10s., 360*l*.; 28 and 30, Northampton-st., u.t. 26 yrs., g.r. 10*l*., r. 68*l*., 435*l*.; 13, Alwyne-villas, Canonbury, u.t. 26 yrs., g.r. 6*l*., r. 36*l*., 250*l*.—By *Jenkins & Sons*: 80, Blackheath-rd., Greenwich, f., 560*l*.—By *Warman Bros.*: 12, Manor-rd., Stoke Newington, f., 1,270*l*.; 18, St. James's-rd., Hackney, u.t. 66 yrs., g.r. 5*l*. 8s., r. 35*l*., 380*l*.; l.g.r. of 20*l*., Bonner-rd., u.t. 65 yrs., g.r. 12*l*., 135*l*.; 27, Northfield-rd., Stamford-hill, u.t. 94 yrs., g.r. 9*l*., 580*l*.; 97, Lordship-rd., u.t. 82 yrs., g.r. 12*l*., 650*l*.; 63, Osbaldeston-rd., u.t. 86 yrs., g.r. 8*l*., r. 48*l*., 485*l*.

MARCH 22.—By *C. W. Davies*: 32, Clifton-st., Finsbury, u.t. 15 yrs., g.r. 7*l*. 8s., r. 65*l*., 305*l*.; 40, Turnpike-lane, Hornsey, u.t. 88 yrs., g.r. 7*l*., 305*l*.—By *J. McLachlan & Sons*: "Prescott Lodge," Clapham, and a plot of land, u.t. 49 yrs., g.r. 31*l*. 10s., 950*l*.—By *Debenham, Tewson, & Co.*: l.g.r. of 203*l*., Burgess, Ashlin, and Brownfield roads, Stratford, u.t. 54 yrs., g.r. 80*l*., 1,880*l*.; 14, 15, and 16, Taylor's-pl., Stepney, u.t. 31 yrs., g.r. 8*l*., 305*l*.; 26, Little Marylebone-st., Marylebone, u.t. 10 yrs., g.r. 14*l*., 365*l*.—By *Dowsett & Co.*: 2 and 13, Elm-mews, Hyde-pk., u.t. 67 yrs., g.r. 16*l*., 325*l*.; 5 and 6, Elm-mews, u.t. 67 yrs., g.r. 13*l*., r. 61*l*. 10s., 400*l*.; 119, Warwick-rd., Kensington, u.t. 83 yrs., g.r. 16*l*., r. 100*l*., 1,270*l*.; 1 to 29 (odd), Agnes-st., Silvertown, u.t. 83 yrs., g.r. 45*l*., r. 273*l*., 1,370*l*.; 2 to 22 (even), Agnes-st., u.t. 83 yrs., g.r. 33*l*., r. 200*l*. 4s., 1,000*l*.—By *Foster & Cranfield*: "Ridge House," The Ridgeway, Enfield, u.t. 86 yrs., g.r. 15*l*. 10s., 600*l*.; 30, Lordship-pk., Stoke Newington, u.t. 81 yrs., g.r. 10*l*. 10s., 755*l*.—By *Bean, Burnett, & Co.*: 18 and 20, East Dulwich-grove, Dulwich, u.t. 91 yrs., g.r. 13*l*., r. 68*l*., 450*l*.

MARCH 23.—By *Alfred Watson*: 45 and 47, Eleanor-rd., Hackney, u.t. 52 yrs., g.r. 10*l*., r. 66*l*., 620*l*.; 214 and 216, Richmond-rd., u.t. 53 yrs., g.r. 13*l*. 10s., r. 80*l*. 590*l*.—By *C. P. Whiteley*: 7, 9, and 11, Britannia-st., King's Cross, u.t. 17 yrs., g.r. 11*l*. 10s., 380*l*.; l.g.r. of 9*l*. 18s., u.t. 15 yrs., with reversion for 2 yrs., Marylebone, 360*l*.—By *Hobson, Richards, & Co.*: No. 40, Tulse Hill, u.t. 20 yrs., g.r. 12*l*., 150*l*.—By *D. Young*: 139 and 143, Hungerford-rd., Camden-rd., u.t. 68 yrs., g.r. 4*l*., 78*l*., 335*l*.; l.g.r. of 16*l*. 16s., u.t. 68 yrs., g.r. [illegible], 205*l*.; "The Hungerford Arms," u.t. 68 yrs., g.r. 50*l*., g.r. [illegible], 1,000*l*.; [illegible] Hungerford-rd., u.t. 68 yrs., g.r. [illegible]; l.g.r. of 12*l*., u.t. 68 yrs., g.r., 1*l*. 12s., 190*l*.; 48, Hungerford-rd., u.t. 70 yrs., g.r. 6*l*., r. 60*l*., 500*l*.; 50, 52, 58 to 68 (even), Hungerford-rd., u.t. 70 yrs., g.r. 5*l*., 3,685*l*.; 70, 74 and 76, Hungerford-rd., u.t. 70 yrs., g.r. 18*l*., r. 126*l*., 1,095*l*.; 18, 20 and 25, Hildrop-cres., u.t. 56 yrs., g.r. 24*l*., r. 165*l*., 1,490*l*.; 36 and 41, Hildrop-cres., u.t. 56 yrs., g.r. 13*l*. 10s., r. 105*l*., 930*l*.

MARCH 24.—By *Messrs. Trollope*: 32, James-st., Buckingham-gate, f., 6,000*l*.—By *Messrs. Chadwick*: "The Ship," Romney-st., Westminster, f., r. 50*l*., 990*l*.; 27, Romney-st., f., r. 30*l*., 565*l*.; "The Rose and Shamrock," Marsham-st., f., r. 40*l*., 800*l*.; 215, High-st., Brentford, f., r. 40*l*., 1,000*l*.—By *Farebrother, Ellis, & Co.*: 8, Buckland-cres., Hampstead, u.t. 60 yrs., g.r. 20*l*., 1,210*l*.—By *C. C. & T. Moore*: 11, Gold-st., Stepney, u.t. 32 yrs., g.r. 2*l*. 17s. 6d., 180*l*.; 13, Cleveland-st., Mile-end, u.t. 278 yrs., g.r. 10s., 345*l*.; 5 to 13 (odd), Burgess-street, Limehouse, u.t. 83 yrs., g.r. 20*l*., 830*l*.; 40, 42, 44, and 46, Ettrick-st., Bromley-by-Bow, u.t. 81 yrs., g.r. 17*l*., 660*l*.; 49 and 51, Waterford-rd., Fulham, u.t. 65 yrs., g.r. 6*l*. 6s., 405*l*.—By *A. J. F. Gibbon*: 25, Victoria-av., Upton-pk., u.t. 94 yrs., g.r. 4*l*. 10s., r. 30*l*., 235*l*.—By *Stimson & Sons*: 57, 59, and 61, Clifton-cres., Peckham, f., r. 72*l*., 825*l*.; 58 to 64 even, Penrose-st., Walworth, u.t. 75 yrs., g.r. 32*l*., r. 211*l*., 1,675*l*.; eight sets of stabling, Penrose-mews, u.t. 75 yrs., g.r. 22*l*., 1,320*l*.; 5 to 8, Orchard-row, Camberwell, u.t. 95 yrs., g.r. 24*l*., 1,250*l*.; 69, College-pl., Camden-town, u.t. 79 yrs., g.r. 9*l*., r. 81*l*. 18s., 600*l*.; 65, Dulwich-rd., Herne-hill, u.t. 73 yrs., g.r. 6*l*., r. 38*l*., 310*l*.; 67, Dulwich-rd., u.t. 52 yrs., g.r. 7*l*. 10s., r. 65*l*., 560*l*.; 43, Shakespeare-rd., u.t. 72 yrs., g.r. 7*l*., r. 36*l*., 285*l*.; 52, Spencer-rd., u.t. 56 yrs., g.r. 7*l*.; 305*l*.; 46 to 52 (even), Effra-parade, Brixton, u.t. 69 yrs., g.r. 12*l*., r. 124*l*. 16*l*., 1,015*l*.; 95 and 97, Railton-rd., u.t. 76 yrs., g.r. 10*l*. 10s., r. 78*l*., 560*l*.—By *Wilkinson, Son, & Welch* (at Brighton): 30, Guildford-st., Brighton, f., 380*l*.; 18 and 21, Waterloo-st., Hove, f., r. 120*l*., 1,630*l*.

MARCH 25.—By *Fuller, Horsey, Sons, & Cassell*: "Albion Wharf," Holland-st., Blackfriars, area 19,000 ft., c., 18,500*l*.; 28, 29, and 30, Lambeth-sq., Lambeth, u.t. 7 yrs., g.r. 25*l*. 4s., r. 88*l*., 210*l*.—By *Geo. Gouldsmith, Son, & Co.*: 20, Rutland-gate, Hyde-pk., u.t. 42 yrs., g.r., 12*l*. 12s., 4,250*l*.; 1, Rutland-mews, u.t. 42 yrs., no g.r., 360*l*.; f.g.r. 44*l*. 2s., with reversion in 37 yrs., Montpelier-row, Knightsbridge, 1,130*l*.; 26, Montpelier-sq., f., r. 135*l*., 2,540*l*.—By *A. & A. Field*: a plot of freehold land, George-lane, Woodford, 150*l*.; 13, Parmiter-st., Bethnal-green, u.t. 37 yrs., g.r. 2*l*. 10s., 225*l*.—By *Baker & Sons*: f.g.r. of 143*l*., with reversion in 85 yrs., Silwood-st., Rotherhithe (16 lots), 3,860*l*.; f.g.r. of 18*l*., with reversion in 85 yrs., Brackton-rd. (8 lots), 390*l*.; f.g.r. of 51*l*., with reversion in 86 yrs., Eugenia-rd. (8 lots), 1,451*l*.

[*Contractions used in these lists.*—F.g.r. for freehold ground-rent; l.g.r. for leasehold ground-rent; i.g.r. for improved ground-rent; g.r. for ground-rent; r. for rent; f. for freehold; c. for copyhold; l. for leasehold; e.r. for estimated rental; u.t. for unexpired term; p.a. for per annum; yrs. for years; st. for street; rd. for road; sq. for square; pl. for place; ter. for terrace; cres. for crescent; yd. for yard, &c.]

PRICES CURRENT OF MATERIALS.

TIMBER.		
Greenheart, B.G. ton	9/0/0	0/0/0
Teak, E.I. .. load	10/10/0	15/0/0
Sequoia, U.S. ft. cu.	2/3	3/0
Ash, Canada load	2/10/0	4/0/0
Birch, do.	3/5/0	4/10/0
Elm, do.	3/10/0	4/15/0
Fir, Dantsic, &c.	2/0/0	3/10/0
Oak, do.	3/0/0	5/5/0
Canada	5/10/0	7/0/0
Pine, Canada red	2/10/0	3/10/0
Do. yellow	2/10/0	5/0/0
Lath, D'ntsic, fath	5/0/0	6/0/0
St. Petersburg	5/0/0	7/0/0
Deals, Finland, 2nd & 1st std 100	8/10/0	10/10/0
Do. 4th & 3rd	7/10/0	8/10/0
Do. Riga	6/10/0	8/0/0
St. Petersburg, 1st yellow	11/0/0	15/0/0
Do. 2nd yellow	8/10/0	10/0/0
Do. white	7/10/0	10/10/0
Swedish	7/15/0	16/0/0
White Sea	8/10/0	18/0/0
Canada, Pine 1st	20/0/0	26/0/0
Do. do. 2nd	14/10/0	16/0/0
Do. do. 3rd, &c.	8/0/0	10/5/0
Do. Spruce, 1st	8/10/0	11/0/0
Do. do. 3rd & 2nd	6/15/0	8/0/0
New Brunswick	7/0/0	7/10/0
Battens, all kinds	3/10/0	15/10/0
Flooring Boards, sq., 1 in. prep. 1st	0/9/6	0/14/6
Do. 2nd	0/7/6	0/11/6
Other qualities	0/4/6	0/8/0
Cedar, Cuba .. ft.	/3½	/4½
Honduras, &c.	/2½	/4
Mahogany, Cuba	/4½	/6½
St. Domingo, cargo av	/4½	2/0
Mexican do. do	/4	/5
Tobasco do. do	/5½	/7
Honduras do.	/5½	/6½
Box, Turkey ton	4/0/0	15/0/0
Rose, Rio	10/0/0	20/0/0
Bahia	9/0/0	18/0/0
Satin, St. Domingo .. ft.	0/0/8	0/1/3

TIMBER (continued).		
Satin, Porto Rico	0/0/8	0/1/6
Walnut, Italian	0/0/3½	0/0/7
METALS.		
IRON—Pig, in Scotland .. ton	2/0/9	2/1/0
Bar, Welsh, in London	6/0/0	6/10/0
Do. do. at works in Wales	5/10/0	6/0/0
Do. Staffordshire, in London	6/5/0	6/15/0
COPPER—British, cake and ingot	49/0/0	50/0/0
Best selected	50/0/0	50/10/0
Sheets, strong	59/0/0	60/0/0
Chili, bars	45/8/9	45/16/3
YELLOW METAL lb.	0/0/5¼	0/0/5½
LEAD—Pig, Spanish .. ton	10/17/6	10/18/9
English, com. brands	11/0/0	11/5/0
Sheet, English, 3 lbs. per sq. ft. and upwards	13/0/0	0/0/0
Pipe	13/10/0	0/0/0
ZINC—English sheet .. ton	25/5/0	0/0/0
Vieille Montagne	25/15/0	0/0/0
TIN—Straits	89/12/6	90/2/6
Australian	89/17/6	90/7/6
English Ingots	93/0/0	93/10/0
OILS.		
Linseed .. ton	18/15/0	19/0/0
Cocoanut, Cochin	24/15/0	0/0/0
Do. Ceylon	22/15/0	0/0/0
Palm, Lagos	22/0/0	0/0/0
Rapeseed, English pale	25/10/0	26/0/0
Do. brown	23/10/0	23/15/0
Cottonseed ref.	18/15/0	19/0/0
Oleine	21/10/0	22/10/0
Lubricating, U.S.	4/0/0	6/0/0
Do. refined	5/0/0	10/0/0
TAR—Stockholm barrel	0/19/0	1/0/0
Archangel	0/12/6	0/0/0

TENDERS.

[Communications for insertion under this heading should be addressed to "The Editor," and must reach us *not later than 12 noon on Thursdays.*]

BARNET.—For building a villa residence at Barnet, for Mr. Chipperfield. Mr. Joseph White, architect, High-street, Barnet:—

Brown	£1,498	Wilmot & Sons	£1,295
Elwood	1,330	Houghton & Son	1,262
Daniels	1,297	Dutcher	1,130

BEDDGELERT (Wales).—Accepted for additions to Chalet, for Sir Edward Watkin, Bart., M.P. Messrs. Thomas Roberts & Son, architects, Portmadoc:—

William Jones, Portmadoc £155 10 0

BLYTH (Northumberland).—For alterations and extensions to Central Hall, for Mr. John Robinson. Mr. Gibson Kyle, architect, 135, Pilgrim-street, Newcastle-on-Tyne. Quantities by Mr. Alfred G. Kyle:—

Brown	£1,650 18	J. Richardson & Co.,	
Lilburn	1,494 10 0	Newcastle*	£1,406 12 0
J. C. Hope	1,430 10 8	* Accepted.	

BRISTOL.—For sewerage works at Brislington, Keynsham, for the Rural Sanitary Authority. Mr. F. Fox, engineer. Quantities by Messrs. A. P. I. Cotterell & A. Barratt:—

E. Ambrose	£4,285	C. Gardiner	£3,395
T. J. Davis	3,706	C. A. Hayes	3,367
W. Merewether	3,597	Love & Waite, Bristol*	3,187
Cowlin & Son	3,573	H. R. Fahey	2,898
Stephens & Bastow	3,399	* Accepted.	

BROMLEY (Kent).—For making-up Waldo-road, for the Bromley Local Board. Mr. Hugh S. Cregreen, Surveyor:—

S. Hudson	£410 8 0	J. Lansbury	£385 4 5
Woodham & Fry	393 0 2	E. Pell & Sons	347 6 5
Mayo & Co.	372 0 0	J. Mowlem & Co.*	327 0 0

* Accepted.

CARNYORTH (Cornwall).—For the erection of a School to accommodate 200 children at Carnyorth, in the Parish of St. Just-in-Penwith, for the St. Just-in-Penwith School Board. Mr. Oliver Caldwell, architect, Penzance:—

Ford & James £2,522 0 0
Maris & Roberts, St. Just, Penzance (accepted) .. 1,899 16 0

Carpenter, Joiner, Plumber, Smith, Painter, and Glazier only.

James Roberts	£611 15	Joseph James	£536 0
J. Gibson	496 10		

HARROGATE.—Accepted for the erection of Wesleyan Schools, Grove-road, Harrogate. Messrs. Morley & Woodhouse, architects, 269, Swan-arcade, Bradford, Yorks. Quantities by the architects:—

Mason's Work.—Jas. Simpson, Harrogate	£697 0 0
Joiner's Work.—Checkley, Harrogate	360 0 0
Plumber's, Glazier's, and Gas Work.—J. Lindley, Leeds	117 0 0
Plasterer.—Laycock, Harrogate	39 0 0
Painter.—Dent, Harrogate	26 0 0
Shepherd, Harrogate	50 0 0
Total	1,289 0 0

LIVERPOOL.—For alterations to Turkish baths at 18, Leigh-street, Church-street, Liverpool, for Mr. Robert Parry. Mr. J. W. Auger, architect, 3, North-view, Edgehill, Liverpool:—

Raffle & Campbell	£520 0	J. & J. Crosbie	£477 0
F. Mayor & Co.	490 0	W. Hall	358 8
W. Stunnett	494 5	W. Hunt	340 0

[All of Liverpool.]

LONDON.—For alterations and decorations to 47, Cromwell Houses, S.W., for Mrs. Morrison. Messrs. Florence & Satchell, architects:—

Marler & Bennett £2,131 1 6

LONDON.—For alterations and repairs (exclusive of fittings), to No. 10, John-street, W.C., for adaptation as a Public Library, for the Holborn District, for the Commissioners. Messrs. Fletcher & Migotti, architects:—

Putnam & Fotheringham	£463	Wells & Son	£373
Sobey	419	King (accepted)	278

LONDON.—For alterations, &c., at "The King's Head" public house, Ebury Bridge, Pimlico, S.W., for Mr. C. Brown. Messrs. Fletcher & Migotti, architects:—

Walker Bros.	£477	Courtney & Fairbairn, Camberwell*	£379
Bell	430	* Accepted.	
Jackson & Jennings	429		

LONDON.—Accepted for building workshops, St. Paul's-road, Camden-road, for Mr. George Corling. Mr. John Young, architect, 3, Great Winchester-street, E.C.:—

Percival Hart, Station Works, West Green £667 0 0
[No competition.]

LONDON.—For alterations, &c., at the Southwark Gasmeter Testing Station, for the London County Council. Mr. Thomas Blashill, Architect:—

William Downs	£580	W. Oldrey & Co.	£496
Co-operative Builders Ltd.	570	G. H. & A. Bywaters	495
Higgs & Hill	540		

LONDON.—Accepted for alterations and painting at Huntingdon House, Hornsey-lane, for Mr. S. W. Francis. Mr. W. Graves, architect, Winchester House, Broad-street, E.C.:—

E. Houghton & Son, Stroud-green £173 0 0

LUTON.—For the erection of factory, King-street, for Messrs. Gaffard & Stadden. Mr. A. E. Smith, architect, Luton:—

Pryer	£1,598 0	Saunders	£1,455 12
Neville	1,490 0	Dunham	1,394 0
Smart	1,445 10		

[All of Luton.]

LUTON.—For the erection of two houses, Cromwell-road, for Mr. W. Cherry. Mr. A. E. Smith, architect, Luton:—

Parkins	£545 0 0	Smart	£495 0 0
Kingham	517 0 0	Wright	477 0 0
Saunders	507 10 6	Pryer	474 10 0

NEATH.—Accepted for the execution of the Maesyrhaf and Melincrythan improvements, for the Urban Sanitary Authority. Mr. D. M. Jenkins, A.M.I.C.E., Borough Surveyor, Gwyn-hall, Neath. Quantities by the Borough Surveyor:—

D. Dodd, Neath £425 0 0

NEWBURY (Berks).—For alterations and additions to Arlington Manor, for the Hon. Sir Francis Jeune. Mr. James H. Money, architect, Newbury. Quantities by Messrs. R. L. Curtis & Sons:—

A. Estcourt	£1,750 0 0	G. Elms	£1,394 0 0
J. Shillitoe & Sons	1,620 0 0	E. James & Son	1,287 10 0
T. H. Kingerlee	1,604 0 0	A. H. Houghton, Newbury*	1,178 0 0
G. Allen	1,510 0 0	* Accepted.	
T. Halliday	1,467 0 0		

NEWPORT (Mon.).—For an extension of the "Cross Keys" Hotel, Newport, Monmouthshire, including dining-hall, &c., for Mr. S. G. Hobbs. Mr. W. Conyers Kirby, architect, Gloucester Bank Chambers, Newport. Quantities by the architect:—

J. Hooper	£1,220	Jno. Jenkins	£1,197
J. Linton	1,180	G. F. Sharrem	1,089
J. T. Morris	1,150	D. Parfitt	1,064
Wm. Price	1,145	Geo. Wilkins	1,031

[All of Newport.]

NEWPORT (Mon.).—For erecting new business premises, Skinner-street, for Mr. Ingleton. Messrs. Habershon & Fawckner, architects:—

T. Webb	£2,557 0	Morgan & Roberts	£2,305 0
Moulton & Brownscombe	2,500 0	J. Linton	2,216 10
C. Lock	2,425 0	E. Richards	2,216 0
Westacott	2,403 0	Blackburn	2,167 0
T. G. Diamond	2,395 0	G. Wilkins	2,150 0
W. A. Linton	2,349 0	W. Moore	2,138 0

[All of Newport.]

NEWPORT (Mon.).—For rebuilding the "Blucher's Arms," Griffin-street, for Mrs. George Jones. Messrs. Habershon & Fawckner, architects:—

G. Wilkins	£1,100 0	T. Webb	£1,036 0
Westacott	1,084 15	W. Price	1,032 0
J. Linton	1,080 0	E. Richards	1,030 0
Williams, Rees, & Son	1,070 0	W. A. Linton	1,025 0
W. Moore	1,060 0	Blackburn	1,028 0
Moulton & Brownscombe	1,050 0	Morgan & Roberts	990 0

[All of Newport.]

NEWPORT (Mon.).—For rebuilding 114, Commercial-street, Newport, for Mrs. Rowe. Messrs. Habershon & Fawckner, architects:—

W. Moore	£742	Westacott	£635
T. G. Diamond	733	Blackburn	633
G. Wilkins	700	W. A. Linton	632
W. Price	698	Williams, Rees	630
T. Webb	695	Morgan & Roberts	625
J. Linton	690	E. Richards	615

[All of Newport.]

NORTHALLERTON.—For the widening of the county bridge, Upleatham, for the North Riding (Yorks) County Council. Mr. Walker Stead, C.E., County surveyor, Court House, Northallerton:—

Parker & Sharp	£442 12 0	W. C. Atkinson	£231 1 0
Isaac Atkinson	276 17 0	Wm. Blackburn, Leven	
White & Cruddas	243 4 6	Bridge, Yarm*	226 10 6

[Engineer's estimate, £240.]
* Accepted.

OSWESTRY.—For the erection of the Oswestry Municipal Buildings. Mr. T. M. Lockwood, architect, Chester:—

Jackson Bros.	£9,930	J. Matthews	£8,728
J. D. Williams	9,700	W. E. Samuels	8,620
Stephens & Bastowe	9,609	T. Martin	8,605
Davies Bros	9,200	W. H. Thomas, Oswestry*	8,597
Gethin	8,898	R. Price	8,308
Kelly Bros.	8,780	J. S. Kimberley	8,231

* Accepted.

PENZANCE.—For the erection of a convalescent home, near Alexandra-terrace, Penzance, for Mr. T. B. Bolitho, M.P. Mr. Oliver Caldwell, architect, Victoria-square, Penzance:—

Reed, Blight, & Co.	£3,833 0 0	Wm. Trounson	£3,141 2 11
Perkins, Caldwell, & Caldwell	3,308 0 0	Richard Walters	3,020 15 0
Richard Hill	3,149 0 0	Arthur Carkeek, Redruth*	2,674 0 0
Joseph James	3,145 15 0		

* Accepted.

RUGBY.—For the construction of a circular gasholder tank and other works thereto. Mr. J. Simpson, engineer:—
B. Cooke & Co., Battersea (accepted) £2,600 0 0

STRATFORD.—For alterations and dilapidations at the "Marsh Gate" Tavern, High-street, Stratford, E., for Mr. A. E. Carter. Mr. Fred A. Ashton, architect, 4, Crooked-lane, E.C.:—

Hearle & Farrow	£442	F. Volter	£372
W. Shurmur	479	W. Watson (accepted)	348
North Bros.	415	Coulsell Bros.	347

SUNDERLAND.—For the erection of a miners' hall, retiring, and reading-rooms, &c., at Silksworth, for the Miners' Association. Mr. Henry Grieves, architect, Albany-chambers, South Shields. Quantities by Messrs. Bordman & Morton, Sunderland:—

Draper & Sons	£3,640 10 2	M. R. Cooper	£3,060 0 6
Robert Allison	3,329 8 8	J. Eltick	3,011 17 10
George Muir	3,249 4 0	T. P. Shafto, Sunderland*	2,915 0 0
C. D. Potter	3,296 0 0		
D. Rankin	3,203 0 0		

* Accepted.

THORPE SATCHVILLE (Leicestershire).—For repairs and alterations at farm buildings, Thorpe Satchville. Messrs. Miles & Beasley, architects, 37, Friar-lane, Leicester:—

Pendleton & Bambury	£150 0	C. Stoughton, Hungarton, Leicester*	£96 15
E. Clarke	101 0		

* Accepted.

WIMBLEDON.—For the construction of roads and sewers on the Wimbledon Park Estate. Mr. William Hunt, surveyor, 5, York-buildings, Adelphi, W.C.—

Contract No. 1.		Contract No. 2.	
Adams	£3,784	Adams	£2,189
Towney & Wimpey	3,479	Nowell & Robson	2,150
Nowell & Robson	3,460	E. Rogers & Co.	2,100
E. Rogers & Co.	3,435	Joseph Mears	2,080
Joseph Mears	3,290	Towes & Wimpey	2,045
Killingback	3,161	Killingback	1,979
Barlow & Roberts	3,025	Barlow & Roberts	1,8[illegible]

SUBSCRIBERS in LONDON and the SUBURBS, by prepaying at the Publishing Office, 19s. per annum (or 4s. 9d. per quarter), can ensure receiving "The Builder," by *Friday Morning's Post.*

The Builder Cathedral Series.

1891.

1. Canterbury	Jan. 3.	7. Salisbury	July 4.
2. Lichfield	Feb. 7.	8. Bristol	Aug. 1.
3. St. Alban's	Mar. 7.	9. Norwich	Sept. 5.
4. Peterborough	April 4.	10. Rochester	Oct. 3.
5. Wells	May 2.	11. Lincoln	Nov. 7.
6. Exeter	June 6.	12. Gloucester	Dec. 5.

1892.

13. St. Paul's .. .. Jan. 2.

14. Hereford	Feb. 6.	20. Worcester	Aug. 6.
15. Chichester	Mar. 5.	21. Bangor	Sept. 3.
16. Ely	April 2.	22. St. Asaph	Sept. 3.
17. Llandaff	May 7.	23. Winchester	Oct. 1.
18. Oxford	June 4.	24. Truro	Nov. 5.
19. Southwell	July 2.	25. St. David's	Dec. 3.

[Further arrangements will be duly announced.]

Post-free FOURPENCE HALFPENNY each, except Nos. 1 and 2, which are *out of print*; but the VIEW, PLAN, AND DESCRIPTION of CANTERBURY and of LICHFIELD have been re-printed, and they can now be had, price ONE SHILLING each set; by post, 1s. 2d.

THE REREDOS, ST. PAUL'S.
Reprinted from "The Builder," January 28, 1888 (15 in. by 11½ in.), on stout paper, unfolded, for framing, 6d.; by post, 8d.

PORTFOLIOS,
for Preserving the Plates unfolded, 2s. 6d.; by post, 3s.

London: Office of "The Builder," 46, Catherine-street, W.C.

PUBLISHER'S NOTICES.

Registered Telegraphic Address, 'THE BUILDER,' LONDON.

CHARGES FOR ADVERTISEMENTS.

SITUATIONS VACANT, PARTNERSHIPS, APPRENTICESHIPS TRADE, AND GENERAL ADVERTISEMENTS.

Six lines (about fifty words) or under .... 4s. 6d.
Each additional line (about ten words) .... 0s. 6d.

Terms for Series of Trade Advertisements, also for Special Advertisements on front page, Competitions, Contracts, Sales by Auction, &c. may be obtained on application to the Publisher.

SITUATIONS WANTED.

FOUR Lines (about thirty words) or under .... 2s. 6d.
Each additional line (about ten words) .... 0s. 6d.

PREPAYMENT IS ABSOLUTELY NECESSARY.

. Stamps must *not* be Sent, but all small sums should be remitted by Cash in Registered Letter or by Money Order, payable at the Post-office, Covent-garden, W.C. to

DOUGLAS FOURDRINIER, Publisher,
Addressed to No. 46, Catherine-street, W.C.

Advertisements for the current week's issue must reach the Office before THREE o'clock p.m. on THURSDAY, but those intended for the front Page should be in by TWELVE noon on WEDNESDAY.

SPECIAL.—ALTERATIONS IN STANDING ADVERTISEMENTS or ORDERS TO DISCONTINUE same must reach the Office before TEN o'clock on WEDNESDAY mornings.

The Publisher cannot be responsible for DRAWINGS, TESTIMONIALS, &c. left at the Office in reply to Advertisements, and strongly recommends that of the latter COPIES ONLY should be sent.

PERSONS Advertising in "The Builder" may have *Replies addressed to the Office,* 46, Catherine-street, Covent Garden, W.C. *free of charge.* Letters will be forwarded if addressed envelopes are sent, together with sufficient stamps to cover the postage.

AN EDITION Printed on THIN PAPER, for FOREIGN and COLONIAL CIRCULATION, is issued every week.

READING CASES. { Now ready. NINEPENCE EACH. By Post (carefully packed), 1s.

TERMS OF SUBSCRIPTION.

"THE BUILDER" is supplied DIRECT from the Office to residents in any part of the United Kingdom at the rate of 19s. per annum PREPAID. To all parts of Europe, America, Australia, and New Zealand, 26s. per annum. To India, China, Ceylon, &c., 30s. per annum. Remittances payable to DOUGLAS FOURDRINIER, Publisher, No. 46, Catherine-street, W.C.

TO CORRESPONDENTS.

R. D. and W.—E. L. G. (we concur in condemning the system you allude to, but we decline to print a letter expressed in such violent and fanatical language).—A. R.—C. S.—J. E.—R. & G.—A. B. B.—W. H. H. (amounts should have been sent).

All statements of facts, lists of tenders, &c., must be accompanied by the name and address of the sender, not necessarily for publication.

We are compelled to decline pointing out books and giving addresses.

Note.—The responsibility of signed articles, and papers read at public meetings, rests, of course, with the authors.

We cannot undertake to return rejected communications.

Letters or communications (beyond mere news-items) which have been duplicated for other journals, are NOT DESIRED.

All communications regarding literary and artistic matter should be addressed to THE EDITOR; all communications relating to advertisements and other exclusively business matters should be addressed to THE PUBLISHER, and *not* to the Editor.

The Builder.

Vol. LXII. No. 2566. Saturday, April 9, 1892.

ILLUSTRATIONS.

Illustrations of Old Chester: IV., Supports under Bishop Lloyd's House, Watergate-row.—Drawn by Mr. T. P. Ivison .... *Double-Page Ink-Photo.*
Norwich Cathedral: View in Interior.—Drawn by Mr. S. K. Greenslade .... *Single-Page Ink-Photo.*
Ely Cathedral: Exterior of East End of Choir.—Drawn by Mr. S. K. Greenslade .... *Single-Page Ink-Photo.*
Design for a Steeple: Awarded the Tite Prize.—By Mr. T. Rogers Kitsell, A.R.I.B.A. .... *Double-Page Ink-Photo.*
Rotherhithe Infirmary: Plans of Alterations and Additions.—Messrs. Newman & Newman, Architects .... *Double-Page Photo-Litho.*

Blocks in Text.

New Offices for the *Athenæum*, Bream's-buildings.—Mr. W. C. Street, Architect .... Page 290

CONTENTS.

Architecture of the Lake Dwellings of Europe 277
...s 279
...al Institute of British Architects 281
...rature and Architecture 284
...strations of Old Chester 285
...erior, Norwich Cathedral, and East End of Choir, Ely 286
...ign for a Steeple 288
...herhithe Infirmary, St. Olave's Union 288
...gazines and Reviews 288
... Architectural Association Spring Visits 289
... London County Council 289
...w Offices for the *Athenæum* 290
...gineering Societies 290
Books: S. A. Russell's "Electric Light Cables and the Distribution of Electricity" (London: Whittaker & Co.); F. Mitchell's "Forty Plates on Building Construction" (London: Cassell & Co.); A. R. Wolff's "Ventilation of Buildings" (New York); P. Paris' "Elatée, La Ville le Temple d'Athéna Cranaia" (Paris: Ernest Thorin); T. Mackay's "Plea for Liberty" (London: J. Murray); E. Curtius and F. Adler's "Olympia" (Berlin: Asher & Co.); "Wiener Vorlegeblätter fur Archäologische" (Wien: A. Hölder); "Fünfzehntes Hallisches Winckelmanns-programm" (Halle: Niemeyer); P. Girard's "La Peinture Antique" (Paris: Quantin); H. Clarke's "London Street Improvements" 291
Architectural Education 292
Lincoln Cathedral Library 293
Removing Old Paint 293
Student's Column.—Warming Buildings by Hot Water, XV. 293
Obituary 294
General Building News 294
Sanitary and Engineering News 294
Foreign and Colonial 295
Miscellaneous 295
Legal 295
Capital and Labour 296
Meetings 296
Recent Patents 296

The Architecture of the Lake Dwellings of Europe.

IT is proposed in this essay to give a rapid survey of the facts already known in regard to this remarkable class of building works, mostly of remote antiquity, which until comparatively recent times were altogether unknown; to trace their extension into many of the countries of Europe, indicate some of the modes of construction adopted, with notes on some of the works discovered on the various sites.

It is now almost an old story, which need only be glanced at, to refer to the winter of the years 1853-4, when a very great drought and continued cold caused an unusual event in the Swiss lakes. Not only the rivers, but the lakes, sank much below the oldest recorded level, and, in consequence, much of the shores that had been covered with water was left high and dry. The inhabitants took advantage of this state of things to reclaim portions of the land, and at Ober Meilen, on the Lake of Zurich, the workmen were surprised to find that the land they were reclaiming was covered by a mass of wooden piles firmly driven into the bed of the lake, but so rotten as to indicate very great age. The piles commenced about 300 paces from the existing shore, and extended parallel to the bend of the lake about 500 paces further into the water until it became suddenly deep. They might be counted by thousands in the portion operated upon. They were driven below and covered by an upper bed 2 ft. thick, consisting of yellowish mud, such as is deposited all over the surface of the lake where not much exposed to the action of the waves. Beneath this is a bed of sandy loam from 2 ft. to 2 ft. 6 in. in thickness, black with organic matter, called the "relic bed" by Swiss antiquaries, and in this the heads of the piles and many antiquities were found. Below this was a bed of clean loam, of great thickness, into which the piles were driven, but nothing was found. The piles are of oak, beech, fir, and birch, from 4 in. to 6 in. thick. Some are whole trunks, but the majority of the sizes named consist of split stems, the ends being either pointed by fire, or in some cases roughly hacked into form by stone implements. Only a few bronze articles were found, the others consisting of stone celts, chisels of varying size, form and material, several being of stone foreign to Switzerland, some of nephrite, and some few articles of flint being also met with, this material being rare in Switzerland. This, the first site met with, proved to be one of the oldest, since it belongs to the age of stone, with evidences of some, but not much, later occupation.

The description given is more or less typical of numberless other discoveries that were made in an incredibly short space of time, in many other of the Swiss lakes, varying only in details of construction, extent, and in the articles found in the "relic beds," which latter have been invariably found beneath the ordinary and most recent deposit. Discovery followed discovery: an eager band of investigators emulated one another in making search, either by excavations wherever possible, or by dredging the lake bottoms, and all were well rewarded.

A map of any Swiss lake, on which the discoveries are recorded, affords ample subject for comment, for the lake dwellings prove to be remarkable in respect to their numbers, indicating the existence of a large population. Almost all along the lake of Neuchatel, the sites which have been found up to the present are at distances averaging about an English mile apart, or fifty sites in all. On that of Bionne four sites are met with within a single mile. On the shores of the little lake of Morat fifteen sites are indicated in Keller's "Lake Dwellings," in a shore-line of about eleven miles. The lake of Geneva is dotted with a remarkable number of sites from the capital quite up to and past Lausanne. These sites are in some cases just opposite to modern villages, suggestive of what is probably a fact,—that, when the lake dwellings were finally given up, their inhabitants settled on the mainland opposite to their old homes.

The discoveries in Switzerland were not likely to remain for long isolated. Investigators in other countries,—Italy, Holland, Germany, France, Great Britain, Austria, and elsewhere,—speedily had discoveries to record; and what seemed at first but a peculiar mode of building of an unknown people, now has spread to the greatest part of Europe, revealing to us an entirely new and unexpected field of study. Since these structures afford, perhaps, the oldest system of building construction at present known, the system claims attention, and the more so since the traditions of early architecture all refer to a time when the grandest features of Classic art had their prototypes in structures of wood. But the buildings of Switzerland are, doubtless, of earlier date and of simpler design than the earliest and most incipient form of the Doric order in its first wooden conception.

Investigators of the lake dwellings soon became aware that various modes of building were adopted, and these will now be referred to. The simplest type consists of a platform supported on piles driven into the shallow sides of the lakes, generally of rectangular form, connexion with the shore being obtained by means of a narrow causeway of piles supporting a timber gangway. On the platform huts were erected, forming the habitations of the tribe or settlement, together with enclosures for cattle. A large hearth was placed in the centre of each hut, bedded upon a layer of clay to prevent the timbers of the platform from becoming ignited, and in some instances there are indications of long occupation, as is evidenced by there being one hearth above an older one at a higher and more recent level. The flowing waters of the lakes passed freely between the piles, and trap-doors in the platforms afforded a ready means of disposal for the refuse of the settlement into the water. By this means a vast amount of *débris*, broken pottery, worked bone, and other articles numberless in quantity have been deposited, all of which help to form the "relic bed" which is met with on the site of each settlement. The piles are found, in most cases, singly, in others close together, generally placed with a certain amount of regularity, in parallel rows, but sometimes in great confusion of position. The points show very distinctly the marks of the implements with which they have been cut, and distinction can be made as to whether with flint, by fire, with bronze, or in the late examples, with iron hatchets. The piles are formed close to the shore in the earliest examples, but the revolution caused by the introduction of bronze is at once marked by the piles being longer, and driven into deeper water. In some instances a settlement of the Stone Age has been found, extended in this way into deeper water; in other instances, fresh formations are found. The piles being cut to a level, the platforms were then laid above them, the beams of support being fastened to them by pins or by mortises, central hollows, or notches. The floors were formed by unbarked stems of trees, in some cases in two layers, and, in one of the Italian examples, of rough split boards. The floor was then covered with clay and gravel firmly pounded down into position; and in some of the Italian examples, which resemble in other respects those of Switzerland very exactly, there is a layer of large pebbles.

In a few cases, the outer line of piles had an upright enclosure of wattles or hurdles above water-line, in order, apparently, to break the force of the waves from the piles. While this advantage would be secured, it would have to be at the risk of the retention of the decaying mass of deposit thrown in from above, and which would have been better washed away.

Another mode of construction of the platforms was for a mass of earth and stones to be brought from the land and thrown into the water, as the site of the intended settlement. By this means a certain amount of earth was deposited to form a mound beneath the water, into which the piles were driven, stones being afterwards deposited between the piles to steady them and keep them better in position. This arrangement is far from uncommon, especially in certain of the Swiss lake, and is known to antiquaries as a "Steinberg." In some examples the "Steinberg" has been brought to the surface, and at Nidau there is evidence of its having been occupied by the Romans. This site has been known for centuries, but the mass of ancient pile work beneath the later deposits has only been observed in the recent years of these discoveries.

While the formation of platforms upon piles has existed from the earliest beginnings quite to the Iron Age, with but little alteration, except in better workmanship, another mode of construction has been noticed in many instances. The platform is carried on a solid mass of sticks, small trees, stems, and such like, in fascines piled together in the water of the lakes, and kept in position by a few piles driven here and there to steady the mass. When it was sufficiently consolidated the platform was laid. This system is found mostly in the smaller lakes, but a high antiquity has been assigned to them which is sufficiently attested by the nature of the articles found.

It is far from improbable that this system is the older of the two, and certainly its simplicity would be likely to commend itself to an early people rather than the elaborate system of felling trees by means of flint implements, with all the labour of sharpening them, driving them into position in the waters of the lake, together with the framework of the carpentry platforms.

Sufficient attention has hardly yet been given by Swiss antiquaries to the difference between the systems named in regard to which is the earlier of the two, but a study of the subject, and of the articles found, can hardly leave a reasonable doubt that the formation of solid platforms of twigs and boughs, readily carried and deposited into position, was the earlier of the two. The insertion of a few guiding piles would readily enough be called for as a necessity, and this would lead in process of time to their entire use for the supporting of the platforms, for the advantage of obtaining a ready output for deposits.

Of the construction of the Dutch terpen, and the crannoges of Ireland and Scotland, mention will be made later.

The dwellings above the platforms were formed of small piles, and the framework filled in with branches, and wattle-covered with plaster inside and out. This is no mere matter of conjecture, for in several instances, quantities of the plastering have been found in the submerged mass of *débris*, with the marks of the wattles remaining. Fire has frequently caused the destruction of the settlements, and in such cases the whole mass of the burnt material is found where it fell. Nor were the surfaces left undecorated, if we may judge by the fact that in one of the sites met with on the Lake Bourget portions were found ornamented with incised lines and concentric circles, while on others the circles, arranged in a row, were filled in with the Fylfot cross. But this site is of late date. At Windisch, the clay coating was seen by the late Dr. Keller to be coloured white and red.

The covering of the huts was of thatch, various portions having been found; white moss was often used to stop the inequalities of walls and roofs. The huts were possibly circular in form in some few instances, but, apparently, for the most part rectangular, traces showing the sizes of the apartments having been met with in many places, in Switzerland and Italy especially. At Schussennied a settlement has been found, abandoned probably by its occupants on account of its being overgrown by peat. It is, at least, completely so overgrown now, and deep beneath it. One of the huts has been excavated, and found to have been about 33 ft. long and 23 ft. wide, divided into two inequal chambers. Other sites have produced indications of buildings of very similar size. In others, a sort of skirting-board is found on the platforms marking the sites of huts. In some places it is evident that they must have stood very close together, with compartments for cattle,—doubtless for security of keeping.

Safety from attack, with convenience for fishing, &c., appears to have prompted this singular and laborious mode of construction, although Switzerland did not possess, even at a remote period, wild animals of great ferocity, and foreign foes might have turned these timber dwellings speedily to ashes. Although many have suffered from conflagration, there is but little or no appearance that this was the work of an enemy. No traces of surprise and massacre, at least, are to be met with, except in the settlement, of late date, at La Tène. The general absence of human remains points forcibly to the peaceful existence of the inhabitants through a very lengthened period. But that they did actually indulge in warfare is apparent from the mass of offensive and defensive weapons which abound in all the sites, early as well as late; while at Estavayer something decidedly like a bronze arrow-head, with a groove for poison, has been found. The lake of Bienne and some other places have produced cups formed out of human skulls,—most probably those of enemies slain in battle.

It could hardly be expected otherwise than that the reports, made at intervals rapidly following one another, of the discoveries taking place in Switzerland, would have the effect of stimulating inquiry in other districts. Italy was the first to follow, by directing systematic inquiry into the subject. This is no more than was to be expected, for records of many chance discoveries were in existence, some of which, notably those made in the works of deepening the harbour of Peschiera, in which remains had been found very analogous to those in Switzerland. Some of these were communicated to Professor Keller, who pronounced upon their general resemblance and the importance of further investigations. But, indeed, inquiry had only to be made to produce evidence of a great many discoveries which had previously been made. These were eagerly sought for by Professor Bart. Gastaldi, who published, in 1862, a small volume full of records of such discoveries. At this early stage, the Anthropological Society of London rendered excellent service by the publication of a translation, by Mr. Harcourt Chambers, of Professor Gastaldi's book, under the title of "Lake Habitations and Prehistoric Remains in the Turbaries and Marl Beds of Northern and Central Italy." This was in 1865. The book is filled with records of discoveries of objects of remote antiquity, which evidently had no relation to, and were of much earlier origin than, any of the antiquities previously known which the prolific soil of Italy has yielded.

Aided by an opportune grant from the Society of Natural Sciences at Milan and the zeal of a number of explorers,—M. Desor, Sig. Stoppani, M. Mortillot, the Abbé Rauchet, Pigorini, Chierici, Strobel, and many others,—investigations were made in all directions, followed by a great number of discoveries. It is neither possible nor necessary that these should be examined in detail, but the general results are as follows. Avoiding to a great extent the larger of the Italian lakes, for the reason which was very soon recognised,—namely, that the cliffs are rocky and so precipitous that no shallow water is to be found or any soil into which piles could be driven,—the lake builders attached themselves to the smaller lakes, where these conditions do not occur.

Several sites around the little Lago di Varese have proved to be those of pile dwellings, while the whole of the Isola Virginia has been shown to be of artificial origin, for its whole area has been found to be filled with piles, the number of which have been estimated to be between 35,000 and 40,000, the area of the piles being now filled in with solid earth, probably, as supposed by Professor Castelfranco, after a fire had consumed the earlier wooden settlement towards the close of the Bronze Age. Articles of remote antiquity, down to other of Roman times, have been found here, the earliest at the lowest level. The small adjacent lakes of Monate, Varano, and Biandrono, and many others have also rewarded the explorers, the objects found, at the latter place, being in many instances in regular sequence from the polished Stone Age to that of Iron.

All the sites found, so far, have been lake dwellings of the Swiss type—placed in shallow water, close to the land, with traces of a bridge across to the latter. But there is another class of buildings to which Italian antiquaries have given the name of terremare. "Mare" is, in fact, the rich, marl-like soil called marl by Prof. Gastaldi. It was noticed at an early period that these sites were to be found in places far removed from where water is now found, or at a higher level; that they had been originally surrounded by a ditch and bank, and that the original platform, supported on the usual piles of a lake dwelling, was sometimes covered by a second platform and piles; and in some few instances, by a third, the whole being now filled in solid by what has proved to be the accumulated rubbish from droppings made from the various platforms. This deposit is now eagerly sought for by the agriculturist for the purposes of manure, and hence the constant discovery of new dwelling sites. A lengthy controversy arose with respect to the mode of erection stated above, which involves the supposition that when the thrown-out refuse came up to the floor-level of the first platform the second then became necessary; after that the third. It is but again the principle by which an Eastern village is now found to be raised on a mound, formed by the nameless droppings of rubbish which cover traces of more ancient dwellings. The weak point of the theory, to us, is, that much of the deposit seems to have been stratified by aqueous agency, and, although this might be easily accounted for in the case of the first platform, in some examples, supposing that there was then some shallow water, yet which would be an impossibility so far as regards the upper ones, except on the hypothesis that, at one time, the country was all at a much lower level, that it sank again and again, and that it has ce been raised up to a level above the sent water-line. But this is not an idea t appears yet to have been discussed, and is only mentioned since such changes of el have occurred again and again in other ts of Italy, and it would account for all earances.

)nly a few of the curious results that have eady been recorded can be glanced at. At telnuovo the devoted explorer, Chierici, nd beneath a Bronze Age terremare, indica-ns of an older settlement. At Lagozza, no mal remains of any kind have yet been nd, but ample evidences of vegetable food the way of hazel-nuts, wild apples, acorns, kinds of wheat, and six-eared barley. ere were also traces of cherry and poppy-ds, &c., while there were many others also nd by Prof. Sordelli of wild flax. At chiera, Prof. F. Unger has recognised the stence of rye, and also the vine. The es of dog, sheep, horse, ox, pig, goat common, and occasionally the bones of n.

Many of the structures are rectangular in m, and are remarkable from the fact that y frequently face the cardinal points, or nearly so as to justify the belief that they re set out to face sunrise at the varying iods of the year when first begun.

)ur observations, so far as Italy is con-ned, must close with a brief reference to exploration of the remarkable terremare Castione, undertaken in 1877 by funds pro-led by the Minister of Public Instruction, l directed by Prof. Pigorini. Judging by area of ground excavated, the settlement sisted of a quadrangular block, with an ntation 30 deg. from east to north. The tral area consists of an enormous number uprights, which supported the wooden tform, the evidence being that the entire a below was once open, and left so as a con-ient place for the deposit of rubbish. Around block was a series of projecting buildings, e square towers of defence. These were med of lengths of timber crossing and re-sing at the angles, and projecting irregu-ly, the internal space of each being filled olid with earth. Beyond was an earthern part and ditch. In process of time, the beneath the platform became filled up, then the builders enlarged the rampart proceeded to erect a second platform ve the first. The recent explorers have red themselves that, although the site once covered with water, it was not so he period when the erection took place, on what was then somewhat rising nd. The earthen rampart is some sort of ence as to this; but the whole structure, its indications of double platforms, has to be excavated from a fairly deep bed of e recent aqueous deposit, which covers all locality. The theory is proposed that the jecting towers were intended to render port to the earthern bank outside them,—dea not involving very profound structural wledge. It is far more likely that the ers were to act as external buttresses to large internal mass of pile work. Wher-r piles have been met with, feebly fixed as y must have been, and with but little, if strutting, except the top platform, held ther, not by nails, but with the rudest ns and mortises with pins, it is not to be dered at that the mass of uprights would suffer deflection. Indeed, every photo-h of the condition of either Swiss or ian piles, taken when first found, readily cates such deflection, and that it must e been a serious matter. Here, indeed, at tione, the remedy proposed has not been cient, for the piles have all sunk out of perpendicular, and are all deflected to-ds the towers.

[ore recent researches have revealed the that late dwellings or terremare are to be d all over the valley of the Po, from ona quite away to Bologna, while the nity of Parma is studded with sites ady discovered. In other directions the of discovery has been great, and is con-tly on the increase. In addition to the nals already noted, there are bones of the bear, fox, dog, wolf, badger, pole-cat, wild boar, donkey, roe deer, fallow deer, reindeer, sheep, hare, wood-mouse, porcupine, wild cat, and hedgehog. The horse is of two kinds, and is not uncommon. The raven, domestic fowl, stork, heron, wild goose, duck, and tortoise, have also been traced.

From Italy to Holland is not a very connected passage; but, in the low-lying lands bordering the North Sea, from West Friesland,—in fact, right away to East Friesland,—there are a great many sites which very closely resemble those of the Italian terremare, with certain differences which are readily noted. They are called Terpen in Holland, and Warfen in East Friesland. Dr. Monro, in his invaluable "Lake Dwellings of Europe," has given an interesting notice of these structures, including a visit to a terp near the town of Dokkum, or about four or five miles from the present seashore. Here, in a flat country he found the terp to consist of a slight elevation, crowed by a small, ancient church and a clump of trees. Workmen were busily engaged in the removal of the elevated mass, where not covered with buildings, for the purposes of manure, and the excavations revealed a section 15 ft. or 18 ft. high, in which he soon detected upright piles of oak in the last stage of decay, while elsewhere was a heap of oak beams recently removed from the diggings. The mass of the mound was stratified. These structures, which are very numerous in the district, appear to be those referred to by Pliny, who, in his "Natural History," describes the wretched race of the Chauci, who construct their cabins or mounds just high enough to be above the level of the sea which covers the entire land twice daily, far and wide, and who, on the receding of the tides, catch the fish entangled in the land.

We have, in the mound described by Dr. Monro, where the uprights were clearly intended to support a timber flooring on which the huts were erected, the same system of erection as in the Italian terremare, and also the same accumulation of earth beneath them, now quite covering the timbers, which is here, as there, highly prized by the agriculturist for manure. The objects found, however, are of later date. Up to the present time no objects of very remote antiquity have been met with, while, indeed, they continue to Mediæval times. Roman Samian ware, Saxon and later coins, tiles, &c., have been found. It is doubtful, too, if any additional discoveries are likely to arise on other sites, since exploration of several have been so completely made, the excavations revealing the entire contents of many of these structures, leading to their entire removal. The whole character of the country is now changed, and the sea now no longer invades it, the sea-walls, erected in Mediæval times, having steadily kept out the ocean, allowing of the cultivation of the land which was once covered by its waters.

In 1883, Dr. Hartmann investigated the prehistoric structures which exist in the Holstein Fen districts, near the Elbe. Here there are artificial mounds from 13 to 23 feet high, covering structures of piles and fascines, the piles being apparently placed to keep the latter in position. The elevation was skilfully adjusted to carry the structure above the tides where the country was open to the flow of the sea, now happily excluded, and it is supposed by Dr. Hartmann to have been based upon a layer of cowdung. Above the first erection, examined in one instance, was a second, and a third above that again, the whole being now covered with a mass of *débris* as in the other cases. The belief in pile dwellings here is not entertained by Dr. Hartmann, but the general resemblance of construction goes far to warrant our idea that here, as in Italy and Holland, the mode of building was similar. The general mass of objects met with relate to very ancient times, but in one of the structures investigated, masses of iron slag were found.

The Rhine district has produced several sites, but the objects found appear to be later than those of Switzerland. That at Bebro, near Mayence, appears to have been in existence in Roman times. At Billingheim, while oak square-cut beams and pottery of late date have been found, prehistoric flint implements have been discovered at a lower level. At Gägelow, North Germany, late objects as well as early ones have also occurred. At Spandau, near Berlin, in what was formerly a lake, piles partly burnt have been exhumed, and the same may be said of many another site, already more or less investigated, in Poland, East Prussia, Livland, in Carinthia and Carniola, Pomerania, and Prussia; in Austria and Hungary; along the Danube, and many more.

At Zahsow, near Cottbus, and at Potzlow, lake dwellings on piles have been found beneath the early constructions called Burgwälle by German antiquaries. In other north-country sites curious examples of circular huts have been discovered; and at Bouslack was the curious structural feature of some of the timbers being tied together with thongs of birch.

One of the most singular constructions was that in the Lake Persanzigersee, where what had once been a small island was surrounded by sixty or more rectangular enclosures, in the water, erected in the usual manner of log huts, with horizontal beams notched at the angles. Upon these platforms had been erected, which contained the huts of the settlement. A bridge connected the island with another mound nearer the shore, which was itself connected to the mainland by a second bridge. The quantity of timber used had been enormous.*

NOTES.

WE have received from Mr. John Waugh, C.E., of Bradford, his report to the Coroner on the fall of the chimney of Messrs. Thornton's mill at Cleckheaton on Feb. 24, by which fourteen persons were killed and a considerable amount of property destroyed. The history of the chimney can leave no surprise at the catastrophe. It was built in 1859 under the superintendence of a hybrid person described as "a joiner and architect." When it was 40 yards in height it was found that it had gone out of the perpendicular by about 7 in. in a south-easterly direction, a circumstance which at once showed either that the foundation was inadequate or that some of the lower portion had been badly constructed, and it ought to have been taken down again and rebuilt under better advice. It was however straightened as it stood (the particulars of the straightening operation are not given). On February 8 of this year the attention of the owner was called to signs of distress in the chimney, and Messrs. Moulson builders of Bradford sent one Harrison to look to it, who said vaguely that "the chimney appeared all right," but advised the renewing of the brickwork where the cracks and the bulge existed, for which purpose considerable portions of the brickwork appear to have been removed on each day and made good with new brickwork Harrison had, on his second visit, practically condemned the chimney, saying "you had better get out a new foundation and build a new chimney"; but this advice seems to have fallen on deaf ears.

"Before leaving for the night of Wednesday, the 24th, Harrison thought it advisable to prop 'the loose brickwork of the bulge' from the boiler-house wall; whilst in the act of performing this operation, he felt the brickwork of the outer shell press against his knees, the chimney then settled down, and finally tumbled over in an easterly direction, destroying about half the adjoining mill, and killing fourteen persons."

Mr. Waugh's Report further says:—

"In the building of a chimney it is customary to select the bricks from the very best kilns in the district, and, further, to carefully inspect such when delivered, and reject the unsound ones. Had this latter course been adopted in regard to this chimney a great proportion used in its construction would have been rejected. In fact, they were, with the exception

* To be continued.

of the firebrick, unfit for the purpose of building a chimney, even if constructed of solid brickwork. They were of various sizes, various material, and differed very much in the degree of burning. I am strongly of opinion that from some cause or another, bad as the bricks were in the first instance, that they, along with the lime, forming about one-fifth of the volume of the bricks, have both undergone a deterioration. I can attribute this marked deterioration of bricks and lime to nothing less than moisture extending over a long period. I have examined chimneys which have fallen by accident, and some by design, but I have never seen such a crushing to powder of the material of a structure as in this instance, and where bricks appeared to be stuck together in any quantity, they could be separated by hand with no effort whatever. . . . . The total weight of the whole structure was about 500 tons, the weight of the two shells above the solid was 480 tons. The outer shell alone weighed 325 tons. The distressed area, including bulge and cracks on the easterly and northerly sides, was equal to half the circumference. Therefore, if the chimney had been vertical the weight above the half the circumference would equal 162 tons, or 6·33 tons per square foot, but the chimney leaned over on this side, and it is impossible to say how much the weight was increased by this fact without a knowledge of the amount of departure from the vertical. Given this crushing weight above (apart from any lateral strains due to vibration) and a solid brick base and foundation below, with the weak places—bulge and cracks—in between, remembering the quality and condition of the brick and the nature of the structure, and the result should have been anything but a surprise. The chimney fell on the calmest day in the whole month, from a combination of causes, and in the following order as regards importance:—1st, bad bricks; 2nd, weak construction; 3rd, deterioration by moisture; 4th, the attempted repairs. Sooner or later, however, it would have fallen, apart altogether from the 4th head. The repairs were too late: the chimney was a doomed structure before either Moulson or his man saw it. In conclusion, I would say this is the second inquiry I have assisted at in regard to the deaths of persons from the fall of chimneys in ten years, making in those *two instances* alone a *death-roll* of *sixty-eight*. My earnest recommendation to the authorities is, that such structures should be annually inspected, from top to bottom, inside and out, by competent persons, and that the owners should be possessed of a certificate as to the safety of the structure as the result of such thorough inspection, such certificate of safety to be produced to Her Majesty's Inspector of Factories when required."

To which we need only add a remark as to the *morale* of false and we might say criminal economy in erecting such a structure. To save expense the chimney was proceeded with, after weakness had already shown itself before it was finished. To save expense the owners apparently refused to listen to the only sensible thing their bricklayer said about it, to have a new foundation and a new chimney. The result has been the loss of fourteen lives as well as the wrecking of part of the property. Most deplorably in this case has "penny wise" turned out to be "pound foolish."

THE *Architectural Review* (Boston) publishes an able article by Mr. R. D. Andrews, on "The Compensation of Architects," which is, in fact, an attack on the percentage system of payment. The main argument Mr. Andrews uses is the same which has been often suggested in our columns, and which must be obvious to every reflecting person, viz., that while other artists, as well as some professional men (as doctors and barristers), can get the value of superior ability in superior fees, the architect can only get this value by an increase of work, by taking in fact more work than he can attend to personally, and making his office an architecture-mill. Mr. Andrews does not forget also the minor objection (detrimental in principle perhaps rather than in practice), that by the per-centage system the financial interests of the architect and his client are directly opposed to each other. Mr. Andrews proposes that the architect should have a salary during the progress of a building, on condition of devoting a specified proportion of his time to it, and urges that it would be more economical in the end to pay out in this manner a sum twice the amount of the usual commission and secure the eminent architect's personal attention to the work. We do not think this idea would be found very practical, and Mr. Andrews seems to forget that there would be the same conflict in that case between the financial interest of client and architect, as it would be obviously to the interest of the latter to prolong the period of construction. What Mr. Andrews does see clearly, and puts well, is that the present system is not only unfair to architects of superior attainments and reputation, but inimical to the interests of art, as it prevents an architect from profiting by superior ability except by taking more work than he can attend to personally. The simplest method by far is for the architect to name a fee for which he will design and carry out the building, just as a painter names the sum for which he will paint a portrait. A man who has achieved a reputation for special genius or ability would then be able to obtain a just return for it without overburdening himself with work he could only do by proxy. There can be little doubt, at all events, that the 5 per cent. system of payment to architects is about the worst that could be devised; but (owing partly to the fact that it is officially recognised by the Institute) the public at all events seem to have an almost superstitious reverence for it, and look suspiciously upon any architect who proposes to be paid in any other way, as a half-caste kind of person who is not to be trusted.

THE outlook in the North is disheartening in the extreme, and, at the time of writing, shows but little sign of improvement. Were the Durham miners to re-commence work at once, it would still be some time before the normal activity prevailed in the district,—trade having been so seriously disturbed. The *Times*, indeed, goes the length of referring to the dispute as having already done more harm than any strike of modern times; and attributes the present deadlock to the want of a strong leader on the men's side. The absence of such a leader is very significant, for it can hardly be said that capable men are not to be found, especially in mining centres. The probability is that the heroes of previous labour disputes recognise the fact that in this case there is but little prospect of victory, and that the only way to ensure peace would be to counsel the unpalatable course of giving in. Such advice as this the majority of the Durham miners are not yet in a mood to listen to, although the proportion in favour of keeping up the strike, as shown by the ballot, is much smaller than at the outset. The last ballot showed 31,483 in favour of continuing the strike, as compared with 43,036 on the previous occasion; but only some 50,000 voted last Saturday out of a total of 92,000. The tone of the strikers at mass meetings held this week is distinctly against accepting any reduction, in spite of the many indications that the state of trade calls for it. The collapse of old-established works, together with the prevailing feeling of insecurity and apprehension, ought to convince them that their action is threatening a permanent stoppage of other industries. The folly of the engineers' strike, which has now lasted ten weeks, is so far recognised, that a number of members of the Amalgamated Society of Engineers are cutting themselves adrift from that body, and resuming work. The obstinacy of the strike committee has produced a widespread feeling of exasperation, and there is every indication that they will be defeated by the gradual defection of their allies.

AS the Metropolitan Railway Company have obtained legislative sanction to subscribe to the capital of the Eiffel Tower at Wembley, this work will, no doubt, be constructed. We assume that the public have not shown a disposition to put money into this work, but we have no doubt that this would not stop Sir Edward Watkin from carrying out his scheme. We have already stated our doubts as to whether this building,—not inside London, but like the Crystal Palace, well outside of the Metropolis,—can be a commercial success; and we are not enamoured of the principle of railway companies becoming partners in affairs outside their own legitimate business. The principle may be carried out to disastrous results, and is not altogether unlike a practice in the City by which trust companies brought out new concerns, and practically took part of the capital.

IT seemed almost beyond hope that w
should be able to lay a finger on an actua
monument of the battle of Marathon. Thi
however, Dr. Studniczka seems to hav
effected in his paper in the last issue (Ban
vi., 4, 1892) of the Prussian Archæologica
Jahrbuch. Every one who has recentl
visited the museum in the Acropolis a
Athens has been struck by the fragment
vividly painted and but little below life-siz
of a mounted horseman, dressed in th
closefitting garb of an Oriental. The
fragments, five-and-twenty in number, D
Studniczka reconstructs, by ingenious com
parison with a plate in the Ashmole
Museum at Oxford, in which is represented
Persian bowman seated on a horse, a
wearing a tiara; he holds a bow i
his left hand, and carries a quiver
his side; the plate is inscribed "Miltiad
Kalos." This plate, Dr. Studniczka show
by a most careful examination of the fra
ments, must have been a fairly good copy
the actual statue in question. We hav
therefore, in these fragments, not only
monument profoundly interesting in itself
one of the greatest decisive battles of the wor
but a piece of archaic sculpture accurate
dateable, and so of the first importance
the history of art. Other papers of inter
in the same issue are a discussion, by
Winnefeld, of the plan and arrangements
the two country seats of Pliny the Young
i.e., Tusci, in the upper valley of the Tib
and Laukenlinum, on the sea-coast. They
described, as will be remembered, in two
his letters to Domitius Apollinadris (v. 6) a
to Gallus (ii., 37). Considering the scantin
of the notice of such structures by Vitruvi
—*i.e.*, private as opposed to public hou
(Vitr. vi., 8),—any help to the reconstructi
of their details is of great value. T
concluding paper, by Dr. Winter, on
vase in the Cook Collection at Richmo
may serve to remind Englishmen that mu
remains yet to be done in the matter of su
publications. The vase, a krater of late sty
represents the adventure of Odysseus w
the Cyclops, and after a fashion so far u
precedented. The escape of Odysseus benea
the ram is a familiar *type* with black-figur
vase painters, but here we have for the fi
time a representation improved, not by t
epic but the dramatic form of the t
Polyphemus, with a huge eye in the centre
his forehead, lies in drunken sleep, while t
Satyrs of Euripides gather round, and t
companions of Odysseus prepare to break t
huge tree-trunks. It is surprising that t
unique vase has so long gone unnoticed.

M. PERROT contributes to the r
number of the *Bulletin de Corresp
dance Hellénique* a long analysis of the st
of the Vaphio cups. His article is illustra
by excellent plates. The two colou
fac-similes of the actual shape of the c
give a better idea of the gold surface t
any we have yet seen, but it seems a pity
republish the designs which the archæolog
public already have in adequate form in
Ephemeris Archæologikè. M. Perrot co
to the conclusion,—not a new one,—t
the cups are the outcome of local Pelop
nesian art, and that they owe little
nothing to foreign, *i.e.*, Oriental, influen
M. Lechat publishes a beautiful little bro
statuette of Aphrodite, recently acquired
M. Carapanos, and devotes most of his pa
to the discussion of the nature of bro
patina. He believes this patina to have be

ot the result of natural decay by exposure air or lapse of time, but to have been arti- ially produced,—he would call it rather enduit," than patina. Plutarch speaks in s life of Pericles (B.C. 159) of a class of tisans at Athens known as βαφεῖς χρυσοῦ orkmen who dyed gold of various colours. ay there not also have been βαφεῖς χαλκοῦ?

FROM a recent issue of the *Manchester Guardian* we get the substance of the port of the City Surveyor to the Art allery Committee, and their remarks there- on, on the subject of the proposed altera- ons to the Royal Institution. It is charac- ristic enough. It attempts in the first ace to depreciate the interior architecture hich is to be destroyed by pointing out at part of the details are plaster. At the ne when the Royal Institution was built it as the fashion to execute in plaster or ment many things which would now be ecuted in a nobler material; but that es not affect the value of the design. it the most noteworthy point is the mission that the space gained by de- oying Barry's galleries would only afford mporary accommodation for about ten ars, after which it is hoped that a more ibitious scheme in the nature of a separate rmanent Gallery may be carried out. So at the Art Gallery Committee of Man- ester propose to destroy the most charac- ristic feature of the interior of a great chitect's building to fit it for temporary use, d having spoiled the building irremediably, leave it for a new one. This is worse and orse, and only renders the proposal the more lefensible.

THE St. Pancras Vestry have now their first reward in the completion of their gent's Park Station with a plant capable a simultaneous output for 10,000 incan- scent lamps of 16-candle power each,—the iole of which has been contracted for by tomers,—and 90 arc lights for street light- of 10 ampères each. The station has n erected on a freehold site of 21,000 are feet purchased by the Vestry for 000l.; the remainder of the houses not uired for the works still contributing their ts. The plant consists of nine dynamos incandescents coupled separately to as ay triple-expansion engines; and two aller dynamos and engines for the arc lights; oiler-house with five boilers, and a storage tery of sixty cells. There is an under- und tank for condensed water containing ,000 gallons; and surrounding the lower tion of the chimney, attached to an iron ning, is a series of corrugated iron plates r which the hot water pumped from the densers flows back to the tank. The maxi- m amount of water required in the day is ,000 gallons, so that as the water is pur- sed of the water company, this innovation cooling will play an important part in the nomy of the station. There are seven ers in the distribution of current addition to the mains, and there i underground sub-station, with two bat- es of fifty-eight cells each, on the open e by the Cobden monument in Camden n. The mains are laid on the three-wire em, the conductors being of copper strips ported on insulators. The culverts are of crete, with asphalted roofs to render them erproof. The street lighting is very good, arc lamps being carried on handsome cast- standards 25 ft. high, and placed centrally he road at about 200 ft. apart. In all the ils great care has been taken by the ry's engineer, Professor Henry Robinson, King's College, to whom the work was usted.

E have received from Mr. Brandreth, architect, a scheme for a Public rks and Construction Stock Exchange, Institution constituting a link between different branches of the builders', the tractors', and the engineers' businesses under the dome of a central hall in London." The further objects which such an Institution might serve are thus stated in Mr. Brandreth's letter or prospectus:—

"A practical and permanent Building and Construction Exchange with a classified exhibition of specifications, plans, samples, models, tarifs, price lists, adjudications, tenders, the latest notices and advertisements relating to work at home and abroad and the leading English and foreign technical papers.

A market for the introduction of new projects, and for dealings in matters relating to the aforesaid trades in all their branches, the sale and purchase of materials by private treaty or public auction.

A financial centre for the negociation of monetary transactions, contracts, agreements, referring to advances, mortgages, purchases and sales of land and building property, on strictly impartial principles and with the least possible expenditure of time and money."

That such an institution would be useful if it could be established and kept going is very probable, but it is not very easy to see where the funds are to come from. Similar attempts have been made before and have not answered practically.

WE learn from the *Magazine of Art* that the Hanging Committee for the Royal Academy Exhibition this year consist of Messrs. Calder Marshall, Brock, Calderon, Gow, and Dicksee; two sculptors and three painters. Architecture, we suppose, is left to take care of itself.

THE Court of Contributors of the Edinburgh Royal Infirmary have, with only three dissentients, approved of a scheme for the extension of the hospital, the cost of which is estimated at 100,000l. The additional buildings will be situated immediately to the west of the present infirmary, and will occupy the site of the Sick Children's Hospital, which has been demolished, and the site now occupied by one of the Schools of the Merchant Company. The Directors of the Sick Children's Hospital have secured the School of the Trades Maiden Hospital, at Rill Bank, which will be adapted to the purposes of the hospital, and additions will be made thereto, for which the ground annexed affords ample scope.

THE *Daily News* of last week printed some letters concerning York House, Strand, and its water-gate,—the latter now lying neglected, in a hollow of the Embankment-gardens. What we believe to be the true story of the house and gate is as follows: In the sixteenth century a town "inn" of the Bishops of Norwich stood next eastwards of Villiers-street. In or about 1535 the inn was exchanged to Charles Brandon, Duke of Suffolk, for St. Bennett Holme Abbey, Norfolk. The house was bought for, or by, Heath, Archbishop of York, *temp.* Mary, but reverting to the crown in her sister's reign, it was let to the Lord Chancellor Egerton, and then to Sir Nicholas Bacon, whose son, Francis, as he himself tells us, was born there. By an Act of May, 1624, King James I. obtains possession of the property, which he grants to the first Duke of Buckingham. Whether Buckingham rebuilt the house or not is not exactly known. Campbell says, in *Vitruvius Britannicus*, that the water-gate was erected by Buckingham when Lord High Admiral of England in 1626. Its design is commonly attributed to Inigo Jones; yet some would ascribe it to Nicholas Stone, the elder, upon evidence contained in the Soane MS. list written by Charles Stoahes of some of his uncle's most eminent works.* Having sold the property for, we think, 30,000l., the second Duke of Buckingham went to live on College-hill, Upper Thames-street. The site was then cleared for building purposes, and York-buildings is now known as Buckingham-street.

* We discussed this matter in an article on June 21, 1879, vol. xxxvii., 677. See also our vols. xii., 252, and xxii., 450, *in re.*

WE have received a number (containing two parts) of the *Zeitschrift für Bauwesen* (Wilhelm Ernst & Sohn, Berlin), a periodical devoted to matters concerning architecture and engineering. Its scope is wide, embracing such articles as timber buildings in Brunswick, the mechanics of railway lines, the drainage scheme of Naples, and a list of buildings, both small and large, erected during 1890 by the State of Prussia, the particulars being carefully arranged under several columns; one devoted to ground plans,—a very interesting and valuable item. The larger buildings,—technical high schools, laboratories, &c.,—and the humbler buildings of the Pfarrhaus class are treated in the same way. The value of the plans would, however, be increased by having scales attached, especially the larger ones. Issued separately from the letterpress is a series of plates illustrating the various articles. Some are reproduced from photographs, others from pen drawings. A very curious house forms one of the plates illustrating the timber work of Brunswick, work from a town and district which is not so well known to Englishmen as other parts of Germany. There are also a number of plans of a large asylum for the insane at Landsberg, and the building of the Berlin Electrical Works, which naturally derive more interest from their plans than from their elevations. Altogether the publication seems well got up and carefully printed.

AT a general meeting of the Royal Scottish Academy held in Edinburgh last week for the purpose of electing Associates, no less than seventy nominations were made. There were twelve vacancies to fill up, four of which were caused by the deaths of four Associates, and the number had to be made up to twelve in terms of the new charter which provides for an increase of the number of Associates. Amongst those nominated were twelve architects, viz., Messrs. H. J. Blanc, Edinburgh; G. Washington Browne, Edinburgh; G. Burnet, Glasgow; Campbell, Glasgow; J. Dunn, Edinburgh; J. Honyman, Glasgow; Kinnear, Edinburgh; W. Leiper, Glasgow; J. Keppie, Glasgow; Sydney Mitchell, Edinburgh; J. Maclachlan, Edinburgh; and Boss, Inverness. Of these four secured the necessary number of votes, viz., Messrs. W. Leiper, Washington Browne, H. J. Blanc, and J. Honyman. Mr. Leiper was one of the first four at the top of the poll, and, therefore, becomes a full participant in the benefits of the Associateship, filling as he does one of the vacancies under the old charter. The other three who are in a similar position are Messrs. John Rhind, sculptor, Edinburgh; A. D. Reid, painter; Edinburgh; and John Lavery, painter, Glasgow.

ROYAL INSTITUTE OF BRITISH ARCHITECTS.

THE eleventh general meeting of this Institute for the present session was held on Monday evening last, the President, Mr. J. Macvicar Anderson, in the chair.

Obituary.

Mr. William H. White said that it was with deep regret that he had to announce the death of Mr. Thomas H. Eagles, Fellow, Professor of Architecture at Cooper's Hill College, and a member of the Institute's Board of Examiners. He also regretted to announce the death of Mr. John Murray, Honorary Associate of the Institute.

Mr. John Slater said he thought that the death of Mr. Eagles, who was a comparatively young man, inflicted upon them one of the most deplorable losses that they had had to record of late. He had only recently taken a seat at the Examination Board, where his services had been of the greatest possible value, owing to his knowledge and attainments being of a kind not common amongst architects. The Board of Examiners would hear of his death with very great regret.

The Examinations.

The President said he had now to report the results both of the recent Preliminary Examination and of the qualifying Examination for candidates for the Associateship of the Institute, which were held during the month of March. For the Preliminary Examination there were 74 new applicants, and six who had been previously relegated to their studies made the total number of applicants 80; 35 of these were examined in London and 13 in Manchester, 29 were exempted in accordance with the regulations, and three did not attend. Of the exempted candidates, 9 were relegated in London, and 3 in Manchester, making 12; 36 candidates passed, and these, with the 29 exempted candidates, the 12 who were relegated to their studies, and the 3 who did not come up for examination, accounted for the total of 80. In the Examination in Architecture, qualifying for the candidature for the Associateship, there were 71 new applicants, besides 21 candidates relegated to their studies on previous occasions, making a total of 92. Of the new applicants, 11 were not admitted on account of their probationary work not being sufficiently good; 70 candidates were examined in London,—and it was no easy matter to accommodate them in the Institute rooms, which presented a very busy sight indeed, 70 men all working at the examination at once,—and 11 in Liverpool, making 81. Of these, 38 candidates passed in London and 11 in Liverpool, making a total of 49 who passed, 32 candidates being relegated to their studies for a further period. The result of the Examination in point of numbers appeared to be eminently satisfactory, and not the least satisfactory feature about it was that a considerable number of the applicants had been relegated to their studies, inasmuch as it showed that the examination was a real one. The names of the successful candidates in this examination were as follows:—

Angel, R. J., Liverpool
Ayling, R. S., London
Bain, J., London
Baker, C. W., London
Blakey, J. W., Liverpool
Breden, A. C., London
Bridgman, N. G., Paignton
Burt, W. H., London
Child, E. H., London
Cleaver, A. W., Leytonstone
Cooper, T., London
Corlette, H. C., Sydney, N.S.W.
Cranfield, S. W., Enfield
Cummings, E. S., Edinburgh
Dobie, W. G., Birkenhead
Ford, G. M., London
Goodman, H., London
Grace, W., London
Greene, W. H., Liverpool
Greenslade, S. K., Exeter
Hack, M. S., Leicester
Hale, A., Birmingham
Harvey, F. M., London.
Hodgson, J. L., jun., Heston Moor
Houston, A. C., London
Howdill, C. B., Leeds
Jarvis, A. W., London
Jones, E. H., Liverpool
Kennedy, D. W., London
Kitchen, L., Manchester
Maclaren, T., London
Mausell, T. G., London
Murray, J., Greenwich
Ough, A. H., London
Passmore, H., Whetstone
Paxton, J., Kilmarnock
Rees, T. T., Birkenhead
Reid, R. A., London
Rix, R. A., Croydon
Sakurai, K., London
Saunders, J., Oldham
Shearman, E. C., Buenos Ayres
Thornton, E., London
Vaughan, W., London
Walker, B., Birmingham
Warburton, A., Bolton
Ward, F. E., Belfast
Watt, J. C., London
Wills, F. R. G., London

M. Chipiez's Model of the Parthenon.

The President said that before the reading of the papers was proceeded with, Mr. Statham would make a short communication in reference to M. Chipiez's model of the Parthenon.

Mr. H. H. Statham said he wished to endeavour to clear up the point which has been raised by M. Chipiez in his letter* in regard to the model of the Parthenon, which was made, as was understood, under his direction, and which had been purchased for America and set up in New York. The two mistakes that he (Mr. Statham) particularly referred to were that the metope sculptures were at the wrong end,—that was to say, the metopes of the east end were under the pediment of the west, and *vice versâ*; and the next was as to the entasis of the columns. In regard to the first, M. Chipiez said that the model was sent over in pieces numbered, and that they must have put it up wrong in New York. They must accept that explanation. With regard to the entasis of the columns, he could not quite understand M. Chipiez's argument. He said that his model was made from a photograph which showed quite as great an entasis as he showed, and that if the photograph which was sent over from America showed a greater entasis, it must have been a mistake made over there. He (the speaker) could only account for that by supposing either that the Americans had remodelled the columns to suit their own ideas, or that the laws of optics were different in Paris and New York. He had brought a pretty large photograph of the Parthenon, and anybody who applied a straight-edge to the uninjured lines of the columns would see that it showed absolutely straight lines, as everybody knew that it must do who knew the facts. The deviation from the curve was less than half an inch in a height of 31·43 ft. The American photograph of the model was taken from the front of the model as it stood in New York, and if one looked at it closely, one would see that although the columns were only half the scale of the photograph of the actual remains, there was quite a visible curve in them, although the actual height was only about 3½ in. in the photograph, and no such curve could show on that scale. He confessed that he could not understand M. Chipiez's explanation. He believed Mr. White had some other photograph to produce, and he should like to know what really was the truth of the matter. It was obvious that the columns as shown in the New York photograph were wrong, and that they showed a degree of entasis which did not exist in the Parthenon, and that they professed to be from a model which was made in Paris, and which was afterwards purchased and set up in New York. He had only one other remark to make, and that was that it appeared to him from M. Chipiez's letter (and Mr. White would correct him if he were wrong), that in furnishing the data for that model he had neglected what was really the best source of accurate information, and that was the book of their distinguished member Mr. Penrose, which contained exceedingly minute measurements from the Parthenon, from which the actual facts of the case could be got. If so, he thought there was some justice in the complaints which had been made, that the French architects, in restoring buildings in that way, did to some extent neglect the information which they might get from English sources, and that they had neglected it in the present case. He saw no reference in M. Chipiez's letter to Mr. Penrose's book, or to his having got any facts from that book. If he had referred to it, he would have got the facts correctly; whereas, so far as he (the speaker) could understand at present, it seemed that he had not.

The Secretary, Mr. W. H. White, said that as he happened to have the honour of knowing personally that distinguished architect M. Chipiez, they would perhaps excuse his taking up a few minutes in reply to the statement made by Mr. Statham. M. Chipiez had sent over a photograph of the model as it was taken in Paris, while it was still in his hands. This model, which was sent over to New York in hundreds of pieces, had to be put together again, and possibly there might have been some errors in putting it together, for, in a letter just received from M. Chipiez, he said:—"I have not furnished any drawings for the existing parts of the Parthenon. In accordance with his contract the sculptor caused the necessary working drawings for those parts of the model to be made by an architect of his own choice, and he did this after the measurements of Mr. Penrose. In the workshop of the sculptor I placed the metopes in their regular order, with the book of Michaelis in my hands." He added that, in the temporary and too hasty putting together of the model at the Exhibition of 1889, the order was inverted by the sculptor, and hence the same inversion occurred, no doubt, at New York. With regard to Mr. Statham's error (if he would excuse his saying so) that the entasis of the columns in the model was determined by photographs of the actual Parthenon, he thought that in his letter M. Chipiez did not state that. The entasis was decided by the drawings provided for M. Chipiez, and not made by him.*

* Published in the *R.I.B.A. Journal* for March 24, p. 229.

* The result seems to be that all the mistakes are admitted, but M. Chipiez denies responsibility for them. If so, why was the model referred to in all the French architectural papers as "M. Chipiez' model?" If the model was supposed to be based on Mr. Penrose's measurements, there has evidently been a mistake in applying them.—H. H. S.

The Construction of the Central Pillars of Milan Cathedral.

An abstract of a paper by Signor Beltrami on this subject was read by the Secretary, Mr. William H. White.

The author said he was glad to supplement
Mr. Somers Clarke's Paper on "The Fall of one
of the Central Pillars at Seville Cathedral,"
with the result of investigations carried on a
Milan Cathedral. The Ministry of Public
Instruction authorised a committee of architects and builders to carry out the investigations, with the object of ascertaining how th
central pillars had been built, the causes c
their decay, and the most satisfactory remedie
to keep them in repair. The south-easter
central pillar was drilled to the depth of
centimètres, boring two blocks of marble, afte
which was a core of common stone (*sarizzo*
The same pillar was drilled through the cour
below, and the *sarizzo* was found at a depth o
35 centimètres. In the north-eastern pillar
the *sarizzo* was met with at depths of 66 and
centimètres in one course, of 58 centimètres i
the course under, and of 28 centimètres in th
course above. Thus proof was obtained tha
the thickness of the facing of marble varie
from at least 28 to 97 centimètres; that t
builders of the Cathedral had meant to ere
the central pillars as solid shafts; and that th
considered the resistance to pressure of t
white marble equal to that of the *sarizzo*
stone. From a list of building mater
(date fourteenth century) preserved in t
archives of Milan, *sarizzo* cost a quarter t
price of the marble, and the author thought t
use of small pieces of marble in the core of t
pillars might be accounted for on the sup
tion that they were too small for decora
purposes. Experiments to test the actual resi
ance of the two materials were made by
Building Construction Department of the Tec
nical Institute of Milan. These experime
proved that the average resistance of the sto
was about $\frac{14}{15}$ of that of the marble, and t
the weight supported by each was $\frac{1}{8}$ of
resistance to pressure, and $\frac{1}{16}$ of its resista
to crushing. Signor Beltrami then turned
the nature and causes of the decay of th
pillars. The white marble came from the quar
of Gandoglia; and its saccharoid texture var
from the granular to the perfectly crystalli
and sometimes to the spathic form,
general structure being spathic. The *sarizzo*
is a stone extracted from the sediments
the glacial period in the northern
of the valley of the Po. Its structure
granitic, much varied in texture. Of these
materials in Milan Cathedral the marble
showed signs of decay, which consisted in fr
tures or fissures perpendicular or tangential to
surface of the pillars. The former were to
attributed to the inequality, or occasio
imperfection, of the surfaces of horizo
contact; or to the oxidation of the iron cla
originally used to bind together with
central mass the moulded blocks forming
surface of the pillars. Such fractures
splits were not, however, to be considered
dangerous, especially when limited to
course of masonry, and ought not, therefore
be made a pretext to tamper with the origi
surface of the stonework. The tangent
fractures and chipping off of the edges of
facing courses were caused by the fact tha
many cases the pressure was transmitted f
course to course along the edge; or else
concentration of the pressure around
periphery of the pillars consequent upon
condensation of the mortar. The pecu
nature of the fissures was due to the spa
structure of the marble; and that defect sh
be considered as a natural consequence of
care taken by the mediæval builders to ob
a perfect surface in the pillars they erec
and to prevent damp from penetrating into
cores of the pillars. Only the larger fract
were to be repaired, such as were dangero
altered the architectural appearance of
masonry, leaving untouched the minor one
testimony of its peculiar structure, its form
decay, and of its age. Signor Beltrami
cluded his paper with a reference to the opi
of Mr. Somers Clarke, F.S.A., that Se
Cathedral "stands far above it" [Milan Ca
dral] "as a specimen of mediæval,"—an opi
Signor Beltrami thought it not easy to dis
as the two buildings were not erected con
porarily, and were not of the same size. In
case he believed Mr. Somers Clarke w
change his opinion were he to verify on
spot that the vaults of Milan Cathedral ar

domes with ribs on their faces;" that its olumns are *not* "quite cut off from the members bove them," and that the windows are *not* in many cases half sham."

Mr. R. Herbert Carpenter, F.S.A., said he ad a letter from Mr. Somers Clarke on this ubject. He wrote:—"What the Signor says bout the materials of the pillars at Milan is ery interesting, and supports my view that had he pillars at Seville been well built and of good tuff, they would have been of ample strength o do their work. The dimensions I gave were aken: (1) from rough measurements of my wn; and (2) from the book issued to ompetitors for the façade, of which I ot a copy at Milan. In answer to the oncluding sentences of the printed paper, have to say—1. That I have visited the athedral of Milan several times. 2. That I annot affirm that the vaults have not the ribs hrough their substance; but I can affirm that hey are domes rather than intersecting vaults. hey are not on the lines of the best ledieval vaults. 3. I respect Signor Belami's statement very much, but I can only firm what every student knows,—that the olumns are quite cut off from the members of e arch above them. A reference to the drawgs I have referred to shows this, outside one's amination of the church itself. 4. The me drawings show the clearstory windows of e centre nave to have their lower part openg into the nave, their upper part opening ove the steep sides of the very domical ults. This is very easily seen as one walks ong the aisle roofs. I very much respect gnor Beltrami for sticking up for so glorious fabric as Milan, and in comparing it with ville I have wished to treat it with all respect, it—facts are facts."

Mr. Alexander Payne proposed a vote of anks be accorded to Signor Beltrami for his per and present of books.

Professor Aitchison, A.R.A., seconded the te of thanks to Signor Beltrami. They were tremely indebted to him for sending them pies of his works. He was one of the most stinguished architects in Italy. They should, thought, elect him as an Honorary Correonding Member.

The vote was passed by acclamation.

rought-Iron Work: The Renaissance Period.

Mr. Starkie Gardner next read a paper on this ject, copiously illustrated by lantern-slides. his preliminary remarks, Mr. Starkie Gardner d he considered the industry of ironworking, e every other art, subject to fixed laws which regulated its growth, development, and y. Its signs of youth were seen in a robust playful vigour when the smith manipulated hot iron with his hammer without any entitious aid, the forms thus obtained being ophisticated and without refinement. The t stage was in introducing organic forms, a decorative, not a superstitions, sense, by use of smiths' tools alone. Its maturity reached when such crude results were no ger deemed satisfactory, and the file, saw, sel, drill, and punch were called in; the inluction of mouldings, tracery, and other hitectural features necessitating more cultion in both designer and executant. Next, ater finish still was required, and the iron to be turned on the lathe, polished, carved, ed, &c., in fact, treated as a precious metal, holly apart from painting in colour or ling. That, as the last step, denoted old and approaching death. After that might e a renaissance, when the process would in again, the phases of development folling, however, with greater rapidity, and n concurrently. In Italy the smith's had made considerable progress during period of Gothic architecture. Church les, its principal expression, were almost ays based on the quatrefoil, which merely a development of the circle, that itself probably suggested by the ct of the leaded roundels with which St. k's and other churches were glazed. The trefoil certainly became the traditional n, and grilles of that design were often nounted by very deep friezes and crestings the richest work. The Doge's Palace and ers seemed to possess nothing more decorathan latticed grilles; these, however, asionally showed a desire for better effect, the fifteenth-century *Casa* had some beaual traceried grilles in the window-heads. e open scale pattern grilles at St. Mark's re copied in 1481 by Pietro Lombardo in the Vendrami Palace. A far more decorative effect was obtained by scrolling up the ends of the scales, as seen in the Manzoni Palace. From these to window grilles of C scrolls placed vertically and in all possible directions was a natural and inevitable development. Under Sansovino the style was at its zenith, and spread far beyond the limits of Venice. Italian smithing reached maturity about the close of the fifteenth century, and was ripened, perhaps, almost to decay when "Vitruvius" and its overwhelming influence, leading to an entire suppression of decorative ironwork in buildings, gave architectural smithing its *coup de grâce*. A renaissance took place when Palladian architecture degenerated, and, though smithing was feeble, it marched onwards to the Italian version of the French rococo. In Germany it was otherwise; the laws of Vitruvius were not current over the border, at least as far as concerned ironwork; the smith had a free hand, and his art had for once an opportunity of showing of what magnificent developments it is intrinsically capable. Considering the advantages, however captivating the work might seem, the result was disappointing; the designs were the same for a palace or a church, the guest-chamber or the grave, and all changes were rung on three leading themes: the thistle, the passion-flower (both introduced in the Gothic Period), and the threaded work. The thistle in the Renaissance had its curving leaves fashioned into rich grilles formed entirely of intertwining scrolls, a grand example of which, from Lübeck, was as late as 1784. The passion-flower, the origin of which seemed to have been the twelfth-century iris, was a favourite as far as the German language was current, and consisted of erect and recurved petals, &c. There was at first no intentional reproduction, but as the work became richer the resemblance became strikingly apparent, and must have been purposely heightened. The flower was invariably combined with the typical threaded work traceable to the early French lattice grilles; and, after relatively simple stages, became elaborated with bewildering complications, as many as 400 threadings having been counted in a single specimen. Examples in the cathedrals and churches extend from 1550 to 1672, and an offshoot of the style showed the sheathing leaves growing in the reverse direction,—a variety much used in grave crosses, and taken originally from an attempt to introduce the snail. In the Baroque style broken scrolls and acanthus leaves were introduced, and following that was the German Louis XV. work. Before turning from German ironwork Mr. Gardner referred to the contemporary locksmiths' work, the designs for which were, he said, far more varied and fantastic than those for grille-work, and he mentioned the carving of even equestrian statuettes out of solid blocks of iron. The remarkable fact about Flemish ironwork was the rapidity with which it developed; but under the Renaissance little was made beyond wall anchors, kitchen utensils, finials, and door furniture, &c., all of which, especially shutter-hinges and fastenings, had quite a peculiar style. At a church at Bruges, however, there was a pair of gates of an interesting style, made in 1690, which constituted an example of an arrested development. The guild and shop signs were remarkable, preserving an altogether Flemish rotundity of curve, though French in details. The Flemish art was most noteworthy, however, for being the parent stock of the magnificent school of Spanish ironwork. Spain seemed to have realised with a rush the great capabilities of iron. First, the Flemish grille was imported into the churches; next,—a bold step,—crestings were added to them, directly borrowed from liliaceous plants; next, the grilles were carried three stories in height; and, finally, the details were translated into their fine new plateresque, and the freest play given to the imagination with the most astounding results. The colossal *rejas*, produced between 1500 and 1600, which screened the *coros*, high altars, and chapels, the author considered the most magnificent specimens of the smith's art extant; not unfrequently they reached a height of 30 ft., and they were divided into several tiers of long balusters, often enriched with leaf work forged and carved out of solid iron. These piers were separated by deep bands of the richest scroll and arabesque work, nothing, apparently, being too ambitious for the smith to successfully achieve. The artificers were known in many cases to have been in holy orders. The extraordinary perfection to which Spanish ironwork had reached was even more apparent in the arms and armour, where, too, the Moorish influence was decided. It declined rapidly with the Baroque, but no country so abounded with it. In the south every house had well-designed balconies and window grilles, &c. In France the Renaissance found the art deeply rooted, and affected its traditions but little; the most beautiful and refined ironwork ever executed was the French late Gothic and early Renaissance work. The pierced steel locks had reached a point beyond which real progress was impossible, and the transition simply meant that such sumptuous works slowly lost Mediæval features and followed Classic models. Under François I., due to Italian influence, an abrupt change was seen in the locks; and the lock covers, instead of being chiselled and formed of layers of pierced work, were embossed in high relief out of single sheets of iron. Bolt cases and knockers were treated in a similar manner. But far more beautiful and satisfactory were the exquisite keys, purse-mounts, flambeaux, &c.; for beauty of design and for refinement they, as a rule, far surpassed Italian work, although usually mistaken for it. During the perfecting of the locksmith's and armourer's work, there appeared to have been little demand for ordinary blacksmith's work; a grille made for Henri II. was a mere series of parallelograms with crescents, but the finials showed more originality of design. The germs of the new school were first discerned under Henri IV., and under Louis XIII. a fully developed style was found, which rapidly developed until it reached its culminating point under Louis XV. During this period nearly every cathedral in France and Belgium seemed to have had new choir and chapel grilles, and the demand for high-class smith's work must have been prodigious. Mr. Gardner then turned to the art in England, which he considered, although enjoying the least consideration in our museums, as the most valuable and interesting to the English. Unfortunately, the art had sunk so low that during the Renaissance it practically was a missing chapter in the development of the native arts. From the practice of fencing in church monuments with iron rails, one might best judge of the state of iron working. The series in the cathedrals was most valuable. During the Renaissance they were no longer made of massive bars, and the traceried cornices and buttressed angles also disappear towards the sixteenth century — only the closely-set lighter bars with small spear points, or sometimes ending with *fleur-de-lis*, remain. The finest series must have been in Westminster Abbey, and several examples were mentioned by Mr. Gardner, including the rail to the tomb of Dean Wotton, 1566, in Canterbury Cathedral. Good examples of a later style existed at Old Chelsea and other churches. Among the rarer objects was the valuable herse or canopy in Tanfield Church, and that in South Kensington Museum from Snarford Church. After describing in considerable detail a fine alms-box in St. George's Chapel, Windsor, door-hinges, especially those at Dartmouth Church, together with the wrought-iron columns there supporting the gallery, Mr. Gardner turned to lock-plates, which, though not rivalling those of France, Belgium, or Germany, began to show, during the Renaissance, design of a higher order. Rich locks, especially of James I. and Charles I. periods, were more often of brass, but the keys were of iron and of the most exquisite finish. After describing in detail specimens of English locksmith's work, the author dealt with flat work, of forged bands cut into arabesques, scrolls, and other figures, of which the so-called cradle of Henry VI. in the Ashmolean is a good example. The gates to the chapel in Farley Castle show the work on a larger scale, while the staircase at Holyrood seems to show what an Elizabethan iron stair might have been. The oldest strap work in a church hour-glass-stand is 1597, with a wheel arabesque design; and another, dated 1636, introduces branches of oak. These and other examples of knockers, work on chests, door and window furniture, &c., show that, though rude and uncared for, the English smithing was full of character, quaintness, and individuality; and, had the architecture shown any disposition to make use of it, might have blossomed into a fine industry.

The President, in inviting discussion, said that there were few subjects possessing a greater charm for architects than that of wrought-iron work. They had had the privilege of listening to an exceedingly admirable paper by an able expert on the subject. He thought the paper possessed a unique value.

Mr. H. H. Statham said he had very much pleasure in moving a hearty vote of thanks to Mr. Starkie Gardner for the interesting sketch which he had given of the history of the subject, and for the interesting series of illustrations which he had shown to them. There were, perhaps, one or two ideas which the paper suggested. One was the absurd mistake which was committed when realistic foliage was introduced into wrought-iron work. Two or three illustrations of that had been shown: they were useful as warnings, in that they were opposed to all true canons for the treatment of the work. Another thing that occurred to him was that considering that a number of the examples were based upon certain vegetable forms,—he alluded to those which were properly conventionalised,—after all, very few of the available forms of the vegetable world had been used as a basis of design in wrought-iron work. The examples which they had been shown, although there was a considerable variety in the treatment of them, really represented but a very few types, when one came to add them up. That fact suggested what a large field there was for new treatment in wrought-iron, and what a scope there was for a far greater variety in design than at present existed. It had often occurred to him, in looking over designs for wrought-iron-work, that one saw very much the same ideas over and over again,—the same kind of leaf, treated more or less satisfactorily, the same use of spirals, with a little variety in the way of working them or placing them, and very little attempt to get anything different from what had been done before. In the illustrations which had been shown by Mr. Gardner, they had seen a great variety of treatment of design from very few types. The types of nature were almost endless, and the aim of the modern worker and designer in wrought-iron should be to make the most of the hints which existed in nature; he should turn to forms which had not been worked out already; he should endeavour to evolve something new in wrought-iron work, of which we did not see much. Modern taste in wrought-iron was very much better than it used to be. We seldom saw things in such bad taste as we saw thirty years ago. Those with a turn for designing wrought-iron work should devote their energies, not only to excellence of execution and to purity of taste, but to the selection of new forms suitable to the material.

Professor Aitchison, A.R.A., said he had great pleasure in seconding the vote of thanks, for personally he felt extremely indebted to Mr. Gardner for showing him those splendid specimens of Spanish ironwork, with which, he was sorry to say, he was entirely unacquainted. He thought this Spanish ironwork was the finest of any ironwork he had seen. There was, doubtless, a peculiar charm about work roughly done on the spur of the moment. Although the rococo work of Louis Seize was not beautiful in itself, still the way in which it had been treated by some of the ironworkers was remarkable. There was an iron screen in one of the churches at Munich which was the most wonderful instance of delicate wrought-iron-work that he had ever seen. It was certainly worthy of a picture being made of it by an accomplished artist. The fine artistic way in which the iron was treated was quite unlike anything that he had seen before, and reminded one of the curled leaves in a young plantation. We of the present day were no doubt like the Athenians,—we were ever looking for something new; and it was the characteristic of every generation that it wanted something different from that which had gone before. But the thing we wanted was to get ironwork properly treated, with such slight variety as the taste of the day might call for. The only other thing he wished to refer to was Mr. Gardner's remark, that in future wrought-iron might be used as a medium for modern architecture. It was, however, too large a subject to attempt to enter on at any length, but he might say that iron had one great peculiarity which we wanted particularly at the present time. There was no doubt that architecture, when it went on again, would take a new development, and that development might possibly take place in the moulding of the material to the shapes that the strains indicated. Iron being a costly material, we were now obliged to give it the shapes that it should have to meet the strains, only at present no architect had been fortunate enough to put these forms into an architectural shape, nor to ornament them characteristically. There certainly appeared to be a vast field for the exercise of invention in the application of new and appropriate shapes of ornament.

Mr. J. Hunter Donaldson, as a visitor, spoke of the great difficulty there was in obtaining photographs of old ironwork in the Italian cities.

The vote was passed by acclamation.

Mr. Starkie Gardner, in reply, said that as a botanist he was quite alive to the endless forms which nature provided from which we might take hints in designing ironwork. But, practically, and as a matter of every-day expediency, one had more or less to follow the styles of ironwork that were recognised. Very few buildings would, he thought, admit of entirely fresh treatment,—entirely fresh departures in their ironwork. They had to be more or less assimilated to the styles and periods in which architects were working.

The proceedings terminated with the announcement that the next meeting would be the annual general meeting, on May 2, to discuss the annual report of the Council.

LITERATURE AND ARCHITECTURE.

ARCHITECTURAL ASSOCIATION.

At the ordinary fortnightly meeting of this Association, held on the 1st inst., Mr. F. T. Baggallay, President, in the chair,

Mr. E. S. Gale, Honorary Secretary, announced a donation to the general fund of the Association of 10*l.* from Mr. J. A. Gotch; and some donations to the Studio and Library. He also announced that a prize of 5*l.* 5s. had been offered by Mr. James Brooks, open to any member of the Association, for the best set of measured drawings of the vaulting of Christ Church Cathedral, Oxford. He moved a hearty vote of thanks to the various donors, which was carried by acclamation.

On the motion of Mr. F. T. W. Goldsmith, a vote of thanks was accorded to Mr. J. Wolfe Barry for permitting the members to visit the Tower Bridge on a recent occasion.

This being the last ordinary general meeting but two of the present session, Mr. E. S. Gale, in accordance with By-law 31, on behalf of the Committee, submitted a list of members willing to serve as officers and members of committee for next session. It would be premature to give this list *in extenso* now, but we may mention that Mr. H. O. Cresswell was nominated by the Committee to fill the office of President. Subject to the terms of the By-law, it is open to members of the Association to nominate other gentlemen to serve as officers or members of committee.

Mr. Horace Townsend then read the following paper entitled "Literature and Architecture":—

Mr. President and Gentlemen,—When last year I had the pleasure and honour of appearing before you in this place, I remember that I had to frankly appeal to your more charitable sentiments in that I came before you bearing but little with me that might prove of material advantage to you, the active professors of an art which has about it much of the practical as well as of the purely æsthetic. You were hospitable enough upon that occasion to receive me with all friendliness and courtesy, and to grant me so full and free a pardon for my first offence, that you yourselves are surely to blame if I have presumed upon those expressions of goodwill to travel to-night yet farther from the straight pathway of rectitude and virtue in that same regard. Your Friday evening meetings here are, I take it, of the nature of educational symposia, and those who are so far dignified by you as to be invited to take prominent part therein should, as a rule, endeavour to add something to the general stock of architectural knowledge.

Judging from the list of subjects upon which, during the session now drawing to its close, you have been enlightened, I am rejoiced to be able to say that I am probably the one striking exception which helps to prove this undeniably meritorious rule. But I may at least lay this flattering unction to my soul, that, were I not to exhibit so striking a contrast to my utilitarian predecessors, you would never perhaps realise how exceedingly edified you had been by them in the past—you all of you, I am sure, have too much of the artistic temperament to be indifferent to the value of the judicious apposition of strength and weakness. And yet, perhaps, though no precisely gaugeable amount of instruction is to be imparted to you this evening, the time devoted to considering, however perfunctorily, the relations of two such leading arts as Literature and Architecture, even if those relations are at present not the most intimate that can be conceived, will be time not wholly misapplied.

In the little journey into the abstract we are about to take, the deviously winding side paths rather than the direct high roads are likely to lead us to the most advantageous spots, and the subordinate phrases and variations will probably in our ears sound more pleasingly than the main theme. The old book-men of the Middle Ages have won the scoffs and sneers of more enlightened generations because it was their pleasing custom to debate at prodigious length as to how many angels could dance on the point of a needle. Owing to the regretable absence of the ubiquitous reporter on these interesting occasions we are debarred from any exact knowledge of the tenor of these discussions. I can myself, though, see no reason to doubt but that they were at least as provocative of material advantage as a modern debate on such subjects as, for example, "whether Architecture is an Art or a Profession," for consider how many side issues of absorbing interest might have been raised, from deliberations concerning the angelic host to the more mundane considerations touching the economic history of the needle itself.

Do not, however, imagine for one moment that I am going to subject you to the risk of incurring the pains and penalties earned by those guilty of even tacitly aiding and abetting the criminal who is in unlawful possession of hard-and-fast theories concerning either literature or architecture. I do not even intend to confine myself over strictly to my text, but merely to consider, somewhat casually perhaps, but I trust not altogether unprofitably, such questions as the conjunction of the names of two of the leading arts may serve to suggest. It will not be unprofitable, in the first place, to indicate such points of comparison as offer themselves between literature on the one hand and architecture on the other. At first I am sure you will all be disposed to say that no two arts could be more dissimilar or have fewer features in common, save, perhaps, such abstract and underlying æsthetical principles as are common to art in general. A little reflection, however, will I think convince you that if they are unfortunately, as I shall later on endeavour to point out, a little less than kind they are, if not more, at least no less than kin, and that certain special artistic faculties nurtured by the follower of one need but the merest differentiation to be of service to the other. Thus the basis of artistic literary form, whether displayed in the guise of poetry, fiction, or the drama, is undoubtedly construction, and the constructive faculty is after all but a specialised and somewhat theorised sense of planning, such as finds its place among the most important and necessary tools of an architect's mental workshop. I remember discussing, not many years ago, the subject of stage-craft with a dramatist who not only stands at the head of his profession in America, but is held in sufficiently high esteem on this side of the Atlantic. "If," said he, "I were to come across an architect who also had taste and talent for literature, I should look to see a better play from him than from ten out of a dozen of our masters of fiction. Constructing a play," he added, "demands, I am convinced, a cognate mental faculty to that required for the planning of a house." One has only to apply this same rule to other branches of literature, in which, though construction may not be of such vital importance as it is to the playwright, it is yet by no means to be slighted, to see that the two arts touch at this point somewhat closely.

Again, somewhat similar limitations are imposed upon both author and architect as regards the medium in which they work. There is a language and grammar of architecture quite as complex and quite as conformable to tradition and general usage as the language and grammar by which the literary artist is, not so much fettered, as strengthened and sustained. The genius of the one, as of the other, is to be found in the skill and aptitude with which old and conventional symbols, some of them by force of association representing concrete or abstract ideas, others serving but as the mean whereby these ideas are linked together, are disposed in so novel and original a manner as to convey to us a new thought or a novel impression. And I may, perhaps, be permitted to parenthetically suggest at this point, that as by this time the dream which has deluded not only our own but other generations, the dream of a new and arbitrarily formed language to usurp the places of those diverse tongues which are undoubtedly a bar and hindrance to the universal exchange of thought, has proved itself to be but the fallacious confusing of the desirable with the possible, so that similar vision which, like a misleading but fair-appearing mirage, has mocked so many otherwise far-seeing and clear-thinking men, that will-o'-the-wisp, if I may be allowed the expression, of a "new architectural style" is destined to a corresponding dissipation under the mist-dispersing rays of reason. "Volapük," the latest of the universal language crazes, is no more ludicrous and abortive an attempt to override deep-seated traditions and conventions than is the essay to provide us with an entirely new order or style of architecture.

But there are other matters of technique wherein the two crafts closely approach one another, though they may, after all, be chiefly classed as subordinate rules of construction. One of the most perfect literary artists of our generation, considered simply as an artist, but one who, because she wrote nominally for young people has had denied to her by the unthinking public her due meed of praise in this respect, always declared that she owed much of her education in those matters of construction which have helped to render her masterpiece the perfectly cut and polished gem of literary art it is now admitted to be, to the latter part of the third letter in Ruskin's "Elements of Drawing," a treatise which is, perhaps, more familiar to you than Mrs. Ewing's "Jackanapes," the little book to which I refer. She clearly saw that the principles there laid down with regard to music, poetry, and painting applied to prose with at least as equal force as to architecture. I need not, to those who are so well versed in Ruskinism as yourselves, dwell upon that consummate literary artist's analyses of the Laws of Principality, Repetition, Continuity, Contrast, Harmony, and so forth, which are there to be found. I can only regret that those incomparable artistic stylists the French have seen the light in this respect so much more clearly than our own writers, and that, however much we may excel them in the imaginative aspect of our modern literature, we are obliged to admit that their constructive ability is of a far higher order. This, I take it, is chiefly due (and this is a point I cannot too strongly emphasise) to the more intimate relationship between the arts, to the better comprehension of the common principles underlying them, which in that nation exist. It is the old story emphasised by each successive "Salon" and each "Academy." We may have an excellent story, but we tell it in a slovenly manner; the French may have no story at all, but, if you will excuse the Hibernicism, they tell it remarkably well. This, however, is perhaps wandering a little too far afield, though, as I warned you when I began, I intended to explore any side-alley that should seem promising as I rambled down the main avenue of my subject.

Let me return for a moment to the application of Ruskinian theories to literature. I cannot do better, perhaps, than take as my concrete example the very story to which I have referred. In "Jackanapes" the law of principality is clearly demonstrated. All the minor characters, touched in with loving fidelity, are yet grouped around the hero in such artistically subordinated a fashion as to cause us to feel that all they do, and say, and feel, serves but to increase the pre-eminence of the principal figure; they all conspire, as has been said by one before me, with one consent to reflect forth the glory and beauty of the noble, generous, recklessly brave, and gently tender, spirit of "Jackanapes." What aunt could fail to dote on such a boy? What village lad refrain from leaving his father's plough and following so inspiring an example to the field of honour? What brother-officer, however seared with sorrow and made taciturn by trial, could hold that dying hand, and not weep for him who begged for the grace of Christ and the love of God as he passed away?

The same story, too, is a good example of the values of the law of repetition and the law of contrast. With the rapid sweeping action of the human lives with which the story is concerned, are finely contrasted the eternal peace and quietude of the village-green; a quietude the abiding sense of which is gained by close attention to the law of repetition; over and over again in constantly, but unobtrusively, recurring sentences the picture of this peaceful old village-green is evoked, for, as Ruskin says, "In general throughout Nature, reflection and repetition are peaceful things."

I have endeavoured to briefly compare, or rather to suggest on what lines a comparison may be drawn between two arts at first glance as widely dissimilar as those we are considering, but have so far confined myself entirely to the actual technique. From such consideration it is not easy to see what practical advantage is to be gained by the student on either side, though perhaps, after due reflection, we may be enabled to recognise that even here material advantage is to be secured by the earnest and thoughtful. One takes a new point of sight from which to view the perspective, and though the lines converge according to the same formula in either case, a very different impression is often conveyed through the retina and optic nerves to the brain. Thus the very question of Principality is apt to assume a new meaning to us in our own art, when we see how it applies to, and the effect it produces in one apparently alien to us. This trick, if you care to apply to it no higher term, is one that has been learnt to perfection by some few architects, who, I fear, are but exceptions to the general rule; though, if we journey across the Atlantic, we shall find that it is the dominant note in the scheme of the American school. Last year I ventured to briefly draw attention to this fact, but upon that occasion I borrowed from the stock of current art terminology or slang, another phrase to express the same meaning. I referred then to the impressionism of much of what is best in Transatlantic architecture, by which, I said, I meant that quality or characteristic of a building which leads the spectator to carry away from it when he departs a more or less vivid impression of some one feature which so dominates the rest as to be thereafter primarily called into imaginative existence by the reminiscent faculties. It may be an entrance, or a gable, or a bay, or a chimney-stack, that is thus insisted upon, not necessarily to the detriment of other features, but to their semi-effacement. Is not this but another exemplification of an artistic truth dwelt upon with such insistent effect by all masters of literary style? The value of repetition, too, is one which is but dimly and sub-consciously recognised by the great mass of architects, though in literature, as has been shown with fine effect by Robert Louis Stevenson in the "Merry Men," for instance, and by Dickens perhaps to excess in nearly all his later novels, it has proved a veritable gold-mine of artistic effect. I need only refer to the Houses of Parliament as a striking example of the power of a countless repetition of details to produce, when employed by the hand of a true artist, and with a sense of the wide difference between this quality and that of mechanical triviality, an effect of reposeful and dignified quietude. Nor are these the only means whereby a study of a sister art may prove of indirect advantage to the architect. I have hinted already that those well-meaning but irrational individuals who persist in looking forward to that problematical millennium when we shall have evolved a new style, may take comfort in its non-appearance by reflecting that our Tennysons and Brownings, our Thackerays and George Eliots, our Carlyles and Ruskins, needed not nor even wished for a new language wherein to express the messages of originality and genius which they have delivered to our ears, and that the search for a new style in architecture is closely akin to the quest for a new language in literature. But, on the other hand, it must not be forgotten that those architects who are content to slavishly reproduce the models of the past, adapting them as little as may be to the requirements of the present, carry with them no message at all, save that of archæological investigation. They put themselves into the position of a poet who would convince us that not only is the language of Chaucer capable of neither extension nor improvement, but that it would be but truckling to the pervasive utilitarian and materialistic spirit of the age to endeavour to alter the exact sequence of ideas, which the Father of English poetry used the linguistic symbols of his time to convey. It is in the underlying sentiment, in the creative thought, clothed though they may be in conventional forms of speech, that true literary and poetic originality consists, and so it must always be with architecture. To be too conservative is as grave a fault as to be too iconoclastic. I remember when the fashion of the day,—healthy in the main, but, as all reactionary fashions are apt to be, not a little exaggerated by its votaries,—led us to turn back for our vocabulary to the earlier forms of our language, and to forsake the superabundant Latinity then prevalent, an enthusiast published a series of sermons in words of one syllable, and mainly of early English origin, to show how true eloquence might go hand-in-hand with absolute archaism. Well, it was exceedingly and cleverly interesting, but it was not literature; and so I venture to believe that a nineteenth-century building, whose chief title to favour is that a ghost of the thirteenth stumbling upon it by accident, between midnight and cock-crow, might be led to think the hand of time had somehow been turned back, and that he was in his own newly-built parish church, is neither more nor less than a deceptive study in archaism; it may indeed be archæology, but it is not architecture. Don't misunderstand me, I beg of you. I do not decry,—I should be the last in the world to decry,—that patient study, that sympathetic assimilation of the records of the past, which is one of the watchwords of our English architectural generation. I only wish to protest against the confusion of the means with the end, against the slavish worship of the word, accompanied by a blind indifference to the spirit which should inform the word; and here it is, in my estimation, that even the casual study of an art outside our own is likely to have a beneficial effect, for, once admitting that the premisses are the same in both, the *reductio ad absurdum* is more apparent in the one than in the other, and, therefore, more salutary.

But, gentlemen, literature has another relation to architecture, or, perhaps, I should say to architects. It is nearly a score of years now since I first entered an architect's office, the world is constantly moving, and so, doubtless, things are not what they used to be in regard to what I am about to touch upon. In my day, however, it was the exception rather than the rule to find an architect's pupil or assistant who was also well read in his own literature. There was much, doubtless, to excuse this in him. He worked at his office all day, and if he were earnest and industrious he spent a majority of his evenings over his drawing-board or his books of professional reference. Nowadays, perhaps, from what I gather, his leisure time is even more fully occupied with studies having direct bearing upon his profession, for examinations appear to be the chief end of architectural man, and we are fast rivalling, as devotees of the Competitive Cult, our almond-eyed friends the Chinese, who have headed us off by a few score centuries in this, as in so many other inventions of our newer civilisation. Let the cause have been what it might, the effect was one to be deplored, and unless things have altered very much for the better in this respect, one to be deplored fully as much in the 'nineties as in the 'seventies. Of all artists an architect is the better craftsman in direct ratio to the width and extent of his general knowledge. One can just barely conceive that a great painter may be ignorant of everything save of a technical knowledge of his craft and of an intuitive knowledge of human nature, but there is hardly a fragment of general information to be acquired, which may not at one time or another be of inestimable service to the architect in the direct line of his profession. The great genius, perhaps, who appears in a decade of centuries is, of course, superior to all rules and regulations, and is, to a certain extent, complete within himself, unless we adopt the meretricious diagnosis of genius as the gift of taking infinite pains. I am, however—and I trust in saying this I do not wound your self-esteem—I am, however, not speaking to a roomfull of geniuses, but rather to a body of men of talent and artistic taste. To such I would say that it is at least necessary in my opinion for an architect to have an appreciation of the higher forms of literature as it is for him to be able to properly calculate the strain on an iron girder. Now, appreciation without familiar knowledge is a contradiction in terms, so that it is evident that a portion of the working day or night should be as sedulously set aside for the assimilation of general literature as for other more definitely and distinctly professional branches of study.

Our contemporary architecture suffers, more than from any other cause, from want of imaginative faculty, and I cannot accuse myself of riding a hobby to death if I maintain that this very want arises from that widespread indifference to imaginative literature, which is characteristic, not of the architect alone, I beg to say, but of the majority of our nominally well-educated and refined upper classes. Imagination is, beyond a certain point, more or less of a habit of mind, and, like all similar functions of the intellect, can be developed or retarded by circumstances and surroundings, quite exterior to, and independent of, itself. We may starve it, or we may feed it, and to carry the analogue a little further, we may stunt its development as effectually, by confining it to one species of food alone, as by depriving it of sustenance altogether. Thus, though the benefit may not be objectively apparent, you may quicken your capacity for original designing quite as successfully by reading and enjoying an act of "Hamlet," or one of "The Idylls of the King," as by committing to memory a chapter of Fergusson or a page or two of Gwilt. Nor, again, should it be forgotten that the narrowness of mind which is the inevitable consequence of an indifference to literature is of all intellectual faults most to be avoided by the architect who, by the very nature of his art, is hidden to enlarge to the very widest extent the horizon of his sympathetic appreciation. Without culture you can hardly hope for refinement, a lack of which quality in your work is, as you all know, one of the most detestable of faults.

And now, gentleman, I have endeavoured, all too imperfectly I fear, to make clear to you to what degree Literature is the creditor of Architecture. But is there not a counter-claim, as law records have it? Is the balance all on one side? I hardly think so, though I must confess that, if the debt *per contra* has not been expressly repudiated, it has at least been but grudgingly acknowledged. If it had not been for the inherent poetry and mystic imagination, for instance, of Nôtre Dame de Paris, we should have never enjoyed what, from some points of view, is the masterpiece of that literary demi-god Victor Hugo, and Quasimodo and Esmeralda would for us have never been. To the same cause, though in a somewhat more indirect manner, those Wizardrics of the North, the "Waverley Novels," owe their very existence, while how much of William Morris and of Rossetti, as we know them, is due to the influence of the late Gothic revival I leave you to judge for yourselves. I doubt, indeed, if much that is characteristic in Browning's later volumes is not due to the subtle influence of the sun-kissed, weather-stained marbles of the Italian Renaissance with which at various critical periods of his poet's life he was surrounded. Finally, there is no manner of doubt in my mind that literature has to thank architecture far more than architecture has to be grateful to literature for the gift of that master of melodious phrase, that great prose poet of the century, John Ruskin. It is architecture itself that the "Stones of Venice" and the "Seven Lamps" have to thank for their existence, and it grows with each year more clear to our eyes that, despite his marvellous rhetoric, despite his riotous wealth of eloquence, Ruskin has impressed the literature of his generation with a seal more enduring than that with which he has stamped its architecture. Ruskin apart, has any literature of an ennobling eloquence been devoted to the service of architecture? To my knowledge, at least, none. We have our Fergussons, our Parkers, our Guilts, but how little else? Trustworthy educational treatises, encyclopædic in style, even if absolutely reliable in fact, are but a poor return for literature to pay you for all she owes to your art. It is surely somewhat humiliating for us to consider that the majority of such architectural works as can claim to be really literature, and not mere samples of book-making, are, as the phrase goes, "made in France" or "in Germany," as the case may be, for we have, alas! no Viollet-le-Duc to adorn his subject with grace of manner and charm of diction, as well as to bring to it the treasured results of a lifetime of patient and laborious investigation. Even the books of that intermediary rank, which act as a sort of link between the professional man and the layman, are much fewer and farther between than should be the case in a country, the average level of whose literary culture is so high as that of England. Nor are the reasons for this difficult of recognition; the fault is not wholly upon one side or the other. It is only within the memory of the last generation that the great majority of architects have caused their own profession to be estimated by the outside world as worthy of that dignified position which is now universally accorded to it, while, on the other hand, outsiders have never felt, for they have never been taught to feel, an interest in architectural technique, comparable to that with which they have ever regarded the technical aspects of painting and sculpture. That something more than mere taste or general education is necessary to enable them to justly estimate an architectural creation, is a somewhat novel idea to the vast majority of the public. This indifferent, well-nigh contemptuous attitude towards the art itself has reacted naturally enough upon its professors, and is curiously reflected in the attitude towards architects assumed by the practitioners of the art of fiction. An essay upon the appearance of the architect in fiction would be almost as brief as the celebrated chapter on "The Snakes in Ireland," and for the same reason. Dickens, however, whose portrait gallery is hung with the counterfeit presentments of representatives of nearly every trade which is to be found within the covers of the London Directory, has not forgotten the architect, and painfully suggestive too, is his method of treating our honoured profession. Mr. Pecksniff, as you will remember, is perhaps the most offensive of the amazingly offensive personages by whom the action of "Martin Chuzzlewit" is carried on; so offensive indeed is he, that he has been declared to be an altogether impossible personage. Certainly he is an absolutely impossible architect, and the ignorance displayed by the author of those details which would have helped to give *vraisemblance* and local colour, as it were to his creation, is little short of surprising. In introducing him to us, as you may remember, the author's remarks that "of his architectural doings, nothing was clearly known, except that he had never designed or built anything, but it was generally understood that his knowledge of the science was almost awful in its profoundity," and further that "Mr. Pecksniff's professional engagements indeed, were almost, if not entirely, confined to the reception of pupils; for the collection of rents, with which pursuit he occasionally varied and relieved his graver toils, can hardly be said to be a strictly architectural employment." And yet but a few pages farther on we find Mr. Pecksniff has evidently been invited to send in a set of competitive drawings for a new grammar-school. Not only does he do this, but he uses for that purpose a set of plans which had been drawn in the course of a very few days by young Martin Chuzzlewit, who, whatever his other valuable qualities may have been, was clearly as ignorant of the practice of architecture or of the principles of design as a new-born babe. And yet these plans are successful, and win the competition. More than this, Mr. Pecksniff, though bereft of the services of his only assistant, and himself engaged in non-professional affairs which take him here, there, and everywhere, somehow manages to prepare the working drawings, and to be present at the laying of the foundation stone by, as you will remember, "the member for the gentlemanly interest." After this, as far as the book is concerned, he ceases even to be nominally an architect, and (for no apparent reason) after he has finished his triumphant career as a hypocrite, becomes a mere begging-letter writer. The one redeeming quality which I can find in the character of this libel on an honourable profession, to whom I have already perhaps devoted too much of your time, is that he recognised the importance of literature to architecture. "Various books," he is reported to have observed upon one occasion, waving his hand towards the wall, "connected with our pursuit! I have scribbled myself, but I have not published."

That Thomas Hardy, the only other novelist of distinction who to my knowledge has made of an architect a seriously-considered character, should have displayed a more intimate knowledge of the subject is not so surprising as, at first glance, would appear, for, before he was a novelist, Mr. Hardy was himself an architect. Much as I admire those works of imagination, with which the distinguished biographer of Wessex folk has presented us, I am at times tempted to regret that he did not remain longer in his original profession, and use, in a measure at least, his literary gifts in her service. We might have lost "The Return of the Native," or even "Tess of the D'Urbervilles," but we should have gained that *lusus naturæ*,—a work of the highest degree of literary merit with the name of a real live architect upon its title-page.

Finally, a word must be given to the periodical literature of architecture, and here, I suppose, I am treading upon somewhat delicate ground. I think, though, that I voice the sentiments of some of you at least, when I declare that ideal provision has not yet been made for us in that respect. Year by year the architectural profession is counting upon its rolls fewer who look upon it as a mere business, and more who regard it as a sacred art. The paths of the contractor and the architect daily diverge more and more, and, though I have no words save of praise for those organs which, at present, represent so worthily the entire community which depends upon the art of building, I do not think that the ideal architectural paper is yet in existence. It will, as I conceive it, when if ever it does arise, concern itself not with architecture alone, but with all those subsidiary arts which she has enlisted in her service, and with those artistic crafts which are subordinate only because they differ in degree and not in kind. It will be, from its inherent interest, the medium which shall bridge over the chasm which now seems to cut off so effectually the architect from the general community, a chasm the existence of which is due only to the hereditary ignorance of the latter, and the hesitation of the former to assume that position which, in the empire of art, is his inalienable right. It will be a model of all that the representative of artists should be, in regard to its printing and its illustration, while in its pages will be found that perfection of literature which is only possible when the men who write concerning an art, of whose principles they are thoroughly cognisant, are also thoroughly informed with the principles of the literary art itself, and have recognised that the two are one and indivisible.

And now, gentlemen, conscious of having trespassed somewhat unduly upon your good-nature and of having taxed beyond the bounds of due discretion your patience, I can, as my excuse, find nothing better to bring forward than the mention of the fact that Literature and Architecture are arts in which I am equally interested, and to which I owe an equal share of my allegiance. I warned you when I began, that of practical suggestion I should have but little to offer you, and I fear that I have onl too well fulfilled my prophecy. But, after all I may be fortunate enough to be wrong in thi gloomy surmise; perhaps, weak and halting as has been my utterance, loosely knit as have been my arguments, random and fortuitous as have been my illustrations, I may yet have added one poor stone to the great House of Art we are all of us, in our several ways, helping to build. You know how the violinist, standing by an open piano and idly drawing his bow across the strings of his own instrument, strikes every now and then a note to which responsive echo is made by the silent strings beside him; so perchance at intervals to-night I have unconsciously touched some chord which may in either your hearts or your brains have set some responsive string vibrating in harmonious accord.

If this be so, and if the memory of those pulsations remains with you even for a little while, my time or yours has not been wholly mis-spent. Let me then, while thanking you for the attention, far beyond my merits, with which you have listened to me, urge on you once more the consideration of what, in my own mind, I have dimly recognized as the text from which to night I have been preaching; that art, namely, is one and indivisible and that he who would be pre-eminent in one must not be absolutely without rank or recognition in the others; that from the architect, as from no other artist, there is required a catholicity of sympathy with all that is great and ennobling in human life; that, with Terence, you ought each one of you to declare that "*Homo sum; humani nihil a me alienum puto.*" "I am an architect, and nothing that belongs to man do I regard as insignificant to me," as we may not unaptly phrase it. How then can you fail to take into your communion that art which is the link between all others, without which we should still be sunk in the apathetic ignorance of the middle ages (for it must not be forgotten that it was the Revival of Learning in Italy which made possible the Renaissance of Art); how, in short, unless you are servitors of literature, can you aspire to be Masters of Architecture?

Looking at the matter from the narrowest nd most direct view, the study of literature is eccssarily enjoined upon you, for the meaning f the architecture of the past can hardly be lear to us until we have a clear conception of he conditions which prevailed when each par-icular style was in process of formation. To hose who are ignorant of what manner of eople that wonderful handful of the human ace were, who leavened the whole mass of the vorld's posterity with the vital germs of all the rts, the shattered fragments which strew the brupt Acropolis must speak but haltingly or in n unknown tongue; to those who have not ppreciated the more material supremacy exer-ised by those ethnical prototypes of our own ation, who held a score of centuries ago the mpire of the world, the arches and the olumns of the City by the Tiber must be ereft of half their meaning; to those who have ot studied that unutterably awful spectacle resented to us by the nightmare-like gloom vhich overspread society in mediæval Europe, he long-drawn aisles and fretted vaults of the othic cathedrals must lose no little of their sad uggestiveness; while to those who are un-itting of the passions and the transports, the ickening vices and the moral excellences of fteenth-century Italy, the legacy it has left to s of such surpassing beauty and symmetrical race must be as a sealed book. Here again ur only guide is literature, and with her to aid ou, you can clothe again those dried skeletons f the past with fair-seeming flesh and make hem speak to you, when to others they would reserve but a Sphinx-like silence, the message f art which which it is theirs to deliver, and ours to interpret to your own time and your wn people.

In the discussion which followed,

Mr. W. Burrell said he had much pleasure in roposing a vote of thanks to Mr. Townsend or his paper, which had been one of great inte-est and suggestiveness. Such papers as that fted them out of the turmoil in which they ere generally engaged. Usually, papers read efore them dealt with some more or less echnical matter relating to the science of con-ruction, but on the present occasion they had ad a literary treat which would be, he thought, ry wholesome for them, for Mr. Townsend's per had served to show them that there were ore things in heaven and earth than were em-aced in their Curriculum. As a matter of urse, the list of things which they had to rn as architects could not include everything ich was necessary to make them men of cul-e, although the study of literature was one the most important aids to that end. Mr. wnsend, as one who had himself practised as architect, and who was now engaged in erary work, thoroughly understood how to at his subject from their point of view. til he (the speaker) had heard Mr. Townsend's per that evening, he had not thought that ere was so close a connexion between the art the architect and that of the play-ight as the gentleman in America, to iom Mr. Townsend had referred, seemed think. As to the little book mentioned Mr. Townsend, entitled "Jackanapes," he e speaker) had read it and had been very ich interested in it; but the statement made Mr. Townsend that Mr. Ruskin's "Elements Drawing" had anything to do with it quite tonished him. He was hardly prepared to ee with Mr. Townsend that Dickens had ogether misrepresented the architectural ofession in his portrayal of Mr. Pecksniff. did not think that Dickens meant to portray yone but Mr. Pecksniff himself; but, never-eless, he (the speaker) was bound to say that ere were still to be found in the profession me gentlemen who were not wholly devoid of me of Mr. Pecksniff's peculiarities. As to the probability of Dickens's story about the com-tition designs for a grammar-school having en gained by a young and inexperienced man, ll, they all new that grammar-schools and her buildings were won in competition, even der present conditions, by young gentlemen ho did not know much about the architectural ofession. He had much pleasure in pro-sing a vote of thanks to Mr. Townsend.

Mr. A. H. Clark, in seconding the vote of anks to Mr. Townsend, said his paper was a ry difficult one to follow in discussion. There emed to be only one thing that could be und fault with in the paper, and that was Mr. ownsend's excess of modesty; but the members of the Association had a far higher opinion of Mr. Townsend's merits than he him-self entertained. Amongst the whole phalanx of truisms to which he had adverted there was none which struck him (the speaker) so much as that concerning the light that literature was able to throw upon old buildings. No one could visit old buildings without feeling that their interest was doubled and trebled if they had been the theme of some of the celebrated writers. With regard to what Mr. Townsend had said in reference to the Renaissance and the parallel which he had drawn between the literature and architecture of that time, it always seemed to him (the speaker) that the Renaissance poets, or the poets who wrote just about the time that the Renaissance archi-tecture was coming to the front, possessed a distinct flavour of the old Roman poets,—so much so, that in reading some of the Renais-sance poets one really seemed, so far as style was concerned, to be reading translations of Virgil. Mr. Townsend had briefly referred to a subject which might, perhaps, with advan-tage have been more fully treated in his paper, viz.: the relation of modern current literature to architecture. Literature owed a very great debt to architecture, although it did not seem to be at all adequately recog-nised. The public, in their estimation of archi-tecture, would always be led, to some ex-tent, by current literature and by the press; but he very much regretted that in the present day the press showed such callous indifference to architecture, such an ignorance of its details, and such a want of appreciation of good work by the best architects of the day. In proof of that, one had only to read those garbled accounts of great public buildings which ap-peared in the daily papers. It was a regrettable fact that while other artistic subjects were treated with due attention, architecture received such meagre treatment; because there was so large a portion of the public who were unable to form their own opinions, or whose opinions, when formed, were not worth anything, and they were ready to lean on the current litera-ture of the day, particularly on the press, and not only to adopt the opinions expressed in the public prints, but to repeat them to their friends. He thought that if architecture were represented in the way it ought to be by the press, the effect on the general public would be very beneficial.

Mr. E. H. Sim supported the vote of thanks. Of course he quite agreed with the general spirit of the paper, but he was afraid that an acquaintance with the story of "Jackanapes" on the part of an architect would not be so good a recommendation to a client as a know-ledge of the price of brickwork. He quite agreed that architecture in the present day was very much overlooked by the press. In the descriptions of new buildings which appeared in the general press, the architect's name was hardly ever mentioned.

Mr. J. C. Stockdale remarked that although it was no doubt true that an acquaintance with the story of "Jackanapes" or any other literary work would not teach a man how to draw a moulding, it should be remembered that imagi-nation played a most important part in archi-tecture. There was no doubt that imagination was of supreme importance to the architect, and that much of the work which now appeared so unsightly would have been improved had the architect drawn his work with a greater amount of feeling and refinement, and that was only to be obtained by a study of literature.

Mr. F. T. W. Goldsmith said be desired to support the vote of thanks to Mr. Townsend, whose paper had not only been of great literary merit, but had treated the subject most com-prehensively. Without question, the wider and more extensive the knowledge possessed by architects of the present day, the better it would be for architecture. So long as the architect was confined to one groove of reading, his work (as affected by such reading) would be biased. He was very glad to hear Mr. Townsend refer to the influence of the imagination on architecture. Mr. Stock-dale had alluded to (an eminent politician (Mr. Goschen, he believed), who had not long ago discoursed on the uses of imagination. Mr. Goschen himself was a man who combined, in a singular degree, a practical, hard-headed knowledge of the world, with the imaginative faculty. He did not think that any architect, with any pretentious to literary taste, could fail to have his work influenced by every book, or even chapter of a book, which he read during the working out of his design. For instance, if the building to be designed had some poetic purpose to serve, and if its architect were studying at the time some eminently un-imaginative book, the practical work which he was reading would have a direct and subtle influence on the general conception of the design and its details. On the contrary, if he allowed his mind to become imbued with the fine imaginings of some great poet through the reading of some distinctly poetic works (not necessarily in rhyme, but such works as those of Mr. Ruskin's, which were emphatically the great poetic works of the age), his design would be brought under such poetic influences, in such a manner as would not, perhaps, be felt by himself, but which would be impressed on every feature of the work. He thought that Mr. Townsend had good reason for the deduction that the literary tendency of architects was in the direction of dramatic rather than in purely literary taste.

Mr. Houston said he thought there was some analogy between what was called the "New Journalism" and the bad architecture that one saw at the present day in Shaftesbury-avenue and elsewhere.

The President, in putting the motion, said he supposed that the analogy, or some of the analogies, between literature and architecture could not have escaped any thinking archi-tect; at the same time he thought it was the first time that the subject had been treated in a paper before them. He thought that some of the analogies referred to by Mr. Townsend were fairly apparent. They were quite accustomed to call the styles of architecture languages, or to use words having that significance. The more one looked into it, the more one saw that what we called styles were languages of which it was necessary to learn the grammar before one could compose in them. He thought there was some little confusion sometimes in the present day between learning the grammar of a style and executing a building in a particular style; it seemed to him that they were two very different things. It seemed to him very useful to learn what other people had done,—to learn the grammar of the old styles,—but it was a very foolish thing to copy old work exactly. The President, in conclusion, said he should like to add his own personal thanks to Mr. Townsend for his paper, which had given them all a great deal of food for reflection, and he had great pleasure in putting the vote of thanks to the meeting.

The vote of thanks was then put and carried by acclamation.

Mr. Townsend, in acknowledgment, replied to some of the points raised in the discussion. In reference to Mr. Burrell's criticisms on what he had said with regard to Mr. Pecksniff, he (Mr. Townsend) was perfectly aware of the fact that many pupils and many assistants did design grammar schools, or buildings of a similar kind, on the foundation stones of which other men's names were placed; but he had never heard of a pupil of three days' duration who was able to make a successful set of competi-tion plans. He merely referred to that point as showing in a very striking way how Dickens, who took such immense pains in his work, even spending days in tramping over London in order to find a suitable name for one of his characters, seemed to have regarded an archi-tect as a man of so low a grade that it was not worth the trouble of making the least inquiry,—which he could easily have done,—as to how he carried on his profession. On the other hand, with regard to his medical and legal characters, Dickens seemed to have taken the greatest pains to be accurate.

GOOD FRIDAY WEEK.—Next week we go to press a day earlier than usual. All communications for the Editor should reach him by *first post on Wednesday morning*; but lists of tenders will be received up to 12 noon of the same day.

THE BEXLEY SYSTEM OF EMPTYING CESSPOOLS.—This system, which we described in detail in the *Builder* for June 18 last year, is becoming increasingly used. Mr. Boulter, the Surveyor of the Local Board of Bexley, informs us that he has now dealt with 700 cesspools without the least of complaint. The Public Health London Act 1891 has been the means of the introduction of the system within the metro-politan area, the Plumstead Board using it both in Plumstead and Eltham. Since we described the system, it has been adopted at Gravesend, Chatham, Richmond, Staines, Enfield, and Chichester; and it is in contemplation to introduce it at Dunstable.

Illustrations.

ILLUSTRATIONS OF OLD CHESTER.*

IV.—SUPPORTS OF BISHOP LLOYD'S PALACE.

THE drawing shows the boldly-designed story-posts which support the over-hanging portion of the old house called "Bishop Lloyd's Palace" in Watergate-row. They appear on a small scale in the marginal sketch appended to the general view of Watergate-street published in the *Builder* of February 27.

INTERIOR, NORWICH CATHEDRAL, AND EAST END OF CHOIR, ELY.

THESE two illustrations are reproduced from two beautifully-executed pencil sketches by Mr. S. K. Greenslade. The exterior of the choir at Ely is one which he kindly placed at our disposal for illustrating Ely Cathedral, but as there was nothing to balance it well among the other Ely drawings, we preferred to give it this week along with the interior of the crossing at Norwich.

The two form interesting examples, in very different ways, of the solidity and monumental character of the earlier forms of Mediæval architecture. In spite of the large amount of window area in the east end of Ely, the massive yet gracefully decorated flanking buttresses give the effect of ample strength and stability, further emphasised by the massive buttresses and pinnacles at the angles of the aisles.

DESIGN FOR A STEEPLE.

THIS is the design, by Mr. T. Rogers Kitsell, for which the Tite prize was awarded this year by the Institute of Architects. The design fulfils the conditions of the bequest, which was to promote the study of Italian or Renaissance architecture, and the design is graceful and satisfactory, if not showing any very new or original features. The treatment of the spire at its junction with the tower is elegant, the curved lines at the base giving lightness and play of line in a manner in keeping with the style. We may suggest that the balustrade over the cornice is in the wrong place. It forms a fence to an inaccessible corner where no one would ever require a fence; whereas the section will show that the window opening, which comes right down to the floor under the spire, is left entirely unprotected. Balustrades have come to be very much a conventional ornament, but they should be placed where there is most semblance of use for them.

ROTHERHITHE INFIRMARY, ST. OLAVE'S UNION.

OUR illustration shows the additions and enlargement recently carried out at the Rotherhithe Infirmary, for the Guardians of St. Olave's Union, and opened by the Chairman of the Board, Augustus Scovell, Esq., on December 16 last.

The new portions of the building are shown in black, the hatched portions showing the building as erected in 1873 by Mr. Snell. The additional accommodation provided consists of a new male block with separation-wards, day-rooms, and duty-rooms for 177 inmates. New female block for 96 inmates; nurses' home for 40 nurses. The enlargement of the laundry, kitchen, receiving-wards, new officer's mess-room, and new dead-house and *post-mortem* room.

The wards are 88 ft. long, 24 ft. wide, and 13 ft. high, and contain twenty-eight beds each, and at the end, separated by disconnecting corridors, are the bath-rooms, lavatories, and w.c.'s. In the disconnecting corridors are the fire-escape doors, which lead on to the escape staircases. The heating is carried out by hot water, and by central hot-air stoves, with vertical flues, which, with the flues provided in the external walls, carry off the vitiated air; the fresh-air inlets are fixed in the external walls, and communicate with the boxes covering the hot-water pipes. In the centre of each block are the day-rooms, duty-rooms, and separation-wards, and the new buildings are connected up with the old by open corridors.

The buildings have been carried out from the designs of the architects, Messrs. Newman & Newman, of 31, Tooley-street, London Bridge, by Mr. J. O. Richardson, of Albert Works, Peckham. The clerk of works was Mr. William Gannaway, and Mr. C. W. Read, the contractor's foreman. The engineering works were carried out by Messrs. Clements, Jeakes, & Co., of Great Russell-street; the lifts by Messrs. Waygood; the sanitary works by Messrs. Tylor & Son and Mr. M. Syer; and the heating by Messrs. Clements, Jeakes, & Co. and Mr. John Grundy. The amount of the contract was 30,857*l*.

* For preceding views of this series, see *Builder* for February 6, February 27, and March 12 last.

MAGAZINES AND REVIEWS.

The *Gazette des Beaux-Arts* includes an article on Opie by Mr. Claude Phillips, giving a fair summary of the painter's merits and defects, with perhaps rather an undue exaltation of the former. We presume French art magazines are about to "discover" Opie as they have "discovered" Lawrence. M. Salomon Reinach contributes a paper on the "Musée des Antiques à Vienne," which he praises as one that in the matter of installation can fear no comparison with any similar establishment in Europe; he also draws attention to the excellent arrangement and editing of the catalogues and guides. Illustrations are given of some of the most remarkable fragments of antique sculpture in the Museum. M. Marcel Reymond endeavours to show that one or two pictures attributed to Raphael are really the works of Cesare de Sesto. M. de Fourcaud gives the second part of a communication on "L'Art Gothique," in which he sums up with the conclusion that the heart and soul of Gothic art is to be found in France, and speaks (naturally enough) with approval of the work on Gothic architecture by Mr. Moore, whom he refers to as "un savant Anglais." French critics should really dis-distinguish between English and American writers; Mr. Moore's book is one that no Englishman would care to own to.

The *Art Journal* gives the second of a series of articles under the title "Outings in India," dealing with Poona and its neighbourhood, and including among its illustrations a reproduction of a photograph "On the River Moota-Moola" giving a remarkably real effect of strong sun-light. The article on "Paris Pleasure Resorts" continues the illustrations of the Marne, and Mr. J. F. Boyes contributes an article on Sir A. H. Layard. Mr. Aymer Vallance's article on the decoration of the house (No. 4) deals with "Furniture," giving some illustrations of furniture which are unexceptionable in taste and refinement of design.

The *Magazine of Art* illustrates a short article on Mr. Stanhope Forbes by reproductions from his two best works, "The Health of the Bride" and "By Order of the Court." The paper on "Artistic Homes" is this month on "Wall-papers," by Mr. Lewis F. Day, and gives some illustrations of mostly fine designs, of which the most original is what is called a "Tile-paper," we presume from its being designed after the manner of tiles; it is said to be designed by "Arthur & Co." Why does not the *Magazine of Art* insist on the real name of the designer being given, instead of the name of a firm? A "company" cannot make a design; it can only sell it when made. Other articles are on Sir George Reid, the President of the Royal Scottish Academy; on "Painter-etching"; and on "The Art Treasures of the Comédie-Française," giving some exceedingly interesting illustrations.

The *Fortnightly Review* contains an article by Sir Robert Ball, "How Long can the Earth sustain Life?" to which some persons, not conversant with the proportions of cosmic time, will possibly turn with some anxiety to find out the probable fate of their immediate descendants, and will be relieved at finding that four million years is the smallest period promised, and that it may be extended to ten million. Considering what an immense space even the period of about four thousand years of human life of which we have anything like historic knowledge appears to us, we may well regard Sir Robert Ball's few million of years as further, at all events, than we can think to the end of; although there is a distinct difference to the mind, no doubt, in regarding the habitable state of the earth as necessarily to terminate within a period calculable on definite data. The data, of course, are the considerations as to the rate of waste of the sun's heat. As long as the sun remains in a gaseous state, it may lose heat, accompanied by shrinkage, without losing temperature; but when once it begins to solidify, then loss of heat means loss of temperature, with no replenishment. So physicists understand it now; and as far as they have got there is no great probability that the conclusions are wrong. Sir R. Ball even suggests as a probability that the dark bodies in the stellar system are more numerous than the luminous ones; that luminosity is but a temporary stage. So stupendous to the human mind, however, are the intervals of time involved, that one thinks rather of the positive than the negative results. If knowledge "grow from more to more," what may not the human intellect have achieved after even a million years from now? So vast are the considerations involved, that one turns with a smile to Mr. Walter Sickert's hysterical splutter about Whistler's pictures in the same number; the "Nocturne in Blue and Silver—Bognor," that is an "immortal canvas," and the man that created it "thereby alone immortal a thousand times over." Poor little paint-pot of a day!

The *Nineteenth Century* contains a well-written article by Sir Henry Wood on "Chicago and its Exhibition," the object of which is partly to reconcile Englishmen with a city which has been painted recently in no very attractive light. From his official connexion with the Exhibition Sir Henry no doubt must be taken rather as an advocate than a judicial critic, but he presents the Exhibition side of the case in an able and persuasive manner.

The *Atlantic Monthly* contains "Some notes on French Impressionism," by Miss Cecilia Warren, serving up again the old argument that the eye cannot rest simultaneously on two things, consequently that "a more open-air impression" is conveyed by a painting which shows only one object distinctly and leaves the rest a blur. It seems to be forgotten by those who use this curious argument that the eye looks from point to point of the picture as it looks from point to point of the real landscape, and has a right to expect some recognisable form in all parts of the painting; not to say that the principle involves the quiet assumption that the world of landscape-painting has been wrong up to the present generation. The article is well written and contains some good criticism in detail.

Scribner's contains an article on the "New Parks of the City of New York," referring to parks laid out in pursuance of an Act passed in 1883, appointing a Commission to secure new parks beyond the Harlem River. The land for three large and three small parks was purchased at a cost of 9,000,000 dollars, after much opposition from economists who objected to the outlay. The large parks referred to are the Pelham, Bronx, and Van Cortlandt Parks, of which some sketches are given, looking very much like park scenery all over the world. There appear to be some interesting old houses on the estates, which have been preserved. The same number contains an article on "Charles Keene of *Punch*," by Mr. G. Somes Layard, written both with enthusiasm and judgment, and including a letter addressed to Keene in 1883 by a Dutch admirer, which in itself is worth getting the number for, on account of its delightful mingling of true enthusiasm with naïveté and broken English.

The *Century* contains a long and carefully considered article by Mr. Edward Robinson on the question, "Did the Greeks paint their sculptures?" going pretty fully into the at present attainable evidence, and concluding that the Greeks probably painted their sculpture fully and strongly; if not realistically, at least as near to realism in flesh tint and colour of draperies as the slightly conventional treatment of the sculptured form is to the natural form. This can hardly be proved to be the case, but we think the available evidence points very strongly in that direction. All we can say is, so much the worse for the æsthetic perception of the Greeks, which must have been less immaculate than was once supposed. We may observe that Mr. Robinson makes the same observation which Mr. Statham made not long since at a discussion at the Institute on the relations of sculpture and architecture, viz.: that the frieze of the Parthenon (the *cella* frieze) was placed in such a position that "much of the labour spent upon its execution was in vain." Mr. Robinson uses this as an argument in favour of strong polychromy, which alone could have made the sculpture intelligible in the position in which it was placed. The same number of the *Century* contains an interesting paper by Mr. E. S. Holden on "The Total Solar Eclipses of 1889," with illustrative diagrams. An article on "Our Common Roads" (meaning we suppose what we call High Roads in England), by M

ILLUSTRATIONS OF OLD CHESTER.—Drawn by Mr. T. P. Ivison.

No. IV.—SUPPORTS UNDER BISHOP LLOYD'S HOUSE, WATERGATE ROW.

DRAWN BY MR. S. K. GREENSLADE.

DRAWN BY MR. S. K. GREENSLADE.

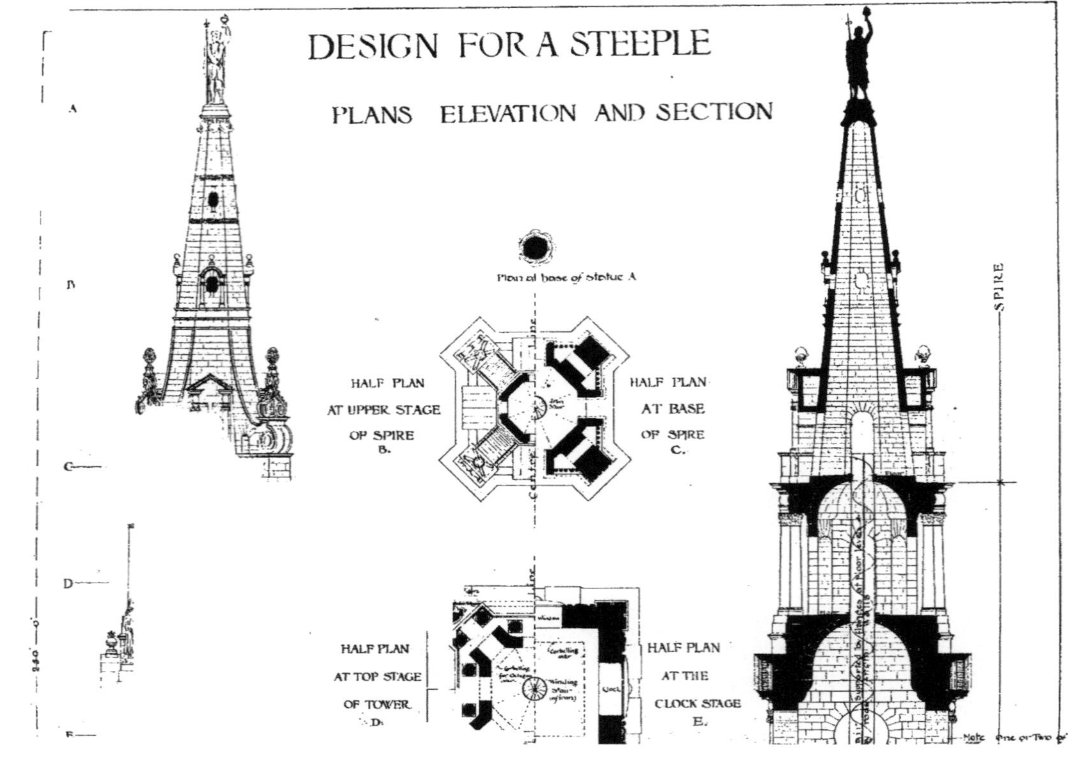
DESIGN FOR A STEEPLE
PLANS ELEVATION AND SECTION
Plan at base of Statue A
HALF PLAN AT UPPER STAGE OF SPIRE B.
HALF PLAN AT BASE OF SPIRE C.
HALF PLAN AT TOP STAGE OF TOWER D.
HALF PLAN AT THE CLOCK STAGE E.
SPIRE
A
B
C
D
E
240

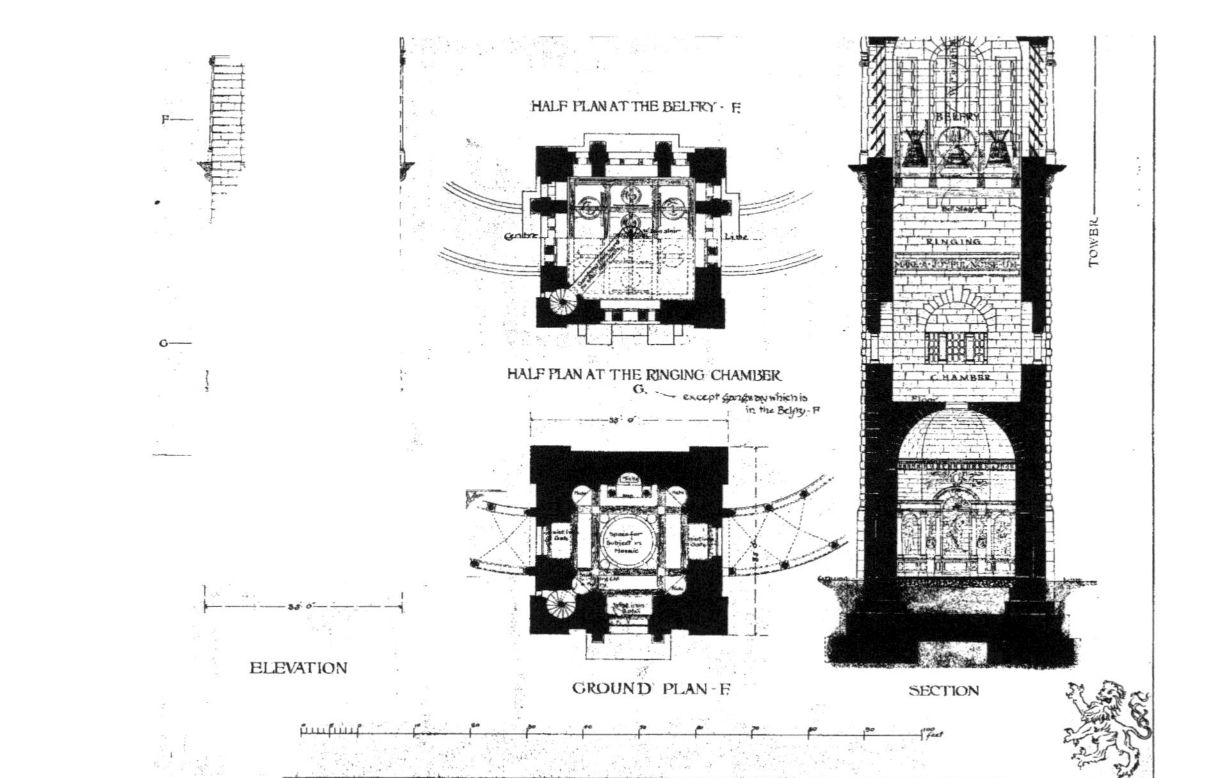

DESIGN AWARDED THE "TITE PRIZE," R.I.B.A., 1892.—BY MR. T. ROGERS KITSELL, A.R.I.B.A.

THE

ROTHERHITHE INFIRMARY: ALT

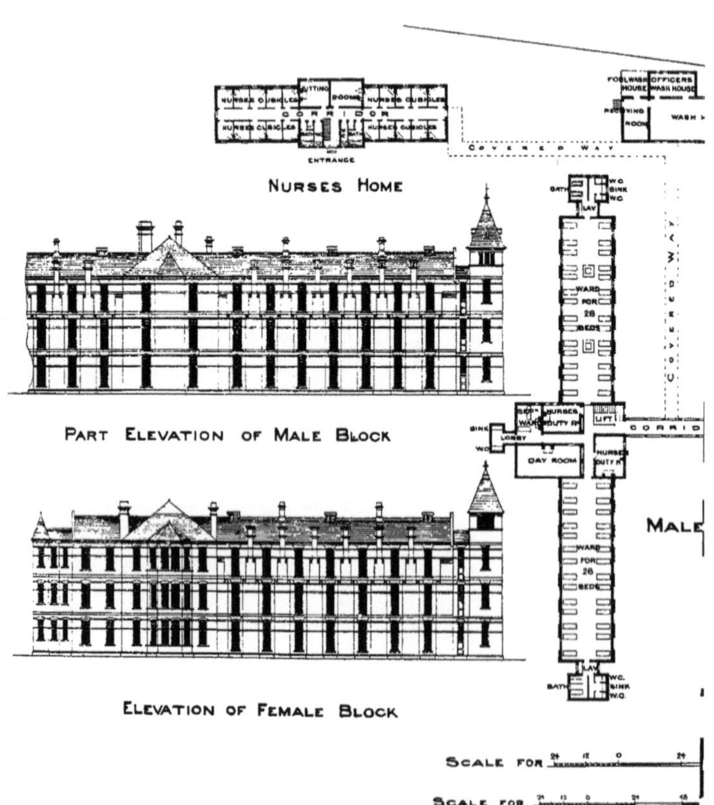

ND ADDITIONS.

SSRS NEWMAN & NEWMAN, ARCHITECTS.

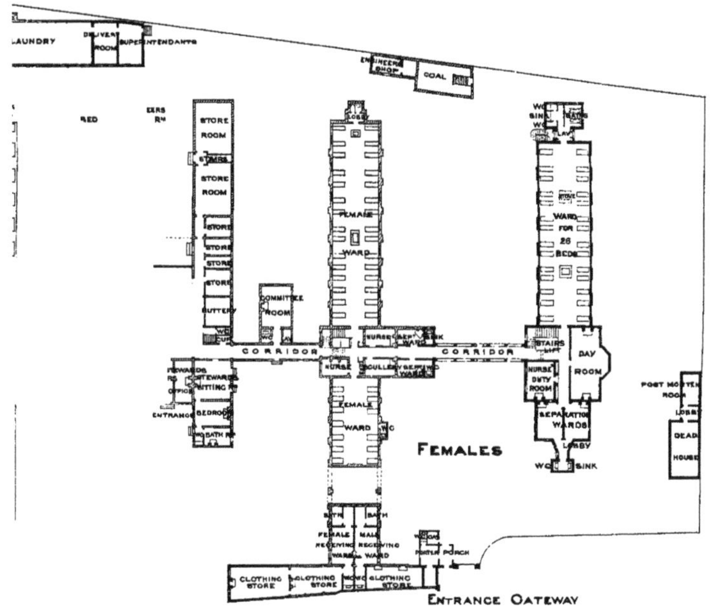

ELEVATIONS

PLANS

PHOTO LITHO SPRAGUE & CO 4 & 5, EAST HARDING STREET, FETTER LANE, E.C.

Isaac B. Potter, serves to show by its illustrations of the state of main roads in the vicinity of great American cities, how discreditably careless and behind the age is the United States civilisation in the matter of the maintenance of roads. Some of the illustrations (apparently taken from photographs) show a state of things almost incredible to an English road surveyor.

Harper's Magazine contains an article on Shakespeare's *Tempest*, or apropos of a French criticism of the play, by Mr. Andrew Lang, with a number of illustrations by Mr. E. A. Abbey. The article suggests some new critical ideas which are worth attention, but we cannot say the same of Mr. Abbey's illustrations, which appear to us singularly poor and weak in conception, except perhaps the one representing Trinculo's first encounter with Caliban. Mr. F. D. Millet's series of articles "From the Black Forest to the Black Sea, continues," and is illustrated by capital sketches of figures and bits of landscape and buildings. Mr. Julian Ralph's article on "Western Modes of City Management" is rather political than municipal, to the perception of an English reader, but is not without interest. A short poem, "In a London Street," may interest English readers as an instance of the fascination which our great smoky capital exercises on some minds.

The *English Illustrated* has an article by Miss Rose G. Kingsley on "A Hampshire Moor," with illustrations by Mr. Alfred Parsons; and "A Look Round Swindon Works," by Mr. A. H. Malan, with illustrations from the workshops. It is a pity the magazine should have admitted such nonsense as "A Middy Hero," of which it is difficult to say whether the illustrations or the text are the more absurd.

The *Antiquary*, in its notes of the month, remarks that "the regularity with which we have to chronicle complete or partial destruction of ancient churches through fire caused by faulty heating flues becomes almost monotonous. This time it is the old parish church of St. Nicholas, Rochester." Some stained-glass windows, a good deal of the roof, and the organ were destroyed; and the *Antiquary* probably does not exaggerate in regard to the frequency of this kind mischief from heating-flues. Among special papers are the conclusion of a series on "Prehistoric Rome," by Dr. Isaac Taylor; one on Norwich Castle by Mr. Mottram; and the third of Dr. Halbherr's papers on "Researches in Crete."

Temple Bar gives the conclusion of an article on B. R. Haydon, chiefly written, as the writer observes, "to direct some sympathetic attention to a very human document," viz., Haydon's autobiography, a book which certainly ought not to pass out of notice.

In the *Cornhill Magazine* the only noticeable article from our point of view is one on "Early Railway Travelling," which gives some details as to the conditions of railway travelling in the earlier days of the art, serving to show what a rude performance it was in comparison with the speed and comfort of modern railway travelling.

The *Revue Scientifique* contains an article on trans-continental railways of South America, by M. Daniel Bellet, giving among other things some account of the proposed railway across the Andes, a bold undertaking, which however will probably be carried out, and which among other results "will bring Valparaiso ten days nearer to Europe."

THE ENGLISH IRON TRADE.—Unfortunately, there is no change to record in the depressed condition of the English iron and allied trades, and the near approach of the holidays prevents any hope of amelioration. From all the pig-iron centres complaints as to the stagnation in business continue to be received. The prolongation of the Durham coal strike has caused a decrease of 85,136 tons in the production of pig-iron in the Cleveland districts, and a reduction of seventy in the number of furnaces in blast. Stocks have been drawn upon to the extent of 43,659 tons; but despite this fact the price has fallen 9d. per ton during the week. The Scotch warrant market is practically lifeless. Manufactured iron is very quiet, and a further weakening of prices is manifested. The tin plate trade shows no change, and the steel trade is dull. Many of the engineers who have been on strike in the Tyne districts are returning to work, but engineering establishments are slack. Ship-building yards are only moderately engaged. The coal trade generally shows little movement, and prices exhibit a certain amount of fluctuation.—*Iron.*

THE ARCHITECTURAL ASSOCIATION SPRING VISITS:

NEWINGTON WEIGHTS AND MEASURES OFFICES.

THE members of the Architectural Association had the opportunity on Saturday last of inspecting the first public testing offices for weights and measures erected in London by the County Council, and a large number availed themselves of the opportunity. The visitors were met by Mr. Spicer and several officers of the London County Council, who explained the purport and working of the various features of the establishment. The plan consists of a good-sized courtyard, with weighbridge, and on one side stabling and coachhouse for the various travelling inspectors; on the other, a weighing-room, treated like a hall, with open-timbered roof, and used for testing the ordinary weights and lineal measures of every-day use in ordinary trades. Beyond this are a room for the examination of jewellers' and apothecaries' weights with balances of various degrees of delicacy, and standard weights from the cental to $\frac{1}{100}$ grain, and beyond this room again, another with exceptionally good light for the testing of measures of capacity, both dry and liquid. Amongst the interesting features of this room are the sandblast machine for marking glass measures of approved fidelity, and various old standard measures of the counties of Kent and Surrey. A vote of thanks to their hosts by Mr. F. T. W. Goldsmith, the honorary secretary, concluded the reception, and the members then proceeded to the second portion of their visit, after remarking on the advance made in the matter of design shown in these buildings beyond the average level of official architecture.

ROYAL SOUTH LONDON OPHTHALMIC HOSPITAL.

The members subsequently visited the new South London Ophthalmic Hospital, designed by Mr. Keith D. Young, with the co-operation and direction of Professor McHardy. It occupies a site on the north-west of St. George's-circus, which, though admirably situated as a house of relief for the sufferers of South London, must have presented considerable difficulties to the designers in scheming the arrangements of the hospital. Professor McHardy met the members, and, in his own attractive and inimitable manner, conducted them over the building, and explained the details of the construction and fitting of the hospital, so that no doubt could exist in the minds of the visitors that careful attention and forethought had been lavishly expended by the doctor and the architect on all the minutiæ of the building, a description of which we hold over until next week.

THE LONDON COUNTY COUNCIL.

The usual weekly meeting of this Council was held on Tuesday afternoon at Spring-gardens, the Chairman, Lord Rosebery, presiding.

The Deputy-Chairman's Salary.—Another futile attempt was made, on the motion of Mr. Elliott, to rescind the resolution of November 7, 1889, fixing the Deputy-Chairman's salary at £1,500. The motion was lost by 64 votes against to 44 votes for,—a majority of 20 against.

The Water Question.—On the recommendation of the General Purposes Committee, it was resolved:—

"That the following be the order of reference to the Special Water Committee:—

The Committee shall prosecute and conduct all needful inquiries and negotiations relative to the supply of water or to companies supplying water in or near London, and shall consider the steps to be taken for acquiring the undertakings now supplying London or for providing a new supply.

The Committee shall conduct any negotiations with the water companies for purchase or otherwise which may be authorised by the Council.

The Committee shall take the necessary steps for the purpose of promoting and conducting conjointly with the Corporation of London the Water Bill of the Council.

The Committee shall conduct the case of the Council before the Royal Commission appointed to inquire into the subject of the London water supply."

The Proposed Amendment of the Building Acts.—The Building Act Committee reported for the information of the Council, that they had appointed a Sub-Committee to consider as to the amendment of the existing Building Acts, and as to other matters, such Committee to consist of the Vice-Chairman of the Council, the Chairman of the Committee, and Messrs. G. B. Holmes, J. Marsland, A. C. Ranyard, R. Roberts, L. Stevens, R. Strong, and H. R. Taylor.

Contracts for Lime.—The Main Drainage Committee, referring to a report which they made to the Council on the 1st ult., on the subject of the tenders for lime, now reported that they had received a letter from Messrs. C. Christopherson & Co., asking that they might be permitted to supply 2,000 additional tons, which they offered to do at 16*s.* per ton, being the same price as had already been accepted by the Council for 2,000 tons of lime. The Committee recommended—

"That, subject to an estimate being submitted to the Council by the Finance Committee as required by the statute, the offer of Messrs. C. Christopherson & Co. to supply 2,000 tons of lime at 16*s.* per ton be accepted, and that the Solicitor be instructed to prepare the contract."

An amendment that the recommendation be referred back, with instructions to the Committee to re-advertise for tenders, was moved by Mr. Goodman and seconded by Mr. Leon, but it only found 16 supporters, and the recommendation was agreed to.

The Brook-street, Limehouse, Scheme.—The Public Health and Housing Committee's Report contained the following paragraph and recommendation:—

"The Brook-street, Limehouse, area comprises two plots of land cleared under a scheme confirmed by Parliament in 1883. The land was advertised for sale by the late Board in 1887, for the erection of artisans' dwellings to re-house 562 persons, but without result. In March, 1890, application was made to the Secretary of State for his consent to a reduction (viz., from 562 to 281) of the number of persons to be re-housed on the area, such reduced number to be accommodated in buildings to be erected on plot 1, and for permission to devote plot 2, which measures only 20 yards in width by 50 in length, to the purpose of an open space. The Secretary of State declined to sanction the reduction, suggesting that as a tentative measure the Council should again advertise plot 1, with the condition of re-housing 281 persons, the disposal of plot 2 being left for future consideration. Accordingly, plot 1 was offered for sale by auction on July 17, 1890, and again on March 24, 1891, but in each case without result. It was thought that the failure to find a purchaser might be due to there being no demand in the neighbourhood for block dwellings, and the Council therefore decided to make application to the Secretary of State, requesting him to sanction the reduction of the number of persons to be re-housed under the scheme to 281, on condition that both plots were used for the erection of cottage dwellings. The sanction of the Secretary of State was obtained to this proposal in due course, and the land was again put up for sale on the 23rd ult. on the altered conditions, but again to no purpose, no offers being made. Taking into consideration the fact that the plots have been put up by the Council four times for sale without result, and that an improvement scheme under Part II. of the Housing of the Working Classes Act, 1890, is now being proceeded with close to the area, with a consequent displacement of persons of the working classes, we are of opinion that a duty is cast upon the Council to see that the erection of dwellings is no longer delayed, and to this end that the Council should itself undertake to erect dwellings on the plots in question. The Housing of the Working Classes Act fully contemplates the possible necessity of the Council itself undertaking building in connexion with an improvement scheme, but provides (1) that the consent of the Home Secretary shall be first obtained, and (2) that the dwellings when erected shall be sold within ten years of completion, unless the Home Secretary otherwise determines. The first step, therefore, is to obtain the consent referred to, and if this is given, to cause proper specifications and estimates to be prepared for the approval of the Council. The recommendation we make at this moment is—

'That application be made to the Home Secretary under section 12 (3) and (5) of the Housing of the Working Classes Act, 1890, for permission for the Council to erect cottage dwellings on the vacant plots on the Brook-street site, in general accordance with the plans which have already been approved by him, and that if such application be granted, proper specifications and estimates be prepared and submitted to the Council.'"

The recommendation was agreed to, and after transacting other business the Council adjourned.

ROBERT BOYLE & SON (LIMITED).—We are informed that the Directors of Robert Boyle & Son (Limited), ventilating engineers, London and Glasgow, have resolved to pay an instalment on account of dividend at the rate of 12 per cent. per annum, free of income-tax, for the half year ending March 31 last.

NEW OFFICES FOR THE *ATHENÆUM.*

From the designs and under the superintendence of Mr. William C. Street, F.R.I.B.A., new premises have been erected at Breams-buildings, Chancery-lane, for the accommodation of the Editorial and Publishing Departments of the *Athenæum* and *Notes and Queries*, also the printing establishment of the Athenæum Press, of which Messrs. Francis & Co. are the proprietors. The upper floors or composing-rooms are well lighted by means of the side and back in Church-passage and ordinary square windows, while the extensive machine-rooms in the basement are lit through the medium of a central wall and pavement lights back and front. The front of the building is Venetian-Gothic in character, and the premises are built of red brick, Portland stone, and Aberdeen granite, the contractor being Mr. B. E. Nightingale, of the Albert Embankment.

Finnish Industrial Exhibition.—It has been decided to postpone the holding of the projected Finnish Industrial Exhibition at Helsingfors until next year.

ENGINEERING SOCIETIES.

The Institution of Civil Engineers.—At the ordinary meeting of this Institution, o Tuesday last, Mr. Berkley (President), in th chair, it was announced that five Associate Members had been transferred to the class o Members, and that fourteen candidates ha been admitted as Students. The monthl ballot resulted in the election of five Member and of thirty Associate Members. Mr. H. A. Roechling, Associate-Member, read a paper o "The Sewage-Farms of Berlin."

Society of Engineers.—A meeting of th

Society of Engineers was held at the Town Hall, Westminster, on Monday evening, April 4, Mr. Joseph William Wilson, jun., President, in the chair, when the adjourned discussion on Mr. Stephen Sellon's paper on "Electrical Traction and its Financial Aspect" was concluded, and a paper was read by Mr. Reginald Bolton, on "The Application of Electricity to Hoisting Machinery." The author dealt with various methods of distributing power to cranes and hoists, and instances of steam, water, and compressed air, ropes and belts, shafting and gear, and stated the comparative advantages of electricity, among which are handiness, cleanliness, quietude, and economy. Some description was next given of the peculiarities of the electro-motor, which converts the electrical energy into rotative movement, and its distinctive characteristics as applied to the duties of lifting and hauling, and the machine is described as admirably effective, simple, and useful, with the minimum of working parts and an extraordinary efficiency. The author contended that the success of the application depended largely upon mechanical considerations, with several electrical conditions, and instanced several unsuccessful instances where these had been neglected; proceeding next to a description of simple mechanical gear, fulfilling all the requirements laid down, and which are embodied in the design of a ship's winch described and illustrated. A safety device, which also forms part of the apparatus, was described in detail, and it was shown how this prevents the overloading and consequent stoppage of the motor, overcoming in the simplest automatic manner the chief danger to their use. Several successful installations were described, and finally the question of first cost was dealt with, and compared with that of other systems. At the close of the meeting, the usual monthly ballot took place, when the following were duly elected, viz.:—As Life Member, Mr. Ernest Docwra; as Members, Messrs. Douglas Allport, junr., James . Mingay, Frederick Lennard; as Foreign Members, Messrs. John A. Rossbach, Edward C. Harvey; as Associates, Messrs. Alfred H. C. lley, William H. Sadler, Arthur S. Harbord, James H. Paul, Maximillian W. H. Clarke, Henry Conradi, Charles N. Spencer, William B. arstin, Lionel C. H. Savory, Henry T. Jackman, John E. Campbell, Frederick Southey, Joseph B. Kimfull, Takeo Nitta, John H. ammar, William P. Lipsett, Henry A. Scott, Augustin Mora, Douglas Clark, Gerard L. Baldwin, Harold L. Phillips, Harold T. Creasy, Alexander A. Rawlins, Alexander M. Furlonge, Cyril D. Bury, Reginald L. Bennett, Whitbread . Silcock.

Books.

Electric-light Cables and the Distribution of Electricity. By Stuart A. Russell. London: Whittaker & Co. 1892.

THIS book belongs to "The Specialists' Series," and may, therefore, be regarded as "caviare to the general" reader. For all that, the "general reader" who cares for such things will find it both more interesting and more intelligible than nine-tenths of the scientific works written expressly for him. Just as school histories seem expressly designed to create a loathing for the study of history, so popular science is, generally, at once obscure and dull; sometimes owing to the ignorance of the writer, but more frequently because he is thinking of his audience, while the specialists writing for specialists think only of their subject,—"And being natural, naturally please."

Mr. Russell begins with a short sketch of the first attempts at cable-laying in the early days of telegraphy, pointing out the causes of their failure, and how they were eventually replaced almost universally by the overhead system. In Chapter II. he comes to the subject of "Electric Light Cables," founding his whole treatment of the subject, with an insistance which is rather amusing, on "Thomson's Economic Law."

No doubt, when electrical distribution was in its infancy, and no one knew what thickness of cable to lay, this law was of some use as a rough guide; it could never be more than that; an exact calculation founded on uncertain data, such as cost of labour, allowance for depreciation, and rate of interest on capital, is little better than waste of time; but now that experience and natural selection have settled the matter, the companies that laid wasteful cables have been crowded out, and the survivors have learnt an economic law, as bees learn geometry, without calculation. Mr. Russell states with admirable clearness the various considerations which modify the application in practice of this law; but he apparently fails to perceive that the existence of these qualifications takes the matter out of the hands of the Professor and puts it into those of the practical engineer. As for the tables he quotes from Professor Forbes, we have tried in vain to discover how they were constructed, nor does a reference to the report of the original papers (Cantor Lectures, 1885) help us. One thing, however, is clear, the tables profess to give the current density in terms *inter alia* of "the cost of laying one additional ton of copper." Now we were told at school that an equation was not solved if the unknown quantity appeared in the result; and since the current density in any particular case involves the section of the cable, and the cost of laying a ton of copper must greatly depend on its length, and therefore on its cross section, the tables lose even the academic value they might otherwise possess.

After a chapter on "Rise of Temperature" and "Fall of Potential" in the mains, which, as before remarked, modifies greatly the conclusions of the preceding chapter, we come to an excellent account of the different systems of distribution, followed again by a discussion of their relative economy, in which we find the advantages and disadvantages of the various systems impartially and graphically set forth. We doubt, however, whether there is in actual work any such system of double accumulators as described on p. 69, and we think Mr. Russell hardly does full justice to Mr. Bernstein's ingenious system.

After this are four practical chapters dealing with questions of insulation, making of joints, and the various systems of cable-laying, to which last he returns more fully in the last four chapters of the book.

All these matters are entered into in full detail and with knowledge evidently at htst hand. The general consensus of authority, and the carelessness of American linesmen, support Mr. Russell in his general condemnation of bare overhead wires, but if he had had any experience of such a system properly carried out, as in Brighton about 1885, he might see reason to qualify the severity of his judgment, and allow that they are, in many cases, at least as satisfactory as overhead cables with heater wires, while they are certainly much cheaper.

With respect to this latter system our author gives good reason for objecting to the Board of Trade regulation that the bearer wires should be insulated, pointing out that it is closely analogous to metal sheathing, which it is universally recognised should be connected to earth.

The remaining chapter of the book treats of internal wiring and the testing of cables and circuits, and is as satisfactory and thorough as the rest. To the many disadvantages of wood-casing that the author has collected we may add one more,—it is a favourite resort of cockroaches.

We hope that in a subsequent edition the test given on pp. 184 and 185, and the accompanying figure 50, may be made clearer; at present we cannot see how two relations can be got by one observation; if a key were placed in the short circuit between the resistances the difficulty would vanish. We think Mr. Russell should note, moreover, that this method is identical with the bridge test, instead of so carefully contrasting the two.

The page or so devoted to the calculation of the insulation resistance of a cell might be cut down to a couple of lines if Mr. Russell would make use of the integral calculus.

Forty Plates on Building Construction. By F. Mitchell. London, Paris, and Melbourne: Cassell & Co.; 1891.

THESE plates, prepared by Mr. Mitchell, the lecturer on building construction at the Polytechnic Institute, should be in the hands of every young student of architecture and building.

Mr. Mitchell has been assisted by other lecturers at the Polytechnic, and, with their help, has produced a series of plates of the very highest value, and certainly superior to any other illustrations of the detailed construction of modern builders' work, that a student can readily find. Specially noteworthy is the care which has been exercised in figuring dimensions and scantlings, and in providing details, for the most part in isometrical projection, showing the various portions of the construction separate from each other, so as to make it easy for a learner to understand the precise articulation of the structure which he is studying.

We should advise all students who work from these plates to draw them out to a very much larger scale, as naturally the drawings here given have been considerably reduced in order to prevent the plates from being unwieldly. The reduction, however, has not seriously affected the clearness of the diagrams, though it has made some of the plates look rather full of work.

We do not suppose that the author intends that these plates should be used entirely without the assistance of a master or of a good text-book, since it would be quite impossible for an unassisted student to comprehend, for example, the meaning of the diagrams given to illustrate the bevels and face moulds for wreathed hand-rails.

One especially good feature of the work is the fact that pains have been taken to bring the diagrams up to date by incorporating illustrations of modern specialised forms of construction.

Ventilation of Buildings.—By Alfred R. Wolff, M.E. New York.

IN this small pamphlet by Mr. Wolff we have, within the compass of an ordinary lecture, what the writer accurately describes as "the terse presentation, in a popular way, of the great general principles underlying the proper ventilation of buildings."

We are glad to find ourselves in accord with the principles herein laid down, most of which we have from time to time drawn attention to in our pages, such as, for example, that temperature is no criterion of the efficiency of ventilation.

A useful feature in the pamphlet is the series of tables which the author gives for simplifying the calculations necessary in applying ventilation. Within the compass of such a pamphlet the author could not, of course, fully describe all that he touches upon, but he has well pointed out the chief factors determining the amount of ventilation, the method, and the warming, which necessarily follows the introduction of ventilation, as well as some general hints, which we completely endorse, as to the expense of various methods and forms of apparatus.

Elatée. La Ville le Temple d'Athéna Cranaia; par Pierre Paris. Paris: Ernest Thorin. 1892. (Bibliothèque des Ecoles Françaises d'Athènes et de Rome, publiés sous les auspices du Ministère de l'Instruction Publique. Fascicule Soixantième.)

M. PARIS' book is practically, as he states in the preface, intended to be a monograph on the ancient city of Elateia, but practically by far the greater part of it is devoted to the discussion of the Temple of Athene Cranaia, to which the city owed much of its fame, and the excavation of which is due to the French School of Archæology at Athens. Reports of the progress of this excavation have, of course, appeared from time to time in the Bulletin de Correspondence Héllénique since the beginning of the work in 1884. Now, for the first time, M. Paris presents us with a valuable summary of the results, preceded by an excellent account of the history of the town in ancient and modern times. Elateia was always second in interest among the towns of Phocis to Delphi, with its world-wide renown; but if we may trust Strabo, it was the largest of all. Pausanias (x., 34) devoted a whole chapter to its history and the discussion of its monuments; and he specially notes the Sanctuary of Athene Cranaia, the seat manifestly of an ancient local cult. It is recorded that the priest was always a young boy, and that he used for his bath a peculiar and ancient form of tub called an ἀσάμινθος; this ἀσάμινθος dates from Homeric days, and M. Paris believes he has found some specimens just big enough to bathe a rather small boy. There is little doubt the tradition must be connected with the famous ceremonial "Bath of Pallas." The book altogether is of great interest in connexion with that early local cult of Athene. The site of the temple itself struck even Pausanias as remarkable; it stood on the crest of a precipitous hill. M. Paris devotes a chapter to its ground-plan and proposed reconstruction. He believes it to have been of similar construction to the so-called Theseion at Athens, but of somewhat earlier date. There is evidence that baked clay was largely employed in its structure, whereas the Theseion was entirely of marble. Only second in interest to the temple itself are a large collection of votive terracottas and inscriptions, which M. Paris discusses in detail.

A Plea for Liberty. An Argument against Socialism and Socialistic Legislation. With an Introduction by Herbert Spencer and Essays by various writers. Edited by THOMAS MACKAY. New and Revised Edition. London: John Murray. 1892.

THIS is a cheap edition of a book which all persons who are interested in the affairs of their time would do well to read. The various writers state their case with clearness and brevity, and in a plain, common-sense style. The faults of Socialism, and the weak points of a system which represses individual freedom, are exposed in a way which any ordinarily educated man should understand. Thus Mr. Herbert Spencer points out what is very apposite at the present time, that every society is apt to take away from the freedom of its members. In trades unions "the regulative agency becomes all powerful. Their members, even when they dissent from the policy pursued, habitually yield to the authorities they have set up." This is perfectly true, and will in time be recognised by working men. Considering that the price of this edition is only 2s., it ought to be very widely read.

Olympia. Die Ergebnisse der von dem deutschen Reich veranstalteten Ausgrabung. Herausgegeben von ERNST CURTIUS und FRIEDRICH ADLER. Textband IV. Die Bronzen und die übrigen kleineren Funde. Tafelband IV. Berlin: Verlag von Asher & Co. 1890.

THIS is the fourth volume in the sequence of the great official work, "Olympia," to whose programme we drew attention about a year ago, but it is the first to appear. It is based mainly on the elaborate studies made by Dr. Furtwangler on the spot, at Olympia, in 1886, —studies which he revised and enlarged during a shorter stay there in 1888. Dr. Furtwängler had for years been second in command (under Dr. Curtius) over the Antiquarium at Berlin, where all the smaller antiquities, vases, terracotta, bronzes, &c., of the Museum, are stored, and there could be no one more competent to undertake the work of elucidating the bronzes of Olympia than he. The task is no light one. In a series of eighty plates he has published and elucidated no less than 1,371 minor objects of antiquity, ranging in date from prehistoric votive offerings to Byzantine jewellery. The antiquities published are as diverse in character as in date. They comprise fragments of statues, statuettes, tektonic fragments, and a vast board of votive offerings of every description in bronze and terra-cotta. Of these, the most interesting are undoubtedly those with mythological subjects,—*e.g.*, Herakles and the Old Man of the Sea (inscribed), Ajax and Cassandra, and Hermes, Achilles and Priam, which designs are all impressed on thin bronze plates. The book, as a corpus of a certain class of discoveries, is essential to all archæological libraries, but its appearance will not arouse such interest as many of the subsequent volumes,—*e.g.*, that on the topography, and that on the architecture, of Olympia, in both of which novel discoveries may be looked for.

Wiener Vorlegeblätter für Archäologische. Ubingen, 1890-91. Mit Unter-stuzung des KK. Ministeriums für Cultur und Unterricht. Herausgegeben von Otto Benndorf. Wien: A. Hölder. 1891.

THIS new issue of the invaluable Vienna "Vorlegeblätter" is divided into two parts. The first consists of a corpus of the works of one Greek vase-painter, and that the most prolific of all,—*i.e.*, Nikosthenes; the second contains plates devoted to the statement of certain archæological problems dealing with vase interpretation. The vase-painter Nikosthenes has special claims to attention. He is, perhaps, of all whose signature we possess, the most decorative, and his work in antiquity attained to an extraordinary popularity. We have no really fine examples in the British Museum (his finest work is in the Louvre), so the "Vorlegeblätter" this time specially appeals to English students. The plates are, as usual, first-rate. Not only are many vases published for the first time, but,—a matter scarcely second in importance,—vases hitherto known in inferior plates are now republished from new and accurate drawings. Even the most recent publications are not reproduced without the most exact revision. The "problem" plates will be a genuine delight to all ingenious archæologists, and should be a lively stimulus to students. A well-known but hitherto unexplained vase is reproduced, and, side by side with it, analogous type-forms which may and should help to its solution. Another form of problem is to publish in one sheet a number of fragments known to have been found together, and leave it to the student to reconstruct the design. This is real actual archæological practice, and training alike for mind and eye.

Funfzehntes Hallisches Winckelmannsprogramm. Scenen des Ilias und Aithiopis auf einer Vase der Sammlung des Grafen Michael Tyskiewicz. Fest-schrift zur Eröffnung des Archäologischen Museums der Friedrichs Universität. Halle-Wittenberg: von Carl Robert. Halle: Niemeyer. 1891.

WE have again and again called attention to the necessity of the prompt publication of important works of Greek art in *private* collections, and collections, from the nature of the case, less accessible to science, and always liable to unnoticed dispersion, and we are glad to find the last Winckelmann's Programm devoted to the reproduction of a truly magnificent red-figured krater in the possession of Count Michael Tyskiewicz. The vase is notable for its perfect preservation, it not only being intact, but every line even of the super-imposed brushwork being preserved with extraordinary freshness. The scenes represented are also of great interest. On the one side Diomede contends with Æneas in the presence of Aphrodite and Athene, on the other Achilles and Memnon fight over the fallen body of Melanippos,—Eos and Athene advance on either side to protect their favourite heroes. All the figures are inscribed, so happily the interpretation is undoubted. The text is as valuable as the plates. We cannot here enter into details, but Dr. Robert, with his usual brilliancy, discusses,—apropos of the figure of Melanippos, a new element in the *type*,—the relation of literature and vase-painting with some new and interesting results.

London Street Improvements. By HENRY CLARKE, Chairman of the Improvements Committee of the first London County Council. 1892.

THIS is a pamphlet containing some practical remarks on the special problems of London improvements, with a map and a list of suggested street improvements. Some of the general remarks on the subject are well worth attention. As usual in this country, the improvements are suggested on mere practical and financial grounds, and take no account of opportunities for architectural effect.

La Peinture Antique, par Paul Girard. Bibliothèque de l'enseignement des Beaux-Arts. Publiée sous la direction de M. JULES COMTE. Paris: Quantin.

ON the general excellence of this series, it is now superfluous to insist. Seven of the manuals have found their way into English translations, and we hope this small handbook on ancient painting will shortly appear in the same form. It is unfortunate that whereas the French volume can be got for 3 f. 50 c., they emerge in England (certainly with some substantial additions) at the comparatively high figure of 10s. 6d. We may note one point in which M. Girard's manual on painting is distinctly in advance of the rest, and that is in the matter of illustration. They have been, M. Girard says in his preface, the object of his special attention, and not in vain. So often these elementary and cheap manuals go on reproducing *ad nauseam* wretched cuts of subjects already thrice familiar, that it is a distinct relief to turn over the pages of a book which gives really excellent reproductions of works of art only brought to light within the last three years, or hitherto only accessible in rare or costly publications. We note,—*e.g.*, p. 104,—the remarkable painted bull of Tiryns and the famous Vaphio gold cups which have so lately appeared in the "Ephemeris Archæologike," the lovely painted plaque with th[e] figure of a warrior, recently discovered in th[e] Acropolis; and the fragments,—if possibl[e] still more beautiful,—of the white cylix wit[h] Orpheus and the Thracian woman, lately pul[b]lished in the *Hellenic Journal*, but reproduce[d] here from original drawings. The book shoul[d] be specially welcome to artists, to whom Gre[ek] vase-paintings are, as a rule, almost unknow[n] but by whom, when known, they are high[ly] prized.

SOME RECENT TRADE CATALOGUES.

Messrs. John Bolding & Sons, of Sou[th] Molton-street, send us a new edition of the illustrated catalogue of plumbers', engineer[s'] and gasfitters' brasswork, valve and earthe[n]ware pedestal closets, sanitary earthenwa[re] gullies, air-chambers, and drain-disconnecto[rs]. The catalogue is a very comprehensive o[ne] extending to nearly 500 pages. It is we[ll] printed and indexed. Its contents include a good variety of excellent valve and oth[er] closets, water waste-preventing cisterns, bath[s], lavatories (the "Paragon" lavatory basi[n] with flushing-rim and quick-waste is one [of] the best things of its kind known to us: o[ne] turn of a lever shuts the waste and fills t[he] basin for use; by reversing the lever the bas[in] is emptied and rinsed), and many other thin[gs] too numerous for mention.

Messrs. Baird, Thompson, & Co., send us th[eir] revised and illustrated catalogue of ventilati[ng] and heating appliances to meet all requireme[nts]. It is clear and concise, and will repay keepi[ng] for reference.

Messrs. J. M. Bennett & Sons, of Ardwi[ck], Manchester, send us a useful little catalogue [of] priced details of stock of logs, dry oak and a[sh] held by them at the present time. The cat[a]logue gives the length and sale contents, a[lso] the number of boards into which each log [is] sawn, also the date of sawing, sawing conte[nts] and the net cost of log,—timber and saw[ing] included. The catalogue will be found [ex]ceedingly convenient by builders, join[ers], cabinet-makers, and others in all parts of [the] country, for in addition to the before-mentio[ned] particulars, there is a table of railway ra[tes] for the conveyance of timber from Ardw[ick] station.

From Woodhouse & Rawson United (L[td]) we have received an illustrated catalogue [of] hydraulic machine tools manufactured by th[em] on the Payne-Gallwey system. It is an [in]teresting and suggestive production, and c[on]tains illustrations and particulars of a g[reat] many appliances likely to be of use to [a] building contractor. The portable hydra[ulic] rivetters will be of great service wherever t[here] is a quantity of ironwork to be built up *in s[itu]*. A hydraulic pile-extractor, figured on page [—] is also worth attention. The catalogue [has] been compiled by Mr. W. Payne-Gallwey.

Correspondence.

To the Editor of THE BUILDER.

ARCHITECTURAL EDUCATION.

SIR,—A foremost place in the April nu[mber] of "*A.A. Notes*" is given to a letter from [Mr.] Thos. G. Jackson, A.R.A., concerning "[The] Training of Architects to the Pursuit of A[rchi]tecture," which said letter has a wider int[erest] and more reaching consequences than is [sur]prised in the publication in which it appea[rs].

Mr. Jackson tells us in his letter that h[e and] the memorialists against registration an[d ex]amination have not been idle, and that o[ne or] more meetings have taken place between [a] half-dozen of those who signed the mem[orial] and some half-dozen members of the A.A. [;] that, at the request of the latter, Mr. Ja[ckson] writes to let "the Association know wha[t has] been and is being done," and he very pl[ainly] and honestly tells us on what grounds [the] memorialists will extend their aid to [the] A.A., and on what conditions; we are [also] promised a volume of essays, setting [forth] the view of "various *artists*, exp[osing] the delusive character of a diploma [ob]tained by examination." The italics ar[e our] own. The conditions of help from this q[uarter] are the giving up of the present schem[e of] studies, which "points definitely to prepa[ration] for the examination of the Institute," [in] return the memorialists will, Mr. Jackson [says], "feel it an honour to help . . . . as vi nd aid in drawing up, facilitating, and super-ising," if we desire it, our scheme of studies; ut unless the A.A. purges itself of the old eaven, the memorialists cannot take any nterest in our programme. In plain language, enounce the Institute and all its works, and mbrace the true faith as set forth by s, the memorialists. Another bait offered s a promised reform of the Architectural chools at the R.A., and the further possi-ility that our schools should be affiliated to hose of the Academy. Mr. Jackson concludes is invitation to forsake the Institute and join is party thus:—"In conclusion, I can only emind you that the future, so far as concerns ny help or co-operation on our part, rests with ou. If you turn your faces the right way, you vill not find us backward in going with you, if ou should think proper to invite our as-istance."

Now, sir, I am curious to know who the half-lozen members of the A.A. are who have ntered into negotiations with Mr. Jackson and is friends, and whether they have been autho-ised to do so, and by whom.

That the present scheme of education in the A.A. is more or less the outcome of the Institute xaminations is patent; that the promoters of he scheme and the examiners and many of the eachers are members of both bodies is per-ectly well known.

That the A.A., by the mouth of its President, n an admirable address, quite recently set orth the new scheme and the claims of the A.A. to the sympathy and aid of the Institute; nd that the Institute in reply made a generous rant to the friends of the A.A. stands re-orded. That many members of the Institute ave, in a very appreciable manner, shown heir interest in the work of the A.A., every nember who cares to inform himself may now. What the gentlemen, who now seek to lestroy the close relationship which exists be-ween the Institute and the A.A., have done or the latter body is not so clear.

If the members of the A. A. are content to be atronised, and to change a very carefully hought out scheme at the invitation of men ostile to the Institute, however distinguished ome of them may be, then they have sadly leteriorated from the vigour, determination, and nanliness they once possessed, and which has ade the A. A. what it is. Everything that the emorialists offer can in time be grafted on to the esent scheme, and in the ranks of the Institute e men every bit as able as those few who and aloof from it to aid with instruction. I ust that before very long the members of the A. may have an opportunity of meeting gether to discuss Mr. Jackson's invitation, and reply to it, and at the same time to hear om the half-dozen of their *confrères* to what tent, and by what right, they led Mr. Jackson suppose that they expressed the voice of the A.; and that at the solicitations of the emoralists the A.A. would go back on their d traditions, and,—renouncing their old sturdy dependence,—lean upon others for support d guidance.

COLE A. ADAMS,
Past-President Architectural Association.

LINCOLN CATHEDRAL LIBRARY.

SIR,—In my letter on this subject it was not y wish to speak with any disrespect of the te Sir Gilbert Scott. Mr. Fergnson refers to is preservation of old work at Ripon, and I ink be might have quoted other places where e was prompted by the same good spirit. Sir ilbert was, indeed, a man of great activity nd intelligence, and by no means anxious to lose his mind against new schools of thought, ut the sad fact remains that, following in the ld grooves, the so-called restorations carried ut under his direction involved the most holesale destruction. His practice having been ost extensive, so, too, was the destruction, nd this was wrought more particularly in our athedrals, from which all fittings not of pproved "Gothic" were cruelly turned out.

April 3, 1892. SOMERS CLARKE.

REMOVING OLD PAINT.

SIR,—I should be much obliged if any of the aders of your paper could give me any informa-on of any process, other than chipping with a isel, of removing old paint from stonework. The se to which I refer is that of some stone pillars in a urch which years ago have had several coats of aint, which it is now wished to remove. I should e very grateful for any information on this bject.

H. F. WHITE.

The Student's Column.

WARMING BUILDINGS BY HOT WATER.
XV.

BOILERS (*continued*).

IN the previous paper the list given applied to saddle boilers having 2 in. to 3 in. water-ways, according to the size of the boiler. Some people prefer a larger water-way than this, especially if a considerable accumulation of dirt is anticipated, but the boiler-makers, for some reason or other, put a considerably higher working value upon these than on those with the smaller water-ways first referred to. This is deceptive, as the mere fact of adding an inch to the water-way does not increase the direct heating surface at all, it adds a trifle to the outer flue surface, though scarcely sufficient to be worth calculating. Some makers actually attribute one-eighth greater total heating value to the boiler for this little addition in the water-way. It would be unsafe to trust to this.

This larger water-way brings us to consider a question that requires every attention when fixing boilers, viz., provision for, and easy access to clean out, any accumulated matter that may collect or be deposited. In almost every case it is dirt, pure and simple, that has to be removed periodically, and the periods have to be regular and moderately frequent if the apparatus is fed with ditch or pond water, as is frequently the case. Then the supply or filling cisterns are just as commonly without lids, and foreign matter of many kinds, leaves, insects, &c., enter, and all go to increase the collection at the lowest point in the apparatus, the boiler.

The provision for the removal of this is a hole drilled at the bottom of the two sides or legs of the boiler in front, and from these holes, say $1\frac{1}{4}$ in., are brought two short lengths of pipe through the brickwork that must exist in front. The front ends of these pipes are plugged. By removal of the plugs, a cane or wire can be inserted, and made to disturb whatever soft dirt deposit there may be in the boiler, and this can be flushed out.

Another and entirely different kind of deposit occurs when the apparatus is fed with what is known as "hard" water, and this water frequently renewed,—that is, water withdrawn and replaced with fresh. This deposit, which is actually carbonate of lime, adheres to the boiler plates tenaciously, and is very hard, and requires very generally to be chiselled off.

This state of things is not common in heating works as, in the first place, the water must be "hard," such as we get from water companies' mains in the South of England, and not surface or rain water. Then, in addition to this, the water must be rather frequently changed, as, although we get a certain quantity of lime deposit from one charge of water, the quantity is so very small as to be harmless and imperceptible. If an apparatus is used for both heating and yielding a supply of hot water in a building, then the trouble will certainly occur if the water be "hard." Kitchen-range boilers that are used exclusively for yielding hot water suffer greatly in this way in London and the South of England.

Boilers are made of cast iron, wrought iron, and copper. The latter material is but seldom used. Cast iron is used to some extent, particularly in small boilers, and its adaptability to larger ones is successfully illustrated in Keith's boilers, which can only be spoken well of. The great fault with articles of cast iron lies with the founder who does not, for reasons known to himself, use a good admixture of metals. It is quite possible to have cast iron of a quality that possesses features quite contrary to what are generally expected. It will not crack if subjected to really violent usage and blows; if struck with moderate care at an edge, the material will burr over instead of particles flying off, and by skilful hammering flat plates can be actually bent a little, and all this without annealling or specially treating, except in the selection of the different brands of pigs. A metal like this is really tough, and shows a most irregular and rough fracture when broken.

Wrought-iron, however, is the material chiefly used at present for boilers of moderate and large size, both of the brick-set and independent kind, the joints being welded. Welded joints are cheaper than rivetted, and are very satisfactory. Of course, very large boilers, like the Cornish pattern, &c., have rivetted joints, as they are too large to be conveniently welded. The general thickness of plate is $\frac{3}{8}$ in. This is a serviceable strength, and can be recommended, but there is no objection to $\frac{5}{16}$-in. plate if the boilers are small. The difference in cost between $\frac{5}{16}$ in. and $\frac{3}{8}$ in. is about 20 per cent. The thicker plate should be used wherever cost will allow, although the writer is in doubt whether it would give 20 per cent. more service than that which is only $\frac{1}{16}$ in. thinner. It is possible that when thinner plates are used they are of a less quality than the others; perhaps some boiler-maker will contradict this if incorrect. It has to be remembered that the majority of boilers fail by an accumulation of dirt causing their fracture, and not from ordinary wear and tear.

There now remains one other feature to be treated, before proceeding with the actual description of boilers, and this is the area of furnace bars needed to effectually work certain sizes and certain patterns. This subject is of importance, though, of course, those who use boilers but little, have no need to calculate the size of furnace-bars required; the boiler maker will supply them with the other fittings of a correct size, with the boiler, if ordered.

This is a question that Hood also treats fully and successfully in his book. His allowance in this respect is 50 square inches area of furnace bars to each 100 ft. of 4-in. pipe, or 100 superficial feet of radiating surface. This allowance only applied to the saddle boiler. The newer forms of boilers having internal flues, &c., do not require so great an area in proportion to the pipe they can effectually heat as is shown in the table given further on. It will be noticed that the area of furnace bars is fixed by the quantity of pipe to be heated, and this, at first sight to the inexperienced, may appear to be a peculiar arrangement. Such, however, is not the case, and a little thought will show that no better plan could be devised. If we tried to decide the area of bars by the width or length of boiler, we should probably get irregular results, and if we calculated by the actual direct and indirect heating surfaces, then we should get exactly the results as calculating by the quantity of pipe, but at unnecessary trouble.

Table showing the area of furnace-bars required for each 100 ft. of radiating surface, with the various kinds of boilers at present in use:—

	Square inches.
With a plain saddle boiler	50
With a saddle boiler having one check or waterway end	45
With a saddle boiler having two waterway ends	40
With a saddle boiler having a tubular flue as fig. 56	40
With boilers as figs. 57 and 58, which have both waterway ends and tubular flues ...	35
If a boiler is fitted with an oval cross-tube, the above figures can be reduced by ...	5 to 10

The above will be seen only to apply to boilers which are brick-set. Independent boilers are always fitted up with bars and the other fittings by the maker. Many independent boilers are worked with a less proportionate area of bars than the above. Keith's Challenge boiler, for instance, only has about 20 square inches of bars per 100 ft. of radiating surface. It is understood that, when speaking of area of fire bars, the spaces between the bars are included.

From the table it will be seen that a plain saddle-boiler, estimated to heat 800 ft. of radiating surface, should have an area of bars of 400 in. (say 24 by 17); but if this same-sized boiler was fitted with an oval cross-tube, its estimated power would be increased to 1,000 ft., but it would not require any greater area of fire-bars.

If the pipes to be used are not 4 in., then allowance must be made as follows:—For 3-in. pipe a fourth less, for 2-in. pipes one-half less area of fire-bars than 4 in. For instance, if we can work 100 ft. of 4-in. pipe with 50 square inches of bars, then the same area will be suited for 133 ft. of 3-in. pipe, or 200 ft. of 2-in. pipe. It was mentioned in the last paper that in calculating the working value of boilers, similar allowance has to be made.

THE FERDINAND'S BRIDGE, VIENNA.—As every-one knows, it was the custom in the Middle Ages to build houses on both sides of bridges, such as was the case with old London Bridge, the Rialto, and the Ponte Vecchio in Florence, and now it is projected to follow this ancient custom in rebuilding the Ferdinand's Bridge across the Danube. It is proposed to line the bridge on both sides with shops, the rents of which would go far towards covering the cost of construction.

OBITUARY.

Mr. T. H. Eagles.—At the meeting of the Royal Institute of British Architects on Monday evening last, as reported in another column, the death was announced of Mr. Thomas Henry Eagles, M.A., F.R.I.B.A., and Professor of Architecture at Cooper's Hill College, Staines. He was elected an Associate of the Institute in 1871 and a Fellow in 1881.

Mr. John Rhind, A.R.S.A.—On the 5th inst., Mr. John Rhind, sculptor, who was recently elected an Associate of the Royal Scottish Academy, died in Edinburgh. He was born in Banff, where his father was a builder, and to that trade he served his apprenticeship. He went to Edinburgh to study architecture; but, having a taste for sculpture, he entered the studio of the late Mr. Handyside, A.R.S.A. In 1858 he commenced practice for himself, and subsequently carried out many works in connexion with Scottish buildings.

Mr. W. J. Beadel, M.P.—We regret to hear that Mr. W. J. Beadel, M.P. for the Chelmsford Division of Essex, died on the 5th inst., after several weeks' illness, at his residence, Hutton Hall, Brentwood. He was born in 1828. Since 1846 Mr. Beadel had been an estate agent and surveyor, and he had served as President of the Surveyors' Institution.

Dr. John Collingwood Bruce, F.S.A.—We regret to learn that Dr. J. C. Bruce, the well-known antiquary, died at Newcastle-on-Tyne on Tuesday last. He was a prolific writer on antiquarian subjects, but will be best remembered by his "Historical and Descriptive Account of the Roman Wall in the North of England." He was in his eighty-seventh year. The *Newcastle Chronicle* of Wednesday last contains a long and interesting memoir of Dr. Bruce and his labours as a minister of religion, philanthropist, and antiquary.

GENERAL BUILDING NEWS.

Additions to Catholic Cathedral, Portsmouth.—On the 31st. ult., the consecration took place of the new additions to the Cathedral church of St. John the Evangelist, in Edinburgh-road, Portsmouth. The building is from the designs of Mr. Joseph S. Hansom, and is in the Gothic style of the Decorated period, cruciform in shape. When completed it will have a tower and spire at the west end, but for the present this portion of the scheme remains in abeyance. The building of the transepts, sanctuary, &c., has been carried out by Messrs. W. R. & C. Light, of Landport, under the superintendence of Mr. J. W. Randle as clerk of the works, and Mr. John Townsend as foreman. The new work consists of the transepts, each 24 ft. wide by 20 ft. deep; the sanctuary, terminating in an apse, 52 ft. long from the eastern arch of the nave, by 26 ft. wide; the Lady Chapel, on the south side of the sanctuary, 30 ft. long by 12 ft. wide; and St. Edmund's Chapel, on the north side, 22 ft. long by 12 ft. wide; while there have also been added a porch and entrance lobby on the south side of the Lady Chapel, and on the Alfred-road side of the Cathedral four confessionals, sacristies, tribune, guardian's room, and other apartments that cover a considerable area, extending across to the school wall, which they join. A covered way leads from these to the Bishop's house. The external walls are of Fareham red bricks, relieved by Portland stone dressings, and the roof is covered with red tiles. In the sanctuary there are thirteen two-light windows, with pointed and tracery heads. In the north transept a five-light window, 32 ft. in height and 18 ft. across, the pointed arch filled with tracery, is constructed, and in the gable of the south transept is a rose-window of floriated design, 18 ft. 6 in. in diameter. Below this a recessed arcading of stonework is formed, which will accommodate a peal of ten of Harrington's tubular bells. The sanctuary walls are flanked by a series of buttresses, each of which is surmounted by a Portland stone pinnacle, with carved crockets and finials and sunk tracery panels. A coping of stone, pierced with a quatrefoil design, also runs round this wall. The apex of the apse is crowned by an ornamental wrought-iron cross. At the outer angles of the transepts are four buttresses, supplied with stone weatherings, and surmounted by carved crocket finials, and the gables are coped with moulded stone, terminating on either side in a carved stone cross. Above the principal windows in the gables are two small quatrefoil lights. At the entrance to the porch is an ornamental wrought-iron gateway, manufactured by Messrs. Jones & Willis, of London. The stone carving, both externally and internally, has been executed by Mr. George Porter, of Chelsea. In the interior the sanctuary is divided from the nave by a rood-screen of wrought-iron, constructed by Messrs. Powell, Hardman, & Co., Birmingham. Around the apse the walls (which, like the other parts of the interior, are faced with Beer stone) are relieved by dark marble columns extending to the ribs of the roof. The ceilings both in the sanctuary and transepts are of wood, groined, perforated, and stained and varnished; in the chapels they are of deal, stained and varnished, with ribbed mouldings. The floors are of wood-block, Duffy's patent. The altar is raised some 3 ft. above the floor of the nave. In the Lady Chapel a carved stone reredos, which formerly occupied the wall at the end of the south aisle, has been placed above the altar. The doors are of panelled oak, and the windows are filled with cathedral-tinted glass with ruby borders.

Additions to General Post Office, Edinburgh. — Extensive additions are being made to the General Post Office, Edinburgh, on vacant ground immediately to the east of that building. When the present Post Office was contemplated, the Office of Works objected to the plans prepared by their local architect, the late Mr. Robert Mathieson, as being beyond the requirements of the department, and it was only owing to pressure being put forth by the local authorities that the design was carried out in its entirety. Two departments,—the Board of Lunacy and the Ordnance Survey,—were accommodated for a time in the new edifice, but these departments had after a short time to make way for the increasing requirements of the Post Office. It is lucky that there is ground left for the addition now urgently required.

Mission Hall, Cardiff.—The memorial stones of a new mission hall were laid at the East Moors, Cardiff, on the 23rd ult. The hall is situated in Carlisle-street, and is designed to accommodate 1,000 worshippers. The large hall is 72 ft. by 48 ft., and a gallery runs round the entire building, supported upon light iron columns, which help to support the roof. In front of the hall is a large class or committee room. The fresh air inlets will be fixed about 7 ft. above the floor level, and exhaust ventilators in the ceiling for the extraction of vitiated air. The cost of the building when completed will be 2,000*l*. Schools are intended to be erected in the rear of the present building, land being reserved for this purpose. The building is being erected by Messrs. Thomas & James, of Cardiff, from the design and under the superintendence of Messrs. Habershon & Fawckner, architects, Cardiff.

The New National Scottish Observatory.—The plans of the new National Scottish Observatory have now been completed, says the *Scotsman*, and the erection of the buildings on Blackford Hill, Edinburgh, will, it is expected, be proceeded with immediately. The plans have been prepared by Mr. W. W. Robertson, of her Majesty's Board of Works. The buildings consist of an observatory proper and transit house, placed along the north front of the site, with detached residences on the south slope. There is also a gatehouse at the entrance, which is to the south side. The Observatory proper will consist of a T-shaped building, with a frontage towards the north of 180 ft. It shows towards the city an unbroken range of flat-roofed central buildings having a mean height of 30 ft., and consisting of a principal story and a basement. These are flanked by octagonal towers of unequal size, crowned with large cylinders of copper,—the larger tower 75 ft. high and 40 ft. in diameter, placed at the east end; and the smaller, 44 ft. high and 27 ft. in diameter, placed at the west end. The design is Italian in style, with an admixture of Greek feeling, says the same journal. The stone employed is freestone, and the basement is built of rusticated ashlar work. The principal story of the central building is pierced with eleven windows. They have carved jambs and lintels, and on the wall spaces between them are carved the signs of the Zodiac. Along the length of the building, over the windows, runs a moulding, and the whole is surmounted by an ornamental balustrade. In the larger tower there are two rows of windows. The lower story windows have pilastered jambs and carved pediments, and the decoration of the upper story windows is after the same style, and has been combined with that of a projecting parapet. In the smaller tower there is one row of windows, which have been similarly treated, and the pediment of the window facing the town has carved upon it a representation of Phaeton driving the chariot of the Sun. The Observatory will be used for physical as well as for astronomical observations. In the towers are to be placed the two large equatorial telescopes. The telescopes are to rest on massive, hollow, brick piers, completely isolated from the surrounding walls and floors. The larger pier is 50 ft. high and 23 ft. square at the base, and both taper towards the seat for the telescopes. A small vault is to be formed in the interior of the larger tower for housing the standard sidereal clocks. The upper stage of each tower will consist of the cylinder of copper in which the equatorial telescopes are placed, and each has an observing aperture extending from the horizon to the zenith. Each will rotate upon a vertical axis so as to admit of its being turned with the telescope. The apartments below the domes will be used as chart rooms, and in the base of the larger tower will be placed a suite of rooms for photographic purposes. The central range of buildings between the towers is to be occupied by laboratory rooms for the astrophysical side of the Observatory work. In the angle between the large tower and the central buildings, at the back, has been placed a turret carrying a spiral stair, and beside it is a smaller turret carrying a lift for convenience in moving apparatus. The flat roof of the central buildings has been adopted to facilitate communication between the towers. In the principal story, beginning at the west end, there will be a room used for spectroscopic work, and to the south of the building, outside this room, will be placed a heliostat, by which the rays of the sun will be reflected into the apartment through a 10-in. aperture in the wall. Next will come the experimenting room, or working laboratory, having three isolated pillars for delicate measuring operations, and there also the mean time clocks will be kept. Then comes an electric room, which will be the centre of the electric system for lighting and scientific purposes. Next will come the mechanics' workshop and cleaning room; and, lastly, the chronograph room. The basement of the range is to be occupied by stores, workshops, and printing room. Southward from behind the central building extends a wing 80 ft. in length and 28 ft. wide. It consists of three floors, and has the entrance to the Observatory on the west side. The basement floor is to be occupied by the heating apparatus, and rooms for the dynamos and accumulators in connexion with the electrical apparatus. The principal floor will contain the library, with accommodation for about 30,000 volumes. Besides the library, this floor will contain the directors' room, ante-room, and computing room. The top floor is to be occupied by a long apartment to be used in connexion with the 15-in. heliostat. It is for spectroscopic and photographic purposes when long distances are required, and insulated rails are fitted up in it so that the delicate instruments in use are free from vibration. The room will be lighted from the roof by skylights, the shutters of which can be closed instantaneously. At a distance of 80 ft. west from the main Observatory, and in line with the north-west front of it, is to be placed the transit house, which is connected with the main building by a covered way. The walls and roof are to be of corrugated iron, covered with curved louvres of tinned steel, with an air space between of about 6 in., the object being to prevent radiation and secure uniformity of temperature between the inside and the outside of the building. The Observatory being above the level at which the water of the Edinburgh and District Water Trust can be supplied by gravitation, a large tank will be provided on the principal floor of the great tower for the storage of water, which will be forced up by a pumping apparatus placed in an underground chamber near the Harrison Arch, and worked by an electric motor with a current supplied from the Observatory. The dwellings will be lighted with gas, but electric light will be provided for the Observatory buildings. The whole Observatory will be heated with hot water from a central furnace. The cost of the building, including fittings, will be about 34,000*l*., and the contract has been entrusted to Messrs. W. & J. Kirkwood, Edinburgh.

Enlargement of Chapel, Brompton Hospital.—The Chapel of the Brompton Hospital for Consumption is undergoing considerable enlargement from designs by Mr. Wm. White, F.S.A., and there has just been re-laid, in the centre of the east wall of the extended chancel, the foundation stone which originally occupied a similar position. The bottle found, containing an inscription in good preservation on parchment, was replaced beneath the removed stone. The ceremony was of the simplest character, only members of the Board, besides the architect, being present. After a few prayers offered by the chaplain, the stone was laid by Mr. T. Percival Beckwith, the chairman of the Board. The chancel will be extended in length and in breadth to about double its former area; a new aisle is added on the north side, and the organ aisle is rebuilt to a similar extent. The dressed stonework of the old chapel is much decayed, but as much as possible of the old work is retained or re-used, incorporated into the new work. The stained glass, given by various benefactors, had got into a bad state, much of the painting having peeled off, and the leadwork being decayed. This is being carefully repaired and made good for replacement in the removed windows.

SANITARY AND ENGINEERING NEWS.

Peasmarsh Sewerage.—The Rural Sanitary Authority of the Rye Union (Sussex), at their meeting on the 29th ult., appointed Mr. H. Bertram Nichols, C.E., of Birmingham, to prepare a scheme and report on the sewerage and sewage disposal of the parish of Peasmarsh.

Royton (Lancashire) Sewerage. — A Local Government Board Inquiry was held at Royton, Lancashire, on the 31st ult. by Colonel Luard, R.E., with regard to the application of the Local Board for permission to borrow the second instalment of money for works already sanctioned by the Local Government Board, and also for sanction of a further loan for the erection of sludge-pressing plant, a refuse destructor, and sundry other works to complete the sewage works now in course of construction. The original sewerage scheme was approved by the Local Government Board two or three years ago, and a loan of 27,500*l*. sanctioned. This sum was chiefly for the sewers of th district, and the subject of the recent inquiry was chiefly to enable the purification works to be completed in the most efficient manner suggested by recent experience. The engineer for the scheme, Mr. Theo. S. McCallum, C.E., of Manchester, explained the general arrangement of the sewers and the details of the works. Nearly one half of the district is now sewered and the work is progressing. The purification process decided upon is the "International," and the settling tanks, filters, &c., are nearly completed. The precipitant will be added to the sewage automatically by one of Keirby's patent mixers. The sludge will be pressed and subsequently calcined in destructor furnaces. The refuse destructor will adjoin the sewage tanks, and the waste heat from the burning of ashpit refuse will be utilised to raise steam for the sludge-pressing. The destructor and sludge-pressing plant is being supplied by Messrs. Goddard, Massey, & Warner, of Nottingham. Jones' fume cremator is to be used. The cost of the sewerage scheme for Royton, the sewage purification works (including fifteen acres of land), and the destructors will be about 51,500*l*. In connexion with the sewage works, several special features have been introduced. The contractor for the tanks, filters, &c., is Mr. S. Johnson, of Pendleton.

FOREIGN AND COLONIAL.

France.—In the large gallery of the National Conservatoire of Arts and Crafts in Paris, a marble bust of Nicolas Appert has been erected. He was the inventor of the process of preserving foods. The bust is the work of the sculptor Roulloau.——The annual exhibition of Pastellistes, and the Black and White exhibition, have just been opened, the former in the Galerie Georges Petit, the latter for the first time is held in the Palais des Arts Libéraux in the Champ de Mars.——It is announced that the Society of the Rose Cross is going to be dissolved owing to the violent discussions between the principal organisers.——The Museum of wood carvings, copies of old works, which was begun in 1888, in the Trocadero, by M. Ravaisson, is going to be re-organised provisionally in the old riding-school of the Louvre. This Museum is replaced by a new collection of similar sculpture in the Trocadero.——On account of the re-organisation of the Service of Historical Monuments MM. Sauvageot and Darcy have sent in their resignations. They have been replaced by M. Vaudremer, member of the Institute, and M. André Michel, art critic.——On Sunday last a hospital was opened in the neighbourhood of Vincennes and Montreuil. It will serve for the suburbs of Paris in that quarter.——During the course of some works carried on under the direction of M. Mazoy, in the Canal of Briarè, the remains of a Roman town have been brought to light. The town, called Gannes, lies between Châtillon sur Loire and Beaulieu. Amongst the things found are some well-preserved pavement, several tools, ornaments, and coins. Owing to the necessity of continuing the work, all traces of the town will have disappeared by the end of the year.——The Society of Amis des Arts have placed in one of the halls of the Evreux Museum a bronze bust of Philippe Rousseau, modelled by M. Gérôme.——The Cardinal-Archbishop Langémeux is about to present to the Cathedral of Reims a great statue of St. Paul. It is in the style of the sculpture of the Roman decadence. The draperies are in bronze, the head, hands, and feet in white marble.——The bust of the poet Pierre Gringoire is to be erected by public subscription. The bust has been executed by M. E. Bussière.——The competition for the Hôtel de Caisse and Salle des Conferences at Meaux has been decided. The first premium has been awarded to M. Perdrigé, the second to M. Simôn, and the third to M. Bondinand.——The Mairie situated in the Rue Drouot, one of the richest centres of Paris, is going to be the object of an important artistic decoration. Independent of the Salle des Mariages which will be decorated with paintings, there is to be placed in the court-yard (an interesting specimen of eighteenth-century work) a group of busts of the principal celebrities of the quarter,—Lamartine, Mirabeau, Pigalle, and Berlioz, and four statues symbolising the nature of their respective talents.

Berlin.—During the last week of the Session the Imperial Reichstag devoted some time to the Inland Navigation question. A Bill had been brought in relating to the construction of the Dortmund-Ems Canal, which is to run in connexion with the proposed great "trans-Prussian" canal.——In the course of a debate on the General Purposes Budget, Herr von Meyer (Arnswalde) proposed that the Government should place in their Budget for 1893-94 an item "to be spent in studentships, &c., for young and talented artists engaged in the study of monumental painting and sculpture." The proposal was coolly received by the Government and strongly opposed by Clerical and German Liberal parties. It hence fell through.——Owing to the bad financial results obtained by the Administration of State Railways, the number of so-called "quick" trains running on the main lines is to be reduced. The Railway Administration intends introducing the mean European time for the time-tables and actual working of all its railroads throughout the country.——Again the foundation-stone for a new church has been laid with royal pomp. The Emperor has given the site for this church, and 200,000 marks of the 380,000 required for its erection. There will be 1,300 seats in the building. Herr F. Schulze is the architect.——The Berlin Chamber of Commerce will meet on the 6th inst. to discuss the preliminary steps that are to be taken in the arrangement of the proposed Berlin International Show for 1896.——The question of altering Berlin's chief thoroughfare, the "Unter den Linden," has again come to the front. The authorities have elected a special committee to decide on a practical plan, according to which the traffic on this thoroughfare can be more conveniently regulated.

MISCELLANEOUS.

Glasgow Institute of Architects: The Building Regulations Bill.—At a quarterly meeting of the Glasgow Institute of Architects, held on the 31st,—Mr. William Leiper, A.R.S.A., in the chair,—a report by the Council of the Institute with regard to the Building Regulations Bill was submitted to the meeting. The Council reported that they had drawn up a petition to Parliament against the Bill, embodying the principal points in the report formerly printed and circulated, that the petition had been lodged in the private Bill Office of the House of Commons, but that an intimation had subsequently been received from the promoters of the Bill that it was their intention to object to the *locus standi* of the Institute. The Council, however, did not consider it incumbent upon them to contest the matter, considering that they had sufficiently performed their duties towards the public in making the views of the Institute known. Attention was called to the inconsistency shown by the promoters of the Bill in respect that at first they had objected to the amendments urged by the Institute, on the ground that the Institute was an interested party, but that when the Institute wished to have an opportunity of bringing its views under the notice of the Committee of the House of Commons before which the Bill is to come, the promoters then objected to the Institute being heard on the ground that it had no interest in the Bill.—The congratulations of the Institute were offered to the President and Mr. Honeyman on their election to the Associateship of the Royal Scottish Academy, which in honouring them did honour to itself and the profession. Mr. W. F. Salmon, vice-president, and Mr. J. J. Burnett were appointed Governors of the Glasgow School of Art for three years, in terms of the new articles of association. After some other business the meeting separated.—*Glasgow Herald.*

The Incorporated Association of Municipal and County Engineers.—The thirteenth Examination, held under the auspices of this Association, was held at the Institution of Civil Engineers, Westminster, on Friday and Saturday, the 1st and 2nd of April, when eighteen gentlemen presented themselves for examination, the written portion of which was taken on the first day. The greater part of the second day was occupied with the *viva voce* division of the Examination. The Examiners were: I., For Engineering as applied to Municipal Work, Mr. Clement Dunscombe, M.A., M.Inst.C.E., Westminster; II., Building Construction, Mr. James Lemon, M.Inst.C.E., Southampton (Past President); III., Sanitary Science, Mr. Charles Jones, M.Inst.C.E., Ealing, W. (Past President); and, IV., Public Health Law, Mr. Joseph Lobley, M.Inst.C.E., Hanley (Past President). The next Examination will be held in October.

International Electrical Exhibition in Moscow.—It is officially announced that La Section Moscovite de la Société Impériale Technique Russe intends holding an international electrical exhibition in Moscow between April 14 and October 14 this year. There will be eight sections, viz.:—1, electric lighting; 2, telegraphy and telephony; 3, electro-technology, the use of electricity on railways, in war, medicine, &c.; 4 and 5, electric motive power; 6, scientific apparatus; 7, new discoveries in all branches of technical science; 8, literature, plans, designs, &c., connected with electricity. The cost of space is 90 francs per square mètre in the main building whether wall or floor, and for detached exhibits 180 francs per square mètre. The charges include the cost of cleaning, watching, catalogues, &c., as well as the installation of mounted exhibits.

Sanitary Conveniences in Marylebone.—On Thursday, the 7th inst., the public convenience which the Vestry have constructed at Oxford-circus was opened for inspection. It is noticeable that accommodation has been provided for women as well as for men. The convenience, which is placed under the centre of the roadway north of the Circus, is so arranged as to cause the least possible hindrance to traffic,—the exterior being a rest of 6 ft. in width, and about 60 ft. in length. The entrance steps at each end are surrounded by an ornamental cast-iron railing. The walls of the interior are faced with white glazed bricks, the floor being of coloured encaustic tiles. In addition to urinals and closets, lavatory accommodation is also provided. The convenience is well lighted during the day by means of pavement lights, and at night by the electric light. For the purpose of ventilation Kite's system has been adopted. The whole of the work has been carried out by Messrs. Finch, from plans prepared by Mr. Tomkins, Surveyor to the Vestry. The total cost is about 2,400*l*.

"The Local Government Journal."—After an existence of twenty years, the weekly journal hitherto known as *The Metropolitan* has changed its title, and will in future be known as *The Local Government Journal*. This change is brought about by the fact that the scope of the paper has outgrown the limited, though large, area of London, and has spread over the whole kingdom, dealing with the news connected with local government of every department all over the country. It is an exceedingly useful journal, and under its new name it will no doubt be increasingly successful and useful.

Square-hole Boring-tools.—We have received the prospectus of a company formed to work the square-hole drill patented in 1890 by Messrs. James Melling and J. R. Hughes. The invention consists of a drill, triangular in section, but working through a square template, and drilling a hole the size of the template. The promoters claim that this drill requires no costly machinery, depending on the shape and action of the drill, which can be fixed in any lathe or machine.

Removals.—Mr. Evelyn Hellicar, architect, has removed his offices from Wellington-street to 10, Serjeants'-inn, Fleet-street.——Messrs. Wheatley, Kirk, Price, & Goulty announce that they have removed from 52 to 49, Queen Victoria-street, E.C.

New Maps of London.—We have received from Mr. Stanford a map of London showing metropolitan railways, tramways, and miscellaneous improvements according to plans deposited at the Private Bill Office up to November of last year. As many of these will probably be carried out sooner or later, this constitutes a map in advance of future improvements. Mr. Stanford also sends us a "County Council Map of London," showing the boundary of jurisdiction of the Council, and boundaries of urban sanitary districts and Boards of Works.

Surveyorship Appointment.—At a meeting of the Hanwell Local Board, held on Tuesday last, Mr. Sidney Barnes, Assistant to the Surveyor to the Ealing Local Board, was appointed Surveyor to the Board. Mr. E. J. Reynolds, late of the same office, has just entered on his duties as Surveyor to the Priern Barnet Local Board.

Eaton Hall.—The Duke of Westminster has commissioned Messrs. Shand, Mason, & Co., of London, to construct an improved pattern steam fire-engine for the protection of Eaton Hall, near Chester, and the numerous farms upon the property. A trained fire-brigade is maintained on the estate.

LEGAL.

LIABILITY OF LANDLORD FOR SANITARY DEFECTS:

CASE UNDER THE PUBLIC HEALTH ACT (LONDON).

In the City of London Court, on Monday, before Mr. Commissioner Kerr and a jury, the case of Gebhardt *v.* Saunders was heard. The action was brought by Mr. Thomas Gebhardt, 9, Tankerville-road, Streatham Common, to recover the sum of £18. 5s. 7d. from the defendants Messrs. Saunders, Hawksford, & Bennet, of 68, Coleman-street, E.C., for which it was contended they were liable (as the plaintiff's landlords) under the Public Health Act of last year.

Mr. Johnston Watson, counsel for the plaintiff, stated that the case was one of some importance, as it was the first which had been tried under the Public Health Act, which came into force on January 1 last. The plaintiff became the tenant of the defendants of the house, 9, Tankerville-road, Streatham Common, at a yearly rental of £47. After he had been in occupation of the house for a little time he noticed bad smells arising from the cellar, and these continued for several months, until the cause was discovered in January last. A quantity of soil had accumulated in the cellar, where it was found that the drain-pipe had become broken, and the sewage went on escaping until there were 3 in. of water and soil covering the whole area of the cellar. The plaintiff communicated with the defendants, his landlords, and also with the Sanitary Inspector of the Wandsworth District Board of Works. The inspector served a notice on the premises, addressed to the "owner or occupier," giving orders for repairs to be done to the drains. These the plaintiff did by calling in his builder, and then it was discovered that the drain-pipe was a 4-in. instead of a 6-in. pipe, and that the pipes were simply laid on the ground instead of on a bed of concrete. This caused the pipes to become irregular, and was the reason which accounted for their breaking. Additional repairs had to be done, and now it was sought to make the defendants liable under the Public Health Act.

COMPETITIONS, CONTRACTS, AND PUBLIC APPOINTMENTS.

COMPETITIONS.

Nature of Work.	By whom Advertised.	Premium.	Designs to be delivered.
*Improving Open Space called "The Maes"	Criccieth Loc. Bd.	6l. 6s.	May 27
*Town Hall and Public Offices	Llanelly Loc. Bd.	50 and 20 guineas	June 18

CONTRACTS.

Nature of Work or Materials.	By whom Required.	Architect, Surveyor, or Engineer.	Tenders to be delivered.
*Sewerage Works	Hambledon R.S.A.	W. N. Lailey	April 12
Alterations at Workhouse	Plymouth Union	H. J. Snell	do.
Granite, &c. Road Metal	Sharnbrook (Bedford) Highway Board	Official	do.
*10-ton Steam Road Roller, &c.	Mile End Old Town Vestry	J. W. Knight	April 13
Police Station, Keith, N.B.	....	F. D. Robertson	do.
Steel-plate Girder Bridge over River Suir, Ireland	Gt Southern & Western Railway	K. Bayley	do.
Caretaker's House, New Penshaw School, Fence Houses	Penshaw and Offerton (U.D.) School Bd.	Official	do.
*Blue Guernsey Granite Spalls	West Ham Union	do.	do.
*Kerbing and Channelling	Hackney Bd. of Wks.	do.	do.
*Gullies, Grates, Manhole Covers, &c.	do.	do.	do.
*Asphalte Works	do	do.	do.
*Sewerage Works	Petersfield R.S.A.	W. N. Lailey	do.
*New Arches, Urinal, &c.	Borough of Brighton	F. J. C. May	April 14
Workhouse Hospital Extension	Cardiff Union	Seward & Thomas	do.
Roadway (3 miles in length), Waterhead, Cumberland	Mr. Marshall	....	do.
*Broken Granite	Norwich Corporation	P. P. Mitchell	April 16
*Sixty Sluice Valves and Eighty Hydrants	Standish-with-Langtree Local Board	Heaton & Ralph	do.
*Laying Water Mains	do.	do.	do.
Seven Through Houses, Midgley, Halifax	....	T. L. Patchett	do.
Flint, &c. Road Metal	Hollingbourn High. B.	J. S. Roper	April 18
*Fire Brigade Station, Dulwich	London County Council	Official	do.
*Wood Paving Works	Wandsworth Bd. of W.	do.	April 19
Shop and Business Premises, Old Market, Halifax	....	Horsfall & Williams	do.
Three Bridges, Kirkmichael, Banff	....	R. Davidson	do.
*Additions, &c. to Town Hall	Shoreditch Vestry	C. Barry	do.
Rag and Block Stone	Gravesend Commrs. of Sewers	Official	April 20
Technical School, Batley, Yorks	....	H. B Buckley	do.
Chapel and School, Thurgoland, Barnsley	....	Geo. Moxon	do.
Additions, &c. to Schools, Swalwell	Whickham Sch. Bd.	T. C. Nicholson	do.

CONTRACTS.—*Continued.*

Nature of Work or Materials.	By whom Required.	Architect, Surveyor or Engineer.	Tenders to be delivered.
Mansion House, Glen of Rothes, N.B.	....	C. C. Doig	April 20
Semi-detached House, Sowerby Bridge, Yorks	....	Utley & Gray	April 21
Thirteen Houses, Sowerby Bridge, Yorks	....	do.	do.
*Police Station, Courts, Offices, &c.	Blackpool Corp.	J. Wolstenholme	do.
Workshops, Gas Tank, &c.	Warrington T. C.	W. S. Haddock	do.
*Drainage of Christchurch Workhouse	St. Saviour's Union, Surrey	Jarvis & Son	do.
Wesleyan Chapel, Crossgates, Leeds	....	Geo. F. Danby	April 22
Widening a Bridge, Waver, near Wigton	Cumberland C. C.	G. J. Bell	April 23
*Sewerage Works	Canterbury Corp.	Official	do.
*New Roads, Sewers, &c. Surbiton	....	S. Mather	do.
*Asphalte Paving	Portsmouth U. S. A.	Official	April 25
*Aberdeen Pitchings	Bermondsey Vestry	do.	do.
Rag Stone and Pit Flints	Sheppey R. S. A.	do.	April 26
*Labourers' Dwellings	Manchester Corp.	J. Allison	do.
School and Class-rooms, near Halifax	Stainland-with-Old Lindley Sch. Bd.	C. F. L. Horsfall & Son	April 27
Sewerage Works	Pocklington U.R.S.A.	G. Rohn	do.
*Completion of New Workhouse	St. Pancras Guardians	A. & C. Harston	do.
*Widening Viaduct, Cardiff	G. W. R.	Official	do.
*Sewerage Works	Worthing Corp.	do.	May 2
*Supply of Materials	War Department	do.	No date
*Gravel, Granite, Siftings, &c.	Royal Hosp, Chelsea	do.	do.
*Making Road on an Estate	....	A. Strong	do.
*Rebuilding Portion of Church Tower, Northamptonshire	....	Talbot-Brown & Fisher	do.
*Shops, Houses, Citadel, &c. Belfast	Salvation Army	W. G. Scott	do.
*Shops, Houses, Citadel, &c. Liverpool	do.	do.	do.
Twenty-three Cottages, Commercial-road, Hanley, Staffs	Overfield & Gossetray	John Taylor	do.
Biscuit Factory and Warehouse, Cardiff	Spillers & Bakers, Ltd.	Veall & Sant	do.
Improvement Works, Westgate-road, Newcastle-on-Tyne	....	Philip Spicer	do.
House and Alterations to Buildings, Reay Garth, near Gilsland	....	T. Taylor Scott	do.
Steam Laundry, Botcherby Bridge	Carlisle Steam Laundry & Carpet Beating Co.	do.	do.

PUBLIC APPOINTMENTS.

Nature of Appointment.	By whom Advertised.	Salary.	Applications to be in.
*Inspector of Nuisances, Surveyor, &c.	Southborough Loc. Bd.	220l.	April 19
*Builder's Clerk	Westminster Vestry	100l.	April 20
*Borough Engineer	Salford Corp.	500l.	April 23

Those marked with an Asterisk (*) are advertised in this Number. *Competitions, p. iv. Contracts, pp. iv., vi., & viii. Public Appointments, p. xxi.*

Section 121 showed that "any costs and expenses which are recoverable under this Act by a sanitary authority from an owner of premises may be recovered from the occupier for the time being of such premises; and the owner shall allow the occupier to deduct any money which he pays under this enactment out of the rent from time to time becoming due in respect of the premises, as if the same had been actually paid to the owner as part of the rent." The plaintiff had paid the rent to avoid a distress, and he, therefore, now claimed for the repairs.

Mr. Rufus Isaacs, counsel for the defendants, did not dispute that there was a structural defect in the house, but he raised the technical objection that the defendants had been served with no notice to do the repairs, and that as the plaintiff chose to do them on his own responsibility, he must pay for them. The owners were only liable for structural defect when notice had been given. The Sanitary Inspector's notice said nothing about there being any defective structures. It only spoke about repairs to drains and stoppage.

Mr. Watson explained that the reason for that was that when the Sanitary Inspector called at the house he only saw the cellar flooded with sewage. When the ground was opened, and the drains laid bare, he saw there was no concrete underneath them, and then he gave orders for the work to be completed properly.

Mr. Isaacs said, if that were so, when the additional work was found to be necessary the Sanitary Inspector should have given notice to the owner. As that was not done, the plaintiff could not recover.

Mr. Watson pointed out that Section 128 provided that notice should be served by leaving it on the premises.

Mr. Isaacs: That is not on the owner.

Mr. Watson urged that it was sufficient.

Mr. Commissioner Kerr, after further argument, said he was inclined to take Mr. Isaac's view of the technical objection that the defendants ought to have had notice. The plaintiff would have to go to the High Court, as the question was one of so much importance. He knew that houses were built very badly in the present day, but legislation was only passed to make landlords do repairs when they had had notice. An Act of Parliament did not necessarily make landlords erect sanitary houses. He non-suited the plaintiff, and allowed the defendants costs.

The jury were therefore discharged without being called upon to give a verdict.

CAPITAL AND LABOUR.

THE LONDON BRICKLAYERS. — The Operative Bricklayers' Society have submitted for the approval of their members a proposed code of working rules for London. It is suggested that the code of rules should come into force on June 1 next. The workmen, we understand, have approved of the proposed code of rules by a large majority, and the code has been submitted to the master builders, who have not yet expressed their views on the subject. Failing compliance with the men's demands, a strike is talked of. The following is the code proposed by the workmen:—

"RULE 1.—The working time for bricklayers in summer shall be nine hours per day for the first five days of the week, and five hours on Saturday. Work to commence at 6.30 a.m., and cease at 5 p.m., except on Saturday, when work shall cease at 12 noon. There shall be allowed half an hour for breakfast each day, and on the first five days of the week one hour for dinner.

RULE 2.—From the second Monday in November and the twelve following weeks the working time shall be 8¼ hours per day for each of the first five days of the week, and 4½ hours on Saturday. Work to commence at 7 a.m. each day, and cease at 4.30 p.m., except on Saturday, when work shall cease at 12 noon. There shall be allowed half an hour for breakfast each day, and on the first five days of the week half an hour for dinner.

RULE 3.—That the minimum rate of wages be 10d. per hour; this clause to apply to all bricklayers wherever employed, and at whatever class of work employed at.

RULE 4.—That no time beyond the above hours be worked except when necessary, and then to be paid at the rate of time and a-half from the ordinary time of ceasing work until 8 p.m., and double time from 8 p.m. until the ordinary time of commencing work next morning. On Saturdays double time to commence from 12 noon, and continue for all time worked until the ordinary time of starting on Monday morning. Bank Holidays and Christmas Day to be paid for the same as Sundays.

RULE 5.—One hour's notice to terminate the engagement on either side, and all wages due to be paid at the expiration of such notice.

RULE 6.—That all bricklayers sent to country jobs be paid London rate of wages, with 1s. per day in addition as country money. Employers to pay lodgings, rail, and 'bus fares to and from, and if the workman is discharged through no fault of his own, his time travelling home to be paid for.

RULE 7.—That payment of wages commence at 12 noon on Saturdays, and to be paid on the job, but if otherwise arranged, walking time at the rate of three miles per hour to be allowed to get to the pay table at 12 noon.

RULE 8.—That no part of a workman's wage be deducted for charitable, benefit club, or insurance purposes, under any circumstances. That the employer shall provide a suitable place on all jobs in which workmen can have their meals.

RULE 9.—The wages earned on Saturday only be kept in hand as back time.

RULE 10.—The London District shall comprise the area contained within a radius of twelve miles from Charing Cross, and in which these rules shall be in force."

MEETINGS.

SATURDAY, APRIL 9.

Edinburgh Architectural Association.—Visit to Yester House and Old Castle, and Nunraw.

MONDAY, APRIL 11.

Society of Arts (Cantor Lectures).—Mr. Bennett H. Brough on "Mine Surveying." III. 8 p.m.

Clerks of Works' Association (Carpenters' Hall).—Annual Meeting. 8 p.m.

TUESDAY, APRIL 12.

Institution of Civil Engineers.—Discussion on Mr. H. A. Roechling's paper on "The Sewage-Farms of Berlin." 8 p.m.

Society of Arts (Applied Art Section).—Mr. C. Purdon Clarke on "English Brocades and Figured Silks." 8 p.m.

Sheffield Society of Architects and Surveyors.—Annual Meeting at the School of Art. Mr. W. H. Bidlake on "Timber, its Growth and Characteristics."

WEDNESDAY, APRIL 13.

Civil and Mechanical Engineers' Society.—Mr. G. M. Lemmi on "The Development of Ordnance." 7 p.m.

THURSDAY, APRIL 14.

Institution of Civil Engineers.—Students' visit to the works of Messrs. Siemens Bros. & Co., at Charlton. 2 p.m.

Dundee Institute of Architecture.—Mr. W. D. M'Kay on "The Art of the Low Countries." 8 p.m.

RECENT PATENTS:

ABSTRACTS OF SPECIFICATIONS.

1,435.—FLUSHING APPARATUS: *W. H. Bodin.*—This specification relates to automatic flushing apparatus for water-closets, urinals, folding, and other lavatories, and the like, and drains. As applied to water-closets, urinals, or lavatories, the apparatus consists of a flushing-pipe and a closed tank at the top thereof, which are normally empty, and a valve or valves arranged to be operated by the movement of the water-closet-seat or by a footboard, so that upon the seat or footboard being depressed one of the said valves is opened and water under pressure flows from the water supply up the flushing-pipes into the tank and compresses the air therein; and upon the seat or footboard being allowed to rise the water supply to the tank is closed and a valve in the flush-pipe opened, allowing the contents of the flush-pipe and tank to be expelled by the compressed air and by gravity, and the basin flushed out. The arrangement and combination of the valves and pistons as applied to different forms of urinals, lavatories, and for drains are fully set out and illustrated in the specification and drawings.

7,138.—ARCHITECTURAL FACINGS: *E. Wehrli.*—This patent relates to the manufacture and use of cast or moulded covering plates, slabs, or the like, of cement or concrete. These slabs can be employed for covering the whole structure of the façade or other part of a building, and are arranged as facings and supported between binding pieces, such as border and cornice pieces, which may be also cast or moulded. These comparatively thin slabs, as well as the binding pieces, are to enable them to be securely held, and to be readily arranged in position, formed at their sides or edges with joints or connexions. The slabs may be provided with insertion pieces for ornamental purposes, or for binding or strengthening them. Any desired colour may be imparted to these slabs, and thus a great variety in the construction of façades and the like may be obtained.

7,145.—FLUSHING BASINS: *W. T. Allen.*—This specification relates to an improved form of automatic basin for flushing water-closets, drains, &c., consisting of a basin of any material fixed or hung on a pivot and placed in a frame or pipe, which receives water from surface drainage or otherwise, and is so weighted that when it becomes filled with water to a certain level, it revolves automatically and discharges the contents into the drain or otherwise for the purpose of flushing the same.

7,209.—WINDOW-FASTENERS: *W. Eddleston.* — This invention relates to improvements in fasteners for securing and bolting windows when the latter are either closed or open, and preventing the same from being moved from the outside. It consists of a rack or recessed bracket on the window-sash, and a bolt on the window-frame, by which the distance the window is open can be adjusted and then secured.

:15.—FIRE-GRATES: *A. J. Boult.*—The object of this ention is to better utilise fuel in heating apparatus the employment of a hollow fire-grate having no ect connexion with the steam boiler, when employed heat such, but adapted to have water circulated rough it to prevent the "burning on" of slag, for ich purpose its hollow bars, forged or wrought of mogeneous metal or material, are wedge-shape in tion, and connected with the transverse carriers or dges either frictionally or by means of screw threads, hollow terminal trunnions being of a different pe in section, and narrower than the bar proper. e advantages claimed for such a grate are fully set by the inventor.

NEW APPLICATIONS FOR LETTERS PATENT.

March 21.—5,493, E. Carter, Automatic Water-closet sinfector.—5,547, A. Boult, Hinges.

March 22.—5,598, J. Anderson, Joiner's Jobbing nch.—5,624, A. Boult, Ventilating Devices for indows.—5,644, A. Lamplough, Sash-fasteners.—47, J. Dungey, Fittings for Gas and other similar pes and Tubes.

March 23.—5,674, A. Thornalley, Fire-grates and oves for Consuming its own Smoke.—5,682, J. White, tomatic Grip Sash-holder.—5,683, J. Harries, Artiial Stone.—5,710, D. Faulkner, Fireproof and Sanitary rtitions or Divisions.—5,732, J. J. A. Lee, Electric ht Fittings.—5,746, A. Morse, Destemper for Walls, lings, &c.

March 24.—5,752, J. Hickling, Tombstones or Monunts.—5,801, S. Cook and J. Chambers, Sash-fasteners.

March 25.—5,830, F. Tunks, Bakers' Ovens.—5,863, Morison, Taps.—5,887, J. Ingram and others, Adtable Sliding Sashes.

March 26.—5,932, J. Kirkman, Water-closets.—5,946, Price, Screws for Joiner's and other use.—5,949, W. len, Means of Rendering Air and Water-tight Sliding shes, either old or new, in dwelling houses, or elseere.—5,957, W. Kinniple, Caissons or Bridges to close d open, or bridge across, and leave clear as required entrances to graving docks, wet docks, harbours, ers, or estuaries, &c.

PROVISIONAL SPECIFICATIONS ACCEPTED.

,215, C. Pyrce, Kilns.—3,446, K. Friedrick, Woodking Tools.—3,644, R. Tootall, Ventilating Fans.—71, M. Piper, Fastenings for Doors, &c.—3,771, H. ttrell and G. Pauling, Device for Preventing the oke Nuisance.—3,905, J. Roots, Suspending, Raising, Lowering Gasaliers, &c.—3,978, S. Jacobs, Fire-grate. 91, G. Nunn, Electrical Call and Indicating Appaus.—4,052, P. Mancheron, Fire-grates.—4,061, G. lliamson, Kitchen-ranges.—4,280, R. Hocking, Watersets.—4,281, W. Shears, Tool employed in working od, such as planes, spoke-shaves, &c.—4,288, E. icher, Machine for Moulding, Paving, Slabs, Building, namental and other Blocks and Bricks.—4,295, J. lin and J. Brown, Construction of Blocks or Bricks Street Pavements.—4,379, J. Shanks, Fittings for ths, &c.—4,445, G. Pawson, Securing Knobs to Brass untings of Door and other Furniture.—4,511, S. rner, Fireproof Floor.—4,518, R. Carey, Hydraulic ts.—4,572, W. Macnamera, Stops for Gates.—4,590, Thrower, Girders.—4,656, R. Harrison, Devices for ning, Closing, and Adjusting Windows, Fanlights, —4,700, T. Robinson, Cross-cut Saw-benches.—4,791, radbear, Closet-fittings.

COMPLETE SPECIFICATIONS ACCEPTED.

(*Open to Opposition for Two Months.*)

581, G. Hayes, Metallic Lathing.—3,539, H. Brunson E. Gillett, Building or Paving Blocks.—3,586, C. strong, Kilns or Ovens for Burning and Glazing itary Ware, &c.

OME RECENT SALES OF PROPERTY:

ESTATE EXCHANGE REPORT.

ARCH 28.—By *George Head & Co*: 9, 11, and 13, e-st., Caledonian-rd., u.t. 58 yrs., g.r. 31*l*. 10s., 285*l*. *Wells & Read*: 70 and 72, Kyverdale-rd., Stoke ington, u.t. 83 yrs., g.r. 13*l*. 10s., r. 75*l*., 790*l*.—By *on & Sons*: 8, Bodney-rd., Hackney, u.t. 80 yrs., 7*l*., 375*l*.—By *Hampton & Sons*: The residence, Agnes," near Basingstoke, and 1½ acres, f., 1,000*l*.; ive f. cottages, 1,225*l*.

ARCH 29.—By *J. C. Platt*: 1 and 3, Adelaide-rd., pherd's-bush, f., r. 110*l*., 1,800*l*.; 64, Carter-st., worth, g.r. 3*l*. 12s. 6d., r. 30*l*., and a l.g.r. of 2s. 6d., u.t. 53 yrs., 475*l*.—By *W. Spearman*: 78, wa-rd., Balham, u.t. 85 yrs., g.r. 7*l*. 10s., 380*l*.—By *Richards*: 3 to 10, Hatch-row, Lambeth, f., r. 16s., 1,630*l*.; 103 to 109 (odd), Glengall-Old Kent-rd., u.t. 82 yrs., g.r. 28*l*., 300*l*.—*ebenham, Tewson, & Co.*: 66 to 70, Leather-lane, orn, f., area 6,955 ft., 6,950*l*.; 28, Brushfield-st., opsgate, f., r. 52*l*. 10s., 900*l*.; a profit rental of 74*l*. ar, Buckingham-rd., Kingsland, u.t. 32 yrs., 1,110*l*.; of 60*l*., with reversion in 89 yrs., Great Turnstile, orn, 1,640*l*.; "The Three Magpies" public-house, 7a. 1r. 12p., f., Harmondsworth, 2,480*l*.; c.g.r. of 11s. 6d. secured on "The Royal William," publice, Dorset-rd., Clapham; and 14 and 16, Kibworthwith reversion to rack rents in 8 yrs., 1,700*l*.; "The nix Brewery," 106, Dorset-rd.; and 9, Kibworth st., Peppercorn rent, with reversion in 8 yrs., 890*l*.; o 116 (even), Dorset-rd., with reversion in 8 yrs. 800*l*.; e Black Horse," public-house, 10, Bedfordbury, ing-cross, f., r. 52*l*. 10s., 1,720*l*.; 37, Queen-sq., msbury, f., r. 165*l*., 2,710*l*.; stabling, f., Ormond-yd., 1,020*l*.; f.g.r. of 10*l*., secured "The Duke of Wellington," public-house, s Pond-rd., Kingsland, f.; and 176, 178, and Culford-rd., with reversion in 12 yrs., 4,110*l*.—*Rogers, Chapman, & Thomas*: l.g.r. of 75*l*. 12s., berland-st., Pimlico, u.t. 45 yrs., g.r. 8s., reversion yrs., 1,738*l*.; l.g.r. of 75*l*., Sutherland-st., u.t. 46 g.r. 9s., reversion for 8 yrs., 1,710*l*.; l.g.r. of 29*l*., erland-ter., u.t. 46 yrs., g.r. 3s., reversion for 10 yrs.; l.g.r. of 10*l*., Lupus-st., u.t. 46 yrs., at Peppercorn, sion for 3 yrs., 208*l*.—By *W. & F. Houghton*: three es and shops, Orford-rd., Walthamstow, f., r. ., 650*l*.; 1 to 4, Church End Cottages, f., r. 78*l*., ; 2 to 5, Church End, Walthamstow, f., r. 80*l*., 1,070*l*.; a block of freehold stabling premises, r. 25*l*., 600*l*.; 1 to 4, Church-ter., f., r. 132*l*. 8s., 1,150*l*.

MARCH 30.—By *Briant & Son*: No. 253, Clapham-rd., f., 1,820*l*.—By *J. Millburn*: 215, Goldhawk-rd., Shepherd's-bush, u.t. 51 yrs., g.r. 6*l*. 8s., 600*l*.—By *E. Grice*: 5, Johnson-st., Commercial-rd., f., 350*l*.—By *R. A. Enright*: 138 and 140, Richmond-rd., Dalston, and a plot of land, u.t. 46 yrs., g.r. 12*l*. 10s., 790*l*.; 27, Sparholt-rd., Crouch-hill, u.t. 54 yrs., g.r. 5*l*. 10s., 275*l*.; 1 to 5, Caroline-cottages, Newington-green, no term given, g.r. 15*l*., 200*l*.—By *R. Tidey & Son*: 24, Bride-st., Barnsbury, and 5 and 7, Dorinda-st., u.t. 30 yrs., g.r. 7*l*. 4s., 100*l*.; an improved g.r. of 18*l*., Brixton, u.t. 9 yrs., g.r. 5*l*. 10s., 40*l*.—By *F. Jolly & Co.*: 14, Dynham-rd., Hampstead, u.t. 90 yrs., g.r. 9*l*. 10s., 265*l*.; 37, Approach-rd., Victoria-pk., u.t. 62 yrs., g.r. 5*l*., r. 40*l*., 470*l*.—By *Trollope & Sons*: 7 to 33 odd, Everard-st., Commercial-rd., f., 1,960*l*.; f.g.r. of 69*l*. 6s., Providence-st., &c., Commercial-rd., with reversion in 27 yrs., 1,800*l*.; f.g.r. of 2*l*., Grove-st., with reversion in 10½ yrs., 150*l*.; f.g.r. of 22*l*. 2s., with ditto in 10½ yrs., 2,000*l*.; f.g.r. of 13*l*. 15s., with ditto in 10 yrs., 805*l*.—By *D. Smith, Son, & Oakley*: 191, High Holborn, f., r. 110*l*., 1,430*l*.; 27 and 29, Great Queen-st., Long-acre, f., r. 146*l*., 3,040*l*.; f.g.r. of 60*l*., Ham-yd., St. James's, with reversion in 32 yrs., 1,460*l*.; 9 and 10, Smith's-ct., and 6 to 9, Ham-yd., f., 1,300*l*.; 21, Scrutton-st., Finsbury, f., r. 40*l*., 640*l*.; 14 and 16, Edna-st., Battersea, u.t. 85 yrs., g.r. 13*l*., 490*l*.; f.g.r. of 3*l*., Sand-st., Woolwich, reversion in 43 yrs., f.g.r. of 27*l*., reversion in 20 yrs., 625*l*.; enclosures of freehold land, 51a. 3r. 27p., Farnborough, a cottage and garden, f., 20*l*., 320*l*.

MARCH 31.—By *D. Young*: 2 to 36 (even), Regent-rd., Herne-hill, u.t. 73 yrs., g.r. 51*l*., 2,380*l*.; 24, Melbourne-grove, Dulwich, u.t. 82 yrs., g.r. 6*l*., r. 30*l*., 290*l*.—By *Newbon & Co.*: 39, Sumatra-rd., Hampstead, u.t. 90 yrs., g.r. 6*l*., rent 30*l*., 235*l*.; 1, Klea-av., Clapham Common, u.t. 93 yrs., g.r. 6*l*. 10s., r. 33*l*., 300*l*.—By *H. Griffin*: 1 to 23 (odd), Benham-street, Battersea, u.t. 74 yrs., g.r. 44*l*. 15s., 1,280*l*.—By *Collier & Henderson*: 23, Heyworth-rd., Clapton, f., r. 45*l*., 655*l*.; f.g.r. of 28*l*., Mentmore-ter., Hackney, with reversion in 82 yrs.; f.g.r. of 13*l*., with ditto in 81 yrs., 1,025*l*.; f.g.r. of 7*l*., with ditto in 81 yrs., 170*l*.; f.g.r. of 21*l*., with ditto in 82 yrs., 525*l*.—By *Battam & Co.*: 4 to 9, Wells-pl., Ealing, f., 660*l*.; 9, 10, and 11, Oak-st., f., 320*l*.; 1 to 8, Charles-st., f., 975*l*.; 17 to 22, Charles-st., f., 820*l*.; Well's-pl., and Charles-st., f.g.r., of 8*l*. with reversion in 30 yrs., 250*l*.; "The Prince of Wales," public-house, Charles-st., f., r. 36*l*., 730*l*.; 17 to 20, Western-rd., u.t. 70 yrs., g.r. 9*l*., r. 88*l*. 10s., 780*l*.; 33, 35, and 37, Lancaster-rd., u.t. 30 yrs., g.r. 3*l*. 16s., 800*l*.—By *P. D. Tuckett & Co.* (at Forest Gate): 30, 36, 41, and 46, Clarence-road, Upton pk., u.t. 92 yrs., g.r. 15*l*. 12s., r. 92*l*., 670*l*.; Forty-eight plots of freehold land, Gipsy-lane, &c., 3,053*l*.

[*Contractions used in these lists.*—F.g.r. for freehold ground-rent; l.g.r. for leasehold ground-rent; i.g.r. for improved ground-rent; g.r. for ground-rent; r. for rent; f. for freehold; c. for copyhold; l. for leasehold; e.r. for estimated rental; u.t. for unexpired term; p.a. for per annum; yrs. for years; st. for street; rd. for road; sq. for square; pl. for place; ter. for terrace; cres. for crescent; yd. for yard, &c.]

PRICES CURRENT OF MATERIALS.

TIMBER.		
Greenheart, B.G. ton	9/0/0	0/0/0
Teak, E.I. ... load	10/10/0	15/0/0
Sequoia, U.S. ft. cu.	2/3	2/0
Ash, Canada load	2/10/0	4/0/0
Birch, do.	3/5/0	4/10/0
Elm, do.	3/10/0	4/15/0
Fir, Dantsic, &c.	2/0/0	3/10/0
Oak, do.	3/0/0	5/0/0
Canada	5/10/0	7/0/0
Pine, Canada red	2/10/0	3/10/0
Do. yellow	2/10/0	5/0/0
Lath, D'ntsic, fath	5/0/0	6/0/0
St. Petersburg	5/0/0	7/0/0
Deals, Finland, 2nd & 1st std 100	8/10/0	10/10/0
Do. 4th & 3rd ..	7/10/0	8/10/0
Do. Riga	6/10/0	8/0/0
St. Petersburg, 1st yellow ..	11/0/0	15/0/0
Do. 2nd yellow	8/10/0	10/0/0
Do. white	7/10/0	10/10/0
Swedish	7/15/0	16/0/0
White Sea	8/10/0	18/0/0
Canada, Pine 1st	20/0/0	26/0/0
Do. do. 2nd	14/10/0	16/0/0
Do. do. 3rd, &c.	8/0/0	10/5/0
Do. Spruce, 1st	8/10/0	11/0/0
Do. do. 3rd & 2nd	6/15/0	8/0/0
New Brunswick	7/0/0	7/10/0
Battens, all kinds	3/10/0	15/10/0
Flooring Boards, sq., 1 in. prep. 1st	0/8/6	0/14/6
Do. 2nd	0/7/6	0/11/6
Other qualities	0/4/6	0/6/0
Cedar, Cuba .. ft.	/3½	/4½
Honduras, &c.	/2½	/4
Mahogany, Cuba,	/4½	/6½
St. Domingo, cargo av	/4½	2/0
Mexican do. do	/4	/5
Tobasco do. do	/5½	/7
Honduras do. .	/5½	/6½
Box, Turkey ton	4/0/0	15/0/0
Rose, Rio	10/0/0	20/0/0
Bahia	9/0/0	18/0/0
Satin, St. Domingo ......ft.	0/0/8	0/1/3

TIMBER (*continued*).		
Satin, Porto Rico	0/0/8	0/1/6
Walnut, Italian ..	0/0/3½	0/0/7
METALS.		
IRON—Pig, in Scotland .... ton	2/0/10	2/1/0
Bar, Welsh, in London	6/0/0	6/10/0
Do. do. at works in Wales	5/10/0	6/0/0
Do. Staffordshire, in London	6/5/0	6/15/0
COPPER—British, cake and ingot	49/0/0	49/10/0
Best selected ..	50/0/0	51/0/0
Sheets, strong ..	59/0/0	60/0/0
Chili, bars	45/12/6	46/0/0
YELLOW METAL lb.	0/0/5¼	0/0/5½
LEAD—Pig, Spanish .... ton	10/15/0	10/17/6
English, com. brands	11/2/6	11/5/0
Sheet, English, 3 lbs. per sq. ft. and upwards ..	13/0/0	0/0/0
Pipe	13/10/0	0/0/0
ZINC—English sheet ...... ton	25/5/0	0/0/0
Vieille Montagne	25/15/0	0/0/0
TIN—Straits	89/15/0	80/17/6
Australian	90/0/0	90/2/0
English Ingots	93/0/0	93/10/0
OILS.		
Linseed ...... ton	18/10/0	18/12/6
Cocoanut, Cochin	24/10/0	0/0/0
Do. Ceylon	22/10/0	0/0/0
Palm, Lagos	23/0/0	0/0/0
Rapeseed, English pale	25/10/0	0/0/0
Do. brown	23/10/0	0/0/0
Cottonseed ref. ..	19/0/0	0/0/0
Oleine	21/10/0	22/10/0
Lubricating, U.S.	4/0/0	6/0/0
Do. refined	5/0/0	10/0/0
TAR—Stockholm barrel	0/19/0	1/0/0
Archangel	0/12/6	0/0/0

TENDERS.

*** Next week communications for insertion under this heading must reach us *not later than 12 noon on Wednesday*, as we go to press a day earlier than usual.

BIRMINGHAM.—For erecting villa residence, Hagley-road, Edgbaston, for Mr. Urban Broughton. Mr. Joseph Lavender, architect, Wolverhampton:—

Moffat & Sons	£1,178	Papcote & Sons	£979
B. Guest	1,050	G. Cave, Wolverhampton* ..	975

* Accepted.

BOSTON (Lincolnshire).—Accepted for the erection of a villa residence, on the West-street-road, Boston. Mr. James Rowell, architect, Boston:—

Building.

C. Jessop, Boston £490 0 0

Plumbing, Painting, Glazing, Gasfitting, and Bell-hanging.

B. F. Parker, Boston 64 0 0

KENT.—Accepted for the repairs of main-roads in Kent 1892-93, for the Kent County Council:—

Section	Contractor	£	s.	d.
Sec. 1, Dartford, 10 m. 0 f. 12 p.	Kent Road Co., Gravesend	£2,733	7	9
Sec. 2, Dartford, 14 m. 7 f. 0 p.	Kent Road Co., Gravesend	2,532	7	6
Sec. 3, Bromley, 9 m. 1 f. 20 p.	Kent Road Co., Gravesend	2,594	11	
Sec. 4, Bromley, 10 m. 3 f. 0 p.	Pelli & Sons, Bromley	1,131	17	6
Sec. 5, Wrotham, 10 m. 0 f. 0 p.	E. B. Chittenden, West Malling	1,220	7	1
Sec. 6, Rochester, 10 m. 6 f. 24 p.	Tuff & Miskin, Rochester	3,025	3	8
Sec. 7, Rochester, 5 m. 0 f. 20 p.	Kent Road Co., Gravesend	555	2	6
Sec. 8, Hoo, 1 m. 3 f. 0 p.	Tuff & Miskin, Rochester	1,657	9	2
Sec. 9, Milton, 7 m. 4 f. 25 p.	Tuff & Miskin, Rochester	894	15	10
Sec. 10, Milton, 9 m. 5 f. 0 p.	Tuff & Miskin, Rochester	915	19	2
Sec. 11, Sheppy, 6 m. 2 f. 34 p.	Tuff & Miskin, Rochester	993	0	0
Sec. 12, Sevenoaks, 12 m. 3 f. 0 p.	E. B. Chittenden, West Malling	1,839	2	6
Sec. 13, Sevenoaks, 13 m. 1 f. 0 p.	E. B. Chittenden, West Malling	1,498	11	8
Sec. 14, Tonbridge, 8 m. 1 f. 0 p.	F. Playfoot, Edenbridge	910	14	0
Sec. 15, Tonbridge, 12 m. 4 f. 16 p.	Kent Road Co., Gravesend	3,774	11	3
Sec. 16, Tonbridge, 12 m. 6 f. 12 p.	W. & G. Arnold, Frant	2,098	12	6
Sec. 17, Tonbridge, 18 m. 2 f. 30 p.	Arnold & Lambert, Frant	3,704	9	9
Sec. 18, Malling, 4 m. 3 f. 20 p.	E. B. Chittenden, West Malling	409	5	4
Sec. 19, Malling, 13 m. 6 f. 34 p.	E. B. Chittenden, West Malling	2,271	15	0
Sec. 20, Malling, 14 m. 4 f. 19 p.	E. B. Chittenden, West Malling	2,303	14	1
Sec. 21, Maidstone, 6 m. 3 f. 22 p.	Maidstone Rural Sanitary Authority	1,144	13	3
Sec. 22, Maidstone, 10 m. 2 f. 29 p.	Maidstone Rural Sanitary Authority	933	5	8
Sec. 23, Maidstone, 6 m. 5 f. 20 p.	J. Ellis & Co., Maidstone	1,419	0	0
Sec. 24, Maidstone, 10 m. 0 f. 30 p.	Kent Road Co., Gravesend	2,078	18	4
Sec. 25, Cranbrook, 3 m. 5 f. 20 p.	W. Lambert, Horsmonden	2,311	10	0
Sec. 26, Cranbrook, 10 m. 4 f. 0 p.	Kent Road Co., Gravesend	1,800	3	4
Sec. 27, Cranbrook, 11 m. 6 f. 20 p.	Kent Road Co., Gravesend	1,633	0	0
Sec. 28, Hollingbourne, 9 m. 3 f. 0 p.	R. L. Knight, Sittingbourne	1,140	13	4
Sec. 29, Hollingbourne, 12 m. 4 f. 0 p.	J. Ellis & Co., Maidstone	1,096	17	6
Sec. 30, Hollingbourne, 15 m. 2 f. 20 p.	Kent Road Co., Gravesend	2,213		
Sec. 31, Hollingbourne, 6 m. 4 f. 0 p.	N. Marley, Detling	759	10	0
Sec. 32, Faversham, 9 m. 2 f. 0 p.	Faversham Highway Board	1,070	8	7
Sec. 33, Faversham, 11 m. 6 f. 0 p.	Faversham Highway Board	1,043	2	6
Sec. 34, West Ashford, 13 m. 7 f. 4 p.	E. B. Chittenden, West Malling	1,448	1	8
Sec. 35, West Ashford, 12 m. 6 f. 9 p.	E. B. Chittenden, West Malling	1,593	1	8
Sec. 36, East Ashford, 9 m. 2 f. 0 p.	R. L. Knight, Sittingbourne	1,375	0	4
Sec. 37, East Ashford, 8 m. 6 f. 0 p.	R. L. Knight, Sittingbourne	802	5	0
Sec. 38, East Ashford, 13 m. 2 f. 0 p.	R. L. Knight, Sittingbourne	956	0	0
Sec. 39, Tenterden, 9 m. 6 f. 27 p.	Tenterden Highway Board	1,618	7	4
Sec. 40, Tenterden, 9 m. 3 f. 27 p.	Tenterden Highway Board	1,789	14	5
Sec. 41, Tenterden, 7 m. 6 f. 32 p.	Tenterden Highway Board	1,193	9	4
Sec. 42, Romney Marsh, 7 m. 2 f. 2 p.	Kent Road Co., Gravesend	843	5	0
Sec. 43, Blean, 6 m. 0 f. 15 p.	T. Ashenden, Canterbury	716	13	3
Sec. 44, Blean, 10 m. 3 f. 14 p.	T. Ashenden, Canterbury	944	12	0
Sec. 45, Thanet, 14 m. 0 f. 13 p.	Kent Road Co., Gravesend	1,174	0	0
Sec. 46, Thanet, 7 m. 6 f. 37 p.	Kent Road Co., Gravesend	970	1	3
Sec. 47, Bridge, 10 m. 5 f. 0 p.	Bridge Rural Sanitary Authority	1,416	6	10
Sec. 48, Bridge, 15 m. 1 f. 30 p.	Bridge Rural Sanitary Authority	1,352	4	2
Sec. 49, Elham, 13 m. 0 f. 20 p.	Elham Rural Sanitary Authority	1,427	0	0
Sec. 50, Elham, 9 m. 2 f. 20 p.	Elham Rural Sanitary Authority	1,075	17	6
Sec. 51, Elham, 10 m. 4 f. 7 p.	Elham Rural Sanitary Authority	1,462	10	3
Sec. 52, Eastry, 8 m. 3 f. 0 p.	Eastry Rural Sanitary Authority	1,633	7	0
Sec. 53, Eastry, 11 m. 7 f. 0 p.	Kent Road Co., Gravesend	1,894	18	4
Sec. 54, Dover, 9 m. 1 f. 0 p.	Dover Rural Sanitary Authority	1,014	10	8
Sec. 55, Dover, 9 m. 2 f. 30 p.	Dover Rural Sanitary Authority	1,060	12	6
Sec. 56, Romney Marsh Level, 3 m. 2 f.	The Lords of Romney Marsh Level	426	5	0

	M.	F.	P.
Total Mileage	566	7	21

	£	s.	d.
Total amount of accepted tenders	83,004	16	5
County Surveyor's estimate	83,709	2	10

LEICESTER.—For additions to shoe factory, for Mr. C. G. Allen. Messrs. Roberts & Gordon, architects, Leicester:—

Clark & Garrett	£705 0		T. C. Tyers	£640 0
T. & H. Herbert	673 10		W. H. Kellett*	631 15
W. J. Iliffe	673 1		* Accepted.	
H. Plant	652 0		[All of Leicester.]	

LONDON.—For the enlargement of the Pakeman-street School, Lower Holloway, by 380 places, for the School Board for London. Mr. T. J. Bailey, Architect:—

G. S. S. Williams & Son	£3,748	Johnson & Co.	£3,378
W. Cregar & Son	3,594	E. Lawrance & Sons*	3,207
Atherton & Latta	3,450		

* Recommended by the Works Committee for acceptance.

LONDON.—For the enlargement of the boys' and girls' departments of the Portobello-road, School, Notting-hill, by eighty places; and for erecting new water-closets for all departments of the School for the School Board for London. Mr T. J. Bailey, Architect:—

Cowley & Drake	£2,888 0 0	F. J. Coxhead	£2,451 14 6
Davis Bros.	2,822 0 0	M. Marsland	2,450 0 0
J. Garrett & Son	2,673 0 0	H. Mallett*	1,981 0 0
J. Derry	2,574 0 0		

* Recommended by the Works Committee for acceptance.

LONDON.—For erecting the first portion of the school on the Swan-street site, Minories, which will provide accommodation for 947 children, for the School Board for London. Mr. T. J. Bailey, Architect:—

John Grover & Son	£10,250	Atherton & Latta	£9,615
William Downs	10,211	D. Charteris	9,567
Clarke & Bracey	10,118	J. T. Chappell	9,484
John Mowlem & Co.	10,098	E. Lawrance & Sons, 14 and 16, Wharf-road, N.*	9,419
Thomas Boyce	9,970		
Kilby & Gayford	9,936		

* Recommended by the Works Committee for acceptance.

LONDON.—For erecting a school-keeper's house and cookery and laundry centre on the Site in Charing-cross-road, Soho, for the School Board for London. Mr. T. J. Bailey, Architect:—

Treasure & Son	£3,148	H. Lovatt	£2,612
J. Longley & Co.	2,914	Staines & Son	2,679
J. T. Chappell	2,791	Holliday & Greenwood	2,570
T. Boyce	2,698	C. Cox	2,515
S. & W. Pattinson	2,686	E. Lawrance & Sons, Wharf-road, N.*	2,432
J. Tyerman	2,486		
M. Marsland	2,043		

* Recommended by the Works Committee for acceptance.

LONDON.—For refitting the water-closets in connexion with the Hollydale-road school, Nunhead, with stoneware troughs and automatic flushing-tanks, and for providing better ventilation to the offices, &c., for the School Board for London. Mr. T. J. Bailey, Architect:—

J. Garrett & Son	£383	L. Whitehead & Co., Clapham-road, S.W.*	£298
J. Smith & Sons	349		
J. Marsland	303		

* Recommended by the Works Committee for acceptance.

LONDON.—For enlarging the infants department of the Victory-place school, Walworth, by fifty-five places, and for carrying out additions and improvements to the existing school, for the School Board for London. Mr. T. J. Bailey, Architect:—

		A.
Hart Bros.	£8,434	£150
Holliday & Greenwood	8,320	..
B. E. Nightingale	8,281	180
J. Derry	8,173	..
W. Downs	8,127	170
Holloway Bros.	8,031	180
Lather Bros.	7,682	141
J. Smith & Sons	7,643	146
J. Marsland, 1, York-street, Walworth, S.E.*	7,610	190

* Recommended by the Works Committee for Acceptance.

A. Deduct if Keene's cement dado, and distempering be substituted for glazed bricks, as taken.

LONDON.—For the erection of a School on the Sussex-road site, Coldharbour-lane, Brixton, to provide accommodation for 798 children, and also for the erection of a schoolkeeper's house and a cookery centre, for the School Board for London. Mr. T. J. Bailey, Architect:—

		A.
James Longley	£18,961	£823
Thomas Boyce	17,283	915
Lathey Bros.	16,916	628
Foster & Dicksee	16,865	871
Holliday & Greenwood	16,798	880
John Mowlem & Co.	16,418	723
Hart Bros.	16,408	650
E. Lawrance & Sons	16,031	905
William Downs	15,988	600
J. T. Chappell, 149, Lupus-street, Pimlico, S.W.*	15,611	720

* Recommended by the Works Committee for acceptance.

A. Amount included in Tender for supplying glazed brick internal facings.

LONDON.—For the erection of a Model Home at Norwood, for the British Home for Incurables. Mr. Arthur Cawston, architect, 15, Queen Anne's-gate, S.W.:—

	Estimate No. 1.	Estimate No. 2.	Estimate No. 3.
Foster & Dicksee	£21,454	£1,247	£1,984
Deacon & Co.	20,698	720	1,395
Lorden	20,500	1,180	1,930
Longley	20,470	1,180	1,878
Sanders	20,072	1,068	1,761
Charteris	19,704	1,143	2,000
Lawrance & Sons	19,654	1,124	1,892

LONDON.—For rebuilding factory at Bermondsey, for Messrs. Shuttleworth & Co. Mr. Arthur Vernon, architect, 29, Cockspur-street, S.W.:—

Cornish & Gaymer	£805	W. Shepherd	£780
W. Brooks	800	Houghton & Son	612
Bullers	795	C. N. Philips	502
Batley	734		

LONDON.—Accepted for decorative works, at "Hohenlohe," Chisletts-road, West Hampstead, for Mr. S. Flatau:—
Greatorex & Co., Limited £135 0 0

LYTCHETT MINSTER (Dorset).—For alterations and additions to school, for the School Board. Mr. H. F. J. Barnes, architect, Poole:—

Orchin	£588	A. Saunders	£352
W. H. C. Curtis	397	G. Baker, Wimborne*	335
T. C. Rigler	378		

* Accepted.

NEWPORT (Mon).—For the erection of a Reading Institute at Blaina, near Newport, Mon. Mr. F. R. Bates, architect. Quantities by the architect:—

A. P. Williams	£1,870	D. Davies	£1,635
T. Rees	1,749	C. Lock	1,650
J. Linton	1,740	W. A. Linton	1,610
W. Bagley	1,697	Morgan & Roberts	1,505
George Wilkins	1,695	Henry Parfitt, Pontnewydd Mon.*	1,390
Alfred Hazel	1,653		
W. Jones & Son	1,647		

* Accepted.

POOLE.—For rebuilding premises, West Quay-road, Poole, for Messrs. Dalston & Co. Mr. H. F. J. Barnes, architect:—

Imms	£1,807 0	W. H. C. Curtis, Market-street Poole*	£1,483 10
Cowlin & Son	1,657 0		
T. C. Rigler	1,513 12		

* Accepted.

WANDSWORTH.—For reconstructing a roadway at the Infirmary, St. John's-hill, New Wandsworth, for the Guardians of the Wandsworth and Clapham Union. Mr. T. W. Aldwinckle, architect, 1, Victoria-street, Westminster, S.W.:—

Mowlem & Co.	£654 0	S. Kavanagh	£505 0
Bradshaw & Co.	603 12	J. Bowles	485 0
W. Neave & Son	580 0	Barlow & Roberts	431 0
G. Neales	560 0	Woodham & Fry	392 0
W. H. Wheeler	556 0		

WANDSWORTH.—For a relief station and residence at Swaffield-road, Garratt-lane, Wandsworth, S.W., for the Guardians of the Wandsworth and Clapham Union. Mr. T. W. Aldwinckle, architect, 1, Victoria-street, Westminster, S.W. Quantities by Mr. Stafford Elmore:—

H. Brown	£2,124	P. Peters	£1,700
J. Allen & Sons	1,995	J. Garrett & Son	1,699
Young & Lonsdale	1,887	E. Houghton & Son	1,684
E. Parsons & Co.	1,850	W. Hammond	1,664
F. V. Windebank & Co.	1,839	Trappitt & Batley	1,580
W. Smith	1,825	W. Wallis	1,560
W. Potterton	1,798	Cowper	1,525
J. Mills	1,720		

WEST HARTLEPOOL.—For the erection of a block of School buildings, for the School Board. Mr. J. Mitchell Bottomley, architect, 12, Albert-road, Middlesbrough:—

Excavator, Bricklayer, &c.—Beattman Bros., Middlesbrough £2,950 0 0
Carpenter and Joiner and Painting.—T. Beetham, West Hartlepool 1,386 0 0
Plumber and Glazier.—L. Robson, West Hartlepool 562 0 0
Plasterer.—H. Tomlinson, Middlesbrough 182 10 6
Seating.—J. Howe 115 0 0

WOLVERHAMPTON.—For erecting offices and seed stores, Riches-street, for Mr. T. Bradburn. Mr. Joseph Lavender, architect, Wolverhampton:—

H. Gough	£648 15	B. Guest*	£633 0
G. Cave	640 0		

* Accepted.
[All of Wolverhampton.]

SUBSCRIBERS in LONDON and the SUBURBS, by prepaying at the Publishing Office, 19s. per annum (or 4s. 9d. per quarter), can ensure receiving "The Builder," by *Friday Morning's Post.*

TO CORRESPONDENTS.

J. F. B. (thanks; not suitable).—J. C. T.—F. J. B.—G. G. S. (shall have attention).

All statements of facts, lists of tenders, &c., must be accompanied by the name and address of the sender, not necessarily for publication.

We are compelled to decline pointing out books and giving addresses.

Note.—The responsibility of signed articles, and papers read at public meetings, rests, of course, with the authors.

We cannot undertake to return rejected communications.

Letters or communications (beyond mere news-items) which have been duplicated for other journals, are NOT DESIRED.

All communications regarding literary and artistic matter should be addressed to THE EDITOR; all communications relating to advertisements and other exclusively business matters should be addressed to THE PUBLISHER, and not to the Editor.

TERMS OF SUBSCRIPTION.

"THE BUILDER" is supplied direct from the Office to residents in any part of the United Kingdom at the rate of 19s. per annum Prepaid. To all parts of Europe, America, Australia, and New Zealand, 26s. per annum. To India, China, Ceylon, &c., 30s. per annum. Remittances payable to DOUGLAS FOURDRINIER, Publisher, No. 46, Catherine-street, W.C.

VOL. LXII. No. 2567. SATURDAY, APRIL 16, 1892.

ILLUSTRATIONS.

"Christ before Pilate": Mural Painting in the Chapel of Maynooth College.—By Mr. N. H. J. Westlake .... *Double-Page Ink-Photo.*
Design for a Chapter-House.—By Mr. John Begg, A.R.I.B.A. .... *Double-Page Ink-Photo.*
Section of Mr. John Begg's Design for a Chapter-House .... *Single-Page Photo-Litho.*
Design for a Stone Railway-Bridge (Awarded the Grissell Gold Medal).—By Mr. Harold Harlock ....*Double-Page and Single-Page Photo-Litho's.*

Blocks in Text.

Red Rock Cantilever Bridge, Atlantic and Pacific Railroad....................Page 303
Old Houses in Great St. Helens, Bishopsgate 304
Remains of Roman Hypocaust, Chester 307
Bradford Small-Pox Hospital.—Morley & Woodhouse, Architects ...... Pages 308, 309
Diagrams in Students' Column: Heating by Hot Water 312
A Keyed Casing for Electric-Light Wires 314

CONTENTS.

he Architecture of the Lake Dwellings of Europe. II......... 299
otes 301
he Red Rock Cantilever Bridge 302
he Royal South London Ophthalmic Hospital 303
ld Houses, Bishopsgate 304
he Sewage Farms of Berlin 304
rchitectural Societies 305
ritish Archæological Association 305
he London County Council.................... 305
emains of Roman Hypocaust, Chester.................... 307
Mural Painting in the Chapel, Maynooth College 307
Design for a Chapter House.................... 307
Design for a Stone Railway Bridge 307
Competitions 307
Bradford Small-pox Hospital 308
The Sanitary Inspectors' Association 310
Books: P. Planat's "Encyclopédie de l'Architecture et de la Construction," (Paris: Dujardin et Cie) 310
Architectural Education 310
"Steam Road Rolling" 311
Removing Old Paint 311
Students' Column.—Warming Buildings by Hot Water, XVI.. 311
Obituary 312
General Building News 312
Foreign and Colonial 313
Miscellaneous.................... 313
Meetings 314
Recent Patents 314
Some Recent Sales of Property 315
Tenders.................... 315

*The Architecture of the Lake Dwellings of Europe. II.**

HE Lake Dwellings of Great Britain form a class far more numerous than at first might be supposed, and now that attention has been drawn to their existence, it is probable that a few more years will add aterially to the lengthening list. The rannoges of Ireland have been noted by Sir '. R. Wilde, Mr. Shirley, and others, and ter, these and many examples in Scotland, y Dr. Monro, whose monograph, published 1882, renders an extended list. They were equently formed on shallow islands, but not nfrequently built up with boughs and deosited material upon the bed of a shallow ke, the area being first enclosed by a frameork of piles to keep the structure in posion. The examples given by Dr. Monro nder full details, and also of the manner in hich several of the sites indicate continuance f occupation, and many structural alteraons. Nevertheless, the objects found, up to e present time at least, do not possess very gh antiquity, and there are records of their cupation to quite recent times.

Various sites in England and Wales have en partially investigated, and among these rtain sites in Holderness, now on dry, or at ost on marshy land, but once covered with ater, appear to be counterparts of the pile wellings of Switzerland, as far as the meagre vestigations have been followed. They ave been met with so late only as 1881 uring some extended drainage works, and iles and relics of apparently great age were iscovered. It is greatly to be hoped that ome one or other of these promising sites ay be systematically explored. In 1886 eneral Pitt Rivers described a remarkable rea in London-wall, which on being laid are by excavations for a new warehouse was ound to be the site of a timbered structure aving many piles and planks. Its existence within the City is subject for comment, and the more so since the objects found were not older than Roman times, possibly later.

London antiquaries have not to be reminded that the entire course of the Walbrook, which enters the City close to this site, is bounded by piles, but which have no reference, so far as has yet been pointed out, to timbered dwellings. But at Southwark, on the shallow banks of the River Thames, a discovery was made which seems to point to a construction very analogous to the Swiss dwellings. In 1866, the late Mr. Wimble reported to the British Archæological Association that a site on the south side of Southwark-street, between the square and Winchester-street, was covered with piles 7 ft. to 11 ft. long, and their heads about 12 ft. beneath the modern level. Masses of Kentish rag had been used to steady them. Wherever the excavations were carried for a new building these piles were found. Mr. Syer Cuming testified at the same time to their existence in what had been the marshy ground of Moorfields, and elsewhere in the north of London.

The articles of the Stone Age are in many cases wrought with very great mechanical skill, and neatly finished, while there are many curious evidences of straight sawing through and the perforation of hard material, most probably by friction caused by rapidly moving a board or a stick for the latter purpose, with sharp sand and water for the cutting material. The labour with which so many thousands of trees were felled, and their trunks pointed to form the piles for the platforms, all indicate a considerable amount of skill of no mean order,—certainly not the work of savages.

But actual ornamentation occurs on some of the pottery, doubtless of late date in the Stone Age, which is fully developed in the succeeding one. Some of the Bronze Age pottery is of elegant form, very neatly turned on the wheel, and ornamented with graceful lines and mouldings, the patterns in some few instances being filled in with a white substance. But the most remarkable development found in Switzerland is the ornamentation of pottery with an inlay of tinfoil. The well-known dish found at Cortaillod is of great beauty, the pattern being of considerable intricacy. A vase found at the same place is similarly ornamented, as is also a few fragments found at La Crasaz, and some other places.

One fragment of pottery found elsewhere was ornamented with fine triangular cuttings of beech fixed to it by asphalt, and either asphalt or, as supposed by Dr. Dom, of Tübingen, an adhesive glue derived from beech bark, was used with charcoal for a black glaze.

The Weavers' art has furnished several really elaborate designs, while one figured by Keller, found at Irgenhausen, is of very great elaboration and artistic beauty. But it is the bronze articles that claim our particular attention. The greatest number are admirably wrought, and present a multiplicity of forms. The fibulæ and other personal ornaments are covered with lines, dots, perforations, &c., while some objects supposed to relate to religious uses are occasionally met with. These consist principally of moon-shaped figures. The cross has been found punctured on crockery at Polado, and a tin cross was found at Peschiera, both, of course, of pre-Christian date. A bronze vase, cast, found in Lake Bouget, is a remarkable article, but many others, bowls, horse-trappings, a chariot wheel, lance heads, &c., demand notice. The swords of bronze are numerous, and of considerable interest, since they agree in many respects with the forms of Roman swords, and also with many of the fine examples found in the north of Europe, having curves at the ends of the handles. The pear-shaped blades are of common occurrence, and found under circumstances that entirely forbid their being considered of Roman date.

The most remarkable group of iron implements yet found are the swords and scabbards from La Tène—the Marin of the older antiquaries. They are ornamented with raised patterns in a variety of ways, all of great interest, and of a style generally called late Celtic. One has three quaint animals in relief. The general resemblance of these articles to four others found at Lisnacroghera, Ireland, has been pointed out by Dr. Monro. It remains to call attention to an interesting discovery recorded in 1890 by Mr. A. T. Evans, M.A., at Aylesford, Kent, where in an interment of a form seldom met with in England, some bronze articles were

* See p. 277, ante.

found ornamented in a style so remarkably like that of the La Tène swords as to fully justify the inference that both works were the production of one people. It is impossible to enter into the arguments that were adduced which seem to show the emigration of a people westward. But, in addition to traces of their presence in Switzerland and England alike, must now be added Lisnacroghera.

The archaic type of the pottery found in all the early settlements has been referred to by many foreign writers, and Dr. Deschmann has pointed out the remarkable resemblance which exists between the early pottery found by Dr. Schliemann at Hissarlik and that which has been met with at the sites of lake dwellings in Laibach Moor, Carniola. There is resemblance also between the jadeite articles found at Troy and similar ones in Switzerland. The latter district has produced many articles of pure copper. In fact, these have been found in such numbers as to give some warrant for the belief in an age of copper as well as of bronze.

The number of sites which have been exploited, or partially so, up to the present time, being so great, it necessarily follows that, since every settlement has been found to be prolific of relics, the quantity of articles found has been enormous. Many examples are scattered abroad, but a large number remain in private collections in Switzerland and in the other countries where the sites occur; while, fortunately, various local museums, notably those of Switzerland, have fine collections, for the most part carefully arranged. In the British Museum is a small but very interesting assortment of articles, one of many things for which the nation is indebted to Mr. Franks. There are examples of almost all the varying relics that have been found.

The objects found on the sites consist of stone and flint implements, scrapers, hatchets, arrow-heads, &c. Pins and many other articles worked in various kinds of bone; clay weights for nets; spindle whorles; pottery, made by hand in the earliest examples, and on the wheel in the later ones, the clay showing gradations of skill in the working, pebbles and many fragments of quartz being found in the earliest, and much better baking in the latest. The Bronze Age produced a vast number of implements of all descriptions and classes, while some few sites in Switzerland have produced worked gold in small quantities.

Flint is not common in Switzerland, and in many sites there is reasonable ground for believing that it was an article of import, as was certainly the obsidion used for scrapers and such-like, which have been found in small quantities. Nephrite or jadeite has already been mentioned.

The articles found on various sites present curious points of resemblance to others met with at distances far removed; there being many points of difference, while the recurrence of some indicate that the sites were occupied mainly by fishermen, others more particularly, perhaps, by hunters.

Weaving utensils are found in some places, while others are destitute of them. Corn and fruits appear in like manner. But it has to be remembered that only a very few sites have been systematically explored, and fewer still in any very extended manner, except the Terpen of the Low Countries, although, their removal having been for agricultural purposes and not for research, it follows of necessity that many relics have been lost. Everything indicates, in the Swiss examples, at least for the most part, a steady and continuous occupation from very remote times until the mode of building over water was abandoned altogether. Some sites are found to be of the stone age, no articles of metal being found, with indications of conflagration and abandonment. The same is observable in others of the bronze age, but many indicate that occupation was continuous, through the earliest to a late period, the relics being in some instances found above one another. In others, the earliest examples of stone, &c., are close to shore, while articles of the bronze period are found farther away.

The Iron Age in Switzerland has produced some fine and remarkable articles; but it does not appear to have been of long duration.

The various articles, when studied in any of the well-arranged museums, where the specimens are of sufficiently comprehensive character, present a remarkably perfect and complete gradation from the rude works of the earliest period of these articles down to historic times,—the latter is marked by the presence of a few Gaulish and other coins, and, lastly, of Roman pottery. Traces of the Roman occupation on the lake-dwelling sites are, however, so very few in number as to warrant the belief that then the practice of occupying them had all but ceased. To indicate the retention of sites in some cases, it has been recorded that some Frankish and German relics have been found; while, as we have seen, the system of construction with but little variation was continued in the Dutch and other settlements, occupied until even later date.

That the first founders of these sites were well advanced in civilisation appears to be proved by the skilful nature of their buildings and the presence of implements, showing that they were good weavers, hunters, and agriculturalists. The latter is abundantly testified to, not alone by the cultivation of wheat of more than one kind, flax, fruits, and even of grapes.

The inquiry has often been made, with reference to these discoveries, as to the period of time when they were erected.

A very cursory examination of the objects found in the sites is sufficient to show that, so far as the Swiss examples are concerned, the dwellings were erected at very various periods, extending from a remote stone age of antiquaries, although Neolithic rather than Palæolithic, to late times, while it is no doubtful conjecture that several of the modern villages which line the margin of the lakes are the representatives from Mediæval times of the sites of remote antiquity which lie buried opposite to many of them deep beneath the waters. We also possess evidences further than that of the objects found which give an idea of the extreme remoteness of time since the foundations of some of these structures were laid. The lake of Zug affords important indications in this direction. In excavating for the erection of the Keltenhof Hotel, in the suburbs of the Town of Zug, on a site among the houses, the workmen came upon a bed of decayed organic matter at a depth of about 5 ft. Piles were also found, and all the usual deposits of a lake dwelling, including evidences that the settlement had been destroyed by fire. The site is 60 ft. distant from the present waters of the lake, and as much as 15 ft. higher than their present level. The excavations showed very clearly that when the piles were driven the site was covered with water. This, too, is not an isolated instance, for further research has shown that there are several more sites around the borders of the lake of Zug, all now being on dry ground, away from the level, and high above its waters. The lake has shrunk materially in its volume, which points to a period of remote antiquity since the settlements were founded. There is no historical evidence whatever of any convulsion of nature that would account for the change, but there is a dim tradition that the waters once were higher.

The articles found on all the sites around the lake of Zug belong for the most part to the Stone Age, which affords further evidence of their great age.

Many of the sites, not alone in Switzerland, but elsewhere as well, are found on dry land covered with a growth of peat, affording evidence of remote antiquity. Thus, to refer to the well-known and important settlement of Rubenhausen, which occupies an extent of about three acres, the site is found to be now 2,000 paces from what was the ancient shore. The growth of peat has so completely encroached upon the waters of the entire lake that the remains of the piles are now covered with a depth of about 6 ft. of that material, which exists above the relic bed, the latter having 3 ft. more of thickness. All this encroachment must have taken place since the piles were placed in position. There are abundant traces that this settlement was consumed by fire.

The observations made by M. Louis Rochat on the lake dwellings found in the neighbourhood of Yverdon, have the same tendency as at Rubenhausen. At Les Uttins also, he describes vast deposited plains which have been formed between the present borders of the lake and the pile dwellings which are now entirely covered, one site being 1,856 yards from the water, and another 2,200; the whole of this mass of added material having been deposited by a little torrent, La Baine, and he makes some weighty observations as to the extreme length of time that must have elapsed to enable the deposit to have been formed. This site has evidently been of long duration, since articles of stone have been found here, as well as a great many of the bronze age.

Several others of the Swiss sites, as we have seen, indicate that the first settlements were made fairly close to the shore; and at a later period, probably owing to the silting up of the lakes, piles were driven beyond the original site into deeper water beyond. The articles of stone do not compare in antiquity to the implements found in drift deposits, but their high antiquity is attested by many facts. Thus, at St. Aubin, flint arrow-heads have been found white with age, and yet in the bronze period they have been resharpened for re-use. In Switzerland, traces of wild animals are found in the earliest period, such as the large ox with large semilunar horns, which has been found in a fossil state in Italy, then contemporary with the mammoth and the hippopotamus. Bison has been found in Wauwyl and elsewhere, urus in several places, bos in all its varieties in early and in late settlements. The great preponderance of wild animals disappears in the Bronze Age, when traces of domestic animals appear, mainly such as now exist. Wheat is small in the early settlements and larger in the later ones, but wild plants do not evidence any change, having undergone no cultivation, and as they appear in the earliest sites so are they now.

These discoveries reveal to us the state of the arts at a remote period. But they also stand as evidence (if any were wanted) of the exceedingly slow nature of the changes which evolution has wrought on the earth's surface. We find, over and over again remains of animals and vegetables which agree with those still on the earth, or of some well-known type of animal easily recognised, but now extinct or absent from the district. We have already spoken of the various varieties of bos and other extinct animals. The beaver, not now in Carinthia and its district, has been proved by discoveries on Laibach Moor to have been common then. The marsh-pig is recognised by its bones in many of the Swiss sites. Wheat of many varieties, as there may be to-day improved by cultivation, but still wheat, has been found in a burnt state in many places. The oak, the fir, the cherry, all the other kinds of timber used in the various constructions, have all been identified, not only on one site, but on many throughout the whole area of the investigations; showing that, at what appears a comparatively remote era in the history of man, the conditions under which he lived were still much the same as in the present day.

Workhouse Extensions, Patricroft, Lancashire.—On the 6th inst., at the fortnightly meeting of the Barton Board of Guardians, Mr. Noah Robinson presiding, the Clerk reported that the Local Government Board had given its sanction to the amended plans prepared by Messrs. Mangnall & Littlewoods, architects, for the workhouse extensions at Patricroft, and that tenders had been invited for the foundations for the first block of buildings. The cost of the proposed alterations, inclusive of land, will be 30,000*l.*

NOTES.

THERE seems some hope that the monument to the Duke of Wellington by Stevens may at last be dragged out from the obscure rner in St. Paul's Cathedral where it can t be seen, and placed where the artist ways hoped and expected it was to go, in a ntral position in the nave. We do not iow what special circumstance may have ompted Sir F. Leighton's letter to the *Times* i the subject at the present moment, but it ems that he has ascertained that we now at ast have the support of the Dean and hapter of the Cathedral, which is the most portant point to be gained, and in that case is only a question of funds. It is hoped at there are a sufficient number of perns in England who feel interest in a great ork of art to subscribe the sum required for oving the monument, which is estimated at out 1,000*l*.*; though of course we are aware at to the majority of Englishmen the subct is of no consequence at all. They have t a monument to Wellington; they can go d look at or take their friends to see; as to ho the sculptor was or what his merits they ostly know and care as little as they do out the unsatisfactory position of the onument. No great monument, could be eated worse than this has been. On the only de on which it is lighted you must stand close der it to see it; on the only side on which u get a comprehensive view the lower portion barred off by a screen, and the sculptures of e upper portion are reduced to dark masses en in outline against the light. In the ave the monument would make a grand ntral object, quite in keeping with the style the cathedral. Then would follow the estion of completing the monument by the uestrian figure at the top. The monument rtainly requires that both in regard to sign and sentiment; the idea was that the gure of the dead warrior below was to be ntrasted with his living presentment above. portrait-figure of the man only will t suit the proportions of the monument; is designed for an equestrian group. Some rsons, we believe think it incongruous to ve a horse in the church, though they would ver be troubled by the incongruity of groque carvings in a Mediæval church. The rse is one of God's creatures (as Kingsley ould have said), and a very noble one, and ry architecturesque in his lines and design. nd as to precedent, have we not the De rezé monument in Rouën Cathedral, with squestrian statue which has stood there r many generations without scandalising y one?

THE recent fall of a piece of stonework from the north-west tower of Lincoln inster may be regarded as fortunate, both as awing the attention of the Dean and hapter to the dilapidated condition of that rt of the fabric, and as diverting it from her more questionable projects. The stone ich fell was a portion of one of the veral mouldings of the octagonal north-west ircase turret of the Perpendicular belfry ge. These mouldings are throughout plied externally, and are kept in their place bond-stones running into the wall at interls. An examination conducted by the thedral mason proves that these bond-stones mostly much decayed, and that the mouldings resting on them, together with much of surface decoration, are in a perilous state insecurity. All portions likely to fall have w been removed, and insecure places have n temporarily pointed and cemented to p further damage. This work, however, s only extended to the west side of the wer, which threatened danger to life; but is only too clear that the stonework of the her three sides is equally decayed, and mands immediate attention. The beauul pierced parapet is in an especially bad ndition, and only needs a strong gale to ng it over bodily. The Dean and Chapter are waiting for Mr. Pearson's report on the tower generally; but there is good reason to believe that the fabric itself is structurally sound, the decay extending no further than the external ornamental features, which, in the lower Norman stages, as well as in the Perpendicular upper storey, are much dilapidated. The most serious structural feature is a crack extending from south to north, and gradually widening along the crown of the barrel vault of a wall passage in the upper part of the Norman screen in front of the tower. This seems to indicate that the front wall is parting from the tower behind it, and that the two will require to be tied together with iron rods, as was successfully done by Mr. Pearson in the south-western tower a few years back. We shall anxiously wait for Mr. Pearson's report. Under the most favourable circumstances, the expenditure required must be large, and will probably effectually stop any unnecessary work.

* Sir F. Leighton and the Dean and Chapter of St l's have already set an example by subscribing 50*l* h.

THE paper by the Rev. A. C. Headlam, on "A newly discovered Byzantine church in Cilicia," read at the meeting of the Hellenic Society on Monday and illustrated by drawings and photographs, introduced to our knowledge a curious and interesting example of a building which seems to form a link between Classic and Byzantine architecture. The plan is a curious mingling of the Basilica form with a kind of hint of the future central treatment of the plan, which was to characterise Byzantine architecture proper. The main supports have the plan of the Roman Basilica pier (approximately), but with the centre emphasised on plan and marked on the design by a tower, where the true Byzantine dome would come. The chancel terminates in an apse, and the aisles in small apses adjoining the chancel arch, but with doors in them opening through into two apartments at each side of the chancel. In the western façade are three doorways which present a strange mixture of Classic and Christian feeling; one of them especially, of which a photograph was shown, has all the general characteristics of a Classic doorway with a cornice and architrave mouldings, and consoles at each end of the cornice, but the architrave is decorated with vine-leaf carving in which all Classic feeling seems to have disappeared, and which may be classed as Byzantine work in point of style and feeling. There seems no reason to suppose, however, that the whole of the work is not of the same date; indeed, it is difficult to see how it could be otherwise. The illustrations, which have been prepared by Mr. Schultz, will be published, we believe, in the Hellenic Society's *Journal*. The locality of this interesting discovery is Koja Kalessi. It is to be hoped that some further discoveries of the same interest are still to be made in the district, which may help to fill up the debateable land between the confines of Roman and Byzantine architecture.

THE result of the international competition for the drainage of Sophia sheds a curious and edifying light upon the way in which things are managed in Bulgaria. The judges consisted of certain officials, two doctors, one geologist, three State engineers, and two civil engineers, the latter a German and an Austrian. Of the twenty-five plans submitted, seventeen were at once excluded, and although none of the remaining eight were declared perfect, their order of merit was announced as follows:—1. "Stoneware" (author, Mr. Momtchiloff, of Sophia). 2. "Circulation pas de stagnation" (Mr. Louis Masson, of Paris). 3. "Properté est la Santé" (Weigand, of Sophia, and Paulsen, of Strasburg). 4. "Tarquinius" (J. and L. Botto, of Rome); whilst the judges recommended the purchase of the other four, which were by Knauff and Grove, of Berlin; Hallenstein and Edwards, of Munich; Brix and Frank, of Wiesbaden; and Aimond, of Paris. So far there seems nothing unusual in the course and result of this competition, but we are now informed that the gentleman, whose design was placed first in the above order, not only was one of the judges, not only attended the meetings, but actually took part in the discussions and deliberations upon his own design. In vain did the German and Austrian (Messrs. Kühn, of Charlottenburg, and Rella, of Btünn), protest and demand Mr. Momtchiloff's exclusion, either as a judge or competitor, and they had to content themselves with refusing to sign the protocol and drawing up a separate statement as a mark of their disapproval of this instance of Bulgarian morals.

WE are glad to note the appearance,—after much too loug an interval,—of a new number of Daremberg & Saglio's invaluable "Dictionnaire des Antiquités" (16, Epi-Eup). Perhaps the most useful article is that by M. Jules Martha, on the Etruscans, which gives an admirably clear *résumé* of the known facts respecting the religion, life, and manners, and especially the monuments, of this problematic people, an account supplementary in many respects to the well-known popular handbook on the subject by the same author. As to the vexed question of origin, M. Martha cites the various hypotheses ancient and modern, and, perhaps prudently, concludes:—"Au milieu de tant cohue d'hypothèses le plus sage est de s'abstenir. Un problème qui comporte toutes les solutions possibles est, a vrai dire, un problème insoluble." Perhaps so, but it is strange in glancing through the bibliography of the subject to miss the great names of Otto Crusius and Hesselmeyer,—will the French ever learn to read German? Other articles of interest are those on the structure and management of ancient stables (equitatio, &c.), which seem to have been surprisingly like modern ones. Pompei furnishes us with the plan of two, and at Mondelein, in Syria, there are substantial remains which may be new to some of our readers. The mythological articles are, as usual, of the weakest.

THE most important paper in the last issue of the *American Journal of Archæology* (vii., 3) is unquestionably that which deals with the excavations at Eretria. The American plan is to divide out the area to be excavated among various members of the School, Dr. Waldstein, the director, holding, of course, in his hands the general supervision of the whole. Dr. Waldstein was most anxious that the Eretria theatre should not be prematurely dragged into the burning controversy about the Greek stage. As, however, it has been freely quoted on both sides during the past year, he has thought it well to issue at once certain sections of the work and a plan of the theatre as far as at present excavated. The section relating to Epigraphy and Topography has been undertaken by Professor Richards, of Dartmouth College, and the all-important *skene* excavated by Mr. Fossum, late of John Hopkins University, appears in the present number. Still, though offering, as far as possible, all new facilities for the solution of the problem, Dr. Waldstein, with commendable caution, declines to take sides. "This reticence," he says, "I thought called for, because, though what may be called the 'orthodox' view of the Greek stage has had adequate exposition, the new views of Dr. Dörpfeld have not yet been supported by a full and systematic account of the numerous data collected by that eminent archæologist in support of his theories. Pending this publication it did not appear to me wise for archæologists who had not access to all the material at the disposal of Dr. Dörpfeld, either to accept his views unconditionally or to oppose them." For all details as to this very interesting theatre, we must refer our readers to the easily accessible *Journal*, only reminding them that in a recent number of the *Athenæum*, Professor Pollard, the present director of the school, reports the supplementary excavation of the eastern portion of the orchestra, and the eastern parodos.

d

THE appointment of a Judge specially to adjudicate on the winding-up of limited companies and of a registrar and official staff should not pass unnoticed. It is of the utmost importance to men of business that the winding-up of companies should be quickly and economically performed. This new departure also emphasises the tendency to the specialisation of legal business which is so marked at the present time. This specialisation cannot stop here; as we have more than once pointed out, patent business should be dealt with by a specially-appointed judge assisted by competent assessors. It would also be very desirable were all cases relating to building contracts, which are referred to the official referees, assigned to one particular referee who also should have the assistance of an architect. What may be called a more pronounced "business" spirit is required in the transaction of the legal work of the country.

THE Crown lease of the Albert Palace, Battersea Park, will be offered for sale at an upset price of 5,000*l*., on the 27th instant, at the Mart. The purchaser will be given a right to take the freehold, at a sum to be agreed upon. It is stated that more than 100,000*l*. have been expended upon this ill-starred property. The hall (Messrs. F. & H. Francis, architects) was opened in June, 1885, the late Sir R. Carden, M.P., being at that time chairman of the Albert Palace Company. Three years later, by order of the Court of Chancery, the property, as covering ten acres of land, and held on two leases from the Commissioners of Works for a ninety-one years' term from 1886, at a ground-rent of 1,425*l*. per annum, was put up for sale by auction. No offer, however, was made upon that occasion (June 7, 1888). In the forthcoming sale will be included all the furniture and equipment, together with the great organ that formerly belonged to Mr. W. Holmes, of Primrose-hill. On July 20 last, the Prince of Wales laid the foundation-stone of the Battersea Polytechnic Institute, to be erected near to the Palace, on a site of rather more than two acres, acquired, we believe, from out of the original grounds of the latter. We published a perspective view of Mr. E. W. Mountford's selected design for the Institute, together with his ground-floor plan, on March 28, 1891. We read in the *Times* that Messrs. Holloway have contracted to erect the larger part of the new buildings for 35,988*l*., and that these will be ready in October of next year.

THE eighth exhibition of the New English Art Club, just opened at the Dudley Gallery, is much less aggressive in style than most of its predecessors, and in fact many of the works exhibited have no special stamp on them of any artistic school, and impress one merely as sketches by artists of the ordinary profession of faith, who have sent in clever studies which they did not care to finish. Thus Mr. James's "A Writing-table" and "Yellow Polyanthus" (3 and 10) are masterly sketches, the flowers especially, but betray no "mission," any more than Mr. Simpson's "From Southwold Pier" (13) or the "Snow Effect, Whitehall" (16), by Mr. Herbert Marshall, who is not a member of the club, and has indeed very little in common with their apparent aims. The English apostle of impressionism does not exhibit, but there are attempts on the part of other exhibitors to "do Whistler," as in Miss Draper's "Green Signal Lamps, Blue Night" (62), and some others. Among works savouring more of the old leaven of the English Art Club is the "Study for a Portrait in the Open Air" (47) by Prince Troubetzkoy (not a member, however), a three-quarter length sketch of a woman, with a most brilliant open daylight effect, which would look however still better if the picture were finished as to detail and texture, instead of being left in a state of splashes. Mr. Theodore Roussel's portraits of Miss Pettigrew and Mr. Bernard Sickert (50 and 57) have strongly-marked character and fine colour in the costumes, but the artist contrives to impart a very unpleasing colour and texture to the faces. There is character also in Mr. Furse's two portraits of ladies (67, 73), though the "lady in a grey dress" is in a position in which she would find it difficult to maintain her balance. The best portrait in the room is that by Mr. George Thomson (82), a genuine pourtrayal of face and action in a powerful but perfectly unaffected style. Mr. Maitland's sketches of London neighbourhoods (14 and 79) are very good, though it is difficult to understand why in "Oakley Crescent" the tree near the foreground should be far fainter in tone and detail than the houses in the middle distance. Mr. Lindner's "Over the Moonlit Sea" (89) is a charming effect, but has too much light for moonlight. Mr. Hope McLachlan's "Bathers" (95) is a fine little work with no eccentricity about it, but the artist is not a member of the club. In short the conclusion from the contents of the exhibition seems to be that the English Art Club has practically abandoned its colours to some extent; that its members are rather backward in exhibiting, and that the merits of the exhibition may be divided pretty equally between members and non-members.

IN the Gallery of the "Nineteenth Century Art Society" Mr. Edgar Barclay is exhibiting a set of small paintings of Stonehenge and its neighbourhood, giving "the stones" (as they are called in the district) from every point of view, and giving also various bits of scenery and building within a circuit of three miles round. Mr. Barclay announces a forthcoming book on Stonehenge, with a new inquiry into its meaning and the ideas originally associated with it. Along with the paintings in the exhibition we find a careful survey of Stonehenge and the ground around it, with pen-and-ink drawings of the remains, which we presume are to form a portion of the illustrations of the book. We fear we cannot feel very sanguine that anyone will now be able to throw any more light on the origin, date, and meaning of Stonehenge, but Mr. Barclay's book, when it comes out, may popularise the study of the subject by bringing before the general public considerations and questions which have mostly hitherto been confined to the transactions of learned societies. In the meantime the oil paintings make a very interesting collection even topographically, and some of them are beautiful little works in an artistic sense also. Among these latter may particularly be named "Storm Clouds" (17) and "Thunder Clouds" (27), two very fine studies which make an effective pair; and "Water Meadows below Amesbury Bridge" (32). Our only complaint is that there is rather a want of light in them; "Stonehenge, Midsummer-day" (22), for instance, certainly does not produce the effect of midsummer. Dull weather at the time of our visit, and a consequent unsatisfactory light, may however have had something to do with this.

A CIRCULAR which is being sent out by "Johnson's Patent Pulley and Lock Manufacturing Co." is an amusing instance of the naïveté with which trading companies propose to associate architects with them in pushing their goods. The circular sets out that "the great success which has lately attended Commercial Companies where the Shares were allotted to the Customers of the Companies—in which case the Shareholders directly influence trade—is the real cause of the large dividends and present high prices of the Shares of such Companies. We lay considerable stress upon the fact that the shares in this Company will be allotted in first instance to the Architectural profession, contractors and buyers of Locks generally, so that most of our Shareholders will be able to influence business to the Company." This is evidently said in entire good faith, and without the least suspicion that there is anything questionable in the position which the company invite architects to take. Are they aware that architects who take their shares are thereby (if the fact is known) disqualified as members of the Institute of Architects?

THE RED ROCK CANTILEVER BRIDGE.

THERE are to be found in the "Transactions of the American Society of Civil Engineers" for last December three papers describing a bridge lately built by the Atlantic and Pacific Railway Company, to carry their line over the Colorado River, at a place known as Red Rock. We are accustomed to find in the contributions made to this Society,—especially when they deal with bridge-work,—descriptions of important undertakings, often executed with great skill and rapidity. The Red Rock Bridge is, however, somewhat an exception to this rule, since it is not a particularly large structure, and, for an American bridge, it was not constructed very expeditiously. Although the work contains many points of interest, its chief importance consists in the lesson it should teach the promoters of such schemes, as well as the engineers who are called upon to carry them out.

The Colorado river over which the bridge passes drains an area of some 230,000 square miles, and is a powerful excavator and disintegrator. During the floods, about eight million cubic yards of earth, in the form of silt are carried away by it in twenty-four hours. Geologically, this may be very satisfactory; but it is to be regretted that such immense power cannot be employed more usefully. Could this rate of excavation be attained in making the Manchester Ship Canal, for instance, it would occupy but a week to do the work that has taken 10,000 men and 100 steam navvies many years to accomplish.

On both sides of the river the railway company had to construct some miles of approaches to their new bridge, and for these surveys and estimates were made, but no soundings and borings were taken across the river, along the line of the bridge, because the authorities hesitated to incur the expense of the necessary appliances for doing such work, it not having been absolutely decided at that time to carry out the scheme. When the railway company made up their mind to proceed with the work everything had to be done in the least possible time, and soundings that had been made in 1881 were accepted as being correct, and, upon this information, the contracts for making the bridge and approaches were let. The work being now commenced, it was thought expedient to employ a professional man to make new soundings and borings, and it was not long before it was discovered that those formerly made, and upon which the design had been based, were so inaccurate that it would be necessary to suspend work. When the new soundings were completed, they indicated the position of the rock to be such as shown by the line marked "supposed rock, 1888," in the above diagram. The first design for the bridge was consequently modified to suit this new condition of affairs; the cantilever system was adopted, it being thought that the east pier would only have to be sunk to a moderate depth before it reached the bed rock. The work was, therefore, again started, and pushed on with the greatest speed. In three months the approach lines were finished, the two west piers were completely built, and most of the stone prepared for the east pier. A considerable portion of the superstructure, which was being prepared by the Phœnix Iron Company, was also constructed in their shops. The work was in this condition when the caisson for the east pier was ready to be sunk. The sinking progressed satisfactorily until a depth of 10 ft. had been reached, and it was then discovered that what was originally thought to be bed rock was only a compact boulder bed, 3 ft. to 4 ft. thick, portions of which could be penetrated by the drill. Below this bed sand and gravel were met with, until, at a depth of 64 ft., the solid rock was reached. It was at once evident that a stronger caisson, sunk to a much greater depth, would be required if a pier was to be made in this position, and the work on the superstructure was, therefore, again stopped to allow the whole scheme to be reconsidered. When it became

›wn what a large ount of work had n done by the Phœnix n Company in con- :ion with the steel- rk, it was thought irable to make no inge in the designs y had been working but to carry out the itilever system, as viously settled upon. s total cost of the dge, without the ap- ach lines, is stated have been 92,500l., i one item of this ex- iditure is 1,600l. for soundings and bor- s. Had these few idreds been spent at proper time, they uld most probably re saved the company many thousands.

n dealing with the erstructure we must nember that the can- vers were originally portioned in accord- e with information cerning the founda- as which was after- rds found to be in- rect. If the bed of river had been as in- ated by the line rked "supposed rock, 8," in the above dia- m, there is no doubt t the positions of the rs were fixed with a regard to economy, hough the centre in is somewhat long. e arms of each canti- er are 165 ft. long, ich gives a central in of 330 ft., or one- lf of the total span. was stated by Mr. binson in his paper t if this span had n reduced to 275 ft., saving in the total ount of metal re- ed for the super- cture would only e been about 1½ per t. The distance be- en the trusses is 25 ft., one-twenty-seventh he span, and it has n shown that this pro- tion gives the same ral stiffness to a tilever bridge that btained in a single s bridge where the ers are placed one- teenth of the span t. Greater stability d have been given the structure by easing the width een the lower es at the piers, s retaining the 25 ft. h at the ends of the tilevers; but this od was objected to use of the extra t it would cause in shops, and also be- e it would necessi- a tie of considerable ion being placed be- en the trusses at the s, which, when alter- its length, due to perature, would tend split the masonry. re the anchor arms antilever bridge are icularly short, the ht of the structure een the piers may sufficient to over- nce the combined and dead loads on shore arms. This is case with the Red

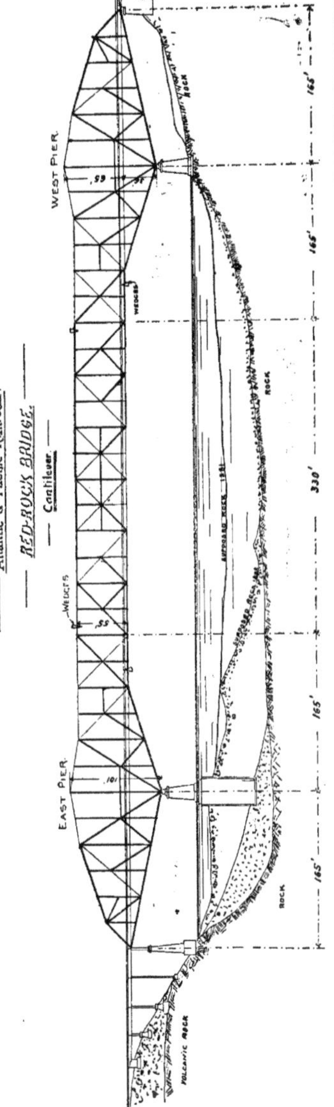

Rock Bridge, and consequently no alterations in the stresses from compression to tension, or *vice-versâ*, can occur in any member of the shore arms.

The material used throughout the structure, except for a few minor parts, is open hearth steel, having a quality almost identical with that adopted for the Forth Bridge.

In building the superstructure at the site, the shore arms had, of course, to be first erected on staging, and when these were finished and anchored down the cantilevers on the river side were built out. The central girders were built by overhang in the same way, until the two halves of each met at a point half way between the piers.

The bridge was completed on June 25, 1891, about twenty months after it was commenced. A considerable portion of this time was lost through the information regarding the nature of the bed of the river being inaccurate, as above alluded to. What extra expense the company was put to from this cause, it is impossible to say, but the amount must have been very large, and those who are responsible for similar undertakings would do well to remember that it is not economical to unduly cut down preliminary expenses, and that it is possible to delay the completion of such works by hurrying too much.

THE ROYAL SOUTH LONDON OPHTHALMIC HOSPITAL.

This new building, which, as we mentioned last week, was recently visited by the Architectural Association, has been in course of erection for the past three years. It is now approaching completion, and has already been opened for out-patients. The building occupies the whole site of the old hospital and that of some adjoining property which was acquired. The whole frontage is about 174 ft. in length, partly towards St. George's-circus, and partly towards the open space at the junction of Waterloo and Westminster Bridge-roads. The site is thus a commanding one, with abundance of light and air, and it may be said to occupy one of the best possible sites for such a hospital, where the out-patients largely predominate, for it is computed that no fewer than 4,000 public vehicles,—omnibuses, tramcars, &c.,—going to almost all parts of London north and south of the Thames, pass the Obelisk in the centre of St. George's-circus every day. The old frontage-line has been set back, so that there is a pavement 22 ft. wide towards St. George's-circus,—a very desirable thing in the interests of the large number of blind or nearly blind out-patients who will use it daily. The building consists of a half-basement, ground floor, and four floors above, with a flat roof on top having an area of about 4,000 ft. super., covered with Claridge's Seyssel asphalte, and a very airy promenade and recreation-ground it will form at certain times of the year for the staff and some of the in-patients.

The half-basement is principally devoted to the purposes of a large and well-lighted, warmed, and ventilated waiting-hall for the out-patients, having a separate entrance in the Waterloo-road. From this waiting-hall, which is provided with sanitary conveniences for both sexes, the patients will ascend by a staircase direct to the surgeons' examination and consulting rooms on the ground floor, and thence will pass into a corridor to the "refractory" or spectacle-room, and thence past the dispensary (where they will get their medicines or lotions) direct into the street by a separate exit, so that patients coming in and going out will not meet each other. The ground floor also includes ophthalmoscope-rooms, bandaging-rooms, dark-rooms, and offices for the staff. There is also an isolation-room and an office for the Secretary closely adjoining the main entrance. The entrance-porch and staff entrance face towards Westminster Bridge-road, and consist of a flight of steps within a recessed archway closed by a Bostwick folding gate. The porch is lined with chocolate and pale-green glazed bricks, of special make, supplied by Messrs. Cliff & Son, of New Wortley.

A notable feature of the arrangement of the building is the devotion of a portion of the ground floor at the Waterloo-road end of the frontage (with a mezzanine floor above) to the purposes of a coffee-tavern or temperance restaurant, so that the poor patients, many of whom come long distances, will be able to get a cup of tea or other light refreshment at a cheap rate. This will be quite distinct from the hospital, however, and will have to be entered from the street. It will not be under the management of the committee of the hospital, though possibly conditions as to the quality and price of the refreshments will be imposed upon the tenant.

The htst-floor is occupied partly by rooms for paying patients, and partly by apartments for the resident surgeon and for the matron. The second and third floors are chiefly devoted to in-patients' wards, with a few private rooms for paying patients. The wards contain seven or eight beds each. The fourth floor is occupied by the kitchen and other domestic offices, and by bedrooms for the servants of the hospital.

There are some noteworthy points about the planning of the hospital. The staircase, for instance, is semi-circular on plan, and is 5 ft. wide, this width, however, being divided into two by a double handrail in the centre, supported on standards, into an up and a down road, with the risers and treads of each differently arranged. There is a separate handrail on each of the wall-sides of the staircase, which has been specially designed for the use of blind or half-blind patients. The water-closets, &c., are built in projecting blocks on each side of the staircase, and are cut off from the main building by cross-ventilated lobbies. In the construction of these blocks of conveniences, iron stanchcons and girders are used as framing and support for the brick enclosing walls. Near these, and also external to the building, is a lift, by Messrs Archibald Smith & Stevens, going up to the top floor. Another point worth note is that there are no square corners or angles in the whole building, the corners of rooms and projections being rounded off, as well as the junctions of walls with ceilings and floors. The building is throughout of fireproof construction, and will be fitted with the electric light. An interesting feature of the arrangements is a system of telephonic and electric communication from all parts of the building, even from the bedside of each patient, to a small lobby where an attendant is always on duty. Mr. Julius Sax fitted up these appliances.

The architect of the building is Mr. Keith D. Young, the general contractor being Mr. William Downs, of Hampton-street, Walworth-road. The red facing bricks of the façade were supplied by Messrs. Lawrence & Sous, Bracknell, and the moulded red bricks in all window dressings, string-courses, and cornices were specially made, to the architect's designs, by Mr. James Brown, of Cannon-street. The terra-cotta was modelled to the architect's designs by Mr. J. C. Edwards, of Ruabon. The whole of the glazed bricks were supplied by Messrs. Cliff & Son. The terra-cotta air-extraction shafts from each room, and the drain-pipes, were made and supplied by Messrs. Doulton & Co. The whole of the plumbing and sanitary fittings are by Messrs. Dent & Hellyer. Messrs. James Slater & Co., of High Holborn, were the contractors for the boilers and heating apparatus, the entire building, in every room, being heated by hot-water coils. The same firm also fitted up the kitchen and scullery with gas-cooking apparatus. The whole of the structural ironwork is by Messrs. W. H. Lindsay, Neal, & Co., of Paddington. Mr. T. Elsley supplied and fixed the gun-metal casements. Messrs. Richardson, Ellson, & Co., supplied the tradesmen's entrance-gate and wrought-iron grilles; Messrs. Murrell, of Chelsea, the wrought-iron screen-gate to out-patients' entrance, exit turnstile, and wrought-iron hand-railing; Messrs. Hayward Bros. & Eckstein the pavement and roof-lights; Mr. J. Gibbons the locks; and Messrs. Hart, Son, Peard, & Co. the general ironmongery. The damp-course work and the floor of out-patients' waiting-hall were executed by Messrs. Pilkington; the *terrazzo* floors by Messrs. Burke & Co.; the parquet floors to public and private wards by Messrs. Turpin & Co.; the slate work for ophthalmoscope rooms, baths, &c., by Messrs. Robert Holland & Co; the dispensary fittings by Messrs. Hawks; the gas-fittings by Mr. Biggs; and the glazing by Messrs. Clark & Sons. The clerk of the works is Mr. H. J. Heathe, to whom, and to Professor McHardy, we must express our thanks for having been shown over the building. Professor McHardy has been the life and soul of the work, and to him are due many details of the hospital. We congratulate him on the near completion of his arduous work.

Old Houses on the South side of Great St Helens, Bishopsgate (attributed to Inigo Jones) now about to be demolished.

Two panels on pilastre in centre of front.

OLD HOUSES, BISHOPSGATE.

WE give a sketch of the houses generally supposed to have been designed by Inigo Jones, which form a part of the south side of Great St. Helens, Bishopsgate, and which are about to be removed. They are of brick, with bands on the pilasters, caps and bases in stone. The wall-jambs, and window-heads are rusticated, and a bold cornice projects over the first-floor window. The original finish, probably a deep cornice carrying the eaves, has been destroyed, and a more modern window-storey built in its place. There are one or two fireplaces and a staircase, which we understand are going to be preserved.

In his "Illustrated Itinerary of the Ward of Bishopsgate," 1862, the Rev. Thomas Hugo, F.S.A., refers to the house in Bishopsgate-street Within named "Crosby Hall Chambers," and says:—

"The front towards the street has lost all its ancient peculiarities, except two beautiful festoons of flowers inserted between the windows of the first and second floors."

He then goes on to say:—

"The north front, which faces an inside court, is very remarkable. The base is composed of rustic work, and the wall above is relieved with pilasters and capitals. The whole of this front is another pleasant specimen of the graceful ease with which the genius of Inigo Jones, for to him I attribute it, could invest ordinary objects with an air of essential beauty. . . . . In a room behind the front last described is a chimney-piece which bears the date 1633, and is a gorgeous specimen of English ornamental work of the earlier half of the seventeenth century."

Mr. Hugo, whose book we cite, as well as his "Last Ten Years of the Priory of St. Helen's" (1865), which we commend to the perusal of our readers, mentions other work in this neighbourhood as by, or reputedly by, Inigo Jones, such as the south entrance to St. Helen's Church, bearing date "1633," and Nos. 11 and 12 in Great St. Helen's, a red-brick house with pilasters of the same material, though the doorways have a somewhat later character (this building must not be confused with Nos. 8 and 9, supposed to be Sir John Lawrence's, and bearing date "1646"). Crosby-square was built in 1677, over that part of Crosby-place that had been burnt in the previous year; between the square and Crosby Hall Chambers lies a pleasant little garden, whose whereabouts Mr. Besant is fearful to find disclosed.

THE SEWAGE FARMS OF BERLIN:

INSTITUTION OF CIVIL ENGINEERS.

AT the eighteenth ordinary meeting of this Institution for the present Session, held on the 5th inst., the President, Mr. George Berkley, in the chair, the paper read was on "The Sewage-Farms of Berlin," by Mr. Herman Alfred Roechling, Assoc.M.Inst.C.E.

Berlin is situated in the sandy plains of North Germany, on both sides of the River Spree, which empties itself into the Havel, at the town of Spandau, about 5½ miles below the city. The Havel is a tributary of the Elbe, and forms a succession of lakes immediately above and below the junction with the Spree, which are picturesque in places, and are a favourite holiday resort of the population. The flow of water in the Havel and in the Spree is very sluggish, and the latter river, in periods of great drought, discharges only about 460 cubic feet per second. The area of the city is about 24½ square miles, and its population at the last census (December 1, 1890) was 1,578,794. The density varies from 220 to 25 persons per acre, each dwelling-house (flat system) being inhabited by an average of sixty-five people. There are about 250 miles of streets, 80 miles of brick sewers, 285 miles of stone-ware pipe sewers, and 55½ miles of pumping mains to the sewage-farms. The Waterworks were purchased (from an English company) by the city authorities in 1874, and the authorities also established their own gasworks, as they could not come to terms with the "Imperial Continental Gas Association." The city provides for its extraordinary expenditure by the issue of loans, the last loan, that of 1886, 2,500,000*l*., was issued above par (101·18); this is an excellent indication of the credit it enjoys in the money market.

After the Franco-German War, Berlin became the German metropolis. Since then it has grown rapidly, and the changes it has undergone have been very marked. Whole districts have been cleared of their old insanitary houses, new streets have been formed, and others have been widened. Many new and elegant buildings have sprung up, the old, abominably-smelling street-gutters, which were practically open sewage-carriers, have disappeared, and under the sway of an intelligent and enterprising City Council, which is the sole municipal authority, Berlin has become one of the finest and best managed cities in the world. It was originally intended to drain the city in the ordinary way by two main intercepting sewers, one on each side of the river, with one common pumping station, and to discharge the sewage, after some slight treatment, into the Spree. A scheme was prepared on these lines in 1861, but it was not accepted, and finally, after numerous experiments respecting the best mode of sewage disposal had been made, the City Council decided to employ sewage-irrigation, and Mr. Hobrecht's new plan for the main drainage of the town was adopted in March, 1873. The works were commenced in August of the same year, and they have been in hand ever since. Under Mr. Hobrecht's scheme the whole area of the town is divided into twelve separate drainage areas, called "radial systems," which are entirely independent one of the other. They have each a pumping station, from which the sewage is raised direct on to the farms, two drainage-districts being in some cases united to one rising-main. The area of these radial systems varies from about 674 acres to 2,117 acres, the total population in such of them as are entirely built over being about 200,000.

The authorities have purchased the whole of the land required for sewage-farming; some of this land lies in the north and north-east, about six miles from the city, and some in the south about twelve miles distant from it. The total area of all the farms has now reached 18,790 acres, of which at present only 11,016 acres are under sewage-treatment; the remainder is, however, being prepared for sewage-farming, and the acreage of the farms is extended as circumstances require. The sub-soil on the farms is, generally speaking, sand, with a preponderance of sandy loam in places, especially on the northern farms, and is well suited for sewage-irrigation. The land is practically level, with small eminences here and there. The sewage of about 112 persons is now treated on each acre of land.

The distribution of the sewage takes place by means of underground cast-iron pipes, which start from the stand-pipes on the rising-mains and terminate on the small summits, where the open earth carriers commence. The whole of the land that receives sewage has been specially prepared for irrigation by levelling and draining. The effluent from the farms is conveyed in open ditches into small streams, which empty into the River Spree, partly above, partly in the city, and partly below it.

The authorities employ a large number of "misdemeanants" in the work on the farms; these are men who have been sentenced for various minor offences to undergo a period of confinement in the House of Correction; they are the loafers of the Berlin streets. From a philanthropic point of view, this course cannot be too highly commended, as it gives the men a chance to get back into regular habits and thus to redeem their character.

The city has spent about 2,906,792*l.* in works of sewerage, and 1,173,648*l.* in the sewage-farms, and about 350,000,000 tons of sewage have been utilised on the farms since the commencement of irrigation. Broadly speaking, the largest acreage in 1889-90 was under cereals, viz., 2,817 acres, then follow the grass plots with 1,785 acres, the roots and green vegetables take the third place with 1,013 acres, and oil-producing plants are cultivated only on 237 acres. There has been a very fair profit on the management of the farms since 1886, but, of course, the amount has not been sufficient to meet the payments for capital expenditure. The deficiency, however, is not a large one, as it has necessitated only an average annual rate of 0·89d. in the £ during the last five years, or a payment of 7·11d. per head of the population per annum. This is a remarkably small amount, and compares favourably with what has been paid in England for sewage-utilisation.

The degree of purification attained has been excellent, as on an average from 95 to 98 per cent. of the organic ammonia contained in the sewage has been abstracted on the farms. This is considerably above the figures quoted by the Rivers Pollution Commissioners as the result of sewage-farming in this country. The farms have had no ill-effect upon the health of the population living on them, and the prejudice against them has almost died out, which is evidenced by the ever-increasing demand for sewage by adjacent farmers and landowners.

On the whole, Berlin is to be congratulated upon the cheap and efficient way in which it utilises the sewage. Where other towns have failed it has succeeded, and that upon a scale at present without a parallel.

ARCHITECTURAL SOCIETIES.

THE ARCHITECTURAL ASSOCIATION (LONDON).—The tenth meeting of the discussion section (late advanced Class of Construction and Practice) was held at the rooms of the Association, on the 6th inst., when Mr. Francis R. Taylor read a paper on "Science applied to Architecture." Mr. Henry Adams, M.Inst.C.E., attended as special Visitor. The paper, which was illustrated by the limelight lantern, was, of course, merely a sketch of this big subject, but was very interesting, and created a good discussion. Votes of thanks were passed to Mr. Taylor and to Mr. Adams for the useful information which they had brought before the class.

EDINBURGH ARCHITECTURAL ASSOCIATION.—At a meeting of the Edinburgh Architectural Association held at 42, George-street on the 7th inst., Mr. Hippolyte Blanc presiding, Mr. A. H. Millar, of Dundee, read a paper on "The Hie Gait and Sautmercat of Glasgow in the Olden Time." Mr. Millar said his purpose was to apply the analytical process and show why Glasgow had taken its present form. There were various theories to account for the present form of the city, but he would confine his attention to the most reasonable of them. The nucleus of the city was the Cathedral, which was built on the side of a hill, around which the houses of the ecclesiastics had been planted. The extremity was the river Clyde, and here had been the colonies of salmon fishers. With the passing and repassing of the ecclesiastics on an errand for fish, and of the fishers for the ministrations at the Cathedral, a footpath would be gradually formed. The footpath would soon become a beaten track, and develop into a road. Artificers, &c., settled in the place, and they also chose the side of the river. There was no trace of the name Sautmercat until about 1600. The name would be given to the place at the Cross round which the salt sellers took their place. There were also lateral extensions by Drygait and Rottenrow, and by Gallowgait and Trongait. Such was the skeleton of the city. The people wended their way on solemn occasions either to the Cathedral or to the other chapels, and the footpaths through the fields had determined the form and fashion of the great city of Glasgow.—About forty members of the Association paid a visit on the 9th inst. to Yester House and the old Castle of Yester, near Gifford. They were received by the Marquis and Marchioness of Tweeddale, by whom they were entertained. Mr. Thomas Bonar, the leader of the party, explained that very little was known of the early history of the old feudal tower, which dated back as far as 1267. Notwithstanding its great antiquity, there still remained evidence enough to show that it must have been a very powerful stronghold, and a castle of the very first importance for the defence of the surrounding district. Tradition had it that it was the last castle that stood out against Cromwell's troops. After that date it fell completely into disuse and decay, owing not only to the effect of time, but to the removal of its stones for building operations by the people of the locality. After discussing at some length its architectural features, Mr. Bonar mentioned that the Castle came into possession of the present family some time in the fourteenth century. The character of the architecture of Yester House was known as Scottish Classic, and resembled such houses as Arniston, Airth, Drum, and others. The building dated from 1740-46.

GLASGOW ARCHITECTURAL ASSOCIATION.—The usual monthly meeting of this Association was held on the 5th inst., the President, Mr. Alexander M'Gibbon, in the chair, when a paper on "Early Irish Architecture" was read by Mr. Charles E. Whitelaw. The Irish examples of pre-Anglo-Norman building were, he said, specially valuable, as of that period England had but a meagre collection. The diminutive size and austere simplicity of the Celtic oratories was to be attributed as much to veneration for some prototype as to poverty and social rudeness. St. Patrick formulated a model, whose dimensions very nearly approached those of the Greek churches of somewhat similar date. Cormac's Chapel, 1127, was about the earliest example of true Norman, in most points similar to English usage, excepting the chancels, that continued to be constructed with square east end rather than semi-circular or polygonal. The round towers were not now considered to date earlier than the ninth century. They range from 50 ft. to 150 ft. in height, and from 40 ft. to 60 ft. in diameter at the base, and have from four to eight stories. Their purpose was undoubtedly for the secure storage of valuables. Mr. Whitelaw showed drawings of Celtic ornament and moulding of features, such as doors and windows, and photographic views. The discussion which followed was opened by Mr. Blane, and at its close the customary vote of thanks was awarded the essayist.

BRITISH ARCHÆOLOGICAL ASSOCIATION.

AT the meeting of this Association on Wednesday, April 6, Mr. C. H. Compton in the chair, it was announced that H.R.H. the Prince of Wales had consented to act as one of the patrons of the Congress of the Association, to be held at Cardiff in August next. Some antiquities recently found at Peterborough and Sibson were exhibited by Mr. Bodger. Among these were some interesting Roman coins, and a Saxon comb, found at a great depth beneath one of the roadways of Peterborough. Mr. Wood exhibited an impression of the sixteenth century seal of the town of Sudbury, Suffolk. Mr. De Gray Birch, F.S.A., sent for exhibition a series of impressions from the seals of Boxley Abbey, Kent, cleverly restored by Mr. Ready. A paper was then read by the Rev. J. Cave Browne, on the seals of Boxley Abbey, all the known examples being referred to and described. On one of the most elaborate of the examples, the heads of St. Benedict and St. Bernard appear within small quatrefoils, placed central upon the shafts of elaborate tabernacle work, while a branch of box in reference to the name, appears on one side. Box still grows on the neighbouring chalk hills, close to the site of the Abbey. Mr. Loftus Brock, F.S.A., described the present condition of the remains of the conventual buildings. The second paper was on the discovery of a Roman hypocaust at Chester. It has been met with in erecting new business premises for Mr. Sykes, who, with praiseworthy regard for the preservation of the remains, has had the work altered to allow of this. The hypocaust, which is in Northgate-street, consists of a large number of square pillars, worked in red sandstone, in excellent preservation. The meeting concluded by the passing of votes of thanks to the author of the paper, and to Mr. Sykes for arranging for the preservation of the remains, so far as they exist on his property.

THE LONDON COUNTY COUNCIL.

THE last meeting of this Council before the Easter holidays was held on Tuesday afternoon last at Spring-gardens, the Vice-Chairman, Mr. John Hutton, presiding.

Payments to Contractors During the Recess.—The Finance Committee's report contained the following paragraphs and recommendation:—

"We have had under consideration the question of making the necessary provision to meet payments to contractors during a recess. At the last Christmas recess, nineteen cheques were drawn, of which six had to be cancelled as not required, and in the interval between the last Council going out of office and the election of the present Council, of the forty-six cheques drawn nineteen were cancelled. With a view of preventing so large a number of cheques being drawn and cancelled, we suggest the adoption of a different course of procedure, as also to meet the difficulty of a contractor, who, although entitled to some payment, but not having done a sufficient quantity of work to cover the cheques drawn, is unable to obtain an advance which he is, under the contract, entitled to on obtaining the certificate of the certifying officer concerned. The only payments likely to be required in the Easter recess are for Mr. Gabbutt, the contractor for Claybury Asylum, 15,000*l.*, and Mr. Hine, the architect, 450*l.*

It is proposed (1) that the Council should authorise the Treasurer to pay the contractor such sums as will be mentioned on certificates signed by the architect, and countersigned by a member of the Council, not exceeding in all (in the present case) the sum of 15,000*l.* and 450*l.*; the Treasurer to take receipts only on forms vouched by the Cashier or other authorised officer in the Comptroller's department. (2) That the certifying officer should have a book of forms of certificate which he would fill up as required, and send, when signed, to the Cashier, who would then obtain the counter signature of the appointed member of the Council, and issue it with the form of receipt to the contractor, who would convey it to the Treasurer and obtain payment. (3) That the Treasurer do receive from the Council, before the recess, orders in favour of certain contractors, and record on each order every payment made on account of that order.

We propose to try this as an experiment for the ensuing Easter recess, so that if found satisfactory it may be brought into general use for all similar occasions. We recommend—

'That the Treasurer be authorised, upon a certificate or certificates of Mr. G. T. Hine (architect), and countersigned by a member of the Council appointed by the Finance Committee, to pay the sums mentioned therein not exceeding the following amounts—Mr. Edmund Gabbutt, for erection of Claybury Asylum, 15,000*l.*; Mr. G. T. Hine, architect, commission at 3 per cent., 450*l.*'"

The recommendation was agreed to without discussion.

Proposed Public Buildings at Battersea.—The Finance Committee also reported as follows concerning an application for a loan by the Vestry of Battersea:—

"We have considered the application of the Vestry of Battersea for the loan of 35,000*l.*, to purchase a site and erect new parochial offices, repayable in 50 years.

The property purchased by the Vestry is situated between Lavender-hill, Eland-road, and Elsley-road, and has a frontage of 163 ft. to Lavender-hill and extends to a depth of 650 ft. Included in the purchase are two houses in Eland-road, which, being part of the same property, the Vestry state that they were compelled to purchase. The price paid for the whole is 8,450*l.*, which the Council's Valuer considers reasonable, and the Vestry apportion on the site for the Vestry offices the sum of 6,000*l.*

The Vestry offices will be provided in the building to be placed on the front portion of the site, and these offices include accommodation for the holding of inquests, approached by a separate staircase. In the rear it is proposed to erect a large hall 98 ft. by 55 ft. 3 in., with a reception-room and a small hall 55 ft. 6 in. by 38 ft. 6 in. underneath this, together with retiring-rooms and the conveniences incidental to such a structure as might be let or used for public meetings, entertainments, &c.

We caused to be notified to the Vestry the fact that there were legal difficulties which prevented our recommending the Council to consent to the loan as applied for, as no authority had been obtained to raise money for the erection of the large halls or coroner's court, and we have since received an explanatory communication from the Vestry and seen a deputation on the subject, and our objections not having been removed, we are unable at present to recommend any advance for these purposes.

The Council's Architect has examined the drawings and specification for the proposed buildings, and apportions the cost as follows: Vestry buildings proper (15,200*l.*), professional and incidental charges (1,300*l.*), and fittings and fixtures (3,000*l.*), making 19,500*l.* Coroner's court and professional charges, 1,400*l.*, and the public halls 10,000*l.*, making a total upon the buildings of 30,900*l.*

The amount which we consider may be now advanced is 19,500*l.* (15,200*l.* and 1,300*l.* and 3,000*l.*) for Vestry offices, and 6,000*l.* for the land, and we accordingly recommend—

'That, subject to the Council hereafter giving its written consent under seal to the borrowing, and subject to all necessary consents and evidence being furnished to the satisfaction of the Solicitor of the Council, the application of the Vestry of Battersea for a loan of 35,000*l.*, to defray the cost of purchasing a site and erecting Vestry offices, be granted to the extent of 25,500*l.*, on condition that the loan is taken up at once, interest being charged thereon at the rate of 3*l.* 10*s.* per cent. per annum, calculated quarterly, and with the principal being repaid by such equal half-yearly payments of principal and interest combined as will repay the amount borrowed as to 6,000*l.* for site within a period of 57 years, as to 16,500*l.* for buildings within 30 years, and as to 3,000*l.* for fittings within 15 years; that it be referred to the Solicitor to take the necessary measures for completing the loan, and that the amount be advanced out of the Consolidated Loans Fund.'"

This led to some discussion, on an amendment moved by Mr. Costelloe, to the effect that the recommendation be referred back to the Committee. He expressed the opinion that, for the purpose specified, a larger loan should be made. It was, he said, very desirable that facilities should be granted for the erection of public halls.

Mr. Harben seconded the amendment.

Mr. Evan Spicer (Chairman of the Finance Committee) said they had taken legal opinion, with the result that, though they regretted the circumstances, they did not feel justified in recommending that a larger loan should be made.

Mr. Westacott said they should endeavour to get the law altered rather than go beyond their present powers.

Mr. Spicer suggested that they should pass the present recommendation, and later on consider a separate application in reference to the halls, &c.

Mr. Costelloe, in view of Mr. Spicer's suggestion, withdrew his amendment.

Mr. Cohen next moved to omit the words "and interest combined."

Mr. Fardell seconded the amendment, which was lost by a large majority. The recommendation was then agreed to.

The Annual Estimates: Grants in Aid of Technical Education.—Mr. Evan Spicer, Chairman of the Finance Committee, next brought up and explained the estimates of the Council's receipts and expenditure for the year ending March 31, 1893. He explained that the total sum required to be raised during the year would be 1,696,034*l.*, of which 1,403,688*l.* would be on the General County Account, and 292,346*l.* on Special County Account. This sum total was the difference between the estimated total expenditure for the year (2,959,330*l.*) and the estimated total receipts (1,263,296*l.*) from all sources other than the rates. This would necessitate a rate of 10·1d. in the pound on General County Account, and of 2·4d. in the pound on Special County Account, making a total rate, outside the City, of 12½d., as compared with 11¾d. in 1891-92, or an increase of ¾d. in the pound. Mr. Spicer concluded a long explanatory statement by moving a series of resolutions, of which the first was as follows:—

"That the estimates now before the Council, of the receipts and expenses of the Council for the year ending March 31, 1893, be approved, and that the Council do hereby estimate the amount that will be required to be raised in the first six months and in the second six months of the said year by means of contributions, to be as follows:—

	In the first six months.		In the second six months.		Total.
General County Account	£701,844	..	£701,844	..	£1,403,688
Special County Account	146,173	..	146,173	..	292,346
	£848,017		£848,017		£1,696,034"

On this recommendation, Mr. Quintin Hogg moved, as an amendment:—

Provided that 30,000*l.*, being part of the amount receivable by the Council under the Local Taxation (Customs and Excise Duties) Act, 1890, be carried over to a suspense account, instead of being applied in reduction of rate, and that such 30,000*l.* when carried over, be dealt with on or before October 1 next, by the Council for any purpose authorised by the above Act; and that a special committee be appointed to consider what action the Council should take under the Technical Education Acts 1889-91, and the Local Taxation (Customs and Excise Duties) Act, 1890, with power to draw up a scheme or schemes for the consideration of the Council."

Mr. Hogg said be moved this amendment because he saw with regret that the Finance Committee proposed to follow the course adopted by the last Council, and to devote no portion of the money coming to them from the Imperial Exchequer to the promotion of technical education. It was clearly the implied, if not the expressed, intention of the Legislature that the London County Council should devote part of the money thus accruing to it to the cause of technical education, as other County Councils had done, instead of applying it to the relief of the general rate. He contended that to help on the cause of technical education was one of the surest ways of relieving the rates, for our workmen would become better skilled in their various trades and able to cope more succesfully with foreign competitors.

Mr. Bantu, as a representative of the skilled artisans in the metropolis, said he was pleased to second the amendment. He thought the matter should not be met by charitable doles, but by some systematic scheme of technical instruction all over London, of which every child might take advantage.

Colonel Hughes, M.P., thought it rather a reproach to the Council that they had not looked at the matter of technical education with sufficient earnestness up to this moment. He supported the amendment.

Mr. Charles Harrison opposed the amendment, and pointed out that by an Act of Parliament the Council were empowered to impose a rate not exceeding a penny in the pound for the purposes of technical education, but he doubted whether there was a single councillor who would propose the increase of the rates to that extent for that object. In his opinion it was premature for the Council to apply funds over which they had absolute discretion in that way, as it was inexpedient to relieve the pressure which otherwise existed on the City Guilds to provide and have their moneys applied for technical education and for works of public utility within the meaning of the report of the Royal Commission on the City Guilds.

Mr. Sydney Webb supported the amendment.

Sir Thomas Farrer said it appeared to him that the County Council were not in default on this question, as Mr. Goschen had suggested i[n] his Budget speech. Mr. Goschen showed dis[-]tinctly in 1871 that the persons who neede[d] assistance in the matter of rates were th[e] towns, and especially the metropolis. Whe[n] they came too look at the way in which th[e] Exchequer contribution was distributed, the[y] found that the towns, and London especiall[y] had not received anything like their fair sha[re] of that contribution.

Dr. Collins supported the amendment, be[-]cause he believed that at the present time th[e] question of technical education in the metro[-]polis was one which was ripening for solution.

Mr. Doubleday also approved the amend[-]ment, as he considered it would provide th[e] quickest way of getting at the funds in th[e] hands of the City Guilds.

Mr. Pickersgill, M.P., oppposed the amend[-]ment, although he admitted that, by th[e] action of the Science and Art Department i[n] curtailing or withdrawing grants to technic[al] schools, on the assumption that all the Coun[ty] Councils would help on the cause of technic[al] education, certain institutions in London wou[ld] suffer great hardship, and their work would b[e] seriously crippled.

Sir John Lubbock said that as treasurer o[f] the Technical Education Association, perha[ps] he might be allowed to say a few words. Th[e] amendment had been appropriately moved b[y] Mr. Quintin Hogg, who had done so much f[or] the technical instruction of London. It w[as] fortunate indeed for London that Mr. Hog[g] had not himself acted on the advice of M[r.] Harrison. The opponents did not den[y] the importance of technical education, an[d] if we wished to maintain our supremacy i[n] commerce and manufactures we must give o[ur] people the same advantages as they enjoye[d] elsewhere. Other counties and cities had appli[ed] their funds to technical education, and he hop[ed] London would not remain behind. It was sa[id] that the Council was not the proper body, b[ut] Parliament had decided that for them. I[t] trusted that the Council would support M[r.] Hogg; for if, on the contrary, they r[e]jected the proposal, it would be a gre[at] discouragement to the cause of educati[on] throughout the whole country.

Mr. Torr claimed that the money of the Ci[ty] Guilds belonged to the ratepayers, and oug[ht] no longer to be wasted in feasting. The Coun[cil] ought to have it, so that they might as soon a[s] possible set to work to establish seriously tec[h]nical education in London.

After some further discussion, the amen[d]ment was adopted, on a show of hands, by [a] large majority.

Mr. Arthur Arnold next moved to amend t[he] amendment by omitting all words betwe[en] "that," in line 1, and "a special committe[e]" towards the latter part of the amendment, [so] as to confine it to the question of the appoin[t]ment of a committee, without setting aside [or] tying up 30,000*l.* or any other sum.

This amendment was seconded by Mr. Hu[b]bard, but was defeated, on a division, by [64] votes against to 39 for,—a majority of 25 again[st] the amendment.

Major Probyn next moved, and Mr. Emd[en] seconded, as a further amendment:—"That it [be] referred to the General Purposes Committee [to] report as to the desirability of devoting at lea[st] 100,000*l.*, derived from the Customs and Exc[ise] duties, for the purposes of technical educatio[n]." The amendment was immediately negativ[ed] and the recommendation of the Finance Co[m]mittee, as amended by Mr. Hogg's additi[on] was approved.

The other recommendations, which were o[f a] formal nature, were then agreed to without d[is]cussion.

The Limit of Height of Buildings, whether old or new Foundations.—The Public Hea[lth] and Housing Committee's report contained t[he] following:—

"The Council, on the 8th December last pass[ed] the following resolution—

'That it be referred to the Building Act Committ[ee] to consider and report whether, with a view to preve[nt]ing the increase of insanitary areas in London, it is de[sir]able that effect should be given to the recommend[a]tions made in 1885 by the Royal Commissioners on t[he] Housing of the Working Classes, with regard to limit[ing] the height of dwelling-houses according to the sp[ace] about them, whether built on old or new foundatio[ns,] and what amendments of the Building Acts are pr[ac]ticable in this direction.'

Shortly after the passing of this resolution, t[he] Building Act Committee reported to the Coun[cil] the amendments which they suggested were requi[red] to the Metropolitan Building Acts, which are m[ade] the subject of a Consolidation Bill. The amendme[nts]

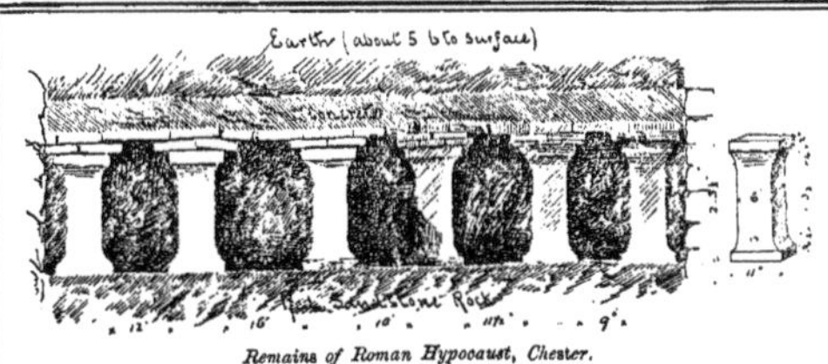

Remains of Roman Hypocaust, Chester.

then suggested included one framed on the principle of a rule prevailing in Liverpool for securing an open space in the rear of all buildings, whether built on old or new foundations, based on an angle of 45 deg., and such an alteration in the law would undoubtedly greatly assist in preventing the creation of slums in the future. It does not, however, go to the length to which your Committee would wish to see an alteration in the law, as it does not deal at all with the air space in front of the building.

Again and again cases have come to our notice, either by complaints from local authorities or private individuals or otherwise, in which it is proposed to erect buildings on old foundations, which from lack of air space would inevitably be insanitary; and beyond warning the builders that proceedings may be taken when the houses are erected to obtain their closing and demolition, perhaps at the cost of the ratepayers, no action has been possible owing to the defective state of the existing law. Any efforts of the Council to abolish narrow and unhealthy courts and yards are constantly frustrated by the fact that the law permits the erection of dwellings of any height so long as they are on old foundations, and we consider that steps should be taken with a view to the insertion of a clause in the Building Acts Amendment Bill dealing fully with this important question. We therefore recommend:—

'That the Council do pass the following resolution That, in the opinion of the Council, it is desirable that a clause should be introduced into the London Building Law (Consolidation) Bill controlling the height of buildings, whether built on old or new foundations, in relation to the street or open space in front of them, and that it be referred to the Parliamentary Committee to give effect to this resolution.'"

Dr. Longstaff, Chairman of the Building Act Committee, objected to the action of the Public Health and Housing Committee in this matter, and opposed the adoption of the report, the consideration of which was adjourned.

After transacting other business, the Council adjourned until Tuesday, May 3.

REMAINS OF ROMAN HYPOCAUST, CHESTER.

WE give a drawing of the remains of a Roman Hypocaust recently discovered behind Northgate-street, Chester. The pillars, of red sandstone, rest on the sandstone rock; the tiles forming the roof vary from 1½ in. to 2½ in. in thickness by about 10 in. on the face; the concrete is about 6 in. deep.

The section shows part of two rows of columns,—the three to the right are 18 in. behind the others. We give in the margin the dimensions of a pillar which has been removed for preservation.

SHAKSPEARE AT STRATFORD-ON-AVON. — The annual series of Shaksperian Memorial Performances at Stratford-on-Avon have again this year, for the fifth time, been undertaken by Mr. F. R. Benson, and will consist of eight representations of Shaksperian plays, including a most interesting revival of "Timon of Athens," a tragedy that has not been seen on the boards since Phelps produced it at Sadler's Wells about twenty-five years ago. The performances commence on Monday, April 18, and will be as follows:—Monday, 18th, and Tuesday, 19th, "A Midsummer Night's Dream;" Wednesday, 20th, "Julius Cæsar;" Thursday, 21st, "Twelfth Night;" Friday, 22nd, and Saturday, 23rd (Shakspeare's birthday), "Timon of Athens." There will be also two matinées, one of "A Midsummer Night's Dream" on Monday, 18th, and one of "Timon of Athens" on Saturday, 23rd. Special trains will be run from London on Friday, the 15th, and Friday, the 22nd. There will also be special trains from Northampton, Birmingham, Wolverhampton, Leamington, and surrounding districts.

Illustrations.

MURAL PAINTING IN THE CHAPEL, MAYNOOTH COLLEGE.

OUR illustration represents the first of a series of fourteen "stations," which go round the choir of the chapel of Maynooth College. Each station, with its accessory ornament, occupies a space of 15 ft. by 8 ft.

The subject of the first station is taken from St. John, xviii., v. 28, &c. Our Lord is before Pilate; in the background are the Jews who will not enter the hall; Pilate, therefore, comes to the atrium to meet them, and there listens to their accusations, &c.

The other thirteen subjects are those now commonly used to complete the pilgrimage of the "Via Crucis." Seven of these are completed.

In the adjoining bay, next to the first station, are the four Major Prophets, with their prophecies of our Lord's sufferings and passion.

Besides these paintings in the lower part of the choir, Mr. Westlake has designed the roof decoration; and the figures (life-sized), ninety-two in number, are from his *atelier*. It is one of the largest painted roofs now existing in a Gothic church, and may be classed with those at Ely and St. Albans, in England; and St. Michael's, at Hildesheim, in Germany. The figures in the sanctuary roof, twenty in number, represent Apostles, Evangelists, and Prophets. Those in the nave comprise Our Lady with the Divine Infant, SS. Michael, John the Baptist, Joseph, Celestine, Patrick, Bridget, and Laurence. Following these are a series of angels with instruments of the passion, &c., whilst the western end contains the principal national saints. Around each saint or angel there is a versicle. The whole of the three hymns, the "Te Deum," "Quam Dilecta," and "Benedictus," are thus given.

Around the scroll and versicle are ornamental foliated borders, in gold and low-toned colour.

The whole of the work is done under the care of Mr. Hague, the architect, of Dawson-street, Dublin, whose designs won the competition which was called some three years ago for the completion of the decoration of the chapel, which has been pushed on with untiring energy by the present President, the Very Rev. Canon Browne, D.D. N. H. J. W.

DESIGN FOR A CHAPTER HOUSE.

THIS design, by Mr. John Begg, was one of those submitted to the Council of the Institute of Architects in competition for the Soane Medallion, and obtained for its author a "medal of merit" as the second best design sent in.* The material was intended to be brick with stone dressings for the exterior, with a lead-covered roof. For the interior work stone and red brick, the latter being proposed for the filling in of the groining. The stalls would be of oak, and the floor of dark grey or black and white marble.

We give the exterior perspective, a reduced copy of the plan, and the section. The treatment of the buttresses, carried right up to the plane of the mullions, with the arch mouldings butting against them, has a very bold effect, and the whole design is very creditable to its author.

DESIGN FOR A STONE RAILWAY-BRIDGE.

THIS is the design for which the Grissell Gold Medal, for constructive work, has been awarded by the Council of the Institute to its author, Mr. Harold Harlock. As the author has sent us no description of his design, we must leave the drawings to speak for themseves. The Grissell medal being given for constructive design, the work is to be judged, we presume, purely from an engineering point of view; though we may suggest that architects, in competing for such a medal, might very well endeavour to improve a little upon the engineering type of design, and see if construction could not be combined with a little more of architectural effect and expression than we usually find in works of this class.

* The design, by Mr. Heber Rimmer, which gained the Soane Medallion, we shall illustrate later on; it is unavoidably postponed for the present.

COMPETITIONS.

TECHNICAL SCHOOL, HEYWOOD, LANCASHIRE.—On the 8th inst., at a meeting of the Technical Instruction Committee held in the Council-chamber, Heywood, the assessor's award was opened and the result made known of the competition amongst architects for plans for the proposed Technical School, Heywood. Mr. Tuke (of Messrs. Maxwell & Tuke), Manchester, was the assessor, and in his award he stated that he had no hesitation in awarding the first premium in the competition to the plans marked No. 2A and No. 2B, alternative plans, sent in by the same author. He experienced some difficulty in deciding upon the respective merits of the plans for the second and third premiums, but he suggested that the premiums should be divided equally between the plans marked No. 3 and No. 10. The Committee resolved, after deliberation, to adopt this suggestion, and the premiums are, therefore, awarded as under:—First, Messrs. Woodhouse & Willoughby, Manchester and Stockport; second and third, Messrs. Butterworth & Duncan, Rochdale, and Mr. F. Brockbank, Liverpool.

FARNWORTH PUBLIC BATHS.—In the limited competition for this work an amount was stipulated for the cost which was not to be exceeded. This condition not being fulfilled by the design at first selected, tenders were obtained for the execution of the buildings according to the design which was placed second in the competition, and as submitted by Messrs. Bradshaw & Gass, of Bolton. These tenders being satisfactory, the work has been put in hand according to their designs.

ROSSIVILLE ASYLUM, N.S.W.—In the competition for Rossiville Asylum (New South Wales), the judges, after no less than twenty sittings, have placed the competitors in the following order of merit:—

1st, Messrs. Sulman & Power, } Sydney.
2nd, Mr. Jno. Kirkpatrick, } Sydney.
3rd, Mr. C. D. Payne, } Sydney.
4th, Mr. — Clarke, Brisbane.
5th, Messrs. McKinnon & Weitzel, Sydney.

The name of Mr. Sulman, whose design in conjunction with Mr. Power is placed first, will be well remembered among our London readers.

BUILDING INDUSTRY, MEXICO.—According to a recent report of the British Consul at Mexico, there were in that city, at the end of 1890, houses worth 19,853,152*l*., an increase of 2,447,866*l*. or 14·3 per cent., since 1888. The increase in value of the same class of property in the small suburban towns of the Federal district during the same period was 126,342*l*., or 20·35 per cent. This development of the building industry is due not so much to any great increase of the population as to the general increase of wealth and a consequent demand for more commodious houses. It has a direct interest to British trade, in having opened a market for foreign building material, which, a very few years ago, did not exist.

LONDON PROPERTIES FOR SALE.—At the Mart, on the 28th instant, the second portion of the City-road Estate, Islington, comprising twenty-four houses, situated in the City-road (western end), Duncan-terrace, Sidney-street, and Goswell-road, being freehold, and yielding a rental amounting, in the aggregate, to about 1,394*l*. per annum. Also, consequent upon the death of Mr. J. J. Keily, twenty-four freehold houses in the same quarter,—including Nos. 1-5, Colebrooke-row,—producing an aggregate rental of 1,545*l*. a year; and Black-horse-yard, with other building sites, tenements, &c., covering a total area of 2½ acres, near to the "Angel" tavern, and lying north and south of the City-road. Many of the houses have large front or back gardens; some of them, being Nos. 2—15, Duncan-terrace, and 391-403 (odd), City-road, are scheduled in the Bill for an extension of the City and South London Electric Railway.

BRADFORD SMALL-POX HOSPITAL.

We give the plans and section of the new isolation wards of this hospital, of which Messrs. Morley and Woodhouse are the architects. The hospital is arranged with two wards, each 72 ft. by 15 ft., which are placed back to back, having a space of 3 ft. between them. Bath-rooms, w.c.'s, slop sinks, and linen shoots are arranged at the end of each ward, and nurses' rooms adjoin the wards at the entrance ends, with supervision windows to each ward. A private ward is also provided. A special feature of the arrangements is an undressing-room for convalescents, where they leave behind hospital clothing, and then pass into a bath-room, and thence into a dressing-room, where their own clothes are put on, and from this room they pass direct into the outer air, thus doing away with all risk of carrying infection away with them. The drainage is divided into two separate and distinct systems; the one for roof and surface-water goes direct into the mains, but all the foul drains empty into disinfecting tanks, which are duplicated, so that whilst one tank is being emptied after disinfection, the other is receiving the drainage, and going through the process of disinfection by an admixture of chemicals.

Special arrangements are made for the destruction of the germs of disease. All the windows are made tight, and the fresh air is let in by three shafts from the outside, carried under floors and into the lowest compartment of the 3-ft. space between the two wards. Above this compartment, and divided from it by flags with open joints, in another compartment are placed the heating pipes, which are very powerful, and from this compartment flues are carried into the wards which conduct the fresh air (warmed in cold weather by contact with the heating pipes last named) into the same through gratings in the floors, one being placed at the foot of each bed. Above the compartment last named is an extracting flue made perfectly air-tight, and into this flue openings are made at the ceiling level of the wards over each bed. A powerful furnace, with honeycomb fire-brick divisions, is placed in the cellar at the end of this flue, and this furnace draws the foul air out of the wards, and it passes through the furnace and out into the open air by a large chimney. Thus all vitiated air from both wards, w.c.'s, bath-rooms, &c. (which are all connected with the flue), passes through a furnace which is heated up to at least 800 deg., and therefore is more than sufficient to destroy all obnoxious germs. The working of the scheme has been properly tested by the anemometer, and it has been found that at least 10,000 cubic feet per hour per patient can be passed through the wards and out through the furnace, and that at the same time in cold weather a temperature of at least 60 deg. can still be maintained in the building.

The contractors for the building were:—Mr. Farnish, mason; Messrs. Wilkinson & Dawson, Joiners; Mr. J. Wood, plumber; Messrs. Cordingley & Sons, plasterers; Messrs. Hill & Nelson, slaters; and Mr. J. Arundel, painter. Mr. Bancroft acted as clerk of works.

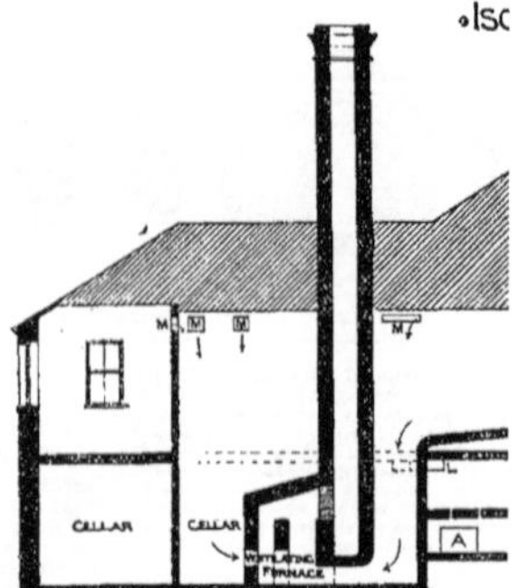

M. GRATINGS AT CEILING LEVEL FOR EXTRACT OF VITIATED AI
A. COLD AIR INLETS.
L. FRESH AIR TO WARDS.

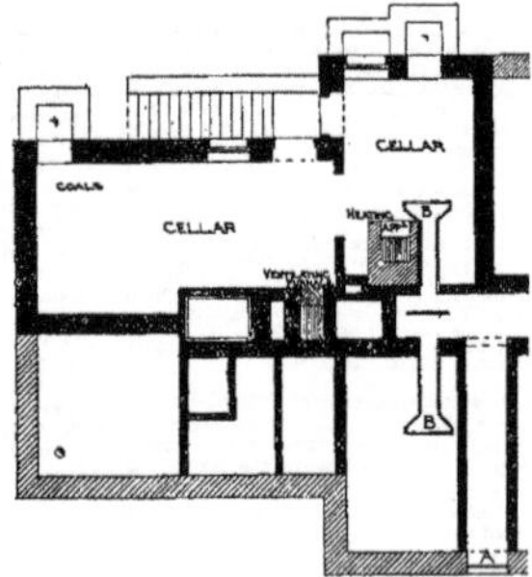

A. COLD AIR INLETS.
B. FRESH AIR FLUES THRO' FLOOR INTO WARDS.

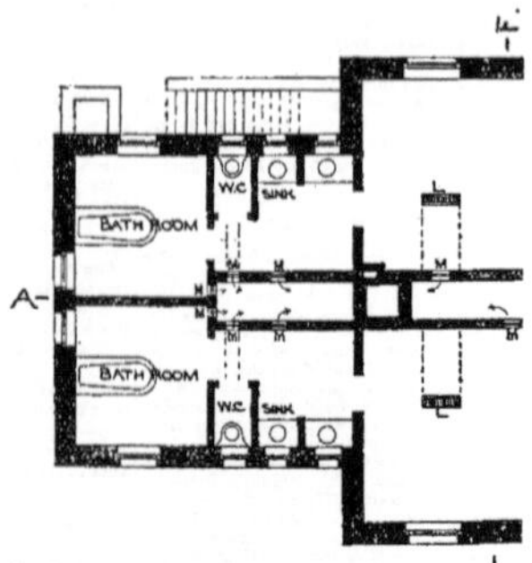

L. GRATINGS IN FLOOR FOR FRESH AIR SUPPLY TO WARDS.
M. GRATINGS AT CEILING LINE FOR EXTRACT OF VITIATED AIR.

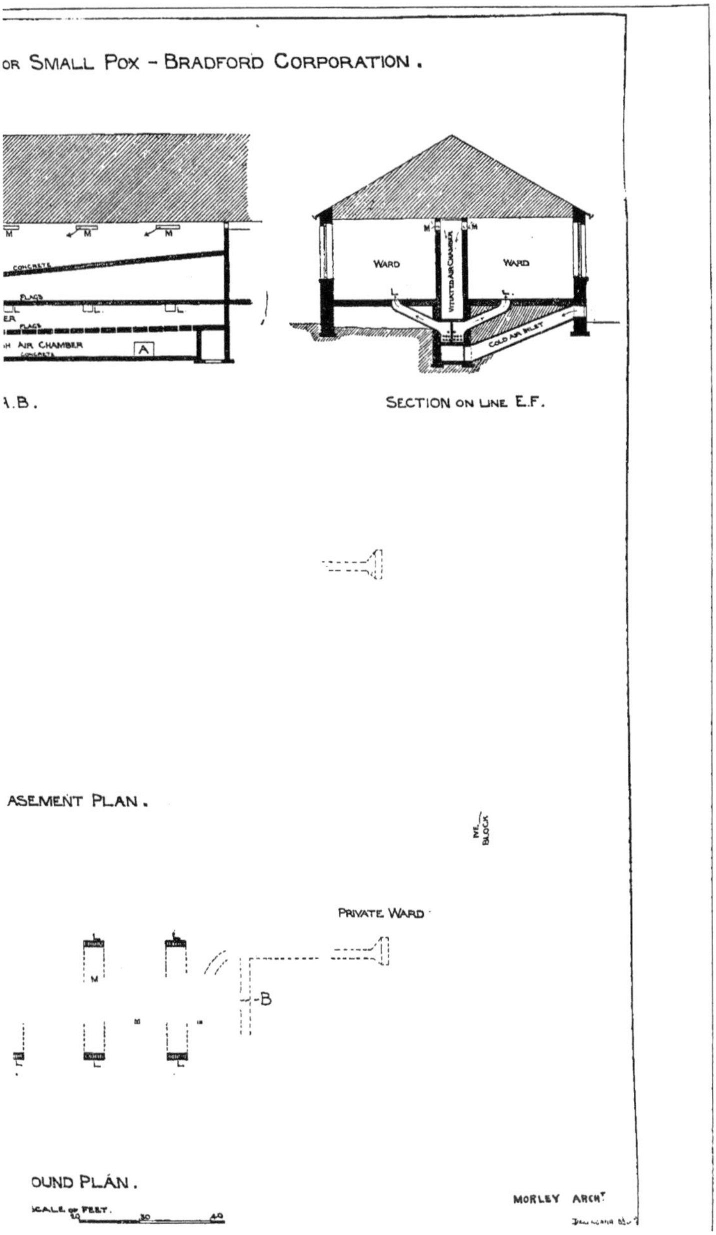

OR SMALL POX - BRADFORD CORPORATION.

M M M
CONCRETE
FLAGS
L L L
ER
FLAGS
H AIR CHAMBER
CONCRETE
A

A.B.

M M
WARD
VITIATED AIR CHAMBER
WARD
L L
COLD AIR INLET

SECTION ON LINE E.F.

ASEMENT PLAN.

PRIVATE WARD

M
B

OUND PLAN.

SCALE OF FEET. 20 30 40

MORLEY ARCH^T.

THE SANITARY INSPECTORS' ASSOCIATION.

An earnest and interesting address was delivered on the 2nd inst. before the members of this Association at Carpenters' Hall, by Mr. J. Davenport, C.E. (Nantwich Union), one of the founders of the North-Western Sanitary Association, Mr. H. Alexander, the Chairman of the Council, presiding. The title chosen for the lecture was "The Sanitary Inspector—His High Calling." The paper claimed not only the sanction of the noblest of sciences,—that of saving human life, for the work of the Sanitary Inspector,—but the sanction of a Divine prescription as express as that which those who seek to save souls obey. A very close parallel was drawn between the canons of sanitary law as developed by science during the last sixty years, and the canons of the Mosaic law. A Divine origin was, in short, claimed for the "laws of health." Isolation of patients, destruction of sources of contagion, and cleansing of the most thorough character, were enjoined by this law, and God himself was declared ready to inspect the results, in the passage, "For the Lord thy God walketh in the midst of thy camp; therefore shall thy camp be whole, that he see no unclean thing in thee and turn away from thee." The leper and every one that was defiled was made responsible for his own isolation, for he must call out with a loud voice, "Unclean!" If any healthy person came near his place of banishment. An infected house must be scraped, and the dust be removed to a special place outside the city; and, if that were not effectual, the house must "be broken down, and the stones, timber, and mortar carried out of the city." Infected garments of woollen or linen, warp or woof, or skin must be burnt with fire. The reward of obedience was immunity from epidemics, the penalty of disobedience, annihilation by them. The penalty was illustrated by reference to plague years in England in the seventeenth century, when 310 per 1,000 (in 1625) and 430 per 1,000 (in 1665), were the horrible death rates of the years of the plague. The reward of obedience was also illustrated. The Great Fire of London so effectually carried out the Mosaic precept, that London has never since had a return of the scourge. At the village of Eyam, in Derbyshire, where a tailor had received a parcel of woollen clothes, the death rate reached its maximum, the tailor and five out of every six of his fellow-villagers dying of the plague in a few months. It was only after the survivors had been induced by two heroic parsons to isolate their village from the rest of the world and to burn every stitch and stick, that the plague was stamped out. In the present century, the visit of the Asiatic cholera in 1831 had been a blessing in disguise, for that epidemic had originated sanitary reform, and thus been the main cause of the advances made since by sanitary science. It had been shown that the death-rate from certain of these diseases was only one-hundredth of the rate of sixty years ago, and in the typhoid classes the mortality had fallen from 1·23 to 0·18, or down to one-seventh. A report of the Local Government Board showed that 250,000 lives were saved in the decade 1871-80, which would have been lost had the death-rate of the previous thirty years been maintained, and counting twelve cases of sickness for one death, three millions of people, or one-ninth of the population, had been saved from sickness, by causes not previously in operation. Their late president, Sir Edwin Chadwick, than whose, no name stood higher in sanitary circles, had calculated the money saving by the improved state of the British Army at 344,000*l.* a year, and a life saving of 40,000 men in ten years. But from him we also knew that there still remained a great deal to do, for even with our reduced death-rate, preventible disease was slaying over 100,000 lives every year, that might be saved with improved sanitation. The sanitary inspector represented to a great extent for the people of his district the present state of hygienic knowledge and to the other functions of his "high calling" he therefore added that of educator. It was in the spirit of study and contemplation that the duties of the sanitary inspector should be undertaken, and if so undertaken he must become a power in the regeneration of the world.

The Chairman, in inviting discussion, said that when they found they could not hope to get Sir Robert Rawlinson to give them an address by reason of his great age and feeble health, he had selected the next best man, well knowing that Mr. Davenport would talk of something better than D-traps and drain-pipes. A vote of thanks was proposed by Mr. West (Walthamstow), who warmly eulogised the paper. Mr. Poulson (Chelsea) seconded the motion, and continued the discussion. He objected to the idea of a Divine origin being ascribed to sanitary laws on account of anything that Moses might have said or done. Moses had learned all he knew from the Egyptians. If they had seen, as he had, at the Natural History Museum, "The Book of Death," they would find out that the ideas of the Egyptians on public purity and sanitation were simply splendid. They had their sanitary inspectors, their sanitary regulations, aye, and their sanitary engineers, whose works spoke of their almost superhuman talent in the remains of the great city of Memphis. The Egyptians were the very antithesis of another ancient people, the Chinese, whose sanitary ideas were beneath contempt. Mr. Thomas (Bermondsey) said he felt as deeply impressed with the importance of his work as any minister of the Gospel did of his ministry, but nothing was to be gained by confusing the calling of the one with that of the other. He had the co-operation of his clergy, and very glad he was of it, because they always left the care of the bodies of the parishioners to the proper officers. He had been so well supported that he had cast down 300 houses to the ground, and twelve more rotten houses would have gone the same way but for the opposition of certain interests. At every meeting of his Board he had repeated the same cry, "the disgraceful state of things still exists in Crosby-row" until, weary of the iteration, they had armed him with the authority asked for. He agreed thoroughly with the spirit of the paper. The motion was supported by Messrs. Edwards, Dee (Westminster), Turner (Greenwich), Goodwin (Richmond), &c., and on being put was carried by acclamation.

Books.

Encyclopédie de l'Architecture et de la Construction. Volume V.; deuxième fascicule. Directeur, P. Planat. Paris; Dujardin et Cie.

The fifth volume of M. Planat's encyclopædia takes us nearly to the close of the letter M, and contains several important articles: "Lombarde," "Louvre" "Lycée," "Mairie," "Maison," and "Moderne (architecture)" among them. It may be questioned whether such a heading as "Modern Architecture," which is so large and extended a subject that it would require a treatise to itself, fairly comes within the proper scope of an article in a publication of this kind. M. Planat, who contributes the article himself, has succeeded, however, in bringing it within reasonable scope and making it fairly representative. He proposes as the object of the article "to indicate rapidly, by some examples, the actual tendencies of architecture in different countries" at the present day. Taking the principal countries alphabetically, "Architecture Anglaise" takes the lead, is treated with more knowledge and sympathy than we find accorded to this country in some other portions of the encyclopædia, and is fairly illustrated. It may be interesting to the reader to notice the buildings which the French critic selects for illustration. Remarking that the variety [of religious sects in England leads to an interesting variety in their religious edifices, M. Planat gives first a view of Mr. Waterhouse's chapel in Mayfair, in which the architect "à fait la marque caractéristique de son talent, et qui permettre de reconnaitre sa main comme on discerne celle d'un peintre." Next comes "L'Église St. Pierre" at Kuddington by Messrs. Bell & Roper, followed by "L'Église St. Jean Baptiste" at Brighton, by Mr. S. J. Nicholl. But that ends the churches! Of Mr. Pearson the editor seems ignorant. We have next the Art Gallery at Sheffield by "MM. Floken & Gibbs" (how is it that French writers *cannot* copy English names correctly?), and following that the interior of Mr. Robson's library at the People's Palace. Then we have the central portion of the Natural History Museum at South Kensington, where "nous retrouvons également l'emploi de ces hautes tours multipliées, sans lequelles il semble qu'il n'y ait pas d'architecture moderne en Angleterre." The same architect's University College at Liverpool follows; then a part of the centre of the Law Courts' façade, apparently copied from a photograph, without the trouble to correct its distortion of lines; not a creditable illustration. The Girls' School at Bristol, by Mr. Gough, "se rattache à ce style de la Renaissance anglaise qui n'est pas sans analogie avec le caractère des constructions allemandes, hollandaises et flamandes;" the Town Hall at Leamington, by Mr. Cundall; the buildings for an insurance company in London, by Messrs. Aston Webb & Bell; the Liberal Club at Leeds, by Messrs. Chorley & Cannon. This is followed by Ascott House, at Leighton, by Messrs. Williams, West, & Slade, as an example of the picturesque style of modern English house; one is sufficient, for "qui a vu un cottage anglais les a tous vus" (!). An entrance-hall interior from Palace Court, Kensington follows, by MM. Harvey and Bernard Smith. That is the end of the English examples. Can it be believed that the name of Mr. Norman Shaw is not even mentioned, nor one of his works illustrated! Mr. Planat has something more to learn about contemporary English architecture. The illustrations, though necessarily on a rather small scale, are mostly very well executed.

Modern German architecture is fairly illustrated; the subject is of course much larger, as it covers far more ground. Of Italian architecture the largest illustration given is that of the new Palais de Justice at Rome. American architecture does not fare well; the design for New York cathedral is shown in a very poor and small illustration, and the Capitol at Washington, which is going rather far back for contemporary architecture. The remarkable development of modern domestic and street architecture in the United States seems to have escaped M. Planat's notice altogether. French modern architecture is omitted, having been treated sufficiently already, we presume, under "France."

M. Dedartein's article on Lombard architecture is a long and very largely illustrated treatise, giving both plans, sections, and a considerable illustration of ornamental details. The history of the Louvre is treated by M. H. Nodet, and the subject of "Lucarne" by M. Rivoalen, "lucarne" of course corresponding to "dormer" in English. As far as it goes this is a good article, well illustrated; but it has the defect that we have noticed in many others of the smaller articles in the Encyclopædia, that it is entirely confined to French examples, without the slightest hint of any others, and is an essay which could only find its proper place in an "Encyclopædia of French architecture," not in an "Encyclopædia of Architecture." In the article on "Lycée," which is really a term peculiar to France, the author, M. Charles Lucas, is more broad in his views, and divides his article into two sections, "France" and "Étranger," though we are bound to say that the latter is by far the smaller section. The buildings in England illustrated are Manchester New College, Oxford; Holloway College, and the Technical Institute in Exhibition-road. The article on "Mairie" is more general in character and in the selection of its illustrations. "Maison," by M. Rivoalen, is a rather shorter article than we should have expected for such a large subject, compared with the length at which less comprehensive subjects have been treated. The illustrations are very inadequate, and are nearly all French; there is a curious travesty of the "Cottage Ouvrier Anglais," professing to be taken from a model in the Exhibition of 1878. Among the practical articles, "Matériel de Chantier" is treated at some length by M. C. Bazin, and "Menuiserie" rather inadequately by "E. R." M. Rivoalen treats of "Metope," which (we need hardly say) he regards as essentially *remplissage*; he omits to give the Greek form and derivation of the word. "Musée" and "Museum" are treated as separate subjects, the former being referred to museums of art, the latter to natural history museums. The most pleasing building under the heading of Musée is that at Laval, an excellent example of the graceful semi-Classic architecture often employed by the French on works of this class. M. H. Saladin contributes a long and elaborate article on Mahommedan architecture, and M. Charles Lucas finishes the volume with a biographical notice of the Mylne family of architects in this country. As a whole, the present volume of the Encyclopædia quite keeps up the standard of the former volumes.

Correspondence.

To the Editor of The Builder.

ARCHITECTURAL EDUCATION.

Sir,—In reply to the letter of Mr. Cole A. Adams, published in your last issue, we should be glad if you would allow us to make it quite clear that "the some half-dozen members of the A. A.," referred to in it, met Mr. Jackson and his friends but once, and at that meeting Mr. Jackson's letter to "A. A. Notes" was not so much as thought of or referred to in any way, and was not written at the request of the "some half dozen," as stated by Mr. Adams.

We will now proceed to give Mr. Adams the information he asks for. The meeting referred to was held on March 15, at 7, Storey's-gate, and the following members of the A. A. were present:—Messrs. C. H. Brodie, H. O. Cresswell, O. Fleming, E. S. Gale, W. Millard, T. E. Pryce, F. M. Simpson, and L. Stokes. The following

MURAL PAINTING: "CHRIST BEFORE PILATE." IN THE C

BLIN.—By Mr. N. H. J. Westlake, F.S.A.

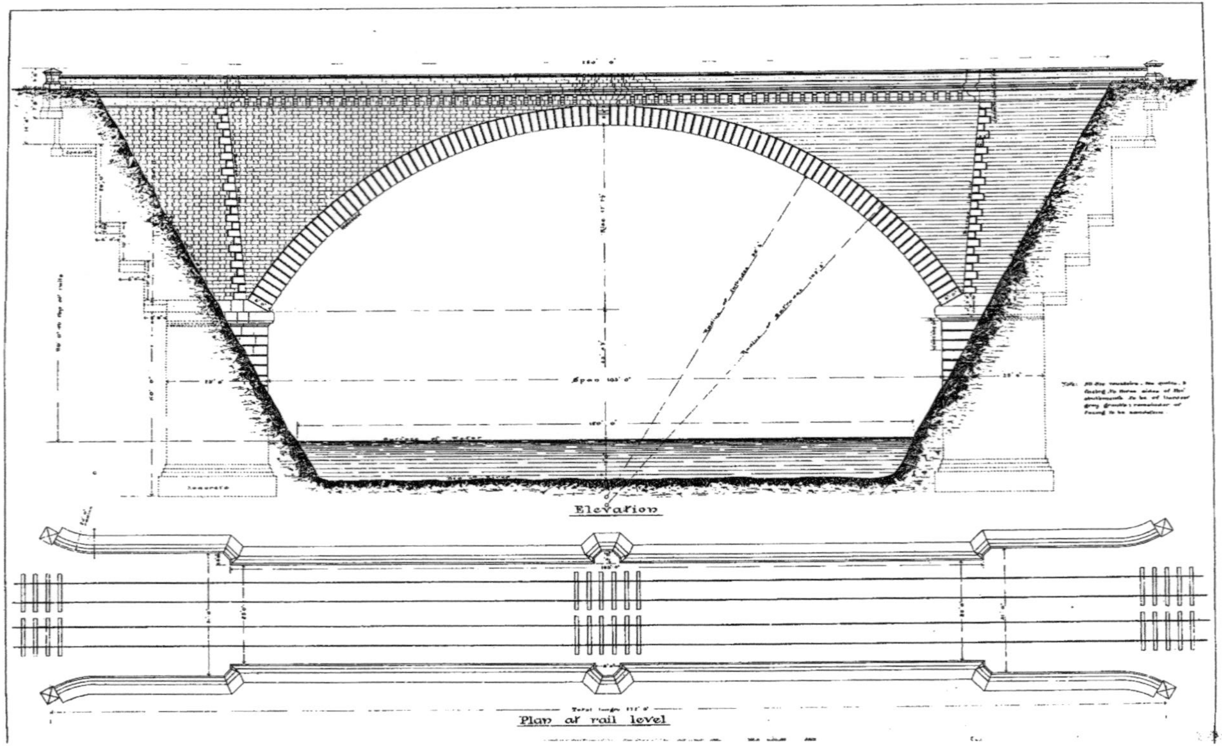

Elevation

Plan at rail level

PHOTO-LITHO SPRAGUE & CO. 4 & 5 EAST HARDING STREET, FETTER LANE, E.C.

DESIGN FOR A CHAPTER-HOUSE.—BY MR. JOHN BEGG, A.R.I.B.A.

Merit, Soane Medallion Competition, 1892.

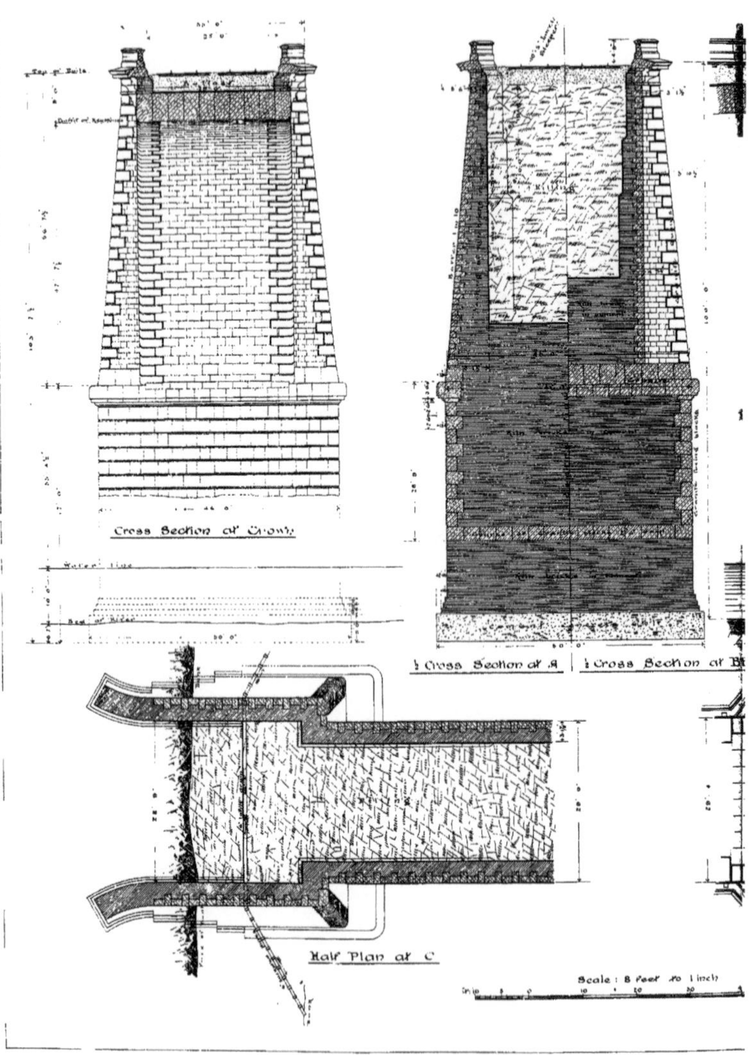

DESIGN FOR A STONE R

Grissell Gold Medal, 189?.

1892

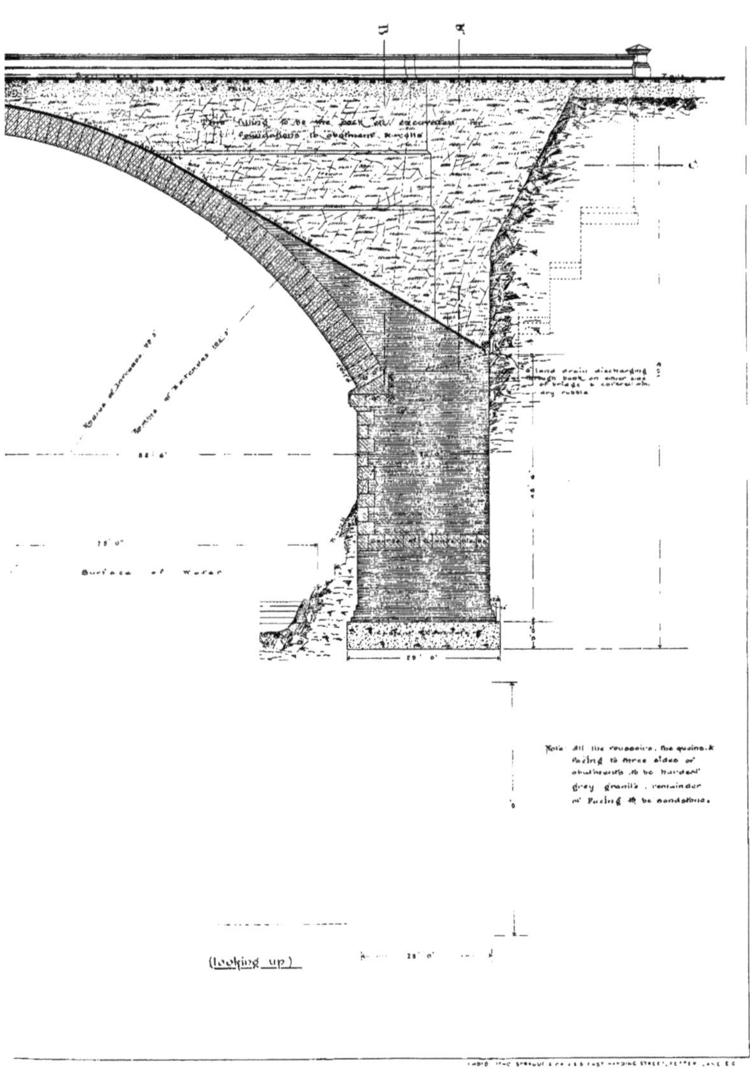

—By Mr. Harold Harlock.

ı-members of the A. A. were also present:— ssrs. R. T. Blomfield, T. G. Jackson, A.R A.. . Macarthey, E. S. Prior, and E. P. Warren; ı met with the object of ascertaining whether not Mr. Jackson and his friends would help ively the work of the A. A. Now, it was st clearly stated and understood that the mbers present simply attended in their vate capacity, and did not represent any one any one's views but their own. Mr. Jackson, refore, was not "led to suppose that they" he some half dozen—"expressed the voice the A. A.," as Mr. Adams assumes.

Mr. Jackson and his friends stated their lingness to help, but stipulated for the olute independence of the A. A. and its eme, and pointed out that this was langered by the frequent reference to the titute examinations made in our Brown k and Curriculum. Other points were cussed, but the independence of the A. A., trangely the very cry that Mr. Adams has v so curiously set up,—was the only one that s insisted upon.

The result of this meeting has since been mally laid before the A. A. Committee. Perps if Mr. Adams had known this he would have troubled you with his letter. We, vever, are glad that he did so, as we now ve it clearly recorded that Mr. Adams intends fight for the good "old traditions" and urdy independence" of the A. A., which is t what most of us desire.

Mr. Adams reminds us,—quite unnecessarily, hat the Institute has made a generous grant the funds of the A. A. We also are aware t several prominent members of the Institute ve likewise helped us generously; but Mr. ams appears to forget that on our subscrip- n list there are also such names as Sir F. ighton, P.R.A., R. Norman Shaw, R.A., Pro- sor Herkomer, R.A., Sir A. Blomfield, A.R.A., fessor Aitchison, T. G. Jackson, A.R.A., ners Clarke, B. Champneys, C. H. Mileham, l others.

Mr. Adams misrepresents Mr. Jackson—no ıbt, unintentionally—when he states that . Jackson wants us to "give up our present eme of studies." This is not the case, as h the exception of a few details, he and his nds generally approved the scheme.

It would be difficult, we imagine, to adopt a re "independent course" or one more calcu- d to serve the best interests of the Archi- ural Association, than to seek advice from apable men, without stopping to inquire to t body they may happen to belong.—We sir, &c.,

. H. BRODIE. WALTER MILLARD.
. O. CRESSWELL. THOS. EDWARD PRYCE.
WEN FLEMING. FRED. M. SIMPSON.
RNEST S. GALE. LEONARD STOKES.

"STEAM ROAD-ROLLING."

IR,—Will you kindly allow me space for a few arks on the letter from Mr. Robert Phillips, County Surveyor for Gloucestershire, published our issue of March 26 last?

r. Phillips makes a broad statement that eam-rolling cannot be defended on economy of ," and afterwards adds "it saves by consolida- without abrasion or trituration one-eighth of metal."

must, therefore, be apparent that if the cost of ng in a cubic yard of material, less the cost of -raking is less than one-eighth of the cost of material when spread on the road, economy is result.

illustration I here give actual figures from my district:—

age cost per cubic yard aterials used on main roads.	£.	s.	d.	Average cost of rolling in one cubic yard of material.	£.	s.	d.
rying, lity, ling, ling, king	0	4	3	Wages of driver, do. 2 sweepers, Water hauling, Coal, Stores, Depreciation of steam roller and water-carts	0	0	9
ading (includ- hauling m depots)	0	1	0				
	£0	5	3		0	0	9
e eighth =	0	0	7⅞	Less cost of after-raking..	0	0	2
					£0	0	7

saving of ⅞ of a penny is therefore made on y cubic yard of stone rolled in by the steam r.

is is taking Mr. Phillip's view, viz., that the g in materials is one-eighth. My own ex- ence, however, is that the saving is very much ter, and that one-quarter would be much nearer the mark. Taking this standard the above calculation would show a saving of nearly 9d. a cubic yard. ALLAN GREENWELL, A.M.I.C.E.

Surveyor to the Frome Highway Authority.

Frome, Somerset, April 8, 1892.

REMOVING OLD PAINT.

SIR,—Referring to Mr. H. F. White's letter in your issue of Saturday, permit me to state that I have found the following a very successful method of removing old paint from stonework. Take a fresh lime shell and strong black soap, mix together into a lather and lay on the paint. The mixture cannot be too strong for this purpose. Allow it to lie for two hours, and if at the end of that time the paint does not come clean away it can lie longer. A brush may be used gently. I hope this may serve Mr. White's purpose.—Yours, &c.,

D. MCARTHY.

SIR,—I beg to recommend the following as a sure remedy:—Three pounds of common washing soda, 4 lbs. of unslacked chalk of grey stone lime dissolved in boiling-water, and made about the thickness of cream, and applied hot with fibre brush and washed off with clean cold water with a fibre scrubbing brush. This applied two or three times will remove the paint and leave the stonework perfectly clean. The materials are cheap, and can be easily mixed in any quantity at the same rate.

GEO. GODBOLT.

The Student's Column.

WARMING BUILDINGS BY HOT WATER.

XVI.

BOILERS: INDEPENDENT.

INDEPENDENT boilers, as the term signifies, are those that need no brickwork in their setting (assuming that the floor upon which they stand is not inflammable), and all that is usually necessary is to place them in position, and connect with the nearest chimney by a pipe. If no brick chimney exists, then the flue pipe is carried up to a sufficient height to form a chimney in itself. The fire-box is situated below the boiler, within an iron casing, in fact, forms a base upon which the boiler rests.

As a rule, these boilers are not used in large undertakings, although there is no reason why they should not be. The boiler, however, in large horticultural works is placed in a pit, and in building works is similarly situated or given a little house or room to itself. In both these cases the brickwork is not objectionable, and it is understood that brick-set boilers are cheaper than the independent kind. In many forms of boilers brick-setting is really necessary to benefit by the flues that can be conducted around their outer surfaces. This cannot be done with independent boilers, and the other surface or shell cannot be made use of. This is the drawback to boilers of this kind, for we are not only unable to conduct the flames or hot gases around to the outer surface as they leave the fire, but this outer surface goes to waste a considerable amount of heat by radiation, if it is not covered with some poor heat-conducting compound.

Reference must again be made to Keith's boilers, as these, in this respect, differ from the ordinary independent patterns. The chief peculiarity in these boilers is that, being made of cast-iron, and in sections, the inner direct heating surfaces can be made of any design to best benefit by the heat; designs such as cannot be made with wrought plates. For instance, the sections of the Challenge boiler are chiefly made much resembling large gratings, the bars of which have a waterway through them from side to side of the jacket. By an arrangement of this kind we get such a great direct heating surface, within a small compass, that it is doubtful if the heated products would be of much value when they eventually escaped. By making such a number of surfaces, all obstructing the free passage of the heat, we can rob the air and gases, and make them of quite a low temperature at the outlet.

Every kind of independent boiler should, if economical results are aimed at, be covered with some bad heat-conducting material. The loss of heat from the outer surface of a boiler, when exposed, is really considerable. Brickwork would effectually prevent this, but independent boilers are intended to dispense with this. Silicate cotton would answer excellently, but it is somewhat difficult of application, upon upright boilers in particular. The material used by the writer is Leroy's composition, which, when once become accustomed to, is easy of application, and decidedly efficacious. We shall have to refer to the subject when speaking of main pipes when they are not used for radiating purposes, but merely to convey hot water to the branches.

There is a little care needed in fixing independent boilers. It is possible to fix a boiler so that the fuel will not burn properly, that is to say, the fire will not "draw"; and, doubtless, most of our readers know that it is quite possible to fix a boiler and its flue pipe, so that it suffers with a down draft.

It takes but little draft to work an independent boiler of any kind, as, supposing it is one having flues within it, these all ascend or incline towards the chimney, very different to fixing an independent or portable cooking range, having flues for the flame to be carried *down* beneath the oven, boiler, &c. If a brick chimney exists, a pipe is carried from the boiler into this chimney, either up through the mouth or bottom aperture, or through the brickwork of the breast. The flue pipe can be carried horizontally or ascending, but, without a skilled opinion, it is not desirable to make the pipe descend anywhere. If the pipe is carried up into the mouth of the chimney the opening must be closed up tightly around the pipe with sheet-iron. If the pipe is carried through the breast, the brickwork is made good around it and the lower opening quite closed up. The rule that has to be followed in fixing close fire-stoves, ranges, and boilers is to complete the work so that all the air passing into the chimney first passes through the fire. There should not be any means whatever for air to pass into the chimney without first passing through the burning fuel. This rule will bear relaxing a little, if necessary, with stoves and boilers which have no descending flues within them, but if it is convenient to strictly adhere to the rule it is better, and the work will then bear criticism.

Every independent boiler is provided with a ventilator arrangement in the ashpit door, which acts as a damper, by regulating the passage of air as the openings are opened or closed. This is correct in principle, but they are often badly fitted and not liked by the average attendant. It is much better to put a proper damper in the flue-pipe, near the boiler, and convenient for use. A throttle-damper (like a throttle-valve), a disc of metal in the pipe operated by a handle outside, is commonly used, but these are not very reliable. A sliding damper, which works in a little square casting, is better. They are cheap and easily obtained.

Independent boilers are more generally used in building works, which accounts for our explaining how they can be connected with existing brick flues, but if no brick chimney can be pressed into service, it becomes necessary to carry the pipe through an outer wall, and up outside to the top of the building. If a glass house, then the pipe need not be carried far; but if a residence or warehouse, the pipe may have to go a great height, and on this account every effort is made to utilise one of the chimneys of the building. In any case, we cannot hope to be free from down draught unless the chimney terminates above the building, and well above its highest part. It is impossible to even briefly treat the subject of down draughts here on account of the many points it involves, but it must be understood that unless a chimney terminates as high as stated, trouble will ensue. If some form of cap or wind-guard can be used and permit of the pipe terminating at some point below this, then it should be considered a fortunate circumstance due to some favourable condition, such as could not be expected to happen every time by any means. If the boiler is situated in a boiler-pit outside a glass-house, the question of down-draught is not considered so much, for, supposing down-draught does occur, it does no harm, and the gusts only last for a moment or two at a time in certain weathers. If, however, the boiler is in a residence, or building of almost any kind, the outbursts of smoke, &c., from the furnace would be intolerable, and would have to be prevented by some means. When using pipe-flues, it is very necessary that the joints be made air-tight. Common putty is best for this, it hardens with heat.

The smallest independent boilers we have are those heated by a gas-burner or lamp-flame, and which have the pipes, &c., complete as fig. 59. These are very useful appliances for the little greenhouses that are attached to small residences. They merely require the gas to be connected, and are then ready for use and act very effectively. If oil is used, no connexion whatever is necessary, but there is a general

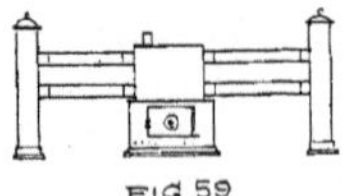

Fig. 59

aversion to oil for heating purposes, as a disagreeable odour is easily obtained. If the stove is of any but very small size, and is heated by gas, it is necessary to have a flue to it to convey away the products of combustion. This flue only requires to be of small size, but if it is to be effective it must be carried in the same manner as a smoke-flue; it is important to note this.

The products of combustion from a gas-burner are water and carbonic acid. Heat is also evolved, but this is more an effect of combustion than a product. In addition to the products named, there are certain gases which are the result of impurities or foreign substances in the gas. The particularly objectionable one of these is sulphurous acid, which comes from the small percentage of sulphur which the gasworks cannot wholly eliminate. This product is very hurtful indeed to plant life, and were it not for this the other and proper products could be borne to a considerable extent. One maker of these little appliances fits them with a purifier (as he terms it) which is intended to intercept and absorb this particular ill product.

There are several gas boilers made that are intended for larger and more practical purposes

Fig. 60

than that just referred to, one, as fig. 60, made by Fletcher & Co., being a good example. Keith also makes a good gas boiler, as fig. 61. Gas boilers are never made very large; it is considered to be more economical to use two or more of them,—a battery, so to speak, if there

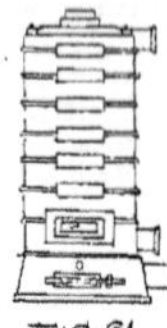

Fig. 61

is much pipe to be heated. Effective flues have to be provided with these larger sizes, and, as a rule, it is considered best if they can be fixed in a little outhouse of some kind, so that any escape of gas may prove harmless. The flue should also be outside the building for the same reason. If the flue exhibits a down-draught, a great deal of trouble will be occasioned by its extinguishing the gas-flame, or causing it to light back in the air chamber, if it be an atmospheric burner. It must not be forgotten that the water product will probably be condensed in the iron pipe, and a tiny stream will be constantly trickling down it. This can be easily disposed of.

These blocks were inadvertently omitted in the last chapter of "Student's Column." They are referred to in the table of the area of furnace bars in various types of boiler, page 293, *ante*.

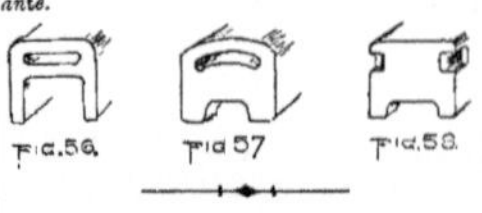

Fig. 56. Fig. 57 Fig. 58.

OBITUARY.

Mr. E. H. Burnell.—We regret that we have to announce the somewhat sudden death of Mr. Edward H. Burnell, F.R.I.B.A., of Bedford-row, W.C., which occurred on the 5th inst. at his residence, 15, Orrett-terrace, Hyde-park. Mr. Burnell carried on for many years an extensive practice as a surveyor in the metropolis and elsewhere. He was the senior member of the Surveyors' Association, and for many years its secretary, and only nine months ago he retired from his appointment as Surveyor to the Skinners' Company, on the ground of failing health, after having filled that office for nearly thirty years. On his retirement the Company unanimously voted him a large retiring pension. He was elected a Fellow of the Institute of Architects in 1877.

GENERAL BUILDING NEWS.

Lincoln Cathedral.—We hear from Lincoln that the committee appointed to consider the form which the proposed memorial to the late Sir Charles Anderson should take, have unanimously decided in favour of the restoration of the chantry chapel of Bishop Fleming in the north aisle of the retrochoir of the Minster. Bishop Fleming died in 1431, but, according to the fashion of the day, his chantry was erected and his monument executed previous to his death. It is a good specimen of Early Perpendicular, having three windows to the north, with rich buttresses and parapets and panelled work. But the whole has been long in a miserable state of squalor and decay, reflecting little credit on the members of Lincoln College, Oxford, of which Fleming was the founder. The proposed work may be a good one in itself, but we fail to see the appropriateness of the restoration of one man's chantry chapel as a memorial to another, at the distance of four centuries and a half, and we shall be curious to know in what way it will be identified with Sir Charles Anderson. The restoration, if done at all, should have been taken in hand by Lincoln College, "in priam fundatoris memoriam."

Poor Law Buildings, Croydon.—The foundation stone of the new Board room, offices, and out-relief station for the Croydon Union was laid on the 5th inst. by Mr. J. Farley, Chairman of the Board of Guardians. The architect is Mr. Fredk. West, of Croydon, and the contractor Mr. Alfred Bullock, also of Croydon. The cost of the building will be about 6,500*l*.

Hospital for Consumption, Manchester.—On the 30th ult. the new out-patient department of the Manchester Hospital for Consumption and Diseases of the Throat and Chest was opened by Miss Balfour. The building is situate in Hardman-street, Deansgate. It is twice the size of the former one, which occupied a portion of the same site. The new waiting-hall (capable of seating 200 patients), the entrance to which is from Hardman-street, is 40 ft. by 40 ft. It is lighted by an octagonal dome 30 ft. in height, which terminates in a turret for the extraction of vitiated air. Round the hall are grouped nine consulting and examination rooms, each having double doors and windows. The new dispensary is placed at the junction of Byrom-street with Byrom-place. There is also a patients' exit therefrom into Byrom-street. Fresh air is admitted into the basement, and after passing over hot-water coils, is driven through underground flues to the various rooms by a fan, the motive power being supplied by a gas-engine. The work has been executed by Messrs. Wilson & Toit, of Hulme, from the designs and under the superintendence of Messrs. Pennington & Bridgen, architects, at a cost of upwards of 2,500*l*.

Wesleyan Church, Wolverton. — The foundation-stones of the new Wesleyan Church which is being erected at Wolverton, North Bucks, were laid on the 2nd inst. The new building will seat about 550 persons, and will involve an outlay of 2,300*l*. The style is Early English, and the architect is Mr. Ewen Harper, of Birmingham, and the builders Messrs. H. & C. Burden, of Chipping Norton.

Club Buildings, Glasgow.—The plans of the new Conservative club-house to be erected at the corner of Bothwell and Wellington-streets, Glasgow, were on the 31st ult. passed by the Dean of Guild Court. The drawings have been prepared by Mr. R. W. Edis, architect, London. The external design of the building is Scotch Renaissance, freely treated, with projecting bays and oriels, and crows'-feet gables, flanked by small turrets. The main entrance in Bothwell-street is flanked with red granite columns. This entrance is on the street level, and leads into an outer hall, from which access is gained to the main ground floor level by a flight of steps. On this floor are the morning or reading-room, 46 ft. by 25 ft., facing Bothwell-street, with two bay windows; the dining-room 73 ft. by 25 ft., with the usual service arrangements communicating with the kitchen, still-room, &c., and the lavatories and cloak-rooms. On the first floor is a smoking-room, 70 ft. by 25 ft. fronting Bothwell-street, with three bay windows. Fronting Wellington-street is a library and private billiard and dining-rooms. On the second floor, above the smoking-room, is the billiard-room, also 70 ft. by 25 ft., and a card-room. There are twenty-five bed-rooms for the use of the members, and, in addition, there are dressing and bath-rooms on a mezzanine floor. In the basement is the kitchen, with a ceiling 22 ft. high, also the servants' hall, sitting-rooms for the maids and men servants, wine cellars, &c. On the mezzanine floor above the basement are the steward's office, close to the servants' and tradesmen's entrance in Wellington-street, housekeeper's rooms, still-room, and still-room maids' sitting-room, upper servants' dining-room, men servants' dormitories, &c. The building is to be of brick, faced with red sandstone, and it is proposed that all the floors shall be of fire-proof construction, and all partitions to be of brick and cement.

Restoration of All Saints' Chuch, Hilton, Dorset.—On the 28th ult. the Church of All Saints, Hilton, Dorset, was re-opened after restoration. The architect for the restoration states that the principal works that have been carried out under the present restoration are the taking down and rebuilding, stone by stone, as before, the whole of the south arcade and the wall of the south aisle as far as the porch. The shoring up of the chancel arch and south wall, &c., to allow the rebuilding of the pier on the south side of the chancel arch, which was crippled and out of the upright. In carrying out this work the pier was found to have contained the steps which formerly led to the rood-loft. The masonry of this pier was in a very unsafe condition, partly from the removal of the ground under the foundations in the formation of vaults and graves to a depth of nearly 6 ft., and also on account of the alterations that have taken place in it at various times. The original openings, at the bottom and top of the staircase, seem to have been walled up, and two more (doorway) openings found, one on the south side of the pier leading from the south transept and one on the west side of the pier, the cell of which was about 3 ft. 6 in. from the floor. All four openings were, when found, walled up, and also the interior of the pier, with solid masonry. All four doorways have now been opened out, and provision made for the stability of the pier by inserting slabs of stone to bond it together, and, in order to obtain a sufficiently firm footing, it was necessary to go down to a depth of 6 ft. below the floor of the church. The perpendicular roofs of the north and south aisles have been reconstructed and restored, care having been taken to preserve and work in again all the old timber that was sound enough to leave. A new open hammer-beam roof of pitch-pine replaces the former roof of the nave, which had a round plaster ceiling, and which was erected about 100 years ago. None of the oak of the original nave roof was found. During the progress of the works a few fragments of Norman architecture have been found. The tower arch has been repaired and made good, where it had been cut away and mutilated for the housing of the gallery timbers. The font, which was formerly placed under the gallery, has been cleaned and repaired, and refixed in the centre of the tower, the walls of which have been pointed and made good, and an ornamental tile floor laid down. The panel paintings of Apostles and Saints, which were before fixed on the north and south walls of the chancel, have been cleaned and placed in oak frames, and refixed on the north and south walls of the tower. The whole of the floors of the nave, aisles, and vestry have been re-laid with pitch-pine block flooring on a bed of concrete. The church has been re-seated with pitch-pine framed open seats. The old pulpit has been cleaned, and the carved panels repaired, and the moulded stone base, which was before buried under the floor, replaced, and the pulpit again fixed on it. A new vestry, with heating chamber under it, has been built on the north side of the tower. The exterior masonry of the church has been repaired and made good. The missing parapet, &c., on the north aisle restored, and the defective gargoyles replaced. The south porch, which projects into the church, has been made good, the floor laid with tiles, and the roof renewed. The porch has a ground roof of Ham Hill stone, and on two of the bosses, at the intersections of the ribs of the tracery, are carved the arms of Milton Abbey and the arms of Abbotsbury. On removing the ivy from off the wall of the south aisle to take it down, certain ornamental panels, with initials cut in them, were found. These have all been replaced as near as possible in the position in which they were found. At the south-east angle of the parapet on the south aisle was fixed a stone sundial, bearing the date 1695. This has been re-fixed in its original position. The roofs of the aisles have been covered with lead ing on false roofs, raised above the old oak ings. The masonry of the tower has been aired, and the defective stonework made good. windows of the south aisle and transept and t window of tower have been filled in with new hedral glazing. The church has been heated h hot-water apparatus by Mr. Pond, of Bland-. The chancel of the church has also been ored by the Ecclesiastical Commissioners, and ew open-timber roof fixed, the chancel fitted up h oak reading-desks and choir-benches, and the r paved with tiles. This part of the work has n done under the direction of Mr. Ewan istian, the Architect to the Ecclesiastical Com-sioners. The whole of the work to the nave, es, &c., has been carried out by Messrs. Merrick oc, of Glastonbury, and under the direction of Walter J. Fletcher, F.R.I.B.A., of Wimborne.

ESTORATION OF THE OLD CHURCH OF HADDING-.—The restoration of the Old Church of Had-gton, which has been in progress for the last hteen months, is, says the *Scotsman*, now all but plete. The church is built on the cruciform n, with aisles in nave and chancel. When the posed restoration of the building was under sideration about a couple of years ago, it was posed not only to restore the nave, but also the ruinous portion of the structure,—the chancel transepts. Owing chiefly to the large expendi-e involved, the restoration of the nave was ne proceeded with. The building is an mple of Late Ecclesiastical Scottish Gothic. the work of restoration, it was necessary to in with the flooring, which has now been brought uch a level as to admit of the bases of the old ars being exposed to view. The former galleries, ich were placed round three sides of the nave, e disappeared, and also the old box-like pews high wooden pulpit. The former entrances on north side of the nave, which were alterations the original building, have been closed up, and ess to the church is now obtained by the west rway, and by a new doorway in the east wall nediately below the central tower. These door-ys open into porches enclosed with oak screen-rk. In the north-east corner of the nave a small ing-room or vestry is screened off by oak-work. d it been possible, galleries would probably e been done away with altogether in the re-red building; but it was found that, without the ra accommodation which they provided, the re-site number of sittings could not be obtained. s accounts for the existence of an east and t gallery in the restored church. That at the t-end, above which is a large stained-glass dow, is devoted to the purposes of sittings; the er, which is on a smaller scale, is partly for the ommodation of the choir and of the organ, with ch the church will for the first time be provided. supporting beams of the galleries rest on stone els with carved foliage, inserted into the nave rs and walls. The sockets are divided into lded panels, while the gallery fronts are of oak, hed with tracery, niches, and carved foliage. galleries are reached by oak stairs, and the gallery is so designed that part of it overhangs, canopy, the marble platform on which the munion-table stands. The church, which accommodate about 1,000, has been re-d in modern style. Open oak-benches been substituted for the former square . The nave is laid with encaustic tiles, e the remaining portion of the floor is laid with l-blocks on a foundation of cement and alt. All the old plaster work has been cleared e walls, and the paint has been removed from pillar, the walls having been pointed and ired where necessary. It was found that ing could be done to alter the construction of plaster ceiling, which, however, has been ured in a tone corresponding with the walls. pulpit stands next the north-east pillar of the , and the font occupies a corresponding ion on the south side. They are executed in hed Corncockle stone. The pulpit rests on polished red marble shafts, which rest on cular disc. It is entered by a staircase h curves round the old pillar, and is enriched perforated tracery, railing, and carved ls. The platform under the east gallery on h the Communion table stands is of polished marble, and the steps to it are of marble. table rests on carved pillars. The font, d near the south-east pillar, rests on two ts of steps in octagonal form, and has polished le shafts, arches, and carved foliage. The lectern carved stone pillar with a spreading carved and capital, and twisted wreath. On the top of haft, and serving as a book-rest, is a polished eagle moulded by Mr. Starkie Gardner, of on. The pulpit, font, lectern, and communion were executed by Mr. W. Birnie Rhind, tor. The organ will have an oak case in ng with the gallery fronts, and enriched with etted pinnacles, tracery, and carving. The ng of the building is by small pipes on the pressure system, and provision has been made ghting the church by gas. Two gifts of stained windows have already been intimated, and restoration of the large window in the south ept is now being proceeded with. The de-ng of the whole work was entrusted to Messrs. & Henderson, architects, Edinburgh. During the progress of the restoration, a doorway leading from the south-east isle to the turret, giving access to the roof, was discovered. The doorway has been carefully restored, and is now in use. Messrs. W. & J. Kirkwood, Edinburgh, were the principal con-tractors, and Mr. Laird acted as clerk of works.

NEW COURT-HOUSE, BIRKDALE, LANCASHIRE.—On the 7th inst. the new court-house which has been erected in Weld-road, Birkdale, by the County Council, was formally opened. The building is in the English Renaissance style, and is constructed of brick, freely relieved with carved stone panels and cornices. Divided into three blocks, the adminis-trative block occupies the centre, on the south side of which is the house for the inspector, while on the north side is the sergeant's house. The central block contains, on the ground floor, charge-office, constables' day-room, and four cells; and on the first floor are the magistrates' room, apartments for solicitors and witnesses, and a court-room, 40 ft. long by 28 ft. wide, with accommodation for nine magistrates. The building was erected from the designs of Mr. William Verity, architect, Wigan, and the contractor was Mr. George Johnson, Sea-forth.

CO-OPERATIVE PREMISES, JARROW.—On the 26th ult. new co-operative premises, which have been erected at the corner of North-street and Market-square, Jarrow, were opened. The new premises occupy the site of the old stores, together with that of two dwelling-houses, and cover an area of about 5,227 superficial ft. They are four stories in height, and contain on the ground floor six shops. On the first floor are flour and grocery warehouse and tea-room, work-rooms for tailors, milliners, and shoemakers, and also a large millinery show-room. There are also cellars in the basement. Communication between the different departments has been provided by staircases and corridors; lifts and hoists being also fixed in various positions. The lecture-hall on the second floor is 84 ft. by 36 ft., and 25 ft. high, and will accommodate between 600 and 700 people. The building is warmed throughout by a low-pressure hot-water heating apparatus, fitted by Messrs. Dinning & Cooke, of Newcastle. The building is to be lighted by electricity. The dynamo will be driven by a 16 horse-power gas-engine, which will also work the hoists, lifts, and other machinery about the premises. The building, which is of red Normandy bricks with Denwick stone dressings, is Renaissance in character, and has on the North-street side a clock-tower about 65 ft. in height. The total cost of the building will be upwards of 7,000*l*. Mr. Pringle, of Gateshead, was the con-tractor. The electric lighting has been entrusted to Messrs. King, Brown, & Co., of Edinburgh, and was carried out under the superintendence of Mr. Alfred Flood; the plumbing and sanitary work, together with the tiling, by Messrs. Tweddle & Co., of Newcastle. The plastering and painting have been in the hands of Messrs. Dodds and Hopper, respectively, both of Jarrow; Mr. George Gordon acting as clerk of works. The whole of the work has been carried out from the plan, and under the supervision, of the architect, Mr. J. Walter Hanson, of Jarrow.

PROPOSED RESTORATION OF BRISTOL CATHEDRAL.—According to the *Bristol Times and Mirror*, the Dean and Chapter of Bristol Cathedral have been considering matters relative to the restoration of the Cathedral. It has been decided to take in hand at once the restoration of the Cathedral as a whole, and not do the work in sections. The plan to be adopted is that of the late Mr. Street, and it is to be carried out under the direction of Mr. Pearson. It embraces the restoration of the central tower, the lady chapel, the re-arrangement of the whole of the choir, involving the restoration of the older lady chapel, and a new organ, that is to be divided, and not to be placed on the screen. An approxi-mate estimate of the cost which Mr. Pearson has furnished is 20,000*l*. Another matter to be taken in hand is the transformation of an apartment at the south end of the cloisters into a vestry for the minor canons, for which work separate estimates have been received.

FOREIGN AND COLONIAL.

FRANCE.—The Government will shortly give com-missions for bronze statues of the following men: Vergniaud, Danton, Casimir-Perier, Ledru-Rollin, and Gambetta. These statues which have been asked for by the Bureau of the Chamber of Deputies, will ornament the Committee-room of the Bourbon Palace, where M. Dalou's bas-relief of Mirabeau and the tiers-etat is.——The large room in the Court of Appeal has just been opened. It was begun by M. Coquart and finished by M. Paul B'oudel, who, after the ceremony was presented with the Legion of Honour.——M. Adrien Moreau artist, has also been decorated on the occasion of the Exhibition of Pastellites.——The jury of archi-tecture is composed as follows, for the Salon des Champs Elysées: MM. Coquart, Pascal, Garnier, Raulin, Daumet, Ginain, Guadet, Mayeux, Normand, Loviot, Vaudremer, Corroyer—supplementary jurors, MM. Ancelet and Paulin.——The administration is going to ask the Municipal Council for the neces-sary funds to carry out the restoration of the Church of St. Eustache, which is one of the most beautiful specimens of the Renaissance. It is calculated that it will require about 430,000 franc to restore it thoroughly.——An interesting e hibition of the works of Mdlle. Abbéma is announced, to be held in the Galerie Georges Petit.——The Municipal Council have just voted the necessary sum for the construction of a bridge over the Seine, between the Pont de Greville and the viaduct of the Pont du Jour. This bridge will connect the quarters of Auteuil and Javel, and will be called the "Pont Mirabeau."——The sculptor Fremiet, the decorator Jambon, and the medal-engraver, Chaplain, have just been elected members of the Commission for the decora-tion of the Hôtel de Ville, in place of MM. Chapu, Lavastre, and Bailly deceased.——The sculptor Etienne Leroux has lately finished a statue of Surcouf, the celebrated sailor, which is to be placed in the town of St. Malo.——The military authorities are proposing to demolish the old forti-fications of Lille, which extend from the Porte St. André to the Porte de Louis XIV. The existin enclosures and the moats are to be replaced by a simple wall with a moat and slope, which will allow the construction of a large exterior boulevard, thus giving light and air to the old quarters of this populous town. In consequence of this plan there will be several large works commenced, namely, the enlargement of the Hospital St. Sauveur, the General Hospital, two large barracks, and the station of the Chemin-de-fer du Nord.——A monu-ment to Dr. Coste is to be inaugurated this week at Villes-en-Michaille (Ain). He was chief sur-geon in the army during the war of the American Independence and the first Revolution.——M. Martel, senator and late minister, has just left a most important artistic collection to the town of St. Omer.——The permanent ex-hibitions of local works of art at Rouen have not been satisfactory during the last two years. The committee have, therefore, decided not to hold them any longer.——The late Duc de Trevise has left to the town of Ajaccio, in Corsica, an in-teresting collection of works of art and historical souvenirs of the time of Napoleon.——An exhibition of modern decorative art of Lorraine is in course of preparation at Nancy.——The death of M. Thomas de Barbarin is announced as having taken place in Paris at the age of seventy-one years. He was a pupil of Delaroche and Scheffer. Since 1846 he has annually exhibited in the Salon.——A young artist of considerable talent, M. Charles Armand Etienne Thomas, has died in Paris, aged thirty-six. He confined himself principally to landscapes and flowers, and had been a pupil of Leclaire. He had obtained a medal of the third class in 1886 for a beautiful composition, entitled "Veille de Fête," bought by the town of Havre. He obtained an honourable mention in the Universal Exhibition of 1889.——We have to notice the death of M. Jules Louis Haro, at the age of thirty-nine. He had studied painting with M. Carolus Duran, and en-graving with M. Hedouin. He was an artist from whom much was expected.

SWEDEN AND DENMARK.—At the last meeting of the Swedish Slöjd, or Handicraft Society, Herr E. G. Folcker read a paper on English wall-papers, illus-trated by numerous specimens of such.——The pro-posal to sell the two wings of the Norwegian Minis-terial Hotel in Stockholm for building purposes is strongly disapproved by a committee appointed to examine into the matter. The building is one of the most imposing in the Swedish capital.——A fine new thoroughfare is in course of construction, running right through the city from the Nybrovik to the Träsk Market. Its construction involves the demo-lition of numerous unsightly "rookeries."——King Oscar has presented to the National Library the valuable and copiously-illustrated work "Hand-buch der Architektur," by Prof. J. Durm, of Carls-ruhe.——The leading land-owning associations of Copenhagen have framed a grand scheme for the rebuilding of a large portion of the old town and the construction of a wide new avenue right through the city.

MISCELLANEOUS.

THE PROJECTED NEW RAILWAY TO LONDON.—The Committee of the House of Commons on the pro-posed extension of the Manchester, Sheffield, and Lincolnshire Railway to London met on Tuesday last, when, after hearing further evidence, the room was cleared and the Committee deliberated. On the readmission of the counsel and parties, the Chairman (Sir Richard Paget) stated (says the *Times* report) that the Committee were unanimously of opinion that the preamble of the Bill was proved, but that, as there were certain incidental matters which would have to be discussed,—such as the report of the Home Office upon the rehousing of the displaced working-class population (the recommendations upon which point the Committee were inclined to accept), together with the reports of the Local Government Board and of the Com-missioners of Woods and Forests,—the Committee would adjourn until April 28, in the hope that nearly all the matters referred to might be satis-factorily arranged in the interval.

COMPETITIONS, CONTRACTS, AND PUBLIC APPOINTMENTS.

COMPETITIONS.

Nature of Work.	By whom Advertised.	Premium.	Designs to be delivered.
*Valuation of Property	Stockport Union	....	May 2
*Town Hall and Public Offices	Llanelly Loc. Bd.	50 and 20 guineas	June 15
*Barrett-Browning Memorial Clock Tower and Institute, Ledbury	The Committee	20*l*. 10*l*.	No date

CONTRACTS.

Nature of Work or Materials.	By whom Required.	Architect, Surveyor, or Engineer.	Tenders to be delivered
*Dwelling, Stores, &c. at Lighthouse, Gibraltar	Corp. of Trinity House	*Official*	April 16
Sewerage Works, Harth'll	Worksop U.R.S.A.	W. T. Brown	April 19
Road Materials (1,500 yds.)	Penarth Local Board	J. Court	do.
Additions to School, West Haddon, Northampton	G. Harday	....	April 20
Dwelling-house, Low Dryburn, Durham	J. F. Bell	W. Cook	do.
Cooperage Works, Blackfriars-road, Elgin, N.B.	G. Gorrad	....	April 21
Five Dwelling-houses, Crownhill, near Plymouth	S. Revell	J. H. Keats	do.
*Broken Guernsey Granite	Vestry of St. Matthew, Bethnal Green	*Official*	do.
Wesleyan Chapel, Stockdale Wath, Cumberland	Wm. Gibson	....	April 22
Brass Foundry and Workshop, Peltone-lane, Halifax	....	Lister & Sons	do.
*New Roads, Sewers, &c. Surbiton		S. Mather	do.
Chapel Gates, Walls, &c. Cemetery	Abergavenny Bur. Bd.	E. A. Johnson	April 23
*Building Manholes, Supply of Granite, &c.	Mortlake Dist. Highway Board	H. Richards	do.
Tower (2nd portion) of Church, Irthlingborough, Northants	Rev. R. Bleese	Talbot-Brown & Fisher	April 24
Street Work	Warrington T. C.	T. Longdin	April 25
Roadmaking and Draining	Hanley Town Council	J. Lobley	do.
*Asphalte Paving	Portsmouth U. S. A.	*Official*	do.
*New Sewer in Oil Change	Commrs. of Sewers	do.	April 26
*Painters' and Plumbers' Work	do.	do.	do.
*Engineers' Work	do.	do.	do.
*Carpenters' Work	do	do	do.
*Paving Works	Willesden Local Board	O. Claude Robson	do.
*Labourers' Dwellings	Manchester Corp.	J. Allison	do.
Brick Sewer	Halifax Corporation	E. R. S. Escott	April 27
*Taking Down and Rebuilding Kingsford Bridge	Essex County Council	P. J. Sheldon	do.

CONTRACTS.—*Continued.*

Nature of Work or Materials.	By whom Required.	Architect, Surveyor or Engineer.	Tenders to be delivered.
*Postal Sorting Office, Sheffield	Com. of H.M. Works	*Official*	April 2[illegible]
Widening Viaduct over River Taff, Cardiff	G. W. R.	do.	do.
*New Lighthouse, Withernsea	Corp. of Trinity House	do.	April 2[illegible]
*Police Station, Courts, Offices, &c.	Blackpool Corp.	J. Wolstenholme	do.
*Foundations of Block I., Record Office Extension	Com. of H M. Works	*Official*	April 2[illegible]
*Roadmaking Works, Drains, &c.	Tonbridge U.R.S.A.	W. Oakley	do.
Additions to School, near Cardiff	Pentyrch Sch. Bd.	Bruce Vaughan	April 3[illegible]
*Wrought-iron Railings	Islington Vestry	J. P. Barber	May [illegible]
*Stoneware Pipe Sewer	do.	do.	do.
*Making-up Part of Pinner-road	Harrow Loc. Bd.	R. R. Capon	May [illegible]
*Entrance Gates and Iron Railings	Bristol S.A.	F. Ashmead	May [illegible]
*Refitting Bath-rooms, &c. Western Fever Hospital	Metro. Asylums Bd.	A. & C. Harston	do.
*Two Shops and Five Houses, Hammersmith	....	F. & W. Stocker	do.
*Painting and Decorating Part of Town Hall	Leeds Corporation	T. Hewson	May [illegible]
*Alteration at Cane Hill Asylum	London County Council Asylums Committee	*Official*	May [illegible]
School Buildings, Broughton, Kettering	....	Hert & Dawson	No date
House, &c. Rose Garth, Gilsland, Carlisle	....	T. Taylor Scott	do.
Rebuilding "Belmont," Exeter	R. B. West	E. H. Harbottle	do.
Dwelling-house and Shop, Stanley, nr. Oldham	J. W. Moffitt	E. F. W. Liddle	do.
New Schools, Tanfield Lea, Newcastle	Tanfield Sch. Bd.	Davidson & Kendle	do.
Weaving Sheds, Brompton, Northallerton	W. & J. Pattison	Thos. Winn	do.
Theatre, Mexborough, Sheffield	....	Geo. White	do.
Six Dwelling-houses, Mosley Bar, Thorpe Hesley	Wm. Mallinson	....	do.
*Temporary Iron Building	Sch. Bd. for London	*Official*	do.
Road-work, Cogan & Llandough	Penarth Loc. Bd.	J. Court	do.
Alterations, "Old Fleece Inn," Gateshead	White & Bennett	B. F. Simpson	do.

PUBLIC APPOINTMENTS.

Nature of Appointment.	By whom Advertised.	Salary.	Applications to be in
*Builder's Clerk	Westminster Vestry	100*l*.	April [illegible]
*Borough Engineer	Salford Corp.	500*l*.	April [illegible]
*Assistant Borough Surveyor	Borough of Maidstone	[illegible]*l*.	do.
*Clerk of Works	Pwllheli Corp.	Not stated	April [illegible]
*Office Assistant	Lambeth Vestry	2*l*.	April [illegible]
*Three District Superintendents	do.	3*l*. 3s.	do.

Those marked with an Asterisk (*) are advertised in this Number. *Competitions*, p. iv. *Contracts*, pp. iv., vi., & viii. *Public Appointments*, p. xviii. & xix.

A "Keyed" Casing for Electric-Light Wires.—The accompanying gives the section of a new construction of electric-light casing, which has been registered by Mr. George G. Sarney. It will be seen that when the casing is used on the walls of buildings, and fixed flush with the plaster, the capping acts as a "key" for it. When so fixed, should it be necessary to look to, or alter the wires, the capping can easily be removed without breaking away the edges of the plaster. In buildings in the

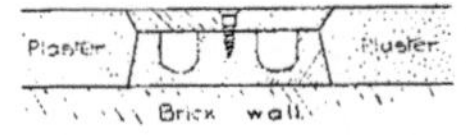

course of erection the casing would serve as a ground for plasterers to gauge to, and it is claimed that it would also prove useful and economical to contractors when wiring buildings after the plastering has been finished; because the chases cut in the walls can be so much smaller than when ordinary casing is used.

Cornwall County Council.—Mr. Silvanus Trevail, architect, has been re-elected Chairman of the County Sanitary Committee, the headquarters of which is to be located at Truro. The Housing of the Working Classes Act, 1890, and other sanitary legislation was under the consideration of the Committee, with the result that it was decided to again call the attention of the various Medical Officers of Health and Sanitary Inspectors of the county to the new duties imposed upon them by these Acts. It was also decided for the Chairman to proceed with the digest of the various medical officers' annual reports preparatory to the June meeting of the County Council.

Sanitary Specialities at Chelsea.—Messrs. Thomas Crapper & Co., of Marlborough-road, Chelsea, have just completed some extensive additions and improvements at their works. The additions include an admirably-lighted and arranged workshop for brass-finishing, &c., the lathes being driven by an 8 horse-power "Otto" gas-engine. There is also a new and very complete foundry for brass, gun-metal, and other castings, and a considerable addition of warehouse room, so that the firm are able to keep in stock a large supply of sheet-lead, pipe, traps, sanitary stoneware and white ware, rain-water goods, closets, urinals, lavatories, &c. In addition, Messrs. Crapper & Co. have been able to materially enlarge their showrooms, enabling them to readily demonstrate the good points of many of their specialities. Amongst these we may single out for special mention the "Kenon" disconnecting trap, which we described in a former volume of the *Builder*; an improved patent self-rising closet-seat, specially adapted for a closet used also as a slop-receiver; an improved and really "silent-syphon" water-waste preventer, fitted with Rawlings's patent silencing air-tubes,—an invention of much merit; and a new pedestal-closet with patent lead connexion, which seems to merit attention.

Relative Wear of Various Floor Materials.—According to the *Thonind Zeitung*, some recent tests with various floor materials as to their relative resistance to wear have resulted as follows:—

	Coefficiency of Wear.
Basalt	7·1
Porphyry	6·7
Granite	8·3
White marble	24·4
White sandstone	72·7
Parquetry slabs from G. Behne, Magdeburg	15·3
Plaster composition by "Rabitz" patent	49·2
Portland cement: One part cement to one part normal sand	15·3
One ditto to two ditto	17·1
One ditto to three ditto	32·4
One ditto to four ditto	53·1
One ditto to five ditto	124·2

It would, therefore, appear that a mixture of cement and sand constitutes the most enduring of floor materials. It should be added that the above tests were carried out on a cast-iron disc coated with emery dust.

London School Board *v.* Charles Wall.—The above action was referred to Mr. Macvicar Anderson, who has just awarded the School Board 208*l*. for deviations made by the contractor in the erection of the Flora Gardens Schools at Hammersmith. The arbitrator decided that each party should pay their own costs.

Surveyorship, Bootle.—We understand that Mr. J. A. Crowther, Borough Surveyor of Nelson, has just been appointed by the Streets and Buildings Committee of the Corporation of Bootle as surveyor of that borough. The salary attached to the office is 350*l*. per annum. There were ninety-three applications for the vacant office.

The Railways of the World.—According to the *Almanach de Gotha*, the total length of the railways open for traffic at the end of last year was 221,534 kilomètres, Germany heading the list with 43,003 kilomètres, France following with 36,697 kilomètres, and Great Britain third with 32,304 kilomètres, whilst the smallest railway net is that of Greece, viz. 602 kilomètres. The average length of railway in Europe per 1,000,000 inhabitants is 642 kilomètres, and the average length per 1,000 square kilomètres, 1,000 kilomètres. Germany possesses 71 kilomètres of railway per 1,000 square kilomètres of area, and 909 kilomètres per 1,000,000 inhabitants; whilst France comes next, with 71 kilomètres and 939 kilomètres respectively, Great Britain being third with 102 kilomètres and 862 kilomètres. Norway comes last as regards length of railway and size of country, viz., 417 kilomètres per 1,000 square kilomètres, but stands comparatively high in proportion to population, viz., 723 kilomètres per 1,000,000 inhabitants. The United States possesses 260,0[illegible] kilomètres of railway, although having one 63,000,000 inhabitants, as against 221,000 kilomètres to 345,000,000 inhabitants in Europe, making no less than 4,127 kilomètres per 1,000,000 inhabitants, and 34 kilomètres per 1,000 square kilomètres of area.

The Euphrates Valley Railway.—A syndicate of German, French, and Austrian financiers h[illegible] applied to the Sultan for a concession for a railway from Scutari to Bagdad through the Euphrates Valley, with an eventual extension to the Persian Gulf and India. The cost of the former railway [illegible] estimated at about 12,000,000*l*.

MEETINGS.

Wednesday, April 20.

British Archæological Association.—(1) Miss Russ[illegible] on "A Discovery in Rome in Relation to Mythology [illegible] Britain." (2) Mr. H. Syer Cuming on "The Ho[illegible] Head: The Nuptial Cup of Sussex." 8 p.m.

Royal Meteorological Society.—Mr. W. H. Dines [illegible] "Anemometer Comparisons." 7 p.m.

Builders' Foremen and Clerks of Works' Institution.—Quarterly meeting of the members. 8.30 p.m.

Friday, April 22.

Institution of Civil Engineers (Students' Meeting).—Mr. E. L. Hill on "The Speed and Power of Locomotives." 7.30 p.m.

Saturday, April 23.

Society of Antiquaries.—Anniversary meeting. [illegible] p.m.

Edinburgh Architectural Association.—Visit[illegible] Callender House.

RECENT PATENTS:

ABSTRACTS OF SPECIFICATIONS.

7,432.—Brick-moulding Machinery: *E. Breeth[illegible]*—This invention relates to improvements in machin[illegible] for moulding bricks. In order to compress clay in[illegible] the moulds, each mould as it is to be filled, is broug[illegible] below an opening in the bottom of a box within wh[illegible] a plunger works, which is forced down when the mo[illegible] is below the opening. When the plunger is raised [illegible] slide at one side of the box is lifted to open a commun[illegible]cation from a pug-mill, or other clay-express[illegible] machinery, and allow the box to be filled with clay. [illegible] the plunger commences to descend the slide is quic[illegible] closed, and the clay within the box is forced dow[illegible]wards by the plunger and into the mould, its return [illegible] the pug-mill being shut off by the slide. All exces[illegible] clay forced downwards is allowed to pass from t[illegible] bottom of the box to the bottom of a second, [illegible] pressure-relieving, box, fitted with a heavily-weigh[illegible] plunger. When the plunger of the pressing-box ag[illegible] rises, the clay in the second box is, by the action of [illegible] heavily-weighted plunger, forced back from it into [illegible] pressing-box, or, if the weight of the plunger is insu[illegible]cient to force the clay back, it is forced downwards [illegible] a positive movement. An arrangement is provided [illegible] prevent injury to the moulds from stones in the [illegible] The specification contains a full description of the c[illegible]struction of the moulds.

7,095.—Size Paint: *A. J. Doult.*—The subject of [illegible] patent is an improved paint, claimed to combine [illegible] lvantages of good quality and economy in cost, fit for e in any weather, and not liable to scale off. It consts of wheat-flour, alum, and water in the following oportions:—1 kilogramme of wheat-flour, boiled as hen used for making ordinary size, 20 litres of water, d 50 grammes of alum dissolved in 2 litres of water.

7,727.—DIVIDABLE TILES: *D. & F. Platt.*—This vention relates to an improved metallic die for use in rming dividable tiles of earthenware, cement, comsition, or other suitable material, and has for its ject the construction of a die in such a manner that les made by the use of the die will have an insertion or sertions cut in them, crossing the tile in any desired rection, and of suitable depths in the top and bottom es of the tile, so that the tiles may be easily divided fore or after firing without chipping or damaging eir back or front faces. Each die is made in two rts, a top and bottom portion. To the face of each rtion is attached, by any suitable means, a metallic ade or plate of suitable shape and size, vertical to the ce of the die, so that these plates, when the dies are tached to a suitable press, and used for making vidable tiles, will cut or form an insertion in both the ont and back faces of the tile.

9,812.—VENTILATING TUBES: *G. Brown.*—This is an vention relating to inlet-ventilators of the description own as "Tobin tubes," designed with the object of plying to the flap or valve of the ventilator an indiitor showing whether the apparatus is open or closed. consists essentially of a combination of the valve or lve-spindle with a disc or plate inscribed with the ords "open" and "shut," or others of a similar port, and a hollow plate or cover with a slot or slit to splay the words or marks inscribed on the disc or ate.

1,062.—CHIMNEYS: *J. M. Barber.*—This specification lates to an improved device for the cure of smoky imneys and the prevention of down-draught, at the me time increasing the up-draught. The inventor aims to be able to dispense with unsightly chimneyts and cowls, and to reduce the consumption of al. These advantages are to be gained by means of centrally-perforated flanged trapezoidal piece of fireay, metal, or the like, fixed at the back of a fire-place st above the register of the stove, so as to allow the gister to be opened or closed, as required.

NEW APPLICATIONS FOR LETTERS PATENT.

March 28.—5,978, H. Hodgkinson, Automatic Door urniture.—5,980, J. Anderson, Automatically Controlg the Ventilators of Greenhouses, &c.—5,984, W. oare, Circular Saws.—5,989, A. Taylor, Dressing Stone. 6,005, S. De Fetruotá and J. Noad, White Lead and rome Pigments.

March 29.—6,037, T. and W. Starkey, Door-catches for lding doors.—6,042, B. Bloom and A. Kotin, Closing ors.—6,067, D. France, Fire grates.—6,080, L. Segenrph, Metallic Facings for Buildings.—6,091, H. Newn, Ventilation of Sewers.—6,104, C. Luther, Cement or ue for Joining Wood.

March 30.—6,138, E. Wild and J. Kent, "In or Out" dicator for Entrance-hall, &c.—6,146, M. Perrett, oves or Fire-places.—6,147, W. Davies, Coin-freed paratus for Use in Connexion with Water-closets.

March 31.—6,200, J. Merrill, Alternating Valve chanism for Flushing.—6,229, J. Kenwood, Soil-pipe ntilation.—6,242, H. Leigh, Securing Doors and Casents.—6,250, G. Sharp, Fasteners for Doors, Windows,

pril 1.—C. Gray, Rapid Door-bolt.—6,290, G. Asher, ndow-fasteners.—6,331, W. Byers, Fixing Glass in hes of Skylights, &c.—6,352, A. Boult, Fasteners for rs.—6,358, H. Ford, Window-sashes.

pril 2.—6,408, W. Waghorne, Chimney-cowls.

PROVISIONAL SPECIFICATIONS ACCEPTED.

206, R. Frost, Joints for Pipes and Tubes in Stonee or Metal.—2,088, H. Penn, Socket-bolts for Doors. 094, J. Bolding, Discharging the Contents of Flush-Cisterns, &c.—2,602, W. Sterling and T. Swann, itary and other Pipes, and an improved method of structing Sewers and Drains.—3,411, C. Formby, nt-brushes.—4,826, P. Pierpoint, Smoke or Ceiling tectors for Chandeliers, &c.—5,004, R. Crompton, ings or Coverings for Walls, &c.—5,291, W. Morton, mental Materials for Decorating Walls, &c.—5,292, Morton, Constructing parts of Walls, Partitions, &c. 437, C. Wallworth, Wooden Flooring Blocks.

COMPLETE SPECIFICATIONS ACCEPTED.

(*Open to Opposition for Two Months.*)

513, J. Thomson, Ventilation and Distribution of rmth by Movements of Air.—7,510, R. Marshall and itzGerald, Air Propelling or Ventilating.—7,640, F. bons, Locks of Window-sashes.—2,033, C. Baker and ers, Composition Material forming Boards, Slabs, &c. ubstitution for Wood or other Materials.

SOME RECENT SALES OF PROPERTY:

ESTATE EXCHANGE REPORT.

APRIL 4.—By *P. Hodson*: F.g.r. of 28*l.*, with reverin 11 yrs., Alfred-pl., Bermondsey, 550*l.*; 9 and 10, don-ter., Wimbledon, u.t. 95 yrs., g.r. 12*l.* 12s., r. 290*l.*; 1, Newington-cres., Newington, u.t. 20 yrs., 7*l.*, 170*l.*—By *Chesterton & Sons*: 57, Holland-rd., ington, u.t. 69 yrs., g.r. 15*l.*, 800*l.*; 61, Belgrave-rd., ravia, u.t. 42 yrs., g.r. 14*l.*, r. 105*l.*, 830*l.*; 64, Inverter., u.t. 55 yrs., g.r. 15*l.*, r. 150*l.*, 1,890*l.*—By *E.* : 61, Greenwood-rd., Hackney, u.t. 59 yrs., g.r. 7*l.*, ; 133, Lewisham-rd., Lewisham, u.t. 13 yrs., g.r. 7*l.*, ; 33, Stafford-rd., Peckham, f., 250*l.*; 21, Dingwall-Wandsworth, u.t. 90 yrs., g.r. 5*l.*, 150*l.*; 27, Glycena-Lavender-hill, u.t. 82 yrs., g.r. 6*l.*, 215*l.*

APRIL 5.—By *Newton & Long*: 62, Middleton-rd., ton, u.t. 47 yrs., g.r. 4*l.*, r. 34*l.*, 275*l.*—By *W. B. lett*: 18, Andover-rd., Holloway, f., r. 26*l.*, 355*l.*—*Debenham, Tewson, & Co.*: "Les Fleurs," Tooting, 67 yrs., g.r. 7*l.* 7s., including the lease of garden nd, 570*l.*—By *Ellis & Son*: "Crescent Lodge," The cent, Denmark Hill, u.t. 60 yrs., g.r. 15*l.*, 850*l.*—By *mbert Son, & Flint*: Nos. 3 and 6, Post-office-ldings, Walthamstow, f., 1,645*l.*—By *Montagu & ason*: 2, Prince's-st., Spitalfields, f., r. 75*l.*, 1,320*l.*; 133, 204 to 207 (odd), Rommany-rd., Gipsy Hill, u.t. ., g.r. 33*l.* 10s., 440*l.*; 214 to 228 (even), Rommany-rd., u.t. 77 yrs., g.r. 44*l.*, 705*l.*; 2141 to 217 (odd), Rommany-rd., u.t. 77 yrs., g.r. 20*l.*, 330*l.*; 119 and 123, Gipsy-rd., u.t. 78 yrs., g.r. 12*l.*, 295*l.*; 125, 127, and 129 Gipsy-rd., u.t. 80 yrs., g.r. 18*l.*, 410*l.*; 163, 165, and 167, Gipsy-rd., u.t. 79 yrs., g.r. 27*l.*, 455*l.*—By *Geo. Goldsmith, Son, & Co.*: F.g.r. of 13*l.*, with reversion in 32 yrs., Montpelier-row, Knightsbridge, 380*l.*; f.g.r. of 7*l.* 7s., with ditto in 36 yrs., Montpelier-pl., 210*l.*; f.g.r. of 56*l.*, with ditto in 34 yrs., Montpelier-row, 1,365*l.*; f.g.r. of 5*l.* 10s., with ditto in 32 yrs., 160*l.*; f.g.r. of 6*l.* 10s., with ditto in 35 yrs., 185*l.*; f.g.r. of 26*l.*, with ditto in 34 yrs., 660*l.*; f.g.r. of 49*l.*, with ditto in 35 yrs., Montpelier-pl., 1,405*l.*; f.g.r. of 14*l.* 14s., with ditto in 32 yrs., 460*l.*; f.g.r. of 7*l.* 7s., with ditto in 36 yrs., 245*l.*; f.g.r. of 60*l.*, with ditto in 8 yrs., Rutland-st., 2,170*l.*; f.g.r. of 55*l.* 10s., with ditto in 34 yrs., 1,630*l.*; f.g.r. of 33*l.* 10s., with ditto in 33 yrs., Montpelier-sq., 1,255*l.*; 7, 8, 9, 19, 26, and 27, Montpelier-row, f., r. 190*l.* 13s. 4d., 2,735*l.*; 18, 19, 20, 23, and 25, Montpelier-pl., f., r. 100*l.* 6s. 8d., 2,375*l.*; 26 to 29, Montpelier-pl., f., r. 127*l.*, 1,940*l.*; 6 and 28, Rutland-st., f., r. 63*l.*, 910*l.*; 5, 9, and 10, Montpelier-mews, f., r. 180*l.*, 2,335*l.*; 8, Montpelier-sq., u.t. 32 yrs., g.r. 14*l.* 14s., 975*l.*; 11, Montpelier-sq., u.t. 37 yrs., g.r. 29*l.* 8s., 590*l.*

APRIL 6.—By *Ventom, Bull, & Cooper*:—35 and 37, Priory Pk.-rd., Kilburn, f., r. 73*l.*, 1,000*l.*; 45 and 47, Priory Pk.-rd., f., r. 75*l.*, 980*l.*; 86 to 92 (even), Priory Pk.-rd., f., r. 141*l.*, 1,820*l.*—By *Driver & Perfect*: 8, Hampton-rd., Holloway, f., 300*l.*—By *Rushworth & Stevens*: I.g.r. of 7*l.* 8s., Tonbridge-st., Euston-rd., u.t. 14 yrs., g.r. 5*l.*, 425*l.*; 161, Essex-rd., Islington, u.t. 10, g.r. 28*l.*, r. 85*l.*, 305*l.*; 160, Hornsey-rd., Holloway, u.t. 51 yrs., g.r. 8*l.* 8s., r. 40*l.*, 300*l.*; 24 and 26, Lothian-rd., Camberwell, u.t. 68 yrs., g.r. 9*l.*, r. 45*l.*, 400*l.*; 36, Chalcot-cres., Regent's Pk., u.t. 43 yrs., g.r. 8*l.*, r. 42*l.*, 200*l.*—By *Farebrother, Ellis, & Co.*: No. 89, Fleet-st., f., area 1,200 ft., r. 300*l.*, 9,050*l.*—By *T. B. Westacott*: 26, Wrotham-rd., Camden-town, u.t. 59 yrs., g.r. 5*l.*, r. 45*l.*, 420*l.*; 85, Marsden-st., Kentish-town, u.t. 56 yrs., g.r. 6*l.* 6s., r. 45*l.*, 320*l.*; 13 and 14, Preston-st., u.t. 56 yrs., g.r. 11*l.*, r. 67*l.* 12s., 380*l.*; 10, Londesborough-rd., Stoke Newington, u.t. 72 yrs., g.r. 8*l.*, r. 50*l.*, 465*l.*; 15, Grove-pk.-rd., Tottenham, u.t. 84 yrs., g.r. 6*l.* 15s., r. 23*l.*, 105*l.*—By *Weston & Sons*: No. 481, Wandsworth-rd., u.t. 30 yrs., no g.r., r. 45*l.*, 520*l.*; 33, 35, 37, 64, and 66, Union-grove, u.t. 32 yrs., g.r. 37*l.*, r. 212*l.*, 1,435*l.*; 47 and 49, Union-grove, u.t. 32 yrs., no g.r., r. 80*l.*, 695*l.*; I.g.r. of 11*l.* 10s., u.t. 32 yrs., g.r. 15s., 210*l.*; 41 and 42, Broad Hinton-rd., Clapham, u.t. 50 yrs., g.r. 9*l.*, r. 50*l.*, 535*l.*; 8, The Grove, u.t. 53 yrs., g.r. 10*l.* 10s., 400*l.*; 148 and 145, Barry-rd., Dulwich, f., r. 52*l.*, 830*l.*; 8, Harold-st., Camberwell, u.t. 70 yrs., g.r. 8*l.*, r. 42*l.*, 375*l.*

APRIL 7.—By *Glover & Harrison*: 10 and 12, Caversham-rd., Kentish Town, u.t. 56 yrs., g.r. 24*l.*, 815*l.*—By *P. H. Clarke*: 18, Charlwood-st., Pimlico, u.t. 33 yrs., g.r. 7*l.* 18s., r. 50*l.*, 430*l.*—By *G. Robins*: 28 and 30, St. Donatt's-rd., New Cross, u.t. 62 yrs., g.r. 8*l.* 10s., 480*l.*—By *Newbon & Co.*: 53 and 55, South-hill-pk., Hampstead, f., 1,065*l.*; 77 and 81, South-hill-pk., f., r. 125*l.*, 1,445*l.*; 3A to 13A (odd), Rectory-rd., Stoke Newington, u.t. 72 yrs., g.r. 62*l.*, 1,000*l.*; 59, Craven-pk., Willesden, u.t. 84 yrs., g.r. 10*l.*, r. 55*l.*, 550*l.*; 108 and 110, Forest-rd., Dalston, u.t. 59 yrs., g.r. 12*l.* 16s., r. 76*l.*, 700*l.*; 112 to 118 (even), Forest-rd., u.t. 50 yrs., g.r. 25*l.* 12s., r. 152*l.*, 1,420*l.*; 18, Canonbury-grove, Canonbury, u.t. 26 yrs., g.r. 7*l.*, 315*l.*; 2 and 5, Stewart's-pl., Clerkenwell, u.t. 49 yrs., g.r. 14*l.*, 400*l.*—By *Stimson & Sons*: 85, 87, and 89, Beckway-st., Walworth, f., 1,010*l.*; 50, Hanover-gardens, Kennington, u.t. 53 yrs., g.r. 2*l.*, r. 35*l.*, 330*l.*; 81, Albert-rd., Peckham, u.t. 55 yrs., g.r. 3*l.* 18s. 6d., 200*l.*; 32 and 34, Brayards-rd., u.t. 76 yrs., g.r. 6*l.* 11s., 385*l.*; 10, Russell-grove, Brixton, u.t. 28 yrs., g.r. 5*l.*, 185*l.*—By *S. Chatwood*: "Silver Leys," Broxbourne, u.t. 89 yrs., g.r. 13*l.*, r. 80*l.*, 900*l.*; 100, Blackthorn-st., Bow, u.t. 62 yrs., g.r. 6*l.*, r. 35*l.*, 300*l.*; No. 402, Hornsey-rd., u.t. 60 yrs., g.r. 9*l.*, r. 40*l.*, 150*l.*; four houses and six cottages, High Bridge-st., Waltham Abbey, f., r. 155*l.* 12s., 2,010*l.*; four f. cottages, Barge-yd., r. 23*l.* 18s., 160*l.*; two cottages, North-pl., f., r. 23*l.* 8s., 330*l.*; twelve f. cottages, Romeland, r. 121*l.* 11s., 1,375*l.*; three copyhold houses, r. 35*l.* 2s., 300*l.*; ten f. cottages, r. 112*l.* 9s., 1,040*l.*; f. house and shop, Market-st., r. 20*l.*, 305*l.*; two houses and a cottage, Sewardstone-st., f., r. 35*l.* 2s., 310*l.*; "The Greyhound" public-house and house adjoining, Sun-st., r. 57*l.* 10s., 1,350*l.*; Copyhold house, Sun-st., r. 28*l.*, 350*l.*; Six freehold houses with shops, r. 132*l.*, 2,475*l.*; Freehold house, Sewardstone-road, r. 27*l.*, 520*l.*; Four villa residences, New-road, f., r. 88*l.* 10s., 1,515*l.*; Freehold residence, "The Laurels," 835*l.*; A plot of freehold land, 170*l.*; Two freehold cottages, Honey-lane, 230*l.*; "Harold House," Waltham-lane, f., r. 30*l.*, 500*l.*; Four freehold cottages, Park-lane, Waltham Cross, r. 45*l.* 10s., 330*l.*

APRIL 8.—By *Weatherley & Haslett*: 38 to 44 (even), Union-rd., Clapham-rd., u.t. 70 yrs., g.r. 24*l.*, r. 160*l.*, 1,230*l.*—By *W. W. Jenkinson*: 2 to 10 (even), Upton-lane, Forest-gate, u.t. 88 yrs., g.r. 50*l.*, subject to mortgage, 180*l.*; 252 and 254, Canbury-pk.-rd., Kingston-on-Thames, u.t. 77 yrs., g.r. 8*l.*, 270*l.*—By *Woods & Snelling*: 15, Mervan-rd., Brixton, u.t. 81 yrs., g.r. 7*l.*, r. 35*l.*, 310*l.*; 14 and 16, Stanfield-rd., u.t. 78 yrs., g.r. 13*l.*, r. 70*l.*, 505*l.*; 4 and 5, Western-rd., u.t. 72 yrs., g.r. 13*l.* 5s., 585*l.*—By *Harris & Bradly*: 21 and 23, Farwig-lane, Bromley, f., r. 23*l.* 12s., 300*l.*; 2 and 3, Payne-st., Deptford, u.t. 70 yrs., g.r. 3*l.* 8s., 330*l.*—By *Charles & Tubbs*: Moor-lane, City of London, f.g.r. of 340*l.*, with reversion in 72 yrs., 7,200*l.*; f.g.r. of 57*l.*, with reversion in 79 yrs., Wimbledon, 1,000*l.*; 1, Bridgewater-sq., Barbican, u.t. 13 yrs., g.r. 20*l.*, r. 114*l.*, 125*l.*—By *Reynolds & Eason*: 91 and 93, Milton-st., City, freehold area 2,052 ft., 3,650*l.*; "Devon House," Devonshire-rd., Greenwich, u.t. 73 yrs., g.r. 4*l.* 10s., 400*l.*; 22, Nailour-st., Islington, u.t. 59 yrs., g.r. 5*l.* 10s., r. 28*l.*, 220*l.*; 22 and 31, Lyon-st., u.t. 52 yrs., g.r. 10*l.*, r. 57*l.* 12s., 425*l.*; 1, Baxter-grove, u.t. 67 yrs., g.r. 3*l.* 10s., 145*l.*; 8, Charles-st., u.t. 60 yrs., g.r. 4*l.* 10s., r. 28*l.*, 220*l.*; 22 and 24, Harcombe-rd., Stoke Newington, u.t. 72 yrs., g.r. 10*l.*, r. 52*l.*, 475*l.*; 3 and 4, Clevedon-rd., u.t. 88 yrs., g.r. 10*l.* 10s., r. 62*l.* 8s., 315*l.*; 45 and 47, Marlborough-rd., Dalston, u.t. 51 yrs., g.r. 7*l.* 10s., 505*l.*; 51 to 60 odd, Parnell-rd., Old Ford, u.t. 70 yrs., g.r. 20*l.*, 620*l.*; 2, Wellesley-rd., Wanstead, freehold, r. 30*l.*, 465*l.*; 35 to 59, Charlotte-st., Shoreditch, f., 1,025*l.*; 69 and 70, Charlotte-st., f., 335*l.*

[*Contractions used in these lists.*—F.g.r. for freehold ground-rent; l.g.r. for leasehold ground-rent; i.g.r. for improved ground-rent; g.r. for ground-rent; r. for rent; f. for freehold; c. for copyhold; l. for leasehold; e.r. for estimated rental; u.t. for unexpired term; p.a. for per annum; yrs. for years; st. for street; rd. for road; sq. for square; pl. for place; ter. for terrace; cres. for crescent; yd. for yard, &c.]

PRICES CURRENT OF MATERIALS.

TIMBER.		
Greenheart, B.G. ton	9/0/0	0/0/0
Teak, E.I. ... load	10/0/0	16/0/0
Sequoia, U.S. ft. cu.	2/3	3/0
Ash, Canada load	2/10/0	4/0/0
Birch, do.	3/5/0	4/10/0
Elm, do.	3/10/0	4/15/0
Fir, Dantsic, &c.	1/10/0	3/10/0
Oak, do.	3/0/0	5/5/0
Canada	5/10/0	7/0/0
Pine, Canada red	2/10/0	3/10/0
Do. yellow	2/10/0	5/0/0
Lath, D'ntsic, fath	5/0/0	6/0/0
St. Petersburg	5/0/0	7/0/0
Deals, Finland, 2nd & 1st std 100	8/10/0	10/0/0
Do. 4th & 3rd	7/0/0	8/10/0
Do. Riga	7/0/0	8/0/0
St. Petersburg, 1st yellow	11/0/0	18/0/0
Do. 2nd yellow	8/0/0	10/0/0
Do. white	7/10/0	11/0/0
Swedish	8/0/0	16/0/0
White Sea	8/0/0	18/0/0
Canada, Pine 1st	20/0/0	26/0/0
Do. do. 2nd	14/10/0	16/0/0
Do. do. 3rd, &c.	8/0/0	10/5/0
Do. Spruce, 1st	8/10/0	11/0/0
Do. do. 3rd & 2nd	6/15/0	8/0/0
New Brunswick	7/0/0	7/10/0
Battens, all kinds	3/10/0	15/10/0
Flooring Boards, sq., 1 in. prep. 1st	0/8/0	0/14/0
Do. 2nd	0/7/0	0/11/0
Other qualities	0/4/0	0/9/0
Cedar, Cuba ... ft.	/3½	/4½
Honduras, &c.	/3½	/4
Mahogany, Cuba	/4½	/6½
St. Domingo, cargo av.	/4½	2/0
Mexican do. do.	/4	/6
Tobasco do. do.	/5½	/7
Honduras do.	/6½	/6½
Box, Turkey ton	4/0/0	13/0/0
Rose, Rio	10/0/0	20/0/0
Bahia	9/0/0	18/0/0
Satin, St. Domingo ... ft.	0/0/8	0/1/3

TIMBER (continued).		
Satin, Porto Rico	0/0/8	0/1/6
Walnut, Italian	0/0/3½	0/0/7
METALS.		
Iron—Pig, in Scotland ... ton	2/1/1	0/0/0
Bar, Welsh, in London	5/17/6	6/0/0
Do. do. at works in Wales	5/7/6	5/10/0
Do. Staffordshire, in London	6/5/0	6/15/0
Copper—British, cake and ingot	45/10/0	49/0/0
Best selected	49/15/0	50/5/0
Sheets, strong	58/0/0	60/0/0
Chili, bars	45/13/9	46/1/3
Yellow Metal lb.	0/0/5½	0/0/5¾
Lead—Pig, Spanish ... ton	10/12/6	10/15/0
English, com. brands	10/17/6	11/0/0
Sheet, English, 6 lbs. per sq. ft. and upwards	12/5/0	0/0/0
Pipe	12/15/0	0/0/0
Zinc—English sheet ... ton	25/10/0	0/0/0
Vieille Montagne	26/5/0	0/0/0
Tin—Straits	90/10/0	90/12/6
Australian	90/15/0	91/0/0
English Ingots	93/15/0	94/0/0
OILS.		
Linseed ... ton	16/7/6	18/12/6
Cocoanut, Cochin	24/10/0	0/0/0
Do. Ceylon	22/0/0	0/0/0
Palm, Lagos	23/5/0	23/10/0
Rapeseed, English pale	24/15/0	25/10/0
Do. brown	23/5/0	28/10/0
Cottonseed ref.	19/0/0	0/0/0
Oleine	21/10/0	22/10/0
Lubricating, U.S.	4/0/0	5/0/0
Do. refined	5/10/0	0/0/0
Tar—Stockholm barrel	0/19/0	1/0/0
Archangel	0/12/6	0/0/0

TENDERS.

(Communications for insertion under this heading should be addressed to "The Editor," and must reach us *not later than 12 noon on Thursdays.*)

ASHTON-ON-RIBBLE (near Preston).—For the erection of a Wesleyan Chapel, to accommodate 850 persons, in Wellington-road, Ashton-on-Ribble. Mr. Walter Barrow, architect, Preston:—

Walker	£3,415	Croft	£3,201
Lucas	3,235	Baldwin (accepted)	3,000

BECKENHAM.—For erecting shop and dwelling-house at Croydon-road, for Messrs. A. C. S. & H. Crowley. Mr. John Farrer, architect, No. 20, Finsbury-pavement, E.C. Quantities supplied:—

W. Smith	£1,237	Bullock	£1,120
Smith & Sons	1,214	Taylor	1,095
Harris & Fagg	1,187	Mid Kent Building Co.	1,085
Mattock Bros.	1,178	G. H. Martin & Co., West Croydon (accepted)	1,073
Palmer	1,150		

BRIGHTON.—For the erection of mission hall and school, Sutherland-road. Mr. W. H. Nash, architect, 42, Ship-street, Brighton. Quantities by architect:—

W. Allfrey	£1,448	Sattin & Evershed	£1,230
W. Taylor	1,235	V. P. Freeman	1,226
A. Wilkinson	1,274	A. R. Lockyer (accepted)	1,200

[All of Brighton.]

CLACTON-ON-SEA.—For alterations to No. 6, North-avenue, for Mr. J. Bearman. Mr. A. W. Hunter, surveyor:—

Mark Potts (accepted) ... £103 0 0

CLACTON-ON-SEA.—Accepted for the erection of villa residence in Rosemary-road, for Mr. J. T. Button:—

Mark Potts, Clacton-on-Sea ... £380 0 0

COVENTRY.—For erecting the Coventry Public Baths. Mr. Harold T. Burgess, and Messrs. Spalding & Cross, joint architects. Quantities by Mr. F. G. W. Buss, 16, Furnival's-inn, W.C.:—

	£.	£. A
Balaam Bros.	18,900	949
F. N. Stephens	18,800	1,170
Gould & Brand	18,179	762
J. T. Wingrove	16,978	967
Reid, Bright, & Co.	16,935	899
Thos. Lowe & Sons	16,550	940
John Allen & Sons	16,417	995
G. F. Smith & Son	16,290	970
C. G. Hill	15,076	824
Chas. W. King	14,600	790

A Extra for carrying the foundations 4 ft. lower.

CREDITON (Devon).—For new frontage to banking premises for the Devon and Cornwall Banking Company, Limited. Mr. Geo. Soudon Bridgman, architect, Torquay:—

W. P. Berry, Crediton* ... £492

*Accepted.

DUNCHIDEOCK (Devon).—For the restoration of rood-screen, Dunchideock Church, Devon, for the Rector and Restoration Committee:—

Herbert Read, Exeter*	£231	Harry Hems	£225

* Accepted.

KINGSBRIDGE (Devon).—For proposed new banking premises and post office, for the Devon and Cornwall Banking Company, Limited. Mr. G. Soudon Bridgman, architect, Torquay:—

J. P. Berry	£3,380	Rabbich & Brown	£3,115
G. Hooper	3,[illegible]	Drew Bros.	2,912
G. Shellabeer	3,230	H. Webber, Paignton*	2,906
J. Finch	3,107	*Accepted.	

LEISTON (Suffolk).—For proposed alterations and additions to Aldringham House, Leiston, Suffolk, for Mr. Frank Garrett. Mr. G. W. Coleman, architect:—

Grimwood & Sons	£2,809	Runnacles	£2,758
Bennett	2,820	Girling & Co.	2,755

LONDON.—For alterations and additions to the "Blakesley Arms," Station-road, Manor Park, E., for Mr. T. Deitesworth. Mr. Fred. A. Ashton, architect, 3, Crooked-lane, E.C.:—

W. Shurmur	£594	F. Voller	£495
North Bros.	514	W. Watson	482
Coulsell Bros.	487	Hostle & Farrow (accepted)	409

LONDON.—For providing and fixing heating apparatus on the low pressure hot-water system for the new school now in course of erection on the Ilderton-road site, Rotherhithe New-road, for the School Board for London. Mr. T. J. Bailey, Architect:—

Russell & Co.	£427	R. H. & J. Pearson	£390
R. Crane	398	T. Potter & Sons*	303
W. G. Hunt	381		

* Recommended by the Works Committee for acceptance.

LONDON.—For providing and fixing heating apparatus, exclusive of radiators, on the low-pressure hot-water system for the under-mentioned new schools now in course of erection, for the School Board for London. Mr. T. J. Bailey, Architect:—

High-street, Plumstead.

Wenham & Waters, Ltd.	£490 0	J. & F. May	£407 0
J. Wontner Smith, Gray, & Co.	430 0	Purcell & Nobbs	392 0
		W. G. Cannon*	385 10

Chisenhale-road, Bow.

Fraser & Fraser	£790 0	Jolly & Attwood	£416 0
R. Dawson & Co., Ltd.	498 0	W. G. Cannon	398 10
Wenham & Waters, Ltd.	435 0	R. Crane*	373 0
J. Wontner Smith, Gray, & Co.	418 0		

Honeywell-road, Wandsworth-common.

J. & F. May	£493 0	R. Crane	£[illegible] 0
Purcell & Nobbs	474 0	Potter & Sons*	423 0

* Recommended by the Works Committee for acceptance.

LONDON.—For altering the "Wheatsheaf" Hotel, Balham, for Messrs. Tucker Bros. Mr. W. Hilton Nash, architect, 5, Adelaide-place, London-bridge:—

H. J. Humphries	£8,153	B. E. Nightingale	£7,118
Lonnell & Sons	7,[illegible]	T. Gregory & Co.	6,945
Edwards & Medway	7,[illegible]	Turtle & Appleton*	6,800
J. Allen & Sons	7,[illegible]	Leeke & Hooker	6,[illegible]
D. Charteris	7,242		

* Accepted.

LONDON.—For the erection of fire-escape stairs at the Rotherhithe Infirmary, for the Guardians of the St. Olave's Union. Messrs. Newman & Newman, architects, 31, Tooley-street, London Bridge, S.E.:—

The Coalbrookdale Co.	£1,441	G. F. Darby & Co.	£720
Hayward Bros. & Eckstein	1,[illegible]	The Constructional Iron Co.	593
T. & W. Cole	[illegible]		
J. F. Clark	[illegible]		

LONDON.—For making roads and laying out grounds at the Rotherhithe Infirmary, for the Guardians of the St. Olave's Union. Messrs. Newman & Newman, architects, 31, Tooley-street, London-bridge, S.E.:—

The Seyssell Asphalte Co. £718 0 0
Hebman & Co. (accepted) 609 0 0

LONDON.—For works at the Chancery-lane Safe Deposit extension, Chancery-lane, W.C., for Mr. Thomas Clarke. Mr. William A. Burr, architect, 65, Chancery-lane, W.C.:—

Tiling.

Doulton & Co. (accepted) £244 0 0

For Brass-work to new Staircase, &c.

Messrs. Comyn Ching & Co. (accepted) £206 7 0

For Marble-work to Steps.

Mullis (accepted) £20 0 0

NANTGAREDIG (Caermarthenshire).—For the erection and completion of stables and laundry, for Mr. F. H. Bath, J.P. Messrs. J. Buckley Wilson & Glendinning Moxham, architects, Swansea:—

Dd. Jenkins	£1,420	Bennett Bros.	£1,025
Thomas Watkins & Co.	1,391	J. D. Williams, Knighton*	995
Hy. Billings	1,075		

* Accepted.

NANTGAREDIG (Caermarthenshire).—For the erection and completion of a lodge, for Mr. B. H. Bath, J.P. Messrs. J. Buckley Wilson & Glendinning Moxham, architects, Swansea:—

Hy. Billings	£544 10 0	Thomas Watkins & Co.	£498 14 0
Bennett Bros.	500 0 0	J. D. Williams, Knighton*	415 0 0
Dd. Jenkins	490 0 0		

* Accepted.

NEATH.—Accepted for the erection and completion of stables near the Gnoll, Neath. Messrs. J. Buckley Wilson & Glendinning Moxham, architects, Swansea:—

D. C. Jones & Co., Gloucester £220 0 0

PLYMOUTH.—For the reconstruction of a portion of the Public Market, in three sections, containing the Corn Exchange, fourteen shops, twenty-five butchers' stalls, and covered entrances to markets. Mr. Charles King, architect, Plymouth. Quantities by the architect:—

A. R. Debnam	£23,161	Tozer & Son	£19,421
G. Shellabeer	22,733	A. W. Coles	19,250
J. P. Berry	21,521	J. Finch	19,064
J. H. Blackell	21,013	A. R. Lethbridge & Son	18,640
Reed, Blight, & Co.	20,142	T. May	18,[illegible]
Wm. Trevena	19,597	S. Roberts*	17,725
Pethick Bros.	19,[illegible]		

* Accepted.

PWLLHELI.—For the construction of outfall-sewer, Pwllheli. Messrs. Thomas Roberts & Son, engineers, Portmadoc:—

Fortescue & Co.	£5,[illegible] 0	Owen Morris	£3,748 0
Griffith Griffiths	4,977 0	Humphrey Thomas	3,207 10

[Engineers' estimate, £3,003.]

REPTON (Derbyshire).—For the erection of a new sanitorium for the school at Repton, for the trustees of Sir John Port's Charity. Messrs. John Shaw & Son, architects, The College, All Saints', Derby. Quantities by the architects:—

W. A. Stevenson	£6,[illegible] 0 0	Jos. Parker	£5,993 0 0
J. Lowe & Sons	5,760 0 0	Arthur Brown	5,[illegible] 0 0
Walker & Slater	5,[illegible] 0 0	Bullock & Barton	5,[illegible] 0 0
Wm. Wood	5,[illegible] 19 10	Joseph Dickin	5,[illegible] 0 0
Geo. Ward	5,[illegible] 0 0	Roger Platts, Etwall*	5,[illegible] 0 0
W. Walkerdine	5,380 0 0	H. Vernon	4,915 0 0

* Accepted conditionally.

SHANGHAI.—For the supply of 16,500 tons of broken granite, 3,000 tons of sand, and 2,000 tons of broken bricks, for the Shanghai Municipal Council. Mr. Chas. Mayne, Engineer and Surveyor:—

Contractor.	Broken Bricks.	Large Granite.	1½ inch Granite.	¾ inch Granite.	Sand.
	per ton.	per ton.	per ton.	per ton.	per ton.
Yung Ming Cheng	2 6½	2 4½	3 3½	3 9½	3 1½
Ling Foh Kee	1 7½	2 4½	3 4	3 9½	2 10½
Joe & Ming Kee	2 4½	2 4½	3 4	3 6½	2 11
Fung Kee	2 3	2 3½	3 3½	3 7½	2 10
Yah Kee & Co.	2 2½*	2 2½*	2 10½*	3 6½*	2 9½*

* Accepted.

SWANSEA.—For the erection and completion of St. Thomas's Vicarage. Messrs. J. Buckley Wilson & Glendinning Moxham, architects, Swansea:—

Hy. Welch	£1,715	Thomas Watkins & Co.	£1,400
J. D. Williams	1,[illegible]	Stephens & Bastow	1,351
D. C. Jones	1,496	John F. Weaver	1,348
Bennett Bros.	1,450	Gustavus Bros.	1,295
D. Jenkins	1,425	Hy. Billings, Swansea*	1,245

* Accepted.

SWANSEA.—For the erection and completion of residence in Sangland, near Swansea. Messrs. J. Buckley Wilson & Glendinning Moxham, architects:—

G. Mercer	£2,034	Thomas Watkins & Co.	£1,750
J. D. Williams	1,886	O. Morris	1,722
D. C. Jones & Co.	1,[illegible]	Hy. Billings	1,635
Glasters Bros.	1,867	Dd. Jenkins, Swansea*	1,600
Bennett Bros	1,770		

* Accepted.

WORMLEY (Herts).—For the erection of new parish room at Wormley, Herts, for the Rev. F. W. Greenstreet. Messrs. Newman & Newman, architects, 31, Tooley-street, London Bridge:—

Archer £441 0 0
G. A. Hunt, Broxbourne (accepted) 413 14 0

SUBSCRIBERS in LONDON and the SUBURBS, by prepaying at the Publishing Office, 19s. per annum (or 4s. 9d. per quarter), can ensure receiving "The Builder," by *Friday Morning's Post.*

TERMS OF SUBSCRIPTION.

"THE BUILDER" is supplied DIRECT from the Office to residents in any part of the United Kingdom at the rate of 19s. per annum PREPAID. To all parts of Europe, America, Australia, and New Zealand, 26s. per annum. To India, China, Ceylon, &c., 30s. per annum. Remittances payable to DOUGLAS FOURDRINIER, Publisher, No. 46, Catherine-street, W.C.

TO CORRESPONDENTS.

A. B. (next week).—W. J. L. (next week).

All statements of facts, lists of tenders, &c., must be accompanied by the name and address of the sender, not necessarily for publication.

We are compelled to decline pointing out books and giving addresses.

NOTE.—The responsibility of signed articles, and papers read at public meetings, rests, of course, with the authors.

We cannot undertake to return rejected communications.

Letters or communications (beyond mere news-items) which have been duplicated for other journals, are NOT DESIRED.

All communications regarding literary and artistic matter should be addressed to THE EDITOR; all communications relating to advertisements and other exclusively business matters should be addressed to THE PUBLISHER, and not to the Editor.

Vol. LXII. No. 2568. SATURDAY, APRIL 23, 1892.

ILLUSTRATIONS.

Designs for Wall-Papers.—By Mr. Walter Crane and Mr. Lewis F. Day .... Double-Page Ink-Photo.
Church of St. John-the-Baptist, Kensington: Western Front.—Mr. James Brooks, Architect .... Double-Page Photo-Litho
Lavenham Guildhall: Details of Porch.—Measured and Drawn by Mr. John S. Corder .... Double-Page Photo-Litho.
Board Schools, Stamford-road, Kettering.—Messrs. Gotch & Saunders, Architects .... Single-Page Ink-Photo.
Lodge, Compton, Sherborne.—Mr. E. Hellicar, Architect .... Single-Page Ink-Photo.

Blocks in Text.

Designs for Ceiling Papers .... Page 323 | Diagrams in Student's Column: Heating by Hot Water .... Pages 326, 327

CONTENTS.

gow Art Galleries Competition 317
nt Excavations in Attic Burying-Places 318
s 319
rescence on Brickwork 321
ssional Chit-Chat 321
Surveyors' Institution 322
petitions 323
itectural Societies 323
gns for Wall-Papers 323
ch of St. John the Baptist, Holland-road, W. 323
The Old Guildhall, Lavenham 323
Stamford-road Schools, Kettering 324
Lodge at Compton, Sherborne 324
Crystal Palace School of Practical Engineering 324
Architectural Education 325
Two Views of Sir Gilbert Scott's Restorations 325
Sir G. Scott and Ripon Minster 326
Steam-Rolling on Roads 326
Student's Column.—Warming Buildings by Hot Water. XVII. 326
Surveyorships 327
Obituary 327
General Building News 327
Sanitary and Engineering News 328
Stained Glass and Decoration 328
Foreign and Colonial 328
Miscellaneous 329
Meetings 330
Recent Patents 331
Some Recent Sales of Property 331
Tenders 331

Glasgow Art Galleries Competition.

IN September last the Association for the Promotion of Art and Music in the City of Glasgow advertised an open competition for the proposed new buildings in Kelvingrove Park, to t about 120,000*l*. Mr. Waterhouse, R.A., assessor, and from the sixty-two designs in in December he selected for the final petition those by Messrs. Simpson & n, Mr. T. M. Deane, Messrs. Malcolm, k, & Rowntree, Messrs. Honeyman & pie (two designs), and Messrs. Treadwell artin. The drawings for the final comion were submitted in the end of March, the award was given on April 13 in ur of Messrs. Simpson & Allen.

he task set to competitors was a hard one. single building were to be combined a ral or Music-hall, Art Galleries, Museum and Galleries, and a School of Art. It ident that this is in a measure to accomate irreconcilables, and that the executive mittee had not a perfectly definite conion of their own requirements from the . A hall for hearing music and a central to "give easy access to all parts of the ding" are not compatible; a school of art students is with difficulty associated with eries and halls requiring unembarrassed ulation for easy-going sightseers. And in nd the art school has had to be abandoned, le no one of the six final designs achieves mplete solution of the central hall. This nfortunate, though scarcely surprising, is largely due to want of clear decision instructions on the part of the committee. "music-hall" with "special attention n to its acoustics" was asked for in the iminary competition. In the final conns this is modified. "The central hall is intended so much for vocal concerts as for umental music, and the better music is d in the courts of the museum and the ure galleries, corridors, and staircases ounding the hall, the more nearly the building meet the object of the promoters." Two only of the six designs really embody this at all, and it is evident that the committee have not clearly defined either to themselves or to their architects "the object of the promoters." Apparently what is required is a hall which shall be at once the centre of the whole building architecturally, a grand reception hall for special functions, and a suitable space for music of the more popular sort, a kind of glorified and grandiose band-stand. It is meant, presumably, to impress the casual visitor on his first entrance, before he proceeds to wander through the galleries; to be for the systematic visitor the centre round which all else is grouped; to be the gathering hall for all when orchestral music is provided; and to be the centre and climax of the whole building when receptions and ceremonial take place. It is evidently neither a concert-room nor a *salle des pas perdus*; equally, evidently, it is capable of a genuine architectural character of its own, and should be the artistic expression of its definite purpose and intention.

The six designs selected, as worked out, differ very greatly in scheme of plan, architectural composition, and, it must be added, in merit. The site is a somewhat special one, a rectangle, in the West-end Park of Glasgow, on the southern bank of the Kelvin. It is immediately below Gilmorehill, the commanding site of the University, which rises steeply on the northern bank. From the north, therefore, the new art galleries will be overlooked from directly above, very much as in Edinburgh the stately Classic buildings of the Mound are overlooked from the Free Church College, so disastrously for their Classic reputation. Three of the six designs rank decidedly above the others, and two are of outstanding merit. We take them in detail in inverse order.

Messrs. Treadwell and Martin's design,—as have five out of the six,—has the central hall running north and south across the site, and approached from either end, the grand vestibule and staircase being to the south, or city, side. The circulation round the museum halls on the ground floor, and art galleries on the first, is complete and most straightforward, forming, with the central hall, two hollow squares, which enclose two museum courts. The plan is thoroughly obvious, but it is not monumental. The central hall does not sufficiently dominate; it is simply a larger room reserved for music, undoubtedly the principal room, but not a central hall. It is destitute of side corridors or aisles on either floor, which precludes all but the outer circulation round the galleries above, and greatly detracts from the ground floor also. The internal museum courts have galleries above, which are entirely cut off from the rest of the building, with out-of-the-way staircases of their own, liable to congestion if used, but more likely to be practically unvisited. The dining and refreshment rooms are separated, which implies an unnecessary double service; they somewhat unnaturally form a sort of internal pendant to the lavatory accommodation, which, on the other hand, is the better for being doubled. Subsidiary staircases are lacking in the east and west blocks, which would certainly be practically desirable. The art school is a small subsidiary annex on the western side. On the whole the plan, though straightforward, is commonplace, a defect which is still more regrettably true of the elevations. The main feature of the composition is the four great angle towers; the style is what presumably passes for "Queen Anne" of the most accepted type, but is sadly far removed from the best work contemporary with Wren's old age; some of the Renaissance detail is extraordinarily out of scale.

Messrs. Honeyman & Keppie, of Glasgow, have two designs included in the six; the plans bear a family likeness, but the elevations are as dissimilar as possible. The central hall, running north and south, divides the building into museum on the east, and art galleries, art school, &c., on the west, the staircases, of which there are four, being scarcely emphasised sufficiently to the east and west of the great hall. The division of the building is not quite natural and confuses the plan, which is in strong contrast to the obviousness noted in the last. Both these plans, however, have first-floor communication from north to south alongside the central hall, which is a great gain; it is managed with much greater skill in one plan than in the other. There is in both a lack of directness in planning, doubtless increased by the mistaken exigencies of accommodating

d

the art school, but which could not fail to detract from the monumental character of the building. Of the elevations the finer is attached to the poorer plan. It is a scholarly design of quiet dignity, strictly Classic througout. It is, however, open to the objection of being quite unsuited to the site. To have Sir Gilbert Scott's Gothic University on the hill-top (flattened to receive it), dominating a strictly Ionic Art-gallery on the plain below, would have been a strange inversion of natural order in architecture, in which we should have had repeated the disastrous effect of roof-lights, above noted, as seen to demonstration in Playfair's Classic buildings in Edinburgh. The central hall in this design is most disappointing; instead of the Classic dignity of the exterior, we have a most commonplace concert-hall, quite unworthy of the building, with disjointed architectural decoration, and an ugly ceiling; the whole has little dignity and less interest. Messrs. Honeyman & Keppie's second design is the exact converse: the central hall is far superior (in spite of its railway-station roof), with arcaded gallery on both floors; it is far less a concert-room, and much more a central hall to the building, both in plan and design. The exterior elevations, on the other hand, are a most curious medley of architecture, full of unexpected "features," for the most part out of place. In spite of considerable dignity in general design, the exterior is robbed of its unity and marred by these ill-studied features and a certain trickiness.

Messrs. Malcolm, Stark, & Rowntree, of Glasgow, have an exceedingly able design on strikingly different lines. The central hall is still north and south, but forms a genuine centre to the composition, with important approaches for all four sides. The main entrance, of course, is from the south, with a lordly vestibule that is distinctly out of scale. The plan is exceedingly clever. The museum is kept quite distinct on the east, with its own galleries and circulation on the upper floor, which is kept, however, secondary in importance. The art galleries, art school, &c., are to the west, for the most part concentrated with much skill on the ground floor, so that the galleries are top-lighted. There is thus no general circulation to provide for, and the art school is less of a difficulty, being placed in the north-west angle. The ingenuity shown in the plan is very great: at the same time it is in some respects by far the least monumental of the six. It possesses four fine approaches, with vistas to the central hall, but otherwise is rather a congeries of galleries most deftly fitted in, but still without a feeling of unity, and with a sense of false balancing in parts: the six picture galleries and one sculpture gallery are huddled together on the ground floor, and would be most monotonous, while the additional galleries eked out on the first floor would be as lost to the ordinary visitor as some of the upper *salons* in the Louvre. The central hall is rather dwarfed by its vestibules, and appears too small, and the whole is unsatisfactory for its absence of all grip of the design as a monumental whole. Out of this unpromising material the authors have contrived symmetrical Classical elevations of much dignity and interest. They are, however, largely helped by screen walls; consequently the whole would appear most undignified from Gilmorehill. Perhaps none of the designs would suffer so considerably from its position as this, as it would be impossible to hide its real want of due symmetry and balance. The perspectives shown damage rather than help the design, which is a pity: especially the interior of the central hall is quite inadequate, though the design in itself is fine, and, while rather too much of the concert hall, is yet, perhaps, the most successful of the six. The actual detail drawing is a most beautiful one, with a charming organ, in great contrast to the others shown.

Mr. T. M. Deane's design is masterly, and certainly disputes the palm with that of the successful architects. The central hall is here reversed, running east and west; it has a vaulted gallery or aisle completely encircling it on either floor, while the main galleries make a grand circulation round the entire building. The main entrance is from the south, with a fine vestibule and grand staircase; subsidiary entrances are provided on the east and west; to the north is the art school, a separate building, but connected so as to allow entrances to the galleries from this side also. The whole plan is most monumental and ably studied; both ground and first floors are equally successful; the library, refreshment-rooms, &c. are most conveniently placed, set so as not to interfere with the admirable circulation. Almost the only criticisms to be passed are on the side entrances, which are somewhat of excrescences in plan and elevation, and on the four subsidiary staircases in the four angles, which are so stowed away as to lose their serviceableness. The elevation is a fine one, admirably rendered in perspective by (presumably) Mr. Raffles Davison. It is, however, somewhat monotonous, and the addition to the four angle towers of two more that are practically identical, and are quite uncalled for, over part of the art school, is a great mistake. The design has evidently been intended to be Scotch in character. It is, however, a curious parallel to Sir Gilbert Scott's attempt (and failure) on Gilmorehill hard by; apparently it is still supposed that a multitude of round angle-turrets scattered broadcast turn a design into "Scotch baronial." The central hall is very fine, but it is quite out of harmony with the object of the building. It is utterly unlike a hall for music or for any of the arts; it is the Salle des Pas Perdus in its extreme form, with huge semicircular transverse ribs and complicated Renaissance vaulting. This probably, and, it may be presumed, the excessive cost of such a design, has prevented its adoption; for, even at the author's estimate, the lopping required to bring it down to 120,000*l.* would have been disastrous to the design.

Messrs. Simpson & Allen's design is also very masterly, especially in plan. The difficulty of the art school has been got over by boldly thrusting it into a basement, a cutting of the Gordian knot that has been successful. The central hall, running north and south, is here most absolutely the centre of the whole composition, which is grouped around it in masterly simplicity; the circulation is complete on both floors, though a little tortuous at the angles; the central courts are part of the design, not smothered up, and the east and west staircases are architectural additions, instead of being stowed away in obscure corners. The merits of the plan are very great; at the same time it has some serious faults. The great central hall is decidedly out of scale, though it barely gives the accommodation asked for. It is impossible to get from the main entrances to the ground floor courts and galleries without absolutely passing through the central hall, which is surely a grievous restriction. On the first floor the complete circulation is only obtained by passing through the refreshment rooms. Moreover, from the practical point of view, there is no wall space provided for the larger exhibits, such as tapestries or the full-sized architectural casts which are the glories of South Kensington and Paris. Still the plan is, on the whole, most able, and is no unworthy outcome of the competition. The elevations of the building are scarcely so satisfactory, though presented in a fascinating perspective, we presume by Mr. Raffles Davison. A want of sobriety and repose, felt in the outline of the plan, is most conspicuous; the due sense of breadth is lost, and the dignity that is missed is but ill made up for by more or less happy inspiration after Mr. Aston Webb. The whole is far too much a casino rather than a gallery of art. The central hall, which, with its adjuncts, completely traverses the building from north to south, is too large in scale on plan; it is still more markedly so in elevation. The flanking museum and gallery wings on either side, instead of being simply treated to be as broad as possible i
feeling, are deeply recessed and overpowere
by angle pavilions, which again are flanke
by towers on the side elevations. The detail
are often equally wanting in repose, especiall
in the north front, where a great porch i
quite unnecessarily projected forward in al
aggressiveness. The whole is amusing, an
likely to be popular, but sadly wanting i
sobriety, and restfulness, and dignity; breadt
and power have been abandoned for the pic
turesque. The central hall is scarcely quite suc
cessful, a double arcade to the upper galler
standing upon a great square-lintelled open
ing below; nor are the great clearstory win
dows and barrel ceiling as interesting as the
might be. The hall does not quite realise it
special character, and is capable of muc
re-study. The whole design, however, is s
completely re-studied from the original com
petition that this further re-study will doubt
less be forthcoming. In any case, it is a ver
wonderful improvement on the same author
design for the Edinburgh Municipal Building
years ago.

On the whole, particularly in view of th
Committee's intimation as to cost, it is diffi
cult to see how any other award could b
made out of the six selected. In a furthe
article we hope to touch upon some of th
designs which were not selected in the six.

RECENT EXCAVATIONS IN ATTI BURYING-PLACES.

THE beginning of the present centu
saw the opening of the first tomb
in the ancient cemetery of th
Cerameicus at Athens. Fro
1800-1812 Fauvel, Gall, Stackelberg, an
others were at work, and some of the fine
results of their earliest excavations a
embodied in Baron von Stackelberg
"Gräber der Hellenen." Naturally, how
ever, according to the fashion of the time
though the excavations were carefully co
ducted, and with a genuine enthusias
for the objects of art found, the top
graphical data noted were meagre, a
for any scientific investigation of t
relative ages of tombs and the objec
buried in them practically useless. Up
1862 little further was done. That year
memorable from the fact that Mr. Daniel,
civil engineer, while making a road from t
Place de la Concorde to the Peiræus, had
cut through the little hill of the Ha
Trias, and in so doing came upon the li
of ancient grave-stones to the south of t
Sacred Way. Rather than deflect his ro
by a few feet, he earned for himself u
enviable notoriety by carting off t
monuments wholesale, shattering many
process of transit. Naturally, his discover
could not be utilised for scientific purpos
From 1862 to 1871 the Archæological Soci
took the matter up and laid bare three oth
parallel rows of tombs, but still chiefly wit
view to the discovery of fresh instances of t
lovely grave-reliefs that had so excited pub
attention. Then came a pause in the
vestigations, till two and a-half years
Dr. Staïs undertook again the excavat
both of the Dipylon site and other buryi
places of Attica, with the definite
tention of establishing the chronolo
of the subject. Dr. Brückner, w
assisted at many of the excavations,
whose name is well known in connexion w
Greek grave-reliefs, took the opportun
afforded by the Carl Winckelmann's Fest
lay before a large gathering of archæolog
the principle data of the subject, and the
sults he believed to be deducible. His rep
is of great interest; it appeared in
"Deutsche Wochenblatt" (No. 50), on wh
the following account is based:—

The consecutive history of graves
grave monuments in Attica begins ab
700 B.C., with the so-called Dipylon peri
The characteristics of this period are, g
simplicity of the tomb and the uniform p
tice of burying, not burning, the body.
the large number of "Dipylon" va

lected from the twenty excavated graves this period, no single one presents ces of burning, and to this fact, no ıbt, they owe their fine state of pre-vation. The grave of this period, then, sents the following appearance: it ısists of an ample trench, in which the ly of the dead man was laid, with room the disposal about him of an abundant play of household utensils,—vases of every pe and size, cups, cylikes, wine-pourers, n, in one instance, a large cooking-pot. lden diadems are the chief personal orna-nt, and the man has his iron sword or ar, the woman her terra-cotta wheel for ıning. Everywhere there is abundant dence of a lively conviction that the dead n had need, in the tomb below the ground, the furniture of his life above.

The grave was then covered in with wood, th was heaped over the covering, but not ıs to level it up,—there always remained a ıch, and this is certainly the intention, for tunately one of these ancient graves has n preserved, with its monument still nding over it. Here it is clear that the nument, a large terra-cotta vase, stood h its foot buried in the trench, and only body of the vase visible above it. The pose of the trench is clear enough,—it was sacrifice to the dead men below, just as ysseus dug his trench and poured into it blood of the black ram, to revive the ls of the heroes. Bones of the sacrificed mals are found in masses about the pylon graves. It is a curious point that the es set up as monuments have holes ough the bottom, and it is conjectured t through these holes the offerings were ıred.

Passing to a grave dating two centuries er the contrast is clearly marked. The side is resplendent with slabs of polished rble, and to the uninitiated would raise h hopes of treasure within,—hopes tain to be disappointed. A single bastron or a lekythos, a chance mirror,—t is all. The splendidly-decorated vases he sixth and fifth centuries B.C. were for ıria, and not for home use. Faith in the l man had perished, and ritual offerings narrowed to a minimum of convention,—a imum strictly regulated by the legislation olon.

hat strikes us most (to go back a little) e contrast between the "Dipylon" mode urial and that known to us through er. In the Dipylon, burial; in Homer, ing: in the Dipylon little outward show, ı provision for the ghost below; in Homer ge memorial mound and a stele, but no orial sacrifice. The ghost banished for to Hades, remote, inaccessible, apart. All spiritual significance of the contrast has brilliantly worked out by Dr. Rohde in "Psyche." About 600 B.C. (*i.e.* a hundred s later than the Dipylon tombs) the influ- of epic thought is apparent: burning lants burial; huge mounds, such as those urva and Velanidesa, are upreared; the ard pomp contrasts with the inward iness. Most striking of all, in place of cenes from *real* life, buryings and battles h appear on Dipylon vases, the huge) vases are decorated with scenes from mythology — Perseus and Medusa, akles and Nessos.

With the fifth and fourth century came magnificent series of grave-reliefs that h so much for the history of art, which belong to the story of the ıence of Pheidias and Praxiteles, and nothing of the convictions of the ivors. Next, suddenly in the third ury B.C. the grave *reliefs* cease. Grave-es still abound, small columns with in-tions, small table-like vases,—*τράπεζαι* t no groups of figures. Cicero tells us he second book De Legibus) the cause,—ıactment of Demetrios between 317 and B.C.: "Sepulcris autem novis finivit um: nam super terræ tumulum noluit statui nisi columellam tribus cubitis ne rem aut mensam aut labellum." Of all e sorts,—the pillar, the table, the vase,—we have instances; the vase, a large sort of wide-mouthed water-vessel, appears not only in actual monuments, but in the representation on later Italy vases.

Athens was sunk very low; she altered the whole fashion of her funeral monuments at the word of the tyrant. Sculpture and decoration only revived, and in very modest form, under Roman rule. Once the conviction in the after-existence of the dead man weakened, if not destroyed, the manner of burial and the form of monument became mere matter of passing fashion.

NOTES.

AS might have been expected, the proposal of the Manchester Corporation authorities to destroy the best interior feature of Sir Chas. Barry's Royal Institution building has been carried. Such propositions always are carried in England, in cases where art is on the one side and the making or saving of money on the other. Those who understand and care for architecture are in a minority, and can only protest; they may have all the reason and knowledge palpably on their side, but when it comes to counting votes the majority will be with the Philistines. In this case the majority was unusually large, fifty-six to six, which we presume represents the proportion of artistic enlightenment in the Manchester Town Council. The names of the protesting six should be given; they were Mr. Alderman J. Thompson, Mr. Alderman King, Mr. Alderman Lloyd, Councillors Abbot, Pingstone, and Milne. These gentlemen deserve the thanks of those interested in architecture for doing their best to preserve one of the not too numerous pleasant bits of modern town architecture, which Manchester is prepared to wipe out in order to get room for a temporary occupation of the building for a few years, when it will probably be deserted for a new gallery. It is a discreditable and stupid affair, and will long be remembered against the Manchester official authorities by those who understand what is the value to a city of any detail that is beyond the ordinary run of architectural commonplace. The wrath of one of the Town Councillors against this journal and its editor for what he called our "insolent" remarks on the subject of the proposed demolition was an amusing feature in the proceedings of the Council meeting, but no doubt the worthy Councillor really felt himself and his colleagues aggrieved: it is so difficult for some people to understand why anyone should feel strongly about a mere effect of architecture when the saving of money or of space is in question.

SINCE the fight about the Royal Institution began, another unfortunate case of architectural muddling in Manchester has been started, in the shape of a proposal to enlarge the Royal Exchange by, as far as we can understand, advancing the whole front wall to the plane of the front colonnade of the portico, and leaving the building with a closed front and a couple of mean-looking side entrances instead of the stately columnar portico and central entrance. The Manchester Royal Exchange is not a building we can quite feel enthusiasm about; it is not refined in detail; but it is a dignified structure in the average classic style, and there is no question that to alter it as proposed would be simply to ruin it architecturally; nothing less can be said. The reason of course is that the area of the building is not large enough for the present demands upon it; but is that a reason for architecturally ruining the façade of one of the most important modern buildings in the city, designed by a Manchester architect? The architect (Mr. Murgatroyd) is himself to be entrusted with the task of destroying the architectural effect of his own building, but we fear that will be rather a poor consolation to him. We wish to emphasise the fact that to alter the building in the way proposed is a kind of operation which cannot be described as remodelling; it is simply destroying the front architecturally. Manchester, though a commercial city, used to have a kind of name as a centre of artistic interest, but she seems resolved on flinging away deliberately whatever reputation of that kind she possessed.

THE Manchester, Sheffield, and Lincolnshire Railway have got their Bill for a new line to London. In technical parlance, the preamble has been "proved." This does not prevent a large number of details,—in this instance of an important kind,—being yet reserved for consideration; but the fact that the Committee have found the preamble proved, means, as we understand in this case, not only that the line may be constructed, but also the terminus, as desired in the Bill. There may be some public safeguards inserted, and a certain number of details; but the site chosen is approved. As that forms an integral part of the undertaking, we hope that care will be taken by the Committee to safeguard, to the full, all public and private rights. Sir Edward Watkin is not a man to look beyond the mere selfish interests of his company, as witness, for example, the way in which Charleywood Common, in Herts, has been severed by the open cutting for the Metropolitan Extension when the line could have been constructed through a tunnel, and this important open space have been left uninjured. No doubt "Lord's" has been generously dealt with by the company, but simply and solely from the point of view of railway policy. Therefore it is the bounden duty of the Committee, before the Bill receives its final sanction, to examine all the clauses with care, and with a view to protect all the rights involved.

THE loss of life at the Hampstead Heath Station of the London and North-Western Railway is surprising only because no accident of a similar kind has recently occurred. The really surprising thing is that accidents are not of constant occurrence at many surburban and metropolitan railway stations where large crowds are assembled. Many of these stations are difficult of access, and the mere weight of the crowd on such staircases as those, for instance, on nearly all the Metropolitan and District stations, is in itself a danger. It is equally surprising that on bank holidays passengers are not pushed on to the line in the insensate rush for the trains which is visible on these days. The bad lighting of many of the approaches to metropolitan and surburban stations is also a source of danger to the public. In fact it is questionable whether the Board of Trade ought not to make periodical surveys of all railway stations. The convenience of passengers may, perhaps, not be within the jurisdiction of that department, but their safety undoubtedly is.

THE idea of having an international exhibition at Berlin in 1896 or 1897 has been coming up again of late. Meetings have been held on the subject by several public bodies, by various guilds and chambers of commerce, and now the municipal authorities of Berlin have elected a special committee of thirty members of the town executive and the Common Council to consider the matter thoroughly, and to decide on what steps the city as such should take, and to what extent, and in what way, pecuniary assistance should be given. Herr von Berlepsch, who holds the Prussian portfolio of Commerce, is also taking interest in the scheme, and has gone so far as to declare that the idea of having an international exhibition at Berlin has the sympathy of the present Government. There is certainly a strong probability of the exhibition being held now, especially as rumour says that both Government and the Municipality will, for once, loosen their purse-strings and try to compete with France as regards liberality. The money question will probably not be the great difficulty, as patriotism will be an ally in that matter; the difficulties will commence in the selection of a site for the exhibition grounds; a conveniently situated site will be most difficult to find, and when found the monotony of Brandenburg's dusty plain will have to be diversified by artificial means.

THE new number of the Prussian Archæological "Jahrbuch" (1892, vii. 1) is so full of good things that it is hard to make selection. Dr. Puchstein, who has done so much for the investigation of early architectural forms, contributes an article, which architects should not miss, "On the column in Assyrian architecture." Briefly, the conclusions he draws (based chiefly on the architectural statements made in cuneiform inscriptions,—of which he thinks sufficient use has not, so far, been made) are these,—that the column was originally an element unknown to Assyrian structures,—that in this respect they offer a marked contrast to Hethite, *i.e.*, Syrian work, for Syria shows an acquaintance with the column that dates from the tenth or eleventh century B.C.,—that the column came to Assyria from Syria by way of a fashion for imitating the Hethite style, which came in about the middle of the eighth century B.C.; but down to the seventh century B.C. the column was regarded as a foreign element, and only employed under exceptional conditions. Dr. Puchstein reserves for a second article the consideration of the special base and capital forms customary in Assyria, and of their relation to the Hethite form from which they are derived.

ANOTHER structural article of interest is that on nautical archæology, which forms in effect a sort of supplement to the article on "Seewesen," which the writer (Herr Ernst Assmann) contributed to Baumeister's "Denkmäler." Herr Assmann draws largely on the British Museum for his illustrations, the collections of which, he thinks, have so far not been made of adequate use. Two articles of special importance are devoted to vase paintings. Dr. Fröhner publishes two Corinthian vases, with Homeric subjects, hitherto unknown in this class of work. One, the most remarkable piece of ceramography that has been published for many years, represents the Greek heroes pouring out of the Trojan horse. We examined the vase, some years ago, in the Oppermann collection of the Bibliothèque Nationale at Paris, with a view to publication, but renounced it owing to its extremely damaged and effaced condition. Dr. Fröhner, however, has succeeded admirably, though the inscriptions still baffle him. Another vase painting published by Dr. Kretschmer, shows Perseus contending with the Bacchantes, a myth hitherto not known on vase paintings. Dr. Hauser contends that the interesting and beautiful bit of archaic sculpture, usually known as the "woman mounting a chariot," and sometimes connected with the frieze of the earlier Parthenon, is in reality the god Apollo. Last, Dr. Maximilian Mayer contributes an article,—valuable in relation to the Vaphio cups,—on the Mycenæ representations of bull contests and capture.

THE "Vereinigung Berliner Architekten" some time since sent a petition to the municipal authorities asking them to consider the advisability of making some alterations in the management of their buildings, so that not only the members of the Municipal Board of Works, but also the "unattached" architects, might have the chance of putting up some of the public buildings. It was hoped that these alterations would tend to give the citizens not only a more practical, but also a more beautiful, set of municipal erections than they could at present boast of. Some fifteen members of the Municipal Board of Works have now sent in a counter petition, according to which they apparently consider their work perfect, and excuse the hideousness of their façades by stating that any embellishment would be a sin against economic considerations. We are under the impression that no extra expenditure need be incurred for the purpose of putting an end to the erection of the worst forms of Berlin official architecture. The so-called "Pomeranian" brickwork, as is used on the simplest Hamburg warehouse, is not only cheaper but more agreeable to the eye than brickwork with poor copies of ornamented Greek mouldings in a bad terra-cotta. If we consider that no less than 180 schools, twenty covered markets and fire-stations, and four hospitals and asylums have been put up under the present head of the Board of Works, and then examine some of the latest planning, we can safely affirm that a change in the management of municipal building affairs can at least not do any harm.

AS we stated in a "Note" in our issue for February 27 last, the Middlesex County Council intend to enlarge, at an estimated cost of 20,000*l.*, the Council Chamber and Sessions House at the Westminster Guildhall. On the date mentioned we gave some particulars of the history of the site and its surroundings: we now append a description of the building itself, which, we fear, will be more or less altered in appearance when the works, now just commencing, are completed. James Elmes, in a work published in 1828,* gives a view of the building, and writes of it as follows:—

"The Guildhall, Westminster, is an insulated structure, designed for the use of the municipality of Westminster, standing on the south side of the ancient sanctuary, near to the Abbey. In this building are held the sessions for the city, and the trials in the court of the High Bailiff, and it afforded accommodation for the various high courts of law and equity during the repairs of Westminster Hall. It is a quadrangular brick building, with recesses at the angles, that give it somewhat the form that continental architects call a Greek cross; and has a tetrastyle portico of the Doric order, with a pediment, in the principal front. The centre of the building is crowned by an octangular tower, with semicircular windows in every face that give light to the principal court below. At each angle is a pier that serves for a buttress, which, with a connecting moulding that runs round the entire building, crowns and connects the whole. On this cornice is a blocking-course, with a light and lofty balustrade, in three panels to each face. The roof meets in a point over the centre of the building, on which is a lantern and vane. It was designed and executed by the late Samuel Pepy (*sic*) Cockerell, Esq., a pupil of Sir Robert Taylor's, and father of the able and travelled architect, Mr. C. R. Cockerell,† who designed the beautiful Ionic chapel of St. George in Regent-street,‡ which is noticed at p. 100 of this work."

It was in this building that, in 1888, the Royal Commission of Inquiry into the proceedings of the Metropolitan Board of Works, presided over by Lord Herschell, held its sittings, which we reported at some length in the volumes of the *Builder* for that year.

THE *Scotsman* draws attention to an act of vandalism in course of being perpetrated on a well-known historical landmark,—the Abbey Craig of Stirling. This grand object in the scenery of the Forth is threatened with something like piecemeal removal for building material and road metal. Many who were sound patriots, as well as men of taste, lamented and protested when the summit of the Craig was crowned by the nondescript form of a National Wallace Monument. They held that, as in the case of a later proposal to perch a monument on the top of Arthur's Seat, nothing could be added by art to the grand handiwork of Nature without spoiling it,—that the Craig itself was the best monument of the national events that had taken place around its base, and of the national heroes who had sheltered in its recesses. Now, however, that the monument is in its place, and that time has begun to mellow its tone, it is found to harmonise with the landscape, in which the Abbey Craig forms so prominent an object, better than many of its critics expected. In any case, those who found fault with its appearance will be as energetically opposed as the most enthusiastic of its promoters to the removal of the monument, along with the magnificent natural pedestal upon which it stands,—the Craig itself. Hardly less than this seems to be implied in the quarrying work in which the Stirlingshire County Council are diligently engaged; and it is quite true that the voice of Scotland was joined to the Town Council of Stirling in arresting the progress of pick-axe and dynamite charge, which have already made ugly scars on the flank of one of the most beautiful and famous of the national high places. An appeal to the county authorities has hardly been received in the spirit which should be looked for in such a quarter, and the weight of opinion of that wider public who are interested in the preservation of the Abbey Craig ought to be brought into play to arrest the work of destruction.

THE proposed alteration of the great thoroughfare "Unter den Linden," at Berlin, will be both an artistic and a practical improvement. The promenade in the centre will remain as before; it will, however, be hemmed in on either side by a broad strip of grass, with flower-beds, and two double rows of trees standing closer together than the present ones. The three carriage-ways and riding-path will be turned into two broad carriage-ways, one on either side of the promenade, and then will come the footpaths, each having an extra 8 ft. added to its present width.

IT is satisfactory to find, as has been already noted in the daily papers, that owing to the English Government having increased th vote for the Chicago Exhibition to 60,000*l.* instead of the 25,000*l.* originally granted, i will no longer be necessary to charge exhi bitors for space in the English Section, whic will be free to all whose claims to exhibit a accepted. This is as it should be.

THE Clerk of the St. Pancras Vestry h sent us a copy of a report which h made on the 21st ult. to the Highways Sewers, and Public Works Committee of tha body, as to the steps taken in the parish o St. Pancras under the provisions of the Publi Health Act (London) for cleansing of foot ways from snow during the winter which i still loth to leave us. As the report possesse some interest, and gives particulars as to cost we extract a few passages from it. Wit regard to the snowfalls in February, we ar told that immediately on the first fall, step were taken to cleanse both the footways an roadways in the principal thoroughfares; an that every man applying for work at th several stone yards was employed thereon, a well as all the men in the ordinary gangs.

"Those workmen of superior grade in th Vestry's regular employ were made foremen ove the newly-formed gangs.

The number of additional men employed was 51[illegible] and the number of ordinary gangs was 426, makin a total of 939.

The cost of the extra men amounted t 280*l.* 16s. 8d.

Carts were employed on day work in removin the snow to the sewer shafts, at a cost o 69*l.* 13s. 9d.

As there were three snowfalls in close successio the work accomplished was twice obliterated, bu as testimony that it was effectively done to th extent of the means available, I may mention tha there were fewer complaints than were ever receive on such occasions, and they were principall unreasonable demands for the footways to b cleansed in bye streets.

On the occasion of the second visitation in th month, 273 additional men were engaged at a co of 103*l.* 6s. 3d.

On account of the severity of the frost, salt w used in some places, but with the caution need for such an expedient, having regard to the adver

---

* "Metropolitan Improvements; or, London in the Nineteenth Century: displayed in a series of engravings of the new buildings, improvements, &c., by the most eminent artists, from original drawings, taken from the objects themselves, expressly for this work by Mr. Thos. H. Shepherd."

† Afterwards Professor Cockerell, R.A.

‡ Latterly known as "Hanover Chapel," and now, by an Act of Parliament passed last session, doomed to destruction.

pinion expressed in a report to the Committee by r. Stevenson some years ago.

The cost of salt was 24*l*. 2s. for 17 tons."

'he officials of the Vestry seem to have cquitted themselves well on the occasion of his, their first experience of fulfilling the uty cast upon them by the new Statute, and ı this respect St. Pancras has shown a good xample to some other parishes, whose ıactivity was almost as masterly under he new as it used to be under the old *égime*. But we are doubtful about the use f salt, and, as the report says in its conluding paragraph, it yet remains to be seen hat will be the effect of a really heavy nowfall, when the clearance of the main oads will form, as it has before, the work of aramount importance.

AMONG the different publications about to be made under the auspices of the 'ereinigung Berliner Architekten, we notice ne which is to be taken in hand by the editor f the *Deutsche Bauzeitung*, which will contain ıe plans, elevations, and sections of all the ıore important Protestant churches in 'russia.

THE penny catalogue of the Birmingham Museum and Art Gallery, recently ssued under the direction of Mr. Whitworth Vallis, is indeed a remarkable pennyworth. t contains long and ably-written critical nd descriptive notes on the various artists hose works are represented, and is well rinted on fairly good paper, and Mr. Wallis alculates that on an edition of 10,000 there ill be a profit of 15*l*. Why are there not uch penny catalogues to the National Gallery, ritish Museum, and South Kensington? 'hey would be of immense service in proiding a better understanding of the objects xhibited among the poorer classes; and hough, of course, such a catalogue in regard the British and South Kensington Museums could only be of a general kind, ealing with groups of objects, general owledge is better than none.

FROM a letter in the *South Wales Daily News*, signed by the Hon. Secretaries of e Cardiff Architects' Society, we regret to that in the conditions of competition for e Town-hall at Llanelly there is a clause oviding that competitors shall quote the s on which they will be prepared to carry the work if appointed, thus making it a comition of terms as well as designs. We had to ice a similar case at Brighton a short time ce. Nothing could be more improper or re calculated to degrade the architectural fession than such a condition, and it is to hoped that no architect will have anything do with the Llanelly Town-hall competia until its promoters agree to rescind the use referred to.

CORRESPONDENT sends us the following charming example of a "prosional" touting letter now in circulation in Iidland town:—

'Gentlemen,—Having opened offices at the ve address I am prepared to wait upon you at time you are desirous of effecting alteras, additions, or erecting new buildings of any d. From an early practical training and a long l successful practice in ——, I am able to design he most economical manner possible, combining with utility. Preliminary advice free of charge. ur support and recommendation earnestly icited.—Yours faithfully,

—— ——."

only remains to add that the author of this scious epistle writes "M. S. A." after his me, and is therefore apparently a member the Society which is endeavouring again to t up a Registration of Architects Bill in der to raise the tone and standing of glish architects.

Ventilation.—Messrs. Baird, Thompson, & Co., orm us that they have obtained the highest ard for improved systems of ventilation (autotic and mechanical), and improved ventilating pliances at the Leather' Trades Exhibition, ndon.

EFFLORESCENCE ON BRICKWORK.

The white, semi-crystalline powdery efflorescence that appears on new bricks after being placed *in situ* has engaged the attention of builders and experts for a considerable time; nevertheless, no rapid effectual remedy has yet been promulgated for preventing the unsightly white patches appearing on a newly-erected wall. The result of some experiments the writer has conducted during the last twelve months may be of value to all builders, as the writer believes he has found the true remedy for the effectual removal and permanent prevention of this disfiguring efflorescence.

In the first place, a few words on the probable causes of the white appearance may not be out of place.

Bricks are naturally porous, and, therefore, readily imbibe moisture and gases. The mortar in which they are set contains two very active ingredients for the incipient evolution of organic life and crystalline formation of mineral substances,—viz., oxygen and lime (an oxide of calcium). The yellow or red colour of the sand mixed with the lime in the preparation of mortar is due to the presence in varying quantities of oxide of iron. This salt,—oxide of iron,—is one that readily gives up a part of its oxygen to any suitable body with which it may be in contact, or it readily acquires a further proportion of oxygen from the air if placed under suitable conditions. The lime also is a body in which the union of the metal (calcium) with the oxygen is not very permanent, the metal uniting with any other suitable compound substance, as, for example, carbon from the air, to form carbonate of lime,—a combination of calcium, carbon, and oxygen, $CaCO_3$, which is a body that is also unstable in composition, readily breaking up and forming new combinations or salts of other metals. Besides the sand,—silica coloured with oxide of iron,—and the lime, there are present in mortar small portions of other bodies, notably sodium salts of some kind. Now sodium (Na) unites with oxygen to form soda (Na_2O), and also with the iodide CO_2 (carbon dioxide) to form carbonate of soda, Na_2CO_3. (There are several other formulæ for this salt, as it varies in the proportions of its constituents, but the above simple form will do for our purpose.) Now, carbonate of soda can exist in the crystalline form when water is combined with it, or it can be a dry anhydrous powder; and this salt when it loses the CO_2 radical becomes Na_2O (oxide of sodium or soda), and if the elements of water have been present in the carbonate, a deliquescent salt, sodic hydrate (NaHO) can be formed. Without going further into chemical questions, deliquescent is applied to a body capable of imbibing moisture, and hence becoming semi-liquid. Suffice it to say that it is with the salts of soda we purpose to deal.

Let us imagine that the soft porous brick has imbibed water from a passing shower of rain, that it dissolves some of the sodium salts in the water, and thereby becomes impregnated with a solution of a salt of soda. Now, as the surface of the brick dries, this salt of soda, or hydrate of sodium, will become dry and converted into the anhydrous sodic oxide (Na_2O) (every one has seen a piece of ordinary mortar crystallised, and washing soda fall to a white powder after some days' exposure to the air) if the weather be dry. This is the white efflorescence that appears on the surface of the brick. If the weather be damp, it will not be positively dry (anhydrous), but appear in minute crystals (as a crystalline carbonate?). In any case, there the white efflorescence is, and it is a positive eyesore to every builder, for the white patch on the surface of the newly-built wall spoils all architectural beauties by its glaring whiteness and irregular patches. So long as any soluble salts of soda remain in the mortar to be dissolved out by the water imbibed by the porous brick, so long will this white efflorescence continue until the supply of soluble soda salt has been dissolved out and brought to the surface.

The nearest approach to a successful remedy the writer has come across amongst the various proposals for removing this disfiguring white efflorescence is hydrochloric acid (HCl). This liquid combines with the Na_2O to form water and chloride of sodium (viz., $2\,HCl + Na_2O = H_2O$ – water + 2NaCl, sodic chloride, *i.e.*, common salt).

As this sodic chloride that is formed is a soluble salt, its presence is not manifested, as it is soluble in water, and, therefore, washed away by every shower of rain. If the efflorescence is due to the presence of NaHO (sodic hydrate), the hydrochloric acid will form sodic chloride and water, as before, only half the quantity of acid being required to effect the re-formation of salts.

The remedy, therefore, would seem to point to saturating the bricks with this acid,—a process that, however, would be expensive, and dangerous to the workmen using such fluid.

Acting on the hint conveyed by the fact that the excess of sodic hydrate in soap-making is expelled from the soap by salting it,—*i.e.*, strewing the surface of the soap as it floats on the ley with common salt,—*i.e.*, sodic chloride,—the writer applied a solution of common salt to the white efflorescence on some bricks that were badly stained therewith. In every instance where such fluid was applied the white efflorescence was instantly removed, and, what is more, has never reappeared, and in obstinate cases three applications, or one application well saturating the bricks with the common salt solution, has sufficed to effect the desired result.

The chemical reaction that takes place is represented below:—

NaCl (common salt) + NaHO (sodic hydrate) produce Na_2O (sodic oxide), and HCl (hydrochloric acid). Now, theoretically Na_2O is the body we wish to expel or convert into something else, and, therefore, we are actually forming the body we are endeavouring to expel, and, *ipso facto*, the acid would be the best body to effect the desired result. One fact, however, stands strongly in evidence against such theory, and that is the remarkable non-appearance of the white efflorescence after the application of the salt solution. This may be accounted for by the fact that the combination between hydrogen and chlorine (HCl) is stronger than between sodium and chlorine (NaCl), and, therefore, the chemical reaction represented above as occurring between the efflorescent and acid occurs only to a limited extent, whereas in the application of the sodic chloride (NaCl) solution, the chlorine in the sodic chlorine readily forsakes that body to unite with the hydrogen (H) in the sodic hydrate, and that although sodic oxide is formed thereby, the simultaneous production of hydrochloric acid also neutralises the effect of the sodic oxide efflorescing. As a solution of common salt is much cheaper than hydrochloric acid, the writer would suggest that the bricks should either be dipped in a pail of such solution before being laid *in situ*, or else be well washed,—impregnated,—with it afterwards.

H. C. Standage.

PROFESSIONAL CHIT-CHAT.*

I propose this evening rather to provoke discussion on certain matters connected with our profession than to enunciate any new ideas; and the fitst topic is that of Architectural Drawing. In doing so, I propose to regard the architect as a business man. The true architect must, of course, be an artist; he must have the feelings and aspirations of an artist; he must be imbued with the importance of making his work beautiful as well as fitting; but the great aim of his drawings must be to convey intelligibly the ideas which he conceives. To do this he is somewhat handicapped, for, unlike the mere painter, he must take no licences; he must set aside pictorial effect in his drawings, and define most accurately the actual and true effect of his buildings when erected; in other words, his drawings are simply the tools by which he works.

An architect must of necessity, for the sake of accuracy and definition, work mainly with the point, and produce his drawings in line,—that is to say, his spaces must be bounded by lines, and not, as the painter's, defined by colour or surface treatment, only because the latter treatment is practically too undefined for drawings which have to be interpreted by rule and compass; but there are lines and lines.

In the days of my pupilage we were taught that an architectural line could hardly be too fine, and I have a vivid remembrance of the magnificent drawings of competition works which were given to us as copies for draughtsmanship; drawings in which the lines were almost imperceptible in their fineness; draw-

* A paper by Mr. E. Appleton, F.R.I.B.A., recently read before the Devon and Exeter Architectural Society.

ings which were fit to be bound up in books, and which would vie with the line engravings of that day.

Now, if we take Euclid's definition of a line (viz., length without breadth) we know that we can only conceive it; it cannot be practically realised.

In drawings of great precision, such as the architect has to deal with, he cannot do without lines, though I remember well once being in Beauvais Cathedral and watching a man making a drawing of the interior, and the only lines he used were simply guide lines for setting out the intersections of the groining and springing of the arcade arches; the whole of the remainder of the work he was putting in with direct colouring. But this was not the sort of architectural drawing I am alluding to; it was simply a picture, and could not have been used for building purposes. And this brings me to a point which I wish to emphasise,—viz., our architectural drawings must not be mere pictures, not even our perspective views, for our aim, if we are truthful men (as every architect should be), should be to pourtray our work as it will appear when it leaves our hands nearly completed. Do not misunderstand me. I do not mean to say that an architect must not make pictures; he ought to be able to do so, both of his own work and the work of others, old and new,—in fact, if he be a true artist, he cannot fail to do so, his very conceptions will be truly picturesque; he will think picturesque, and his thoughts will take form in his pencil, but his drawings must not be pictures only.

Who of us can say that our clients have not been misled by pretty drawings, that the realisations of our designs have frequently not come up to what was shown on our drawings? This, no doubt, has partly arisen from the fact that the drawings have been made from one point of view only, by the simple front or side elevation, without considering what the effect would be in perspective; but apart from this, the present tendency and practice of architects is to give a fictitious picturesque effect, even to their geometrical drawings. In some cases these effects are very subtle, and the client is deceived. How often do we not see false and impossible shadows given, picturesque surface treatment and broken lines,—such surfaces and such broken arrises as, if we found them in any of our new work, we should make the contractor take it down? Now, this kind of work I can call by no other name than deception. The test of how a new building will appear is best conveyed by photography (except as regards colour). By that we get the best effect of light and shade, projection and perspective, and in making an architectural drawing we should honestly consider "How will it appear when it leaves my hands, brand new, if photographed?"

In my opinion, great mischief has resulted in the modern system of etching with pen and ink in architectural drawings, instead of as, in former days, of tinting them. I am quite aware that this mode of execution is very seductive; a good etched drawing is most charming, most picturesque, but as a simple architectural drawing, most delusive. You have only to take up any number of our professional illustrated journals at haphazard to prove what I affirm. Then, again, the very system so much now in vogue of drawing with coarse lines is deceptive, and does not give the correct appearance (when finished) of new buildings, for the coarse lines give the effect of impossible shadow; there is no such thing as a line in nature, and though, as I said, lines must be used by the architect, for the purpose of accurate definition, to work by, yet these lines must be reduced to a minimum if we wish to show as nearly as possible by a drawing what the actual appearance will be.

To my mind the coarse, thick line drawings of the present day have a very slovenly, crude, and unrefined appearance; they look more like the production of a carpenter working with a broad pencil than that of an educated architect. We hear a good deal about vigour nowadays, but vigour is apt to degenerate into vulgarity.

If, then, you desire, as architects, to show faithfully by your drawings how the buildings you design will actually appear when they leave the builder's hands, let me urge the abandonment of etched, coarse line, pictures. If you must, or wish to work with the point, then do as the old line engravers did, work with such delicate, fine lines as will produce texture of surface almost like simple tinting; but you will, doubtless, say (or think) this is far too laborious a process for these go-a-head days, and would not pay. Well, then, I would say, do not etch at all in dealing with your purely architectural drawings. If we respect our craft, if we are true, honest men, and if we are real artists we must not, we dare not, give a false, delusive, deceptive effect to our drawings, or we shall surely rue the day and hear our clients say:—"I am disappointed with the result of the work; it does not look like what I thought it would from your drawing."

One of the most conscientious draughtsmen I have known was the late W. Burges; his drawings for architectural purposes, such as elevations and sections, were as near perfection as possible, consisting, as they did, of simple, fine, firm lines bounding the spaces, parts, and details without any surface treatment or shadows; little notes were put to denote particulars, such as "these stones to be bedded in cement, these to be joggled, this iron bar to be fixed with molten lead, these beams to be pinned with oak pins," and so on, which greatly reduced the labour of the quantity surveyors in arriving at the exact quality of work intended.

The late Mr. F. P. Cockerell, one of the most accomplished architects of the day, worked with fine, firm lines frequently without shades or shadows, sometimes tinting his drawings with raw sienna, putting in his shading and shadows with sepia, in which case the lines of the drawing were almost imperceptible.

I know it is exceedingly tempting, when making an architectural drawing, to give a crispness and a thereby dazzling effect,—it makes it look picturesque. By all means do this, if you please, in making sketches of old buildings for your own delectation; but not with drawings intended to be worked from and shown to your clients as representations of what their building will be.

I need not lay stress upon the infinite importance of great accuracy, even in the smallest matters of detail, to insure which it is a good plan to figure profusely every part of a drawing, whether elevation, section, or plan, and by so doing (when the drawings are being made) much labour is saved hereafter, both to oneself and the builder, by not having to resort to a scale; moreover, the scale cannot always be read sufficiently accurately; the thickness of all walls, heights of floors, width of openings and spaces, depth of strings and cornices, scantlings of timbers, centres of arches, projection of parts, outside and inside total dimensions, direction, and scantlings of joists, &c., should all be carefully figured, and it is a good plan to work from axis lines, in order to check dimensions,—in fact, the more a drawing is figured, the less likely are errors to creep in, and the more readily will all the work be set out. To my mind it is not fair to put the builder to the trouble of using a scale upon drawings, nor to throw the responsibility of taking dimensions upon him. I think, too, it is a good plan to put as many drawings as possible on each sheet; it saves a vast amount of trouble in compassing parts and dimensions. Quantity surveyors will tell you how greatly it helps them in their work. It will be found very useful, as, no doubt, you have frequently experienced, to prepare drawings showing one half of the external elevation and one half of the internal elevation, side by side, by which means the proper execution and fitting together of parts may be readily seen; the nature of the materials used should also be shown by simple tinting, showing, for instance, what parts are intended to be of brick, what of stone, what of timber; and with the elevations should be sections of the walls, if there are any details of construction to be indicated. The scale of general drawings must be left to the judgment of the architect, but I think it will be found to save a great deal of trouble if the elevations and sections are made to a large scale,—say $\frac{1}{4}$ in. to a foot, or even $\frac{1}{2}$ in. to a foot, as before hinted. Notes on drawings greatly facilitate their correct interpretation; in fact, time and labour spent upon drawings, in careful figuring and noting, is well spent, and saves much trouble hereafter.

Before concluding, let me say a word upon the value and importance of making true perspective sketches of the work in hand, not only of the entire building from various points of view, but also of the leading details. How very different a capital, for instance, looks on an elevation drawing, to what it appears in perspective; how disappointing frequently is a broach spire when viewed on the angle. In the elevation drawing the junction of the octagonal spire with the square tower looks perfect, the lines flowing into each other with ease and grace, but when seen on the angle there is frequently an abruptness and want of assimilation of parts. So, too, a circular or curved bay looks perfectly right in elevation, but when viewed at an angle the window heads and cornices are overhanging in a most uncomfortable manner.

Let me repeat, for I lay great stress upon the importance of it, make sketches in perspective to a good large scale of all leading details before finally adopting them, such as windows doors, carving, cornices, strings, capitals, terminals and last, though not least, of internal effects, both of form and light and shade, remembering that work will be subject to very different conditions when viewed inside a building and by artificial light; shadow and shade are very different indoors to what they are outside. We lose shadow, for the most part, and must design accordingly.

Much might be said about harmony of colouring in our buildings. We are too often apt to lose sight of this, with the result that many modern buildings are wanting in repose. Violent contrasts of colour in materials give a building a crude, harsh, vulgar appearance, lacking what artists term "breadth;" the eye is distracted by patches of colour, and is unable to take in the whole treatment. There is no doubt that the charm of old buildings greatly arises from the mellowing of time and weather.

I think this is a strong argument in favour of tinting our drawings in colours, rather than etching them, because the absence of colour in etching is liable to mislead us as to the real effect.

THE SURVEYORS' INSTITUTION:

EXAMINATIONS FOR THE PROFESSIONAL ASSOCIATESHIP.

The following Student Candidates have passed the Examination for the Professional Associateship:—

Bate, W. H.
Brinkworth, R. E.
Brown, G. T.
Burder, R. E. C.
Child, C., jun.
Cooke, L.
Crookes, C. R.
Druce, E.
Elgar, W. R.
Evered, G. E.
Everett, A. S.
Finn, F.
Foster, J. H. F.
Haigh, T. F.
Hales, A. J.
Hankinson, F. H.
Jarman, F. W.
Johnson, B. M.
Knight, G. E.
Little, H.
Morris, R. P.
Ouvry, P. A.
Parker, F. W.
*Raffety, H. W.
Scott, T.
†Squire, G. R.
Weatherhead, D. W.
Wells, W. H.
Whitaker, E. V.

* Special Prize, 1892. † Institution Prizeman, 1892.

The following Non-Student Candidates have also passed the Examination for the Professional Associateship:—

Allen, J. P.
Amos, F.
Barker, G. L.
Bevan, S.
Davies, D. T.
Debenham, F. B.
Ellis, A. E.
Flight, A.
Ford, S.
Fox, C. E.
Gardner, G.
‡German, G., Jun.
Griggs, H. J.
Hellicar, G. T.
Jarrett, T. W.
Johns, P.
Lucas, J. A.
McCarthy, H. R.
Macer, A. T.
Maughan, J.
Mollenfeld, J. H.
Menzies, R.
Mew, R. H.
Miller, G. F.
Morrish, H. K.
Newman, S. F.
Ovenden, C.
Prall, H. A.
Price, R. A.
Skipper, H. H.
Thomas, E. M. D.
Tory, J. E.
Venning, A. J. M.
Wheeler, J. H.
Wilson, J. H.
Wing, G. S.
Woods, A. G.

‡ Driver Prize, 1892.

The results as regards the Fellowship Examination will, it is hoped, be announced next week.

Danish Antiquities.—As is generally known, the southern part of Denmark is very rich in antiquities from the Stone, Bronze, and Iron Ages, and, since the war with Germany, it was the custom to send such antiquities to the Museum at Kiel. However, the Danish press in Northern Schleswig having protested against sending these valuable archæological relics into Germany, local museums for their preservation are now being formed in various pa[rts]. As an illustration of the movement, it may be mentioned that of the 133 antiquities sent to the Kiel Museum during the last half of 1891, only one came from South Jutland, and this was of doubtful origin, a potter's disc.

The "Pine" Ceiling Paper.

The "Vine" Ceiling Paper.

COMPETITIONS.

NEW BOARD SCHOOLS, PENRITH.—We ear that the designs sent in under the motto Experience" have been selected as the best by he Penrith School Board for the new schools in runswick-road, Penrith, from amongst sixteen ets submitted in open competition. The author roved to be Mr. Geo. Dale Oliver, F.R.I.B.A., f Carlisle, who has accordingly been appointed rchitect for the new schools.

THE DESIGNS FOR THE NEW COINAGE.—he *Pall Mall Gazette* announces that, in ccordance with the report of the Committee ppointed by the Treasury, the coinage has een entrusted to two competitors. They are Ir. Thomas Brock, R.A., and Mr. Edward J. oynter, R.A. Mr. Brock's design has been osen for the head of her Majesty which will pear on all the new coins. One of his reses has also been absolutely accepted. It s intended for the two-shilling piece, but it thought likely that it will be adopted for her coins. Mr. Brock's "St. George and the agon" for a second reverse has also been cepted, but his design has been returned to e studio for a slight modification which has en suggested. Mr. Poynter's designs for all e other reverses have been selected.

ARCHITECTURAL SOCIETIES.

BIRMINGHAM ARCHITECTURAL ASSOCIATION. A meeting of this Association was held on the th inst. at the Birmingham and Midland stitute. The following gentlemen were cted as officers for session 1892-93:—esident, W. Hale, F.R.I.B.A.; Vice-President, Barry Peacock; Hon. Treasurer, C. E. Baten; Hon. Librarian, H. Beck; Hon. Secretary, rbert R. Lloyd, A.R.I.B.A.; Council, W. H. lake, M.A., A.R.I.B.A., H. H. McConnal, .I.B.A., W. Hawley Lloyd, T. Naden, Rawson Bewlay, S. F. Harris, and C. Silk. C. E. Bateman then read a paper on astle Bromwich Church," in which he debed, with considerable minuteness, the disery which he has recently made, that within eighteenth century pseudo classical buildare the remains of a much earlier Gothic ch, which was apparently chiefly, if not irely, a timber building. The remains of earlier church, which are still *in situ*, are roof of the nave, with its supporting oak amns, clearstory, and gable ends, all framed extraordinarily massive oak timbers, the pret nave being merely a plaster case to the lier work, with aisles and chancel probably lt on the lines of the original aisles and ncel, but in brick and stone, in the fashion the eighteenth century, in place of the ber Gothic work. Mr. Bateman illustrated paper with an elaborate series of measured wings of the church, and gave extracts from parochial accounts, proving the dates of the ious works carried out from time to time. A of thanks, proposed by Mr. Newton, was ported by Messrs. Bidlake, Naden, Double-, Harrison, Peacock, and Hale, who each erred to the great value of the discovery made by Mr. Bateman, and to its great interest to both architects and archæologists.

DUNDEE INSTITUTE OF ARCHITECTURE.—At the meeting of the Dundee Institute of Architecture, Science, and Art, on the 14th inst., a lecture was delivered by Mr. W. D. M'Kay, R.S.A., Edinburgh, on "The Art of the Low Countries." Mr. Charles Ower presided, and there was a fair attendance. At the outset the lecturer said in two at least of the fine arts,—painting and architecture,—the Low Countries were a treasure-house hardly second to Italy itself. Certainly no part of the world contained such a mine of artistic wealth within so narrow a compass; nor had any lands exhibited such a full measure of artistic activity in the development of painting as did Belgium and Holland during the first half of the seventeenth century. He then proceeded to treat his subject from the painter's point of view. Photographs illustrative of several of the paintings to which the lecturer referred were exhibited, and at the conclusion Mr. M'Kay was, on the motion of the chairman, awarded a hearty vote of thanks.

Illustrations.

DESIGNS FOR WALL-PAPERS.

THESE are three recent designs for wall-papers. That marked A, by Mr. Walter Crane, is founded on an alternating grouping of peacocks and cockatoos; one of the many new fancies which Mr. Crane has contributed to wall decoration of this kind. We confess that we are not altogether in favour of the adoption of birds or animals in wall-papers, unless they are very highly conventionalised, and conventionally interwoven, as one may say, with the design; these of Mr. Crane's seem a little too much as if merely *placed* where they are on the wall, they do not sufficiently grow into or out of the design, in spite of the clever attempt to unite them with it by conventionalising their tails. As a whole, however, it is a rich and effective wall covering, with a strongly-marked character of its own.

The paper marked B, designed by Mr. Lewis F. Day, is named the "Florentine," from the use of the Florentine fleur-de-lis as the centre ornament of the panels formed by the rich Romanesque foliage. It is a relief paper, produced in rich effects of colour and gold as in the old Venetian leathers, and in this form can be appropriately used in combination with oak or painted dados. The paper is only suited to a large and somewhat sumptuous class of interior, but it is a fine powerful design, one of the best recent ones that we have seen of this kind.

The design marked C, also by Mr. Day, consists of a paper marked "The Artichoke," being founded on that vegetable, with a frieze of very different character, distinguished by the introduction of a small snake as an element in the design, and hence called the "Serpent" frieze. Though a frieze should always show a sufficiently marked contrast with the wall surface below, it may perhaps be a question whether the frieze and the wall pattern in this case are not too much at variance in style and detail; they have not the appearance of having been designed together. The frieze is, however, a very graceful and rather novel design in itself.

All the papers illustrated were designed for, and are manufactured by Messrs. Jeffrey & Co., the well-known makers of Islington. We append also cuts of two other recent designs made for the same firm, the "Vine" and the "Pine," intended for ceilings.

CHURCH OF ST. JOHN THE BAPTIST, HOLLAND-ROAD, W.

THE elevation we publish this week is the western façade, a plan to a small scale being added. All the church is finished with the exception of the turret porches at the west end. The building is of great height. It is situated between houses, so is, therefore, difficult to get a good view of; the west end abuts on to the Holland-road.

The church is in the Early Pointed style; the exterior is faced with Ancaster rag rubble work, the dressings of the windows, copings, &c., being of Bath stone. The roofs of the aisles are covered with lead, and the remainder of roofs with green slates. The internal surface of the wall is formed with Bath stone, and the whole area of the church is covered with stone groining. The arches are all richly moulded.

The chancel is raised four steps above the nave floor, and the altar five steps more above the chancel floor, the pavings of these portions being of encaustic tiles and brown and blue Ancaster stone. The organ is placed in a tribune over the north aisle of the chancel. On the south side is the Lady chapel. A large stone and painted panel reredos is about to be erected behind the high altar. The paving of the passages in nave and aisles is of stone, with wood blocks under the seats. The church is warmed by Mr. Grundy, and consists of hot air in conjunction with hot water.

The total length of the building as at present completed is about 151 ft., and breadth 67 ft., interior height to groining, 55 ft., exterior to ridge of roof, 75 ft., the length of the chancel is 58 ft.

During the progress of the building, the Architectural Association paid a visit to the works.

The architect of the building is Mr. James Brooks.

THE OLD GUILDHALL, LAVENHAM.

THE old Guildhall at Lavenham, of which we publish a sheet of measured drawings and details by Mr. J. S. Corder, stands at the south side of the Market-place, at the corner of Lady-street, and has a frontage of 48 ft. to the former and 27 ft. to the latter. These dimensions refer to the main structure, though it is probable that the buildings abutting on it, and now used as cottages, were at one time connected with it.

The hall consists of a ground-floor with cellars underneath one portion, and an overhanging upper storey, ceiled at the plate level, the roof space over being lighted by small windows in the gable ends. The construction is as follows:—The walls to cellars and up to ground-floor line are very thick, and built of brick and rubble united by mortar, as are also the massive chimneys. On this substructure was placed oak framing ingeniously morticed and tenoned together and pegged with oak pins, the interstices of the framework being filled with clay and chopped straw and wattles intertwined, and the durability of this construction is marvellous.

The first floor overhangs the ground floor 18 in., and this is continued on both frontages by means of an angle beam and corner post, the joists being framed into the former, and showing at right angles to the wall all round; thus carrying the framing above, which rests on a beam beautifully carved with twisted leaf pattern. The roof would be covered with either tiles or thatch.

All the windows, except the small lights under the overhanging fitst floor, were in the form of projecting bays, but of these only one exists, namely, that on the ground floor to Lady-street. The gables originally projected over the wall face and had carved barge-boards, but only that to the porch remains.

On the exterior is an elaborate corner post, on which is carved a small full-length effigy of John, the fifteenth Earl, its noble founder, in plate armour. He stands on a pedestal or buttress beneath a cusped and crocketed canopy, the underside of which is groined in imitation of stone roofing. In his right hand he grasps a distaff, on which may be seen some unspun yarn, and in his left bears the scroll or charter of the Guild. The post is richly decorated with sunk tracery and Tudor floriations.

Entering by the porch, at the corners of which are two angle posts of similar design to the one above mentioned, but having beneath the canopies, in place of effigies, two lions sejant rampant, emblematical of the Corpus Christi, we find ourselves in the main hall of the Guild,—a room without a fireplace, 20 ft. by 17 ft., with elaborately-moulded beams and joists overhead. It was here that the merchants met and transacted business.

On either side of the hall are two smaller rooms, offices of the Guild, each having a large open fireplace.

In the rear of the left hand one was probably the kitchen, from the vast size of the fireplace, being over 10 ft. in width.

The central hall communicates with the staircase by a door immediately opposite the entrance. This staircase leading to the first floor is formed of solid balks of wood, sawn through diagonally, and resting on bearers. The arrangement of the rooms above follows that below, a small room being over the porch. Two of these rooms have large open fireplaces.

In the room to the right of the central hall are remains of linen pattern panelling, and doubtless the whole of the walls on the ground floor were covered with this, or similar material. The upper rooms probably showed the timber framing inside, plastered between the studs.

The doorways are all Tudor-headed, those on the ground floor having carved spandrels; the doors were ledged and boarded, hung on massive band hinges, of which several examples exist. The outer door of the porch was probably a large one, with a smaller door cut in the centre, similar to examples which still exist in the town.

The windows were filled with glass in lead quarries, and, in the upper lights, rich blazonings and coats of arms were doubtless inserted.

Beneath the principal staircase to the first floor is a brick stair leading to the cellar: this is a most interesting apartment, about 16 ft. 10 in. by 31 ft. 9 in., 7 ft. 3 in. high; lighted by three small iron-barred windows. In the walls of the cellar are small recesses about 2 ft. wide and 1 ft. 2 in. deep, arched over with Tudor heads in brick, and having seats in them 1 ft. 3 in. above the floor, but for what purpose they served remains doubtful. Besides these there are other recesses for lamps and cupboards.

After the Guild was abolished, the building passed successively through the stages of town-hall, prison, and workhouse; falling into private hands, it was converted into cottages, and finally a granary and wool-store.

The building is now the property of Mr. W. C. Quilter, M.P., who is restoring it with a view to its future preservation. J. S. C.

STAMFORD-ROAD SCHOOLS, KETTERING.

THESE schools are the first of those erected by the School Board for the town of Kettering. They include the large mixed school, the smaller infants' school, and the offices for the use of the Board. The accommodation is for rather more than 1,100. The class-rooms are all on the ground floor, and are grouped round two central halls; they are in every case lighted from the left, except in one of the infants' rooms, where left-hand lighting is not of so much importance. Half of the class-rooms in the mixed department accommodate sixty children, the other half forty, and on each side there are two rooms communicating, so that a pupil-teacher may take a class under supervision. There is also a cookery class-room placed outside the main group, and accessible for classes in the evening without throwing the whole school open. The corridors are broad, and communicate directly with the cloak-rooms. The master has his private rooms over the boys' cloak-room; the mistress has hers in the central block, near the offices; and the infants' mistress has hers over the infants' cloak-room. The w.c.'s for the children are in detached buildings in the playgrounds; those for the teachers adjoin their own quarters. The offices comprise a waiting-room and clerk's office on the ground floor, and a board-room and committee-room upstairs.

The heating and ventilation are by warm air on the *plenum* system, the engineers being Messrs. Ashweil & Co., of Leicester. The fresh air is taken in at the traceried openings of the tower, and is driven by a fan along large corridors under the ground-floor, and then up a shaft into each of the class-rooms. At the base of each shaft is a battery of steam-pipes, which warms the air as it commences its ascent, and the supply can be regulated by valves. The air thus impelled into the class-rooms is then expelled by the same force up extract shafts into a large trunk in the roof, and so out through the turret. The air is taken in at a comparatively high level, as being likely to be purer. The other stages of the tower are devoted to a clock and a bell.

The building throughout is of red brick, with dressings of Weldon stone. The exterior is in Leicester sand bricks; the interior in hard-pressed bricks from Kettering, painted and colour-washed. The cloak-rooms and corridor have a high dado of glazed bricks. The roof is covered with Broseley tiles, except to the inner parts surrounding the central hall of the mixed school, where the pitch is kept flatter in order not to obstruct the light to the clearstory windows more than possible; the roofs here are slated, but the change in covering is not visible from any point of view. The floors throughout are of pitch-pine wood blocks.

The works are being carried out by Mr. A. Barlow, of Kettering, from the designs of the architects, Messrs. J. Alfred Gotch, F.S.A., and Charles Saunders, Mr. W. J. Vinnell being the clerk of works.

LODGE AT COMPTON, SHERBORNE.

THIS lodge has lately been built almost entirely by workmen on the estate, from the designs and under the superintendence of Mr. Evelyn Hellicar. The walls are in coursed rubble work, brought to a fairly smooth face, of a capital walling stone quarried on the property. The moulded work and quarries are in stone from the neighbouring Ham-hill quarries, and the roof is covered with red Broseley tiles.

CRYSTAL PALACE SCHOOL OF PRACTICAL ENGINEERING.

THE distribution of certificates awarded to the students of the Crystal Palace School of Practical Engineering took place on the 13th inst., Mr. John Aird, M.P., presiding.

Mr. F. K. J. Shenton, the Superintendent of the Science and Art Department of the Crystal Palace, having read a report setting forth the result of the examinations,

Mr. Aird addressed the students. He said (we quote from the report in the *Standard*) that it was a great pleasure to him to note the progress which had been made, and also to observe the further efforts which had been put forth by the Crystal Palace Company to develope and encourage good work by providing increased conveniences and comforts for both teachers and pupils. It was very gratifying to observe in the report that in regard to Mechanical Engineering, 41 of the students had passed out of 52 available, and he was sure it must be a pleasure to all who had the welfare of the School at heart to see that with a maximum of 288 marks Mr. H. J. Lintott should have been successful with 251 marks. He was followed very closely by Mr. J. B. E. Gwira with 248 marks, and by Mr. A. Edwards with 244 marks. That was a most satisfactory result, and said a great deal for the earnestness of purpose of many of the students of the college. Comparing the progress made now with that of the year 1888 he found that the number of students had increased from 73 to 112. As to the advantages of the School, he might, having some little knowledge of the matter, assure the parents and friends of the students that he did not think any more complete engineering school could be arranged. Nor did he think that any engineering school offered such advantages as could be obtained there for those students who really intended to work. Having been through the workshops, he was able to bear testimony to the perfection of the work there exhibited, whether it related to practical construction or the preparation of plans, &c. He did not think that any occupation offered such vast interest to young men as by its means they not only secured a position for themselves, but were so placed that they could do much good to the world at large. He could only hope that the Crystal Palace School of Engineering would continue to prosper in the way it had done in the past. In 1888 he put forward a suggestion that the time was rapidly approaching when, in the interest of the country, it would be desirable that there should be again a great International Exhibition. He not only communicated that suggestion to the Press, but had an interview with the Council of the Society of Arts upon the subject. Great attention was given to it by the Duke of Abercorn and others associated with him; but the Duke afterwards wrote him stating that after having given the matter careful consideration the Council had come to the conclusion that it would be premature to take any steps at that time, as it was doubtful whether an International Exhibition could be arranged with advantage until 1894 or 1895. What he now wished to put forward for consideration was that four years had now elapsed since then, and that although the suggestion might have been premature then, it might not be so now. In fact, he held that such an exhibition was necessary if the country was to hold its own in the trading world, and such an exhibition could not be held to be complete unless advantage was taken of the Crystal Palace, with its extensive grounds, for the purpose. He threw it out as a suggestion to Mr. Shenton and Mr. Wilson that it might be worth while for the students who had shown such great capacity in drawing to devote some of their spare time in devising some general scheme by which the exhibition, if carried out, might be held in the grounds of the Palace.

Mr. J. G. Rhodes, in moving a vote of thanks to the examiners, mentioned that the Board of the Crystal Palace Company, at a meeting held on the previous day, had passed a vote for the installation of an electric plant in connection with the School, for the benefit of the students who were making electric engineering their special study.

Mr. J. Day, Mr. C. W. Best, and Mr. Milne having acknowledged the compliment, the certificates were distributed, and Mr. J. Wilson (the Principal of the School) having offered a few observations, the ceremony closed with a vote of thanks to Mr. Aird.

CO-OPERATIVE STORES, SHIREMOOR, NORTHUMBERLAND.—New co-operative stores were opened at Shiremoor on the 6th inst. by Mr. T. Burt, M.P. The front of the building is 70 ft. The grocery and drapery shops occupy the full length of frontage, and are divided by a central entrance, with staircase leading to the first floor. At the rear of the front shops are flour shops, milliners' rooms and goods warehouse, beneath which is a cellar. On the first floor is the hardware and boot department, 45 ft. by 30 ft., tailors' and tea rooms. The flour warehouse is over the flour shop. The committee-rooms, manager's-office, and check-office are at the east end, and are also provided with separate side entrance and staircase. There are also a stable, &c., at the back. The total cost will be 3,000*l*., and the work has been carried out from the designs of Messrs. Davidson & Bendle, architects, Newcastle, by Messrs. M. Hogarth & Sons, builders, Choppington.

A.—COCKATOO AND PEACO(

B.—"THE FLORENTINE"

C.—"ARTICHOKE" PAP

DESIGNE

A.

B.

DESIGNS

DESIGNED BY MR. WALTER CRANE

IGNED BY MR. LEWIS F. DAY

IEZE, "THE SERPENT"
s F. DAY

C.

PAPERS

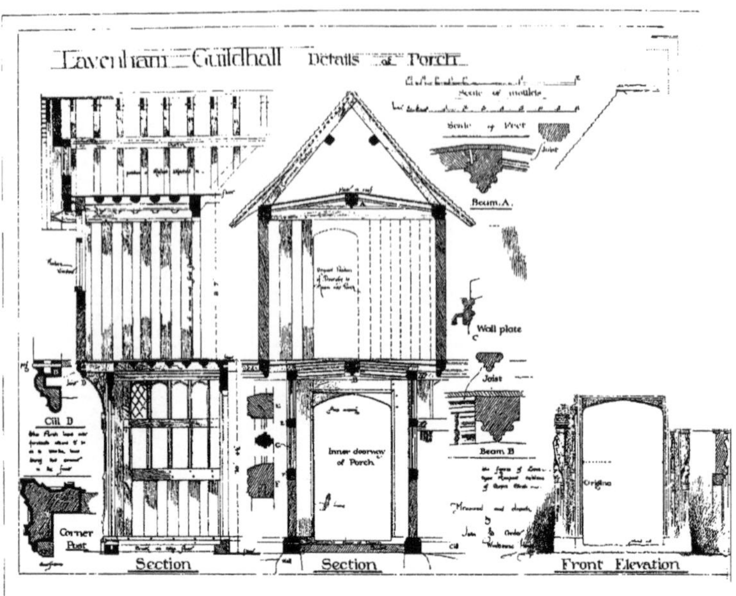
Lavenham Guildhall Details of Porch
Scale of moulds
Scale of Feet
Beam. A.
Wall plate
Joist
Beam B
Inner doorway of Porch
Cill D
Corner Post
Section
Section
Front Elevation

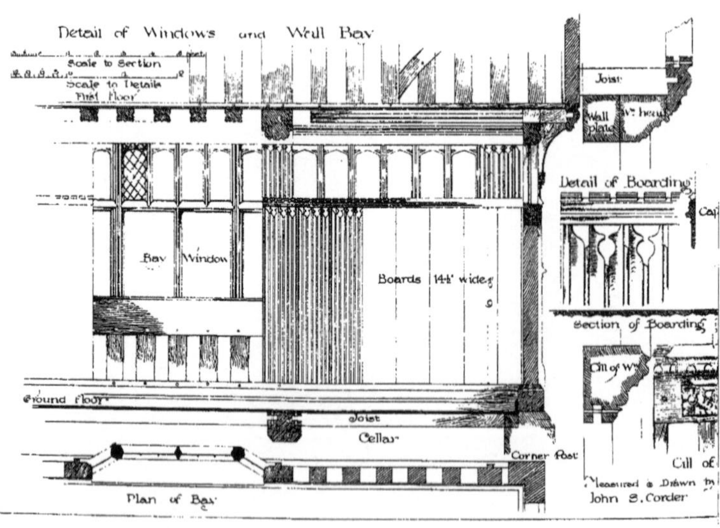
Detail of Windows and Wall Bay
Scale to Section
Scale to Details
First Floor
Joist
Wall plate
Detail of Boarding
Bay Window
Boards 14½" wide
Section of Boarding
Ground floor
Joist
Cellar
Corner Post
Cill of
Plan of Bay
Measured & Drawn by
John S. Corder

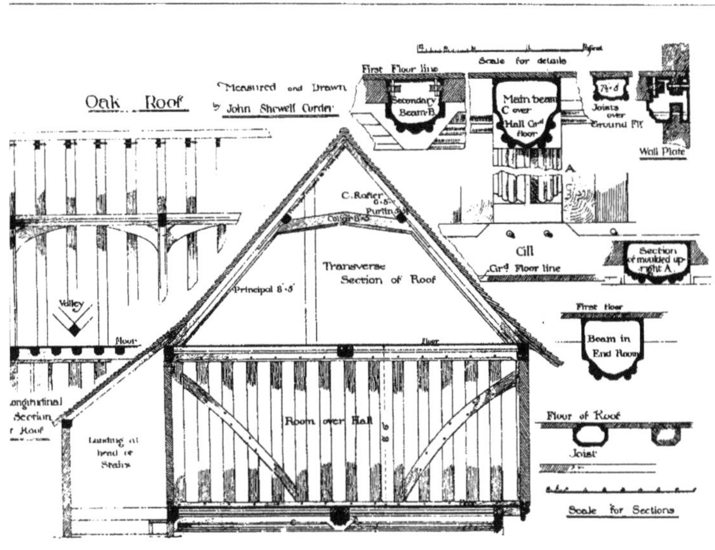
Oak Roof
Measured and Drawn by John Shewell Corder
Scale for details
First Floor line
Secondary Beam B
Main beam C over Hall Grd floor
Joists over Ground Flr
Wall Plate
C. Rafter
Purlin
Collar
Cill
Grd Floor line
Section of moulded upright A
Transverse Section of Roof
Principal 8·5
Valley
Floor
First floor
Beam in End Room
Longitudinal Section of Roof
Room over Hall
Landing at head of Stairs
Floor of Roof
Joist
Scale for Sections

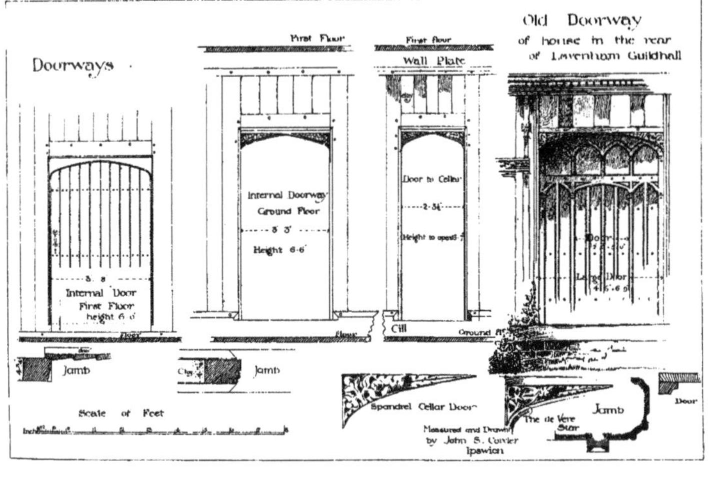
Doorways
Old Doorway of house in the rear of Lavenham Guildhall
First Floor
First floor
Wall Plate
Internal Door First Floor height 6 6
Internal Doorway Ground Floor
Height 6·6
Door to Cellar
Cill
Ground Flr
Floor
Jamb
Jamb
Scale of Feet
Spandrel Cellar Door
The de Vere Star
Jamb
Door
Measured and Drawn by John S. Corder Ipswich

PHOTO LITHO SPRAGUE & Cº

Stamford - Road Schools, for the
Kettering School - Board.
Gotch & Saunders
Architects 1891
STAMFORD ROAD

Lodge at Compton for Col. Goodden. J.P.

Church of S. John ye Baptist

Holland Road : Kensington

Elevation of Western Front.

James Brooks, Architect.

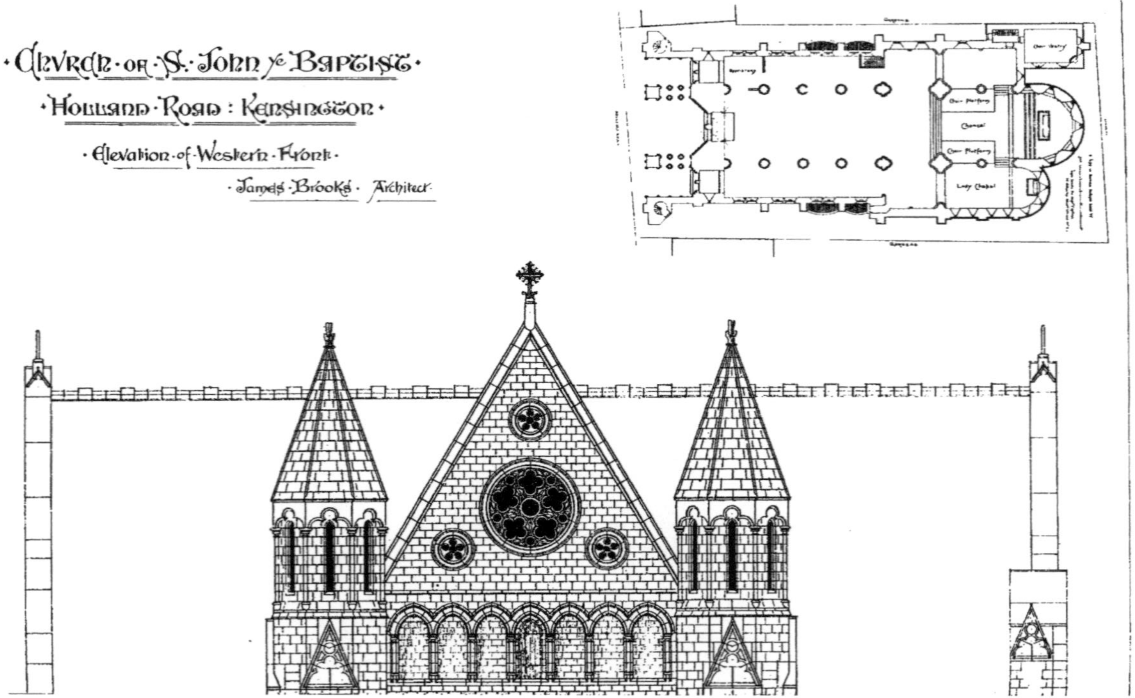

PHOTO-LITHO. SPRAGUE & Cº 4 & 5 EAST HARDING STREET FETTER L

Correspondence.

To the Editor of THE BUILDER.

ARCHITECTURAL EDUCATION.

SIR,—I must again trespass upon your luable space, but the answer of Messrs. C. H. odie, H. O. Cresswell, O. Fleming, E. S. le, W. Millard, T. E. Pryce, F. M. Simpson, d L. Stokes is in many respects so at riance with what Mr. Jackson stated in his ter to "A.A. Notes," and with my letter to *Builder* of the 9th inst., that I ask your rmission to reply to it, and then, as far as am concerned, to trouble you no more in e matter.

These gentlemen state that, "the some half-zen members of the A. A.," referred to in my ter, met Mr. Jackson and his friends but *ce*. I find in Mr. Jackson's letter he dis-otly mentions *two* meetings with his friends d some members of the A. A. Again, they te that the letter in "A. A. Notes" was *not* ritten at their request. Mr. Jackson says, have been asked by some of your members let the Association know what has been, and being, done, &c." Discrepancy somewhere!

These gentlemen state that they met Mr. ackson and his friends with the object of certaining whether they would help actively e work of the A.A., and that they did not present any one or any one's views but their m. This I am glad my letter has brought rth. On reference to the "Brown Book" I d that no less than six of these gentlemen e members of the Committee of the A.A., two the number editors of "A.A. Notes"; that r. Millard was the *only* unofficial member esent at the meeting at Storey's-gate; and at, though these gentlemen were quite un-thorised to enter into negotiations with the emorialists, they yet laid the result of their liberations *formally* before the Committee of e A.A., and six of them would, in their *autho-sed* capacity, have a vote in Committee upon e very subjects they discussed in their *un-uthorised* capacity with the Memorialists. ere they elected to serve on the Committee of e A.A. for such purposes as these?

That Mr. Jackson and his friends were, as I ferred, led "to suppose that they expressed e voice of the A. A." by those they met, would no matter of surprise, finding that they in-uded the past President of the A. A., who had ought the new educational scheme to the rth, and five other members of the Committee the A.A.

I do not forget (as these gentlemen fear) that the list of subscribers were the well-known ames that these gentlemen recite; but that es not affect my meaning as to the greater ligation the A. A. is under to the Institute d its members, and I contend that my marks were perfectly just on that point. On ference to the list of donations lately pub-hed, I find that the Institute, members of the me, and members of the A. A. subscribed out 1,300*l*., and those outside the ranks of th bodies about 80*l*.

I am told that I misrepresent Mr. Jackson hen he states that he wants us to "give up r present scheme of studies." Mr. Jackson ys, "Your printed scheme of education, in ite of a show of disclaiming it, points finitely to preparation for the Examination of e Institute. While this remains in your ges we cannot take any interest in your ogramme," and again, "If all this were rept away, &c.," tolerably conclusive evidence, think, of what Mr. Jackson meant.

A few words in conclusion. On reference to e "Brown Book," I find that out of the list of e members, ninety-six are Fellows, and 193 ssociates of the Institute, roughly 25 per cent. the total number; are they to renounce the stitute at Mr. Jackson's invitation? Mr. ckson, of course, sees the importance of inning over the A.A. to the views of the emorialists, and tells us that the A.A., if it pleased to use it, held in its hand e key of the situation." I quite agree, it believe I am rightly interpreting the ice of the majority of our members if I y that we intend to keep it; that we do not prove the alternative set forth by the Memo-alists; that we do not consider these eight ntlemen were serving the best interests of e A.A. in what they did, and, lastly, that fore any of these gentlemen seek re-election, ey should place their views without delay and without reservation before the A.A. electorate, so that we may know upon whom to rely and where we stand.

COLE A. ADAMS,
Past President A.A.

TWO VIEWS OF SIR GILBERT SCOTT'S RESTORATIONS.

SIR,—If Mr. Somers Clarke's two letters in the *Builder* had been confined to the subject of the proposed removal of Sir Christopher Wren's library at Lincoln, his case against the Dean and Chapter would have been stronger than it now stands, prejudiced by wholesale denunciation against all who undertake under the name of "restoration" any necessary repair, alteration, or adaptation of our ancient buildings to modern use for fear lest their historical value should be impaired.

Scott the restorer and Grimthorpe the destroyer alike fall under his ban. There is something so obviously uncanny in this combination that it must surely be the result of a belief that the one view they had in common was a mistaken one rather than an objection to their mode of action. Scott and Grimthorpe both had reparation and adaptation to modern use in view.

The school to which Mr. Somers Clarke has allied himself has a negative theory and do-nothing policy.

Upon what principle can a judgment of the theory and practice of this school be formed, or their results gauged?

May it not be found in the old saying, "The man that does the most good does the least harm," and "The man that does nothing, does nothing but harm."

Mr. Clarke acknowledges that Sir Gilbert Scott preserved much old work, and, as the country is full of examples of his skill in not only preserving the fabric of our ancient buildings in imminent danger of destruction, but also in bringing to light many architectural features of intense historical interest, such as the apse of the south aisle of Chester Cathedral, I think, in his case, the verdict must be that he had an excellent record of good deeds to weigh against his misdeeds, which Mr. Clarke characterises as "wholesale destruction" as "extensive as his practice," words strong enough to convey the impression of his worthiness to stand in a niche with Lord Grimthorpe, whereas the reference is only to "fittings."

That this charge is to a slight extent true in respect to Sir Gilbert's early work is manifest, and no one deplored the fact more deeply than himself in his latter days, when he endeavoured to preserve everything of historical value.

He often remarked on the strange irony of fate which brought to his own door the fault which he always sought to overcome in himself and others.

Sir Gilbert spent a life in inspiring a love for ancient art and history, and in creating the science by which it might be shown in the preservation of our ancient buildings.

Being but a man and beset by tremendous difficulties, his practice was not always abreast of his theory, and so his critics, regardless of the greatness of his work, sought in every litttle failing an excuse for leaving the field of action for the school of thought. A new school, forsooth, only founded on the old truth, and to which the saying may well be applied, "What is new in it is not true, and what is true is not new," for the new leave-alone principle must in time, by the sheer force of its masterly inactivity, bring about the very evil which the old principle seeks to avoid.

If this new principle had been in vogue when Sir Gilbert Scott first drew attention to the need of "restoration," he would have been snubbed, and our cathedrals would not only have remained melancholy monuments of neglect, but in many cases would have been by this time both towerless and roofless; or if they had succeeded in their endeavours to prevent architects engaging in this work, the cathedrals might have fallen into the hands of distinguished builders, and shared the fate of St. Albans, which owes much of its treatment indirectly to the action of the Anti-Restoration School, whose early attacks were made against Sir Gilbert Scott as architect to the Abbey. Partly owing to the violence of this attack, and partly owing to the action of Lord Grimthorpe in preventing Sir Gilbert making the investigation necessary for the restoration of the west portals, the work was delayed. His death came, and Lord Grimthorpe, the great anti-restorationist, prevailed.

Leaving the new school to the enjoyment of this triumph, I would ask, why those who are alike interested in the preservation of our ancient buildings, should not start from this excellent standpoint to a practical consideration of the subject by bringing it to bear upon the undoubted fact that our old buildings can neither be allowed to become ruinous or be kept as curiosity shops.

If, then, they must be touched, some practical rules should be laid down as to their treatment, and a supply of professional men capable of treating them should be maintained. If an anti-restoration theory prevails, the result must be that the race of architects capable of dealing with ancient buildings will die out for want of employment, and the present idea that an architect is an architect, and, therefore, capable of undertaking every class of architectural work, which is now sadly too prevalent, would be still more universal.

To prevent such a lamentable event as this the matter should be taken up by the Institute and Architectural Association, and the subject of the treatment of ancient buildings made a special subject of study, and opportunities given to the public of knowing to whom such work can be safely entrusted.

ARTHUR BAKER, F.R.I.B.A.
21, *Lower Phillimore-place, Kensington, W.*

SIR,—I think few lovers of old architecture who had not the advantage of studying under Sir G. Scott will share Mr. Somers Clarke's evident awe at the mention of his name. I withstood him while he lived to the utmost of my poor ability, and venture to hope I did so with some small success. I do not feel now in the least called upon to speak of him with bated breath. I should mention that I had no personal acquaintance with him whatever, or perhaps I might have come under the remarkable influence he seems to have exerted over all, or almost all, he knew. But when Mr. Somers Clarke speaks of his cruelty to cathedrals, I am tempted to send you the following list, if only for the warning it may prove to some who contemplate "restorations."

At Canterbury he was called in shortly before his death, and though he put forward a scheme for the destruction of the noble carved stalls, he had no opportunity of carrying it out. At York the two fires of 1829 and 1840 left little to destroy. At Winchester he restored the wretched screen which replaced Inigo Jones's Palladian work. He practically rebuilt Bangor to a design of his own composition, carefully wiping off every ancient feature. Bristol was dealt with by Street. Mr. Christian is responsible for Carlisle. But Scott rebuilt Chester, wholly destroying the exquisite charm of antiquity which made it one of the loveliest of cathedrals. At Chichester he rebuilt the spire, altering the design, in spite of his own stipulations and the opposition of the local folk. He was a near-sighted man, and probably was unable to recognise the result of the alteration. He was also singularly ignorant of proportion, for which, indeed, he seems to have had no eye whatever, and even if he could have seen his new spire, would have considered it quite as good as the old one. He also built a new reredos, but it is so unpleasing in design, so heavy, and so incongruous, that every one will be glad it was never completed, and will possibly be removed as an eyesore. His reredos at Ely is much lighter. Exeter, "restored" in 1876, is not much the worse, but the reredos is very heavy and of poor design. Gloucester was undertaken in 1865, Scott's most rampant period. Nothing ancient that could be "restored" away was left, though the Council of the Archæological Institute intervened on behalf of history and old art. The reredos here also is his, very costly and gorgeous, but not lovely. Hereford had been pretty thoroughly mauled by Wyatt, Scott's worthy predecessor, but in his later days Scott acknowledged that he did things at Hereford which he almost regretted. There is little, except a reredos, of his work at Lichfield. Lincoln, Llandaff, and Manchester escaped him; but between 1873 and 1877 he completely remodelled Newcastle. He does not seem to have touched Norwich. At Oxford, the east end is wholly a conjectural "restoration," its historical features having been carefully obliterated by Scott. Peterborough escaped him, being reserved for a worse fate; but at Ripon he worked his will. He rebuilt the west end, put in new windows of his own design, renewed the vaulting, and made a wooden vaulting for the nave. He does not seem to have carried on Cottingham's destructive work at Rochester, which has been left for Mr. Pearson, if funds do not fail, as I hope they will. At St. Albans, Sir Gilbert commenced the vandalic operations now being carried out by Lord Grimthorpe. St. Asaph's was rebuilt in 1868 and the following years, nothing of interest from the old church being preserved. At St. David's, Scott had an opportunity he was not slow to seize. There was no one on the spot to meddle. He pulled down the front and rebuilt it from a design of his own. He pulled down the Perpendicular east end and made it Early English. He rebuilt the tower and raised the roof. At Salisbury, what traces of antiquity Wyatt had left Scott scrupulously removed. In his "Recollections" he regrets some of the work he carried out here, and throws the blame on others. Southwell was reserved for another "restorer." Wakefield had suffered much at his hands, as has been set forth by Mr. Micklethwaite, but some of the alterations were improvements. Salvin tinkered Wells, but Scott rebuilt the Chapter-house at Westminster, the cloisters, where he removed the traces of the *Scriptorium*, and the greater part of the north side. At Worcester little could be done, but that little Scott did. Perkins had been before him, and now the cathedral may be described as their joint work. At Durham we have some of the worst of all his vandalisms. The choir-screen would be a frightful eyesore anywhere, and is peculiarly out of place in this church.

Such is, I think, a complete list of the cathedrals "restored" by the late Sir G. G. Scott, but any of your readers who wish for categorical information will find it in the "Reminiscences," a kind of apology. Had I kept silence while he was yet alive I might be ashamed to speak out now, but I never hesitated to protest against his doings, his very principles appearing to me to be radically wrong.

W. J. LOFTIE.

SIR G. SCOTT AND RIPON MINSTER.

SIR,—No doubt Sir G. Scott preserved much Mediæval work at Ripon. But he gratuitously destroyed the ancient ritual arrangement of the choir, by moving the sedilia a bay east, and setting the altar against the very low-silled east window,—a place which it assuredly never occupied before. Let us hope this may be soon remedied, together with the similar barbarism at Bristol.

The Lincoln scheme (now happily in abeyance through the need of repairs to the north-west tower), seems to have arisen from the wish of a rich implement-maker to get a view of the Minster from his new house—in great measure at other folks' expense.

VIATOR.

STEAM-ROLLING ON ROADS.

SIR,—My broad statement is based on the cost for several years of steam-rolled roads and seven steam-rollers used by urban and rural authorities. It is my experience; your correspondent's may be different.

Twenty years' cost-keeping teaches me to place no reliance in single isolated experiments. One of the long jumps last week was reported at 23 ft., but this does not prove that all men jump that distance.

Waste in consolidation is governed by weather, crushing-power, and binding qualities of the materials. Many tests with various materials resulted in my figures. Mr. Greenwell may have equal reasons for his estimate.

I must object to any cost calculated on per cube yard of material as misleading; it should be per yard superficial rolled.

Many wheel-rolled roads are maintained with 80 tons of limestone per mile. If Mr. Greenwell can roll a mile of road for 3*l*., he has beat the record.

ROBERT PHILLIPS,
County Surveyor for Gloucestershire.

The Student's Column.

WARMING BUILDINGS BY HOT WATER. XVII.

INDEPENDENT BOILERS (*continued*).

THE subject of gas boilers cannot well be left without referring to an ingenious introduction of Mr. Fletcher's. This is a water-heater, or boiler, as fig. 62. The peculiarity consists in the quantity of solid metal (copper, in this instance,) pins projecting from the lower heating surface. Mr. Fletcher, in a paper read before the Gas Institute meeting, describes how he has ascertained by experiment that flame never has actual contact with surfaces which are at or below 212 deg.,—the temperature of boiling water. He adduced in evidence several facts to show that surfaces at this heat had a sort of repelling action, and

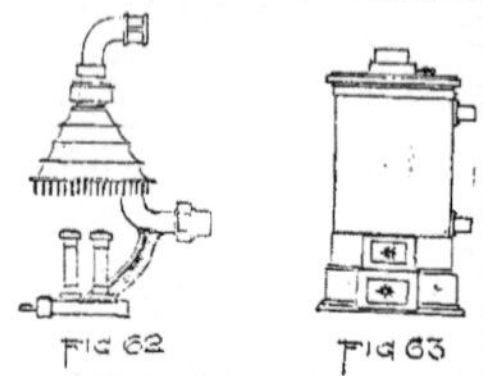

FIG 62 FIG 63

between the flame and the surface there always exists a thin film or space, to the disadvantage of the water receiving the full benefit of the heat. The remedy proposed, and which he has brought into practice, is to furnish the heating surface with these solid pins, protuberances, or gills (all can be adopted to the same end), as, when flame is applied to their free extremities, it has ready contact, owing to the much higher temperature that they (the extremities) can be raised to.

It will be seen that although we cannot get a surface, having water on one side of it, hotter than 212 deg. (and rarely this with boilers), if solid rods or projections extend from this surface sufficiently far, we can get their extremities red hot, although at their other ends they are in contact with water. Mr. Fletcher makes his rods about 1½ in. long; this permits the extremities to attain about 500 deg., and flame has actual contact at this temperature, and the greater and more effective heat so obtained is readily transferred to the water by conduction. Now, the peculiar effect of these rods does not end here. It has been common knowledge for many years that the affinity of water for heat,—its heat-absorbing power,—is 2½ times greater than a plain heating surface can impart the heat to it. This power of water is met with these rods, which, being solid, go to increase the heat-receiving surface to the extent named without increasing the water-surface. In other words, if the flat bottom of this little heater be a superficial foot, the addition of the rods make the actual heat-receiving surface some 2½ ft., and the superficial foot of water-surface resting on the flat bottom is quite able to absorb all the heat of this greater heat-collecting area. There is now advertised a boiler-tube made upon this principle having a series of flanges inside it, where the flame and heated gases have contact, and the makers contend that these flanges, which are solid, and simply additions to the heat-receiving surface, add fully 30 per cent. to the boiler-tube's effectiveness. Mr. Fletcher's experiments showed a really great difference between boilers that had the rods and those that had not. The length of the rods has a limit, as when the heat received is more than the water can dispose of, the extremities perish.

This little gas-boiler would require to be fixed in a house or little structure by itself, like the others. There must be free ingress of air for combustion, and equally free outlet for the products of combustion. This provision of inlet and outlet ventilation must, however, be unattended by violent draughts, or the flame will be blown out, or caused to "light back." In the former case, a disagreeable effect might

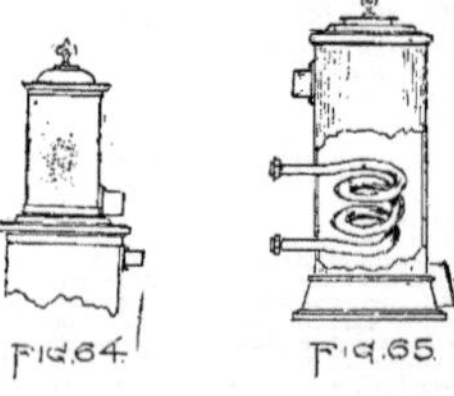

FIG.64 FIG.65

be experienced when re-lighting the burner by the explosion of the unburnt gas that may have collected.

INDEPENDENT BOILERS FOR COKE FUEL.—It will not be possible to enumerate more than a few of these, having distinct features peculiar to themselves. The number is too great to speak of them all. About the smallest and least expensive we have is what is generally termed the "Star," as fig. 63; it is, however, unsafe to give some of the old patterns, as this is, any specific name, for a similar design of boiler may be found in every maker's list, but not more than two will name it alike. This is a useful little boiler for small purposes, for heating a greenhouse or carriage-house, or for two or three coils in an entrance-hall. Its size does not admit of taking a charge of fuel to last many hours without attention, but it can be had with an extension, or fuel chamber, at top, as fig. 64. They are also made with sloping sides,—that is, slightly conical, which assists the free movement of the fuel in its falling to replace that which is consumed below. These boilers are made to heat from 150 ft. to 700 ft. of 2-in. pipe (theoretical quantity), and can have the pipe sockets on right or left side or at back, as desired; the smoke-nozzle can be on top or at back.

Fig. 65 represents a distinct form of small boiler, if it can be termed such, the heat-receiving surface being a coil of rather small pipe, as shown. A coil is undoubtedly effective, for it presents a greater surface to the fire in comparison to the quantity of water it holds than any other water-heater; it has the advantage of being wholly direct heating surface in contact with hot fuel. The drawback to coils is, however, that accumulation of deposit cannot be readily removed, even if some sort of provision is made for it. With this particular pattern accumulated dirt may soon do harm, as the pipe is small, and would be readily filled. Deard's coil boiler, to which we may presently refer, is considered successful, the pipes being 3 in. and 4 in.

The next description of boiler to notice is Messenger's "Loughborough," as fig. 66. The

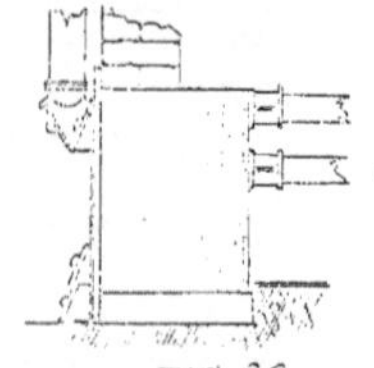

FIG.66

peculiarity of this boiler, as every reader must know, is its being adapted for building in the wall of the greenhouse. When it is so fixed the stoking, &c., is all conducted outside, and the flue-pipe is similarly placed; but the opposite side of the boiler projects inside the house, and the pipes are there connected. By this arrangement there is practically no loss of heat from the boiler, and the whole of the circulating-pipes do good service in radiating heat. The only loss of heat is from the front surface, which faces outward. The writer cannot see any reason for making waterway fronts with these boilers. Messrs. Kinnell's "Horseshoe" boiler, of a somewhat similar design to the "Loughborough," has an air chamber in front, by which the air which enters the fire is heated; this is in lieu of the waterway front, and seems a very good idea. Another good form of boiler for building in the thickness of the wall is Jenkins & Sons' "Ivanhoe." This has a fire-brick front, as fig. 67.

A very good pattern of boiler, made by all makers, is the "dome-top," as fig. 68. This is a very good and serviceable form of upright boiler, and has had general use and approval for many years. This boiler has a waterway top, and is the first we have shown with the flow-pipe starting vertically, which is decidedly the best way for it to start if the works are of any magnitude. It is unnecessary to describe this boiler in detail, the illustration gives what

FIG.67 FIG.68

is needed in this respect, but there is one feature in the drawing which requires special alluding to.

The feature in question is the waterway shown carried down below and beneath the fire-bars. This arrangement, owing to the increased cost it incurs, is not generally adopted, but it certainly has pronounced advantages. In the usual way, the waterway terminates exactly level with the fire-bars all round, except where the stoking-door comes; it is arched here, as is necessary. Terminating the boiler at this point means that the lowest point of the boiler, where dirt accumulates, comes exactly where the very greatest heat is felt, and where it can bring about the most harm, and what aggravates matters is that a weld joint has to exist at this important point. If the waterway is carried below, as shown, the accumulation of deposit occurs below the point where heat is felt, and the dirt, being at this low point, can do no harm; but i dition to this, it is so much easier remove the dirt from this flat surce than it is from the cylindrical space gher up. Added to this is the gain effected the absence of welds and joints immediately ar the glowing fuel—it is better to keep them ray from this point. Welded joints are, as a le, strong and very serviceable, but exceptions this rule are not uncommon. If a boiler of is type is used for the supply of hot water at ps, and the water it heats is "hard," the aterway bottom is a very great advantage, and nnot be over-estimated. The hard deposit is ns almost entirely kept away from the heated ints where it so readily causes damage, and e removal of the deposit is facilitated. This rd deposit is difficult enough to remove at any ne, but particularly so with cylindrical boilers ving the waterway ending level with the fireirs. The waterway bottom forms a sort of ttling bed for sedimentary or precipitated atter of every description, as very little can there to the vertical surfaces just round the e-box. It will be understood that matter posited anywhere else than just where the eat heat is felt does little or no mischief.

There are several effective shapes of independent boilers that are not of vertical design, we have hitherto referred to, but are rizontal, as fig. 69, for example. These are

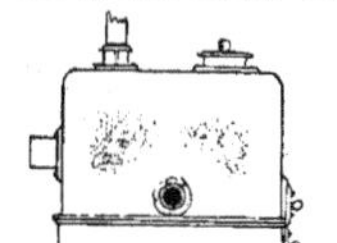

FIG. 69.

arly all much like square saddle boilers, aced upon iron bases, and furnished with the cessary furnace fittings, making them independent of brick setting. The illustration ows one with waterway front and back, with p-feeder. This is a very good form of boiler, n be fed to last the night without attention, t a deal of heat can be radiated and lost m its exterior if not covered, or if not fixed a little close brick chamber. It could have smoke-nozzle on top, if desired. This style boiler is made to heat up to 2,000 ft. of 2-in. , and if fitted with internal flue or cross-s, is still more powerful. It is a boiler the ter has used, and given every satisfaction. quare boiler can be cleared out with comstive ease.

SURVEYORSHIPS.

RANTHAM.—The *Leeds Mercury* says that Mr. J. Gamble having resigned the post of Borough veyor, on his appointment as second officer of Metropolitan Fire Brigade, the Grantham Town ncil received eighty applications for the vacancy. of that number three candidates were selected interview by the Council. They were:—Messrs. eph Evans, of Wolverhampton; Thos. W. nks, West Bromwich; and Frank Bagshawe, rogate. The first-named gentleman was unaninly appointed. The post is worth 200*l.* per um. Mr. Evans has been engaged as chief stant to the Borough Surveyor of Wolverpton.

IEREFORDSHIRE.—The *Liverpool Post* says that H. T. Wakelam, M.Inst.C.E., who has been veyor to the Garston Local Board for four years t, has been selected, out of eighty-four canates, for the office of Surveyor to the Hereford-e County Council.

OBITUARY.

MISS AMELIA B. EDWARDS.—We regret to see, he *Times* of the 16th inst., the announcement the death of this lady. Up to the year 1880 was best known to the public as a novelist, since that date her attention has been mainly oted to archæological and especially to Egyptian jects, on which she wrote frequently in the umns of the *Times* and the *Academy*. Miss wards also contributed articles on Egyptology to "Encyclopædia Britannica," and wrote for the erican supplement to that work an account of ecent Archæological Discoveries in Egypt." The ndation in 1883 of the Egypt Exploration Fund largely due to her efforts, and she has been for e years its honorary secretary; indeed, as was arked by one of the speakers at the recent eting of that Fund, reported in the *Builder* for rch 19 last, she was the life and soul of its work. Egyptology was the subject of a very numerous course of lectures delivered by her in the winter of 1889-90, in the United States.

MR. WILLIAM CHAFFERS, F.S.A., the veteran antiquary, who died a few days ago, aged eighty, at his residence at West Hampstead, in comparative obscurity and oblivion, was, says the *Times*, very little known, even through his standard works and useful life, to the present generation of art collectors. Mr. Chaffers will be principally remembered by the following works:—(1863), "Marks and Monograms on Pottery and Porcelain" (seventh edition); "Hallmarks on Plate," illustrated with tables of date letters; (1865-1886), "Handbook of Marks and Monograms on Pottery and Porcelain" (ninth thousand); (1889), "The Keramic Gallery of Pottery and Porcelain," with numerous illustrations, 2 vols.; (1887), "Gilda Aurifabrorum," a history of goldsmiths and their marks on plate, &c.

GENERAL BUILDING NEWS.

PROPOSED MEMORIAL HALL, LIVERPOOL.—It is proposed to erect a "People's Hall" for Liverpool, in memory of the late Mr. Clarke Aspinall, to be situated at the corner of Byrom-street and the Old Haymarket. Messrs. Ware and Rathbone, of Liverpool, are the architects, and their designs show that the hall will be built of salmon-coloured terra-cotta, relieved by broad bands of red, and the roof covered with green slates. On the ground floor there will be a café 80 ft. by 40 ft., reading-room 50 ft. by 30 ft., billiard-room 55 ft. by 36 ft., smoking-room 55 ft. by 35 ft., committee-rooms, lavatories, &c., while the frontage will be occupied by several shops. Part of the basement is to be utilised as a gymnasium. The first floor will be occupied by the great hall—104 ft. by 75 ft., with accommodation for 2,500 people; small concert-room, 50 ft. by 35 ft., capable of seating 300 persons; various committee and retiring-rooms. The remaining space on the second and third floors not occupied by the upper parts of the great hall and small concert-hall will be devoted to committee-rooms, &c. A large lift is to be placed at one end of the building, for the convenience of the people attending the hall.

NEW CHURCH, PAISLEY.—The memorial stone of the new Original Secession Church, now in course of erection in Wellmeadow, Paisley, was recently laid by Mr. Wm. Dunn. The church is in the Gothic style, and is being built of Auchinlea stone. It will be seated for 500 persons, while underneath the church there will be three halls, capable of accommodating 60, 80, and 350 respectively. Owing to the site being between two tenements, no light can be obtained from the sides, but, besides a two-light window in the frontage and a three-light at the south end, there will be a large amount of borrowed light from the roof. These will all be of cathedral tinted glass. The entrance is from Wellmeadow by a flight of ten steps, leading to a vestibule, from which there are two passages to the area seats. There will be, besides, a stair leading to a small gallery at the north end of the church, the pulpit, which will be more of the character of a platform, being at the other end. The interior of the church will be finished in red pine. At the south end a small building will be erected, attached to the main edifice, and will comprise the minister's vestry, ladies' room, heating apparatus, &c. The whole structure is estimated to cost about 3,000*l.* Mr. T. G. Abercrombie, Paisley, is the architect.

PROPOSED ISOLATION HOSPITAL AND PUBLIC MORTUARY, PLYMOUTH.—According to the *Western Morning News*, so soon as plans, which have been prepared by Mr. G. D. Bellamy, the Borough Engineer, have been finally approved by the Local Government Board, some definite progress will be made in the erection of both an isolation hospital and a public mortuary for Plymouth. The provision of an isolation hospital for the borough has become a necessity for the due carrying out of the Infectious Diseases (Notification) Act, 1889. The present temporary wooden structure at Mount Gould is unfitted to the requirements of the borough. It is on the site of this building that it is proposed to erect the new premises. The site covers nearly ten acres, and varies from 100 ft. to 175 ft. above sea-level, it being on slate rock. The new premises will be approached from the Higher Mount Gould-road, which is now being widened by the Corporation. On entering the hospital grounds, the porter's lodge will be found just within the gates, and further up the path, on the left will be the administration block. Local limestone will be used and Portland cement will serve for the exterior. In this block there will be bed-room and living-room accommodation for the matron and nurses; the medical officer's quarters and the servants of the hospital will be also housed here. A distinct building is proposed to be erected as an isolation pavilion. This will be divided for the use of male and female patients. In either portion of the building will be a ward, measuring 24 ft. by 18 ft., which will take two beds, and a nurses' and duty-room, so placed that a complete oversight of the patients will be obtainable. Each wing, also, will have a ward, measuring 36 ft. by 18 ft., attached, capable of accommodating three persons. The height of these rooms will be 13 ft., with ordinary plaster ceiling. The southern side of the pavilion will be provided with a verandah. More in the centre of the site will be two ward pavilions, one to accommodate twelve and the other sixteen patients, and there will be attached the customary nurses' duty rooms, bath room, and other conveniences. The area of the land will allow for the erection in the future of two additional wards. All the premises will be on one floor, raised above the level of the surrounding ground so as to allow for the free circulation of air under the building. The floors will be of wood block paving, which will be saturated with paraffin wax and will rest on concrete. The subordinate erections proposed include two laundries, one for the staff, and the other for patients. At the extreme rear will be a public disinfecting apparatus, which will serve for the use, not only of the patients in the hospital, but of those residing in the borough whom it may not be necessary to remove, but whose garments may need treatment. Disinfection is to be effected by the use of steam. Near by will be a comparatively small mortuary, with a room adjoining for post-mortem examinations. The new public mortuary will be near the old cellarage, which has served the purpose for so many years. This is situate near Vauxhall-street, and the new premises will be on some property belonging to the Corporation, lying between Vauxhall-street, Sutton Wharf, and West Quay. It has been planned to serve a population of 100,000, and will consist of a mortuary chamber, lighted from the top, and large enough to take twelve bodies. The block of buildings will face the road with a façade of red brick, with stone dressing. The caretaker's quarters will consist of four rooms. An entrance at the side of this building will give access to the coroner's court and the mortuary. The coroner's court will be approached from the entrance by a covered way, which will be continued from front to back, linking the buildings together. The measurement of this room will be 17 ft. by 16 ft., and it will be possible to shut off a portion of this with folding doors. From this enclosed portion of the court a door will lead to the coroner's private room, which will have a separate approach to the mortuary. The death chamber will be divided into two compartments, one being for infectious cases. At the rear of the mortuary there will be a room, 15 ft. by 12 ft., for the holding of post-mortem examinations. A small store-house and a shell-room will be adjacent.

GIRLS' INSTITUTE, MANCHESTER.—A technical institute for girls was opened at Ancoats on the 9th inst., by the Countess of Aberdeen. The site of the institute, which adjoins the Ancoats Hospital, contains about 1,260 square yards, the greater portion of which is covered by buildings, with its main frontage to Mill-street. The *Manchester Courier* says that the ground floor contains a large restaurant fronting Mill-street, which will accommodate several hundred girls, a cooking and other class rooms, together with a large cooking kitchen, scullery, and pantries. The lavatories are arranged on one side of the central court or area, and are well lighted and ventilated. In the front basement under the restaurant is a gymnasium, well lighted, containing a dressing-room and also a gallery at one end for the use of the public. The other portions of the basement contain private wash baths and various class-rooms. On the first floor is an entertainment room capable of seating 700 to 800 persons; there is also a committee-room and social and class-rooms on this floor. A caretaker's house, containing a living room, bedroom, and scullery, is provided in the second floor. The staircases and corridors are of ample width and are fireproof, and a hoist is provided for easy access to all parts of the building. The laundry and wash-house are placed over the boiler-house and heating chamber, which form a separate block of buildings at the rear of the institute, but which are connected therewith by a covered corridor and staircase. The corridors, staircase, walls, and walls of baths are lined with glazed brick dados. The cost of the works will exceed 8,000*l.* The architects were Messrs. Darbyshire & Smith, of Manchester.

WORKMEN'S INSTITUTE, DEEPCAR, YORKSHIRE.—On the 11th inst. the Earl of Wharncliffe opened at Deepcar the Lowood Institute. The total cost of the building was 1,500*l.* On the ground floor are a billiard-room, a smoke-room, committee-room, and conveniences. A caretaker's residence, fitted with cooking apparatus, is added. Upstairs there is a lecture-room and reading-room. The contractors for the work were Messrs. Joseph Martin & Sons, of Sheffield; Mr. Joseph Esherby was the carpenter and joiner; the plasterer and slater, Messrs. Hodkin & Jones; and the plumber, Mr. Corrie. The building was erected from the designs of Mr. W. J. Gardiner.

CHURCH SCHOOL, BARRY, GLAMORGAN.—On Easter Monday memorial-stones were laid of a new Church school for Barry parish. The building, which will occupy a site near the parish church, will be 60 ft. in length, 27 ft. in width, and 21 ft. to the ceiling. It will be of Gothic design, the material to be used being Cattybrook brick outside and stone inside, with brick facings. The seating accommodation will be for 200, and the structure will be heated by a special apparatus, with chamber running underneath. The architects are Messrs. Kempson & Fowler, of Llandaff, and the contractor Mr. F. Small, of Barry, the cost of the work being about 900*l*.

PROPOSED FEVER HOSPITAL, STOKE NEWINGTON. —The nine acres of land at Stoke Newington which some members of the Metropolitan Asylums Board were anxious to purchase as the site of a fever hospital are to be used for building purposes. On the day that the proposition came before the Asylums Board in the first instance, the plans for laying out the grounds for building were approved by the Hackney Board of Works, the local authority in the matter. When these have obtained the further sanction of the London County Council, the actual work will be commenced.—*City Press.*

ADDITIONS, JEDBURGH PARISH CHURCH.—The recent additions to this church, which include chancel, vestry, organ-chamber, chancel furniture in oak, and stone and alabaster pulpit, were formally dedicated on the 7th inst. The works have been carried out by Messrs. Brunton, Jedburgh, to designs by Mr. P. MacGregor Chalmers, architect, Glasgow.

CLAYBURY ASYLUM, WOODFORD, ESSEX.—Messrs. Reed, Blight, & Co., Limited, contractors, Plymouth, have been selected by the London County Council to carry out the alterations and additions to Manor House, Claybury Asylum, Woodford, Essex, from plans by Mr. G. T. Hine, architect. The amount of the accepted tender is 8,995*l*.

MARLBOROUGH HOUSE.—We learn that alterations are about to be made at Marlborough House, for H.R.H. the Prince of Wales. All possible precautions will be taken against fire, and Messrs. Mark Fawcett & Co. have received the order to construct the floors with their special fireclay tubes, the same as are now being used at the New National Portrait Gallery.

ALTERATIONS TO ST. MARY'S CHURCH, WAINFLEET, LINCOLNSHIRE.—It has been decided to carry out the following works at Wainfleet St. Mary's Church:—To take down and rebuild the north arcade, put new roofs to nave and north aisle, add new organ-chamber on north side of chancel, and to restore tower windows, in accordance with plans prepared by Mr. J. B. Corby, architect, Stamford. Nine builders sent in tenders, and that sent by Mr. J. T. Turner, of Wainfleet, was accepted at 973*l*.

SANITARY AND ENGINEERING NEWS.

SEWERAGE, ASH-NEXT-SANDWICH.—The Sewerage and Sewage Purification Works for Ash have just been completed. The system of purification adopted is that of the International Water and Sewage Purification Company, Limited. The engineers for the works are Messrs. Charles H. Beloe, M.Inst.C.E., and Frank E. Priest, A.M.Inst.C.E., of Westminster, and the contractors were Messrs. G. H. Denne & Son, of Deal.

WATER-SUPPLY, RUGELEY.—An artesian-bored tube well, yielding 120,000 gallons per day continuous pumping, has been completed for the town of Rugeley in little over four weeks. The depth is 152 ft. and 5 in. in diameter. After passing a few feet of alluvial deposits, the conglomerate beds were reached, from which the water is obtained. The town of Burnam, near Taplow, is having similar work carried out by Messrs. C. Isler & Co., of London.

HARBOUR WORKS, ARDROSSAN.—There has just been completed at Ardrossan, Ayr, a new dock and other harbour extensions. The additions include a wet dock about 10 acres in extent, a tidal basin of 5 acres, an extensive entrance channel, a considerable extension of the quay accommodation for passenger steamers outside the dock, and a breakwater 1,320 ft. in length. The new dock and outer basin occupy the site of an old tidal harbour. This has been deepened to the uniform depth of 18 ft. below low-water level, and divided into two portions—wet dock and tidal or outer basin—by means of a cross-pier, 80 ft. wide. In constructing the walls of the dock a portion of the Montgomerie pier has been removed, but as much of it as could be utilised has been widened from 30 ft. to 165 ft., in order to give the necessary railway and other facilities on the north side of the new dock and tidal basin. At the end of the pier as it now stands the Lanarkshire and Ayrshire Railway Company have erected a station. The old quay walls on the north and south sides, which were taken advantage of in constructing the new dock, have been underbuilt with concrete. The walls on the east and west sides of the dock are new, and have been constructed of rubble concrete. The new dock is 700 ft. long and 620 ft. broad. It is separated from the new tidal basin by a quay 80 ft. wide, with a connecting passage for vessels 60 ft. wide near the north-west corner of the dock. This passage is provided with gates of green-heart timber, and with strut-gates behind for protection in stormy weather. The new outer or tidal basin is 500 ft. long and 370 ft. broad. The old walls on the south and west sides, having very shallow foundations, were discarded, and new walls constructed of rubble concrete have been built in front of the old quay walls. These walls were constructed in lengths of from 60 ft. to 100 ft. inside cofferdams, the new walls here, as elsewhere being founded on the rock. The new breakwater, which is 1,320 ft. long, has been constructed of concrete. At the southern extremity it is founded on a rock, which forms the north boundary to the entrance channel. The new pier, which takes the place of the old Montgomerie Pier, has accommodation on the south-side for a large steamer, and on the north side for two passenger steamers. The old pier on the south side of the outer basin has been replaced by a new erection, which extends 20 ft. further into the water than the old structure, and has been carried down to the rock. The accommodation at this pier has been improved, and will be further improved when the Glasgow and South-Western Company complete the erection of a new pier station, which is now in progress, for the accommodation of their Arran and Belfast traffic. The hydraulic machinery for the equipment of the dock has been supplied and erected by the Hydraulic Engineering Company, Limited, of Chester. In connexion with the extensions, a tract of land, about 700 ft. wide, has been reclaimed from the sea, the material excavated from the harbour having been used for this purpose, and a portion of this reclaimed ground is used as the site of the Lanarkshire and Ayrshire Railway Company's station for the town of Ardrossan. The harbour extensions were designed by and carried out under the superintendence of Messrs. Strain, Robertson, & Thomson, civil engineers, Glasgow and Westminster, while the works have been completed by Messrs. Lucas & Aird, contractors, London.

SEWERAGE OF WHITBY AND ELLESMERE PORT.—The sewerage of Whitby and Ellesmere Port, Cheshire, has recently been completed by the Wirral Sanitary Authority. The work was rendered all the more necessary by the great increase in the population of Ellesmere Port through the construction of the Manchester Ship Canal. The sanitary condition of the place was becoming exceedingly defective. The total length of the sewers constructed is about 5,000 lineal yards. They are laid with stoneware pipes supplied by Messrs. Doulton & Co., ranging in diameter from 9 in. to 18 in., and provided with Stanford's joints. Flushing-tanks and all other modern appliances are provided, and the manholes are furnished with deodorising baskets fitted with polarite. The work, which has cost 4,250*l*., was designed by Mr. Charles H. Beloe, the Engineer to the Authority, assisted by Mr. Frank E. Priest, and has been executed, under their superintendence, by Messrs. Young & Sons, contractors. The clerk of works was Mr. Geo. McIlwaine.

STAINED GLASS AND DECORATION.

MEMORIAL WINDOW, MANCHESTER CATHEDRAL.—The westernmost window on the south side of the Manchester Cathedral is now being filled in with the Chadwick memorial, by Messrs. Heaton, Butler, & Bayne, of London. The subject of the window is "Moses Coming Down from the Mount," which will fill the five lights of the clearstory. In the tracery is the inscription, "Moses coming down from the mount," the rest of the tracery being filled with the passion flower and foliage. In the centre division Moses appears bearing the tablets of the law, and to his left, in the two centre compartments, the subjects are "The Sacrifice" and "The Golden Calf." The corresponding windows to his right are occupied by a banner-bearer and foliage.

STAINED GLASS WINDOW, ST. GILES' CATHEDRAL, EDINBURGH.—One of the two-light clearstory windows on the south side of the choir of St. Giles' Cathedral has just been filled with stained glass. In the one light is placed the arms and in the other the crest of the Worshipful Goldsmiths' Company, surmounted by their motto—"To God only be all glory." These are placed within canopied ornament. The work was executed at the studios of Messrs. Ballantine & Gardiner, Edinburgh.

WINDOW, KIRKWALL TOWN-HALL.—A large stained glass window has been placed in the Town-hall of Kirkwall. The window consists of three lights, divided by a transom. The left-hand light, being the gift of Shetland to Kirkwall, shows a figure of Henry St. Clair, one of the Earls of Orkney and builder of Kirkwall Castle. At the base of the centre light appears—"Erected by public subscription. Thomas Peace, Provost. 1892." It contains a figure of James III. presenting a charter to Kirkwall. The third light—the gift of Sheriff and Vice-Admiral Thoms—contains the figure of King Hakon Hakonson. Above the transom are placed the arms of Shetland, Orkney, and Sheriff Thoms, the whole surmounted in the centre light by the Royal arms of James III. impaled with those of his spouse, Queen Margaret of Denmark. The windows were executed at the studios of Messrs. Ballantine & Gardiner, George-street, Edinburgh.—*Scotsman.*

MEMORIAL WINDOW, ST. PHILIP'S CHURCH, HULME.—St. Philip's Church, Chester-street, Hulme, has been presented with a stained glass window as a memorial of the late Mr. Herbert Birley. The window, which has been designed and executed by Messrs. T. Thomason & Co., of Manchester, contains three lights, the left-hand subject representing "Eli instructing Samuel," the centre depicting "The Good Samaritan," and the right hand subject representing "Christ blessing little children." Surmounting the whole are figure of angels, embellished with tracery.

FOREIGN AND COLONIAL.

FRANCE.—The President of the Republic ha signed the decree authorising the erection of the statue of Balzac on the Place du Palais Royal.——1,720 pictures have been admitted to the Salon thi year. The number was 1,733 last year.——It is announced that the Gare de Lyon at Paris is to be completely transformed and increased to double its present size, according to plans prepared by M. Noblemaire, the engineer to the company. The scheme will take five years to carry out, and wi cost about eleven million francs.——A new hospit for aged paupers is to be built at Pantin, ne Paris.——The Council of State has before it recommendation to extend the railway from S Lazare to Molineux, Courbevoie, &c., up to th Esplanade des Invalides. The terminal statio would be placed near the Quai d'Orsay, adjoining the Ministry of Foreign Affairs.——The Académie des Beaux-Arts has not awarded the Duc prize this year, because the only design sent in does not conform to the conditions.——The statue of Clément Marot, the poet of the Renaissance period, it to be inaugurated in June, at the town of Cahors. ——An art exhibition is to be open at Cognac during June.——The works begun some years ago for the formation of a port at Marmande, or the Garonne, have just been completed.——A fire broke out a few days ago in one of the chapels of the Cathedral of Dol, but was fortunately got unde before much damage had been done. The church is a fine monument of thirteenth-century work, containing some splendid oak stalls, an episcopa throne of the fifteenth century, and the remarkable tomb of Bishop Thomas James, executed in 150 by Jean Juste.——A fire has nearly destroyed th ancient and curious church at Avon, near Fontainebleau. It contained the tombs of Monaldeschi Ambroise Dubois, Bezout, and Daubenton. Th high altar, which dated from the time of Louis XIII. was entirely destroyed, as well as the sacerdota ornaments lately given by Queen Anne of Austria ——We hear at the last moment, with much regret of the death of an architect of great talent, M Alphonse Crépinet, at the age of sixty-six. H was a Government architect, entrusted with th care of the Hôtel des Invalides, and it was he wh carried out in 1868, with great skill, the restoratio of the dome of that building. In the competitio for the Paris Opera House his design w classed next to that of M. Garnier; his desig for the Hôtel de Ville was one of the mo remarkable, and M. Thiers had commissione him to make the plan for the Parliamenta Palace which he had intended to have built at S Cloud. At the time of his death M. Crépinet was bu with the plans for the Opéra Comique, in accor ance with a commission from the Minister of Publ Works.——The publication is announced of t posthumous memoirs of the painter Eugè Delacroix.——The Minister of Public Instructio will shortly lay before the Chamber of Deputies h financial scheme for providing for the rebuilding o the Opéra Comique.

BERLIN.—In the course of a debate on the petitio of some seventy-five artists that the municipalit should set aside a sum of money in their Budget fo the purchase of works of art, one of the city cou cillors, Herr Kyllmann, spoke in a most spirited wa in favour of the proposal, and even went so far as t say that it was high time that the City of Berli should no longer be subject to the reproach that a the art treasures the citizens had the benefit o seeing belonged either to the Crown or to th nation, and that the city as such did next to nothin in the matter. He was not only in favour of th municipal buildings having some works of art i them, but also that the city should establish good municipal art collection in a similar way a such cities as Leipsic or Cologne had don Thanks to this speech the councillors have decide on having a fairly large sum put down for th purchase of works of art in 1892-93.——Owin to the unsatisfactory results of the various co petitions for Government Prizes and Studen ships held under the auspices of the Prussia Royal Academy, the Minister of Educational Affai has now made some radical alterations in the ve unpopular regulations referring to them. The will no longer be the preliminary examinatio within the walls of the Academy, and then a dist bution of ideal subjects to be worked out at hom by the candidates. The competition will simp be in the form of an application tendered, togeth with examples of work already done. As regar the examples of work to be sent in by candidat for the architectural studentships, it is interesti to note that they need simply consist of drawin or photographs of any buildings put up or in cour of erection from their designs, one drawing in pe spective being the only compulsory adjunct. Ca didates must be Prussians by birth, and mu not have entered their thirty-third year of lif The value of the studentships has also be altered. There will now be an annual arc tectural one, having a value of 165*l*., stead of a biennial one of 330*l*.——Acco o their report for 1891, the managers of Great Berlin Tramway Company (which has of a total length of over 240,000 mètres) have discussing the advisability of introducing icity as a motive power instead of horses. have come to the conclusion to postpone their ion for several years, so as to be able to see levelopment of the electrical traffic in other s. They do not consider any of the present ms perfect, there would be great local diffi- e to contend with, and they shun the expenses periments as their concession to run the lines a short one.——Owing to the several railway ents caused by faults of overworked railway nts, the Minister of Public Works has sent a gent reminder to those responsible that he will use of his powers without leniency whenever e of over-work comes before him.——Herr fessen, the librarian of the "Arts and Crafts ty," read a paper on the taste shown in and in work of this class. The meeting was attended by members and visitors.——The sion of the General Post Office in the Leipziger se will not be commenced this year, owing to ecessary funds not having been voted. This reat pity, if only on account of the excellent office museum, which is terribly cramped in ark rooms of the old building.

RWAY.—The Norwegian Government has pre- d a bill with plans to the Storthing for erecting Government Offices in Christiania. There are designs, the one principally suggested being of Herr Lenschow, the so-called "H" shaped ing, and a "rectangular" one by Herr Bull, ity architect, and awarded second prize in the etition. However there is but little difference cost between the two plans, about 10,000l., total cost being estimated at 200,000l. It is ntended to locate in this building the offices e Central Statistical Bureau, and those of our, lighthouse, canal, road, agriculture, forests. Provisionally a sum of 15,000l. ed for the building, which will be situated on ite of the old city hospital, now to be pulled .——We have on previous occasions referred e disgraceful manner in which the competition signs to a museum at Bergen was conducted e "fathers" of that city, and, as a closing the Norwegian Association of Architects Engineers has now issued a formal letter rotest against the same, particularly against entirely ignoring the suggestions of that sentative body as to the competition.——The by Professor L. Dietrichson, "The Norwegian Churches," to which we have previously red, is the object of a highly-laudatory article e *Centralorgan für die Interessen des Real- wesens.*——Arrangements are being made for installation of a municipal electric central n in Throndhjem, in order to light the streets ectricity.

NICH.—The following sums are to be devoted ilding purposes on the Bavarian Government ads: (1) for the Eger railway station extension 70,000l.; (2) for the new central station at berg some 250,000l.

IA.—The competition for a design of a new ge system for the city has been decided by an sing jury, consisting of the Mayor, several arian civil engineers and medical men, and a an and Austrian specialist (Ingenieur Rella, inn, and "Stadtbaurath" Koehn, of Charlot- rg). None of the twenty-five designs sent in considered suitable, and hence no first premium iven. The four designs considered best, how- received awards. Their authors are Mr. tchiloff, of Sophia; Mr. L. Masson, of Paris; s. Weigand & Paulsen, of Sophia and Strass- ; and the Botto Bros., of Rome.—*Central der Bauverwaltung.*

TERNATIONAL BUILDING EXHIBITION IN LEM- .—From August 30 to September 20 this year ternational building exhibition will be held in berg, Galicia, which is intended to illustrate resent-day efficiency of the building industry, specially the progress which has been made in manufacture of both the older-fashioned and building materials. Applications for space d be made on a specially-printed form, which be obtained gratis from Die Komitee der ewerblichen Ausstellung in Lemberg, Ring- , 30. The reception of exhibits will begin on ist 10, and terminate on August 25, 1892.

PE TOWN, SOUTH AFRICA.—The *Cape Times* e 30th ult. says that some serious defects in rainage having been discovered at Government e, the official residence of his Excellency Sir y and Lady Loch, extensive alterations are carried out in the sanitary arrangements, the design of Mr. Corben, late of Southamp- Chief Sanitary Inspector of the Municipality ape Town.

OPOSED RESTORATION OF BRISTOL CATHEDRAL. quoted a paragraph last week from a Bristol , which stated that the restoration of the edral (under Mr. Pearson) was to be carried out ording to the plans of the late Mr. Street." Pearson writes to say that this is a mistake, hat Mr. Street left no plans for any restora- and no record of what his ideas were on the ct.

MISCELLANEOUS.

A TIMBER-TRADE VIEW OF THE EXAMINATION IN ARCHITECTURE.—The *Timber Merchant*, a trade journal published at Liverpool, in its issue for the 16th inst., under the heading "Awkward Sizes," refers to the examination held under the auspices of the Royal Institute of British Architects the other day, and says:—"The candidates seeking to be admitted as Associates of the Institute were examined on a variety of useful subjects, but to the list we think one other could very appropriately have been added. We think they might have been questioned as to what are the general and usual sizes of sawn wood imported into this country, and by dividing the subject into two, it could have been made even more interesting and beneficial. The students might have been asked as to what are —firstly, the standard dimensions of sawn wood imported into the West Coast Ports, and, secondly, into the East Coast Ports. A large number of our readers will already see our drift, for builders and contractors are, from experience, painfully aware that very many architects are comparatively ignorant of the standard sizes of sawn wood, and consequently often specify, in quantities, very awkward dimensions of timber. This causes more irritation amongst builders and contractors using Canadian timber than perhaps amongst those who chiefly use Swedish wood, for the sizes of the former wood are much more limited in number than are those of the latter. Spruce comes generally in three sizes, 7, 9, and 11 by 6, and pine deals are also largely of the same dimensions. Swedish, Norwegian, and Russian wood varies in thickness from 1½ in. to 4 in., and in widths from 4 in. to 12 in. We have not referred to boards, as they do not concern our present point. Now, we affirm that architects should be tolerably well acquainted with the standard sizes of these different woods, and that they should specify only such dimensions as can readily be sawn from them without waste of material and money. Especially should they know the sizes of Canadian woods, for the reasons briefly given. It is very annoying to the builder when he finds spruce floor joists specified 6 in. by 3 in., or 5 in. by 2½ in.; or spruce ceiling joists, 3½ in. by 2 in.; or spruce spars, 3½ in. by 2½ in.; yet these and other awkward sizes are constantly met with in quantities. A knowledge of the standard sizes of spruce would dispense with such specifications, and prevent the display of much bad temper, and the utterance of hard and impolite expressions. The lot of a builder and contractor is sufficiently worrying, without his being needlessly harassed by specifications of timber which he knows cannot be obtained without incurring a deal of extra cutting, and a deal of waste."

SEA DEFENCES AT LANCING.—An inquiry was held on Tuesday last, the 19th inst., by Mr. Arnold Taylor, Inspector of the Local Government Board, at the Town Hall, Worthing, when the scheme for providing sea defences for the frontage of Lancing was considered. Mr. R. F. Grantham, M.Inst.C.E., explained the plans and estimates, and the features of the proposed system of groynes. The system, when carried out, will form, together with the series of groynes erected some years ago to the eastward of Lancing, a complete defence for a length of frontage of two miles. The groynes are generally 300 ft. long, and are placed at from 400 ft. to 500 ft. apart. It is claimed for this system that it is the most economical form of defence in such situations, costing about 12s. per lineal foot of frontage. The Inspector determined to recommend sanction for a loan for the purpose.

ANEMOMETERS.—At the meeting of the Royal Meteorological Society, on Wednesday evening, a paper was read on "Anemometer Comparisons," by Mr. W. H. Dines. This was a report on a valuable series of experiments, which have been carried out at the request of the Council of the Society with the view of obtaining a direct comparison of the various anemometers in common use, so that some opinion might be formed as to which type of instrument is the most suitable for general purposes. The Meteorological Council have defrayed the cost of the work. The anemometers which were compared were:—1. Kew-pattern Robinson. 2. Self-adjusting Helicoid. 3. Air-meter. 4. Circular pressure plate (1 ft. in diameter). And 5. A special modification of tube anemometer. Most of these instruments are of the author's own invention, as well as the apparatus for obtaining automatic and simultaneous records from all the instruments upon the same sheet of paper. It appears that the factor of the Kew-pattern Robinson is practically constant, and must lie between 2·00 and 2·20. The Helicoid anemometer is quite independent of friction for all excepting light winds, and different sizes read alike, but it is not so simple in construction as the cup form. The air meter consists of a single screw blade formed of thin aluminium, and made as nearly as possible into the exact shape of a portion of a helicoid. A similar instrument with a larger blade, and with the dial protected from the weather, would probably form a useful and correct anemometer. It would be light, and offer a very trifling resistance to the wind. The oscillations of the pressure-plate must have been considerably damped by the action of the floating weight, but as it was they were sufficiently violent. It seems probable that the remarkably high values sometimes given by the Osler Pressure-plate may be due to the inertia of the moving parts. The tube anemometer appears to possess numerous advantages. The head is simple in construction, and so strong, that it is practically indestructible by the most violent hurricane. The recording apparatus can be placed at any reasonable distance from the head, and the connecting-pipes may go round several sharp corners without harm. The power is conveyed from the head without loss by friction, and hence the instrument may be made sensitive to very low velocities without impairing its ability to resist the most severe gale.

THE ENGLISH IRON TRADE.—Unfortunately, there cannot be recorded any amelioration of the depressed condition of the English iron market. Prices show little variation, but new orders are not forthcoming, and the continuance of the Durham miners' strike prevents business in the Cleveland district, where not a single furnace is working on Cleveland pig, and only five in all are in blast. Manufactured iron is still in limited request, and the demand for steel is slack. There is, however, some improvement in the inquiry for tin-plates. Engineers and iron-founders continue to experience only a moderate enquiry, but shipbuilding yards are fairly active. The coal trade is tolerably active. —*Iron.*

MOSAIC AT ATHENS.—In the atrium of a Roman house recently excavated at the Piræus an unusually fine mosaic pavement has been laid bare, of which a large Medusa head occupies the centre. The head, 60 centimètres high, has abundant hair, and on the forehead two wings, like those of the *petasus* of Hermes, and is flanked by serpents. The inscription which runs round it is a reproduction of verses 741-2 of the fifth book of the Iliad, describing the Medusa on the shield of Athena. In the same ruins was found a terra-cotta antefix bearing in the centre a Gorgoneum, but dissimilar from the above, as it is of savage and repulsive appearance, with the tongue hanging out of the mouth.—*Athenæum.*

"THE BRITISH CLAYWORKER."—This is the title of a new monthly journal especially devoted to all products of which clay is the raw material,—bricks, tiles, terra-cotta, earthenware, porcelain, faïence, drain-pipes, sanitary ware, &c., &c. The contents of the number are varied and interesting, one of the features being the first of an intended series of articles entitled "Modellings in Clay," of which the subject is Mr. Thomas Minton, J.P., Chairman of Minton's, Limited, of whom a portrait is given. Brick and tile-making machinery, and new forms of kilns, are included among other items of technical interest described and illustrated.

TRADE CATALOGUES.—Messrs. R. Waygood & Co.'s abridged Catalogue of Lifts, Hoists, and Cranes, recently issued by them, contains, within a small compass, a very useful series of illustrated and priced descriptions of their well-known lifts and hoists for all purposes. It may be truly summed up in the words *multum in parvo.*—Messrs. G. B. Kent & Sons send us their "Painting Brush List," for March, 1892. It includes all kinds of tools for decorators, painters, and glaziers, and is illustrated and priced. This catalogue also is of small bulk, although it is very complete and useful.—Messrs. George Waller & Co. send us illustrated catalogues of their specialities in sanitary machinery and appliances, including cesspool-pumps and vans, as used in the "Bexley" system of emptying cesspools, already fully described by us. The catalogues also include air-tight covers for sewerage systems, inspection and man-hole covers, side-entrance covers, ventilators, gullies, penstocks, tide-flaps, drain and gully cleaning tools, &c., &c.

THE LONDON COUNTY COUNCIL AND THE TRAMWAYS.—It is stated by the *Times* that the Board of Trade have appointed Sir Frederick Bramwell as referee in the arbitration proceedings between the London County Council and the London Tramways Companies as to the former taking over control of the tramways.

LONDON PROPERTIES FOR SALE.—On May 18 next, by order of the Ecclesiastical Commissioners, will be put up for sale, at the Mart, the site (about 3,900 square feet) and materials of the St. Mary Magdalen (Old Fish-street) Church, in Knightrider-street. The church was destroyed by the fire that broke out in an adjoining block of warehouses on December 2, 1886. In our issue of December 11 of that year we gave a history, with an illustration, of the church, as re-built by Wren, and a description of the walls and interior as they stood after the fire. About eighteen months ago it was stated that a large number of ferns had sprung up amongst the *débris* on the floor. The parish has been united, we believe, with that of St. Martin, Ludgate, whose church is one of the four that are specially exempted from demolition under the powers to which public attention is just now directed in the case of St. Dunstan's-in-the-East. The organ, to which we adverted in our article, was by Green, and reconstructed, in 1857, by Messrs. Gray & Davison; it was cleaned for removal, together with some other relics, to St. Martin's.—On the 28th and 29th inst., in 250 lots, some freehold ground-rents, amounting to 2,400l. per annum, secured upon about 600 houses on the South Bermondsey estate, and covering more than 30 acres. On the 27th inst., will also be let on lease for 80 years, at the Mart, the final portion of the London-wall estate belonging to Sion

COMPETITIONS.

Nature of Work.	By whom Advertised.	Premiums.	Designs to be delivered.
*Valuation of Property	Stockport Union	....	May 2
School, Teachers' House, &c.	Wombwell (Barnsley) Sch. Bd.	....	May 23
*Town Hall and Public Offices	Llanelly Loc. Bd.	50 and 20 guineas	June 18

CONTRACTS.

Nature of Work or Materials.	By whom Required.	Architect, Surveyor, or Engineer.	Tenders to be delivered.
Stone Retaining Walls, &c.	Brighouse Local Board	J. Parkinson	April 26
*Painters' and Plumbers' Work	Commrs. of Sewers	Official	do.
*Engineers' Work	do.	do.	do.
*Carpenters' Work	do.	do.	do.
*Paving Works	Willesden Local Board	O. Claude Robson	do.
*90 ft. 12 in. Pipe Sewer	Fulham Vestry	J. P. Norrington	April 27
Sewerage Works	Halifax Corporation	E. R. S. Escott	do.
Isolation Hospital, Bruntcliffe-lane	Morley Corporation	M. H. Sykes	do.
Gasholder and Iron Tank	Leeds Corporation	Official	do.
*Aberdeen Granite Pitchings	St. George-in-the-East Vestry	do.	April 28
*Police Station, Courts, Offices, &c.	Blackpool Corp.	J. Wolstenholme	do.
School and Out-offices	Haltwhistle Board Sch. Trustees	H. Watson	do.
Excavations and Masonry Work, Porth	Ystradyfodwg Loc. Bd.	J. W. Jones	do.
Works at Hospital Grounds	Plymouth Corp.	H. D. Bellamy	do.
Church Schools, Radcliffe-lane, Pudsey	....	C. S. Nelson	do.
Sewering, Paving, Channelling, &c.	Elland Local Board	G. Hepworth	April 29
*Foundations of Block 1., Record Office Extension	Com. of H. M. Works	Official	do.
*Roadmaking Works, Drains, &c.	Tonbridge U.R.S.A.	W. Oakley	do.
Additions to County Asylum, Exminster	Devon County Asylum	E. H. Harbottle	April 30
Cattle Houses, Mount Whitleigh Farm, St. Budeaux, Devon	S. W. Adams	....	do.
Additions to Schools	Pentyrch (co. Cardiff) School Board	Brice Vaughan	do.
*Repairs to Public Baths	Commrs. P. B. & W., Greenwich	— Dinwiddy	do.
Stone Chimney, Thornhill Briggs Mills, Brighouse	....	G. Hepworth	May 2
Causeway, near Midland Railway Bridge	Altofts Local Board	W. Wilkinson	do.
Buildings, Electric Light Station	Manchester Corp.	Official	do.

CONTRACTS.—*Continued.*

Nature of Work or Materials.	By whom Required.	Architect, Surveyor, or Engineer.	Tenders to be delivered.
*Dredging	Torquay Local Board	Official	May
Canal Work (Contract No. 3)	Manchester Ship Canal	do.	do.
*Road Works	Aldershot Local Board	do.	do.
*Removal, &c. of Sludge Cake	Richmond Main Sewerage Board	W. Fairley	do.
Alteration of Premises, Torpoint	Plymouth Co-op. Soc.	H. J. Snell	do.
*Distempering, Cleansing, &c.	Managers Poplar, &c. Sick Asylum	G. E. Hobson	do.
*Entrance Gates and Iron Railings	Bristol S.A.	F. Ashmead	May
*Roadmaking Works	Lewisham Bd. of Wks	Official	do.
*Two Shops and Five Houses, Hammersmith	....	F. & W. Stocker	do.
*Painting and Decorating Part of Town Hall	Leeds Corporation	T. Hewson	May
*Slaughterhouses, Cattle Market, &c.	Aberdare Market Co.	T. Roderick	do.
*Concrete Gasholder Tank	East Grinstead Gas & Water Co.	Official	do.
*Police Station and Lock-up House, &c.	Breconshire C. C.	do.	May
*Alteration at Cane Hill Asylum	London County Council Asylums Committee	do.	May
Culvert, Embankment, &c. Wheatley	Halifax High Level Ry. Co.	Utley & Gray	do.
*New Police Station, Clacton-on-Sea	Essex C. C.	H. Stock	May 1[illegible]
*Dwelling, Stores, &c. at Lighthouse, Gibraltar	Corp. of Trinity House	Official	May [illegible]
*Parish Room and North Transept	St. Stephen's Church, Twickenham	Mawson & Hudson	No date
Hotel, Blaydon-on-Tyne	Edward Adams	....	do.
House and Shop, Stanley, co. Durham	J. W. Moffitt	R. P. W. Liddle	do.
Schools, Tanfield Lea, Newcastle	Tanfield Sch. Bd.	Davidson & Beadle	do.
Additions to School, St. Philip's	Bristol Sch. Bd.	W. L. Bernard	do.
Alterations and Additions to Premises, Carlisle	J. Thompson	G. D. Oliver	do.

PUBLIC APPOINTMENTS.

Nature of Appointment.	By whom Advertised.	Salary.	Applications to be in.
*Clerk of Works	Pwllheli Corp.	....	April [illegible]
*Engineering Assistant	Belfast Corp.	250l.	April [illegible]
*Office Assistant	Lambeth Vestry	9l.	April [illegible]
*Three District Superintendents	do.	1l. 3s.	do.
*Inspector of Sewerage Works	Horsham Loc. Bd.	2l.	May [illegible]
*Inspector of Sewerage Works	Southend Loc. Bd.	2l.	No date

Those marked with an Asterisk (*) are advertised in this Number. Competitions, p. iv. Contracts, pp. iv., vi., & viii. Public Appointments, p. xx.

College. It consists of an area of 1,440 ft. superficial, having a frontage to Philip-lane, and is at present occupied by the Cripplegate Ward Schools, to be vacated by next Midsummer-day. On October 20, 1853, we published a view, taken from the court, of the gateway of the old College, which was pulled down twelve months afterwards.—On May 11, by an order in Chancery, *in re* Hope v. d'Hedouville, some freehold property covering two acres, and comprising 126 houses, cottages, and shops, in Lever-street, Central-street, and thereabouts, in St. Luke's parish, yielding an aggregate rental of 2,064*l*. per annum.—And in June, by direction of the late Mr. F. R. Leyland's executors, the house No. 49, Prince's-gate, whose interior has been richly decorated under the superintendence of Mr. Jeckyll, Mr. Norman Shaw, and Mr. James McNeill Whistler. The main staircase, leading from the ground floor, was brought hither from Northumberland House by Charing Cross.

CLOCK, HURWORTH-ON-TEES.—A new public clock has been fixed here. The clock has Lord Grimthorpe's gravity escapement and maintaining power, compensation pendulum, and all the latest improvements inserted. The hours are struck upon the fine tenor bell of about 18 cwt., and the Cambridge chimes upon four bells. All the bearings are of gun metal, screwed into the frame, and the dial or motion wheels of gun metal, cut and polished on the engine. Messrs. Wm. Potts & Son, of Leeds, were the makers.

"SHOULD GAS COMPANIES DO ALL GAS-FITTING?"—This question formed the title of a paper read by Mr. W. H. Anson, of Columbus, Ohio, at the eighth annual meeting of the Ohio Gaslight Association, held at Columbus on March 16 and 17 last. The proceedings of the meeting are fully reported in the *American Gaslight Journal* for April 11. Mr. Anson answered the question with a decided affirmative, on the ground that the so-called "gas-fitters and plumbers" in that part of the world are generally merely plumbers, with no proper knowledge of gas-fitting and its requirements. He concludes his paper with these words:—"The taking in hand of internal fitting by gas companies would, I think, have a tendency to decrease, instead of increase, their liability for damages because of leaks, explosions, &c., for by doing so they can greatly improve the character of the work, thus lessening the chances of accidents. Many accidents have been caused by carelessness on the part of plumbers, and very few are caused by bad work on the part of the gas companies. Damages have been recovered by individuals from gas companies as the result of an accident caused by the ignorance or carelessness, or both, of plumbers, simply because it was the gas company's product which was contained in the pipes. If a gas company is assumed to be financially responsible for all the accidents occurring through the poor work of the professional fitter, then, I think, the sooner they take in hand this branch of their business the better. Gas companies should enlist the co-operation of the architect, the contractor, the builder, the owner or agent, and the manufacturer of and dealer in all gas appliances. The co-operation of these individuals with the gas companies would be of more pecuniary benefit to the latter than the combined efforts, as now put forth, of the united kingdom of plumbers. For they, especially the dealers and manufacturers, are sufferers with the gas companies at the hands of the plumbers. In view of all these and many other considerations, I am of the opinion that gas companies should do all gas fitting." In the discussion which followed, Mr. Anson's views were fully endorsed by all the speakers.

FATAL CRUSH AT HAMPSTEAD HEATH RAILWAY STATION: EIGHT LIVES LOST.—On Easter Monday evening, shortly after six o'clock, the railway station at Hampstead Heath was somewhat suddenly besieged by a dense crowd of holiday-makers on their way home. The day had been fairly fine, and the Heath had consequently been thronged with people, but shortly before the time named the weather became threatening, and large numbers of the holiday-makers hastened to the station. A staircase leading down to the platform was packed with people when, it is said, some one fell at the foot of the stairs, this caused others to fall, and in the result eight persons (two women and six boys) were crushed or trampled to death through the pressure of the surging and undisciplined crowd behind and above. Of course there will be a coroner's inquest into the circumstances of the disaster, but there can be no doubt that, as the *Times* says, "the practical lesson which should be learnt from the accident is that the whole system of railway accommodation at stations in or near populous towns requires consideration, and that the companies themselves cannot be accepted as the best judges of its adequacy for all the requirements which it may be called upon to fulfil."

STREET IMPROVEMENTS AT SHEFFIELD.—At the meeting of the Sheffield Town Council on the 13th inst., Alderman W. J. Clegg moved "That the Corporate Common Seal be affixed to agreements for the purchase of land and premises in Watson-walk, belonging to Messrs. Cockayne, Messrs. Birks, Sir Henry Watson, and the trustees of Mr. William Watson, at not exceeding the prices mentioned in the report of the sub-committee of the Improvement Committee, and presented to that Committee on April 4, 1892." This notice was the result of a discussion which took place at a meeting of the Improvement Committee on April 4. On the latter day a sub-committee of the Improvement Committee made a report to the effect that the widening of Watson-walk to a street of 42 ft. wide could be carried out at a cost of 47,000*l*.; the re-sales of property would probably realise 10,000*l*., leaving the net cost 37,000*l*. To this would have to be added 1,000*l*. for making the new street and 250*l*. for the purchase of tenant rights. The Improvement Committee discussed the report, Alderman Clegg moved that the Council be recommended to adopt agreements for acquiring the needful properties. This motion was not carried, and Alderman Clegg intimated that he should bring the matter forward at the next Council meeting. The motion was then carried, after long discussion, by a majority of one vote only. The *Sheffield Daily Telegraph* criticises the scheme and says it would have been better to widen the High-street.

WARMING AND VENTILATION OF FACTORIES.—The *Eastern Evening News* of the 25th ult. describes Messrs. Harmer's new clothing factory in St. Andrew's Broad-street, Norwich, which is warmed and ventilated on the Blackman-Smead system. This we are told is "an elaborate system of ventilation, introduced by an American company, and one which has not before been tried in this country. At the rear of the premises there is a square iron chamber containing a number of steel tubes through which the air is drawn, being cleansed on its way by passing through sieves of gauze, whose efficacy is attested by their blackness. A large fan forces the air up a brick shaft running from the basement to the top. Another fan at the top of the building is at work extracting the air which has been used. In this way a constant circulation is kept up throughout the whole building, and the air of the factory is changed every half-hour. By the same apparatus the temperature can be carefully regulated, the heat being applied, not directly to the air itself, but to the outside of the steel tubes. A walk through the premises is sufficient to demonstrate how great are the advantages of this system as compared with the old method of heating the air over and over again by flues or steam-pipes."

MEETINGS.

SATURDAY, APRIL 23.

Society of Antiquaries.—Anniversary meeting. [illegible] p.m.

Edinburgh Architectural Association.—1. Visit to Callender House and Grounds, including the Roman Remains of the Antonine Wall. 2. Visit to Town and Churchyard of Falkirk.

MONDAY, APRIL 25.

Surveyors' Institution.—Mr. E. G. Wheler on "Leases to Limited Liability Companies." 8 p.m.

Leeds and Yorkshire Architectural Society.—Presentation of Annual Report and election of officers. 7.30 p.m.

TUESDAY, APRIL 26.

Institution of Civil Engineers.—Mr. James Swinburne on "Electric-Light Measuring Instruments." 8 p.m.

Royal Institution.—Professor T. G. Bonney on "The Sculpturing of Britain—its later Stages."—I. 3 p.m.

Society of Arts (Foreign and Colonial Section).—Sir Edward Braddon on "Australasia: its Progress and Resources." 8 p.m.

WEDNESDAY, APRIL 27.

Civil and Mechanical Engineers' Society.—General Meeting for the Presentation of the Report, Election of Council, &c. 7 p.m.

Society of Arts.—Professor R. Wallace on "Egyptian Agriculture." 8 p.m.

Paul's Ecclesiological Society — Rev. F. E. ...man on "The Cross in its Connexion with the ..." 7.30 p.m.

THURSDAY, APRIL 28.

...itution of Electrical Engineers.—Mr. A. P. Trotter ...the Light of the Electric Arc." 8 p.m.
...ety of Antiquaries.—8.30 p.m.
...al Institution. — Professor Dewar on "The ...stry of Gases." I. 3 p.m.

FRIDAY, APRIL 29.

...itution of Civil Engineers (Students' Meeting).— ... H. Vaughan on "The Steam-Hammer and its ...on to the Hydraulic Forging-Press." 7.30 p.m.
...itute of Certified Carpenters.—7.30 p.m.

RECENT PATENTS:

ABSTRACTS OF SPECIFICATIONS.

...1.—DRILLING-MACHINES: *J. Melling.*—This is an ...tion relating to the adaptation to an ordinary ...ng or boring machine, of vertical or horizontal ... of a triangular or spade-shape tool or cutter ...ned with a templet. The inventor constructs a ...able nose-piece or chuck, which may be fitted ... spindle-head of the drilling-machine and rigidly ...n the same manner as an ordinary drill or bit. ...nose-piece is bored, so that the shank of the ...r cutter fits loosely. A centre is fitted inside ...re of the nose-piece or chuck, which corresponds ... countersunk centre in the shank of the tool. A ... is provided in the shank, passing transversely ...gh it, and corresponding with a similar hole in the ... or chuck, so that a pin may be passed through ... The hole in the shank of the tool or cutter is, ...ver, bored sufficiently large as to be perfectly free ... pin. When in use for drilling or boring a square ...ygonal hole, the oscillatory or lateral movement ... tool or cutter is compensated by the free move... of the shank upon the centre and within the nose ...ck, the function of the pin being to drive or rotate ...ol in unison with the spindle-head.

...07.—ELECTRIC LIGHT FITTINGS: *W. E. Dow.*— ...nvention relates to a drop more particularly de... to be used for incandescent electric light lamps, ... is also applicable for many other purposes.

...92.—DOOR-FASTENINGS: *W. Worrall.*—This speci...n relates to an improvement in fastenings for ... windows, gates, &c. A steel spring, made pre...y of half-round section, having its flat side rivetted ... end to the catch plate of bolt, latch, or other ... fastener, the loose end being turned upwards, ...g the spring, which has a sunken indent or lip ... the place where the action of the bolt, lever, or ...usually ends. Each of these have a protruding lip ... end, which, on the fastener being pushed to its ...ity, engages with the sunken indent and cannot ...eased until the free end of the spring is pressed

...98.—FIRE-PROOF FLOORS: *F. H. Willis and R. ...*—This patent relates to a system for constructing ...oof flooring with iron or steel joists, or other ...m for carrying the load, with arched fire-clay or ... incombustible material and lintels formed with ...ting tongues to rest on the bottom flanges of the ... and to protect the under side of the same from ...tion of fire: the lintels also forming centreing for ...ncrete, which fills in the spandrels of the upper ...f the fire-clay arched lintels, thus protecting the ... portions of the joists from fire. The underside of ...ntels are toothed to form a key for the ceiling ...r.

...4.—DOOR-KNOBS: *W. E. Riley.* — This Invention ...s to improvements in the construction of knobs ...or-handles, and to the means of holding them ... spindles by means of a screwed socket passing ...gh the front of the knob and over the end of the ...e, accurately adjusting its position and holding it ... the spindle, so that the strain required to turn ...indle is taken mainly by the neck of the knob.

...3.—WINDOW-SASH FASTENER: *T. McCulloch.*— ...ash-fastener which is the subject of this patent ...ts of a casing containing a bolt, also a loose catch ... a hinge. The case is mortised into the lower ...w-sash, flush with the surface, the catch with ... being mortised into the upper window-sash. To ..., the loose hinge catch is dropped over and down ...he case, and the bolt is shot through the loose ... catch. A lid is then shut down, forming a cover ... the case.

NEW APPLICATIONS FOR LETTERS PATENT.

...il 4.—6,468, S. Jefferies, Machinery for Making ... and similar articles from Plastic Clay.

...il 5.—6,511, W. Morrison, Roof Ventilators.

...il 6.—6,606, H. Sutcliffe, Domestic Fireplaces.— ... T. Potter, Construction of Fireproof Floors.— ... W. Hindle, Automatic Let-off and Container for ...-closets.—6,638, W. Ward & Sons, Ltd., and W. ... Brick-making Machinery.—6,654, O. Westblad, ...g Tiles.

...il 7.—6,663, H. Eggert, Hot-air Jet for Stoves.— ... J. Walker, Draught Excluder for Doors, &c.— ...S. Hellyer, Covers of Means for Closing Man... ...of Drains or Sewer Connexions, &c.

...il 8.—6,745, V. Smidth, Hydraulic Cement for ...ng Purposes.—6,758, C. Berle, Door-closer.—6,761, ...lliams, Preventing Down-draughts in Chimneys.— ... H. Winrow, Tile and Other similar Presses.— ... G. Ayling, Portable Scaffold for the Use of ...ators, &c.

...il 9.—6,860, G. Sparling and F. Solomon, Lock or ...ner for Securing Window-sashes.—6,866, R. ...chka, Planes.

PROVISIONAL SPECIFICATIONS ACCEPTED.

...8, C. Francione and J. Baconnet, London.—3,401, ...nty, Covering Roofs and Gutters for Houses and ... Buildings.—3,686, J. Lodge, Brick Kilns.—3,739, ...ockmann, Tools and their Handles.—4,373, T. Wal... ...nd J. Hodgkins, Caps or Terminals for Chimneys. ...1, A. Bromley, Open Fire-grates.—4,918, E. Peters, ...ney-tops or Terminals.—4,969, H. Thorpe, Gas ...ets.—5,010, J. Grundy, Ventilator and Chimney... —5,054, H. Ransome, Band-sawing machines.— ... J. Johnson, Screw-drivers.—5,254, A. Lamplough, ...asteners.—5,390, J. Hamblet, Paving-bricks.— ... A. Boult, Hinges.—5,633, T. Harris, Artificial ...—6,732, J. J. and A. Lee, Electric Light Fittings.—5,533, F. Tunks, Bakers' Ovens.—5,887, J. Ingram and others, Adjustable Sliding-sashes.—5,949, W. Allen, Rendering air and water-tight sliding-sashes, either old or new in dwelling-houses or elsewhere.—5,950, W. Kinniple, Caissons or Bridges, to close and open, or bridge across, and leave clear, as required, the entrance to graving docks, wet docks, harbours, &c.

COMPLETE SPECIFICATIONS ACCEPTED.

(Open to Opposition for Two Months.)

5,709, O. Clausen, Fire-clay and Magnesian Bricks, and in Kilns for fixing same.—5,731, W. Currie, Golf Club Head.—5,890, W. Trousdale and J. Thompson, Bolt for Lavatory and other doors.—9,440, W. Horn, Metallic Lathing for walls of Buildings.—10,231, J. Warman and F. Collyer, Sash-fasteners.—1,730, W. Beddows, Planes. —2,496, F. Phelps and H. O'Brien, Carpenters' Planes.— 4,159, H. Anstie, Sash-fasteners.—4,301, A. Illidge, Sash-fasteners.—4,496, J. Holliday, Artificial Stones.—4,525, H. Fitzpatrick, Glass-bricks.—4,540, G. Graham, Building or Paving Blocks.

SOME RECENT SALES OF PROPERTY:

ESTATE EXCHANGE REPORT.

APRIL 11.—By *C. R. Cross*: 47, 48, and 49, Aschurch-grove, Hammersmith, u.t. 97 yrs., g.r. 21*l.* 10s., 860*l.*—By *Warlters & Lovejoy*: 65, Maplin-st., Mile End, u.t. 42 yrs., g.r. 3*l.* 10s., 165*l.*; 19, Matlock-st., Stepney, u.t. 34 yrs., g.r. 3*l.* 5s., 245*l.*; 9, King John-st., u.t. 51 yrs., g.r. 3*l.* 15s., 235*l.*—By *Protheroe & Morris*: 1, Gothic Villas, Woodford, f., r. 22*l.*, 310*l.*—By *Rutley, Son, & Vine*: 41 and 43, Judd-st., Euston-rd., and Workshop, u.t. 15 yrs., g.r. 50*l.* 13s. 6d., r. 205*l.*, 855*l.*; a plot of freehold land, Surrey-rd., Peckham-rye, 37*l.*; 36, Dartmouth-pk.-rd., Dartmouth-pk., u.t. 70 yrs., g.r. 9*l.*, 410*l.*

APRIL 12.—By *Ramsay & Co.*: "Lime Cottage," York-grove, Peckham, u.t. 22 yrs., g.r. 5*l.*, r. 28*l.*, 150*l.*; 1, 3, and 5, Gervase-st., Old Kent-rd., u.t. 16 yrs., g.r. 9*l.*, r. 70*l.* 4s., 195*l.*; 12 to 16, Tenda-rd., Bermondsey, u.t. 60 yrs., g.r. 17*l.*, r. 118*l.*, 785*l.*—By *Eastman Bros.*, 29, Houston-rd., Forest-hill, f., 350*l.*—By *Walker & Runtz*: A plot of land, Vauxhall-rd., Westminster, area 19,000 ft., 25,800*l.*; 11 and 13, Little Compton-st.; and 1 to 4, Star-ct., Soho, f., area 3,700 ft., 1,705*l.*; 108 to 114 even, Brougham-rd., Dalston, u.t. 52 yrs., g.r. 40*l.*, 535*l.* By *C. & H. White*: No. 364, Kennington-rd., c., 705*l.*; 32, Studholme-st., Peckham, u.t. 82 yrs., g.r. 5*l.*, 250*l.* By *W. Hall*: 11, Glengall-ter., Old Kent-rd., f.r. 40*l.*, 755*l.*; 8, Glengall-ter., f.r. 36*l.*, 725*l.* By *A. Booth*: 15, Somerfield-rd., Finsbury-pk., u.t. 74 yrs., g.r. 6*l.* 6s., r. 40*l.*, 385*l.*; i.g.r. of 60*l.*, Hilldrop-rd., Camden-rd., u.t. 61 yrs. at a peppercorn, 1,200*l.*; Hilldrop-cres., i.g.r. of 12*l.*, u.t. 61 yrs., at a peppercorn, 240*l.*—By *Driver & Co.*: 25a, Lisle-st., Leicester-sq., and stabling, &c., f., 2,450*l.*; 23, Lisle-st., f., r. 65*l.*, 1,310*l.*; f.g.r. of 21*l.*, Norman-rd., Kensington, with reversion in 81 yrs., 500*l.*; f.g.r. of 42*l.*, Bramber-rd., with reversion in 81 yrs., 920*l.*; f.g r. of 6*l.*, with reversion in 81 yrs., 145*l.*; f.g.r. of 52*l.*, with reversion in 81 yrs., 1,095*l.*

APRIL 13.—By *J. T. Bedford & Co.*: 10, Wigmore-st., Cavendish-sq., u.t. 4 yrs., g.r. 32*l.*, 365*l.*—By *J. Nicholson & Son*: 1, Wilson-st., Mile-end, u.t. 70 yrs., g.r. 6*l.*, r. 30*l.*, 310*l.*; "The Red, White, and Blue" beer-house, Wilson-st., u.t. 70 yrs., g.r. 8*l.*, r. 36*l.*, 385*l.*; 43 to 49 (odd), Walden-st., Whitechapel, u.t. 15 yrs., g.r. 10*l.*, r. 128*l.*, 690*l.*; 9 to 17 (odd), Pole-st., Stepney, u.t. 24 yrs., g.r. 17*l.* 10s., 750*l.*; 38, 40, and 42, Hubbard-st., Stratford, u.t. 78 yrs., g.r. 10*l.* 10s., 235*l.*

APRIL 14.—By *Deverell & Co.*: 8 and 10, Bismark-rd., Highgate, f., r. 68*l.*, 960*l.*; 8, Carleton-rd, Tufnell-pk., u.t. 60 yrs., g.r. 10*l.*, r. 60*l.*, 435*l.*—By *C. C. & T. Moore*: No. 289, East India Dock-rd., f., r. 36*l.*, 710*l.*; 1, Marmaduke-pl., and 45, Langdale-st., St. George's-in-East, f., r. 45*l.* 10s., 360*l.*; 23 and 24, Freeman-st., Spitalfields, f., 720*l.*

[*Contractions used in these lists.*—F.g.r. for freehold ground-rent; l.g.r. for leasehold ground-rent; i.g.r. for improved ground-rent; g.r. for ground-rent; r. for rent; f. for freehold; c. for copyhold; l. for leasehold; e.r. for estimated rental; u.t. for unexpired term; p.a. for per annum; yrs. for years; st. for street; rd. for road; sq. for square; pl. for place; ter. for terrace; cres. for crescent; yd. for yard, &c.]

PRICES CURRENT OF MATERIALS.

TIMBER.		
Greenheart, B.G. ton	6/0/0	0/0/0
Teak, E.I. ... load	10/0/0	15/0/0
Sequoia, U.S. ft. cu.	2/3	3/0
Ash, Canada load	2/10/0	4/0/0
Birch, do.	3/5/0	4/10/0
Elm, do.	3/10/0	4/15/0
Fir, Dantsic, &c.	1/10/0	3/10/0
Oak, do.	3/0/0	5/5/0
Canada	5/10/0	7/0/0
Pine, Canada red	2/10/0	3/10/0
Do. yellow	2/10/0	5/0/0
Lath, D'ntsic, fath	5/0/0	6/0/0
St. Petersburg	5/0/8	7/0/0
Deals, Finland, 2nd & 1st std 100	8/10/0	10/0/0
Do. 4th & 3rd ..	7/0/0	8/10/0
Do. Riga	7/0/0	8/0/0
St. Petersburg, 1st yellow ..	11/0/0	16/0/0
Do. 2nd yellow	8/0/0	10/0/0
Do. white	7/10/0	11/0/0
Swedish	8/0/0	16/0/0
White Sea	8/0/0	18/0/0
Canada, Pine 1st	20/0/0	26/0/0
Do. do. 2nd	14/10/0	16/0/0
Do. do. 3rd, &c.	8/0/0	10/5/0
Do. Spruce, 1st	8/10/0	11/0/0
Do. do. 3rd & 2nd	6/15/0	8/0/0
New Brunswick	7/0/0	7/10/0
Battens, all kinds	3/10/0	15/10/0
Flooring Boards, sq., 1 in. prep. 1st	0/8/0	0/14/0
Do. 2nd	0/7/0	0/11/0
Other qualities	0/4/0	0/9/0
Cedar, Cuba .. ft.	/3½	/4½
Honduras, &c.	/3½	/4
Mahogany, Cuba.	/4½	/6½
St. Domingo, cargo av.	/4½	1/0
Mexican do. do	/4	/5
Tobasco do. do	/5½	/7
Honduras do. .	/5½	/6½
Box, Turkey ton	4/0/0	13/0/0
Rose, Rio	10/0/0	20/0/0
Bahia	9/0/0	18/0/0
Satin, St. Domingo ...... ft.	0/0/8	0/1/3

TIMBER (continued).		
Satin, Porto Rico	0/0/8	0/1/6
Walnut, Italian ...	0/0/3½	0/0/7
METALS.		
IRON—Pig, in Scotland .... ton	2/1/2	0/0/0
Bar, Welsh, in London	5/17/6	6/0/0
Do. do. at works in Wales	5/7/6	5/10/0
Do. Staffordshire, in London	6/5/0	6/15/0
COPPER—British, cake and ingot	49/0/0	49/10/0
Best selected ..	50/0/0	50/10/0
Sheets, strong ..	59/0/0	0/0/0
Chili, bars	46/2/6	46/10/0
YELLOW METAL lb.	0/0/5	0/0/5½
LEAD—Pig, Spanish .... ton	10/13/9	0/0/0
English, com. brands	10/15/0	11/0/0
Sheet, English, 5 lbs. per sq. ft. and upwards ..	12/5/0	0/0/0
Pipe	12/15/0	0/0/0
ZINC—English sheet ...... ton	25/10/0	0/0/0
Vieille Montagne	26/5/0	0/0/0
TIN—Straits	92/0/0	92/10/0
Australian	92/12/6	93/2/6
English Ingots	93/15/0	94 0/0
OILS.		
Linseed ...... ton	18/7/6	18/12/6
Cocoanut, Cochin	24/10/0	0/0/0
Do. Ceylon	22/0/0	0/0 0
Palm, Lagos	23/3/0	23/10/0
Rapeseed, English pale	24/10/0	25/0/0
Do. brown	23/0/0	0/0/0
Cottonseed ref. ..	19/0/0	0/0/0
Oleine	21/10/6	22/10/0
Lubricating, U.S.	4/0/0	5/0/0
Do. refined	5/0/0	15/0/0
TAR—Stockholm barrel	0/19/0	1/0/0
Archangel	0/12/6	0/0/0

TENDERS.

[Communications for insertion under this heading should be addressed to "The Editor," and must reach us *not later than 12 noon on Thursdays.*]

BECKENHAM.—Accepted for the erection of extension to dairy premises at Beckenham-road, Beckenham, for Mr. J. Broomfield. Mr. J. P. Chost, architect:—
A. & W. Garnar, Peckham £700 0 0
(No competition.)

BOURNEMOUTH.—Accepted for making-up roads, &c., under sec. 150 of the Public Health Act, 1875. Mr. F. W. Lacey, C.E., Borough Surveyor:—
G. Troke, Winton, Bournemouth £1,530 6 2
Tar-Paving Footpaths.
Bradshaw & Co., London .... Schedule Prices.
Wood-Block Crossings.
Bradshaw & Co., London £309 7 6

BUSHEY (Herts).—For erecting house for Mr. J. Herkomer. Messrs. J. E. K. & J. P. Cutts, architects:—
C. Brightman, Watford £1,150 0 0

BUSHEY (Herts).—For additions to photo-etching electric-light studio, for Messrs. André & Co. Messrs. J. E. K. and J. P. Cutts, architects:—
C. Brightman .... £335 | I. Darvill £310

CHIGNAL (Essex).—For erecting a pair of cottages. Mr. Ed. Mawhood, architect, Chelmsford:—
H. Gozzett .... £267 10 0 | J. Norrington, Broomfield* £225 0 0
W. Samms .... 240 0 0 |
A. Harman .... 225 0 0 |
* Accepted.

CO. DURHAM.—For erecting new laundry and washhouse, at the Durham County Lunatic Asylum. Mr. William Crozier, A.M.I.C.E., County Architect, Shire-hall, Durham. Quantities by Mr. J. Ezra Miller, 1, Tunstall-road, Sunderland:—
Thos. Dickinson.... £8,000 0 0 | John Shepherd...... £7,088 0 0
M. R. Draper ...... 7,614 11 5 | Geo. Marshall & Son, 7,007 18 6
Geo. Grudon & Son.. 7,135 14 9 | W. C. Atkinson, Stockton-on-Tees*. 6,918 5 5
Joseph Elliott...... 7,125 0 0 |
*Accepted.

Sub-Tenders.
Adam & Co., Ltd., Birmingham (Plaster instead of Glazed Bricks) £446 10 0
Threlkeld & Wallace, Newcastle (Plumber and Smith and Ironfounder) 672 12 6
Emley & Son, Newcastle (Iron Roof, Plumber, Smith, and Ironfounder) 1,309 0 6

GUILDFORD.—For proposed Police Buildings, Guildford. Mr. W. G. Lower, architect, Guildford:—
J. Longley & Co. .... £7,200 | Smith & Sons £5,900
Brown Bros. .... 6,700 | P. Peters 5,850
Stephens, Bastow, & Co. .. 6,290 | Higlett & Hammond...... 5,775
Reed, Blight, & Co. ...... 6,044 | R. Wood 5,725
Gammon & Son .... 5,990 | J. Bottril 5,690
Geo. Strudwick .... 5,973 | G. Kemp 5,579
T. H. Kingerlee .... 5,967 |

LITTLE WALTHAM (Essex).—For additions to Little Waltham Schools. Mr. R. Mawhood, architect, Chelmsford:—
G. Milbank £103 10 0
G. Holland, Great Leighs (accepted) 102 0 0

LONDON.—For erecting and completing warehouse and stabling, at Storehouse Wharf, Brand-street, Ratcliff, E., for the Free Trade Wharf Company. Mr. Charles Dunch, architect. Quantities by Mr. James F. Wesley, 294, Romford-road, Forest-gate:—
J. Greenwood .... £6,098 | Stimpson & Co. £4,854
J. Morter .... 5,067 | Brown, Son, & Bloomfield 4,820
B. E. Nightingale .... 4,985 | Ashby & Horner 4,702
Harris & Wardrop .... 4,958 | Munday & Sons 4,552
Lawrance & Son .... 4,936 | Perry & Co. 4,529
Ashby Bros. .... 4,918 | Scharien & Co. 4,483

LONDON.—For pulling down and rebuilding "The London Apprentice" public-house, Oldstreet, E.C., for Mr. George Eeles. Mr. Joseph G. Needham, architect, 11, Powerscroft-road, Clapton, N.E. Quantities supplied by Mr. J. F. Bewley:—

		Old materials.
J. Ivory	£6,083	£35
W. Shurmur	5,896	100
S. Goodall	5,883	30
Walker Bros.	5,790	50
Spencer & Co.	5,674	30
Coulsell Bros.	4,763	70

[Surveyor's estimate, £4,540.]

LONDON.—For repairs, &c., to Nos. 27, 29, 31, 33, 35, 37, and 39, Lucas-street, Commercial-road, E., for Mr. Frederick Garner. Mr. Joseph G. Needham, architect and surveyor, 11, Powerscroft-road, Clapton, N.E.:—
Walker Bros. .... £504 | J. F. Holiday £375
N. Thomas .... 480 | Worden & Easton 320
Coulsell Bros. .... 375 | A. & F. Wilson (accepted) .. 273

LONDON.—For repairs and decorations to No. 26, Goodge-street, Tottenham-court-road, W.C. Mr. F. West, architect, Croydon:—
E. Williams .... £237 0 | Waddington & Co. £198 10
T. A. Cooper .... 220 10 | Gardiner & Llewlyn 180 0

LONDON.—For alterations and additions to the Shoreditch Town-hall. Mr. C. Barry, architect. Quantities by Messrs. Russell & Young:—
Faulkner .... £6,077 | Smith & Son £5,522
Mitchell .... 5,600 | Colls & Sons 5,445
Nightingale .... 5,564 | Steed 5,420
Coulsell .... 5,556 | Houghton 4,973
Chesham .... 5,549 |

PLUMSTEAD.—For laying 2,940 feet of 12 in. pipe sewer in Church Manorway. Mr. H. H. Church, architect, Woolwich:—
Woodham & Fry .... £1,098 | Nichols 747
Ossenton .... 835 | Rackham & Bentham* 694
* Accepted.

PLUMSTEAD.—For drainage works, in Genista-road, Shooter's-hill. Mr. H. H. Church, architect, Woolwich:—
Girling .... £165 | Farmar & Gregory £160
Rackham & Bentham ...... 163 | * Accepted.

PLUMSTEAD.—For drainage works and forming road on The White Hart Estate. Mr. H. H. Church, architect, Woolwich:—
Girling .... £210 | Rackham & Bentham £185

PORTMADOC.—For kerbing, channelling, and tar-paving. Messrs. Thomas Roberts & Son, engineers:—
O. Lister £2,487 0 0
John Lees, Bangor (accepted) 1,839 10 0
[Engineers' estimate, £1,870.]

QUAKER'S YARD (Glamorgan).—For the erection of a truants' school, outbuildings, &c., for the South Wales and Monmouthshire Joint School Boards. Mr. W. H. Dashwood Caple, architect, 1, St. John's-square, Cardiff. Quantities by the architect:—
John Lewis .... £7,260 | Osborne & Co. £6,350
H. Willcock .... 7,220 | Stephens, Bastow, & Co., Montpelier, Bristol*.... 6,279
D. J. Davis .... 7,100 |
Henry Welsh .... 6,650 |
* Accepted.

SOUTHEND (Essex).—For new sewage works, for the Southend Local Board:—
Contracts Nos. 1, 2, and 3.
J. Neave .... £3,265 4 0 | Dupont £2,310 1 3
Rackham & Bentham .... 2,985 6 11 | W. Buxton 2,257 14 0
G. Bell .... 2,802 15 9 | C. W. Killingback & Co., Camden Town* 2,213 5 6
E. & W. Iles .... 2,376 10 9 | Beeks 2,186 15 4
* Accepted.

SOUTH SHIELDS.—For the erection of houses and shops, for Mr. B. Chapman, in Wester-lane, South Shields. Mr. Henry Grieves, architect, Albany-chambers, South Shields:—

Jas. Yelling	£2,700 0 0	Goodwin & Son	£2,130 0 0
R. Summerbell	2,600 0 0	A. Ross, South Shields (accepted)	2,066 0 0
W. J. Robertson	2,478 12 4		

STOCK (Essex).—For erecting house and shop. Mr. Ed. Mawhood, architect, Chelmsford:—

H. Gozzett	£950	E. West	£843
F. Johnson	875	Choat & Son, Chelmsford*	796
W. Pincham	873	* Accepted.	

WAINFLEET (Lincolnshire).—For the restoration of St. Mary's Church, Wainfleet, Lincolnshire. Mr. J. B. Corby, architect, Stamford:—

J. M. Thompson & Sons	£1,906 0 0	Walter & Hensman	£1,648 0 0
S. Sherwin	1,867 0 0	Thos. Elmes	1,608 19 3
A. Wood	1,857 0 0	E. Bowman	1,374 0 0
Rodd & Son	1,810 16 1	J. T. Turner, Wainfleet*	1,328 2 5
S. F. Halliday	1,690 0 0	*Accepted for part of the work.	

WALTHAMSTOW.—For the erection and completion of new cookery room and teachers' room at the south-west end of the Higham Hill Girls' School, for the Walthamstow School Board. Mr. W. A. Longmore, architect, Bridge Chambers, Hoe-street, Walthamstow. No quantities supplied:—

Calnan	£700	Coulsell	£593
Coxhead	674	Walling	588
Evans	615	Kelland	535
Amey	567	Challis (accepted)	425

WATFORD (Herts).—For new oak ceilings to chancel and transepts of St. Matthew's Church, Oxhey, Watford. Messrs. J. E. K. & J. P. Cutts, architects:—
E. Robinson, Bloomsbury, London £435 0 0

WOOLWICH.—Accepted for erecting five dwelling-houses in Brewer-street, and two in Eleanor-road. Mr. H. H. Church, architect, Woolwich:—
Builder's work.—Coombs £2,715 0 0
External mason's work.—Ransom 140 0 0

WOOLWICH.—For alterations and additions to the "General Havelock" Tavern, for Mr. G. H. Campbell. Mr. H. H. Church, architect, Woolwich:—

Munday & Sons	£2,136	Holloway	£1,730
Multon & Wallis	1,997	Battley (accepted)	1,545

For Pewterer's work.

Helling	208	Sanders & Sons	£191 15
Warne	203 0		

WOOLWICH.—For erecting additional offices for the Woolwich Local Board of Health. Mr. H. H. Church, architect, Woolwich:—

Proctor	£965	Nightingale	£826
Chapman	909	Munday & Son	811
Multon & Wallis	866	Young & Lonsdale	797
Battley	[illegible]	Hart	795
Woodward	839	Holloway (accepted)	792

WOOLWICH.—For rebuilding Kent-House, Powis-street, for Messrs. Garrett & Co., Limited. Mr. H. H. Church, architect, Woolwich:—

Treasure & Son	£14,890	Nightingale	£12,355
Allen & Sons	14,350	Chapman	12,350
Kirk & Randall	13,858	Yolling & Lonsdale	11,998
Balaam Brothers	12,759	Holloway	11,719
Woodward & Co.	12,700	Munday & Son (accepted)	11,640

Aldringham House, Leiston.—In the list of tenders for alterations at Aldringham House, Leiston, in the *Builder* of 16th inst., p. 315, the name of the firm who sent in the lowest tender was, by a mistake of our printers, given as "Girling & Co." It should have been "Girling & Coe."

SUBSCRIBERS in LONDON and the SUBURBS, by prepaying at the Publishing Office, 19s. per annum (or 4s. 9d. per quarter), can ensure receiving "The Builder," by *Friday Morning's Post.*

TO CORRESPONDENTS.

J. S.—M. J. L. (we cannot publish such a very elementary inquiry).—H. H.—"Waterproof" (inquiry should be addressed to a manufacturer of the material). "Another Member A.A." (we cannot publish letters not authenticated by name or address).—"Architect and Surveyor" (ditto).

All statements of facts, lists of tenders, &c., must be accompanied by the name and address of the sender, not necessarily for publication.

We are compelled to decline pointing out books and giving addresses.

Note.—The responsibility of signed articles, and papers read at public meetings, rests, of course, with the authors.

We cannot undertake to return rejected communications.

Letters or communications (beyond mere news-items) which have been duplicated for other journals, are NOT DESIRED.

All communications regarding literary and artistic matter should be addressed to THE EDITOR; all communications relating to advertisements and other exclusively business matters should be addressed to THE PUBLISHER, and not to the Editor.

PUBLISHER'S NOTICES.

Registered Telegraphic Address, 'The Builder,' London.

CHARGES FOR ADVERTISEMENTS.

SITUATIONS VACANT, PARTNERSHIPS, APPRENTICESHIPS TRADE, AND GENERAL ADVERTISEMENTS.

Six lines (about fifty words) or under .... 4s. 6d.
Each additional line (about ten words) .... 0s. 6d.

Terms for Series of Trade Advertisements, also for Special Advertisements on front page, Competitions, Contracts, Sales by Auction, &c. may be obtained on application to the Publisher.

SITUATIONS WANTED.

FOUR Lines (about thirty words) or under .... 2s. 6d.
Each additional line (about ten words) .... 0s. 6d.

PREPAYMENT IS ABSOLUTELY NECESSARY.

*** Stamps must not be sent, but all small sums should be remitted by Cash in Registered Letter or by Money Order, payable at the Post-office, Covent-garden, W.C. to

DOUGLAS FOURDRINIER, Publisher,

Addressed to No. 46, Catherine-street, W.C

Advertisements for the current week's issue must reach the Office before THREE o'clock p.m. on THURSDAY, but those intended for the front Page should be in by TWELVE noon on WEDNESDAY.

SPECIAL.—ALTERATIONS IN STANDING ADVERTISEMENTS or ORDERS TO DISCONTINUE same must reach the Office before TEN o'clock on WEDNESDAY mornings.

The Publisher cannot be responsible for DRAWINGS, TESTIMONIALS, &c. left at the Office in reply to Advertisements, and strongly recommends that of the latter COPIES ONLY should be sent.

PERSONS Advertising in "The Builder" may have *Replies addressed to the Office,* 46, Catherine-street, Covent Garden, W.C. *free of charge.* Letters will be forwarded if addressed envelopes are sent, together with sufficient stamps to cover the postage.

AN EDITION Printed on THIN PAPER, for FOREIGN and COLONIAL CIRCULATION, is issued every week.

Now ready.

READING CASES, { NINEPENCE EACH. By Post (carefully packed), 1s.

TERMS OF SUBSCRIPTION.

"THE BUILDER" is supplied direct from the Office to residents in any part of the United Kingdom at the rate of 19s. per annum Prepaid. To all parts of Europe, America, Australia, and New Zealand, 26s. per annum. To India, China, Ceylon, &c., 30s. per annum. Remittances payable to DOUGLAS FOURDRINIER, Publisher, No. 46, Catherine-street, W.C.

The Builder Cathedral Series.

1891.

1. Canterbury	Jan. 3.	7. Salisbury	July 4.
2. Lichfield	Feb. 7.	8. Bristol	Aug. 1.
3. St. Alban's	Mar. 7.	9. Norwich	Sept. 5.
4. Peterborough	April 4.	10. Rochester	Oct. 3.
5. Wells	May 2.	11. Lincoln	Nov. 7.
6. Exeter	June 6.	12. Gloucester	Dec. 5.

1892.

13. St. Paul's .. .. Jan. 2.

14. Hereford	Feb. 6.	20. Worcester	Aug. 6.
15. Chichester	Mar. 5.	21. Bangor	Sept. 3.
16. Ely	April 2.	22. St. Asaph	Sept. 3.
17. Llandaff	May 7.	23. Winchester	Oct. 1.
18. Oxford	June 4.	24. Truro	Nov. 5.
19. Southwell	July 2.	25. St. David's	Dec. 3.

(Further arrangements will be duly announced.)

Post-free FOURPENCE HALFPENNY each, except Nos. 1 and 2 which are *out of print;* but the VIEW, PLAN, AND DESCRIPTION of CANTERBURY and of LICHFIELD have been re-printed, and they can now be had, price ONE SHILLING each set; by post, 1s. 3d.

THE REREDOS, ST. PAUL'S.
Reprinted from "The Builder," January 28, 1888 (18 in. by 11½ in.), on stout paper, unfolded, for framing, 6d.; by post, 8d.

PORTFOLIOS,
for Preserving the Plates unfolded, 2s. 6d.; by post, 3s.

London: Office of "The Builder," 46, *Catherine-street, W.C.*

The Builder.

Vol. LXII. No. 2560. Saturday, April 30, 1892.

ILLUSTRATIONS.

St. Peter's College, Radley : New Cloisters and Proposed New Chapel.—Mr. T. G. Jackson, A R A, Architect .... *Double-Page Ink-Photo.*
Bedroom Furniture and Fixtures, House in Lennox-gardens.—Mr. Arthur Cawston, Architect .... *Single-Page Ink-Photo.*
Drawing-Room, "Brooklands," Weybridge.—Mr. Reginald T. Blomfield, Architect .... *Single-Page Ink-Photo.*
Houses of Parliament, Melbourne : West Elevation, Longitudinal Section, and Plans.—Mr. P. Kerr, Architect .... *Two Double-Page Ink-Photo's.*

Blocks in Text.

Diagrams in Student's Column : Heating by Hot Water .... Page 343

CONTENTS.

…cture at the Royal Academy 333
…etch Designs for the Glasgow Art Galleries 335
.... 336
…w Gallery Exhibition 338
…t-Union of London 339
…ool Engineering Society 339
Archæological Association 339
…oisters and Proposed New Chapel for Radley College 340
…m Fittings at 99, Lennox-gardens 340
…r of Drawing-room, "Brooklands," Weybridge 340
… of Parliament, Melbourne 340
Books: A. S. Murray's "Handbook of Greek Archæology, &c." (London: Murray); "Les Artistes Célèbres" (Paris: Librairie de l'Art); "Plain Handicrafts" (London: Percival & Co.); A. Cartault's "Terres Cuites Grecques Photographiées, &c." (Paris: Colin et Cie); Barr Ferree's "Christian Thought in Architecture" (New York: American Society of Church History); W. D. Douglas's "The Geometrical Problem Solved" (Cardiff: D. Douglas & Co.); Oxborrow and Money-Kent's Universal Office Manual (London: 17, Victoria-street, S.W.) 340
Architectural Education 342
"Glasgow Art Galleries 342
Student's Column.—Warming Buildings by Hot Water. XVIII. 342
Obituary 343
General Building News 344
Sanitary and Engineering News 344
Foreign and Colonial 344
Miscellaneous 345
Legal 346
Meetings 346
Recent Patents 346
Some Recent Sales of Property 347

Architecture at the Royal Academy.

HE collection of architectural drawings at the Royal Academy is somewhat more heterogeneous, perhaps, than usual, and does not present anything which can be singled out as of special and marked interest. It contains …ver a great many interesting drawings, …he general level of draughtsmanship is … kept up. The hanging is somewhat …ised in its arrangement, and the …nce of either carelessness, ignorance …partiality is perhaps stronger than …l. Which of these qualities is …he ascendant it is of course impos… to surmise unless we knew (which no …loes) under whose direction the drawings …eally selected and hung. As we have …dy noticed, the Hanging Committee this …did not include an architect, and how … sculptors and painters are able to judge …chitecture we know only too well. The …*it* goes that one well-known painter … superintended the conclusion of part …e architectural hanging excused him… for having skied some small drawings … of sight by the plea that "they …ed the wall better so," that being …ently the main object. There is evi… of either incapacity or carelessness in …ejection of some drawings of which we … and the acceptance of some others; and …me of the rejected drawings were hung …side some of the accepted ones, the … would be rather curious. Lastly, how… we cannot but think that there is an …us element of unfairness in the manner …hich the drawings representing one or … of the largest buildings in progress …pparently deliberately put on one side …ounted aloft. We noticed this last year …e case of Mr. Mountford's view of the …ield Municipal Buildings, which was the … important new building of that year, …he drawing of which was placed where …e could see it. We find again this year …lrawing of the most important new building of the year, Mr. Webb's completion of the South Kensington Museum, put on one side at an angle of the room, and one of the non-accepted designs given the central place. There is an obvious intention in this, and though of course it is always possible that the accepted and executed design for a building may not be the best artistically, we cannot see any valid excuse for the treatment in this case. Generally speaking we believe there is a widespread feeling of dissatisfaction among architects with the way the architectural exhibits at the Academy are dealt with; the acceptance or rejection of a drawing is regarded by many (as an architect remarked to us the other day) as "a mere toss-up"; and we cannot but feel strongly that if there is to be any pretence on the part of the Academy of treating architecture as an art on the same level with painting and sculpture, the Hanging Committee ought invariably to include one of the architect members who would be known to be responsible for the hanging, and exhibitors would then know in whose hands they were. As it is, no one has any idea who selects and arranges the architectural drawings; the whole thing is done in a corner, and there is consequently a general feeling of distrust in regard to it.

Once again we point out that the system of exhibiting architecture at the Academy is radically wrong. The room set apart specially for architecture is too small to provide space for any such drawings as would really give the facts and structure of an architectural design. Preference is given to picturesque views of buildings on a small scale, which, regarded as pictures, are of course of little interest in comparison with the other pictorial exhibits, and with the space allotted no other system is possible. With the public such drawings may be more popular than true architectural delineations of a building, although even this popularity is so limited that the room is generally nearly empty; but an academy of arts ought to lead the public taste, not follow it, and some consideration ought to be given to what is of interest and value to architects and to serious students of the art of architecture. In Paris an architect can exhibit a whole set of drawings giving the plan, section, and detailed treatment of a single building, and that is the true way to illustrate architecture by drawings. In the case of architecture the picture of the building is not the real thing, it is only a representation of it, being thus in an entirely different class from the other pictorial exhibits. On the French system of exhibiting a complete set of constructive drawings, we have before us the facts and the genesis of the architectural design; instead of a mere picture of it; we can see how the architect has dealt with the problem constructively as well as artistically. The drawings do not represent the mere appearance of the building, but they represent the work itself, and we can put together the architectural treatment of it from the drawings. Until this system is accepted at the Royal Academy, the architectural section of the exhibition must always remain a thing of merely superficial interest, and mere draughtsmanship take the precedence of design properly so-called, as it obviously does at present. The majority of architects who exhibit depend upon a draughtsman to put their idea into a shape in which it is likely to prove acceptable; a most vicious system. But for anything better than this the space allotted is wholly inadequate. Architecture, the central art, is allowed to be cornered instead of taking its proper position, and until the Royal Academy awake to the fact that art does not mean pictures merely but design in every sense, there is no hope of an improvement. Whenever that principle is realised, it will be recognised that the space allotted for architecture is too limited to serve any good purpose, and it will then be seen that architecture must have more space, in order to meet its claims for exhibition adequately. We fear however that it will be long before the perception of this necessity takes any root in the minds of the majority of Royal Academicians. The majority of the Academicians are painters, and think art means pictures; a heresy in which the public are only too ready to follow them. Architects have some right to complain, for they at least have wider views, and are interested in painting and sculpture,—while the painters and sculptors for the most part think of no art but their own. So things

d

are, and for the present one can only make the best of it.

The three central points of the walls are occupied respectively by Mr. Waterhouse's "Examination Hall, Yorkshire College, Leeds" (1751), Mr. Pearson's view of Truro Cathedral as it will appear when (or if) completed (1687), and Mr. Belcher's geometrical elevation of the competition design for the completion of the South Kensington Museum (1809). No plans are given with any of these. Mr. Waterhouse's Examination Hall is a solid-looking brick building with stone dressings introduced a good deal in the way of flat bands, which form a feature in the upper story of the towers. The entrance front takes the form of two square towers with corbelled-out turrets on the upper stage, and slated spires square on plan; between which is, on the upper floor level (we presume from the appearance of the exterior design that there are two floors), a large Perpendicular traceried window of the orthodox type marking the end of the hall. The side of the building is treated with two ranges of traceried windows of the same type between buttresses, but with segmental arched heads, and a strongly-marked corbelled cornice over. The building has a solid and monumental appearance: the drawing is executed in water-colour in Mr. Waterhouse's well-known and effective if rather heavy style. The drawing of Truro Cathedral is a beautiful water-colour drawing, but gives a false impression of the tone of the exterior of the building, giving it the appearance of a breadth and quietness of tone in the masonry which is not the effect which the actual building has. The general effect in the drawing is fine, the western towers group well with the central one, but they are perhaps rather deficient in power and character themselves; a little more solid wall left in the lower portion would have given them more. The delicate detail about the south porch is carefully touched in the drawing, and contrasts well with the plainer portions of the design. On the whole however the best parts of the cathedral are those now executed; the completion of the nave will not add much to the architectural interest of the cathedral beyond taking away the painful appearance of incompleteness from the eastern portion.

Mr. Belcher's elevation of his design for the South Kensington Museum is an unusual and original piece of design, but very much wants a plan to furnish the key to it. This is a point on which we have spoken so often and so strongly that it becomes wearisome to have to repeat it every year. It is a quasi-Classical elevation, with a long row of columns on the ground story of rather abnormal tenuity. We see no reason why the proportion of the Classic column should not be modified at pleasure and in the desire to get a new effect and expression from the feature, but in this instance we cannot but think that the long row of very thin columns would have a weak effect, and when we find the upper story again striped down with thin columns or pilasters (it is difficult to say which at some points), one feels that this feature has been repeated rather to superfluity. The two cupolas are elegant in design, and so is the upper portion of the tower, though we certainly do not like the columns corbelled out from the plain mass of wall, below the line where the chief decorative treatment of the upper stage begins; they look as if stuck on, and carry nothing but a slight projection suggestive of a balcony. The detail elevation (1,675) is a very fine piece of work, and a kind of drawing of which we wish to see more in the architectural room. The sculptural decoration above the ground-floor windows, between the columns, is very original: over each keystone is a shield with the name of an eminent artist, and two female figures, one on each side of the shield, holding up a symbolic accessory; the shield with the name of Chantry is flanked by two nude figures holding up a statue; in the next compartment Mr. G. F. Watts is commemorated, and an easel and brushes symbolise painting; in the next is the name of Gottfried Semper, and two figures hold up a model of a Classic building. Whether however it was well to show these figures carved in stone built into a red brick wall which occupies the plain spaces is a question; it looks piquant and unusual, but it detaches the sculpture too much from the architecture and destroys the appearance of breadth and repose. The drawing is a beautifully executed one, and quite a model for the getting up of detailed elevations. Whether the design could really be quoted as in keeping with existing portions of the museum which are completed externally (which was we think a a requirement in the competition), may be a question.

As before observed, Mr. Aston Webb's perspective of his South Kensington design (1,716) hangs in one of the angles. It was illustrated and commented upon by us at the time of the competition. The building seems to group in a very satisfactory manner, and suits its site; in another Academy exhibition we hope we may see some illustrations of the further treatment of the building in detail design and in construction. Occupying the position balancing this, at the other angle of the room, is a view of the front of "Gosford House N.B., as completed" (1790), by Mr. W. Young, a design carrying one back to the old days of "Classic" mansions. The entrance is approached by two flights of steps at each end of a terrace carried on a rusticated arcade, which represents apparently the principal floor level of the central part of the house. A great mass of wall rises behind this, broken up by pilasters which are not very happily placed, and pierced with three great round-arched windows divided horizontally at the springing by an entablature carried on a couple of small columns. A pediment occupies the centre of the skyline, with a balustrade on each side crowned at the extremities with lions, and behind the pediment is a low octagon crowned by a circular dome. At each side of the central mass we have wings in orthodox fashion; a square mass in the centre of each wing with lower recessed portions at each side, one of which connects it with the main central building. The front is absolutely symmetrical, and has the dignity of the old-fashioned type of "mansions of the nobility and gentry," but the want of a plan renders it absolutely impossible to form any real judgment as to the treatment of the building: what is the central block, and what do the three large windows light? And what are the functions of the symmetrical side blocks? Do they lend themselves conveniently to the arrangement of the plan, or is the whole simply an architectural screen? These are questions which the design at once suggests, and to which no answer is given.

The exhibition contains another illustration from a mansion on a great scale, this time an interior, "Hewell Grange; interior of Hall" (1629), by Mr. Thomas Garner. This is a very large central hall with a ponderous flat panelled oak ceiling, the ends of the beams carried on carved brackets. The height of the wall is divided halfway by a band of carved ornament running round. On the left is an arcade with marble columns opening from the centre of the side of the hall, a large square-headed opening with pilasters facing it on the other side. The first floor galleries are seen above, with intermittent arcaded openings with marble shafts, leaving solid piers at intervals, and across the end of the gallery is a similar but uninterrupted arcade, through which are seen the arches of a larger arcade in a further part of the building. The lower part of the wall is panelled, the upper part hung with tapestries or carpets. The drawing, a water-colour, is a fine and rich one, and the whole effect exceedingly sumptuous, but there is an impression conveyed that the scale of the apartment is exaggerated, and that it can hardly be really so large as it is made to appear here, where it suggests the central hall of a great hotel rather than of a private house.

The Sheffield Municipal Buildings is illu[strated] by Mr. Mountford in several drawing[s]. A view of the principal staircase (1,67[?]) shows a wide and dignified staircase-hall, th[e] first floor portion carried on arches, with [an] open arcade on the principal landing, th[e] design of which is carried round the wall [on] the other sides, the pilasters between th[e] arches supporting a large panelled cove ov[er] which is a lantern. The general effe[ct] is fine and spacious, but we cannot sa[y] that the details are interesting. The Surre[y] street front of the building is shown i[n] another drawing (1,737), and makes a ver[y] agreeable architectural composition, in whic[h] the author has succeeded in indicating th[e] multiple nature of the uses of the buildin[g] while preserving a sufficient degree of arch[i]tectural unity. The view towards the churc[h]yard, the front at the opposite side from th[e] last mentioned, is not quite so satisfactory i[n] this respect, and appears somewhat too muc[h] like a group of buildings put together acc[i]dentally, and the end of the council-chamb[er] might have claimed a rather more strikin[g] architectural treatment. The staircase turr[et] adjoining it comes in well, and makes a go[od] feature in the façade.

The front of the Royal College of Mu[sic] at South Kensington, by Sir A. W. Blomfi[eld] (1636), is one of the important new buildi[ngs] illustrated, and one which suffers much fro[m] want of a plan, as the elevation gives th[e] idea that the architect has been restricted [to] treatment mainly of a utilitarian characte[r]. The building may be suitable for the site a[nd] for its purpose, but the elevation can har[dly] be said to present much architectural inte[rest] in itself.

Prominent features in the room are t[he] large decorative panels, hung at each [end] above the strictly architectural drawin[gs]. One of these is Mr. J. Babb's "Am[...] Caprarii—frieze" (1,678), a design of the sa[me] type which its author has previously [ex]hibited at the Academy, consisting of a pr[o]cession of figures in a yellowish tone relie[f] on a dark ground, and with painted arch[i]tectural decoration forming horizontal border[s] above and below. The present one is a pr[o]cession of young men and goats arranged in [a] purely decorative manner; the general effe[ct] is pretty and suitable to its position, thou[gh] the figures are abnormally thin. The oth[er] work referred to is one of a more serious ty[pe], "Decorative Panel: Youth; the Toilers a[nd] the Idlers" (1796), by Mr. Gustav Natorp; [a] wall-painting with a moral. There are [no] accessary decorations, the design consisti[ng] simply of figures of men and women, nu[de] and somewhat conventionalised in colou[r], against a light indication of sky as a bac[k]ground; the figures are not too mu[ch] modelled, but the whole kept flat in effe[ct]. The composition is arranged in two slopi[ng] lines descending towards the centre (t[he] reverse of a pediment composition), "t[he] blank space in the background in t[he] centre serving to divide off the t[wo] groups distinctly, the toilers on the l[eft] and the idlers on the right. The who[le] composition is agreable and suggestive, and [the] effect truly decorative; there is however o[ne] mistake, to our thinking, in drawing the recu[m]bent "idler" figure near the centre as [a] partially foreshortened, the feet recedi[ng] somewhat. As all the other figures are [as] nearly as possible in a flat plane, the result [is] to give this particular figure the appearan[ce] of having the legs too short and the feet [too] small.

Other drawings in the Architectural Ro[om] we will notice in future numbers.

LECTURES AT UNIVERSITY COLLEGE.—The foll[ow]ing lectures on Archæology are announced: F[ive] lectures on the "Mediæval Archæology of [the] West," by Professor Stuart Poole, on Mondays, fr[om] May 2 to May 23; five lectures on "The Relati[on] of Religion and Art in the Middle Age," by [Mr.] Maurice Hewlett, on Mondays, from May 30 [to] June 27; six lectures on "Mediæval Archæol[ogy] of the East," by Professor Stuart Poole, on Thu[rs]days, from May 5 to June 9; and four lectures [on] "Art in India," by Mr. J. Kennedy, on Thursd[ay], June 16, Friday, June 17, Thursday, June 23, [and] Friday, June 24.

HE SKETCH DESIGNS FOR THE GLASGOW ART GALLERIES.

OF the sixty-two designs submitted for this competition, fifty-one only are included in the public exhibition of the drawings, and of these veral are anonymous. It is unfortunate at the preliminary conditions left competi-s the option of withdrawing their designs, it cannot be too strongly insisted that full blicity is essential to a rightly-conducted npetition. It is strange that architects ould fail to see this, and should have with-awn their work when invited by the com-ttee to exhibit.

It must be confessed that of these fifty-one arge proportion is frankly bad; it is some-at disappointing to find nearly one-half luded in this sweeping category. The dness, of course, is of varying degree; ich of it arises from ignorance of planning, an art in the higher sense, not less capable artistic inspiration than an elevation; much it, too, arises palpably from simple inex-rience. This last is almost welcome, for e cannot but feel that an important compe-ion, such as this, may be of genuine educa-nal value. What is not welcome is the gressive badness of experienced incapacity, tawdry "Classic," the unspeakable aronial," or the atrocity of a Leicester-uare "Alhambra."

It is abundantly evident that the com-ttee's unfortunate instructions, or, rather, k of explicit definition, as to the central ll, have completely misled the majority of competitors, who have most naturally erpreted it as a concert-hall. That this, crucial feature of the whole design, should ve been left so vague and ill-defined in the ginal instructions is the most unsatis-tory point about the competition; it must ve occasioned many murmurs and heart-rnings that could, and should, have been oided.

Mr. J. J. Burnet's design is, in point of an, exceedingly able and well studied; it is ewhat unaccountable that it should not e been included in the six selected. The tral hall is here placed lengthwise, east west, as in Mr. Deane's design; the in entrance is from the south, with a sidiary entrance from the north or river ; the administration and school of art grouped to right and left in the south nt, so that, by recessing the main entrance the building proper, an exceedingly in-ious yet obvious arrangement has been ned, in which the three separate entrances ed for to these distinct departments are uped together most conveniently. From vestibule, which is really part of the seum, the circulation is uninterrupted complete round the entire building on h floors, with entrances to the central l on all four sides below. The whole n is dignified and broad, with ch skill shown in its adjustment and binations, even to the basement service the galleries and schools of art. Its f defect is that the central hall, which is kly a hall for music, and rather long for its th, is too much cut off on the first floor, destitute of all circulation commanding while on the ground floor it is not quite py that the main approaches should be at sides. This would detract considerably n its impressiveness on entering. The vations to this design are evidently sketches sufficiently studied, and rather forbidding heir sketchiness. The style is a dignified dern Classic, that would, however, require re study to make the building as attractive it might be. The four thin towers round central hall recall rather obviously Mr. skin's (perhaps cheap) criticism of King's llege Chapel, "a table upside down."

Mr. G. Washington Browne's design may grouped with Mr. Burnet's in that it also bines the entrances to the building proper n those to the school of art and the inistration; these form, however, a arate block thrown forward on the south nt, and connected with the main building by a vestibule. The central hall is here elliptical, with gallery or corridor all round it on both floors; to the right and left are the museum and art galleries in most straightforward simplicity, with an admirable circulation for the public. The staircases are not adequate, but the plan is otherwise an able one. It is, however, doubtful if an oval hall would be of sufficient dignity; it is certainly disappointing here in section. The elevations are less successful, being disjointed and overpowered, in spite of two towers, by the huge roof of the central hall; some of the detail is seriously out of scale.

Mr. W. J. Anderson has also an exceedingly good design, which does much credit to the younger school of Glasgow architects. The art school and administration are similarly grouped with a main entrance, but in this case to the north: the great hall and galleries are thus a complete whole, with the same uninterrupted circulation, and a satisfactory sense of unity. The central hall is square, with great bays on all four sides, two of which are separated off by columns into aisles, and restore the hall to the rectangle. The section of the hall is poor, but the design as a whole is very good, the elevation to the south being very fine. To the north the art school, &c., are most unnecessarily large, which leads to a quite exaggerated vestibule; but the semicircular entrance is very good indeed. The north elevation is scarcely successful, and the side façade is marred by the disjointed connection of the museum proper and north block. These defects, however, could doubtless have been greatly overcome (particularly as the art school has been ultimately abandoned), had the author been accepted for a second study.

In a totally different category comes the remarkable design of Mr. Wm. Leiper. Here the plan, though in detail artistic and with a certain poetry about it, has been somewhat fatally sacrificed. It is open to much criticism for its want of broadly thought-out circulation, its galleries that are *culs-de-sac*, its staircases to the north that are too hidden away; nearly one-third of the site is left vacant "for future extension," which makes the plan lopsided. But the building would have been beautiful, full of poetry and character. The elevations are most studied, broad and dignified, yet each with a special interest of its own. The style adopted is Italian Gothic, more especially Venetian, and with a certain almost Oriental feeling, full of poetry and charm; the entrance to the east, which more directly serves the museum and galleries, is particularly good. In the south front the central feature is a finely-proportioned dome over the entrance-vestibule; on the north is a flatter dome, with behind it two beautiful octagonal towers flanking the great hall, containing staircases and ventilation shafts. The angles of the building are emphasised with turrets, thoroughly in keeping with the style. It is, however, doubtful whether a more important motive might not have been adopted, to which the plan, with its square-angle rooms, would have lent itself most readily. The façades have a tendency to run on *ad infinitum*, with no very evident termination, a criticism which, however, is equally true of the old buildings on whose inspiration Mr. Leiper has worked. The museum courts are very interesting in section, and the great hall would be very fine, with galleries round it on both floors, a semicircular arcade below and traceried triforium above. In plan the hall itself is very skilful, though with an almost ecclesiastical feeling about it; it is arranged for orchestra, but could easily have been modified to suit the committee's revised conditions. One cannot but regret that a design so artistic and full of poetry was not admitted among the six, in spite of plan. It is probably an instance where the personality of the assessor counts for much.

Another design to be noted for its elevations is that of Mr. A. N. Paterson. Here the plan is good, with continuous circulation and very well-placed staircases; it is not big enough in conception, being too much cut up, and the parts too small, but is well-balanced and clear. The central hall is purely a concert-room, but is interesting in section. The elevations are distinctly noteworthy, as being the only attempt, and a very interesting one, to treat the building in monumental Scotch architecture; the whole is dignified and good, if somewhat too cautious in design. The central motive on the northern front is a fine Scotch tower, but all the elevations are carefully studied, restrained, and effective.

Mr. J. A. Campbell's design, though wholly different, is also very able and refined in elevation. The plan is scarcely successful, the outer circulation being incomplete, and the galleries too much cut up into small and monotonously similar rooms; the museum courts enclosed within the outer galleries are practically isolated. The central hall, both in plan and section, is very good, with galleries round it on both floors. The elevations are broad in feeling, and interesting in point of architecture, the style being Modern Classic, somewhat French in character. The semi-dome that covers one end of the great hall is distinctly theatrical and out of harmony,—a distant reminiscence on a small scale of a feature that has been made typically French by the great roof of the Paris Opera. Two towers flanking the great hall are the central motive in the south front; they are scarcely high enough to be as elegant as might be; the sculpture shown is greatly out of scale; the side elevation is very good. Messrs. Honeyman & Keppie have yet a third design, in plan not essentially differing from the two designs included in the six selected. The elevations are classical, broad, and restrained. The central feature is a dome which is not very obvious in plan, but is very good in outline and design. It distinctly recalls the dome recently added by Dr. Rowand Anderson to Edinburgh University.

Messrs. Morris & Hunter have adopted an oval hall (which, as shown in section, is singularly uninteresting), and have spread the museum over the whole ground floor. A maximum of floor space is gained at the cost of all sense of unity or assured design; nor would the lighting be always satisfactory. On the first floor the arrangement of the picture galleries is monotonous in the extreme, and the general circulation is quite interrupted (save for a narrow corridor) by the art school. The elevations on the other hand are very broad and dignified Renaissance, a trifle dull perhaps, and not always true to plan, but with a genuine character of their own. To the park front is a fine terrace, approached by stairs in a semi-circular portico.

Messrs. Chorley & Connon have a disappointing design in uninteresting Classic, with an overpowering pediment on a dozen columns. Behind this gigantic pediment is a (square) dome that cannot be called beautiful, with similar roof to the angle pavilions of the building. The central hall is oval and quite isolated on the first floor, as are also the upper galleries to the museum halls, with separate staircases of their own. The circulation, however, is very straightforward; the school of art is relegated to the basement.

Mr. T. L. Watson's design is strongly Byzantine, both in plan and elevation, and is an interesting piece of work. The central hall is approached from three sides, and forms a genuinely central feature; the galleries around it are grouped in rather haphazard fashion, with little sense of a circulation for the public.

A design more original than reasonable is that of Mr. J. Wallace, who has elected to preserve a passage-way (at present existing) across the centre of the site; the main entrance is accordingly at the east-end, with a lordly vestibule and an enormous development of the school of art and administration. The central hall, a concert-room pure and simple (no longer central), is grouped with the museum to the west of this passage-way; the museum is, in consequence, grievously confined. Otherwise, however, the plan is skilful, and the elevations are exceedingly good, strictly Classical, well-designed, and stately, with a very successful dome over the vestibule.

In reviewing this competition from the broader standpoint of the architectural profession generally, one or two matters certainly call for criticism. Allusion has already been made to the indecisive and misleading instructions issued in regard to the central hall. This is the most serious blunder of the competition, and naturally provokes severe comments. The first and foremost duty of a Committee is to issue precise and definite instructions, in common fairness to competitors. In the present instance nearly all have misinterpreted the principal requirement, and many of the designs have been thrown out in consequence. Either the Committee did or did not know their own minds; if they did, they should have given unmistakable expression to their wishes; if they did not, they should have said so plainly, and left the competitors a free hand.

In the next place, public exhibition of the drawings should be not optional, but a condition of competition. If, for fear of misappropriation of ideas, it is impossible to have the designs on public view after the first competition, which would be the best solution; at any rate, all should be ultimately exhibited together. In no other way can the fairness of the award be vindicated; in no other way can the genuine educational value of an important competition be turned to use.

Further, the assessor's report should be made public, and be detailed. There is, of course, safety in silence, but, for the good of all concerned, a full and thorough report by the assessor should be invariably published. It is not too much to ask a well-paid assessor to take the trouble; to most of the competitors it is their only consolation; while to all it is the best instruction to be gained from the competition. In this case the report of Mr. Waterhouse has been published, but it is very meagre.

For a competition of this importance, it is open to question whether a single assessor, however eminent, should be appointed sole judge. No one questions for a moment the ability, the eminence, or the impartiality of the assessor in this case; a committee of experts might, however, have been more open to some artistic considerations that are very valid. The temptation to design "up to" an assessor's personal predilections (real or presumed) is great. As a matter of fact, the award has been given to a design that embodies, skilfully enough, the latest "London fashion." The commercial capital of the North, grey, grimy, and damp, yet palatial Glasgow, has an architectural character of its own that is well worth studying. It is a pity that the new Art Galleries will hardly be in keeping with this character.

NOTES.

THE conditions upon which the Durham coal-owners are prepared to resume work are, as had been anticipated, based upon an immediate reduction of 10 per cent. on the wages paid at the time work was suspended. Indeed, it would not have been surprising if the loss they have suffered in the interim had caused them to stipulate for a further reduction. The rate arrived at may be revised after July 31, if either masters or men establish the necessity for such revision, but the Association suggests the immediate formation of a Wages Board, to deal with the question, in order to prevent a recurrence of suspension of work during its discussion. Surely the disastrous effects of the present mode of procedure must by this time be apparent to all engaged in the contest, even without the lesson of the engineers' strike. This has dragged along for weeks and months, inflicting incalculable hardships upon businesses and individuals, and is only just coming to a termination. Certainly the two contests are of an entirely different nature, but each appeals for the adoption of conciliatory measures for the prevention of unnecessary conflicts in the future. Mr. Burt told the Miners' National Union Conference on Monday that, although the Durham men were doubtless acting perfectly within their rights in refusing arbitration, they had made a mistake. With characteristic bluntness he explained the difference between arbitration resulting in reductions and strikes having a similar termination, and showed the necessity of abandoning the latter unsatisfactory system. The advice given contrasted very strongly with the reckless defiance of economic laws which has recently been advanced by certain labour leaders. "Turn it how you will," asserted Mr. Burt, "demand must ultimately control the market." It is to be hoped that moderate counsels will prevail, and that work will soon be resumed, as the distress in the district is very keen, and the loss daily becoming more serious.

THE appointment of a Royal Commission to decide upon the question of a teaching university for London is a satisfactory step. No doubt those who strongly favoured the new charter for the proposed university will see in it only a hindrance to the quick establishing of a university. But it is much better that the scheme should be thoroughly considered in all its bearings, and in a somewhat wider manner than is possible in the judicial proceedings before the Privy Council when the grant of the charter was opposed. Those who favour the creation of this new university will probably find that the report of the Commission will, in the end, serve to strengthen the university when it is established. Such a university, if wide and thorough in its teaching, should do not a little to improve the education of the architects of the country.

IT appears to be contended by some patentees and patent agents that Mr. Goschen has not gone far enough in the reduction of the fees on patents. This contention is natural; persons interested in patents would, of course, like to have no fees on patents. No remission of taxation ever occurs without those who gain by it thinking that more might have been done for them. There is a good deal to be said for making patent fees as low as possible, and even for their entire abolition. On the other hand, the fact that the fee on the renewal of patents causes a considerable number of patents to lapse is not one altogether to be regretted in the public interests. The tendency to patent every trifling improvement in every trifling thing is not to the public advantage, and if the patent fees prevent the renewal of a certain number of patents one may be pretty sure that the patents are of no very great value, and that it is as well that they should be thrown open to the public without restriction.

RAILWAY time-tables are getting very bulky, but they are, at the same time, certainly becoming rather less puzzling than they used to be. The small type and other economies of space are gradually giving way to bolder figures and less abbreviated, and, consequently, more lucid directions; the desired information being far more easily obtained now than formerly, both in "Bradshaw" and in some of the companies' guides. It will be noticed that the Midland Guide for the ensuing month exhibits a marked improvement in this respect, no fewer than sixty additional pages being used as a consequence of the complete re-arrangement of the tables and the employment of larger type and bolder figures. Another improvement is the adoption of italic figures for trains that only run on certain specified days of the week. This system has been in use for some time on the London and North-Western and one or two other lines, and might with advantage be adopted by all compilers of railway guides. The attention is thereby at once arrested and drawn to the exceptional circumstances connected with the running of the train, whereas,—as many know to their cost,—these "traps" are often easily overlooked, even by constant travellers, when ordinary type is used. Many would hail with considerable satisfaction the general substitution of larger figures for the microscopic type which tries the eyesight in some of the time-tables.

THE *Times* has recently printed several letters relative to the proposed destruction of St. Dunstan's-in-the-East, upon the union of that parish with All Hallows, Barking, under the Union of Benefices Act.* Some writers, it appears, are ready to sacrifice as a peace-offering to the Commissioners under the Act, one of Wren's two neighbouring churches: St. Mary-at-Hill, and St. Margaret Pattens, Rood-lane, which latter has a lofty octagonal leaden spire, virtually Gothic in form. All seem to be agreed upon saving the steeple, at any rate, of St. Dunstan's. For this there are precedents, as witness Wren's tower of St. Mary Somerset, in Upper Thames-street, conspicuous for its eight pinnacles in shape of angle and side pedestals, carrying, respectively, vases and obelisks capped with balls; and the fifteenth-century tower of All Hallows Staining, by Mark-lane. A model of the latter was included in Mr. Birch's "Old London," prepared for the International Health Exhibition of 1884. All Hallows escaped from the Great Fire; but the body of the fabric fell down five years afterwards, and was then re-built. Since the untoward fate of St. Antholin's spire has been cited in the correspondence, we may direct attention to a passage in a letter from Major H. A. Joseph, C.C., and churchwarden of St. Antholin, printed in the *Times* of April 21. He says:—

> The parishioners with great regret consented to the removal of their church. They, however, worked hard for, and obtained the retention of, the spire, supposing it to be one of Wren's. When it was found to be a modern structure the consent of the parishioners was obtained for its sale. . . .

It will be interesting to learn what proofs were found for upsetting a current belief. We have always understood that the stone spire of St. Antholin, which is shown upon the bas-belief that has been set up in Sise-lane, Watling-street, to mark its site, was designed by Wren. Hatton (1708) says so, adding that it was "built by Mr. Cartwright"; the late George Godwin, in his "Churches of London," vol. i. (1838), with many other writers, speaks of it as having been due to Wren. In Mr. Andrew T. Taylor's illustrated monograph upon "The Towers and Steeples designed by Sir Christopher Wren" (1881), based upon the essay which gained the medal of the Royal Institute of British Architects, we read:—

> St. Antholin (or St. Anthony), Watling-street, was erected in 1682, and was the only stone spire, pure and simple, which Wren carried out. . . . It was pulled down in 1875. One cannot but deeply regret the loss of this spire, unique in its way amongst Wren's works; especially as it could very well have been allowed to remain, and, indeed, did remain for a short time after the church was pulled down. . . .

However, less mercenary considerations did not prevail, and the tower, after standing for, we think, two years only, followed the church. In one of his letters to the *Times* Canon Venables writes (25th instant) that the whole edifice was Wren's work, and that sometime back the spire, having been damaged by lightning, was rebuilt, and its apex unduly blunted. (The apex was somewhat in shape of a Corinthian capital, 154 ft. above the ground). But the re-building, upon the original lines, did not constitute a modern structure, as commonly understood. The steeples of St. Mary-le-Bow and St. Bride's, Fleet-street, have both, if we remember aright, been in part re-built. Of other churches by Wren that have been removed in pursuance of the Act, we recall to mind, St. Matthew, Friday-street; St. Benet, Gracechurch-street: St. Dionis Backchurch; St. Mildred, Poultry; St. Mary Somerset; All Hallows, Bread-street, successor to that

* See "Note" as to this in our issue of November 2[illegible] last.

erein Milton was baptised; and St. :hael, Queenhithe, whose spirelet and ıe are replaced above the new rectory-ıse for St. James, Garlickhithe, in Upper ımes-street.

NEW kind of casing for electric-light . wires has been patented by Mr. Thomas ith. In general form it is like the ordi-y wood casing in common use; the grooves 'eceive the cables are made by rolling iron, ›ther metal, from sheets of such thickness t the wire can be slipped into place and l there by the spring of the metal. The ers are made to spring or slide on or off, can be made to any design. The grooves covers are varnished with some suitable ılating substance, but in practice it will :ainly be found to chip off in places, and casing will not, therefore, add to the in-ıtion resistance of the circuit in the way t ordinary wood-casing does; on the other ıd, if a sufficient number of fuses are ›loyed, the risks from fire will be less than ɜn wood is used. In the event of the ering of the cable failing, the leakage and sequent local heating will take place irely within an incombustible case, and ›re the heating can possibly become gerous the fuses must go.

CCORDING to the Vienna local press, . the Duke of Cumberland has notified :he authorities of the "Austrian Museum" that city that he will soon require them return the collection of antiquities which ıg George V. of Hanover, soon after his ıronement, lent them for exhibition. This ection of some eighty-two objects, known the "Welfenschatz," is considered to be exceedingly valuable one, and includes a ch-admired reliquary not unlike the tykoff one at the South Kensington seum. The collection has a somewhat ›resting history dating as far back as 1173, first abode being in the St. Blasius Church Brunswick. Among the various journeys collection made, we notice one from over, to England in 1803, on account of expected invasion of the French. On g George V. losing his throne, the collec-"disappeared" for some eighteen months, urn up again at Vienna in September, ', after it had been officially made out to he deposed monarch's private property.

DESCRIPTION of the large steel dome of the proposed Government Buildings :he Chicago Exhibition will be found in January volume of the *Transactions* of American Society of Civil Engineers. structure, which is 118 ft. diameter, is of the tallest iron or steel domes in the ıd, its total height being 235 ft. It is orted by sixteen columns, under each of h there are fifteen timber piles. The :mum weight that can come on each of piles is 14 tons, the wind pressure being erable for no less than 90 per cent. of load. In order to secure good founda-, it was specified that test piles should riven to ascertain the probable length would be necessary, and these were ɪn until they would not sink more than under a hammer weighing 2,500 lbs. ɪg 25 ft. In making the calculations the ses were first found in the dome proper, afterwards in the columns supporting it. as assumed to start with that the struc-was a braced arch, hinged at the crown ends,—the ends being at the springing —although, as a matter of fact, the ribs all riveted up at these points. The ical loading was taken at 50 lbs. per re foot on the horizontal projection of dome, and a horizontal wind pressure of bs. per square foot was also allowed for.

the last number of the *Journal* of the Franklin Institute there is a paper by Elmer G. Willyoung, on "Resistance dards: their Manufacture and Adjust-t." The author first states the qualities which should be possessed by the material of which a resistance standard is made. It should have high specific resistance: it should not change its resistance in time, nor be acted upon chemically by the medium in which it is enclosed; it should have as small a temperature coefficient as possible. Dr. Matthiessen, who was chairman of the sub-Committee (of the Committee on Electrical Standards of the British Association) from 1862-65, decided that an alloy of some sort would most closely fulfil the required conditions. He found a considerable time change in many of the alloys examined; zinc always seems to crystallise out from alloys containing it, changing the homogeniety of the wire, and, at the same time, its resistance. Dr. Matthiessen suggested that in other cases the time change is due to a process of gradual annealing. It is worthy of note that when the original platinum-silver coils, finally adopted by the British Association, were examined last year, it was found that even their resistance had increased by 0·06 per cent. Resistance may be permanently changed by temporary change of temperature; in 1889 Bergmann found that if coils of copper, aluminium, and zinc are kept at a temperature of 300 deg. C. for one hour and then cooled, a permanent increase of resistance takes place which is as great as 6·8 per cent. in the case of magnesium, though with German silver there is a decrease of 0·2 per cent. The specific resistance of a substance obviously varies with its density; if a wire is wound on a spool whose diameter is less than eight times that of the wire, the resistance increases from 0·5 to 2 per cent., falling again, however, as the wire slowly anneals. From some results obtained by Drs. Feusner and St. Lindeck in 1891, it appears that an alloy consisting of copper 70 parts and manganese 30 parts has a temperature coefficient of 0·004 per cent., while an alloy of copper 73 parts, manganese 24 parts, and nickel 3 parts has a *negative* coefficient of 0·003 per cent.; it therefore seems that by taking proper proportions of these three metals an alloy may be obtained with the coefficient zero. All things considered, however, Mr. Willyoung regards platinum-silver as the most satisfactory material yet used. In conclusion the author describes a modification of the Carey-Foster method of measuring a resistance.

IN the same number of the *Journal* above referred to there is also a paper by Wm. S. Aldrich "On the Variable Action of Two-coil Solenoids." Experiments were carried out upon "(1) The combination (the differential coil-and-plunger of Silvanus P. Thompson's classification), consisting of two solenoid coils as two parts of one coil, traversed by a pulsating current of variable intensity in each part, and giving rise to a resultant magnetic field from the combination of the two variable-intensity electromagnetic stresses of like character, and constant in direction. (2) The combination operating as two distinct solenoids, producing resultant stresses in the ether medium from the two variable-intensity electro-magnetic stresses of opposite character and constant in direction." The results obtained are shown by means of some carefully-drawn diagrams.

AMONGST the principal sales set down for the coming season is that of Apethorpe, the Northamptonshire seat for 300 years past of the Mildmays, and their descendants the Earls of Westmoreland. Extending over nearly 8,500 acres of Willybrook Hundred, it lies near to King's Cliffe, midway between Oundle and Stamford, and within the district formerly covered by Rockingham Forest. In 15 Hen. III. Ranulph Brito obtained grant of Apelthorpe, or Aypthorpe, Manor, out of the Royal demesne, at a yearly rent of 10*l.*; of the house built in that reign some remains, including a fireplace, are, we believe, extant. In Edward VI.'s time it reverted from Lord Mountjoy to the Crown, and was next exchanged to Sir Walter Mildmay, Knight, Chancellor of the Exchequer to Queen Elizabeth, and founder, in a house of the Black Friars, of Emmanuel College, Cambridge.* His son, Sir Anthony (by his wife, sister to Sir Francis Walsingham), entertained here James I. on his first coming into England, and introduced George Villiers to the King. Stow relates in his "Chronicle":—

> "Ye 27th of Aprill ye King removed from Burleigh towards Hinchingbrooke, to Sir Oliver Cromwell's, and in ye way hee dined at Sir Anthony Mildmays."

To the early sixteenth-century house Anthony added a larger quadrangle, having a screen or cloister along one side, to the building whereof James I. gave some timber. This quadrangle resembles that of Rushton, in the same county, as enlarged by Sir Thomas Tresham, of which we gave a description and illustration on October 27 and November 3, 1888.† Anthony and his wife, Grace Sheringham, rest beneath a sumptuous tomb, carrying figures of Justice, Wisdom, Charity, Devotion, and Hope, in the parish church (1617-21). Their daughter and sole heir, Mary, married Francis, Lord Burghersh and Earl of Westmoreland, eldest son of Lady Mary Fane, who had been restored, 1604, to the ancient dignity of her house as Baroness Le Despencer. Of their eldest son, Mildmay, second Earl of Westmoreland, a portrait, by Van Dyck, was hung at Apethorpe; the two full-length paintings of Philip and Mary are, says Bridges, supposed to have been done by Holbein; yet Holbein died,—of the plague it is believed,—in 1543. His will bears date October 7, and was proved on November 29 of that year. The pictures may be by Sir Antonio More, who painted other portraits of Mary and her consort, and followed the latter into Spain. Apethorpe justly ranks amongst the best examples of its kind in England. A plate of the principal front will be found in J. P. Neale's "Views of Seats," 1820. Our article "Round Stamford," of October 17, 1885, is illustrated with several details of the exterior and interior of the house and the church. Near to Apethorpe are Rockingham Castle, originally built *temp.* the Conqueror, in the chapel of which William Rufus called his great council of bishops and abbots who renounced Anselm; Fotheringhay; and Cotterstock Hall, built by one Norton, the friend of Dryden, who here composed his last work, the "Fables," and passed the final two summers of his life.

IN the course of next month the Hummums Hotel, Covent Garden, together with "Rockley's" Restaurant (in the same building), will be offered for sale by auction, with possession. A company was formed in October, 1888, to acquire the premises then newly rebuilt for Mr. Harry Smith, by Messrs. Peto Brothers, from the designs of Messrs. Wylson & Long, architects. The present hotel stands at the south-western corner of Russell-street, Covent Garden, on the site of Small's (latterly Rigg's) Bagnio, which is cited in Hutton's "New View of London" (1708), and formed the scene of the reputed appearance of Parson Ford's ghost, as related by Dr. Johnson to Boswell. The Bagnio had supplanted a popular place of resort known as Mrs. Dubois's, afterwards the "Three Chairs" tavern. The Hummums,—a corruption of the Arabic, *hammam*, a bath,—and Pero's, in St. James's-street, were amongst the earliest hotels opened in the town. We gave a detailed description of the new premises in our issue of January 7, 1888.

THE Society of Watercolours has a very good exhibition, though we do not agree with some of the critics that it is better than

* *Ob.* 31 May, 1580: his tomb is in the south-aisle of St. Bartholomew's the Great, West Smithfield. He was son of the Thomas Mildmay, lord of the manor of Chelmsford, whose tomb forms an illustration to our review, April 18, 1891, of Mr. Fred. Chancellor's book on "The Ancient Sepulchral Monuments in Essex."

† See also Mr. J. A. Gotch's paper on "A Building Squire of the time of Elizabeth" printed in our columns of April 20, 1889: and our review, July 21, 1883, of his work upon Tresham's Buildings in Northamptonshire.

usual, or even quite so good. Mrs. Allingham's non-appearance is a serious loss; on the other hand there is a drawing by Mr. Tadema, which has not happened often of late. This is "Calling the Worshippers" (179); a young woman in a leopard skin, a piece of carving, marble flooring and wall, a charming silver vase, and the corner of a temple up the steps, make the picture, which is fully worthy of the painter's unique reputation in this class of subject. Mr. Alfred Hunt exhibits a view of "Grasse" (104) which is one of of the most beautiful water-colours he has ever painted; the sense of mere pigment seems etherealised away, and we look into air and sunlight. Mr. H. Moore also has never done a finer and more powerful water-colour of sea than his "Pack Clouds Away" (84). Mr. Albert Goodwin has attempted a very difficult effect in "Salisbury Close" (14), a bright summer night with a mingling of sky light and lamp light; it is a remarkable work, and seems to come out more as it is studied. Mr. Tom Lloyd has a picture of a Thames garden gate where the "lord of the manor" (a little boy) comes out to admire the swans; the two figures make a harmony in blue and saffron: the swans are admirably painted; his "Reapers" (120), a kind of semi-decorative horizontal composition, is a finer work in feeling and colour; one of his best. Among the old school of landscapes may be mentioned Mr. A. D. Fripp's "Isle of Portland" (111), and Mr. G. A. Fripp's "Cleve Mill" (106); and "Penrhyn Castle" (85); Mr. Cuthbert Rigby's "Under Wetherlam" (16), Mr. Philip's "Crags of Glenogle" (140); Mr. Rigby has also a very fine snow picture (155), and Mr. Eyre Walker, in "When sweet summer airs do blow" (88), has succeeded in getting really the light of summer: nowadays we too often see pictures called "summer" with no sunlight in them at all. Other landscapes by the same artist are among the best of the exhibition. Mr. R. W. Allan has been painting Eastern scenes; his "Golden Temple, Amritsar" (114) is admirable as a representation of architecture under a tropical sun; "On the Beach at Madras" (267) is another Indian study; there are also some excellent drawings of Scotch scenery by him. Mr. Rooke and Mr. S. J. Hodson contribute some architectural subjects, and Mr. H. Marshall has painted the Mansion House and its surrounding in a mist. Among other architectural subjects Mr. R. Little makes a capital little picture out of the "Greek Church, Bayswater" (38), in snow, Mr. Herbert Marshall has also very successfully treated "The Embankment" (22) on a winter evening. Mr. Thorne Waite's finest work is "Changing Pasture, Aldborough" (61). We regret to see the increase of large drawings of an essentially vulgar type in the exhibition, such as 156 and 102 and others. These are the kind of things to engrave in the *Graphic*, no doubt, but not for an exhibition which has such traditions as the Society of Water-colours has, and ought to cling to.

THE NEW GALLERY EXHIBITION.

THE exhibition of this year is not up to the standard of most of its predecessors. Mr. Burne-Jones, whose works have been usually the great attraction of the New Gallery, does not exhibit, and others among the prominent exhibitors are hardly at their best.

The finest work in the collection is Mr. Adrian Stokes's landscape, "Roman Campagna; Early Spring" (143), showing the undulating sward of the Campagna, with a forsaken quarty and a clump of small trees on the right, the back of a Roman aqueduct just showing in the distance over the horizon made by the uneven ground, and a sky full of light and air above it, the blue just broken by a thin fleecy cloud. A landscape more real in all its details is not often seen; it looks as if one could walk into it, and yet this is no mere realism, the artistic balance of the whole is perfectly kept. It is a real pleasure to see such a landscape as this. Among the more prominent figure pictures a high place must be given to one hanging near this, Mr. Collier's "Gretchen" (140). Goethe's heroine is shown in her night dress, looking at the casket, at the moment of her reflection that everything with men turns on gold, and "Ach, wir Armen!" The figure is backed by a delightful old German cabinet, painted with great care. Gretchen is, as Goethe imagined her, a lower-class girl, with handsome but somewhat coarse features and a profusion of reddish hair; the face is a little wanting in definite expression, but the whole conception is at all events not commonplace. The figure is lighted by artificial light, the effect of which is well conveyed.

Mr. Watts's "Sic Transit" (77), which holds the place of honour in the West Gallery, is one of those pictures of his which look like an attempt to say in painting what is better said in poetry. As a painting it is not interesting. A shrouded dead figure is laid out on a bier, while on the floor are strewn various emblems of the occupations of life,—armour, a lute, and other objects, the metal painted in a subdued rich tone, as of things that have the *patine* of age on them; but of the whole one feels that there is more moral than pictorial power about it. The very reverse is the case with Mr. Tadema's "A Silent Greeting" (15), in which the thought is of the slightest, but the pictorial effect perfect. A Roman in soldier's dress is going out at a door facing the spectator, just laying his hand in farewell on the hand of a woman seated inside the door; beyond is seen the blue sky and brightly-lighted wall; a building, yellow in the sunshine, opposite. The great charm of the painting is its carefully-wrought and perfect harmony of colour, in which sense it affects one like a perfectly-balanced musical composition, without a discordant note in it, and yet there is no appearance of contrived effect about it. Near this is Mr. Poynter's "When the World was Young" (10) a small study for the picture in the Royal Academy; and the same artist's "White Roses" (13), a half length of a woman backed by foliage which, as well as her face, seems hard and artificial in texture and colour; in this respect we much prefer the artist's figure seated in a Greek window, "Chloe" (57), with a tortoise lyre in her hand; there is a flush of life in the face which is certainly wanting in the lady of the white roses.

Sir J. Millais' figure entitled "Sweet Emma Moreland" (69), if we are to accept it as a representation of Tennyson's fancy, seems a curious instance of the failure resulting from giving an ideal name to a figure too closely copied from a model which does not answer to the ideal. The face is a fine one, richly painted; the hands are large, coarse, and bony, and as much out of keeping with the character of the face as with the title of the picture. The only other figure picture in the West Gallery (except portraits) which is worth a thought is Mr. A. Moore's "A Rèvery" (104—so spelt in the catalogue), a seated figure of a woman facing the spectator, backed by a rather too busy mural decoration which interferes a little with the breadth of the painting; the figure and the composition have the artist's usual grace and completeness, though is is hardly one of his best works.

Mr. Kennedy's "Jonah" (142) in the north gallery is incomprehensible; it seems to be a struggle going on in a Viking ship, but what the meaning or point of it is we cannot pretend to understand. Mr. Brighton's "Black-eyed Susan" (132) is a pretty figure in the foreground of a coast landscape, but much too refined for the idea suggested by the title. Mr. R. W. Macbeth has made a brilliant study of flowers in "An Alsatian Flower Stall" (166), and the picture has a marked character of its own. In "Bedtime" (139), an interior with a woman and child looking out at the moonlight, Mr. Philip Burne-Jones has realised a very true effect of a moonlit interior. The north gallery shows two "conscientious nudes" (as the French students say), Mr. Fowler's "Spirit of the Morning" (180), a kind of Venus Anadyomene in which the nudity is more evident than the poetry, and Mrs. Swynnerton's "Mater Triumphalis" (187), a portentously stout and thick figure with a crown at her feet, well painted but by no means attractive, and not very clear in its apparently ideal meaning.

In portraits the exhibition is stronger. In the west gallery Mr. Richmond's portrait of "The Venerable Archdeacon Wilson" (48) is more successful than his "Mrs. Marsden Smedley" (55), a lady in a white dress with a green-lined cloak; a graceful figure, but hard and mechanical in execution. Mr. Shannon's "Lady Skelmersdale" (92), seated with a violin in her hand, in a white dress, shows a noble and queenly head and a beautifully-drawn right hand and arm; but what a waist! It is almost like a fashion-plate, and appears exaggerated from what is possible in life; an artist should rather have erred from nature (if this be nature) the other way, and refused to paint a woman like a wasp in figure. His portrait of "Mrs. Wordsworth, principal of Lady Margaret Hall Oxford" (99) is one of the finest portraits in the exhibition, both in character and colour. Mr. Collier's "Mrs. W. H. Foster" (137), in a satin dress with a richly-coloured screen behind her, is a powerful piece of work. Mr. Shannon's "Mrs. Chapman" (158) is perhaps his best portrait, with a very finely-painted head. Mr. Herkomer has two "presentation portraits," "Sir Gabriel Stokes" (181) and "The Rev. T. E. B. Mayor" (185), belonging to that class of realistic portraits in which the dark costume leaves little chance for pictorial effect, and everything is concentrated on the expression of the head, which is very powerfully given in both cases. The exhibition includes two portrait heads of M. Paderewski, one by Mr. Tadema and the other by the Princess Louise; the former, representing the great pianist facing the spectator and apparently in in the act of playing (though the hands are not visible), is a splendid piece of painting, but does not seem to convey the concentration of expression of the face of a great executant intent upon his work. Mr. Watts has also a fine portrait of Mr. Walter Crane.

The exhibition contains a good many small landscapes of interest, and two or three large and important works, besides the fine one by Mr. Stokes to which we have already referred. Landscape painting at the New Gallery generally tends rather to the study of special and unusual effects rather than to the representation of nature under ordinary atmospheric circumstances. Mr. P. Burne-Jones has another good moonlight effect in "The Harvest Moon" (26). Mr. Parton's "In the Autumn Sunshine" (30) does not seem necessarily to suggest autumn, the trees at least rather suggest spring than autumn. Mr. Christie's "The Wreck" (59) is a small painting with a definite style (rather impressionist in its leanings) and fine colour. In "A Riverside Pastoral" (71) Mr. Calvert seems to have been "doing Corot" secondhand—not unsuccessfully. Mr. Frank Walton's "In Opulent June" (80) is one of the old school of straightforward landscapes, prosaic perhaps the modern school would call it; but it realises its title in the sunlit effect and the rich heavy masses of foliage. Mr. David Murray has a small but fine and poetic landscape "Gathering Mists" (91), with one dark tree like a ship at anchor on the plain, and a beautifully faintly-lighted aërial western sky. In the north room we have a contrast between the old and new in Mr. Wimperis's "Way Across the Marsh" (127) and Mr. McLachlan's "Evening" (128), hung next to each other, both good in their way. Mr. North's winter scene, with no title but a verse (136), is a remarkable work, somewhat different from his usual range of effect; a bright but misty landscape with the first hint of coming spring in it. Mr. Padgett's "Moonrise over the Marshes" (148) has a character of its own. Mr. David Murray sends a large and powerful work "A Hampshire Haying, 1891" (175), representing only too well the characteristics of that terrible autumn of last year; a thunder-cloud hangs over the right of the scene, on the left a hay cart is being dragged home over flooded meadows, the hay blown back by the wind which roars also through the trees on the right; the scene is dashed here and there by that strong sunlight which often produces such startling effect when half the sky is overcast with a thunder-cloud: it is a powerful rendering of a wild and striking moment of storm. Mr. H. W. B. Davis has a large twilight landscape, "Approaching Night" near Calais, and Miss Anna Alma-Tadema contributes a very charming study of sky—fleecy white clouds hovering amid the blue. In the South Gallery is a very fine study of sea by Mr. Tristram Ellis, "In Mediterranean Waters" (222), with a long blue swell rolling through the picture; Mr. Henry Moore contributes a very windy sea-piece in his best style; and Mr. Albert Goodwin exhibits one of his ideal scenes, "The Rich Strand" in the "Faërie Queene," where dwelt Marinell, and where all things ric nd rare were cast up by the sea. As a Spenerian landscape it is not to the purpose to say hat it is not like any scene in this world, for he Spenserian landscape is of the world of omance; but it is a fine and imaginative work, he more to be remarked on because painters o seldom attempt to illustrate Spenser, who is ch in subjects for painting nevertheless.

The sculpture this year is not very important, he most noticeable thing is Mr. Simonds's ountain, with a mermaid on the top playing n a pipe, and sea lions grouped symmetrically eneath looking up at her. This is a variation om the usual form of aquatic subject for a ountain; the mermaid indeed is a well-worn iece of furniture in fountain design, but this not a conventional mermaid, but a figure eated and modelled in a very spirited manner, pecially in the bold curves of her double fishils (they make mermaids' extremities double ow,—see Mr. Jacomb-Hood's picture in the outh Gallery). Mr. Mullins's "Comus and the ady" is a very well-composed group, though e lady is rather too naïve for Milton's highed and high-minded creation. Mr. Dressler's lt bronze figure of a "Girl tying up her ndal" repeats very pleasantly an old Classic pe of sculptural design.

THE ART-UNION OF LONDON:

NNUAL MEETING AND PRIZE-DISTRIBUTION.

THE fifty-sixth annual meeting and prizestribution of the Art-Union of London was ld in the Adelphi Theatre on Tuesday afteron last. In the absence of the President (the arl of Derby), the chair was taken by Mr. John ackrell, Chairman of the Finance Committee.

The annual report of the Council, read by e Secretary, Mr. R. W. Harrison, contained e following passages:—

"At the close of the fifty-sixth year of the ciety, the Council have pleasure in reporting a ntinuance of the support which the society has ceived in various parts of the world.

The Council, with the object of giving earlier cilities to prize-winners for the selection of ctures in the May exhibitions, have convened the nual meeting for the day on which it used to be ld in former years, and earlier than in the past w years. Although this arrangement was duly nounced to all the society's representatives, many them have apparently not observed the date, as, the close of the list a number of returns had ll not come to hand, representing a considerable duction from the expected total of subscripns. . . . .

In 1890 the Council foresaw that they could not g hope to have the services of their valued cretary, Mr. Watson, and in view of the importce of having a successor to him experienced in e peculiar duties of the office, they engaged as assistant-secretary Mr. R. W. F. Harrison, at t time assistant-secretary to the City Guilds chnical Institute. In the course of last summer, . Watson, who had served the society faithfully forty-six years, desired to retire and enjoy well-earned repose to which his long labours the society's service entitled him, and Council were glad to have at hand so cellent and competent a successor as Mr. rrison has proved himself to be. They ret to have to report that in December last, hin three months of his relinquishing his active ties, Mr. Watson died, at the advanced age of enty-nine. Mr. Watson's retirement necesated some reorganisation of the office, which, ning at a time when all the operations for the suing year had to be prepared, naturally occaned some difficulty in carrying on the complex l widely-ramified work of the society; and ing regard to these circumstances, the Council gratulate the members upon the issue of the r's operations.

The change of secretary offered a favourable ortunity for a reorganisation of the system of ounts, and the Council thought it best in the rests of the society to appoint a firm of prosional accountants as auditors of the society's ounts. They accordingly appointed the firm of ssrs. Prideaux, Booker, Frere, & Co. to act in s capacity, and the books are now kept under ir supervision. The accounts for the past year l be audited and printed and circulated among members, with the full report of the Coun- . . . .

he amount available for prizes, after providing for annual work given to every subscriber and the other enses of the year, enables the Council to award the owing prizes:—

work of art of the value of 100*l*.
works " " " 45*l*.
" " " " 35*l*.
" " " " 20*l*.
" " " " 15*l*.
} to be selected by the prize-winners.

arge bronzes, the 'Warrior,' after H. Thornycroft.
10 large Doulton ware jugs, the copyright of the society.
10 " " beaded vases " "
10 " " Burslem vases " "
10 " " Burslem 'Rose' vases.
10 repoussé bronze 'Bellerophon' vases.
20 portfolios of 10 engravings, to be selected by the prize-winners.

Twenty-five artists' proofs of a fine mezzotint, engraved by Mr. F. McCulloch after the diploma picture of Sir John Millais, Bart., R.A., and entitled by him a 'Souvenir of Velasquez.' The proofs are signed by Sir John Millais and by the engraver, and the Council have every belief that this fine work will be found a most valuable acquisition by those who are fortunate enough to obtain it;

Making, with the prizes given to unsuccessful members, 292 prizes.

The Council have suffered several losses since the last annual meeting. Early last summer they had to deplore the death of Mr. Edwin Henry Lawrence, who had been their colleague for many years, and later in the year they lost an old and valued member of their body in Mr. George Wallis, for nearly thirty years Keeper of the South Kensington Museum. Mr. Wallis was born at Wolverhampton in 1811, and was one of the earliest Art Masters of the old Schools of Design. He was a Deputy Commissioner of the Exhibitions of 1851 and 1862, and was appointed Keeper of the Art Collections at South Kensington in 1863. His life was spent in the endeavour to improve and promote the art industries of the country.

The pressing claims of other business have deprived them of the assistance of Sir Philip Cunliffe Owen and Mr. T. E. Collcutt, and of the valuable services of one of the Honorary Secretaries, Mr. H. J. Francis, who, however, continues to give them the benefit of his co-operation as a member of Council. They consider themselves very fortunate in having obtained the consent of Mr. T. Buxton Morrish to undertake the duties of the Honorary Secretaryship, rendered vacant by the retirement of Mr. Francis, and in retaining the very valuable services of Mr. John Sparkes as Honorary Secretary.

To fill vacancies on the Council, Mr. J. T. Bennett Poë and Mr. L. B. Sebastian have been elected . . . .

The Royal Naval Exhibition, held last year, afforded an opportunity, of which the Council were happy to avail themselves, for the exhibition of the original oil-painting by Maclise of 'The Death of Nelson,' from which the popular plate, issued to the members of the Society in 1876, was engraved. The picture attracted much attention in the exhibition, and at the request of the Committee of the Naval Exhibition now being held at Liverpool, it has been lent by the Council for the gallery of that exhibition.

For the coming year the Council have been fortunate enough to secure the copyright of this year's Academy picture by Mr. W. Robert Macbeth, A.R.A., who is now engaged upon an etching of the work on the commission of the Council. The picture represents the ancient and picturesque town of King's Lynn, seen from across the river, towards which a number of fisher-folk in the foreground are hurrying to catch the last ferry-boat, which waits on the tide below. . . . .

The advantages offered by the society can only be brought adequately before the public by zeal and energy on the part of the Council's representatives in various parts of the world; and the special thanks of the members are due to several representatives, many of them old friends to the society, who have succeeded in recruiting an increased number of subscribers. Mr. F. G. Bonsor, of Balham, has surpassed himself with a return of 139 subscribers. The Council hope that his example may serve to stimulate others to still greater efforts in the future.

Various circumstances, above referred to, somewhat hampered the Council in the preparations for the year's work, and occasioned delays which cannot but have hindered the efforts of their representatives in distant parts of the world. Nevertheless, several of the returns received from their Colonial representatives show an advance upon the lists of last year. . . . .

No undertaking responds more quickly to the fluctuations of the general prosperity than one like that of the Art-Union of London, and the commercial depression which has been so marked a feature of the past year, especially in London, has not been without its effect upon the society's operations. In spite of these drawbacks, several of the society's friends have succeeded in securing an increase in their number of subscribers."

The Chairman, in moving the adoption of the report, said he thought that on the whole it was very satisfactory, especially in view of the circumstance of the loss of Mr. Watson's services, whose retirement and death they deeply regretted. He thought they were exceedingly fortunate in his successor, Mr. Harrison.

Mr. J. W. Butterworth, F.S.A., seconded the motion, which was unanimously agreed to.

On the motion of Mr. Butterworth, seconded by Mr. T. O. Donaldson, a hearty vote of thanks was accorded to the honorary secretaries, Mr. John Sparkes and Mr. T. Buxton Morrish, who were both, from unavoidable causes, absent from the meeting.

On the motion of the Chairman, a vote of thanks was given to Messrs. A. & S. Gatti for their kindness in granting the use of the theatre for the meeting.

The drawing for the prizes was then proceeded with, the principal prize falling to Mrs. M. Sutherland, of Beckenham.

LIVERPOOL ENGINEERING SOCIETY.

THE thirteenth ordinary meeting of the present session was held at the Royal Institution on Wednesday, April 20, Mr. John T. Wood, President, in the chair.

After the usual routine business, including the nomination of the Council and Officers for the ensuing session, a paper was read by Mr. H. Percy Boulnois, M.Inst.C.E., entitled "Refuse Destructors."

After describing house refuse, and the different methods of collection, the lecturer recapitulated the various methods at present adopted for the ultimate disposal, and gave an interesting description of the manner in which the greater portion of the refuse of Liverpool is barged away to sea, and sunk in deep water. The lecturer then proceeded to describe in detail, and with diagrams, the various destructors which are now being erected in different parts of the country, and gave a fully detailed description of the twelve-cell destructor, on the "Fryer" principle, which he had recently erected for the Corporation of Liverpool, and a new method of charging which had been adapted thereto. In conclusion, the lecturer stated his opinion that the burning of town refuse was at present the best and most sanitary method known for dealing with such material, and, although the cost may be slightly in excess of other methods of disposal, the safety of such an operation, from a sanitary point of view, more than counterbalances any small increase in the amount of cost for its disposal.

The discussion upon the paper was adjourned until the next meeting.

BRITISH ARCHÆOLOGICAL ASSOCIATION.

AT the meeting of this Association on the 20th inst., Mr. J. W. Grover, F.S.A., in the chair, Mr. F. Williams reported the discovery of further portions of a Roman hypocaust at Chester, and exhibited photographs of the remains, and also of a curious open timber roof of fifteenth-century work, which exists as part of the old buildings adjoining the site, which, it is feared, will have to be shortly removed. Mr. Earle Way exhibited a fine sixteenth-century bronze medallion of Faustina the Elder. Italian work, which was described by Mr. Allan Wyon, F.S.A. It is cast and not struck, the size being too large to admit of the latter process. Mr. de Gray Birch, F.S.A., exhibited illustrations of the sculpture on the font of Winchester Cathedral. Mr. C. J. Williams described a curious example of pottery made at Southwark. Mr. Marriage exhibited a perfect bowl-shaped vessel of light-coloured pottery, of Roman date, found probably at Rhodes. A paper was then read on "The Hog's Head: the Nuptial Cup of Sussex," by Mr. H. Syer Cuming, F.S.A., Scot. It was descriptive of an old custom, once common in the county,—and apparently confined to it,—of drinking the health of the bride, at wedding festivals, from a vessel made in the form of the head of a hog. Various examples of these vessels were described, some being of silver, but mostly of pottery; but one, formerly kept at Elstead, is of pewter. Several of the speakers, in the discussion which followed, spoke of other forms of these cups, and Mr. Way described one in the form of a pig, with a movable head, which formed the cup. The custom is now obsolete. The paper was read, in the author's absence from illness, by Mr. Loftus Brock, F.S.A. A second paper on "A Recent Discovery in Rome in connexion with Mythology in England," by Miss Russell, was then read. Some few months since, a Roman mosaic pavement was discovered on the Cælian Hill, Rome, on which the Evil Eye was represented, attacked by various forces. Miss Russell pointed out the general resemblance of the design to various cup and ring markings in England, which are traversed by a parallel line like a javelin, and suggested that these markings were charms against the Evil Eye.

Illustrations.

NEW CLOISTERS AND PROPOSED NEW CHAPEL FOR RADLEY COLLEGE.

RADLEY COLLEGE, near Abingdon, has lately become the possessor of the old mansion and park of the Bowyers, which it had before occupied as a tenant. When the tenure of the College was uncertain, it housed itself in buildings of a temporary character, with the exception of the fine old house which was occupied by the Warden and some of the Masters, and by the dining-hall. Having now acquired the ownership of the property, the College has begun to replace its temporary buildings by others of a more substantial kind, for which Mr. T. G. Jackson has been employed as architect. An infirmary has been built of a very complete type, and on a somewhat novel plan, and a long range of cloisters, with studies and dormitories above, connects the various rows of buildings with themselves and with the Chapel. A new chapel, to seat 300, is now about to be erected to meet the growing requirements of the school, which has increased, and is still increasing, in numbers under the present Warden.

BEDROOM FITTINGS AT 29, LENNOX-GARDENS.*

THIS illustration shows how such useful and unromantic accessories to a bedroom as a boot-cupboard, a medicine-chest, wardrobes, are mixed up with Italian *casone* fronts and delightful nick-nacks of all sorts in the bedroom.

It will be remembered that a casone is a chest about 4 ft. long, 2 ft. high and wide, made to contain the valuables, which in Italy are presented to a bride by her parents. Many exquisitely-carved old specimens exist in South Kensington Museum.

The front and ends shown in the drawing over the chimneypiece, and which now give interest to the cupboards containing the more practical treasures of an English lady's room, were rescued from Messrs. Wright Bros., in Wardour-street, and bear many marks of the vicissitudes of their lengthened career.

All the other fittings are in hard wood painted white; they were made by Messrs. Jackson, of Rathbone-place, and arranged by Mr. Arthur Cawston, the architect.

INTERIOR OF DRAWING-ROOM, "BROOKLANDS," WEYBRIDGE.

THE illustration shows the interior of a drawing-room, forming part of some extensive alterations and additions carried out at the house in 1889-1890. The two rooms were thrown into one by means of the arcade. The lady who appears to be stepping out of the wall, is really a lift-size portrait on the wall. A view of the entrance front of the house as altered, and of a design for the billiard room, were in last year's Academy. The architect was Mr. Reginald Blomfield; Mr. Thomas Hunt, of Hoddesdon, was the contractor for the work.

HOUSES OF PARLIAMENT, MELBOURNE.

THE Houses of Parliament, Melbourne, which are not yet finished, though for some years past work has been almost continuously carried on there, are situated on a hill at the east end of the city, in Spring-street. The Parliament Houses, when completed, will occupy an approximately square space, the actual dimensions being 320 ft. by 312 ft., the site is a portion of the Parliament Gardens, a small reserve, on the laying out of which considerable skill has been expended.

The principal entrance is opposite the end of Bourke-street, up a great flight of steps, 140 ft. wide. These lead to a decastyle portico, 140 ft. long, consisting of nine bays; from each end of the portico doorways lead to the offices, committee-rooms, &c.; and from the centre of the portico three doorways open into the entrance vestibule, 44 ft. square, the lower portion only of which has yet been completed; over this vestibule a double stone dome, 46 ft. in external diameter, will eventually be erected, surmounted by a stone lantern, the topmost portion of which will be 218 ft. above the ground. Immediately behind the entrance vestibule is the Queen's Hall, 85 ft. long by 45 ft. wide, and 54 ft. high; on either side of the Queen's Hall lie the two Chambers, and at its east end is the Library; it serves, therefore, as a ready means of communication between these, the three most important centres. Across the east end of the Queen's Hall runs an elegant loggia, supporting a small gallery. This loggia forms portion of the direct line of communication between the Chambers, and the gallery over serves to connect the reporters' galleries belonging to them.

The Legislative Council-chamber is on the south side of the Queen's Hall. The portion of the floor reserved for the use of members only measures 44 ft. by 30 ft.; and the extreme size of the chamber, including the galleries at the sides and ends, is 72 ft. by 42 ft.; the height of this chamber is 38 ft.

The Legislative Assembly Chamber is on the north side of the Queen's Hall. The portion of the floor reserved for the use of members only measures 46 ft. by 40 ft.; and the extreme size of the chamber, including the galleries at the ends, is 72 ft. by 40 ft.

From the east end of the Queen's Hall access is gained through a small lobby to the central library, on either side of which, and communicating with it, are the two side libraries; these three libraries occupy the centre of the east frontage of the site, and additional libraries on either side will eventually be erected. The central library is 41 ft. square; the central portion of it is carried up on columns to a height of 46 ft., and carries a highly-ornamental dome; the remaining portions of the central library form a gallery at the first-floor level round the central portion. The two side libraries are each 49 ft. by 23 ft., and are 18 ft. high.

The refreshment and billiard rooms are over the side libraries, and are each 49 ft. by 23 ft., and are 24 ft. high.

The north and south frontages will be occupied by committee-rooms, offices, &c. These have not yet been erected, temporary accommodation in the meantime having been provided in a wooden building.

The external architecture consists throughout of a single Roman Doric order, standing on a bluestone rusticated basement, and is surmounted by an attic. This order embraces both the floors (principal and first) of which the building consists, each inter-columniation including a doorway or window-opening on each floor.

The internal architecture of the entrance vestibule consists, so far as it has been at present executed, of a single composite order, with coupled attached columns, standing on high pedestals.

The internal architecture of the Queen's Hall is in two orders,—the lower being Ionic, and the upper Composite. Above the upper order the ceiling is deeply coved, and is pierced so as to form a clearstory; this lights the hall. The centre portion of the ceiling is elaborately coffered, highly enriched, and profusely ornamented.

The internal architecture of the Legislative Council Chamber belongs to the Corinthian order; the ceiling over the centre portion is vaulted and coffered, and the ceilings over the end portions are vaulted; domed ceiling-lights cover the side galleries

The internal architecture of the Legislative Assembly Chamber is executed in the Ionic order, and this chamber is covered by a coffered, coved, and enriched ceiling.

The architecture of the interior of the central library is in two orders, the lower being Doric and the upper Ionic; and the central portion is surmounted by pendentives carrying a highly ornamental coffered dome, pierced with openings to light the space below.

The west front, which is the portion last completed, has been executed in beautiful white and very hard sandstone from Mount Difficult in the Grampian Ranges, near Stawell, and it is intended eventually to complete the building in this material.

As we observe that the so-called architectural journals of Australia are very indignant with us for some occasional depreciatory comments on the existing state of Australian architecture, we give this illustration of one of the most important Government buildings recently erected in an Australian city, and our readers can form their own opinion on it.

We may observe that a design for the Melbourne Houses of Parliament, by Messrs. Knight & Kerr, was published in the *Builder* for September 8, 1860, but appears to have been never carried out. The present building appears to be based on the same design, somewhat altered and modified. The architect of the building in its present form is Mr. P. Kerr.

* "Sussex-gardens" on the plate was a mistake in reading the MS. title, not discovered till too late for altering the plate title.

Books.

Handbook of Greek Archæology, Vases, Bronzes, Gems, Sculpture, Terra-cottas, Mural Paintings, Architecture, &c. By A. S. MURRAY, LL.D., F.S.A., Keeper of Greek and Roman Antiquities in the British Museum. With numerous Illustrations. London: Murray, Albemarle-street. 1892.

THE market has been of late flooded with manuals of Greek Archæology, but so far they have all been avowedly of second-hand character,—just so many *pis-allers* translated from the French or German, and somewhat perfunctorily posted up to date. It is a relief to turn from such books,—useful, even indispensable, as they have hitherto been,—to Mr. Murray's work, which is stamped with originality, or, to define more closely, idiosyncrasy. The book had its origin, the author tells us in his preface, in the Rhind Lectures given in Edinburgh in 1887. Books based on lectures are apt to be tiresome, but we may say at the outset that the author has entirely succeeded in shedding that mixture of the "preacher and the play-actor" which makes the lecturing personality intolerably irritating in print.

Archæology has suffered from its own inherent complexity. It is required of the archæologist that he be two men, the art critic to appraise, and the man of science to interpret. Mr. Murray holds, and perhaps rightly, that "the artistic element must be the first consideration in Greek archæology," but he is too wise not to allow that interpretative study must go along with technical appreciation. In characterising the book as a whole, what we feel is that its strong side is a minute and most diligent technical criticism, its weak side constructive and scientific interpretation; very few minds combine the two faculties. For this reason, perhaps, we think it will be read with more both of pleasure and profit by the advanced than by the elementary student; indeed, we are sure there are few professed archæologists who will not gain much from every chapter, and will not thank the writer for the persistently personal angle which compels the reader in salutary fashion to shift his own point of view. At the same time the book suffers, as Mr. Murray's are apt to do, from a certain want of subordination of detail, very puzzling to the beginner who lacks landmarks. It is, however, easy enough to get a *coup d'œil* from the manual of some fallaciously clear Frenchman, and then the full corrective value of Mr. Murray's deliberative proceedings will be duly felt. One example may suffice: "The rule of the black figure vases is to represent the eyes of men as circular, those of women as an almond shape," so the handbook universally, "but this distinction was not much observed in the early art of Asia Minor, as we see in the pottery of Naucratis, Daphnæ and Camirus, where Asiatic influence was felt; there the almond eye is conspicuous in men as in women," ... Mr. Murray, with a precise differentiation that ... valuable.

The whole section on vases seems to ... the most valuable in the book, specially the portion on the primitive period,—doubly valuable to the English student, because he ... here, for the first time, in popular and accessible form, the results of English excavation at Daphnæ and Naucratis, and he can examine the originals themselves in the British Museum. Of course, it is easy to wish details otherwise; ... hold ourselves, *e.g.*, that unquestionably painted vases were in actual use, but we do not think the story cited on p. 72 as evidence, is of the smallest value. Asklepios is recorded in an inscription to have mended a broken vase for ... boy. His pious master presented the vase to the Temple. "We are entitled to conclude," says Mr. Murray, "from the value attached to the vase that it had been painted with a design, probably one of great beauty." Not at all, the point was the glory of the god, not the grandeur of the vase. Fortunately, there are few "conclusions" of th... precarious character. Again, when illustrations are so numerous, it is hard that we are given no instance of a real masterpiece of the ear... fine red period,—*e.g.*, the remarkable Mæna...

THE I

1842

T. G. Jackson. Archt. fect. Mar. 20 1892

DRAWING-ROOM: "BROOKLANDS," WEYBRIDGE.—Mr. Reginald T. Blomfield, Architect.

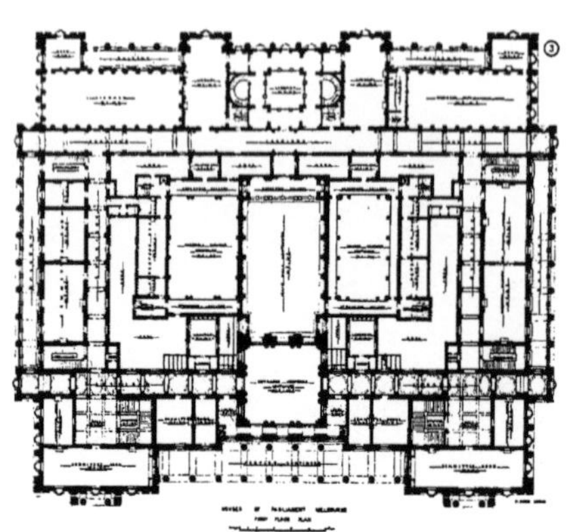

HOUSES OF PARLIAMENT, MELBOURNE.

MR. P. KERR, F.R.I B.A., ARCHITECT.

HOUSES OF PARLIAMENT, MELBOURNE.

MR. P KERR, F.R.I B.A., ARCHITECT.

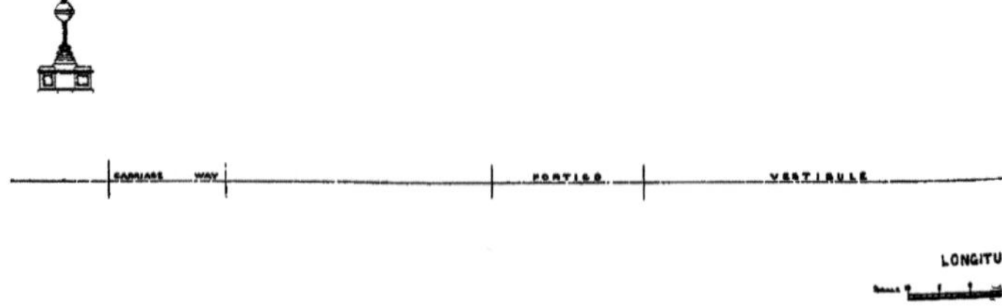

1892.

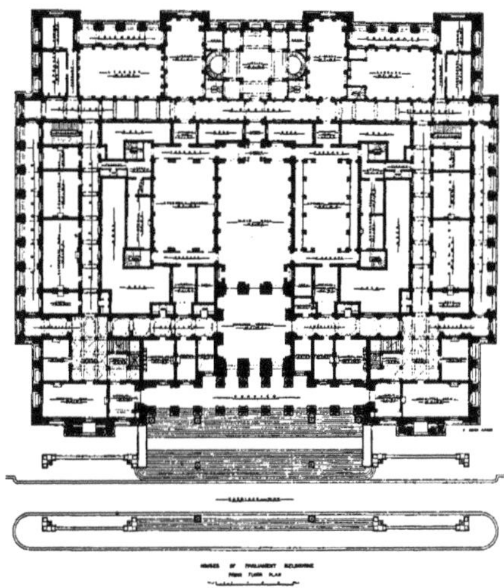

MAIN HALL | LOBBY AND CORRIDOR | LIBRARY

TION

PHOTO-LITHO SPRAGUE & CO 4 & 5, EAST HARDING STREET, FETTER LANE, E.C.

ance of Hieron, or some sample of Euphronios t his best. An artist glancing over the book rould form from the illustrations a needlessly ow estimate of the merits, as to fine design, of ireek vase-painting. While speaking of illustrations we may note that the reproductions re, as a rule, excellent; those of vases in red nd black are a new and most desirable feature n a handbook. Some admirable plates come rom the author's large book on sculpture; only few,—*e.g.*, slab from the Harpy tomb (fig. 69), re cruelly harsh.

We said at the outset that we felt interpretaion to be the weak side of the book, and a cerain fatality seems to compel Mr. Murray here nd there to waste most valuable space on ssues hopelessly doubtful. Who knows and vho cares whether the wretched design from a ella (p. 142) represents an effete type of the 'udgment of Paris or not? The writer himself as not much ground for confidence in the nterpretation he is going to propose, and yet it ccupies four and a half pages (!), just because he writer loves it as a troublesome child. Again, Mr. Murray has something like a mania or the conjectural restoration of lost works of rt; a harmless pastime it may be for the dvanced archæologist if out of work, but vaste of time for the student. Why encourage im in twisting such sand-ropes by tabular views f the subjects of the paintings in the 'Lesche." There was no space, we are told, or that most dateab'e, most *real* branch of rchæology, numismatics, and yet there are lost ages that we sigh over. The chapter on rchitecture is slight, but, perhaps, sufficient or its purpose. It is odd though, in discussing he transit from hut-shaped house to hut-shaped emple to find no reference to Mr. J. G. Frazer's lelightful article (in the *Journal of Philology*) n the circular Hestia-Vesta temples, and their rigin in the Græco-Italic hut-house.

The critic is bound to note blots and omisions; but, all said and done, the book is an dmirable piece of work, and no self-respecting tudent can leave it unread.

Les Artistes Célèbres: Velasquez, par PAUL LEFORT; *Antoine Watteau*, par G. DARGENTY; *Gerard Terburg*, par ÉMILE MICHEL; *Les Brueghel*, par ÉMILE MICHEL; *Gavarni*, par EUGÈNE FORGUES; *Abraham Bosse*, par ANTHONY VALABREQUE. Paris: Librairie de l'Art; 29, Cité d'Antin.

HIS series of thin volumes, in their artistically esigned parchment covers, form a portion of very admirable collection of brief biographical nd critical treatises on eminent artists, each lustrated with a good many engravings after he artist's principal works, some coarse in xecution but sufficient for purposes of refeence and description, and by a certain number f fac-similes of original drawings, which have special value as being in many cases represntations of works of which the originals are ot well known or easy of access. As the two st issued (those on the Brueghels and on A. osse) one dated in the present year, we may resume that the series, former volumes of which e have noticed some time since, is still in proress, and when complete it will form a very seful and interesting set of artistic biographies, opular in form and pleasant to read, but each ne written by a learned and competent critic.

M. Lefort regards the great Spanish painter especially the apostle of naturalism, the irit which has had such a revival in recent rench art, but in which he declines to see that nger to art which some see in it. Those who ke this view he says, "forget that art being a onvention can only exist through convention, nd that the artist himself is only worthy of e name in proportion as something of his wn personality mingles itself with his manner f understanding, feeling, and interpreting ature." In other words, the so-called realists re only, after all, indulging in a new form of onvention. This, though sounding somewhat aradoxical, is no doubt true in a sense. nstead of the convention of conception, which ave rise to purely unreal and theatrical repreentations of historical events or of Nature, the chool of Velasquez, and of the moderns who ollow him, adopt a realism of conception, ith a conventionalism of representation or technique. The event, as in Velasquez' oble picture of the "Surrender of Breda," is presented as it might have happened, but e method of painting does not aim at realistic inuteness of detail, at anything like deception of the eye: it is the artist's rendering of nature through painting, in accordance with his own special faculty of perception and execution.

M. Lefort regards the celebrated picture of his younger period, "Les Buveurs," as containing the germ of all the remarkable qualities of Velasquez. One peculiar quality in this celebrated work is that while it is antique or classic (in a way) in its leading idea and grouping, it is frankly realistic as to the figures taken separately; there is no attempt at ideal beauty; the figures are ordinary types of humanity, repulsive even (some of them); they have the air of being an ancient bacchanalian group translated into the human semblance of the painter's own period. The more essential point to be noticed is that it is essentially an artist's picture; there is nothing to interest or attract one in the incident or the personages, the attraction is in the grouping and treatment, representing exactly that kind of power which can be exhibited through painting alone, and the attraction and suggestiveness of which it is absolutely impossible to define in words: there is a harmony about it which appeals to the eye as music to the ear, but which is equally indefinable in both cases. In his portraits, especially those of his later days, what we feel impressed by is rather the remarkable power and mastery of execution without laboured finish, execution to which, as M. Lefort remarks the painter "has brought a boldness and freedom absolutely disdainful of unnecessary detail and accessories. Yet in spite of his apparent negligence the effect is always obtained, and the effect he wanted and aimed at." The fac-simile illustrations in the volume are few; they include a characteristic pen sketch of a coach and horses seen in perspective from the rear (another of Velasquez' peculiarly painter-like qualities is his love of experiments and *tours de force* in foreshortening), and two heads of that scoundrel the Duc d'Olivarez, reproduced respectively from an etching by Velasquez and an engraving attributed to him.

It is like going into another world to turn to M. Dargenty's volume on Watteau; though Watteau was a far more versatile painter than is realised by those who only judge him by the "Fête Champêtre" pictures to which he chiefly gave himself. These indeed have qualities of the highest order in composition, drawing, even in imaginative power, which many ordinary gallery-goers overlook because the subjects are of a light and frivolous order. But he could have done pretty nearly what he pleased, had not the fashion of the day led him into the pleasant paths of "Fêtes Champêtres." The tolerably numerous fac-similes from his studies in this volume are sufficient to show this. The author commences his biographical sketch with a brief sketch of the state of France at the time. "Oublions le passé! Le bon côté des choses, voilà ce qu'il faut voir; heureux, voilà ce qu'il faut être. Rattrapons le temps perdu; la vie est court, coulons la bonne. La Grèce, Rome? Sans doute: les grand dévouements, les nobles sacrifices, les vertus austères? Oui, certes; mais nous foulons le sol du Gaule! Nous sommes les enfants frivoles de cette vieille mère facile et gaie! . . . . Voilà ce que pensait la France quand Watteau se mit à peindre; son génie est de l'avoir deviné, sa gloire est de l'avoir traduit." There is the case in a nutshell. An artist of genius paints the life of his day; it may be a frivolous life in itself, but his genius will show itself all the same. His real power of figure-drawing is somewhat masked by the stiff and unnatural costume in which the figures in his usual scenes are dressed, but his studies of figures in more dégagé costume give quite a different impression. It is curious to read, in connexion with the prevalent style of his pictures, that he was a sombre and melancholy man in ordinary temperament and manner.

Watteau's Fêtes Champêtres are at all events more elevating subjects than Pierre Brueghel's horrible moral fantasies, which are an instructive contrast to Watteau. The latter treated light subjects so as to give them a serious artistic value; P. Brueghels treated serious subjects in a manner that is a travesty of all idea of art in the true sense. Jean Brueghel,—"Velvet" Brueghel,—was of course an artist in a very pretty way. It is curious to contrast the portraits of the two men with their works. They give the impression, with their fine chivalrous-looking heads and military bearing, of artists whose natural tendency would have been towards a far higher class of subjects.

Terburg, of whom M. Michel gives a well-illustrated account (so far as pictures depending so much on colour can be illustrated in cuts), may be said to have been intellectually an artist of the same type as Watteau, one who treated the society of his day in an artistic sense. Unfortunately, he had a graver (certainly) but a less graceful and *spirituel* society to depict, and his feeling is bourgeois compared with that of Watteau, but it is extraordinary what an air of grandeur, and an amount of suggestion of a story, he gets out of a group of two or three plain Dutch people in their heavy stiff costume. The figure of the large young woman with her back to the spectator in the celebrated picture of "The Satin Dress" (M. Michel calls it "La Remontrance Paternelle") is one of the most unforgettable things in painting, as far as expression and suggestion are concerned; a novel might be based on it.

The volume on Abraham Bosse gives a large number of engravings from his curious half-grotesque figures of various types of society and professions of his day, and that on Gavarni gives a number of fac-similes from his inimitable sketches of character.

Plain Handicrafts; being Essays by Artists setting forth the Principles of Design and Established Methods of Workmanship. A guide to elementary practice, with a preface by G. F. WATTS, R.A. Edited by A. H. MACKMURDO. London: Percival & Co.

THIS little book is issued by the National Association for the advancement of Art, one of the principal objects of which has been to promote an artistic spirit in what may be called every-day work-objects of ordinary use. The artists concerned in it are Mr. Selwyn Image, who writes "On the Design and the Study of Nature;" Mr. Lethaby ("Cabinet-making"); Mr. E. Roscoe Mullins ("Modelling" and "Carving"); Mr. Ernest W. Gimson ("Plaster-work"); Mr. Reginald Blomfield ("Metal-work"); Miss May Morris ("Embroidery"), and Mr. Heywood Summer ("How to make Stencil Plates and how to use them"). Though it is a thin little volume of only sixty-three pages, it will thus be seen that it contains the opinions of some very accomplished artists in several important branches of art.

Mr. Watts's short preface takes the line that "it is a social demand, rising into a religious duty, to make every endeavour in the direction of supplying all possible compensating consolation for the routine of daily work, because so mechanical and dreary." . . . . "The boy encouraged to imitate some natural object will ever after see in that object something unseen and unknown to him before, and he will find the time he formerly did not know what to do with—a state of being that continually drives thousands to the congested metropolis—henceforth full of pleasurable sensations." What drives thousands to the "congested metropolis" is, we fancy, in the main an idea that they will somehow get on there, though they cannot get on in the country, which proves in most cases a delusion; but in the main sense of Mr. Watts's remark we thoroughly agree. Of the other essays perhaps the most practical useful is Mr. Lethaby's on cabinet-making, with its little sketches showing how to fashion simple pieces of furniture. "Do not pretend," he says, "to cleverness or originality" (this is for the young workman employing his leisure in making things for himself), "consider place, use, size, strains, and other conditions of shape, make, and service. For, by putting your work together in the best practical way; by smoothing a surface, or rounding an edge as thought will suggest, you will reach the beauty of pleasant form, because you will have sound, sensible form." The suggestive sketches bear this out, unless we may take exception to the wavy outlines of the supports to the bench (fig. 7) which we do not quite see the advantage of, even in appearance. Mr. Gimson in his chapter on plaster work gives a wholesome piece of advice as to staying within the limits of plaster, and condemns the practice of teaching modelling in our schools from examples of carving; it may be excellent training, but tends to lead him into wrong ways of designing. Both this and Mr. Blomfield's paper would have been the better for a few sketches to explain more fully to the eye what is meant; but Mr. Blomfield's is a most practical paper apart from this, and concludes with some excellent advice as to the spirit in which natural forms should be adopted for use in the material. It is just here that a sketch would have come in well; beginners do not always understand the meaning of directions in regard to a principle of working, though the meaning may be perfectly obvious to more experienced minds. Miss Morris gives a few illustrations chiefly of a practical kind as to the use of the needle in embroidery, and Mr. Heywood Sumner's chapter on the use of stencil plates is accompanied by some illustrations showing the adaptation of natural forms to the conditions of stencil work, without which the directions could hardly have been intelligible.

The book, as far as it goes, is one of the most useful and sound little works of the kind that has been published; and should be of use for others besides those whose lives especially want brightening. It might well be in the hands of all children as soon as they are come to an age to feel interest in making things for themselves, and learning to make them in the right way.

A. CARTAULT. *Terres Cuites Grecques Photographiées d'après les Originaux des Collections Privées de France et des Musées d'Athènes.* Paris: Colin et Cie. 29 pl. fr. 25.

THIS book is only mentioned by way of warning. It is little more than a specious snare set for the unwary, who are wholly unacquainted with recent investigations as to the authenticity of a certain class of terra-cottas. Not only does M. Cartault pay no manner of attention himself to the arguments by which M. Reinach has convinced, we may safely say, the whole scientific world, but he—and it is for this that we quarrel with him—suppresses all mention of a literature of whose existence he cannot well be ignorant. Glancing over the plates we find, *e.g.*, No. xviii., the Thetis seated on a dolphin, with the helmet of Achilles, and no word to hint that this manifestly modern forgery has ever been suspected; upwards of a dozen others out of the twenty-nine stray plates might be cited. After such evidence of incapacity it is not necessary to dwell on the shortcomings of the annoyingly pompous text.

Christian Thought in Architecture. By BARR FERREE. New York: American Society of Church History. 1892.

THIS is a reprint of a paper read by the author before the Society named on the title-page, and is a consideration of the extent to which Christian feeling is represented or symbolised in Gothic architecture. The ideas embodied in the paper are not new—in fact are rather old—to English readers. In regard to one point we may observe that the author is no doubt correct in upholding the view that the cross was not deliberately selected as the typical plan of the church for any symbolical reason; that it was evolved by natural steps from the ritual requirements of the early church, which first pushed out the side chapels from which the transept gradually developed. But it does not therefore follow that the frequent inclination of the choir northward was not symbolical. Although the *origin* of the cross form was not symbolical, there is no doubt that a symbolism of the cross was tacked on to it by the mediæval mind, and when once that idea was adopted the temptation to carry it further into detail was natural enough. The explanation that the peculiarity arose from careless setting out of the plan is hardly tenable, since there is no setting-out problem so easy and natural as that of aligning a long narrow building correctly on its axis.

The Geometrical Problem Solved. By W. D. DOUGLAS, of Cardiff. Cardiff: David Douglas & Co.

A SMALL manual designed for scientists and students, purporting to illustrate graphic methods of dividing any angle into any number of equal or fractional parts. The plan is ingenious, and described by fifteen propositions, in which the measuring or dividing of arcs of circles is rationally introduced as the most approximate method of geometrically dividing up a given angle, and as the author claims that the problems indicated in his book are infinite, so there is also no limit to the division of the angles discussed. The treatise is, however, more likely to be useful in setting out workshop drawings full size than when drawn to scale on a drawing-board, and would have been more suitable for a paper on the Transactions of a Mathematical Society than as a special text-book for students.

Oxborrow and Money-Kent's Universal Office Manual. London: Published by the authors, 17, Victoria-street, S.W.

THIS work contains a sensible treatise on counting-house and business routine, an exemplification of book-keeping on the modern double-entry system, and a number of specimen account-book page rulings and examples suitable for every description of business. The authors, in their preface, disclaim any desire to pose as exceptionally-qualified instructors of those who conduct their business on systematic principles, their work being primarily intended for the guidance of the, we fear, very large body of traders whose opportunities for acquiring sound business knowledge have not been great. We can cordially recommend the work. The lessons inculcated by it will, if taken to heart and acted upon, not only save many a man from filing a petition in bankruptcy, but will start him on the high road to success. The specimen pages of account-books include builders' prime-cost books (with separate sections for materials and wages), analyses of materials used and wages paid, summaries of materials and wages, workers' time record, manufacturers' cost-book, &c. The way in which these and other account-books should be kept is lucidly explained. The cost of the book, which is very well got up, is 5s.

Correspondence.

To the Editor of THE BUILDER.

ARCHITECTURAL EDUCATION.

SIR,—In reply to Mr. Cole A. Adams, may I try to clear up one or two points on which there appears to be some misunderstanding?

The two meetings referred to by Mr. Jackson in his letter to *A.A. Notes* had nothing whatever to do with one another.

The first was held at my office, as already stated. The second was held at Barnard's Inn, when about fifty architects, *all members of the Art Workers' Guild*, were present. It was this meeting that asked Mr. Jackson to inform the A.A. as to what was being done, and not the first.

What Mr. Adams says about my being "the Past-President of the A.A. who had brought the new educational scheme to the birth," ought to have been sufficient guarantee that I was not likely to try and strangle the child,—as he infers,—before it was even a year old. However, as there seems to be some doubt upon this point, I wish to state clearly that no such idea ever entered my mind.

Mr. Jackson did not suggest any such thing as sweeping away our present curriculum at our meeting; if he had, he would not have been listened to for a moment by any of the members of the A.A. who were present. On this point I am quite clear.

I am of opinion that the scheme we have started with so much trouble, and with which "the some half-dozen" have been so intimately connected, is a very good one, and with this Mr. Jackson generally agreed. The one point to which he took exception was,—not the scheme itself, as Mr. Adams states,—but the fact that it "*points* definitely to preparation for the Examinations of the Institute." Omit this pointing (which consists of some few paragraphs and foot-notes), amend your scheme in one or two small details, and we will help you, if you like, and your students can then go in for the examinations or not as they may elect. This is what Mr. Jackson told "the some half-dozen." In his letter to *A.A. Notes*, however, he puts his views into words so very different to those he used to us that, without some satisfactory explanation,—which I hope will be forthcoming,—it would obviously be quite impossible for the Association to accept his offer as it may at first sight appear to be laid down in *A.A. Notes*.

These, I have reason to believe, are generally speaking, the views of "the some half-dozen" members of the Association who met to confer with Mr. Jackson and his friends on the 15th inst.; and I venture to think that the general body of members of the A.A. will consider that we *were* serving their best interests in acting as we did.

LEONARD STOKES.

"GLASGOW ART GALLERIES."

SIR,—I have read your criticism upon my design for the above, and I am not sure whether i
means,—on the average,—praise or the reverse
You say it is one of two of "outstanding merit,"
and go on at first to give it what seems to be a full
measure of praise; but did you get sorry for wha
you said? For in the latter part the lash is laid o
pretty hard.

If my design be a curious parallel to Sir G
Scott's "failure" at Gilmore-hill, it is quite acci
dental. I never heard of, nor saw,—either in prin
or reality,—the place; and as to the Central Hall
it was intended to be "*monumental*," and *not* like
music-hall,—if "The Oxford" or "The Pavilion"
be the orthodox thing. But I think I read correctl
the intentions of the Committee, as every one, in
cluding, I believe, Mr. Waterhouse, admired it
The vaulting is not "complicated," and I shoul
be glad to know how a span of 70 ft. may b
covered *in fireproof construction* in any simpl
manner, except with a roof like Cannon-stree
Station? You should not have drawn you
criticisms from my internal perspective view o
this, as I am quite aware it was a poor drawing.

As to style, what is one to do? Please to re
member the cruel fact of a competition, we can onl
select what we believe will be most popular. It i
seldom one can really consult one's own taste, o
practise the style he thinks most true. In thi
Mr. Waterhouse was the assessor; he won't hav
Classic. My father and I made a design for th
Imperial Institute, which most people admitted t
be fine; it would not do. We tried another styl
at South Kensington with equally bad luck, and no
this,—of which I had much hope,—"with tower
scattered broadcast," as you say, to produce "th
Scotch baronial": all no use. Do let me know wh
you think is right and *fin de siècle*, so that I may d
better the next time.

Anyhow, I must say for my design that it is n
copy, either of Sir Gilbert Scott or Mr. Aston Webb
and I do not think my late friend and respecte
master, William Burges, A.R.A., would have bee
ashamed of his pupil on account of his latest effo
at least.

THOS. MANLY DEANE.

3, *Upper Merrion-street, Dublin*, April 23, 1892.

*** We admired Mr. Deane's design, and did n
intend to suggest otherwise; nor did we mean t
imply that he had copied Scott. We did imply th
neither Scott in his Glasgow University nor M
Deane in his Art Gallery design had succeeded i
being genuinely Scotch in character. The centr
hall we said was "very fine," but not a "hall f
music." This Mr. Deane admits. "Complicate
vaulting" was not intended in a depreciator
sense.

As to the latter part of Mr. Deane's letter, we c
only say that it is a melancholy confirmation
what we have often said as to the evil effect of co
petitions on architecture, the object being, as M
Deane so frankly admits, not to produce the be
possible architecture but to secure the appoin
ment. The "assessor" system in this respe
seems to increase the evil—"So-and-so is t
assessor; what is his favourite style? Let us go
for that." Truly a melancholy state of things f
the art of architecture.—ED.

The Student's Column.

WARMING BUILDINGS BY HOT WATE

XVIII.

INDEPENDENT BOILERS: BRICK-SET BOILER

AMONG types of independent boilers w
may mention first Keith's Challen
Boiler (fig. 70), which is well-know
and for those purposes to which it is adapt
it is decidedly successful. The peculiarity
in its internal construction, which, as befo
referred to, presents a very large area of dire
heating surface in a comparatively small spac
It is a cast boiler, and built up in sections
the illustration shows, and it can be seen th
the power of the boiler can be increased, or t
reverse, within certain limits by the addition
removal of some of the sections. The low
sections which constitute the furnace are co
voluted inside, which about doubles the area
surface compared to flat plates. The upp
sections are more complex, being partly co
voluted, and also having cross water-way b
extending from side to side. Other devices
a similar nature are resorted to to increase t
interior heat-receiving area. The fact of t
parts being cast-iron permits of these varieti
of surfaces being easily obtained in the man
facture, a result that would be difficult a
costly to obtain (to this extent) with wroug
plates.

If desired, the sections can be arranged
the feeding-door to be placed at a high
position, so that the boiler may be charg
with coke to last several hours. This, howev

s not desirable if the full power of the boiler s needed. In fact, every boiler is at a disadvantage in being filled up in this manner with uel, as the black mass in the upper part of the oiler effectively prevents the plates at that art receiving the heat that should be imparted o them, and the boiler is worked almost wholly y the glowing fuel in contact with the plates t bottom.

A boiler of this character must necessarily e coated with non-conducting compound, or urrounded with brickwork, to prevent loss of eat, and with a boiler having such a large lirect heating surface, with comparatively little water, there should always be two or more flow ipes and returns. This boiler is made to heat p to 7,000 ft. of 4-in. pipe.

The last boiler of the independent order to e mentioned, is by the same maker, and

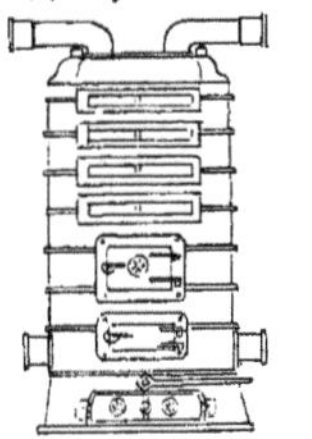

Fig 70

ermed the "Python," as it is of a horizontal hape, and can be shortened or lengthened by he withdrawal or addition of sections. Fig. 71 hows the boiler in front elevation, but with the ront casting, and its fire-doors, &c., removed. This boiler has a convoluted inner surface, top nd sides, and a multiplicity of other heating urfaces, chiefly in the form of cross water-way ars. This, and also the last boiler mentioned, as fire-bars that, by the movement of a lever andle outside, set up a rocking motion to clear he bottom of the fire and assist in preventing linker-forming. This arrangement prevents he too frequent opening of the stoking-doors. 'his is the most powerful boiler made, and is

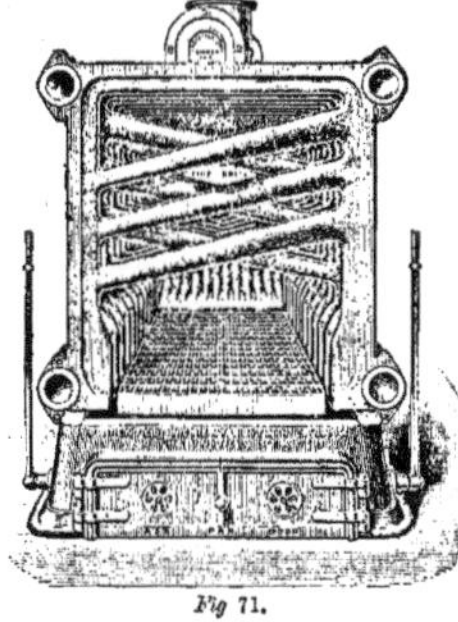

Fig 71.

sed for such works as public washing and ming baths and laundries.

The automatic damper, or draught-regulator own in the flue-nozzle at back, is worth scribing, as it acts upon a good and reliable inciple. This damper is practically an nott's ventilator in its action, opening into e flue or chimney and permitting air to pass , in variable quantity according to the extent at its flap is open. The flap or door is nicely votted at its lower edge, and by the use of a tle balance weight it swings to and fro with ry little impulse. Now, it is probably known most of the readers that the draught in a imney is very irregular, even within the ce of a few minutes, at one moment being ong and another moment rather slack. This ick irregular action is generally due to wind, t a slower, but just as inconvenient irregularity is brought about by careless or insufficient attention to the fire. If an ordinary damper is left open a little too far and the attendant absents himself, a deal of annoyance may be experienced by the fierce burning of the fire, &c., and this automatic damper obviates this.

If we make an opening in a chimney a short distance above a stove or boiler, we shall find that an inrush of air immediately sets in through this aperture, and the current of air through the fire below will be reduced proportionately. Now, the automatic damper is this opening, but its balanced door or valve regulates the amount of air that passes in. If the fire commences to burn fiercely, the draught in the chimney at once becomes strong, but its strength in this case defeats itself, as it causes the valve to open and the inrush of air robs the fire below of draught which at once checks its fierceness. With the abatement of the fierceness, the draught in the chimney also slackens, and this allows the valve to wholly or partially close until called upon to act again. Any irregularity of draught caused by wind, and which would make the fire burn badly, is checked by the same means. Whether the fire or whether the wind is the cause of excessive draught in the chimney, this valve checks it just the same. (The draught in a close-fire kitchen-range can be regulated in precisely the same manner by inserting an Arnott's valve in the chimney-breast.)

Brick-set Boilers. — The shape that necessarily takes precedence in this description is the "saddle" boiler. It is one of the oldest forms we have, cheap to make, effective (up to a certain size), and its shape is calculated to benefit by the heat evolved from the fire. The addition of water-way ends front and back

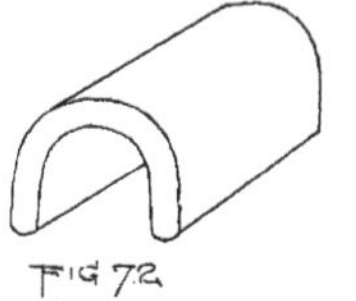

Fig 72

makes it as nearly perfect as a wrought boiler can be. When, however, we require a great quantity of pipe to be heated it is more economical in results to have some one of the more complex forms of boiler, which present a greater heating surface within a restricted area.

It will be noticed that with the saddle boiler, fig. 72, at a point about half way up, the plates begin to describe a half circle over the top, both outside and inside. This, in the writer's opinion, is a disadvantage, not so much inside, however, as outside.

With the outside flue, or indirect heating surface, it has been explained that plates which come beneath the source of heat are practically valueless, owing to flame and heated gases having no efficient contact with surfaces beneath them (unless the flue be choked somewhat, when an objection of another kind presents itself). In addition to this, these surfaces always have a collection of dirt upon them, which by itself would prevent a ready transfer of heat to the water. A square shape, as fig. 73, would give

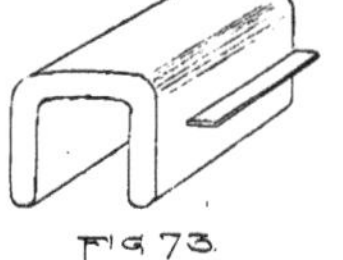

Fig 73.

better results, as the inside and more effective direct heating surface would be increased and the vertical surface outside would be added to; vertical surface, notwithstanding its low value, being more useful than a surface beneath the source of heat. By having the boiler of this shape, the flame can be led up and down its length as usual, but along the side, the midfeather being central, as shown. The top, the useless surface, need not be made use of except to support the brickwork above, and this would reduce the cost of fixing. Most of the newer shapes, which follow the saddle somewhat, are of square cross section, and the top outer surface is not used except in the way just mentioned.

In fixing saddle-boilers (ordinary shape) there are two methods in common use, one being adapted for the smaller sizes and the other and more usual method for small and large sizes alike. The former method is to fix the boiler so that heat and heated products escape from beneath the boiler at all points, and so envelope the boiler without being specially conducted by flues to this end. It is a very effective method. Fig 74 shows in

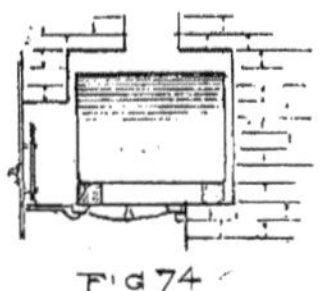

Fig 74

longitudinal section the boiler so fixed; it is set upon four fire-bricks, one at each corner, these raising it three inches above the fire-bars. By this means the draught in the chimney causes the heated gases to pass from the fire-box under the sides, and then embrace the outer surface of the boiler, as a moderately close-fitting arch is thrown over. The space between the boiler and the brickwork of the arch would be, say, three inches.

The illustration shows the chimney leading off from the centre at top, this can commonly be arranged and gives the best results; if, however, the chimney must be carried up at the back, then feathers must be introduced to keep the heat from inclining towards that point too much. It will be noticed that only a narrow space is left between the boiler and brickwork at front and back. The object of this is to prevent the too free escape of heated gases at these high points, as otherwise we should not get heat to pass under the lower sides. This space in question should be 1 in. to $1\frac{1}{2}$ in. If the chimney was carried up at the extreme back, the boiler could be butted tight against the brickwork at that end. A damper to regulate the draught would have to be fitted in the brick chimney immediately where it starts at from the top. This is the usual, and the best and most convenient position for it. This method, as mentioned, is only suited for small boilers, as will be readily understood. It possesses a disadvantage in the fact that when the fire has been going slowly for a little time without attention, the passage-ways beneath the lower side edges of the boiler become choked with ash, &c., and the outer indirect heating surface has little of the heat. The less useful spaces at each end of the boiler would be more active then, but it would not do to stop or omit them. Boilers fixed in this manner will more quickly fail with accumulated dirt, than when they are fixed with their lower edges level with the fire bars.

OBITUARY.

Mr. R. J. Johnson, F.R.I.B.A.—We regret to hear of the death of Mr. Robert James Johnson, F.R.I.B.A., F.S.A., of Newcastle-on-Tyne and York. He died, after a long illness, on the 18th inst., at Tunbridge Wells, aged 60. He was elected an Associate of the Royal Institute of British Architects in 1861 and a Fellow in 1865.

Sir Gilbert Scott's Restorations.—We are compelled to hold over several letters on this subject, which will appear next week.

Steam Tree-felling and Cross-cutting Machinery.—Some fourteen or fifteen years ago Mr. Allen Ransome, of Chelsea, took out a patent for a steam tree-felling machine, and we were present at some practical trials of it made on the Roupell-park estate, Tulse-hill. (See *Builder* for January 19, 1878, p. 71, for an account of the trials). *Engineering* for last week (April 22) contains a description and illustrations of a new and improved form of tree-felling machine which is free from some of the difficulties experienced in the use of the old machine. By a simple mechanical contrivance, the machine can be partially rotated on its axis when required for cross-cutting.

GENERAL BUILDING NEWS.

LABOURERS' DWELLINGS IN MANCHESTER.—In the Ancoats district of Manchester, by the side of Jersey-street, a disused cotton-mill has just been converted into a dwelling-house in flats. The total accommodation is for 149 families. The block is seven stories in height. The total cost of the undertaking has been about 20,000*l.* All the old windows of the mill have been replaced with modern sashes. From top to bottom, both front and back, there are a series of iron balconies to which access is obtained from the staircases, four in number, and which have been erected at each corner of the building. These are of concrete and iron. The walls of the building are from 3 ft. thick at the bottom to 2 ft. at the top. Every floor is covered with concrete, resting on brick arches. Each room has a good light. In front of each window is a sink, with a supply, night and day, of hot and cold water. Self-cleansing water-closets are provided, and there are dust-shoots on all the floors. The balconies do not run from end to end of the structure. Each staircase and each landing has its separate balcony. There is a large playground at the back of the building, one end of which is to be converted into a drying-ground. A washhouse, with coppers, hot and cold water, &c., has also been provided. Two clubrooms, both apart from the main structure, are being fitted up for the use of the males and females. Each has separate conveniences. The clubroom for the men is 40 ft. 6 in. by 18 ft., that for the women 58 ft. 6 in. by 18 ft. 6 in. Baths have also been provided for both sexes, each supplied with hot and cold water. Every dwelling has a cupboard. A double system of ventilation has been provided for the water-closets. Mr. C. J. Maycock, of Manchester, was the architect, and the work has been carried out for the Manchester Labourers' Dwellings Company, Ltd.

TRADE SCHOOL, BRUTON, SOMERSET. — The opening of the new buildings of Sexey's Trade School, Bruton, took place on the 19th inst. The buildings have been erected from designs by Mr. George J. Skipper, of Norwich, by Messrs. Francis & Sons, of Castle Cary, and cost over £3,000. They consist of a master's residence, with principal schoolroom, class-rooms, chemical laboratory, workshops, dining-room, cloak-room, lavatory, &c. The laboratory has been fitted for twenty students. Gas and water are laid on. The workshop is fitted with benches, &c.

PROPOSED SALVATION ARMY "CITADEL," ABERDEEN.—This proposed block of buildings, the plans of which have just been approved of, will occupy a site at the east end of Castle-street, with a frontage of 160 ft. The barracks have been designed in the Scottish Baronial style, and the whole building will be of blocked stone, finely axed. Almost the whole of the ground and basement floors will be occupied as shops, several of which will be the largest in Aberdeen, being about 40 by 80 ft., and about 20 ft. high. On the first floor, and to the south of the tower, there will be a hall capable of accommodating 2,000 persons, the three front windows forming features in the front elevation. Over the front entrance of the building there will be oriel windows hung on projecting corbels, and the block at its chief corners will be flanked by round towers, about 100 ft. in height. A prominent feature of the building will be a large tower. At the foot of the tower there will be the grand entrance to the Citadel, an archway 20 ft. wide by 30 ft. high, with massive piers, and an arch containing ornamental stones, on which it is proposed to put the initials and crests of leading men who are taking an interest in the erection of the building, which is estimated to cost about 15,000*l.*, and has been designed by Mr. James Souttar, architect, of Aberdeen.

PARISH BUILDING, ALL SAINTS', PLYMOUTH.—The corner-stone of the new Parish Building for All Saints', Plymouth, was laid on the 23rd inst. by Mr. Shelly, of Plymouth. The cost of the building will be about 1,250*l.*, and it is to be completed by October next. The materials for the structure are the same as used in building the vicarage by Mr. John D. Sedding five years ago—namely local limestone and red brick. Mr. Edmund Sedding, of Plymouth, is the architect, and Mr. Blowey of the same town is the builder.

CONVENT OF MERCY, GRANARD, CO. LONGFORD. On the 21st inst. the ceremony of laying and blessing the foundation-stone of the Convent of Mercy, Granard, was performed by the Rev. Dr. Woodlock. The general plan of the building comprises an entrance-hall and staircase, with parlours and reception-rooms, community-room, &c.; culinary apartments, cells, and a suitable oratory placed in a convenient position. The architect is Mr. Wm. Hague, of Dublin, and the contractor Mr. P. Kelly, of Longford.

REOPENING OF HANMER CHURCH, FLINTSHIRE.—On the 19th inst. the parish church of Hanmer, in the detached portion of Flintshire, which was almost destroyed by fire in 1889, was reopened, after restoration, by the Bishop of St. Asaph. The church, says the *Birmingham Gazette*, was not insured, but immediately after the fire steps were taken for its reconstruction, Messrs. Bodley & Garner, of London, being the architects entrusted with the work, the estimated cost being about 10,000*l.* The architects have been able, by means of photographs, to reproduce the ceiling of the north aisle, and, with the exception of the chancel, the restoration has been carried out, as far as possible, upon conservative lines. The chancel has not been restored, it being decided to build one more in character with the rest of the church. The new chancel is larger than the old, and an organ-chamber and vestry have been added. The pulpit and font are the work of Mr. Forsyth, from designs by Mr. Bodley, and the screen was entrusted to Mr. Douglas, of Chester.

COUNTY TRUANTS' SCHOOL, QUAKER'S-YARD, GLAMORGAN.—Tenders have just been accepted for the erection of a Truants' School at Quaker's-yard, Glamorgan. The buildings will provide a large schoolroom, with a portion divided off at one end by a sliding partition, forming a class-room, dining-hall, plunge-bath, three dormitories, drill-shed, and workshop. In addition, a laundry, with drying and ironing room, will be provided, with top lights, and supplied with stored rain-water; a reception-room for new-comers, and a disinfecting-room, with separate entrance from the outside. There will be three entrances to the buildings. At the main entrance, for the Board and visitors, there will be a large vestibule and hall. The superintendent has a wing of the building to himself, with all necessary conveniences and private staircase. Two other staircases will be provided, both of Forest stone, one in the boys' hall and the other in the servants' hall. The dormitories will be provided with inspection-chambers, entered from the master's rooms. On the same floor and under the matron's supervision will be sick and convalescent sitting-rooms. Adjoining the former, but disconnected, and with separate staircase entrance and conveniences, will be provided a room for the reception and isolation of cases of infectious diseases. The matron and staff will be accommodated with private apartments. The linen and store-rooms will be kept aired by means of pipes from the heating apparatus. It is proposed to heat the main building by hot-water, and the cooking will be done by steam. In the disinfecting-room will be a steam disinfecting machine. The water to the plunge-bath and lavatory will be warmed by an injection of steam, and the wash tubs in the laundry will have a continual supply of hot water, kept at a given temperature throughout washing operations by the same means. There being no sewer to connect the drainage to, it is proposed to collect and filter it. Provision will be made for a board-room, and an office for the superintendent and waiting-room will adjoin the main hall. A fire hydrant will be fixed on each floor. The walls will be built of local stone, the front and sides faced with hammer-dressed random ranged work, relieved with box-ground stone and buff, and red terra-cotta and brick bands. It is proposed to use plain "hit-and-miss" inlets and Kite's patent automatic exhaust ventilators. The building is designed in the Italian Renaissance style, and the plans, which were selected in open competition, have been prepared by Mr. W. H. Dashwood Caple, architect, of Cardiff. The design and plans have been approved by the Home Office and the Education Department. The tender of Messrs. Stephens, Bastow, & Co., of Bristol, has been accepted at 6,279*l.*

LIBERAL CLUB, BACUP.—On the 9th inst. the foundation stones of a new Liberal Club were laid at Hempsteads, Bacup, Lancashire. The club will be built of stone,—parpoint facing and stone dressing,—and the style will be English Renaissance. The new building contains, on the ground floor, a vestibule, with screen doors leading into the corridor. On the right-hand side is a billiard-room, 27 ft. by 21 ft.; on the left-hand side is the news-room, 27 ft. by 21 ft., with an octagon projecting window at the angle; at the back of these two rooms is the steward's serving-room, lavatory, and kitchen, with a side entrance and staircase to be used for public entertainments only, and which leads to the large assembly-room. The first pair floor is approached by a staircase 4 ft. wide, and contains a public room, 51 ft. by 29 ft., capable of holding 400 to 500 people, with a raised platform at one end, and having a retiring-room, lavatory, &c., adjoining; lavatories and steward's bedrooms are also on this floor. The second pair floor contains a billiard-room, 51 ft. by 27 ft. Adjoining is a committee-room, card-room, and lavatories. Messrs. Mangnall & Littlewoods, of Manchester, are the architects, and the premises will cost about 4,000*l.*

SANITARY AND ENGINEERING NEWS.

THE INCORPORATED ASSOCIATION OF MUNICIPAL AND COUNTY ENGINEERS.—This Friday and Saturday (April 29 and 30) the Incorporated Association of Municipal and County Engineers will hold a meeting at Nottingham. Papers will be read, (1) "On Municipal Works in Nottingham," by Mr. Arthur Brown, the Borough Engineer; (2) "On Public Health Acts Amendment," by Mr. W. Spinks; and (3) "On County Management of Main Roads," by Mr. James Robinson, County Surveyor of Hampshire. Visits will be paid to the sewage farm, the epidemic hospital, and other places.

THE TUNNELS UNDER THE CLYDE AT GLASGOW.—Work on the Glasgow Harbour tunnels has been proceeding without interruption since last autumn, according to *Industries*. Only about 100 ft. of the west tunnel remain to be driven, while the heading of the east tunnel has been advanced about 60 ft. from the south bank. The material encountered is boulder-clay on the south side, thinning off to sand and gravel. No large boulders have yet been met. The maximum progress of the shields in the clay has been 2 ft., and in the sand 3 ft. The air-pressure has never exceeded 160 lb. The shields are 17 ft. in diameter by 7 ft. in length, the shells being built up of two ½ in. plates and 3½ in. by 3½ in. angles. The rams are of cast-steel, and worked under a water pressure of 1,000 by means of two hand-pumps attached to the shield itself. In the west tunnel a brick wall forms the entrance to the air-chamber, while in the east tunnel a stiff steel diaphragm is used.

WINCANTON SEWERAGE.—The Wincanton Rural Sanitary Authority have called in Mr. A. P. I. Cotterell, Assoc. M. Inst. C.E., of Bristol, to advise them as to what may be done to improve the purification of the sewage at their disposal works. Mr. Cotterell has visited the town, and recommended the adoption of the International Sewage Purification Co.'s system, with polarite filter beds, but with a new form of precipitating tank not hitherto used in this country. The tank is constructed like a circular well, about 25 feet deep, and the sewage is conducted by a pipe to the bottom, precipitating as it slowly rises. The sludge which collects at the bottom is pumped out daily without emptying the tank. The top is covered in, and the sewage is not, therefore, open to the action of the sun's rays. These tanks are, it is stated, already in successful operation on the Continent, and we are informed that experiments made in England have produced very satisfactory results, much superior to those from the usual form of tank. The Sanitary Authority are now considering the report.

FOREIGN AND COLONIAL.

FRANCE.—MM. Gustave Moreau and Carolus Duran have been appointed members of the Conseil Supérieur des Beaux-Arts, in place of the late M. Delaunay and of M. Bonnat who has become President of the Société des Artistes Français.——By a decision of the Minister of Public Instruction, the "Prix de Salon" given each year to a painter, a sculptor, an architect, or an engraver alternately, will henceforth be known as the "Prix de Paris." The prize cannot be given to an artist older than 32, and is accompanied by a sum of 10,000 fr. payable in two annuities, to enable the holder to travel for two years.——An exhibition of the works of Raffet is to be opened at the Galérie Georges Petit, the proceeds to go towards a monument, consisting of a column surmounted by a bust, and surrounded by French soldiers.——M. Maze Leucier has left to the Carnavalet Museum a curious collection of snuff-boxes belonging to political celebrities of the revolutionary period.——The École des Beaux-Arts has set apart a special room for the valuable collection of manuscripts and drawings offered by Madame Lesoufaché, the widow of the architect who died two years ago.——A fine ceiling attributed to Mignard has been fixed in one of the rooms of the Gobelins Museum; it represents Apollo playing the lyre. It is said to have formed the ceiling of Lebrun's atelier.——There is talk of building a large military hospital near Issy, to replace the St. Martin and Gros Caillou hospitals which are now inadequate.——The first stone of a large boys' school has been laid at Meudon.——A bronze statue of Rouget de l'Isle was inaugurated last Sunday at Choisy-le-Roi.——There has just been opened at the Hôtel de Ville at Paris an exhibition of the designs sent in by MM. Courselle Dumont, Delance, J. Ferry, Prouvé, and Simas for the second competition for the decoration of the Salle des Banquets. The decision will be made known during the week. The design of M. Delance appears to us far superior to the others.——The second competition for the Beaumarchais statue is also to be settled shortly. The three designs in competition are by MM. Allouard, Clausade, and Lormier.——There has been installed in the Palais des Beaux-Arts a collection of the views of old Paris, executed by M. Hoffbauer, and which formed, some years ago, the diorama of "Paris à travers les ages" exhibited at the Champs Elysées. These views have been presented to the Paris municipality by M. Firmin Didot, the well-known publisher.

BERLIN.—The Special Committee of members of the Town Executive and the Common Council elected by the Municipal Authorities of Berlin to consider matters relating to the proposed opening of an International Exhibition in that city, has decided in favour of the scheme, and has recommended that the greatest possible assistance be given to those entrusted with the arrangement of the exhibition. The committee will now consider in what form the assistance is to be given. The Imperial Chancellor has now also assured the Chamber of Commerce of the Government's interest and aid. It may therefore now be taken for granted that the exhibition will come off. The German public seem to be greatly in favour of th[illegible] lea, and the press throughout the country has ıken it up warmly. Some doubt, however, still xists as to the feeling in the German trades. ontinental exhibition at the large international hows, at the national and the various local ones, as of late been felt as a great burden, especially as he exertions made have not had much commercial esult. —— There is still a probability of the mperor's idea of having further alterations made the vicinity of his "Schloss" being carried out, spite of the enormous expenditure which would ave to be covered by the profits off another ttery.——The Bill put before the Prussian 'Landtag" relating to the extension of the overnment Railway System proposes that some inety millions of marks shall be spent in the ourse of a few years on "special extensions." f this sum 26,000,000 marks will be required for ew lines, some 44,000,000 marks for the extension nd alteration of existing ones, and 10,000,000 marks r rolling stock.——The municipal authorities ave decided to erect a so-called "Provincial" useum in which some local collections and several braries are to have room found for them. A iitable site for the museum building has been ound, and a competition for designs (three prizes, ,500. 1,500, and 1,000 marks) is to be opened.—— 'he Municipal Authorities of Berlin have for some me back been paying attention to the various dvantages and disadvantages of cremation. They ave now decided to introduce cremation in the funicipal burial-grounds, and hence all unlentified corpses, as well as those of paupers, &c., aving no relations or friends who might be dverse to this mode of proceeding, will henceorward be thus disposed of. Instead of using the sual urn, a zinc box some 15 cm. cube will be used s a receptacle for the ashes, and the numbers or ames relating to the contents will be marked on mall copper plates, which are to be enclosed with ne remains, as well as in black figures or letters n the outside. The apparatus necessary for the urning process has been ordered. The Schneider ystem is to be used.

VIENNA.—The "International" Theatrical and Iusical Exhibition is to be officially opened on Iay 7.

SWITZERLAND.—The committee in charge of the ffairs pertaining to the proposed erection of a large lock containing concert and assembly rooms for urich are apparently not satisfied with the result f the (second) competition lately held for the urpose of obtaining a suitable design. Herr runo Schmitz, of Berlin, who took the first prize both competitions, is not likely to have the rection of the block, as Messrs. Fellmer & Helmer, ne Vienna theatre specialists (who have put up ne new municipal theatre at Zurich last year), d Professor F. Bluntschli, of Zurich, have now en invited to tender designs. It is true that uno Schmitz's work is to serve as a basis for the signs, but that will give but little satisfaction to e architect or his friends. Apparently Messrs. llmer & Helmer are favourites of the committee, they were invited at once after the issue of the mpetition; Professor Bluntschli was only invited er the Swiss architects had expressed their gust. That the German professional journals by no means very gentle in their criticism on behaviour of the committee is only natural.—— me thirty designs were sent in for the competin for the design of a Tell Monument at Altdorf. e first prize (2,500 francs) was given to the ilptor, R. Kissling, of Riesbach, Zurich.

INFORMATION FOR EMIGRANTS. — The April culars of the Emigrants' Information Office, and new annual editions of the penny and other ndbooks, with maps, which have just been issued, w the present prospects of emigration. Branch ces are now organised at Bradford (Yorks), Bury Edmunds, Cardiff, Devizes, Glasgow, Hereford, mington, Leeds, Liverpool, and Reading, mostly connexion with Free Public Libraries, where all above publications and other information may be obtained. This is the best season of the r to go to Canada, and there is likely to be a d demand for farm labourers, and to a extent for general labourers and navvies for mechanics in the building trades. New South Wales and Victoria mechanics are wanted, except in a few districts, and in toria especially the depression is great. The eensland Government withdrew their free ssages last February, so that now all except ninated and indented emigrants have to pay fares. There is no demand whatever for chanics in Queensland, many carpenters, mbers, and general labourers have been out work, and no one should go there at present the chance of finding employment. Western stralia offers free and reduced passages to tain classes of emigrants, but free passages farm labourers have just been suspended. rk there has been much brisker than for ne time past, and there is a demand for a ited number of farm labourers, men in the building trades, miners, and labourers on railways and lic works. In Tasmania the chief demand is for ers, farm labourers, and a few country blackths; the new silver mines at Zeehan on the st Coast are giving employment to considerable nbers of miners, railway navvies, and small ers. In various districts of New Zealand there is a demand for farm and station hands and for miners. Cape Colony and Natal offer reduced passages to mechanics, female servants, and others, for whom there is a limited demand. Government Labour Bureaus have recently been opened in New South Wales, Queensland, and New Zealand. Emigrants on arrival should apply to the head offices at Sydney, Brisbane, or Wellington, or to one of the country branches, which are very numerous. The warnings already issued by the Emigrants' Information Office against emigration to South America still hold good. Intending emigrants are especially strongly warned not to go to Brazil at the present time.

MISCELLANEOUS.

BUILDERS' CLERKS' BENEVOLENT INSTITUTION: ELECTION OF PENSIONERS.—A special general meeting of the donors and subscribers took place on Tuesday last, at the offices of the Institution, 21, New Bridge-street, E.C. The President, Mr. Colin G. Patrick, who occupied the chair, stated that as there were but two candidates, it had been decided that the election should be by show of hands. The candidates were Mr. William Marcham, and Mrs. Mary E. Robb, and after some particulars respecting each had been given by the President, they were elected in due course, the former to the Clerks' Pension of 25*l.* per annum, and the latter to the Widows' Pension of 20*l.* per annum. A vote of thanks was accorded to the chairman at the close of the business.

A NEW IRISH SEAL.—A new great seal for Ireland has been completed by Mr. Allan Wyon, chief engraver of her Majesty's seals, to take the place of the seal designed on the accession of the Queen, which is now worn out. The new seal is an exact replica of its predecessor, and is similar in all respects to the great seal of England, save that in the exergue a harp with shamrock leaves takes the place of the trident-head and sprays of oak, which form the distinctive mark of the English seal. The material is silver, the weight of the whole about 15 lb., and the diameter of the impression is 6¼ in. —*Irish Builder.*

THE NOVELTY THEATRE, GREAT QUEEN-STREET. —This property, having a lease for 69 years unexpired, will, by order of the mortgagees, be offered for sale at the mart, on May 20 next. The premises have a second frontage, with entrances, in Parker-street. They were built from the plans and designs of Mr. Thomas Verity, architect; the theatre was opened on December 9, 1882, under its present style; but for an interval was known as Jodrell's. We may supplement the tale of celebrated residents in Great Queen-street, as given in the guide-books, by stating that Mr. Frederick Crace, who formed the collection of maps, plans, prints, and drawings of London,—purchased from his son, Mr. John Gregory Crace, for the British Museum,—lived for a while in the house on the southern side, into which Sir Godfrey Kneller removed from the Piazza, Covent Garden; and that the *Mercurius Politicus* for the week November 19—26, 1657, contains an advertisement of the robbery, from the Earl of Chesterfield's, in this street, of certain "pictures" in gold and in jewelled cases.

THE SANITARY INSTITUTE'S EXAMINATION FOR INSPECTORS OF NUISANCES.—At an examination for Inspectors of Nuisances, held in London by the Sanitary Institute on April 8 and 9, 105 candidates presented themselves. Questions were set to be answered in writing on the 8th, and the candidates were examined *vivâ voce* on the 9th. Sixty-eight candidates were certified to be competent, as regards their sanitary knowledge, to discharge the duties of Inspector of Nuisances.

CHICAGO EXHIBITION, 1893.—The *Journal of the Society of Arts* announces, on behalf of the Royal Commission for this Exhibition, that, her Majesty's Government, having increased the grant placed at their disposal for the purposes of the British Section from 25,000*l.* to 60,000*l.*, they can dispense with any charges for space at the Exhibition, and will return to the intending exhibitors the amounts already paid on that account. The available space in the General Manufactures Building is now almost entirely filled. In the Agricultural Building, and in the Machinery Building, space is still available. All applications for space must be made upon forms to be obtained from the Secretary of the Commission, at their offices, John-street, Adelphi, London. The French Chamber of Deputies have just voted 130,000*l.* as a grant for the proper representation of France at the Exhibition.

FRENCH ROAD-MAKING.—The British Vice-Consul at Dieppe, in his last report, says that the roads which surround the docks, and the national roads which lead out of the town on the east and on the west, have been made with an exceptionally good quality of stone, of singular hardness and durability, which was brought from Cherbourg. In fact, it is so hard that it will cut glass. It is broken up into macadam, and forms splendid material for making roads. Her Majesty's Consul at Cherbourg mentioned this stone very favourably in his report for 1890, and its use has proved so satisfactory in Dieppe, that the Vice-Consul thinks it might be worth inquiring whether it could be employed on some of our English roads, where a lesson in road-making might be learnt with advantage from the French *cantonnier*. The material is usually marble, flint, stone, or gravel, and whatever is used must be of the best quality and cleansed from all foreign substances. The stone must be broken up so that each piece may pass through a ring 2½ in. in diameter. It is then spread evenly over the road, the interstices being carefully filled in with smaller pieces, so that the whole is smooth and free from abrupt eminences and depressions. A steam-roller then crushes and levels the whole, after which a superficial layer of clay and earth completes the work. In Normandy, where the roads are perfect, they are made slightly convex, with a trench on each side, and are diligently scraped to keep them dry. One of the most important ingredients used in road-making is a little chalk, which helps to bind and consolidate the macadam or small stones into a firm and hard mass. If too much chalk were used it would render the roads sticky after frost.—*Times.*

ROBINSON'S IMPROVED PLASTERING.—A demonstration of the qualities and modes of application of Robinson's "Fireproof Cement and Paragon Plaster" was given at a new building (No. 48, Chancery-lane) on Saturday, the 23rd inst., by permission of the architects (Messrs. Somers Clarke and J. T. Micklethwaite) and the builders (Messrs. Langdale & Hallett). One of the advantages claimed by the manufacturers, and apparently with justice, is that by the use of the "Paragon Plaster" the plasterers "can commence in a room in the morning and completely finish it before the day is out, without previously having been in to first coat." The next day there is a hard surface, which continues to harden, until the result is a wall or ceiling which will withstand damage even from the exercise of a considerable amount of force, as was demonstrated in our presence on the ceiling of a room which had only been finished a week previously. The manufacturers claim that walls, ceilings, battened or strapped walls and stoothed partitions which are coated with this material will never crack. Used pure, the "Paragon" plaster lays on the ceiling like gauged putty. Floating coats can be used with or without sand, but if sand is used it must be clean sharp river or pit sand. Finished with a thin coat of Robinson's "No. 1" cement, this plaster makes admirable work. Messrs. Robinson & Co. are also introducing a new and simple form of lathless ceiling, in which their "Paragon" plaster is laid between and is carried by the joists, a light temporary centreing of floor-boards being required until the plaster has set. Where rolled-iron joists are used, the bottom flange supports the plaster; in the case of wooden joists, fillets or cleats are nailed on to serve as bearings. Messrs. Robinson's specialities will be on view in the room in Chancery-lane, to which we have referred, up to the end of this week.

RECENT SANITARY CATALOGUES.—Messrs. Young & Marten, of the Caledonian Works, Stratford, have sent us their new illustrated catalogue of plumbers' brasswork, cast-iron and earthenware goods, and other requisites for sanitary work. It consists of 96 pages of well-arranged and well-printed illustrated letterpress. It is a very complete and useful production, and contains an abundance of good things. From this category, however, we must exclude the appliance represented by fig. 91, on page 40, which is no other than the old-fashioned and now generally-condemned pan-closet, with its abominable filth "container." We had hoped that the pan-closet was rapidly becoming a thing of the past, so far as new "installations" of it are concerned; it has disappeared from the catalogues of some manufacturers and merchants, and we can only regret that Messrs. Young & Marten express their willingness to supply it, in these days of supposed sanitary enlightenment. We shall no doubt be told that manufacturers and merchants are "compelled" to make and supply this bad old form of closet; some years ago we were told by a manufacturer that he was compelled to make and stock it for his country and foreign trade, and that he "regretted" that its sale averaged a dozen a week. Messrs. Young & Marten also send us their "Tariff No. 16," which is the most complete they have yet issued, containing as it does 120 pages of illustrated letter-press and a few pages of chromo-lithography. It includes illustrations, descriptions, and prices of a large selection of stock articles, including traps, waste-preventing flushing cisterns, cowls, ventilators, brasswork, plumbers' tools, pumps, baths, water-closets, lavatories, urinals, leaded glasswork, oils, colours, varnishes, chimney-pieces, tile hearths, stoves, grates, ranges, locks, door furniture, builders' ironmongery, &c. Both these catalogues will be found exceedingly useful in every builder's office.

THE ENGLISH IRON TRADE.—There continues to be little of note stirring in the iron trade, which maintains its lethargic condition. The Durham coal-miners' strike seems as far off settlement as ever, and while this prevails business must necessarily be withheld. Prices throughout the trade are fairly upheld; but the orders coming forward are extremely limited. In the steel trade, the furnaces at Barrow have been re-started. Tinplates remain dull. The return to work of the engineers

COMPETITIONS, CONTRACTS, AND PUBLIC APPOINTMENTS.

COMPETITIONS.

Nature of Work.	By whom Advertised.	Premium.	Designs to be delivered.
*Extension of Queen's Parade	Kingston-upon-Thames Corporation	21l. & 10l. 10s.	June 13
*Municipal Technical School	Manchester Corp.	Not stated	Aug. 2

CONTRACTS.

Nature of Work or Materials.	By Whom Required.	Architect, Surveyor, or Engineer.	Tenders to be delivered.
Alterations to Workhouse, Ponteland	Castle Ward Union	W. Lister Newcombe	May 3
*Thirty-one Houses, Penrhiwceiber, Glam.	Cyn Cynon Building Club	C. Bailey	do.
Granite Road Metal	Glows Town Council	Official	do.
*Broken Granite	Middlesex C. C.	do.	May 4
*Reclamation Works	Lewisham Bd. of Wks	do.	do.
Boundary Walls &c. for S. Pontypridd	Llanwonno School Bd.	do.	do.
Schools, House, &c. Westmoor	Longbinton Sch. Bd.	Wm. Hope	do.
Linoleum Works, Extension to Offices, &c. Northallerton	Tarpaulin, Brattice Cloth, and Linoleum Co. Lim.	....	do.
Schools, House, Offices, &c.	Knottingley (Leeds) School Board	J. M. Greaves	do.
Villa, Stabling, Walls, &c. Cogenhoe, Northampton	....	W. H. Dyer & Sons	do.
Sewerage Works	Chester-le-Street U.R.S.A.	D. Balfour	May 5
Public Hall and Institute, Treharris, Glam.	Treharris Public Hall & Institute (Lim.)	....	do.
*Gasholder Tank in Concrete	Caterham and District Gas, &c. Co.	C. W. Anderson	do.
Cast-iron Water-pipes, Valves, Hydrants, &c.	Blaydon Local Board	Michael Hawdon	do.
Large Additions to Hydropathic Establishment	Harrogate Hydropathic Co.	J. Lane Fox	do.
*Slaughterhouses, Cattle Market, &c.	Aberdare Market Co.	T. Roderick	do.
*Concrete Gasholder Tank	East Grinstead Gas & Water Co.	Official	do.
*Cleansing and Painting Station Roofing St. Pancras	Midland Railway	do.	May 6
*Extension of Fitting Shop, Manchester	do.	do.	do.
*Extension of Gas Works, Chelmsford	do.	do.	do.
*Building for Electric Light Machinery, Derby	do.	do.	do.
Whinstone Road Metal (1,300 tons)	Great Driffield Loc. B.	do.	May 7
*Police Station and Lock-up House, &c.	Breconshire C. C.	do.	do.
Asphalting or Tar Pavement (3,800 yds.)	South Gosforth L. B.	C. J. Banff	do.
*Painting, Repairs, and Alterations to Infirmary	St. Marylebone Guar.	Official	May 9

CONTRACTS.—Continued.

Nature of Work or Materials.	By Whom Required.	Architect, Surveyor, or Engineer.	Tenders to be delivered.
*Wood Paving Blocks	St. Marylebone Vestry	Official	May
*Supply of Road Materials	Kingston-upon-Thames Corporation	do.	do.
Enlargement of School, Waunarlwydd	Swansea School Board	do.	do.
Additions to School, &c. Pentre	Ystradyfodwg Sch. Bd.	J. Rees	do.
Hotel, Craigellachie, Elgin, N.B.	....	C. C. Doig	May
*Painting, &c. Workhouse	Strand Union	W. S. Cross	do.
*Making-up and Paving Roads	Fulham Vestry	W. Sykes	May
*Boundary Wall	do.	J. P. Norrington	do.
*Pipe Sewer, &c.	do.	do.	do.
*Wood Paving, &c.	do.	do.	do.
Rebuilding "Royal Oak," Machen, Newport (Mon.)	Griffiths, Bros. (Lim.)	E. A. Lansdowne	do.
Golf Club House, Stotfield, Elgin, N.B.	....	A. & W. Reid	do.
*Iron and Stoneware Pipe Sewers	Watford U.R.S.A.	Urban Smith	May
*Sewerage and Drainage Works	St. Albans Corp.	Official	May
*New Wards, Staircase, Bath Accommodation, &c.	Stoke-on-Trent Guar.	do.	May
*Painting and Decorating Town Hall	Leeds Corporation	do.	May
*Sheds, Latrines, &c. Penzance	Admiralty	do.	May
*Sewerage Works	Fareham Loc. Bd.	do.	May
*New Class-room at Girls' School	Walthamstow Sch. Bd.	W. A. Longmore	May
Settling Tanks and Sewerage Works	Methley Loc. Bd.	J. Richardson	May
*Iron Swing Bridge	Sandwich Corp.	A. J. Catt	May
Warehouse and Offices, Bridge-street, Bristol	Lindrea & Co.	H. J. Jones	No date
Forty-three Houses, Gilfach Goch, near Bridgend	Evanstown Bldg. Soc.	Official	do.
Additions to Workhouse	Stoke-upon-Trent Union	do.	do.
Residence for Chief Constable, St. Giles'-street	Northampton Corp.	do.	do.
Semi-detached Villas, South Wylam, Newcastle-on-Tyne	Williamson & Gibson	....	do
Smith's Shop, Additions to House, &c. Watergate, Ripperholme, Halifax	....	Raymond Berry	do.
Alterations, "Old Golden Lion" Hotel, Leeds	Henry France	T. Winn	do.
Chapel and Schools, Rotherham	....	Thomas Howdill	do.
Two Shops, Weather, Sheffield	T. Blow	A. Appleby	do.
*Painting Works, Woolwich	War Department	Official	do.
*Schoolmaster's, &c. Quarters, Warwick	do.	do.	do.

PUBLIC APPOINTMENTS.

Nature of Appointment.	By whom Advertised.	Salary.	Applications to be in
*Clerk of Works	Wakefield Corp.	Not stated	May
*Assistant Inspector of Nuisances	Plymouth T. C.	80l. rising to 110l.	May

Those marked with an Asterisk (*) are advertised in this Number. Competitions, p. iv. Contracts, pp. iv., vi., & viii. Public Appointments, p. xx. & xxi.

on the Tyne who have been on strike is to be recorded with satisfaction. Ship-building is rather depressed, except on the west coast. The coal trade is rather quiet.—*Iron.*

EDINBURGH ARCHITECTURAL ASSOCIATION.—On the 23rd inst. about twenty members of this Association paid a visit to Falkirk and Callendar House and grounds, the latter being thrown open to them by Mr. Forbes of Callendar. The excursionists afterwards visited the Antonine Wall, which runs through Callendar grounds.

THE LONDON WATER QUESTION.—Apart from the fact that our water charges are unfair, and our supply not what it should be, advocates of the tedious process of a Royal Commission should bear in mind that London is growing at an alarming rate, and, as the sources of supply are not being increased, the quality of the water will deteriorate as the quantity required increases. We are now face to face with the fact that we are asking the London water companies to supply us with eight million gallons daily more than we required last year. Every day we postpone the solution we are nearing the great water famine.—*Local Government Journal.*

ENAMELLED METAL.—Messrs. Angles Ward & Co. send some specimens of coloured enamel on thin metal, representing a process which they have patented and by which they claim that colour can be applied in this way much more cheaply than by any other process. Of course the value of the special system entirely depends on this, as enamelling on metal is nothing new. The specimens sent are very poor in design, but they seem to show that good colour effects may be produced by the process, in the hands of a good designer.

FORTHCOMING EXHIBITION OF INDIAN METALWORK.—An exhibition of Indian metalwork is to be held at the Imperial Institute early in June next. The Maharajah of Jeypore is sending a very complete collection, and it is expected that his example will be followed by the rulers of other feudatory states. The British authorities, as well as private owners in India, have been specially invited to contribute any artistic specimens in their possession. Many collectors at home promise interesting exhibits, and the show of armour and weapons ought to be unique. There is to be a section solely for the purpose of discovering how dealers can meet the increasing demand for metalware manufactured in our Eastern Empire. Some valuable jewellery will be displayed in a separate apartment. A suite of fine rooms has been set apart for the exhibition, and an experienced committee, with Surgeon Lieutenant-Colonel Hendley as its honorary secretary, is actively engaged in the work of organisation.—*Iron and Coal Trades Review.*

THE EARLY DAYS OF KEENE'S CEMENT.—Looking casually through the number of the *Printers, Stationers, and Kindred Trades' Effective Advertiser* for March, we met with a few lines referring to the early days of Keene's cement in a biographical notice of Mr. E. G. Tomsett, a well-known printer and a prominent supporter of the printing trade charities, who is now connected with Lloyd's *Register of Shipping.* Mr. Tomsett, it is stated, "was born at Alfort, near Fort Charenton, in France, where his father had settled a few years previously in conjunction with Mr. R. Keene, the inventor of Keene's patent cement, and set up a factory for turning out large quantities of cement, mosaic pavement, and imitation alabaster, for clock pedestals, then coming into favour." It is stated that Messrs. Keene and Tomsett found it necessary to carry on their business in the part of France referred to "in consequence of some quarries of a particular stone, essential to their business, being there." Mr. Tomsett and his family left France in 1848.

A BIG RAFT.—It is understood that the idea of towing large quantities of logs in cigar-shaped rafts is becoming very popular on the Pacific coast, and is giving, generally, success. The inventor of the Joggins system, Mr. H. H. Robinson, of St. John, N.B., is constructing a large raft of timber at Fort Bragg, for the Fort Bragg Redwood Company, and which, when completed, will be transported to San Francisco. The raft will carry a crew, and will consequently be equipped with rudder and steering gear, besides a complete code of signals for night and day use, anchors, chain, &c. The affair will be 360 by 36 ft. at the centre, and will contain 3,000 piling sticks.—*Timber.*

LEGAL.

LAW REPORTS IN "THE BUILDER."—The *Building and Engineering Journal* (Melbourne) for March 19 last says that at the last meeting of the Builders' and Contractors' Association of New South Wales, Mr. Murray suggested that a small committee should be formed for the purpose of collating all law records relating to building suits. Mr. Murray instanced a case in which he had searched the London *Builder* for eleven years back to find a case parallel to the one in which he was then engaged, and had succeeded in finding such an instance, and, although this particular case was unknown to the lawyers, the judge who was conducting Mr. Murray's case admitted the *Builder* as evidence, and Mr. Murray won his suit.

MEETINGS.

MONDAY, MAY 2.

Royal Institute of British Architects.—Annual General Meeting, to discuss the Annual Report of the Council. 8 p.m.

Royal Institution.—Annual Meeting. 5 p.m.

Victoria Institute.—Sir C. Wilson on "The Past and Present Water Supply of Palestine." 8 p.m.

Society of Engineers.—Mr. S. H. Cox on "Dry Crushing Machinery." 7.30 p.m.

Society of Arts (Cantor Lectures).—Dr. Percy Frankland on "Recent Bacteriological and Chemi[cal] Research in Connexion with the Fermentati[on] Industries." I. 8 p.m.

Liverpool Architectural Society.—Annual Gene[ral] Meeting: President's Closing Address.

TUESDAY, MAY 3.

Institution of Civil Engineers.—Further discussion [on] Mr. James Swinburne's paper on "Electrical-Meas[ur]ing Instruments." 8 p.m.

Institute of Builders.—Dinner at "The Mon[ico]," Piccadilly-circus, W. 6.30 p.m.

Royal Institution.—Professor T. G. Bonney on "T[he] Sculpturing of Britain,—its Later Stages." II. 3 p.[m.]

Society of Biblical Archæology.—8 p.m.

Glasgow Architectural Association.—Mr. A. Fryers [on] "Half-Timber Work." 8 p.m.

WEDNESDAY, MAY 4.

Royal Archæological Institute.—Mr. F. C. J. Spur[rell] on "Early Painting and Colours from Medum." 4 p.[m.]

Society of Arts.—Mr. James N. Shoolbred on "[The] Bradford Corporation Electricity Supply." 8 p.m.

Builders' Foremen and Clerks of Works' Institutio[n].—Ordinary meeting. 8.30 p.m.

THURSDAY, MAY 5.

Institution of Mechanical Engineers.—Ordi[nary] General Meeting. (1.) Inaugural Address by [the] President, Dr. W. Anderson. (2.) Two papers to [be] read. 7.30 p.m.

Royal Institution.—Professor Dewar on "[The] Chemistry of Gases."—II. 3 p.m.

Society of Antiquaries.—8.30 p.m.

FRIDAY, MAY 6.

Architectural Association.—Members' *Soirée.*

Institution of Mechanical Engineers.—Ordi[nary] General Meeting (continued). 7.30 p.m.

Royal Institution.—Captain Abney on "The Sensi[tive]ness of the Eye to Light and Colour." 9 p.m.

SATURDAY, MAY 7.

Edinburgh Architectural Association.—Visit [to] Pitteadie Castle (ruin), Seebeld Tower.

RECENT PATENTS:

ABSTRACTS OF SPECIFICATIONS.

8,020.—NAILS: *A. Chandler.*—This patent refer[s to] an improvement in horticultural nails, which for[m a] kind of bracket or support to clip the branches or li[mbs] of trees and plants, and secure the same to the w[all,] fence, or trellis work. On or over the head of [a] suitable nail a form of soft metal, such as lead, is fi[xed,] provided with a finger, rectangular and flattened [of] sheet metal. Two modes of fixing this soft metal t[o the] nail are given in the specification. The nail [thus] formed can be driven in in the usual way, and th[e] finger part can be bent round or over the branc[h or] limb of the tree or plant by means of the thum[b or] finger without injury to the tree or plant.

480.—KILNS: *H. Warrington.*—This specificatio[n de]scribes an improvement in ovens for bricks, earthen[ware,] porcelain, and similar materials. The improvement [con]sists in forming such ovens in the form of two

:utrie chambers, which can be either placed in com- nunication with one another, or isolated as required.

9,710.—VENTILATORS: *E. Copland.*—The object of this nvention is to produce a ventilator combining the dvantages of the sliding and the hopper form of entilation without their disadvantages. The inventor roposes to make the ventilator of the sliding form, roviding it with the requisite means for raising and owering, and on the inside of the window or other lace to which the ventilator may be placed is securely ttached a hopper immediately in front of the sliding 'entilator, the hopper being open at the top, and closed ir-tight at the sides and front. By this construction he entering air is directed towards the ceiling or top of he room, or other place, while the entry of air can be egulated at will.

323.—FLOORS: *A. F. Whittome.*—This invention con- ists of an improved method of laying solid wood-block loors, formed with pieces of fir or other timber, ectangular on the upper surface, either bevelled, or therwise on the lower edges. The essential feature onsists in the method of keying or securing the adjoin- ng pieces together, which is effected by cutting liagonal grooves in edges at each of the four angles of he block, and inserting a rectangular tongue in such a nanner as to key together the four angles of each of the our blocks adjoining, and by this means to obtain the ffect of a solid continuous floor. Each block may be edded in sand on a foundation of concrete.

NEW APPLICATIONS FOR LETTERS PATENT.

April 11.—6,900, R. Gibbs and E. Maddock, Ventila- ors and Chimney-cowls.—6,910, F. Pigott, Manufacture f Greenhouses and all other Buildings requiring Sash- lars and Construction of the Sash-bars.—6,920, A. ohnson, Window-fastener.—6,938, G. Laurence, chool Buildings.—6,940, G. Hayes, Construction of Buildings and Fire-proofing same.—6,947, A. Brookes, Iinges.—6,950, S. Hellyer, Water-closets, &c.—6,956, J. Iarris, Closet-fittings.

April 12.—7,008, W. Hayes, Electric Light Fittings.— ,016, J. McFarlane and W. Edger, Electric Fittings.— ,023, T. Riley, Hinge with Pin and Plate.—7,034, F. Villis and R. Astley, Constructing and Fixing Fireproof- loors.—7,053, W. Wythe, Window-shades.—7,071, W. Beaumont, Pneumatic Apparatus for Wood-working lachinery.—7,084, W. Bodin, Paints, &c.—7,085, B. nd E. Joberns, Brick-making Machines.

April 13.—7,106, G. Haynes and F. Mott, Fasteners or Window-sashes.

April 14.—7,205, A. Leo, Portable Collapsible Ladders. ,224, H. Thompson, Grates or Stoves.—7,225, D. IacDonald and others, Sash-locks.—7,248, H. and J. Varrington, Bricks for Building Purposes.

April 16.—7,270, R. Huppertsberg, Artificial Bituminous Stone.—7,278, D. Sutherland, Automatic Flushing Apparatus.—7,280, J. Simpson, Waste Water- losets.—7,308, J. Briggs, Kilns for Burning Limestone, Cement, &c.—7,312, W. Hull and others, Burglar Alarm Devices.

PROVISIONAL SPECIFICATIONS ACCEPTED.

5,644, A. Lamplough, Sash-fasteners.—5,647, J. Dungry, Fittings for Gas and other similar Pipes and Tubes.—5,801, S. Cook and J. Chambers, Sash-fasteners. -6,037, T. and W. Starkey, Door Catches for holding loors.—6,042, B. Bloom and A. Kotin, Closing Doors.— ,104, C. Luther, Cement or Glue for joining wood.— ,170, G. Bartlett, Water-closets.

COMPLETE SPECIFICATIONS ACCEPTED.

(Open to Opposition for Two Months.)

9,892, S. Gratrix and brother, and H. Blocklesby, Flushing Cisterns.—10,045, S. Wilde, Clip to prevent indows rattling.—10,073, J. Bennett, Roof Tile and ethod of laying and fixing the same on roof framings. 11,013, C. Lewin, Automatic Safety Fastenings for indow-sashes or other Sliding Sashes and Panels.— ,221, W. and R. Smith, Chimney-cowl or Ventilator.

SOME RECENT SALES OF PROPERTY:

ESTATE EXCHANGE REPORT.

APRIL 20.—By *Crafter, Harris, & Co.*: "The Coopers' rms," Old Kent-rd., f., 2,250*l.*; an improved rental of *l.*, Boundary-rd., Walthamstow, u.t. 65 yrs., with version, 550*l.* By *Dann & Lucas*: An enclosure of ilt land, Horton Kirby, Kent, 1a. 0r. 32p., 260*l.*; a plot freehold pasture land, 1a. 1r. 10p., 165*l.*

APRIL 21.—By *Prince & Lewis*: 63 to 79 (odd), Banstead- .; and 39, Tappersfield-rd., Nunhead, u.t. 84 yrs., g.r. *l.* 10s., 500*l.*—By *E. & H. Lumley*: Nos. 95 and 164, ew Bond-st.—Corporation lease, 31,600*l.*; "The White on" public-house, Brook-st., Hanover-sq.; and 13, 14, d 15, Avery-row—Corporation lease, 3,800*l.*—By *insell & Rowe*: The residence, "Broughton," untain-rd., Norwood, u.t. 45 yrs., g.r. 17*l.*, 0*l.*—By *J. H. Hibbard*: 167, Elderfield-rd., apton, u.t. 86 yrs., g.r. 4*l.* 10s., 205*l.*; 41, Caven- sh-rd., Harringay, u.t. 95 yrs., g.r. 7*l.* 7s., r. 34*l.*, 330*l.*— *Newbon & Co.*: 44, 46 and 48, Mayton-st., Holloway, t., 68 yrs., g.r., 15*l.* 15s., r. 96*l.*, 735*l.*; 31, Brunswick- ., u.t. 58 yrs., g.r. 7*l.*, r. 27*l.*, 205*l.*; 59, Chalton-st., mers Town, u.t. 36 yrs., g.r. 15*l.*, r. 65*l.*, 245*l.*; 107 and 9, Shakespeare-rd., Stoke Newington, u.t. 60 yrs., g.r. *l.*, r. 56*l.*, 495*l.*; 227, Markhouse-rd., Walthamstow, f., 5*l.*; 19, Albert-rd., f., 355*l.*—By *Jenkins & Son* (at eptford): 5 and 7, St. James's-rd., New Cross, u.t. 72 s., g.r. 14*l.* 14s., r. 84*l.*, 900*l.*; 72 and 74, Shardeloes-rd., t. 72 yrs., g.r. 8*l.* 10s., r. 56*l.*, 525*l.*

APRIL 22.—By *Jones, Lang, & Co.*: Nos. 70 and 70A, ldermanbury, f., area 1,700 ft., r. 400*l.*, 10,700*l.*; 72, ldermanbury, f., area 940 ft., r. 415*l.*, 5,300*l.*—By *Baker Sons*: 4, High-st., Whitechapel, f., 3,720*l.*; "The rown and Anchor" beer-house, St. Albans, f., r. 25*l.*, 5*l.*; "Albert Villa," Fallow-lane, Finchley, f., 700*l.*— *y Furber, Price, & Furber*: i.g.r., of 63*l.*, Aldenham-st., mers Town, u.t. 30 yrs., g.r. 24*l.*, 480*l.*; i.g.r. of 50*l.*, astings-st., Burton-cres., u.t. 14 yrs., g.r. 15*l.* 15s., 250*l.*; .r. of 30*l.*, Jeffrey's-st., &c., Camden Town, u.t. yrs., g.r. 7*l.*, 340*l.*; No. 333, Wandsworth-rd., 58*l.*, and a g.r. of 11*l.*, u.t. 42 yrs., g.r. 26*l.*, *l.*; a profit rental of 60*l.*, South Hill-pk., Hamp- ead, u.t. 63 yrs., 1,000*l.*; 499 and 501, High-rd., iswick, u.t. 69 yrs., g.r. 12*l.*, 735*l.*; "The Duke of mbridge" public-house, Cale-st., Chelsea, u.t. 16 yrs., r. 4*l.*, r. 60*l.*, 450*l.*; King's-rd., i.g.r. of 35*l.* 10s., u.t. 61 s., g.r. 1*l.*, 625*l.*; i.g.r. of 27*l.* u.t. 64 yrs., g.r. 1*l.*, 480*l.*; i.g.r. of 63*l.*, Claribel-rd., Brixton, u.t. 22 yrs., g.r. nil, 730*l.*; 20, Rush-hill-rd., Lavender Hill, u.t. 79 yrs., g.r. 6*l.*, r. 32*l.*, 265*l.*—By *Field & Sons*: 90, Park-st., South- wark, f., r. 50*l.*, 780*l.*; 19, 20, and 21, Lent-pl., f., r. 85*l.* 16s., 760*l.*; 65, Mervan-rd., Brixton, u.t. 81 yrs., g.r. 7*l.* 7s., r. 32*l.*, 270*l.*; 2, Whitecross-st., Borough, u.t. 16 yrs., g.r. 8*l.*, r. 20*l.*, 21*l.*; 53 and 54, Woolwich-rd., Belvedere, Kent., u.t. 70 yrs., g.r. 9*l.*, r. 30*l.* 10s., 200*l.*; 156, High-st., Borough, u.t. 10 yrs., g.r. 150*l.*, r. 395*l.*, 660*l.*

[*Contractions used in these lists.*—F.g.r. for freehold ground-rent; l.g.r. for leasehold ground-rent; i.g.r. for improved ground-rent; g.r. for ground-rent; r. for rent; f. for freehold; c. for copyhold; l. for leasehold; e.r. for estimated rental; u.t. for unexpired term; p.a. for per annum; yrs. for years; st. for street; rd. for road; sq. for square; pl. for place; ter. for terrace; cres. for crescent; yd. for yard, &c.]

PRICES CURRENT OF MATERIALS.

TIMBER.		
Greenheart, B.G. ton	9/0/0	0/0/0
Teak, E.I. .. load	10/0/0	15/0/0
Sequoia, U.S. ft. cu.	2/3	3/0
Ash, Canada load	2/10/0	4/0/0
Birch, do.	3/5/0	4/10/0
Elm, do.	3/10/0	4/15/0
Fir, Dantsic, &c.	1/10/0	3/10/0
Oak, do.	3/0/0	5/5/0
Canada........	5/10/0	7/0/0
Pine, Canada red	2/10/0	3/10/0
Do. yellow	2/10/0	5/0/0
Lath, D'ntsic, fath	5/0/0	6/0/0
St. Petersburg	5/0/0	7/0/0
Deals, Finland, 2nd & 1st std 100	8/10/0	10/0/0
Do. 4th & 3rd ..	7/0/0	8/10/0
Do. Riga	7/0/0	8/0/0
St. Petersburg, 1st yellow ..	11/0/0	15/0/0
Do. 2nd yellow	8/0/0	10/0/0
Do. white	7/10/0	11/0/0
Swedish	8/0/0	16/0/0
White Sea	8/0/0	18/0/0
Canada, Pine 1st	20/0/0	26/0/0
Do. do. 2nd....	14/10/0	16/0/0
Do. do. 3rd, &c.	8/0/0	10/5/0
Do. Spruce, 1st	8/10/0	11/0/0
Do. do. 3rd & 2nd..........	6/15/0	8/0/0
New Brunswick	7/0/0	7/10/0
Battens, all kinds	3/10/0	15/10/0
Flooring Boards, sq., 1 in. prep. 1st	0/8/0	0/14/0
Do. 2nd........	0/7/0	0/11/0
Other qualities	0/4/0	0/9/0
Cedar, Cuba .. ft.	/3½	/4½
Honduras, &c.	/3½	/4
Mahogany, Cuba.	/4½	/6½
St. Domingo, cargo av	/4½	2/0
Mexican do. do	/4	/6
Tobasco do. do	/5½	/7
Honduras do..	/5½	/6½
Box, Turkey ton	4/0/0	13/0/0
Rose, Rio........	10/0/0	20/0/0
Bahia	8/0/0	16/0/0
Satin, St. Domingo ....ft.	0/0/8	0/1/8

TIMBER (continued).		
Satin, Porto Rico	0/0/8	0/1/6
Walnut, Italian..	0/0/3½	0/0/7
METALS.		
IRON—Pig, in Scotland ....ton	2/1/2	0/0/0
Bar, Welsh, in London........	5/17/6	6/0/0
Do. do. at works in Wales	5/7/6	5/10/0
Do. Staffordshire, in London	6/5/0	6/15/0
COPPER—British, cake and ingot	48/10/0	49/0/0
Best selected ..	49/10/0	50/0/0
Sheets, strong..	59/0/0	0/0/0
Chili, bars	45/2/6	45/10/0
YELLOW METAL lb.	0/0/5¼	0/0/5¾
LEAD—Pig, Spanish ....ton	10/10/0	10/11/3
English, com. brands	10/15/0	10/17/6
Sheet, English, 3 lbs. per sq. ft. and upwards ..	12/5/0	0/0/0
Pipe	12/15/0	0/0/0
ZINC—English sheet ......ton	23/10/0	0/0/0
Vieille Montagne..........	26/5/0	0/0/0
TIN—Straits	94/7/6	94/17/6
Australian	94/7/6	94/17/6
English Ingots	96/0/0	96/10/0
OILS.		
Linseed ......ton	18/5/0	18/10/0
Cocoanut, Cochin	24/10/0	0/0/0
Do. Ceylon	22/0/0	0/0/0
Palm, Lagos	22/5/0	22/10/0
Rapeseed, English pale	24/10/0	25/0/0
Do. brown	23/0/0	0/0/0
Cottonseed ref. ..	19/0/0	0/0/0
Oleine	21/10/0	22/10/0
Lubricating, U.S.	4/0/0	6/0/0
Do. refined	5/0/0	10/0/0
TAR—Stockholm barrel	0/19/0	1/0/0
Archangel	0/12/4	0/0/0

TENDERS.

[Communications for insertion under this heading should be addressed to "The Editor," and must reach us *not later than* 12 *noon on Thursdays.*]

ANGLESEY.—For work on the Marquis of Anglesey's Estate, Anglesey. Mr. Wm. E. Jones, architect, Graig, Llanfair, P.G.:—

Farm House, Dairy, and Cattle Sheds, Caeuchaf.

D. Owen	£970	Thos. Griffith	£780
W. O. Daniel	827	R. Owen & Sons, Pentraeth*	700
John Owen	815		

* Accepted.

Cattle Sheds, Cefn Poeth, Llangefni.

Lewis Parry	£262	0	W. & O. Pritchard	£200	0
G. Parry	230	10	Thos. Jones	179	4
John Pritchard & Son	220	0	Thos. Griffith, Tynygongl, Anglesey*	170	0
John Owen	214	0			

* Accepted.

Farm Buildings, Budlu Penymynydd.

L. Parry	£797	0	Owen Thomas	£520	0
W. & O. Pritchard	705	0	Thomas Griffith, Tynygongl, Anglesey*	510	0
John Owen	600	0			
G. Parry	520	17			

* Accepted.

Cattle Sheds, &c., Carnauddu, Gaerwen.

Lewis Parry	£536	0	Griffith Parry, Llanddeniolfab (accepted)	319	15
W. & O. Pritchard	386	0	John Pritchard & Son	317	0

AYLESBURY.—For the erection of a new farm-house, for the Trustees of Harding's Charity. Mr. W. F. Taylor, architect, Aylesbury:—

Webster & Cannon	£635	0	G. Green	£577	0
S. Grist	588	18	Ball & Mayne	530	0

[All of Aylesbury.]

EVIE (Orkney).—For erecting Volunteer Artillery Drill Hall and Instructor's cottage, Evie, Orkney, for Colonel J. W. Balfour. Mr. T. S. Peace, architect, Kirkwall:—

Gerimal & Shurrie	£815	0	J. Taylor	£694	8
Jas. M. Chalmers & Son	760	0	Saml. Firth, Harray*	613	0
J. Garrioch	694	0			

* Accepted.

LONDON.—For pulling down and rebuilding No. 3, Palace-street, and altering and repairing Nos. 1, 3, and 5, Buckingham Palace-road, and No. 1, Palace-street, S.W., for Mr. John Gooch. Mr. Geo. Edwards, architect, 52, Cannon-street:—

Martin Wells & Co.	£1,899	Knight	£1,750
Barnett	1,896	Drake	1,648
C. Wall	1,873	Stimpson & Co.	1,623
Staines & Son	1,864	Ward & Lamble	1,611
Stevens	1,849	Scharien & Co.	1,483
Leslie & Knight	1,796		

LONDON.—For alterations at No. 44, King William-street, for the Aerated Bread Company. Mr. Geo. Edwards, architect, 52, Cannon-street:—

C. Wall	£576	Scharien & Co.	£338
Weld & Lamble	421		

LONDON.—For the erection of a new warehouse, for Messrs. Blenkiron & Son, Bexton. Mr. Frank E. Smee, architect, 12, West Smithfield, E.C.:—

Minton & Co.	£490	Lamb	333
Johnson	368	Hawtrey & Son	320

LONDON.—Accepted for making-up road, &c., at Peckham Rye. Mr. F. A. Powell, surveyor, Kennington-road:—

J. Bowles, Mendip-wharf, Battersea.............. £349 10 0

LONDON.—For alterations and additions to the "Swiss Stores," Cranbourne-street, W.C., for Mr. E. Maddick. Mr. H. I. Newton, architect, 49, Victoria-street, Westminster, S.W.:—

Edwards & Medway	£670	C. Deering & Son	£628
J. Milroy	650	R. Lamble, Kentish Town*	621

*Accepted.

LONDON.—For rebuilding the "Green Man" public-house and two shops, Old-Kent-road, S.E., for Mr. G. Homer. Mr. Bruce J. Capell, architect, 70, Whitechapel-road, E. Quantities by Mr. Max Clarke, 4, Queen's-square, Bloomsbury:—

	Public-house.	Shops.	Total.
Mills	£5,300	£2,970	£8,270
Todd	5,134	2,845	7,979
Harris & Wardrop	4,989	2,744	7,733
Whitehead	4,980	2,650	7,630
Jerrard	4,679	2,593	7,272
Courtney & Fairbairn	4,642	2,534	7,176
Young & Lonsdale*	4,631	2,544	7,175

* Accepted.

LONDON.—For erecting the new Church of St. Barnabas, Dulwich. Messrs. Oliver & Leeson, architects, Bank Chambers, Newcastle-on-Tyne:—

				Alternative.		Fencing.			Total.	
Botterill	£6,200	0	0	£589	0	£300	0	0	£7,053	0
J. P. Groome	5,955	17	0	320	0	600	0	0	6,873	0
Mid-Kent Bldg. Co.	6,156	0	0	444	0	178	0	0	6,778	0
Wm. Purniss	5,928	19	0	—		717	3	8	6,646	0
Jackson Bros.	5,628	0	0	554	15	430	0	0	6,612	0
R. E. Nightingale	5,742	0	0	468	0	394	0	0	6,604	0
W. J. Mitchell	5,819	0	0	276	0	350	0	0	6,445	0
Cornish & Garner	5,458	0	0	554	0	277	0	0	6,289	0
Reed, Blight, & Co.	5,379	0	0	298	0	323	0	0	6,000	0
P. Houghton	5,055	0	0	575	0	349	0	0	5,970	0
Jos. Ellistre	5,150	0	0	443	0	307	0	0	5,900	0
J. C. Bowyer	5,129	0	0	338	0	226	0	0	5,606	0
J. W. Sawyer	4,769	0	0	650	0	220	0	0	5,636	0
W. Wallis	4,987	0	0	300	0	243	0	0	5,530	0
Wm. Shepherd	4,975	0	0	342	0	216	0	0	5,532	0
W. H. Lorden & Son	4,910	0	0	349	0	240	0	0	5,499	0
Wm. Brooks	4,860	0	0	250	0	350	0	0	5,460	0
Goddard & Son	4,681	17	0	207	3	287	0	0	5,172	0
Trappitt & Batley	4,685	0	0	83	10	363	0	0	5,131	10
Richardson	4,065	9	9	260	0	251	10	3	4,577	0

LONDON.—For alterations to Nos. 195 and 197, New Cross-road, for the London and South-Western Bank. Messrs. Truefitt, architects, 5, Bloomsbury-square. Quantities by Messrs. Morris, Brane, & Son:—

Bunning & Son	£2,378	Higgs & Son	£1,940
Faulkner	1,892	J. Hunt	1,089
Legg	1,888	Balaam Bros*	1,935
Bryan & Son	1,831		

* Accepted.

LONDON.—For building new coffee factory, Bermondsey, for Messrs. W. S. Shuttleworth & Co. Mr. Arthur Vernon, architect, 29, Cockspur-street, Charing-cross:—

Cornish & Gaymer	£805	W. Shepherd	£700
W. Brooks	800	Houghton & Son	612
J. Bullers	785	C. N. Philips*	591
R. G. Battley	734		

* Accepted.

LONDON.—For alterations at "The Pelican," Southwark-street, S.E. Mr. W. Seckham Witherington, architect, 79, Mark-lane, E.C.:—

Mills	£2,190	Courtney & Fairbairn	£2,061
Sheffield Bros.	2,079	Spencer & Co.	2,050

LONDON.—For erecting proposed middle-class dwellings and shops, Green Lanes, Stoke Newington, for Mr. R. Tomlinson. Mr. Horace E. Davey, architect, Saxon-road, Selhurst, S.E. Quantities by Messrs. W. Heelis & A. F. Wrightson, Budge-row:—

Holloway Bros.	£34,415	L. & H. Roberts	£32,793
Colls & Sons	33,800	W. Downs & Co.	32,777
Patman & Fotheringham	33,081	Burman & Sons	32,600
Dearing & Sons	33,500	Kilby & Gayford	32,434
F. & H. F. Higgs	33,420	Wilmot & Sons (too late)	32,226
Perry & Co.	32,967	T. Knight, Sidcup	32,209
Lawrence & Sons	32,909		

LONDON.—For the erection of the New Central Public Library, in the Peckham-road, for the Commissioners of Public Libraries for the Parish of Camberwell. Mr. R. P. Whellock, architect, 45, Finsbury-pavement, E.C. Quantities by Messrs. Franklin & Andrews, 25, Ludgate-hill, E.C.:—

Holliday & Greenwood	£11,377	Avard	£10,360
Brooks	11,200	Tucker	10,350
Downs	10,909	Nightingale	10,223
Holloway Bros.	10,698	Balaam Bros.	10,145
Scharien	10,438	W. Richardson	10,000
H. L. Holloway	10,437	Kirk & Randall	9,920
Young & Lonsdale	10,436	J. O. Richardson	9,358
Allen & Sons	10,365	R. & E. Evans*	8,795

* Accepted.

LONDON.—Accepted for fitting up stores at 11 and 12, New Bridge-street, E.C. Mr. Alexander Gordon, architect, 101, Queen Victoria-street:—

G. H. Martin & Co., West Croydon.................... £493

LONDON.—For repairs at the Licensed Victuallers' Asylum, Old Kent-road, London, S.E. Mr. W. F. Potter, architect:—

Courtney & Fairbairn	£480	B. Cook & Sons	£230
R. Eddie	448	Walker Bros., Poplar*	171
S. Hayworth & Sons	324	W. Wythe	150
Ditcham & Co.	233		

* Accepted.

Restoration of Stone-cornice and Coping-stones to Matron's House.

	Stone.		Cement.	
W. Wythe	£180	0	£73	0
Courtney & Fairbairn	141	10	75	10
Ditcham & Co.	127	0	50	0
S. Heyworth & Sons	119	16	58	8
R. Eddie	113	0	56	0
B. Cook & Sons	110	0	46	10
Walker Bros., Poplar*	107	0	50	0

* Accepted to execute the work in Portland stone.

LONDON.—For pulling down and rebuilding No. 189, Upper-street, for Mr. Loewe. Messrs. Henson & Whitehead, architects, 7, Finsbury-square, E.C.:—

Coombs	£880	Houghton	£772
Chessum	790	Marshall	750

LONDON.—For alterations and additions to Nos. 9 and 10, Norland-terrace, Notting-hill. Mr. C. L. R. Tudor, architect, 81, Lancaster-road, Notting-hill. Quantities by Mr. C. J. Ford, 4, Mitre-court, Fleet-street, E.C.:—

Watts	£1,088	Nash	£740
Colley	797	Tozer	739
Cowley & Drake	756	Moody (accepted)	730

LONDON.—Accepted for the erection of new Wesleyan Chapel and vestries at Upton-park. Mr. F. Boreham, architect, 73, Finsbury-pavement, E.C.:—

William Jelley, Wood-green £3,033 0 0

MARGATE.—For painting and decorating at the Royal Assembly Rooms, Margate. Mr. W. Graves, architect, Winchester House, E.C. :—

Bowyer	£630	Brown	£420
Houghton	573	Parsmor	395
Pitman	495	London	390

NEASDEN (Middlesex).—Accepted for the erection of eight villa residences in Lansdowne-grove, for Mr. R. Richards. Mr. Thos S. Stephens, architect, Acton :—

H. G. Heywood £3,200 0 0

SHEFFIELD.—For new roof and other works, at the Ruskin Museum, Meersbrook Park, Sheffield :—

T. Lowe & Son	£747	6	6	C. Skelton	£649	4	0
Ash, Sun, & Biggin	680	0	0	T. Fish & Son, Nottingham*	603	8	8
Chadwick	678	0	8	S. Warburton	534	0	0
Chambers & Son	665	18	8				
J. Eshelby	650	18	8	* Accepted.			

[Borough Surveyor's estimate, £600.]

STOCKPORT.—For the construction of a bridge over the river Mersey, near Wellington bridge. Mr. A. M. Fowler, engineer, 45, Great Underbank, Stockport :—

Masonry.

Smith	£6,283	0	4	C. A. Rigby & Co.	£5,351	13	8
T. & W. Meadows	5,980	0	0	Townsend & Watson	5,293	0	0
J. Broadhurst	5,803	0	0	D. Eadie, Stockport*	4,965	0	0
Dyson	5,084	0	0	* Accepted.			

Ironwork.

Stockton Forge Company	5,889	13	1	Cleveland Engineering Company	£4,626	6	5
Heenan & Froude	5,650	17	0	Jesse Tildesley	4,580	0	0
Maylock Bros.	5,391	0	0	Shewell & Co.*	4,553	0	10
Peter Smith	4,767	5	0	* Accepted.			

SURBITON.—For erecting and completing a pair of villa residences in the Ditton-road, Surbiton, for Mr. Davis Rands. Mr. R. Lane Pearce, architect, 100c, Queen Victoria-street, E.C. :—

Oldridge & Sons	£1,234	R. House & Son	£967
W. H. Gaze	1,145	Adkins Bros., Surbiton*	955

* Accepted subject to modification.

SURBITON.—For making roads and sewers on the Cranes Estate, Surbiton. Mr. Mather, surveyor :—

Cooke & Co.	£3,188	10	8	Killingback	£2,495	0	0
Neal & Co.	3,082	0	0	Atkins	2,395	9	0
Marlow & Roberts	2,989	0	0	Rigby	2,308	6	0
Bentley	2,901	0	0	Bowles	2,234	12	0
Jarvis	2,875	0	0	Hunter	2,200	0	0
Woodham & Fry	2,827	0	11	W. Cunliffe, Kingston-on-Thames*	2,193	1	7
Kavanagh	2,470	4	6	* Accepted.			

WALTON-ON-NAZE.—Accepted for constructing new Pyrne terrace, restoration, &c., No. 5 Contract. Mr. S. B. Goslin, engineer :—

B. Cooke & Co., Battersea £1,400

SUBSCRIBERS in LONDON and the SUBURBS, by prepaying at the Publishing Office, 19s. per annum (or 4s. 9d. per quarter), can ensure receiving "The Builder," by *Friday Morning's Post.*

The Builder Cathedral Series.

1891.

1. Canterbury	Jan. 3.	7. Salisbury	July 4.
2. Lichfield	Feb. 7.	8. Bristol	Aug. 1.
3. St. Alban's	Mar. 7.	9. Norwich	Sept. 5.
4. Peterborough	April 4.	10. Rochester	Oct. 3.
5. Wells	May 2.	11. Lincoln	Nov. 7.
6. Exeter	June 6.	12. Gloucester	Dec. 5.

1892.

13. St. Paul's .. .. Jan. 2.

14. Hereford	Feb. 6.	20. Worcester	Aug. 6.
15. Chichester	Mar. 5.	21. Bangor } 22. St. Asaph }	Sept. 3.
16. Ely	April 2.	23. Winchester	Oct. 1.
17. Llandaff	May 7.	24. Truro	Nov. 5.
18. Oxford	June 4.	25. St. David's	Dec. 3.
19. Southwell	July 2.		

[Further arrangements will be duly announced.]

Post-free FOURPENCE HALFPENNY each, except Nos. 1, 2, 3 and 4, which are *out of print*; but the VIEW, PLAN AND DESCRIPTION of CANTERBURY, LICHFIELD, ST. ALBAN'S, and PETERBOROUGH, have been reprinted, and they can now be had, price EIGHTPENCE each set; by post, 10d.

THE REREDOS, ST. PAUL'S.
Reprinted from "The Builder," January 29, 1888 (18 in. by 11½ in.), on stout paper, unfolded, for framing, 6d.; by post, 8d.

PORTFOLIOS,
for Preserving the Plates unfolded, 2s. 6d.; by post, 3s.

London: Office of "The Builder," 46, Catherine-street, W.C.

PUBLISHER'S NOTICES.

Registered Telegraphic Address, 'The Builder,' London.

CHARGES FOR ADVERTISEMENTS.

SITUATIONS VACANT, PARTNERSHIPS, APPRENTICESHIPS TRADE, AND GENERAL ADVERTISEMENTS.

Six lines (about fifty words) or under .... 4s. 6d.
Each additional line (about ten words) .... 0s. 6d.

Terms for Series of Trade Advertisements, also for Special Advertisements on front page, Competitions, Contracts, Sales by Auction, &c. may be obtained on application to the Publisher.

SITUATIONS WANTED.

FOUR Lines (about thirty words) or under .... 2s. 6d.
Each additional line (about ten words) .... 0s. 6d.

PREPAYMENT IS ABSOLUTELY NECESSARY.

*** Stamps must *not* be sent, but all small sums should be remitted by Cash in Registered Letter or by Money Order, payable at the Post-office Covent-garden, W.C. to
DOUGLAS FOURDRINIER, Publisher,
Addressed to No. 46, Catherine-street, W.C.

Advertisements for the current week's issue must reach the Office before THREE o'clock p.m. on THURSDAY, but those intended for the front Page should be in by TWELVE noon on WEDNESDAY.

SPECIAL.—ALTERATIONS IN STANDING ADVERTISEMENTS or ORDERS TO DISCONTINUE same must reach the Office before TEN o'clock on WEDNESDAY mornings.

The Publisher cannot be responsible for DRAWINGS, TESTIMONIALS, &c. left at the Office in reply to Advertisements, and strongly recommends that of the latter COPIES ONLY should be sent.

PERSONS Advertising in "The Builder" may have *Replies addressed to the Office,* 46, Catherine-street, Covent Garden, W.C. *free of charge.* Letters will be forwarded if addressed envelopes are sent, together with sufficient stamps to cover the postage.

AN EDITION Printed on THIN PAPER, for FOREIGN and COLONIAL CIRCULATION, is issued every week.

Now ready.

READING CASES, { NINEPENCE EACH. By Post (carefully packed), 1s.

TERMS OF SUBSCRIPTION.

"THE BUILDER" is supplied DIRECT from the Office to residents in any part of the United Kingdom at the rate of 19s. per annum PREPAID. To all parts of Europe, America, Australia, and New Zealand, 26s. per annum. To India, China, Ceylon &c., 30s. per annum. Remittances payable to DOUGLAS FOURDRINIER, Publisher, No. 46, Catherine-street, W.C.

TO CORRESPONDENTS.

W. B. C. T.—J. D. W. (too late).—G. C., "Ferrozone" is, we believe, a persalt of iron. "Polarite" is a preparation of li[...] The "International" system is in use at, amongst other p[...] Acton. For an account of the works there and of the whole pr[...] see *Builder* for April 9, 1887, p. 534.—"Bricks and Mortar" [...] week).—W. H. W. (next week).—F. W. L. (we cannot insert items twice).

All statements of facts, lists of tenders, &c., must be accomp[...] by the name and address of the sender, not necessarily for publica[...]

We are compelled to decline pointing out books and g[...] addresses.

Note.—The responsibility of signed articles, and papers re[...] public meetings, rests, of course, with the authors.

We cannot undertake to return rejected communications.

Letters or communications (beyond mere news-items) which [...] been duplicated for other journals, are NOT DESIRED.

All communications regarding literary and artistic matter sh[...] be addressed to THE EDITOR; all communications relatin[...] advertisements and other exclusively business matters shou[...] addressed to THE PUBLISHER, and not to the Editor.

Vol. LXII. No. 2570. SATURDAY, MAY 7, 1892.

ILLUSTRATIONS.

Cathedrals of England and Wales: XVII., Llandaff (West Front).—Drawn by Mr. C. E. Mallows .... *Double-Page Photo-Litho.*
Plan of Llandaff Cathedral.—Measured and Drawn by Mr. John H. James .... *Double-Page Photo-Litho.*
Cartoons for a Window.—Designed for Euston Church, Suffolk, by Mr. H. Ellis Wooldridge .... *Double-Page Ink-Photo.*
Monument in St. Neot's Church, Huntingdonshire.—Mr. Frederick A. Walters, Architect .... *Double-Page Ink-Photo.*

Blocks in Text.

Llandaff Cathedral: Supposed Chancel Arch of Bishop Urban's Church ....Page 358
First Bay of Nave, Llandaff Cathedral 358
Chapter House, Llandaff Cathedral 359
West Door, Llandaff Cathedral ....Page 3'0
The Ancient Choir Screen, Canterbury Cathedral 363
Diagrams in Students' Column: Heating by Hot Water 363, 364

CONTENTS.

Royal Academy Exhibition 349
ts of Building-Stones 351
es 352
hitecture at the Royal Academy.—II. 353
ter from Paris 354
Surveyors' Institution: Result of Fellowship Examination 355
rporated Association of Municipal and County ngineers 355
Architectural Association Spring Visits 356
hitectural Societies 356
London County Council 357
The Institute of Builders: Annual Dinner 357
Competitions 357
Llandaff Cathedral 358
Cartoons for Stained-Glass Windows, Euston Church 360
Monument to the late Mrs. Rowley, St. Neots 360
The Steeple of St. Antholin's 361
Architectural Education 361
Sir Gilbert Scott's Restorations 361
The Grissell Medal Competition 362
Safety of Ladders 362
Christ's Hospital 363
Student's Column.—Warming Buildings by Hot Water. XIX. 363
Obituary 364
General Building News 364
Sanitary and Engineering News 364
Foreign and Colonial 365
Miscellaneous 365
Capital and Labour 365
Meetings 365
Recent Patents 365
Some Recent Sales of Property 366
Tenders 367

The Royal Academy Exhibition.

CAREFUL examination of the array of pictures at Burlington House justifies the conclusion that this year's is an exhibition of more than usual interest. No doubt a good many mpant specimens of commonplace are deited on the line by Academicians who re outlived their reputation; but these s are counterbalanced by the presence of a d many very clever and interesting works men who are not Academicians, as well as some eminent R.A.'s who are quite at their t in the present exhibition.

e picture of the year is unquestionably .Orchardson's "St. Helena, 1816; Napoleon tating to Count Las Cases the history of campaigns" (173). Mr. Orchardson is one the few English painters of the day whose rks, admirable and conscientious as they in execution, have an intellectual interest te beyond that which arises from mere ll in technique. The figure of Napoleon the cocked hat and grey overcoat has been nted hundreds of times, well, badly, and ifferently: Mr. Orchardson has endeavoured show the man without his war-paint. cording to a frequent practice with this nter, there are but two figures on this her large canvas, each of which is the plement or balance to the other. Napoleon, he ordinary dress of the period, stands in middle of the floor, his arms behind him, face fixed on the large map which lies for moment above the others on the floor, t down at one end by a book, and at the er by a sheathed sword. His countenance resses intent recollection and concentra-1, as he endeavours to recall on the map the mory of one of his marches over the ntry it represents; and the look of power his face is curiously blended with a certain garity; giving the character of a man om you might fear but not respect. This o mere conventional "historical painting;" figure is a brilliant realisation which will e in the memory of all who are capable of appreciating its power. Las Cases sits at his desk in a corner of the room, waiting with upturned face for the next communication from his chief. The accessories, not numerous or elaborate, are most carefully painted, and it hardly seems possible to find a fault in this truly memorable work.

The President, in his own very different manner, is at his best, too, in "The Garden of the Hesperides" (204). The composition of the picture, of course, is essentially decorative. The three maidens, draped respectively in red, saffron, and green, are reclined with their heads nearly meeting against the magic tree; the serpent (not a conventional dragon) coils in friendly fashion round one of them and turns its head to her caress; the head, by the way, is somewhat mixed with the dark purple sea in the distance, and does not quite stand out from it. The colour harmony of the draperies is perfect and the attitude of the figures graceful; only is there something harsh and crude in the tones of the foreground foliage. Besides this, Sir F. Leighton exhibits "The Sea Gave up the Dead Which Were in it" (115), a repetition of his study for a decorative painting for St. Paul's, and which seems to us a gruesome and unhappy conception: "At the Fountain" (156), a half-length draped figure rather hard and mechanical in design and treatment; a "Bacchante" (257), leaping along in a leopard-skin dress (a much finer piece of colour, but surely the left hand, stretched as it is towards the spectator, should be larger than it is drawn,—the perspective of the arm seems the wrong way about); and "Clytie" (489), a small landscape in which the heroine, on an altar in the foreground, passionately worships the god of day setting over a mountain, and illuminating the rolling clouds with a brassy splendour which effectually kills Mr. Furse's portrait of the Bishop of Oxford hung above it.

In their usual neighbourhood in the Third Gallery appear the chief works of Mr. Tadema and Mr. Poynter, the rival classicists. In Mr. Tadema's picture, "A Kiss" (258) is a very innocent one offered to the sweetest of little children by one of a group of Greek ladies at the top of a marble stair which leads to a bathing resort, as we see by the one or two figures swimming in the water and undressed on the beach below. A great marble balustrade, and an inscription in bronze relief on the side of the stair wall, most carefully drawn in very sharp perspective, are characteristic of the painter's preferences. Mr. Poynter's "When the World was Young" (265) hardly answers to its title; it has been absurdly called in some of the papers a Greek interior; it is Roman in every detail, in the design of the mosaic floor, in the painted decoration under the window, in the marble columns carved with foliage in relief; and the Roman world was anything but "young" in the days of these decorative details. Two very pretty maidens are seated on the floor playing with knuckle-bones; a third sits half dozing in the window; figures and decorations are alike solidly and learnedly painted, with uncompromising care; the picture is one of the best its artist has produced.

Mr. Watts's large picture (164) is a bewildering mistake, and the title, "She Shall be Called Woman," suggests at once an absolute refusal to concur. This colossal bronzed figure, half seen through circling vapours, and with head upturned so that only the chin is visible, is apparently intended as a kind of typical representative of ideal woman; as far as it can be seen at all, a rather terrible ideal. This is the snare into which this remarkable painter not infrequently falls, of thinking more of expressing a meaning than making a picture. Mr. A. Moore in his one picture "Lightning and Light" (672), represents, perhaps, the opposite error of thinking only of pictorial effect and being content with no meaning; but as painting, after all, is painting, this mistake is the least mischievous of the two. Sir John Millais' much-talked-of work is a winter landscape, "Blow, blow, thou Winter Wind" (211), a hillside with the beginning of a snowstorm. It is a disappointing work with very fine passages in it, especially the wild look of the distant part of the landscape half seen through whirling snow, but the foreground is more realistic than powerful, and the tree very hard and metallic-looking. His other landscape, "Halcyon Weather" (142), a quiet pool in a wood, with a wooded distance beyond, is admirable in detail, but does not give us the summer-like impression as a whole. His best work is the pretty little child portrait named from the flower she holds, "The Little Speedwell's Darling Blue" (256), which contrasts happily with the seated child's white frock and fair complexion. There is obvious reference to Reynolds in the attitude and placing of the child. The tree and landscape are most happily touched in, just indicated and left in subordination. A little more of that subordination in the landscape previously mentioned would probably have made all the difference in its effect.

It is to be hoped that Mr. Stanhope Forbes will not believe the critics who tell him that "Forging the Anchor" (287) is his best work. It is his largest, and it is a fine pictorial subject powerfully treated, but it (necessarily) exhibits nothing like the varied discrimination of character which charmed us in "The Health of the Bride" and "By Order of the Court." Mr. Brangwyn's "Convict Ship" (307) is hung too high to be well seen, but it does not appear to be among his successes, and is not either agreeable in colour or very pointed or intelligible in motive. Nor can we congratulate Mr. Crofts much on his two pictures in the same room, "The Gunpowder Plot: the Conspirators' last Stand at Holbeach" (311) and "Charles I. at Edge Hill" (331). Perhaps the subjects are deficient in interest in comparison with some others which he has treated; at any rate, considering that they are Mr. Crofts' work, they are disappointing. Battle pictures are not at their best this year; Mr. Laslett J. Potts has a splendid subject in the "First Sight of Moscow" (609), but it is only a very average Napoleonic picture, and one cannot afford an average one now. The military picture of the year is Lady Butler's "Halt on a Forced March: Peninsular War" (27), a curious example of the power which real knowledge of and sympathy with the subject will lend to a picture hard in execution and deficient in pictorial effect. It is *real*, and therein lies its strength. The prominent object is a gun-carriage and horses, with wounded men propped on the carriage under various conditions of suffering. One of the leading horses has just dropped dead or exhausted.

Mr. Waterhouse's "Circe Poisoning the Sea" (20) is weird enough; a long lank figure (apparently too long) in clinging drapery, standing on tiptoe on the water and dropping the poison in a thin stream from the lip of a shallow glass vessel. The uncanny look of the face reminds one of Mr. Burne Jones's "Mermaid." Mr. Waterhouse's other contribution is "Danaë" (924) helped out of her box on the shore by men who are as old-world as the crew of the Ulysses ship last year, but "Danaë" looks too modern to group with them. Much is made of the antique brass-bound box, and not much of the sea. Mr. F. D. Millet has abandoned his Georgian ladies and interiors for Puritan figures, in "Between Two Fires" (12), and paints figures and details as well as ever, but there is not the same completeness about it as we are accustomed to in his favourite class of subjects. In the same room hangs Mr. Leslie's only work, "Queen Rose of the Rosebud Garden of Girls" (60), a set of pretty English girls on the terrace and steps of a garden, with a straight line of hedge behind; grace and prettiness there is in the figures, but the whole *facture* of the picture is dry, hard, and flat, there is no sensation of air and life. Mr. Briton Riviere paints a lion with a Cupid riding on his back (his face to the tail), under the title "A Master of Kings" (46), the lion looks rather long, but he is a grand beast, and there is fine colour and a real element of imaginative creation in the work, which is far superior to "The Haunted Temple" (38), where the realism of the tigers in the foreground rather clashes with the idea of the supernatural. That is the difficulty of combining animal painting with ideal and especially supernatural subjects. Among other things to be noted in Gallery I. (we exclude landscape for the present) are Miss M. Dicksee's picture of Angelica Kauffman at Reynolds's studio (the head of Angelica is one of the most bright and charming things in the exhibition), and Mr. Boughton's twilight winter scene "The Home-light" (66).

Mr. Frank Dicksee produces under the title "Leila" (97) a very brilliant and successful study of a blonde eastern girl in bright red embroidered draperies, oddly set off by its next neighbour, Mr. H. Mosier's "Last Moments" (96), one of the "harrowing" order of pictures, in which dirt and desolation are predominant; pathetic, but pictorially repulsive. In the same room is Mr. Dicksee's pretty and impossible diploma picture, where a modern girl and her little sister, clutching up their classic draperies, are hurrying away from the bank in a quiet reach of the upper Thames where they have been disturbed in bathing by the alarming apparition of a Norse galley suddenly rowing up the stream from Henley Regatta: at least that is the general impression conveyed. There are so few painters who, like Mr. Tadema, give a really antique air to figures in an antique scene. Mr. Prinsep does not, in his large picture of "The Broken Idol" (368), where a Christian slave is brought before his mistress in the atrium for having "renversed" an idol in a fit of holy indignation. We have the usual thing; Christian slave pointing upwards, modern lady in Roman dress looking touched and puzzled; the master of the slaves is the only real-looking figure. Artists who are going to paint Roman ladies of the Empire should read Mr. Swinburne's "Faustine" fitst.

Mr. Riviere's "Dead Hector" (242) is another failure in a poetic sense; there is the naked corpse of a man on his face, and there are jackals, but we do not realise that it is Hector; it is painted for the jackals. In "A Day of Mortification" (88), where a lady going to church orders the dogs to stay at home, the balance is complete and the picture a success. Mr. Marks's "The Great Auk's Egg" (228), shown by one old connoisseur to another, is also a perfectly balanced work of its kind, in its author's best way.

The centre place facing the President's "Hesperides" is occupied by M. Bouguereau's "Distraction" (250), a maiden and cupid, one of those perfectly executed academical works which yet remain mediocre in their very perfection. Galleries III. and IV. present us with two noteworthy nudes, Mr. Jacomb-Hood's "Summer" (219) and Mr. Hacker's "Syrinx" (344), a curious contrast in treatment. Mr. Hacker's figure is conventional in design, the figure reduced to "Classic" lines, but realistic in colour; Mr. Jacomb-Hood's is realistic in drawing, without even beauty in the head and face, but conventional in colour, a study of a white body against whiter drapery thrown behind on the rocks. It is an unusual and interesting work, though the Syrinx will probably have the popular vote.

Among works of pure imagination there are few more interesting than Mr. Arthur Hughes triptych "Viola d'Amore" (893-4-5), a real little allegorical poem in painting. A girl in the first picture tunes the viol, looking brightly up to the open window, where are seen the blue sky, the may-blossoms, and the birds; in the second she sits on a terrace, holding the instrument, but a winged cupid behind handles the bow, and she sits amazed at the sound; in the third she is in her room at evening, an embroidered curtain making a kind of suggestion of a bridal veil floating over her head, the viol is drooped in her hand and a spray of yellow flowers is grasped with it. The three scenes are full of charming bits of detail, though the whole is far too refined in thought to be popular; one is almost surprised to find it in the Academy, and then to compare it with some academicians' works on the line! Miss Henrietta Rae has also done well in her "Mariana" (557), Tennyson's Mariana, a beautiful woman seated at the window with a weary look; among the details may be noticed the delicate way in which the embroidery and ornaments on the bosom of the dress are indicated. Mr. Solomon's "Orpheus" (666) is a large ideal work in which the size is more striking than the ideality; Mr. Arthur Hacker's "Annunciation" (901), another large work the ideal class, is far superior to this, but fa in what should be the central point interest, the face of the Virgin, which deficient in expression.

Among figure subjects of more pros meaning are two noteworthy works in Galle XL, Mr. La Thangue's "After the Gal (977), a big painting of a small boat in whi an injured man from a wreck is being scull home, and which is a capital study of rou seafaring figures in full daylight; and M Melton Fisher's "A Summer Night" (1,02 a most clever representation of figures group by lamplight in a verandah overlooki Venetian waters, and containing some tema ably pretty women. This is a picture of t "new school," in which detail is indical rather than suggested. In regard to bc it is a question whether they are i far too large for the interest of the subje and the same remark applies to Mr. F. Ha clever and brilliant interior of a "vet. surgery (apparently), with a number of bott and knick-knacks, and the vet. preparing prescribe for a fat King Charles which l come there as "The Result of High Livin (1,041). The execution is brilliant and cle to a degree; but is it worth all this canvas

Among works in the way of *genre* painti which justify themselves by their subject a scale is Mr. Bridgeman's spirited "La Tennis Club" (102), a thoroughly Engl scene by an artist American by birth a French by education. Mrs. Forbes's " Minuet" (343) should be looked at for originality of design and colour; Miss Bi "Orphans" (374), an orphan-school sce and (in a much more serious key) Mr. Tebb "Alone" (511), an interior with one sea figure of a girl in mourning, marl both by true pathos and very and careful painting. Mr. J. R. Re "The Mate of the *Mermaid's* Weddi (513) is a good crowded scene of fishing to life, rather recalling Mr. Fildes's "Vill Wedding" some years ago; many of figures are admirable studies, and one is g to find that the painter has cast aside th unfortunate experiments in a violent sys of colouring which had threatened to s him altogether not long since. "A Bit a Yarn" (660) by Mr. C. T. Garlan admirable for the varied expression in three children's faces.

Among pictures dealing prominently w architecture two by Mr. Woods should be missed by any visitor interested in ar tecture, "The Church of the Frari School of San Rocco, Venice" (157), mirably solid and brilliant in its paint and a more interesting because more unu subject, "In the Belfry of the Campanile St. Marks" (233); there is also a good st of the "Grande Mosque de Tangiers" (by M. Emile Wauters. We may men here also one admirable piece of still painting by Miss Catherine Wood (Mrs. R Bright), "Onions" (317), a piece of imitat painting perfect in its way, and justified the pithy quotation from Browning—

—"Paint these
Just as they are, careless what comes of it!"

Portraits are not perhaps striking this y but include a good many thoroughly ones. Mr. Herkomer's large group of traits under the title "A Board of Directo (458) is one of the most important work this class; and among others we may spec name Mr. John Collier's brilliant but s what too stagey portrait of "Miss J Neilson" (210), Mr. Tadema's remark vivid likeness of "Mr. Alfred Waterhou (222), Mr. Ouless's "Herbert C. Gibbs (305), noteworthy for its simplicity style and pose; and Miss Anna B ska's "Portrait de l'Auteur" (502 frank piece of Bohemianism, repe in colour but wonderfully spirited in racter and execution. Two pictures w might be portraits but are not called so sh not be overlooked, Miss Gulland's head ca "Honeysuckle" (438), a very fine piec colour, and Miss Mary Field's charming ngth called "Daisy" (491), a picture which ıth for colour generally and for the fine pe painting of a very sweet face, merited more central position than it has obined.

We had nearly passed over the finest ıimal painting by far in the room, Mr. wan's "Thirst" (454), a picture of two opards drinking. The remarkable element Mr. Swan's animal pictures is the way in hich he realises the action and life of vage animals in their wild state. His opards are not as taking animals as cture-book leopards in pretty attitudes, but e sprawl of the one facing the spectator, s forepaw and shoulder splayed outward in s eagerness to stoop to the water, has someing thoroughly animal about it not to be sily forgotten. But we must turn to ndscapes, of which there are some very fine amples this year, and many more or less orth study.

The landscapes of the year afford, taken together, an interesting exemplification not ıly of the inexhaustible variety of nature, ıt of the variety of ways in which nature ay be regarded in painting. They might be assed under the heads of pictures simply presenting nature, and pictures representing e painter's method of translating nature, ough we will not venture to follow ıt the classification in detail in regard the pictures exhibited. Perhaps the ost powerful work of the year is Mr. rett's "The Isles of Shomer and Skokham" 96), in which this painter has surpassed himlf in the treatment of sea. He has quitted at representation of calm sunlit sea of hich we have had perhaps rather too many petitions, and shows the sea rolling in dark am-crested billows under a fresh breeze, ıth a realism in regard to movement, colour, d reflected skylight, which is extraordinary. e exhibits several other works which are r the most part repetitions of effects with hich he has familiarised us. Mr. H. oore's principal work, "Perfect Weather r a Cruise" (19), gives fortunate evidence t he has entirely recovered from the nful accident which incapacitated him m painting for some time. Sea pictures erwise are not very numerous, but atten-ı should be given to one by Miss A. J. ılters, "A Bright Gleam from the West" 3), which is remarkable for the truth tenderness of its aërial effect and the tle tones of light on the water. Mr. W. B. Davis's paintings rank as landpes, though the animal painting in them f nearly equal importance. His "Springe" (191) is beautiful in its rendering the delicate light on the slopes of the disce; his "Summer Time" (665), with sheep the foreground under strong light, is pers a little too hard in the foreground, ugh we thank him for not shirking sunlight some painters of "summer" do), but the hadow of Evening" (671) is an almost fect work of its class; it shows the foreund sloping down from the spectator, dowed from the western sun, which lights the rising land beyond with a calm warm iance; the whole thing is as true as it be. Mr. Davis has never been seen to more antage than this year. Mr. David rray's principal work is "The White at" (919), an expanse of level meadows f flooded, under an empty summer sky; we do not realise the effect of heat gested by the title. "The River Road" 9) is a finely composed landscape, with a s of dark trees and a bridge on the right; ı is one of the school of landscapes comed, as one may say, from one side, of which ther and very fine example is Mr. C. E. son's "Evening Shadows" (460), a beau-l specimen of the purely natural landscape ct, in which the painter is transcriber ıer than translator. There is a taste at sent for flat level landscape with a large , as in Mr. Murray's "White Heat" just ntioned, and Mr. East gives a fine example it in "Hayle, from Lelant" (104), where centre of the canvas is occupied by the t sands of a nearly empty tidal river or estuary, the houses gleaming warm in the sunlight in the distance. Mr. Logsdail, who has not been much seen as a landscape-painter, produces a somewhat similar class of effect in "Venice from the Public Gardens, Early Morning" (125), a very pleasant work. Mr. MacWhirter's "June in the Austrian Tyrol" (120) is remarkable as a painting of a profusion of bright wild-flowers occupying the banks in the foreground; it is a *tour de force*, but gives rather too much that impression, and does not quite convince us of its truth. Nor does Mr. Parsons's "The Flowers appear on the Earth" (184), they seem rather to appear on a surface of green baize, displaying none of the texture of grass. Mr. H. G. Hewitt's "November" (367) is a landscape of great merit by an artist whose name is not familiar to us. Mr. East's "Autumn Afternoon" (591) is one of the pleasantest of the quieter landscapes of the year; and Mr. W. L. Wyllie's "Spanish Armada" (691) should not have been overlooked among sea-pieces. Mr. Arnesby Brown's "Low Land" (988) is a very good work of decidedly French tendencies, one of those in which the interest lies as much in the idiosyncrasy of the painter's treatment as in the scene itself; the same might be said, though in rather a different sense, of Mr. North's "Druidscombe, Somerset" (602) which has a great charm about it, but it is not nature so much as nature idealised. Mr. Adrian Stokes's "Sunset, Roman Campagna" (475) contains a fine sunset effect, and would strike one more perhaps if it were not so entirely dominated in our recollection by his much more powerful Campagna landscape in the New Gallery. Mr. Vicat Cole's large picture of "Westminster" (306) may we suppose be classed as a landscape; as such we do not like the general tone of it, which is muddy and disagreeable, and we object even more strongly to the theatrical and stagey painting of the Victoria tower, which is loaded with yellow in order to get a sunlight effect, to the extent of making the main lines of the tower appear as if gilt as well as the lantern. As a painting of a great building it is a thing that no architect could regard with satisfaction. We may also class with landscape Mr. A. Goodwin's remarkable illustration of the scene in Dante's *Inferno* where Virgil and Dante attempt to enter the city of Dis. Here, as in the poem itself, we are in a sense out of contact with nature, but it is worth while to try to realise in painting some of Dante's lurid and tremendous scenes; the attempt has not been often made (partly no doubt on account of its extreme difficulty), and on the whole Mr. Goodwin has been successful; he has produced a grand and striking effect which assists us in realising Dante's conception, and if a picture does that the attempt is justified, though it is moving no doubt on dangerous ground for painting. Mr. Goodwin has some special faculties for illustrating Dante, and we should not be sorry to see some further attempts at it from his hand.

There are many smaller pictures of interest besides those we have named, and in the process of going through these notes we have been more than confirmed in our first impression, that this year's Academy is one of great and varied interest. Of sculpture we will say something on another occasion.

THE 19TH CENTURY ART SOCIETY.—Saturday, the 14th inst., has been appointed for the Private View of the Summer Exhibition (the twenty-seventh) of the 19th Century Art Society at the Conduit-street Galleries, and the exhibition will open to the public on Monday, the 16th inst. We are informed that the Society has been recently considerably strengthened by the enrolment of many additional well-known artists as members. With the view of enabling the members to exhibit their works in a thoroughly adequate and advantageous manner, the requisite alterations and improvements have been carried out by throwing the Maddox-street Galleries into those already occupied by the Society, thus forming one of the most important and attractive suites of galleries in London.

TESTS OF BUILDING-STONES.

WE have received an excerpt from the current volume of "Minutes of Proceedings of the Institution of Civil Engineers," entitled "Building-Stones of Great Britain—their Crushing Strength, and Other Properties," by Mr. Thomas Hudson Beare, B.A., B.Sc., Assoc.M.Inst.C.E., which is deserving of notice as an example of how elaborate "tests" may be carried out on stone, and yet may possess but little practical value. Seeing that the excerpt is merely a pamphlet, thirty-one pages in length, including the appendices, it will readily be understood that the author deals with a comparatively small number of building-stones. We do not find in it a single reference to any of the building-stones of Wales. Tests on the following properties of English and Scotch stones are recorded: crushing strength, density, absorptive power as a test of weathering, effects of low temperature, and, lastly, an inquiry into the behaviour of stone under gradually increasing pressures, with a view to determining the modulus or co-efficient of elasticity. The author commenced work by applying to various quarry-owners for samples, instead of obtaining them from the quarries himself. All the specimens were carefully prepared in the form of cubes, 2¼ in. in the side, before being experimented with. The crushing tests were carried out in the large Greenwood & Batley testing-machine belonging to the laboratory of University College, London, which is a horizontal machine of 100,000 lbs. capacity. In every case, except two, the specimens were placed in the machine in such a way that the pressure was applied on the bedding faces,—*i.e.*, the axis of pressure was perpendicular to the planes of the quarry-bedding. The author shows,—and this is decidedly the most interesting part of his communication,—that the practice of interposing sheets of lead, or thin pieces of soft wood, between the dies of the machine and the specimens to be tested, does not yield a fair result. Of course, it is not the first time that this has been pointed out,—a paper on the subject was read to the British Association a few years since, whilst Professor Unwin, in his "Testing of Materials of Construction," also deals fully with it, and the question has received much attention in America; but Mr. Beare's observations are especially useful, as being additional evidence derived from direct investigation. His experiments indicate that, by using lead, there is an enormous reduction of strength, varying from 36 to 55 per cent., and the stronger the stone the greater the loss. Therefore, he prepared the surfaces of the stone with a thin layer of plaster of Paris only, and applied them directly to the steel faces of the dies of the testing machine. It is a pity, however, that the author was unable to deal with samples of larger dimensions than 2¼ cubic inches. Such small pieces do not fairly represent the lithological and other physical features of any class of stone, so that the majority of the tests recorded can have but little practical value. Large blocks of stone used for ordinary building purposes very frequently have a number of minute—microscopic—fractures running through them for short distances, which considerably weaken the material as a whole, and 2-in. cubes are not sufficiently large to reveal the effect of these. But even supposing the tests were satisfactory in that respect, it is difficult to deduce much of practical value where the results on the same stone vary from 288 tons to 460 tons per square foot, as they do in Gunnerton sandstone; 341 tons to 579 tons as in Corsehill; 171 tons to 245 tons as in white Grinshill stone; 395 tons to 546 tons as in white Mansfield; 383 tons to 703 tons as in a yellow magnesian limestone; 74 tons to 128 tons as in Corsham Down Bath stone, &c., &c. Yet the author informs us that "the figures for crushing loads are very closely concordant." True enough, the granites give higher results than dolomites,

dolomites than sandstones, and sandstones than limestones, but no elaborate tests were required to carry conviction on those heads. In speaking of the absorption of water tests, the author states that "the relative amount of absorbed water must be a very good guide to the relative weathering power of stones, since it shows to what extent deleterious agents in rain-water and fogs will penetrate the stone," which, as we have on previous occasions pointed out, is a very unfounded, though prevalent, notion.

NOTES.

THE *conversazione* of the Royal Society, held at the Society's apartments, Burlington House, on Wednesday last (the 4th inst.), although successful so far as the attendance of a large number of influential scientists was concerned, was a little disappointing in regard to the exhibits. Many of these latter were by no means novel, and included minor discoveries whose chief claim for space consisted, apparently, in their startling ocular results, or the noise they made. The really interesting portion of the exhibits were chiefly in the domain of electricity, as usual. Amongst the more prominent, we noticed the various electrical apparatus shown by Captain Holden, R.A. One consisted of a high-speed chronographic pen with automatic re-setting attachment, the object of which is to take a number of successive records of short intervals of time on a revolving drum or moving surface, under as nearly as possible the same conditions. Another was an improved compensated voltmeter, on the hot-wire system, a very simple instrument. Mr. W. Crookes, F.R.S., showed some experiments with electrical currents of high potential and extreme frequency, which were somewhat similar to the celebrated demonstrations of M. Tesla. The physiological action of the high frequency current is feeble, and Mr. Crookes in dealing with a current having an electromotive force of about 100,000 volts, the frequency of alternation being 1,000,000 per second, to show its harmlessness caused it to pass through his body, and then communicated it to bystanders, who experienced merely a slight shock on its application. Mr. J. Wimshurst exhibited some interesting phenomena connected with Leyden jars with wire coatings; and Professor Oliver Lodge, F.R.S., produced interference bands by projection, electric sparks in and to water, illustrating lightning effects, multiple flashes, &c. An electric chronograph, designed for the measurement of the velocity of projectiles, and small periods of time in physiological research, was shown by the Rev. F. J. Smith, M.A.; and Messrs. Pyke & Harris had some high tension apparatus. Dr. G. Gore, F.R.S., exhibited a remarkable electrolytic formation of copper in the form of wires, produced during the ordinary process of electrolytic refining of copper. A selection of the proof plates to the first memoir of the Archæological Survey of Egypt, which, we learn, will be published very shortly, were shown on the wall of the Council room by Mr. Percy E. Newberry, by permission of the committee of the Egypt Exploration Fund. Mr. A. P. Maudslay showed photographs of ancient Central American monuments and buildings, some of which have been recently described in our columns. The Royal Geographical Society and Mr. J. T. Bent had rather an extensive series of finds from Zimbabwe ruins, Mashonaland; there was also a small model of a circular temple at the same place. This temple is built of small blocks of granite, without mortar; it is 280 ft. in diameter; the walls are 32 ft. high and 17 ft. thick in parts, and the solid round tower is 34 ft. high. Various photographic, astronomical, natural history, and other objects were also exhibited.

AMONG the cases submitted to the Board of Trade in 1889, under the "conciliation" clause of the Railway and Canal Traffic Act, was a complaint by the Liverpool Chamber of Commerce and others of undue preference in the rates from Birkenhead to Birmingham. Meetings between the complainants and the railway company's representatives were held at the offices of the Board of Trade, but no satisfactory settlement could be arrived at, and the Board gave the matter up as being too wide and complicated a problem for them to deal with. The rates complained of were those charged by the Great Western Railway for the carriage of grain; but the principle involved was one of general interest, it being alleged that Birkenhead traders were prejudiced owing to the rates from that port to Birmingham being unduly high as compared with those from Bristol and Cardiff. The case has now been submitted to the Railway Commissioners, and they gave judgment on Monday last, to the effect that the action of the railway company did not constitute an undue preference under the Act. Taking all the facts of the case into consideration, this cannot but be regarded as a satisfactory decision, although the Birkenhead traders certainly had a strong case. From Cardiff and the Bristol Channel ports the Great Western have to compete with various other means of conveyance, and must either charge comparatively low rates, or allow their competitors to carry the whole of the traffic. If they were compelled to regulate their rates from these ports to Birmingham by those in force from Birkenhead, they would simply throw away the former traffic and nobody would be benefited. If they had overstepped their Parliamentary powers in the Birkenhead rate, a different decision would have been given; but it did not appear that the rate is in itself excessive, and Mr. Justice Wills expressed himself satisfied that the Liverpool traders were able, notwithstanding the difference in rates, to compete effectively in the Midland markets with the traders in the West. We should be very sorry to see any trade, unfairly prejudiced by a railway company, make an ineffectual appeal to the Commissioners; but they are clearly right in looking at such matters from all points of view,—not excepting that of the consumer, to whom the maintenance of effectual competition is often both a benefit and safeguard.

THE two interesting speeches at the Royal Academy dinner were Mr. Balfour's and Professor Butcher's, the latter of which, full of clever and piquant points of criticism in regard to art and literature, came rather as a surprise. His remarks on "the cult of the meaningless," and his story of a critic of the new school who explained to him the artistic object of a certain portrait—"Think away the head and face, and you get a residuum of pure colour"—are much to the point at present. In literature, for which he spoke, Professor Butcher said that such a principle, form without substance, meant sure decay. Art and literature are not quite parallel cases, but the warning in regard to art is certainly needed just now. It is refreshing to find in Mr. Balfour an ardent politician whose political fighting has not deadened his love of art. His lament over the fact that such monstrous things as the Charing-cross Station and railway viaduct should be allowed there at all to spoil a site with such opportunities as the Thames Embankment, will come home to the sympathies of many of our readers. But when Mr. Balfour laments, further, that the "great public," whose property such a site is, cannot make its voice heard, we fear he was attributing to the great public perceptions which it does not possess. The great public of England is absolutely indifferent to any question of architectural beauty, and would ask no questions about the ugliest railway viaduct than whether it was convenient and safe; on those conditions, it may be as ugly as any engineer likes to make it, for all the public care.

THE action of Macleod *v.* Thrupp, whi
was tried this week before Mr. Justi
Wills and a special jury, exemplifies the gre
care necessary in putting a value on proper
when money is to be lent on the security
it. The action was by a lady against h
solicitors to recover a sum which she had lo
by reason of the property which was t
security for the loan proving not to be
sufficient value when realised. The su
advanced was 3,100*l.*, in 1879, the securit
two sets of property in Fulham; both pr
perties, when sold in 1890, realised togeth
only 1,360*l.* The opinion of a surveyor h
been taken as to the value of the first securit
he advised that 2,500*l.* might be lent upon
and he estimated the value of the buildin
on it to be 3,200*l.*, there being
addition the security of the freeho
site. The jury returned a verdict f
the plaintiff for the difference betwe
the sum advanced and that which the pr
perty fetched when sold. But the poi
which we desire to emphasise is the gre
caution required by professional men wh
advising on these matters. House propert
as we all know, is liable to fluctuations, b
the figures which we have given above,
printed in the report of the case, appear
show that a margin for contingent shrinka
in the value of the property had not been,
in this case at least,—properly taken in
account.

THE new platform at Euston Station f
some of the local traffic has, undoubtedl
helped to make the despatch of the longer d
tance traffic both easier and more convenie
to passengers. But this new local platfo
is at present inconvenient for those using
as there is no connexion by means of a brid
between it and the main platform. Not o
passenger in ten can discover the local boo
ing-office,—a mere shed near the gate for t
departure of cabs from the arrival platfor
Moreover, not every local train leaves fr
the new platform, so that there must alwa
be confusion with the present makesh
arrangements. But in any event, a bric
should connect the new platform so t
passengers may enter in the usual mann
and cross directly to the new departu
platform.

THE case of the London County Counci
Pearse, heard before Mr. Baron Poll
and Mr. Justice Williams, settles the mat
(which we had regarded as already settl
whether a builder's movable office on wheel
a structure within the meaning of the Build
Act. The plaintiffs contended that the c
came within the Act, but the two Judges b
concurred on Tuesday in giving judgment
the defendant. The judgment appears to
to be in accordance with what we should d
the common sense of the matter.

IN districts which are fortunate enough
be within the area allotted to an e
tricity supply company it is almost
common to wire the houses for the elec
light as to fit them with the necessary
pipes. A natural consequence of this is t
new systems of wiring are constantly be
devised, and Messrs. Cook, Smythe, & Pa
have patented a "fire-proof system of c
ductors" which are usually arranged on
concentric principle. An inner metallic t
or rod is kept apart from an outer tube
means of glazed earthenware rings or st
and the combination, which forms the
conductors, is mechanically protected b
third tube. Wherever rods would be u
for hanging pictures or curtains, &c., t
conductors may be employed. This syst
like that adopted by some of the supply c
panies in their mains, relies upon air for
insulating material. In practice, the i
lation resistance has not been found to b
high as was anticipated, but within a
building better results may be obtained.
convenience of this form of conductor n
not be pointed out, but it is not free f
risk. It would not be considered pruden
hang weights from gas-pipes, and, tho

lectricity cannot leak like gas, any undue train might bring the positive and negative ıads into dangerous proximity.

)N the 26th of last month the Duke of Devonshire laid the foundation-stone of t. Werbergh's, Derby. For this church, to e erected at an estimated cost of 9,000*l.*, Sir .rthur Blomfield was chosen architect, as we nnounced on June 14, 1890. The old church, 'hich yet stands by Wardwick, at foot of riar-gate, and once belonged to Derley Abbey, as, — like its more famous neighbour All aints',—a Gothic tower, rebuilt after the orm of 1602, with a later nave and chancel fter the Tuscan order. Here are a monuent by Chantrey; and a font cover, a brazen elican "in her piety," latterly serving for a ctern, given in 1711 by Charles Benskyn. oswell tells us that Dr. Johnson set out ith Mrs. Porter on horseback from Biringham to be married in Derby. It is not enerally known that the wedding took place this church. The register contains an try, dated July 9, 1735, thus:—

"Mar. Saml. Johnson, of ye Parish of S. ary's, in Lichfield, and Elizh. Porter, of ye Parish S. Phillip, in Birmingham."

aving adverted to the history of bridgeapels in our illustrated articles of November and 29, 1890, and a "Note" on March 28 llowing, we may say here that the chapel, ith a floor-space of about 45 ft. by 15 ft. on . Mary's-bridge across the Derwent, which as used in turn for a Presbyterian meetingouse (*temp.* Charles II.), a residence, and a rpenter's shop, was re-fitted and licensed r service in 1873. A view of it will be und in Fullarton's Gazetteer (1843). Dr. rasmus Darwin practised for the last twenty ars of his life in a fine Elizabethan house, w, or lately, No. 15, in Tenant-street. In the ammar-school, founded, 1170, by William ardant, Bishop of Lichfield, and William Barbâ Aprilis, were educated Joseph 'right, painter, and Flamsteed, our first stronomer Royal. The school, which cently returned to its original situation at Helen's, claims also Thomas Linacre, nder of the Royal College of Physicians, two Archbishops — Juxon and Vernon rcourt—amongst its *alumni*.

HE Danish Art School of Needlework and Embroidery gave a private view on nday, the 2nd, at 12, Queen's-road, Bayser. The school is in connexion with Royal Technical College for Ladies at enhagen, and classes are held in emidery, Swedish wood-carving, art weaving, lace-making. The embroideries were ıer ordinary: inferior in design to the e class in South Kensington, and perhaps xecution. In the wood-carving and metalk there were many very nice things, ecially some paper-knives in metal inlay. old Celtic designs in the woodwork and al inlay were quaint and charming, and work was beautifully finished. In an er room visitors were initiated into all mysteries of the hand-loom, and very tty it was to see the shuttles flying swiftly and fro, and hear the sweet foreign accents the Swedish ladies, who explained the rking of the looms. Very pretty; and looms would undoubtedly look very turesque in a boudoir; but we cannot erstand anyone with much artistic feeling ing a whole day weaving a chamber towel, ich after all is not artistic, it is merely a d piece of woven stuff with a conventional der at each end, which border could as l be done in a machine. Embroidery, of rse, is an art; weaving merely requires ctice, and, given a pattern, anyone with inary perceptions could do it. The pat- ıs seemed to us very commonplace, with exception of one or two pieces of tapestry; represented a marriage scene, in the centre altar with three lighted candles, the bride bridegroom on each side in Swedish s, and attended by four solemn storks, are supposed to bring good luck to the py pair.

IN our columns of the week before last we gave a short notice of the death of Mr. R. J. Johnson. A few words more on his work and career will not be out of place. His work was remarkable for the way in which it was carefully thought out to the smallest detail, whilst in house-planning, in which he was remarkably successful, convenience was combined with great charm of invention. Preferring the study of architecture to that of civil engineering, he was apprenticed to Mr. Middleton, the father of Professor Middleton, of Cambridge. He was afterwards in the office of Sir Gilbert, then Mr. Scott. Returning to the north, he purchased the business of Mr. Dobson, a man well known in times past in Newcastle. In that city he practised with much success, and was appointed Diocesan Surveyor to the Dioceses of Durham and Newcastle. Among the churches he built or repaired, may be mentioned the repair and refitting of St. Nicholas, now the Cathedral of Newcastle; the Chapel at Castle Howard; Monkwearmouth Parish Church; Cramlington Church; St. Hilda's, Whitby; St. Matthew, Newcastle; Transept of Hexham Abbey Church. Among secular buildings should be named Hodgkin's Bank, the College of Science, the Northern Insurance Office, and the Tyne Commissioners offices, all at Newcastle,—the last in conjunction with Mr. J. J. Stevenson. Among houses, Haughton Castle, on the North Tyne; Urpeth Lodge, Chester-le-Street; Provost Watson's house, Hawick; Mr. Pease's house, Pendover, Newcastle. Mr. Johnson was one of the very few men standing quite in the front rank of the profession, who continued to practise in the country instead of being absorbed in the great vortex of London.

ARCHITECTURE AT THE ROYAL ACADEMY.—II.

1618; "Edginton Priory Church, Wilts. View showing restoration of ancient parish altar;" Mr. C. E. Ponting. This is hung too high to be well seen; it is an interior view of a fourteenth-century church executed in sepia, and showing the restored altar at the farther end. Perhaps a detail of the altar restoration would have been more to the purpose; little of it can be seen in the drawing.

1619; "Hall, Buller's Wood, Chislehurst"; Mr. Ernest Newton. A pendrawing of a moderate sized hall of a country house with pedimented doors and a ceiling divided into four by two beams or soffits at right angles; rather a mechanical kind of division; the surfaces of the ceiling are divided up into panelling in which hexagonal figures predominate. A certain character is given to the large window on the right by the introduction of a large arched rib spanning two of the lower compartments of the window. Altogether a pleasant bit of homely quiet domestic work.

1620; "Design for Boat-house and Entrance-lodge;" Mr. C. E. Mallows. A picturesque little pen-drawing of a boat-house of Gothic predilections close to the arch of an (apparently) mediæval bridge, but this may be only to keep up the fitness of things. The most characteristic point in the building is the way in which the entrance from the garden is scooped out of it, as it were, with the wall running in obliquely under the upper story of the building.

1,622; "Bronze Doors, Adelphi Bank, Liverpool"; Mr. W. D. Caroë. This is a well-executed tinted elevation drawing showing an attempt (unusual enough!) to make something artistic of a bank entrance. The doors are designed in panels with small sculpture subjects, the relevance of which to a bank is not apparent on this small scale, but might be if we could see the details. The fanlight space is filled in with colonnettes with a scroll ornament behind. In the masonry design of the doorway the twisted columns and their capitals seem hardly in keeping, either in style or proportion, with the carved brackets over them; a side elevation is rather wanted to show the working of the design. The whole thing is original, but a little wanting in refinement of detail; the bronze doors are the best part.

1,623; "Warnham Lodge Sussex;" Messrs. Batterbury & Huxley. This is, as appears from the small plan judiciously appended, an addition to an existing old house. It is a long block of black and white work on a solid basement wall, the timbers kept vertical, and a certain character given by the row of little carved posts which run all round just above the solid wall; but why cut these into the shape of buttresses, which is the last thing they can be compared to? The gables and the tall mass of brick chimney are effectively placed, and the whole is a picturesque bit of Domestic architecture of its kind.

1624; "Design for a Window, Jesse Haworth Memorial Church, Walshaw"; Mr. W. Pape. A three-light window, with the transfiguration represented in the three large centre panels, subjects from the New Testament in smaller panels below, and kneeling angels with trumpets in the heads of the lights; these latter are the most pleasing bit of the work, which is satisfactory but presents nothing original in idea or treatment.

1625; "Retable for St. Alban's Church, Teddington," Mr. A. H. Skipworth. This is a really original bit of design in a very cleverly executed pencil drawing with a little tinting. It should have been hung lower. There are octagonal colonnettes at each end, with a twisting ornament on them which gives them a certain character. Within these is a broad band of decorative work, foliage intermingled with sacred emblems, which runs horizontally along the whole design and is returned vertically within the colonnettes. Angels are introduced at the angles, and a further line of foliage enrichment and moulding above the wide band completes the design. Without the least pretentiousness, this is a really original and refined little bit of ecclesiastic decorative work.

1,626; "Design for Altar Cross, Carshalton Church;" Mr. Reginald Blomfield. Metal cross and candlesticks shown on a dark ground. The angles between the arms of the cross are filled in with a light scroll connecting the arms, and making an approximate quatrefoil with a leaf form apparently (cannot be well seen) in each of the four spaces. The wide heavy base gives a look of monumental security.

1627; "House in Connecticut, U.S.A." Mr. E. J. May. This seems a picturesque house, drawn in Mr. May's well-known style; a tower-like mass projects in the centre of the front, giving a marked character to the house, and the employment of three gables of the same size along the return side gives an architectural breadth to this part. Mr. May employs his favourite device of a window at the outer meeting angle of two walls, which is piquant but rather unconstructive. By the way, one of Vitruvius's reasons why the triglyphs could not have originally represented windows is that they were placed at the angle of a building, "where no one would place a window;" but we have altered many things since Vitruvius.

Numbers 1,628 and 1,629 we have already described; No. 1,630, "The Mount, near Wolverhampton," by Messrs. Grayson and Ouse, is a fine pen-drawing by Mr. Raffles Davison showing a central hall with a strongly-marked first-floor string carried round it, with the balustrade of the landing along one side. The ground-floor shows a considerable amount of architectural picturesqueness in the manner in which nooks and staircase openings are contrived out of different arches, and the corbelled-out balcony above is a picturesque feature of which the most is made in the drawing, which is an unusually good one, and with more effect of light and shade and consequently more power of contrast than its clever draughtsman usually allows himself.

1,631; "St. Paul's Cathedral," by Mr. H. H. Statham, is the original drawing for the lithograph published in January last as one of the *Builder* series of Cathedral illustrations; we merely note its presence here.

1,632; "Albion Church, Ashton-under-Lyne;" Mr. John Brooke.—This is a well-executed pen-drawing of a church in the received Gothic style, with the tower and spire forming the prominent object at the nearest angle. The stair-turret at the angle is well arranged and forms an effective feature in the tower. A small plan shows that the church is one of those designed with narrow side-aisles for passage only; flying buttresses are introduced over them.

1,633; "Ambone from the Cathedral, Salerno;" Mr. F. D. Bedford. Apparently a very good and effective piece of pencil drawing, hung too high to be well seen. It shows a large spacious square ambo with a rich inlaid balustrade, supported on columns, three on each face.

1,634. "St. Peter's Church, Newton-le-Willows, Lancashire." Messrs. Demaine & Brierley. A church which derives a certain marked character from its large low square west tower, which is apparently oblong on plan with three large windows towards the nave roof and two on the other face. The drawing cannot be well seen, but there seems a general breadth about the treatment of the building which gives it a satisfactory effect as a whole. A plan is appended.

1635; "Chapel. Ridley Hall, Cambridge"; Mr. W. Wallace. Rather a heavy drawing of rather a heavy building, but it has the proper treatment of a college chapel in a somewhat ordinary Gothic style. The only feature of any originality is the turret at the south-west angle, the lantern of which is effective.

To No. 1,636 we have already referred.

1,637; "The Ulster Bank. College-green, Dublin," by Mr. Thomas Drew, shows that in Dublin the good old faith in Classic orders and pediments as the proper adjuncts and architectural characteristics of a bank is still retained. This is not however a common-place Classic front; there is a good deal of richness and originality in the decorative treatment of details, and one very effective point in the manner in which the top story between the large columns is set back, so that the latter, which are engaged columns below, become at their upper portion free columns with a deep shadowed recess behind shaft and capital. This is a distinctly original and picturesque incident. The capitals are not of regulation Classic type, but with a Renaissance freedom about them. The ground-floor is a plain rusticated wall, forming a good base to the whole. The spectator who is at first tempted to pass this by as one of the many bank fronts of the columnar type will find, on looking into it, that it is not a common-place piece of work at all, and differs materially from the average front of which it seems a type.

1,638; "Competition design for the Birmingham General Hospital; Corner of the Administrative Block;" Mr. W. H. Bidlake. We presume this was not a drawing sent in for the competition, but sent here to illustrate the picturesque qualities of the building. It shows a corner out of a large building, which groups very well without appearing unduly decorative for a hospital; the entrance to the administrative block, which of course is a legitimate occasion for a little architectural treatment, is marked by a projecting bay in stone with pilastered windows in the middle story, an open arcaded porch (an arch on each face of the semi-octagon) below, and a lightly treated open loggia or balcony above. The rest of the building that is shown is in brick. The main interest of the drawing is as a piece of architectural water-colour work, in which respect it shows an artistic freedom of execution and a feeling for colour which place it quite above the work of the "architectural draughtsman" as too commonly understood.

1,639; "New Organ for the Church of St. Mary, Bottesford;" Mr. G. C. Horsley. This is rather a hard pen drawing, nor do we think the design shows by any means as much freedom and effectiveness as the author's admirable organ-case sketch of last year; the general idea is more like the usual organ-case type. The best point in it is the bold large treatment of the foliage filling up the spaces on each side of the lower portion of the organ, flanking the keyboard. The same large free character is maintained in the scrolls on the top, but this kind of free semi-naturalistic treatment is better suited to fill in a space bounded by decisive lines than to be treated free as a scroll, in which case it gives a rather too ragged outline.

1640; "Design for a Town House," Mr. Herbert Baker. A dignified design of Italian type, with a strongly marked cornice, and a wide band of carved decoration in relief between the first and second floor windows. The tier of first-floor windows is given dignity and connexion by pediment heads and by niches between the windows, which would, however, have looked much better if filled with the sculpture, without which they have no meaning; and on paper at least sculpture can be introduced *ad lib.* The heavy square mass of the solid porch projecting outward to the pavement is rather an eyesore, and seems to want connecting more closely with the main design.

LETTER FROM PARIS.

IN spite of the serious considerations occasioned by the attempts and threats of the Anarchists, the Salon had a brilliant opening on "varnishing day," a profitable one for the Société des Artistes Français, thanks to the fashionable crowd which collected on an occasion more consecrated to spring fashions than to art. The formal opening took place on April 30, when, in place of M. Bonnat, who was kept away by a domestic loss, M. Paul Dubois and M. J. P. Laurens did the honours of the Salon to the President. The example set by the new Salon has not been without its effect, and the old establishment showed, this year, various improvements in its interior arrangements. Tapestries and hangings abounded, and the Salle de Conversation has been adorned with shrubs and flowers, and tapestries from the national collection, and the hanging line for the paintings has been kept lower. Lastly, in the central area occupied by the sculpture, a semicircle of trellis has been formed opposite the main staircase, which produces a good effect as a background to the principal sculptures.

The exhibition seems one of about average excellence. Some account of it will be given in a future number of the *Builder.* It may here be observed, however, that among the principal attractions of the year are the two ceilings, by M. Bonnat and M. Benjamin Constant, intended for the Hôtel de Ville, and a somewhat pretentious allegorical picture of the sculptor Carpeaux dying in the midst of his works, which descend from their pedestals to do homage to their creator. Among the sculptures are noticeable the decorative fountain of M. Peynot and the monument to Cabanel by M. Mercié.

Paris now possesses a third Salon rejoicing in the pompous title of "L'Union Libérale des Artistes Français." This new exhibition, which is to be open till June 20, contains about 600 works; but the result hardly justifies the new venture, for the collection includes little of interest, and the "Christ aux Outrages" by M. Groux, which the jury of the Salon made a mistake in refusing, is the only really powerful work to be seen there. The decorative studies of M. Mellocheau deserve notice however, and the still-life paintings by M. H. Stevens. The rest are below the level of the worst pictures of the ordinary Salon.

The "Black and White" exhibition is this year installed in the Palais des Arts Libéraux. It is divided into six sections: Black and white drawings; pastels and water-colours; modern engravings; old engravings; Japanese art, and sculpture. Altogether there are about 2,500 works, far too many, for the exhibits really worth study are lost amid a crowd of mediocrities. We may mention only the drawings by M. Renouard, the charcoal landscapes by M. Osbert, the rather mannered pastels of M. Carrier-Belleuse, and M. Sirouy's engravings after Prud'hon and Delacroix.

The first international photographic exhibition is also to be found at the Champ de Mars, near the entrance from Avenue Rapp. This very curious exhibition is divided into seven groups intended to illustrate the history of photography, its commencement, its progress, and its application to scientific, artistic and industrial pursuits.

Now that the Salon of the Champs-Elysées is open, the smaller exhibitions lose much of their interest, but the different special exhibitions of the past month deserve a word of recognition. First we may name the Pastellistes, among whom M. Besnard is still the defiant leader. Beside the works of this artist, open to much criticism but always original and interesting, may be named the contributions of MM. Jas. Tissot, Whistler, Billotte, Duez, and Lhermitte, as well as two fine studies by M. Puvis de Chavannes.

A small exhibition at the Georges Petit gallery is devoted to the works of six painters grouped under the denomination of "Les Inquiets." It may be said that every artist who loves his art and studies nature is an "Inquiet," always analysing his work and demanding of himself whether he has succeeded, so that the special assumption of the title seems hardly fair. Then there is the small exhibition which Mdlle. Louise Abbema forms every year at the Georges Petit gallery, the *résumé* of her work of the year, always full of charm, truth, and grace. At M. Durand Ruel's gallery we have had also a third exhibition of "peintres graveurs," where MM. Bracquemond, Guérard, Gœneutte, Hellen, and Lepère occupy a considerable place. Among the collection we may mention the very characteristic works in the Japanese manner by M. Henri Rivière, whose powerful execution shows great delicacy and sincerity. Etchings by the late Mr. Keene are also to be seen here, the fine qualities of which command great admiration.

Lovers of art have also been specially attracted by the too short exhibition of the works of Raffet, organised to raise funds for a monument to this remarkable artist, who perfectly understood how to represent in painting and lithography the military types of France. More than 500 subjects were got together in this exhibition, which was only open for seven days, and which served to bring before us, with a splendid mastery of style, the wars of the Revolution, the First Empire, and the Algerian and Roman campaigns. Most of the scenes composed by Raffet are very well known, but this exhibition brought out from private collections drawings entirely unknown and unpublished, in which Raffet reveals himself as the true painter of the French army, superior to Horace Vernet, Bellanger, De Neuville or even Meissonier, if not in drawing, at least in vigour and energy of representation.

Two new second competitions for the Hôtel de Ville decoration have just been decided. One is for the Salle des Banquets; the names of the five competitors have already been given, but no prize was awarded and the competition was cancelled, with a consolation fee of 2,500 francs to each competitor. It is to be hoped this will be a lesson to the authorities, who seem to wish for these eternal competitions for artistic work in Paris, which cost a great deal of money, and from which the highest class of artists stand aloof.

The object of the second competition is for the erection of a statue of Beaumarchais on the Boulevard of the same name. M. Allouard's sketch was charming in its aristocratic grace; but he has not received the prize, which has been awarded to M. Clausade's rather trivial figure. M. Clausade is a pupil of M. Falguière.

The *Builder* has recently spoken of the windows in the Church of St. Gervais, which have been seriously damaged by the recent dynamite explosions. We are now able to announce that the Service of Historical Monuments is going to make a valuation for the restoration, the expenses of which are to be defrayed by the Government. The sum required will be about 3,000 francs.

The gifts to the Musée du Louvre are becoming more and more frequent. We hear that M. Léon Moreaux has just made a donation of six fine pictures of the Dutch school, by Hondecoeter, Weenix, Téniers the younger, Ruysdäel, Adam Rynaeker, and Van Huysum. A few days ago the Museum received from M. le Député Clémenceau a curious portrait of Madame de Lamballe, by Gabriel, taken as the unfortunate Princess was on the way to the scaffold. M. Gerspach, Director of the Gobelins Tapestries, has in his turn offered to the section of the "moyen âge" a very rare Venetian mosaic of the twelfth century. We have also to announce the opening, which will shortly take place, of a new hall consecrated to Punic inscriptions, where will be gathered the votive steles, or funeral emblems, which are almost all the historical monuments that Carthage has left us. Paris is soon to have a new panorama, which has been painted by MM. Poilpot and Dupaty, the ordinary executors of this class of paintings, which are more commercial than artistic. This panorama, which is situated near the Palais de l'Industrie, represents the terrible naval combat, in which the French vessel "Le Vengeur" preferred sinking herself to surrendering. The scene is made rather too realistic for those who have not their sea legs, by a moving foreground representing the oscillation of the sea.

The recent death of the painter Andrieu, who was the favourite pupil of Eugène Délacroix, and the trustee of many of his sketches, necessitates a public sale of many of the master's works. Among the number will be seen nearly all the sketches of the fine paintings that he executed in the Salon de la Paix, in the Hôtel de Ville. It is also M. Andrieu who possesses the notes written from day to day by Délacroix, and which contribute true memoirs of the greatest interest from the point of view of the history of Art. The memoirs which are announced as shortly to be published are very voluminous, and they will complete the corre ondence of Délacroixthat Philippe Barty pub- ·hed some years ago. We may mention that the ıadémie des Beaux-Arts has just nominated r. Burne Jones as Corresponding Member in e place of Mr. Alma Tadema, who is now reign associate.

M. Bonnat, Member of the Institute, has just stained a great loss in the death of his brother- -law, the painter, Enrique Mélida, after a long ness. He died at the age of fifty-five. M. élida was born at Madrid; he obtained a medal the third class in 1860, and the cross of the ·gion of Honour at the Universal Exhibition 1889. He was an artist of talent, devoted to s art, very conscientious, and much beloved the world of painters. In the Palais de ndustrie last year, he exhibited a number of markable pictures, and he also occupied an ıportant place amongst foreign artists.—We ve also heard with much regret of the ath of M. Jules Eugene Monnier, architect, e of the most devoted members of the ciété Central, of which he was secretary from 82 to 1889. Very modest and very hard- orking, Eugène Monnier was much appreciated ıongst his colleagues, both as a scholar and a learned man. He first came into notice in e works of the church of St. Laurent, under e direction of Constant Defeux, after having en the pupil of Guenepin. He took part after- ırds in the construction of the Vaudeville, ilt by Auguste Magne, and he became suc- ssively diocesan architect to Vannes, and xpert" in connexion with courts of justice at ris. These positions secured him the re- ect of every one. We may mention amongst works the restoration of the Château of lzac, the construction of the flèche of the urch of Vanves, the transformation of the âteau of Praslin at Auteuil, the Hôtel de lzac, at Paris, the monument to Voltaire at Claude (Jura), and the very picturesque ıdio of his friend and compatriot, the old inter, Jean Gigoux. Monnier interested him- f much in the art of drawing. He founded 'eral prizes for its encouragement in the partment of the Seine, and every year, at time of the Congress, the Central Society re able to award, thanks to his liberality, a dal to the instructor who had most dis- guished himself. We may add that he con- buted most powerfully to the Caisse de fense Mutuelle, and that up to the moment is last illness he did not cease to give his nt for the good of the Corporation. Eugène ınier was born at Lure (Haute Saône) in). His early death has been a great grief is numerous friends and fellow workers.

THE SURVEYORS' INSTITUTION:

ESULT OF FELLOWSHIP EXAMINATION.

HE following candidates have passed the owship Examination:—

ɔombe, E.	Merry, A. W.
:kett, F. H.	Mitchell, G. S.
le, H.	Muller, J. J.
eroy, A.	Ogden, M. G.
y, H. T.	Osenton, G., Jun.
ey, E.	Palamountain, J. W.
ard, A. N.	Preston, S. D.
y, O. H.	*Richardson, O. A.
n, A. E.	Savill, E.
an, H. H.	Slater, C. F.
er, A.	Walker, J. A.
ward, F. G.	Webster, H. C.
p-Smith, J. F.	Young, H. A. L.
in, T.	

* Crawter Prize, 1892.

INCORPORATED ASSOCIATION OF NICIPAL AND COUNTY ENGINEERS:

MEETING AT NOTTINGHAM.

VERY successful meeting of the Midland ıties' District of this Association was held ottingham on Friday and Saturday, April nd 30.

ıe members assembled at the Exchange at noon on Friday, where they were ally received by the Mayor (Mr. R. ıugh), who made some remarks expressing ppreciation of the great usefulness of these ıatetic meetings of the Association, which le the borough and county engineers and ɜyors of the country to interchange ideas experiences, and to see a great variety of :s of municipal and sanitary engineering in ess.

aving said his words of welcome, the Mayor gned the chair to Mr. T. de Courcy Meade, of Hornsey (President of the Association), who cordially endorsed some remarks made by the Mayor as to the ability with which the present Borough Engineer of Nottingham (Mr. Arthur Brown, M.Inst.C.E.), had carried out certain works of municipal engineering in the borough. The members of the Association, said Mr. Meade, always looked upon Nottingham as being one of the first towns in the kingdom in regard to matters of municipal engineering.

Some formal business having been transacted, including the re-election of Mr. Davis (County Surveyor of Shropshire) as District Honorary Secretary,

Mr. Arthur Brown, Borough Engineer of Nottingham, read a paper on "Municipal Works in Nottingham." At the outset he dealt with the subject of street subways, the necessity of which was now, he contended, becoming greater than ever. It did seem, he said, to be somewhat of a blot on our boasted civilisation that when a pipe had to be taken up, in a busy and crowded thoroughfare, the system usually adopted was to tear open the street, whatever might be the class of pavement, lay in the pipes, and then "make good" the surface. Those two little words,—"make good,"—covered a lot of ground, but were somewhat misleading; it was as much an engineering impossibility to immediately restore the paving over a newly-filled-up trench to its original condition, as it was a physical impossibility to heal a serious wound on a human body without leaving a scar. The first subways constructed in this country were in London about the years 1860-62, and the first subway outside the metropolis was constructed in Nottingham in the years 1861-62, in Victoria-street and Queen-street; these were followed a year or two later by subways in Lister-gate and Market-street, and in the year 1886 the author designed and carried out subways in Albert-street and Wheeler-gate. To show the value of such works in the street called Victoria-street, in which is situated the General Post Office, it was stated that there are, besides the gas and water pipes and connexions, no fewer than six pipes containing telegraph wires in this subway, that not one single stone was disturbed in this carriage-way for twenty-five years, and that in that period not one single penny was spent on repairs in this street. Mr. Brown next proceeded to describe some subways which are now being constructed under his direction, on what is known as the "Condemned Area." This site, which has an area of about 12,500 square yards, was declared an unhealthy area, and was purchased under the Artisans and Labourers Dwellings Act, 1875; it was covered with a wretched and disreputable class of property, and was very much overcrowded. Plans hung upon the walls showed the area and the method of laying out the site for building purposes. The streets form on plan the letter Y. The street on the west side is 48 ft. wide, and that on the east side 50 ft. wide, while the short length of street forming the tail of the letter Y is 60 ft. wide. The subway proper is 10 ft. wide and 8 ft. 6 in. high, with semicircular arch, and is ventilated by means of gratings at the surface level of the street about 48 ft. apart, also by three side entrances and by an open grating in the refuge at the lower end of the 60-ft. street. The sideways, which form the means of communication between the subway and the vaults, are placed ordinarily about 40 ft. centre to centre, and are 4 ft. high and 3 ft. wide. The sewer is constructed under the floor of the subway, and is a 15-in. earthenware pipe, with Hassall's patent single lined joint. Under the causeways on each side of the streets vaults are constructed, which are each 8 ft. 6 in. wide by 9 ft. 3 in. long, and about 7 ft. high; these vaults are rented by the purchasers of the building lots adjoining. The floor of the subway is laid with cement concrete brought to a smooth surface, and the floors of the sideways and vaults are laid with bricks. Along and under each sideway is laid a 9-in. pipe with a Buchan's disconnecting trap and air inlet, and beyond is a right- and left-hand junction for receiving the drainage from the properties. In the subway are fixed brackets, upon which may be placed pipes containing telegraph and telephone cables, the gas, water, and any other pipes being laid on the floor of the subway, or on iron standards fixed to the floor of the subway. At convenient distances hydrant chambers are built over certain of the sideways, in which are placed the fire hydrants and valves. By this method of construction access can be obtained to, and any alterations and additions made to, sewers, gas, water, and other pipes, and the house connexions therewith; and the fire hydrants and valves can be examined, repaired, and renewed without taking up or disturbing one single stone in the surface of the street. The life of the iron pipes and connexions in the subway is practically everlasting, as there is no rust, and the expense of relaying mains, and especially gas services, through this cause is saved. In the execution of the works very considerable difficulty was encountered in consequence of the number of rock cellars which were met with during the operations. A plan hung on the wall gave but a faint idea of the network of these curious cellars. One cellar is 370 ft. long, and would hold a regiment of soldiers; on the site of all the main walls borings were made 10 ft. deep in order to discover these cellars; the bulk of them are within a few feet of the foundation-walls of the subways, and these walls, of course, had to be carried down to the solid. Nottingham was in olden times, said Mr. Brown, called "Snotteyn-ham," which means the town of caves, and the name was singularly appropriate. As there is considerable doubt in the minds of some engineers as to the possible effects of a very severe frost on the water-pipes in the subway, Mr. Brown mentioned that during the somewhat severe frost in the early part of this year, the maximum, minimum, and 10 o'clock a.m. temperatures inside the Albert-street subway were taken, and the similar and corresponding readings were taken outside the subway. The results of these observations were given in a table, together with the maximum, minimum, and 9 a.m. temperatures at the observatory at the Nottingham Castle. The lowest reading in the open air at the Water Offices, outside the subway, was 19·2 on February 19, and the lowest readings in the subway, 40·7, 41·0, and 41·0 on January 16 and 17 and February 19; the highest reading outside the subway was 53·4, on February 7, and the highest reading on that day in the subway was 45·8, so that for a range of temperature outside of 34·2, there was only a range of temperature of say 5 deg. inside the subway, so that there is not the least chance, even with the present rigorous English winters, of the thermometers in the subways going down to anywhere near freezing point. The minimum temperature at the observatory at the Nottingham Castle, on February 19, was as low as 13·0, showing what the temperature was outside the town. As regards cost, it was, of course, rather heavy; the cost of the subway proper, including side-entrances, sideways, and everything appurtenant to the subway itself, was about 10*l.* per lineal yard. This does not include the cost of the sewer, as this would be common to any method of forming streets with or without subways, nor does it include the cost of the concrete foundation for roadway. The vaults under the causeways cost about 20*l.* each, and there being vaults under each causeway they cost, therefore, about 12*l.* per running yard of the street; these vaults are let on a rental of 1*l.* each per annum, or 5 per cent. on the outlay. The subways proper cost about 3,000*l.*, and there are 169 vaults, costing about 3,380*l.*; 3½ per cent. interest on 3,000*l.* is 105*l.*, but the profit on the vaults is 1½ per cent., as the money is borrowed at 3½ and 5 is charged, and this equals say 50*l.*, so that it resolves itself into this question, is it worth 55*l.* per annum to have subways in the two new streets referred to? The author of the paper thought there can be only one answer to the question, and that it must be in the affirmative. He did not urge that Town Councils should incur immediately a large expenditure of money on laying down subways in all existing streets: that would be impossible from its cost, but that in the case of new main streets, and where main thoroughfares are improved and widened, the opportunity should be seized to lay down subways, in order to minimise as much as possible the evils resulting from the continuous taking up and relaying of streets.

Turning next to notice the sewerage works, Mr. Brown said it was not necessary for him to give any lengthened description of the sewerage system of the borough, or of the sewage farm, those subjects having been somewhat exhaustively treated in a paper read by him before a meeting of the Association in Nottingham in 1885, and also in a paper read by the late Mr. Tarbotton at Hanley, in 1886. A reference to those papers would give all the information required on the subject. Attention was called in those papers to one of the difficult problems which Borough Engineers have to face in some large towns, that is, what is to be done with the large amount of liquid and semi-liquid manufacturing refuse which is delivered from works where such processes as bleaching and dyeing are carried on? The subject is one which is of considerable interest, and the problem has been recently occupying the attention of the author and that of the Town Council. The total sewage flow of the borough in dry weather is about 6,125,000 gallons in twenty-four hours; of this quantity about 2,125,000 gallons per day gravitate down to the farm, and the remaining 4,000,000 gallons per day have to be pumped; the larger portion of the low-level sewage is brought down the Leen Valley sewer, and it is in the valley of the Leen where the principal difficulty regarding the manufacturing refuse is encountered. The river Leen is a small tributary of the river Trent, is 13¼ miles long, measured along its course, and the area of its watershed is about 40½ square miles. The flow of this river, of course, fluctuates very much, according to the seasons; gaugings were taken in the early part of 1891, and the lowest was on January 15, which was 901,549 cubic feet, or 5,634,681 gallons per day, and the highest gauging, taken during a somewhat heavy rainfall, was on January 24, and showed a discharge of 6,162,976 cubic feet, or 38,293,600 gallons per day. The normal discharge of the river in ordinary weather would be from 15 to 16 million gallons per day. On the banks of this river Leen, or contiguous thereto, there are about twenty-four bleach and dyeworks, of which number seventeen discharge their waste waters into the river Leen, or into the tributaries and brooks, or into special surface-water sewers in connection therewith, and the remaining seven have been permitted to discharge their waste waters into the Leen Valley sewer previously referred to. The water used by the bleachers, &c., is not taken from the river Leen, but is pumped from copious springs in the magnesian limestone, in which strata water particularly suitable for bleaching and dyeing processes abounds in large quantities. The works are not concentrated in one particular district, but are scattered about in the valley of the river, and the distance from the uppermost works to the lowermost works, measured along the course of the Leen, is not less than four miles. The waste waters turned into the river from these works is about 3,000,000 gallons per working day when the local trades of lace and hosiery are fairly good. The processes of bleaching differ in various districts according to the nature of the goods. The following, however, is the method adopted at one of the largest works in this district:—The goods to be bleached are first passed through cold water and then boiled in caustic soda (sodium hydrate NaHO) and crich lime; they are then run through a solution of bleaching powder (chloride of lime) and afterwards washed and run through a weak solution of sulphuric acid which is called "sours"; they are then boiled in carbonate of soda and soap, washed and run through chloride of lime, washed, and again run through "sours" (dilute sulphuric acid), and a final washing completes the operation. In some works strong liquor ammonia is used as an alkali instead of carbonate of soda, and in all cases, of course, very large quantities indeed of soap are used in the operations. The chloride of lime in the waste waters effects a precipitation of the soap and other solids when these waters reach the river Leen, and the result is the accumulation of the offensive and noxious slime and mud on the banks of the river. The filthiness of the water and banks of the river appears to be an invitation to the residents on the banks to still further pollute the river by throwing in all manner of rubbish, &c. The existence of the various mills on the river tends to aggravate the difficulty, and render the precipitation more effectual as the damming up of the water to provide head for the water-wheels forms a succession of settling ponds. To make matters still worse, the river Leen does not deliver direct into a fast-flowing river of large volume, like the Trent, but enters the Nottingham canal, which flows through a densely populated part of the town, and does not reach the river Trent for upwards of two miles. In this canal, which is practically stagnant water, the deposition of mud and slime is continually going on, and in warm weather the nuisance is considerable. The normal discharge of the river Leen is from 15 to 16 million gallons per day; the discharge between 6 a.m. and 6 p.m., which would include the bleach and dye water, would in round figures be about 9 million gallons; the waste water from the works is, therefore, about one-third of the total flow of the river between the hours named. The problem is to effect the purification of the river, and the solution of this problem is not a very easy one. However, in reporting on this question to the Town Council, there appeared to the author to be three methods of solving the difficulty. 1. To connect the bleach and dye works in the district with the system of sewers, and allow their waste waters to mix with the ordinary sewage and flow down the main intercepting sewer; eventually it would be pumped and delivered on to the sewage farm, and therefore purified by broad irrigation on land. 2. To connect the waste waters from the works referred to with an entirely new and independent sewer, and conduct these foul waters to some convenient site and purify the same by precipitation and filtration. 3. To compel owners of works to abstain from polluting the river, and put down on their own works a plant or apparatus for purifying their waste waters, either by precipitation or filtration, or both. The first scheme would involve somewhat heavy engineering works, but nothing of any very particular difficulty; it would be necessary to increase the pumping plant at the pumping station, to provide an additional pumping main, and to buy about 225 acres of additional land at the sewage farm; this would make the total area of the sewage farm 1,134 acres for say nine million gallons of sewage per day. The author said he was perfectly well aware that there are several very grave objections to this scheme; in the first place the three million gallons of bleach and dye water has very little if any manurial value; this, however, may be as truly said of the greater part of the sink washings from more than half of the property in the town; further, it was a matter of doubt whether the bleach and dye waters when mixed with the ordinary sewage would have any harmful effects on the crops at the farm. Having given analyses of waste waters from various bleach and dye works, and also of mud from the bed of the river Leen, made by Dr. E. B. Truman, the Borough Analyst, the author proceeded to discuss the alternative means of dealing with the problem to be solved, and concluded his paper by describing the new Epidemic Hospital, which appears to be one of the most complete buildings of its kind in the country.

[We will resume our account of the meeting in our next.]

THE ARCHITECTURAL ASSOCIATION SPRING VISITS:

THE NEW TRAVELLERS' CLUB.

THE sixth spring visit of the Association took place on the afternoon of Saturday, April 30, when a large number of members assembled to inspect the new Travellers' Club, Piccadilly, designed by Messrs. Thomas & Frank Verity. Mr Frank Verity kindly met the party, and gave an interesting description of the aims and objects of this interesting addition to the architecture of Clubland, and the difficulties met with in its design. The site is at the corner of Piccadilly and White Horse-street, and, as it overlooks the Green-park, the situation is an ideal one for a club. The entrance is from the new street, and leads into a spacious hall with grand staircase. The morning-room faces Piccadilly, and the coffee-room is placed on the right of the entrance facing White Horse-street. The first floor is occupied by a reading-room in front, and a two-table billiard-room and card-rooms at the back and side. The upper floors are devoted to bedrooms. A basement and sub-basement floors accommodate lavatories, kitchen, and offices. The work is hardly sufficiently advanced for an opinion to be formed of its aspect at completion. There are, however, scagliola columns and pilasters on the staircases, and glass mosaic pavings and portions of marble bands to the stairs visible. The front and side elevations are treated in Palladian Renaissance style, and are executed in Ham Hill stone, the present colour of which is a pleasant variation in the grey tone of most stone buildings in London. There is quiet dignity about the elevations, which is very pleasing. The building appears to be well planned and well lighted on all the upper floors, and this has been successfully contrive in spite of difficulties with adjoining owners a to light. The work has been executed b Messrs. A. Bush & Sons, and Mr. A. W. Earl has acted as the clerk of works.

ARCHITECTURAL SOCIETIES.

THE EDINBURGH ARCHITECTURAL ASSOCIATION AT LINLITHGOW PALACE.—On Saturda last a deputation from the Edinburgh Archi tectural Association visited Linlithgow in con nexion with the proposed repairing of th ancient Palace. The deputation was met i the Palace-grounds by the Provost and Magis trates, the Town Clerk, and several of th members of Town Council. The object of th visit (says the *Scottish Leader*) was to assis the Town Council in the preparation of a state ment as to what is actually necessary for th repair and preservation of the old structur Accompanied by the local officials, the visitor made a minute inspection of the various part of the building, and Mr. Ross, one of th deputies, submitted a number of written sug gestions as to how the proposed repairs migh be effected, and as to what was necessary fo the proper preservation of the historical fabri It is expected that steps will now be taken t have these suggestions brought under th notice of Parliament, and an endeavour mad to induce the Government to augment th grant of 500*l.* voted recently for the repair o the Palace. In connexion with the subjec certain important letters have been receive by Mr. Ferguson, Town Clerk. Lord Rose bery wrote:—"I am in receipt of you letter. I have urged Mr. Munro Ferguson t take the line that if the Duke of Cumberlan sequestrated the property of the Earl of Living stone for taking part in the Rebellion of 171 when the Duke of Cumberland's soldiers burne down Linlithgow Palace, it would be fair t apply the proceeds of the one to the repair o the other. That seems to me simple fairne and common sense." In his communicatio Mr. Munro Ferguson, M.P., says:—"This is bu one of the many examples where Scotla suffers from London Departments, where offici regard for our national buildings is not to distinguished from that indifference which pr vailed too generally amongst us for 200 or 3 years. A better spirit has arisen in our tim and it is good to see Linlithgow leading t way towards the restoration of the finest of t ancient palaces of Scotland. Your action worthy of every support, and your exam cannot be too widely followed." Letters ha also been received from Mr. M'Lagan, M. Mr. Sinclair, M.P.; Mr. Fraser-Macintosh, M. and others, all promising to give the obj their heartiest support.

LEEDS AND YORKSHIRE ARCHITECTU SOCIETY.—A general meeting of this Soci was held on the 29th ult., at the Law Institu Mr. W. H. Thorp, the retiring President, in t chair. The hon. secretary, Mr. W. Carby H read the annual report and balance-she which were adopted. The report was of favourable character, the Society having had successful year. There had been a gratify increase in the number of associates; t lectures were of great merit, and listened to better audiences than usual; the library h been considerably increased, and now contain most of the standard works appertaining to t profession. The Society, anxious to further t education of its younger members, had mad grant of 10*l.* 10*s.* to the Yorkshire Coll towards the payment of a lecturer on sanit science. The financial condition of the Soci is satisfactory, there being a considera balance at the banker's. The Travell Studentship, with 5*l.* 5*s.* added by the Preside was awarded to Mr. T. Denton Brooks, having submitted the best set of drawin Before the meeting concluded, Mr. Hobson p posed a vote of thanks to the retiring Presid for the very able manner in which he fulfilled his duties during the past two yea Mr. Beevers seconded the proposition, wh was supported by Mr. Hall. The Presid suitably replied.

SOCIETY OF ENGINEERS.—At a meeting of Society of Engineers, held at the Town Hall, W minster, on Monday evening last, Mr. Jos William Wilson, jun., President, in the chai paper was read by Mr. Samuel Herbert Cox, "Dry Crushing Machinery."

THE LONDON COUNTY COUNCIL.

THE London County Council resumed its eekly meetings on Tuesday last, the Chair-an, Lord Rosebery, presiding.

Tenders.—Tenders were received (*a*) for the rection of a fire-brigade station at East Dul-ich, (*b*) for repairs and alterations to the as-meter testing station at Spitalfields, (*c*) for ie erection of a gymnasium at Battersea-park, ad (*d*) for the erection of a gymnasium and iree bathing shelters at Victoria-park. (The sts are given on another page, under the eading "Tenders.")

The Limit of Height of Buildings, whether ı old or new Foundations.—The Public [H]ealth and Housing Committee's report on iis subject (published in the *Builder* for pril 16) was again on the *agenda*, but it was iled out of order, as not being within the erms of reference of the Committee.

The Shaftesbury Memorial Fountain, Picca-illy-circus.—The report of the Improvements ommittee contained the following paragraph ı reference to the fountain which is to be rected on one of the "islands" at Piccadilly-rcus.

"On January 14, 1890, the Council assented to ie appropriation, for the purpose of the Shaftes-ury Memorial Fountain, of the remaining vacant pace at Piccadilly-circus. Since that date the culptor, Mr. Alfred Gilbert, has been engaged pon the work, and we are now informed that the ountain is almost ready to be placed *in situ*. It ierefore becomes necessary for the Council to onsider the question of (1) connecting the water-ipes with the fountain, (2) forming the founda-ons for the memorial, and (3) building ie enclosing wall or balustrade in com-liance with the provisions of the Metropolitan nprovements Act, 1889. We have ascertained iat the cost of connecting the pipes with the ater main in the subway in Piccadilly-circus will e about 80*l*., and of forming the foundations and ilding the balustrade about 930*l*. It is possible iat this estimate will be considerably reduced. We minded the Memorial Committee that it would be cessary for this work to be done; and that Com-ittee has expressed its regret at its inability, wing to lack of funds, to undertake the work, and as asked the Council to do it. We freely admit iat this is by no means an unreasonable quest, having regard to the fact that if the site e not appropriated to the Shaftesbury Memorial untain, the obligation under the Act of laying ; the piece of ground as an ornamental enclo-e and of building the enclosing wall would rest irely upon the Council. We are confident that refusal of the Council to incur this expenditure uld preclude the Memorial Committee from cing the fountain upon the site, and the double portunity of providing for a much-needed amentation of Piccadilly-circus, and for a per-uation of the memory of the public man after om the Avenue was named, would be irre-vably lost. We may add that the Highways nmittee has given its consent to the connexion the pipes with the water main in the subway at Circus. We recommend:—

That, subject to an estimate being submitted to the ncil by the Finance Committee, as required by the ute, the Council do authorise us to provide for the nexion of the necessary water pipes with the ntain and the formation of the foundations upon ch the memorial will be placed, and the building of balustrade around it.'"

he recommendation was agreed to without cussion.

sebery-avenue.—The Improvements Com-tee also reported as follows as to a proposal the extension of Rosebery-avenue to Essex-d, Islington:—

'We have had before us a letter from the stry of Islington, suggesting that the Council uld undertake the continuation of Rosebery-nue along Owen's-row and Colebrooke-row into ex-road. The Vestry states that such a thorough-as that proposed would afford considerable ef to the congested traffic at the 'Angel,' and the advantages to be derived from the forma-of the new street would be very great. We e asked the Vestry whether, in the event of the ncil agreeing to undertake the work, it would prepared to contribute towards the cost, but the try states that in its opinion the new street ld be a County improvement, and that the cost uld be defrayed by the Council. Having ard to the unwillingness of the Vestry to con-ute towards the cost, we are not prepared to ise the Council to carry out the proposed im-vement. We therefore recommend,—

That the suggestion that Rosebery-avenue should be inued to Essex-road be not at present entertained he Council.'"

'he Council concurred in this recommenda-.

The other reports were disposed of by five minutes past four,—that is to say, all the reports had been gone through in an hour and five minutes, an event unprecedented in the history of the Council, as the Chairman remarked. But the sitting was by no means over. The *agenda* paper was full of "notices of motion." Some of these were withdrawn, but the others were not all disposed of when the Council adjourned at seven o'clock. The only one we need notice is that concerning

The "Fair Wages and Hours" Clause,—as to which Mr. Leon moved:—

"(*a*) That in future the 'fair wages and hours' clause be inserted in the contracts made with contractors instead of as heretofore being only put into the tender form, and that a penalty be imposed on breach.
(*b*) That 'fair wages' shall mean such rates of wages, and 'fair hours' such hours as have been agreed upon in each occupation between employers and the London Trades Unions concerned."

Mr. John Burns moved, as an amendment:—

"That all the contractors be compelled to sign a declaration that they pay the trade union rate of wages, and observe the hours of labour and conditions recognised by the London trade unions, and that the hours and wages be inserted in and form part of the contract by way of schedule, and that penalties be enforced for any breach of agreement."

Mr. Goodman seconded the amendment, and after considerable discussion the debate was adjourned.

THE INSTITUTE OF BUILDERS:

ANNUAL DINNER.

THE annual dinner of the Institute of Builders was held in the Egyptian Saloon of "The Monico," Piccadilly-circus, W., on Tuesday evening last, the President, Mr. Herbert Henry Bartlett, in the chair.

The President proposed the toasts of "The Queen," "The Prince and Princess of Wales and the other members of the Royal Family," and "The Navy, Army, and Auxiliary Forces." Colonel Trollope, in responding to the last toast, said he very much regretted the absence that evening of Colonel Stanley Bird, who had caught a chill and was unable to be present.

Mr. H. T. Ashby proposed the toast of "The Houses of Parliament," coupled with the name of Major L. H. Isaacs, M.P., who, in reply, said the next Parliament would have some very difficult subjects to deal with, which would concern the general community, and particularly contractors and builders. One of the most important questions which would have to be disposed of was that of the proper relations between capital and labour, and in regard to that question there was certain to be a big fight. Up to the present time capital had been able to assert its claims, and labour had been compelled to relinquish some of the absurd demands which it had made. A short time ago a strike of the carpenters had to be endured by the masters, and he now understood that at no very distant date they would have to face another strike on the part of the bricklayers. It was quite clear that strikes could not go on in that piecemeal fashion, and that there must be a genuine attempt on the part of all concerned to bring those strikes to something like an end.

The President, in proposing the toast of "The Institute of Builders," said although they were not all members of the trade, he thought they must all take an interest in the calling, as it was one which affected them all. The tastes and requirements of man had so developed, and his ideas of a perfect habitation had become so complex, that a large number of different branches of the trade had been called into existence. We could not do without our houses, and it was important to us that those houses should be properly constructed. And as it seemed to be a modern idea that everybody should belong to a society, not for the purpose of self-glorification, but for aid, and for the benefit of their class, it came to pass that the builders formed a society. That society had grown and had become an Institute, and had found it necessary to obtain a charter; and now it was in a position to meet on equal terms with other corporate bodies. The ramifications of the building trade were so extensive that a surprisingly large proportion of the legislation proposed, in one way or another affected their interests, and the self-sacrifice of those gentlemen who gave their time on behalf of the Institute was deserving of all honour. There were committees and sub-committees in connexion with the Institute, and the matters which were dealt with affecting the trade were very many. The President next referred to the Parliamentary work of one session, and proceeded to say that it was necessary to thoroughly discuss any proposed legislation, for they did not know how a little word, insidiously slipped into an Act, might affect their interests. They had in connexion with the Institute a library, and although he did not like to appear to be begging, he was sure the Library Committee would be glad to receive any volumes which gentlemen could give. Under the able President who preceded him, they had had a series of winter lectures which had been given with a view to the discussion of important subjects in connexion with the trade, and he hoped that those lectures would be started again. The building trade gave employment to more men than any other trade in the country, and it had been found necessary to keep abreast of what was going on. When they were beset on all hands by labour agitators, by curtailments of power, by constantly-increasing Parliamentary requirements, and the continual encroachments that labour was making upon capital,—and to his mind, notwithstanding the way in which some of the labour leaders regarded it, capital was the very staff of labour,—they felt that a body ought to exist which should adequately represent the important interests of their trade, and which should be so much in the trust and confidence of its members that it should at all times speak with authority and power.

Mr. Thomas F. Rider, President of the Central Association of Master Builders of London, then proposed the toast of "The Architects and Surveyors," coupled with the names of Mr. Thomas Blashill and Mr. T. F. Franklin.

Mr. Blashill, in responding for the architects, said that some portion of his professional career had been devoted to matters of arbitration, and he had always thought that there were two ways of dealing with differences: either to make those differences worse, or to lessen them, so that the end might be agreement. He was sure that all those present that evening hoped and wished to agree. The building trade might always rely upon the sympathy of the architectural profession, and he was very confident that those present would do what was right and proper in reference to the questions which were agitating their minds.

Mr. T. F. Franklin having responded for the surveyors, Sir John Colomb, M.P., proposed the toast of "The President," who replied.

The last toast, that of "The Visitors," was then proposed by Mr. J. Mowlem Burt, coupled with the name of Mr. W. H. Strudwick, who briefly replied.

Amongst the gentlemen present (besides those already named) were Messrs. F. J. Dove, H. A. Hunt, J. Norton, Joseph Randall, W. E. Stoner, Thos. Gregory, Wm. Brass, H. Gough, E. S. Henshaw, H. I. Sanders, Woodman Hill, Richard S. Henshaw, J. Hill, Basil Peto, T. M. Rickman, L. J. Maton, Frank May, J. Howard Colls, and R. Neill, jun.

COMPETITIONS.

THE GLASGOW FINE-ART GALLERIES DESIGNS.—The five designers whose plans were rejected in the final competition for the new art galleries, concert-hall, and museum at Kelvingrove, have lodged, through Dr. David Murray, of Messrs. Maclay, Murray, & Spens, an objection to the design which was accepted by the Executive Committee of the Association for the Promotion of Art and Music in Glasgow. The ground of the objection is that Messrs. Simpson & Allen's design does not conform to the conditions which were laid down for competing architects by the Committee. In these conditions it was stated that the central hall was to contain a minimum of 10,000 square feet, and the objectors allege that, according to the figured dimensions on the accepted design, it only contains 7,312 ft. 6 in. The difference is made up by including in the central hall what, it is maintained, are vestibules or corridors. In the final instructions to competitors, one of the clauses stated—"The central hall is not intended so much for vocal concerts as for instrumental music, and the better music is heard in the courts of the museum and the picture-galleries, corridors, and staircases surrounding the hall, the more nearly will the building meet the object of the promoters." It was also laid down that the central hall and the corridors and approaches were to be dis-

e

tinguished in the plans by different colouring. On these conditions the objectors base their allegation that the successful designers have included in their measurements of the central hall floorage which is not a part of it. The committee have forwarded the objection to Mr. Alfred Waterhouse, R.A., who acted as their assessor. The Glasgow Institute of Architects have also the matter under consideration.—*Glasgow Herald.*

New Free Church, Ayr.—St. Andrew's Free Church congregation, Ayr, recently invited a number of architects to furnish designs for a new church to be erected on a site on Bellevue estate, near to Park Circus East. Seven sets of designs were sent in, and were submitted to the adjudication of Mr. Hippolyte J. Blanc, A.R.S.A., Edinburgh, who recommended the adoption of design "B," and which recommendation the deacons' court endorsed. The author of that design is Mr. John B. Wilson, Glasgow. The style of the building is modern Gothic. The form of plan suggested is that of a nave with two wide side aisles, the accommodation in the area being for 492, and in the gallery over each aisle and at the end of the nave, further accommodation for 268 is found. There is to be a spire, which will rise to the height of 140 ft. The cost of the building, without reckoning the spire, will be about 4,000*l.*

Schools, Woolpit, near Stowmarket.—In a competition among four selected architects for new schools for the School Board of Woolpit, near Stowmarket, the design submitted by Mr. Frank Whitmore, architect, Chelmsford, has been accepted by the Board.

Laying-out New Park at Newport (Mon.)—Twenty-five sets of plans for this work have been sent in. The first premium of 50*l.* has been awarded to Mr. Mawson, landscape gardener, Windermere, the cost of carrying out his scheme being estimated at 10,761*l.*

Illustrations.

LLANDAFF CATHEDRAL.*

ON the difference in the sites of English and Welsh cathedrals, Professor Freeman says:—"Founders of Welsh cathedrals, unlike their English contemporaries, seemed to seek their dwellings in remote places rather for retired contemplation than for any active government of the Church, in sites suited rather for Cistercian abbeys than for cathedral churches." The English sees in several instances were removed to cities of greater importance, whilst the Welsh remain where they were originally founded to this day. There is no reason to believe that the cities of St. David's and Llandaff were at any time of greater importance than at present in a military or commercial sense, though the ecclesiastical population both in proportion and in actual numbers has no doubt declined. Some remains of the original clergy houses can still be seen, either in foundations or in walls, or built into modern work.

The situation of the Cathedral is one of great beauty, and in a way unique. It is surrounded on the south and west sides by wooded hills, and elsewhere by pleasant fields and meadows, which give to the Cathedral a character more distinctly rural than any other in the country. In this respect it differs from most of its English fellows, for whilst they, as a rule, are the centre and nucleus around which a busy city has grown, here at Llandaff, the "City" is little more than a village, consisting mainly of the ruined Bishop's Palace, the Deanery, and the Clergy-houses, and a few untidy, deserted-looking streets, all of which are to the south and west of the Cathedral, and high on a hill above it. From this hill a steep and picturesque lane, shaded with trees, leads down to the west front, and past it to meadows bounded by the river Taff, from which the city takes its name.

Taking Llandaff as a whole, there is little in its external appearance, except its beautiful west front, that is suggestive of a cathedral. In the absence of any central feature, such as a tower or lantern, or of transepts, or of collegiate buildings (for the ruined Bishop's palace has no connexion with the Cathedral, and might, indeed, be the ruins of a castle, so little is there to mark its original purpose), the whole fabric might well be taken at first sight, externally at least, for an enormous parish church.

The feature which is immediately noticed by a student of architecture, and which gives th Cathedral its unique character, is the long a except at one point, unbroken plan, compris the nave, choir, and presbytery under one ro

The Supposed Chancel Arch of Bishop Urban's Church. From a pencil drawing by G.M.

First Bay of the Nave, Llandaff. From a Pencil Drawing by G.M.

* This series of Illustrations of the Cathedrals of England and Wales was begun in our issue of January 3, 1891. A list of those already illustrated, with particulars of future arrangements, will be found on page 368.

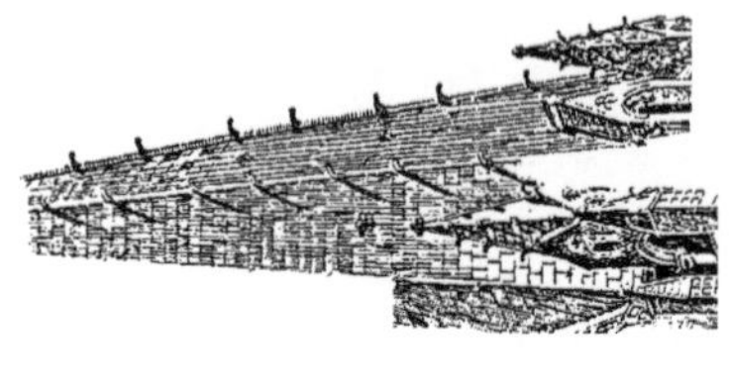

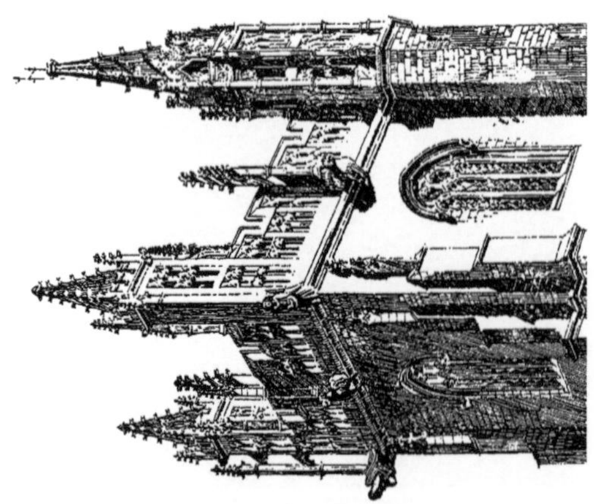

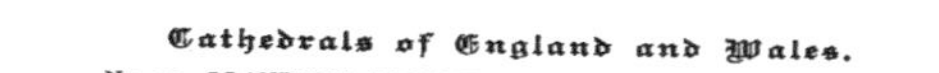

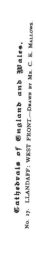

Cathedrals of England and Wales.

No. 17. LLANDAFF: WEST FRONT.—Drawn by Mr. C. E. Mallows.

PHOTO-LITHO. SPRAGUE & Co 4 & 5 EAST HARDING STREET FETTER LANE, E.C.

THE

GR

Scale of 10 5 0 10 30 50

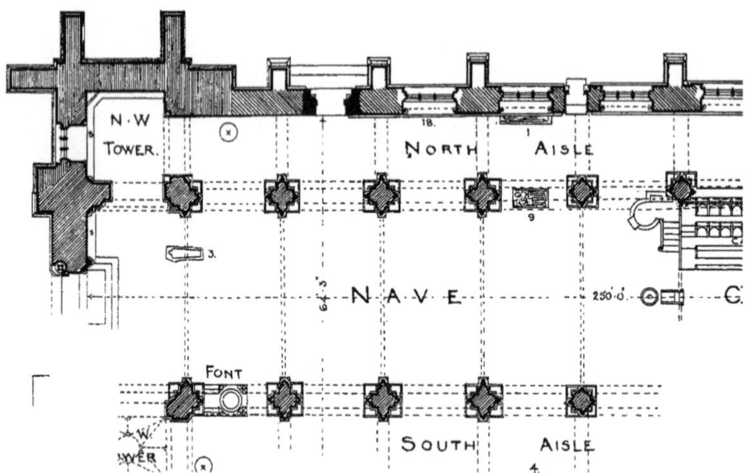

Monuments.

1. Said to be St. Dubritius 1st B: of Llandaff.
2. " " " " Teleiau or Teilo . 1200.
3. 13th Century Coffin discovered.
4. Said to be Bishop Henry de Monmouth. 1323.
5. Bishop de Breuse 1287.
6. " Brumfield 1391
7. " Marshall 1496.
8 A coffin Lid Unknown.
9 Sir. Wm. Matthew. and His Lady 1528.
10. " Do. " standard bearer. to Edward IV 1500.
11 Christopher Matthew & Lady 1500
12 An Emaciated Lady 14th Cent:
13 Lady Audley early 15th "
14 Bishop Coplestone 1827 on Wall.
15. Benjn. Hall Esq. Hensol Castle 1817.
16 Rt. Hon. John Nicholl. D.C.L. 1853.
17 Dean Conybeare . 1857.
18 Hy. Thomas Esquire 1863 in recess
19. Bishop Ollivant. 1882.
20 John Prichard Archt. of Restoration 1886

a Stair up to Library.
b Hagioscope or Squint.
C.C Squint above. (Norman.
d 14th Cent. Reredos removed from Pres
e.e. Signs of destroyed Arches
S Stone Seats
× Stoves.
✦ Stair up to leads.

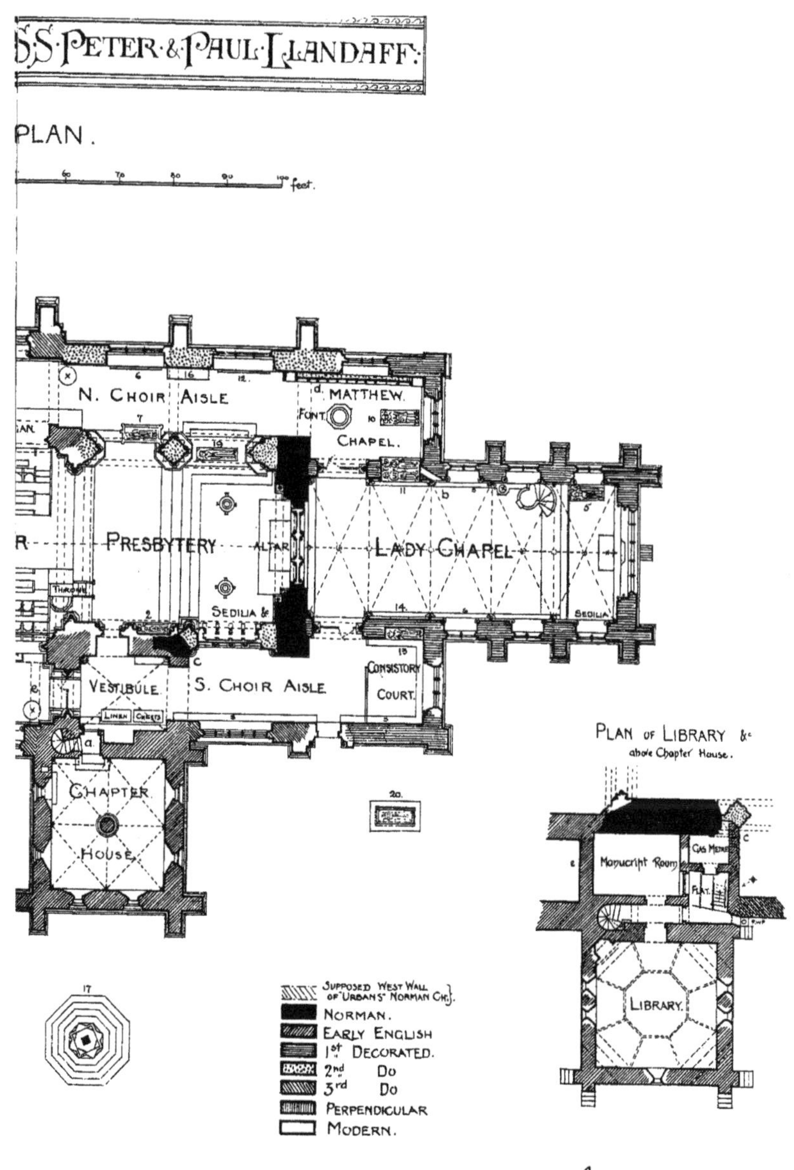
S·S·PETER·&·PAUL·LLANDAFF·
PLAN.
60 70 80 90 100 feet.
N. CHOIR AISLE
MATTHEW
FONT
CHAPEL.
PRESBYTERY
ALTAR
LADY CHAPEL
SEDILIA
THRONE
VESTIBULE.
S. CHOIR AISLE
CONSISTORY COURT.
LINEN
CHAPTER HOUSE.
PLAN OF LIBRARY &c above Chapter House.
Manucript Room
GAS METRE
FLAT.
LIBRARY.
SUPPOSED WEST WALL OF "URBAN'S" NORMAN CH.
NORMAN.
EARLY ENGLISH
1st DECORATED.
2nd Do
3rd Do
PERPENDICULAR
MODERN.
John H James.
mens et delt.. 1892.

INK-PHOTO SPRAGUE & Co 4 & 5 EAST HARDING STREET FETTER LANE, E.C.

CARTOONS FOR A W NDOW.—DESIGNED FOR EUSTON CHURCH, SUFFOLK, BY MR. H. ELLIS WOOLDRIDGE.

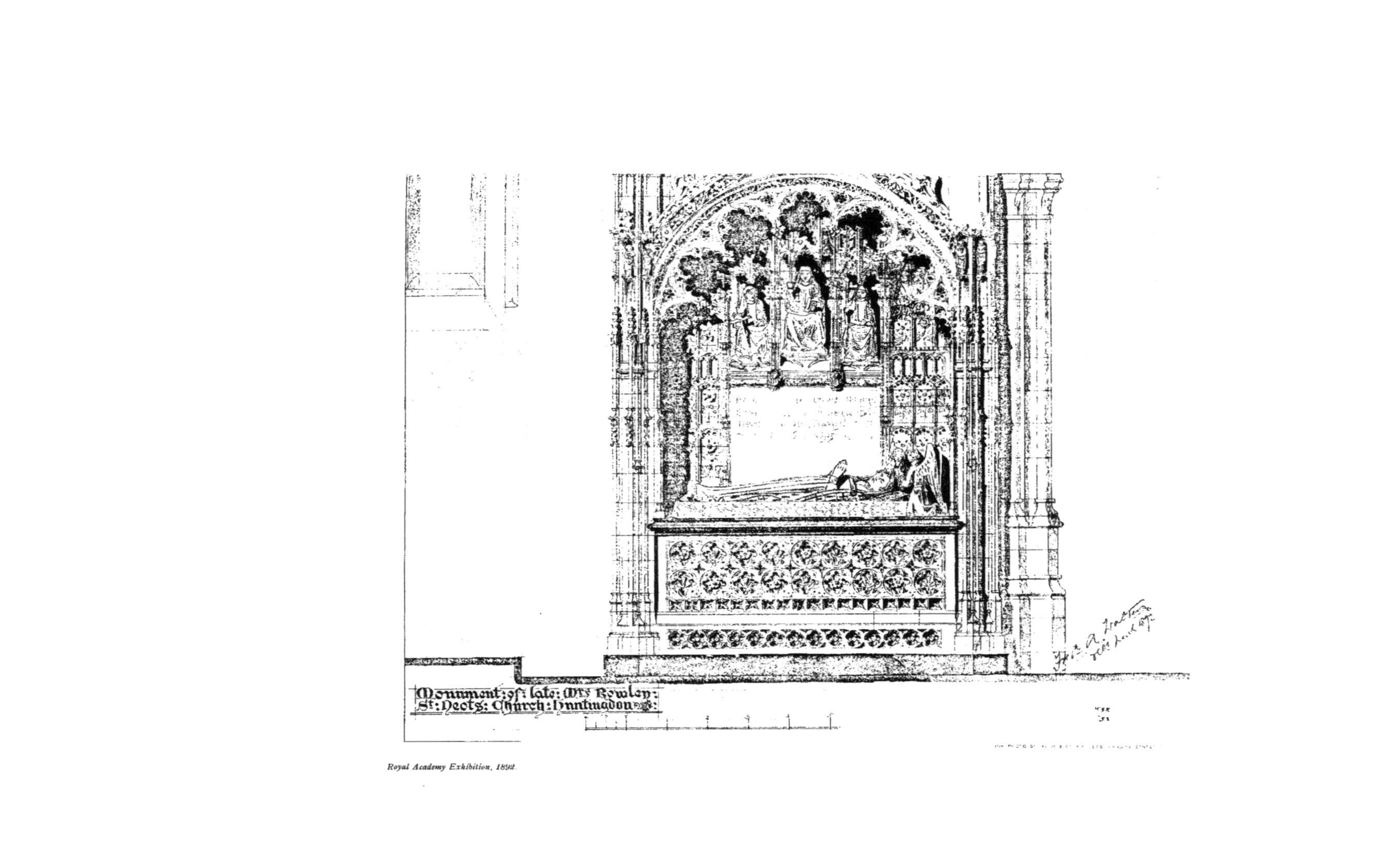

Monument: of: late: Mrs Rowley:
St: Neots: Church: Huntingdon:

Royal Academy Exhibition, 1892.

e Lady-chapel projects at the east end at a wer level. The aisles extend the whole length the church, and include one bay of the Lady-apel. The one break in this line is the apter-house, which projects on the south side om the second bay westward of the presbytery sle; on the plan it is a little suggestive of transept. Another most strongly-marked aracteristic is the absence, before mentioned, any transepts or central tower. "In this spect," Professor Freeman says, "it is unique nongst Cathedrals of South Britain, and has t few parallels amongst churches of equal ze, even when not designed as episcopal es, as the present Cathedral of Manchester, orchester Abbey, and the churches of Boston, Lincolnshire, and of S. Michael's, at ventry."

In Llandaff, again, there is but the difference detail between the nave and choir, viz., in e plan of the piers, in the arch mouldings, d in the treatment of the shafts dividing the ys; and the only difference externally be-een the latter and the presbytery is in the rangement of the clearstory. Hence the ex-rnal appearance loses a great deal in effect, e long line of roof unbroken, except where e Chapter-house occurs, and the general inness and flatness of the treatment is very satisfactory, and must have been still more in its original state, for the addition of the ttresses in the recent restoration helps to a eat extent to relieve what would otherwise be e general monotony.

The ecclesiastical foundation of the See is id to be the oldest now existing in Great itain still remaining upon its original site; t, although there is plenty of evidence to ow what the original building was like (for a inute description of it appears in "Liber andavensis"), no stone of an earlier building an that founded by Bishop Urban in 1120 w remains. The original S xon church was ost likely entirely destroyed to make room r its Norman successor, the principal remains which are the large Early Norman arch hind the high altar, and which is one of the ost effective features of the interior, and a rtion of a window and wall on the south side the presbytery, part of which has been cut vay in a very curious manner by the Decorated cade.

The large Norman arch was, doubtless, the ancel arch of Bishop Urban's church, and his ve stood where the presbytery now is, whilst e site of his choir is now occupied by the esent Lady-chapel. Judging from this, the iginal Norman church must have been a ry small one, although, as the re-ains indicate, of a somewhat elaborate aracter. There is a theory that these mains are but a portion of a much larger urch extending as far as the present west ont, but the later work in the porches at the stern end is much too advanced in detail to mit of the idea that they formed any portion Urban's work; the latter is more likely to ve consisted of only nave and choir without ntral tower or transepts, as no signs of these ving existed eastward of the present Presby-ry remain. Some foundations have, indeed, en found on the north side near the presby-ry aisle, but what they originally formed is ly very conjectural. There are more definite lications, however, on the south wall of the esent presbytery, which seem to point to the ct that a Norman tower of an irregular lygon shape existed over the present Early glish vaulted bay into the Chapter-house; e core of the walls of this bay is evidently rman, although the facing is Transitional. e walls here are very thick, and seem by eir strength to have been built for a tower. e extent of Urban's church may have been e bay westward of this part.

Bishop Urban died in 1133, and there seems have been an interval of about fifty or sixty ars before building operation were again mmenced. The external walls of the nave d choir, including the two Norman doorways, attributed to Bishop Henry, of Abergavenny, o held the See from 1193 to 1218, the nave d choir and the vaulted bay to the Chapter-use being built during the latter years of his e, and that of his successor William Prior, of uldcliff, whose death is recorded in 1229. e work carried out by these prelates is by the most beautiful and interesting in the ole building, and well repays careful study. e detail is especially good and pure of its te, and is marked everywhere with great lividuality, notably in the arch-molds and

the manner in which these die upon the piers at the springing. The accompanying sketch illustrates this, and also the difference in the detail between the nave and choir before mentioned. The sketch shows the first bay of the nave with the last choir pier and the first pier of the nave.

As already observed, the chief beauty and the most attractive portion of the Cathedral is to be found in the west front. It was built at a time when the Early English style was at its best, and is entirely free (with the exception, perhaps, of the porch) from the slight Romanesque feeling which still lingers in the details of the nave and choir.

It is interesting to compare this front with that of Saint Remi at Rheims; the similarity of the treatment is very evident, the proportion and grouping of the windows in the middle stage is almost identical, and appears to suggest that the architect at Llandaff and Saint Remi was one and the same man.

The interior design of this portion, both in detail, arrangement, and proportion, is admirable; it gains a great deal in dignity by the difference in height between the level of the nave floor and of the ground outside, there being a fall of several feet at this point. The additional height thus gained is given to the stage occupied by the three great central lights, whose internal cill reaches nearly to the tympanum of the semi-circular doorway outside, the loss of proportion to the lower internal stage being made up by the depth below the external ground line. The manner in which the different proportions of the exterior, and interior, necessitated by the two levels, are managed so as to give effect of dignity and good proportion to each, is very ingenious, and deserves close attention.

From the fact that traces of the springing of arches exist in the eastern bay of the aisle on each side of the choir, Professor Freeman believes that they were originally the western arches of a pair of towers, the position of which would have been similar to those at Exeter, except that at the latter they are separated by the aisles from the church itself, whilst here they would have been built over them. If these towers ever existed, the Early English church would have consisted of two steeples flanking the choir, with two larger ones at the west front. This would have contributed a great deal to break up the general monotony of the design. Soon after the nave and choir were completed the Chapter-house was added by Bishop William de Burgh, chaplain to Henry III. (consecrated 1244 and died 1253), and probably completed by William de Radnor, 1256-1265. It is transitional from Early English to Decorated in style, clearly later than the nave and choir, having deeply-recessed lancet windows, with foliated heads. The plan is very unusual,—if not unique,—amongst Chapter-houses, for where they are usually either rectangular or polygonal in plan, here it is square and vaulted, in four compartments, with a plain central pillar. It has an octagonal upper story, finished with a high pyramidal roof.

During this time Urban's nave and choir existed, but on the completion of the Chapter-house his choir was removed, to make room for the next and last addition,—the Lady-chapel,—which was built about the latter half of the thirteenth century, and consequently is Early Geometrical in date. It was founded by Bishop de Breos, who was Bishop of Llandaff from 1265 to 1287, and whose tomb is in the Lady-chapel on the north side of the altar. This part of the Cathedral is fortunate in being to-day in practically the same condition as that in which its founder left it. It is a very good example of the period to which it belongs; but, by reason of its tall and narrow proportions, is in strong contrast to the rest of the work, and somewhat out of harmony with it. It is vaulted in stone of five bays, with Purbeck marble vaulting shafts, and has some good carved bosses at the intersection of the groins. The whole detail is of a very simple and refined character. The external treatment is somewhat plainer, with long and narrow two-light windows between the buttress, these latter have three stages; the lower one has a gablet or pediment at the height of the window-sill, and the upper one carried up to and terminating in the deep stone parapet which finishes the sides. The whole is covered with a low-pitched modern roof, considerably spoiling the external appearance. But, taken generally, the effect of this delightful building is quiet and dignified.

On the completion of the Lady-chapel, a complete repair and remodelling of the aisles was undertaken. It was apparently from one uniform design throughout, and originated at the east end of the aisles, the work there being contemporary with that of the Lady-chapel. In some parts the original walls were left standing, in others completely reconstructed from the ground. This work was so slowly carried out that it extended through the remaining portion of the thirteenth century, and probably through the whole of the fourteenth, when the present aisle windows, with their ogee heads and reticulated tracery, were inserted. It was at this time that all indications were destroyed, so far as the aisles are concerned, of the bases of the supposed towers. The earliest portion of Decorated date is that comprising the two bays of the aisle on the north side of the presbytery, and the work commenced but never completed in the re-building of Bishop Urban's nave.

Two arches were finished on the north side, but on the south the eastern one only; the next arch on this side was just started, leaving the head of a Norman arch and the commencement of the next one above, the latter cutting into the head of a Norman window just above the springing, and leaving the western jamb and the greater portion of the arch intact. This peculiar stopping of the Decorated work, and the mixture of the Norman with it, forms one of the most interesting points in the Cathedral.

The north-west or "Jasper Tudor" tower and some tracery in the eastern windows of the aisles were the only additions of the Perpendicular period. The former was erected by Jasper Tudor, Earl of Pembroke, afterwards Duke of Bedford, and uncle of Henry VII. The Early English tower, contemporary with the west front, was probably destroyed at this time, but much of the old work in the lower portion was used in the re-construction of the new Perpendicular tower, and the latter still rests upon the original walls on the east and south sides.

The building of this tower was the last event in the architectural history of the Cathedral, until the first of those changes occurred which ended in the shameful state of neglect and decay in which Deans Bruce Knight and Conybeare found it, and from which they were the means of bringing it to the present,—on the whole,—satisfactory condition.

Few cathedrals have suffered more since Reformation days than Llandaff, for its history from that time until about thirty years ago is one of gradual ruin, spoliation, and decay. It was in such a dilapidated and unsafe condition in the year 1718 that the removal of the see to Cardiff was for some time seriously entertained. Storms, literal and figurative, have waged around its walls, playing havoc with its beauty, terminating in that of November 27, 1703, which destroyed the upper part of the north-west tower and a large portion of the nave. It was then left practically to the mercy of the weather for years, and in a pitiable state of decay, the walls of the nave and aisles were ivy-grown, and grass grew on the nave floor, whilst the aisles themselves were roofless.

A worse misfortune, however, awaited the Cathedral when it fell into the hands of Wood, the well-known Bath architect, about the middle of last century. A sum of about £7,000 was spent in converting the presbytery and the four eastern bays of the nave into what has been aptly compared to a Bath pump-room, but what was said by the architect to be a reproduction of an Italian temple. This incongruity existed for nearly one hundred years, until the movement for the complete restoration of the Cathedral commenced, as just mentioned, under Dean Bruce Knight in 1843; this restoration included the rebuilding of the presbytery, choir, and nave, and the external completion of the Chapter-house.

One or two other points of interest remain to be noticed; of these, the principal is the ruined Bishop's palace, which stands on the top of the hill on the south-east side of the Cathedral. It was, apparently, mainly of the Decorated style, and very strongly fortified, and, as the remains indicate, had more the character of a castle than a palace,—indeed, it is commonly mistaken for the former. The greater portion,—nearly the whole,—was destroyed by fire in his wars against Henry IV. by Owen Glendower, who is responsible for the loss of many of the architectural beauties of Llandaff and elsewhere in the county. The old gateway, which forms such a picturesque adjunct to the Cathedral, and some ruined walls, are all be left standing of this, at one time, stately palace.

At no period in the history of the Cathedral does there appear to have been any cloisters, and there are but few stones left of its collegiate buildings. The principal of the latter class was the Archidiaconal Castle, said to have been of great magnificence. This was also destroyed at the same time as the Bishop's Palace, and by Owen Glendower. This castle formerly stood on the north-west side of the church opposite Jasper Tudor's Tower. In Browne Willis's time (the first half of last century), there was also standing to the north-east of the castle a prebendary and a treasury house, but both in very bad repair, and soon to be pulled down; and exactly east of the Cathedral, outside the graveyard, there was formerly standing a small college for the Vicars choral.

Llandaff once possessed a famous campanile, which stood about 120 yards south-west of the west front. There were but few such towers in the country, others being at Evesham, Chichester, and Salisbury; the latter, however, was destroyed by Wyatt in the beginning of this century.

Judging from an old description of the tower at Llandaff, which appears in "Liber Landanvensis," it was evidently of considerable size and fine design. The ground plan measured 42 ft. square, and the doorway,—that is, the wooden door itself,—was 13 ft. high and 7 ft. broad. The famous "Great Peter" bell of Exeter formerly hung here, but was taken down in the fifteenth century by Jasper Tudor, and exchanged to Bishop Courtenay, of Exeter, for five smaller bells.

Another interesting relic of the Cathedral as it existed before the visitation of Wood is the painting on wood from the back of the Bishop's throne, which formed part of the Decorated choirs-tails, these latter, according to Browne Willis, were very refined in detail, and of an elaborate character. The painting represents the assumption of the Virgin Mary with seven attendant angels.

At the top of the picture on either side is an angel playing on an instrument of music, probably intended to mark her welcome into heaven. At the foot, on the left side, is an angel holding an escutcheon, on which are painted the arms of the Bishop and See, and on the right a full length portait of the Bishop himself, having a scroll coming from his mouth, on which is written the hexamter line:—

O Virgo scandens sis
Marshall cœlica pandens.

The history of this painting is very curious; during the Rebellion it narrowly escaped destruction, and was partly defaced by being covered with lamp-black. It was taken from its position during the alterations of last century, and built in the wall over Wood's Classic portico, where it was discovered by some workmen during subsequent alterations. It was then carefully cleaned and repaired, and is now on the staircase of the palace of the present Bishop. The Decorated altar-screen, which was removed to make way for the present modern one, is an excellent example of the work of that date; it was erected by Bishop Marshall, and is contemporary with the choir-stalls just mentioned. It now stands in the east end of the north presbytery aisle.

Llandaff Cathedral does not possess many monuments or tombs, although there are some deserving notice. Of these one is Decorated in style, and is on the north side of the Lady-chapel, and in the second bay from the west-end. It is of alabaster, and has nine canopied niches on each side, each containing a small figure of a saint; the whole tomb is in an unusually complete state of preservation. The tomb of Saint Teilo (whose statue is in the vesica of the tympanum of the west doorway) is interesting locally as being the tomb before which it was formerly the custom for people making purchases of land, &c., to swear to their bargains. Two curious tombs are those of Lady Audley, who is in a long robe and close muffler, with two monks bearing escutcheons at her feet, and of an emaciated figure in a winding sheet, who fell a victim to disappointed love in the fifteenth century. C. E. M.

CARTOONS FOR STAINED-GLASS WINDOWS, EUSTON CHURCH.

THESE lithographs are reproduced from cartoons made by Mr. H. Ellis Wooldridge for windows which are now being executed by Messrs. Powell, for Euston Church.

The design is entirely executed in brown and stain on white glass, leaded in squares of equal size. The subject, as will be seen, is the visit of the three Maries to the sepulchre of Christ, on the morning of the Resurrection.

MONUMENT TO THE LATE MRS. ROWLEY, ST. NEOTS.

THIS monument, in the form of a canopied altar tomb, is now being carried out from the signs of Mr. Frederick A. Walters, F.S.A., by r. Thos. Earp, of Lambeth, and will, on com-etion, be erected on the south side of the terior of the chancel of the Parish Church of ;. Neots, Hunts, of which the deceased lady's ving representative is the lay rector. The osition chosen is west of the sedilia and out-de the altar rails. The effigy in white alabaster habited in an heraldic mantle over the other arments worn, and rests on a moulded slab of ark Derbyshire fossil marble, of which aterial is also the step or plinth on which the onument stands. The whole of the rest of e work is executed in Beer stone. Above the rge arch supporting the canopy are floating ngels bearing the family shields of the lady nd her husband, while at her head, in the cess, is her own lozenge-shaped shield as a idow. The five niches surmounting the anopy contain figures of Our Lord in Majesty ttended by angels. The rose and lily are, by pecial desire, largely introduced in the carving, nd for the same reason the heart, emblematic f charity, over the main arch of canopy.

Correspondence.

To the Editor of THE BUILDER.

THE STEEPLE OF ST. ANTHOLIN'S.

SIR,—Referring to your "Note" in last week's umber as to the former Church of St. Antholin, Vatling-street, I may inform you that the spire ras undoubtedly the work of Wren.

About sixty years ago the upper part was ound to be dangerous, and it was rebuilt y John Griffith; but my father, who resided the parish in 1823, informed me that it as reduced in height, I think, about 15 ft. he capital which formed the apex was, I lieve, removed to a garden somewhere in the iburbs.

In the bas-relief on the Memorial in Size-ne, I have endeavoured as nearly as possible o produce the original proportions of the spire. t may be interesting to remark that, in conse-uence of an irregularity in a notice calling a Vestry meeting, my father and I were enabled o rescind a resolution to remove the tower as well as the church; and matters went so far as to excavate the inside of the tower, and reinter some of the human remains oused in the church, which were placed n specially-made boxes. But a parishioner, feeling that the site of the church would realise a much larger sum if the tower was removed, obtained an order in Council, and great astonishment was expressed both in the parish and outside when such order was signed. A deputation waited on the Ecclesiastical Commissioners, I think I may say *headed* by the former respected Editor of the *Builder* (Mr. George Godwin), who took great interest in the matter, to endeavour to get the order rescinded, but we were told it was impossible. The remains were, therefore, removed from the tower to the City of London Cemetery at Ilford, and the tower demolished.

I may say authoritatively that no doubt was ever expressed as to the spire being Wren's work.

The church as well as the spire was very interesting, on account of the elliptical dome set on an irregular octagon occasioned by the angle of the street.

If any of your readers take any interest in the matter, I shall be pleased to show them the drawings taken before the church was removed.

J. DOUGLASS MATHEWS.

11, *Dowgate-hill, E.C.*
May 4, 1892.

ARCHITECTURAL EDUCATION.

SIR,—Since writing the letter which you kindly printed in your last issue, I have re-ceived the accompanying communication from Mr. Jackson, which, as it clears up a confused point in the correspondence under the above heading, I venture to hope you will kindly pub-lish. I also send you the conclusion the in-formal meeting, held in my rooms on March 15, arrived at on the principal point then under consideration, as this is referred to in Mr. Jack-son's letter. I hope these documents may satisfy Mr. Adams and those of your readers who have been able to follow this correspon-pondence.

LEONARD STOKES.

7, *Storey's-gate, S.W.*, May 3, 1892.

"DEAR MR. STOKES,—I am sorry to hear from you that my letter which was published in the *Notes* of the Architectural Association has been understood in a sense that I certainly never in-tended it to bear.

Nothing was farther from my thoughts than to suggest you should make a clean sweep of your whole scheme and draw up a new one from the very beginning. The greater part of your plan seems to me excellent, though no doubt in some details you yourselves might admit it capable of improvement. For instance, I thought it attempted rather too much in including certain branches of study, of which only a smattering could have been obtained within the limits of your course, and which I thought might therefore be left out till more essen-tial things had been mastered. These are mere matters of minor detail.

The only thing of which I should like to see you make a 'clean sweep' is the pointed *reference* in your *Brown Book* and curriculum to the Examinations of the Institute.

Believing as I do, and as all those with whom I am in sympathy believe,—yourself I am happy to think among them,—that the Student who works to *pass* and not to *know* is working in the wrong way, and with the wrong motive, and will never in that way qualify himself for an architect, I cannot feel any sympathy with an educational plan which contemplates examination as its goal.

When we met at your rooms we drew up and agreed to certain points.* My letter was not in-tended to do more than reinforce what we then agreed to.

I wish I had heard of the need of an explanation in time for publication in your journal (*A. A. Notes*), but I shall be glad if you will make this letter public among the members of the A. A., or in any other quarter that you may think proper.

In conclusion, I must express my regret, not un-mixed with surprise, that some of your members should imagine I had ventured in any way to attack the independence of the Architectural Association, or, as one writer in your *Notes* puts it, to 'dictate your future course of procedure.' I cannot see how such an interpretation can be put on anything I have said or done. I was asked by you and others whether I would help your educational scheme, and I naturally replied that I could not join in it so long as it pointed towards examination, which I consider a misfortune. Surely this is not dictation. The Association is at perfect liberty to go its own way without any regard to me or my opinions; but when I was invited,—it matters not whether formally or informally,—to say on what under-standing I would join you, I could not do otherwise than state my own views for what they were worth, and explain the conditions on which I should be glad to co-operate with you. I fail to see why this should, in Mr. Adams's words, have caused the Association 'surprise, astonishment, and indig-nation.' I may surely claim for myself that inde-pendence which the Association very properly values in its own case.—Yours very truly.

T. G. JACKSON.

14, *Buckingham-street, W.C.*, April 28, 1892."

* The following is the principal point referred to above:—That the instruction given by the lecturers and instructors in the studio should be directed solely to a thorough architectural training, without special reference to preparation for any examinations.—L. S.

SIR GILBERT SCOTT'S RESTORATIONS.

SIR,—Mr. Loftie, in his letter published in your issue for April 23, says that Sir Gilbert Scott "put forward a scheme for the *destruction* of the noble carved stalls" at Canterbury Cathedral. The stalls at the west end of the choir are of the time of Charles II., the canopies being profusely ornamented with wreaths of palm branches, swags, and cherubs, with the Royal arms in full relief over the doorway. These canopies Sir Gilbert Scott proposed to *remove* and place in the nave, in order to expose the rich stone screen, the work of Prior Henry de Estria, which is now completely hidden by them. This screen, the existence of which is known to few, resembles the side screens of the choir in general design, but is more elaborate in detail, having the spandrels of arches filled with richly-carved diaper work, also painted panels between the arched openings. The space between the cills of the arcade and the elbows of the stalls is filled with oak boarding and decorated, and the stalls of the prior and sub-prior have had canopies of stone. The original colouring of the screen is mostly in a perfect state of preservation, and agrees with traces of colouring still to be seen on the south choir screen at the back of one of the canopied monu-ments,—showing that this colouring was continued all round the choir. See illustration, p. 362.

Mr. Loftie remarks that at Gloucester Cathedral "nothing ancient that could be 'restored' away was left,"—a sweeping statement, leaving the erro-neous impression that there is very little of the ancient work untouched.

Sir Gilbert Scott's work was chiefly confined to the choir, where he put new seats in front of the stalls, bringing back to their original places the ancient arcaded fronts and "shades;" he also removed the galleries.

The uninteresting modern screen at east end was taken down, and replaced with a reredos and side screens. The only work done externally was to the porch, which was in such a state of decay that repairs were absolutely necessary to prevent the features from utterly disappearing.

Mr. Loftie also says that Manchester Cathedral "escaped" from Sir Gilbert Scott, but he has over-looked the fact that the ancient choir-screen, which had been cast aside as a thing of no value, was replaced by Sir G. Scott in its original position, and had it not been for him this fine oak screen would probably have been destroyed before now.

JOHN MEDLAND.

SIR,—The two letters, one from Mr. Loftie and one from Mr. Arthur Baker, printed side by side in your columns of April 23, and which seem to have been called forth by my humble effort to defend Wren's Library at Lincoln, are amusing and in-structive reading.

Mr. Loftie is such a champion on my side, that he has not even had time to be correct in his facts.

It is, however, but too true that most of the buildings to which he refers have, in one way or another, been murdered under the pretence of restoration. Galvanised corpses are left.

But—poor Mr. Baker—what can we say for him! He entirely misses the point, and is evidently living in the uttermost regions of outer darkness.

Curiously enough, the monstrosity erected, under the plea of restoring the south aisle, at Chester Cathedral, which Mr. Baker so much admires, was one of the pieces of gratuitously destructive restoration I had in my mind when I was mention-ing Sir Gilbert as a man whose name must inevitably be classed—in time—with that of Wyatt.

At the same time, I speak of my old master, Sir Gilbert, with the highest esteem. In working so much destruction, he believed he was doing right. He spared neither time nor trouble. His ardent love for, and delight in, the buildings he was wreck-ing under the name of restoration, could not be exceeded. Had he lived in these days, I feel con-vinced that "repair," and not "restoration," would have been his watchword. A watchword which, it seems, Mr. Baker is quite unable to understand.

SOMERS CLARKE.

SIR,—It is scarcely correct to say "Worcester was the joint work of Sir Gilbert Scott and Mr. Perkins." Sir Gilbert was only called in to finish the choir and pave the nave. Perkins did the work of restoration; he saved the tower from the fate that befel Chichester, taking out and rebuilding two large piers. Perkins secured the stone vaulting that had been condemned as hopeless years before, and that narrowly escaped being substituted for wood.

Some of the mistakes that were made were not the fault of the architect, but of the authorities of the cathedral,—*e.g.*, the geometrical west window, which ought to have been curvilinear. I have seen Perkins's design for the window in that date of style, and a magnificent design it was; but he was overruled.

Perkins was a man of retiring disposition, and was consequently overlooked; yet clever he cer-tainly was.

Blunders were made; but I think some of our important modern men would blunder more and worse, had they the work.

W. LUNN.

Malvern, April 27, 1892.

SIR,—I would not for a moment question Mr. Loftie's right to his own opinion, on matters of principle and taste, or of the artistic power of any artist whether he be dead or living; but I do feel at liberty to protest against an author who has gained a reputation as an historian, passing from history to romance without giving his readers fair notice, and especially so when the deviation is made at the expense of the memory of that good and great man under whose spell it was my privi-lege to remain for sixteen years.

During the sixteen years I not only had an opportunity of witnessing Mr. Loftie's animosity to Sir Gilbert Scott, but of judging of the inaccuracy of both his past and present accusations.

Their inaccuracy is of two degrees,—the mitigated and the unmitigated.

Of the latter class are the statements: First, as regards his sight, which, far from being imperfect, was particularly keen; his fondness for fine and delicate drawings, and his appreciation of the finest detail on buildings being proverbial.

Then, as to his work, Messrs. Slater & Carpenter's reredos, at Chichester, is put to his credit or rather discredit.

He is said to have "restored the wretched screen at Winchester," whereas, being so wretched as to be only fit for destruction, it was replaced by a screen designed by Sir Gilbert. The restoration of the west front of Lichfield Cathedral is entirely omitted, and Scott and Lord Grimthorpe at St. Albans, and Cottingham and Pearson at Rochester, are pitched in company into the anti-restorationists' Gehenna without one word of proof of the justice of their joint or separate committal. One comparison should be sufficient to show that the work of Scott and Lord Grimthorpe was of an utterly different nature. Scott brought up the western end of the south wall of the nave, which was so much out of the

A. Masonry painted to imitate carved compartments. B. Carved diaper, gilt, on pale blue ground.

The Ancient Choir Screen, Canterbury Cathedral; portion showing Stall and Remains of Canopy. (*See Mr. Medland's letter, page* 361).

perpendicular as to be in danger of falling, without the least interference with the old work, and thus preserved this magnificent specimen of Mediæval architecture which would otherwise have been totally destroyed; whereas Lord Grimthorpe pulled down Norman work, which was so strong that it required blasting, in order to carry out his own designs, and yet in the eyes of Mr. Loftie these are both "Vandalic operations."

To the former class I have ascribed the term mitigated, as I take the inaccuracies to lie rather in the meaning he intends to be attached to some of his terms rather than to the terms themselves. For instance, the word re-building which he frequently uses might, in ordinary parlance, refer to a partial re-erection of a building, or to an operation necessary to preserve a building, the old design and materials being reused, whereas Mr. Loftie uses it always as implying destruction of what was to supply something new and different.

"Scott rebuilt Chester, wholly destroying the exquisite charm of antiquity."

In this case "the exquisite charm of antiquity" was, unfortunately, caused by a decay of the facing of the walls, which, in the case of St. John's Church, Chester, where no restoration was attempted, caused the fall of the tower. And the "rebuilding" consisted of the absolutely necessary work of renewing the face of the walls with sound stone, every detail of the new work being made exactly after the pattern of the old. Mr. Loftie's statement infers that the removal of the old stones was unnecessary; but he says nothing either in support of this, or to show how he would have had the charm of antiquity preserved, or whether he would have allowed it to extinguish itself in its antiquity.

Again, the work at St. Asaph is spoken of as re-building, whereas the actual rebuilding was confined to only a portion of the wall and roof of the choir, which was a necessary work, and resulted in some archæological discoveries of great interest, the rest of the work being mainly the repairing and beautifying of the interior, and I may safely challenge any one who knew the cathedral before and after it fell into Sir Gilbert's hands to compare its present unfavourably with its past condition.

Again, at St. David's an unscrupulous use is made of the word rebuild. The rebuilding of the tower being only partial and confined to the piers, which were so rotten that the tower must have collapsed if Sir Gilbert Scott, with wonderful engineering skill, had not shored up the upper part of the tower and removed and rebuilt the piers one by one, and thus preserved the tower. And yet Mr. Loftie, though a professed lover of antiquity, allows his animosity to Sir Gilbert to transform this into an evil deed.

I regret that I have not time to deal with all the examples quoted by Mr. Loftie, but I think I have given fair specimens of the inaccuracy of his statements. ARTHUR BAKER, F.R.I.B.A.

SIR,—I have just been shown in the *Builder* of the 22nd a letter from Mr. A. Baker, a former clerk of the Scotts. He says that in the early days of the restoration of this Cathedral I prevented Sir G. Scott from examining the closed and brick rebuilt west fronts of the porches, to find remains of the original ones, with a view to restoring them. It is impossible that he can be ignorant that the Committee, and on my motion, expressly authorised him (or possibly by that time Mr. J. O. Scott) to spend 100*l*. in that very investigation. The result was that they pulled down the whole of the two closed-up fronts, up to the top of the vaulting, and left the walls above supported on timber, which it would have cost twice as much to build up again if I had not restored the whole properly; and that they found nothing of any value. They did find some pretty bits of carving, which we did our best to keep as relics, but they gradually perished into dust.

Before that I one day found Longmire, the contractor for the defined works under the Committee, pulling something else to pieces. I asked him what for. He answered that Scott wanted to investigate something or other. Well, I said, I have no objection; but remember it has nothing to do with the contract, and we shall not pay for anything done without our order, as the contract says. And we heard no more of that, or any other such thing, until we had the application I have mentioned.

St. Albans, May 2, 1892. GRIMTHORPE.

THE GRISSELL MEDAL COMPETITION.

SIR,—In the *Builder* of April 16, I see that you publish the drawings which have won the Grissell Gold Medal for 1892. Will you kindly allow me space to criticise these drawings, and also to make a remark or two as regards the general conditions of the competition?

First, then, as regards the structure. The geological features of the cutting, over which the bridge is to be built, seem to have been ignored, and huge, unbeautiful (except perhaps to the contractor), and, to my mind, criminally wasteful abutments have been designed, where there was not the slightest need for any at all, nature having herself supplied rock sides to the cutting from which the arch should spring direct. I have roughly estimated the cost of the abutments as pe[r] drawing, and consider that they would requir[e] at least 5,500*l*. to prepare for and build A "flying arch,"—so often met with [in] Brunel's railway works,—would have bee[n] all that was required: footings, of course, woul[d] have been needful if the rock was soft, and perhaps, a pad of concrete beneath them. A muc[h] flatter curve, on the equilibriated principle, woul[d] have looked better, been safer, and saved in the sprandrel walls, although this latter would probably have been counterbalanced by the increase of span. Another point where I think Mr. Harlock has been guilty of waste is in the depth of his arch stones. The keystone of Cabin John Bridge, in America, with a span of 220 ft., is 4 ft. 2 in.; that of the Grosvenor Bridge at Chester (200 ft. span) is 4 ft. I think that both Molesworth and Trantwine would have been satisfied with 3 ft. 6 in. in the present case. If "architectural features" were sought by this excessive depth, I think they might have been gained another way, viz., by making the outside arch quoins *only* of greater depth, and feather-headed, both for appearance sake and also for getting some bond and level foundation for building the sprandrel walls from.

Now, secondly, as regards the general conditions of the competition. Would it not have been well to state that economy of design, within the limits of safety, would be a most essential feature, to be considered in making the award? If this is not done in future, of what use at all is a design for this class of work. I take it that the prize drawings should be such that they would be suitable for actual constructional purposes, and not merely made up of eyeable lines, pleasing colours, and "architectural effects" on paper. Railway work, as at present carried out, is done on the safest and cheapest possible lines. If ornamentation is needful, let it take a third place, safety and cheapness ranking before it. To ensure economy in the future, I think it would be well to make each competitor send in quantities, and an estimate for his design. If this is not done I feel sure that wasteful drawings will be the result.

H. H. HUMPHREYS,
Stud. Inst. C.E.

P.S.—I had better add, perhaps, that I was not a competitor, nor, as far as I know, were any of my friends or acquaintances.

SAFETY OF LADDERS.

SIR,—As a test question in regard to the safety of ladders, permit me through your columns to pu[t] the following:—

A ladder 60 ft. long and weighing 3 cwt., whos[e] centre of gravity is one-third of the way from th[e] foot, stands on a rough pavement and leans agains[t] a rough wall, its foot being 12 ft. from the wall. Will some one show by a graphical method of solution how near the top of the ladder a man weighin[g] $1\frac{1}{2}$ cwt. can ascend, the coefficient of friction fo[r] the pavement and the wall being $\tan^{-1}\frac{1}{6}$.

W. J. W.

CHRIST'S HOSPITAL.

IR,—Fourteen years having elapsed (copying m a widely-circulated statement) since a Royal nmission reported that "for a thorough reform he management and discipline of Christ's Hosal we think that its removal from London is inpensable," and the Privy Council scheme which ame operative on January 1, 1891, providing ction 63) that the Hospital Schools for 1,170 olars of both sexes "shall be maintained within onvenient distance from the City of London," I sume the public may expect soon to hear of nething being done. Can anyone give any inmation? BRICKS AND MORTAR.

The Student's Column.

ARMING BUILDINGS BY HOT WATER. XIX.

BRICK-SET BOILERS (*continued*).

THE most customary way to set a saddleboiler, especially of medium and large size, is to provide flues up and down along its exterior as follows:—The iler is placed upon a level with the furnacers, the height of this point being fixed by the sition of the door, &c., of the furnace tings that are furnished for the job. The ont of the boiler comes up tight against the ickwork front (against which the iron furnace ont is fixed), and the joint between the boiler d brickwork must be a thoroughly sound and ht one to prevent the draught and flame king a short cut this way into the upper flue; e fig. 75.* This brickwork should be 9 in. ick.

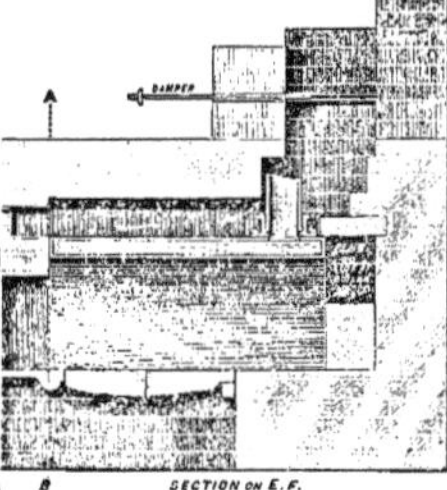

SECTION ON E.F.

Fig. 75.

There is frequently a difficulty in tting the iron front and fittings to ld securely against the front brickork, owing to several causes. Firstly, the pansion and contraction of the metal, and, ain, the opening and shutting of doors, and e of stoking tools, are the chief causes of the rk getting loose. This happens especially if e fittings are merely secured with holdfasts the brickwork. The object in referring to is is to explain a method of securing the front ich will not only keep the fittings in place der the roughest of usage, but which will tend keep the front brickwork tight against the iler also, as is so necessary, as just mentioned. is method is to have iron rods or stays tending from the iron furnace front right rough along the sides of the boiler and pping round its furthest end. These can be sily tightened up by having the front ends ming through holes, screwed, and with nuts them.

From the illustration it will be seen that evious to the boiler being placed in position, base is built up, and it is arranged that the ickwork extension of the fire-box at back (for e bars do not extend the whole length of iler) is exactly level with the top surface of e fire-bars. The bars are also exactly level with e dead or dumb plate in front, the front ends the bars coming just level with the front of e boiler as shown. Sometimes, when it is sired to place the boiler lower than usual, or do with a shallower boiler-pit, the bars and ck brickwork are kept level, as just explained, t some two to four inches below the lower edge of the furnace door, instead of being level with it. This inequality is made up by having the dumb-plate sloping, as fig. 76.

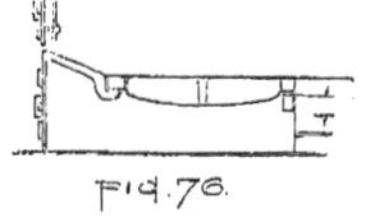

FIG. 76.

The common use of the dumb-plate now is to complete the furnace bottom from the bars to the front; it is a solid and strong plain plate, as bars are not needed here, and brickwork would do, only that clear way must be left beneath, the space below being the ashpit. The dumbplate is sometimes used in the manner originally intended,—viz., to place a charge of coal upon, that it may dry and volatilise some of its lighter gases, which, passing over hot fuel, are consumed, the charge of fuel being afterwards pushed on, a considerable reduction in smoke and waste products being the result. It will be noticed in fig 75 that, from extreme front to back, the furnace bottom is quite level. This is how it should be in the usual way, and simplifies the stoking and reduces the chances of rough usage.

The furnace-bars usually occupy about twothirds the area of the fire-box with a plain saddle-boiler, but the area varies with the pattern of the boiler, as has been fully explained (Art. XV.). The rear ends of the bars are sometimes made to rest on the brickwork with a light flat bar beneath, or they may be supported on a stronger bar, clear of the brickwork, as shown. In any case, their upper surfaces have to be quite level with the brickwork in question. The front extremities rest upon the rebated edge of the dumb-plate, or in some cases the dumb-plate has no rebated edge, and both this plate and the fire-bars rest upon a strong bar which extends from side to side. This latter method is not so good as the former, not so neat, and no stronger, for the dumbplate being supported by the brickwork at each of its ends, will carry the fire-bars well. The fire-bars are kept forward, as shown, so that the inner and direct heating surface of the boiler may have the fullest benefit of the heat and heated gases, &c., before passing away at the back into the flues.

The rear end of the boiler does not reach to the back wall by some 5 in. to 8 in. (according to size of boiler); this space forms the passageway for the heated products from the furnace to the flues of the boiler. There is, however, some brickwork built in this space with the object of guiding the heated gases in the directions they are intended to go. In this space between the boiler-end and the wall at the back is firstly built a fire-brick bridge, as shown in fig. 75, extending about halfway up the back of the boiler; and as marked in fig. 77, which

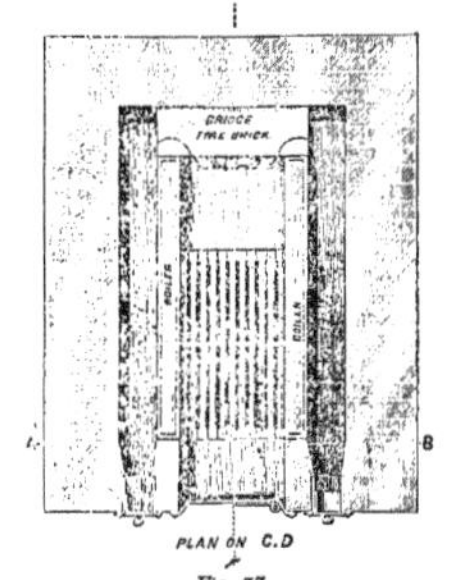

PLAN ON C.D

Fig. 77.

shows the fixing work in plan, say 6 in. above the level of the fire-bars. The object of this "bridge" is, firstly, to prevent the fuel working from the fire-box into the flues; and, secondly, to check the too free escape of the heated gases, &c. As mentioned, this bridge extends as nearly as possible half-way up, as shown at fig. 75, and also in the sectional elevation to be shown directly. With small boilers, a thick fire-brick slab is used for this purpose, but the space at back should be tolerably roomy; no harm will result as would happen if we made the other flues too wide. The action or direction of the flame at this point is to hug the boiler, to cling to it, we may say. This last illustration shows the two box soot-doors that have to be provided for cleaning the lower parts of the flues; another sootdoor is provided over the top of the boiler in front.

At a point outside the boiler, a little above where it commences to describe a circle, two mid-feathers have to be provided, one on each side, as fig. 78; they are marked "brick." The

SECTION ON A.B.

Fig. 78.

object of these feathers is to divide the flueway round the boiler into three; they extend from the extreme back to within about 5 in. to 7 in. of the front of the boiler, as shown in dotted lines in the first illustration. From the last drawing just shown, it will also be seen that their position is a few inches above the brick bridge, or, in other words, there is a clear way for flame and heat to pass over the brick bridge and into the flues each side of the boiler underneath the feathers. This is shown by arrows on both figs. 75 and 77. After the flames have traversed the length of these flues to the front, they enter the top flue together, there being provision made for this by terminating the feathers some inches short of the front of the boiler, as shown in dotted lines at fig. 75.

They then pass along the top of the boiler from front to back, and into the chimney at the rear. It is supposed that with a low chimney and low draught the heated products have lost most of their heat after having made this journey.

To make the explanation as clear as possible, we have spoken of the flame and gases finding their way through these flues; of course, it is understood they are impelled or carried by the draught induced in the chimney.

This last drawing is in section and elevation across the front ends of the furnace-bars, and it will be noticed that the brickwork forming the bottom of the flues is also exactly level with the fire-bars and the rest of what may be called the base. The side flues are, as a rule, say, 4 in. for boilers up to 3 ft. 6 in. in length, and 4½ in. up to 5 ft., and 5 in. up to 7 ft. This is large enough, as we must always remember that flame, and heated gases and products, heat by contact only; that is, they must actually impinge against or touch an object, to heat it effectually.

It may be as well to explain the customary way of making the arched flue-way over the boiler, this method requiring no woodwork supports and suiting all sizes alike. After building up the brickwork at the sides to the point where the boiler begins to arch over, dry ashes are obtained and laid over the top to a thickness that agrees with the size of the flue required. The brickwork is then carried over, resting upon this bed of ashes, and when it is set the ashes are raked out.

The final point to be mentioned is the second bridge, which is carried over, extending from mid-feather to mid-feather each side, and above the other bridge at back. This bridge is seen in the first illustration. It is introduced to prevent the flame taking a short passage up at the back of the boiler into the chimney, which will probably exist just there. Some make this bridge by carrying an iron bar from side to side, about 5 in. or 6 in. above the lower

* This and figures 77, 78, 79, are from the catalogue of akins & Son, Rotherham.

bridge, and building brickwork on this to the required shape and extent. This is not a good plan, for, unless the bar be a piece of small stout girder iron, it will contort or sag down, and cause very bad results. It is best to arrange to throw an arch over from feather to feather.

Fig. 79 shows the boiler finished complete,

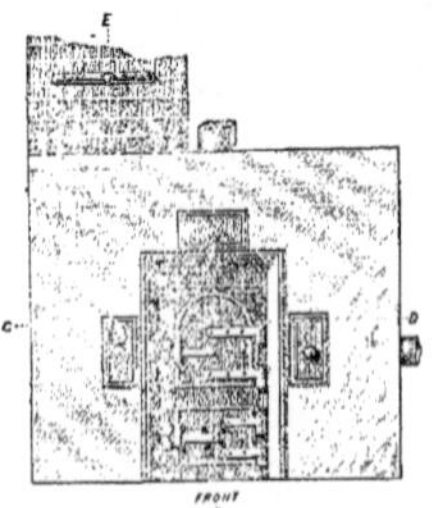

Fig. 79.

the boiler itself being out of sight, of course. Boilers can be had with waterway mid-feathers if desired; also the lower bridge at the back can be formed in the boiler with a waterway through it, and when the boiler is arranged to be fed through the top, by a proper feed-hole provided, it can also have a waterway front. The fixing of the saddle boiler has been dwelt upon rather fully, but it is necessary information, and goes far towards making a man competent to fix almost any other boiler.

OBITUARY.

MR. LUMB STOCKS, R.A.—We regret to hear that Mr. Lumb Stocks, R.A., died last week at his residence in Holloway, after a short but sharp attack of influenza. For many years he practised the art, now almost extinct, of line engraving, and his copies of Maclise's cartoons were published by the Art Union of London.

MR. F. J. ROBINSON, F.R.I.B.A.—We regret to hear of the death of Mr. Frederick Josias Robinson, of Derby. He was articled to the late H. J. Stevens, Fellow, and after passing some time in the office of Sir Gilbert Scott he entered into partnership with Mr. Stevens. He was fifty-eight years of age, and died from pneumonia supervening on a bad attack of influenza.

MR. GEORGE BIDLAKE.—On the 18th ult., Mr. George Bidlake, of Leicester, and formerly of Wolverhampton, died suddenly at Broadstairs, at the age of sixty-two. Mr. Bidlake was born in London, and educated at Merchant Taylors' School. He was afterwards articled to Mr. Kendall, a city architect, and was a student of the Royal Academy, where he won silver medals for his measured drawings of the Banquetting House, Whitehall, and for a design for a stamped drugget. Subsequently, he commenced practice at Wolverhampton, in which neighbourhood most of his works have been carried out. These comprise, amongst many other buildings, the Town Halls of Pontypool, Oswestry, Sutton Coldfield, and Bilston; workhouses at Dudley and Forden; Tettenhall College, Handsworth Grammar School, Lichfield Museum, Wellington Market, South Staffordshire Hospital Extension; Queen-street Chapel, Wolverhampton, and many other chapels and churches; additions to Albrighton Hall and numerous houses in the counties of Stafford, Worcester, and Salop. Mr. Bidlake retired from practice in 1872, removing at the same time to the neighbourhood of Leicester, where he resided until the time of his death.

GENERAL BUILDING NEWS.

VILLAGE-HALL AND CLUB, WARNHAM, SUSSEX.—A village-hall and club was presented to the village by Mr. H. Harben, of Warnham Lodge, on Monday, May 2. The land upon which the building is erected was given by Mr. C. T. Lucas, of Warnham Court. The building consists of a hall about 51 ft. long and 24 ft. wide, reading-room 25 ft. by 20 ft., smoking-room 25 ft. by 17 ft. 6 in., artistes' rooms and caretaker's apartments. The hall has a semi-circular iron roof, the walls being lined with glazed coloured bricks in patterns. For the exterior, a simple treatment of the half-timbered style common to many parts of Sussex has been adopted. The building has been erected from the designs of Messrs. Batterbury & Huxley, architects, London, by Messrs. J. Potter & Son, builders, of Horsham, at a cost of about 3,500*l.*

CHOIR STALLS, PLYMSTOCK CHURCH, NEAR PLYMOUTH.—Some new oak choir-stalls have been placed in this church, made by Messrs. Luscombe from the designs of Messrs. Tait & Harvey, architects, of Exeter.

NEW CHURCH, WYBUNBURY, CHESHIRE.—On the 25th ult., the Duchess of Westminster laid the foundation-stone of a new church at Wybunbury, Cheshire. From stones which have been from time to time unearthed in course of excavation, it has been ascertained that no less than four churches have been built on the same site, the first existing probably about 1130. The church now in course of progress is being built on a slab of Portland-cement concrete covering the entire area. The work is being done by Messrs. Treasure & Son, of Shrewsbury and London, from the designs of the architect, Mr. James Brooks, of London.

CHAPEL, ST. MARGARET'S HOUSE OF MERCY, ROATH, CARDIFF.—On Saturday last the Bishop of Llandaff opened the new chapel situate in the grounds of the St. Margaret's House of Mercy at Roath, Cardiff, which is worked by the St. Margaret's Sisterhood, East Grinstead. The chapel consists of a nave and sanctuary with a small vestry. Accommodation is provided for sixty adults. The building is Early English in style. The material is native stone, with box ground stone dressings and weatherings. Internally the walls are plastered. The tile floors are from Messrs. Smith & Co., Coalville. The windows are glazed with lead lights and cathedral glass by Mr. S. Evans, West Smethwick. The ironmongery and gas-fittings are by Messrs. Brown & Co., of Birmingham. The whole of the works have been carried out by Messrs. Shepton & Son, of Cardiff, from designs and under the superintendence of Messrs. Veall & Sant, architects, of the same town.

CONSERVATIVE CLUB, CHORLTON-CUM-HARDY, LANCASHIRE.—On the 23rd ult. the Chorlton-cum-Hardy Conservative Club was opened by Lady Egerton of Tatton and Mr. J. W. Maclure, M.P. The new building has been erected at the corner of Manchester and Wilbraham-roads, on a site covering an area of 2,000 square yards, from the designs and under the superintendence of Messrs. Darbyshire & Smith, architects, of Manchester. The principal entrance occupies a central position facing Wilbraham-road, and the various clubrooms are situated on the right and left of the entrance. The billiard-room, which is 40 ft. long and 26 ft. wide, contains two billiard tables, and is supplied with lavatory accommodation. The card-room and bar adjoin the billiard-room. At the other end of the buildings are the secretary's room, lavatories, and committee and reading-rooms; the two latter rooms being divided by a movable partition. The public hall, which is capable of holding about 800 persons, occupies the whole of the first floor, and is provided with both ladies' and gentlemen's retiring-rooms. The public and platform entrances are separate from the club entrance and from each other. A connexion is made between the club and hall for the use of members. A cooking-kitchen is also provided in the basement, with a hoist connecting the kitchen with the club and rooms above. A caretaker's house has been erected at the rear of the club. The exterior of the building is faced with Accrington red pressed bricks, relieved with Edwards's Ruabon buff terra-cotta. The roofs are covered with Buttermere green slates. The heating apparatus is on the low pressure hot-water system, and supplied by Messrs. Leech Bros. Mr. Owen Williams is the general contractor for the works. The cost of the buildings and furniture will be over 4,000*l.* The building is provided with a clock tower.

PAROCHIAL INSTITUTE, WOODHOUSE, LEEDS.—A working-men's institute, which has been erected by the Misses March, has just been opened at Woodhouse, near Leeds. The building is faced with pressed bricks, having Bradford stone dressings, the roofs being covered with Buttermere green slates. The two entrances from Cathcart-street give access on the ground floor to a reading-room and a recreation-room, each about 28 ft. by 20 ft. There is also a small lecture-room behind these two rooms, 31 ft. by 23 ft., fitted up with a platform. A large tea-making-room adjoins. A committee room, lavatories, and caretaker's house complete the accommodation on this floor. Near the two entrances are two stone staircases leading to the large lecture-hall on the first floor. This room is 70 ft. by 40 ft., and will accommodate about 600 people. The platform is constructed in sections, the permanent portion being large enough for ordinary occasions, while the enlargement makes it suitable for dramatic and other performances. The roof bindings are moulded, and spring from moulded stone corbels. Air trunks are fixed in the ceiling to carry away the vitiated air, which is extracted by one of Boyle's air pumps placed in an octagonal turret. The ground falling rapidly from front to back, the opportunity has been taken to construct a covered playground in the basement, which is lined with white glazed bricks, and lighted through an arcade of semi-circular arches. Messrs. Smith & Tweedale, of Leeds, were the architects, and Councillor Hannam has erected the building from their designs.

NEW CATTLE MART, GATESHEAD.—On the 25th ult. the new cattle mart for auction purposes was opened at Redheugh, Gateshead, by Messrs. T. and I. Maughan & Co. The mart is situated about fifty yards from the Gateshead entrance to the Redheugh Bridge, and is within a short distance of the Newcastle Cattle Docks. It covers an area of about 1,350 superficial yards, and it has been laid out and erected by Messrs. Geo. Scott & Son, contractors, of Newcastle, under the personal supervision of Mr. T. Nelson. The sale mart proper,—which is covered in, and lighted from the roof,—is about 36 ft. square, and the sale space is about 24 ft. square. The whole of the pens and stakes are cemented throughout, and the whole of the alleys and the sale space are paved with cement blocks.

CORPORATION PUBLIC BATHS, STAFFORD.—The formal opening of the new baths recently erected in the borough of Stafford took place on the 19th ult. The elevations of the bath to the river and to Greengate-street are in the half-timbered style, the material generally used being red brick. A clock tower, at present without a clock, is used as a shelter for the fire-escape. Within, there is a main swimming-bath, 83 ft. by 33 ft., and a ladies' swimming-bath (which at some future time may be used as a brine plunge bath), 60 ft. by 18 ft. The greatest depth of the large bath is 6 ft., and of the small 5 ft. 6 in. Each bath has a roomy gallery, and a suite of private baths opens on to the ladies' gallery. A suite of private baths for gentlemen is also attached, and there is a set of rooms and baths for the Turkish bath. There is provision for a number of private brine baths, which can be put in use as soon as the brine at the north end of the town becomes available. The cost of the whole is about 6,000*l.*, and the designs were by the Borough Surveyor, Mr. W. Blackshaw.

WESLEYAN CHAPEL, SHADWELL, LEEDS.—The foundation-stones of a new Wesleyan Chapel at Shadwell were laid on the 27th ult. The design of the new chapel is by Mr. Geo. F. Danby, architect, Leeds. The building is to be constructed of stone, with an interior lining of bricks, and the edifice will be in the Decorated Gothic style, with open timbered roof. A large class-room and minister's vestry will be provided. The whole of the woodwork will be of varnished pitch-pine, and the roof will be covered with Welsh slates.

BOARD SCHOOLS, BRECON.—The corner-stone of the new Board schools in Mount-street, Brecon, was laid by the Mayor of the Borough, Colonel Morgan, on the 15th ult. The accommodation will be for 198 infants, in three rooms on the ground-floor, where are also all the cloak-rooms and lavatories; the mixed schoolroom and two class-rooms for 110 boys and 119 girls being above. Mr. E. H. Lingen-Barker, of Hereford, is Architect to the Board, and the contractor of these schools is Mr. B. Jenkins, of Brecon, whose contract amounts to 2,586*l.*

SANITARY AND ENGINEERING NEWS.

WATER SUPPLY, BISHOP'S CASTLE.—A Local Government Board inquiry was held at Bishop's Castle, Shropshire, on the 28th ult., by Col. Luard, R.E., on an application of the Corporation for sanction to borrow 4,000*l.* for works of water supply. Water will be collected on the hills about six miles west of the town, and brought in by gravitation. The engineer for the works is Mr. W. Wyatt, of Shrewsbury.

SEWERAGE, ABERGWYNFY, SOUTH WALES.—The Sanitary Authority of the Rural Sanitary District of the Neath Union in the counties of Glamorgan and Brecon, having applied to the Local Government Board for sanction to borrow 7,500*l.* for works of sewerage and sewage purification, an inquiry was held on the 20th ult. at Abergwynfy by Major-General Henry Darley Crozier, R.E., when evidence was given in support and against the granting of the loan. The scheme was virtually approved of by the opposing side, the main contention being that the work should not be done by the Rural Sanitary Authority, but by the New (Local) Board when formed. The process recommended is the International Company's process by "Ferrozone" and "Polarite," and is the first instance of its being introduced into Wales. The sewage will be conveyed to the outfall works by gravitation. The precipitating tanks are constructed for either the "quiescent" or "continuous flow," and a patent arrangement is to be applied to the polarite filters for automatically cleaning the top layer of sand without having to remove the same off the beds for washing. The engineer for the scheme is Mr. W. E. Clason Thomas, of Neath.

BUILDING TRADE WAGES IN GENEVA.—According to a recent report of the United States Consul at Geneva on labour and wages in French Switzerland, carpenters, joiners, masons, &c., generally work by the hour, ten forming a day, for which they receive 4s. 2d. to 5s. When paid by the piece the rates are fixed so that they earn from 4s. to 5s. 7½d. a day. In these trades there are unions of employers and workpeople who fix prices and avoid difficulties and strikes, which, however, have broken out occasionally. Locksmiths and plasterers earn about the same wages, but in some cases more, viz., 5s. 7½d. to 6s. 3d. a day.

FOREIGN AND COLONIAL.

FRANCE.—In a cellar in the Rue de la Reine Blanche (Quartier des Gobelins) a large stone tomb has been discovered, containing bones, pieces of money of the time of Dagobert, and arms. The Service of Historical Monuments is taking steps to find out if an ancient Mirovingian cemetery did not exist in this neighbourhood, where for twenty years important archæological remains had been discovered. ——The General Council of the Vosges has just voted the necessary funds for the erection of a museum in the house of Joan of Arc at Domrémy. The Council have charged their President to petition the sculptor Antonin Mercié to hasten the completion of the statue of Joan of Arc at Domrémy.——A committee has been formed in the Department of Indre-and-Loire for the erection of a statue of Joan of Arc at Chinon. This Committee has just appealed to the sculptors for models one-fifth size, which will be the object of a competition open till July 15. The statue will be 2·40 m. high.——The town of Toulouse has just opened a Museum of Decorative Art in the beautiful edifice known as the Collège Saint Reymond. This museum contains the Greek, Gallo-Roman, and Renaissance treasures which were before crammed into the Museum of Painting. It is M. Romestin, Inspecting Architect of Historical Monuments, who has turned the edifice into its present use.——M. Diehl, Professor of the Faculty of Letters at Nancy, is charged with a mission to Tunis to study the ancient Roman inscriptions and the principal monuments of the Byzantine period.——The jury on the open competition for the construction at Biarritz of an Etablissement de Bains de Mer has just given its judgment for the first degree. Out of twenty-four designs sent in, four have been selected; these are by MM. Felix Calinaud, architect in Paris; Galinier et Curvale, architects at Toulouse; Métivier, architect of the Department of Gers; and Nodet, architect in Paris.——The Academy of Beaux-Arts has just chosen the subject for the Bordina Prize, to be awarded in 1894—"Continue the history of engraving on medals in France from the end of the fifteenth century to 1890." For the Troyon Competition, the prize of which will be awarded in 1893, the Academy has chosen as subject, "The border of a pond in a wooded valley, with animals; effect of sun and storm clouds."——The celebrated panorama of the battle of Champigny, by the artists De Neuville and Detaille, which attracted such crowds a few years ago, is going to be parcelled out, and the fragments sold separately.——The artist Weerts has just finished a great allegorical ceiling, ordered by the State for the decoration of the Hôtel de Monnaies in Paris, and which symbolises the triumph of the Universal Exhibition of 1889.

MISCELLANEOUS.

COMPLETION OF THE WIDENING OF LUDGATE-HILL.—According to Colonel Haywood's report for last year to the City Commissioners of Sewers, the widening of Ludgate-hill (southern side), which was begun twenty-seven years ago, will shortly be effected in its entirety. The claims, amounting to nearly 83,500*l.*, in respect of Nos. 5, 7, and 9, have been ultimately settled for 32,000*l.*, the Commissioners giving up the surplus land of Nos. 1 and 3, Ludgate-hill, together with Nos. 1 and 2, St. Paul's-churchyard. These premises will be taken down within a few weeks' time, and the frontage set back in alignment with the new houses recently built. A well-known firm of tea and coffee dealers have already removed to other premises in St. Paul's-churchyard, and Dollond, the optician's,—a business established in 1750, at No. 1, Ludgate-hill,—is re-opened in a shop lower down. The average width of the street was 43 ft. In 1866 they arranged with the London, Chatham, and Dover Railway Company for a widening of the lower part of the hill on the making of the bridge and viaduct. In course of the next five years the properties Nos. 51—71 (odd), as far eastwards as St. Martin's-court, had been acquired; in 1889 the block Nos. 37 to 47, and 5, St. Martin's-court, between the court and Pilgrim-street, was demolished, the block Nos. 11 to 35, between Pilgrim-street and Creed-lane, having been taken (in two portions) in the meanwhile. A conspicuous feature of the new buildings, by St. Martin's-court, is the City Bank, of which we published an illustration on 22 August last. The bank was planned and designed by Mr. T. E. Collcutt. From reports of the meetings of the Commissioners we gather that the sums expended upon the purchase of interests in the various properties will have amounted to about 375,000*l.* for, we think, 39 houses; a total that is subject to abatement, if the capitalised value of the ground-rents, estimated at 4,000*l.* a year, with other recoupments, be reckoned. Messrs. Joseph & Smithem were the architects of the two blocks of shops and offices at the corner of Creed-lane and by Pilgrim-street.

A NEW DREDGING PROCESS.—A further trial of the new dredger built by Messrs. Simons & Co., Renfrew, for the New South Wales Government, and which is to be used in Sydney Harbour, took place on April 12 in the presence of a number of people interested in harbour construction. The two suction pipes through which the sand, &c., is lifted, measure 20½ in. in diameter, and when the centrifugal pumps were in full operation drew up and deposited in the hoppers dredgings from the bed of the river at the rate of 1,000 tons an hour, or about double the quan'ity guaranteed in the contract.—*Iron and Coal Trades Review.*

DISSOLUTION OF PARTNERSHIP. — Mr. R. W. Hitchins asks us to say that he has dissolved partnership with the firm of Messrs. F. Jones & Co., Perren-street, Kentish Town.

SCAVENGING IN NEW YORK.—The *Engineering Record* (New York) for April 16 says:—"We are glad to note that the New York Street-cleaning Bill, which was prepared in accordance with the recommendations of the advisory committee of citizens, has become a law. Under its provisions, the streets will be cleaned by a permanent corps of trained labourers, applicants for appointment in which must pass an examination as to character and physical fitness."

ELECTRIC ORGANS.—The new Hope-Jones system of electric organ control is to be called into requisition at All Saints' Church, Bristol. Mr. W. G. Vowles is about to build an additional choir organ, and to entirely reconstruct the present instrument in accord with Mr. Hope-Jones's patents, in such a manner that the whole of the organ can be controlled from a movable key-desk which will be placed at the entrance to the chancel.—*Electricity.*

THE KENNEDY DRY PRESS BRICK MACHINE. — Some months ago (November 14, 1891, p. 372) we noticed what we believe was the first public exhibition in this country of an American invention known as the Kennedy Dry Press Brick Machine. The exhibition took place at Southall Brickworks, Middlesex, and a large variety of clays were tried, including the white clay of Cambridgeshire, and slate from North Wales, from all of which bricks of very good form were moulded and turned out at the rate of four per minute, computed to yield 26,000 per day. Since then, the prospectus of a Syndicate has been issued. Mr. Nichols, the proprietor of the Thames Pottery Brick and Tile Works, near Southend, at the mouth of the Thames, has erected a complete working plant in a permanent building some 60 ft. by 25 ft. on the ground plan, and two stories high. The steam is brought from a boiler previously in use at 100 yards distance away to a steam-engine of apparently about 12-horse-power, fixed within the new building. The crusher which pulverises the clay, the hopper-elevator which carries the powdered clay to the sieve on the upper story, and the brick-making machine, which is seated on the ground floor, are each driven direct by separate belting from the engine. On Tuesday last the directors assembled at the brickworks to receive a large party of practical brickmakers, and other visitors, who came to see the operations. Besides the local brick-earth, other clays were tried, including clay from Bridgewater forwarded by Messers. Major & Co., and a remarkably adverse kind of fuller's earth sent by Mr. Lloyd Price of Bala. The latter pulverised into dust so fine that it filled the hopper-room, and came out by the windows like a fog. By slacking the speed of the crusher and the addition of a small percentage of moisture, bricks were, however, moulded from it. The chief feature in the results of the Kennedy machine is that drying before burning is eliminated. The bricks are smooth-faced all over, but an indentation or frog could be put on one or on both sides, if desired.

SMALL-POX HOSPITAL, BRADFORD. — Messrs. Morley & Woodhouse, the architects for this building, ask us to state that the scheme for the building (in regard, we presume, to heating and ventilation), illustrated in the *Builder* of April 16, is patented by them in conjunction with Mr. E. Oldroyd, the heating engineer, and they wish this to be known in order that no one may inadvertently make use of it. While we are happy to publish the statement, we feel, however, some doubt whether the patentees will find that they have power to protect the planning and arrangement of a building by patent. The law on the subject may still be doubtful, but precedents are against it.

A NEW STRAIGHTWAY VALVE.—Messrs. Beck & Co. send us an illustration and description of the Handy Straightway Valve, a double-disc valve operated by a detachable lever instead of the ordinary wheel: the position of the lever showing the degree of opening of the valve. It is designed for low pressures, as more compact than the ordinary globe valve, and for such a purpose seems likely to be useful and convenient.

WORKMEN'S DINNER.—On the 30th ult. Messrs. Marsh, Son, & Gibbs, of the Bath Stone Works, Box, entertained about 100 of the men and youths employed at their stone quarries at Rudloe and Corsham, at a repast at Rudloe. The dinner was presided over by Mr. R. J. Marsh, the senior partner in the business, the vice-chair being filled by Mr. F. H. Gibbs. After the dinner, various toasts were proposed and songs contributed.

THE ENGLISH IRON TRADE.—Little change has occurred in the English iron market during the past week; the demand generally is of a hand-to-mouth character, although there is an improvement in the demand for crude iron in Cleveland. The returns for this district show a reduction of stocks amounting to 75,000 tons. The production exhibits a decrease of 101,951 tons on the month. There are only four furnaces in blast, all on hematite. Manufactured iron is in restricted inquiry, and the tinplate market remains very dull. In steel there is very little doing, and rails are easier. Both shipbuilders and engineers continue slack. The coal trade generally is not over active.—*Iron.*

CAPITAL AND LABOUR.

BIRMINGHAM.—The dispute at Birmingham between the master-builders and the bricklayers and their labourers still continues. The bricklayers demand an increase of pay from 8½d. an hour to 9d., and the labourers ask for 6½d. an hour instead of 5½d. The strike has now entered on its fifth week.

CARDIFF.—A serious dispute has arisen in Cardiff affecting about 3,000 carpenters, joiners, plasterers, bricklayers, masons, and plumbers. After protracted negotiations, a strike has been resolved on. The questions at issue are piece-work, sub-contracting, and importation of prepared stone and joinery. The masters have signified their willingness to grant an advance of ½d. per hour. The men demand 1d.

HARROGATE.—The *Leeds Mercury* says that the building trade at Harrogate is now practically at a standstill, the stonemasons being out on strike for an advance of wages. The masons only gave a week's notice before going out, and the master builders maintain that such a short notice is unjust, as they are fairly entitled to a month's notice before any alteration should be made in the rate of payment.

STAFFORD.—The bricklayers of Stafford came out on strike on Monday morning for a rise of wages from 7d. to 7½d. per hour. The *Birmingham Gazette* says that the officials of the Union met the heads of the different firms during the day, with the result that the advance was conceded by all except one contractor.

WORCESTER.—The bricklayers of Worcester still remain out for an advance from 7½d. to 8d. per hour. The house decorators and painters have accepted the ½d. advance which the masters offered when 1d. was claimed. Over 200 bricklayers' labourers came out on Monday for an advance from 4½d. to 5d., but they decided to accept the masters' offer of an immediate rise to 4¾d., and an advance to 5d. in May of next year.

MEETINGS.

SATURDAY, MAY 7.

Sanitary Inspectors' Association (Carpenters' Hall).—Mr. Frederick T. Poulson on "The Circulation of Rain Water." 8 p.m.

St. Paul's Ecclesiological Society.—Visit to St. Paul's Cathedral. 2.15 p.m.

Edinburgh Architectural Association. — Visit to Pitteadie Castle and Seafield Tower.

MONDAY, MAY 9.

Surveyors' Institution.—Professor G. E. S. Boulger on "The Scientific Study of Timber." 8 p.m.

Society of Arts (Cantor Lectures). — Dr. Percy F. Frankland on "Recent Bacteriological and Chemical Research in Connexion with the Fermentation Industries." II. 8 p.m.

Clerks of Works' Association (Carpenters' Hall).—Monthly meeting. 8 p.m.

TUESDAY, MAY 10.

Institution of Civil Engineers.—Mr. A. P. Trotter on "The Distribution and Measurement of Illumination." 8 p.m.

Royal Institution.—Mr. Frederick E. Ives on "Photography in the Colours of Natute." I. 3 p.m.

WEDNESDAY, MAY 11.

Society of Arts.—Mr. G. L. Addenbrooke on "Uses and Applications of Aluminium." 8 p.m.

Civil and Mechanical Engineers' Society.—Annual Dinner, Holborn Restaurant.

THURSDAY, MAY 12.

Institution of Civil Engineers.—Students' visit to the Beckton Gasworks, the Northern Outfall Sewer, the Victoria and Albert Docks, and the P. & O. ss. *Oceana.* (Leave Fenchurch-street at 9.18 a.m.)

Institution of Electrical Engineers.—(1) Continuation of discussion on Mr. A. P. Trotter's paper on "The "Light of the Electric Arc." (2) Dr. J. H. Gladstone and Mr. W. Hibbert on "The Cause of the Changes of Electro-motive Force in Secondary Batteries." 8 p.m.

Royal Institution. — Professor Dewar on "The Chemistry of Gases."—III. 3 p.m.

Society of Antiquaries.—8.30 p.m.

Edinburgh Architectural Association.—Annual Meeting; President's Valedictory Address. 8 p.m.

Dundee Institute of Architecture.—Mr. James Thomson on "Modern Sanitary Plumbing and its Defects." 8 p.m.

FRIDAY, MAY 13.

Architectural Association.—Nomination of Officers. Paper by Mr. C. R. Ashbee on "The Relation of the Architect to the Workman." 7.30 p.m.

Institution of Civil Engineers. — Students' visit to Woolwich Arsenal, the Works of the London Electric Supply Corporation, Deptford, and the Tower Bridge. (Leave Charing-cross at 9.40 a.m.)—Students' annual dinner at the Holborn Restaurant 7.30 p.m.

COMPETITION, CONTRACTS, AND PUBLIC APPOINTMENTS.

COMPETITION.

Nature of Work.	By whom Advertised.	Premium.	Designs to be delivered.
*Municipal Technical School	Manchester Corp.	....	Aug. 2

CONTRACTS.

Nature of Work or Materials.	By whom Required.	Architect, Surveyor, or Engineer.	Tenders to be delivered.
Residence, Hetton-le-Hole, Sunderland	Wesleyan Methodist Connexion	J. Shields	May 10
Road Construction, Woodhouse	Handsworth Loc. Bd.	W. H. Lancashire	do.
Flagging, Paving, &c.	Plymouth Corporation	G. D. Bellamy	do.
Three Cottages, Calcots, Elgin, N.B.	....	A. & W. Reid	do.
*Kerbing and Channelling	Hackney Bd. of Works	J. Lovegrove	May 11
Sewerage Works	Ystradyfodwg Loc. Bd.	J. W. Jones	do.
Offices and Stables, Kirkdale, &c.	Lancs. & Yorks. Ry.	Official	do.
Granite Road Metal, Kerbing, &c.	East Stonehouse L. B.	do.	May 12
*Cleaning and Painting Works, E. E. F. H.	Met. Asylums Bd.	Jarvis & Sons	do.
Alterations and Additions to Library, Brightside	Sheffield Corporation	C. F. Wike	do
Additions, Westfield Mills, Yeadon, Yorks	Edwd. Denison	Geo. Foggitt	do.
Road Work and Drainage, Maindy, Pentre, Rhondda Valley	"General" Booth	Edwin Jones	do.
*Construction of Lavatories, &c. &c.	Brighton Town Council	F. J. C. May	May 13
*Removing Street Refuse by Barge	Vestry of St. Giles, Camberwell	Official	do.
*Removing Dust by Barge	do.	do.	do.
*Road Materials	Folkestone Corp.	J. White	May 14
*Wood Paving Blocks	do.	do.	do.
*Masons' Works, Stockeld Park, Wetherby	R. J. Foster	T. H. & F. Healey	do.
House, Llantrisant, Glam.	Howell Davies	A. O. Evans	do.
Iron Lattice Girder Bridge, Forres, N.B.	Forres Police Commrs.	Gordon & McBey	do.
*Stonework, Town Hall	Bermondsey Vestry	Official	May 16
*Painting Iron Railings	St. Marylebone Bur. B.	do.	do.
*Paving Works	Vestry of St. Giles, Camberwell	do.	do.
Wesleyan Chapel and School Buildings, Newbridge, Cornwall	....	J. W. Trounson	do.
Wesleyan Chapel and Schools, Church Fenton, near Leeds	Rev. Harvey Field	J. H. Brearley	do.
Thirteen Houses and Two shops, Town End, Morley	....	T. A. Buttery	do.
Electric Lighting, Western Shore	Southampton Corp.	J. G. W. Aldridge	do.

CONTRACTS.—*Continued.*

Nature of Work or Materials.	By whom Required.	Architect, Surveyor, or Engineer.	Tenders to be delivered.
*Sewerage and Drainage Works	St. Albans Corp.	Official	May 17
*Supply of Materials	London County Council	do.	do.
*Roadmaking Works	Lewisham Bd. of Wks	do.	do.
*Making-up Roads	Brentford Loc. Bd.	J. M. Strachan	do.
*Broken Granite	do.	do.	do.
*Supply of Road Materials	Maidstone U. S. A.	W. C. Scoones	do.
*Kerbing and Channelling	Cheshunt Local Board	F. Bennett	do.
Two Homesteads, Blairmore, N.B.	Alex. Geddes	Geo. Sutherland	do.
*Cleaning and Painting Works, East F. H.	Met. Asylums Board	K. D. Young	May 18
*Reconstruction of Stratford Viaduct, Stroud	Gt. Western Ry.	Official	do.
New School, Eastleigh, Southampton	S. Stoneham Sch. Bd.	Mitchell, Son, & Gutteridge	do.
Chapel, Mossfab, near Abergavenny	Wm. Williams	....	May 19
*Painting and Decorating Town Hall	Leeds Corporation	Official	do.
*Sheds, Latrines, &c. Penzance	Admiralty	do.	May 20
*Painting Works, Caterham Asylum	Metro. Asy. Bd.	do.	do.
*Construction of Two Filters, &c.	Dorking Water Co.	J. Mansergh	May 21
*Semi-detached Villas, Barnet	....	W. H. Mansbridge	May 23
*Enlargement of P. O. Southampton	Commrs. of H. M. Wks	Official	May 31
*Dock Gates	Barry Railway Co.	J. Wolfe Barry	June 11
*Married Soldiers' Quarters, Eastbourne	War Department	Official	No date
*Oak Telegraph Arms	G. P. O.	do.	do.
*Alterations, &c. to Buildings, Machinery, &c. at Baths	Chelsea P. B. & W. Com.	do.	do.
*Cast-iron Pipes	Bishop's Castle T. C.	W. Wyatt	do.
Waterworks, Whittle Dene	Newcastle & Gateshead Water Co.	Official	do.
Additions and Alterations, Embleton Hall, Northumberland	Dr. Fenwick	Boolds & Hardy	do.
Two Houses, Burley, Leeds	....	Chas. Fluerty	do.
Two Shops, Westbar, Sheffield	T. Blow	A. Appleby	do.
Eight Houses, Intake, Sheffield	J. H. Strong	....	do.
Restoration of Church, Peudoylan, near Peterstone-super-Ely	....	Bruton & Williams	do.
Three Houses, Commercial-road, Newport, Mon.	Henry Fry	Newland & Hunt	do.
Street Improvement Works	Mirfield Loc. Bd.	F. H. Hare	do.

PUBLIC APPOINTMENTS.

Nature of Appointment.	By whom Advertised.	Salary.	Applications to be in.
*Assistant Inspector of Nuisances	Plymouth T. C.	80*l.* rising to 110*l.*	May 19
*Head Master	Coalbrookdale School of Art	....	No date

Those marked with an Asterisk (*) are advertised in this Number. *Competition*, p. iv. *Contracts*, pp. iv., vi., & viii. *Public Appointments*, p. xx., & xxi

RECENT PATENTS:

ABSTRACTS OF SPECIFICATIONS.

7,547.—KILNS: *J. Morton.*—This invention relates to a new construction of kiln to be used for burning retorts, pipes, or fire-clay slabs, but it may also be used to burn bricks for other fire-clay articles. The primary part of the invention has reference to the roof of the kiln, and consists of a new method of covering in the roof by means of a suitable number of sections or arches, each section being composed of two springer beams, each end of which is connected by bolts to angle-iron shaped plates, and from these the archways are built up and composed of fire-brick slabs, each having formed on its upper surface notches or slots for taking hold of the flange projecting from the inner side of the springer beams, such beams being tied together by a tie-rod, which is made with a loop by which to lift the arch. It will be seen that all the ironwork is outside the kiln, and free from the direct action of the fire, whilst the kiln can be easily uncovered by lifting the several sections or arches.

7,887.—COWLS: *J. C. Waterhouse.*—This specification relates to chimney cowls, the object of the improvements being to lubricate the upper portion of the revolving spindle which carries the vanes, and also to adjust the flint-bearing upon which the foot of the spindle tests. The inventor places within the upper spindle-bearing a series of carbon plugs, commonly called "metaline," which provides a smooth and noiseless bearing, and as the bearing which contains these oilless carbon plugs is situated near the top of the main spindle, it forms a strong support, and steadies the spindle. The flint-bearing is placed upon a set screw in the flint-box, so that it can be adjusted, and preferably a washer is placed between the flint and the foot of the spindle for the latter to rest upon.

8,324.—SASH FASTENERS: *W. Smith and J. Claydon.*—The great advantage claimed for this improved sash-fastener is that the window can be opened for a short distance, and still be fastened by it. Upon the upper rail of the bottom sash is screwed down a plate in which revolves freely a perpendicular pin in the thickness of the sash rail, a circular hole having been drilled to allow for such easy working, and a coiled spring being arranged around this pin. Upon the bottom tail of the upper sash is screwed a flat hinged metal flap, the tree portion of which is bent down at its end at right angles to the remaining portion. Another part, homogeneous with the part screwed down, traverses the oblique face of the top rail, and is additionally screwed to the side of this rail by one screw. The hinged portion is pierced upon both its faces with a long slot and also with two holes respectively at right angles to these slots. The movable pin beforementioned is attached to the lower sash-rail, which terminates at the top with a flat head provided on each side with projections capable of fitting into the circular holes before referred to in the hinged plate. When it is required to fasten the windows, the hinged plate is brought down upon the lower sash-rail, and the revolving pin slightly raised and turned at right angles across the slot, when the projecting point will fall into the circular holes and be firmly held there by means of the coiled spring below.

1,961.—WATER AND GAS PIPE HOOKS: *W. H. Dransfield.*—This patent refers to a method of manufacturing water or gas pipe hooks by first rolling or forging a bar or strip of steel or other suitable material, tapering towards each edge, and having a rib or web projecting from one side along the centre, and next cutting off wedge-like transverse sections from the same and bending up the wide end into the form of a "bill" or hook. Another modification of the invention is also described.

2,997.—HEATING APPARATUS: *W. Matthews and Others.*—This invention relates to apparatus for heating buildings and structures by radiation from metallic pipes internally supplied with heated water, air, or steam. The inventors form the pipes with an elliptical, flattened, hour-glass-shaped, sinuous, or other suitable cross-section, which will give a larger radiating surface than a circular cross-section for similar sectional areas. In addition, they form longitudinal gills, flutings, or corrugations in or upon the pipes, in order to increase the radiating surfaces. Compact radiators may be formed in the usual manner from a tier range, or series of such pipes inter-connected by means of branch pipes, for the purpose of securing the circulation of the heated fluid therein.

NEW APPLICATIONS FOR LETTERS PATENT.

April 19.—7,436, 7,437, and 7,438, G. Gibson, Sash Locks.—7,386, A. Palethorpe, Combined Draught Preventors and Door-springs.—7,401, H. Leigh, Vapour-burners or Plumbers' Torches.—7,432, J. Bounon, Cowl.

April 20.—7,486, J. Robertson, Construction of Roofs, Floors, and similar Structures.—7,492, H. Oppenhemier, Electric Bells.—7,502, W. Thompson, Plaster for Building purposes.

April 21.—7,522, G. Ballard, Edging Tile or Brick.—7,533, J. Duckett and others, Construction of Kilns or Ovens for Drying and Burning Bricks, &c.—7,554, H. Bridson, Siphon Cisterns.—7,558, B. Hellmann and others, Stoves.

April 22.—7,631, E. Waller and C. Solfiin, White-lead.

April 23.—7,660, F. Carter, Tiles.—7,685, R. Mushet, Ventilators and Chimney Cowls.—7,686, L. Bertholet, Securing Doors.—7,692, H. Replogle, Spirit-level.—7,715, J. Bühlmann and A. Mosele, Scaffolding-frame and Trestles, usable also for other purposes.—7,719, S. Théraizel & F. Grand Montagne, Artificial Marble.

PROVISIONAL SPECIFICATIONS ACCEPTED.

2,137, C. Crompton and G. Taylor, Window-catch.—2,547, H. Baxter, Windows.—3,403, W. Pates, Water-closets.—4,269, F. Fitton, Treads for Stairs, Steps, &c., with or without devices for advertising, lighting, or ventilation.—5,446, T. Burrow, Stoves.—5,682, J. White, Holders for Sliding Sashes.—5,710, D. Faulkner, Fire-proof and Sanitary Partitions or Divisions.—5,752, J. Stickling, Construction of Tombstones or Monuments.—5,946, W. Price, Screws for Joiners' and other use.—6,261, P. Schmahl, Mounting Window-sashes and means or apparatus for Opening, Closing, and Holding the same in place.—6,358, H. Ford, Window-sashes.

COMPLETE SPECIFICATIONS ACCEPTED.

(Open to Opposition for Two Months.)

7,229, G. Cooper, Self-acting Hook for Holding Doors or Gates.—9,107, G. Barnes, Connecting Union for Electric-light Fittings.—14,608, J. Hanson, Window-sashes and frames.—5,346, M. Martin, Rule and Plumb-level.

SOME RECENT SALES OF PROPERTY:

ESTATE EXCHANGE REPORT.

APRIL 25.—By *D. J. Chattell*: 16, Stockman's-row, Chiselhurst, f.r. 25*l.*, 800*l.*—By *G. F. Flower*: 21, Albert-st., Pentonville, u.t. 55 yrs., g.r. 6*l.*, 270*l.*—By *Moss & Jameson*: 98, Stebbington-st., St. Pancras, u.t. 52 yrs., g.r. 7*l.*, 410*l.*—By *Elliott, Son, & Boyton*: 31, Montagu-sq., Hyde Pk., u.t. 12 yrs., no g.r., 1,700*l.*; 3 to 6, Church-ter., Lambeth, u.t., 30 yrs., g.r., 21*l.* 6s., r. 125*l.*, 1,040*l*; 89 to 92, Cornwall-rd., u.t. 30 yrs., g.r. 18*l.* 14s., r. 172*l.* 18s., 1,000*l.*; 8, Mason-st., u.t. 30 yrs., no g.r., r. —*l.*, 315*l.*—By *E. E. Croucher & Co.*: F.g.r. of 28*l.*, with reversion in 74 yrs., Oscar Villas, Broadstairs, 660*l.*; f.g.r. of 15*l.*, with ditto in 173 yrs., Wrotham-rd., 310*l.*; f.g.r. of 27*l.* with ditto in 75 yrs., Ramsgate-rd., 600*l.*; 21, St. Paul's-rd., Camden-town, u.t. 5 yrs., g.r. 10*l.*, r. 38*l.*, 230*l.*

APRIL 26.—By *Jones & Son*: 11, 12, and 23, Dalgleish-pl., Limehouse, f., 565*l.*; warehouse and stabling, Gloucester-st., f., 100*l.*; 1, 2, and 3, Clarendon-pl., Camberwell, u.t. 34 yrs., g.r. 9*l.*, r. 96*l.* 14s., 470*l.*—By *Debenham, Tewson, & Co.*: 47 to 53 (odd), St. John-st., West Smithfield, f., area 2,400 ft., 3,650*l.*—By *Norton, Trist, & Gilbert*: 10, The Crescent, Surbiton, f., 1,600*l.*—By *F. Jolly & Co.*: F.g.r. of 28*l.*, Church-rd., &c., Tottenham, with reversion in 29 yrs., and 3 freehold houses in Moselle-pl., 1,860*l.*—2, Chestnut-rd., f., r. 20*l.*, 270*l.*; "Vernon Cottage," Summerhill-rd., f., r. 22*l.*, 300*l.*; 116, Charles-st., Stepney, u.t. 32 yrs., g.r. 3*l.* 3s., 250*l.*; 87, King Edward's-rd., Hackney, u.t. 47 yrs., g.r. 6*l.*, r. 38*l.*, 350*l.*—By *A. Chancellor*: "Sussex Villa," Bracknell, with stabling and ground, f., 1,000*l.*—By *Bean, Burnett, & Co.*: [illegible] Grove-pk.-gardens, Chiswick, f., 695*l.*; 301, Old-st., and 45, Coronet-st., City of London, 2,820*l.*; 97, Riversdale-rd., Highbury, u.t. 78 yrs., g.r. 8*l.* 8s., r. 84*l.*, 270*l.*; 31, Michael's-grove, Brompton, u.t. 35 yrs., g.r. 2*l.*, r. 95*l.*, 995*l.*

APRIL 27.—By *Inman, Sharp, Harrington, & Roberts*: "Portland Lodge," Atkins-rd., Clapham, u.t. 32 yrs., g.r 5*l.*, r. 50*l.*, 280*l.* By *Inman & Co.*: 15, Loudoun-rd., St. John's Wood, u.t. 45 yrs., g.r. 10*l.*, r. 63*l.*, 750*l.*; 1 Queen's-rd., u.t. 27 yrs., g.r. 5*l.*, r. 52*l.* 10s., 465*l.*—By *Wood & Kirby*: 31, Winchester-st., Pimlico, u.t. 38 yrs., g.r. 9*l.*, 450*l.*—By *Hobson, Richards, & Co.*: 28, Buckland Cres., Hampstead, u.t. 59 yrs., g.r. 16*l.*, 1,200*l.*; 50 and 51, Doddington-grove, Battersea, u.t. 60 yrs., g.r. 8*l.*, r. 68*l.* 10s., 310*l.*; 14, 16, and 18, Spanby-rd., Bow, u.t. 61 yrs., g.r. 10*l.* 10s., r. 93*l.* 12s., 610*l.*; "The Myrtles," Jeptha-rd., Wandsworth, u.t. 90 yrs., g.r. 17*l.* 15s., r. 35*l.*, 340*l.*—By *H. J. Bliss & Sons*: [illegible] Stamford-grove East, Clapton, f., r. 26*l.*, 345*l.*; 54, Beulah-rd., Walthamstow, f., r. 27*l.* 10s., 315*l.*; 23, 24, and 25, Emma-street, Hackney, u.t. 42 yrs., g.r. 9*l.* 9s., 385*l.*—By *D. Young*: 2, St. Barnabas Villas, Lambeth, u.t. 50 yrs., g.r. 8*l.*, r. 44*l.*, 405*l.*—By *Toplis & Harding*: F.g.r. of 16*l.* 10s., Tennyson-rd., Kilburn, with reversion in 95 yrs., 405*l.*; f.g.r. of 22*l.* 8s., Kemble-road, with ditto in 84 yrs., 540*l.*; f.g.r. of 14*l.* with ditto in 93 yrs., 340*l.*; No. 43a, Peckham Rye, f.s. and f.g.r. of 10*l.* 10s., with ditto in 48 yrs., 400*l.*; l.g.r. of 70*l.*, Riding-house-st., Marylebone, u.t. 24 yrs., 620*l.*—By *E. & S. Smith*: No. 340, Gray's-inn-road, f., r. 63*l.* 12s., 950*l.*; 5, Upper Chadwell-st., Myddleton-sq., u.t. 20 yrs., g.r. 9*l.*, r. 48*l.*, 256*l.*; 29 and 31, Cloudesley-rd., Islington, and 10, Islington-pl., u.t. 25 yrs., g.r. 36*l.*, 165*l.*; 72, Margaret-st., Clerkenwell, u.t. 23 yrs., g.r. 7*l.* 10s., r. 27*l.*, 125*l.*; l.g.r. of 10*l.*, Upper Yardley-st., u.t. 23 yrs., 100*l.*; 2 and 3, Noble-st., u.t. 23 yrs., g.r. 22*l.*, 235*l.*—By *Jones, Lang, & Co.* (at Banbury): freehold land, 24a. 3r. 2p., King's Sutton, Northants, 1,000*l*; "Tomes Farm" and 55a. 2r. 10p., f. and c., 1,600*l.*; c. and f. land, 30a. 2r. 5p., 1,000*l.*; the dairy ground, 24a., f., 1,000*l.*; the residence called "Hollands" and cottages, 200*l.*; f. and c. cottages, r. 13*l.* 10s., 210*l.*; "The Bell Inn" public-house, f., r. 50*l.*, 1,110*l.*; f. plot of land, 1a. 1r. 31p., r. 12*l.* 15s., 120*l.*; c. and f. residence, with grounds, 350*l.*; f. farm-yard, nine cottages, f., and seven cottages, c., 345*l.*

APRIL 28.—By *G. B. Hilliard & Son*: "North Weald Lodge," near Ongar, and 64a. 2r. 7p., 1,125*l.*; A freehold er-house, in Wood-lane, 127*l.* 10s. — By *Messrs. Trollope*: F.g.r. of 48*l.*, Chepstow-place, Bayswater, with reversion in 66 yrs., 1,615*l.*; i.g.r. of 18*l.*, Priory-st., Camden-town, u.t. 32 yrs., no g.r., 280*l.*—By *C. C. & T. Moore*: 27, 29, and 31, Ricardo-st., Poplar, u.t. 67 yrs., g.r. 7*l.* 10s., 375*l.*; 24, Burghley-rd., Hornsey, u.t. 87 yrs., g.r. 6*l.* 6s., r. 24*l.*, 250*l.*; 54, Lessada-st., Bethnal-green, u.t. 40 yrs., g.r. 3*l.* 8s., 170*l.*; 29 and 31, St. Dunstan's-rd., Mile-end, u.t. 57 yrs., g.r. 7*l.* 9s., 290*l.*—By *Newbon & Co.*: 23, Hayling-rd., Stoke Newington, u.t. 80 yrs., g.r. 5*l.* 10s., r. 28*l.*, 230*l.*; 23 and 25, John Campbell-rd., Kingsland, u.t. 75 yrs., g.r. 12*l.*, 530*l.*; 24, ersley-rd., Stoke Newington, u.t. 82 yrs., g.r. 6*l.* 6s., 5*l.*; "The Good Intent" beer-house and stabling, edmore-st., Holloway, u.t. 18 yrs., g.r. 33*l.*, 265*l.*; six houses in Nightingale-st., Marylebone, u.t. 29 yrs., no g.r., 550*l.*; 46, Malvern-rd., Hornsey, u.t. 85 yrs., g.r. ., r. 30*l.*, 260*l.*—By *Stimson & Sons*: 148 and 150, ong-lane, Bermondsey, f., r. 100*l.*, 1,500*l.*; an improved rental of 20*l.* 10s., Brixton-rd., u.t. 7½ yrs., 73*l.* 10s.; to 73 (odd), Chadwick-rd., Peckham, u.t. 65 yrs., g.r. *l.* 16s., 2,300*l.*; 1 to 8, Victoria-rd., f., r. 370*l.*, 4,800*l.*; 2 and 24, Beresford-st., Walworth, u.t. 58 yrs., g.r. *l.*, 690*l.*; No. 81, Drury-lane, f., r. 83*l.* 4s., 650*l.*; 3, dney-rd., Stockwell, u.t. 50 yrs., g.r. 6*l.*, r. 32*l.* 10s., 0*l.*; 201, St. George's-rd., Peckham, u.t. 70 yrs., g.r. ., r. 26*l.*, 170*l.*—By *Baker & Sons*: F.g.r. of 28*l.*, Ilderton-rd., Bermondsey, with reversion in 85 yrs., 828*l.*; g.r. of 25*l.*, Ilderton-rd., with ditto in 85 yrs., 650*l.*; g.r. of 513*l.*, Ilderton-rd., with ditto in 85 yrs., 13,972*l.*; g.r. of 60*l.*, Cranswick-rd., with ditto in 85 yrs., 614*l.*; f.g.r. of 150*l.*, Bramcote-rd., with ditto in 85 yrs., 3,875*l.*; f.g.r. of 120*l.*, Delaford-rd., with ditto in yrs., 3,037*l.*; f.g.r. of 80*l.*, Ablett-rd., with ditto in yrs., 2,002*l.*—By *Chinnock, Galsworthy, & Co.*: Nos. 391 to 403 odd, City-rd., f. 10,160*l.*; 2 to 15, uncan-ter., f., 12,360*l.*; a Plot of Freehold Land, Torrens-st., area 3,196 ft., 880*l.*; a Plot of Freehold Land, Goswell-st., area 5,200 ft., 2,000*l.*; 302, Goswell-rd., f., r. 38*l.*, 900*l.*

APRIL 29.—By *Protheroe & Morris*: "Shanklyn Villa," sborn-rd., Buckhurst Hill, u.t. 91 yrs., g.r. 4*l.* 10s., r. *l.*, 275*l.*—By *Phillips, Lea, & Davies*: 1 to 4, Pear Tree-., Clapton, f., r. 57*l.* 4s., 410*l.*—By *W. A. Blakemore*: .g.r. of 6*l.*, Clifton-ter., Finsbury Park, with reversion in 76 yrs., 133*l.*; 1, Southerton-rd., Hammersmith, u.t. 74 yrs., g.r. 6*l.*, 300*l.*; No. 438, Fulham-rd., u.t. 44 yrs., g.r. 18*l.*, r. 50*l.*, 305*l.*—By *P. Hodson*: 2 to 14 (even), Pleasant-passage, Holloway, u.t. 42 yrs., g.r. 25*l.*, 525*l.*; 18, Eden-grove, u.t. 36 yrs., g.r. 22*l.*, 175*l.*; 56, Chichester-rd., Kilburn, u.t. 65 yrs., g.r. 5*l.*, 370*l.*; 10, Lyrne-st., Camden Town, u.t. 47 yrs., g.r. 7*l.*, r. 55*l.*, 460*l.*—By *Chinnock, Galsworthy & Co.*: 1 to 5, Colebrook-row, City-rd., f., 4,780*l.*; 73 to 379 (odd), and 383 and 387, City-rd., f., 7,100*l.*; 53, 355, 357, 359, to 363 (odd), City-rd., f., 7,040*l.*; 41 to 345 (odd), 349, 350, and 351, City-rd., f., 6,000*l.*; No. 366, Goswell-rd., f., area 2,650 ft., 1,090*l.*—By *Baker & Sons*: F.g.r. of 91*l.*, Bramcote-rd., Bermondsey, with reversion in 85 yrs., 2,382*l.*; f.g.r. of 14*l.*, Ablett-st., with ditto in 35 yrs., 395*l.*; f.g.r. of 162*l.*, Barkworth-rd., with ditto in 85 yrs., 3,979*l.*; f.g.r. of 80*l.*, Verney-rd., with ditto in 85 yrs., 1,461*l.*; f.g.r. of 59*l.*, Varcoe-rd., with ditto in 85 yrs., 1,498*l.*; f.g.r. of 46*l.*, Rotherhithe New-rd., with ditto in 85 yrs., 1,097*l.*; f.g.r. of 0*l.*, Cranswick-rd., with ditto in 86 yrs., 1,442*l.*; f.g.r. of 26*l.* 12s., Credon-rd., with ditto in 85 yrs., 651*l.*—By *R. Reid*: 46 and 47, Berwick-st., Oxford-st., , r. 200*l.*, 3,600*l.*; No. 228, Uxbridge-rd., f., 860*l.*; , Bloomfield-ter., f., 910*l.*; 10, Girdlers-rd., West Kensington, u.t. 73 yrs., g.r. 4*l.*, r. 50*l.*, 650*l.*; 24 to 32, Cardross-st., Shepherd's Bush, f., r. 117*l.*, 970*l.*; f.g.r. of 20*l.*, nslett-rd., Kensington, with reversion in 86 yrs., 495*l.*; g.r. of 30*l.*, Sinclair-rd., with ditto in 85 yrs., 800*l.*; g.r. of 19*l.* 10s., Davisville-rd., Shepherd's Bush, with reversion in 84 yrs., 460*l.*; f.g.r. of 6*l.* 10s., with ditto in yrs., 160*l.*; f.g.r. of 10*l.*, Purcell-st., Fulham, with ditto in 86 yrs., 200*l.*

[*Contractions used in these lists.*—F.g.r. for freehold ground-rent; l.g.r. for leasehold ground-rent; i.g.r. for improved ground-rent; g.r. for ground-rent; r. for rent; f. for freehold; c. for copyhold; l. for leasehold; e.r. for estimated rental; u.t. for unexpired term; p.a. for per annum; yrs. for years; st. for street; rd. for road; sq. for square; pl. for place; ter. for terrace; cres. for crescent; yd. for yard, &c.]

PRICES CURRENT OF MATERIALS.

TIMBER.		
Greenheart, B.G. ton	9/0/0	0/0/0
Teak, E.I. ... load	10/0/0	15/0/0
Sequoia, U.S. ft. cu.	2/3	3/0
Ash, Canada load	2/10/0	4/0/0
Birch, do.	3/5/0	4/10/0
Elm, do.	3/10/0	4/15/0
Fir, Dantsic, &c.	1/10/0	3/10/0
Oak, do.	3/0/0	6/5/0
Canada	5/10/0	7/0/0
Pine, Canada red	2/10/0	3/10/0
Do. yellow	2/10/0	5/0/0
Lath, Dantsic, fath	5/0/0	6/0/0
St. Petersburg	5/0/0	7/0/0
Deals, Finland, 2nd & 1st std 100	8/10/0	10/0/0
Do. 4th & 3rd ..	7/0/0	8/10/0
Do. Riga	7/0/0	8/0/0
St. Petersburg, 1st yellow ..	11/0/0	15/0/0
Do. 2nd yellow	8/0/0	10/0/0
Do. white	7/10/0	11/0/0
Swedish	8/0/0	16/0/0
White Sea	8/0/0	[illegible]
Canada, Pine 1st	20/0/0	26/0/0
Do. do. 2nd	14/10/0	16/0/0
Do. do. 3rd, &c.	8/0/0	10/5/0
Do. Spruce, 1st	8/10/0	11/0/0
Do. do. 3rd & 2nd	6/15/0	8/0/0
New Brunswick	7/0/0	7/10/0
Battens, all kinds	3/10/0	15/10/0
Flooring Boards, sq., 1 in. prep. 1st	0/8/0	0/14/0
Do. 2nd	0/7/0	0/11/0
Other qualities	0/4/0	0/9/0
Cedar, Cuba ..ft.	/3½	/4½
Honduras, &c.	/2½	/4
Mahogany, Cuba	/4½	/6½
St. Domingo, cargo av	/4½	2/0
Mexican do. do	/4	/5
Tobasco do. do	/5½	/7
Honduras do..	/5½	/6½
Box, Turkey ton	4/0/0	13/0/0
Rose, Rio	10/0/0	20/0/0
Bahia	9/0/0	18/0/0
Satin, St. Domingo ......ft.	0/0/6	0/1/8

TIMBER (*continued*).		
Satin, Porto Rico	0/0/8	0/1/6
Walnut, Italian ..	0/0/3½	0/0/7
METALS.		
IRON—Pig, in Scotland ......ton	2/1/0	0/0/0
Bar, Welsh, in London	5/17/6	6/0/0
Do. do. at works in Wales	5/7/6	5/10/0
Do. Staffordshire, in London	6/5/0	6/15/0
COPPER—British, cake and ingot	48/0/0	49/0/0
Best selected ..	49/10/0	50/0/0
Sheets, strong ..	59/0/0	0/0/0
Chili, bars	45/7/6	45/15/0
YELLOW METAL lb.	0/0/5	0/0/5½
LEAD—Pig, Spanish ....ton	10/8/9	10/11/3
English, com. brands	10/12/6	10/15/0
Sheet, English, 8 lbs. per sq. ft. and upwards ..	12/0/0	0/0/0
Pipe	12/10/0	0/0/0
ZINC—English sheet ......ton	25/10/0	0/0/0
Vieille Montagne	26/5/0	0/0/0
TIN—Straits	94/7/6	94/17/6
Australian	94/7/6	94/17/6
English Ingots	96/0/0	96/10/0
OILS.		
Linseed ......ton	17/17/6	18/0/0
Cocoanut, Cochin	24/0/0	0/0/0
Do. Ceylon	21/17/6	22/0/0
Palm, Lagos	23/0/0	0/0/0
Rapeseed, English pale	24/0/0	24/5/0
Do. brown	22/15/0	0/0/0
Cottonseed ref...	19/0/0	0/0/0
Oleine	21/10/0	22/10/0
Lubricating, U.S.	4/0/0	5/0/0
Do. refined	5/0/0	10/0/0
TAR—Stockholm barrel	0/19/0	1/0/0
Archangel	0/13/6	0/0/0

TENDERS.

[Communications for insertion under this heading should be addressed to "The Editor," and must reach us *not later than* 12 *noon on Thursdays*.]

BEVERLEY.—For the erection of an infirmary for sixty patients adjoining the workhouse. Messrs. Hawe & Foley, architects, Beverley, Yorks. Quantities by the architects:—

J. Constable	£3,375 0	Geo. Downs	£3,034 2
G. & R. Pape	3,360 0	Richard Potts	2,994 12
G. Jackson & Son	3,100 0	Jno. R. Foley, Beverley (accepted)	2,987 0
R. Stephenson & Son	3,075 0		

BOXMOOR (Herts).—For erecting new stabling at "The Bell," for Messrs. Salter & Co., Lim. Mr. C. P. Ayres, architect, Watford:—

Timberlake	£265 10	Waterman	£247 0
Turner, Lim.	250 0	Dove & Co., Watford*	246 0

* Accepted.

BRANDON (Suffolk).—For the erection of a steward's house, at Brandon Park, Brandon, for the Baron de Barreto. Mr. Edward S. Mansergh, surveyor, 28, Mount-street, Grosvenor-square, W.:—

W. Saint	£815	Benjamin & Robinson	£734
Sanitation Company Ltd.	773		

BRISTOL.—For the erection of new premises, Baldwin-street, for Messrs. Bartlett & Co. Mr. Henry Williams, architect, 28, Clare-street. Quantities by Mr. A. Barratt, Somerset Chambers, Corn-street, Bristol:—

J. Wilkins	£1,670	G. H. Wilkins	£1,548
Cowlin & Son	1,643	R. Wilkins & Son	1,545
J. Bastow	1,627	W. Church	1,540
J. E. Davies	1,575	Eastabrook & Son*	1,498
C. A. Hayes	1,570	E. Love	1,473
Stephens, Bastow, & Co.	1,568	H. A. Forse	1,300

[All of Bristol.]
* Accepted.

CASTLE DONINGTON (Derby).—For providing and laying cast-iron mains for water supply at Castle Donington, for the Shardlow Union Guardians. Mr. Geo. Hodson, engineer, Abbey-buildings, Princes-street, Westminster, S.W. Quantities by Mr. F. W. Hodson:—

Jones & Fitzmaurice	£1,999 0 0	Hy. Vickers	£1,905 0 0
Chas. Green	1,979 10 0	Price & Shardlow, Nottingham*	1,780 0 0
G. F. Todd	1,919 6 2		

* Accepted.

GRAYS (Essex).—For the construction of sewers, tanks, cottages, buildings, &c., for the Grays-Thurrock Local Board. Mr. W. H. Radford, engineer, Nottingham:—

Price	£36,841	Neave	£33,444
Cook & Co.	34,500	Dickson	33,428
Bell	33,960	Rackham & Bentham	32,048
Lloyd	33,731	Band	28,500

Iron Pipes, &c.

Abbot & Co.	£3,356	Stanton Company	£3,038
Neave	3,229	Clay Cross Company	2,942
Butterley Company	3,092	J. & S. Roberts	2,927
Cochrane & Co.	3,065		

GREAT WRATTING (Suffolk).—For erecting new granary, &c., at Great Wratting Hall, for the trustees of the late Right Hon. W. H. Smith. Mr. C. P. Ayres, architect, Watford:—

Arber	£894 0	Mason, Haverhill*	£869 10
Jarvis	887 0		

* Accepted.

GUILDFORD.—For the construction of main sewers, tanks, buildings, &c., for the Corporation of Guildford. Mr. C. N. Lailey, Borough Engineer:—

Contract No. 1.—Sewers.

Stephens, Bastow, & Co.	£38,526	Osenton	£25,174
Peters	36,452	Neave	24,689
Green	36,000	Hayward	24,195
Finnegan	36,500	Cook & Co.	21,900
Band	29,440	Nicholls	20,186
Dickson	26,308	Cunliffe, Kingston*	18,647
Peattie & Axtell	24,215	Morgan & Co.	18,496
Hall	26,000	Rowles	14,800
Bentley	25,736		

* Accepted.

Contract No. 2.—Tanks, Engine-house, Cottages, &c.

Hall	£14,000	Peattie & Axtell	£10,845
Dickson	13,282	Nicholls	10,831
Neave	12,488	Peters	10,695
Bentley	12,395	Hayward	10,581
Osenton	12,319	Cook & Co.	10,289
Finnegan	12,167	Band	9,850
Stephens, Bastow, & Co.	12,126	Cunliffe, Kingston*	8,785
Morgan & Co.	10,934	Rowles	6,915

* Accepted.

HANLEY (Staffs.)—For making a road and draining park, for the Town Council. Mr. J. Lobley, Borough Engineer and Surveyor:—

Contract No. 1.—Outer Circle-road.

W. Vaughan	£5,480	F. Barke	£3,640
H. Holloway	4,408	George Wild, Hanley*	2,831
Jones & Fitzmaurice	3,786		

* Accepted.

Contract No. 2.—Land Drainage.

W. Vaughan	£2,195	John Gott	£1,396
Jones & Fitzmaurice	1,734	George Wild	1,389
W. Williams	1,459	F. Barke, Stoke-on-Trent*	969
H. Holloway	1,443		

* Accepted.

IRTHLINGBOROUGH.—Accepted for rebuilding the second portion of the church tower, Irthlingborough. Messrs. Talbot-Brown & Fisher, architects, Wellingborough:—
E. Brown & Son, Wellingborough £890 0 0

LEYTON.—For constructing three additional concrete sewage tanks (lined with blue bricks), penstock chambers, &c., for the Leyton Local Board. Mr. William Dawson, engineer:—

Howard	£3,945	Neave	£3,648
Bell	3,787	Jackson, Leyton*	3,456

* Accepted.

LLANDILO.—Accepted for rebuilding Rutland House, Llandilo, for Mr. W. Williams. Mr. D. Jenkins, architect:—
Phillip Jones & Son, Swansea £315 0 0

LLANDILO.—For building six houses at Alan-road, Llandilo, for Mrs. W. Lewis, Canton. Mr. D. Jenkins, architect:—

Thomas Brothers	£1,554	Alfred Meredith, New-bridge-on-Wye*	£1,374
Price & Dankins	1,550	Benj. Davies	1,367

* Accepted.

LLANDYSSIL.—Accepted for water supply to Llynewydd Mansion, for Colonel Lewes. Mr. D. Jenkins, surveyor, Llandilo:—
John Jones, Red Lion, Ornich, Llandyssil £360 0 0

LLANGATHEN.—Accepted for the completion of Court Henry Church, for Miss Saunders. Mr. D. Jenkins, architect, Llandilo:—
Benj. Jenkins, Brecon £310 14 6

LONDON.—For alterations and additions to No. 24, London-road, Forest Hill, S.E. Mr. J. Randall Vining, architect, 89, Chancery-lane, W.C. Quantities supplied:—

Drew & Cadman	£897	Black & Son	£788
W. Johnson & Co.	875	H. C. Bowyer	739
C. Sprockley	840	R. G. Battley (accepted)	733

LONDON.—For alterations to milk-shed and stables, Christian-street, Commercial-road, for Mr. Harris. Mr. John Taverley, architect, 4, Leman-street, Whitechapel:—

Paulton	£364 0	C. Henry	£258 10
H. Gunn & Co.	325 0	H. Buck	257 0
M. J. Ingle	292 0	J. Lundy & Co.	250 0
Holly & Co.	285 0	Morgan & Son	237 17
Jefrays	275 0	J. P. Groome	223 15
H. Palmer	274 0		

LONDON.—For gasfitters' work at the "Lion," Junction-road, Upper Holloway:—

Conolly & Co.	£198 0	Biggs & Co.	£177 10
Hodges & Co.	184 0	Winn (accepted)	160 0

LONDON.—For erecting "model dwellings" in Radstock-street, Battersea, S.W., for Mr. E. Purchase. Messrs. Saville & Martin, architects, Dacre House, Arundel-street, Strand, W.C. Quantities supplied:—

Bates	£2,210	Young & Lonsdale	£1,793
Dearing & Son	2,150	Goodall	1,773
Toms	1,943	Gould & Brand	1,718

LONDON.—For alterations and pewtering at "The Eagle," Great College-street, Camden-town, for Mr. Sams, under the direction of Messrs. Thorpe & Furniss, architects, 164, High-street, Camden-town:—

Watts & Co.	£113 14 6	Edwards	£88 10 0
Helling	93 0 0	H. & F. Warne*	73 2 0

* Accepted.

LONDON.—For repairs to Nos. 7 and 8, Hatfield-place, Lambeth, S.E., for the Lambeth Estate Co. Ld. Mr. C. P. Ayres, architect, Watford:—
Holliday & Greenwood ...... £337 | T. Turner, Ld., Watford* .. £312
* Accepted.

LONDON.—For repairs to No. 23, Cornwall-road, Lambeth, S.E., for the Lambeth Estate Company, Limited. Mr. C. P. Ayres, architect, Watford:—
Holliday & Greenwood .... £483 | T. Turner, Ld., Watford* .. £427
* Accepted.

LONDON.—For the erection of first portion of residental flats to be called "Palace Mansions," Addison Bridge, Kensington. Mr. Fredk. Hemings, architect, 20, Bridge-row, E.C. Quantities by Mr. Alfred Boxall, 6, John-street, Adelphi:—

		A*
Pink, Fryer, & Co.	£29,870	£196
Gregory & Co.	29,787	350
Nightingale	29,680	270
Killby & Gayford	29,230	261
Stevens	29,150	200
Smith & Co.	28,787	393
Bush & Sons	28,139	178
Perry & Co.	27,976	100
Green†	27,357	450

* Extra for fireproof floors.
† Accepted with slight alterations.

LONDON.—For pulling down and rebuilding the "White Hart" tavern, King's-road, Chelsea, for Mr. F. W. Chamberlain. Messrs. Dickinson & Paterson, architects, 5, John-street, Adelphi. Quantities by Mr. F. Thomson, 5, Great James-street, Bedford-row:—

Turtle & Appleton	£7,990	Burman & Son	£7,200
Ansell	7,731	Edwards & Medway	6,890
Harris & Wardrop	7,695	Bates	6,784
Marks	7,540	Dearing & Son, Canonbury (accepted)	6,300
Godden	7,280		

LONDON.—For alterations at the "Haberdashers' Arms," Battersea, S.W., for Mr. A. A. Solomon. Messrs. Fletcher & Migotti, architects:—

Littlefield	£550 0	Salt	£454 0
Walker Bros.	510 0	Courtney & Fairbairn*	437 0
Jackson & Jennings	476 10		

* Accepted.

Pewtering and Counter.

Edwards	£132 0	Williamson*	£72 10
Warne	125 10		

* Accepted.

LONDON.—Accepted for alterations to the "Rose and Crown" tavern, Charing-cross-road. Messrs. Dickinson & Paterson, architects, 5, John-street, Adelphi, W.C.:—
W. Hearn & Co., Bayswater £1,332 10 0

Counter and Pewter Work.
Heath £187 0 0

LONDON.—For alterations to the "Waterloo" tavern, Haymarket, for Mr. F. A. Rhodes. Messrs. Dickinson & Paterson, architects, 5, John-street, Adelphi:—

Dearing & Son	£690	Edwards & Medway, Kennington, S.E. (accepted)	£485
Godden	645		

LONDON.—For re-building Nos. 28, 29, and 29A, Wimpole-street, Cavendish-square, for Mr. Samuel Lithgow. Mr. C. H. Worley, architect. Quantities by Mr. R. C. Gleed:—

G. H. & A. Bywaters	£17,530	E. Lawrance & Sons	£16,956
Simpson & Son	17,000		

LONDON.—For alterations and additions to No. 26, Welbeck-street, Cavendish-square, for Mr. Lewis W. Thomas. Mr. C. H. Worley, architect. Quantities by Mr. R. C. Gleed:—

Simpson & Sons	£2,137	E. Lawrance & Sons	£1,925
G. H. & A. Bywaters	2,087	Scrivener & Co.	1,808
Wm. Downs	2,070	Keyes & Head	1,770

LONDON.—For alterations and additions to Nos. 88 and 90, Norfolk-terrace, Bayswater, for Mr. A. C. James. Mr. C. H. Worley, architect. Quantities by Mr. R. C. Gleed:—

E. Toms	£2,520	E. Lawrence & Sons	£2,390
Wm. Dowse	2,525	H. & E. Lea	2,113
Scrivener & Co.	2,453	Keyes & Head*	1,870

* Reduced and accepted.

LONDON.—Accepted for rebuilding Nos. 67, 69, and 71, Oxford-street. Mr. Robert J. Worley, architect. Quantities by Mr. R. C. Gleed:—
Perry & Co. £4,070 0 0

LONDON.—For the erection of a Fire-Brigade station at East Dulwich, for the London County Council. Mr. Thomas Blashill, Architect:—

Holliday & Greenwood	£10,877	G. Munday & Son	£10,716
H. L. Holloway	10,864	Stimpson & Co.	10,250

[Referred to the Fire Brigade Committee.]

LONDON.—For repairs and alterations to the gas-meter testing station, Spitalfields, for the London County Council. Mr. Thomas Blashill, Architect:—

G. H. & A. Bywaters	£1,724	Higgs & Hill	£1,680
E. Lawrance & Sons	1,720	Co-operative Builders, Ltd.	1,640
Hall, Beddall, & Co.	1,700	Holloway Bros.	1,254

[Referred to the Public Control Committee.]

LONDON.—For the erection of a children's gymnasium and three bathing shelters at Victoria-park, for the London County Council. Mr. Thomas Blashill, Architect:—

A. Wallis	£767	H. Faulkner, jun.	£695
F. & F. J. Wood	730	J. Garrett & Son	620

[Referred to the Parks and Open Spaces Committee.]

LONDON.—For the erection of a children's gymnasium at Battersea-park, for the London County Council. Mr. Thomas Blashill, Architect:—

W. Akers & Co.	£511	H. Faulkner, jun.	£487
A. Wallis	499	J. Garrett & Son	463

[Referred to Parks and Open Spaces Committee.]

NORTHAMPTON.—For additions to a school at West Haddon, for the Heygate Schools Trustees. Messrs. Ingman & Shaw, George-row, Northampton :—

Richman & Leatherland	£125 0	Smith & Palmer, West Haddon (accepted) £112 10
A. Marsh	118 0	

NOTTINGHAM.—For proposed additions to Ilkeston-road Board Schools, for the Nottingham School Board. Mr. A. H. Goodall, architect, Market-street, Nottingham :—

T. Barlow	£2,475 0	J. Oscroft	£2,115 0
Gilbert & Gabbitass	2,330 0	J. Cooper	2,114 0
A. B. Clarke	2,256 0	F. Wartnaby	2,113 0
Emerson & Franks	2,245 0	J. Shaw	2,111 0
J. Hutchinson	2,230 0	G. A. Pillatt	2,109 0
G. Bell & Son	2,226 0	R. Keeling	2,090 0
J. Attenborrow	2,156 0	Thos. Cuthbert, Nottingham*	2,039 0
J. F. Price	2,154 4		
F. Evans	2,140 0		

* Accepted.

PLYMOUTH.—For the erection of five dwelling-houses at Crownhill (Knackersknowle), for Mr. Sampson Bevell, of Truro. Mr. J. H. Keats, architect, 34, Bedford-street, Plymouth. Quantities by the architect :—

Lapthorn & Good	£2,970 0	F. C. Ambrose	£2,166 0
E. Shoolake	2,592 0	J. Finch	2,180
J. Taylor	2,529 0	J. Cobb	2,147 0
J. Julian	2,400 0	G. Shellabear	2,065 0
A. R. Lethbridge & Son	2,382 0	Reed, Blight, & Co.	2,025 0
Watkins, Bryant, & Co.	2,338 0	W. E. Blake	1,850 0
T. May	2,198 5	A. N. Cole, Plymouth*	1,753 0
Trant & Son	2,191 0	E. G. Good	1,644 7

* Accepted.

RICHMOND.—For proposed new shop at the corner of Kew and Church roads, Richmond. Mr. Frank E. Smee, architect, 12, West Smithfield, E.C :—

W. Lamb £278 0 0

[No competition.]

RICKMANSWORTH (Herts).—For alteration at Highfield, for Mr. Rd. Warwick. Mr. C. P. Ayres, architect, Watford :—

Waterman	£334	Brown & Sons	£294
T. Turner, Ld.	301	Dove & Co., Watford*	285

* Accepted.

RICKMANSWORTH (Herts).—For various repairs to the brewery house, for Messrs. Salter & Co., Limited. Mr. C. P. Ayres, architect, Watford :—

Brown	£445	Dove & Co.	£403
Waterman	448	Turner, Limited, Watford*	389

* Accepted.

SOUTHAMPTON.—For the erection of offices, &c., in the Ogle-road, for Mr. F. Page. Mr. A. W. Galbraith, architect, 22, Portland-street, Southampton. Quantities by the architect :—

H. J. Sanders	£3,[illegible]	Reed, Blight, & Co.	£3,47[illegible]
H. Stevens & Co.	3,842	Morgan, Istel, & Morgan	3,432
P. Crook & Sons	3,[illegible]	J. W. Roe & Co.*	3,[illegible]
J. Dyer & Son	[illegible]		

* Accepted.

SUTTON-IN-ASHFIELD.—For the proposed erection of twelve cottages, George-street, Sutton-in-Ashfield, for Messrs. Heath & Johnson. Mr. A. H. Goodall, architect, Market-street, Nottingham :—

R. Keeling	£2,593 0 0	J. Cooper	£2,280 0 0
J. Oscroft	2,519 17 8	Goodband & Franks	2,244 17 0
G. Bell & Son	2,424 0 6	J. F. Price	2,203 0 0
G. A. Pillatt	2,409 0 0	W. Savage	2,193 0 0
J. Hutchinson	2,348 0 0	C. Coulton	2,085 0 0
Thos. Cuthbert	2,320 0 0	Chambers & Padgett, Sutton-in-Ashfield*	2,075 0 0
H. Vickers	2,309 0 0		

* Accepted.

TORQUAY.—For additions to vestry and transept, S. Mary Church, Torquay, Devon. Mr. Geo. H. Fellowes Prynne, architect, 6, Queen Anne's-gate, Westminster, London, S.W. Quantities by Mr. R. Henry Hale, 6, Duke-street, Strand, W.C. :—

Messrs. E. L. Luscombe	£1,298	Fred. Mathews	£640
John Parker	770	Alfred Harris, S. Mary Church, near Torquay*	£591. 17s. 6d.
Edward Bovey	760		

* Accepted.

TUNBRIDGE WELLS.—Accepted for a residence at Gipps Cross, near Tunbridge Wells, Kent, for Mr. C. W. Powell. Mr. C. E. Powell, architect. Quantities by Mr. R. C. Gleed :—

Wallis & Son, Maidstone £1,633 0 0

WANSTEAD (Essex).—For the erection and completion of new residence and stables at Wanstead, for Mr. J. Richardson. Mr. Geo. Blowers, architect and surveyor, 46, Queen Victoria-street, E.C. :—

Holland	£1,479	W. T. Nichols	£1,077
Barker	1,455	Chas. L. Cole*	1,050
Graves	1,075		

* Accepted.

WATFORD.—Accepted for temporary bridge, restoring walls, &c., in yard at Cannon Brewery, for Messrs. Benskin & Co. Mr. C. P. Ayres, architect, Watford :—

Dove & Co., Watford £261 10 0

WELLINGBOROUGH.—Accepted for erecting house, Hatton Park, Wellingborough. Messrs. Talbot-Brown & Fisher, architects, Wellingborough :—

George Henson, Wellingborough £1,[illegible] 14 9

WELLINGBOROUGH.—For erecting public swimming-baths, Wellingborough (exclusive of engineering works). Messrs. Talbot-Brown & Fisher, architects, Wellingborough :—

Green Bros., Palmerston-road, Northampton £1,463 0 0

WELLINGBOROUGH.—For erecting twelve cottages, Stanley Estate, Wellingborough, for the Wellingborough Co-operative Society. Messrs. Talbot-Brown & Fisher, architects, Wellingborough :—

George Henson, Wellingborough £2,382 0 0

WORKSOP.—For laying a sewer at Harthill, for the Union Rural Sanitary Authority. Mr. W. T. Brown, surveyor, Sherwood-road, Worksop :—

L. Dearden	£315 17 6	C. Buckle, Harthill*	£255 0 0
C. Askin	300 0 0	J. M. Herring	194 10 0
Thos. Meakin	274 0 0		

* Accepted.

Rebuilding 189, *Upper-street.*—Mr. R. Maskall, builder, &c., 180, New North-road, writes calling our attention to an error in last week's list of tenders for this job. The name of the lowest tenderer should have been "Maskall," not "Marshall." The mistake was not ours.

SUBSCRIBERS in LONDON and the SUBURBS, by prepaying at the Publishing Office, 19s. per annum (or 4s. 9d. per quarter), can ensure receiving "The Builder," by *Friday Morning's Post.*

TO CORRESPONDENTS.

J. S. H. (letter forwarded as requested).—"Lover of Fair Play" (should have enclosed his name and address. We cannot print communications not so authenticated).—C. C.—J. B.—E. T. S. (it is a piece of architects' bad grammar, of which unfortunately we get too much. What the writer meant to imply is obvious enough).—T. F. L.—B. & Co.—W. W. L.—F. C. S. (too small).—J. P. (we cannot insert tenders without amounts, unless they are at per schedule of prices).—J. W. T. (we do not insert such items).—E. H. & Son (too late).—O. A. J. (we cannot understand your letter).

All statements of facts, lists of tenders, &c., must be accompanied by the name and address of the sender, not necessarily for publication.

We are compelled to decline pointing out books and giving addresses.

NOTE.—The responsibility of signed articles, and papers read at public meetings, rests, of course, with the authors.

We cannot undertake to return rejected communications.

Letters or communications (beyond mere news-items) which have been duplicated for other journals, are NOT DESIRED.

All communications regarding literary and artistic matter should be addressed to THE EDITOR; all communications relating to advertisements and other exclusively business matters should be addressed to THE PUBLISHER, and *not* to the Editor.

TERMS OF SUBSCRIPTION.

"THE BUILDER" is supplied DIRECT from the Office to residents in any part of the United Kingdom at the rate of 19s. per annum PREPAID. To all parts of Europe, America, Australia, and New Zealand, 26s. per annum. To India, China, Ceylon, &c., 30s. per annum. Remittances payable to DOUGLAS FOURDRINIER, Publisher, No. 46, Catherine-street, W.C.

The Builder Cathedral Series

1891.

1. CANTERBURY	Jan. 3.	7. SALISBURY	July 4.
2. LICHFIELD	Feb. 7.	8. BRISTOL	Aug. 1.
3. ST. ALBAN'S	Mar. 7.	9. NORWICH	Sept. 5.
4. PETERBOROUGH	April 4.	10. ROCHESTER	Oct. 3.
5. WELLS	May 2.	11. LINCOLN	Nov. 7.
6. EXETER	June 6.	12. GLOUCESTER	Dec.

1892.

13. ST. PAUL'S .. .. Jan. 2.

14. HEREFORD	Feb. 6.	20. WORCESTER	Aug. 6.
15. CHICHESTER	Mar. 5.	21. BANGOR	Sept. 3.
16. ELY	April 2.	22. ST. ASAPH	Sept. 3.
17. LLANDAFF	May 7.	23. WINCHESTER	Oct. 1.
18. OXFORD	June 4.	24. TRURO	Nov. 5.
19. SOUTHWELL	July 2.	25. ST. DAVID'S	Dec. 3.

[Further arrangements will be duly announced.]

Post-free FOURPENCE HALFPENNY each, except Nos. 1, 2, 3, and 4, which are *out of print*; but the VIEW, PLAN, AND DESCRIPTION of CANTERBURY, LICHFIELD, ST. ALBAN'S, and PETERBOROUGH, have been re-printed, and they can now be had, price EIGHTPENCE each set; by post, 10d.

THE REREDOS, ST. PAUL'S.

Reprinted from "THE BUILDER," January 28, 1888 (15 in. by 11½ in.), on stout paper, unfolded, for framing. 6d.; by post, 8d.

PORTFOLIOS,

for Preserving the Plates unfolded, 2s. 6d.; by post, 3s.

London: Office of "THE BUILDER," 46, *Catherine-street, W.C.*

The Builder.

Vol. LXII. No. 2571. SATURDAY, MAY 14, 1892.

ILLUSTRATIONS.

Design for Municipal Buildings, Bury, Lancashire, by Mr. F. H. Tulloch .... *Double-Page Ink-Photo.*
Tonbridge School Chapel.—Messrs. James Brooks & Son, Architects .... *Double-Page Photo-Litho.*
New Reredos, St. Botolph's, Boston, Lincolnshire.—Mr. W. S. Weatherley, Architect .... *Double-Page Ink-Photo.*
Design for Memorial to Mary Tudor, St. Mary's Church, Bury St. Edmunds.—Mr. A. E. Street, Architect .... *Single-Page Ink-Photo.*
Design for Chimneypiece, St. Margaret's, East Grinstead.—Mr. A. E. Street, Architect .... *Single-Page Ink-Photo.*

Blocks in Text.

Remains of Early English Hall, Lincoln .... Page 374
Westminster Guildhall or Sessions House, now in course of demolition 376
Ancient Processional Cross, St. Oswald's, Durham .... Page 379
Diagrams in Student's Column: Heating by Hot Water 385

CONTENTS.

Architecture at the Paris Salon 369
Notes 371
Architecture at the Royal Academy.—III. 373
Early English Hall, the Close, Lincoln 374
Exhibition at Carpenters' Hall 374
Magazines and Reviews 375
The Royal Institute of British Architects 376
The Guildhall or Sessions House, Westminster 376
Ancient Processional Cross, St. Oswald's, Durham 379
The Scientific Study of Timber 379
Design for Bury Municipal Buildings 380
School Chapel, Tonbridge 380
New Reredos, St. Botolph's Church, Boston, Lincolnshire 380
Design for Memorial to Mary Tudor 381
Chimney-piece, East Grinstead 381
Municipal Engineers at Nottingham 381
The London County Council 382
Liverpool Engineering Society 382
Architectural Societies 383
The Sanitary Inspectors' Association 383
The Architectural Association *Soirée* 383
Architectural Association 384
Sir Gilbert Scott's Restorations 384
Mr. Baker on St. Albans 384
Boston Church 384
Grissell Medal Competition 384
Student's Column.—Warming Buildings by Hot Water, XX. 385
Obituary 386
General Building News 386
Sanitary and Engineering News 386
Stained Glass and Decoration 387
Foreign and Colonial 387
Miscellaneous 387
Meetings 388
Recent Patents 388
Some Recent Sales of Property 389

Architecture at the Paris Salon.

HE extent of wall space covered by architectural drawings at the Salon is enough to make a conscientious critic somewhat anxious. Two large rooms are filled with strainers (the framed drawing is not *de rigueur* in the architectural department), the whole of one side of the gallery flanking the great central hall of the Palais de l'Industrie, and two-thirds of the opposite side. Nor is it possible to make a selection out of the numbers very easily, or to settle at a glance what to pass over. There is a defiant equality of excellence in the drawing, for the most part, which renders selection difficult at first sight. Indeed, while one complains that architecture is cut short of room at the Royal Academy, one may at the *Salon* rather be inclined to smile at the liberality of space which allows of the exhibition of a whole set of half-a-dozen or more large geometrical drawings to illustrate one of the commonest of red and yellow brick villas, "La Marouette," by M. Saintier. But if the space is abused in some such cases, for the most part the liberality in this respect is a clear gain, as it enables architects to send drawings in which all the detail can be well and clearly made out, and the final effect of the building far better estimated than it can be from the small drawings with which English architects are obliged to content themselves.

As usual, the proportion of restorations is very large—the kind of things that are at once turned out of our Royal Academy, as matters of no kind of value; and along with these are a number of studies for buildings,—"projets," the drawings of works executed or commissioned being by far the least numerous. At the Academy the preference seems to be for representations of executed works, as far we can judge by the logic of facts; at all events we see this year some very bad drawings hung of executed buildings, and we know of at least one very fine drawing of a restoration which has been refused. Either tendency might be defended. It may be urged on the one hand that the architectural portion of an annual exhibition should represent the work that has been carried out in the year. It cannot be denied on the other hand that restorations and ideal designs represent the kind of work which can be shown in drawings and in no other way, and that architects are so commonly restricted in their artistic ambition in the conditions of actual building that they may very well be glad to have opportunities of showing what they could produce if fate were kinder to them. Whether there are a large number of drawings of executed work sent in and refused we have no means of knowing; but we surmise that the character of the Paris architectural exhibition results from the tastes of the exhibitors as much as from the inclinations of the jury.

The place of honour is supposed to be in the two enclosed rooms rather than along the gallery. There we may notice first M. C. N. Normand's large coloured geometrical drawing giving his idea of the restoration of the Parthenon before the invasion of the Persians; *i.e.* the supposed Parthenon on the site afterwards just crossed by an angle of the Erectheion. M. Normand shows us the front of a hexastyle Doric temple with a strongly-marked necking to the columns and a large and clumsy echinus, the triglyphs painted blue and the metopes painted with a geometric arrangement of the "honeysuckle" ornament; the back of the pediment is painted dark red with only a sun in the centre. It is not easy to see why the metopes should be supposed to be treated with flat painting in this temple, when metope sculpture was already known to have been used in more ancient examples. The drawing shows the other supposed objects of the Acropolis at the period, so far as they come within the line of sight; among other things, small temples or shrines cut after the manner of the timber-like rock-cut tombs of Asia Minor; a very doubtful suggestion. We can hardly imagine such structures getting deliberately made at Athens contemporaneously with such far-advanced Doric as the main temple shown in the drawing. Other details shown, "après les résultats des dernières fouilles," look also far too archaic in form and colouring for the assumed period, the drawing seems to include types of very different periods in fact. But it is a highly interesting study, accompanied by large detail drawings, a plan of the Acropolis, and a section of the restored Parthenon with a colossal Athene not too archaic for the situation. The section represents the Temple with an entirely closed roof and no lighting.

M. Espouy, whose name is well known now in connexion with Classic restoration drawings, exhibits a pretty restored view of the Wingless Victory temple, looking from the platform down to the plain, and a fine set of drawings of a restoration of the Basilica of Constantine. He gets a rich effect with the colouring of the coffered vaults; he fills the large windows with lattices in two well-known Roman forms; he restores the façade towards the Via Sacra with red marble columns on the ground-floor and green marble pilasters in the upper stage, with red spandrils to the arches; the large piers are crowned with equestrian groups. This is all possible and probable, but the painting of the surfaces of the pendentives with a kind of Pompeiian scheme of ornament—thin columns and wreaths—looks improbable and certainly architecturally out of keeping with the rest.

The room contains a couple of Mediæval restorations, that of the château of Josselin (Morbihan), by M. Lafargue; a long narrow strip of building of which it may be said that it is a "castle" on the outer side and a "château" on the inner side; the drawings are large and powerfully coloured: and M. Roussel's restoration of the Porte Tournisienne at Valenciennes, a building the plan of which shows a long rectangle with flat walls and small angle turrets at one side, and the other side covered by two immense three-quarter circle turrets filling up nearly the whole flank of the building.

Besides restorations, we find in the two principal rooms various more or less important drawings of a purely illustrative order. The largest are M. H. Boussac's elevations of the remains of the vestibule and tomb of Auna, at Thebes, a careful drawing showing the wall paintings as existing. M. Georges Chedanne exhibits, under the title "Etudes d'Architec-

d

ture Italienne," two beautifully-executed water-colours of Renaissance detail, a marble tomb with a recumbent figure, and a portion of the carved decoration of the cloister of the Sistine chapel. Draughtsmen who are interested in; the production of truthful effects of colour and texture in water-colour should look at these, which are executed to perfection. Among the illustrative drawings may be mentioned also M. Gaida's drawings of the paintings of the west cupola of the Cathedral of Cahors, the property of the "Ministère de Justice et des Cultes," we presume drawings officially commissioned. M. Gaida gives a drawing of the whole cupola in line, which is divided into eight compartments by bands of decoration, while in the spaces are painted shrines each containing a draped figure; the head of the shrine is formed of two trefoil arches, which clash awkwardly with the heads of the painted figures. There is a complete set of coloured drawings giving the effect of the paintings as existing.

Two designs for practical work in the principal rooms call for notice. One is M. Marcel's "Palais du Senat Roumain," shown in a number of very large drawings. It is a heavy Classic building with a certain power and individuality about it. The plan, on a site forming an irregular trapezium, largest in the rear, shows a central state block running from front to back, consisting of a grand vestibule, a great Salle des Pas Perdus with aisles, and finally the theatre-shaped Senate-house at the back. The corridor communication to the subsidiary departments is entirely unbroken all round, a cross corridor running between the Senate House and Salle des Pas Perdus. The front elevation, an immense tinted monochrome drawing, shows a pediment with a colossal Ionic order of very thick unfluted columns, and thin base mouldings which seem crushed under the weight of the columns. On the other hand, there is an immense plinth moulding in the wings which is utterly out of scale with the rest of the mouldings. The wings are treated with a solid rusticated basement and a Tuscan order of pilasters above. The Salle des Pas Perdus shows a second larger pediment in the rear of the front one. There is an unquestionable power and solidity in the design, but the details, as already implied, are coarse and wanting in scale.

The other design referred to is that of a "Hôtel et Maison à Loyer" at Paris, by M. Escalier. The plan shows clever treatment of an awkwardly shaped site; the exterior designs are of very refined Italian type, the maison à loyer exhibiting the best and most refined style of Paris street architecture of this class. The fronts are shown in perspective in the most beautifully delicate shaded line drawings. There is not a pen-drawing in the Academy architectural room which would not appear coarse beside these.

M. Cordonnier's "Palais de la Bourse pour Amsterdam" is also in one of the separate rooms; it is shown in an immense line and tinted elevation drawing of florid Renaissance type with very coarse detail, great bulbous rusticated voussoirs and plinth stones, &c., and gables with all kinds of scrolls and nine-pin pinnacles. The tower is badly designed, with a heavy corbelled out stage half-way up its height; and on the other hand the ground-floor arcade along the façade is too light in detail for the superstructure. Whether this is a building to be executed or only a competition design is not stated.

Launching out into the wide sea of drawings in the galleries of the great hall, and taking first some of the restoration drawings, we notice a large and fine geometrical drawing by M. Dubois of the restoration of the lanterns of the great staircase at the château of Chambord, carried out last year. From the subsidiary drawings we gather that the lantern was entirely rebuilt, there is nothing to show from what data; it is in keeping with the general style of the château, though the spotty effect of the circles and diamonds of black marble introduced is not agreeable. M. Charles de Wulf has a good set of complete geometrical drawings of a restoration of Hadrian's Villa at Tivoli, accompanied of course, in the French manner of thorough illustration of these things, by complete measured drawings and a bird's-eye view of the existing remains. An interesting restoration is that by M. Boonen of the Arch of Hadrian at Athens; he restores the upper portion, as others have done, with a small colonnade of three columns and an entablature cross-wise across the ends of the main cornice, resting partially on the main order of flanking columns below. M. C. Wable exhibits an interesting restoration of the manoir of Courboyer, showing its L-shaped plan with the little chapel fitted diagonally into the outer angle, and the round tower restored with its projecting gallery with little arrow slits all round, and the conical roof over, giving it somewhat the appearance of a humming-top. There is, one must confess, a good deal of family likeness about these early château restorations, which are always to be found among the Salon architectural exhibits, though they are not this year so numerous as usual.

Among the numerous "Projets," studies for buildings, we can only name a few of those which present some special feature of character or originality. One of these is M. Denues' "Etude Théorique" for a Hôtel de Ville, a good Classic elevation in which the three circular-headed doorways in the ground story are alternated with similar blank arches filled in with elegantly-designed tablets for *affiches*. M. Trilhe exhibits a design for a monument to commemorate the reconstitution of the "Service d'Architecture" of Paris under Haussmann, appropriate enough to its subject; a blank wall with an Ionic order and inscription spaces between, with square pavilions at intervals surmounted by trophies; there is (unusually enough here) no plan to show whether any and what use is to be made of the space behind the wall. M. Simon's design for an "Église de Village avec Presbytère" is a semi-Romanesque kind of building with a slated spire of somewhat Swiss character setting oddly upon it; the complete working drawings of the spire, &c., are given, the principal elevation is tinted with the landscape in the rear to produce the effect of a perspective,—a method of treatment which French draughtsmen are fond of, and which has its recommendations. This is a very complete set of drawings, but as an example of the picturesque in modern church architecture it almost sets an Englishman's teeth on edge. One must allow something for national habits of design, but generally it seems to us (and various examples in this year's Salon would illustrate this view) that the French architects, while they nearly always succeed in classic work, invariably fail when they attempt the picturesque. M. Tronchet's "Projet d'Eden" is an Eden with the serpent in it; a great glass-house with dancing figures in stained glass in the semi-circular end of the building, a kind of mixture of Crystal Palace and Casino; not without ability, but essentially vulgar. A very different thing is M. Belesta's design for a museum for Nantes (presumably a competition design). This is a charming set of sketch elevations, showing a rusticated basement with arched windows all round, and an order above on the front elevation; the side elevation is a blank wall with angle pavilions and broken by an intermediate pavilion (not central) which marks the end of a cross corridor. The building is graceful and suitable for its purpose, and the design in complete relation to the plan. M. Pachianu's "Projet" for a library for Lyons has considerable merit; the main façade has three large semi-circular arches over which are large shrines for sculpture, with a broken pediment and reclining sculptures on each side; a horizontal line of attic wall connects the whole of these details by a common background; the design is unusual, effective, and suitable for its purpose. Another very able "Projet" is that by M. Hannotin for a "Rendezvous de Chasse," evidently in connexion with a great man's domain, for it is palatial in size for its object. There is a great centre pavilion with one large room and very lofty high-pitched hip-roof, the wall design is Classic but a suitable picturesque effect is given to it by strongly marked and broken up rusticated treatment; the centre pavilion is balanced or accompanied by small brick and stone pavilions of somewhat similar character but of quieter treatment, of course entirely symmetrical in arrangement (that goes without saying in French design of this kind), but the whole thing is a success, because it combines architectural dignity and a certain palatial air with a treatment which suitably expresses its object, as the hunting or shooting pavilion on a great scale, and there are few better studied designs in the collection. M. Bruneau's study for a Lyric Theatre is too much like a kind of glorified conservatory, clever, but not sufficiently monumental for a theatre. M. Rixson's "Projet de Maison Suburbaine" is a tremendously big elevation of a modern château; there are several designs of this kind for imaginary town or suburban houses, and for the most part we may say they are much more commonplace than the designs of a similar kind which find place in the Royal Academy Architectural Room. Among other enormous "projets," apparently competition designs, is M. Loyau's "Un Casino," without merit of any kind that we can see; M. Mougenot's "Concours du Collège d'Epinal," carefully planned but an enormous barrack architecturally,—indeed there seems to be a kind of understanding among French architects to make scholastic and collegiate buildings as repellent as possible in appearance, giving them the aspect of prisons and barracks, as if education could have no connexion with architectural beauty or attractiveness, which is surely as mistaken a view of the matter as could possibly be entertained. These great establishments in France are generally well planned and very complete in a sanitary sense, but they are most uninviting-lookin[g] buildings. M. Guyon's "Concours pour l[a] Construction de l'Ecole Boule" is no bette[r] in this respect. M. Delmar's design for [the] Hôtel de Ville for Nice has merit, but th[e] treatment of the ground-story arcade is no[t] in keeping, in point of style and detail, wit[h] that of the upper portion of the design.

Among the drawings of buildings execute[d] or to be executed is a fine and large set b[y] M. Huot for the "Hôtel des Postes et Télé[-] graphes" at Marseilles. This covers a larg[e] irregular site, and though plain is treate[d] with some architectural dignity. The en[-] trance is through a great arcaded vestibul[e] and the principal façade has large circula[r] staircase turrets at the angles with a balcon[y] and small cupola over them, which ar[e] architecturally effective; a square tower a[t] the extreme back angle of the site (probabl[y] facing the sea) is terminated by an iron cag[e] erection apparently intended for an elec[-] tric lighthouse, it is of purely utilitaria[n] design and looks an odd adjunct to th[e] architecture. There are a number of phot[o-] graphs of interiors added, besides the com[-] plete geometrical drawings.

M. Rives's new entry to the establishmen[t] of Veuve Crespin et Dufayel is shop archi[-] tecture *in excelsis*, showing a tremendou[s] archway filled up with glazing and gimcrac[k] ironwork, and a dome and details apparentl[y] inspired by the front of the central 1889 exhi[-] bition building at the lower end of the Cham[p] de Mars. Of M. Wable's design for a Pala[is] des Art Décoratifs for the site of the Cour d[es] Comptes we know not whether it is a mer[e] *projet* or has a chance of execution, but it is [a] fine and pompous kind of design which look[s] well in the bird's-eye view perspectiv[e]. M. Parent's "Hôtel Exécuté Avenue [de] l'Alma" is a very meritorious example [of] the Paris residence, well and compactl[y] planned, designed with a central open cou[rt] elliptical on plan, and a boldly sweepin[g] staircase cleverly worked into an angle of th[e] plan. It is shown partly by a cleverly

:ecuted section with the portion beyond the ane of section drawn in perspective. rchitecturally a little more might have ɪen made of the elliptical courtyard, which a little too much broken up into bits and not eated with sufficient breadth; but the whole worth the study of those engaged on town ɔuses. The street façade is of a quiet type Classic design. Another Paris hôtel (rue allu) is shown by M. Dézermaux, of what ight be called a coarse type of Elizabethan ɪsign; the wooden details of doors and antel are separately shown in drawings hich would certainly not be admitted into e Royal Academy (bad as are some of the ings admitted there), and which are absotely without interest of any kind. In the an of the house we notice that the prinpal w.c. is in the centre of the house, close the drawing-room wall. We thought rench architects were unlearning these sanitary devices of house-planning by this me. Another domestic design shows the ngitudinal section of a house entrance-hall hich is decorated (?) by great circular aques of red marble at regular distances on e upper portion of the wall, with wreaths ɪrtially encircling them. We can fancy the te of anyone who sent in such a "notion" interior decoration to the Academy! M. apaume's drawings for a "Refuge-Ouvroir ɔur Femmes" show a well-arranged plan on triangular site, with quiet characteristicallyeated elevations in coloured brick. M. Farge ows a creditable treatment of a railwayation front at Almeria.

Among decorative designs, which are not ımerous and not mostly good, M. Parent nds a set of drawings of a "cheminée onumentale" for a great house, a study polychromatic decoration; the drawings e splendidly executed, but the design would ɔt find much admiration on this side of the aannel, and the colouring is crude and owy; blue and gold predominating. M. ionnois sends a design for a monument ɪmmemorative of the siege of St. Jean-de ɔsne in 1636, consisting of a thick column stele with the model of a conventional stle on the top; this part is well treated, t the stone carved cannons worked into the se of the design are clumsily introduced and t decorative in effect. M. Bobin's monument mmemorative of the piercing of the Isthmus Suez, shown in a slight perspective view, based on Egyptian details, but is suitable the situation and object. Another comɪmorative design is that of M. Legrand for fountain to the memory of Germain Pilon. ɪis is triangular on plan, with a three-niched ɪle crowned by a group of female figures, d the statue of Pilon in one niche; the sin and stele are stone or marble and the ures bronze; the enormous bronze consoles ɪich seem to ramp on the edge of the basin posite the three angles of the centre angle are very coarse in effect, architecral details entirely misplaced. While eaking of decorative design we may menɪn one pleasing though very unassuming loured drawing by M. Hista of the wall coration executed in the library of the culté de Médecine at Paris; it consists ɪrely of a wall decoration and ornamental eze, but it is agreeable in colour and in oroughly good taste.

The collection contains numerous drawings d sketches illustrative of existing ancient ɔrk, many of them of much excellence. nong these is a drawing of monumental e, finish, and solidity, by M. Honoré, a loured elevation of one of the doorways d bronze doors of the façade of the thedral of Pisa; a superb piece of illustive work of its kind. M. Gayet's great of drawings and restoration of the Coptic nvent of Assouan is one of the most narkable sets of illustrative drawings, a great scale and got up with imɪnse care and labour. Another coloured vation drawing gives with the most nute care the remarkable façade of ancient church at Gisors; this is by Boutron. Among sketches and illustive drawings of a less conventional order are M. Stoughton's charming tinted drawings of the Loggia of the Hôtel d'Écoville at Caen; M. Sirot's "Souvenirs des Forticarions de. Valenciennes"; M. Conin's sketches of Eastern and Spanish buildings in bright and free-executed water-colours; and M. Breffendille's excellent set of water-colour sketches under the title "Souvenirs de Voyage," giving views of portions of St. Mark's, the Alhambra, a ceiling in the Pitti Palace &c., the last a splendid sketch of a very difficult subject to treat adequately in water-colour.

NOTES.

BERLIN is apparently about to follow the example set by Vienna, and appear to the world as "Gross-Berlin." There has of late years often been some serious contemplation of the question of an extension of the city limits, and the various architectural and engineering societies have given the matter their attention. A bulky literature already exists on the subject, and the local press has spasmodically devoted a good deal of space to the subject for a few weeks every year. The whole question has been until now considered as one of the far future. Now we suddenly hear that the Government has been quietly taking action in the matter, and that the first decisive step has been taken by the Governor of the Province of Brandenburg, in which the "County" of Berlin lies. He has asked the municipal authorities to consider the advisability of an extension of the city boundaries, and to send in their views as soon as convenient. The Government is much in favour of the extension, while the Municipality rather shuns the outlay which the improvements necessary in the newly-acquired districts of "Gross-Berlin" would at first require. The sanitary arrangements, water and gas supply, the street paving, and the fire protection service would swallow enormous sums during the first decade. Probably the extension of the boundaries will take place sooner than is generally expected, and we should not be surprised if the matter were arranged prior to the opening of the great international show that will take place some four years hence. The step taken by the Governor of Brandenburg is a very important one, and practically means that (1) rapid action is required on the part of the Municipality, and that (2) the Government expects an affirmative reply. A so-called municipal loan of seventy millions of marks (some 3,500,000*l.*) has to be arranged for this year, so that the executive Council may be able to carry out the various extensions and improvements they propose to make in the course of the next four years, *i.e.*, until the close of the financial year 1895-96. Estimates show that a sum somewhat over one hundred million marks is in reality required, but owing to various circumstances the whole sum is not to be asked for at once. Among the expenses to be incurred we notice the following:—(1) Some thirty-three million marks for the extension of the sewerage system; (2) twenty-three millions for the extension of the municipal waterworks; (3) six millions for the extension of the gasworks; and (4) eight millions for new bridges over public waterways. Some extension of the public slaughter-houses will cost four millions, the erection of some more covered markets five millions, while of the single buildings not belonging to an extensive scheme, a new lunatic asylum is alone to cost 2,860,000 marks, and an epileptic hospital 3,460,000 marks. We hope that where so much money is to be spent for building purposes, some attention will be paid to architectural features, so that it may not be said that other eyesores have been erected in the shape of municipal buildings.

THE second reading of a Bill of a noticeable character was not carried last week in the House of Commons. We refer to the Local Authorities (Purchase of Land) Bill. The astonishing thing is that sensible men could be found to support a measure of so unreasonable a character. To empower County Councils to purchase land whenever it should appear to the public advantage was a thoroughly unbusinesslike proposal, for there is nothing more necessary than that the objects for which land may be compulsorily acquired should be absolutely definite and clearly for the benefit of the public. But the further provision that a County Council might have land valued, but need not purchase for twenty years, and even at the end of that time not purchase, but have another valuation, was a proposal which would put an end to all security of property, and be a block to improvement. The provision that the unearned increment of the land between the time of the valuation and of the purchase should not belong to the owner for the purpose of compensation would also have made landed property near towns absolutely worthless for the purposes of private property, for men do not buy property any more than other things without a hope, at least, that it will increase in value, and thus enlarge the capital invested in it. It is also obvious that County Councils must have become land speculators pure and simple, whilst the door would have been opened to various forms of fraud. A more mischievous measure than this of Mr. Haldane has seldom been seen.

THE Committee of the House of Commons has quite rightly sanctioned the Bill for a tramway across Westminster Bridge to a point on the Embankment to the west of Charing Cross. This action has displeased, among others, the *Times* newspaper, which makes itself ridiculous by urging, as one reason why the Bill should not have been sanctioned, that the beauty of the Embankment will be spoilt by tramcars. There really is no more ugliness in a tramcar than in one of the numerous contractors' wagons which are continually rattling up and down the Embankment, but, if beauty is to be considered before the convenience of the public, there are plenty of eyesores in London which the *Times* might well devote its attention to. As a matter of fact, there cannot be a doubt that this tramway will be a convenience to large numbers of persons, and must, sooner or later, be extended to Blackfriars. Our objections are in no way lessened to the County Council becoming proprietors of this and other tramways, for reasons which we have more than once stated, but that is a matter between members of the Council and their constituents: for the moment we, like the Committee of the House of Commons, have only to consider whether this piece of tramway is required in the public interest, and it certainly is. If the County Council lose money over it by allowing their employés to work shorter hours for higher rates of pay than trading companies, so much the worse for the County Council and the ratepayers. The public as wayfarer is not concerned with the pecuniary results.

A CASE of some importance under the Metropolitan Local Management Act of 1862 was decided by the Court of Appeal last week. In the case of the London County Council *v.* Cross, the latter had been charged, before Justices sitting at Hampstead, with having unlawfully erected a building beyond the general line of building in a particular road. The matter was brought before the magistrates on October 28, 1891. On April 27 of the same year the building had reached to the joists of the first floor. The Justices also found, as a fact, that Mr. Cross began to erect the house before April 27. It was conceded that, by law the complaint should be made within six calendar months from the time that such complaint arose. The question, therefore, had to be decided, When did the matter of complaint arise? In the Divisional Court, Mr. Justice Smith held that the offence did not begin till the architect had given his certificate; while Mr. Justice Denman thought that the matter of complaint did not arise until the completion of the building. The Court of Appeal, however, did not agree with the Divisional Court, and considered that the offence was committed when the builder began to build beyond the proper line without the consent of the local authority. It followed, therefore, that the County Council had not brought the proceedings before the Justices within the necessary six months, and, therefore, the Court of Appeal dismissed the proceedings against Mr. Cross. This is not the only case which throws some light upon this point, but it is the latest, and in it all the previous cases are carefully examined. It lays down a plain and sensible rule that anyone can understand, and therefore, in the future, no difficulties should arise on this point, if the local officials keep a watchful eye on new buildings.

A MEETING of the Horse Accident Prevention Society was held on Tuesday at Cannon-street Hotel, "to protest against the decision of the Commissioners of Sewers to repave Wormwood-street, St. Mary-axe, Barbican, Bridewell-place, and St. Paul's-churchyard, with asphalte instead of wood." The meeting was a very representative one of the omnibus companies, carriers, and other owners of horses. Among the statistics given we note the following figures:—1. Of 1,180 coachmen asked as to which pavement they considered the most dangerous, 1,045 considered that asphalte took the lead. 2. That official research in the City had shown that twice as many horses fell on asphalte as on wood. 3. That in 1890 the engines of the Berlin Fire Brigade were delayed by the falling of their horses once in every 110 miles when running on asphalte, and only once in every 750 miles on wood, macadam, and granite. These figures seem conclusive in regard to the greater danger of asphalte. On the other hand, we must repeat what we have before said, that wood pavement is in a sanitary point of view the most undesirable pavement possible for a crowded city.

THE third exhibition of art brass and copper work and smiths' work, under the auspices of the Company of Armourers and Braziers' is being held this week in the hall of the Company at 81, Coleman-street. The object of the exhibition appears to be to encourage and to mark the advance of brass work from year to year, and for this purpose the Company purchases each year representative exhibits; with lapse of years these purchases will become very interesting and valuable, and the advance must appear more marked than it is at present. The Company deserves praise for its efforts to emphasise the name of the designer and the craftsman, and for giving preference to the work designed and made by one hand. A very liberal list of prizes, ranging from 10*l.* to 2*l.*, has attracted over 400 exhibitors, and many of these are women. The work of the following schools is well represented by numerous exhibits:—The Lyzwick School of Art, Keswick; Keswick School of Industrial Art; the Birmingham Guild of Handicraft; the Birmingham Municipal School of Art; the Birmingham Jewellers' Technical School; the Corstorphine Brass Class, Midlothian; the Guild and School of Handicraft, Mile-end. The merit of several of the exhibits is of a distinctly high character, though it is to be feared that the majority do not reach a very high standard. The different uses of brass and copper are most distinctly shown, and the results of the different methods of workmanship form a most useful study for the architect or any other craftsman. We have not space to refer in much detail to the exhibits, but the wide range of the work may be gathered from the fact that there are no fewer than eighteen classes, which include specimens of hammered hollow ware, repoussé work, hammered work as applied to ornament, brazing, engraving, etching, chasing, damascening, specimens of hollow-spun ware, saw-piercing, cored and *cire perdue* casting.

IT is stated that William Pitt's verses printed (and now for the first time) in the current number of the *National Review* were inspired by the prospect and associations of Coombe Wood, Surrey. The wood lies between Richmond-park and Wimbledon Common, and at present belongs to, we believe, the Duke of Cambridge. The Domesday Survey cites two manors here, since united: the one, of about 210 acres, as held of the Queen's fee by Humfrey, the chamberlain and collector of Queen Maud's woolcess; the other, 300 acres, and afterwards known as Comb-Nevil, held of the King by one Ansgot. King John granted the joint property to Hugh Nevil, his justice of the forests and treasurer; in Edward I.'s time it was held by William de Nevil. Having reverted to the Crown on the Duke of Somerset's attainder, it was granted by Queen Elizabeth to William Cecil, Lord Burghley, and then, at Cecil's request, to Thomas — Vincent, of Stoke d'Abernon, who rebuilt the manor-house. In 1753 the trustees of John Spencer, created Lord Spencer of Althorp, in 1761, bought it of the Harveys. Here, after some years' residence, died Lord Liverpool in 1828. From some springs on this estate Wolsey laid a water-supply for his palace at Hampton Court, by way of Surbiton and so beneath the Thames. The original pipes, being of lead, were moulded in lengths of 25 ft. apiece, with an overlay along the seam.*

THE colliers, or charcoal-burners, of Croydon formed a favourite object for the jests and gibes of our satirists,—Barkley in his "Eclogues," and Crowley, for instance,—and comic dramatists in the sixteenth and seventeenth centuries. Grimme, the Collier of Croydon, figures in Robert Edwards's "Damon and Pythias," first acted in 1566, and a later comedy is entitled "Grim, the Collier of Croydon; or, the Devil and his Dame, &c." (1662). In Queen Elizabeth's time, indeed, the inhabitants were for the most part smiths and charcoal-burners, who gathered their wood in the forests round about, remains of which at Norwood, Addington, Carshalton, and Beddington have survived to our own day. Their trade flourished until as late as *circa* 1780, London being their chief market. In Collier's Water-lane, leading from the London road to Thornton-heath station, stands an old-fashioned tenement, bearing, on the Parchmore-road front, the date "1590," latterly a farm-house which, together with its land, is about to be taken for building purposes. Known as Collier's Water-farm, it forms, we believe, the last memorial here of the charcoal-burners. It is the traditional home of Francis Grimes, the collier, who is said to have come off victorious in a dispute with Archbishop Grindal, who had taken umbrage at the clouds of smoke which at times invaded the precincts of his palace, by the parish church. A wooden cross, now decayed, inscribed "In memorium (*sic*) Francis Grimes, Collier," stands in an orchard behind the house. "Collier's Field" appears in the plan attached to Mr. J. C. Anderson's interesting book, published two years ago, upon the award of the Commissioners to enclose the Croydon commons, with the occupiers' names for the period 1793-1803.

THERE seems to be, comparatively speaking, a lull in building operations in Oxford just now. The only new building of importance at present in progress is Manchester College, situated at the back of Holywell-street, and not far from the recently-completed Mansfield College. The roof timbers are now being fixed, but it is early yet to judge of the design. When the new Municipal Offices are erected, a picturesque but now sadly dilapidated building will disappear,—Nixon's School at the back of the Corn-market. There is a goo[d] deal of effective detail about the little buil[d]ing, which is entirely of wood and plaste[r] and those who designed it have evidentl[y] been at work in some of the villages roun[d] Oxford, where much good work in window[s] and doorways still remains in houses of a[n] otherwise humble character. We shall hop[e] to give a sketch of Nixon's School shortl[y] made within the past few days.

* See an illustration in Brayley's "Surrey": 1841.

IN an interesting letter in the *Times* [o]f Saturday last, under the title "Fro[m] Tideway to Tideway," Mr. Rudyard Kiplin[g] comments in very plain language on th[e] municipal management of New York, and, i[n] fact, on American conditions of life generall[y]. He catalogues "the three pillars of moderatel[y] decent government" as regard for human lif[e], justice criminal and civil, and good road[s]. With his remarks on the first two head[s], which are trenchant enough, we are n[ot] directly concerned; but those on the Ne[w] York streets are satisfactory from the poi[nt] of view of the patriotic "Britisher," an[d] ought to make grumbling Londoners mor[e] contented with their lot. Kerbstones risin[g] from 2 in. to 6 in. above the level of pavement[s], tram lines from 2 in. to 3 in. above street level[s], building materials scattered half across th[e] street, &c., are among the evidences of "slove[n]liness, sordidness, and want of capacity," which have roused in Mr. Kipling a fee[l]ing of contempt which is healthy enoug[h] but will not make him popular in th[e] country in which he is travelling. As [a] set-off to this picture may be taken th[e] description of the suburbs of St. Pau[l], Minnesota, in the same letter, which i[s] charming, and quite bears out the testimon[y] of a writer in one of the American magazine[s] to which we referred a little while sinc[e]. As Mr. Kipling's letters to the *Times* [o]n *voyage* are marked "To be continued," w[e] recommend our readers to look out for them, for Mr. Kipling is one of those writers (no[t] too numerous) who combine power of litera[ry] style with a keen practical observation [of] those little things (so-called) which often [go] so far to determine both the picturesque a[nd] the sanitary character of a city or a distric[t].

WE have received a copy of *The Arc[hi]tectural Record*, a quarterly periodi[cal] published in New York, and which appea[rs] to contain some good writing on architectur[e], and has also a considerable number of illu[s]trations. Unfortunately, however, the pub[li]cation seems to be characterised by th[e] absence of common honesty in regard to t[he] appropriation of other people's proper[ty] which we so often have to complain of [in] American publications. We find among t[he] illustrations four drawings which have be[en] published in the *Builder*, viz.: Messrs. Kem[p]son & Fowler's "Church at Pentre, Glamo[r]ganshire," Mr. Aston Webb's "Fren[ch] Protestant Church and Parsonage, London," Mr. Jas. Neale's "St. Peter's Bushey-heath," and Messrs. Truefitt & Truefitt's "Schwep[pe] & Co.'s Factory, Malvern." No ackno[w]ledgment of the source whence these a[re] taken is made, but we can have no reaso[n]able doubt that they are plundered fr[om] our pages, without the ceremony of sayi[ng] "with your leave" either to us or to t[he] original owners of the drawings, who mig[ht] be supposed to have some right to be consult[ed] in the matter. We cannot observe, by t[he] way, that any reference is made to th[e] illustrations, or any special use made [of] them; they are just introduced, apparent[ly] for the pleasure of plundering when th[ere] is no legal power to prevent it.

THE attack which has been made on [Mr.] Madox Brown in the Manchester To[wn] Council, arising out of dissatisfaction w[ith] his last fresco at the Town Hall, seems pe[cu]liarly ungracious. Mr. Madox Brown [has] now been engaged for many years on [the] painting of the only series of important de

:ive mural paintings in an English public ilding which is in the way of comple- n, and it appears that these have been rried out at the very inadequate re- neration, for such work, of 320*l*. per :ture. His last work of the series s now been made the object of a vulgar d violent attack in the Council, by a mber who admitted that he knew nothing out art. We have not seen the picture, d do not know its merits, but a painter who s done such work as Mr. Brown has done the Town Hall deserves at least to be ticised with the utmost respect. The cision of the Town Hall Committee, that r. Brown should be requested to exhibit etches of his pictures before proceeding th them, is not in the least unreason- le or unusual in itself; at the Paris itel de Ville every artist has been required submit preliminary sketches of his rk for the decorations, and the Manchester wn Hall Committee would have been quite stified in making that a condition at the tset. But to spring it upon the veteran inter now, near the close of his series of rks, and as the sequel to a coarse and lgar attack upon him, is at the least, a culiarly unfortunate and ungracious kind proceeding.

THE bright May days of the early part of the week, in Paris at least, showed the ench capital at its best, and nothing could more charming than the effect, last Sunday rning, of the foliage in the Tuileries rdens (in many shades of green, but all ght and vivid), contrasted with the many tues glistening white in the sunshine—the ghtest lighted of all showing, by a happy ance of "composition," against the darkest mp of trees; the two fountains, one in the eground and one in the middle distance as n from the Tuileries end, *jaillissants* (no glish word gives it so well) between the sses of trees. A damsel with a bright red shade goes down the walk, giving the tist the one spot of bright colour needed to ve point to the picture. Beyond the gardens e obelisk of the Place de la Concorde makes pillar of silver in the bright misty sunlight, d, far beyond, the great mass of the Arc de toile just shows its outline in the extreme stance. What a vista! How full of the pression of a refined and artistic civilisa- n. But alas! one turns one's eyes a little athward to take in more of the garden ne, and there, rising above the bright es, is the great spidery, lanky, unmeaning mework of the Eiffel tower, spoiling the le of everything, intruding the associations vulgarity and commercial display—the of of the Philistine planted in fair Paris. w long are the Parisians going to leave it re to discredit their æsthetic sense?

ARCHITECTURE AT THE ROYAL ACADEMY.—III.

1,643; "Barton Pines, Paignton, Devon;" . F. M. Simpson. This has very much the k of an old house; we presume it is a new , an example of that rather over-acted plicity which seems to be a charm to many ver architects nowadays. It is a house with reat deal of wall, small windows with very all panes opened in the wall here and there, bles with stone ball finials. From the plan it ms to be an addition to an existing house, ence perhaps the manner of treatment, but old portion is not seen in the view. There pleasant old-world feeling about it, but it y be questioned how much this is owing to manner of the drawing.

1,644; "The Queen's Tower. Imperial In- tute;" Mr. Thos. E. Collcutt. A fine coloured wing of the tower with just the dormers and bles of the roof at the foot of it. The main ject is to show the crowning stage of the wer, which has an octagon stage cleverly con- cted with the angles of the square sub-struc- re by what may be called Classic buttresses d flying buttresses; the octagon stage is open the four cardinal sides; above is a circular m with thin pilasters alternating with le lights all round, and defined horizontally by bands of red and white masonry; a lead dome with a little circular lantern rises above. There is a little too much of the strip-pilaster work, all down the substructure of the tower, and on the octagon and dome of the cupola; *toujours perdrix*, an overdose of a form of detail which is not very recondite in its signification. At the distance when the eye loses these pilasters a little, the whole makes a fine group, effectively treated in water-colour drawing.

1,646; "Mosaic Pavement of Staircase and Hall, and Copper Balustrade, 9, Chester-field-gardens;" Mr. G. Aitchison. The drawing does not indicate the texture of mosaic, but looks like inlay; the principal design consists of a border of black conventional dolphins on a white ground (dolphins play a part in other painted decorations of the same house), and in the centre white scroll work of Renaissance type on a black ground, with smaller panels at the end. These and other smaller panels are arranged in reference to the position of doors shown on the plan; the whole will have a satisfactory effect but presents nothing very special in detail. The stair baluster, executed in hammered copper, is shewn with a large free Renaissance scroll design repeating its general *motif* in each compartment, but with difference of detail.

1,647: "Sketch for the Unfinished Side of the new Quadrangle, King's College, Cambridge;" Mr. G. F. Bodley. We cannot say that the architects who are Academicians are doing much for the architectural room this year. This is a part of an elevation of a quadrangle building of which it is really difficult to say anything except that it is in domestic or collegiate Gothic style, has bay windows at intervals with gablets over them and a tier of small windows between them, and a gate-tower of the usual collegiate class, with an oriel over the arched gateway. The style of thing is in perfectly good taste, but it is difficult to find any interest in it.

1,648; "Glenlyon House, Perthshire;" Messrs. W. Dunn and R. Watson. An elevation, treated with the effect of a perspective in regard to the landscape, of an exceedingly simple country house with plain windows and a round cone-capped tower at one angle, in which is apparently the garden entrance. Before it apparently is a hedge cut as a paling, at least this is the impression conveyed. The level lines contrast well with the undulating country shown in the rear, and the whole has the charm of simplicity appropriate to a medium-sized country house.

1,651; "A Street Corner;" Mr. Clarence Coggin. A corner house with a treatment of the gable on each face with Dutch Renaissance details; it is a somewhat hard little pen-drawing, but effective as an idea for a brick corner house.

1,652; "Design for Stained Glass;" Mr. W. Griffiths. A very pretty little coloured drawing with a figure representing "Industry," entirely free from conventional Mediævalism; an indication of drapery and trees over it forms a background to the figure. The detail is very delicately drawn on the small scale adopted, and the colour effect harmonious and with a certain individuality about it.

1,654; "Two of a Series of Windows for the Imperial Institute, representing the Arms of the British Empire, with Figures of Aborigines;" Mr. Clement Heaton. Designs for Classic round-arched windows of considerable originality. The lower portion has a wide coloured border with arabesque ornament, interrupted at the angles in one case, and at the centre of the sides in the other, by winged heads or masks on dark grounds; the angle treatment is the best. In the centre of the white glass within the border is a large kind of trophy design, an architectural shrine with base mould, corbels, and cornice having a circle in the centre in which emus are introduced in one design and a kangaroo in the other, and below the circle are seated aboriginal African and Australian figures back to back. The semicircular heads of the windows are treated in much the same way. The general effect is truly decorative, and the attempt to give the designs a symbolical signification is of course a distinct merit. The only query is whether the centre portion of the design, being decidedly architectural in character and detail, does not look out of place and unsupported when hung in this way, as it appears to be, within an expanse of white glass and without any appearance of constructional connexion with the frame design.

1,656 and 1,661 may be taken together, as they are by the same author and are hung together, and both represent the same "House at Northwood." The former is a pleasant little bit of what may be called humorous treatment of a small country-house, with a bulbous finial, like a pumpkin on end, stuck on the roof of a projecting apse; and a round rusticated arch losing itself against the wall of the "apse" which contains, as the plan shows, the staircase. No. 1661 is a rather rough pencil-sketch of the back of the same house with a more sober treatment, and an indication of clipped and shaped hedges, and bushes standing up in the middle of a formal garden. Plans are appended. The house is picturesque, but we can hardly think the two drawings merited the very good place which has been given to them.

1,657; "Municipal Buildings, Bury;" Mr. F. H. Tulloch. This drawing is shown in one of our lithograph illustrations this week, but in a different tone from the prevalent one of the drawing, which is worked in Indian ink, a tone that is apt to get rather heavy in ink-photo. It represents part of a design submitted in competition for the Bury Municipal Buildings, and is one of the best pieces of design and drawing among this year's Academy architecture. The contrast between the rich frieze and the plain turrets which intercept it is very picturesque; not less so the open lanterns of the turrets with their short colonnettes. The employment of short colonnettes seems to have been made intentionally a feature in the design, and gives a unity of character to it. We regret that there is no plan to explain the intention of this portion of the design, but at any rate it is an admirable piece of architecture, and one cannot but regret that it is not to be carried out.

1,658; "A Renaissance Ceiling;" Mr. J. J. Shaw. This may be called a satisfactory ceiling of its type; it contains rather heavy but rich-looking Renaissance scroll-work and ornamental figures in what appears to be a large cove, with many-winged harpy-like figures filling up the angles; a strong moulding and circle of ornament on the gold ground of the large centre panel, with little circles at the side. This is very mechanical, and the design would have been more attractive with a plain gold centre panel and nothing else.

1,659; "Firsdene, Lickey, Bromsgrove;" Messrs. Bateman & Bateman. This is a very nice watercolour, fine in tone and treatment, of a quiet stone country house with red roofs and gables of varying sizes facing a lawn, at the side of which is a clipped hedge and terrace. The windows are simple mullioned ones introduced where they are wanted. There is a pleasing English feeling about the whole, and the drawing deserved far more to be hung on the line than some of those that have attained that capriciously-conferred honour.

1,662; "House and Studio, Holland Park;" Mr. G. D. Oliver. There is a certain sober whimsicality in the manner in which the modillioned cornice of the house part is stopped against Gothic-shaped buttresses flanking the bay window of the studio and billiard-room (one over the other); apparently the studio portion is an addition to a regulation street house, the two parts seem to have no relation to each other except in plan, and evidently "that's the humour of it."

1,664; "Sketch for a house;" Mr. Dudley Newman. A pleasant rapid sketch for a brick country house, with a feeling for colour in the drawing; unfortunately the lines are not all upright, a defect even in a rough sketch when we are dealing with architecture.

1,665; "Proposed Group of Almshouses, Lytton, Wilts;" Mr. C. E. Ponting. Apparently on toned paper; very red houses with a gable at each end of the front with windows supporting its soffit, the wall (or partition) below the windows touched with white body colour for the plaster (that is what gives part of the character to the drawing), and these partitions again supported on window-panes, according to a prevalent fashion. There is no plan to show the meaning of the large arched doorway in the centre of wall, which suggests the idea that a carriage was to be provided as one of the appendages of the almshouses, and this is the coach-house. It is a pretty and picturesque little drawing, however.

1,666; Design for New Municipal Buildings, Oxford;" Mr. Thos. Davison. This is a pleasantly composed design shown in a good pen drawing, though it consists really of little more than the putting together of features which have come

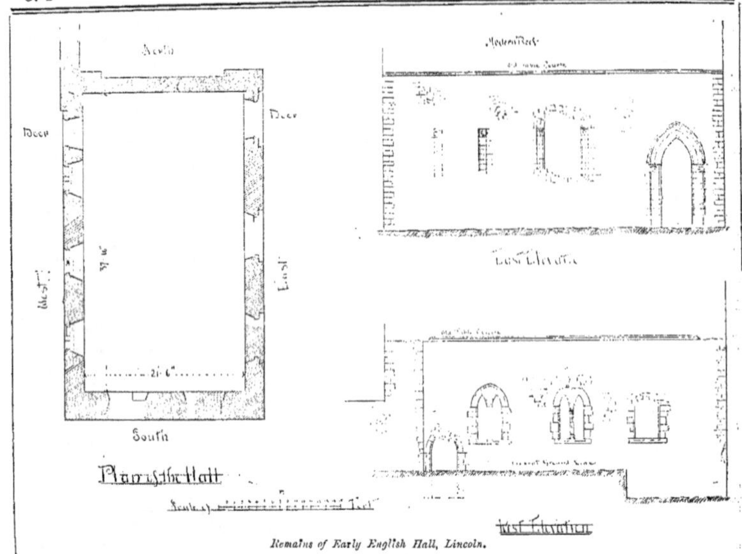

Remains of Early English Hall, Lincoln.

into common use in architecture lately, and suggests the idea of being like a great many other buildings, though it is an agreeable example of its type. There is no plan, consequently nothing to render the design intelligible.

1,667; "Design for Painted Glass," Mr. E. J. Chapman. Apparently a good bit of treatment of stained glass for a Renaissance building, in the Rococo Renaissance style, in light stain on white glass set in squares: too high for detail to be seen.

1,668; "St. Marylebone General Dispensary;" Mr. Beresford Pite. Evidently a bit of old building somewhere in the decayed portions of ancient Rome, patched up and furnished with doors and windows for modern use. In this sense the drawing is effective, but has an unhappy and desolate appearance, quite out of keeping with one's idea of a dispensary, as a place of relief to the bodily ailments of the afflicted.

EARLY ENGLISH HALL, THE CLOSE, LINCOLN.

OF the group of houses recently pulled down at Lincoln to afford a better view of the Minster from the north-east, only one had any claim to antiquity. The others were common-place tenements of the last or the present century, the loss of which there is no reason to deplore. The one exception was known as "The College House," being in fact the shell of a thirteenth century hall, in which the college of vicars and the other officers of the cathedral were entertained by the dean and canons on the appointed "feeding days," according to a fixed rotation, so many days being allotted to each dignitary. At first these "feedings" were given in the houses of the residentiaries; but it was soon found more convenient to receive the guests in a common hall or refectory erected for the purpose. More than one such appears to have been built, as "halls" are spoken of in the plural, "aulae," in the directions for lighting the fires, which, as formerly at Westminster School, and other similar foundations, were kindled on the eve of All Saints' Day, October 31, and extinguished on Easter eve, without any reference to the time of year when it fell. That which has recently been discovered, and discovered only to be destroyed, is the only one of these halls, of which there is any trace. It belonged to the early part of the thirteenth century and afforded a very good example of the domestic architecture of that period. When its original use had passed away, this hall, in common with many such structures,* was converted into a small dwelling-house by the introduction of floors and partitions. The windows were blocked up, modern sashes inserted, and little was left to indicate the architectural character of the building beyond the mutilated arched doorway of entrance (of which a sketch is given) and a single blocked lancet light in the southern gable. When these houses passed by purchase from the Dean and Chapter to Mr. Shuttleworth, and their demolition was begun, directions were given to the contractor to deal very carefully with this house, and to preserve every feature of antiquity. These instructions were complied with, and an opportunity was thus afforded to Mr. W. G. Watkins (son of Mr. W. Watkins, architect, of Lincoln) to measure and take careful drawings of every part. Some of these drawings are given as illustrations of this paper, and as a record of an interesting building now entirely destroyed.

The hall was 37 ft. 10 in. long by 21 ft. 6 in. broad, the walls being 20 ft. high to the table course. It ran from north to south, having its chief elevation, or "showside," to the east, and the plainer elevation, or "backside" to the west. On the east side, at the northern extremity, was the chief entrance: an arched doorway, 4 ft. wide in the clear by 11 ft. high,—a good example of a plainish Early English archway, with chamfered orders and nook shafts, of which only the foliaged capitals remained. On this side there were distinct traces of two largish windows, of which the jambs, the foliaged capitals, bases of the shafts, and, in the northern window, the springing of the arch remained. The west side was plainer. There was a door of simpler design opposite to the chief door, and three windows, not opposite to the others, smaller and destitute of their ornamental features. Two of these, having been built up in the wall when the hall was turned into a house, were almost perfect. Of the third, only the jambs and sill remained. They showed two lancet lights, with a shaft between, combined under one arch, the tympanum being unpierced. The central window of the three was the most perfect and exhibited its old arrangements very clearly. They had never been glazed, the jambs not having been rebated for glass, but were closed with wooden shutters, of which the hooks remained, shutting-to against the inner face of the window-shaft, left flat to receive them, the outer face being semi-octagonal. The holes in the jambs showed that the openings were protected by vertical and horizontal bars, of the latter of which one still remained in its place. In the south gable end were traces of two windows, and evidence of a door in the north wall communicating with what was probably the kitchen further north. This had been almost entirely destroyed, but on the west side part of the wall remained, containing one lancet window. The table-course on which the roof had rested was formed of very large slabs, 18 in. broad.

It would have been very desirable if so interesting an example of Early Domestic architecture could have been preserved. But after the removal of the floors and partitions it was in so ruinous a state that to have secured its preservation would have involved its almost complete rebuilding, and have destroyed its value as an architectural document. All the moulded stonework and other architectural fragments have been carefully put by for re-erection.

* The Bishop's Palace at Hereford, and a portion of the Deanery at Winchester, are formed out of Mediæval halls. The now unhappily demolished Guesten Hall at Worcester was converted by floors and partitions into the modern Deanery.

EXHIBITION AT CARPENTERS' HALL.

THE Worshipful Company of Carpenters is exhibiting this week, at its hall in London Wall, a collection of examples of woodwork, furniture, carving, and specimens of handicraft. This is a larger exhibition than the annual one, and takes place every four years. This corporation is noted for endeavours to maintain its connexion with the trade whose name it bears, and its good work is done in a methodical manner. The British Institute of Wood-carvers at Chapel-street owes much to the company, which exercises some control in its management. Both Kings College and University College classes of construction have been largely endowed also by the company. The Institute at Stratford is now well known, wi

:s swimming-bath and institute and handi-raft classes, and is a great boon to a densely-opulated neighbourhood, and its success peaks volumes for it.

To encourage interest in this exhibition, rizes are offered for models in constructive arpentry, ornamental carpentry, specimens of oinery, carving, handwork, and the loan of bjects illustrating the arts of joinery and carv-ng has been invited. In the constructive car-entry division a first prize and silver medal as been awarded to Mr. E. Langdon, who con-ributes a model, carefully made, of a flying and aking shore. The flying shore would, in our pinion, have been better had the lowest struts een in the same plane with the other two. Ir. C. Rochester takes a second prize with a iodel of staging for carrying a steam crane. his is a framing in two stages with four cor-er posts. It is braced in a sound manner nd would be probably strong enough for ractical purposes; theoretically, however, the ruts carried into the centre of the corner post ith no abutting timber behind it is inadvisable. ome of the struts are carried down to the vel of the second staging in a better manner, it these require a stiffening piece from the orner post half way down.

There are more carefully and elaborately ade models, about 9 in. long, of entrance gates, ade by Mr. Benjamin Holmes. It seems a pity encourage this style of work, as it is too small be joinery, and hasn't the finish of cabinet ork; it would merely produce finnicking work. e note that prizes have been awarded to them. model of shoring for capital and springing one of a church, carefully made in oak by Mr. . E. Cutler, takes a second prize and bronze edal. An illustration of something very similar opears in Viollet le Duc's Dictionary. The st of these exhibits are interesting models of ofs and scaffoldings, centreing, &c. Mention ould be made of Mr. Daniel Bryant's model self-supporting queen-post partition, which kes a second prize and bronze medal.

In the joinery division there are five models staircases amongst others. The first prize d medal falls to Mr. Geo. Welch, who exhibits circular stair with circular well. The lines these stairs are very true and the workman-ip good.

Mr. Alfred Wort secures the second prize ith a model of geometrical staircase with liptical well. Mr. C. W. D. Boxall gains the st prize and medal for handrailing. Mr. . J. Johnson and Mr. S. G. Lidstone take izes for casements and sashes, and Messrs. T. Aston and Silas Evans prizes for lantern-hts. Mr. E. Young also receives a second ize and medal for some good models of otions of sills to sashes, with a view to the clusion of the weather and the removal of ndensation.

The exhibits of carving are numerous and in-resting. Mr. A. Halliday takes a first prize d silver medal for a carved oak chair-back, ry properly in low relief. The carving and es are vigorous. A second prize has been arded to Mr. Charles Stephens' somewhat me carved oak frieze for chimney-piece. Mr. A. Vogt takes a first prize and silver medal r a vigorous carved capital of a column in ft wood; and a similar distinction is awarded Mr. Anthony Smith for a carved bracket. e of the most interesting exhibits is the case Mr. James Osmond, which receives a first ize and silver medal. The contents are of tistic merit of no mean order, and comprise gorous models in clay, carved wood panels, d fan sticks, all in hard wood, the signs being Renaissance in character. We not care for the subject of the centre bject, labelled "The Cronies;" but, at the me time, the expression on the old lady's ce is wonderfully rendered. A second prize es to Mr. James Osmond for a study of a gro's head. The face has been sand-papered, d, though this in the ordinary way must be precated, it renders the shiny appearance a negro face very effectually. Honourable ention and an award has been given to Mr. . B. Harrison for a carved satinwood clock-se; the workmanship of this is excellent and e carving of some merit, but the attempt to eat a clock-case design architecturally is more ten than not unsuccessful, and this design is exception, the faults of proportion being parent in several cases.

A small table in this room shows a few speci-ens of the useful kind of instruction to be tained at the Company's Institute at Strat-rd.

The smaller room adjoining contains the loan collection, and much interest is attached to this portion. Most noticeable is an English armoire, lent by Mr. Seymour Lucas, which is labelled "English Gothic Armoire, date about 1500," which may be safely considered of an earlier date. The tracery work is of great beauty. Mr. W. H. Spiller contributes a carved oak Italian chest, date about 1600, and an interesting case of inlaid guns and powder-flasks. Professor Banister Fletcher also contributes some objects of interest, among them a carved chair of the Caroloan period.

A carved bracket in this room, by Mr. E. T. R. Boreman, takes a first prize and silver medal. The execution is excellent. There are some interesting specimens of work done by the Wood-carving Classes at Kings College. The reproductions of old furniture which are exhibited and executed by the Chiswick School of Arts and Crafts are interesting. The reproduction is exact and slavish; even the date, 1670, is carefully inserted. We hope tricks of this sort will not mislead the careless observer. We understand that the judges were Mr. Seymour Lucas, A.R.A., Professor Roger Smith, and Banister Fletcher, and Messrs. Bartlett, Hill, Ryder, Howard, and Aumonier. The exhibition is well worth a visit.

MAGAZINES AND REVIEWS.

THE *Gazette des Beaux-Arts* opens with an article by M. Henri Béraldi on Raffet, of the recent exhibition of whose works something was said in our Paris Letter last week. M. Béraldi considers that Raffet will take a place in art history beside such masters as Délacroix and Meissonier. Some interesting sketches by Raffet accompany the article. M. Paul Lefort contributes an article on "Zurbaran," with a number of illustrations from drawings in various museums; and M. A. Renan has an article which will be interesting to architects on the old city of Tlemcen, "the Pearl of Algeria," with illustrations of some of its Arabic architecture. "Le Musée des Artistes Contemporains," by M. Léonce Bénédite, deals with the present and possible future of the Luxembourg, which he considers by no means in a flourishing condition. The Museum is too small, and frequent promises that it should be enlarged have never been carried out. Foreign countries are badly represented; the country of "Leighton, Burne-Jones, Watts, Tadema," &c., is represented only by a work of a second-rate landscape-painter, Wyld (this was evidently written before the thrilling incident of the addition of Mr. Whistler's picture), and the museum is debarred by its regulations from hanging more than three works by any one painter, so that a fourth work, however superior, is condemned to rejection in advance. The duty of such an institution as the Luxembourg, M. Bénédite urges, is to be absolutely eclectic, and to give full representation on equal terms to all schools and all countries. The number concludes with an article by M. A. Gayet on "La Sculpture Copte" with one or two curious illustrations.

The first article in the *Art Journal* is devoted to two notices of the late Mr. F. Leyland's collection of works of art, by Mr. Val Prinsep and Mr. Lionel Robinson, in which far too much importance is attached to the tastes and supposed influence of a self-made millionaire whose predilections in art were of a very one-sided nature, and who probably had not known nearly so much about art as he professed or was credited with by a clique of artists of a certain school to whom he played the part of patron. The article is very well illustrated by engravings of some of the well-known pictures of Rossetti and Mr. Burne Jones which were in his collection, and of some of the rooms in the house decorated by Mr. Whistler. An article on Mr. David Murray by Miss Marion Hepworth Dixon is accompanied by reproductions from his leading pictures of the year. Mr. Charles Holme writes an article on old Japanese pottery containing a good deal of information, and illustrated by examples the majority of which are rather curious than beautiful.

In the *Magazine of Art* "The Royal Academy" is the subject of an article by the editor, in the course of which some strong but perfectly true remarks are made as to the narrowness of the Academy in refusing admittance within its ranks to artists in black and white—pen artists as they may be termed. Keene, it is observed, was admirably praised by the President in his speech at the annual banquet, "and his praises have been sung by the whole artistic universe. Yet he was not thought fit to enter Burlington House." Messrs. John Tenniel, Linley Sambourne, and Edwin Abbey are equally unrecognised. But the fact is, as we have already observed in speaking of architecture, that the majority of the Academicians are people who think (or act as if they thought) that art means painting. The article is illustrated by some reproductions of pictures of the year, and (which is of more interest) by the studies made by Sir F. Leighton for the "Hesperides," "Bacchante," and "At the Fountain." An article on "Press-day and Critics," with portraits, is a new departure which will interest a good many readers, while others may be rather surprised to find among the "art-critics" some accomplished literary men whose knowledge of art is not generally supposed to be very deep. Mr. G. T. Robinson contributes an article to the "Artistic Homes" series on the decoration of ceilings, with illustrations of some very charmingly ceiled rooms from old Renaissance houses. Other articles are a short one on Mr Wedmore's book on Méryon, and one on "The Dixon Bequest at Bethnal-green," by Mr. R. Jope-Slade.

The Antiquary contains, in its "Notes of the Month," a great many items of interest, and this department of the publication, which is being gradually expanded, is likely to become one of its most attractive features. Mr. J. Romilly Allen contributes a paper on "Archæology and Philosophy," in the course of which he urges, and rightly, that there should be a photographic department in connexion with all great archæological museums, "and every object should be permanently identified by means of photography." A strong article (unsigned) refers to "Doings at Lincoln Cathedral" in relation of course to the threatened demolition of Wren's cloister, in which the writer laments, and with reason, the extent to which Mr. Pearson has allowed himself to become identified with the removal and so-called "restoration" of ancient work. The writer avers that Wren's cloister is really the most valuable side of the four, inasmuch as the other three sides have been more or less modernised, whereas Wren's work is entirely original and remains just as it was built. It is probable, in our opinion, that the check given to the proposal by the discovery of serious dilapidations in one of the western towers will have the effect of preserving Wren's cloister by affording a decent pretext for backing out of a piece of work which has been so generally condemned. Other articles deal with "Bookbinding," "Ancient Leicester," "The Discovery of the coffin of Mrs. Margaret Godolphin in Breage Church, Cornwall," &c., &c.

The *Edinburgh Review* gives an article on "Dr. Schliemann's Last Excavations" sympathetic in tone, but admitting an element of good luck in his career, and a power of making the most of his successes. The *Review* admits that in his early days Schliemann was tempted into indulging in mere guesses which afterwards turned out to be untenable, but regards these as of no more importance in respect of the main quality of his work "than the first errors in an uncorrected proofsheet." The same number of the *Review* contains an article on "The Municipal Administration of London," not very favourable in its views of the London County Council. The attempt to govern London by a "committee of one hundred and thirty-seven people" the *Review* considers to be fraught with the gravest inconvenience, and speaks elsewhere of the necessary result of attempting to govern the affairs of London by "a number of small committees," in which there is no demand of personal responsibility. The fluctuating nature of the Council is regarded as another serious evil; "three years is but a short time" in which to make due acquaintance with the problems to be dealt with. The *Review* charges the "Progressists" with endeavouring to increase the popularity of London by increasing its attractiveness and lowering its rents, thereby increasing the already too great tendency to flock into London. "The keep the labourer on the land" is one of the great difficulties of the day, and the present policy of the County Council tends rather to increase than to diminish it. At all events the *Review* would not recommend the principle of building municipal dwellings and letting them at rents below the cost price. Rather it would recommend the Council to see

The Westminster Guildhall or Sessions-House, now in course of Demolition.

to it that no insanitary dwellings are allowed to be let at all; which latter is certainly a wholesome recommendation. The recent defeat of the moderate candidates the *Edinburgh Review* considers to have been due not so much to the influence of any definite principle in voting, as to the fact that the right sort of candidates were not forthcoming on the moderate side, and that there were few who appeared personally to be worth voting for. In conclusion, the *Edinburgh Review* urges that, in the conduct of the business of London, responsibility, economy and efficiency should be the three watchwords of the day.

The *Nineteenth Century* contains an article on "Stevens and the Wellington Memorial" by Mr. Walter Armstrong, which is appropriate just now, and is intended to show the public "how unique a thing deans and Parliament men have hidden away in a corner of St. Paul's." Mr. Armstrong possibly a little exaggerates Stevens. He admits, indeed, at the close, that Stevens invented no new method or detail, he worked with the materials left to him by the Renaissance, but claims for him, and we think rightly, a remarkable power of unity of conception, as illustrated especially in the Wellington Monument. It is a whole thing, one idea which is all in keeping; and a great idea. In stating that Stevens had a power of design only second to that of Michelangelo, it should be remembered however that Michelangelo came first, and that Stevens annexed his style and manner a good deal; some people think, too much. Nor is it quite true to say that Stevens was irreproachable in his treatment of detail. Some of the smaller decorative detail of the Wellington monument is not good, as decoration, not truly architectural in character. But then painters know so little what decorative detail really means in this connexion.

The *English Illustrated Magazine* contains an article by the Dean of Gloucester, under the title "The Vanished Abbey," on the ancient Abbey of Evesham and what is known of it. The article is illustrated by sketches by Mr. Detmar J. Blow and Mr. E. H. New. The sketch given of Evesham Tower is hardly satisfactory, the other illustrations are good sketches and of some interest.

Scribner has a good article on "Rapid transit in cities," by Mr. T. C. Clarke, the first of a series. "The Problem" is the subject of this article, the solution is to be given in another number. One point of the paper is that the writer endeavours to show, and does show to some extent, that the means for giving more rapid transit by street railways are nearly always commenced by a ring round the city, and that in all cases this is found to have been a mistake, and to require correcting by cross lines, as Paris and London are now endeavouring or wishing to correct it the moral being that rapid transit must take people where they want to go, and not where they do not want to go. In London the cross connexion is at present made by omnibuses. The writer thinks the travelling on the underground railway very small compared with the great population of London, which perhaps is true. "Unter den Linden" is a pleasantly-written article on the great Berlin promenade and its frequenters, Mr. Shaler's "Sea and Land" is a very interesting article, illustrated, on the action of the sea on coast formations, and the fourth number of Mr. Apthorp's "Paris Theatres and Concerts" is both entertaining and useful, giving an insight into the system of Paris theatre management in relation to the public.

The *Century* devotes an article to "Architecture at the World's Columbian Exposition," from which it appears that a great deal of thought has been bestowed on the consideration of the design of the principal buildings, of some of which we have given illustrations, though we may question whether they will excite quite the same admiration among European architects as Mr. Van Brunt, the author of the article, claims for them. Mr. Van Brunt is, we believe, one of the architects of the five principal structures, who, it is interesting to know, are all connected professionally with Mr. Hunt, the leading architect, as former pupils or assistants, a fact which will no doubt tend to promote a certain unity of architectural feeling in the structures to be erected. "Homesteads of the Blue Grass," in the same magazine, is a paper on old American houses of a certain district, with illustrations.

In the *Atlantic Monthly* the only article of special interest to our readers is one on "Private life in Ancient Rome," by Miss H. W. Preston and Miss Louise Dodge. It includes a description of the Roman house and its daily use.

The *Quarterly Statement* of the Palestine Exploration Fund is an interesting number, containing a report on "Excavations at Tell el Hesy" by Mr. F. J. Bliss, with plans, and engravings of a good many objects discovered; a letter from Herr Schick on "Recent Discoveries at Nicophorieh," with drawings of some interesting sarcophagi and architectural details, and a "Narrative of a journey to Palmyra" by the Rev. G. B. Post.

The *Essex Review* for the April quarter contains the second of the articles on "Essex Churches," dealing with St. Michael's, Woodham Walter; the article is by Mr. F. Chancellor, and is accompanied by a plan and a pretty sketch of the picturesque little church. The first of a set of articles on Parish Registers, by Mr. Robert H. Browne, is on the register of the same church, followed by one on that of Alphamstone, by Mr. C. Golding. Under the general heading of "Notes and Queries" a good deal of interesting information is collected.

THE GUILDHALL OR SESSIONS HOUSE, WESTMINSTER.

IN the *Builder* for April 23 (p. 320) we referred to what we then spoke of as the "enlargement" of this well-known building. We now regret to learn that the building is being demolished, and that a totally new building of quite a different character is to be erected on its site, from a design by Mr. F. H. Pownall, the County Surveyor for Middlesex, for the use of the Middlesex County Council.

The Westminster Guildhall was erected, according to Elmes and Shepherd's "Metropolitan Improvements" (1828), by Samuel Pepys Cockerell, father of Professor C. R. Cockerell, R.A. The book does not mention the date of the erection of the building, but we believe it was about the year 1804. We have thought it would be of interest at the present time to reproduce Shepherd's engraving of it from the book mentioned.

THE ROYAL INSTITUTE OF BRITISH ARCHITECTS:

THE ANNUAL REPORT.

THE annual general meeting of the Royal Institute of British Architects was held on the 2nd inst. We make the following extracts from the annual report, as adopted by the meeting:—

The Council have held twenty-one meetings since the announcement of their election at the first general meeting in June, 1891, previous to which two Council Meetings were held, making in all twenty-three meetings since the publication of the last Annual Report on May 7, 1891. Committees of the Council have also met for the consideration of matters connected with (1) Professional Practice, (2) Finance, (3) the Alliance of Non-Metropolitan Societies, (4) the grant of funds in furtherance of the Educational Scheme of the Architectural Association, and (5) the award of the Royal Gold Medal.

During the official year (from the beginning of May, 1891, to the end of April, 1892) 6[illegible] Fellows have been elected, 29 of whom were previously members in the class of Associates, and 51 Associates have been elected. The number of Fellows is now 610, as against 560, and the number of Associates 794, as against 784 at the corresponding period last year. One Hon. Associate—Mr. Henry T. Boodle—has been elected, and the number is now 67. Five Hon. Corresponding Members—Dr. William Dörpfeld (Athens), Baron Max von Ferstel (Vienna), His Excellency Osman Hamdy Bey (Constantinople), Professor Carl König (Vienna), and Herr Otto Wagner (Vienna)—have been elected, and the number is now 49. H.H. the Maharaja of Jeypore, G.C.S.I., has been elected an Hon. Fellow.

The losses by death, in the class of Fellows, ince the issue of the last Annual Report, have een:—Isaac Barradale (Leicester), Edward H. lurnell, Thomas Henry Eagles, M.A., Philip C. Iardwick, F.S.A., Robert J. Johnson, F.S.A. Newcastle), Harry Oliver, Alexander Peebles, lfred Porter, Frederick J. Robinson (Derby), dward J. Tarver, F.S.A., C. J. Toxward (Wellington, N.Z.), Thomas Verity, and Vincent W. 'oisey (Bristol). In the class of Associates: V. W. Kendall Clarke, Henry Curzon (Tenbury), Ienri C. Elworthy (St. Leonards-on-Sea), and . Russell Walker (Edinburgh). In the class of Ion. Associates: Sir John Coode, K.C.M.G.; he Rt. Hon. William Cavendish, Duke of Devonshire, K.G.; Sir John Hawkshaw, F.R.S.; he Prince Victor of Hohenlohe-Langenburg; and 'ohn Murray, F.S.A. In the class of Hon. Corr. Members: Antoine Nicolas Bailly (Paris), Professor Giovan B. F. Basile (Palermo), and Cavaliere Pietro Rosa (Rome). In the class of Hon. Fellows: Professor E. A. Freeman, D.C.L. Obituary notices of nearly all the above-mentioned members have appeared in the *Journal of roceedings*.

At the general meeting, held on January 18 st, addresses of condolence with her Majesty e Queen and his Royal Highness the Prince Wales, Patrons of the Institute, on the elancholy death of his Royal Highness the uke of Clarence and Avondale, were voted; id the business of the Special General Meeting hich was summoned for the same evening was ostponed out of respect for the national loss.

The Preliminary Examination was held in ovember, 1891, and March, 1892, in London and Ianchester. The Intermediate Examination of 5 Probationers last November, and 22 last onth, was held in London. The number of *robationers* is now 320, and the number of *udents* (all of whom were previously Proationers) is 41.

The Examination in Architecture, to qualify r candidature as Associate, was held last ovember in London, and this Spring in ondon and Liverpool, at which latter centre r. John Slater attended for the Oral Examination. The names and addresses of the 26 andidates (out of 40 admitted) who passed in November were reported to the General Meeting of December 14, 1891; those of the 49 candidates (out of 81 admitted) who have just passed were reported to the General Meeting of April 4, 1892.

Statistics of the Examinations of 1891-92 are here given in a tabular form:—

The Preliminary Examination.

Dates.	Admitted.	Not passed.	Relegated for periods	Passed and Registered.
Nov., '91	74 {21 Exempted, 48 Examined, 5 did not attend .... }	3	6	60
March, '92 ..	80 {29 Exempted, 48 Examined, 3 did not attend .... }	—	12	65
—	154 (8 did not attend)	3	18	125

The Intermediate Examination.

Dates.	Probationers admitted.	Relegated for periods.	Passed and Registered.
Nov., '91	16	5	11
March, '92 ..	22	9	13
—	38	14	24

The Examination in Architecture.

Dates.	Applied.	Admitted	Not passed.	Relegated.	Passed.
Dec., '91	48	40	—	14	26
March, '92 ..	92	81	—	32	49
—	140	121	—	46	75

The Council think it worthy of attention that 140 applications were made in 1891-92 to be admitted to the Examination qualifying for candidature as Associate, the number of such applications during the preceding official year having been 106; while the number of passed candidates was 75, as against 49 in 1890-91, and 54 in 1889-90. During the kalendar year 1891 the number of candidates who passed amounted to 50, amongst whom Mr. John Begg most highly distinguished himself, and was awarded the Ashpital Prize. At the same time the Board of Examiners highly commended Mr. Owen Fleming and Mr. Joseph William Twist (South Shields), also passed candidates in the Examinations of that year.

A Statutory Examination for the office of District Surveyor of London, and of Building Surveyor under local authorities, was held in November, at which two applicants presented themselves, neither of whom passed. The April Examination was held on the 28th and 29th ult., when six candidates presented themselves for examination under the Metropolitan Building Act, 1855, four of whom obtained certificates of competency to act as District Surveyors in London, viz:—John Albert Gill Knight (*Associate*), 40, St. Luke's-road, Clapham, S.W.; George Arthur Lansdown, 5 and 7, Warwick-street, Charing-cross; Frank John Waldemar Leverton, H.M. Office of Works, Whitehall; Robert Williams (*Associate*), 8, John-street, Adelphi, W.C. One candidate also presented himself for examination under other Acts, but the Council were not recommended to grant him a certificate of competency.

At the request of the Committee of the Architectural Association the Association scheme of education in course of establishment was discussed by the Institute, after a full explanation of it had been given by Mr. Frank Baggallay, President of the Association, at a General Meeting held last June; and at the adjourned Meeting in July a resolution was passed by the Institute authorising the Council to consider and decide in what manner and to what extent pecuniary assistance should be given towards the establishment and carrying out of the Association scheme. The matter having been previously discussed by a Special Committee and reported on by the Finance Committee of Council, final consideration was given to it by the Council at the end of last December, when they decided "That a sum of three hundred pounds (£300) be granted to the Architectural Association (London) in support of the A. A. Educational Scheme, such payment to be made in three equal annual instalments: on Jan. 30, 1892, Jan. 31, 1893, and Jan. 31, 1894, but that the grant of the instalments of 1893 and 1894 respectively be conditional on the A. A. Educational Scheme being then still in operation." This decision was reported to the Institute on January 25 last, and the first instalment of £100 was duly paid to the Architectural Association and acknowledged.

The Council having been asked by the Siamese Legation in London to consider and report on a draft curriculum of architectural study, which was submitted to them, for Siamese students resident in England, and desirous of becoming architects in their own country, sent, in reply, three papers of comments and suggestions prepared respectively by the Chairman of the Board of Examiners in Architecture, by the Professor of Architecture at the Royal Academy of Arts (London), and by the Master of the Architectural School of that Academy, which were offered for the consideration of the Siamese Legation, and duly acknowledged.

The Devon and Exeter Architectural Society and the Dundee Institute of Architecture, Science, and Art have been admitted to alliance with the Institute,—the number of such allied societies being now thirteen.

The Royal Gold Medal, 1891, for the promotion of architecture was presented to Sir Arthur W. Blomfield, A.R.A., for his works as an architect, on June 22, 1891. By a resolution of the Institute, passed on March 7, 1892, Monsieur César Daly, *Hon. Corr. Member* (Paris), was elected Royal Gold Medallist for the current year, for his literary works in connexion with architecture; and General Sir H. F. Ponsonby, G.C.B., has written signifying the approval of the award by her Majesty the Queen. This having been communicated to Monsieur Daly, he has accepted an invitation to attend in London next June to receive the Medal from the hands of the President.

The annual Deed of Award of Prizes and Studentships was presented to the Institute on January 18 last, and published at length in the *Journal* of the 28th of the same month. At the presentation of prizes held on January 25 the President delivered an Address to Students on the Art of Planning; and the Hon. Secretary a Critical Notice on the designs and drawings submitted. The public exhibition of the drawings, which lasted from January 15 to 25, included the work as Pugin Student for 1891 of Mr. Sidney K. Greenslade. A selection of drawings which had obtained prizes was forwarded to those of the Allied Societies who applied for them, and an exhibition of the same was held in Newcastle, Dundee, Glasgow, Liverpool, Sheffield, Leeds, Leicester, and Birmingham, under the respective charge of the Societies in those centres. The sum of money for foreign travel given under conditions with the Soane Medallion was increased last year to 100*l.*, and the minimum period of travel was also increased to six months. The successful competitor for the Tite Prize has now to travel in Italy for a period of not less than four weeks.

The pamphlet of subjects and conditions for the Prizes and Studentships of 1891-92 was published early in March. It will be seen therein that some notable modifications have been made in the programme and conditions of the Owen-Jones Studentship, which is now an annual Studentship, open to members of the profession under thirty-five years of age; and the Council have announced that in the examination of candidates' work preference will be given to that exhibiting acquaintance with the application of colour as a means of architectural expression, not alone by the use of pigments, but also in the juxtaposition and combination of different coloured materials.

Pursuant to Resolutions passed at the last Annual General Meeting, the Council appointed a Special Committee to "inquire whether it is not possible under By-law 9* for a small body of members to exclude from the Fellowship of the Institute qualified persons approved by the Council, although a large majority of the members of the Institute approve of the election; and if so, to suggest steps for the amendment of the anomaly." The Committee they appointed—consisting of Messrs. Arthur Cates, *Vice-President*, F. T. Baggallay, James Brooks, Thomas M. Rickman, Lacy W. Ridge, R. Phené Spiers, and Paul Waterhouse, members of their own body; with Messrs. H. C. Boyes, E. T. Hall, E. B. I'Anson, and J. G. Finch Noyes, *Fellows*, and Messrs. Charles Henman and Wm. Woodward, *Associates*—have sent up a unanimous Report, to which the Council have given their general approval, and which they propose to submit to the Institute at the General Meeting to be held on June 13, 1892.

The Institute Paper of "Suggestions for the Conduct of Architectural Competitions" has, for a considerable period, engaged the attention of the Competitions Committee, whose recommendations having been submitted to the Council were considered and approved by them. The amended Paper was brought before a General Meeting of the Institute on March 7 last, when a Resolution was passed that "The principle of the amended Paper of Suggestions for the Conduct of Architectural Competitions be adopted; and that it be left to the Council to issue the same as an Institute Paper, after due consideration of the suggestions made at that Meeting." The Council having since done so, the Paper will be shortly issued.

A Bill to provide for the Registration of Architects was read a first time in the House of Commons on March 2, 1892, and the second reading of it is announced for June 2. The Council have taken the necessary steps to oppose it.

The Art Standing Committee have held eleven meetings since their election in June, 1891, making, since the issue of the last report, twelve in all. Under the provisions of the By-law the Council appointed as additional Members of the Committee Mr. Alma Tadema, R.A., Mr. C. B. Birch, A.R.A., Mr. Ernest George, Mr. Leonard Stokes, and Mr. Alfred Waterhouse, R.A.; and in the course of the year they have filled up vacancies in the Committee by appointing Mr. W. Kidner, Mr. W. S. Weatherley, and Mr. T. J. Flockton (Sheffield). The Committee elected Mr. Waterhouse, R.A., Chairman, and Mr. R. Herbert Carpenter, F.S.A., Vice-Chairman; they also appointed Mr. W. D. Caröe, M.A., and Mr. Beresford Pite, Hon. Secretaries.

The subject of the disfigurement of Somerset House,—the possibility of taking action to deal with the building recently added to it by the authorities of King's College and to prevent the further addition of such works,—has largely occupied the attention of the Committee; and on their recommendation the Council, with the concurrence of the Institute at its meeting of November 2 last, entered into

* By By-law 9, Fellows are elected by ballot, one black ball to six white ones excluding from election.—ED.

communication with the First Commissioner of H.M. Works and Public Buildings, forwarding at the same time the resolution passed at that meeting. By the reply of the First Commissioner, dated December 16, 1891, it appeared that the Office of Works had no power to prevent the addition which was then in course of erection at the eastern end of the river front of Somerset House. By a subsequent letter, dated March 22, 1892, the Council were informed by the First Commissioner that in the event of the authorities of King's College proposing to advance their buildings towards the Embankment, the Government had the power (1) to prevent any erection which would interfere with the light and air of Somerset House, (2) to require that any additional structures forming part of the river front of Somerset House should not be erected without their assent, and (3) to control any buildings proposed to be erected on the triangular piece of land at the south-east corner of King's College site. The correspondence on this subject has been published in the *Journal of Proceedings*.

The proposed demolition of Lauderdale House, Highgate, has been inquired into by the Committee, and some of their members were deputed to visit the old house and report thereon. It was decided that certain portions and fittings of interest might with advantage be retained, as examples of joinery of the period, in any building to be erected in the park"; and the Council approved the Committee's recommendation. It is a matter of satisfaction to know that by the action of the London County Council the house will be preserved.

The threatened destruction of Bourne Old Hall, Lincolnshire, was considered by the Committee, and the Council addressed the Directors of the Great Northern Railway as to the architectural interest of the Hall and the advisability of preserving it if possible. The arrangements of the new line have now been made in a manner that will preserve the building.

The works of external repair to Gray's Inn Hall, in the removal of the stucco and the revealing of old brick and stone work underneath, have had careful consideration; and the Committee recommended the Council to take steps for the preservation of Emanuel Hospital, Westminster, by petitioning that the requisite assent of the authorities be withheld for its removal, and, failing success, to obtain the mention of this important matter in Parliament. St. Mary Woolnoth Church, and Grey Friars, Bedford, have also received the careful attention of the Committee with a view to their preservation. The Council, as far as possible, have adopted the Committee's recommendations in these matters.

The Committee have undertaken the arrangement of three Ordinary Meetings of the Institute during the Session. Those already held, dealing with the subjects of "Sculpture and Sculptors' Methods in relation to Architecture," and with "Stained Glass," have proved of considerable interest to the general body. The Committee hope that this series of meetings for the consideration of new and revised processes of decorative art may be continued and extended in Sessions to come; and the Council congratulate the Institute on the great success that has attended the efforts of the Committee in this direction.

The Literature Standing Committee have held ten meetings since their election in June, 1891, making since the issue of the last report eleven in all. The Council appointed as additional Members of the Committee, Mr. J. D. Crace, Mr. T. H. Eagles, M.A. (since deceased), Mr. R. F. Grantham, Mr. B. Ingelow, and Colonel Lenox Prendergast. The Committee elected Professor Aitchison, A.R.A., Chairman, and Mr. Alex. Graham, F.S.A., Vice-Chairman; they also appointed Mr. Paul Waterhouse, M.A., and Mr. R. Elsey Smith, Hon. Secretaries. . . .

The Sessional Papers presented and read during the official year are:—

The *Journal of Proceedings* of 1890-91 (vol. vii.) contained 468 pages, with two double-page plates and a few illustrations in the text; and twelve numbers have already appeared of the volume for 1891-92. The Committee express themselves greatly indebted to a large number of gentlemen for leading articles and reviews of notable works, and especially to Messrs. Wyatt Papworth, A. E. Street, M.A., Paul Waterhouse, M.A., J. D. Crace, and R. F. Grantham, for valuable assistance repeatedly rendered.

The annual volume of *Transactions* [vii. New Series] contained 416 printed pages with ten double-page plates, 195 illustrations in the text, and a frontispiece portrait of Mr. Alfred Waterhouse, R.A., the ex-President. With it was issued an Index to the volumes of the original series (1836-1884), printed at the sole cost of Mr. Arthur Cates. The Index was originally compiled by the Librarian, Mr. Alex. Beazeley, and presented by him to the Council; and he also prepared the work,—some sixty pages quarto,—for press, in consultation with Mr. Cates. . . . .

By a resolution of the Council, confirmed at the last Annual General Meeting, the management of the Reference Library and Loan Collection of Books was intrusted to the Literature Standing Committee, and has been arranged for by the present Committee for the first time. They have had under their consideration the attendances of the Library officers, the recommendations for purchase of books and the examination of new purchases and presentations, the preparation of reviews of the most important works for the *Journal of Proceedings*, and the desirability of increasing the facilities possessed by country members for borrowing books from the Loan Collection. At the present time the Committee have under consideration the desirability of increasing the available accommodation in the Library.

The old Council-room having been partly fitted with bookcases is now used for the purposes of the Library. . . . .

The Library has been kept open on Saturday afternoons until 6 p.m. from October 1, 1891, to the end of March, 1892, but the Librarian reports only forty-two attendances during the twenty-five afternoons in that period. It has not been proposed to keep the Library open after 2 p.m. on Saturdays during the six months between April and September both inclusive.

The attendances of readers in the Library during the year numbered 3,482 (details whereof are given in a table in the report). From the report of the Librarian to the Literature Committee it appears that during the twelve months from April 1, 1891, to March 31 of the present year the additions to the Library amounted to 172 volumes and 104 pamphlets, and to the Loan Collection 29 volumes and 7 pamphlets, exclusive of parliamentary papers, reports, and transactions of societies, parts of works issued in a serial form not yet completed, and trade lists. The number of volumes presented to the Library was 98, and to the Loan Collection 7. Of pamphlets, 101 were presented to the Library and 7 to the Loan Collection. Of drawings, engravings, and photographs 172 sheets were presented. There were also presented 2 medals, one of the Paris Exhibition, 1889, and one of the Paris Société Centrale des Architectes. The number of tickets (exclusive of renewals) issued for admission to the use of the Library and Loan Collection was 107 (last year 91). The number of volumes issued on loan was 1,131 (last year 945). The attendances of members of the Architectural Association as readers in the Library were 280 (last year 304), and the number of issues on loan (both these items being included in the gross returns above given) was 86 (last year 117).

The Practice Standing Committee have held 11 meetings since their election in June, 1891, making since the issue of the last Report 12 in all. The Council appointed as additional members of the Committee Mr. Henry Currey, Mr. Arthur Cates, Mr. Gruning, Mr. Hansard, and Mr. Tabberet. The Committee re-elected Mr. Currey, Chairman, and Mr. Cates, Vice-Chairman; and Mr. T. M. Rickman and Mr. E. T. Hall, Hon. Secretaries. Besides incidental business of minor importance, the Committee have carefully reconsidered the Conditions of Contract in the amended form in which they were returned by the Institute of Builders, and have completed a further revised form of Contract and Conditions, which they are now sending back to the Institute of Builders for further consideration and conference.

They have given great attention to and have produced a draft Bill for the codification and amendment of the technical portions of the Metropolitan Building Act, which document has been forwarded by the Council to the Local Government Board, to the London County Council, and to the Commissioners of Sewers of the City of London. The Council trust that this work will receive at the hands of the public authorities that consideration and weight which is due to it as coming from a body of experts who have applied their special knowledge to the very technical subject of safeguarding the public in the important matter of building.

The Committee have also considered and reported upon the London Building Law Consolidation Bill put forward by the Local Government Board, and the amendments to that Bill put forward by the London County Council. The questions discussed in these Bills, suggestions, and amendments have been explained on behalf of the Committee by one of their Hon. Secretaries, Mr. Edwin T. Hall, at a General Meeting of the Institute on February 8, 1892.

In the matter of the Draft Bill prepared by the Local Government Board for the purpose of consolidating the enactments relating to the construction and use of buildings in London, the Council, through the President of the Institute, have submitted to the President of the Local Government Board some general observations on the Building Law now in force; and they have urged the necessity of amendment as well as of consolidation, which latter is all that is proposed by the Draft Bill in question. The Council are of opinion that, to make legislation on this important subject useful and effective, the introduction of an amendment Bill simultaneously with a consolidation Bill is imperative, at least, if the requirements of the present day are to be satisfactorily met. The Council have further urged the Local Government Board to make the use of fire-resisting materials compulsory in the construction of important and extensive buildings in the metropolis.

In connexion with these matters the Council have to report that at the beginning of last June, Mr. Cates was asked by them to attend before the Lords' Committee on the London Sky-signs Bill, but that their Lordships were content to accept the evidence he had given, on behalf of the Institute, before the Commons' Committee on the Bill; and the Bill then passed.

The Science Standing Committee have held nine meetings. The Council appointed as additional Members of the Committee Mr. A. C. Bulmer Booth, Mr. G. A. Pryce Cuxson, Mr. Frederic R. Farrow, Mr. Kidner, and Mr. P. Gordon Smith. The Committee re-elected Mr. Lewis Angell, Chairman, and Mr. Henry Dawson, Vice-Chairman; and Mr. Henry Lovegrove and Mr. William C. Street, Hon. Secretaries.

The Committee's Report on "Light and Air" was published in the *Journal of Proceedings*, and an invitation addressed to members of the Institute and other readers of the Journal to forward observations and suggestions in the matter of the several clauses of the Report. The Committee have expressed a hope that there may be an early reform of the present law of light and air, and that questions affecting the rights of owners of property in respect to adjacent buildings may be settled upon an intelligible and equitable basis.

The Committee have been principally engaged in making arrangements in connexion with the General Meeting of the Institute on May 16, when it is proposed that the important subject of the proper introduction and fitting of the electric light in domestic work is to be the subject of discussion. Mr. W. H. Preece, F.R.S., has kindly consented to open the proceedings with an address on the "Art of Interior Illumination," and a Sub-Committee have visited different places with a view to gather information, and to present a Report upon the various details connected with electrical installations.

The Committee have visited the recent Building Exhibition, and had under consideration some new building materials and mechanical appliances, and they propose to bring such of them as appear to merit special consideration before the Institute as soon as an opportunity can be afforded for the purpose. . . .

The revenue account of ordinary funds for the year ended December 31, 1891, duly audited and signed by Mr. Joseph S. Hansom, *Fellow*, and Mr. Reginald A. Crowley, *Associate*, the auditors appointed at the last Annual General Meeting, is submitted with the report. It shows total receipts amounting (with a balance of 31*l*. 13s. 3d. brought forward from last year) to 5,457*l*. 7s. 1d. The total expenditure was 5,214*l*. 0s. 5d., leaving a balance of 243*l*. 6s. 8d., of which the sum of 185*l*. 0s. 2d.,—made up of the balance brought from the Revenue Account of 1890, and a portion of the balance of the Revenue Account of 1891,—has been transferred to the Exceptional Account (for defraying expenses connected with the recent enlargement of premises.) The remainder, viz.

58*l.* 6s. 6d., has been carried to the Revenue Account for 1892.

The revenue account of trust funds for the year ended December 31, 1891, duly audited and signed by the auditors before named, together with the balance-sheets of ordinary and trust funds, were also submitted with the report. . . .

The Council further submit an account of exceptional expenditure during the years 1890 and 1891, and during the three months of the year 1892. From this it appears that the sum of 1,146*l.* 15s. has been expended on the purchase of eighty-four shares in the Architectural Union Company, Limited, thus increasing the number of shares held by the Institute in that Company to 222, of which twenty pertain to the trust funds; while a sum of 2,180*l.* 18s. 6d. has been expended on the additions and alterations to the Institute premises, upon new fittings and furniture, and upon a new lease. . . . .

HAMPSTEAD HEATH STATION.—The directors of the London and North-Western Railway Company have selected Messrs. Kirk & Randall to carry out the work of enlarging and altering this station, the scene of the late disaster, and the contractors have undertaken to complete the whole before the Whitsuntide holidays.

ANCIENT PROCESSIONAL CROSS, ST. OSWALD'S, DURHAM.

LITTLE is known of this cross, except that it was discovered in a package found in a mail-coach in an hotel yard in Durham, about thirty odd years ago. It was then sold to a Mr. Caldcleugh, whose widow subsequently presented it to St. Oswald's Church.

It is, probably, of late fifteenth-century workmanship. A similar one is now in the British Museum.

Figures and emblems are of "white" metal, the cross and arms being gilded. The silver nop and ebony shaft are modern.

THE ENGLISH IRON TRADE.—Quietness still prevails in the English iron market, although the probable early termination of the Durham coal miners' strike gives a healthier tone to business. Cleveland pig is 9d. lower, the decline being occasioned by the prospective settlement of the dispute. Manufactured iron is still in limited inquiry, and very little is doing in tinplates; but a better tone is apparent. There is but little change to chronicle in the steel trade; but in the north-west, ship-plates, angles, and tin-plate bars are all lower. Engineers and shipbuilders are only moderately employed. The coal trade generally is quiet. —*Iron.*

THE SCIENTIFIC STUDY OF TIMBER: SURVEYORS' INSTITUTION.

AT the ordinary general meeting of the Surveyors' Institution, held on Monday evening last, Mr. R. C. Driver, President, in the chair, Professor G. E. S. Boulger, F.L.S., F.G.S., read a paper on this subject. We extract some portions of it:—

It is, I think, a simple statement of fact to say that at present engineers, surveyors, and even timber-merchants recognise most kinds of converted timber (of which alone I am about to speak this evening), not only as to kind, but also even largely as to quality, by methods obviously and confessedly empirical.

In standing timber we often have foliage, flower, or fruit to guide us, in addition to that most important character, the ramification, or caulotaxis; and in unconverted timber we have the bark and often various superficial indications of internal disease or defect, or of probable inferiority. All these indications are absent in converted timber. Not only are we generally, at present, dependent upon "rule-of-thumb" but for many of the ordinary purposes of business we must, no doubt, necessarily, for the sake of rapidity of work, continue to be so. In the examination of wood, once for all, however, as in the testing of the comparative utility of various species or varieties in the inquiry as to the value of new foreign or colonial timbers, or in the selection by sample of large quantities of timber for important works of construction, a more thorough and more scientific estimate might well be applied, and it would be well if more uniform methods of testing were adopted. In any work of construction, for example, it is not only desirable, but practically essential, that the minimum strength of the materials employed, that strength which alone should be reckoned upon, should be known. The approximate durability of timber,—the only material with which I am concerned,—is also a matter of supreme practical importance; and, although, as the conditions under which it may be placed will vary, it is not possible to foretell this exactly, it may be very closely approximated,—more closely than has hitherto been usually done.

It might seem unnecessary to insist that, for any accurate knowledge of timber it is at least just as well to be acquainted with the latest results of scientific investigation into its minute structure, and even into its physiology and pathology. At the present day, moreover, when exact methods have, with the advance of science, found their way into so many branches of trade, one need not fear ridicule in advocating the use even of the microscope in such investigation. If, however, we turn to most of the recognised manuals for professional students, we find the information about the minute structure, growth, physiology and pathology of timber either altogether absent, extremely meagre, or hopelessly antiquated and inaccurate. In Tredgold's "Carpentry," as edited by Mr. E. W. Tarn in 1886, this part of the subject is professedly based upon Rhind's "History of the Vegetable Kingdom," a work published in 1840, and, even then, not very satisfactory. In Mr. Thomas Laslett's "Timber and Timber-trees" (Macmillan, 1875), a generally admirable work, the account of the general anatomy of timber, though having the advantage of a few illustrations, is but meagre, as it is also in the extremely accurate and valuable, though anonymous, "Notes on Building Construction," issued by Messrs. Rivingtons (Part III., chapter v.). In the late Dr. Franklin B. Hough's "Elements of Forestry" (Chicago, 1882), this part of the subject is treated in a very elementary manner though with fair accuracy of statement, but far too briefly.

It is not, I think, asking too much in the direction of scientific education to require that those practically concerned with timber should know as much about its microscopic structure as is contained in the admirably illustrated first chapter of Professor Marshall Ward's excellent little book, "Timber and Some of its Diseases" (Macmillan, 1889). Dr. Robert Hartig's little book, translated by Dr. Somerville as "Timbers and How to Know Them" (Nimmo, 1890), though containing rather minute descriptions of the microscopic appearance of 76 different woods, some of which, such as the rose, the vine, and the barberry, cannot be called timber, has in it no general exposition, beyond a glossary, as to the structure of wood. Such microscopic examination of woods will prove useful not only in the specific identification of timbers, but also in the more difficult and often even more important discrimination between varieties of a single species. The same species from different districts, or grown under different conditions, may yield timber varying considerably in character, and, not improbably, in quality; and, though such differences will often be found, on the careful examination of the trees in bark, branching, leaf, flower, and fruit, to correspond to slight botanical distinctions, for practical purposes it is most important that such distinctions should be correlated with those of the timber. It is, therefore, useful to have a comprehensive classification of woods, based exclusively on characters presented by converted timber.

The difficulties in the way of such work are numerous. As regards not a few valuable exotic woods, some of which, such as the "Ballow" of North Borneo, or the "Pink Ivory" of Natal, may at no distant date come into use, either for constructive or ornamental purposes, we are as yet altogether ignorant of the botanical characters or position of the trees from which they are derived. As to others, even well-known native species, uncertainty is introduced by the ambiguity of the names used for them in commerce, and in some cases botanists have increased rather than diminished this ambiguity by minimising or altogether overlooking the facts of variation. The willow-wood, for instance, used in England, valuable from its non-resinous, and consequently uninflammable, character, its lightness, freedom from splinters, and durability whether in air or water, is mainly the product of *Salix alba*, though partly *S. Russelliana*, whilst, according to Mather, *S. fragilis*, the redwood willow, or stag's-head osier, produces the best timber, and is used in Scotland in ship-building, and in France the wood of *S. Caprea*, our goat-willow, is preferred. Poplar wood, again, is but little used in this country, though in France and Germany both *Populus canescens* and *P. fastigiata* are used for packing-cases, and *P. tremula* for flooring, as is *P. monilifera*, the most rapid-growing species, in Switzerland and North Italy. We, however, import from New York increasing quantities of a wood sometimes known in Liverpool as American, or yellow poplar, and at other times as American whitewood, or canary whitewood. This is no poplar, but the tulip-tree (*Liriodendron tulipifera*), a member of the magnolia family. Grown only for ornament in Europe, in America this tree is largely used for rafters, wainscots, roof-shingles, boxes, furniture, and turnery. The nature of the soil is said to have so marked an influence on the wood that in West Virginia three varieties are distinguished as "white," "blue," and "yellow poplar." The yellow alone is commonly shipped to this country, coming from moister, low-lying ground. It comes in waney logs or large planks, commanding a price equal to Quebec yellow pine (*Pinus Strobus*), and is now valued, for staining or polishing, by cabinet-makers, shop-fitters, and coach-builders. Its name, "whitewood" might cause confusion with the spruce (*Picea excelsa*), the "whitewood" or "white deal of the Baltic trade; but the confusion among the coniferous woods themselves is quite sufficient without any new element of discord. Dr. F. B. Hough[*] and Mr. W. Stevenson[†] both speak of the varieties of *Liriodendron* as unrecognisable by outer characters and as purely due to soil, but F. A. Michaux[‡] terms the more valuable "yellow wood" *L. tulipifera*, var. *obtusiloba*, indicating that there is a difference at least in the foliage as well as in the wood. The name "tulip-wood," used by Mr. Stevenson, is unfortunate, being commonly applied to the handsome Brazilian wood of the Lythraceous *Physocalymma floribunda*, though a Meliaceous wood of New South Wales, that of *Owenia venosa*, and *Harpullia pendula*, in the same colony, have received the same name. Carpenters call all white deal "spruce," red and yellow deals from the Baltic "fir," and similar woods from America "pine," though both the last, at least, are products of species of Pinus. Take as a sample of confusion the trade name "yellow pine." In New Zealand, *Dacrydium Colensoi* yields a useful timber, so called. In British Columbia *Pinus ponderosa* yields "yellow pine;" in Quebec, *P. mitis*; in Nova Scotia, *P. Strobus* or *P. rubra*; and in the middle and southern United States, *P. australis*, to say nothing of "yellow deal" from *P. sylvestris* in Europe, and some half a dozen different "yellow woods."[*] If we conversely take a single species, the wood of which comes to market under a variety of names, we find an equally confusing ambiguity. *Pinus sylvestris*, familiar to us as the Scots (*anglice* "Scotch") Fir, it is proposed by Mr. Hurst, in his edition of Tredgold, to call "Northern Pine" in consideration of its wide distribution in Northern Europe. Most writers on timber treat the varieties of this timber as if they were due solely to soil and climate. Thus, Mr. Stevenson says of it:—[†]

"On poor soil, at great elevations, it becomes a diminutive shrub; and in low situations, where it is a lofty timber tree, the wood on poor sandy soil is light, almost without resin, and of little duration; while on soils of a colder and more substantial nature it is red, heavy, and of great durability. It appears, also, that the same soil will produce both white-wood and red-wooded trees; but, generally speaking, the former is found on the plains and the latter on the hills. . . . . The quality of the timber . . . . is dependent on the soil and climate. That grown in the south is thick-barked, carrying a great amount of sapwood, whilst that grown in the north is the reverse. Again, that grown in the south is hard and resinous, with live or red knots when converted, whilst that grown in the north is soft and non-resinous, with a large number of black or dead knots. . . . Such was the ignorance, in even high quarters, on this subject one hundred years ago, that the French Minister of Marine, in 1785, seeing the fine fir masts imported from Riga, sent out a M. Barbé, a master mast-maker of Brest, to obtain seeds of the trees, which, upon being planted, produced, to the surprise of the French authorities, the common Scotch fir.

In addition to this geographical difference in the quality of the wood there is a local one, arising out of the nature of the soil. . . . . Wood grown upon dry, elevated land, will be harder and more resinous than that grown on low, wet, or swampy soil. . . . ."

In trade it is recognised that red deal is superior to yellow, the best timber having its annual rings not more than $\frac{1}{10}$ in. across, and the autumn wood of a bright red, whilst inferior varieties are honey-yellow and over-resinous. Though only known in commerce by the names of their ports of shipment, there are undoubtedly distinct and important botanical varieties of this species. Without going as far as the Baron de Morogues of Orleans, who recognised no less than fourteen distinct varieties among the pines of Savoy alone,[‡] after the long and careful study of thirty different forms by the late M. de Vilmorin, at Les Barres, between 1821 and 1862, we can hardly deny the importance of the five main types which he made out.[§] These are grouped in two divisions:—(1) with ascending branches, var. *rubra*; (2) with horizontal branches, var. *vulgaris*. Division 1 includes three sections:—(A) with close, pyramidal branching, as in some of the Riga pines; (B) with scattered branches and a symmetrical top, as in other Riga pines; and (C), with scattered branches, often very large and unsymmetrically developed, as in the Hagenau or German pine. Division 2 includes two sections: (D) with the branches in layers, tapering irregularly, as in the Geneva pine; and (E), thick and compact, as in the Briançon pine, that of the Higher Alps. Of these sections M. Vilmorin prefers the first (A), to which belong the pines of Smolensk, Vitebsk, Tchernigov, and Volhynia. Our Scots pine, which is inferior, is intermediate between sections B and C.

In English oak and elm, and in the false acacia or locust (*Robinia*), the question of slight botanical variation is also one of importance. It is commonly said that, of our two commoner varieties of oak, *Quercus pedunculata* yields the better timber. This opinion is probably based upon the fact that this variety generally presents a longer unbranched bole, thus yielding more straight timber of fair dimensions. Laslett, for example, whilst stating that the timber of *Q. sessiliflora*, sometimes called the Bay oak, is a little less dense and compact than that of *Q. pedunculata*, owns that, apart from dimensions, the two timbers so much resemble each other that "few surveyors are able to speak" positively as to the identity of either."[‖]

In concluding his paper, the lecturer said a few words as to the exhibition of timber, and illustrative specimens for educational purposes. Assuming that it is desirable that students, whether intending to be land agents or surveyors, should learn to recognise familiarly the woods commonly grown and employed, and to judge of their condition as to soundness and durability, he could only say that, at present, though we examined in that subject, there were but scanty facilities for the student to acquire such knowledge. The small timber museum at Kew was mainly of Colonial woods, and could hardly be called systematic; other specimens were lost sight of in the great general collection of economic products; nor did the collections of the Natural History Museum in Cromwell-road adequately fulfil this purpose. The requisite specimens need not occupy much space, as the number of species and varieties important to surveyors was not large.

* "Elements of Forestry," p. 251.
† "The Trees of Commerce" (1889), p. 101.
‡ "The North America Sylva" (Philadelphia, 1865).

* Including the Coniferæ *Podocarpus latifolius* and *P. elongatus* of South Africa, besides several dicotyledonous angiosperms, some of which are used as yellow dyes.
† *Op. cit.*, pp. 155 and 159-163.
‡ "Forestry and Forest Products," Edinburgh, 1885, p. 200.
§ "Pine Plantations on the Sand-wastes of France." By Dr. J. Croumbie Brown, pp. 103 *et seq.*
‖ "Timber and Timber-trees," p. 44.

Illustrations.

DESIGN FOR BURY MUNICIPAL BUILDINGS.

THIS fine drawing of part of a competition design submitted by Mr. F. H. Tulloch for the Bury Municipal Buildings hangs in the Architectural Room at the Royal Academy, and is referred to in our notes on "Architecture at the Royal Academy" on another page.

SCHOOL CHAPEL, TONBRIDGE.

THE plan of this chapel is arranged on the same lines as our old Collegiate institution, viz., choir-wise, with a central passage about 13 ft. between the stalls. The dimensions of the building between the internal face of the walls are 155 ft. long by 36 ft. wide. Accommodation is provided for about 450 boys, twenty masters, and stalls at the west end for twelve other or head masters. On the south side of the nave a Founder's Chapel forms an important feature in the design; there are four openings or arcades into the nave. This chapel is arranged for early services, and for the use of the families and servants of the masters, and for visitors the accommodation given is for about eighty-four. By this arrangement the boys and masters are completely separated from the other portion of the congregation; at the west end of this aisle is a large vestry for the choir and clergy. The main entrance is by a cloister of four bays running the entire length of the south side of the head master's house; the ceiling is groined by fan vaulting, and the walls are arcaded. At the west end is a staircase giving access to the organ-chamber, which occupies the upper part of the cloister, with three openings into the chapel. There is at the west end of the nave a large entrance for the boys connected with their playground.

The style of architecture adopted is that which prevailed in the latter part of the fifteenth century. The nave is vaulted in stone (and forms an important feature in the design), with a timber and lead roof over. The two turrets at the east end are staircases to give access to the roofs. These are to be covered with copper. The materials of the walls, both inside and outside, are to be the brown Ancaster stone ashlar. The estimated cost, with fittings, is about 17,000*l*.

The architects are Messrs. James Brooks & Son, and the drawing is hung in this year's Royal Academy Exhibition.

NEW REREDOS, ST. BOTOLPH'S CHURCH BOSTON, LINCOLNSHIRE.

THIS reredos, or eastern screen, was unveiled and dedicated by the Bishop of Lincoln in November, St. Andrew's day, last year. It bears the following inscription:—"In honour of Our Blessed Lord, and in memory of her brother, Walter Scrivener, this reredos was erected by Maud Scrivener, MDCCCXCI." The work is carried out as shown in our illustration, excepting that the upper niches are at present vacant.

The centre panel contains the scene of the "Last Supper"; those at the sides, "Moses Lifting up the Serpent," "Abraham Offering Isaac," "Jonah and the Fish," and "Elijah's Ascension." The seated figures are SS. Gregory, Augustine, Jerome, and Ambrose. The single figures shown on the drawing are Our Lord, St. Peter, St. Paul, and the Evangelists; and in the wings, Joshua, Samuel, David, and Isaiah.

St. Botolph, abbot and confessor, the patron

Royal Academy Exhibition, 1892.

DESIGN FOR CHIMNEY PIECE, ST MARGARET'S, EAST GRINSTEAD.—Mr. A. E. Street, F.R.I.B.A., Architect.

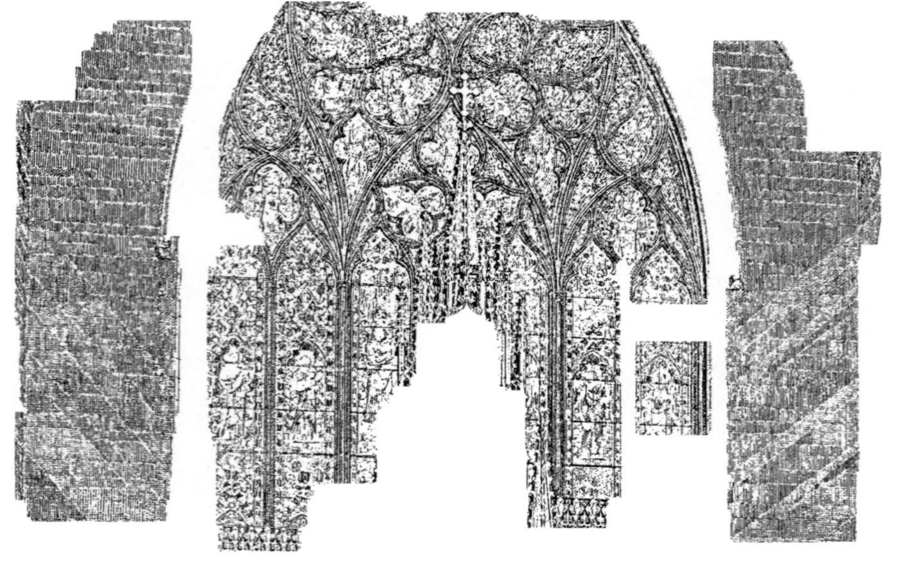

NEW REREDOS: ST. BOTOLPH, BOSTON, LINCOLNSHIRE.—Mr. W. Samuel Weatherley, Architect.

saint and founder of the church and monastery, is placed in the topmost niche. "His remains were buried here until translated to Ely and Westminster." The thirty-six small niches it has been proposed to fill with saints, either local or associated with Lincolnshire dedications.

The work has been executed by Mr. Elwell, of Beverley, from the design of Mr. W. Samuel Weatherley, architect, of London. This completes the oak-work east of the stalls, which has been in progress some time under the same architect's superintendence.

DESIGN FOR MEMORIAL TO MARY TUDOR.

THE Society for the Protection of the Memorials of the Dead contemplate the erection of memorial tombs to Mary Tudor and Cardinal Beaufort in the Church of St. Mary, Bury St. Edmunds. The design for the first-named, here illustrated, is to be carried out in polished Hoptonwood stone with bronze cross and canopy.

The design is by Mr. Arthur E. Street, and the drawing from which the illustration is taken is hung in the Royal Academy Exhibition.

CHIMNEY-PIECE, EAST GRINSTEAD.

THIS chimney-piece, designed by Mr. Arthur E. Street, will stand in the Assembly-room which is shortly to be built in connexion with the new buildings of St. Agnes School, East Grinstead. The materials will be polished Hoptonwood for the lower and local sandstone for the upper part.

MUNICIPAL ENGINEERS AT NOTTINGHAM.

WE now resume and conclude our report of the Midland Counties District meeting of the Incorporated Association of Municipal and County Engineers, held at Nottingham on April 29 and 30.*

After the reading of the paper by Mr. Arthur Brown (the greater part of which we gave in our last), the members adjourned to inspect the subways therein described, and were much impressed by the excellence of the work. One of the subways was converted for the nonce into an elongated banqueting chamber, and here the visitors were entertained at luncheon by Mr. Brown (the Borough Engineer) and Mr. John Parker (Surveyor to the Basford Rural Sanitary Authority). The guests included Alderman Sir John Turney, Alderman Blackburn, Councillor G. Clarke, and Mr. F. Messom, the contractor. Illuminated by electric light, and decorated with flowers, this subterranean luncheon-chamber presented an appearance which was likened by some of the visitors to "a glimpse of fairydom." On ascending to the surface, the party witnessed a test by hydraulic power of a short length of stoneware drain-pipes fitted with Hassall's patent safety joint. The pressure was gradually applied by a pump until 00 lbs. to the square inch was registered. At this pressure the pipe cracked, but the joint remained intact. The result was regarded as exceedingly satisfactory, for of course no such internal pressure in a drain-pipe would occur in practice. We gave a description of Hassall's patent joint, which appears to be an exceedingly efficient and reliable one, in the *Builder* for September 26, 1885, p. 417.

The members then returned to the Exchange Hall, where Mr. William Spinks, Assoc.-Mem. Inst. C.E., and Lecturer on Sanitary Engineering at the Yorkshire College, Leeds, read a paper on "Public Health Acts Amendment: Some Suggestions in Relation to Private Improvements." He said that since the Association discussed the question of Private Improvements in 1886, he had had a great deal of correspondence, not only with surveyors and Clerks to urban authorities, but also with property owners and agents, and many of the cases they had brought under his notice had occurred to him as being worth recording. During the past five years the Association had had a considerable influx of new members, and it would be well to ascertain the experiences and opinions of the new blood before any attempt was made to recast the sections of the Public Health Act which dealt with Private Improvements. As the Council had invited the co-operation of members in the work they had in hand, the author had revised the remarks he made in 1886 upon "Suggested Remedies for the defects of the 150th Section, Public Health Act, 1875," and extended them in the directions dictated by the experience he had recently acquired. Most surveyors in their practice, in carrying out the section, had met with cases that were not apparently provided for, and which, being recurrent, it would seem to be desirable for legislation to be enacted, so as to embrace the most important points. Of course it would be impossible to frame an Act of Parliament to meet all exceptional and unusual cases, and one that would justly satisfy the various interests and parties involved. In the author's opinion reform was required in the direction hereafter pointed out. The interpretation of the term "street" should be made still more clear, and should include any road dedicated to the use of the public, whether built upon or not, even if it was not in the ordinary and popular sense a street. A road might be an important thoroughfare, largely used, and in a deplorable condition so far as the surface was concerned,—might be confined within walls or other fences, and fronted by agricultural land. There should be no doubt as to the powers for dealing with cases of this character. As to boundaries, in some instances roads had boundaries running down the centre, crossing them diagonally, or along the building line; possibly the adjoining authority might be a rural one. The present method of dealing with these cases was by mutual agreement. For the purposes of private improvements a street of this character should be placed under the exclusive management of one of the authorities, who should be able to deal with it precisely as if it was wholly within the district of that authority, and they should have the same rights against the frontagers for the recovery of expenses as if the whole street and premises fronting, adjoining, or abutting, were entirely within the district. These conditions obtained within the area governed by the Metropolis Management Acts, and appeared to be a sensible provision, and the most satisfactory that could be made. As to notices, Mr. Spinks said he thought it would be generally admitted, and the cases that had been before the courts proved that the present method of service was altogether unsatisfactory and unreliable, however great pains might have been taken to be precise. The Manchester method of publication was by posting in the street and advertising in the newspapers, the posting being witnessed a given number of times, and a copy of the bill and advertisement being endorsed and filed for proof of publication if contested. This was considered sufficient notice to the owner, and the system might, with advantage, be made universal. There should be no option in the notice as to who should do the work. The system of allowing the owner to do it was bad, besides being impracticable. It was impossible to complete half a street. How could a man lay half a sewer, and what sort of a surface would there be if each half was laid at different times? The specification on the notice should be comprehensive and exact, and state the whole of the intended works required by the authority to be carried out, and they alone should carry out the work accordingly, and be responsible for its due and proper fulfilment. As to the character of the works required to be done, at the present time it was customary for an authority to adopt a hard and fast line throughout its district for the method of completing private streets, without any regard to the character of the property abutting on to different streets, or to the necessities of such streets. Such a system was manifestly unfair and absurd. Mr. Spinks cited an illustration of how this system worked in a suburb of Manchester, and exhibited a diagram showing (*a*) wide streets leading from one populous district to another: these were much traversed, and partially fronted by shops; (*b*) short cross streets, fronted by small houses, having no vehicular traffic but costermongers' carts, doctors' carriages, &c.; (*c*) *culs-de-sac*, fronted also by small houses; and (*d*) roads and avenues, fronted by detached and semi-detached villa residences. The whole of these roads were apparently, be said, completed exactly alike, the surfaces flagged and paved, whereas the surface of the main road was macadamised. The common-sense view to take of cases like these, was, that each street should have been dealt with according to its necessities. The streets (*a*) being main arteries of traffic, and means of communication between one populous locality and another, and being fronted by important property, required strong foundations and durable surfaces, and the materials and workmanship should be of the best throughout. Streets (*b*) being streets which ran crosswise between main thoroughfares, and only having light traffic, or being fronted by cottage property, required lighter foundations and less excellent surfaces, but these, on sanitary grounds, should be impervious. Streets (*c*), courts, alleys, *culs-de-sac*, passages, &c., should be formed with impervious surfaces, such as flags or asphalte. Streets (*d*) were roads amongst better-class residential property, such as suburban roads and avenues in parks, &c. Having regard to the quality of the property, and the convenience and comfort of the inhabitants residing on this class of road, it might be desirable to complete these surfaces with macadam, asphalte, or gravel. Mr. Spinks said he was aware that the foregoing suggestions were surprisingly radical, and a complete reversal of present methods, and that some might see difficulties in administering such powers. His proposal was that each authority should declare that they would divide all incompleted or intended private streets into four such classes, and then to fix the standard of materials and finish required in each class. Of course there would be many objections to a body of citizens fixing for their fellow citizens such standards, inasmuch as committees were so subject to outside influences and pressure, as well as being guilty of sympathy with suffering property owners, and oftentimes the "outs" became the "ins," followed by a ruthless reversal of policy. To obviate all that, an impartial tribunal was suggested, such as an Inspector of the Local Government Board, who, after the declaration by the authority, should hold a public inquiry, and after viewing the character of the streets of the district, should take evidence as to the most suitable materials the locality afforded, and then fix the respective standard for each class of street, which should afterwards be adopted throughout the district. If after publication of notice to do the work the owner objected and considered the works excessive, an appeal to the magistrates, assisted by a professional assessor, would decide under which class the particular street in question would come. The great object should be for an authority to arrive at a satisfactory understanding with the owners before the works were commenced, and thus prevent disputes arising after completion which ought to have been cleared up at the outset. At the present time the owner was rather arbitrarily dealt with, having no remedy until Section 257 came into operation, and some such suggestions as the foregoing, if carried into effect, would afford him all the protection which was rightly his due, and by proceeding in the manner described there would be no difficulty in doing that equitably between the parties, as both the proposed courts would be open and impartial, and their decisions would only be arrived at after hearing and weighing the evidence of both parties. If it were left to the owner to have the right of appealing against the proposed works on the grounds of their being unreasonable, then appeals would be incessant, because there were so many owners who considered the interest of their own pockets as paramount, and not the comfort and health of the inhabitants occupying their houses; and to that class of men a cartload of gravel or ashes spread on a street made it a reasonable surface, and any expenditure beyond that he looked upon as downright extravagance. It should be remembered that, in large towns especially, the street was after all the playground of the children, amongst whom, unfortunately, in our manufacturing districts the death rate was so abnormally high. A child with its nostrils so close to the surface breathed and inhaled mephitic odours arising therefrom, which at the height of an adult person became dissipated in the air; so that on sanitary grounds it was imperative that the surfaces of this class of streets should not be precipitating tanks nor filter beds, but should be clean, dry, and impervious. It might be urged that to classify the quality of the surfaces of streets would inflict undue hardships on property, and would be inequitable in its

* See last week's *Builder*, pp. 355-356.

incidence; but on the other hand it should not be forgotten that when a man took land for building purposes on a main thoroughfare he generally did so with an eye on the "main chances," knowing very well that the traffic and the business it brought all tended to enhance the value of the property when erected; consequently it was better able to bear the increased burden of superior roadmaking. After dealing with the questions of estimate and preliminary apportionment, partial works, and the method of executing works, Mr. Spinks proceeded to speak of the sewers. He said it would be much simpler and more satisfactory if the cost of all sewers were charged direct to the district rates. The clean water that came into the town did so in pipes, the cost of which was charged to a common fund, but immediately the water was fouled and became sewage, the owner of the property had to provide means of carrying it away so far as was coextensive with his premises. The reasons for that anomaly had never been made clear. If the authority alone was responsible for the construction of sewers, surveyors would not feel hampered in designing them for private streets, nor would the question as to how far the sizes were reasonable ever be raised. If it should be found impossible to revise the existing system, powers should be given to an authority to contribute, if necessary, towards the cost of sewers in certain cases; for example, if for the purposes of a sewerage scheme it was desirable to construct an intercepting or trunk sewer in a private street, then the excess cost of such a sewer over one sufficient for the requirements of the street itself should be borne by the authority. The author had had a case of that sort in a road running along the boundary of one portion of his district, and that course was followed. It should also be made plain to the surveyor that he must only design sewers sufficient for the necessities of the street he was dealing with. The author knew several cases where sewers had been made as large as 3 ft. by 2 ft., when by no possibility could more sewage enter than would be discharged by a 9-in. pipe, and the defence for that had been that it was customary in the district to build sewers large enough for a man to traverse. Such reasoning was ridiculous, and the costs incurred through such ignorance should be thrown upon the right shoulders. The size of the sewer did not, so long as it was adequate for the duty it had to perform, in any way enhance the value of the property, and to expend money in sewers excessive in size and beyond actual requirements was wasteful, and an imposition upon property owners. After speaking of the method of dealing with old sewers, Mr. Spinks concluded by some remarks on levels, repairs, measurement of frontages, paving apportionments, and other subjects, for which we have not space.

In the afternoon the members visited the very successful sewage farm, 1,000 acres in extent, belonging to Nottingham, and situate at Stoke Bardolph. We are obliged to reserve a description of this farm for a future number.

In the evening the members dined together at the "George" Hotel, and some good speeches bearing on professional topics were made, Mr. Hodson in particular referring in terms of condemnation to the growing practice of public bodies declining to grant superannuation allowances to old officials even after many years of meritorious service at very inadequate salaries.

On the second day of the meeting (Saturday, April 30) the members assembled at nine o'clock in the Shire Hall (Mr. De Courcy Meade, President, in the chair) for the purpose of discussing the two papers read on the previous day. General approval was expressed at the character of the municipal engineering works at Nottingham, as described by Mr. Brown, and especially of the new subways, and it was agreed that the Corporation took a very enlightened and liberal view as to such matters. Mr. Spinks's paper was strongly criticised, and his proposals, both as to road formation and sewer construction, were condemned as impracticable. Admitting that there were difficulties to be encountered, it was the general opinion that things were much better as they are than they would be if Mr. Spinks's proposals became law.

Lord Belper, Chairman of the Nottingham County Council, having taken the chair, Mr. James Robinson, County Surveyor of Hampshire, read a paper on "County Management of Main Roads." This chiefly dealt with matters of administration and finance. The writer was of opinion that inasmuch as the county authority had to provide the funds for the maintenance of the roads, they should have the first voice in the expenditure of those funds, and that could only be secured by the repeal of sub-section 2 of section 11. The roads could then be maintained either direct by the county authority (sub-section 1), or by agreement under sub-section 4. In the former event, power, if thought fit, could be given to the urban authority to appeal to the Local Government Board if they considered the roads were not being kept in a satisfactory condition.

In the course of a long and interesting discussion, in which Lord Belper, Mr. Hooley (County Surveyor of Nottingham), Mr. Davis (County Surveyor of Shropshire), and several other speakers took part, it seemed to be pretty generally agreed that many of the difficulties and disputes which now arise between county authorities and local authorities could be prevented by a friendly interchange of views between the respective surveyors, coupled with a desire on the part of the authorities to be reasonable in their requirements. Votes of thanks to the readers of the papers were heartily agreed to.

The proceedings of a very successful meeting were concluded in the afternoon by an excursion. Taking train to Mansfield, the visitors had a pleasant drive of ten or twelve miles to Welbeck Abbey, the seat of the Duke of Portland, by whose permission the conservatories and gardens, the picture gallery, the riding school, the stables, and certain of the subterranean passages and roadways for which the place is famous, were shown to the visitors. We may mention that a long description of these remarkable works was published in the *Builder* for September 22, 1888, under the title of "Welbeck Abbey and its Tunnels."

THE LONDON COUNTY COUNCIL.

The usual weekly meeting of this Council was held on Tuesday last, the Chairman, Lord Rosebery, presiding.

Tenders were opened for certain building works at the Cane Hill Asylum. We publish the particulars elsewhere. There were only three tenders sent in.

The Chairmanship.—Lord Rosebery reminded the Council that his occupancy of the chair was only of a temporary character, pending the framing of a scheme of organisation, and also with a view of enabling the Council to get into its work. Both of these objects had now been attained. As regarded the scheme of organisation, that had been agreed to by the Committee on the previous day, with a minority of only two against it. And, as regarded the Council getting into its work, it was clear from what occurred last week, when they got rid of all the reports in an hour and five minutes, that it did not need any further assistance in the conduct of its business. He hoped that now that things were so far settled the Council would consider as soon as possible the question of appointing his successor.

Electric and Cable Railway Schemes.—The Parliamentary Committee submitted a long report in reference to the electric and cable schemes which are now under the consideration of a Joint Committee of Lords and Commons. They recommended that certain propositions should be submitted to the Joint Committee indicating the attitude of the Council. These propositions were:—

"1. That the size of the tunnels of the lines should be sufficient to allow in the future of an interchange of traffic with existing railway lines.

2. That underground lines should not follow the line of existing streets, but should go from point to point, the depth below the surface being such as to avoid injury or inconvenience to buildings in the line of the railways.

3. That the companies should only be allowed to acquire the right of forming the tunnels, without acquiring any absolute freehold in the soil, paying compensation for actual damage only."

The Committee held that the formation of more than one line between the north and south of London should not be encouraged, and they recommended the insertion of a clause giving the Council compulsory powers of purchase of the undertakings, sixty years,—in place of twenty-one years, as in the case of the tramways,—being allowed, to enable those who find the capital in the first instance time to obtain remuneration for their outlay.

Mr. Saunders moved as an amendment:—

"That the suggestion that only one such line should be constructed between north and south London be omitted, and that evidence be placed before the Joint Committee showing the importance of continuing into the country electric and cable lines which may pass under London, in order to relieve the congestion of population and encourage building in the suburbs, and that, subject to the above, the course recommended by the Committee be approved."

The amendment was seconded by Mr. Beachcroft, and after some discussion was agreed to, and the report of the Committee as amended was adopted.

Brooke's Market, Holborn. — The Public Health and Housing Committee reported as follows as to this insanitary area:—

"The Council on October 13 last, in the resolution which committed it to the preparation of a scheme for the improvement of the area in Brooke's-market, expressed the opinion that the Holborn District Board should contribute at least one-half of the total net cost of the improvement, and the District Board were duly informed thereof. A communication has now been received from the Board to the effect that they are willing to contribute one-half of the cost of the scheme provided such half does not exceed 3,000*l.*, and that the Council undertake to advance that amount to the Board on loan, the repayment being spread over a period of thirty years. The estimated net cost of the scheme is 5,950*l.* We are advised by the solicitor that the District Board cannot contribute towards the cost of the scheme without an order of the Home Secretary, and that it will be therefore necessary to apply to the Home Secretary for an order directing the amount to be contributed by the Board. We consider that the offer of the Board is a reasonable one, and, apart from the question of a loan to the Board of the amount contributed, which will doubtless come before the Finance Committee in the usual way, we recommend—

'1. That the Council do, subject to an order from the Home Secretary, accept the offer of the Holborn District Board to contribute one-half of the net cost of the London (Brooke's-market, Holborn) Improvement Scheme, 1891, such half not to exceed 3,000*l.* in all.

2. That the solicitor be instructed to apply to the Home Secretary for an order directing the amount of the contribution by the District Board in accordance with section 46 (6) of the Housing of the Working Classes Act, 1890, having regard to the offer above mentioned.'"

The recommendations were agreed to.

Structural Alterations in Theatres and Music-halls.—The Theatres and Music-halls Committee reported as follows:—

"Under section 11 of the Metropolis Management and Building Acts Amendment Act, 1878, the late Board was empowered in some cases to require proprietors of theatres and certain music-halls in use at the time of the passing of the Act to remedy structural defects. Such power has since been transferred to the Council. When alterations were found necessary at any premises, it was the custom of the late Board, and the practice has been continued by the Council, before serving the sealed notice authorised by this section of the Act, to order a draft notice to be forwarded to the owner of the premises, containing a list of the alterations considered necessary, accompanied by a letter informing him that the Committee to whom the matter was referred would be willing to consider any objections to such notice, which he might transmit by a certain date, and that in the event of his forwarding such objections the Committee would be prepared to hear him thereon.

We have now to report that complaints have been made from time to time by persons connected with places of public entertainment coming within the scope of this section, that, in the event of alterations being considered necessary at their premises, the first intimation they usually receive (under the above system) of such alterations being required was through the medium of the public press, which they considered extremely unsatisfactory. We have therefore taken the matter under consideration, and we recommend—

'That in future, in lieu of the service of a draft notice, the Clerk do forward a statement of the suggested alterations required at any premises to the owner of those premises, and do request him to send his observations thereon, and that the matter be not reported to the Council until the service of the sealed notice is recommended by the Committee.'"

The recommendation was agreed to.

Quantity Surveyors and their Remuneration.—On the motion for the reception of the Asylums Committee's report, Mr. Rober[illegible] asked whether the quantities for the additional buildings at the Claybury Asylum had been taken out by one of the quantity surveyors appointed by the Council, and, if not, whether the quantity surveyor employed was to be paid at the rate which the Council's surveyors were paid.

Mr. M'Dougall, in the absence of the Chairman of the Committee, replied that the Claybury Asylum was commenced before the co[illegible]

tion of the London County Council, and for the additional buildings it had been thought desirable to employ the same architect and the same quantity surveyor as were originally employed. He could not say what was the remuneration of the quantity surveyor.

The "Fair Wages and Hours" Clause in Contracts.—The notices of motion standing on the agenda in reference to this question were not reached until nearly seven o'clock, and their discussion was again adjourned until next week.

LIVERPOOL ENGINEERING SOCIETY.

THE annual general meeting of this Society was held on the 4th inst., at the Royal Institution, Mr. John T. Wood, President, in the hair. The meeting was numerously attended.

The election of the Council and officers for the ensuing session, commencing in October next, was the first business. Mr. Robert E. Johnston, M.Inst.C.E., was elected President, and Messrs. H. P. Boulnois, M.Inst.C.E., and Prof. H. S. Hele Shaw, M.Inst.C.E., were elected Vice-Presidents.

The adjourned discussion upon the paper ead at the last meeting by the City Engileer of Liverpool, Mr. H. P. Boulnois, M.Inst.C.E., entitled "Refuse Destructors," was hen opened by Mr. John Price, who stated that he had seen most of the refuse destructors n the country at work, and was very much in avour of their use. He agreed with Mr. Boulnois in considering that refuse destructors vere in almost all cases the best and only neans of getting rid of house refuse successully.

Mr. George Farren stated that he had xamined the Liverpool Corporation's destructor, nd was very much impressed with it.

Mr. Maginnis criticised very freely the present nethod of dealing with ashpit refuse, which, e stated, is in most places very much behind he times.—Mr. E. R. Window dealt principally rith an improved method for the collection of shpit refuse.

Dr. Tatham, of Manchester, dealt with the ubject as to how far destructors gave rise to a uisance to the surrounding district.

Various other speakers followed, and Mr. oulnois replied to the various points raised in he discussion.

A vote of thanks was accorded by acclaman to Mr. Boulnois for his valuable paper.

ARCHITECTURAL SOCIETIES.

EDINBURGH ARCHITECTURAL ASSOCIATION. On the 7th inst. the members of this Associan, under the leadership of Mr. Thomas Ross, hitect, visited the old castles of Pitteadie d Seafield, both situated in the parish of nghorn. Pitteadie, says the *Scotsman*, is a n in a state of tolerable preservation, hough totally neglected. The castle is proached through a quaint round-arched teway containing the carved arms and tials of William Calderwood, of Pitteadie, th the date 1686. The castle itself is conerably older than the gateway or than the e of William Calderwood, and existed in 09. The castle appears to have been someat modernised about the time that Calderod built the gateway. Previously the rance-door appears to have been on the first or level, which was reached probably by a der from the outside, but this arrangement s changed, and a door was constructed on ground floor and other improvements ected. The members walked from Pitteadie Seafield Castle, a lofty ruined tower standing the sea-shore between Kirkcaldy and Kingn, passing on the way through the farmading of Grange, once the residence of kcaldy of Grange. Of the house of Grange hing appears to be left, and the only morial remaining to show that the place was residence of some one of at least the rank a laird is the dovecot. Seafield stands on bare sea-shore; the tower, exposed to blasts which sweep the Forth, is not so l preserved as its neighbour at Pitteadie; it still remains in a sufficient state to give a d idea of the kind of accommodation to be nd in such structures, where defence was of re consequence than comfort. Seafield was lt by a family of the name of Moultray. The e of its building is not known, nor when y acquired the lands; but they were there in 3, and must have been in possession before t time.

GLASGOW ARCHITECTURAL ASSOCIATION.—The usual weekly meeting of this Association was held in the rooms, 114, West Campbell-street, Glasgow, on the 3rd inst., the President, Mr. Alexander M'Gibbon, in the chair. A paper was read by Mr. Arthur J. Fryers on "Half-timber Work," illustrated by photographs and plates of old work. Mr. Fryers reviewed the subject briefly from an historical standpoint, and passed on to describe more fully the cottages of Surrey. He then went over the various points to be noticed in the detail of this class of work, such as the framing and filling-in, the roofs and barge-boards, the doors and windows, and the chimneys with their ingle-nooks. He concluded by considering its adaptability to present-day requirements, and strongly advocated its use in Scotland, it being quite capable of standing the climate, and also as giving a very picturesque effect. Mr. Robert Hamilton opened the discussion which followed, after which a vote of thanks was awarded the essayist.

LIVERPOOL ARCHITECTURAL SOCIETY.—At the closing meeting of the session of the Liverpool Architectural Society, Mr. T. H. Harrison, the President, delivered an address upon "The Sciences as related to Art."

THE SANITARY INSPECTORS' ASSOCIATION.

THE paper read at the meeting of this Association held on the 7th inst. at Carpenters' Hall, London Wall, Mr. Hugh Alexander presiding, was "The Story of a Rain Drop," by Mr. Poulson, Sanitary Inspector, Chelsea. Prefacing his story by quoting the dictum of the reader of a former paper to the effect that "If the knowledge now possessed by sanitary experts could be made to thoroughly permeate the masses of the people, and if the sanitary laws were enforced, the physical, moral, and spiritual condition of the people of this country might undergo a complete transformation," the lecturer, in metaphorical language, showed the important functions performed in Nature's economy by a drop of rain. Chemistry, and particularly the discovery, by synthesis, a century ago, of the composition of water, by Sir H. Cavendish, had taught us that water was not an element, as believed for thousands of years, but a combination of two gases, hydrogen and oxygen, coming together in the proportion of 16 parts of the latter to 2 of the former, in 18 parts. The formation of vapours, born of the sun and the sea, and their behaviour under the influence of currents of air from the Arctic or the Torrid regions; proximity or distance from mountains, trees, or grass; and the different forms of hail, ice, hoar-frost, fog (white in the country, but a rich yellow in the metropolis) were interestingly traced. The practical effect of the power possessed by water of absorbing oxygen and carbon, and of being absorbed in varying proportions by alluvial soil, chalk, and sandstone, produced very beautiful effects in stalactitic caverns, but deleterious effects on human health. In Derbyshire, the enlargement of the thyroid gland of the throat (the disease known as "Derbyshire neck") was an outcome of these varying relations upon each other of the soil and the rain. By its cohesive predilections, its fluidity, and its weight, rain formed the rivers, lakes, streams, and springs which were the sources of our water-supply. Before it reached the consumer river-water required to be filtered, and carried by mains and service-pipes into our houses and our cisterns; and in every varying situation it had to be studied and analysed to find out how it had been affected by or had affected the channels through which it had passed. Dr. Moncton Copeman had discovered that pure Spanish lead, from which all the silver originally alloyed with it had been eliminated, when employed for pipes, readily combined with the chemical elements of the water, and greatly prejudiced health in certain districts by lead poisoning. The course of the rain-drop was traced until it reached the tanks and reservoirs of one of the London water companies at West Molesley. The various processes and the apparatus of filtration were described, beds of sand, shells, and gravel, in all 8 ft. thick, being insufficient, in many cases, to remove the lime taken up from the rocks, as proved by the furry incrustations we found in the interior of our kettles. The enormous importance of the knowledge of such facts would be gathered by considering certain astounding totals with regard to our water-supply which had been given in a recent report by General Scott, one of the examiners. London took from the Thames daily, 89,272,600 gallons; from the Lea 55,766,185; from springs and wells, 26,088,624; and a small supply (752 gallons) from Highgate pond, making a daily total of 171,727,721 gallons for 5,692,879 persons, or 30·06 gallons per head. The length of main-pipes required for this colossal distribution is 4,678¾ miles, more than half through the world. The engines required for pumping this water numbered 184 with a total force of 21,659 horse-power. For drinking purposes alone, 104 filtering-beds, with an area of 1,021½ acres of storage, are required for 215,792,000 gallons of filtered water, the unfiltered stock in store amounting to 1,300 millions of gallons more. The sources of supply and the characteristic qualities of water in different districts were described, and a curious fact was noted, to which the observations of the official examiners, Drs. Crookes Odling, and the late C. Meymott Tidy testified that in December, 1890, Thames water was found to have a peculiar faint taste, due to fog.

A brief discussion arose on the proposal of a vote of thanks to Mr. Poulson, which was accorded by acclamation.

The meeting subsequently considered a circular which had been sent round to members, notifying the arrangements proposed for the visit to Paris by the Association at Whitsuntide. It is proposed to leave London at 9 a.m. on Thursday, June 2, by the Newhaven and Dieppe route, but some of the members desired to spend the 2nd prox. in London, and to cross the Channel by the night service. An influential committee of the Society of Hygiène of France has been formed, which includes MM. Cacheux, Fèret, and Jottrain, of the Paris Municipal Council, and Drs. E. Monin, J. de Pietra Santa, and other gentlemen; and the Committee of the Sanitary Inspectors Association co-operating will include Mr. H. Alexander (Chairman of Council), and Messrs. Raymond, Tidman, Edwards, and Watson. In addition to the conferences, the programme includes a banquet given to the Englishmen by the French society, and visits to the sewers of Paris, the irrigation fields at Gennevilliers, workmen's dwellings at Passy, night lodging-houses, the Aultre disinfecting station, Montsouris reservoirs, crematorium of Père la Chaise, cellular prison of La Santé, the Catacombs, and the Eiffel Tower.

THE ARCHITECTURAL ASSOCIATION *SOIRÉE*.

THAT always well-attended annual gathering, the Members' *Soirée* of the Architectural Association, was held in the Westminster Town-hall on Friday, the 6th inst., when, under the auspices of the A. A. Lyric Club, there was produced what was described on one page of the programme as a "burlesque," and, on the succeeding page, as "Ye ryght pleasaunt Tragedie," entitled "The Princess' Idea," written by Mr. Theo. Moore ("after Tennyson and Gilbert"). The *dramatis personæ* were:—*Prince Hilarion*, Mr. A. Brumwell Thomas; *Florian*, Mr. Ernest Rhütz; *Cyril*, Mr. T. Honnor; *Melissa*, Mr. J. P. Sutton; *Hildebrand*, Mr. A. C. Bulmer Booth; *Gama*, Mr. J. Douglas Scott; *Foreman*, Mr. C. H. Brodie; *Princess Ida*, Mr. H. Seton Morris; *Lady Blanche*, Mr. Theo. Moore; and *Lady Psyche*, Mr. Percy D. Smith. Scene i. of Act I. was supposed to represent the Association's Studio in Great Marlborough-street. Cyril, Florian, and Hilarion (students or assistants) are discussing with some freedom the hardships inflicted upon them by "the principals," and express their determination to

"——— strike for better times all round :
More cash and shorter hours,—more things found."

In the course of further discussion, however, Hilarion and Florian disagree, one taking his stand on "art" and the "art-cult," the other on "good old common-sense." They draw swords, and are engaged in mortal combat when the "principals" (Hildebrand, an architect, and Gama, a surveyor) enter. The fight with swords ceases, but a wordy conflict ensues between the assistants and their masters, and the vulgarity of Gama, the surveyor, leads Florian to refer to him contemptuously as

"A man who dabbles in the sordid mixtures
Of ancient lights and party-walls and fixtures."

The scene ends with the strike of the assistants, and the resolve of Hildebrand and Gama to engage lady assistants. Scene ii. opens before "Castle Adamant" (a Ladies' College of Architecture), presenting in its *façade* a grotesque specimen of "eclecticism" in design, combined with a *reductio ad absurdum* of "sanitary plumbing." Before this *façade*, two of the "sweet girl graduates," Melissa and Psyche, are in the act of tossing-up as to which of the two shall "black-in" a lot of competition sections, when the Principal of the College, Lady Blanche, enters, and sentences them to write "a schedule of dilapidations." After a dance by one of them, there enters the Princess Ida, described on the programme as "a latter-day Jenny Wren," who sings a song, in which she expresses the intention of herself and her fellow lady students of architecture to "have nothing to do with drains, nor anything practical." At this point Hildebrand and Gama arrive, seeking an interview with the Lady Blanche for the purpose of engaging lady assistants. They withdraw for private converse, and Hilarion, Florian, and Melissa enter, Hilarion singing a song to Ida, with whom he is in love, though she disdains his suit, preferring to devote her life to architecture. Florian speaks of himself as "a lover of art" with "a thousand a year," and is denounced by Melissa as one of those who, having "his own pocket lined, drivels in the *Times* about surveying work being *infra dig.*, and wants to stop everybody else from getting a living." (This denunciation, it should be stated, was warmly applauded by the audience.) Scene ii. concludes soon after the announcement that "the ladies are called out and embodied into a great force of architects." Scene i. of Act II. represents "works" in progress under the superintendence of Ida, and in charge of a foreman (Mr. C. H. Brodie), who in the intervals between 12 and 3 on a Saturday afternoon has been drinking "not wisely but too well" pending the arrival of the members of the A.A. on a "Spring Visit." The experiment of lady assistants not proving satisfactory, the male assistants on strike, and their masters, talk matters over, with the result that the strike comes to an end, and Scene ii. opens with a combined attack of principals and assistants on Castle Adamant, resulting, as the "bill of the play" puts it, in the "defeat of the ladies by the men, and the capture of the men by the ladies," and all ends well, after a song in which each of the leading characters sings a verse, the lines falling to Florian proclaiming him to be

"—— An Arty-crafty man,
Break-up-the-A.A. young man,
A sign-a-memorial, high-dictatorial
Certain-I'm-right young man."

Hildebrand, on the other hand, declares that he is

"An iconoclastic, City-bombastic
Pull-down-Wren's-churches old man."

There were many other songs and a few dances, and some striking hits were made concerning some of the professional topics of the hour. All the actors acquitted themselves very well, and at the close, they and the author were called before the curtain. The incidental music was played by the A.A. String Band. Mr. F. T. W. Miller acted as stage manager, and the scenery was painted by Mr. Percy D. Smith.

Correspondence.

To the Editor of THE BUILDER.

ARCHITECTURAL ASSOCIATION.

SIR,—I must ask you to be good enough to let me trespass once more upon your valuable space, which, when I last wrote, I had no intention of doing; but the letters from Mr. Leonard Stokes, and the one from Mr. Jackson, addressed to the latter, in which he explains himself, demand some remarks from me.

Mr. Jackson says, "Nothing was further from my thoughts than to suggest you should make a clean sweep of your whole scheme, and draw up a new one from the very beginning." If in this or in any other respect I have misinterpreted Mr. Jackson's meaning, I offer my apologies. To anyone who cares to study the correspondence which has passed, the opportunity is open, but, in the light of what I have learnt since Mr. Jackson's letter first appeared in A.A. *Notes*, I see nothing (with the above exception) of importance that I care to revise or omit. What I wrote was written with careful consideration, and I contend it has been a fair commentary on the matter before us.

Mr. Jackson's letter was perfectly frank; he stated that he wrote it, and had attended two meetings at the request of some of our members, who took his view. When I asked in your columns who those members were, and on whose authority they acted, a letter appeared, signed by eight gentlemen, members of the A.A., and also of the Institute, stating that they met Mr. Jackson but *once*, and that the letter was not written at their request. As to their authority to enter into negotiations with the memorialists, they candidly admitted they had none, and that they only represented their own particular views. Puzzled at the discrepancy between Mr. Jackson's assertions and the answer of these gentlemen, I again pressed for particulars. Then Mr. Stokes replied, "The two meetings referred to by Mr. Jackson in his letter to A.A. *Notes* had nothing whatever to do with one another."

"The first was held at my office, as already stated. The second was held at Barnard's-inn, when about fifty architects, *all members of the Art Workers' Guild*, were present. It was this meeting that asked Mr. Jackson to inform the A.A. as to what was being done, and not the first." The italics are those of Mr. Stokes.

A natural inference from the foregoing surely is—*then no members of the A.A. were present*: the natural comment, "What business was it of the members of the Art Workers' Guild to interfere in our concerns?" So, to clear up the matter, I wrote and asked Mr. Stokes whether he and any other members of the A.A. were at this last meeting. He tells me that he, Mr. Simpson, and, perhaps, one or more were there. This information should have been given at once; it would only have been fair to Mr. Jackson, and due to the Association to have done so.

That I was not alone in the view I took of Mr. Jackson's letter is apparent, *vide* statement by the Committee, letter from the President-elect, and a letter from one of the eight members who met Mr. Jackson and his friends, and letters of approval from many quarters. Then Professor Kerr,—I believe the senior of all the Past Presidents living, who has always taken a keen interest in the A.A., said at the Institute last Monday; "Indeed, they (the memorialists) are now attacking the Architectural Association, and seem almost likely to split it up,—a result which I am sure everybody here would deprecate." And even Mr. Stokes, writing on behalf of himself and the others, says of Mr. Jackson, "he puts his views into words so very different to those he used to us that, without some satisfactory explanation,—which I hope will be forthcoming,—it would obviously be quite impossible for the Association to accept his offer as it may at first sight appear to be laid down in A.A. *Notes*."

That there could be any objection to any members of the A.A. meeting Mr. Jackson and his friends with a view to seeing how the A.A. might be strengthened and its scheme of studies improved, I, for one, should never have raised. But when we learnt from Mr. Jackson his account of what the outcome of these particular meetings was intended to be, I confess to very great surprise. That Mr. Stokes, who must have known equally with Mr. Jackson what took place, should, after perusing the letter, have suffered it to appear in A.A. *Notes*, without the slightest comment or contradiction whatever, is to me astonishing; thereby, I maintain, he implied an assent. It now becomes the duty of every loyal member of the A.A. to support the Committee, and to see that the candidates standing for election on the House list, receive an unmistakable mandate to maintain its independence, continue the old policy of the A. A., and not receive help from any quarter whatsoever, the conditions of which it would be a dishonour to accept. When it is remembered that the A. A. asked the Institute to help forward their scheme; accepted their aid, also the liberal contributions made by members of the Institute; how, with any consistency, can they at the bidding of the memorialists reverse their policy and at the same time maintain self-respect?

COLE A. ADAMS.

SIR GILBERT SCOTT'S RESTORATIONS.

SIR,—I have already occupied so much of your space that I must apologise for adding another word to the controversy "on Sir Gilbert Scott's Restorations."

Although Mr. Somers Clarke has exhibited the weakness of his cause in taking refuge in epithets and personal opinions, he has done a service in giving the watchword of his party in the word "Repair." A most excellent word, and if every one understood it in the same sense, and applied it in the same manner, there would be no further need of controversy.

The question still remains, What does Mr. Clarke mean by the term "repair"?

I send a drawing of the tower of Chester Cathedral before it was restored, and I should like Mr. Clarke to send you another for publication, showing how he would have repaired it, bearing in mind that the outside casing was rotten, and the inside of the wall liable to fall to pieces without proper support from the outside facing, as in the case of St. John's Church, and also that the whole of the original design and detail of the tower, up to the top of the cornice, could be ascertained from the remaining perfect stones.

With regard to the restoration of the apse of the south aisle, I hope an opportunity may soon arise of your readers seeing Sir Gilbert Scott's report. I quite admit that this is a work upon which differences of opinion may well exist, but I should prefer to hear opposing opinions expressed in argument founded on a knowledge of facts rather than in epithets.

Lord Grimthorpe's letter is very satisfactory, as he owns to having prevented Sir Gilbert Scott getting information which he required; this is a second case, as the one to which I referred he appears to have forgotten. I spoke only of what occurred before Sir Gilbert's death, as after he died I fell ill, and knew little of what happened. If Lord Grimthorpe had allowed Sir Gilbert Scott to spend 100*l*. in investigating, I should have been aware of it, as the investigations would have been made by myself.

ARTHUR BAKER, F.R.I.B.A.

MR. BAKER ON ST. ALBANS.

SIR,—Mr. Baker's last letter, saying that I "pulled down Norman work at St. Albans which was so strong that it required blasting, in order to carry out my own designs," is as false in every possible way as his previous one which I exposed last week; and as another, nearly two years ago, in another architectural paper, intimating that I somehow made away with the small relics which I had got the Committee to allow 100*l*. to search for, and which fell into dust soon after they were exposed to view, as Chapple told me.

After these specimens of his veracity, any one must have a singular taste and judgment who believes a word he writes. And any one who wants to know what was really done in pulling down ruinous and unsafe Norman work, of which a great deal came down as mere dust, in baskets, and rebuilding it in the same style* may read it in my Guide-book of "The Cathedral and its Restoration," which has been current here ever since, besides sundry letters in the *Times* exposing other people equally veracious, the chief of whom had to confess at last that he had never seen what he professed to criticise.

GRIMTHORPE.

May 8.

*** What Lord Grimthorpe refers to was merely a misapprehension as to the precise point at which difficulty was experienced in pulling down the old work. It does not affect the fact that he deliberately destroyed a Norman feature of peculiar interest, and replaced it by a thing looking like a piece of engineers' railway station design. He refers for a true account of his doings to his "Guide-book," which is, as he says, "still current," and a very curious specimen of uncharitableness and self-laudation it is, to be sold as a guide-book to a church dedicated to a faith of which charity and humility are supposed to be cardinal virtues. Of its "veracity" we will give one typical example. It contains the statement, which Lord Grimthorpe had previously made in the *Times*, that this journal had characterised his west front at St. Alban's as "not fit for a Methodist chapel," the words being in both cases put in quotation commas as our *ipsissima verba*, and he repeated the "quotation" again in an article in *Murray's Magazine*. The real words printed in the *Builder* were as follow:—

"The general look of the whole front may perhaps be best indicated by saying that it is very much the sort of Gothic which one sometimes meets with in competition designs for the larger class of Dissenting chapels,—effective in a showy way, but totally devoid of refinement." †

This, it will be admitted, was a reasonable and moderate way of putting it; and in order to misrepresent the journal which criticised his architecture, Lord Grimthorpe put in print an absolute falsehood, which he has twice repeated in print since. After this we may say, in his own words (*supra*), that "any one must have a singular taste and judgment who believes a word he writes," or credits him with any claim to pose as the apostle of "veracity."—ED.

BOSTON CHURCH.

SIR,—A paragraph in a local newspaper stated that the west door of Boston Church is being restored. A few days ago I paid a short visit to this fine old building, when to my dismay I discovered it was a rebuilding instead of a restoration. In vain I looked for some few fragments of the original work of which there were plenty in existence only six months ago, but not one was to be found, base, shafts, cap, jamb, arch, and crockets ruthlessly swept away, not a particle left behind of the original work. Such is the so-called restoration of a once most magnificent doorway.

AN OCCASIONAL VISITOR.

GRISSELL MEDAL COMPETITION.

SIR,—Your correspondent, Mr. Humphreys, has not fully considered the conditions of the competition, or my design for the same.

The conditions stated that the banks were to be "of sandstone rock." To quote an authority on the subject, "Rock is the best foundation, if homogeneous, but if cracks are found it cannot be relied upon, and is inferior to other materials." In the absence of reliable information, the experienced engineer adopts the least advantageous view.

The "criminally wasteful and unnecessary" abutments were spread out at the base, by means of battering walls, in order to lessen the pressure per foot super. on the foundations, and at the same time add a minimum of weight. This seems to have been overlooked by your correspondent. As to their being "unbeautiful," Mr. Humphreys may find it a profitable task to put them into perspective, and then reconsider his opinion.

With regard to the other criticisms, the reasons for dimensions of keystones, voussoirs, abutments, &c., are clearly shown on my third sheet of stra[illegible]

* ?!—ED.

† *Builder*, August 11, 1883; page 172.

d details, which was not published by you,* and fancy not seen by Mr. Humphreys.
With reference to the conditions, my only complaint is that the time allowed was too short. This has been remedied this year, and I trust will be in future, as I am sure better designs will be the result; after having worked out my strains, &c., I found far too little time remained for the designing of "eyeable lines and architectural effects."

HAROLD HARLOCK.

The Student's Column.

WARMING BUILDINGS BY HOT WATER.

XX.

BRICK-SET BOILERS (*continued*).

THE description (and fixing) of the plain saddle-boiler was completed in the last paper, and the next, and nearest design is as fig. 80. This is practically a saddle-boiler

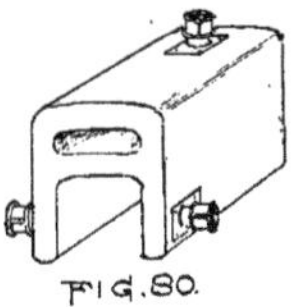

FIG. 80.

with flue-way carried through the top of it from front to back, as shown. The particular advantage of this top flue is that the flame and heat are thus brought beneath a heating-surface,—a horizontal surface that comes over the source of heat being of so much greater value than one that bounds it on the side, or one that comes beneath. To illustrate the method of fixing this boiler, some makers' lists show it in section, with the flame first passing through this flue from back to front and then passing over the top of the boiler to the chimney. So far as conducting the flames into this top flue at the back immediately they leave the fire, no objection can be raised, it being the best plan; but when the flame issues from this flue in front, it would be much better to carry it down and along each side, so as to benefit by the vertical surfaces. Some of the more powerful boilers have iron feathers provided expressly to do this, and it is undoubtedly the best way. In any case, the flame should go through the top flue first. This style of boiler is made with two top flues through it, one above the other, but it is not, to the best of the writer's belief, in great demand.

It should be explained that the few representative boilers now being referred to, are not the only patterns worth recommending by any means. They are merely a representative few that have seen good service, and therefore can be safely referred to.

The next and nearest approach to the last boiler is Fig. 81, a very powerful and efficient

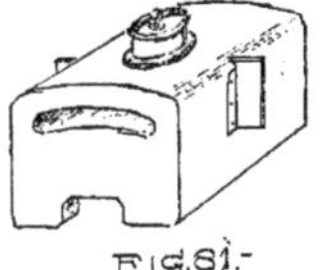

FIG. 81.

boiler. It is practically a saddle, with water-way ends front and rear, and a flueway through the top. In fixing this it is arranged for the flame to first enter the top flue at the back, and, as it leaves the front to be conducted down and along the sides under the midfeathers provided, and as the arrows indicate. This, as already explained, has to have a top feeder, as the waterway front does not admit of feeding from this point. A boiler of this shape will, in the larger sizes, heat up to 4,000 ft. of 4 in.-pipe, and it can be well adapted for shallow drainage, i.e., when the boiler-pit cannot well be made deep owing to water being found in the earth too near the surface). The top surface of this boiler is not usually made use of; the brickwork rests upon it and the feeder nozel projects through above. A soot-door would have to be provided opposite the top flue, for the easy removal of the dust or soot which will readily accumulate in it.

A good boiler, somewhat like the last in general character, is as fig. 82. This, like the

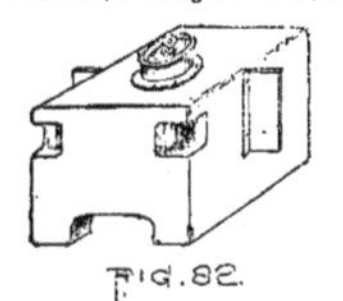

FIG. 82.

last, is not confined to one maker. It is to all intents a saddle-boiler with water-way ends, but the flue-way through the top is made in two distinct passages, as will be seen at fig. 83,

FIG. 83.

which is the elevation, in section, just through the feeding-nozzle. It will be noticed in this boiler that the top flues do not extend quite to the front, but have their sides cut away back some inches. This permits of the boiler front being butted tight up against the front brickwork, and no intervening brickwork to give direction to the flame is needed. In this boiler, as with the last, the flame, as it leaves the top flues in front, is taken down beneath the midfeathers shown, so that it may operate on the vertical sides. The top is not used except to support brickwork; this being all that it is good for, as before-mentioned. Two top soot doors would be needed (in front) in this case.

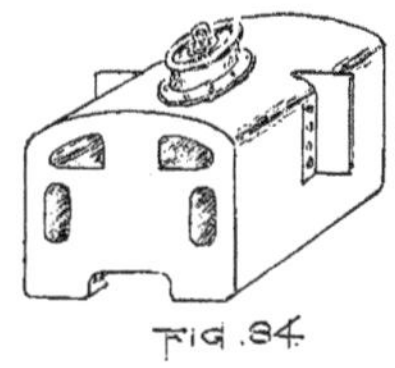

FIG. 84.

Fig. 84 represents a still more powerful boiler, owing to its having an additional pair of flues through it, but this, let it be noted, necessitates a tolerably efficient chimney, which can only be gained by having it a sufficient height. (Chimneys will be treated separately.) With this boiler, the flames, as they leave the boiler, enter the two lower side-flues by an entrance provided in the fire-box. From these, as they make their exit in front, they are conducted into the top flues. After passing along these and out at the back, they are brought along and beneath the feathers, and pass from there to the chimney. It is a shallow boiler suited for shallow drainage, but having a high power, if the chimney is suited. This must end our list of horizontal boilers, although there are very many more almost, if not quite, equally deserving of mention. It is strange how certain pattern boilers will be in favour in certain districts, but not elsewhere; and again a certain pattern may have a great demand for a certain period, then cease almost entirely; it may revive again or it may not. Every boiler-maker can give peculiar experiences in this way.

The next form of boiler to be noticed is of an upright character, quite different to those already mentioned, as fig. 85. This is a very efficient form of boiler, and is particularly well adapted for those building works that extend up several floors, and which have an enormous pressure exerted in the boiler, that is, of course, at the lowest point. A cylindrical shape is best adapted to withstand a pressure. This pattern well fulfils what is so desirable in a boiler, viz., a shape that will envelope the fire, and it nearly approaches the inverted basin-shape that Hood spoke so highly of years ago. This has a top feeder, and is adapted for taking a charge of fuel. The hole shown in the front of the drawing is the flue-way from the interior of the boiler, and the brickwork is arranged so that the flame is caused to take the direction indicated by the arrows. The grating over the hole is merely to keep the fuel from falling through into the flues.

The lower front edge may be level with the rest of the boiler bottom, or it may have a little arched opening as fig. 85; this arched aperture

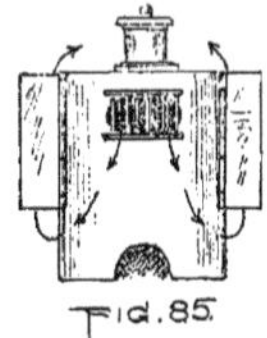

FIG. 85.

being just behind the stoking-door, and for the passage of the stoking tools into the fire-box. If this arched way is not provided, the boiler is propped up on fire-bricks and a stoking aperture thus provided for. Sometimes the feeding door, which is shown on top, projects from the top edge towards the front. This latter arrangement is for such times when the fuel cannot be shovelled in at the top. This boiler is practically fixed in a circular brickwork chamber, of such a width that the feathers reach each side tightly. Water-way mid-feathers can be had if desired. They add considerably to results.

Wagstaff's segmental boiler is well worthy of notice. This is made in two shapes, the shape most known being of the ordinary saddle outline, as fig. 86. It is a cast boiler and the

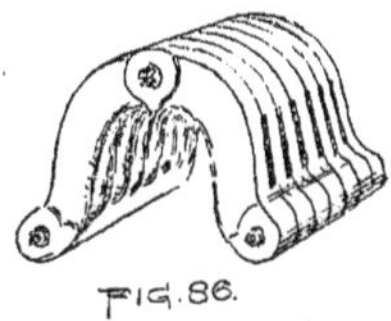

FIG. 86.

sections are bolted together as shown. The form of the sections makes the interior deeply convoluted, which adds materially to the heating surface. Between each section will be noticed a vertical slot-like opening, the object of this is as follows. The boiler is not intended for flues in the ordinary way, but is placed on the customary level base with fire-bars suitably provided; the brickwork is then carried over it corresponding to the shape of the boiler, but leaving from 3 in. to 4 in. between. The front and back ends come tight against the brickwork.

When this boiler is in use, the heated products escape through the slots or fissures at the sides between the sections, and then, in their passage to the chimney, envelope or embrace the outer surface.

The reader is recommended to obtain lists of Weeks & Co.'s tubular boilers and Deard's coil boilers; both have novel features, and are in general use. For large purposes where a simple old pattern boiler may be preferred, the "Trentham" or Cornish boiler can be inspected with advantage.

* The figuring and other details would not have been visible when the drawing was reduced to the size of our page.—ED.

OBITUARY.

DR. JAMES THOMSON.—We regret to hear of the death of Dr. James Thomson, Emeritus Professor of Civil Engineering in Glasgow University, which occurred on the 8th inst. According to the *Times*, he was born in Belfast in 1822. His father was Professor of Mathematics in the Royal Belfast Academical Institution, and subsequently became Professor of Mathematics in Glasgow University. Many still alive remember the college career of his two sons, James Thomson and William Thomson (now Lord Kelvin). James Thomson chose the profession of a civil engineer, serving his apprenticeship in the works of the late Sir William Fairbairn. He began practice in Belfast, and held the office of engineer to the Belfast Water Commissioners. In 1857 he became Professor of Civil Engineering in Queen's College, Belfast. In 1872 he was elected to fill the Glasgow chair.

GENERAL BUILDING NEWS.

SCIENCE AND ART SCHOOLS, WESTON-SUPER-MARE.—On the 9th inst. the foundation stone of the new building in Church-road, Weston-super-Mare, to be used as a school for science and art teaching, was laid by Lord Dungarvan. The building is Renaissance in style. The lower story is being built in local blue limestone, but the upper portion will be in Bath stone with faience panels. On the ground floor will be a science lecture-room, 36 ft. by 20 ft., with chemical laboratory and apparatus-room attached; three workshops, 20 ft. by 16 ft., for plumbing, wood and stone carving, and modelling respectively, also a master's room and lavatories, &c. These rooms are all 16 ft. in height. On the upper floor, which will be approached by a temporary wood staircase until the front portion of the building is carried out, will be two art rooms, each 60 ft. by 20 ft., one for elementary and the other for advanced work; also a small conservatory in which to keep plants in use for flower painting, &c. The building will be fireproof, having a concrete and iron floor. The contract has been let to Messrs. Theo. Palmer & Son, who are carrying it out under the immediate superintendence of the architects, Messrs. Price & Wooler, of Weston-super-Mare. The *Daily Graphic* of the 11th inst. gives a small view of the building, and two other illustrations connected with the ceremony of laying the foundation-stone, but omits to mention the name of the architect. We are surprised that a paper avowedly devoted to art should thus follow the bad example of most other daily journals, which seem rarely to think the architect's name worth mention.

PAROCHIAL BUILDINGS, NEWCASTLE.—On the 3rd inst., the new parochial buildings which have been erected in connexion with Jesmond Parish Church, Newcastle, were opened by Mr. N. G. Clayton. The style of the building is a free treatment of Tudor. The external walling is composed of specked rubble, with stone dressings. A ventilation turret is placed over the main hall roof. The architects for the work are Messrs. Plummer & Burrell, and the contractor Mr. S. B. Burton. The slating has been executed by Messrs. Kirk & Dickinson, the painting and glazing by Messrs. Robertson & Son, the plumbing by Mr. McPherson, and the heating by Messrs. Dinning & Cooke, all of Newcastle.

SHERWOOD FREE CHURCH, PAISLEY.—On the 21st ult., the new Free Church erected at Greenlaw, on the Glasgow-road, Paisley, was formally opened. The building is of red sandstone. The extreme length within walls is 74 ft. by 52 ft., having a recess in front over the vestibule, with one at the north end, immediately behind the pulpit. Entrance is obtained through a doorway in the centre of the south front, which leads into a vestibule, 30 ft. by 9 ft., subdivided by two ornamental screens, glazed with lattice glass. A gallery extends round three sides of the church, with a recess behind the south gable; and the roof, which has timbered principals, enriched with mouldings and arched ribs, rises to a height of 55 ft. above the level of the floor. A square tower, with pinnacles and octagonal spire, is situated at the south-east corner. The tower is 120 ft. high. At the corresponding corner an octagonal turret, 48 ft. in height, is erected. In the centre of the south gable is a traceried and cusped window, having eight vertical lights, divided by moulded mullions and transomes with arched heads. The side fronts have gablets, forming eastern and western transepts, with two lancet and rose windows in each. The area of the church has two-light and the gallery three-light side-windows with cusped heads, whilst the chancel, or organ recess, is lighted by single windows in side and a three-light window in back with arched heads. To the back of the church the hall, the vestry, and the mission-house have been placed. Mr. James Donald, of Paisley, is the architect. The total cost of the buildings will amount to over 4,000*l*.

CO-OPERATIVE SLAUGHTER-HOUSES AT BRADFORD.—The Bradford Provident Industrial Society, Limited, has recently erected new slaughter-houses, cattle-sheds, stables, &c., at Dudley-hill. They are built on a plot of ground, 3,790 square yards in extent, and have frontages into Bolton-lane, Cutler Heights-lane, a new street which is to be called Industry-street, and another thoroughfare, to be known in future as Bank-road. All the buildings are faced with stone, and special attention, it is said, has been given to drainage and ventilation. The yards and sheds are paved with setts. The total amount of the contracts is 4,175*l*. The following contractors have executed the works, from plans and specifications prepared by Messrs. Rycroft & Firth, architects:—Masonry, Messrs. John Moulson & Son; joinery, Messrs. K. Wilkinson & Sons; plumbing, Mr. Charles Nelson; concrete work, Messrs. T. Cordingley & Son; slating, Mr. Thomas Nelson; painting, Mr. Wm. Townson; ironfounders' work, Messrs. Taylor & Parsons. Mr. F. Moulson was clerk of the works.

RAILWAY STATION, BINGLEY, YORKSHIRE.—A new station on the Midland Railway at Bingley has for some time been in course of construction, and it will be opened about the beginning of July. The new station buildings have a frontage of over 100 ft. to Wellington-street, which will be considerably widened to form an entrance. The plans have been designed by Mr. C. Trubshaw, the Company's architect, and the works are being carried out by Mr. C. Murgatroyd, contractor, Idle, under the superintendence of Mr. Austin, clerk of works to the Company. The site is a short distance from the present station, which, when no longer required, will be removed, and a large goods warehouse, 174 ft. by 40 ft., erected in its place. Mr. Trubshaw has designed a stone building for the offices and public rooms. An awning of glass and iron projects 18 ft. from the frontage, and, passing under it, the passengers will enter a porch 12 ft. in width, lined with enamelled brick, the dado of chocolate-brown, and the upper portion of a light buff. On the Wellington-street level there is a booking-hall, 30 ft. by 20 ft.; a booking-office with two windows, 30 ft. by 12 ft.; a telegraph-office; and a parcel-office, 38 ft. by 25 ft. In continuation of the porch, an iron-girder footbridge, 14 ft. in width, is being erected over the lines. It will be lighted by side-lights, and roofed with zinc. The descent to the platform is by stairs on either side of the bridge. For the easy transfer of luggage from the parcel office down to the platform, a sloping passage has been designed. Below the level of Wellington-street, on the down-line, there is a range of rooms, including the sanitary accommodation; a general waiting-room, 28 ft. by 12 ft.; a porters' and lamp room; and other rooms and offices; and first-class and third-class ladies' waiting-rooms, each 19 ft. by 12 ft., with entrance-lobbies of enamelled brick. The buildings on the opposite, or the up, platform comprise a general waiting-room, 28 ft. by 12 ft., and two classes of ladies' waiting-rooms, first and third, each being 19 ft. by 12 ft. The platforms are 3 ft. above the level of the rails, and are each some 190 yards in length. On each side is an awning, glazed with glass and supported by iron pillars.

ST. PATRICK'S NEW SCHOOLS, WIDNES.—These schools in connexion with St. Patrick's R.C. Church were formally opened on the 2nd inst. The material used is St. Helen's pressed brick, with Rainhill stone dressings. All landings, steps, &c., are of Yorkshire stone. The schools, with the playgrounds, stand on 875 square yards of land. The architects are Messrs. Sinnett, Sinnett, & Powell, Liverpool, and the contractor was Mr. Geo. E. Mulholland, of Liverpool, and Great Crosby. The total cost of the buildings has been about 4,500*l*. The schools are built to accommodate 750 scholars.

CONSERVATIVE CLUB, ROATH, CARDIFF.—On the 4th inst., Mr. J. M. Maclean, M.P., re-opened the premises of this club, which have been rebuilt and enlarged, from the designs of Messrs. Veall & Sant, architects, Cardiff. The chief architectural feature is the principal entrance, which is in the Italian Renaissance style, executed in Forest of Dean and Corsham Down stone, richly moulded, and with massive corbels carrying a balcony over the entrance, in the pediment of which the arms of the club have been carved by Mr. Wormleighton, of Cardiff. The club consists of a large assembly-room, kitchen, private room, and committee-room on the first-floor; billiard-room, smoking-room, reading-room, and bar on the ground floor, with a good entrance-hall and staircase. In the basement is extensive cellarage and a skittle-alley. The whole of the works have been carried out by Mr. R. Dinham, contractor, Cardiff, under the personal superintendence of the architects. The specialists employed have been Messrs. Brawn & Co., for the ironmongery and gas-fittings; Mr. S. Evans, for the lead lights; Messrs. T. Thomas & Sons, Cardiff, for the lift; whilst Messrs. Jones & Willis supplied the memorial brass which has been erected on the staircase.

NEW CHURCH, NEW KILPATRICK.—On the 8th inst. the Temple Church, New Kilpatrick, erected on a site on the farm of Temple of Garscube, granted by Lady Campbell, was opened. The new church is cruciform in plan, having nave, aisles, and transepts, with a deep chancel behind. The internal length is about 80 ft., and the breadth between the transepts 64 ft. The style of the architecture is Gothic, and the stone is rock-faced red freestone. The approach is from the Crow-road, and the main entrance is through an open porch, thence into an inner vestibule, from which access is had to the area of the church. The inner vestibule, which is the lower portion of the tower, contains a staircase leading to the back gallery. The area, including the transepts, is seated for 460 worshippers, and the back gallery for sixty. The church is principally lighted from windows in the clearstory, which is supported on stone arches carried on stone pillars, having ornamented moulded capitals and bases. The chancel is raised a few steps above the level of the floor of area of church, and partly screened off by a parapet stone wall with ornamental wrought-iron railing on top. The pulpit is of oak. The chancel is fitted up with oak stalls for the choir. The tower, rising to a height of 80 ft., is provided with a bell-chamber designed for a chime of bells. There is also vestry and session-house accommodation. The total cost is 3,500*l*. The church was designed by Mr. Henry Higgins, jun., architect, Glasgow, under whose superintendence the work has been carried out. The following were the tradesmen who executed the work:—Mason, Mr. W. M'Gaw, Mary-hill; joiner, Mr. W. Anderson, Glasgow; slater, Messrs. A. & D. MacKay, Glasgow; plumber, Messrs. Stalker & Daye, Glasgow; plasterer, Messrs. J. & A. Williamson, Kirkintilloch; glazier, Messrs. M'Culloch & Gow, Glasgow; painter, Messrs. John Orr & Sons, Glasgow; heating, Messrs. M'Cormick & Sons, Glasgow; gas fittings, &c., Messrs. Buchans & M'Intyre, Glasgow.

PROPOSED NEW BANK FOR ROTHERHAM.—The Sheffield Banking Company, Limited, have decided to increase their accommodation at Rotherham, and a new bank is about to be erected. The new building is to be erected on the site of the existing bank, including the vacant land on the south side fronting the Market Hall. The building will be a stone structure with a granite base, and will have a frontage of about 72 ft. on the east side, and about 42 ft. on the south side, with main entrance on the east. The ashlar in the outer walls will be obtained from the new red sandstone quarry at Canklow, belonging to Mr. Chas. Green, the contractor for the whole of the works. The foundation will be composed of a thick bed of Portland cement concrete, and the basement walls will be lined with either white-glazed or salt-glazed bricks in cement, backed with concrete walling. The main banking-room will be about 36 ft. by 27 ft. Adjoining this will be ante-rooms and manager's room. The manager's house will occupy the site of the present building. The plans have been prepared and the work will be carried out by Messrs. Hadfield, Son, & Garland, architects, Sheffield. The clerk of the works is Mr. W. Kaye, of Doncaster.

SANITARY AND ENGINEERING NEWS.

SEWERAGE, POCKLINGTON (YORKSHIRE).—The Vestry of the Township of Pocklington, near Hull, has consulted Mr. D. Balfour, (M.Inst.C.E.,) Newcastle-on-Tyne, as to a scheme of main sewerage and sewage disposal for the town of Pocklington, and he has accordingly submitted plans and report.

WATER SUPPLY, HENLEY-IN-ARDEN.—The question of a water supply for Henley-in-Arden is now in a fair way of being settled. At the last meeting of the Stratford-on-Avon Rural Sanitary Authority, it was announced that a local company had been formed, and that Mr. J. E. Willcox, C.E., of Birmingham, had been called in to advise and to submit a scheme for the provision of a supply of pure and wholesome water for the town.—*Leamington Spa Courier.*

SEWERAGE WORKS, HORNSEY.—Colonel Charles Henry Luard, R.E., one of the Inspectors of the Local Government Board, held an inquiry at Hornsey, on Tuesday, with respect to sanction to borrow 9,191*l*. for works of sewerage. Mr. T. de Courcy Meade, M.Inst.C.E., who had prepared the scheme, explained the plans, and afterwards conducted the inspector over the line of proposed works. Colonel Luard expressed his approval of the scheme, and promised to report to the Local Government Board in due course.

WATER SUPPLY, CHESHUNT.—A Local Government inquiry was held at Cheshunt, Herts, on the 5th ult., by Major-General Carey, R.E., on the application of the Cheshunt Local Board, for sanction to borrow 3,100*l*. to complete the scheme of water-supply now being carried out. After the inquiry General Carey visited the works, and will report in favour of the application. The total cost of the works will be 32,000*l*. The engineer is Mr. T. Bennett, Assoc.Mem.Inst.C.E., Engineer and Surveyor to the Local Board.

ALTAR AND REREDOS, BELCHAMP ST. PAUL'S.—On the 2nd inst. the Bishop of St. Albans dedicated a reredos and altar which have been erected in the Church at Belchamp St. Paul's, Suffolk. The reredos and altar are of oak, and have been executed by Mr. Harcourt Runnacles, of Halstead, from the designs of Mr. Arthur Blomfield Jackson, architect, London.

CHICAGO EXHIBITION, 1893.—The Royal Commission announce that applications for space in the British Section can only be received up to Saturday, May 21. Any applications received after that date will be filed, in case of any space becoming hereafter available, but will not be included in the first allotment.

STAINED GLASS AND DECORATION.

WINDOW, ST. MICHAEL'S, BELGRAVE, LEICESTER. —St. Michael's Church, Belgrave, Leicester, has just received three further windows from the studios of Messrs. Mayer & Co., of Munich. They are situated in the east end of the church, and represent in the largest the Crucifixion, and the two smaller ones St. Peter and St. Paul.

STAINED-GLASS WINDOW FOR SELBY ABBEY.—The window on the west side of the north transept of Selby Abbey has just been filled with stained glass by the Rev. Canon Harper, of York, to the memory of the late Mrs. Harper. The window, which is a circular-headed one, is occupied by one subject, "The Crucifixion." The window is crowned with a canopy. The work has been executed by Messrs Clayton & Bell, of London.

MEMORIAL WINDOW, CRICH CHURCH.—A window to the memory of the late churchwarden, Mr. James Lee, has been placed in the north aisle of Crich Church. The subject, "The Great Physician" (our Lord healing the sick) is painted in three lights, under canopies, upon a base. The window is from the studio of Mr. T. W. Camm, of Smethwick.

FOREIGN AND COLONIAL.

FRANCE.—The Government has just bought an important picture by M. Puvis de Chavannes, "the beheading of St. John the Baptist." This work will be placed in the museum of the Luxembourg, where it will hang as a companion picture to the "Pauvre Pecheur" by the same master.——The sculptors Boucher, Falguière, Barrias, Dalou, Marquests and Steiner, have been commissioned to execute statues of Danton, Gambetta, Ledru Rollin, Vergniaud, Casimir-Perier, and Berryer, which are to ornament the Palace of the Chamber of Deputies.——The Museum of Woodcarving which has been temporarilly installed in the Trocadèro, is to be reorganised in the Louvre, in the old Salle de Menage.——The posthumous exhibition of the works of Ribot has just been opened in the Ecole des Beaux-Arts.——The Minister of Public Instruction has just instituted a commission, charged with the preparation of the works (in regard to artistic matters) for the International Conference which is to be held in Paris, 1893.——MM. Gerôme, Bonnat, Puvis de Chavannes, Carolus Duran, Dagnan-Bouveret, and Benjamin-Constant have accepted the work of examiners, for the works sent to Paris by the young American painters, anxious to obtain the prize founded by the Club of Arts at Philadelphia. This prize, which is called the "Prix de Paris," consists of an annual sum of 900 dollars for five years.——A hospital for consumptives is shortly to be built near Dourdan (Seine et Marne) on the plan of that at Falkestein.——Some workmen have just discovered some interesting objects on the north side of the hill of Montmatre. A monumental stone ornamented with sculpture and inscriptions, and some pewter pots very finely worked.——On Thursday last at Bois-le-Roi (Seine et Marne) the statue of "Olivier Métra," the musical composer, was inaugurated, the statue is by Ludovic Durand.——There are several acts of vandalism which have been committed lately. The church of Gizy-les-Nobles près d'Auxerre (Yonne) has been pillaged. The altar, the ornaments, the statues, have been completely shattered. Near Saint Florent has been destroyed a magnificent dolmen, much prized by archæologists, as being amongst the historical monuments, and at Troyes (Aube) the Hotel de la Préfecture has been destroyed by an incendiary.——The commission for the preservation of historical buildings has saved from demolition several forts in the north, the château de Selles, a curious Carlovingian bastille, the gate of Notre Dame, a bijou of the Renaissance, the gate of St. Sepulchre and the tower of Abancourt, which dates from the fifteenth century. At Lille they are trying to save the most ancient Lillois monument, the "Noble Tour," and also the gates of Gand and Roubaix, almost unique specimens of military architecture of the thirteenth century.——An artistic exhibition is announced to be held at Rheims, from October 1 to November 7.

An exhibition of industrial art has just been opened at Lille. It will be closed on August 1.——The painter Marcel Briquiboul has just died at the age of fifty-five. He was a pupil of Leon Cogniet, and of Gleyre. He obtained a medal of the third class at the Salon of 1863. The death is also announced of Léon Gobron the painter, he made a certain reputation in the works of industrial art. —The well-known caricaturist Grévin, is just dead. He had for a long time contributed to the *Journal Amusant*, and the *Charivari*, and he created the museum of wax figures which bears his name. He died at the age of sixty-five years.——We have also to mention the death of Louis Charles Marion one of the oldest members of the Sociétié Centrale des Architects. M. Marion was born at Mezieres in 1802. In 1820 he entered the studio of Duban, and assisted in the building of Notre Dame de Lorette, and to the establishment of the first line in France, in 1820, which ran from St. Etienne to Lyons.

BERLIN.—The annual "Salon" is to be opened on the 15th inst. The halls of the provisional "Landes Ausstellungs Palast," near the Lehrter Bahnhof, will again be used for this exhibition this year.——A large exhibition of objects relating to the interior arrangement of dwellings is to be opened this summer. The "furniture" group will have the lion's share of space at this show.——The model of a very interesting building for colonial purposes is on exhibition. It shows an iron skeleton with wall-surfaces of thin plates of compressed bamboo shavings. The weight of the building is comparatively light.——From an English point of view, but slow progress has been made during the last three years on the new home for the Imperial Parliament. This is due to the thoroughness with which all work relating to the delineation of the mouldings and the sculptural decoration is done. Not only has much labour been spent on the preliminary studies necessary, but it has also been customary to make several attempts with full sized plaster models before deciding on the minutest details. The local papers now state that a great stride is to be made this year, and further, that to pacify the grumbling as to slow progress, the outside scaffolding is to be taken down this summer, thus showing the façade and the iron and glass cupola. As the hoarding, however, will still remain in position, both laymen and art critics should be warned not to form conclusions on the general proportions too rapidly, as was done in the case of Garnier's French Opera-house at Paris. The advisability of taking down the scaffolding before the windows and doors are fixed is doubtful if importance be attached to criticism, and no practical points come into consideration. The building will not be ready until the end of 1894 at the earliest.——The Berlin "Architekten Verein" has decided to re-edit the book "Berlin und Seine Bauten," which they published in 1878 on the occasion of the biennial gathering of the amalgamated societies of architects and civil engineers held in the capital that year. As great changes have been made in Berlin in the last fifteen years, the book is quite out of date now. An editorial staff of twelve members is to have the new edition ready in 1894, in which year a similar gathering at Berlin has been planned. This year's gathering takes place at Leipsic.——The Schinkel collection of the Royal Technical College contains a valuable set of the deceased architect's designs for the mounting of operas and dramas played at the Court Theatres of Berlin. Some seventy of these have been sent to the Vienna Theatre and Music Exhibition, together with some architectural drawings of the Court Theatre Schinkel built.——A competition, opened for the purpose of obtaining a suitable model of an oven to be adopted for artisans' dwellings, has been decided. The "programme" required that the oven could be used both for cooking and for heating purposes without contamination of the air, and that the supply of fuel necessary should be small. The sum of 50*l*. was devoted to two prizes. A competition for the best essay on the ventilation of artisans' dwellings was a failure, as no prize could be awarded.——The proposed harbour for inland water traffic, which will be situated in the south-western district (am Urban), is to be taken in hand this summer.——A new lunatic asylum is to be built at a cost of some 140,000*l*.——The official *Central Blatt der Bauverwaltung* publishes Bruno Schmitz's design for the Zürich Assembly and Concert Rooms, and expresses regret at the bungling of the Swiss managing committee in the matter.——A meeting of some sixty gentlemen interested in Germany's representation at the Chicago show took place last week. Herr Wermuth, the Imperial Special Commissioner, made some statements which show that Germany's interests are being well taken care of at the Exhibition. Besides having an official exhibition building of its own and a so-called German village, the Empire is to have 100,000 square feet of floor in the Palais d'Industrie, and 30,000 ft. in the "Electrical Building," thus making a total of 218,000 square feet. The Government has, as before stated, raised their grant for exhibition purposes, a satisfactory rate of freightage has been arranged, and the insurance dues are to be reasonable.——The increase in the number of persons deriving benefit from the education given at the Royal Technical Colleges of Germany is again a large one this session. This year's total is 6,110; last year the corresponding number was 5,362. Of the 6,110, no fewer than 4,885 are immatriculated students, and of this number 1,886 fell to the Berlin College.

HOLLAND.—A report has been published by the Züyder-Zee Commission as to the possibility of reclaiming a large part of the Zee from the sea. The Commission recommends that the Zee be cut off from the waters of the North Sea near the island of Wieringen. The area to be reclaimed is to be cut in four divisions by dykes, these are to be drained off and filled up separately. The total of the estimates for the work shows a figure of 190,000,000 gulden, and the time required is calculated at thirty-two years.

VIENNA.—On Saturday last the "International" Musical and Theatrical Exhibition at Vienna was opened by the Emperor of Austria with all due ceremony, though scarcely with the pomp expected, owing to various unpleasant hindrances having occurred at the last moment. The Exhibition, as we have before stated, has had a home found for it in the old Prater Park Rotunda, and in some provisionally-erected buildings on the grounds adjacent to this hall. The show has by no means a complete appearance as yet, the non-Austrian countries, with England at the head of the list, having apparently vied in giving the public the best collection of empty show-cases on opening day. Of the specially-erected buildings, Herr Marmorek's Concert Hall, containing some fourteen hundred seats, Messrs. Fellmer and Helmer's Model Theatre, and a reproduction of a part of Old Vienna, are greatly admired, and have received the praise of the Austrian daily and technical press.

BULGARIA.—A competition for the design of a commercial college at Rustschuk, which is to be built at a cost of 240,000 fr., has been decided. M. Braug, an Austrian, resident in Sofia, obtained the first prize (Zeitschritt des Oestr. Ing.-und Arch-Vereines).

MISCELLANEOUS.

ARTISTS' GENERAL BENEVOLENT INSTITUTION.—The seventy-seventh annual dinner of the Artists' General Benevolent Institution was held on the 7th inst., at the Hotel Métropole. The Chairman, Viscount Powerscourt, in proposing the toast of "Prosperity to the Artists' General Benevolent Fund," said that in 1891 212 persons had been relieved from the fund, in sums varying from 70*l*. down to 10*l*., at a total cost of 4,403*l*., the working expenses being only 352*l*. Since the institution of the society in 1814 it had administered a sum of 96,556*l*. The Orphan Fund was in a most prosperous condition, and was entirely self-supporting. The hon. treasurer (Mr. A. Waterhouse, R.A.) announced the receipt of subscriptions amounting to 2,363*l*. 9s.

FIRE-PROOF PAINT.—According to the *Droguen-Zeitung* the following is an excellent formula for making a fire-proof paint:—A quantity of freshly-burnt unslaked lime of the best quality is completely slaked; skim-milk, or, failing this, water is added until the mixture becomes of the consistence of syrup. To each 10 kilogrammes (1 kilogramme = 2·2 lb.) of this lime-milk are added, under continual stirring, the following, in a powdered condition: 2 kilogrammes of alum, 1½ kilogramme of the common commercial potash, and 1 kilogramme of common cooking-salt. If a perfectly white shade is desired a small quantity of plaster of Paris is added. Lamp-black gives, according to the quantity incorporated, shades of colour varying from light grey to deep black. The colour-additions are always to be admixed last. The whole is then run through a moderately-fine wire sieve, after which it is passed through an ordinary paint-mill in the same manner as oil colours. Finally, the compound must be heated to 100 deg. Celsius. It is then applied as hot as possible to the surface which is to be protected. Before heating, the mixture may be brought to a suitable thickness by the addition of skim-milk or water. The compound must be used in painting in the same way as oil colours. For ceilings or damaged walls an addition of white sand to the mixture is recommended.

THE SANITARY INSTITUTE.—At an examination for Local Surveyors and Inspectors of Nuisances, held at Derby on April 28 and 29, five candidates presented themselves as local surveyors, and thirty-six candidates presented themselves as inspectors of nuisances. Questions were set to be answered in writing on the 28th, and the candidates were examined *vivâ voce* on the 29th. The following four candidates were certified to be competent, as regards their sanitary knowledge, to discharge the duties of local surveyors:—Messrs. Joseph Goddard, Chapel-en-le-Frith; William Samuel Green, Idrigehay, Derby; Henry James Kilford, borough surveyor, Ilkeston; and Mason Outram, Dronfield, Sheffield. Seventeen candidates were certified to be competent, as regards their sanitary knowledge, to discharge the duties of inspector of nuisances.

BUILDERS' HARDWARE AND SANITARY PLUMBING IN FRANCE.—According to a recent report of the United States Commercial Agent at St. Etienne on "The French Market for American Produce," there is an apparent need in that country for builders' hardware of a light and tasteful description, the bolts, hinges, knobs, locks, and window-fastenings used, throughout nearly the whole of France, being of the same patterns and weights as those in vogue a century ago. The widespread necessity for good sanitary plumbing is perhaps the most real and urgent material want of France. Outside of Paris and Nice there are not 300 houses or hotels furnished with decent water-closets or sanitary plumbing. To find a good market in France there must be intelligent unremitting effort, and, if the business be large, the expenditure of much money. Circulars, illustrated catalogues, posters, and ornamental agents will not do, but hard personal work, combined with newspaper advertising, will create and hold a market.

THE WORKS OF MESSRS. SIEMENS BROS. & CO., LIMITED, WOOLWICH.—No. 4 of the *Manufacturers' Engineering and Export Journal* (published at 22, Paternoster-row) is a special issue, and it devotes no fewer than fifty pages to an interesting and well-illustrated account of the rise and progress of the extensive establishment of Siemens Bros. & Co., electrical engineers, Woolwich. The account is prefaced by an excellent portrait of the late Sir

COMPETITIONS, CONTRACTS, AND PUBLIC APPOINTMENTS.

COMPETITIONS.

Nature of Work.	By whom Advertised.	Premium.	Designs to be delivered.
*Illuminated Clock Tower	New Sarum T. C.	20l. and 5l.	June 28
Intermediate and Technical School, Aberdare	Building Committee	25l.	June 20
Church, Sheffield	Rev. M. Parkin	....	Aug. 1
*Municipal Technical School	Manchester Corp.	200l. 150l. 100l. 75l.	Aug. 2
*New Masonic Hall	Newcastle-upon-Tyne Central Masonic Hall Co. Ltd.	50l. 25l.	No date

CONTRACTS.

Nature of Work or Materials.	By whom Required.	Architect, Surveyor, or Engineer.	Tenders to be delivered.
*Masons' Works, Stockfield Park, Wetherby	R. J. Foster	T. H. & F. Healey	May 14
*Supply of Road Materials	Maidstone U.S.A.	W. C. Scoones	May 17
*Kerbing and Channelling	Cheshunt Local Board	F. Bennett	do.
Reservoir, Earlsburn	Falkirk & Larbert Trustees	Leslie & Reid	do.
Cast-iron Pipes and Castings	Edinburgh Water Trsts.	do.	do
Excavating and Pipe Laying	do.	do.	do.
Alterations and Additions to Houses, Retford	....	C. D. Ogle	do.
Dry Dock and Pontoon Jetties, Mode Wheel	Manchester Ship Canal &c. Co.	*Official*	do.
*Roadmaking Works	Lewisham Bd. of Wks	do.	do.
*Widening Railway between Crewe and Sandbach, &c. &c.	L. & N. W. Ry. Co	do.	do.
*Wrought-iron and Wire Fencing, Battersea Park	London County Council	do.	do.
Lodge and other Buildings	Newcastle-on-Tyne Crp.	do.	May 18
Cast-iron Pipes, Hydrants, &c.	Nelson Corporation	do.	do.
Exhauster, Boiler and Pump House, and Chimney	Leeds Corporation	do.	do.
*Goods' Shed, Ledbury	G. W. R. Co.	do.	do.
Lunacy Wards, &c. Workhouse	Stoke-upon-Trent Guardians	C. Lynam	do.
Road Work, Cambuslang	Lanark Lower Ward Committee	Crouch & Hogg	do.
Additions to Board Schools, Fulwell, near Sunderland	Fulwell School Board	J. Shields	May 19
Workhouse Work, Stoke Damerel, Devon	Commissioners	*Official*	do.
*Wood Paving Works	Vestry of St. John's, Hampstead	do.	do.
*Brick Sewer, &c.	do.	do.	do.
*Painting and Decorating Town Hall	Leeds Corporation	do.	do.
*Sheds, Latrines, &c. Penzance	Admiralty	do.	May 20
Battery, Drill Shed, &c.	do.	do.	do.
Residence, Laverock Loch, Elgin, N.B.	....	A. & W. Reid	May 21
Dwelling-house, Cwmtaff, Merthyr Tydfil	Trustees of the Meyrick Estate	J. Williams	do.

CONTRACTS.—*Continued.*

Nature of Work or Materials.	By whom Required.	Architect, Surveyor, or Engineer.	Tenders to be delivered
*Block of Buildings, Aberdare	Constitutional Club Buildings Co. Lim.	T. C. Wakeling	May 23
*Cleansing Works, &c. at Schools, Southall	St. Marylebone Guar.	*Official*	do.
Isolation Hospital, Garland's Asylum	Committee Cumberland & Westmoreland Asy.	G. D. Oliver	do.
Granite and Limestone	Cardiff Corporation	W. Harpur	May 24
*Making-up and Paving Road	Fulham Vestry	W. Sykes	do.
*Rustic Band Stands in Parks	London County Council	*Official*	do.
*Broken Granite	Hackney Bd. of Works	do.	May 25
Electric Lighting, Leeds	Yorkshire, &c. Electricity Co.	do.	May 26
*Public Baths	Ipswich U.S.A.	F. W. Coltman	May 27
*Semi-detached Villas, Barnet	....	W. H. Mansbridge	May 28
*Road Materials	Hendon U.R.S.A.	R. A. Wilson	do.
*Concrete Sea-wall, Promenade, &c.	Filey Loc. Bd.	*Official*	do.
*New Lighthouse, Withernsea	Trinity House Corp.	do.	May 30
*Portland Cement, Macadam, & Chippings	Toxteth Park L. B.	J. Price	do.
*Sewerage Works	Chard R.S.A.	C. N. Lailey	May 31
*Painting Works, &c. Workhouse	Paddington Guar.	A. & C. Harston	do.
*Rebuilding of P. O. Southampton	Commrs. of H.M. Wks	*Official*	do.
*Stoneware Drain Pipes	Enfield Loc. Bd.	W. Kitteringham	June 1
Fifty Cottages, near Abertillery, Mon.	Griffiths Building Club	E. A. Lansdowne	do.
*Repairs and Drainage Works at Workhouse	Newhaven Union	W. A. Mole	June 3
*Repairing and Painting Old Buildings, &c.	St. Olave's Union	Newman & Newman	June 9
*Dock Gates	Barry Railway Co.	J. Wolfe Barry	June 11
*Sewerage Works	Chepstow Loc. Bd.	C. B. Walker	June 13
*Married Soldiers' Quarters, Eastbourne	War Department	*Official*	No date
*Internal Painting, &c. Anglesea Barracks	do.	do.	do.
*Purchase and Pulling Down Old Houses	Sch. Bd. for London	do.	do.
*Cast-iron Pipes	Bishop's Castle T. C.	W. Wyatt	do.
Eighteen Cottages, Blaengarw, near Bridgend	Evan Griffiths	Wm. Thomas	do.
Residence, Ben Rhydding, Leeds	....	F. J. Dodgshun	do.
Stables, &c. Headingley, Leeds	J. Nicholson	B. Wilson	do.
Inn, Wheatley Green, Durham	Newcastle Breweries, Ltd.	S. Oswald & Son	do.
Business Premises, Hanley, Staffs	Granger & Smith	Elijah Jones	do.
*Pair of Villas, Brockley	....	E. Clarke	do.

PUBLIC APPOINTMENTS.

Nature of Appointment.	By whom Advertised.	Salary.	Applications to be in.
*Assistant Inspector of Nuisances	Plymouth T. C.	80l. rising to 110l.	May 19
*Surveyor and Estate Agent	Gt. Western Ry. Co.	300l.	May 28
*Clerk of Works for Waterworks	Bishop's Castle T. C.	....	May 30
*Clerk of Works	Gt. Northern Hosp.	3l. 3s.	No date
*Head Master	Coalbrookdale School of Art	....	do.

Those marked with an Asterisk (*) are advertised in this Number. *Competitions, p. iv. Contracts, pp. iv., vi., & viii. Public Appointments, p. xx.*

William Siemens, F.R.S., and by portraits (no doubt equally good as likenesses) of Mr. Carl Siemens and Dr. Werner von Siemens. The establishment at Woolwich, which covers an area of 7½ acres, is described and very fully illustrated by some thirty photo-engravings specially made for the purpose, showing the interiors of the many busy machine-shops and of other departments. The manufacture and laying of submarine cables are described, and the account concludes with an illustrated description of many of the instruments and appliances made at Woolwich.

FUNERAL REFORM ASSOCIATION. — The fifth monthly meeting of the Funeral Reform Association was held last week in the Church House, Westminster. Among those present were the Archdeacon of London, in the chair, the Hon. D. Fortescue, Gen. Lowry, Rev. T. B. Johnston, Rev. R. B. Ransford, Dr. W. T. Greene, Dr. Septimus Gibbon, Dr. W. Squire, Mr. Vigers, Mrs. Leigh Hunt Wallace, and Miss Bayley. The Archdeacon said that London and other great towns needed more cemeteries within convenient reach, and each cemetery should be conducted as a natural underground purifier, where the dead are dissolved by the action of the earth and air, instead of being preserved in durable coffins. The extra cost of more numerous spaces required by such sanitary burial could be met by the abandonment of the prevalent extravagances of funerals.

DESIGNS FOR FLOORCLOTH AND LINOLEUM.—Messrs. M. Nairn & Co., floorcloth and linoleum manufacturers, of Kirkcaldy, announce that in response to their invitation of January last, 470 competitors, residing throughout the United Kingdom, the Continent, and America, have sent in 1,080 designs for competition. With the assistance of Mr. A. F. Brophy, of London, they have decided that the prizes should be awarded as follows:—Class A: 1st prize, "Autrim," Mr. R. A. Boyd, London; 2nd prize, "Aristophanes," Mr. Andrew Forrester, Edinburgh; 3rd prize, "Only a Pansy Blossom," Mr. John Cone, Hipperholme, near Halifax. Class B: 1st prize, "Meadowsweet," Mr. W. H. Edmead, London; 2nd prize, "Esperance," Miss E. C. Brothers, Canterbury; 3rd prize, "Aristophanes," Mr. Andrew Forrester, Edinburgh. Class C: 1st prize, "Help One Another," Mr. J. H. Park, Kidderminster; 2nd prize, "L. N. Z.," Mr. Isaac Jones, London; 3rd prize, "Meadowsweet," Mr. W. H. Edmead, London. Class D: 1st prize, "Carton," Mr. T. B. Widdowson, Leicester; 2nd prize, "Tattingstone," Mr. P. Claude Hooper, Ipswich; 3rd prize "Aristophanes," Mr. Andrew Forrester, Edinburgh. Class E: 1st prize, "Meadowsweet," Mr. W. H. Edmead, London; 2nd prize, "Antrim," Mr. R. A. Boyd, London; 3rd prize, Figure with Fleur-de-lis, Monsieur D. Van Walle, Paris. Messrs. Nairn add that several unsuccessful drawings of merit have been purchased by them, and the remainder have been returned to the senders.

SCAVENGING AND REFUSE DISPOSAL.—Under the auspices of the Sanitary Institute and the Norfolk County Council, a lecture was delivered on Saturday last on "Scavenging and the Disposal of Refuse and Sewage" at Blackfriars Hall, Norwich, by Mr. T. de Courcy Meade, M.Inst.C.E. The lecture was well attended, principally by intending candidates for positions as Inspectors of Nuisances. The lecturer went very fully into the question of the collection and disposal of refuse. He described the "Street Orderly" system which has been in use in the City of London many years, and then gave some interesting figures as to various methods and the cost of removal of street refuse, watering streets, and the use of the rotary brushes and other machines for the cleansing of streets and the removal of snow. He described at length the various systems now in use for the collection and disposal of house refuse, dealing very fully with the subject of refuse cremation and other systems in use throughout the country. Commencing with "Fryer's "Destructor," Mr. Meade described the various systems which have been tried with more or less success in the principal towns in England and Scotland, and he also described the Fume Cremator which is used in connexion with the destructor, and the various improvements which have taken place in furnaces for destroying refuse. The furnaces known as the "Perfectus" Destructor, the Horsfall Destructor, the system devised by Mr. Young, of Glasgow, that of Mr. Heeley, the new furnace invented by Mr. Whiley, of Manchester, and others, were fully dealt with. The midden system was also described, and the lecturer concluded with a short description of the various systems now adopted for the purification of sewage. A few questions which had been given by the lecturer were printed and distributed amongst the students by Mr. Widdows, the Principal of the Technical School at Norwich. At the conclusion of the lecture, a vote of thanks was given to the lecturer, and a request was made that he would have the principal portions of his lecture transcribed and printed for the use of those interested.

MEETINGS.

MONDAY, MAY 16.

Royal Institute of British Architects.—Mr. W. H. Preece, F.R.S., on "The Art of Internal Illumination of Buildings by Electricity." 8 p.m.

Society of Arts (Cantor Lectures). — Dr. Percy F. Frankland on "Recent Bacteriological and Chemical Research in Connexion with the Fermentation Industries." III. 8 p.m.

TUESDAY, MAY 17.

Institution of Civil Engineers.—(1) Further discussion on Mr. A. P. Trotter's paper on "The Distribution and Measurement of Illumination." (2, time permitting), Professor W. C. Roberts-Austen on "The Measurement of High Temperatures." 8 p.m.

Society of Arts (Applied Art Section).—Mr. William Simpson on "Mud, A Material for Architecture in Persia and the East." 8 p.m.

Statistical Society.—Mr. J. S. Jeans on "The Recent Movement of Labour in Different Countries in Reference to Wages, Hours of Work, and Efficiency." 7.45 p.m.

Royal Institution.—Mr. Frederick E. Ives on "Photography in the Colours of Nature." II. 3 p.m.

WEDNESDAY, MAY 18.

British Archæological Association.—Mr. Cecil T. Davies on "Merchants' Marks of the Fifteenth and Sixteenth Centuries." 8 p.m.

Society of Arts.—Captain W. De Abney on "Colour Blindness." 8 p.m.

Royal Meteorological Society. — Three papers to be read. 7 p.m.

Builders' Foremen and Clerks of Works' Institution.—Ordinary meeting. 8.30 p.m.

THURSDAY, MAY 19.

Society of Arts (Indian Section).—Mr. J. A. Baines on "The Administration of the Imperial Census of 1891 in India." 4.30 p.m.

Society of Antiquaries.—8.30 p.m.

Royal Institution. — Professor Dewar on "The Chemistry of Gases."—IV. 3 p.m.

FRIDAY, MAY 20.

Royal Institution.—Mr. J. Wilson Swan on "Electro-Metallurgy." 9 p.m.

RECENT PATENTS:

ABSTRACTS OF SPECIFICATIONS.

5,389.—DRAIN VENTILATION: *I. Shone.*—This invention relates to improvements in the ventilation of drains and sewers. According to the specification, sewer and drain gases are diluted with fresh atmospheric air, and are discharged into the atmosphere so diluted. The dilution is effected by introducing fresh air into the conduit, trap, or other device by which the foul gases given off from the sewage in a drain or sewer are discharged into the air. The gases so diluted will, it is urged, be far less noxious in all respects than sewer gases as ordinarily discharged from a drain. Stand-pipes are used for introducing the fresh air, and the inventor proposes that gas lamp posts should be utilised, where possible, for such stand-pipes.

7,650.—GLAZING ROOFS: *G. Emerton.*—This invention is described as a simple and cheap means for securing glass in roofs, skylights, and the like, without the aid of putty. A longitudinal groove is ploughed out of each side of the bars of the roof, the groove extending the whole length of the bar. A sheet of metal or other suitable material is then taken, and with it the open or outer surface of the bar is covered, being forced into the grooves on both sides. Below the grooves are spread the lateral edges of this sheet, at right angles or thereabouts of the bar, projecting as far as may be desired. The pieces of glass are slid one by one into the complementary grooves of the two opposing bars from and through the bottoms, and when one piece has attained its desired position it is secured by a disc, pivotted eccentrically on the side of one or both the bars above the groove, therein acting as a cam. In the upper, or intermediate cams, a projection is made by which the lower edge of this piece of glass is held and retained. The next piece of glass is then slid along the grooves until its upper edge passes the desired distance under the lower edge of the upper piece, when it, in its turn, is secured in position by one or more similar clams, and so on with the remainder of the glass. To remove the glass the process is reversed.

8816.—DOOR LATCHES: *W. M. Trousdale.*—This specification refers to what is described as an improvement in latches, applicable to door locks or doors without locks, and consists in making a rectangular triangle shaped latch, having the face and nose rounded and vertically pivotted to swivel parallel with the door, the latch being so weighted or acted on by a spring, and resting on a staple, that the point of the latch, or latch part, just projects sufficiently far beyond the face of the door as to form a secure hold of the box staple fixed on the inside of the door jamb, when the door is shut. In withdrawing the latch the inventor applies a tang, curved and going through the door and working on a pivot, arranged as to the latch so that when the tang is raised it swivels the latch, and withdraws it from the box staple. This tang has handles at each end hanging downwards on each side of the door, or so arranged that on opening the door on entering, the hanging handle is pressed forward, swivels and withdraws the latch, and by the same pressure opens the door; the reverse action occuring on withdrawing the hanging handle, the hanging handle being pulled, which swivels, and withdraws the latch, and the same pulling action continued pulls open the door. Various forms of this latch are given in the diagrams attached to the specification.

9,319.—DAMP IN WALLS: *W. P. Thompson.*—This invention relates to a process for the manufacture of chemical preparations with which walls of houses are coated for the purpose of preventing the damp from penetrating. The process consists in first coating the wall with a thick solution, and then with a thin one, thus forming a covering through which water cannot penetrate. The first solution is composed of stearine, saponified with caustic potash, acetic acid, and salicylic acid. These substances are heated in water to boiling point. A little phenic acid is added to destroy the unpleasant odour of the soap. The thin solution is composed of alum, chloride of calcium, and salicylic acid, diluted with water, and a little phenic acid is also added. Any suitable colouring matter may also be added to these solutions. It is claimed that water runs off walls so coated, as it does off sheets of glass, without rendering them damp, and that the appearance of the coated stones does not change at all, and they are thus prevented from becoming dirty.

NEW APPLICATIONS FOR LETTERS PATENT.

April 25.—7,728, W. Johnson and J. Coultner, Tieing Walls, Chimney-shafts, Piers for Bridges, and other brick or similar structures.—7,732, F. Brooke, Furnaces of Kilns.—7,774, J. Bloomfield, Plaster.—7,784, F. Volante, Window-fastening device.

April 26.—7,802, D. Richmond, Flushing Water-closets, Urinals, &c.—7,804, A. and A. Budde, Traps for Sewers or Drains.—7,827, T. Halbourne, Bakers' Ovens.—7,843, J. Landes, Machines for Sharpening and Setting Saws.—7,849, W. Reid, Method of Manufacturing Malms, Stocks, and other Bricks.—7,850, E. Warner and J. Curry, Mortar.—7,882, M Goodwin, Ventilating Cowl for drawing off obnoxious gas or air.

April 27.—7,895, T. Baylis, Paving Bricks, Paving Tiles and Quarries.—7,896, E. Prestage, Saw-setting Appliance.—7,900, J. Major, Domestic Grates, and the mode of setting them.—7,907, W. Pryke and W. Palmer, Eaves Gutters.—7,927, J. Cartland, Hinges.—7,941, P. Geraud, Cutting Stone, and machinery and accessories therefor.—7,949, F. Fortescue, Fastener for Sashes, &c.—7,964, O. Fuller, Plumb-level.—7,973, J. Hamblet, jun., Paving Bricks or Blocks.

April 28.—7,998, J. Handley, Drain and Sewers Pipes.—8,017, O. Bremnox, Ships' Ventilators.—8,021, G Bray, Extension-ladders.—8,036, H. & H. Warrington, Bricks for building purposes.—8,040, G. Meager, Construction and Fittings to Window-sashes.—8,050, O. Imray, Corrugated Sheet Metal Pipes.—8,070, J. Mitchell, Planes.

April 29.—8,076, T. Whitehead, Chimney-cowls and Extracting-ventilators.—8,078, H. Leggott, Sitting-room Fire-ranges.—8,087, F. Bergmann, Automatically Closing-doors, &c.—8,122, H. Jodicke, Channelling Bricks, Artificial Stones, &c.—8,124, H. Border, Floor and Manhole Chamber for Drains.

April 30.—W. Tithecott, Balance-pulley for hanging Side-sashes of Bay and other Windows.—8,178, J. Rockett, Automatic Valve to prevent waste of water under pressure.—8,199, B Goldmann, Dryer for Paints, &c.—8,203, E. Hole, Sash-fastener.

PROVISIONAL SPECIFICATIONS ACCEPTED.

3,749, F. Fitton, Ventilation.—5,033, A. Ransome, and-sawing Machines.—5,156, P. Field, Sash-fastenings r Windows or Doors.—5,180, J. Johnstone, Screw-rivers.—5,493, E Carter, Disinfecting Apparatus for Vater-closets.—6,250, G. Sharp, Fastener for Doors, Windows, &c.—6,331, W. Byers, Fixing Glass in Skyghts, Roofs, &c.—6,352, A. B. ult, Fasteners for Doors, indows, &c.—6,608, T. Potter, Construction of Fireroof Floors.—6 681, J. Walker, Draught Excluder for oors, Windows, &c.—6,779, A. Winrow, Tile and other milar Presses.—7,205, A. Leo, Portable Collapsible adders.

COMPLETE SPECIFICATIONS ACCEPTED.

(*Open to Opposition for Two Months.*)

8,287, J. Hodgson and E Sheard, Coating the surfaces Walls and Buildings with Sand or other similar aterial.—10,395, J. Morris, Roofing Tiles.—15,981, . Green, Windows.

SOME RECENT SALES OF PROPERTY:

ESTATE EXCHANGE REPORT.

MAY 2.—By *Weatherall & Green*: The residence, Langsmead," near Godstone, and 113a. 2r. 13p., f., 500l.—By *Dolman & Pearce*: 23, Winchester-rd., ampstead, u.t. 72 yrs., g.r. 4l., r. 60l., 700l.; 25 and 33, Vinchester-rd., u t. 72 yrs., g r. 8l., r. 136l., 1,570l.—By *rodie, Timbs. & Baker*: 96, North-st., Edgware-rd., u.t.) yrs., g.r. 10l. 10s., r. 45l., 225l.; 6, Cambridge-rd., unnersbury, u.t. 69 yrs., g.r. 8l. 3s., 265l.; 28 and 30, ambridge-rd., u.t. 69 yrs., g.r. 6l., r. 70l., 580l.—By *urtis & Sharp*: 43 to 49 (odd), Austin-rd., Battersea, , 580l.; 33 and 35, Henley-st., u.t 76 yrs., g.r. 5l. 10s., 30l.; 61 to 67 (odd), Hibbert-st., u.t. 69 yrs., g.r. 10l., 550l.;) to 22, Tisdale-pl., Walworth, u.t. 18 yrs., g.r. 9l. 11s.; l to 81 odd, Tisdale-pl., u.t. 18 yrs., g.r. 30l., 750l.; 22 nd 24, Lingford-st., Battersea, u.t. 23 yrs., g.r. 4l. 10s., 50l.; 2 and 4, Austin-rd., u.t. 22 yrs., g.r. 6l., 175l.—y *Rutley, Son, & Vine*: 115, Stanhope-st., Hampstead-l., u.t. 31 yrs, g.r. 22l., 165l.; 3, Great Percy-st., King's ross, u.t. 27 yrs., g.r. 3l. 10s., 490l.; 39, Blundell-st., aledonian-rd., u.t. 58 yrs., g.r 5l 10s., r. 39l., 240l.—By *astman Bros.*: Eight plots of freehold land, Byne-rd., ydenham, 530l.; three plots of freehold land, Wiverton-d., 225l.; 58, Colfe-rd., Forest Hill, u.t. 84 yrs., g.r. 4l., 40l.; 31, Kemble-rd., u t. 84 yrs., g r. 5l. 10s., 230l.

MAY 3.—By *E. Millard*: "The Crown Inn," Oxted, urrey, f., r. 44l. 10s., 1,600l.; 22 and 24, Larkhall-lane, lapham, f., r. 45l. 12s., 800l.—By *C. N. Philips*: 89, 1, and 97, Canterbury-rd., Kilburn, u.t. 65 yrs., g.r. 15l., 740l.—By *Debenham, Tewson, & Co.*: No. 55, Stamford-hill, with grounds, f., 2,240l.; 18, Camden-rd., Camden-town, u.t. 84 yrs., g.r. 7l., r. 94l. 2s., 900l.; 55, 57, 61, 63, and 67, Highgate-rd., Kentish-town, f., r. 240l., 2,380l.; 41, Old Compton-st., Soho, and 46 Dean-st., f., area 980 ft., subject to an annuity of 20l., life aged 61 yrs., 1,600l.—By *Humbert, Son, & Flint* (at Watford): House and shop and plot of land, Capel-rd., Bushey, f., 600l.; 1 and 2, Victoria-villas, Croxley-green, f., 448l.

MAY 4.—By *Weatherall & Green*: 68, Bonner's-rd., Victoria-pk., u.t. 62 yrs., g.r. 5l. 5s., r. 35l., 310l.; 48, Eleanor-rd., Hackney, u t. 65 yrs., g.r. 6l. 10s., r. 35l., 270l.; 167 to 171, Elwin-st., Bethnal-green, u.t. 30 yrs., g r. 22l. 10s. 990l.—By *R. Tidey & Son*: 30, Benyon-rd., Kingsland, u.t. 35 yrs., g.r. 6l., 325l.; 86, Benyon-rd., u.t. 35 yrs., g.r. 8l. 10s., 330l.—By *Segrave & Taylor*: 8 to 16, Walker-st., Bermondsey; and 21, Staple-st., with reversion in 2 yrs. to r. of 200l. a year, 1,750l.; 13 to 21, Oak Cottages, Bowes-pk., f., r. 152l. 2s., 1,255l.—By *Humbert, Son, & Flint*: 85, Bishopsgate-st. Without, f., area 1,750 ft., 3,000l.; 16 and 18, Palace-ct., Bayswater, f., and stabling, 9,550l.; By *E. S. Dallas*: 17 and 17B, Manchester-st., King's Cross, f., r. 200l., 4,500l.; 20, Liverpool-st., f., r. 38l., 620l.; 20, Red Lion-st., Clerkenwell, f., r. 80l., 1,510l.; 15, 16, 18, 19, 20, Manchester-st., King's Cross; 19, 21, 22, and 23, Liverpool-st., f., r. 392l., 7,610l.

MAY 5.—By *Fuller & Fuller*: An improved rental of 100l., Porchester-ter., Hyde-pk., u.t. 29 yrs., 1,650l.; 94 to 104 (even), Rosoman-st., Clerkenwell, 1A, 1, and 2, Hardwick-st., u.t. 18 yrs., g r. 23l., r. 303l., 1,200l.; 16 and 20, Landrock-rd., Crouch-end, u.t. 97 yrs., g.r. 12l., r. 68l., 540l.—By *Cooper & Goulding*: "Benhilton Cottage," Sutton, f.r. 39l., 480l; "Farm House," Roxborough-rd., Harrow, and 1a. 0r. 12p., f., r. 45l., 790l.: a plot of f. land, 200l.—By *Henry & Latchford*: 37, Bromfelde-rd., Clapham, u.t. 70 yrs., g.r. 6l. 10s., r. 44l., 400l.—By *Newbon & Co.*: 339, York-rd., Battersea, u.t. 69 yrs., g.r. 6l., r. 25l., 250l.; 28, Aberdeen-pk., Highbury, u.t. 63 yrs., g.r. 13l., 1,510l.; 32 and 34, The Broadway, Hackney, and a l.g.r. of 10l. u.t. 45 yrs., g.r. 19l., 620l.; i.g.r. of 50l., Duncan-rd., u.t. 45 yrs., g.r. 15l., 525l.; l.g.r. of 12l., Lowman-rd., Holloway, u.t. 71 yrs., g.r. 5l., 100l.; 13, Kingsdown-rd., u.t. 66 yrs., g.r. 7l., r. 34l., 250l.—By *Stimson & Sons*: 76, Lavender-rd., Battersea, u.t. 49 yrs., g.r. 4l., 235l.; 2 freehold houses, Grey's-hill, Henley-on-Thames, 250l.; 121, Northcote-rd., Wandsworth, f., r. 80l., 490l.; i.g.r. of 6l. 15s., with reversion in 84 yrs., 165l.; 10 to 16 (even), Benfield-st., Battersea, u.t. 65 yrs., g.r. 20l., 600l.; 100 and 102, Culvert-rd., u.t. 61 yrs., g.r. 6l., 310l.; 74 to 84 (even), Carpenter-st., u.t. 79 yrs., g.r. 22l. 10s., 320l.; 1 to 9 (odd), and 32 and 34, Sheepcot-lane, u.t. 84 yrs., g.r. 6l., 510l.—By *Worsfold & Hayward* (*at Dover*): The "Greyhound" public-house, Union-row, Dover, f., r. 18l., 470l.; 25, Trevanion-st., f., r. 18l., 315l.; "The Marine Livery Stables," f., 1,600l.; 13 and 13A, Cannon-st., f., r. 80l., 1,720l.; 13, Woolcomber-st., 13, Military-rd., and 3, Adrian-row, f., 716l.; 3, Albany-pl., u.t. 88 yrs., g.r. 1l., 185l.; three freehold cottages and a stable, Barfrestone, Kent, 305l.; a copyhold meadow, Alkham, Kent, 1a. 3r. 20p., 64l.

MAY 6.—By *Driver & Perfect*: 62, Wrotham-rd., Camden Town, u.t. 59 yrs., g.r. 7l., r. 40l., 330l.; 14, Elm-rd., u.t. 59 yrs., g.r. 8l., r. 40l., 320l.; 1A Murray-st., u.t. 52 yrs., g.r. 10l., r. 45l., 450l.—By *Baker & Sons*: 56 58, 60, 66, and 68, Weymouth-st., Hackney, f., r. 166l., 1,985l.; i.g.r. of 26l., Harvest-rd., Holloway, u.t. 50 yrs., g.r., 2l., 410l.—By *E. Evans*: 7, Palace-rd., Norwood, u t. 62 yrs., g.r., 9l. 9s., 125l.; "Clarendon" and "Drayton" Villas, Queen's-rd., u.t. 68 yrs., g.r. 17l. 8s., 380l.; 6 and 8, Hartland-rd., Kentish Town, u.t. 38 yrs., g.r. 8l., r. 72l. 16s., 380l.; 24, Grafton-st., u.t. 43 yrs., g.r. 5l., r. 32l. 10s., 270l.; 19, Disraeli-rd., Forest Gate, f. 445l.; two plots of freehold land, Raynes-pk., 70l.; eight plots of freehold land Draycot Grove, Surbiton, 106l.; 3, 6 to 9, 11 to 17 odd, Peak Hill Gardens, Sydenham, u.t. 83 yrs., g.r. 81l., 1,090l.

[*Contractions used in these lists.*—F.g.r. for freehold ground-rent; l.g.r. for leasehold ground-rent; i.g.r. for improved ground-rent; g.r. for ground-rent; r. for rent; f. for freehold; c. for copyhold; l. for leasehold; e.r. for estimated rental; u.t. for unexpired term; p.a. for per annum; yrs. for years; st. for street; rd. for road; sq. for square; pl. for place; ter. for terrace; cres. for crescent; yd. for yard, &c.]

PRICES CURRENT OF MATERIALS.

TIMBER.			TIMBER (*continued*).		
Greenheart, B.G. ton	[illegible]	[illegible]	Satin, Porto Rico	[illegible]	[illegible]
Teak, E.I. load	[illegible]	[illegible]	Walnut, Italian	[illegible]	[illegible]
Sequoia, U.S. ft. cu.	[illegible]	[illegible]	METALS.		
Ash, Canada load	[illegible]	[illegible]	Iron—Pig, in Scotland ton	[illegible]	[illegible]
Birch, do.	[illegible]	[illegible]	Bar, Welsh, in London	[illegible]	[illegible]
Elm, do.	[illegible]	[illegible]	Do. do. at works in Wales	[illegible]	[illegible]
Fir, Dantsic, &c.	[illegible]	[illegible]	Do. Staffordshire, in London	[illegible]	[illegible]
Oak, do.	[illegible]	[illegible]	Copper—British, cake and ingot	[illegible]	[illegible]
Canada	[illegible]	[illegible]	Best selected	[illegible]	[illegible]
Pine, Canada red	[illegible]	[illegible]	Sheets, strong	[illegible]	[illegible]
Do. yellow	[illegible]	[illegible]	Chili, bars	[illegible]	[illegible]
Lath, Dantsic, fath	[illegible]	[illegible]	Yellow Metal lb.	[illegible]	[illegible]
St. Petersburg	[illegible]	[illegible]	Lead—Pig, Spanish ton	[illegible]	[illegible]
Deals, Finland, 2nd & 1st std 100	[illegible]	[illegible]	English, com. brands	[illegible]	[illegible]
Do. 4th & 3rd	[illegible]	[illegible]	Sheet, English, 3 lbs. per sq. ft. and upwards	[illegible]	[illegible]
Do. Riga	[illegible]	[illegible]	Pipe	[illegible]	[illegible]
St. Petersburg, 1st yellow	[illegible]	[illegible]	Zinc—English sheet ton	[illegible]	[illegible]
Do. 2nd yellow	[illegible]	[illegible]	Vieille Montagne	[illegible]	[illegible]
Do. white	[illegible]	[illegible]	Tin—Straits	[illegible]	[illegible]
Swedish	[illegible]	[illegible]	Australian	[illegible]	[illegible]
White Sea	[illegible]	[illegible]	English Ingots	[illegible]	[illegible]
Canada, Pine 1st	[illegible]	[illegible]	OILS.		
Do. do. 2nd	[illegible]	[illegible]	Linseed ton	[illegible]	[illegible]
Do. do. 3rd, &c.	[illegible]	[illegible]	Cocoanut, Cochin	[illegible]	[illegible]
Do. Spruce, 1st	[illegible]	[illegible]	Do. Ceylon	[illegible]	[illegible]
Do. do. 3rd & 2nd	[illegible]	[illegible]	Palm, Lagos	[illegible]	[illegible]
New Brunswick	[illegible]	[illegible]	Rapeseed, English pale	[illegible]	[illegible]
Battens, all kinds	[illegible]	[illegible]	Do. brown	[illegible]	[illegible]
Flooring Boards, sq., 1 in. prep. 1st	[illegible]	[illegible]	Cottonseed ref.	[illegible]	[illegible]
Do. 2nd	[illegible]	[illegible]	Oleine	[illegible]	[illegible]
Other qualities	[illegible]	[illegible]	Lubricating, U.S.	[illegible]	[illegible]
Cedar, Cuba ft.	[illegible]	[illegible]	Do. refined	[illegible]	[illegible]
Honduras, &c.	[illegible]	[illegible]	Tar—Stockholm barrel	[illegible]	[illegible]
Mahogany, Cuba	[illegible]	[illegible]	Archangel	[illegible]	[illegible]
St. Domingo, cargo av.	[illegible]	[illegible]			
Mexican do. do.	[illegible]	[illegible]			
Tobacco do. do.	[illegible]	[illegible]			
Honduras do.	[illegible]	[illegible]			
Box, Turkey ton	[illegible]	[illegible]			
Rose, Rio	[illegible]	[illegible]			
Bahia	[illegible]	[illegible]			
Satin, St. Domingo	[illegible]	[illegible]			

TENDERS.

[Communications for insertion under this heading should be addressed to "The Editor," and must reach us *not later than 12 noon on Thursdays.*]

BLACKPOOL.—For the erection of a police-station, offices, cells, &c., for the Corporation. Mr. J. Wolstenholme, Borough Engineer, Town-hall Blackpool:—

William Ives & Co.	£10,819	Wm. Hy. Dean	£9,558
John Walmesley	10,650	Clement Wallworth	9,500
Joseph Fielding & Sons	9,973	Wm. Eayrs & Co.	9,297
Samuel Warburton	9,797	Saml. & James Whitehead, Oldham (accepted)	8,900
Thomas Riley	9,797		

BOURNEMOUTH.—For making new road, &c., in Durley-chine, for the Town Council. Mr. F. W. Lacey, Borough Engineer and Surveyor:—

C. Pike	£1,092 7 0	G. Toke	£806 13
W. H. Saunders & Co.	927 11 0	G. T. & W. Budden, Parkstone*	762 12.
J. Edwards	879 4 0		

* Accepted.

BOURNEMOUTH.—For painting the promenade pier for the Town Council. Mr. F. W. Lacey, Borough Engineer and Surveyor:—

	Whitelead Paint.	Torbay Paint.
F. T. Cutler	£240 0 0	£240 0 0
J. J. Dacombe, Bournemouth*	272 5 0	236 10 0

* Accepted.

BRIGHTON.—For the erection of Public Elementary Schools, Elm-grove, Brighton, for the Brighton and Preston School Board, U.D. Mr Thomas Simpson, 16, Ship-street, Brighton, and Mr. John W. Simpson, 10, New Inn, Strand, W.C., joint architects:—

Killby & Gayford	£12,934 0	J. T. Chappell	£12,061 0
Dean	12,763 0	Reed, Blight, & Co.	11,961 0
Stimpson & Co.	12,646 0	P. Peters*	11,506 15
Longley & Co.	12,375 0		

* Accepted.

BRIGHTON.—Accepted for alterations to the high altar and pulpit, and carving in baptistry, at the Church of the Sacred Heart, West Brighton, for the Rev. S. A. Donnelly. Mr. Joseph Stanislaus Hansom, architect, 27, Alfred-place West, South Kensington:—

R. L. Boulton & Sons, Cheltenham £330 0 0

CANE HILL (Surrey).—For erecting additional buildings, and for alterations, at the Cane Hill Lunatic Asylum, for the London County Council. Mr. G. T. Hine, architect:—

Nudd & Son	£16,656	Reed, Blight, & Co.	£15,416
Kirk & Randall	16,362		

KNAPHILL (Surrey).—For the erection of a pair of cottages at Knaphill, Surrey, for Mr. Alfred Mitchell. Mr. A. J. Sturges, architect and surveyor, Guildford:—

P. C. May	£560 0 0	Charles Thompson	£520 0 0
John Faggetter	532 0 0	Gay Bros., Knaphill*	489 18 0
James Gosden	519 10 0		

* Accepted.

LLANFAIR P.G. (Anglesey).—Accepted for constructing new reservoir, providing hot-water, &c., for Plasnewydd Mansion, for the Marquis of Anglesey. Mr. W. E. Jones, architect, Graig, Llanfair P.G.:—

J. A. Hornby, Menai Bridge £384 0 0

LONDON.—For the erection of a residence and stables, Hornsey-lane, for Mr. H. H. Barrett. Mr. W. Graves, architect, Winchester House, Old Broad-street. Quantities by Mr. J. W. Bailey, 85, High-road, Kilburn:—

Williams & Son	£3,878	Palman & Fotheringham	£3,573
Turtle & Appleton	3,850	Nightingale	3,587
Hall, Bedall, & Co.	3,798	Bowyer	3,441
Grover & Son	3,754	Killby & Gayford	3,439
Stimpson & Co.	3,742	H. & E. Lea	3,427
Scrivener & Co.	3,740	Kearley	3,381
Burman & Sons	3,733	Davies	3,390
Lawrence & Sons	3,716	Gould & Brand	3,331
Macfarlane Bros.	3,606	Toms	3,210
Simpson & Son	3,600	Scharien & Co.	3,191
Harris & Wardrop	3,598	E. Houghton & Son	3,192

LONDON.—For constructional ironwork and stone front at St. Olave's Chambers, Old Jewry. Mr. Delissa Joseph, architect, 17 and 18, Basinghall-street, E.C.:—

Ironwork.

M. T. Shaw & Co. (including fixing)	£264 10 0
R. Moreland & Son (without fixing)	228 0 0
Rownson, Drew, & Co. (including fixing)*	230 0 0

* Accepted.

Portland and Bath Stone Front.

C. W. Matthews	£874 0 0
Webber & Corben	[illegible] 0 0
F. J. Barnes (accepted)	487 0 0

LONDON.—For repairs, additions, new drainage and sanitation to the premises, No. 31, Trevunter-road, South Kensington, for Mr. M. Dodsworth, under the supervision of Messrs. Rogers, Chapman, and Thomas, F.S.I., surveyors, &c., 56, Belgrave-road, S.W.:—

Stimpson & Co.	[illegible]	Howlett & Sons	[illegible]
Whittaker	[illegible]	E. D. Hook*	[illegible]
Lorden & Son	[illegible]	W. Marks	[illegible]
Henry Smith & Son	[illegible]		

* Accepted.

LONDON.—For the erection of a billiard-room and alterations, for the Constitutional Club, Grange-road, Bermondsey, S.E. Mr. L. R. Ford, architect, Railway Approach, London Bridge:—

Almond	[illegible]	Preston	[illegible]
Russell	[illegible]	Bullers*	[illegible]
Wells	[illegible]	White & Co	[illegible]
Fairhead	749		

* Accepted.

LONDON.—Accepted for forming roads, footways, sewers, manholes, &c., complete on the Clock House estate, Tottenham, London, N., for the executors of the late Mr. Joseph Mark. Messrs. Foster & Co., architects:—

W. M. Webster, White Hart-lane, Tottenham £3,600

LONDON.—Accepted for building six villa residences on the Clock House estate, Tottenham, London, N. Messrs. Foster & Co., architects:—

W. M. Webster £3,100

LONDON.—For the enlargement of the Columbia-road School, Bethnal Green, by 398 places, and also for erecting a new house for the schoolkeeper and carrying out other works, for the School Board for London. Mr. T. J. Bailey, Architect:—

W. Gregar & Son	£13,365 0 0	W. M. Dabbs	13,[illegible] 0 0
J. Willmott & Sons	14,335 0 0	J. Grover & Son	12,944 0 0
F. J. Coxhead	14,323 6 11	Killby & Gayford,* 87, Worship-street, Finsbury, E.C.	12,940 0 0
Co-operative Builders, Limited	13,727 0 0		
G. S. S. Williams & Son	13,992 0 0		

*Recommended by the Works Committee for acceptance.

LONDON.—For the enlargement of the Infants' department of the Queen's Head-street School, Islington, by 220 places, and also for improving the drainage of the schoolkeeper's house, for the School Board for London. Mr. T. J. Bailey, Architect:—

C. Dearing & Son .. £2,815 0 0
F. J. Coxhead 2,778 4 9
D. Charteris 2,768 0 0
L. Whitehead & Co. 2,672 0 0
John Garrett & Son, 40, Old Town, Clapham, S.W.* .. £2,640 0 0

* Recommended by the Works Committee for acceptance.

LONDON.—For carrying out drainage and sanitary works in connexion with the Gideon-road School, Lavender-hill, for the School Board for London. Mr. T. J. Bailey, Architect:—

Holloway Bros. £498 0 0
John Garrett & Son, No. 40, Old Town, Clapham, S.W.* 300 0 0

* Recommended by the Works Committee for acceptance.

LONDON.—For pulling-down and rebuilding Nos. 85 to 89, Park-street, Limehouse, for Mrs. Rosher. Messrs. Baggalley & Bristowe, architects:—

Lee £5,924
Rowe Bros. 5,400
Lemon £5,293
Jelly 4,498

LONDON.—For supplying 9in. 6in. 3in. wood blocks for street paving purposes, for the Vestry of St. Pancras:—

	Pitch Pine. £. s. d.	Yellow Deal. £. s. d.	Jarrah. £. s. d.
Bellew & Co.	10 0 0	7 17 0	—
Ellis	9 18 9	7 14 8	14 9 6
Rowe Bros.	8 10 0	8 12 8	19 10 0
Knight & Co.	7 17 6	6 10 0	—

LONDON.—For distempering and other works at the Infirmary of St. Pancras, Dartmouth Park-hill, for the Guardians of St. Pancras:—

J. Dixon £1,195 0
Capell 798 0
Darnall 769 0
Wall & Co. £750 0
Rowe Bros. 745 0
Bangs 742 15

LONDON.—For making and fixing furniture and fittings at the new workhouse, Pancras-road, for the Guardians of St. Pancras:—

Hines £330
Wall & Co. 323
Isom 319
Rowe Bros. £290
J. Dixon 272

NEWPORT (Mon.).—For new Congregational Schools, London-street, Maindee, Newport. Messrs. Habershon & Fawckner, architects, 39, Bloomsbury-square, London:—

A. Hazell £935
J. Linton 917
W. Price 895
E. Richards 892
T. Webb 785
W. M. Blackburn 767
W. A. Linton 760
Moulton & Brownscombe .. 730
T. G. Diamond £745
Dyson Parfitt 744
Morgan & Roberts 740
W. Moore 738
G. F. Sharrem 735
R. Williams & Son (withdrawn) 598

[All of Newport.]

NEWPORT (Mon.).—For rebuilding business premises, 132, 133, Commercial-street, Newport, for Mr. A. W. Bland. Messrs. Habershon & Fawckner, architects, 39, Bloomsbury-square, London:—

E. Richards £4,999
Moulton & Brownscombe.. 4,950
W. Jones & Son 4,947
T. G. Diamond 4,898
C. Lock 4,879
G. Wilkins £4,830
W. Price 4,820
W. M. Blackburn 4,797
Morgan & Roberts 4,785
J. Linton (accepted) 4,760

[All of Newport.]

NORTH ADELAIDE (South Australia).—Accepted for new altar at St. Dominic's Convent, North Adelaide, South Australia. Mr. Joseph S. Hansom, architect, 27, Alfred-place West, South Kensington:—

R. L. Boulton & Sons, Cheltenham.................. £230 0 0

NOTTINGHAM.—For erecting lavatory to Children's Ward, and bath-room and water-closet to Men's Receiving Ward, at the Nottingham Union Workhouse. Mr. A. H. Goodall, architect, Nottingham:—

R. Fisher £152 7 0
H. Vickers 148 0 0
R. Keeling 129 18 0
Emerson & Franks........ 129 0 7
J. Hutchinson 126 0 0
G. Caulton 121 10 0
J. J. Adams.............. 123 12 2
Thos. Cuthbert £123 11 0
J. Attenborrow 122 11 0
Gilbert & Gabbitas...... 122 3 0
W. Gell & Son............ 122 0 0
F. Warinsby 121 6 6
J. Cooper* 120 0 0

* Accepted.

PRETORIA (Transvaal).—For the erection of Bank and Mint buildings, for De Nationale Bank der Z.A.R. Beperkt. Messrs. Emley & Scott, architects, Pretoria and Johannesburg. Quantities by the architects:—

J. Parslow £15,296
J. Clark 15,076
J. Munro 14,780
J. J. Kirkness* 14,027
H. Williams................ £14,569
Hallyburton & Co. 14,490
Murdoch & Haldane 14,400

[Architects' estimate, £15,527.]

* Accepted.

PWLLHELI.—For kerbing, channelling, and paving footways. Messrs. Thomas Roberts & Son, engineers, Portmadoc:—

Griffith Griffith........ £1,697 9
Evan Humphrey 1,156 0
W. & R. Jones, Pwllheli* £1,120 0

* Accepted.

SOUTHEND.—For the erection of new business premises, Southend, for Mr. A. Martin. Mr. E. Wright, architect:—

Baker & Wiseman £3,160
Darke & Sons 3,077
Rowe Bros. 2,930
West £2,918
Dupont, Colchester* 2,889

* Accepted.

[Architect's estimate, £3,092.]

STANLEY (Co. Durham).—Accepted for the erection of dwelling-house and shop, for Mr. J. W. Moffit. Mr. E. F. W. Liddle, architect, 24, Collingwood-street, Newcastle-on-Tyne:—

Woodall & Wilson, Gateshead.................. £674 0 0

TORQUAY.—For additions and alterations to the Torbay Hospital, Torquay. Messrs. Habershon & Fawckner, architects, 39, Bloomsbury-square, London:—

Jackson, Bros. £10,200 0 0
Wm. Mills 9,897 0 0
Stephens & Bastow. 9,450 0 0
R. R. Facey........ 8,850 0 0
J. C. Parker 8,379 0 0
Stephens & Son 7,990 0 0
F. Matthews 7,981 0 0
R. F. Yeo.......... 7,948 0 0
W. W. Sanders £7,947 2 5
Reed, Blight, & Co., Limited 7,897 0 0
W. Goss 7,813 0 0
E. P. Bovey........ 6,678 0 0
W. H. Gooding 6,276 10 0
J. Chubb, Torquay* 6,201 0 0

* Accepted.

TYNEWYDD (Wales).—For erecting new schools to accommodate 300 children at Tynewydd, Ogmore Vale, near Bridgend, for the Llangeinor School Board. Mr. George F. Lambert, architect, Bridgend. Quantities supplied by the architect:—

William McGaul £5,250
David Jenkins 4,800
Daniel Price 4,697
William Lissiman........ 4,500
D. C. Jones & Co., Gloucester (accepted)........ £4,150
Stephens & Bastow 4,190
Thomas Roberts 4,080

WORTHING.—For the erection of two houses and shops in the Railway Approach-road, for Mr. W. Frost. Mr. Reata. W. Moore, architect:—

J. Binker £1,180 10
Inkpen & Sons 1,180 0
G. Baker £1,165 8
W. W. Sandell* 1,148 12

* Accepted.

SUBSCRIBERS in LONDON and the SUBURBS, by prepaying at the Publishing Office, 19s. per annum (or 4s. 9d. per quarter), can ensure receiving "The Builder," by *Friday Morning's Post.*

TERMS OF SUBSCRIPTION.

"THE BUILDER" is supplied DIRECT from the Office to residents in any part of the United Kingdom at the rate of 19s. per annum PREPAID. To all parts of Europe, America, Australia, and New Zealand, 26s. per annum. To India, China, Ceylon, &c., 30s. per annum. Remittances payable to DOUGLAS FOURDRINIER, Publisher, No. 46, Catherine-street, W.C.

TO CORRESPONDENTS.

C. O.—W. H. R.—W. G.—W. P. T. & Co.—W. W. (thanks).—"Crusi" (It is impossible to say without an examination of the work, or a detail drawing of the windows).—A. L. L. (too late to find any space this week).—F. [illegible] F.—J. [illegible] (we cannot publish tenders without amounts).—J. A. (ditto).

All statements of facts, lists of tenders, &c., must be accompanied by the name and address of the sender, not necessarily for publication.

We are compelled to decline pointing out books and giving addresses.

NOTE.—The responsibility of signed articles, and papers read at public meetings, rests, of course, with the authors.

We cannot undertake to return rejected communications.

Letters or communications (beyond mere news-items) which have been duplicated for other journals, are NOT DESIRED.

All communications regarding literary and artistic matter should be addressed to THE EDITOR; all communications relating to advertisements and other exclusively business matters should be addressed to THE PUBLISHER, and *not* to the Editor.

The Builder.

Vol. LXII. No. 2572. Saturday, May 21, 1892.

ILLUSTRATIONS.

Sheffield Municipal Buildings.—Mr. E. W. Mountford, Architect:—
Grand Staircase .... *Double-Page Ink-Photo.*
Surrey-street Front .... *Double-Page Ink-Photo.*
View towards Churchyard .... *Double-Page Ink-Photo.*
Music-Room, "Highlands," Putney Heath.—Mr. W. D. Caröe, Architect .... *Double-Page Photo-Litho.*

Blocks in Text.

Diagrams in Student's Column: Heating by Hot Water .... Pages 401-405

CONTENTS.

w Chapters in Greek History 391
e Competition for the Christchurch New Cathedral, Victoria, B.C. 392
tes 393
chitecture at the Royal Academy.—IV. 394
nch Art of the Year 395
e Royal Institute of British Architects 396
e Nottingham Sewage Farm 399
e Architectural Association's Spring Visits 399
ffield Municipal Buildings 400
sic Room, "Highlands," Putney Heath 400
e Architectural Association 400
Architectural Societies 402
The London County Council 402
Royal Meteorological Society 402
Books: S. Bottone's "Guide to Electric Lighting" (London: Whittaker & Co.); G. R. Redgrave's "History of Water-Colour Painting in England" (London: Sampson Low, Marston, & Co.); W. H. White's "Architect and his Artists" (London: Spottiswoode & Co.); "Royal Academy and New Gallery Pictures" (Office of *Black and White*); P. Lindley's "New Holidays in Essex" (London: 30, Fleet-street) 403
The Architectural Association 403
Boston Church 404
St. Peter's Church, Bushey Heath 404
Student's Column.—Warming Buildings by Hot Water, XXI. 404
Surveyorship 405
Obituary 405
General Building News 405
Sanitary and Engineering News 406
Stained Glass and Decoration 406
Foreign and Colonial 407
Miscellaneous 407
Meetings 408
Recent Patents 408
Some Recent Sales of Property 409

New Chapters in Greek History.

WE have been asked more than once, "Is there any readable book that gives the outcome of all these recent excavations?" and up to the present time we have had always to reply the negative and dismiss the dejected quirer with references to Jahrbuchs and illetins which we know perfectly well he s neither time nor inclination to consult. ofessor Gardner has, we are sure, supplied very real need in the work now issued.* My endeavour," he says in the preface, has been to set forth briefly and, if possible, a way tending to interest all phil-Hellenes, gains which the excavations of the last enty years have brought us in regard to our owledge of Greek history, using the word his-y in the widest sense, as covering not only litical events but all sides of the activity of nation. I have written," he goes on to r, "not for archæologists, but for the ordi-ry educated reader, for those who are quainted with the literature, or the history, the art of Greece, and who wish to fill up lacunæ, or to learn in what directions spade is increasing our acquaintance with cient Hellas."

The book is in part a reprint. A consider-le portion of chapter iv., the Palace at yns; vi., Ancient Cyprus; vii., Naucratis d the Greeks in Egypt; viii., the excava-ns in the Athenian Acropolis; ix., Olympia d its Festival; xv., the successors of Alex-der, have already appeared in the *Quarterly view*; chapter ix., on reliefs and inscrip-ns of Athenian Tombs, in the *Contem-ary;* xi., on Spartan Tombs and the ltus of the Dead, in the *Fortnightly;* parts i., on the Verification of Ancient History d on Recent Discoveries and the Homeric poem, in *Macmillan's*. On the other hand, the chapters on Phrygia and Troas, Mycenæ and the islands, Epidaurus and Ancient Medicine, Eleusis and the Mysteries, and Dodona and the Oracles, are mainly new. With the exception of the last chapter on the Successes of Alexander all the published articles are carefully revised up to date.

No one but a thoroughly furnished archæologist could travel with comfort over a field so wide as the mere enumeration of the titles of the chapters indicates; no mind but one exceedingly wary and well-balanced could keep a safe foothold among pitfalls so precarious. Professor Gardner is all these things, and, most of all, he is a man of peace, contending steadfastly enough for the truth, but with little instinctive love of conflict. Naukratis, Mycenæ, Troy,—their very names are as the trumpet to the archæological war-horse; in Professor Gardner they stir the steady glow of a scholar's enthusiasm, but no heat and fury of the battle. How rigidly, too, he can resist what must have been temptation is shown by the significant fact that there is no chapter on that red rag, the Greek theatre.

We naturally turn first to see what Professor Gardner has to say on the question of supreme interest for the moment,—the relation of the Schliemann discoveries to the Homeric poems. The chapters that precede we need not dwell on in detail; they present admirable summaries of the explorations of Professor Ramsay in Asia Minor, and of the details of the Schliemann excavations. The account of these last was, in the main, written before the appearance of the English edition of Dr. Schuchardt's book. It is interesting to compare Professor Gardner's view with that presented by Dr. Leaf in his admirable preface to the English version. The issue,—for issue there is,—stands thus:—"Mr. Monro and Mr. Leaf are both disposed to think that most of the Homeric poems were composed by Achæans before the Dorian conquest, and taken to Asia by the colonists." "This," writes Professor Gardner, "I cannot concede; for it seems to me certain that the poets who wrote them were speaking of a past which lay some distance behind them." To put it a little more fully, Dr. Leaf holds that there is, at all events, a possibility that the oldest parts of the "Iliad" at least may be actual survivals in their present form from Achæan and pre-Dorian days. "This view, setting aside philological arguments as a working hypothesis, certainly relieves the archæologist of grave difficulties; the poems are then allowed to depict actually and as contemporaries what they pretend to depict,—*i.e.*, the Achæan age. We understand at once how they can present, with such vivid life a state of manners and customs which must have been utterly unknown to the Ionians of the coast of Asia Minor." These Ionians were eager traders, democratic, full of enterprise, ever intent on widening their horizon, the very antipodes of the Homeric Achæans, ancient families, aristocratic, patriarchal, conservative, stay-at-home. That an Ionian could depict such an age in life-like fashion is an assumption, Dr. Leaf holds, that strains all probability; for it not only assumes a trained historic imagination, but involves actual archæological study such as is absolutely foreign to the genius of a young and rising nation. We confess we are with Dr. Leaf. The whole of Professor Gardner's argument for the wide chronological gap that separates the writer of the Homeric poem from the age he depicts is vitiated by this assumption of a certain archæological consciousness in that writer or writer's mind. Anachronisms, Professor Gardner writes, "were kept out of their epic poems on the same principle on which a writer of pastoral idyls in our day would avoid the mention of the telegraph or telephone." We must register our distinct conviction on the opposite side, as we believe, with Dr. Leaf, that the writers describe in reality the age they profess to describe,—an age as regards the earliest parts of the poem contemporary with themselves, depicted by no effort of historic imagination; and, further, that this age is the age of the builders of the beehive tombs. On this supposition the Homeric poems are brought into close and actual contact with the Mycenæ excavations, — a contact far closer than Professor Gardner will allow. So temperate, however, is his tone here, as always, that a misconception we believe to be somewhat fundamental scarcely vitiates at all his interesting account of the facts.

* "New Chapters in Greek History. Historical results recent excavations in Greece and Asia Minor." By rcy Gardner, M.A., Litt.D., Lincoln and Merton fessor of Classical Archæology and Art, Oxford; late ney Professor of Archæology, Cambridge, with strations. London: John Murray, Albemarle-street. 2.

The chapter on ancient Cyprus is a record of shame for England. We need not tell again the melancholy tale of the Cesnola excavations: perhaps the only civilised Government which would have tolerated such proceedings is the English; we wilfully tore up a chapter in ancient history committed to our charge, and civilised Europe is not likely to let us forget it. The Cyprus Exploration Fund is doing what it can with meagre resources to wipe out by private effort the public blot, but large sums are needed, and scarcely likely to be forthcoming before the excavations can be in an adequate way completed. Something, however, has been done. Three classes of tombs—Primitive, Phœnician, and Græco-Roman have been cleared out; the plan of the Temple of Aphrodite at Paphos has shown us how widely different was an Oriental sanctuary from a Greek temple; and a number of richly-painted terra-cotta statues have taught us something of the art of a people who thought more of dress than its wearer,—an art so languid that it imitated the style of any one of the more living arts of the nations round.

The story of Naukratis is told with special fulness and vivacity. The excavations there owed much to the zeal and scholarship of Mr. Ernest Gardner, and Professor Gardner's interest is rightly and naturally personal as well as professional. At Naukratis, we English have redeemed something of the prestige that we lost at Cyprus, and we have discovered most where we looked for least. Time, which has destroyed all that was splendid in the temples of Naukratis,—the marble pillars, the cultus statues, the dedicated vessels of gold and silver,—has made some amends by preserving to us their rubbish-heaps. As the temples became too full of votive offerings, dedicated and usually inscribed by the Greek traveller who had reached Egypt in safety, the temple officers would dig a trench, break up the anathemata for economy of space, and bury those they judged superfluous. From these trenches thousands of fragments of vases (many now in the British Museum), painted and inscribed, have been rescued. Before visiting these treasures, or referring to the official report and its plates, every reader will do well to run through Professor Gardner's interesting historical and topographical sketch, he will save himself much wandering in the bye-paths of ancient history, and he could not take a safer guide.

The chapter on the excavations of the Acropolis is largely in substance a review of that very Dörpfeldian book, "Mythology and Monuments of Ancient Athens." To this book the most generous justice is done, though Professor Gardner himself refuses to give anything like exclusive attention to the voice of the charmer. He is not the least convinced by Dr. Dörpfeld's arguments as to the preservation down to the times of Pausanias of the "old Athene Temple." Still less does he hold with Miss Harrison that when Pausanias speaks of the Temple of Athene Polias, and the treasures it contained, he intends not, as all writers have hitherto supposed, a part of the complex building called the Erechtheion, but this most ancient Temple of Athens." He goes on to say, "at the same time she is obliged to allow that the very archaic wooden figure of Athene, which the people of Athens guarded as their most important and venerable treasure, was preserved under the roof of the Erechtheion thus acknowledging in her theory a weakness which if not fatal is at least serious." The fact is, we believe, that Miss Harrison considers the supposed Athene was originally no Athene at all, but an old stock image belonging to a cult that existed long before Athene came to the Acropolis, an image, namely, of *Gaia*-Pandrosos, the early form of the goddess known as Demeter, and worshipped at Athens as at Thebes in primitive Pelasgian days, just such an image as that of which Tertullian pertinently remarks "the Karian Ceres which is a formless effigy, and consists of an unhewn and shapeless stock." Such an image would rightly be housed in the old museum of cults, the Erechtheion.

The remaining chapters may be dealt with more briefly. In the account of Olympia so much space is given to the Athletic contests that its careful reading by large numbers of educated Englishmen to whom the bulk of archæology is unsympathetic may be taken as assured. Professor Gardner is an acknowledged authority on the subject. The two next chapters are to be taken in conjunction, and had we had the ordering of the book we should certainly have reversed their sequence. "Spartan Tombs and the Culture of the Dead,"—a most valuable and well-nigh complete study,—should have preceded "Reliefs and Inscriptions on Athenian Tombs." Beautiful—universally admired as they are—Athenian grave-reliefs have, as the author fully recognises, a coldness and emptiness of faith that is disappointing. "One closes the Corpus of Sepulchral Inscriptions with a feeling of surprise—surprise that a people so gifted as the Athenians should be so helpless and tongue-tied in the presence of death." We have written so lately on the subject of Athenian beliefs, as reflected in tombs and burial customs, that we cannot do more than say that the account of the Cultus of the Dead is admirable,—only noting that we do not think Professor Gardner allows sufficient weight to the influence of the art type of the Spartan on the Athenian reliefs. The chapter in Epidaurus is to us the least satisfactory of all, the account of the monuments, ground plan, and chiefly of the inscriptions is good and full, but Professor Gardner ignores wholly a book which he can scarcely have left unread; the "Isyllus" of Dr. Wilamowitz Moellendorff, a book of which it is not too much to say that it revolutionises wholly our views of the cult of Æsculapius. Professor Gardner seems still to hold (and we feel sure he must have his ground for so doing, only he nowhere states it) the old view we thought exploded of the late rise of the cult of the god—whereas Wilamowitz traces him back to the earliest days of primitive Thessalian worships. The chapters on Eleusis and Dodona, which might well have opened the book, are delightful reading. On the delicate ground of the mysteries the writer holds an even path between the absurd credulities of Warburton and the brilliant but too destructive rationalism of the great Lobeck. He points out in interesting fashion that in the Sekos of Eleusis we have the only one and ancient parallel to a Christian church or a place for the assembling of the worshippers. He also shows that the excavations have made clear that no elaborate scenic effects, such as the ascent and descent from and into subterranean chambers, could have been attempted. Into the complex question of the stratification of the various temples, wisely, in a book for popular use, he does not enter. In taking leave of a delightful book, we can only emphatically record that what the author has attempted he has attained. To use his own apt phraseology, he has fulfilled the mission of the archæologist—he has furthered not only the *veri*fication but the *vivi*fication of ancient history.

THE COMPETITION FOR THE CHRISTCHURCH NEW CATHEDRAL, VICTORIA, B.C.

THE drawings submitted in this competition have recently been exhibited at the Church House. The fourteen sets of drawings received, six being by Colonial and eight by English architects, have been judged by the assessor, Sir Arthur Blomfield, but the purport of his award has up to the present been purposely concealed.*

Briefly summarised, the conditions ask for a stone church in the Gothic style, to seat 1,200. The cost is to be limited to 30,000*l.*, and the design is to be capable of being carried out in three sections. Three premiums were offered, of 150*l.*, 100*l.*, and 50*l.* The assessor has selected the three best designs, we are told, and the final selection will be made by the Committee on the spot.

The three selected competitors will be required to prepare further plans and specifications, and the cost will be made a condition of payment of premium. No premium is to be awarded if the cost is 10 per cent. beyond the stated sum.

The site is on the top of a hill, which can be seen from the bay in approaching the town.

In the absence of the award of the assessor, we have made our own selection, and this has been the easier, owing to the low standard of design which marks the majority.

There is one design, that of "Old and New," which stands far beyond all others in artistic treatment, and there are two others which are good in a less degree, under the mottos "Ars" and "Duomo."

The arrangement of the plan of "Old and New" comprises a nave of three bays with north and south aisles, which are to be retained for monuments unless extra seats are required, and for this purpose the windows are kept high. The nave is entered from a porch with west and north doors. There are also north and south transepts of small projection, and these are respectively flanked by the morning chapel and the vestries. The choir is surrounded by choir aisles, and the ambulatory at the back of the altar is prolonged into one walk of the cloisters, which surround a courtyard with a fountain in the centre. This is placed immediately behind the morning chapel, and on the opposite side of the cloisters to the west a rectangular chapter-house is placed. The variety of the plan is likely to lead to good elevations, and there is no disappointment in that respect. The west elevation is flanked by two towers which are kept plain in character. They are relieved by two rich staircase turrets placed against them, and finished with timber flèche roofs. The whole of the west end between these two turrets is occupied by a two-light traceried window of much beauty of design. A flat arch below, spanning the whole width over the west doorway, is also a noticeable feature. Above the window a gable encloses a figure-subject of the Crucifixion. The gable is surmounted by an open stonework tower, standing on the piers of the porch through which is apparent a slender spirelet. The treatment of the west end is original and the lines of the steps that approach the entrance enhance the beauty that the design undoubtedly possesses. The angles of the transepts and the east end are each marked by a turret. The architectural quality of this design is much in advance of the remainder and, in our opinion, to this must be assigned the first place.

The second place we should assign to the design by "Ars," which is treated in a plain Early Gothic style of a severe type, but the proportions are, in most cases, good. The plan shows a nave of six bays, north and south aisles. The entrances are from the west front and a south porch. A north entrance porch also leads into the transept. A central tower and spire marks the intersection of nave and transepts. The chancel is in three bays, and is furnished with return-stalls for the clergy. There are also choir aisles, and a passage at the back of the altar. It is proposed to build an octagonal chapter-house at the south-east corner, with entrance from the choir-passage.

The third place we should assign to "Duomo," though it cannot be called a very good design. The fault of the design is the massive, ill-proportioned exterior appearance of the domical covering, which has not been at all happily treated. The plan shows a narthex at the west end, with entrance from north and south, and a small circular baptistery in the west wall. The nave is in six bays, with north and south aisles, and a dome in wood marks the intersection. The south transept has an entrance porch and a gallery

* Sir A. Blomfield considers that it would be hardly right to make the award public in this country before the Committee at Victoria, by whom he was commissioned as assessor, can have received it and sanctioned its publication; and in this of course we entirely concur with him.

nd a morning chapel and the Bishop's vestry re on this side of the chancel. The chapter-ouse is at the east end. The choir appears to e too small. "Old and New" is really the nly design of first-class merit; and those eyond the three we have mentioned do not resent any qualities to call for serious con-ideration or description. The exhibition robbed of much interest by the inevitable bsence of the assessor's award and the names f the architects who have sent in designs. Ve shall await the issue of the award with ome interest.

NOTES.

A SIGNIFICANT feature of the recent discussion between Lord Salisbury and the labour delegates on the eight hours ques-ion was the unanimity with which all the peakers deprecated strikes. The unfortu-ate people involved in the Durham miners' ispute have certainly good reason to enounce in unmeasured terms this bar-arous and, as it has proved, wholly abortive ethod of endeavouring to settle wages uestions. The strikers themselves,—that is o say, the majority of them,—only very eluctantly recognised the futility of their emand for the old rate of wages, and it was ot until last Saturday week that they mpowered the Federation Board to try and rrange matters on the best obtainable terms. 'he Board offered, on behalf of the men, to esume work at a reduction of 7½ per cent.,—recisely the terms submitted to them by the wners at the commencement of the dispute; ut it was shown that it was now too late in e day to take that figure as a basis for ettlement. Weeks and months of dead loss, wing greatly to the unreasoning hostility of e strikers, has placed the coal-owners in a r worse position than when they declared a ½ per cent. reduction imperative; while e men have sacrificed an immense sum wages unavailingly and unnecessarily. at they are beginning to recognise that eir policy has been a mistaken one is idenced by an expression on the part of e Federation Board of their willingness, at e earliest possible moment after re-starting ork, to recommend the formation of a Wages oard for the settlement of all wages ques-ons in the future. Such boards have proved ccessful in various industries throughout e country,—and, we believe, in other dis-icts, in the coal trade itself,—and the sooner e Durham colliers protect themselves in is way from the possibility of the recur-nce of such a disastrous conflict as this, the tter it will be for them and the country at rge. There can be no doubt, however, that e mischief already done is to a great tent irreparable. For one thing, so much outside" coal is getting a footing in places retofore drawing their supplies wholly from e Durham pits, that some of the latter will ver again, probably, have an output equal that of the past, while the actual damage stained at other pits through the compul-ry stoppage of various necessary operations ill also have the effect of preventing many the men from resuming their work when a ttlement is arrived at. The miners' latest ggestion is the withdrawal of all previous fers, and the submission of the matter to en arbitration.

THE concession obtained by Mr. Blundell Maple in regard to cheap trains on the etropolitan Railway, and, in consequence, the Manchester, Sheffield, and Lincoln-ire Railway at the London end, when com-leted, is of importance. The maximum fare r five miles and under, including return, is d., and for longer distances in proportion. his concession rendered any further dis-ssion of a new clause in the Manchester, heffield, and Lincolnshire Railway Com-anies' Bill on its third reading last week nnecessary. This increase of facilities for orkmen's locomotion will certainly make this railway extension popular among large numbers of artisans, though it will in no way lessen the dislike with which the residents in the neighbourhood of St. John's-wood regard, and must continue to regard, the placing of a new terminus in this locality. Advantages of this kind procured for the artisan classes by Members of Parliament on the Conservative side, and such legislation as the recent Factory Act, are noteworthy, because they show that the interests of the working man are not neglected, even if he is not represented by members of his own class.

MR. LAWSON TAIT, the well-known Birmingham surgeon, last week unveiled a fountain and clock tower at Willenhall, which has been erected by the inhabitants to the memory of Dr. Joseph Tonks, who died at the early age of thirty-five. Among many suitable remarks, Mr. Tait, in his speech at the dinner given in the evening, threw out the useful and somewhat original suggestion that, instead of the senseless practice of erecting monuments to the dead in cemeteries, it would be a more useful tribute to their memory to erect drinking fountains and clock towers in the streets, place pictures in public buildings, and make improvements in schools. This is a suggestion which is worth taking to heart, and, though it might lead to the production of objects of indifferent taste at first, it must lead to useful results from a sanitary, if not always from an æsthetic, point of view. In the long run it would certainly lead to a more varied, and probably a higher, form of art than we find among the tombstones in the majority of churchyards and cemeteries. The rapidity of the growth of opinion in favour of cremation must help to the formation of new views of the construction of memorial to the dead; and, seeing that cremation is advocated solely on sanitary grounds, it must eventually become associated with other public sanitary measures like fountains, public buildings, playing-fields, public gardens, and the like. At present the memorials which are not raised in the churchyards and cemeteries go to the decoration of the church itself, but, while these need not be neglected, the town-hall, public library, market-place, and the streets, should not be forgotten. Even in the matter of restoration and preservation, there are many public objects such as market crosses, tolbooths, sundials, and bridges, which are falling to decay more from lack of thought of their guardians than wilful negligence, and the preservation of which would be more interesting and useful memorials of fellow-townsmen than the monotonous structures raised to them in the cemeteries.

THE first important step taken by the "Architekten Verein" of Berlin as regards the alteration of the general building regulations of 1887 was taken last week. The nature of the alterations thought necessary, from the architects' and land-proprietors' points of view, was described by Herr Heim. The main points for alteration, according to his report, refer to (1) the proportion of ground that may be covered by buildings on small sites, (2) the planning of basement floors, (3) the maximum height of the top floor of a house above the street level (at present only 17·5 mètres), and (4) the more lucid wording of the disputed paragraphs of the present code. The proposals of the Architekten Verein (as well as those of the Vereinigung Berliner Architekten) will probably receive due consideration by the Government Board of Works when the alteration of the code is under their consideration, but we scarcely believe that concessions will be made where the owners of land and their professional advisers would most wish it, even at the cost of lesser light and air and a worse hygiene for the city. The authorities will probably grant facilities where they are least expected,—*i.e.*, in those paragraphs which were framed to ensure the "fire protection" of the city. Some of these paragraphs are practically of little use, as, for example, that which requires each house to have a passage through which a fire-engine, fully horsed and manned, can be run into a courtyard, a facility which no firemen have ever made use of. This regulation, which has caused endless trouble to architects, will probably be expunged, while, on the other hand, a provision for two staircases to all tenement mansions may be substituted.

THE case of The Churchwardens and Overseers of Norwood *v.* Salter, which was decided by Mr. Justice Hawkins and Mr. Justice Collins a few days ago, settles an important practical point of rating law. Without going into technical details, and into the construction of some Acts of Parliament, which, like a good many statutes, are obscure, it is sufficient to say that by the Poor Rate Assessment Act, 1869, the owner of houses under the annual value of 8*l*. can contract with the parish to pay the rates instead of the occupiers, receiving in return a certain sum in the nature of discount. The object of this arrangement is twofold: the parish gets its rates with certainty and without difficulty, and the ratepayer in return for his responsibility gets a small pecuniary advantage. The question which the Court had to decide was whether, when the annual value of the house rose above 8*l*. (in the present instance it reached 11*l*.) during the period of the agreement, the occupier, and not the owner, could be charged with the rates. The Court decided in effect that the increase in the annual value nullified the agreement, and that the occupier, on whom the primary liability for the payment of rates falls by the general law, became *ipso facto* as responsible as if no arrangement had been made. If this decision proves, as we think it may, inconvenient in practice, some member of Parliament will have to remedy it by a statute.

FROM May 5 to 8, 1842, the great fire of Hamburg raged, and left a large part of the city proper in ruins. Last week the fiftieth anniversary of the rebuilding of the city was celebrated, and due regard was taken of all those who had so earnestly laboured at the time to overcome the difficulties of rapid reconstruction, and at the same time to improve the portions of the town which were destroyed. Amongst the hardest workers were the members of the "Special Building Commission," which included the civil engineer, W. Lindley, and the architect, G. Semper. This Commission, which was but three and a half years in existence, did wonders. Under its direction a very valuable survey of the site was made, the streets were newly laid out, new building regulations framed, public and private buildings rebuilt, and various improvements, including the first laying of a good sewerage system, the construction of gas and water works, and the reconstruction of harbour and canal embankments, carried out. Mr. Lindley was the member of the Commission to whom Hamburg owes the original plan of the reconstruction of the streets destroyed. Unfortunately, the great extension of road traffic was not foreseen, and hence the city at present has to complain of having too narrow thoroughfares. The development of Hamburg since 1842 is something remarkable, especially in the last decade. What with its new free harbour, which is continually being extended, and its excellent Board of Works, which pays attention to the artistic as well as the practical side of every improvement taken in hand, Hamburg may be said to hold its own as the finest of the Continental commercial ports.

WE regret to hear that there has been a serious proposal entertained to alter and add to the east end of the fine parish church at Wrexham. Of course we should maintain, as we have always maintained, that if there is a real necessity to enlarge an ancient church to accommodate an increased congregation, practical requirements must take the lead. But, if we are to take the very full report of a recent vestry meeting given in a copy of the *Wrexham Advertiser* which has been forwarded to us, as a guide, it seems very doubtful whether the circumstances can be said to constitute a practical necessity. The main point in favour of the alterations seems to be that the Vicar wishes to get the organ removed to the east end, and there is not space for it there at present. In the present day, when an organ can be arranged to be played from any part of the church by electric connexion, there is not nearly so much reason for the eastern position as there used to be; the organist can sit with the choir, though the organ remain at the other end, and can thus hear them and regulate his accompaniment accordingly, and there is no doubt that the effect of the organ itself is far better at the west end of the church than in an organ-chamber or aisle near the chancel. The present position of matters is that a resolution was carried to the effect "that the further consideration of the plans and report be postponed for two months [one of which has now nearly run out], and that the Wardens obtain in the meantime an elevation and plan of the proposed alterations at the east end, and also consult a leading organ-builder as to the advisability of removing the organ from the west to the east end of the church." The architects who have been consulted are Messrs. Middleton, Protheroe, & Phillot; the head of the firm is the well-known Slade Professor of Fine Art, and we should hope that under such advice all possible respect would be paid to the claims of the ancient structure, and that nothing would be done in any case which would architecturally disfigure the church; but we very much doubt whether there are sufficient grounds for meddling with it at all. A correspondent at Wrexham assures us that the congregation is not increasing in numbers, owing to the fact that many who lived in the town are drifting out to the suburbs.

CORONERS' juries are not always the best guides in technical and professional matters, but a recommendation attached to a verdict recently given by a jury in America is hardly to be wondered at. During a high wind last April a building in course of erection in Chicago was blown down, six persons being killed and several more injured. At first the disaster was looked on as a natural result of the exceptional force of the wind, it apparently not occurring to anyone that, even for the short time that buildings are in course of construction in Chicago, they might be at the mercy of a gale springing up. The coroner's inquest, however, has brought to light some unpleasant facts, and the jury has had the courage to return a verdict in accordance with the evidence. The "architect" is said to have been simply a contractor, and therefore, presumably, with no professional training. The work was found to have been improperly carried out, and the inspection, which should have been made by the public authority appointed for the purpose, is described as having been a "mere pretence." The jury have, accordingly, found the accident to be due to criminal carelessness on the part of the Commissioner of Buildings, two of the inspectors of the Building Department, and the owner and architect of the building, and the case will be presented to the grand jury. The recommendation of the coroner's jury is that architects should be required to take out licences after proving their competency, but as no architect appears to have been employed in the case under notice, the recommendation has somewhat the appearance of a *non sequitur*.

ON June 21 will be offered for sale, at the Mart, the Lavington and Beechwood House Estates, of about 3,100 acres, in West Sussex, lying within Rotherbridge Hundred and the Rape of Arundel. Lavington (or more correctly Woolavington) and West Lavington parishes consist of certain scattered portions. In the Conqueror's day the manor, being nine hides, was held of Earl Roger de Montgomeri by Ivo, and of Earl Godwin by a Godwin. It subsequently passed to the D'Albinis and Fitzalans, and has become part of the honour of Petworth. The large house built here by a Garton in 31st Elizabeth was replaced with a smaller one, after J. Lewis's designs, in 1794, by John Sergeant, who had succeeded to the property on marriage with Charlotte Betteswerth. In the churchyard at West Lavington Richard Cobden was buried. This property, standing above the valley of the Rother, and comprising portion of the timber-covered Downs, commands a fine view over the Weald.

IN a "Note" on November 16, 1889, we printed a brief description of Her Majesty's Theatre, which, together with the "United Hotel," is about to be demolished to make way for, it is said, a new hotel. The site has been that of an opera-house for nearly two hundred years, one having been opened by Betterton on April 19, 1705. The former house on this site is worthy of remembrance as that wherein some of Handel's works, including several of his operas, "Israel in Egypt" and "Belshazzar," and, we believe, "Acis and Galatea," were first performed in London.

AT the Vienna Exhibition a gold medal for painting has been awarded to Mr. John R. Reid for his painting "The Shipwrecked," the same very powerful work, we presume, which was exhibited at the Royal Academy three or four years ago. This is the fourth gold medal which Mr. Reid has received during the past five years, the others being, Berlin 1887; Paris, 1889; Munich, 1890.

THE *Manchester Guardian* published on Tuesday a map of the drainage basin of the river Irwell, showing by varied shading which districts have undertaken sewage schemes, which have completed them, and which are still persisting in polluting the river. The districts have been thus classified in a Report recently presented to the Mersey and Irwell Joint Committee by their chief inspector. The local boards which pollute the Irwell are, according to the map, Whitworth, Ramsbottom, Bury, Radcliffe, Little Lever, Kersley, Failsworth, Droylsden, and Gorton.

ARCHITECTS in Wales (or some of them) seem to have an eye to business in a sense which is not to be approved, if we may judge from the prospectus of the "Wales and West of England Girder Company" which has been sent to us. Five of the directors are architects, and the circular states that the company "will be in a great measure co-operative in its transactions, embracing as it does architects, engineers, contractors, builders, iron merchants, &c., and therefore the Directors have every confidence in its success." Further on it is stated that "the Directors will give the preference in allowing shares to Consumers or Professional men who can introduce business to the Company." As far as the "professional men" are concerned that means, of course, that they are to specify the Company's iron work for use in their clients' buildings, in order to swell the profits of the Company of which they are shareholders. None of the "Director" architects, we are glad to find, are members of the Institute.

BARRETT BROWNING MEMORIAL, LEDBURY.—The competition for the Barrett Browning memorial at Ledbury has resulted in the selection of the design by Mr. Brightwen Binyon, of Ipswich; that by Mr. Lunn, of Malvern, being placed second. The designs will be exhibited for a few days at the Town-hall at Ledbury.

ARCHITECTURE AT THE ROYAL ACADEMY.—IV.

1,669; "Reredos for Grayingham Church, Lincolnshire;" Mr. A. H. Skipworth. A very delicate little water-colour drawing; over the centre portion, in which is a sculpture of the Crucifixion, is a projecting semi-octagon canopy of Late Gothic form and general detail; the side panels are filled with pierced ornament with a blue ground behind, which is only partially orthodox, and partially a free floral detail. Two narrow niches divide the centre from the side panels. This is a delicate and original bit of work.

1,671; "Mosaic Pavement at Torcello;" Mr. A. C. Blomfield. Not exactly what is generally understood by mosaic, it is rather a marble inlay, of unusual colouring, the effect of which is well conveyed in the water-colour drawing.

1,672; "An Artist's House at Croydon;" Mr. C. Henman. It has three plans showing how the studio is connected with the house off a landing of the staircase, in a convenient fashion yet so as to keep it a little apart: the small house is compactly planned, but there is not anything in the design which especially marks it out as an artist's house, the architectural treatment being a common enough type of country-house picturesque. The studio window rightly makes a point in the exterior design.

1,674; "Cloisters, Xanten, Germany;" Mr. H. W. Brewer. This and 1,694 ("Choir, Xanten") are drawings which have appeared in our pages, or rather they are the pencil forms of drawings executed in ink for this journal. The subjects will be found in the *Builder* for April 5 and May 3, 1890. The pencil drawings are admirable specimens of effect produced without labour, being in fact very slight and free in execution, but quite complete in effect.

1,675 we have already noticed; 1,676 "Porch: Modena Cathedral," and 1,677, "Doorway, Genoa Cathedral," both by Mr. F. W. Bedford, are among the drawings, we presume, which were skied by the painter R.A. who wished to "cover the walls" in a symmetrical manner; they are probably good sketches, but cannot be seen. 1,678, the large frieze by Mr. Babb, we have already referred to; 1,679, the staircase of the Sheffield Municipal Buildings, to which we have also referred, is published in the present number.

1,680; "Staircase, Buller's Wood, Chislehurst"; Mr. Ernest Newton. A pleasantly-treated simple staircase interior, with an arcade of two arches over the first landing, carried on a column seated on the newel, and which is made to show up effectively, white against the shadowed portion of the upper staircase. The drawing is a slight but very artistically-executed one by Mr. Raffles Davison.

1,681; "Design for Memorial to Mary Tudor, St. Mary's Church, Bury St. Edmund's;" Mr. A. E. Street. We published a lithograph from this drawing on May 14, to which we can refer the reader for the design, though it does not give the colour and marble texture, which are very well rendered in the drawing. This is a very interesting variation on the sarcophagus type of tomb, with what we take to be a bronze cross and canopy affixed to the top of it, in relief from the curved surface of the marble. The three small plaques in the side of the monument are filled up with yellowish veined marble, which we suppose has some purpose of taking inscriptions or engraved symbols, not indicated on the drawing; as mere plaques they cannot be said to have any decorative value, in regard to form at least, though the colour harmonises well with that of the darker marble. But in the main this is a very interesting and well considered piece of work. Perhaps the brackets at the end have a little too much the suggestion of being clamps to hold the whole together.

1,682; "Corner of a Drawing-room"; Mr. J. Armstrong Stenhouse. The title is we believe a blunder of the Academy catalogue, and is that of another drawing which was not hung, the real title of this being 'Interior of Hall and Ball-room." It is a pretty little water-colour drawing of part of a long room with an open hammer-beam roof, ornamented with pierced panel work. The mullions shown in the large window at the end cut very awkwardly into the circular arch of the window, but the general style and tone of the little drawing are admirable.

1,684; "Competitive Design for Municipal Buildings, Oxford;" Mr. Halsey Ricardo. A sketch competition design for Oxford Municipal

is the reason we are specially informed that is a "new" one.—It is shown in a pleasant sunny-looking pencil sketch, rather spoiled by the rough and ready manner of indicating the trees.

1,698; "Altar Cross for Private Chapel, Welbeck Abbey;" Mr. H. Wilson. This is a fine piece of work and a grand drawing; Mr. Wilson's power of indicating texture and surface with the brush is remarkable, witness the drawing of the brass work here. The upper portion of the cross is treated in light enamel decoration, with circles of darker colour in the centre of the arms; at the crossing of the arms is a larger circle within a square, with the angles filled up with beaten ornament. The massive brass stem is also relieved by a circular enamel plaque affixed to it half way up, shewing the expulsion from Eden, and in the base the serpent and the tree are introduced in a richly coloured enamel following the lines of the brass work and contrasting finely with it. This is the finest drawing of decorative work in the room.

1,704; "Dining-room, house at St. Sebastian, Spain;" Mr. R. S. Wornum. A capital little water-colour drawing of a quiet but original bit of interior treatment of the wall of a room. The mantel is oak, and the room panelled with oak to a height half-way between floor and frieze; the mantel is carried up with ornamental panelling to the frieze; beneath it is a richly-carved sub-mantel and pilasters, enclosing a plain white marble chimney-piece contrasting well with the wood. The plaster frieze is pleasantly treated in delicate mouldings in relief, forming variously shaped panels.

1,707; "Aisle Window, Blackburn Church: sketch design"; Mr. Ion Pace. A pretty three-light window with Old Testament subjects in panels under architectural canopies of the accepted type; the scheme and contrast of colour is effective.

1,703; "Interior of a Library in London;" Mr. G. Aitchison, A.R.A. A little coloured elevation of a library with bookcases of an Elizabethan pattern ending in an entablature two-thirds of the height of the room, over which an effective wall-paper is delicately indicated. The chimney-piece is in a light grey marble with panels of darker and richly-coloured marble. The effect of the whole is very tasteful and harmonious, though showing nothing new or original.

1,701; "Interior of Nave, Gloucester Cathedral;" Mr. C. E. Mallows. This is the drawing published as part of our illustrations of Gloucester Cathedral in the *Builder* for Dec. 5, 1891. It comes out very well on the walls; being a pen drawing somewhat boldly and strongly executed it is none the worse for being hung a little high.

1,710: "Stained-glass Window, with Early Renaissance detail;" Mr. Clement Heaton. This is an unusual window design; a kind of conventional Renaissance tabernacle is erected on the window, leaving some space at each side; in the lower compartment of the architectural frame (which looks a little too like a fireplace) is a representation of the Nativity, in the upper more lofty arched compartment the worship of the Magi; over the cornice is a small shrine by way of "attic," in which an angel is seated. The space between the architectural frame and the edge of the window is filled with a string of knots of foliage on white glass ground, somewhat of the type of the modelled foliage in the jamb of the Baptistery of Florence doors; realistic sprigs connected on a sort of string. This is not good decorative design, though it is in keeping historically. The general effect of colour is good.

1,709; "One of a Series of Windows, South Side, British Church, Moscow;" Messrs. Ward & Hughes. A lofty two-light window treated in two stories, the upper showing the marriage at Cana, the lower the raising of Lazarus, each subject going through the two lights and divided by the centre mullion. It is notable for the good drawing and design of the figures and draperies, especially in the Lazarus subject, in which there is more of movement and expression in the figures than is commonly found in stained-glass design. The subjects are crowned with conventional representations of Gothic vaulting as frequently introduced as a canopy to niches.

APPOINTMENT. — Mr. Reginald G. Pinder, of Bournemouth, has been appointed Architect to the School Extension Committee of that town.

FRENCH ART OF THE YEAR.

A CERTAIN special interest attaches to the Salon of this year, from an architect's point of view, owing to the presence of a larger proportion than usual of pictures avowedly studied and painted as ceiling or mural decorations, for the Paris Hôtel de Ville and other buildings. The French seem now to have fully adopted the system of executing such paintings on canvas (and fixing them in their place afterwards, so that the large compositions executed for this purpose can be hung in a miscellaneous picture exhibition and judged along with the rest as framed pictures, before being finally placed *in situ*. This is convenient for those who wish to study such decorative paintings collectively, though it is hardly fair to the pictures themselves that they should be seen apart from the architectural framework for which they are intended; at least, it would not be fair if the paintings had the true character of mural decorative art. Unfortunately most of them have not, they have the character of easel pictures much more than of mural pictures, and really look more in place in an exhibition than they will on the walls they are intended for, except in the case of ceiling paintings which, painted to be seen horizontally, have to be hung vertically at the Salon, with rather curious results. This system of painting on canvas and then fixing up the pictures has the advantage of avoiding the chances of injury to the paintings from damp in the walls or efflorescence on the plaster, but on the other hand it removes the paintings from that intimate and monumental relation with the construction which seems the very essence of mural painting; and we cannot help thinking that the system has a bad effect upon the artists, and leads them to forget the true conditions of mural painting, and to indulge in vagaries on which they would hardly have ventured under the sobering limitations of fresco painting on the actual wall surface.

M. Benjamin Constant's "Paris Conviant le Monde À Ses Fêtes," the painting for the central ceiling compartment of the Salle des Fêtes of the Paris Hôtel de Ville, though odd enough in idea, is perhaps the most successful work of its class in the exhibition. It has the merit of being painted as a picture on a limited plane, and not a perspective *di sótto in su*, as are many of the other decorative designs. "Paris" is represented as a lady in a ball dress seated in the clouds, and partially relieved against a break of blue sky, but the figure is kept so faint as to lose all realism and appear rather a suggestion than a figure. Below, geniuses, in masses of drapery with a yellow glare, blow trumpets. The effect is somewhat violent in colour, but it is brilliant and decorative. The mistake is the introduction of a bit of the façade of the official buildings at the top of the Place de la Concorde, in the lower corner of the picture, the building being quite out of place in such a composition and appearing crushed beneath an allegorical figure leaning over it. It would have been much better if this realistic architecture had been omitted; it is out of the scheme. But otherwise, this is a brilliant and effective piece of work, though there will always be the difficulty of knowing which way up to look at it when it is in its place on the ceiling.

That is the mischief of ceiling painting, and the only defence for the system of painting in upward perspective from the eye (*di sótto in su*), which is a rampant sham, but at least one knows which way to look at it.

M. Ferrier exhibits a compartment for the ceiling of the same rooms, "Les Fleurs," also bright in colour, two women below cut off by the frame, and a girl flying in mid-air with a basket of roses; not bad as decoration, but fancy it on the same ceiling with Benjamin Constant's painting! The collocation will be absurd; they belong to two different worlds of painting. Then we have M. François Flameng's immense, brilliant, and very cleverly-drawn ceiling for a private mansion, "Dans l'Olympe," the gods and goddesses drawn with their feet towards the spectator, and a circular temple in the angle appearing to stick out into space; a conventional representation of the Signs of the Zodiac forms a circle concentric with this across the middle of the picture. Some of the figures are admirable, that of Mars especially, seated on steps, and when the composition gets into its proper place on the ceiling it will be a fine thing of its kind, though the wrong kind. On like principle does M. Moreau-Néret design "for a terminus hôtel" a ceiling surrounded by a trellis fence in upright perspective, and "Abondance," "La Chasse," "La Pêche," and other such personages playing in the blue sky. Then we have another Hôtel de Ville ceiling, M. Morot's "Les Danses Françaises à Travers les Ages," representing the dance of different centuries and costumes up to the modern waltz, carried out on clouds by figures in the costumes of the various periods; cleverly painted, but we fear amusing in a sense not intended by the painter.

A curious and clever experiment in decorative painting is that by M. Ruel, "L'Art Présentant à la Ville de Moscou la Peinture et la Sculpture Française," in which the figures of Painting and Sculpture are treated as if they were modelled figures executed in silver (life-size), and two little boys with symbolical shields occupy the centre of the composition in front of the principal seated figure. This is absolutely decorative, that and nothing more, and as a new experiment in decorative painting is worth attention. Among other decorative paintings are M. Aubert's "Patriarchs, Prophètes," a processional decorative composition of the pure school, in one plane and on a gold ground (rather dull though!); M. Bertaux' clever design for a stained-glass ceiling,—but here again we have this system of vertical perspective, a row of foreshortened columns in the side panels of the glazing,—the centre panel showing flying figures which are spirited and effective; M. Debon's "Famille, Travail, Exercise, et Repos," a wall-painting for the Mairie of Saint-Maurice, in which modern figures are treated in a sufficiently conventional manner, and which tells its story well; and M. Ehrmann's lunette figures for spandrel spaces in the Salle des Fêtes of the Hôtel de Ville, representing Bretagne and Auvergne. These are very successful, well contrasted, combining decorative effect with spirit and meaning. But a vertical spandrel like this is no doubt a much easier problem than a ceiling. Finally, M. Tony Robert-Fleury has painted for the Hôtel de Ville a figure representing "Architecture," a richly-draped finely-modelled woman who holds a pair of compasses and leans on a carved Renaissance pedestal; this is a fine work both in design and colour, but impresses one as not powerful and monumental enough for a figure symbolical of architecture, and the head is small for the body, which adds to this impression. Change the "attributes," and the figure would better represent "Painting."

At the Salon one looks for M. Tattegrain's picture as at the Academy one looks for Mr. Orchardson's. His work this year is a remarkable revival of a historical scene. "The Entry of Louis XI. into Paris, August 30, 1461." The picture is explained by a quotation from the chronicles of Jehan de Troyes It is a street scene in Old Paris, showing the ancient houses, the crowd of sightseers, and the humours of the show; the three girls dressed as mermaids, standing in a tank of water; in the background on the other side of the street is a representation of the crucifixion by three men tied on crosses, which formed part of the show; in the centre of the street Louis XI. on horseback, and the knights in armour who formed part of the procession. Every detail in the picture is carefully studied, every figure in the crowd; perhaps the whole looks a little too clean and respectable for a Mediæval crowd in a Mediæval city. The other important historical picture is M. Detaille's representation of the marching out of the small garrison which defended Huningue against the Austrians in 1815, and were received with honours by their conquerors on evacuating the town. The scene is finely rendered; the brilliant uniforms of the Austrians contrast effectively with the poor array of the small band of defenders. Another fine picture of the historical class is M. Chicotot's "Mort de Pierre Corneille," the old dying man seated in a chair and his daughter kneeling by him: a picture perfectly simple in its composition and truly pathetic in expression. M. Kratké has added one to the numerous pictures of the retreat from Moscow, under the title "Novembre 1812"; a snow landscape in the fall of the day, with the long columns of men straggling in parallel lines over the snow; a painting in which there is a tragic realism. M. Motte sends a painfully real picture of the destruction of the Swiss Guard at the Tuileries on August 10, 1792. A finer and more impressive war picture, because one with a poetic idea in it, is M. Rouffet's "Le Chemin de la Gloire," a bare landscape cut across by an equally bare high road, at one side of which lie a dead cavalry soldier and, a little apart from him, his dead horse, while in the distance a troop of cavalry disappear over the hill. This is one of a class of pictures in which the French excel, and of which we have unfortunately so few to show among us; pictures which are interesting not only for their execution but for the thought which underlies them. M. Roussel's large painting, "Le Corps de Marceau Rendu à l'Armée Française," is a fine and impressive one of its kind; it is divided into two main groups, that of the officers awaiting the return of the body of their brilliant comrade, and that of the group who approach in the middle distance with his bier borne upon their shoulders; the spectator involuntarily identifies himself with the group in the foreground; the composition is natural and unforced, and tells its tale completely.

Among the figure pictures of the more imaginative class are some which detach themselves from the mass of paintings as of special interest. M. Gerôme's "Ils Conspirent" is a curious and original treatment of the subject; a long bare room nearly in darkness, at the further corner of which are three men seated at a table lighted by a single candle, two of them with their backs to the spectator; of the third only the profile is partially seen, but the expression of something sinister going on is completely conveyed. Nude studies are not quite as numerous or as unmeaning and devoid of point as we often find them. Among the more poetic works of this class the finest perhaps is M. Lœwe-Marchand's picture from Dante of "Myrrha" (*Inferno*, canto xxx.), a naked figure crouched in the foreground of a rocky gorge; in the background Dante and Virgil turn back to look at her; the figure is finely painted and the face darkly expressive of evil passion; this is a poetic conception and not a mere figure study. Benner's "Printemps," a figure reclined on the grass partly in shade but with the head in full sunlight, is one of this painter's usual pretty idyllic conceptions. "Phœbe s'Éveille," by M. L. Berthault, is a fine composition of ideal figures; M. Bouguereau's "Le Guêpier," a half-nude nymph persecuted by a crowd of little Cupids, is as pretty and scholar-like as usual with him. M. Cabane's "Nymphe" (325) is a fine example of nude painting with no particular meaning or sentiment, but striking from the richness and freedom of its execution. M. Raphael Collin's "Au Bord de la Mer," a party of girls dancing in a ring on the seashore, is one of a class of works in which idealism is sought for not in the conception of the subject but in the mode of execution; the figures are faint and dream-like in execution, and thereby removed from real life; but the painter has spoiled all by giving to these nude figures the pinched waists which come of the artificial conditions of tight dresses, a curious and unhappy intrusion of realism into what should be an ideal scene. M. Henri Martin, too, in his allegorical paintings, adopts a method of execution peculiarly suited to such subjects; we have not real bodies so much as suggestions, and this gets over a great intellectual difficulty of allegorical painting, in which frank realistic execution of figures is wont to contrast, sometimes almost absurdly, with the poetic character of the thought intended to be conveyed. Moreover, M. Martin's method of execution leads him into very fine prismatic though subdued effects of colour. He has not equalled this year his remarkable "Chacun sa Chimère" of last year, but "L'Homme entre le Vice et la Vertu" is a fine example of a painting with a moral, in which the moral has not been allowed to kill the painting, as too often happens.

The taste for medical and hospital pictures seems to have subsided again, at least we only noticed one this year; large pictures of scenes in primary and middle-class schools (educational art, one may call it) seem to be taking their turn in fashion. We do not find this type interesting. Among the immensely large pictures which are found only at the Salon may be noted M. Luminais' "Passage de la Meuse par les Francs au IVe Siècle," one of the "Gaulois" pictures, a raft propelled across a river with a crowd of men, a warrior with sword drawn and leather shield standing in front—a spirited picture, but spoiled by the bad painting of the water. M. Deully's "Orphée" is theatrical, but a new treatment of the subject, and M. Salgado's large painting, "Jésus," a single white-robed figure in a dim twilight landscape, has a certain power and pathos. Among paintings of subjects of real life a very charming one is M. Debat-Ponsan's "À La Saint Roch; Vieille Coutume du Midi," apparently the priest coming out to bless the cattle, remarkable for admirable painting of peasantry and cattle, with the cathedral standing up as a background. M. Lœnhardt paints with pathos a group of Huguenot prisoners (women) on a tower at Aigues-mortes, who were separated from their husbands and kept in semi-starvation; a powerful picture of the historical class. M. Richir's "Misère," a poor pianist in an obscure corner of a brilliant ballroom; M. Richemont's "Sacrifice," an interior with two ladies burning old letters, a painting of the modern flat and thin school of execution, very well drawn and lighted; Mr. Walter Gay's "Messe en Brétagne;" are pictures with a distinctive character in idea or treatment. M. E. Michon paints a ghastly picture of the realities of a bull-fight; Mr. Bridgman contributes the unusual subject (for him) of a very beautifully-painted nude figure, "Le Songe;" and M. Lavery's "Une Équestrienne," a life-size painting of a lady on horseback, which has been seen in London, holds it place splendidly here, and looks all the better for being exhibited in a larger room, and with more space to see it than when it was in Bond-street.

The average of portraits for the year is good, and there are some remarkable ones. Among these may be mentioned M. Bonnat's uninviting but very powerful portrait of M. Renan, and the same artist's "Mdme. L. N——," apparently in rivalry of Carolus Duran, a lady in a sumptuous dress of purple velvet with a yellow-lined cloak; M. Brouillet's portrait of "Mdme. A. B——" in a white dress with the head thrown out brilliantly against a red background; M. Chartran's portrait of the reigning Pope, a very spirited and expressive performance; M. Choppart-Mazeau's portrait of his mother, an old lady in a fur cloak, painted in full daylight in the open air; M. Paul Dubois' half length of a young lady, noteworthy for its dignified composure of attitude and expression; M. Ferrier's characteristic portrait of a little girl in a green dress standing before a half opened door; Mdlle. Fornier's fine though slightly theatrical portrait of a noble looking young lady in a primrose-coloure[d] dress holding a greyhound; Mdlle. Houssay['s] "Mdme. la Comtesse A——," remarkable f[or] the intellectual expression imparted to a plai[n] but interesting face; M. Renouf's "Mdm[e]. X——," noticeable for the same kind of excellence; M. Salgrado's frankly realistic portrai[t] of a man lounging with his hands in hi[s] pockets,—one of the *dégagé* order of portraits and last but certainly not least, M. Benjamin Constant's portrait of "M. Auguste L——," [a] man in shooting dress seated on or leanin[g] against the end of a table with a gun, a do[g] beside him. Few would put down to th[e] account of M. Benjamin-Constant this sobe[r] looking portrait, so quiet and subdued in colour but it is one of the most lifelike and real thing[s] in the exhibition, and another proof of th[e] versatility of this remarkable artist.

Where, O where, is the great school of Frenc[h] landscapists gone? The great men are de[-]parted, and seem to have left no successo[rs]. What strikes one especially is the dull an[d] deadly colour of nature, the lack of air an[d] sunlight in the majority of the landscapes. I[t] is among some of the cattle painters in th[e] Salon that we find the most vivid and rea[l] open-air effects, as in M. Merlot's "Troupea[ux] dans les Marais de la Somme," which may b[e] contrasted in this way with M. Marais' "A[u] Retour" which hangs as a pendant to it, wher[e] the cattle are forcible and solid enough, bu[t] that is all. Again and again we find the sam[e] dull sky and livid colours in what i[s] supposed to be the verdure. Those i[n] which architecture or buildings are com[-]bined with landscape are the best, fo[r] buildings the French painters of the da[y] generally treat well. M. Liepvre essays a large decorative landscape for a staircase; w[e] do not like the notion of decorative landscape but this one is something of a success, being bright in tone and not too realistic. M. Besnard, the king of the Impressionists, at all events does not shirk light and colour; he is repre[-]sented only by one landscape, "Etang d[e] Sologne" which is vigorous enough. There is tenderness of colour and light in M. Dieterle's "Le Calvaire de Criquebeuf-en-Caux," a scene f high downs with a crucifix and a kneeling gure in the foreground. M. Gaillard's "Un oin de Pré en Fleurs" is as hard as if they ere paper flowers, and again there is a contrast ith its pendant, M. Grivolas' "Buissons des oses," which has the freshness of nature. M. uillemet's "La Seine à Conflans" is a good ealistic landscape, and M. Louchet's "La Seine la Frette" has higher qualities, and is note-orthy for the harmony of the whole lines ade by sky and land in the composition. [. Pointelin's "Jura" is a landscape with me of the poetry of nature in it; and [. Quignon's "Avoines en Fleurs," a sketch of ndulating meadow country, is a really fine ork, which we are glad to see the State has ad the discernment to purchase. M. Schutz-erg's "Les Bords de la Seine en Hiver" is a ood real scene in its effect and lighting. But nong such a large collection of paintings there e really very few landscapes that would give use to any one accustomed to our modern nglish landscape school, in which at least e are far ahead of the French though it only of recent years that this could said. We may as well make the most it, for it is only in this department of ainting that we can pretend to beat them, cluding sea-pieces under the general head landscape. The Salon sea paintings are ven more bewildering than the landscapes. M. Kuwasseg's "Coup de Mer à Trégastel" e water is more like ice; the sense of move-ent is lost. M. M.-Auguste Flameng paints a ip in a gale, "Marine," which at once leads e to ask whether the painter ever *saw* the a, much less sailed on it. Certainly he never w sea like that, nor a ship seated on it in the traordinary way in which his craft is repte-nted. The whole things reminds one of the odel ships on inflated paper seas which are metimes made as toys.

It is curious to note that on going over to the ew Salon in the Champ de Mars one loses to great extent this impression of dull and airless ndscape. The New Salon is to some extent questionably impressionist in its tendencies, d the impressionists delight in painting fects of light, and seek for them. As regards oice of subject there is a prevalence also of uthern landscapes and of their strong effects light and shade. Generally speaking, how-er, the Salon of the Champ de Mars hardly jus-ies its separate existence. It has had a great ss of course in Meissonier, and now it may be id that the lion of its exhibitions is M. Carolus uran, who however is really in direct opposi-on to what are supposed to be its prevalent tistic methods, and would be more in place in e old Salon. He exhibits, as usual, a collec-n of his brilliant and powerful portraits of dies in whom the interest of portraiture is vided with that of dress, or rather the por-ait is a portrait of the dress as well as of e lady. The finest is the portrait of the Comtesse de C——," in lilac satin against e background of an "old gold" velvet screen. ere are other portraits by this artist of the me degree and kind of excellence, and a ady of a semi-nude figure which is as fine in way as the painting of the silks and satins. e New Salon has also its large decorative inting, by M. Puvis de Chavannes, a great nvas entitled "L'Hiver," and intended r the Hôtel de Ville. It consists as usual groups of figures mostly of great grace d admirably grouped, and a landscape, inted in flat tones and with as little possible of realistic truth, in the rear. The ddle distance is partially occupied by trees nearly equal distances and with bare straight rtical stems, which may be supposed to be corative or to give a decorative character to e landscape, but which are not beautiful nor ggestive of nature. We have also M. rmillac's large decorative picture for the cuité de Médecine of Lyons, which would t have been painted, or not painted it is, had not M. Puvis de Chavannes led the y. It is a scene *en plein air* in a garden by e river side, with a bridge on the right robably local scenery) and groups of learned n in more or less academic garments attered about it, balanced or contrasted by her groups of women and children, leaving wever plenty of open space between the ures. It is a picture in a flat fresco-e style, and in that sense decorative, t (like that of Puvis de Chavannes) ficient in warmth of colour for a really deco-tive work. M. Béraud, who astonished us t year by a painting of Christ in a Parisian club-room, has repeated the same kind of idea this year in a picture of the Descent from the Cross, the body being taken down reverently by French *ouvriers*, one of whom shakes his fist at the wicked city below him which evidently takes the place of Jerusalem in the tragic drama: a Parisian lady kneels and clasps her hands with an expression of agony and contrition at the sight of the dead body. To say the truth, though we thought last year's picture striking in spite of its extraordinary combination of real and ideal, we doubt the wisdom in any sense, artistic or otherwise, of repeating the idea, and it very narrowly escapes the borders of bad taste, some would say irreverence. "Les Nautes Parisiens à l'Epoque Gallo-Romaine," by M. Delance, is another decorative painting intended for the Salle d'Audience of the Tribunal de Commerce, representing the ancient Paris quay and the unloading of a galley, but the painter does not succeed in giving reality to the scene or rendering it very interesting.

One of the most prominent and clever pictures in the New Salon is an interior with four life-size figures, by an American lady, Miss Lee-Robbins, under the title "Five o'Clock;" probably it is really a set of portraits, under which category it is defensible; as a mere *genre* picture it is far too large for the subject. Mr. Sargent's "Carmencita" is here, looking even more brilliant and powerful than it did at the Academy, as it is in a better light. Mr. Whistler is pretty largely represented. M. Lhermitte has followed the lead of M. Béraud by introducing a figure of Christ seated at table in a workman's cabaret, under the title "L'Ami des Humbles," a fine picture, but this use of a sacred figure to produce what may be called a cheap sensationalism is much to be deprecated, and it is to be hoped we shall see no more of it. Among other things to be specially noted are M. Dagnan-Bouveret's portrait of a lady in white; M. Damoye's large landscape, "Un Marais"; M. Edelfeldt's portrait of Prince Charles of Sweden; Miss Foss's "Ouvrière Fleuriste," an interior with a life-size figure (the artist is an American); M. Gandara's "Entre la Coupe et les Lèvres"; M. Karbowski's "L'Anniversaire," a cemetery scene of decking a tomb, with many figures, intended as a decorative painting for the Mairie of Nogent-sur-Maine; M. Mathey's "Portrait de Mdlle. M——"; M. Parrot's "Baigneuse," a figure seated on the bank of a stream in full sunlight; and M. Rondel's "Portrait de Madame H. R——."

The attempt to keep up two Salons is more and more obviously a mistake; there are sufficient important works in the two to make a splendid collection if they were kept together, and the average level of both exhibitions suffers by the division. On the other hand the New Salon contains many very charming small landscapes which would be crushed under the numbers and inferior lighting of the Champs Elysées exhibition; and the real part for the New Salon, with its admirably lighted rooms, to take, would be to restrict the wall space and make it an exhibition of cabinet pictures, such as would not be seen to advantage in the larger Salon. It would have a *raison d'être* then; it has none now, as it can hardly be said to represent any special tendencies.

Sculpture is but poorly represented at the Champ de Mars, and architecture practically not at all; the old Salon completely holds its place in these two departments. The two most noticable facts about the sculpture exhibition at the old Salon are that M. Falguière does not exhibit, and that M. Gerôme appears as a sculptor, with two curious and very highly-finished works, neither of which however can be called satisfactory. One is "Billone" (Bellona), a figure with the flesh parts in ivory and the armour and draperies in bronze; the figure has her mouth wide open as if screaming, a cobra reared at her side repeats the action; the thing is sensational and un-sculpturesque. M. Gerôme's other work is Pygmalion and Galatea, at the moment when the statue comes to life; still standing on the block on which she has been modelled, she turns to kiss the sculptor, who, clad in a working tunic, stretches up to her embrace; the marble of the female figure has been tinted slightly, and the hair nearly realistically tinted, but this is not overdone; the decorative effect is very good; the failure of the work is that, while splendidly modelled, it is utterly deficient in beauty and sentiment, Galatea being a very ordinary female model; the poetry of the legend has been entirely lost, and we see only an atelier study. Of the sculpture generally it may be said that it is not up to the highest level for the Salon, though there are many works which would give the artist a first-rate place in the Royal Academy sculpture-room. The central work is the half-size model by M. Peynot for his great monument "A la Gloire de la République" for the town of Lyons; a fountain with a column in the centre, with groups of figures planted against it on three faces, a fountain basin below with figures of Neptune and Amphitrite, and the female figure representing the Republic seated on the prow of a ship above. The half-size model gives the figures life-size or rather more. This is a grand work and very finely composed in a decorative sense. The same sculptor exhibits marble groups of the "Four Quarters of the Globe" for the château of Vaux-le-Vicomte, also a very fine and serious work. M. Mercié has a beautiful figure of "Le Regret," a heavily-draped female figure leaning on a tomb and placing flowers on it; apparently a monument; the treatment of the drapery and the indication of the pose of the figure within it are in the highest style of sculpture. M. Marqueste exhibits a spirited group of a centaur and a female figure under the title "Nessus," but the subject is rather grotesque from the point of view of the present day. M. Frémiet exhibits a fine alto-relief equestrian statue of the Constable Oliver of Clisson. An American sculptor, Mr. French, exhibits a fine bronze alto-relief, "L'Ange de la Mort et le Sculpteur," the figure of Death, heavily draped and with part of the drapery forming a kind of hood and throwing the head into shadow, arrests the sculptor in the midst of his work: it is intended as a monument for the tomb of a sculptor. M. Lombard has a finely-composed group of Samson and Delilah, and M. Hugues a powerful work entitled "Victoire;" a warrior who has conquered but is fainting from his wounds, supported by a companion. This is an illustration of the quality of original thought and conception which gives so much interest to a collection of French sculpture. There are a good many works, no doubt, which are simply finely-modelled figures, but there is a considerable proportion of subjects which show original thought either in the idea or the treament. M. Charron's "Sommeil de l'enfance" is one of these, an infant sleeping with a finely-modelled and draped figure of an angel playing a violin beside him, in illustration of the lines:—

> "Il dort paisiblement; sur le viole d'or
> Son ange interprétant l'harmonie éternelle
> Enchante son sommeil, l'abrite de son aile:"

here the sculpture is a poem in itself: so also is the late M. Christophe's figure of the man clutched in the embrace of the Sphinx,—

> "Dans l'eclair d'un baiser qui vaut l'eternité."

This is a marble group of which, if we remember right, the plaster model was exhibited in a previous year. M. Rougelet's "Hero and Leander," again, is no mere group of figures, it is remarkable for the intensity of expression in the faces, which yet does not transgress the conditions of sculptural art. M. Chevalliand's "Génie de la Liberte," a bronze male figure *adossé* on a pillar or stele, is a spirited work, intended for a commemorative monument of the "Federation Brétonne et Angevine de 1790"; the architectural portion is designed by MM. Deperthe, the architects. The French sculptors set ours a good example in this respect, in almost invariably going to an architect for the design of the subsidiary details; nor is the architect's name and his share in the work ever overlooked.

DISCOVERY OF AN AZTEC CITY.—A party of Mexican labourers, while digging in the extension of the Santa Cruz Canal, Arizona, came upon what is believed to be an old Aztec city. They struck the first ruin in cutting through the desert about 20 ft. below the surface, where it had doubtless been covered up by sandstorms. Everything about the old building had been wonderfully preserved, owing to the alkali in the sand. The first building disclosed consisted of a triangular structure about 300 ft. in length and 200 ft. in width. The roof had caved in, but the wooden pieces by which it was held together were sound. They were pulled out of the old wall, and are on exhibition at Tucson. In the building was a stone trough in sections, held together with cement. There were eighteen bodies in the building, all of them of medium size, and their flesh was mummified. — *Anglo-American Times.*

THE ROYAL INSTITUTE OF BRITISH ARCHITECTS:

THE ART OF INTERNAL ILLUMINATION OF BUILDINGS BY ELECTRICITY.

AT the ordinary general meeting of this Institute on Monday evening last, the minutes of the previous meeting having been read and confirmed,

The President (Mr. J. Macvicar Anderson) said that happily there was no preliminary business to stand in the way of the subject which was to come before the meeting and occupy their attention that evening. That subject was one of great interest not only to the public but to the architectural profession. That meeting had been arranged for by the Science Standing Committee, and he would ask Mr. Lewis Angell, the Chairman of the Committee, to say a few words by way of introducing the lecturer.

Mr. Lewis Angell said that as Chairman of the Science Standing Committee he had very much pleasure in introducing Mr. Preece to the meeting,—not that Mr. Preece needed any introduction. Notwithstanding his many engagements, he had been good enough, at the request of the Committee, to prepare a paper for their instruction. Of course the reputation of Mr. Preece as a scientist and as a specialist in electricity was well-known to them all. Electric lighting was at present making such rapid strides, and there was so much demand for it, that the Science Committee felt that the Institute should, as far as possible, be kept abreast of the subject. It was not desired that the discussion should run very much into the scientific and mechanical details connected with the generation and distribution of electricity, but rather that it should be directed to the artistic aspect of the question, so that the members might learn what was the most elegant and useful way of using the electric light in order to get good effects without paining the eye or offending the taste by violent contrasts, garish blazes, and deep shadows,—defects which had been only too apparent in many installations. It was desirable that architects should get out of the hands of the mere workman and gas-fitter, who had, as a rule, very little appreciation of the delicacies of light and shade and of the decorative harmonies. There was one practical point, however, to which architects must give their serious attention, and that was the steps to be taken to avoid danger in the use of the electric light. As an aid to their study of the question, Mr. Preece had been kind enough to provide the Science Committee with a working specification, which would, no doubt, be printed as an appendix to his paper.

Mr. W. H. Preece, F.R.S., Electrician to the Post Office, who was very heartily received by the meeting, then read his paper "On the Art of Internal Illumination of Buildings by Electricity." The following is an abstract of the paper:—

The art of internal illumination of buildings, the author considers, is just born, and will be an art in the future. Electricity is rendering theatres bearable and houses healthier, while the architect is brought face to face with a new art, in which the aid of the electrician is required to solve some of the difficulties. History is silent as to the origin of tallow, pitch, wax, and oil, but gas as an illuminant came in with the present century. From the earliest days history, whether culled from paintings or writings, teaches that lights have been dim and crude until the middle of the present century. Light, by whatever means generated, follows the same laws, and is due to the rapid rhythmic undulations of the medium called ether that fills all space. Wherever there is light there is heat, and the hope of the philosopher to supply light without any heat at all is at present but a dream. Light cannot be produced without heat, and the higher the temperature the brighter the light. Colour varies with the rate of vibration of the ether, while changes of colour are due to the changes of wave-motion of the ether. Light may become so intense that all sense of colour is lost, and very bright illumination causes all colours to appear whitish. If light emanates from a point, its intensity diminishes with the square of the distance. The candle is the British standard source of light, and the bright surface produced by it at a distance of 1 ft. the standard illumination by which to measure the amount of light distributed by any other means. This standard Mr. Preece calls a "lux." The great problem is to diffuse light throughout a room so that it be distributed uniformly over the working surfaces with an intensity of a lux. Sixteen-candle glow lamps suspended 8 ft. above the floor and fixed in 8 ft. squares, effect this very well; and groups of four such lamps fixed 16 ft. high produce a similar result. The light a lamp gives is owing to the expenditure of energy in its carbon filament; an electric current is driven through this filament by electric pressure, its resistance is overcome, it is intensely heated by the proceeding, and the result is pure unadulterated light. The energy expended per second by an *ampere* (the standard current), driven by a *volt* (the standard pressure), is called a *watt*. A sixteen-candle glow lamp takes sixty-four watts, which, assuming the lamps to be fixed 8 ft. high, means that one watt per square foot of surface is required to secure ample illumination from lamps so fixed. Therefore, in designing the normal illumination of rooms, Mr. Preece takes the floor area in square feet and divides it by sixty-four, which gives the number of sixteen-candle power lamps required, fixed 8 ft. high,—these being increased or diminished according to the purposes of the room, its form and height, &c. The adaptability of the eye to nearly every degree of light is very great, and it is almost impossible for it to Judge accurately of the amount of light present; but it is not as a mere source of light that the glow lamp is superior to the gas-burner. The former can be put anywhere, and used without the adventitious aid of match or fire. It does not vitiate nor unnecessarily warm the air, and it simplifies the problem of ventilation, while it lends itself above all to the æsthetic harmony of furniture and decorations. Electric light is not always absolutely safe; security is to be obtained only by good design, perfect materials, first-clats workmanship, and rigid inspection. Imperfect materials erected by cheap contractors lead to many disasters; on the other hand, it is stated no fire has occurred in buildings fitted up under the rules and regulations, and inspected by the officers, of the insurance companies in this country. Mr. Preece advocates keeping everything as much as possible in view, and not hiding the conductors under wainscots or floors or above ceilings. The glow lamp excited by three watts per candle is at present the most perfect source of domestic light, and when the patent expires,—in a year or two,—will be obtainable at one-third the present price. It is scarcely fair, Mr. Preece thinks, to say all light should come from the side of a room, as Lord Beaconsfield stated in "Lothair" when describing the lighting of Belmont. The House of Commons is one of the best-lighted chambers in London, and is lighted from the roof, a false glass ceiling excluding the heat and glare, and admitting only the light. What is wanted is to avoid the glare of the incandescent filament in the eyes, and to prevent the lamp from being too obtrusive; it can be shaded from the eye without its effectiveness being destroyed, and without the flow of light being obstructed or its quality being deteriorated. Judging from the Crystal Palace Exhibition, at which several leading firms have not exhibited, the electric light fitter has not seized upon the spirit of the age,—which is the rule of science over mere conventional æstheticism. Two exhibits at the Crystal Palace, however, especially deserve, the author considers, inspection. The one is a Tudor ribbed ceiling erected by Messrs. Allen & Mannooch, who have applied glow lamps to the moulded intersecting pendants in such a way that the feeling of the artist is maintained by day, and is rather intensified, and not marred, by the artificial illuminant at night. The other is a bold attempt of Messrs. Rashleigh, Phipps, & Dawson to design in ironwork the whole of the fittings of a dining-room, so that they shall, in combination, convey an idea. The artist (Mr. Reynolds) has attempted to symbolise the solar system, the centre light over the table representing the sun, and the brackets on the walls the planets. A survey of the Royal Academy pictures, the author thinks, affords instructive study. There are many interiors, but few into which artificial light has been introduced. Having described several pictures in which artificial light has been introduced with more or less successful results, Mr. Preece, in conclusion, said he considers that Science is advancing with giant strides. Science has subdued nature so as to bring it within the compass of the human intellect, and Art must follow the knowledge thus acquired. These two being the chief instruments of modern civilisation, the architect and engineer must work hand in hand.

Mr. John Slater, in proposing a vote of thanks to Mr. Preece for his paper, said it was exactly ten years ago since the Institute meeting-room was first lighted by electricity, but not without many difficulties in the regulation of the intensity of the current,—difficulties which had been overcome by the invention of the Sellon-Volckmar storage cells or batteries. Science, as Mr. Preece had said, had made great strides during the past ten years, but he (the speaker) was inclined to agree with him in thinking that no very great advance had been made in the way of artistic illumination by electricity. It was true that the theatres had had an entirely new world of possibilities opened to them, and that by the use of electric lamps in all sorts of positions they were able to get effects which would never have been dreamt of twenty years ago. Referring to the present Crystal Palace Exhibition, he thought there were some things ther which were absolutely wrong. For example, ther were candelabra with imitation candles, havin incandescent lamps at the tops; this was a striking exemplification of the length of absurdity t which some people would go in their adhesion to old and past customs and ways. No doub everyone who had seen the interior of th House of Commons at night would agree tha it was a most admirably lighted interior; but ther the lights which actually lighted that chambe were all hidden behind the ground-glass ceiling so that none of the glare from the lights reache the eye, and the light was perfectly diffused That seemed to him to be the sort of thing i the way of artificial illumination that should b generally aimed at, whether in public or privat rooms. But he could not understand why M Preece should praise the lighting of the Hous of Commons, and at the same time condem as he had done, the use of ground-glass incan descent lamps. He (Mr. Slater) thought tha unless we used low-power lamps, which we not economical, we were bound, in some way o other, to screen off the direct glare of the fila ment of heated carbon. If Mr. Preece could tel them how the glare could be avoided withou any diminution of the effectiveness of the light they would all be very much obliged to him Mr. Preece had alluded to the attempts which had been made, at the Crystal Palace and else where, to accentuate the architectural forms o a ceiling by having incandescent lamps placed at the junction of the mouldings, or in little hollows. That undoubtedly was an exceedingly effective means of illumination, but it could not be denied that it was also, to a certain extent a very extravagant method of lighting, becaus the reflectiveness of the ceiling was altogether lost. In conclusion, Mr. Slater said that h thought the Science Committee, in conjunction with Mr. Preece, were deserving of the bes thanks of the meeting for having given them such an extremely artistic evening.

Mr. Henry Dawson seconded the vote c thanks, said that Mr. Preece was eminently deserving of their thanks for the very valuabl and practical paper which he had given t them. He was glad to hear him emphasise th necessity of having good work, properly super vised, if danger from fire were to be avoided and he thought it was a matter for congratula tion that electricity could not be adulterated and that the use of electric lighting woul promote health and cleanliness by saving th air of our rooms from becoming over-heate and vitiated.

Mr. Sidney Vacher said that the discussio seemed to have a tendency to become limite to such details as the relative advantages o ground and unground glass. He should like t see the question discussed on a broader basi How, for instance, would they light the Churc of Sta. Sophia at Constantinople?

Mr. T. Tayler Smith said he thought tha the subject had been introduced at a ver fitting time, because we were now acquainte with the technical necessities which were th foundation upon which we might work t produce pure art, truthfulness of design, an consistency of purpose. He thought it w fortunate that they now had in the electr lighting industries a very different set o people to those who were launched out on th introduction of the gas industry. It w lamentable to see hanging over the footwa lamps 3 ft., 4 ft., or 5 ft. in diameter shieldi three or four fish-tail burners.

Mr. W. Bainbridge Reynolds said that in lesigning electric-light fittings, the quality of novement or unrigidity which differentiated he electric light from all other methods of ighting was one which should, he thought, be xpressed in the design of the fittings, and consequently he thought that the best position or a glow-lamp was vertical and pendent.

Mr. E. Manville, Mr. R. C. Crompton, Mr. ston Webb and Mr. Joseph Goddard, having poken, the President put the motion for a vote f thanks, which was carried by acclamation.

Mr. Preece, in reply, said he was much bliged to the meeting for thanking him, but e, in his turn, had to thank the audience for istening to him so attentively. He was rather orry that his paper had not been more fully riticised, for there had been very little criticism indeed of any consequence, if he excepted hat of the gentleman who complained that he subject had not been dealt with on a suffiiently broad basis, and who wanted to know ow they would light the Mosque of Sta. Sophia t Constantinople? He was reminded, by that emark, of Mr. Dick, in "David Copperfield." Mr. Dick lived in a small room near Charingross, with which he was very well satisfied. Somebody, alluding to the smallness of the partment, told him that "there wasn't room o swing a cat there," to which Mr. Dick eplied, "I don't want to swing a cat." Neither did English architects want to conider, at present, how to light up Sta. Sophia; hey had to consider how best to light their wn English interiors. Mr. Slater had twitted im with the fact that while he had objected o strongly to ground glass as an obstruction to ight, he spoke approvingly of the lighting of he House of Commons, which was entirely hrough ground glass. It was quite true that he House of Commons was admirably lighted, he light being well diffused and distributed. But then Mr. Slater had probably never seen he gas-bill: he (Mr. Preece) *had*, and he knew ow large it was and what a serious waste it epresented. There was quite six times as nuch energy wasted in lighting the House of Commons than was really necessary. But people id not want to have the light directly in their yes, and the problem to be solved was, ow to avoid that in an interior which was to e lighted effectively and without glare, and, t the same time, with some regard to cost. He as not an advocate for ceiling lighting, except hen the lights could not be put anywhere else. hat was wanted was that the lights should so disposed or arranged that they should irly distribute the light in every direction. conclusion, Mr. Preece referred to a number the things exhibited in illustration of his per, and said a few words as to the electric hting of the Institute meeting-room, which, said, was not as efficiently lighted as it ight be.

On the motion of the President, a vote of anks was accorded to the several firms who nt exhibits to the meeting, viz., Messrs. Benm & Froud; Messrs. Faraday & Son; Messrs. alter Glover & Co.; Messrs. Laing, Wharton, d Down; Messrs. Strode & Co.; The Planet lectrical Engineering Co.; and the Taylernith Electric Co.

The meeting terminated with the announceent that the next meeting of the Institute r the present session will be held on Monday, ay 30, when papers will be read on "Castings Metal," &c. This meeting has been arranged r by the Art Standing Committee.

THE NOTTINGHAM SEWAGE FARM.

DURING the recent Midland Counties Disict Meeting at Nottingham of the Incorporated ssociation of Municipal and County Engineers, visit was paid to the Borough Sewage Farm at toke Bardolph, as we mentioned. The following escription of the farm has been kindly furished to us by Mr. Arthur Brown, M.Inst.C.E., e Borough Engineer:—

The question of utilising the sewage of the rough, and thus preventing the pollution of e river Trent, was forced upon the Corporan as early as the year 1870. The riparian ners naturally objected to the sewage of the wn of Nottingham being passed direct into e river, and threatened the Corporation with injunction to restrain them from further lluting the river Trent. The Corporation, cognising the absolute necessity for an improvement being made in the condition of the ver, immediately set to work to obtain the necessary powers to enable them to commence operations. At this time, which was previous to the extension of the borough in 1877, the town of Nottingham was encircled by other outlying parishes, the sewage from which either delivered into the river Trent or into the river Leen, a tributary of the Trent. Parliamentary powers were obtained, and a joint Sewerage Board was formed, which consisted of members from the Town Council of Nottingham and from the various Local Boards of the parishes referred to.

The first step was to construct an intercepting sewer to pick up the sewage from the various districts; this was done about the year 1873.

The joint Sewerage Board had in the meantime thoroughly discussed the question of methods of purification, and, after visiting the principal towns in England, decided to adopt that of broad irrigation and downward filtration on land. For this purpose land to the extent of about 640 acres was leased at what was known as Stoke fields, about five miles from Nottingham. The rent asked for the land was at the rate of 5*l*. per acre for a sixty years' lease, and it was found impossible to obtain the land for less than this rent, although a large portion of it was then only let at from 30s. to 35s. per acre. The rent is certainly very heavy, but the Corporation have the small consolation of knowing that they are not treated any worse than other towns when they have to buy or lease land for a similar purpose.

The dry weather flow of sewage is about 6,125,000 gallons per day of twenty-four hours. Of this quantity, 2,125,000 gallons flow down by gravitation; the remainder, however, has to be pumped. The length of the outfall sewer (from the point where the gravitation and pumping mains meet) down to the farm is about four miles, and the sewer is constructed of various shapes to suit the exigencies of the case; where it is in tunnel the sewer is a 5 ft. barrel sewer; where it passes through low-lying meadow lands it is 7 ft. wide by about 4 ft. high, with a flat top of York landings. For a length of 1,000 ft. through meadow lands the sewage is carried through iron syphons in duplicate, each 42 in. in diameter, and 1,000 ft. long. The ruling gradient of this outfall sewer is about 2 ft. per mile, and the discharging capacity is about 25 million gallons per day, so that ample provision has been made for the growth of the town.

The farm, as at present laid out,* has an area of 640 acres. An additional area of 269 acres has just been purchased from Earl Manvers, in order to provide additional land for farming purposes; this land is now being under-drained and laid out by the Borough Engineer, and will shortly be ready to receive sewage. The land is eminently suitable for irrigation, and is a natural filter which cannot be surpassed. There are on the top from 9 in. to 12 in. of light arenaceous soil; then about 1 ft. 6 in. to 2 ft. of fine sand, with very fine gravel; then 1 ft. 6 in. of fine gravel; then 12 in. of fine sand and lastly comes a bed of river gravel, varying from fine to coarse. The land being meadow land, near the river Trent, was fairly level, but still a considerable sum of money had to be spent on levelling the surface, uprooting hedges, and generally preparing the ground to receive the sewage.

Of the total acreage of 640 acres, about 130 acres were laid out as a filtration area, which was divided into plots, and upon which the sewage is delivered in turn in winter time, at night, and at other times and seasons when there is an overplus of sewage to be dealt with. This area is deep-drained, and has main drains of from 9 in. to 12 in. diameter, laid about 6 ft. deep, and being about two chains apart; the "feeders," laid "herringbone" fashion, are of 4-in. agricultural pipes, and on this area are 10 ft. apart. The main drains on the remainder of the farm are laid four chains apart, and the "feeders" 20 ft. apart. For the drainage of the 640 acres of land, about 400 miles of pipes of various sizes were laid.

The carriers for delivering the sewage on to the land are laid at such a level as to command all the land on the farm, and at numerous points in the side of these carriers are wooden sluices, which, when opened, allow the sewage to be delivered on to the land. The carriers are formed of earthwork lined with Portland cement concrete about 6 in. thick; they have stood remarkably well, and are in as good a condition now as they were when first constructed twelve years ago. The concrete was composed of cement and gravel, the latter being found on the ground. The distributing channels, which are opened by the plough, are formed on the crown of a very slight ridge, and these convey the sewage from the carriers over the land.

About 340 acres of the farm consist of ordinary arable land, 140 acres are permanent pasture, and 30 acres are occupied by the homestead, &c. Italian rye-grass occupies about 70 acres, and, in suitable weather, is cut about every six or seven weeks. Some of the rye-grass is made into silage, and is much relished by the cattle.

It was very soon realised by the Corporation that it was exceedingly difficult, and practically impossible, to sell the produce grown upon the farm, and acting upon the advice of their excellent farm bailiff, Mr. James Avis, they decided to keep and rear a large stock of cattle, so that the bulk of the produce should be eaten on the farm. Experience has shown that this is the only way to make sewage farming a success. Profitable it can never be, but this method reduces the loss to a minimum.

The stock of cattle on the farm at the present time is:—Beasts, 340; sheep, 300; pigs, 80; farm horses, 35; and young horses, 20. Of the beasts, about 90 or 100 are milch cows, nearly the whole of the milk from which is sent to London.

The land takes the sewage well, and the effluent could not be better. No difficulty has been experienced in dealing with the sewage during the severe winters of the past three years, and there is not the slightest sign of the land becoming clogged.

Although the sewage farm has been in operation for twelve years, not a single complaint has ever been made of any nuisance arising from the operations of utilising the sewage on the land. The neighbouring village of Burton Joyce closely adjoins the farm, and owners of property there have evidently confidence in the farm being carried on without any nuisance, as they are building villa residences within a stone's-throw of the farm.

* Under the direction of the then Borough Engineer, the late Mr. M. O. Tarbotton.

THE ARCHITECTURAL ASSOCIATION'S SPRING VISITS:

THE NEW NATIONAL PORTRAIT GALLERY.

THE seventh visit of this season was made on Saturday afternoon last to the New National Portrait Gallery, now being erected from the designs of Mr. Ewan Christian. Owing to ill-health and consequent absence at Eastbourne, Mr. Ewan Christian was unable to be present, but Mr. Henry Christian kindly met the members of the Association, and explained the design of the Gallery very fully to them, and afterwards conducted the party over the building.

The design of the National Gallery has been preserved with great care in the new east front, but, owing to the great difference in levels, it was found impossible to continue that design further than the staircase block of the New Portrait Gallery, which is from that portion entirely different in style and treatment from the other part. This variation was also found desirable, inasmuch as the windows of the National Gallery would be far too small for the purpose for which the Portrait Gallery has been designed, and the arrangement in floors necessitated larger windows for giving the only light available. The basement is devoted to lavatories, stores, engine-rooms, and engineer's apartments, and large galleries, which, even in this position, are well lighted. The long narrow gallery to the left of the main staircase is to be devoted to sculpture. This staircase gives access to all the galleries in the main block intended for the exhibitition of portraits, which are arranged on both sides of a wide corridor, lighted at each end.

The entire building is as nearly fireproof as a building can be made, even to the roofs of the large galleries on the top floor, which are of iron and concrete. The building is heated by hot air conducted by very large flues over the entire building, so designed as to be under the complete control of the engineer and attendants. After the members had carefully inspected the works under Mr. Henry Christian's guidance, a cordial vote of thanks was accorded to him for his kindness in attending.

Illustrations.

SHEFFIELD MUNICIPAL BUILDINGS:

GRAND STAIRCASE AND TWO EXTERIOR VIEWS.

THESE three drawings in illustration of the Sheffield Municipal Buildings, showing the grand staircase and the two long sides of the building, are all hung in the architectural room of the Royal Academy, and were mentioned in our notes on architecture at the Royal Academy. As to the building generally sufficient information has from time to time been given in our columns, which it would be superfluous to repeat here.

The view of the staircase represents only the general scheme, the details have hardly been matured as yet (so Mr. Mountford informs us) and may be considerably modified. The walls are intended to be lined with polished Hopton Wood stone below, the arches being of Mansfield stone; the steps of Sicilian marble, the balusters of alabaster, their bases and capping of red marble. Everything in the building is to be English, except this said Sicilian marble. The columns will mostly be of red Devonshire marble.

It may be noted that the statue of Vulcan for the summit of the tower, and that of the Queen for the principal entrance, are now nearly completed by Signor Raggi.

MUSIC ROOM, "HIGHLANDS."

THIS room has been designed as an addition to "Highlands," Putney-heath, for Dr. Longstaff.

Its size is 48 ft. by 22 ft., with an ingle nook at one end, and recessed alcove with second fireplace at the other, and a recessed bay with a music-gallery over. The mantelpiece is of Weldon stone and polyphant, by Mr. Hitch, of Kennington.

The floor has been specially constructed for dancing purposes. Evans & Swain's patent fireproof construction has been adopted throughout.

Over the room are billiard-room and smoking-room.

The work was executed by Messrs. Turtle & Appleton, of Wandsworth, from the designs of Mr. W. D. Caröe.

THE ARCHITECTURAL ASSOCIATION:

NOMINATION OF COMMITTEEMEN.

THE ordinary fortnightly meeting of this Association was held on the 13th inst., in the meeting-room of the Royal Institute of British Architects, Mr. F. T. Baggallay, President, in the chair.

The minutes of the previous meeting having been read and confirmed, Mr. E. S. Gale, honorary secretary, read a list of members nominated for election, and he also announced a list of donations to the general fund, amounting in all to 100*l*. 15*s*., including 20*l*. from G. T. Hine. He moved a vote of thanks to the donors, which was carried by acclamation, after a few words by the Chairman.

The Chairman said he had a great deal of pleasure in moving a hearty vote of thanks to the members of the A. A. Lyric Club and to the other gentlemen who contributed to the success of the entertainment at the recent *Soirée* of the Association. This was also agreed to by acclamation.

On the motion of Mr. F. T. W. Goldsmith, honorary secretary, votes of thanks were accorded to (1) Mr. Blashill, Architect to the London County Council, for kindly allowing the members to visit the Newington Weights and Measures Offices; (2) to Mr. Keith D. Young, for permitting them to visit the new Royal South London Ophthalmic Hospital; and (3) to Mr Frank Verity, for giving them permission to visit the New Travellers' Club.

The President said he had, with very much regret, to announce, in accordance with By-law 35, that three casual vacancies had occurred on the Committee. They were most of them aware, to a certain extent, through *A.A. Notes*, that the cause of those vacancies was the resignation of Mr. Owen Fleming, Mr. T. E. Pryce, and Mr. Leonard Stokes. The Committee regretted those resignations very much; but without entering any further into the matter at that stage, he would call upon Mr. Pryce to make a personal explanation.

Mr. T. E. Pryce, who was received with loud applause, said he wished to ask the President a series of questions, of which he had given him notice, and he wished to ask those questions before he made his statement.

The President said he thought it would be better if Mr. Pryce made his statement first and asked his questions afterwards.

Mr. Pryce said he should prefer to have the answers to his questions first.

The President: Very well then: ask your questions.

Mr. Pryce said the first question he had to ask was, whether it was not a fact that one of the chief charges made against the staff of *A.A. Notes* was the publication of a letter from Mr. T. G. Jackson, expressing views which were not those of the Committee, and which the Committee could not endorse?

The President: Not altogether.

Mr. Collard rose to order. He said that the meeting had assembled to hear Mr. Ashbee's paper. Was that to be deferred to the end of a long list of questions such as the one which had been asked?

The President said that in accordance with the By-laws they were bound to announce that the vacancies on the Committee had occurred, and it would not be in accordance with custom if they did not allow the gentlemen concerned to make any personal explanations which they wished to make.

Mr. Pryce said his second question was whether it was not alleged as one of the reasons for altering the staff of *A. A. Notes* that it was desirable to bring that publication more under official control than it had hitherto been?

The President: Yes.

Mr. Pryce next asked whether the Committee, having received the resignation of the staff, was responsible for the publication of Mr. Earle's letter in the last number of *A. A. Notes?*

The President said that the acting Editor (Mr. F. R. Farrow) was alone responsible: the Committee and Manager had no knowledge of it. The Committee did not endorse the letter.

Mr. Pryce further asked whether the Committee knew of the prominent position which that letter occupied, and whether the Committee would have approved of the insertion of the letter if they had known of it?

The President, in reply, said that the present Manager had always declined to take a position of censorship over the *Notes*, and he simply occupied the position of Manager *pro tem.*, in the same sense as there was a publisher to a journal. The intention was to afford some control over the *Notes* by the future President, who had not yet come into office. The acting Editor, in fact, took the sole responsibility for the insertion of Mr. Earle's letter.

Mr. Pryce said he regretted that he had to make a somewhat disagreeable statement. The members were aware, from certain statements which had appeared in *A.A. Notes* and other journals, that a certain meeting took place some time ago at Mr. Stokes's rooms. With the calling of that meeting he had nothing whatever to do. The meeting was called for the express purpose of doing good to the Association, and the members who attended that meeting included, besides himself, Mr. Cresswell, Mr. Gale, Mr. Brodie, Mr. Millard, Mr. Fleming, Mr. Stokes, and Mr F. M. Simpson. There were other gentlemen present, some of whom had been heard in that room. There were Mr. Jackson, Mr. Blomfield, Mr. Macartney, Mr. Prior, and Mr. Warren. Now he (Mr. Pryce) thought those who knew him well would not say that he was a "Memorialist" in the slightest sense, for he disapproved very strongly of the course which the "Memorialists" had taken in connexion with another body. But those gentlemen were men of very high attainments, and included the late John Sedding, who, he believed, would have been at the meeting in question had he been alive, for his help was always most willingly given when the Association was in need of it. The members of the Association who attended the meeting were all extremely anxious to enlist the services of some of the gentlemen he had named for the benefit of the Association. Would they not all like to have men like Mr. Blomfield, Mr. Jackson, and Mr. Norman Shaw in their Studio, criticising their drawings, and helping them with their great and varied e: perience? For his own part he thought th: any steps that they might have taken to g the assistance of those gentlemen in the wo of the Association were deserving of approv and thanks, and that the willingness of t gentlemen in question to help them should n be perverted and misrepresented as an effo on their part to forward their views with rega to another body. He had fully and truly stat the motives by which those who called and a tended the meeting were actuated. They meta discussed certain matters, one of which w the question of the alteration of the wordi of the preface to the A. A. curriculum. Ve little alteration was necessary, but it was the same time proposed to lighten the ship omitting one or two subjects. The propositio of that meeting were brought before the Co mittee of the Association, perhaps not in t best possible way. The Committee reject the main proposition, but with regard to t others, he did not think they had any stro feeling. In the meantime, certain lette appeared in *A.A. Notes* and in the *Builder*. M Cole Adams in particular wrote to the *Build* He (Mr. Pryce) thought it was rather foolish discuss such questions in the public prints, an for his own part he had refrained from joinin in the correspondence. Those letters had u doubtedly exercised a certain amount of i fluence. Then followed the action of t Committee directed against *A.A. Notes* for t publication of Mr. Jackson's letter. A resol tion was passed calling for the resignation one of the Editors of that publication, and was plainly hinted which of the Edito was required to resign. Another reso tion was passed nominating Mr. Farr to act in his place. Now there was no dou that the Committee had acted distinctly with its rights, but the question was how far t exercise of those rights was for the good of t Association. He believed that the Committ had adopted a line of policy which would detrimental to the Association's interests. T Committee were, of course, for the time bei absolute masters of the Association; but thought it behoved them to take carefully in consideration any such violent course as th had recently pursued. He thought it was pret clearly explained to the Committee that t staff of *A.A. Notes* would be likely to sta together; but that did not have any effect the judgment of the Committee, whose acti had the appearance of a desire to absolute bind them to any policy which might be pr mulgated by the Institute. ("No, no!") We that was a matter of opinion. No one wou say that he was an anti-Institute man, but the same time he was bound to say that he d not want to see the Association made simply feeding ground for the Institute or any oth society. He extremely regretted the action the Committee, because he felt that it wou keep the distinguished gentlemen whom he h named out of touch with the Association, a prevent them from helping them in any wa These were the chief reasons which caused h to send in his resignation as a member of t Committee, and he earnestly begged the me bers to consider the matter carefully bef they endorsed the action which had been tak by the majority of the Committee.

Mr. Woodthorpe: But the proposal was cut out the word "Institute" from the "Bro Book" altogether.

Mr. Pryce, continuing, said he need not en more into detail, but would only say that t action of the majority of the Committee, endorsed, would keep away from the servi of the Association eminent men like Mr. Ja son, Mr. Blomfield, Mr. Macartney, and othe The question was whether they might not able to see their way to comprehend eve body,—to be catholic in the true sense of t word, and to continue their work for the p fession at large and not in the interests of t policy of any one society. Those who conven the meeting wanted the Association to rep sent all shades of opinion in the professi and for that reason they had gone out of th way to attempt to get the active co-operati of the eminent men whose names had be mentioned. The majority of the Commit had not backed them up in that laudable eff and he regretted it very much.

Mr. Farrow said that Mr. Pryce had rai two points, the first by his questions, and second by his explanation of the reason of resignation. His questions had been direc practically against the last number of *A*

YARD.—Mr. E. W. Mountford, F.R.I.B.A., Architect.

MUSIC ROOM: "HIGHLANDS," PUTN

PHOTO-LITHO SPRAGUE & Cº 4 & 5 EAST HARDING STREET, FETTER LANE, E.C.

tes, for which, as the President had said, he r. Farrow) was wholly responsible. He ould like to ask Mr. Pryce, as a past Editor of *A. Notes*, whether it was not a fact that ring his editorship of that publication he d never refused to insert any letter sent to n by a member of the Association, except on e occasion when he requested the writer to ' the matter before the Committee?

Mr. Pryce said he was not finding fault with insertion of Mr. Earle's letter so much as th the way in which it was inserted. One of e great grievances of the Committee against e late Editors of *A.A. Notes* was that they erted a letter from a prominent man whose ews were not in accordance with their own, d that was the reason why a change in the itorial staff was insisted upon. Now, the mmittee having changed the staff because . Jackson's letter was inserted, the result s the insertion of a letter fifty times more proper, and in a much more prominent posi- n. He alluded to Mr. Earle's letter, which s inserted in the form of a leaflet.

Mr. Farrow said he would ask whether, if an itor of *A.A. Notes* received a letter from a mber of the Association, he was not bound publish it if he could possibly do so?

Mr. Pryce said he would not go out of his y to publish it as a leaflet.

Mr. Slater rose to order. He wished to know ether the question before the meeting was t of the rival views of Mr. Farrow and Mr. ce as to the management of *A.A. Notes*?

he President said he thought that they t allow the explanations to proceed.

Ir. Farrow said that Mr. Earle's letter was an tioneering letter. Mr. Earle was on the ouse List" for election as a member of the mmittee, and he (Mr. Farrow) would have sidered it a gross breach of duty on his t, as acting Editor of *A.A. Notes*, if he had pressed a letter from a member on the eve an election. The letter was sent as an ctioneering letter with a view of influencing e election, and therefore he felt that must insert it. He was quite willing to stify his action in that respect before any eeting of the Association. The other point hich Mr. Pryce had raised was in his explana- on why he had resigned his seat on the Com- ittee. He had told them that he resigned cause the action of the Committee had lost em the services of Mr. Jackson and other ninent men who might have been willing to sist the Association in its educational work.

Mr. Pryce: That is one of the details of it; is not everything.

Mr. Farrow, continuing, said Mr. Pryce had t told the meeting upon what terms the sistance of Mr. Jackson and his friends was be obtained. It was all very well for Mr. ryce to say that they should have the assist- ice of Mr. Jackson and his friends; every one as agreed upon the desirability of securing e help of Mr. Jackson, Mr. Norman Shaw, d other gentlemen, but they were not all greed upon the price which they were asked pay for that assistance. What that price as, was clearly indicated in Mr. Jackson's tter inserted in *A.A. Notes*. His terms were, effect, "Cut away from the Institute, and we ll help you." It was true that in a subsequent tter, addressed to Mr. Stokes and printed in e *Builder*, Mr. Jackson had tried to explain ay the offensive terms of his first letter. The mmittee's view of the situation was very early indicated in their statement which peared in the current number of *A.A. Notes*. e Association refused to bind itself either to e Institute, to the Academy, or to any other dy, but sought to maintain a position of inde- ndence. The position which Mr. Jackson uld have them take up was not an inde- ndent one. Mr. Jackson wished them to here to his views, one of which was that the mbers of the Association must not go in for e Institute Examination.

Mr. Pryce: Distinctly not.

Mr. Farrow: Well, the members had all had *A. Notes*, and they could read Mr. Jackson's ter for themselves. As to the request made the Committee that one of the Editors should ign, Mr. Pryce had not told the meeting that at was not the first occasion on which objec- n had been taken on the Committee to the y in which *A. A. Notes* had been conducted. was true that the Committee had previously ssed no resolution upon the subject, the reso- ions proposed by members of the Committee ving been withdrawn out of courtesy to the itors, but on the understanding that some heed would be paid to the expressed desire that *A.A. Notes* should be conducted in the interests of the Association at large. When the Committee recently suggested that one of the Editors should resign, they did not wish to make any invidious distinction, but they thought it desirable that at least one of them should represent a set of opinions not then represented on the editorial staff. He was quite aware that there was a section of members of the Association who were prepared to pay the price which Mr. Jackson asked for the help of himself and his friends, but he ventured to think that the members of the Association, as a whole, were not prepared to pay that price; and therefore the Committee did not think that *A.A. Notes* should be carried on merely as an exponent of one side of the question. Mr. Pryce had remarked that he did not wish the Association to be the feeding-ground for any one society. Nor did the Committee; they wanted the Association to be a feeding-ground for all societies, including the Academy, if the Academy would only help them, and would give them some little credit for the work which they did in the Association. Some of them might be aware that there was a petition now in course of signature asking the Academy to reform its Schools, so that they might be made more useful to the architectural student. The present members of the Committee of the Association, if they were re-elected, desired to maintain the Association as an independent body; they did not think that the Association, which had its own proper work to do, should bow down to the Academy or any other society, to Mr. Jackson, or to anybody else. They desired that a free representation of the diverse opinions which existed in the Association should be found in *A.A. Notes*, the journal of the Association, and they desired that the educational work of the Association should be fitted to prepare a man for the Institute Examination if he wished to go in for it, for entering the Academy schools, or for enabling him to pass any other test of his knowledge.

Mr. Leonard Stokes, who was received with loud applause, said it was his desire, if possible, to leave on one side all personal matters. He only wished to say that in retiring from the Committee he was acting up to the best of his lights. He should regret it if he were mistaken, but he had felt it an imperative duty to make some protest against the course which the Committee had taken in these matters. He and some of his friends met Mr. Jackson, as they knew. There were other men behind Mr. Jackson. He (Mr. Stokes) and those members of the Association who met at his rooms were anxious, if possible, to get Mr. Jackson and other gentlemen of eminence to help them in their work at the Association. There had been a great outcry raised to the effect that the independence of the Association would be sacrificed; but, of course, they were not going to take Mr. Jackson's terms if they did not like them. It was the unfortunate discussion of these matters in the newspapers which had raised all that storm about their ears. Now, it was one thing to secure Mr. Jackson's assistance, and it was another thing to buy off his active opposition. He (Mr. Stokes) had authority to tell the meeting that Mr. Jackson and Mr. Norman Shaw had under consideration a scheme of their own which they intended to start, though, as he happened to have heard indirectly, they would much prefer to help the Association, because it would be less trouble to them. The terms which some members had been so frightened about were very simple, and the idea that the Association was to lose all its independence was a mere bogey. All that Mr. Jackson and his friends said was that it was desirable that no reference should be made in the "Brown Book" to the Institute Examination, and they also suggested the omission of certain words in the "Brown Book." They desired to help in the work of giving a thorough training to young architects. But it was stated in the "Brown-book" that it was the object of the Association to obtain a good training for young architects. There was no desire to alter the Curriculum. He did not think that anyone had had much more to do with the Curriculum than he had; but he,—and he believed the Committee itself would acknowledge the fact,—thought the amount of work which had been set for young men to do must be lightened. Mr. Jackson suggested that they should lighten it by omitting such subjects as Chemistry and Geology. Now, if they could see their way to fall in with Mr. Jackson's views, they would secure his help; but, if not, they would lose it and that of Mr. Norman Shaw, who had both said that they would help provided they would simply omit the reference to the Examination. The gentlemen he had named held that the right thing for a young architect to get was a thorough training. Surely the Institute and everybody else would endorse that! The question whether a young man afterwards passed the Examination or not was not very important, provided that he had a good training. Mr. Jackson had said that if the Association provided the training, it was nothing to him if young men did go in for the Examination: let them do what they liked. He (Mr. Stokes) laid it down as a fact that they in the Association established the Curriculum with the only object of providing a sound training for young architects. In that Curriculum, asterisks were put against certain subjects which were necessary to be taken up by those who wished to pass the Institute Examination. But was it necessary that those asterisks should continue to be inserted? The Committee said that it did not want to lean either on the Institute or on the Academy. Mr. Farrow had said that they ought to help young men to get into the Academy, but yet the Committee would not allow a petition to lie in the rooms of the Association asking the Academy to reform its Schools! Surely there could have been no objection to the Academy improving its schools. The Committee were asked to sign in their corporate capacity, but they declined to do so. He demurred to Mr. Farrow's statement that the views of only one party in the Association had been represented in *A.A. Notes*; at any rate, if any members felt that their views had not been put forward therein, it was their own fault, for, as a rule, whatever was sent to the Editors for insertion was inserted. During his term as Editor, he could say that only one article that had been sent for insertion was suppressed, and that was a rabidly anti-Institute article. As to the Committee's statement in *A.A. Notes* that Mr. Jackson demanded that the Association should alter its scheme to suit his (Mr. Jackson's) anti-Examination theories, there was no adequate foundation for it; nor was there any justification whatever for saying that Mr. Jackson desired to convert the Association into the mere tool of the "Memorialists." He thought it was very unfair that the Committee should have made such a statement in the pages of *A.A. Notes*.

Mr. Owen Fleming said that as one who had been on the editorial staff of *A.A. Notes* from the first, he strongly protested against the statement that that publication had been conducted in a one-sided manner.

Mr. F. T. W. Goldsmith said that while he thought it was to be regretted that the incidents which they had been discussing had occurred, he thought it was satisfactory that the meeting should have heard the broad and comprehensive statement which Mr. Stokes had made; and he was sure that they were beginning to see that these differences, which had excited so much ill-feeling on both sides, were, apparently, diminishing in intensity, and things were acquiring a more normal condition than at first seemed likely.

The discussion was continued by Messrs. Brodie, Earle, Beale, A. H. Clark, Dicksee, and others, and eventually the meeting was brought to a close by the re-nomination as members of the Committee of those gentlemen who had been already nominated, but who had, in consequence of the differences discussed, declined to accept the Committee's nomination, viz., Messrs. C. H. Brodie, T. E. Pryce, F. M. Simpson, and L. Stokes. Messrs. Owen Fleming, Gerald Horsley, W. J. N. Millard, E. J. May, and A. W. Cooksey were also nominated as Committeemen, in addition to those nominated in the "house-list."

The discussion of these matters having occupied nearly two hours, the reading of Mr. C. R. Ashbee's paper on "The Relation of the Architect to the Workman" had to be postponed, the President expressing the regrets of the meeting to Mr. Ashbee, who kindly promised to attend and read the paper on a future occasion.

Messrs. Lansdown, Bartlett, Beale, and Rickards having been appointed scrutineers of the voting-papers, the meeting terminated.*

---

* Two letters bearing upon the subject of this meeting will be found in another column.—ED.

ARCHITECTURAL SOCIETIES.

NORTHERN ARCHITECTURAL ASSOCIATION STUDENTS' SKETCHING CLUB.—The annual meeting of this Club was held on the 12th inst., at Newcastle. The annual report showed that meetings were held during last summer at Durham Cathedral and Castle, Morpeth Church, Tynemouth Priory, Ovingham Church and Prudhoe Castle, and Chester-le-Street Church and Finchale Abbey. A new series of meetings were arranged, and will start at Seaton Delaval Hall this Saturday, the 21st inst. The Committee were appointed as follows:—Messrs. R. B. Dick, J. W. Twist, J. W. Boyd, and Edmund Rich, Mr. C. G. Errington being re-elected secretary.

SHEFFIELD SOCIETY OF ARCHITECTS AND SURVEYORS.—The annual meeting of this Society took place on Tuesday evening, the 10th inst., at the School of Art, Mr. C. J. Innocent, President, in the chair, and there were also present Messrs. T. J. Flockton, F. Fowler, E. M. Gibbs (Vice-President), W. F. Hemsoll, J. B. Mitchell-Withers, C. Hadfield (Hon. Sec.), and a large number of members. The Secretary's and Treasurer's reports were read and adopted. A ballot took place for the election of President, Officers, and Council for the coming year, Messrs. E. Winder and J. B. Mitchell-Withers, jun., acting as scrutineers. Mr. C. J. Innocent was re-elected President, and Mr. E. M. Gibbs, Vice-President, Mr. C. Hadfield Hon. Sec., and Mr. J. B. Mitchell-Withers Treasurer; and the old Council,—Messrs. E. M. Gibbs, T. J. Flockton, W. H. Lancashire, W. F. Hemsoll, and W. C. Fenton,—were re-elected for the coming session. The Secretary announced, in terms of regret, the recent decease of Messrs. J. McInery and J. F. Wightman, Fellows of the Society. A very interesting and scientific paper on "Timber, its Growth and Characteristics," was read by Mr. W. H. Bidlade, M.A., of Birmingham. The paper was well illustrated by diagrams and specimens of various kinds of wood. The lecturer gave a graphic illustration of the structure and growth of various kinds of timber. He also alluded to the various kinds of damage to which timber was liable when used in building construction from dry and wet rot, and other causes. At the close of the paper an interesting discussion took place, and a hearty vote of thanks was awarded to Mr. Bidlake on the motion of Mr. J. B. Mitchell-Withers, and supported by Messrs. Hadfield, Winder, and H. W. Lockwood.

GLASGOW INSTITUTE OF ARCHITECTS.—On the 13th inst. in the Bath Hotel, Glasgow, Mr. William Maclean, who acted from 1868 till 1889 as Secretary of the Glasgow Institute of Architects, was presented with a testimonial. Mr. William Leiper, A.R.S.A., President, presided. The testimonial took the form of a bust in bronze of Mr. Maclean, executed by Mr. Pittendreigh Macgillivray, A.R.S.A.

THE LONDON COUNTY COUNCIL.

THE usual weekly meeting of this Council was held on Tuesday afternoon last, the Chairman, Lord Rosebery, presiding.

Tenders.—Tenders for iron fencing at Battersea Park were opened by the Chairman. We print the list elsewhere.

Loans to Local Bodies.—On the recommendation of the Finance Committee, sanction was given to the following loans:—To Camberwell Vestry, 20,000*l.*, for contribution towards the purchase of land for the extension of Peckham Rye, term 48 years; to the Hackney District Board of Works, 1,500*l.* for the purchase of land, erection of mortuary, &c., 30 years; to Rotherhithe Vestry, 3,800*l.* for granite paving, 20 years; to the Wandsworth District Board of Works, 3,500*l.* for purchase of site for store depôt, 35 years; to the Islington Baths Commissioners, 5,000*l.*, for the erection of baths in Hornsey-road, 30 years; to the Stratford-by-Bow Baths Commissioners, 3,850*l.* and 7,550*l.*, for completion of baths, 30 and 10 years; and to the Managers of the Central London District School, 2,200*l.*, for the erection of buildings at Hanwell, 30 years.

Sewage Sludge and Sludge Ships.—The Main Drainage Committee reported that during the week ending May 7, 23,000 tons of sludge were taken to sea from the Northern Outfall at Barking, the estimated amount then remaining in stock being about 6,000 tons. On the subject of the general superintendence of the Council's fleet of sludge-vessels, the Committee reported as follows:—

"We are considering the arrangements to be made for the working of the whole fleet of sludge vessels belonging to the Council, when they are all completed and delivered. As the Council is aware, three are now in use, and the other two will be delivered very shortly. We are of opinion that one of the first things necessary for the proper and efficient working of the ships is the employment of a thoroughly experienced nautical man, holding a master's certificate, as general superintendent of the whole fleet. The person appointed would be required to communicate and advise, when requisite, with the Committee, and to relieve the other masters respectively when off duty. He should, moreover, be a person who has had charge of large bodies of men, and should possess good administrative as well as executive abilities. We think that the services of a suitable person could be obtained for a salary of 4*l.* a week, which is the same as that paid to the masters of the vessels, with an additional allowance of 2*l.* a month. We recommend:—

'That the Council do sanction the appointment of a general superintendent of the vessels as above described, and that an advertisement be at once issued inviting applications for the office.'"

This recommendation was agreed to.

Brockwell Park.—The Parks and Open Spaces Committee reported that

"In the plan for the purchase of Brockwell Park, the line of boundary cut off a corner of the walled-in garden, and as we are laying this out as an old-fashioned English garden, we think it desirable that the garden should be preserved intact. There is also a very narrow entrance to the park from Herne-hill, which is the principal approach, and we think that a corner plot of land adjoining should be secured so as to form a better entrance. We propose that offers of 220*l.* and 200*l.* respectively should be made for these two plots, and we recommend,—

'That, subject to an estimate being submitted to it by the Finance Committee, as required by the statute, the Council do authorise the Committee to incur an expenditure of 420*l.* on capital account for the purchase of two additional plots of land to be added to Brockwell Park.'"

The recommendation was agreed to.

Alexandra Palace and Grounds.—The same Committee also reported that they were in communication with the Middlesex County Council and other bodies, and were considering the terms upon which the Alexandra Palace estate could be obtained as a public park. In the meantime, as the Council had decided to oppose the Bill now being promoted by the owners of the Alexandra Palace estate, because it proposed to repeal a clause in one of their Acts which prohibited them from building on 127 acres of the land, the Committee now reported that the repealing clause had been withdrawn, and they therefore recommended,—

"That, subject to the omission of the clause for repealing the prohibition to build on 127 acres of the Alexandra Palace grounds, the Council do withdraw its opposition to the Bill promoted by the owners of the Palace."

This was agreed to, after some discussion.

North Park, Eltham.—The same Committee further reported:—

"We have given consideration to the question of purchasing as a public park the remaining portion, 118 acres in extent, of North Park, Eltham. The Valuer estimates the cost of this property at 35,400*l.*, and, having regard to its distance from the populous parts of the county, we are not prepared, as no contributions have been offered by the local authorities or other bodies, to advise the expenditure. We recommend—

'That no further steps be taken with reference to acquiring the remaining 118 acres of North Park, Eltham.'"

Mr. Evan Spicer moved that the matter be referred back for reconsideration; but, after some discussion, in the course of which it was stated that the land is Crown property, and has recently been leased by the Office of Woods and Forests for a short term of years to a golf club, the amendment was withdrawn, and the recommendation agreed to with the addition of the following words:—"until the local authorities or other bodies are prepared to offer some adequate contribution."

Alterations at the Cane Hill Asylum.—The Asylums Committee reported as follows:—

"We have to report that we have considered the three following tenders received for the further additions, alterations, and other works at the Cane-hill Asylum, viz.:—

Reed, Blight, & Co., Plymouth ...	£15,416
Kirk & Randall, Woolwich	16,562
Rudd & Son, Grantham...............	16,666

It will be observed that the lowest of these tenders is 2,056*l.* in excess of the expenditure of 13,360*l.* authorised by the Council for the works under this contract. This additional amount, we are informed, will not cause any excess in the total estimates for the enlargement of this Asylum already submitted and approved. We recommend—

'That the Committee be authorised, pursuant to the provisions of section 254 of the Lunacy Act, 1890, to accept, subject to the Secretary of State's approval, the tender of Messrs. Reed, Blight, & Co., at the sum of 15,416*l.*, provided that they agree to the insertion in the contract of the condition that they will pay the London rates of wages and observe such hours of labour as are generally accepted in London as fair in the trades they employ.'"

This was agreed to, after some discussion.

Appointment of Resident Engineer, Blackwall Tunnel.—The Report of the Bridges Committee contained the following paragraph:—

"The Engineer has informed us that the time has now arrived when a second resident engineer should be appointed to assist in the supervision of the Blackwall Tunnel works. The Council, in December last, decided to appoint two engineers, and one has been already appointed. At the time of selecting candidates, we saw Mr. Hay and Mr. Fitzmaurice, both of whom had had experience in work carried out under pneumatic pressure. The gentleman selected for the first appointment was Mr. Hay, and it was understood at the time that the second appointment should be reserved for Mr. Fitzmaurice, who is highly recommended by Sir Benjamin Baker. He was resident engineer on the foundation work of the Forth bridge, which was put in under air pressure of 30 lbs. to 35 lbs. on the square inch, and he has a thorough knowledge of hydraulics, knowledge which will be largely required in manipulating the shield during the construction of the tunnel. We therefore recommend—

'That, subject to an estimate being submitted to the Council by the Finance Committee as required by the statute, Mr. Maurice Fitzmaurice be appointed to fill the vacant post of resident engineer, at a salary of 600*l.* per annum, to supervise the works in connexion with the construction of the Blackwall Tunnel.'"

This was agreed to without discussion.

The "Rate of Wages and Hours" Clause in Contracts.—The remainder of the sitting was taken up with the resumed debate on this question, which has been before the Council for two or three weeks. Mr. John Burns, as we have already reported (see *Builder*, May 7, p. 357), has the following motion before the Council:—

"That all contractors be compelled to sign a declaration that they pay the trades union rates of wages and observe the hours of labour and conditions recognised by the London trades unions, and that the hours and wages be inserted in and form part of the contract by way of schedule, and that penalties be enforced for any breach of agreement."

To this a large number of amendments were on the *agenda*, including that of Mr. Roberts, which was taken first by the ruling of the Chairman.

Mr. Roberts moved, as an amendment to Mr. Burns's motion,

"That a Special Committee be appointed to consider in what manner the Council can require its contractors to pay all employed on work for the Council the standard rate of wages."

Mr. Yates seconded the amendment, which, after a long debate, was voted upon, the result of the division being that the amendment was lost by 3 votes,—52 members voting for it and 55 against it.

Mr. Costelloe then moved a further amendment, which was still under discussion when the clock struck seven and the Council adjourned.

ROYAL METEOROLOGICAL SOCIETY.

THE usual monthly meeting of this Society was held on Wednesday evening, the 18th inst., at the Institution of Civil Engineers, 25, Great George-street, S.W.; Dr. C. Theodore Williams, M.A., President, in the chair. Mr. B. E. C. Chambers, Mr. R. Law, F.C.S., Dr. W. A. Sturge, and Dr. E. Symes Thompson were elected Fellows of the Society. Five honorary members were also elected, viz.:—M. A. D'Abbadie, Dr. W. H. von Berold, Dr. R. Billwiller, M. N. Ekholm, and Professor P. Tacchini. The following papers were read. (1) "Raindrops," by Mr. E. J. Lowe, F.R.S., F.R.Met.Soc. The author has made over 300 sketches of raindrops, and has gathered some interesting facts respecting their variation in size, form, and distribution. Sheets of slate in a book form, which could be instantly closed, were employed; these were ruled in inch squares, and, after exposure, the drops were copied on sheets of paper ruled like the slates. Some drops produce a wet circular spot, whilst others, falling with eater force, have splashes around the drops. he same sized drop varies considerably in the nount of water it contains. The size of the rop ranges from an almost invisible point to iat of at least 2 in. in diameter. Occaonally large drops fall, that must be more or ss hollow, as they fail to wet the whole surice enclosed within the drop. Besides the rdinary rain drops, the author exhibited diarams, showing the drops produced by a mist oating along the ground, and also the manner i which snow flakes, on melting, wet the ates. (2) "Results of a comparison of Richard's .némographe with the Standard Beckley .nemograph at the Kew Observatory," by Mr. . M. Whipple, B.Sc., F.R.Met.Soc. This istrument is a windmill vane anemometer, nd is formed by six small wings or vanes of luminium, 4 in. in diameter, inclined at 45 deg., vetted on very light steel arms, the diameter of hich is so calculated that the vane should take exactly one turn for a mètre of wind. Its inning is always verified by means of a whirlig frame fitted up in an experimental room, here the air is absolutely calm, and, if necesary, a table of corrections is supplied. The ecording part of the apparatus differs entirely rom any other anemometer, and is called the .némo-Cinémographe, and in principle is as ollows:—The pen, recording on a movable aper, is wound up at a constant rate by means f a conical pendulum acting as a train of heel-links, whilst a second train, driven by the an, is always tending to force it down to the ower edge of the paper; its position, therefore, governed by the relative difference in the elocity of the two trains of wheel-work, being t zero when the air is calm, but at other times t records the rate of the fan in mètres per econd. The author has made a comparison of his instrument with the Standard Anemometer t the Kew Observatory, and finds that it gives xceedingly good results. (3) A paper was also ead on the "Levels of the River Vaal, at Kimerley, South Africa; with remarks on the ainfall of the Watershed," by Mr. W. B. ripp.

Books.

Guide to Electric Lighting. By S. BOTTONE. London: Whittaker & Co. 1892.

R. BOTTONE addresses himself, as we find from the title-page, to "householders and amateurs," and, as ppears elsewhere, "to all who lay any aim to an intelligent knowledge of their rroundings"; that is, his aim is partly actical and partly educational. From neither int of view can he be said to have succeeded. ie householder who should try to install the ectric light in his own house, relying on the eagre and not over-trustworthy information to found in this book, would find his experient an expensive one; nor, after he had called an electrical engineer to set things right, ould he find the "Guide to Electric Lightg" of much use in meeting the occasional fficulties that generally arise in private installations.

The amateur fares rather better; he is supied with some useful tables, and with details specting primary batteries which, however it of place in a treatise on electric lighting, ay well be of service to him.

It is the gentleman in search of "intelligent iowledge" who is most to be pitied if he falls to Mr. Bottone's hands. Mr. Bottone is very nd of the word "intelligent." A reader of is class wants a clear exposition of the prinples and elements of electrical science as pplied to electric lighting; he does not want inute details (such as the specific gravity of e sulphuric acid in a cell) and trade illustraons of various machines, obsolete and otherise; he is probably a man of some education, nd when he reads "the resistance becomes dditive; *in other words, we must add the sistances of each of the cells together*;" will e disposed to ask how many resistances *each* f the cells may possess; he may even have ome acquaintance with applied mathematics, nd form a low estimate of an instructor who p. 45) measures "angular velocity" in feet per inute; or he may be so constituted that the curacy of the information conveyed in the ntences,—"If lighting lamps known as arc mps (to be described further on) be his inten-on, the preference will lie with machines hich are series wound. If, on the contrary, inandescent lamps are in view, the shunt wound or compound wound dynamos will be indicated,"—will insufficiently compensate him for the irritation produced by the sentences themselves.

Passing from the consideration of style to that of matter, it is as well to say plainly that when Mr. Bottone writes on dynamos, he is writing on a subject that he does not understand. If this appears to anyone a hard saying, let him read the calculations given on p. 46, and try to imagine the mental picture of a dynamo in the mind of a man to whom it seems sense.

There is a plentiful crop in this book of the errors usually found in writers whose physical ideas are in a fluid condition. Thus we have "electric energy in the form of current," "transformed into mechanical energy in the form of motion," and, again, "the conversion of mechanical energy into electricity." We are told that a "conductor becomes heated in proportion to the amount of current it has to carry, and to the resistance which it presents to the passage of that current." "Electricity itself is another form of motion," and that "the term *watt* has been introduced to indicate the amount of electrical energy contained in one volt by one ampere."

Even in describing the practical details of dynamo construction the author contrives to make mistakes; for example, he calls the collector rings of an alternator "commutators" (apparently because they do *not* commute the currents), and speaks of them as "insulated from one another, but each (*sic*) connected to the opposite ends of the armature wires."

There is one class of readers, however, to whom we can heartily recommend this book—Mr. Bottone refers to them as frequently raising the question: "Can a dynamo be driven by an electric motor which is *itself* actuated by the current from a battery?" To this species of "intelligent reader" the errors of which we have given examples will be of no importance; and they will, in accepting the author as their instructor, be under the guidance of an intelligence superior to, but not far removed from, their own.

A History of Water-Colour Painting in England. By GILBERT R. REDGRAVE. London: Sampson Low, Marston, & Co. 1892.

THIS is one of the South Kensington series of "Art Text-books," and gives a succinct account of the leading English water-colour painters, prefaced by a short chapter giving a very brief and concise history of the early art of water-colour painting. After that the book proceeds a good deal in the way of a dictionary of water-colour painters, the names succeeding each other in capitals as headings of paragraphs in which a short account of the artist and his method is given. Girtin and his methods are treated of at rather more length than most of the names, and the author gives evidence that Girtin's available palette was more varied than is usually supposed, and that no less than fifteen pigments can be enumerated among those he used, "a number," observes the author, "which would probably satisfy most of the water-colour painters of the present day, and far in excess of those in common use by the earlier masters of the art." It is interesting to know this, but we must say that Girtin's drawings do not in general produce the impression of the use of any such variety of colour. Some account is also given of the rise of the two leading Water-colour societies, which breaks in on the regularity of the biographical dictionary treatment. The main value of the book, however, is as a conveniently-sized reference-book for information about the date and artistic leanings and position of any water-colour artist about whom the reader may require information: it is more for that purpose than to read through. Some critical estimate of each painter, however, is given; these critical notes are written with sound judgment and perception, and the book fulfils very well its object of furnishing a "text-book" in regard to English water-colour painting.

The Architect and his Artists: an Essay to Assist the Public in Considering the Question,—Is Architecture a Profession or an Art? By William H. White, F.R.I.B.A. London: Spottiswoode & Co. 1892.

THIS is an amplification of a paper read by Mr. White at a provincial architectural society, some part of which in its original form was printed in our columns. There is a great deal of good sense in the paper, which those who are tempted to be exclusively "æsthetic" in architecture would do well to read; but we fail to see the point of the title, which is not such as to predispose the reader in favour of the book. Mr. White combats, with much spirit and sense, the modern idea of some gentlemen that an architect should be solely a designer of artistic buildings, and that the engineer can look after construction and drains and the surveyor after surveying; but his title phrase "the architect and his artists," seems rather to imply that the converse arrangement may be upheld, and that the architect who is a practical man may be assisted by subordinate artists. That is what it practically comes to in many cases, but surely the situation is not an ideal one.

Royal Academy and New Gallery Pictures; 1892. London: Published at the Office of *Black and White.*

THIS is the best illustrated memorial of the principal pictures of the year that we remember to have seen. The selection has been well made, and the reproductions are exceedingly good, many of them really being charming little engravings, and much more than mere memorials. The illustrations are prefaced by a brief history of the Royal Academy, with portraits of and biographical notes on the work of the leading painters. Any one who wants an interesting and valuable memorial of the contents of the two leading exhibitions of the year cannot do better than purchase the *Black and White* book.

New Holidays in Essex. By PERCY LINDLEY. London: 30, Fleet-street.

THIS sixpenny guide-book, which can be carried in the pocket, gives a map of Essex, with some routes of interest marked on it, and some information, accompanied by illustrations of places to be looked at. It will be very useful to those who wish to take walking or cycling excursions in the county.

Correspondence.

To the Editor of THE BUILDER.

THE ARCHITECTURAL ASSOCIATION.

SIR,—As Mr. Pryce and Mr. Stokes referred, at the meeting last Friday night, to some resolutions passed at the informal meeting held at Mr. Stokes's rooms, and as they omitted to explain the main point in the resolutions which the Committee objected to, and as on Friday last individual members of the Committee were debarred, by the rules of procedure, from replying or further elucidating the resolutions referred to, we think it right that the Association should know the main point that the Committee objected to, and its reasons. The Committee were asked to pass a resolution to eliminate altogether from the Brown Book and Curriculum all reference whatever to the Institute Examinations, and Mr. Stokes informed them, unless this was done, Mr. Jackson and his friends would have nothing whatever to do with the Association, though they had previously promised to assist. This reference in the Brown Book is made only to give to those students who desire to enter for the Institute Examinations information as to subjects necessary for them to take up, but it is clearly stated "that the aim of the Association courses is to help members to fit themselves for their work as architects." We failed to see why Mr. Jackson and his friends should take exception to this, and we thought that if we gave way we should only be taking a side in the controversy between the Memorialists and the Institute. In his subsequent letter to *A.A. Notes*, Mr. Jackson explained more clearly what his views and intentions were in this respect, and to these the Committee could not assent. It is worthy of mention that the Royal Institute have just voted to the A.A. scheme 300*l.* *without any reservations or conditions whatever.* Mr. Stokes was hardly fair in charging the Committee with narrow-mindedness and bias in refusing to sign the petition to the Royal Academy with reference to the proposed reform of the Academy Schools, because he omitted to explain the terms of that petition, and, as he had already resigned before it was considered, he could not know what occurred. The Committee did give the matter the fullest consideration, but they came to the conclusion that as it contained many statements with which they did not agree, and about which there would probably be much difference of opinion in the Association, it would be wrong for them to sign it in their corporate capacity, and so pledge the name of the Association without first giving the members an opportunity of expressing an opinion upon it. This they were willing to do, and offered to publish it in *A.A. Notes*, so that the members might have an opportunity of discussing it, but the promoters objected to this course on the ground that it was a private document and could not be published in the manner proposed. Under these circumstances, the Committee felt that they ought not to sign it as a body, or to allow it to be placed in the Studio for signature by individual members, as by doing so it would create the impression that they approved of it.

With regard to *A. A. Notes*: as it had for some time past given too great and exclusive prominence to a particular set of opinions, we asked for the resignation of one of the Editors, and, in order that there may be some official control over the journal, we passed a resolution making any future President manager—as he would be, for his term of office at any rate, the elected representative of the Association. This view formerly received Mr. Stokes's active support. We believe that the Association can only continue to be useful by maintaining the independent position which it has always held and defended, and which no one who knows its temper can suppose for a moment that it will sacrifice. It must not lean either upon the Institute or upon the Academy alone, or upon any support less broad than that of the whole body of architects and students of architecture in the country. It must recognise in its curriculum all tests, whether by examination or otherwise, of progress and efficiency, established by the Institute or by the Academy or by any other recognised authority.

This is the position we thought, and still think, the Association should maintain.

(Signed)

H. O. Cresswell.
E. W. Mountford.
Edmund Woodthorpe.
F. R. Farrow.
Hampden W. Pratt.
Willm. Burrell.
E. S. Gale.
F. T. W. Goldsmith.

Sir,—The whole of the difficulty of the A.A arises from one cause, and the only question the members of the A.A. are called upon to decide by their votes is the following:—

Is the assistance of the Memorialists worth the price demanded by them for such assistance?

The price demanded is, that the A.A. shall purge itself from all connexion with the Examination scheme, and refuse to assist its members in preparing for same, thereby cutting itself off from the large body of members of the profession which considers an Examination desirable.

Mr. Stokes and those who think with him say this price is not too great; but in my opinion the aim of the Association should be to enable its members to learn every branch of study necessary for an architect, and to hold an independent position free from dictation by any one.

I should much appreciate the assistance of the Memorialists, and regret that they should deem it necessary to demand such payment for it, but as they do so, in such unqualified terms, I must decline to accept it, and the members of the A.A. must decide for themselves.

William Burrell.

9, *Adam-street, Adelphi*, May 19, 1892.

BOSTON CHURCH.

Sir,—It is hardly worth while replying to the anonymous correspondent in your last issue except to state that the restoration now being carried out is not to the west door, but to the wall, arcade, and plinth courses of tower.

The work to the west door was completed in 1890 and, therefore, it is impossible to understand what original work existing "only six months ago" be looked for in vain.

If your correspondent had applied to me I should have been pleased to give every information in my power; I mention this because it must be known to him that the late vicar, Canon Blenkin, who would readily have explained what had been done, died last February.

W. Samuel Weatherley.

20, *Cockspur-street, London*.

ST. PETER'S CHURCH, BUSHEY HEATH.

Sir,—In your issue of the 14th inst. (page 372) you complain with reference to the above and other drawings which were published in the *Builder*, and now appear in the New York quarterly, the *Architectural Record*. You write:—"We can have no reasonable doubt that they are plundered from our pages, without the ceremony of saying 'with your leave' either to us or to the original owners of the drawings, who might be supposed to have some right to be consulted in the matter." I agree with you. My drawings were not sent to the *Architectural Record* or to any other journal excepting your own, and no permission was asked or given by me that they should appear in the *Architectural Record*.

James Neale, F.S.A.

10, *Bloomsbury-square, W.C.*

The Student's Column.

WARMING BUILDINGS BY HOT WATER. XXI.

BUILDING WORKS—GENERAL INFORMATION—QUANTITIES.

In treating of the heating of buildings the various phenomena relating to circulation, radiation, &c., are governed by precisely the same natural laws as in glass-house works. The circumstances and general conditions and the general points to be considered are, however, so different, that it becomes almost a distinct calling from horticultural works, and in many cases a man who can execute one may be almost at a loss with the other. The difference is as great as with those works for the supply of hot water for baths and domestic purposes, this being a quite distinct branch of practice.

One peculiarity of buildings works is the pressure that manifests itself when the pipes extend up two or more floors of a building; a pressure that needs consideration in many ways, particularly as to the joints of pipes, &c., which must be capable of withstanding it.

The pressure comes about in this way. When pipes extend any distance above a boiler, and they are charged with water, the weight of this water must be pressing downwards towards the boiler, and we learn from any work upon hydrostatics that the pressure so exerted is 1 lb. per square inch for every 2 ft. 4 in. height. In other words, if a pipe of 1 square inch area and 2 ft. 4 in. high, be filled with water, its contents will weigh 1 lb. If the pipe was set up on its end the weight of its contents, 1 lb., would be pressing upon what it was supported by. It is very necessary to avoid the notion that the pressure is in any way associated with the heat; it is merely weight of water. An apparatus extending, say, 42 ft. in height, would cause a pressure of 18 lbs. to be exerted upon every square inch surface in the boiler, or in the pipes near the boiler. As we rise above the boiler the pressure decreases in like ratio, that is, every 2 ft. 4 in. above the boiler the pressure become 1 lb. less, until we arrive at the top, where the pressure is *nil*. It is only vertical height that counts; it matters not how the pipes may be carried, the distance from the supply cistern at top to the boiler at bottom, in a vertical line, is the sum of the pressure exerted. It may be noted that the pressure is identically the same whatever the size of pipe, whether they be, say, 1 in. or 4 in.; but the reader is referred to my elementary work on Hydrostatics for those details.

It should be mentioned, as there is an idea rather prevalent that the size or area of the feed-cistern in some way governs the pressure, that this impression is wrong. The contents of this reservoir make no difference in pressure except as to its height. If in one case a very shallow cistern was used, and in another instance a very high cistern, and this latter filled quite full, then the higher cistern would bring a greater pressure to bear, but only 1 lb. for every 2 ft. 4 in. of its height, the same as in a pipe. If we wanted to get the exact pressure we should measure from the level of the water in the cistern to the centre of the boiler, the shape or extent of the cistern need not be considered. It may be well at the same time to explode the idea that pressure assists the circulation. It does not do so, yet at the same time as a high pressure means a high apparatus, a good circulation is always (or nearly so) obtained when a good pressure exists. It is, however, the height of the apparatus that increases the motive power, the pressure is merely a consequence, and has no active part in aiding circulation. If the pressure was down one pipe and up the other it would be a different thing, but the pressure is equal down all pipes, irrespective of whether the water has to travel up or down them.

The strain upon the boiler and pipes need not have any injurious effect. It makes care necessary in jointing the pipes as just mentioned, and when the apparatus extends a good height, the shape of the boiler has to be considered. Many a saddle boiler has been bulged inside by this cause, as it must be remembered that, say, 10 lb. pressure per square inch amounts to between two and three tons per square foot. Of course the larger the boiler the greater likelihood of its becoming misshapen by the strain. If the vertical height of the apparatus is mentioned to the boiler-maker he will say if the boiler selected is suitable.

If an apparatus burst throught this great strain or pressure of water, no harm would ensue unless anyone be near enough to be scalded by the outrush of hot water (supposing it to be hot). The fracture would be merely a fissure and no expansive or rending force would be felt. If the apparatus had its expansion pipe and other outlets closed, an explosion would occur, which would have very different results.

In works of this kind there is, we may say, never any lack of motive-power or strength of circulation. The extent to which the pipes always run vertically gives us this. It is so different to horticultural work in which vertical pipe is absent. When the mains are quite vertical, which is often the case, the circulation is so rapid sometimes as to carry the water right past the branches, ignore them, so to speak, and provision has frequently to be made to obviate this. Sometimes the provision is in the form of stop-valves; but a natural and simple arrangement, if found necessary, is to joint the pipe at every branch, as Fig. 87.

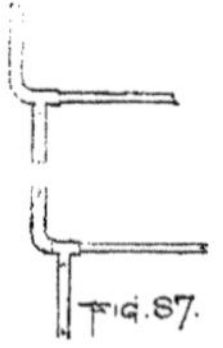

Fig. 87.

The size of the mains differs more in these works than with horticultural apparatus. They vary from 1½ in. to 3 in. or even 4 in. The former size is only suited for moderate-sized works, but with vertical pipes it is quite astonishing what a quantity of hot water small pipes can deal with. When these mains are not used for radiating purposes, they should be covered carefully, as already described. There should be no loss of heat. Where cost will admit, it is best to err towards having mains of sufficiently full size; it is a real gain, provided they are covered and cause no loss of heat. It will have been gathered that the higher the apparatus extends, the smaller the mains may be, to give certain results; but never run the risk of their being too small.

The water-supply to these works is provided for by a cistern of the necessary capacity, as per the rule already given. Sometimes the water is added by hand, but in these works it is usually a ball valve that automatically makes good the loss. The particular objection to these articles is, that at the best, they are not very reliable, and in fulfilling this duty, the demand for water being so small, they get stuck and out of order for want of regular use. They should be looked to regularly. It is a not uncommon practice to terminate the upper extremities of the main flow and return in a small tank; it is a very good plan, and in several little ways is found a convenience. If the apparatus is hand-filled, the water is put into this tank, which will answer as a filling cistern. In many cases the highest part of the circulating pipes may be a coil, and no tank is ermissible. The tank is only suggested when onditions are quite favourable.

The discharge of air from the apparatus is uite different to anything we have yet spoken f. It is practically impossible to use air-pipes; hey would sometimes have to be 60 ft. long, s it would be imperative that they reach up to point above the level of the supply-cistern, nd as we should require one from every ranch of pipes and every coil or radiator, the xpense would be great, and they would be isible in all directions. The customary rrangement is to use air-cocks, one at each ighest point; if pipes, one at each furthest xtremity; if coils or radiators, then one upon he extreme top of each of these. The ordinary orm of air-cock is as fig, 88, but a new one

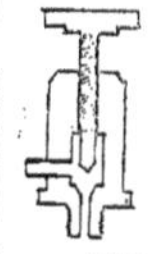

FIG. 89 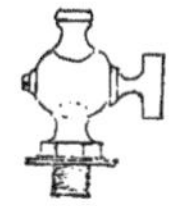   FIG. 88.

aving several good features has been introuced, as fig. 89 (section). Air-cocks need egular attention about once a fortnight, as air s continually finding its way into the appaatus, and collects at the highest points. When pening air-cocks to discharge air, it is necesary to hold a cloth over, as we cannot tell vhether the air is all out until water issues, nd the issue of water under pressure, however ittle, may do damage to wall-papers or decoraions, &c.

When an apparatus is wholly devoid of air ipes, it is very desirable to have an expansion ipe at some point. It is not absolutely necesary, as the cold supply-pipe and cistern allow or the actual increase in bulk of water, but if he apparatus overheats, and other such ossible happenings, the expansion-pipe beomes useful. It is never a great expense.

QUANTITIES.

A cubical contents table is about the only ractical means of arriving at the quantity of ipe needed in works of this character. There s a rule which is based upon the area of glass windows), the deperdition or loss of heat by alls (certain thicknesses, materials, and osition), and the degree of ventilation, &c. his rule, however, is rarely, if ever, resorted o. If it were discussed here, it would involve o many points, particularly as to aspects and entilation, as to complete the rest of these apers by itself.

Hood, when he gave his excellent though omplex rule to the world, applied it almost holly to glass-house work which it is well lapted for, but he also, unfortunately, enavoured to make it apply to building works y allowing so many cubic feet of air per erson occupying the room or place. It will be en what a weakness this introduces in the t that, firstly and chiefly, the number of ople has no relation to the size of the apartent. A small lecture-room may be calculated have an average of 200 people in it, yet some ivate reception-rooms would be nearly as rge and yet not exceed an average of 20 occunts. A rule founded this way will not work all satisfactorily unless a variety of allowces be made, with doubtful results. It would better to calculate the wall and window face, but this is not so good as basing calcutions on cubic contents.

In arriving at quantities in these works there always some guesswork introduced and lowances needed,—in fact, the tables given by writers are subject to this. In the use of e following table it must be seen that, firstly, e glass or windows are of ordinary area or mber; secondly, that the ventilation is rmal (except in drying-rooms, &c., where usual ventilation is allowed for). The place be heated must not be naturally damp or posed by being an addition to a main ilding, or standing out so that it is liable to eater cooling influences than ordinary. Again, nsideration must be given as to whether the iler fire has skilled or indifferent attention. buildings, particularly residences, the tendant is very commonly a page-boy or manservant, who only knows that the fire must not be allowed to go out. All these things occur readily to the mind after a little experience. It is hard to say what allowance is necessary in these different cases, but supposing all of them to exist at once, it would necessitate doubling the quantity of pipe given in the following table.

This table is based upon the water in the pipes being at a temperature of 180 deg. F., and the lowest external temperature 20 deg. F. Ordinary conditions: A foot length of 4-in. pipe is as nearly as possible a superficial foot of surface; for 3-in. pipe add one-third: for 2-in. pipe the quantity must be doubled:—

Temperature required.	Quantity of 4-in. pipe required for every 1,000 cubic feet capacity in a brick-built room. Windows as usual.	Some of the uses for which the heat may be required.
Deg. Fah.	Feet.	
50	6	Coach-houses, &c.
55	7	Work-rooms, &c.
60	8 to 9	Churches, bedrooms.
65	10	Living-rooms.
70	35	Drying-rooms, herbs, paper, &c. Free ventilation. This heat when empty and dry.
75	46	
80	60	
100	110	Drying-rooms for moist articles, laundry-work, &c. Full ventilation. This heat when empty and dry.
110	140	
120	180	

For the higher temperatures given good attention at the boiler is necessary, and the water kept at or as near boiling-point as possible. The allowance necessary if pipes are in channels with gratings over (or coils beneath floors) is the same as with glass-house work,—viz., one-third more pipe needed. This commonly occurs in church work which has either lines of pipes in channels, or stacks of pipe here and there beneath the floor, with gratings over. The latter causes a very disagreeable amount of heat to be felt by those whose seats are near these openings.

SURVEYORSHIPS.

NELSON (LANCASHIRE).—Mr. J. W. Bradley, of the Borough Engineer's office, Leicester, has received this appointment, the salary of which is 250*l*. per annum. There were ninety-three applicants for the appointment. The office became vacant by the appointment of the present Surveyor (Mr. J. A. Crowther, formerly of Leeds), as Borough Surveyor of Bootle.

OBITUARY.

DEATH OF AN OLD DISTRICT SURVEYOR.—The death of Mr. H. J. Hammon took place recently. He was appointed in 1853 District Surveyor of St. Luke's, Old-street with the Liberty of Glasshouse-yard, when there was a fierce contest with Mr. F. W. Porter, afterwards elected to the Holborn District. Mr. Hammon was in his eighty-second year, and for some years resided near Battle, Sussex. It is expected that the District will be added to one of the adjoining ones.

MR. GEORGE FREETH ROPER.—At the moment of going to press we hear with regret of the death of Mr. George Freeth Roper, whose name will be familiar to many of our readers. He died on the 14th inst., aged forty-nine.

GENERAL BUILDING NEWS.

REBUILDING OF ST. WERBURGH'S CHURCH, DERBY.—On the 26th ult., the Duke of Devonshire laid the foundation-stone of the new Church of St. Werburgh, Derby. Sir Arthur Blomfield is the architect, and in his plans for the new structure the present tower, chancel, and organ chamber, which are of comparatively modern date, are preserved intact. The new nave is to consist of five bays, and the total length will be 88 ft. 8 in., the width being 62 ft. 2 in. The body of the church will be 60 ft. high, with an open hammer-beam roof. The chancel will be 40 ft. 6 in. by 27 ft. At the end of the chancel there will be a seven-light window, with a carved reredos below. The walling will be of Coxbench stone, which from the exterior will be rock-faced, and in the inside hammer-dressed. The dressings will also be of Coxbench stone, except in the case of the finer parts of tracery, which will be worked in Hollington stone. The roof will consist of green slates with lead gutters, and stone-embattled parapets. The entire area of the nave will be paved with wood blocks, whilst the chancel, which will be divided from the nave by a dwarf screen, will have a tiled floor with steps of Portland stone. The seating accommodation will be for 878 persons. The contract for the building was let to Messrs. Shillitoe & Sons, of Bury St. Edmunds, and the total cost has been estimated at between 11,000*l*. and 12,000*l*.

POLICE STATION, CATHCART.—Plans by Mr. Davidson, of Paisley, for a new police station at Cathcart, near Glasgow, have been approved by the County Committee. The style adopted is Scotch, and, as part of the building is three stories in height, it will be quite a prominent building in the district, where (as yet) the houses are principally of one and two stories.

HALIFAX MARKETS AND ARCADE.—These works have now let, and the contract for covering the roofs has been secured by Messrs. Helliwell & Co., of Brighouse and London, for their well-known patent system of glazing without putty. The architects are Messrs. Leeming & Leeming, of London.

RESTORATION OF PARISH CHURCH, GIGGLESWICK, YORKSHIRE. — The ancient Parish Church of Giggleswick, near Settle, has just been re-opened by the Bishop of Richmond, after extensive restoration. The work, which has cost some 3,500*l*., has been carried out from the designs of Messrs. Paley, Austin, & Paley, architects, of Lancaster, the contractor being Mr. H. Brassington, of Settle. The work done includes the construction of an organ chamber and vestry, the erection of a heating apparatus chamber, the re-roofing of the entire fabric with oak and lead, the pointing of the stonework, the re-seating of the interior, and the erection of several stained-glass windows in the od of the church and the clearstory.

NEW LIBRARY FOR SOLICITORS, EDINBURGH.—The new library for the Society of Solicitors in the Supreme Courts of Scotland, was opened on the 12th inst. by the Lord Justice-General of Scotland, the Right Hon. J. P. B. Robertson. The site of the library is in the Cowgate, to which it shows a frontage of 150 ft., and as the Cowgate is at a much lower level than Parliament-square, the Society's premises, says the *Scotsman*, have been put in the topmost stories of the building, so that the top or main story is on the same level as the floor of Parliament House, with which it is connected by a bridge, which is a continuation of the corridor between the Inner and the Outer Houses. The four lower stories have been turned into artisan dwelling-houses, with shops on the basement. On the main or top-floor, beginning at the west end, is an entrance-hall, lighted by four stained-glass windows. A staircase, executed in teak, leads from the hall to the flat below, and facing the entrance is the reading-room, 30 ft. by 22 ft. East of the entrance hall is the main library, measuring 74 ft. by 42 ft., with arched ceiling. Each side is divided into five alcoves, and the bookcases have been made part of the architectural features of the room. Each block is terminated by pilasters facing the interior of the room, and from the tops of these spring a series of elliptical arches supported on moulded and carved trusses. The windows are to be of stained glass. A gallery with ornamental iron railing runs round three sides of the room. Beyond the library, entering off it to the eastward, is the Society's hall, 40 ft. by 26 ft.; librarian's room and other accessories. The second story, entered from the staircase in the vestibule, is taken up with book stores, repairing and sorting rooms, consulting rooms for members of the Society, and heating apparatus. There is accommodation in the library and stores for about 70,000 volumes. The architect has been Mr. James B. Dunn, of Edinburgh, whose design was selected in competition. The cost of the site and building has been close on 30,000*l*.

ST. BARNABAS' CHURCH, BELFAST.—On the 7th inst., the memorial-stone of St. Barnabas' Church, Duncairn-gardens, Belfast, was laid by the Mayor of Belfast. The church is being carried out in the Early English style. The materials used are red perforated brick, with white Scotch stone dressings. The church when completed will consist of a nave 70 ft. long by 27 ft. wide, with north and south aisles, divided from the same by a series of moulded arches carried on cut-stone piers. The chancel, which is approached by an arch springing the full width of the nave, provides accommodation for clergy and choir. The church at present being built will seat 550 persons, but when the north aisle is added accommodation will be provided for 770. The contract is being carried out by Mr. Thomas M'Millan, of Belfast, from the plans and under the superintendence of the architect, Mr. Henry Seaver, also of Belfast.

RESTORATION OF WOODHAM MORTIMER CHURCH, ESSEX.—The re-opening, after restoration, of St. Margaret's Church, Woodham Mortimer, by the Bishop of St. Albans, took place on the 27th ult. With the exception of the south wall and the east end, the whole of the church, says the *Essex County Chronicle*, has been rebuilt. A new arcade takes the place of the north wall, and the old north transept has been replaced by an aisle. In the roof of the aisle are two dormer windows. The church has now also the addition of a new vestry; the old gallery and organ-loft, which stood at the west end of the church, have been pulled down, and the organ has been enlarged and repaired by Fincham & Co., of London, and placed in the transept. Previously there was no west window, but in the course of the alterations an old one was found beneath the plaster, and it has been opened up and restored. Two windows,—one a Norman and the other Decorated,—were also discovered in the south wall after the plaster was stripped off, and they have been opened up. The old-fashioned high-backed pews have been replaced by modern benches of oak; the floors and aisles are laid with blocks of wood, and a new heating apparatus has been put in. The church furniture is of oak, the altar-table and rails and the pulpit and lecterns being made of old carved oak. The roof is of yellow deal, panelled and ribbed, with a plain cross on the chancel beam. In the east end is a three-light window with stained glass, the subject being the Nativity. The tracery is filled in with angels bearing instruments of music. At the side of the altar is another painted glass single-light window. At the south side of the chancel is a two-light window (replacing a single light) with two figures, St. Peter and St. John. The west window has two painted-glass lights representing the figures of Charity and Purity. The painted glass windows are the work of Messrs. Heaton, Butler, & Bayne, of London. The restoration has been carried out by Mr. H. Gozzett, sen., at a cost of about 1,750*l*. The architect was Mr. Sidney Gambier Parry, of Westminster.

PROPOSED RECONSTRUCTION OF THE COUNTY BUILDINGS, EDINBURGH.—It is proposed to reconstruct the Edinburgh County Buildings, and, according to the *Edinburgh Evening News*, several members of the Justices of the Peace of Edinburgh, being dissatisfied with the plans prepared for the County Council, had new designs prepared for them by Mr. M'Farlane Cameron, architect, of Edinburgh. It is proposed to bring the frontage forward to the present line of pavement, leaving a small area light only at the north-west corner. A large entrance from George IV. Bridge is provided. The front is treated in Palladian Classic, and the lines of the present building have been retained. It is proposed to ask support from the Town Council in the matter.

CATHEDRAL OF ST. MACARTAN, MONAGHAN.—According to the *Freeman's Journal*, the Cathedral of St. Macartan, Monaghan, is fast approaching completion. It is a Gothic structure, and the foundation-stone was laid more than twenty years ago by the late Bishop M'Nally. The building was designed by the late Mr. M'Carthy, but since 1883 it has been in the hands of Mr. Hague, who has been responsible for the spire and the larger portion of the interior fittings and embellishments. The spire springs from a tower built against the southern transept of the church to the height of 245 ft., and is furnished with cathedral bells. Internally, there are five altars,—the high altar, surmounted by a baldachino, and the four side altars, each with a reredos of interlaced marbles. The flooring and balustrades of the sanctuary, the choir, the side-chapels, and the baptistry are in mosaic of fourteen varieties of Italian marble. The statuary is from Carrara. On the western façade of the Cathedral is the statue of St. Macartan. The western door is flanked by two statues of SS. Peter and Paul, and its tympanum is filled by a bas-relief in marble, representing Our Lord committing the keys of Heaven to St. Peter. In the colonnade of the northern transept are statues of seven saints. On the corresponding colonnade of the southern transept stand seven figures of personages interesting to the people of Clogher. On the southern front of the tower is a figure of Our Lord. There are seven stained-glass windows in the apse around the high altar, and in the four side chapels the altars are surmounted by stained-glass windows. The oak furniture of the Cathedral has been supplied by Messrs. Brien & Keating, of Wexford. The Cathedral organ is the work of the Messrs. Telford, of Dublin. The stained-glass windows were executed by Messrs. Cox, Buckley, & Co., London and Youghal; Messrs. Early & Powells, Dublin; and Messrs. Mayer & Co., of London and Munich. The decoration of the Cathedral walls is the work of Mr. Mannix, of Dublin.

CHANCEL, PARISH CHURCH, UPHILL.—The parish church of Uphill, Somerset, was re-opened on the 10th inst., after the building of a new chancel, in addition to which new choir and clergy vestries, organ chamber, north and south porches, have been erected, and the nave reseated with oak seats. The architect for the work is Mr. G. F. Burr, of Hastings; and the contractor Mr. Charles Addicott, of Weston-super-Mare. The cost has been about 1,650*l*. The wrought-iron gates to the chancel-screen, which is of oak and carved chestnut, were executed by Mr. George Wilson, of Birmingham, from the designs of the architect.

PUBLIC BATHS AND PUBLIC HALL, CHEETHAM HILL, NEAR MANCHESTER.—Land has just been purchased and plans approved for the erection of public baths and a public hall in the Bury Old-road, Cheetham, Manchester. Messrs. Booth & Chadwick, of Manchester, are the architects. The public hall will be built on the higher and the baths on the lower land, but all the principal entrances will be from Cheetham Hill-road. The first-class swimming-bath will have a water area of 54 ft. by 27 ft., and the second-class bath one of 75 ft. by 24 ft. The latter will be surrounded by a balcony. The pavilion in which it is situate is so arranged as to be capable of being used as a gymnasium in the winter months. There are twenty slipper-baths and three waiting-rooms. A residence for the superintendent will be situate over the ticket office and entrances to the baths, and in connexion with this department there is to be a tower for a public clock. The laundry and boiler-house are centrally situate between the two large swimming-baths, and the fall of the land will enable the boiler-house to be approached on the street level from Back Halliwell-lane. The public hall will be on the ground-floor level, and will be practically a separate building. The principal room will have a clear floor area of 64 ft. by 42 ft., and there will be a balcony gallery in addition. There will also be five retiring and cloak rooms, with lavatories, &c., attached, a refreshment-room, serving-room, and a cellar kitchen. There will be an entrance-hall leading to the public-room; and the retiring-rooms for ladies and gentlemen will be placed to the right and left of it. Additional doors for occasional exit are provided from the public hall and from the large second-class bath pavilion. The design of the buildings is based on the Italian style, with some of the earlier features of the Elizabethan introduced in the windows, &c. The main fronts will be faced with Ruabon stock bricks and terra-cotta. The public hall will have a panelled ceiling, and be lighted by a series of mullioned windows.

RAGGED SCHOOLS, MANCHESTER.—The new buildings for Charter-street Ragged School and Girls' Home, Manchester, were opened on the 28th ult. by the Baroness Burdett-Coutts. The new buildings are situated on a plot of land lying between Ashley-street and Charter-street. On the ground floor at the corner of Ashley-lane and Little Nelson-street is a mission-hall capable of accommodating 500 persons, with two public entrances in Ashley-lane and a platform entrance in Little Nelson-street. On the first floor, above the mission-hall, is a school-room to accommodate 700 children, with two class-rooms in addition to accommodate 40 each. The infants' school is placed on the ground floor, with an entrance through a yard from Charter-street, and an entrance for the teachers and visitors from Little Nelson-street. The room is 63 ft. long, and will accommodate 500 infants. The whole of the roof is of glass. There is a gallery for infants at one end of the room, which is to be divided off from the rest of the room by a movable shutter, and there is a platform at the other end. The Girls' Home provides accommodation for about forty young women. The girls' sitting-room is 32 ft. by 20 ft., lit with three bay windows facing the south and east. This room is heated with one of Shorland's ventilating stoves. On the first floor of the home is provided a wash-house. The girls' kitchen is provided with a cooking range. The hot water for the kitchens and bath is generated in a boiler in the basement, and the water is circulated in copper pipes to the wash-houses, lavatories, kitchens, and baths. The materials used for the exterior are second brick with red dressings, and the walls inside have been pointed and colour-washed. The general contract for the work has been carried out by Messrs. Peters, of Rochdale, from the plans and under the supervision of Messrs. Maxwell & Tuke, architects, of Manchester.

CHURCH OF ST. GILES, LULSLEY, WORCESTER.—On the 25th ult. the foundation-stone was laid of the Church of St. Giles, Lulsley, Worcester, which is being built near the site of the old church. The church is to be built of a red sandstone from a local quarry at Blackswell. The architects are Messrs. H. Rowe & Sons, of Worcester, and the builder is Mr. T. Collins, of Tewkesbury.

SANITARY AND ENGINEERING NEWS.

LEOMINSTER WATER EXTENSION SCHEME.—On the 10th inst., the Corporation of Leominster received the Local Government Board's sanction to the water extension scheme which was laid before Mr. T. Codrington, C.E., last June. The engineer for the scheme is Mr. John W. B. Rooke, the Borough Surveyor.

DRAINAGE, WHITCHURCH, CARDIFF.—At a meeting of the Cardiff Rural Sanitary Authority, held at their offices, Queen's-chambers, Cardiff, on the 11th instant, a scheme of drainage for the Parish of Whitchurch, prepared by their surveyor, Mr. William Fraser, was considered and referred to a sub-committee. The scheme is estimated to cost 6,200*l*., and includes over six and a half miles of stoneware pipes ranging in size from 9 in. to 18 in. in diameter, with all necessary manholes, ventilators, and automatic flushing tanks, &c., having an outfall by eight connexions into the Ystradyfodwg and Pontypridd main sewer, which passes through the district of the authority, emptying into the Bristol Channel near Rumney.

SEWAGE DISPOSAL, LUDLOW.—The Corporation of Ludlow is now considering the question of adopting a scheme of sewage disposal. In 1861 the town was sewered by the late Mr. T. Cunley, C.E., and a system of disposal, involving deodorisation and filtration, was then adopted. Since 1861, however, sanitary science has advanced, and the sewage tanks have been pronounced by Government Inspectors obsolete and out of date. The Corporation has lately made application to the Local Government Board for permission to extend the boundaries of the Borough, and the Local Government Board have held a preliminary inquiry, the outcome of which is the Board has now sent the Corporation a map with a suggested boundary marked on it, with an intimation that it will be willing to entertain an application based on this, provided the Corporation can show that it has at the time of the application an efficient system of sewage disposal which can be made available not only for the present borough, but for the areas proposed to be added. The Corporation has passed a resolution that it will provide such a system, and has referred the question to a Committee to consider the details.

EXTENSION OF WATER SUPPLY, ROTHESAY, BUTE.—On the 13th inst. the Rothesay Municipality opened the new extension and filter-works at Ascog Loch. The extension includes not only the erection of filters, but the raising of the loch by means of a puddled embankment, which raises the storage area 6 ft. above the former level. The engineers for the work were Messrs. Leslie & Reid, of Edinburgh, while the contractor was Mr. John Murray, Maryhill. The total cost of the work, including stripping the margins of the loch and beaching, is expected to be between 7,000*l*. and 8,000*l*.

SEWERAGE WORKS AT HENDON.—On the 14th inst. the Chairman of the Hendon Local Board, Mr. John Warburton, opened the new pumping station, which has been erected near Cool Oak-lane, to deal with the sewage from what is known as the Station district, forming part of the Low Level area. The latter comprises about 1,100 acres. It has become necessary to drain this district in consequence of the complaints made by the Regent's Canal Company, who own the Brent reservoir, at Hendon, and into which pollution from the houses in the Station district forced its way when the cesspools overflowed. The Thames Conservators also complained of the same state of things, the river Brent being a tributary of the Thames. The Board instructed their engineer, Mr. S. S. Grimley, A.M.I.C.E., to prepare the necessary drawings for the works, and in June, 1891, the tender of Mr. James Dickson, of St. Albans, was accepted for the sewer, which was constructed with Hassall's double-lined pipes, 18 in. diameter, surrounded with portland cement concrete. The tender of Mr. Joseph Meston, of Westminster, was accepted for sewering and making up three roads leading to the outfall sewer, and the tender of Messrs. Crossley Brothers, of London and Manchester was accepted for the machinery. The total cost of the works has been 6,358*l*., being well within the engineer's estimate. Although the outfall sewer had to be laid about 8 ft. below the high-water mark in the Canal Company's reservoir, and closely adjacent thereto, and during the wet year of 1891, the leakage from all sources is not more than one four-thousandth part of the capacity of the sewer. The machinery consists of two 7-h.p. (nom.) Crossley's "Otto" gas-engines, with tube ignition and all the latest improvements giving out about 11½-h.p. on brake. Each gas-engine drives a set of three-throw plunger-pumps, 18 in. by 10 in., by means of Victoria belting through counter-shafting 3¼ in. in diameter, working in gun-metal bearings bolted to pump-frames. Each set of pumps will throw 350 gallons per minute, or over 500,000 gallons in twenty-four hours, into the high-level gravitating sewer through a 9-in. rising main about 800 ft. long, at a speed of thirty revolutions per minute. The sewage flows about a mile and a-half through the gravitating sewer to the outfall works where it is treated on the ferrozone and polarite process of the International Water and Sewage Purification Company.

STAINED GLASS AND DECORATION.

WINDOW, ST. JOHN'S CHURCH, LONGSIGHT, MANCHESTER.—A new three-light east window has been inserted in the chancel of St. John's Church, Longsight. The subject is the transfiguration of Our Lord, He being the central figure of the upper portion, with Moses and Elias on either side. Below are the figures of SS. Peter, James, and John, one in each light. The whole of the masonry of the east wall is new. The works were designed by and have been carried out under the superintendence of Mr. Medland Taylor, Messrs. Heaton, Butler, & Bayne being the artists by whom the window was executed, and Messrs. Ekis & Hinchliffe the masons who did the stonework.

NEW WINDOWS, ST. ANDREW'S CHURCH, RADCLIFFE, LANCASHIRE.—On the 17th ult., the windows in the octagonal-shaped chancel of the Church of St. Andrew, Radcliffe, which had been filled with stained glass, were unveiled and dedicated. The twelve lights forming the seven windows have been filled with the following subjects from Our Lord's passion:—1. The supper in the house of Simon. 2. The entry into Jerusalem. 3. Christ purging the temple. 4. The institution of the Holy Eucharist. 5. Washing the disciples' feet. 6. The agony in the garden. 7. Christ before Caiaphas. 8. Behold the Man. 9. The way of the Cross. 10. The Betrayal. 11. The Crucifixion. 12. The Entombment. In each case the subject fills the whole light as far up as the spring of the arch, the rest being led in with shields enclosed in foliated ornament th border. The tracery above each window conins an angel holding a shield upon which is shown me instrument of the passion. The windows have en executed by Messrs. Jno. R. Lee & Co., imited, of Birmingham.

FOREIGN AND COLONIAL.

FRANCE.—A picture in the Champs Élysées tion has been cut with a pen-knife; the picture is . Vibert's "Médécin Malade." It is not known ho has committed this act of vandalism.——M. amille Krantz, deputy of the Voges, member of e jury at the Universal Exhibition of 1889, has en nominated General Commissioner for the rench Government at the International Exhibition Chicago in 1893.——The section for French orks of art at the Chicago Exhibition will be ened on May 1, 1893, and closed on October 30. —The fifty-ninth session of the Archæological ongress of France will be held this year at rléans. It will begin on June 22, and last till the d of the month.——An exhibition of paintings by . Huet is to be held in the Galerie Georges Petit. —M. J. Prevost has just offered to the Luxemourg Museum a picture by M. Weisz, called Femme du Masque."——The picture by M. douard Detaille, "Sortie de la Garrison de uningue," has been presented to the nation by a erson unknown, but who is supposed to be an merican. The picture is to have a place in the uxembourg.——At last the fees for the architects ho have reconstructed the Hôtel de Ville have been efinitely settled. This work has cost 26,646,686f., ot counting the work of artistic decoration.—— hey are shortly to proceed with the enlargement the Musée du Louvre, by taking in the quarters ccupied by the Prefecture of the Seine since 1879. —The State has just bought for the Louvre a ne portrait of Eugène Delacroix, by Gericault. —A monumental door is to be placed on the ôtel Carnavalet. This door is in a very fine style, d is the last vestige of the church of Saint tienne des Grés.——Several French artists,—MM. ublet, Castellani, Duez, Ferrier, Flameng, Gervex, uillemet, J. P. Laurens, Rochegrasse, Merson, oll, &c.,—are proposing to execute a panorama of tance for the Chicago Exhibition. It will include e country, types, and manners and customs of e French provinces.——A discovery has been ade near Versailles of an amphora, containing a rge quantity of Gallo-Roman money.——The eneral Council of Var has voted 400,000 francs for e enlargement of the Asylum of Pierrefeu, which as built in 1882, and which was the object of a ry important competition, the first prize having en awarded to MM. Violet and Geyler.——The w railway to Crémaillère from Aix-les-Bains is to opened in September next.——The death is announced of the sculptor, Louis Vidal. He was rn at Nimes in 1831, and was a pupil of Barye, d received medals in 1861 and 1863. In latter ars he had lost his sight.

BERLIN.—The question of a further alteration of e neighbourhood of the Imperial "Schloss" has en formally dropped, and the "Schlossplatz" is assume the same aspect as was planned at the ne of the first lottery which was opened for the rpose of raising money for the improvement of e site; and the memorial monument to Emperor illiam I. will have a place found for it on the east ie, under the windows of the Schloss. According the *Cologne Gazette*, this monument is now to be rried out by the sculptor Reinhold Begas and the chitect Ihne.——There are a number of monuents in course of erection in the country. The e to be erected on the historical Kyffhauser had foundation stone laid by the Duke of Schwarzrg-Rudolstadt on the 10th inst., this being the niversary of the Peace at Frankfort-on-Main. runo Schmitz is the architect.——The competition r the models of the sculptural parts on Bruno hmitz' Soldiers' and Sailors' Monument at Indianolis has apparently been decided in favour of a rlin sculptor, Herr Nikolaus Geiger (*Nordd. lg. Ztg.*). This is the second piece of monuental sculpture to be done in Berlin for America. e first piece was the Washington Monument for iladelphia, which was in the hands of Professor dolf Siemering. The bronze parts of this lossal monument are already for the most part in nerica.——The private view of the Berlin salon s on Friday. The local papers considered the ow to be a fair one on the whole, although the old ilt of the Berlin art exhibitions, *i.e.*, the ranking quantity above quality, has been made by the nging committee with the purpose of filling their lls. The sculpture hall excites much interest, rtially, perhaps, on account of the huge size of the aibits.——The official "Architekten Verein" has d a debate on the selection of a suitable site for International Exhibition, and will give a prize 25*l.* for the best proposition made, if accomnied by a rough plan of the grounds as proposed. ree sites are deserving of attention at present, , one in an outlying suburb, Wilmersdorf, (2), in the Treptow Park, and (3), another on the ge Review grounds in the south-west of the y.

MISCELLANEOUS.

THE CONVERSION OF GAUGE ON THE GREAT WESTERN RAILWAY.—The *Engineer* for May 13 contains an interesting article on this subject. At midnight this Saturday, May 21, the entire section of the line from Exeter to Falmouth, a distance of 113½ miles, will be closed to traffic, and handed over to an army of 3,500 platelayers, who will alter the permanent way to the narrow-gauge system. The whole of the work will be so far completed in forty-eight hours that the line will be opened for traffic again on Monday. With the conversion of the Exeter and Falmouth line the broad-gauge system ceases to exist in England. The broad-gauge rail on the mixed lines from Paddington to Exeter, from Truro to Penzance, and from Tavistock Junction to Lidford, will, it is true, be suffered to remain for the present, but it will be removed subsequently as occasion offers.

THE CONCENTRATION OF POPULATION IN GREAT CITIES.—The *Lancet* of May 14, contains the first part of a lecture on this subject, recently delivered at University College, London, by Dr. G. V. Poore. It is full of suggestive points. Quoting from a paper read by Dr. Gould, of Washington, before the recent International Congress of Hygiene and Demography, he says that only half a century ago the urban population of the United States was 8·5 per cent. of the whole, while to-day the urban population constitutes 29 per cent. of the whole. The American city, says Dr. Gould, "creates itself with appalling suddenness," and it is probable that Chicago, with its 1,200,000 inhabitants, having doubled its population in the last ten years, may be said in this particular matter to have beaten the record. It must not be forgotten, however, adds Dr. Poore, that London has more than doubled its population in the last half century; that Cardiff has risen from 80,000 to 130,000 inhabitants in the last ten years; that Barrow-in-Furness, Eastbourne, Bournemouth, West Ham, and Croydon, are all instances of towns (and other instances could easily be given), which have sprung into existence within the memory of many people now living. One of the undoubted consequences of the concentration of population in towns is deterioration in physical health. The disease-rate and the death-rate are both higher in urban than in country districts. The Registrar-General's returns show that for every 100 deaths in country districts there are about 120 deaths in towns. Dr. Poore deprecates the increasing tendency towards the erection of lofty tenement dwellings, and thinks that the comparatively low death-rate which London has hitherto enjoyed is to be attributed to the fact that, as a rule, each family has had a house of its own.

INNOCUOUS WHITE-LEAD.—The Patent Innocuous White-lead Company (T. B. Freeman) send us a pamphlet of testimonials from chemists and others in regard to their "non-poisonous white-lead paint," which is stated by Professor Church to be "practically insoluble, so far as the lead is concerned in water or acids, and non-poisonous, and that it possesses the merits of ordinary white-lead as a pigment without its drawbacks." A paint of which this can be said should prove a great boon to painters.

THE TRADES' MAIDEN HOSPITAL, EDINBURGH.—The Trustees of the Trades' Maiden Hospital of Edinburgh have acquired Ashfield, a residence situated to the south of the city, which, with additions thereto, is to be adapted to the purposes of the Institution. Ashfield was designed by Mr. David Macgibbon as a residence for himself, and is an adaptation of the Scottish Baronial style. It stands in about two acres of ground facing to the south and looking out upon Blackford Hill. The situation is a fine one, and there is ample scope for any future additions that may be necessary, and the style is one whigh lends itself to such being carried out in a manner which should add to the *tout ensemble*. The sum received by the trustees from the managers of the Sick Children's Hospital for the premises at Rill Bank was 17,000*l.*, and the price paid for Ashfield is 9,000*l.*, leaving a sufficient margin for the necessary alterations and additions.

THE LYRIC THEATRE.—Another of the London new theatres,—the Lyric, in Shaftesbury-avenue,—has just been placed in the market. This theatre, erected for Mr. H. J. Leslie, from the plans and designs of Mr. C. J. Phipps, architect, was opened on December 17, 1888. Its site covers 14,200 ft. superficial, of which 10,000 is held by an eighty years' lease, running from 1886, at a ground-rent of 1,164*l.*; the remainder, with the buildings thereon, being freehold. The frontage to the Avenue is 148 ft. long. The upper floors are occupied as residential chambers. We gave a full description of the fabric in our issue of December 22, 1888.

THE DANGERS OF BARE COPPER UNDERGROUND ELECTRIC MAINS.—Our contemporary, *L'Electricien*, published, on April 16, an article with the above title, referring to the explosion which had recently taken place in a manhole belonging to the Edison Company, in the Rue Taitbout (Paris). The statements contained in the article in question were such that, in view of the large use to which the bare copper system has been put in England, it would be imagined that English engineers would (unless in the case of the Edison Company there had been culpable negligence) have experienced similar difficulties. We are informed, however, that this is not the case, and that, with the exception of explosions resulting from coal gas leaking into the conduits, no difficulties of the kind indicated have been encountered with the bare copper system in England. Such a thing as carbonising of, or deposition of, copper salts on the conductors is, in ordinary working, unknown. Where any section of the main has got to earth through breaking of the copper, the latter has, of course, generally been eaten through; but such an accident as this cannot fairly be attributed to the demerits of the system, and is, of course, entirely the fault of the workmanship. The growth of the bare copper system of underground mains has been so rapid (there being over 100 miles now laid in England) that, on reading our contemporary's article, we were inclined to conclude that the formations referred to were of so unusual a nature as to be unfairly described as a danger to which bare underground mains are frequently subject, and that they were rather the result of careless and inefficient engineering. We are glad to find that our opinion is confirmed by those who have had most experience with this class of work in England.—*Electrical Plant.*

CHICAGO EXHIBITION.—We are informed that the new building which is now in course of erection for the headquarters of the British Royal Commission will be generally characteristic of the best type of English half-timber houses of the sixteenth century. It is proposed to use terra-cotta somewhat largely in the lower story, with red brick facing and mullioned windows, so that the building may be a typical example of an old English house. The upper portion will be of half-timber construction, with overhanging and projecting gables. The plans and designs for the whole building have been prepared by Colonel Robert W. Edis, F.S.A., the honorary architect to the Royal Commission; and the whole of the internal fittings and furniture will be executed from his designs by Messrs. Johnstone, Norman, & Co.

THE PRODUCTION OF TIN PLATES IN THE UNITED STATES.—Owing to the strenuous efforts now being made in the United States to establish the manufacture of tin plates there, to the exclusion of the British product, the report on the subject just presented by Colonel Ira Ayer, agent of the American Treasury Department, is of special interest. The report of Colonel Ayer covers the period from July 1, 1891, to March 31, 1892, the former date being the day on which the McKinley tariff came into operation. The annexed statement shows the production of tin and terne plates by quarters:—

Quarter ended	Works Established.	Tin Plates.	Terne Plates.	Totals.
		lbs.	lbs.	lbs.
Sept. 30, 1891 ..	5	152,489	674,433	826,922
Dec. 31, 1891 ..	11	215,911	1,193,910	1,409,821
Mar. 31, 1892 ..	19	1,099,656	1,904,431	3,004,087
Totals	..	1,468,056	3,772,774	5,240,830

According to Colonel Ayer's report the average annual imports of British tin and terne plates for the three years ended June 30, 1890, amounted to 678,000,000 lbs. In the year ended June 30, 1891, the imports were 1,058,000,000 lbs. This large increase of 380,000,000 lbs. was due to larger importations in the first six months of 1891 to avoid the new duty of 2·2 cents. per lb. imposed by the McKinley tariff. It is stated that, if the imports for the current year are made to meet only the actual wants of the United States, they will not exceed 300,000,000 lbs. For the eight months up to February 29, 1892, they amounted to only 177,000,000 lbs. The quantity of tin plates imported in the year ended June 30, 1891, which were used in the manufacture of exported articles, and upon which a drawback was paid, was 150,000,000 lbs. In 1890 it was 150,000,000 lbs., and in 1889 it amounted to 166,000,000 lbs. It is a stipulation of the McKinley tariff that, if after six years after the introduction of that tariff the quantity of tin plates made in the United States exceeds one-third of the quantity imported, the present duty of 2·2 cents. is to be maintained. Taking the figures given above as a basis, it is estimated by Colonel Ayer that the American manufacturers, in order to make the duty on tin plates perpetual after October 1, 1897, must produce in any one of the six years up to that date 50,000,000 lbs. of tin and terne plates.

ELECTRIC RAILWAY IN SIAM.—The contract for the electrical plant of the electric railway in Siam has gone to the United States, the Short Electric Railway Company of Cleveland, Ohio, being the successful competitors. The contract includes two 65-h.p. generators and six cars with a 20-h.p. motor to each car. It has been the custom lately for some of our authorities to congratulate this country on having allowed the Americans to go ahead of us in the application of electricity to industrial purposes. The line of argument taken is that the advances being made in this field are so enormously rapid, that we shall do well to let the Americans go a bit ahead to show us the way, and so we shall

COMPETITIONS, CONTRACTS, AND PUBLIC APPOINTMENTS.

COMPETITIONS.

Nature of Work.	By whom Advertised.	Premium.	Designs to be delivered.
*Illuminated Clock Tower	New Sarum T. C.	20l. and 5l.	June 28
*Municipal Technical School	Manchester Corp.	200l. 150l. 100l. 75l.	Aug. 2
*New Masonic Hall	Newcastle-upon-Tyne Central Masonic Hall Co. Ltd.	50l. 25l.	No date

CONTRACTS.

Nature of Work or Materials.	By whom Required.	Architect, Surveyor, or Engineer.	Tenders to be delivered.
Three Blocks Artisans' Dwellings, Salford	Lancs. & Yorks. R. Co.	Henry Shelmerdine	May 24
Baths and Public Rooms	Manchester Corp.	Official	do.
*Paving, Granite, Channel, &c.	Strand Bd. of Works	do.	May 25
*Broken Granite	Hackney Bd. of Works	do.	do.
*Broken Granite, Lime, and Cement	Mile End Old Town Vestry	J. M. Knight	do.
*Construction of Brick Culvert	Borough of St. Helen's	G. J. C. Broom	do.
Granite and Whinstone Paving	Gateshead Corporation	J. Bower	do.
Rebuilding "William IV." Inn, Newport, Mon.	Phillips & Sons, Lim.	W. Gardner	do.
Wesleyan Chapel and Schools, Blaina, Mon.	Rev. Joseph Wells	F. R. Bates	do.
Twenty-five Miners' Dwellings, Wheal Agar, Illogan, Cornwall	Lord Robartes	Silvanus Trevail	May 26
Central Station Electric Lighting Plant, Mains, &c.	Yorkshire House-to-House Electricity Co. Lim.	Official	do.
Twenty Houses, Craghead, Chester-le-Street	Craghead Colliery	J. W. Routhwaite	May 27
Villa, "The Whins," Stotfield, Elgin, N.B.	....	A. & W. Reid	do.
*Public Baths	Ipswich U.S.A.	Thos. W. Cotman	do.
New Church, Omagh, Ireland	Very Rev. B. M'Namee	Wm. Hague	May 28
*Erection of House, Surbiton	A. R. Upjohn	A. Mason	do.
*Road Materials	Hendon U.R.S.A.	R. A. Wilson	do.
*Concrete Sea-wall, Promenade, &c.	Filey Loc. Bd.	Official	do.
*Sundry Repairs, Painting, &c.	Central London Sick Asylum	do.	May 30
Brick Intercepting Sewer	Burslem Corporation	F. Bettany	do.
*Sewerage Works	Chard R.S.A.	C. N. Lailey	May 31
*Wood Paving Works	Commrs. of Sewers	Official	do
*Enlargement of P.O. Gravesend	Commrs. of H.M. Wks	do.	do.
*Supply of Timber	Eton Union	do.	do.
*Making-up Carriageways	Kensington Vestry	Wm. Weaver	do.
Main Drainage (Contract No. 10)	Manchester Corp.	J. Allison	do.
*Refitting W.C. Rooms, Western Hospital	Met. Asylums Board	A. & C. Marston	June 1
Alterations to Church, Kildare, Ireland	Very Rev. Dr. Murphy	Wm. Hague	do.
*Extension of Old P.O. Woolwich	Commrs. of H.M. Wks	Official	do.
Wooden Viaduct, Elliot Pit, Rhymney Valley	Powell Duffryn Coal Co	....	do.
*Alterations, &c. Northern Hospital	Met. Asylums Board	Pennington & Bridgen	June 2
*Station Buildings, Leicester	M. R. Co.	Official	June 3
*Painting, &c. Station Buildings, Sheffield	do.	do.	do.

CONTRACTS.—Continued.

Nature of Work or Materials.	By whom Required.	Architect, Surveyor, or Engineer.	Tenders to be delivered.
*Sewerage Works	Wakefield U.R.S.A.	F. Massie	June 3
*Repairs and Drainage Works at Workhouse	Newhaven Union	W. A. Mole	do.
*Making-up Carriageway and Tarpaving Footways	Hendon Local Board	S. S. Grimley	June 6
School Work, near Chesterfield	Brimington (U.D.) S.B.	Official	do.
Penmaenmawr Stone	Northwich High. Bd.	do.	do.
*Tar and Asphalte Paving	Tottenham Loc. Bd.	J. E. Worth	June 7
*Sewerage Works	do.	do.	do.
*Officer's House, Freshwater Gate (I. W.)	Admiralty	Official	do.
*Cottages, Lewisham	....	Dyer, Son, & Hilton	do.
*Repairing and Painting Old Buildings, &c	St. Olave's Union	Newman & Newman	June 9
*School Buildings, Horsham	The Governors	A. Vernon	do.
*Works and Repairs, Plymouth District	War Department	Official	June 10
*Dock Gates	Barry Railway Co.	J. Wolfe Barry	June 11
*Sewerage Works	Chepstow Loc. Bd.	C. R. Walker	June 13
*Extension of School	Grays Thurrock Sch. B.	Geo. Waymouth	do.
Chancel, &c. Parish Church, Talley, near Llandilo	Rev. J. H. Lloyd	....	June 14
*Painting Barracks, Aldershot	War Department	Official	No date
*Road Works, Constructing Stables	do.	do.	do.
*Internal Painting, &c. Anglesea Barracks	do.	do.	do.
*Painting, &c. Warwick	do.	do.	do.
*Schoolmaster's, &c. Quarters, Worcester	do.	do.	do.
*Working Sandstone Quarry	Manchester Ship Canal Co.	do.	do.
Methodist Sunday Schools, Risca, Mon.	....	Thos. Howdill	do.
Twenty-seven Cottages, Blaengarw, near Bridgend	Ocean Collieries	David Griffiths	do.
Inn, Wheatley Green, Durham	Newcastle Breweries, Ltd.	S. Oswald & Son	do.
Stables, &c. Alma-road, Headingley, Leeds	Joseph Nicholson	T. Butler Wilson	do.
Bank Premises, Ashburton, Devon	Capital and Counties Bank, Ltd.	J. W. Rowell & Son	do.
Conservative Club, Bacup	....	Smith & Cross	do.
Large Concrete and Brick Tank, Mill Dale, near Burslem	....	Ford & Slater	do.
Three Lobbied Houses, Heron-street, Fenton, Staffs	Richd. Woolley	Elijah Jones	do.
Church Work, Salt, near Stafford	....	N. Joyce	do.
Pumping Machinery, Mill Dale, near Burslem	....	Ford & Slater	do.

PUBLIC APPOINTMENTS.

Nature of Appointment.	By whom Advertised.	Salary.	Applications to be in.
*Clerk of Works for Waterworks	Bishops Castle T. C.	....	May [illegible]
*Sanitary Inspector	Holborn B. of W.	2l. 10s. weekly	June [illegible]
*Borough Surveyor & Inspector of Nuisances	Borough of Welshpool	110l.	June [illegible]
*Head Master	Coalbrookdale School of Art	....	No date

Those marked with an Asterisk (*) are advertised in this Number. *Competitions, p. iv. Contracts, pp. iv., vi., viii., & ix. Public Appointments, p. xx.*

avoid those difficulties which they overcome by the light of experience. There would seem, however, to be one counterbalancing disadvantage at any rate, for whilst we are waiting, our more pushing cousins are establishing a very good connexion for the sale of electrical appliances abroad.

PUBLIC WORKS, NELSON, LANCASHIRE.—On the 17th inst. Mr. Rienzi Walton, Local Government Board inspector, opened an inquiry at Nelson into an application by the Corporation for sanction to borrow 10,000l. for electric-lighting purposes, 10,000l. for purchasing a cemetery, 7,500l. for the erection of a public library and technical school, and for the appropriation of land now possessed by the Corporation as a site for the technical school.

PUBLIC WORKS, MANCHESTER.—On the 17th inst. Mr. S. J. Smith, one of the inspectors of the Local Government Board, held an inquiry in the Mayor's Parlour at the Town Hall, Manchester, respecting the application of the Town Council to borrow the sum of 150,000l. for purposes of electric lighting, and 12,000l. for providing a public library for the Openshaw district.—Mr. J. W. Southern, chairman of the Libraries Committee, said it was proposed to erect library buildings to cost 15,000l. It was estimated that the fittings would cost 1,750l.—Mr. James W. Beaumont, the architect, submitted plans of the proposed library. He stated that it was expected the building would be completed in twelve months.—Alderman Sir John Harwood then gave evidence relative to the application to borrow 150,000l. for electric lighting purposes. He stated that the Corporation had had the matter of supplying the electric light under consideration for the last ten years. In 1890 they got an order from the Board of Trade and confirmed by Parliament empowering them to supply electric lighting. They invited four eminent electrical engineers to prepare plans for the installation, each being paid 100 guineas, and their reports were submitted to experts. It was finally determined to adopt the scheme of Professor Dr. John Hopkinson, who had been employed by the Corporation to carry out the work. The site on which they intended to erect the works was situated in Dickenson-street, off Portland-street.—Dr. Hopkinson then explained the plans for the installation. The immediate outlay, he said, would be 78,715l. In addition there was the cost of the site and the cost of the additional machinery, which would absorb the whole of the 150,000l.—The inquiry having been completed, the Inspector visited the sites.

THE ENGLISH IRON TRADE. — Comparatively little change has taken place in the English iron market since last week, but in the Cleveland district there has been more inquiry for No. 1 pig-iron owing to a prospective early increase in the Swedish tariff. In all the pig-iron centres trade is very dull, and quotations remain practically unchanged. In the finished-iron trade business is confined to hand-to-mouth requirements, and there is little alteration of note in the steel trade. Shipbuilding material continues to prove the chief article inquired for. The tinplate trade is slightly brisker, but values remain low. Engineers and shipbuilders show little fresh life. The coal trade generally is quiet.—*Iron.*

MEETINGS.

MONDAY, MAY 23.

Society of Arts (Cantor Lectures). — Dr. Percy F. Frankland on "Recent Bacteriological and Chemical Research in Connexion with the Fermentation Industries." IV. 8 p.m.

TUESDAY, MAY 24.

Institution of Civil Engineers. — Professor W. C. Roberts-Austen on "The Measurement of High Temperatures." 8 p.m.

Society of Arts (Foreign and Colonial Section).—Col. Howard Vincent, M.P., on "The Extension of Colonial Trade." 8 p.m.

WEDNESDAY, MAY 25.

Guild and School of Handicraft.—Mr. J. S. Thornton on "Slöyd." 8 p.m.

Society of Arts.—Mr. F. E. Ives on "Researches in Photochromy." 8 p.m.

FRIDAY, MAY 27.

Architectural Association.—Mr. C. R. Ashbee on "The Relation of the Architect to the Workman." 7.30 p.m.

RECENT PATENTS:

ABSTRACTS OF SPECIFICATIONS.

8,878.—SASH-CORD FASTENERS: *J. W. Mumby.*—This invention relates to what is described as an improved method for securing the sash-cords of windows to the sash-frames, and an improvement in the construction of moulds employed in the manufacture of appliances for the purpose. The appliance for securing the sash-cord consists of two lugs cast to, and forming part of, a bracket mounted between the lugs, and carried eccentrically on a through pin is a swing catch, the outer edge being grooved and serrated for the purpose of holding the cord when threaded between the lugs and the serrated catch. The improved mould for the casting of the fastener is constructed so that several may be cast at the same time, the mould being formed in three parts, the two outer ones forming the box, and the inner one the core, having recesses on each side of it of the size and shape of the lugs. A continuous recess along its edge forms the brackets, which are to be divided afterwards. The core is placed in the recess in the box, the latter being held by an eccentric handle. The mould for forming the swing catches has a double core, in order to form the serrated grooves, and to facilitate stripping of the castings. The boxes have troughs formed in them into which the molten metal is run, and a series of holes in the troughs communicate with the interior of the boxes and the cores.

9,152.—LOCKING WINDOW-SASHES: *G. Chisholm, Jun.*—This invention relates to an improved means for locking and unlocking, automatically, window-sashes, and providing means by which the sashes may be locked on the inside with the top sash partly open or down, and at the same time prevent the sashes being opened from the outside. The inventor mounts in the central bead of the window, at the junction of the upper and lower sashes, a metal plate having provision formed on it for carrying a small double-armed rocking lever, and also provided at its top end with a small bevelled guard plate, which protects the wood of the upper sash. The rocking lever is caused to engage by means of its shape with a pivotted double-armed bracket secured to the top of the lower sash, and in openings formed in a metal plate secured to the inside face of the upper sash. This plate has two or more of such openings formed in it, one above the other, at any desired distance apart. The whole is such that the upper sash cannot be moved unless the locking lever is out of gear with it, which can only be effected by raising the lower sash, which, to prevent its being raised from the outside, is provided with a suitable sill lock.

7,646.—WINDOW-SASHES: *F. J. J. Gibbons.*—This specification refers to an improvement in the locks of window-sashes. It consists more particularly in the combination with the lock proper of devices by which the key is locked in its lock until the sashes themselves are locked in the desired position by the protrusion of the lock-bolt, and also of an indicator by which it is rendered impossible for the lock to be left unlocked without the indicator showing it. The lock itself has a bolt, consisting of two parts, pivotted together at an angle. The operative nose of the bolt is pivotted to one part, and the end of the other part is screwed, its thread being engaged by a socket rotatable in the lock-case by an external webless key.

3,531.—METALLIC LATHING: *G. Hayes.*—This invention relates to lathing formed of sheet metal, and having at intervals throughout tongued apertures. It consists of a sheet metal lathing formed with corrugations throughout, and in the hollows of the corrugations (as they appear to its front or receiving face) are tongued apertures in line lengthwise; the corrugations, with the tongues turned over backward from the openings in a direction lengthwise the hollow, and towards the next opening in line. It further consists of a corrugated sheet of metal lathing having tongued apertures of special shape in the hollows of the corrugations appearing to its receiving face, as shown in the drawings accompanying the specification.

NEW APPLICATIONS FOR LETTERS PATENT.

May 3.—8,292, G. Graham, Artificial Stone Blocks.—8,327, H. Hunt, Fire-grates.—8,346, W. Hewitt and A. Suart, Brickmaking Machinery.—8,352, C. Borgner, Construction of Bricks.—8,381, C. Behn, Ventilation of House-Drains.—8,384, H. Hunt, Mantelpieces for Fireplaces.

May 4.—8,403, S. Johnson, Attaching Door-knobs to Spindles.—8,460, W. Hewitt and A. Suart, Compounds for Paving or Covering Roads, Paths, or Floors, and for Manufacture of Paving-bricks or Blocks. — 8,472, C. Hawkes, Covering for Walls, &c.—8,477, X. Charles, Kiln or Drying Apparatus.—8,481, H. Berthold, Self-closing Door-hinge.

May 6.—8,580, T. Carlaw, Window-fittings.—8,583, T. Fawcett, Making and Pressing Bricks, and in moulds therefor, and in Clay-mixing or Grinding pans employed therein.

May 7.—8,706, S. Moore, Electrical Fittings, such as ceiling roses and cut outs.—8,714, A. Boult, Pipe Connexions.

PROVISIONAL SPECIFICATIONS ACCEPTED.

4,448, T. Jackson, Grates and Fireplaces.—5,939, A. Taylor, Dessing Stone.—6,067, D. France, Firegrates.—6,136, E. Wild and J. Kent, "In or Out" Indicator for Entrance Halls, &c.—6,200, J. Merrill, Alternating Valve Mechanism for Flushing.—6,403, W. Waghorn, Chimney-cowls.—6,606, H. Sutcliffe, Domestic Fireplaces.—6,663, H. Eggert, Hot-air Jet for Stoves.—6,716, S. Hellyer, Covers or Means for Closing Man-holes of Drains or Sewer-connexions and the like.—6,866, R. Zawischka, Planes. — 6,920, A. Johnson, Window-Fastener.—7,034, F. Willis and R. Astley, Fixing Fireproof Floors.—7,486, J. Robertson, Roofs, Floors, and similar Structures.—7,522, G. Ballard, Edging Tile or Brick.—7,660, F. Carter, Tiles.—7,683, R. Mushatt, Ventilators and Chimney-cowls.

COMPLETE SPECIFICATIONS ACCEPTED.

(Open to Opposition for Two Months.)

10,177, T. Starkey & Son, Door Springs.—11,101, M. Syer, Syphon Water Waste Preventer.—1,416, F. Edwards, Concrete and Iron Beams or Beams composed of similar Materials.—5,353, E. Stoctler and F. Alexandre, Smoothing Iron with Removable Handles.—6,091, H. Newton, Ventilation of Sewers.—6,654, O. Westblad, Roofing Tiles.

SOME RECENT SALES OF PROPERTY:

ESTATE EXCHANGE REPORT.

MAY 9.—By *Schofield & Evans*: 1 to 7, Francis-pl., Westminster, u.t. 3 yrs., 140*l.*; 17 to 25, Coburg-row, u.t. 5¾ yrs., g.r. 21*l.*, 220*l.*; 9 to 14, Alma-ter., Wandsworth, u.t. 35 yrs., g.r. 20*l.*, and l.g.r. of 13*l.*, same term, [illegible]*l.*; "The Woodman" public-house, f., and the residence, "Elm Lodge," Wimbledon, 1,500*l.*

MAY 10.—By *Ellis & Son*: F.g.r. of 30*l.* 18s. 6d., South Lambeth-rd., Vauxhall, with reversion in 20 yrs., 1,880*l.*—By *W. Simmonds*: 1, Farnell-mews, Kensington, u.t. [illegible] yrs., g.r. 8*l.*, r. 50*l.*, 640*l.*—By *F. J. Bisley*: 7 and 9, Adford-rd., Rotherhithe, u.t. 83 yrs., g.r. 9*l.*, r. [illegible] 16s., 180*l.*; 1 to 7 odd, Westlake-rd., u.t. 61 yrs., g.r. [illegible], r. 104*l.*, 830*l.*; 128, 136, 138, and 140, Rotherhithe New-rd., u.t. 61 yrs., g.r. 13*l.*, 1,290*l.*; 130 and 132, Rotherhithe New-rd., u.t. 61 yrs., g.r. 12*l.*; and a l.g.r. [illegible]4*l.*, same term, 590*l.*; 118, 120, and 122, Creek-rd., Deptford, f., r. 78*l.*, 725*l.*; 22, James-st., f., r. 26*l.*, 175*l.*; [illegible] and 96, Drummond-rd., Bermondsey, u.t. 52 yrs., g.r. [illegible] 3s., 705*l.*—By *Rogers, Chapman, & Thomas*: "The Hermitage," School House-lane, Wimbledon; 1 to 7 and 11 to 14, West-pl.; and Timber-yd., 2,200*l.*; the freehold residence "Clairville," 1,080*l.*; [illegible] to 36, West-pl., f., 1,150*l.*; 3, Torrington-pl., Gordon-[illegible], u.t. 31 yrs., g.r. 10*l.*, 1,140*l.*—By *E. & H. Lumley*: three plots of land, 1a. 3r. 33p., f., West-hill, Putney, [illegible]70*l.*; "The Orphanage," and a plot of land, f., 950*l.*; plot of land, 0a. 2r. 12p., f., 630*l.*—By *Thurgood & Martin*: F.g.r. of 204*l.*, High-st., Croydon, with reversion in 86 yrs., 4,405*l.*; Freehold rent-charge of 5*l.* a year, 135*l.*; the f. residence, "Ottinge," Whytecliffe-rd., Purley, r. 65*l.*, 1,860*l.*; "Stamford House," London-rd., Croydon, f., r. 50*l.*, 605*l.*; "Field View," f., r. 40*l.*, [illegible]*l.*

MAY 11.—By *W. S. Morris*: 1A, 1 to 23 odd, Richard's Cottages, Acton, f., 1,500*l.*—By *Barker & Cathie*: No. [illegible]3, High Holborn, u.t. 33 yrs., g.r. 60*l.*, r. 180*l.*, 1,490*l.*—By *Harman Bros.*: 1, St. John's-lane, Smithfield, f., r. [illegible]*l.*, 900*l.*; 392, Uxbridge-rd., Shepherd's Bush, u.t. [illegible] yrs., g.r. 20*l.*, r. 75*l.*, 640*l.*; 404 and 406, Uxbridge-rd., u.t. 82 yrs., g.r. 45*l.*, r. 179*l.*, 1,375*l.*; 2, London-rd., Hackney, u.t. 67 yrs., g.r. 6*l.*, 300*l.*—By *Glover & Harrison*: 1 and 2, Lawn Cottages, Tooting, f., 675*l.*—By *A. & R. Beal*: 99 to 113 odd, Dawes-rd., Walham Green, f., r. 505*l.*, 5,350*l.*—By *Rushworth & Stevens*: 5, [illegible] and 7, Bond-st., Pentonville, u.t. 27 yrs., g.r. 15*l.*, r. [illegible]4*l.*, 910*l.*; 119, Pembroke-st., Islington, u.t. 57 yrs., g.r. 6*l.* 10s., r. 34*l.* 4s., 275*l.*; 121, Pembroke-[illegible], u.t. 57 yrs., g.r. 6*l.* 10s., r. 34*l.* 4s., 250*l.*; [illegible] Church-lane, Hornsey, u.t. 91 yrs., g.r. 9*l.*, r. 52*l.* 10s., [illegible]0*l.*; 7, Ashmount-rd., u.t. 88 yrs., g.r. 6*l.* 10s., r. 36*l.*, [illegible]5*l.*—By *Battam & Co.*: 28, Brandenburgh-rd., Chiswick, u.t. 71 yrs., g.r. 7*l.* 7s., 250*l.*; 42, Kensington-pk.-gardens, Notting-hill, u.t. 58 yrs., g.r. 21*l.*, 1,400*l.*; 13, Poplar-grove, u.t. 84 yrs., g.r. 6*l.*, r. 47*l.* 10s., 460*l.*

MAY 12.—By *Drew & Son*: "Mount Ararat House," Richmond, and 2a. 3r. 20p., f., 9,000*l.*—By *W. W. Jenkinson*: 10, Queen-st. East, Greenwich, f., r. 10*l.* 8s., [illegible]*l.*; a plot of freehold land, East-st., 40*l.*—By *T. G. Wharton*: L.g.r. of 42*l.*, Spencer-st., Canonbury, u.t. 26 yrs., and reversion for one year, 570*l.*; l.g.r. of 180*l.*, Harold-rd., Upton-pk., u.t. 67 yrs., g.r. 15*l.*, 2,875*l.*—By *Single*: 27 and 29, Princes-rd., Notting-hill, u.t. 48 yrs., g.r. 16*l.*, 460*l.*—By *Hards & Bradly*: 88, Herbert-rd., Plumstead, and plot of land, f., 1,000*l.*; 7 to 13 [illegible]d. Oglander-st., Peckham, u.t. 83 yrs., g.r. 20*l.*, r. 104*l.*, 250*l.*—By *Charles & Tubbs*: 1 to 8, Hutley Cottages, Finchley, u.t. 91 yrs., g.r. 22*l.*, 750*l.*—By *Farebrother, Ellis, & Co.*: No. 45, Lincoln's-inn-fields, f., area 6,100 ft., 15,750*l.*—By *Newbon & Co.*: [illegible] g.r. of 40*l.*, Cornwall-rd., Southwark, with reversion in 29 yrs., 1,025*l.*; f.g.r. of 22*l.* 10s., with ditto in 29 yrs., 550*l.*; an improved rental of 40*l.*, King's-rd., Camden Town, u.t. 58 yrs., 700*l.*; 51, College-st., Barnsbury, u.t. 24 yrs., g.r. 6*l.* 10s., r. 40*l.*, 250*l.*; 27, Upper Ogle-st., Great Portland-st., u.t. 35 yrs., g.r. [illegible], r. 60*l.*, 450*l.*—By *C. C. & T. Moore*: 45, Digby-rd., Homerton; and 25, Berger-rd., f., 620*l.*; [illegible] to 91 (even), and 101, Chapel-st., Stratford, f., 1,010*l.*; [illegible] to 18 (even), Queen-st., Stratford, f., 1,200*l.*; 122 and [illegible], Tower Hamlets-rd., Forest-gate, f., 360*l.*; 43, Addison-rd., Kensington, u.t. 29 yrs., g.r. 8*l.*, 820*l.*—By *Stimson & Sons*: 30 to 38 (even), West-st., Mile-end, and 2, 4, and 6, Ann-st., f., 1,060*l.*; Nos. 126 and 128, New Cross-rd., u.t. 68 yrs., g.r. 12*l.*, 685*l.*; 196, Stanstead-rd., Forest-hill, u.t. 91 yrs., g.r. 8*l.*, r. 38*l.*, 270*l.*; No. 2, "Acre House," Brixton-hill, u.t. 11 yrs., g.r. 10*l.*, [illegible]0*l.*; 8, The Ter., Peckham, u.t. 370 yrs., no g.r., 1,700*l.*; [illegible], 16, and 18, Basing-rd., u.t. 81 yrs., g.r. 11*l.* 5s., 360*l.*; [illegible]0 and 292, Commercial-rd., Old Kent-rd., u.t. 17 yrs., g.r. 10*l.*, 300*l.*—By *Messrs. Chadwick*: F.g.r. of 21*l.* 10s., Grove-pk., Camberwell, with reversion in 63 yrs., 610*l.*; f.g.r. of 15*l.* 12s., Grove-pk., with reversion in 67 yrs., [illegible]0*l.*; f.g.r. of 24*l.*, ditto in 67 yrs., 710*l.*; f.g.r. of [illegible]*l.* 16s., ditto in 70 yrs., 870*l.*; f.g.r. of 12*l.* 7s. 6d., ditto in 80 yrs., 355*l.*; f.g.r. of 31*l.*, Chadwick-rd., Peckham, with reversion in 64 yrs., 80[illegible]*l.*; f.g.r. of 60*l.*, ditto in [illegible] yrs., 1,695*l.*; f.g.r. of 80*l.*, ditto in 77 yrs., 2,371*l.*—By *Wilkinson, Son, & Welch* (at Brighton): The freehold residence "Oaklands," Hayward's-heath, 2,800*l.*; three freehold plots of land, 4a. 0r. 29p., 1,390*l.*; "Boltro Farm," and 1a. 1r. 20p., f., 615*l.*

MAY 13.—By *Reynolds & Eason*: 1 and 3, Devas-st., Bromley-by-Bow, f., 300*l.*; 146, Boleyn-rd., Kingsland, and "Arundel Arms," profit rental 32*l.* 10s., u.t. 57 yrs., [illegible]5*l.*; 183 and 185, Broke-rd., Clapton, u.t. 81 yrs., g.r. [illegible]*l.*, r. 56*l.*, 500*l.*; 28, St. Peter's-rd., Mile-end, u.t. 38 yrs., g.r. 3*l.* 8s., 320*l.*; 7, Balcombe-st., Dorset-sq., u.t. [illegible] yrs., no g.r., r. 100*l.*, 840*l.*—By *Driver & Perfect*: 93 and 99, Junction-rd., Holloway, u.t. 59 yrs., g.r. 20*l.*, r. [illegible]0*l.*, 1,750*l.*; 103, Junction-rd., u.t. 59 yrs., g.r. 10*l.*, r. 70*l.*, 730*l.*; 17, St. John's-pk., u.t. 59 yrs., g.r. 2*l.*, [illegible]0*l.*; a plot of freehold land, Brook-rd., r. 10*l.*, 175*l.*—By *Herring, Son, & Daw*: F. stabling, &c., Dorset-st., Spitalfields, area 1,800 ft., 975*l.*; 343, Brixton-rd., Brixton, u.t. 59 yrs., g.r. 15*l.* 10s., 810*l.*; Freehold ground rents of 8*l.* 15s., Brighton-ter., with reversion in [illegible]½ yrs., 2,300*l.*; F.g.r. of 81*l.* 10s., with reversion in [illegible]½ yrs., 2,935*l.*—By *Norton, Trist, & Gilbert*: 34 and 36, Beckenham-rd., Penge, u.t. 70 yrs., g.r. 25*l.*, 675*l.*; 3, Livington-grove, u.t. 70 yrs., g.r. 8*l.*, 255*l.*; 1 to 14, Brunswick-pl., Anerley-rd., u.t. 72 yrs., g.r., 60*l.*, 1,730*l.*

[*Contractions used in these lists.*—F.g.r. for freehold ground-rent; l.g.r. for leasehold ground-rent; i.g.r. for improved ground-rent; g.r. for ground-rent; r. for rent; f. for freehold; c. for copyhold; l. for leasehold; e.r. for estimated rental; u.t. for unexpired term; p.a. for per annum; yrs. for years; st. for street; rd. for road; sq. for square; pl. for place; ter. for terrace; cres. for crescent; yd. for yard, &c.]

PRICES CURRENT OF MATERIALS.

TIMBER.		
Greenheart, B.G. ton	8/0/0	9/0/0
Teak, E.I. load	9/10/0	15/0/0
Sequoia, U.S. ft. cu.	2/3	3/0
Ash, Canada load	2/10/0	4/0/0
Birch, do.	3/5/0	4/10/0
Elm, do.	3/10/0	4/15/0
Fir, Dantsic, &c.	1/10/0	3/10/0
Oak, do.	3/0/0	6/5/0
Canada	5/10/0	7/0/0
Pine, Canada red	2/10/0	3/10/0
Do. yellow	2/10/0	5/0/0
Lath, D'ntsic, fath	5/0/0	6/0/0
St. Petersburg	5/0/0	7/0/0
Deals, Finland, 2nd & 1st std 100	8/0/0	9/10/0
Do. 4th & 3rd	7/0/0	8/0/0
Do. Riga	7/0/0	8/0/0
St. Petersburg, 1st yellow	11/0/0	14/10/0
Do. 2nd yellow	8/0/0	10/0/0
Do. white	7/10/0	10/10/0
Swedish	7/10/0	15/10/0
White Sea	8/0/0	17/10/0
Canada, Pine 1st	20/0/0	28/0/0
Do. do. 2nd	14/10/0	16/0/0
Do. do. 3rd, &c.	8/0/0	10/5/0
Do. Spruce, 1st	8/10/0	11/0/0
Do. do. 3rd & 2nd	6/15/0	8/0/0
New Brunswick	7/0/0	7/10/0
Battens, all kinds	2/10/0	15/10/0
Flooring Boards, sq., 1 in. prep. 1st	0/8/0	0/14/0
Do. 2nd	0/7/0	0/11/0
Other qualities	0/5/6	0/7/6
Cedar, Cuba ft.	/3½	/4½
Honduras, &c.	/3½	/4
Mahogany, Cuba	/4½	/6½
St. Domingo, cargo av	/4½	2/0
Mexican do. do	/4	/6
Tobasco do. do	/5½	/7
Honduras do.	/5½	/6½
Box, Turkey ton	4/0/0	13/0/0
Rose, Rio	10/0/0	20/0/0
Bahia	9/0/0	18/0/0
Satin, St. Domingo ft.	0/0/8	0/1/3

TIMBER (continued).		
Satin, Porto Rico	0/0/8	0/1/0
Walnut, Italian	0/0/3½	0/0/7
METALS.		
Iron—Pig, in Scotland ton	2/0/10	2/0/11½
Bar, Welsh, in London	5/17/6	6/0/0
Do. do. at works in Wales	5/7/6	5/10/0
Do. Staffordshire, in London	6/5/0	6/15/0
Copper—British, cake and ingot	48/0/0	49/10/0
Best selected	49/10/0	50/10/0
Sheets, strong	58/0/0	58/10/0
Chili, bars	46/7/6	46/15/0
Yellow Metal lb.	0/0/5	0/0/5⅜
Lead—Pig, Spanish ton	10/10/0	10/11/3
English, com. brands	10/12/6	10/15/0
Sheet, English, 6 lbs. per sq. ft. and upwards	12/0/0	0/0/0
Pipe	12/10/0	0/0/0
Zinc—English sheet ton	25/10/0	0/0/0
Vieille Montagne	26/5/0	0/0/0
Tin—Straits	95/7/6	95/17/6
Australian	95/7/6	95/17/6
English Ingots	97/10/0	98/0/0
OILS.		
Linseed ton	18/10/0	18/15/0
Cocoanut, Cochin	24/0/0	0/0/0
Do. Ceylon	21/17/6	22/0/0
Palm, Lagos	22/5/0	22/10/0
Rapeseed, English pale	25/5/0	0/0/0
Do. brown	23/15/0	0/0/0
Cottonseed ref.	19/0/0	0/0/0
Oleine	21/10/0	22/10/0
Lubricating, U.S.	4/0/0	6/0/0
Do. refined	6/0/0	12/10/0
Tar—Stockholm barrel	0/19/0	1/0/0
Archangel	0/12/6	0/0/0

TENDERS.

[Communications for insertion under this heading should be addressed to "The Editor," and must reach us *not later than 12 noon on Thursdays.*]

ABINGDON.—For the repairs, refitting, and redecoration of the Manor-house, Shippon, on the Duchy of Cornwall Estate. Mr. J. G. T. West, architect, Abingdon:—

Hutchings & Osborne ... £1,180 | Thatcher & Stroud ... £1,020

ACTON.—Accepted for additions to 1, Goldsmith's-gardens, for Mr. A. T. Pocock. Mr. A. B. Christy, architect, 30, Great St. Helens, E.C.:—

Geo. Hooper, Acton ... £496 0 0

APPLEFORD (Berks).—For alterations and repairs to "The Carpenters' Arms," Appleford, for Messrs. Townsend. Mr. J. G. T. West, architect, Abingdon:—

Cox & Holloway ... £398 16 | T. Barrett ... £319 0

ASHTON-UNDER-LYNE.—Accepted for building five shops in St. Michael's-square, for Mr. John Fletcher, Springfield, Ashton-under-Lyne. Messrs. T. George & Son, architects, Old-square, Ashton-under-Lyne. Quantities by the architect:—

Excavator and Bricklayer.—J. Gibson & Son, Dukinfield	£850	0	0
Stonemason.—Thomas Crackston, Ashton-under-Lyne	684	0	0
Carpenter and Joiner.—Elijah Holmes, Dukinfield	624	0	0
Plasterer and Slater.—Robert Newton, Symondly, Glossop	153	0	0
Plumber and Glazier.—G. H. Coup, Ashton-under-Lyne	195	0	0
Painter.—P. M. Mellor, Ashton-under-Lyne	30	0	0

BEDFORD.—For building new shops on the forecourts of Nos. 50, 52, 54, and 56, Bromham-road, Bedford, for Messrs. Smith & Barnes. Mr. Wm. Barnard Davis, architect:—

W. Haynes	£804	T. Dawson	£693
G. Harrison	773	T. H. Coleman*	685
G. E. Fathers	755	* Accepted.	

BOURNEMOUTH.—For erecting the new "Granville" Temperance Hotel. Messrs. Lawson & Donkin, architects. Quantities supplied:—

Barrow & Entwistle	£8,780	Jones & Son	£8,125
Saley & Son	8,717	McWilliam & Son	7,790
Jenkins & Son	8,497	Curtis, W. H. C.	7,770
George & Harding	8,370	J. W. Lucas	7,694
Reed, Blight, & Co.	8,250	Hayward, Penton & Hayward	7,497
H. J. Sanders	8,200	T. H. Kingerlee	7,467
F. Hoare & Son	8,187		
Chinchen & Co.	8,147		

BROMLEY (Kent).—For the erection of a Chapel and gatehouse and laying-out the cemetery, Burnt Ash-lane, for the Plaistow Burial Board. Messrs. Wadmore, Wadmore, & Mallett, architects, 35, Great Saint Helens, E.C. Quantities supplied by Messrs. C. Stanger & Son:—

	Kentish Stone Random.	Ditto All Coursed.	Red Brick Facing.
R. A. Lowe	£3,084 0 0	£3,229 0 0	£2,983 0 0
Rowe Bros.	2,860 0 0	3,080 0 0	3,000 0 0
Love Bros.	2,775 0 0	2,925 0 0	2,865 0 0
Wm. Downs	2,700 0 0	2,720 0 0	2,630 0 0
J. Otway	2,636 0 0	2,681 0 0	2,451 0 0
F. P. Duthoit	2,512 0 0	2,736 0 0	2,305 0 0
Wm. Grubb	2,500 0 0	2,634 0 0	2,479 0 0
Thos. Crossley	2,458 0 0	2,540 0 0	2,310 0 0
R. Avard	2,348 0 0	2,453 0 0	2,280 0 0
G. J. Jones	2,337 16 8	2,488 10 9½	2,269 5 2
T. D. Graty, Bromley, Kent*	2,209 0 0	2,420 0 0	2,149 0 0

* Accepted.

Carriage Drives and Paths.

Mayo & Co.	£540 0 0
J. Jackson	500 0 0
Pell	497 0 0
T. Lansbury, Bromley, Kent (accepted)	463 0 0

Oak Fencing.

	For 86 Rods.	Per Rod for Extra.
Ellis Bros.	£268 15 0	£3 2 6
Murray Marshall	263 14 0	2 19 0
Beadle Bros.	249 8 0	2 18 0
Taylor & Brooker	243 0 0	2 18 6
Roland Bros.	211 15 0	2 9 3
Avard	210 0 0	2 8 10
Barrett, Bromley*	207 13 1	2 8 3½

* Accepted.

BRENTFORD.—For the construction of a new road near Clifden House, for the Brentford Local Board. Mr. J. H. Strachan, Surveyor:—

Mowlem & Co.	£320 0 0	W. Parker	£246 0 0
Nowell & Robson	321 0 0	John Ball, Chiswick*	233 1 2
Holce & Co.	250 0 0	* Accepted.	

[Surveyor's estimate, £260.]

BRENTFORD.—For the supply and delivery of 1,400 yards of blue Guernsey granite, for the Brentford Local Board. Mr. J. H. Strachan, Surveyor:—

	Per yd. s. d.		Per yd. s. d.
Fennings	15 7	Mowlem & Co. Westminster*	14 9
Nowell & Robson	15 6	* Accepted.	
Lemaire	14 11		

BRENTFORD.—For making-up the undermentioned roads, for the Brentford Local Board. Mr. J. H. Strachan, Surveyor:—

	Glenhurst-road.	Avenue-road.	Mercury-road.
Mowlem & Co.	£754 0 0	£436 0 0	£305 0 0
Nowell & Robson	731 0 0	442 0 0	199 0 0
Holte & Co.	680 6 8	399 6 10	188 0 0
W. Parker, Brentford	600 0 0	*355 0 0	151 0 0
John Ball, Chiswick	*543 0 2	358 11 2	*154 19 4
Surveyor's estimates	600 0 0	382 0 0	180 0 0

* Accepted.

BRENTFORD.—Accepted for the supply and delivery of 1,400 yards of Kentish flints, for the Brentford Local Board. Mr. J. H. Strachan, Surveyor:—

G. Pearce, Brentford ... 5s. 4d. per yard.

BRISTOL.—For new warehouse and offices, for Messrs. Liodren & Co. Mr. Herbert J. Jones, architect, 12, Bridge-street, Bristol:—

E. Gay	£3,186	W. Galbraith	£2,970
J. E. Davis	3,162	J. Perrott	2,936
W. Church	3,043	W. Cowlin & Son	2,878
Stephens, Bastow, & Co.	3,030	E. Walters	2,831
Eastabrook & Sons	2,998	R. Wilkins & Sons	2,749
G. Humphreys	2,988	G. H. Wilkins (accepted)	2,678

[All of Bristol.]

CANNING TOWN.—For paving Victoria Dock-road, Canning Town. Mr. Lewis Angell, M.Inst. C.E., Borough Engineer:—

W. Hirst	£8,363 2 6	Mowlem & Co.	£7,406 0 0
Nowell & Robson	7,932 2 6	W. Griffiths	6,936 11 3
Turner, Son, & Evanson	7,654 15 0	E. Parry	6,138 10 0
R. Cooke & Co.	7,590 0 0	J. Biggs	6,030 17 1
O. G. Rutty	7,578 0 0	Woodham, Fry, & Fry, Greenwich*	5,606 7 6
J. Jackson	7,477 0 0	* Accepted.	

CANTERBURY.—For sewage farm extension Works and new Storm sewers, for the Corporation of Canterbury. Mr. Frank Baker, C.E., engineer, Vernon House, Canterbury:—

Contract No. 1.—Supply of Stoneware Pipes, &c.

Pipes.

	24-in.	18-in.	15-in.	12-in.	9-in.	6-in.	4-in.
G. Jennings*	6 0	3 0	2 3	1 1½	0 8½	0 4½	0 3½
T. Wragge & Sons	5 5	2 7½	1 8½	1 0	0 8	0 4	0 3
Cliffe & Son	5 0	2 9	1 9½	1 0	0 7	0 4	0 3
Stiff & Son	6 8	3 0	2 3	1 1	0 8	0 4	0 3
Doulton & Son	7 0	3 0	2 3	1 1	0 8	0 4	0 3

Gully Traps.

	18-in.	15-in.	12-in.	9-in.	6-in.
G. Jennings*	20 0	15 0	11 3	7 6	5 6
T. Wragge & Son	21 0	15 0	9 6	5 6	3 3
Cliffe & Son	21 0	..	..	..	..
Stiff & Son	17 6	14 0	9 0	6 0	2 9
Doulton & Co.	20 0	16 0	13 6	6 0	2 9

Contract No. 2.—Wrought Iron Fencing, Gates and Fixing.

	Fencing. Per yard.	Field Gates.
Drury & Biggleston	4 3	£4 0
Bayliss, Jones, & Bayliss	3 1	7 10
Hill & Smith*	2 8	6 0

Contract No. 3.—24-in. Cast-iron Pipes, &c.

	Pipes.* Per ton.	Special Castings. Per cwt.
Staveley Iron Company*	£4 16 6	9 0
Stanton Ironworks	4 12 3	8 10
Newton Chambers	5 0 0	11 0
Clay Cross Company	4 15 0	10 9
Butterley	6 1 0	10 10

Contract No. 5.—Sewage Tanks, Storm Outfall, and other Works.

Cooke & Co.	£2,950 9	Johnson & Co., London*	£2,819 0
W. J. Adcock	2,834 0		

* Accepted Tenders.

GRAFTON (near Hereford).—For building villa residence at Grafton, near Hereford. Mr. W. W. Robinson, architect, Hereford:—

Bowers & Co., Hereford ... £435 0 0

GUILDFORD.—For the erection of St. Saviour's permanent Church-room and temporary church. Mr. Miles, architect, Bournemouth. No quantities:—

May	£1,445	Downs	£1,325
Lunn	1,395	Mitchell Bros.	1,298
Higlett & Hammond	1,387	Robert Smith	1,298
Smith & Sons	1,374	Thos. Swayne	1,218
Stanley Ellis	1,372	[All of Guildford.]	

HALESWORTH.—For the enlargement of and improvements to the Rifle Hall. Messrs. Bottle & Olley, architects, Great Yarmouth:—

Hindes & Son	£734 0 0
B. Howard & Sons, Halesworth (accepted)	661 10 0

HEREFORD.—For erecting hop-kiln and stores, Burghill, Hereford. Mr. W. W. Robinson, architect, Hereford:—

Andrews & Rudge	£330 0	Andrews & Son	£246 15
Davies	265 0	Powis, Wellington, near Hereford*	225
Lloyd	247 0		

* Accepted.

HEREFORD.—For the erection of four semi-detached villa residences, Hereford. Mr. W. W. Robinson, architect, Hereford:—

Reuben Taylor, Hereford ... £1,380 0 0

HEREFORD.—For additions to Beechwood, Hereford. Mr. W. W. Robinson, architect, Hereford:—

Beavan & Hodges, Hereford ... £543 0 0

HOLYHEAD.—For the erection of two cottages at Blackbridge, Holyhead, for Miss Adenne. Messrs. Arthur Baker & H. Kohl Hughes, architects, Bangor:—

Owen Morris, Carnarvon (accepted) ... £719 0 0

HORNSEY.—For repairs and painting at the "Priory," Hornsey, for Mr. Williams. Mr. E. J. Paine, architect, 11, Great James-street, W.C.:—

Ellingson & Co.	£645	E. Houghton & Son	£568
Harris & Wardrop	613		

KETTERING.—For erecting Broughton School, near Kettering, Northamptonshire. Messrs. Hart & Dawson, architects, 21, King-street, Wakefield. Quantities by the architects:—

C. Sharman	£1,130 0 0	Woolford & Son	£968 6 4
A. Barlow	1,114 1 9	W. Clow	885 10 0
J. Grant	1,099 4 3	Abraham Mansell, Thrapstone*	822 13 0
S. Hipwell	1,046 19 0	Thos. Whitney (withdrawn)	778 10 0
A. Claypole	1,029 9 7		
G. Henson	985 0 0		

* Accepted.

LEIGHLINBRIDGE (co. Carlow).—For new chancel, chapels and sacristy, to the Parish church of Leighlinbridge, near Bagenalstown, co. Carlow. Mr. W. G. Doolin, M.A., architect, 20, Ely-place, Dublin. Quantities by Mr. D. W. Morris:—

Messrs. Morrison Bros., Bagenalstown* ... £1,475 0 0

* Modified amount accepted.

LONDON.—For rebuilding No. 142, Oxford-street, W. Mr. A. E. Hughes, architect. Quantities by Mr. Henry Lovegrove, 24, Budge-row, E.C.:—

		Old Material.
Wall, Beddall, & Co.	£6,120	—
Williams & Son	5,977	£10
Faulkner	5,583	—
Patrick & Son	5,340	20
H. & E. Lea	4,993	20
Holloway Bros.	4,853	—
Woodward & Co.	4,708	28

LONDON.—Accepted for the erection of bakery, Field-place, Clerkenwell. Mr. J. Henry Richardson, architect, Shepherd's-bush:—

G. Veale & Co. ... £430 0 0

LONDON.—For repainting a portion of Leadenhall Market, for the Corporation of the City of London. Mr. Andrew Murray, City Surveyor. Quantities by Mr. H. Lovegrove:—

W. J. Lister & Co.	£893	0	0	Pollips & Binker	£840	0	0
Lidstone & Co.	890	0	0	Hoeps	820	0	0
Holliday & Greenwood	877	0	0	Kirkaldy & Son	798	0	0
Harrison & Spooner	847	0	0	Collis Willmott*	779	3	4

* Accepted.

LONDON.—Accepted for the erection of stabling at Chiswick, for the West Metropolitan Tramway Co. Mr. J. Henry Richardson, architect, Shepherd's-bush. Quantities by Mr. Henry Lovegrove, 96, Budgerow, E.C.:—
Chamberlen Bros. £584 0 0

LONDON.—Accepted for decorative works at "The Waterloo" Tavern, Haymarket (second contract), for Mr. F. A. Rhodes. Messrs. Dickinson & Paterson, architects, 5, John-street, Adelphi:—
Edwards & Medway £111 13 0

LONDON.—For ornamental and wire fencing at Battersea-park, for the London County Council. Mr. Thomas Blashill, Architect:—

L. Faulkner & Sons	£654	0	0	Hill & Smith	£591	8	4
The Iron Wire, Wire Rope, and Fencing Co.	616	12	9	R. Holliday	527	0	0
				Johnson, Bros., & Co.	515	0	0
				M. McVey	497	19	9

LONDON.—To reinstatements, reparations with fire-proof floor, &c., after fire, the upper portion of stable buildings in the rear of No. 1, Upper Tollington-park, for Mr. C. King. Mr. Geo. Carter, architect, 513, Holloway-road:—
Wood, 62, Hampden-road, N. (accepted) £825 0 0

LONDON.—For proposed residences in the Green-lanes, Hornsey, N. Mr. Geo. Carter, surveyor, 513, Holloway-road:—
Messrs. Horne & Chaffey £3,300 0 0

LONDON.—For gas fittings to be done at the "Victory" public house, Barlow-street, Locksfields, Walworth:—

Biggs & Co.	£250	0	Winn*	£200	0
Hodge & Co.	211	18			

* Accepted.

NANTWICH.—For the erection of hotel buildings and baths at Shrewbridge Hall for the Nantwich Brine Baths and Hotel Company, Limited. Messrs. Mackmurdo, Hornblower, & Walters, architects, London and Liverpool:—

Hotel (exclusive of works in Old Hall).

Holme & Green	£12,442	Hughes & Stirling	£11,400
Browne & Backhouse	12,285	J. Mathews	10,838
Wm. Tomkinson & Son	12,073	Wm. Brown & Son*	10,216

* Accepted.

Baths.

Browne & Backhouse	£3,000	Hughes & Stirling	£2,650
Holme & Green	2,969	J. Mathews	2,435
Wm. Tomkinson & Son	2,943	Wm. Brown & Son*	2,363

* Accepted.

NORTH FINCHLEY.—For the erection of shop, dwelling-house, and stores at North Finchley. Mr. F. D. Thomson, architect, Woodside-park, North Finchley:—

Cooper	£2,487	Voller	£1,898
Brown & Swalland	1,869	Wheeler & Co.	1,535

STRATFORD.—For making-up Warton-road, Stratford. Mr. Lewis Angell, M.Inst. C.E., Borough Engineer:—

Cooke & Co.	£2,486	G. J. Anderson	£1,908
Nowell & Robson	2,453	W. Griffiths	1,900
G. G. Butts	2,390	J. Jackson, Plaistow, E.*	1,899

* Accepted.

WOLVERHAMPTON.—For the erection of a villa-residence and stabling, Avenue-road, Wolverhampton, for Mr. S. Larkinson. Mr. J. Lavender, architect:—

B. Guest	£1,362	7	G. Cave	£1,278	0
H. Willcock	1,255	0	H. Gough (accepted)	1,150	0

[All of Wolverhampton.]

WOLVERHAMPTON.—For building board school for infants at Moseley Village, near Wolverhampton, for the Wednesfield School Board. Mr. Geo. H. Stanger, architect. Quantities by the architect:—

H. Dorse & Son	£1,433	0	0	C. E. Borton	£1,225	0	0
H. Lovatt	1,419	0	0	Thos. Tildesley	1,200	0	0
J. Moore & Son	1,389	8	1	Hy. Gough, Wolverhampton*	1,150	0	0
H. J. Hunter	1,350	0	0				
H. Willcock	1,300	0	0				

* Accepted.

WORTHING.—For building a house at Worthing, for Dr. Gosling. Mr. Alfred M. Butler, architect, 16, Finsbury-circus, E.C. Quantities by Mr. Geo. Fleetwood, 15, Furnival's-inn, E.C.:—

R. C. Blaker	£2,411	0	W. Gladding	£2,321	0
N. A. Roome	2,368	0	McCormick & Sons	2,784	0
Chas. C. Cook	2,358	0	Geo. Baker, Worthing*	2,028	15

* Accepted.

SUBSCRIBERS in LONDON and the SUBURBS, by prepaying at the Publishing Office, 19s. per annum (or 4s. 9d. per quarter), can ensure receiving "The Builder," by *Friday Morning's Post.*

TERMS OF SUBSCRIPTION.

"THE BUILDER" is supplied DIRECT from the Office to residents in any part of the United Kingdom at the rate of 19s. per annum PREPAID. To all parts of Europe, America, Australia, and New Zealand, 26s. per annum. To India, China, Ceylon, &c., 30s. per annum. Remittances payable to DOUGLAS FOURDRINIER, Publisher, No. 46, Catherine-street, W.C.

TO CORRESPONDENTS.

W. M.—A. S. (We will endeavour to give you the information if it is not too far back).—H. H. (We have not space to continue the correspondence).—"One who was there."—G. H. M. & Co. (too small).—R. M. B. (It is not necessary to go farther into the matter; all our readers know the facts).—W. H. (We do not insert tenders without amounts).

All statements of facts, lists of tenders, &c., must be accompanied by the name and address of the sender, not necessarily for publication.

We are compelled to decline pointing out books and giving addresses.

NOTE.—The responsibility of signed articles, and papers read at public meetings, rests, of course, with the authors.

We cannot undertake to return rejected communications.

Letters or communications (beyond mere news-items) which have been duplicated for other journals, are NOT DESIRED.

All communications regarding literary and artistic matter should be addressed to THE EDITOR; all communications relating to advertisements and other exclusively business matters should be addressed to THE PUBLISHER, and *not* to the Editor.

PUBLISHER'S NOTICES.

Registered Telegraphic Address, 'THE BUILDER,' LONDON.

CHARGES FOR ADVERTISEMENTS.

SITUATIONS VACANT, PARTNERSHIPS, APPRENTICESHIPS TRADE, AND GENERAL ADVERTISEMENTS.

Six lines (about fifty words) or under .... 4s. 6d.
Each additional line (about ten words) .... 0s. 6d.

Terms for Series of Trade Advertisements, also for Special Advertisements on front page, Competitions, Contracts, Sales by Auction, &c. may be obtained on application to the Publisher.

SITUATIONS WANTED.

FOUR Lines (about thirty words) or under .... 2s. 6d.
Each additional line (about ten words) .... 0s. 6d.

PREPAYMENT IS ABSOLUTELY NECESSARY.

*** Stamps *must not* be sent, but all small sums should be remitted by Cash in Registered Letter or by Money Order, payable at the Post-office, Covent-garden, W.C., to
DOUGLAS FOURDRINIER, Publisher,
Addressed to No. 46, Catherine-street, W.C.

Advertisements for the current week's issue must reach the Office before THREE o'clock p.m. on THURSDAY, but those intended for the front Page should be in by TWELVE noon on WEDNESDAY.

SPECIAL.—ALTERATIONS IN STANDING ADVERTISEMENTS or ORDERS TO DISCONTINUE same must reach the Office before TEN o'clock on WEDNESDAY mornings.

The Publisher cannot be responsible for DRAWINGS, TESTIMONIALS, &c. left at the Office in reply to Advertisements, and strongly recommends that of the latter COPIES ONLY should be sent.

PERSONS Advertising in "The Builder" may have *Replies addressed to the Office,* 46, Catherine-street, Covent Garden, W.C. *free of charge.* Letters will be forwarded if addressed envelopes are sent, together with sufficient stamps to cover the postage.

AN EDITION Printed on THIN PAPER, for FOREIGN and COLONIAL CIRCULATION, is issued every week.

Now ready.

READING CASES, { NINEPENCE EACH. By Post (carefully packed), 1s.

The Builder Cathedral Series.

1891.

1. CANTERBURY ..	Jan. 3.	7. SALISBURY	July 4.
2. LICHFIELD	Feb. 7.	8. BRISTOL	Aug. 1.
3. ST. ALBAN'S	Mar. 7.	9. NORWICH	Sept. 5.
4. PETERBOROUGH ..	April 4.	10. ROCHESTER	Oct. 3.
5. WELLS	May 2.	11. LINCOLN	Nov. 7.
6. EXETER	June 6.	12. GLOUCESTER	Dec. 5.

1892.

13. ST. PAUL'S .. .. Jan. 2.

14. HEREFORD	Feb. 6.	20. WORCESTER	Aug. 6.
15. CHICHESTER	Mar. 5.	21. BANGOR .. .. }	Sept. 3.
16. ELY	April 2.	22. ST. ASAPH .. }	
17. LLANDAFF	May 7.	23. WINCHESTER	Oct. 1.
18. OXFORD	June 4.	24. TRURO	Nov. 5.
19. SOUTHWELL	July 2.	25. ST. DAVID'S	Dec. 3.

(Further arrangements will be duly announced.)

Post-free FOURPENCE HALFPENNY each, except Nos. 1, 2, 3, and 4, which are *out of print;* but the VIEW, PLAN, AND DESCRIPTION of CANTERBURY, LICHFIELD, ST. ALBAN'S, and PETERBOROUGH, have been re-printed, and they can now be had, price EIGHTPENCE each set; by post, 10d.

THE REREDOS, ST. PAUL'S.
Reprinted from "THE BUILDER," January 28, 1888 (18 in. by 11½ in.), on stout paper, unfolded, for framing, 6d.; by post, 8d.

PORTFOLIOS,
for Preserving the Plates unfolded, 2s. 6d.; by post, 3s.

London: *Office of* "THE BUILDER," 46, *Catherine-street, W.C.*

Vol. LXII. No. 2573. SATURDAY, MAY 28, 1892

ILLUSTRATIONS.

Church of St. Mary Woolnoth, City: Interior.—From a Water-Colour Drawing by Miss A. Fooks .... Double-Page Ink-Photo.
Illustrations of Old Chester: V., "The Lady's Bower," Watergate Row South.—Drawn by Mr. T. P. Ivison .... Double-Page Ink-Photo.
New Municipal Buildings, Bath: Perspective View.—Mr. J. M. Brydon, Architect .... Double-Page Photo-Litho.
Design for Church of St. Peter, Drogheda.—Mr. T. L. Watson, Architect .... Double-Page Photo-Litho.

Blocks in Text.

Premiated Design for Baths and Public Hall, Cheetham, Manchester.—Messrs. Booth & Chadwick, Architects .... Page 417
Plan of Design for Baths and Public Hall, Cheetham .... Page 418
Ancient Font at St. Andrew's Hospital, Northampton 423
Diagrams in Student's Column: "Heating by Hot Water" .... Page 423

CONTENTS.

The Dictionary of Architecture" 411
he Right of Quantity Surveyors to Receive Fees 412
otes 412
rchitecture at the Royal Academy.—V. 414
he Barrett-Browning Memorial Competition, Ledbury 415
oyal Academy Sculpture 416
ncorporated Association of Municipal and County Engineers 416
aths and Public Hall, Cheetham, Manchester 416
he Royal Commission on Metropolitan Water Supply 418
Interior of Church of St. Mary Woolnoth 420
Illustrations of Old Chester 420
Municipal Buildings, Bath 420
Design for Proposed R. C. Church of St. Peter, Drogheda 420
The London County Council 422
Competitions 422
British Archæological Association 422
Ancient Font at St. Andrew's Hospital, Northampton 423
Student's Column.—Warming Buildings by Hot Water, XXII. 423
General Building News 424
Sanitary and Engineering News 424
Foreign and Colonial 424
Miscellaneous 425
Legal 425
Capital and Labour 425
Meetings 425
Recent Patents 426
Some Recent Sales of Property 426

"*The Dictionary of Architecture.*"

THE completion of the "Dictionary of Architecture" is an event which certainly calls for special notice in our columns. It has been in progress for forty years, during the rhole of which period the original plan and haracter of the work have been rigidly adred to, and the last volume* issued is concted on the same lines as the first. It is rtainly rare to find a work of this kind, iich has been spread over so many years, rried out so completely on a plan definitely ed from the date of its first publication.

To the concluding volume a preface is efixed giving a short account of the manner which the work was first started, and it ay be of interest to some of the younger neration which has sprung up since the mmencement of the work, to recapitulate iefly its history. The Dictionary, of late ars especially, has been practically the ork of Mr. Wyatt Papworth, and it was to s action that we are indebted for the first itiation of the idea. In 1848 he issued a rcular letter setting forth the plan of proposed "Society for the Promotion ! Architectural Information, intended for e Revival and Restoration, Investigaon, and Publication of Knowledge in rchitecture, and the Arts connected thereith;" and a meeting was held at 10, Carolinereet, Bedford-square, on the 4th of May of e same year. A committee, comprising ost of the leading architects of the day, as appointed, and the name of the "Archiectural Publication Society" was adopted. 'he first publication of the Society consisted f detached "Essays and Illustrations," but he real plan of the Dictionary arose out of he preparation by Mr. Wyatt Papworth of "List of Terms" proposed for an Encyclopædia of Architecture. This List of erms afforded a practical suggestion for the framework of such an encyclopædia, and the committee as existing in 1852 were of opinion that the carrying out of an encyclopædia on the lines thus suggested would be a work of so much usefulness that it ought to be commenced forthwith. The Committee in question numbered thirty people, of whom only six have survived to see the completion of the proposed labour. The names are given in the preface; the six survivors referred to are, we presume, Mr. Ewan Christian, Mr. H. B. Garling, Professor Kerr, Professor Hayter Lewis, Mr. Wyatt Papworth, and Mr. W. W. Pocock. Among the other names were those of Sir Charles Barry, Professor Cockerell, Professor Donaldson, Mr. George Godwin, Mr. I'Anson, Mr. John Woody Papworth, and Mr. (afterwards Sir) William Tite. The opinion of this committee was that it would be impolitic to enter upon a publication of a large encyclopædia to be issued in successive parts, extending over a long series of years, "creating the apprehensions and exhausting the patience of subscribers," and that therefore the project should be carried out as a dictionary of explanation and reference, with incidental woodcut illustrations, "so arranged as to be completed in about three years at the present terms of subscription." What actually happened was that the Dictionary was continued on the proposed basis as a work of reference and explanation only, but that its completion has occupied forty-four years instead of the three years calculated on, and certainly with that concomitant result of "creating the apprehensions and exhausting the patience of subscribers," which was supposed to constitute the special obstacle to the bringing out of an encyclopædia on a larger scale. In fact to many, especially of the younger generation, the "Dictionary of Architecture" became a kind of myth, heard of vaguely now and then, but the origin of which was lost in the mists of pre-historic times.

The causes of this extraordinary delay seem to have been, in the first place, the care taken in collecting correct information and in revision of the matter when in type; the system adopted of extreme condensation and repeated revision caused a disproportionate amount of labour over every page, and often the sacrifice of a large amount of collected material. This was a delay of a creditable nature, consequent on the determination to have all the information as correct as possible. But the main cause of the interminable dragging out of the Dictionary has been want of funds, arising partly out of the fact that the architectural profession did not support and subscribe to the work to by any means the extent which had been expected. The list of subscribers is certainly not a long one for such a work. We presume that many architects considered the publication a dry one, that they did not care about accurate information so much as about artistic illustrations, and accordingly took no interest in the publication. In this they certainly made a mistake, which has delayed and crippled the production of a work for standard reference which in its own way is of the highest value. It is no doubt due to this deficiency of funds that the Dictionary has during many years, we believe, been left practically to the labours of Mr. Papworth, who in 1858 was relieved of the duties of hon. secretary which were undertaken by Mr. Cates, in order that he might devote his undivided attention to the actual work of the Dictionary. This we presume we may take as an admission that practically the work is the result of Mr. Papworth's study and researches, though we believe he has consulted and received assistance from others to a certain extent.

It is hardly possible that any one man should be able to treat all subjects for a work of this kind with the same degree of success, and if the work had been an encyclopædia of the extended type such a *tour de force* would be manifestly impossible. As the object of the Dictionary, however, is confined to the explanation of terms and the collection of information as to the further sources of study in regard to each subject, this is a matter of study and industry rather than universal genius, and the numerous papers by Mr. Papworth which have been published from time to time in our columns and in the *Transactions* and *Journal of Proceedings* of the Institute of Architects are sufficient to show that Mr. Papworth possesses in an unusual degree that kind of passion for research, and carefulness in the looking up and recording of facts, which form peculiar

* "The Dictionary of Architecture," issued by the chitectural Publication Society. With illustrations. ol. viii. 1892.

qualifications for dictionary work. It might be expected that certain subjects which lie specially within Mr. Papworth's favourite line of studies would be better or more fully treated than others; but on the whole a very impartial attention seems to have been given to all classes of subjects. In the preceding volume of the Dictionary we noted some curious errors, partly of a literary kind, but these seem to have been rather accidental than essential characteristics. What they did show is that the practical extinction of the large committee of revision which formerly sat upon and sifted everything before finally passing it for press was a great loss to the Dictionary, and that in a multitude of councillors there is safety, at any rate comparatively, from minor errors and inaccuracies.

Taking it all in all, however, the "Dictionary of Architecture" is a very remarkable monument of patience, care and industry, and when Mr. Cates says, in his leaflet accompanying the concluding volume, that "as a dictionary of explanation and reference the work stands alone," he is saying no more than may be legitimately claimed for it. We have remarkable illustrated dictionaries of architecture, in which the articles take the form of extended literary essays on each of the subjects handled; but the "Dictionary of Architecture" is really, so far as we know, the only work on an extended scale the object of which is simply to convey information as to facts, put in the most concise form, and accompanied by a reference to the titles of works from which detailed information can be obtained. This last is one of the most useful features in the Dictionary. Under each subject we find a list of books, periodicals (with dates), or other publications from which the subject can be studied. It must be admitted that these lists too often omit the more recent publications, partly because of the slow rate of progress of the Dictionary, partly we think from an element of the *laudator temporis acti* on the part of the author or editor, whichever we are to call him. We have noticed on another occasion Mr. Papworth's tendency to go a good many years back for his references and authorities, and ignore recent books and recent numbers of periodicals. Thus under the word "Theatre," we find reference to "Donaldson" on the form of the Greek theatre, but none to "Dörpfeld" or "Gardner." It may of course be replied that as "Theatre" comes in the earlier pages of the concluding volume of the Dictionary, the article must have been written some years ago, before the recent controversy had made itself felt. We fear that in a general way the Dictionary will be found in this respect always a few years out of date, and if ever a second edition of it should be issued, it will of course have to be brought up to date in this respect. However, all the numerous references to early and standard works and ancient publications retain their full value, and if the Dictionary had been produced as quickly as the original promoters intended it is obvious that it would now be much more out of date than it actually is.

The scope of the Dictionary includes every term that refers to anything connected with or relating to architecture, including of course eminent architects, and also eminent towns or places of architectural interest. Thus we find in two or three pages such a variety of subjects as "Tite," "Trieste," "Triforium," "Triglyph," "Trilithon," "Trimming joist," a set of words which includes a tolerably wide category of subjects. The Dictionary also serves as a repository and preservative of some ancient words which are nearly forgotten, and may in that way convey some unexpected information. How many of our readers ever heard of "Twichyngropes," or can tell of what place "Tysdrus" was the ancient name? As far as we have observed, no opinions peculiar to the Dictionary are advanced upon any of the subjects; it is confined to the statement of ascertained facts, or of opinions only as matters of history, as held at a certain time or place, or by this or that eminent writer. This is really a wholesome reaction against the modern tendency to issue, as Dictionaries, what are really a string of independent essays embodying individual opinions.

In short the "Dictionary of Architecture" is a Dictionary pure and simple, a work to give information. It will be found deficient in regard to new facts or new opinions of the last few years, but it is a mine of information for all time preceding that, and information which we believe will be found to be exceptionally accurate and reliable. The work is beautifully printed on a large two-columned folio page, and is in every sense a monumental production, and one on the completion of which we may sincerely congratulate Mr. Papworth and his supporters. The cost of such a work of course puts it entirely out of reach of popular circulation; there are now in fact, we are informed, only twenty copies purchasable beyond those which are due in advance to subscribers,* and the Committee are under a distinct pledge not at any time to allow the issue of copies at less than the original subscription price, so that the market value of the book will always be retained. We hope, however, that the available public sale will not always be restricted to the aforesaid twenty copies, and that there may be a prospect of a second edition on the present sumptuous scale, but with such revision as will bring it as closely up to date as possible.

* Mr. Gates gives a list of the principal Institutions and Libraries in which the Dictionary is to be found, which it may be convenient to reprint here for the benefit of those who may wish to consult it. Mr. Cates's list is as follows—"Among learned bodies and Public Institutions may be named,—the Athenæum Club, the London Institution, the Royal Academy, the Inner Temple, the Middle Temple, the Surveyors' Institution, the House of Commons, the Commissioners of H.M. Works, the Lords of the Admiralty, the Carpenters' Company, and the Institute of France, Paris. The work will be found also in the City of London Library, Guildhall; the National Art Library, South Kensington: the Patent Office Library; the Libraries of the University of Glasgow, the University of St. Andrew's, the Queen's Colleges at Belfast, Cork, and Galway; King's College and University College, London; the Thomason College, Roorkee, Bengal; the Massachusetts Institute of Technology, Boston, U.S.A.; in the Signet Library, Edinburgh; also in the Free Public Libraries of Birmingham, Glasgow, Leeds, Liverpool, Manchester, and Sheffield; of Boston, U.S.A.; and of Melbourne, Victoria."

THE RIGHT OF QUANTITY SURVEYORS TO RECEIVE FEES.

IT may be doubted if any point of practical importance has given rise to more legal disputes than that in regard to the payment of quantity surveyors for work done to enable builders to tender for work which has to be performed. In the well-known case of Evans v. Carte, which occurred in 1882, Lord Coleridge remarked that "it is quite monstrous that the employer should pay for the quantities,—that is, that he should pay for what it is the duty of the architect to do." In other words, he considered that the employment of a quantity surveyor was altogether improper. We have, however, now for our guidance a case definitely and clearly decisive on this point, differing materially from the *obiter dictum* of Lord Coleridge. We refer to North v. Bassett (Law Reports, 1, Q.B., 1892, p. 333). In the course of his judgment, Mr. Justice Mathew observed, "What is the usage which, upon these facts, it is sought to set up? It is one which I should have thought to be notorious—a usage that the fees of the quantity surveyor are paid by the builder whose tender has been accepted by the building owner. *This is a sensible and convenient usage;* it brings all the people together,—the builder, the building-owner, and the quantity surveyor,—and they all assent to it." Mr. Justice Smith says more briefly, "This kind of tripartite agreement is a sensible and convenient one." Here are two of the ablest and most shrewd judges on the bench, each noted for his commercial knowledge and common-sense, who approve of this usage.

The action was brought by a quantity surveyor against a builder in respect of fees. It was a case of the most ordinary character, but it is of first-rate professional importance, because the Divisional Court not only thus emphatically approved of this notorious custom, but also sustained it as being good law. Therefore, until a Court of Appeal upsets the case, it must be regarded as making the custom valid, and, in a sense, proving the existence of it. But, unfortunately, there exist some discordant elements. In 1888, the case of Priestley v. Stone came before the Court of Appeal. This was an action by builders against a quantity surveyor for damages caused by his negligence in preparing an inaccurate bill of quantities. The Court of Appeal held that such an action could not be brought, because there was no privity of contract between the two parties. Lord Justice Lindley said:—"There was no privity of contract between the builders and the quantity surveyor. The custom relied on as to privity between them was not proved, and, even if proved, the custom would probably be held to be unreasonable and bad. . . . . The real truth was, that the defendant was employed by the architect, and not by the builders." But if there is no privity, either by contract or custom, as seems to be the opinion of the Court of Appeal, how can there be a right to recover for fees against the builder? No doubt, in North v. Bassett, Mr. Justice Mathew remarked that "I am convinced that the Court of Appeal in Priestley v. Stone never meant to say that this usage was a bad one," and Mr. Justice Smith made a remark to the same effect. But this is rather a cavalier way of treating the judgment of the higher Court, or rather the expression contained in it.

It is possible that the decision of the Court of Appeal might well be supported so far as the particular case before it was concerned, because there was no proof of negligence on the part of the quantity surveyor. But the observations in regard to the relationship of the quantity surveyor and the builder are of importance, and cannot be lost sight of, for these seem to go farther than the case before the Court of Appeal, and in a sense to indicate a principle. Therefore there is still a skeleton in the cupboard; behind the clear and definite case of North v. Bassett there is the ominous shadow of Priestley v. Stone. For the present the Courts must act upon the decision of Mr. Justice Mathew and Mr. Justice Smith, but we shall be surprised if, some day, when the amount in dispute is large, the question is not taken to the Court of Appeal. Until, however, this event occurs, the decision, North v. Bassett, which is in accord with a long-continued practice, must be regarded as a binding decision. But it should be borne in mind that North v. Bassett was a case in which the work was done by the builder. We have yet cases such as our old friend Moon v. Guardians of the Witney Union, decided so long ago as 1837, where the contract has gone off. In that case it is by no means so clear that the building owner can be made liable for the fees of the quantity surveyor, though, perhaps, the balance is in favour of the contention, because the practice of employing a quantity surveyor is becoming more and more known to the general public, and is not regarded by them as so unreasonable as by the Lord Chief Justice of England.

NOTES.

WE have received the Chief Engineer's annual report of the National Boiler and General Insurance Co., Limited. It is a readable and instructive pamphlet. Of course, practically every boiler user has his boilers insured, for of all the assurances that can be effected by the payment of a small annual premium, this, to a manufacturer, is as satisfactory as any. If there are any power users whose boilers are uninsured, then let it be a first and instant duty to remedy this state of things. This is very safe advice to give, but if further impressing is needed, let this report be perused. The information it contains is applied chiefly

recommending the purposes of the com-
ıy, of course, but in doing this the
ıgineer has gone out of his way to
ıke his report comprehensive, and much
ıeresting and valuable information of
technical character is included. It is
ssible that many boiler users do not know
ıt in addition to the expense of replacing
ı boiler and recompensing the injured, when
explosion occurs, there is a considerable
elihood of a Board of Trade inquiry under
ı "Boiler Explosions Act." The result of
s may be a heavy penalty imposed, if ordi-
ry care and thorough and regular inspections
qualified men have not been resorted to.
e insurance of a boiler removes this risk,
the necessity of periodical inspection is
ın remembered by someone else besides the
ır, and an insurance inspector is certain
be a qualified man. The causes of ex-
sions and fractures may be summed up as
lows:—Defective conditions, external cor-
ion, internal corrosion, general deteriora-
n (which must occur to every boiler),
ernal grooving, mistake, negligence, over-
ssure, deficiency of water, deposit, mal-
ıstruction, weakness of tubes, safety-valves
perfect or improperly used or fixed, with a
idue of causes difficult to ascertain. This
ı formidable list, but does not embrace all,
l the "causes difficult to ascertain" repre-
ıt a fair total by themselves.

N extract from a report of the Highways, Sewers, and Public Works
mmittee of the St. Pancras district which
have received, contains some observations
ıut materials for roads, a matter on which we
re still to seek the most perfect method. The
od paving of Euston-road (by the Henson
eet Wood Paving Company) has been
ten up after lasting eleven years, the
ıgest of any mode of paving with
t wood, and the chairman of the com-
ttee (Mr. Jos. Thornley) asks the Works
partment "in consequence of the unsatis-
tory experiences we have had with yellow
ıl," to reconsider the decision to pave
tenham-court-road with that material, and
se an Australian hard wood. As a middle
se, pitch pine is to be used. A quotation
ı a report on wood pavements in Australia,
ever, shows that even with the Australian
d woods, it is strongly recommended that
pavement of streets in Sydney with wood
cks be entirely discontinued. The prin-
ıl reason given is that "the analysis shows
t the blocks in actual use here have
orbed an amount of organic filth which is
e in comparison with the short time
ng which they have been laid, and which
istributed throughout the blocks in such a
ıner as shows that their complete impreg-
on is only a matter of time." Again
report continues:—"So far as the
ful researches of your Board go, the
ous, absorbent, and destructible nature of
d must, in their opinion, be declared to be
nediable by any process at present known;
were any such process discovered, would
ı effectual unless it were supplemented by
ther which should prevent fraying of the
." This opinion from Sydney, where
can command a far superior style of
l for pavement to what we can econo-
lly use here, is certainly significant.
own opinion has been for some time
that wood pavement will have to be
doned, before long, on sanitary grounds;
what is to satisfactorily take its place
o not yet see. Asphalt is sanitary and
t, but the cruelty to horses which it
lves is a consideration which we have no
t to pass over.

appears that the Improvement Sub-Committee of the Manchester City Council
, whether by intent or only by a happy
ıidence, struck an effective side blow at
proposed architectural defacement of the
chester Exchange building by walling up
portico. The Sub-Committee have re-
nended that a new building line should
opted from the Conservative Club along
s-street to Market-street. The effect of this, we understand, will be to constitute the Exchange portico, with the approaches thereto projecting beyond the present solid portion of the Exchange building, an intrusion on the street, and with that status it will be there on sufferance. This will put the Corporation in a position to veto any conversion of present air-space into solid building by the filling up of the spaces between the octastyle portico as proposed. The line of Cross-street can never be made quite direct,—a small mercy for which the number who are thankful will probably increase, as very straight streets are very dreary. The recommendation of the Sub-Committee has to be sanctioned by the General Committee and the Council, but it is expected that this will be done. It is certainly a new and ingenious strategical way of defeating a proposed architectural blunder.

IT appears that there is to be some question as to repairs to Linlithgow Palace, under the department of Scottish Parks and Pleasure grounds. In view of this, as we learn from a recent number of the *Glasgow Herald*, the Edinburgh Architectural Association have circulated among Scottish Members of Parliament their own report of the condition of the palace and the repairs necessary to it. Their circular is to some extent an anti-restoration circular, as they take special care to point out all the parts of the building which are in good condition and have no need of repair, though we think it contemplates or suggests rather too much nevertheless. For the restoration of the fountain in the centre of the quadrangle, "the most unique thing of its kind in great Britain" (as a matter of grammar we may observe that a thing cannot be "the most unique"—it is "unique" or it is not) "there is ample material for guidance; and the names of the figures that filled the few vacant niches on the exterior of the building are known." We fear this points to a sham restoration of fountain and figures, which will have no interest, and only introduce a false element into the building. In their recommendations as to the necessary repairs the Association are on safer ground, and we entirely agree with them that the building should be roofed without delay.

THE case of Pendarves *v.* Monro, reported in the current number of the Law Reports, should be noted, though it does not lay down a new legal principle, but simply emphasises and exemplifies one which has been for some time in existence. Article 41 of Roscoe's "Digest of the Law of Light" states that "when a right is claimed in respect of windows in a new building coincident, wholly or in part, with windows in an old building, the owner thereof must show clearly that the new windows are coincident with and contain the area of those which have acquired the right to light." This principle was enunciated by, among other cases, that of Fowler *v.* Walker, and it is this principle which Pendarves *v.* Monro emphasises. The identity of the old and new windows was not proved. "By reason of the omission," said Mr. Justice North in his judgment, "to keep any plan, there is no evidence which satisfies me that any part of an old window can be identified with any part of an existing window." In the work from which an extract has been given, the author states, in the note to article 41, that when a building is to be pulled down, a plan showing the position of ancient lights should be made and kept with the title deeds. The place in regard to which the dispute in this last case arose was in Sardinia-place, Lincoln's-Inn-fields, and the old houses were pulled down in 1872; therefore, being buildings in the centre of London, it was eminently desirable that plans should have been kept. The occupier of the building from 1869 to 1872 made an affidavit giving particulars of the old windows, and stating that he believed that the new windows "cover in whole or part the ancient lights." But, as we have seen, this was not enough,—the evidence was too vague. The practical result, therefore, is that without a plan it is almost impossible to establish a right to light in respect of windows in a new building which have not themselves acquired a right, but are alleged to have such a right in respect of old windows in a demolished building, with which they are alleged to be identical.

IT is generally conceded that the electric light is the best of all, at least for the theatre. But it is no use having a good thing without the intelligence to use it aright. Naked lights, whether electric or otherwise, are unpleasant unless very far removed from the eye, nor is it desirable that the *auditorium* should be more brilliantly lighted than the stage. The neglect of such obvious considerations at Covent Garden provoked some correspondence in the *Morning Post* last week, happily concluded on Saturday by a letter from Sir Augustus Harris promising to "encase the offending lamps in soft salmon surah silk"—what an ear Sir Augustus has for alliteration!—and that "on German opera nights the lights will be turned out." But why only on German opera nights? Is Italian opera unworthy to be seen as well as heard? or are we to understand that the "music of the future" is a matter chiefly of *chiaroscuro*?

OUR New York contemporary, *Engineering News*, illustrates a monolithic concrete floor recently introduced by Mr. C. F. Terney, of 59, East 106th-street, New York. Concrete floors have been used in some large buildings in Philadelphia, in which the spaces between the beams have been filled in solid: but in the newer arrangement tubular spaces of an oval section, the longer axis being horizontal, are run parallel with the beams. Working in this way, it has been found that great strength is obtained with a comparatively small amount of material. The method of construction is described as follows:—"A temporary floor is suspended from the beams to support the concrete while setting, and a very rich concrete is laid upon it to a depth of several inches. The tubes are made of rich concrete, and vary in size according to the span of the beams, and their spacing and the total depth of the floor. The tubes are made in short lengths and in halves, and when laying them the joints are well cemented, and the outside is flushed all over with grout. The upper and lower halves of the tubes break joint with each other. The space at the sides of and above the tubes is filled with concrete of a cheaper grade than that used for the lower layer and the tubes." The tubes are placed near the upper surface of the floor. This is done so that there may be larger transverse area in the extension than in the compression plane, the compressive strength of concrete being greater than its tensile strength; the ratio assumed by the designer of the floor being 8 to 1. The inside dimensions of the tubes vary from 12½ in. and 9 in. for floors of 20 ft. to 30 ft. span, with 8 in. beams, spaced 5 ft. 9 in. apart, down to 7 in. and 4½ in. for floors of 14 ft. to 18 ft. span, with 5 in. beams, spaced 3 ft. 6 in. apart. The safe loads per square foot of floor are said to vary through the wide range of from 130 lbs. to 570 lbs. in some sample floors tested. The inventor computes the strength of the construction to be as follows:—In a floor of 20 ft. span, with 7 in. I-beams of 15½ lbs. per foot, and spaced 4 ft. apart, a load of 200 lbs. per square foot can be sustained with a factor of safety of 4. The total depth of the concrete would be 9½ in., and four tubes would be used, with cross sections 5½ in. by 8½ in. The total cost of such a floor is about 56 cents (say 2s. 4d.) per square foot, which is said to afford a saving of 25 per cent. in price over ordinary construction.

THE *Times* correspondent, writing from Paris on the 19th instant, announces that in making a cutting at Andresy for a new railway line between Argenteuil and Mantes, an extensive Merovingian cemetery has been uncovered, dating from the sixth century. Andresy (or, rather, Andresis), lying fourteen miles distant north-west from Paris, stands upon the right bank of the Seine, near to Conflans, and opposite to the forest of St. Germain (which the Seine surrounds upon three sides), and just below the confluence of the Oise with the Seine. The Frankish dominion established in Gaul by Clodion and his son-in-law Merovæus, in the former half of the fifth century, included Artois, and extended from the Rhine to the Somme. On the death, in 511, of Clovis, grandson to Merovæus, whose conquests advanced further to the west and south, and comprised Burgundy and Aquitaine, the kingdom was divided amongst his four sons. Of these, Childebert I. reigned at Paris, Clothaire I. at Soissons, and Clodomir in Orleans. From 558 to 561 Clothaire I. reigned, alone, at Paris; and so did Childebert II. during the interval 575—584. After his victory over the Alemanni at Tolbiac, Clovis, influenced by his wife, Clothilda, embraced the Christian faith, together with 3,000 of his warlike subjects. "The new Constantine"—in the words of Gibbon—was baptised by Bishop Remigius in the Cathedral of Rheims. The first interment of a king of the Merovingian dynasty in St. Denis was that of Dagobert the Great, in 638.

THE Langdon Abbey estate, in East Kent, extending over about 654 acres, is to be offered for sale. The manor formerly belonged to the ancient barony of Averenches (Folkestone), of which it was held by service of one knight's fee and ward to Dover Castle, by the family of Auberville, of Westenhanger. William de Auberville so held it, *temp.* Richard I. He founded here, in 1192, an abbey—since a priory—for some white Premonstratensian canons whom he brought from Leiston, in Suffolk, and dedicated it to the Virgin and St. Thomas-the-Martyr. At the Suppression, having a yearly gross income of 56*l.* 6s. 9d., it was surrendered voluntarily by Abbot William Sayer and his band of ten monks. A list of the abbots, with a print of their seal, will be found in Hasted's "Kent," 1799, folio. King Henry VIII. gave the manor of West Langdon, with the priory site, to Archbishop Cranmer; it was subsequently possessed by, in turn, the families of Thornhill, who re-instated the house, called "Abbey Farm," Master, Furnese, and Coke. St. Mary's Church, described by Hasted as being in ruins, was rebuilt in 1869. In the vicinity are Shebbertswell (Shepherd's-well), or Sibertswould, so named after a Saxon owner, Sibert, where, according to vol. i. of C. Greenwood's "Epitome of County History," 1838, 4to, the manor-house was built by Inigo Jones; and Waldershare, its mansion attributed to Jones also. But if, as it is said, Waldershare was built, *circa* 1705, for Sir Henry Furnese, it could not have been erected in Jones's lifetime, for that architect died in 1652.

ANOTHER selection of Mdme. Ronner's paintings of cats is on view, at the Goupil Gallery. The painting of cats is not the highest mission of art; if it were, Mdme. Ronner would be the greatest artist of the day, since her painting, as far as cats go, is simply perfection; the cats seem to be alive, and the various expressions of the kittens, so unconsciously humorous and so difficult to catch, are charming. A life's close study could alone have enabled the artist thus to understand and reproduce the very life and feeling, one may say, of the cat tribe. Though the cats are the essential portion of the pictures and the chief object of the artist's studies, it must be observed also that all the accessories to the larger pictures are painted with great force; in "Un Bout de Toilette," "Les Antiquaires," "Amateurs of Jewels," the old casket, the tapestry, the jewels, and laces are beautifully finished.

Manchester Society of Architects.—The first of the summer series of sketching visits was paid on the 14th inst. to Astbury Church and Moreton Hall, Cheshire, under the leadership of Mr. A. H. Davies-Colley, A.R.I.B.A.

ARCHITECTURE AT THE ROYAL ACADEMY.—V.

1,712; "Sheffield Municipal Buildings: Council Chamber;" Mr. E. W. Mountford.—Hung rather high; it shows a room with a flat ceiling divided into compartments with pendants at the crossing lines of the leading mouldings, the compartments filled in with tracery. The room is wainscotted to the foot of the large traceried windows, which come down lower at the end than at the sides. As far as one can judge from the drawing, the proportions look rather low for the area of the room. A richly-decorated cove connects the ceiling with the wall.

1,714; "Interior, New Church, Miles Platting, Manchester;" Mr. Leonard Stokes. A very fine pen drawing of a very original design. The aisles are for passage only, the church being practically one-aisled, the lofty piers are apparently of hexagon plan with the point towards the nave; they support ponderous plain-soffited wall arches springing from a lintel between pier and outer wall; the piers have thin cap-mouldings on each side, between which the vaulting ribs spring from the surface of the pier; for base-mould there is only a set-off. The piers are connected with the wall half-way up by cross lintels worked into a kind of coffer shape and with bas-reliefs in panels on the sides; if these are a bond to the construction, as may be supposed, their form looks rather out of place in that position, they have no constructive expression. The sculpture, we understand, represents the Stations of the Cross. The roof is a simple quadripartite vault. Statues decorate the piers on the side towards the nave, and the chancel arch has a broad splay decorated with sculpture in niches. The whole is a very remarkable and novel architectural conception.

1,715; "Somerville Memorial Free Church, Keppoch-hill, Glasgow;" Mr. W. G. Rowan. A slight but well-tinted sepia drawing of a picturesque group of buildings, the plain tower with angle buttresses and a lantern stage, with short slated spire over, forming the centre of the group. What we take to be schools or a meeting-hall at the side, a plain low building, groups well with the rest, and sets off by contrast the richer treatment of the church gable at the other side of the tower. A plan would have been an improvement; there is plenty of room on the paper for it.

1,716; Mr. Webb's South Kensington design, we have already referred to; 1,719, "Mausoleum Windows, Hertingfordbury Church," by Mr. Jas. Fisher, shows a two-light window of quiet and unobtrusive colour, with a figure of an angel in each compartment, one of them St. Michael weighing souls, an antique superstition which is surely out of place in a modern window; the saint has rather too much the appearance of being in "Court dress." The drawing of the brackets on which the principal figures stand, as if they *projected* in perspective, is a mistake in stained-glass design.

1,721; "Dining-room and Library;" Messrs. Ernest George & Peto. The dining-room merely shows a bit of the woodwork and cornice; the library is a very good bit of perspective sketch lightly tinted in brown with a panelled ceiling in straight-lined geometric pattern with pendants, the walls are mostly plain, and are cross-lined as if divided into large squares, but what this represents it is not easy to see. The white marble chimney-piece has a wooden overmantel with long upright panels partially carved, and an entablature above. Over the two doors the woodwork is carried up to the cornice and decorated with a moulded balustrade, which seems a very unmeaning ornament in such a position. By the same architects is

No. 1,722; "Country House, Dorset;" an imitation Old English house of plain character with mullioned windows and a doorway flanked with columns, and with little pyramids on the attic, which are also repeated at the feet of the principal gables. The garden front is diversified by two bay windows, and what we take to be the servants' quarters front (there is no plan) is treated picturesquely, with an arcade under the end gables, and a little open balcony and arch above the door. If people wish to make believe to have an old house of the seventeenth century nothing could be better for the purpose.

1,723; "Portal, Sta. Maria Maggiore, Bergamo;" Mr. T. MacLaren. A very clear sunny little water-colour drawing.

1,724; "New Wing to St. Agnes School, East Grinstead;" Mr. Arthur E. Street. A plain stone Gothic building with a great deal of solid wall-surface and high-pitched red-tiled roofs; a point in the design is made by carrying a broad band of similar red tiling along the wall, half way up the building, confined by string-courses. The building is solidly built, pleasing and unpretentious, and shown in a very good water-colour drawing, but absence of a plan makes it impossible to understand properly the meaning of its disposition.

1,725; "School Chapel, Tonbridge;" Messrs. James Brooks & Son. This was published in the *Builder* for May 14, to which we may refer the reader. The design shows the traditional idea of a school or college chapel, carried out with some touches of new and original treatment.

1,726; "St. Augustine's Church, Brinksway;" Messrs. Preston & Vaughan. A pleasing design for a small country church, with a little bell turret with a timber upper stage, which is picturesque, but looks out of scale with the rest of the building, *i.e.*, too small in scale and parts, it looks as if it had been designed to half the scale of the rest of the drawing. The drawing is apparently a very good one, hung too high to be properly seen.

1,727; "New Parish-room and School, All Saints', Plymouth;" Mr. Edmund Sedding. The architect seems to have caught something of the feeling of his late talented brother in the treatment of the staircase which leads to the upper floor, with porch over the top landing, but the detail of the building is rather coarse.

1,728; "Institute of Chartered Accountants: Portion of Elevation;" Mr. John Belcher. A large elevation in pencil on grey paper touched with white. Heavily rusticated piers between the ground story windows, with winged terminal figures over them, crossing a kind of plain frieze space between two string-courses, on which are painted on the wall surface the names of various towns; the second story is perfectly plain masonry with cornice windows inserted, the upper story a heavy Tuscan order supporting the under side of the large cornice, the orthodox architrave and frieze being omitted. The large and rich modillion cornice, however keeps its place pretty well. A frieze of figures is introduced under the windows of this story, interrupted by the lower part of the columns. The rusticated treatment of the upper story windows is rather wild, but the whole is an interesting treatment of old materials in a novel manner.

1,731; "Interior of Turkish Bath, Avery Hill;" Mr. Thomas W. Cutler. This is part of the *matériel* of "Cutler *v.* North," and shows what complete and elaborate work the defendant in that *cause célèbre* had done for him. It is a brilliantly-executed little water-colour showing an octagon room with Arabic foliated arcade and a ceiling divided out in one of the well-known forms of Arabic geometrical pattern; through the archway opposite the spectator is seen a further apartment in the same style. The prevalent tone of the decoration seems rather too blue, if the drawing represents it rightly.

1,732; "Grandtully Castle, Perthshire, as added to;" Mr. Thomas Leadbetter. There seem to be "two Richmonds in the field;" we published recently (March 12) a drawing of Grandtully Castle as intended to be added to, by another architect; we know not which is the right man. This is a very disagreeable rough scratchy pen drawing, and there is no indication, either by plan or otherwise, which is new and which is old, the whole looking equally time-worn and dilapidated in the drawing.

1,733; "Selsdon Park: garden front as altered;" Mr. W. F. Unsworth. It is the same here; there is no indication of what Mr. Unsworth has done to the house, what is his, and what is not. It is a neat but somewhat hard pen elevation of a long terrace front of a Late Gothic house, with a ground floor arcade in the centre portion, and a tower-like mass on the left, which groups effectively with the rest.

1,734; "Municipal Buildings, Bath;" Mr. J. M. Brydon. This is the perspective view of the new Municipal Buildings which we publish in the present number, and to which we refer the reader in place of any description here. Considered entirely apart from the circumstances in which the design was made, this might be considered, perhaps, somewhat tame and wanting in architectural invention for an important new building of the kind. But when we consider that this was a building intended to group with and keep up the traditions of Wood's old buildings, we cannot but congratulate Bath on having obtained a new Municipal Building which so completely harmonises with the architectural associations of the modern city, and which is in itself dignified and stately in composition. The introduction of the quartercircle on plan at the angles, with the order and the band of sculpture on the walls, is an effective incident which, while it is a touch above the level of Wood, is quite in harmony with the general spirit of his work. The drawing, in pen line, is an admirable one.

1,735; "New Travellers' Club, Piccadilly;" Messrs. T. & F. T. Verity. This is orthodox club architecture, with a Corinthian order of pilasters running through the fitst and second floors, and a cornice and an attic over. We mention it as a design of a well-known new club, but we are at loss for anything to say about the architecture more than we have said.

1736; "View of the End of the North Transept of Westminster Abbey as restored;" Mr. J. L. Pearson R.A. This is a view from nearly the same point as that by Mr. John Begg, which was published in our first number of this year, and to our mind not so good a drawing. It appears to be either a pencil or a crayon-shaded drawing helped out with slight washes of Indian ink, and has a very finished look, but the tone is dull and melancholy. The architectural features of the restoration, on which we have before commented, are carefully shown, but the character of the whole is not so well conveyed as in our published illustration just referred to, especially in regard to the effect of the heavy angle buttresses and their pinnacles.

1,738; "Proposed Roman Catholic Church;" Messrs. Goldie, Child, & Goldie. An exterior perspective of a satisfactory church of the orthodox Gothic type, of reddish stone with a very solid-looking low square tower at the crossing. The colour of the drawing is rather harsh and inharmonious.

1,739; "Proposed Houses at Ledbury;" Mr. George C. Grocock. A pen drawing of rather a pretty and picturesque group of semi-detached small houses; each with an octagonal projecting bay which has only a row of small windows at top and bottom, the remainder being solid wall; the introduction of a half-timbered gable on the centre line of the block, and therefore alf belonging to one house and half to the ther, is rather an illogical treatment.

1,740; 'St. Michael's Roman Catholic hurch, Newcastle-on-Tyne;" Messrs. Dunn, ansom, & Dunn. An interior of a solid rthodox late Gothic church, satisfactory nough architecturally, but not made the best f by the drawing, a pen drawing which has een too heavily lined, and without apparently ny eye for effect or any feeling for touch in his kind of drawing.

1,741; "Design for St. Bride's Foundation nstitute;" Mr. Thomas Garratt. This is a ell-executed and effective water-colour drawng, showing the proposed new building as een from the corner of some neglected churchard or some such enclosure overlooking the treet, and which forms the foreground. The ew buildings are apparently meant to be brick nd terra-cotta, and are effectively shown in he drawing, but the handling of the drawing oes for more in the effect than does the archiectural design.

1,742; "Design for Parish Church of St. Peter Drogheda;" Mr. T. L. Watson. This is pubshed in the present number, and, as will e seen, represents a satisfactory and wellomposed exterior of geometric Gothic type, nd a good deal recalling the churches which cott used to build in this style. The tower nd spire are finely proportioned and group ell with the church. As in the case of No. 740, the design owes very little to the ability f the draughtsman, the drawing being in a oor hard scratchy style, with no artistic feelg about it.

1,743; "'Kaikoura', Calne;" Messrs. Russell Gibson. This is hung too high to be well seen, but we have a lithograph of it before us, which will be published among our illustrations in due time, and which shows it to be a picturesque country house of Gothic type, with some characteristic bits of detail about it. Among other things, an open square wooden gallery or gazabo is curious planted out over the angle of the house on a double arrangement of timber corbelling, one beam partly seated on the wall, the others crossing it from the other wall. The house has a very decided look of a dwelling uitable for a mountainous neighbourhood, in which the drawing shows it. The authors are to be commended for adding plans.

1,744; "Flats at Earl's Court-square;" Mr. R. A. Briggs. This is a good example of the effect which may be produced in a very plain utilitarian building by massing and grouping the windows. Two bays run right up the end of the building, the strong projecting cornice going round them; they are connected by light balcony railings, the solid floors of the balconies making deep shadows between the bays. There is a mass of unbroken wall immediately round the corner, and then the main entrance with a series of windows over it up to the cornice, and a segmental pediment. There is character and architectural effect in this, and as the drawing is an admirable one, the building gets full justice.

1745; "Exeter Cathedral;" Mr. H. Needham Wilson. This is the view of Exeter Cathedral which was made by Mr. Wilson for the *Builder* Series of Cathedrals, and was published by us in June, 1891; it is balanced by Mr. Horsley's drawing of Ely Cathedral (1756), executed for the same series, and published on April 2 of this year.

1750; "Pedestal for the Ayr Burns' Statue;" Messrs. Morris & Hunter. The designing of pedestals for sculpture is so much neglected in this country that it is gratifying to find an example of a pedestal carefully studied by an architect, and recognised as a thing worth exhibition at the Academy. The treatment of the pedestal is simple, but the mouldings (the stumbling-block of sculptors) are very carefully designed, so as to give solidity to the base and refinement to the upper portion. Beneath the crowning moulding of the pedestal runs a little kind of frieze of carved ornament in low relief, formed of foliage intertwined with scrolls bearing the names of towns connected with Burns's life; below on each face is a decorative nail-head for hanging wreaths on at anniversaries, each of which has a monogram worked on it: on the lower part of the pedestal are bas-reliefs in bronze affixed to the stonework. Larger details are given of all the architectural portions, and a small sketch of the complete pedestal and status (Mr. G. A. Lawson is the sculptor). The whole is a carefully-studied sheet of architectural detail very well applied for its purpose.

1,752; "Frieze of the Sciences;" Mr. F. Murray. This is a sumptuous coloured elevation representing the upper portion of a marble internal wall and cornice, above which rises the architrave of a door in darker marble, and above on either side of the door-head are symbolical figures, draped, one with a maxillary sphere and one with a shield and coat-of-arms. A child figure or genius stands over the door. The figures are relieved from a lunette with a blue ground. The effect of the whole is rich; the tawdry gilded ornament over the upper part of the door architrave is a defect.

1,753; "Design for a chapter-house;" Mr. Heber Rimmer. This is the perspective of the design for which its author received the Soane medallion of this year, and on which we have already commented.

THE BARRETT-BROWNING MEMORIAL COMPETITION, LEDBURY.

It is the intention of the inhabitants of Ledbury to erect a memorial to their illustrious townswoman, Elizabeth Barrett-Browning, who was the daughter of Mr. Edward Moulton Barret, of Hope End.

Having secured a corner site in the centre of the town, and opposite the old half-timber Market-hall, with frontages of 30 ft. 9 in. and 36 ft. to the Homend (the principal street) and Bye-street respectively, the Memorial Committee invited architects to submit designs in open competition for a Clock-tower and Institute. In response to the committee's advertisement, forty-five sets of drawings were sent in, and these have this week been publicly exhibited at the Market-hall.

Amongst the "Conditions" issued to architects, the following may be noted:—The clock-tower to stand at the angle of the two frontages, and the centre of the dials to be 45 ft. from the ground. A vestibule, reading-room (33 ft. by 19 ft. 6 in.) and library annexe to be provided on the ground floor, two class-rooms and lavatory on the first floor, and caretaker's rooms above. The entrance preferred near the angle of the streets. The cost not to exceed 1,600*l*. The selection to rest with the Committee (as already stated in our columns). Mr. Brightwen Binyon has gained the first premium of 20*l*., and the second premium of 10*l*. has been awarded to Mr. Lunn, of Malvern.

The conditions virtually determine the plan, and nearly all the competitors show identically the same arrangement, with, perhaps, the exception of Messrs. Guy Dawber and Langton Dennis, who have rather gone out of their way to make a simple matter complicated. The design of the elevations, and the grouping of the tower and the rest of the building, thus becomes of decisive importance. In the grouping, however, there is again a general unanimity, the majority showing a large gable supporting the tower towards the Homend, balanced by two smaller gables, facing Bye-street. The tower designs are very varied.

A visitor to Ledbury is at once impressed with the quiet, homely character of the town, with its many half-timber gables, its fine, though somewhat rambling, church, and its picturesque timber Market-hall supported on massive chestnut posts. It is an old-world place whose romance has not yet been stifled.

It is, therefore, disappointing, almost exasperating, to notice how many of the competitors have submitted designs of a pretentious and fussy character, altogether out of harmony with the quiet surroundings. Either, it must be supposed, these architects have not taken the trouble to inspect the site or acquaint themselves with the town, or else having eyes they yet see not.

This does not apply to Mr. J. E. Newberry's quiet design, which, although not being very original or striking, would yet at once incorporate itself into the town. A simple square stone tower stands at the angle, and large, half-timber gables, with brick lower stories, face the two streets. But the half-timber upper story of the tower looks heavy, and mars the general design, and its semi-tipped gables present a very ugly sky-line. Walking down the Homend one would see the Memorial Tower clear against the sky, and its outline is therefore an important matter. Messrs. Radclyffe & Watson, of Birmingham, send a quaint and clever design, which is one of the best there. The extended base of the lantern tower is pierced on two sides by ogee archways, over one of which is a niche for a memorial statue. In the middle stage, the square plan below grows into a half-timber octagon by bold curved splays at the angles, and this again becomes constricted by an inverted ogee curve to a smaller octagonal lantern, with ogee roof. The upper story of the main building is of half-timber, and the roof is hipped back from both façades.

Messrs. Guy Dawber & Langton Dennis are represented by the most artistic set of drawings of the exhibition. Their plan, however, is not happy except for the direct light it affords to the reading-room. The staircase, which has to be reached by crossing the reading-room, is cramped, and, having no well-hole, would not obtain much light from the lantern placed at the top. The "tower" is tile-hung, and does not extend to the ground, being developed by corbels from the angle of the building. Its upper story is suggestive of an Italian campanile,—a pyramidal roof supported by a colonnade,—and is a pleasing and clever piece of design. The main roofs are hipped back as in the last design, and the awkward outline thus occasioned is not so well corrected by the projecting dormers. The result is that as the roof lines slope up towards the tower, the tendency of the tower to look top-heavy is enhanced.

Mr. Brightwen Binyon's design both in plan and grouping follows the general type before described. It is a little jerky in outline. Thus in the elevation facing the Romend the ground storey projects, the first floor recedes, while the gable one projects again. So too in the tower, which after rising without interruption for nearly 40 ft. carries a corbelled out half timber stage, covered with a truncated pyramidal roof, from which rises an oblong lantern, with louvres, and whose roof is adorned with wrought iron cresting. A little more quaintness would bring the design more into harmony with its surroundings. The plan is well proportioned and convenient; the entrance vestibule is spacious and well lighted. It is questionable if the caretaker can be trusted with a dust shoot from his house on the top floor to the basement, as he will probably use it as a shoot for vegetable and other refuse.

Mr. Binyon proposes to face the building with best red local bricks, with red sandstone dressings. A band of terra cotta or carved brick round the tower about 6 ft. above the ground will illustrate some subject taken from Mrs. Browning's poems. On the side of the tower next Bye-street is a drinking fountain. The estimate of cost is 1,600*l*.

It is a little difficult to understand the committee's choice in their award of the second premium. The lower part of the tower and building generally is of brick with stone dressings, and of rather commonplace design. The gables are half timber. The upper part of the tower—or rather upper *half*, for it is divided exactly in the middle of its height by a broad weathering—is entirely of stone of a florid Gothic character, with traceried window and crocketted pinnacles grouped in pairs and engaged to the sides of the tower.

Space does not allow a detailed notice of the more important designs of the remainder. Mr. A. Ardron sends a boldly-drawn design, showing a brick tower surmounted by a timber lantern. A half-timbered gable faces the Homend, and an ornamental plaster one overlooks Bye-street.

Mr. J. Johnstone has a well-proportioned tower, but of a too monumental character, and in the perspective drawing the sky apparently forms part of the design. The staircase oriel window is not satisfactory. A design of an ecclesiastical character is submitted by Mr. C. R. Ashbee. The angle buttresses of the tower look very wiry.

Messrs. W. Cook and W. G. Lewton send good examples of tower design, though in the latter the lantern looks too heavy for its supports. The designs of Messrs. Crouch & Butler, Houston & Houston, and J. W. Boyd are too ambitious, and miss the sentiment of the place, and so too does the "Greek Design" of Mr. G. S. Hill.

ROYAL ACADEMY SCULPTURE.

THE central work of the year is unquestionably Mr. Onslow Ford's "Shelley Memorial," a work at once poetic in feeling and decorative in effect. On a slab or sarcophagus of dark veined marble lies the naked body of the drowned poet, a laurel sprig in bronze encircling the head. The base of the composition, in the same marble, is brought out in front in a semi-circular pedestal on which sits a partially-draped female figure, the muse of lyric poetry(?), leaning with the right arm on a lyre, the left hand stretched out as if commanding attention. On the pedestal behind sit, back to back, two winged lions, whose wings support the slab on which the body of the poet rests; the modelling of the head and mane seems suggested by Stevens's celebrated little lion figures which decorate the railing of the British Museum. The only portion of the design which rather jars with the rest is a too realistic bronze tree, with bare branches and rounded bright fruit, which grows from the pedestal at the back, and rather clashes with the ideal and perfectly sculpturesque character of the rest of the work. The bright bronze plaque with the name of Shelley engraved on it, and some bronze festoons bearing small inscriptions, also standing out brightly from the dark marble, increase the decorative effect of this very original monumental conception.

Mr. Alfred Gilbert's chief work is a posthumous bust, or rather half-length, of the late Baron Huddlestone in his judicial robes. It is in gilded bronze, and the head is very forcibly modelled. Mr. Gilbert also exhibits a striking half-length in the same manner of execution, of Sir George Birdwood, holding in his hand a small Indian idol, to which he seems to be calling attention. Here also the head is remarkably expressive. An odd little nude statuette called "Tragedy and Comedy," a man holding a comic mask and at the same time looking down in alarm at an insect on his leg, which appears (from the action of the limb) to have stung him. It is a little sculptor's joke, not quite in the happiest vein. A superb chain of office for the Corporation of Preston, completes Mr. Gilbert's contributions to the exhibition. It is modelled with that largeness of style and multiplicity of detail which characterises Mr. Gilbert's work of this class, and in this respect is worthy of the best period of the Renaissance, but it looks rather an uncomfortable chain to wear.

Mr. Harry Bates's bas-relief, of "The Story of Endymion and Selene—How she conveyed him in a sleep to old Mount Latmos" is one of the most successful works this artist has produced. It is in low relief, and the car of Selene is drawn by two horses with wings on their feet, whose heads are modelled on the type of the Parthenon horse. The head and torso of Endymion are reclined in the arms of Selene, who sits on the right of the composition, her drapery making a moon-like outline round her head. The legs and feet of Endymion point forward towards the horses' heads, making a level line which is of great value in the composition as a contrast to the curved lines of the Selene figure, and as impressing on the whole group a sentiment of repose. The same sculptor's Memorial of the late James Tennant Caird, a bronze alto-relief figure of an angel in full flowing drapery writing on the top of a memorial slab, is fine in idea and in its spirited action, but the indication of the figure beneath the drapery is rather incomplete and the hips in fact seem lost, there is no place for them under the modelling of the drapery, which moreover is somewhat too disturbed in its folds and hollows. A beautifully-modelled little silver figure for a door-knocker is also defective in relation to its purpose, as there is no indication in it of anything to knock with, unless it be the heels of the little figure. A knocker should leave no doubt of its function; there should be something which is obviously meant to knock with, and there is no indication of that here.

Mr. Adrian Jones's great pyramidal group of "Duncan's horses," in the middle of the central hall, composed of three fighting horses, is spirited and energetic, but the subject is hardly worth the space it occupies and the talent rather to our thinking, thrown away upon it. Among the other works in the Central Hall, Mr. A. Drury's "Harmony," a nude female playing the violoncello and singing with open mouth at the same time, is rather odd in effect than beautiful, and some of the modelling of the figure seems more masculine than feminine in type; the bow-hand is fine and nervous, but the violoncello does not combine happily with a life-size ideal figure. Mr. Fehr's seated half-draped female under the title "Favourites" (the favourites being birds) looks as if the author had studied the feeling and spirit of Mr. Ford's work a good deal, especially in the head; it is a pleasing and graceful work, but hardly rises above that level. Miss Beatrice Browne's "Pearl" is one of those fancies about the pearl on which there has been rather a run of late years both in sculpture and painting; this is a nude figure of a young girl reclined in a rather uneasy attitude within a colossal oyster-shell; it is a carefully-executed piece of work, but fails in not being beautiful, and beauty is the one excuse for this kind of fancy; the face is plain and un-*spirituel*, and the head uncomfortably posed. Mr. G. W. Wilson exhibits an effective and pleasing model for a wall fountain; an architectural alcove with Renaissance type of ornament, at the back of which stands a pretty female figure holding the conventional urn for the water to flow from.

To return to the Lecture-room, we find among the larger works in the middle of the room Mr. G. Frampton's "Children of the Wolf," we presume the infants Romulus and Remus carried home by the peasant who found them. A fine figure of a man; but there is a want of imagination in the work; it might be any stalwart man bringing home any two babies; there is not the slightest attempt to give special character to the children who certainly ought to show signs of their brutal bringing up, but they are two as innocent round-faced babes as one could wish to see. Power of modelling without power of imagination, which is at the root of so much of the shortcoming of English sculpture. Mr. Albert Toft's nude figure, "Fate-led," which was exhibited in plaster last year, is here in marble and seems considerably improved from the original model; the face conveys rather the idea of somnambulism, but it is a figure with an idea expressed in it. Mr. Fehr's little "Morning," a bronze statuette of a nude figure with her hair blown in the breeze, is a pretty conception.

Architects may look with interest on Mr. Pegram's two reliefs for the main entrance of the Imperial Institute, "Industry" and "Britannia," and feel glad that a sculptor of so much ability is employed on a class of work too often left to the race of "carvers." "Britannia" is the most original figure of the two, and the most powerful; "Industry," who winds a skein off a turning drum or reel, is awkwardly posed on the edge of a seat, with one leg stretched right across the panel and the other doubled back, an indication of the sea forms a horizontal line of broken up surface on the background of the panel. Still this is sculpture distinctly above the general level of decorative architectural sculpture in this country.

Mr. Onslow Ford's "Gordon Memorial Shield," presented to Miss Gordon by the Corps of Royal Engineers, is an interesting bit of decorative metal work; it takes the general shape of a form of shield familiar in Renaissance paintings, with an alto-relief of a naked St. Michael slaying the dragon, in an oval in the centre; around the margin are small figures of children intermixed with chased ornament; the central group is the only portion which seems to have any symbolical reference to the subject of the shield.

Among the smaller works of the year Miss Ruth Canton's bronze head of "Azrael, the Angel of Death" has fine poetic character. Miss Esther Moore's "Head of a Boy" is a work with distinctive character, also Mr. Pomeroy's noble and dignified bust of "Miss A. Broke," a bust treated in a decorative manner, with a band of conventional floral ornament surrounding the base. Miss Beatrice Angle's bust of "A Bacchante," and Mr. Partridge's "A Dream," a very low bronze relief of a head in profile, should not be passed over. Among animal subjects are several very clever little bas-relief studies of horses by Mr. Gilbert W. Bayes, especially "Carting Sand—France," in which there is a novelty of style and execution; and Mr. J. M. Swan exhibits two small bronzes of an "African Panther" and a "Lioness Drinking" which exhibit (the former especially), the same forcible realisation of animal character and action which we see in his paintings.

INCORPORATED ASSOCIATION OF MUNICIPAL AND COUNTY ENGINEERS.

THE following gentlemen having satisfied the Examiners at the Examination held in London on the 1st and 2nd ultimo, certificates have been granted them by the Council:—

Anderson, J. R., London.
Andrews, C. P., London.
Ball, J. B., London.
Bradshaw, J. B., Gateshead.
Cross, F. W., Walsall.
Fitton, G., Reading.
Hills, H. J., London.
Lloyd, C., Chatham.
Shackleton, C. W., Coseley.
Veit, L. J., Ipswich.
Yates, F. S., York.

The next Examination will be held in Leeds, on Friday and Saturday, September 29 and October 1.

BATHS AND PUBLIC HALL, CHEETHAM, MANCHESTER.

THE design we publish for the New Baths and Public Hall, at Cheetham-hill, Manchester, was selected by the Baths Committee of the Manchester Corporation, out of a number of designs submitted in open competition.

As will be seen from the ground plan, the site is very irregular in shape, with a good frontage to Cheetham Hill-road and another smaller frontage to Back Halliwell-lane. It has a fall of about 12 ft. from the highest to the lowest point. Advantage has been taken of this conformation of the site to place the Public Hall on the higher portion thereof, and the Baths on the lower, the Boiler House, Laundry, &c., being at the lowest point easily accessible for coals, &c., at the street level.

The first-class swimming-bath will have a water area of 54 ft. by 27 ft., and the second-class bath one of 75 ft. by 24 ft. The latter will be surrounded by a balcony for the accommodation of spectators on the occasion of swimming-fêtes. The pavilion in which it is situated is so arranged as to be capable of being used as a gymnasium in the winter months. The first-class swimming-bath is so planned that it can be used by ladies on such days as may be set apart for that purpose; and a special dressing-room has been provided for their accommodation. There are twenty slipper-baths and three waiting-rooms, and these will be classified as ladies' and men's first and second-class. A commodious residence for the superintendent will be situate over the ticket-office and entrances to the baths, and in connexion with this department there is a handsome tower for the reception of a public clock.

The public hall is to be on the ground-floor level, and be practically a separate building, designed to be capable of being used for

Premiated Design for Baths and Public Hall, Cheetham, Manchester: Perspective View.—Messrs. Booth & Chadwick, Architects.

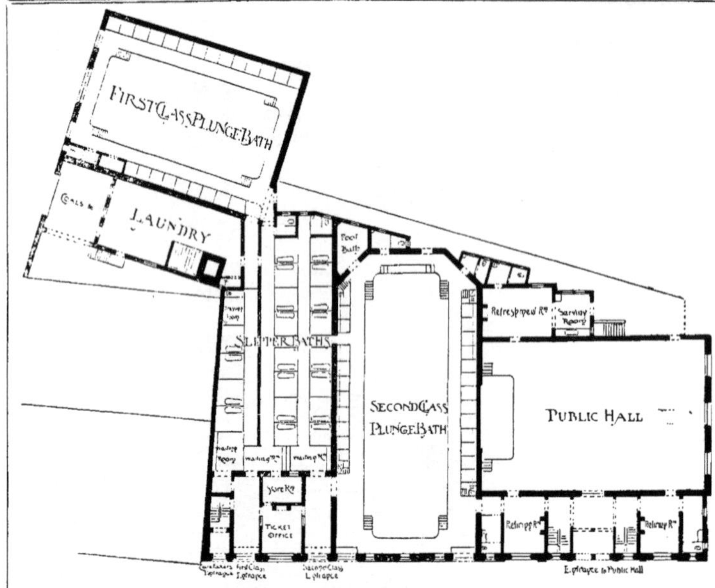

Plan of Baths and Public Hall for Cheetham, Manchester.—Messrs. Booth & Chadwick, Architects.

lectures, public meetings, conversaziones, concerts, bazaars, dramatic performances, dances, and all other proper purposes. The principal room will have a clear floor area of 64 ft. by 42 ft., and there will be a balcony-gallery in addition. There will also be five retiring and cloak-rooms, with lavatories attached, a refreshment-room, serving-room, and cellar kitchen. There will be a fine entrance-hall, leading to the public-room; and the retiring-rooms for ladies and gentlemen will be placed to the tight and left of it; and these will, by being placed close up to the main road, secure the large hall against the noise and disturbance arising from street traffic.

Additional doors for occasional exit are provided from the public hall and from the large second-class bath pavilion.

The architects are Messrs. Booth & Chadwick, of Manchester, who have received instructions to prepare the necessary working drawings, and to obtain tenders for the erection and equipment of the building.

THE ROYAL COMMISSION ON METROPOLITAN WATER SUPPLY.

THE Royal Commission on Metropolitan Water Supply consists of Lord Balfour of Burleigh (Chairman), Sir G. B. Bruce, C.E., Sir A. Geikie, D.Sc., LL.D., F.R.S., Professor J. Dewar, M.A., F.R.S., Mr. G. H. Hill, C.E., Mr. J. Mansergh, C.E., and Dr. W. Ogle, with Mr. Francis Gaskell as Secretary.

The Commission has held two sittings for the taking of evidence. It commenced its inquiries with the River Lea and the two companies that draw a great part of their supplies from that river,—the New River Company and the East London Company. When the sittings are resumed, the Lea Conservancy will be heard, and then the companies that draw their supplies mainly from the Thames. There are maps on the walls of the room to elucidate the evidence as to the local position of intakes and wells. The Commissioners have before them printed statements and tables which have been furnished by the companies; also communications from the Lea Conservancy and from the local authorities in the districts referred to. The latter statements, from the questions that were founded upon them, appear to suggest that the water of the Lea is not always sufficient for the navigation and for the companies, that the water is polluted by the manure and other traffic carried on upon it, and that the wells in the Lea Valley, from which the companies obtain large supplementary supplies, have affected, or may affect, the wells of the local authorities. The main object of the companies was to show by expert evidence that their wells are practically inexhaustible, without affecting any other existing wells. The examination of the witnesses was mainly directed to the explanation of the companies' printed statements and figures, and in particular to the testing of the data for estimating the consumption of water per day per head of the population, the actual supplies from all sources, and specially the possible future supplies from the wells that have been sunk, and others that are projected.

The New River Company.

Mr. James Searle, for twelve years Clerk of the New River Water Company, was the first witness. He was told by the Chairman that he need not go through a history of the Company, because that was dealt with fully enough in the first eight paragraphs of the printed statement which had been handed in. Asked about the increase in the number of houses in the district supplied by the Company, he said that was also set out in the statement. From 1851 to 1871 the total increase was 31,000 houses; from 1871 to 1891, 35,000; making for forty years 66,568, or a yearly average of 1,664. The growth had been fairly steady, but in the last two years there had been a considerable falling-off, and the reason was that the Metropolitan district was to a great extent filled up, and the building was now chiefly in the Hornsey and Edmonton parishes. He afterwards explained that by "houses" he meant "supplies," and that in a block of buildings each separate tenement would be called a house; so that the yearly addition was 1,664 tenements. A private house let off in rooms would be called one house, because there would be but one rated occupie but each set of rooms separately rated w called a "supply" or a house, and therefo the Company's return of the number of hous would not coincide with that of the census. T average daily supply in 1891 was set down 33,028,000 gallons, of which 22,500,000 we derived from the Lea, and the remaini 10,500,000 gallons from the Chadwell sprin and from wells. The average increase in t period of forty years was taken as an index the probable increase during the next for years with the object of showing that the Com pany possessed the means to meet the deman arising from increase of population. T Chairman, however, asked, "Would not the tr way of looking at it be to endeavour to find o what the average increase to the new rat would be, rather than to deduce it from t average of the past?" The average daily co sumption had been 24,440,000 gallons in 187 and it was now 33,000,000; and, said the Cha man, "If you apply that ratio of the 33 million which is the present consumption, would it n be fairer to say that in twenty years the increa would have been 44 millions, if the ratio taken from the 33 millions now, rather th applying the same ratio of increase to the millions as you do to the 24 millions?" T witness did not think the increase would be fast. The present consumption per head, 2 gallons, was taken as the basis of the estima for the future. Not quite half the district w under constant supply. The consumption p head had increased with the growing desire f comfort and luxury; but the full effect of th had been already felt, as water-closets an baths were now fitted in all new houses, an had been freely used for 15 or 20 years. D weather in summer and continued frosts winter were without equal in the strain th put upon the company. The largest supply a single day had been 42 million gallons, an that occurred in January, 1891. The Compa had sunk wells without Parliamentary powe because they were all put down on land th had been purchased.

Mr. Joseph Francis, Engineer to the Ne River Company, said that for twenty years l had superintended the construction of the wells. Chadwell spring now yielded about 2,000,000 gallons a day, and the wells 8,500,000; but the daily available supply from these sources was estimated at 34,000,000 gallons, or 23,500,000 more than was now taken. The 34,000,000 was arrived at by taking what each well could do, and had done for weeks together, pumping day and night, taking each well separately, and then adding the results together. The witness gave particulars of the wells, which we summarise in the following table: The first column gives the depth in feet, and the second the depth of the borehole from the surface for each well that has one, and the third the year of completion. In the case of Turnford Well, the well was first sunk into the chalk with borehole, and the deep boring was done from 1875 to 1880. The last column gives in millions of gallons the details of the estimate of 34,000,000 gallons as the available daily supply. Amwell Marsh was given as 2,800,000 gallons, and Hoddesdon as 2,160,000. The letter (*h*) indicates that the wells have headings:—

	Well. ft.	Boring. ft.	Year.	Million galls. daily.
Broadmead	26 ...	831 ...	1879 ...	1½
Amwell End............	72 ...	·419 ...	1848 ...	1½
Amwell Hill (*h.*)......	90 ...	160 ...	1848 ...	3¼
Amwell Marsh (*h.*)...	109 ..	392 ...	1885 ...	2¾
Rye Common (*h.*) ...	204 ...	— ...	1886 ...	3¾
Hoddesdon	54 ...	403 ...	1868 ...	2⅛
Broxbourne	197 ...	— ...	1886 ...	4½
Turnford (*h.*)	167 ...	1,001 ...	1867 ...	3¾
Cheshunt (*h.*)	130 ...	157 ...	1846 ...	¾
Hoe Lane, Enfield (*h.*)	192 ...	— ...	1886 ...	3½
Betstile......	142 ...	300 ...	1872 ...	½
Highfield (*h.*)	178 ...	— ...	1887 ...	3
Campbourne	213 ...	— ...	1888 ...	3⅛

The general policy of the Company was to bring in the supply from the wells to supplement that from the Lea and the Chadwell spring. All the wells are in use except Cheshunt. Broad Mead well had yielded 1,500,000 gallons daily for seven weeks together. The figures by no means represented what could be got out of the wells by working the engines a little faster. There was connexion between the Turnford and the Cheshunt wells, which were a mile apart, and that was the reason why Cheshunt was put down at 750,000. Anwell Hill and Anwell Marsh to some extent affected each other; but the quantities named were given when both were at work, as they had been for a few weeks together. Only in the cases named did the pumping at one point affect the supply at another. He did not think there was any ground for complaint that their pumping operations had depleted other wells in the district, except so far as it affected any spring in the immediate neighbourhood of a well. The Chairman read a statement by the Cheshunt Local Board that the pumping operations of the New River and the East London Companies had drained two artesian wells sunk by the Board, and one artesian well of the Waltham Gas Company. These wells, 150 ft. deep and driven into the chalk, were three years ago overflooded, but now the water did not rise within 50 ft. from the surface, unless the pumping ceased for a long time. The witness did not understand that, because the level of the water in the Company's well had never sunk 50 ft. or anything like that, and the Board's Surveyor had reported the yield as satisfactory and the level as unaltered. He afterwards explained that they pumped down to the depth of 60 ft. or 70 ft., and when they stopped pumping the water rose, and the level was unaltered. The County Council of Hertford had informed the Commission that many of the rivers of the county now rose considerably below the point at which they had their source twenty years ago, and were much reduced in volume, that the volume of many natural springs was much diminished, and that the water-levels of the county were materially lower than in the past. Of these complaints the witness had not heard. Nor had he heard of a complaint by the Enfield Local Board, who were advised by their Surveyor that the lowering of the water-level in the chalk was due to the sinking of deep wells by the New River and the East London Companies. From Turnford Well northward, he said, there had been no lowering whatever of the level in the chalk during the fifteen or twenty years he had noticed or taken the levels. There had been no lowering of it since the new wells had been sunk. These replies suggested to Sir G. B. Bruce the question whether between Turnford and London there had been a falling of water; and the answer was that under London there had been a considerable falling off, and that influence extended up towards Enfield. Under London it was nearly 18 in. a year; and the standard water-level had been for some years falling. The Company had old wells they were not using now at Hampstead Heath and Hampstead-road, and at these wells they had the opportunity of measuring the water-line. It was sinking there although they were not pumping. The fall of water in the upper valley of the Lea no doubt arose from increased drainage. Fields were drained and the water that would otherwise water-log the upper part was drained off into the springs, and that accounted for rivers rising lower down. The water was taken off so much more rapidly than before that the upper ground did not get so well saturated. He had no doubt that the quantities of water named for each well could be depended upon, supposing all were pumped together continuously. There would not be a general depression, but a local cone of depression at each well. There would not be danger of pollution from surface water, because the surface was covered with drift clay, sand, and soil, so that the water was filtered before it could get downward. He did not think that any wells the East London Company could sink in their district would affect the yield of the New River Company's wells; taking into account percolation and area, there seemed to be plenty of water for both for many years. "There must be a limit somewhere," said Mr. Hill; and the witness rejoined: "Yes, but we find that what we pump has practically no effect upon the surface level, and therefore it is evident that a very much larger quantity could be pumped without doing any appreciable harm." If the pumping were more than the supply, the level in the chalk might be lowered; but he had no fear that the demands of the companies would have that effect. Having investigated the matter carefully, they were quite satisfied that the water they were pumping would not go to feed springs or streams or rivers, except in local cases; the water was really passing down towards the south-east end of London, and it did not get into the rivers at all. The pumping would not affect the river Lea itself, but it would affect the Thames at Woolwich. There was no diminution in the discharge of the river Lea compared with a few years ago; and this was shown by a return put in giving the discharge at Fields Weir for each month of the year from 1880 to 1891. Mr. Mansergh pressed upon the witness the point that the wells were to be relied upon for four times the supply they yielded now. The witness said that was hardly it. They wanted an average of 47,250,000, and they had got 56,000,000. The 34,000,000 a day from the wells might be wanted only for a few days during the year. "But in a very dry season it would be longer than a very few days?" "Yes, but we never find that the maximum lasts very long." The 34,000,000 was not what it was proposed to draw every day; it was merely a store to meet any excessive claim that might come. The company had power to take 22,500,000 gallons from the Lea at a point a mile below Hertford, and he had never known a time when that quantity could not be got. The river Lea people had not complained that too little was left for navigation. Wet or dry seasons did not make an appreciable difference in the quantity obtainable from the river; the level of the water in the wells varied with the seasons to the extent of a few feet. The water from Belstile was pumped into a reservoir; with that exception, all the water from the Lea, Chadwell Spring, and the wells was conveyed to London by the river, which was covered in for three miles, and partly so for a mile and a half. There was great expense in keeping it open in time of frost; but the full quantity could always be got through. The river was fenced almost throughout its course; surface streams did not run into it; and it was patrolled and watched and carefully guarded against pollution. The water given by the Chadwell Spring varied very much. The average was about 3,500,000 in the twenty-four hours; but 2,500,000 was the average for last year. For a short time it has been under 500,000 in dry seasons. The figures of 4,500,000 given to the Commission twenty-five years ago was rather too high. The river water may not always be so clear as the well water, but it is equally good for domestic consumption after it has been filtered. The lowering of the water level under London he attributed to the increased pumping that had taken place from under London itself, and the difficulty that the water had in getting down there, through the restrictions in the channels in the chalk. After wet seasons the level was higher in the chalk; after dry seasons it was somewhat lower; but changes did not follow immediately, and it was difficult to trace the connexion between rainfall and the level in the chalk, except in a general way. Asked what was the condition of the lower part of the Lea in summer time, he said there was always plenty of water in it. Reminded that Mr. Binnie had told a former Commission that the effect of the increased abstraction of water was "to reduce it in summer time to a stagnant pond," he replied that Mr. Binnie did not say there was a want of water, but that it was stagnant. The movement of the traffic would give plenty of circulation in the water if it was only kept free from sewage matter. "Of course, if you put sewage into it, it takes a very large flood to keep it always clear. There is no want of water at all." Pressed by the Chairman, the witness said the companies always left the navigation quantity, but sometimes took all that remained. There was always left as much as the traffic could need, and it was enough to keep the water from being stagnant, providing large quantities of sewage were not turned into it. The Chairman asked for the minimum discharge from the Lea at any period within the last five or ten years; but the witness had only the monthly averages, and one was as low as 44,000,000, although the daily average in that year (1887) was 104,000,000. At such a time the New River Company would still take its 22,500,000; but the East London Company, having storage reservoirs, would not take much from the river. Questioned as to the population and the nature of the country above the company's intake, Mr. Francis said that Luton was eleven miles above it, and the sewage of the town was kept away from the river by being taken to a sewage farm on high ground. The general character of the country through which the Lea ran was purely agricultural. The Lea Conservancy took great pains to prevent anything like pollution. There was a manure traffic in barges, and it went on to a small extent above the intake; but the navigation did not extend much above the intake, for it stopped at Hertford. It would be possible for each company to store about 10,000,000 gallons a day during the winter months of the surplus water of the Lea, but there was no scheme in hand; indeed, it would be possible for them to store 365 times 10,000,000 gallons, but, the Chairman pointed out, the storage would have to be at the rate of 20,000,000 gallons a day for half the year. Still, nothing had been done because well-sinking was a much simpler way of obtaining a supply. But, for all that, he wanted to test the storage plan. There was room at Walthamstow for reservoirs which would cost 300,000*l.* or 400,000*l.* The reservoirs would not be of great depth, and there would be no danger from a great head of water. The reservoirs would want puddling, because the London clay does not extend so far. "We know it is not as happy a site as we should like," but the Company had carefully considered the possibility of having to erect reservoirs. In the area from which the water-supply was derived, the increase of population was very slow, and it had been more than met by the increased precautions of the Conservancy in diminishing population. He did not agree with the statement that during flood time the water was exceedingly bad. The worst time was just at the commencement of the flood, and means were taken to shut it off partially or wholly. As soon as the first flush was over, the water was not bad. There was a good deal of sand and clay in it, but it was not polluted. It would not be true that the condition of the flood waters was "as bad as the main drainage outfalls at Crossness." The flood water at their intake was never bad; it was turbid with sand, clay, and chalk; but it had not the offensive smell or the bad colour of sewage. The water from the wells was filtered with the water from the river, not because it needed it, but because it was cheaper to bring it along the river channel than to lay separate pipes. The New River water stood highest amongst the river-derived waters, and the river-borne pollution from navigation was gradually decreasing. The flood water, when stored, would be good water, provided you did not take just the top of the flood; and he did not think that the bulk of the water would have to be rejected on account of the pollution brought down by heavy rains. Tottenham, Enfield, Ware, Cheshunt, and Hoddesdon had independent supplies.

[*Continued on page* 420.

Illustrations.

INTERIOR OF CHURCH OF ST. MARY WOOLNOTH.

AS our readers are aware, there has been some foolish talk about pulling down this fine church in consequence of its insanitary condition owing to the mass of human remains beneath the floor, it being apparently considered in these days preferable to destroy a remarkable church rather than go to the expense of removing the remains of the burials of the past. It is to be hoped this absurd and discreditable proposal will not be really carried out.

The site has been occupied by a church for many centuries; the building preceding this one was injured in the fire of London, and repaired by Wren; why soon after this it was pulled down no one seems to know. The present church was designed by Wren's pupil Hawksmoor; the exterior, heavy and castellated as it is in appearance, has nevertheless a kind of defiant originality in the treatment of the principal façade. The interior, one of the most convenient (for congregational purposes) and one of the moss architectually effective church interiors in London, is a Greek cross on plan, with shallow arms, and three Corinthian columns at each angle (as shown in the drawing), with a segmental dome over the central area. The view shows part of the interior as it was remodelled by Mr. Butterfield in 1876, when the galleries were removed, but in order to preserve their fine carved fronts the architect bethought him of the happy idea of fixing them as an architectural feature round the walls; their original use is sufficiently obvious to tell the history of the change.

The church was built in 1716. Among the persons connected with its history was the Rev. John Newton, the joint author with Cowper of the "Olney Hymns," who was rector of the church for twenty-eight years, and was buried there in 1807. The lithograph is from a monochrome watercolour drawing by Miss A. Fooks.

ILLUSTRATIONS OF OLD CHESTER.*

V.—THE LADY'S BOWER, WATERGATE-ROW SOUTH.

THIS very interesting little court, with its covered gallery, measuring only about 16 ft. by 14 ft., is in this series illustrated for the first time, as it is very little known, and has fallen into a dilapidated state, much to be regretted. In the view no attempt has been made at restoration except the removal of a wall under the gallery and abutting against the column, to form a passage for the convenience of a house in the rear, and the introduction of mullions in the windows, which have been modernised. All the woodwork is oak, elaborately carved. In the adjoining mansion, now in the occupation of Mr. Maddon, cabinet maker, are some interesting remains, including a noble fireplace of great height, now almost hidden, and a pendant of great beauty, and at the back of this tenement is a house before alluded to, in which are remains, including fragments of stained glass, a fine old stone fireplace, and other carvings, which will form subjects for future illustrations, when the whole will be fully described, with some account of the distinguished Cheshire family who originally made it their town residence.

THOMAS P. IVISON.

MUNICIPAL BUILDINGS, BATH.

THIS is the amended perspective view of Mr. J. M. Brydon's accepted design for the new Municipal Buildings at Bath, the elevations and plan of which we published on January 9 of this year. We did not then give the perspective in accordance with Mr. Brydon's express wish, as he was not satisfied with it in its original form.

We gave a very full description of the design and plan in our review of the competition designs on December 26 of last year, to which it is unnecessary to add anything here; we may mention again that the block on the right or south wing contains the municipal offices proper, and that on the left or north wing contains the technical schools. The plans for the whole are in hand, and will be carried out substantially as in the competition design.

The drawing from which the illustration is taken is exhibited at the Royal Academy.

* For preceding views of this series, see *Builder* for February 6, February 27, March 12, and April 9 last.

DESIGN FOR PROPOSED R. C. CHURCH OF ST. PETER, DROGHEDA.

THE illustration shows a drawing submitted in competition for an Irish church several years ago.

The church was designed to take the place of an existing structure on the same site, and the Sacristy and other buildings shown on the right of the drawing had been built as an addition to this older church, and were to be preserved in connexion with the new church, and this to a small extent controlled the design.

The internal dimensions of the proposed church were as follows:—Total length, 138 ft.; width over aisles, 58 ft.; ditto over transepts, 88 ft.; and height, 52 ft. 6 in. The spire was 220 ft. high. Confessionals were provided in the nave between the buttresses of side walls.

Mr. T. L. Watson, of Glasgow, is the designer, and the drawing is at present in the Royal Academy Exhibition.

THE ROYAL COMMISSION ON METROPOLITAN WATER SUPPLY.

(*Continued from p.* 419).

Mr. Ernest Collins said he was the engineer in charge of the distributing works of the New River Company, and was responsible for the tables laid before the Commission. The average supply per head per day for all purposes, trade and domestic, was 27·10 gallons in 1872, 28·77 in 1881, and 28·49 in 1891. Constant supply had been introduced, and extended to 17,557 houses in 1881, and in 1891 to 68,000, out of a total of 154,568. The increased consumption from 1871 to 1881 was partly due to the bad state of the fittings in Shoreditch. In 1883 the company made great efforts to suppress waste; and it now employed thirty-eight waste inspectors, while Deacon's meters were largely used to detect flow at night. An average of 28 gallons per head per day ought to be taken as the maximum consumption for trade and domestic purposes for the New River district. Fifteen years ago a directly-supplied closet was quite exceptional. Now every 20*l.* house had a water-closet, and houses above 25*l.* had often two, and a bath. Future increase would perhaps bring more efficient means of checking supply. London, he thought, could not be compared with any other town, because London had more baths and water-closets. The consumption had reached 32½ gallons per head per day in July, 1887, and 32 in July and August, 1884. The average was arrived at by dividing the total by the number of supplies and estimating seven and a-half persons to each. The figures had been tested by experience. It was reckoned that about a quarter of the supply went for trade purposes, including railways and breweries and street watering. He put 28 gallons per head as the maximum, because there was still great waste going on that could be prevented. The constant supply was the most economical with proper fittings, but the intermittent without them. People who had put on proper fittings on notice were impatient for constant supply, and the Company were obliged to give it,—when perhaps only ten houses out of fifty were ready for it. The consequent waste he estimated at 3,000,000 gallons a day.

Mr. Edmund L. Morris, engine-superintendent, gave evidence as to the capacity of the engines at the wells. At most there were two sets of machinery; but the stand-by power was in the number of wells, at which, in the aggregate, the quantity of water pumped was only one-third of what could be pumped. Mr. Morris has also charge of the filtering operations, which he described in detail. He said there was no test other than that of colour for the efficiency of the filtration. When the sand was scraped off a filter-bed it was washed until it was quite clear of foreign matter, and then it was used again. Sir A. Geikie asked, "Can you be sure that you take away all the organic material?" and the answer was, "All the particles are separated and washed, and it is thoroughly cleaned."

The Chairman remarked that this concluded the evidence put forward as specially referring
to the New River Company; but at the n
sitting Mr. Francis was requested to furnis
plan showing for each well the normal leve
the saturation, the level to which the wa
rises after pumping has been stopped for so
time, and then the level to which the wa
must be pulled down by pumping to give
quantities mentioned in the table.

The East London Company.

Mr. W. B. Bryan, Engineer to the E
London Company, was asked to describe
company's intakes. He said that at Chingf
Mill they had two intakes,—a high-level int
at the mill-head to supply their high-level re
voirs, and one at the tail of the mill to sup
the low-level reservoirs. They took out of
stream flowing past their works on the aver
32,000,000 or 33,000,000 gallons a day. In t
of drought, the amount of water that pas
below the intakes was not very great; bu
was never reduced to nothing. The navigat
having a prior right, was always full.
witness was reminded that the average quan
taken was 36,000,000 in 1891, and 37,000,00
1890, and he assented to the statement that
New River Company might, if they chose, t
over and above their 22,500,000, one-half
what was taken by the East London Co
pany; except so far as the latter took wa
when the river was in flood for storage in th
large reservoirs. The Conservancy took
much water as they required for the navi
tion, and the East London Company never
jected to the Conservancy taking its
amount. It might be that it had taken "o
as much water as was necessary for the p
sage of the traffic," but he was not aw
that any complaints had been made
his Company. He estimated that it wo
be safe for his company to take 30,000,
gallons a day from the Lea. It had ta
nearly its full amount from the Thame
9,750,000 for four weeks in 1885; and he
lieved it might safely have taken 10,000,0
The quality of the water at the point at wh
they got it was improving; and it was not tal
when the river was in flood, when the Compa
relied upon its large storage reservoirs in
valley of the Lea. Field's Weir is at the ju
tion of the Stort and the Lea, and the quant
of water passing over it after the New Ri
Company had taken its allowance was s
before the River Lea Committee to be 15,30
gallons a day; but the witness said that
quite a mistake, due to the erroneous wa
which the gaugings had been taken. This
the Chairman to remark: "What we wan
know is the minimum quantity going over
weir for a certain number of days or week
the summer." The witness said he could
every day for twelve years; and he mentic
a day in August, 1887, when the quantity
22,185,000, and another in October, 1
when it was 30,000,000. But, in 1
two wells were in process of construct
and water was pumped into the river,
it would not exceed 1,000,000 gallons
day. The most adverse condition to
encountered was a prolonged frost, follo
a dry summer. Then the Company must d
upon its wells and its storage reservoirs.
at the worst it might count on get
20,000,000 a day out of the river. If 40,000
a day were required, 20,000,000 would be ta
from the Lea, 10,000,000 from the Thames,
the remainder from the wells and the stor
The full storage capacity was 910,000
gallons. There was no means of telling w
was taken daily from the River Lea. W
the Lea was in flood the intakes were absolu
closed, sometimes for a week together
sometimes longer. On the Lea works t
were about twenty-five acres of filter-beds,
the maximum out of use at any time was a
three acres. The pumping machinery wa
a high-class and doing splendid duty, and t
was adequate stand-by power. The ta
furnished to the Commission showed that
average daily supply had increased 10,000
gallons a day in eleven years, but it was
mated that in the future the increase woul
only 2,000,000 gallons a day in five ye
The increase was now all in the Essex dist
The average population per house in the Lon
district was about 7.62; in the Essex distri
was only 6·1. The company took the pop
tion, and divided it by the number of supp
to get the average of each house or supply.
number of supplies in 1891 was 172,310.
was believed that 33 gallons per head per
was an excessive estimate for the next f

ILLUSTRATIONS OF OLD CHESTER.—Drawn by Mr. T. P. Ivison.
No. V.—"THE LADY'S BOWER," WATERGATE ROW SOUTH.

PERSPECTIVE VIEW OF NEW MUNICIPAL B

Royal Academy Exhibition, 1892.

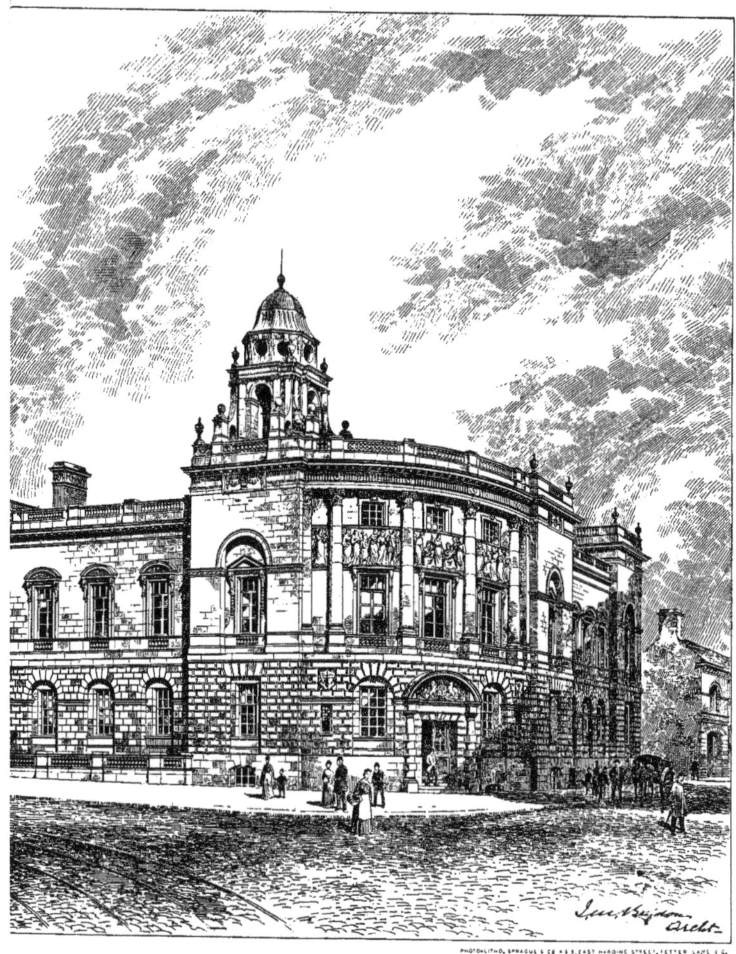

PHOTO-LITHO, SPRAGUE & Co 4 & 5, EAST HARDING STREET, FETTER LANE, E.C.

BATH.—Mr. J. M. Brydon, F.R.I.B.A., Architect

Design for
New Parish Church
of Saint Peter Drogheda.
Mr. T. L. Watson, F.R.I.B.A. Architect

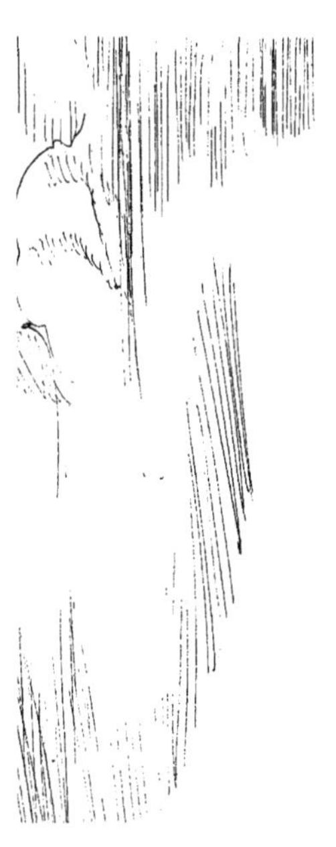

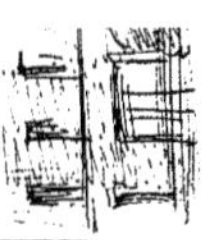

years, because so much water was now wasted through the absolute carelessness of the poorer classes. Then immigrants washed their clothes by putting them under the tap, and letting the water run for two or three days. There were portions of the district in which the consumption was as high as 70 gallons per head per day. Thirty inspectors were employed in checking waste, and, while it was watched, the night line would be reduced, but it would rise again to the day line in the following week. The yearly increase in the number of supplies culminated in all London in 1885, and then it was checked with the decrease in jerry-building. It was most difficult to estimate what the population was at any particular time in such a district, because the population was so migratory, and one or two big strikes would reduce it very much. It was impossible to tell what the East-end of London would be like in a few years time, because a check must come to the increase of the population within the Metropolitan area. In West Ham the sites for new houses were limited, and if the population went further east, to Barking, it would be in the district of another water company. In wealthier districts the consumption per head was less than it was in poorer districts; and he had found it the same in Blackburn. In the Company's district there were 80,000 or 90,000 houses at a water rental of less than 15s., and that indicated that the rental was weekly. When a house got dirty the occupants would change into a clean one, and it was difficult to know how many were actually occupied at any given time. The witness was requested to furnish the Commission with a return of the number of gallons of water used per head per day, and to prepare it with a "keen appreciation of the importance which was attached to it." The pollution of the Lea from its traffic was infinitesimal, and the bulk of the traffic stopped below the Company's intakes. The two Companies pay an annual sum for securing the sanitary supervision of the river, and immediate attention to any reported pollution. The Conservancy have informed the Commission that there are thirteen sewage-treated towns above the East London intake, and sixteen towns—eight sewage and eight cesspool —above the intake of the New River. The witness said he knew only about Hertford and Cheshunt. In the latter case the effluent was now carried for several miles into the Company's intercepting drain, which discharges it some miles below the intakes. Hertford used a precipitation process, and the effluent flowed through a ditch to the Lea. No doubt, said the witness, the organic impurity in the East London water was greater than in the New River, for two reasons: first, their intake was in a better position; and, secondly, they had a greater admixture of well-water. The difference was about 50 per cent. on the average; and it was mainly due to the well-water. The present and the possible yield of the Company's wells and springs was the subject of many questions. In the Company's statement the daily average of water taken from wells and springs was set down at 3,681,000 gallons. Mr. Bryan now gave the quantities pumped from the wells as follows:—

		Gallons.
Waltham Abbey	......	800,000
Chingford	......	500,000
Walthamstow	......	400,000

The remainder, which would be nearly 2,000,000, he said, came from the springs at Hanworth. In the statement it was said that the existing wells would yield 11,000,000, and from other wells "some of which are being sunk," they could get 13,000,000. This statement elicited from the witness the story of the Hanworth springs, and led to important questions. At Hanworth, four miles past Hounslow, and two miles north of the Thames, there were gravel springs which yielded 2,000,000 gallons a day. It is lifted by centrifugal pumps, so it is difficult to say the exact amount. A trench around the filter beds was being puddled, on account of the pressure of land water. It was found to be a volume of good water. Ou Mr. Bryan's advice, tunnels were driven to collect it. It was a permanent supply. There was a bank of clay which held up an immense amount of water in a gravel bed of 70 or 80 square miles. The water was running on its way to the Thames. Pumping did not seem to have any effect upon it. The water flowed over the edge of the bank in four or five places. It was simply a small portion of the surplus that was taken. "Where does it come from?" was asked. From a large area which is permeable, and is little built upon. "Then, practically, it is surface water?" said the Chairman. Yes, it is. The water has been analysed several times, and the Local Government Board gave permission to use it four years ago. The following conversation ensued:—

The New River Company tell us they are pumping, on the average, 8,500,000 gallons a day. So it comes to 10,000,000 or 11,000,000 a day from the chalk wells. In your statement you say that from the Company's existing wells in the Lea valley you can get 11,000,000. That is about 9,000,000 more than you are taking now?—Yes.

And from other wells, "some of which are now being sunk," you think you can get 13,000,000?—We do.

Thus you propose to take 20,000,000 more than you are taking now?—Yes.

And the New River Company propose to take 23,500,000 more?—Yes.

So that the two propose to draw daily 44,000,000 more from the chalk than now?—Yes. From our present wells we have taken continuously 7,000,000 daily.

For how long?—Until the pumps gave out, for three or four months at a time. Some of it we pumped to waste and some we ran into our filter beds. From the Lea Bridge well we have pumped continuously for six months, and we have had as much as 3,500,000 a-day passing to the last day.

During the construction of the well at Waltham Abbey there were complaints of depression in four public wells at Waltham Abbey and Cheshunt, but Mr. Bryan found the explanation to be that their pumps were out of order. In reply to further questions he said,—I think it is safe to assume that we and the New River can take 44,000,000 gallons more, because there is an immense volume of water running to waste in a south-easterly direction into the Thames, down towards Purfleet, Grays, and that neighbourhood. Our wells immediately fill up when we cease pumping. At Lea Bridge we have 6,000 ft. of tunnel, and as soon as we cease to pump the water fills the tunnels quickly, and, as soon at it reaches the shaft, it comes up the shaft at the rate of 40 ft. an hour. At Walthamstow the action is very rapid. At Waltham Abbey our pumps are drowned by about 140 ft. of water. We cannot reduce the level with our existing pumps to nearer than 128 ft. from the bottom of the well. It is difficult to make any estimate of what we are pumping when we have got workmen down below. On this the Chairman said, "And that makes it difficult for us to form an estimate of what you have really been doing." The following occurred in subsequent conversation:—

You have powers to sink wells beyond those you have exercised?—Yes.

What length of headings have you driven?—At Waltham Abbey about 600 ft.; at Walthamstow about 600 ft.; at Lea Bridge about 6,000 ft. At Lea Bridge we have driven headings at a very low level. The chalk was so hard it had to be blasted with dynamite. After driving 1,000 ft. and finding no water, we abandoned the lower heading, and came up 60 ft. higher. All complaints of our affecting previously existing wells have been groundless, and at present they are drawing all the water that is needed. Of the 910,000,000 gallons, 600,000,000 can be drawn off by gravitation.

Have you formed any idea what would be the effect of getting these 44,000,000 gallons extra from the chalk?—As far as my district is concerned, I do not see how it can affect the surrounding country. There is the London clay, which is a very compact mass, lying between the Thanet base and the surface, so that, whatever water comes from below, it cannot affect the surface close to our wells. I cannot see how the abstraction of any amount of water from the chalk underneath the London clay, so far as the London clay extends, can affect either the surface springs or the country generally.

I suppose there is a limit to the quantity to be got from the chalk?—I should think there is.

There must be a point at which you would begin to draw on the streams from the surface, must there not?—The streams have no connexion with the wells where the London clay is.

I am speaking of where you have the chalk?—We have not any chalk in our district; there is no outcrop of it in my Company's district. All down the valley, if you dig 2 ft. you come to the water from 2 ft. to 3 ft. in the gravel.

How are the wells lined?—We support them with cylinders 15 ft. in diameter at the surface. We seal these into the London clay, so as to absolutely exclude any water from the gravel.

With respect to the depletion of the Lea, the Chairman quoted a letter from the Conservancy to the Company on March 17, stating that there was difficulty in keeping the navigation below Old Ford up to a proper head, and that at Limehouse Cut the navigation had been stopped at times for want of water. The witness said that up as far as Chingford the Lea was always full. The Thames tides went into the Limehouse Cut, and left a considerable deposit of mud. The Conservancy had filled up a compensation reservoir, which had been constructed by the Company. The tide used to flow in and out, and thus the reservoir acted as a flushing tank, but the Conservancy had filled up the reservoir with dredgings. An extra 5,000,000 a day would be nothing in six or seven miles of river. Neither would it place the Company in difficulty, because they had always sufficient water in their storage reservoirs, and they had never objected to the Conservancy taking their full amount.

The witness further stated that the East London Company has secured excellent sites for more storage reservoirs. Turbid water is not taken. In flood and rainfall the intakes are shut down until the water is in good condition; and they have never been unable to fill up their reservoirs a few days after a flood.

Sir F. Bramwell said he had been consulted on these matters by the East London Company. He handed in a table prepared from the publications of Mr. Lass, which showed that from 1881 to 1890 the houses or supplies of the East London Company's district had increased from 130,086 to 167,989. He also produced another table giving corresponding figures for all the eight companies. The estimate of 33 gallons was, he thought, largely in excess of what it ought to be; including the trade supply of 6,000,000 or 7,000,000, the estimate ought to be from 25,000,000 to 27,000,000 at the utmost. The East London would do with this supply without stinting anybody if it had the same assistance from the local authorities as other companies had. The average price or cost of the East London Company's whole supply was 4·187d. per 1,000 gallons; and for the eight companies, including the East London, the figure was 7·116d. Where the customers acted with reasonable fairness, the constant supply system took the least water; and waste arose mainly from carelessness and indifference. The East London Company was peculiarly situated in its power to pump from the chalk large quantities of water running to the river or the sea. He could not conceive that any amount of pumping would ever affect places in the district,—Luton for example.

Professor W. Boyd Dawkins said he had made it his business to master in detail the geology of the district, and in particular the area of the chalk and the area of the London clay. The water which the East London Company obtained from wells, sunk mostly through the London clay, was obtained from the rainfall which came upon the chalk; and the area of the chalk in the Lea valley was about 275 miles, including outliers. On this area 1 in. of rainfall a year would give 11 million gallons a day; and there was a percolation of not less than 10 in. a year. The chalk was an enormous porous sponge, the upper half being more porous than the lower half, and the whole something like 400 ft. in thickness. The streams were on the surface of this mass, which was more or less saturated. At Mimms, south of Hertford, all the surface-water went through three or four swallow-holes bodily into the chalk, proving in that case the capacity of the chalk to take 20 square miles of surface drainage. The chalk was full of swallow-holes in which that sort of thing went on, and, therefore, 10 in. was a very moderate amount of percolation. To the east, in the valley of the Roding, the Company could intercept water on its way down to the line of the Thames, and so largely increase their supply. He had seen water passing from the chalk into the Thames, and he was fully persuaded there were vast masses finding their way through it, to say nothing of certain large isolated springs which came bodily into the Thames. These masses did not come through the London clay; they came through the chalk. The surface of the chalk was extremely irregular, especially under London. He showed by a section from Sevenoaks to the line of the Thames the gradual descent of water from an altitude of 172 ft., and said it was the same on the other side of the river. There was a general lowering of level due to increased drainage, which might also diminish percolation; but that did not apply to wells in London that had been sinking a long time, because water could not get to them to compensate for what was taken out. That would not happen to the Company's wells, because they were nearer to the area of the exposed chalk, and the yield of these wells showed that there was certainly very much more water in the district than there was under London in the chalk. The Company had wells with a capacity of 4,000,000 to 5,000,000 gallons a day, but no well under London had produced much more than a fourth of that. This underground water certainly came from the surface of this area, and possibly adjoining areas. "Then," said the Chairman, "rainfall and percolation cannot be the bases of estimates." Pumping on a large scale would have some effect on the surface drainage, and probably on the streams; but the area was so extensive that a large amount of water might be taken without much danger to the surface.

Mr. Wm. Topley, F.R.S., F.G.S., said the water at the Lea Bridge well was largely derived from the tertiary sands, and this source of supply could be more largely utilised. If this water were not pumped it would go to feed the general supply in the upper part of the chalk under London, which found its way down to the Thames and flowed out along the Thames. The gravels of the Lea were in direct communication with the sands of the tertiary beds. He saw no reason why a large amount of water should not be drawn from the gravels of the Lea. All along there was gravel underneath and along the sides of the river, and whenever it was tapped it was water-logged. If any harm was done by taking that water it would be to the river lower down. What was done at Lea Bridge was a capital example of what could be done by developing old wells and making new ones in the Roding and Stort valleys. It was impossible to say what would or would not happen, but none of the existing wells were sufficiently near the outcrop to be a source of danger to the neighbours of the East London Company. There seemed to be something exceptional in the Lea valley in the large amount of water that could be drawn, and in the wells not affecting each other. Two wells in the Stort valley might, perhaps, yield 3,000,000 gallons between them. Of course, there must be a limit beyond which it would be unsafe to go, but he did not think the proposals of the Company would reach that limit.

Mr. J. H. Barnes, C.E., handed in tables showing the monthly flow of the Lea from 1880 to 1891 at Field's Weir, and, asked for the lowest, said it was twenty-one millions in September, 1891.

Mr. W. C. Young, consulting chemist to the Lea Conservancy, handed in analyses of water from the intakes made in 1884, 1886, and 1891, and said they showed a considerable diminution in organic pollution; but the Chairman, remarking that analyses taken at such an interval did not convey any idea to the mind, preferred to examine Mr. Young as the witness of the Conservancy rather than as the witness of the Company, and, therefore, deferred further questions until the case of the Conservancy is taken.

The Commission will resume its sittings on the 30th inst.

THE LONDON COUNTY COUNCIL.

THE usual weekly meeting of this Council was held on Tuesday afternoon at Spring-gardens, the Chairman, Lord Rosebery, presiding.

The Water Question:—Mr. Dickinson, the Deputy-Chairman, reported that the Committee of the House of Commons which was considering the question had expressed their willingness to pass the London Water Bill, provided it was limited to conferring powers to conduct inquiries and negotiations and to promote Bills in Parliament, and to pay all the necessary expenses thereof; but that they were not prepared to constitute as the Water authority either the Council or the Joint Committee of the Council and the City Corporation, as was proposed by the Bill. The effect of that decision was to give to the Council all the powers originally asked for by them, but to deny to the Corporation for the present year the representation sought by them on a Joint Statutory Committee. Under the circumstances, therefore, the Corporation's representives had asked to be permitted to consider what action should be taken, and the matter had consequently been adjourned, in order that they might decide whether or not they should insist upon the Bill being abandoned, or would proceed with its promotion in the altered form.*

Organisation of the Council's Work.—The Vice-Chairman (Mr. John Hutton) presented a long report by the Special Committee on Organisation and the methods of conducting the Council's business. The Committee made a number of detailed recommendations, the first of which was the creation of a new Committee, to be called the Establishment Committee. Other recommendations were as follows:—

"That, with respect to officers charged with technical or professional work under the control of a single Committee, and who are not heads of departments, all recommendations for their appointment shall be made direct to the Council by that Committee after consultation with the Deputy-Chairman.

That, with respect to officers charged with technical or professional work under the control of particular Committees, more than one in number, and who are not heads of departments, all recommendations for their appointment shall be made to the Council by such Committees jointly after consultation with the Deputy-Chairman.

In cases where the work of the officials is not confined to particular Committees, the questios of appointment shall be dealt with by the Establishment Committee as a matter falling under the reference to them."

The recommendations were agreed to after some discussion, in the course of which Mr. Hutton strongly urged the necessity, in the interests of economy and efficiency of administration, no less than in the interest of the health of the Council's *employés*, of obtaining a site and erecting new and adequate municipal buildings. The central building in Spring-gardens was totally inadequate to the needs of the staff and its work, and it now had to be awkwardly and expensively supplemented by a number of scattered houses. The inconvenience of this scattering of the staff was very great. Another thing was that many of their *employés* were now working in rooms which were positively unhealthy.

The "Rate of Wages and Hours" Clause in Contracts.—The discussion of this question was resumed. As we have already informed our readers, Mr. John Burns raised the question by the following motion:—

"That all contractors be compelled to sign a declaration that they pay the trade union rates of wages and observe the hours of labour and conditions recognised by the London trade unions, and that the hours and wages be inserted in, and form part of, the contract by way of schedule, and that penalties be enforced for any breach of agreement."

To this Mr. Costelloe moved last week the following amendment:—After the first word "That" to insert the words "except as regards work intended by the Council to be done outside London."

Mr. Sydney Webb seconded this amendment, and, after a long discussion, the amendment was negatived by 73 to 32.

The further discussion of the matter was adjourned to a special meeting fixed for Friday afternoon, the 27th, at 3 p.m.

The Council adjourned at 7 o'clock.

COMPETITIONS.

HIGHER GRADE SCHOOL, WINCHESTER.—In this competition, we understand that the successful competitors are Messrs. Pink, Farrow, & Nisbett.

WILLESDEN FREE LIBRARY.—We are informed that the designs of Messrs. Newman & Newman, of London Bridge, have been selected in competition for the new free library to be built at Willesden-green.

BURSLEM BOARD SCHOOLS.—We understand that in the recent competition for new schools at Hill Top and Longport, for the Burslem School Board, the plans of Mr. A. R. Wood, of Tunstall, were adopted, and that he has been appointed to carry them out. The Longport school is intended for 400 boys and girls, and the Hill Top school for 400 boys, with re-arrangement of the Board-room and Offices.

* At the sitting of the Parliamentary Committee on Wednesday, Mr. Littler, Q.C., on behalf of the London County Council, said that that body desired to proceed with the Bill in its altered form, which was subsequently ordered to be reported to the House for third reading.

BRITISH ARCHÆOLOGICAL ASSOCIATION.

AT the meeting of this Association on Wednesday, May 18, Mr. J. W. Grover, F.S.A., in the chair, the progress of the arrangements for holding the Congress at Cardiff were detailed. Mr. Loftus Brock, F.S.A., exhibited a series of articles which had been found in recent years in various parts of London, in proof of the existence of a settlement on the site of the City in prehistoric times. The articles consist of bones split for the extraction of the marrow, bone spear-heads hacked into shape by flint implements, and pottery not worked on a wheel. The chairman produced an old Bible covered with embroidery in silver and colours, most probably the work of the nuns of Little Gidding. Mr. Wells reported the discovery of prehistoric remains which have been made in cutting a watercourse on the Wray Park estate, Maidenhead, on land which had once been a bog. At a depth of 7 ft. or 8 ft. the antlers of red deer, used as a pick, have been met with, together with a portion of a human skull, flint implements, and a stone axe, which, after having been cut and polished, had been repolished at a later date. Many hazel-nuts were also found, and cockle shells, the latter being refuse of food. The chairman spoke of a ford which appears to have existed at Maidenhead in Roman times, and probably for a period long anterior. Mr. Earle Way exhibited a small collection of Egyptian antiquities, the principal of which was a cone of a foundation deposit, with an inscription. A paper on "The Merchants' Marks of England" was then read by Mr. R. Davis. This was an exhaustive treatise, in which the rise of the use of merchants' marks was traced from early times to our own. Old Acts of Parliament were cited in which Merchants, 1420, were to make barrels with a sign; and others required Goldsmiths to have their marks while in action. Old documents were produced in which certain witnesses had affixed their marks, the latter being distinctive and not a common sign. Thumb marks from the actual thumb of the witness were also noticed. Arms and marks were sometimes used by the same individual when qualified to bear arms, and the instance of Wm. Canynge and some others were mentioned; while the shield of John Terry, 1524, in St. John's Church, Maddermarket, Norwich, bears his arms, those of the Mercers' Company, and his Merchants' mark. Many of these marks are based upon a cross, apparently in token of good faith. The paper was illustrated by drawings of over 500 examples from monumental crosses, documents, stained glass, and seals.

Correspondence.

To the Editor of THE BUILDER.

ANCIENT FONT AT ST. ANDREW'S HOSPITAL, NORTHAMPTON.

SIR,—This font is of admirable workmanship, though now much worn by its 300 years of desecration and exposure. It was found in a midden immediately outside what I believe to have been the southern doorway of the ancient priory church, or chapel of the Augustinian Canons of St. Andrew's, of which the present St. Andrew's Hospital grounds, extra parochial, formed the country house. Their town house, famous as that in which Thomas A'Beckett, Archbishop of Canterbury, took refuge after the stormy scene with Henry II. in the castle, was situated near the river, upon the site of the London and North-Western railway-station, closely adjoining the castle hill.

The font is of late twelfth-century character, and of Barnacle stone. These quarries,—still discernible as "hills and hollows,"—so the local term for such ground runs, became exhausted towards the end of the thirteenth century. This is sufficient, even without the clear architectural evidence, to prove the antiquity of the object in question. It has, I am told, though this cannot well now be seen, as it serves as a flower-basket or stand, no drain. This proves it never to have been accommodated to the Protestant form of baptism. According to the Catholic rite, the water of baptism is blessed but once a year (on Holy Saturday), and a drain would have been sure to "weep" in that time. It is thus only necessary in Catholic churches to bale out the fonts once a year. In the Protestant rite the priest blesses the water at each baptism, and if a drain were not pro-lded, it would be necessary to bale out the water at every christening. The absence of drain thus proves this font, thrown out f the church into the midden (in which, hree hundred years after, it was found) pon the dissolution of the priory by Henry VIII., and the desecration and ain of the church which it once adorned, —never to have served for the Protestant rite. There further remain clear traces of the hinge nd staple of a wooden cover for securely ocking up the font, as is required by the Catholic rubrics to this day. Of the building

rom which this font has been removed, *i.e.*, he Priory church of St. Andrew, considerable emains, as I believe, exist in the farm buildings ately in the occupation of Mr. J. Perkins, and ow the property of the Hospital of St. Andrew. These appear to me of very early character, probably like the neighbouring churches of Earl's Barton and Brixworth, of pre-Conquestal date. The nave, aisles, and transept can be dearly traced, and only the quire or sanctuary, nd part of the north-wall of the nave, have entirely disappeared. An hour's digging would ecover at least the general plan of its eastern ermination. GEO. GILBERT SCOTT, F.S.A.

The Student's Column.

WARMING BUILDINGS BY HOT WATER.

XXII.

COILS AND RADIATORS.

THE distinction between a Coil and a Radiator is not at all clearly defined, unless we rely upon the fact that the former usually has its pipes fixed horizontally and the atter vertically. At the same time, if we fixed a coil on one of its ends, as is done sometimes, it would scarcely constitute it a radiator. For the information of those who have not used these latter articles, it may be explained that they are, to all intents and purposes, coils, but with pipes of an ornamental character, always having the pipes fixed vertically; and, by ordinary decoration, they can be made of sufficiently good appearance to need no casing. They are also cast of such a section as to hold but little water, so that results are more rapidly obtained, but, of course, they just as rapidly cool as the fire goes down.

Radiators are practically the outcome of experiences gained with the ordinary horizontal pipe-coils. In the first place, these latter appliances are at the best of times ugly; this necessitates their being surrounded by a case, solely with the idea of hiding them, unless in an unimportant position. The case, however inexpensive, generally costs more than the coil; sometimes, when well-finished, four or five times as much. Then the case goes a good way towards neutralising the effects of the coil, as it will be understood that more heat is obtained from exposed pipes than those encased in any way. The coil case also introduces another bad feature by usually making it an impossible matter to dust and keep the pipes clean, and the horizontal pipes lend themselves to the collecting of dust more readily than vertical ones. The difference in heat diffusion between a clean pipe and one coated with dust is sufficient to surprise some people, but if it be remembered that dust is wholly composed of poor heat-conducting materials, as fibre, wool, cotton, grit (silica), &c., no wonder need be felt. Dust is almost as effective as silicate cotton in preventing the dispersion of heat.

The fact that horizontal pipes collect dust and vertical ones do not, has led to the general adoption of the latter arrangement with the tubes of radiators. Horizontal coils, in cases as just mentioned, are great sufferers in this respect, and so are pipes in channels, &c., and even exposed coils and pipes are sometimes allowed to get covered with dust, and the results are lessened accordingly.

With nearly all the present radiators the necessity of a case is supposed to be obviated by their being cast of a design equal in appearance to a casing itself, and if additional finish is needed, they can be fitted with marble tops. Nearly all the makers' lists show them also made in pedestal or columnar form as well as flat, and other shapes to meet different requirements. As regards appearance, they can always be picked out in two or more colours if desired, and it has been already explained that the ordinary decorative paints and colours have no prejudicial effect upon heat diffusion. Bronze powders and gold leaf are not however to be recommended, except to a very limited extent.

The last point in particular to be mentioned respecting radiators is that they hold but little water. By this is meant that a certain superficial area of radiating surface has less water in it than the same area of a round pipe. It can be seen that the less water an apparatus contains the quicker it will become heated up, and it is quite possible to get the same area of radiating or heat-giving surface (capable of furnishing the required temperature) by radiators with one-half or almost one-third the water that would be held if the radiating media

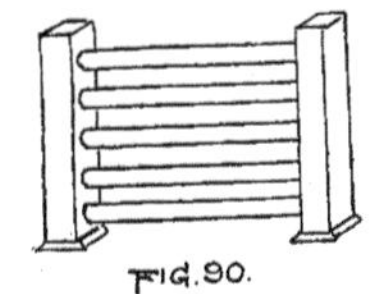

FIG. 90.

consisted of the ordinary 4-in. pipes. It is, however, necessary to again mention that, although the small amount of water is heated the quickest, it is also the quickest to become cool as the fire goes down. The small amount of water also shows any irregular stoking, as the degree of heat radiated is rendered irregular also; when the body of water is large, these effects are not noticeable, the water acts as a reservoir or medium for the storage of heat.

With glasshouse works the 4-in. pipe is decidedly the best; the results are rendered as equable as it is possible to get them. The same applies to any of those places where heat is required night and day regularly. When, however, quick results for just a matter of a few hours are needed, smaller pipes are used, as, for example, a 2-in. pipe, although so much less superficial surface of a 4-in. pipe, does not hold more than about a fourth of the water, and the results are quicker in proportion. Where quick results, and also good appearance, are needed, nothing can excel some of the forms of radiators.

The common form of coil is as fig. 90, being a pair of cast ends, with pipes inserted as

FIG. 91

shown. The joints between the pipes and box ends are either made with yarn and lead, or more commonly, perhaps, with borings (the rust joint). A good coil can be made up by using one of the different forms of patented joints, in which an india-rubber collar is the jointing material. These joints are not expensive, and the saving of time is considerable. They also have a good appearance, and are expansive (this will be referred to again). Space will not permit of giving details of all the different forms of radiators introduced; reference to the advertisement columns of this and other papers will furnish all the details required in this respect; but to illustrate the difference between the ordinary box-end coil just shown and the more modern appliances referred to, fig. 91 will make it plain what an improvement has been made.

There are several radiators made and arranged so that fresh air can be introduced and caused to pass over the heated surfaces and so be warmed. These are generally termed ventilating radiators, but they have no particularly active effect in causing ventilation. If outlet or exhaust ventilation exists (either by ventilating flues or the ordinary fire-place opening), then the inflowing fresh air will enter by way of these openings, and it will be warmed by contact with the hot surfaces.

There is one point in connection with these ventilating radiators that needs discussion, which is their effect upon the moistness of the air. This subject was dealt with somewhat fully when speaking of the necessary saturation of the atmosphere in glass houses, but it may be mentioned here that, when provision is made to increase the temperature of inflowing air we

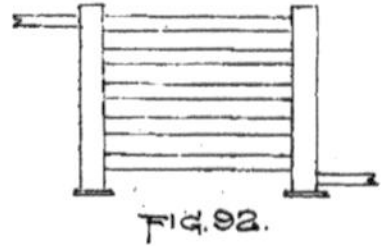

FIG. 92.

ought, at the same time, to provide for the increase of moisture that it needs and should have, in ratio with the heat it attains. This is provided for by some makers, who make the top castings of a trough-shape to hold water, with an ornamental cover over. The temperature air attains by contact with these pipes, however, is not so great as to demand this provision of moisture in every case; the engineer must use his judgment in this respect. In hot-air works, where air is heated by contact with stoves and flue-pipes, the moisture question is very important.

Amongst hot-water fitters there exists a considerable difference of opinion as to how coils,

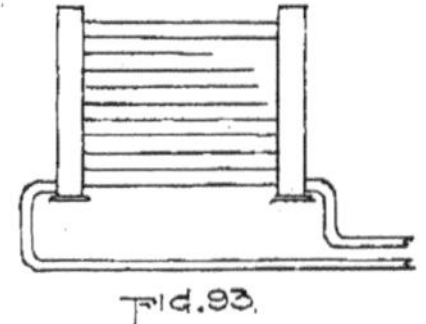

FIG. 93.

&c., should be connected; that is, at what point in the coil the pipes should be inserted. Many seek to get one pipe at the top and one at the bottom, as fig 92, but there is no occasion for this, if both pipes are connected at the bottom, the coil will heat just as effectivel It must not be supposed that because both pipes are at a low point the hot water will pass in and then out without the top portion of the coil getting hot. The coil will beat just as well as one pipe at the top and one at the bottom, which is supposed to possess the advantage of causing the water to circulate right through, as it certainly does. There is one advantage this latter method has, in the fact that if the top

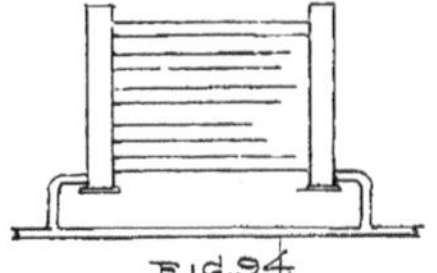

FIG. 94.

pipe is carried from the extreme top, probably no air-cock will be needed.

If a single coil or radiator is on a branch flow and return, the connexion may be made as fig. 93. If it should be one of a series on a branch service, then fig. 94 is a good method. This latter way gives all the radiators, from the first to the last, a chance of getting hot without much interval in their times of heating. If we had, say, four radiators, and caused the water to circulate through the first one before it had any opportunity of getting to the second, and through the second before affecting the third, we should cause very irregular results indeed.

Seeing what advantage radiators have under

certain conditions, it is to be expected that a hot-water pipe with full area of surface, but holding less water, will be introduced for those works needing rapid results. It would be a very simple matter and certainly useful in many cases where pipes have necessarily to be used, yet where heat is required at the shortest notice. It could be made of a section that would the least readily collect dust.

GENERAL BUILDING NEWS.

DUNBLANE CATHEDRAL.—During the past three years this cathedral has been undergoing a complete restoration, and will be re-opened,—it is hoped by the Queen,—in September next. The nave, as our readers are aware, has been roofless for about 250 years past, and the choir, with the chancel arch built up as a gable, has been used as the parish church till the present restoration was commenced. The choir was considerably restored about twenty years ago, but not sufficiently to prevent continuous decay which threatened the structure. There are still many unfinished details which must remain until sufficient funds are subscribed to complete the work. A new organ, worthy of the proportions of the restored cathedral, and enclosed in a fine oak case, is being built by Mr. Eustace Ingram, of London, and will be erected in a chamber on the north wall of the choir, over one of the side chapels. The whole cost of the work, exclusive of the organ, will be about 20,000*l.* The architect is Dr. Robertson, of Edinburgh.

VOLUNTEER DRILL HALLS, EXETER.—On the 23rd inst. the Duke of Cambridge opened the new drill halls which have been built for two of the branches of the Volunteer forces in Exeter. One of the buildings has been erected for the accommodation of the First Rifle Volunteers. It occupies the site of the old theatre in Bedford-circus and a portion of the city wall. The hall is 100 ft. long and 50 ft. wide, with a gallery at one end capable of accommodating 200 persons. In the basement under the hall there is a shooting-gallery 90 ft. long, a large armoury, and large store-room. On the west side of the building is an entrance hall and staircase, with an orderly-room on the ground floor 27 ft. by 18 ft., and over the orderly-room off the landing of the stairs an officers' room and a sergeants' room. A clerk's office and an adjutant's office adjoin the orderly-room. On the extreme west side is a dwelling-house. The roof of the hall is of slate, with a large centre skylight. The other roofs are of red tile. The other building is situated in Friar's-walk, Holloway-street. The architect was Mr. S. Wilkinson, and the builders were Messrs. Tree & Bolley, of Exeter.

NEW WESLEYAN CHURCH, LICHFIELD.—On the 20th ult. the Rev. Dr. Stephenson (President of the Wesleyan Conference) opened a new church which has been erected in Tamworth-street, Lichfield. The building has been constructed by Mr. Williams, of Tamworth, from the designs of Mr. Thomas Guest, architect, Birmingham. The new building will accommodate upwards of 300 people, and is to cost about 2,000*l.* It consists of nave, aisles, and chancel, two vestries, and an organ chamber. Stained glass has been introduced into the chancel windows.

EXTENSION OF PREMISES, BRISTOL.—Extensive additions are now in course of erection for Messrs. J. S. Fry & Sons, cocoa and chocolate makers. The new building has three frontages, that to Union-street being 55 ft.; Nelson-street, 125 ft.; and Little St. James' Back, 66 ft. A portion of the ground and first floors will be used as offices, the remainder of the building as a factory. In addition to a well-lit cellar, lined with white glazed brick, there are five floors, constructed with cast-iron girders and columns. The fronts up to the second floor are built with granite from the West of England Granite Quarries, Penryn; the remaining portion being built of Cattybrook buff bricks, with red Mansfield frieze, strings, &c. The whole is being carried out from the designs and under the superintendence of Mr. Richard Milverton Drake, architect, of Bristol.

BOARD SCHOOLS, KINGSWOOD, BRISTOL.—On the 20th inst. the new board schools at Kingswood were opened by Mr. Campbell-Bannerman, M.P. They are designed to accommodate 834 children, and have been erected at a cost of 8,000*l.* The building is a semi-Gothic gabled structure, occupying a frontage at Warmley-hill of 150 ft., or a total frontage to the main road of 175 ft. The inner construction of the schools is on the class-room system, each standard having a separate class-room allotted to it. They are divided into three divisions, for boys, girls, and infants, and around the exterior of the building play-yards are provided. The work has been carried out by Mr. J. Perrott, of Bristol, from designs by Mr. W. T. Bernard, also of Bristol.

NEW CHURCH, EDINBURGH.—On the 18th inst. the foundation-stone was laid of St. Cuthbert's new Parish Church, Edinburgh. The site, at the west end of Princes-street-gardens, and near the junction of Princes-street with Lothian-road, has, says the *Glasgow Herald*, been occupied for centuries by a succession of church buildings. The fabric which has recently been dismantled was erected about the middle of last century, and was mainly a parallelogram, measuring externally 98 ft. by 71 ft., while the new fabric has an internal length of 101 ft. and a width of 63 ft. Transeptal projections are formed on the north and south sides, and choir accommodation is afforded in the apse, 38 ft. deep and 33 ft. wide, forming an extension of the nave. The only part of the former church allowed to remain is the tower, the lower part of which will form a porch entrance from the west end, and leading from it will be a vestibule of about 66 ft. long by about 17 ft. wide. From this vestibule egress doors are also provided, and two staircases lead to the gallery above. In addition, there are two staircases at the east end leading to the galleries in the transepts, and doors of egress are also provided there and on the ground floor of the transepts. The eastern staircases are enclosed within tower projections, which are designed to be carried up above the roof to a height of 100 ft. in the form of campaniles. Externally the structure is designed in a phase of the Renaissance. The side façades are divided into a series of bays with square-headed and corniced windows on the ground-floor, the gallery level being defined by a cornice and string-course treatment, upon which rest the windows for the main lighting of the church. These windows are circular-headed, with archivolt moulding springing from panelled pilaster imposts. The transept projections are treated in a similar way, but with the windows grouped, and the upper part terminated in pediment form. The juncture of the roof with the wall-head is treated with ornamental cornice and parapet. At the east end, the apsidal treatment of the end of the church forms a feature, the main horizontal lines being continued from the main building. Its upper stage is divided by pilastered treatment in low relief, marking it into a series of bays, in each of which a moulded and corniced window supplies the lighting of the interior. The upper part of the apse is treated with panelled parapet-decorated cornice, and in semi-dome form the roof returns to the main gable line of the church, which is elevated in pediment form to receive it. The roof will be covered with lead, ribbed and panelled. The accommodation in the new church will be nearly equal to that in the church demolished, namely, about 2,000. The cost is estimated at between 18,000*l.* and 19,000*l.* The mason work is at present being carried out by Mr. White, builder, and the carpenters are Messrs. Beattie & Sons. Mr. Hippolyte Blanc, of Edinburgh, is the architect.

CONGREGATIONAL CHURCH, LAUGHARNE, CARMARTHENSHIRE.—On the 17th inst. the new Congregational Church at Laugharne was opened. The building is erected in the main street. The architects were Messrs. George Morgan & Son, Carmarthen, and the builder was Mr. James Rees, of St. Clears.

PUBLIC OFFICES, SLAITHWAITE, YORKSHIRE.—On the 19th inst. Mr. W. Varley laid the corner-stone of new offices intended for the use of the Slaithwaite Local Board. The buildings will form a block at the corner of Lewisham-road and Station-road, and are being erected from plans prepared by Mr. J. B. Eagland, architect, Slaithwaite.

NEW CHURCH, SMETHWICK.—On the 24th inst. the Lord Bishop of Lichfield consecrated the new Church of St. Michael's Mission at Smethwick. The church is situate in Crockett's-lane, adjoining the Central Board Schools. It is in the Early English style. The interior is formed of nave and aisles, with baptistry and double porches at the west end, chancel raised some 4 ft., morning chapel, north transept, and organ chamber. Underneath the chancel is a parish-room, 47 ft. by 35 ft., and also a vestry on the same level. The church will accommodate 650, and the cost, including 500*l.* for the site, has been 5,600*l.* Mr. H. Willcock was the builder, the architect being Mr. A. E. Street.

PARISH CHURCH, MORETON-IN-THE-MARSH.—The Bishop of Gloucester and Bristol has just re-opened this parish church after considerable improvement and enlargement, from the plans of Mr. E. H. Lingen Barker, of Hereford. Three galleries have been pulled down, the chancel has been extended 10 ft. eastwards, the south aisle 7 ft. southwards, and a chancel aisle added on the south side.

TECHNICAL AND FISHERY SCHOOL NEAR DUBLIN.—A technical and fishery school is about to be erected at Ringsend, near Dublin. The Earl of Pembroke has generously placed a sum of 4,000*l.* at the disposal of the Pembroke Township Commissioners to carry out the necessary works. The plans of Mr. W. Kaye-Parry, M.A., architect, of Dublin, have been selected in open competition for the proposed buildings, which will be commenced forthwith.

THE DECORATION OF THE LEEDS TOWN-HALL.—The Corporate Property Committee of the Leeds Corporation met yesterday, and considered a number of tenders sent in for the decoration of the Leeds Town-hall. A list of eight tenders was reduced to two,—namely, those of Messrs. Dobie & Sons, Edinburgh, and Mr. J. Bookbinder, London. These were with reference to the Victoria-hall and vestibule only. The Committee appointed a deputation to visit various buildings in other town which had been decorated by these firms, and to report.—*Leeds Mercury* (May 25).

SANITARY AND ENGINEERING NEWS

SEWERAGE WORKS, KING'S NORTON.—On Friday, May 20, Mr. Rienzi Walton, M.Inst.C.E., one of the Engineering Inspectors of the Local Government Board, held an inquiry at King's Heath as to an application by the King's Norton Rural Sanitary Authority to borrow 10,500*l.* for works of sewerage and sewage disposal for the village of King's Norton and the surrounding district. The scheme, which was prepared by Mr. Robert Godfrey, A.M.Inst.C.E., the Engineer and Surveyor to the Authority, was fully set forth and explained by him to the Inspector, after which he was subjected to a severe cross-examination by Mr. Hugo Young, barrister, on behalf of several landowners and by Mr. J. S. Pritchett, barrister, on behalf of Messrs. Baldwin, the owners of Sherborne Mills. The scheme, which provides for deposition, filtration, and irrigation, was supported very fully by the evidence of Mr. E. Pritchard, M.Inst.C.E., and much of the opposition to it was based on the fear that it was the intention of the Authority to establish a "destructor" on part of the site. After a protracted inquiry, the inspector was driven round the district to be dealt with, and to the land proposed to be utilised as a sewage farm. The Inspector will make his report to the Local Government Board in due course.

FOREIGN AND COLONIAL.

FRANCE.—On Sunday the "Bourse du Travail" was opened. It has been built by M. Bouvard, and is situated in the Place de la République, at the corner of the Rue du Chateau d'Eau and Rue de Bondy.——The statue of Marshal Ney, which was erected on the very spot (in the Avenue de l'Observatoire) where the hero of Moskova was shot, is shortly to be taken down to make room for the extension of the line from Paris to Sceaux. The statue will be re-erected further on, in the Boulevard St. Michel.——The prizes for the open competition for the statue of Claude Chappe, inventor of the aërial telegraph, have been awarded. The first prize has been awarded to MM. Damé (sculptor) and Farcy (architect), and they are to execute the work. The second prize has been given to M. Boisseau, and the third to M. Pezieux. This monument is to be erected on the Boulevard St. Germain, near the Ministère de la Guerre.——The Archæological Society of Auteuil and Paris are going to erect busts and commemorative bas-reliefs which are to be placed on houses which have been inhabited by celebrities, such as Franklin, Victor Hugo, Boileau, Molière, Racine, &c. On the other hand, we hear that the house occupied by Lamartine, near the Trocadéro station, is likely to be demolished.——The museum of Carcassone has just been enriched by a magnificent portrait of the poet Joseph Chenier, and also several relics belonging to André Chenier, who was executed in 1793.——Madame la Duchesse d'Uzès, who is known in the artistic world under the name of "Manuela," has just given one of her works, a marble statue of the Virgin Mary, to the church of Poissy. This statue was inaugurated on May 19.——It is announced that the beautiful Château de Montrabech, near Lezignan (Aude) has been destroyed by fire, a great number of precious documents have been lost; a few works of art and some Gobolins tapestry was all that was rescued.——The artistic exhibition of Tours, which opened on May 19, is to close on August 31. That at Troyes, opened at the same time, is to be closed on June 30.——A National School of Agriculture is to be opened at Rennes.——The sculptor Rodin has been commissioned to erect the monument at Nancy to the memory of the painter Claude Gelée, called "Lorraine." It is to be unveiled on June 6.——The Municipal Council of Rouen are erecting a statue of Gambetta in the place which bears the name of the famous orator. —— A discovery has been lately made at Rouen in the court-yard of the famous Hôtel de Bourgtheroulde; in demolishing a little construction which served as a porter's lodge, the sill of a window was brought to light, covered with sculptures, interesting both from an artistic and historical point of view. This decoration consists of an escutcheon, with bands and garlands of flowers supported by children, all in high-relief. The demolition of the little battlements has also revealed the existence of a gallery of half-timber work of the style of the sixteenth century, leaning on a low arcade, like those which are to be seen on the old houses in Rouen.——At Châlons-sur-Marne, some rare medals have been discovered, on one of which is the portrait of Posthumius, Emperor of the Gauls, who was assassinated in 267.——The artistic world at Havre has just lost one of its best painters, M. Lanfant, at the age of seventy-eight years.

BERLIN.—In a hall adjoining the premises occupied by the annual salon, there is an exhibition of the models sent in by sculptors for the competition which has been opened for the purpose of obtaining a suitable design for the Frederick Memorial Monument on the battle field at Wörth.——An enterprise has been started the object of which is to publish, in the cheapest possible form, the majority of all designs sent in for the numerous architectural competitions held annually in Germany. Each number of the publication appears as soon as ossible after a competition has been decided. Until now the only publications of competition rawings were the small woodcuts in our contemoraries or the very expensive lithographic folios of n architectural bookseller.

HAMBURG.—In connexion with the fiftieth anniersary of the rebuilding of Hamburg after the reat fire of 1842, a description of the conflagration nd work of reconstruction has been written by Herr Faulwasser, an architect. The total loss curred by the fire was at the time estimated at 35,000,000 marks; the payment to firemen, 34,000 marks; and the clearing of the site and its aterways, about 690,000 marks. Although the re retarded Hamburg's development for several ears, it certainly was of a great benefit to the own, and caused it to have its present stately ppearance and good bill of health.

MISCELLANEOUS.

SANITARY LEGISLATION A CAUSE OF OVERROWDING IN CITIES.—Dr. G. V. Poore, in the conluding portion of his paper on "The Concentraion of Population in Cities" (appearing in the *Lancet* of May 21) says:—"It needs to be pointed ut that the overcrowding of our cities, which is dmittedly the greatest of all sanitary evils, is the irect result of sanitary legislation. When, some orty years since, it was recognised that waterarried sewage inevitably poisoned the wells, no ttempt was made to protect the wells from pollution; but the surface wells were compulsorily losed, the inhabitants were sold in bondage to the ater companies, and the houses were compelled to ollute our rivers. These measures have given a atal facility for overcrowding, and wherever a line f sewers is taken the speculative builder follows; or, not being hampered by questions of waterupply or filth disposal (the sanitary authorities elieving him of all responsibilities in this matter), e is able to erect buildings without any curtilage, nd of any height, almost, that he chooses. Be it bserved that this state of things is not limited to ondon or the big towns. The notion that houses re as well without curtilage as with it has infected he country, as anybody may see for himself hen travelling by railway . . . . We have ngendered a stingy habit of mind towards the uestion of space round houses, which almost mounts to a national insanity."

INFECTION BY TELEPHONE.—The possibility of nfection by the use of the telephone mouthpiece by uccessive speakers has been hypothetically disussed before now. A Dundee correspondent rings forward some facts in support of the possiility of such an occurrence. Dr. Anderson, the Medical Officer of Health for Dundee, who has had he matter submitted to him, has given a very ensible answer, which sums up the position in practical manner: "If a person who is suffering rom sore throat of an infectious nature brings his outh into close, or even near, relation to the outhpiece of a telephone instrument, I think, in he act of speaking and expiration of air from the ungs and throat, it is possible that infectious articles might adhere to the instrument. I think instrument which is so much exposed to the uman breath should be frequently cleansed, hether the instrument be in a public or private oom; and perhaps the simplest and most conenient cleanser is warm water and carbolic or anitas soap."—*British Medical Journal*.

PICTURES OF 1892.—The *Pall Mall Gazette* issues wo books of reproductions from pictures of the ear, one with prints in various tones of colour, the ther in black. The latter, which seems to have een only a secondary issue when the first was out print, is in some respects the best, as the tints ed in the other edition are not all well chosen; me of the landscapes being printed in treated nky tones very much at variance with our associations with the tones of natural scenery.

BRITISH ASSOCIATION FOR THE ADVANCEMENT OF CIENCE.—It is announced that the next annual neral meeting will be held at Edinburgh, comencing on Wednesday, August 3. The Presidentect is Sir Archibald Geikie, LL.D., D.Sc., For. c. R.S., F.R.S.E., F.G.S., Director-General of e Geological Survey of the United Kingdom, rresponding Member of the Institute of France.

PARQUETRY FOR HOSPITAL FLOORS. — The urge Ward of the London Temperance Hospital, ampstead-road, which was opened by the uchess of Westminster on the 11th inst., has en laid with Bassants' patent ½-in. parquet flooring 1,700 ft. of which were required. Mr. Bassant s likewise just received a contract for 7,000 ft. of s patent ½-in. teak parquet flooring for three ards and nurses' rooms at the East London ospital.

RECONSTRUCTION OF BONAR BRIDGE VIADUCT, THERLAND.—On the 20th inst. a special meeting discuss the rebuilding of the fallen viaduct at nar Bridge was held at Ardgay, Ross-shire, by e joint committee of the Ross and Sutherland unty Councils. Mr. Charles P. Hogg (of Messrs. ouch & Hogg, civil engineers, Glasgow), subtted plans prepared by that firm, which were opted. The new bridge will be composed of bowing steel girded for three spans of 140 ft., 105 ft., d 70 ft. respectively, resting on masonwork at either end, and supported by stone piers in channel. There will thus be a clear waterway of 315 ft. instead of 260 ft., as formerly. The roadway will be 25 ft. wide, and will have a hardly perceptible gradient, but the approach from the Ross-shire side will have a gradient of 1 in 30.

THE CONVERSION OF GAUGE ON THE GREAT-WESTERN RAILWAY.—In connexion with this notable operation, which was accomplished at the end of last week, the *Engineer* of the 20th inst. gives some interesting particulars of the first broad-gauge train used by the public, which ran on July 4, 1838. Our contemporary also gives illustrations and descriptions of two of the early broad-gauge engines.

THE SANITARY INSTITUTE.—We hear that Sir Charles A. Cameron, F.R.C.S.I., D.P.H., Medical Officer of Health, Dublin, has accepted the Presidentship of the Congress of this Institute to be held at Portsmouth in September next.

DRAIN-PIPE TEST AT NOTTINGHAM.—In our report of the proceedings of the meeting of the Incorporated Association of Municipal and County Engineers at Nottingham, it should have been stated that the stoneware drain-pipes used in the new subways in that town (and of which we recorded a test on p. 381, *ante*) were manufactured by Messrs. John Knowles & Co. We were not informed of this at the time, or we should have mentioned it.

A NEW AUTOMATIC SELF-FLUSHING CLOSET.—Messrs. John Knowles & Co., of King's-road, St. Pancras, are now showing what they claim to be "the first and only double-action self-flushing water-closet." It is named the "Presto," and is a closet of the "wash-out" type, although the automatic arrangement can be applied to hopper or any other flush-out closets. By a simple method of gearing, the seat is slightly depressed when sat upon. Directly the person rises from the seat the closet is flushed. This is the first action. The second action is brought into play when the closet is used as a slop-sink or urinal. The seat is of course turned up for either of these purposes, inducing a preliminary flush, and the full flush is obtained by returning the seat to its normal position. The mechanism is exceedingly simple, and appears unlikely to get out of order, the flushing-cistern being discharged by means of a rod or chain connecting it with the seat-action.

CHISWICK LAND AND KENTISH TOWN FREEHOLDS.—Mr. Walter Hall, of Chancery-lane, offered to a crowded auction room on Wednesday last, at the Mart, City, about nine acres of freehold building land (together with a mansion thereon), having a long frontage to the "Duke's-avenue." The bids started at 10,000*l.*, and, by degrees, reached the sum of 13,500*l.*, at which they stood for some time, when the auctioneer stated that he exercised his discretion of buying in the property, as he could do better by private negotiation. The shop property at Kentish Town, with frontages to the main Highgate and Fortess roads, was eagerly competed for, and eight of the ten lots offered were sold, realising a total of 4,210*l.*

MEMORIAL WINDOW, MANCHESTER CATHEDRAL.—A new stained-glass window, in memory of three members of an old Manchester family,—the Grays, of Ancoats and Seedley,—has, says the *Manchester Courier*, just been erected in the library of Manchester Cathedral. The window is of four lights, and illustrates the text, "They found Him in the Temple, sitting in the midst of the doctors, both hearing and asking them questions." The work has been done by Messrs. Heaton, Butler, & Bayne, of London.

ARTISANS' DWELLINGS AT ESSEN.—In the course of some proceedings relating to the welfare of German artisans, some interesting information was given by Herr Krupp's representative. Herr Krupp had in 1891 rented dwellings situated in closest proximity to his works to no less than 3,659 of his workmen. The erection of these habitations cost him over 11,000,000 marks, and the ground about 1,200,000 marks. After deduction of all running expenses, such as repairs, &c., the money spent brought an income of about 2·1 per cent. Of some other 500 dwellings erected in outlying districts the income was 2·5 per cent. Owing to the special facilities offered, some seventy of the men already owned their houses.

LEGAL.

ALLEGED BREACH OF CONTRACT:

RICHARDSON *v.* MATHEWS.

THIS was an action tried in the Lambeth County-court, and brought by Mr. J. O. Richardson, builder and contractor, Peckham, against Mr. Mathews (of the firm of Ashton, Green, Mathews, & Co.), slate merchant, St. Mary Axe, to recover the sum of about 9*l.*, being the extra cost incurred by plaintiff in executing 145 squares of slating in consequence of an alleged breach of contract by the defendant. Mr. Robertson, barrister, appeared for the plaintiff, and Mr. T. Poulter, barrister (instructed by Messrs. Hunter & Downes), for the defendant.

Plaintiff's evidence was given at the sitting of the court on Tuesday, the 17th inst., when the case was adjourned until Tuesday last, when Mr. Mathews and other witnesses were heard for the defence. The claim was for extra cost incurred by the plaintiff (beyond the price quoted by the defendant) in executing the slating in question, and for the hire of tarpaulins, &c., rendered necessary by the alleged breach of contract by the defendant.

For the defence, it was contended that there was no contract.

It appeared that the plaintiff wrote to the defendant asking for a quotation for 145 squares of Penrhyn slating, no time being named for the execution of the work. The defendant offered to do the work at 22s. 3d. per square. The plaintiff wrote to the defendant on a Friday accepting that price, and requiring the defendant to commence the work on the following Monday. The defendant was unable to comply with that request, and said that three days was not sufficient and reasonable notice for a work of such magnitude; that they had not a sufficiency of the particular-sized slates required for the work in stock; and that it would take ten days or a fortnight to get them from the quarries.

Evidence was called by the defendants to show that it was unreasonable and unusual to expect work of the magnitude in question to be done at such short notice. The witnesses examined were Mr. C. W. Jones (the defendant's manager), Mr. S. R. Parker (a member of the firm of Patman & Fotheringham, builders), Mr. Alexander (a builder carrying on business in Bow-road), Mr. C. J. Devereux (manager for Messrs. Jarvis, builders, Hackney-road), and a member of the firm of Roberts, Adlard, & Co., slate merchants. These witnesses all deposed that it was the custom for builders, when about to tender for a work, to ask for quotations for certain materials from the merchants who dealt in those materials. The builder whose tender was accepted usually wrote at once to the merchant whose quotation best suited him, saying that he had obtained the contract and would probably want the material in about three, four, or six months, as the case might be. Within a week or two of the time arriving for roofing-in, it was usual to give the merchant another reminder, so that he might be fully prepared. The two or three days elapsing between Friday and Monday was not adequate notice for a work of the extent in question. The mere giving of a quotation by a merchant did not constitute a contract. Quotations of that kind were given by merchants every day.

Counsel for the parties having addressed the Judge, he immediately found for the defendant, with costs. He held that the defendant had not, in giving his quotation to the plaintiff for the work, entered into any contract, and therefore he had not committed any breach of contract.

CAPITAL AND LABOUR.

BRICKMAKERS' STRIKE IN WEST LONDON.—The strike of brickmakers in the Shepherd's-bush and Acton districts, which has now been in progress, we understand, for about seven weeks, still continues. The men ask for an increase of 9d. per thousand in the price paid for moulding, which, if granted, would, the masters say, entail an increase in the price paid for other processes involved in manufacture. The London Conciliation Board have endeavoured to bring both parties to an agreement, but without success. Two meetings have taken place at the London Chamber of Commerce, Botolph House, Eastcheap, at which representatives of the masters and men have met. The number of stools idle is about sixty. Therefore there must be between five and six hundred men and boys concerned. The Kent and Essex and the Cowley Brick-masters' Association have expressed their sympathy with the masters, and have, we are informed, entered into an arrangement with the Shepherd's-bush and Acton masters to make for them all bricks they require, so that the probabilities are that unless the strike very soon collapses, no bricks will be made in the strike districts this season.

MEETINGS.

MONDAY, MAY 30.

Royal Institute of British Architects.—Four papers on "Castings in Metal." (1) Mr. Alex. Graham, F.S.A., "On the Application of Metals to Architectural Design in all Countries." (2) Mr. C. Krall "On the Precious Metals." (3) Mr. H. Longden "On Castings in Iron and Brass." (4) Mr. Herbert Singer "On Castings in Bronze." 8 p.m.

Surveyors' Institution.—Annual General Meeting, to receive the Report of the Council, &c. 8 p.m.—Annual Dinner, Holborn Restaurant. 6.30 p.m.

TUESDAY, MAY 31.

Institution of Civil Engineers.—Annual General Meeting, to receive the Report of the Council and to elect the Council and Officers for the ensuing year. 8 p.m.

Society of Arts (Applied Art Section).—Mr. William De Morgan on "Lustre Ware." 8 p.m.

WEDNESDAY, JUNE 1.

Royal Archæological Institute.—(1) Rev. Precentor Venables on "A Roman Villa lately discovered at Lincoln." (2) Mr. C. E. Keyser on "Some Mural Paintings at Little Horwood Church, Bucks." 4 p.m.

British Archæological Association.—Mr. J. H. Macmichael on "The Greybeard." 8 p.m.

COMPETITION, CONTRACTS, AND PUBLIC APPOINTMENTS.

COMPETITION.

Nature of Work.	By whom Advertised.	Premium.	Designs to be delivered.
*New Masonic Hall	Newcastle-upon-Tyne Central Masonic Hall Co. Ltd.	50l. 25l.	No date

CONTRACTS.

Nature of Work or Materials.	By whom Required.	Architect, Surveyor, or Engineer.	Tenders to be delivered.
*Wood Paving Works	Commrs. of Sewers	Official	May 31
Brick Gasholder Tank, Parkgate	Rawmarsh (Sheffield) Local Board	do.	do.
Various Buildings on Aberlour Estates, Balvenie, N.B.	John Alcock	....	do.
Residence, Rubislaw, Den South, Aberdeen	....	Matthews & Mackenzie	do.
Ten Cottages New Tredegar	Powell Duffryn Colliery Co.	Aaron Davies & Son	do.
Work at Totnes Club, Totnes, Devon	Committee	....	do.
Shop, Four Cottages, Warehouse, &c. Hopkinstown, Pontypridd	D. & W. Thomas	F. Gibson	June 1
Flagging and Asphalting	Halifax School Board	Official	do.
*Supply and Fixing Venetian Blinds	Met. Asylums Board	do.	do.
*Roadmaking and Paving Works	Hammersmith Vestry	H. Mair	do.
Infant School, Kaegarw, Mountain Ash, Glam.	Llanwonno Sch. Bd.	A. O. Evans	do.
Wards at Joint Hospital	Calverley (Bradford) Hospital	W. & J. B. Bailey	do.
Two Scrubbers, with Mains, Valves, &c.	Tynemouth Gas Co.	W. Hardie, Jun.	do.
Cast-iron Pipes (750 yards)	do.	do	do.
*Alterations, &c. Northern Hospital	Met. Asylums Board	Pennington & Bridgen	June 2
*Painting and Repairs at Schools	St. George-in-the-East Guardians	Wilson, Son, & Aldwinckle	June 3
*Iron Escape Staircases at Workhouse	do.	do.	do.
Additions and Repairs to Manse, Aboyne, N.B.	....	Matthews & Mackenzie	do.
Sixty Houses, Burnhope Colliery, Newcastle-on-Tyne	Ulrick A. Ritson	J. W. Rounthwaite	do.
Additions to School, Kinellar, Aberdeen	J. J. Tindal	....	do.
*Repairs and Drainage Works at Workhouse	Newhaven Union	W. A. Mole	do.
Pianoforte Shop and Warehouse, &c. King's Cross, Halifax	....	Raymond Berry	do.
*Sewerage Works	Wakefield U.R.S.A.	F. Massie	do.
Four Through Houses, Lightcliffe, Halifax	....	Raymond Berry	June 4
Restoring Bacton Church, near Pontrilas Station, Hereford	J. G. Monro	Nicholson & Son	June 6
*Making-up Carriageway and Tarpaving Footways	Hendon Local Board	S. S. Grimley	do.
*Tar and Asphalte Paving	Tottenham Loc. Bd.	J. E. Worth	June 7
*Sewerage Works	do.	do.	do.
*Officer's House, Freshwater Gate (I.W.)	Admiralty	Official	do.
*Science and Art School	Gravesend Town Coun.	do.	do.
*Trial Boring, 200 ft. deep	East Cowes Local Bd.	Lemon & Blizard	do.
Thirty-three Houses, Merthyr Tydfil	Stewart Building Club	John Williams	do.
*Brick Sewers	St. Pancras Vestry	W. N. Blair	do.

CONTRACTS.—*Continued.*

Nature of Work or Materials.	By whom Required.	Architect, Surveyor, or Engineer.	Tenders to be delivered
*Painting, &c. Works	Whitechapel Union	B. J. Capell	June 7
*Nurses Rooms, &c.	do.	do.	do.
Wesleyan Chapel and School, Church Fenton	Rev. H. Field	F. W. Dixon	do.
*Making-up Roads	Fulham Vestry	W. Sykes	June 8
*Erecting Cart Lodges in Board's Yard	Greenwich Bd. of Wks	Official	do.
*School buildings, Horsham	The Governors	A. Vernon	June 9
*Works and Repairs, Plymouth District	War Department	Official	June 10
*Drainage Works, Castle Cary	Wincanton U.R.S.A.	E. Cousins	June 13
*Laying, &c. Cast-iron Pipes	Newark Corporation	E. Ross	do.
*Covered Service Reservoir	do.	do.	do.
*School Building at Crossness	London County Council	Official	June 14
*170 tons Cast-iron Pipes	St. Anne's-on-Sea L.B.	H. Bancroft	do.
*New Sewer	Harrow Loc. Bd.	E. R. Capon	do.
*Painting, &c. Workhouse, Fulham-road	St. George's Union	H. Saxon Snell	do.
*Waterworks, Lockerley Hall, Hants	F. G. Dalgety, Esq.	Cyrus Combes & Parsons	June 15
*Additional Hall at Workhouse	St. Saviour's Union	E. M. Whitaker	June 16
Cemetery Chapels, Entrance Lodge, &c. Ryecroft, Walsall	Walsall Corp.	Official	June 1
*Erection of an Office for the Board	Reading Sch. Bd.	C. Smith & Son	June 18
*Higher Grade Board School	Wolverhampton S. B.	T. H. Fleming	June 24
Red Fir Telegraph Poles	G. P. O.	Official	do.
*Additional Asylum Buildings, Banstead	London County Council Asylum Committee	G. T. Hine	June 2
Improvements to Sligo Harbour	Harbour Commrs.	Official	July
*Malt Kiln, Store, &c. Canterbury	Messrs. Flint & Sons	....	No date
*Making Roads, East Grinstead	East Court Estate	Official	do.
*Road Works, Constructing Stables	War Department	do.	do.
*Manufacture of Universal Bed Rest	Medical & Surgical Appliances Co. Lim.	....	do.
Five Cottages, Heudrefoding, near Cardiff	Mr. Thomas	....	do.
New Church, Barry Dock	....	Kempson & Fowler	do.
Restoration of Kingston Church, near Plymouth	....	Edmund Sedding	do.
Chapel and School, Woodbourne-road, Attercliffe, Sheffield	....	Alfred Appleby	do.
Alterations and Extension of the English Church, Dowlais, S. Wales	....	E. A. Johnson	do.
Chancel, Vestries, &c. St. John's Church, Yeadon	....	Messrs. Healey	do.
Two Vestries, &c. Schoolroom, Sheepbridge	United Methodist Free Church Society	....	do.

PUBLIC APPOINTMENTS.

Nature of Appointment.	By whom Advertised.	Salary.	Applications to be in.
*Clerk of Works for Waterworks	Bishops Castle T. C.	....	May 30
*Sanitary Inspector	St. Pancras Vestry	120l.	June 1
*Surveyor and Inspector of Nuisances	Cheshunt Loc. Bd.	250l.	June 7
*Assistant, Borough Engineer's Office	Stockton-on-Tees Corp.	150l.	do.
*Road Foreman	Islington Vestry	40s. weekly	June 9
*Geometrical Drawing and Estimating and Lecturer in Architecture	Royal Indian Engineering College	450l. &c.	No date

Those marked with an Asterisk (*) are advertised in this Number. *Competition*, p. iv. *Contracts*, pp. iv., vi., viii., ix., & xxv. *Public Appointments*, pp. xx. & xxi.

Builders' Foremen and Clerks of Works' Institution.—Ordinary meeting. 8.30 p.m.

THURSDAY, JUNE 2.

Society of Antiquaries.—8.30 p.m.

FRIDAY, JUNE 3.

Guild and School of Handicraft.—Mr. John Gamgee on "The relation of the skilled handicraftsman to physical discoveries." 8 p.m.

SATURDAY, JUNE 4.

Edinburgh Architectural Association.—Annual Excursion, Drumlanrig Castle.

RECENT PATENTS:

ABSTRACTS OF SPECIFICATIONS.

5,890.—BOLTS: *W. M. Trowsdale and another.*—This patent relates to an improved bolt for lavatory and other doors. It is screwed on the inside of the door, the section of the bolt being cylindrical, and the end set off from the back plate to allow for a working joint having a conical corner, on the neck of which a pivotted drop piece works, having a collar fixed on it to prevent it coming off, the drop-piece being held in the vertical position by its own weight. There is on the boss of the drop-piece, at right angles to the knob, an arm acting as a locking-piece conjointly with the back plate, which has two elongated slot holes, one to lock the bolt when shot into the staple, the other to prevent it being shaken out of its position when not in use, the door being recessed to allow the arm to work freely in it. On the inside architrave of the door-frame a bolt staple is fixed, covering a lever, which works clear of the face of the architrave, and is made large enough to allow for the revolving movement, being shaped to suit the bolt, and elongated so as to admit the bolt if in course of time it should sag. When the door is closed the bolt comes in a straight line with the edge of a lever connected with an indicator, or otherwise, and above the centre, so that when the drop-piece is lifted the bolt may be shot into the staple. The drop-piece of the bolt, when released by the hand, will revolve downwards, and the arm on the boss of the drop-piece will revolve upwards, and lock itself in the elongated slot-hole on the lock-plate by its own weight, thus fastening itself so that it cannot be opened from the outside. The bolt may be easily withdrawn by lifting the pivotted drop-piece, and drawing into the former position. The bolt may be used with or without an indicator.

10,029.—DOOR PIVOTS: *B. Mädler.*—This invention relates to door pivots. In swing doors having rising pivots, it is needful to provide a device which enables a suitable adjustment of the two inclined sliding surfaces relatively to each other when the doors, in consequence of the greater wear of the one sliding surface, cease to have the desired amount of swing purchase, or when the proper position of the door is to be maintained as it closes. According to the specification this is effected by adapting the upper sleeve or socket which surrounds the pivot proper to be turned and to be fixed in the desired position. The lower sleeve or socket is immovably fixed in the pan, whilst the upper sleeve or socket has an arm placed in a recess formed in the lower edge of the door, and a part of which is bent upwards in order to fit it to the rear edge of the door. Through the medium of this arm, the upper sleeve or socket can be turned a little. In the upwardly bent part is formed a slot, which enables it to be displaced below the head of a screw in the adjustment. By tightening this screw, the arm, and, therefore, the upper sleeve or socket can be fixed in the desired position. The arm does not protrude at any point beyond the edge of the door, and the inner surface of its upwardly bent part and the corresponding surface of a piece of metal which receives the screw and is let into the door, have the axis of the pivot proper for their common centre.

1,736.—PLANES: *W. Beddows.*—This invention relates to improvements in side planes, or those planes which are known as "side-rabbets," and are employed for smoothing quirks, bevelled shoulders, and grooves in woodwork. The object of the invention is to so construct side-rabbeting planes that they shall be of the requisite thinness, and capable of smoothing the sides of very narrow grooves. Furthermore, that the irons or bits of such plane shall be retained in place in the stock, and yet be so arranged as to be capable of ready removal therefrom for the purpose of sharpening, and be of a shape suitable for sharpening. For this purpose the stock, which is made preferably of iron, steel, or gunmetal, is formed with a specially-contrived bed or groove extending obliquely from the upper part to the lower edge of the stock, inclining transversely from point to back, and canted laterally, the groove terminating in a mouth formed at the side of the stock, and which may be at any suitable angle to the bottom edge of the stock. Into the bed or groove thus formed the plane iron, which is slender, is received, and is retained in position by any suitable means, the cutting edge of the plane-iron being inclined at an angle to suit the inclination of the mouth. The planes can be made right or left handed.

13,824.—SLIDING DOORS: *H. Champness.*—This invention relates to improvements in the construction, and also in the fastening, of sliding or other doors. It consists essentially in so hanging a shutter as to cover the top or open half of the door by cords and weights, the cords passing over pulleys, and the weights sliding in casings fixed to the outside of the door. The fastening of the door is effected by means of a pawl actuated by a lever, a lock preventing the lever being raised. This lock also fastens the shutter.

NEW APPLICATIONS FOR LETTERS PATENT.

May 9.—8,777, J. Brittain, Grinding Cement, &c.—8,781, A. de Muralt, Spring-Bolt Door Locks.—8,783, A. de Muralt, Door Locks.

May 10.—8,790, B. Fowell, Boilers for Heating Public Buildings and Greenhouses.—8,795, G. Moeckel, Arches for Ceilings and Vaults.—8,811, A. Peterson, Window Fasteners.—8,825, E. Jones and Others, Sash Fasteners and Regulators.—8,826, W. Dielitzsch, Door-Check.—8,865, V. Lewes, Manufacture of Glass.—8,875, N. Brandt, Closets.—8,883, J. Gibbons, Sash-Lifts or Fasteners.

May 11.—8,889, F. Willis and R. Astley, Fireproof Floor and Stairs.—8,899, R. Wyatt, Water-Waste Preventer for Water-Closets, &c.—8,910, J. Longworth, Closing and Latching Doors.—8,938, J. Cronk, Window Sashes and their Frames.

May 12.—8,985, Yates, Haywood, & Co., and the Rotherham Foundry Co., Limited, Adjustable Fire Grates.—9,010, S. Newton and J. Partington, Spring and Lever Door Hinge for Double and Single Doors.—9,052, G. Hall, Letter-Boxes for use on Private Dwellings.

May 13.—9,077, L. Cresswell, Fireplaces and Grates for Dwelling-houses.—9,093, W. Allen, Water and Burglar Proof Sash-fastener.—9,095, W. Allen, Hand Machine for rapidly Trimming Wall-papers, &c.—9,115, A. Boult, Skylights.—9,130, J. Milner, Water-closets.—9,142, A. Fyfe, Combined Building-block and Electric Insulation.

May 14.—9,154, W. Texhauer, Sliding Windows.—9,157, M. McNamara, Flushing-cisterns.—9,170, J. Woodcock, Syphon for Flushing tanks.—9,180, J. Thompson and R. Pollock, Central Ejector or Injector Ventilators.—9,191, T. Durrans, Nails.—9,193, H. Bracewell, Devices or Means for Retaining Windows or Doors in a more or less open position.—9,209, R. Astley, Construction of Fireproof Floors.

PROVISIONAL SPECIFICATIONS ACCEPTED.

3,896, W. Fox, Mitre Cutter or Trimmer.—4,878, W. Sterling, Sanitary and other Pipes and an Improved Method of Constructing Sewers and Drains.—5,863, D. Morrison, Taps.—6,229, J. Kerwood, System of Soil Pipe Ventilation.—6290, G. Asher, Window Fasteners.—6,571, W. Morrison, Roof Ventilators.—6,338, W. Ward & Son, Ltd., and W. Ward, Brick Making Machinery.—6,940, G. Hayes, Buildings, and Fire-proofing same.—6,950, S. Hellyer, Water-Closets.—6,956, J. Harris, Closet Fittings.—7,053, W. Wythe, Window Shades.—7,280, J. Simpson, Water Waste Closets.—7437, 7438, G. Gibson, Sash Locks.—7728, W. Johnson and J. Coultner, Tying Walls, Chimney Shafts and other Brick or similar Structures.—7,849, W. Reed, Malms Stock Bricks, &c.—7,978, J. Hamblett, Junior, Paving Bricks or Blocks.—8,021, G. Bray, Extension Ladders.—8,036, H. & H. Warrington, Bricks for Building Purposes.—8,076, T. Whitehead, Chimney Cowls and Extracting Ventilators.

COMPLETE SPECIFICATIONS ACCEPTED.

(Open to Opposition for Two Months.)

9,531, J. Giraud and J. Marini, Working Stones, Apparatus for shaping them into Cornices, or any other shape.—12,083, J. Hart-Davies, Blocks for Street or other Paving.—5,067, H. Angles, Imitation Faience Tiles or the like.—5,624, A. Boult, Opening and Closing Windows.—7,225, D. Macdonald, Sash Locks.

SOME RECENT SALES OF PROPERTY:

ESTATE EXCHANGE REPORT.

MAY 12.—By *Hards & Bradly*: A plot of freehold land, Barry-rd., Peckham, 250l.

MAY 14.—By *Rushworth & Stevens* (at Hastings): 8, Whiterock-gardens, Hastings, u.t. 85 yrs., g.r. 20l., r. 90l., 850l.

MAY 16.—By *J. & W. Johnson & Co.*: Nos. 182 and 184, Hackney-rd., f., 2,050l.—By *Ventom, Bull, & Cooper*: 270 and 270A, Belsize-rd., Kilburn, u.t. 81 yrs., g.r. 33l., r. 92l., 750l.—By *Mullett, Booker, & Co.*: 15, Lancaster-gate and stabling, Hyde-pk., f., 4,300l.; No. 46, Hyde-pk.-sq., u.t. 41 yrs., g.r. 20l., 4,000l.; 28, Kensington-pk.-gardens, u.t. 86 yrs., no g.r., 1,050l.—By *Trafford & Davison*: 208, Regent-st., profit rental of 120l., u.t. 9 yrs., 860l.; 5 and 7, Seymour-st., Deptford, u.t. 52 yrs., g.r. 4l. 10s., 385l.; 31 to 33, Strickland-st., u.t. 53 yrs., g.r. 8l. 8s., 905l.—By *Ball, Norris, & Hadley*: Three plots of freehold land, Walpole-rd., Bromley, 495l.; 47, Chelsham-rd., Clapham, u.t. 70 yrs., g.r. 9l. 10s., r. 70l., 710l.—By *Ellwood & Fuller*: I.g.r. of 21l. 11s., Burton-cres., u.t. 14 yrs., g.r. 15l., 1,375l.—By *Fleuret, Sons, & Adams*: 1 to 4, Spotted Dog-cottages, Willesden-green, u.t. [illegible] yrs., g.r. 4l., r. 80l. 12s., 400l.—By *M. Searle*: I.g.r. of 49l. 10s., Pownall-rd., Dalston, u.t. 53 yrs., 660l.; I.g.r. of 34l. 5s., Brougham-rd., u.t. 53 yrs., 460l.; f.g.r. of 50l., Langton-rd., Camberwell, with reversion in 68 yrs., 1,180l.; 30 and 32, Neckinger-rd., Bermondsey, u.t. 20 yrs., g.r. 7l. 10s., r. 57l. 4s., 210l.; 85 and 105, Abbey-st., f., r. 52l., 700l.; 57, Maltby-st., f., r. 56l., 1,400l.; 134, 136, and 138, Abbey-st., f., r. 97l., 1,310l.

MAY 17.—By *Eastman Bros.*: 10, Priory-villas, Sydenham, u.t. 83 yrs., g.r. 11l., r. 65l., 800l.—By *Debenham* eeson, & Co.: "The Lodge," 40, Gibson's-hill, Norod, and 3a. 0r. 22p., f., 3,500l.; freehold house and bling, London-st., Kingston-on-Thames, r. 70l., 1,400l. By *Chinnock, Galsworthy, & Co.*: 5 and 6, Albert-pl., nsington, f., r. 154l., 2,700l.; 228, Regent st., u.t. 28 ., g.r. 96l., 13s. 6d., r. 280l., 6,800l.; 7, Swallow-, Oxford-st., u.t. 25 yrs., g.r. 4l. 4s., r. 105l., 2,020l.— *Lound & Howitt*: 10 and 11, Park-pl., St. James's, "The Pk. Hotel," f., r. 440l., 10,000l.—By *Dowsett & .*: "St. Boniface House," Ventnor, Isle of Wight, d 3a. 1r. 7p., f., 4,000l.—By *Weston & Sons*: 6, Balm Ct.-ter., Balham, f., r. 85l., 1,200l.; 44, Sydney-rd., ockwell, u.t. 50 yrs., g.r. 5l. 5s., r. 34l., 250l.; 19, 23, Knatchbull-rd., Camberwell, u.t. 83 yrs., g.r. 18l., 124l., 1,300l.

MAY 18.—By *J. Baker & Sons*: Seven cottages and a ot of land, Edgware, f., 1,020l.—By *R. A. Enright*: Grovedale-rd., Holloway, u.t. 81 yrs., g.r. 5l., r. 28l., 5l.—By *Horne, Son, & Eversfield*: I.g.r. of 80l., inster-sq., Bayswater, u.t. 60 yrs., g.r. 2l., 1,670l.; .r. of 72l., Princes-sq., u.t. 60 yrs., g.r. 2l., 1,550l.; .r. of 188l., Edward-st., St. Pancras, u.t. 29 yrs., g.r. l., 2,230l.; 10, Manor-pk.-rd., Finchley, u.t. 88 yrs., r. 6l., r. 19l., 70l.—By *T. B. Westacott*: 4 and 6, Hampn-rd., Holloway, f., r. 52l., 640l.—By *J. Hibbard & ns*: 45, Mildmay-pk., Stoke Newington, u.t. 59 yrs., r. 8l., r. 48l., 540l.; 19, Statham-grove Villas, u.t. 82 ., g.r. 6l. 10s., 205l.; 41, Digby-rd., u.t. 83 yrs., r. 7l., r. 36l., 355l.; 20, Pyrland-rd., Canonbury, t. 58 yrs., g.r. 8l. 8s., r. 50l., 500l.; 42, Mayle-st., Islington, u.t. 69 yrs., g.r. 5l., r. 24l., 195l.— *Glover & Harrison*: 28 to 34 even, East-rd., West am, f.r. 100l., 1,000l.; "Woodford Villa," Ripon-rd., umstead, f.r. 32l., 525l.—By *Rushworth & Stevens*: and 3, Clare Villa, Merton, f.r. 46l. 16s., 285l.; 11, oodville-cres., Harrow-rd., u.t. 71 yrs., g.r. 7l. 10s., 42l., 320l.; 87 to 93 odd, Weedington-rd., Kentish own, u.t. 67 yrs., g.r. 25l. 4s., r. 136l., 1,040l.; and 100, Carlton-rd., u.t. 58 yrs., g.r. 12l., r. 68l., 520l.; and 47, Parchmore-rd., Thornton Heath, u.t. 72 yrs., r. 16l., r. 64l., 500l.—By *D. Young*: 35, Guildford-rd., ambeth, u.t. 50 yrs., g.r. 10l., 1,000l.; 23, Keplar-rd., rixton, u.t. 77 yrs., g.r. 6l. 10s., r. 30l., 260l.; 33, 35, nd 37, Keplar-rd., u.t. 77 yrs., g.r. 19l. 10s., r. 90l., 780l. —By *Walford & Wilshin*: "Claremont," "Dorset Villa," nd an unnamed Villa, Addington-grove, Sydenham, 1,370l.; "Silverbirch" and "Maude" Villas, r. 62l., 650l.; 75 and 77, Catford-hill, Catford, u.t. 71 rs., g.r. 10l., r. 42l.; and a l.g.r. of 5l., same term, 380l.

MAY 19.—By *D. Watney & Sons*: No. 257, Edgware-., f., r. 57l., 2,000l.; 261, Edgware-rd., f., r. 80l., 600l.; 61 to 69 (odd), Defoe-rd., Tooting, u.t. 86 yrs., r. 25l., 600l.; 6, Church-ter., f., 320l.; 1 and 2, Sidney-illas, f., 630l.; Brightwell-cres., a plot of f. land, 135l.— *King & Chasemore*: "Lutwicke," Slinfold, Sussex, od 61a. 0r. 1p., f., 2,700l.; "Battles," and 30a. 1r. 22p., 1,125l.; "Little Slifehurst Farm," Kirdford, and a. 2r. 8p., f., 600l.—By *C. C. & T. Moore*: 6, Westbury-illas, Forest-gate, long leasehold, g.r. 4l. 10s., 370l.; and 22, Shap-st., Kingsland, u.t. 11 yrs., g.r. 3l. 13s., 0l.; 36, How-st., u.t. 13 yrs., g.r. 2l., 100l.; 28, How-, u.t. 37 yrs., g.r. 2l. 5s., 165l.—By *Bray, Young, & o.*: 30, 32, and 34, Auckland-rd., Clapham, f., r. 94l., 5l.; 25, Charles-st., Portland Town, u.t. 36 yrs., g.r. ., r. 82l., 225l.; 55, York-st., Bryanstone-sq., u.t. yrs., g.r. 10l. 10s., 380l.—By *Rogers & Temple*: 11, St. ildred's-rd., Westgate-on-Sea, f., r. 95l., 1,480l.—By *. J. Bliss & Sons*: "Laurel Cottage," in High-st., leet, Hants, f., 360l.; 21, 22, 23, and 24, Marian-st., ackney, u.t. 58 yrs., g.r. 5l., 830l.; 17 and 19, Ashwell-., Bethnal-green, u.t. 65 yrs., g.r. 6l. 6s., 630l.; 16 and , Wennington-rd., u.t. 65 yrs., g.r. 5l., 460l.; 9 15 odd, Chisenhale-rd., Old Ford; and 78 and 80, ewardstone-rd., Bethnal-green, sold before auction.— y *Newbon & Co.*: 70 and 71, Roman-rd., Barnsbury, .t. 66 yrs., g.r. 12l., r. 64l., 610l.; 78, Barnsbury-rd., .t. 25 yrs., g.r. 5l., r. 46l., 295l.; 3, 4, 19, 20, and 22, lwyne-sq., Canonbury, u.t. 44 yrs., g.r. 67l. 10s., r. 07l. 10s., 1,800l.; 12, Kempsford-gardens, Kensington, .t. 74 yrs., g.r. 6l., r. 50l., 525l.; 17, Haselrigge-rd., lapham, u.t. 70 yrs., g.r. 5l. 10s., r. 34l.; 308, Balham igh-rd., Balham, u.t. 50 yrs., g.r. 5l., r. 36l.; and four lots of freehold land, Hereward-rd., Tooting, 1 lot, 600l.— y *Stimson & Sons*: 14, Carson-rd., Dulwich, f., 800l.; 6 to 82 (even), and 96 to 102 (even), Kimberley-rd., eckham, u.t. 81 yrs., g.r. 36l. 16s., 1,440l.; 25, 27, 65, to 2, 74, and 76, Barset-rd., u.t. 83 yrs., g.r. 64l., 1,450l.; 4, Longton-grove, Sydenham, u.t. 59 yrs., no g.r., r. 2l. 10s., 500l.; 13 to 16, High Cross-ter., Tottenham, .t. 85 yrs., g.r. 19l. 10s., 440l.; 69 to 75 (odd), 11 and 113, Wellbourne-rd., u.t. 15 yrs., g.r. 27l., 690l.; , 61, 62, and 64, Walcot-sq., Kennington, u.t. 15 yrs., .r. 42l., 410l.; 31 to 34, Edward-st., Bermondsey, f., 10l.; 353 to 361 (odd), Southwark-pk.-rd., u.t. 40 yrs., .r. 16l., 1,010l.; 1 to 33 (odd), Litlington-st., u.t. 50 rs., g.r. 66l. 3s., 1,390l.; 20 and 28, Litlington-st., u.t. 9 yrs., g.r. 9l., 225l.; 1 to 7 (odd), Clare Hall-pl., and g.r. of 5l., u.t. 39 yrs., g.r. 25l., 350l.; 2 and Clare Hall-pl., u.t. 39 yrs., g.r. 9l., 190l.; 99 and 301, Rotherhithe New-rd., u.t. 40 yrs., g.r. 1l., 40l., 810l.—By *A. Robertson*: 101 and 103, East Surrey-rove, Peckham, f., r. 46l. 16s., 485l.; 111 and 113, amden-grove North, f., r. 54l. 12s., 565l.; 22, 24, and , Mann-st., Walworth, u.t. 59 yrs., g.r. 9l., 835l.; 29, ann-st., u.t. 60 yrs., g.r. 4l. 5s., r. 41l. 12s., 250l.; 205, ill-st., u.t. 58 yrs., g.r. 4l. 10s., r. 36l. 8s., 260l.; 8 and , Belvedere-rd., Lambeth, u.t. 31 yrs., g.r. 15l., r. 64l., 0l.—By *Hards & Bradly* (at Deptford): 4 to 7, Payne-., Deptford, f., 705l.

MAY 20.—By *Messrs. Aldridge*: 21 and 23, Livingtone-rd., Thornton Heath, u.t. 89 yrs., g.r. 8l., 166l.— y *H. Gibson*: Twenty-one freehold cottages in Half-oon-yd., St. Albans, 515l.—By *Curtis, Rogers, & Co*: g.r. of 30l., Lennox-villas, Willesden, u.t. 82 yrs., 520l.; g.r. of 45l., Nicosia-rd., Wandsworth Common, u.t. 87 rs., g.r. 2l., 850l.—By *Foster & Cranfield*: The Residence, Beaulieu," Winchmore Hill, and 10a. 1r. 25p., 6,800l.; he freehold residence "Elmhurst," Bycullah-rd., nfield, 1,310l.—By *Reynolds & Eason*: 137, 139, nd 141, Jubilee-st., Mile End, u.t. 8 yrs., g.r. . 10s., 120l.; 157, Jubilee-st., u.t. 8 yrs., g.r. 2l. 5s., 65l.; 7, 38, and 39, De Beauvoir-sq., Kingsland, u.t. 27 yrs., .r. 13l. 18s., r. 101l., 510l.; 40 to 46, De Beauvoir-sq., .t. 26 yrs., g.r. 35l., r. 239l., 1,200l.; 53 to 61 odd, St. eter's-st., Mile-end, u.t. 37 yrs., g.r. 15l., r. 160l., ,275l.; 15, St. Peter's-rd., u.t. 38 yrs., g.r. 3l. 6s., r. 2l., 345l.; 9 to 19 odd, Chicksand-st., White-hapel, and 19, 21, and 23, Spelman-st., u.t. yrs., g.r. 31l. 10s., r. 318l. 10s., 1,880l.; 4, and 5, Hutchinson's-av., Aldgate, f.r. 67l. 10s. 0l. By *Baker & Sons*: "The Limes," Grafton-rd., Harrow, f.r. 90l., 740l.; 1 to 7, Queen's-ter., f., 550l.; three copyhold cottages, Crown-st., 180l.; a detached house in Greenford-rd., r. 19l. 10s., 210l.; "Wolsey House," High-st., copyhold, 1,900l.; three plots of freehold land, "Mount-pk. Estate," 615l.; freehold land, 5 a., Mundesley-on-Sea, 840l.

[*Contractions used in these lists.*—F.g.r. for freehold ground-rent; l.g.r. for leasehold ground-rent; i.g.r. for improved ground-rent; g.r. for ground-rent; r. for rent; f. for freehold; c. for copyhold; l. for leasehold; e.r. for estimated rental; u.t. for unexpired term; p.a. for per annum; yrs. for years; st. for street; rd. for road; sq. for square; pl. for place; ter. for terrace; cres. for crescent; yd. for yard, &c.]

PRICES CURRENT OF MATERIALS.

TIMBER.		
Greenheart, B.G. ton	9/0/0	9/0/0
Teak, E.I. .. load	9/10/0	15/0/0
Sequoia, U.S. ft. cu.	2/3	3/0
Ash, Canada load	2/10/0	4/0/0
Birch, do.	3/5/0	4/10/0
Elm, do.	3/10/0	4/15/0
Fir, Dantsic, &c.	1/10/0	3/10/0
Oak, do.	3/0/0	5/5/0
Canada	5/10/0	7/0/0
Pine, Canada red	2/10/0	3/10/0
Do. yellow	2/10/0	5/0/0
Lath, D'ntsic, fath	5/0/0	6/0/0
St. Petersburg	5/0/0	7/0/0
Deals, Finland, 2nd & 1st std 100	8/0/0	9/10/0
Do. 4th & 3rd ..	7/0/0	8/0/0
Do. Riga	7/0/0	8/0/0
St. Petersburg, 1st yellow ..	11/0/0	14/10/0
Do. 2nd yellow	8/0/0	10/0/0
Do. white	7/10/0	10/10/0
Swedish	7/10/0	15/10/0
White Sea	8/0/0	17/10/0
Canada, Pine 1st	20/0/0	26/0/0
Do. do. 2nd	14/10/0	16/0/0
Do. do. 3rd, &c.	8/0/0	10/5/0
Do. Spruce, 1st	8/10/0	11/0/0
Do. do. 3rd & 2nd	6/15/0	8/0/0
New Brunswick	7/0/0	7/10/0
Battens, all kinds	5/10/0	15/10/0
Flooring Boards, sq., 1 in. prep. 1st	0/8/0	0/14/0
Do. 2nd	0/7/0	0/11/0
Other qualities	0/5/6	0/7/6
Cedar, Cuba .. ft.	/3½	/4½
Honduras, &c.	/3½	/4
Mahogany, Cuba	/4½	/6½
St. Domingo, cargo av.	/4½	2/0
Mexican do. do.	/4	/6
Tobasco do. do.	/5½	/7
Honduras do. ..	/5½	/6½
Box, Turkey ton	4/0/0	13/0/0
Rose, Rio	10/0/0	20/0/0
Bahia	9/0/0	18/0/0
Satin, St. Domingo .... ft.	0/0/8	0/1/8

TIMBER (*continued*).		
Satin, Porto Rico	0/0/8	0/1/6
Walnut, Italian ..	0/0/3½	0/0/7
METALS.		
Iron—Pig, in Scotland .... ton	2/0/9	0/0/0
Bar, Welsh, in London	5/17/6	6/0/0
Do. do. at works in Wales	5/7/6	5/10/0
Do. Staffordshire, in London	6/5/0	6/15/0
Copper—British, cake and ingot	48/10/0	50/0/0
Best selected ..	51/0/0	51/10/0
Sheets, strong ..	58/0/0	59/0/0
Chili, bars	46/12/6	47/0/0
Yellow Metal lb.	0/0/5¼	0/0/5¾
Lead—Pig, Spanish .... ton	10/11/3	10/13/9
English, com. brands	10/12/6	10/15/0
Sheet, English, 3 lbs. per sq. ft. and upwards ..	12/0/0	0/0/0
Pipe	12/10/0	0/0/0
Zinc—English sheet ...... ton	25/15/0	26/0/0
Vieille Montagne	26/5/0	0/0/0
Tin—Straits	97/15/0	98/5/0
Australian	97/15/0	98/5/0
English Ingots	91/0/0	99/10/0
OILS.		
Linseed ...... ton	18/0/0	18/5/0
Cocoanut, Cochin	24/0/0	0/0/0
Do. Ceylon	22/0/0	0/0/0
Palm, Lagos	22/5/0	22/10/0
Rapeseed, English pale	25/10/0	0/0/0
Do. brown	23/10/0	0/0/0
Cottonseed ref. ..	19/0/0	0/0/0
Oleine	21/10/0	22/10/0
Lubricating, U.S.	4/0/0	5/0/0
Do. refined	6/0/0	12/10/0
Tar—Stockholm barrel	0/19/0	1/0/0
Archangel	0/12/6	0/0/0

TENDERS.

[Communications for insertion under this heading should be addressed to "The Editor," and must reach us *not later than 12 noon on Thursdays*.]

ABERGAVENNY.—Accepted for the construction of a chapel, entrance gates, boundary wall, &c., at the new cemetery, for the Burial Board. Mr. E. A. Johnson, architect, Abergavenny. Quantities by architect:—
J. D. Williams, Knighton £1,523 10 0

BOURNEMOUTH.—Accepted for erecting the "Granville" Temperance Hotel, corner of Yelverton-road and Richmond-hill, Bournemouth, for Messrs. Colman and others. Messrs. Lawson & Donkin, architects and surveyors, Bournemouth. Quantities supplied:—
T. H. Kingerlee, Oxford £7,467 0 0
[For full list, see last week's *Builder*, p. 409.]

CRAWLEY (Sussex).—For the erection of a new church at the Id. Crawley, Sussex. Mr. W. Hilton Nash, architect, 5, Adelaide-place, London Bridge, E.C.:—

Norman	£2,298	P. Peters	£2,167
Row and Bros.	2,474	Cook & Sons, Crawley*	2,159

* Accepted.

CREDITON (Devon).—For a pair of labourers' cottages, for General Sir Redvers Buller, C.B., V.C. Mr. J. Widgery, architect, Downes Estate, Crediton:—
W. Dart, Crediton (accepted) £445 | W. Berry £440

EASTLEIGH.—For the erection of Infants' School, offices, and boundary-wall, Cranbury-road, Eastleigh, for the South Stoneham School Board. Messrs. W. H. Mitchell, Son, & Gutteridge, architects, Southampton:—

T. H. Kingerlee	£2,994 0 0	Crook & Son	£2,637 0 0
W. R. & C. Light ..	2,857 0 0	W. C. Mears	2,658 12 0
W. Franklin	2,806 6 5	Molyneux, Ireland, & Morgan, Southampton*	2,634 0 0
H. Stevens & Co.	2,780 0 0		
J. Nichols, Exors. of	2,748 0 0		

* Accepted subject to confirmation by the Educational Department.

EAST MOLESEY.—For the erection of a pair of cottages at Summer-road, East Molesey, Surrey, for Mr. F. W. Last. Mr. Walter J. Ebbetts, architect, Savoy House, 115, Strand, W.C.:—

Wheatley & Son	£510	Pettitt	£487
Potterton	508		

EDINBURGH.—For 750 tons of dry sand, cast-iron pipes, and special castings, for the Edinburgh and District Water Trustees. Messrs. J. & A. Leslie & Reid, C.E., 72A, George-street, Edinburgh:—

D. Y. Stewart & Co. ..	£3,590 16 11	R. Maclaren & Co. ..	£3,438 1 2
Macfarlane, Strang, & Co.	3,469 6 3	R. Laidlaw & Son, Glasgow*	3,442 16 11
Cochrane, Grove, & Co.	3,460 12 7		

* Accepted.

For Laying and Jointing Foregoing.

Henderson & Duncan	£1,858 14 1	John McKnight & Son	£3,316 6 0
R. R. Stewart	4,578 4 0	James Young & Sons, Edinburgh*	3,294 0 0
John Best	3,869 13 10		

* Accepted.

FAREHAM (Hants).—For erecting the new Capital and Counties Bank, Fareham. Mr. W. Wallace, architect, 27a, Old Bond-street, London. Quantities by Mr. F. Thompson, 5, Great James-street, Bedford-row, W.C.:—

Steven & Son	£4,830	Stallard, G.	4,630
Cooke, J. H.	4,829	Blackman	4,460
Light, W. R., & Co.	4,797	Hall, T. P., Southsea*	4,490

*Accepted.

GREAT MALVERN.—For additions to "Holly Mount," for Mr. Benson Rathbone, J.P. Messrs. Mackmurdo, Hornblower, & Walters, architects, London:—
William Porter .... £1,310 | Thomas Brond, Malvern* . £1,275
* Accepted.

Hot Water Work.

William Birbeck, Worcester (accepted) £101 0 0

HITCHIN (Herts).—For alterations and additions to mansion and for the erection of stabling, at King's Walden, Hitchin (exclusive of foundations and drainage), for Mr. T. F. Harrison. Messrs. Beeston & Burmester, architects, 30, Lincoln's Inn-fields, W.C. Quantities by Mr. C. Fitzroy Doll:—

	Mansion. £.	New Stabling. £.	Totals. £.	Time. Weeks.
Coll's & Son	17,480	6,760	24,240	52
Gillow & Co.	16,570	5,990	22,960	60
Trollope & Son	16,449	6,440	22,889	45
Jones & Son	16,900	5,950	22,850	60
Pattinson & Co.	16,737	6,079	22,816	40
Simpson & Son	16,737	6,000	22,737	65
Green, T. L.	15,785	6,265	22,050	70
Bell & Son	15,597	6,097	21,694	42
Wm. J. Adcock, Dover*	14,800	5,700	20,500	65

* Accepted.

LEEDS.—Accepted for the erection of Church schools, Pudsey. Mr. C. S. Nelson, architect, Royal Insurance-buildings, 10, Park-row, Leeds:—

Mason, &c.—Thomas Wood, Pudsey	Total amount of accepted tenders, £1,680 0 0.
Joiner, &c.—Thomas Hatton, Pudsey	
Plumber, &c.—Joseph Scant, Pudsey	
Plasterers.—Joseph Laycock & Sons, Stanningley	
Slater.—Frederick Thompson, Stanningley	
Painter.—John Nicholson, Pudsey	

LONDON.—For re-erecting the water-closets of the Infants' department of the Neckinger-road School, Bermondsey, at a further distance from the School building, for providing stoneware troughs and automatic flushing tanks, and also for adapting the existing water-closets and urinal for a coal and wood store, for the School Board for London. Mr. T. J. Bailey, Architect:—

John Garrett & Son	£406	F. & H. F. Higgs	£383
J. Deffy	340	H. Mallett, 233, Clapham-road, S.W.*	298
Lecks & Hooker	308		

* Recommended by the Works Committee for Acceptance.

LONDON.—For the erection of a school to provide accommodation for 605 children on the site in Mulgrave-place, for the School Board for London. Mr. T. J. Bailey, Architect:—

J. T. Chappell	£19,591	Lathey Bros.	£17,080
Holloway Bros.	18,489	E. Lawrance & Sons	17,038
J. Mowlem & Co.	18,430	Hart Bros.	17,005
Thomas Boyce	17,709	W. Downs, Hampton-street, Walworth-road, S.E.*	16,622
Holliday & Greenwood ..	17,756		
J. Marsland	17,520		
D. Charteris	17,498		

* Recommended by the Works Committee for acceptance.

LONDON.—For the erection of a block of stabling on the South side of Edwardes-square, Kensington, for Mr. John Crowle. Mr. Charles R. Guy Hall, architect, 14, St. Alban's-road, Kensington:—

John Douglas	£1,735	John Barker & Co.	£1,273
Stafford Hill	1,580	J. B. Hayden	1,257
Leslie & Co.	1,334	Chas. F. Kearley (accepted)	1,119

LONDON.—For rebuilding No. 47, Maddox-street, W., for Messrs. G. & W. Lawrence. Mr. W. A. Williams, architect, 156, Regent-street, W. Quantities by Mr. C. W. Brooks:—

Lowe	£7,745	Gregory & Co.	£7,539
Harris & Wardrop	7,643	E. A. Roome, 112, Clarence-road, Lower Clapton* ..	7,485
Chappell	7,549		

* Accepted.

[Burmantofts' estimate of £900 for the whole front in faience ware accepted.]

LONDON.—For the erection of stables, with dwelling-rooms, at Lansdown-mews, Guilford-street, for Messrs. R. Dolling & Sons. Mr. P. Cuffey, architect:—

		A.*
Falten	£895 0 0	£40 0 0
Worsley & Co.	783 0 0	43 15 0
Brown & Harris	750 0 0	—
Wells & Son	740 0 0	—
Woodrow & Pitcher, 43, Millman-street, W.C.	731 16 0†	26 0 0

* Additional for brickwork in cement. † Accepted.

LONDON.—For Alterations, &c., to "Whitwell Arms," Canning Town, for Messrs. Mann, Crossman, & Paulin:—

J. & H. Cocks	£389	J. G. Smith (accepted)	£301
Inkpen & Son	321	S. Salt	294
G. Barker	318		

LONDON.—For alterations, additions, and repairs to 61, High-road, Kilburn, for Mr. James Stewart. Mr. Edward Harnot, architect, 8, John-street, Adelphi:—

Smith	£1,640	Eady	£1,341 18 3
S. J. Dainton (accepted) ..	1,500		

LONDON.—Accepted for the erection of residence and studio in Cadogan-gardens, Chelsea, S.W., for Mr. Mortimer Menpes. Messrs. Mackmurdo, Hornblower, & Walters, architects, London:—
H. J. Wright, Chelsea £3,915 0 0
[Exclusive of decorative works.]

LONDON.—For alterations and additions to Messrs. Carter, Paterson, & Co.'s Depot, High-street, Deptford. Mr. Wm. Eva, architect, 10, Union-court, E.C.:—

Harris & Wardrop	£495	Salt	£394
Burman & Sons	486	Chafen, 20, Trundley's-road, Deptford (accepted)	357
Godfrey & Son	454		

LONDON.—For rebuilding the "Sir Isaac Newton" public-house, High-street, St. John's Wood, N.W. Mr. Thomas Durrans, architect, 44, Upper Baker-street, N.W.:—

H. C. Clifton	£4,930	T. Stevens	£4,596
Staines & Son	4,880	C. Dearing & Son*	4,539
Macklelow & Co.	4,920		

* Accepted.

LONDON.—Accepted for new front, &c., to the "Moorgate Tavern, Moorgate-street, E.C., for the Brewery Assets Corporation (Limited). Mr. H. I. Newton, architect, 40, Victoria-street, Westminster, S.W.:—
B. Plummer, City £490 0 0

LONDON.—For erecting the Roman Catholic Church of the Sacred Heart, West Battersea (Contract B, superstructure, excepting aisles and tower). Mr. Fredk. A. Walters, architect. Quantities by Mr. John H. Lofting, 4, Great Queen-street, Westminster:—

F. & H. F. Higgs	£6,900	Thos. Gregory & Co.	£6,187
Tuttle & Appleton	6,690	Jas. Longley & Co., Crawley*	6,175
Holloway Bros.	6,681		
Stimpson & Co.	6,660		

* Accepted.

LONDON.—For painting and cleaning works at the Casual and Receiving Wards, Bear-yard, Lincoln's Inn-fields, for the Guardians of the Strand Union. Mr. Wm. S. Gross, architect, 18, Outer Temple, Strand, W.C.:—

J. D. Hobson	£701 7 8	G. Dorrell & Co.	£445 0 0
Graham & Graham	645 0 0	C. Beach	387 0 0
Chas. Wall	549 0 0	J. Parker & Co.	378 0 0
Foster & Son	517 18 0	McLachlan*	359 0 0
G. H. Rowe	465 0 0	R. Beed	347 0 0
W. Wright	449 10 0	G. W. Stewart & Co.	341 16 8
V. Roger	446 4 0		

* Accepted.

LONGTOWN (Cumberland).—For church fittings, &c., to Kirk-Andrew's Church, Longtown, Cumberland. Mr. Temple L. Moore, architect. Quantities by Mr. John B. Lofting, 4, Great Queen-street, Westminster:—

Martin	£1,298 3 6	Elwell	£1,163 7 6
Longley	1,250 0 0	Court & Henderson	1,054 0 0
Black	1,207 0 0	Davidson	1,031 3 0

RINGWOOD (Hants).—For residence at Ringwood, Hants, for Mr. J. Cogan Conway. Messrs. Lawson & Donkin, architects and surveyors, Bournemouth:—

McWilliam & Son	£1,995	W. Hoare	£1,650
Barrow & Entwisle	2,065	Hayward, Fenton, & Co.	1,640
T. H. Kingerlee	1,995	W. H. C. Curtis, Poole*	1,585
Joseph White	1,950	H. Tuck	1,580
W. E. Alexander	1,796		

* Accepted subject to modification.

SHOTLEY BRIDGE.—For rebuilding a farmhouse at Medomsley Grange Farm, for Mr. Jas. Hunter, Aulon's Hill, N. R. Messrs. John Smith & Son, architects, Rose Cottage, Shotley Bridge:—

Milborn & Gibson	£472 16 0	Taylor & Robinson,	
J. F. Thompson & Co.	418 17 7	Medomsley*	£416 14 8

* Accepted.

SOUTH SHIELDS.—For alterations and additions to the business premises of Messrs. J. & G. Carruthers, Ocean-road, South Shields. Mr. Henry Grieves, Architect, Albany-chambers, South Shields:—

Brown, Robt.	£456 8 2	Goodwin & Son, South	
Robertson, W. J.	465 18 4	Shields*	413 16 0

* Accepted.

SOWERBY BRIDGE.—Accepted for the erection of a floor oil-cloth manufactory in two divisions, together with warehouse, engine and boiler-houses, and approach-road, on the site of the Calder Chemical Works. Mr. T. L. Patchett, architect, Halifax:—

Masonry and Brickwork.—Nathaniel Calpan & Son, King Cross, Halifax	£819 0 0
Carpenter and Joiner.—James Lister, Hebden Bridge	690 0 0
Plumber and Glazier.—James Stafford, Sowerby Bridge	120 0 0
Slater and Plasterer.—George Whiteley, Sowerby Bridge	130 0 0
	£1,759 0 0

(Iron beams, troughs, &c., from Belgium.)
(Foundation work already in, and stone, slates, and bricks provided by proprietor.)

TANFIELD (Durham).—Accepted for the erection of schools at Tanfield Lea, for the School Board. Messrs. Davidson & Bendle, architects, 33, Grainger-street West, Newcastle-upon-Tyne:—

A. & R. Davis, Burnopfield, Co. Durham £2,023 4 11½

WALTHAMSTOW.—For the erection and completion of Additional class-room accommodation adjoining to the Pretoria-avenue Schools, for the Walthamstow School Board. Mr. W. A. Longmore, Architect, 7, Great Alie-street, Whitechapel:—

Baffett & Power	£485	R. & E. Evans	£440
Amey	454	Kelland, Stoke Newington*	426
Watling	449		

* Accepted.

[Architect's estimate, £440.]

WOOLWICH.—For additions to the Woolwich Polytechnic. Mr. M. H. Church, architect, Woolwich:—

Chessum & Sons	£1,050	Young & Lonsdale	£957
Munday & Son	1,015	Mutton & Wallis	949
H. Brown	998	Holloway	923
Chapman	980		

The Builder Cathedral Series.

1891.

1. CANTERBURY	Jan. 3.	7. SALISBURY	July 4.
2. LICHFIELD	Feb. 7.	8. BRISTOL	Aug. 1.
3. ST. ALBAN'S	Mar. 7.	9. NORWICH	Sept. 5.
4. PETERBOROUGH	April 4.	10. ROCHESTER	Oct. 3.
5. WELLS	May 2.	11. LINCOLN	Nov. 7.
6. EXETER	June 6.	12. GLOUCESTER	Dec. 5.

1892.

13. ST. PAUL'S .. .. Jan. 2.

14. HEREFORD	Feb. 6.	20. WORCESTER	Aug. 6.
15. CHICHESTER	Mar. 5.	21. BANGOR	Sept. 3.
16. ELY	April 2.	22. ST. ASAPH	Sept. 3.
17. LLANDAFF	May 7.	23. WINCHESTER	Oct. 1.
18. OXFORD	June 4.	24. TRURO	Nov. 5.
19. SOUTHWELL	July 2.	25. ST. DAVID'S	Dec. 3.

(Further arrangements will be duly announced.)

Post-free FOURPENCE HALFPENNY each, except Nos. 1, 2, 3 and 4 which are *out of print*; but the VIEW, PLAN, AND DESCRIPTION of CANTERBURY, LICHFIELD, ST. ALBAN'S, and PETERBOROUGH, have been re-printed, and they can now be had, price EIGHTPENCE each set; by post, 10d.

THE REREDOS, ST. PAUL'S.
Reprinted from "THE BUILDER," January 28, 1888 (15 in. by 11½ in.), on stout paper, unfolded, for framing, 6d.; by post, 8d.

PORTFOLIOS,
for Preserving the Plates unfolded, 2s. 6d.; by post 3s.

London: Office of "THE BUILDER," 46, Catherine-street, W.C.

SUBSCRIBERS in LONDON and the SUBURBS, by prepaying at the Publishing Office, 19s. per annum (or 4s. 9d. per quarter), can ensure receiving "The Builder," by *Friday Morning's Post.*

TERMS OF SUBSCRIPTION.

"THE BUILDER" is supplied DIRECT from the Office to residents in any part of the United Kingdom at the rate of 19s. per annum PREPAID. To all parts of Europe, America, Australia, and New Zealand, 26s. per annum. To India, China, Ceylon, &c., 30s. per annum. Remittances payable to DOUGLAS FOURDRINIER, Publisher, No. 46, Catherine-street, W.C.

PUBLISHER'S NOTICES.

Registered Telegraphic Address, 'THE BUILDER,' LONDON.

CHARGES FOR ADVERTISEMENTS.

SITUATIONS VACANT, PARTNERSHIPS, APPRENTICESHIPS TRADE AND GENERAL ADVERTISEMENTS.

Six lines (about fifty words) or under .... 4s. 6d.
Each additional line (about ten words) .... 0s. 6d.

Terms for Series of Trade Advertisements, also for Special Advertisements on front page, Competitions, Contracts, Sales by Auction, &c. may be obtained on application to the Publisher.

SITUATIONS WANTED.

FOUR Lines (about thirty words) or under .... 2s. 6d.
Each additional line (about ten words) .... 0s. 6d.

PREPAYMENT IS ABSOLUTELY NECESSARY.

*** Stamps *must not* be sent, but all small sums should be remitted by Cash in Registered Letter or by Money Order, payable at the Post-office, Covent-garden, W.C. to
DOUGLAS FOURDRINIER, Publisher,
Addressed to No. 46, Catherine-street, W.C.

Advertisements for the current week's issue must reach the Office before THREE o'clock p.m. on THURSDAY, but those intended for the front Page should be in by TWELVE noon on WEDNESDAY.

SPECIAL.—ALTERATIONS IN STANDING ADVERTISEMENTS or ORDERS TO DISCONTINUE same must reach the Office before TEN o'clock on WEDNESDAY mornings.

The Publisher cannot be responsible for DRAWINGS, TESTIMONIALS, &c. left at the Office in reply to Advertisements, and strongly recommends that of the latter COPIES ONLY should be sent.

PERSONS Advertising in "The Builder" may have *Replies addressed to the Office, 46, Catherine-street, Covent Garden, W.C. free of charge.* Letters will be forwarded if addressed envelopes are sent, together with sufficient stamps to cover the postage.

AN EDITION Printed on THIN PAPER, for FOREIGN and COLONIAL CIRCULATION, is issued every week.

Now ready.

READING CASES, { NINEPENCE EACH. By Post (carefully packed), 1s.

TO CORRESPONDENTS.

W. L. N. (amount should have been sent).—J. J. A. (we do know).—T. F.—G. M. L.—P. P. & Co.—U. S.—

All statements of facts, lists of tenders, &c., must be accompanied by the name and address of the sender, not necessarily for publication.

We are compelled to decline pointing out books and giving addresses.

NOTE.—The responsibility of signed articles, and papers read at public meetings, rests, of course, with the authors.

We cannot undertake to return rejected communications.

Letters or communications (beyond mere news-items) which have been duplicated for other journals, are NOT DESIRED.

All communications regarding literary and artistic matter should be addressed to THE EDITOR; all communications relating to advertisements and other exclusively business matters should be addressed to THE PUBLISHER, and not to the Editor.

VOL. LXII. No. 2574. SATURDAY, JUNE 4, 1892.

ILLUSTRATIONS.

Cathedrals of England and Wales: XVIII., Christchurch, Oxford.—Drawn by Mr. Roland W. Paul .... *Double-Page Photo-Litho.*
Plan of Christchurch Cathedral, Oxford.—Measured and Drawn by Mr. R. W. Paul .... *Double-Page Photo-Litho.*
Christchurch Cathedral, Oxford: View across the Lady Chapel.—Drawn by Mr. R. W. Paul .... *Single-Page Ink-Photo.*
Christchurch Cathedral, Oxford: View across the North Transept.—Drawn by Mr. R. W. Paul .... *Single-Page Ink-Photo.*
Remains of the Shrine of St. Frideswide, Christchurch Cathedral, Oxford.—Measured and Drawn by Mr. R. W. Paul .... *Double-Page Ink-Photo.*

Blocks in Text.

The Chapter House, &c., Christchurch Cathedral, Oxford .... Page 440
Capitals, Christchurch Cathedral, Oxford 441
Sculpture on Base of an Ancient Cross, Christchurch Cathedral, Oxford 441
Sculptured slab in Chapter House, Christchurch Cathedral, Oxford .... Page 442
Poppy-heads to Stalls, Latin Chapel, Christchurch Cathedral, Oxford 442
Diagrams in Student's Column: "Heating by Hot Water" 444, 445

CONTENTS.

Inland Navigation in Russian Europe 429
Notes 431
Architecture at the Royal Academy.—VI. 432
Letter from Paris 434
The Royal Institute of British Architects 434
[T]he Royal Commission on Metropolitan Water-Supply 436
[T]he Relation of the Architect to the Workman 437
[Th]e London County Council 439
[B]uilders' Benevolent Institution 439
[O]xford Cathedral 440
The Architectural Association 442
Books: Laxton's "Builders' Price-Book for 1892" (London: Kelly & Co.); Lockwood's "Builders', Architects', Contractors, and Engineer's Price-Book for 1892" (London: Crosby Lockwood & Son); Spon's "Architects' and Builders' Price-Book" (London: E. & F. N. Spon); J. Imray & C. H. W. Biggs' "First Principles of Mechanical Engineering" (London: Biggs & Co.); W. L. Baker's "The Beam" (London: Chapman & Hall); "Palliser's Specification Blanks" (New York: Palliser, Palliser, & Co.); "Popular Map of England and Wales" (Edinburgh: W. & A. K. Johnston); M. D. Burke's "Brick for Street Pavements" (Cincinnati: R. Clarke & Co.); G. M. Lawford's "House Drainage Hydro-mems" (London: G. Gill & Sons); H. G. Assiter's "Notes on the Public Health Act" (London: Crosby Lockwood & Son); A. A. Macdonell's "Camping Out" (London: G. Bell & Sons) 443
Victoria Cathedral Competition 444
A Question of Building Penalty 444
Fire-brick 444
Student's Column.—Warming Buildings by Hot Water, XXIII. 444
Surveyorships 445
General Building News 445
Stained Glass and Decoration 446
Foreign and Colonial 446
Miscellaneous 447
Capital and Labour 447
Meetings 447
Recent Patents 448
Some Recent Sales of Property 448

Inland Navigation in Russian Europe.

USSIA in Europe is happily provided by Nature with numerous broad, deep, and long rivers, navigable to a greater distance than is found practicable in any other European country, which, with their tributaries, have a collective length of 53,000 statute miles. These rivers act as the conduits of four great rain catchment basins flowing respectively into the Baltic Sea, the Arctic Ocean, the Caspian Sea, and the Black Sea. Art, with comparatively little effort, has contrived by the construction of a few short canals connecting the different navigable river systems here and there, and at one point or another canalising for a short distance some of these natural avenues, to provide for placing in direct intercommunication the whole of the mileage of this magnificent system of inland waterways. This system of inland navigation is placed under the control of the Ministry of the Ways of Communication. Of the official computation of 53,000 miles, there is, however, so far,—up to the beginning of 1890,—only 42,935 miles of inland navigation actually included under the jurisdiction of this body. The active function of the Ministry of the Ways of Communication is discharged by a department known as the Superintendence Bureau of Navigation. Of the 42,935 miles of inland navigation administered by the Bureau, 9,758 miles are stated officially as being only capable of navigation by rafts, 20,268 miles as being navigable by boats, leaving 12,559 miles of waterways without any definite specification. The canalised portion of natural rivers is given as being 2,392 miles, the collective length of the purely artificial canals being 1,336 miles, this making the trifling proportion in relation to the whole mileage of 3,728 miles of artificial and semi-artificial waterways.

By far the most important of the Russian arterial waterways are certainly those which form links in the several through chains of navigation which connect the Baltic Sea at St. Petersburg with the Caspian Sea at Astrakhan. Of these there are three, in each of which that majestic waterway, the Volga, or, as the Muscovites style that river, "The Ocean's Nurse," is the principal factor. Rising in the Valdai hills, some 200 miles east by south of St. Petersburg, at 550 ft. above the sea level, it traverses the provinces of Tver, Jaroslav, Kostroma, Nijni-Novgorod, Kazan, Simbirsk, Samara, Saratoff, and Astrakhan, where it enters the Caspian Sea, which, being 113 ft. below the sea level, makes the total fall of the Volga, from its source to its *débouchure*, 663 ft., which, distributed over a sinuous course of over 2,000 miles (of which 1,794 are navigable), averages the mild gradient of less than 4 in. per mile.

The Volga, with its tributaries, the chief of which are the Oka and the Kama, forms the main avenue for the chief industrial region of Russia, comprising twenty-one provinces, inhabited by 40,000,000 people, out of a total population of Russia in Europe of 90,000,000. The navigation of the Volga and its chief tributaries, according to the varying degrees of latitude, is open for a period of from 199 to 220 days, the navigation usually being closed about the middle of November. During this period of open navigation some 55,000 voyages are made by barges, rafts, and steamers, the aggregate tonnage ascending and descending being 5,000,000. The upward freights consist mainly of grain, timber, mineral oils, and Eastern produce, the downward cargoes being chiefly metals, minerals, textiles, and other manufactured products. M. Nicolas de Sytenko, Engineer to the Russian Government, and a member of the Aulic Council, in a memorandum published in 1890, while admitting that there are no official statistics available, computes that, as an inside estimate, the volume of traffic on the Volga during the open season amounts to 2,900,000,000 ton-miles. Besides several thousands of craft of various dimensions plying on the Volga, there is a fleet approaching 900 steamers, partly engaged in the towing of barges and partly in the conveyance of cargoes. In connexion with the traffic of the Volga and its tributaries there are some 5,000 large barges built yearly, many ranging from 300 to 500 tons, and a considerable number with a remarkable capacity, vieing with ocean steamers,—5,000 to 6,000 tons. Very few of these survive more than one voyage, when they are broken up for firewood. Although, as the crow flies, the Baltic Sea and the Caspian Sea are only separated by an interval of 1,250 miles, the inland navigation from Astrakhan to St. Petersburg is twice that figure; the route by the Marie Canal system, the one most in vogue, being 2,507 miles in length. We in this country, who send 8,000,000 tons of coal yearly to London by rail from the Midlands at forty miles per hour, are apt to smile at the speed with which the phlegmatic Russ is content on the Volga navigation. This slow rate of progression largely explains the reason why most of the vessels are broken up after a single voyage. After making due allowance for passing through locks, rapids, and other hindrances, the average voyage for sixteen hours per diem is twenty-four miles,—say, including the stoppages, one mile and a half hourly. This slow speed along 2,507 miles of navigation,—say twenty-four miles during each twenty-four hours, — averaging 105 days, coupled with a doubtful chance of obtaining a return cargo, has led to this general destroyal of these craft after a single journey.

What is known as the Marie Canal system is in effect a continuation of the navigation of the Volga from Rybinsk, which place is an extensive emporium for the commerce of the western provinces of European Russia, and finds, during the open navigation season, employment for 100,000 men and 5,000 craft. From the Caspian, the line of navigation by the Volga to Rybinsk is 1,794 miles. The distance from Rybinsk to St. Petersburg by the Marie Canal system is 713 miles. The principal traffic on the Marie Canal system consists of grain for St. Petersburg, and, notwithstanding the construction of railways connecting the fertile basin of the Volga with the Baltic ports during the last thirty years, the volume of traffic conveyed upon this navigation system has been doubled during that period. Fully recognising the growing expansion of traffic between the Volga grain districts and the Baltic Sea, the Ministry of Ways of Communication have decided to improve the Marie Canal system. The present locks of the Marie system for vessels 139 ft. 2 in. long, 28 ft. beam, with 4 ft. 8 in. draught are being superseded by locks of superior dimensions, namely, 227 ft. 6 in. in length, 34 ft. 2 in. beam, with 5 ft. 10 in. draught. The facilities thus being provided will enable vessels carrying 655 tons of grain to proceed right through to St. Petersburg without breaking bulk at Rybinsk, and thus save the cost of transhipment.

The second route, connecting Astrakhan with St. Petersburg, proceeds from the Volga a little above Rybinsk, whence it utilises its affluent, the River Mologa, thence by the River Tschagodolska, the Lake Volksjoe, the River and Lake Sominko, and the canalised River Voltzine—where the summit level is attained at an elevation of 570 above Lake Ladoga. Thence falling to the Ladoga Canal and proceeding by Lake Kronpino, it enters the Marie Canal system, after a course of 466 miles from the Volga. This route is far inferior to the Marie Canal system, which it falls into, though shorter, as it but affords passage for boats 63 ft. in length, 14 ft. beam, and the light draught of 2 ft. The last route to be mentioned as being a through chain of inland navigation between the Caspian and the Baltic Seas, though not the least in importance, and the first in a historic sense, was initiated through the enterprise of Peter the Great in 1698, after his famous tour of discovery throughout Europe in search of knowledge likely to be of advantage in the betterment of his own country. That monarch was induced by two considerations to connect by a series of short canals the navigable lakes and rivers intervening between Astrakhan and his newly-formed capital and Port of Petersburg, now denominated St. Petersburg. The principal object was the conveyance from the Caspian Sea to his new seat of Government of the rich products of Persia and the Orient generally. The other and equally important motive was that the provision of such facilities as would be thus afforded would also be of material advantage in a military sense, eventually as a valuable factor in defensive operations. This system commences from the Volga at Tver, a fortified city, the capital of the Government bearing that name, and an *entrepôt* for the commerce between Moscow and St. Petersburg. Proceeding from Tver by the river Twertza to the water-parting between the Baltic and Caspian catchment basins, which is traversed by the Twersk and Tsninsk Canals, it follows the river Msta, upon which the town of Vijni-Volotchok, is situated, from which the system is named, thence continuing by other rivers till it arrives at the Ladgosky Canals, which join the Neva at Schlüsselberg. The length of this system is 539 miles, of which only 31 miles are artificial waterways. It is navigated by trains of barges and rafts, and accommodates vessels 119 ft. in length, 28 ft. beam, but with only 2 ft. 2 in. draught. This shallowness has led to this route being, to a large extent, superseded by the Marie system.

The St. Petersburg or Pontiloff Ship Canal, which was opened for traffic on May 27, 1885, affords direct access to St. Petersburg for large vessels which had previously to load from or discharge into lighters in the Cronstadt roadstead. It extends from the Fortress of Cronstadt, which is situated on an islet at the head of the Gulf of Finland, to the Port of Goutouyeff, on an island of that name at the mouth of the Neva, immediately in front of St. Petersburg. This maritime canal, including about one mile of the Neva, is 18¼ miles in length, with a branch canal of 2¼ miles connecting the main line with the Catherinkoff mouth of the Neva, thus making in all 20½ miles. The minimum bottom width of the Pontiloff Canal is 210 ft. and the depth 22 ft. This navigation saves at least ten days' delay in arriving at St. Petersburg, and saves expenses equal to more than the amount of freight between that city and the United Kingdom. The total cost, including wharves at Port Goutouyeff and Pontiloff, has been 1,325,000*l*. The works were commenced in 1878 and completed in 1884. A small charge is made for the use of the wharves at Goutouyeff and Pontiloff. Three basins, with a collective area of 430 acres, have been formed by widening the canal for the accommodation of the import and export trade.

The White Sea and the Baltic Sea are connected by inland navigation, but the route is very circuitous. Vessels can ascend the river Dwina from Archangel to its affluent the Suchona, thence the navigation is continued by canals which connect the Lakes Kubinskoe, Bielozersk, Onega, and Ladoga, from which latter access is obtained to the Neva, and thence to the Gulf of Finland. A project has been under consideration since the time of Peter the Great for making a more direct avenue by way of Lake Onega which would save 1,000 miles, the present route being about 1,500 miles. The canal contemplated by the Russian Government is intended for the passage of barges of about 100 tons, and is computed to cost from 750,000*l*. to 1,000,000*l*.

Like the Baltic and Caspian Seas, the former sea and the Black Sea have been connected by several systems of inland navigation. The first of these was the enterprise of Stanislaus, the last King of Poland, about 1790, who made a canal which connects a tributary of the Western Bug with one of the Dnieper, this navigation being known as the King's Canal. Another inter-sea connecting canal is of Polish inception, connecting the river Stchava and the river Pripet, thus providing passage from the Niemen to the Dnieper, and consequently connecting the Baltic and Black Seas, the former at Memel and the latter at Kherson. This navigation is thirty-four miles in length, and affords an outlet for the agricultural produce of the intervening region principally to the Baltic Sea. This is known as the Oginsky Canal. A third route is formed by the Western Dwyna or Düna, thence by its affluent the Ulla, which is connected by a canal about thirty miles in length with a tributary of the Beresina, which is an affluent of the Dnieper. This connecting link is known as Beresinski Canal, which thus performs the function of placing Riga, on the gulf of that name, in connexion with the Black Sea at Kherson.

At the beginning of the eighteenth century Peter the Great devised the Ivanhoff Canal, to provide a passage from the Black Sea to the Caspian Sea, by uniting the Don with the Volga *viâ* Lake Ivan. This was realised at the beginning of the present century, but the passage from the Gulf of Taganrog to the Volga Delta at Astrakhan is too devious to be of practical use. A much more practicable project has received the approval of the Russian Government for the connexion of the Black Sea with the Caspian Sea by means of a navigable canal, a little over thirty-five miles in length, traversing the water parting between the Don and the Volga, which is formed by the Surpa Hills. The deepest cutting will be across the Surpa ridge, averaging 140 ft., and can be effected without difficulty. The Volga-Don Canal is estimated to cost 2,800,000*l*. It involves the construction of thirteen locks, which are to be constructed so as to contain at one time a couple of vessels of 210 ft. in length, 42 ft. in breadth, with 7 ft. draught. The Caspian Sea trade has attained dimensions that Peter the Great never dreamt of. The execution of the Volga-Don Canal, on the lines contemplated, would create trade of much larger proportions, and would largely restore Astrakhan its former prestige as the chief *entrepôt* for the commerce between Russia and Persia and the East generally.

Among recently-completed Russian canals is that connecting the rivers Vytegra and Kovja, which forms an additional link in the chain of navigation between the Caspian Sea and the Baltic. It was completed in July, 1886, at a cost of 350,000*l*. The surface width is 70 ft., the depth 7 ft., and the line of navigation 15½ miles. In 1887 the Russian Government raised 2,500,000*l*. for the bisection of the Isthmus of Perekop, which connects the Crimea with the mainland of South Russia. The line of navigation will be 73 miles, the surface width 12 ft., and the depth 12 ft. The works were commenced during 1888 under the direction of M. Louis Coiseau, one of the chief engineers of the Suez Canal. The total outlay is estimated at 8,000,000*l*. The voyage from Odessa to Maripol, round the Crimean Peninsula, is 434 nautical miles, while the Perekop Canal will lessen the distance to 295 nautical miles. The works were announced to be completed in 1893, but this is very doubtful, as the Russian Exchequer has more demands upon it than can be complied with. The *Gazette Russe* in the spring of 1891 commented severely on the neglect of the upper waters of the Volga navigation, which have become shallow through silt.

The primary reason for making the Perekop Canal has not been the exigency of commerce, but the necessity of quicker transit of the fuel required by the Black Sea Fleet from the Donetz collieries, and as affording greater security for coaling in emergency than by the open route around the Crimea. The capital outlay on the Perekop Canal would be much better applied and would be more in consonance with the wishes of the traders of Russia, if devoted to the efficient maintenance and improvements of the inland waterways. The roads of the Russian Empire, with the exception of that from St. Petersburg to Moscow, which is probably unrivalled in the world, are in a wretched condition. This, to a large extent, arises from their being covered with ice and snow for many months in the year, when sledge travelling is universal.

Space forbids a more detailed account of the extensive system of the inland waterways of Russia, but there is one, probably the longest inland navigation anywhere, situated within the limits of the Russian Empire which could not well be passed over without mention. There is a considerable volume of traffic between St. Petersburg and Pekin in the exchange of the several products of the two countries. In Transbaikalia, on the confines of the Mongolian frontier of China, there is a produce exchange of which the world in general hears but little.

The Russians and the Chinese, who are both zealous guardians of their respective frontiers, have effected a definite delimitation of the boundary-line by a long timber structure, which is the scene of the brokerage transactions concerned in the exchange of produce. One narrow exit on the north side of this international mart opens into the Russian dominions, another, on the south side, opening into the Chinese. That portion of the town on the north side contains the Russian community of Kiakhta, and that on the south the Chinese one of Mai-ma-tchin. At sunset a bell is rung, when transactions cease, and both parties retire within their respective boundaries. The Chinese chiefly transport their goods to Mai-ma-tchin on camels; it is five days' journey from Pekin to the Great Wall of China, and forty-five days more for the crossing of the Great Mongol Desert. From Kiakhta the goods are conveyed by water on the Salenga River, thence by the Lake Baikal, and *viâ* Irkutsk, by the Angara (or Upper Tunguska) to Yeniseisk, where that river enters the Yenisei. Here the break of sixty miles occurs, the goods having to be carried by land from Yeniseisk to Makoffskio-Ostwg, whence an avenue is formed by the Ket River to its confluence with the Obi River, which is traversed until that river is joined by the Irtish. From this point the Irtish is ascended as far as Tobolsk, which is a considerable centre for the inter-trade between Europe and China. A little above Tobolsk the route is continued from the Irtish by the Iset River, connected with the Tchusovaya River, which falls into the Kama River some twenty miles above Perm, the principal emporium of the Russo-China trade. The Kama joins the Volga near Spask, at a point fifty miles below Kasan on that river, the chief *entrepôt* for the inter-commerce between European Russia, Siberia and Bokhara. The length of this navigation system cannot be recisely stated, but, as the distance taken the crow flies from St. Petersburg to iakhta is 2,500 miles, it cannot well be less ian 4,000 miles. The caravan track from lai-ma-tchin to Pekin is 1,050 miles. It ight be said that a conveyance involving ,000 miles of inland navigation and 1,000 iles of overland transit would be so costly s to be prohibitory. Taking the two ex-remes of St. Petersburg and Pekin, the sea oute between the Peiho and the Neva, or ie Yellow Sea and the Gulf of Finland, *vid* ie Behring Straits and the Arctic Ocean, is bout 12,500 miles, and if by the Straits of lalecca and the Suez Canal, then the voyage ould be about 9,500 miles. This circuitous avigation traverses the greatest land-locked rea in the world, and collects and distributes raffic from regions remote from any sea-port.

NOTES.

ROBBING Peter to pay Paul is not a sensible way of doing business, but it is the principle on which the London County Council appear to be about to act in the xecution of work. The motion of Mr. Burns, amended by Sir T. Farrer, was carried n Friday last, and it pledges the Council to blige all contractors to pay the rate of vages and observe the hours of labour ecognised by the trade unions in the place vhere the contract is to be executed. Of ourse contractors will have no objection o this, since they will make the County Council, if necessary, pay a larger sum for the vork to be done. The persons who will uffer are the ratepayers of London: in other vords the general community of the Metro-polis will be to some extent taxed for the enefit of a particular class who happen t the present moment to be the most energetic ection of the electorate. This is simply nother form of protection, and does not in he least differ in principle from the old rotection abolished by Sir Robert Peel, which protected the agriculturalists of the ountry at the expense of the general com-unity of Great Britain. In the days of gricultural protection the farmers and land-ords were the strongest electoral force, now n the management of the affairs of the netropolis the artisan is the most powerful orce. The result of such a system of pro-ection is not to produce either better work or reater comfort for the artisan. For the naster must pay high wages simply because is so laid down by the Council, not because he workman is better, and this same high ate of wages will attract more men to the netropolis, so that the competition among the vorkmen is increased. After a certain period f time the folly of this system will probably e perceived by the general community of ondon.

WHEN we last alluded to the Durham miners' strike, there seemed to be very probability of an early settlement of his disastrous dispute; but two weeks more ave passed, and still no work is being done. When the men got so far as to offer to accept n immediate reduction of 10 per cent., it vould have been a satisfactory termination if he masters could have seen their way to llow a resumption of work on this basis. It ppears, however, that they were unable to o so, and it is not for any one unacquainted vith the extent of their losses to impute lame to them for the firm attitude which hey have taken up, though it was impossible o repress a feeling of disappointment at the ailure of negotiations which approached o nearly to a settlement of the ques-ion at issue. The proportion in favour of continuance of the strike had gradually windled down till a large majority vere in favour of a compromise; but the allot last Saturday on the question of sub-nitting to the full 13½ per cent. reduction, esulted in a majority of no fewer than 1,026 for resuming an attitude of non-urrender. The distress in the district must y this time be very acute,—though the statements with regard to its extent are rather confusing. The *Colliery Guardian*, for instance, remarks in a leader: "Possibly the case is overstated when, in the petition forwarded this week by the Cleveland Ironstone Miners' Association, it it said that 28,000 human beings are on the verge of starvation." While in an article on the subject in the very same issue (May 27) we read: "There cannot be less than 27,000 men idle through no fault of their own, and, with their families, some 140,000 persons must be on the verge of starvation." It must be regarded as fortunate that the mediation of the Bishop of Durham has been accepted, and we may now venture to predict an early settlement of the dispute with a much greater degree of certainty than before. Bishop Westcott,—who happens to have been presiding at a meeting of the Arbitration and Peace Association only this week,—is respected by both parties, and, in spite of being *ex officio* a royalty owner, can be trusted to approach the subject with impartiality, combined with a benevolent earnestness which will, we trust, result in healing the breach. [Since this was put into type, we are glad to learn that the mediation of the Bishop has been successful, and that the masters have agreed to reopen the pits at the 10 per cent. reduction originally proposed by them.]

THE Committee of the House of Commons which had under consideration the London Council's Bill in which this question of "betterment" was again raised, this time in reference to the proposed bridge at the west end of Cromwell-road, threw out this clause by the casting-vote of the chairman. The manner in which the principle of "betterment" was to be applied was by means of a rate on certain owners who might have been assumed to benefit by the bridge. It is just as well that the committee refused to sanction this principle, for the House of Commons itself had already done so, and there is no reason to suppose it would not have done so again. As we have more than once said, if the principle of "betterment" is to be allowed, it must be sanctioned by the Legislature and made applicable to the whole of England. But if this principle is adopted, it seems difficult logically to refuse to enlarge the principles of compensation. Thus, at present, persons get no compensation if the prospect or view of a house is spoilt by a work in respect of which property may be compulsorily taken. If, then, the vague "betterment" principle is to become law, it would be unfair not also to introduce an equally vague "worsement" principle. The more the question is looked at in a practical light, the more difficult also does the just application of any such principle appear, and, therefore, however specious it may seem at first sight, we are convinced it will never commend itself to the general sense of the community.

ALTHOUGH the Earl of Wemyss's amendment on Monday last, to make the provisions of the Water Companies' (Regulation of Powers) Bill applicable also to corporations which supplied water, was withdrawn,—and with good reason, as it would have led to an indefinite postponement of the measure,—the tone of the debate on the amendment was such as to leave no doubt that the question of regulating the powers of water-supplying corporations will be raised again before long. As Lord Grimthorpe pointed out, in the case of companies supplying water the corporation was always on the spot to watch the action of the companies; but when the corporation held the water-supply in its hands, there was no controlling power whatever over them, and any resistance to their action could only be made by a small man fighting a battle against a great corporation; a most unfair position for the consumer who had any cause of complaint. Water is a necessary of life and health, and in regard to the latter point the health of separate members of the community, or at all events the sanitary condition of separate houses, is a matter in which the community at large is practically interested. One house reduced to an insanitary condition for want of water may lead to disease which will affect or infect others in the neighbourhood: and as there is a growing tendency in the present day towards the theory that the water supply of a town should be undertaken by the municipal authorities, there is good reason for the demand that such authorities should be tied down from manipulating or cutting off the water supply in an injurious manner by any arbitrary and ill-judged exercise of official rights.

ON Friday, May 27, Dr. Oliver Lodge read before a full meeting of the Physical Society an interesting paper, reviewing the attempts that have been made to ascertain the relative motion of the ether and the earth. After pointing out the difficulties that arise in explaining astronomical aberration on the undulatory theory, and the consequent necessity of assuming that the ether is not stagnant, he proceeded to give an account of the various experiments that have been devised by Maxwell and others to prove that there must be at least a partial flux of ether with respect to the earth. The results were for the most part negative, though with great ingenuity it was shown that some that appeared negative were consistent with either hypothesis. The final conclusion was that the problem must still be considered unsolved. Without going into details, the question that naturally occurs to an outsider is: If the ether is not carried along with the earth, why should it move with the sun? and if it does not move with the sun, why take the earth's velocity in its orbit as the velocity of the earth relative to the ether?

THE Post Office service is gradually being released from many of the trammels which have so long hampered it, a large instalment of reforms being given to an appreciative public on June 1. Foremost among these is the abolition of the fee for re-directing letters,—no charge being now payable provided the letter is re-posted within twenty-four hours after delivery, and that it has not been opened. This regulation applies to letters only, and it will be advisable to procure a copy of the new rules for information as to exceptions and definitions. Under the latter heading mention may be made of the new classification of book-post matter, which is considerably extended, and now covers a much larger number of commercial, literary, and other documents than heretofore. The Post Office authorities are to be congratulated on their efforts to increase the efficiency and popularity of the service,—a policy contrasting very strongly with that which has been pursued in this Department in the not very remote past.

THE concessions referred to in the foregoing paragraph are rapidly reducing the number of counts in Mr. Henniker Heaton's formidable indictment of the Post-Office a year or two ago; but the "Member for Australia" is one of those indefatigable persons to whom such proverbs as "half a loaf is better than no bread" afford no excuse for slackening of exertion. The goal of "Imperial Penny Postage" is being more vigorously aimed at than ever, and in a pamphlet just circulated, Mr. Heaton gathers up and reiterates the forcible arguments which he has been persistently pressing upon the Government and the Postmaster-General for some years past. Although, of course, a strictly non-political question, our modern Postal reformer is evidently sorely disappointed at finding the Dissolution almost upon us without the change for which he has toiled so hard being accomplished by the Government of which he is a supporter. He has gone so far as to offer to furnish Bank guarantees against loss for a period of three years; but there seems to be some special obstacle which hinders the desired reform, the nature of which is not apparent.

The whole question, we should judge, turns upon the cost of transmission from shore to shore; for, as we are relieved of the distribution of outgoing letters in return for free delivery of those we receive, inland and foreign conditions are really equal in all respects, plus cost of conveyance abroad. Mr. Heaton argues that we are paying far more than we ought for this service; and that it should not cost the 150 per cent. above the inland rate which is now charged is evident from a comparison with the ridiculously low rates for the postage of newspapers, &c. If the loss on the postage of printed matter is so small that we can afford to carry 4 oz. of printed matter to any part of the world for a penny, the day cannot be far distant when a letter weighing half an ounce will cost no more. The point upon which we think Mr. Henniker Heaton is building too much is the great increase of correspondence he anticipates between emigrants and their friends. Probably commercial correspondence would increase considerably with a reduced postage; but we venture to suggest that it is frequently less a question of the few cents for the postage, than a disinclination for letter-writing, that affects the frequency with which the emigrant and "the old folks at home" correspond with each other.

THE daily papers state that the Terrace (which consists of sixteen houses) along the southern side of Kensington-road, and covering about four acres in all, was sold a few days ago for 170,000*l.* We are authoritatively informed that the purchase, being for building purposes, includes only Nos. 1—7 (Shaftesbury House) and the two cottages numbered 8 and 9. These houses have large gardens extending to Cheniston-gardens in the rear; whilst that of Shaftesbury House, No. 7, reaches much farther southwards. They have had many celebrated inhabitants. At No. 1 lived Sir Henry Cole, K.C.B.,—died April, 1882,—who was educated in the Blue-coat School, and to whom was due most of the success of the Exhibition in 1851. No. 6 was the home,—and, we understand, the last home,—of John Leech, where they show the screened attic he had made to lessen the annoyance by street-music, from which he suffered. Into No. 7, a home of the third Earl of Shaftesbury, author of the "Characteristicks"—but since rebuilt—Sir David Wilkie removed, in 1824, from No. 24, Lower Phillimore-place, on the opposite side of the main road. Coming up to London in 1805, Wilkie lodged in Chelsea; at No. 11, Norton- now Bolsover-street, Marylebone; and at No. 10, Sol's-row, by the southern end of Hampstead-road. In 1811, the year of his election as R.A., he went to a friend's house, No. 11, in Lower Phillimore-place, and shortly afterwards removed, with his mother and sister to No. 24. From Norton-street he sent, as Haydon tells us, his "Blind Fiddler" to the Academy Exhibition of 1806; and there he painted his "Village Politicians." At Kensington he did some of his best work, including the "Chelsea Pensioners" (1822) for the Duke of Wellington, and now, we believe, at Apsley House; the "Reading of the Will"; "Duncan Gray": "Blind Man's Buff"; the "Penny Wedding"; and the "Rabbit on the Wall." In 1825 he left the Terrace for a three years' stay on the continent,—a visit which wrought a change in both his style and class of subjects. For some while before he left England in 1840 for a tour in the East, Wilkie had occupied the present Maitland House, next to the barracks: in his day it stood in Vicarage-place, Church-street, Kensington.

ON Monday next Lord Rosebery will formally open Brockwell Hall Park. The park, about 78 acres in extent, lies on the rising ground between the road from Herne-hill to Lower Norwood,—to which it has a long frontage, lined with elm trees,—and Lower Tulse-hill. To the north lies that part of Water-lane which is now called Dulwich-road, and lies over the course of the Effra river. Six years ago the park was to have been taken over for building purposes, but after protracted negotiations has been secured for the public enjoyment. At the hual meeting of the Brockwell Park Committee, held on April 9 last, it was announced that the total purchase moneys, 119,500*l.*, are derived from the following contributions:—The Charity Commissioners, 25,000*l.* out of the surplus funds of the City Parochial charities; the vestry of Lambeth, just within which parish the estate lies, 20,000*l.*; the vestries of Camberwell and Newington, 6,000*l.* and 5,000*l.*; the Ecclesiastical Commissioners, 500*l.*; Mr. J. J. B. Blackburn, owner of the adjoining property, 2,000*l.*; and the London County Council, 61,000*l.* The last-named payment and that by the Charity Commission are made as including, in each case, a contribution of 12,500*l.*, which would otherwise have been payable in respect of Raleigh Park, Brixton, in the event of failure to secure this larger area: see our "Note" of September 3, 1887, and our report on August 3, 1889, of the Council's meeting of the previous Tuesday. Brockwell Hall was built, 1810, for John Blades, a glass dealer on Ludgate-hill, after the designs of D. Riddle Roper, architect. In 1829 the property, originally 60 acres, passed to Joshua Blackburn, his son-in-law.

THE groups of buildings at the head of the Mound immediately to the west of the Free Church College in Edinburgh, extending westward to and including Ramsay Lodge, have been acquired by a syndicate for the purpose of erecting on the site a set of chambers, to be used as students' quarters, studios, &c. The site is one of the finest in Edinburgh. From its high position overlooking Princes-street-gardens, the new buildings will form a conspicuous feature in the view looking southwards from that street. The existing buildings possess no architectural character, although an attempt was made by the proprietor, the late Lord Murray, to give some architectonic expression to the portion comprising Ramsay-gardens and Ramsay Lodge. The matter was placed in the hands of the late Mr. Billings, who attempted to improve Ramsay Lodge by the doubtful expedient of throwing out a heavy iron balcony. He also carried out a battlemented terrace in front of Ramsay-gardens, with a castellated lodge at its east end, but one morning, after heavy rain, the terrace and new lodge slipped into the valley below, and since then nothing further has been done to beautify the site. Ramsay Lodge was built by Allen Ramsay, the poet, as a residence for himself, and from the oddness of its form was known as "Allen's Luggy."* In Ramsay-gardens resided the late well-known editor of the *Scotsman*, Alexander Russell. At one time, it is stated, the Government was desirous of obtaining Ramsay-gardens as a site for military quarters, for which purpose it is most suitable, owing to its proximity to the Castle, but the negotiations for a purchase fell through. The chief drawback to the situation is the steepness of the access, which during a severe frost is rendered impassable to vehicular traffic. The plans for the new buildings have been prepared by Messrs. Sydney Mitchell & Wilson, and show a picturesque group, a conspicuous feature of which is a tower surmounting an archway over Ramsay-lane, which intersects the line of frontage. We understand that it will be some time ere actual building operations are commenced.

THE accommodation placed at the disposal of the Royal Commission on Metropolitan Water Supply cannot be deemed creditable to the authorities,—at any rate, so far as the room in which the inquiry is being held is concerned. This room is an awkwardly-shaped apartment on the third floor of Trafalgar-buildings, Charing Cross, at the Whitehall corner of Northumberland-avenue, in the building which was the temporary home of the National Liberal Club, and the room in question, if we mistake not, was the former grill-room of the Club. If the grill had been there this week the room could hardly have been warmer. The room is low in proportion to its size, and certainly inadequate to accommodate between fifty and sixty persons, the number present when we looked in on Monday afternoon. The sun was shining brightly and warmly on the windows, which had to be opened in order to avoid asphyxiation; and, to exclude the direct glare of the sun, the crimson blinds had to be drawn. The opening of the windows admitted not only air, but the noise of the street traffic, so that it was very difficult at times to hear the Commissioners' questions and the witnesses' answers; the drawing of the crimson blinds, which the sunbeams half penetrated, had the effect of imparting to the proceedings a hue strikingly in keeping with the *couleur de rose* view which some of the companies' witnesses seem inclined to take of the question, or of suggesting (most unwarrantably, no doubt) that the witnesses,—who sit facing the blinds, with the full red glare in their faces,—were blushing at the shortcomings of the companies, or were addicted to stronger libations than they themselves are concerned in supplying. Seriously, however, we think it is greatly to be regretted that no better accommodation could be provided for the holding of this important inquiry,—which affects the well-being of the whole of the inhabitants of London, and which is, indeed, of national importance,—than the room which we have described.

* Luggy—a wooden basin used for porridge and soup.

IT appears that there is some feeling in Berlin that German characters should be used in lieu of Latin ones on the new set of street-nomination plates which are about to be fixed at the corners of the thoroughfares in that city. This novelty would be a great nuisance to those non-Germans who visit th Prussian capital, and are not well acquainted with the German language. In a city which delights in the constant increase of non-German visitors and tourists, such so-called "patriotic" pettiness as is only shown in Russia need not make itself prominent. The German characters are even more unsuited for street signs that the Russian or Polis ones, on account of their elaborate lines. A Russian character can, at all events, be deciphered at some distance, even if it is no understood.

ARCHITECTURE AT THE ROYAL ACADEMY.—VI.

1,755; "Nos. 190 and 191 Queen's Gate, Sout Kensington;" Mr. F. G. Knight. This is th drawing published in the *Builder* of Feb ruary 13 of this year. The houses are goo examples of the modern brick London architec ture. The fronts are very simply treated, bu the variations in the treatment of windows an other details give a certain interest to ever part, and it is noticeable how the same features —the bay window, the porch, the gable, &c.,— are varied so as to give each house a distinc character, yet keeping them sufficiently in har mony with each other as two contiguous stree fronts.

1,757; "Design for Free Library, Stok Newington;" Mr. Ernest Rüntz. This is very nice unpretending little coloured elevatio in brick, to which interest is given by the treat ment of the windows in accordance with neces sities of the interior. A plan is added.

1,759; "Nymans, near Crawley;" Mr. Leonar Stokes. This is a sensible way of showing th additions to a house; a plan is given showin the added portions in black, and a sketch of th original house given in the corner. The ol house was an oblong mass with an entranc door flat in the wall and a single bay windov marking the dining-room, on one side of it. Th architect has thrown out a square porch whic rises above into a short tower breaking the lin of the eaves; the bay is finished with gables i concave curves and a spare panel of carving o the front face; a similar gable is added to th extension on the right; to right of this a large wing is thrown out, of which the ground floor is a billiard-room with an open verandah round it forming circular pavilions at the angles; these are only on the ground floor. Is there enough light for the billiard-room? is the only question. The plan shows various smaller internal alterations. The house has been given character and picturesqueness, in a reserved and quiet manner. The projections of the eaves appear to have been increased, giving a strong shadow. We recommend others who exhibit drawings of additions to old houses to follow Mr. Stokes's example, and send drawings which show intelligibly what the additions are.

1,758; "Drawing of the Crucifixion at St. Rémi, Rheims;" Mr. J. P. Seddon. A small but apparently careful copy in colour of this curious and interesting piece of ancient stained glass, in which the crucified figure occupies the centre long panel, the arms extending on two cross panels, over two saints in the side panels. Beneath the feet of the crucifix are the symbols of the cross and a face probably representing the sun, the symbol of Christ as the light of the world.

1,760; "The Tate Library, Brixton;" Mr. Sidney R. J. Smith. This is a pen perspective effectively executed, giving some additional interest thereby to a design which is suitable and solid-looking, but not of very much architectural interest.

1,761; "Coats Memorial Church, Paisley: Entrance Front;" Mr. Hippolyte J. Blanc. A pencil perspective sketch executed in a masterly manner, with firm yet free touch. It shows the west end of a Gothic church approached by a very lofty flight of steps, at the top of which is a triple porch of somewhat Continental character, a large west window above, and the whole flanked by octagonal turrets which spread out the composition and add much to the effect of the whole, but there is no plan to show their function. Presumably they are stair turrets. The lower portion of a tower is shown in the rear. The whole is a very powerful composition, though the west window strikes us as of rather coarse design.

1,762; "No. 191, Queen's Gate, South Kensington: Hall and Staircase;" Mr. F. G. Knight. This is the interior published in the *Builder* of March 17, to which we refer the reader. It is a pleasant bit of staircase architecture, but it seems a pity to repeat in these days the old illogical use of a square block of architecture mounted on the top of a column.

1,765; "Church of the Good Shepherd, Gospel Oak: South-east View;" Messrs. James Brooks & Sons. A beautifully-executed pen drawing, showing the exterior perspective of a church in true Gothic spirit, but without being a mere copy of old Gothic. As the grouping of the building is peculiar, it is a great pity that a small plan was not added to explain it. It appears to present a nave with three aisles of nearly equal height, all terminating in gables, and low narrow side-aisles for passage. The buttresses are treated in an unusual and very massive manner, in lines sloping outwards between the set-offs. There is a double-gabled transept, against which the low lean-to aisles stop; the middle aisle of the nave is flanked by turrets partly attached into the walls. The windows are simply treated in Early Gothic style, with a little geometric tracery in the heads of some of them. The remarkable point about the church is the look of monumental massiveness and solidity which it presents.

1,766; "Part of Second Court, St. John's College, Cambridge;" Mr. W. H. Thorp. An artistic little sketch, with a good deal of haracter in it.

1,767; "Convent of Sta. Paula, Seville, Spain:)oorway;" Mr. A. N. Prentice. A coloured levation, "measured and coloured on the spot" nd as such of value and highly creditable to he artist. It shows a Gothic doorway in thin ourses of darker and lighter bricks, with a road band of elaborate tiled (?) ornament over ;, with circular medallions painted with small gure subjects. This and the decoration in the pandrels of the arch are very carefully and inutely shown, and the drawing is a valuable ecord of design and colour.

1,768; "Battersea Polytechnic Institution;" Ir. E. W. Mountford. As a drawing this is ot very effective in execution, and seems to ave been hurriedly executed; it is drawn in pen nd tinted in a rather showy style in Indian nk. The grouping, with the two narrower Elizabethan-like gables grouped in the centre, and the larger straight-lined gables at the end wings, is effective, and the three stories are well contrasted in the intervening portions of the front, in regard to the treatment of the windows; the ground story has a large semicircular headed window in each bay, above are two long windows coupled, and the upper story, just under the roof, has small circular windows between Elizabethan-like pilasters. For an institution of this kind it is a dignified and suitable front, but just falls short of being architecturally interesting, for which the style of the drawing may be partly to blame.

1,769; "Cottages, Eaton Hastings, Berks;" Messrs. Ernest George & Peto. Very charming cottages in a simple unpretending Old English style, with the form of low mullioned windows which is more conducive to domestic happiness in humble life than any other form; we cannot give a reason, but we are convinced that it is so. Whether the ornaments of balls and nine-pins on the top or at the foot of the gables add to the effect may be questioned. They are simple enough ornament, undoubtedly, but just a little worn-out.

1,770; "New Premises, Heath-street, Hampstead;" Mr. Keith D. Young. Not very attractive at first sight, but this is a capital little water-colour drawing, and shows a good solid treatment of shop-fronts with three-centred arches over the large windows; and the octagon turret over the angle gives a certain distinctive character to the block, which is carried out in brick with light-coloured stone dressings.

1,771; "Pastoral Staff for the Bishop of St. Asaph, designed by the late J. D. Sedding;" Mr. H. Wilson. The drawing is by Mr. Wilson, and is a water-colour drawing which is quite a study in colour and texture. The staff takes the orthodox form of a knop with a crook and a little sculpture subject (Christ's Charge to Peter) within the crook; but the details are treated with the freedom and originality usual in the late Mr. Sedding's work. Above the knop is a little shrine of two stories of niches with small figures in them, the spandrels over the niches being filled up with delicate foliage of a more unconventional type than in Mediæval work. The side face of the crook is lined out up the centre by a small continuous ornament of repeated leaves on either side of a stem, interrupted at intervals by jewels. The whole is a very refined piece of work.

1,772; "Reredos in South Transept, St. Alban's, Teddington;" Mr. A. H. Skipworth. A pencil elevation showing a square panel above the altar, of the same width, with a late Gothic moulding and the usual "perpendicular" square flower enrichment, and an enriched cornice with angels and shields; above this are three niches with canopies, and figures on octagonal pedestals, which are designed in imitation of work in Henry VII.'s Chapel; this was done "by request," so the architect is not responsible for the choice. This part of the work, however, appears rather heavy in comparison with the cornice below, which does not seem to give it sufficient support. A panelled screen the height of the vaulting impost of the church forms a background to the whole.

1,775; "The Wern, Tremadoc, N. Wales: alterations and additions"; Messrs. Douglas & Fordham. This is one of Mr. Hodkinson's fine sepia drawings; there is nothing to show what are the alterations and what is original; the greater part of the house is in a solid Gothic style with mullioned windows, the porch on the left and the portion to left of it, with lofty mullioned windows, appear like part of an old Jacobean house; but what is new and what is old we can only conjecture. It seems extraordinary to us that so many architects in these cases should be content (apparently) with merely getting a good draughtsman to make a drawing which "will get into the Academy," and leave the reason and method of their work entirely unintelligible.

1,776; "Mission Hospital, Jerusalem;" Mr. Beresford Pite. This is a frame of very prettily-executed coloured geometrical drawings, two sections, elevation and plan. The work is treated in an Oriental style, with wooden verandahs ornamented by pierced work in the upper part, and there is a low eastern-looking dome over the entrance-hall. The plan is that of a pavilion hospital with large wards for men and smaller ones for women on the opposite sides of the corridors, an isolation ward and private ward divided up into small rooms or cubicles. Whether the arrangement of the administration portion in similar blocks on each side of the entrance, but not closely connected, would be convenient, may be a question. There is a refreshing originality about the work and the manner of showing it in the drawings.

1,778; "Bury Municipal Buildings;" Mr. A. N. Bromley. This gives the perspective view of the building accompanied by a small plan. The site is triangular, and the reception rooms occupy the greater portion of the principal front. The Sessions-house is in the centre of the building parallel with the main front, and the principal committee-rooms in convenient proximity with it in an adjoining portion off one of the main corridors. The defect of the plan is that the all-round communication is not complete, being blocked at one angle. Architecturally the building is effectively grouped as a whole, but the details are rather commonplace.

1,780, "Design for Stained-glass Window: Tree of Jesse;" by Mr. G. W. Rhead. This is a pencil drawing showing only the linear design without the colour; it is to be commended both for the well-filled effect of the design, and for the conventional and decorative treatment of the "tree," which takes the form of branching scroll-work of Early Gothic character: Jesse "trees" are too often treated in a too realistic manner.

1,781; "Monument to the late Mrs. Rowley, St. Neots;" Mr. F. A. Walters. This is the design which was published in the *Builder* of May 7, and is a fine modern example of a monument in a Mediæval form. The monumental figure lies under a richly-foiled canopy arch, with a lofty and richly-decorated ogee gable rising over it, terminating in a finial which forms part of the bracket for the central figure of the group in niches at the top of the composition. The space above and on either side of the ogee is divided by mullions which rise into pinnacles dividing the niches at the top. Angels are sculptured in bas relief here, holding shields, their figures and wings crossing and breaking up the vertical lines of the mullions. The effect of the whole ought to be very fine and decorative in execution. The figures are nearly life-size.

1,783; "Stables, Pewsham, Wilts;" Mr. C. E. Ponting. Two drawings executed on brown toned paper and whitened where the plaster covering occurs on the building, as in another drawing by the same architect, already referred to. The stables are quietly picturesque in appearance, but owe something of their effect to the manner of execution of the drawings, which gives a certain degree of exceptional character.

1,784; "Design for a Small Country House;" Mr. G. C. Horsley. Two small elevations, slightly tinted, and two plans, and (a detail often forgotten) the north and south point shown in connexion with the plans. The design is of a quiet cottage-like type with mullioned windows.

1,785; "Convent of St. Marcos, Leon, Spain: Façade;" Mr. A. N. Prentice. This is a delicate little coloured elevation of a façade of plateresque architecture, with a "fronton" looking something like a big timepiece breaking the line over the central arch, but a delightful and interesting specimen of Spanish Renaissance of this type. The drawing, stated in the margin to have been measured and coloured on the spot, is executed with remarkable delicacy, and is a high credit to the patience and taste of its author.

1,786; "Nos. 39 and 40, Margaret-street, Cavendish-square;" Mr. F. L. Pearson. Street fronts in red brick, with a variegated skyline formed by a large scroll at each side and two semicircular gablets in the middle. On the ground floor a shallow segmental arch is carried right across each front, grouping the door and ground-floor windows under it, and offering an apparent support to the balconies. The windows are treated with brick mullions and brick mouldings over them, the whole being carried out conscientiously in a brick style which is suitable, but of which the details are not very interesting. One is always glad, however, to see a complete brick front for a street house, as a protest against the inferior and patchwork effect of "brick with stone dressings."

A NEW CLOCK has just been fixed at the new training stable, Newmarket, to the order of Captain Heston, of Stetchworth-park. This clock was made by Mr. J. W. Benson, of Ludgate-hill. It shows time upon a dial 3 ft. 3 in. diameter (illuminated by electric light), and strikes the hours upon a 2-cwt. bell.

LETTER FROM PARIS.

A few days since the posthumous exhibition of the works of Ribot was opened at the Ecole des Beaux-Arts. By general consent this exhibition, which is closed to-day, is one of the finest and most interesting exhibitions for some time past. The collected works were not numerous; the 150 pictures and 170 drawings had been carefully selected, and formed a compendium of the work of the old artist who was great and original, and showed a sincere love of Nature, even in his mistakes. We had his copies of Watteau, done in the period of his early struggles; then his studies from everyday life, humble interiors, peasant girls at work; small pictures valuable for the minute care expended on their execution. His portraits also must be mentioned, so powerful in their light and shade effects, and a few great pictures as vigorous as those of Ribeira. Then the drawings and studies showing the inner work of his artist life, his knowledge and his industry combined. This fine exhibition has added much to his posthumous renown.

Though the Salon of the Champs Elysées has still a month to remain open, the members of the Société des Artistes Français are already organising the jury for their next year's exhibition. The painters propose to appoint, for three years, sixty jurors chosen from among those who have received honours and those who have exhibited at least five times. Twenty members from among these would be chosen by lot each year. It remains to be seen whether this arrangement will give any more satisfaction to the easily dissatisfied tribe of artists.

In the section of engraving, the médaille d'honneur has been given, by thirty-one out of fifty-two votes, to M. Paul Mauron. This artist, a native of Avignon, has exhibited this year two fine lithographs, a "Tête de Mérovingien," after J. P. Laurens, and "La Tentation," after Bourgonnier.

At the Hôtel Drouot there has been a sale recently of the works of the painter Andrieu, not very much known except as a pupil of Delacroix who had acquired the art of copying in a curious fashion the style and colouring of his master. One result is that a good many drawings were sold on this occasion under the name of Delacroix, which were probably only clever repetitions of the work of that master. The regular picture dealers kept in the background and left to some amateurs the satisfaction of having, as they supposed, obtained original works by Delacroix at a very low price. Among the works sold were a whole series of sketches of the decorations executed by him for the Salon de la Paix in the old Hôtel de Ville. These pictures, the authenticity of which is not disputed, have been purchased by the Municipality, which has rightly wished to obtain and preserve these unpublished documents of a fine work by the master, now destroyed.

It is announced that the house in the Rue de Furstenberg, where Delacroix long lived and worked, has been distinguished by a marble slab affixed to it, recording the date of his birth and death. His studio still exists and is now occupied by a talented painter, M. Maillard.

A Parisian journal has published recently a decorative composition commissioned by the Government from M. Joseph Blanc, and which is to be reproduced at the Gobelins manufactory. It appears to be intended that this tapestry should figure at diplomatic audiences, and should accompany M. le Président on his journeys, in order to decorate the places where official receptions are held in his honour. It is a curious idea, and it hardly seems that the head of the State ought to require, to keep up his personal prestige, a "toile du fond," as they say in the theatre, packed up amid the Presidential luggage and displayed wherever he stops on his journey; a kind of accessory which will be more likely to create a smile than to impress the imagination of the crowd. It is said, however, that the procedure is not without precedent, and that in former days the Kings of France, when they went about, were followed also by their State tapestries which successively adorned all the châteaux where they stayed. In the present day of plainer manners travelling decorations can hardly be considered a necessity, and M. Carnot, who in his tastes and character is simplicity itself, would be the last person to wish for such accompaniments. As for the composition of M. Blanc, it represents in the centre (always according to aforesaid journal) the monogram of the Republic surrounded by the collar of the Order of the Legion of Honour. On each side of the central *motif* is seated an allegorical figure, the one representing Truth, the other Justice. Above, a child or genius with difficulty restrains the ardour of the emblematic bird of Gaul, represented in full crow. At the bottom reposes a lion, emblem of the popular power,* kept in restrain, by chains of flowers held by two Cupids. Flags and attributes relating to Agriculture, Commerce, and the Arts, fill up the composition. Taking into consideration, however, the proverbial slowness of work at the Gobelins, it will probably be four or five years before this piece of official decoration is completed, and it is generally thought that it will prove to be an "immeuble" in the literal sense, and will never enter in its travels.

The Louvre has acquired for the department of modern sculpture two fine busts by Carpeaux, that of M. Delaborde of the Institut, and that of M. Fiocre, who, under the second Empire, was a brilliant operatic star. The Cluny museum has obtained a curious miniature in oil representing Benvenuto Cellini, and some splendid Arab textiles of the Byzantine epoch, resembling those preserved in the treasury of St. Sernin at Toulouse.

The mortuary dépot constructed at Père la Chaise has just been inaugurated. It is the first establishment of the kind in Paris, and is expected to be of great service to the poorer classes of the population. The general style is naturally very sober; the interior arrangements are most carefully carried out. The floor in the halls is in mosaic; the walls, painted in oils, are bordered with a wainscot of black marble. All the work has been directed by the architect, M. Formigé, who has for a long time been studying similar establishments in other countries. In the Church of Notre Dame des Champs a mural decoration has just been inaugurated. It has been executed by M. Joseph Aubert, and represents "The Glorification of Our Lady of the Fields," the patron of horticulturists and the cultivators of the environs of Paris. This important work has been under the direction of M. Ginain, architect. It is announced that the new Minister of Public Works, M. Viette, has the firm intention of carrying out the study of metropolitan railway working, already begun by his predecessor. Will some happy solution come to him soon? We can hardly think so, though the Minister has expressed his willingness to present it to Parliament by the end of June. We may notice in passing, that the pictures, pastels, and sketches of Mdme. Bertha Morisot are now on view in the Boussod-Valadon Gallery in Boulevard Montmatre. Mdme. Morisot was sister-in-law of the painter Manet, and one of his best pupils.

The recent death of the painter on enamel, Claudius Popelin, has been a serious artistic loss. Popelin was born at Paris in 1825, and studied first under Picot and Ary Scheffer, and made his début in the Salon in 1852 by a remarkable picture, "Dante reading his poems to Giotto." From 1860 he gave himself almost exclusively to enamel painting, and produced in this form his portraits of Julius Cæsar, Pico de la Mirandola, Napoléon III., &c., and a composition called the "Renaissance of Literature," which gained him a medal in the 1865 Salon. He had not exhibited since 1867, but continued to execute remarkable enamels. He published also various works, notably one entitled "Cinq Octaves de Sonnets," illustrated by engravings of his own. He leaves a son, M. Gustave Popelin, also a painter of great talent, who gained the Prix de Rome in 1882.

The English Iron Trade.—The news of the termination of the Durham miners' strike will be welcomed on all sides, as there is now a probability of business returning to its normal level. By the intercession of the Bishop of Durham the masters have been induced to accept an immediate reduction of 10 per cent. With the near approach of the holidays there is little doing in the English iron market. In most of the crude-iron centres a quiet tone is observable; but rates, generally, are firm. Manufactured iron is in sluggish request. Tin-plates are in fair demand; but the steel market shows little inquiry. Shipbuilders and engineers are only moderately employed. The coal trade generally exhibits fair movement.—*Iron*.

* Tennyson came near anticipating this emblem, in the picture symbolising The People in the "Palace of Art,"—

"Here played, a tiger, rolling to and fro
The heads and crowns of kings."

The present emblematic animal seems to be, however, "a very gentle beast, with a good conscience."

THE ROYAL INSTITUTE OF BRITISH ARCHITECTS:

CASTINGS IN METAL.

The fourteenth general meeting of this Institute for the present session was held at Conduit-street on Monday evening last, the President, Mr. J. Macvicar Anderson, in the chair.

The minutes having been confirmed, the Secretary read a long list of gentlemen nominated for election as Fellows, Associates, and Honorary Corresponding Members.

The President said that as they had a somewhat full programme to get through that evening, he should not venture to occupy their time with any remarks of his own. There were no fewer than four papers to be read, the first of which would be by Mr. Alexander Graham. Before calling upon Mr. Graham he wished to intimate with regret that Mr. Alfred Gilbert was unable to be with them on that occasion; he much regretted his inability to attend. An interesting letter had also been received from Mr. Alma Tadema, regretting his inability to be present.

Mr. Alexander Graham, F.S.A., then read a paper giving an interesting historical outline of the application of metals to architectural design in all countries.

The Precious Metals.

Mr. C. Krall followed with a paper on working in the precious metals. The following is an abstract:—

The structural and main features of architecture being never, or very rarely, cast in precious metals, the author dealt with those of furniture, decoration, and articles of use, in which gold and silver had been employed in all ages down to the present. It was surprising, on investigating what parts of such work should be cast as against parts made of hammered plates, to find how limited the legitimate use of casting in precious metal was; while, apart from its intrinsic value, the quality of the heavier cast silver and gold work was very inferior to wrought. First among the legitimate uses of cast work was high relief sculptured work, that was, all such parts which would first be modelled in clay or wax, and which, to work by hand, meant a great deal of costly and tedious handwork, and necessitated a number of solder lines. Thus a figure or animal 4 in. high, with legs and arms or wings projecting, would be cast. Secondly, the decorated mouldings with patterns that repeat, and all such parts which, offering resistance, required greater thickness of metal than could easily be worked out of sheet-metal. Thirdly, the number of repeating ornaments, perforated borders, and crestings, of which a few copies only were required, and which would not justify the engraving of a steel die for stamping. A figure, 18 in. high, however, would rarely be cast, particularly when modelled in high relief. This would be embossed out of thin plate, as a whole or in sections, and soldered together or nailed down to the wooden or other foundation,—a process used by the ancients, and in Byzantine art as well in the present day. Precious metal was never cast in its pure and soft state, but was used in its harder alloys, the composition varying according to the colour and the amount of hardness desired. The process of casting flat work, mouldings, and ornament, was by the sand moulds; that of hollow work, with sand cores and by the wax process. The latter was the better for uniform thickness. By sand moulds the thickness varied greatly, which caused the thicker parts, in cooling, often to fall in, which was very detrimental to the work, and often impossible to correct. Knowing what parts should be cast, the designer would work with great advantage, and in many cases effect an easier and cheaper working. Silver and gold work was not now, he was glad to say, estimated chiefly by its weightiness; the lighter it was, the more carefully it must be made, so as to be strong in all its parts. In designing silver and gold work it must be borne in mind that even plain mouldings did not always turn out satisfactorily in cast work; and that for all better work they were made in flat or turned up in sections of wrought tough metal and joined together. Mouldings suitable for stone or wood should not be introduced. Old work should be examined, much of which was to be found in the museums, and in which it would be found that the mouldings affording the greatest charm were mostly very indistinct and often mere repetions of lines or combinations of squares and und wires, with now and then a hollow and twisted wire between. The old goldsmiths ad no lathes and no machinery; they filed, graved, swatched, or rolled their mouldings; nd for tracery work soldered one plate above gether, with a round wire sometimes laid ver it. Mr. Krall concluded by exhorting signers to study the old work and learn its ysteries, and to let designs be carried out nder its influence; then, whether cast or rought, or made by any other process, the ork would give satisfaction, and give delight oth in the present and in the future.

Castings in Iron.

Mr. H. Longden read the third paper, on stings in iron. He said that in the usual rocess of iron-founding, wooden models were ade by skilled model-makers, whose training as quite apart from that of a carpenter or binet-maker. The sides of the model or any lieved parts must not be square, but slightly stripped" or bevelled to ease the draught from e sand. The model was laid on a board on e floor of the foundry which was covered ith sand, a cast-iron casting box, called the bottom box," which was put on the board ver the model, and the foundry sand sifted pon the model, first through fine riddles until e whole surface of the model was equally overed with it, and then through a coarser ddle. The sand was carefully and evenly mmed with iron rammers until the box as filled. The whole was then turned over, nd the board which was cramped to the ox taken off, and the "top box" was put n, and the filling with sand and ramming rocess was repeated until the model was ompletely enclosed in evenly, lightly, and yet rmly rammed sand. The making of the hannels through which the molten iron was to e run into the sand matrices was an important atter, and had to be carefully arranged. The top box" was then removed and the model ken out, leaving a beautiful impress of the rnament, if any in the sand, which was carelly dusted over with fine-ground charcoal. Where the surface of a casting was to be full of rnament, the model was often put in again nd evenly pressed upon the charcoal to give e fine surface seen on good castings; and this ust be done with perfect accuracy of "register," e slightest inaccuracy blurring the impress. e two boxes were then cramped together ain with iron cramp and wedged with wooden dges. Casting with cores was another kind moulding, and one requiring much skill and tience. If a great number of castings were quired, instead of a wooden model cast-iron odels were used. Wooden models were somenes carved, and at others made the groundork of modelling in wax or in gesso if the effect sired were specially soft. There was also a very etty process called "reversing" by which a sting may be made from a solid block in aster or wood. The choice of the iron for stings was an important matter, different ixtures being used for different castings. ost of the iron now used was smelted from e ore by "hot-blast," but when great strength d tenacity were wanted the older fashioned old-blast" was still utilised. When the iron s melted in the cupola, or furnace, the casting gan. The furnace was "tapped" near the ttom with an iron bar, the white hot molten n ran down a spout prepared for it into lles of iron protected from being burnt by nd. The ladles were carried by the moulders the casting boxes and the molten metal ured through the gates or channels into the ace prepared for it in the casting boxes. hen the iron had been long enough in the nd to set, the top box was taken off and the sting taken up with the tongs, the loose sand out it removed, the gates knocked off, and it s reared up to cool until the next morning. st-iron some time ago had fallen into a rtain disrepute; but with the further study of terials it had been found that it had qualis of cheapness and usefulness as well as reproducing a suitable model with perfect ecision and delicacy. In designing for castn, it was to be remembered that when the odels were paid for, enrichments cost nothing suitably applied. This facility for ornament, hough a temptation to the unwary, in the nds of a master produced fine results. The nament, if applied, should rarely rise to much lief. A front for a fire must have a due prortion between its parts; the bars must be of e right plan and section; a grating must be irly even in the thicknesses of the parts; a casting should not be enclosed with heavy mouldings like a frame; and many other rules, simple and reasonable, could be learnt from any competent founder. Mr. Longden concluded with the opinion that respect for the real conditions of the work to be done, as was always the case, would produce a finer effect than clever *tours-de-force*, such as imitating wrought-iron, stone, or wood in cast-iron.

Castings in Bronze.

This was the subject of the fourth and last paper, read by Mr. Herbert Singer, and of which the following is an abstract:—

The author considered the subject of bronze castings a very wide one; the most ancient metallic objects yet discovered having been made of it. Pure bronze was simply nine parts of copper and one of tin. A vast number of alloys, however, were produced for different purposes, and the Japanese were said to use 200 distinct alloys; delicate colours depending on the alloy used. The author, having referred to the ancient knowledge of the existence of tin in Great Britain, was of opinion that the proportion of five parts copper and one tin was the alloy of the bronze implements of the ancients. It gave a hard substance, but would not suit many of the bronze productions of the present day. The brothers Keller, who worked in France in 1699, used for their alloy 91½ parts of copper, 5½ parts of zinc, 1¾ of tin, and 1¼ of lead for statuary work; others used only about 82 parts of copper. The sculptors during the Renaissance were often their own founders, and generally used a metal of good quality, in order that their work might not be injured in the casting. Having referred to the alloys of brass and the contraction inevitable in the use of copper, Mr. Singer thought bronze statuary would be a more exact reproduction of the sculptor's model if an alloy similar to bismuth could be found that would give no contraction. If bismuth were not so expensive it could be used with great advantage in the composition of bronze. The subject of alloy led to that of soldering. The Romans had not used solder, but it evidently had been used by the Saxons. The alloy for gold solder was silver, for silver solder silver and brass, and for bronze a mixture with brass made a good solder. The two processes of casting bronze into any required form were known as the "sand" and the "*cire perdue*." The founders of early ages used the wax, or latter process; but it had not been and was not so much practised in France as in Italy, perhaps because a very fine sand could be found near Paris by which the best castings by the "sand" process could be produced. This sand was also much exported, both to England and America. Mr. Singer then proceeded to describe moulding by the sand process. For statues of more than life-size it was necessary to have a lofty foundry in order to raise the large flasks from the pit in which the large pieces of metal were cast. The pit should be at least 12 ft. square and 10 ft. to 12 ft. deep. The flask for a statue 10 ft. in height would weigh 5 tons or 6 tons and should be so constructed of plates that it could be increased or reduced in size to suit the dimensions of the model. The model to be cast being then placed in the flask partly filled with sand, the preparation of the mould was commenced. The making of the mould, which had been well described by Mr. George Simonds as the concave or negative imprint from which the positive or convex imprint was to be obtained, would sometimes take three months, according to the number of pieces. The core had then to be prepared, and was a rough copy in sand of the original model, slightly reduced in size over the whole surface; the difference between the size of the core and the model giving the thickness of the bronze casting. The core was held in place by iron bars so as to leave half an inch of space between the exterior face of the model and the interior face of the mould. The mould and core being thoroughly dried, the flask was then lowered into the pit, and the molten metal run in. The flask, if all had gone well, being unscrewed, and the runners, or channels, which conveyed the metal to different parts of the mould being cut off, there should be but little work to complete the bronze statue. For the "*cire perdue*" or "lost wax" process a very different method was followed. After describing the old process adopted by Cellini of building up the core first, Mr. Singer dealt with the present mode in which the plaster moulder and the bronze founder relieved the sculptor of the mechanical part of the work. The sculptor modelled the work in clay or wax, the plaster moulder reproducing it in plaster, making probably several copies; one was handed to the bronze founder, whose first duty was to make an exact reproduction in moulder's wax, with a core inside it. He might effect this with a gelatine or a piece-mould,—according to the subject. If a piece-mould, the work was laid down and the lower part covered with clay; upon the upper part the liquid plaster, of the consistency of thick cream, was moulded into appropriate forms fitting together; the whole being protected and kept together by one large outside piece. The upper part being completed, the work was turned over, the clay from the lower part removed, and it was treated in the same way as the upper part. If using gelatine, the moulder covered the work with clay of the thickness the gelatine needed to be, and on the clay he formed two coats of plaster to keep the work steady. The clay was then removed, and the gelatine poured into the place it had occupied,—a mould of gelatine being the result. Having, whether by the piece-mould or gelatine method, obtained a complete mould the moulder formed a core inside it. The mould being taken apart, the core was pared down to allow as much space between it and the mould as the metal should occupy. The mould being put together again with the pared core inside, the wax was poured in, producing an exact reproduction of the original model. The wax was then handed to the sculptor, who removed all seams and generally "touched it up." Being returned to the moulder, he then made the mould to form the metal, which mould was composed of a substance, kept secret by most founders, applied in layers until there was a tolerably thick coating all over the work. A cage made of iron was then formed round the work, and sand rammed between the spaces. The whole being placed in a muffle, the wax was melted by means of gas, the mould thoroughly dried, and, while still hot, taken out of the cage, and, if necessary, placed in an iron flask and the metal poured in. It only remained to open the mould, remove the core, clean the casting, take off the runners, and apply the patina. An eminent sculptor had described the wax method of bronze-founding as an art, the sand as a trade. He (Mr. Singer) considered that an exaggeration. For some work, and where cost was an object, the sand process was the best. For others, especially where casting of the highest excellence was required, the wax process was the one to use.

A discussion followed, in which Messrs. J. M Brydon, Onslow Ford, George Simonds, Starkie Gardner, G. Aitchison, H. H. Statham, W. White, Sidney Vacher, and H. R. Pinker took part, and a vote of thanks to the readers of the papers having been carried by acclamation, Mr. Singer and Mr. Alexander Graham replied to some of the points raised in the course of the discussion, of which we will give a summarised report next week.

It was announced that the next meeting of the Institute (which will be a business meeting) will be held on Monday, June 13.

THE ROYAL COMMISSION ON METROPOLITAN WATER-SUPPLY.

THE Commissioners have held three sittings this week, and their inquiries have been mainly on the lines indicated in last week's *Builder*, with respect to the two companies first taken in hand. As the New River and the East London Companies* draw their primary supplies from the Lea, its conservators followed the companies with evidence as to the quantity and quality or purity of the water. The witnesses put forward by other companies were examined upon statements previously sent in by the companies at the request of the Commission. The examination in each case resolved itself into a rigid scrutiny of facts and figures as to present and future sources of supply, storage capacity, areas for filtration, machinery for pumping, actual and prospective supplies in proportion to population, the methods of ascertaining the population, and hsing the average of supply per head per day, and the data for determining the growth of population, the increase in the use of water for baths and closets, the waste by neglect and bad fittings, and the saving to be effected by vigilant inspection under present

* For report of evidence relating to these companies see last week's *Builder*, pp. 418 *et seq.*

or more stringent regulations. Many questions were put as to what constitutes a house or a supply, and the means of arriving at the average population for each. In some cases the facts which have been ascertained for small areas have been found to concur with the result arrived at by dividing the estimated population by the number of supplies. The estimates taken, it was said, were those of the Registrar-General; and Dr. Ogle thereupon remarked that for the whole of London the Registrar-General uses the figures of the water companies; that there are no census returns of tenements; that a house is not a tenement; and that in one of the Peabody buildings there are 716 tenants. The Chairman of the Commission, Lord Balfour of Burleigh, appears to regard it as a matter of vital importance to ascertain with all the accuracy possible the actual population of a company's district and the actual supply, so as to test the stated averages of consumption, and in this way to obtain correct data for estimating the probable requirements of the future.

The Lea Conservancy.

The points to which the examination of witnesses was directed were two—the sufficiency of the water to meet the requirements of the navigation and the present demands and any future demand of the water companies; and the pollution or purity of the water. The witnesses were Mr. Geo. Corble, Clerk; Major Flower, Sanitary Engineer; Mr. Job Child, Engineer; and Mr. Young, Consulting Chemist; who, however, was offered as the witness of the East London Water Company rather than of the Conservancy.

From the evidence of Mr. Corble, it appeared that last year there had been a correspondence between the Conservancy Board and the water companies about the supply of water, and the Board also received complaints from traders of the shortness of water in the lower reaches of the navigation. Only once during last summer was the full quantity of water reserved for the navigation passed down, and on that day the water in the lower reaches was exceptionally low. The Board had at all times to consider their obligations to the water companies, and they never took more water than was necessary for the navigation, nor allowed any to run away that the companies might want. The conservators and the companies accommodated each other on "give and take" principles, and did not enforce legal rights. The Conservancy for a long time was unable to obtain a substantial conviction for the pollution of the river with sewage, because the magistrates leaned to the side of the towns; but now proceedings could be taken before a county court judge, and that had been done in one case with a good result. There was a diminution in the barge manure trade which was partially diverted to the railway. A good deal of gas lime was brought up the river; and from these there was a little pumping at night time; but the barge owners are prosecuted if they are caught at it. These things are above the East London intake, but below that of the New River.

Major Flower was examined in much detail as to the actual or possible sources of pollution, and he stated how the sewage of many towns and villages was disposed of. He said there was no pollution above Hertford, and at Hertford it was local and did not affect the water at the intakes. It was below the New River intake and fifteen miles above the East London. He had condemned it strongly as "black, filthy, and shining" before the Rivers Pollution Commission in 1886, and the treatment had not altered since. The Conservancy had not remonstrated against the discharge of malting water. A map exhibited and professing to show "recognised pollutions" represented things unfairly. It was a "most unfair map." There were eighty-seven black dots above the intake of the East London; and he did not recognise them; they did not exist as pollutions, although they might exist as possible sources of pollution, if people neglected their duty. The water of the river was at one time deteriorating, but now it was improving. The sources of the tributaries were lower down the valley; and he thought that was due, not to pumping from the chalk, but to the rainfall. He had seen the Lea above Luton so dry that you might put it into a 6-in. pipe. The East London's source of supply was perfectly sound and satisfactory; there was no pollution which affected the company's water. There was practically no sewage pollution above the New River intake.

Mr. Child was examined as to the records of the flow over Childe's Weir, and was desired to give the lowest flows for certain definite limited periods, the chairman remarking that, whilst there was doubt about averages, there was none about a minimum. Excepting at Ware, below the junction of the Manifold ditch, he had never observed any signs of sewage contamination. His analysis of various samples did not indicate any serious pollution of such a character. There was some evidence of slight contamination by organic matter of vegetable origin in some places from the Stort, the Ash, and the Lea, above Hertford, and this was accounted for by the fact that the rivers were there very full of vegetation. Immediately below the Ware Mill Lock, and for some distance further down, the Lea, especially in hot weather, presented every appearance of sewage pollution. The water was dark, and had an offensive odour, and there were many pieces of black, slimy substance seen floating on the surface. This was caused by the discharge of the effluent from the Hertford sewage works into the Mainfold ditch, which joined the river Lea just below the Ware Mill Lock. The effluent from these works was extremely weak in sewage matter, and the effect upon the appearance of the river was much worse than would be expected. He had no doubt that this was due to the development of sewage fungus in the cutting which conveyed the effluent from the works to the ditch. This growth appeared to possess the property of absorbing the albumenous matter, and also the chlorides and other inorganic matter from the effluent, and of giving them up to the water when decomposing or disturbed. Its decomposition was also accompanied by the formation of sulphuretted hydrogen and sulphide of iron, which produced the unpleasant odour and dark colour of the water. The black, slimy mass found floating on the river below the Manifold Ditch was this fungus in a decomposed state. Analysis of the water from above and below the ditch showed the effect of the sewage effluent, and this, although generally slight, was unmistakeable. The point below the ditch at which the samples were taken was not in the main stream of the river, but in a practically stagnant pool. Lower down the river, below the junction with the main stream, nearly all trace of the pollution was lost. He was of opinion that although this pollution was objectionable locally, it did not affect the quality, as regarded the quantity of organic matter present, of the water of the river at the intake of the East London Company at Ponders-end. In 1891 he made analyses of samples of water taken above and below each tributary or probable source of pollution to ascertain the condition of the water of the Lea as regarded the quantity of organic matter in solution. The results showed that the river was at the time in a remarkably pure condition, that the tributaries did not add to the amount of organic matter, that no appreciable pollution reached the river from the sewage farms, and that the water at the intakes contained less organic matter than the water at the sources of the Lea and the New River. He had no hesitation in saying that the water at the East London intake had improved of late years, and that throughout the year it was generally of excellent quality as regarded freedom from organic matter. In April of this year he had made a series of analyses which showed that there was a sudden increase of organic matter in the water below the junction of the river Stort, but it was of vegetable origin, and was of no importance, and the amount gradually diminished until at the East London intake it was little more than one-third of a grain per gallon, which was appreciably less than in 1891. On both occasions the weather had been fine and dry for about three weeks before the samples were taken. The analyses, therefore, showed the normal condition of the water when unaffected by floods; and they conclusively proved, by the small quantity of organic matter present in solution, the excellence of the water as a source of public supply. He had also analysed samples of water after filtration and samples of that from the well, and submitted the detailed results.

The witness was examined, or rather cross-examined, at considerable length as to the time and manner of the selection of the samples, and also as to analytical tests. His theory as to the action of the fungus was founded upon actual experiment; but for a long time it was a puzzle to him. He did not think there was a process known which would remove soluble organic matter; and it was this which promoted the growth of the sewage fungus. He had not heard of the sewage fungus anywhere else. It improved the water up to a certain point, and then polluted it. Asked to explain the statement that other analyses showed the East London water to contain on the average 50 per cent. more organic matter than the New River, he said he did not believe it was so.

The West Middlesex Company.

The statement submitted by this company gave a history of the undertaking from the incorporation of the company in 1806, and a description of the works. The twenty-first paragraph was as follows:—

"In 1886 an agreement was made with the Thames Conservancy by which, in consideration of a further payment of 1,000*l*. per annum, they granted the company permission to take from the river a daily quantity of 4½ million gallons in addition to the 20 millions now allowed to be taken under the original agreement with the City Corporation, whose duties in this respect were afterwards transferred to the Thames Conservators."

The intake of the Company is at Hampton, from the Thames, and the water gravitates from the river to the engine wells through two 48-in. cast-iron pipes. Here are three engines and eleven boilers; the engines are capable of pumping 59,750,000 gallons in twenty-four hours. The engines pump the water into the reservoirs at Barnes, a distance of eight miles and a half, through two 36-in. mains. At Barnes there are four reservoirs capable of storing 117,500,000 gallons. The water is admitted at one end of the reservoir, and drawn off at the other, so as to allow as long a time as possible for subsidence. There is a filtering area capable of dealing with 39,000,000 gallons in twenty-four hours, taking the rate of filtration at 2½ gallons per square foot per hour. The filtered water is conveyed to the engine wells at Hammersmith by gravitation through two 36-in. cast-iron pipes laid in the bed of the river. At Hammersmith there are ten engines, with thirty-two boilers, and 35,877,280 gallons can be supplied in twenty-four hours. All these engines pump against an average head of 175 ft. during the day and 195 ft. at night. There are four service reservoirs,—Campden-hill, Kensington; Barrow-hill, by Primrose-hill; Harlesden-lane, Willesden; and Platt's-lane, Kiddespore, by Finchley-road,—with an aggregate capacity of 13,422,000 gallons. At Barrow-hill, three pumping engines, with eight boilers, raise the water to Kiddespore reservoir, and can pump 5,175,000 gallons in twenty-four hours, pumping against a maximum head of 150 ft. The works occupy over 96 acres of land, and the Company has over 7 acres of spare land.

The number of "supplies" in 1891 was 74,482, being an increase of 49,284 since 1851. The additions in periods of five years, going backwards, had been 6,702, 10,191, 9,471, 5,902, 5,885, 5,135, 2,998, and 3,000. In periods of ten years, going backwards, the additions had been 16,893 15,373, 11,020, and 5,998. The most important paragraphs in the statement are those which relate to the estimate of increased supply required in forty years' time. The directors say that, although they have always endeavoured, and with success, to anticipate and provide for the requirements of the future, they have not, until requested by the Commission, turned their attention to the question of what their policy would be at such a distant period as forty years hence. They claim indulgence "when attempting, in the short time allowed, to answer a question such as no municipal authority or board of directors would think of dealing with without much more consideration and assistance." They add that there are in the Company's district 5,820 acres outside the Metropolitan area, which may at some future time be built over; but it is considered that there is not any probability of more than half this space being covered within the next forty years. This 2,910 acres, with an average of twelve houses to an acre, would give 34,920 houses. Over the Company's district, including Marylebone and parts of St. Pancras and Paddington, the present average is 7¾ persons per house. The following is a tabular synopsis of the figures and estimates given. The estimates (*a*) are based on the assumption that half the area outside the Metropolis will be covered in forty years. The estimates (*b*) are based on the assumption that the same increase that has taken place since 1851 will continue for the next forty years:—

	1891.		40 years.		1931.	
Houses	74,482	+	34,920	=	109,402	(*a*)
	74,482	+	49,284	=	123,766	(*b*)
Population...	577,235	+	270,630	=	847,865	(*a*)
	577,235	+	381,952	=	959,187	(*b*)

Supply per head per day last year... 29 gallons.
Average, last ten years.................. 27·6 „

	Persons.			Gallons.
(*a*)	847,865	at 29 gallons	=	24,588,000
	„	„ 28 „	=	23,740,000
(*b*)	959,187	„ 29 „	=	27,816,433
	„	„ 28 „	=	26,857,236

Daily quantity now authorised... 24,500,000

The directors think it not improbable that they may, by negotiation with another company, acquire a part of the unexhausted right as authorised by the Thames Conservancy Act of 1878; and, in addition, they are advised by expert engineers and other scientific authorities that a much greater quantity than that now authorised could be taken from the Thames, even at times of exceptional drought, without involving the necessity of any additional provision for storage by the companies, and without injury to any interest. The directors further think that by constructing reservoirs when required by the increased demand, double the quantity might be taken without reducing the flow of the river more than has already been done and without affecting any water level that may be thought desirable by the Thames Conservators or other authority, and the supply thus taken would be free from the objections which might be urged against water taken in times of flood. The directors are also advised that an enormous quantity can be derived from wells sunk in the chalk area, the water from which now finds its way direct to the sea, and that a large supply may also be obtained from the gravel beds.

The witnesses examined on behalf of the West Middlesex Company were Sir W. H. Wyatt, Chairman, Mr. Harvey, Mr. Wybroo, and Mr. Willis. Mr. Harvey estimated the storage capacity at 8½ days' consumption; the Chairman called it 7½ days, making certain allowances. As to organic impurity, the water was 30 per cent. better than it was in 1868. Mr. Wybroo said the number of supplies increased from 1880 to 1884, when building speculation was at its height; but since then the rate of increase had fallen, and last year it was lower than in any of ten years following 1876.

We will next week continue our report of the evidence.

Now that the question of London water supply is engaging so much attention, Mr. Edward Stanford, of Cockspur-street, Charing-Cross, has very opportunely issued a "Water Supply Map of the County of London," showing the boundry of the jurisdiction of the London County Council, and the areas supplied within the county by the various water companies, distinguishing the areas under constant supply. The map will be found very useful in following the proceedings of the Royal Commission.

THE RELATION OF THE ARCHITECT TO THE WORKMAN,

AS ILLUSTRATED BY THE WORK AND METHODS OF THE GUILD AND SCHOOL OF HANDICRAFT.*

YOU have asked me to speak to you on some subject bearing on the practical work which, as an architect, I am engaged in, and to illustrate it, if possible, by reference to the actual processes of production followed in the carrying out of this work.

So I have chosen as my title "The Relation of the Architect to the Workman," and shall try and give you a few ideas that I have sought to work upon now for some years, and such insight as I am able to upon this theme, illustrating it not so much by actual instances of work produced, as by description and explanation of the system of work that has made this production thus far possible, and would seem to tend to its further encouragement.

I shall arrange my subject broadly, therefore, under two heads, the first more theoretical, the second, inasmuch as it is intended to illustrate the first, of a more practical character, and having definite application to such materials as it would seem convenient in the course of a brief hour to touch upon.

On the threshold of my subject, I would say that this relation of the architect to the workman, the right understanding of it and its application to one's work as an artist, seems to me to be the most important part of that larger subject often called "The Relation of Architecture to Life." I suppose to most of us here, the relation of architecture to life is a question fraught with meaning in more senses than the narrow one of our own bread-and-butter; but I would challenge each one of you to put his interpretation on the question, and to ask himself what it actually means to him in the everyday humdrum of things. How he feels it; whether in the multitude of great architectural work, whether in the poverty of good building, whether in the absence of style, whether in the eclecticism of choice, whether in his dealings with clients, with builders, with workmen, or how? How as an English architect, and as a private individual?

For my part, I think the relation of architecture to life in modern times cannot but be regarded but as of the slightest. To *our* life, as architects, it means much, and always will; to our life as a nation it means little,—unfortunately for us. As a nation, we have small sympathy for, and scarce any understanding of, architecture, and what sympathy and understanding there is, is limited to a few in the profession and their supporters. As a nation, we love *show* and *vulgarity*, with its concomitant, cheapness; we love poverty of construction and its symbol, the iron girder; we love *hurry* and its resultant, the ill-considered moulding. We have not the great sympathy which could build the cathedral and forget the name of the architect; or the great power of reserve that could leave, in the consciousness of their harmonious development, the hundred details of the building to the craftsman. Architecture is no longer democratic, no longer understanded of the people: it has lost its corporate significance. As a nation, we do not love architecture; we are content to let our mouldings be struck with compasses, and our subtlest details be evolved by the office-youth; and we firmly believe, that when the assessor of the Royal Institute of British Architects has told us, or our representatives, the local committee, that this set of plans is the best we can possibly expect for the money, that it is good architecture we have got, and we thereupon proceed to what is called "merge the premium in the percentage."

I was comparing lately the conditions of some recent modern competition clauses, and the ethical frame of the English mind which these portrayed, with the document issued by the Florentines for the rebuilding of their cathedral in the year 1294. The British parallel, as it is familiar to most of you, I shall not give; the Florentine being less so, I will give you a portion of. Here is the key-note of it:—

"Since the highest mark of prudence in a people of noble origin is to proceed in the management of their affairs so that their magnanimity and wisdom may be evinced in their outward acts, we order Arnolfo, Head Master of our Commune, to make a design for the renovation of Santa Reparata in a style of magnificence which neither the Industry nor the power of man can surpass, that it may harmonise with the opinion of many wise persons in this city and state, who think that this Commune should not engage in any enterprise unless its intention be to make the result correspond with that noblest sort of heart which is composed of the united will of many citizens."

It was this "united will," this "noblest sort of heart," which those old burghers felt could only be expressed by Architecture,—the mother art. It seems somewhat of a mockery to speak of Architecture as actually being the mother art nowadays. Look at the walls of the Royal Academy at this moment,—is it true? Look at Gower-street,—is it true? Look at Greater London, "the desert of London town, grey miles long," "the desert of London town, mirk miles broad,"—is it true? Look at the public-house, the restaurant, the Nonconformist chapel, the average shop, the suburban villa, the Board school, the railway junction, the pit village, the factory town, and ask again,—is it true? When that phrase was invented, building and architecture were synonymous terms; *we* draw a subtle distinction, and say with truth, Yea, those be buildings: what we wish to deal with is architecture,—the art of the Chief Builder,—αρχι τεχτων,—the essence of building. Possibly what we say is true in a double sense, but the truth is a bitter one.

Now, I do not say these things as a tirade at existing circumstances. Tirades are futile and unnecessary to us as practical men, but I say them in order to point at ways that, by the energy mainly of the young architect, may be bettered, and at facts existing in modern life which, if rightly understood by him, will give him the opportunity of bettering them. Having spoken therefore of the national sympathy for architecture, I now regard the architect in his relation to existing things.

To me it seems that this divorce of architecture from the national life leaves its mark on him, and injuriously. He is not, if I may say so, and using the expression in the largest sense, sufficiently educated, not sufficiently,—if one may put it in the famous term of the Italian Renaissance,—humanist. His scope and sympathies in the first place are not wide enough, and then his technical training is not sufficiently all embracing. He finds that his "profession" or "art,"—I use either word,—is only becoming recognised as one of the polite arts or professions. It does not stand by the law, or the work of the doctor, or the schoolmaster, or the many services of the State, or the University in the public eye. Its position is doubtful, and it ministers in the main to the private comfort of wealthy men, not to the common heart of a great people.

As regards his method of work, he feels himself but a link in the productive chain. He sits in his office and makes designs, and he has a connexion through specifications with contractors who carry them out; and he frequently anathematises a man of straw, who is known to him under the name of "The British Working-man," when they are not carried out properly. My contention is, therefore, that the architect as yet is not sufficiently educated in his relation to the "body social." It is, perhaps, unfair to say that he is (in a non-political sense) too conservative, but he has not that wide training in life which should make him sympathise with the greater movements of his time. His training is a narrow one, in the four walls of an office. He does not touch life directly, as the doctor or the clergyman; he does not get glimpses into men and manners like the lawyer.

Here, then, we ask ourselves, If this be true, how can it be best remedied? And we are brought face to face with the question of the relation of the architect and the workman. The architect has to understand his position *as* a workman in relation to other workmen; more than this, he has to feel his responsibilities in organising and directing their work; and more than that still, he should feel some direct responsibilities likewise in training and educating them. Thus only will he deserve his title as architect or chief builder.

I will return to the consideration of this directly in detail, staying for a moment to consider the question in its bearing on a question very dear to all of us,—*style*, the language of architecture. The architects of the later nineteenth century have settled the question of style; they have almost ceased to dogmatise; the Battle of the Styles has been fought out, and a rough-and-ready compromise has been made between eclecticism and originality. That is style in its external sense; but I believe we have gone deeper: the inner question of the origin of style is what we have now to solve. The origin of style lies not in the theories, not in the forms, of art, but in the social relations of men to men, in their state of society, in their habitude to one another, in the leisure they may have for the thinking out of problems and the creation of forms. In short, the origin of style is a social, not an artistic question. The question of style, therefore, is solving itself for the young architect, and will do so more and more as he grasps his relationship to the workman and the body social.

I repeat, then, that the young architect has to feel that he is a workman in a privileged position, in the position of giving other workmen their line of work. He is to be the "chief master of our Commune;" to fulfil this high function rightly he must come into close and direct relationship with his fellows in every possible way.

Barry, I believe, once suggested that it would be a good thing for an architect with capital to invest it in building operations, and such work as might be in connexion with architecture. That suggestion was a very wise and far-seeing one. Barry's age was, perhaps, not fully ready

---

* A paper read on the 27th ult. before the Architectural Association by Mr. C. R. Ashbee, M.A., as elsewhere mentioned.

for it, but it has been and is being at the present day acted upon by architects in various ways. Regarding capital as the force that binds workmen together, regarding also the other great cohesive forces which were undiscernible to Barry,—the workmen's movements, &c., which are tending to a reconstruction of industry at the present day; regarding also the advisability, nay, necessity, of commencing (especially for the young architect) in the *ministering arts, the crafts*, in other words, rather than in the mother art direct; and regarding in the last instance the necessity of the frank recognition of the architect's connexion with industry, Barry's suggestion, which implies the closer union of the architect to the body social, we might all set before us.

But I would give this suggestion more definiteness, and at the same time limit it. I would like to see applied to it the system of the old Craft Guild; or such conditions as were possible of a society that produced the greatest architecture of all time. In this society we find the right relation,—a more human relation between the architect and the workman.

Now, it seems to me that there are three ways in which we are approximating to what was good in the old system. Three phases of modern developments which it behoves especially us younger men to study, and which all of them comprehend,—this better relation of architect and workman upon which I would seek to fix your attention to-night. These three things I might term "Craft-Guild, Potentialities," and they may be distinguished as follows: There is—

1. The existing connexion of architects with trade for artistic purposes.

2. The workmen's movements that are daily convulsing industry.

3. The educational movement that is making progress with rapid strides.

I will take them in order.

First of all, the existing connexion of architects with trade for artistic purposes,—the architect and the shop, let us call it. In the relation of the architect to tradesmen we see these guild potentialities. We see it among the men employed by some of the leading architects,—his builders, his furniture makers, his painters, and so forth. I will put it plainer. In some cases the architect is in a position in which he can place his building with a particular builder with whom he has worked for years; or, if the contract is to be competed for, he can limit it to some three or four of those who have worked for him and whom he can trust. In this the guild element enters. In some cases an architect, or group of architects, support a business in which stuffs, or furniture, or materials are produced specially from their designs, and to serve the purpose of their buildings. I use the word *support* advisedly, for, if their work is conscientiously done, more money of theirs goes into these businesses than ever comes out of them. Here, again, the guild element enters. In some cases, again, the leading architects attract round them various small workmen,—painters, carvers, sculptors, ironworkers,—men of some special ability, whom they have met with in the course of their professional experience, and to whom they continue to give small jobs in one or other of their works. Here, above all, the guild element enters because of the educational element, and because there is a constant and direct relationship between the employing architect and the producing craftsman.

Now, it seems to me that we younger men have to take up this side of the professional tradition, one might almost call it, and develops it. Here is a portion of our heritage that is worth having; in this there lies a future.

We should get into closer touch with our builders, our carvers, our decorators. We should welcome, instead of glancing at them with the eye of false shame, the efforts of architects to work through the ordinary distributive agencies of the shop; and, above all, we should unite to us a body of men,—young men, if possible,—who are capable of ministering to the various crafts dependent upon architecture.

The step from this to the completed Craft Guild is a social one, and one that time must bring. The atoms at present are distributed, but the personality of the architect should unite them. Their interests, at present, are discordant. A loses what B gains; the architect has it in his power to make them harmonious by uniting them with him. Their training at present is incomplete, and each, if left to himself, would ruin the ensemble; the architect, as having the grasp of the whole, has it in his power to teach, and to so give each his place that left to himself he shall be trusted to understand his own limitation. I am a painter, and must feel the relation of these reds to the whole scheme of colour; I am a joiner, and must understand that this panelling must range with the architectural treatment of the frieze and cornice; and so forth.

I should be as opposed as any man to the idea that the architect should be connected in any way with trade or with dealing, or should receive any remuneration other than that professionally established for professional services, or for purely artistic work of his own hands in connexion with it; but inasmuch as the architect's work is productive, so he should be in immediate touch with production: but I hold that an architect should have a workshop at his back and come into constant relation with a body of men in various crafts educated with and by him.

2.—Then we come to the next point,—the workmen's movements,—the great underlying questions of the development of industry, its re-organisation, the evolution of co-operation and co-operative societies,—(a purely Mediæval repetition in many respects). These things the young architect should study, and should learn to make use of and not to shun.

The real interests of the day are, and probably will be for the next decade or so, social: not political, not artistic, not directly educational. I hold it the duty of the young architect, if he wishes to get more into touch with life, to learn to take an intelligent interest in these workmen's movements. The knowledge or interest of the architect in them at present is often limited to the "strike clause" in the contract. I know it is the opinion of many artists, professional men of standing, that the art may take care of itself, that social questions and ethics have no place whatever in art; and they accept the teaching of what may be called the reaction,—an inevitable one,—to the doctrines of John Ruskin. They hold that all the architect should care about is the final work produced. Does it or does it not conform to his design,—no matter how it has been produced? This may be right enough for the landscape painter or the artistic antiquarian, but I hold it to be absolutely and fundamentally false for the architect. I insist that the architect is in the position of the highest producer, and so should he bear the responsibility of the highest production.

He should study it, get to see its bearing on his work and those that work under him; he should seek to unite them co-operatively as producers, and without middlemen between them and him. There is nothing so painfully instructive to one as reading the habitual tone of scornful unsympathy expressed by the leading building papers whenever a question relating to workmen's movements, strikes, and industrial struggles come forward. These papers, presumably, express professional opinion, but they are unreservedly biassed in favour of the employer as against the employed. It is for the young architect to study better these relations of capital and labour. If he does, he will see that there is no real antagonism between capital and labour: that the apparent antagonism of the present day is in the first instance, one in the *degree of remuneration for services*; in the second instance, in the *degree of control* between master and men.

3. Now to my last factor in modern movements, to which also lie guild potentialities,—the educational developments. The old apprenticeship system is dying out. It still remains in a somewhat unsatisfactory condition in architecture; and in such crafts as bookbinding, that have in them some of the old-world element undestroyed by the machine, where the hand still holds, and which have not yet quite sunk into the slough of industrial despond; but for the most part it is finished. Side by side with it we see a new growth,—the technical school, which is even offering to take its place.

But the technical school never has taken and never can take its place. The technical school must be either a combination of primary education, as in the case of the Welsh intermediate schools, and so aim at the more harmonious education of the child; or be a continuation of the work in life, as is the case with such classes at polytechnics and technical institutes which seek something other than merely to "gild the leisure of the clerk." It can never, as far as we can at present see, tea the actual trade itself as an apprentice shou learn it; and certainly, according to t Technical Education Act, it may not ev profess to teach it.

Edward Bellamy, in his "Looking Backwar made the trenchant statement that, in the n state, a new force must take the place of t "master's eye" of the old trade system. Tl new force was "the perfectness of the organi tion." I would accept this entirely, insistin only that perfectness of organisation compri "humanism."

Now, with the apprenticeship system dyi with the technical schools admittedly n fulfilling requiring conditions, and with t organisation of industry imperfect, what the educational outlook, as far as the arcl tect is concerned? We have, it see to me, to recognise that the apprenti ship system, regarded educationally, has be destroyed by subdivision of labour, and is this subdivision of labour that we arc tects have to grapple with, and that we, virtue of our position, can be of service We must help in the educational side of th re-organisation of industry that is taking place, not only in our own immediate art, b in all the handicrafts subordinate.

I would urge you all to consider how far it not within the scope of the profession, entering more into the study of the crafts, approaching more the men in their movemen by working more in workshops and less offices, to supply somewhat that which is want educationally, to enter into this educatio movement in its humanist and its techni side which we see going on on all hands. Y yourselves are entering into it in a most excell manner at the Architectural Association; it being taken up by the County Councils in m parts of the kingdom; and it may said to be living, from the Universities do to the Board Schools. We architects shou take it up for the future of the profession a all that depends on it.

I have now indicated the three main lines which it would seem to me that in dealing w the question of the relation of the architect the workman we younger men, having in mi the greater and more comprehensive devel ment of the profession, have to look,— development, in fact, more in conformity w the ways and methods of the Mediæval gui Let me now sum up the position of the arc tect as I conceive it should be, in his relation the workman,—an architect's ideal, if I may allowed the term.

We should, in the first place, then, regard o selves more as workmen on whom fall the dut of production and of organisation, and less gentlemen of the office. As far as our o training goes, we should draw as little possible, but with our hands work as m as possible; or, rather, I should say, we sho seek to express our detail designs as m as possible *in actual material* and not paper,—that is to say, in the worksh Working thus in the workshop, we sho grow into the sympathies of the wo shop, and then seek to develope our posit as organisers and employers of indust We should train up a body of men with t it is only by educating workmen in architectu principles, and ourselves in the relation of handicrafts to our work, that style,—real livi style,—not the shell of it in a modern Got church or Queen Anne mansion,—can co At present we act as a disintegrating for and tend to keep the craftsmen asunder. have sense enough to see that we can get bet work from them when they act as units th when they are under the control of a contrac or a big firm. It should be our effort to sec the advantages of freedom and spontaneity work which a guild system would give wi out losing those advantages of business meth and order which the present system ensu We ought, in fact, not to use a good craf man as an artistic convenience, as we tempted to do at present; but we should h him, bind him to us,—as it were, take him i partnership with us,—and so take more respo bility for the *man* and less responsibility the *work*. By so doing we shall avoid that wa which at the present day always tends to c vert the good craftsman into the bad emplo of labour. The architect, more than any ot person, has the blame of this; the archite more than any other, ought to strive prevent it.

It is not for me to pretend to lay down a

sys e that shall even pretend to meet those difficulties, I merely say that some efforts at reorganising of industry, in so far as it affects architecture, on the principles of the Craft Guild, seem to me to be the right ones; and that the ideas which I have endeavoured to set before you contain the main principles that have guided my own creative work in the Guild and School of Handicraft since I took my degree and served my apprenticeship. I will now give you, in a few words, the method and system of the creative and educational work of the Guild and School, in which, if nothing else has been done, at least we have made an attempt to establish a more healthy relation between the workman and the architect.

That closes the more theoretical part of my subject, and I should now like to sketch out for you, in a few words, what the ways and methods of the Guild and School of Handicraft are. You must understand that this Guild and School is not a thing that has been suddenly created in a doctrinaire manner. It has grown up in a perfectly harmonious and gradual way in the course of a short period of time,—five years, though. But its growth claims to be spontaneous. It was not pre-conceived as a system, and then established in the manner that Rousseau and reformers of his type would seek to establish a thing; but it has grown up by two or three men coming to work and read together, and then, feeling that they had to make their work a little more practical, taking up work with their hands. That has led to the establishment of the *School* on the one hand, and the *Guild* or workshop on the other. The Guild and School, therefore, has two distinct parts: first it is a productive workshop, conducted on the lines of an industrial partnership, in the same way as some of the northern co-operative societies are conducted,—such, for instance, as the Woodhouse Mills in Huddersfield; secondly, it is a school in which are trained workmen,—men and boys,—who are still at work at home. We also train elementary teachers in various forms of handicraft. We therefore consider that we have two lines of teaching going on in the school: one where the young artisan is taught, and the other where the elementary teacher is taught,—that is, the teacher who is going to teach the artisan of the future. Of course, the school is and always must remain a small concern, and we regard it as a hunting-ground for our future artisans. We entirely disapprove of the sale of anything in the nature of school-work. We consider that that is wrong. It is, I know, being done all over the country. But we hold that no school-work must be sold; that the school is educational, and must not be regarded as directly productive in any sense whatever. The result is, we give vigour to our workshop. It is in the workshop where the Guild is established, and it is in the workshop where we carry on the training of the apprentice when he passes out of the school. When he is bound apprentice he is bound to the society as a corporate body. He is taught his trade, or craft, in the production of work of which I have brought a few specimens for you this evening. I have not been able to bring any specimens of work which bear more particularly upon architecture, because one cannot bring in a cab, panelling of rooms, or other large and important pieces of work relating to building. I have brought some specimens of leather work; one little specimen of woodwork treated with *gesso*; some specimens of hammered copper, specimens of hammered gold and silver work, castings, metal-turning, hammered hollow-ware, &c. There are also two printed volumes: one, the Transactions of the Guild and School, which contain addresses by many eminent artists, delivered at our workshop, and taken down by a reporter and thus preserved; the other is the Manual of the Guild and School of Handicraft, published three days ago, which contains the latest expression of our work. I have brought copies of each of these books, and I should like to be allowed to present them to the Association. As regards the way in which we work, however, the Guild has as yet no place where it exhibits or displays its things, and the reason is that the workmen of the Guild are anxious, in the way I have mentioned in the theoretical part of my paper, to work with architects. Therefore, the bulk of the work which is done there is done in connexion with architects, who come and visit the workshop and talk with the men. Of course, most of my own work goes there, and it is always a delight for me to see the whole thing, from top to bottom, if I can possibly manage it, passing through the Guild workshop, because one feels that one has there men whom one has trained up into an understanding of their craft and of the right treatment of materials. Therefore, there is always going on a good deal of work which is either architectural work or work for architects. As regards the place itself, I can only say that I hope you will come and pay it a visit, and see it for yourselves. We have got an old eighteenth-century house, built by Gibbs, that we have had our eye upon for many years. It was formerly in a park by itself, but it is now built round, although it has a nice garden at the back. We have laid out a lawn and have built our workshops along the lawn; there is thus always a pleasant outlook, and the work is, therefore, done under better conditions than usually prevail in a London workshop. I shall now be very happy to answer any questions which you may care to put to me about any of the processes in detail, but I refrain from going into a practical description of these processes for fear of wearying you with technicalities. In conclusion, I would only repeat my invitation to you to come and see the place for yourselves, and not only I, but all my colleagues, will be only too happy to welcome you.

[An interesting discussion ensued, the speakers being Messrs. H. O. Cresswell, Leonard Stokes, Sidney Vacher, E. W. Mountford, A. E. Bartlett, Sidney Tugwell, and the Chairman, and Mr. Ashbee replied to some of the points raised. We are obliged to defer our report of the discussion until next week.]

THE LONDON COUNTY COUNCIL.

The "Rate of Wages and Hours Clause" in Contracts.—A special meeting of this Council was held on Friday, the 27th ult., to consider this subject, which was adjourned from the previous meeting of the Council, as mentioned by us last week. The following motion, it will be remembered, had been moved by Mr. John Burns:—

"That all contractors be compelled to sign a declaration that they pay the trades union rates of wages, and observe the hours of labour and conditions recognised by the London trades unions, and that the hours and wages be inserted in and form part of the contract by way of schedule, and that penalties be enforced for any breach of agreement."

Mr. Beachcroft asked whether counsel's opinion had been taken as to the legality of the stipulations proposed, in the event of the motion, or its substance, being carried.

The Chairman (Lord Rosebery), in reply, said that the questions had been submitted to an eminent counsel, Mr. Meadows White, Q.C., who had given an opinion, in which he said:—

"I may say generally that I do not see anything in stipulations defining the *minimum* of wages or the *maximum* of hours which would be held contrary to law or so far opposed to public policy as to be illegal. . . . . This case is, I think, without precedent. The subject is therefore not free from doubt, but I am of opinion, on the whole, that a clause could be framed so as to secure the right to liquidated damages for breach of such stipulations. . . . I should advise that liquidated damages should be specially stipulated for in each care, and that it would not be prudent to rely on a general stipulation applicable to all the stipulations in the contract. There would be nothing contrary to law in a stipulation entitling the Council in the event of breach to determine the contract, but, of course, such a stipulation would be subject to the usual incidents of forfeiture clauses, and I think that a provision that the Council might themselves pay to workmen underpaid or not paid according to the terms of the stipulation and recover or deduct the amount would be valid. . . . It would avoid many difficulties if a schedule of wages could be agreed upon, framed on the proposed principle, or that reference could be made to some authority or existing scale of wages, rather than to leave the language indefinite."

Sir Thomas Farrer moved, as an amendment to the motion, to omit the word "London," and to insert after the words "trades unions," the words, "in the place or places where the contract is to be executed." He said as Mr. Burns's motion stood, and according to the construction put upon it, there could be no doubt that they would be compelled to apply London trade union rates and rules to the country contracts. That seemed to him to be a most objectionable thing to do. Mr. Burns proposed by his resolution to prevent Londoners getting the benefit of the cheaper labour in the country. Another important aspect of the question was that the adoption of the resolution would keep country contractors from tendering. That meant they were going to exclude country contractors and country workmen from London work. (Mr. Burns: Why not?) Because it would be setting one class of workmen against another.

Lord Monkswell pointed out the impracticability of London rates and conditions of labour being imposed all over the country. The contractor would rather let his men work in the country, and they in London did not wish them to crowd up London. Many people would be put to great inconvenience for no reason. He also objected because the local workmen who might still be employed outside London would be made into a privileged class who would receive higher wages than their fellow workmen working for the local needs only.

After a long discussion, in the course of which Mr. Burns's motion was strongly supported by Mr. Martineau, Chairman of the Asylums Committee, and other speakers, on the ground that it would result in good work and so be productive of true economy, the amendment was carried by a majority of 10, sixty voting for it and fifty against.

Mr. Costelloe and Mr. H. P. Harris moved further amendments, which were negatived, and eventually Mr. Burns's motion as amended was agreed to, and it was resolved that it should be referred to a Special Committee to consider how best to give effect to the resolution. It was also agreed to refer the following proposed additions to the resolution standing in the name of Mr. Stockbridge on the agenda paper, viz.:—

(1.) Should any workman in the employment of the contractor be not paid the schedule wages then the Council shall be at liberty to deduct from the money payable to the contractor under the contract a sum equal to double the amount of such deficiency, and the Council shall be at liberty out of such sums so deducted, to pay the contractor's workmen any deficiency in their proper wages, for the whole of the past term of the contract.

2. The contractor shall undertake to keep proper time books and wages books in connexion with the contract work, and such books shall at all times be open to the inspection of such person or persons as may be appointed by the Council for this purpose, and the contractor shall, under a penalty, be bound to make and deliver to the Council, whenever required, a declaration that the hours and wages set out in the time and wages books are correct, and that he has paid the several sums charged therein.

Mr. Leon had given notice to add to the resolution the words:—

"But London rates of wages shall be paid by every contractor to all workmen employed on any London County Council work within twenty miles of London."

He asked that these words should also be referred to the committee, and the suggestion was adopted.

The Council then adjourned.

At the ordinary weekly meeting of the Council on Tuesday last, Lord Rosebery presiding, there was little business of special interest to our readers, except the nomination of the Special Committee on Contracts to consider the foregoing matter. It was resolved that the following members should constitute the Committee, viz., Messrs. Hood Barrs, Branch, Burns, C. Harrison, Lyon, Roberts, and H. R. Taylor.

After transacting other business, the Council adjourned over the Whitsun recess.

BUILDERS' BENEVOLENT INSTITUTION:

ELECTION OF PENSIONERS.

THE seventy-sixth election of pensioners in connexion with this Institution took place on Thursday, the 26th ult., Mr. B. E. Nightingale, President, in the chair.

There were six candidates,—two men and four women,—and there were vacancies for one man and one woman.

The successful candidates were William Rowland, 579 votes, first application; and Margaret A. Richardson, 3,626 votes, being her seventh application.

Votes of thanks were given to the scrutineers (Messrs. T. Stirling and T. F. Rider), and to the President, and the meeting terminated.

DISSOLUTION OF PARTNERSHIP.—Messrs. Tolley & Son, architects and surveyors, 86, Cannon-street, inform us that they have dissolved partnership by mutual consent as from March 25 last. Mr. Tolley retires from practice, and Mr. James Tolley, jun., will carry on the business under the old style of "Tolley & Son." Mr. Tolley retains his appointment as District Surveyor for Sydenham.

Christchurch Cath^dl, Oxford — The Chapter House, etc. from E.

Illustrations.

OXFORD CATHEDRAL.*

SERVING both as the Cathedral of the diocese and as the Chapel of the College, Christchurch Cathedral holds a unique position amongst our episcopal buildings. The changes it has undergone since its foundation have each left their mark on the fabric, lend a large amount of interest to its plan and detail, and give a fairly clear record of its gradual development from early times to the present.

In dimensions, it is the smallest of our cathedrals, its total internal length, with the modern bay added to the nave, being but 175 ft. Its position, too, well set back from all the principal approaches, and much hidden by the great buildings of Wolsey's College, deprive it of that importance and dignity which is generally associated with a cathedral-church. But it possesses a picturesqueness quite its own, and the peculiar form which the plan takes east of the crossing is a point of great interest,—an interest which is increased in the light of recent discoveries. With the exception of the west walk of the cloister and three western bays of the nave, the church remains much as it was at the Dissolution. The monastic buildings have necessarily fared worse, as they were, with the exception of the refectory and the Chapter-house, destroyed to make room for Wolsey's new works.

Founded originally in the beginning of the eighth century by King Didan, and existing as a nunnery under his daughter, Frideswide, it was, three centuries after, converted into a monastery of Secular Canons, and later of Canons Regular of St. Augustine, and so remained until the sixteenth century, when Cardinal Wolsey obtained its suppression, for the purpose of founding the college which was to bear his name, and which is now represented chiefly by his alterations to the Cathedral, and the great "Tom" Quad, with its hall and unfinished cloisters, standing between the Cathedral and the present main street. The peculiarities of plan, and the curious mixture of detail, have afforded, and still afford, much matter for discussion and research, although of late something has been done which tends to clear up the mystery which enveloped the north-eastern portion of the church. The original church of Didan and his daughter, afterwards Saint, Frideswide, was doubtless a humble structure, and, if not of wood, was of small dimensions. At the commencement of the eleventh century the nuns of St. Frideswide were massacred and the church burnt; and afterwards additions were commenced by King Ethelred II. About 1120 further additions were made by Prior Guimond, and the consecration took place sixty years afterwards (1180). In these cases it was probably the endeavour, so far as was possible, to keep the original church, sanctified as it had become by the presence of St. Frideswide's burial, as an integral part of the structure, and it is this point which makes the ground plan at the present time one of so much peculiarity and interest.

The church now comprises a nave of four bays with aisles (and a modern bay or vestibule westward), a central tower, a north transept of three bays with a western aisle, a south transept of two bays, and an eastern chapel dedicated to St. Lucy, and a choir of four, the central alley of the presbytery being carried one bay beyond. On the north side of the north choir aisle are two aisles of later date, the first being the Lady Chapel, of thirteenth-century date, and the outer, or north, aisle, known as St. Katharine's, or the Latin Chapel. Both these aisles occupy in their western bays the site of the eastern aisle of the choir. It should be noted that, although the nave and south transept are at right angles, the eastern arm bends to the north, and the north transept, being at right angles with the choir, turns a little westward. The projecting portion of the presbytery is not in line with the rest, turning a little more to the north.

In 1887 Mr. J. Park Harrison, to whom we are indebted for much information with regard to the discoveries, had excavations made outside the east wall of the north choir aisle and Lady Chapel. The result was the finding of foundations of three apses, in all probability forming the eastern termination of the Early church which Didan founded. It will be noticed on reference to the plan that these foundations coincide with two rough arches which still exist in the east wall of the aisles, and there are distinct traces of a central arch now nearly covered by the Norman buttress. How far this wall is ancient is difficult to say. At first sight it appears early, and the fact of the new Norman choir having been built south of what was the south aisle of the Saxon church, seems to point to the fact that it was intended to keep the original building temporarily at least. There is no reason, however, to suppose that the Norman design was not completed. The vaulting shafts of the north aisle still remain, and also the angle of this aisle with the east aisle of the north transept. In addition to this a chapel was thrown out eastward from the northernmost bay of the east transept aisle, and it is quite possible that the north aisle of the Saxon church might have been retained, occupying as it would the space immediately north of the north aisle of the choir. Whether or not this was the case, any of the original building which might have been standing was swept away in the thirteenth century.

And it is here that we find the first evidence of something unusual in the plan. The two eastern bays of the Lady Chapel are 2 ft. wider than the others. At first sight this is apparently Decorated work, but on closer examination it will be found that the vaulting shafts including the one at the north-east angle are Early English. Bearing in mind that this aisle stood on the site of the Saxon church in which St. Frideswide was buried, it is not impossible that this widening was necessary to increase the accommodation for worhippers at the shrine of St. Frideswide. It so happens that the foundation-wall of this addition would be clear of the older foundation of the Saxon building, the early foundations not being considered strong enough to bear the newer and heavier load. This addition was the Lady Chapel, and occupied a similar position to the "Elder Lady Chapel" at Bristol, which was also an Augustinian house.

The next alteration was in the fourteenth century, when the chapel at the north-east

* This series of illustrations of the Cathedrals of England and Wales was begun in our issue of January 3, 1891. A list of those already illustrated, with particulars of future arrangements, will be found on page 450.

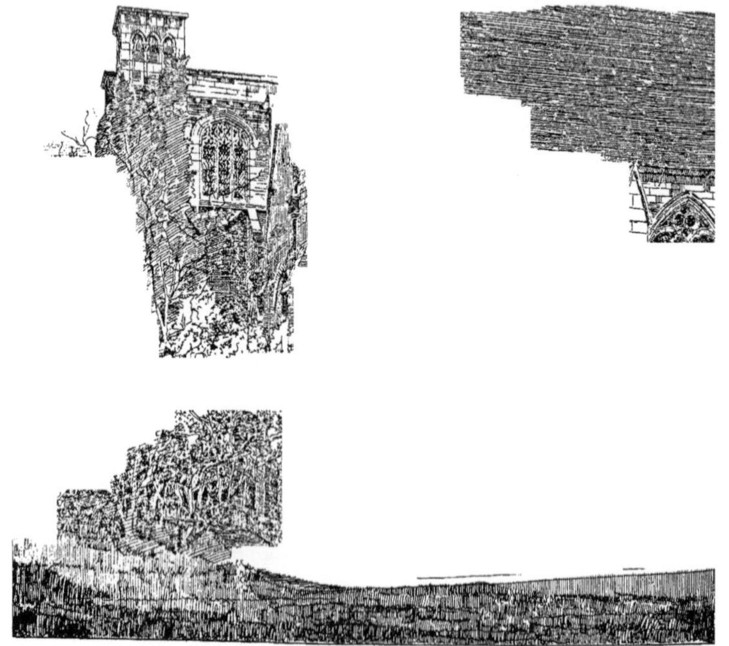

Cathedrals of

No. 18. CHRISTCHURCH, OXFORD: FROM

ɪd and Wales.

.TH-EAST.—Drawn by Mr. Roland W. Paul.

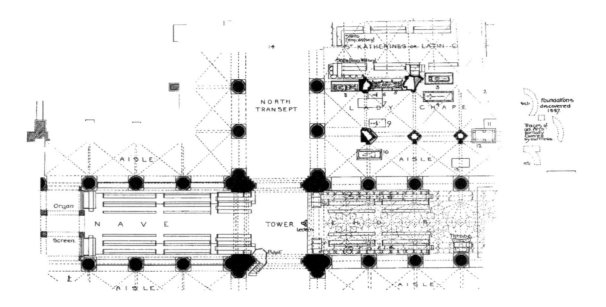

Christchurch Cathedral Oxford.

Ground Plan.

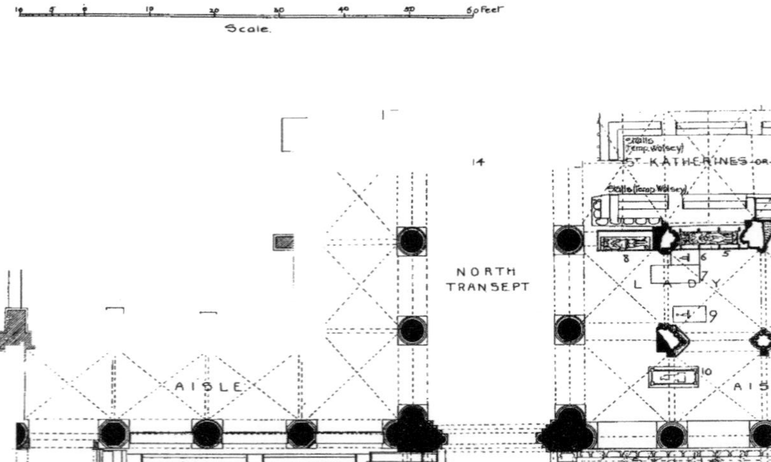

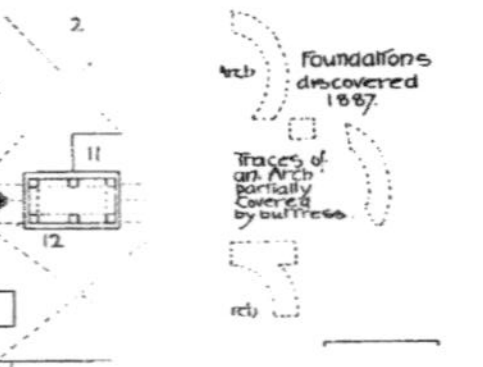

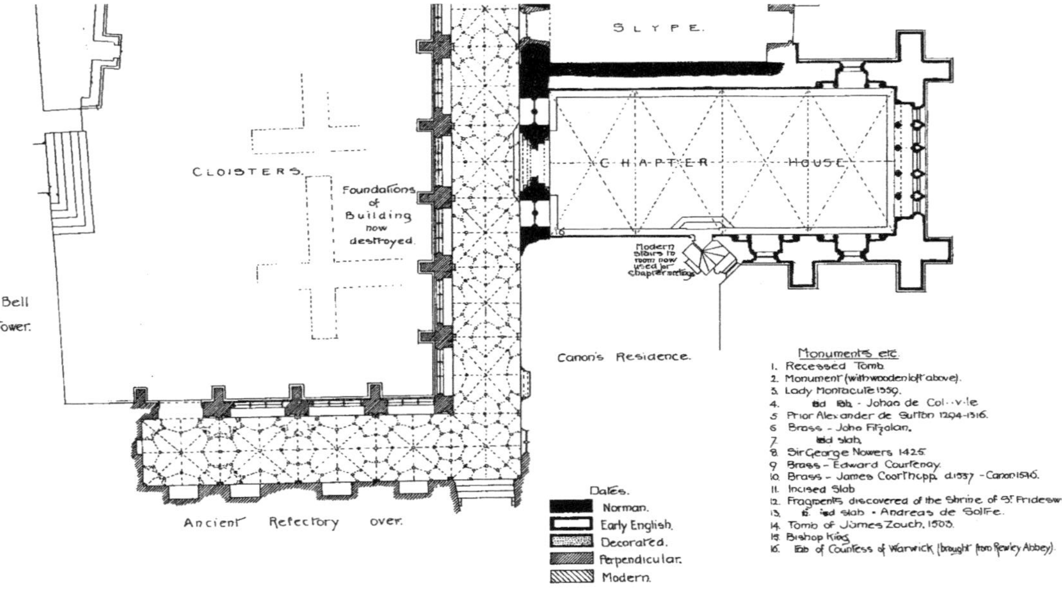

SLYPE.
CHAPTER HOUSE.
CLOISTERS.
Foundations of Building now destroyed.
Bell Tower.
Modern stairs to room now used for Chapter sittings
Canon's Residence.
Ancient Refectory over.
Dates.
Norman.
Early English.
Decorated.
Perpendicular.
Modern.
Monuments etc.
1. Recessed Tomb.
2. Monument (with wooden loft above).
3. Lady Montacute 1559.
4. - Johan de Col··v·le
5. Prior Alexander de Sutton 1294-1316.
6. Brass - John Fitzalan.
7. slab.
8. Sir George Nowers 1425.
9. Brass - Edward Courtenay.
10. Brass - James Coorthopp d.1557 - Canon 1546.
11. Incised Slab
12. Fragments discovered of the Shrine of St. Frideswide.
13. slab - Andreas de Solfe.
14. Tomb of James Zouch. 1503.
15. Bishop King.
16. of Countess of Warwick (brought from Rewley Abbey).
Roland W. Paul 1892.
PHOTO-LITHO SPRAGUE & Co. 4 & 5 EAST HARDING STREET FETTER LANE, E.C.

CHRISTCHURCH CATHEDRAL, OXFORD: VIEW ACROSS THE LADY CHAPEL.

CHRISTCHURCH CATHEDRAL, OXFORD: VIEW ACROSS THE NORTH TRANSEPT.

B
South Side
This fragment of a clustered shaft is now lying on the shrine & has been placed here as suggesting its former position.
Section
modern
floor level.
modern
We
G
E
Section of End shewing the interpenetration of mouldings at angle.
East side.
A
De
SP
Sketch of Angle (inside).
Section of Arch mouldings (taken at angle just above springing)
Cornice Moulding (at G see section)
Scale for Elevation
Scale for Mouldings &

INK-PHOTO SPRAGUE & Co. 4 & 5 EAST HARDING STREET, FETTER LANE, E.C.

...S OF THE SHRINE OF S. FRIDESWIDE.

angle of the transept was removed, the north wall of the Lady Chapel opened out, and a very beautiful chapel was erected of equal length with the Lady Chapel, and now known as St. Katharine's or the Latin Chapel. About this time also the eastern termination of the chapel on the east side of the south transept was removed and a large three-light window,—with tracery of somewhat similar design to those at Dorchester Abbey,—was added. This chapel is known as St. Lucy's Chapel, and is now the baptistery, with a modern font.

The south transept is of three bays, as the north; the southernmost bay, however, is of two stories, the lower being formed by the slype which leads from the cloister to the cemetery eastward, and the upper being a gallery approached by a stair from the inside of the transept which was formerly a communication between the church and the dormitory. The same arrangement, in a slightly modified form, exists at Bristol, but there the Chapter-house immediately adjoins the transept and there is no slype.

With the exception of the rich pendant roof of the choir and Presbytery, the additions made in Perpendicular times were chiefly confined to the insertion of windows and doors, and the rebuilding of the Cloister Court. The outer wall of the north nave aisle appears to have been rebuilt at this time, and the vaulting here is in cement, and a bad imitation of earlier work.

The general character of the interior is one of simplicity. Only the aisles and the choir are vaulted. The nave, transepts, and tower have wood ceilings of late date. The peculiar arrangement of the arcades,—the caps being at two levels, carrying an upper and a lower series of arches,—will be best understood by reference to the view of the interior of the transept (see lithograph). The caps themselves vary much in character, the earlier ones being in the choir, with some curious carving, resembling Saxon ornament, while those in the nave are more fully developed, bordering on Early English foliage. It is thought that some of

Christchurch Cathedral Oxford – Cap in Choir.

Christch. Cathedl Oxford. Caps in Nave.

these Early caps are portions of Ethelred's church. They are more worn, and have the appearance of having belonged to a building that had been ruined and exposed to the

weather, and afterwards incorporated in a larger scheme. The whole series of these caps, from east to west, form a very interesting study of the progress of carving. The view across the transept which we give shows some of these caps.

Christchurch Cath. Oxford. Base of a Cross formerly built in buttress of S Lucy's Chapel, now in Sacristy in N Transept
Sketch shewing subjects: Adam & Eve and Abraham & Isaak
11½ deep
1' 10"
Plan of top of Pedestal with holes for shaft: etc.
Portion of one side. ? Moses receiving Tables of the Law.

The most important of the monuments are all in the north-eastern portion of the church, standing in close proximity to the shrine of St. Frideswide. The most interesting objects here now are the remains of the shrine itself. Some fragments of what appears to be Forest marble, with delicate carving, were found, forming the sides of a well in the yard south-west of the Cathedral, and they have been set up under the easternmost arch between the Lady Chapel and the north choir aisle, stone having been used to fill in the missing parts. A portion of the plinth formed a step with the carved portion turned inwards, and another was found built in a chimney in "Tom" quad. This interesting piece of work is probably the shrine which was in course of construction in 1270, and to which St. Frideswide's relics were removed in 1289. It measures 7 ft. in length by 3 ft. 6 in. in breadth, and consists of an arcade of two arches at the sides, and one at each end. There was no vaulting inside, the arch moulds being repeated on the inner face, and mitreing with a slightly projecting cornice moulding which served as a ledge in which the upper part of the structure, containing the shrine proper, was fixed. The spandrels throughout are filled with very beautifully carved foliage—the carving being very naturalistic, and suggesting a later date than is ascribed to it. The plants represented are: on the south side, the greater celandine, maple, and columbine; on the north side, ivy, oak, and sycamore; at the east end, vine and fig; and at the west end, white thorn and bryony.* It should be noticed that the foliage at the angles takes the form of pastoral staves, either by accident or design. The intermediate spandrels on the north and south sides are circular in form, with beads in the centre. A large portion of the plinth has been found, showing a series of quatrefoils with beads of queens on the south side, and at the west end, that of a bishop. Very delicate foliage is worked on a little roll moulding at the angle, and foliage instead of a head occupies the centre and end panels on the longer sides. Much of course is still missing, and considering that the fragments already found came from places some distance apart, it is difficult to organise a search in any one particular part of the fabric with any hope of finding more.

After the shrine the most interesting monuments are those arranged under the arcade between the Lady Chapel and St. Katharine's Chapel. Under the east arch is a large stone tomb richly panelled, with a staircase at its western end leading to an upper chapel or loft, constructed of wood, and of later date than the tomb. It is supposed by some to have been a watching-chamber to guard the shrine of the saint, as at St. Albans, but at present there is no satisfactory evidence as to where the shrine itself stood, and it seems more likely that the loft was used as a chantry chapel in connexion with the tomb below. In the next bay westward, is the beautiful tomb of Elizabeth, Lady Montacute, who died in 1359, and who gave Christchurch Meadow to the Priory for the founding of a chantry. The effigy itself is a very fine piece of workmanship, the ornament on the dress being rendered in *gesso* and coloured. On each side of the tomb are six standing figures, which are excellent examples of the costume of the period, and which will be found, as well as the principal effigies, finely engraved in Hollis's "Monumental Effigies."

The next tomb westward is that of Prior Alexander de Sutton, 1294-1316. The effigy of Purbeck lies under a canopy composed of three gables supported on shafts of Purbeck. There were formerly figures at the angles, but only one,—at the north-west angle,—remains at all complete, and still has a little of its original colour. A tomb, with the recumbent effigy of a knight,—said to be Sir George Nowers, a companion of the Black Prince, occupies the next bay, which is actually the old eastern aisle of the transept. These two last-mentioned monuments were shown in a sketch given in *Builder*, August 9, 1890, in our account of Oxford, and also some of the caps from Prior Sutton's tomb. In the floor of the Lady Chapel are several stones of interest. Two contain brasses,—one to John Fitzalan, 1452, and another to Edward, son of Hugh Courtenay. Immediately south of Lady Montacute's monument is a stone with a large cross in the centre, and the following remains of a marginal inscription in Lombardic characters:—

JOHAN : DE : COL . , V . LE : GIST : ICI : DIEV : (illegible) MCCC (or MERCI) . POVR : LAME PRIER : DIS : JOVRS : DE : PARDON : AVER : AMEN.

In the adjoining north aisle of the choir is a stone commemorating, "Andreas de Soltre Quondam rector Ecclesiæ de Kalleyn."

In this aisle is also a fine brass to James Coorthoppe, Canon of Christchurch 1546, and Dean of Peterborough, who died in 1557.

Under the north window of the transept is a

* The names of the plants are given in an appendix to two sermons by the Very Rev. H. Liddell (late) Dean of Chichester, as identified by Mr. Druce, of Oxford.

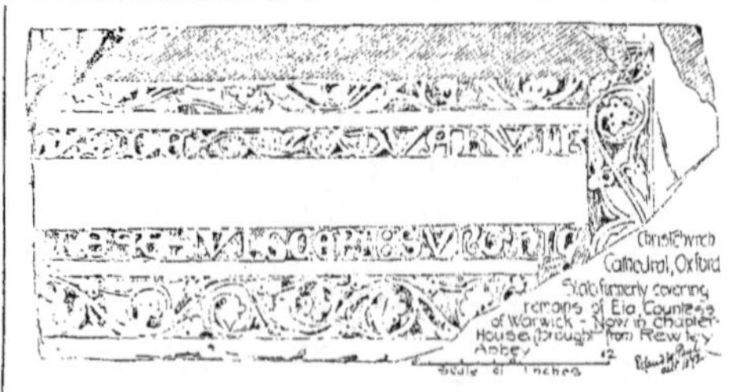

small altar tomb to James Zouch, who died in 1503, and near St. Lucy's Chapel, a monument to Bishop King, the first Bishop of Oxford, who died in 1557. It is not, however, in its original position, having been removed from the choir.

In the Latin Chapel are some stalls, *temp.* Wolsey, and probably forming part of his choir fittings. The poppy-heads are very elaborate. We give two, showing the way the Cardinal's hat and tassels were worked into the design. The windows of the Latin Chapel are shown in the view of the exterior, with their flowing tracery. Some of the glass is of the same date, and includes figures of SS. Frideswide, Margaret, and Catherine, Etheldreda (?) and the Virgin and Child. In the borders are various animals, monkeys being introduced both here and in the glass now in St. Lucy's Chapel. This latter is a fine example of reticulated tracery with elaborate cusping. The glass, too, is interesting, of early fourteenth-century date, and including representations of St. Cuthbert (with St. Oswald's head), St. Blaze, St. Martin (giving his cloak to a poor man at the gate of Amiens), the murder of Beckett, and St. Augustine preaching to his clerics.

The upper floor over the slype, which forms a portion of the south transept, as before mentioned, is now used as a small museum, and contains several specimens of early stonework and carving, found from time to time. Amongst these is the base of a cross with sockets, central shaft, and two side brackets for figures. (See illustration on page 441).

In the Chapter-house, which is a fine specimen of Early English work, is some interesting old glass, of Wolsey's time and later. The entrance to the Chapter-house is Norman, and just within, lying on a stone bench, is the slab which covered the remains of Ela, wife of Thomas de Newburgh, Earl of Warwick, and daughter of William Longspée. It was brought here from Rewley Abbey, and is an interesting specimen of its date (thirteenth century). The cloisters have been extensively restored. All the vaulting is modern except that in the south walk and the two southern bays of the east walk. There are some foundations, evidently of some important building, still visible in the garth. They would seem, however, to have no connexion with any of the portions now in existence. The interior of the Cathedral has been restored, and new choir fittings and a reredos put up. The pulpit is a fine specimen of Jacobean work. Some good modern stained glass, from designs by Mr. Burne-Jones, should not be overlooked. It is placed in the eastern windows of the aisles and in that at the west end of the south aisle.

THE ARCHITECTURAL ASSOCIATION:

ELECTION OF OFFICERS FOR 1892-93.

THE last meeting of this Association for Session 1891-92 was held on Friday, the 27th ult., Mr. F. T. Baggallay, President, in the chair.

On the motion for the confirmation of the minutes of the previous meeting, one or two members took exception to one or two passages in the minutes as read, and on the suggestion of Mr. Leonard Stokes it was decided to postpone the confirmation of the minutes until after Mr. Ashbee had read his paper.

Mr. C. R. Ashbee then read a paper on "The Relation of the Architect to the Workman," which we print on another page, deferring the discussion until next week. A hearty vote of thanks was given to Mr. Ashbee for his paper, and for kindly coming a second time with it, under the circumstances mentioned in the *Builder* for May 21, p. 401.

The Travelling Student's Notes.

Owing to want of time, Mr. Kotaro Sakurai, the A. A. Travelling Student of last year, did not read the "Notes" of his tour, but they appear *in extenso* in the new number of *A. A. Notes.* We can only find space for a brief summary of Mr. Sakurai's paper. The author commenced by expressing his thanks to the members for having awarded the Studentship to him last year. He travelled in Somersetshire, commencing his tour on July 7. The first two weeks were spent at Wells, in studying the cathedral and its precincts. The chief glory of the cathedral, he said, lies in its interior. The staircase to the Chapter-house he characterised as "one of the most unique" pieces of work that he had ever seen; while for ingenuity of design, attained with graceful effect, few if any, can equal the Lady Chapel. The parish church of St. Cuthbert possessed a magnificent western tower of remarkably bold design for the period in which it was erected. Besides the ecclesiastical buildings, there are many examples of domestic work, both in the cathedral precincts and town. While at Wells, the author took trips to Glastonbury and Croscombe; the latter place is well worth a visit, for, besides the beautiful church, rich in Jacobean woodwork, there are many old houses, among which is a bay window of a quaint type. He also visited the village of Cheddar, alliteratively known for its cliffs, caves, and cheese, to which two more "C's" of equal interest might be added,—the Church, and the Cross: the former contains a good deal of woodwork and a rich stone pulpit. The hexagonal market cross, of simple design, has been restored recently. The author's next halt was at Langport, which (although not containing much of interest, except the church, whose chancel is considered to be above the average) is a good centre for visiting the numerous churches in the neighbourhood. Those at Curry Rivell, Long Sutton, and High Ham are specially noteworthy for richness of oak-work. At Muchelney there are considerable remains of the Benedictine Abbey of SS. Peter and Paul, founded by Athelstan in 939. Most of the existing parts date from not long before the Dissolution of the monasteries,—*i.e.*, a portion of the richly-panelled cloisters, the kitchen, the ante-room, and a large chamber over, with a fine mantel-piece and linen pattern panelling round part of the wall. Close by is a fifteenth-century thatched cottage, long used as the vicarage house. Huish Episcopi is the nearest church to Langport, and perhaps the most important one in the neighbourhood, as it has one of the best towers of the "Taunton type." The charm of the structure consists chiefly in its elegant details, admirable execution, and the delightful colour of the Ham Hill stone employed. The church at Martock, a typical old country town, is a large structure of the usual local type. The nave of six bays, covered with an elaborate tie-beam roof, is a good specimen of late fifteenth-century work, but perhaps not quite equal in merit to the enthusiastic description of Mr. Freeman, who says:—"The nave is a notable instance of the idea of a great parish church, thoroughly worked out,—a nave as perfect in its own style as the nave of a cathedral." The chancel is undoubtedly that of the older church, and contains five lancet windows at the east end and a curved brace roof. On the south side of the church there is a fourteenth-century manor-house, retaining the original arrangement of the hall (with a good roof), kitchen, and offices, in a perfect state. While staying at Martock the author visited the churches at Kingsbury Episcopi and Stoke-sub-Hamden. The former has a tower almost identical, though somewhat inferior in detail, to that of Huish Episcopi, but the church, itself with its fine rood-loft and screen, is much better in every respect to the last-named. Stoke-sub-Hamden Church, cruciform without aisles, was originally Norman, but now combines work of every period; from Early Norman to Late Perpendicular. The author next went to South Petherton, and saw the house known as "King Ina's Palace," the hall of which has been much restored. He next visited Barrington Court, Montacute House, Odcombe, Preston, and Yeovil. In conclusion, Mr. Sakurai sums up the characteristic features of Somersetshire architecture, speaking highly of its domestic work, but criticising what he calls the "confectionery-like" treatment of many of the church towers, and also expressing the opinion that the position of the towers,—almost invariably at the west end of the nave,—was a most difficult one for the production of an agreeable composition. He had rarely met with any truly successful *façade* thus designed (he did not say this of Somersetshire only); the ends of the aisles, as a rule, formed very awkward terminations, and the arrangement necessitated the use of a large west window in the lower stage of the tower, where the appearance of solidity was much needed.

On the motion of the President, a hearty vote of thanks was given to Mr. Sakurai for permitting his paper to be merely "taken a read," instead of reading it, as usual.

Minutes, &c.

The meeting then reverted to the question of the minutes, which were ultimately confirmed, after one or two emendations suggested in the course of a rather heated discussion, which principally turned on the question of the validity or invalidity of the nomination, made and received at the previous meeting (see *Builder* for May 21, p, 401), of Mr. Gerald C. Horsley as a member of the Committee. It appeared that in the view of the Committee, Mr. Horsley is not a member of the Association, and therefore his nomination to serve on the Committee was invalid. It seems that some months ago Mr. Horsley (for some reason which was not stated) wrote to the secretaries resigning his membership. The receipt of that letter, it appears, was duly entered on the minutes at the time. But it was stated by Mr. Stokes that, at the request of the Committee, he had an interview with Mr. Horsley, in order to induce him to withdraw his resignation. The result of that interview was that Mr. Horsley verbally withdrew his resignation of membership, and Mr. Stokes said he distinctly recollected reporting Mr. Horsley's withdrawal of resignation to the Committee. The majority of the Committee appeared to have no recollection of this, although Mr. Pryce and Mr. Brodie said they distinctly remembered Mr. Stokes reporting the result of his interview with Mr. Horsley. At any rate, there was no entry on the minutes mentioning Mr. Horsley's withdrawal of resignation, and the majority of the Committee, or the officers (the matter was not made quite clear), had, since the meeting at which Mr. Horsley was nominated to serve on the Committee, decided that his nomination was not valid, and that any votes given to him would be lost, whatever might be his position on the poll. It was pointed out by Mr. Stokes and other speakers that this was a very unfortunate circumstance; that it was a pity that some member of the Committee had not taken objection to Mr. Horsley's nomination when it was made at the previous meeting; and that Mr. Horsley himself was present at the meeting when he was nominated, and, in answer to a question from the President, said he would be willing to serve,—which (said Mr. Stokes) showed that Mr. Horsley himself was quite under the impression that he was still a member of the Association.

Three new members were nominated for election, and the following gentlemen, nominated at a previous meeting, were duly elected, viz., Messrs. W. G. Horseman, J. W. Hoult, E. O. Sachs, G. W. Stone, P. J. Groom, A. M. Sinclair, A. W. Moore, A. Hannaford, R. T. Grove, A. R. Dannatt, H. W. Anderson, and G. F. Grover.

Among the donations to the library was Part XXIII. of "The Dictionary of Architecture," presented by the Architectural Publication Society. A vote of thanks was accorded to the donors.

On the motion of Mr. F. T. W. Goldsmith, a hearty vote of thanks was given to Mr. Ewan Christian for permitting the members to visit the new National Portrait Gallery, as reported in the *Builder* for May 21, p. 399.

Travelling Student for 1892.

The President announced that two sets of drawings had been sent in for the A.A. Travelling Studentship, and the Committee was of opinion that the Studentship should be awarded to Mr. Thomas Arthur Sladdin, and that a second prize of 5*l.* should be awarded to Mr. E. A. Richards. Whilst regretting that there was not a larger number of competitors, the Committee wished to express their high appreciation of the excellence of the drawings sent in.

Election of Officers and Committee.

The President having called for the report of the scrutineers of the balloting papers,

Mr. Beale, one of the scrutineers, said he wished to be allowed to make a personal explanation. He said he happened to be the proposer of Mr. Horsley as a member of the Committee, and he felt that some discredit would attach to him (Mr. Beale) unless he said that he had no reason to suppose that Mr. Horsley was not a member of the Association at they time; furthermore, he was quite sure that Mr. Horsley believed himself to be a member of the Association. Under the Committee's ruling, he (Mr. Beale) and his fellow-scrutineers were of opinion that the balloting-papers were all invalid and that the election was void, and therefore they did not think that there was sufficient ground for presenting their report.*

The President said that the voting papers were not invalid and the election was not void. The only thing would be that any votes given to Mr. Horsley would be lost.

Mr. Beale said he was sorry that he could not present the report.

The President: You must present the scrutineers' report, if you please, or one of the other scrutineers must do so.

Mr. Beale: I am sorry I cannot.

The President: I call upon the meeting to support the chair (loud and long-continued applause).

Mr. Beale: Sir, as it is the evident wish of the meeting, I comply with your request, but it is entirely under protest. I feel that I am presenting a report on invalid voting papers.

The President then read the report of the scrutineers on the result of the voting, which was as follows:—

President: Mr. H. O. Cresswell.

Vice-Presidents.—Mr. Paul Waterhouse, 444 votes, and Mr. E. Woodthorpe, 391 votes.

Committee: F. T. Baggallay, 421; E. W. Mountford, 421; F. R. Farrow, 375; W. Burrell, 301; L. Stokes, 301; W. J. N. Millard, 272; E. J. May, 265; A. W. Earle, 246; A. O. Bulmer Booth, 232; and W. D. Caröe, M.A., 228.*

Hon. Treasurer: Mr. Hampden W. Pratt.

Hon. Librarian: Mr. J. W. Stonhold.

Hon. Secretaries: Messrs. Ernest S. Gale and Mr. F. T. W. Goldsmith.

On the motion of Mr. Cresswell, President-elect, a vote of thanks was accorded to the scrutineers; and on the motion of Mr. Leonard Stokes, a hearty vote of thanks was given to the retiring President, and to the retiring Vice-Presidents (Messrs. F. R. Farrow and E. W. Mountford) for their services during the past year. Mr. Baggallay was highly eulogised by Mr. Stokes for the indefatigable manner in which he had discharged the exceptionally onerous duties of the year, especially in connexion with the first year's working of the new curriculum.

Mr. Baggallay having briefly replied, the meeting terminated.

* Mr. Sydney Beale has sent us a long letter, detailing the reasons of this action taken by the scrutineers, to which we cannot give space: we may merely mention that there appears to have been a difference of opinion as to whether Mr. G. C. Horsley, who had early in the year resigned membership, had or had not formally withdrawn his resignation, as he had been invited to do. The scrutineers counted the votes under the impression that those for Mr. Horsley were valid, while it was stated afterwards at the meeting that Mr. Horsley was not a member. The scrutineers therefore considered the lists were informal or invalid. —ED.

* The number of votes recorded for the unsuccessful candidates was not announced, but, in answer to a question by Mr. Dicksee, the President stated that Mr. Horsley had not received a sufficient number of votes to place him amongst the first ten candidates.

The Annual Dinner.

The work of the session was brought to a close very amicably and pleasantly by the annual dinner, which was held at the "Criterion" on Tuesday evening last, Mr. Baggallay in the chair. The toast of "The Queen and Royal Family" having been duly honoured,

The Chairman proposed "The Royal Academy," which he spoke of as the only body, besides the Association, which had ever done anything for the training of architects. Although there was no doubt that the Academy might do more, admission to its Architectural School was rightly looked upon as of the greatest educational advantage to a young architect. He regretted that there was no Academician or Associate present to respond for the toast, which he coupled with the name of Mr. H. L. Florence, a former gold medallist and travelling student of the Academy.

Mr. H. L. Florence, in responding, said he regretted that they had not the advantage of the presence of some member of the Academy, who might have been asked to respond to the toast. He noticed that the toast appeared on the list as "The Royal Academy." He should have preferred to reply for "The Royal Academy of Arts." He could conceive such an academy, in which Architecture would take her rightful place as an elder sister of the Arts, and not be a mere Cinderella.

The next toast was "The Royal Institute of British Architects," proposed by the Chairman, and coupled with the name of Mr. J. M. Brydon, who replied.

The toast of the evening, "The Architectural Association," was proposed by Mr. W. Hale, President of the Birmingham Architectural Association, who said he was a member of the London Association forty years ago, in the days when it used to hold its meetings in Lyon's Inn Hall. With the toast was coupled the name of Professor Kerr, the first President of the Association, who, in reply, made an interesting speech contrasting the Association as it was forty-five years ago and as it is now.

The other toasts were "The Visitors," proposed by F. T. W. Goldsmith and coupled with the name of Mr. Knowles, President of the Northern Architectural Association; "The Instructors and Studio Visitors," proposed by Mr. Leonard Stokes, and responded to by Mr. E. W. Mountford and Mr. Holmes; "The President-Elect" (Mr. H. O. Cresswell), proposed by the Chairman; and "The Retiring President and Officers," proposed by Mr. Cresswell and coupled with the names of Mr. F. T. Baggallay and Mr. E. S. Gale. During the evening some excellent singing was given by members of the A.A. Lyric Club.

NEW SURVEYS OF LONDON PARISHES. — The Vestry of St. Mary, Newington, have commenced a re-survey of the parish for drainage purposes, and we understand that Mr. Alfred Mark, who has recently been engaged upon similar work, under Mr. Charles Mason, Surveyor to St. Martin's Vestry, Charing-cross, has been entrusted with the work, which will bring the whole of the plans of the district (632 acres in extent) up to the present date. Mr. Mark previously prepared a new map of the Parish of Islington, under Mr. J. Patten Barber, Chief Surveyor to the Vestry.

Books.

Laxton's Builders' Price-Book for 1892. Seventy-fifth edition. London: Kelly & Co.

Lockwood's Builder's, Architect's, Contractor's, and Engineer's Price-Book for 1892. Edited by FRANCIS T. W. MILLER, A.R.I.B.A. London: Crosby Lockwood & Son.

Spon's Architects' and Builders' Price-Book. By W. YOUNG, Architect. London: E. & F. N. Spon.

THE demand for these books finds sufficient proof in their regular re-appearance year by year, as also in their steady increase in bulk. The veteran "Laxton," now in its seventy-fifth edition, numbers about 760 pages, of which nearly 200 are devoted to trade advertisements. We have already stated our opinion that tables of prices might and should be drawn up in a more scientific manner than is attempted in any book we know, and we are therefore unable to express unqualified approbation of the works before us, in which the old system is still followed. At the same time, we are glad to notice that within these limits a real effort is made to write the books up to date, and to keep the prices tolerably coherent. Specially noticeable is this in respect of the new kinds of wood now used in joinery, and in the matter of new sanitary appliances. The demand for the latter has greatly increased of late, from the awakening of the public intelligence to the vital importance of sanitation, and the large space given to them in these pages is well employed. It would be convenient to be told whether the prices set out for the various patent fittings include in all cases the same percentage of profit, or whether they are merely list prices subject to varying discounts.

One of the uses of a price-book should be to assist builders in calculating prices for themselves, to meet the multitude of cases which arise wherein the stereotyped items do not apply. This function cannot be adequately discharged without a carefully-prepared analysis of a large number of prices, showing the elements of which they are made up. In "Laxton" last year a chapter appeared entitled, "On the Adaptation of a Price-book to Meet Varying Rates of Wages," which was certainly a step in the direction we have indicated. The approximate proportions of labour and materials were there given in the cases of several trades, each trade being treated as a unit. Thus the cost of labour in bricklayers' work was put at one-third of the whole, in carpenters' and joiners' work at two-thirds, and so on. This is obviously very rough, and we are not concerned at the moment to say how near to accuracy these ratios may come. But it was a welcome effort, and we regret to see that this year, so far from being carried further, it is abandoned,—although the compiler of the carpenters' prices seems to be unaware of the fact (p. 99). We may be asked, why, when the books are to all appearance satisfactory to the trade, depart from the present system? We reply that the trade does not rely on them for serious pricing. It is, indeed, something of a misnomer to call them price-books. They are a compendium of handy information on matters connected with building, and would command a sale if there were not a single price in them. To say nothing of tables of weights of materials, tables for calculating weekly wages, tables for ascertaining the value of leases, annuities, &c., model conditions of contract, the Metropolitan Buildings Acts, with cases and decisions thereon, the By-laws of the London County Council and the list of District Surveyors, we may obtain from these volumes instruction in mensuration, in the art of measuring builder's work of all kinds, in perspective drawing, and in classical design. Nay more, we may here learn that "few men realise the importance of trifles: stored, they make one man's fortune; neglected, they cause another's ruin. There are few trades in which this occurs more frequently than in the builder's" ("Laxton," p. 399). Notwithstanding the apparent plethora of price-books, there still remains room for one which shall not only give tables of prices, but shall examine and explain the principles on which they are based, and the methods by which they are arrived at.

The First Principles of Mechanical Engineering. By JOHN IMRAY and C. H. W. BIGGS. London: Biggs & Co., 1892.

To write a book on Mechanical Engineering without using any but simple mathematics is a much more difficult task than most people would imagine, since laborious and tedious description is the penalty to be paid for despising algebraical formulæ, and the result, instead of being a scientific treatise, is but a popular hand book on the subject. Valuable information may, however, be given even in this way, and the authors have left but few subjects untouched between such limits as the mechanics of antiquity and modern screw-cutting gear. A good deal is said about mechanical drawing, materials and stresses, sources of mechanical power, and such subjects, and although the book contains but little that is original, yet the explanations and descriptions, besides being well illustrated, are always written in a clear and simple manner, suitable for the class of readers for which the work has been prepared.

The Beam, or Technical Elements of Girder Construction. By William Lewis Baker, A.M.I.C.E. London: Chapman & Hall, Limited. 1892.

One of the first things that should be mastered by the student commencing to study engineering is the strength of girders and beams under the various conditions of loading to which they may be exposed, and in the above little book this subject is treated in a very clear manner, and without employing complicated algebraic formulæ. Commencing with an explanation of the elementary principles, the author shows how to ascertain the stresses in cantilevers and beams, and also how the different parts of cast-iron and plate girders should be proportioned to resist these stresses. The methods of computing the stresses in simple lattice girders are also dealt with, and by a series of well-chosen examples the author illustrates what calculations are most frequently required in the ordinary practice of the architect and engineer, and students wishing to become acquainted with the elements of the subject could not do better than to study carefully this little book.

Palliser's Specification Blanks. New York: Palliser, Palliser, & Co.

This is a specimen of one of the skeleton forms of printed specification published by Messrs. Palliser & Co., of New York, the object of which is of course to shorten specification writing (which is a gain) and to take a good deal of the thinking out of the architect's hands, which is not a gain. The skeleton in this case is rather too much filled up, and moreover is not suited for English practice, which would require a form for itself differing from that of the States. We do not much approve however of skeleton specifications, except those which an architect draws up and lithographs or prints for his own use. If that is carefully done it saves the trouble of writing over again permanent requirements and forms a memorandum also, and it then represents the architect's own practice derived from his own thought and experience, and he is likely to leave it so far open as to leave room for the specification of the special requirements of each separate building. But a published form of specification only tends to do away with individuality of work and to save an architect the trouble of thinking out fully the carrying out of his work; and we do not think any architect of original power and ability will ever care for published specification forms. They may be useful to those gentlemen who at present (we believe there are not a few) leave the quantity surveyor to write the specification: but even they will want an English and not a New York edition.

Brick for Street Pavements: an Account of Tests made of Bricks and Paving-Blocks, with a Brief Discussion of Street Pavements and the Method of Constructing them. By M. D. Burke, C.E. Cincinnati: Robert Clarke & Co. 1892.

A large part of the contents of this pamphlet was included in a report made to the village authorities of tests of material to be used in paving streets at Avondale, of which the author was "village engineer" (we presume "village" has not precisely the same meaning in the States as here). The tests were made upon specimens of granite and of various bricks, and the results of chemical analysis, absorption tests, and of crushing, transverse strength, and abrasion tests are given. The specimens are numbered in the tables, and a description of the quality of each specimen given in the text, referring to the tabular number. The object of the pamphlet is, as a sequel to these tests, to recommend the use of brick as a pavement, as the best substitute for granite in an economical sense. With a hard brick this may be worth trying, but in regard to towns it is not of course a noiseless pavement, and that (in a comparative sense) is almost a *sine quâ non* nowadays. Engineers and road-surveyors will, however, in any case find the statistics of interest.

Popular Map of England and Wales: in cloth case. Edinburgh: W. & A. K. Johnston.

This is one of the best cheap and portable maps of England that has been issued. It is a very full one, admirably engraved, and on a scale about double that of the usual larger type of atlas map. A detailed map of the environs of London is added in the margin. The map folds into a sufficiently small case to carry in the pocket. It is sold either mounted or unmounted, at the price of 1s. and 2s. respectively, but we should recommend the mounted map as the better economy. These folding maps, on mere paper, always tear after a short usage, even of the most careful kind.

House Drainage Hydro-mems. By G. M. Lawford. London: Geo. Gill & Sons.

This very small publication consists simply of a card printed on both sides and made to double up so as to go easily into the pocket. It contains tables of velocity, inclination and discharge of house drains, weight of lead pipes, water pressure, and cisterns' capacities and usual stock sizes, with a few general memoranda. It is very useful as a reference card for data which are often wanted and not easily carried in the memory.

Some Notes on the Public Health Act, with an Appendix on London Fog and Smoke. By Harry G. Assiter. London: Crosby Lockwood & Son.

This is one of the numerous commentaries on the spirit and bearings of the Public Health Act, which have appeared since that Act was passed, and gives a useful *résumé* of its provisions and of their practical results when put into action. The author adds a short essay on the smoke question, which he has taken up a good deal, in which he urges the application of legal restriction against creating smoke to domestic fireplaces as well as to factories. Mr. Assiter can see (what some people cannot) that the public will not accept stoves or anthracite coal as a substitute for the open fire, and falls back upon the recommendation of a modification of the present system of combustion, which he observes "is not a difficult matter;" but he does not say what modification he proposes, which rather takes away the point from the whole essay.

Camping Out. By Arthur A. Macdonell, M.A. London: G. Bell & Sons. 1892.

We do not know why this book has been sent to us, as it has no sort of relation to our special subjects of interest; but for any of our readers who want to make a boating and camping-out holiday we can recommend it as a readable book, with a great many useful suggestions for novices in open-air living.

Correspondence.

To the Editor of The Builder.

VICTORIA CATHEDRAL COMPETITION.

Sir,—My attention has been called to the fact that my designs for the new cathedral at Victoria, British Columbia, were published in the *Building News* last week.

May I ask room to state that this has been done entirely without my knowledge and consent, and much against my wishes.

The Author of the Design marked "New and Old."

June 1, 1892.

A QUESTION OF BUILDING PENALTY.

Sir,—In June, 1891, a builder entered into a contract for the erection of a building which was to be completed by October of the same year under a heavy penalty. This building was not completed for the following reasons:—

1. There was an extra depth of excavation, and consequently an extra quantity of foundation, owing to bad and insecure ground.

2. The architect gave orders for commencing the building before the land was properly conveyed, thereby preventing the builder from proceeding with the works.

3. Various alterations were ordered to the interior walls.

4. Iron built girders were ordered in lieu of wood framing, causing many weeks delay.

5. A very glaring mistake in the quantities, whereby a quantity of extra work was caused.

6. Numerous alterations at completion, caused by the local authorities objecting to pass the building till alterations had been done to the satisfaction of the surveyor.

7. Delay in getting details from the architect, some of which were not delivered, but had to be prepared by the builder long after the works were specified to be completed.

The architect has given the proprietors a final account and also a certificate, less the error in quantities. The proprietors now object to pay the builder unless he will allow the amount stipulated to be paid if the building was not completed within the specified period.

Are the proprietors entitled to deduct this sum where it is not the fault of the builder, but owing to the numerous alterations?

Who should the builder apply to for the amount of the error in quantities?

If any of your readers would kindly give their views, it would oblige,

A Contractor.

FIRE-BRICK.

Sir,—Will you be good enough to allow me the assistance of your pages to inquire what make of fire-brick is considered to be the best in the market; and the means of ascertaining and procuring a report of the refractory qualities of any make of fire-brick?

J. C. Kenwood.

The Student's Column.

WARMING BUILDINGS BY HOT WATER.

XXIII.

EXAMPLE BUILDING WORKS.

In the following few examples it has to be mentioned, as was done when giving examples of horticultural works, that it may never fall to the reader's lot to erect an apparatus like any one of them; but by describing, and also illustrating, one or two methods of carrying out the works, great assistance can be rendered to the unskilled. The principles are thus made more clear, and once the principles are grasped, nothing else can be gained except by actual experience. The examples are merely supposed requirements, and the possibly best way of meeting them. It is impossible to do more than this, as there are but very rarely two works anyway resembling one another.

Fig. 95 shows a convenient little arrangement (it can hardly be called an apparatus) to give

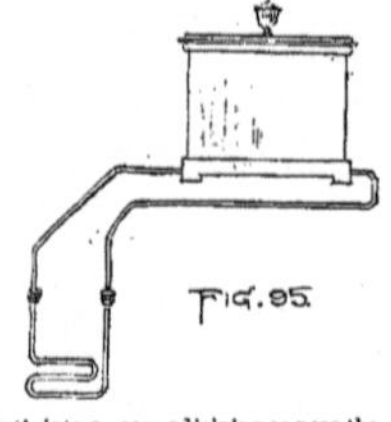

warmth into a room adjoining or near the place where the fire is. The coil is supposed to be at the back of an ordinary open-grate fire, and furnishes heat to a few feet of pipe or a small radiator, which, however, should not be far away. This drawing shows a coil of three ½-in. pipes, the top pipe being continued upwards as the flow, and the lower one forming the return. Two unions are shown just above the fire-box to facilitate the removal of the coil if eventually it becomes fractured. There is no doubt it will fail one day if it has much usage, as dirt will find its way into the pipes, and eventually fill up the lower one, and cause it to split. If steam quality tube is used, it will last very well for several years, only having use in the winter. A piece of copper tube for the coil would do well.

It is hard to suggest what actual work this little appliance is capable of doing, it depends upon several things. Firstly, the size of the fire; if it is a fire-box holding a good thickness of fuel, that is a mass of fuel deep from front to back, very effective results are obtained. If the fire-box has wholly fire-brick at back and sides (as with all good modern grates), it helps matters, and the attention to the fire will affect the heating of the pipes. In putting pipes, containing water, in the fire of an open grate, we introduce a cooling influence that may completely spoil the utility of the grate, for it must be particularly noted that the combustion effected in an open fire is very different to that in a close stove or boiler, with the important assistance it has by the draught that is induced. With a close stove the draught passing through the fuel (and not over it as it does with a grate fire) causes combustion to proceed briskly irrespective of cooling influences, and this speed of combustion can be regulated, just as may be required, by the damper.

If the grate fire-box is not a large one, three pipes will have a deadening effect upon the fire, and two or one pipes only must be used for small requirements. The uses of this arrangement are that a radiator can be put into a neighbouring room, which is perhaps of such a size as not to be heated by its own fireplace; or it may be used to introduce a little warmth into a room that is not used regularly. If the coil was in a large fire it might be made to heat sufficient radiating pipe for the warmth a billiard-room should always have when out of use.

The water-supply may be provided for by a little cistern in any convenient place where it is not seen, or, the radiator may be fitted with a little vase filling cup at top as shown. This latter article then acts as an air vent. In any case an air-cock will be needed at the highest point in the radiator to allow for the escape of air as it is being filled. No stop-cock would be required with this apparatus; but a draw-off service (for emptying purposes only) might be found useful if it can be conveniently placed.

The next example, fig. 96, illustrates two radiators in connexion with a small independent

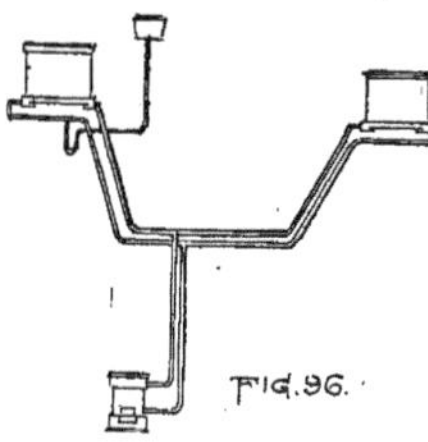

boiler, for heating an entrance hall or other similar purpose. Of course, coils or hot-water pipes could be used in place of the radiators, if so desired. There is scarcely a better purpose to which heating works can be put than this. The great gain that is effected by providing warmth in an entrance hall cannot be over-estimated. This part of the house, with the staircases leading from it, has been likened to an artery, as it furnishes a constant current of air to the rooms and places that lead off from it. It must be known by everyone that in nearly all cases the greater part of the air entering a house (and the volume is great) enters by the doors and openings it can find on the ground floor. This inflow is necessary, as the chimneys in a house require air, also the occupants of course, and the house itself can well be likened to a great chimney, for an upward current of air, as a rule, always manifests itself inside. These conditions, perhaps, do not exist, or at any rate to such an extent when a good system of ventilation is provided; but this, unfortunately, is absent in too many cases.

Assuming that a considerable volume of air finds its way into the house by the best route it can, the larger proportion will pass through the entrance hall, and, as a rule, this part of the house is very cold; all doors in the vicinity have disagreeable draughts to them; and the staircases are in quite as bad a state. By introducing heat in the entrance hall, a really important benefit is obtained. The heating medium should be placed as near the outer doors as possible, so as to contribute its warmth to the incoming air. By this means the hall is made agreeable if not quite warm; the air entering the rooms is tempered, and that which passes up the staircases goes to make the upper parts of the house less cold. By keeping the boiler fire alight through the night, the very disagreeable degree of cold experienced in the halls and staircases at early morning is prevented. Engineers are particularly cautioned against using the same quantity of radiating surface in an entrance hall as they would in a toom, if they want to make a success of the job. These places are not usually expected to be of as high a temperature as a room; but, notwithstanding this they require 50 per cent. more pipe. The necessity for this is due to the air of the hall being in tolerably rapid motion always; being taken by the rooms, and particularly the staircases, leading from it. If the gain effected was generally known, no residence of any pretension would be without heat in the entrance-hall.

In this example a small, independent boiler is shown, which would be situated in a cellar or basement room below. From the boiler is carried an inch flow and return service, by the best route (observing the principles already dwelt upon), and the pipes can be carried first to one radiator and then on to the other, or can be taken to a central point and branched each way as shown. If the pipes be carried first to one radiator, and then on to the other, the connexion to the first would have to be as fig. 94 (Art. XXII.), or the second coil would be much longer than the first in heating.

In branching the services as illustrated, a little better rise should be given to the pipes which extend furthest, so as to equalise results each way. There would be no need for stop-cocks in a little apparatus like this. The cold supply would be provided by a small cistern as shown, either filled by hand, or with a ball valve. If the latter, the cistern should only fill just an inch or two, so as to allow for the expansion of water when heating. An air-cock would have to be fitted in each radiator, and cleaning plugs, and an emptying cock should be provided to the boiler.

The pipes from the boiler should be 1 in., as just mentioned, but there would hardly be need for the branch to each radiator to be more than $\frac{3}{4}$ in. It will be seen that the cold supply-pipe has the customary dip in it to prevent the heated water circulating into the cold-water tank. The way in which this acts has been fully explained, and does not need repeating here.

SURVEYORSHIPS.

Salford.—A meeting of the General Purposes Committee of the Salford Town Council was held on the 27th ult., at the Salford Town-hall, presided over by the Mayor, Mr. Alderman Keevney, for the purpose of appointing a Borough Engineer and Surveyor, in the place of Mr. A. Jacob, who has retired. Out of the large number of applicants for the position, the following five candidates were selected to appear before the committee:—Mr. Geo. J. C. Broom, Borough Engineer of St. Helens; Mr. J. Corbett, engineer, Manchester, who lately resigned his office as a Salford councillor; Mr. H. C. Marks, Borough Engineer of Dewsbury; Mr. H. T. Marten, deputy Borough Surveyor of Bradford; and Mr. John Price, Engineer and Surveyor to the Toxteth Park Local Board, Liverpool. The voting resulted as follows: — Price, 22; Corbett, 21; Marks, 18; Broom, 13; and Marten 12. The selection of Mr. Price will come before the next meeting of the Council for confirmation.

GENERAL BUILDING NEWS.

The Proposed Exchange Alterations, Manchester.—The Improvement Committee of the Manchester City Council met on the 25th ult., and had under consideration the plans submitted by the Directors of the Manchester Royal Exchange for the extension of the building in Cross-street. In view of the proposed alterations, the Sub-Committee had recommended the adoption of a new building line in Cross-street, the practical effect of which would be to put an end to the present scheme of the Directors. The Committee gave their full and unanimous approval to the proposal of the Sub-Committee. The new building line for Corporation-street, from Market-street to Hanging-ditch, was also approved.—*Manchester Guardian.*

Proposed Parish Buildings and Club, Burton-on-Trent.—Lord Burton, having presented the town of Burton-on-Trent with the present St. Paul's Institute and the adjoining club premises for municipal buildings, has consented to erect a new church institute. The site selected for the building is at the corner of the Grange field. The building will be practically divided into two portions, viz., the club and the Sunday-school. The chief entrance for Sunday-school and parish purposes will be from St. Paul's-square, while the club premises will have a separate entrance, also from the square. The main entrance will lead direct to the lecture-hall, 66 ft. by 40 ft., which is to have walls of coloured brickwork and a panelled plaster ceiling. There will be a raised platform at the end, and retiring-rooms will be provided, these being approached by a separate staircase and entrance. On the same hoor will be the parish-room, 38 ft. by 22 ft., and a large kitchen. A side entrance will be provided to the lecture-hall, and access will be given therefrom to the boys' and girls' yards, which will be fitted up with the necessary offices. At the south end of the building will be the caretaker's residence. Cellars will be built under the parish kitchen and class-room. A staircase near the side entrance will give access to the upper floor of the Sunday-school and parish-rooms, and over the lecture-hall three class-rooms, each 17 ft. by 16 ft., and a teacher's reading-room in connexion with the general library of the club, will be provided. On the same floor will be a class-room, 40 ft. by 33 ft., and a smaller one leading from it. The club premises will be over the parish-room. The club-room will consist of a reading-room, 27 ft. by 22 ft.; a billiard-room, 44 ft. by 22 ft.; club-room, 25 ft. by 15 ft.; and library, 30 ft. by 12 ft. There will also be the Secretary's room and lavatory. The staircases in the public parts of the building are to be of stone, and all the floors will be fireproof. The height of the rooms will vary from 15 ft. to 20 ft. The main corridors will be 7 ft. wide, and screens with folding swing doors will be fixed inside all outer entrance doors. Siemen's patent regenerative lamps are to be used for lighting purposes, and there will be open fireplaces in the class-rooms and club-rooms, and hot water pipes for heating will be laid over the whole building. Block floors will be laid throughout. Messrs. Thomas Lowe & Sons, of Burton-on-Trent, whose tender for 9,925*l.* has been accepted, will be the builders. The work will be carried out from the plans prepared by Mr. Reginald Churchill, architect, Burton-on-Trent.

Addition to Schools, Middleton, Lancashire.—Extensive additions are being made to the Parish Church Schools, Middleton, consisting of two large class-rooms, new entrances, cloak-rooms, staircases, and offices. The external walls will be faced with South Ouram parpoints, relieved at all openings with dressed Huddersfield stone. The floors to cloak-rooms, &c., will be fireproof, and the interior woodwork pitch-piue. The works will be carried out by Messrs. Grundy & Sons of Middleton, under the supervision of Mr. T. A. Fitton, architect, of Middleton.

Restoration of St. Lawrence Church, Jersey.—On the 18th ult. the old parish Church of St. Lawrence, Jersey, was re-opened after restoration. The work, which was begun in 1889, has been completed under the direction of Mr. John E. Trollope, of Messrs. Giles, Gough, & Trollope, of London. The old church, says the *Jersey Express*, dating from 1199, had been allowed for centuries to fall into decay. Both the exterior and interior of the edifice have undergone renovation. The contractors were Messrs. Woodsford & Harris, and Mr. Cuzner has done the flooring and pewing. The passages are all floored with oak blocks, the remaining portion of the floor being in deal blocks. The pulpit and font are the gift of Mr. Elias Collas, of La Folie. Two stained-glass windows have been placed in the chancel, both representing scenes in the life of St. Lawrence. There has been acquired a new oak lectern and two oak sanctuary chairs, designed by Mr. John E. Trollope, and executed by Mr. Harry Hems, of Exeter.

Miners' Hall, Silksworth, Durham.—On the 21st ult. the corner-stones of the new Miners' Hall at Silksworth were laid by Mr. Samuel Storey, M.P., and other gentlemen. The new building will occupy a central position in the village, and will cost about 4,000*l.* The building will be of red brick, with stone dressings, having a length of 80 ft. by 45 ft. wide, and height inside 30 ft., the height from the hoor to the vane on the turret which will surmount the roof being 66 ft. 6 in. There will be an entrance hall with a check office on the right-hand side, and a committee-room on the left. At the far end of the hall there will be a platform, with a lobby on each side, in addition to two retiring-rooms on the right of the platform. There will be a gallery above the check office and committee-room. On the right-hand side of the building, on the ground level, will be a reading-room, with a billiard-room above. There will also be a heating chamber, and offices and conveniences. The window of the gallery will be filled with lead lights. Mr. Henry Grieves, of South Shields, is the architect, and the contract is being carried out by Mr. T. P. Shafto, builder, of Sunderland.

Restoration of Brignall Church, Yorkshire.—On the 12th ult., the Church of St. Mary, Brignall, was opened, after restoration, by the Bishop of Ripon. Funds did not admit of the renovation of the exterior, and where such actual repair has been done was necessary to preserve the structure from decay. The three lancet lights of the east window have been filled with stained glass from the studio of Mr. C. E. Kempe, of London, representing the Crucifixion and St. Mary and St. John, which, together with the pulpit and reredos, is the gift of Miss Easton, of West Layton Manor. The architects for the restoration were Messrs. Johnson and Crawford-Hick, of Newcastle-upon-Tyne, and the contractors were:—For mason and general repair, Mr. J. Kyle, Barnard Castle; woodwork, Mr. R. Snaith, Darlington; plumbing and glazing, Mr. C. Hedley, Barnard Castle; carring, Mr. R. Hedley, Newcastle-on-Tyne; gilding, Mr. R. Halfnight, Sunderland.

ENLARGEMENT OF SCHOOLS, IDLE.—A memorial-stone of a new wing to the Church schools at Idle, Yorkshire, was laid on the 14th ult. by Mr. C. J. Vint, of Bradford. An assembly hall is being erected, and a re-arrangement of the old schools is being made. The cost of the additions and alterations will be about £1,600. Messrs. Kendall & Bakes, of Leeds and Idle, are the architects.

CONGREGATIONAL CHAPEL, BEDWAS, MONMOUTHSHIRE.—A new Congregational Chapel has just been erected at Bedwas. The building is 39 ft. long by 34 ft. wide, and it has accommodation to seat 320 people. The plans of the new chapel were prepared by Mr. Edmund Jones, Caerphilly, and the contractor was Mr. Thomas Rossiter, also of Caerphilly.

NEW CHURCH, APPERLEY BRIDGE, YORKSHIRE.—The foundation-stone of a new church for Apperley Bridge and Greengates was laid on the 7th ult. by Mr. John W. Garnett, of Greengates House. The new edifice is situated at the top of Apperley-road, in the parish of Eccleshill. Besides chancel, organ chamber, and choir vestry, there will be sitting accommodation provided for about 300 persons. The building is from the plans of Messrs. Kendall & Bakes, architects, Leeds. The estimated cost, including furnishing, is about 3,000*l*.

BANK PREMISES, ST. HELENS.—The enlarged premises of the Manchester and Salford Bank in St. Helens have just been completed. The old premises have been enlarged by the addition of the adjoining shop and a public-room. The dados and counters and desks are of polished walnut. A consulting-room for the manager is enclosed with glazed panel screens, and lighted by a dome. The heavy columns and girders necessary to carry the first and second floors of the building have been relieved by fibrous plaster, and cornices of the same material form a panelled ceiling. A strong-room has been formed of concrete walls 18 in. thick. Outside, the front of the building has been faced with Aspatria (Cumberland) stone. The total cost has been 2,200*l*. Messrs. J. & W. Gaudy, St. Helens, were the architects, and the builder was Mr. R. H. Davies; Messrs. Critchley Bros. & Co. have executed the decorations in the bank and the lighting of the building.

PRIMITIVE METHODIST CHAPEL, RIPLEY, YORKSHIRE.—On the 27th ult. the memorial-stones were laid of a new Primitive Methodist Chapel on the Nottingham-road, Ripley. The architect is Mr. H. Gill, of Nottingham; and the contractor Mr. Ellis, also of Nottingham. The estimated cost of the chapel is 2,000*l*., including Sunday-school premises for 300 children. The chapel accommodation is for 450 persons.

EPISCOPAL CHURCH, STRANRAER, WIGTOWN.—On the 25th ult. the new Episcopal Church of St. John, Stranraer, was opened. The church is erected at the corner of London- and Bellevilla-roads. It is seated for 180 worshippers. The building is in the Gothic style, built of whinstone, with red free-stone facings. The entrance is at the south-west corner, facing London-road. The interior consists of a nave, with chancel at the east end. Within the altar-rails there are seven Scriptural panels in oak. Mr. J. C. Macfarlane, Stranraer, was the architect, and the work was executed by local contractors.

SCHOOL BUILDINGS, &c., LEEDS.—On the 27th ult. the Right Hon. W. L. Jackson, M.P., laid the foundation-stone of a new Sunday-school and Parochial Institute for All Hallows', Burley, Leeds. The Sunday-school will accommodate 1,100. There will be separate departments for boys, girls, and infants, and also a number of class-rooms. The boys' schoolroom will measure 50 ft. by 30 ft., and 34 ft. high. It will be lighted by windows on three sides. The girls' schoolroom will be 60 ft. by 30 ft. That portion of the building to be used as a parochial institute will be entered from Hartwell-road. On the second floor there will be a large assembly-room. The architects are Messrs. Kelly & Birchall, of Leeds, and the contractors are Messrs. Wood & Airey. The total cost of the undertaking is estimated at about 3,000*l*.

REBUILDING OF FALSTONE CHURCH, NORTHUMBERLAND.—The small church of Falstone, on the Scottish border, was almost entirely destroyed by fire in December, 1890, only the walls of the tower and a height of 3 ft. or 4 ft. from the ground of the main walls of the church escaping destruction. It has just been rebuilt from plans prepared by Messrs. Plummer & Burrell, architects, of Newcastle, together with the addition of a small chancel. Messrs. Martinson & Welton were the builders. The stained-glass three-light traceried east window, by Messrs. James Powell & Sons, of London, was the gift of Mr. Thomas Spencer, and the memorial font, by Messrs. Jones & Willis, was the gift of Miss Pictou. The plumbing and iron-founder's work has been executed by Mr. Scott, of Byker; the tinted glazing by Mr. Baguley, of Newcastle; the painting by Mr. Forbes, of Birtley, North Tyne; the green Westmoreland slating is by Mr. C. Nicholson, and the oak parclose screens, the pulpit, and the reredos dado were the work of Mr. Ralph Hedley, of Newcastle, from designs by the architects. The bell was founded by John Taylor & Co., of Loughborough, Leicestershire. The church is heated with a Musgrave stove with a descending flue. The aisles and chancel are laid with mosaic work by Mr. J. F. Ebner, of London, borders, monogrammes, and symbols being inlaid in the chancel flooring, this work being executed by Italian and Venetian workmen. The lamp pendants and brackets, communion rails, and pulpit reading-desk are supplied by Messrs. Hart, Son, & Peard, of London. The choir-seats and reading-desk and the external doors are all of oak. The church is internally ceiled with a waggon-vaulted boarded roof, divided into panels by longitudinal and transverse mouldings, having bosses at their intersection, and with a moulded and quatrefoiled pierced cornice course. Buttresses have been introduced to the exterior of the church and to the old tower. The door hinges, vestry and other fittings, are made from the architects' designs.

RESTORATION OF PARISH CHURCH, HERRINGWORTH, LINCOLNSHIRE.—The Bishop of Peterborough re-opened, on the 19th ult., the parish church of Herringworth, which has undergone restoration, under the superintendence of Mr. H. M. Townshead, architect, of Peterborough. The fabric has been under repair during the last nine months, and the work has been executed by Mr. S. Halliday, builder, of Stamford. The chancel has been restored at the cost of Mrs. Tryon, of Bulwick Hall, as a memorial of her late husband. There is a new pitch-pine roof in the chancel. In the nave the greater part of the roof is new, and is mainly of oak. The roof has been releaded. The seats are of pitch-pine. The old Jacobean pulpit has been restored. The nave has been refloored with wooden blocks. The screen has been restored, and the galleries in the church removed. The upper part of the steeple has been rebuilt. During the progress of the work part of an old Norman font was found in the wall of the chancel, and the relic is to be inserted in some conspicuous place in the building.

STAINED GLASS AND DECORATION.

MEMORIAL WINDOW, THORPE SATCHVILLE CHURCH, LEICESTERSHIRE.—A stained-glass window, consisting of three lights and tracery, the subject of which is "The Crucifixion," has been placed in the east window of Thorpe Satchville Church, near Melton Mowbray, to the memory of Martha Madeline, the late wife of Mr. Edmund Arthur Paget. The work has been carried out by Messrs. Winfields, Limited, of London.

MEMORIAL WINDOW, PARISH CHURCH, YARDLEY, WORCESTERSHIRE.—A stained-glass west window, placed in Yardley Parish Church in memory of the late Mr. Joseph Barrows, was unveiled on the 1st ult. The window is by Messrs. John Hardman & Co., and has been erected under the superintendence of Mr. J. A. Chatwin. The subject illustrated is that of our Lord coming in glory with His saints and angels to judge the world.

MEMORIAL WINDOW, JEDBURGH PARISH CHURCH.—A stained-glass window has just been put into the east end of the north aisle of Jedburgh Parish Church in memory of the late Mr. and Mrs. Charles Anderson, of Glenburn Hall. The window is composed of two pointed lights, with cusped circle above, and is by Messrs. Clayton & Bell, London.

STAINED-GLASS WINDOW, PARISH CHURCH, BODMIN, CORNWALL.—A stained-glass window has recently been erected in the south aisle of Bodmin parish church by Mr. George Henderson, J.P., of Bodmin, in memory of his wife. The window has been made to correspond in form as nearly as possible with two others recently unveiled as military memorials. In the upper lights of the old tracery figures of angels have been inserted bearing scrolls. The four long lights are occupied by the following full-length effigies:—1, Saint Anna, the aged prophetess; 2, St. Mary, the Blessed Virgin; 3, St. Elizabeth, her cousin, mother of St. John the Baptist; 4, St. Mary of Bethany. Above them are canopies, surmounting groups illustrative of the Parable of the good Samaritan. The window has been supplied by Messrs. Clayton & Bell, London.

THE TURNERS' COMPANY.—The Worshipful Company of Turners announce that they will offer this year, according to custom, their silver medal, five guineas, and the Freedom of the Company, for the best specimen of Turning in Wood or Pottery. Objects for competition are to be delivered at the Mansion House during the week ending Friday, October 21. Further information as to the competition may be obtained from Mr. Edgar Sydney, 53, Gresham House, the Hon. Secretary to the Competition Committee.

FOREIGN AND COLONIAL.

FRANCE.—The National Gobelins Manufactory has just executed a tapestry for the National Library, the designs for which have been painted by the artist, J. B. Lavastre. This tapestry symbolises "Mechanism."——The Académie des Beaux-Arts has awarded the "Jean Reynaud" prize to the painter Joseph Blanc for his work "The Battle of Tolbiac," which is in the Panthéon.——A Roman mosaic formed of black and white cubes has been found at Lyons on the rope railway to Fourvières. A fine mosaic has recently been found at Saint Colombe-les-Vienne (Rhone). This mosaic represents "the works of the field," and the allegories of the Seasons framed in a rich border.——In destroying the foundations of a house at Cahors (Lot) the workmen have brought to light the ruins of a Roman habitation, the walls of which bear traces of fresco painting, and the halls are paved with mosaic. They have also found some potteries, money, and many interesting things in bronze and marble.——The wooden suspension bridge of St. Pierre at Toulouse has been entirely destroyed by an incendiary.——The work of arranging the historical museum in the house of Joan of Arc at Domremy (Vosges) is shortly to be commenced. The sketches of the paintings of Lenepveu at the Panthéon are to be placed there, also the original casts for the statues of Joan of Arc, by Chapu, Frémiet, Paul Dubois, Chatrousse, and Pezieux. There are also to be some tapestries made especially for this object at Gobelins from the designs of M. Puvis de Chavannes, and the collection will contain the principal portraits of John of Arc, from the equestrian statue which is in the museum at Cluny to the picture of Ingres, with the pictures which represent her in all the most stirring events of her life.——The line from Argenteuil to Nantes has just been opened. It passes through a very rich and picturesque part of the country, crossing the Oise by a very strong metal viaduct and going over the Seine on a stone bridge.——The Society of "Souvenirs Français" has commissioned M. Ridel, architect, of the town of Laval, to design a monument, which is to be erected in the town, in memory of the last battle fought by the army of the Loire, January 18, 1871. The monument is composed of a tumulus, ornamented with a figure of "La Patrie" veiled and surrounded with palms. The execution of the sculpture is confided to M. Eugène Legueult, sculptor. The inauguration is fixed for the month of September.——An inhabitant of Toulouse, who has recently died, M. Maury, has left his fortune to his native town. Amongst many other charitable works, he has created two annual prizes for painting and sculpture, and one prize for architecture, which are to be distributed equally every year.——The new line from Grasse to Nice has just been opened.——There is a project to build a large military hospital at St. Cloud, to replace the one now in Paris; the scheme is being violently opposed by the inhabitants of this pretty town, which is such a favourite resort with tourists.——A statue of Lazare Carnot, grandfather of the President, has just been inaugurated at Carnot (Algeria).——The Prince of Monaco has just bought the magnificent domain of Bonrepos, one of the most beautiful of Tarn and Garonne.——We regret to learn the death of M. Eugène Chenantais, architect, at Nantes. He was late president of the Society of Architects of the Loire Inférieure, and member of the Central Society, the congresses of which he followed with great interest.

NORWAY.—The death is announced of Herr Nordan, a prominent Christiania architect. The coffin was born to the grave by eight leading architects.——An electrical exhibition has just been held in Christiania, and it is contemplated to hold an industrial exhibition there next year.——Work has now been commenced on the new Customs House in Christiania. The cost of the building itself is estimated at 26,000*l*., and the total cost of the entire establishment complete at about 56,000*l*. The work will occupy about three years.——The Storthing has decided upon the erection in Christiania of an historical museum. The frontage will have a length of 83 mètres, and there are to be three storys with basement. The entire cost of the structure is estimated at about 36,000*l*.——The ancient timber church at Hustad, in Throndhjem's Amt, purchased by the Society for the Preservation of Ancient Norwegian Monuments, is to be thoroughly repaired by Herr Hoflund, architect.

SWEDEN.—The catholic community in Stockholm has acquired a site for its projected cathedral at a cost of 16,000*l*. It is said that the funds required for the edifice are also secured. It is estimated that the building of it will occupy five years.——A monumental chapel is to be raised over the remains of the late Capt. John Ericsson, the famous inventor, in the cemetery at Fillipstad, and two premiums of 400 ks. and 200 ks. are offered for the best designs.——New barracks are to be erected in Stockholm for the Horse Life Guards at a cost of 120,000*l*.——The Society of Artists in Stockholm has arranged a grand lottery of pictures, in order to raise funds for a new exhibition building, to which all leading Swedish artists have contributed, including Prince Eugen.——The Swedish Crown Office has decided to purchase the site of the former Swedish Theatre or Opera House, Stockholm, for a sum of 25,000*l*.

—A company has been formed for the purchase of the Circus in Stockholm, in order to rebuild it so as to form an industrial and art exhibition building with winter gardens. Plans, &c., for the new buildings have been prepared by Herr G. Lindgren, a well-known Stockholm architect.——A new so-called "villa suburb" is in course of being built three and a-half kilomètres from Stockholm on the sea shore.

DENMARK.—The death is announced of Professor Ove Petersen, a prominent Danish architect and a member of the Copenhagen Academy of Arts. He was the son of a porter in the Ministry of Finance, and rose step by step to his high position by his natural genius.——Prof. Meldahl, the present architect to the so-called Marble Church or Cathedral in Copenhagen, upon which work has been in progress at intervals for over a century, has discovered twenty-three drawings in the archives of the ministry of the interior, showing that the French architect, Jardin, was not the original designer of this great edifice, but that this honour belongs to the Danish Col. Eigtved, the builder of Amalienborg Palace. He made his design to the church in 1754, or two years before Jardin, but the leading artistic idea is the same in both. The idea, says Prof. Meldahl, is the same as that underlying the design for the projected Berlin Cathedral.——It appears from a communication to the Rigsdag that the Danish Government has under consideration some very large building schemes in the ensuing years, considering its limited resources. They include a new National Library, to cost 122,000*l.*, exclusive of site; a new Metropolitan school; enlargement of the Theatre Royal; a new technical college for teachers; a new observatory; removal of the arsenal to a more convenient site (at a cost of 120,000*l.*); new barracks for the Life Guards (to cost 45,000*l.*); and finally there are the old plans for the re-building of Christiansborg Palace, a new House of Parliament, and new central railway station.

BERLIN.—The result of the competition for a suitable model of the memorial monument to Emperor Frederick III., which is to be placed on the battlefield of Woerth, shows three sculptors, classed first and equal. They are Herr Baumbach, Herr H. Hidding, and Professor R. Maison. The architect, Herr Pfann, one of the winners of the Great Memorial Competition, assisted Professor Maison in the conception of his design, whilst the architectural draughtsman, Herr Rieth, helped Herr Hidding. Both architects are members of the *atelier* of the new Houses of Parliament in course of erection.——The foundation-stone of the new central railway station at Cologne has been laid, with some ceremony.——An "artists' home" is to be erected in Rome, at the expense of the Prussian Government, for the benefit of artists and art students. The cost of Herr Genick's design, which is still subject to Ministerial approval, is estimated at about 400,000 francs. Besides ample accommodation for artists, who will only make a short sojourn in the "Holy City," there will be twenty-four large *ateliers* for resident painters and sculptors, and a mutual reception and exhibition hall.——The fashionable summer resort, Wiesbaden, is to have a new theatre. Designs were invited from Messrs. Fellmer and Helmer (Vienna), Messrs. Semper and Krutisch (Hamburg), and Professor Freuzen (Aix-la-Chapelle). Their work has been criticised by the Prussian Royal Academy of Works. Although isolated, the proposed building will be difficult to plan on account of the position of the site selected.——Another huge terminus station is to be erected in Germany. This time it is Dresden that wishes to compete with places like Frankfort. A competition for the design has been opened. From the "programmes" we see that the building will cost 275,000*l.*, the prizes offered have a total value of 1,000*l.*, the sending-in day is September 1, and the assessing jury will comprise of nine very prominent architects and engineers.——The Frankfort Baron Rothschild has offered the town of Osnabrueck some 6,000*l.* for its historical Imperial goblet. The Prussian Government will, however, try to prevent the sale.

ST. PETERSBURG.—An international competition for the design of a new bridge over the River Newa has been opened. There will be three prizes,—(1) 6,000, (2) 3,000, and (3) 1,500 rubels, and some extra prizes if the assessors think fit. The River Newa is 650 mètres broad at the point where the bridge is to cross it. Six million rubels are at the disposal of the authorities for building purposes. The sending-in day is in the middle of October. The French language can be used (Centralblatt der Bauverwaltung). The bridge will be a most important feature in the city; it will commence just opposite the Marble Palace and replace the old wooden one now in use.

DOVER HARBOUR.—The Admiralty Pier having been transferred to the Dover Harbour Board, Mr. Edward Druce, who formerly held the position of Resident Engineer in charge of the pier under the Board of Trade, has retired upon a pension, and the maintenance of the pier has been placed under the care of Mr. A. T. Walmisley, of Westminster, the Engineer to the Dover Harbour Board.

MISCELLANEOUS.

EDINBURGH ARCHITECTURAL ASSOCIATION. — The annual general meeting of this Association was held on the 26th ult. in the Architectural Hall, George-street, Edinburgh, Mr. W. W. Robertson, Vice-President, in the chair. In his report, the Treasurer stated that the membership was now 278, and the balance in hand 176*l.* The reports of the other office-bearers were submitted and approved. Mr. Robertson intimated a new departure of the Association in the fact that the institution would be housed next year in the Royal Institution, where a new field of usefulness would be entered upon in connexion with the School of Applied Art, in which the members of the Society were so much interested, and which the Association had undertaken to support in every possible way. The increased advantages of the Association would be only equalled by the increased opportunities of usefulness which the new scheme opened up to them. The following office-bearers were elected:—Past President, Mr. J. Kinross; President, Mr. W. W. Robertson; Vice-Presidents, Dr. R. Anderson, LL.D., and Mr. T. Ross.

OCKWELLS MANOR HOUSE.—In a "Note" on April 6, 1889, we adverted to the then contemplated sale by auction of the Ockholt, latterly Ockwells, Manor-house and grounds, about 21½ acres, in Bray parish, Berkshire. The sale was effected on June 4 of that year, at a bid of 2,500*l.* That same property, together with a farmhouse and 360 acres of land, will again be put up at auction, at the Mart, in July next. To what we said before as to the antiquity of the house, we may now add that it was built by John Norreys, Master of the Wardrobe to King Henry VI. and Esquire of the body to Edward IV., but not quite completed by him in 1465. For by his will of that year,—he died in 1467,—he bequeaths "to the full building and making uppe of the chapell, with the chamber adjoyning, within my mannor of Okholt, in the parish of Bray, not yet finished,—xl. *li.*" A correspondent, writing to the *Gentleman's Magazine* of December, 1798, says that a considerable portion of the house, damaged by fire, was in ruins, to his own knowledge, twenty years previously. But the entrance-hall, the paved cloisters beyond, the great hall with minstrel's gallery, and some other interesting portions of the building, have been preserved.

THE NICARAGUA CANAL.—From a report just issued, it appears that last year a sum of 875,000 dols. was expended on the Nicaragua Canal works. The canal itself has now been completed for one mile to a depth of 17 ft., and a breadth of 270 ft. Of the ship railway, twelve miles have been completed.

HORNSEY MAIN ROADS ARBITRATION. — The Order of the Local Government Board on the reference from the Hornsey Local Board and the Middlesex County Council for the determination of the amount to be paid to the Board by the Council in respect of the cost of maintenance and repair during the year ending March 31, 1891, of the main roads within the Hornsey district (mileage about 2¾ miles) has only just been received, although the inquiry by Mr. Thomas Codrington, M.Inst.C.E., F.G.S., one of the Government Inspectors, was held so long ago as in the month of December last, occupying two whole days. The counsel engaged were Mr. Alexander Macmorran for the Board, and Mr. Alexander Glen for the Council. Mr. T. De Courcy Meade, M.Inst.C.E., Engineer and Surveyor to the Local Board, Professor Henry Robinson, M.Inst.C.E., Mr. E. Purnell Hooley, Nottingham County Surveyor, and Mr. F. Smythe, Surveyor to the Finchley Local Board, gave evidence on behalf of the Board, and Mr. F. H. Pownall, Middlesex County Surveyor, on behalf of the Council. The Council had offered to pay towards the cost of maintenance nineteen-twentieths of the amount, including establishment charges, but not exceeding the County Surveyor's estimate,—viz., 2,730*l.*,—of the net cost reasonably and properly expended, and offered their cheque accordingly, which was returned by the Board. The Board claimed to be repaid the total amount expended, including establishment charges. The amount awarded is 3,221*l.* 5s., being 491*l.* 5s. in excess of the amount offered. The costs incurred by the Local Government Board,—27*l.* 14s. 4d.,—are to be paid one half by each party, who bear their own costs of the reference. No reasons for the terms of the award are given. The accounts presented included a sum for footways according to the well-known Warminster case. The Hornsey Local Board, at their meeting held on Monday last, unanimously passed the following resolution:—"That the Streets Committee be and are hereby empowered to give instructions and make all necessary arrangements in regard to the amount to be paid to the Board by the Middlesex County Council in respect of the maintenance and repair and improvement of the main roads in the Board's district during the year ending March 31, 1892, and in regard to the negotiations and communications with the Council thereon, and, in case arbitration of the Local Government Board has to be resorted to, the instructing of counsel and engaging of skilled witnesses and otherwise."

FORESHORE IMPROVEMENTS, SOUTHPORT. — According to the *Southport Visitor*, the object of the Foreshore and Improvement Committee of the Southport Town Council, so far as relates to the scheme for the construction of a marine park and lake, and the effecting of other improvements on the north foreshore, may be said to be practically accomplished, and the formal opening of the park and lake by the Mayor, Alderman Dr. Pilkington, will take place on the 20th inst. The improvement scheme included, in addition to the construction of a marine park and lake, the widening of Nevill-street bridge, and the removal from it of the old lattice girders, as well as the widening of the promenade from the bridge to Seabank-road, and the continuation of the lower promenade from the pier to a point opposite Seabank-road. The width of the bridge has been increased to 86 ft., and has been cleared of all obstructions; the promenade itself has been widened to 40 ft., the carriage-way to 36 ft., and the footpath on the opposite side to 10 ft. This extends for over a quarter of a mile on the north side of the pier. The work of laying out the marine park into ornamental gardens and lawns is being executed by the Corporation's head gardener, Mr. Halewood. At the foot of the park, and separating it from the lake, is the lower promenade, 50 ft. wide, approached by five sloping pathways. It is laid with concrete, asphalted over. The lake is 27¼ acres in area. It is 920 yards long and over 200 yards across at the widest part, and there will be a uniform depth of 3 ft. of water. The lake can be emptied by means of two rows of outlet pipes 24 in. in diameter, and water can also be admitted by this means. The slopes are formed of concrete, and there is a footpath round three sides of it laid with the same material. The lower promenade is protected from the lake by iron railings. The harbour is 60 yards long by 60 yards wide, and the main landing-stage is 250 ft. in length by 50 ft. wide; whilst the small landing-stage fronting the boat-house is 180 ft. long and 24 ft. wide. At the entrance to the landing-stage is a ticket-office. The boat-house is a red brick building, the outside walls of which are relieved by rows of white enamelled bricks. The roof is railed round, and will be used as a promenade. The first boat-shed is 50 ft. square. The next boat-shed is 96 ft. long and 50 ft. deep, and beyond this is a cushion-room and a lumber-room. The promenade over the building is planked and caulked all the way along, except the portion over the cushion-room and lumber-room, which is laid with corrugated tiles. The boat-house is surmounted at one end by a large iron tank of 25,000 gallons capacity, standing on pillars. This will contain a supply of water for street-watering purposes. Another feature of the scheme has been the erection of a pavilion in the Marine Park. The roof of this building forms part of the promenade, and is supported by iron pillars. The inside walls are lined with white enamelled bricks, with rows of grey bricks at intervals. It is 220 ft. long and 48 ft. wide in the centre; it will hold about 1,500 persons, and will contain ample lavatory accommodation. The whole of the work has been executed under the direction of the Borough Surveyor, Mr. William Crabtree. The setting-out of the ground has been done by his son, Mr. Walter Crabtree, and since June last the Assistant Borough Surveyor, Mr. R. P. Hirst, has had the general supervision of the carrying out of the work.

CAPITAL AND LABOUR.

STRIKE OF BRICKLAYERS, REDDITCH.—According to the *Birmingham Gazette*, three months since the bricklayers of Redditch and district gave their employers notice that they should on June 1 require an additional ½d. an hour, their present rate of wages being 7d. per hour. It seems, however, that the masters declined to accede to the demand, and the result is that the whole of the men came out on the 31st ult. The number is about 70, and this throws out of employment a corresponding number of labourers. At the present time the building trade is extremely brisk in Redditch, and it is regrettable that the men and the employers have not been able to arrive at an amicable arrangement.

MASONS' STRIKE AT NELSON, LANCASHIRE.—On the 23rd ult., in consequence of the strike of masons and wallers in Nelson and district, about 200 labourers were prevented from resuming employment. At the request of the workmen, a conference took place between representatives of the masters and the men, but with no result, the masters adhering to their resolution not to concede the advance in wages from 8d. to 8½d. an hour until after the expiration of three months' notice, whilst the men were equally determined to adhere to the seven days' notice, which expired on the 21st ult.

MEETINGS.

SATURDAY, JUNE 4.

Edinburgh Architectural Association.—Annual Excursion, Drumlanrig Castle.

WEDNESDAY, JUNE 8.

Toynbee Hall, Whitechapel, E.—Mr. A. Waterhouse, R.A., on "The Architecture of the Thirteenth and Fourteenth Centuries." 8 p.m.

COMPETITION, CONTRACTS, AND PUBLIC APPOINTMENTS.

COMPETITION.

Nature of Work.	By whom Advertised.	Premium.	Designs to be delivered.
*New Masonic Hall	Newcastle-upon-Tyne Central Masonic Hall Co. Ltd.	50l. 25l.	No date

CONTRACTS.

Nature of Work or Materials.	By whom Required.	Architect, Surveyor, or Engineer.	Tenders to be delivered.
Flagging, Paving, &c.	Plymouth Corp.	G. D. Bellamy	June 7
Baptist Chapel, Barry, Glam.	Committee	....	do.
Covered Playground, &c. Board School, Caldewgate	Carlisle School Board	T. Taylor Scott	do.
*Officer's House, Freshwater Gate (I.W.)	Admiralty	Official	do.
Iron and Steel Work	N. & R. Co.	do.	do.
Sewering, Levelling, Paving, &c.	Mountain Ash L. B.	do.	do.
*Trial Boring, 200 ft. deep	East Cowes Local Bd.	Lemon & Blizard	do.
Offices, Store Rooms, &c. Pentre Rhondda	Ystrad Gas, &c. Co.	A. O. Evans	June 8
*Supply of Lime and Cement	Mile End Old Town Vestry	J. M. Knight	do.
Pipe Sewers, Manholes, &c.	Tynemouth R.S.A.	A. S. Dinning	June 9
Road Metal	East Stonehouse L. B.	Official	do.
House and Stable, Rosserow, Cwmbach, Aberdare	....	John Evans	June 10
Hotel, Treharris, South Wales	T. Jones	T. Roderick	do.
*Supply of Men and Horses for Watering Streets, &c.	Borough of Brighton	F. J. C. May	do.
*Supply of Portland Cement	do.	do.	do.
Ironwork, &c.	Cambrian Ry. Co.	Official	June 11
Additions, &c. to Hotel, Aberlour, N.B.	....	C. C. Doig	do.
Artificial Lake, Pontefract Park	Trustees	J. H. Greaves	do.
Technical School, Free Library, &c.	Darwen Corp.	J. Lane Fox	June 13
Sewage Works	Hanley Corp.	Jos. Lobley	do.
*Laying, &c. Cast-iron Pipes	Newark Corporation	H. Role	do.
*Covered Service Reservoir	do.	do.	do.
Boundary Wall, &c. St. Mark's, Leeds	....	Borough Engineer	June 14
*Unclimbable Hurdle Fencing and Gates	London County Council	Official	do.
*Six New Water Vans	Boro' of West Ham	L. Angell	do.
Additions, &c. Macallan Distillery, Speyside, N.B.	....	C. C. Doig	do.
*170 tons Cast-iron Pipes	St. Anne's-on-Sea L.B.	H. Bancroft	do.
Vicarage House, &c. Talloug, Brecon	Rev. J. Williams	W. & T. Williams	June 15

CONTRACTS.—Continued.

Nature of Work or Materials.	By whom Required.	Architect, Surveyor, or Engineer.	Tenders to be delivered.
Alterations, &c. Gasworks	Leeds Corporation	Official	June 15
Water Supply, Parkmore, Dufftown, N.B.	....	Gordon & McBey	June 16
Vicarage House, Goytre, Abergavenny	Rev. J. D. James	E. M. Bruce Vaughan	do.
*Public Baths	Bilston Township Com.	C. L. N. Nelson	do.
*Erection of an Office for the Board	Reading Sch. Bd.	C. Smith & Son	June 18
Electric Lighting Works	Hanley Corp.	Jos. Lobley	June 20
*Reconstructing Bridge at Pontllogell	Montgomeryshire C.C.	Official	do.
*Filter Tunnel	Derby Corporation	T. & C. Hawksley	do.
*Sewers, Painting Work, &c. &c.	Acton L. B.	D. J. Ebbetts	June 21
*Higher Grade Board School	Wolverhampton S. B.	T. H. Fleeming	June 24
*Additional Asylum Buildings, Banstead	London County Council Asylums Committee	G. T. Hine	June 27
*Church, Crewe	....	Hicks & Charlewood	No date.
*Building Warehouse	....	T. F. Shaw	do.
*Green English Oak, Elm, and Ash	London Road Car Co. Ltd.	Official	do.
Suspension Bridge over River Wear, near Leamside	....	A. C. Chapman	do.
Rebuilding Inn, Shire Moor, near Backworth	R. Emmerson & Sons	Philip Spicer	do.
Additions to Large Works, Carlisle	Hudson, Scott, & Sons	G. Dale Oliver	do.
Dwelling-houses, &c. Stanley, Durham	Mrs. Stokoe	G. A. Kerrich Walker	do.
Hall, Market, Shops, &c.	Abertillery (Mon.) Market Hall Co.	Alfred Swash	do.
Restoration of Tower of Moulton Church, Northamptonshire	Committee	Edmund Law	do.
Reform Club, Wigan	do.	F. W. Simon	do.
Wood and Iron Erections, Netherfield-road, Liverpool	....	G. Dalton & Sons	do.
Five Cottages, Underwood, Plympton, Devon	W. J. Moon	Mr. Avery	do.
Twelve Houses, Armley, Leeds	....	C. F. Wilkinson	do.

PUBLIC APPOINTMENTS.

Nature of Appointment.	By whom Advertised.	Salary.	Applications to be in.
*Assistant, Borough Engineer's Office	Stockton-on-Tees Corp.	150l.	June 7
*Surveyor	Bermondsey Vestry	250l. &c.	June 15
*Sanitary Inspector	Plumstead B. of W.	3l.	June 21
*District Surveyor	County Borough of Sheffield	140l.	No date

Those marked with an Asterisk (*) are advertised in this Number. Competitions, p. iv. Contracts, pp. iv., vi., & viii. Public Appointments, p. xviii.

SATURDAY, JUNE 11.

Architectural Association.—Visit to new Music School, Harrow, Mr. E. S. Prior, architect; and to other school buildings and houses at Harrow. Meet at Harrow Church at 3 p.m.

Junior Engineering Society.—Visit to the Works of the Patent Victoria Stone Co., Stratford. 3 p.m.

RECENT PATENTS:

ABSTRACTS OF SPECIFICATIONS.

10,045.—WINDOWS: *S. J. Wilde.*—This Invention relates to an appliance to prevent windows rattling. It is a clip formed in two separate parts, of brass or other metal, one part being fixed to the meeting-rail of the lower window-sash by means of screws, and the other to the meeting-rail of the upper sash in like manner. The appliance is stated to be self-acting, and can be used in conjunction with any sash-fastener.

10,106.—VENTILATORS: *E. Hatton*—This refers to an invention for attaching an apparatus to hopper-shaped wall or window ventilators, or to any ordinary sashes and sliding frames for the interruption of smuts and dirt, the avoidance of draught, and for automatically cleaning the gauze forming a part of the apparatus. To carry the invention into effect, there is fixed on the top of a hopper-shaped ventilator a plain or corrugated wire gauze or perforated screen or cover for diffusing the air, avoiding draughts, and preventing smuts from passing into the room, the gauze being automatically cleaned by means of a brush kept in contact with the gauze when opening or closing the ventilator. At the sides a flexible tube is fixed, to prevent draughts from passing between the stationary and working parts.

11,013.—SASH-FASTENERS: *C. E. Lewin.*—This invention claims to be a strong, simple, and self-gripping burglar-proof appliance for window-sashes, sliding panels, ventilators, and other fittings where it is desired that such fittings should be rendered secure from one side or from rattling. The invention consists in the use of curved or cam-like pieces of material suspended or supported upon a point placed at such a position in relation to its outline that its own weight, or a spring, or electro-motive force, or other suitable available force, causes the cam to press with an initial force against the frame of the window or other like part, not being the same part as that to which the cam itself is suspended or supported. The cam is fixed in such a position that the attempted opening or moving of the sash or sliding part will cause the cam fastener to tend to revolve around its point of support, thus causing a reaction between the two objects to which the cam is fixed and that to which it is caused to bear when revolved by the movement of the part first mentioned.

5221.—COWLS: *W. T. & R. Smith.*—This patent refers to what is described as an improved chimney top, cowl, or ventilator, the essential features of which are the employment of two vertical tubes or channels placed more or less parallel with each other, but not absolutely side by side, and not necessarily both of the same dimensions or contour externally or in cross-section. The top end of the one of the tubes or passages, intended to be the lower tube when finished, is bent or curved, or diverges from the vertical in any desired manner, and joins the upper tube at or about its centre. At this point suitable baffle plates are provided in such a manner, relatively to each other, that a down-draught entering the top of the upper tube is prevented from passing down the lower tube, as both ends of the upper tube being open, the down-draught passes harmlessly through it. At the same time, the baffle-plates do not obstruct the passage of the smoke or vitiated air, but provides a curved passage therefore from the lower to the upper tube, and this will there be met by the down-draught in the upper tube, in which case it would be carried thereby through and out at the lower end of the upper tube, consequently the down-draught in the upper tube, however severe, would tend to improve rather than deteriorate the up-draught in the lower tube.

NEW APPLICATIONS FOR LETTERS PATENT.

May 16.—9,217, J. Izod, Ornamentation in Clay, for architectural and other purposes.—9,235, J. Rymer-Jones, Refractory and Non-conducting Bricks, Blocks, Tiles, Slabs, and Pipes.—9,251, J. McGlashan, Ornamentation and Decoration of Walls, Ceilings, &c.—9,258, J. Julbi, Hardening of Plaster, and the development of colours mixed therewith.—9,264, E. New, Device for Loading Brick from Machine.—9,279, F. Miller, Laying Wood Pavements.

May 17.—9,293, J. Brown, Chimney-pots.—9,332, A. Boult, Pavements.

May 18.—9,408, C. Taylor, Heating or Warming Dwelling-houses, Warehouses, Buildings, &c.—9,421, J. Jones, Construction of Casement Window-frames and Sliding-sashes.—9,427, J. Jeffreys, Jointing Cast-iron Pipes.—9,449, W. Williams, Hot-water Apparatus for Heating Greenhouses, Baths, and Buildings, &c.—9,462, H. Doulton and C. Morris, Joints for Earthenware Pipes.

May 13.—9,642, J. Castle, Mills for Grinding Cement, &c.

May 20.—9,685, R. Bocock, Siphon Cistern for Flushing Water-closets.

May 21.—9,660, W. Jones, Water or other Closet Seats and Frames.—9,698, J. Grubb, Sliding Gas Pendants.

PROVISIONAL SPECIFICATIONS ACCEPTED.

6,147, W. Davies, Coin Freed Apparatus for use in connexion with Water-closets.—6,440, J. Hunt, Roof Gutters.—7,008, R. Heyes, Electric Light Fittings.—7,071, W. Beaumont, Pneumatic Apparatus for Wood-working Machinery.—7,631, E. Waller and S. Sniffin, White Lead.—7,744, J. Bloomfield, Plaster.—8,384, H. Hunt, Mantelpieces for Fireplaces.—8,472, C. Hawkes, Covering for Walls, &c.—8,477, X. Charles, Kiln or Drying Apparatus.—8,583, F. Fawcett, Machinery for Making and Pressing Bricks and in Moulds therefore, and in Clay Mixing or Grinding Pans employed therein. 8,706, S. Moore, Electrical Fittings, such as Ceiling Roses and Cut Outs.

COMPLETE SPECIFICATIONS ACCEPTED.

(Open to Opposition for Two Months.)

9,819, W. Pain, Carpenters' and Joiners' Hammers. 10,270, R. Hodges and F. Lilley, Door Indicators.—12,049, W. Deeming, Pipes for Sanitary and other purposes.—5,698, J. Henderson, Joiners' Jobbing Bench. 7,502, W. Thompson, Plaster for Building Purposes.

SOME RECENT SALES OF PROPERTY:

ESTATE EXCHANGE REPORT.

MAY 23.—By *Jenkins & Sons*: 51 and 53, Cranfield-rd., Brockley, u.t. 74 yrs., g.r. 8l. 15s., 450l.—By *Elliott, Son, & Boyton*: No. 148, Oxford-st., u.t. 49 yrs., g.r. 120l.; 5,200l.; No. 38, Great Portland-st., u.t. 38½ yrs., g.r. 35l., r. 160l., 1,560l.; 75, Great Portland-st., u.t. 39 yrs., g.r. 30l., r. 150l., 1,530l.; 77, Great Portland-st., and 26, Riding House-st., u.t. 39 yrs., g.r. 35l., r. 210l., 2,150l. —By *Wagstaff & Warman*: 278, Essex-rd., Canonbury, u.t. 25 yrs., g.r. 9l., 225l.—By *Beale & Capps*: 29, Blagrove-rd., Notting Hill, u.t. 74 yrs., g.r. 7l., r. 36l., 300l.

MAY 24.—By *J. C. Platt*: 57 to 63 odd, Nasmyth-st., Hammersmith, u.t. 78 yrs., g.r. 20l., 635l.—By *J. N. Goatley*: "Milford Lodge," Belmont-rd., Twickenham, u.t. 63 yrs., g.r. 10l., 60l.; "Abney House," u.t. 63 yrs., g.r. 16l. 16s., 90l.; 2, Carlton-villas, u.t. 63 yrs., g.r. 7l. 10s., 90l.; "Percy Lodge," u.t. 63 yrs., g.r. 10l., 50l.; Grove, Heath, and York-villas, u.t. 63 yrs., g.r. 22l. 10s., 240l.; "Sion House," Manor-rd., u.t. 66 yrs., g.r. 10l. 10s., 85l.; "Park Villa," and "Vine Lodge," Belmont-rd., f., 415l. —By *J. H. Hunter*: 82, Mountgrove-rd., Finsbury-pk., u.t. 74 yrs., g.r. 10l. 10s., r. 45l., 285l.; 67, Finsbury-pk.-rd., u.t. 74 yrs., g.r. 9l. 9s., r. 40l., 385l.; 58 and 60, Finsbury-pk.-rd. u.t. 74 yrs., g.r. 18l. 18s., r. 89l., 745l. —By *A. Booth*: 64 and 66, Boston-st., Hackney, f., r. 44l. 4s., 320l.—By *C. & H. White*: 27 to 37 (odd), Nutbrook-st., Peckham, u.t. 85 yrs., g.r. 30l., 915l.; 22 and 24, Hampton-rd., Holloway, u.t. 75 yrs., g.r. 14l., 200l.—By *R. Tidey & Son*: 135, Isledon-rd., Holloway, u.t. 67 yrs., g.r. 7l. 15s., r. 40l., 315l.; 14 and 16, Cook's-rd., Walworth, u.t. 61 yrs., g.r. 5l., r. 69l., 525l.; 141 and 143, Lorimore-rd., u.t. 61 yrs., g.r. 6l., r. 83l., 610l.; 4 to 16 even, Heron-st., u.t. 61 yrs., g.r. 14l., 1,770l.—By *W. & F. Houghton*: "Brook's Croft," and 4½ acres, f., Walthamstow, 2,650l.; an enclosure of land adjoining, 5a. 3r. 25p., 2,350l.; a plot of freehold land, High-st., 1,260l.; 12, and 14, Vallentin-rd., f., 510l.; 8, Bythorn-st., Brixton, u.t. 72 yrs., g.r. 5l., 200l.; 10, Glendall-st., u.t. 72 yrs., g.r. 10s., 270l.—By *Furber, Price, & Furber*: F.g.r. of 9l. 9s., Turtle-rd., Wandsworth, with reversion in 86 yrs., 185l.; f.g.r. of 15l. 15s., Cumberland-villas, ditto in 86 yrs., 315l.; f.g.r. of 25l., Warple Way, ditto in 91 yrs., 425l.; 365, Wandsworth-rd., and 1, Southville, f., 1,180l.; 11, Southville, f., r. 40l., and a f.g.r. of 5l., with reversion in 4 yrs., 630l.; f.g.r. of 5l., Southville, with ditto in 4 yrs., 330l.; f.g.r. of 6l., with ditto in 4 yrs., 280l.; f.g.r. of 81l., with ditto in 4 yrs., 3,910l; 110 and 118, Cleveland-st., Fitzroy-sq., f., r. 95l., 1,875l.; "Norfolk House," Kew-rd., Richmond, u.t. 77 yrs., g.r. 27l. 10s., r. 155l., 1,900l.; f.g.r. of 20l., Paul-st., Finsbury-sq., with reversion in 18 yrs., 1,350l.; f.g.r. of 9l., Bradley-st., Wandsworth-rd., with reversion in 46 yrs., 210l.; f.g.r. of 31l., Dawlish-st., Wandsworth-rd., with reversion in 45 yrs., 920l. By *Humbert, Son, & Flint* (at Watford): "Linden Villa," Chalk Hill, Bushey, f., r. 40l., 700l.; eight plots of freehold land, Merry Hill-lane 120l.; a plot of freehold land, 75l.; 118, 120, and 122, High-st., Watford, and seven cottages, f., 1,632l.

MAY 25.—By *A. Savill & Son*: Roydon Mill and 13a. 2r. 30p., f., Roydon, Essex, 1,800l.; "Grove Lodge," and "Baker's Farm," Sawbridgeworth, 142a. 3r. 18p., f., 6,900l.; "The Butcher's Arms," c., Hermon-hill, Wanstead, 770l.—By *E. Tomkins*: No. 13, "Caton Lodge," Streatham-hill, u.t. 56 yrs., g.r. 42l., r. 350l., 3,525l.—By *W. B. Hallett*: 78, Gloucester-st., Pimlico, u.t. 41 yrs., g.r. 10l., r. 60l., 660l.; 20, 24, and 26, Brackenbury-rd., Hammersmith, u.t. 71 yrs., g.r. 21l., r. 90l., 615l.—By *Woods & Snelling*: 13, Fleur-de-Lis-ct., Fetter-lane, f., r. 40l., 700l.; "Wildersdale," Alderhill, Sidcup, u.t. 83 yrs., g.r. 10l., r. 65l., 700l.; 7, Cargreen-rd., Norwood, u.t. 74 yrs., g.r. 13l. 13s., r. 50l., 250l.—By *F. Jolly & Co.*: 88, Shakespeare-rd., Acton, f., 300l.; 21 and 22, Albion-sq., Dalston, u.t. 46 yrs., g.r. 14l., 700l.; 24, Stainsby-rd., Poplar, u.t. 39 yrs., g.r. 5l. 10s., r. 45l., 450l.; 149, Graham-rd., Hackney, u.t. 64 yrs., g.r. 8l., r. 40l., 380l.—By *Talbot & White*: 83, 85, and 87, Coutts-rd., Mile End, u.t. 30 yrs., g.r. 10l. 10s., 300l; 89 to 115 (odd), Coutts-rd., u.t. 30½ yrs., g.r. 40l., 1,400l.; 2, St. Thomas-rd., u.t. 30 yrs., g.r. 3l. 15s., 115l.—By *Prothero & Morris*: "The Ferns," Lime-grove, New Malden, f., 1,050l; The Residence, "Roselands," Billericay, and 7a. 2r. 18p., f., 700l.—By *W. Hall*: 4, Highgate-rd., and 1, Fortess-rd., Highgate, f. 800l.; 6, Highgate-rd., f., r. 33l., 565l.; 3 to 9 odd, Fortess-rd., f., r. 120l., 2,080l.; 112, Upper Fore-st., Edmonton, u.t. 11 yrs., g.r. 6l., r. 50l., 65l.—By *Inman & Co.*: 9, The Grove, St. John's Wood, u.t. 20 yrs., g.r. 6l. 6s., 350l.; 40, Capland-st., Marylebone, u.t. 28 yrs., g.r. 4l., r. 23l. 8s., 95l.; 63, 79, and 81, Princess-st., u.t. 48 yrs., g.r. 16l. 10s., r. 96l., 975l.; 57 and 59, Salisbury-st., u.t. 28 yrs., g.r. 10l., 400l.; 10A, 10 to 18, Weston-pl., u.t. 47 yrs., g.r. 27l. 10s., 1,310l.; 32, Carlisle-pl., u.t. 47 yrs., g.r. 4l., 160l.; 56, Richmond-st., u.t. 29 yrs., g.r. 5l. 10s., 155l.; 6, Nightingale-st., u.t. 29 yrs., g.r. 3l. 3s., 150l.; I.g.r. of 40l., Little Grove-st., u.t. 23 yrs.,

…o g.r., 455l.; l.g.r. of 26l. 16s., Salisbury-st., &c., u.t. 29 yrs., g.r. 9l. 2s., 230l.; l.g.r. of 58l. 9s., Nightingale-st., u.t. 29 yrs., g.r. 27l. 13s., 380l.; l.g.r. of 50l., Carlisle-st., u.t. 29 yrs., g.r. l. 3s., 710l.; l.g.r. of 39l. 18s., Richmond-st., &c., u.t. 29 yrs., g.r. 16l. 16s., 310l.; l.g.r. of 10l., Hatton-st., u.t. 29 yrs., no g.r., 160l.; l.g.r. of 82l., Little North-st., u.t. 29 yrs., g.r. 32l., 560l.; l.g.r. of 52l., Orcus-st., u.t. 29 yrs., g.r. 20l., 330l.; l.g.r. of 58l. 8s., Orcus-st., u.t. 29 yrs., no g.r., 700l.; l.g.r. of 16l., Orcus-st., u.t. 29 yrs., 215l.; l.g.r. of 14l. 10s., Richmond-st., u.t. 29 yrs., no g.r., 190l.; l.g.r. of 22l. 10s., Henry-st., St. John's Wood, u.t. 27 yrs., no g.r., 320l.

MAY 26.—By *Thurgood & Martin*: 1 and 3, Edith-grove, Brompton, f., r. 120l., 1,850l.; f.g.r. of 5l., Edith-grove, with reversion in 34 yrs., 205l.; f.g.r. of 7l., Edith-grove, ditto in 34 yrs., 870l.; f.g.r. of 7l., ditto in 34 yrs., 355l.; "Grove House" and "Grove Cottage," Seymour-pl., f., r. 105l., 1,630l.; a plot of freehold land, 410l.; 24, St. Leonard's-ter., Chelsea, u.t. 6 yrs., g.r. 7l., r. 42l., 120l.—By *C. R. Cross*: 2, Kildare-gds., Bayswater, u.t. 59 yrs., g.r. 8l., r. 72l., 950l.—By *Osborn & Mercer*: C.g.r. of 20l., Kensington, with reversion in 60 yrs., 350l.—By *J. A. Smith*: F.g.r. of 10l. 10s., Seymour-pl., Battersea, ditto in 14 yrs., 800l.; 185, The Grove, Hammersmith, u.t. 61 yrs., g.r. 5l., 360l.—By *C. C. & T. Moore*: 2 to 7, Homerton-ter., Hackney, f., 1,580l.; 11 to 15, Homerton-ter., f., 1,300l.; "South and East View" and "Avenue Cottage," 116, Morning-lane, f., area 25,500 ft., 1,150l.; "The Rookery," Clapham Common, f., r. 120l., 2,740l.; 177 to 185 (odd), Eastfield-st., Limehouse, f., 360l.—By *Rushworth & Stevens*: 4, Bennett-st., Piccadilly, f., r. 200l., 3,600l.—By *Newbon & Co.*: No. 71, Newington-causeway, and four cottages, f., 2,400l.; 69, Eden-grove, Holloway, f., r. 32l., 370l.; 46, Loraine-rd., f., r. 0l., 635l.; one-fourth share in 169 to 179, Upper-st., Islington, c., r. 1,696l. 13s. 4d., 6,350l.; 70, 72, and 74, Marquis-rd., Canonbury, u.t. 54 yrs., g.r. 15l., r. 180l., 1,790l.; 9, James-pl., and 1 to 6, Pear Tree-ct., Clapton, f., r. 106l. 4s., 750l.; 76, King Edward-rd., Hackney, u.t. 46 yrs., g.r. 8l. 15s., 440l.; 36 and 37, Hall-st., City-rd., u.t. 50 yrs., g.r. 12l., r. 76l., 680l.—By *Briant & Sons*: No. 136, Fenchurch-st., f., r. 491l., 8,300l.; 204 and 205, Blackfriars-rd., Blackfriars, f., r. 133l., 2,420l.; 11, Eagle-ct., Clerkenwell, f., r. 40l., 560l.; 6, Flodden-rd., Camberwell, u.t. 24 yrs., g.r. 11l., 460l.; 8 and 10 Albion-st., Rotherhithe, f.r. 38l. 7s., 450l.; 34, Clarence-st., f. 150l.; f.g.r. of 35l., Jamaica-rd., Bermondsey, with reversion in 36 years, 630l.—By *Stimson & Sons*: 159, Bancroft-rd., Mile End, f. 300l.; 7, Lammas-pk.-rd., Ealing, u.t. 05 yrs., g.r. 6l., r. 28l., 300l.; f.g.r. of 64l., Ware-st., Kingsland, with reversion in 40 yrs., 1,600l.; f.g.r. of 32l., Oxford-ter., Islington, ditto in 65 yrs., 840l.; f.g.r. of 32l. Chamberlain-st., Regent's-pk., ditto 41 yrs., 800l.; f.g.r. of 27l., Great Chapel-st., Westminster, ditto 59 yrs., 760l.; f.g.r. of 21l., Earl's Court-rd., &c., Kensington, ditto, 68 and 63 yrs., 800l.; f.g.r. of 18l. 10s., London-rd., Clapton, ditto, 88 yrs., 675l.; f.g.r. of 17l. 10s., Lansdown-hill, Norwood, ditto, 24 yrs., 470l.; f.g.r. of 12l., Grove-lane, Camberwell, ditto, 76 yrs., 300l.; f.g.r. of 2l., Ives-st., Chelsea, ditto, 31 yrs., 105l.; l.g.r. of 60l., Holland-rd., Brixton, u.t. 30 yrs., 950l.; l.g.r. of 15l., Hackford-rd., u.t. 7½ yrs., g.r. 5l., 31l.; Nos. 94 and 96, Upper Kennington-lane, c., r. 97l., 1,296l.; 100, Upper Kennington-lane, c., r. 45l., and c.g.r., 780l.—By *Debenham, Tewson, & Co.*: F.g.r. of 150l., Bush-lane, Cannon-st., with reversion in 71 yrs., 4,600l.; "The Cock Hotel," Sutton, f., r. 210l., 10,100l.; "The Red Lion," Parliament-st., Westminster, f., 10,250l.; "The Red Lion," Duke-st., Manchester-sq., f., 2,860l.; "The Volunteer" Public-house, Baker-st., u.t. 9 yrs., g.r. 20l., 710l.; 4, Tregunter-rd., Kensington, u.t. 45 yrs., g.r. 9l., r. 100l., 900l.; 8, Orchard-st. Portman-sq., u.t. 21 yrs., g.r. 20l., r. 131l. 10s., 1,350l.; 37 to 43 (odd), Westminster-bridge-rd., u.t. 41 yrs., g.r. 8l., r. 473l., and stabling in Whitehorse-yd., 3,550l.—By *Farebrother, Ellis, & Co.*: Six freehold cottages, Chaseside, Enfield, 620l.; f.g.r. of 22l. Iffley-rd., Hammersmith, with reversion in 73 yrs., 560l.; f.g.r. of 78l., Kilmarsh-rd., ditto, 73 yrs., 1,930l.; f.g.r. of 143l., Sutherton-rd., ditto, 73 yrs., 3,469l.; f.g.r. of 62l., Glenthorn-rd., ditto, 73 yrs., 1,834l.—By *Messrs. Woods* (at Putney): 81 and 83, Chelverton-rd., Putney, u.t. 94 yrs., g.r. 15l. 10s.; and 9 to 15 (odd), Erpingham-rd., u.t. 82 yrs., g.r. 24l., 2,150l.

MAY 27.—By *C. P. Whiteley*: 138 and 140, Portland-st., Walworth, u.t. 76 yrs., g.r. 10l., 360l.; 18, 20, 26 to 32 even, Aylesbury-st., u.t. 16 yrs., g.r. 17l. 5s., 615l. By *White & Sons*: "Warwick Villa," Holmwood-common, Dorking, f., 1,000l. By *Baker & Sons*: F.g.r. of 29l. 10s., Forster-rd., Croydon, with reversion in 78 yrs., 560l. By *R. Reid*: 97, Dean-st., Soho, f., 740l.; 56 to 59, Bolingbroke-grove, Wandsworth-common, f., r. 130l., 1,475l.; 49, Edith-grove, Brompton, u.t. 72 yrs., g.r. 4l., r. 40l., 430l.; l.g.r. of 90l., Whitcombe-st., Pall Mall, reversion in 82 yrs., 2,250l. By *E. Owers*: 13, Crossfield-rd., Hampstead, u.t. 86 yrs., g.r. 5l., 885l.; 27, Gascony-av., u.t. 83 yrs., g.r. 10l. 10s., r. 42l., 257l. By *A. & A. Field*: 23, Sceptre-st., Mile End, f., r. 33l. 16s., 235l.; 26, Sidney-st., u.t. 2 yrs., g.r. 3l.; 46, Clark-st., u.t. 5 yrs., g.r. 3l. 5s.; 14, Blakesley-st., u.t. 6 yrs., g.r. 3l., 125l.; 319, St. Leonard's-rd., Bromley-by-Bow, u.t. 50 yrs., g.r. 8l., 60l.; 19, Carlton-rd., Mile End, u.t. 34 yrs., g.r. 3l., 185l.; 23, St. Thomas-rd., u.t. 58 yrs., g.r. 5l., 120l.; 6, 7, and 8, Markfield-rd., Tottenham, u.t. 70 yrs., g.r. 13l. 10s., 165l.; 19 and 21, Royston-st., Bethnal Green, u.t. 32 yrs., g.r. 6l., 425l.; 6A, 5 to 16, Reliance-sq., Shoreditch, f., 2,035l.; 18, 20, and 22, St. Paul's-rd., Limehouse, u.t. 33 yrs., g.r. 20l., 360l.; 187, Plimsoll-rd., Finsbury-pk., u.t. 85 yrs., g.r. 5l. 15s., 265l.; f.g.r. of 12l., Norton-st., Bethnal-green, reversion in 162 yrs., 296l.; f.g.r. of 8l., ditto in 61 yrs., 200l.; 53, Manilla-st., Millwall, f., 210l.; 1, 2, and 3, Manor Cottages, f., 415l.—By *A. Prevost & Son*: Nos. 83 and 2A, The Cres., Peckham-rye, u.t. 12 yrs., g.r. 14l., 75l.; l.g.r. of 128l., Nunhead-cres., u.t. 13 yrs., g.r. 48l., 460l.; No. 192, Commercial-rd., E., u.t. 8 yrs., g.r. 5l., r. 50l., 115l.; f.g.r. of 29l., The Portway, West Ham, reversion in 73 yrs., 587l.; f.g.r. of 51l., Dirleton-rd., ditto in 73 yrs., 1,110l.; f.g.r. of 8l. 10s., The Portway, ditto in 74 yrs., 150l.; f.g.r. of 37l. 5s., Church-st., ditto in 5 yrs., 615l.; 1 and 2, Roslyn-cottages, and 50 and 52, The Portway, f., 490l.; 53, Church-st., f., r. 22l., 420l.

[*Contractions used in these lists.*—F.g.r. for freehold ground-rent; l.g.r. for leasehold ground-rent; i.g.r. for improved ground-rent; g.r. for ground-rent; r. for rent; f. for freehold; c. for copyhold; l. for leasehold; e.r. for estimated rental; u.t. for unexpired term; p.a. for per annum; yrs. for years; st. for street; rd. for road; sq. for square; pl. for place; ter. for terrace; cres. for crescent; yd. for yard, &c.]

PRICES CURRENT OF MATERIALS.

TIMBER.

Greenheart, B.G. ton	9/0/0	0/0/0
Teak, E.I. ... load	9/10/0	15/0/0
Sequoia, U.S. ft. cu.	2/3	3/0
Ash, Canada load	2/10/0	4/0/0
Birch, do.	3/5/0	4/10/0
Elm, do.	3/10/0	4/15/0
Fir, Dantsic, &c.	1/10/0	3/10/0
Oak, do.	3/0/0	5/5/0
Canada	5/10/0	7/0/0
Pine, Canada red	2/10/0	4/10/0
Do. yellow	2/10/0	5/0/0
Lath, D'ntsic, fath	5/0/0	6/0/0
St. Petersburg	5/0/0	7/0/0
Deals, Finland, 2nd & 1st std 100	8/0/0	9/10/0
Do. 4th & 3rd ..	7/0/0	8/0/0
Do. Riga	7/0/0	8/0/0
St. Petersburg, 1st yellow ..	11/0/0	14/10/0
Do. 2nd yellow	8/0/0	10/0/0
Do. white	7/10/0	10/10/0
Swedish	7/10/0	15/10/0
White Sea	8/0/0	17/10/0
Canada, Pine 1st	20/0/0	26/0/0
Do. do. 2nd	14/10/0	16/0/0
Do. do. 3rd, &c.	8/0/0	10/5/0
Do. Spruce, 1st	8/10/0	11/0/0
Do. do. 3rd & 2nd	6/15/0	8/0/0
New Brunswick	7/0/0	7/10/0
Battens, all kinds	3/10/0	15/10/0
Flooring Boards, sq., 1 in. prep. 1st	0/8/0	0/14/0
Do. 2nd	0/7/0	0/11/0
Other qualities	0/3/6	0/7/6
Cedar, Cuba .. ft.	/3½	/4½
Honduras, &c.	/3½	/4
Mahogany, Cuba	/4½	/6½
St. Domingo, cargo av	/4½	2/0
Mexican do. do	/4	/5
Tobasco do. do	/5½	/7
Honduras do. ..	/5½	/6½
Box, Turkey ton	4/0/0	13/0/0
Rose, Rio	10/0/0	20/0/0
Bahia	9/0/0	18/0/0
Satin, St. Domingo ... ft.	0/0/8	0/1/6

TIMBER (continued).

Satin, Porto Rico	0/0/8	0/1/6
Walnut, Italian ..	0/0/3½	0/0/7

METALS.

Iron—Pig, in Scotland .... ton	2/1/0	0/0/0
Bar, Welsh, in London	5/17/6	6/0/0
Do. do. at works in Wales	5/7/6	5/10/0
Do. Staffordshire, in London	6/5/0	6/15/0
Copper—British, cake and ingot	48/10/0	50/0/0
Best selected ..	51/0/0	51/10/0
Sheets, strong ..	58/0/0	59/0/0
Chili, bars	46/7/6	46/15/0
Yellow Metal lb.	0/0/5½	0/0/6
Lead—Pig, Spanish .... ton	10/15/0	10/17/6
English, com. brands	11/0/0	11/2/6
Sheet, English, 3 lbs. per sq. ft. and upwards ..	12/0/0	0/0/0
Pipe	12/10/0	0/0/0
Zinc—English sheet ...... ton	25/15/0	26/0/0
Vieille Montagne	26/5/0	0/0/0
Tin—Straits	97/15/0	98/0/0
Australian	98/0/0	98/2/6
English Ingots	100/0/0	101/0/0

OILS.

Linseed ...... ton	18/0/0	18/2/6
Cocoanut, Cochin	24/0/0	0/0/0
Do. Ceylon	21/17/6	22/0/0
Palm, Lagos	22/5/0	22/10/0
Rapeseed, English pale	25/0/0	25/10/0
Do. brown	23/10/0	0/0/0
Cottonseed ref. ..	19/0/0	0/0/0
Oleine	21/10/0	24/10/0
Lubricating, U.S.	4/0/0	5/0/0
Do. refined	6/0/0	12/10/0
Tar—Stockholm barrel	0/19/0	1/0/0
Archangel	0/12/6	0/0/0

TENDERS.

[Communications for insertion under this heading should be addressed to "The Editor," and must reach us *not later than 12 noon on Thursdays.*]

AYLESBURY.—Accepted for alteration and additions to house in New-street, Aylesbury, for Messrs. E. & F. Middleton. Mr. Guest Luckett, architect, Aylesbury:—
Jewell £140 0 0
[No competition.]

BIRTLEY (near Newcastle-on-Tyne).—For main sewerage and sewage disposal works for the town of Birtley. Mr. D. Balfour, engineer, 3, St. Nicholas Buildings, Newcastle-on-Tyne:—

Alex. Meston	£6,160	12	1	Robert Hudson, jun.	£4,038	0	0
John Band	4,950	0	0	John Carrick	3,966	0	0
William Kennedy ..	4,797	0	0	Thomas Dixon, Houghton-le-Spring (accepted).	3,914	0	0
Kell & Groves	4,583	12	8				
George Robson	4,464	8	3				

BOURNEMOUTH.—Accepted for furniture, &c., for the New Municipal Offices, Bournemouth. Mr. F. W. Lacey, Borough Engineer and Surveyor:—
J. J. Allen, Bournemouth £492 13 11

Cupboards, Desks, Counters, &c.
Spring & Sons 320 2 6

BURTON-ON-TRENT.—For erecting St. Paul's Church Institute, Burton-on-Trent. Mr. Reginald Churchill, architect:—

Hunter	£11,600	Walker & Slater	£10,200
Chamberlain Bros.	11,495	Hodges	9,930
Varlow	10,775	Lowe & Son, Burton*	9,925
Stevenson	10,400	* Accepted.	

FOREST HILL.—For the erection of works for the Victoria Printing Works Company:—

Wells	£1,660	Dorpell & Co.	£1,275
Waddington & Co.	1,369	Whitwick & George	1,152

HANLEY (Staffs.).—For erecting premises, Trinity-street, Hanley, Staffs., for Messrs. Grainger & Smith. Mr. Elijah Jones, architect. Quantities by the architect:—

A. & H. Salt	£2,492	J. Longden	£2,083
N. Bennett	2,385	Clarke	2,030
C. Cornes	2,120	A. Hall	2,010
G. Ellis	2,110	T. Godwin, Hanley*	1,990

*Accepted.

HANLEY (Staffs.).—For the erection of three houses, Heron-street, Fenton, for Mr. Richard Woolley. Mr. Elijah Jones, architect, 10, Albion-street, Hanley. Quantities by the architect:—

H. Goodwill	£1,050	0	A. Hall	£920	0
Challenor & Hughes	967	17	Embrey	843	0
C. Cornes	925	0	T. Minks, Fenton*	842	0

* Accepted.

HIGH WYCOMBE.—Accepted for rebuilding the Rye Paper Mills (first contract). Mr. Arthur Vernon, architect, 29, Cockspur-street, London:—
C. H. Hunt £4,983 0 0

HYTHE (Kent).—Accepted for alterations, &c., to the "Swan" Hotel, Hythe, for Mr. T. Elliott. Mr. H. I. Newton, architect, 49, Victoria-street, Westminster, S.W.:—
W. N. Martin, Ramsgate £471 0 0

KEW.—For additions to the west wing of the Kew Observatory, for the Kew Committee of the Royal Society. Mr. John Lessels, architect. Quantities by Mr. Thos. Massey:—

Gascoyne & Blake	£797	C. Eldridge	£632
Lansdown & Co.	646	J. Dorey & Sons	540

LEAVESDEN (Herts).—For alterations and additions to workshops at the Leavesden Asylum, for the Metropolitan Asylums Board. Messrs. A. & C. Harston, Architects, 15, Leadenhall-street, E.C. No quantities supplied:—

Windebank	£979	C. Miskin, St. Albans*	£940

* Accepted

LONDON.—For the completion of re-construction of St. Pancras Workhouse, Pancras-road, for the Guardians of the Poor of the Parish of St. Pancras. Messrs. A. & C. Harston, Architects, 15, Leadenhall-street, E.C. Quantities by Messrs. Corderoy & Selby, 19, Queen Anne's Gate, Westminster, and Mr. W. T. Parthing, 46, Strand, W.C.:—

Shillitoe & Son	£57,500	Lawrance & Son	£54,042
Reed, Blight, & Co.	54,802	Leslie & Co.	53,930
Mark Patrick	58,200	W. Brooks, Folkestone*..	50,861
Kirk, Knight, & Co.	56,648	* Accepted.	

LONDON.—Accepted for alterations and repairs, No. 99, Dean-street, Soho, W. Mr. G. Alexander Wright, surveyor:—
Turtle & Appleton, St. John's Hill, S.W. £224 1 0

LONDON.—For converting the large schoolroom of the Infants' department of the Kender-street School, Hatcham, into a hall; for erecting two additional classrooms to provide accommodation for 100 infants to take the place of the schoolroom, and for carrying out other works, for the School Board for London. Mr. T. J. Bailey, Architect:—

John Garrett & Son	£3,157	0	0	T. McCormick & Sons	£2,388	0	0
F. & H. F. Higgs....	2,493	0	0	F. J. Coxhead, Leytonstone*	2,385	9	9
J. Willmott & Sons	2,423	0	0				

* Recommended by the Works Committee for acceptance.

LONDON.—For erecting a laundry centre and technical room in connexion with the Stanley-street School, Deptford, and for carrying out other works, for the School Board for London. Mr. T. J. Bailey, Architect:—

John Garrett & Son	£3,309	0	0	F. J. Coxhead	2,692	7	9
L. Whitehead & Co.	2,866	0	0	James Smith & Sons	2,655	0	0
F. & H. F. Higgs....	2,804	0	0	Norris & Luke, No. 52, Grovedale-road, Upper Holloway*.	2,488	0	0
John Willmott & Sons	2,733	0	0				

* Recommended by the Works Committee for acceptance.

LONDON.—For the enlargement of the Bell-street School, Edgware-road, by 1395 places, and for carrying out other works, for the School Board for London. Mr. T. J. Bailey, Architect:—

B. E. Nightingale	£12,344	J. T. Chappell	£11,618
S. & W. Pattinson	12,106	John Willmott & Sons ..	11,476
Foster & Dicksee	11,781	John Mowlem & Co., Westminster, S.W.*	11,436
Thomas Boyce	11,700		

* Recommended by the Works Committee for acceptance, less the sum of 1,883l. for the erection of schoolkeeper's house with technical room and laundry centre, which the committee propose to omit from the contract for the present.

LONDON.—For providing and fixing heating apparatus on the low pressure hot-water system for the enlargement of the Holmes-road school, Kentish Town, which is now in course of erection, and for the existing infants' department, for the School Board for London. Mr. T. J. Bailey, Architect:—

W. G. Cannon	£730	10	G. Davis	£635	0
Rosser & Russell	749	0	Purcell & Nobbs	634	0
J. Fraser & Son	746	0	J. Wontner Smith, Gray, & Co., 81, Finsbury-pavement, E.C.*	618	10
J. & F. May	739	0			
C. P. Kinnell & Co.	650	0			

* Recommended by the Works Committee for acceptance.

LONDON.—For alterations and additions to the "Blue Boar" public-house, High-street, Stratford, E., for Mr. Geo. Kidd. Mr. James F. Wesley, architect and surveyor, 284, Romford-road, Forest-gate, E. Quantities by Mr. Geo. Francis, Prince's-road, Buckhurst-hill, Essex:—

Harris & Wardrop	£1,950	0	Alfred Reed & Son....	£1,834	15
Walker Bros.	1,890	0	W. Watson	1,656	0
Wm. Gregar & Son......	1,868	10			

LONDON.—For alterations and fittings to the "Old Justice" public-house, Southwark Bridge-road, S.E., for Mr. W. Robertson. Mr. Fred. A. Ashton, architect, 3, Crooked-lane, E.C.:—

Hearle & Farrow	£796	W. Watson	£712
W. Shurmur	792	Coulsell Bros.	658
F. Voller	730	Snow & Co. (accepted)	564

LONDON.—For alterations and additions to the "Royal Hotel," Leytonstone-road, Stratford, E., for Mr. Wm. Dorton. Mr. Fred. A. Ashton, architect, 3, Crooked-lane, E.C.:—

Hearle & Farrow........	£2,799	Walker Bros.	£2,198
W. Shurmur........	2,515	W. Watson	2,175
Coulsell Bros.	2,446	J. & H. Cocks (accepted) ..	2,150
F. Voller........	2,295	J. & F. Bane........	1,889

LONDON.—For the erection of dwellings, Peacock-street, Newington-butts, for Mr. A. Rickarby. Mr. F. A. Powell, architect, 344, Kennington-road, S.E.:—

Young & Lonsdale	£806	Newton	£725
Downs	798	Burman........	690

LONDON.—For the erection of flats, Ardville-road, Brixton, S.W., for Mr. J. Roycroft. Mr. E. L. Schneider, architect:—

F. & H. F. Higgs	£1,569	Taylor........	£1,485
Young & Lonsdale	1,524	Cowper	1,300

LONDON.—For the erection of artisans' dwellings, Bristol-street, Burton-road, Camberwell, S.E., for the Tenant Co-operators, Limited. Messrs. Goodey & Cressall, architects, 20, Bishopsgate-street, E.C.:—

Clarke & Bracy	£3,580	G. Dobson	£2,970
B. E. Nightingale	3,490	Co-operative Builders, Brixton*	2,896
Stimpson & Co.	3,337	* Accepted.	
F. Dupont........	2,975		

LONDON.—Accepted for new fitting, &c., to the "George," East Harding-street, Fetter-lane, E.C., for the Burton and Lincoln Breweries, Limited, Burton-on-Trent. Mr. H. I. Newton, architect, 49, Victoria-street, Westminster, S.W.:—
H. S. & W. Close, Lincoln £583 0 0

LONDON.—For alterations and additions to No. 58, South Molton-street, W., for The Tayler Smith Electric Lighting Co. Mr. T. Tayler Smith, architect. Quantities by Messrs. Bushell & Crosier, 22, Great James-street, Bedford-row, W.C.:—

Sayers, Thos.	£733	11	5	Bettley, B. G.†	647	0	0
Shoolbred & Co.*	728	0	0	† Time not stated.			

* Accepted.

LONDON.—For pulling down and rebuilding No. 81, Bishopsgate-street Within, for Mr. Arnold Gabriel. Mr. Lewis Solomon and Mr. E. Carrington Arnold, architects:—

Wm. Downs	£2,680	Scott	£2,448
Barlow & Roberts	2,679	Coulson	2,423
Holloway Bros.	2,640	Patman & Fotheringham	2,361
Besson	2,455	C. N. Philips	2,333

MIDDLETON (near Manchester).—For extensions and improvements to the Parish Church Schools, Middleton, near Manchester. Mr. T. A. Fitton, architect, Middleton:—

Young, Tinker, & Young £1,127		0	Thomas Jackson	£1,030	0
E. Partington & Sons ..	1,052	0	John R. Mallekin	1,029	12
Jonathan Partington ..	1,050	0	J. Grundy & Sons*	1,017	0

* Accepted.

MIDDLETON (near Manchester).—Accepted for extensions to Kid Clough Dye Works, Middleton, near Manchester. Mr. T. A. Fitton, architect:—
Wm. Pollitt £1,500 0 0

MIDDLETON (near Manchester).—Accepted for erecting three cottages at Slattocks, near Manchester. Mr. T. A. Fitton, architect:—
E. L. Grindrod, Rochdale........ £467 0 0

MIRFIELD (near Halifax).—For street improvement works at Mirfield, for the Mirfield Local Board. Mr. F. H. Hare, Surveyor, Town Hall, Mirfield, Halifax. Quantities by Mr. Hare:—
Garforth Bros. £1,121 3 9
William Oates, Mirfield (accepted)........ 1,049 9 4

NEWMARKET.—Accepted for the erection and completion of a stable block at "Wellington Villa," Newmarket, for Mr. Christopher Turner. Messrs. Bushell & Crosier, architects, 22, Great James-street, Bedford-row, W.C.:—
H. J. Linzell, Newmarket £156 10 0
[No competition.]

NEWMARKET.—Accepted for the erection and completion of four cottages on Cheveley-road, Newmarket, for Mr. Christopher Tarpey. Mr. Charles Crosier, architect, Newmarket. Quantities by Mr. Henry Bushell, 22, Great James-street, Bedford-row, W.C.:—

H. J. Linzell, Newmarket £530 11 0
(No competition.)

ORPINGTON (Kent).—For decorative repairs to Aynscomb House, Orpington High-street. Mr. St. Pierre Harris, architect and surveyor, 1, Basinghall-street, E.C.:—

Glassup Bros	£145 0	Taylor	£108 0
Owen	120 10	Somerford & Son*	99 10

* Accepted.

ORPINGTON (Kent).—For additions and repairs to residence at Orpington. Mr. St. Pierre Harris, architect, 1, Basinghall-street:—

Knight*	£609 0	Somerford & Son	£578 0
Lowe	579 18	Stebbings & Pannell*	480 0

* Accepted.

ST. ALBANS.—For about a mile and a quarter of 12 in. and 9 in. sewers, under the direction of the City Surveyor:—

J. Jackson	£1,888 8 8½	S. Capper	£1,082 10 6
J. Dickson (accepted)	1,840 0 0		

ST. PAUL'S CRAY (Kent).—For erecting detached private residence at Sandy-lane, for Mr. T. H. Nash. Mr. St. Pierre Harris, architect, 1, Basinghall-street. Quantities by Messrs. C. Stanger & Son:—

Norris & Son	£2,872	Holt & Son	£2,530
Crossley	2,842	Gregory & Co.	2,480
Knight	2,789	Somerford & Son	2,395

SIDCUP.—For the erection of eight cottages at Sidcup. Mr. Arthur Vernon, architect, 29, Cockspur-street, Charing-cross:—

Black	£3,250 0	Pearce	£2,547 0
Joyce	3,244 0	Barker	2,494 0
Lindfeld	3,225 0	Morgan	2,490 0
Munter	2,900 0	Trappit & Bartley	2,460 0
Payne	2,861 0	Peters	2,440 0
Dutholt	2,789 0	Yelford	2,470 0
Richardson	2,757 0	Harris	2,140 0
Groome	2,730 0	Sayers	1,985 0
Minton	2,649 0	Gale	1,880 0
Furness	2,600 0	Sunley	1,757 10
Heathfield	2,307 0		

SURBITON.—For erecting a house on the Crane's Park Estate, Surbiton, for Mr. A. R. Upjohn. Mr. A. R. Mason, architect, 27, High-street, Kingston-on-Thames:—

A. H. Harris	£3,980	G. C. Mortimer	£3,160
H. Faulkner, jun.	3,287	R. Nicholes	3,030
J. Piler & Son	3,204		

SURBITON-HILL.—For erecting and completing twelve houses for Mr. F. Butler. Mr. T. Timberley, architect:—

Dunn	£3,000	Rease	£2,984
Tomkinson	2,934	Jarvis, Surbiton*	2,975

* Accepted.

WAKEFIELD.—Accepted for drainage and other works for the Wakefield Rural Sanitary Authority. Mr. Frank Massie, Engineer, Tetley House, Wakefield:—

East Ardsley Drainage.—Contract No. 3.
George Wilson £96 17 6

Shitlington Drainage.—Contract No. 3.
Doleman & Booth 178 16 6

Stanley Drainage.—Contract No. 3.
Doleman & Booth 306 7 10

Stanley Drainage.—Contract No. 4.
F. W. Denholme & Co. 54 18 3

Isolation Hospital.—Disinfecting House.
W. Richardson 150 19 2

WALTHAM CROSS.—For kerbing and channelling certain roads at Waltham Cross, for the Cheshunt Local Board. Mr. Thos. Bennett, Surveyor:—

Thos. Porter	£987 0 0	Thos. Adams	£765 1 0
Jas. Bloomfield	931 9 8	John Jackson	749 6 10
Jno. Mowlem & Co.	9.7 0 0	W. Griffiths, Kingsland-road, N.*	738 5 2
Jas. Dickson	882 11 0		

* Accepted.
[Surveyor's estimate, £743.]

SUBSCRIBERS in LONDON and the SUBURBS, by prepaying at the Publishing Office, 19s. per annum (or 4s. 9d. per quarter), can ensure receiving "The Builder," by *Friday Morning's Post.*

TERMS OF SUBSCRIPTION.

"THE BUILDER" is supplied DIRECT from the Office to residents in any part of the United Kingdom at the rate of 19s. per annum PREPAID. To all parts of Europe, America, Australia, and New Zealand, 26s. per annum. To India, China, Ceylon, &c., 30s. per annum. Remittances payable to DOUGLAS FOURDRINIER, Publisher, No. 46, Catherine-street, W.C.

TO CORRESPONDENTS.

E. W. T. (the preservation of the general design is not affected by such a detail as that; a little variety in detail is even preferable).—J. B. (the proposal is absurd, as wheeled traffic in crowded streets cannot keep to a straight line).

All statements of facts, lists of tenders, &c., must be accompanied by the name and address of the sender, not necessarily for publication.

We are compelled to decline pointing out books and giving addresses.

NOTE.—The responsibility of signed articles, and papers read at public meetings, rests, of course, with the authors.

We cannot undertake to return rejected communications.

Letters or communications (beyond mere news-items) which have been duplicated for other journals, are NOT DESIRED.

All communications regarding literary and artistic matter should be addressed to THE EDITOR; all communications relating to advertisements and other exclusively business matters should be addressed to THE PUBLISHER, and not to the Editor.

PUBLISHER'S NOTICES.

Registered Telegraphic Address, 'THE BUILDER,' LONDON.

CHARGES FOR ADVERTISEMENTS.

SITUATIONS VACANT, PARTNERSHIPS, APPRENTICESHIPS TRADE, AND GENERAL ADVERTISEMENTS.

Six lines (about fifty words) or under .... 4s. 6d.
Each additional line (about ten words) .... 0s. 6d.

Terms for Series of Trade Advertisements, also for Special Advertisements on front page, Competitions, Contracts, Sales by Auction, &c. may be obtained on application to the Publisher.

SITUATIONS WANTED.

FOUR Lines (about thirty words) or under .... 2s. 6d.
Each additional line (about ten words) .... 0s. 6d.

PREPAYMENT IS ABSOLUTELY NECESSARY.

*** Stamps *must not* be sent, but all small sums should be remitted by Cash in Registered Letter or by Money Order, payable at the Post-office, Covent-garden, W.C. to

DOUGLAS FOURDRINIER, Publisher,
Addressed to No. 46, Catherine-street, W.C

Advertisements for the current week's issue must reach the Office before THREE o'clock p.m. on THURSDAY, but those intended for the front Page should be in by TWELVE noon on WEDNESDAY.

SPECIAL.—ALTERATIONS IN STANDING ADVERTISEMENTS or ORDERS TO DISCONTINUE same must reach the Office before TEN o'clock on WEDNESDAY mornings.

The Publisher cannot be responsible for DRAWINGS, TESTIMONIALS, &c. left at the Office in reply to Advertisements, and strongly recommends that of the latter COPIES ONLY should be sent.

PERSONS Advertising in "The Builder" may have *Replies addressed to the Office,* 46, Catherine-street, Covent Garden, W.C. *free of charge.* Letters will be forwarded if addressed envelopes are sent, together with sufficient stamps to cover the postage.

AN EDITION Printed on THIN PAPER, for FOREIGN and COLONIAL CIRCULATION, is issued every week.

Now ready.
READING CASES, { NINEPENCE EACH. By Post (carefully packed), 1s.

The Builder Cathedral Seri

1891.

1. Canterbury	Jan. 3.	7. Salisbury	Ju
2. Lichfield	Feb. 7.	8. Bristol	A
3. St. Alban's	Mar. 7.	9. Norwich	Se
4. Peterborough ..	April 4.	10. Rochester	O
5. Wells	May 2.	11. Lincoln	N
6. Exeter	June 6.	12. Gloucester	D

1892.

13. St. Paul's .. .. Jan. 2.

14. Hereford	Feb. 6.	20. Worcester	Au
15. Chichester	Mar. 5.	21. Bangor .. .. }	Se
16. Ely	April 2.	22. St. Asaph .. }	
17. Llandaff	May 7.	23. Winchester	Oc
18. Oxford	June 4.	24. Truro	N
19. Southwell	July 2.	25. St. David's	De

(Further arrangements will be duly announced.)

Post-free FOURPENCE HALFPENNY each, except Nos. 1, and 4, which are *out of print;* but the VIEW, PLAN, AND DESCRI of CANTERBURY, LICHFIELD, ST. ALBAN'S, and PE BOROUGH, have been re-printed, and they can now be had, EIGHTPENCE each set; by post, 10d.

THE REREDOS, ST. PAUL'S.
Reprinted from "THE BUILDER," January 28, 1888 (15 b 11½ in.), on stout paper, unfolded, for framing, 6d.; by post, 8d.

PORTFOLIOS,
for Preserving the Plates Unfolded, 2s. 6d.; by post, 3s.

London: Office of "THE BUILDER," 46, *Catherine-street, W.*

The Builder.

Vol. LXII. No. 2576. — Saturday, June 11, 1892.

ILLUSTRATIONS.

The Three Temples at Sbeitla, North Africa: Restoration by Mr. Alexander Graham, F.S.A. .... *Double-Page Ink-Photo.*
"Rivernook," Wraysbury.—Mr. T. E. Collcutt, Architect .... *Double-Page Photo-Litho.*
Retable for St. Alban's Church, Teddington.—Mr. A. H. Skipworth, Architect .... *Single-Page Ink-Photo.*
Reredos for Grayingham Church, Lincolnshire.—Mr. A. H. Skipworth, Architect .... *Single-Page Ink-Photo.*
Working Men's Unionist Club, Ayr.—Messrs. Morris & Hunter, Architects .... *Single-Page Ink-Photo.*
Church of St. Jude, Preston.—Mr. R. Knill Freeman, Architect .... *Single-Page Ink-Photo.*

Blocks in Text.

Thompson and Lee's Safety Arrangement for Jib-Cranes .... Page 459
Plan of "Rivernook," Wraysbury .... Page 461
Diagrams in "Student's Column": Heating by Hot Water .... Pages 463, 464

CONTENTS.

The Restoration of the Choir of Peterborough Cathedral 451
Notes 452
Architecture at the Royal Academy.—VII. 454
The Application of Metals to Architectural Design 455
The Royal Commission on Metropolitan Water-Supply 456
A Safety Provision for Cranes 458
Magazines and Reviews 459
The Three Temples at Sbeitla, North Africa 460
House at Wraysbury 461
Retable for St. Alban's Church, Teddington 461
Reredos for Grayingham Church, Lincolnshire 461
Working Men's Unionist Club, Ayr 461
St. Jude's Church, Preston 461
The Architectural Association 462
Architectural Societies 462
British Archæological Association 462
Election of Fellows, R.I.B.A. 463
Hornsey Main Roads Arbitration 463
"A Question of Building Penalty" 463
Fourteenth and Fifteenth Century Screens 463
Student's Column.—Warming Buildings by Hot Water, XXIV. 463
General Building News 464
Foreign and Colonial 465
Miscellaneous 465
Competitions, Contracts, and Public Appointments 466
Capital and Labour 466
Meetings 466
Recent Patents 466
Some Recent Sales of Property 467
Tenders 467

The Restoration of the Choir of Peterborough Cathedral.

N Thursday in last week, June 2, a special service of much stateliness was held in Peterborough Cathedral, in the presence of a very large congregation, for the dedication, by the Archbishop of Canterbury, of the costly furniture and adornments which have been added to the choir since its formal re-opening in October, 1890.

The character of these additions, from their costliness and elaborate workmanship, demands a special notice. The whole of them have been designed by Mr. Pearson, R.A., who has thus set the stamp of his architectural ability on the decoration of one of our noblest cathedrals, which his engineering skill had already saved from a threatened ruin. Much as has been already done for the substantial repair of the fabric in the taking down and rebuilding the central tower with its sustaining piers and arches, and in the under-pinning of the north aisle and transepts, at the cost of more than 31,000*l.*, the struts which still extend their unseemly bulk at various points of the fabric, especially at the north-east corner of the Eastern Chapel, indicate that this most essential work is by no means complete, and that a large expenditure will be still needed before the Cathedral can be said to be in a state of complete security. The west front especially, the chief glory of the edifice, causes much anxiety. The façade is leaning outward bodily, and the whole calls for speedy attention to forestall possible disaster of no ordinary seriousness. This careful survey, we understand, Mr. Pearson will commence as soon as he can be provided with the necessary scaffolding, which, as our readers do not require to be informed, "means money," and a good deal of it. May it be forthcoming. The eastern angle of the chapel beyond the apse or "new building," as it has been commonly called since it was first erected more than four centuries ago, the ceiling of which is one of the most admirably-designed examples of fan-tracery in the kingdom, evidently from the same hand as King's Chapel, Cambridge, has also given way, through the failure of the foundations, and requires underpinning and repair. When we add that the masonry of the gables of the transepts is in many places insecure and requires extensive repairs, and that the corner turrets of the central tower, which has now a painfully squat appearance reminding one of Winchester, still have to be built, it will be seen that the Dean and Chapter have much on their hands before the external works are finished. We have said nothing of the building of the south-western tower, which is so urgently needed to balance its sister to the north, and complete the harmony of the western prospect. For this long-desired work no very large sum would be required, and we have often hoped, and hope still, that one of our northern millionaires, when he catches sight of the unfinished design as he passes by on the railway, may be fired with the desire of immortalising himself by undertaking it.

But it is time that we pass from what remains to be done, to that which is the proper subject of this article, viz., what has been done by way of internal decoration.

Under this head we have to speak of the Bishop's throne, the choir pulpit, both presented by the present Dean, Dr. Argles, the choir pavement,—also the gift of the same munificent benefactor, who had previously given large amounts to the works of material restoration, and the cleaning of the stonework of the nave,—the choir stalls, presented by various donors, together with the litany desk and other minor matters.

The throne and pulpit are both placed, somewhat unusually, outside the ritual choir,—which has been brought back from the eastern limb to its ancient place in the first two bays of the nave,—against the south-east and north-east piers, respectively, of the great eastern lantern arch. This position was rendered almost necessary by the throwing open of the transepts,—as at Westminster Abbey and Norwich,—for congregational purposes. However advantageous this arrangement may be for the accommodation of hearers and worshippers, to throw the transepts into the choir without any intervening screens, is as injurious to the general effect of the building as it is contrary to the intentions of the original builders. Light iron grilles, similar to those which occupy a like position across the lesser transepts at Lincoln, would have satisfied the eye without materially interfering with sight or hearing. When so much still remains to be done, and the inflow of funds is naturally not so plentiful as in the first enthusiasm of the movement, we hardly like to suggest fresh expenditure; but there is hardly any work which would be more rewarding in general effect. Screens are even more urgently required for the arches on either side of the constructional choir, which, now that it is denuded of all furniture and fittings, looks painfully naked and open. Grooves in some of the huge Norman columns show where such screens once stood, and where it is to be hoped they will ere long stand again. Though we cannot profess to be admirers of Blore's woodwork which, however admirable in material and workmanship, shows a fatal want of recognition of the difference between wood and stone to work in, we should have been glad if, when Dean Monk's choir, dating from 1830 (the year, one may say, from which dates the first commencement of the movement for cathedral restoration), was dismantled, the fronts of his strangely-designed stalls had been used to screen off the aisles. They have been so employed on the north side of the nave to form choir and clergy vestries in the aisle, and that with an effectiveness which makes us the more regret their removal from the choir.

To turn from noting deficiencies to the description of the costly works dedicated last week. The first to challenge attention is the new throne, which, from its position, is conspicuous in the eastward view almost as soon as the cathedral is entered. This has been executed in oak by Mr. Thompson's workmen at the cost of 1,250*l.*, and, as we have said, has been the gift of the dean. "It was not every dean," the bishop remarked at the luncheon, "who wanted to build a throne for his bishop." Though the conventional type of an episcopal throne, as a choir stall of greater loftiness and richness, has been maintained, Mr. Pearson has given a degree of originality to his design, by omitting the front legs of the canopy, which rests on curved supports coming forward from the back. The canopy is very lofty, ending in a tall, crocketed spirelet reaching halfway up the triforium, and comprises three tiers of rich tabernacle work, connected by delicate pierced fenestrations. The angles of the principal canopy are accentuated by square turrets of pierced work,—*lanterns* we may almost call them,—also ending in spirelets. The niches of the canopy contain statuettes of abbots and bishops of Peterborough. In the lower tier are Saxulf, the first abbot, Cuthbald his successor, De Seez the builder of the choir, Benedict the builder of the nave, St. Hugh of Lincoln (of which diocese Peterborough formed part till the Reformation changes), and lastly, John Chambers, the last abbot and first bishop. In the upper canopy are figures of Bishop Dove,—a favourite preacher with Queen Elizabeth, who called him "the Dove with silver wings,"—and of Bishop White Kennett, the eminent antiquary and historian.

Against the corresponding pier on the north is the pulpit. The body is of circular outline, ornamented with panelling and tabernacle work of somewhat excessive richness, and broken by projecting niches containing figures of the Apostles St. Paul, St. Peter, St. John, and St. James. Between these are wide panels, with carvings in high relief of Our Lord's parting Commission to His Apostles, the Day of Pentecost, and Saxulf Preaching to the Gyrvians. The pulpit rests on an elaborately-carved polygonal base, with niches containing statuettes of four of the Abbots connected with the building of the Cathedral. The figure-carving of the pulpit is by Mr. Hitch, who is responsible for the greater part of the carving at Truro Cathedral; that of the throne, we believe, was executed at Peterborough, under Mr. Thompson's superintendence, by his own workmen.

Passing westward, and entering the ritual choir, the whole range of stalls, nineteen in number, has been completed on the south side, filling the two bays of the arcade comprised within the limits of the choir. On the north side only seven stalls have as yet been erected, leaving twelve to be made up. There are also six return stalls at the west end, three on either side of the entrance. Eighteen of these stalls having been given since 1890, were included in the service of dedication. They exhibit semi-hexagonal canopies, with ogee, crocketed, and traceried gablets, flying buttresses and pinnacles rising into elaborately carved niches with ogee pediments containing statuettes, the design finishing in a lofty crocketed spirelet. The ornamentation of the lower canopies is rather crowded, and suffers from excess of richness. In common with the throne and the pulpit, the carved work is somewhat too profuse and "busy," and a quieter and bolder design would have been more effective. The wearied eye craves for repose. The two terminal stalls at the west end for the dean and vice-dean are loftier and more elaborate in treatment. They are three stages in height, with two tiers of statuettes, and have taller spires. The sides of the terminal stalls flanking the entrance bear panels carved with legends from the history of the abbey,—the wonder-working arm of St. Oswald, the apparition of the angel to Ethelwold, &c. The canopies of all the stalls are groined within, with bosses at the intersection of the ribs. The statues in the niches present a sculptural record of the history of the fabric in its successive representative personages, from Peada, the founder of the monastery, to Archbishop Magee and Deans Saunders and Perowne. Other statues illustrate the history of the Church of the O. T. and N. T., as represented by the Patriarchs and Prophets, the Apostles and Evangelists. The selection and arrangement is the result of careful study, and will repay examination. The fronts to the central range of stalls on each side are relics of the old Benedictine choir, now once more restored to their original place and use. The ogee panelling and traceried work, divided by small buttresses and crocketed pinnacles of remarkable beauty, has been made good from the traces left after the Puritans had brutally torn off the carved work, leaving the plain wood behind. The new stall-fronts have followed the same model: we wish their hue could have been adopted. The whole of the new woodwork looks painfully raw. But this is an evil that time will mend. We must not forget to mention a handsomely-carved Litany desk executed in oak, the gift of Mrs. Rigg, the daughter of the late Archdeacon Davys, which stands in the centre of the choir.

The most distinctive feature in the refitting of the choir is the sumptuous pavement of tessellated work and inlaid marbles, which as long as the Cathedral stands will perpetuate the name and record the munificence of Dean Argles and his daughter. This pavement has been designed by Mr. Pearson, and carved out by Italian workmen under the superintendence of Mr. Robert Davison, of London. The whole of the marbles employed are from Italian quarries, of rich and varied hues, contrasting and yet harmonising. The cost has been little, if at all, short of £2,000, the original estimate, we need hardly say, having been largely exceeded. The pavement is divided into sections, increasing in richness of material and complexity of design as it advances eastward. The ritual choir and the lantern space are paved with tesseræ of a subdued red, green, and white, arranged in a geometrical pattern, the low tone satisfying the eye without distracting it. The floor of the eastern limb is divided into three chief sections corresponding to three bays of the arcade, the sanctuary and altar-space forming a fourth section in which the decoration culminates. The bays are separated by steps of polished marble of various kinds, the first step being of the black Frosterly marble flecked with white madrepores, familiar to us in the Chapel of the Nine Altars at Durham; the two next are of Levanto marble of a reddish-brown with white veinings. The remaining steps, as well as those of the footpace of the altar, are of pure Pavonazzo with exquisite veinings. The design of the pavement of the first two bays is the same. Four large parallelograms of Pavonazzo are set in a framework of deep red porphyry, the intervening cruciform space being occupied by interlacing bands of cream-coloured tesseræ forming circles and lozenges on a tesselated ground of red and black. The third bay, though of much more elaborate design, is hardly so effective. The design comprises three square compartments laid transversely from north to south, each containing four panels of Cipollino, framed in bands of "opus Alexandrinum," made up of squares, triangles, and diamonds, of brilliantly-coloured marbles, which are again set in a broad border of mosaic of white squares on a light green ground. The design of this bay strikes us as too much scattered and somewhat deficient in decision of outline. Bolder lines would have been more effective. The fourth bay shows a system of interlacing bands, enclosing alternately large and small octagonal spaces, the small octagons being filled with rich plaques of marble, the larger being divided into eight triangular panels of marble mosaic of varied patterns. At either extremity of this bay is a long panel of intersecting circles, filled with rich mosaic. The altar footpace, and the three steps, are as yet unfinished. They are to be inlaid with rich mosaic enclosed in marble bands. The pavement north and south of the altar is of "opus sectile," exhibiting hexagons of Pavonazzo, between lozenges of a rich marble resembling our English serpentines. The entire design is finished on the outside with a long band of red marble extending the whole length of the Presbytery. Though, as we have said, the pavement might have proved more effective if greater simplicity and boldness of outline had been adopted in some parts, it must be acknowledged to be a magnificent work, which calls forth admiration both for the elaborateness of the design and the richness and beauty of the materials employed.

The reredos, side screens, altar rails, and credence-table are still deficient, and wait the liberality of future donors. The place of the two first-named is temporarily supplied by rich hangings. Behind and over the altar is a tester of crimson and orange velvet, plain but effective. On either side are curtains of a dull green, entirely excluding the view of the apse and of the chapel beyond, which is to be regretted.

Among the *desiderata* enumerated is the reconstruction of the organ. We observe that it is proposed to place it in the triforium as at Canterbury. This may be necessary but it is much to be regretted. An organ enclosed in a case, such as men were once able to design and might design again is a grand and beautiful object, and when placed, as we hold it ought always to be placed, on architectural as well as musical grounds, on the centre of the choir screen it is of inestimable value as breaking the protracted vista, suggesting something beyond, and creating "that mystery of things half seen," which, as the late Mr Street has truly said, "is the secret of many of the greatest successes of mediæval architecture." When the funds allow the Chapter to undertake the choir screen, which is one of the first wants of the Cathedral, to hide the plain and ugly backing of the screen stalls, we hope that no foolish outcry for an unbroken view from end to end, which our Cathedrals never had nor were intended to have, will prevent their putting the organ in its proper place, over the entrance to the choir, provided it is in any way practically possible from the organ-builder's point of view. The difficulty of course arises from the increased size of modern organs, especially in the department of the pedal, which includes the largest pipes in the instrument. But we think it may be possible, if the difficulty is fairly faced; and it would be better to reduce the contemplated size of the organ to some extent in order to get it into this position, as it is unquestionabl that a rather smaller organ in the centra position is more effective than a larger on placed in the triforium, while the archi tectural effect of the organ in the triforiu position is of course entirely non-existent.

NOTES.

TWO very important resolutions ar to be brought forward at th meeting of the Institute o Monday night, by Mr. Charle Barry and Mr. Searles-Wood, both having fo their object to provide that within a limite period it shall be declared that every candi date for Fellowship of the Institute shall b an Associate, or shall have passed an examina tion qualifying him for Associateship, "excep in such special cases of age, merit, or dis tinction as shall justify the Council in dispensing with such examination unde Section 3 of the Charter." The reason fo the movement is that at present men jus past the prescribed age of thirty may b qualified to be elected as Fellows, and tha it is an anomaly that a man wh before that age would have had to enter th Institute through the medium of the exami nation for Associateship should, by merel waiting till he is thirty, be able to evad that test and enter as a Fellow. The Counci have received various memorials in recom mendation of this policy. That the presen condition of things is an anomaly there ca be no doubt; but the proposal is practicall very much the same as a proposal for th examination of candidates for Fellowshi though it is perhaps a better way to put i The proposal has a great deal of support, w believe, from provincial members especially.

MISS OCTAVIA HILL, in a letter the *Times* of Tuesday, makes an el quent but we fear fruitless appeal against th passing of the Manchester and Sheffiel

Railway Bill by the House of Lords. After noticing that Parliament is asked to sanction the sudden and irrevocable destruction of a residential district of comparative quiet, against the strong representations of the London County Council, "the only body which can judge of London as a whole," Miss Hill continues:—

"This railway proposes to destroy two squares; to invade acres of space covered with cheap, pleasant houses with gardens; if constructed it would in a great measure cut off the whole poor district of Lisson-grove from its natural playground, —Regent's Park,—which at present is approached by pleasant wide streets with little traffic, safe for small groups of children to traverse alone, wide breathing spaces, now bright with laburnum and lilac hanging over the low garden walls.

I believe the line to have been thus planned with the sole view of its being cheap to the promoters.

It has been said that these leases will fall in in about fifteen years, and that the public has no security that when they fall in the ground may not be more thickly covered. That is no doubt true, but that is no reason why fifteen years of healthy life with gardens and good air should be snatched away by Parliament,—years which will distinctly influence the life of many a child now three or five years old."

There could hardly be a more forcible and touching plea put in against this last attempt to destroy the comparative quiet and repose of a whole district of London. As we have said, we fear the appeal is hopeless now. Years hence, when London has all been turned into one racketting-ground of noise and traffic and piled-up buildings, people may begin to find out, when it is too late, that there are more vital interests to the comfort of life than rapid locomotion, and that in search of that convenience London has been made all but unbearable as a place of residence either for poor or rich.

THE inquest on the death of the two men who were killed in the extraordinary railway collision at Birmingham has resulted in a verdict of manslaughter against the driver of the Midland train, and no other verdict seems possible on the evidence. The length of time (nearly an hour) which the jury occupied in arriving at this verdict was probably owing to a natural reluctance (to bear hardly on a driver who appears to have a good record of long service with his Company; but as the evidence leaves no doubt that the signals were open for the London and North-Western train, and as it was proved that they were (of course) so constructed that they could not be open for both lines, there is no room for doubt that the Midland driver was going against his signals. According to the evidence of Mr. Loveday, the chief inspector of traffic for the Midland Railway, there are "confusing elements" in respect to the signals near the junction, which appear to alter their position owing to the curve and the interposition of a chimney. In that case some responsibility, not very easily to be defined, would seem to be placed on the company. The more serious matter is that, as far as the signalman at Duddeston Mill-road box could judge, the Midland driver paid no attention to his "caution" signal; and that he did not act as if he had seen it is obvious from the remainder of the evidence. It remains to be seen whether this was actually a case of culpable carelessness, or whether it is one of those instances which will occur at times, in railway traffic as in other matters, when the human machine unaccountably fails for a moment; when the eye sees what it expects to see, or does not see what it does not expect. Such momentary fallacies do happen from time to time, even to very careful and methodical men; whether this was one of them it is difficult to say; the trial may throw more light on it.

IT is clear that Mr. Goschen's change in the incidence of the patent duties has not in the least satisfied those persons who are interested in this subject. We have recently received a circular from a Patent Law Reform Association, which appears to be composed chiefly of Lancashire men. The subject cannot adequately be dealt with in a very short space, but the fact is clear that the question has now reached the point whether any but nominal patent duties are to be any longer in existence. The duty of about 7*l*. in the United States must be regarded as merely nominal. It may be that the increase of patents under a nominal duty would compensate the Exchequer for the loss in actual amount on each patent. It is questionable whether a patentee, more than an author, should be taxed for the purposes of revenue; but, be that as it may, it is well that we should not hide from ourselves that the time has now come when the point above stated has been arrived at. The issue between moderate and nominal duties will obviously have to be decided early in the life of the next Parliament.

IT is noticeable that in the recent Report of the Select Committee on Theatres there is no suggestion of the advisability of any general regulations to promote the safety of theatres, applicable to the whole kingdom, which would surely be desirable, instead of leaving each municipality to formulate its own regulations according to its own perceptions. It may be added that in addition to fire-resisting construction and good planning for exits, it would very much increase the confidence of audiences if the rule were followed which has been established in Berlin and some other continental cities, of compelling the management to keep on the premises a "fire-watch" composed of men who are retired firemen, familiar with the best methods of guarding against fire or combating it if it arises. The few recently-built theatres in London are as safe in regard to structure and planning as such buildings can be made, but the existing majority are only as safe as they can be made without entire rebuilding; and the knowledge that there was always, by legal regulation, a sufficient number of competent and experienced firemen on the premises would tend to give audiences that feeling of security that the building would be properly looked after, in the event of any accident, which does more than anything else to check panic.

BROCKWELL-PARK, Herne-hill, was formally opened on Monday morning last, amidst the rejoicings of the neighbourhood, by Lord Rosebery, Chairman of the London County Council, who commended the action taken by that and other bodies in saving this important "lung" to the neighbourhood, which is fast being covered with bricks and mortar. In addition to the new colony of houses which has sprung up at the top of Milkwood-road, opposite Herne-hill station, we notice that on Herne-hill itself, between the church and Poplar-walk, four new roads have already been marked out, so that this hitherto semi-rural neighbourhood will soon be materially changed, and there is likely to be ample need for the park as a breathing-space in the near future. Hardly had Lord Rosebery left the park when an event occurred which cast a gloom over the remainder of the day. Mr. T. L. Bristowe, M.P. for the Norwood Division of the Borough of Lambeth, in the midst of whose constituency the park is situated, and who had taken a prominent and active part in its acquisition, was suddenly taken ill, and died in the park after the lapse of a few moments. Mr. Bristowe's death at the very moment of the full fruition of his efforts in an important work has elicited widespread feelings of regret amongst men of all parties in his constituency.

THE threatened demolition of Emanuel Hospital, Westminster, is much to be regretted on more grounds than one. Not only is it a very interesting and picturesque old building, a peculiarly favourable specimen of its date, but the ground in connexion with it keeps an open space where open space is much wanted. The region neighbouring on Victoria-street is rapidly becoming a collection of enormous heaps of building, the height of which is quite out of proportion to the ground they cover; and it is on that account all the more desirable that any unbuilt space in the vicinity should be preserved intact. We are glad to see, therefore, from a letter in the *Times* of Thursday, from Messrs. Horne & Birkett, the solicitors representing some of those who are opposed to the removal of the building, that an application has been made to Mr. Justice Chitty on behalf of the Dean of Westminster and others for leave to appear and submit arguments why the building should not be demolished, and that this application has been assented to. It is to be hoped that the result will be the preservation of the hospital and its grounds as now existing.

THE great controversy between the Prussian Royal Academy and the "Verein Berliner Künstler" as to the management of the Berlin Art Exhibitions has been settled by compromise, neither body receiving the Government permission necessary for independent action. The "Verein Berliner Künstler" and the Prussian Academy will henceforward mutually arrange all the official art exhibitions which are held, each body being equally represented in the management. The Government reserves the right of revising the "programme" of the exhibitions, and also of deputing a representative to watch the proceedings of the joint committees. The "Verein" will, to a certain extent, incur the pecuniary risk of future exhibitions; they are to be managed with the capital of this society, which will have the benefit of any profits, but also the responsibility for deficits. The Government support consists of a loan of the halls of the Landes-Ausstellungs-Palast free of charge, and the vote of a substantial sum for purchases. A committee of connoisseurs (selected by the Minister of Education, &c.) will act as advisor to the Government as regards the purchase of exhibits, and the Emperor is to be requested to act as patron. The art exhibitions are henceforward to be of more national interest than the usually purely local ones held under auspices of the Academy. At certain intervals large international exhibitions, similar to last year's, will be arranged. It is to be hoped that under the new rule more attention will be paid to architecture, which has hitherto been very badly provided for in German art exhibitions.

WE note with pleasure that the German Emperor has selected Sir John Everett Millais to be a holder of the Order "Pour le Mérite" (Arts and Science Division, Foreign Section). It is the highest Prussian distinction, and is only given with the consent of the Knights of the most honourable order.

A DISCOVERY of very great interest has been made at Silchester, Hants, during the excavations that have been going on, on the site of the Roman city. This is the complete ground-plan of an Early Christian basilica of small dimensions, situated near the south-east corner of the Forum. As the earliest example of a Christian place of worship in the British Isles its value is great, and lends additional interest to the discoveries that are being made at Silchester. We hope to give a ground-plan and some more particulars next week.

THE new market for fruit, vegetables, and flowers, which is to be opened on the 13th inst., in West Smithfield, completes the tale of central markets erected by the Corporation, under statute. It will supplant Farringdon Market, and takes the place of one that was built, for the same goods, in Farringdon-road, opposite, but which, before its completion, the Corporation decided to open for the sale of fish, and which was so opened in May, 1883, having cost altogether 450,000*l*. As the fish traffic resulted in a heavy loss, the building was converted, by Mr. A. Peebles, the then City architect, and at a further cost of 12,000*l.*, for the sale of poultry and provisions. Of the works for a new fruit market, as planned and designed by Mr. Peebles, we gave descriptions in our columns on September 13 and November 1, 1890. Messrs. Rudd & Son, of Grantham, took the contract, at 41,973*l.* for the basement and sub-structure. The super-structure was estimated to cost 15,500*l.* On February 28, 1885, we adverted to the establishment by the London Riverside Fishmarket Company of a fish market at Shadwell.

IT is stated that St. Mary's Hospital, Paddington, is to be added to, at an estimated cost of 100,000*l.*, as a memorial to the late Duke of Clarence. The present hospital, enlarged a few years ago, was built in 1845-9, of red brick with stone dressings, after the designs of Mr. J. H. Wyatt and Mr. Thomas Hopper; according to Cassell's "Old and New London:" in William Robins's "Paddington, Past and Present" (its preface dated in 1853), we read that Mr. Hopper was the architect, and made no charges for his professional labour. The entire plans were for five separate divisions, or blocks, with a total capacity of 380 beds.

A NEW form of cowl for chimneys and other minor ventilation, has been patented by Messrs. Wheeler & Sons, for which considerable merits are claimed, and which may fairly be classed as a good specimen of revolving cowls on the archimedean screw principle. The chief features of the cowl are the use of twin blades to the screw, the introduction of coned louvres within the wind-blades to prevent the admission of rain and snow, and careful provision for decreasing the friction of working parts, which is always the weak point of revolving cowls. The use of phosphor bronze for bearing surfaces, and the reduction of bearing points to one by careful balance of the cowl, tend to the reduction of friction.

THE vitality of some of the popular errors about the history and development of architecture is extraordinary. The notion that Gothic vaulting arose from an imitation of trees has been exposed and laughed at by every competent architectural critic for years back, and it is needless to say here that it is an idea which no one could entertain who had given the slightest intelligent study to the history of the development of Gothic vaulting. Yet in a critical article in the *Times* of the 6th inst. on the life and works of Gustave Doré,—an article, moreover, which as far as its notice of Doré's work goes is marked by a very sound spirit of criticism,—we are told, in reference to Doré's appreciation of Gothic architecture, "that he loved to go wandering in the forest solitudes of the Vosges, under those colonnades of stately stems with their arching foliage which had furnished the Gothic architects with their designs" (!) When are we to be rid of this nonsense? The writer of the article in question is evidently a man of education and thought in regard to some forms of art; let him, before he next refers to architecture in print, read any illustrated sketch of the development of Mediæval vaulting, by a competent exponent of architectural history, and he will then perhaps realise that architecture is not a subject to be dragged in for literary illustration without some knowledge of the scientific facts of its history and development.

THE development of new proposals for plundering the architectural profession under the name of "competition," has been going on fast of late years. It is always of interest to note a new feature. The last we hear of has been furnished to us in the form of the conditions for a limited competition to which some eminent Dublin architects have been invited. We suppress all names, as it has not been publicly advertised; but after giving the particulars for the building the instructions proceed;—

> "It is to be understood that no fees or commission are to be payable to any architect who may send in plans as above, and that the building committee do not bind themselves to adopt any of the plans that may be submitted."

This really deserves the distinction of being the best joke of the kind that has yet been made; it is difficult to decide whether it is the offspring of pure audacity or pure innocence; or is it a characteristic development of Irish humour?

ARCHITECTURE AT THE ROYAL ACADEMY.—VII.

1,788; "New Tower, St. Mary's Church, Lynton;" Mr. H. Wilson. A water-colour drawing of a very original church tower, showing how its author has been trained in the school of the late J. D. Sedding, whose work he seems to be carrying on in the same artistic spirit. The tower is nearly plain up to the belfry stage, where coupled traceried windows are inserted, with a statue over the dividing mullion; a low-pitched leaded roof of concave outline projects its eaves boldly, and the buttresses stop flat under them; the wrought-iron gargoyles at the angles look a little thin and out of keeping with the solidity of the rest. The angle staircase turret appears to penetrate the roof and finishes in a small lantern a little too suggestive of a pigeon-house; but the whole is picturesque and original.

1,789; "East Window, Skelton-in-Cleveland Church, Yorkshire;" Messrs. Shrigley & Hunt. A five-light window with a figure of Christ in the centre light on a rather larger scale than the figures of saints in the other lights, which we think a mistake; the general colour-effect of the window is very good, and the architectural canopies are treated with due subordination and mass well with the whole; but here again we have canopies which project in perspective and leave platforms in perspective for the figures to stand on, which is contrary to the true principle of stained glass; and having this appearance of bulk, there seems nothing adequate to support them.

1,791; "Figures from the Workmen's Window, Law Courts, Birmingham;" Mr. P. H. Newman. We published these figures in the *Builder* for July 25, 1891, with the decorative adjuncts to one figure only. The effect of the whole is very rich, and interesting as an unusual introduction of Renaissance architectural detail in stained glass; but the effect of the heavily-coloured perspective niches is here again very solid for a surface intended to transmit light, and the boots, aprons, braces, and other details of working-men's costume have an odd effect in stained glass. If it were determined to treat the figures as realistic types of working-men this could not be avoided, and the conundrum has been solved perhaps as well as it could be under these circumstances; but we should have preferred emblematic to realistic figures for a window. These would have been quite suitable for wall painting; a window is another affair entirely.

1,793; "'In Heaven their Angels Always Behold the Face of My Father': Design for a Stained-glass Window for Rydal Church;" Mr. Henry Holiday. This is a true example of decorative stained-glass, entirely clear of realism or perspective; the design is made up of winged children's figures (the purple wings furnishing a valuable element in the colour design), bearing scrolls with texts, the figures and scrolls intertwined with foliage, with a sky background. This is an unusual and very fine and successful piece of stained-glass design.

1,794; "Portion of the East Window of Bath Abbey;" Miss Emma Knight. A very fine and powerful illustration of old stained glass, giving almost the rich effect of the glass itself, at least to an extent seldom produced by pigments.

1,797; "Design for a Window at All Souls' College, Oxford;" Messrs. James Powell & Sons. A Renaissance window in small square leadings, of which the border is an admirable piece of ornamental design; in the centre is an architectural niche with a figure of Wren in his habit as he lived, with a panel with arms and supporters below the niche. The mistake of this is that this architectural erection seems to be hung in air in the middle of a white space, and has nothing to support it, nor is the figu in blue coat and buckled shoes happy in effec A medallion portrait with a less architectur framing would have been better for a window.

1,798; "The Baptistery, Florence; Zodia Panel in Pavement;" Mr. R. W. Schultz. very careful pencil-drawing, slightly tinted places, showing the pavement on plan, with th joints of the main slabs carefully marke This affords an admirable study for real dec rative work in pavement inlay; the artist h attempted no more in his representation of th signs of the Zodiac than is quite within th powers of inlaid work; and though the desig is generally symmetrical, there is an enti absence of that minute care for symmet which would tend to give the design mechanical hardness.

1,800; "Design for a large Town House; Mr. Arthur Bartlett. A very pretty and origin design, shown in a tinted pencil-drawing; it not easy to see, however, what can be th function of the little windows between nich and colonettes which form the only openin in the mass of wall on the ground floor. Arch tecturally the effect is charming, but how do it fall into the plan, and what becomes of a entertaining room on the ground floor? A pl might have solved the riddle, but none is give The upper portion shows a recessed centre wi mullioned bay windows running through tw stories and stopped by the soffit of a balco connecting the end wings. The lanterns ov the wings are the least happy features, a seem out of place and unmeaning.

1,802; "Glasgow Art Gallery, Competiti Design;" Mr. A. N. Prentice. A curious b very picturesque design of somewhat Spani character. The centre feature is a circul tower with a conical roof and lantern, risi from a square central block, and flanked circular turrets which sit on the angles of th square. The rest of the building is a long na extending both ways, with a transept term nating in an apse abutting against it. Th ground story is kept quite plain, only brok by entrance-doors, the upper story rich treated with rows of small circular-head windows very deeply recessed, and the eav projecting in an immense cove over. Th transept is kept quite plain, affording a ba for the ornate treatment right and left of The author seems to have been strongly infl enced by his sketching tour in Spain, and t whole look of the building is as if designed f a hot country (the presumable roof-lighting kept out of sight behind a balustrade on t roof); one certainly could not fancy it Glasgow; but it is a brilliant architectural co ception nevertheless.

1,803; "River Nook, Wraysbury;" Mr. T. Collcutt. This is published among the plates our present number, to which we refer t reader. By Mr. Collcutt's courtesy we enabled also to give the plan of the hou which is not shown on the drawing at t Academy.

1,804; "Drawing-room Ceiling, Ashridge Mr. T. Strethill Smith. It is impossible to de boldness and vigour to this ceiling design, b that is all it can claim. It has all the wo and most rampant vulgarities of Louis Qui taste; immense cartouches with the usual g shoulder-knot kind of feature dear to the perio bundles of instruments and other things sti ing out from the margin, heavy garlands f tooned horizontally, &c. The centre portion occupied by a copy of Guido Reni's "Auro a composition quite out of place on a ceili and the ragged outline of the frame whi surrounds it has a very bad effect. The auth has reproduced faithfully and with spirit t characteristics of one of the worst periods decorative taste.

1,805; "Convalescent Home, Chatham," a 1,806, "House at Royston, Herts;" in o frame, by Mr. John Belcher, may be tak along with 1,813, "Studio, Melbury-road;" a 1,814; "Mark Ash, Abinger," also in one fra and by the same architect: four small wat colours of characteristic and pretty litt buildings. In 1,813 and 1,814 the figures evidently wrongly placed or wrong in th catalogue; 1,814 is the studio; it is to t architect's credit that it is quite obviously even without any plan. "Mark Ash" is exceedingly pretty specimen of a small coun house treated in "picturesque cottage" style.

1,808; "Flixton Hall, Suffolk;" Mr. F. Wade. This is apparently an addition to a ri old Elizabethan house: a plan is given showi the extent of new and old work. The additio consist of a large conservatory forming the main garden entrance, new garden fronts to the drawing-room and morning-room, and a very extensive return wing of lower buildings in the same ornate style, containing kitchen and other offices, and another conservatory towards the garden court. The house is in the richest Elizabethan style, of brick with stone dressings, panelled balustrades, cut brick chimneys and pinnacles, but as all the work shown in the perspective view is new, we cannot tell how far this is a carrying on of the design of the original, or how far it is a creation of a modern Elizabethan house. If the latter, it is very completely done and in a very rich and pleasing style, though it cannot be said to present any originality of idea or detail. The octagon turret above the garden entrance is a very pleasing and picturesque feature. The drawing, a large water-colour in the true "architectural draughtsman" style, is weakly executed and not good enough to do full justice to the building.

1,811; Caer-hun, North Wales;" Mr. T. M. Lockwood. A good sepia drawing of an exceedingly solid stone house with mullioned windows, this portion contrasted with the half-timber work of the secondary portions of the house, which seem to shelter behind the solid mass of the other portion. If, however, this is a new house all built at the same time, it has too much the appearance of two different buildings of different dates. There is no plan to give any explanation on this head.

1,812; "St. Bartholomew the Great, E.C., the New Transepts;" Mr. Aston Webb. Three fine solidly-executed line drawings in one frame, showing the interiors of the two transepts and an exterior view of the north transept and porch. In the north transept the triforium arcade is carried round, with three lancet windows over, which show cusped heads externally, but internally are masked by arches with traceried heads divided into two lights by (apparently) Purbeck or other marble shafts, which are shaded darker in the drawing. In the south transept the triforium arcade is stopped, and the end wall above the main arcade occupied by three large two-light windows with geometrical tracery in the heads. The drawings are by Mr. C. E. Mallows.

1,815; "Gloucester Cathedral, Interior of Choir;" Mr. C. E. Mallows. This is the drawing published in the *Builder* of Dec. 5, 1891, as one of the illustrations of Gloucester Cathedral.

1,816; "Design for a Window, Trinity College, Oxford;" Messrs. Jas. Powell & Sons. This is another example of a Renaissance architectural shrine with a figure hung in the middle of white squared glazing; but it is less open to objection than No. 1,797, because the architectural framing of the figure is treated in a more light and decorative manner and with less of architectural formality and squareness. Still, even here, the niche is too much as if hung in air. Apart from this objection, the design is graceful and effective in its dealing with decorative details which have the sanction of precedent, though they are anything but pure in taste.

THE APPLICATION OF METALS TO ARCHITECTURAL DESIGN:

ROYAL INSTITUTE OF BRITISH ARCHITECTS.

THE following is an abstract of Mr. Alexander Graham's "Historical Sketch of the Application of Metals to Architectural Design," read at the meeting of the Institute on the 30th ult., as an introduction to the three papers* read by Messrs. C. Krall, H. Longden, and H. W. Singer on "Castings in Metal":—

The application of metals to the adornment of buildings might be traced to a very remote period of the world's history. The exact period when the work of the hammer and chisel was supplemented by acquaintance with the earthen mould was not recorded, but tradition attributed this distinction to Phrygia. The art was, however, probably known to the Israelites in the time of Moses. The beating of copper must have been familiar to the earliest races, and the leathern shield with its studs of glittering copper was probably the earliest piece of decoration applied to buildings. The earlier founders made their castings as thin as possible, and attached them to a wood foundation with pins of metal; and this would account for the scarcity of ancient examples, whether in copper or in bronze. It was doubtful whether the Phrygians made any progress with their invention, but it spread with rapidity in other countries. The walls of Babylon were defended by a hundred gates of bronze, and metal was extensively used both for the construction and adornment of buildings in Chaldæa and Assyria. The gates of Balawat, composed of plates of beaten bronze, made for Shalmaneser II., about 850 B.C., were now to be seen in the British Museum. Philostratus said that the palaces of the kings of Babylon were "covered with bronze which caused them to glitter in the sunshine." The use of metals applied to buildings in Persia appeared to have been restricted to covering their brick and timber construction with thin plates, sometimes adorned with work in *repoussé* and inlays of gold. At the present day the gates of the Mosque at Ispahan were covered with laminæ of silver, adorned with inscriptions and arabesques in gold. The forging of metals for decorative purposes preceded the casting in moulds. We had to turn to the Egyptians for the earliest artistic representations of the human form. They first used pure copper, being ignorant of the fact that by the admixture of a little tin its hardness could be increased. Among the metals in common use among the Egyptians was *asimu*, or electrum. There was a dearth of skilled workers in Judæa, and we learn from the book of Samuel that "there was no smith found thoughout the land of Israel"; and this was probably the cause of their defeat by the better armed Philistines. The Phœnicians, who had at their command the commerce of the then known world, were able to place at the disposal of Solomon those who were the most skilled in metal-work, and amongst them Hiram of Tyre. The resources of the men who cast and chased and worked those masses of brass and silver, and even of gold, for Solomon, must have been equal to our own, though the methods might have been different. The date of this manufacture was a century before the birth of Homer, and a century and a half before the building of Carthage by Dido. Among the Greeks the application of the metals to decorative purposes was restricted. Copper and bronze and the precious metals were mere playthings in the hands of the Roman, and the traditions as to metal-work that had been maintained in Assyria and Egypt had been strengthened in his hands by an increased love of art and by the natural aspirations of a wealthy community. During the long period of the so-called Byzantine and Romanesque styles the same methods prevailed; there was an extension of art knowledge, but an absence of invention or originality. The most beautiful works at this period had their origin in strong religious sentiment, but they belonged rather to the arts of the jeweller and the goldsmith than to those pertaining to structural adornment. In France the bronze gates of the Church of Saint-Denis showed that the art of casting was familiar in that country as early as the twelfth century. The names of the artists in metal formed the history of metal-work during the most stirring centuries of the Christian era; and most of these masters in art were architects at that happy period of the world's history in which architecture was regarded as the art *par excellence*, to which all others were kept subordinate. At the Reformation the dry bones of art refused to be reanimated into life; the English Revolution effected nothing worth recording for the goldsmith or metal-worker; and the Restoration brought with it but few works of art, except perhaps the statue of James II. in Whitehall-gardens. The Gothic revival gave little more than a few improved patterns of gas-standards and altar-rails, but it enriched our literature with many valuable works on every known branch of metal-work. To architects the interest of metal castings was in their use in the adornment of buildings; and lessons from past history were of little practical value unless turned to account for the benefit and delight of mankind.

In the discussion which followed the reading of this and the three other papers mentioned,

Mr. J. M. Brydon, in moving a vote of thanks to the readers of the four papers, said that Mr. Graham's interesting introductory historical sketch had invested the subject with a sort of literary halo. Mr. Krall, with his intimate knowledge of the precious metals, had told them of many processes, but the substance of his remarks seemed to be that there was very little casting resorted to in the treatment of the precious metals, although there were occasions when cast-work was employed; but even when cast-work was employed, the artists very skilfully adapted the means to the end, so that when the work was produced it was very difficult to distinguish the wrought-work from the cast. Mr. Longden, as a practical ironfounder, had very ably and very lucidly described to them the *technique* of casting in iron. There were several gentlemen in that room who were not so very old as not to be able to remember that in the years following the Gothic revival it was considered to be quite the correct thing to scoff at anything cast, and to shrug one's shoulders at everything except wrought-iron; but we heard of the greatest artists in the world working in cast metal-work. Mr. Longden had, however, omitted to mention Alfred Stevens's magnificent castings. Mr. Singer had discoursed of practical bronze casting, and had explained the difference between sand castings and the wax process. It seemed to him (the speaker) that the great difference between the one and the other was that the wax process gave much more intimately the touch of the sculptor himself than the sand process did.

Mr. Onslow Ford, A.R.A., said the real difference between sand casting and the wax process, from the sculptor's point of view, was that the bronze produced by the sand process was five times removed from the original model, whereas the wax casting was only twice removed from it; and those two removes were so slight that a casting, when perfect, had the appearance, even to the artist who made the model, of being an exact reproduction of his design in bronze. Mr. Singer, in his paper, had said he hoped that we should be able in time to produce castings as good as those which were produced in the fifteenth century; but he (the speaker) should like to say that Mr. Singer had produced castings as fine as any that had ever been done in any period of the world's history.

Mr. George Simonds said that Mr. Singer had spoken of the sculptors of the Renaissance, Cellini and others, adopting the extremely laborious and risky process of first modelling the core and then making their wax over that, afterwards covering it with a mould, and firing and casting it, so that if anything went wrong the work would be lost, and the whole thing would have to be recommenced. But although they worked thus on many occasions, they were perfectly well acquainted with the process of making the piece-mould, and they had the replica of the original work to fall back upon in case anything should go wrong. Cellini himself gave a long description of both processes. Mr. Singer had referred to casting work by the two processes combined. That was a very important thing, and, as far as he (the speaker) knew, Mr. Singer was the first who had done it. It seemed an obvious thing to do when making a large statue for outdoor purposes,—or, indeed, for indoor purposes,—because in such cases it was obviously a fearful waste of time and expense to use the *cire perdue* process throughout. In the statues that were put up all over England it was not worth while to cast a man's coat by the *cire perdue* process, but it was worth while to cast his head and hands by that process. He fully endorsed what Mr. Onslow Ford had said as to the excellence of the castings produced by Mr. Singer.

Mr. J. Starkie Gardner said the four papers had been so excellent that there was really nothing to say about them in the way of criticism. With regard to one point raised in Mr. Graham's paper, he thought they must take it that metal was originally cast, and not beaten. They could not go beyond the prehistoric bronze period, and all the metal that they found of prehistoric date was cast metal, and, as far as they knew, it was all cast by something approaching to the sand process,—*i.e.*, it seemed to have been cast in a mould of rather porous stone, which, of course, in the case of simple castings was equivalent to the loamy sand now used. Mr. Krall had said that the value of the precious metals was formerly much greater than it was now, but he did not know what authority there was for that statement. So far as his (the speaker's) reading went, the precious metals of antiquity were of rather less value relatively than they were at the present time. Cast-iron was very much appreciated during the Renaissance, and he (the speaker) questioned whether Inigo Jones ever used anything but cast-iron, for he could not find examples of wrought-iron

* Abstracts of these papers were printed in last week's *Builder*, pp. 434, 435.

in any of his buildings; and Wren, as they all knew, used cast-iron for his railing round St. Paul's Cathedral, not because it was cheaper, for it cost 12,000*l*., but because it was the very finest thing that he could do there. He thought no wrought-iron railing that could be put round the Cathedral could possibly look so noble and dignified as the present cast-iron railing. When properly used, cast-iron was not a brittle substance; it was only when we tried to do too much with it that it failed. There were many specimens of modern cast-iron work that were good and appropriate. As instances, Mr. Starkie Gardner mentioned the railing outside the New Travellers' Club and the park gates at Hyde Park Corner.

Professor Aitchison, A.R.A., said he had great pleasure in seconding the vote of thanks to the readers of the papers. Their friend Mr. Gilbert, the great sculptor, once told them that they made a great mistake in using bronze so little in their architectural work, and that where ornament was to be frequently repeated it could be modelled by our best sculptors and produced in bronze at a very small cost,—at a less cost, in fact, than it could be carved in stone. He (the speaker) happened at the time to have some internal work to do, and the owner wished all the capitals of a certain part to be alike. About a dozen of them had been ordered, but there were more to do, and it struck him that bronze could be successfully used for the purpose. Mr. Gilbert was kind enough to model one of those capitals for him, and they were cast in bronze and put up at a lower price than those which had been carved in mahogany. Bronze stood well in any climate, even in our own. It was true that it became ink-black in London, but still, it preserved its form, and was not made sufficient use of, considering that architects could now avail themselves of the skill of some of our best sculptors for modelling it. The objection to its use for the highest work of fine art,—the undraped human figure,—was that although it was almost imperishable if left alone, it was melted down in times of trouble. Thus several of Michelangelo's celebrated statues had been turned into halfpence or into cannon. So far as cast-iron went, they knew a good deal about it, but he was afraid that although they knew a good deal about it they did not make nearly the use of it that they might; and though he believed he was opposed to the views of most of the members of his profession, he still looked forward to a time when it would be used to a very much greater extent than it had been. He looked forward to the style of architecture of the world,—the civilised world, at any rate,—being entirely modified by its use. When brick, stone, and rubble were almost the only materials to be had, it was necessary that arched and domed forms should prevail; but now that we had a material that was enormously stronger in cross-strain than stone or marble, it seemed to him that our architecture should naturally take the form of the old post and lintel of the Greeks. Although he believed cast-iron could not be cast with the perfection of bronze, and could not be chased,—so that ornament on it might not be perfect,—still, when it was used on a large scale, it was obvious that in a thing that was removed many feet or many yards from the eye, elaborate fineness would be absolutely thrown away. Where columns 50 ft. or 60 ft. high were used, it certainly seemed unnecessary that they should have the same perfection in the finish of the ornament that would be required were they close to the eye. In concluding his remarks, Professor Aitchison recalled some interesting historical points connected with metal-working and metal-casting.

Mr. H. H. Statham asked Professor Aitchison how many centuries he would give for the duration of a monumental work of architecture in cast-iron? He once asked Sir Benjamin Baker how long the Forth Bridge would last, and the answer was that with proper care it ought to last five centuries. Now, mild steel, the material used for the Forth Bridge, would probably last a good deal longer than cast-iron, but even five centuries was a comparatively short period in the life of a monumental work of architecture in brick or stone.

Mr. William White, F.S.A., said he thought that if ever architecture should become iron, it would cease to be architecture.

Mr. Sydney Vacher said he had understood, from a gentleman who contemplated adorning a public work of his with bronze statuary, in place of either stone or terra-cotta, that, taking into consideration the fees which the sculptor would charge, his founder's bill would be so large as to prevent him from employing bronze statuary instead of statuary in other materials. It would be interesting if the meeting could be afforded some idea as to the percentage of difference of cost between executing statues from the clay in marble and executing them in bronze.

Mr. Pinker, in reply to the question raised by Mr. Vacher, said that bronze was certainly much cheaper than marble.

Mr. Singer said as to the relative cost of bronze castings compared with other materials, it compared most favourably with, and was far cheaper than, marble, and he only wondered that that metal was not more used for architectural enrichment, as, when a repeat of the same ornament occurred, the cost would be but little.

Mr. Onslow Ford, A.R.A., said it might interest the meeting to know that, if the same bust were carved in marble, and also cast in bronze, it would cost in marble, including the marble and the labour of producing it, from 35*l*. to 50*l*.; whereas in bronze it would cost from 20*l*. to 25*l*. He thought that was about the proportion.

The President having put the vote of thanks to the meeting, it was carried by acclamation, and,

Mr. Alexander Graham acknowledged the compliment on behalf of the readers of the papers. He said that the only point raised which he had to answer was that mentioned by Mr. Starkie Gardner with reference to early castings. He (Mr. Graham) had never for a moment doubted that the primitive races were acquainted in some way or other with the fusion of ore, but he had always doubted whether they were acquainted with the art of finishing the metal, whatever it was, into form, otherwise than beating it with a hammer.

The meeting then terminated.

THE ROYAL COMMISSION ON METROPOLITAN WATER SUPPLY.

WE resume our report of the evidence tendered before this Commission,* giving first analyses of the statements submitted to the Commission on behalf of the London Water Companies, in compliance with the request which the Commission had addressed to them, and then explanations offered by the witnesses called in support of the statements. In a conversation which took place at the last sitting, the Chairman said the Commission did not expect that any conclusions they might come to would be absolutely free from discussion, but they felt strongly they ought to narrow the field of inevitable discussion as much as possible, especially on such points as population, number of gallons per head, and area to be built over,—points on which all who had watched the inquiry would see that there was an "unusually wide scope for conjecture and for estimate." In order to secure the strict relevance and utility of the evidence, the Commission must receive in advance the fullest information, in writing or in print, of the points that witnesses were going to deal with; and, subject to that condition, the Commission would err on the side of letting in evidence rather than excluding it, especially on the larger branch of the inquiry, the geology of the Thames and Lea basins, and the available supplies of water. Mr. Hollams, on the part of the Water Companies, rather complained of the Companies being put upon their defence, and said it was for the County Council to support its vague accusations. The Chairman repudiated the idea of there being any accusation, but Mr. Hollams maintained it was for the County Council to justify the necessity for the Commission, and suggested that the County Council's witnesses ought to be cross-examined by counsel. But the Chairman would not hear of that. Mr. H. L. Cripps, on behalf of the County Council, said the justification for the Commission was the growing feeling in London that inquiry was really called for; and he suggested that the county of Hertford, represented by Sir Richard Nicholson, should precede the London County Council by tendering evidence on the conflicting claims of the London Water Companies and the county of Hertford to the water supplies of that county. The Chairman, however, desired first to hear the London County Council on the points involved in the first part of the enquiry,—population, requirements, present supply,—and then to take the larger question. Mr. Hollams complained that the Companies did not know what the London County Council's "case" was; and the Chairman said "We want to know, in the first instance, what everybody's case is, before everybody knows what everybody else's case is; and I am going to stick to that." Then Mr. Hollams claimed, and the Chairman conceded, the right of reply and refutation.

The Grand Junction Company.

This Company's statement named the successive sources of its supply,—Paddington, Chelsea, Kew Bridge, and Hampton, on the border of Sunbury in Middlesex. There are two intakes,—one at Hampton, and the other a mile higher up on an island opposite Kenton Court, Sunbury. Filters, reservoirs, and machinery are all adequate to any possible increase of demand in the near future. Besides the intakes, the Company has works, used for ten years, for the natural filtration of Thames water, which is passed through extensive beds of gravel and sand and then pumped into the reservoirs. The number of "supplies" of all kinds at the end of 1891 was 57,535; and the quantity of water pumped in the year (deducting for slip in the pumps) 6,203,000,000 gallons, or 17,000,000 a day. This is 7,500,000 short of what the Company may take. Constant supply prevails over four-fifths of the service, and will soon embrace the whole. With good fittings, constant supply does not materially increase demand. Of the 57,535 supplies, 34,626 are within and 22,909 outside the county of London. These figures include 5,000 unoccupied houses. "The Census returns show 7·7 inhabitants for each town supply, and 5·4 for each suburban supply." (We quote these words because of a statement, mentioned last week, by Dr. Ogle, who is at the head of the Statistical Department of the Registrar-General's office, that the Registrar-General takes his figures from the Companies.) There are, therefore, continues the statement, 266,620 persons within and 123,708 outside the county of London; total, 390,328; or, deducting for unoccupied houses, 350,000. If the rate of building for the last ten years is continued for forty years (which is considered impossible), the population would reach 584,969, for whom 24,500,000 gallons would give 42 gallons per head. Tables support the conclusion that the population in both districts will not increase in the future as it has done in the past. The average number of persons per house within the Metropolis has fallen from 8·2 to 7·7, and the numbers of houses and of people have diminished in some parishes. In the suburbs the average per house has fallen from 5·6 to 5·4 in the past ten years. Within the Metropolis the number of supplies has actually decreased. The prevention of waste would make the present supply go further, but only a moderate supervision is exercised, because the supply is in excess of the demand. The storage is sufficient for seven days' consumption. Although five Companies take daily 100,000,000 gallons from the Thames, the lowest summer level remains unchanged. The Company are satisfied that they could, like others, augment their present resources by large supplies from the gravel beds and the underlying chalk. They have promoted a Bill to do this, but it was rejected by the Commons on the second reading. Official reports prove the good quality of the water now supplied, and the death-rate in the Company's districts is low. Taking the census returns of inhabited houses and population in six parishes,—St. James, St. George, St. Marylebone, Paddington, Kensington, and Hammersmith,—for 1881 and 1891, an appended table shows the average per house reduced from 8·2 to 7·7. The local averages are 9·4, 6·9, 9·2, 8·1, 7·5, and 7·0. The figures are also given for nine extra-metropolitan places, and show a reduction from 5·6 to 5·4.

Mr. Fraser, the Company's engineer, was called, and explained that the natural filtration process was a totally different thing from the gravel bed supply of the East London Company. The filtration process was simply passing the river water through gravel beds.

* See *Builder*, pp. 418, 435, *ante*. It should be stated that in last week's *Builder*, page 436, second column, the scientific evidence as to the condition of the water in the Lea was (as mentioned in an introductory paragraph) given by Mr. W. C. Young, Consulting Chemist to the Conservancy Board, whose name was accidentally omitted at the commencement of his evidence, after that of Mr. Child.

The process was used only when the river water was bad. The witness held that the maintenance of the level of the river was a proof that it was not depleted by the Companies, although the Chairman held that the level was rather governed by the lock below. The present supply for all purposes, according to the figures, was 48 gallons per head per day. It was a high figure, no doubt,—11 higher than any other Company, and 17 higher than the New River. The quantities were right, the numbers of supplies were right, but the Company had no means of checking the population returns. The district included clubs and railway stations, which were large consumers. The Carlton Club was supplied by meter.

The Chelsea Company.

The Chelsea Company mentioned in their statement that they first took water from the Thames at Ranelagh. They were compelled by the general Act of 1852 to remove their intake above the influence of the tide; and they then got powers to take the water from the Thames at Seething Wells, Kingston. Next, to avoid discolouration from sudden floods in the Mole, in 1875 they removed the intake to West Molesey, four miles higher up the Thames. There are now four subsidence reservoirs, holding 140,000,000 gallons, sufficient for a supply of two weeks. The water is invariably bright and clear; few complaints are received from customers; and when bad colour is complained of it is found to be due to dirty cisterns or local causes. The reports of Messrs. Crookes, Odling, & Tidy, and of Dr. Frankland show the Company's water to be good throughout the year, and this is largely due to the capacity of the storage reservoirs, and the extensive filtration area. The average daily supply during the last twenty years is shown by a table to have varied from about 8,500,000 gallons to over 10,000,000 in 1885 and 1887, and 9,250,000, 9,500,000, and 9,750,000 in the last three years; and the number of supplies has risen from 27,949 to 35,630. Last year the maximum daily average for the month was 10,838,290 gallons in July, and the minimum, 9,351,607 in March. The daily average per head of the population was 34·6 gallons. The population of the district on December 31 was set down at 287,362 persons, and the number of houses supplied was 36,250. Shut in by the river and other Companies, the district contains only 523 unoccupied acres, chiefly in Fulham, and on these 10,500 houses may be built. Forty or fifty years hence there may be a total of 46,770 houses, which, at eight persons per house, will give a population of 375,000, and, at 35 gallons per head, will give a daily requirement of 13,125,000 gallons, or, say, a maximum of 15,000,000 gallons. The high average of eight persons per house is taken purposely. According to the Census returns for 1881, the average number of persons per house was 7·3, and in 1891 it had fallen to 7·1. Eight persons per house is a very full number to allow over the whole district. An average of 35 gallons per head is a very liberal estimate, because in the class of property likely to be built in the new district it is estimated that the outside quantity used will be 25 gallons per head, inclusive of trade supplies, road watering, &c. The eventual maximum of 15,000,000 is, therefore, a very full figure. The Company have power to take 24,000,000 gallons from the Thames during the twenty-four hours, and under an agreement with the Thames Conservancy they may take 2,000,000 more, making 26,000,000. This is more than double what is now taken, and 7,000,000 more than the estimated possible future maximum. The Company have machinery, capital, and spare land to meet increasing requirements.

Mr. Richard Hack, engineer, stated that the Company had abstained for as long as ten days together from taking water from the Thames. Three years ago all the four reservoirs were cleaned out, and, as a rule, one a year was done. The depth of the deposit was 4 in. or 5 in. The rate of filtration was 1¾ gallons per square foot of filtering area, the recognised rate being 2½ gallons. The area of filtration was the reason of the specially good quality of the Chelsea water. The filtering beds were cleaned out every eight or ten weeks. The Company had experimentally taken water from the gravel 100 ft. from the margin of the river, and from a sample, Dr. Tidy had pronounced it to be spring water. There were no buildings near to pollute this water. The object in taking it would be to prolong the time the intakes from the river might be closed. The limitation on the river supply applied to each twenty-four hours; and one day's deficiency could not be made up by excess on another day; but if 3,000,000 gallons were taken from the gravel it would not be part of the river supply. The gravel area averaged 8 ft. or 10 ft. in depth, overlying the clay down the valley from Windsor.

Mr. A. C. Gill, a district engineer, said that in the returns empty houses were balanced by a delay of six months in reckoning new houses. He thought the census taken at Easter was misleading, because many persons would be out of town; but he was reminded that many of the residents of St. George's, Hanover-square, were out of town eight months in the year, so that the Easter census would fairly approximate to the average. He admitted the importance of discrimination in speaking of houses, tenements, and supplies, and on this point had a long conversation with Dr. Ogle, who referred to model dwellings as a disturbing element in estimates and approximate returns. With rigid inspection, there was no reason why constant supply should lead to greater consumption, but, with the Company's surplus of water, waste was not of great consequence.

Mr. G. H. Gill, the Secretary, said the Companies' Act gave them the power to take water from any springs on their own land.

The Southwark and Vauxhall Company.

In the statement submitted by this Company, the following figures are given: 24,500,000 gallons may be taken daily from the Thames; 3,000,000 can be obtained from "collecting works" at Hampton,—"natural filtration works," which cover an area of 39¾ acres; 3,000,000 may be obtained from the well at Streatham. 30,500,000 is thus the total quantity available. 10,500,000 may be obtained from seven wells yet to be sunk. 43,000,000 gallons is, therefore, the prospective supply. 25,000,000 gallons is the estimated requirement in 1932 for a possible population of 1,215,457, at 25 gallons per head, 18½ or 19 for domestic supply, and 6 for trade supply. The Thames, it is said, could afford a much larger quantity than is at present abstracted from it, not only from the daily flow, but by storage in reservoirs, which would be constructed as required. "All the sources and statistics point to the fact that the Company has sources of supply within itself, or at its doors, which will meet all requirements for a period far beyond that for which any reliable estimate can be formed. Neither would the Company be at any difficulty in raising the capital for the extra works as they become necessary, the experience of the past proving that the increased revenue is more than sufficient to meet the increased interest on dividends which will become payable on the increased capital." The object of the works in progress at Streatham is to obtain an auxiliary supply from the chalk. A boring has been sunk through the chalk to a depth of 1,142 ft. With the temporary machinery 1½ gallons were pumped daily for weeks. The maximum depression it has been possible to effect in the level of the water has been from a depth of 48 ft. to a depth of 97 ft. from the surface. It is, therefore, inferred that a supply of from 3 to 4 millions can safely be estimated as available from this source after the completion of the works in the course of next year.

The present total supply is 23,653,412 gallons daily, which, with an average population of 841,989, equals 28·09 gallons per head, of which 5·89 is for trade purposes, leaving 22·20 for the actual domestic supply. In the districts constantly supplied (now 87,310 "supplies" out of 113,781), the waste-water-meters show the progressive reduction of the supply per head for domestic purposes only to 24·71 for 1887, 20·72 for 1888, 19·57 for 1889, 18·53 for 1890, and 19·70 for 1891. It is in this experience that the future estimate for domestic supply is reduced to 18½ gallons.

Full details are given as to storage, pumping, and filtering. At Hampton are three storage reservoirs that hold 20,000,000 gallons; a new one is proposed, to hold from 50,000,000 to 60,000,000 gallons. The filtration works cover 39¾ acres; three filters 3½ acres; an extension will make this filtering area 7½ acres. At Battersea are reservoirs for 46,000,000 gallons, and 11½ acres of filters; at Nunhead, reservoirs for 18,000,000; at Forest Hill, reservoirs for 1,000,000 gallons.

Mr. J. W. Restler, engineer, in his evidence mentioned that one of the reservoirs at Hampton was being converted into filters, and thus the storage was reduced to 60,000,000 gallons, equivalent (as the Chairman said) to less than three days' supply; but (said the witness) there were in addition 21,000,000 gallons of filtered water stored. That would add a day's supply, although the storage of filtration water could not be "depleted to nothing at all;" but the company did not lay any stress on storage. The intakes from the Thames were never closed completely. "You take flood water at all times?" "Yes, we have to take it." But this involved no disadvantage as regarded quality. Of course, the filters were clogged more rapidly, and they had to be cleaned more frequently. The early flood water was the worst that had to be dealt with, but the draught of it was minimised, because at times of flood the "natural collecting works" gave one-half the supply. These works were used in two ways. Water was taken from the ballast beds first, without any water from the river. The ballast beds were also charged by means of pipes directly from the river. The Thames water was often let into the gravel bed; but in times of flood this was quite unnecessary, because there was so much water in the ballast itself that 10,000,000 or 12,000,000 gallons a day could be pumped without difficulty. This water did not come from the river, because the level in the ballast was higher than the level in the river. At that point the river was coated over with a very thin suspended clay,—a sort of puddled surface. The sides of the river seemed to be practically tight. Sometimes this water was pumped into subsiding reservoirs, but as a rule into filters. Dr. Tidy had described it as magnificently pure water; and, seen through a 2-ft. tube, it was clearer than the ordinary artificially-filtered water. He did not regard this as Thames water, although ultimately it might find its way into the river much lower down. He thought the Thames itself flowed through the centre of a ballast bed, which extended from about Staines right down almost to the metropolis. The whole bed was charged with water, and it must at some time have got charged from the Thames, but he did not think there was any direct connexion, certainly in that neighbourhood, between the Thames and this ballast water. When building operations threatened the purity of this source of supply, this company and the Grand Junction constructed a puddle wall between the Thames and the outcrop of the ballast, at the northern end of the works. That reduced the quantity to be obtained from them; and so it was put down at 3,000,000 gallons instead of 5,000,000 gallons; but the lower side remained unaffected by the wall; and on that side any sources of pollution were too remote to affect the water. Describing the works at Streatham, the witness said the level of the ground was 110 ft. above ordnance datum; the well itself was 10 ft. in diameter down to 148 ft. from the surface; it was 9 ft. in diameter down to 191 ft. from the surface; it was 7 ft. 6 in. down to 244 ft. from the surface. When the sinking was being made, the water broke in at a depth of 212 ft. from the surface. It was really in the Thanet sand formation the water was found; the cylinders were carried down to, but were never actually sealed into, the chalk. The cylinders are in a bed of flints, practically on the chalk; but, of course, overlying the chalk. From that point a 30-in. boring was taken through the chalk to a depth of 813 ft. Then there was some 24-in. pipe, which went through the sandy chalk and marl. Below that, a length of 20-in. pipes go through the upper green sand and the gault to 937 ft. Below that, again, there is a line of 18-in. pipes, which are all in the gault. They go right through the gault; and at 1,073 ft. is reached a sort of red sandstone. There the boring was reduced to 15 in., and it went down to 1,094 ft. 6 in. After leaving the chalk, the whole boring was lined down to the bottom of the gault. There was a 4 in. boring,—a trial boring, really,—and that was taken down to 1,271 ft. That was also in the sandstone. There were no faults met with till quite the last few feet, and it was just a point whether it was the old or the new red sandstone. It was not green sand; the lower green sand was never found at all. There were just traces of what was supposed to be the lower green sand after the gault, but only traces. The machinery was put down primarily with the object of draining the well, so as to get cylinders into the chalk and drive headings. The capacity of the pumps was under two millions a day, and, running them hard, the water could never be got lower than 98 ft. from the surface, so that the water was depressed by pumping 49 ft. Water was not being pumped from the Streatham well. The official sanction had just been received to use it as a source of supply. When the machinery was up, he had no doubt they would get 3,000,000 gallons a day. The seven wells that were to give 1,500,000 gallons daily were not sunk yet. Some fourteen years ago the advice of a number of eminent geologists was taken as regarded the best positions and the quantity of water that might be derived, and this estimate was based upon the reports they sent it. The Company had power to sink wells anywhere, and to take water therefrom. The Company's storage would be small for the large quantity of water used if it were not for the 10,000,000 or 12,000,000 gallons of naturally filtered water obtained when it was most needed.

Asked by Professor Dewar to explain why in December, 1891, the company's water was the only water that was turbid on six occasions, he said it was a difficult matter to trace, because they did not know of the analysis until a month after it was made. The same as to February, 1891. It was not that there was any lack of filtering area. If it was coincident with the taking in of flood water, it would look as if that was the explanation. On days when he had expected a chance of turbidity, because the filtration was working at its maximum, there had not been complaints, and for days when he thought they were all right complaints had come a month afterwards. The extension of the filters would reduce the chance of this trouble, although he would not say it was due to bad filtration. Sometimes he had thought it was due to samples being taken from points at which the water had been lying stagnant in the main. The points and the dates could be traced, and Professor Dewar remarked that it was certainly strange that the complaints should occur only in the case of this company. The average rate at which the filters worked was two and a half gallons per square foot, but at Hampton it sometimes reached three gallons. There did not appear to be any relation between the turbidity and the rapid working of the filters.

Dr. Ogle asked the witness to explain the curious fact that the amount per head given by this company was only about half that given by the Grand Junction. He said the Grand Junction gave constant supply, in reliance upon the house-to-house inspection of fittings. If this company did the same, its supply would be from 58 to 60 gallons per head. But the company checked its whole supply by waste-detection meters,—automatic registers,—which detected an enormous amount of waste that would never be seen otherwise,—waste from underground pipes and broken services, and numberless other causes. In addition, the company kept a check on the fittings by regular inspection. There would be less consumption on the intermittent system if the fittings were as good as for constant supply; but with better fittings the consumption was lessened by constant supply. It would be infinitely less if there were the same control over fittings that there was in the Midlands and the North. In some fairly respectable, small houses of £27 or £28 a year, where proper care was taken of the fittings, the supply was only 6·73 gallons per head per day. These houses had closets, but not many had baths. Baths and hot-water supplies did not much affect the consumption, and there would be an ample margin for them if waste could be checked. If the waste-meter system were adopted universally throughout London, the average consumption could be reduced to 24½ gallons. It was specially difficult to give constant supply economically in this company's poorer localities. If the water were shut off, the people would steal the fittings and sell them.

Mr. Joseph Lucas, called as a geologist, said in the course of his evidence that there were no scientific means whatever for forming an opinion that would be worth the paper it was written upon as to the quantity of water that could be obtained from the Streatham well. Still, he believed it was probable the 3,000,000 gallons expected would be raised when the machinery was completed, in eight months' or a year's time. The Streatham well water, he believed, came from the Wandle, which had a volume of 17,000,000 to 20,000,000 gallons a day. The pumping dried artesian wells at Tooting, but that only prevented the water running to waste in the Wandle.

Mr. Wm. Topley supported the opinion that it was probable the well would yield 3,000,000 gallons daily. The pumping affected a well at Teddington and one at Anerley.

The Lambeth Company.

This Company's statement is a descriptive and historical review occupying twelve closely-printed foolscap pages, and divided into sixty-seven paragraphs, which include several statistical tables. The principal source of supply is the Thames, from which 24,500,000 gallons may be drawn daily, and this may be augmented by from 6,000,000 to 8,000,000 gallons from the gravel beds, which were discovered and utilised in a manner analogous to that described in the case of the East London Company. From 7,000,000 to 8,000,000 gallons are taken when the Thames is in flood and the river intake closed. Borings have been sunk to the chalk, and reported on as favourable sites for wells, but none have been sunk, as there is a large margin in the present supply, and larger quantities can be taken from the Thames and impounded in storage reservoirs to meet future needs and to tide over periods of flood on drought. At West Molesey, where the 24,500,000 gallons may be taken, the capacity of the pumping power is 42,500,000 gallons, and of the subsidence storage 125,000,000 gallons. The filtering area at Ditton is 9½ acres; and the capacity of the covered reservoirs for filtered water is 28,750,000 gallons. There are large margins of pumping power at Ditton and at Brixton Hill. As far as this company is concerned, there is no need for a supply from Wales or any distant source. The company can meet any demand likely to arise in its district for the next forty years. A great saving can be effected in the present consumption by the prevention of waste. It is believed that by the use of waste meters and by inspection, the consumption is now 7,000,000 gallons less daily than it would have been with the same population in 1871. The following are daily averages in gallons for the last three years:—

	Pumped.	Per Supply.	Per Head.
1889 ...	18,235,739 ...	204 ...	29·17
1890 ...	18,776,432 ...	205 ...	29·35
1891 ...	19,736,466 ...	213 ...	30·36

The following figures exhibit the decrease in the average daily consumption:—

	No. of Supplies.	Population.	Gallons per Head.
1871 ...	45,000 ...	295,000 ...	44·04
1881 ...	69,123 ...	483,861 ...	36·76
1891 ...	93,703 ...	655,921 ...	30·36

Mr. S. H. Louttit, Secretary and General Manager of the Company, said that the gravel-beds extended from the river for some miles inland. The Company were entitled to take the 8,000,000 gallons from the gravel in addition to the 24,500,000 gallons from the river. The water was not practically abstracted from the Thames. At a long inquiry by the late Mr. J. T. Harrison, in 1880, the question of this underground water was gone into very fully, and Mr. Harrison and Col. Hildyard, his assessor, concluded that the water came from the direction of the Bagshot sands, and came under these gravel beds in very large quantities. During the severe frost of 1890-91, in eight days 54,760,000 gallons of this water were pumped, and there was no trace of exhaustion or diminution at the end of that period. The chance of pollution was very remote, the nearest building to this source of supply being a cottage three-quarters of a mile away. Chertsey was six miles from the intake, and the pollution from that district would flow into the Wey. The largest average daily quantity of water ever pumped was 22,561,743 gallons, in the week ending January 23, 1891. The calculation of the future available supply depended partly upon the estimate of what could be saved, which was pretty well known. The constant supply question had been gone into scientifically, and every district with constant supply was under one of Deacon's waste meters. These gave daily records of the water passed, and their use, coupled with inspection, showed what could be saved. It was from the experience thus gained he concluded that, taking the whole district, 22 gallons per head per day was an ample supply. Some divisions recently inspected gave 19·53 per head, and, as compared with the half year ending March, 1891, the half year of the greatest frost, it was a reduction of a gallon per head. In four new districts in Streatham, the average was 21·16. The saving by constant supply for the past twenty years amounted to 75·91 gallons per supply. At the rate of supply of 1871, the present total would have to be increased by 7,112,843 gallons, to 40 gallons per head; and yet the supply was better now than it was then. When great waste was discovered in a meter division it was inspected, and defects remedied, and that generally brought the average down to 12 or 14. After a short time it went up to 18 or 20, and then another inspection brought it down again. The meter supply, and that for road water and sewer flushing was about 23 per cent of the whole supply, or 6·36 gallons per head per day, and this made the total 26·87. In the past, when consumption was largest, there were great complaints about pressure, because water would not reach the upper services; but there were no such complaints now. Supplying statistics that had been asked for, the witness said that 22,561,743 gallons was the highest daily average for a week,—that ending January 23, 1891; 20,557,884 gallons was the daily average for December, 1890, and January and February, 1891; 20,268,231 gallons was the daily average for July, August, and September, 1887; 20,439,600 gallons for July, August, and September, 1889; 20,420,820 gallons, for January, February, and March, 1891; 28,411,025 gallons might be required in 1931 to give 25 gallons per head per day; 30,500,000 gallons were now obtained from the Thames and the gravel beds, and this is "irrespective of the water that can be obtained from the chalk. The directors are advised that they can obtain 3,000,000 gallons per day from a well at Selhurst, where they have just sunk a boring." In a final explanation on the statistical question Mr. Louttit said he had taken a population of eight persons per supply in constant supply divisions, and that was a reasonable figure, considering that the supplies were in the most thickly-populated parts of the district. The census returns of inhabited houses confirmed the correctness of the returns submitted by the companies in a remarkable manner. The population worked out at exactly seven per house in the Lambeth Company's district.

Mr. T. F. Parkes, the Company's Engineer, said he desired to emphasize what had been said as to Companies having more control over fittings. If they had as much as provincial Corporations and Companies, the reduction of waste would be facilitated. The Company ought to prescribe the fittings to be used, and not the builder. He would have the fittings brought to be stamped by the Company as approving of them. He would not limit the supply to the fittings of any selected tradesman, but would have free trade in fittings provided they were efficient according to a recognised standard.

In answer to Mr. Mansergh, he said that of the 19,000 000 or 20,000,000 gallons supplied from Brixton, about 9,000 000 gallons were supplied by gravitation, and the balance was pumped to Streatham, Selhurst, Norwood, or Rockhill, which was a maximum lift of 387 ft., to which must be added 25 ft. more over a standpipe.

Questioned by Professor Dewar as to the water being turbid on nine occasions in February, he said the filters were acting perfectly, and something must be due to the place where the samples were taken. This was the cab-rank in St. George's-road, and it was not near a dead end, but it it was in the centre of the main.

Evidence concerning the Kent Company was then taken. We have a report of this in type, but must defer it until next week for want of space.

After the Whitsuntide holidays, the Commission will hear the cases of the Hertford County Council and the London County Council, which are expected to traverse that of the companies as to the sufficiency and fitness of their resources.

ASSISTANT-SURVEYORSHIP, NEATH. — At a meeting of the Neath Rural Sanitary Authority on June 8, the salary of the Assistant-Surveyor was increased from 104*l.* to 120*l.* per annum.

Thompson and Lea's Safety Arrangement for Jib-Cranes.

A SAFETY PROVISION FOR CRANES.

THE erection of modern edifices, particularly those of great height,—which so many now-a-days are,—has involved the increased the use of "Scotch" derrick-cranes for the hoisting of materials. The accidents which happen with these cranes are quite different from those which occurred in the days of the hod. But it is only when the nature of the accidents with the derrick is considered over any extensive series that one sees that it is not so much from the load being dropped, or by any failure of the heaving-chain or gear, that accidents occur, as it is from what at first sight seems a minor source altogether. It is the jib-chain of the derrick which is most frequently in trouble. The danger from the jib is twofold. If it comes down by the run, it smashes interior staging or external scaffolding and walls, and everything in its way. If it be suddenly brought up by a check-chain, the whole derrick may be canted, and there is worse wreckage still. It is granted that these accidents are infrequent; they are nevertheless very ugly matters when they do occur. The chief source of evil in the "jib-chain," or the chain which passes from the head of the jib to the top of the derrick-mast, is not so often from breakage as from the chain being unavoidably short, and therefore apt to run off from the drum. No effective remedy for this has hitherto been provided. The most that has been attempted has been to put a second loose chain lower down between the jib and the mast. This is no real security, but a delusion.

What has now been done by Messrs. Thompson and Lea is a very simple and efficacious arrangement introduced into the ordinary metal head of the jib, whereby the instant that the jib-chain breaks or ceases to hold, the heaving-chain takes up the jib and maintains it as well as the load at the end of it. What is done is this:—The pulley over which the heaving-chain runs has ratchet teeth attached to each side, and in the stirrup to which the jib-chain is usually fastened there is a hooking-on rod provided with a spring at one end and a lever at the other attached to the two pawls which work into the ratchet teeth. When the jib-chain is holding on, the spring is drawn home and the pawls are kept out of contact with the ratchet teeth. But if the jib-chain breaks or becomes loose, the spring, being released from compression, pushes forward the lever, and the pawls engage with the ratchet. Thus the pulley is immediately gripped and the links of the heaving-chain are imprisoned in the pockets of the pulley, the jib being thereby as firmly grasped in its angle of position as it was by the jib-chain itself. The merit of this invention is that the remedy for the accident is so close at hand, and that of two chains running side by side, the one takes up the work of rescue the instant the other gives way. The spring is not a cumbrous affair, the side ratchets add very little to the dimensions of the pulley, the stirrup is no longer than the one in ordinary use, as the rod and the spring work within it, and the lever and pawls within the head in the space behind the pulley. (See illustration.)

In some tests of the appliance which were made on Wednesday on the Albert Hall Estate by the contractor for the new buildings of the Royal College of Music, a three-ton derrick crane, fitted with the safety appliance here described, was employed. The jib was 45 ft. long, of 10½ in. timber, and weighed 15 cwt. A large block of stone was slung on the end of the heaving-rope, and the jib-chain, hauled taut, was secured at the drum end by a hemp rope. The chain on the drum was then unwound, so that the rope held the jib. This rope was then cut with a hatchet, and the metal head of the jib did not fall 6 in. before the spring lever and pawls had acted, and the jib was firmly held by the heaving-chain on the pulley. This experiment was repeated many times with the like results. A model derrick, showing a modification of the invention to cranes in which wire ropes are employed was also experimented with, and gave equally successful results.

MAGAZINES AND REVIEWS.

The Gazette de Beaux Arts contains an article by M. Edmond Pottier on "The Salons of 1892," a well-studied and thoughtful piece of criticism. The writer maintains, at the outset, that two conclusions are to be drawn from the present condition of French art as shown in this year's exhibitions; first, that the study of the art of the past has not shut the eyes of artists to modern subjects; secondly, that the restlessness of modern art does not represent "une marche aveugle vers les abimes," but that there is a vital principle to be discerned in it. The various nude studies of the present period, M. Pottier regards as the direct legacy from Greek art; the very names of classical legends or personages appended to them indicate this; the varieties of treatment are great, but the true source of inspiration is the same in all. In connexion with this portion of the subject M. Pottier urges that a closer study of the silhouette figures in Greek vase-painting is worth the modern painter's attention. The taste for allegory shown at present in French art is a kind of reaction against the influence of realism; M. Benjamin Constant's decorative picture shows a desire to escape from the commonplace and prosaic treatment of allegory: "The ideal is eternal." In summing up, M. Pottier concludes that modern French art is under the domain of two distinct influences; the great style of Italian Renaissance, coupled with a research after special effects of colour and lighting derived from the great Dutch painters. M. Salomon Reinach contributes an article on the museum of antiquities at Vienna, with some fine illustrations of early Mediæval sculpture. M. Germain Bapst has an interesting article on "La Décoration Théatrate à la cour de Louis XIV.," giving curious illustrations of the rich but preposterous costumes designed for ideal characters on the French stage of the period; "Diana" in a gorgeous flounced dress, with feathers on her head, and a bow and arrow in her hand; and other extravagances of similar type.

The *Revue des Deux Mondes* has its article on the Salon, starting with a view the very reverse of that of M. Pottier in the *Gazette*, and regarding contemporary art as of an anarchist or nihilist character. There is too manifest a struggle to astonish, to gain notice from the press, and the *Revue* recommends the artists to live more to themselves and to the thoughtful study of their art, and think less of the public and the journalists; advice certainly not uncalled for in France at present. The old Salon it notes as "less unquiet" in its aims than the new. The *Revue* makes the same comment which we made in regard to the paintings for ceiling decorations at the old Salon,—that it is impossible to judge rightly of them when hung on a wall, in a perfectly different position from that in which they are intended to be seen.

In the *Art Journal* an article on "Some English Shrines," by Mr. Vernon Blackburn, gives descriptions of shrines in various English Cathedrals,—that of the Black Prince at Canterbury; Bishop Hatfield's, at Durham; Wykeham's, at Winchester; Edward the Confessor's at Westminster; with illustrations by Mr. Symington, which give the chief value to the article. "The Private Art Collections of London" this month deals with Sir John Pender's collection at Arlington-place, with illustrations of some of the rooms and pictures, the latter including Sir F. Leighton's popular and pretty "Phœbe." Mr. R. J. Slade contributes an article on "Mr. Thorne Waite," and Mr. Claude Phillips commences some articles on the summer exhibitions at home and abroad which are well illustrated, and as thoughtful criticisms are welcome reading in comparison with the foolish and malevolent literary onslaughts on painters which seem the fashion of the day.

In the *Magazine of Art* the Editor gives a review of the Royal Academy — somewhat *couleur de rose*. The first page is occupied with an endeavour to justify Mr. Watts's "She Shall be Called Woman," but we fear it is unconvincing. That Mr. Watts has formed a very lofty intellectual and moral ideal of the art of painting we all know—honour to him for it; but it is no less evident that his ideal has occasionally led him to forget the realities of pictorial representation. An article on "Scenic Art," by Professor Herkomer, is of rather special interest. He attacks the conventional arrangement and lighting of the stage, and gives two pictures of the actor as seen from the gallery and the actor as seen from the stalls, to show the absurdity of anyone posing for an audience distributed over so large a vertical angle. Quite true, but the question is, how is a house to pay without galleries except at a higher average of prices? Professor Herkomer also gives sketches of the face as lighted from the footlights and the face in diffused light; and explains that his own abandonment of footlights at his Bushey Theatre was originally only a happy accident. We rather doubt, however, if footlights will be disestablished. They have the advantage at all events of separating very completely the players from the audience, leaving the players more isolated from the spectators and consequently with a feeling of greater freedom. To remove the footlights would be like taking down a wall of partition. "The Pupil of the Eye as a Factor of Expression," by Dr. Wilks, is a short practical paper from the physiological point of view, which may be suggestive to painters. In another article Mr. W. F. Dickes replies to his critics in regard to his theories on Holbein's "Ambassadors" picture.

In the *Antiquary* Mr. Ward continues his "Notes on Archæology in Provincial Museums," dealing in this number with Shrewsbury. A short article called "The Antiquary among the Pictures" suggests a review of archæological lore as exhibited in Royal Academy pictures but in fact it does not draw any attention to questions of archæological correctness in painting, which might very well and usefully occupy such a journal as the *Antiquary*, but is mere chit-chat without even an attempt at criticism; a kind of writing that is of little value. Mr. Henry Barber contributes an article on the Cistercian Abbey of Maulbronn, with birds-eye views (from old representations) and a plan.

The *Fortnightly* contains an interesting and learned astronomical article by Mr. W. Huggins on "The New Star in Auriga," and a remarkably insolent and violent article on "The Royal Academy Exhibition" by Mr. G. Moore, whose qualifications for the assumption of the status of an *ex cathedrâ* critic may be sufficiently estimated by the fact that he proclaims Mr. A. Moore and Mr. Whistler the two greatest artists of the day, whose non-acceptance by the Royal Academy into its ranks is the *teterrima causa* of Mr. Moore's wrath against that body. The grouping together of two painters of such opposite aims as representing the highest achievements of art is amusing; one might almost be inclined to say that if Mr. A. Moore is right Mr. Whistler must be wrong, and *vice versâ*. Some of the writer's criticisms on individual artists and individual pictures are just enough; but the whole tone of the article is offensively typical of the spirit in which literary men seem nowadays to think they have the right to dictate about art. The same number contains an equally one-sided and conceited article on "The Two Salons," signed Elizabeth Robins Pennell. In the eyes of these two modest critics, it should seem, nearly all painters are fools, and all exhibitions contemptible. The tendency of reviews to the publication of this kind of literary abuse of contemporary art is a very disagreeable sign of the times.

The *Nineteenth Century* contains an article by the gifted lady who writes under the name of "Vernon Lee," on "The Tuscan Sculpture of the Renaissance," an article which however is rather ingenious than convincing. It is a comparison between Greek and Renaissance sculpture, with the object of proving that the latter is more truly decorative sculpture; that the Greeks only sought to give the human form correctly in a manner based on clay modelling, while the Tuscan sought for the decorative effect of the figure. It is noticeable that the writer only refers to Greek sculpture as work in the round, and appears to have entirely forgotten the Parthenon frieze, to which not the slightest reference is made. Such an omission is in itself sufficient to very much weaken the argument; and we may add that if Vernon Lee really believes that the Greek Doric style of architecture consisted of "little more than the imitation of the original carpentering," she has a good deal to learn on that subject.

The *National Review* publishes an article by Mr. E. J. Gibbs on "London and Rome," a comparison of the two cities in regard to wealth, influence, and agreeableness. Mr. Gibbs brings forward reasons for thinking (as we have always thought) that the immense wealth of Rome under the Empire has been little realised, and that it was positively and not only comparatively as great as that of London, while its standard of luxurious living was incomparably higher (or lower); and that in population Rome was more on a par with London than at first appears, the suburban districts not counting as part of Rome, as in these days they count as part of London. In comparing the advantages of life in the two cities Mr. Gibbs emphasises the fact that in ancient Rome every citizen could have the run of bathing establishments on such a scale of luxury as the world has never seen equalled, for the payment of an entrance fee equal to about half a farthing.

In the *English Illustrated* we find another of those articles on great railway workshops which are now becoming rather a fashion, each railway taking its turn apparently; now it is "The Midland Railway Locomotive Works at Derby," by Mr. C. H. Jones, an assistant locomotive superintendent of the Midland, with illustrations from photographs taken by Mr. Scotton, the company's official photographer. Though there has been a good deal of this lately, we like to see such such articles, which may give the readers of popular magazines a little better idea than they have at present of the colossal and varied labour which underlies the daily work of a great railway establishment.

In the same number is an article on "Dunster and its Castle," by Mr. Graham Wallas, with illustrations by Mr. E. W. Charlton.

In the *Revue Générale* the greater part of M. Trogan's "Lettre de Paris" is occupied with the leading pictures in the two Salons, and though this is a mere magazine article written in a somewhat light-hearted style, it contains in a bantering way much good sense and sound criticism, as well as some happy hits, and is quite worth reading in both senses. Over the tendencies of some of the leading works of sculpture M. Trogan is melancholy; M. Gerôme's "Bellona" suggests to him a sign for a dentist, a patient opening the mouth wide; and the colour statues represent "L'art du boudoir. Qu'on nous redonne les Dianes de Falguière"; and one cannot but echo the wish.

In *Scribner's Magazine* Mr. Shaler gives his second article on "rapid transit in cities," giving "the solution" of the problem. His solution is apparently electric railways in the streets. This, however, pre-supposes (after the horses have ceased to be frightened by them) streets of sufficient width to allow for this along-side of the ordinary traffic. In many cities the streets where rapid transit is most demanded will not admit of this; and it is too late to rebuild them. The American's objection to underground railways is neatly put—"Americans do not like to go underground until they are dead."

The *Century* has an article on Budapest, under the title "The Rise of a New Metropolis." It is illustrated by sketches by Mr. Joseph Pennell, which convey some idea of the remarkable manner in which this city has attained, in so short a life, to the appearance of a first-class modern city. An article on "Early Political Caricature in America" contains many reproductions of old carricatures, remarkable for vigour and malice, though a good deal of their point is necessarily lost now.

To *Harper's Magazine* Professor Waldstein contributes an article on "Funeral orations in stone and wood," relating especially to the bas-relief of "The Mourning Athene from the Acropolis," which forms the frontispiece to the number, and which is a curious mixture of archaic style and comparatively late or "modern" sentiment. The knowledge we now have of the existence of an archaic or "pre-Raphaelite" school in later Greek art might have been supposed to furnish the explanation of this; but Professor Waldstein is disposed rather to regard the bas-relief as the work of a sculptor trained originally in the earlier and stiffer technique, but who had entered into the more poetic sentiment of the later day. He would suggest about 470 B.C. as the probable date of the work.

In the *Atlantic Monthly* is a continuation of the interesting article on "Private Life in Ancient Rome" by two ladies, to the first part of which (in the preceding number of the same magazine) we have already referred. In the same number is a pretty little poem in praise of "Nuremberg," by Julia R. C. Dorr.

The *Cornhill Magazine* includes a short article on "Curiosities in our Cathedrals," a readable summary of some out-of-the-way peculiarities in the design or the contents of various cathedrals which are not popularly known, though familiar to archæologists.

All the Year Round includes a fairly good article on "The Loan Collection of Pictures at the Guildhall," followed by a pleasantly-written chapter on "Florence in Spring."

The English Iron Trade.—With the intervention of the Whitsun holidays the English market remains very quiet. In Cleveland, many of the works will be started as soon as a sufficient supply of coke can be obtained; but work will not be in full swing for some weeks. No. 3 G.M.B. is firm at 41s. 9d. There is practically no change to record with regard to any of the other pig-iron centres. In tinplates the volume of business passing is fair; but the manufactured-iron trade continues dull. Steel works are also inactive. Shipbuilders are less brisk, and engineers remain dull. The coal trade is rather quiet.—*Iron*.

The New Cross-country Railway.—At Chesterfield, on the 7th inst., Mrs. William Arkwright performed the ceremony of cutting the first sod of the projected trunk railway line, which is to cross England from sea to sea. The new railway, which is 175 miles in length, will form a connecting link between the eastern and western coasts.

Illustrations.

THE THREE TEMPLES AT SBEITLA, NORTH AFRICA.

As we have commented strongly on the procedure of the Hanging Committee of the Academy this year in regard to architecture, especially with reference to some of their rejections, we may give point to our criticism by mentioning that this interesting restoration of three Roman temples from existing remains, by an architect who has given special attention to the illustration of ancient Roman work, is one of the drawings which the person who looked after the hanging of the architectural drawings (whoever he was) considered not worth a place. The rejection of a drawing such as this, by an architect who can not only bring archæological learning to the subject but can make his own drawings, while space is found for commonplace houses bearing the names of men who have to pay a draughtsman to make a drawing for them, is discreditable only to the Academy, not to Mr. Graham, whose work would no doubt have found a good place among the architectural exhibits of the Salon, though it did not recommend itself to the eye of the carpenter in the Royal Academy architectural room.

Mr. Graham sends us the following article in respect to the site and restoration of the temples:—

"A glance at a map of North Africa is necessary to give the reader an idea of the geographical position of Sbeitla. Three days' journey from Tunis, either along the coast by way of Soussa or across country by Zanfour, brings the traveller to Kairouan, and a ride of about seventy miles from that holy city in a south-westerly direction enables him to reach the banks of the pretty stream that once skirted the walls of the ancient city of Sufetula. The modern name of Sbeitla is an Arab corruption, as that of Sbiba, some thirty miles further north, represents the original name of Sufes. Whether this word Sufes was associated in old times with *Suffetes*,—the two supreme magistrates who ruled over Carthage, and whose title bears a resemblance to the Hebrew *Shofetim*, mistranslated in the Bible, Judges,—is open to doubt. The history, however, of Sufetula is so intimately interwoven with the progress of Christianity in North Africa, and with the first disastrous encounter of a Christian population with the followers of Mahomet, that European as well as Arab historians have given it a special place in their records. Edrisi, the Arab geographer of the twelfth century, tells us that "Sobeitala was, before the Arab invasion, the town of Gerges (Gregory), King (prefect) of the Romans of Africa; it was remarkable for its extent as well as for the beauty of its situation, for its abundant water, for the mildness of its climate, and for its wealth; it was surrounded by orchards and gardens. The Musselmans conquered it during the first year of the Hegira, and put the great King Gerges to death." Other writers tell us that this Gerges, sometimes written Gregorius, had revolted from the Byzantine Empire, and had made himself ruler of the whole country from Tripoli to Tangiers, making Sufetula his capital. With the appearance of the Arabs in this remote corner of North Africa commenced the struggle for supremacy between the representatives of Christianity and the followers of Mahomet. The city, having no walls of defence, soon succumbed to the invader. Gregorius was slain, and the treasure of a numerous and wealthy population passed into the hands of the victorious army. With this calamity the records of Sufetula cease, and Christianity in Africa received a blow from which it never recovered.

The monumental remains are extensive, though it would be difficult to define the exact boundaries, owing to the absence of external walls. The lines of streets and the foundations of numerous buildings, both public and private, can be traced for nearly a mile in one direction, and somewhat less than half a mile in another. Its ruined edifices, many of them of noble proportions, bear ample testimony to the wealth and importance of Sufetula prior to the Arab invasion. The principal monument that has withstood the ravages of time and the neglect of more then twelve centuries, consists of a range of three temples, placed side by side and partly attached. They may be assigned to the

THE THREE TEMPLES AT SBEITLA, NORTH

—Restoration by Mr. Alexander Graham, F.S.A.

Plan of Ground Floor
Plan of First Floor

Royal Academy Exhibition, 1892.

PHOTO-LITHO, SPRAGUE & Co. 4 & 5, EAST HARDING STREET, FETTER LANE, E.C.

CHANCEL LEVEL
NAVE LEVEL
Scale
A. H. Skipworth Architect.
5 Staple Inn. London –

al Academy Exhibition, 1892.

INK-PHOTO SPRAGUE & Co

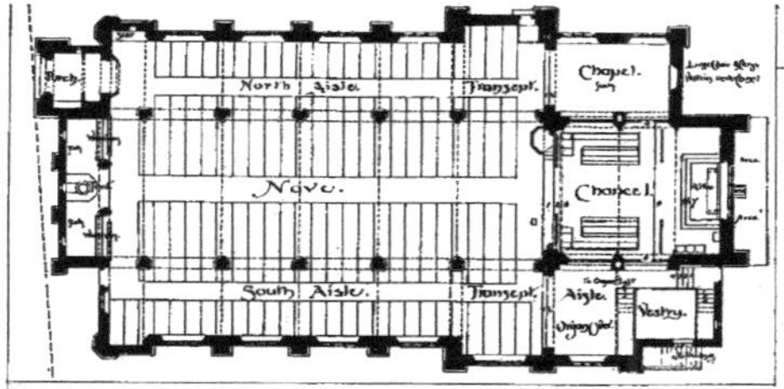

North Aisle. Transept. Chapel. Nave. Chancel. South Aisle. Transept. Aisle. Organ Chl. Vestry.

CHURCH OF ST. JUDE, PRESTON.—MR. R. KNILL FREEMAN, F.R.I.B.A., ARCHITECT.

INK-PHOTO SPRAGUE & Cº 4 & 5 EAST HARDING STREET FETTER LANE E.C.

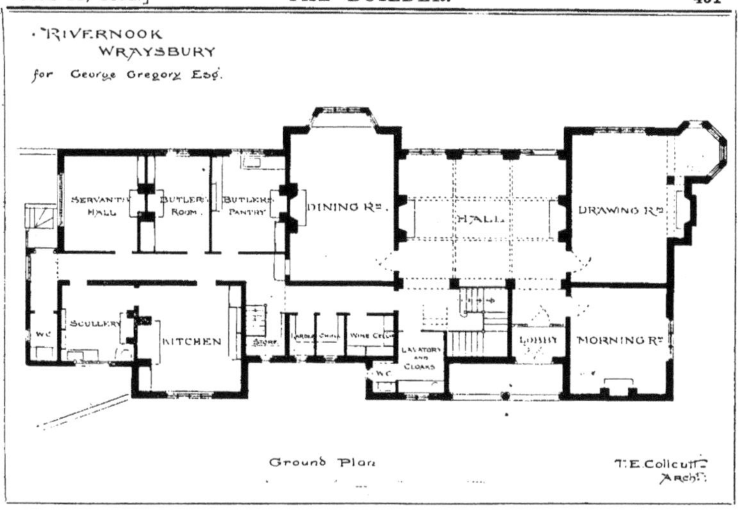

reign of Antoninus Pius, A.D. 138-161. The porticoes formed nearly the whole of one side of a large walled enclosure, measuring about 240 ft. square, to which access was obtained through a monumental gateway facing the temples. This gateway, in very fair preservation, is still standing. The back walls of the three temples formed the back of the enclosure, and behind them ran one of the main streets of the city. The central edifice is of larger proportions than the two that flanked it, and is of a more ornate character. Its order is Composite, the others being Corinthian. They are all tetrastyle and pseudo-peripteral. The cella of the middle temple has engaged columns at the sides and back, but the others have pilasters only. The back walls of the three temples, the entire cella of the central one and a greater part of the flank walls of the side ones are still standing. The porticoes are overthrown, but the bases of many of the columns are in position as well as the lines of steps. The broken monolith shafts, which were more than 30 ft. high, with their enriched capitals and huge fragments of sculptured ornament, lie piled up one on another in a majestic and imposing mass. The enclosure appears to have been paved with immense slabs of stone, which are still visible some 4 ft. below the present surface. Around it was a colonnade and, from the general appearance of the remains and the number of *frusta* of shafts of varying dimensions, it is reasonable to suppose that there were other shrines or votive monuments within the enclosure. The entrance, as already stated, was through a gateway of three arches, and within the gateway was a portico connecting the colonnades on either side. It was evidently intended that the entrance should face the central temple; but, for some unaccountable reason, it is fully 20 ft. to the west of the central line or axis of the enclosure. The custom of enclosing sacred edifices with walls of defence originated at some remote period when temples were used as depositories for the treasure of a city, as well as for affording shelter to women and children in times of invasion. At Carthage, for instance, the chief temple in the city, dedicated to Æsculapius, stood within the citadel. The Parthenon at Athens was within the walls of the Acropolis, and the temple of Jupiter in Rome was in the capitol. At Balbec also there is an enclosure commonly called the *Hieron*, bearing some resemblance, though on a larger scale, to this one at Sufetula.

The illustration is a restoration of the three temples and of a portion of the enclosure, being the result of actual measurement on the spot and of sketches of the details of the architecture. It is satisfactory to know that the Société des Monuments Historiques is keeping a watchful eye over these interesting remains as well as over the other ruined edifices and inscribed stones, and that in course of time our knowledge of this ancient city and of the important part it played in the spread of Christianity during the rule of the Byzantine Emperors may be largely extended.

The appearance of Sufetula, as it was in the fourth and fifth centuries, is easy to imagine. Situated on rising ground, at a point where the great highway from Carthage to the interior intersected the main road from Theveste seawards, its position was a commanding one. A fertile soil, forests of pine-trees, and a never-failing river of pure water that ran by the city walls, contributed to make Sufetula a place of delight for the wealthy colonists of North Africa. To-day it is a dreary, unpeopled spot, lying "remote, unfriended," in the midst of a trackless country. The waters are still there,—a perennial stream, pure as crystal, but the trees are gone, the plains are arid or clothed with rough herbage, and all signs of habitation have long since passed away. Yet, in spite of prevailing desolation, this spot, so far removed from human dwellings,—its ruined fanes outlined sharp against the sky, its weird stones standing ghost-like on the outstretched plain, the stillness of the air broken only by the babbling of the waters,—has much to charm the eye and quicken the imagination.

ALEX. GRAHAM, F.S.A."

HOUSE AT WRAYSBURY.

THIS house is being built near Egham Lock, from the designs of Mr. T. E. Collcutt, the materials employed being red brick, stone, and oak; the bricks are of special make, from the Cranleigh brick works, and work six courses to the foot in height. Mr. Messum, of Twickenham, is the builder.

The drawing is exhibited at the Royal Academy.

RETABLE FOR ST. ALBAN'S CHURCH, TEDDINGTON.

THIS retable, designed by Mr. A. H. Skipworth, will be executed in either Clunch or Ancaster stone, and will be partially coloured and gilded. Mr. L. A. Turner will carry out the work, the modelling of the angels being most probably entrusted to Mr. Dressler.

The drawing is exhibited at the Royal Academy.

REREDOS FOR GRAYINGHAM CHURCH, LINCOLNSHIRE.

THIS reredos is of oak, slightly stained and partially coloured, gilded, and silvered. The centre panel, in copper gilt, is the work of Mr. Conrad Dressler. The woodwork was executed by Mr. L. A. Turner, of Orde Hall-street, from the designs of the architect, Mr. A. H. Skipworth.

The drawing is exhibited at the Royal Academy.

WORKING MEN'S UNIONIST CLUB, AYR.

THIS club, which has been opened this week, is built from the designs of Messrs. Morris & Hunter. The large bay window in the end on the ground-floor forms part of the club reading-room; the three windows above light the ante-rooms attached to the hall, and the centre one opens on to the balcony as a convenience for open-air speeches when required. The half-timber gable above forms part of the club-master's residence.

There are three distinct exits with separate staircases from the hall. The club contains, besides the hall, a billiard-room, recreation-room, and reading-room. The hall will seat 600 people. The cost of the whole was limited to 2,500*l.*, hence the building has necessarily been kept plain and simple in its architecture.

ST. JUDE'S CHURCH, PRESTON.

THIS church is now approaching completion for the new parish of St. Jude's, Preston. The general character of the design is that of late Decorated Gothic. The walls are carried out with smooth-faced Yorkshire parpoints and Rainhill stone dressings, the interior dressings also being in Rainhill stone. The total accommodation is for 645 persons, and, in addition, there are chapels on the north and south sides of the chancel, which may be used for seating. The organ is placed in the gallery over the south chapel. The chancel floor is well raised, and choir vestries, &c., provided underneath. The clergy vestry is at the east end of the south chapel, and connected with the choir vestries by a passage and steps. The baptistery is at the west end, and the main porch and entrance at the north-west corner, with smaller entrances at the south-west corner and north-east end of north aisle. The design is by Mr. R. Knill Freeman, of Bolton and Manchester. The contractor for the whole of the work is Mr. Thomas Croft, of Preston; the sub-contractors being Messrs. Tullis (mason); Mr. W. Whiteside (joiner); Messrs. Walmsley (plumbers and glaziers); Mr. Cook (plasterer and painter); and Messrs. Bradshaw & Son (slaters). The heating by hot water has been carried out by Mr. Seward; and the choir-stalls, &c., of oak, by Messrs. Bell & Copeland; all of Preston.

THE ARCHITECTURAL ASSOCIATION:

THE RELATION OF THE ARCHITECT TO THE WORKMAN.

IN the discussion which followed the reading of Mr. Ashbee's paper* on this subject,

Mr. H. O. Cresswell said he had great pleasure in proposing a vote of thanks to Mr. Ashbee for his paper, especially as he had attended twice there to read it. Considering that they in the Association had been discussing educational methods a good deal of late, it was very interesting to them to have a paper from what he might call an entirely fresh mind,—in other words, from a gentleman who had not been following the ways and work of the Association, but who looked upon the education of the architect from a somewhat different standpoint. Mr. Ashbee had introduced them to the workman's side of the question, and perhaps with advantage, for they were possibly a little too much inclined to look at it from the employer's or contractor's point of view alone. He did not know how they would get on with the communal system, and in general he was hardly prepared to follow some of the theories enunciated by Mr. Ashbee without having had the opportunity of reading the paper. He thought there was a great deal in it, but that it wanted more consideration before he felt able to discuss it with very much profit. He thought their sympathies were very much with Mr. Ashbee on the question of the desirability of young architects mixing with workmen, and seeing work in the workshops, and he hoped that the Association would be able to do something to bring its members more in contact with workmen. Probably the Guild and School of Handicraft might be able to give them some assistance in that direction. Mr. Ashbee had spoken against architects working too much upon paper. They had, he (the speaker) was afraid, been accustomed to think too much upon paper, and no doubt, if they could think with materials rather than on paper, they would be able to take a wider grasp of their work; but in dealing with buildings pure and simple, it was difficult to see how they could be dealt with on any other material than paper. If one was considering the planning and arrangement of a building, or if one had to make details of the masonry work of that building, he failed to see a better method of working them out than on paper, unless they adopted the mason's method of setting out the work on boards, which, after all, came to pretty much the same thing. He trusted that the members of the Association would have an opportunity of visiting the workshops of the Guild and School of Handicraft, where they might learn much that was useful.

Mr. Leonard Stokes said he should like to be allowed to second the vote of thanks, especially as it was partly his (the speaker's) own fault that Mr. Ashbee had to come there a second time. He thought they could not be too grateful to Mr. Ashbee for the lucid and somewhat new light in which he had put the whole question before them. As he had said, our modern life must of necessity have a great influence on modern architecture. A great deal of the work produced now was merely in supply of a demand for cheap grandeur, which became cheap vulgarity. The great idea of the present day was to make a show. Possibly that might be a fault of our social system, and it was for architects to endeavour to persuade their clients to be a little more reserved,—to accept designs for buildings which showed far greater reserve than much of the stuff which was now built. It was very difficult to persuade a client that a simple design was better than an elaborate one. The uneducated client thought that an elaborate thing was the best. Of course, the question of style came in. "Style" was an odious word, but if they went to work conscientiously he thought they could let style alone. So long as a building was a good one, it did not matter what the style was. As to what Mr. Ashbee said about young architects mixing with workmen, he (the speaker) thought that was a matter of great importance. It was very desirable that workmen should become more in touch with the architect and the designer. As matters were ordered at the present time, the workmen never, or hardly ever, got sight of the architect's drawings. The bricklayer was set to work in one place, the mason in another, and the carpenter in another, but they were all working in ignorance of each other's work, and had no idea of what the building would be like as a whole when finished. How could they, under such circumstances, be expected to take any very lively interest in their work? He thought it would be a very desirable, although a very simple, step in the right direction to allow the workmen to look at the drawings occasionally. Let them put it in the contract, if they liked, that the workmen should be allowed to look at the drawings once a week. Many of Mr. Ashbee's remarks, on such questions, for instance, as apprenticeship, and the possibility of architects being able to get at the labour market directly, without the intervention of the middleman, were of great interest. He thought it would be a great good if the architect could more often come into contact directly with the individual workman who was to carry out work from his designs. In conclusion, he desired to express the thanks of the meeting to Mr. Ashbee for having brought down so many interesting specimens of the Guild and School of Handicraft.

Mr. Sydney Vacher said he should like to say something on the opposite side of the question. If an architect could go direct to the trained workman, why could not the public? Why have an architect at all? As to the architect consulting the workman, he failed to see the advantage of it. Would they have the British sailor consulted about the handling of a man-of-war? Must not the architect, like the commander of a vessel, be the responsible head, and must not each of them be able to rely on implicit obedience to orders? Was it not the first duty of the architect to supply the best building he could for his client? While he could not assent to all the propositions laid down in Mr. Ashbee's paper, he (the speaker) was delighted to see the work of the Guild and School of Handicraft, because it was educating the workman; and if they could find a workman who had originality, they should give him a suggestion, and leave him to work it out. Of course, that method of procedure was not possible with regard to the whole work of everyday building. While it helped to educate the workman, it also helped to educate the architect, who naturally felt bound to keep in touch with what was going on. Above all, it helped to educate the public, and that was what was wanted more than anything else. It had been said that the present was an age of show, but every age had been an age of show. No doubt one evil of the present day was that we lived too fast; we were too fond of living beyond our means. Everyone was trying to obtain gorgeous show or smartness for a minimum of expenditure, and but few would pay for the real thing. That was the complaint everywhere. There was another thing which struck him, and that was whether, if these schools and guilds became very powerful, would not they be attacked by the modern unionism? Mr. Ashbee had said that apprenticeship was being killed by the modern subdivision of labour, but in his (the speaker's) opinion apprenticeship was being killed by modern unionism,—it was being killed by the enormous number of unskilled workmen who were driving down the standard of work to a dead level. One was constantly hearing of the difficulty of taking boys as apprentices by builders; the men struck against it. It seemed to him that the technical schools were now attempting to supply a real substitute for the workshop training of apprentices; and he thought that sooner or later the Government might have to take steps for the compulsory education of the craftsman. One suggestion he might make, arising out of the work of the Association, was this: that, if any members found themselves, as the result of their work in the classes, unlikely to succeed as architects, owing to inability to grasp theoretically, that was to say, on paper, either the artistic or the constructional part of the work,—perhaps both,—why should they not turn their attention to craftsmanship? Many men who now spent their lives as clerks or assistants would have a much finer position if they became craftsmen. By the Committee of such a school as Mr. Ashbee's, such men should be welcomed, and when successful, as they became known, many architects would be only too glad to employ them, giving to a craftsman in each trade a share of a building, just in the same manner as in Scotland the architect, instead of giving out his work to one contractor, gave it to many.

Mr. E. W. Mountford said he fully agreed with Mr. Ashbee that the interests of the work man and the interests of the architect were identical. He agreed, too, with the previous speaker that modern trades unionism had many faults, and that it did a great deal of harm in some respects; but in other respects it did a great deal of good. He believed that every step towards improving the wages of workmen and (up to a certain point) shortening their hours of labour was a step in the right direction. Those who had had the misfortune to work with builders, generally in a small way of business, who employed non-union men, to whom they paid less than the union rate of wages, knew, to their cost, that such men were, as a rule, utterly incapable of producing really good work. In his experience, men who got higher wages undoubtedly did a higher class of work than the men who got low wages, and it was always best to entrust building work to good firms of contractors who were known in the trade as paying the highest wages. Such firms retained a large staff of men who were capable of doing the best work. There was one point on which he could hardly agree with Mr. Ashbee, and that was when he said that an architect should do as little as possible on paper. It was no doubt desirable that the architect should be able to model a little, but he thought it was quite out of the question for an architect to become sufficiently conversant with the whole of the many trades concerned in building to be able to explain to the workman, in the material itself, how every detail of the work should be executed. To properly learn any one of the trades concerned in building was the work of almost a lifetime. Although an architect might, perhaps, learn to be a decent bricklayer in the course of a few years, he could not possibly expect to become a good mason unless he gave up many years to the work. But, of course, without being able to do the work himself, he ought to know how it should be done, and in order to give his instructions to the workmen, he was bound to have recourse to drawing-paper or tracing-paper. He cordially supported the vote of thanks to Mr. Ashbee for his paper.

The discussion was continued by Messrs. A. E. Bartlett and Sidney Tugwell; and the Chairman (Mr. F. T. Baggallay) having put the motion for a vote of thanks to Mr. Ashbee, which was carried very heartily, Mr. Ashbee replied to some points raised in the course of the discussion, and the meeting proceeded to consider the affairs of the Association, as reported in our last.

* Printed *in extenso* in last week's *Builder*. See pp. 437 *et seq.*

ARCHITECTURAL SOCIETIES.

EDINBURGH ARCHITECTURAL ASSOCIATION.—By permission of Messrs. R. Irvine and D. Harris, the Sketching Class of this Association will meet at Royston House, Carolina Park, Granton, at three o'clock on the afternoons of Saturdays June 11, June 25, July 2, and July 16, to make measured drawings and sketches of the south front of the mansion. The Class will be conducted by Mr. J. Watson and Mr. J. N. Scott.——The members of the Association had their annual excursion on the 4th inst. The destination this year was Drumlanrig Castle, in Nithsdale, permission having been obtained from the Duke of Buccleuch to inspect the building. A company of some thirty-five gentlemen proceeded by express train to Elvanfoot, and a drive was then commenced. A stop was made at the village of Durrisdeer, where the party were met by the Rev. Mr. M'Kenzie. The old manse was first inspected, and Mr. M'Kenzie explained that it was supposed to be of pre-Reformation date. The church proper only dates from 1699, and is a very plain building. In the tower there are the notable "Queensberry marbles," and these were viewed with much interest. The sculptor of these works is unknown, but they date from about the middle of last century. The vault below is the burial-place of the ukes of Queensberry. After lunch the party roceeded to Drumlanrig, the pink sandstone le which occupies such a commanding posi-on above the right bank of the Nith. Mr. ohn M'Lachlan, who acted as leader of the xcursion, gave some account of the castle nd its history. The builder, he said, of rumlanrig Castle was William, first Duke f Queensberry, and the erecting, which egan about 1680, lasted for over ten years. egarding the building, the arrangement was imple and dignified. It consisted of a great quate, 146 ft. by 120 ft. externally, with an nside space of 77 ft. by 57 ft. The double ircular staircase to the front entrance was omparatively new, but a similar staircase ormed part of the original design. The hollow quare of the building had four staircases lead-ng to the various flats, an arrangement some-what similar to those of Linlithgow Palace, aroline Park, and Heriot's Hospital. The rchitect of the building was unknown. The ompany subsequently went over the house and fterwards drove through the Drumlanrig roods and along the banks of the Nith. From Mennock Bridge the drive was continued up he Mennock Water to Wanlockhead and on o Leadhills, where the party dined.

GLASGOW ARCHITECTURAL ASSOCIATION.—The opening meeting of the season (1892-3) vas held on Tuesday evening in the N. B. Station Hotel, George-square, the hon. President in the hair. Mr. Alexander McGibbon delivered his Presidential address, the subject being "Current Architectural Criticism." A few remarks by he hon. members present concluded the usiness meeting. The meeting then resolved tself into a smoking concert, during which Mr. Alexander McGibbon was presented with a hand-ome old Dutch cabinet and set of silver plate rom the past and present members of the Asso-iation, as a mark of their esteem of his long nd faithful services as secretary. Mr. W. I. Anderson made the presentation on behalf of he members.

BRITISH ARCHÆOLOGICAL ASSOCIATION

AT the meeting of this Association on une 1, Mr. J. W. Grover, F.S.A., in the hair, Mr. Barrett exhibited several sketches f various armorial bearings of old members f the Trinity House, and read an elaborate aper on the history of the Company, the aterials for which he had obtained from arious State papers, the archives of the Com-any having been burnt in 1714. The lost istory thus recovered referred to many curious oints of sixteenth and seventeenth century istory, including the establishing of light-ouses along the coast of England, the Com-any having a patent for doing so. The origin as from a fifteenth-century guild, which was corporated in 1573. The Company's arms ere those of Sir T. Sport, the first Master, who ied in 1541, and who is buried in Stepney hurch. Enormous sums were spent by the ompany in helping to man the fleet in times national peril, details of which were rendered. addition, many particulars were given of the ompany's work in freeing captives from the arbary corsairs, whose ravages round the oasts of England and Ireland is no creditable age of English history. Mr. Loftus Brock, .S.A., exhibited some curious examples of eatly-turned alabaster found on the site of yzacus, of Greek workmanship. The chair-an described several remarkable flint imple-ents, of prehistoric date, one of which, found him at Stonehenge, was carbonated and hite from long exposure. Mr. Earle Way hibited several examples of bellarmine jugs und at Southwark, including some of earlier ate than the middle of the sixteenth century. r. Barrett exhibited a very fine Grès de Flandres g, dated 1691. A second paper by Mr. Mac-ichael was then read, entitled "The Grey-ard." The author traced the origin of this ce common brown ware jug from early times, d produced several examples, which showed e progress of the form to its full develop-ent, when, by the addition of the head and oad, square-cut beard, the shape was supposed resemble the portly form of the obnoxious rdinal. These vessels were made in very rge quantities in almost every town of the Low ountries, and imported into England. A col-tion of the designs of the cartouches which orate the sides were exhibited. These show, almost every case, the arms of the various ties of manufacture.

Correspondence.

To the Editor of THE BUILDER.

ELECTION OF FELLOWS, R.I.B.A.

SIR,—It is proposed to alter the present system, and dispense with the ballot.

I beg to suggest as an alternative that the existing system be retained, with the provision, however, that in the event of any candidate being blackballed, he shall have the option of a further chance with voting-papers, but only upon his own requisition.

The cost of the voting-papers and postage, addressing, &c., would in an isolated case be not much less than 10*l*.

A proposition has been made that the elections shall be by show of hands (unless three members should demand that voting-papers be issued).

In either case I think the cost of the voting-papers, &c., should be paid by the candidate only when unsuccessful.

"SUUM CUIQUE."

June 6, 1892.

HORNSEY MAIN ROADS ARBITRATION.

SIR,—It would no doubt prevent a good deal of misunderstanding, as well as needless litigation and expense in the future, if you would allow me, as the Chairman of the Highways Committee of the Middlesex County Council, to supplement the paragraph which appeared in the *Builder* under the above heading [p. 447, *ante*], by stating that the Hornsey Local Board claimed 4,098*l*. 18s. 4d., the total amount expended by them for the maintenance of about two miles and three-quarters of main roads for one year; the award of the Local Government Board was, as mentioned, 3,221*l*. 5s. The important fact, however, is omitted, that the award is 877*l*. 13s. 4d. less than the amount claimed by the Local Board.

Without this explanation, local authorities throughout the country are likely to form a most erroneous judgment with reference to this case.

H. R. WILLIAMS.

6, *Lime-street, E.C.*, June 8, 1892.

"A QUESTION OF BUILDING PENALTY."

SIR,—The letter under the above heading in last week's *Builder* should be carefully noted by all contractors, and replying to this we should say "A Contractor" had better refer to the contract he entered into, for from recent experience in a somewhat similar case, in which we were mulcted in a loss, we found that everything depended on this.

In our case delay was caused—1. By the carpenters' strike. 2. By additional work. 3. By our being unable to proceed for want of details and instructions.

The contract we had entered into allowed extra time for delay caused by "general lockouts," "strikes," or from any cause whatever which in the opinion of the architect was beyond the control of the contractor."

Now, this looked all right on the surface, but the fact was, the architect was brother to the employer, and we found to our cost that it was not a question of strikes, lockouts, or other cause whatever, but the opinion of the architect; and, having to choose between an action for fraud on the ground that the certificate was given contrary to facts,—and a loss, —we were advised not to throw good money after bad.

The lesson we have learned from this is, not to put ourselves into the hands of any one man or firm; and we think the conditions agreed on between the Royal Institute of British Architects and the master builders of London are to prevent unfairness on either side, and that builders should not sign any other.

OTHER CONTRACTORS.

SIR,—In answer to your correspondent on p. 444 *ante*, I consider that the penalties in his case cannot be enforced, but before anybody could definitely decide all the points raised the whole of the documents should be inspected.

On the one question of the errors in the quantities it is necessary to know whether they were prepared by the architect or by an independent surveyor, and whether paid for by the builder or by the employers.

HENRY LOVEGROVE.

26, *Budge-row, E.C.*, June 8, 1892.

FOURTEENTH AND FIFTEENTH CENTURY SCREENS.

SIR,—I shall be much obliged to any reader of the *Builder* who will inform me where I can see good specimens of church screens of the fourteenth or early fifteenth centuries.

B. RUCK-KEENE.

Copford Rectory, Colchester.

The Student's Column.

WARMING BUILDINGS BY HOT WATER.

XXIV.

EXAMPLES OF BUILDING WORKS.—*Continued.*

THE next example that may be suggested, is as fig 97. This is an apparatus extending away from the boiler in two different directions, for the purpose of heating two rooms of different size and in different manner. Taking the boiler first, this is shown having two flow pipes off the top, and each flow has a stop valve near the boiler, as shown.

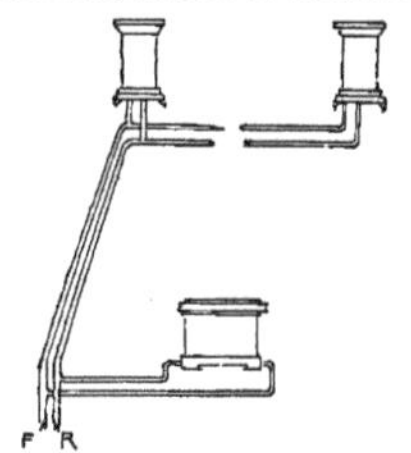

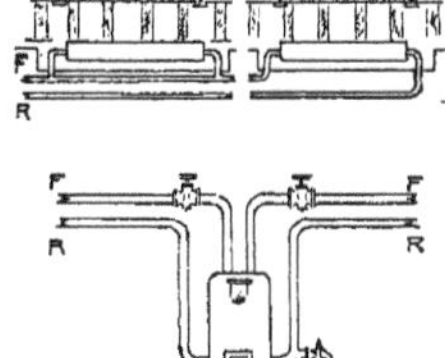

FIG. 97.

When it is convenient to have two flow pipes in this manner, it is as well to use them, although one flow, which is immediately branched in two directions, has no bad features; in this latter case the single pipe should be a size larger. In an apparatus such as this, especially as it does not appear to be extending far in height, the main or general services should be $1\frac{1}{4}$ in.; 1 in. might do in some cases, but is not recommended. The returns are usually brought right back to the boiler, although there would be no objection to their being branched into one, if they met at some distance from the boiler (this is not the case in the example given). If the two services terminate in a single return, it would be well to have this of a size larger pipe, as suggested with a single flow. An emptying cock and cleaning plugs must be provided to the boiler, and when placing the boiler there must be room enough in front of it for the cleaning and stoking tools to be used.

Each flow-pipe should have a stop-valve in it, so as to regulate the heat in either direction as occasion may require, and also to check the possible inclination one service may have to work more freely than the other. Hitherto we have suggested giving the longest service a greater rise (if possible) so as to equalise results, and this may be done in this case if convenient, but stop-cocks must be provided as well. We cannot suppose that both rooms want to be heated at the same time and to the same extent always, and on this account alone the stop-cocks are needed.

The service shown as proceeding to the left, goes to heat a large room, requiring three radiators,—a billiard-room, for instance. Speaking of billiard-rooms, let the reader be cautioned against putting pipes or coils under the billiard-table, nothing more improper could be done. If the pipes in question are sufficient to heat the room, they will pull the table to pieces. The writer was once consulted respecting a billiard-room that some one had attempted to heat by a single radiator placed under the table. Fortunately for the table, the radiator was not a large one, it failed to heat the room and did no injury; but even with this insufficient heat the players complained of the heated air ascending from under the table, and coming directly to the face when in the act of resting on the board to play. No heating appliances should be under a billiard-table.

The illustration is intended to show the radiators placed around the room, in corners, or at most convenient points. They must not, however, be too near wainscotted or similar woodwork, or the heat will injure it. The radiators are shown of different shapes, but this is settled by the general conditions; the method of connecting them, however, requires a little explanation.

The nearest radiator is shown connected by a distinct branch flow and return from the main service; this is the best way to treat this one. The next, in the left-hand corner, is connected to the flow only as shown, and as described in Article XXII. The last radiator on the right has the main flow and return directly connected with it; it really forms a terminal to these pipes, as illustrated. Each of these radiators would need the usual air-cock on the top. There would be no need for a stop-valve to each, as although one may heat quicker than the other, the whole three would soon become of an even temperature. The mains with this apparatus should be 1½ in., but the pipes or branches from the mains into the radiators need only be 1 in., or ¾ in. will do sometimes.

The service to the right may be supposed to furnish heat to a smaller room, but one of such a character that radiators, however good in appearance, would be objectionable. In this case the radiating media must be put out of sight, and this example shows it placed beneath the floor. In a new building, arrangements can be made for pipes to be carried whichever way may be most suitable, but such works as these are more often put in residences already occupied, but which have certain rooms that should have a regular heat, or which the ordinary fire-places are not successful in heating. This latter trouble often occurs. There are numbers of rooms, even as large or larger than billiard-rooms, that have only one fireplace, which cannot heat the whole of the room, although it may be large enough to cause an intolerable heat at the end where it is situated.

The writer's usual plan when the heating-pipes have to be beneath a floor is first to see that the room below is an unimportant one,—a kitchen or servants' offices; then to cut away the plaster of the ceiling, and secure an ordinary pipe-coil with box ends up to the joists. Immediately above the coil, on the top side of the joists, a suitable sized hole is cut in the floor-boards, and a brass grating laid in. The pattern of the grating should be open, yet strong enough to bear being stood upon. Branch flow and return pipes enter the box ends of the coils as shown, but, with coils lying flat, it is best to let the flow-pipe enter at a point as far removed from the return as possible, so as to ensure the passage of hot water through all the pipes. (It is not as if the coils stood upright, when it is recommended to connect all pipes at the bottom only, as the heated water then readily finds its way through the top pipes without any special provision).

Thus far the arrangement is sufficient to heat the room, as although the coils are on the ceiling of the room below, all the heat would come up through the joists and gratings, but there are two things further to consider. First, the coils would have an exceedingly bad appearance below, and secondly, and most important, all the impure air and possible odours (if a kitchen) will come through with the most undesirable speed imaginable. The coils must be boxed in below, this will totally hide them and will make the ceiling sound, and, when whitened, of ordinary appearance except for the square box projections that must exist. To do away with these boxes the joists would have to be cut through and trimmed to make a space for the coil; this would be a somewhat expensive and troublesome undertaking. Notwithstanding the box below, which quite shuts off communication between the room above and below, the spaces between the joists should be soundly stopped also, or air may be drawn this way from disagreeable sources. When this is done, the coil will heat the air of the room only, it will be practically a coil in a box, or well, sunk in the floor, but, if convenient or desirable, a fresh-air conduit could be led to it from outside. There would be then a rapid inflow of

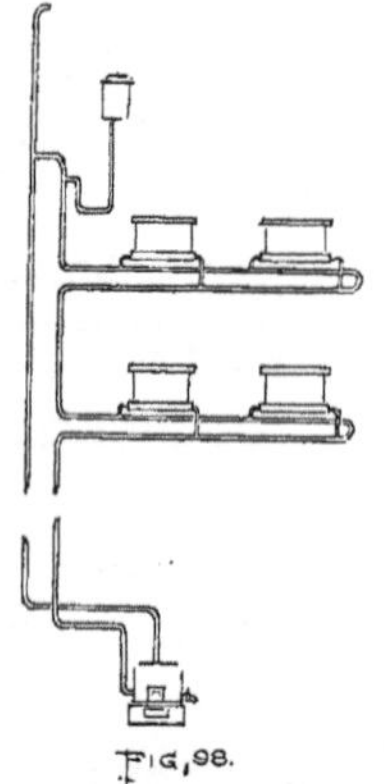

FIG. 98.

air, warmed by contact with the coil, and an inlet of this kind always goes to reduce the disagreeable draughts at doors and windows.

Air-cocks would have to be put upon the highest points of the coils, and when requiring attention could be got at by removing the gratings. If this is inconvenient, small tubes can be carried from the same points, but either up or down, whichever is best, and terminating with cocks.

With an apparatus like this, an expansion pipe should be provided; ⅜ in. would do, and the proper point for it to start from, would be in the flow-pipe somewhere between the two stop-cocks. The cold supply would be provided for by a good-sized cistern fixed at any point from 1 ft. to 4 ft. above the top of the highest radiator. The supply-pipe might be led into any of the return-pipes with the necessary dip or syphon.

Doubtless many of our readers have heard that it is proper in some instances to connect all radiating pipes, coils, &c., to the main return service only. This is correct in some cases, but in none of the examples yet given is it necessary or desirable. The methods shown are as good as any. The idea of putting all radiating media on the main return, arises from the argument that the service-pipe which has the greatest weight of water in it, or connected with it, should be the one that has the water

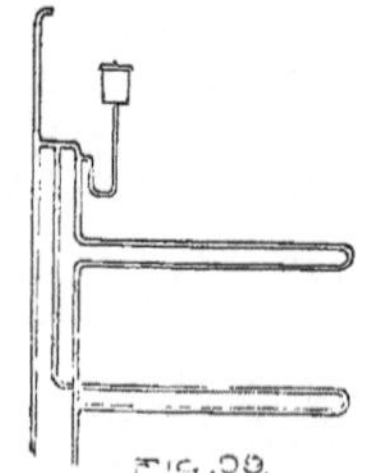

FIG. 99.

descending within it when at work. In other words, if the flow-pipe had a greater bulk of water in connection with it than the return, it would tend to be an obstacle to the upward direction of the water when it goes to rise up this pipe, and having a greater amount of water to displace than there is in the teturn-pipe, it might bring about a reversed or retrograde circulation.

This theory is broken down a great deal now, yet, at the same time, when an appar extends in a vertical direction a good hei and the engineer has any fear of such a res he may put his coils all on the return, as fig for instance. This shows an apparatus wit boiler in the basement, but going to heat corridors or rooms a floor or two above. I was feared the upper coils (or pipes) wo give better results than the lower, then circulation to each could be equalised running the services as in fig. 99. If it is desired to make the connexions wholly with

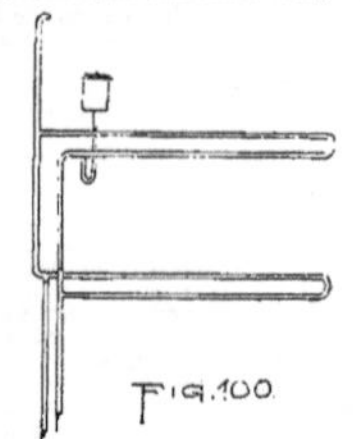

FIG. 100.

return pipe, then it could be carried out as fig. 100, which is, perhaps, the most customa way of doing it now.

GENERAL BUILDING NEWS.

ENLARGEMENT OF TULLIE HOUSE, CARLIS —On the 26th ult. the Mayor of Carlisle laid t foundation-stone of the enlargement of Tu House, Carlisle. Tullie House, which dates fr the end of the seventeenth century, is situate Abbey-street, and will be used as a museum, and new wing will be built at right angles with Abb street, to include rooms for the School of Art, t Public Library, with lending and reference depa ments, a general reading-room, a boys' readin room, class-rooms for technical instruction, and Fine Art Gallery. It is estimated that the c will be 12,000*l*. The scheme was devised by M C. J. Ferguson, who prepared sketches embodyi his suggestions, and Mr. Howard Smith, the Ci Surveyor, prepared the detailed drawings. Up the basement of the new building will be a boy reading-room. On the ground floor will be t Public Library, class-rooms for technical instru tion, and a lecture theatre to seat 200 student Upstairs will be the School of Art, with its vario elementary and advanced class-rooms, painti studio, and picture galleries. The chief contrac have been taken by Messrs. J. & W. Baty, f bricklayer's and mason's work; Mr. H. Court, ca pentry and joinery; and Messrs. R. M. Ormerod Sons, fireproof flooring. Mr. Howell is clerk of work We published in the *Builder* of May 9, 1891, so drawings of Tullie House as proposed to be adapt for a free library and school of art, which we furnished to us by Mr. Ferguson.—After t foundation-stone of the enlargement of Tull House was laid, the Mayor's-drive on the boulevar round the Sauceries was inaugurated, and the ne Recreation-ground in Botchergate was dedicated the public. The Mayor's-drive was commenc from plans prepared by Mr. McKie, the then Ci Surveyor, and has been finished by his success Mr. Howard Smith. It is a roadway formed fro Eden Bridge round the Sauceries. It is abo 1,200 yards in length, and along both sides of are planted trees. There is a project for continui the "Drive" round the Sheep Mount, and if this carried out a bridge will be built across the riv Caldew, a short distance above its confluence wi the Eden. The new recreation-ground is off Fus hill-street, and is over an acre in extent.

PUBLIC BATHS, SALFORD.—On the 2nd inst., t Mayor of Salford (Mr. Alderman Keevney) open the public baths recently erected by the Salfo Corporation in Regent-road. The baths a situated at the corner of Regent-road and Derb street, and have been erected from designs pr pared by Messrs. Mangnall & Littlewoods, arch tects, of Manchester. The design is Renaissance character, the material for the elevation being r terra-cotta and the best pressed bricks fro Ruabon. The principal entrances are in Derb street, the manager's residence over them formi a central feature to the elevation in that stree The first-class entrance is at the right-hand doo way, which leads to the first-class swimming-bat the first-class gentlemen's slipper-baths, and t ladies' slipper-baths. The left-hand entrance is f the second-class bathers, and leads to the secon class swimming-baths and second-class me slipper-baths. The first-class embraces vapou baths, cooling-rooms, and shower-baths. The bat rooms are 8 ft. by 6 ft. 6 in. There are ten fir class slipper-baths and eighteen second-class f gentlemen. The ladies are provided with four first-class slipper-baths and eight second-class. The first-class swimming-bath has a water area of 58 ft. by 25 ft. The second-class swimming-bath has a water area of 75 ft. by 28 ft., the depth being 5 ft. 9 in. at the deep end, and 5 ft. at the shallow end in each case. The contractors were Messrs. Robert Neill & Sons, of Strangeways, and the total cost of the buildings is about 11,000*l.*

Board School, Edinburgh. — On the 3rd inst., a new school for the Edinburgh School Board was formally opened by Lord Reay. The school is situated at Sciennes-place, and is the largest and most completely equipped of the schools erected by the Board. The total cost of the buildings was stated by the convener of the Building Committee to be about 21,626*l.*, and he claimed that in all its arrangements and equipment the Board had by no means neglected economy while securing the greatest efficiency. The accommodation of the school, including all the class-rooms and the lecture-room, he explained, was calculated at 10 square ft. for juveniles and 8 square ft. for infants, and amounted to 1,682 places; but, including the swimming-bath and gymnasium, the total accommodation was 1,985. Taking the total accommodation as for 1,985 children, the cost per scholar was barely 10*l.* 17s. 11d. The building was designed by and carried out under the superintendence of Mr. Robert Wilson, the architect for the School Board. (We take the foregoing particulars from the *Scotsman*).

Memorial Church, Sunderland.—On the 18th ult. the Bishop of Durham (Dr. Westcott) laid the foundation-stone of St. Hilda's Church, Sunderland, which is being built as a memorial to the late Bishop Lightfoot. The church will be situated near the junction of Westbourne-road and Clanny-street, Millfield. It will be erected at an estimated cost of 5,072*l.* The nave will be 62 ft. 6 in. long, by 21 ft. wide, and, in addition, there will be two side aisles, two transepts, and a baptistry. Twelve pillars will be erected in the interior of the building, the majority of them being subscribed for by various local societies. The glass for three lancet windows at the east of the church has been presented by the Misses Halcro, of Sunderland. The church will be surmounted by a spire, rising to a height of 134 ft. from the level of the ground. Accommodation will be provided for 505 persons, and there is to be a morning chapel running along the east of the south transept. The architects are Messrs. Hicks & Charlewood, Newcastle-on-Tyne.

Girls' Home, Ballysillan, Belfast. — The opening of the Victoria Voluntary Homes for the Shamrock Lodge Girls at Ballysillan took place on the 19th ult. The new buildings are approached from the Crumlin- and Oldpark-roads. The entrance lodge is situated on the Ballysillan-road. The main buildings are arranged in a hollow square. In the middle of the front is placed a square tower, finished with a pyramidal roof and copper vane. The principal doorway is placed below. From the inner porch access is obtained on either side to the principal schoolrooms. The west wing contains practically a distinct house, with the board-room, parlour, kitchen, and pantries on the ground floor. A corresponding wing on the south side for the industrial school department is arranged for 40 children. Behind it stands the hospital, complete in itself, having separate kitchen, scullery, and yard. The upper stories of all these buildings form a series of dormitories, with bath-room and lavatories attached. The rear of the entire block is occupied by the laundry, smoothing and drying rooms, heated from the boiler-room adjoining. A dairy and general storehouses complete these offices. A small engine with a pump attached, is used for forcing up the water supply to a cistern placed in the tower. At a short distance from the central building stands the Forster Green Home. It is so planned as to be complete in itself, and accommodates thirty girls. On the ground floor access is obtained through a porch and hall, from which open the dining-room, mothers' room, and the playroom. A bath-room, with lavatories, is attached to the last-named. Behind these are the kitchen, scullery, pantries, and yard. The upper floor is used for dormitories. A play-shed is arranged for use in wet weather. The buildings have been carried out in red brick, with Dumfries mullions and sills. The plumbing has been executed by Mr. John Dowling. Mr. Robert Corry, Donegall Pass, has carried out the works, and Messrs. Young & Mackenzie, of Belfast, are the architects.

FOREIGN AND COLONIAL.

France.—At the Champs Elysées Salon this year nothing in the sculpture or architectural exhibits has been deemed worthy of the *grande médaille d'honneur.* On the other hand, in the section of painting, after three tours of inspection, the award has been bestowed on M. Albert Maignan, by 163 votes out of 324. The other awards have been distributed between MM. Vayson, Roybet, Henner, Benjamin Constant, Raphäel Collin, and Henri Martin. M. Maignan, who has exhibited an Apotheosis of Carpeaux, is a pupil of M. Luminais. He obtained a medal of the third class in 1874, one of the second in 1876, a first-class in 1879, and a gold medal at the Universal Exhibition in 1889. He was decorated in 1883.——In architecture MM. Cordonnier and Charles Normand have obtained medals of the first class; MM. Chédanne, Lafargue, Hannotin, and Gaida the second; MM. Tisandier, Nizet, Tropey-Bailly, Boussac, Loyau, and Escalier the third: honourable mention has been awarded to MM. Bévière, Bobin, Coulon, Dalmas, Desnues, Dezermeaux, Giroix, Guénot, Guyon, Legendre, Lépouzé, Mauber, Mougenot, and Paul Normand.——At the École des Beaux Arts the Fortin d'Ivry prize has been given to M. Bonis. ——Several fires due to malevolence have destroyed a great quantity of wood in the most picturesque part of the forest of Fontainebleau.——In the Georges Petit Gallery an exhibition of 100 pictures has just been opened for a charitable object. They are works chosen from the most celebrated masters, from the time of Rubens and Rembrandt to Meissonier, Millet, and Corot. This exhibition is organised under the presidency of the Duc d'Aumale. —— They have lately inaugurated a statue of Pascal Duprat, at Mont de Marsan (Landes). The statue is the work of M. Labatut. ——Etienne Arago, recently dead, has left as a legacy to the museum at Versailles, two busts in terra-cotta, by Carrier-Belluse, of the astronomers Mathieu and Paul Langier. —— M. Waldeck Rousseau has offered to the Luxembourg Museum a picture by M. Gervex, which was exhibited in the Salon of 1885, entitled "Meeting of the Jury of Painting."——MM. Français, Bonnat, Jules Breton, Daumet, and Roty have been appointed to represent the Académie des Beaux-Arts at the ceremony of inaugurating the monument of Claude Lorraine at Nancy.——An exhibition of the works of the painter Antoine Richard is to be opened on the 15th inst. at Châlon-sur-Saône.——It is announced that, on the occasion of the approaching visit of the President to Nancy, the corporation of sculptors of that town will offer to M. Carnot an armchair richly carved in walnut-wood and covered with a fine tapestry in which the arms of Lorraine are woven. This work has been executed by M. Donot, sculptor.——The death is announced of M. Frederic Grosslande, portrait painter. He was born at Geneva, but had been naturalised many years. He exhibited at the Salons annually from 1872 to 1888 studies of heads and portraits in pastels, executed with a certain amount of talent.——The sculptor Bonnassieux, member of the Institute, one of the oldest professors at the Ecole des Beaux-Arts, has lately died at the age of 81. He was born at Panissière (Loire), in 1810, and obtained the Prix de Rome in 1836. He then obtained a second medal in 1862, a first in 1864, a second in 1868, and a new first medal at the Universal Exhibition of 1855, at which time he was decorated. His well-known religious views made him the official sculptor of the Catholic clergy, and it is to him that we owe the colossal statue of Notre Dame de France, which commands the Vallée du Puy (Haute Loire); it was made from the bronze of the cannons taken at Sebastopol. He also assisted at the decoration of several of the Paris churches, notably that of St. Augustin. He has contributed nothing to the Salons for some time.——We have also to announce the death of the painter Jaumot, who died at Lyons at the age of 78. He received medals in 1849 and 1859.

Berlin.—Herr von Forckenbeck, who has been Lord Mayor since 1878, died last week. His funeral was one of great civic state. During the fourteen years he held office, Berlin has seen a marvellous development, and also great improvements in all matters relating to municipal management.——The value of the prizes to be offered for the coming competition for designs of the proposed Provincial Museum has had to be raised from 250*l.* to 400*l.*, owing to dissatisfaction expressed in architectural circles as to the low figure of the premiums.——Some very interesting buildings for the Army Commissariat Department have been completed. In the main block there will be room to store 70,000 cwt. of oats. Owing to the great losses the forage departments have lately had through fires in their store-houses, great precautions have been taken against the outbreak and spread of a conflagration. Each of the seven stories of the main building is divided into two separate risks, and each compartment has a separate system of sprinklers. It appears, however, that for some inexplicable reason wood has been used for all the floors.——On the recommendation of the sanitary inspectors the Police President will probably now prohibit ladies from kindly acting as voluntary street scavengers. There is to be a restriction as to the length of ladies' trains.——The historical Castle Church at Wittenberg, the restoration of which has cost some 45,000*l.*, will be reopened by the Emperor in the autumn. Professor F. Adler has had charge of the works.

Munich.—The International Art Exhibition, which has now become an annual institution, has been opened by the Prince Regent with the usual ceremony. The local press considers this year's show to be a good one.——The buildings for the Bavarian National Museum, which are to be erected on a fine site near the so-called "English Garden," will cover a superficial area of some 8,600 square mètres. The new block is to cost about 220,000*l.*, and some five years will have to elapse until the halls will be ready for the reception of the exhibits (*Deutsche Bauzeitung*).

Stuttgart. — Again a competition has been opened with a great philanthropic object in view. This time it is a competition for designs of some large buildings, in which 400 or 500 railway servants and their families are to dwell. Each tenement,—consisting of two rooms, a kitchen, w.c., lobby, and a share of the staircase landing,—is to have an area ranging from 75 to 80 square mètres; those with three rooms from 90 to 95 square mètres. Much importance will be attached to the laying out of the ground which stands at the disposal of the authorities, as, besides the dwelling-houses, there are to be general washhouses, baths, stores, and a preparatory school to be found room for. The competition excites much interest throughout those parts of Germany where the artisans' dwellings question has been mooted.

Switzerland.—Whilst at the past competitions for designs of new post-office buildings in Geneva and Lucerne the number of designs sent in was large, the assessors who have had to decide on the merits of the work tendered at the Zurich Post-office competition have only had twenty-seven to select from. They have not found any one of the twenty-seven deserving of the first prize, and have only been able to give five minor awards. The most valuable of these went to M. Eugen Meyer, a Swiss architect resident in Paris.

MISCELLANEOUS.

Christ Church Cathedral, Oxford.—We are informed that the grave marked as Dr. Pusey's grave in our plan of Christ Church last week, in the external angle of choir and south transept, is in reality that of Philip Pusey, a son of Dr. Pusey. The latter was buried in the nave of the Cathedral.

Forthcoming Sales.—At the Mart, on the 21st instant, by order of the late Mr. W. B. Waterlow's trustees, various residential and building estates in the neighbourhood of Reigate and Redhill, comprising those known as High Trees, on the west side of Redhill Common,—the house built of stone, in the Italian mode, for its late owner,—and, with frontages to the Common, Fairlawn, The Mount, Blackstones, and Earlswood Cottage; together with High Trees Park, and other lands adjacent. In July: The Barwhillanty estate, of nearly 4,000 acres in the stewartry of Kirkcudbright, Galloway, and situated in the parishes of Parton and Crossmichael. The latter parish lies between the rivers Urr and Dee, to the north-west is Parton — a district famous for its Celtic and Pictish remains. At Carlisle, on an early date, the Springkell estate, in county Dumfries, just across the border, and about ten miles distant from Carlisle. It embraces an area of 14,000 acres, divided amongst fifty-one farms, yielding an annual rental of, say, 11,000*l.* The mansion house, built, we believe, about 100 years ago, for Sir William Maxwell, stands on the famed Kirtle-water, which flows for some miles between Eskdale and Annandale. Gretna, or rather Graitney (*olim* Meg's-hill) is a farmstead, near to Springfield, a village established by Sir William Maxwell. One of the first inhabitants of that new settlement was Joseph Paisley, a tobacconist, — often wrongly described as having been a blacksmith,—whose memory is associated with the "Gretna Green" marriages since the passing of Lord Hardwicke's Act in 1754. Paisley died in 1814: his business, after that kind, was carried on here by his grand-daughter's husband.

Patent Office Report for 1891.—According to the Comptroller-General's ninth report, for the year 1891, the general business of the Patent Office was represented by applications for 22,888 patents, being the highest total since the new procedure under the Act of 1883; designs, 21,950 (22,553);* and trade marks, 10,787 (10,258). Of the patents, 15,484 came from persons residing in England and Wales, 1,177 from Scotland, 134 from Canada, 1,466 from Germany, and 2,364 from the United States. Sales of the Office publications yielded a receipt of 6,142*l.* 13s. 7d., and a surplus of 100,339*l.* 6s. 7d. is declared out of gross receipts amounting to 203,520*l.*, the patent fees alone being 181,777*l.* 4s. 8d. The largest number of patents applied for under the old law was 6,241, in the year 1882, and of them two-thirds remained in force to the end of the fourth year. The ratio for the year 1890, under the new Act, is a little less than one-half. In virtue of a Royal charter dated August 11, 1891, the Institute of Patent Agents was incorporated; it had a total number of 236 names upon the register of agents on December 31 last. For the re-building of the Patent Office, as already begun in Took's-court, a sum of 21,703*l.* is taken on account in the estimates, for new works and purchase of premises.

Sweden and the Chicago Exhibition. — The Swedish Society of Engineers in New York is urging Swedish manufacturers to participate in the Chicago Exhibition, and has, to that end, offered a prize for the best essay, "Ought Sweden to Exhibit in Chicago," which is to be distributed in Sweden and America.

* The corresponding figures for the preceding year are enclosed within brackets.

COMPETITIONS, CONTRACTS, AND PUBLIC APPOINTMENTS.

COMPETITIONS.

Nature of Work.	By whom Advertised.	Premium.	Designs to be delivered.
*Public Baths	Walsall Corp.	50*l.* 30*l.* & 20*l.*	July 14
*Schools	Norwich Sch. Bd.	50*l.* 25*l.*	July 26
*Local Board Offices, &c. &c.	Bexhill Loc. Bd.	50*l.*	Sept. 1

CONTRACTS.

Nature of Work or Materials.	By whom Required.	Architect, Surveyor, or Engineer.	Tenders to be delivered.
Sixty Cottages, Aberdare Junction	Carne Town Cottage Co. Limited	....	June 14
*Six New Water Vans	Boro of West Ham	L. Angell	do.
*Coal Stage, &c. Skipton	Midland Railway Co.	Official	June 16
*Cleansing and Painting Goods Depot, Bristol	do.	do.	do.
*External Repairs to Workhouse	St. Saviour's Union	Jarvis & Son	do.
Workshop, &c. Blackfriars-road, Elgin, N.B.	....	J. Jamieson	do.
Additions and Alterations to Church, Stanwix, Carlisle	....	C. J. Ferguson	do.
Twenty Houses, Tredegar Junction	Tredegar Junction Building Club	W. Edwards	do.
Widening of Bridge, Botcherby, near Carlisle	Cumberland C. C.	G. J. Bell	June 17
Long Boundary Wall, &c.	Halifax Corporation	E. R. S. Escott	June 18
Cottages, &c. Barrows Green, near Widnes	J. W. Wareing	....	do.
*Stonework, Town Hall	Bermondsey Vestry	Official	June 20
*Repairs, Painting, &c. Relief Offices, &c.	St. Marylebone Guar.	do.	do.
*Shaft Sinking, Tunnelling, &c.	Manchester Corporation Waterworks	G. H. Hill	do.
Memorial Hall and Assembly Rooms, Llandovery	C. P. Lewis	....	do.
*Guernsey Granite, Gravel, and Flint	Borough of Croydon	W. Powell	June 21
Villa, Nairn, N.B.	J. B. Leslie	C. C. Doig	do.
*Concrete Pavement in situ	East Ham Local Bd.	W. H. Savage	do.
*Brickwork, Erection of Chimney Shaft	Manchester Corporation Waterworks	Official	June 22
Abbatoirs, Cattle Sheds, Houses, &c. North Dean	Halifax Industrial Soc. Ltd.	Horsfall & Williams	do.

CONTRACTS.—*Continued.*

Nature of Work or Materials.	By whom Required.	Architect, Surveyor, or Engineer.	Tenders to be delivered
Two Cottages, Penrose Farm, Sennen, Cornwall	Henry Laity	....	June 22
Heating Arrangements, &c. Hospital, Easington	....	Lamb, Armstrong, & Knowles	do.
Street Improvements	Ystradyfodwg Loc. Bd.	J. W. Jones	do.
*Making-up and Paving Streets	Fulham Vestry	W. Sykes	do.
Dwelling-house, Moorville, Cumberland	John Elliott	....	June 25
*Hire of Steam Roller	West Sussex C. C.	Official	June 27
*Rebuilding Broadbourne Bridge, &c.	do.	do.	do.
*Painting Works, Infirmary	Fulham Union	do.	June 30
*Rebuilding Ystrad Bridge	Brecknockshire C. C.	do.	July 2
*School Premises, New Swindon	The Committee	W. Whincops	No date.
*Green English Oak, Elm, and Ash	London Road Car Co. Ltd.	Official	do.
Biscuit Factory and Warehouse, Cardiff	Spillers & Bakers, Ltd.	Veall & Sant	do.
Schools, Knutsford	Lord Egerton of Tatton	Preston & Vaughan	do.
New Church of St. John, Crewe	....	Hicks & Charlewood	do.
Farm Buildings, Cwm Cerwyn, near Maesteg, S. Wales	Edward Knox	....	do.
New Church, Horrabridge, Devon	....	G. H. F. Prynne	do.
Sinking and Walling Shaft, near Wakefield	Hemsworth Colliery Co.	....	do.
Engine House and Seatings	do.	....	do.
Shops, Westbar, Sheffield	R. S. Whitworth	W. H. Lancashire	do.
Club Premises	Walkley Conservative Club	....	do.
*Painting Works, Kingston and Tower of London	War Department	Official	do.

PUBLIC APPOINTMENTS.

Nature of Appointment.	By whom Advertised.	Salary.	Applications to be in.
*Surveyor	Bermondsey Vestry	250*l.* &c.	June 15
*Foremen of Works (3), Lagos	Crown Agents for Colonies	250*l.* to 300*l.* &c.	June 18
*Sanitary Inspector	Plumstead B. of W.	2*l.*	June 21
*Instructor in Geometrical Drawings and Lecturer in Architecture	Royal Indian Engineering College	400*l.* &c.	No date

Those marked with an Asterisk (*) are advertised in this Number. *Competitions, p. iv. Contracts, pp. iv., vi., & viii. Public Appointments, p. xx.*

BRITISH MINERAL PRODUCTION.—The "Mineral Statistics of the United Kingdom" for 1891 show that the total value of the minerals raised last year was 91,238,032*l.*, against 92,794,481*l.* in 1890, which is a decrease for 1891 of 1,556,449*l.*, or 1·46 per cent.; the decline extending to nearly all branches of mineral production. The principal item of output was coal, of which were obtained 185,479,126 tons, or 4,264,836 tons (2·34 per cent.) more than in 1890, when the production was only 181,614,288 tons. The value of the coal output declined by 854,181*l.*, or 1·14 per cent., the figures being 74,090,816*l.*, against 74,953,997*l.* in 1890. Of iron ore, 12,777,689 tons were raised, valued at 3,355,860*l.*, compared with 13,780,767 tons, valued at 3,926,445*l.* This shows a falling-off in 1891 of 1,003,078 tons, or over 7 per cent., in quantity, and of 570,585*l.*, or 17 per cent., in value. Of the output of stone, the value only is given, amounting to 8,693,743*l.*, against 8,708,691*l.* in 1890; decrease, 14,948*l.*, or 0·17 per cent. The quantity of clays (excepting ordinary clay) obtained in 1891 was 3,222,035 tons (value, 943,896*l.*), against 3,308,214 tons (value, 899,166*l.*) in 1890. Thus, although the quantity raised in 1891 decreased by 86,170 tons, or 2·6 per cent., compared with 1890, the value increased by 44,730*l.*, or nearly 5 per cent. The production of slates and slabs amounted to 415,029 tons, against 434,352 tons in 1890; the values were 987,000*l.* and 1,027,235*l.* respectively; the decline being 19,323 tons, or 4·4 per cent., in quantity, and 40,235*l.*, or 3·9 per cent., in value. Of gypsum, 151,708 tons (valued at 60,038*l.*), against 140,293 tons (valued at 57,991*l.*), were obtained; decrease, 11,415 tons, or 7·55 per cent., and 2,047*l.*, or 8·4 per cent., respectively.

"HYLONITE."—This material, some specimens of which have been forwarded to us by Mr. H. Brockmann, the London agent of MM. Schreiber & Co., is a preparation of wood pulp, to be used in place of plaster or stucco for decorations, or for wall covering. The special value claimed for it is that it is guaranteed to stand any amount of heat "without shrinking, bending, or losing its original shape." "Paper stucco" is another material of the same class claiming the same heat-resisting qualities. If this resistance to heat is realised under test no doubt this is a very useful material for lining buildings which are intended to be specially fire-resisting. As far as decorative effect is concerned, the examples of ornament appear to be very deficient in sharpness as compared with plaster or stucco. This difficulty may be met to some extent by designing specially for the material, as is often done for cast-iron. At all events, in a practical sense the material seems worth attention.

DEDICATION OF THE CATHEDRAL BELLS, NEWCASTLE.—On the 7th inst. the new peal of bells recently placed in the belfry of St. Nicholas's Cathedral, Newcastle, were formally dedicated. There are ten bells in the new peal, exclusive of the major or hour bell. Messrs. John Taylor & Co., of Loughborough, have had the casting of the bells and the re-casting of the major.

HOMES FOR SAILORS IN THE EAST-END, LONDON.—A new branch institute, in West India Dock-road, of the British and Foreign Sailors' Society, of which the Duke of York is patron, is to be known as the Albert Edward Sailors' Rest. The freehold of a disused public-house, called the "Jolly Sailor," with a messuage at the back, have been bought by the society, who appeal for contributions in aid of their work, both at home and abroad, which they began about seventy-five years ago, on board of H.M.S. *Speedy*. In 1856 the society's labours were greatly promoted by the late Prince Consort's active co-operation. On December 5, 1888, the Duke of Cambridge re-opened the institute in Mercers'-street, Shadwell. Of the Scandinavian Sailors' Home, by the East and West India Docks, we gave an account in our number of June 25, 1887. The Home in Well-street, Wellclose-square, stands, we believe, on the site of the Brunswick Theatre, which replaced the Royalty Theatre burnt in 1826.

CAPITAL AND LABOUR.

THE THREATENED STRIKE IN THE LONDON BUILDING TRADE.—As the outcome of the demands of the London bricklayers as to hours and rate of wages (published in the *Builder* for April 9, p. 296), the London Association of Master Builders, feeling the practical inconvenience that would arise if the men of the different trades had varying hours for commencing and leaving off work, at a conference held with the representatives of the bricklayers on May 25 announced that they could give no reply to the demands of the men until a conference could be held between the representatives of all the trades and of the employers, with a view of agreeing upon one code of working hours and rules. This conference has now been arranged, and will take place a few hours after these lines are published, the representatives of the masters having agreed to meet, at 2 o'clock on Friday, June 10, three delegates from each of the following trades, viz., bricklayers, masons, carpenters, plumbers, painters, plasterers, smiths (including fitters and bell-hangers), and labourers. In spite of some rather wild talk which has appeared in some of the newspapers, we trust that both sides will exhibit a conciliatory spirit, and that a strike may be averted.

THE STRIKE IN THE CARDIFF BUILDING TRADES.—According to the *Western Mail*, the carpenters and joiners of Cardiff who have been concerned in the strike in the building trade there have agreed to accept the 8½d. offered by the masters, and to eliminate their free labour clause. This action, however, does not affect the other trades, for from the first the carpenters and joiners have held aloof from the allied trades.

MEETINGS.

SATURDAY, JUNE 11.

Architectural Association.—Visit to new Music School, Harrow, Mr. E. S. Prior, architect; and to other School buildings and houses at Harrow. Meet at Harrow Church at 3 p.m.

Incorporated Association of Municipal and County Engineers.—Eastern Counties District Meeting at Peterborough.

Junior Engineering Society.—Visit to the works of the Patent Victoria Stone Co., Stratford. 3 p.m.

St. Paul's Ecclesiological Society.—Visit to Chesham Bois and Chesham.

Edinburgh Architectural Association.—The Sketching Class to meet at Royston House, Caroline Park, Granton, to make measured drawings and sketches of the south front of the mansion. 3 p.m.

MONDAY, JUNE 13.

Royal Institute of British Architects. — Business Meeting—(1) To receive the Report of the Scrutineers on the Election of the Council, Standing Committees, &c. (2) To receive and consider the Report of By-law 9 (Election of Fellows) Special Committee. 8 p.m.

Society of Engineers.—7.30 p.m.

Clerks of Works' Association (Carpenters' Hall).—Monthly meeting. 8 p.m.

TUESDAY, JUNE 14.

Incorporated Gas Institute.—Twenty-ninth Annual Meeting. 11 a.m.

Society of Biblical Archæology.—8 p.m.

WEDNESDAY, JUNE 15.

Incorporated Gas Institute. — Twenty-ninth Annual Meeting (*continued*). In commemoration of William Murdoch and the centenary of gas lighting, a "Murdoch" lecture will be given by Professor Vivian B. Lewes on "A Century of Work on the Development of Light from Coal Gas." 10 a.m.

Builders' Foremen and Clerks of Works Institution.—Ordinary Meeting. 8.30 p.m.

Royal Meteorological Society. — Two papers will be read. 7 p.m.

THURSDAY, JUNE 16.

Incorporated Gas Institute. — Twenty-ninth Annual Meeting (*continued*). 10 a.m.

Society of Antiquaries.—8.30 p.m.

RECENT PATENTS:

ABSTRACTS OF SPECIFICATIONS.

7,229.—SELF-ACTING HOOK: *G. Cooper.*—This patent refers to an invention for retaining doors, gates, or for any other purpose where a self-acting hook is required, to fasten back and release when required. The inventor provides a circular plate with a barrel containing a buffer and spring. There is a slot in the sides of the barrel for the purpose of sliding screws, working a hook. There is also a screw below the slot for holding the hook in position. This part is fixed on the skirting or other position above the floor line. A plate with staple and releaser lets go the hook.

11,175.—FLAP VENTILATORS: *S. S. Robson.* — This specification refers to an improvement in flap ventilators, the object of which is to produce a noiseless flap distinct from those now in use. The inventor uses asbestos paper, which is, of course, uninflammable and noiseless. It is fixed to the ventilator in the same way as the ordinary flaps in use.

14,608.—WINDOW-SASHES: *J. Hanson.*—This refers to an invention intended to be applied to carriage windows and the like, to prevent rattling or noise. One edge of the window-frame is provided with a corrugated slip corresponding in pitch to another corrugated slip contained by a metal case, and let into the groove of the door stile. To this case are attached inclined springs upon which the loose slips work in such a manner that when the window is raised the corrugated slip slides up the inclined spring, so taking the grip off the window and allowing it to be raised without friction. When the window is stopped, the loose slips drop down the inclined springs and block the window.

4,871.—PIPE CONNEXIONS: *T. Robinson.*—The object of this Invention is to make a perfect air and liquid tight joint between the earthenware outlet-pipe of water-closet basin, or other sanitary appliance, and th leaden soil-pipe in connexion with the drains, and to enable such joint to be readily opened and closed. To the end of the outlet-pipe is attached a metal conical ring grooved inside, and provided with three screws and an internal lip for the end of the pipe to abut against. To the end of the leaden soil-pipe is soldered a partially conical metal ring provided with a flange. A flat ring, or collar, made in two halves, is passed over the outlet pipe and abuts against the base of the conical ring. By means of bolts the earthenware pipe and the soil-pipe are firmly united together.

5,746.—DISTEMPER: *A. T. Morse.*—This specification relates to what is claimed to be an improved distemper for interior house decoration and other work. The specification states that it is a non-poisonous self-binding distemper, complete in itself and ready for use by mixing merely with water without the addition of size or other ingredients. The chief ingredients are gilders' whiting, gelatine, oxide of zinc, and sulphate of manganese.

NEW APPLICATIONS FOR LETTERS PATENT.

May 23.—9,732, H. Martin, Tool for Forming a Recess in Bricks or other articles which can be moulded in clay or other similar substance.—9,755, R. Pancoast, Ventilators or Chimney-cowls.—9,761, W. Allen, Ventilating Buildings.—9,762, W. Allen, Window-frames.

May 24.—9,790, J. Shaw, Window-fastener.—9,826, E. Torrey, Plumbers' Waste-pipe Traps.—9,847, W. John, Facing Bricks or Tiles.—9,853, L. Lecellier, Automatically Released Latch or Bolt for Locks.

May 26.—9,908, G. Addy and W. Johnson, Self-releasing Safety Grindstone Rest.—9,924, W. Bosley, Self-fixing Expansion Block for Flushing Sewers.—9,950, J. McHardy and W. Garland, Wood-carving and Moulding Machines.—9,951, E. Ramsbottom, Window-fittings.—9,974, H. Majewski and W. Beyenbach, Artificial Marble.—9,980, C. Hill, Door-stops and Draught-excluders.—9,996, G. Gwillim and H. Swan, Tool or Apparatus for Carving Wood, Stone, or other material, or for boring or drilling holes in the same.—10,031, W. Gabriel, Hanging Windows.—10,038, B. Pitt, Open Firegrates.

May 27.—10,087, W. Slade, Catch for Sliding Doors or Sashes.—10,089, H. Dodd, Window Respirator and Draught-check.—10,111, J. Williams, Caps, Pots, or Tops for Chimneys, Ventilating-shafts, &c.—10,123, H. Doulton and S. Leech, Terra-cotta and like materials, and in apparatus therefore.—10,132, J. Riordan, Sash-fastener.

May 28.—10,160, J. Baines, Artificial Stone.—10,179, D. Paul, Firegrates and Register-grates.—10,224, G. Tweedy, Chimney-pots and Cowls.

PROVISIONAL SPECIFICATIONS ACCEPTED.

6,285, C. Gray, Door-fasteners.—7,016, J. McFarlane and W. Edgar, Incandescent Electric Lamps.—7,802, D. Richmond, Flushing Water-closets, Urinals, &c.—8,078, H. Leggott, Sitting-room Fire-ranges.—8,122, H. Jodicke, Channelling Bricks, Artificial Stones, &c.—8,203, E. Hole, Sash-fasteners.—8,327, H. Hunt, Fire-grates.—8,346, W. Hewitt and H. Suart, Brick-making Machinery.—8,403, S. Johnson, Attaching Door-knobs to Spindles.—9,052, G. Hall, Letter-boxes for use on private dwellings.—9,154, W. Teschauer, Sliding Windows.

COMPLETE SPECIFICATIONS ACCEPTED.

(Open to Opposition for Two Months.)

9,885, R. Tapscott, Self-closing Water-taps.—10,661, W. Pilkington, Kilns for Annealing Plate-glass.—12,444, R. Rosoman, Ventilators.—12,801, J. Hartis, Syphon Flushing Cisterns.—4,408, C. Dobbs, Scoria or Slag Blocks for Paving, &c.—7,804, A. and A. Budde, Traps for Sewers or Drains.—7,850, E. Warner and J. Curry, Mortar.—7,907, W. Pryke and W. Palmer, Eaves Gutters.

SOME RECENT SALES OF PROPERTY:

ESTATE EXCHANGE REPORT.

MAY 30.—By *H. J. Bromley*: "Ada" and "Maude" Villas, Sydenham, u.t. 66 yrs., g.r. 11*l*., r. 58*l*., 250*l*.; 13 and 15, High-st., u.t. 13 yrs., g.r. 5*l*. 8s., 265*l*.; 85 to 97 odd, Ormside-st., Old Kent-rd., u.t. 61 yrs., g.r. 17*l*. 10s., 470*l*.—By *Weatherall & Green*: 75, Claybrook-rd., Fulham, u.t. 88 yrs., g.r. 5*l*. 5s., r. 28*l*. 12s., 180*l*.—By *Broad & Wiltshire*: "Clovelly," The Avenue, Grove-pk., with grounds, f., r. 210*l*., 3,100*l*.; a plot of f. land, Bromley-rd., 430*l*.—By *Bean, Burnett, & Co.*: "Isleworth House," Isleworth, and 19 acres, f., 11,000*l*.; "The Black Boy" public-house, Mile-end-rd., f., r. 115*l*., 2,050*l*.; 171 to 179, Mile-end-rd., f., r. 193*l*., 2,930*l*.—By *Hampton & Sons*: "Rockville," Cosham, Hunts, and 4½ acres, f., 3,800*l*.—By *Farebrother, Ellis, & Co.*: f.g.r. of 28*l*., reversion in 59 yrs., Newington-green, 840*l*.; f.g.r. of 19*l*. 10s., Mildmay-grove South, ditto in 59 yrs., 492*l*.; f.g.r. of 10*l*., Aden-ter., Hornsey, ditto in 53 yrs., 262*l*.; f.g.r. of 7*l*. 4s., Burma-rd., Green-lanes, ditto in 57 yrs., 195*l*.; f.g.r. of 30*l*., "Triangle Cottages," Hackney, ditto in 68 yrs., 549*l*.; a plot of f. land, Shooter's Hill, 4a. 1r. 20p., 470*l*.; 9, Cosmo-pl., Southampton-row, f., r. 86*l*. 5s., 1,430*l*.; 13, Cosmo-pl., f., r. 87*l*., 1,400*l*.; f.g.r. of 104*l*. 10s., Queen-sq., Bloomsbury, reversion in about 800 yrs., 3,365*l*.—By *Reynolds & Eason*: F.g.r. of 173*l*. 5s., Blantyre-st., Chelsea, reversion in 420 yrs., 4,100; f.g.r. of 300*l*. 2s., Seaton-st., ditto in 420 yrs., 7,160*l*.; 61, 63, and 65, Seaton-st., f., r. 96*l*., 1,330*l*.; freehold rental of 75*l*., Cheyne-walk, u.t. 420 yrs., 1,640*l*.; 73, Oakley-street, u.t. 69 yrs., g.r. 2*l*., r. 70*l*., 850*l*.; 45, Oakley-sq., u.t. 73 yrs., g.r. 7*l*. 10s., r. 95*l*., 1,600*l*.; 47, Oakley-st., u.t. 73 yrs., g.r. 7*l*. 10s., r. 75*l*., 1,200*l*.

MAY 31.—By *Segrave & Taylor*: 5, 7, and 9, Farrer-st., Brixton, u.t. 28 yrs., g.r. 9*l*., 277*l*. 10s.—By *R. A. Notley*: 3, Charlton-st., Fitzroy-sq., u.t. 23 yrs., g.r. 18*l*., r. 80*l*., 800*l*.—By *Kelf & Son*: 5 to 8, West-rd., Tottenham, u.t. 74 yrs., g.r. 22*l*., 560*l*.; 47, Prospect-pl., Edmonton, u.t. 56 yrs., g.r. 5*l*. 5s., r. 19*l*., 150*l*.—By *Messrs. Trollope*: the f. residence, "St. Helen's," Hampton Wick, 3,700*l*.—By *Messrs. Foster*: "Oakleigh," Thetford-rd., Malden, f., r. 45*l*., 790*l*.; f.g.r. of 16*l*., Villiers-rd., Willesden, with reversion in 94 yrs., 330*l*.; f.g.r. of 15*l*., Brownlow-rd., ditto in 94 yrs., 295*l*.; a perpetual rent charge of 4*l*. 8s. 7½d., Blackburn, 87*l*. 10s.—By *Debenham, Tewson, & Co.*: 7, Blue Cross-st., Leicester-sq., f., r. 75*l*., 1,070*l*.; f.g.r. 139*l*. 17s. 6d., Trigon-rd., Lambeth, reversion in 32 yrs., 4,750*l*.; f.g.r. of 51*l*. 9s., Granville-rd., Kilburn, ditto in 70 yrs., 1,180*l*.; f.g.r. of 151*l*. 4s., Netherwood-st., ditto in 75 yrs., 3,660*l*.; f.g.r. of 50*l*., Charles-st., Stamford-hill, ditto in 81 yrs., 1,000*l*.—By *Ventom, Bull, & Cooper*: 230 and 232, Gray's-inn-rd., u.t. 18 yrs., g.r. 64*l*., r. 140*l*., 600*l*.; 46, 47, 49, 50, and 51, Myddleton-st., Clerkenwell, u.t. 19 yrs., g.r. 20*l*., 1,000*l*.; 2 and 3, Garnault-pl., u.t. 19 yrs., g.r. 10*l*., r. 75*l*., 450*l*.; 5 to 8, Garnault-mews, u.t. 19 yrs., no g.r., 110*l*.; 14, Mabledon-pl., St. Pancras, u.t. 14 yrs., g.r. 21*l*., r. 50*l*., 110*l*.; 1 to 6, Southampton-buildings, Euston-sq., u.t. 15 yrs., g.r. 12*l*., 460*l*.—By *J. G. Hammond, junr.*: 24, 26, and 28, South-pk.-hill-rd., Croydon, f., r. 140*l*., 3,450*l*.; 25, 27, 33, and 35, Birdhurst-rd., f., r. 220*l*., 3,125*l*.; the f. residence, "Homeleigh," Hayling-pk.-rd., r. 120*l*., 1,600*l*.; "St. Sidwell's," Main-rd., f., r. 50*l*., 900*l*.

JUNE 2.—By *P. Hodson*: 5 and 6, Ralph-st., Holloway, u.t. 76 yrs., g.r. 9*l*., 240*l*.—By *Deverell & Co.*: 6, Raveley-rd., Kentish Town, u.t. 77 yrs., g.r. 3*l*., r. 44*l*., 500*l*.; 23A, Bickerton-rd., u.t. 84 yrs., g.r. 6*l*., r. 40*l*., 395*l*.; 57, Bartholomew-rd., Camden-rd., u.t. 66 yrs., no g.r., 775*l*.; 15, Fitzroy-rd., Regent's-pk., u.t. 70 yrs., g.r. 8*l*., 540*l*.—By *Newbon & Co.*: "Bellevue House," Bellevue-rd., Southgate, f., r. 85*l*., 520*l*.; 63, Judd-st., Euston-rd., u.t. 14 yrs., g.r. 18*l*. 18s., r. 65*l*., 185*l*.—By *T. Wright*: 2, Surreyville-gardens, Barnes, u.t. 89 yrs., g.r. 10*l*., r. 63*l*., 680*l*.; 14, Studland-st., Hammersmith, u.t. 75 yrs., g.r. 5*l*., r. 39*l*., 290*l*.; 18, Acacia-rd., Sydenham, f., 305*l*.; 95, Goodrich-rd., Dulwich, u.t. 87 yrs., g.r. 6*l*., r. 26*l*., 165*l*.—By *Wilkinson, Son, & Welch* (at Brighton): "North House," Gloucester-pl., Brighton, f., 3,000*l*.

(*Contractions used in these lists.*—F.g.r. for freehold ground-rent; l.g.r. for leasehold ground-rent; i.g.r. for improved ground-rent; g.r. for ground-rent; r. for rent; f. for freehold; c. for copyhold; l. for leasehold; e.r. for estimated rental; u.t. for unexpired term; p.a. for per annum; yrs. for years; st. for street; rd. for road; sq. for square; pl. for place; ter. for terrace; cres. for crescent; yd. for yard, &c.)

PRICES CURRENT OF MATERIALS.

TIMBER.		
Greenheart, B.G. ton	9/0/0	0,0 0
Teak, E.I. .. load	9/10/0	15/0/0
Sequoia, U.S. ft. cu.	2/3	3/0
Ash, Canada load	3/10/0	4/0/0
Birch, do.	3/5/0	4/10/0
Elm, do.	3/10/0	4/15/0
Fir, Dantsic, &c.	1/10/0	3/10/0
Oak, do.	3/0/0	5/5/0
Canada	5/10/0	7/0/0
Pine, Canada red	2/10/0	3/10/0
Do. yellow	2/10/0	5/0/0
Lath, D'ntsic, fath	5/0/0	6/0/0
St. Petersburg	5/0/0	7/0/0
Deals, Finland 2nd & 1st std 100	8/0/0	9,10 0
Do. 4th & 3rd	7/0/0	8/0/0
Do. Riga	7/0/0	8/0/0
St. Petersburg, 1st yellow	11/0/0	14/10/0
Do. 2nd yellow	8/0/0	10/0/0
Do. white	7/10/0	10/10/0
Swedish	7/10/0	15/10/0
White Sea	8/0/0	17/10/0
Canada, Pine 1st	20/0/0	26/0/0
Do. do. 2nd	14/10/0	16/0/0
Do. do. 3rd, &c.	8/0/0	10/5/0
Do. Spruce, 1st	8/10/0	11/0/0
Do. do. 3rd & 2nd	6/15/0	8/0/0
New Brunswick	7/0/0	7/10/0
Battens, all kinds	3/10/0	15/10/0
Flooring Boards, sq., 1 in. prep. 1st	0/8/0	0/14/0
Do. 2nd	0/7/0	0/11/0
Other qualities	0/3/6	0/7/0
Cedar, Cuba ..ft.	/3½	/4½
Honduras, &c.	/3½	/4
Mahogany, Cuba	/4½	/6½
St. Domingo, cargo av	/4½	2/0
Mexican do. do	/4	/5
Tobasco do. do	/5½	/7
Honduras do.	/6½	/6½
Box, Turkey ton	4/0/0	13/0/0
Rose, Rio	10/0/0	20/0/0
Bahia	8/0/0	18/0/0
Satin, St. Domingo ft.	0/0 8	0/1/3

TIMBER (*continued*).		
Satin, Porto Rico	0/0/8	0/1/6
Walnut, Italian	0/0/3½	0/0/7
METALS.		
Iron—Pig, in Scotland ton	2/1/7	0/0/0
Bar, Welsh, in London	5/17/6	6/0/0
Do. do. at works in Wales	5/7/6	5/10/0
Do. Staffordshire, in London	6/5/0	6/15/0
Copper—British, cake and ingot	46/10/0	50/0/0
Best selected	51/0/0	51/10/0
Sheets, strong	56/0/0	59/0/0
Chili, bars	46/7/6	47/0/0
Yellow Metal lb.	0/0/6¼	0/0/6½
Lead—Pig, Spanish ton	10/15/0	10/18 3
English, com. brands	11/0/0	11/2/6
Sheet, English, 3 lbs. per sq. ft. and upwards	12/0/0	0/0/0
Pipe	12/10/0	0/0/0
Zinc—English sheet ton	25/15/0	26/0/0
Vieille Montagne	26/5/0	0/0/0
Tin—Straits	99/7/6	99/10/0
Australian	99 10/0	99/12/6
English Ingots	101/0/0	101/10/0
OILS.		
Linseed ton	18/0/0	18/2/6
Cocoanut, Cochin	24/0/0	0/0/0
Do. Ceylon	22/0/0	0/0/0
Palm, Lagos	22/5/0	22/10/0
Rapeseed, English pale	25/0/0	0/0/0
Do. brown	23/5/0	0/0/0
Cottonseed ref.	19/0/0	0/0/0
Oleine	21/10/0	22/10/0
Lubricating, U.S.	4/0/0	6/0/0
Do. refined	6/0/0	12 10/0
Tar—Stockholm barrel	0/18/0	1/0/0
Archangel	0/12/6	0/0/0

TENDERS.

[Communications for insertion under this heading should be addressed to "The Editor," and must reach us *not later than 12 noon on Thursdays.*]

BURWASH (Sussex).—For the erection of stabling, out-buildings, and greenhouse, for Mr. A. Jarvis. Mr. H. Percy Monckton, architect, 32, Walbrook, E.C.:—

S. Lusted & Son	£558 9 6	T. Dray*	£448 5 0
S. Piper	520 0 0		

* Accepted.

CHILWORTH (Surrey).—For erecting bakehouse and stable, Chilworth, Surrey, for Mr. R. Coe. Messrs. Peak & Lunn, architects, Guildford:—

H. Brown	£229 10 10	Parsons	£192 18 0
Etherington	202 16 0	Downes, Guildford*	180 0 0
Edwards	196 0 0		

* Accepted.

GATESHEAD.—For laying down and constructing sewerage works at Dunston, for the Local Board. Mr. John Dinsdale, surveyor, Whickham, Gateshead:—

Thos. Heaton	£317 1 10	John J. & J. Robson, 95, Osborn-road, Jesmond, Newcastle*	£233 1 6
Geo. Edward Simpson	297 14 3	William Adamson	226 13 2
Gustavus Bailey	290 10 1		
W. Scott	281 7 8		
Nicholson & Elliott	269 10 0		
Noble & Waugh	254 3 6		

* Accepted.

GUILDFORD.—For extension of Walnut Tree Close Roadway, Guildford, for the Earl of Onslow. Messrs. Peak & Lunn, architects, Guildford:—

Cunliffe	£365	W. Smith & Sons	£291
Robt. Smith	305	G. A. Franks, Guildford*	282

* Accepted.

GUILDFORD.—For alterations to 123, High-street, Guildford. Messrs. Peak & Lunn, architects, Guildford:—

May	£237 0 0	Billimore	£198 0 0
Strudwick	228 0 0	Higlett & Hammond	182 8 0
Johnson	209 0 0		

[All of Guildford.]

GUILDFORD.—For erecting new house, Edgeborough-road, Guildford, for Mr. M. Colebrook. Messrs. Peak & Lunn, architects, Guildford:—

Downes	£1,950 0 0	Brown Bros.	£1,791 7 6
Mitchell Bros.	1,927 0 0	Kingerlee	1,790 0 0
S. Ellis	1,872 0 0	Botterill & Son	1,743 0 0
R. Smith	1,849 0 0	W. Smith & Sons	1,685 0 0
May	1,810 0 0	R. Pink, Milford*	1,662 0 0
Higlett & Hammond	1,796 0 0		

* Accepted.

GUILDFORD.—For alterations at the Old Barracks, Guildford, for Mr. Geo. Trimmer. Messrs. Peak and Lunn, architects, Guildford:—

Higlett & Hammond	£526 0	Billimore	£463 0
Diamond & Sons	501 0	Ellis, Guildford*	449 0
Johnson	466 8		

* Accepted.

GUILDFORD.—For erecting dairy and stable buildings, Guildford, for Mr. Lymposs. Messrs. Peak & Lunn, architects, Guildford:—

Billimore	£276 0	R. Smith	£260 0
Johnson	273 15	Higlett & Hammond	258 0
Coker	260 0	Edwards, Shalford*	214 10

* Accepted.

GUILDFORD.—For erecting a pair of cottages, Ludlow-road, Guildford, for Mr. McWharrie. Messrs. Peak & Lunn, architects, Guildford:—

Strudwick	£464	Elliott	£375
Higlett & Hammond	427		

[All of Guildford.]

KEARSNEY (Kent).—For alterations and additions to house, for the Rev. J. W. Ewing. Mr. H. Percy Monckton, architect, 32, Walbrook, E.C.:—

W. T. Adcock	£196	T. J. Chamberlain	£180

LEATHERHEAD.—For erecting house and shop at Leatherhead, for Mr. John Symonds. Mr. F. Dibble, architect:—

Edser	£1,637 0	Lee	£1,549 10
Hamblin Bros.	1,630 0	Brown Bros.	1,473 0
Colls & Son	1,624 0	W. H. Batchelar	1,452 10

LONDON.—For works in connexion with the Distillery-lane sewer, Fulham, for the Vestry of the Parish of Fulham. Mr. J. P. Norrington, Surveyor:—

Towner & Wimpey	£387 0	J. Mears*	£315 0
R. Mullett	377 0	S. Saunders	232 10
G. Parry	325 0		

* Accepted.

LONDON.—For wood-paving, Harwood-road, Fulham, for the Vestry of the Parish of Fulham. Mr. J. P. Norrington, Surveyor:—

	Creosoted.	Plain Deal.
J. Biggs	£4,150 0	£3,800 0 0
Turner & Co.	4,090 0	3,750 0 0
Improved Wood-Paving Co.	4,013 0	3,824 0 0
E. Parry	3,880 0	3,500 0 0
Fell & Co.	3,518 11	3,288 16 6

LONDON.—For boundary wall, for the Vestry of the Parish of Fulham. Mr. J. P. Norrington, Surveyor:—

Keefe	£279 12 6	Parry	£259 0 0

LONDON.—For alterations at "The Crown" public-house, 179, Pancras-road, N.W., for Mr. H. F. Forster. Mr. W. Beckham Witherington, architect, 79, Mark-lane, E.C.:—

Larke & Sons	£664	Courtney & Fairbairn	£547
Spencer & Sons	597	Rowe Bros.	500

LONDON.—For the erection of new factories and offices at Messrs. Grindley & Co.'s tar and resin distillery, Poplar, E. Mr H. Percy Monckton, architect, 32, Walbrook, E.C.:—

W. B. Briant	£1,384 10	Harris & Wardrop*	£1,183 0
Harrison & Spooner	1,189 0		

* Accepted.

Ironwork.

Croggon & Co.	£506 10 8	F. Braby & Co.*	£469 10 0
Gospel Oak Co.	494 0 0		

* Accepted.

LONDON.—For the erection of a new police-station at Plumstead, for the Receiver for the Metropolitan Police District. Mr. John Butler, Architect, New Scotland-yard. Quantities by Mr. W. H. Thurgood:—

Hart Bros.	£4,825 0	Higgs & Hill	£4,394 0
Nightingale	4,795 0	Garlick & Horton	4,253 0
Holloway	4,606 0	Scrivener & Co.	4,237 0
Perry & Co.	4,695 0	Grover & Son	4,200 0
Gardener	4,507 18	Chappell	4,170 0
Ansell	4,600 0	Lathey Bros.	4,120 0
Willmott & Son	4,440 0		

LONDON.—For new drainage at Christchurch Workhouse, for the Guardians of the St. Saviour's Union, Surrey. Messrs. Jarvis & Son, architects:—

Charles Blyton	£1,472 0 0	Irwin Wallas	£921 0 0
Tom Turner, Limtd.	1,134 0 0	Johnson & Co.	873 0 0
F. C. Stokes & Co.	1,105 0 0	Pettitt & Axtell	859 0 0
George Newton	907 0 0	Joseph Cowper*	722 0 0
Matthew Brodie	966 7 8		

* Accepted.

LONDON.—For rebuilding No. 61, Cheapside, for the Aërated Bread Company, Limited. Mr. Geo. Edwards, architect, 62, Cannon-street:—

J. Knight	£2,670	Leslie & Co.	£2,243
C. Wall	2,435	Ward & Lamble	2,221
Martin Wells & Co.	2,488	T. Stevens	2,178
O. Craske	2,389	Stimpson & Co.	2,173
Colls & Son	2,270	Scharien & Co. (accepted)	2,118

LONDON.—For erecting and completing new warehouse and stables situate at Storehouse Wharf, Ratcliff, E. Mr. Chas. Dunch, architect. Quantities by Mr. J. F. Wesley, 294, Romford-road, Forest-gate:—

J. Greenwood	£5,098	Stimpson & Co.	£4,854
J. Morter	5,047	Brown, Son, & Bloomfield	4,820
B. E. Nightingale	4,985	Ashby & Horner	4,702
Harris & Wardrop	4,958	Munday & Sons	4,552
Lawrance & Son	4,936	Perry & Co.	4,529
Ashby Bros.	4,918	Scharien & Co. (accepted)	4,483

LONDON.—For the erection of proposed Rectory House, St. Olave's, Old Jewry. Mr. Ewan Christian, architect. Quantities by Mr. J. O. Abbott:—

Dove Bros.	£4,395	Ashby & Horner	4,100
Holloway Bros.	4,352	Holland & Hannen	3,990
Charteris	4,330	B. E. Nightingale	3,893
Cornish & Gaymer	4,272		

LONDON.—For the erection of proposed Albert Palace Mansions, for Mr. J. Halley. Mr. W. J. Chambers, architect:—

Martin Wells & Co.	£12,550	Holloway Bros.	10,914
Riggs & Hill	11,640	Oldeney & Sons	10,900
Garlick & Horton	11,464	Chappell	10,377
H. & E. Lea	11,218	Turtle & Appleton	10,384
Prestige & Co.	11,060	B. E. Nightingale	10,21
Kirk & Randall	11,044		

LONDON.—For several works in building new church-house, and restoration to the Church of St. Mary, Clapham. Mr. J. Francis Bentley, architect. Quantities by Mr. A. O. Gate:—

Colls & Sons	£20,584	Higgs & Hill	£19,893
Lawrence	20,280	Nightingale	19,300

LONDON.—For rebuilding No. 16, Newman-street, Oxford-street, W., for Dr. Kirby. Messrs. F. W. Porter & Hill, architects:—

Staines & Sons	£5,509	Allen & Sons	£4,920
Perkins	5,430	B. E. Nightingale	4,863
Woodward & Co.	5,420	Worsley	4,813
T. Rider & Son	5,347	W. Downs	4,800
A. & H. Bywaters	5,230	J. Morter	4,784
D. Charteris	5,185		

LONDON.—For superstructure and finishings in Great Trinity-lane, E.C., for Mr. W. M. Gray. Mr. H. Cowell Boyes, architect:—

Brown, Son, & Blomfield	£8,379	Colls & Sons	£7,691
J. Smith & Son	8,147	Grover & Son	7,680
B. E. Nightingale	8,122	Cubitt	7,620
Kilby & Gayford	7,934	Ashby & Horner	7,516
T. Boyce	7,890	Patman & Fotheringham	7,363
M. Patrick & Son	7,727	Gould & Brand	7,258

LONDON.—For re-instating, after fire, Brandram's Wharf, Rotherhithe, S.E., for the Liverpool, London, and Globe Insurance Company:—

Hunt	£3,468	Lee	£4,7[illegible]
Marsland	5,165	Smith & Son	4,[illegible]
Clarke & Bracey	4,933	Nightingale	4,5[illegible]

LONDON.—For proposed new drill hall, offices, &c., Clapham, for Lieutenant-Colonel A. J. Bowen, Commanding. Mr. [illegible] A. Briggs, architect:—

Harrison & [illegible]	£6,232	Turtle & Appleton	£5,872
Balaam Bros.	6,0[illegible]	Kirk and Randall	5,7[illegible]
H. L. Holloway	5,[illegible]	Nightingale	5,770
Holloway Bros.	5,[illegible]		

LONDON.—For iron escape-staircase at the Workhouse, Old Gravel-lane, E., for the Guardians of the parish of St. George-in-the-East. Messrs. Wilson, Son, & Aldwinckle, architects, 1, Victoria-street, Westminster, S.W.:—

T. & W. Cole	£[illegible] 0 0	The St. Pancras Iron Work Company*	£510 0 0
The Lion Foundry Company	621 17 6		
T. Potter & Sons, Ltd.	[illegible] 0 0		

* Accepted.

MAIDENHEAD.—For erecting St. Mary's new R.C. Schools, for the Rev. John Watson. Mr. F. [illegible] A. Walters, architect, 4, Great Queen-street, S.W. Quantities by Mr. John R. Lotting, 4, Great Queen-street, S.W.:—

Longley & Co.	£2,078	Cooper & [illegible]	£1,972
Gregory & Co.	2,014	Bottrill & Son, Reading*	1,767
[illegible] & Sons	1,998		

* Accepted.

PLASHET.—For painting and repairs at the Industrial Schools, Plashet, for the Guardians of the parish of St. George-in-the-East. Messrs. Wilson, Son, & Aldwinckle, architects, 1, Victoria-street, Westminster, S.W.:—

G. E. Todd	£676	T. White & Son*	£473
J. Holland	593		

* Accepted.

RIPLEY (Surrey).—For additions to business premises, Ripley, Surrey, for Mr. Richard Green. Messrs. Peak & Lunn, architects, Guildford:—

Whitbourn	£468 0 0	Johnson	£[illegible] 0 0
Pullen	440 0 0	Billimore	[illegible] 0 0
Young	440 0 0	Higlett & Hammond,* Guildford	353 0 0
Brown	424 0 0		

* Accepted.

SWANSEA.—For the erection of two shops and premises, Alexandra-road, Swansea, for Mr. Jacob Jenkins. Mr. H. C. Portsmouth, architect, Swansea. Quantities by the architect:—

David Jenkins	£1,795 0 0	Thos. Watkins & Co.	£1,[illegible] 0 0
Bennett Bros.	1,785 0 0	Lloyd Bros.	1,[illegible] 0 0
Thos. Richards	1,785 13 11	R. Billings	1,370 0 0

[All of Swansea.]

WALTHAMSTOW (Essex).—For the erection of a new police station at Walthamstow, for the Receiver for the Metropolitan Police District. Mr. John Butler, Architect. Quantities by Mr. W. H. Thurgood:—

Gardener	£5,003	Chappell	£4,6[illegible]
Hart Bros.	4,[illegible]	Grover & Son	4,6[illegible]
Riggs & Hill	4,[illegible]	Scrivener & Co.	4,[illegible]
Holloway	4,770	Lathey Bros.	4,5[illegible]
Wilmott & Sons	4,730	Morter	4,457
Garlick and Horton	4,6[illegible]		

WIMBORNE.—For alterations and additions to stabling, &c., at Canford Manor, Wimborne, Dorsetshire, for the Right Honourable Lord Wimborne. Messrs. Romaine-Walker & Tanner, architects:—

Cornish & Gaymer	£8,[illegible] 0 0	Lovett	£7,791 0 0
Boyce	7,[illegible] 10 0	McWilliam, Bournemouth	7,036 17 7
Holloway Bros.	7,[illegible] 10 0		
Nightingale	7,791 0 0		

The Builder Cathedral Series.

1891.

1. Canterbury	Jan. 3.	7. Salisbury	July
2. Lichfield	Feb. 7.	8. Bristol	Aug. 1.
3. St. Alban's	Mar. 7.	9. Norwich	Sept. 5.
4. Peterborough	April 4.	10. Rochester	Oct. 3.
5. Wells	May 2.	11. Lincoln	Nov. 7.
6. Exeter	June 6.	12. Gloucester	Dec. 5.

1892.

13. St. Paul's .. .. Jan. 2.

14. Hereford	Feb. 6.	20. Worcester	Aug. 6.
15. Chichester	Mar. 5.	21. Bangor } 22. St. Asaph }	Sept. 3.
16. Ely	April 2.	23. Winchester	Oct. 1.
17. Llandaff	May 7.	24. Truro	Nov. 5.
18. Oxford	June 4.	25. St. David's	Dec. 3.
19. Southwell	July 2.		

[Further arrangements will be duly announced.]

Post-free FOURPENCE HALFPENNY each, except Nos. 1, 2, 3, and 4, which are out of print; but the VIEW, PLAN, AND DESCRIPTION of CANTERBURY, LICHFIELD, ST. ALBAN'S, and PETERBOROUGH, have been re-printed, and they can now be had, price EIGHTPENCE each set; by post, 10d.

THE REREDOS, ST. PAUL'S.
Reprinted from "The Builder," January 28, 1888 (15 in. by 11½ in.), on stout paper, unfolded, for framing, 6d.; by post, 8d.

PORTFOLIOS,
for Preserving the Plates unfolded, 2s. 6d.; by post, 3s.

London: Office of "The Builder," 46, Catherine-street, W.C.

SUBSCRIBERS in LONDON and the SUBURBS, by prepaying at the Publishing Office, 19s. per annum (or 4s. 9d. per quarter), can ensure receiving "The Builder," by *Friday Morning's Post*.

TERMS OF SUBSCRIPTION.

"THE BUILDER" is supplied DIRECT from the Office to residents in any part of the United Kingdom at the rate of 19s. per annum PREPAID. To all parts of Europe, America, Australia, and New Zealand, 26s. per annum. To India, China, Ceylon, &c., 30s. per annum. Remittances payable to DOUGLAS FOURDRINIER, Publisher, No. 46, Catherine-street, W.C.

PUBLISHER'S NOTICES.

Registered Telegraphic Address, 'THE BUILDER,' LONDON.

CHARGES FOR ADVERTISEMENTS.

SITUATIONS VACANT, PARTNERSHIPS, APPRENTICESHIPS TRADE, AND GENERAL ADVERTISEMENTS.

Six lines (about fifty words) or under .... 4s. 6d.
Each additional line (about ten words) .... 0s. 6d.

Terms for Series of Trade Advertisements, also for Special Advertisements on front page, Competitions, Contracts, Sales by Auction, &c. may be obtained on application to the Publisher.

SITUATIONS WANTED.

FOUR Lines (about thirty words) or under .... 2s. 6d.
Each additional line (about ten words) .... 0s. 6d.

PREPAYMENT IS ABSOLUTELY NECESSARY.

*** Stamps must not be sent, but all small sums should be remitted by Cash in Registered Letter or by Money Order, payable at the Post-office, Covent-garden, W.C. to DOUGLAS FOURDRINIER, Publisher, Addressed to No. 46, Catherine-street, W.C.

Advertisements for the current week's issue must reach the Office before THREE o'clock p.m. on THURSDAY, but those intended for the front Page should be in by TWELVE noon on WEDNESDAY.

SPECIAL.—ALTERATIONS IN STANDING ADVERTISEMENTS or ORDERS TO DISCONTINUE same must reach the Office before TEN o'clock on WEDNESDAY mornings.

The Publisher cannot be responsible for DRAWINGS, TESTIMONIALS, &c. left at the Office in reply to Advertisements, and strongly recommends that of the latter COPIES ONLY should be sent.

PERSONS Advertising in "The Builder" may have *Replies addressed to the Office, 46, Catherine-street, Covent Garden, W.C., free of charge*. Letters will be forwarded if addressed envelopes are sent, together with sufficient stamps to cover the postage.

AN EDITION Printed on THIN PAPER, for FOREIGN and COLONIAL CIRCULATION, is issued every week.

Now ready.

READING CASES, { NINEPENCE EACH. By Post (carefully packed), 1s.

TO CORRESPONDENTS.

E. H. B. (thanks, not required).—Karnac (if the correspondent who writes on this subject from the "Science and Art Department" will kindly send us a legible signature, we will reply to his letter).—C. T. T.

All statements of facts, lists of tenders, &c., must be accompanied by the name and address of the sender, not necessarily for publication.

We are compelled to decline pointing out books and giving addresses.

NOTE.—The responsibility of signed articles, and papers read at public meetings, rests, of course, with the authors.

We cannot undertake to return rejected communications.

Letters or communications (beyond mere news-items) which have been duplicated for other Journals, are NOT DESIRED.

All communications regarding literary and artistic matter should be addressed to THE EDITOR; all communications relating to advertisements and other exclusively business matters should be addressed to THE PUBLISHER, and not to the Editor.

The Builder.

Vol. LXII. No. 2576. Saturday, June 18, 1892.

ILLUSTRATIONS.

The Queen's Tower, Imperial Institute.—Mr. T. E. Collcutt, F.R.I.B.A., Architect .... *Double-Page Ink-Photo.*
Design for Frieze.—By Mr. Arthur Gwatkin .... *Double-Page Ink-Photo.*
Wall Decoration, &c., Chapel of St. James, San Miniato.—Drawn by Mr. G. C. Horsley .... *Single-Page Ink-Photo.*
Pulpit, San Cesareo, Rome.—Drawn by Mr. G. C. Horsley .... *Single-Page Ink-Photo.*
Pewsham House, Wilts.—Mr. C. E. Ponting, F.S.A., Architect .... *Double-Page Ink-Photo.*

Blocks in Text.

Illustrations of Sand Used in Ancient Mortar .... Page 471
Ironwork in the South Kensington Museum 473
The House of the Tradescants and Elias Ashmole, Lambeth 474
The Tower Bridge: Diagrams Showing Erection of Footways .... Page 476
Plan of Early Basilica at Silchester 478
Diagrams in "Student's Column": Heating by Hot Water 485

CONTENTS.

Proposed Changes at the Institute 469
The Composition of Ancient Mortar 470
Notes 472
Architecture at the Royal Academy.—VIII. 475
The Tower Bridge 476
The Architectural Association's Visit to Harrow 477
Discovery of an Early Christian Basilica at Silchester 478
The Royal Institute of British Architects 478
The Institution of Civil Engineers 478
The London County Council 479
Central Tower, Imperial Institute 480
Design for a Frieze 480
Wall Decoration, Chapel of St. James, San Miniato 480
Pulpit, San Cesareo, Rome 480
Pewsham House, Wilts 480
Competitions 480
The Royal Commission on Metropolitan Water Supply 480
Municipal Engineering at Peterborough 482
Fourteenth and Fifteenth Century Screens 484
Lewisham Parish Church 484
Students Column.—Warming Buildings by Hot Water, XXV. 484
Surveyorships 485
General Building News 484
Foreign and Colonial 486
Stained Glass and Decoration 487
Miscellaneous 487
Capital and Labour 488
Meetings 488
Recent Patents 488
Some Recent Sales of Property 488

Proposed Changes at the Institute.

HE discussion of a proposed change in the mode of election of members occupied a very crowded meeting at the Institute last Monday, the report of which is by this time in the hands of members. The question arose in regard to the adoption of the report of the Special Committee which had been appointed to consider the present conditions of election as provided for under By-law No. 9. The By-law runs as follows:—

"Elections shall take place at Business meetings only, and, except as herein otherwise provided, by ballot, in which at least ten Fellows shall join; and the proportion of one black ball to six white shall exclude from election. At every election the meeting shall appoint two subscribing members as Scrutineers, and they shall superintend the ballot.

(*a*) In the case of candidates for the class of Fellows the election shall always be by ballot."

The two next sub-sections (c and *d*) provide for the occasions on which balloting may be dispensed with, the fourth states distinctly that no exception is allowed in the case of Fellows—

"(*d*) An Associate being eligible, and desiring to become a Fellow, must go through all the forms prescribed for the election of a Fellow."

The reasons for the appointment of the Committee were given in resolutions of the Annual General Meeting of May 4, 1891—

"That a Committee be appointed to inquire whether it is not possible under By-law 9 for a small body of members to exclude from the Fellowship of the Institute qualified persons approved by the Council, although a large majority of the members of the Institute approve of the election; and if so, to suggest steps for the amendment of the anomaly.

That it be left to the Council to appoint the Committee, such Committee to be a general one, and not exclusively composed of members of the Council."

The Committee consisted of Messrs. Frank T. Baggallay, James Brooks, Thomas M. Rickman, Lacy W. Ridge, R. Phené Spiers, Paul Waterhouse, Henry Cowell Boyes, Edwin T. Hall, Charles Henman, E. B. I'Anson, J. G. Finch Noyes, and Wm. Woodward, with Mr. Arthur Cates as Chairman. They have reported that the present system of the election of Fellows is open to abuse, that it gives facilities for a small minority of members to enforce conditions of membership which have not been recognised by the majority, and takes up valuable time at a business meeting, and that the fitness and qualification of candidates can only be investigated by a confidential body of limited numbers, such as the Council; but the pith of the report, the essential point of the position taken up, perhaps lies most particularly in the following paragraph:—

"That, in the opinion of your Committee, the Royal Institute, in accepting a Royal Charter, placed itself under an obligation to admit to membership, in the class appropriate to their standing, all British subjects who, being willing to join, are duly qualified, and are prepared to exercise their profession in an honourable manner, in accordance with the conditions of membership imposed by the Charter and By-laws; and that herein the Royal Institute differs from any body of limited membership or from any club formed for private and social association among its members."

The recommendations of the Committee in detail are in the hands of all members of the Institute; we need only observe here that they amount to this: That after some special provisions for investigation of the claims of every candidate for election as a Fellow, the election shall ultimately be made at the general meeting by show of hands, unless a requisition be presented, signed by not less than three subscribing members (the majority of whom must be Fellows), demanding that the votes of the whole number of members should be taken by voting-papers. This is the proposal referred to in the letter of "Suum Cuique" in our last number.

At the meeting on Monday it was moved by Mr. Cates and seconded by Mr. H. C. Boyes that the Report should be received and adopted, and that the Council be requested to prepare modifications of the By-law in accordance therewith, and take the steps necessary to obtain the desired alterations. After a long discussion, this was carried by a large majority, a majority probably larger than it would otherwise have been, owing to an anonymous printed whip which was sent round to all those members who were thought likely to support the new rule: we presume at least that this was the motive, as it was not sent to everyone. It seems to be unknown whence this circular emanated or by whose authority it was sent, but the sending round of a whip of this sort anonymously and on no one's specified responsibility is a piece of very bad taste on the part of whoever did it, and a line of proceeding which we hope will not be repeated, or will receive no attention if it is. If any members or any party in the Institute are desirous of supporting a special measure and of bringing together those whom they think likely to support it, let them do so openly and put their names to their document; then it is all fair and straightforward. In this case it was evidently circulated anonymously in the hope that those who received it would imagine it was official, and this is not a creditable piece of tactics.

We are not prepared to say that the proposed change is undesirable (nothing of course is final until the By-law in its new form is really passed), but we are of opinion that the resolution in favour of it was passed hurriedly at a meeting which was not duly representative of both sides of the question, and that the subject needs more consideration. The ostensible reason for the proposed change is that it is asserted that the ballot has been misused of late to keep out members who ought to have been elected, but who were obnoxious to a minority of persons who had combined accordingly to keep them out. One may say, as the senators did to Brabantio, "To vouch this, is no proof;" it is only common talk; nor, if we understand what is meant, are we by any means sure that those who are supposed to have been thus excluded were desirable members or would have been an honour to the Institute. Mr. Brydon, who, in a very able speech, moved that the consideration of the question should be postponed until the more important question of the conditions under which Fellows should be elected (to which we referred last week) had been settled, observed that out of two hundred and three ballots for Fellows during the past five years there had only been thirteen rejections, a proportion which does not look as if there had been any excessive use (or abuse) of the power of black-balling. Mr. Brydon objected also to the theory propounded in the report of the Committee, that every person who was a *bond-fide* architect and prepared to carry on his profession in accordance with the requirements of the Institute had a right to election; he wished that election should be an honour only to be obtained by those whose works had shown them to be worthy of it, and that "F.R.I.B.A." should carry with it the same kind of testimony to ability in architecture which "R.A." is supposed to give to the possessor of that title. Here he was obviously illogical, in comparing two institutions which are not on the same kind of basis. The Royal Academy is a body of limited numbers, whose members are supposed to represent the *élite* of the artists of the day, admitted to membership on the ground of their special distinction; we do not say that it does as a fact represent the best of the artists, but that is the principle on which elections are supposed to be made. The Institute of Architects is a body unlimited in numbers, and which, besides being concerned with "the advancement of the art of architecture," is a body representing the interests of the profession, and which has the duty of considering and to some extent adjudicating on disputed questions of professional practice. It is therefore quite a different class of institution from the Royal Academy, and the reasoning which applies to the one does not necessarily apply to the other. It is desirable that all who are admitted to membership of the Institute should have given evidence of a certain standard of knowledge and ability; but, within that restriction, the position taken in the committee's report, that all *bonâ fide* architects who comply with the requirements of the Charter and By-laws have a right to expect election if they desire it, is not unreasonable or illogical in substance, though it might perhaps have been more carefully and less comprehensively worded. It would hardly be right, at all events, that candidates who come under that category should lose election because a minority black-bailed them from reasons, for instance, of personal dislike. That would be a sufficient reason for blackballing a candidate for a club, which is a social institution; but an institute of professional men, as the committee rightly observes, is not the same thing as a club, and reasoning which applies to the one case does not necessarily apply to the other.

At the same time we very much doubt whether the ballot has been used against candidates at the Institute for no better reason than personal dislike; at all events there is nothing to prove it. As Mr. Belcher (who supported Mr. Brydon's motion) observed, there may have been very good reasons for the not very large amount of black-balling which seems to have caused so much consternation. We should be inclined to go further than Mr. Belcher, and to add that there have been elections (we will not say many) which had better not have been made, and cases where candidates who received a large percentage of adverse votes would have been black-balled three times over if all who voted had known as much about them as some did. There may be such a thing, too, as a sense of general policy and fitness of things, to influence voting, apart from any personal feeling. One speaker at the meeting, who is exceedingly fond of posing as Indignant Virtue, inveighed against the idea of black-balling a candidate because he was a member of a certain Society which shall be nameless, and asked if that was not personal motive. It is nothing of the kind, not necessarily at all events. It appears to us that those who have been active members of a Society which includes all kinds of hangers-on to the skirts of the profession among its members, and which in its corporate capacity has done all it can to injure the Institute, have earned about as good a right to be black-balled in Conduit-street as any man could wish for, and though the present policy of the directors of the Institute in this respect may be very Christian (in the sense of "if a man smite thee on the one cheek turn to him the other also"), it is a somewhat pusillanimous policy, and not the way to keep up the high standing and dignity of the central professional body.

The case between the system of election of Fellows as existing and the system which it is proposed to substitute for it may be summed up thus. At present the Council enter into inquiries as to a candidate and recommend him (if they are satisfied) for election; but the election depends on the vote of the general body. That appears to us to be on principle a very good and wholesome arrangement; the Council and the proposers of the candidate are supposed to do all they can to see that the candidate is a fit and proper person, but the possibly wider knowledge embodied in the general meeting has a chance of operating. The drawback to this is said to be that, according to the present arrangement of the ballot, a small minority have a power of excluding a man whom the Council wish to see elected, and moreover that this power of the minority may be and has been exercised from personal motives. We have seen no proof of the latter supposition, and we rather doubt it. If however, the minority has too great a power, it seems a simple matter to raise the proportion of "blacks" for excluding. On the other hand, we maintain that there may be and have been instances in which the adverse minority knew more or perhaps (even) were better judges than the Council. The best wisdom of the combined Institute cannot be supposed necessarily always to reside in the Council: figures and averages are against the probability of such a chance.

On the other hand the Council now propose to make arrangements for greater efficiency of inquiry into the status of any candidate, and having done so, merely to ask the general meeting to ratify their decision by a show of hands. That is now done in the election of Associates, but then Associates have passed a tolerably stringent and comprehensive examination, so that the cases are not parallel. This proposed regulation would no doubt do away with all opportunity for unfair frustrating of an election, but it has the disadvantage of constituting the Council a kind of irresponsible Vehm-Gericht with the election all in their own hands, the general body having only to take the candidates the Council give them. In a general way we have no doubt the Council would put forward the right men and keep back the wrong ones; but we do not know that members as a body will be altogether willing to part with their right of voting. And there are other features in the scheme open to objection. The Council propose, when a provincial candidate is not a member of his local Architectural Society, to enter into a confidential inquiry about him from that Society. As Mr. Pite very truly observed in the course of the discussion, is such a local Society likely to report fairly on a man who, from whatever cause, does not enrol himself with them? We certainly do not think such an arrangement would be popular with provincial architects, or would be likely to influence them towards wishing to be candidates for membership of the Institute.

On the whole therefore it appears to us that while the objections to the present system are not proved to have any ground in fact, and may be imaginary, the objections to the proposed system, so far as they go, are real and obvious, and that the minority who on Monday voted for postponing the matter for further consideration were in the right even on the merits of the case. But there would have been an additional reason for not coming to a resolution at the moment. The resolution which was to have been proposed by Mr. Chas. Barry, but which there was no time to go into, is really the key of the situation, and ought to have been considered first. The substance of this resolution, as we have already noted, was to the effect that for the future candidates for Fellowship should be Associates who had passed the examination qualifying them for Associateship, in order to avoid the present anomaly by which candidates can avoid the Associateship examination altogether by waiting till they have passed the prescribed age of thirty, except in cases in which the Council might see occasion to abrogate the rule in consequence of the known standing and ability of the candidate. This, of course, practically amounts to the institution of the examination test for Fellowship, except in special cases; but it is not very easy to see how the Institute can stop short of this after laying so much stress on the Associateship examination. The candidates who would come up for election under this arrangement, we may safely conclude, would not include all those who under the present *régime* would be put up for election by the Council. At all events, it seems pretty clear that if this subject is to be seriously discussed, it should be discussed and settled before, and not after the proposed alteration of by-law 9. For if it were settled in the affirmative, all necessity for the other rather complicated machinery would be at an end, and Fellows could be elected by show of hands on the same principle that Associates now are. It is possible that when the alteration in the by-law, to which the vote of Monday night must naturally lead, comes to be finally laid before the meeting, there may be a requisition for a general vote of all members by voting paper. And in that case it may be found that the majority of members will take the view which has been already suggested, that the question involved in Mr. Barry's resolution should be settled before any further legislation is entered on. That would certainly be the most logical course.

THE COMPOSITION OF ANCIENT MORTAR.

THE chemical composition of the mortar employed in the construction of our old castles, abbeys, and churches has hitherto not received that attention which the subject certainly deserves, and which, moreover, in these days of scientific investigation it might reasonably have expected.

To the antiquarian and the admirer of old buildings it must be interesting to know how far the permanence of a structure is due to the massive character of its proportions, and how far to the superior quality of the mortar employed, while to the architect and the builder the subject must be of the greatest importance and of practical use.

In the former papers the writer has drawn attention to the inquiry, and in this communication desires to add the results of eight complete analyses of average specimens of the mortar authentically obtained from the buildings named in the table at the close of this article; also some illustrations showing the character and appearance of the sand employed in the mortar. The original photos were taken from microscopic slides by Mr. Albert Ashe, chief assistant to the writer, and in each case the sand was separated from the mortar by the removal of the lime and other salts with the aid of hydrochloric acid.

It should be mentioned that the analyses in the table represent, as far as possible, the average composition of the mortar, and not that of isolated pieces,—the samples analysed being prepared from the ground-up portion of a great number of small particles taken from different parts of the ruins, except in Nos. 2 and 4. In arranging the results the total amount of lime is first stated separately, and then, for convenience of reference, the proportions assumed to be present as carbonate, caustic, sulphate, and otherwise combined are added at the bottom of the table.

The largest quantity of lime (34·46 per cent.) occurs in specimen No. 6 from Glastonbury Abbey, and the smallest quantity (10·59) in No. 7 from Glendalough Church (in ruins), County Wicklow. A large proportion of lime, however, does not necessarily imply that the mortar is of the highest quality; for

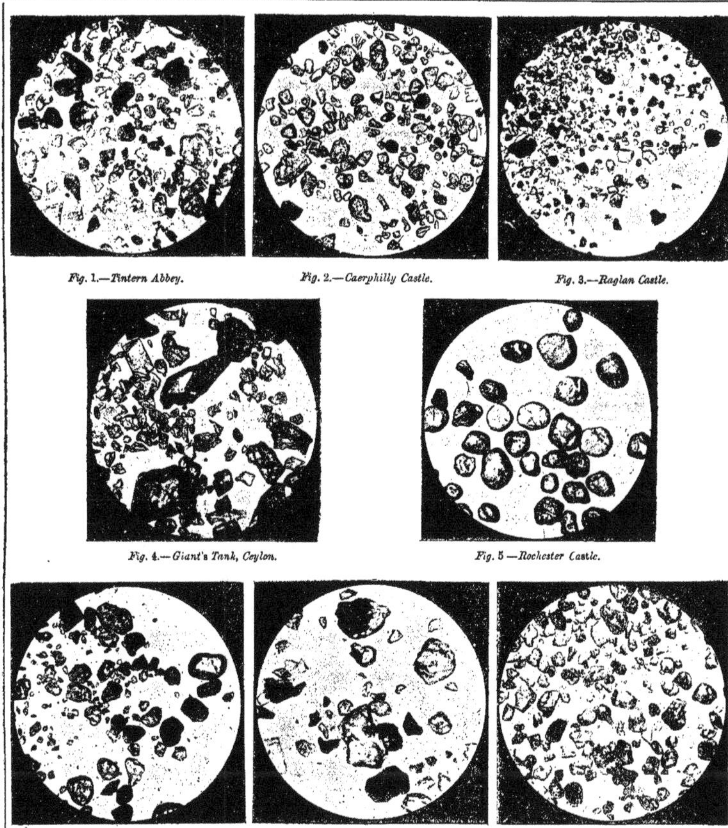

Fig. 1.—Tintern Abbey. *Fig. 2.—Caerphilly Castle.* *Fig. 3.—Raglan Castle.*

Fig. 4.—Giant's Tank, Ceylon. *Fig. 5.—Rochester Castle.*

Fig. 6.—Glastonbury Abbey. *Fig. 7.—Glendalough Church, Ireland.* *Fig. 8.—Corfe Castle.*

Illustrations of Sand used in Ancient Mortar.

instance, in specimen No. 2, from the leaning tower of Caerphilly Castle, Mon., there is only 13·39, yet the splendid character of the mortar is amply proved by the fact that it withstood the attempted destruction in the time of Charles II., and still remains in its leaning position.

Again, No. 4, representing the mortar used in the construction of the anicut of the Giant's Tank in Ceylon, more than 600 years ago, contains only 16·24 of lime; while in No. 1, from Tintern Abbey, on the banks of the Wye, the proportions of lime are 18·84. Both these specimens are certainly very superior in quality. Those who are acquainted with the beautiful ruins of the Abbey are aware that the four gable ends remain intact to the present day, and that this stability is not by any means due to the massive character of the walls; indeed, quite the contrary, for each gable carries a large window, so that the permanence of the gable is due to the tenacity of the mortar in holding the fragile structure together, thus withstanding the force and action of the combined effects of wind and water for so many centuries.

On the other hand, No. 5, from Rochester Castle, represents, on the whole, an inferior mortar, though the lime amounts to as much as 28·67 per cent., while that from Corfe Castle, No. 8, with 31·05 of lime, is, on the whole, decidedly a superior mortar.

Indeed, the present appearance of these two old castles is a good indication of the quality of the mortar used in their construction.

Of Rochester Castle, practically only the keep remains, and that still stands by virtue of its massiveness rather than by any excellence of its mortar.

Of Corfe Castle, the late George Godwin, in his prize essay "On the Nature and Properties of Concrete," tells us that Smeaton visited it, and found that its solidity did not consist in having been built with large hewn stones throughout, for the filling in of the walls consisted of rough rubble and fragments from the quarries, the interstices being entirely filled up with mortar poured in a fluid state, and the whole mass had in time become thoroughly cemented together. As a consequence, when the castle was destroyed in 1646, the walls when blown up did not fall into small pieces, but were split up into huge masses, which rolled bodily down into the moat below, where they remain still intact, the native builders finding it easier to obtain fresh stones from the nearest quarry rather than from these masses of cemented masonry.

As regards the actual proportions of lime, therefore, the requirements of good mortar would suggest that much more depends on the quality than on the quantity of the lime employed. Before passing on to other points, it may be remarked that, in all these analyses, the proportion of caustic lime is practically unappreciable, and that most of the lime exists now as carbonate; also, that after allowing for the lime as sulphate, there still remains an excess of lime which is probably present in combination with gelatinous silica and alumina, — as existing in Portland cement.

The proportion of magnesia is very small in all these eight specimens, the amount being less than ½ per cent., except in that from Caerphilly Castle, where we find 1·87. It is interesting to bear this in mind after what has been written in reference to the presence of magnesia in some Portland cement used in the Aberdeen harbour works.

The proportions of oxide of iron and alumina are higher in the specimens of good mortar, such as Nos. 2, 6, 4, 1, and 8, than in Nos. 5 and 7, which represent the inferior quality, while No. 3 may be regarded as of medium quality, and has 1·35 oxide of iron and ·80 alumina.

Sulphuric acid is 1·37 in No. 1 and ·26 in No. 8, both specimens being regarded as of superior quality.

Chlorine varies considerably, the higher quantities being, doubtless, due to local circumstances, such as proximity to the sea or tidal rivers, but the variations are of no consequence in this particular inquiry.

The relative amount, however, of gelatinous silica soluble in a 10 per cent. solution of caustic soda is a point of considerable importance in determining the quality of a mortar. For the information of other investigators, it may be here stated that two grammes of the finely-ground mortar were first evaporated with HCl. acid to complete dryness in a water bath, the insoluble residue was then treated with dilute hydrochloric acid, and the total insoluble matters filtered off, burned, and weighed. This was then boiled for half an hour with 100cc. of a 10 per cent. solution of caustic soda, which dissolves all the gelatinous or amorphous silica, leaving the crystalline and coarser sand unaffected, and if this latter be weighed the difference between the original weight gives the amount of so-called soluble silica. It is in this form that most of the silica exists in Portland cement, the actual figures being from 20 to 22 per cent.

It will be noticed that this gelatinous silica is highest in specimen No. 2, namely, 9·85, which is very nearly half as much as occurs in the best Portland cement.

No. 8 comes next, with 7·50; then No. 4, with 7·10; and No. 1, with 6·20; also No. 6, with 6·10; afterwards No. 3, with 4·10; No. 7, with 3·90; and last, No. 5, with only 1·60 per cent.

In the analysis of limestone intended for making lime for building purposes, it would be desirable to specially determine the amount of gelatinous silica present,—inasmuch as the best building limes no doubt possess to a considerable extent the properties of a cement.

We now come to the proportions of sand, which form the subject of the illustrations, and it will be noticed how very much they vary in quantity, in size, and general character, as observed through a microscope. No. 7 specimen contains 72·08, while No. 6 contains only 13·70.

Specimens 1 and 2 contain respectively 51·67 and 49·12; No. 4 has a little more, 55·45; while No. 5 has a little less, 45·62; then comes No. 3, with 34·78; and No. 8, with 29·51 per cent.

When we examine the size and character of the sand, the illustrations are particularly useful.

Fig. 5 is specially interesting, showing the smooth, rounded nature of the sand in the mortar from Rochester Castle; while in figs. 2 and 4 the variation in size of the particles, as well as the much sharper edges, are easily seen. In Raglan Castle, fig. 3, the granules are very small; while, in Glastonbury Abbey, fig. 6, and Glendalough Church, fig. 7, the particles are much larger, and present a more rounded appearance. The same power of magnifying was observed in all the specimens, and the sand was specially removed from the mortar without any grinding-up of the sample, in order to preserve the original appearance as far as possible.

Having now briefly reviewed the characteristics of the eight specimens, what are the practical conclusions to be drawn from these analyses?

1. That the actual amount of lime present in a mortar may vary very considerably, but that within certain limits the *quality* of the lime is of as great importance as the quantity,—indeed, a smaller quantity of well-prepared good lime is much more effectual than a larger quantity of a badly-prepared or naturally inferior lime.

2. That the proportions of sand may also vary considerably, even in really good mortar, and that while it is always desirable that it should be rough, irregular in size, and with sharp edges, rather than be smooth and round, still that, on the whole, the quality of the sand is not of so much importance as the quality of the lime.

3. That the presence of oxide of iron and alumina in a form readily combined with silica is not to be objected to in good building lime, indeed, that the purest limestones are by no means the best for making superior lime for building purposes.

4. That the higher the proportion of amo phous or gelatinous silica soluble in alka the better the quality of the mortar, and, this kind of silica is associated originally wi the lime, rather than with the sand, becomes of the greatest importance that t character and composition of the lime i tended to be used should be fully inquire into; and the best possible quality in t neighbourhood always selected by t architect and used by the builder.

JOHN HUGHES, F.C S.

Analyses of Ancient Mortar.

	No. 1. Tintern Abbey.	No. 2. Caerphilly Castle.	No. 3. Raglan Castle.	No. 4. Giant's Tank, Ceylon.	No. 5. Rochester Castle.	No. 6. Glastonbury Abbey.	No. 7. Glendalough Church, Ireland.	No. 8. Corfe Castle.
Probable date of erection, about A.D.	1269.	1200.	1290.	1250.	1088.	1240.	Not known.	1000.
Water (lost at 212° F)	1·72	2·60	1 36	1·18	·36	4·90	·55	2·42
Combined water	3·98	7 73	4·06	2·66	1·48	4·94	2·92	4 02
Lime **	18 84	13·49	30·68	16 24	28·07	36·46	10 59	31·05
Magnesia	·32	1 87	·25	·38	·18	·45	·43	·28
Potash	·02	·22	·15	·20	·16	·33	·25	·20
Soda	·27	·29	·45	·17	·24	1 18	·13	·15
Oxide of iron	1·99	3·61	1·35	2 20	·40	3 00	1·58	·95
Alumina	1·36	1·34	·80	2·65	·30	1·45	·71	·15
Sulphuric acid	1·37	·34	·86	·58	·29	·59	·32	·26
Carbonic acid*	12·13	9·53	21·01	11·11	20 00	25·06	6·40	22 86
Chlorine	·13	·01	·15	trace.	·10	·88	·14	·65
Gelatinous silica, soluble in alkali	6·20	9·85	4·10	7 10	1·60	6·10	3·90	7·50
Insoluble matters (sand)	51·67	49 12	34 78	55·45	45 02	13 70	72 08	29 51
	100·00	100 00	100·00	100·00	100 00	100·00	100·00	100·00
* Equal to carbonate of lime	27·56	21·66	47·75	25·25	46 81	56·05	14 54	51 95
** Lime present as carbonate	15·43	12·13	26·74	14 14	26·21	31·69	8·14	29·09
** Lime present as caustic	·78	·56	·84	·50	·56	·56	·84	·28
** Lime present as sulphate	·95	·23	·60	·40	·20	·02	·22	·18
** Lime present as silicate and otherwise combined	2·18	·57	2 50	1·14	1·70	3 39	1·39	1·50
	18 84	13 49	30 68	16 24	28 07	36·46	10·59	31·05

NOTES.

A LARGE and influential meetin was held at Bristol on Monda last to consider the question c raising funds for the restoratio of the Cathedral. The Bishop of the Dioces presided, and in the course of the pr ceedings a report from Mr. Pearson on th state of the Cathedral was read. Mr. Pea son reports the tower to be in a sound cond tion with the exception of the dilapidation c the exterior surface of the masonry, whic could be refaced by taking out two o three stones at a time, retaining all th old ones that were good, except in th upper part of the tower, where the pier between the openings are so thin that i would be necessary to take this part dow and rebuild it. The Lady Chapel required considerable amount of repair, in renewal o parapets and pinnacles and repair of externa walling generally, and internally the wester archway into the north transept required t be opened out and restored to its origina condition, with Purbeck shafts, caps, vases, &c The floor should be taken up and a concret bed formed under it and the old paving relaid In regard to the re-arrangement of the choi we extract the following memoranda fron Mr. Pearson's report as printed in the *Bristo Times and Mirror*:—

"The choir still retains the arrangement neces sitated when the nave was wanting, but whic arrangement is now wholly inappropriate. Wan of space led to the eastern Lady Chapel being in cluded in the choir, with the altar-table against it eastern wall, and the stalls occupying a place so fa eastward as to leave practically no space for th especial functions of a cathedral, such as ordina tions and other gatherings of the clergy. The stall are of simple character, with canopies devoid o tabernacle work and less enriched than those o many a parish church; they were reconstructed som years ago, the old misereres and sundry othe interesting fragments of ancient carving being re used. Although it is impossible not to feel certain amount of regret that this Cathedral should not possess more important stalls; still, as prac tically reproducing the ancient treatment and pre serving to some extent the ancient carvings, m feeling is that they might be preserved, and tak their proper place just east of the crossing. . . . It will be found necessary to remove the organ on bay westward, in order to bring the organist int direct communication with the choir. As a part c this general scheme of re-arrangement, the hol table will be moved to what was obviously the positio intended for it, *i.e.*, one bay west of the Lady chapel It should be new and much larger and more elevate than the existing altar table, which is so small an is raised so little above the general level of th cathedral that it adds no dignity to the east enc The removal of the altar table will render necessar the erection of a screen to separate it from th eastern part of the cathedral; this screen should b of sufficient height to give importance to the alta and its surroundings, and should be of stone, enriche with sculpture. The choir will need side-screens these might be of metal, excepting those enclosing th sanctuary, which should be of stone. Sedilia and cre dence, also in stone, might be attached to these, wit a seat for the Bishop on the north side. A weste screen of open character would mark the entranc to the choir. The floor of the choir is at preser on the same level as that of the nave, and the wan of elevation is severely felt. I propose to raise th choir three steps at its western end, and by th addition of other steps eastward, to raise the alta table nine steps above the nave floor. The floor c the choir should be of marble, using up the ol marble squares now in the choir. The steps, too should be of marble. A new and sufficiently digni fied Bishop's throne is especially required."

A resolution in favour of the scheme o restoration, as proposed by Mr. Pearson was carried nearly unanimously.

THE second *soirée* of the Royal Society was held in the rooms at Burlington House on Wednesday last, the 15th inst., when the company was received by Lord and Lady Kelvin. It is generally the case that many of the exhibits at the second *soirée* have already been shown at the first, but this year there were a great number of new things, though but few were of such a character as would interest our readers. Amongst these few we may mention an instrument for drawing parabolas, exhibited by Mr. R. Inwards, which consists of a species of link-work, so contrived that a pencil attached to one part of it is always equidistant from a pivot representing the focus of the parabola, and from a steel straight edge representing its directrix. Mr. F. C. Penrose showed some water-colour drawings of Greek temples, &c., at Athens, as they appeared in 1847, illustrative of his investigations on the Orientation of ancient Greek Temples. There were eight drawings in all,—the Propylæa, the Temple of Wingless Victory seen from the Propylæa, the Parthenon seen from the north-west, sketch of part of the west front of the Parthenon, the east front of the Parthenon, the north portico of the Erechtheum, the Theseum,—east portico, and the Temple of Jupiter Olympius seen from the north-east. Mr. W. M. Flinders Petrie exhibited facsimile drawings from the pavement of the Palace of Chuenaten, at Tell-el-Amarna (1400 B.C.), which pavement was discovered by him during excavations last winter. It is the only one of the kind known in Egypt, and is especially remarkable for the realistic treatment of the plants depicted, not being in the conventional style familiar in ordinary Egyptian art. A number of additional proof plates to the first memoir of the Archæological Survey of Egypt were shown by Mr. Percy E. Newberry, including drawings of the tombs of Chnemhotep I. and II., and of Ameni, unfinished lotus-bud column, &c., from Beni Hasan. We learn that four coloured "Goupil" plates will accompany each of the three volumes Mr. Newberry has in hand, in addition to the ordinary illustrations. There were a number of drawings representing wall-paintings, also from Beni Hasan tombs, which furnish us with the fullest, and by far the most curious, representations we possess of the daily life of the ancient Egyptians of the Middle Kingdom. There is hardly an incident in ordinary life that is not here delineated. Mr. W. Crookes showed an apparatus for producing the flame of burning nitrogen, proving that nitrogen is a combustible gas. There were a number of other electrical and natural history objects on view, but they were not such as to call for special comment.

AS will be seen by our report of the proceedings at the meeting of the London County Council on Tuesday, both Vauxhall and Lambeth Bridges are to be rebuilt in the course of the next few years. The former has quite outgrown its capacity to serve the traffic passing over it, especially since the new Vauxhall station of the London and South-Western Railway has been opened. Its numerous piers are also highly obstructive to the river traffic, and are not over-secure, the foundations being subject to a heavy scour at certain states of the tide. Lambeth Bridge it is proposed to rebuild first, owing to its greater insecurity. We shall not be sorry to see the last of this bridge, which is one of the ugliest on the river. That the creation of such an engineering commonplace should ever have been permitted at a spot just above the Houses of Parliament was not creditable to the authorities of that day, and we are not sorry that it has turned out to be a failure, although erected comparatively speaking only a few years ago. We trust that the London County Council will model their new bridges on such types as London Bridge and the new Putney Bridge, and not perpetrate a repetition of such architectural monstrosities as Blackfriars or (still worse) Hammersmith Bridge.

A REMARKABLE circumstance connected with the promotion of the Lancashire, Derbyshire, and East-Coast Railway, is the complete absence of anything like serious opposition to the scheme. It can hardly have been that a line upwards of 150 miles in length was looked upon as "not worth powder and shot," and if some of our existing lines had been as considerately dealt with, and had required as little ammunition of this sort, for clearing away obstacles at the preliminary stages of their existence, the shareholders would have been in a far better position than they are. Years ago it was estimated that the money *wasted* on the formation of railways in this country amounted to at least 12,000,000*l*. The absence of opposition to the new line, will, it is supposed, allow of its being constructed at a total cost of about 43,000*l*. per mile,—a lower figure than that for most similar undertakings. The average for the United Kingdom is nearly 45,000*l*. per mile,—a striking contrast to the cost of colonial lines, which range from 6,866*l*. for South Australia, to 14,559*l*. for New South Wales. Of course there are certain easy sections of our own lines which were equally low; the York and Scarborough, for instance, which was constructed at a cost of 6,000*l*. per mile, and the Northampton and Peterborough branch of the London and North-Western, forty-seven miles in length, the total cost of which was 429,449*l*. The new east and west line will be more expensive from an engineering point of view, as thirteen tunnels and nine viaducts will be required. There is another east and west scheme, by-the-bye, that we hear nothing about, although the connecting links have for some time been completed. There is now direct cross-country communication between the Midland main line at Bedford aud their west branch at Broome (just above Evesham), over the East and West Junction lines *viâ* Olney, Towcester, and Stratford-on-Avon. The last section was completed a year or more since, and a regular service of goods traffic has been passing over the new route for months past, but it has not yet found a place in "Bradshaw."

A VERY sensible and practical proposal was made by Sir Alfred Hickman at the meeting at the Board of Trade on Tuesday regarding the new railway rates. The suggestion was that the railway companies should publish, at a moderate cost, the distances between all their stations, to enable any one to calculate the legal rates between any two points without difficulty. Quite recently we noticed that the Educational Society of Bombay had just published a set of tables giving the shortest distance between any two railway-stations in India; and, upon inquiry, failed to find anything obtainable giving similar information with regard to this country. The fact of this demand being made, affords one more proof of the probable value that will attach to the new schedules of maximum rates, as compared with the antiquated jargon of the Acts which they supersede. Under the old *régime* a knowledge of the distances from station to station was of very little benefit to a trader, and very little more, perhaps, even to the railway companies' rate officials. Otherwise this information would have been pressed for and obtained long ago, but it was of no use whatever in the absence of a clearly defined classification and schedule. In the future, however, all this will be very different. There is but little doubt, judging from the remarks made at Tuesday's conference, that the railway companies will be allowed an extension of time for the publication of their new rates,—*i.e.*, from August 1 next to January 1—and it would be very convenient if the required distance tables could be compiled during the interval.

WE are very glad to see that, as reported in another column, the threatened extensive strike in the building trades of London has been averted, and that, as we ventured to hope would be the case, conciliatory councils prevailed on both sides. Let us hope that we shall go on smoothly now for some time to come.

THE various examples of wrought and other ironwork at South Kensington Museum have recently been re-arranged in an upper gallery between the two architectural courts. The fine gates from Hampton Court, and cases containing specimens of locks, keys, and bolts, chiefly foreign, are arranged down the centre, and on the balconies, and against the walls on either side, brackets, grilles, candlesticks, some domestic utensils, and one or two specimens of English ecclesiastical work. Of these latter the most interesting are the old hinges of late twelfth-century work from the door which formerly led from the south transept to the slype at St. Alban's Abbey. This slype has now been removed, and we must be thankful, under the circumstances, that so interesting a relic has been preserved. There is also a portion of a hearse of fifteenth-century date from Snarford Church, Lincolnshire, and a screen of hammered iron from St. John's Church, Frome, but their proper place is distinctly in their several churches. While it is always good to see ancient work preserved in our national collection, it is still more important for objects of local interest such as these to be kept in the places to which they belong, and for which they have been designed. They are meaningless where they are, and the local interest which would otherwise surround them is gone. Amongst the other

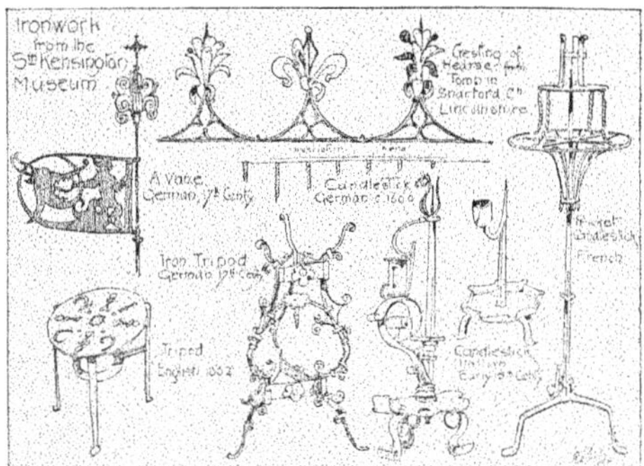

examples of interest are two gondola prows some good Italian grilles, several French and German candlesticks, a delicately-worked iron tripod in one of the centre cases, and another —English—dated 1662. There is also a quaint vane of German work, and two fine wrought-iron crosses. Some of the foregoing we herewith illustrate.

THE nights of June are shorter than those of any other month; and, therefore, the new departure in lighting omnibuses will not, for some months to come, be put to any severe test. If, however, the Lithanode and General Electric Company and Messrs. Willing are able to accomplish the half of what they promise, their prudence in selecting the present time for their earlier installations is superfluous. We wish, and anticipate, all success to the undertaking. The problem of devising a battery of reasonable weight and low resistance, which shall not be interfered with by the jolting of an omnibus, does not seem insuperable, and Messrs. Willing and the Lithanode Company appear to have solved it most successfully. A battery of five cells, weighing only 3 lbs. apiece, maintaining an e.m.f. of 10 volts for fifteen or twenty hours while a current of 1 ampère is being taken from it, is certainly something to be proud of; and the efficiency of the 5 c.-p. lamp is also high, being 2 watts per candle. But even if the cell in practice is only used for twelve hours, and the lamp fall for part of that time to 4 c.-p., few people will be found to grumble, and all will be glad to get rid of the greasy, smoky oil or the flickering candle which is the rule in these not too luxurious conveyances. The first installation of the light will be with the Road Car Company's omnibuses. The L.G.O.C. will, doubtless, also take it up as soon as it has been proved a success.

ON Saturday last, the 11th inst., several members of the Junior Engineering Society availed themselves of an invitation to visit the new works of the Patent Victoria Stone Company at Stratford Market Station, E. They were conducted over the premises by Mr. Harry Rogers, the secretary and manager. The shed in which the washed, crushed granite is stored as it arrives from the Groby quarries was first visited. Near by were seen the machines designed for incorporating the crushed granite with Portland cement; the water used in the process is automatically gauged. A considerable part of the company's business consists of the manufacture of paving-stones, and this section naturally attracted the greatest share of attention. After being well mixed up, the concrete for making the stones is laid in slab moulds lined with zinc. The secretary and manager explained that the granitic concrete slabs, after setting, are turned out of the moulds, and steeped for about ten days in a solution of silicate of soda, by which process they become indurated. Considerable space is occupied by the large "silica-tanks," in which the slabs are immersed. The silicate of soda solution is made by boiling Farnham stone (quarried in beds of Upper Greensand age, at Farnham, in Surrey) with 70 per cent. caustic soda, previously made into a solution with water; the silica of the stone dissolves, and the solution is diluted for use to the required strength. The slabs when taken out of the solution are scoured with water and stacked in yards, where they are kept for some months before being sent away from the works. A large number of stair-treads, landings, and troughs were also observed in process of manufacture on Saturday; and several small tests as to the strength of the material were carried out. The visit concluded with the inspection of the cement store and engine, boiler, and solution houses, and after the usual votes of thanks, the members dispersed.

MR. C. DRURY E. FORTNUM'S second magnificent gift, this time in money as well as in kind, to Oxford University, as accepted in Convocation on the 7th instant, will result in the erection of a new Ashmolean Museum, on, we presume, the ground near to the Taylor Building, and in the conversion of the existing museum into an extension, with a capacity, it is expected, of 100,000 books, of the Bodleian. The last-named was re-constructed in 1610 by Thomas Holt, of York, architect, for Sir Thomas Bodley, who further bequeathed funds for its enlargement with a third story, begun in 1613, the year of his death: the library had been founded nearly two hundred years earlier, by Humphrey, Duke of Gloucester. The Schools, built here in or about 1578, having been gradually absorbed by the library, are now replaced by the building planned and designed by Mr. T. G. Jackson, of which we published illustrations on August 9, 1890. The Ashmolean was built under, we believe, Wren's superintendence, for the Tradescant and Ashmole collections formerly housed in "Tradescant's Ark," South Lambeth, of which the site and once-famed botanical garden (four acres) were sold eleven years ago for 16,150*l.*, and converted into building lots.* Elias Ashmole's own collection consisted mainly of manuscripts and coins, but he lost part of them, together with his library of books, through a fire in the Temple, London. The contents of the Ashmolean, including the Arundel marbles, and the Etruscan antiquities presented by Chevalier Castellani, have lately been re-arranged. In 1888 Mr. Fortnum made a gift to the Museum of a considerable portion of his own collection,—gathered to exemplify the progress of art work from a remote period to the decline of the Renaissance, and stored in his residence at Stanmore. In a pamphlet published at Oxford in 1881, the late Rev. Greville J. Chester draws a heavy and detailed indictment against the University for ill treatment of the treasures in its keeping. There were grounds for his charge, albeit somewhat warmly expressed; but of late years the authorities, whose pecuniary resources in this direction are limited, have done much to dissipate the reproach. In our "Note" of October 25, 1890, upon the opening of the New Cast Museum, we referred to the signal advantages now to be enjoyed at Oxford by students of archæology.

The House of the Tradescants (and afterwards of Elias Ashmole), Lambeth; as it appeared circa 1810. From the view in the "Fauntleroy" Pennant, Soane Museum.

ON the 27th instant will be opened to the public, St. Anne's, Soho, churchyard, which is being laid out as a recreation ground by the Metropolitan Public Gardens Association, a faculty having been granted, in terms of the Open Spaces Act, by Dr. Tristram, Q.C., Chancellor of London. The church can be best seen from Wardour- and Dean-streets. It was finished in 1686, according to a stone on the west face, north side, of the tower. On the south side is Hazlitt's tombstone; he died September 18, 1830; and, just above it, the monument, carrying an urn, that Walpole set up and inscribed in memory of Theodore, King of Corsica (and near to his grave), who died in the parish on December 11, 1756, a few days after his release from King's Bench prison. John Wright, an oilman in Compton-street, saved the King's remains from a pauper's burial. Here, too, was buried (1816) David Williams, founder of the Literary Fund that originated in a meeting, whereat Benjamin Franklin was present, of a small club at the Prince of Wales's tavern in Conduit-street, 1773. St. Anne's parish had been taken out of St. Martin's in 1678. Standing in what had been Kemp's-field, the church has a good interior and a fine east window. The original spire, shown in B. Cole's plate for Maitland's "History of London," 1756, consisted of a cupola carrying an octagonal lantern, with a heavy finial over it, and was removed in June, 1800. The present spire is surmounted with a singular spherical-shaped dial-piece. S. P. Cockerell, architect, rebuilt the tower about ninety years ago, in terms of an Act to that intent, of May 28, 1802. Malcolm, in vol. ii. of his "Londinium Redivivum," 1803, refers to the "monstrous copper globe;" in the "Dictionary of National Biography," the "ugly tower" is ascribed to Henry Hakewill, but is not cited under his name in the "Dictionary of Architecture." We read in Mackeson's "Guide" that Wren completed the church, which has been lately restored by Sir A. W. Blomfield. William Croft was the first organist; the later organ, by John Gray the elder, was rebuilt by Walker about twenty-five years since. In Dean-street, the home of Mrs. Thrale (Piozzi) when, as a girl, she came to the town, was "Jack's" coffee-house, since "Walker's" hotel. At the dispersal on April 19, 1888, of the late George Godwin's collection of historical chairs, with other relics, was bought, for two guineas and a half, "Dr. Johnson's banner-screen, from Jack's coffee-house, Dean-street, Soho."

* See also the *Builder* of January 8, 1881; and Smith's "Antiquities of London and its Environs." There is a view of the house in the "Fauntleroy" Pennant, Soane Museum.

WE learn that Mr. W. M. Flinders Petrie will most probably be appointed to the Chair of Egyptology recently founded by the late Miss Amelia B. Edwards, in University College. The foundation states that no official in the British Museum, and no one over forty years of age, shall be eligible for the post.

THE fourth part of Mr. Gotch's series of illustrations of "Architecture of the Renaissance in England"* is just issued, and includes illustrations and description of Cranborne Manor House, Canons Ashby, and other old places of much interest. As we have before said, we propose to consider the work more in detail when all the six parts have appeared.

* B. T. Batsford.

AT the Fine Art Society's Gallery is to be seen Mr. Wyllie's large and very fine and interesting painting of the battle of Trafalgar, the most important work which this fine painter of marine subjects has produced. Near the centre of the picture the *Victory* is prominent, with the Ftench ship *Redoubtable* locked to her by an entanglement in the rigging. Other historical ships are shown in the picture, which has been carefully studied from available records. The day was a sunny day with little wind, but a long heavy swell on the water, one can almost see the roll of the ships on it; the sea was even more finely given perhaps, in a small painting, perhaps a study for this, which the artist exhibited, if we remember right, at the Royal Academy a year or two ago. This painting of a great event in modern English history is well worth a visit. It is a curious coincidence that the room in which it is exhibited formed part of a house in which Nelson once lived. At the same galleries are also to be seen a collection of water-colour drawings of "Devonshire" by Mr. Henry B. Wimbush, a little too much of the "pretty vignette" order, but interesting nevertheless; and a small collection of "Early English Water-Colour Drawings," including examples of Barret, Morland, Gainsborough, Reynolds, F. Wheatley, Hamilton, Cipriani, and others. Among them is an interesting drawing by Kneller, on brown paper, the lights touched with white, called a portrait group, and showing Kneller's method of making studies for his pictures.

THE collection of small paintings of Venice by Mr. Mortimer Menpes, at Messrs. Dowdeswell's gallery, is perhaps the best thing this artist has done. The small studies of bits of Venice architecture are painted with great force and truth of colour, and the larger view of the façade of St. Mark's under late afternoon light is a remarkably real and forcible piece of architectural painting. Among the small works specially noticeable are "A Vista" (7); "Santa Maria, della Salute" (16); "A Family Wash" (25), the white clothes hung out to dry contrasting with the sunlit walls behind; and "Humble Quarters" (28), the lower portion of an old crumbly marble palace.

THE Ameer of Bokhara is to be added, apparently, to the list of energetic sanitary reformers. He has ordered a cleansing of the city, described by the *Times'* correspondent as a nursery of disease and infection; and on hearing that there was a revolt against this order on the part of the dirt-loving inhabitants, "His Highness at once commanded the execution of every subject who did not carry out the new sanitary regulations within a week." We ought to have the Ameer of Bokhara to deal with the landlords of insanitary property in London.

ARCHITECTURE AT THE ROYAL ACADEMY.—VIII.

(CONCLUDING NOTICE.)

1,817; "Pewsham House, Wilts;" Mr. C. E. Ponting. This drawing is published in the present number. It appears a very pleasing reminiscence of the style of the seventeenth century English country house, to which has been added the formal garden proper to the period, but not with entire copyism of old details. In the period to which the architecture of the house belongs, the garden would have been bordered by alternately clipped pyramids and little shock-headed round bushes; the less formally trimmed trees and the alternate vases are an improvement on this.

1,818; "Baroda Museum: Pavilion;" Mr. R. F. Chisholm. One of Mr. Chisholm's applications of the Hindu style to modern Indian buildings, of which some others have been seen in the Academy in former years. This is a brown shaded pen elevation with a central pavilion, or rather double pavilion with a recessed entrance between, with slender pillars and brackets in the form common in Indian architecture; an external stair in three flights leads up to the entrance. The side portions are kept much lower, with an open arcade with segmental arches on brackets in the ground story, a frieze of figures and elephants above that, and a very high roof with two stories of dormers. Small pavilions form a stop to each end. It is an architecture which, being flat and destitute of mouldings, must depend very much on colour for its effect, which is not of course shown in this drawing, but the adaptation of the architectural style of the country to buildings erected there by English architects, though there may be a difference of opinion about it, is at all events an experiment of interest. It is contrary, of course, to the general precedent of history, which for the most part shows us the conquering nation imposing their own style of architecture on the conquered. As, however, we have no style to impose, there is the less to be said about that.

1,823; "Design for Bucharest Houses of Parliament;" Messrs. Williams, West, & Slade. A tinted elevation (no plan) in a rather French style of Renaissance with a large pavilion in the centre and a smaller one at each end, all covered by high domical roofs. Pilasters or engaged columns are run through both stories with a rather too perpendicular effect; the ground story has pedimented windows placed in the middle of each compartment or wall, with no architectural connexion, the upper storey large semi-circular headed windows, giving the impression that this is the principal storey. The authors may be credited with spirit in going so far afield in a competition, though we cannot think Bucharest has lost seriously by not having the building carried out.

1,824; "Proposed Gallery for British Art;" Mr. Sidney R. T. Smith. We have already illustrated the design for this. The architecture of the building, like that of the last-named, does not rise above the merest Classic respectability, and we may point out that the rather common-looking lean-to roofs of the loggie between the centre and the wings go far to deprive the façade of the one good quality, dignity, which it might otherwise boast.

1,826; "All Saints' Church, Penarth, Glamorgan;" Messrs. Seddon & Carter. Three cleanly-executed pen-drawings of a church in Early Gothic style, which is to be praised for the simple and unpretending character of its architecture, but we cannot like the effect of a row of small gables over the aisle, at right-angles with the centre roof of the nave. It is in contradiction to the spirit of three-aisled design, and has (we know not why) a kind of Dissenting-chapel look; not that we profess any sectarian prejudices, but Dissenting Gothic as a rule is not the best modern Gothic. The west end is the best part of the building.

1,827; "Design for a Timber Spire;" Mr. W. Percival. We believe we remember this drawing as one of a set which either earned the prize or a good place in one of the Institute Grissel medal competitions. It is a clever and picturesque piece of design, but perhaps has, for a timber spire, a little too much the aspect of masonry details slightly modified for wooden treatment, rather than of forms or treatment originally suggested by wood.

1,828; "Ferguslie Park, Paisley;" Mr. Hippolyte T. Blanc. A rather curious house, it seems a mixture of "Scottish baronial" with more English types; corbelled out turrets and corbie-step gables, combined with respectable-looking bay windows and a conservatory with Classic pilasters. It is not otherwise than effective, but the circular turrets seem intrusions and have not much meaning. No plan is given. The drawing is one in Mr. Raffles Davison's most "linear" style—rather too much so in this instance.

1,829; "Design for a Frieze;" Mr. A. Gwatkin. A boldly-designed scroll on a red ground, in which, as in other instances, the author has hit very happily the mean between realism and a too formal convention. The thin lines along the centres of the large leaves serve to define the scroll line well, and the edges of the serrated leaves are allowed a little freedom.

1,832; "Design for East Window, St. Margaret's Church, Lowestoft;" Mr. E. Frampton. A design for a Perpendicular five-light window of some originality. Two circles are formed in the centre, extending over the width of three lights, by rows of cherub heads, the upper of which forms a framework for a figure of Christ; at the foot of the centre light is a figure of St. Michael weighing souls (we have before referred to this as a Mediæval superstition quite out of place in a modern window); in the side lights are groups of kneeling figures directed towards the centre of the window; the small upper lights of the tracery are treated as niches for small figures of saints. The drawing and colour are good, though the effect of the drawing is a little hard as a representation of stained glass.

1,836; "Temple of Mithras; the Vestibule;" Mr. W. Stirling. This is an interesting bit of imaginative work, an interior in pencil, belonging to no special style, showing a round-arched arcade on a pier surrounded by four small columns of a kind of quasi-Classic type, but with symbolic capitals of no recognised type; around the walls are bas-reliefs, connected by a sculptured serpent which waves along the wall, and twists its neck into a circle in the foreground in which stands a female figure in alto-relief. On a little altar-like stand in the foreground four figures of boys support a fourfold candle-bearer with a symbol in the shape of an egg in the middle. This drawing looks as if it were a result of Mr. Lethaby's book on "Architecture, Mysticism, and Myth." It is a very original bit of work, only we cannot help thinking the door into the *penetralia* should have had more importance and a more mystic look about it; the conception rather breaks down at that point.

1837; "Interior View of a Hall;" by the same artist as the last-named, also a pencil interior, with a plan, apparently a small bit of executed work. It shows part of a hall with a solidly-built fireplace and ingle-nook, and part of a timber gallery over, of which the balustrade is decorated with delicate and prettily-designed floral ornament, apparently on successive squares of stamped leather tacked on. The author has a style of his own in handling the pencil.

1,839; "Reredos, All Saints, Richards Castle;" Mr. R. Norman Shaw. There is not much architectural design in this, the interest of which consists chiefly in the paintings of saints on the reredos and the inner sides of the open doors: the paintings are divided by bars with a simple Mediæval incised ornament. A wall diaper of Mediæval design occupies the space below the doors, which appears too large in scale for the situation, and rather clashes with the scale of details and figures in the reredos.

1,840; "Selby Abbey Yorkshire; Restoration of Old Glass of great East Window, according to the original design;" Messrs. Ward & Hughes. The design of the glass of this great seven-light traceried window, as restored here, has a grand effect; it shows a series of small richly-coloured figures, imbedded in rich decoration, one above the other up each light; the design fills up the space well and produces a very fine total effect; according to a memorandum on the drawing the existing portions of old glass are distinguished by a red line, but the drawing is too minute, being a good deal above the eye, for this to be made out. At the base of the window a large-scale figure reclines, extending across the three centre lights.

1,843; "Design for West Window, Jesse Haworth Memorial Church, Walsham"; Mr. William Pape. The general design only can be made out; the figure groups, which extend in bands across the window, seem not sufficiently supported by the lighter colour and detail above and below them. The design of the window itself is not very satisfactory; it looks like two three-light windows with tracery heads, divided by a single lancet-shaped compartment.

1,844; "Ambo, San Cesareo, Rome;" Mr. J. C. Horsley. This is the drawing published in the present number; a pencil drawing, with slight tinting to show the colouring of the inlaid marbles, red in the pulpit panels and green in lower ones; the panels of the pilasters are very delicately inlaid with coloured mosaic. The bold character of the twisted shafts in the pulpit is remarkable. The drawing is an admirable one, complete in effect, though but slightly executed.

1,847; "Mosaic Pavement at Murano;" Mr. A. C. Blomfield. A careful coloured drawing of a curious bit of pavement showing Byzantine influence; it is in two halves, and represents on one side what may be called we suppose a cockatrice, a half bird half beast creature, on the other side two more harmless-looking birds drinking out of a vase. The birds and other parts of the design are outlined in black tesseræ, and coloured with yellow, two tones of red, &c. It is a curious and interesting piece of work.

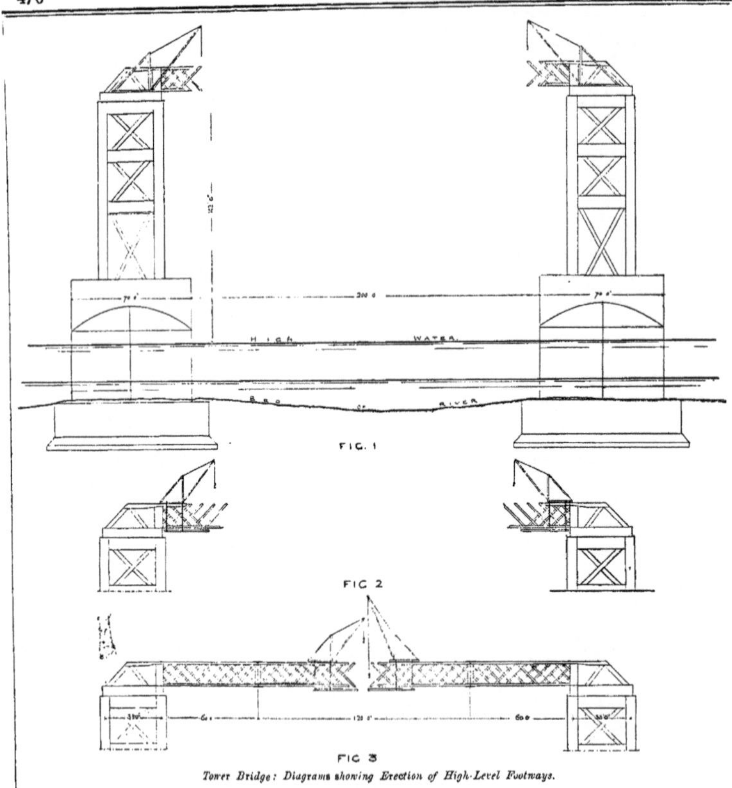

Tower Bridge: Diagrams showing Erection of High-Level Footways.

1,848; "Kirklevington Grange, Yorkshire: additions;" Mr. E. J. May. A small plan shows the extent of the additions (Mr. May is one of the architects who never forgets the plan), which practically make a new entrance-front to the house, a long centre block with a projecting porch and room over, and return wings with large shallow bay windows carried through two stories and crowned with a balcony with small console-like buttresses at the angles of the balustrade, which give a little special character. The work is in general a reproduction of the English seventeenth-century domestic style now so much in vogue, save that the windows are treated and spaced unsymmetrically on the central portion of the front. There is a restful feeling about this kind of house architecture, though there is rather a look of pretended archaism about it, which is increased by the architect's style of drawing, which is original and entirely his own, but gives a somewhat aged and time-worn look to the building in the illustration, which the actual structure would probably not bear out.

1,849. "Design for Stained Glass; Angels Appearing to the Shepherds;" Mr. A. L. Duthie. There is a refreshing originality about this bit of design for stained glass, in which we seem to get clear of the element of the "shop" which is too apparent in much stained glass work of the day, including a good deal of what is exhibited (in drawings) at the Academy. The design is divided into two groups, the Angels above and Shepherds below, separated by conventional clouds forming a concave curve bending upwards towards the sides of the window. In both groups there is the same *motif* of action spreading, as it were, from the centre to the sides, the shepherd group starting apart from the centre, the lines of the angel figures taking the same general arrangement. The angel figures are designed with great boldness and freedom, in a manner quite distinct from the usual stiff and formal stained-glass angel (who seems kept in stock and cut out when wanted), and the colour effect is fine and unusual; the design is quite out of the conventional track.

In reference to the subject of stained glass we may observe that when our Royal Academy has come to recognise that there are other forms of art besides painting and sculpture, one of its efforts should be to endeavour to provide the means of exhibiting a certain quantity of actual stained glass by transmitted light, so as to represent the real work of the stained glass artist instead of a mere drawing of it on a small scale. There will have to be great changes at the Royal Academy, no doubt, before such a thing will be considered possible or within its scope; but the changes will have to come sooner or later, if the Academy is to keep its place as a true Academy of Arts, in the eyes of a generation becoming gradually more enlightened as to what Art means.

THE TOWER BRIDGE:

METHOD OF ERECTION OF THE HIGH-LEVEL FOOTWAYS.

THE great progress that has been made during recent years in bridge-building, is chiefly due to the introduction of mild steel, and to the adoption of the cantilever system of construction. In America and other countries where bridges have often to span wide and deep rivers, the cantilever system is very extensively used, but the bridges that are required in England are seldom of sufficient magnitude to render this form of design necessary. Occasions, however, sometimes occur, where it is most desirable to follow this principle, and few better examples of its application could be found than the high level footways of the Tower Bridge.

These footways had to be erected over the busiest part of the Thames, and the river authorities would not, of course, allow any staging being put up that would interfere with the shipping interests, even if it had been desirable for the building of the bridge. No experienced engineer would, however, consider staging necessary for such a purpose, because by designing these footways on the cantilever principle it would be almost as easy to build them out horizontally without any external support, as to erect them on the ground in the contractors' yard.

The clear span to be bridged over was only

about 240 ft., but the difficulties of construction were somewhat increased by the work having to be built at a height of nearly 150 ft. above high water, and immediately over a part of the river always crowded with vessels. The way in which the cantilevers were built out from their supports on either side of the river, and the central girders erected between them, was briefly as follows. After the steel columns on each of the large masonry piers were completed, cranes were placed on the top of them by which the first portions of the footways could be put into position (fig. 1). When this part of the work was finished and securely anchored down at the shore end, a travelling-stage, carrying a small band crane, was placed on the overhanging portion (fig. 2). The lower part of this stage projected forward to form a platform upon which men could stand to bolt up the steelwork as it was put into place, piece by piece, by the crane above them.

The second length of the cantilevers being completed, the travelling stage, with its crane, was drawn forward ready to build another length in front of it. In this manner the cantilevers were soon entirely erected, and projected 60 ft. beyond the columns on each side of the river, and were ready for the end portions of the central girders to be attached to them. These girders, which are 120 ft. long, are suspended to the ends of the cantilevers by steel links, but during erection their top and bottom booms had to be temporarily connected to those of the cantilevers to allow them being built by the overhang method previously adopted. Before this could be done careful measurements had to be taken across the river, because the central girders, having been entirely finished by Messrs. Wm. Arrol & Co., the contractors, in their works at Glasgow, there was no place where any adjustment in the lengths could be made, and it was therefore necessary that the ends of the girders should be placed exactly in their right positions, to ensure the two halves just meeting

The distance between the ends of the cantilevers having been ascertained, the central girders were commenced on both sides of the river, the first portions being fixed in such a position that when each half was completed they would just touch, if the temperature was such as might be expected, in the middle of the day on which it was thought everything would be ready to make the final connexion.

When these temporary connexions were all made, the erection of the girders was proceeded with, and when completed, the two halves were found to be about ¼ in. apart at a temperature of 60 deg. Fahr., and so nearly opposite to each other both in elevation and plan that no difficulty was experienced in connecting them together on the first occasion when the weather became a little warmer. As quickly as possible after the booms had been bolted together the temporary plates which were connecting the ends of the girders and cantilevers, were removed, and the central spans were then supported only by the suspension links at their ends, and free to expand or contract according to the variations of the temperature.

The total weight of steelwork in the footways is about 600 tons, and from the above description it will be seen that this was built and finished without any staging whatever being required to support it during the process of erection.

THE EXETER DIOCESAN ARCHITECTURAL AND ARCHÆOLOGICAL SOCIETY held its annual meeting on the 10th inst., at the College Hall, South-street. The chair was occupied by Canon Edmonds, and afterwards by the Rev. W. T. A. Radford. A paper was read on Domes, by Mr. E. Ashworth, commencing with that of the Pantheon, the work of Agrippa, so indefatigable a builder in the Augustan age of Rome. Other early domes were considered, and the progress of the cupola-covered churches of Byzantium under Justinian described, culminating in the Church of St. Sophia in the sixth century, which has been imitated in numerous mosques that adorn Constantinople. The introducing of Byzantine work into Italy, in St. Mark's Venice, and St. Antonio, Padua, and its appearance in the South of France, were illustrated. The domes reared by the Mogul Emperors in India as mausolea were next exhibited. The officers were elected, and a concluding part to Vol. V., Second Series, of the "Transactions," was issued.

THE ARCHITECTURAL ASSOCIATION'S VISIT TO HARROW.

THE first of the summer visits was made on Saturday, June 11, to Harrow-on-the-Hill, where Mr. Owen Fleming had arranged for the members to visit several of the school buildings as well as two private houses.

Assembling at 3 o'clock in the well-known churchyard, commanding perhaps the most extensive and beautiful views in Middlesex, a short visit was paid to the parish church. Unfortunately the vicar was prevented from meeting the party,—as he had intended,—so that no description or history of the church was forthcoming, but several items of interest were soon noted by the members. There is a good twelfth-century font, it is circular, with characteristic Norman decoration on the bowl, which is supported on a short base, having a shallow spiral decoration. The whole is of Purbeck marble, and in wonderfully good preservation.

Both the north and south doorways are examples of the Early Decorated period, with good labels and arch mouldings. That on the north still retains an original door with an oak lock of Brobdingnagian proportions.

The flat roof is an example of fifteenth-century work, having good detail in many parts, while a good effect is obtained by placing canopied figures under each truss against the walls. Unfortunately this roof has been somewhat lavishly varnished, with a result that can hardly be considered satisfactory.

On one of the nave piers is an original memorial brass to the founder of Harrow School, commencing thus:—

HEARE LYETH BURYED THE BODYE OF IOHN LYON LATE OF PRESTON IN THIS PISH YEOMAN DECEASED THE IIIth (*sic*) DAY OF OCTOBER 1592 WHO HATH FOUNDED A FREE GRAMMAR SCHOOL IN THIS PISH TO HAVE CONTINUANCE FOR EVER. * * *

On the wall of the south aisle are hung two brasses of sixteenth-century date. The mode of hanging them framed in oak suggested that they were "Palimpsests," and an examination of the backs proved this to be the case, as they were evidently both part of a much larger, earlier brass of rich workmanship and design, as portions of a border with small figures under canopies were easily recognisable.

The western tower shows signs of early work, the outlines of two round arches, now blocked up, but visible internally, being apparently very Early Norman work, if not earlier. Externally, there are remains of a Norman doorway with zig-zag mouldings.

The clearstory windows are being gradually filled with stained glass, the subjects being chosen to illustrate events connected with the history of the parish. The first of these windows commemorates the restoration of church lands to Harrow, A.D. 825.

On leaving the church, a short visit was paid to the old schoolroom, which is now used for prayers only, and although Harrovians may consider it convenient enough for this purpose, the low, narrow, and worn seats (they cannot be termed benches) would probably be regarded with contempt by any modern School Board child. The wood panelling is carved all over with names of "Old Boys," in the traditional style, and the name of Byron, under the window, to the right of the headmaster's seat, is pointed out to visitors. The library, by the late Sir G. Gilbert Scott, was next visited. Externally it has plenty of colour, obtained by the use of variously coloured bricks and stone, and although, on close inspection, some of the detail is not quite in accordance with modern ideas, yet, seen from below, with its background of thick foliage, it groups well with its surroundings.

Crossing the road, a few minutes were spent in the speech-room, erected from designs by the late William Burges. It is to be regretted that it is still unfinished, and also lacks the colour decoration, which it was presumably intended should be added, which gives the cast-iron columns and bare wooden vaulting a rather cold expression. Few of those who enter this building are aware that it contains an organ. The organist's seat and key-boards are below the front of the platform, but the instrument itself is placed along the straight wall, being principally below the level of the platform, along the back of which a plain wooden panelling extends, which hides all indications of its existence. Possibly the architect considered that the recognition of an organ in the design would give to music undue predominance. If, however, music was not recognised in the speech-room, Harrow now possesses a building devoted entirely thereto in the new music school, designed by Mr. E. S. Prior. This building contains a lecture-room, surrounded by corridors, off which are placed the practising-rooms. These are all provided with double doors, double windows, and separated from each other by hollow walls. In the corridors are lockers for music and racks for violin-cases. Under the platform of the lecture-room a baud-room is provided. The rooms are warmed by hot water, and ample provision made for ventilation by means of flues, which, with the double doors and windows, is absolutely necessary.

On the hill above the Music School is the Museum and class-rooms in connexion with it, erected to commemorate the Headmastership of Dr. Butler. The building was designed by Mr. Basil Champneys, and is of red brick, with ornamental features and carving executed in bright "rubbers," which soft material has, unfortunately, already suffered at the hands of its constant frequenters, who could not resist the temptation when such an easily "worked" material was placed ready to hand.

An external staircase is carried from the ground level to the top story, and forms a pleasing feature in the design, being enclosed by an arcade carried by short carved brick columns. On the top floor the museum consists of two top-lighted saloons, side by side. The collections are not fully arranged yet, but an interesting feature is the collection of Egyptian and Grecian antiquities from the collection of Sir Gardner Wilkinson. A portrait of Dr. Butler, by Prof. Herkomer, hangs in one of the galleries. There are three floors below the museum, on each of which are two class-rooms fitted with modern desks and other appliances, and a waiting-hall, intended for the boys before the arrival of the Master. This, the custodian seemed to think, quite superfluous

Opposite to this building, and near the speech-room, a house, by Mr. T. G. Jackson, was noticed.

Having completed the visits to buildings in connexion with the school, the party proceeded to a house designed by Mr. Prior for Dr. Stivens. There was an old house standing further back from the road; this was pulled down and the old bricks used for the facing of the new house, being, however, relieved by terra-cotta of a pinkish tint, which is used for window-dressings, cornices, balusters, &c. Internally, the house is conveniently arranged; the entrance-hall is a few steps lower than the principal floor, thus admitting of a consulting-room being placed so as to be easily accessible from the entrance, yet quite distinct from the family rooms.

Another example of Mr. Prior's work completed the programme. This consisted of a billiard-room recently added to a house on the Mount Park Estate, which, by the kindness of Mrs. Cator, the members were permitted to see. The room is a large one, and is end-lighted by two large windows in deep recesses at each end of the table. In addition to these there is a central glass dome internally, although externally only a steep tiled roof with the upper part glazed is the only indication of a top light.

The room is really more than a billiard-room, being devoted as well to the exhibition of a fine collection of Japanese and Oriental curios as well as to a collection of stuffed birds, &c., for which deep cabinets with glazed fronts have been arranged in each corner of the room. This being the last place to be visited, the party then broke up.

The next visit is announced for the 25th inst. It will be a whole-day visit to Canterbury.

WESLEYAN CHAPEL, CUDWORTH.—The Wesleyan Memorial Chapel was opened at Cudworth a few days since. The chapel, which is in the Renaissance style, is 39 ft. long and 35 ft. wide inside and capable of accommodating 200 persons on the ground floor. Preparation is made so that a gallery can be erected over the front vestibule; also an orchestra behind the rostrum at any future time. There are ministers' vestry, class-room, &c., provided at the rear of the building. The roof of the chapel, which is partly open-timbered, is of stained and varnished pine. the remaining inside woodwork is of pitch-pine varnished. Fresh air is admitted through inlet shafts, and the foul air carried away through an extract ventilator fixed on the roof. The work has been executed from the designs of Mr. Charles T. Taylor, architect, of Oldham.

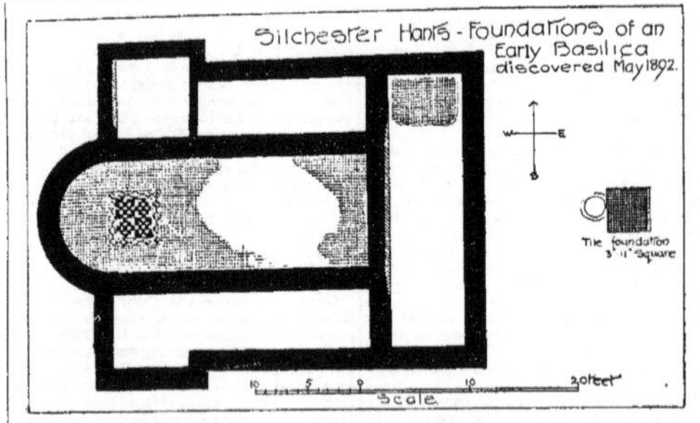

DISCOVERY OF AN EARLY CHRISTIAN BASILICA AT SILCHESTER.

As we mentioned in a note last week, a highly-interesting discovery has been made on the site of the Roman city of Silchester, in Hampshire, the excavation of which has this year been resumed. By the kind permission of Mr. St. John Hope we are enabled to give a plan of the foundations of the early basilica which has been found on the same *insula* as, and south-east of, the Forum—nearly in the centre of the city. Its apse or chancel faces west, and is flanked on either side by rudimentary transepts. Narrow aisles flank the centre portion of the church, and across its east end runs a narthex. The whole building is on a small scale, the total length being but 42 ft., outside measurement. The width of the nave is 10 ft., the aisles 5 ft., and the narthex 6 ft. 9 in. The whole of the centre portion of the church has been paved with inch-square red tile tesseræ. In front of the apse is a square of finer mosaic, 5 ft. square, in black and white checks, with a border of coloured lozenges. There are some remains of paving in red tesseræ in the northern end of the narthex. About 11 ft. east of the church is a foundation of brick about 4 ft. square, perhaps formerly the base of a fountain, in connexion with which the pit on its western side, lined with flints, was probably used. This discovery of what is generally supposed to be the earliest example we have of a Christian church in Britain will increase the interest already taken in the excavations at Silchester. Some notes on the results of previous excavations will be found in the *Builder*, January 10, 1891, and January 16, 1892.

THE ROYAL INSTITUTE OF BRITISH ARCHITECTS:

ELECTION OF COUNCIL.

AT the business meeting of this Institute, held on Monday evening last, Mr. J. Macvicar Anderson, President, in the chair, numerous donations to the library and collection were announced.

The President, having read the report of the scrutineers appointed by the annual general meeting to direct the election of the Council for the year of office 1892-93, announced that the Council, consisting of thirty-six members, for the official year, and the auditors for the official year, were duly elected as follows:—

President.—Mr. John Macvicar Anderson [unopposed].

Vice-Presidents.—Professor George Aitchison, A.R.A., Mr. James Brooks, Mr. Henry Currey, and Mr. Campbell Douglas (Glasgow) [unopposed].

Hon. Secretary.—Mr. Aston Webb [unopposed].

Members of Council.—Messrs. Thomas Edward Collcutt, Ernest George, Arthur Oates, John Slater, B.A Lond., William Emerson, Alexander Graham, F.S.A., Richard Phené Spiers, F.S.A., Thomas Blashill, Wyatt Papworth, John Alfred Gotch, F.S.A. (Kettering), Henry Louis Florence, John Belcher, Richard Herbert Carpenter, F.S.A., John Holden (Manchester), Lacy William Ridge, John McKean Brydon, Edward Augustus Gruning, and Octavius Hansard.

Associate Members of Council.—Messrs. Paul Waterhouse, M.A. Oxon., and Thomas Miller Rickman, F.S.A.

Presidents of Allied Societies.—Messrs. Thomas Harnett Harrison (Liverpool Society), William Hale (Birmingham Association), William Leiper, A.R.S.A. (Glasgow Institute); George Bertram Bulmer (Leeds and Yorkshire Society), Charles John Innocent (Sheffield Society), Thomas Drew, R.H.A. (Royal Institute of Ireland); Robert Evans (Nottingham Society), Henry Crisp (Bristol Society), and Edward Salomons (Manchester Society).

Representative of the Architectural Association (London).—Mr. Herbert Osborn Cresswell.

Auditors.—Messrs. Lewis Angell, M.Inst.C.E., and William Woodward.

The result of the election of Standing Committees was next declared.

Fifteen Fellows, thirty-four Associates, and three Hon. Corr. Members were elected, and the meeting afterwards proceeded to discuss the question of the method of electing Fellows.

The meeting terminated at 11 p.m. with the announcement that the sixteenth and final meeting of the session will be held on Monday, June 27, when the Royal Gold Medal for Architecture will be presented to M. César Daly, Hon. Corr. Member.

THE INSTITUTION OF CIVIL ENGINEERS:

ANNUAL REPORT.

THE annual general meeting of this Institution was held on May 31, Mr. H. Hayter (Vice-President) being in the chair, in the absence, from indisposition, of Mr. Berkley, President.

The Report of the Council for the Session 1891-92 commenced by stating that the objects of the Institution were so widely known, had been so frequently referred to, and appeared to be so largely appreciated, that they might be passed over without comment. The constitution had remained unchanged since December 2, 1878, when the class of Associates was divided into two groups,—one being civil engineers, to whom corporate privileges were granted, and who were distinguished by the title "Associate Members," the other being non-corporate Associates, described as "persons able, from their connexion with science or the arts, or otherwise, to advance professional knowledge."

The Council had carefully guarded the admission of new members to every class, and the qualifications of all candidates had been subjected to rigid scrutiny. It was believed that a strict inquiry into each candidate's career was better than any system of examination. Members were again urged not to attach their names to the recommendation of any one for election or for transfer, unless thoroughly satisfied that the candidate was in all respects, professionally and socially, eligible. With regard to the changes in the roll of the Institution, it was stated that fifty-nine Associate Members had been transferred to the class of Member, and that there had been elected three Honorary Members, twenty-eight Members, 324 Associate Members, and seven Associates, while four Associate Members had been restored to the register. These additions together amounted to 366. After deducting 145 names from deaths, resignations, and erasures there was an increase of 221, bringing up the total number on the register to 5,371, as against 5,150 at the corresponding date last year.

This enumeration was irrespective of the Students, of whom 200 had been admitted during the year, as against 166 for the previous twelve months; but during this period 106 Students had become Associate Members, and 140 had disappeared from the list, so that the number now on the books was only 868, whereas last year the number was 914. Thus, including Students, the total number on the books was now 6,239, as against 6,064 twelve months ago.

During the financial year ending March 31, 1892, the receipts amounted to — Income, 20,070*l.* 17s. 3d.; Capital, 5,186*l.* 7s.; and Trust-Funds, 930*l.* 19s. 8d., making a total of 26,188*l.* 3s. 11d., as compared with 24,274*l.* 8s. 11d. for the previous twelve months. The disbursements were—General expenditure, 15,038*l.* 14s. 6d.; capital, 7,497*l.* 5s. 3d.; and trust-funds, 821*l.* 1s. 5d.; together, 23,357*l.* 1s. 2d. Capital expenditure extraordinary amounted to 1,612*l.* 13s. 9d., mainly for the purchase of the lease of No. 27, Great George-street, against which there was a set-off for rents of 251*l.* 5s., whilst there had been transferred from the current receipts 1,361*l.* 8s. 9d. to effect a balance. The purchase of the lease of No. 27, Great George-street was deemed advisable, having regard to the question of re-building, still under consideration. The capital receipts included a bequest of 500*l.*, free of legacy-duty, under the will of Sir John Hawkshaw, which, although unconditional, had been added to Capital. These several receipts had been invested in Debenture Stocks of British railway companies, of the nominal or par value of 7,000*l.* The balances to the credit of the Institution at the beginning and at the end of the financial year were respectively 6,755*l.* 2s. 8d. and 8,224*l.* 16s. 8d.

Allusion had been made on several occasions to the fact that, as the corporation included all classes of civil engineers, it must be expected that the "Minutes of Proceedings" would be gradually modified and developed, so as to meet the wants of its more diversified membership.

Having regard to these considerations, it would be found that, in Constructive Engineering, five papers have been read. Two of these, —"The Bishop Rock Lighthouses," by Mr. W. T. Douglass, and "The Illumination by Gas of Tory Island Lighthouse," by Mr. D. C. Salmond, referred to sea-coast works of supreme importance to every maritime nation. The three communications on "Portland Cement" and "Portland Cement Concrete," by Messrs. Bamber, Carey, and Smith, related to a material fast becoming indispensable to the constructive engineer. Two papers directly connected with Municipal Engineering were submitted for discussion, namely, — on "The Sale of Water by Meter in Berlin," by Mr. Henry Gill, and on "The Sewage-Farms of Berlin," by Mr. H. Alfred Roechling. Both bore witness to the advanced condition of sanitary matters in the capital of the German Empire. The elaborate paper by Mr. Alex. R. Binnie "On Mean or Average Annual Rainfall," must also be classed with this branch of engineering, as referring to one of the data upon which the Waterworks Engineer based his calculations. Mining and Metallurgical Engineering were represented by the paper on "Gold-Quartz Reduction," by Mr. A. H. Curtis. As the modern processes of ore-reduction were accomplished by the aid of machinery, the efficient conduct of the operations was directly dependent upon the engineer. In regard to Mechanical Engineering, the memoir on "Weighing-Machines," by Mr. Wilfrid Airy, opened up entirely new ground, while that on "Petroleum Engines," by Professor W. C. Unwin, was mainly an exhaustive study of a particular machine. Electrical Engineering was represented by a paper on "Electrical Measuring-Instruments," by Mr. James Swinburne. Finally, reference was made to some questions of importance belonging primarily to the domain of physics, and which required to be attentively studied by engineers; especially was this the case in respect to the operations connected with the Measurement of Light and of Heat, dealt with in the papers by Mr. A. P. Trotter, on "The Distribution and Measurement of Illumination," and Professor W. C. Roberts-Austen, on "The Measurement of High Temperatures."

To the Authors of some of the above communications the Council had had pleasure in making the following awards: — A George Stephenson Medal and a Telford Premium to Mr. Alex. R. Binnie; Telford Medals and Telford Premiums to Mr. A. P. Tro'ter and Mr. W. T. Douglass; and Telford Premiums to Messrs. H. Alfred Roechling, A. H. Curtis, W. Airy, H. Gill, and Professor W. C. Roberts-Austen.

Among the papers which had been deemed suitable for printing without being discussed, those of Mr. F. Fox, on "The Hawarden Bridge," and Mr. Alfred W. Szlumper, on "The Widening and Improvement Works of the London and South-Western Railway," belonging strictly to Constructive Engineering; closely related were "The Building-Stones of Great Britain, their Crushing Strength and other properties," by Professor T. H. Beare, "Stresses and Deflections in Braced Girders," by Mr. A D. Stewart; and "Practical Astronomy as applied to Land Surveying," by Mr. R. H. B. Downes. The description of "The Nagpur Waterworks Extension," by Mr. E. Penny, and of "The Southampton Waterworks," by Mr. W. Matthews, affected the municipal engineer, while Mechanical and Electrical Engineering were respectively dealt with in the papers by Professor W. C. Unwin, on "The Transmission and Distribution of Power from Central Stations by Compressed Air;" and Dr. C. B. Sheibner, on "The Florence and Fiesole Electric Railway."

In respect of these communications, Telford medals and Telford premiums had been adjudged to Messrs. F. Fox and Alfred W. Szlumper; and Telford premiums to Messrs. Sheibner, T. H. Beare, W. C Unwin, E. Penny, A. D. Stewart, R. H. B. Downes, and W. Matthews.

The Howard Quinquennial Prize had been awarded to Sir Isaac Lowthian Bell, Bart., F.R.S., M Inst.C.E., for his treatise on "The Principles involved in the Manufacture of Iron and Steel"

The papers read at Supplemental Meetings of Students had shown in nearly every case evidence of having been prepared with care. Three, at least, were of high merit, and, with four others above the average, had been deemed worthy of publication, either in whole or in part, in the "Minutes of Proceedings." For the seven papers above referred to, the Council had had satisfaction in awarding,—the Miller Scholarship to Mr. H. B. Ransom, for his paper on "Fly-wheels and Governors," and Miller prizes to Mr. C. H. Wordingham, E. L. Hill, D. Carnegie, G. H. Sheffield, J. B. Ball, R. J. Durley.

Understanding that there was a dearth of professional men in the Engineer Volunteer Corps, the Council expressed the hope that young civil engineers, whose education rendered them peculiarly fitted to fill the vacancies and to be of service to their country, would come forward in larger numbers than appeared to be the case at present, so as to prepare themselves by the necessary military training to give their aid in any National emergency.

The Report having, after discussion, been adopted, cordial votes of thanks were passed to the President, to the Vice-Presidents, to the Members of Council, to the Auditors, and to the Secretaries and Staff.

The scrutineers, to whom a vote of thanks was passed by acclamation, announced that the following gentlemen had been duly elected to serve on the Council for the ensuing year:—

President: Mr. Harrison Hayter.

Vice-Presidents: Mr. Alfred Giles, M.P., Sir Robert Rawlinson, K.C.B., Sir Benjamin Baker, K.C.M.G., LL.D., F.R.S., and Sir Jas. N. Douglass, F.R.S.

Other Members of Council: W. Anderson, D.C.L., F.R.S., J. Wolfe Barry, Alex. R. Binnie, E. A. Cowper, Sir Douglas Fox, J. C. Hawkshaw, M.A., Charles Hawksley, Sir Bradford Leslie, K.C.I.E., George Fosbery Lyster, James Mansergh, Sir Guildford L. Molesworth, K.C.I.E., W. H. Preece, F.R.S., Sir Edward J. Reed, K.C.B., F.R.S., M.P., William Shelford, and Francis W. Webb.

THE ENGLISH IRON TRADE.—There is little alteration to note in the English iron market. In Cleveland the works are slowly being started; there are now six furnaces in blast out of the eighty stopped for want of coke. Prices are easier. In manufactured iron there is still little doing; but in tin plates a fair amount of business is reported. Steel is in sluggish demand; but the prospects of new work are rather more encouraging. Shipbuilders continue quiet, and engineers are only moderately employed. The coal trade remains fairly active.—*Iron.*

THE LONDON COUNTY COUNCIL.

THE London County Council resumed its weekly meetings, after the Whitsuntide holidays, on Tuesday afternoon last, when the Chairman, Lord Rosebery, presided.

A Vacant Seat.—The Chairman announced that he had received a formal communication from the Clerk stating that the bankruptcy of Mr. Ernest Bowen Rowlands, one of the members for Central Finsbury, had been officially notified in the *Gazette*. It was therefore necessary to fill up within fourteen days the vacancy thus caused.

The Opening of Brockwell Park.—The Chairman referred to the sad death of Mr. Bristowe, M.P., on the occasion of the opening of Brockwell Park (as mentioned by us in a "Note" last week), and it was resolved unanimously to authorise the Chairman to communicate to the family of Mr. Bristowe the profound regret of the Council at the untimely death of that gentleman.

A Paucity of Tenders.—The third item on the *agenda* was thus stated: "To receive tenders for the erection of a school building at Crossness" (for the children of the workmen employed at the Southern Outfall Sewage Works), but the Chairman announced that only one tender had been received. Under the circumstances he thought it would not be advisable to open that tender, but that the whole matter should be referred to the Main Drainage Committee for reconsideration. This suggestion was agreed to, it being understood that the Committee were not to open the solitary tender sent in.

The Proposed Alterations at Shoreditch Town Hall.—One of the paragraphs of the Finance Committee's report was as follows:—

"The Vestry of Shoreditch recently applied to the Council for sanction to their borrowing 5,500*l.* for the purpose of carrying out certain additions and alterations to their Town Hall required by the Theatres Committee of the Council to comply with the regulations as to places used for music and dancing. It was pointed out to the Vestry by the solicitor that the Council could only sanction the cost of such additions to the offices of the Vestry as were required to meet the reasonable office necessities of the Vestry when acting under the Metropolis Management Acts, and that the proposed expenditure did not appear to be within this limitaion. The Vestry have since withdrawn the application. It occurs to us, however, that there may be cases in which it might be desirable to have the powers of vestries and district boards under the Metropolis Management Acts enlarged, so that should occasion arise they may be able to build halls which could be used for meetings of the ratepayers for public and other purposes in which the inhabitants of the locality take an interest. We therefore recommend:—

'That it be referred to the Local Government and Taxation Committee to consider and report whether it is desirable that Parliament should be asked to amend the Metropolis Management Acts, so as to permit the Vestries and District Boards, where desirable and requisite, to provide for the erection of large halls for places of public meeting and other public purposes of the ratepayers and inhabitants of the district.'"

On the motion of Mr. Moss, it was resolved to add, at the end of the recommendation, the following words, viz., "and for the maintenance and alteration of such halls." The recommendation, as thus amended, was agreed to.

Decision to Purchase Hackney Marsh.—The Parks and Open Spaces Committee brought up a report in which they set out at length their report of November last,* recommending that the Council should offer 50,000*l.* for Hackney Marsh, including common, manorial, and other rights. That offer, it was now reported by the Committee, was declined by the vendors, but negotiations had since been entered into with the local bodies, and as the result, the lord, the commoners, and other owners of rights, who had combined for the purposes of selling the marsh, were now prepared to accept 75,000*l.*, which sum could be raised as follows:—The Council, 50,000*l.*; the Hackney District Board, 15,000*l.*; contribution by the lord of the manor, 5,000*l.*; and local and other contributions to be obtained, 5,000*l.*; making a total of 75,000*l.* "The question of the acquirement of Hackney Marsh," added the Committee, "is one for all London, and not for the East-end only, as, apart from the local use which can be made of it for games, it forms a splendid open space at the eastern boundary of the county." They accordingly recommended—

"That, subject to a supplementary estimate of 10,000*l.* being submitted to the Council by the Finance Committee, as required by the statute, and subject to the Hackney District Board entering into an agreement to contribute 15,000*l.*, and to the lord of the manor contributing 5,000*l.*, and to 5,000*l.* being raised from other sources, the Council do purchase Hackney Marsh for the sum of 75,000*l.*, such sum to include the rights of the commoners, the lord of the manor, and other owners, the Council's contribution of 50,000*l.*, being contingent on the necessary statutory authority being obtained."

* Printed *in extenso* in the *Builder* for November 21, 1891, p. 389.

After the discussion of an amendment (moved by Mr. Lloyd), to refer the whole matter back to the Committee with a view of obtaining further information, but which was rejected by a large majority, the recommendation was agreed to.

Recreation Ground at Fulham.—A further report of the Parks and Open Spaces Committee contained the following paragraph and recommendation:—

"The Council will remember that it agreed to contribute 5,625*l.* to the cost of purchasing ten acres of land for a recreation-ground at the corner of Crown-lane and Fulham-palace-road, such contribution being contingent on the Vestry of Fulham laying it out within twelve months from the date of the Council's vote. It was represented to us, however, some weeks ago, that the Vestry only obtained possession of the ground on March 8 last, and on that plea they asked for an extension of time for six months, which the Council on our recommendation granted on April 12 of the present year, attaching the condition, however, that no gravel should be removed from, nor dustbin or other offensive refuse deposited on, the ground. On visiting the place on May 18 last, we found that a quantity of gravel had been removed and sold, and that some very offensive material had been deposited in the hole whence the gravel had been taken. We at once communicated with the Vestry, to the effect that they were not complying with the terms of the Council's resolution granting conditionally an extension of time for the laying out, and received in reply an assurance that the sale of the gravel and the deposits of foul matter should be stopped. Provided that this promise is adhered to, we recommend:—

'That the Council do grant an extension of time to the extent of twelve months from March 8 last, to the Vestry of Fulham, to lay out the recreation-ground at the corner of Crown-road and Fulham Palace-road, on condition that no earth, gravel, or sand be removed from the land, and no dustbin or other offensive refuse deposited thereon.'"

Mr. Fred Henderson moved, as an amendment, that the matter be referred back, he and other speakers animadverting in strong terms on the way in which the Vestry had broken faith with the Council. After some further discussion, however, Mr. Henderson withdrew this amendment, and seconded the following, moved by Mr. Costelloe:—

"That the consideration of the recommendation be deferred, and that the Committee be instructed to require from the Vestry of Fulham an explanation of the removal of the gravel in breach of the agreement, an account of its value, and to satisfy the Medical Officer of the Council as to the condition of the matter used to fill in."

This amendment was agreed to almost unanimously.

Proposed Re-building of Vauxhall and Lambeth Bridges.—The Report of the Bridges Committee contained the following paragraphs and recommendations:—

"*Vauxhall Bridge.*—The question of the rebuilding of this bridge is engaging our attention, and the information that has been laid before us points to the fact that the bridge must be rebuilt. The bridge now requires to be repaired, the carriage-way being in a very unsatisfactory state. We have, therefore, had an estimate prepared showing what the cost of the works will be, pending the rebuilding of the bridge five years hence. The estimate reaches a sum of 2,400*l.*, which includes an amount for repaving the roadway with wood. We therefore recommend—

'That, subject to an estimate being submitted to the Council by the Finance Committee, as required by the statute, a sum of 2,400*l.* be expended for keeping Vauxhall Bridge in repair during a period of five years.'

"*Lambeth Bridge.*—The condition of this bridge is such that the Council will have to obtain powers in the next session of Parliament to rebuild it. The rebuilding will, it is estimated, occupy a period of two years, but it is necessary for the bridge to be repaired before the works are commenced. The works which now must be carried out are repairing the carriage-way and re-puttying and painting the strands of the cables, which will cost about 170*l.* We recommend—

'That, subject to an estimate being submitted to the Council by the Finance Committee, as required by the statute, Lambeth Bridge be repaired, at a cost of about £170.'"

After some discussion, in the course of which exception was taken to the proposed paving of Vauxhall Bridge with wood, the gradients being so steep, both recommendations were referred back, and after transacting some other business, the Council adjourned.

Illustrations.

CENTRAL TOWER, IMPERIAL INSTITUTE.

THIS is the drawing of the tower exhibited at the Royal Academy, except that the sky has been re-sketched by the architect, as that in the original drawing failed to reproduce sufficiently in lithographing. The tower is now being erected, but as it is impossible to build more than about 2 ft. in one week, it will be some months before it is entirely finished.

The facework is in Portland stone, with occasional bands of red brick; the roof will be covered with copper. Besides a large tank to serve the fire hydrants, there will be a peal of ten or twelve bells.

The contractors are Messrs. Mowlem & Co., and the architect Mr. T. E. Collcutt.

DESIGN FOR A FRIEZE.

THE motive of this design by Mr. Arthur Gwatkin is the yellow horned poppy, and the foliage is evolved from its leaf forms.

The statement on the margin of the print, that it is in the Royal Academy Exhibition, is however only what ought to be the case and not the actual fact. The Royal Academy contains a drawing by Mr. Gwatkin entitled "Design for a Frieze," of the same shape and the same type of design as this one, and as we knew that this one was sent to the Academy, and had no occasion to examine the drawing at the Academy minutely till this week, we naturally concluded that this was the drawing. Mr. Gwatkin drew our attention to the mistake too late to alter the printing on the lithograph. Why we say that the statement "ought" to have been true is that this is a better and more elaborated design than the one hung at the Academy, and that they should have rejected the best design and hung the one which is certainly of less merit and interest, is only another of the eccentricities of hanging at the Architectural Room.

WALL DECORATION, CHAPEL OF ST. JAMES, SAN MINIATO.

THIS is from a drawing by Mr. G. C. Horsley. The lower part of the decoration is of marble, comprising a throne and panelling. The subject of the Annunciation is painted on canvas, and the picture is surrounded by a small gilt moulding; the trees and sky are painted in fresco on the wall.

PULPIT, SAN CESAREO, ROME.

THE pulpit is one of the most beautiful of the works of the "Cosmati" school remaining in Rome. It is of marble, carved, and inlaid with glass mosaic. The large disc of marble on the wall of the stair is of porphyry. The illustration is from a drawing by Mr. G. C. Horsley which is exhibited at the Royal Academy.

PEWSHAM HOUSE, WILTS.

THIS house is now in course of erection in one of the prettiest parts of Wiltshire. Externally it is faced with Cattybrook bricks, with Ham Hill stone dressings, and the roof covered with Ruabon tiles.

The internal fittings are mainly of deal, the most notable exception being the principal staircase, which will be oak. The arrangements include a large top-lighted billiard-room on the first floor. The principal rooms on the ground level have their floors laid with wood blocks.

Stabling is about to be commenced. The work is being carried out by Messrs. Light & Smith, of Chippenham, from the designs and under the superintendence of Mr. C. E. Ponting, F.S.A., Marlborough.

The drawing is exhibited at the Royal Academy.

PRESENTATION FOUNTAIN FOR AYR.—On the 11th inst. the fountain presented to the town of Ayr by Mr. Steven, of Skeldon (of Steven Bros. & Co., architectural ironfounders, London and Glasgow), was formally handed over to the Town Council by that gentleman.

COMPETITIONS.

INFECTIOUS DISEASES HOSPITAL FOR WEST FIFE.—At a meeting at Dunfermline, on the 11th inst., of a joint committee appointed by the burgh and county local authorities, it was resolved to adopt the plans of Messrs. Charles S. Johnstone and David B. Burnie, architects, Edinburgh, for an infectious diseases hospital for the district. There were seventeen designs sent in. The hospital is to be built on a site acquired from the Earl of Elgin at Milesmark, and is, with furniture, to cost nearly 6,000*l.*

COTTAGE HOSPITAL, GALASHIELS.—Some time ago, says the *Scotsman*, a scheme was set on foot for providing a Cottage Hospital for Galashiels and neighbourhood, for the treatment of patients suffering from non-contagious diseases. The Committee obtained plans and estimates, which were submitted to a meeting of the subscribers held on the 11th inst. in the Burgh Court-room. The Committee had selected, on the recommendation of Mr. Blanc, architect, Edinburgh, the plan by Mr. Wallace, architect, Edinburgh, which will give accommodation for fourteen beds, with all the other accessories for an hospital such as that required for Galashiels. The estimated contract cost was 2,600*l.* for building, without the fittings and furniture. It was agreed to proceed with the undertaking at once, on the plans selected, with such modifications as might be desirable.

THE ROYAL COMMISSION ON METROPOLITAN WATER SUPPLY.

WE continue our report* of the evidence tendered before this Commission.

The Kent Company.

This Company's statement began by citing the letters patent granted, in 1701, by William III., to certain persons, conferring on them for five hundred years the exclusive privilege of breaking up the streets in certain manors to lay water-pipes. The monopolists constructed the Ravensbourne Waterworks, which were in operation till 1808. Next year the Company was incorporated, and acquired the patent for 65,000*l.* The manors included Greenwich, Deptford, and adjoining districts, which have now a population of 165,000. From time to time the limits of supply have been extended, till they embrace an area of 178 square miles, of which thirty are in the county of London and the remainder in Kent. About 1835 the available flow of the Ravensbourne proved insufficient. Then were sunk deep wells which yielded abundant supplies of good water. The river was superseded, and the district wholly supplied from the chalk wells in 1862. The supply, obtained from deep wells and borings in the chalk, is fed by rain falling on the North Downs and on the chalk district lying between them and the river Thames. The mass of the chalk, which is from 500 ft. to 600 ft. thick, forms an immense underground reservoir, the overflow from which breaks out in numerous springs along the valleys of the Ravensbourne, the Gray, and the Darenth, whilst many springs flow directly into the lower Thames at Erith, Northfleet, and elsewhere, where the river flows across the chalk formation. The chalk and other permeable strata which drain into it form a large catchment area, of which it is estimated that at least 110 square miles contribute to the supply in this Company's district. The rainfall on this area varies from 24 in. per annum in the Thames Valley to 36 in. on the North Downs, which rise to an elevation of from 700 ft. to 800 ft. above sea level. The heavy rainfall on the hills of the chalk escarpment may be assumed to give a percolation of 10 in. instead of 6 in., and this would give a daily discharge of 44,000,000 gallons. Beyond the chalk downs, there is a considerable area of lower greensand in the neighbourhood of Westerham, and this town is supplied from a well in that formation. The water from the greensand is excellent, and has been sought for in vain, and at great expense, by deep borings under London. This Company might obtain a large quantity either by borings through the gault or by wells in the out crop. Paragraphs on these supplies are quoted from the reports of former Commissions. That of 1869 said that this reservoir in the chalk did not feed the Lea or the Thames above Hampton, and that it would probably yield 30,000,000 gallons a day; that the water from the greensand was soft and good, but there were then n[o] means of estimating its quantity; an[d] that the chalk wells might be increased i[n] Kent without interfering with the springs i[n] the valleys above London. The Company ar[e] assured that they can obtain from the old chal[k] area, from the new chalk area, and from th[e] lower greensand 53,000,000 gallons daily. Larg[e] quantities escape into the Thames from th[e] chalk, the Thanet sand, and porous Woolwic[h] and Reading beds along a line from Deptford past Erith and Northfleet to Cliff, and it ha[s] been estimated by Mr. Barlow and Mr. Anstea[d] that 60,000,000 gallons a day from the chal[k] could be obtained by an intercepting tunne[l] along this line. The following are the Com[pany's] pumping stations and wells in use, thei[r] estimated daily yield in gallons, and th[e] capacity of the pumping machinery (excludin[g] the well at Westerham and a bore-hole in th[e] chalk at Dartford available for use in thos[e] districts):—

	Yield.	Pumping power.
Deptford (3)	8,000,000	12,000,00[0]
Crayford (3)	3,500,000	5,000,00[0]
Shortlands (2)	2,250,000	2,250,00[0]
Orpington (2)	2,500,000	3,750,00[0]
Wilmington (1)	4,000,000	4,000,00[0]
Plumstead (1)	800,000	1,200,00[0]
Totals	21,050,000	28,200,00[0]

Average daily supply for 1891	13,534,00[0]
Maximum (January 28, 1891)	17,000,00[0]
Number of houses and other supplies, 1891	76,75[illegible]
Average per head of population, in galls.	29[illegible]
Number of supplies under constant service (38 per cent.)	44,27[illegible]
Company's area in square miles	17[8]

Testimonies to the chemical superiority o[f] the chalk water are quoted from the Chemica[l] Commission of 1851, the Rivers' Pollution Com[mission], Professor Frankland, and Dr. Alber[t] Bernays. The latter said he would not recom[mend] the adoption of any chemical process fo[r] the softening of the water. The Company'[s] limits not being coterminous with registratio[n] districts, and many houses in rural districts no[t] being supplied by the Company, an exact cal[culation] of population to supplies is hardl[y] possible. Tables show that since 1850 the average daily supply has doubled in seven[,] thirteen, and twenty years. The present supply may, perhaps, be doubled in thirty-six years. By 1912 another 6,500,000 gallons may be needed to make the total 20,000,000 gallons daily. Taking increase of supplies as a guide, and allowing 30 gallons a head, 6,000,000 gallons more would be required in twenty years. Add 6,000,000 gallons for a margin between average and maximum, and a possible maximum of 26,000,000 is reached. The present yield is 21,000,000 gallons, and by additional pumping machinery and mains, 8,000,000 gallons more could be provided without resort to other known and accessible sources. With improved fittings the supply per head could be reduced from 30 gallons to 28. The Company therefore claim to be able to provide abundance of water of the highest quality for the population in its district for many years to come, and, if necessity should arise, it could tap water-bearing strata estimated to yield from 50,000,000 to 60,000,000 gallons a day.

Mr. Alexander Dickson, the Secretary of the Company, called the attention of the Commissioners to the Company's monopoly in the supply of a portion of its district. After a long examination as to the method of arriving at the population, the number of houses or supplies, and the average supply per head per day, he expressed the opinion that with proper fittings and proper control, such as was exercised in Manchester and Liverpool, the average per head could be greatly reduced. Of the 30 gallons, 24 gallons were estimated to be for domestic use and six for trade, and, comparing these with several provincial returns, there seemed to be a very large margin for saving. The witness gave the maximum supplies (asked for in each case by the Chairman) for a week, a month and three months. The three months covered the drought of 1877, and the highest point reached was 16,180,000. The highest week and month were in the period. The prolonged frost of 1890-91 produced the highest day, the 28th of January, when the supply reached 17,000,000 gallons, the week averaged over 16,000,000 gallons; and the month nearly 15,500,000 gallons. The ratio of increase of supplies was less now than it was five or ten years ago. A difficulty in basing estimates for

* See *Builder*, pp. 418, 435, 456, *ante.*

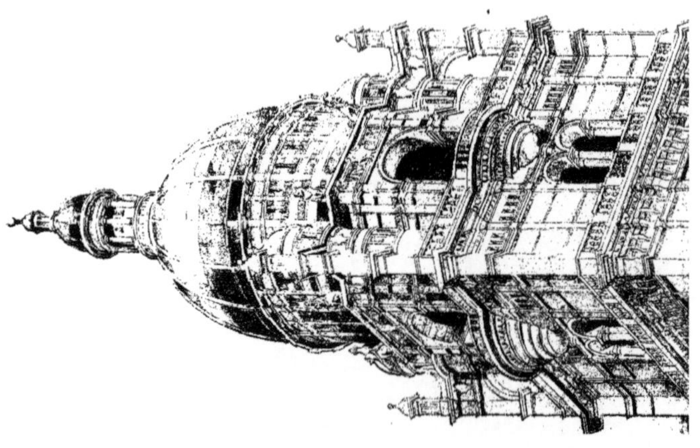

THE QUEEN'S TOWER, IMPERIAL INSTITUTE.—MR. T. E. COLLCUTT, F.R.I.B.A., ARCHITECT.

Royal Academy Exhibition, 1892.

Royal Academy Exhibition, 1892.

DESIGN FOR ERIEZE

R. ARTHUR GWATKIN.

INK-PHOTO SPRAGUE & Co 4 & 5, EAST HARDING STREET, FETTER LANE, E.C.

INK-PHOTO SPRAGUE & Cº 4 & 5, EAST HARDING STREET, FETTER LANE, E.C.

Royal Academy Exhibition, 1892.

Royal Academy Exhibition, 1892.

INK-PHOTO SPRAGUE & Cº 4 & 5, EAST HARDING STREET, FETTER LANE, E.C.

the future upon the past arose from the frequent enlargement of the Company's district, and this involved detailed explanations. Constant supply was being extended slowly, because difficulty was found in getting fittings altered, and the Company desired to avoid what had had to be done at Liverpool and Croydon,—turning off the water to avoid the waste. They thought steady advance was the best in the public interests; and, as far as it had gone, constant supply had resulted in a saving in some districts. The greatest difficulty occurred in times of prolonged drought and prolonged frost, when the public ran away with the supply and it passed beyond control. Cases of deliberate waste were very numerous, such as keeping open the valve of a closet, and there had been several prosecutions and convictions. Asked as to Dr. Bernays' discouragement of softening by chemical process, and Dr. Frankland's description of a method of doing it, the witness said the Company had met with no evidence to prove that water so softened was improved for domestic or dietetic purposes.

Mr. Wm. Morris, Engineer to the Company, was pressed on the point whether the Company could by any means get daily the estimated 44,000,000 gallons out of the chalk, and he said "possibly not the whole, but three parts of it." No doubt that would have a very considerable effect in diminishing the flow of the springs that feed the Ravensbourne, the Cray, and the Darenth. No experiments had been made to determine what could be got out of the greensand. The wells at Deptford were within 200 yards of each other, and pumping from one affected the level in the others, but not largely. No complaints had been received by the Company except with regard to shallow wells supplying houses in the immediate vicinity. Mr. Barlow's estimate of 60,000,000 gallons was given in evidence before the Commission of 1869. The storage capacity of covered service reservoirs was 10,500,000 gallons. A storage reservoir for 3,000,000 gallons had just been completed at Eltham, so that the aggregate was about a day's supply. At Deptford, working two wells continuously night and day, they had got 8,000,000 gallons a day. The witness was asked by the Chairman to supply the greatest quantities taken out of the wells consecutively in three months, six months, and a year. It was at the instance of this Company that the Lambeth Company was restrained in its Act of 1883 from sinking a well "in any part of the water lands" of the Kent Company. "Were you apprehensive that they might take water from you?" "Well, we have a very good supply, and we thought others might like to have as good."

This week the Commissioners have met twice. The greater part of Monday's sitting was devoted to an examination of Mr. A. R. Binnie, C.E., Chief Engineer to the London County Council; but the examination was confined to the statistical question of the relation between supply or consumption and population, in the past, the present, and the future. Tuesday was occupied with the evidence of the Secretary, the Engineer, and the Consulting Chemist of the Thames Conservancy; and the witnesses gave a good deal of definite information as to the relation between the Conservancy and the companies, the amounts of water that may be taken by them, and the measures adopted to prevent the pollution of the Thames and its tributaries.

Consumption and Population.

On Monday, Mr. W. B. Bryan, of the East London Company, was recalled, and handed in a statement of the water supplied for trade and non-domestic purposes, and it amounted to 21·06 per cent. of the total supply. He produced also a table showing for four parishes, wholly supplied by the Company, the number of "supplies" and the number of houses, according to the census of 1891. These are the figures:—

	"Supplies."		Houses.
London district:—			
Bethnal-green ...	19,141	....	17,109
Poplar...............	8,962	....	10,173
Country district:—			
Leyton	11,506	....	10,714
Walthamstow ...	8,799	....	7,977

He also furnished a table of the rainfall at six points for the years 1875 to 1891. In connexion with this table, he said the rainfall was not always followed by a corresponding discharge at Fieldes' Weir, because much depended upon the time of the year when the rain came. If much rain was to come now, with all the grass in the valley very long, it would scarcely reach the river at all. If the rain came in the early spring it would make a very considerable difference in the amount flowing over Fieldes' Weir. Referring to the table of supplies and houses, Dr. Ogle stated that the census returns of houses were not yet published, and the number of houses at Poplar, instead of being 10,173, was 7,404. The Chairman wanted to know what allowance ought to be made for uninhabited houses, and the witness suggested that the Commission should wait until the census returns are published. Dr. Ogle stated that the population of Bethnal-green and Poplar was 185,515, which, divided by the number of supplies, gave 6·6 as the number of persons per supply. The population of Leyton and Walthamstow was 90,252, which, divided by the supplies, gave 4·4. It had been previously stated that the number of county supplies was 68,310, and of London supplies 104,000. Multiplying the latter by 6·6, and the former by 4·4, and adding the results together, Dr. Ogle arrived at a population for the whole district of 989,696, and the witness said, "That is evidently wrong." Dr. Ogle continued that the average daily supply in 1891 was 40,282,200 gallons, which, divided by the population, gave 40·7 gallons per head per day. The witness said that Poplar and Bethnal-green were not to be compared with Whitechapel and St. George's-in-the-East, and therefore Bethnal Green and Poplar are not fair representatives of the urban parishes. After further conversation between Dr. Ogle and the witness, the Chairman said, "It is quite clear that this will require a great deal of investigation before we can usefully go on discussing the result. We must endeavour to get it as accurately as we possibly can in the face of the undoubted difficulties which exist." The witness offered, if time were allowed, to have every supply in the district counted,—that is, the number of persons for each ascertained,—and he said it would take a month or six weeks to do it. After consultation, the Chairman said the Commission thanked the witness for the offer, but would not accept it at present, but they must find some method of getting more accurate information on this important point of the number of supplies in a given district, and the number of people in the same district. They would take a little time to consider how it could best be done, and then probably ask the companies for definite information on a uniform basis.

Mr. A. R. Binnie, Chief Engineer of the London County Council, was then examined at great length in reference to a voluminous statistical compilation, occupying, with explanations, some eighty printed foolscap pages. He dealt with "Municipal London,"—the County Council area; "Greater London,"—that of the Metropolitan Police, 701 square miles; "Water London,"—the area supplied by the Water Companies, 514½ square miles; "Registration London," practically Municipal London, without Penge. Municipal London was the "Inner Ring;" the "Outer Ring" was that larger area which the Census returns called "Greater London,"—the police district. He had endeavoured to obtain accurate information as to population and the supply per head, and asked the Companies for data for 1861 and 1871, believing at the time that the data for 1881 and 1891 were in the official reports of the Companies. But now he doubted it. He found the same difficulty the Commission was finding in unravelling this question. He could not reconcile the populations with the number of houses supplied, and both with the quantity of water said to be supplied by the Companies. On the assumed accuracy of the populations of the Companies' areas, he had worked out calculations which he afterwards abandoned; and he embodied tables which reduced the assumed basis to an absurdity. To take an example from one table. In 1891, 182,456,905 gallons were supplied by the Companies. At 30 gallons per head per day, 6,081,896 persons were supplied. It was clear that that population did not exist in Greater London, or any other district supplied by the Companies. At 32½ gallons per head, the population would be 5,614,059; but that was an impossible population, because Greater London contained only 5,633,000. At 35 gallons per head, we get a population of 5,213,054,—more likely to be correct. The fact that the Companies' districts and the registration districts are not co-extensive, makes it difficult, if not impossible, to get anything but an estimate.

The Chairman remarked that from the average daily consumption for 1891 of 182,456,905 gallons, there would have to be some deduction made, in order to allow for slip in the valves, and short stroke in the pumps.

Witness: There should not be.

Why not?

Because we have had for years past the statements made by water companies that they supplied so much as a total quantity of water, and I say, as an engineer, that they must have known that these quantities were either correct or incorrect. No engineer could make such a mistake as that.

Then the figures supplied to us were in the first instance, as we understand, without any such reductions?

Some of them, I am told, were so.

The Chairman said that the East London claimed a reduction of 10 per cent., the Grand Junction, 7½, and one or two other companies, 5.

The witness: The reduction is perfectly correct, and every engineer would make it. The only complaint I have to make is that all the returns that have been made to the water examiner have been hitherto false statements, and knowingly false statements.

The Chairman said he would prefer "incorrect statements," but the witness said "No engineer would return the quantity of water pumped without deducting the slip, which he must know. No pump discharges the theoretical quantity of water."

The Chairman consulted with the other Commissioners and said there might be some misunderstanding about this, and they wished to avoid any allegations of wilful misstatement.

The witness rejoined that he could not but remark on statistics on which he had had to base his calculations up to the period of the inquiry. Then followed a minute description and comparison of tables, without which the evidence would be unintelligible. Starting from a present population of 5,185,000 in Water London, the witness estimated that in 1941 the population would be 12,373,243, and that the consumption, at 35 gallons per head per day, would be 433,063,505 gallons. In Bradford he had been totally unable to reduce the amount per head per day to much below 35 gallons for strictly domestic purposes. The rates per head per day were much higher in some of the chief cities of France, Germany, and America. In Dublin it was 47, Glasgow 50, and Edinburgh 40. London was far behind in the appliances for the public distribution of water for ornamental, sanitary, and cleansing purposes, and compared with Paris it was deplorably in the background. Paris used about 18 gallons per head per day for public purposes,—twenty times as much as London. But for the fact that 35 gallons appears to be the present actual rate of consumption, he would have preferred to base his estimates on a total consumption of 40 gallons per head per day. In conclusion, the witness asserted that the West Middlesex and Chelsea Companies were precluded by statute from taking more than 20,000,000 gallons a day from the Thames.

The Conservators of the Thames.

The first witness for the conservancy was Mr. James H. Gough, secretary, and he was examined upon a carefully-prepared narrative which he explained and amplified by many details. The historical portion explains the successive relations of the Companies to the Corporation, and then to the Conservancy, and the present relation may be summed up in the following table:—

	A.	B.		C.
Southwark and Vauxhall...	£3,000	20	+	4½
Lambeth	3,000	20	+	4½
Grand Junction	3,000	20	+	4½
West Middlesex	3,000	20	+	(4½)
Chelsea	2,500	20	+	(2)
East London	2,000	10		—
		110		20
				110
				130

The first column, A., gives the annual contributions of the Companies to the Conservancy.

The second column, B., in millions of gallons, the water that may be taken from the Thames under the 1852 agreement with the Corporation; and in the case of the East London, under the Act of 1867.

The third column, C., the extra quantities

which may be taken under the 1886 agreement with the Conservancy (the legality of which Mr. Binnie questions as to the West Middlesex and the Chelsea).

The following are the principal passages in the statement of Mr. Gough, which constituted the framework of his evidence:—

The condition of the works on the Thames above Staines, when handed to the Conservators, was so bad, and their reconstruction so costly, that the water income of 12,000*l.* was insufficient. A debt of 100,000*l.* had been incurred for the purpose of the works. After some negotiation the Companies consented to pay in the aggregate a further sum of 4,500*l.* One of the terms of the arrangement of 1886 was that the Conservators should enter into agreements with the five Companies, allowing them to draw 20,000,000 gallons daily in excess of the 100,000,000 permitted by the agreements of 1852, such additional quantity to be divided as in the table, or, in the aggregate, 120,000,000 gallons, which, with the 10,000,000 gallons allowed to the East London Company, makes a maximum draught from the river by these Companies of 130,000,000 gallons daily. The first payments under the agreements of 1886 became due in January, 1888, and, immediately after, the auditor appointed by the Local Government Board to examine the Water Companies' accounts raised a question as to the legality of the payments by the Chelsea Company and the West Middlesex Company. Sir Henry James was appointed to arbitrate, and he decided in favour of the legality of the agreements. Whilst the decision of the Arbitrator has set at rest the question of the legality of the agreements, it is worth notice that the two Companies in question have not reached the quantity of 20,000,000 gallons daily provided for in the original agreements, nor are they likely to do so for some considerable time. It has been found by gaugings taken at Teddington Weir that only in a few and most exceptional cases in the driest seasons known has the discharge at Teddington Weir fallen below 200,000,000 gallons in one day, and that after the abstraction of the water companies' supply. Even in these cases no detriment to the navigation or the amenities of the river has been experienced as a consequence of the abstraction of the water, which in dry seasons is at its maximum, exceeding, as it has done, 100,000,000 gallons in a day, and the Conservators are advised that no such detriment would ensue if the quantity abstracted were, even at those exceptional times, increased to the maximum of 130,000,000 gallons. In addition to the six Metropolitan Water Companies there are a few Local Authorities and Companies who are enabled by statute to draw water from the river; these are:—The Oxford Corporation, for the supply of the City of Oxford; the South-West Suburban Water Company; the West Surrey Water Company. In all these bodies are enabled to draw the following maxima supplies from the river:—

	Gallons.
Oxford Corporation	5,500,000
West Surrey Water Company..	3,000,000
South-West Suburban Water Company	1,000,000
Total...........	9,500,000

And the grand total of water which by statute or under the agreements can be taken from the Thames is:—

	Gallons.
Metropolitan Companies	130,000,000
Other Authorities and Companies	9,500,000
Total.........	139,500,000

in respect of which the Conservators receive at the present time the sum of 18,115*l.* per annum.

The Conservators are of opinion that under existing circumstances this maximum quantity should not be exceeded. It has not escaped the Conservators' attention that the average daily supply of one Company to its consumers (the Southwark and Vauxhall Water Company), as reported by the Water Examiner of the Metropolis, has recently often exceeded the maximum of 24,500,000 gallons allowed to be taken from the river. The Conservators have called upon the Company for explanations, and are assured that the excess, if any, is taken from sources other than the Thames, and that the quantity taken from the river has not reached the authorised maximum. The subject is continuing to receive the close attention of the Conservators. They desire to express their agreement with the views stated by the Committee of 1867 on the East London Water Bill, and by the Royal Commission of 1869, that it is quite possible to provide for a greatly enlarged demand by the storage of flood waters in reservoirs in the valley of the Upper Thames. They are prepared to adduce evidence on this point. In the year 1867 a Committee of the House of Commons on the East London Water Company's Bill reported that "if at any future period the increase of population should render it necessary to make provision for a greater supply of water than could be conveniently drawn from the Thames in a dry season, it could be adequately made by storing up in reservoirs in the valley of the Thames a portion of the flood water which now yields in a single day a sufficient supply for the whole year." The Royal Commission on Water Supply, 1867, 1868, and 1869, which was presided over by the Duke of Richmond, reported that when efficient measures were adopted for excluding the sewage and other pollutions from the Thames, and for ensuring perfect filtration, water taken from that source would be perfectly wholesome and of suitable quality for the supply of the Metropolis. The sixth report of the Rivers Pollution Commission, dated June 30, 1874, took a radically different view of the subject, and reported that the Thames should as early as possible be abandoned as a source of water for domestic supply, basing their opinion on the grounds that the Thames received the sewage of a large number of towns and other inhabited places, as well as pollution of other kinds. All opinions agree on one point, and that is, the necessity for the exclusion of pollution from the Thames; and the Conservators feel that they are able to show by facts that that exclusion is now accomplished, and that, whilst twenty years ago there was possibly room for a divergence of opinion on the subject, no such reason now exists. At first, after the passing of the Acts against pollution, difficulties in deciding between competing schemes, in raising the necessary funds, and in selecting suitable sites, confronted the Local Authorities in all parts of the river, and caused delays; but since 1874, difficulties have diminished, works by degrees have been completed, and year by year the Conservators have found the river improving in purity. Every town on the main river has taken steps to prevent the discharge of its sewage into the stream, and all, with the exception of Staines, which is now dealing with the question, and, to a limited extent the Chertsey District, have completed their works, and are passing into the river either no discharge, or effluents which are so free from pollution as to satisfy the rigorous analysis of the Conservators' Chemist, Mr. C. E. Groves, F.R.S. Of the towns which have so completed works there are, above the intakes of the water companies, on the main river, Oxford, with a population of 45,741; Abingdon, 6,557; Wallingford, 2,989; Reading, 60,054; Henley, 4,913; Maidenhead, 10,607; Windsor, 12,327; Eton, 2,490; total, 145,687. There are,—on the tributaries,—Cirencester with a population of 7,441; Old Swindon, 5,545; New Swindon, 27,295; Earley, 4,461; Wokingham, 2,060; High Wycombe, 13,435; Slough, 5,427; total, 65,664, thus making the total population of these towns above the intakes, 211,351. The following towns below the intakes of the Companies have, in consequence of pressure brought by the Conservators, diverted the sewage of their districts from the Thames or its tributaries:—On the main river,—Surbiton, with the population of 10,052; Kingston, 27,059; Teddington, 10,025; Twickenham, 16,026; Isleworth, 12,973; Brentford, 13,736; Chiswick, 21,964; total, 111,835. On the tributaries,—Ealing, with a population of 23,978; Hanwell, 6,139; Willesden, 61,266; Acton, 24,207; Finchley, 16,639; Hendon, 15,835; Harrow, 5,725; Pinner, 2,519; Epsom, 8,417; total, 164,725, making a total population of these towns below the intakes, 276,560. No less than 683,100*l.* was the cost of the works executed by the towns above the water intakes, and 653,832*l.* below that point.

[Owing to pressure on our space, we are obliged to defer, until next week, the concluding portion of our summary of Mr. Gough's statement on behalf of the Thames Conservators, as well as some notes of the evidence subsequently given by Mr. Gough, Mr. C. J. Moore, the Engineer to the Conservancy, and Mr. C. E. Groves, Consulting Chemist.]

MUNICIPAL ENGINEERING AT PETERBOROUGH.

A VERY successful and well-attended Eastern Counties District Meeting of the Incorporated Association of Municipal and County Engineers was held at Peterborough on Saturday, the 11th inst. The members, to the number of about sixty, assembled in the Guildhall, where they were received by the Deputy-Mayor (Mr. Councillor Herbert), in the unavoidable absence of the Mayor. The Deputy Mayor, in the course of his words of welcome, said that while they did not profess to have anything remarkable in the way of sanitary works in Peterborough, they had nothing to be ashamed of, particularly in view of the fact that the borough was only incorporated nineteen years ago. The citizens of Peterborough were very much indebted to the public spirit of the original members of the Corporation, who found the city without any sewerage system and without any wholesome water supply, and at once set to work to provide both. The result of the energy and public spirit thus displayed by the members of the first Corporation of the borough had been to greatly improve the health and to lessen the death-rate. He hoped that on a future occasion the members of the Association would have time to visit the waterworks at Braceborough, some fourteen miles distant.

Mr. T. de Courcy Meade, the President of the Association, expressed the thanks of the members for the Deputy Mayor's words of welcome.

On the motion of Mr. Barber, seconded by Mr. Radford, Mr. Buckham, Borough Surveyor of Ipswich, was re-elected Honorary District Secretary.

Sewerage, Paving, &c.

Mr. J. W. Walshaw, Borough Surveyor of Peterborough, then read a paper on "Municipal Work in Peterborough," in the course of which he said:—

The Borough of Peterborough is situate on the banks of the river Nene, which divides it into two portions, the larger being in the county of Northampton, of which it forms the eastern extremity, and the smaller in the county of Huntingdon; it lies on the borders of the great Fen country, but is chiefly known on account of its grand old cathedral.

The population of the borough at the last census was 25,172, being an increase of 4,061 during the preceding ten years; the rateable value is 106,350*l.*

The main line of the Great Northern Railway passes through the town, and the Midland, Great Eastern, and London and North-Western Railway Companies have joint stations here. The river Nene is navigable, and much timber and farm produce is brought by barges and discharged at the several railway wharves. It is due to the great railway accommodation that the town owes its prosperity. The trade is principally in malt, timber, agricultural produce and machinery, and the Great Northern Railway Company have engine-works, and employ a large number of men.

The town obtained a Charter of Incorporation in 1874; previously it was governed by Improvement Commissioners. Upon coming into office, the newly-formed authority found sanitary matters in a deplorable condition, especially in those parts of the borough which had not been included within the Commissioner's district; hundreds of houses were drained into cesspools, privies running into open vaults; and the water supply to the whole borough was taken from wells, many of which were not more than 8 ft. deep, and in close proximity to cesspool and privy vaults. There were twelve public pumps in the centre of the town, the whole of which, with one exception, have been left out of use; they are available, however, in cases of emergency. I am pleased to state that there has been no occasion to use them.

Upon coming into office the Town Council took immediate steps, both with respect to water-supply and drainage, and called in Mr. J. Addy, C.E., to prepare a scheme and report upon the subject; these were adopted, and the works proceeded with without delay. I may here add that at that time the sewage ran into the river, and that the authorities were threatened with an injunction to restrain them from permitting this to be continued.

The sewers are laid in straight lines, with

manholes at junctions and regular intervals; the inclinations are fairly good, with the exception of that of the intercepting sewer, part of which has a fall of 1 in 2,249, and requires periodical attention. All the old sewers, where practicable, have been retained for surface-water, and they are also used as storm overflows. The sewers are ventilated by open manholes at street levels; they are flushed by means of wooden discs, which are placed in the block on the outlet side of the manhole, and allowed to remain there until the water, which is run in from the town mains at various points, rises to a considerable height; the disc is then suddenly withdrawn and a good flush obtained. A large quantity of flush water is also run into the sewers which is not held up. Notwithstanding these arrangements, we have, especially in the autumn months, complaints of smells arising from the manholes; I suppose this is the general experience where similar means of sewer ventilation are adopted. Several cast-iron shafts, varying in diameter from 4 in. to 6 in., have been erected against buildings and trees; where these shafts are fixed near to the manholes they are often the means of preventing the escape of offensive smells from them, but this is not the case where they are more than ten or twelve yards away.

The sewage is treated by broad irrigation on a farm containing 300 acres, and situate about half-a-mile from the borough boundary; the whole of it reaches the farm by gravitation; that from the Huntingdonshire part of the borough, and from a low-lying portion on the Northamptonshire side of the river, has to be pumped. Upon reaching the farm the sewage runs into two small tanks with gratings fixed at the outlet end, to prevent paper and other solid matter passing on to the land; from the tanks it is carried through the farm by open concrete conduits, and distributed upon the land by slackers with sliding doors.

The straining tanks are emptied every three weeks; the mud is thrown into pits having earth sides; it is turned from one pit into another, and thus becomes stiff enough to cart away; as a rule I find a sale for the sewage mud at 3d. per cartload; occasionally it is given away.

About 100 acres of the farm are grass, of which 70 acres are let annually from April to December, at an average rental of 5*l*. per acre, and 30 acres are kept by the Corporation for grazing and hay for the horses belonging to them. Willows are grown on 21 acres; some of them are sold on the land at 10*l*. to 11*l*. per acre; such as are not so disposed of are cut and peeled by our own workmen, and I always find a ready sale for them at a price of about 12*l*. per ton on rail here.

Rye grass is grown upon about 20 acres; much of this is cut green, carted to the Corporation yard, and sold at 4d. per sack; that not cut for sale is made into hay, but the hay so made is not of very good quality. The remaining portion of the farm is under cultivation, and we grow fine crops of wheat, oats, beans, mangolds, potatoes, &c. Our last year's farming operations were very successful; the profit, not allowing for interest on capital borrowed for the purchase of the land and the laying out of the same, was 1,030*l*.; this left a balance in hand of 145*l*., after paying all pumping expenses and for sewage distribution, &c. The farm cost 132*l*. per acre, and the sum of 6,000*l*. has been spent upon it in roads, laying-out, conduits, levelling, &c.

Roadways.—There are about 30 miles of roadway in the borough, of which 1¼ miles are paved; 5½ miles are main road, the cost of maintaining which is paid by the County Council of the Soke of Peterborough. About forty-five years ago the central part of the town was paved with random granite setts laid on sand, with joints filled in with similar material. The paving was in a bad condition before the commencement of the drainage and waterworks excavations; but matters were made much worse by reason of the numerous disturbances of the old setts. For some years the Town Council were desirous of improving affairs, but their borrowing powers were exhausted, and the work had to be delayed. The first new paving to be executed was in 1884, when, as an experiment, about 600 yards of wood was put down in a narrow, busy street; the system adopted was similar to that at Norwich, viz., without a concrete foundation; the cost was 5s. 6d. per yard; the paving gave great satisfaction, and was renewed last year, after having been down seven years; the total quantity of wood paving here is about 2,500 square yards. In a portion of one of the streets so paved creosoted blocks were used; I am of opinion that they are an improvement upon ordinary deals, but they have not been down sufficiently long to enable me to give a decided opinion. In 1888 powers were obtained for borrowing the money required for repaving the remaining portion of the then paved streets with 5 by 3 granite setts laid on 6 in. of cement concrete, grouted in with pitch and oil; the works were extended over a period of two years, and the sum expended was a little over 8,000*l*. The whole of the materials were contracted for, the paving done by the square yard, and the rest of the work executed by the Corporation workmen. The cost was between 10s. and 11s. per square yard. Those acquainted with the streets of Peterborough three years ago cannot but be struck with the altered appearance of them to-day. We have put down two short lengths of tarred macadam,—one with granite, the other with slag; that of the latter material has been the more successful, and I am about to extend it. A 12-ton steam roller is used on the macadamised roadways.

Footways.—Whilst the paving works were in progress, new footways were put down in the same streets; they are of concrete, with 12-in. by 6-in. granite edging. The bottom layer of the concrete is 2½ in. in thickness, and composed of 4 parts local gravel to 1 part Portland cement; the top layer is ¾ in. thick, and consists of 1 part Portland cement to 2 parts gravel; several materials have been mixed with cement for the top layer, viz., slag, granite, and gravel; that made with slag is the most durable, but its slipperiness is objectionable, and I have discontinued using it; I find the best material to be local gravel, free from sand, and granite sand in equal quantities. The work is carried out by our own workmen, and the cost is about 2s. 6d. per square yard. The main portion of the other footways is formed of tar and gravel, with 12-in. by 3-in. York edging; they cost 1s. 3d. per square yard. The Corporation have twelve horses in their town stables; these are supplemented by teams from the farm, and others are hired as required at 6s. 6d. per day for horse, cart, and man.

Building Bye-Laws.—Two years ago the "Model Building Bye-Laws" were adopted. They have effected a great improvement in the smaller class of dwelling-houses, both with respect to the thickness of walls and amount of open space required. A few of the clauses are felt to be stringent, more especially that with respect to the thickness of walls of houses where the space within the roof is so constructed as to be used as a box or lumber-room. It appears to me to be somewhat excessive to require the walls, for their full height, to be increased in thickness from 9 in. to 13½ in., when the space intended to be utilised in the roof does not necessitate the walls being of a greater height than they would otherwise have been.

House Refuse.—A periodical removal of house refuse is in operation in the borough,—there are two collections weekly in the centre of the town, and one collection elsewhere; the average number of loads collected weekly is 90, and the number is increasing. I regret to say that the disposal of the collected matter is not so satisfactory as the collection, for it is deposited in disused gravel pits, &c., a great part of which will some time or other become building land.

Cottage Hospital.—Eight years ago a cottage hospital for cases of small-pox only was erected on the sewage farm; during that period it has only been used on five occasions, one of them of recent date. The Rural Sanitary Authority have joint use of the hospital, for which they pay a yearly rental of 30*l*.; the cost of it was under 500*l*., and it will accommodate eight patients. We in Peterborough have great reason to congratulate ourselves upon our comparative freedom from this terrible disease. We have a Goddard & Massey's disinfecting stove at our store yard; it is used after all cases of infectious disease, free of charge.

Death-Rate.—The average death-rate of the borough for the past ten years has been 14·7, for the previous eight years the average was 20·7. The Compulsory Notification of Diseases Act is in operation here.

Public Library.—The Public Library Act has been recently adopted, a suitable building has been taken on a seven years' lease, and is now being fitted up at a cost of about 400*l*.

Public Lighting.—The gas-works are in the hands of a company; they supply and erect the public lamps wherever required, at a distance not exceeding 60 yards apart; the price of gas for public purposes is 3s. 2d. per 1,000 cubic feet, for private purposes 3s. 4d. There are 642 public lamps, of which fifty-nine consume from 14 to 21 cubic feet of gas per hour; the remainder are regulated to consume 5 cubic feet each per hour; the charge for cleansing, lighting, and maintaining the ordinary lamps is 15s. each per annum, and the larger ones 20s. About two-thirds of the total number of lamps are not lighted during the summer months and moonlight nights, excepting when such nights fall upon a Saturday or other special occasion. Last year the bill for public lighting amounted to 1,847*l*.

Cattle Market.—The cattle market is owned by the Corporation; they purchased it about eighteen months ago, at a cost of 15,000*l*., and have found it a remunerative investment.

Municipal Buildings.—I cannot ask you to congratulate Peterborough upon the character of its municipal buildings; this is our Guildhall; our offices are scattered about here and there. We have expended all our means upon more urgent matters. I do, however, hope that when next the Association visits Peterborough,—which I trust may be at no distant date,—the meeting may be held in a building of a more pretentious character, and more befitting the dignity of a corporate town.

Water Supply.

Mr. John C. Gill, Assoc.-M.Inst.C.E., Waterworks Engineer to the Corporation of Peterborough, next read the following paper on "The Water Supply of Peterborough:"—

Peterborough was incorporated as a municipal borough in 1874, and previously to this date the water-supply, derived from shallow wells, was insufficient and impure. The Improvement Commissioners, as the Urban Authority before the town was incorporated, had been compelled to consider the advisability of providing an adequate supply of pure water from some extraneous source, but no active steps in this direction had been taken. In the meantime, outbreaks of zymotic diseases were frequent, and could be distinctly traced to the presence of organic impurities in the water used for domestic purposes.

The Corporation, with admirable promptitude, determined immediately upon its establishment to introduce simultaneously an abundant water-supply and a new system of drainage, and in August, 1874, within six months of the date of the Charter of Incorporation, instructions were given for the preparation of schemes for both purposes. The water-supply then introduced and since extended is the subject of this paper.

Summary of Works.—The works, which were opened in 1879, consist of:—1. A pump-well 63 ft. deep, 5 ft. 6 in. in diameter. 2. Three 6-in. tube-wells discharging into pump-well. 3. A pair of 120 horse-power rotary beam engines. 4. Four pumps of the bucket and plunger type. 5. Two "Lancashire" boilers,—shell 26 ft. long by 7 ft. diameter. 6. Buildings, consisting of engine-house, boiler-house, stores, workshop, and engineers' cottages. 7. A rising main from pumps, 7 furlongs in length. 8. A covered reservoir, of one million gallons capacity. 9. A delivery main, 18 in. in diameter and 14 miles long. 10. Thirty-three miles of distributing mains. 11. The necessary valves, hydrants, wash-outs, and fittings. The total cost of these works has been 91,118*l*.

The Water and its Source.—The water is drawn from wells sunk in a piece of land adjoining a branch of the Great Northern Railway, in the parish of Wilsthorpe, Lincolnshire, about three miles from Bourn, and fourteen miles from Peterborough. The original well from which the water is pumped is 5 ft. 6 in. in diameter, lined with cast-iron cylinders, and when the yield from this well became, through the increased requirements of the borough, inadequate for its supply, three 6-in. tube wells were sunk, from which the water is discharged into the original pump-well. The wells penetrate the oolite formation and strike the water-bearing strata at an average depth of 53 ft. 6 in. from the surface. From this depth the water rises with considerable force; in one instance a stone weighing 6¾ lb. was ejected from the top of one of the tubes. Before reaching the water a bed of argillaceous limestone, 8 ft. thick, abounding in marine fossils, was passed through, and between this rock and the water-bearing strata the estuarine clays, 27 ft. in thickness, were pierced. The first experimental boring was made in 1875, and on September 6 in that year the water rushed up the hore-hole in large volumes, and was projected in the form of a fountain to a height of 15 ft. above the surface. The yield on September 21, fifteen days after being first tapped, was at the rate of 420 gallons a minute from the 4-in. bore, and gave a velocity of 770 ft. per minute at 3 ft. above the surface. The original pump-well, 5 ft. 6 in. in diameter down to the water-bearing rock, and thence continued by five 6-in. bore-holes, gave sufficient water until the year 1885, when, because of contracts entered into for supplying the railway companies, additional sources of supply became necessary. Three tube-wells were therefore sunk with a bore of 6 in. in diameter down to the water-rock, and continued to a distance varying from 9 ft. to 15 ft. in the different wells, with a diameter of 5 in. A solid drawn copper tube lines the bore down to the water-rock, into which it is sealed. At the top of each tube a stop-valve is fixed, and by this means the quantity of water drawn from the wells may be regulated according to the consumption in the town. When only one of these extra wells is required, the other two may be shut off entirely, thus preventing the water running to waste. The daily yield of these three 6-inch tube wells, gauged on November 12, 1888, was as follows:—No. 1 well, 674,818 gallons; No. 2, 681,108; No. 3, 810,320; total, 2,166,246 gallons. The cost of the three wells, including all labour and materials, was 649*l*. 13s. 11d. The total quantity of water drawn from all the wells during last year was 511,546,955 gallons, or an average throughout the year of 1,401,498 gallons a day.

The Engines, Pumps, and Boilers.—The engines are of the rotary beam type, with single cylinders 32 in. in internal diameter, and 6 ft. stroke of piston. The steam and exhaust valves are gun-metal, of the ordinary double-beat equilibrium type, the various grades of expansion being obtained by making the cams for operating the steam valves with an increasing tread, so that by sliding them on the shaft by means of suitable screws and gearing, which may be operated while the engine is in motion, the valves may be kept open for a longer or shorter period of admission of steam, and the speed of the engines thus regulated. Each fly-wheel is 20 ft. in diameter, and weighs 20 tons. The crank-shaft where in fly-wheel is 15 in. in diameter, and 12 in. at the necks. The throw of the crank is 3 ft. The beams are of wrought iron, 24 ft. in length, and 4 ft. in depth at the centres, the rolled plates of which the beams are formed being 1½ in. thick. To each beam are connected the rods of two main water-pumps, condenser air-pump, feed-pump for boilers, and air-pump for charging air-vessel. The main pumps, four in number, are of the bucket-and-plunger type. Each pump has a cylinder 1 ft. 5½ in. in internal diameter, with a stroke of 3 ft. The bucket is made of gun-metal, with a valve of the double-seated equilibrium type, with white-metal seatings. The diameter of the plunger is 1 ft. ⅞ in. The pumps draw their water through two suction-pipes,—the two pumps on each engine being fed by the same pipe. These pipes are 1 ft. 6 in. in hore from the wells to the outward pumps, and 1 ft. 3 in. from the outward to the inward pumps. All the pumps deliver their water into the same delivery main which conveys the water direct to the town, the surplus over the consumption being accumulated in the reservoir. Two boilers of the "Galloway" type supply the steam for actuating the engines. The shell of each is 26 ft. long by 7 ft. in diameter. They are fed by water from the condenser hot well, which is at a temperature of 95 deg. to 100 deg. Fahr., when it enters the boilers. The engines, pumps, and boilers were made and erected by Messrs. Galloway & Sons, of Manchester, whose contract was 9,000*l*.

The Reservoir.—The reservoir is constructed on Obthorpe Hill, an elevation about seven furlongs from the pumping-station, having a summit level of 160·2 ft. above Ordnance Datum. It is a brick structure, encased in concrete, and made water-tight with an outer shell of puddle. The covering is formed by segmental brick arches, springing from transverse walls, built with arched openings upon piers. The floor is of concrete, finished smooth with cement. The reservoir is rectangular in plan, 120 ft. long inside by 89 ft. 6 in. wide, with a depth when full to overflow level of 16 ft., and a capacity of 1,000,000 gallons. The height of water in the reservoir is shown on a dial at the engine-house by means of an electrical water-level indicator supplied and fitted by the Silvertown Company. The overflow level of the reservoir is 135·1 ft. above the ground level at the Guildhall, Peterborough. The cost of the reservoir and fittings was 7,356*l*. 12s. 9d.

Delivery and Distributing Mains.—The 18-in. delivery main, 14 miles in length, is laid in all the straight sections with pipes 12 ft. long, with bored and turned joints; in other parts the ordinary lead joint is used. The price per ton for the ordinary cast socket pipes was 5s. less than for those with bored and turned joints, yet the extra labour and materials used in making the lead joints caused the total cost of the finished main to be 1s. 4d. per yard run higher where the lead joints were used than in the lengths laid with pipes that were bored and turned. The bored and turned joints were used entirely throughout the delivery main, except at the bends, and have been eminently satisfactory during the thirteen years the main has been in work. The distributing mains, 33 miles in length, are of various sizes, from 12 in. down to 4 in., and are connected up in circuits so as to avoid dead ends as much as possible. Fire hydrants are fixed at an average of 90 yards apart, and sluice valves at all junctions and other places where required. The contract for supplying the pipes was let to Messrs. Cochrane, Grove, & Co., of Middlesborough, and the sluice valves, hydrants, &c., were supplied by Messrs. Alley & MacLellan, of Glasgow. The total original cost of the delivery main was 36,456*l*. 13s. 4d., and of the distributing mains, 16,654*l*. 1s. 1d.

The district supplied by these works comprises several villages adjoining the main pipes, or the boundaries of the borough, and contains altogether a population of 29,300. The four railway companies who have works at Peterborough are supplied from these waterworks, and together consume about 750,000 gallons a day. The total daily consumption of water, taken on an average throughout last year, was 1,401,498 gallons. Excluding the water sold in bulk to the railway companies, this gives a daily consumption of twenty-two gallons a head for all purposes.

Mr. Isaac Shone next read a paper on "The Shone System of Town Drainage," but a summary of this, as well as a condensed report of the discussion which followed the reading of the three papers, we must postpone, for want of space, this week.

Owing to rain, only a few of the party visited the sewage-farm, under the guidance of Mr. Walshaw, the Borough Surveyor.

Correspondence.

To the Editor of The Builder.

FOURTEENTH AND FIFTEENTH CENTURY SCREENS.

Sir,—The Rev. B. Ruck-Keene's query suggests a very tall order indeed!

Confining myself entirely to the county in which I write (Devonshire), of fourteenth-century stone screens there is—Bishop Stapeldon's (A.D. 1308–26) rood-screen in Exeter Cathedral; a screen of about the same date at Ottery St. Mary; and the beautiful fifteenth-century rood and parclose screens at Totnes Church. The detail on these latter screens is so similar to those to the Lady Chapel and side chapels abutting it in Exeter Cathedral, that they are probably the work of the same hands. At Awliscombe and Paignton there are also stone screens of the same date.

Of oak screens, Devonshire stands well to the fore. Just to the left, on entering the Cathedral from the west, is St. Edmund's Chapel, now more commonly known as the Consistory Court. It is divided from the north aisle by a Decorated screen (A.D. 1340),—the oldest in the Cathedral. The screens that form lines of demarcation between the aisles of the nave and those of the choir date from a little later period. There are no fourteenth-century oak screens, so far as I am aware, in churches in the diocese. It seems that nearly all the county's efforts in the fourteenth century were directed to transforming our Norman-Transition Cathedral into a Decorated one. One hundred years later, however, people having had time to breathe, the wave of restoration went through Devonshire,—from east to west and north to south. There are some very beautiful fifteenth-century oak screens in the cathedral choir. The city of Exeter only boasts of one other fifteenth-century oak-screen; it is now in St. Mary's Steps Church, but was formerly in (the now destroyed) St. Mary Major's.

There are fifteenth-century screens at Pinhoe, Stoke-in-Teignhead, Poltimore, Littleham (near Exmouth), Broadwood Widger, St. Saviour's (Dartmouth), Staverton, Bradninch, Cullompton, Feniton, Payhembury, Plymtree, Colebrook (a very curious parclose), Down St. Mary, Lapford (rather late), Stockleigh Pomeroy, Atherington (late, and the only instance of an original rood-loft gallery in the county), Swimbridge, Sheldon, Halberton, Alphington, Chudleigh, Comb-in-Teignhead, Dunchideock, Haccombe, Kenn, Kenton, Talaton, Shirwell, Berry Pomeroy, Churston Ferrers, Broad Hempston, Ipplepen, Torbrian, Woolborough, Bovey Tracey, Ilsington, Manaton, St. Michael's (Honiton), North Leigh, Ashprington, Blackawton, Harburton, Rattery, Hartland, Kingsbridge, Aveton Gifford, North Bovey, Bow, Cruwys Morchard, Bampton, Bridford, Holberton, Little Hempston, East Down, Denbury, Chulmleigh, Chivelstone, Cornwood, Calverleigh, Burrington, Burlescombe, Buckland Monachorum, Buckerell, Welcombe, Ugborough, Stokenham, Slapton, Sherford, Holne, North Huish, Kentisbeare, Sampford Peverell, Portlemouth, Rattery Plymstock, North Petherwin, Petertavy, North Molton, Musbury, Littleham (near Bideford), King's Nympton, South Milton, Dodbrooke, Marwood, and Buckland-in-the-Moor.

These names occur to me, but there are doubtless other churches in the county in which fifteenth-century oak screens, or portions of such screens, still exist.

Of all those now mentioned, by far the most beautiful and ornate is that at St. Paul's, Staverton, upon the banks of the river Dart. It consists of a continuous run of seventeen bays, in all 50 ft. long from north to south. It is groined on both sides, and there is a rood-loft the entire length, 6 ft. 9 in. wide. The gallery front, facing westward, is richly canopied. The height of the screen is 15 ft. It has recently been restored, at a cost of about 1,000*l*., by an anonymous donor, through the medium of the Rev. S. Baring-Gould, and under the direction of Mr. F. Bligh Bond, architect, of Bristol. The actual work itself was carried out by myself and sons. Harry Hems.

Exeter, June 11, 1892.

LEWISHAM PARISH CHURCH.

Sir,—I learn from the minute-book of the trustees for rebuilding the parish church of Lewisham in 1774, that the architect of the new church was Mr. George Gibson, and that the builders selected were Oliver Burton & Co. I should be much obliged if any readers of the *Builder* could inform me whether representatives of the above are now living. Leland L. Duncan, F.S.A.

June 14, 1892.

The Student's Column.

WARMING BUILDINGS BY HOT WATER.
XXV.

JOINTING AND SUPPORTING PIPES.—CHIMNEYS.

THE general method of jointing hot-water pipes, when there is a large number of joints to be made, is by what is known as the rust joint. For small works there is now a more general application of the rubber ring, or some of the different forms of expansion joints, these latter being now made in considerable variety and having many good features. Joints are also made with red and white lead and yarn, but this is a more expensive joint; it, however, is not so rigid as the rust joint, and fulfils a use in this respect as will be seen directly. It is a joint also used with small works, as the little extra expense is then trifling, and it is convenient both in application and in obtaining the materials. The rust joint is cheapest but not convenient, unless the works are on a large scale, or several jobs are being carried on at once. There are other different joints, workmen sometimes making a joint specially their own. The writer once saw a joint made with old tarred cord and nothing else, and this withstood a pressure of 30 lbs. per square inch.

There is a distinction between horticultural and building works in the question of joints, in the fact that the former, in having no height, produces no pressure, and almost anything will make a water-tight joint, if it does not make a lasting one. With building works, the pressure, if the height be anything to speak of, quite precludes the use of the plain rubber ring, and the other joints (rust, &c.) must be allowed to set thoroughly hard before the apparatus is charged. This, it is understood, applies to cast-iron heating pipes and coils; what wrought pipe may be used has screwed joints, and will bear very heavy pressures.

The rust joint is made by mixing iron borings (these can readily be procured at about 9s. per cwt.) with some sal-ammonia and sulphur in a powdered form. The addition of these two latter materials to the borings causes a chemical action to set in, and the iron rusts into a hard and solid mass. The rusting process takes place quickly, but it is some days before the action entirely ceases, and this brings about very disagreeable results when the workman is not experienced. The borings, during the change they undergo by the addition of the two substances named, expand somewhat; that is to say, the mass of material exerts an expansive force while the chemical action is proceeding. The result of this is that, as the action chiefly takes place after the borings are caulked into the socket, there is every probability of the socket splitting if the joint is not made by a skilled man. There have been vast quantities of pipe spoiled in this way, and it is somewhat fair evidence of experience when a man makes rust joints which remain sound, and do not injure the sockets.

Workmen have different ways of caulking in this material. The socket is, we may say, never filled with borings only; there is always some yarn used. Some workmen caulk the socket half-full of yarn, the remaining half with borings; sometimes it is three-fourths yarn, just finished off with borings, or it may be the socket is packed with two or three alternate layers of the two materials. A good workman makes his joint quite watertight with the yarn alone, but this material needs sustaining with the iron borings which go to complete and make the joint permanent. Two-thirds yarn and one-third borings make a good joint.

The proportions of the materials added to,—say, 100 parts of borings, are one part powdered sal-ammonia and two parts powdered sulphur, the whole being moistened and thoroughly mixed. It requires to be made from one to two hours before it is used; but the weather will affect it in this respect. It cannot usually be kept longer than one day without becoming hard and unfit for use.

The red and white lead joint is made by taking the latter material, which is a sticky mass, and adding the dry red lead to it until the mixture is of the consistency of putty. Some of this mixture is taken, and has boiled oil added until it is quite liquid, and the ends of the pipes are painted with this, otherwise the putty material will not adhere. Usually the joint is made by caulking in alternate layers of yarn and lead, the yarn first, and finishing with the lead, and when dry it is a sound and durable piece of work.

The rubber-ring joint is now considerably in favour, as it has many good features, chiefly by its convenient application to certain purposes. A considerable trade is now done in small boilers, which are sent out for amateurs' greenhouses, complete with the pipes, &c., and are so constructed that the purchaser can erect the whole of the apparatus himself. The joints of these pipes, both with the boiler and with one another, are commonly made with a plain rubber ring, and for this purpose it is a great convenience. Then, again, in some large works, temporary lines of pipes are sometimes needed, and for this purpose the rubber ring is a positive boon, as it can be used with any ordinary description of pipe. Occasionally permanent works of a large character are carried out with this joint, but it is not a usual practice.

The particular convenience of the rubber-ring joint is the expeditious way in which it can be used. It consists of a ring of round india-rubber, full ½ in. thick, the size varying with the size of the pipe, of course. This ring, which is a little smaller than the pipe, is stretched just on the spigot end of the pipe and this is then forced into the socket. Its passage in causes the ring to roll, and by the time the spigot is pushed home, the ring joint is half way up the socket, as fig 101 (section). Instead of stretching the ring on to the spigot, a ring expander can be had, which, when one

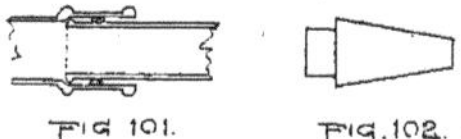

FIG 101. FIG.102.

end is placed in the pipe, permits of the ring being rolled up it, on to the pipe, and this prevents it being put on in an irregular manner or twisted. The tube expander is as fig. 102. This joint is totally wanting in rigidity, and the pipes need to be well supported.

This, and the following joint, are what is termed "expansive." What is really meant is, that it is elastic, and, considering that every variation in the temperature of the water brings about a movement in the pipes (expansion and contraction), the necessity of such a joint becomes obvious. With the rust and also the red and white lead joint, some provision is always made for this, if the pipes extend any distance. With short services no provision is needed. With the two joints named, a long, loose socket is provided here and there, and so packed that the pipes can move to and fro in it to a trifling extent. One firm of growers uses rust joints, but uses a rubber ring for every sixth joint. The expansive force is not extensive, that is to say in a 100-ft. run of pipe we may never get more than 1 in. total extension in length, but the force is certain and irresistible; so much so that brickwork has often been displaced by the thrust. The rubber joints allow for this, and act very successfully.

There are several forms of patented joints that have rubber as the jointing material, and which possess the elasticity just spoken of. It is not necessary to describe them all, but Jones's patent, as fig. 103, can be described as

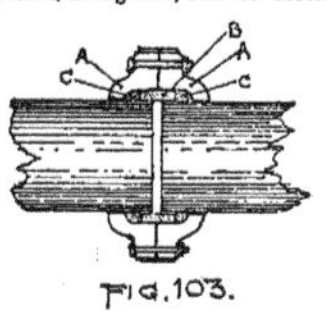

FIG.103.

an example. This consists of two cast collars, A A, an iron ring B, two rubber collars C C, and the whole brought together with the bolts shown. This joint has the advantage of being used without socketed or special shaped ends to the pipes, any plain pipe can be jointed, and if the pipe was badly or roughly cut, a joint might still be well made. This saves waste of cut pipe, as some of the patented joints depend upon one of the ends being made to suit the other. A joint like this (fig. 103) permits of any length of pipe being taken out and replaced with new, if needed, without disturbing the remainder. This would prove very convenient if, after laying down a long run of pipe, a bad leakage was found somewhere in the middle. With the ordinary joints, a mishap like this is provided for by putting running,—*i.e.*, loose,—sockets here and there. All kinds of rubber joints are more expensive than the rust joint; but if anyone wishes to compare the cost between the two, let it be remembered that a rubber joint can be made in an exceedingly short space of time.

PIPE SUPPORTS.—In nearly all horticultural works the supports are little piers of brickwork, and for such purposes nothing better is needed. It is essential that the brick piers be on a good foundation, or their own weight and the weight of the pipes may cause them to sink, with the most disagreeable results, even if the joints in the pipes did not become fractured. For those situations where the pipes are seen iron supports can be used, these (as fig. 104) being of better appearance and very safe; they are also exceedingly cheap, being mere plain castings.

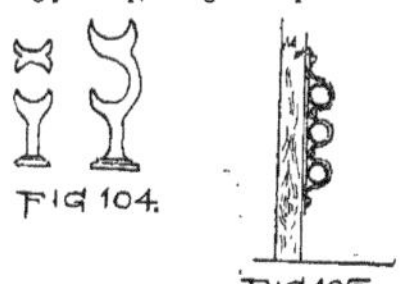

FIG 104. FIG.105

When pipes are carried along a wall or woodwork they are sometimes strapped on as fig. 105. There is nothing unworkmanlike in this.

When the runs of pipe get somewhat extensive, then, in addition to elastic joints, there must be some provision on the supports themselves, to allow for the movement that takes place. With brick piers a piece of small iron pipe, or round rod-iron, will form a frictionless bearing, or if iron supports are used they can be purchased as fig. 106, or a smith can make something with rollers for the pipes to rest upon. If such a provision is not made there is every probability of some harm ensuing; but, as just mentioned, this need not be thought of with medium and small sized works.

CHIMNEYS.—Reference has been made to these from time to time in the previous papers, and very little remains to be said. We have fully pointed out the necessary features with

FIG.106.

chimneys in building works, but there needs to be given the rules usually followed in making the chimneys to boilers attached to glass-house works, those which stand away from buildings. In giving the following sizes it is supposed the chimneys are brick built, not sheet-iron pipe. Earthenware pipes, however, answer very well for this purpose as a rule.

The minimum height of chimney should not be less than the length of the flues that lead up and down the boiler,—that is to say, a 4-ft. saddle boiler, having flues once up and down its length, should have an 8-ft. chimney. If the boiler was one having the flues traversing its length three times, then it should have a 12-ft. chimney. Let it be clearly understood that these are minimum heights. If we made the chimney of less height than this, the draught in it would be insufficient to carry away the smoke or gases, and cause a proper degree of combustion in the furnace. Sometimes a chimney a little lower will work passably well, but it is best to calculate, as just described, for a minimum height.

Every opportunity should be taken to have a higher chimney wherever possible; better and more reliable results are attained; but of course in private gardens the chimney, beyond certain limits, is strongly objected to on account of its unsightliness in most cases. With professional growers, sightliness may probably be the last thing to be considered, profit has more consideration, and higher chimneys are the rule.

The area of the chimney should bear some relation to the size of the boiler, and the following sizes are reliable—

		Area of chimney in square inches.
For Trentham boilers	8 to 10 ft. long	400
" Saddle "	6 ft. long ...	300
" " "	4 ft. 6 in. long	250
" " "	3 ft. or smaller	200

These areas are for the minimum height chimneys just referred to. As the height is increased the area can be reduced. For low chimneys the area cannot be too roomy, it is essential; and at the point where the flues from the boiler enter the chimney, the passage should not be choked in anyway. It will be understood that as the height of chimney is increased, the draught is more keen and a less area will answer, but small area must be avoided with very low chimneys. If the height of chimney was double the minimum given, then the area could be reduced, say, one fourth.

SURVEYORSHIPS.

SALFORD.—At the monthly meeting of the Salford Town Council, held in the Salford Town-hall on the 1st inst., the Mayor, Mr. Alderman Keevney, as Chairman of the General Purposes Committee, as well as the Selection Committee, proposed the adoption of Mr. John Price (the Engineer and Surveyor to the Toxteth Park Local Board, Liverpool) as the Borough Engineer and Surveyor of Salford, at a salary of 500*l.* per annum, and that he devote the whole of his time to the duties of the office. Mr. Linsley seconded. Mr. Alderman Walmsley proposed, as an amendment, that Mr. Joseph Corbett, of Broughton, be appointed the Borough Engineer and Surveyor. Mr. Alderman Bailey seconded the amendment. After some discussion the amendment was carried, 30 voting for it and 26 against. The recommendation of the General Purposes Committee was therefore rejected. The amendment then became the substantive motion, against which Mr. Snape moved an amendment that the name of Mr. H. C. Marks (the Borough Engineer and Surveyor of Dewsbury), one of the candidates, be substituted for that of Mr. Corbett. Mr. Hamblett seconded. On a second vote being taken, 25 voted for the amendment and 29 against. The substantive resolution was then adopted, appointing Mr. Corbett to the office.

GENERAL BUILDING NEWS.

MUNICIPAL BUILDINGS, CROYDON.—On the 9th inst. the Mayor of Croydon laid the foundation-stone of the Municipal Buildings, Croydon, which are being erected at a cost of £80,000. The principal front (we quote from the *Local Government Journal*) will be 285 ft. long, the side frontage being 170 ft. The municipal buildings block will extend for a distance of 160 ft. towards the High-street. The entrance is in the centre, and leads to a large hall on the ground floor. From this hall staircases lead to the lower ground floor and to the first floor. Right and left on each floor branch corridors 10 ft. wide, lighted from two large open areas, giving access to the various departments as follows:—On the lower ground floor, Borough Engineer's drawing offices, plan and samples rooms, offices for the Building Inspectors, water and sewers foremen, offices for the Medical Officer of Health, Sanitary Inspectors and Clerks, Road Surveyor's offices, Inspectors of Weights and Measures offices, three waiting-rooms, and a muniment-room. On the ground floor to the left of the entrance are the public and private offices of the Borough Engineer, with access from the latter to the drawing offices by a spiral staircase, to the right of the entrance are the rates offices of the borough, comprising the accountant's department. On the first floor is the Town Clerk's department containing a large public office, three small private offices for clerks and the Town Clerk's private room. The remainder of the Borough Accountant's department is on this floor, viz., his private office, a large public office, a small private office, and a room for auditors. On this floor will also be the Council Chamber, with galleries for the public and for reporters. Adjoining is the Mayor's parlour, a large ante-room, and two committee-rooms. On each floor are cloak-rooms and lavatories. There are also strong-rooms, and rooms for books and papers in connexion with several of the departments. Rooms for the hall-keeper will be on the floor above formed in a portion of the roof. The session courts are behind the municipal buildings. They will be on the ground-floor level. The court for the borough bench and quarter sessions is 50 ft. by 40 ft.; the county-court is 40 ft. by 30 ft., both top-lighted. Near to the former are rooms for the magistrates, the magistrates' clerk's offices, and a large room for the grand jury at quarter sessions. There are also rooms for the county-court judge, barristers, &c., with cloak-rooms and lavatories. Beneath the courts are rooms for prisoners and police, which will connect, by a corridor and subway, with the police-station, to be built on the opposite side of the new street, and by a staircase with the dock in the large court. The public library forms a continuation of the Municipal Offices block towards the High-street, but the front of the former is recessed 45 ft. from that of the latter; in the angle so formed stands the tower, about 150 ft. high. The lower part forms a vestibule from which a short flight of steps leads to a central-hall, on the left of which is the lending library, on the right the reading and news room, and opposite is the librarian's room. From the vestibule stairs lead down to the magazine-room, a workroom, stores, &c. Open areas, 12 ft. and 18 ft. wide, with retaining walls to the roads faced with ivory-tinted glazed bricks, will afford light to all rooms at this level. A corn market completes the group on that portion of the site nearest to the High-street. It is proposed to warm the buildings by steam radiators fed with fresh air from the exterior, and to draw off the spent and vitiated air by the chimney shaft from the furnace of the boilers, supplemented by extraction fans in a shaft or trunk which will be connected by openings from each room. The style of the design is modern Renaissance, freely treated. The materials of the exterior are red bricks, with Portland stone dressings and green Westmoreland slates for the roof covering. Mr. Samuel Page, of Croydon, has undertaken the contract for the foundations and lower ground floor. Mr. E. W. Nightingale is the clerk of the works. The architect is Mr. Charles Heuman, of Croydon and London.

BOWES MUSEUM, BARNARD CASTLE, DURHAM.—The Bowes Museum, Barnard Castle, the foundation-stone of which was laid by the late Countess of Montalbo, wife of the late Mr. John Bowes, of Streatlam Castle, in November, 1869, was opened to the public on the 10th inst. by Sir Joseph W. Pease, Bart., M.P. According to the *Leeds Mercury*, the structure is in the style of the French Renaissance. The south, or principal, front is 300 ft. in length; the central dome and the two turrets are carried to a considerable height above the main building, which has an elevation of about 85 ft. East and west are wings, the length of each of which is 130 ft., and the front is set back 38 ft. within these wings. The entrance-hall is 42 ft. square; the walls are of polished freestone, and the floor of marble mosaic. The main doorway is 24 ft. 6 in. high by 20 ft. 6 in. wide, and the doors are of iron. The steps of the principal staircase, which are 52 in number, are of polished Peterhead granite, and hang out of the wall 8 ft.; twelve polished red granite columns support this staircase, the landings of which are of stone from the Craigleith Quarries, Edinburgh. The basement and top floors are appropriated to residential purposes. The rooms on the third floor are filled with collections of pottery and porcelain, glass, carved ivory, crystals, silversmiths' work, &c. On the second floor the rooms to the left form the library. In the large room on the right of the staircase, 42 ft. square by 25 ft. high, are hung a number of paintings, chiefly foreign landscapes, which were executed by the foundress of the museum. The picture-gallery, which is entered from the first room, consists of a suite of three rooms, the entire length of which is 204 ft., and the width 44 ft. In the roof are three lights, each of which is 41 ft. 6 in. by 20 ft. The sculpture-gallery on the first floor is under the picture-gallery, and is of the same dimensions. The building was commenced in the spring of 1870. Mr. Joseph Kyle, of Barnard Castle, was the builder; Monsieur Jules Pellechet, of Paris, and the late Mr. John Edward Watson, of Newcastle-on-Tyne, were the joint architects.

THE NEW FRUIT AND VEGETABLE MARKET IN THE CITY.—On the 13th inst. the Lord Mayor opened the new fruit, vegetable, and flower-market erected at the junction of Charterhouse-street and Farringdon-road. The new market has cost 70,000*l.*, exclusive of the value of the site, and of this sum 41,000*l.* has been laid out on the substructure and for basement works, under an agree- with the Great Northern Railway Company. The market has a frontage to Charterhouse-street of about 370 ft., and to Farringdon-road of about 184 ft. Of this area, representing about 54,000 ft., the building now erected occupies 30,000 ft. super., leaving ample room for extension when required. The main vehicular and footway extrance to the new building is in the middle of the Charterhouse-street front, and is 33 ft. wide. The avenue from this entrance, running parallel with Farringdon-road, and dividing the market equally, is of a like width; and a further entrance, 16 ft. wide, for carriages and pedestrians is placed at the north end of the Farringdon-road front. Two footway entrances, 8 ft. wide, are provided on the Charterhouse-street front, and one on the Farringdon-road front, all three affording access to gangways of a like width, traversing the market from south to north and west to east. The building is designed of iron and glass. The height of the building to the plate level is 28 ft., and to the ridge 46ft. The basements under this and adjoining markets will be occupied by the great Northern Railway Company, whose lines of rail and platforms will traverse the entire length from Charles-street to Snow-hill. The area of these basements is about 100,000 ft. Large hydraulic lifts are designed to raise the market produce brought by the railway companies to the markets above, and inclined roadways for horse traffic are provided as means of access from the basement to the street level. The late Mr. Alexander Peebles, City Architect, drew up the designs of the market, which has been constructed by Messrs. Rudd & Son, of Grantham, and Messrs. Perry & Co., of London. The execution of the work was carried out under the superintendence of the City Surveyor, Mr. A. Murray.

PRIMITIVE METHODIST CHURCH, GATESHEAD.—On the 6th inst. the foundation-stones were laid of a new church for the Primitive Methodists, Gateshead. The building is situate in Durham-road, and has a frontage also to South-street. There are three entrances, the two principal being from Durham-road. The church is 61 ft. in length and 42 ft. wide, with a gallery round three sides, and will accommodate about 620. The organ and choir are placed in a gallery behind the rostrum, and raised about 8 ft. above the church floor, with entrance from South-street. Under the choir gallery is a large church vestry, with ministers' vestry adjoining. There are two staircases to the gallery. The principal staircase leading from the entrance hall is so planned as to give communication with the schools and lecture hall adjoining. The church is being built with stone, and has been designed, to harmonise with the schools, in the Early English style, with a tower over the entrance porch, connecting the two blocks. The seating, rostrum, gallery front, and internal fittings generally are to be carried out in pitch-pine. The buildings are to be heated by hot water on the low pressure system, and are being carried out from plans and under the supervision of the architects, Messrs. Davidson & Bendle, of Newcastle, at a cost of about 3,250*l.* Messrs. Haswell & Waugh, Gateshead, are the contractors.

NEW YORKSHIRE PENNY BANK, LEEDS.—On the 1st inst., the foundation-stone was laid of the new Yorkshire Penny Bank in Leeds. The site is at the corner of Infirmary-street and Toronto-street, immediately behind the new General Post-office. The new bank, says the *Leeds Mercury*, will occupy an area of 1,315 square yards, with a frontage to Infirmary-street of 103 ft., and to Toronto-street of 115 ft. The designs are a treatment of Domestic Gothic. The tower at the angle of the building is terminated by an open stage, covered by a pyramidal roof of red tiles, surmounted by an octagon turret. Inside the tower there is to be a stone staircase and a lift, giving access to the two suites of offices on the first and second floors. The basement will contain cellars, clerks' rooms, and other apartments, as well as the heating, ventilating, and lifting apparatus. The business of the bank will be conducted on the ground floor, where there will be a large room, entrance to which will be obtained from Infirmary-street. The whole of the internal walls of this room are to be arcaded. On the same floor are rooms for the manager, clerks, inspectors, and other officials, and a safe-room. A large room for the use of the board of directors will occupy a part of the same floor. The second floor will be let off as offices, and the third will be utilised as storage-rooms. The building, which is now above the ground, is to be erected entirely of Morley stone, with red-tiled roof. Special attention has been paid to the lighting and heating and to the sanitary arrangements. The lavatories and other conveniences will be disconnected from the sewerage system, and the supply of hot and cold water to all parts will be ample. The banking-room is to be heated by warm air, which will be driven inside by a fan, the same power supplying cool air in the summer season. The various lifts in the building will be worked on the high-pressure hydraulic system. Throughout the floors are to be constructed of iron and concrete, and the materials generally will be as far as possible fireproof. The architects are Messrs. Perkin & Bulmer, Leeds. Messrs. Nicholson & Son, Leeds, hold the contract for the erection of the superstructure, including the masons', bricklayers', and joiners' work; and Mr. Evans has made the foundations and the basement. It is estimated that the buildings, including the land, will cost between 30,000*l.* and 40,000*l.*

MARCROSS CHURCH, GLAMORGANSHIRE.—We are informed that this very ancient and most interesting church, situated on the coast not far from Nash Point, and St. Donatt's Castle is about to be restored. The Norman chancel arch and porch doorway, together with the leper window in the chancel were the subjects of much interest to the members of the Archæological Society, who visited the church a few years back. The work of restoration has been entrusted to Messrs. Kempson & Fowler, architects, Llandaff. This restoration may, no doubt, be necessary, practically, but we fear it will greatly diminish the "interest" of archæologists in the church.

FOREIGN AND COLONIAL.

FRANCE.—It is announced that, on account of the opposition of a certain number of architects who composed the section of architecture in the Champs Elysée Salon, and who have not received the summons for the vote of the Medal of Honour, the sub-committee has resolved to cancel the negative ballot of May 30, and proceed with a new election this week.——The Society of Fine Arts of Departments has just held its annual réunion at the École des Beaux-Arts, under the presidency of the Minister of Public Instruction.——The special commission charged with the awarding of the three prizes called "de l'Institut," at the Salon des Champs Elysées, has given them as follows:—M. Henri Royer, the Henri Lehmann prize, for the encouragement of good classical studies; M. Moteleya, the Brizard prize, for landscape or sea painting; and the Maxime David prize, for the best miniature painting, has been awarded to Madame H. Richard.——The competition instituted by the National Society of French Architects for young French architects, between the ages of eighteen and twenty-four, has just been decided in the Palace of the Bourse du Commerce. The competition was for a lodging-house in the Batignolles quarter, which was to contain all the latest inventions for comfort and hygiene. Out of thirteen interesting designs, the jury decided to give the first prize to MM. Colas and Daudanne; the second to M. G. Madaule, and the third to M. Paul Martin, of Moulins; a first mention to M. Bierry, and a second mention to M. Déjean.——Ninety-two painters have taken part in the open competition for the decoration of the Mairie of Montreuil-sous-Bois. The exhibition is open at the Hôtel de Ville in Paris, and the judgment will be given in the course of next week.——We hear of fresh fires in the forest of Fontainebleau, principally in those parts which are planted with pines, and covered with heather.——The Government has just offered to the Museum of Troyes a beautiful picture by M. Adrien Moreau, entitled "In the Park."——At Marseilles a monument has just been inaugurated to the memory of the Abbé Dassy, who founded the schools for the blind, and the deaf and dumb. The monument, which has been paid for by subscription, is the work of Falguière.——On the suggestion of M. Charles Garnier, the committee for the monument which is to be erected by subscription to the memory of Alphand, has chosen the environs of the Bois de Boulogne, and more especially the great avenue which leads to it. M. Formigé, the architect who is execute the work, has been instructed to study the spot, and choose the best site.——The death is announced of M. William Haussoulier, painter and engraver, pupil of Paul Delaroche. He received medals at the Salons of 1866-1884 and 1889.——On Sunday last in Paris there was a solemn inauguration of the new Roumanian Church, which was found to be the old chapel of the Dominicans of the Rue Jean-de-Beauvais. This edifice, which ad been abandoned by the order from the time of their expulsion from France in 1882, has been entirely transformed and richly decorated.——The Minister of War has given up the idea of having a military hospital in the park of St. Cloud.—— August 1 is the last day for the sending in designs for the competition for the erection at Lilles, in the Square Jussieu, of the monument to the memory of Achille Testelin, who, during the Franco-German war, organised the national defence in the North of France.

VIENNA.—The municipal authorities have opened a competition for plans for the future arrangement and improvement of the city, including the extension of the drainage system, the regulation of the canal, the erection of warehouses, the building of railway lines, &c. The time granted to competitors is twelve months. Premiums* will be given not only for "whole designs," but also for parts of the general scheme, points of detail, &c. The competitor does not require so much knowledge of the locality as outsiders might be led to believe. The plans obtainable with the "programme" would suffice.

CAIRO.—A competition for designs for a new drainage system has been opened. Some thirty candidates sent in work, and a jury consisting of a French, a German, and an English expert, after coming to the conclusion that none of the schemes submitted could be adopted unaltered, have now made a rough sketch of what they consider desirable. An Egyptian Government Department will now work out the proposed scheme in detail, and it is hoped that the excavators can be put into motion this winter. Some 12,500,000 ftancs are to be spent.

THE NEW MUNICIPAL BUILDINGS, BOMBAY.—The *Bombay Gazette* of the 7th ult. says that, with the exception of the central tower and dome, the masonry work of the new Municipal Buildings, Bombay, has long since been finished, and now the decorative work is being proceeded with. The general ornamental work is all Indian, being composed of Indian animals, birds, and foliage, all worked into fanciful designs in relief. The balcony over the main porch is flanked by two-winged Venetian lions, rampant and holding between their paws weather vanes, while over the council chamber a rampant lion holds between its paws a shield bearing the arms of the Corporation. (These lions, we understand, were carved by Mr. Harry Hems, of Exeter.) From the terrace over the third floor, the central gable on the front tapers to a point from which rises an allegorical female figure, 13 ft. high, representing "Urbs Prima in Indis," below which is a circular panel bearing the arms of the Corporation. The lions are now all in position, and the statue of "Bombay" will soon be in position over the main structure with outstretched wings and holding aloft in her raised hand a full-rigged ship. It is intended to plant small gardens in front of the eastern and western wings of the building, facing respectively the Hornby and Cruickshank roads, while the ground between the wings will be laid out with shrubs and flower-beds and will have a fountain playing in the centre. Almost all the carved work in the buildings was designed and modelled at the Bombay School of Art and executed by skilled Telegu carvers. The architect of the buildings is Mr. F. W. Stevens, C.I.E., F.R.I.B.A., of Bombay.

STAINED GLASS AND DECORATION.

WINDOW, NORTON CUCKNEY CHURCH. — A stained-glass window has just been placed in Norton Cuckney Church, Mansfield. It is the east window of the church, and contains subjects of the Baptism, Crucifixion, Resurrection, and Ascension of Our Lord. The work was designed and executed by Messrs. Warrington & Co., of London.

MEMORIAL WINDOW, MANCHESTER CATHEDRAL. —A new stained-glass window, which has been placed in the south side of the nave of Manchester Cathedral, to the memory of the late Dean Oakley, was formally presented to the Dean and churchwardens at Manchester Cathedral on the 26th ult. The window is a representation of the "Magnificat." It has been executed by Messrs. Burlison & Grylls, of London.

DECORATIONS AT HAWORTH CHURCH. — This church was re-opened on the 29th ult., after having been temporarily closed, chiefly for extensive mural, &c., decorations, which have been designed by Messrs. Powell Brothers, of Leeds. The whole of the walls of the chancel, nave, and aisles are painted a warm vellum tint, diapered richly in colours and in gold, introducing significant emblems, —the cross, crown of thorns, lily, &c, borders, and other ornaments being also carried around the arches, and other salient features in the architecture. In addition to this general ornamentation, the upper portions of the chancel walls are further enriched with groups of angels, some singing and some bearing musical instruments; and similar angelic attendants follow on above the large eastern window, whilst the spaces to right and left of this window are devoted to the Evangelists. At the west end of the church a large wall space has been painted with a representation of Our Lord's entry into Jerusalem, and above the arch leading into the chancel is the final event on Mount Calvary. The figures of this picture are almost life-size, upon a "flat" or "dead" gold background. Some considerable colour has also been introduced into the wooden roofs throughout, chiefly in the form of spots and bands of brilliant colour, with lines of pure gold. In most cases the girders and the principals end in shields, and advantage has been taken of this to introduce here a scheme of heraldic emblazoury, embracing the arms of the principal Sees, and of the colleges and halls of Oxford and Cambridge.

MISCELLANEOUS.

SALE OF BOOKS UPON ARCHITECTURE AND OTHER ARTS.—The library of Mr. Wyatt Papworth, together with other collections, was sold by auction a few days since by Messrs. Puttick & Simpson. The lots realised, as a rule, but low prices. Amongst those that fall within our own province may be cited the following:—Octavo size: J. Fergusson's "Illustrated Handbook of Architecture," 2 vols., and a volume of his "History of Architecture," 1*l.* 6s. (George); vols. i. and ii. of Ruskin's "Modern Painters," 1851, 1*l.* 4s. (Newton); the *Archæological Journal*, 1844-91, in the original numbers, 5*l.* (Sotheran); vols. i.-iv. of the "Antiquarian Itinerary," large paper, 1816, and others, 1*l.* (George); Jackson and Chatto's "Treatise on Wood Engraving," 1838, 1*l.* 1s. (Edwards); Viollet-le-Duc's "Dictionnaire Raisonné," &c., Paris, 1854-68, 7*l.* 5s. (Quaritch); Ackermann's "Repository," the three series, 41 vols., 1809-28, 9*l.* (Parsons); T. H. Turner's "Domestic Architecture in England," 4 vols., 1851, 2*l.* 14s. (Lugsher); Fergusson's "History of Indian and Eastern Architecture," 1876, 1*l.* 8s. (Batsford); and Knight's "Cyclopædia of London," 1851, Shepherd's "Metropolitan Improvements," with views, 2 vols., with other similar volumes, fourteen in all, 4s. (Parker). Quarto size: W. Smith's "Particular Description of England in 1588," with views, edited by Wheatley and Ashbee, a subscriber's copy, 12s. (Harris); two sets of Stothard's plates to illustrate the "Pilgrim's Progress," 1*l.* 11s.; J. O. Halliwell's "Ancient Inventories of Furniture, Tapestry, Plate, &c.: Illustrative of Domestic Manners in England in the Sixteenth and Seventeenth Centuries" (twenty-five copies privately printed), 9s. (Harris); Morant's edition, being the third, of T. D. Whitaker's "History and Antiquities of the Deanery of Craven," 1878, 10s. (Bull); R. Ackermann's "Westminster Abbey," 2 vols., coloured plates, 1812, 1*l.* 10s. (Fawcett); his "Microcosm of London," 3 vols., 104 coloured plates by Pugin and Rowlandson, 1808, 5*l.* 7s. 6d. (Fawcett); R. & J. Brandon's "Analysis of Gothic Architecture," 2 vols., 1847, 1*l.* 4s. (Batsford); A. Pugin's "Gothic Ornaments," with Harding's illustrations (and an autograph letter of Pugin inserted), 1831, 15s. (Massey); J. B. Papworth's "Select Views of London," coloured plates, scarce, 1816, 2*l.* (Fawcett); and C. Clarkson's "History, &c., of Richmond, Yorkshire," 1821, 1*l.* 10s. (Quaritch). Folio size; vols. i. to v., in two volumes, of the "Vernon Gallery of British Art," large paper, 2*l.* 17s. (Roche); J. Walker's "Itinerant in Great Britain and Ireland," first edition, 180 engravings, 1799, 1*l.* (George); T. Chippendale's "Gentleman and Cabinet Maker's Directory," 160 copper plates, a fine copy of this scarce work, 1754, 14*l.* (Forrester); D. Wyatt's "Metal Work and its Artistic Design," many coloured and plain plates, 1852, 1*l.* 6s. (Quaritch); F. T. Dollman's "Priory of St. Mary Overie, Southwark," 1881, 6s. (Parsons); J. Gibbs's "Book of Architecture," 150 plates, 1728, 1*l.* 4s. (Batsford); A. Basoli's "Compartimenti di Camere per uso degli Amatori," &c., 1827, 1*l.* 13s.; J. Fergusson's "Rock-cut Temples of India," and "Illustrations of Ancient Architecture in Hindostan," in one volume, tinted plates, 1845-8, 3*l.* 14s. (Batsford); "Disel and Corvinus: Erste und Zweite Fortsetzung Herrlicher Garten und Furstgebäude," 92 plates, Augsburg, 6*l.* 17s. 6d. (Quaritch); the Domesday Survey, Record Commission Publication, 2 vols., 1783, "Inquisitio Eliensis, Liber Winton," &c., 4*l.* 10s. (Jebb); and "Churches of Moscow," some of the plates coloured, letterpress in Russian, an incomplete copy of a rare book, Moscow, 1850, 1*l.* 14s. (Batsford). Six pounds were bid for eighty-one original plates of Morland's sketches, with ten of Craig's landscapes, with animals, 1824; and a copy of Ainsworth's "Jack Sheppard," with portrait and plates by Cruikshank, 3 vols., first edition, 1839, was bought for 6*l.* 5s. (Horn).

EFFECTS OF THE ZONE RAILWAY TARIFF.—From an official report just issued on the working of the Zone tariff in Hungary during the two first years of its introduction, viz., August 1, 1889, to July 31, 1891, as compared with the two preceding years, we learn that in the former period 35,328,300 passengers were carried, yielding receipts amounting to 25,041,400 florins, as against 12,752,300 passengers and 19,660,700 florins respectively in the two preceding years. Thus there was an increase in the number of passengers of 177 per cent., and in the receipts of 27 per cent. Of the former, 3,500,700 passengers fall upon the period August-December, 1889; 11,716,400 on the year 1890, and 7,358,900 on the seven months January-July, 1891. These increases show that further increases may be calculated upon. The directors of the Kaschan-Oderberg Railway, too, have issued a report, showing that even on this short line, running through poorly-inhabited districts, there is a marked increase of passengers and earnings since the adoption of the zone system.

PETERBOROUGH CATHEDRAL.—Mr. Hitch, whom we named last week as the sculptor of the pulpit at Peterborough, writes to say that the carving on the bishop's throne was his work also, as well as most of the figure work on the stalls.

PROPOSED DOCK IMPROVEMENTS, LIVERPOOL.—At the weekly meeting of the Mersey Dock and Harbour Board, held in the Revenue-buildings, Channing-place, Liverpool, on the 2nd inst., the recommendation of the Committee of Works, to spend 180,000*l.* extra in the improvement of the Canada, Huskisson, and adjoining docks, for the accommodation of Atlantic liners and other large vessels, was again under consideration. Mr. Kennedy, Chairman of the National Steamship Company, said that, with regard to the width of entrance, he thought it desirable to give 100 ft. He was informed that the difference between that and the lesser width would only be 5,000*l.*, and this, in an expenditure of 180,000*l.*, was not worth considering. That ships of the future would be longer and broader he had little doubt, but that they would be deeper in proportion he had very grave doubt, and he thought it would not be well to spend more money on depth than was absolutely necessary. Ships would be deeper, but not in proportion to the increased length and breadth of beam, and while he would be quite prepared to vote for the proposed expenditure, he should like that if the Committee, after further consideration, found the extreme depth unnecessary, they should have power to revise their opinion. The recommendation of the Committee was adopted unanimously.

MONUMENT TO COLUMBUS, NEW YORK.—The monument to be erected in the Central Park, New York, by the Italian residents of the United States, in commemoration of their countryman Columbus, is, we learn from the *Il Progresso Italo-Americano*, almost completed. It has been executed at Rome, from the designs of Cætano Russo, and will be conveyed to America in an Italian war-ship some time next month. The monument is 77 ft. high. The pedestal, consisting of terraced steps with four octagonal buttresses, is of red Italian granite. Against the second or die portion of the pedestal rest, on opposite sides of the monument, two figures, each 10 ft. in height, consisting of a winged statue of the Genius of Columbus contemplating the globe, and a carving of an Alpine eagle in an attitude of defending the arms of the United States and Genoa. From the top of the die springs a shaft of the same red granite, terminating in a capital of white Carata marble, and surmounted by a statue of the great navigator, chiselled from red granite, and 12 ft. high. On the main base of the monument two bronze bas-reliefs, 10 ft. long by 2 ft. wide, represent "The First Sight of Land," and the "Landing on San Salvador Island." The shaft is ornamented with fac-similes in bronze of the prows of Columbus's fleet,—the *Pinto*, *Nina*, and *Santa Maria*,—and bears the inscription, "A. Christofero Colombo," also in bronze. The ceremony of unveiling the monument (the cost of which is not stated) will take place on October 12 next, fittingly to celebrate the 400th anniversary of the discovery of the New World; and also, we are told, "in grateful acknowledgment of the Italians who have begun life anew, and made homes for themselves within the borders of the great Republic."

REREDOS, BERROW, SOMERSET.—An oak reredos has been erected in the parish church here to the memory of the late Vicar, the Rev. C. R. Jervis Pearson. The architect, Mr. J. Houghton Spencer, sends us the following remarks on the symbols employed:—"The centre portion, which is raised above the sides, is divided into five arch-shaped cusped compartments bearing early Christian symbols, carved in boxwood, standing in advance of diapered oak panels. The centre symbol is taken from the catacomb of St. Agnes, and is formed of the equal-armed St. George's and St. Andrew's crosses combined, with the bow of the Greek letter 'rho' attached to the latter. The St. Andrew's and St. George's crosses, respectively corresponding to the Hebrew letters 'aleph' and 'tau,' occupy the extreme right and left panels, and the 'alpha' and 'omega' the panels next to the centre; the former alluding to the saying of the Rabbins, 'Ab Aleph usque ad Tau,' corresponding to the Greek, 'I am Alpha and Omega, the beginning and the end.' The central symbol of the interlacing crosses before described, with the bow of the 'rho' attached to the St. Andrew's cross, or 'chi,' combines the Hebrew with the Greek idea by the evident allusion in this symbol to the Greek name of Christ, 'Christos.' Three equal-armed crosses, referring to the name of Christ, were employed in the early centuries of the Christian era, and were continued in use by the Eastern Church, and preferred to the

* Two of 10,000 florins, three of 5,000, three of 3,000, and a number of minor ones having a total value of at least 20,000 florins.

COMPETITION, CONTRACTS,

COMPETITION.

Nature of Work.	By whom Advertised.	Premium.	Designs to be delivered.
*Public Baths	Walsall Corp.	50*l.* 30*l.* & 20*l.*	July 16

CONTRACTS.

Nature of Work or Materials.	By whom Required.	Architect, Surveyor, or Engineer.	Tenders to be delivered.
Addition to House, Headingley, Leeds	....	W. Hill & Son	June 21
*Concrete Pavement in situ	East Ham Local Bd.	W. H. Savage	do.
Granite Paving and Kerbing, Elgin, N.B.	Borough Authorities	D Mackintosh	do.
Villa Residence, Nairn, N.B.	J. B. Leslie	C. C. Doig	do.
Street Lighting and Drainage Works	Wimborne & Cranbourne Guardians	*Official*	do.
*New Station, Thatcham	G. W. R. Co.	do.	June 23
Additions to Fever Hospital, Leadgate	Lanchester Joint Hospital Board	J. W. Rounthwaite	do.
Business Premises	Leadgate Indus. and Prov. Soc. Lim.	....	do.
Three Houses, Houghton-le-Spring, Darlington	Geo. Parkinson	....	do.
Model Lodging House, Southmoor	....	J. W. Rounthwaite	June 24
Street Works	Cardiff Corporation	*Official*	do.
Grand Stand, Stalls, Offices, &c. Cardiff	Cardiff & South Wales Horse Show Com.	do.	do.
*Paving Works, Iron Posts, &c.	Romford Local Board	do.	June 25
Repairs, &c. Several Schools	Mynyddislwyn Sch. B.	do.	do.
House, Cilfynydd, Pontypridd	....	A. O. Evans	do.
Schools (S. Columba), Southwick	....	Frank Caws	do.
Extension of Cattle Market, Thrapston	....	Siddons & Sons	do.
Alterations and Repairs to Farmhouse, &c. Prowse's Luscombe Farm, Harberton, Devon	Robt. Harvey	W. M. Tollit	do.
Cottage, &c. Sandridge, Barton, Devon	Baroness De Virte	Michelmore & Son	do.
*Hire of Steam Roller	West Sussex C. C.	*Official*	June 27
*Rebuilding Bradbourne Bridge, &c.	do.	do.	do.
Schools, Out Offices, &c.	Goole School Board	W. Watson	do.
*Iron and Stoneware Pipe Sewers, &c.	Watford U.R.S.A.	Urban Smith	do.
Cottage, Bishopmill, Elgin, N.B.	....	C. C. Doig	June 28
Additions to Station, &c. Beidlington	N. E. R. Co.	W. Bell	June 29
*1,000 tons Broken Granite	Halton Local Board	E. H. Capon	do.
*Making-up Road	Ealing Local Board	C. Jones	June 30
*Industrial School, Lichfield	Burton-on-Trent and Walsall School Bd	R. Stevenson	do.
*Twelve Cottages and Club House	Clee Hill Dhu Stone Co.	*Official*	do.
*Enlargement, &c. of Warren Bridge, Writtle	Essex County Council	do.	do.
*Painting Works, Infirmary	Fulham Union	do.	do.
*Rebuilding Ystrad Bridge	Breconshire, U.R.S.A.	do.	July 2
Water Supply, Braithwaite, near Keswick	Cockermouth C. C.	Mr. Wilson	do.
*Chapels Caretakers' Houses, &c. at Cemetery	Oxford Loc. Bd.	W. H. White	July 4
*Palm House (chiefly Iron), Battersea Park	London C. C.	*Official*	July 5
*Schools for about 1,050 children	Brighton and Preston Sch. Bd.	J. W. Simpson	do.
*Surface Water Drains, &c.	Leyton Loc. Bd.	W. Dawson	do.
*Dispensary, Bermondsey	St. Olave's Union	Newman & Newman	July 7
*Police Station	Shrewsbury Corp.	J. Johnson	July 8
*Taking-down and Rebuilding Walls, &c.	South Hornsey L. B.	M. W. Jameson	July 13
*School Premises, New Swindon	The Committee	W. Whinoup	No date.
*Painting Works, Kingston and Tower of London	War Department	*Official*	do.
House, Caerphilly	....	Bruton & Williams	do.
Welsh Church, Pontycymmer, Llangeinor	Rev. David Phillips	do.	do.
Restoring Church, Llanwarney, near Cowbridge, Glam.	....	do.	do.
*Woodlands Park Schools	Tottenham Sch. Bd.	C. Bell	do.
*Repairing and Re-decorating Chapel	Sutherland - avenue Wesleyan Chapel	J. W. Chapman	do.
Water Supply, Moreton Pinkney	Brackley R.S.A.	W. J. Treadwell	do.
Schools, Residence, &c. Ystalyfera, Swansea	....	Wilson & Moxham	do.
Shop and Houses, Walker-road, Newcastle-on-Tyne	J. H. Brannan	B. F. Simpson	do.

PUBLIC APPOINTMENT.

Nature of Appointment.	By whom Advertised.	Salary.	Applications to be in.
*Road Surveyor	Hackney B. of W.	2*l.* 10*s.*	July 4

Those marked with an Asterisk (*) are advertised in this Number. Competition, p. iv. Contracts, pp. iv., vi., & viii. Public Appointment, p. xxi.

form known as the Latin cross, which the Latin, or Western, Church, afterwards insisted upon employing, as being, so it is stated, a probable form of the instrument of His suffering."

SHERBORNE WATERWORKS.—The Local Board of Sherborne, Dorset, upon the recommendation of their Engineer, Mr. Thos. Farrall, have decided to adopt Jennings & Brewer's electrical apparatus to indicate and register in the engine-house of the waterworks pumping station the varying levels of the water in the storage reservoir.

CAPITAL AND LABOUR.

SETTLEMENT IN THE LONDON BUILDING TRADES.—We are glad to learn that at the conference between masters and men, representing all trades, held on Friday, the 10th inst., and to which we referred in our last, after a discussion of five or six hours it was agreed:—1. That the working hours in summer shall be fifty per week. 2. That during fourteen weeks in winter, commencing on the first Monday in November, the times for the first three weeks shall be eight and a half hours per day, during the eight middle weeks eight hours per day, and the three following weeks eight and a half hours daily. 3. That the present rate of wages for skilled artisans and labourers shall be advanced ½d. per hour. 4. That overtime, when worked at the request of the employer, but not otherwise, shall be, from leaving-off time until 8 p.m., time and a quarter; from eight p.m. until ten p.m., time and a half; after ten p.m., double time. No overtime shall be charged until a full day has been made, unless time has been lost through stress of weather. On Saturdays the pay from noon until four p.m. shall be time and a half, after four and during Sundays double time. Christmas Days and Good Fridays to count as Sundays. 5. The employers shall give one hour's notice, or pay one hour's money, on determining the engagement. All wages to be paid at the expiration of such notice, or walking time if sent to the yard. 6. That men who are sent from the shop or yard, or sent to the country, shall be allowed for their expenses 6d. per day for any distance over six miles from shop or job, exclusive of travelling expenses or lodging money. 7. That payment of wages shall commence at noon on Saturdays and be paid on the job. But if otherwise arranged, walking time at the rate of three miles an hour to be allowed so as to get to the pay table at noon. 8. That employers shall provide, where practicable and reasonable, a place to have meals in on the work, and a labourer to assist in preparing them. 9. That the wages earned after leaving off time on Fridays and Saturdays only, shall be kept in hand as back time. 10. That the term "London district" shall mean a twelve-mile radius from Charing-cross. 11. That six months' notice on either side shall terminate the foregoing resolutions, to expire on the first Monday in November. The foregoing resolutions shall come into force on the first Monday in November next, but the increase of pay to bricklayers shall commence on July 1 next.

THE STRIKE IN THE CARDIFF BUILDING TRADE.—The arrangements made between the Master Builders' Association and the carpenters and joiners, through the general secretary, have fallen through, the masters refusing to discharge men who were employed by them during the strike, and who do not belong to any union. The masters have now withdrawn their offer of an advance of ½d. per hour.

MEETINGS.

SATURDAY, JUNE 18.

Liverpool Engineering Society.—Excursion to Thirlmere Aqueduct.

Glasgow Architectural Association.—Visit to Largs.

Dundee Institute of Architecture.—Excursion to Perth and Scone Palace.

TUESDAY, JUNE 21.

Society for Preserving Memorials of the Dead.—Tenth Annual Meeting, Bishop's Stortford.

WEDNESDAY, JUNE 22.

Society for Preserving Memorials of the Dead.—Tenth Annual Meeting (continued).

FRIDAY, JUNE 24.

Institute of Certified Carpenters (Carpenters' Hall).—Monthly meeting 7.45 p.m.

SATURDAY, JUNE 24.

Edinburgh Architectural Association.—The Sketching Class to meet at Royston House, Carolina Park, Granton, to make measured drawings and sketches of the south front of the mansion. 3 p.m.

RECENT PATENTS:

ABSTRACTS OF SPECIFICATIONS.

10,177.—DOOR-SPRINGS: *T. & W. A. Starkey.*—This specification refers to an improvement in springs for closing doors by means of an ordinary spiral spring, with suitable ends attached, which may be of any metal adapted for the purpose. The inventors take an ordinary spiral spring, one end being fastened firmly to the door-jamb, the other end fitting to a circular collar or disc, having ratchet teeth formed on its face, which closely fit into another disc fastened to the door, and by means of a lever in the form of a wire pin placed in holes on the side, the upper disc is turned so as to uncoil the spring. Thus the teeth, by rising over each other, pass round and increase the pressure the spring exerts on the ends which are attached to it.

10,526.—DOOR-FASTENINGS: *A. Hodge.*—This patent relates to an arrangement which the inventor prefers to call a bolt-lock and key. The arrangement is also available for use by means of a bolt having no handle. The invention comprises:—firstly, the arrangement on the slip-bolt of friction or gearing surfaces, material, or teeth suitable for the key to act on; secondly, the addition to the bearing frame or case of the bolt of bearing parts, or one or more journals, in or on which the key may move; thirdly, the key, so formed at the part or parts that actuate the bolt with friction or other device, as above mentioned, that in putting it into or taking it out of its bearings, it so revolves the bolt as alternately to free and replace the handle in or on its terminal positions or notches, and in turning or revolving the key in or on its bearings it acts as a gear or pinion to slide the bolt longitudinally.

10,994.—PORTABLE BUILDINGS: *G. Espitallier.*—The object of this invention is a new type of building, constructed entirely of cardboard, cellulose, or other compressed substances, with the introduction or insertion into such substance of a sheet of metal, thus increasing the rigidity, and requiring that the thickness of the various substances should be only a few millimètres. This new type of building, while presenting the various advantages of similar structures, is said to be capable of being very easily moved, in consequence of the lightness of its parts and the facility with which it can be erected.

6,091.—SEWER VENTILATION: *H. E. Newton.*—The object of this invention is to ventilate sewers from their lower grades, and at the same time destroy by heat any deleterious sewer gases and the germs contained therein. This is effected by means of an appliance of peculiar construction, fully described and figured in the specification, placed near the base of an uptake shaft, up which the objectionable gases are drawn by the action of the apparatus. The uptake shaft is bulbed at a certain height, so as to form a chamber containing the ventilating apparatus. Within this chamber is placed a perforated spherical shell constructed of fireclay, or other material that will resist intense heat, its upper part being formed as a lid. A perforated false bottom covers the bottom part of the interior of the shell, forming a chamber below the false bottom, to receive a Bunsen or other gas-burner, the air being supplied to the burner from without the shaft. The space within the shell between the false bottom and the cover is loosely packed with asbestos.

6,654.—ROOFING TILES: *O. R. Westbad.*—This invention relates to roofing tiles having a free surface of a symmetrical shape in the longitudinal direction of the tile. This free surface can, therefore, be either of regular hexagonal, elongated hexagonal, square, or rhombic form, the longitudinal direction going along a diagonal. The tiles do not lie loose upon each other, as has hitherto been the case, but are provided at the under side with ribs along half their periphery, the ribs being adapted to engage in corresponding grooves near the upper edges of the tiles placed beneath.

NEW APPLICATIONS FOR LETTERS PATENT.

May 30.—10,236, J. Gordon, Sash-fasteners.—10,248, J. Voce, Lead Lights.—10,253, J. Turner, Seasoning or Preserving wood.—10,272, W. Manizer and Others, Sashes and Casements capable to open inside or outside. 10,280, J. Reap, Tool for Cutting Wood to Mitre or other Angles.

May 31.—10,300, W. Naylor, Cords for Hanging Window Sashes.—10,311, W. Wheeler, Water Waste Preventing Cisterns for Flushing Purposes.—10,319, S. Keeling and J. Smith, Water-closet Cistern Pulls.—10,336, W. Briggs, Flushing Water-closets.—10,341, H. Sankey, Decorating Walls.—10,389, F. Weldon, Temporary Bridges, and other-like structures.

June 1.—10,397, J. Shaw, Window-sash Fastener.—10,407, J. Shaw, Reversible Window-sashes.—10,419, F. Itaker, Casement Stay and Fastener, Combined.—10,455, J. Gastrell, Fastening Devices for Windows and Doors.—10,460, W. Carrington, Bricks for the Copings of Walls.

June 2.—10,476, W. Horn, Dry Docks.—10,373, C. Hibberd & R. Lowman, Window-sashes.—10,632, M. Laffont, Material suitable for Building and Architectural Purposes, &c.

June 3.—10,547, A. Wilcockson, Water-closets.—10,574, W. Maxfield, Stove made of Dutch Tiles, &c.—10,578, J. Palmer, Sewer-gas Destructor.—10,592, M. Tayleure, Mitreing Plane or Machine.—10,601, A. King, Ventilators.—10,613, G. Davies, Window Jack or Scaffold.—10,626, A. Shill, Testing Drains, and for disinfecting purposes.

June 4.—10,657, H. Sully, Ceiling Roses for use with Electric Light Fittings.—10,675, H. Take, Brick Cutting Tables.—10,705, F. Underhay, Supplying Water to Water-closets.

PROVISIONAL SPECIFICATIONS ACCEPTED.

5,674, A. Thornalley, Fire-grates and Stoves for Consuming their own Smoke.—7,554, H. Bridson, Siphon Cisterns.—7,882, M. Goodwin, Ventilating Cowls for Drawing off Obnoxious Gas or Air.—8,040, G. Meager, Window-sashes.—8,985, Yates, Haywood, & Co., and the Rotherham Foundry Co., Limited, Adjustable Fire-grates.—9,209, R. Astley, Construction of Fire-proof Floors.—9,217, I. Izod, Ornamentation in Clay for Architectural and other purposes.—9,251, J. MacGlashan, Ornamentation and Decoration of Walls, Ceilings, &c. —9,258, J. Julhe, Hardening of Plaster and the Development of Colours mixed therewith.—9,427, J. Jeffreys, Jointing Cast-iron Pipes.—9,542, I. Castle, Mills for Grinding Cement, &c.

COMPLETE SPECIFICATIONS ACCEPTED.

(*Open to Opposition for Two Months.*)

14,948, H. Selling, Paint.—6,358, H. Ford, Window-sashes.—8,124, R. Border, Floor and Man-hole Chamber for Drains.—8,157, W. Tithecote, Balance Pulley Side-sashes of Bay and other Windows.

SOME RECENT SALES OF PROPERTY:

ESTATE EXCHANGE REPORT.

JUNE 7.—By *J. & R. Kemp & Co.*: F.g.r. of 10*l.*, Branch-pl., Hoxton, reversion in 42 yrs., 220*l.*; l.g.r. of 18*l.*, Caledonian-rd., Islington, u.t. 51 yrs., g.r. 3*l.*, 245*l.*; l.g.r. of 23*l.*, u.t. 52 yrs., g.r. 6*l.*, 280*l.*; l.g.r. of 132*l.*, Hampstead-rd., u.t. 26 yrs., g.r. 32*l.*, 1,225*l.*; l.g.r. of 65*l.*, Mornington-cres., u.t. 27 yrs., g.r. 21*l.*, 505*l.*; l.g.r. of 170*l.* 9s., Euston-st., &c., St. Pancras, u.t. 27 yrs., g.r. 26*l.* 12s., 1,520*l.*; l.g.r. of 16*l.*, Stockwell Pk.-rd., Clapham, u.t. 37 yrs., 245*l.*; "Belmont Wharf," York-rd., King's-cross, u.t. 29 yrs., g.r. 280*l.*, 1,300*l.*; 10, Oakley-sq., St. Pancras, u.t. 51 yrs., g.r. 14*l.*, 500*l.* — By *J. W. Neighbour*: 1 and 2, Domingo-st., St. Lukes, f., r. 95*l.* 4s., 1,180*l.*; 1a, Domingo-st., f., r. 28*l.* 12s., 510*l.*; 32, Baltic-st., f., r. 27*l.* 6s., 230*l.*

JUNE 8.—By *Randall, Beard, & Baker*: "Runnymede," Leicester-rd., f., r. 32*l.*, 400*l.*—By *Harman Bros.*: 124, Brook-rd., Stoke Newington, u.t. 85 yrs., g.r. 6*l.* 10s., r. 32*l.*, 330*l.*; 21, Grazebrook-rd., u.t. 47 yrs., g.r. 7*l.* 7s., 490*l.*; 43, Lordship-pk., u.t. 81 yrs., g.r. 9*l.* 9s., 630*l.*; 91, Darenth-rd., Stamford-hill, u.t. 91 yrs., g.r. 10*l.*, 645*l.*—By *R. J. Collier & Henderson*: 10 to 24 even, and 36, Pembury-rd., Clapton, u.t. 52 yrs., g.r. 53*l.*, r. 460*l.*, 3,110*l.*—By *Baxter, Payne, & Lepper*: Part of the "Pinkhurst Park Estate," Bromley, Kent, containing 28a. 0r. 11p., f., 8,535*l.*; two f. cottages and 2a. 1r. 18p., near Farnborough, Kent, 500*l.*

JUNE 9.—By *Gilders Bros.*: F.g.r. of 96*l.*, Sandilands-rd., Fulham, reversion in 90 yrs., 1,836*l.*; f.g.r. of 120*l.*, King-st., Walthamstow, ditto in 90 yrs., 2,295*l.* By *A. Chancellor*: 26, Strawberry-hill-rd., Twickenham, f., 810*l.* By *C. C. & T. Moore*: 35, Claremont-rd., Forest-gate, u.t. 84 yrs., g.r. 8*l.* 16s., 395*l.*; 58, Montpelier-rd., Peckham, u.t. 65 yrs., g.r. 6*l.* 5s., r. 32*l.*, 315*l.*; 5 to 15 odd, Quickett-st., Bow, u.t. 81 yrs., g.r. 16*l.* 19s., 600*l.* By *Stimson & Sons*: 52 to 60 even, Salcott-rd., Clapham, f., r. 167*l.* 4s., 1,805*l.*; f.g.r. of 7*l.* 10s., Abberville-rd. North, reversion in 88 yrs., 155*l.*; l.g.r. of 8*l.*, Brooklands-rd., Wandsworth, u.t. 17 yrs., 70*l.*; an improved rental of 48*l.*, Clarendon-st., Camberwell, u.t. 34 yrs., 510*l.*; 2 and 4, Woodland-ter., Dulwich, u.t. 88 yrs., g.r. 12*l.*, 330*l.*; 2, Belmore-st., Wandsworth, u.t. 17 yrs., g.r. 4*l.* 10s., 52*l.* 10s.; 1 and 3, Percy-pl., u.t. 35 yrs., g.r. 5*l.* 10s., 250*l.*—By *Messrs. Cronk*: 19, Granville-rd., Sevenoaks, f., r. 80*l.*, 1,400*l.*—By *Rutley, Son, & Vine*: 43 and 51, Burghley-rd., Highgate-rd., u.t. 75 yrs., g.r. 9*l.*, 820*l.* — By *Newbon & Co.*: 21, Fremont-st., f., 565*l.*; 19, Fremont-st., u.t. 70 yrs., g.r. 4*l.*, r. 32*l.*, 325*l.*; 7, Beatrice-rd., Walthamstow, f., r. 26*l.*, 265*l.*; 6, Milford-ter., Tottenham, f., r. 26*l.*, 240*l.*; 34 to 40, Arthur-st., Chelsea, u.t. 17 yrs., g.r. 120*l.*, 65*l.*; 50, Rhyl-st., Kentish-town, u.t. 58 yrs., g.r. 6*l.*, r. 28*l.*, 230*l.*; 20 and 22, Lupton-st., u.t. 75 yrs., g.r. 14*l.* 14s., r. 82*l.*, 865*l.*; 25, Campdale-rd., Tufnell-pk., u.t. 82 yrs., g.r. 10*l.* 10s., r. 50*l.*, 450*l.*; 5 and 8, Lynton-ter., Hornsey, u.t. 86 yrs., g.r. 15*l.*, r. 80*l.*, 610*l.*; 77, Mountview-rd., Crouch-hill, u.t. 85 yrs., g.r. 11*l.* 10s., r. 55*l.*, 770*l.*; 1, Rising-hill-st., Pentonville, u.t. 50 yrs., g.r. 10*l.*, 300*l.*

JUNE 10.—By *Westmore & Young*: 20, Thicket-rd., Anerley, f., 950*l.*—By *Norton, Trist & Gilbert*: "Rose Cottage," Walton, Suffolk, c., r. 14*l.*, 290*l.*; 9 and 10, New-street, Gravesend, f., 275*l.*; 15 and 16 New-st., and 18a, Berkeley-rd., f., r. 66*l.*, 420*l.*; 36 and 38, Bardon-rd., Walthamstow, u.t. 85 yrs., g.r. 6*l.* 10s., r. 46*l.* 16s., 290*l.*—By *E. Robins & Hine*: 93 and 95, Princess-st., Edgware-rd., u.t. 49 yrs., g.r. 11*l.* 10s., r. 90*l.*, 895*l.*; 66 and 68, Carlisle-st., u.t. 49 yrs., g.r. 11*l.*, r. 60*l.*, 515*l.*; No. 229, Harrow-rd., u.t. 454 yrs., g.r. 9*l.*, r. 105*l.*, 1,640*l.* By *Osborn & Mercer*: Two freehold cottages with gardens, near Chertsey, r. 13*l.* 17s. 4d., 235*l.*; freehold cottage and garden, Lyne, r. £7*l.* 16s., 150*l.* *Furber, Price, & Furber*: 6, 8, 16 to 22 even, 30, Aberdeen-rd., Highbury, u.t. 66 yrs., no g.r., r. 216*l.*, 2,775*l.*; 45, Aberdeen-pk., u.t. 63 yrs., g.r. 10*l.*, r. 120*l.*, 1,180*l.*; 38 and 39, Aberdeen-pk., u.t. 64 yrs., g.r. 20*l.*, r. 165*l.*, 1,480*l.*; 42 and 43, Aberdeen-pk., u.t. 63 yrs., g.r. 4*l.*, r. 50*l.*, 530*l.*; 18, Burnaby-gardens, Gunnersbury, u.t. 94 yrs., g.r. 8*l.* 8s.; r. 36*l.*, 300*l.*: 1 to 12, West-st., Leytonstone, u.t. 60 yrs., g.r. 48*l.*, r. 226*l.* 4s., 950*l.*; i.g.r. of 85*l.*, Aberdeen-rd., Highbury, u.t. 66 yrs., g.r. 20*l.*, 1,310*l.*; i.g.r. of 111*l.*, u.t. 72 yrs., g.r. 60*l.*, 1,030*l.*; i.g.r. of 100*l.*, u.t. 66 yrs., no g.r., 2,020*l.*; i.g.r. 58*l.*, u.t. 66 yrs., g.r. 52*l.*, 85*l.*; 103B and 103C, and 4 and 6, Norfolk-rd., Dalston-lane, u.t. 90 yrs., g.r. 10*l.* 8s., r. 158*l.*, 1,250*l.*; 8 and 10, Norfolk-rd., u.t. 90 yrs., g.r. 12*l.* 12s., r. 63*l.*, 470*l.*; 24, Great Percy-st., Clerkenwell, u.t. 28 yrs., g.r. 6*l.* 17s., r. 56*l.*, 290*l.*; 13, Claverton-st., Belgravia, u.t. 40 yrs., g.r. 10*l.* 10s., r. 85*l.*, 650*l.*; 31 and 33, British-st., Bow-rd., f., 795*l.*; 16 and 18, Stafford-rd., f., 640*l.*

[*Contractions used in these lists.*—F.g.r. for freehold ground-rent; l.g.r. for leasehold ground-rent; i.g.r. for improved ground-rent; g.r. for ground-rent; r. for rent; f. for freehold; c. for copyhold; l. for leasehold; e.r. for estimated rental; u.t. for unexpired term; p.a. for per annum; yrs. for years; st. for street; rd. for road; sq. for square; pl. for place; ter. for terrace; cres. for crescent; yd. for yard, &c.]

PRICES CURRENT OF MATERIALS.

TIMBER.		
Greenheart, B.G. ton	9/0/0	0/0/0
Teak, E.I. ... load	9/10/0	15/0/0
Sequoia, U.S. ft.cu.	2/3	3/0
Ash, Canada load	2/10/0	4/0/0
Birch, do.	3/5/0	4/10/0
Elm, do.	3/10/0	4/15/0
Fir, Dantsic, &c.	1/10/0	3/10/0
Oak, do.	3/0/0	5/5/0
Canada	5/10/0	7/0/0
Pine, Canada red	2/10/0	3/10/0
Do. yellow	2/10/0	5/0/0
Lath, D'ntsic, fath	5/0/0	6/0/0
St. Petersburg	5/0/6	7/0/6
Deals, Finland 2nd & 1st std 100	7/10/6	9/10/0
Do. 4th & 3rd	7/0/0	8/0/0
Do. Riga	6/10/6	8/0/6
St. Petersburg, 1st yellow	10/10/6	14/10/0
Do. 2nd yellow	8/0/0	9/10/0
Do. white	7/10/0	10/0/0
Swedish	7/0/0	15/0/0
White Sea	8/0/0	17/0/0
Canada, Pine 1st	20/0/0	26/0/0
Do. do. 2nd	14/10/0	16/0/0
Do. do. 3rd, &c.	8/0/0	10/0/0
Do. Spruce 1st	8/10/0	11/0/6
Do. do. 3rd & 2nd	6/15/6	8/0/0
New Brunswick	7/0/0	7/10/0
Battens, all kinds	3/10/0	15/10/6
Flooring Boards, sq., 1 in. prep. 1st	0/8/0	0/13/6
Do. 2nd	0/7/0	0/11/0
Other qualities	0/3/6	0/7/6
Cedar, Cuba ..ft.	/3¼	/4½
Honduras, &c.	/3¼	/4
Mahogany, Cuba	/4¼	/6¼
St. Domingo, cargo av	/4¼	2/0
Mexican do. do	/4	/6
Tobasco do. do	/5¼	/7
Honduras do.	/5¼	/6¼
Box, Turkey ton	4/0/0	13/0/0
Rose, Rio	10/0/0	20/0/0
Bahia	9/0/0	18/0/0
Satin, St. Domingo ...ft.	0/0/6	0/1/3

TIMBER (*continued*).		
Satin, Porto Rico	0/0/8	0/1/6
Walnut, Italian	0/0/3½	0/0/7
METALS.		
Iron—Pig, in Scotland ... ton	2/1/5	0/0/0
Bar, Welsh, in London	5/17/6	6/0/0
Do. do. at works in Wales	5/7/6	5/10/0
Do. Staffordshire, in London	6/5/0	6/15/0
Copper—British, cake and ingot	48/10/0	50/0/0
Best selected	51/0/0	51/10/0
Sheets, strong	58/0/0	58/10/0
Chili, bars	46/3/9	46/10/0
Yellow Metal lb.	0/0/5	0/0/0
Lead—Pig, Spanish ... ton	10/12/9	10/15/0
English, com. brands	10/17/6	11/0/0
Sheet, English, 3 lbs. per sq. ft. and upwards	12/0/6	0/0/0
Pipe	12/10/0	0/0/0
Zinc—English sheet ... ton	25/15/0	26/0/0
Vieille Montagne	26/5/0	0/0/0
Tin—Straits	102/10/0	103 0/0
Australian	102/10/0	103 0 0
English Ingots	102/10/0	103 0/6
OILS.		
Linseed ... ton	18/7/6	18/12/6
Cocoanut, Cochin	23/15/0	0/0/0
Do. Ceylon	21/15/0	0/0/0
Palm, Lagos	22/5/0	22/10/0
Rapeseed, English pale	24/15/0	25/0/0
Do. brown	23/5/0	0/0/0
Cottonseed ref.	19/0/0	0/0/0
Oleine	21/10/0	22/10/0
Lubricating, U.S.	4/0/0	6/0/0
Do. refined	6/0/0	12/10/0
Tar—Stockholm barrel	0/19/0	1/0/0
Archangel	0/12/6	0/0/0

TENDERS.

[Communications for insertion under this heading should be addressed to "The Editor," and must reach us *not later than 12 noon on Thursdays*.]

ABERDARE.—For the erection of thirty houses at Cwmaman, for the Cwmaman Building Club. Mr. G. A. Treharne, architect, 7a, Cardiff-street, Aberdare:—

T. Jones Davies	£165	W. C. Webber	£150
Summers	160	W. E. Hales, Briton Ferry*	150

* Accepted.

ABERTILLERY (Monmouthshire).—For the erection of new market and hall, Abertillery. Mr. Alfred Swash, architect, 3, Friars Chambers, Newport, Mon. Quantities by architect:—

Bagley	£4,551 7 5	Stephens, Bastow, & Co.	4,100 0 0
W. A. Linton	4,350 0 0	Thos. G. Diamond	4,000 0 0
John Linton	4,250 0 0	A. P. Williams, Abertillery*	3,900 0 0
B. Williams & Son	4,236 0 0		
Thos. Webb	4,210 0 0		
Edwyn Richards	4,190 0 0		

* Accepted.

ASHBURTON (Devon).—For the erection of bank premises, for The Capital and Counties Bank (Limited). Messrs. J. W. Rowell & Son, architects, Newton Abbot, Devon:—

G. Shellabear	£3,200 0 0	Brook & Ash	£2,326 0 0
W. Trevena	3,100 0 0	Rundle Bros.	2,264 4 5
J. Finch	2,591 0 0	J. H. Fooden	2,199 0 0
Rabbich & Brown	2,572 0 0	F. A. Stacey	2,190 0 0
E. Andrews	2,500 0 0	W. H. Gooding	2,124 0 0
Steer	2,386 0 0	H. Stevens, Ashburton (accepted)	2,061 14 6
Goss Bros.	2,350 0 0		

BEVERLEY (Yorks).—Accepted at schedule of prices for alterations and repairs to the vicarage, North Dalton, for Mr. L. J. Hobson, M.D. Mr. A. Hobson, architect, North Dalton, Beverley, Yorks:— M. Gage, Driffield, Yorkshire.

CARLISLE.—Accepted for the erection of a boiler-house and chimney-shaft, at Fusehill Workhouse, for the Guardians of Carlisle Union. Mr. H. Higginson, architect, Carlisle. Quantities by the architect:—

R. Johnston, *Builders' work*	£380 0 0
J. Bindson, *Joiners' work*	25 0 0
D. Stansfield, *Ironfounders' work*	26 0 0
J. Wilson, *Plumbers' work*	5 18 0
C. J. Nanson, *Slaters' work*	14 18 0
D. Canning, *Glaziers' and Painters' work*	5 18 0
[All of Carlisle.]	£457 14 0

CARLISLE.—Accepted for the erection of semi-detached villa residences, Howard-place. Mr. H. Higginson, architect, Carlisle. Quantities by the architect:—

J. & R. Bell, *Builders' work*	£700 0 0
Jos. Forster, *Joiners' work*	398 0 0
J. Wilson, *Plumbers' work*	92 0 0
C. J. Nanson, *Slaters' work*	55 0 0
Jas. Harrington, *Plasterers' work*	131 0 0
Kirk & Robley, *Painters' and Glaziers' work*	60 0 0
[All of Carlisle.]	£1,436 0 0

COCKINGTON (Devon).—For the erection of a manager's house, cottage, and other buildings at the South Devon Fruit Farm. Messrs. J. W. Rowell & Son, architects, Newton Abbot:—

G. K. Smale	£786	Vanstone & Mumford, Torquay*	£669
C. Cocks	749		
Brown & Pocke	673		

* Accepted.

CROYDON.—For warehouse and offices, George-street, Croydon, for Messrs. John Thrift & Sons. Mr. Alfred Broad, architect, 27, Dingwall-road, Croydon. Quantities by the architect:—

James Smith & Sons	£3,673	A. Bullock	£3,366
D. Waller	3,650	E. P. Bulled & Co.	3,350
W. Marriage	3,650	S. Page	3,340
Maides & Harper	3,587	M. Taylor	3,125
W. Holt & Son	3,500	E. J. Saunders, Croydon*	3,000
D. W. Barker	3,461		

* Accepted.

ENFIELD (Middlesex).—For the supply of 300 yds. 12-in. stoneware pipes and 200 yds. of 15-in. pipes, for the Enfield Local Board of Health. Mr. W. Kitteringham, Engineer and Surveyor:—

	12-inch.	15-inch.
Doulton	2s. 8½d.	4s. 8d. per yard.
Doulton	4s. 8d.	6s. 9d. "
Knowles	2s. 6¼d.	4s. 4½d. "
Wragg & Sons	2s. 6½d.	4s. 4½d. "
Albion Clay Co.	2s. 6½d.	4s. 4½d. "
Ingby & Co.*	2s. 5½d.	4s. 3½d. "
Jenning & Co.*	5s. 6d. less 40 p.c.	9s. 6d. less 25 p.c. per yd.
Woodward & Co.*	2s. 5d.	4s. 2d. per yard.
Eastwood & Co.*	1s. 7½d. per pipe	2s. 6½d. per pipe.
Couper Bros.*	2s. 5½d.	4s. 4d. per yard.
Ellistown Colliery Co.	2s. 8½d.	4s. 4½d. " (too late)
Smith	£38 2s. 9d.	£43. 17s. 6d. lump sum.

* Disqualified for not sending sample pipe.

GRAYS (Essex).—For extensions and alterations at Quarry Hill Schools, for the Grays Thurrock School Board. Mr. Geo. Waymouth, architect, 23, Moorgate-street. Quantities by Mr. J. C. Goodchild, 81, Finsbury-pavement:—

J. Brown	£1,700	Sharpe & Son	£1,443
H. R. Rous	1,671	H. J. Carter, Grays*	1,400
Scharien & Co.	1,533	J. Webb	1,375
G. Jackson	1,480		

* Accepted.

LONDON.—For refitting bathrooms and ward sculleries at the Western Fever Hospital, Seagrave-road, Fulham, for the Metropolitan Asylums Board. Messrs. A. & C. Harston, Architects, 15, Leadenhall-street, E.C.:—

F. Islip	£1,722 0 0	Leslie & Co.	£1,276 0 0
H. Haynes	1,507 10 0	M. Brodie	1,239 0 0
Clements, Teakes, & Co.	1,520 0 0	Wenham & Waters	1,081 0
Burn Bros.	1,369 9 6	Peattie & Axtell	1,070 0
Benham & Son	1,350 0 0	S. Finch & Co., 82, Belvedere-road, Lambeth*	1,047 0
T. Knight	1,317 0 0		
F. G. Minter	1,300 0 0		

* Accepted.

LONDON.—For painting and repairs at the Paddington Workhouse, Harrow-road, Paddington, for the Guardians of the Poor of the Parish of Paddington. Messrs. A. & C. Harston, architects, 15, Leadenhall-street, E.C.:—

T. Stroud	£663	McMillan & Houghton	£303
E. Proctor	517	Hilder & Edge, 17, Bridle-lane, Golden-square, W.*	286
G. Foxley	379		

* Accepted.

LONDON.—For trial boring into the chalk at the workhouse, Fulham Palace-road, Hammersmith, for the Guardians of the Fulham Union. Mr. Alfred Saxon Snell, architect, London:—

Baker & Sons	£940 0	Tilley & Sons, Walbrook, E.C. (accepted)	£847 10
Docura & Sons	909 10*		

* Tubes to have plain Joints.

LONDON.—For steam boilers, heating, and hot and cold water apparatus, gas-fitters' work, and kitchen fittings, at the workhouse, Fulham Palace-road, Hammersmith, for the Guardians of the Fulham Union. Mr. Alfred Saxon Snell, architect, London:—

Clements, Jeakes, & Co.	£7,080 0	May Bros.	£5,773 0
Rosser & Russell	5,020 0	Baffy & Sons, Regency-street, Westminster*	3,400 0
Bradford & Co.	3,972 6		

* Accepted.

LONDON.—For the erection of two dwelling-houses and shops in the Kennington-road, S.E., for Mr. Eddie E. Salkeld. Mr. E. Clarke, architect, 11, Queen Victoria-street, E.C. Quantities by Mr. B. Swinstead, 22, Wellington-street, Strand, W.C.:—

W. Larter & Son	£2,948	J. Hoare & Son	£2,885
S. & W. Pattinson	2,929	M. Patrick & Son	2,870
Young & Lonsdale	2,908	W. Jelley	2,553
Balaam Bros.	2,900		

LONDON.—For rebuilding house and workshop in the rear of No. 51, High-street, Marylebone. Mr. T. Thomas Durrans, architect, 44, Upper Baker-street, N.W.:—

J. Edgar	£1,875	J. Myring & Co.	£1,682
Manktelow & Co.	1,800	Staines & Son	1,679
C. Dearing & Son	1,095	H. C. Clifton	1,458
T. Stevens	1,687		

LONDON.—For the erection of proposed St. Mary's Mission-hall, North-end-road, Fulham, for the Rev. C. B. Foy. Mr. E. F. Roberts, architect:—

S. Powell	£3,500	S. F. Patterson	£2,681
E. Swan	3,408	Chessum & Co. (received by telegram)	2,635
H. Roffey	3,300	Thos. Boudon	2,376
Turner & Withers	2,955	John Bryant	2,330
Leslie & Co.	2,694		
Clark & Co.	2,690		

LONDON.—Accepted for warming and ventilating St. Michael's Schools, Ebury-square, London, for the Rev. Canon Fleming:— John Grundy £140 0 0

LONDON.—For bar-fittings and fixtures at the "Denmark Arms" public-house, Barking-road, East Ham, E., for Mr. A. Smith. Mr. Fred. A. Ashton, architect, 3, Crooked-lane, E.C.:—

Fittings.

Walker Bros.	£448	W. Shurmur (accepted)	£437

Fixtures.

Jas. Johnston	£442	Walker Bros.	£237
W. Shurmur (accepted)	343		

LONDON.—Accepted for new shop-front and fittings, &c., at 324, High-road, Kilburn, for Mr. A. Jacobs:— Oldrey, Albert Works, Kilburn £203 0 0

LONDON.—Accepted for new shop-front and fittings, &c., at 254, Oxford-street, for Messrs. Fearn & Griffiths:— Oldrey, Albert Works, Kilburn £144 10 0

LONDON.—Accepted for decorations and painting, &c., at The "Duke of York," Victoria-street, Pimlico, for Messrs. Baker Bros. Messrs. Saville & Martin, architects:— Oldrey, Albert Works, Kilburn £192 10 0

LONDON.—For new storeroom at 22, Dorset-street, Baker-street, W., for Messrs. Day, Son, & Hewitt. Mr. W. F. Potter, architect:—

Polden	£235	F. Dawes, Peckham-rye*	£145
H. H. Evans	188		

* Accepted.

LONDON.—For rebuilding Nos. 99 and 101, and for alterations to No. 103, High-street, Kensington, for Messrs. Deffy & Tome. Mr. Josiah Moule, architect, 71, Guildford-street, Russell-square, W.C.:—

Stimpson & Co.	£8,950	Spencer & Co.	£8,475
J. T. Chappell	8,834	Patman & Fotheringham	8,423
Grover & Son	8,734	B. E. Nightingale	8,330
C. F. Kearley	8,517		

LONDON.—For pulling down and rebuilding the "Prince of Wales" public-house, with new skittle-alley, for Messrs. Thorne Bros., Nine Elms-lane, S.W. Messrs. Lee & Pain, architects, 62, Lincoln's Inn-fields. Quantities supplied:—

Lawthorne	£3,329	Lathey Bros.	£3,149
Holloway Bros.	3,189	Watson	2,975
Turtle & Appleton	3,175		

LONDON.—For fitting up new offices in St. Bride-street, E.C., for the London Society of Compositors. Mr. Alfred Saxon Snell, architect, London:—

L. H. & R. Roberts	£2,731	Dove Bros., Tokenhouse Buildings, E.C.*	£2,596
The Co-operative Builders	2,643	C. Dearing & Son	2,556
H. Wall & Co.	2,640		

* Accepted.

LONDON.—For alterations to the "Carnarvon Castle" public-house, Notting-hill, for Mr. J. Tindall. Mr. J. H. Richardson, architect, Shepherd's-bush, W.:—

Chamberlen Bros.	£769	Lyford*	£725
Ransom	767		

* Accepted.

Pewterers' Work.

Sanders & Son (accepted) £83 17 0

LONDON.—For additional new tea warehouse for Messrs. Brooke, Bond, & Co., to be erected under the superintendence of Messrs. Dunk & Bousfield, 9, Billiter-square, E.C.:—

Hall, Beddall, & Co.	£4,230	Jerrard	£3,832
Colls & Sons	4,220	G. Munday & Sons	3,805
Rider & Sons	4,219	Holloway	3,700
E. Lawrance & Sons	4,015	Morter (accepted)	3,646

LONDON.—For alterations to No. 227, Strand. Messrs. Saville & Martin, architects, Dacre House, Arundel-street, Strand. Quantities by Mr. E. J. Sadgrove, 22, Surrey-street, Strand:—

H. B. Oldrey	£2,511	Gould and Brand	£2,325
S. Goodall	2,349	E. Toms	2,248
C. Dearing & Son	2,343		

LONDON.—For rebuilding No. 33, Great Castle-street, W. Mr. W. Hunt, architect. Quantities by Mr. H. Lovegrove, 26, Budge-row, Cannon-street, E.C.:—

Bulled & Co.	£2,040	Nightingale	£1,788
F. Saunders	1,995	Jas. Smith & Sons	1,779
Wm. Downs	1,887	J. Allen & Sons	1,735

LONDON.—For the erection of new church and schools at Griffin-road, Plumstead, for the Right Rev. Dr. Butt, Bishop of Southwark. Mr. A. H. Kersey, architect. Quantities by Mr. J. Theodore Carew:—

Faulkner	£8,669	B. E. Nightingale	£7,387
Holliday & Greenwood	8,014	Patman & Fotheringham	7,279
Oathwaite	7,995	H. L. Holloway	7,170
Scott	7,930	J. Smith & Sons	7,079
Jerrard	7,845	Kirk & Randall	6,642

LONDON.—For the erection and completion of new church of St. Jude's, Sursfield-road, Balham. Mr. E. Elton Hankins, architect. Quantities by Mr. Alfred Doxall:—

F. & H. Higgs	£2,448	Gregory	£2,088
Holloway Bros.	2,284	B. E. Nightingale	2,053
Lorden	2,121	Johnson	1,987
Turtle & Appleton	2,103		

LONDON.—For alterations and additions to the "Royal Oak" public house, St. John's-road, Holloway. Messrs. Saville & Martin, architects, Dacre House, Arundel-street, Strand. Quantities by Mr. E. J. Sadgrove, 22, Surrey-street, Strand.

E. Toms	£2,862	Scrivener & Co.	£2,795
S. Goodall	2,848	Dearing & Son	2,718
Ward & Lamble	2,822	Gould & Brand (accepted)	2,097

LONDON.—For redecoration, repairs, and sanitary works to the Battersea Park-road Baptist Tabernacle and Schools, for the Rev. W. Stott and Deacons. No quantities. Work to be completed in a month from June 13:—

J. Allen & Son	£623 0	Thos. Kemp	£355 0
Doyly & Co.	411 12	G. Howard, Victoria-road, Battersea Park*	324 9
C. Tavener	428 0	* Accepted conditionally.	
Lathey Bros.	425 0		

LONDON.—For rebuilding "The Garrick" public-house, Green-street, Leicester-square. Messrs. Saville & Martin, architects, Dacre House, Arundel-street, Strand. Quantities by Mr. E. J. Sadgrove, 22, Surrey-street, Strand:—

S. Goodall	£3,750	Spencer & Co.	£3,450
R. Perkins	3,635	D. Payne	3,421
J. Anley	3,522	Gould & Brand*	3,230
F. Saunders	3,510	* Accepted.	

MAIDENHEAD.—For alterations and additions to Chalk Pit House, Maidenhead, for Mr. Wilbey. Mr. Edwin Clare, architect:—

Porter	£3,132	Silver	£2,569
Toms	2,743	Norris	2,520
Lovell	2,885	Shurmur	2,403
Cooper & Son	2,590	Oldrey	2,320

MONTGOMERY.—For alterations and additions to a Residence at Montgomery. Mr. Edward Parke, architect, Newtown:—

N. Davies	£175	T. Ll. Evans, Montgomery*	£120
A. Watkin	168	* Accepted after revision.	

TEIGNMOUTH.—Accepted for additions to "The Hill," for Mr. Mountford-Spencer. Messrs. J. W. Rowell & Son, architects, Newton Abbot:—

Geo. Hayman, Teignmouth £385 0 0

TREF EGLWYS (Montgomeryshire).—For a vicarage house and stabling, for the Rev. Evan Edwards. Mr. Edward Parke, architect, Newtown:—

R. C. Phillips	£1,437 0	E. H. Williams, Llanbrynmair*	£1,108 10
Morris & Sons	1,329 0	* Accepted after slight revision.	
J. W. Swain	1,209 0		

WASHINGTON (Co. Durham).—Accepted for school building, at the Dame Margaret Home for Waifs and Strays at Washington, County Durham. Messrs. Plummer & Burrell, architects, Newcastle:—

T. Hunter, Washington £365 2 7

The Builder Cathedral Series.

1891.

1. CANTERBURY	Jan. 3.	7. SALISBURY	July 2.
2. LICHFIELD	Feb. 7.	8. BRISTOL	Aug. 1.
3. ST. ALBAN'S	Mar. 7.	9. NORWICH	Sept. 5.
4. PETERBOROUGH	April 4.	10. ROCHESTER	Oct. 3.
5. WELLS	May 2.	11. LINCOLN	Nov. 7.
6. EXETER	June 6.	12. GLOUCESTER	Dec. 5.

1892.

13. ST. PAUL'S .. .. Jan. 2.

14. HEREFORD	Feb. 6.	20. WORCESTER	Aug. 6.
15. CHICHESTER	Mar. 5.	21. BANGOR	Sept. 3.
16. ELY	April 2.	22. ST. ASAPH	Sept. 3.
17. LLANDAFF	May 7.	23. WINCHESTER	Oct. 1.
18. OXFORD	June 4.	24. TRURO	Nov. 5.
19. SOUTHWELL	July 2.	25. ST. DAVID'S	Dec. 3.

[Further arrangements will be duly announced.]

Post-free FOURPENCE HALFPENNY each, except Nos. 1, 2, 3, and 4, which are *out of print*; but the VIEW, PLAN, AND DESCRIPTION of CANTERBURY, LICHFIELD, ST. ALBAN'S, and PETERBOROUGH, have been reprinted, and they can now be had, price EIGHTPENCE each set; by post, 10d.

THE REREDOS, ST. PAUL'S.

Reprinted from "THE BUILDER," January 28, 1888 (18 in. by 11½ in.), on stout paper, unfolded, for framing, 6d.; by post, 8d.

PORTFOLIOS,

for Preserving the Plates unfolded, 2s. 6d.; by post, 3s.

London: Office of "THE BUILDER," 46, Catherine-street, W.C.

SUBSCRIBERS in LONDON and the SUBURBS, by prepaying at the Publishing Office, 19s. per annum (or 4s. 9d. per quarter), can ensure receiving "The Builder," by *Friday Morning's Post.*

TERMS OF SUBSCRIPTION.

"THE BUILDER" is supplied DIRECT from the Office to residents in any part of the United Kingdom at the rate of 19s. per annum PREPAID. To all parts of Europe, America, Australia, and New Zealand, 26s. per annum. To India, China, Ceylon, &c., 30s. per annum. Remittances payable to DOUGLAS FOURDRINIER, Publisher, No. 46, Catherine-street, W.C.

PUBLISHER'S NOTICES.

Registered Telegraphic Address, 'THE BUILDER,' LONDON.

CHARGES FOR ADVERTISEMENTS.

SITUATIONS VACANT, PARTNERSHIPS, APPRENTICESHIPS TRADE, AND GENERAL ADVERTISEMENTS.

Six lines (about fifty words) or under .... 4s. 6d.
Each additional line (about ten words) .... 0s. 6d.

Terms for Series of Trade Advertisements, also for Special Advertisements on front page, Competitions, Contracts, Sales by Auction, &c. may be obtained on application to the Publisher.

SITUATIONS WANTED.

FOUR Lines (about thirty words) or under .... 2s. 6d.
Each additional line (about ten words) .... 0s. 6d.

PREPAYMENT IS ABSOLUTELY NECESSARY.

*** Stamps must not be sent, but all small sums should be remitted by Cash in Registered Letter or by Money Order, payable at the Post-office, Covent-garden, W.C. to

DOUGLAS FOURDRINIER, Publisher,
Addressed to No. 46, Catherine-street, W.C.

Advertisements for the current week's issue must reach the Office before THREE o'clock p.m. on THURSDAY, but those intended for the front Page should be in by TWELVE noon on WEDNESDAY.

SPECIAL.—ALTERATIONS IN STANDING ADVERTISEMENTS or ORDERS TO DISCONTINUE same must reach the Office before TEN o'clock on WEDNESDAY mornings.

The Publisher cannot be responsible for DRAWINGS, TESTIMONIALS, &c. left at the Office in reply to Advertisements, and strongly recommends that of the latter COPIES ONLY should be sent.

PERSONS Advertising in "The Builder" may have *Replies addressed to the Office,* 46, Catherine-street, Covent Garden, W.C. *free of charge.* Letters will be forwarded if addressed envelopes are sent, together with sufficient stamps to cover the postage.

AN EDITION Printed on THIN PAPER, for FOREIGN and COLONIAL CIRCULATION, is issued every week.

Now ready.

READING CASES, { NINEPENCE EACH. By Post (carefully packed), 1s.

TO CORRESPONDENTS.

D. D. H. (matter for a daily paper rather than for us).—W. W.—F. C.—J. H. S.—B. St. A. B. (sent too late).

All statements of facts, lists of tenders, &c., must be accompanied by the name and address of the sender, not necessarily for publication.

We are compelled to decline pointing out books and giving addresses.

NOTE.—The responsibility of signed articles, and papers read at public meetings, rests, of course, with the authors.

We cannot undertake to return rejected communications.

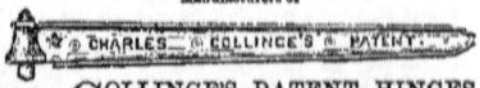

Letters or communications (beyond mere news-items) which have been duplicated for other journals, are NOT DESIRED.

All communications regarding literary and artistic matter should be addressed to THE EDITOR; all communications relating to advertisements and other exclusively business matters should be addressed to THE PUBLISHER, and not to the Editor.

The Builder.

VOL. LXII. No. 2577. SATURDAY, JUNE 25, 1892

ILLUSTRATIONS.

Glasgow Art Gallery Competition: Design Submitted by Messrs. Honeyman & Kepple:—

Perspective View and Plan .... *Double-Page Ink-Photo.*

Detail of Central Part of South Elevation .... *Double-Page Ink-Photo.*

Mosaic Pavement of Staircase Hall, and Copper Balustrade, at House in Chesterfield-gardens.—Mr. G. Aitchison, A.R.A., Architect .... *Double-Page Ink-Photo.*

Flats at Earl's Court-square.—Mr. R. A. Briggs, Architect .... *Double-Page Photo-Litho.*

Blocks in Text.

North Transept, Christchurch Priory, Hants.—Drawn by J. A. Pywell .... Page 499 | Capitals of Arcading, Christchurch Priory, Hants.—Drawn by J. A. Pywell.. Page 500

Diagrams in "Student's Column": Heating by Hot Water........ Pages 507, 508

CONTENTS.

Oxford Municipal Buildings Competition 491
The Further Report of the Committee on Town Holdings 493
Old Pictures at the Burlington Club 494
Notes 495
The Imperial Institute 497
Architectural Societies 498
Competitions 498
Christchurch Priory, Hants 499
The Incorporated Association of Municipal and County Engineers 499
The Shone System of Town Drainage 501
Competition Design for the Glasgow Art Galleries 502
Mosaic Pavement—House in Chesterfield-gardens........ 502
Flats, Earl's Court-square 502
The Royal Commission on Metropolitan Water-Supply 503
Sanitary Samples at Highgate 505
Society of Engineers 505
The London County Council 506
The Status of the Architect at the R.I.B.A. 507
Changes at the Institute 507
Is the Provision of Warmth and Ventilation Compulsory in Workrooms 507
Devonian Screens 507
Student's Column.—Warming Buildings by Hot Water. XXVI. 507
General Building News 508
Foreign and Colonial 509
Miscellaneous 509
Meetings 510
Recent Patents 510
Some Recent Sales of Property 511

Oxford Municipal Buildings Competition.

THE erection of new Municipal buildings in a city like Oxford,—a city of such special character and associations both in a historic and an architectural sense,—is an event of more than usual interest. Although the project is solely that of the Municipality, and does not in any way directly concern the University, one cannot but desire that so important an addition to the old and stately University town should be such as will be in harmony with its surroundings, and be not merely a convenient building for the transaction of municipal business, but an architectural addition to one of the most architecturally beautiful cities in the world. It is gratifying to find that the final competition for the Municipal buildings at Oxford shows at least a possibility of the combination of both elements, the practical and the architectural.

As our readers will remember, this is a competition on the dual system, a sketch competition first and a second trial of strength among a limited number of selected competitors afterwards, which is so much the fashion in France, and has lately been adopted in a good many instances in England; the architects in the second competition, in this as in most similar cases, receiving each a fee for his work. The present competition suggests the question, on which it is worth while to say a word, whether this duplicate system presents sufficient advantages to render its adoption desirable as the normal system of architectural competition. A good many architects object, and not without reason, that it is in reality inflicting double work on the best competitors. This objection would hardly apply, perhaps, if the word "sketch" were interpreted in a more literal sense. If the first set of plans were no more than is generally understood by that word, no doubt a large number of competitors would be saved the vexation, inherent in the ordinary form of competition, of having thrown away much time and labour on getting up a complete set of drawings on a chance which has brought them no return. But competitors themselves will hardly allow of this interpretation. Each competitor hopes to attract attention to his first set of plans, and possibly to surpass others, by putting a good deal of work into them, and turning out a more or less finished set of drawings on a small scale. In the present competition the original sets of drawings in the first competition are (very rightly) hung along with the completed sets. We have thus a direct opportunity of comparing them, and it is obvious at once that the plans at all events might just as well have been selected on the basis of the first as the second competition. The scale is the same in both ($\frac{1}{8}$ in. to the foot), and except that the second set are in most cases rather more neatly and carefully drawn than the first, there is little difference between them, and either would do equally well as a basis for classifying them according to merit. One or two of the plans have, it is true, been materially altered and improved in the second edition (the competitors having been allowed full liberty in this respect), but these improvements do not affect the relative merit of the different plans, and could just as well have been developed (as they no doubt would have been) in making the working drawings; so that as far as plan goes the result is merely that the selected architect has to make out his plans three times instead of twice. In regard to the elevations the matter is different. In the first competition the elevations were to the same scale as the plans, in the second they are to double the scale; and the comparison of the two sets of elevations shows forcibly how much easier it is to produce a decent and attractive-looking elevation on a small than on a large scale. Among the five designs there is only one (No. 5) in which the small scale elevation does not produce a far more favourable impression than the large scale one; an elevation which seems picturesque, well-filled, even rich in effect, on the small scale, looking comparatively thin and hard on the large scale, and the detail in some cases not bearing out the promise given by its rougher indications on the smaller scale. Perspective drawings, from a point of view fixed by the instructions, are required in the second competition; but there is only one instance (No. 2) in which the perspective gives a better or more favourable idea of the design than was afforded by the first set of sketches. The small-scale sections of the first set show all that was required to form an opinion as to the treatment of the interior; and therefore the conclusion is that the whole competition might have been as well settled on the basis of the first set of small scale plans and sections and one large-scale elevation, and would have come probably to the same result in the final selection. The Corporation could still of course have remunerated the five best competitors, and 100*l*., or ·2 per cent. on the estimated outlay of 50,000*l*., is certainly not an extravagant premium for any set of sketch plans which merit serious consideration, without the extra labour of preparing a second set.

The Corporation undertook to select from the first set of sketch-plans a number not exceeding five for the second competition, and have selected the maximum number. The scheme of the required building includes a large Town-hall or music-room; a smaller Assembly-room to be used for meetings for which the Town-hall is too large, or as a supper room when the Town-hall is used for a ball; a police department, with a large parade room in addition to charge-room, cells for prisoners, and other usual requirements; a Sessions Court with its necessary rooms for judges, jurors, barristers, witnesses &c.; Municipal Offices, Council Chamber, Mayor's Parlour, Committee-rooms, and offices for City Engineer, water, rates, Medical Officer, pay office &c.; and the usual offices, kitchen, scullery, porter's room &c. The scheme also includes a public library to form part of the building architecturally, but to be separate from it and self-contained in regard to plan. The site is a difficult one to treat, as it presents only two street frontages, a principal one to St. Aldate-street and a side one to the narrow Blue Boar-lane; the rest is hemmed in with houses and a good deal encumbered with rights of light, so that the use of internal courts for light is a necessity. The principal entrance must naturally be in St. Aldate-street; and as the existing Town Clerk's offices at the north-west angle of the site are to be retained and to communicate

d

with the new buildings, this approximately fixes the position of the Council-chamber and Mayor's parlour, which ought to be within easy reach from the Town Clerk's office; while the library site is fixed, by the instructions, at the south-west angle; at least it is strongly recommended that it should be there, and all the competitors have adopted the suggestion.

We will offer a few remarks on the designs, taking them in the order of numbering. No. 1 arranges the parade-room and police department on the ground floor in a large central block running west and east (*i.e.* at right angles to the principal front) and the Town-hall partly over the parade-room; the library forms a long block along Blue Boar-lane with the assembly-room over it. This lane forms an obtuse angle with St. Aldate-street, so that there is a little contrivance desirable to make a good joining of the two façades; in this case the oblique line is stopped short before reaching the angle and set back to a line at right angles with St. Aldate-street, the re-entering angle being filled up with a staircase turret. Between these two blocks is a long irregular courtyard with an entry from the street, from which courtyard is the entrance to police department, Sessions-court, and stairs to the Town-hall gallery; the Sessions-court is on the first floor in the rear of the Town-hall. This courtyard loses a good deal of space and is not otherwise a good arrangement. There are two entrances in St. Aldate-street, one near the library, beside which is the stair to the assembly-room, the other near the other end of the front, and a corridor runs parallel with the front, with a cross corridor from the entrance, leading to the principal staircase. The Council-chamber is properly placed, internally and near the Town-clerk's offices, on the first-floor; the principal committee-room opens out of it in the interior part of the building. But though the main departments are arranged in good relative positions as regards one another, the whole plan wants system and has mistakes in detail; *e.g.* the position of the ladies' and gentlemen's cloak-rooms, with the doors close to each other and directly facing the assembly-room doors on the other side of the corridor, is absurd. The engineer's drawing-office faces St. Aldate-street and has a west light (slightly south-west) which is not good, but three out of the five competitors have made this mistake. The design is of a late Gothic character; the Town-hall front or end is somewhat recessed and has a large traceried window, with lower buildings forming a screen in front of it; the small scale elevation is very prettily sketched and looks well, but the large one shows but commonplace detail, and the perspective is almost puerile in manner and execution.

No. 2 is far superior, and we should rank it as the second best of the five, in design if not in plan. Here the library is treated also as an oblique block parallel with Blue Boar-lane, but wider than in No. 1, and the Town-hall placed over it; the assembly-room is on the first-floor in the middle of the principal front, that and the large committee-room giving three large windows as the main feature in the central block parallel to St. Aldate-street. The connexion between the oblique blocks and the front is well managed, the library block being returned at right angles to its flank, but provided with a very large segmental bay window the lines of which serve to divert the eye from the change of angle between the two portions of the building. The principal entrance is in the middle of the St. Aldate-street front, and from this a long corridor runs as a backbone to the very back of the building, leading on the first floor to the Sessions-court block in the rear, the public entrance to which is from Blue Boar-lane, behind the library. The parade-room is on the basement under a glass roof, over which on the other stories is a large area for light. In respect both of areas and corridors the plan is wasteful, and the aforesaid front-to-back corridor is a promenade which might have been avoided, and makes the Justice's room (if he is supposed to enter at the principal entrance) a kind of *ultima Thule*. A broad cross corridor runs parallel to St. Aldate-street, and on the first floor a fine use is made of this, which is treated as a state corridor lined with columns and connecting the council-chamber and Mayor's room at one end with the Town-hall at the other, while the assembly-room and large committee-room also open out of it, so that for a large fête the whole are connected by this columned corridor. Unfortunately, the ladies' and gentlemen's cloak-rooms also open direct out of the same corridor; a great blunder. The front also is not the best place for a committee-room, nor, as before observed (though for another reason), for the engineer's offices. The design is a freely-treated Gothic, with a mingling of classic feeling in some details: the effect is got mainly by the arrangement and treatment of the windows, with little decoration. The end of the Town-hall facing St. Aldate-street is treated as a large gable with an effectively designed window, and a very good feature is the treatment of the flank of the library and Town-hall. On the elevation the library front appears a mass of large windows, but these are grouped under lofty wall-arches in such a manner as to have a satisfactory and sufficiently solid effect in perspective. Corresponding to the piers of this large wall arcade are internal buttresses which serve as nuclei for bookcases, and the inner ends of which carry the columns of the side galleries of the Town-hall above, and a kind of clearstory wall which rises above and behind the library wall, and is connected with it by deep buttresses with bold scroll consoles at the top. This treatment of the flank is a very good bit of subsidiary architecture. The perspective, a pen and ink drawing touched with a light and free hand, has an exceedingly picturesque and characteristic effect.

No. 3 covers the ground very much, leaving very small areas for light; in other respects the interior lighting is cleverly managed, but the areas would be very like wells. The Town-hall is arranged parallel to the principal front, with complete corridor communication all round it, but the advantage is rather discounted by the fact that the principal staircase is not sufficiently central, in relation to the Town-hall, for access to these corridors, being near the north-west angle of the Town-hall, and visitors would have to circulate all round the corridors to get access to the further side of the large room. The Sessions-court stairs from Blue Boar-lane would no doubt afford an additional access, but it is not convenient at a large gathering to have two different street entrances for the same portion of the audience. The provision for internal communication by this arrangement of corridors is very complete but somewhat circuitous in character, and the corridors run away with a good deal of space. The author has divided the levels on his section, placing the Council-chamber and Sessions-court on the principal front, half-way above the Town-hall floor level, and divided by the principal committee-room, which projects in the centre of the front, and is connected with both so as to make a suite. This might be convenient on occasion, but the rooms are too high up in the building; the placing of the assembly-room on a different level from the Town-hall would materially interfere with its proposed use as a supper-room in connexion with a ball, and the council-chamber and assembly-room are too distinct in their uses and functions to be properly placed as pendants to one another in either plan or design. Moreover, the front to the principal thoroughfare is not the place for council-chamber and committee-room, in which quiet is especially desirable. The Mayor's-parlour, on the other hand, might better have been placed facing the street, so as to have an outlook, instead of looking only a small interior well. The Sessions-court department is arranged behind the Town-hall, with external access from Blue Boar-lane. On the ground-floor is marked a gentlemen's lavatory and cloak-room for Town-hall receptions, which is well placed, but we failed to discover any similar provision for ladies. The elevation is Gothic with a character of detail which seems to have been intended for terra-cotta; if so, we have another example of the fact that the contemplation of terra-cotta is a temptation sometimes to the use of a rather exuberant character of detail; the heads of the window-lights, for instance, are decorated with small inverted carved scrolls or consoles, one on each side, with a pendant in the centre, which is rather too much for the situation; it makes a bad line for the head of the light, and has rather a pie-crust appearance. The perspective is carefully but somewhat heavily executed, and does not aid much in recommending the design. The author has made a considerable change in the disposition of the plan since the first competition, in which the Town-hall was placed east and west, and is now turned round, as observed, parallel with the principal elevation; the alteration is a distinct improvement. The space allotted to the library seems rather small.

The author of No. 4 has been evidently aiming at a design of "Oxford character," as shown especially in his short square staircase tower with heavy pinnacles at the angles and a lantern connected with them by flying buttresses; the upper portion of the tower is decorated with blank tracery. The entrance, however, is badly managed; for some inexplicable reason the actual entrance, to north of this staircase tower, is masked by a screen wall ending in a pier like a gate-pier, and the actual setting-down place in the street is at some steps in front of the staircase tower, so that people alighting from carriages would have to walk from what may be called the entrance gate, round the angle of the staircase tower, to get under cover in the entrance. Imagine how people would bless the architect for this when there was a large entertainment on a rainy night! The library is placed to the south of the staircase tower, turned more towards the principal front than in the other designs, the parade-room behind it, with the end towards Blue Boar-lane, and the Town-hall over the parade-room. As the platform of the Town-hall room is at the inner or north end of the hall, this brings the main staircase and the platform end in close contiguity, which is not what is wanted; the main staircase should adjoin the public end of any large entertaining-room: the platform should have been put at the Blue Boar-lane end, with its own entrance from the street for those whose place is on the platform. The council-chamber and Mayor's-room are well placed, the former within the building parallel with the main front, the latter on the other side of the corridor, on the main front; the principal committee-room is cleverly got in off the corridor which leads to the Sessions-court at the back of the building, but it is thus a long way from the Town Clerk's offices, which is not convenient. The engineer's offices are placed with a north light, looking towards an internal area to the north of the new buildings. The assembly-room is on the second floor, reached from the central staircase tower, and with a small reception or ante-room between it and the stairs: in view of the point in the instructions already referred to, as to the use of the assembly-room in connexion with the Town-hall, this is a worse position than in No. 3, as it is a whole story above the Town-hall floor instead of half a story. The design may be called Collegiate Gothic, with mullioned windows, with niches between them on the principal floor; there are some characteristic bits of detail, such as the treatment of the roof-balustrade, but the details generally seem rather large and coarse in character, and show an uncertainty as to scale; for instance, the traceried window in the lower part of the tower, which lights the staircase, gives the impression to the eye of being much smaller than the scale shows it to be by measurement. The perspective is a slight but cleverly executed pen sketch which looks well, but in which detail is merely indicated in the roughest manner.

No. 5 is the only really first-class plan of the set, and is one of the best arranged plans we have ever seen in a competition. The arrangements for internal communication are admirable and most compact, with no waste of space in needless corridors; indeed, almost the only fault we should be disposed to find with the plan is that one or two of the corridors (or at all events one,—that leading to the Sessions-court department from the central cross corridor) are insufficient in width; they are barely five feet in width by scale. This only applies, however, to a small portion of the plan. The central entrance in St. Aldate street leads to a square central staircase hall with a staircase with a central lower flight and side return flights above, the ladies' and gentlemen's cloak-rooms are placed on the ground floor with their respective entrances on either side of the lower flight of the staircase, which projects slightly into the hall: this is the only plan in the collection in which this important detail is properly arranged. The water and rates offices are placed in the front to left of the entrance, the latter close to the entrance, as it should be; the engineer's offices are cleverly planned in the same position as in No. 4, with a north light for the drawing office. The ground plan is cut in two by a corridor separating the front from the back portion and entered from Blue Boar-lane, which corridor forms the public access to staircases to the public galleries of Town-hall, Sessions-court, and Council-chamber, which are thus contrived so that one street entrance serves for all. The entrance to the library is at the south-west angle, with an angle turret over it making a feature in the design. This corridor runs at right angles to Blue Boar-lane and therefore obliquely across the building, and behind it the line of building is turned obliquely to the line of the principal frontage. The central portion of the ground floor here is occupied by the parade-room. On the principal floor the Town-hall occupies the position over the parade-room and extending forward over the public corridor before mentioned. The entrance wall of the Town-hall room is very cleverly treated with projections and a large alcove towards the central hall, so as to mask the turn in the line of building and bring the rear side of the central hall parallel with the front side. The Sessions-court department is between the Town-hall and Blue Boar-lane, and connected with the central hall by a corridor, the one which we referred to as being too narrow; but as after all this corridor is only for official communication with other parts of the building (the Sessions-court having its own access from the street), perhaps it is sufficient for its real purpose; it looks rather cramped on the plan. The Sessions-court has its own small central hall out of which the various rooms open, and the justices' room is reached by the other narrow corridor running towards Blue Boar-lane from the central hall, leading to a private room overlooking the lane and outside the Sessions-court department, but opening into the court. The assembly-room is in the centre of the main front, opening from the central hall, and adjoining it a short corridor leads to another small square lobby from which open the doors to the council-chamber (over the engineer's offices), the committee-room in front of the building, and the corridor leading past the door of the Mayor's-room (in front) and to the Town Clerk's offices, the Town Clerk and Mayor thus being in immediate contiguity, and the council-chamber department arranged *en suite* in connexion with its own lobby or vestibule, shut out from the more public part of the building but easily reached from it. The central hall is not over large and runs away with no unnecessary space, and the manner in which everything is grouped in connexion with it cannot be too highly praised. There is a little drawback in having the committee-room facing the street, that is the only criticism that can be made. Another committee-room opens out of the passage to the justice's-room, and this being intended also to serve as a grand jury-room when wanted, its door faces the passage to the Sessions-court department. The manner in which almost everything seems to have been got just into its right place on this difficult and confined site is a triumph of planning, and must have cost the author no little trouble and thought.*

The elevations are in a style partaking a little both of the Jacobean and Elizabethan manner; the St. Aldate-street front is symmetrically treated; the centre block has three large windows between pilasters which mark the assembly-room; the corbelled-out bay-windows of the Mayor's-room and principal committee-room are balanced by similar windows to the library on the other side. The Blue Boar-lane front is simply treated, but a pleasing architectural point is made by an arcade of three large arches on the ground story, the wall behind being set back a little; through one of these is the public entrance to the Sessions-courts, &c., through another the entrance to the basement. The principal front is finished with gables over the bay-windows, decorated with colonnettes and ornamental features belonging to the style, and a larger gable in the centre treated in a similar manner; the feature in the centre of this is too *rococo* in style, and would bear paring down a little; it is in character with some old work in Oxford, but we do not see why old detail which is in a corrupt taste should be repeated now. The gables on the side portion also, though they have windows which light attics, have a little too much the appearance in the perspective view of being carried up for ornament only, in the upper portion at least: for which also, no doubt, there is plenty of precedent.

The front of this design looks rather costly in comparison with others; but apart from that point, which of course will have to be considered, there can be no question between this and any other set of drawings sent in. As far as plan is concerned no other can be considered in the running with it; as far as design goes No. 2 has the merit of producing a very picturesque building at probably less cost, and is a design which we should be very glad to see erected, as architecture, though it cannot have the dignified effect of No. 5. We may add that the drawings in the latter set are beautifully executed, but we do not know that they owe any special advantage to that fact; the incontestible superiority is in plan, in which drawing does not count.

The promoters of the competition made one mistake, in not attaching the architects' reports to the drawings; on which account it is impossible to understand what the several architects propose in the way of ventilation, which cannot be sufficiently indicated on plans and sections except when detailed to a larger scale. This is a serious omission; the architect's report should always be appended to competition drawings when public criticism is invited. On the other hand we must praise the Corporation for their commonsense in putting up the designs for public criticism before they had made their final selection. Generally speaking, one is only invited to criticise competitions after the selection has been made, and when in consequence it is too late for criticism to be of much practical value. As at present intended, the final decision will be made at the Council meeting to be held on the 29th of this month.

THE ENGLISH IRON TRADE.—The approach of the General Election, and the uncertainty which generally precedes the usual quarterly meetings, are not conducive to a considerable augmentation of business in the English iron market, and the condition of trade shows but little amelioration. In Cleveland there is a slight improvement noticeable in the demand, and most of the furnaces are again in blast. The hematite pig-iron trade is also a trifle brighter, on account of an increase in the consumption by steel-makers. Generally, however, the crude-iron branch remains quiet, and manufactured iron continues dull. The steel trade is a trifle better, and the inquiry for tinplates is still fair. Shipbuilders and engineers exhibit little alteration. The coal trade is fairly brisk.—*Iron.*

* There can be no doubt of the authorship of this design; but we do not choose to suggest names as long as they are still officially private.

THE FURTHER REPORT OF THE COMMITTEE ON TOWN HOLDINGS.

IT is to be regretted that the final report of the Committee of the House of Commons on Town Holdings, which was appointed for the first time in 1886, and has been reappointed during succeeding sessions, has been issued when the country is interested in little else than the General Election. Politicians who should study this report will be wholly concerned with the register of electors, and a document of considerable value is likely to be passed over without the full attention which should be given to it. The main point to which the present report refers is that portion of the reference to the Committee which was concerned with "the question of imposing a direct assessment on the owners of ground-rents and on the owners of increased values imparted to land by building operations and other improvements."

A primary reason for taxing any kind of property is that it has hitherto escaped taxation, and is a proper subject for taxation. It has been shown over and over again that things should not be taxed if the obtaining of the money is a cause of difficulty and annoyance. As regards ground-rents and ground landlords, it has been contended by all reasonable men that they are indirectly taxed; that is to say, though the occupier is the person who pays the tax to taxgatherer, yet, in consequence of the law of supply and demand, the ground landlord pays his share indirectly. In other words, it has been contended that he is already taxed. The Committee agree with this view, as will be seen from the following extracts from their report:—

"The idea that ground-rents are a class of property which at present escapes assessment for the purposes of local taxation is, of course, quite erroneous. The basis of all rating is the whole annual value of the building and of the land on which it stands, regarded as one entire property. In the ordinary case of a house subject to a ground-rent, and let by the owner to the occupier at a rack-rent, the several interests of the ground landlord, of the owner of the house, and of the occupier, constitute together the subject-matter of an assessment which is made upon the property as a whole. There appears to have been a popular impression that ground-rents constitute a subject-matter of assessment hitherto untouched, and that a new and fresh source of revenue for local purposes would be "tapped" by imposing a direct assessment on such ground-rents, in addition to the present assessment of the whole property. But this view was found not to bear examination. It was soon seen that the assessed value of the house includes that of all the various interests above enumerated, and that to put a direct assessment on the ground-rent in addition to the existing assessment of the house, would be to rate a certain portion of the value twice over. This would result in an obvious inequality in the burthen of taxation as between different properties. Thus in the case of two houses of equal value standing side by side, if one were leasehold and the other freehold, the leasehold would bear a larger share of local taxation than the other, as, in addition to the rate on its entire value paid by the occupier, there would be a further distinct rate levied on the ground-rent."

The actual conclusion is, perhaps, more concisely stated in the following paragraph from another portion of the report:—

"Upon the whole, the conclusion we have arrived at is that in the inception of the ground-lease allowance is made on account of the existing and contemplated rates, and that the amount of such allowance is deducted from the ground-rent, which might otherwise be charged, and that to the extent of such allowance the owner of the ground-rent indirectly bears the burden of rates, in the sense that if this burden were remitted he would be able to obtain a ground-rent increased by the amount so allowed for. Similarly, the house-owner gets from the occupier a lower rent than he would have obtained if it had not been for the obligation undertaken by the tenant to pay the rates."

The Committee then proceeds to consider whether the present occupiers have to bear new and unexpected burdens, that is to say, whether they are burdened with charges which were not contemplated when they became tenants. The result is thus stated, "from these various considerations we conclude that the number of present occupying tenants who entered into their bargains before the rates now said to be new and unexpected burdens were first imposed must be very small." The result of the inquiries of the Committee thus shows that occupiers are not the illused persons which some individuals are continually declaring them to be, and it is equally clear that the case for any taxation of ground-rents and ground landlords wholly fails. But with a considerable want of logic the Committee, nevertheless, propose a change, for they recommend in their summary that, "Under all future contracts, local laxation shall be equally divided between occupiers and owners, and that each owner should have the right of making a proportionate deduction from his superior landlord." We have already pointed out that the Committee find that the ground landlords at present bear a share of local taxation. Why, then, is the recommendation made? Because, say the Committee, "it is desirable that the real and apparent incidence of local taxation should be as far as possible identical." This reason does not, in our judgment, warrant the making of so large a change which is thus described in greater length.

"We are, however, of opinion that it possessed some advantages of great practical weight. It will impose a portion of the rates, in the first instance, and ostensibly, on the persons who already bear a part of the real burden; it will reduce the importance of the difficult questions arising in connexion with the 'shifting of taxation,' and the still more difficult question how far such doctrine is limited by the various causes known as 'economic friction.' It is not easy to make the abstract reasonings of economists, however well founded, clear to the minds of the great mass of those who have to pay rates; and, in our opinion, the change would do much to remove the sense of injustice which, whether rightly or wrongly, is no doubt at present very widely entertained, by making it clear that at least some share of the local rates is paid by owners."

The change will necessarily involve owners of ground-rents in uncertainty as to the annual amount which they will receive, and it will cause many practical inconveniences. Moreover, the Committee admit that when a new class of direct ratepayers is created they must be represented on local bodies administering rates. They pass airily over a difficult question by stating that, "We see no insuperable difficulty in framing a scheme by which the right to vote could be claimed by those owners who are liable to pay their share of the rates under the new system." The difficulty may, indeed, not be insuperable, but it is a substantial difficulty, and one not easy to overcome. Surely, therefore, seeing that this change is only proposed to remedy an imaginary and not a real grievance, the game,—to use a colloquial expression,—is not worth the candle. The change is not required in the public interest, and we do not believe that the Legislature will ever sanction it, having regard to the fact that the Committee, on their own showing, are unable to prove that there is any real sound and pressing reason in its favour. To enter into the reasons advanced by the numerous witnesses for and against the change would be useless; what we are concerned with is the finding of a semi-judicial body: a finding which has also been arrived at by the great bulk of reasonable and clear-headed men. It has further to be borne in mind that, in some senses, the ground-landlord and the receiver of the rack-rent by no means benefit, except infinitesimally, in the result of the expenditure of rates. "It is difficult," say the Committee, "to point out the pecuniary benefit conferred upon owners by the ordinary current expenditure of the community on such purposes as the cleansing, lighting, and watering of streets, the relief of the poor, or public elementary education."

"On the other hand, speaking generally, expenditure upon public improvements of a permanent or remunerative character, such as the construction of new thoroughfares or new systems of drainage, the erection or freeing of bridges, or on other similar works, undoubtedly benefits owners as well as occupiers, but the extent to which all such owners derive a benefit from this expenditure varies greatly according to the proximity of their reversionary interests. The owner of a reversion ninety years distant or more (and consequently of no actuarial value) would derive no appreciable advantage from a great public work, whilst the same work might confer a substantial pecuniary benefit upon the owner of a reversion falling in within twenty years or less, and, of course, all sorts of cases intermediate between these two may and do occur."

Therefore, seeing that both the rack-renter and the occupier have, in making their bargains with their respective lessors, taken into consideration the general incidence of rates in calculating the ground rent and the rack-rent respectively, it would appear from the foregoing extract that, if anything, it is the rack-renter and the ground landlord who have reason to complain, rather than the occupier. Upon no single ground, at any rate, does the Committee find any reason for a change in the present system of taxation, except upon the purely sentimental one of making the actual incidence of local taxation more plain to the community at large.

We have said enough to make this portion of the report plain to all our readers. It is time to say a word on another part of it, which touches on the taxation of vacant building land. This is one of these specious proposals which, until they are submitted to a close examination, appear to have some merits. The Committee analyse the arguments and reasons, pro and con, with so much levity that it is impossible to give anything like a *précis* of them. It must suffice to state that the proposal to tax vacant building land is rejected in its entirety. It is said that by taxing vacant land of this kind more of it must be forced into the market, so that the rent of town houses would be lessened by the supply being enlarged. But the answer to this is that as soon as land is really "ripe," the owners put it on the market. There is no advantage in keeping it vacant longer than is necessary. Moreover, there is an initial difficulty. Before vacant building land can be taxed, the question has to be answered,—viz., "What is vacant building land?" A moment's thought will show the difficulty of the question. For example, is a pleasure-ground or large garden vacant building land? Again, say the Committee, "Great difficulties must arise, as all land near towns grows imperceptibly into building land," and thus it is difficult to define the time at which land can be said to become building land. Again, also, the Committee can see no distinction between vacant land and empty houses, and if a measure to tax the former becomes law, it must be followed by one to rate the latter. In the result we therefore have these conclusions arrived at:—

"As regards the argument drawn from the benefit to vacant building land from public local expenditure, it does not appear to us that so much of the expenditure as is devoted to current purposes can have any direct effect in increasing the value of such land, nor is such expenditure undertaken with any such object. The purpose of such local expenditure is, as it appears to us, the benefit and convenience of the inhabitants. As regards permanent improvements, it must be borne in mind, as pointed out by some of the witnesses, that streets and sewers are generally constructed at the expense of the persons interested in the land they are designed to develope, and, as regards improvements of a more public character, such as embankments, bridges, and parks, although, no doubt, they benefit the immediate locality, we do not think that the vacant land within the municipal limits can be said generally to derive any appreciable benefit, such as to form a valid ground for imposing special taxation."

Further, the Committee point out that such taxation would not benefit the working classes by enlarging the supply of houses; they show that it is a tax on capital, and is at variance with all received axioms of taxation, and would be most difficult to levy, and they, therefore, reject the proposal. Thus they throw over the suggestions, of which a good deal has of late been heard, to tax the "unearned increment," a principle which could not be confined to one species of property, and upon which economists of high authority differ. Moreover, it is important to bear in mind that what may be termed extraordinary methods of raising money for the purpose of local expenditure can at the best only be justified,—if, indeed, they can be justified,—because there are either no other more legitimate means of taxation or because the increase of taxation is very great. But a return procured by the Chairman of the Committee shows that out of the fourteen most important towns in the country the rates have risen in the pound in seven, and fallen in six, towns. In London the rate has risen, but if in Manchester and Newcastle it has fallen, has its rise been legitimate in the Metropolis? In other words, the true course for municipal and local bodies to pursue is to endeavour by economical and efficient administration to keep down the increase of rates, rather than to seek new methods of raising money. Be that as it may, the report, of which we have given some of the most important points and conclusions, shows clearly that many of the methods now suggested for raising fresh local taxes cannot be justified.

OLD PICTURES AT THE BURLINGTON CLUB.

THE collection, at the Burlington Fine Arts Club, of pictures "by Masters of the Netherlandish and allied schools of the XV. and early XVI. centuries" is a really remarkable one in regard to the interest and power of many of the works contributed, some of them bearing the names of artists who are at all events not popularly known, and some of whose works will surprise many to whom the names of the painters are not very familiar. But in another sense the collection ought to be interesting to those who are interested in architecture and decoration, for many of the paintings contain, in the costumes of the figures, splendidly-executed designs for textiles, and not a few of them illustrate the architectural ideas of the day in the buildings which form backgrounds to the scenes represented.

Among the paintings which are remarkable for their adjuncts none is more so than the painting of "St. Jerome in his Study" (7A) by Antonello da Messina, of whom the catalogue note says, "date of birth unknown, but may have been early in the fifteenth century." This is a truly remarkable little painting, not only in regard to the fine painting of the figure seated in the back part of the interior with side face to the spectator, and the light full upon his expressively and powerfully-painted head, but also in the extraordinary elaboration of all the detail surrounding the central portion of the scene. On the right we look through a door into a vaulted hall with two rows of columns, though which hall roams the traditional lion which was the companion and attendant of the saint. Through two windows in two portions of what we may call the back scene (for the whole very much resembles a set scene on the stage) is seen a distant landscape and figures on the most minute scale and painted with the most careful exactness. Concerning the interior itself, the catalogue quotes Sir J. E. Robinson to the effect that "the two-light window, divided by a slender central shaft, is known in Spain as the *ajimez* window. The type is quite peculiar to the districts of Spain in question. . . . There cannot be a doubt that the interior here depicted with so much verisimilitude, was carefully copied from an existing building, probably the house of one of the rich merchants of Valencia." In the picture of the holy women at the Sepulchre (11), attributed, though we should think very doubtfully, to John Van Eyck, we see in the background the painter's idea of the houses and towers of Jerusalem, with the mosque of Omar doing duty for the Temple. In the two curious Madonna pictures labelled "Early Flemish School" (13 and 16), we see a peculiar feature in the shape of low stone walls with crops of flowers on the top; on one of these, in 16, the Virgin is seated. No. 13 presents a study of Renaissance façade of rather curious detail on the right. In the centre of the wall, over the fireplace, is a little gem of a painting in its way, a "Virgin and Child Enthroned" (14) labelled on the owner's frame "Mabuse," but reduced in the catalogue to the more modest and doubtful claim of "School of Roger van der Weyden." The small figure is seated under a Late Gothic canopy so forcibly painted as to seem almost in relief; the Virgin has an elaborate crown, the jewels in which still make tiny points of light in the picture; her flowing and luxuriant hair has been painted with the greatest care, and seems still fresh from the brush. The architectural canopy is decorated in the upper part with sculptured figures only about a quarter of an inch high, but in which the features and details of drapery are all quite sharp and distinct. The whole picture is less than six inches in height. It is hard and formal of course, but one cannot help contrasting the conscientious labour betowed here with the easy fame won in these days by painting "impressions" and "nocturnes." Near this is one of the most splendid pieces of costume painting in the collection. "S. Victor with a Donor" (17), by Hugo Van der Goes. The armour of the saint, the blue velvet vest, the cloak with fur collar, are painted with marvellous truth and force, and the cope of the ecclesiastic who kneels beside him is painted with equal power, and is a fine and sumptuous piece of design as well. In this case there is dignity too about the face and figure of the saint; in others of the paintings, as in Nos. 13 and 16, it is curious to note how the whole skill of the painter, the whole feeling for beauty, seems to have gone away into the accessories, leaving the faces of the figures utterly devoid of grace or expression, and the figure of the Holy Child, which is the centre and supposed object of the whole painting, looking more like a monkey than a human infant. This is the same puzzle that we see in Japanese art up to the present day; the power to paint decorations and inferior forms of life highly developed, while the painter's capabilities and his sense of beauty alike seem to desert him as soon as he comes to deal with the human face and form. It is a curious paradox in art, and might form a subject for inquiry as to the causes, social or philosophical, which lie behind it.

In the picture labelled as of "The School of Hans Memling" and representing "Virgin and Child Enthroned" (23), the design of the throne is of some interest. It is described in the catalogue as of "red and white marble," which we think is a mistake; it is wood and white marble; if the other material were taken to be red marble we can only say it shows much worse painting of material than is usual in pictures of this school. The artists of the Netherlands School were very fond of painting wood and carefully showing all the details of the grain, as will be seen in other paintings where the object is undoubtedly of wood; the same kind of execution is seen in the more massive portions of this throne, and the compilers of the catalogue seem to have been misled into describing it as marble merely because the combination of wood with marble seemed an odd and unusual one. The upper (marble) portions of the throne are finished at each side by a curious finial bent round and with a bunch of grapes sculptured as if hanging from it, while a small angel figure stands on the upper side of the scroll. Altogether this throne is a curious and interesting piece of work.

The picture of the school of Roger van der Weyden (29) should be noticed for the remarkable painting of the distant town and cathedral seen through an open window, and which is almost like a view through a telescope; notice the minute but carefully-painted figure, so small as to be only just discernible, of a man on a ladder painting the wall of one of the houses. Lucas de Heere's portrait of Lady Jane Grey should not be passed over (32). The Virgin and Child by Mabuse (39), a splendid example, is interesting architecturally from the curious design of the throne, with its short thick pilasters and large capitals, and the four stone consoles in the front on which the floor of the picture seems to be supported. Another painting, called "Mabuse" on the frame but denied as such in the catalogue (41), has a most elaborate architectural background of Roman and Renaissance detail. The genuine Mabuse, No. 42, a triptych, with the Virgin enthroned in front of a landscape, gives an elaborate Mediæval stone castle in the middle distance, contrasted with the half-timber houses of the peasantry adjoining it, and (strange feature in a Dutch picture) we see a garden with *winding* walks and a *rustic* bridge. In the picture described as of the "School of Geeraert David" (46) the student of decorative design will find a "cloth of estate" covering the virgin's throne, which furnishes a splendid wall-paper design. Among the paintings of more purely artistic interest may be mentioned the fine portrait of a man by Bartel Bruyn (52), and the portrait of a lady by Nicolas Lucidel "called Neuchâtel" (53), a beautiful face in which the sweet mouth and bright eyes are all the more expressive, perhaps, from the subdued and rather flat and delicate manner in which the rest of the face is painted. The costume of this half-length figure is a perfect study for artistic design and patience and refinement of execution.

The whole exhibition is one for which we ought to feel real gratitude to the Burlington Fine Arts Club.

NOTES.

WE give in another column some particulars as to the work done at the Imperial Institute, which seems now to be considered to have reached a certain recognisable stage on its road to completion, to be marked by receptions and other such formalities, though there is a great deal to be done yet, both externally and internally. From the architectural point of view there is little to criticise in the interior treatment of the rooms and corridors, which, without being ornate or disproportionately expensive, is substantial in construction and agreeable in appearance, except in the case of the large plaster pendants to the ceiling on one of the principal rooms, a piece of gimcrack which we regret to meet with in a building of this importance. In the corridors and in others of the rooms the plaster decoration is kept of a tolerably flat character, in low relief and refined in detail; the mosaic pavements of the corridors have a good appearance, the Hopton Wood stone with which the lower portion of the walls is lined looks very well and shows a finish almost like marble. The doors are well designed, though simple, and everything is in good taste. The large brackets under the principal stairs form a good architectural feature, and a welcome exception to the fashion of sticking stone stairs and landings out from a wall with no support in an architectural sense, and not quite enough in a constructive sense. The front entrance is decorated, as we have already had occasion to remark, with some bas-relief sculpture of a higher class than is usual in what is somewhat cynically called "architectural sculpture." Mingled with this prominent sculptured detail we notice a small repeating ornament formed of conventionally indicated boy figures with the extended arms crossed. Is this the last reduction to commonplace of Blake's sublime design of the morning stars singing together? We constantly meet with this *motif* now, and it seems to be taken from Blake, but we have never seen it reduced to a mere pattern before. In regard to the exterior generally, it may be said that it is a graceful and elegant building on a large scale, but not a grand one; which, with its dimensions, it might have been. The reason for this appears to reside to a great extent in the character of the detail employed, which is not of the most truly masonic character; there is an undefinable appearance about it as if all the parts were fitted together like joinery, as if it were a piece of cabinet-making on a colossal scale. The deeply-recessed arches on the ground floor, in the portions between the centre and wings, have a fine effect, and this portion will look much better when the intended sculpture in the now bare spandrels and panels is executed. That a building is entirely refined in detail and that there is absolutely nothing of bad or tawdry taste in it, is indeed much to say, and this praise the building fully merits; but we cannot call it a great or striking piece of architecture.

THE soirée given by the President of the Institute of Architects and Mrs. Macvicar Anderson at South Kensington Museum on Wednesday was very well attended; the precise number of guests was, we are informed, 1,145. Among the guests present was M. César Daly, to whom the Institute Gold Medal is to be presented on Monday evening. The string band of the Royal Artillery discoursed music in the Italian Court, and in the theatre a musical entertainment of a less every-day order was given by the Royal band of Hand-bell Ringers, whose performance was a remarkable display of the apparently easy execution of music under difficulties, by the manipulation of bells which have to be continually changed, lifted, rung, and put down again to lift the next pair. The Elizabethan dress of the ringers (we presume a tacit claim for the antiquity of the institution) gave an element of picturesque in the performance, which was increased by the graceful and easy and practised action with which the manipulation of the hand-bells was carried on. From a musician's point of view, no doubt, the result is not of much importance, but the performance is a very pretty and pleasing one, and an example of the manner in which difficulties can be vanquished by practice. The Elizabethan costume, with the ruff, and the beard cut in fashion to match, showed how easily and completely the man of the present day may be transformed into the semblance of another age by judicious treatment: the group of bell-players might have come off Shakspeare's stage.

THE last quarterly report of discoveries in Greece, issued in the *Mittheilungen* of the German Institute at Athens (1892, XVII., 1), contains a good deal of interesting news. In the recent excavations at Epidaurus, an inscription has come to light which promises to be of great architectural importance. Mr. Stais is to publish it very shortly; he believes it to contain the statement of accounts for the building of the famous Tholos of Polycleitus; he further claims that the inscription settles not only the precise date, but also the purpose of this hitherto very enigmatical structure. It has been a fascinating problem for so long, that the solution will be eagerly looked for. Besides this, Mr. Kabbadias, who directed the excavations at Epidaurus, has cleared out the greater portion of the gymnasium, and also the small Roman theatre. The great theatre of Polycleitus is now completely cleared, and the seats have been built up again wherever the original stone slabs could be found.

AT Mycenæ, Mr. Tsountas has made considerable progress with his excavation of the second great "beehive tomb," and it bids fair to be as impressive a spectacle as the better known "treasury of Athens." The *dromos*, or entrance passage, is, however, built of much smaller blocks. Sufficient architectural fragments have been found to restore conjecturally the façade of the entrance. To the right and left of the gate stood half-columns, the one remaining capital of which shows a marked resemblance to that of the Lion Gate. The architrave consists of a frieze decorated with circles, and a cornice in which runs a spiral ornament. Photographs of the façade in its present state, and of the various architectural fragments, have been taken by the German Institute, and are now available to the public. Excavations have been begun to the north of the Lion Gate, but, so far, nothing of much importance has come to light. The same number contains a valuable paper,—far too detailed for summary,—

by Dr. Bruno Sauer, on ancient Naxian sculptural art. Since his paper on the disposition of the Parthenon pedimental figures, Dr. Sauer's name may be held as a guarantee of the ability of his work. He here pursues the same method,—a method too long neglected,—*i.e.*, a close and careful analysis of the technical procedures of sculpture, and he succeeds in dating, with a high measure of probability, many Naxian monuments hitherto vaguely classed as "archaic." Another paper by Dr. Paul Wolters will be read with special interest in England, for it settles, we trust for ever, the vexed question of whether the colossal Melos head in the British Museum be Zeus or Æsculapius. Dr. Wolters publishes a statuette found at Epidamus, representing an unquestioned Æsculapius, for the god leans on a snake-entwined staff, the type of face, *mutatis mutandis*, is precisely that of the Melos head; in fact, the pose of the Melos head can only satisfactorily be explained by supposing it to have belonged to a statue standing in the attitude of the Epidamus statuette. The analogy is made clear by a plate showing the two heads side by side, reduced to the same scale.

THE account given in the *Times* of the deputation to Mr. Gladstone last week on the subject of "the eight hours" question is truly edifying reading. One knows not whether to admire most the preposterous nature of the proposals made by the representatives of labour, or the scarcely veiled insolence with which the veteran statesman who received the deputation at his house was made to understand that the representatives of labour had it in their power and intention to injure his immediate political prospects, if he did not accept their terms. With politics, of course, we have nothing to do; but we are glad to observe that a statesman who has shown himself only too ready to make promises to the constituencies who could bring him into power, in this instance at least refused to be bullied, or to put common-sense and logic on one side to secure the support of the representatives of labour. The deputation, however, has had one good result; we know now in unmistakable language what the advocates of an eight hours movement really want. We have it on their own statement that they wish for an enactment to interfere with the private life of employés after they have left the workshop, and to make it penal for them to take work home and pursue their trade there in order to make a little more money. The trades represented in the deputation do not wish to work more than eight hours; consequently no one else shall do so. After this, the opinion that an employer would make more money out of eight hours work than out of ten hours seems only a mild form of eccentricity.

THE case of Henthorn *v.* Fraser, which is reported in the current number of the *Law Reports*, contains a decision of some practical importance in regard to the sale of property. These were the short facts. H., who lived in Birkenhead, called at an office in Liverpool to negotiate for the purchase of some houses belonging to S., who handed him a note giving him the option of purchase for 750*l.* within fourteen days. Next day, between 12 and 1 o'clock, S. posted to H. a letter withdrawing the offer. This letter was received after 5 p.m. Meanwhile, H., at 3.50, had posted an unconditional acceptance of the offer, which was delivered in Liverpool after office hours, and not received by S. until next morning. The question, of course, arose, Was the acceptance or the withdrawal of the offer binding. The Court of Appeal answered that the acceptance was binding, for two main reasons. In the first place, the Court held that a person making an offer must be considered as continuously making it; or, as we should prefer to say, not withdrawing it until the withdrawal is brought to the mind of the person to whom the offer was made. Here, when the offer was accepted, the withdrawal had not come to H.'s mind. The second reason was thus stated by Lord Herschell:—"Where the circumstances are such that it must have been within the contemplation of the parties that, according to the ordinary usages of mankind, the post might be used as a means of communicating the acceptance of an offer, the acceptance is complete as soon as it is posted." Testing the facts by this rule, it is clear that H. had made a binding and valid acceptance, and that the withdrawal of the offer by S. was too late.

THE Salford County Borough Council seems to have perpetrated what is commonly called a "job" in the election of their new Borough Engineer. They advertised for applications and referred them to a sub-Committee, whence they came before the General Purposes Committee, which selected Mr. Price, of Liverpool, and passed a resolution recommending his appointment, at a salary of 500*l.*, as Borough Engineer and Surveyor. At the Council meeting the Mayor proposed the adoption of this recommendation, remarking that it had been a constitutional usage that the action of the Committees should be supported, and that Mr. Price was head and shoulders in front of all the other candidates; in fact, the Selection Committee thought there was no other candidate in the running. Upon which a member of the Council proposed Mr. Corbett, of Broughton, a candidate who had not been either first, second, or third in the selection of the Committee, and thirty Councillors voted for him and only twenty-four in support of the Committee's choice. Now Mr. Corbett was an ex-Councillor. The gross unfairness of such a proceeding, after inviting public candidature, and after the best man had beeen practically appointed on his merits, it is unnecessary to point out. We really thought the time had gone by when such a method of proceeding would be tolerated in any important public body; but Salford seems to be a survival of Little Pedlington.

TRINITY COLLEGE, the three-hundredth anniversary of which will be celebrated at Dublin in July, was founded under letters patent issued on March 3, 1591, by Queen Elizabeth, who about the same time fitted up the Castle as a residence for the Lord Lieutenants, who had formerly occupied Thomas Court. But as early as 1311 John Leck, archbishop of the See, had obtained a Bull from Rome for the establishment of a university school in Dublin; his successor, Alexander de Bicknor, accomplished the design, and set up a school of learning in St. Patrick's Cathedral, which, however, gradually declined. For a new site the mayor and citizens gave the dissolved monastery of All Hallows on Hoggin,—since College-green, granted to them by Henry VIII. The present buildings consist of three quadrangles, erected in the Classic styles, chiefly after Sir William Chambers's plans and designs. The outer quadrangle, known as Parliament-square, and with a principal front in the Corinthian order, 380 ft. in length, along the whole east side of the Green, has an interior area of 316 by 212 ft.; on its north and south sides stand the chapel and the theatre. The next court is the Library-square, 265 by 214 ft., having the library on one side. To the east of Library-square was built the printing-office, in the Doric style, as founded by Dr. Stearne, Bishop of Clogher.

A PROSPECTUS is issued from the Leadenhall Press of "London City Suburbs," designed for a companion volume to "London City," by the Rev. W. J. Loftie, F.S.A., which we noticed on November 29, 1890. As in the earlier book, the illustrations will be engraved from original drawings by Mr. Wm. Luker, jun. Mr. Percy Fitzgerald contributes the letter-press. Whether he drew up the prospectus we know not; its writer makes us somewhat apprehensive as regards the text. Of the specimen views now printed one shows the pond by the old mile-stone at the top of Heath Mount, an elevation which geologists tell us was laid before the Righi mountain had been formed under water. In the background we see a glimpse,—more should be rendered visible,—of "Upper Bowling Green House," latterly the "Upper Flask" tavern, memorable to readers of "Clarissa," and a resort of the Kit-Kat Club. In 1750 it was converted into a private residence, and has been inhabited by George Stevens the commentator on Shakespeare, and by Coleridge. Another view at Hampstead shows the block of wooden cottages which stand near to Wildwoods, by the "Bull and Bush." The scene, "In Regent's Park," requires amendment; the hirers of boats are excluded from the narrow waters there, and are not allowed to land and lie about on the banks. The picture of Greenwich Park presents the Hospital and the Royal Naval School, the latter occupying what used to be the Palace of Delight, built by two queens,—Anne of Denmark and Henrietta Maria,—of which there is a scarce plate, dated 1637. A succeeding generation may turn to this book if desirous to learn what was the aspect of the suburbs at this day.

THE Census Report published on July 10 last gives the London population as 4,211,056, compared with 3,815,544 in 1881. Four little maps published by the *Lancet* a fortnight since demonstrate in a striking shape how an increase of almost a million in the past twenty years is distributed. The diagrams show an increase at Battersea, and at Fulham, of nearly twice the former population; whilst the populations are more than doubled at Hampstead, Wandsworth, and Camberwell. The change of footpaths and walks into roads, the covering of gardens with houses, go on apace: they who, taking thought, look around and forward, discern the necessity for open spaces here and there to break the continuity of London's monstrous growth. In one of her powerful, yet temperate, appeals, printed in the *Times* some months ago, Miss Octavia Hill pleaded that surely the landless should be enabled to derive some enjoyment from the land.

WE have no wish to say hard things of railway officials who make a blunder after perhaps long years of good service, but we certainly think the signalman who was unquestionably responsible for the accident at Bishopsgate has been remarkably fortunate in finding a jury to return a verdict of accidental death under the circumstances. The accident was confessedly the direct result of the omission of the signalman in the north box to signal a train, and the line being left consequently unblocked. This is one of the curious eccentricities of juries in such cases. There may have been plenty of extenuating circumstances to urge in palliation of the signalman's neglect, but it was a clear and admitted case of neglect of duty, and a verdict of manslaughter has not unfrequently been returned on less decisive evidence than this. In sympathy for the signalman, the jury seem rather to have forgotten sympathy with the victims, and care for the safety of the public.

THE question of providing some means for the safety of persons falling into the water near the Thames Embankment, by providing something along the face of the Embankment which they can catch hold of, has been again before the County Council. The Engineer had suggested life buoys with ropes attached, placed on the Embankment; but unless these were fixed so that there was considerable difficulty in getting them loose, they would quickly be stolen, and if they were not easily got at they would be useless in an emergency, so the suggestion does not seem a very practical one. The Committee have ordered that lines of steel wire with wooden floats should be placed in three bays of the Embankment, and "if found useful for the purpose of saving life" the method should be extended to the whole Embankment; but it is not very apparent how this is to be tested. Is an *employé* of the Council to be thrown into the Thames to ascertain if he can save himself by the wire? Or does any member of the Council intend to make the experiment in the public interest? It is time that something were settled and carried out about this matter, for the long bare wall is a hopeless barrier to any one who falls into the river, and is not a good enough swimmer to reach one of the steps; and the matter has been talked of for years and nothing done.

ABOUT ten years ago, a movement was set on foot for the purpose of erecting a monument in Edinburgh to John Knox. The model of a proposed statue was prepared by Mr. D. W. Stevenson, R.S.A., which was afterwards exhibited in the Glasgow Exhibition, but sufficient funds were not subscribed to enable the project to be carried out. After paying expenses, including the cost of the model, a sum of about 90*l*. remains, and it is now proposed that this amount should be augmented to 200*l*. wherewith to provide a statue of the Scottish Reformer to be placed in one of the niches of the National Portrait Gallery. A Committee has been formed for furthering the project.

THE weekly journal called *Invention* is a very interesting miscellany of news, but we must protest against the rather free use which it makes of matter taken from our columns, without a word of acknowledgment. On two recent occasions it has appropriated matter from our pages, not very great in amount, it is true, but if the matter was worth taking its source should have been acknowledged.

THE annual exhibition of the Home Arts and Industries Association, which has been open from the 16th to the 20th of this month, at the Royal Albert Hall, is more interesting as an exposition of the excellent work which this society is doing than as a show of art workmanship. To those who are not well acquainted with the Association and its work, we may say that it endeavours to nourish home arts and industries as a source of recreation and pleasure by encouraging the work of the many handicraft classes which are springing up all over the country, chiefly with the object of employing to advantage the leisure time of the youth of town and country. By means of grants of money, as funds allow, and by furnishing good designs for execution, this work is carried out, and it certainly deserves the success which seems to attend it. The exhibition does not, and can hardly be expected to, contain many exhibits of real excellence. The objects seem to show that efforts have been made to copy, sometimes slavishly, good designs, and the workmanship is apt to be cramped and devoid of that simplicity, freedom, and vigour which should be a characteristic of art-workmanship. We are probably right in thinking that the work having been done to good designs is due to the Society's care. Amongst the many schools, representing all parts of the United Kingdom, may be mentioned the Ruskin Linen Industry, the Balmoral School, the Alexandra Technical School at Sandringham (in which the Princess of Wales is so keenly interested), and Mrs. Alfred Waterhouse's brass school at Yattendon. The Langdale Linen Industry has an interesting exhibit of their material, embroidered with good conventional designs and capital workmanship in coloured wools, whilst Bangor was represented by slate plaques and other useful articles. We noticed a carved hard-wood panel by J. Phillips, of Altrincham, which for execution and design was much above the average in quality; it was exhibited in connexion with the Sandbach School. The list of schools exhibiting is a long one, but the exhibition is extensive in its range, and includes articles of carved wood, leather work, *repoussé* and hammered metal work, wrought-iron baskets, pottery, and furniture, all of which testify to the excellent work the Association is doing, in which we wish it all success.

THE IMPERIAL INSTITUTE.

ON Saturday, the 18th inst., what may be called a "Press view" of the buildings of the Imperial Institute, as far as they are at present completed, took place. Although we have from time to time during the last five years described the progress of the building,* the following particulars may here be placed on record.

The building has a frontage of about 750 ft. towards Imperial Institute-road, one of the new roadways which have been cut from east to west across what were the Royal Horticultural-gardens,—of late years the scene of the very popular and useful exhibitions known briefly as "The Fisheries," "The Healtheries," and "The Colonies," or Indian and Colonial Exhibition. It was indeed, we are told, in consequence of the great interest excited throughout the British empire by the display at the Colonial and Indian Exhibition of 1886, which illustrated the vast wealth in natural products and the commercial and industrial resources of our various colonies and of India, that the idea was conceived of a permanent institution, designed firstly to afford a thorough and living representation of the progress made in the development of those resources, and, secondly, to serve as a national memorial commemorative of the fiftieth year of the reign of her Majesty. With that end in view, the buildings include, or will include, conference-rooms, reference libraries, exhibition galleries, and a large central hall. These features of the Institute will be supplemented by reading, writing, smoking, and refreshment-rooms for Fellows, who will practically have a club-house for their convenience.

The principal entrance is in the centre of the *façade*, and the portal is 17 ft. wide by 23 ft. 6 in. high. Above it, and for some distance each side of it, will stretch a frieze sculptured by Mr. Pegram in low relief consisting of emblematical figures, with the Queen in the centre. Entering this portal, the visitors were received by Sir Frederick A. Abel, the Secretary to the Institute, and by Sir Somers Vine, the Assistant Secretary, and by them were conducted over the building. The apartment seen through the stone casements on the right as one enters is a general waiting-room for the lifts, cloak-room, &c.; that on the left is the post-office, telegraph, telephone, and inquiry office. The shaft for carrying on the building operations of the central tower at present intersects the main structure. The large unfurnished room at the back is the shell of the vestibule to the proposed great hall. The vestibule will be temporarily used as a general conference hall, and was used on Saturday last as a luncheon-room.

The principal floor is that first reached from the entrance. In the west corridor are the British-American and British-Australasian Conference Rooms (these Rooms are nearly finished), the Council Chamber, and the Secretarial and clerical offices. In the east corridor are the British-Indian and British-African Conference Rooms, the writing, reading, and news rooms, and the temporary library. The windows at the end of each corridor respectively indicate the interior approaches to the contemplated Conference Hall and Library.

The east stairway, by which access is gained to the upper floors, is nearly completed. The walls are lined with Hopton Wood stone, polished (the largest use yet made of this stone in one building, probably), the balustrade and rail being of polished Belgian marble. This stairway gives a very good idea of what the grand stairway on the west side of the vestibule will be like; the latter is intended to be more richly ornamented. The arms of various colonies, and a record of the objects and date of founding of the Institute, are introduced into the coloured glass of the windows.

The first floor has the Fellows' Dining Room as the first apartment to attract notice. The rooms in the east corridor are for the present assigned to the Exhibition of Indian Art Metal Work; they will eventually be used for the Commercial Intelligence Department and commercial conferences. The rooms of the west corridor will be adapted for use by various societies whose objects are kindred to those of the Imperial Institute. Here also will be the conference rooms of the groups of Crown Colonies. The Fellows' Dining Room is panelled in English oak which was carved and worked at Dunmow, in Essex, and is pointed to as a practical illustration of the feasibility and advantages of village industry; the artizans engaged upon it share the profits. Above this room on the second floor is the Public Dining Room and Restaurant (this room will eventually be decorated in a similar manner to the Fellows' Dining Room); and above that again are the kitchens and serving rooms.

On the second floor, the rooms in the east corridor will probably be occupied for some time by certain societies who are seeking the accommodation which the Institute affords for carrying on their work. The rooms in the west corridor and on the south side will be mainly used as sample examination rooms. The two large rooms at the south-west corner will be a map-room and the Fellows' smoking-room. The balcony which leads to the west tower will also be a pleasant smoking lounge in fine weather.

The ground floor will be principally devoted to the stowage of samples in bulk, the portions underneath the main entrance being arranged for certain offices, &c. The two colonnades which are eventually to connect the main building with the side galleries (the old arcades which flanked the Horticultural Gardens) will bring this floor, the arcades, and the lower floors of the central and north galleries to a uniform level. The stores in bulk on the ground floor of the main building will be arranged to be as near as possible to the location of the Index Collections in the galleries.

The engine-room, boiler-house, and dynamo-chambers for providing the heating and lighting of the buildings are at the rear of the central gallery, and immediately underneath what will be the floor of the Great Hall. The steel boilers are Galloway's make, and the whole of the electric-light machinery and fittings are the work of Messrs. Allpress & Belshaw. When fully developed the Institute will be in a position not only to supply motive and dynamo-power for its own wants, but also those of the surrounding institutions. All the gas, water, and sanitary main-pipes are carried along a walking subway in the basement. There are over fifty hydrants throughout the building, and there will always be ready a large supply of water from the tanks in the towers, exclusive of that obtained from the water company.

The Central Tower is now approaching the stage when it will present an effective appearance (see illustration in last week's *Builder*). It has been built without the aid of any exterior scaffolding whatsoever. The plain shaft-like portion indicates the position of the water-tanks. The lantern-chamber now rising above the first balcony (about 200 ft. from the ground) is that where the suggested peal of bells would be accommodated. The Prince of Wales has accepted the offer of an aged Australian lady to provide and completely equip a perfect peal, which is to be rung on the Queen's Birthday and Accession-day, and on the birthdays of the immediate members of her Majesty's family. The alarming statements lately current to the effect that a subsidence of this tower had taken place were grossly exaggerated; the fact is that the compression on the clay bed of this vast weight,—now over 5,000 tons,—is only half an inch, and less than what had been naturally expected.

The Lower Floor Intermediate Gallery has been allotted to the Australian and African and other Colonies. Several of the Colonial Governments are only waiting for the clearance of this gallery by the builders, to commence the work of fitting the cases and installing the collection.

The installation of the British Indian Court,—including Ceylon,—(formerly known as the East Arcade) is sufficiently advanced to afford an appreciable notion of the manner in which this important branch of the Institute's work will be carried on. In accordance with the views which have from time to time been indicated, it has been decided that the scheme to be adopted in the arrangement of the

* The following Illustrations of the building have appeared in this journal, viz., Mr. Collcutt's design as submitted in competition, *Builder*, July 2, 1887; plans and detail of *façade*, July 9, 1887; large perspective view, January 5, 1889; and view of central tower, last week, June 18.

collections representing the economic products of India and the Colonies should have a commercial and industrial, rather than a scientific, bearing. It has consequently been arranged to adopt, in the arrangement of the Collections, the system of grouping economic products which has already been pursued in the preparation of similar collections for exhibition in the Indian Section of the Institute, under the auspices of the Department of Revenue and Agriculture of the Government of India; the following being the general headings of the groups:—1. Foods and Food-Stuffs; 2. Stimulants, Beverages, and Narcotics; 3. Oil Seeds, Oils, Soap, and Perfumery; 4. Drugs, Medicines, and Chemicals; 5. Gums and Resins; 6. Dyes, Tans, Mordants, Pigments, and Paints; 7. Fibres and Fibrous Plants; 8. Hides, Leather, and Horns; 9. Canes, Bamboos, and Grasses; 10. Timbers; 11. Minerals; 12. Domestic Products. Each of these groups is, naturally, subject to subdivision into sections, according to the system which was pursued in the Economic Courts of the Colonial and Indian Exhibition of 1886. This system of grouping renders it, of course, unavoidable that certain products which are applied to more than one use should appear more than once in the collection; thus turmeric receives application as a condiment, as a dye, and as a medicine; hence, specimens of turmeric have to be included in three different groups. Following this system, the form of the collection will be two-fold, *i.e.*, there will be the "Index Collection" (as seen in the court and galleries) on the one hand, which will be illustrative of, and correspond to, a complete Catalogue or Dictionary of Economic Products, and the "Commercial Collection" (stored on the ground-floor of the main building), on the other hand, which will consist, in part, of samples in bulk—corresponding to the specimens included in the Index Collection, and, in part, of products of known or anticipated commercial utility in all stages of preparation and manufacture.

The general method in which the Index Collections are to be arranged is as follows:—(*a*) In air-tight receptacles with glass fronts, and also vessels entirely of glass, in which the samples will be well displayed, and the form of which admits of their compact arrangement and exhibition. The receptacles will bear sufficiently descriptive labels, with reference numbers to the "Dictionary" and to the "Commercial Collection;" (*b*) Cases in which these specimens will be conveniently exhibited, and which are so arranged that any one of the receptacles may readily be abstracted for closer inspection. These cases are so constructed as also to afford accommodation for larger samples, or for small models, and to admit of the display, in connexion with the specimens, of diagrams, maps, or other auxiliary means of illustration and explanation.

The space available in the Institute renders it out of the question that many of the samples in bulk (forming the Commercial Collection), should be openly exhibited, or that they should even be stored in packages in the same locality where the Index Collection is situated; they are therefore to be stored in the commodious rooms on the ground-floor of the main building, close to the galleries containing the Index Collections, and communicating by means of a lift to the second floor of the Institute, where the "Sample Examination Rooms" are situated. The samples are to be stored in air-tight canisters of sheet tin, each tin being marked with the scientific name and Dictionary Number of the sample it contains; in addition a supplementary "Store Number" will be instituted, that number being repeated on the labels of the samples in the other division of the collection, so that any person desiring to closely inspect and to handle a particular sample in bulk would only have to take note of its "Store Number" in the exhibited collections.

In order to render the establishment of this representation of products of continuous service to India and the Colonies, and to those engaged in commerce with them, or practically interested in the application of such products to industrial purposes, every facility will be given to merchants, manufacturers, and scientific workers, to examine samples and to be supplied with specimens of those which interest them, and with all available information concerning them.

It is stated that the authorities of the Imperial Institute are fully alive to the importance of combining, with a comprehensive and progressive representation of the economic resources of India and the Colonies, systematic arrangements for the submission of samples to valuation, and for the analytical and other chemical or physical examination of products which are either new or else but imperfectly known, and also of making arrangements, from time to time, for practical experiments with a view to ascertain the adaptability of new products to practical purposes. When the operations of the Institute are sufficiently advanced, its regular income adequately increased, and its equipment fairly developed, it is intended that the latter should include an experimental department, where commercial valuations and scientific investigations connected with products displayed in the collections can be efficiently carried out.

Another very important branch of the operations necessary for a thorough utilisation of the collections of natural products, which will be taken in hand as soon as the supply and arrangement of these are sufficiently far advanced, is the holding of conferences in connexion with particular groups of products, with a view of considering existing commercial, scientific, and technical knowledge relating to them; the directions in which it needs development; the results of scientific or technical experiments which are new or little known, and other subjects of commercial and industrial importance connected with the development and utilisation of the natural resources of the Colonies and India.

The large quadrangles will lend themselves to a variety of useful purposes. Musical afternoons and evenings will probably be arranged. In the east quadrangle, and adjoining the Indian Court, will be erected the Indian Pavilion (the gift of one of the Indian Princes), in which tea, coffee, and other light refreshments will be served.

As our readers know, the general contractors for the building are Messrs. John Mowlem & Co., of Grosvenor Wharf, Grosvenor-road. The marble mosaic pavement of the principal floor was laid down by Messrs. Burke & Co., of Newman-street, who also executed the marble work of the staircase and the marble chimney-pieces in Rooms 18 and 19. Other mosaic work was executed by Messrs. De Grelle, Houdret, & Co., and by Messrs. Rust & Co., Ltd. The lifting machinery, designed and erected by Messrs. Archibald Smith & Stevens, consists of eleven hydraulic lifts with pumping-engines and power storage plant. There are two passenger lifts running from the ground to second floors, three lifts for reception and distribution of coals and general stores, three appropriated to the kitchen department, one for delivery of refuse from the engine and boiler house, one heavy machine capable of raising a ton up the central shaft of the east tower, and designed for dealing with stores and large objects for the museum, and, finally, a three-ton lift for raising extra large exhibits to the upper floor of the great gallery running east and west. All these are supplied by water at 700 lbs. pressure per square inch. This water is pumped by an engine into a weighted receiver or accumulator, wherein it is stored at the required pressure, and drawn off as required by any of the lifts. Immediately this occurs the accumulator by automatic mechanism starts the pumps, which run till the accumulator is again full, when it automatically stops them till more water is required. All the water employed is returned by the lifts to the pumping machinery for re-use, and is therefore not wasted, but kept constantly circulating. The cost of working the system is consequently only that of the coal burnt, and the labour of stoking, no other attendance being required. In its outlines the system is similar to that adopted by the London and other hydraulic power supply companies, and to that on which the lifts for the Electric Railway are worked. The fire-protection of the buildings has been provided for by the installation of a powerful stationary steam fire-engine with quick-steaming boiler, which will be used in conjunction with a tank in one of the towers, to supply the large number of hydrants fixed throughout the buildings. A new and improved method of running out the fire-hose has also been adopted. The whole of the fire arrangements are being carried out by Messrs. Shand, Mason, & Co., of Upper Ground-street, Blackfriars. The stained glass has been executed by Messrs. Clement Heaton & Co. The casements and stoves were supplied by Mr. Thomas Elsley, and the grilles and ornamental ironwork by Messrs. Potter & Sons. Mr. C. F. Murray painted the panels of the staircase ceiling, and Mr. Julius Sax has provided the electric bells and speaking-tubes.

The architect of the buildings is Mr. T. E. Collcutt, F.R.I.B.A.

ARCHITECTURAL SOCIETIES.

LIVERPOOL ARCHITECTURAL SOCIETY.—Classes have been held during the session which has just concluded, for the benefit of the student members, the subjects bearing directly on the Institute examinations. The classes were well attended, and the students have by their interest shown that the Committee's efforts have been appreciated. The following are the subjects, with the lecturers:—Sanitation, Dr. D. Harrisson and Mr. T. Harnett Harrisson, F.R.I.B.A. (President). Mouldings, Features, and Ornament, Mr. C. E. Deacon, F.R.I.B.A. History of Architecture, Mr. H. W. Keef. Building Construction, Mr. G. Ware. Specifications and Quantities, Mr. H. L. Beckwith, F.S.I. By-laws and Public Health Act, Mr. J. Dod. An examination was held at the close of the session, in which Mr. Lawrence Hobson, to whom the Council will award the prize, distinguished himself most highly. Meetings have been started, and will be continued every week during the summer months, conducted by Mr. C. E. Deacon, at Bebington, for the purpose of preparing measured drawings of the old church.

MANCHESTER SOCIETY OF ARCHITECTS.—The second of the summer series of sketching visits was paid on Saturday, the 18th inst., to Prestbury, under the leadership of Mr. H. E. Stelfox, A.R.I.B.A.

GLASGOW ARCHITECTURAL ASSOCIATION.—A party of about twenty-two members of this Association visited Largs on the 18th inst. On arriving, the party was met by Mr. T. G. Abercrombie, architect of the new U.P. church now being erected by Mr. John Clark, of Curling Hall. Mr. Abercrombie conducted the party over the church, which is still unfinished. Thereafter he kindly showed the members through Curling Hall, to which he lately made a large addition. The company then proceeded to the half timber lodge and gardener's house, recently erected for Mr. E. Philippi, from designs by Mr. A. J. Fryers, architect, Paisley. The new parish church was next visited. Mr. Balfour, of Messrs. Steel & Balfour, the architects, kindly went over the building with the party. After tea, some sixteen of the party visited the Montgomery monument in the Skelmorlie aisle, situated in the old churchyard. This concluded the excursion, and the party returned to town, having spent a very enjoyable day, despite the unfavourableness of the weather.

COMPETITIONS.

NEW BUILDINGS FOR THE STAFFORDSHIRE COUNTY COUNCIL.—In this competition, in which Mr. J. Macvicar Anderson, President R.I.B.A., was the assessor, 63 sets of plans were submitted. The premiums were awarded by the assessor as follow:—First, "M.," 150*l.*, Mr. Henry T. Hare, A.R.I.B.A., London. Second, "Expert," 100*l.*, Messrs. Treadwell & Martin, London. Third, "Acoustics," 50*l.*, Messrs. Cooksey & Cox, London. The architect has yet to be appointed by Council. All plans are retained at present, as under the conditions, the Council have power to exhibit the same. Meantime the names of all the competitors, except the three whose designs have been selected for the premiums, remain unknown.

WESLEYAN CHAPEL, BARNARD CASTLE.—In the competition for this chapel, the design by Messrs. Morley & Woodhouse, architects, Bradford, has been selected. The chapel will cost about 3,500*l.*

WALSALL PUBLIC BATHS.—By a printers' error in an advertisement which appeared in the last two issues of the *Builder*, the date for sending in designs in this competition was given as July 10 instead of Saturday, July 16.

FREE LIBRARY, BIRMINGHAM.—On the 5th inst., the Mayor of Birmingham opened the new Branch Free Library at Bloomsbury, Birmingham. The building has been erected at a cost of 3,700*l.*, from designs by Messrs. Cossins & Peacock, on a triangular piece of land abutting on the Saltley-road. It has a terra-cotta front, and, in addition to the news-room and lending library, a reference library on a small scale has been provided.

North Transept, Christchurch Priory, Hants.—From a Drawing by Mr. J. A. Pywell.

CHRISTCHURCH PRIORY, HANTS.

THE north transept of Christchurch Priory is a curious and in the highest degree interesting example of Norman decoration. On the north-east angle is the Norman turret, the whole surface of which is occupied with arcading interlacing, and other methods of decoration.

The lower story is occupied by the wall-arcading, which also runs round the transept, the spandrels over the arches being filled with fish-scale ornament. Above the string-course is a second arcade, the stone of which is much decayed. The arches of both arcades are moulded, and the lower ones contain a herring-bone ornament between the mouldings on the front face, and traces are also to be seen of it in the upper arches.

Springing from these is a lattice ornamentation which forms a net of large rope-like bands girting the masonry and seemingly holding it together, though in reality carved from it. A third arcade runs round the top story, above which is a dog-tooth string moulding.

The drawings of capitals (see next page) show those to the lower arcade. The shafts are also ornamented, two of them by interlacing, the rest being fluted. The flutings are of four different kinds, which are again varied by being continued spirally round the shafts or by being mitred in front or on angle. Portions of the lower arcade have been carefully restored; the upper portions are 800 years old, J. A. P.

THE INCORPORATED ASSOCIATION OF MUNICIPAL AND COUNTY ENGINEERS.

IN the course of the discussion which followed the reading of the papers read at the Peterborough meeting of this Association,*

Mr. Buckham asked whether the manholes in Peterborough were constructed so as to be made use of as flushing-chambers? In his own district he had found that a very convenient

* See page 482, *ante*, for two of them, viz., "Municipal work in Peterborough," by Mr. Walshaw, the Borough Surveyor, and "The Water Supply of Peterborough," by Mr. J. C. Gill, Waterworks Engineer to the Corporation. For the substance of the third paper, by Mr. Isaac Shone, on "The Shone System of Town Drainage," see succeeding columns of this Issue of the *Builder*.

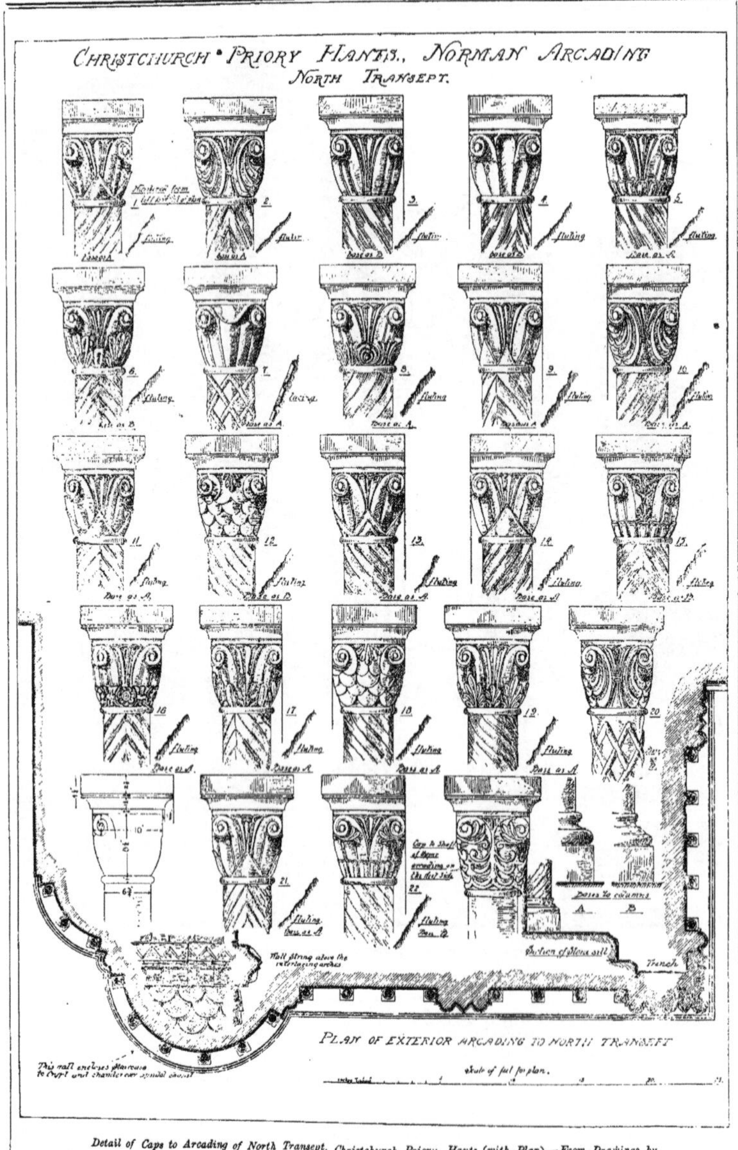

Detail of Caps to Arcading of North Transept, Christchurch Priory, Hants (with Plan).—From Drawings by Mr. J. A. Pywell. (See page 499.)

and economical course. He should also like to ask Mr. Gill whether, in laying his pipes for the water supply, he had tried any other methods of jointing besides those mentioned in his paper? As to Mr. Shone's paper, he begged to express his thanks to that gentleman for so kindly acceding to his request to read a paper on his system of drainage, which he (Mr. Buckham) was prepared to say, from his experience of it at Ipswich, was particularly applicable to the drainage of towns in the Eastern counties, because it was peculiarly fitted to cope with the low levels and flat districts which there abounded, and could be applied to the lifting of sewage in certain situations with more satisfactory results than any other system with which he was acquainted. Moreover, with its aid, the engineer would be able to provide his sewers with adequate and necessary gradients, and could get his sewage lifted without having to buy land for pumping-stations. It had been said by many people that Shone's ejectors were, after all, nothing more than pumps. True, but they were pumps which would do what no other pumps could do, and they were perfectly automatic in action, and the cost of their maintenance was very little.

Mr. C. F. Gower, M.Inst.C.E., Ipswich, said that as a visitor, not being a member of the Association, he should like to bear his testimony to the success of the Shone system as applied at Ipswich. Mr. Shone, in his paper, had referred to the "separate" system. In theory he (the speaker) greatly approved of the "separate" system, and had carried it out in practice, but he found that it entailed a great deal of trouble and difficulty in actual working, and as far as his experience went he could only advise engineers to stick to one system of sewers.

Mr. R. A. MacBrair (Lincoln), referring to footways, said that Mr. Walshaw had referred to slag concrete as being the most durable, but as being objectionable from its slipperiness. His (the speaker's) experience was that the paving slabs made with slag were the least slippery of any. It struck him that the price named by Mr. Walshaw for horse, cart, and man (viz., 6s. 6d. a day) was very low.

Mr. E. J. Silcock (King's Lynn), in moving a vote of thanks to the readers of the papers, said that the best testimony to the efficiency of the works which had been carried out in Peterborough was the striking diminution in the death-rate from 20·7 to 14·7.

Mr. Robert Godfrey (King's Norton), in seconding the motion, referred to the vexed question of sewer ventilation, and the best method of effecting it. He strongly urged that the only real solution of the question would be found in an alteration of the law so as to compel every house or other building which used a sewer to contribute to the ventilation of that sewer by a ventilating-pipe or shaft. Let all the houses by all means be safeguarded against the admission of sewer-air, but do not let them escape their share towards ensuring that the sewer shall contain no foul air. The system of relying only upon ventilating grids in the surface of the roadway had been tried and found wanting. Such grids were, and must necessarily be, comparatively few and far between, and in undulating towns, those at the low level would become inlets, and those at high level outlets. Even when there was no nuisance from these grids, people whose houses were near them were always nervously apprehensive of harm, and fancied it existed when perhaps it did not. No man liked to have a sewer ventilating grid directly opposite to his door, and the only real solution of the difficulty would be found in a law compelling every house to do its part towards the ventilation of the sewers.

Mr. Barber having read a few words in support of the motion,

Col. Jones, V.C., referred to the sewage system of Berlin, in which, he said, a great deal of difficulty had been overcome by the adoption of the radial system, whereby the sewage was taken out into different districts. It seemed to him that the Shone system was particularly applicable to a radial disposition of the main outfall sewers.

Mr. O. Deacon Clarke, late Municipal Engineer at Rangoon, testified to the success of the Shone system in that town. When the works were designed they had a population of 150,000, which had since increased to 180,000, and it had been found quite easy to provide for the increased population much more economically than would have been possible on any other system.

The vote of thanks to the readers of the papers having been carried,

Mr. Walshaw briefly replied to some of the questions raised during the discussion. He said that the manholes were not constructed so as to be used as flushing-chambers. The daily flow of sewage was about 750,000 gallons. As to the cost of carting, 6s. 6d. a day was a low figure, and it was due to the fact that Peterborough is in an agricultural district. The reduction of the death-rate which had been alluded to was undoubtedly entirely due to the sanitary works which had been carried out. Before those works were executed, there used to be 600 cases of typhoid fever treated in the infirmary alone every year.

Mr. Gill, in replying, said that no other joints for pipes had been tried. Bored and turned joints were often regarded as very good in theory, but not in practice: here was a case in which their success in practice was unqualified.

Mr. Shone also replied, and the meeting terminated.

After luncheon, some of the members visited the sewage farm, as mentioned by us last week.

A very successful meeting of the Northern Counties and Yorkshire District of the Association was held at Scarborough on Saturday last, when the members were received by the Mayor. Papers were read (1) by Mr. Joseph Petch, the Borough Surveyor, on "Scarborough, its Progress and its Public Works in Recent Years," and (2) by Mr. William Millhouse, Water Engineer, on "Scarborough Waterworks." Subsequently the members visited some of the public works of the town. We are obliged for want of space to defer a report of the proceedings until next week.

THE SHONE SYSTEM OF TOWN DRAINAGE.*

ALTHOUGH much has been written, printed, and spoken about this system, yet it is feared that there are still to be found municipal engineers, surveyors, architects, Medical Officers of Health, and others interested in sanitary engineering works, who are more or less imperfectly acquainted with its principles and *modus operandi*. The inventor of the system is, therefore, much obliged to your Honorary Secretary for the Eastern Counties, Mr. E. Buckham, M.Inst.C.E., for inviting him to read a paper on it at this meeting. The author assented all the more readily to prepare this paper because he is satisfied that Mr. Buckham (having investigated the system for himself, and having, as the result of that investigation, recommended the Corporation of Ipswich to adopt it, in connexion with the drainage of Stoke, which is a part of Ipswich, and for which it was deemed by him to be specially suitable), as an honest conscientious engineer, became anxious that the merits of the system should be communicated, if possible, to his co-workers in this Association through the medium of a short paper upon it.

The author contends that by the aid of this system, house-drains and sewers can be laid in low-lying, flat, and tide-locked habitable areas, on the most perfect hygienic principle which it is possible or necessary for the practical sanitary engineer to carry out. Not only can drains and sewers be laid down by hydraulic and sanitary rules in low-lying, flat town areas, but they can also be so laid, by the aid of this system, in undulating town areas, in an endless variety of ways.

A few engineers in the past, strange to say, treated the Shone system as if its object was simply to lift sewage in opposition to the most economical pumps extant; and, accordingly, these gentlemen entered into elaborate calculations to try to prove, to their own satisfaction at least, that lifting sewage by compressed air was less efficient than lifting it by steam power direct in the ordinary way. The inventor remonstrated, too often in vain, with these engineers who elected thus to regard the system. But, happily, the discussions which have arisen from time to time between its advocates and opponents have greatly helped to elucidate the intrinsic merits of the system. The process, however, of silencing prejudiced and incompetent critics, and converting opponents into supporters, has been as long as it has been painful and laborious. But the author is now thankful to say that at last he is no longer under the necessity of defending the system against the attacks of opponents. The fact is, they have all caved in and disappeared before the indisputable evidences which have been afforded from time to time by the numerous and various works carried out on the system, in support of the claims originally set forth, in its favour.

The primary object aimed at with the Shone system, is to get as high a degree of sanitary efficiency in connexion with the every-day working of house-drains and sewers as it is possible. The question which relates to the difference between the cost of lifting water by steam pumps, and ejectors worked by compressed air, is one of secondary importance. The ejector system may in certain cases involve you in the purchase of a little more fuel per annum than a steam pump, but, on the other hand, comparatively large and deeply-laid sewers, discharging into one steam pumping station, would be more costly initially and annually, and they would involve you in a larger number of sewage-gas nuisances, and withal a larger number of preventible deaths, than would obtain by dividing a town or district into a number of separate automatic drainage districts on the Shone system. The author regards his ejectors more in the light of life-saving apparatus than as economical sewage lifters; because we are told by the highest medical authorities, that decomposed putrid sewage, whether it be in vertical or horizontal cesspools, gives off gas which is prejudicial to public health; that foul drains, sewers, and cesspools cause an incalculable number of preventible deaths and cases of sickness. No sanitarian will attempt to contradict this statement in these days; and yet it is surprising to observe with what comparative indifference even professional sanitary engineers occasionally treat those who venture to propound simple, scientific, and practical remedies for the prevention of unsanitary drainage and sewerage works. You all know that the only effectual way to place house-drains and sewers in a satisfactory sanitary condition, is to cause them to be self-cleansing and to be properly ventilated. You also know that, in order to render drains and sewers carrying sewage self-cleansing, they ought to be adjusted in size and inclination to suit the volume of sewage which they are intended to carry, so that the velocity of the sewage when the period of maximum flow obtains shall be, if possible, 2·5 ft., but never less than 2 ft. per second. If we call the 2·5 ft. 100 per cent., then it is evident that 2 ft. would only be $\left(\frac{2 \cdot 0 \times 100}{2 \cdot 5} = \right)$ 80 per cent. In other words, no drains or sewers should be designed or carried out which would permit of the velocity efficiency being less than 80 per cent. of the 2·5 ft. per second—the velocity now universally considered to be necessary to render drains and sewers self-cleansing. Drains and sewers thus designed, if they are also efficiently flushed and ventilated, will be as reasonably perfect, from a sanitary point of view, as it is possible and necessary for the practical municipal engineer and surveyor to make them. If drains and sewers are not thus designed, they will become drains and sewers of deposit, and consequently unsanitary.

The velocity of 2·5 ft. per second, however, applies only when drains and sewers are used for the carrying of sewage proper, on what is called the "separate system." When drains and sewers are used as the carriers of sewage and rainfall, on what is called the "combined system," a greater velocity than 2 ft. 6 in. per second must be insured, to preserve them in a self-cleansing condition; because the rainfall carries with it road *detritus*, and this adheres more or less tenaciously to the drains and sewers, and, by degrees, consolidates on their inverts, rendering the process of self-cleansing impossible, even by the most systematic and liberal use of flushing water.

Mr. Julius Adams, C.E., Chief Engineer to the Board of City Works, and Consulting Engineer to the Board of Health, Brooklyn, U.S.A., states in his book on "Sewers and Drains of Populous Districts" (after acquiring considerable experience of town drainage on the combined system):—"As easily carried in memory,

---

* From a paper by Mr. Isaac Shone, read at the Eastern Counties' District Meeting of the Incorporated Association of Municipal and County Engineers at Peterborough, on the 11th inst., as elsewhere mentioned.

the following will represent about the falls which will preserve circular sewers free from deposit, provided they run half full":—

For	6-inch	diameter	a grade of	1 in 60
"	9	"	"	1 in 90
"	12	"	"	1 in 200
"	15	"	"	1 in 250
"	18	"	"	1 in 300
"	24	"	"	1 in 400
"	36	"	"	1 in 600
"	42	"	"	1 in 700
"	48	"	"	1 in 800

Here we see Mr. Adams's practical experience tells him that a sewer which is used for both sewage and rainfall, even in comparatively well scavenged towns, must have a grade which shall be sufficient to give a velocity, when the sewer is half full, equal to about 3·75 ft. per second, which is 50 per cent. *more* than we consider necessary to render *sewage sewers* self-cleansing.

It will be interesting, not to say instructive, to compare the gradients at which Mr. Julius Adams considers the following sized sewers should be laid, on the combined system, with the gradients at which they might be laid, to insure a velocity of 2·5 ft. per second, on the separate system, *i.e.*, according to the author's improved Hydraulic Sewerage Tables, which are now in the press, and which will shortly be issued to the public.

	Combined System.	Separate System.
	1 in.	1 in.
6-inch sewer	60	150
9 " "	90	248
12 " "	200	350
15 " "	250	458
18 " "	300	570
24 " "	400	805
36 " "	600	1309
42 " "	700	1575
48 " "	800	1849

The foregoing comparison shows that the difficulties in the way of an engineer draining a low-lying, flat town of any extent, of its sewage and rainfall discharges combined, in one set of drains and sewers, to one outfall or pumping-station, so that the drains and sewers may be maintained in a self-cleansing, and consequently sanitary condition, are physically insuperable,—*i.e.*, at a reasonably permissible cost. Equally insuperable would be the difficulties, if he had to drain such a town on the separate system, were the whole of the sewage conducted to one outfall or pumping-station.

For scientific, sanitary, and economic reasons the author has long advocated the adoption of the separate system, in preference to the combined system, in all new drainage projects, providing, of course, that the works are carried out throughout on sound sanitary principles, and providing the drainage of the sewage proper cannot be conducted, say, to a sea outfall, through drains and sewers which will carry the sewage separately, or in combination with the rainfall, at a perfectly satisfactory self-cleansing velocity. But some of you may be disposed to say what other engineers have said in effect before,—viz., that all sanitary engineers nowadays lay down sewers at gradients which will secure "self-cleansing" velocities. This we know they do to the best of their abilities; but we also know that many engineers call sewers designed by them self-cleansing sewers if they are laid at gradients suitable to their size, regardless of the volume of sewage available to them. We have known engineers, for example, advise sanitary authorities to the effect that a 24-in. sewer laid at a gradient of 1 in 805 was laid at a self-cleansing gradient, which was literally true, if only the volume of sewage estimated to be available to the sewer had been sufficient to half-fill it; but, inasmuch as the sewage available was barely sufficient to half-fill a 6-in. pipe laid at a gradient of 1 in 150, the velocity of that volume of sewage flowing on the invert of the 24-in. sewer would not exceed 1·16 ft. per second, giving only 46 per cent. efficiency, instead of 100 per cent.! In this case, as in many others, the engineer laid the sewer at the best inclination at which he was able to lay it owing to the natural configuration of the ground! It is in this way that the so-called English water-carriage system of sewage removal from houses and towns has wrought so much unsanitary mischief all the world over.

A 24-in. sewer is $\left(\frac{24^2}{6^2}=\right)$ 16 times more capacious than a 6-in. pipe, and consequently, all things being equal, it will hold sixteen times more foul air, and it will require sixteen times more water to flush it, than would be required to flush the 6-in. sewer. Moreover, the 24-in. sewer would cost roughly five times more than the 6-in sewer! These statements tend to show that we ought in all cases reasonably possible, to recommend the adoption of the separate system of town drainage. Again, the cost of treating sewage conducted to the outfall on the separate system is reduced to a minimum. The value of sewage discharged on the Shone system,—where the separate system of drainage is adopted in connexion with it,—if it is utilised as liquid manure upon land suitable for irrigation purposes, must necessarily be much greater that it can be when it is discharged into drains and sewers on the combined system.

But it would be impossible for the author to explain his views fully on these matters, in the compass of a paper like this, without taking up much more of your time than he is entitled to do. He will, therefore, content himself by saying that the most important part of the work of a sanitary engineer is to drain houses of their sewage discharges in such a way as to cause the minimum unsanitary nuisance *en route* to the outfall. And the way to do this, as he has already stated, is to lay down all drains and sewers by hydraulic rule. If the hydraulic rule cannot be acted upon by trusting to natural gravitation drainage, then recourse should be had to artificial or mechanical means,—such as can be obtained from the adoption of the Shone system. . . .

The following towns have applied the Shone system, more or less, in *its entirety*, viz.: Henley-on-Thames and Beaumaris (at these places automatic flush-tanks, and the author's new system of ventilating sewers, were not used), Rangoon, Hampton Wick, and Wallingford. The improved system of ventilating sewers was not applied at Rangoon, for the reason that it was not invented at the time when those works were designed. But at Wallingford is to be found the most complete example of drainage works on the Shone system. There the public sewers have automatic flush-tanks and air inlets at their heads, and there also all the manhole covers are sealed, and the nozzle sewer ventilators are connected with each ejector station.

You all know that complaints of sewage-gas nuisances arising from perforated manhole covers over street sewers are all but ubiquitous, and these nuisances are intensified when house connexions are being formed with new drainage works. At Wallingford, however, such nuisances have been rendered non-existent, not a single case of complaint having been made up to the present time. . . .

But, occasionally, objections are raised to the system on the score of first cost. The following statement, which may be relied upon, will, however, serve to show that, even in point of first cost, the Shone system is to be preferred to the ordinary gravitation drainage. For example, the following towns were drained on the ordinary system, viz.: Margate (where hydraulic pumping is resorted to), Southport, and Llandudno, and the cost per head amounted to 4*l*. 7s., 6*l*., and 7*l*., respectively; or an average of 5*l*. 15s. 8d. At the following places, drained on the Shone system, the approximate cost per head has been as follows:—

	Cost per head.		
	£.	s.	d.
Beaumaris	3	0	0
Henley-on-Thames	3	15	0
Wallingford	3	9	0
Hampton Wick	3	7	6
Average	3	7	10
Rangoon	2	2	4

The chief object in view in giving you these costs is to show your Association that high-class sanitary drainage works, on the Shone system, may be carried out at home and abroad, at fairly low prices per head of the population. In point of fact, the author knows cases where the ordinary gravitation plan has been carried out at prices which are more than double those at which the same extent of sewerage work could have been carried out on the Shone system.

[We give elsewhere a brief report of the discussion which followed.]

REMOVAL.—Messrs. Pugin & Pugin, architects, have removed their offices to St. Hubert's, Brook-green, London, W.

Illustrations.

COMPETITION DESIGN FOR THE GLASGOW ART GALLERIES.

WHEN criticising the various designs submitted in this competition, we took occasion to comment on the vagueness of the instructions issued by the Committee, which left competitors to find out, or guess, important particulars which ought to have been clearly specified. A comparison of the plan by Messrs. John Honeyman & Keppie, which we now publish, with that selected, well illustrates the consequent perplexities of competitors. The authors of this design understood the Committee to mean that the central-hall was to be a "concert-hall,"—as it is called in the conditions,—provided with the usual accommodation for orchestra or other performers, and capable of being used apart from the rest of the building without any interference with the access to the museum and art galleries. They also understood that the floor area of this Hall was not to be less than 10,000 superficial feet,—that minimum being clearly specified.

In order to gain their object, Messrs. Honeyman & Keppie run spacious corridors along each side of the hall, connected at the south end by the entrance-hall, and at the north end by a cross corridor. These side corridors are 22 ft. wide, and are divided by arches into a series of domical bays, each lighted from the centre. Three of these on each side are open to the hall, from which direct access is thus obtained to the art galleries on the one hand and the museum on the other. These departments have also independent entrances, and are so arranged that they may be kept entirely isolated from each other or otherwise, at pleasure. It now appears that the Committee did not wish any such classification, and it is a pity they did not say so distinctly at first. As will be seen from the elevation, there are no side windows in the galleries on the first floor. These extend right round the building, and are lighted from above. As there are no corner pavilions or other excrescences above the roof line, there is nothing to interfere with the proper lighting of all the galleries, and the whole space is utilised. We understand that this design cost less per superficial foot of area covered than any of the others.

Though this design was formally sent in as Messrs. Honeyman & Keppie's, we believe that practically it represents Mr. Honeyman's idea of the treatment of the problem, and as such is an interesting example of the taste and predilections of the older Classic school of Glasgow architects, among whom Mr. Honeyman has long held an honoured position. The design is at variance with recent architectural proclivities, but it is a fine and dignified building in itself, and, if erected, might possibly have commanded more permanent appreciation than some public buildings which are more in accordance with the latest architectural fashions.

MOSAIC PAVEMENT, HOUSE IN CHESTERFIELD-GARDENS.

THIS is a pavement of black and white mosaic for the staircase hall of Lord Leconfield's mansion in Chesterfield-gardens.

The large panel at the foot of the stairs is filled with floral ornament in white on a black ground, with a border of black dolphins on a white ground. The parts at the sides of the first flight are Powdered with circular and oblong panels filled with red and green porphyry, bordered with black and white mosaic. The corridor to the morning and business rooms has red mosaic grounds in addition to the black and white.

The balustrade to the staircase is entirely of hammered copper, burnished, and consists of openwork panels of floral ornament between turned copper balusters. The balustrade finishes against copper newels on the ground floor, and runs into marble pedestals on the first floor. It contrasts well by its lightness with the marble lining of the well-hole, the marble columns, and the marble balustrade; and its colour is heightened by contrast with the green Genoa marble of the cornice and capping of the marble balustrades.

FLATS, EARL'S COURT-SQUARE.

THIS block of flats has been lately built at Earl's Court-square. As the site was limited in

COMPETITION DESIGN FOR

GLASGOW ART GALLERY.

MESSRS. HONEYMAN & KEPPIE, ARCHITECTS.

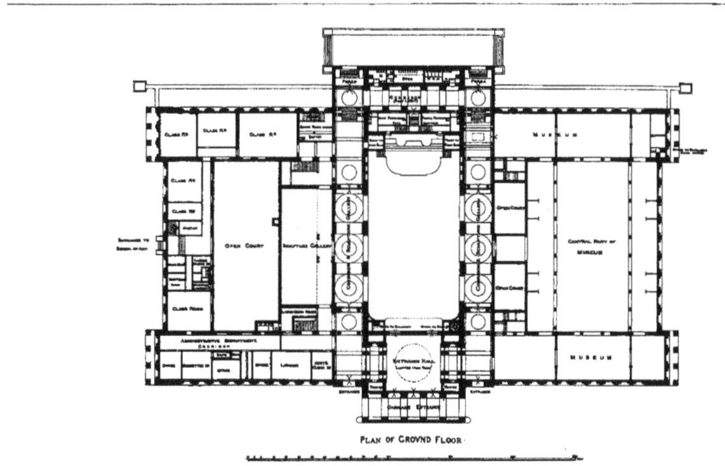
PLAN OF GROVND FLOOR

COMPETITION DESIGN FOR GLASGOW AI

RY.—Messrs. Honeyman & Keppie, Architects.

MOSAIC PAVEMENT OF STAIRCASE-HALL, AND COPPER BALUSTRADE.

Royal Academy Exhibition, 1892.

DETAIL OF RAILINGS IN HAMMERED COPPER
TO INCH SCALE

'USE IN CHESTERFIELD GARDENS.—Mr. G. Aitchison, A.R.A., Architect.

Flats at Earls Court Square. S.W.

for J Douglas. Esqre

R.A.Briggs. F.R.I.B.A. Archt

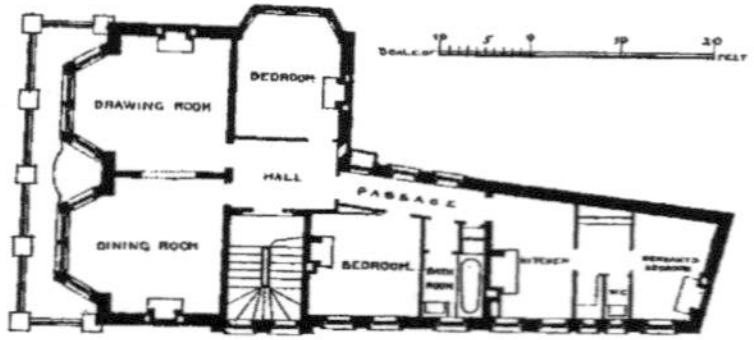

DRAWING ROOM
BEDROOM
HALL
PASSAGE
DINING ROOM
BEDROOM
KITCHEN
W.C.

Scale of 10 5 0 10 20 Feet

FIRST FLOOR PLAN

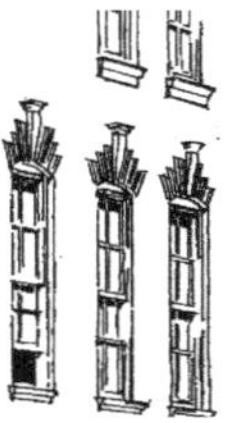

PHOTO-LITHO. SPRAGUE & Cº 4 & 5, EAST HARDING STREET, FETTER LANE, E.C.

" Exhibition 1892

size, great care was necessary in the anning to obtain the necessary accommodation. The walls are faced with red bricks, d the dressings up to the 1st floor are of ortland stone; the large roof cornice and toins, being of cement, were proposed by the chitect to be painted white. The roofs are led. Mr. R. A. Briggs prepared the designs, hich were carried out by Mr. J. Douglas, under is superintendence.

The drawing is exhibited at the Royal cademy.

THE ROYAL COMMISSION ON METROPOLITAN WATER-SUPPLY.

We resume our report* of the evidence given efore this Commission by continuing our ummary of Mr. Gough's statement† on behalf f the Thames Conservators. It had been rged, he said, that in times of very high ood the sewage farms become over-taxed, nd that they do not work efficiently, with the esult that impurities find their way into the iver. The Conservators have had this consideration under their notice, but remark that, n floods of the description referred to, the iver flow is twenty times greater than in dry eather, and that consequently the increased ollution is relatively hardly appreciable. The onservators employ two Chief Inspectors, two ssistant-Inspectors, and four River-keepers, ho, although they have other duties to perorm, devote a very large proportion of their me to the inspection of the sewage works eferred to before, and to the detection of any ases where the law as to pollution may be fringed. In the course of the year these fficers make as many as 2,900 inspections in he aggregate, and it is very rarely that ases are found where steps, even by way of orrespondence, have to be taken by the Conservators. On the tributaries there are five maller towns at some distance from the river, hich have not diverted their sewage; these re:—Highworth, 3½ miles from the river, with 302 inhabitants; Faringdon, 3 miles from the ver, with 3,141 inhabitants; Witney, 7 miles om the river, with 3,110 inhabitants; ynsham, ½ mile from the river, with 2,076 nhabitants; and Uxbridge, on the River Colne, 8 miles from the River Thames, with 8,206 inhabitants. In the case of Faringdon, the Local Authority disclaim all responsibility in connexion with the pollution. Notices have, therefore, been served on the householders. In the four other cases the Conservators have taken proceedings, but the justices have refused to convict, presumably on the ground that the pollution was not likely to reach the Thames. It is an offence only to pass sewage into a tributary *in such a manner that the same is carried, or is likely to be carried, into the Thames*. Great difficulty has been experienced in satisfying Courts of Justice that the sewage is so carried into the river, and the Conservators submit that it is necessary the law should be so amended as to make it penal to discharge sewage or offensive or injurious matter into any tributary of the Thames without qualification. There are three authorities, Hampton, Hampton Wick, and Richmond, below the Water Companies' intakes, who, although they are now executing works, have not finally completed them. In consequence of pressure used by the Conservators, the Sanitary Authority of Guildford, with a population of 14,319, which is beyond the Conservators' jurisdiction, is about to execute works to divert the sewage of that town from the River Wey, at an estimated cost of 27,325*l*. There are a considerable number of places which are within the jurisdiction of Rural Sanitary Authorities, and in the great majority of instances the sewage of these places has been diverted from the river. The efforts of the Conservators have not been confined to the discovery of drains from towns or centres of population, whether large or small, but have also been directed to the prevention of sewage contamination from isolated houses, mills, and farms. There are a considerable number of paper-mills on the tributaries, but it is most rare to detect any discharge from them, and on the few occasions when a discharge has been detected, it has not been of a serious kind. The Conservators have caused the diversion of pollution from 750 scattered houses or farms, and at the present time their officers have difficulty in finding any fresh cases to report of the kind. Although it may be doubted whether suds and sink-water are pollution within the meaning of the Act, the Conservators call upon owners and occupiers of the premises to stop the discharge without delay. In the great majority of instances, earth closets are used on houseboats and on those launches which have any conveniences of the kind. In ordinary circumstances, the owners of the vessels deposit the contents of the closets on land, under arrangement with landowners, and at Henley Regatta, when a large number of these vessels are brought together on a comparatively small section of the river, and it would be difficult to find a place of deposit, the Conservators specially provide four punts to go round at night to collect excreta and refuse of all kinds, and thus guard against any pollution of the river on that occasion. No clear case of pollution from houseboats has been detected, and there is every reason to believe that the law is generally observed. In January, 1884, the Conservators gave instructions that no inhabited houseboat should be allowed to lie in the river between Chertsey Bridge and Hampton Ferry; that is to say, within a distance of from five to seven miles above the intakes of the water companies. Offensive substances falling or thrown into the river are removed before they putrify and pollute the river. With some inappreciable exceptions, the river is no longer contaminated by sewage, and the principal objection to the use of river water for dietetic purposes can now no longer be urged against it. During the last twelve or fourteen years the weirs have been much improved, their sectional area increased, and mode of construction modified so as to admit of the greatest possible aëration of the water and its consequent improvement in quality. During the past year the Conservators had a large number of samples of river water, taken under different meteorological conditions at various points of the stream, not the most favourable for yielding samples of the best quality. The samples were analysed by Mr. Groves, who reported that they were all samples of a good potable river water. It is the view of the Conservators that the Thames forms a source of water supply perfectly suitable in quality for the Metropolis, and that it has not failed in quantity in the driest seasons, whilst, even in those seasons, it is capable of being supplemented by storage to an extent quite sufficient to meet the necessities of London for any measurable period in the future. These are considerations affecting the maintenance of the river which are of great importance to the public who use it. The charge of the river above Staines was not devolved upon the Conservators at their own instance, but, in the year 1866, that part of the river being in an insolvent condition, the President of the Board of Trade invited them to undertake its control, in addition to that of the district below Staines, which was already vested in them. Until recent years, when the contributions were increased, the Conservators have conducted their operations above Staines under the strain of constant financial difficulty. Every available shilling has been expended in the restoration of the river, and much important work remains to be done by degrees, as the state of the funds each year will admit. Difficulty has always been found in balancing the income and expenditure on the upper river, and the Conservators have frequently been compelled to forego the construction of works which nothing but shortness of funds would have made them consent to delay. The revenue received by the Conservators independently of the water companies has, fortunately, during the past twelve or fifteen years increased in amount, owing to the fact that the river has become one of the most important pleasure grounds of the Metropolis, but the traffic which has thus grown up has not proved itself equal to support the river independently of extraneous aid, nor in the opinion of the Conservators is it likely ever to do so. If no funds were left to the Conservators besides the river tolls and the few minor sources of income, there would be barely enough to pay the charge for the debt and the lock-keepers' wages. No further improvements could be contemplated, and it would not be within the competency of the Conservators to prevent the present works from falling, in a very short time, into decay. The staff of inspectors could not be retained, and the inevitable consequence would be that the provisions of the Acts for keeping order on the river would become a dead letter. The necessity of keeping the river pure from pollution for drinking purposes would indeed have ceased, but as a resort for health and pleasure, the river ought to be maintained in its present satisfactory condition, and without proper supervision there would be great risk of losing very much of what has been gained in this respect during the past twenty-five years. Thus the abandonment of the river as a source of water-supply, if accompanied by the corresponding loss of revenue without compensation elsewhere, would practically entail the abandonment of the river as a playground for the metropolis, and the Conservators urge upon the Commissioners the importance, or rather necessity, of some provision being made in this event, to enable them to continue the work they have carried out during the past quarter of a century for the benefit of the public.

Mr. Gough also handed in the following particulars respecting the sewage works of towns and other places on the Thames and its tributaries, above the companies' intakes and below them. After the name is given the population; then the description of works, with their area in acres. Where three figures are given, the first is the highest level of the farm, the second the lowest, and the third the level of the river at the nearest point. Lastly is given the geological formation of the farm; but the latter details are omitted in respect of places below the intakes:—

Above Intakes, on Main Stream.

Oxford, 45,741; irrigation farm at Littlemore, about 334 acres; 224, 190, 177; coralline oolite.

Abingdon, 6,557; irrigation farm, 44 acres, ½ mile south of the town; 169, 164, 162; Kimmeridge clay.

Wallingford, 2,989; Shone's system, 10 acres, ¼ mile west of the town; 154, 152, 141; upper green sand.

Reading, 60,054; irrigation farm, about 700 acres, 1½ miles south-west of the town; 128, 124, 121 (River Kennet); chalk.

Henley, 4,913; Shone's system, 5 acres, 1½ miles north of the town; 145, 135, 101; chalk.

Marlow, 4,764; no sewage works; cesspools in use; chalk.

Maidenhead, 10,607; partly irrigation and partly filter-beds; a large amount is pumped up to florist's land adjoining, and is used over the land; about 20 acres and florist's land; close to town; 105, 75, 70; chalk.

Windsor, 12,327; A, B, C system, about 20 acres at Ham Island, above Old Windsor Lock; 58, 55, 48; chalk.

Eton, 2,499; irrigation, about 30 acres at Eton Wick; 67, 64, 61; chalk.

Staines, 5,060; drainage chiefly into cesspits; no works; subject under consideration; gravel.

Chertsey, 9,215; no sewerage works; drainage into cesspools and tubs, which are emptied by the Rural Sanitary Authority, and contents taken to sewage depots, and subsequently used as manure.

Weybridge, 3,027; no sewerage works; contents of tubs, &c., taken to sewage depots; Bagshot sands.

Sunbury, 4,297; no sewerage works; drainage into cesspools; gravel.

Above Intakes, on Tributaries.

Cirencester, 7,441; irrigation, 57 acres, 3 miles south of the town at Tudmore; 310, 305, 270 (Thames or Isis); cornbrash.

Old Swindon, 5,545; irrigation, about 200 acres, 1 mile south of the town; 350, 340, 335 (river Ray); Kimmeridge clay.

New Swindon, 27,295; irrigation, 50 acres,—farm comprises 100 acres, but only 50 used; 305, 295, 290 (river Ray); Kimmeridge clay.

Wokingham, 2,060, irrigation, 8 acres, 500 yds. from the town; 10 acres, ½ mile north-west of the town; 3 acres, at back of union; 171, 165, 133 (river Lodden); London clay.

Wycombe, High, 13,435; 190, 188, 180 (river Wye); chalk.

Slough, 5,427; irrigation; 10 acres at Dorney; 71, 70, 61 (Thames); chalk.

Highworth, 3,302; no works; two large cesspools, which are emptied when full and sewage distributed over land.

Witney, 3,110; no works; drainage into river Wenwash, above 5 miles distant from Thames.

Faringdon, 3,141; no works; drainage into stream ditch, about 3 miles from Thames.

Uxbridge, 8,206; precipitation and filtration; 6 acres; 100 highest level; 95 level of river Colne; chalk.

Guildford, 14,319; chemical filtration and irrigation; 18 acres (works in progress); distance, 12 miles from Thames.

Walton, 6,572; irrigation; 60 acres; 35 highest level; 27 level of river; gravel.

The following places drain into cesspools:— Shrivenham, 721; Binsey, Wytham, Littlemore, Headington, Cowley, which are on coralline oolite, and calcareous clay; Steventon, 924, on

* See *Builder*, pp. 418, 435, 456, 480, *ante*.
† Ibid., p. 481, *ante*.

gault; Sutton Courtney and Eynsham, on the Oxford clay; Wargrave, 1,882, Remenham, Cookham, 6,851, Datchet, and Chalvey, on the chalk; and Shepperton, on gravel. At Steventon there is one farm which drains into a brook which runs into the Thames, but the provision of a cesspool is promised. A small amount of drainage from Datchet runs into a ditch which flows into the Thames near Wraysbury.

Below Intakes, on Thames.

For the following places the levels and geological formations are not stated as they are below the intakes and do not affect the water supply:—

Kingston, 27,054; Surbiton, 10,052; and Hampton Wick; works on the A B C system, 3 acres.

Teddington, 10,025; works, precipitation, filtration and irrigation, 22 acres.

Twickenham, 16,026; works, filtration, 4 acres.

Richmond, 22,684; Petersham, 566; Kew, 1,670; Mortlake, 6,330.

Barnes, 6,001; works, precipitation and filtration, 11 acres; outlet at Mortlake.

Isleworth, 12,973; works, Candy's process and irrigation, 22 acres.

Brentford, 13,736; works, precipitation and irrigation, 3 acres.

Chiswick, 21,964; pumping station, precipitation, 5½ acres.

Hampton, 5,822; drainage at present into cesspool (scheme lately adopted and to be carried out).

East Molesey, 4,666; cesspool drainage at present; scheme for drainage under consideration; waiting Local Government Board's report.

Ealing, South, 3 acres, precipitation and special.

Acton, 24,207; 5¾ acres; Candy's process, discharge into the River Thames at Chiswick.

Below Intakes, on Tributaries.

Ealing North, 23,978; 22 acres; pre., fil., and irr., r. Brent.

Hanwell, 6,139; 12 acres; pre. and irr., r. Brent.

Willesden, 61,266; 18 acres; pre., fil., and irr., r. Brent.

Finchley, 16,639; 72 acres; chemical p. and irr., formerly into the Brent and now into the Lea.

Hendon, 15,835; 23 acres; International Water and Sewage Purification Company's system, into the Brent.

Harrow, 5,725; 28½ acres; two irrigation farms, into Brent.

Pinner, 2,319; 6½ acres; irrigation farm, Yealing Brook and River Crane.

Epsom, 8,417; 120 acres; irrigation field, Hogg's Mill River.

New Malden, 3,437, 9 acres; p. and irr., Hoggs Mill river.

Cranford, 503, 2½ acres; farm, f. and irr., river Crane.

Alperton, 8½ acres; farm, p. and irr., river Brent.

Stanmore, 1,312, 8½ acres; irrigation farm, river Brent.

Southall, 3,784, and Norwood, 6,681, 11 acres; irr. and f. works, river Brent.

Esher, 1,193, Claremont, Thames Ditton, 2,956, and Long Ditton, 2,315; 26 acres, p. and irr. works; river Mole.

Tolworth and Hook, 9 acres; p. and irr. works; Hoggs Mill river.

Harmondesworth, 1,812; tank, sewering; solids used as manure; Duke's river.

In the course of his evidence, Mr. Gough said that the Companies that were unlimited by Act were the Southwark and Vauxhall, the Lambeth, and the Grand Junction, and the Companies that were limited were the East London, the West Middlesex, and the Chelsea. The Conservancy considered that the effect of granting the extra 20,000,000 gallons would not prejudicially affect the river. The actual amount taken from the river at the intakes varied from about 90,000,000 to 105,000,000 gallons. The quantities taken were furnished by the Companies; and the Conservancy had no check. In the return of sewage farms, the geological formation was taken from the geological map, which did not show what the top soil was; but that he could supply. The Conservators' local officer reported that there was no pollution whatever coming into the Thames from Marlow. Three or four years ago the effluent from Oxford was not satisfactory; this was represented to the Oxford Corporation, and they improved it at once. If the inspecting officer of a district observes that an effluent is at all of a doubtful character, he reports it, and sends up samples. A sample is sent to Mr. Groves for analysis, and if on analysis it is found to be of an indifferent character a representation is made to the authority under whose jurisdiction the farm is. Oxford was reported in September, 1887, again in August, 1888, as "not good" and "bad;" in December, 1889, as "good;" and in February, 1891, as "fair." There are from thirty-six to fifty inspections a year of the same places. A total of about 2,900 inspections are made in the year. There are two inspectors. The upper navigation down to Staines is under Lieut. Bell, assisted by Mr. Green, who is a land surveyor; the district from Staines to the western limit of the Metropolis is under Mr. Little, with Mr. Drummond as assistant, and each is helped by two river-keepers. The officers go up the tributaries to a distance of ten miles measured in a direct line from the Thames. Abingdon works very satisfactorily. Wallingford has given trouble; the sewage was stopped, but not in a satisfactory manner; but lately the authority has completed a system since which there have been no bad reports. When asking about the Reading works,

The Chairman said: We should like to know exactly how many inspections have been made of the effluent, how many times it has been reported upon unfavourably, and what the results of any communications have been. We should also like an estimate of the amount of time the staff of the Conservators can really devote to inspections consistently with the discharge of their other duties.

Speaking of Windsor, the witness said that Ham Island had a lock cut on one side and the river on the other; the sewage was treated chemically in tanks by the A.B.C. process; and in the last five or six years the effluent had not been sufficiently bad to be reported upon and to be analysed.

The Chairman: Who judges as to whether it is what you call "sufficiently bad?"

Witness: The inspector, if he observes anything which he thinks it his duty to bring under the notice of the Conservators, takes a sample and reports it, and it is sent to the analyst at once; I send it on.

Do we understand that no effluent is analysed unless you get a bad report upon it?

The Conservators have not regularly analysed the samples until the samples are reported upon by their officer as being of such a character as to require analysis.

Then, for five years the works of Windsor have gone on absolutely without check?

They have not been analysed.

I mean absolutely without check beyond the test of the eye?

Yes, and the observation of the officers.

Mr. Mansergh: And of the nose, probably?

Yes, and of the nose.

In the case of each town above the intakes, the witness continued, there was an actual effluent into the river. In the case of Highworth, the Conservators took proceedings, but they were not able to obtain a conviction. It is now reported that the sewage is distributed over the land, so that no pollution is coming into the Thames. Farringdon is situated on a hill; the sewage passes into a tributary of the river, which is called a stream ditch. The Conservators have had a great amount of trouble with this case. They have corresponded with the local authority, who disclaim any liability. They say that the drains are private drains, and they quote the decision of the High Court with regard to Staines, — that they have no power to compel the individual owners of drains to divert their sewage. The Conservators have accordingly obtained a list of all persons who have sewage drains and who discharge their sewage drains into the stream ditch, and have served notices, after analysis of samples taken, upon those various individuals requiring them to divert the flow of the sewage from their drains into this stream ditch. These notices will shortly expire, and thereupon the Conservators propose to take proceedings before the magistrates to enforce compliance with the law as to pollution. In the case of Windrush, five miles from the Thames, the Conservators have taken proceedings and have failed to obtain a conviction. In the case of Eynsham, cesspool drainage was general, but there was a small discharge into the ditch at Eynsham Wharf. The Conservators have proceeded against the Rural Sanitary Authority, and were not able to obtain a conviction, but they are watching with the view of obtaining a sample which will enable them to try again. It is not always easy to obtain a conviction by local magistrates. The Conservators several years ago twice took proceedings against Uxbridge for the pollution of the Colne. The magistrates refused to convict, and on the second occasion imposed all the costs upon the Conservators, on the ground that it was not proved that the pollution was likely to reach the Thames at a distance of 8½ miles. On more than one occasion the Conservators have been met by scientific evidence that pollution was not likely to be carried into the Thames. The Conservators have often felt that it ought to be an offence to pass any pollution into a tributary within the watershed of the Thames. The Conservators have watched Staines from the commencement in 1866. They have taken samples and obtained convictions, but the convictions led to no useful result, and they decided to proceed against the Local Board in the High Court. The Judges decided that the Local Board were not liable, because there was a prescriptive right for the individual owners of drains to discharge into their drains. Counsel then advised that the only step to take was to serve notices on the individual owners of the drains. This was in 1888, so that it took twenty-two years to get to that point. Drains had to be broken open and samples taken at the discharge of the small drains into the large drains. On the expiry of the first set of notices proceedings were commenced, and on June 20, 1891, the Local Government Board received a petition from inhabitants praying the department to hold an inquiry. The magistrates adjourned the summonses. The inquiry was held on September 26, and on December 15 the Local Government Board issued an order requiring the Staines Local Board to provide sufficient sewers within six months. The Local Board propose to comply with the order by having a system of cesspools, and they will have carts to empty the cesspools and convey the material away, unless the Local Government Board should interfere, and say that that is not a sufficient dealing with the question. The only power of the Conservators was to say that there should be no pollution passing into the river. Some years ago Weybridge proposed to have sewage works, but the Conservators opposed, on the ground that the sewage was likely to be washed out of them into the river. Paper mills are most carefully watched, and the slightest impurity is easily detected and reported at once. There are some thirty or forty above all the intakes. There are a fellmonger's works at Wokingham, from which blood occasionally passes into the river. The 750 scattered houses or farms have also to be watched. They discharge into tributaries or drainage ditches. In dry weather there is no discharge, but at flood times there is risk of pollution being washed into the river. If the inspectors see a possibility of pollution, occupiers are called upon to divert it, and they do it mostly by cesspools, sometimes by sealed tanks, from which it is pumped out in dry weather and distributed over farms. The Conservators have prohibited inhabited house-boats lying between Chelsea Bridge and the intakes of the Companies. There are 167 vessels registered as house-boats, and 47 as dressing-places and storage for boats' gear. There is a mark outside a house-boat which shows that it has been registered. There is no power to go on board house-boats to inspect them, but it is made a condition of their having places at Henley Regatta that they shall allow inspection. They have on board earth pans and patent closets, the contents of which are taken on shore and dug into the soil. There are 393 registered steam-launches, and on the majority there are no conveniences of any kind. Out of the total amount paid by the water companies, about 3,500*l.* may be apportioned as fairly chargeable in respect of inspection for pollution purposes. The thirty-seven villages or towns named are all that have at any time been suffered to pollute the river. The County Council map shows many places that have been actually dealt with, and which are no longer sources of pollution.

Mr. C. J. Moore, Engineer to the Conservancy, produced a table showing for the nine years 1883 to 1892 the daily flow at Teddington Weir after the water had been abstracted by the companies. The following abstract gives averages, *maxima* and *minima*:—

	Millions of gallons.
Average Annual volume of discharge......	447,041·0
" Monthly " "	37,253·5
" Daily " "	1,224·0

Maximum volume of discharge:—

	Millions of gallons.		Millions of gallons daily.
In a year (1883)...	659,657·4	=	1,807·3
(a) 6 months	466,639·3	=	2,578·1
(a) 3 months	367,235·0	=	4,080·3
(a) 1 month	174,575·0	=	6,234·8
(a) 7 days	60,865·0	=	8,695·0
(a) 24 hours	9,640·0		

Minimum volume of discharge :—

	Millions of gallons.		Millions of gallons daily.
In a year (1890)...	261,915·6	=	717·6
(b) 6 months	76,925·6	=	420·3
(c) 3 months	26,215·2	=	284·9
(d) 1 month	6,517·3	=	210·2
(e) 7 days...........	1,257·3	=	179·6
(f) 24 hours.........	153·9		

(a) All in 1883. (b) June to Nov., 1890. (c) July, Aug., and Sept., 1887. (d) Aug. 1885. (e) Aug., 1887. (f) Aug., 1887.

Having regard to these minima, the present authorised maximum abstraction of 130,000,000 gallons could not be safely increased in dry weather. If 500,000,000 gallons were coming down the river and 100,000,000 gallons were taken out, he estimated that the abstraction would lower the surface about 4½ in.; the abstraction of 130,000,000 would make a further difference of about 1½ in. The effect would diminish as you went down the river, and at Hammersmith would be lost. A half-tide weir is being built at Richmond, and that will maintain a level of about half-tide up to Teddington. The Richmond people have complained of the exposed foreshores, the low-water level having been considerably lowered. This was due to the removal of bridges and obstructions in the lower part of the river, and to dredging for the removal of shoals and the improvement of the navigation. Reminded by the Chairman that the figures he had given were smaller than those adopted by the Commission of 1869, the witness said he thought it had always been assumed until lately that there was more water in the river in dry seasons than was actually the case. The witness handed in a table showing the volume of the discharge at Teddington Weir for the years 1813 to 1891 inclusive, with the addition of the quantities abstracted by the companies, and the equivalent rain-fall for the drainage area of 3,766 square miles above Teddington. The yearly averages were: Gaugings at the weir, 447,042,000,000 gallons; abstraction by the companies, 30,896,000,000 gallons; actual volume of discharge, 477,937,000,000 gallons. This discharge is equal to 347,333 gallons per square mile of the water shed per diem; and that is equivalent to a rainfall of 8·7 in. per year. In this way the volume of discharge seemed to vary from a maximum rainfall of 12½ in. in 1883 to a minimum of 5·4 in. in 1890. The minimum could be partly accounted for by the fact that there was not the full average rainfall, and that there was a very severe frost, during which the river ran very low. For the three driest consecutive months in every year of the nine years there was an average flow of 429,000,000 gallons per day, which might be called the ordinary summer flow. This was what was left after the companies had taken their quantities.

The Commission then proceeded to take the evidence of Mr. Groves, Consulting Chemist to the Conservancy; but we must break off here for the present.

SANITARY SAMPLES AT HIGHGATE.

THERE is now approaching completion, at the Highgate Depôt of the Hornsey Local Board, situate on the great North road of the old coaching days, what is intended to be a permanent exhibition of sanitary appliances, together with a standard reference museum of samples of materials and fittings. The establishment of this useful exhibition and museum is an interesting event, and reflects much credit on the Hornsey Local Board, whose enlightened policy in regard to sanitary administration generally has been noticed on previous occasions in these pages. Under section 18 of the Public Health Acts Amendment Act of 1890, the Board, in common with other local authorities, have power, under certain conditions, to execute, by their own officers and staff, any works necessary to put a dwelling-house into a healthy and habitable condition, and to charge the cost upon the owner. It is not proposed by the Board to adopt the course of doing such works themselves except under very special circumstances, as they have a wholesome desire to refrain from unnecessary interference with ordinary traders, but in all cases they will closely inspect and carefully test the efficiency of such works. The increased attention that has been devoted to sanitary matters of late years is, it seems (in the district of the Hornsey Local Board, at any rate), beginning to tell, and people are showing a laudable desire to feel assured that the houses in which they live are in proper sanitary condition, and that the appliances in use are adapted to their various purposes. In their anxiety for information, inhabitants of the district are constantly writing to the officials of the Board to know what are the best types of appliances and the best modes of fitting them; and so numerous have these demands become that the Board determined to make the experiment of establishing a typical exhibition of the best sanitary appliances and samples, and to confide the direction of the work to their Engineer and Surveyor, Mr. T. De Courcy Meade. A couple of advertisements in the *Builder*, inviting the co-operation of manufacturers and others willing to exhibit, elicited a very large number of offers of help, and a selection having been made, the result is that four large rooms, having an aggregate floor-space of 325 square yards, are now devoted to an exhibition to which nearly all the leading firms of manufacturing sanitary engineers are contributors of appliances of all kinds. Not only is the floor-space well filled, but the walls and division screens are well covered with exhibits. No charge is made for space, but the exhibitors will no doubt be expected to keep their stands always "up to date." An exceedingly useful feature of the exhibition consists not only of standard stamped samples of lead-piping and other materials, but of full-size sections showing the proper construction and sanitary arrangements of a healthy house. By way of negative teaching, showing what to avoid, a number of horrible examples of bad plumbing work are shown in section; and D-traps and other bad old contrivances filled with hard deposited matter, and 9-in. drain-pipes completely choked with tree-roots which have entered at the joints made with clay instead of cement, convey lessons likely to be impressed upon the memory of all beholders. The exhibition (which will be open free of charge to visitors on every working day) cannot but prove of great educational value to the residents; and it is even hinted that many builders and their workmen,—and possibly some architects,—may there learn not only how to produce good work, but how to avoid bad work. We have not space now to attempt a detailed notice of the exhibits: that we must reserve for another occasion; but we must congratulate the Hornsey Local Board upon their excellent idea, and Mr. Meade and his assistants upon the way in which it has been carried out. The exhibition is now practically filled up, but Mr. Meade would nevertheless be glad to hear from anyone who has anything new and special that might be deemed worthy of a place in the collection, which is now being catalogued.

SOCIETY OF ENGINEERS:

FOREIGN SEWAGE PRECIPITATION WORKS.

AT a meeting of the Society of Engineers held at the Town Hall, Westminster, on the 13th inst., Mr. Joseph William Wilson, jun., President, in the Chair, a paper was read by Mr. Albert Wollheim, on "Foreign Sewage Precipitation Works."

In the introduction to his paper the author compared and traced the development of sewage precipitation works in this country and abroad, and stated that as yet there were only very few works of the kind in existence abroad. Then taking for the first part of his subject the works of Germany, he reviewed and detailed the existing legislation for the prevention of river pollution. Unlike England, Germany possessed no statutory legislation for preventing the pollution of its water-courses. There are only in existence Ministerial decrees, rescripts, and reports of scientific bodies.

The most important precipitation works of Germany are those at Frankfort-on-the-Maine (population 160,000). Ever since the year 1885, when the canal works and port were completed, the trade of the town has increased to an enormous extent, and a thorough system of sewerage and sewage disposal is therefore of the first importance to the town. The system of water-closets, drains, and sewers was commenced over thirty years ago under the late Mr. W. H. Lindley, and completed by his son, Mr. W. Lindley, the present city engineer, who has also designed the precipitation works. These are situated on the left bank of the Maine, the sewage from the right bank being conveyed across by two wrought-iron syphons, 3 ft. 6 in. diameter, with a total discharging capacity of 800,000 gallons per hour. The precipitation tanks are covered in, and will consist of two groups of six subdivisional tanks each, but only four subdivisions are as yet constructed. They are each 270 ft. long by 17 ft. average width, and 6 ft. 10½ in. average depth of water. Each sub-division holds 250,000 million gallons, and as the present daily dry weather flow is 6,000,000 gallons, the existing tank capacity is 16 per cent. of the total daily flow. The whole volume gravitates to the works, and in dry weather overflows continuously at the outlet end. But as the high-water mark of the river is considerably above the ordinary water level in the tanks, special adjustable high-water dams have been provided at the tank outlets, which enables the sewage to be backed up in the tanks and sewers for some hours without, however, causing floodings in the town. During exceptionally heavy floods, when there is danger of backing up the sewage too high in the town, two powerful centrifugal pumps with 20-in. suctions can lift the effluent into the river, and thus keep down the tank water level. The sludge is pumped up periodically into sludge drying pits capable of holding an aggregate of 1,000,000 gallons of liquid sludge. The precipitants used are lime and sulphate of alumina, and the quantities are adjusted by means of Lechner and Spohr's patent automatic electric gauge, which continually transmits to the precipitant house, and records on a revolving drum the height of the sewage in a bay formed at the tank inlets where the chemicals join the sewage. In concluding his description of the Frankfort works, the author drew attention to some important experiments carried out by Mr. Lindley, bearing on the displacement of water in tanks. These tend to show that in summer the incoming sewage glides along the top, in winter it immediately falls to and glides along the bottom towards the outlet end. In both cases the body of water in the tank remains more or less undisturbed. To remedy this Mr. Lindley has devised a falling dam to be fixed in front of the outlet, which has the effect of deflecting and distributing the incoming stream throughout the tank.

The Roeckner-Rothe system of circular upward flow tanks, as distinguished from the rectangular longitudinal system was next described. The Roeckner-Rothe system has been somewhat simplified by Herr Kniebuehler, City Engineer of Dortmund. His tanks are huge circular brick wells sunk into the ground, the sewage being led into the conical bottom where it deposits the sludge, the clarified effluent rising and overflowing continuously all round the top. The sludge is pumped up periodically without disturbing the continuous working. A complete installation on this system is at work at Dortmund.

The author concluded his paper with a brief *résumé* of what has been done in the United States to prevent river pollution. It would appear that the States, with their vast area and innumerable rivers and streams carrying large volumes of water, have not experienced any difficulty from the discharge of raw sewage until a short time ago. The country is just now beginning to stir in the matter. This accounts for the fact that only three precipitation works have been constructed. The largest are those at Worcester (Massachusetts). In the Worcester works, which were designed by Mr. Allen, the City Engineer, well-known English types have been followed, the tanks having been planned somewhat after the Coventry tanks. The tank walls are constructed of small rubble bedded in Portland cement, and faced with vitrified bricks, the copings being composed of granite chippings and cement. The chemicals used are lime and sulphate of alumina. Only a portion of the city drains to the works at present, the daily flow being about 3,000,000 gallons. In this connexion the author gave a table showing the number of gallons of water per head supplied to various towns throughout the States, from which it appears that 100 gallons per head is by no means an uncommon figure. An intimate acquaintance, he said, with American home and industrial life was necessary in order to comprehend how such high figures could be reached.

The paper was illustrated by a large number of diagrams.

VISIT TO THE SOUTH METROPOLITAN GAS-WORKS.

The excursion which the members of this Society made down the river on Tuesday last,

June 21, was more particularly interesting on account of the visit to the South Metropolitan Gasworks at East Greenwich, where the largest gasometer in the world is now being erected. The party were landed at the great coal stage, where in the hydraulic room they were entertained at luncheon, Mr. Tysoe, the Supetiutendent of the works, presiding, in the unavoidable absence of Mr. George Livesey. Inspection was thereafter made of the engine-house and the machinery therein for exhausting the gas from the retorts and passing it on under pressure to the washers, scrubbers, and purifiers, and finally through the meters into the mains. The order, quietness, and efficiency were greatly admired. The retort-houses were next taken, and here the process of gas-making was seen carried on by hand at the floors, and by staging for the tiers of retorts one above the other. Mechanical means, too, of charging and of drawing were shown. Other departments were also inspected, and high appreciation invariably expressed. The marked peculiarity of the East Greenwich Works is that they are fundamentally based upon the most modern knowledge and experience, and have not been built up successively from foundations laid in former stages of the general progress of gas manufacture. The South Metropolitan Gas Company possess several large works which originated in such earlier circumstances, and have been kept in touch with advances by modifications and improvements,—namely, Vauxhall, Bankside, Old Kent-road, and Rotherhithe; but East Greenwich is an entirely new station. When the amalgamation of the Phœnix Company with the South Metropolitan took place in 1880, the whole of Blackwall Point was acquired, with an area of over 110,000 acres, of which something like 100,000 acres have been retained for present and future works, and which latter can adequately provide for a long series of years complete extension of gas supply to meet increased demands. Another important feature of this site are the advantageous facilities for the supply of coal,—the raw material of the manufacture. Vessels of from 1,000 to 1,500 tons burden can discharge at the landing-stage, whilst on the other hand the surplus coke from the manufacture can be tipped from the waggons on the railway by the river wall direct into the barges for sale.

The immediate interest of the day, however, centred on the large gasometer erecting in the marshes. The storage of gas is one of the most important considerations, not only in regard to the skill of the engineer in the required constructions, but still more so in the fact that the larger the gasholder the less the cost in proportion to the quantity stored within it. The material, however, must be thin, because the gasometer must not be heavy, as it has to be raised by the very moderate pressure of the gas within it. Nevertheless, the gain of economy is so great as to have tempted one very practical and prudent man to carry magnitude, in this instance, far beyond any previous attempt. The Vauxhall works have a gasometer of 3,000,000 cubic feet capacity, and the existing gasometer of the East Greenwich works will contain 8,500,000 cubic feet of gas. The new gasometer will store 12,000,000 cubic feet, and its diameter is no less than 300 ft. The tank in which it will float is raised above the marshland by a circular embankment of concrete, and is 303 ft. 6 in. across; its depth at the internal wall is 32 ft. to the rest-blocks. Its thickness is 4 ft. 6 in. at the bottom, and 3 ft. 6 in. at top. The gasometer is of telescopic type, and will rise to a height of 180 ft. in six lifts. The surface of such a gigantic and lofty object presented to the wind is enormous, and a mere ring of independent columns, as employed by the old engineers would be utterly inadequate for its support. In the first place, there is no cohesion between the loose columns, and under strong winds the pressure is concentrated on one or two of them alone at the rear, whilst the lateral columns have no stress brought upon them at all. The bracket system of supports, extending from the gasometer to the vertical standards in the surrounding ring, was introduced by Mr. Livesey some years ago at Rotherhithe, and these may be well seen from the decks of the river steamers. This primitive idea has been now developed at East Greenwich into a remarkable engineering structure of enormous strength and coherence. The columns have given place to wrought-iron standards, with their bases firmly embedded in the concrete wall of the bank. A projection on the face of each standard is bevelled on either side, and the two rollers attached to the end of each of the gasometer brackets,—which are set somewhat diagonally, instead of directly radially,—rub against these faces; and thus is distributed some of the wind pressure upon every standard in the whole series. A wrought-iron coping or continuous circular girder, 22 in. in breadth, surmounts the whole circle of standards, and combines them in perfect mutual and united support. The inter-spaces between the standards are finished with strong open wrought-iron lattice-work, so that the final condition is that the wind's pressure on the gasometer will be transferred to a surrounding enormously strong and rigidly fixed wrought-iron cage, built up to the height of 60 ft. from the ground, and above which two-thirds of the gasometer will extend skyward.

The strength of wind which has thus been provided against is 56 lbs. to the square foot, the highest reliable strength of wind record obtainable by the ordinary anemometer, and notably in excess of the 45 lbs. to the square foot usually taken as maximum storm-pressure. There is no doubt that in hurricanes and cyclones there are pressures beyond this, but they occur so rarely, and even then along such limited lines, that, for practical purposes, they may be neglected.

On the return journey, the party landed at the north pier of the Tower Bridge, and were conducted over the works by Mr. Cruttwell, the resident engineer for Mr. J. Wolfe Barry, and by Mr. Tuit, the representative of the contractors, Sir William Arrol & Co. We published some particulars of the construction of this bridge, illustrated by diagrams, in last week's *Builder*.

THE LONDON COUNTY COUNCIL.

The usual weekly meeting of this Council was held on Tuesday afternoon, at Spring gardens, the Chairman, Lord Rosebery, presiding.*

Finance: The Council's Accounts for 1891-92.—The Finance Committee reported that Mr H. Lloyd Roberts, the Auditor appointed by the Local Government Board to audit the accounts of the Council for the year ended March 31, 1891, completed his audit and gave his certificate on May 21, 1892. The Committee append a copy of his report, which they regard as very satisfactory, and as calling for no special observation, the alterations required by the auditor involving questions of book-keeping only, and not allowance or disallowance of any item. Two paragraphs from the Auditor's report may be quoted, as showing the extent of the Council's financial operations and obligations:—

"The balance in the hands of the Council at the commencement of the year was the sum of 912,503*l.* 16s. 9d.; their receipts within the year amounted to the sum of 3,332,309*l.* 10s. 6d., and their expenditure to the sum of 3,698,770*l.* 1s. 1d.; leaving an available balance of 546,043*l.* 6s. 2d. in their hands at the end of the year.

The amount of the Metropolitan Consolidated Stock issued by the late Metropolitan Board of works and by the Council outstanding at March 31, 1891, was 28,834,325*l.* 16s. 11d., and the balances of loans outstanding at the same period were, in respect to loans contracted by the late Metropolitan Board of Works, 153,533*l.* 6s. 8d., and in respect of loans contracted by the former counties of Middlesex and Surrey and taken over by the County of London, 589,260*l.*, resulting in a liability of the Council as to stock and loans of the sum of 29,577,119*l.* 3s. 7d."

Proposed Widening of the South End of Tottenham Court-road.—On the recommendation of the Parliamentary Committee, it was resolved, after some discussion,—

"That we be authorised, in conjunction with the Improvements Committee, to endeavour to arrange with the promoters of the Hampstead, St. Pancras, and Charing-cross Railway, for the clearance of the site of Bozier's-court, on the understanding that the Council will contribute a sum not exceeding half the net cost of such clearance."

An Additional Assistant Medical Officer of Health.—On the recommendation of the Public Health and Housing Committee, it was resolved:—

"That an additional Assistant Medical Officer of Health be forthwith appointed, at a salary of £500 per annum, rising to 600*l.* per annum by two annual additions of 50*l.* each."

Alterations of Claybury mansion-house.—The Asylums Committee's report contained the following paragraph and recommendation:—

"We have further to report that the tender of Messrs. Reed, Blight, & Co., of Plymouth, for alterations to the mansion-house, which the Council on April 12 last authorised us to accept, amounted to 8,995*l.*, and that the sum authorised by the Council, on our recommendation, to be expended on this work, viz., 10,000*l.* (7,500*l.* for building, and 2,500*l.* for furniture, &c.) will therefore be insufficient. The explanation for the estimate being thus exceeded is, we think, that the labour market is at the present time in so unsettled a state. We recommend—

'That, subject to an additional estimate being submitted by the Finance Committee, we be authorised to expend a further sum of 2,000*l.*, not exceeding 12,000*l.* in all, in converting the mansion-house into an annexe to the main asylum for the accommodation of fifty male paying patients.'"

This was agreed to without discussion.

Additions at Cane Hill Asylum.—The same Committee's report contained the following paragraphs:—

"On May 17 last the Council authorised us to accept Messrs. Reed, Blight, & Co.'s tender, amounting to 15,416*l.*, for the above, provided that they agreed to the insertion in the contract of the condition that they would 'pay the London rate of wages, and observe such hours of labour as are generally accepted in London as fair in the trades they employ.' Messrs. Reed, Blight, & Co. intimated their willingness to agree to such a condition being put in their contract, if by that it was understood that the rate of wages recognised at the time of the acceptance of the contract were to be paid during its continuance, and that in the event of an increase of the union rates of pay, they would be compensated by the Council for the extra amount they would consequently have to allow their workmen. We saw Mr. Reed, and informed him that our reading of the Council's resolution differed from his, and that the rate of wages paid and hours of labour observed were to be those which are from time to time accepted in London as fair in the trades employed. Mr. Reed thereupon respectfully declined on behalf of his firm to complete the contract. We accepted this decision, and informed him that his firm would not be prejudiced thereby, inasmuch as the condition was not in the form of contract to which they tendered, but was imposed subsequently.

Though it is most pressing that the buildings and works under this contract should be at once proceeded with, we think, looking to the difficulties that may arise, it advisable not to again issue advertisements until the terms of the 'wages' clause have been definitely fixed by the Council."

These paragraphs gave rise to considerable discussion, and eventually the matter was referred back to the Committee to re-advertise for tenders as soon as possible.

Contracts for Work at Asylums.—The same Committee also reported,—

"We are unable to proceed with the provision of infirmary accommodation at Banstead Asylum, and the installation of the electric light at Claybury Asylum, as, though the forms of contract have been prepared by the Solicitor, he cannot complete them until the terms of the 'wages' clause have been definitely settled by the Council. This, we understand, may take some time, and, as it is most urgent that both these works should be commenced at the earliest possible moment, we recommend—

'That we be authorised to obtain tenders for the provision of infirmary accommodation at Banstead and for the lighting of Claybury Asylum by electricity, conditionally upon clauses being inserted by the Solicitor in the respective contracts binding the contractors to pay the trades union rates of wages and to observe such hours of labour as are generally accepted in London as fair in the trades they employ.'"

Lord Monkswell moved, as an amendment, to omit the words "trades' union," and to insert, after the words "rates of wages," the words, "agreed upon between employers and the recognised trades' unions." This was ruled out of order, however, and the recommendation of the Committee was agreed to.

Further Works at Claybury Asylum.—The concluding paragraph and recommendation of the Asylums Committee were as follow:—

"We have further to report that we have approved estimates for making roads, draining land, preparing airing-courts, building a mortuary, cow-houses, piggeries, stabling, cottages, fence, and greenhouses, and extending electric lighting to mortuary and farm buildings, amounting (together with the commission to architects and salaries of clerk of works and incidental expenses) to 25,000*l.* We have also approved the sketch plans submitted of the cowhouses, piggeries, stables, and cottages. The whole of these works are essential to the completion of the Asylum, and we therefore recommend—

'That, subject to the usual estimate being submitted by the Finance Committee, and to the approval of the Home Secretary being obtained to the plans of the farm buildings, we be authorised to provide at Claybury Asylum the buildings and works above enumerated, at a cost not exceeding 25,000*l.*'"

* Lord Rosebery has since resigned the Chairmanship, the reorganisation of the Council's Committees, &c., having now been effected.

The recommendation was referred to the Finance Committee.

Proposed Residential Chambers at the Westminster End of the Victoria Embankment.—The first paragraph and recommendation of the Building Act Committee's report were as follow:—

"We have had before us an application of Mr. Keeling, on behalf of Mr. J. Sarl, for approval by the Council of an amended plan for consent to the erection of a block of residential chambers on the Victoria-embankment, and adjoining St. Stephen's Club. The site now vacant was sold and conveyed by the late Metropolitan Board on July 2, 1880, for 3,500*l.*, to Messrs. Hansom & Whichcord, who covenanted with the Board not to build or erect any erection or building whatsoever of which the front next the Embankment should be in advance of the line marked "line of building frontage" on the plan in the conveyance (which is a continuation of the line of frontage of St. Stephen's Club), or any erection or building whatsoever, except such as should be faced with stone or marble, or such also as should be in strict accordance with such elevations and plans as should be submitted to and approved by the Board, or their successors, before such erection or building was commenced. The Solicitor advises that the Council can insist that the buildings shall not be erected in advance of the line of frontage marked on the plan on the conveyance, and can also insist that no building shall be built except in accordance with the elevations and plans submitted to and approved by the late Board, provided the Council exercises its powers reasonably, and not in such a manner as practically to prevent the land being utilised to advantage as building land. Your Committee have also had before them a letter from the Receiver of Police, strongly urging that the buildings proposed to be erected on this site should be kept back to the line of frontage of the police offices recently erected. The First Commissioner of H.M. Office of Works also expresses an opinion that if the building as proposed is erected, it will have a detrimental effect upon the Houses of Parliament, and further that the height of the Club building was reduced considerably below that designed by the owners on account of the objection raised by that department, and that it would be a great satisfaction to the Office of Works if the highest part of the new building could be kept down to the top of the level of St. Stephen's Club. In this view your Committee concurs, and under all the circumstances we see no reason to approve of any deviation from the line of frontage shown on the plan in the conveyance of the property by the late Board, more particularly as the building as now designed would be higher and in advance of the adjoining club-house, and would in our opinion spoil one of the finest views in London. We recommend,—

'That the application be not granted.'"

This was agreed to without discussion.

Proposed School Building at the Crossness Outfall Sewage Works.—The Main Drainage Committee's report contained the following paragraph in relation to a matter mentioned by us last week in our report of the Council's proceedings:—

"At the meeting of the Council on Tuesday last the Chairman suggested that as only one tender had been received for the erection of the school building at Crossness, although the work had been duly advertised, the tender should not be opened, but that the subject should be referred to us. That suggestion was acted upon, and the matter has accordingly been under our consideration. We think in view of all the circumstances, and after conference with the Solicitor, that, before deciding to take any other step, it will be best to open the tender which has already been sent in. We therefore recommend,—

'That the tender be opened by the Council, and referred to us for consideration and report.'"

This was agreed to, and the Chairman accordingly opened the tender, the amount of which he stated to be 2,270*l.* The name of the tenderer was not announced.

The London Water Question.—The Special Water Committee presented the following report and recommendations:—

"The Royal Commission on Metropolitan Water Supply having expressed a wish to be furnished with some indication of the views of the Council on the subject of the inquiry, the accompanying memorandum has been prepared by the Deputy-Chairman of the Council, and carefully considered by us in conference with him. It is based on resolutions passed by us after consideration of tables prepared by the Engineer, with reference (*a*) to the number of years upon which estimates, having reference to the future water supply of London, should be based; (*b*) the population for which provision should be made, and (*c*) the quantity of water which should be supplied per head per day. The views which we entertain on these points would, no doubt, have greater weight with the Commission if the matter were considered by the Council. We therefore append the Deputy-Chairman's Memorandum to this report, and recommend,—

'That the Council do confirm and adopt the opinions and conclusions expressed therein:—

1. That in making any estimates having reference to the future water supply of London, such estimates should be based on a period of fifty years from the present time.

2. That in dealing with the question of a source or sources of water which shall meet the requirements of London and its neighbourhood for fifty years, provision should be made for supplying a population of at least 12,500,000.

3. That in calculating the quantity of water required per head per day, the amount at present supplied by the companies should be increased by at least 10 per cent., and in no case should it be less than 35 gallons.'

With reference to the progress of the inquiry before the Commission, we report, for the information of the Council, that the Commission has now held seven sittings, and that, in addition to witnesses on behalf of the Water Companies and from the Thames Conservancy, the Chief Engineer of the Council was examined on Monday last, and scientific witnesses on behalf of the Council as to the quality of the water will be examined on Monday next.'"

The recommendations of the Committee were agreed to after some discussion, and having transacted other business, the Council adjourned shortly before six o'clock, the paper having been cleared an hour earlier than the usual time of adjournment.

Correspondence.

To the Editor of THE BUILDER.

THE STATUS OF THE ARCHITECT AT THE R.I.B.A.

SIR,—In view of last Monday's meeting at the R.I.B.A., and of the meaning of the result obtained (I venture to think not in the most straightforward manner), I would suggest that the time has come to discuss the desirability of the R.I.B.A. availing itself of the clause in its Charter giving it power to create new classes of subscribing members, on the following lines:—

Two new classes should be created, the first to be called "Architect Fellows," or some similar title, the qualification for this class being mainly the architectural beauty, refinement, and skill they show in their executed works. This, I consider, would be acceptable to very many, for until the body that should represent the mass of gentlemen practising as architects and surveyors in these kingdoms honours the leading men who practise the art of pure architecture, how can it expect to hope to raise the status of the general practitioner?

The other new class, to be called "Surveyor Associates," and to be open to gentlemen who are trained to, and follow the calling of, quantity surveyor, but who "practise in bricks and mortar" (that most felicitous term which we owe to one of our eminent Fellows). The qualification of these gentlemen to be the skill in planning and common-sense excellence shown in their works.

A reform like this, I think, would do much to improve the situation at the R.I.B.A. and raise the status of the architect.

SYDNEY VACHER.

CHANGES AT THE INSTITUTE.

SIR,—Will you permit me to emphasise the opinion expressed in your article of last week upon the election of Fellows of the Institute,—that they should be nominated from the ranks of examined Associates?* I cannot but consider that the Examination scheme, if it is to be supported with the same determination that has hitherto been directed towards it, demands this. I would maintain that no distinct examination for Fellows can be established. Candidates would not present themselves. The examination for Associates is valuable, inasmuch as to pass it, affords a *bona fides* that the candidate is an architectural student who has elected to follow architecture as a livelihood, and is, therefore, a fit person to become a member of a guild representing the craft. Without such a test it might be that he was only a surveyor, say, if he resided in London, or an auctioneer if in the country. To show that you possess some knowledge of materials, and would not treat stone, iron, and wood in precisely the same way, is to give some assurance that you may one day be an architect. This a student should be able to give at the end of his articles. But when seven years has elapsed, to ask a man to furnish a sample of his maturer skill and proficiency, towards no end whatever, is what no modest craftsman would do. Neither is it likely that he would possess so little respect for himself as to display his wares to be turned over by he knows not whom, and thrown back to him. I am not sure that it would not be less invidious were the Fellowship altogether abolished, and Membership only remain. But, things remaining as they are, it is clear that the member who has rendered himself eligible for Associateship after the manner prescribed, is the fittest, I had almost said the only possible person, to become a Fellow. At least let him have a voice as to who shall be elected over him.

AN ASSOCIATE.

* We expressed no opinion: we said we did not see how the Institute could avoid that conclusion.

IS THE PROVISION OF WARMTH AND VENTILATION COMPULSORY IN WORKROOMS?

SIR,—In addition to the above question, I would like to ask,—if compulsory, who is responsible for their introduction? I am induced to ask these questions, as I have been informed that at a certain West-end establishment some two dozen girls have to perform their daily work in a room in which there is no chimney, and therefore no means for providing warmth and ventilation, either by the usual open fire, or by other and more modern means. Ventilation is sought to be obtained by a skylight and a hole in one of the side walls; but generally these let in cold draughts, especially in winter, and are, therefore, more frequently closed than open. To obtain some little warmth in winter the gas is often lighted, as also a couple of gas stoves (without flues), and naturally the ventilators are closed. The influence upon the health of the workers, boxed up in such an apartment, can readily be imagined; one of them has just had to leave, her ailment having, no doubt, been aggravated by spending many days and evenings in this modern building, which has now been in existence over eighteen months. Are there many workrooms of this class in the metropolis?

M. R.

[*** By perusing the Factory Acts and the Public Health Acts, our correspondent will probably be able to answer his own question. It is the duty of factory inspectors to see that the provisions of the law are obeyed by owners of factories and workshops, and information of any clear infringement of the law should be given to them.]

DEVONIAN SCREENS.

SIR,—Mr. Hems, in his letter of last week calling attention to these interesting relics of wood-carving, enumerated the chancel screen at Holbeton as a fifteenth-century work. Knowing the screen well, I would point out to him that this is a unique Devonshire example of a particularly ornate description, and is of sixteenth-century date. It never had a cove, and was never intended to have one; but, apart from that, the original treatment in the upper portion, usually filled with tracery, but in this case filled with bunches of foliage of singular boldness, makes this screen of great architectural value, if only as a link between fifteenth-century and Jacobean screens.

E. S.

Plymouth.

The Student's Column.

WARMING BUILDINGS BY HOT WATER.

XXVI.

IRREGULAR FORMS OF APPARATUS—CONCLUSION.

TO carry the pipes of an apparatus in any way contrary to the principles laid down is, of course, never recommended, yet at the same time it is very commonly permissible if there is no possible means of doing otherwise. As an example, we can refer to the occasional practice of dipping a pipe, in greenhouse work, if a doorway has to be passed. In the ordinary way, the pipes are carried round the house some 12 in. above the floor level, and to pass beneath a doorway opening means a dip in a pipe of at least this distance. This would be effected as in fig. 107

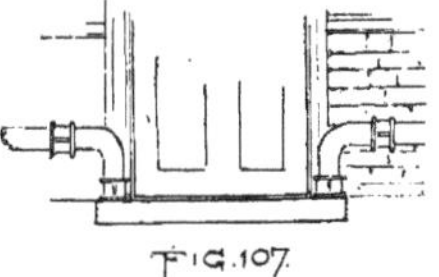

FIG. 107.

but instead of carrying a pipe beneath the path tiles, a special pipe of square design can be obtained, and this would lay flush with the floor.

Now, a dip in a pipe creates an obstacle to the free circulation in a way that will be described directly, and considering the low speed of circulation or motive power that we get in horticultural works, it is very little indeed that we dare attempt in this direction. With building works the circumstances are different, for the speed at which the water moves is so much greater. It will be seen that with works extending up only 2 ft. or 3 ft. the circulation is sluggish enough to be an objection at all times if the services extend any distance and a fair degree of heat is required at the further extremities; and if we introduce anything to make the circulation still slower, trouble will most probably ensue, even supposing the dip does not entirely destroy efficiency.

According to the present accepted theory, the circulation of water in any apparatus depends upon the difference in weight of hot and cold water; the water in one pipe being heavier than the water in the other, and causing the latter to ascend. With an apparatus as fig. 108,

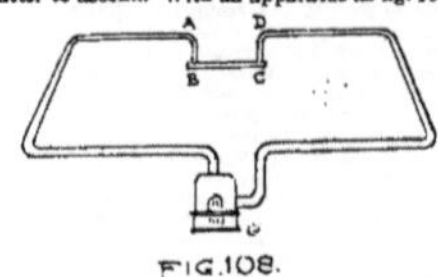

FIG. 108.

which we may suppose is a single pipe carried all the way round a house, we should have to pass a doorway somewhere, and the dip necessary to effect this is shown. (Let it be clearly understood that this is quite an imaginary arrangement, to illustrate the subject under discussion).

This apparatus can be carried, and would work in quite an ordinary manner, to the point marked A, and so it would to C if it did not have to rise again; but from C to D the water is colder and heavier than it is between A and B, and consequently it would tend to bring about a retrograde movement,—a movement in the contrary direction to what the water takes from the boiler to A. It is plain that the farther the water travels from the boiler the cooler it becomes, owing to its losing heat, as it is required to do; consequently the column of water C, D must be colder than that from A to B, and its greater weight naturally opposes the movement of water in an upward direction. A very well-known writer upon heat, in dealing with the circulatory action of heated water, adopts an ingenious method of making the subject clear, by spacing off the pipes in lengths of imaginary temperatures, as figs. 109 and 110.

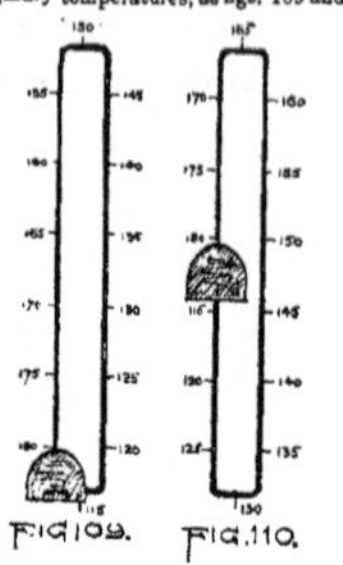
FIG. 109. FIG. 110.

By allowing a certain difference in weight to each space the theory can be very clearly dealt with.

With fig. 109 we have a difference in mean temperature in the two columns of water of 33 deg. This may be called 33 grains (the actual difference is a greater weight than this), the water in the return-pipe bringing about the circulation by it being thus much heavier than the water in the flow. By increasing or decreasing the height of the pipes the motive power will be increased or decreased proportionately. If we plan an apparatus as fig. 110 and space it off, we find in theory that we get an equal weight in each pipe, and we may suppose that the water would fail to circulate either way. By the same reasoning, we may expect a circulation more or less efficient by putting more pipe above the boiler than in the last cut, or, a reversed circulation if we carried the pipe further down below. This makes the theory plain, and in making dips in pipes it will be seen that, if of no great depth, they would prove no serious obstacle in building works, but in the average glass-house apparatus they are better avoided. As before mentioned, if, in these latter works, a dip did not actually stop the circulation, it would render the circulation more sluggish, and in long runs of pipe this is a great drawback.

Occasionally a boiler has to exist between two houses, which, being on rising ground, may bring one house a trifle lower than the boiler itself. This being the case, the more common plan adopted, to permit of the pipes in this

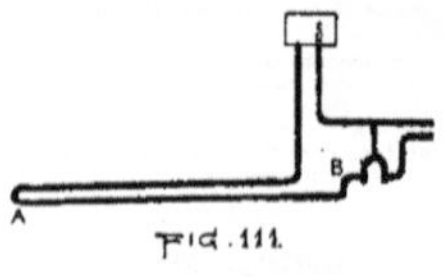

FIG. 111.

house being so low, is to use a tank as fig. 111. The further use of the tank is to act as a feed cistern and air exit. The service from the right of the boiler is supposed to go to heat the house that is of sufficient height, the service to the left is carried as shown, the flow to the tank by the most direct route, and the return acting as the radiating media. By thus circulating up to a higher point than usual, we get a more efficient circulation, a higher motive power, which is always sufficient to make the apparatus work well if the rise of the return-pipe to the boiler does not exceed, say 18 in. It will be understood that the tank shown is not absolutely necessary. If we carried pipe up to this height with a feed-cistern beside it, it would amount to the same thing, but would not have such a workmanlike appearance. The tank should have a cover to keep dirt from entering, as it fulfils the purposes of a supply-cistern as explained.

Occasionally, when a boiler is fixed somewhat centrally to the work, a tank is made use of, having a flow-pipe to it from the boiler, but having several returns running in different directions. The flow would be carried to the tank by the most direct route, as just explained, the returns acting as the radiating pipes. It is said in favour of this plan that it allows of the freest possible escape of air, and it is further suggested by those who recommend the plan, that by the use of wooden plugs in the return pipes where they leave the tank, the need of stop-cocks is dispensed with. Certainly by the use of a tank, placed in the highest position it can be, we get a better or stronger circulation, as will be understood.

The chief trouble experienced in works that depart from the regular form, is air dislodgment. It may appear an easy matter to many to get rid of air that, it is admitted, does get in the pipes, and which must exist in the pipes before they are first charged, but every man with experience knows that air dislodgment partakes of the nature of a problem sometimes, and the solution is not discovered in a moment. In the illustration, fig. 111, the return would descend to the point A, and then take an ascending direction all the way to the boiler, and, at first glance, there would be, apparently, no need for an air-pipe at all. This, however, is not the case, an air-pipe should be provided at B, not that there would be much use for it when the apparatus was once full and working well, but when charging the apparatus with water, there would be every probability of air being locked in the lower pipe between A and B, with ill results. In the same way an air vent would have to be provided both sides of the dip in figs. 107 and 108. It has to be particularly remembered also, that although an apparatus may perhaps be filled easily when first charging it, it does not follow that it can be filled as easily after it has had water once in it, for when emptying it will be practically impossible to get the water out of any dips there may be in the pipes, and these collecting points will prove obstacles to the free escape of air as the water is filled in again, unless, of course, air vents are provided.

This completes the papers upon "Warming Buildings by Hot-water," and our last suggestion to those who have the giving out of these works, is to ascertain that the people entrusted with the work are capable and experienced; and to those who execute the works, let it be an ambition to be master of the subject. This advice is, of course, good in all cases, but with hot-water works it is especially good, for it is really wonderful what perplexing difficulties a little want of knowledge may bring about, and what expense and trouble may be incurred in remedying such errors.

GENERAL BUILDING NEWS.

New Theological College, Edinburgh.—On Wednesday of last week, being the centenary of the repeal of the penal laws affecting the Episcopal Church of Scotland, a new Theological College in connexion with that church, was opened with fitting ceremony. The building is situated within its own grounds, in an appropriately retired spot about 100 yards to the westward of St. Mary's Cathedral. The nucleus of the building consists of a mansion house, called Coat's Hall, which was designed by the late Mr. David Bryce in the Scottish Baronial style, for the late Mr. Napier, sheriff of Peebles-shire. Considerable additions have been made to the original structure, including a beautiful little chapel. The college contains accommodation for twenty resident students. The adaptation of the original building, and the additions thereto, have been carried out in a thoroughly satisfactory manner by Messrs. Sydney, Mitchell, & Wilson, architects, Edinburgh.

Board School, Baildon, Yorkshire:—A new Board School, built at a cost of 2,750*l.*, including site, by the Baildon School Board, at Tong Park, was opened on the 11th inst. by Mr. Edward Holden, of Baildon. The new buildings, for which Messrs. W. & J. B. Bailey, of Bradford, have prepared the plans, are to accommodate 220 scholars.

Schools, Darnall, Yorkshire.—On the 4th inst. the Archbishop of York opened the new schools which have been erected in connexion with Darnall Parish Church. The new school building has two stories, the lower one for boys, the upper one for girls, while the infants are in the old school, which has been remodelled so as to give the requisite accommodation in an improved way. The rooms in the new building are arranged for Sunday-school purposes as well as for large parish meetings, &c. Accommodation for day-school purposes has been provided for 240 boys, 240 girls, and 212 infants. Block flooring of teak has been laid, and movable partitions have been placed between the school-room and the class-rooms, by which 600 persons may be seated in one room for meetings. The architect is Mr. C. J. Innocent, of Sheffield, and the contractors Messrs. George Longden & Son, Neepsend. All the buildings are of stone, walled in courses, and with ashlar dressings. The amount of the contract, including asphalting yards and boundary walling, is 3,912*l.*

Church and Schools, Poolstock, Wigan.—On the 4th inst. the foundation-stone of the Mission Church and Schools of St. James's, Poolstock, Wigan, was laid by Mrs. T. Brown, Shelley House, Wigan. They are to accommodate about 250 children, and will cost 1,500*l.* The architects are Messrs. Heaton & Ralph, of Wigan.

New Church, Bonane, Co. Kerry.—On Ascension Day the dedication of the new Church of Bonane took place. The church was designed by Mr. Daniel O'Connell, Derrynane House, and built by Mr. Daniel Foley, Sneem. The church consists of a nave, 70 ft. by 21 ft., and a sanctuary terminating in a pentagonal apse.

Congregational Buildings, South Shields.—On the 6th inst. the foundation-stone was laid of a new Congregational school and hall, to be built adjoining the Ocean-road Church, South Shields. The building will be raised upon the vacant ground on the east side of the church, and completes the original scheme. The ground floor will contain the hall, 74 ft. by 36 ft. 6 in., and 20 ft. high, with raised platform and ante-rooms at the far end, and having tea and boiler rooms beneath. On the first floor, which will be approached by a stone staircase from the main entrance, is an infants' school, 30 ft. by 25 ft., and eight class-rooms. The heating is to be by hot-water piping, with ventilating coils for the admission of warm air. The contract for the work has been let to Mr. George Goddard, Westoe, and Mr. J. H. Morton, South Shields, is the architect.

Tower, Waddesdon Church.—On Wednesday was dedicated the rebuilt tower of Waddesdon Church, Bucks. It is an unusually fine tower of the fourteenth century, of massive proportions, and contains a peal of eight cast steel bells. It had been in a critical condition for some years, and when taken down, it was with difficulty that accidents were avoided. The interior of the walls was disintegrated throughout, having been built with earth and rubble for mortar. Enormous buttresses had been erected, which, however, failed to afford support to it, for the foundation of the tower, though 6 ft. deep, rested on 2 ft. of soft, wet clay. The tower has been rebuilt as nearly as possible upon its old lines, but with new western doorway, a west window under the old curtain rib, and a turret staircase at the south-east corner. In the pulling down, portions of an old turret staircase were found embedded in the wall. The turret and tower alike are finished with battlements. The old vane is fixed in the centre of the lead roof. The total cost has been about 1,900*l*. Two hundred tons of lime were used in the work. Great care has been taken to protect and preserve the weathered surface of the old stones as far as possible. The new stone for dressed work is from the Hornton and the Ham-hill quarries, with local limestone for walling. Mr. Sherwin, a local builder, who has been clerk of works at Baron Rothschild's mansion in the same parish, obtained the contract, the architect being Mr. William White, F.S.A.

CONSERVATIVE CLUB, FAILSWORTH.—The foundation-stones of the Failsworth Mowbray Conservative Club, which is to take the place of the "Mowbray" Conservative Club in Failsworth, were laid recently by Sir John Mowbray, Bart., M.P., Mr. R. G. C. Mowbray, M.P., and other gentlemen. The new building, apart from the furnishings and extra items, will cost 1,450*l*. It will be faced with Accrington plastic bricks on the two principal entrances, interspersed with stone and red Ruabon terra-cotta dressings. The contractors were, for excavating and brickwork, Messrs. S. & J. Smethurst; masonry, Mr. Joseph Clough; carpenter and joiners' work, Mr. J. W. Kent; slating, Mr. J. Jackson; plumbing, glazing, and painting, Mr. J. Whittle; plastering, Mr. J. Hall. The whole is being erected from the designs, and under the superintendence, of Mr. Charles T. Taylor, architect, of Oldham.

WORKMEN'S DWELLINGS, BIRMINGHAM.—Plans have been prepared, and building operations will immediately be commenced, for the erection of three shops and sixty-eight workmen's dwellings at Vauxhall, a densely-populated district of the city of Birmingham. The erection of these houses at the present time will meet a much-felt requirement, as a great number of dilapidated and unsanitary buildings have recently been demolished in this locality. A new street is in course of formation which will form frontages for a portion of these residences. The total cost of the buildings is estimated at about 11,000*l*. The contractor is Mr. Williams, and the architect, Mr. J. Statham Davis, both of Birmingham.

NEW CHANCEL, POPLAR CHURCH.—On the 5th inst. the newly-formed chancel of Poplar Church was opened. The work just finished forms one of the six sections of the work of restoration now being carried out in the church. In the sanctuary the east window has been covered over and new windows have been formed. A new dossal and hangings surround the walls at the end of the chancel, and a new altar table with retable of marble has been provided. The old choir stalls have been added to, and the chancel floor has been raised above the floor further westward. The new floors are of marble. The old wooden pulpit has been removed, and an open pulpit of bronze and iron put in its place. The cost of the works just finished will be about 600*l*. The general contract has been carried out by Mr. J. Kemp Coleman, of Poplar. The pulpit was executed by Messrs. Strode & Co., of Regent's Park, from the designs of the architects, Messrs. J. & S. F. Clarkson, Great Ormond-street, W.C.

THE NEW ADMIRALTY BUILDINGS.—Messrs. Mark Fawcett & Co. inform us that their fireproof and ventilating floors have been selected for the above buildings, and that the contract for the whole of the floors, ceilings, roofs, domes, &c., with the constructional steel work, connected therewith, has been placed with them.

SANATORIUM, LADYWELL, NEAR ECCLES.—On the 15th inst., the Mayor of Salford (Alderman P. Keevney) opened the new Ladywell sanatorium or hospital for infectious diseases, which has been erected at a total cost of 50,000*l*., at Ladywell, near Eccles. The hospital is situated on the Eccles New-road, and has been erected by Messrs. R. Neill & Sons, Salford, from the designs of Messrs. Maxwell & Tuke and Messrs. E. & F. Hewitt, of Manchester. The hospital is divided into isolated blocks and pavilions. The three pavilions include six centre wards, each being 45 ft. by 26 ft., containing six beds each, and six convalescent wards, 120 ft. by 26 ft., containing eighteen beds each. There are thirty-three nurses' bedrooms. The hospital is heated with steam, and steam is applied to all the disinfecting, washing, and cooking apparatus; also to work the laundry engine, electric-engine, and pumps. A hydraulic lift is provided to raise patients to the upper stories. There are verandahs and gardens for the convenience of patients, and space is left for an extension of the sanatorium.

PROPOSED PUBLIC BUILDINGS, BATH.—At the Bath Guildhall, on the 14th inst., Mr. S. J. Smith, C.E., Local Government Board Inspector, held an inquiry into the application of the Corporation to borrow 6,000*l*. for purchasing three houses in the Abbey Churchyard, for the site of a proposed extension of the Pump-room, and to borrow 35,000*l*. for the purpose of erecting new municipal buildings. With regard to the first application, evidence was given by Mr. Radway, chairman of the Baths Committee, as to the increased number of bathers and takings at the baths, and the need of providing additional accommodation for the visitors. Alderman Gibbs objected to the proposal as unnecessary, though he agreed that something should be done to protect the Roman remains. The application with regard to the municipal buildings was supported by Alderman Murch (ex-Mayor), Alderman Gibbs, Colonel Ford (senior magistrate of the city), Mr. Stone (town clerk), and others, the plans being explained by Mr. J. M. Brydon, the architect. With regard to the objections to the new buildings encroaching on the pavement near the Abbey, the inspector said he would have the building-line shown on the pavement in chalk.

WESLEYAN SUNDAY SCHOOL, HARROGATE.—On the 16th inst., the memorial-stones of a Wesleyan Sunday school were laid at Grove-road, Harrogate. The cost of the chapel and school will be about 5,000*l*., but the chapel will not be proceeded with yet. The architects are Messrs. Morley & Woodhouse, of Bradford. The contractors are—mason's work, Alderman Simpson (Harrogate); joiner, Mr. Checkley (Harrogate); and plasterer, Mr. Laycock (Harrogate).

SANITARY AND ENGINEERING NEWS.

THE PLUMBERS' REGISTRATION BILL.—At a special meeting of the Glasgow Master Plumbers' Association, the Plumbers' Registration Bill, as amended by the Select Committee of the House of Commons, and the Blue Book containing the evidence taken by the Committee, were submitted. The Association entirely approved of the amended Bill, and resolved to petition Parliament in its favour.

CRAVEN ARMS WATER SUPPLY.—This matter has occupied the attention of the authorities for the last seven years. Various schemes have been propounded, but, from unforeseen difficulties, none of them could be carried out. It is hoped, however, that a satisfactory solution of the difficulty has at last been found. A trial boring has just been completed, and pumping from it kept up day and night for a fortnight. The quantity pumped was over 50,000 gallons a day, more than three times the quantity required for the present supply of the district. Mr. Wyatt, of Shrewsbury, is the engineer, and Messrs. Timmins, of Runcorn, the contractors.

FOREIGN AND COLONIAL.

FRANCE.—We mentioned last week that, on account of some disputes, the voting at the Champs Elysées Salon for the awarding of the medal of honour in the architectural section was postponed. Another election was held last Saturday, and, after two tours of inspection, the medal was awarded, by 98 votes out of 103, to M. Louis Marie Cordonnier, artist of the Palais de la Bourse at Amsterdam. This young architect, who lives at Lille (Nord) is a pupil of his father and M. André.——The jury of the École des Beaux-Arts, in the superior competition of anatomy, has awarded the Huguier prize to M. Guilmant, pupil of MM. Bouguereau and Gabriel Ferrier.——The Raigecourt-Goyon prize has been awarded to M. Marius Ferrets for his picture, "Départ des Pirogues pour la Pêche," which was exhibited at the Champs Elysées Salon.——The Institute have not been able, on account of poverty of materials, to award the Bordin prize this year, the subject for which was "Develope the National Characteristics of French Sculpture from the Thirteenth Century to the Revolution."——A curious exhibition of the geographical documents of the sixteenth century has just been opened at the National Library, on the anniversary of the fourth centenary of Christopher Columbus.——The sea painter Léon Haskman has just opened an exhibition of his works at 39, Boulevard des Capucins, under the title "L'épopée de la Mer."——The monument to the memory of Stendhal has just been inaugurated. The monument, which is in the Montmartre Cemetery, is of grey granite, decorated with a bronze medallion of Stendhal by David Angers, fils.——A petition has lately been addressed to Government for the removal of the Polytechnic School to the buildings of the Lycée Lakanal at Bourg-la-Reine, near Sceaux.——Ninety-two artists have taken part in the open competition for the decoration of the "Salle des Mariages" of the Town Hall of Montreuil-sous-Bois. The decision will take place next week.——M. Maurice Yvon is nominated architect of the French Colonies at the International Exhibition at Chicago.——*A propos* of the recent inauguration of the statue of Claude Lorraine at Nancy, the German journals remark that it is a long time since a commemorative monument has been raised to this painter in the environs of Munich.——A company of engineers and learned Frenchmen is shortly to start for Sardes in Asia Minor, for the purpose of excavating.——Last week the bust of the satirical poet Crinon was inaugurated at Vraignes (Somme). The bust is the work of M. Georges Tattegrain, and the model was exhibited in the Salon des Champs Elysées this year.——July 15 is the last day for sending in designs for the open competition for the statue of Joan of Arc in the town of Chinon.——It is announced that an artistic exhibition will be opened at Nice on January 10 next, and closed at the end of March.——The spire of the Church of Bourmont has been completely destroyed during a storm.——The town of Vichy is organising an industrial and artistic exhibition to be held in the buildings of an old hospital; it will be opened on July 1.——The town of Périgueux (Dordogne) has just acquired a beautiful mosaic, which was discovered in the environs last year, and which is of a pure style of Archaic Greek. The mosaic is composed almost entirely of geometric designs.——M. J. Blass, political draughtsman, attached to several Parisian journals, especially the *Caricature* and the *Pilori*, has just died at the age of forty-five years.——M. Alcide Loron, landscape painter, has just shot himself. The suicide is attributed to unhappiness. He was thirty-nine.——We have also to mention the death of M. Jean François Delarue, member of the Central Society of Architects, who died in Paris at the age of seventy-two. He was a pupil of Moreau and Heurteloup. To him we owe the church of St. Cloud, that of Croissy, the gate of Randon at Grenoble, the restoration of the château of La Sauzinière, at Nantes, and numerous other works. He was a Chevalier of the Legion of Honour.

MISCELLANEOUS.

THE "EIFFEL" STAIR TREAD.—This is a leaden stair tread crossed by furrows leaving raised squares arranged diamond-wise, the special feature of which is that whilst the lead is in a molten state numerous small lengths of iron, brass, steel, or white metal tubes are inserted vertically in the thickness of the lead and finishing level with it. The surface of the lead affords a good foothold when new; as it is worn down and more or less polished by the traffic the rings of harder metal are left protruding slightly above the surface, and keep up a roughened surface. The sample of the tread submitted to us seems a thoroughly sound thing, the harder metal being firmly incorporated with the lead, and the invention is worth attention as a means of preventing the slippery state to which stair-treads, which are satisfactory when first laid down, are often reduced when worn. Mr. F. Fitton, of Rochdale, is the inventor.

PETERBOROUGH CATHEDRAL.—Mr. Hitch writes to us again to say that he did not claim the carving *en masse* on the Bishop's Throne as his work, but only the figure sculpture, the decorative carving being by Mr. Thompson's workmen.

CUTTING OFF THE WATER SUPPLY.—The President of the Local Government Board and the Home Secretary have under their notice a question of serious moment, which has arisen since the Public Health (London) Act, 1891, has been put in force. Since the new Act came into operation the Chelsea Water Company has increased its "cutting-off" action nearly sixfold, and during the past two months the District Medical Officer of Health, in his report to the Chelsea Vestry, states that no fewer than twenty-one occupied houses have had their water supply cut off. The Public Health Act, section 49, provides that a water company which has cut off the water supply from a house for non-payment of rate or other cause is required to give notice thereof within twenty-four hours after cutting off the supply to the Sanitary Authority of the district. Section 48 of the same Act provides that an occupied house without proper and sufficient supply of water shall be a nuisance liable to be dealt with summarily under the Act, and, if it is a dwelling-house, shall be deemed unfit for human habitation. The water company, therefore, in exercising the power it has under the Waterworks Clauses Act, 1847, creates a nuisance, liable to be dealt with summarily under the Public Health Act. This is an anomalous state of affairs, for it is one which might seriously affect the public health.—*British Medical Journal.*

THE NEW CENTRAL ELECTRIC STATION IN COPENHAGEN.—The central electric station, erected by the municipality of Copenhagen, has been opened. At present it can only supply about 17,000 lamps, but it may be enlarged so as to supply 40,000. The cable rut, on the treble wire system, is 90 kilomètres in length. At present the steam-engines are three,—one 330 and two of 550 h.-p. each. Each engine works two dynamos. There is also a battery of accumulators, capable of supplying 3,000 lamps for three hours. The electrical plant has been delivered by Messrs. Siemens & Halske, and the steam-engines and boilers by Messrs. Babcock & Wilcox, London and Glasgow. The cost of the establishment is 142,000*l*.

BUILDING LAND AT HASTINGS.—As will be seen by an advertisement in another part of this week's *Builder*, Messrs. E. & H. Lumley will offer for sale on Thursday next, the 30th inst., fifty plots of building land on the St. Helen's Park Estate, Hastings.

NEW PARK AND STREET IMPROVEMENTS AT DEWSBURY.—The Corporation of Dewsbury has just received the Local Government Board's sanction for the borrowing of 41,250*l*. This sum is to be expended in the purchase and laying out of

COMPETITIONS, CONTRACTS, AND PUBLIC APPOINTMENTS.

COMPETITIONS.

Nature of Work.	By whom Advertised.	Premium.	Designs to be delivered.
*Public Baths	Walsall Corp.	50l., 30l., & 20l.	July 16
*Town Hall	do.	21l. and 10l. 10s.	July 18
*Construction of Sand-guard and Widening Marine Parade	Borough of Blackpool	20l.	July 29
*Infectious Diseases Hospital	Keighley Corp.	15l. and 10l.	July 30

CONTRACTS.

Nature of Work or Materials.	By whom Required.	Architect, Surveyor, or Engineer.	Tenders to be delivered.
*Hire of Steam Roller	West Sussex C. C.	*Official*	June 27
*Rebuilding Breadboorne Bridge, &c.	do.	do.	do.
*Iron and Stoneware Pipe Sewers, &c.	Watford U.R.S.A.	Urban Smith	do.
*Painting Exterior, Chase Farm School	Edmonton Union	Mr. Knightley	June 28
*Supply of Materials	St. Martin-in-the-Fields Vestry	C. Mason	do.
Sliding Partitions, &c.	Plymouth School Bd.	*Official*	do.
Sewering, Levelling, Paving, &c.	Rastrick Local Board	do.	June 29
Lodge, Forres, Elgin, N.B.	Trustees of Forres Leanchoil Hospital	Mr. Dorrell	do.
Cementing, &c. Old Durham-road	Gateshead Corp.	J. Bower	June 30
*Whitewashing, &c. at Infirmary	St. Saviour's Union	Jarvis & Son	do.
*Repairing Roofs of Workhouse	do.	do.	do.
Alterations and Additions to Stores, Wadebridge	....	W. T. M. Mear	do.
Workmen's House, Cymmer Collieries Porth	Committee	....	do.
Stores, Otley	Leeds Indus. Co-op. Soc. Lim.	....	do.
Stores, Church-street, Hunslet	do.	....	do.
Additions, &c. Girls' National Schools, Ripon	....	T. Butler Wilson	do.
*Industrial School, Lichfield	Burton-on-Trent and Walsall School Bd.	R. Stevenson	do.
Asphalting (5,300 sq. yds.)	Halifax Corp.	E. R. S. Escott	July 2
Infants' School, New Tredegar	....	James & Morgan	do.
Shop, Dynas Powis, Cardiff	Geo. Hopkins	W. H. D. Caple	do.
Retort Fittings, Hydraulic Mains, &c.	Sheffield United Gas Light Co.	F. W. Stevenson	do.
*Private Street Improvements	Beckenham Local Bd.	G. B. Carlton	July 4
Brick Gasholder Tank, &c.	Cromer Gas & Coke Co. Lim.	J. Church	do.
*Chapels, Caretakers' Houses, &c. at Cemetery	Oxford Loc. Bd.	W. H. White	do.
*Deepening, &c. Cubitt Town Dry Docks	The Co.	F. E. Duckham	do.
Repairs, &c. Cemetery Chapel and Curator's Office	Carlisle Burial Board	*Official*	do.
*York Paving and Broken Granite	Bermondsey Vestry	do.	do.
*Supply of Road Material	Lewisham B. of W.	do.	July 5
*Pipe Sewers, &c.	East Ham Local Bd.	—Savage	do.
*Oak Cleft Fencing	Barking Town L. B.	C. J. Dawson	do.
*Granite Kerb	do.	do.	do.
*Tarpaving	do.	do.	do.
*Stoneware Sewers and Drains, &c.	do.	do.	do.
*8,000 tons of Lime	London C. C.	*Official*	do.
Road Improvements, Barnton, Frodsham	Daresbury High. Bd.	John Swinton	do.
Iron Castings, &c.	Carlisle Gas Com.	J. Hepworth	do.
*Surface Water Drains, &c.	Leyton Loc. Bd.	W. Dawson	do.
Cast-iron Valve Tower, Valves, &c. also Footbridge, Upper Edwick	Baildon Local Board	B. Walker	do.
*Kentish Flints	Southend Local Board	P. Dodd	do.

CONTRACTS.—*Continued.*

Nature of Work or Materials.	By whom Required.	Architect, Surveyor, or Engineer.	Tenders to be delivered.
Service Reservoir and other works	Plympton St. Mary R.S.A.	B. J. Shier	July 6
*Asphalte and Wood Paving Works	Ves. of St. Margaret, & St. John, Westminster	G. W. R. Wheeler	do.
*Construction of Embankment Wall, &c.	Fulham Vestry	J. P. Norrington	do.
*Making-up and Paving Road	do.	W. Sykes	do.
*Painters' Work and Repairs at Infirmary	Chelsea Guardians	A. & C. Harston	do.
*Three Shops, Kingston-on-Thames	....	F. & W. Stocker	do.
Infectious Diseases Hospital	Wortley U.R.S.A.	G. A. Wilde	July 7
*Erection of Waiting Room, Whitechapel	Baths & Washhouses Com.	B. J. Capell	do.
*Making-up Waldeck-road	Ealing Loc. Bd.	C. Jones	do.
*Sinking, &c. Three 12 ft. Wells	Tonbridge Water Works Co. Lim.	*Official*	do.
*Sorting-office, Tunbridge Wells	H. M. Works	do.	July 8
School Extensions	South Shields Sch. Bd.	J. W. Hanson	do.
*Water-tight Dam for Reservoir, &c.	Brymbo Steel Co. Lim.	*Official*	July 9
Villa, Grantown, Elgin, N.B.	....	G. Sutherland	July 11
*Police Station, Braintree	Essex County Council	H. Stock	July 14
*Labourers' Dwellings	Manchester Corp.	Spalding & Cross	do.
*Concrete Floor, &c. Leavesden Asylum	Met. Asy. Bd.	*Official*	July 15
*Paving and Kerbing Footpaths	Maldon U.S.A.	P. M. Beaumont	July 16
*Draining Temple-street	Strood Estate Co. Lim.	W. Banks	July 19
Works, Hartwell House, near Exeter	C. R. Collins	J. Jerman	No date.
Two Detached Villas, Llandaff	....	Llewellyn & Price	do.
Club Houses, St. Hilda's, Darlington	....	Clark & Moscrop	do.
Sinking Trial Shaft, Hipperholme, Halifax	....	Raymond Berry	do.
*Whitewashing, &c. Works at Infirmary	Mile End Old Town Guar.	*Official*	do.
*House, St. Leonard's-on-Sea	Miss Waterhouse	G. T. Redmayne	do.
*Residence, with Stabling, &c. Bournemouth	....	R. G. Pinder	do.
*Restoration of Warnbrook Church	The Vicar	G. H. Gordon	do.
Masonry Work at Court House, Carlisle	....	G. Dale Oliver	do.
School Buildings, Blackwell-road, Carlisle	....	do.	do.
Wing, Tower, Dining-hall, &c. Aspatria, (Cumbld) Agric. College	Dr. H. J. Webb	T. Taylor Scott	do.
Banking Premises, Bradford Old Bank, Tadcaster	....	Bromet & Thorman	do.
Two Houses, Armley, Leeds	Joseph Proctor	F. W. Rhodes	do.
Six Through Houses, Armley Lodge Estate, Leeds	....	J. Eastwood	do.
Additions, &c. Wheatfield Lodge, Headingley, Leeds	J. Nicholson	T. Butler Wilson	do.
Granite Road Metal (250 tons)	Hanslope High. Surv.	*Official*	do.
School Buildings, Longport, Staffs.	....	A. R. Wood	do.
Workhouse Infirmary	Stafford Union	Geo. Wormal	do.
*Chapel, Gray's-Inn Gardens	....	....	do.

PUBLIC APPOINTMENTS.

Nature of Appointment.	By whom Advertised.	Salary.	Applications to be in.
*Temporary Clerk of Works	Fulham Vestry	3l. 3s.	June 29
*Clerk of Works	Met. Asy. Bd.	4l. 4s.	June 30
*Engineering Assistant	Leicester Corp.	200l.	July 4
*Road Surveyor	Hackney B. of W.	2l. 10s.	do.
*Teachers	Proposed Indian Handicraft School	....	July 30
*Accountant Clerk, Director of Works Department	Civil Service Commrs.	....	Aug. 4
*Assistant Instructor in Geometrical Drawings	Royal Indian Engineering College	250l.	No date

Those marked with an Asterisk (*) are advertised in this Number. Competitions, p. iv. Contracts, pp. iv., vi., viii. ix. & xxiii. Public Appointments, p. xx.

public park, and in street improvements. The park is to cost 33,250l., and will be laid out in accordance with the design prepared by Mr. Henry C. Marks, Assoc. M. Inst. C.E., the Borough Engineer and Surveyor, which includes ornamental waters, lodges, and three miles six furlongs of drives and promenades.

NEW LANDING STAGE, HOLYHEAD.—The new landing-place erected at Holyhead, at a cost of about 2,500l., was declared open by Commander E. Scobell Clapp on the 20th inst. The pier is about 220 ft. long, with an "L" arm 60 ft. long. It is 23 ft. high from low water spring tide, and 12 ft. wide from the corner of the Newry yard, and 9 ft. from there to the shore end. The pier is paved on the top with stone pitching, having a hand-rail of rod iron on the side, and a wall at the extreme end, with cement coping, about 4 ft. high. It has a double landing-place. Mr. Corton was the engineer, and Mr. Williams was the contractor.

THE SOCIETY OF ARTS.—The Council have awarded the Society's Silver Medal to the following, among other readers of papers during the Session 1891-2:—At the Ordinary Meetings: To Prof. Silvanus P. Thompson, F.R.S., for his paper on "Measurement of Lenses;" to Mr. G. H. Robertson, F.C.S., for his paper on "Secondary Batteries;" to Prof. Vivian B. Lewes, for his paper on "Spontaneous Ignition of Coal, and its Prevention;" to Mr. Robert S. McCormick, for his paper on "The Trade Relations of Great Britain and the United States;" to Captain W. de W. Abney, C.B., F.R.S., for his paper on "Colour Blindness;" and to Mr. F. E. Ives, for his paper on "Composite Heliochromy." In the Applied Art Section: To Mr. William Morris, M.A., for his paper on "The Woodcuts of Gothic Books;" to Mr. C. Purdon Clarke, C.I.E., for his paper on "English Brocades and Figured Silks;" and to Mr. William de Morgan, for his paper on "Lustre Ware." Thanks were voted to Mr. James Dredge, for his paper on "The Columbian Exposition at Chicago, 1893." Mr. Dredge being a member of Council, and, therefore, under the usual practice of the Council in such cases, not eligible for the award of a medal.

RENOVATION OF THE ROUND ROOM OF THE MANSION HOUSE, DUBLIN.—According to the *Freeman's Journal*, the historic Round Room of the Mansion House, Dublin, has recently undergone renovation. The work was entrusted to Messrs. Sibthorpe & Son, of Dublin. The ceiling of the room has been remodelled to a considerable extent. Immediately below the ceiling is the new cornice, which is formed of fibrous plaster. There are sixteen circular windows, underneath which are fitted leaded lights of tinted cathedral glass. On either side of these windows are thirty-two circular shields, representing every county in Ireland, and in which are shown the arms of the four provinces and principal towns, with wreaths of shamrock. The architectural details below the original and larger cornice have been coloured in white and gold. The architrave is supported by several new pilasters in enamelled wood, coloured in red and gold with festoons. The walls and railings of the balcony are stained in old gold with ornamental gilding. The drapery hangings of the balcony are new. The dais has also been improved. Mr. C. Ashlin, architect, afforded a good deal of assistance in the carrying out of the details. The whole alterations were carried out under the plans of Mr. Spencer Harty, Borough Engineer.

STAINED GLASS WINDOW, CHRIST CHURCH, CLIFTON.—The large west window of Christ Church, Clifton, Gloucestershire, has been filled in with stained glass, the gift of Mr. W. A. F. Powell. The window is a triplet of lancet-headed lights, the central one being more than 25 ft. in height. The subject selected illustrates "The Te Deum." The window has been designed and executed by Messrs. Joseph Bell & Sons, of Bristol.

MEETINGS.

SATURDAY, JUNE 25.

St. Paul's Ecclesiological Society.—Visit to the Churches of Crayford and Dartford.

Edinburgh Architectural Association.—The Sketching Class to meet at Royston House, Carolina Park, Granton, to make measured drawings and sketches of the south front of the mansion. 3 p.m.

MONDAY, JUNE 27.

Royal Institute of British Architects.—(1) Presentation of the Royal Gold Medal to M. César Daly, Hon. Corr. Member. (2) Reading of a description of the collection of architectural drawings by Palladio and others, originally obtained by the Earl of Burlington, and now lent by the Duke of Devonshire. 8 p.m.

WEDNESDAY, JUNE 29.

Builders' Foremen and Clerks of Works' Institution.—Half-yearly meeting of the Directors. 8 p.m.

THURSDAY, JUNE 30.

Dundee Institute of Architecture.—Annual Business Meeting. 8 p.m.

SATURDAY, JULY 2.

Edinburgh Architectural Association.—The Sketching Class to meet at Royston House, Carolina Park, Granton, to make measured drawings and sketches of the south front of the mansion. 3 p.m.

RECENT PATENTS:

ABSTRACTS OF SPECIFICATIONS.

8,500.—BRICK MAKING: *F. & C. Roper.*—This invention relates to improvements in dies or moulds for making bricks, and has for its object to provide an improved passage for the clay from the box into or around the die, and also a self-acting contrivance for moistening the clay and die near the outlet. The invention consists in the construction of tapering guide frames for use in connexion with brick mills and the like, whereby the clay will pass with greater ease and regularity into the die, without being broken by contact with clay left in the angular recesses. Also in the construction of metal frames for brick dies, with a grove running round for the purpose of moistening the clay, by a small supply of water on its passage to the outlet. The inventor sets perforated rods for making holes in bricks, in perforator bars, placed at an angle, so that the rods will maintain an uniform converging direction towards the centre of the outlet, and the clay pass smoothly over them.

11,209.—BRICK, &C., PRESERVATIVE: *H. Aitken.*—An invention to prevent or lessen the destruction or deterioration of stone, brick-work, plaster, mortar, or stucco, or the like. It consists in the use of corrosive sublimate or bichloride of mercury, preferably in the form of a strong solution. The inventor considers that the deterioration in the above materials arise from living organisms, and gives various substances to destroy the same.

11,435.—BUILDING BLOCKS: *F. W. Holloway.*—Improvements in building blocks for arches, &c. The object of the invention is to form from stone, concrete, or other suitable materials, blocks of such uniform shapes of their respective class as by the aid of key blocks, comprise when set in mortar or other adhesive materials, arches without any cutting. Each block or voussoir being a repetition in shape formed respectively with upright or sloping joint beds, with ledge or bearing so that each will fit the adjoining block. The claim as set out in the specification is for:—First: Blocks or voussoirs, for use in building arches, or horizontally bridging openings in brickwork, being moulded or formed with steps, and vertical or sloping joint beds, the depth of such blocks or voussoirs being made to correspond with any required number of courses of brickwork. Secondly: In blocks or voussoirs, the formation of furrows, frogs, or other indents in the joint-beds, by which to bind the work in a manner more effectually to resist lateral pressure.

5,067.—TILES: *H. Miralles y Angles.*—This invention consists in imitation tiles to be used in place of porcelain, faïence, or other tiles for wall decoration and like purposes, the imitation tiles having the same size and general aspect as the ordinary tiles in the same designs, colours, and lustre, but made of paper, or card cut to the proper size, and printed or lithographed, and stuck on a backing of pasteboard, wood, sheet metal, or other backing, not clay, suitable for giving them the necessary strength. If relief is desired, it may be effected in any suitable way, so that the imitation tiles may not differ in appearance from those they are desired to resemble. They are covered with any suitable transparent varnish.

6,745.—CEMENT: *V. F. L. Smidth.*—The object of this invention is to manufacture from ordinary cements, especially portland, a cheaper cement, from which can be prepared mortar having the high qualities of cement mortar, but being in cost of production equal to, or lower than, ordinary lime mortars. The inventor grinds together ordinary cement and a quantity of the same admixture as that which is generally used in the preparation of cement mortar to produce a powder called sand cement, of a similar degree of fineness as that of ordinary cement. This sand cement is then to be used in the same way as ordinary cement, mortar being prepared by mixing one part of sand cement with one or more parts of the ordinary admixture. By grinding together, *e.g.*, one part of ordinary cement and three parts of sand, four parts of sand cement are produced, and from these a mortar can be prepared in the proportion of one part of sand-cement and three parts of sand, so that out of the one part of ordinary cement sixteen parts of mortar are prepared, when, under ordinary circumstances, only four to five parts of mortar would have been prepared out of one part of cement.

NEW APPLICATIONS FOR LETTERS PATENT.

June 7.—10,717, J. Short, Chambers for Drying Bricks, &c.—10,718, C. Judson, Doors, Grates, &c., Shutters, the improvements being specially applicable for use in connexion with elevators.—10,724, W. Wheeler, Water-waste Preventing Cisterns for Flushing Purposes.—10,755, W. Ward & Sons, Limited, and W. Ward, Brick Presses.—10,801, S. Croff, Machines for the Manufacture of Nails and Screws.—10,813, A. Sailer, Construction of Bridges.—10,815, G. Glasson, Sash-weight and Method of Hanging Sashes.

June 8.—10,831, E. Buller, Guard for Preventing Persons' Fingers, Clothing, &c., being shut between the Inside of Doors and Frames.—10,867, S. Jenkinson, Attaching Table Tops to the Frames thereof.

June 9.—10,911, O Hass, Hermetical Closures for Doors.—10,914, T. Riordan, Door Bells.—10,918, V. Aston, Balancing Window-sashes.—10,927, H. Birkbeck, Process for Preparation of a Material for Building or other purposes.

June 10.—10,963, J. Day, Drainage and other Socket-pipes to Facilitate Jointing.—10,964, W. Smyrk, Sash-fastenings.—10,974, A. Walker, Buttons for Doors, &c.

June 11.—10,991, A Selig, Bakers' Ovens.—11,009, W. Steele, Securing Doors in one direction only.—11,022, T. Winter, Cowl.—11,025, J. Blane, Wooden Blocks for Covering Floors, &c.

PROVISIONAL SPECIFICATIONS ACCEPTED.

2,912, H. Fenning, A new T-square and Drawing-easel for the use of Architects, Engineers, and Surveyors.—7,224, H. Thompson, Grates or Stoves.—7,692, H. Kepslogle, Spirit-level.—7,900, J. Major, Domestic Grates.—9,142, A. Fife, Building Block and Electric Insulator.—9,847, W. John, Facing Bricks or Tiles.

COMPLETE SPECIFICATIONS ACCEPTED.

(Open to Opposition for Two Months.)

11,102, J. Parker, Window-sashes, &c.—11,617, J. Severn, Kilns for Heating or Burning Pottery, &c.—6,860, G. Sparling and F. Solomon, Lock or Fastener for Securing Window Sashes.—8,352, C. Borgner, Bricks.—8,881, C. Behn, House Drains.—8,725, G. Moeckel, Arches for Ceilings and Vaults.

SOME RECENT SALES OF PROPERTY:

ESTATE EXCHANGE REPORT.

June 13.—By *G. A. Wilkinson & Son*: "The Wheatsheaf" Public-house, Rotherhithe, f., r. 50*l*., 755*l*.; 298, 300, 334, and 336, Rotherhithe-st., f., r. 82*l*. 3s., 800*l*.; "Aaruna Wharf," area 5,328 ft., f., 1,850*l*.; f.g.r. of 55*l*. 10s., Wilson-st., Battersea, reversion in 60 yrs., 1,445*l*.; f.g.r. of 30*l*., Villa-rd., Brixton, u.t. 80 yrs., g.r. 8*l*., 550*l*. By *Ranch & Parkhouse*: 52, 53, and 54, Grovedale-rd., Holloway, u.t. 81 yrs., g.r. 15*l*. 15s., 600*l*. By *T. B. Westacott*: 13 and 14, Murray-st., Camden Town, u.t. 52 yrs., g.r. 16*l*., 600*l*.; 3, Rochester-rd., u.t. 50 yrs., g.r. 6*l*., 520*l*.; 60, Camden-rd., u.t. 38 yrs., no g.r., r. 55*l*., 625*l*. By *A. Young*: 9, Rydon-cres., f. Clerkenwell, 870*l*. By *E. Millard*: 40, Northside, Clapham Common, f., 1,450*l*.—By *E. Wood*: 3, Botolph's, Sevenoaks, u.t. 84 yrs., g.r. 14*l*., r. 65*l*., 550*l*.; 78, Newington-green-rd., Stoke Newington, u.t. 60 yrs., g.r. 7*l*., r. 42*l*., 350*l*.; "Upton Villa," Mackenzie-rd., Beckenham, f., r. 35*l*., 440*l*.; 50, Duke's-rd., Chiswick, u.t. 76 yrs., g.r. 4*l*., 155*l*.; 104, 112, and 114, Wynford-road, Barnsbury, u.t. 26 yrs., g.r. 6*l*., 335*l*.; 92, 94, and 98, Wyndford-rd., u.t. 26 yrs., g.r. 6*l*., 330*l*.—By *Ventom, Bull, & Cooper*: Freehold land, 4 acres, Camberley, 600*l*.

JUNE 14.—By Chinnock, *Galsworthy, & Co.*: 3, The Chase, Clapham, u.t. 83 yrs., g.r. 12*l*., r. 55*l*., 570*l*.; 7b and 7a, Northwick-mews, Maida-hill, u.t. 31 yrs., g.r. 15*l*., r. 70*l*., 300*l*.; 3, Milner's-mews, Edgward-rd., u.t. 25 yrs.: g.r. 5*l*. 5s., r. 25*l*., 190*l*.—By *Jones & Son*: 29, Church-row, Limehouse, f., r. 36*l*. 4s., 300*l*.; a plot of freehold land, Church-row, 395*l*.—By *Giddy & Giddy*: A plot of freehold land, Skinner's-lane, Ashtead, 310*l*.—By *C. W. Davies*: 13, Parkfield-st., Islington, u.t. 13 yrs., g.r. 4*l*. 17s. 6d., r. 34*l*., 110*l*.; 46, Barnsbury-st., Barnsbury, u.t. 17 yrs., g.r. 2*l*., r. 40*l*., 250*l*.; 100 and 104, Riverside-rd., Highbury, f., r. 75*l*., 820*l*.—By *Geo. Head & Co.*: 1 to 9 (odd), Loates-lane, Watford, f., 740*l*.; 10, 12, and 14, Charles-st., f., 400*l*.; 6 and 8, Charles-st., f., 280*l*.—By *Walton & Lee*: F.g.r. of 17*l*., East Cowes, Isle of Wight, reversion in 750 yrs., 420*l*.; f.g.r. of 28*l*. 18s., ditto in 750 yrs., 720*l*.; f.g.r. of 34*l*., ditto in 750 yrs., 860*l*.—By *Debenham, Tewson, & Co.*: "Park House," Holly Pk., Crouch-hill, and 0a. 3r. 26p., f., 2,850*l*.; 91, 93, and 95, High-st., Wandsworth, and 1 to 7, Newton-lane, f., r. 230*l*., 4,700*l*.; "The Globe" public-house and warehouse, Derby-st., King's-cross, u.t. 12 yrs., g.r. 26*l*. 5s., 1,220*l*.; 12, 13, and 14, Derby-st., u.t. 12 yrs., g.r. 60*l*., r. 121*l*., 170*l*.; 67, Liverpool-st., u.t. 43 yrs., g.r. 6*l*., r. 48*l*., 510*l*.; 4, Chesterfield-st., u.t. 43 yrs., g.r. 6*l*., r. 48*l*., 520*l*.—By *Rogers, Chapman, & Thomas*: 25, Masbro'-rd., Brook-green, u.t. 73 yrs., g.r. 8*l*. 1s., r. 45*l*., 355*l*.; 75, Cumberland-st., Pimlico, u.t. 41 yrs., g.r. 9*l*., 400*l*.; 2 and 4, Rigault-rd., Fulham-rd., u.t. 85 yrs., g.r. 12*l*., r. 58*l*., 420*l*.

JUNE 15.—By *G. J. Smith*: 13, 15, and 17, Princess-rd., Regent's-pk., u.t. 48 yrs., g.r. 24*l*., r. 157*l*. 10s., 1,460*l*. By *E. Morris & Co.*: 48, Hilldrop-rd., Camden-rd., u.t. 61 yrs., g.r. 10*l*., 565*l*.—By *D. Young*: 29, 31, and 33, Iovill-rd., Walworth, u.t. 58 yrs., g.r. 15*l*., r. 97*l*. 10s., 665*l*.; 65, Fentiman-rd., Clapham-rd., u.t. 36 yrs., g.r. 7*l*. 10s., 340*l*.; 30, Dalberg-rd., Brixton, u.t. 83 yrs., g.r. 7*l*. 7s., 320*l*.; 12 and 14, Dalberg-rd., u.t. 77 yrs., g.r. 14*l*. 14s., r. 72*l*., 650*l*.

JUNE 16.—By *Gillow & Co.*: "Elmwood," Atkin's-rd., Clapham, f., 3,000*l*.—By *J. T. Ayton*: 25 and 26, Beaumont-sq., Mile End, u.t. 36 yrs., g.r. 9*l*., 650*l*.; Nos. 327, 329A, and 331; and 1 to 6, Govey's-pl., u.t. 13 yrs., g.r. 136*l*., 80*l*.—By *A. G. Thomson & Co.*: 31, Moreton-ter., Belgravia, u.t. 38 yrs., g.r. 8*l*., 535*l*.—By *Driver & Perfect*: 113 and 115, Neville-rd., Stoke Newington, u.t. 72 yrs., g.r. 10*l*., r. 52*l*., 425*l*.—By *G. B. Hilliard & Son*: "North End Place Farm," Great Waltham, f., 231a. 1r. 1p., 4,350*l*.; "High House Farm," Stapleford Abbotts, 52a. 2r. 6p., f., 1,100*l*.; an enclosure of f. land, 2a. 1r. 17p., 65*l*.; "Holbrook's Farm," Mountnessing, 34a. 3r. 13p., f., 700*l*.—By *Stimson & Sons*: 26, Glengall-rd., Old Kent-rd., f., r. 36*l*., 620*l*.; "The Belle Vue" beerhouse, Clapham-rd., u.t. 18 yrs., g.r. 10*l*. 10s., r. 85*l*., 660*l*.; 2, Clapham-pk.-rd., u.t. 16 yrs., g.r. 5*l*. 5s., r. 45*l*., 260*l*.; 42, Stockwell-pk.-rd., u.t. 32 yrs., g.r. 10*l*. 10s., 300*l*.; 68 and 70, Union-grove, u.t. 52 yrs., g.r. 14*l*. 10s., r. 80*l*., 530*l*.; "Vine Cottage," Surrey-rd., Peckham, f., 130*l*.; 22 and 27, Brunswick-sq., Camberwell, u.t. 49 yrs., g.r. 20*l*., r. 82*l*., 595*l*.; 52, Coldharbour-lane, u.t. 20 yrs., g.r. 8*l*., r. 60*l*., 260*l*.; 52, Aldred-rd., Kennington, u.t. 32 yrs., g.r. 5*l*., 155*l*. By *Vernon & Son*: 46, Portland-st., Stepney, u.t. 16 yrs., g.r. 6*l*., r. 26*l*., 115*l*.; "Harewood Downs Farm," Chalfont St. Giles, and 156a. 0r. 38p., f. and c., 4,200*l*.; an enclosure of f. land, 20a. 0r. 17p., 780*l*.; an enclosure of f. land, 10a. 3r. 18p., 860*l*.; an enclosure of f. land, Great Missenden, 4a. 3r. 33p., 520*l*.—By *H. J. Bliss & Son*: 43 and 45, Ellesmere-rd., Bethnal Green, f., r. 72*l*. 16s., 800*l*.; 63, St. George's-av., Tufnell-pk., u.t. 75 yrs., g.r. 7*l*. 7s., r. 45*l*., 490*l*.; "The Prince of Prussia," Harford-st., Mile-end, and 28 and 29, Cologne-st., u.t. 62 yrs., g.r. 20*l*., 1,450*l*.; 147A and 149, Cambridge-rd., Bethnal-green, u.t. 5 yrs., g.r. 20*l*., 20*l*.; an i.g.r. of 33*l*., Reynold's-rd., West Ham, u.t. 80 yrs., g.r. 16*l*. 10s., 250*l*.; an i.g.r. of 27*l*., Union-rd., u.t. 80 yrs., g.r. 16*l*., 240*l*.; f.g.r. of 37*l*., Eastfield-st., Limehouse, reversion in 30 yrs., 605*l*.—By *Newbon & Co.*: 13 to 23 (odd), Free-grove-rd., u.t. 64 yrs., g.r. 48*l*., r. 252*l*., 2,165*l*.; 8, 10, 16, 29, 38 and 40, Digby-rd., Finsbury-pk., u.t. 83 yrs., g.r. 37*l*. 9s., r. 221*l*., 1,865*l*.; 35, 37, and 43, Brownswood-pk., u.t. 83 yrs., g.r. 22*l*. 1s., r. 122*l*., 980*l*.; 68, Springdale-rd., u.t. 78 yrs., g.r. 6*l*., r. 35*l*., 305*l*.; 131, Grosvenor-rd., Canonbury, u.t. 57 yrs., g.r. 7*l*. 7s., 535*l*.

JUNE 17.—By *Cane & Co.*: 73 and 75, Nunhead-lane, Peckham, u.t. 71 yrs., g.r. 10*l*., r. 57*l*. 4s., 310*l*.—By *Cooper & Goulding*: "Torr Villa," Wood-green, with stabling, f., r. 60*l*., 1,100*l*.—By *Reynolds & Eason*: 284, Albany-rd., Camberwell, f., r. 36*l*., 410*l*.; 12 and 13, Widegate-st., City of London, f., r. 70*l*., 900*l*.; 183, St. John-st., Clerkenwell, f., r. 55*l*., 610*l*.; 11, Hatton-yd., Hatton-wall, f., 420*l*.—By *Montagu & Robinson*: Freehold rent-charge of 17*l*. 10s., Bromley-by-Bow, 440*l*.; one-third share of a f.g.r. of 47*l*., High st., reversion in 26½ yrs., 730*l*.; 8 and 10, Union-st., Stratford, f., 330*l*.; 33 and 34, New-st., f., 100*l*.—By *J. A. & W. Tharp*: 27, 29, and 31, Hare-st., Bethnal-green, u.t. 83 yrs., g.r. 22*l*. 10s., r. 174*l*. 12s., 1,325*l*.; 33, Hare-st., u.t. 83 yrs., g.r. 7*l*. 10s., r. 65*l*., 475*l*.; 164, 166, 168 to 178 even, Brick-lane, u.t. 79½ yrs., g.r. 51*l*., r. 440*l*. 16s., 3,930*l*.; 2, Code-st., u.t. 79½ yrs., g.r. 7*l*., r. 52*l*., 385*l*.; 5, Pedley-st., and 1, 2, and 3, Collyer's-pl., u.t. 76 yrs., g.r. 15*l*., r. 115*l*. 14s., 750*l*.; 6, Pedley-st. and stabling, u.t. 85 yrs., g.r. 24*l*., r. 135*l*., 1,200*l*.; 7, 8, and 9, Pedley-st., u.t. 85 yrs., g.r. 12*l*., r. 109*l*., 1,060*l*.; 2 to 12 even, Eckersley-st., u.t. 85 yrs., g.r. 24*l*., r. 158*l*. 12s., 1,180*l*.; 15, 17, and 19, Moss-st., u.t. 68 yrs., g.r. 25*l*., 680*l*.; 100 to 110 and 118 to 130 even, Abbott-rd., Bromley-by-Bow, u.t. 81 yrs., g.r. 65*l*., r. 364*l*. 10s., 2,805*l*.; 39, Ettrick-st., u.t. 81 yrs., g.r. 10*l*., r. 57*l*. 4s., 345*l*.; 2 and 3, Monkham's-ter., Woodford Wells, u.t. 57 yrs., g.r. 5s., r. 64*l*., 660*l*.

[*Contractions used in these lists.*—F.g.r. for freehold ground-rent; l.g.r. for leasehold ground-rent; i.g.r. for improved ground-rent; g.r. for ground-rent; r. for rent; f. for freehold; c. for copyhold; l. for leasehold; e. for estimated rental; u.t. for unexpired term; p.a. for per annum; yrs. for years; st. for street; rd. for road; sq. for square; pl. for place; ter. for terrace; cres. for crescent; yd. for yard, &c.]

PRICES CURRENT OF MATERIALS.

TIMBER.		
Greenheart, B.G. ton	9/0/0	0/0/0
Teak, E.I. ... load	9/10/0	15/0/0
Sequoia, U.S. ft. cu.	2/3	3/0
Ash, Canada load	2/10/0	4/0/0
Birch, do.	2/5/0	4/10/0
Elm, do.	3/10/0	4/15/0
Fir, Dantsic, &c.	1/10/0	3/10/0
Oak, do.	3/0/0	5/5/0
Canada	3/10/0	7/0/0
Pine, Canada red	2/10/0	3/10/0
Do. yellow	2/10/0	3/0/0
Lath, D'ntsic, fath	5/0/0	6/0/0
St. Petersburg	5/0/0	7/0/0
Deals, Finland 2nd & 1st std 100	7/10/0	9/10/0
Do. 4th & 3rd ..	7/0/0	8/0/0
Do. Riga	6/10/0	8/0/0
St. Petersburg, 1st yellow ..	10/10/0	14/10/0
Do. 2nd yellow	8/0/0	9/10/0
Do. white	7/10/0	10/0/0
Swedish	7/0/0	15/0/0
White Sea	8/0/0	17/0/0
Canada, Pine 1st	20/0/0	26/0/0
Do. do. 2nd	14/10/0	16/0/0
Do. do. 3rd, &c.	8/0/0	10/0/0
Do. Spruce, 1st	8/10/0	11/0/0
Do. do. 3rd & 2nd	6/15/0	8/0/0
New Brunswick	7/0/0	7/10/0
Battens, all kinds	3/10/0	15/10/0
Flooring Boards, sq., 1 in. prep. 1st	0/8/0	0/13/6
Do. 2nd	0/7/0	0/11/0
Other qualities	0/5/6	0/7/6
Cedar, Cuba .. ft.	/3½	/4½
Honduras, &c.	/3½	/4
Mahogany, Cuba.	/4½	/6½
St. Domingo, cargo av	/4½	2/0
Mexican do. do	/4	/5
Tobasco do. do	/5½	/7
Honduras do..	/5½	/6½
Box, Turkey ton	4/0/0	13/0/0
Rose, Rio	10/0/0	20/0/0
Bahia	9/0/0	18/0/0
Satin, St. Domingo .... ft.	0/0/8	0/1/3

TIMBER (continued).		
Satin, Porto Rico	0/0/8	0/1/6
Walnut, Italian ..	0/0/3½	0/0/[illegible]
METALS.		
Iron—Pig, in Scotland ...... ton	2/0/11	2/0/11½
Bar, Welsh, in London	5/17/6	6/0/0
Do. do. at works in Wales	5/7/6	5/10/0
Do. Staffordshire, in London	6/5/0	6/15/0
Copper—British, cake and ingot	48/10/0	49/10/0
Best selected ..	50/15/0	51/5/0
Sheets, strong..	57/0/0	58/0/0
Chili, bars	46/3/9	46/5/0
Yellow Metal lb.	0/0/5	0/0/0
Lead—Pig, Spanish .... ton	10/10/0	10/12/6
English, com. brands	10/15/0	10/17/6
Sheet, English, 3 lbs. per sq. ft. and upwards ..	12/0/0	0/0/0
Pipe	12/10/0	0/0/0
Zinc—English sheet .... ton	20/15/0	26/0/0
Vieille Montagne	26/5/0	0/0/0
Tin—Straits	103/5/0	103/7/6
Australian	103/5/0	103/7/6
English Ingots.	105/0/0	105/10/0
OILS.		
Linseed ...... ton	18/10/0	18/12/6
Cocoanut, Cochin	22/15/0	0/0/0
Do. Ceylon	21/15/0	0/0/0
Palm, Lagos	22/5/0	22/10/0
Rapeseed, English pale	24/10/0	25/0/0
Do. brown	23/0/0	0/0/0
Cottonseed ref. ..	19/0/0	19/5/0
Oleine	21/10/0	22/10/0
Lubricating, U.S.	4/0/0	5/0/0
Do. refined	5/10/0	12/10/0
Tar—Stockholm barrel	0/19/0	1/0/0
Archangel	0/12/6	0/0/0

TENDERS.

[Communications for insertion under this heading should be addressed to "The Editor," and must reach us *not later than 12 noon on Thursdays.*]

ABERDEEN.—Accepted conditionally for additions to a school, Kinellar, for the School Board for the Parish of Kinellar. Mr. Robert Thomson, architect, Ferryhill, Aberdeen:—

	£	s.	d.
Mason's Work—James Harper, Aberdeen	87	10	0
Carpenter's Work—William Edwards, Blackburn, Kinaldie	50	0	0
Slater's Work—Wm. W. Milne, Aberdeen	13	0	0
Plaster Work—James Simpson, Aberdeen	13	0	0
Total	£173	10	0

BILSTON.—For proposed alterations to the Bilston Public Baths, new iron roof and engineering and laundry fittings, for the Township Commissioners. Plans and specifications by Mr. C. L. N. Wilson, C.E., Township Engineer:—

Builders' and Engineering Work.

Davies & Hall	£2,721	Morrell Bros., Bilston* ..	£2,340
E. Marchant	2,583	*Accepted.	

[Engineer's estimate, £2,500.]

CHUDLEIGH (Devon).—For building stables, &c., for Mr. John Whiteway. Mr. S. Segar, architect, Newton Abbot:—

Jas. Widdecombe	£217	Wm. Shapley	£177
Robt. Collings	185	Mardon & Turner	152

DEVONPORT.—For erecting business premises, Tavistock-street, for Messrs. H. J. & E. A. Boolds. Mr. H. G. Luff, architect, Devonport. Quantities by Mr. John H. Dwelley, Plymouth:—

Julian	£1,760	0	Jenkin & Son	£1,513	0
Lapthorne & Good	1,740	0	G. Shellabear	1,495	0
A. R. Lethbridge & Son	1,565	0	Littleton	1,425	0
A. R. Debnam	1,519	0	S. Roberts*	1,330	0
G. Smith & Son	1,515	15	* Accepted.		

EALING.—Accepted for alterations and repairs to the Congregational Church and Manse, Ealing Green. Mr O. Ashby Lean, architect and surveyor, 31, Finsbury Circus, E.C.:—

Messrs. H. & A. J. Jones, Ealing £362 17 6

EAST COWES.—For making trial boring for proposed waterworks. Messrs. Lemon & Blizard, engineers, 9, Victoria-street, Westminster, and Southampton:—

Charles Chapman .. £417	0	0	Exors. of E. Timmins £225	0	0		
Baker & Sons 415	15	0	Le Grand & Sutcliffe.. 200	0	0		
C. Isler 310	0	0	Duke & Ockenden.... 196	0	0		
W. Hill & Co. 280	0	0	W. Brown 190	0	0		
R. T. Batchelor 231	9	7	T. Tilley & Sons* 179	3	0		

* Accepted.

KINGSTEIGNTON (Devon.).—For building brick kilns and drying lofts over, for Messrs. Hexter, Humpherson, & Co., Kingsteignton. Mr. S. Segar, architect, Newton Abbot:—

Joseph Steer	£759	William Mills	£734
Lewis Bearne	746	Frank A. A. Stacey*	717

*Accepted.
[All of Newton Abbot.]

LEEDS.—Accepted for the erection of three houses and a shop at Rodley, for Mr. Reuben Gaunt. Mr. J. P. Kay, architect, 30, Park-square, Leeds. Quantities by the architect:—

Masons—Ormerod & Wood, Farsley ......
Joiners—Ingle Bros., Apperly Bridge ......
Slater—Fredk. Thompson, Stanningley ......
Plasterer—Wilfred Busfield, Farsley ......
Plumber—Ed. Rhodes, Farsley ......
Painter—Wilfred Davidson, Calverley ......
} £973 15 0

LEYTONSTONE.—For new bottling store-house and stables at Leytonstone, for Messrs. Combe & Co., Limited. Mr. B. Elson, architect. Quantities by Mr. J. F. Bull:—

Williams	£4,707	H. & E. Lea	£3,933
B. E. Nightingale	4,490	Bush	3,891
Worsley	4,210		

LONDON.—For additions to the Northern Hospital, Winchmore-hill, for the Metropolitan Asylums Board. Messrs. Pennington & Bridgen, architects:—

L. Bentley	£13,880	Wall & Co.	£10,378
G. E. Todd	10,779	Randall & Co.	10,241
Dixon & Co.	10,569	Wm. Shurmur	9,690
Godson & Co.	10,409	Wm. Brass & Son	9,577

LONDON.—For the erection of the "Birdcage" public-house, Stamford Hill. Mr. H. S. Tyack, architect:—

J. Hicks	£9,551	W. Smith	£7,917
W. Colwell	8,090	Walker Bros.	7,894
Burham & Son	8,826	T. Boyce	7,769
Harris & Wardrop	8,670	W. Shurmur	7,720
F. & F. J. Wood	8,542	Coulsell Bros.	7,743
W. Evans	8,462	F. Voller	7,292
Holliday & Greenwood	8,377	S. Goodall	7,283

LONDON.—For rebuilding Nos. 88, 89, 90, and 91, Drury-lane, W.C., for Messrs. Hart, Son, Peard, & Co. Mr. R. Fabian Russell, architect. Quantities by architect:—

J. Mowlem & Co.	£6,750	Jerrard	£5,575
Williams & Son	6,666	W. Downs	5,347
Dove Bros.	6,365	B. E. Nightingale	5,285
Ashby Bros.	5,840	W. Smith	5,100
Chappell	5,597	Tuttle & Appleton	5,044

LONDON.—For new warehouse, at Old-street, Shoreditch, for Mr. J. Strickland. Mr. M. N. Inman, architect:—

Co-operative Builders	£3,967	Holloway Bros.	£3,550
Atherton & Latta	3,895	J. Chessum & Son	3,526
W. Shurmur	3,843	Pink, Fryer, & Co.	3,495
Clark & Bracey	3,727	J. Grover & Son	3,458
J. Simpson & Son	3,669	Patman & Fotheringham..	3,351
J. H. Johnson	3,567		

LONDON.—For erecting warehouse at Bateman's-row, Shoreditch, for Messrs. Clark, Hunt, & Co. Mr. W. Gilbee Scott, architect:—

W. Dabbs	£3,654	W. Shurmur	£3,294
W. Johnson & Co.	3,619	Creaton & Co.	3,272
T. Boyce	3,556	Godfrey & Co.	3,272
R. Rayner	3,492	G. E. Todd	3,194
S. Goodall	3,384	Harris & Wardrop	3,193
J. Bentley	3,341	J. Chessum & Son	3,149

LONDON.—Accepted for the erection of engine and boiler houses, at Meredith Wharf, Bankside, for the City of London Electric Lighting Company, Limited. Major-General Webber, C.B., Engineer:—

Wm. Shurmur £6,610 0 0

LONDON.—Accepted for the erection of seven shops at West End-lane, Hampstead. Mr. Delissa Joseph, architect, 17 and 18, Basinghall-street, E.C. Quantities by Messrs. Bushell & Co., 22, Great James-street, Bedford-row, W.C.:—

George Neal, Kilburn £5,500 0 0

[No competition.]

LONDON.—For alterations at 48, Brewer-street, W., for Mr. F. Byrne. Messrs. Wimperis & Arber, architects:—

Wetherilt, Lee, & Martin..	£2,673	Giles	£2,485
Prestige & Co.	2,602	Turner, McKay, & Ashpole	2,330
Johnson	2,505	Hocking	1,760
G. H. & A. Bywaters	2,498	Hilder & Edge (accepted)..	1,823

LONDON.—For alterations to premises in Brixton-road and Tunstall-road, S.W., for Messrs. Peter & Evans. Mr. G. Warren Cooper, architect, Bedford-row House, Bedford-row, W.C.:—

E. J. Saunders £1,050 0 0
E. Triggs, The Chase, Clapham (accepted) 900 0 0

LONDON.—For additions and alterations to Nos. 327, 329, 331, 333, 335, 337, 339, 341, 343, 345, 347, Kentish Town-road, N.W., for Mr. W. W. B. Rodger:—

Hoare	£12,637	Hilder & Edge	£6,830
Lawrence	11,000	Ball*	5,930
Marchant & Hurst	9,029	* Accepted.	

LONDON.—For the erection of dwellings at Bear-yard, Lincoln's Inn-fields. Mr. J. Hamilton, architect:—

F. Britten	£1,570	S. Heyworth & Son	£1,419
J. Beale	1,535	W. Shurmur (accepted)	1,395

STRAWBERRY HILL (Middlesex).—For new system of drainage and various sanitary alterations at the City and Metropolitan Police Orphanage. Messrs. John Butler & Son, architects:—

McSwiney	£1,121 0	Kent, Chelsea*	£909 0
Beattie	1,023 16	* Accepted.	

LONDON.—For re-building premises, for the Bottle Seal Co., Eagle Wharf-road. Messrs. J. Butler & Son, architects:—

Kent	£1,125	Garlick & Horton*	£1,068
Lathey	1,149	* Accepted.	

LONDON.—For certain painting and other works at the Infirmary, Fulham-road, S.W., for the Guardians of the St. George's Union. Mr. H. Saxon Snell, architect:—

Flew & Co.	£936	H. Wall & Co.	£435
Henry King	640	Lilly & Lilly, Whitcomb-street, W.C.*	427
Thos. Nye	580	* Accepted.	
J. J. Thompson	444		

LONDON.—For an additional story to Messrs. Goodall & Son's factory, Great College-street, Camden Town, N.W. Mr. Silvester Capes, architect. Quantities by Mr. Alfred Hoxall.

B. E. Nightingale	£940	Lawrence & Sons	£819
Scrivener & Co.	853		

MAIDSTONE.—Accepted for warming the new mansion, "Springfield," Maidstone, by pure warm air. Messrs. Alfred Waterhouse & Son, architects:—

John Grundy £300 0 0

MYTHOLMROYD (Yorks).—Accepted for the erection of a 30-ft. span bridge at Marshaw Bridge, Cragg. Mr. Sam Shaw, engineer, Dewsbury:—

S. & T. H. Riley, Greetland, near Halifax £292 5

NEW TREDEGAR.—For the completion of ten cottages, Uchdir-road, for the Powell Duffryn Colliery Company. Messrs. Anton Davies & Son, architects, Pontlottyn, Cardiff:—

J. W. Evans £1,005 0
J. C. Davies, Pontlottyn, via Cardiff* 977 15
* Accepted.

SWANSEA.—For the erection of three shops in High-street, Swansea, for Mr. F. Knight. Mr. H. C. Portsmouth, architect, Castle-buildings, Swansea:—

Williams	£2,280 0 0	Richards	£1,700 14 2
Jenkins	2,000 0 0	Bennett Bros	1,690 0 0
Billings	1,937 10 0	Weaver, Swansea*	1,595 0 0
Thos. Watkins & Co.	1,725 0 0	* Accepted.	

TARRANT HINTON (Dorset).—For the restoration of Tarrant Hinton Church, Dorset. Mr. Alfred W. N. Burder, architect, Loughborough:—

E. Abley	£1,225	Crook & Son	£940
Jacob Long & Sons	1,060	F. J. Merrett & Son	889
R. Wilkins & Son	1,030	J. S. Kimberley, Banbury*	841
* Accepted.			

SUBSCRIBERS in LONDON and the SUBURBS, by prepaying at the Publishing Office, 19s. per annum (or 4s. 9d. per quarter), can ensure receiving "The Builder," by *Friday Morning's Post.*

TERMS OF SUBSCRIPTION.

"THE BUILDER" is supplied DIRECT from the Office to resident in any part of the United Kingdom at the rate of 19s. per annum PREPAID. To all parts of Europe, America, Australia, and New Zealand, 26s. per annum. To India, China, Ceylon, &c., 30s. per annum. Remittances payable to DOUGLAS FOURDRINIER, Publisher, No. 46, Catherine-street, W.C.

PUBLISHER'S NOTICES.

Registered Telegraphic Address, 'THE BUILDER,' LONDON.

CHARGES FOR ADVERTISEMENTS.

SITUATIONS VACANT, PARTNERSHIPS, APPRENTICESHIPS TRADE, AND GENERAL ADVERTISEMENTS.

Six lines (about fifty words) or under .... 4s. 6d.
Each additional line (about ten words) .... 0s. 6d.

Terms for Series of Trade Advertisements, also for Special Advertisements on front page, Competitions, Contracts, Sales by Auction, &c. may be obtained on application to the Publisher.

SITUATIONS WANTED.

FOUR Lines (about thirty words) or under .... 2s. 6d.
Each additional line (about ten words) .... 0s. 6d.

PREPAYMENT IS ABSOLUTELY NECESSARY.

*** Stamps must not be sent, but all small sums should be remitted by Cash in Registered Letter or by Money Order, payable at the Post-office, Covent-garden, W.C. to

DOUGLAS FOURDRINIER, Publisher,
Addressed to No. 46, Catherine-street, W.C.

Advertisements for the current week's issue must reach the Office before THREE o'clock p.m. on THURSDAY, but those intended for the front Page should be in by TWELVE noon on WEDNESDAY.

SPECIAL.—ALTERATIONS IN STANDING ADVERTISEMENTS or ORDERS TO DISCONTINUE same must reach the Office before TEN o'clock on WEDNESDAY mornings.

The Publisher cannot be responsible for DRAWINGS, TESTIMONIALS, &c. left at the Office in reply to Advertisements, and strongly recommends that of the latter COPIES ONLY should be sent.

PERSONS Advertising in "The Builder" may have *Replies addressed to the Office*, 46, Catherine-street, Covent Garden, W.C. *free of charge.* Letters will be forwarded if addressed envelopes are sent, together with sufficient stamps to cover the postage.

AN EDITION Printed on THIN PAPER, for FOREIGN and COLONIAL CIRCULATION, is issued every week.

Now ready.

READING CASES, { NINEPENCE EACH. By Post (carefully packed), 1s.

TO CORRESPONDENTS.

C. B. H. (we cannot publish mere insinuations of that kind). W. J. (shall have attention, certainly).—A. H. K. (it is against our rule to comply with such requests).—W. M. B. (too late).—T. E. K (next week).

All statements of facts, lists of tenders, &c., must be accompanied by the name and address of the sender, not necessarily for publication

We are compelled to decline pointing out books and giving addresses.

NOTE.—The responsibility of signed articles, and papers read at public meetings, rests, of course, with the authors.

We cannot undertake to return rejected communications.

Letters or communications (beyond mere news-items) which have been duplicated for other journals, are NOT DESIRED.

All communications regarding literary and artistic matter should be addressed to THE EDITOR; all communications relating to advertisements and other exclusively business matters should be addressed to THE PUBLISHER, and not to the Editor.

Lightning Source UK Ltd.
Milton Keynes UK
UKHW021005031218
333381UK00015B/2254/P

9 780260 006639